The "Athenaeum" Portrait of
GEORGE WASHINGTON

By GILBERT STUART

(*Reproduced on opposite page*)

This was the last of three original portraits of George Washington by Gilbert Stuart, and was painted in 1796. It was not finished and Stuart refused to dispose of it, using it for making many copies. It is generally accepted as the standard portrait, and a reproduction of this portrait in poster size was placed in every school room in the United States by the United States George Washington Bicentennial Commission. This portrait of George Washington and the companion portrait of Martha Washington are owned by the Boston Athenaeum, and are exhibited in the Museum of Fine Arts at Boston.

The "Athenaeum" Portrait of George Washington
By Gilbert Stuart

HISTORY

OF THE

GEORGE WASHINGTON

BICENTENNIAL CELEBRATION

VOLUME I

Literature Series

1 9 3 2

UNITED STATES

GEORGE WASHINGTON BICENTENNIAL COMMISSION

WASHINGTON, D. C.

UNITED STATES GEORGE WASHINGTON BICENTENNIAL COMMISSION

PRESIDENT OF THE UNITED STATES
Chairman

VICE PRESIDENT OF THE UNITED STATES

SPEAKER OF THE HOUSE OF REPRESENTATIVES

United States Senate

SIMEON D. FESS, *Vice Chairman*
Ohio

ARTHUR CAPPER
Kansas

CARTER GLASS
Virginia

MILLARD E. TYDINGS
Maryland

House of Representatives

WILLIS C. HAWLEY
Oregon

JOHN Q. TILSON
Connecticut

JOSEPH W. BYRNS
Tennessee

R. WALTON MOORE
Virginia

Presidential Commissioners

MRS. ANTHONY WAYNE COOK
Pennsylvania

MRS. JOHN DICKINSON SHERMAN
Colorado

HENRY FORD
Michigan

C. BASCOM SLEMP
Virginia

WALLACE MCCAMANT
Oregon

ALBERT BUSHNELL HART
Historian
Massachusetts

JOSEPH SCOTT
California

Director
REPRESENTATIVE SOL BLOOM
New York

PREFACE

THIS is the first of a series of three volumes containing literature prepared and issued in connection with the Celebration of the Two Hundredth Anniversary of the Birth of George Washington. Other volumes in the general report of this Commission contain material of various and related kinds, but the present series, of which this is Volume I, is restricted to re-publication of historical pamphlets that have had wide distribution.

Of major importance are the "Honor to George Washington" pamphlets, edited by the Historian of the Commission, Dr. Albert Bushnell Hart. These fifteen studies include the principle phases of General George Washington's life and those elements of his career which chiefly contributed to his character and made possible his great achievements. It is important to note that in these pamphlets the authors have presented authentic information, obtained after most painstaking and thorough research. The method of compilation is calculated to facilitate the work of students, as well as for the accommodation of the casual reader.

Naturally, a thorough investigation was made of all available books, pamphlets and other material relating to the life and times of George Washington. In covering so wide a field, it was necessary not only to study the requirements of selection, but also in condensation to guard against the omission of essential data. In this work of investigation and arrangement, the Commission has had the benefit of the scholarly and patriotic services of Dr. Hart, Dr. John C. Fitzpatrick, Editor of the Definitive Writings of George Washington and of George Washington's Diaries, and David M. Matteson, Historical Assistant of the Commission, with a capable staff of men and women working under their direction.

"The George Washington Programs and Program Papers," originated by and prepared under the direction of Mrs. John Dickinson Sherman, were especially designed to assist patriotic societies, clubs and similar organizations as well as schools, colleges and other educational institutions, in preparing material for special George Washington program events. This series has proved exceedingly popular and has formed a basis for thousands of addresses, articles and discussions in connection with the Celebration.

"The George Washington Appreciation Course," by Miss Hazel Nielson, was designed especially for use in teaching the history of George Washington, and was used as a suggestive guide for teachers and student-teachers in the schools and colleges of the United States. This was one of the most important and helpful pamphlets in all the material furnished to the public.

"The George Washington Atlas," edited by Lawrence Martin, Chief, Division of Maps, Library of Congress, is of special value in its relation to other items of contents, as it affords an opportunity to follow the course of historical records.

"The Highlights of the Writings of George Washington," compiled by David M. Matteson, speak for themselves. They were selected from the more important documents concerned in the career of George Washington.

The character of the "Religious References in the Writings, Addresses and Military Orders of George Washington," compiled by Mr. Matteson, and "The Educational Views of George Washington," by Walton C. John, Senior Specialist in Higher Education, United States Office of Education, and Alma H. Preinkert, Assistant Registrar, University of Maryland, based on his diaries and addresses, is indicated by their titles, and both pamphlets have contributed importantly to the popularity of the material issued by the Commission.

In the remaining sections of this volume are presented other valuable contributions, including plays which have had wide and popular acceptance, especially among the boys and girls of the United States.

The facts are given fully in a style that is clear, concise and direct. No effort has been made at literary embellishment. No labored composition has been attempted to give grace to the text. The readers may be assured that the primary purpose of these studies of George Washington's life has been to achieve the greatest historical authenticity and to insure permanent educational value. They were offered to the public in full confidence that they supplied in convenient and compact form the most useful and enlightening data upon the life and time of George Washington that can be found in the vast literary memorabilia relating to our greatest American.

SOL BLOOM,

DIRECTOR,

UNITED STATES GEORGE WASHINGTON
BICENTENNIAL COMMISSION

CONTENTS

HONOR TO GEORGE WASHINGTON AND READING ABOUT GEORGE WASHINGTON

PAMPHLET No. 1

FRONTIER BACKGROUND OF WASHINGTON'S CAREER

By David M. Matteson

Part I

PERIOD OF WASHINGTON'S YOUTH

Part II

WASHINGTON'S CONTACT WITH THE INDIANS

SELECTED AUTHORITIES

PAMPHLET No. 2

WASHINGTON THE MAN OF MIND

By Albert Bushnell Hart

Part I

PRACTICAL EDUCATION

CONTENTS—*Continued*

CONTENTS—*Continued*

CONTENTS—*Continued*

CONTENTS—*Continued*

PAMPHLET No. 7

WASHINGTON AND THE CONSTITUTION

By DAVID M. MATTESON

Part I

PRELIMINARIES OF THE CONVENTION

Part II

RESULTS OF THE CONVENTION

SELECTED AUTHORITIES

PAMPHLET No. 8

WASHINGTON AS PRESIDENT

By ALBERT BUSHNELL HART

Part I

WASHINGTON'S DOMESTIC POLICY (1789-1797)

Part II

WASHINGTON'S FOREIGN POLICY (1789-1797)

CONTENTS—*Continued*

CONTENTS—*Continued*

CONTENTS—*Continued*

PAMPHLET No. 13

WASHINGTON AS ENGINEER AND CITY BUILDER

By Lieut. Col. U. S. Grant 3d, U. S. A.

Part I

GEORGE WASHINGTON, ENGINEER

Part II

GEORGE WASHINGTON, CITY BUILDER

CONTENTS—*Continued*

CONTENTS—*Continued*

PROGRAMS AND PAPERS PORTRAYING THE PERSONALITY, CHARACTER, AND ACHIEVEMENTS OF GEORGE WASHINGTON

PROGRAM ONE

FAMILY RELATIONSHIPS OF GEORGE WASHINGTON

PROGRAM TWO

HOMES OF GEORGE WASHINGTON

PROGRAM THREE

YOUTH AND MANHOOD OF GEORGE WASHINGTON

PROGRAM FOUR

THE MOTHER OF GEORGE WASHINGTON

PROGRAM FIVE

GEORGE WASHINGTON THE MAN OF SENTIMENT

PROGRAM SIX

GEORGE WASHINGTON THE MAN OF ACTION IN MILITARY AND CIVIL LIFE

PROGRAM SEVEN

GEORGE WASHINGTON THE CHRISTIAN

CONTENTS—*Continued*

CONTENTS—*Continued*

THE GEORGE WASHINGTON ATLAS

---

* *Spelling as in the original manuscript.*

CONTENTS—*Continued*

List of Illustrations

PUBLICATIONS OF THE UNITED STATES GEORGE WASHINGTON BICENTENNIAL COMMISSION

The commemorative volumes issued by the United States George Washington Bicentennial Commission contain the complete history of the George Washington Bicentennial Celebration.

LITERATURE SERIES

The literature series, of which this is the first volume, consists of volumes I, II and III, and contains the publications of the United States George Washington Bicentennial Commission, issued in connection with the Celebration of the Two Hundredth Anniversary of the Birth of George Washington. These volumes present authentic historical information concerning George Washington, which was obtained after the most painstaking research.

FOREIGN PARTICIPATION

The series on Foreign Participation contains the activities of the Celebration in 81 foreign countries, divided into sections as follows: Western Europe, Eastern Europe, Near East, Far East, Canada, Mexico, Central America, South America, West Indies, and Africa.

ACTIVITIES OF THE CELEBRATION

The series on the Activities of the Celebration contains the report of the National Organizations, States, cities, towns, and communities, including municipal activities and programs given by religious, fraternal, patriotic, educational and other groups.

UNITED STATES GEORGE WASHINGTON BICENTENNIAL COMMISSION
WASHINGTON, D. C.

Honor To George Washington

and

Reading About George Washington

A Series of Fifteen Pamphlets

———

Edited

Dr. Albert Bushnell Hart

Titles of Pamphlets of the series

Honor to George Washington
and
Reading About George Washington

INTRODUCTION

THE series of pamphlets under the general title "Honor to George Washington" is divided into distinct subjects, each of which is expertly treated. This arrangement follows a systematic plan of development. It was considered advisable to deal with the life of Washington in this series of pamphlets by episodes and phases rather than in the usual historical order.

There are in existence a bewildering number of "lives of Washington" which chronicle significant events in his life, and most of these books are generally available to all readers. But to know George Washington, to place a proper valuation upon his character and services, and to appreciate those elements of his manhood which contributed to the sum of his greatness, we must study Washington by episodes in his life and by phases of his character. More important still is the fact that the material appearing in this series, and in all other publications of this Commission, has the seal of historical authenticity. Every statement and reference has been examined with the utmost care by the eminent historians of the Commission.

The readers of these chapters will find much material that is new, or that has been rescued from literary obscurity. They will find that these compilations have been arranged for the convenience of the student, as well as the casual biographical reader. The judgment of the Commission in so compiling and publishing these studies of George Washington has been amply vindicated by the tremendous demand for the work and by the intelligent and sympathetic comment that has come from students generally.

GEORGE WASHINGTON
From a portrait by Saint Mémin

Frontier Background of Washington's Career
By David M. Matteson
Part I
Period of Washington's Youth

GEORGE WASHINGTON
By Charles Willson Peale
*The "Virginia Colonel" portrait, painted at Mount Vernon in 1772,
when Washington was 40 years of age. The original hangs in the Lee
Memorial Chapel of Washington and Lee University at Lexington, Va.*

In many respects young Washington was a backwoodsman of the same type as the eager spirits from the coast colonies who were pushing out into central New York and the mountain regions of Pennsylvania, Maryland and the Carolinas. Most of those regions he visited in the course of his life. He invested a good part of his fortune in western lands, then far beyond settlement. He was a frontiersman but at the same time he foresaw the growth of mining and manufacturing and transportation which were to make those frontier regions, then peopled only by scattered Indian tribes, equal in wealth and prosperity to the seacoast states. From the beginning of his active life to his last days, the mind of Washington was bent on bringing his state of Virginia and all the western region into populous, prosperous, and enduring communities. A frontiersman by descent and education, he was always pushing to raise the community in which he lived into a stable social and economic situation. To understand Washington therefore, it is necessary to know accurately how frontiersmen from 1732 to the end of the Revolution lived and worked and associated with their fellow men.

FRONTIER LAND SYSTEM

Twenty years before Washington's birth, there came to Virginia the first governor of the colony who interested himself in the development of the frontier. Governor Alexander Spotswood was an energetic, far-sighted man who set himself to the task of bringing in a class of active immigrants and developing the resources of the back country. Much of the colony even in the tide-water region was still undeveloped. The rivers were the natural highways and a large part of the population lived on or close to those rivers, particularly the wealthy land owners and slave owners who were the political, social, and economic leaders of the colony. The main crop was tobacco which speedily exhausted the land and made it necessary to clear new areas. It was difficult for men without money in hand to buy land and the middle class farmers were always at a disadvantage. The region between the tide-water heads of the rivers and the mountains contained few settlers. Even the Valley of Virginia between the Blue Ridge and the Alleghenies, the garden spot of Virginia, was still unsettled.

A FRONTIERSMAN BY NATURE

 HAT George Washington became the foremost figure in the colony of Virginia and afterwards in the United States of America was not due to chance or to the favor of powerful men or to wealthy marriage. The rise of Washington to responsibility, to fame, and to leadership was the outcome of conditions in the colony of his birth and growth which gave opportunity to a young man of character and ability. If Washington had been born in Massachusetts he would have made a fortune in shipbuilding and foreign commerce and trade which gave the largest opportunities in that colony. Had he been a Pennsylvanian he would have been one of the spirited group which included Franklin and Reed and Morris in developing a commercial community. As a descendant of three generations of planters on Virginia soil he accepted the conditions of his time and place. Only it was in him from youth upward to make the best of those conditions, to improve them and to aid in creating more permanent and prosperous conditions for the colonies.

SPOTSWOOD'S EXPEDITION (1716)

Though the Valley previously had been entered from the north, Governor Spotswood's company of gallant gentlemen in 1716 was the first organized one to surmount the Blue Ridge, at Swift Run Gap, and to reach the South Shenandoah River. One of the members of the party, John Fontaine, kept a journal of the expedition which called itself "Knights of the Golden Horseshoe":

"5th [of September]—A fair day. At nine we were mounted; we were obliged to have axe-men to clear the way in some places. We followed the windings of the James River, observing that it came from the very top of the mountains. We killed two rattlesnakes during our ascent. In some places it was very steep, in others, it was so that we could ride up. About one of the clock we got to the top of the mountain; about four miles and a half, and we came to the very head spring of James River, where it runs no bigger than a man's arm, from under a large stone. We drank King George's health, and all the Royal Family's, at the very top of the Appalachian mountains. About a musket-shot from the spring there is another, which rises and runs down on the other side; it goes westward, and we thought we could go down that way, but we met with such prodigious precipices, that we were obliged to return to the top again. We found some trees which had been formerly marked, I suppose, by the Northern Indians, and following these trees, we found a good, safe descent. Several of the company were for returning; but the Governor persuaded them to continue on. About five, we were down on the other side, and continued our way for about seven miles further, until we came to a large river, by the side of which we encamped. . . . 6th.— We crossed the river, which we called Euphrates. . . . We drank some healths on the other side, and returned; . . . We had a good dinner, and after it we got the men together, and loaded all their arms, and we drank the King's health in Champagne, and fired a volley—the Princess's health, in Burgundy, and fired a volley, and all the rest of the Royal Family in claret, and a volley. We drank the Governor's health and fired another volley. We had several sorts of liquors, viz., Virginia red wine and white wine, Irish usquebaugh, brandy, shrub, two sorts of rum, champagne, canary, cherry, punch, water, cider, &c. . . . 7th—At seven in the morning we mounted our horses, and parted with the rangers, who were to go farther on, and we returned homewards; . . ."

FRONTIER ROUTES

The Washington estates when George Washington was a boy were all on or near the tide rivers, but at the time of Washington's birth the population was pushing out to the frontiers of the Carolinas, Virginia, Maryland, and Pennsylvania; and Governor Spotswood had still another idea in his mind with which Washington was later to be concerned. Spotswood said that "The Chief Aim of my Expedition over the great Mountains in 1716, was to satisfy my Self whether it was practicable to come at the Lakes," in order to trade with the Indians and check the French advance in the Mississippi Valley. However, the more immediate result was the settlement of the Shenandoah Valley. Non-English settlers came to Pennsylvania from the beginning; they were encouraged by the proprietary, and were soon found in the region west of the Susquehanna. Thence through York, Cumberland, and Adams counties to the Maryland line following an Indian trail, later developed into the Monocacy Road, the pioneers came into Maryland about 1729. The route crossed the Ridge by Crampton's Gap, in the region later made famous by the Antietam campaign, and then across the Potomac by a ford above present Harper's Ferry. Though there may have been earlier attempts, the first permanent settlement of the Valley began in 1727.

THE PENNSYLVANIA DUTCH

That portion of the Valley drained by the Shenandoah, the part with which Washington was first acquainted and where his own lands were, was settled mostly by Germans. Benjamin Rush in 1789 noted the special characteristic of these "Pennsylvania Dutch," and it is interesting to trace in them possible influences upon Washington's own traits as a scientific farmer, as described in another pamphlet in this series.

"In settling a tract of land, they always provide large and suitable accommodations for their horses and cattle, before they lay out much money in building a house for themselves. The barn and stables are generally under one roof, and contrived in such manner as to enable them to feed their horses and cattle, and to remove their dung, with as little trouble as possible. The first dwelling house upon this farm is small, and built of logs. It generally lasts the life time of the first settler of a tract of land; and hence they have a saying that 'a son should always begin his improvements where his father left off'—that is, by building a large and convenient stone house.

"They always prefer good land or that land on which there is a large quantity of meadow ground. From an attention to the cultivation of grass, they often double the value of an old farm in a few years, and grow rich on farms, on which their predecessors of whom they purchased them, have nearly starved. They prefer purchasing farms with some improvements to settling a new tract of land.

"From the history that has been given to the German agriculture, it will hardly be necessary to add that a German farm may be distinguished from the farms of the other citizens of the state, by the superior size of their barns; the plain, but compact form of their houses; the height of their inclosures; the extent of their orchards; the fertility of their fields; the luxuriance of their meadows, and a general appearance of plenty and neatness in everything that belongs to them."

FOREST LANDS

The insistence on good land usually meant rich forest growth, likely to be a limestone area, but also meadowland. Washington in various places in his Diaries estimates the probable value of land much on this basis. For instance: "March 13 [1748] Rode to his Lordships Quarter about 4 Miles higher up y. River we went through most beautiful Groves of Sugar Trees and spent ye. best part of y. Day in admiring ye. Trees and richness of ye Land." October 13, 1770: "The Lands we travelld over today till we had crossd the Laurel Hill (except in small spots) was very mountainous and indifferent, but when we came down the Hill to the Plantation of Mr. Thos. Gist, the Ld. appeard charming; that which lay level being as rich and black as any thing could posibly be; the more Hilly kind, tho of a different complexion must be good, as well from the Crops it produces, as from the beautiful white Oaks that grows thereon, the white Oak in generl. indicates poor Land, yet this does not appear to be of that cold kind." October 15: "The Lands which I passed over to day were generally Hilly, and the growth chiefly white Oak, but very good notwithstanding; and what is extraordinary, and contrary to the property of all other Lands I ever saw before, the Hills are the richest Land; and the Soil upon the Sides and Summits of them, being as black as Coal and the Growth, Walnut, Cherry, Spice Bushes, etca." October 30: "A Mile or two below this we Landed, and after getting a little distance from the River we came (without any rising) to a pretty lively kind of Land grown up with Hicky. and oaks of different kinds, intermixed with Walnut, etca. here and there." November 5: "This is a good Neck of Land the Soil being generally good; and in places very rich. Their is a large proportion of Meadow Ground, and the Land as high, dry and Level as one coud wish. The growth in most places is beach intermixed with walnut, etca., but more especially with Poplar (of which there are numbers very large). The Land towards the upper end is black oak, and very good; upon the whole a valuable Tract might be had here, . . ." September 8, 1784: "I . . . recrossed . . . to a tract of mine on the Virginia side which I find exceedingly Rich, and must be very valuable—the lower end of the Land is rich white oak in place springey; and in the winter wet.—the upper part is exceedingly rich and covered with Walnut of considerable size many of them."

THE SCOTCH-IRISH

Mixed with these Germans were some Scotch-Irish, but for the most part the latter continued on to the upper part of the Shenandoah and over the watershed to the southern slope of the Valley. For this there is a probable reason in the character of the people. Logan, Penn's agent, in 1724 wrote of the Scotch-Irish as "bold and indigent strangers, saying as their excuse, when challenged for titles, that we had solicited for colonists and they had come accordingly." Again, in 1727: "They say the Proprietor invited people to come and settle his country; they came for that end, and must live. Both they and the Palatines pretend that they will buy, but not one in twenty has anything to pay with. The Irish settle generally toward the Maryland line, where no lands can honestly be sold till the dispute with Lord Baltimore is decided." In 1730 Logan wrote that the Irish alleged that "it was against the laws of God and nature, that so much land should be idle while so many Christians wanted it to labor on and raise their bread." The Germans, while many of them were originally squatters in the Valley, would pay for the land if the alternative was to move on. They were, in other words, permanent settlers by instinct. With the Scotch-Irish the reverse was true: they were in the van of the pioneers not only because of their adventurous spirit, but because of their unwillingness to acknowledge the rights of the holders of great grants.

Washington himself had an experience with such adventurers. They had squatted on land he claimed in southwestern Pennsylvania, and after he had ineffectually endeavored personally to compromise with them in 1784 he went to law and ousted them. September 14, 1784: "This day also the People who lives on my land on Millers Run came here to set forth their pretensions to it; and to enquire into my Right—after much conversation and attempts in them to discover all the flaws they could in my Deed &ca.—and to establish a fair and upright intention in themselves—and after much councelling which proceeded from a division of opinion among themselves—they resolved (as all who lived on the land were not here) to give me their definite determination when I should come to the land, which I told them would probably happen on Friday or Saturday next." September 19: "Being Sunday, and the People living on my Land, *apparently* very religious, it was thought best to postpone going among them until tomorrow." September 20: "Dined at David Reeds, after which Mr. James Scot and Squire Reed began to enquire whether I would part with the Land, and upon what terms; adding, that tho' they did not conceive they could be dispossessed, yet to avoid contention, they would buy, if my terms were Moderate. I told them I had no inclination to sell; however, after hearing a great deal of their hardships, their Religious principles (which had brought them together as a Society of Cededers) and unwillingness to seperate or remove; I told them I would make them a last offer . . . they then determined to stand suit for the Land; . . ." September 22: "I set out for Beason Town, in order to meet with, and engage Mr. Thomas Smith to bring

ejectments, and to prosecute my Suit for the Land in Washington County, on which those, whose names are herein inserted, are settled."

MIXED FRONTIER ELEMENTS

These Scotch-Irish were not the only border settlers; there was a mingling of Germans, English, Scots, some Huguenots, and even a few Catholic-Irish, Hollanders, and Swedes. Of this mixture Roosevelt has written: "A single operation, passed under the hard conditions of life in the wilderness, was enough to weld together into one people the representatives of these numerous and widely different races; and the children of the next generation became indistinguishable from one another. . . . Their grim, harsh, narrow lives were yet strangely fascinating and full of adventurous toil and danger; none but natures as strong, as freedom-loving, and as full of bold defiance as theirs could have endured existence on the terms which these men found pleasurable. Their iron surroundings made a mould which turned out all alike in the same shape. They resembled one another, and they differed from the rest of the world—even the world of America, and infinitely more, the world of Europe—in dress, in customs, and in mode of life."

HARDSHIPS OF WASHINGTON'S EXPEDITIONS

Washington's frontier relations, in both peace and war, had a large influence upon his development and policies. His experiences with the Indians in the warfare with the French, and his interest in western development, are treated in other articles of these pamphlets; here the purpose is to give some idea of the character and life of these frontiersmen with whom he was brought in contact, first in the Valley and later in present West Virginia and western Pennsylvania. Washington in his account of the journey to the French commandant on the upper Ohio in 1753 illustrates the hardships encountered by those who traversed the wilderness. December 23, 1753: "Our Horses were now [after leaving Venango on the return] so weak and feeble, and the Baggage so heavy (as we were obliged to provide all the Necessaries which the Journey would require) that we doubted much their performing it; therefore myself and others (except the Drivers, who were obliged to ride) gave up our Horses for Packs, to assist along with the Baggage. I put myself in an *Indian* walking Dress, and continued with them three Days, till I found there was no Probability of their getting home in any reasonable Time. The Horses grew less able to travel every Day; and the Cold increased very fast; and the Roads were becoming much worse by a deep Snow, continually freezing: Therefore as I was uneasy to get back, to make Report of my Proceedings to his Honour, the Governor, I determined to prosecute my Journey the nearest Way through the Woods, on Foot.

"Accordingly I left Mr. *Vanbraam* in Charge of our Baggage: with Money and Directions to Provide Necessaries from Place to Place for themselves and Horses, and to make the most convenient Dispatch in Travelling.

"I took my necessary Papers; pulled off my Cloaths; and tied myself up in a Match Coat. Then with Gun in Hand and Pack on my Back, in which were my Papers and Provisions, I set-out with Mr. *Gist,* fitted in the same Manner, on *Wednesday* the 26th.

"The Day following, just after we had passed a Place called the *Murdering*-Town (where we intended to quit the Path, and steer across the Country for *Shannapins* Town) we fell in with a Party of *French* Indians, who had lain in Wait for us. One of them fired at Mr. *Gist,* or me, not 15 steps off, but fortunately missed. We took this fellow into Custody, and kept him till about 9 o'clock at Night; Then let him go, and walked all the remaining Part of the Night without making any Stop; that we might get the start, so far, as to be out of the Reach of their Pursuit the next Day, since we were well assured they would follow our Tract as soon as it was light. The next Day we continued travelling till quite dark, and got to the River [Allegheny] about two Miles above *Shannapins*. We expected to have found the River frozen, but it was not, only about 50 Yards from each Shore; The Ice I suppose had broken up above, for it was driving in vast Quantities.

"There was no way for getting over but on a Raft; Which we set about with but one poor Hatchet, and finished just after Sunsetting. This was a whole Day's Work. Then set off; But before we were Half Way over, we were jammed in the Ice, in such a Manner that we expected every Moment our Raft to sink, and ourselves to perish. I put-out my setting Pole to try to stop the Raft, that the Ice might pass by; when the Rapidity of the Stream threw it with so much violence against the Pole, that it jerked me out into ten Feet Water: but I fortunately saved myself by catching hold of one of the Raft Logs. Notwithstanding all our efforts we could not get the Raft to either Shore; but were obliged, as we were near an Island to quit our Raft and make to it.

"The Cold was so extremely severe, that Mr. *Gist* had all his Fingers, and some of his Toes frozen; but the water was shut up so hard, that we found no Difficulty in getting-off the Island, on the Ice, in the Morning, and went to Mr. *Frazier's*."

THE VALLEY OF VIRGINIA IN 1748

One of the largest landgrants in Virginia was the Northern Neck grant owned by Lord Fairfax, one of the few titled Englishmen to make his home in Virginia. Lord Fairfax was Washington's patron, and selected the youth in 1748 for his first experiences on the frontier. This was more than twenty years after the first movement into the Valley. The settlement, especially of the northern part, was fairly rapid, since there was at that time no Indian trouble. The settlers and the remaining Indians continued as quiet neighbors until 1753; the fact that the pioneers were from Pennsylvania is said to have been a reason for this—a reflex of Penn's comparatively enlightened policy. Against settlers from eastern Virginia, however, the "Long Knife" men, the Indians showed animosity. In 1753 the Indians, after a visit by western tribe emissaries, left the Valley, which, if the settlers could have read the signs, would have been recognized as meaning trouble. By 1734 the inhabitants were demanding a seat of justice nearer than Fredericksburg which was the shire town of Spotsylvania County, within the vast bounds of which the Valley was included. In that year Orange County was formed, but still including land on both sides of the Blue Ridge, and five justices were named for the Valley region. Finally, in 1738, the region west of the Blue Ridge was organized by itself in two counties, Frederick on the north and Augusta on the south.

The upper portion of the Valley was opened later than the lower end and, as stated above, by Scotch-Irish rather than Germans. John Lewis, father of Thomas, one of the surveyors of the Fairfax line, was the first of the race. He settled near present Staunton, probably in 1737. Though Washington's relations were less intimate with this section, yet as he was commander of the frontier it was during the war under his control and frequent inspection. But the Valley throughout was still the pioneer land when Washington first visited it. Settlements "were widely separated and large areas of country entirely destitute of inhabitants." Game abounded; and though there were not many Indians living there, it was still a war trail for the perpetually contending northern and southern tribes.

WASHINGTON WITH A TRANSIT
(1748)

Washington records some of the experiences and impressions of frontier conditions that he met in his first survey expedition in 1748, when for the first time, so to say, he saw life in the raw. "*Tuesday* [March] *15th* We . . . return'd to Penningtons we got our Supper and was lighted into a Room and I not being so good a Woodsman as ye rest of my Company striped myself very orderly and went in to ye Bed as they called it when to my Surprize I found it to be nothing but a Little Straw-Matted together without Sheets or anything else but only one thread Bear blanket with double its Weight of Vermin such as Lice Fleas &c I was glad to get up (as soon as y. Light was carried from us) I put on my Cloths and Lay as my Companions. Had we not been very tired I am sure we should not have slep'd much that night I made a Promise not to Sleep so from that time forward chusing rather to sleep in y. open Air before a fire as will appear hereafter. . . .

"*Wednesday 16th* We . . . Travell'd up to Frederick Town [Winchester] where our Baggage came to us we cleaned ourselves (to get Rid of y. Game we had catched y. Night before) and took a Review of y. Town and thence return'd to our Lodgings where we had a good Dinner prepar'd for us Wine and Rum Punch in Plenty and a good Feather Bed with clean Sheets which was a very agreeable regale . . .

"*Saturday 26* Travelld up ye [Patterson's] Creek to Solomon Hedges Esqr one of his Majestys Justices of ye. Peace for ye County of Frederick where we camped when we came to Super there was neither a Cloth upon ye. Table nor a knife to eat with but as good luck would have it we had knives of [our] own. . . .

"*Monday* [April] *4th* . . . we did two Lots and was attended by a great Company of People Men and Women and Children that attended us through ye. Woods as we went showing there Antick tricks I really think they seemed to be as Ignorant a Set of People as the Indians they would never speak English but when spoken to they speak all Dutch . . ."

He wrote, probably a year or so later, when again in the Valley surveying: "since you receid my Letter in October Last I have not sleep'd above three Nights or four in a bed but after walking a good deal all the Day lay down before the fire upon a Little Hay Straw Fodder or bairskin whichever is to be had with Man Wife and Children like a Parcel of Dogs or Catts and happy's he that gets the Birth nearest the fire there's nothing would make it pass of tolerably but a good Reward a Dubbleloon is my constant gain every Day that the Weather will permit my going out and some time Six Pistoles . . . I have never had my cloths of but lay and sleep in them like a Negro except the few Nights I have lay'n in Frederick Town"

THE MORAVIANS ON THE FRONTIER (1747)

During these early years of the Valley settlement, Moravian missionaries made visits to the outlying members of their flocks, and have left in their diaries a valuable record of what they saw and felt in western Maryland, Shenandoah Valley, and on the south branch of the Potomac, to which the settlements had extended, and where Washington surveyed in 1748. Schnell records in 1747: "July 6th—In the evening we came to the Patomik River, being very tired. We stayed with an Englishman over night. Our poor lodging place reminded us that Jesus had also lain in a stable. . . .

"July 8th. Since we learned that we would not find a house today for thirty miles, but only mountains and bad roads, we took a man with us who conducted us over the mountains. It was a way the like of which I have not seen in America. In the evening we came to an Englishman with whom we stayed over night. . . .

"I visited a place called 'Betessens Creek' [Patterson's Creek], where many German's live, interspersed among Low Dutch [Hollanders] and English New Lights. The High Germans are a poor people, internally as well as externally. . . .

"July 12th, . . . Many complained about their forsaken condition, that they had not been to the Lord's Supper for four years for want of a minister. The people asked us to come again if possible. We had much pity for them. . . .

"July 22nd. . . . In the evening we came to a German. When he heard that we were from Bethlehem and I a preacher, he asked us for our own sakes to return to Pennsylvania at once, as a notice had been posted on the courthouse that all preachers should be arrested who traveled without a passport from England."

A MISSIONARY OF THE FRONTIER (1748)

In 1748 Gottschalk made the journey, Washington being then in the vicinity.

"On March 14-25 [o. s. and N. s.], . . . In the evening I came to the last house, that of an Indian trader [Polk, on the Maryland side of the Potomac], beyond which there was no house for forty miles. It was a very disorderly house. The man was not at home. I asked the Lamb to protect me and it was done.

"On March 15-26, I arose early, being very glad and thankful to the Lord for having delivered me from this house. The Saviour gave me grace to speak to several people, who had conducted themselves very badly the night before.

"I continued joyfully on my way. Today I crossed the high North Mountain, the appearance of which everywhere was terrible. If one is down in the valley he cannot look up to the high, steep mountains without shuddering. And if one is up on the top of the mountains, the deep valleys, in which no bottom but only the tops of the trees are seen and the rushing of the water is heard, are also awe inspiring. The last and highest mountain is called 'High Germany,' and immediately after it is a deep valley, called 'Devil's Alley,' because it looks so terrible. But the Lamb helped me through safely with my horse. . . .

"On March 16-27, I asked the Lord very urgently that, as I was to enter Virginia today for the first time, he should show me the right persons and places. I had hardly entered the house again when Abraham Degart offered to take me to 'Bateson's Creek,' where we arrived late, but safely, in the evening.

"On March 17-28, I went up to the South Branch [of the Potomac]. I had to climb a terrible mountain, and at the same time it rained very hard. I came to an Englishman, Daniel Onar, who showed me much love, and soon afterwards to a German, named Kasselman, in whose house I felt a peculiar grace.

The people sat around me and gave me an opportunity to speak to them. They would have liked to give me a horse to Matthaes Jochem, if it had been possible to take it across the South Branch. The weather being so bad Mr. Kasselman accompanied me three miles, he took me across the South Branch and assisted me in getting a horse from an Englishman, named Collins. Kasselman said to him: 'Mr. Collins, here is a friend, who would like to hire one of your horses. Let him have one, and if he runs away with it, I will pay you for it.' Whereupon the Englishman was not only immediately willing to give me one of his horses, but also asked me to preach in his house to the English people living there. I replied that I would be willing to speak as well as I could, if there were people willing to hear of the Saviour, and I appointed a sermon for the 18-29th, at four o'clock. Then I rode away. During the night it became so dark that I could no longer see the way. I went astray several times, and finally, late at night, eight miles this side of Matthaes Jochem's, I came to a German, named Heiter, with whom I stayed over night.

RIVAL DENOMINATIONS (1748)

"On April 3-March 23, I came to the real German settlement, and among others to a man named George Daehlinger, at whose house Bro. Schnell lodged and preached. The congregation [of the Brethren] is known and loved there as little as the Saviour himself. I found that the people in that district are not pleased with the preaching of the Brethren, but become angry and bitter about it. When they learned afterwards that Bro. Schnell was a Herrnhutter, they wanted to pick a quarrel with Daehlinger, because he did not only not arrest him, but allowed him to preach and even helped him along with his horses. I felt the bitter, hostile and sarcastic spirit of the people in that district very much, and as the conditions were the same at Cedar Creek and in some respects even worse, I did not have the heart to preach to these people, but left again on the next day. The door at these two places is really closed."

MORAVIAN JOURNEY TO NORTH CAROLINA (1753)

In 1753 a more extensive journey was undertaken by a party of fifteen from Bethlehem to the proposed Moravian settlement at Wachovia (Winston - Salem), North Carolina.

"On October 13, . . . When the storm was over, we started at twelve o'clock midnight and traveled several miles farther to the next creek. We passed a little town, called 'Carl Isles' [Carlisle, Pa.], consisting of about 60 houses and inhabited mostly by Irishmen.

"On Sunday, October 14, about 4 o'clock in the morning, we pitched our tent four miles this side of [beyond] 'Carl Isles,' in order not to be an eyesore to the Irish Presbyterians. We lay down for several hours and

slept well and peacefully. After breakfast the brethren were shaved. The rest of the time we spent happily in our tent. At noon we ate pork and dumplings. . . . Towards evening we went three miles farther to the widow Tennent's tavern. This night we stayed on the other side of the creek. Several people came to us, who lodged in the tavern, to see what kind of people we were. We inquired of them about the way. They were very obliging towards us. . . .

"On October 19, . . . The brethren secured bread and hay and brought it to the 'great road' where the other brethren waited with the wagon. . . . We bought several bushels of oats, but had to wait several hours till it had been threshed. Several Germans came to us, of whom we inquired about the way. They gave us bad news, that beyond 'Augusti' Court House the way is so bad that we would hardly be able to proceed. . . .

"On October 24, . . . Three miles farther we came to 'Augusti Court House' [Staunton], a little town of some twenty houses, surrounded by mountains on all sides. This whole district is settled by Irish and English people. Immediately behind 'Augusti Court House' the bad road begins. . . . The road ran up and down continually, and we had either to push the wagon or keep it back with ropes which we had fastened to the rear. There was no lack of water, for every two miles we met creeks. We pitched our tent eight miles this side of 'Augusti Courthouse,' close to a spring and an old dilapidated house. Bro. Loesch went to several plantations to buy feed for our horses. But the people had none themselves. However, they were very friendly and regretted that they could not help us.

"On October 25, . . . In the evening we pitched our tent upon a height. We had to fetch water from a considerable distance. Bro. Gottlob had preceded us half a mile to a free negro, who is the only blacksmith in this district. He had his horse shod. The negro and his wife, who was born in Scotland, were very friendly towards Bro. Gottlob and related to him that not long ago they had removed hither from Lancaster County. . . .

"On October 26, . . . Although it is very hilly here, yet it is a fruitful county. It has a few stones, but consists of the fattest, black soil. It is settled mostly by English and Irish people. Bro. Gottlob and Nathanael preceded us several miles and stayed, a mile and a half across the North Branch of the James River [near present Lexington], with Mr. Brickstone, a well-to-do man, who removed to this place a few years ago . . ."

SETTLEMENTS BEYOND THE VALLEY

This was the condition of the Valley of Virginia before the outbreak of the French and Indian War. Though still pioneer, it was not by that time the extreme western line. Mention has been made of the settlements on both branches of the upper Potomac. Dr.

Thomas Walker, exploring into Kentucky in 1750 under a contract for a settlement, says: "16th March. We kept up the Staunton to William Englishes. He lives on a small Branch, and was not much hurt by the Fresh. He has a mill, which is the furthest back except one lately built by the Sect of People who call themselves of the Brotherhood of Euphrates, and are commonly called the Duncards, who are the upper Inhabitants of the New River, which is about 400 yards wide at this place. They live on the west side, and we were obliged to swim our horses over. The Duncards are an odd set of people, who make it a matter of Religion not to Shave their Beards, ly on beds, or eat flesh, though at present, in the last, they transgress, being constrained to it, they say, by the want of a sufficiency of Grain and Roots, they have not long been seated here. I doubt the plenty and deliciousness of Venison and Turkeys has contributed not a little to this. The unmarried have no Property but live on a common Stock. They don't baptize either Young or Old, they keep their Sabbath on Saturday, and hold that all men shall be happy hereafter, but first must pass through punishment according to their Sins. They are very hospitable."

This settlement was near the mouth of the Little River in present Pulaski County, Va. A few days later he helped Stalkaner raise his house on the Holston River. This was put down in Fry and Jefferson's map of 1751 as the most western habitation, and this and the Dunkard settlement were on the western side of the Alleghenies. There was further activity in this region up to 1755. The inhabitants on the branches of the Potomac and Patterson's Creek were in present West Virginia; and there were attempted settlements on the westward-flowing Greenbrier and Cheat. To the north and south of Virginia the frontier line was being pushed forward also. Washington's interests were concerned with western Pennsylvania, much of which was claimed by Virginia, as well as with his native colony. There, however, at the outbreak of hostilities, the frontier line was still east of the mountains, though there were various trading posts, including some of the Ohio Company, on the western waters. For instance, when Washington reached Venango on his journey to the French commandant, he found the French occupying the house from which they had driven the English trader Frazier.

INDIAN RAIDS (1755-1758)

Following Washington's Fort Necessity expedition, and especially after Braddock's defeat in 1755, the frontier was ablaze between Carolina and New York. In the north and south, the Iroquois and Cherokees being friendly to the British, the forays of the French Indians were held in check; but across the line throughout its length in Virginia and Pennsylvania the hostile tribes made raid after raid, destroyed the outlying settlements, and brought terror to those even in the well-settled regions.

Such petitions as the following to the Virginia Assembly are illustrative: "April 3, 1758 . . . That a Memorial of John Smith, late Captain of a Company of Rangers on the Frontiers of this Colony, . . . was read, setting forth That in June, 1756 the said Smith, then in Fort Vauss [Vass] in Augusta, with a small Party, was attacked by the Enemy, which (after having defended it till he had but three Men left) he was at length obliged to surrender: That the Enemy then most inhumanly murdered his eldest Son before his Face, and carried him Prisoner to the Shawnese Towns and French Forts, and from thence to Quebec, where he was put on Board a Cartel Ship and carried to England. . . . That he has lost three Sons and great Part of his Fortune in the Service of his Country."

"March 20, 1761 . . . A Petition of Mary Ingles setting forth that in the Year 1756 she was with her Husband in Fort Vaux [Vass], in Augusta, when he was killed and she carried away into Captivity by the Indians, amongst whom she was barbarously treated; and on her Return into the Colony she found her House and her whole effects burned, and was thereby reduced to the utmost Distress, since which she has been supported entirely by the charitable Contributions of the Welldisposed, and praying Relief of the House, was presented to the House and read."

WASHINGTON ON THE RAIDS

Washington describes rather emotionally the state of affairs in a letter to Dinwiddie, April 22, 1756: "Your Honor may see to what unhappy straits the distressed inhabitants as well as I, am reduced. I am too little acquainted, Sir, with pathetic language, to attempt a description of the people's distresses, though I have a generous soul, sensible of wrongs, and swelling for redress. But what can I do? If bleeding, dying! would glut their insatiate revenge, I would be a willing offering to savage fury, and die by inches to save a people. I see their situation, know their danger, and participate their sufferings, without having it in my power to give them further relief, than uncertain promises. In short, I see inevitable destruction in so clear a light, that, unless vigorous measures are taken by the Assembly, and speedy assistance sent from below, the poor inhabitants that are now in forts, must unavoidably fall, while the remainder of the country are flying before the barbarous foe. In fine, the melancholy situation of the people, the little prospect of assistance, the gross and scandalous abuses cast upon the officers in general, which is reflecting upon me in particular, for suffering misconducts of such extraordinary kinds, and the distant prospects, if any, that I can see, of gaining honor and reputation in the service, are motives which cause me to lament the hour, that gave me a commission, and would induce me, at any other time than this of imminent danger, to resign without one hesitating moment, a command, which I never expect to reap either honor or benefit from; but, on the contrary, have almost an absolute certainty of incurring displeasure below, while the murder of poor innocent babes and helpless families may be laid to my account here!

"The supplicating tears of the women, and moving petitions from the men, melt me into such deadly sorrow, that I solemnly declare, if I know my own mind, I could offer myself a willing sacrifice to the butchering enemy, provided that would contribute to the people's ease."

MAURY ON THE INSECURITY OF THE FRONTIER (1756)

Reverend James Maury was one of those to bring the matter earnestly to the attention of the Burgesses. He wrote, February 10, 1756: "Not to mention the repeated Acts of Hostility and Violence, committed on our Fellow-subjects, in the remoter Parts of this Colony, by those bloody Instruments of french Policy, the Indians; nor the great Extent of country, on both Sides the Alleghenies, now almost totally depopulated by them; which are Facts long since notorious to all: I beg Leave to inform You, that such Numbers of People have lately transplanted themselves hence into the more southerly Governments, as must appear almost incredible to any, except such, as have had an Opportunity of knowing it, either from their own Observation, or the credible Information of others, or both. From the waters of Potomac, James and Roanoke Rivers on the eastern Side of the above-mentioned Ridge of Mountains, nay from the same Side of the blue Ridge, hundreds of Families have, within these few Months past, removed, deserted their Habitations, & conveyed themselves & their most valuable Movables into other Governments. . . . And they, Sir, notwithstanding those Measures, & all others, which have yet been pursued with the Views, still look upon our Frontiers to be in so insecure & defenseless a State, as to justify their Apprehensions, that the same bloody Tragedies, which were acted at the Expence of their Neighbours last Summer, will, if they stay, be reacted the insuing at their own. If only fifty Indians, which they believe to be as many as were upon our Borders in the Southwest last Year, of which they, perhaps, are the best Judges, made such Havoc & Desolation; drove off upwards of two Thousand Head of Cattle & Horses to support themselves & the Enemy at Duquesne, besides what they wantonly destroyed; & if so contemptible a Band depopulated & ravaged so large a Tract of Country; they suspect, much greater Numbers, animated & tempted by the extraordinary Success of those few, will e'er long renew the same Hostilities, &, consequently, much greater and more extensive Mischiefs insue. And certain it is, should that be attempted, & no effectual Methods pursued to defeat the Attempt, many Parts of the Colony, now several Miles within their Frontiers, will shortly become frontier in their Turn. . . . It is generally believed by the most prudent & discerning in this Part of the Country, that, during the present Troubles, nothing will put a Stop to this prevailing Humour of removing southerly, because nothing will convince the People they are safe, but a Line of Forts, extended quite across the Colony, as a Barrier against Incursions of the Barbarians."

CHAIN OF FRONTIER FORTS
(1756-1758)

This remedy of a line of forts was adopted in both Virginia and Pennsylvania. The Virginia General Assembly, by an act of March, 1756, ordered a chain of forts from Cacapon River in present Hampshire Co., W. Va., to the south fork of the Mayo River in present Halifax Co., Va. A council of militia officers at Augusta on July 27, 1756, which Washington did not attend, designated the location of the forts, which with four already built were to be the guard line. These were, however, not adequately manned; and they neglected the best means of defense, through offense, since, in spite of Washington's pleadings, no adequate provision was made to employ the services of the friendly Indians, who alone could offset the raids. These public forts were not the only defensive points, however. Boughter says that there were some seventy-five forts and stockades, major and minor, along the Virginia frontier from the Forks of the Ohio to Carolina; some withstood the Indian attacks, others, like Fort Vass mentioned above, succumbed. They did not stop the incursions, and by the end of 1758 the frontier had been driven in all along the line. The fact that one of the most important of the fortifications was at Winchester indicates the depth of the terror.

Washington as commander-in-chief of the Virginia forces was in the midst of all the trouble; in fact, as the above letter shows, felt a heavy responsibility for the conditions, though he was for the most part helpless to alter them. These years of trial, coming when he was still in young manhood, receptive to external surroundings and influences, not only helped to build his character but gave him a valuable knowledge of the frontier state of mind, which was useful later in life both in war and in peace. The personal phase is treated in other articles in this series, especially those on the Indian contacts and on his colonial military training.

WASHINGTON'S IMPRESSIONS (1784)

Washington was again in the West in 1770. His last visit was in 1784 when Indian troubles prevented him from going down the Ohio. The fourteen years had witnessed the Revolution, which in the West had been another series of Indian conflicts and these, indeed, continued for another ten years. His comments at this time on the squatters on his Pennsylvania lands have been given above; and in his general comments on the tour, which had this time the development of trans-alleghenian transportation as one of the motives, he wrote, October 4, 1784: "And tho' I was disappointed in one of the objects which induced me to undertake this journey namely to examine into the situation quality and advantages of the Land which I hold upon the Ohio and Great Kanhawa—and to take measures for rescuing them from the hands of Land Jobbers and Speculators—who I had been informed regardless of my legal and equitable

rights, patents, &ca.; had enclosed them within other Surveys and were offering them for Sale at Philadelphia and in Europe.—I say notwithstanding this disappointment I am well pleased with my journey, as it has been the means of my obtaining a knowledge of facts—coming at the temper and disposition of the Western Inhabitants—and making reflections thereon, which, otherwise, must have been as wild, incohert., or perhaps as foreign from the truth, as the inconsistency of the reports which I had received even

from those to whom most credit seemed due, generally were."

This was prophetic of the need of just such knowledge in the years to come when as head of the new nation one of the problems he had to meet was the character and points of view of these same frontiersmen, in the consideration of Indian affairs, foreign affairs, westward extension, and that developing democracy so closely associated with them and the children who inherited their spirit.

Part II
Washington's Contact with the Indians

SURVEYING TRIP (1748)

Washington's connection with Indians began in 1748 on his first survey expedition beyond the Blue Ridge. He records in his diary that on March 23 at Cresap's (present Oldtown on the upper Potomac) "we were agreeably surpris'd at y. sight of thirty odd Indians coming from War with only one Scalp We had some Liquor with us of which we gave them Part it elevating there Spirits put them in y. Humour of Dauncing of whom we had a War Daunce." He describes "there manner of Dauncing . . . in a most comical Manner." This was merely incidental and Indians were not at that time numerous so far eastward.

CARRYING WARNING TO THE FRENCH (1753)

In November, 1753, he was sent by Governor Dinwiddie to deliver to the French commandant on the Ohio a letter of protest and warning for encroaching on territory which Virginia claimed. This was land which, most emphatically, the Indians also claimed, and from which the English rather than the French were likely to push them back; for the English settled while the French did little more than trade. It was part of Washington's task to gain their confidence, to enhance their restlessness over the French intrusion, to make them forgetful of the past harrying by the English, and to prevent too much inquisitiveness concerning the colonial intentions.

He with Gist, a sturdy frontiersman who was his guide, met the Indians at Logstown, a trading post on or near the Ohio at Big Beaver Creek—chiefs of the Delawares, Shawnees, Senecas, and others, including the Half-King, the most important Indian of the region and just then unfriendly to the French—, had speech with them and gave wampum; and a party of them, including Half-King, conducted him first to the Indian town of Venango (at present Franklin, Pa.) and then to Fort Le Boeuf (near

present Waterford), where he delivered his letters on December 12 and received a reply. The French attempted to separate the Indians from the Virginians; but the party held together until Venango was reached on the return trip on December 22.

In his speech to the Indians at Logstown he said: " 'Brothers . . . I am sent, with all possible Dispatch, to visit, and deliver a Letter to the *French* Commandant, of very great Importance to your Brothers, the *English*; and I dare say, to you . . . because His Honour our Governor treats you as good Friends and Allies; and holds you in great Esteem.' . . . He [Half-King] returned . . . and came with . . . other Sachems to my Tent, and begged . . . to know on what Business we were going to the *French*? this was a Question I all along expected, and has provided as satisfactory Answers to, as I could; which allayed their Curiosity a little."

At Venango: "We found the *French* Colours hoisted at a House from which they had driven Mr. *John Frazier*, an *English* subject. . . . Capt. *Joncaire* sent for the Half-King, as he had just heard that he came with me: He affected to be much concerned that I did not make free to bring them in before. I excused it in the best Manner I was capable, . . . But another Motive prevented me . . . I knew he was Interpreter, and a Person of great great Influence among the *Indians*, and had lately used all possible Means to draw them over to their Interest; therefore I was desirous of giving no Opportunity that could be avoided. When they came in, there was great Pleasure expressed at seeing them. He . . . applied Liquor so fast, that they were soon rendered incapable of the Business they came about [to return the French speech belt], notwithstanding the Caution which was given. . . . The Half-King came to my Tent, quite sober, . . . I fain would have prevented him speaking any Thing till

he came to the Commandant [at Fort Le Boeuf], but could not prevail. . . . The King . . . offered the *French* Speech-Belt . . . which Monsieur Joncaire refused to receive; but desired him to carry it to the Fort to the Commander. . . . We found it extremely difficult to get the *Indians* off Today, as every Stratagem had been used to prevent their going-up with me."

At Fort Le Boeuf: "As I found many Plots concerted to retard the *Indians* Business, and prevent their returning with me; I endeavor'd all that lay in my Power to frustrate their Schemes, and to hurry them on to execute their intended Design. They accordingly pressed for Admittance this Evening, which at length was granted them privately, . . . The Half-King told me, that he offer'd the Wampum to the Commander [Le Gardeur de St. Pierre], who evaded taking it, and made many fair Promises of Love and Friendship; . . . The Commandant ordered a plentiful Store of Liquor, Provision, &c., to be put on Board our Canoe; and appeared to be extremely complaisant, though he was exerting every Artifice which he could invent to set our own *Indians* at Variance with us, to prevent their going 'till after our Departure. Presents, Rewards, and every Thing which could be suggested by him or his Officers.—I can't say that ever in my Life I suffered so much Anxiety . . . But I urged and insisted with the King so closely upon his Word, that he . . . set off with us as he had engaged." When he and Gist had finally reached Frazier's post on the Monongahela after their perilous foot journey from Venango, he concluded the diary with the dry remark that "I went-up about three Miles . . . to visit Queen *Aliquippa* [Delaware], who had expressed great Concern that we passed her in going to the Fort. I made her a Present of a Matchcoat and a Bottle of Rum; which latter was thought much the best Present of the Two."

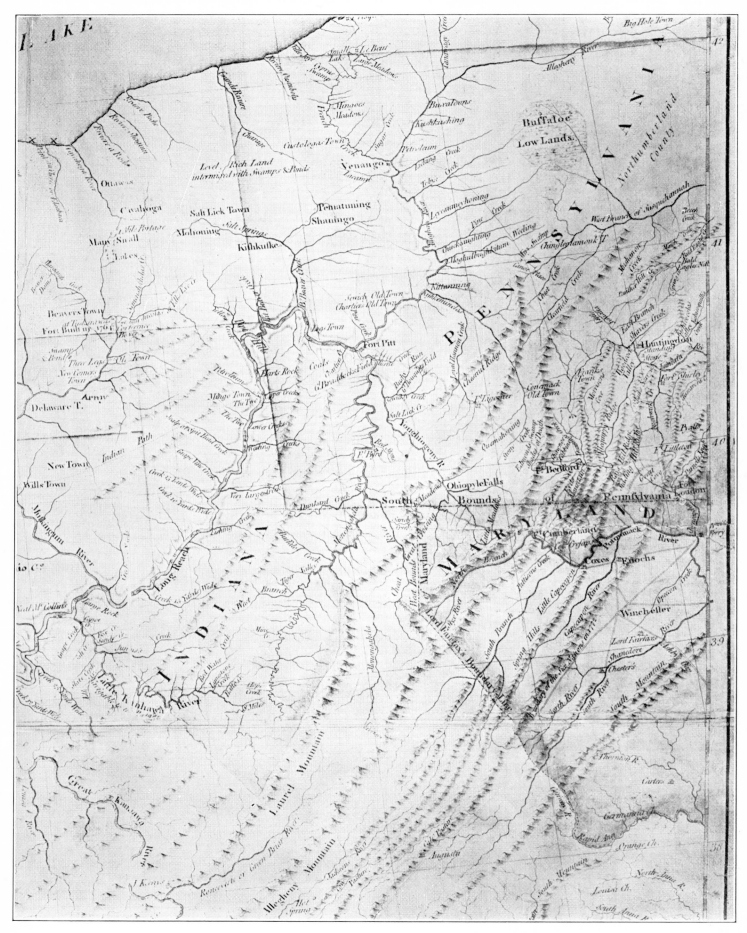

THE INDIAN FRONTIER IN WASHINGTON'S YOUTH
From Thomas Hutchins, Map of the Western Parts, 1778

FORT NECESSITY EXPEDITION (1754)

In April, 1754, Washington's command, marching to complete the fort at the Forks of the Ohio, was met at Cresap's by the news that the French had driven the English away. The works in French hands became Fort Duquesne. Here also a speech and belt from Half-King were delivered and a council of war at Fort Cumberland decided to continue the advance to the Monongahela to assist the Indians, "whose interest is as dear to us as our lives." During the next months, and until Washington surrendered to the French at Fort Necessity, contact with the Indians was continuous, and all possible efforts were made to win their alliance, or neutrality at least, in the forthcoming struggle with the French. Results were not good, however, and the Indians were critical of Washington's conduct of affairs.

Washington's journal of this expedition was captured by the French, and is known only through a French translation of it. The original, if it still exists in the French archives, has not been unearthed. According to this document he went forward from Fort Necessity and held a council with the Indians June 18-21, Half-King with others of the Six Nations, Shawnees, and Delawares, who indicated their unfavorable intentions. "We . . . have been informed that you threaten to destroy entirely all your brethren the Indians, who will not join you on the road; wherefore we who keep in our own towns, expect every day to be cut to pieces by you. We should be glad to know from your own mouth whether there be any truth in that information, . . . We know the French will ask us on our return, of what number our brethren are whom we went to see? Therefore we desire you, by this belt, to let us know it, as also the number of those whom you expect and at what time you expect them, and when you intend to attack the French, that we may give notice thereof to our town, and know also, what we are to tell the French."

WASHINGTON'S APPEAL TO THE INDIANS (1754)

Washington replied: "The English do not intend to hurt you, or any of your allies; . . . they . . . sent an army to maintain your rights; to put you again in possession of your lands, and to take care of your wives and children, to dispossess the French, to maintain your rights and to secure the whole country for you; for these very ends are the English arms now employed: it is for the safety of your wives and your children that we are fighting; and as this is the only motive of our conduct we cannot reasonably doubt of being joined by the rest of your forces to oppose the common enemy. Those who will not join us shall be answerable for whatever may be the consequence, we only desire your brethren to choose the side which seems most acceptable to them. . . . as we have drawn the sword in your cause and in your defence, hesitate

no longer, delay not a moment, but put all your wives and children under our protection, and they shall find plenty of provisions; in the meanwhile set your young men and your warriors to sharpening their hatchets, to join and unite with us vigorously in our battles. The present, my Brethren, which I offer you is not so considerable as I could wish, but I expect in a short time, a quantity of goods, . . ." This speech was to the Six Nations; to the Delawares who were believed to have gone over to the French already a similar answer was made. "After this the Council broke up and those treacherous devils [the Delawares], who had been sent by the French to act as spies, returned, though not without some stories prepared to amuse the French, which may be of service to make our own designs succeed."

There is further evidence, in a letter to Dinwiddie on June 12, that he was fast learning his Indian lore and other diplomacy: "Queen Aliquippa desired that her son, who is really a great warrior, might be taken into council, as he was declining and unfit for business, and that he should have an English name given him. I therefore called the Indians together by the advice of the Half-King, presented one of the medals, and desired him to wear it in remembrance of his great father, the King of England, and called him the name of *Colonel Fairfax*, which he was told signified *the first of the council*. This gave him great pleasure. I was also informed, that an English name would please the Half-King, which made me presume to give him that of your Honour, and called him *Dinwiddie*; interpreted in their language, *the head of all*." Half-King, who remained loyal, died before the end of the year.

IN THE BRADDOCK CAMPAIGN (1755)

Washington held no official position in the Braddock campaign, he was merely a volunteer aide to the general; but his knowledge of the region and his earlier acquaintance with the Indians and their methods of warfare and thought, made his advice of great value even though Braddock would not or could not always profit by it. The French had won ascendancy over the Indians of the region and Braddock's force was without natives except a few as guides, the others who joined from time to time meeting with such a reception that they speedily departed; so that the defeat was due not to a surprise but to the fact that a force using Indian tactics in the forest defeated an army made up largely of British regulars unable or at least unwilling to adopt the only warfare possible in the region. No diary was kept during the expedition, at least none is now known to exist; and there is nothing in the published letters on Indian connections with the march.

ON THE FRONTIER (1755-1758)

During the next three years Washington's task as commander in chief of the Virginia forces was to guard the frontier from Indian raids, with headquarters at Fort Cumberland and Winchester, and inspections of the inadequate line of "little paultry forts" beyond. The raids continued, however, and the pioneers were pushed back so that the frontier line when the French and Indian War ended was far within its position before that conflict. There were some Indians with the Forbes expedition against Fort Duquesne in 1758, Washington, who commanded the Virginia force of the army, having stressed the importance of it; but, except for the annihilation of Grant's detachment in a rash advance, there was no fighting.

No diaries are available for this period. Many letters were written on his task, the importance of which he fully realized, writing on August 14, 1755, "that it requires more experience than I am master of, to conduct an affair of the importance that *this* is now arisen to;" and again, April 7, 1756: "Our detachments . . . have sought them [Indian raiders] diligently, but the cunning and vigilance of Indians in the woods are no more to be conceived, than they are to be equalled by our people. Indians are only match for Indians; and without these, we shall ever fight upon unequal terms." On unequal terms the fight continued; the only available savages were the Cherokees and other southern tribes, and they did not accept to any extent the offers made to them, though Washington continued to "advise, as I often have done, that there should be neither trouble nor expense omitted to bring the few, who are still inclined, into our service, and that, too, with the greatest care and expedition. A small number, just to point out the wiles and tracks of the enemy, is better than none." The little reliance that could be put in the colonial militia to check the flight of "a people overcome with fear and consternation at the inhuman murders of these barbarous savages" is made evident by his letters and memoranda.

CHEROKEES AND CATAWBAS (1756-1757)

Later in the year 1756, when Cherokees and Catawbas were expected under a promise to Virginia commissioners, he expressed his pleasure: "They will be of particular service—more than twice their number of white men. When they arrive, which I pray may be *soon*, we may deal with the French in their own way; and, by visiting their country, will keep their Indians at home. . . . Those Indians who are now coming should be shewed all possible *respect*, and the greatest *care* taken of them, as upon them much depends. 'Tis a critical time, they are very humoursome, and their assistance very necessary! One false step might not only lose us *that*, but *even* turn them against us. All kinds of necessary goods, &c., should be got for them." But Major

Lewis brought only seven Cherokee men and three squaws when some four hundred were expected. When eleven Catawbas appeared: "we undoubtedly might have had more of them, had the proper means been used to send trusty guides to invite and conduct them to us; but this is neglected . . . Indian goods are much wanted." "When I spoke about scalps, I had the Indians chiefly, indeed *solely,* in my view, knowing their jealous, suspicious natures are apt to entertain doubts at the least delay and a suspension of rewards causes a dissatisfaction and murmuring among them, which might be productive of bad events at this critical juncture."

Though there were other such dribblings of Indian allies, evidently more than one false step was taken and savage doubts entertained; for, he wrote on May 30, 1757: "We receive fresh proofs every day of the bad direction of our Indian affairs. It is not easy to tell what expenses have arisen on account of these Indians, how dissatisfied they are, and how gloomy the prospect of pleasing them appears, while we pursue our present system of management." He described the French system of single control; "whereas, with us it is everybody's business, and no one's, to supply. Every person attempts to please, and few succeed in it, because one promises *this,* and another *that;* and few can perform any thing, but are obliged to shuffle and put them off, to get rid of their importunities. Hence they accuse us of perfidy and deceit!"

The unsatisfactory conditions not only continued but augmented, so that after the Forbes expedition the Cherokees became actively hostile. They not only raided the frontier themselves but captured Fort Londoun on the Little Tennessee River in their territory; although Washington wrote at the end of 1757 that "the sincere disposition the Cherokees have betrayed to espouse our cause heartily has been demonstrated beyond the most distant doubt; and, if rewarded in the manner in which that laudable and meritorious disposition entitles them to, would, in all human probability, soon effect a favorable change in the present (apparently) desperate situation of this poor unhappy part of his Majesty's dominions."

IN THE FORBES EXPEDITION (1758)

Washington's chief concern in 1758 was with the Forbes expedition. Cherokees for this began to assemble at Winchester early in the year. There were five hundred of them there by April, and to retain them a speedy campaign was essential. "Without this, I fear the Indians will with difficulty be restrained from returning to their nation before we assemble, and, in that event, no words can tell how much they will be missed. . . . The Indians are mercenary: every service of theirs must be purchased: and they are easy offended, being thoroughly sensible of their own importance." "They

say that they did not leave home with an intention of staying any considerable time, that they can see no appearance of our being able to take the field . . . they would go home and be back again by the time they are wanted," he added in May. He wrote Forbes on June 19 that *"all* except those who came last . . . [have returned] home. . . . Now . . . we shall be left to perform without them a march of more than 100 miles from an advanced Post . . . a great part of which will be over mountains and Rocks, and thro' such Defiles, as will enable the Enemy, with the assistance of *their* Indians, and Irregulars, and their superior knowledge of the country, to render extremely arduous, unsafe, and at best, tedious, our intended Expedition; unless we also can be assisted by a Body of Indians; who I conceive to be the best if not the *only* Troops fit to cope with Indians in such grounds. . . . The Southern Indians, of late, seem to be wavering; and have, on several occasions, discovered an inclination to break with us. I think it will admit of no doubt, that, if we should be unsuccessful in this Quarter, which Heaven avert! the united force of several powerful nations of them might be employed against us; and that such an acquisition to the Enemy would enable them to desolate our Southern Colonies, and make themselves masters of that part of the continent, is not to be questioned. Wherefore, that nothing should be omitted that might contribute to prevent so dreadful a calamity, I suggest the idea of sending a proper person immediately to the Cherokee nation; who may not only heal the differences which now subsist, but get a Body of them to join the army on their march, and no person, surely, who has the interest of our important cause at heart wou'd hesitate a moment to engage in such a Service, on the event of which our all, in a manner, depends." But it was the desertion of the Indian allies of the French, and not the presence of those of the English, that settled the campaign.

ON THE LAND SELECTION TRIP
(1770)

Washington's next journey to the frontier was in October and November, 1770, when he went to inspect and locate bounty lands beyond the Alleghenies for himself and fellow officers of the Virginia regiment. His trip took him to Pittsburgh, then down the Ohio with Capt. William Crawford to the Kanawha, and up the lower reaches of that branch. During seven years of peace the frontier line had again advanced, in disregard of the Proclamation of 1763; and the Indians had also by treaties, which they probably did not understand, relinquished land on the southern side of the Ohio as far as the mouth of the Kanawha. Conotocarious, which was his Indian name, inherited from his great-grandfather, with George Croghan the Indian agent, received a speech and string of wampum from chiefs near Pittsburgh, had Indians to accompany him

down the river, encamped at Mingo Town, below present Steubenville, underwent further down a "tedious ceremony" with another party under the leadership of a companion of the trip in 1753, and on his return left the river at Mingo Town and returned to Pittsburgh by land. He recorded his impressions of the Indians on the Ohio, who viewed "the Settlement of the People upon this River with an uneasy and jealous Eye, and do not scruple to say that they must be compensated for their Right if the People settle thereon, notwithstanding the Cession of the Six Nation's thereto." This was the treaty for Fort Stanwix in 1768; the Cherokees had also made cessions south of the Ohio; but the Shawnees, Delawares, and Mingoes had not participated. As, he continued, the settlers were constantly advancing, "how difficult it may be to contend with these People afterwards is easy to be judgd of from every day's experience of Lands actually settled, supposing these to be made; than which nothing is more probable if the Indians permit them, from the disposition of the People at present." Lord Dunmore's War in 1774, in which Washington had no share, was probably here anticipated.

INDIANS AND THE REVOLUTION-
ARY ARMY (1775-1783)

During the Revolution, Indian policy was important; first of all was the question whether the natives should be employed as auxiliaries. Both sides claimed to depreciate their enlistment; in the end both sides did use them. They participated both as British and American allies in the Burgoyne campaign, but their conduct under the British, especially in the murder of Jane McCrea, as it aroused the resentment of the people, was of far more influence on the outcome than the few hundred Oneidas under Gates. Washington, with the knowledge gained in early frontier warfare, had no doubt as to the proper policy. He wrote Schuyler, April 19, 1776: "You, who know the temper and disposition of the savages, will, I doubt not, think with me, that it will be impossible to keep them in a state of neutrality. I have urged upon Congress the necessity of engaging them on our side, to prevent their taking an active part against us, which would be a most fatal stroke under our present circumstances." His letter to the President of Congress of the same date repeats this advice; and on May 25, 1776, Congress declared it highly expedient to engage the Indians. In 1778 the Congressional Committee of Conference with Washington having so advised, the Board of War wrote that, "seeing these Gentlemen have fully discussed the matter with General Washington, and upon the maturest deliberation recommend it," some four hundred Indians might be employed; Congress so voted on March 4. Washington on March 13 wrote: "Divesting them of the savage customs exercised in their wars against each other, I think they may be made of excellent use as scouts and light troops, mixed with our own parties."

Whatever may have been done under these resolves, the Indians rendered no essential aid. Washington's policy of use was, after all, a limited one. While writing Schuyler, May 15, 1778, his regrets that the disposition of the Indians was "not generally favorable," he also regretted the arrival at Valley Forge of a party of Indians. "All appearances at this time are opposed to the supposition of any speedy offensive movement . . . there will be very little of that kind of service in which the Indians are capable of being useful. . . . I leave it to your judgment to assign such reasons as you shall deem best calculated for the change and satisfy them. I should think however, a good way might be, to inform them, with proper comments, of the [French] Treaties . . . and that in consequence of them, affairs have taken such a turn, as to make it unnecessary to give them the trouble, at this time of coming to our assistance."

The Indians all along the frontier, under the influence of the British agents and loyalist commanders, as well as natural desire, raided throughout the war; such events as the Wyoming massacre in 1778, and the Mohawk Valley incursions, left Washington "thoroughly impressed with the necessity of offensive operations against Indians, in every kind of rupture with them." An expedition to break the power of the hostile Iroquois was carefully planned and carried out; Sullivan, who was given the command in 1779 after Gates declined it, was instructed by Washington that "the immediate objects are the total destruction and devastation of their settlements, and the capture of as many prisoners of every age and sex as possible. . . . that the country may not be merely *overrun*, but *destroyed*. . . . When we have effectually chastised them, we may then listen to peace, and endeavor to draw further advantages from their fears." With the campaign against the Cherokees and Clark's operations in the Northwest, Washington had no direct connection.

ON THE FRONTIER (1784)

Washington made his last journey to the West in September of this year, intending to descend the Ohio for another inspection of the Kanawha lands. He gave it up because of the hostility of the Indians; and they were still intermittently on the warpath when he became President. "[September] 14*th*. . . . Colo Willm. Butler and the officer Commanding the Garrison at Fort Pitt, a Capt. Lucket came here—as they confirmed the reports of the discontented temper of the Indians and the Mischiefs done by some parties of them—and the former advised me not to prosecute my intended trip to the Great Kanahawa, I resolved to decline it."

PRESIDENTIAL POLICY (1789-1797)

The Federal Constitution gave the national government power over Indian affairs, and it was one of the duties of Washington's administration to organize this control. Besides the western Indians, the relations with what was left of the Iroquois and with the southern tribes, especially the Cherokees and Creeks, had to be settled. Delegates from these nations were induced to come to New York and Philadelphia. Brant, Cornplanter, and Red Jacket with the Iroquois and McGillivray with the Creeks were received by Washington, feted, including entertainment by the Tammany Society, treaties made with them there and elsewhere, and peace maintained during Washington's rule. The western problem was difficult. Expeditions under Harmar and St. Clair were defeated, and Washington, irritated especially by what he considered St. Clair's neglect of due precautions, after due consideration of available men appointed Wayne to lead a new expedition. This Revolutionary veteran, in spite of being known as "Mad Anthony," made his preparations and advance with thoroughness and care and by his complete defeat of the Indians at the battle of Fallen Timbers on August 20, 1794, opened the West to peaceful penetration for more than a decade.

President Washington's policy toward the Indians, as stated in his messages, was that "aggressors should be made sensible that the Government of the Union is not less capable of punishing their crimes than it is disposed to respect their rights and reward their attachments;" that "they should experience the benefits of an impartial dispensation of justice;" that "the mode of alienating their lands, the main source of discontent and war, should be so defined and regulated as to obviate imposition and as far as may be practical controversy concerning the reality and extent of the alienations which are made;" that "commerce with them should be promoted under regulations tending to secure an equitable deportment toward them, and that such rational experiments should be made for imparting to them the blessings of civilization as may from time to time suit their conditions;" that "the Executive of the United States should be enabled to employ the means to which the Indians have been long accustomed for uniting their immediate interests with the preservation of peace;" that "efficacious provisions should be made for inflicting adequate penalties upon all those who, by violating their rights, shall infringe the treaties and endanger the peace of the Union;" and that "a system corresponding with the mild principles of religion and philanthropy toward an unenlightened race of men, whose happiness materially depends on the conduct of the United States, would be as honorable to the national character as conformable to the dictates of sound policy."

LO THE POOR INDIAN!

To Edmund Pendleton he wrote, January 22, 1795: "They [the Indians], poor wretches, have no press through which their grievances are related; and it is well known, that, when one side only of a story is heard and often repeated, the human mind becomes impressed with it insensibly. The annual presents, however, to which you allude, are not given so much with a view to purchase peace, as by way of contribution for injuries not otherwise to be redressed. These people are very much irritated by the continual pressure of land speculators and settlers on one hand, and by the impositions of unauthorized and unprincipled traders, who rob them, in a manner, of their hunting, on the other. Nothing but the strong arm of the Union, or, in other words, adequate laws can correct these abuses. But here jealousies and prejudices, (from which I apprehend more fatal consequences to this government, than from any other source,) aided by local situations, and perhaps by interested considerations, always oppose themselves to efficient measures."

Thus did he sum up the impression acquired during an experience of almost half a century with the Indians as friends and as enemies.

Selected Authorities

BURNABY, ANDREW—*Travels through the Middle Settlements . . . 1759 and 1760.* London, T. Payne, 1775. (Other eds.)

DINWIDDIE, ROBERT—*Official Records.* 2 vols. Richmond, Va. Hist. Soc., 1883-84. (*Collections* of Va. Hist. Soc., N. s., Vols. III-IV.)

DODDRIDGE, JOSEPH—*Notes, on the Settlement and Indian Wars, of the Western Parts of Virginia and Pennsylvania.* Wellsburgh, Va., for the Author, 1824. (Various later eds.)

FITZPATRICK, JOHN C.—*George Washington, Colonial Traveller, 1732-1775.*— Indianapolis, Bobbs-Merrill, 1927.

FORD, WORTHINGTON CHAUNCEY—*George Washington.* 2 vols. New York, Scribner, 1900. (Especially Vol. I, chs. iii-vi, viii.)

GABRIEL, RALPH HENRY—*Lure of the Frontier (Pageant of America, Vol. II).* New Haven, Yale University Press, 1929.

HULBERT, ARCHER BUTLER—*Colonel Washington.* Marietta, Ohio, 1902.

JONES, DAVID—*Journal of Two Visits made to . . . Indians on the . . . Ohio . . . 1772 and 1773.* Burlington, N. J., 1774; reprint, New York, J. Sabin, 1865.

KEMPER, CHARLES E.—"Early Westward Movement of Virginia"; in *Virginia Magazine of History and Biography,* Vols. XII-XIII, 1905-6.

KERCHEVAL, SAMUEL—*History of the Valley of Virginia.* 4th ed., rev., Strasburg, Va., Shenandoah Publishing House, 1925. (1st ed., 1833.)

KOONTZ, LOUIS KNOTT—"Washington on the Frontier"; in *Virginia Magazine of History and Biography,* Vol. XXXVI, p. 307, 1928.

MACLEOD, WILLIAM CHRISTIE—*American Indian Frontier.* New York, Knopf, 1928.

MCCLURE, DAVID—*Diary, 1748-1820.* New York, 1899.

"Moravian Diaries of Travels through Virginia"; in *Virginia Magazine of History and Biography,* Vols. XI-XII, 1903-5.

RICHARDSON, JAMES, ED.—*Compilation of the Messages and Papers of the Presidents.* Vol. I. Washington, Govt. Printing Office, 1896. (Other eds.)

ROOSEVELT, THEODORE—*Winning of the West.* Vol. I. New York, Putnam, 1889. (Later eds.)

RUSH, BENJAMIN—"Account of the Manners of the German Inhabitants of Pennsylvania"; in *Essays,* Philadelphia, Bradford, 1798. (Reprint, Pennsylvania-German Society, *Proceedings,* Vol. XIX, 1910.)

SPOTSWOOD, ALEXANDER—*Official Letters.* 2 vols. Richmond, Va. Hist. Soc., 1882-85. (*Collections* of Va. Hist. Soc., N. S., Vols. I-II.)

TURNER, FREDERICK JACKSON—*Frontier in American History.* New York, Holt, 1920. (Especially the first essay, "Significance of the Frontier in American History.")

WASHINGTON, GEORGE — *Diaries, 1748-1799.* Ed. by John C. Fitzpatrick. 4 vols. Boston, Houghton Mifflin, 1925. (Contains the journals of 1753, 1754, 1770, 1784.)

WASHINGTON, GEORGE—*Writings.* Ed. by Worthington Chauncey Ford. 14 vols. New York, Putnam, 1889-93.

WAYLAND, JOHN WALTER—*German Element of the Shenandoah Valley of Virginia.* Charlottesville, Va., the Author, 1907.

ZEISBERGER, DAVID—"Diaries relating to the First Missions in the Ohio Basin"; in *Ohio Archaeological and Historical Quarterly,* Vol. XXI, p. 1, 1912.

WASHINGTON AS A SURVEYOR
From an engraving by G. R. Hall, after a drawing by F. O. C. Darley

Washington the Man of Mind
By Albert Bushnell Hart
Part I
Practical Education

GEORGE WASHINGTON
From the Gilbert Stuart painting known as the "Vaughan" portrait.

VARIETY OF EDUCATION

EORGE WASHINGTON was not an educator: all the world knows that he was a soldier and a statesman, and the Father of his Country—"first in war, first in peace, and first in the hearts of his countrymen." So much has been said about Washington as a soldier and statesman that it is hard to realize him as a live human being, associating with other gentlemen and ladies of his own period; as occupying his mind with problems of his plantation and neighborhood.

It is not an overstatement to say that Washington was the best-educated man in the United States of his day. One proof of his intellectual power is the small extent to which he became educated through books and letters, for he had very little schooling. When he had barely finished his sixteenth year he started out to make his own living; and from that day on he was busy with other things than going to school, reciting, listening to teachers, reading books, and passing examinations.

Washington was the best-educated man of his time because he was educated in many different ways. However slight his book learning, he did acquire that magnificent handwriting which is so characteristic of the man of affairs and intelligence. Everybody knows that Washington had a library—possibly a larger library than was possessed by any other gentleman in Virginia. He read books on military tactics; he read books on agriculture; he also had books of history and general literature.

In another form of education Washington throughout his life was self-educated by his habit of recording things that went on about him and of writing copious letters. Perhaps as many as 20,000 letters are in existence which contain his sentiments, most of them signed with his magnificent hand. In addition, during many years of his life Washington regularly kept diaries, which are elsewhere described.

Some modern so-called biographers attempt to make out that Washington was a slow young man, rather hardheaded, but gloomy, disappointed, discouraged, and unhappy because he was not getting on well. On the contrary, he was the liveliest, handsomest, most successful young man in Virginia. It was no accident that made him first General of the Continental Army and then President of the United States. The trouble with this so-called modern school of Washington biography is that those who write it suppose that Washington was the kind of man that they would have been if they had been Washington.

George Washington was from youth accustomed to associate with people of education and refinement. His own house was a model of hospitality and high living and lofty thinking. He was one of the busiest men that ever lived, and kept educating himself by the tasks that he set for himself. His field surveys he continued from time to time to within a few hours of his death. His travels, in which he learned so much about his countrymen and about the times, continued until the end of his days. No man in the United States had been in so many places at the time of his death as George Washington; had met so many people; had had such experiences of conversation and friendship. No American met in his own country so many cultivated foreigners. That is, there was no other American who

17

had such an opportunity of education by actual contact with the things and people that count.

EDUCATION OF OTHER PEOPLE

George Washington was greatly interested in education, as is shown by the way in which he spent money and time and thought upon the education of the young people for whom he was responsible. Among them, of course, were the Custises, the children and grandchildren of Martha Washington. To them Washington was not simply a stepfather—they were as his own children; throughout his life he was interested in their welfare and he left property to them as though they had been his own. He sent George Washington Parke Custis to Princeton College. Trouble arose, but young Custis was still of the opinion that he was a student at Princeton. The college authorities had a very different opinion; they said that whatever he might have been previously, he was no longer a student. That led Washington to write a letter, in which he reflected upon the possible opportunities for young Custis. First of all, he said the natural place would be the College in New England (Harvard). Yale he excluded from consideration, probably because it was too orthodox.

He not only sent his kindred—he sent several sons of others, paid their expenses, and was glad to do it because he so believed in education. In a statement by Washington of what he thought constituted a good booklearning, he includes a knowledge of French, in which he himself was deficient. Washington thought about education; he advised education; he practiced education.

EDUCATION OF AFFAIRS

Outside of books and colleges Washington had enjoyed the education of a man intensely busy with things of great importance. He was the first professional engineer in the colonies and the United States. He began his training at sixteen as a surveyor; he continued it as a road engineer, for he took part in the making of Braddock's Road, which was the first highway west of the headwaters of the Potomac River. He suggested routes beyond, leading across the mountains. The Baltimore and Ohio Railroad later made use of the route.

Besides his interest as a builder of roads and discoverer of routes, he was interested in steam navigation, and probably was present at the first trial of Rumsey's power boat. He examined Fitch's model of a steamboat. He was a leader in internal improvements, especially of the Potomac River. He drained part of the Dismal Swamp. He was among the first to suggest the possibility of a canal along the lines of the present Erie Canal from the upper waters of the Hudson to the Great Lakes; and he added the suggestion, revived by President Hoover, that there should also be a system of canals connecting the Great Lakes with the Ohio River and its tributaries.

AUTHORSHIP

Part of his works, leaving out the Diaries and the General Orders, have been published in an edition of fourteen volumes. The United States George Washington Bicentennial Commission is issuing a complete series of George Washington's Writings in twenty-five volumes, which will not include the Diaries.

Those diaries are a special mark of Washington's education because, although he did not record his feelings and expectations and views, he did tell from day to day where he was, the people with whom he associated and the people he visited. For George Washington was a man always educating himself by the society in which he moved.

As a public man, Washington was an author of state papers which will go down to posterity as among the ablest utterances of the human mind. The main source of our direct knowledge of Washington is his own thoughts especially as revealed in private and intimate letters.

THE ORGANIZER

Washington, throughout his life, was a man accustomed to statements of high principles in a high way. Take, for instance, sentences from his addresses to the people and private letters after the Revolution while the question of a federal government was still pending: "Today one nation; tomorrow thirteen." "Influence is no government." You have a whole political dictionary applied in that sentence. That Washington was an educated man is shown also by the tributes of various orders, learned societies and colleges as indicated by an accompanying list. In education he sat in the seats of the mighty.

George Washington was an educator because in his life he set forth what an American gentleman could be. He used every means within his power to make him understand better the world about him and his fellow men. George Washington first educated himself; then he educated the young people connected with him so far as he could reach; and eventually he educated all the people of the United States of America by his lofty character and the power of expression which marks him as one of his country's great writers. "There is one glory of the sun, and another glory of the moon, and another glory of the stars: for one star differeth from another star in glory." The glory of Washington, however, is not that of the sun or of the moon, but of the solar system, for he was one of the most many-sided men who ever lived.

Nowadays people pay little regard to the mythical Washington, a combination of Hercules, Napoleon Bonaparte, and Little Lord Fauntleroy, who always spoke in balanced periods. This majestic personality is chiefly the creation of Parsons Weems, who by his unrivalled skill in historical romance

created an artificial figure which has been accepted by a large number of people as though it was founded on facts.

The real Washington was the public man—the character most in our minds; the pioneer, the explorer, the soldier, the statesman, the patriot, the high model for mankind. The longer one lives and the more one studies American history the greater does that figure rise, great in its patience. Washington was a founder, an organizer. He could have set up a university or a social science association or an engineer's club or a Rockefeller Foundation. He had within him that incomprehensible power which enabled him to run anything from a flour mill to the United States of America.

THE INTELLECTUAL WASHINGTON

A Washington less considered than the myth, the statesman, or the home man, is the intellectual George Washington. Such a subject divides itself naturally into three parts: Washington's early training; his writings and their value; and the influence upon his country and mankind of his high standards of character and statesmanship. Of all the contributions made by the American Revolution to mankind, the two greatest are George Washington's character and George Washington's intellectual power.

Of late years we have been learning something about a third kind of Washington, the private gentleman and man of affairs. We see him riding his plantation; reproving the overseers, benevolently dosing his slaves, buying lottery tickets, on which he almost invariably lost, speculating in land, shipping his crops, buying dresses for Mrs. Washington and "Patsy Custis," "6 little books for Children beginning to Read," "1 fashionable dressed baby to cost 10 shillings," "a Box Gingerbread Toys and Sugar Images and Comfits." On the other hand, if George Washington were alive today he would be the president of locomotive works, or a railroad, or steel works.

INTELLECTUAL INFLUENCES

Of the influences upon the early development of Washington's mind, the most significant are his home, his school, his association with cultivated people, and the training of responsibility. As to Washington's home life if, as some of the neighbors of the mother of Washington thought, she was fond and unthinking with her son, she did not spoil him, and George Washington was not the only great man of the time whose mother smoked a pipe (customary to old ladies) and quarrelled with the doctor and imagined she was neglected by her very faithful son and whose vigorous traits of character reappear in her offspring. In her pioneer life she was a strong, energetic, and forcible woman. A strong influence on Washington was that of his half brothers, Lawrence and Augustine, well-to-do men of culture. From Lawrence he inherited the splendid country seat of Mount Vernon, which in itself is the evidence of the good breeding and refinement of the occupant.

To modern college graduates it is humiliating to notice how little proper schooling Washington had: he possibly had a tutor, who might or might not have been an indentured convict servant; and another who was a clergyman. He may also have gone to one or two ordinary schools, where he studied the three R's and a little "Latten." The most important result of his early schooling, on which we have no real information, was the acquisition of that fine handwriting, which is such a reproach to men of the present day.

One useless embellishment Washington spared himself: he never learned to accept the canons of spelling which were then forming; he preferred to spell glue "glew," and window "winder," and indeed, what is the use of being the father of one's country, if one must accept the children's abnormal notions of the way to spell their own language. It is not all of an English style to write with perfect grammar, nor is it all of education to go to college. It should be noted however that throughout his life Washington felt the need of education, and used all his influence to supply for his stepson and nephews and young friends the advantages which he had missed.

CRITERIONS OF EDUCATION

His notions of college education are set forth in a letter of January 2, 1771, with relation to young Custis:

"Had he begun, or rather pursued his study of the Greek Language, I should have thought it no bad acquisition; but whether [if] he acquire this now, he may not forego some more useful branches of learning, is a matter worthy of consideration. To be acquainted with the French Tongue is become a part of polite Education; and to a man who has [the prospect] of mixing in a large Circle absolutely [necessary. Without] Arithmetick, the common [affairs of] Life are not to be managed [with success. The study of Geo]metry, and the Mathe[matics (with due regard to the li]mites of it) is equally [advantageous. The principles] of Philosophy Moral, Natural, &c. I should think a very desirable knowledge for a Gentleman." In Washington's accounts appears: "Dr. James Craik, paid him, being a donation to his son, George Washington Craik, £30." The two sons of his brother Samuel he had educated at a cost "of near five-thousand dollars."

Later in life, in 1788, he was chosen chancellor of William and Mary College, an honorary position; and earlier, after first declining, he appears to have accepted membership in the governing board of Washington College, Maryland.

EDUCATION BY NEIGHBORS

Much more important for Washington's own intellectual development was his early association with cultivated people. Nowhere in America was there a more settled and aristocratic society than in Virginia; and

young Washington was made welcome by such families as the Fairfaxes, Carlyles, the "Carters of Shirley, Nomoni and Sabine Hall," the Lees of Stratford, the Byrds of Westover. The father and two brothers of Washington were educated at the school of Appleby in England. As soon as his public career began, he was brought into close association with the most highly educated statesmen of the time, Thomas Jefferson, a former student of William and Mary, and James Madison, a student of Princeton, and during his presidency he was intimate with John Adams, a graduate of Harvard, and Alexander Hamilton, student of Columbia. From the period of Braddock's campaign to the end of his life, his house was a constant resort for the most highly educated and interesting Americans and foreign visitors, and it is not remarkable that he escaped from his early faults of writing and became a man of cultured thought and of strong, keen, and agreeable expression.

EDUCATION BY RESPONSIBILITY

Washington was not only a cultured man, he was a highly educated man, educated chiefly by the experience of great responsibilities, the best of all educative systems. It is unfortunate that by the term "educated" man or woman people nowadays mean one who has had the training of schools or colleges. How many people we all know who are really educated without large acquaintance with books. Education is the training of one's individual powers, so that one may meet a new problem or new conditions, and apply to them the whole body of one's past experience. The educated man is the man who knows how to do things, even things that have never been done before. General Grant was an educated man who applied the experience of a lifetime to great military problems; but General Grant's West Point training was a small part of his education, and he used to say that he never read books; yet he showed in his last months a wonderful power of writing. Henry Ford, once a laborer, developed into what a wit calls an "automobillionaire," is an educated man. Even such a pursuit as the management and manipulation of a trust requires intellectual training. Washington was a man who knew how to make his surroundings educate him. In Braddock's army he was the largest man; in the government of Virginia under Dinwiddie he was the most aggressive man; in the second Continental Congress, the plain and quiet Colonel Washington was one of the most respected men; and from the beginning to the end of his life, Washington never threw up a responsibility because he felt that he had not the training to fulfil it.

Washington's responsibilities began early: at sixteen years old the modern American boy begins to wonder whether he could pass an examination for college; at sixteen Washington was starting out as a surveyor in the western wilds, where he camped and slept on the hard ground, and ate coarse food and

was proud of his doubloon a day. At twenty he became the heir to Mount Vernon; at twenty-one the dauntless agent of the colony of Virginia to the French frontier; at twenty-three he was the bravest figure on Braddock's field; at twenty-six he was married in blue and silver, adorned with scarlet, and wearing gold buckles; and henceforward to the Revolution he continued to be the type of the active-minded Virginia planter, head of a great family. Possibly the future General and President got some experience of life through his own responsibility for his own kindred; as for instance, niece Harriet, who he says showed "no disposition . . .to be careful of her cloathes . . . dabbed about in every hole and corner, and her best things always in use." "She costs me enough."

Washington's career as a statesman may be said to have begun after his election to the House of Burgesses of Virginia in 1758. For years he remained constantly a quiet, unassuming member of that body, containing so many men both of distinction and experience. It was years before he realized his remarkable powers of judgment and statesmanship.

SECRETARY AND TUTOR (1785)

After the war Washington tried to combine a tutorship with a secretaryship. "My purposes are these—To write letters agreeably to what shall be dictated. Do all other writing which shall be entrusted to him. Keep Accts.—examine, arrange, and properly methodize my Papers, which are in great disorder.—Ride, at my expence, to such other States, if I should find it more convenient to send, than attend myself, to the execution thereof. And, which was not hinted at in my last, to initiate two little children (a girl of six and a boy of 4 years of age, descendants of the deceased Mr. Custis, who live with me and are very promising) in the first rudiments of education. This to both parties, would be mere amusement, because it is not my wish that the Children should be confined. If Mr. Falconer should incline to accept the above stipend in addition to his board, washing and mending,—and *you* (for I would rather have *your opinion* of the gentleman than the *report* of a thousand others in his favor) upon a close investigation of his character, Temper and moderate political tenets (for supposing him an English man, he may come with prejudices, and doctrines of his Country) the sooner he comes, the better my purpose would be promoted."

SELF-EDUCATION OF A PUBLIC MAN

Except the *Journals* of 1753 and 1754, none of Washington's early writings affected the public mind. In 1775, then forty-three years old, he was put into a position which proved that of the greatest responsibility in the whole country. Benjamin Franklin was a world-renowned literary man, Hutchinson had already published several volumes of his history, read far and wide, Francis Hopkinson was about to begin his excellent satirical writings; the press abounded in controversial discussion of the issues of the Revolution, both grave and gay. No one could have predicted that the writings of George Washington would be read when all the others, except Franklin, were almost forgotten. Indeed, his speech of June 16, 1775, is the statement of a great man, little aware of his own greatness.

"Mr. President, though I am truly sensible of the high honor done me in this appointment, yet I feel great distress from a consciousness that my abilities and military experience may not be equal to the extensive and important trust. However, as the Congress desire it, I will enter upon the momentous duty and exert every power I possess in the service and for the support of the glorious cause. I beg they will accept my most cordial thanks for this distinguished testimony of their approbation. But lest some unlucky event should happen unfavorable to my reputation, I beg it may be remembered by every gentleman in the room, that I this day declare with the utmost sincerity I do not think myself equal to the command I am honored with."

No sooner had Washington become the General of the Continental Army, than he was compelled to become not only an author but the head of a literary bureau. As the war went on, he was not only commander of the army but virtual head of the government. Having a vast acquaintance among both military men and civilians, his mind was filled with the most important public questions, upon which he must express himself, and he knew no form of expression that was not vigorous. No wonder that in the Revolutionary correspondence we find a real intellectual growing power, working up to a consciousness of an ability to express his thoughts worthily.

EDUCATION OF SECRETARIES

The correspondence in Washington's own hand was vast, but the General Orders and manifold letters written by secretaries must have been many times more numerous. For a long time Washington found it difficult to attach to himself a young man with suitable power of expression. Indeed throughout his life the secretaries and assistants were convinced that they themselves composed Washington's letters. If however the secretaries are the authors of the compositions which went to presidents of congress, governors, states, heads of armies, men influential in assemblies, and personal friends, then Washington not only secured a very high but a very even quality of secretary, for from beginning to end the letters have the same characteristics. It is notable, that with the exception of Hamilton, whose literary power is undeniable, none of the young men who came close to Washington, wrote for

themselves the powerful sentences which they thought they wrote for Washington.

The truth is that Washington, realizing the responsibility, set himself carefully to the work of composition, as he did to every other task that came to him. He wrote, he reflected, he corrected, he rewrote, until he had struck out a style of his own, which may be detected in nearly all his important communications. It was not his custom to dictate letters; he never had Napoleon's facility of keeping four secretaries busy at once. It was his habit to reread letters carefully before answering them, then to write with his own hand a rough draft. In many cases these were rewritten a second time by his own hand, in others by secretaries.

After the end of the Revolution, Washington realized the historical importance of his correspondence, and secured the preparation of books of copies. In this process he made some small changes in the text, and the result is that the same letter sometimes exists in two forms in Washington's hand, and in a third form in copy. Hence some of his editors have been accused of maltreating the letters and suppressing important passages. Excellent Jared Sparks was pained that the father of his country should misspell or make false grammar and hence Sparks's edition of Washington's Writings often planed down letters and deprived them of their vigor. Nevertheless the real life and go of the spirit which indited them are plainly evident.

A few examples will illustrate the various types of Washington letters. Military letters are very numerous and chiefly formal, directing the disposition and movement of troops. Military correspondence on technical questions was very often prepared by a secretary from a draft or suggestion of Washington. Many of these military letters show remarkable pith, as for example, his answer to the letter sent him by the British Commissioner, addressed "Mr. Washington." "The letter is directed to a planter of the state of Virginia. I shall have it delivered to him at the end of the war; till that time it shall not be opened."

RESPECT FOR EDUCATION (1790)

The same interest in education is shown in a speech to Congress in 1790.

"Nor am I less persuaded, that you will agree with me in opinion, that there is nothing which can better deserve your patronage than the promotion of science and literature. Knowledge is in every country the surest basis of public happiness. In one, in which the measures of government receive their impression so immediately from the sense of the community, as in ours, it is proportionably essential. To the security of a free constitution it contributes in various ways; by convincing those who are intrusted with the public administration, that every valuable end of government is best answered by the enlightened confidence of the people; and by teaching the people themselves to know,

and to value their own rights; to discern and provide against invasions of them; to distinguish between oppression and the necessary exercise of lawful authority, between burthens proceeding from a disregard to their convenience and those resulting from the inevitable exigencies of society; to discriminate the spirit of liberty from that of licentiousness, cherishing the first, avoiding the last, and uniting a speedy but temperate vigilance against encroachments, with an inviolable respect to the laws.

"Whether this desirable object will be the best promoted by affording aids to seminaries of learning already established, by the institution of a national university, or by any other expedients, will be well worthy of a place in the deliberations of the legislature."

PLANS FOR A UNIVERSITY (1795)

What was to give the necessary opportunity of a genuine college education? For years a plan was in Washington's mind which he thus expressed with the intention to back up the plan with his own money. "I have greatly wished to see a plan adopted, by which the arts, sciences, and belles-lettres could be taught in their *fullest* extent, thereby embracing *all* the advantages of European tuition, with the means of acquiring the liberal knowledge, which is necessary to qualify our citizens for the exigencies of public as well as private life; and (which with me is a consideration of great magnitude) by assembling the youth from the different parts of this rising republic, contributing from their intercourse and interchange of information to the removal of prejudices, which might perhaps sometimes arise from local circumstances."

As appears in his own statements of the convictions in his mind: "The Federal City, from its centrality and the advantages, which in other respects it must have over any other place in the United States, ought to be preferred, as a proper site for such an university. And if a plan can be adopted upon a scale as *extensive* as I have described, and the execution of it should commence under favorable auspices in a reasonable time, with a fair prospect of success, I will grant in perpetuity fifty shares in the navigation of Potomac River towards the endowment of it."

"It has been represented, that a university corresponding with these ideas is contemplated to be built in the Federal City, and that it will receive considerable endowments. This position is so eligible from its centrality, so convenient to Virginia, by whose legislature the shares were granted and in which part of the Federal District stands, and combines so many other conveniences, that I have determined to vest the Potomac shares in that university.

"Presuming it to be more agreeable to the General Assembly of Virginia, that the shares in the James River Company should be reserved for a similar object in some part of

(21)

Mount Vernon June 17th 1788

My dear Sir,

I received your letter of the 25th of May, just when I was on the eve of departure for Fredericksburgh to pay a visit to my mother from whence I returned only last evening. —

The information of the accession of South Carolina to the New Government since your letter, gives us a new subject for mutual felicitations. — It was to be hoped this auspicious event would have had considerable influence upon the proceedings of the Convention of Virginia; but I do not find that to have been the case. — Affairs in the Convention, for some time past, have not worn so good an aspect as we could have wished: and, indeed, the acceptance of the Constitution has become more doubtful than it was thought to be at their first meeting

The purport of the intelligence, I received from my private letters by the last Nights mail, is, that every species of address & artifice has been put in practice by the Antifederalists to create jealousies & excite alarms. — Much appears to depend upon the final part which the Kentucke members will take; into many of whose minds apprehensions of unreal dangers, respecting the navigation of the Mississippi & their organization into a separate

rate State, have been industriously infused. — Each side seems to think, at present, that it has a small majority, ~~however it shall turn~~ from whence it may be supposed that the majority, however it shall turn, will be very inconsiderable. — Though, for my own part, I cannot but imagine, if any decision is had, it will be in favor of the adoption. — My apprehension is rather that a strenuous ~~possibly~~ successful effort may be made for an adjournment; under an idea of opening a correspondence with those who are opposed to the Constitution in other States. Col° Oswald has been at Richmond, it is said with letters from Antifederalists in New York & Pensylvania to their Co-adjutors in this State. —

The Resolution, which came from the Antifederalists (much to the astonishment of the other party) that no question should be taken until the whole Plan should have been discussed paragraph by paragraph; and the remarkable tardiness in their proceedings (for the Convention have been able as yet only to get through the 2d or 3d Section) are thought by some to have been designed to protract the business until that time when the Assembly is to convene, that is the 23d instant, in order to have a more colorable pretext for an adjournment. — But notwithstanding the resolution, there has been much desultory debating & the opposers of the Constitution are reported to have gone generally into the merits of the question. — I know not how the matter may be, but a few days will now determine

I am sorry to find not only from your intimations, but also from many of the returns in the late Papers, that there should be so great a majority against the Constitution in the Convention of New York — and yet I can hardly conceive, from motives of policy & prudence they will reject it absolutely, if either this State or New-Hampshire should make the 9th in adopting it — as that measure which gives efficacy to the system, must place any State that shall actually have refused its assent to the New-Union in a very awkward & disagreeable predicament

By a letter which I have just rec'd from a young Gentleman who lives with me but who is now at home in New-Hampshire; I am advised that there is every prospect that the Convention of that State will adopt the Constitution almost immediately upon the meeting of it. — I cannot but hope then that the States which may be disposed to make a secession will think often and seriously on the consequence —

Col° Humphreys who is still here, occupied with literary pursuits, desires to be remembered in terms of the sincerest friendship to you & yours. — Mrs Washington & the family offer, with me, their best compliments to Mrs Knox & the little ones — You will ever believe me to be, with great esteem & regard

My dear Sir
Yr affect & obed't Serv't

G: Washington

General Knox.

that State, I intend to allot them for a seminary to be erected at such place as they shall deem most proper. I am disposed to believe, that a seminary of learning upon an enlarged plan, but yet not coming up to the full idea of an university, is an institution to be preferred for the position which is to be chosen. The students who wish to pursue the whole range of science, may pass with advantage from the seminary to the university, and the former by a due relation may be rendered cooperative with the latter."

The best proof of the educative ability of Washington is that he was the leading man of his time in advocating a reorganization of education in the United States. As he put it: "The time is therefore come, when a plan of universal education ought to be adopted in the United States. Not only do the exigencies of public and private life demand it, but, if it should ever be apprehended, that prejudice would be entertained in one part of the Union against another, an efficacious remedy will be, to assemble the youth of every part under such circumstances as will, by the freedom of intercourse and collision of sentiment, give to their minds the direction of truth, philanthrophy, and mutual conciliation." He was much disturbed at a practice of sending young Americans overseas—nearly all to England—for a genteel education.

FAMILY LETTERS

His private letters which stand side by side with his formal and often indignant protests are equally characteristic. Take this one to his wife, June 18, 1775: "My Dearest, I am now set down to write to you on a subject, which fills me with inexpressible concern, and this concern is greatly aggravated and increased, when I reflect upon the uneasiness I know it will give you. It has been determined in Congress, that the whole army raised for the defence of the American cause shall be put under my care, and that it is necessary for me to proceed immediately to Boston to take upon me the command of it.

"You may believe me, my dear Patsy, when I assure you, in the most solemn manner, that, so far from seeking this appointment, I have used every endeavor in my power to avoid it, not only from my unwillingness to part with you and the family, but from a consciousness of its being a trust too great for my capacity, and that I should enjoy more happiness in one month with you at home, than I have the most distant prospect of finding abroad, if my stay were to be seven times seven years. But as it has been a kind of destiny, that has thrown me upon this service, I shall hope that my undertaking it is designed to answer some good purpose."

VIGOR OF EXPRESSION

Although Washington was never a talking member of the Virginia Assembly or of the Continental Congress, he did have a power of vigorous expression which made itself felt in letters, in council, and in conference; perhaps we might say that the temperateness of his more studied writings disappears. Thus in 1754, at the time of his capture of a body of French, he wrote: "If the whole Detach't of the French behave with no more Resolution than this chosen Party did, I flatter myself we shall have no g't trouble in driving them to the d—— Montreal."

When the Connecticut line broke on the landing of the British in New York in 1776, a contemporary wrote: "I dont know whether the New Engd. Troops will stand there, but I am sure they will not upon open Ground. I had a Specimen of that yesterday. Here two Brigades ran away from a small advanced party of the Regulars, tho' the General did all in his power to convince them they were in no danger. He laid his Cane over many of the Officers who shewed their men the Example of running. These were militia, the New England continental Troops are much better."

Another authority said the General damned them for cowardly rascals. Upon the Tories he fixes the unfavorable term of "execrable paracides." When he went to Boston to take command of the army in 1775, he wrote back, "I have made a pretty good slam among such kind of officers as the Massachusetts Government abound in." When Lee retreated at Monmouth, it is recorded that "Washington swore like an Angel." In 1778 he wrote to his friend Harrison, a most vigorous denunciation of the state of public feeling.

There were some occasions when mild and stately language did not express all the presidential mind. In a Cabinet meeting in 1793 Jefferson tells us that "The President was much inflamed; got into one of those passions when he cannot command himself; ran on much on the personal abuse which had been bestowed on him; defied any man on earth to produce one single act of his since he had been in the government, which was not done on the purest motives; that he had never repented but once the having slipped the moment of resigning his office, and that was every moment since; that *by God* he had rather be in his grave than in his present situation; that he had rather be on his farm than to be made *Emperor of the world*; and yet they were charging him with wanting to be a King. That that *rascal Freneau* sent him three of his papers every day, as if he thought he would become the distributor of his papers; and that he could see in this, nothing but an impudent design to insult him."

After the defeat of St. Clair in 1791, Washington fairly broke down before his secretary and said: "And yet, to suffer that army to be cut to pieces, hacked, butchered, tomahawked, by a surprise, the very thing I guarded him against! O God, O God, he's worse than a murderer! How can he answer it to his country? The blood of the slain is upon him, the curse of widows and orphans, the curse of Heaven!" But then he added, "General St. Clair shall have justice, I will hear him without prejudice, he shall have full justice."

Washington's private letters during his administration are still numerous, but he was at the same time more occupied and geographically nearer to the men to whom he would naturally write; but he kept up his habit of correspondence, also of journal keeping, for he was always exact in private matters and memoranda to the very end of his life.

INTELLECTUAL INFLUENCE OF WASHINGTON

In this survey of the field of Washington's intellectual life, it appears that rather by force of circumstances than by any preparation he was compelled to learn the art of expression. Certainly in public, in private, on matters financial, commercial, military, and civil, he was the most active minded and effective writer of his time. As years passed by, his own greater experience of life and the confidence of the American people gave more and more weight to what he said, so that great state papers like the Farewell Address have come to have in the minds of the American people almost the force of law.

The intellectual influence of Washington, however, is far wider than its immediate effect upon the generation in which he lived. First of all he is an author who is still read. Some of his public papers, such as the letter to the governors, his first inaugural, his Farewell Address, are classics in American history, well known by school children. His letters, part of them gathered into two formal editions, others scattered through many works, are a fundamental source for every writer of history of his time. No man of his time, in public or private life, whether statesman or poet or historian, except perhaps Benjamin Franklin, has had anything like his influence upon the minds of his countrymen.

Washington was a great writer; he was a great writer in the actual amount of his literary composition thought by posterity worthy of preservation; he was a great writer in the millions who have read and pondered his words; he was further a great writer in the power of brief and memorable statement, which has caused little fragments from his writings to be embedded in the literature of our race.

Washington is also a great writer in the noble aims and purposes which he sets forth. Probably no man ever lived who was further from sordidness and pettiness which can be found even in some very great characters. In his private life he needed no assertion of his personal dignity; he was the foremost citizen of Virginia. In his public life he needed no restraint of anything that he might say lest it should make him unpopular; his reputation in his own lifetime was beyond attack. Hence there was no risk in setting forth patriotic standards of life; but had those later expressions lost him his generalship or his presidency he would nevertheless have used them. If his mind was bent upon a great plan, he knew instinctively what his countrymen intended to do and would do. He did not plead for nationality, for economy, for honesty, for public spirit, for self-sacrificing rulers: those things seemed to him the natural principles of a gentleman. For himself he knew no other standards.

Washington was a great writer because of his clear and forcible forms of expression. The fashion of his time was one of orotund periods and large words, and from that fashion he did not deviate; but out of that somewhat unnatural style he causes the voice of Jove to speak; he had an innate sense of form, of propriety, of what was too much, what was too little. His letters and his public writings express his mind, nobody ever found them ambiguous, nobody ever found him trying to say what two parties might each construe according to its own preference.

To sum up, George Washington, surveyor, frontiersman, soldier, planter, commander of the armies of the United Colonies, and President of the United States, was a great writer and a great intellectual influence in his essential and absolute truthfulness. He said what he thought, he withheld nothing that seemed to him necessary to say. The soul of courtesy, writing with the most admirable reserves and delicacy on such difficult occasions as the censure of Benedict Arnold, he wrote things as he saw them; and the essential element of truth in the main shines through every letter. He had a right to say of himself: "I do not recollect that in the course of my life I ever forfeited my word, or broke a promise made to anyone."

Part II
Literary Records

GEOMETRY (1745)

"One of the Seven Sciences, and a very useful and Necessary Branch of the Mathematick; whose Subject is greatness; for as Number is the Subject of Arithmetick, so that of Geometry is Magnitude, which hath its beginning from Point, that is a Thing Supposed to be indivisible, and the Original of all Dimension. By it is explained the Nature, Kind and Property of continued Magnitude that is a Line, a Superficies and a Solid of which in their proper Order.

SURVEYING

"Is the Art of Measuring Land and consists of 3 Parts 1st, The going round and Measuring a Piece of Wood Land   2d. Plotting the Same and 3d To find the Content thereof."

GEOGRAPHICAL DEFINITIONS

"Defin. 1st. The Globe of the Earth is a Spherical Body Composed of Earth and Water &c. Divided in to Contenants Islands and Seas.

"2d. A Continent is a great Quantity of Land not Divided nor Separated by the Sea wherein are many Kingdoms and Principalities; as Europe Asia Africa is one Continent and America Another.

"3d. An Island is such a Part of the Earth that is environed round with Water as the Island of great Britain, Ireland, Barbadoes and Jamaica. . . .

"The Provinces of North America are

New France	Virginia
New England	Carolina North and
New York	South
Pennsylvania	Terra Florida
New Jersey	Mexico or New
Maryland	Spain

"The Chief Islands are

Icelands	Porto Rico
Greenland	Jamaica
Colofornia	Barbadoes and the rest
Hispaniola	of the Caribee Isc-
Cuba	lands"

INSCRIPTION ON A FLY LEAF OF A LATIN TRANSLATION OF HOMER

"Hunc mihi quaeso (bone Vir) Libellum
Redde, si forsan tenues repertum
Ut Scias qui sum sine fraude Scriptum.

Est mihi nomen,
Georgio Washington,
George Washington,
Fredericksburg,
Virginia."

SELECTIONS FROM RULES OF CIVILITY AND DECENT BEHAVIOUR IN COMPANY AND CONVERSATION COPIED OUT BY WASHINGTON
(1745)

"1st Every Action done in Company, ought to be with Some Sign of Respect, to those that are Present. . . .

"3d Shew Nothing to your Friend that may affright him.

"4 In the Presence of Others Sing not to yourself with a humming Noise, nor Drum with your Fingers or Feet. . . .

"6th Sleep not when others Speak, Sit not when others stand, Speak not when you Should hold your Peace, walk not on when others Stop. . . .

"8th At Play and at Fire its Good manners to Give Place to the last Commer, and affect not to Speak Louder than Ordinary . . .

"17th Be no Flaterer, neither Play with any that delights not to be Play'd Withal.

"18th Read no Letters, Books, or Papers in Company but when there is a Necessity for the doing of it you must ask leave: come not near the Books or Writings of Another so as to read them unless desired or give your opinion of them unask'd also look not high when another is writing a Letter. . . .

"21st Reproach none for the Infirmaties of Nature, nor Delight to Put them that have in mind thereof.

"22d Shew not yourself glad at the Misfortune of another though he were your enemy. . . .

"26th In Pulling off your Hat to Persons of Distinction, as Noblemen, Justices, Churchmen &c make a Reverence, bowing more or less according to the Custom of the Better Bred, and Quality of the Person. Amongst your equals expect not always that they Should begin with you first, but to Pull off the Hat when there is no need is Affectation, in the Manner of Saluting and resaluting in words to keep to the most usual Custom . . .

"29th When you meet with one of Greater Quality than yourself, Stop, and retire especially if it be at a Door or any Straight place to give way for him to Pass . . .

"33d They that are in Dignity or in office have in all places Preceedency but whilst they are Young they out to respect those that are their equals in Birth or other Qualitys, though they have no Publick charge. . . .

"35th Let your Discourse with Men of Business be Short and Comprehensive. . . .

"39th In writing or Speaking, give to every Person his due Title According to his Degree & the Custom of the Place. . . .

"44th When a man does all he can though it Succeeds not well blame not him that did it. . . .

"52d In Your Apparel be Modest and endeavour to accomodate Nature, rather than to procure Admiration keep to the Fashio[n] of your equals Such as are Civil and orderly with respect to Times and Places . . .

"56th Associate yourself with Men of good Quality if you Esteem your own Reputation; for 'tis better to be alone than in bad Company . . .

"58th Let your Conversation be without Malice or Envy, for 'tis a Sig[n o]f a Tractable and Commendable Nature: And in all Causes of Passion [ad]mit Reason to Govern . . .

"62d Speak not of doleful Things in a Time of Mirth or at the Table; Speak not of Melancholy Things as Death and Wounds, and if others Mention them Change if you can the Discourse tell not your Dreams, but to your intimate Friend . . .

"64th Break not a Jest where none take pleasure in mirth Laugh not loud, nor at all without Occasion, deride no mans Misfortune, tho' there seem to be Some cause . . .

"72d Speak not in an unknown Tongue in Company but in your own Language and that as those of Quality do and not as yᵉ Vulgar; Sublime matters treat Seriously . . .

"79th Be not apt to relate News if you know not the truth thereof. In Discoursing of things you Have heard Name not your Author always A [Se]cret Discover not . . .

"82d Undertake not what you cannot Perform but be Carefull to keep your Promise . . .

"89th Speak not Evil of the Absent for it is unjust . . .

"[1]05th Be not Angry at Table whatever happens & if you have reason to be so, Shew it not but on a Chearful Countenance especially if there be Strangers for Good Humour makes one Dish of Meat a Feas[t] . . .

"108th When you Speak of God or his Atributes, let it be Seriously & [with] Reverence. Honour & Obey your Natural Parents altho they be Poor

"109th Let your Recreations be Manfull not Sinfull.

"110th Labour to keep alive in your Breast that Little Spark of Ce[les]tial fire Called Conscience.

"Finis."

ACROSTIC TO "FRANCES ALEXA—"

"From your bright sparkling Eyes, I was undone;
Rays, you have more transparent than the sun,
A midst its glory in the rising Day,
None can you equal in your bright array;
Constant in your calm and unspotted Mind;
Equal to all, but will to none Prove kind,
So knowing, seldom one so Young, you'l Find
Ah! woe's me, that I should Love and conceal,
Long have I wish'd, but never dare reveal,
Even though severly Loves Pains I feel;
Xerxes that great, was't free from Cupids Dart,
And all the greatest Heroes, felt the smart."

LETTER TO A YOUNG FRIEND (1749)

"Dear Friend Robin: . . . My place of residence is at present at his Lordship's, where I might, was my heart disengaged, pass my time very pleasantly as there's a very agreeable young lady lives in the same house, (Colonel George Fairfax's wife's sister.) But as that's only adding fuel to fire, it makes me the more uneasy, for by often, and unavoidably, being in company with her revives my former passion for your Lowland beauty; whereas, was I to live more retired from young women, I might in some measure eliviate my sorrows, by burying that chaste and troublesome passion in the grave of oblivion or etarnall forgetfulness, for as I am very well assured, that's the only antidote or remedy, that I ever shall be relieved by or only recess that can administer any cure or help to me, as I am well convinced, was I ever to attempt any thing, I should only get a denial which would be only adding grief to uneasiness."

LETTER TO HIS SISTER-IN-LAW (1749 or 1750)

"I heartily Congratulate you on the happy News of my Brothers safe arrival *in health* in England and am joy'd to hear that his stay is likely to be so short. I hope you'll make Use of your Natural Resolution and contendness as they are the only remedys to spend the time with ease and pleasure to yourself. I am deprived of the pleasure of waiting on you (as I expected) by Aguee and Feaver which I have had to Extremety since I left which has occasioned my Return D[own]."

EXPERIENCES AT BARBADOS (1751)

"[Oct.] *7th.* . . . Saw many fish swimming abt. us of which a Dolphin we catchd. at Noon but cou'd not intice with a baited hook two Baricootas which played under our Stern for some Hours; the Dolphin being small we had it dressed for Supper . . .

"*20th.* A Constant succession of hard Winds, Squals of Rain, and Calms was the remarkable attendants of this day which was so sudden and flighty we durst not go under any but reef'd Sails and those that we cou'd D R [double reef] At 6 A M put abt. to the Eastward A sloop that for the two preceding Days was [in] sight of us hung out a Signal but wheth[er] distress or not we are uncertain; if it had [been we] were incapable of relieving them by ye contrs. of [the wind?] . . .

"[30th] This Morning arose with agreeably assurances of a certain and steady trade Wind which after near five Weeks of buffiting and being toss'd by a fickle and Merciless ocean was glad'ening knews: the preceeding night we separated from sloop abe mentioned . . .

"[Nov. 2d] We were grea . . . larm'd with the cry of Land at 4 A: M: we quitted out beds with surprise and found ye land plainly appearing at [a]bout 3 leagues distance . . .

"[4th. Early this morning came Dr. Hilary, an eminent physician recommended by Major Clarke, to pass his opinion on my brother's disorder, which he did in a favorable light, giving great assurance, that it was not so fixed but that a cure might be effectually made. In the cool of the evening we rode out accompanied by Mr. Carter to seek lodgings in the country, as the Doctor advised,] and was perfectly rav . . . the beautiful prospects which on every side presented to our view The fields of Cain, Corn, Fruit Trees &c in a delightful Green. We return'd without accomplishing our intentions. . . .

"*6th.* . . . Receiv'd a Card from Majr. Clarke wherein our companys were desir'd to Dinner to morrow and myself an invitation from Mrs. Clarke and Miss Robts. to come and see the seprts fir'd being gunpd. . . .

"*9th.* We receiv'd a card from Majr. Clarke inviting us to dine with him at Judge Maynards on the Morrow he had a right to ask being a Member of the Club call'd the Beefstake and tripe instituted by himself. . . .

"[10th] . . . After Dinner was the greatest Collection of Fruits I have yet seen on the Table there was Granadella the Sappadilla Pomgranate Sweet Orange Water Lemmon forbidden Fruit apples Guavas &ca. &ca. &ca. . . .

"*15th.* Was treated with a play ticket by Mr. Carter to see the Tragedy of George Barnwell acted: the character of Barnwell and several others was said to be well perform'd there was Musick a Dapted and regularly conducted by Mr. . . . .

"*17th.* Was strongly attacked with the small Pox: sent for Dr. Lanahan whose attendance was very constant till my recovery, and going out which was not 'till thursday the 12th of December. . . .

"[Dec.] *22d.* Took my leave of my Br. Majr. Clarke &ca. and Imbar[ked] in the Industry Captn. John Saund[ers] for Virginia wai'd anchor and got out of Carlile Bay abt. 12. . . . How wonderful that such people shou'd be in debt! and not be able to indulge themselves in all the Luxurys as well as necessarys of Life Yet so it happens Estates are often alienated for the debts . . . Hospitality and a Genteel behav[ior] is shewn to every gentlemen stranger by the Gentlemen Inhab[itants. . . .] Taverns they have none but in their Towns so that Travellers is oblig'd to go to private houses however the Island being but abt. 22 Miles in length and 14 in width preven[ts] their being much infested with ym. . . . There are few who may be calld midling people they are either very rich or very poor for by a Law of the Island Every Gentn. is oblig'd to keep a white person for ten Acres capable of acting in the Militia and consequently those persons so kept cant but [be] very poor. . . .

"[Jan. 29?, 1752] Early this Morning . . . Wind sprang up at Sp. Et. made Sail under easy Gales past the Cape abt. Sun's Rising and got to the Mouth of York River abt. 11 P. M. and was met by a pilot boat."

DIFFICULTY OF WRITING (1754)

"I think I can do no less than apologize, in some Measure, for the numberless Imperfections of it. There intervened but one Day between my Arrival in Williamsburg, and the Time for the Council's Meeting, for me to prepare and transcribe, from the rough Minutes I had taken in my Travels, this Journal; the writing of which only was sufficient to employ me closely the whole Time, consequently admitted of no Leisure to consult of a new and proper Form to offer it in, or to correct or amend the Diction of the old."

LIFE ON THE PLANTATION (1773)

"Where, how, or with [whom] *my time is Spent.*

"[July] 1*st*. Doctr. Craik and his Companion went away before Breakfast, and Doctr. Rumney after Dinner. Miss Molly Manley came in the afternoon and stayd all Night. Rid with Mrs. Washington to the Ferry Plantn.

"2. At home all day alone.

"3. Rid into the Neck and by Muddy hole. Miss Moly Manley went home in the Afternoon.

"4. At home all day. Mrs. Peake and her daughter dind here.

"5. Rid with Mrs. Washington to Muddy hole, Doeg Run, and Mill Plantations.

"6. At home all day. Mr. Peake dined here.

"7. Rid to Muddy hole, Doeg Run, and the Mill. Mrs. Barnes and Molly McCarty came.

"8. At home all day. Colo. Fairfax and Mrs. Fairfax came in the aftern. to take leave of us and returnd again. Dr. Craik also came and stayd all Night.

"9. Dr. Craik went away in the Morning Early, Miss Molly McCarty in the Afternoon. Mrs. Washington and self went to Belvoir to see them take Shipping. Mr. Robt. Adams and Mr. Mattw. Campbell dined here."

MRS. WASHINGTON (1775)

"I thank you for your frequent mention of Mrs. Washington. I expect she will be in Philadelphia about the time this letter may reach you, on her way hither. As she and her conductor, (who I expect will be Mr. Custis, her son,) are perfect strangers to the road, the stages, and the proper place to cross Hudson's River (by all means avoiding New York,) I shall be much obliged in your particular instructions and advice to her. I do imagine, as the roads are bad and the weather cold, her stages must be short, especially as I expect her horses will be pretty much fatigued; as they will, by the time she gets to Philadelphia, have performed a journey of at least four hundred and fifty miles, my express finding of her among her friends near Williamsburg, one hundred and fifty miles below my own house."

EXAMPLE OF WASHINGTON'S HUMOR (1779)

"Dr. Doctr., I have asked Mrs. Cochran & Mrs. Livingston to dine with me to-morrow; but am I not in honor bound to apprize them of their fare? As I hate deception, even where the imagination only is concerned; I will. It is needless to premise, that my table is large enough to hold the ladies. Of this they had ocular proof yesterday. To say how it is usually covered, is rather more essential; and this shall be the purport of my Letter.

"Since our arrival at this happy spot, we have had a ham, (sometimes a shoulder) of Bacon, to grace the head of the Table; a piece of roast Beef adorns the foot; and a dish of beans, or greens, (almost imperceptible,) decorates the center. When the cook has a mind to cut a figure, (which I presume will be the case to-morrow,) we have two Beef-steak pyes, or dishes of crabs, in addition, one on each side the center dish, dividing the space & reducing the distance between dish & dish to about 6 feet, which without them would be near 12 feet apart. Of late he has had the surprising sagacity to discover, that apples will make pyes; and its a question, if, in the violence of his efforts, we do not get one of apples, instead of having both of Beef-steaks. If the ladies can put up with such entertainment, and will submit to partake of it on plates, once Tin but now Iron—(not become so by the labor of scouring), I shall be happy to see them; and am, dear Doctor, yours."

OPINION OF ARNOLD (1780)

"Arnold's conduct is so villanously perfidious, that there are no terms that can describe the baseness of his heart. That overruling Providence, which has so often and so remarkably interposed in our favor, never manifested itself more conspicuously than in the timely discovery of his horrid intention to surrender the Post and Garrison of West Point into the hands of the Enemy. I confine my remarks to this single act of perfidy; for I am far from thinking he intended to hazard a defeat of this important object, by combining another with it, altho, there were circumstances which led to a contrary belief. The confidence and folly, which has marked the subsequent conduct of this man, are of a piece with his villany; and all three are perfect in their kind."

WORSHIP OF SUCCESS (1782)

"However it may be the practice of the World, and those who see objects but partially, or thro' a false medium to consider *that* only as meritorious which is attended with success, I have accustomed myself to judge of human Actions very differently and to appreciate them by the manner in which they are conducted, more than by the Event; which it is not in the power of human foresight and prudence to command."

POETRY AND FICTION (1783)

"I must beg leave to say a word or two about these fine things you have been telling in such harmonious and beautiful numbers. Fiction is to be sure the very life and Soul of Poetry—all Poets and Poetesses have been indulged in the free and indisputable use of it, time out of mind. And to oblige you to make such an excellent Poem on such a subject, without any materials but those of simple reality, would be as cruel as the Edict of Pharoah which compelled the children of Israel to manufacture Bricks without the necessary Ingredients."

ADVICE TO PEOPLE ABOUT TO BE MARRIED (1783)

"I never did, nor do I believe I ever shall, give advice to a woman, who is setting out on a matrimonial voyage; first, because I never could advise one to marry without her own consent; and, secondly, because I know it is to no purpose to advise her to refrain, when she has obtained it. A woman very rarely asks an opinion or requires advice on such an occasion, till her resolution is formed; and then it is with the hope and expectation of obtaining a sanction, not that she means to be governed by your disapprobation, that she applies. In a word, the plain English of the application may be summed up in these words: 'I wish you to think as I do; but, if unhappily you differ from me in opinion, my heart, I must confess, is fixed, and I have gone too far *now* to retract.' "

GLIDING DOWN THE STREAM OF LIFE (1784)

"From the clangor of arms and the bustle of a camp, freed from the cares of public employment and the responsibility of office, I am now enjoying domestic ease under the shadow of my own vine and my own fig tree; and in a small villa, with the implements of husbandry and lambkins around me, I expect to glide gently down the stream of life, till I am entombed in the dreary mansion of my fathers."

MONEY MAKES THE MARE GO (1785)

"That a man of character & knowledge may be had for *very high wages,* there can be no doubt—money we know will fetch anything & command the services of any man; but with the former I do not abound."

AGREEMENT WITH THE GARDENER (1787)

[Philip Barter, the gardener, binds himself to keep sober for a year, and to fulfill his duties on the place, if allowed] "four dollars at Christmas, with which to be drunk four days and four nights; two dollars at Easter, to effect the same purpose; two dollars at Whitsuntide, to be drunk for two days, a dram in the morning, and a drink of grog at dinner, at noon. For the true and faithful performance of all these things, the parties have hereunto set their hands, this twenty-third day of April, Anno Domini, 1787.

　　　　　　　　　　　　　　his
　　　"PHILIP BARTER　X
　　　　　　　　　　　　mark
　　　"GEORGE WASHINGTON

"Witness:
　　George A. Washington,
　　Tobias Lear."

Part III
Washington Sayings

PERSONAL

Clothes—"An invoice of clothes . . . As they are designed for wearing-apparel for myself, I have committed the choice of them to your fancy, having the best opinion of your taste. I want neither lace nor embroidery. Plain clothes, with a gold or silver button, (if worn in genteel dress,) are all I desire."

Impartialities—"To please everybody is impossible; were I to undertake it, I should probably please nobody. If I know myself I have no partialities. I have from the beginning, and I hope I shall to the end, pursue to the utmost of my judgment and abilities, one steady line of conduct for the good of the great whole. This will, under all circumstances, administer consolation to myself, however short I may fall in the expectation of others."

Plain and elegant—[His secretary had spoken of the rich and elegant style in which the state carriage was fitted up.] "I had rather have heard that my repaired coach was plain and elegant, than rich and elegant."

Posterity—"I had rather glide gently down the stream of life, leaving it to posterity to think and say what they please of me, than by any act of mine to have vanity or ostentation imputed to me."

Envious of none, pleased with all—"Envious of none, I am determined to be pleased with all; and this, my dear friend, being the order for my march, I will move gently down the stream of life, until I sleep with my fathers."

Fatigue of the war—"I feel now, however, as I conceive a wearied traveller must do, who, after treading many a painful step with a heavy burthen on his shoulders, is eased of the latter, having reached the haven to which all the former were directed; and from his house-top is looking back, and tracing with an eager eye the meanders by which he excaped the quicksands and mires which lay in his way; and into which none but the all-powerful Guide and Dispenser of human events could have prevented his falling."

Work well done—"The work is done, and well done."

Rectitude—"I give you a proof of my friendship, if I give none of my policy or judgment. I do it on the presumption, that a mind, conscious of its own rectitude, fears not what is said of it, but will bid defiance to and despise shafts, that are not barbed with accusations against honor or integrity; . . ."

CHARACTER

Character—"Characters and habits are not easily taken up or suddenly laid aside."

Character—"A good moral character is the first essential in a man. It is, therefore, highly important to endeavor not only to be learned but to be virtuous."

Error—"Error is the portion of humanity, and to censure it, whether committed by this or that public character, is the prerogative of freemen."

Indecision—"Accident may put a decisive blunderer in the right; but eternal defeat and miscarriage must attend the man of the best parts, if cursed with indecision."

Highest bidder—"Few men have virtue to withstand the highest bidder."

Candor—"My duty therefore to his Majesty, and the Colony whose troops I have the honor to command, obliged me to declare my sentiments upon the occasion with that candor and freedom of which you are witness. If I am deceived in my opinion, I shall acknowledge my error as becomes a gentleman led astray from judgment, and not by prejudice, in opposing a measure so conducive to the public Weal as you seem to have conceived this to be. If I unfortunately am right, my conduct will acquit me of having discharged my duty on this important occasion; on the good success of which, our all, in a manner depends."

Openness—"As I never say any thing of a Man that I have the smallest scruple of saying *to him*, I would not be understood to mean *by this being between ourselves* that any part of it that effects Mr. Sands should be hid from him. You are perfectly at liberty if you think it necessary to communicate these my Sentiments to him."

Gentleman—"I feel everything that hurts the sensibility of a gentleman."

Promise—"I never wish to promise more than I have a moral certainty of performing."

Foibles—"I shall never attempt to palliate my own foibles by exposing the error of another."

Vice—"Discourage vice in every shape."

Variable minds—"Men's minds are as variant as their faces."

HUMAN NATURE

Secrecy and despatch—"Secrecy and despatch may prove the soul of success to an enterprise."

Disclosures of time—"Time will unfold more than prudence ought to disclose."

As they are—"We must bear up and make the best of mankind as they are, since we cannot have them as we wish.'

Right education—"The best means of forming a manly, virtuous and happy people, will be found in the right education of youth. Without this foundation, every other means, in my opinion, must fail."

Enmity—"The most certain way to make a man your enemy is to tell him you esteem him as such."

Let your hand give—"Let your hand give in proportion to your purse."

Example—"Example, whether it be good or bad, has a powerful influence, and the higher in Rank the officer is, who sets it, the more striking it is.'

Misfortunes—"It is our duty to make the best of our misfortunes."

Extremes—"Men are very apt to run into extremes."

Perseverance—"To persevere in one's duty and be silent is the best answer to calumny."

Resentment — "Resentment, reproaches, and submission seem to be all that would be left to us."

Misspent hours—"Every hour misspent is lost forever, and . . . future years cannot compensate for lost days at this period of your life. This reflection must show the necessity of unremitting application to your studies."

Two edges—"It has however, like many other things in which I have been involved, two edges, neither of which can be avoided without falling on the other."

Imagination—"The thinking part of mankind do not form their judgment from events; and that . . . equity will ever attach equal glory to those actions, which deserve success, as to those which have been crowned with it."

Always together—"Men, who are always together, get tired of each other's company; they throw off that restraint, which is necessary to keep things in proper tune; they say and do things, which are personally disgusting; this begets opposition; opposition begets faction; and so it goes on, till business is impeded, often at a stand."

Foresight—"I urged . . . that the man, who wished to steer clear of shelves and rocks, must know where they lay."

Golden Rule—"It is a maxim with me not to ask what, under similar circumstances, I would not grant."

Fruit of vanity—"There is no restraining men's tongues or pens, when charged with a little vanity."

SITTING FOR HIS PORTRAIT (1785)

"*In for a penny, in for a pound*, is an old adage. I am so hackneyed to the touches of the painter's pencil, that I am *now* altogether at their beck; and sit, 'like Patience on a monument,' whilst they are delineating the lines of my face. It is a proof, among many others, of what habit and custom can accomplish. At first I was as impatient at the request, and as restive under the operation, as a colt is of the saddle. The next time I submitted very reluctantly, but with less flouncing. Now, no dray-horse moves more readily to his thill than I to the painter's chair. It may easily be conceived, therefore, that I yielded a ready obedience to your request and to the views of Mr. Pine."

RELIGION

Providence — "The determinations of Providence are always wise, often inscrutable; and, though its decrees appear to bear hard upon us at times, is nevertheless meant for gracious purposes."

Protection of the Almighty—"I consider it an indispensable duty to close this last solemn act of my official life, by commending the Interests of our dearest country to the protection of Almighty God, and those who have the superintendence of them to his holy keeping."

Vital religion—"I shall always strive to be a faithful and impartial patron of genuine vital religion."

God—"It is impossible to reason without arriving at a Supreme Being."

Religion and government—"True religion affords government its surest support."

Conscience—"Conscience again seldom comes to a man's aid while he is in the zenith of health, and revelling in pomp and luxury upon illgotten spoils. It is generally the *last* act of his life, and comes too late to be of much service to others here, or to himself hereafter."

Church going—"That the Troops may have an opportunity of attending public worship, as well as take some rest after the great fatigue they have gone through; the General in future excuses them from fatigue duty on Sunday (except at the Ship Yards, or special occasions) until further orders."

FRIENDSHIP

True friendship—"True friendship is a plant of slow growth; to be sincere, there must be a congeniality of temper and pursuits."

Company—"The Company, in which you will improve most, will be least expensive to you."

Bad company v. *solitude*—"It is better to be alone than in bad company."

Courteous to all, intimate with few—"Be courteous to all, but intimate with few; and let those few be well tried before you give them your confidence."

Praise from a good friend—"Although the friendship of your father may oblige him to see some things through too partial a medium, yet the indulgent manner in which he is pleased to express himself respecting me is indeed very pleasing; for nothing in human life can afford a liberal mind more rational and exquisite satisfaction, than the approbation of a wise, a great, and virtuous man."

Correspondence—"To correspond with those I love is one of my highest gratifications."

Relieving anxious friends—"I shall ever be happy to relieve the anxiety of parted friends."

Absence and friendship—"The friendship I have conceived will not be impaired by absence."

PUBLIC SPIRIT

Justice—"The due administration of justice is the firmest pillar of good government."

Thinking — "From thinking proceeds speaking, thence to acting is often but a single step. But how irrevocable and tremendous!"

Public support—"The voice of mankind is with me."

Factions—"It is also most devoutly to be wished, that faction was at an end, and that those, to whom every thing dear and valuable is entrusted, would lay aside party views and return to first principles. Happy, happy, thrice happy country, if such was the government of it! But, alas, we are not to expect that the path will be strowed with flowers. That great and good Being, who rules the Universe, has disposed matters otherwise, and for wise purposes I am persuaded."

Danger in congested population—"The tumultous populace of large cities are ever to be dreaded."

LOVE OF COUNTRY

Liberty—"Liberty, when it begins to take root, is a plant of rapid growth."

Lives, liberties, and properties—"Let us have one [government] by which our lives, liberties and properties will be secured."

Let your heart feel—"Let your heart feel for the afflictions and distresses of every one."

Reply to a proposal to abandon the patriot cause—"I yesterday, through the hands of Mrs. Ferguson of Graham Park, received a letter of a very curious and extraordinary nature, from Mr. Duche, which I have thought proper to transmit to Congress. To this ridiculous, illiberal performance, I made a short reply, by desiring the bearer of it, if she should hereafter by any accident meet Mr. Duche, to tell him I should have returned it unopened, if I had had any idea of the contents; observing at the same time, that I highly disapprove the intercourse she seemed to have been carrying on, and expected it would be discontinued. Notwithstanding the author's assertion, I cannot but suspect that the measure did not originate with him; and that he was induced to it by the hope of establishing his interest and peace more effectually with the enemy."

Estimation of one's country—"To stand well in the estimation of one's country is a happiness, that no rational creature can be insensible of."

Gray and almost blind—"Gentlemen, you will permit me to put on my spectacles, for I have not only grown gray, but almost blind, in the service of my country."

Recognizing difficulties—"While we do not underrate difficulties on one hand, we should not overrate them on the other; nor discourage ourselves from a very important undertaking by obstacles, which are to be surmounted."

Basis for prosperity—"Nothing but harmony, honesty, industry, and frugality are necessary to make us a great and happy people."

Pro Patria—"The welfare of the country is the great object to which our cares and efforts ought to be directed."

Love of country—"The love of my country will be the ruling influence of my conduct."

GOVERNMENT

Constitutional power—"The power, under the Constitution, will always be in the people."

Nepotism—"My political conduct in nominations, even if I were uninfluenced by principle, must be exceedingly circumspect and proof against just criticism; for . . . no slip will pass unnoticed, that can be improved into a supposed partiality for friends or relations."

Influence—"Influence is no government."

Principles for a Burgess—"You have, I find, broke the ice. The only advice I will offer to you on the occasion (if you have a mind to command the attention of the House,) is to speak seldom, but to important subjects, except such as particularly relate to your constituents; and, in the former case, make yourself perfectly master of the subject. Never exceed a decent warmth, and submit your sentiments with diffidence. A dictatorial stile, though it may carry conviction, is always accompanied with disgust."

MILITARY

Plea for regular troops—"An army formed of good officers moves like clockwork; but there is no situation upon earth less enviable, nor more distressing, than that person's, who is at the head of troops which are regardless of order and discipline, and who are unprovided with almost every necessary. In a word, the difficulties, which have for ever surrounded me since I have been in the service, and kept my mind constantly upon the stretch, the wounds, which my feelings as an officer have received by a thousand things, which have happened contrary to my expectation and wishes; . . . induces . . . a thorough conviction in my mind, that it will be impossible, unless there is a thorough change in our military system, to give satisfaction to the public."

Preparedness—"To be prepared for war is one of the most effectual means of preserving peace."

Courage—"We must not despair; the game is yet in our own hands; to play it well is all we have to do."

Earning liberty—"Remember, officers and soldiers, that you are fighting for the blessings of liberty."

Cruelty to war animals—"Could the poor horses tell their tale, it would be a strain still more lamentable."

REORGANIZATION

Desire for peace—"I pray devoutly that we may both witness, and that shortly, the return of peace."

Cultivating peace—"My policy has been to cultivate peace with all men."

Inglorious peace—"A patched-up inglorious peace, after all the toil, blood, and treasure we have spent."

The clock—" . . . lamenting . . . the fatal policy . . . of the States of employing their ablest men at home . . . compare . . . to . . . a clock . . . the smaller parts of which they are endeavoring to put in fine order without considering how useless . . . unless the great Wheel, . . . which is to set the whole in motion is also well attended to."

The Confederation—"Today one nation, tomorrow thirteen."

Downfall imminent—"If no change comes about our downfall is as plain as A B C."

Release—"The scene is at last closed. I feel myself eased of a load of public care."

War a plague to mankind—"As the complexion of European politics seems now . . . my first wish is to see this plague to mankind banished from off the earth, and the sons and daughters of this world employed in more pleasing and innocent amusements, than in preparing implements and exercising them for the destruction of mankind."

Sea power—"To an active external commerce the protection of a naval force is indispensable."

Part IV

Academic, Municipal, and Fraternal Honors
held by George Washington

1752, November 4—Entered Fredericksburg Lodge of Freemasons (though a minor).

1774, June 15—Society for Promoting Useful Knowledge, attends a meeting at Williamsburg.

1776, April 3—Harvard Degree of LL.D.

1780, January 19 — American Philosophical Society at Philadelphia, elected member; accepts, February 15; certificate is dated March 22.

1781, January 31 — American Academy of Arts and Sciences at Boston, elected honorary member.

April 26—Yale Degree of LL.D.; diploma is dated September 12.

December 17—Society of the Friendly Sons of St. Patrick at Philadelphia, adopted member.

1782, June 27—Freedom of the City of Albany, N. Y.

1783, June 19—President - General of the Society of the Cincinnati; continued in office through reelection rest of life.

July 4—University of Pennsylvania Degree of LL.D.

November 27—Marine Society of New York, honorary member; certificate is dated November 28.

1784, January 13—Charleston (S. C.) Library Society, honorary member.

May—Member of the Board of Visitors and Governors of Washington College, Chestertown, Md., which, with his consent, was named after him in 1782.

June 24—Honorary member of Alexandria Lodge of Freemasons.

December 2—Freedom of the City of New York.

1785, July 4—Philadelphia Society for the Promoting of Agriculture, honorary member.

November—South Carolina Society for Promoting and Improving Agriculture and Other Rural Concerns, honorary member.

December 17 — Trustee of proposed

Alexandria Academy, attends meeting. Academy incorporated in 1786, with Washington named as a trustee until the first annual election by the supporters of the Academy.

1788, January 18—Chancellor of William and Mary College, date of vote of Visitors and Governors in convocation; honorary life position.

April 28—Appointed first Master in charter of new Lodge of Freemasons in Alexandria.

December 20—Elected Master of the Alexandria Lodge.

1789, March 7—Honorary member of Holland Lodge of Freemasons, New York City.

June 24—Washington College Degree of LL.D.

1790, September 2—Brown Degree of LL.D.

1795, March 25—Board of Agriculture of Great Britain, foreign honorary member.

Selected Authorities

COOLIDGE, CALVIN—*Birth of George Washington* (address, February 22, 1927). Washington, Government Printing Office, 1930.

COOLIDGE, CALVIN, "Washington and Education"; in National Education Association, *Proceedings*, 1926, p. 706.

CUSTIS, GEORGE WASHINGTON PARKE—*Recollections and Private Memoirs of Washington*. Philadelphia, Flint, 1859. (Other eds.)

EVANS, LAWRENCE B., ED.—*Writings of George Washington*. New York, Putnam, 1908.

ELIOT, CHARLES WILLIAM—*Four American Leaders*. Boston, American Unitarian Association, 1906.

FORD, PAUL LEICESTER—*True George Washington*. Lippincott, 1896.

LODGE, HENRY CABOT—*George Washington* (American Statesmen, Library ed.). 2

vols. Boston, Houghton Mifflin, 1898. (Especially Vol. II, ch. vii.)

MITCHELL, SILAS WEIR—*Washington in his Letters*. Philadelphia, Lippincott, 1903.

OSBORN, LUCRETIA PERRY, ED.—*Washington speaks for Himself*. New York, Scribner, 1927.

PARTON, JAMES, ED.—*Words of Washington*. Boston, Osgood, 1872.

PENNIMAN, JAMES HOSMER—*Washington as a Man of Letters*. 1918.

POTTER, ELIPHALET NOTT—*Washington a Model in his Library and Life.* New York, Young, 1895.

RUSH, RICHARD—*Washington in Domestic Life.* Philadelphia, Lippincott, 1857.

Sayings of Washington; the Best of his Wit and Wisdom. Philadelphia, Winston, 1913.

SCHRODER, JOHN F., ED.—*Maxims of Washington; Political, Social, Moral, and Religious.* New York, Appleton, 1855. (Also a reprint.)

TONER, JOSEPH M.—"Some Account of George Washington's Library and Manuscript Records"; in American Historical Association, *Annual Report for 1892*, p. 73.

WASHINGTON, GEORGE — *Diaries, 1748-1799.* Ed. by John C. Fitzpatrick. 4 vols. Boston, Houghton Mifflin, 1925.

WASHINGTON, GEORGE—*Writings.* Ed. by Worthington Chauncey Ford. 14 vols. New York, Putnam, 1889-93.

WASHINGTON, GEORGE—*Writings.* Ed. by John C. Fitzpatrick. Washington, U. S. George Washington Bicentennial Commission, 1931—.

WISTER, OWEN—*Seven Ages of Washington.* New York, Macmillan, 1907.

GEORGE WASHINGTON

Houdon Statue, Capitol, Richmond, Va.

Tributes to Washington
By Albert Bushnell Hart
Part I
Personal Appearance (1759-1799)

GEORGE WASHINGTON
From the Portrait by Wertmueller

ANONYMOUS BRITON (1790)

IT was not necessary to announce his name, for his peculiar appearance, his firm forehead, Roman nose, and a projection of the lower jaw, his height and figure, could not be mistaken by any one who had seen a full-length picture of him, and yet no picture accurately resembled him in the minute traits of his person. His features, however, were so marked by prominent characteristics, which appear in all likenesses of him, that a stranger could not be mistaken in the man; he was remarkably dignified in his manners, and had an air of benignity over his features which his visitant did not expect, being rather prepared for sternness of countenance. . . . his smile was extraordinarily attractive. It was observed to me that there was an expression in Washington's face that no painter had succeeded in taking. It struck me no man could be better formed for command. A stature of six feet, a robust, but well-proportioned frame, calculated to sustain fatigue, without that heaviness which generally attends great muscular strength, and abates active exertion, displayed bodily power of no mean standard. A light eye and full—the very eye of genius and reflection rather than of blind passionate impulse. His nose appeared thick, and though it befitted his other features, was too coarsely and strongly formed to be the handsomest of its class. His mouth was like no other that I ever saw; the lips firm and the under jaw seeming to grasp the upper with force, as if its muscles were in full action when he sat still."

ANONYMOUS (1798)

"It was in the month of November, 1798, I first beheld the Father of his Country. It was very cold, the northwest wind blowing hard down the Potomac, at Georgetown, D. C. A troop of light-horse from Alexandria escorted him to the western bank of the river. The waves ran high and the boat which brought him over seemed to labor considerably. Several thousand people greeted his arrival with swelling hearts and joyful countenances; the military were drawn up in a long line to receive him; the officers, dressed in regimentals, did him homage. I was so fortunate as to walk by his side, and had a full view of him. Although only about ten years of age, the impression his person and manner then made on me is now perfectly revived. He was six feet one inch high, broad and athletic, with very large limbs, entirely erect and without the slightest tendency to stooping; his hair was white, and tied with a silk string, his countenance lofty, masculine, and contemplative; his eye light gray. He was dressed in the clothes of a citizen, and over these a blue surtout of the finest cloth. His weight must have been two hundred and thirty pounds, with no superfluous flesh, all was bone and sinew, and he walked like a soldier. Whoever has seen in the Patent Office at Washington, the dress he wore when resigning his commission as commander-in-chief, in December, 1783, at once perceives how large and magnificent was his frame. During the parade, something at a distance suddenly attracted his attention; his eye was instantaneously lighted up as with the lightning's flash. At this moment I see its marvellous animation, its glowing fire, exhibiting strong passion, controlled by deliberate reason.

"In the summer of 1799 I again saw the chief. He rode a purely white horse, seventeen hands high, well proportioned, of high spirit; he almost seemed conscious that he bore on his back the Father of his Country. He reminded me of the war-horse whose neck is clothed with thunder. I have seen some highly-accomplished riders, but not one of them approached Washington; he was perfect in this respect. Behind him, at the distance of perhaps forty yards, came Billy Lee, his body-servant, who had perilled his life in many a field, beginning on the heights of Boston, in 1775, and ending in 1781, when Cornwallis surrendered, and the captive army, with unexpressible chagrin, laid down their arms at Yorktown. Billy rode a cream-colored horse, of the finest form, and his old Revolutionary cocked hat indicated that its owner had often heard the roar of cannon and small arms, and had encountered many trying scenes. Billy was a dark mulatto. His master speaks highly of him in his will, and provides for his support."

JOHN BELL (1779)

"General Washington is now in the forty-seventh year of his age; he is a tall well-made man, rather large boned, and has a tolerably genteel address; his features are manly and bold, his eyes of a bluish cast and very lively; his hair a deep brown, his face rather long and marked with the small pox; his complexion sun-burnt and without much colour, and his countenance sensible, composed, and thoughtful; there is a remarkable air of dignity about him, with a striking degree of gracefulness."

JEAN PIERRE BRISSOT DE WARVILLE (1791)

"You have often heard me blame M. Chastellux for putting too much sprightliness in the character he has drawn of this general. To give pretensions to the portrait of a man who has none is truly absurd. The General's goodness appears in his looks. They have nothing of that brilliancy which his officers found in them when he was at the head of his army; but in conversation they become animated. He has no characteristic traits in his figure, and this has rendered it always so difficult to describe it; there are few portraits which resemble him. All his answers are pertinent; he shows the utmost reserve, and is very diffident; but, at the same time, he is firm and unchangeable in whatever he undertakes. His modesty must be very astonishing, especially to a Frenchman."

BARON CROMOT DU BOURG (1781)

"General Washington came to see M. de Rochambeau. Notified of his approach, we mounted our horses and went out to meet him. He received us with that affability which is natural to him and depicted on his countenance. He is a very fine looking man, but did not surprise me as much as I expected from the descriptions I had heard of him. His physiognomy is noble in the highest degree, and his manners are those of one perfectly accustomed to society, quite a rare thing certainly in America."

PRINCE DE BROGLIE (1782)

"General Washington is now about forty-nine years of age. He is tall, nobly built and very well proportioned. His face is much more agreeable than represented in his portrait. He must have been much handsomer three years ago, and although the gentlemen

who have remained with him during all that time say that he seems to have grown much older, it is not to be denied that the general is still as fresh and active as a young man."

MARQUIS DE CHASTELLUX (1781)

"In speaking of this perfect whole of which General Washington furnishes the idea, I have not excluded exterior form. His stature is noble and lofty, he is well made, and exactly proportionate; his physiognomy mild and agreeable, but such as to render it impossible to speak particularly of any of his features, so that in quitting him you have only the recollection of a fine face. He has neither a grave nor a familiar face, his brow is sometimes marked with thought, but never with inquietude; in inspiring respect he inspires confidence, and his smile is always the smile of benevolence."

GEORGE WASHINGTON PARKE CUSTIS (1826)

"General Washington, in the prime of life, stood six feet two inches, and measured precisely six feet when attired for the grave. From the period of the Revolution, there was an evident bending in that frame so passing straight before, but the stoop is attributable rather to the care and toils of that arduous contest than to age; for his step was firm, and his carriage noble and commanding, long after the time when the physical properties of man are supposed to be in the wane.

"To a majestic height, was added correspondent breadth and firmness, and his whole person was so cast in nature's finest mould as to resemble the classic remains of ancient statuary, where all the parts contribute to the purity and perfection of the whole.

"The power of Washington's arm was displayed in several memorable instances: in his throwing a stone from the bed of the stream to the top of the Natural Bridge; another over the Palisades into the Hudson, and yet another across the Rappahannock, at Fredericksburg. Of the article with which he spanned this bold and navigable stream, there are various accounts. We are assured that it was a piece of slate, fashioned to about the size and shape of a dollar, and which, sent by an arm so strong, not only spanned the river, but took the ground at least thirty yards on the other side. Numbers have since tried this feat, but none have cleared the water."

JOHN HUNTER (1785)

"The General is about six feet high, perfectly straight and well made; rather inclined to be lusty. His eyes are full and blue and seem to express an air of gravity. His nose inclines to the aquiline; his mouth is small; his teeth are yet good and his cheeks indicate perfect health. His forehead is a noble one and he wears his hair turned back, without curls and quite in the officer's style, and tyed in a long queue behind. Altogether he makes a most noble, respectable appearance, and I really think him the first man in the world.

. . . When I was first introduced to him he was neatly dressed in a plain blue coat, white cassimir waistcoat, and black breeches and boots, as he came from his farm. . . . The General came in again, with his hair neatly powdered, a clean shirt on, a new plain drab coat, white waistcoat and white silk stockings."

MARQUIS DE LAFAYETTE (1824)

"The person of Washington, always graceful, dignified and commanding, showed to peculiar advantage when mounted; it exhibited, indeed, the very *beau ideal* of a perfect cavalier. The good Lafayette, during his last visit to America, delighted to discourse of the 'times that tried men's souls.' From the venerated friend of our country we derived a most graphic description of Washington and the field of battle. Lafayette said, 'At Monmouth I commanded a division, and, it may be supposed I was pretty well occupied; still I took time, amid the roar and confusion of the conflict, to admire our beloved chief, who, mounted on a splendid charger, rode along the ranks amid the shouts of the soldiers cheering them by his voice and example, and restoring to our standard the fortunes of the fight. I thought then, as now,' continued Lafayette, 'that never had I beheld so *superb a man*'."

SENATOR WILLIAM MACLAY (1791)

"In stature about six feet, with an unexceptionable make, but lax appearance. His frame would seem to want filling up. His motions rather slow than lively, though he showed no signs of having suffered by gout or rheumatism. His complexion pale, nay, almost cadaverous. His voice hollow and indistinct, owing, as I believe, to artificial teeth before his upper jaw, which occasions a flatness."

CAPTAIN GEORGE MERCER (1759)

"Though distrusting my ability to give an adequate account of the personal appearance of Col. George Washington, late commander of the Virginia Provincial troops, I shall, as you request, attempt the portraiture. He may be described as being as straight as an Indian, measuring six feet two inches in his stockings, and weighing 175 pounds, when he took his seat in the House of Burgesses in 1759. His frame is padded with well-developed muscles, indicating great strength. His bones and joints are large, as are his hands and feet. He is wide shouldered, but not a deep or round chest, but is broad across the hips, and has rather long legs and arms. His head is well shaped though not large, but is gracefully poised on a superb neck. A large and straight rather than a prominent nose; blue-gray penetrating eyes, which are widely separated, and overhung by a heavy brow. His face is long rather than broad, with high, round cheek-bones, and terminates in a good firm chin. He has a clear though rather colorless pale skin, which burns with the sun. A pleasing, benevolent, though commanding countenance, dark brown hair, which he wears in a cue.

"His mouth is large and generally firmly closed, but which from time to time discloses some defective teeth. His features are regular and placid, with all the muscles of his face under perfect control, though flexible and expressive of deep feeling when moved by emotions. In conversation he looks you full in the face, is deliberate, deferential and engaging. His voice is agreeable rather than strong. His movements and gestures are graceful, his walk majestic, and he is a splendid horseman."

JEDIDIAH MORSE (1789)

"General Washington in his person was tall, upright, and well made; in his manner easy and unaffected. His eyes were of a bluish cast, not prominent, indicative of deep thoughtfulness, and when in action, on great occasions remarkably lively. His features strong, manly, and commanding; his temper reserved and serious; his countenance grave, composed, and sensible. There was in his whole appearance an unusual dignity and gracefulness which at once secured him profound respect, and cordial esteem. He seemed born to command his fellow men."

ABBE CLAUDE C. ROBIN (1781)

"Tall and noble stature, well proportioned, a fine, cheerful, open countenance, a simple and modest carriage; and his whole mien has something in it that interests the French, the Americans, and even enemies themselves in his favor."

DR. JAMES THACHER (1778)

"The personal appearance of our Commander in Chief, is that of the perfect gentleman and accomplished warrior. He is remarkably tall, full six feet, erect and well proportioned. The strength and proportion of his joints and muscles, appear to be commensurate with the preeminent powers of his mind. The serenity of his countenance, and majestic gracefulness of his deportment, impart a strong impression of that dignity and grandeur, which are his peculiar characteristics, and no one can stand in his presence

without feeling the ascendancy of his mind, and associating with his countenance the idea of wisdom, philanthropy, magnanimity, and patriotism. There is a fine symmetry in the features of his face indicative of a benign and dignified spirit. His nose is strait, and his eyes inclined to blue. He wears his hair in a becoming cue, and from his forehead it is turned back and powdered in a manner which adds to the military air of his appearance. He displays a native gravity, but devoid of all appearance of ostentation. His uniform dress is a blue coat, with two brilliant epaulettes, buff colored under clothes, and a three cornered hat with a black cockade. He is constantly equipped with an elegant small sword, boots and spurs, in readiness to mount his noble charger."

DR. JAMES THACHER (1779)

"Yesterday I accompanied Major Cavil to headquarters, and had the honor of being numbered among the guests at the table of his Excellency, with his lady, . . . It is natural to view with keen attention the countenance of an illustrious man, with a secret hope of discovering in his features some peculiar traces of excellence, which distinguishes him from and elevates him above his fellow mortals. These expectations are realized in a peculiar manner, in viewing the person of General Washington. His tall and noble and just proportions, cheerful open countenance, simple and modest deportment, are all calculated to interest every beholder in his favor, and to command veneration and respect. He is feared even when silent, and beloved even while we are unconscious of the motive. . . . In conversation, his Excellency's expressive countenance is peculiarly interesting and pleasing; a placid smile is frequently observed on his lips, but a loud laugh, it is said, seldom if ever escapes him. He is polite and attentive to each individual at table, and retires after the compliment of a few glasses.

EDWARD THORNTON, OF ENGLISH LEGATION (1792)

"His person is tall and sufficiently graceful; his face well formed, his complexion

rather pale, with a mild philosophic gravity in the expression of it. In his air and manner he displays much natural dignity; in his address he is cold, reserved, and even phlegmatic, though without the least appearance of haughtiness or ill-nature; it is the effect, I imagine, of constitutional diffidence. That caution and circumspection which form so striking and well known a feature in his military, and indeed, in his political character, is very strongly marked in his countenance, for his eyes retire inward (do you understand me?) and have nothing of fire of animation or openness in their expression."

HENRY WANSEY (1795)

"The President in his person is tall and thin, but exact; rather of an engaging than a dignified presence. He appears very thoughtful, is slow in delivering himself, which occasions some to conclude him reserved, but it is rather, I apprehend, the effect of much thinking and reflection, for there is great appearance to me of affability and accommodation. He was at this time in his sixty-third year . . . but he has very little the appearance of age, having been all his life long so exceeding temperate."

ISAAC WELD (1797)

"His chest is full; and his limbs, though rather slender, well shaped and muscular. His head is small, in which respect he resembles the make of a great number of his countrymen. His eyes are of a light grey colour; and in proportion to the length of his face, his nose is long. Mr. Stewart, the eminent portrait painter, told me, that there were features in his face totally different from what he ever observed in that of any other human being; the sockets for the eyes, for instance, are larger than what he ever met with before, and the upper part of the nose broader. All his features, he observed, were indicative of the strongest and most ungovernable passions, and had he been born in the forests, it was his opinion that he would have been the fiercest man among the savage tribes."

Part II

Character and Service

DELEGATE JOHN ADAMS (1775, 1776)

"I can now inform you that the Congress have made choice of the modest and virtuous, the amiable, generous and brave George Washington, Esquire to be General of the American army, and that he is to repair, as soon as possible, to the camp before Boston. This appointment will have a great effect in

cementing and securing the union of these colonies.

"There is something charming to me in the conduct of Washington. A gentleman of one of the first fortunes upon the continent, leaving his delicious retirement, his family and friends, sacrificing his ease, and hazarding all in the cause of his country! His views are noble and disinterested. He declared, when he accepted the mighty trust,

that he would lay before us an exact account of his expenses, and not accept a shilling for pay."

"I congratulate you, Sir, as well as all the Friends of Mankind on the Reduction of Boston, an event which appeared to me of so great and decisive importance, that the next Morning after the Arrival of the News, I did myself the honour to move, for the Thanks of Congress to your Excellency and that a Medal of Gold Should be Struck in commemoration of it. Congress have been pleased to appoint me, with two other Gentlemen to prepare a Device."

PRESIDENT JOHN ADAMS (1799)

"I have seen him in the days of adversity, in some of the scenes of his deepest distress and most trying perplexities; I have also attended him in his highest elevation and most prosperous felicity; with uniform admiration of his wisdom, moderation, and constancy. . . . Malice could never blast his honour, and envy made him a singular exception to her universal rule. For himself he had lived enough, to life and to glory. For his fellow-citizens, if their prayers could have been answered, he would have been immortal. For me, his departure is at a most unfortunate moment. . . . His example is now complete, and it will teach wisdom and virtue to magistrates, citizens, and men, not only in the present age, but in future generations, as long as our history shall be read."

REPRESENTATIVE FISHER AMES (1800)

"However his military fame may excite the wonder of mankind, it is chiefly by his civil magistracy that his example will instruct them. Great generals have arisen in all ages of the world, and perhaps most in those of despotism and darkness. In times of violence and convulsion, they rise by the force of the whirlwind, high enough to ride in it, and direct the storm. . . . But such a Chief Magistrate as Washington appears like the pole star in a clear sky, to direct the skilful statesman. His presidency will form an epoch, and be distinguished as the age of Washington. Already it assumes its high place in the political region. Like the milky way, it whitens along its allotted portion of the hemisphere. The latest generations of men will survey through the telescope of history."

JOHN BELL (1779)

"He has an excellent understanding without much quickness; is strictly just, vigilant, and generous; an affectionate husband, a faithful friend, a father to the deserving soldier; gentle in his manners, in temper rather reserved; a total stranger to religious prejudices, which have so often excited Christians of one denomination to cut the throats of those of another; in his morals irreproachable; he was never known to exceed the bounds of the most rigid temperance; in a word, all his friends and acquaintances universally allow, that no man ever united in his own person a more perfect alliance of the virtues of a philosopher with the talents of a general. Candour, sincerity, affability, and simplicity, seem to be the striking features of his character, till an occasion offers of displaying the more determined bravery and independence of spirit. General Washington having never been to Europe, could not possibly have seen much military service when the armies of Britain were sent to subdue

us; yet still, for a variety of reasons, he was by much the most proper man on this continent, and probably any where else, to be placed at the head of an American army. The very high estimation he stood in for integrity and honour, his engaging in the cause of his country from sentiment and a conviction of her wrongs, his moderation in politics, his extensive property, and his approved abilities as a commander, were motives which necessarily obliged the choice of America to fall upon him."

WILLIAM PAULETT CARY (1789)

"A stranger to profusion, yet generous in every instance where liberality was a virtue; during the late troubles, his fortune was employed in succouring merit, rewarding bravery, promoting discipline in the soldiery, and subordination to the new established government, in the citizens. At a time when the calamities incident to a state of civil warfare, fell heavy on all ranks, but principally on the middle class of his countrymen, his beneficence, which seemed to shun the public eye, would in all probability be lost in oblivion, but for the voice of those whom he freed from the accumulated miseries of famine, sickness and imprisonment.

"In whatever light we view the character of this truly great man we are struck with fresh cause for esteem and admiration: we every moment discover new and shining traits of humanity, of wisdom, and disinterested heroism: we see united in him the distinguished virtues of a good citizen, an experienced general, an upright senator, and a wise politician; we behold him rising superior to every mean consideration of self-love, hazarding his fortunes in the cause of freedom, cheerfully submitting to bear the name of rebel, and braving an ignominious death, to which he would inevitably have fallen a sacrifice, had Britain triumphed in the contest: we behold him furnishing an example the most interesting to humanity, and capable of nerving the palsied arm of age, or even of cowardise itself . . ."

DELEGATE ABRAHAM CLARK (1777)

"I believe the General is honest, but I think him fallible."

DELEGATE SILAS DEANE (1775)

"General Washington will be with You soon, possibly by the Time You receive This. His Election was unanimous, his acceptance of the high Trust, modest and polite, his Character I need not enlarge on but will only say to his honor, that he is said to be as fixed and resolute in having his Orders on all Occasions executed, as he is cool and deliberate, in giving them."

GENERAL NATHANAEL GREENE (1775, 1776)

"His Excellency, General, has arrived amongst us, universally admired. Joy was visible on every countenance, and it seemed

as if the spirit of conquest breathed through the whole army. I hope we shall be taught, to copy his example, and to prefer the love of liberty, in this time of public danger to all the soft pleasures of domestic life, and support ourselves with manly fortitude amidst all the dangers and hardships that attend a state of war. And I doubt not, under the General's wise direction, we shall establish such excellent order and strictness of discipline as to invite victory to attend him wherever he goes."

"Greater powers must be lodged in the hands of the General than he has ever yet exercised. . . . I can assure you that the General will not exceed his powers, though he may sacrifice the cause. There never was a man that might be more safely trusted, nor a time when there was a louder call."

COLONEL ALEXANDER HAMILTON (1778)

"The general I always revered and loved ever since I knew him, but in this instance he rose superior to himself. Every lip dwells on his praise, for even his pretended friends (for none dare to acknowledge themselves his enemies) are obliged to croak it forth."

DELEGATE ALEXANDER HAMILTON (1783)

"The Commander was already become extremely unpopular, among almost all ranks, from his known dislike to every unlawful proceeding; that this unpopularity was daily increasing and industriously promoted by many leading characters; that his choice of unfit and indiscreet persons into his family was the pretext, and with some the real motive; but the substantial one, a desire to displace him from the respect and confidence of the army, in order to substitute General ————, as the conductor of their efforts to obtain justice. Mr. Hamilton said that he knew General Washington intimately and perfectly; that his extreme reserve, mixed sometimes with a degree of asperity of temper, both of which were said to have increased of late, had contributed to the decline of his popularity; but that his virtue, his patriotism and firmness, would, it might be depended upon, never yield to any dishonorable or disloyal plans into which he might be called; that he would suffer himself to be cut to pieces."

PRESIDENT JOHN HANCOCK (1775)

"The Congress have appointed George Washington, Esqr., General and Commander in Chief of the Continental Army. His Commission is made out and I shall Sign it to morrow. He is a Gentleman you will all like. I submit to you the propriety of providing a suitable place for his Residence and the mode of his Reception. Pray tell Genl. Ward of this with my Respects, and that we all Expect to hear that the Military Movements of the Day of his Arrival will be such as to do him and the Commander in Chief great honour. . . . General Washington will set out in a few Days. . . . Pray do him every honour. By all means have his Commission read at the head of the whole Forces.''

DELEGATE PATRICK HENRY (1774)

"When Patrick Henry was asked 'whom he thought the greatest man in Congress,' he replied: 'If you speak of eloquence, Mr. Rutledge of South Carolina is by far the greatest orator, but if you speak of solid information and sound judgment, Colonel Washington is unquestionably the greatest man on that floor.' "

EX-PRESIDENT THOMAS JEFFERSON (1814)

"His mind was great and powerful, without being of the very first order; his penetration strong, though not so acute as that of a Newton, Bacon or Locke; and as far as he saw, no judgment was ever sounder. It was slow in operation, being little aided by invention or imagination, but sure in conclusion. Hence the common remark of his officers, of the advantage he derived from councils of war, where, hearing all suggestions, he selected whatever was best; and certainly no general ever planned his battles more judiciously. But if deranged during the course of the action, if any member of his plan was dislocated by sudden circumstances, he was slow in a readjustment. The consequence was, that he often failed in the field, and rarely against an enemy in station, as at Boston and York. He was incapable of fear, meeting personal dangers with the calmest unconcern. Perhaps the strongest feature in his character was prudence, never acting until every circumstance, every consideration, was maturely weighed; refraining if he saw a doubt, but, when once decided, going through with his purpose, whatever obstacles opposed. His integrity was most pure, his justice the most inflexible I have ever known, no motives of interest or consanguinity, of friendship or hatred, being able to bias his decision. He was, indeed, in every sense of the word, a wise, a good, and a great man. His temper was naturally irritable and high-toned; but reflection and resolution had obtained a firm and habitual ascendency over it. If ever, however, it broke its bonds, he was most tremendous in his wrath. . . .

"On the whole, his character was, in its mass, perfect, in nothing bad, in few points indifferent; and it may truly be said that never did nature and fortune combine more perfectly to make a man great, and to place him in the same constellation with whatever worthies have merited from man an everlasting remembrance. For his was the singular destiny and merit of leading the armies of his country successfully through an arduous war, for the establishment of its independence; of conducting its councils through the birth of a government, new in its forms and principles, until it had settled

down into a quiet and orderly train; and of scrupulously obeying the laws through the whole of his career, civil and military, of which the history of the world furnishes no other example.''

REPRESENTATIVE HENLY LEE (1799)

"Will you go with me to the banks of the Monongahela, to see your youthful Washington, supporting, in the dismal hour of Indian victory, the ill fated Braddock; and saving by his judgment and his valour; the remains of a defeated army, pressed by the conquering savage foe? or, when — oppressed America nobly resolving to risk her all in defense of her violated rights—he was elevated by the unanimous voice of Congress to the command of her armies? . .

"Who is there that has forgotten the vales of Brandywine—the fields of Germantown—or the plains of Monmouth? Every where present, wants of every kind obstructing, numerous and valiant armies encountering, himself a host, he assuaged our sufferings, limited our privations, and upheld our tottering Republic. . . .

"Possessing a clear and penetrating mind, a strong and sound judgment, calmness and temper for deliberation, with invincible firmness and perseverance in resolution maturely formed, drawing information from all, acting for himself, with incorruptible integrity and unvarying patriotism: his own superiority and the public confidence alike marked him as the man designed by heaven to lead in the great political as well as military events which have distinguished the era of his life. . . .

"First in war, first in peace, and first in the hearts of his countrymen, he was second to none in the humble and endearing scenes of private life: Pious, just, humane, temperate, and sincere; uniform, dignified, and commanding; his example was as edifying to all around him as were the effects of that example lasting.

"To his equals he was condescending; to his inferiors kind, and to the dear object of his effection exemplarily tender: Correct throughout, vice shuddered in his presence, and virtue always felt his fostering hand; the purity of his private character gave effulgence to his public virtues. . . . Such was the man for whom our nation mourns.''

TUTOR EBENEZER GRANT MARSH OF YALE (1800)

"Resolute and undejected in misfortunes, he rose superior to distresses, and surmounted difficulties, which no courage, no constancy, but his own, would have resisted. His letters during his most gloomy prospects, announce a hero, conscious of his danger, but still deriving a well grounded hope from the resources of his own mind. His valor was never unequal to his duty or the occasion. He attempted things with means that appeared totally inadequate, and successfully prosecuted what he had boldly resolved. He was never disheartened by difficulties, but

had that vigor of mind, which, instead of bending to opposition, rises above it, and seems to have a power of controlling even fortune itself. His character combined a cool and penetrating judgement and prompt decision, caution and intrepidity, patience and enterprise, generous tenderness and compassion, with undaunted heroism. . . .

"In no situation did Washington appear more truly great than at the helm of our federal government. Here he displayed an astonishing extent and precision of political integrity, an incorruptible heart, a constant attention to the grand principles of rational liberty, and an invariable attachment to his country. His genius was equal to the most enlarged views, and minute details, of civil policy. A vigorous mind, improved by the experience and study of mankind, dexterity and application in business, a judicious mixture of liberality and economy. Steadiness to pursue his ends, and flexibility to vary his means, marked his administration. He guided the passions of others, because he was master of his own.''

REPRESENTATIVE JOHN MARSHALL (1799)

"Our Washington is no more! The Hero, the Sage and the Patriot of America—the man on whom in times of danger, every eye was turned, and all hopes were placed—lives now, only in his own great actions, and in the hearts of an affectionate and afflicted people. . . .

"More than any other individual, and as much as to one individual was possible, has he contributed to found this our wide spreading empire, and to give to the western world its independence and its freedom. . . .

"Having effected the great object for which he was placed at the head of our armies, we have seen him convert the sword into the plowshare, and voluntarily sinking the soldier in the citizen. . . .

"We have seen him once more quit the retirement he loved, and in a season more stormy and tempestuous than war itself, with calm and wise determination, pursue the true interests of the nation and contribute, more than any other could contribute, to the establishment of that system of policy which will, I trust, yet preserve our peace, our honour and our independence.''

CHIEF JUSTICE JOHN MARSHALL (1804)

"The day finally came when his work was finished, and he could be, as he phrased it, 'translated into a private citizen.' Marshall describes the scene as follows: 'At noon, the principal officers of the army assembled at France's [sic] tavern; soon after which, their beloved commander entered the room. His emotions were too strong to be concealed. Filling a glass, he turned to them and said, "With a heart full of love and gratitude, I now take leave of you: I most devoutly wish that your latter days may be as prosperous and happy, as your former ones have been glorious and honorable." Having drunk, he added: "I cannot come to each of you to take my leave; but shall be obliged to you, if each of you will come and take me by the hand." General Knox, being nearest, turned to him. Incapable of utterance, Washington grasped his hand, and embraced him. In the same affectionate manner he took leave of each succeeding officer. In every eye was the tear of dignified sensibility, and not a word was articulated to interrupt the majestic silence, and the tenderness of the scene.' "

EX-MINISTER GOUVERNEUR MORRIS (1799)

"Born to high destinies, he was fashioned for them by the hand of nature. His form was noble—his port majestic. On his front were enthroned the virtues which exalt, and those which adorn the human character. So dignified his deportment, no man could approach him but with respect—none was great in his presence. You have all seen him, and you all have felt the reverence he inspired. . . . His judgement was always clear, because his mind was pure. And seldom, if ever, will a sound understanding be met in the company of a corrupt heart. . . . In him were the courage of a soldier, the intrepidity of a chief, the fortitude of a hero. He had given to the impulsions of bravery all the calmness of his character, and, if in the moment of danger, his manner was distinguishable from that of common life, it was by superior ease and grace. . . . Knowing how to appreciate the world, its gifts and glories, he was truly wise. Wise also in selecting the objects of his pursuit. And wise in adopting just means to compass honorable ends."

DELEGATE ROBERT MORRIS (1777)

"Remember, my good Sir, that few men can keep their feelings to themselves, and that it is necessary for example's sake, that all leaders should feel and think boldly in order to inspirit others, who look up to them. Heaven, no doubt for the noblest purposes, has blessed you with a firmness of mind, steadiness of countenance, and patience in sufferings, that give you infinite advantages over other men. This being the case, you are not to depend on other people's exertions being equal to your own. One mind feeds and thrives on misfortunes by finding resources to get the better of them; another sinks under their weight, thinking it impossible to resist; and, as the latter description probably includes the majority of mankind, we must be cautious of alarming them."

JEDIDIAH MORSE (1789)

"It is hoped posterity will be taught, in what manner he transformed an undisciplined body of peasantry into a regular army of soldiers. Commentaries on his campaigns would undoubtedly be highly interesting and instructive to future generations. The conduct of the first campaign, in compelling the British troops to abandon Boston by a bloodless victory, will merit minute narration. But a volume would scarcely contain the mortifications he experienced and the hazards to which he was exposed in 1776 and 1777, in contending against the prowess of Britain, with an inadequate force. His good destiny and consummate prudence prevented want of success from producing want of confidence on the part of the public; for want of success is apt to lead to the adoption of pernicious counsels through the levity of the people or the ambition of their demagogues."

GOVERNOR AND COUNCIL OF NORTH CAROLINA (1790)

"We congratulate ourselves with equal sincerity in beholding you, Sir, in the high department which your virtues merited, and to which your country unanimously and gratefully appointed you. The importance of your situation receives additional dignity by the veneration your Country possesses for your character, and from a confidence that every power vested in you by the Constitution will be exerted for the happiness and prosperity of our country. . . . We have just received the happy information of your recovery from a disorder which threatened your life; a life we may truly say as necessary as dear to us:—With grateful hearts we return thanks to the great Disposer of events for this beneficent mark of his attention in preserving you. May it long be shewn in continuing you among us, and when the awful day comes which is to separate you from us, may you receive the reward of those virtues, which he only can give."

AN OFFICER (1777)

"Our army love their General very much, but they have one thing against him, which is the little care he takes of himself in any action. His personal bravery, and the desire he has of animating his troops by example, make him fearless of danger. This occasions us much uneasiness. But Heaven, which has hitherto been his shield, I hope will still continue to guard so valuable a life."

TIMOTHY PICKERING (1811)

"To the excellency of his *virtues* I am not disposed to set any limits. All his views were upright, all his actions just."

SENATE OF THE UNITED STATES (1799)

"With patriotic pride, we review the life of our Washington, and compare him with those of other countries who have been preeminent in fame. Ancient and modern names are diminished before him. Greatness and guilt have too often been allied; but his fame is whiter than it is brilliant. The destroyers of nations stood abashed at the majesty of his virtue. It reproved the intemperance of their ambition, and darkened the splendor of victory. . . . Let his countrymen consecrate the memory of the heroic General, the patriotic Statesman, and the virtuous Sage; let them teach their children never to forget that the fruit of his labours and his example, are their inheritance."

PRESIDENT SMITH OF NEW JERSEY COLLEGE (1800)

"Washington was always equal to himself. There was a dignity in the manner in which he performed the smallest things. A majesty surrounded him that seemed to humble those who approached him, at the same time that there was a benignity in his manner that invited their confidence and esteem. His virtues, always elevated and splendid, shone only with a milder light by being placed in the vale of retirement. He was sincere, modest, upright, humane; a friend of religion; the idol of his neighbors as well as of his country; magnificent in his hospitality, but plain in his manners, and simple in his equipage. . . .

"His whole character was consistent. Equally industrious with his plough as with his sword, he esteemed idleness and inutility the greatest disgrace of man, whose powers attain perfection only by constant and vigorous action, and who is placed by providence in so many social relations, only to do good. Every thing round him was marked with a dignified simplicity. . . . The virtues and the talents which, in other instances, are divided among many, are combined in him."

WILLIAM SULLIVAN (1797)

"The following are recollections of Washington, derived from repeated opportunities of seeing him during the last three years of his public life. He was over six feet in stature; of strong, bony, muscular frame, without fulness of covering, well formed and straight. He was a man of most extraordinary physical strength. In his own house his action was calm, deliberate, and dignified, without pretension to gracefulness, or peculiar manner, but merely natural, and such as one would think it should be in such a man. When walking in the street, his movement had not the soldierly air which might be expected. His habitual motions had been formed before he took command of the American armies, in the wars of the interior, and in the surveying of wilderness lands, employments in which grace and elegance were not likely to be acquired. At the age of sixty-five, time had done nothing toward bending him out of his natural erectness. His deportment was invariably grave; it was sobriety that stopped short of sadness. His presence inspired a veneration, and a feeling of awe, rarely experienced in the presence of any man. His mode of speaking was slow and deliberate, not as though he was in search of fine words, but that he might utter those only adapted to his purpose. It was the usage of all persons in good society to attend Mrs. Washington's levee every Friday evening. He was always present. The young ladies used to throng around him, and engage him in conversation. There were some of the well-remembered belles of that day who imagined themselves to be favorites with him. As these were the only opportunities which they had of conversing with him, they were disposed to use them. One would think, that a gentleman and a gallant soldier, if he could ever laugh or dress his countenance in smiles, would do so when surrounded by young and admiring beauties. But this was never so; the countenance of Washington never softened; nor changed its habitual gravity. One who had lived always in his family said, that his manner in public life was always the same. Being asked whether Washington *could* laugh: this person said, that this was a rare occurrence, but one instance was remembered when he laughed most heartily at her narration of an incident in which she was a party concerned; and in which he applauded her agency. The late General Cobb, who was

long a member of his family during the war, (and who enjoyed a laugh as much as any man could,) said, that he never saw Washington laugh, excepting when Colonel Scammel (if this was the person) came to dine at headquarters. Scammel had a fund of ludicrous anecdotes, and a manner of telling them, which relaxed even the gravity of the commander-in-chief."

MILITARY SECRETARY TENCH TILGHMAN (1777)

"If it please God to spare the life of the honestest man that I believe ever adorned human nature, I have no doubt of . . . [freedom]. I think I know the sentiments of his heart, and in prosperity and adversity I never knew him utter a wish or drop an expression that did not tend to the good of

his country, regardless of his own interest. He is blessed wherever he goes, for the tory is protected in person and property equally with the whig; and indeed I often think more, for it is his maxim to convert by good usage and not by severity."

VIRGINIA INSCRIPTION ON THE HOUDON STATUE (1784)

"The General Assembly of the Commonwealth of Virginia have caused this statue to be erected as a Monument of Affection and Gratitude to George Washington, who, uniting to the Endowments of the Hero the Vitrues of the Patriot, and exerting both in establishing the Liberties of his Country, has rendered his Name dear to his Fellow Citizens, and given the World an immortal Example of true Glory."

Part III
World Status

"AMERICAN GENTLEMAN NOW IN LONDON" (1779)

"General Washington, altho' advanced in years, is remarkably healthy, takes a great deal of exercise, and is very fond of riding on a favorite white horse; he is very reserved, and loves retirement. When out of camp he has only a single servant attending him, and when he returns within the lines a few of the light horse escort him to his tent. When he has any great object in view he sends for a few of the officers of whose abilities he has a high opinion, and states his present plan among half a dozen others, to all which they give their separate judgments: by these means he gets all their opinions, without divulging his intentions. He has no tincture of pride, and will often converse with a centinel with more freedom than he would with a general officer. He is very shy and reserved to foreigners, altho' they have letters of recommendation, from the Congress. He punishes neglect of duty with great severity, but is very tender and indulgent to recruits until they learn the articles of war and their exercise perfectly. He has a great antipathy to spies, although he employs them himself, and has an utter aversion to all Indians. He regularly attends divine service in his tent every morning and evening, and seems very fervent in his prayers. He is so tender-hearted, that no soldiers must be flogged nigh his tent, or if he is walking in the camp, and sees a man tied to the halberds, he will either order him to be taken down, or walk another way to avoid his sight. He has made the art of war his particular study; his plans are in general good and well digested;

he is particularly careful always of securing a retreat, but his chief qualifications are steadiness, perseverence, and secrecy; any act of bravery he is sure to reward, and make a short eulogium on the occasion to the person and his fellow soldiers (if it be a soldier) in the ranks. He is humane to the prisoners who fall into his hands, and orders everything necessary for their relief. He is very temperate in his diet, and the only luxury he indulges himself in, is a few glasses of punch after supper."

CLAUDE BLANCHARD (1781)

"This day General Washington, who was expected, arrived [at Newport] about two o'clock. He first went to the *Duc de Burgoyne*, where all our generals were. He then landed; all the troops were under arms; I was presented to him. His face is handsome, noble and mild. He is tall (at the least, five feet, eight inches). In the evening, I was at supper with him. I mark as a fortunate day, that in which I have been able to behold a man so truly great."

JEAN PIERRE BRISSOT DE WARVILLE (1791)

"He shows the utmost reserve, and is very diffident; but, at the same time, he is firm and unchangeable in whatever he undertakes. His modesty must be very astonishing, especially to a Frenchman. He speaks of the American war as if he had not directed it; and of his victories with an indifference which strangers even would not affect. I never saw him divest himself of that coolness by which he is characterized, and become warm but when speaking of the present state of America. . . . He spoke to

me of M. La Fayette with tenderness. He regarded him as his son; and foresaw with a joy mixed with anxiety, the part he was about to play in the revolution preparing in France."

PRINCE DE BROGLIE (1782)

"His physiognomy is mild and open. His accost cold although polite. His pensive eyes seem more attentive than sparkling; but their expression is benevolent, noble and self-possessed. In his private conduct, he preserves that polite and attentive good breeding which satisfies everybody, and that dignified reserve which offends no one. He is a foe to ostentation and to vain-glory. His temper is always even. He has never testified the least humor. Modest even to humility, he does not seem to estimate himself at his true worth. He receives with perfect grace all the homages which are paid him, but he evades rather than seeks them. . . .

"Mr. Washington's first military services were against the French in the War for Canada. He had no opportunity for distinguishing himself, and after the defeat of Braddock, the war having crossed the river St. Lawrence, and the Virginia militia of which he was a Colonel having been sent home, he was not kept in active service; whereupon he retired to his plantation where he lived like a philosopher.

"His estate was quite distant from the seat of the English government, the real hotbed of the insurrection; and his wise character withheld him still further from mixing in its movements, so that he had but little share in the first troubles.

"On the breaking out of hostilities with

the mother-country, every body wished a chief who joined a profound sagacity to the advantage of having had military experience. All eyes turned toward Washington, and he was unanimously called to the command of the army. The course of events justified the choice. Never was there a man better fitted to command the Americans, and his conduct throughout developed the greatest foresight, steadiness and wisdom."

LORD BYRON (1818-1821)

"Can tyrants but by tyrants conquer'd be,
  And freedom find no champion and no child
Such as Columbia saw arise when she
  Sprung forth a Pallas, arm'd and undefiled?
Or must such minds be nourish'd in the wild,
  Deep in the unpruned forest 'midst the roar
Of cataracts, where nursing Nature smiled
  On infant Washington? Has Earth no more
Such seeds within her breast, or Europe no such shore?"

"Not so Leonidas and Washington,
  Whose every battle-field is holy ground,
Which breathes of nations saved, not worlds undone.
  How sweetly on the ear such echoes sound!
While the mere victor's may appal or stun
  The servile and the vain, such names will be
A watchword till the future shall be free."

"Great men have always scorn'd great recompenses; . . .
  George Washington had thanks and nought beside,
Except the all-cloudless glory (which few men's is)
  To free his country."

"While Franklin's quiet memory climbs to Heaven,
  Calming the lightning which he thence had riven,
Or drawing from the no less kindled earth
  Freedom and peace to that which boasts his birth;
While Washington's a watchword, such as ne'er
  Shall sink while there's an echo left to air."

PHILLIPS CALLBECK (1775)

[American armed vessels took prisoners on the island of St. John's and pillaged defenceless inhabitants. Such conduct, however, could not fail to excite the indignation of the commander-in-chief and he released the captives immediately, and orders were given for restoring the goods. The following note was written by Mr. Callbeck, one of the captured officials.]

"I should ill deserve the generous treatment, which your Excellency has been pleased to show me, had I not gratitude to acknowledge so great a favor. I cannot ascribe any part of it to my own merit, but must impute the whole to the philanthropy and humane disposition, that so truly characterize General Washington. Be so obliging, therefore, as to accept the only return in my power, that of my grateful thanks."

MARQUIS DE CHASTELLUX (1781)

"I wish only to express the impression General Washington has left on my mind; the idea of a perfect whole, that cannot be the produce of enthusiasm, which rather would reject it, since the effect of proportion is to diminish the idea of greatness. Brave without temerity, laborious without ambition, generous without prodigality, noble without pride, virtuous without severity; he seems always to have confined himself within those limits, where the virtues, by clothing themselves in more lively, but more changeable and doubtful colours, may be mistaken for faults. This is the seventh year that he has commanded the army, and that he has obeyed the Congress; more need not be said, especially in America, where they know how to appreciate all the merit contained in this simple fact. . . .

"It will be said of him, AT THE END OF A LONG CIVIL WAR, HE HAD NOTHING WITH WHICH HE COULD REPROACH HIMSELF. If anything can be more marvellous than such a character, it is unanimity of the public suffrages in his favour. Soldiers, magistrates, people, all love and admire him; all speak of him in terms of tenderness and veneration. Does there then exist a virtue capable of restraining the injustice of mankind; or are glory and happiness too recently established in America, for Envy to have deigned to pass the seas?"

PETER S. DU PONCEAU (1778)

"General Washington received the Baron [Steuben] with great cordiality, and to me he showed much condescending attention. I cannot describe the impression that the first sight of that great man made upon me. I could not keep my eyes from that imposing countenance—grave, yet not severe; affable, without familiarity. Its predominant expression was calm dignity, through which you could trace the strong feelings of the patriot, and discern the father as well as the commander of his soldiers. I have never seen a picture that represents him to me as I saw him at Valley Forge, and during the campaigns in which I had the honor to follow him. Perhaps that expression was beyond the skill of the painter; but while I live it will remain impressed on my memory. I had frequent opportunities of seeing him, as it was my duty to accompany the Baron when he dined with him, which was sometimes twice or thrice in the same week."

COUNT AXEL DE FERSEN (1780)

"I was at Hartford, . . . with M. de Rochambeau. . . . M. de Rochambeau sent me in advance, to announce his arrival, and I had time to see this man, illustrious, if not unique in our century. His handsome and majestic, while at the same time mild and open countenance perfectly reflects his moral qualities; he looks the hero; he is very cold; speaks little, but is courteous and frank. A shade of sadness overshadows his countenance, which is not unbecoming, and gives him an interesting air."

LOUIS, COUNT DE FONTANES (1800)

"The people who so lately stigmatized Washington as a rebel, regard even the enfranchisement of America, as one of the events consecrated by history and past ages. Such is the veneration excited by great characters. He seems so little to belong to modern times, that he imparts to us the same vivid impressions as the most august examples of antiquity with all that they accomplished. His work is scarcely finished when it at once attracts the veneration which we freely accord to those achievements only that are consecrated by time. The American revolution, the contemporary of our own, is fixed forever. Washington began it with energy, and finished it with moderation. He knew how to maintain it, pursuing always the prosperity of his country; and this aim alone can justify at the tribunal of the Most High, enterprises so extraordinary.

"His administration was as mild and firm in internal affairs as it was noble and prudent toward foreign nations. He uniformly respected the usages of other countries, as he would desire the rights of Americans to be respected by them. Thus in all his negotiations, the heroic simplicity of the President of the United States, without elevation or debasement, was brought into communication with the majesty of Kings. He sought not in his administration those conceptions which the age calls great, but which he regarded as vain. His ideas were more sage than bold; he sought not admiration, but he always enjoyed esteem, alike in the field and in the Senate, in the midst of business as in the quiet of retirement."

MEMBER OF PARLIAMENT CHARLES JAMES FOX (1794)

"And here, Sir, I cannot help alluding to the President of the United States, General Washington, a character whose conduct has been so different from that, which has been pursued by the ministers of this country. How infinitely wiser must appear the spirit and principles manifested in his late address to Congress, than the policy of modern European courts! Illustrious man, deriving honor less from the splendor of his situation than from the dignity of his mind; before whom all borrowed greatness sinks into significance, and all the potentates of Europe (excepting the members of our own royal family) become little and contemptible! He has had no occasion to have recourse to any tricks of policy or arts of alarm; his authority has been sufficiently supported by the same means by which it was acquired, and his conduct has uniformly been characterized by wisdom, moderation and firmness."

MINISTER CONRAD A. GERARD (1779)

"I have had many conversations with General Washington. . . . I have formed as high an opinion of the powers of his mind, his moderation, his patriotism, and his virtues, as I had before from common report conceived of his military talents and of the incalculable services he has rendered to his country."

CHEVALIER ANNE C. DE LA LUZERNE (1784)

"The estate of General Washington not being more than fifteen leagues from Annapolis I accepted an invitation that he gave me to go and pass several days there, and it is from his house that I have the honor to write to you. After having seen him on my arrival on this continent, in the midst of his camp and in the tumult of arms, I have the pleasure to see him a simple citizen, enjoying in the repose of his retreat the glory which he so justly acquired. . . . He dresses in a gray coat like a Virginia farmer, and nothing about him recalls the recollections of the important part which he has played except the great number of foreigners who come to see him."

JOSEPH MANDRILLON (1782)

"Imposing in size, noble and well proportioned, a countenance open, calm and sedate, but without any one striking feature, and when you depart from him, the remembrance only of a fine man will remain, a fine figure, an exterior plain and modest, a pleasing address, firm without severity, a manly courage, an uncommon capacity for grasping the whole scope of a subject, and a complete experience in war and politics; equally useful in the cabinet and in the field of Mars, the idol of his country, the admiration of the enemy he has fought and vanquished; modest in victory, great in the reverse; why do I say reverse! very far from being subdued he has made every misfortune contribute to his success. He knows how to obey as well as command, he never made use of his power or the submission of his army to derogate from the authority of his country or to disobey its commands."

PETER IVANOVITCH POLETICA (1812)

"All the life of this man, worthy of eternal praise, can be compared to the cleanest of looking glasses. If one can not say that he was always above the situation he occupied, one can however assert that in any case he was always adequate to it. In his private life, Gen. Washington was always a loving husband, ardent and steadfast friend, a just master and a pious christian."

ABBE CLAUDE C. ROBIN (1781)

"He has ever shown himself superior to fortune, and in the most trying adversity has discovered resources till then unknown; and, as if his abilities only increased and dilated at the prospect of difficulty, he is never better supplied than when he seems destitute of everything, nor have his arms ever been so fatal to his enemies, as at the very instant when they thought they had crushed him for ever. . . .

"Old men, women, and children, press about him when he accidently passes along, and think themselves happy, once in their lives, to have seen him—they follow him through the towns with torches, and celebrate his arrival by public illuminations. The Americans, that cool and sedate people, who in the midst of their most trying difficulties, have attended only to the directions and impulses of plain method and common sense, are roused, animated, and inflamed at the very mention of his name: and the first songs that sentiment or gratitude has dictated, have been to celebrate General Washington."

COMTE DE SEGUR (1782)

"One of my most earnest wishes was to see Washington, the hero of America. He was then encamped at a short distance from us, and the Count de Rochambeau was kind enough to introduce me to him. Too often reality disappoints the expectations our imagination had raised, and admiration diminishes by a too near view of the object upon which it had been bestowed; but, on seeing General Washington, I found a perfect similarity between the impression produced upon me by his aspect, and the idea I had formed of him. His exterior disclosed, as it were, the history of his life: simplicity, grandeur, dignity, calmness, goodness, firmness, the attributes of his character, were also stamped upon his features, and in all his person. His stature was noble and elevated; the expression of his features mild and benevolent; his smile graceful and pleasing; his manners simple, without familiarity. . . . Washington, when I saw him, was forty-nine years of age. He endeavored modestly to avoid the marks of admiration and respect which were so anxiously offered to him, and yet no man ever knew better how to receive and to acknowledge them. He listened, with an obliging attention, to all those who addressed him, and the expression of his countenance had conveyed his answer before he spoke."

CHEVALIER DE SILLY (1781)

"Man is born with a tendency to pride and the further he progresses in his career in an elevated rank the more his self love nourishes this vice in him but so far this Washington although born with every superior quality adds to them an imposing modesty which will always cause him to be admired by those who have the good fortune to see him; as for esteem he has already drawn to himself that of all Europe even in

the heart of his enemies and ours—'tandem oculi nostri, videuntur honorem et virtutem.' "

FRANCIS ADRIAN VAN DER KEMP (1800)

"Washington's character was from his first entrance in public life through its whole course not only unimpeached but highly revered by all, who were admitted to his acquaintance. His active prudence was guided by his intrepid courage:—his vigilant mind, never appalled in the most distressing emergence, was always enliven'd by a manly devotion, and all these virtues, with a vivid sense of his own intrinsic value, were only equalled by his modesty. Remembering that he was a man, Washington made every reasonable allowance for the frailities of human nature, pardon'd its weaknesses, and pity'd her follies, as often they were not blackened by vices, or the Public welfare did not require the infliction of a severer punishment. . . .

"We wrong this eminent man M. H.! [my hearers] in considering him alone as a General. Washington's claims, as a statesman, on our on Posterity's respectful regard, are equally solid. We Americans, assent with all heart to this self-evident truth. Lett Foreigners—to appreciate the solidity of our judgment, consider maturely Washington's admonitions—when he divested himself of the supreme command—dijudicate our Constitution, as a part of his egregious workmanship, and scrutinise his letter to the Individual states, as President of the Convention, and none of them will longer hesitate to go over in the steps of Columbia's sons. A constitution is adopted, and Washington unanimously chosen President of the United States. Here once more this great and good man sacrifices the delights of his retirement to the toils of a laborious life, for the benefit of his Country—with the same inimitable disinterestedness. What a large—what an immense field of glory for him, of stupefying amazement for us see I here opening!

"The sight of the General in his brightest glory is lost in the radiancy of this new Politic Luminary. Mine eyes are weakening—bedimmed—bedewed, but my heart in the same moment joyfully expanded by its benign all vivifying influence."

CHARLES VARLO (1784)

"I crossed the river from Maryland into Virginia, near the renowned General Washington's, where I had the honour to spend some time, and was kindly entertained with that worthy family. As to the General, if we may judge by the countenance, he is what the world says of him, a shrewd, good-natured, plain, humane man, about fifty-five years of age, and seems to wear well, being healthful and active, straight, well made, and about six feet high. He keeps a good table, which is always open to those of a genteel appearance. He does not use many Frenchified congees or flattering useless words without meaning, which savours more of deceit than an honest heart; but on the contrary, his words seem to point at truth and reason, and to spring from the fountain of a heart, which being good of itself, cannot be suspicious of others, till facts unriddle designs, . . .

"I have travelled and seen a great deal of the world, have conversed with all degrees of people, and have remarked that there are only two persons in the world which have every one's good word, and those are—the Queen of England and General Washington,

which I never heard friend or foe speak slightly of."

HENRY WANSEY (1794)

"I confess, I was struck with awe and veneration, when I recollected that I was now in the presence of one of the greatest men upon earth—the GREAT WASHINGTON—the noble and wise benefactor of the world! . . . Whether we view him as a general in the field vested with unlimited authority and power, at the head of a vic-

torious army; or in the cabinet, as the President of the United States; or as a private gentleman, cultivating his own farm; he is still the same great man, anxious only to discharge with propriety the duties of his relative situation. His conduct has always been so uniformly manly, honorable, just, patriotic, and disinterested, that his greatest enemies cannot fix on any one trait of his character that can deserve the least censure."

Part IV
Principal Official Appointments (1749-1799)

1749, July 20—Official Surveyor of Culpeper County, Va., through examination and commission by William and Mary College.

1752, November 6—District Adjutant-General with rank of major in Virginia Militia. The initial appointment was to the Southern District, but at his request early in 1753 Governor Dinwiddie assigned him to the Northern District in November of that year.

1753, October 31—Dispatched by Governor Dinwiddie with message to the French commandant on the Ohio.

1754, March 15—Lieutenant-Colonel of the Virginia Regiment (Colonel Fry), and sent with troops to complete the fort at the Forks of the Ohio.

June 4—Announcement of appointment as Colonel, on death of Fry. Resigned before the end of the year.

1755, May 10—Aide-de-Camp, appointed by General Braddock; a volunteer position without rank.

August 14—Colonel of the Virginia Regiment and Commander in Chief of Virginia Forces. This gave him no authority over regular officers commanding provincials on the frontier.

1756, February-March—Trip to Boston to secure a decision on rank of provincials from Governor Shirley, who commanded the British forces in America.

1758—Participated in the Forbes expedition.

July 24 — Burgess for Frederick County, first election; reelected, May 18, 1761.

December—Resigned commission as Colonel of the Virginia Regiment and Commander in Chief of Virginia Forces.

1762, October 25 — Vestryman of Truro Parish in Fairfax County; also elected for Fairfax Parish, March 28, 1765, but did not serve, being reelected to Truro soon after.

1763, October 3—Warden of Pohick Church of Truro Parish.

1765—Justice of the Peace (see 1770).

July 16—Burgess for Fairfax County, first election; reelected December 1, 1768; September 14, 1769; December 4, 1771; July 14, 1774.

1766—Trustee of Alexandria.

1770, October—Justice of the Peace for Fairfax County; so given in a list of this date; time of appointment not stated, but his ledger mentions attending court at Alexandria as early as June 18, 1765.

1774, July 5—Member of Fairfax County Meeting.

July 18—Chairman of County Meeting at Alexandria that adopted the Fairfax County Resolves; appointed to carry resolves to the Provincial Convention; also member of the Fairfax County Committee of Safety.

August 1-6—Member of First Virginia Provincial Convention; attends as Burgess and special delegate.

August 5—Elected by the Provincial Convention delegate to the First Continental Congress.

September 5-October 26—Attends the Congress at Philadelphia.

1775—Field Officer of the Independent Companies in several counties in Virginia.

February 20—Member of Second Provincial Convention; elected for Fairfax County.

March 20-27—Attend Virginia Provincial Convention at Richmond.

March 25—Chosen by the Provincial Convention delegate to the Second Continental Congress.

May 10-June 22—Attends the Congress at Philadelphia.

June 15—Elected by Congress General and Commander in Chief of the Army of the United Colonies.

June 16—Accepts the election.

June 19 — Commissioned as Commander in Chief.

July 3—Takes command at Cambridge, Mass.

1783, December 23—Surrenders commission to Congress at Annapolis.

1784, December 20-29—Attends upon the Maryland Legislature at Annapolis as Virginia representative for joint legislation on Potomac Improvement.

1787, March 28—Virginia Delegate to the Federal Convention; accepts appointment.

May 25—President of the Federal Convention; unanimously elected.

1789, February 4—President of the United States; elected by unanimous vote for the term 1789-1793.

April 30—President of the United States; inaugurated at New York.

1790, July 16—Act for establishing permanent seat of Government; President Washington authorized by act of Congress to appoint commissioners and direct their activities in locating the district, laying out the city, selecting sites for public buildings, etc.

1791, March 28-30—Commission to lay out the Federal District; first meeting at Georgetown.

March 30—Proclamation of boundaries of District.

1792, December 5—President of the United States; reelected by unanimous electoral vote.

1793, March 4 — Second inauguration at Philadelphia.

September 18—Lays cornerstone of the Capitol at City of Washington.

1797, March 4 — Second Presidential term expires.

1798, July 4—Lieutenant General and Commander in Chief of the Armies; appointed by President Adams.

July 13—Accepts appointment.

(See also pp. 28, 91.)

Selected Authorities

The biographies, biographical sketches, scenarios, addresses, and short comments on Washington run into the thousands; a classification of the most important of these will be found in Pamphlet 15 of this series. Comments printed during Washington's lifetime or soon after are, of course, long out of print and to be found usually only in the large libraries. Several of the books listed below bring together some of these early utterances; but for the most part, unless the tribute is in a work specially devoted to Washington, it is likely to be in a mass of unrelated material and not accessible. Hence the particular value of the present pamphlet. Three of the other books listed below are bibliographies, which will help to open up contemporary material for those desiring to search further.

BAKER, WILLIAM S.—*Bibliotheca Washingtoniana; a Descriptive List of the Biographies and Biographical Sketches.* Philadelphia, Lindsay, 1889. (Arranged chronologically.)

BAKER, WILLIAM S., ED.—*Character Portraits of Washington as delineated by Historians, Orators and Divines, selected and arranged in Chronological Order with Biographical Notes and References.* Philadelphia, Lindsay, 1887.

BAKER, WILLIAM S., ED.—*Early Sketches of George Washington, reprinted with Biographical and Bibliographical Notes.* Philadelphia, Lippincott, 1894.

CHANNING, HART AND TURNER.—*Guide to the Study of American History.* Boston, Ginn, 1912. A classified bibliography including books on the period of Washington.

HOUGH, FRANKLIN B., ED.—*Washingtoniana: or, Memorials of the Death of George Washington, . . . with a List of Tracts and Volumes printed upon the Occasion.* 2 vols. Roxbury, Mass., the Author, 1865.

MERRIAM, GEORGE ERNEST, ED. — *More precious than Fine Gold: Washington Commonplace Book.* New York, Putnam, 1931.

SAWYER, JOSEPH DILLAWAY.—*Washington.* 2 vols. New York, Macmillan, 1927. (Especially Vol. II, chs. xl, xli.)

STILLWELL, MARGARET B. — *Washington Eulogies; a Check List.* New York, Public Library, 1916.

TUCKERMAN, HENRY T.—*Character and Portraits of Washington.* New York, Putnam, 1859.

GEORGE WASHINGTON ON HIS FARM
From a painting by Chappel

Washington the Farmer
By David M. Matteson
Part I
Land and Crops and Stock

GEORGE WASHINGTON
From an engraving by Amos Doolittle, after a portrait by Joseph Wright

INTEREST IN FARMING

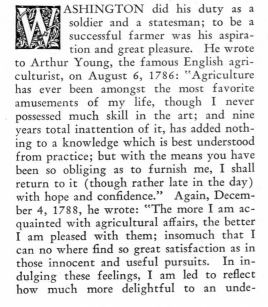

WASHINGTON did his duty as a soldier and a statesman; to be a successful farmer was his aspiration and great pleasure. He wrote to Arthur Young, the famous English agriculturist, on August 6, 1786: "Agriculture has ever been amongst the most favorite amusements of my life, though I never possessed much skill in the art; and nine years total inattention of it, has added nothing to a knowledge which is best understood from practice; but with the means you have been so obliging as to furnish me, I shall return to it (though rather late in the day) with hope and confidence." Again, December 4, 1788, he wrote: "The more I am acquainted with agricultural affairs, the better I am pleased with them; insomuch that I can no where find so great satisfaction as in those innocent and useful pursuits. In indulging these feelings, I am led to reflect how much more delightful to an undebauched mind, is the task of making improvements on the earth, than all the vain glory that can be acquired from ravaging it, by the most uninterrupted career of conquest." Nor were these sentiments simply polite expressions to harmonize with the known belief of his correspondent. Similar phrases are mixed throughout his correspondence, and are exemplified by the actions and observations recorded in the diaries.

Washington was always land hungry, and added various tracts to the original home fields; so that in the end he owned some 8,000 acres, divided into five farms and woodlands. He also carried on fisheries, a ferry, and a mill attached to the holdings.

On this land Washington practiced not only farming in its restricted extent but stock raising, including horses, mules, sheep, cattle, and hogs, as well as hounds, and forage crops for the stock; horticulture; landscape gardening; and, what was particularly unusual in Virginia at this time, the improvement of farming implements and the building of barns and other shelters.

WASTEFUL FARMING IN VIRGINIA

The system of culture to which Washington, the planter, was born was one of extension only with a single crop basis of tobacco production, the rank growth of which and the rude slave labor that looked out for it, soon exhausted the land and compelled abandonment of worked lands and clearing of new fields to be in turn subjected to nature's ravages. Destructive farming was the rule; conservation was unknown. This was not unreasonable in colonial or even later times; Washington well discussed the question in 1791. "The aim of the farmers in this country (if they can be called farmers) is, not to make the most they can from the land, which, is or has been cheap, but the most of the labour, which is dear; the consequence of which has been much ground has been scratched over and none cultivated or improved as it ought to have been; whereas a farmer in England, where land is dear, and labour cheap, finds it his interest to improve and cultivate highly; that he may reap large crops from a small quantity of ground. That the last is the true, and the first an erroneous policy, I will readily grant; but it requires time to conquer bad habits, and hardly any thing short of necessity is able to accomplish it. That necessity is approaching by pretty rapid strides." Mount Vernon was a plantation composed of five distinct farms, and he owned other great land holdings; but he cultivated none of these holdings himself. They were either under managers, or leased, or in case of much of the western property remained during his life wild lands.

WASHINGTON'S SCIENTIFIC FARMING

Though Washington was born with these "bad habits," he took pains not only to eradicate them in his own farming, so far as possible, but to furnish through his results an example to his fellows. He was always the practical farmer, without the resources of the scientific side of the work, as we now know such; but he made up for it in the course of years by agronomical experiments, from the results of which he built up his own theories, and in the end became America's first "scientific farmer." His Diaries are full of his experiments: tests of plowing and ditching; tests of a variety of seeds in various soils and combinations of fertilizers; tests of treatment of seeds before planting; tests of miscellaneous crops and rotation of crops; tests of grafting; tests of vegetables; tests of stock raising, of grazing land, and breeding; tests of tools and shelter; tests of labor, white and black.

TOBACCO

Like all other planters in lower Virginia in colonial times, his crop at first was tobacco, and more tobacco; but from the first this one-crop system displeased him, originally, perhaps, because his land was not of the best quality for this crop; but more because of its effect on the soil, the special labor requirements, and the complications of its marketing. He appears to have been the first large planter to change out of the tobacco routine. Still, in 1759 he made 37,000 pounds of it, and in 1763 almost 90,000 pounds; but by 1773 it had fallen to 5,000 pounds, and it was never a main crop thereafter, though he continued to raise a small quantity down to 1789. He wrote in 1792: "The history, however, is this—a piece of land is cut down, and kept under constant cultivation, first in tobacco, and then in Indian corn (two very exhausting plants), until it will yield scarcely anything;—a second piece is cleared, and treated in the same manner; then a third, and so on, until probably, there is but little more to clear. When this happens, the owner finds himself reduced to the choice of one of three things—either to recover the land which he has ruined, to accomplish which, he has perhaps neither the skill, the industry, or the means—or to retire beyond the mountains—or to substitute quantity for quality in order to raise something. The latter has been generally adopted, and, with the assistance of horses, he scratches over much ground, and seeds it, to very little purpose, as you may suppose, . . . The practice above-mentioned applied more particularly to the tobacco States, which, happily, are yielding more and more every year to the growth of wheat; and as this prevails the husbandry improves." Elsewhere he wrote that he soon discontinued the growth of tobacco; "except at a plantation or two upon York River, I make no more of that article than barely serves to furnish me with goods."

WHEAT FARMING

Wheat became his substitute as the chief crop; and, in spite of other plans, so remained. In 1769 he sold 6,241 bushels, but later he milled the wheat himself and sold the flour. He had two mills close to Mount Vernon, and accepted customs grinding from his neighbors. Most of the flour went ultimately to the West Indies; and from it the greatest part of the farm revenue probably came. He experimented widely in the culture, tried various ways to prevent rust or

the Hessian fly from spoiling the crop, tried various plows and made a plow on his own plan. He also invented a barrel drill. He estimated the proper time to begin reaping and the progress of the cradlers, invested in threshing machines and had a threshing floor in his new round, or many-sided, barn instead of outside as was the accepted custom.

All these matters receive notice in the statements of the Diaries. July 25, 1768, he noted that he "took Wheat of three differt. degrees of Ripeness . . . and observd after they had lain 2 or 3 days in the sun . . . by wch. it evidently appears that to cut Wheat Knot green is not only safe but the most desirable state it can be cut in; . . . The question is, whether it may not be better to begin while the Wheat is colouring from the upper joint, as the grain will loose but little (if any) than to cut in an overripe state, when it may loose a good deal more by shattering. For my part I am clear it is better to cut it green and shall have no reluctance to practice where the whole cannot be cut at the exact period one woud choose it."

REAPING WHEAT

July 15, 1769, he observed that "it appeard evident that 10, and sometimes 9, Cradlers (according as the Wheat was thick or thin) were full suff. to keep the rest of my hands employ'd; and it likewise appeard, that it was evidently to my advantage to employ my own hands to Cradle the Wheat rather than to hire any at all, as these may be got for 2 Shillgs. or half a Crown a day, whereas the Wages of the White Cradlers are exorbitantly high. But if Wheat of different kinds are sowed so as to prevent the Harvest coming on at once, it is my opinion that hirelings of all kinds may be dispensed with. The Rakers in the generality of the Wheat is sufficient to Rake and bind after a Cradle, and the rest of the hands can manage (after the water Carriers and Cooks are taken out) to get the Wheat into convent. places and attend the Stackers. Two, and sometimes three, Stackers will Stack as fast as it is cut and I am of opinion that two brisk hands is sufft. for this purpose. From experience it has been found advantageous to put the Cradlers and their attendants into at least 3 Gangs. The Stops and delays by this means are not so frequent, and the Work much better attended to, as every Mans work is distinguishable, and the whole Cradles not always stopping for every little disorder that happens to each respective one, as is the case when they cut altogether."

RAISING GRAIN

Besides wheat he raised other grains—corn, oats, barley, rye, buckwheat, which last was also plowed under as a fertilizer—but these were mainly for domestic consumption. Corn gave him much trouble, as his land, not being especially fertile, was not favor-

able for the crop. At times he had to purchase corn to make up the quantity necessary for the slaves' food allowance. The plantation was almost self-sustaining, for he cultivated hay crops of various varieties, including alfalfa which he called lucerne, and the more common vegetables—roots and legumes. He wrote, December 4, 1788, that he "planted a large quantity of potatoes," and was, in spite of a poor crop, "more and more convinced of the prodigious usefulness of this root, and that it is very little, if any thing, of an exhauster. I have a high opinion also of carrots." For home consumption he also raised flax and the early diaries mention hemp, but not cotton.

INVENTION OF A DRILL PLOW

He spent the greatest part of the day March 26, 1760, in making a new plow of "my own Invention," and "she answered very well in the Field in the lower Pasture." Years later, April 8, 1786, he "Rid a little after Sun rise to Muddy [hole], to try my drill plow again which, with the alteration of the harrow yesterday, I find will fully answer my expectation, and that it drops the grains thicker, or thinner in proportion to the quantity of seed in the Barrel. The less there is in it the faster it issues from the holes. The weight of a quantity in the barrel, occasions (I presume) a pressure on the holes that does not admit of a free discharge of the Seed through them, whereas a small quantity (sufficient at all times to cover the bottom of the barrel) is, in a manner sifted through them by the revolution of the Barrel." Later on, October 19, 1787, he sowed "Wheat with a Barrel 6 feet long perforated with holes, strapped round with leather bands in order with intention to drop the Wheat in clumps 6 Inches Square; but the leather not binding equally alike in all parts, it discharged Seeds from the Sides and sowed it broad; . . . not having time to try new experiments to alter it, the Season for sowing this grain being far advanced, I directed that it should proceed as it was."

Washington was always readjusting and rebuilding. For example, December 30, 1769, he 'Rid to my Mill with [John] Ball, and agreed with [him] to Build her." This and the race occupied much of his attention during the next month. On September 22, 1770, he "Receivd from Edwd. Snickers the Mill stones he was to get for [me] which were thinner by two Inchs. than what were bespoke." Snickers lived in the Blue Ridge, and the stones probably came from there.

AGRICULTURAL EXPERIMENTS

Again he was testing seed grain, November 30, 1785, when he was "On the Wheat which was . . . from the Cape of Good Hope, . . . I determined to try an experiment, and accordingly on three Rows . . . I cut it within 4 Inches of the ground." The next season, April 10, 1786, he "Began also to sow the Siberian Wheat . . . in the

ground laid apart there for experiments."
At another time he "Began to Sow . . .
wheat steep'd in Brine and allum"; this was
to check the rust. He also experimented
with methods to check the "bugs" and the
Hessian fly. Fertilization had his attention
early. He mixed his "composts," April 14,
1760, in a box with ten apartments, in which
he put soil, sand, marle, mould, clay, and
manure of various kinds, in recorded mixture, and planted in each division three
grains of wheat and as many of oats and
barley, "all at equal distances in Rows, and
of equal depth (done by a machine made
for the purpose)". Two weeks later he
recorded the result. He had great faith in
river mud as a fertilizer, but nature not
being kind enough to distribute it as in the
case of the Nile, he found an unsurmount-
able difficulty in getting it from the bed
of the river to the land.

RAISING STOCK

His interest in stock was one of Washington's important characteristics as an
agriculturist, especially after his war experience had made him acquainted with conditions in the northern states. He saw the
advisability of using oxen to supplement
draft horses and wrote, June 18, 1792:
"Were we to use horses less, and oxen more,
on our farms (as they do in the New England States), we should, unquestionably,
find our account in it." His chief experiment was with mules. From the King of
Spain he received a "Royal Gift," a jack,
and lighter Malta animals, a jack and two
jennies, from Lafayette. With these he
propagated. He wrote on December 4,
1778: "The Spanish jack seems calculated to
breed for heavy slow draught; the others for
the saddle, or lighter carriages. From these,
altogether, I hope to secure a race of extraordinary goodness, which will stock the
country. Their longevity and cheap keeping
will be circumstances much in their favor.
I am convinced, from the little experiments
I have made with the ordinary mules (which
perform as much labor, with vastly less feeding than horses), that those of a superior
quality will be the best cattle we can employ for the harness; and indeed in a few
years, I intend to drive no other in my
carriage." There is no record, however, that
he ever rode and drove any of the get, rather
than behind or aback the offspring of his
great Arabian stallion Magnolia; but the
inventory of his estate included 60 mules.

In the improvement of cattle and swine
he did not show much interest, though he
had many of both, and did his own slaugh-
tering. He considered, however, that the
raising of stock for meat would be a profitable enterprise and spoke of the regrettable
lack of pasturage land in the South. "No
more cattle," he wrote Young, November 1,
1787, "is raised than can be supported by
lowland meadows, swamps, &c., and the tops
and blades of Indian corn; as very few persons have attended to sowing grasses, and
connecting cattle with their crops."

SHEEP RAISING

Wool was the most important textile material and Washington paid much and increasing attention to his sheep, the raising
of which was not at all common in the
South. He found it unusually troublesome,
especially during his own long absences.
Hence he wrote, December 4, 1788: "I cannot help thinking that increasing and improving our breed of sheep, would be one
of the most profitable speculations we could
undertake; especially in this part of the continent, where we have so little winter, that
they require either no dry fodder, or next to
none; and where we are sufficiently distant
from the frontiers, not to be troubled with
wolves or other wild vermin, which prevent
the inhabitants there from keeping flocks.
. . . So persuaded am I of the practicability
and advantage of it, that I have raised near
200 lambs upon my farm this year." He
was thoroughly appreciative of the value of
improving the breed: "But the great impedi-
ment is the British statutes [preventing export of breeding animals]; these discourage
men of delicacy . . . Others, however, less
scrupulous, have attempted to import English rams with success, and, by this means,
our flocks, in many places, are much improved—mine, for instance, though I never
was concerned, directly nor indirectly, in the
importation of one, further than by buying
lambs which have descended from them."

Part II
Organization and Labor

THE ENGLISH SYSTEM

It is evident from Washington's numerous letters to the great English agricultural
expert, Arthur Young, that he considered the
English system as the model for American
agriculture, particularly in the matter of
rotation of crops. In the 1787 letter he
wrote: "There are several (among which I
may class myself), who are endeavoring to
get into your regular and systematic course
of cropping, as fast as the nature of the
business will admit; so that I hope in the
course of a few years, we shall make a more
respectable figure as farmers, that we have
hitherto done."

MANAGER BLOXHAM

Washington had been his own manager,
with overseers for the separate farms, except
when away during the Revolution, at which
time a distant relative, Lund Washington,
was in charge. It was with the above ideal
in view that he decided to engage a practical
English farmer as manager or bailiff, in the
person of one James Bloxham with whom he
entered into a year's agreement, May 31,
1786, by which Bloxham was to "suggest
such plans for the improvement of the said
Washington's Farms, and the stock . . .
which are on them as to him shall appear
most conducive to his interest . . . attending particularly to the care and management
of the Stock of every kind, both in Winter
& Summer—as well those for the use and
benefit of the farms, and for family consumption, as those which may be fatted for
the Market—That he will use his utmost
endeavours to encrease, and properly distribute, the Manure on the farms; and also
will improve to the best of his judgment,
the implements of husbandry necessary
thereto—and will instruct, as occasion may
require, and opportunities offer, the labourers therein how to Plow, Sow, Mow, Reap,
Thatch, Ditch, Hedge, &c. in the best
manner."

This arrangement evidently did not prosper at first for Washington wrote, August 6,
1786: "He has the appearance of a plain
honest farmer,—is industrious;—and, from
the character given of him by a Mr. Peacy
. . . is understanding in the management
of stock, and of most matters for which he
is employed. How far his abilities may be
equal to a pretty extensive concern, is questionable. And what is still worse, he has
come over with improper ideas; for instead
of preparing his mind to meet a ruinous
course of cropping, exhausted lands, and
numberless inconveniences into which we
had been thrown by an eight year war, he
seems to have expected that he was coming
to well organized farms, and that he was to
have met ploughs, harrows, and all the other
implements of husbandry, in as high taste as
the best farming countries in England could
have exhibited them. How far his fortitude
will enable him to encounter these disappointments, or his patience and perseverance

will carry him towards the work of reform, remains to be decided."

He expressed similar sentiments to Peacy, adding that the farmer seems to expect farms in the condition where "there would have been no occasion for his Services." Bloxham on his part wrote on July 23, 1786: "I should bee glad if you could get a Clever Little Deasant D plow which must go without a weeal for the Land is not Level and to be Shoor to make him Light and Deasant and be Shoor to make him turn the worke well for they have som most shoking Plows that Ever was Seen in the world. . . . I Rot in my other Letter to my wife to Com over but I thinke it not worth while for I think thatt I Shall not Stay no Longer than my yeare is up which is the first of next may for things Are verey Desagreable to Do Bisness it is imposable for any man to Do Bisness in any form . . . this Contey is verey pore and there is no chance for any Body to Do any god . . . thear is another thing Which is very Disagreable these Black People I am Rather in Danger of being poisind among them which I think I Shall Leave the Contrey ass son Ass I Can." Matters evidently improved later, for his wife and family came over; and he remained with the General until 1791 and then settled on his own land.

WHITE LABOR AND SLAVES

It is doubtful whether Bloxham was considered the responsible manager of the farms during the President's absence. At first various relatives served in this office; and from 1793 outsiders were employed for the rest of Washington's life. To these he wrote precise instructions and expected equally complete reports each week. The overseers of the various farms and the master workmen were usually white, indentured servants for the most part. They were of all kinds and of various motives and faults, and planter Washington dealt with them according to their deserts, with many comments thereon in the diaries. Thus, January 28, 1760, he "Severely reprimanded young Stephen's for his Indolence," but a few days later "Found Richd. Stephen's hard at Work with an ax—very extraordinary this."

The plantation laborers and most of the lower grade artisans were slaves. Washington considered them more economical than white paid laborers would be. Hence he wrote, June 18, 1792: "But high wages is not the worst evil attending the hire of white men in this country; for being accustomed to better fare than, I believe, the labourers of almost any other country, adds considerably to the expence of employing them; whilst blacks, on the contrary, are cheaper, the common food of them (even when well treated) being bread made of Indian corn, butter-milk, fish (pickled herrings) frequently, and meat now and then; with a blanket for bedding." He was a just master, but he required industry and obedience; and when his slaves, or his indentured

white servants, ran away he advertised or otherwise took measures to procure their return.

In his diary for July 15, 1786, appears a long comment on the method of wheat harvesting, ending: "But as neither rain nor dews will hurt the grain . . . and as there is allways work enough on the Plantations to employ the hands in (such as succouring and hoeing of Corn, pulling flax, weeding the vines, Pease, etca., etca.,) supposing the interruptions above mentioned to happen, no labour need be lost."

MODERN FARMING METHODS

Mention has already been made of Washington's interest in farming utensils and their improvement. He ordered special plows from England, and corresponded with Young about other agricultural instruments. While in New York as President, January 22, 1790, he called "on the Baron de Polnitz, to see the operation of his (Winlaw's) threshing machine," which he describes, and adds: "Upon the whole, it appears to be an easier, more expeditious, and much cleaner way of getting out grain than by the usual mode of threshing; and vastly to be preferred to treading, which is hurtful to horses, filthy to the wheat, and not more expeditious." In 1797 he built a thresher on plans furnished by William Booker, but it was not satisfactory, and probably was junked, for Washington as much as later captains of industry was not slow to discard tools and methods proved to be inefficient. His advanced position in American husbandry is also shown by his building. He built a brick barn after a plan drawn by Arthur Young and wrote, December 4, 1788, "The building of a brick barn has occupied much of my attention this summer. It is constructed according to the plan you had the goodness to send to me; but with some additions. It is now, I believe, the largest and most convenient one in this country." This is probably the many-sided "round" barn described above.

DIFFICULTIES OF IMPROVEMENT

He was in advance of his time in the use of improved implements and shelters, but could not carry his help along with him, hence a pessimistic letter to Henry Lee, October 16, 1793, in which he admits that the model of a thresher brought over by the English farmers "may also be a good one, but the utility of it among careless negroes and ignorant overseers will depend absolutely upon the simplicity of the construction; for, if there is any thing complex in the machinery, it will be no longer in use than a mushroom is in existence. I have seen so much of the beginning and ending of new inventions, that I have almost resolved to go on in the old way of treading, until I get settled again at home, and can attend myself to the management of one. As a proof in point, of the almost impossibility of putting the overseers of this country out of the track

they have been accustomed to walk in, I have one of the most convenient barns in this, or perhaps any other country, where thirty hands may with great ease be employed in threshing. Half of the wheat of the farm was actually stowed in this barn in the straw, by my order, for threshing; notwithstanding, when I came home about the middle of September, I found a treading-yard not thirty feet from the barn-door, the wheat again brought out of the barn, and horses treading it out in an open exposure, liable to the vicissitudes of weather. I am now erecting a building for the express purpose of treading. I have sanguine expectations of its utility."

INTEREST IN SHRUBBERY

In the article on Mount Vernon, Washington's horticulture and gardening are discussed. He was constantly on the alert for trees or shrubs that could be utilized in beautifying the grounds, and was also in receipt of an endless line of gifts of that kind. The diaries, especially those between the Revolution and the presidency, contain many remarks on this topic, such as, on April 13, 1785: "Planted and sowed in boxes . . . Six buck eye nuts, brought with me from the Mouth of Cheat river; . . . Six acorns, which I brought with me from the South Branch. These grew on a tree resembling the box Oak, . . . Eight nuts from a tree called the Kentucke Coffe tree; . . . Ten acorns sent me by Colo. Josiah Parker . . . which I . . . suppose to be those of the live Oak. . . . A scarlet triangular berry the cover of which opens in 3 parts and looks well upon the Shrub. . . . Berry of a Shrub, brot. from the Western Waters with me. . . . a seed brot. from the same place. . . . Seed of a cluster of Red Berrys which looks pretty, and if I recollect right grows on a vine." Later he describes some of the results. "The blossom of the Crab tree is unfolding [May 9], and shedding its fragrant perfume. That of the black Haw has been out some days; and is an ornamental flower being in large clusters, tho' individually small upon single foot stems. They are white with a yellowish cast. The flower of the small berry thorn is also good looking, the tree being full of blossom, which is not much unlike the blossom of the apple tree, but quite white." "The Guilder Rose in my Garden [May 13] has just got into bloom." "The Wood honeysuckle [May 14] wch. has been in bloom about 8 days is an agreeable looking flower and deserved a place in my Shrubberies." "Planted, or rather transplanted [May 1, 1786], from the Box sent me by Colo. Washington of So. Carolina, 6 of the Sweet scented, or aromatic shrubs." "Planted . . . [June 29] 25 of the Paliurus, very good to make hedges and inclosures for fields. Also . . . adjoining the Pride of China Plants . . . 46 of the Pistatia nut in 3 rows. And in the places where the Hemlock pine . . . were dead . . . the Seeds of the Piramidical Cyprus, 75 in number, all of which with others were presented to me by Mr. Michaux, Botanist to his Most Christn. Majesty."

CONTINUING INTEREST

After Washington returned to Mount Vernon on retirement from the Presidency he was, naturally, less active. He even rented out one of the farms to a nephew and

he had written to Young on December 12, 1793, about the conditions under which he would rent out all the farms except the Mansion House one. It was in reference to this that Richard Parkinson, an English farmer and possible superintendent, came to Mount Vernon in 1798. He was by no means favorably impressed and no agreement resulted.

In later years Washington records little on the farms; but his interest did not decrease. Only a few days before his fatal illness, he prepared a plan for a rotation of crops to apply to all his farms for several years. That last illness resulted from exposure in riding out to the farms. To the last he was the husbandman, the agricultural expert, and the farmer on a large scale.

Part III
Washington's Scientific Farm Methods

CRITICAL TRANSACTIONS IN PORK (JANUARY, 1760)

"*Tuesday*, 1. Visited my Plantations and receivd an Instance of Mr. French's great love of Money in disappointing me of some Pork, because the price had risen to 22/6 after he had engaged to let me have it at 20/.

"Calld at Mr. Possey's in my way home and desird him to engage me 100 Bar'ls of Corn upon the best terms he could in Maryland.

"And found Mrs. Washington upon my arrival broke out with the Meazles.

"*Wednesday*, 2d. . . . Fearing a disappointment elsewhere in Pork I was fein to take Mr. French's upon his own terms and engaged them to be deliv'd at my House on Monday next.

"*Tuesday*, 8. . . . Got a little Butter from Mr. Dalton, and wrote to Colo. West for Pork.

"In the Evening 8 of Mr. French's Hogs from his Ravensworth Quarter came down, one being lost on the way—as the others might as well have been for their goodness.

"Nothing but the disappointments in this Article of Pork which he himself had causd and my necessities coud possibly have obligd me to take them.

"*Wednesday*, 9th. Killd and dressed Mr. French's Hogs, which weighd 751 lbs neat.

"Colo. West leaving me in doubt about his Pork yesterday obligd me to send to him again to day, and now no definitive answr was receivd—he purposing to send his overseer down tomorrow, to agree abt it.

"*Thursday*, 10th. . . . Colo. West wrote me word that he had engagd his Pork. Killd the Beeves that Jack brought down two of which were tolerable good.

"*Friday*, 11th. Deliverd Stephens two Hogs in part of his Year's Provisions weight, 69 [and] 90, [or] 159. He had one before of 100 lbs. weight. Two Hogs were also reservd for Foster of the following weight,

90	100
83	100
	97
173 which with	90
	387

that were cut out and salted makes up 719 lbs and accts. for Mr. French's 8 Hogs; showing the loss of weighing meat so soon killd, which cannot be less than 5 pr. Ct."

INVENTION OF A PLOW (1760)

"*Wednesday*, [March] 19. . . . Peter (my Smith) and I after several efforts to make a plow after a new model—partly of my own contriving—was feign to give it out, at least for the present."

AGRICULTURAL BOOKS (1760)

OCTOBER 24. New Kent County, York River.

"I have at different times sent for Hale's Husbandry but never yet got it, which I begin to attribute to a wrong description of the Title, having never till lately seen the Book; you will know it now by 'A Compleat Body of Husbandry compiled from the Original Papers of the late Thomas Hale Esqr, . . .'"

SYSTEMATIC FISHING (1768)

AUGUST 25. Potomac River.

"Hauling the Sein upon the Bar of Cedar Point for Sheeps heads but catchd none. Run down below Mouth of Machodack and came to."

MAY 14. King William County.

"Went to my Plantation in King William by Water and dredgd for Sturgeon, and catched one."

MAY 16. New Kent, on York River.

"Fishing for Sturgeon from Breakfast to Dinner but catchd none."

FISHING—DINNER AT FISH HOUSE (1772)

"[JULY] 25. Went a fishing and dined at the Fish House at the Ferry Plantation."

FISHING SHORES OF ESTATE (1772)

"[JUNE] 30. My Brother and Family set of home, Mr. Tilgham also. After Breakfast I rid with Mr. Byrd in the Forenoon to my Meadow at Doeg Run and to the Mill, and in the Afternn. went to Sound the Depth of the sevl. Fishing shores from Posey's to Gilbt. Simpson's."

A MONTH AT HOME (1769)
OCTOBER

"*Where & how my time is Spent.*

"1. Dined at Belvoir with Mrs. Washington and Patcy Custis. Returned in the Evening.

"2. Colo. Carlyle and two Daughters, Captn. Brady, and Captn. Posey, dined here.

"3. Rid to Muddy hole, Doeg Run, and Mill.

"4. Rid to Alexandria to see how my Carpenters went on with my Ho. Returnd to Dinr.

"5. Went after Blew Wings with Humphrey Peake, killd 3 and returned by Muddy hole.

"6. Went a hunting but found nothing. After which Rid to Muddy hole, Doeg Run, and the Mill.

"7. At home all day.

"8. Likewise at home all day. In the afternoon Mr. Robt. Alexander came.

"9. Went a fox hunting and finding a Deer the Dogs run it to the water, but we never see it. Mr. Alexr. went home.

"10. Went to Captn. Posey's to Run the lines of the Land he bought of Mr. Marshall. Dind there.

"11. At home all day.

"12. Rid to Muddy hole, Doeg Run, and Mill. Captn. Posey dined here.

"13. Captn. Marshall came over here and dined, and I rid with him round his Land.

"14. Went a Fox hunting. Started a Dog Fox by old Palmer's and Run it back of Mr. Clifton's and there catchd it. Went afterwards into the Neck. Mr. Matthew Campbell dined here.

"15. At home all day alone. My Brother Charles came at Night.

"16. Went up to Court and returnd at Night.

"17. Went to Court again and returnd. Mr. Fairfax and Mr. Magowan came here.

"18. Went a Fox huntg. with Mr. Fairfax and Mr. Magowan. Found and killed a Dog Fox.

"19. Rid to Muddy hole, Doeg Run, and Mill, after Mr. Fairfax went away.

"20. At Home all day.

"21. Rid to Muddy hole, Doeg Run, and Mill. Mr. Magowan went to Colchester.

"22. At home all day—alone.

"23. Went to Posey's Sale. Returnd at Night with Colo. Mason, Mr. Ross, Mr. Sebastian, Mr. Harrison, Mr. Magowan, and Colo. Mason's Son George.

"24. Went to the Sale again. Mr. Harrison and Mr. Sebastian and Mr. Magowan came home with me, also Robt. Alexander. Found Doctr. Rumney here.

"25. Went to the Sale again. Mr. Harrison and Mr. Magowan returned home with me.

"26. At home all day, Mr. Harrison went away in the Afternoon.

"27. Rid to Muddy hole, Doeg Run, and Mill; also to my New purchase of Posey's Land. Mr. Stedlar went away.

"28. At home all day. Mr. Magowan went home.

"29. At home all day. Captn. McCarty came in the Afternoon.

"30. Set out on my journey to Williamsburg and reached Colo. Henry's Lee's to a Late Dinner.

"31. Set out from thence abt. Nine Oclock and reached no further than Peyton's Ordy. on Aquia. being stopt by Rain."

A FARMER'S LIFE (JULY, 1770)

"2. Went into my Wheat field after dinnr. Mr. Davis a Midshipman dined here.

"3. One of the Boston's Midshipman breakfasted here. Between breakfast and Dinner I went into my Harvest field.

"4. Went into my Harvest field between breakfast and Dinner.

"5. Sir Thomas Adams and Mr. Glasford, his first Lieutt., Breakfasted here. Sir Thos. returnd after it; but Mr. Glasford dined here, as did the 2d. Lieutt. Mr. Sartell, Mr. Johnston of Marines, Mr. Norris and Mr. Richmore, two Midshipmen.

"6. At home all day. Mr. Stedlar came to dinner. Mr. Wallace, Purser to the Boston, came in the afternoon and purchased and killed my Bull—the 4 quarters of which weighed 710 lbs. Nett.

"7. At home all day. In the afternoon Mr. Edward Smith came.

"8. Went to Pohick Church and returnd to Dinner. Mr. Smith went to Colo. Fairfax's and returnd to Dinner, and Mr. Stedlar went away after Breakft."

THE MILL AND TUMBLING RUN (FEBRUARY, 1771)

"Where & how my time is Spent.

"1st. At the Mill in the forenoon and afternoon. Doctr. Rumney came here before Dinner and stayd all Night.

"2. At the Mill and where my People was at work on the Race in the forenoon and afternoon. Mr. Rutherford and Price Posey came here in the Evening. . . .

"6. Rid to my Mill by the Ferry in the forenoon and afternoon. Price Posey came here this Evening. . . .

"7. Price Posey went away. I rid to the

Mill and Dam at the head of the Race in the forenoon and afternoon.

"8. Rid to my Mill and Tumbling Dam in the forenoon and afternoon. Doctr. Rumney dind here and went away afterwds.

"9. Attempted to go a hunting, but prevented by Rain. Rid to the Mill in the fore and afternoon.

"10. At home all day. Mr. Val Crawford came to Dinner."

FARM ROUTINE (APRIL, 1771)
"Remarks and Occs.

"*5th.* Turn'd the Water of Doeg Run into my Mill Race, which seemed to afford Water enough for both Mills, one of which is constantly employd in Grinding up my own wheat.

"10. Began to Haul the Sein, tho few fish were catchd, and those of the Shad kind, owing to the coolness of the Weather. Many Shad had been catchd on the Maryland shore.

"11. Obliged to send a hand to the Mill to assist in Packing, etca.

"17. Began to Plant Corn at my Mill Plantation.

"20. Began to Plant Ditto at Muddy hole.

"25. Began Ditto at Doeg Run.

"25. The Herring began to run in large Shoals, but were checkd again by the cool weather."

GOING TO TOWN (MAY, 1771)

"2. Set out with Colo. Bassett for Williamsburg, and reachd Town about 12 O'clock. Dined at Mrs. Dawson's and went to the Play.

"3. Dined at the Speaker's and went to the Play; after wch. Drank a Bowl or two of Punch at Mrs. Campbell's.

"4. Dined at Mrs. Campbell's (and paid for Dinner and Club), and went up to Eltham with Colos. Bassett and Lewis.

"5. At Eltham all day.

"6. Returnd to Williamsburg by 11 Oclock with Colo. Bassett and Colo. Lewis. Dined at Mrs. Vobes; and Suppd at Anderson's.

"7. Dined at Mrs. Dawson's and Spent the Evening at Anderson's.

"8. Dined at Southall's with Colo. Robt. Fairfax and some other Gentlmn., and went to the Play."

HARVESTING (JULY, 1772)

"*3d.* Began my Wheat Harvest at Muddy hole and Doeg Run, in the following manner, Viz. At Doeg Run with the two Davy's, and two Sons of Brummil, as Cradler's; and the Wheat being rather green, no regular assortment of Cradlers was allotted to them as yet.

"At Muddy hole, Palmer (who did not work himself, but only acted as an Instructer) and Six of the youngest Cradlers began.

"6. Began in the Neck with Mike and Tom, and three White Men; but as hands were Shifted from place to place there were sometimes more and sometimes less in each Field."

A FARM INVENTORY (NOVEMBER, 1785)

"*Tuesday, 15th.* Went to my Neck Plantation and completed the Acct. of my Stock there, except that of the Hogs, which stand thus:

Horses

A grey dray Stallion		1

Buck a Sorrel,	16 yr. old		
Gilbert a black,	17 Do.		
Randolph a Grey,	7 Do.		
Doctr. a Grey	7 Do.		
Prentice a Bay	10 Do.		
Jolly a Black	9 Do.	Working	
Dick a White	12 Do.	Horses	
Grunt a Bay	9 Do.		
Pompey a Bay	14 Do.		
Diamond White	9 Do.		
Possum Grey	10 Do.		
Jack Black	10 Do.	12	

Carried over 13

Kit—a black Mare 5 yrs.			
Fly Dark brown			
Patience			
Betty White Stockg	9 Do.	Working	
Punch grey flea bittn.		Mares	
Jenny light grey	9 Do.		
Brown	11 Do.		
Fanny Black	9 Do.		

Overseer Black		9

A brown Horse		5	
Bright Bay rising		3	
Black Do		3	
Brown Mealy Co'd	Do.	3	
Black	Do.	3	Unbroke
Black Small	Do.	3	Horses
Ditto	Do.	2	
Iron Grey	Do.	2	
Black bald face	Do.	2	
		9	

A Grey Spring Colt		1

Dark bay	9	
Sorrel	5	
Brown	6	
Black—rising	3	Unbroke Mares
Dark brown	3	
Grey	3	
Black rising	2	7
Black Spring Colt	1	

In all 40

Cattle Bulls y'g		3
Working Oxen		7
Fatting Steers in Corn field		5
Cows		41
Heifers	6 yrs old	6
	3 yrs old	15
	2 yrs old	11
	1 yr old	7
Spring—Cow Calves		19 58

Steers ....full grown 18
4 yrs old 2
3 yrs old 4
2 yrs old 7
1 yr old 3
Spring Bull calves 11 45

159

Cows brot. to the Home
for Milk and to go back 8

Total Cattle 167

Sheep

Rams 7
Ewes 92
Weathers 12
Ditto in Corn field 16

127

Weathers brot. to Ho. Ho. 42

169

Tools and Implemts.

A Waggon Saddle and
Gier for 4 Horses 1
An Oxe Cart—good 1
Ditto—not good 1 2

Oxe Chains 2
Belts for Tongues 2
Yokes, Rings &ca.
Bar Shear Plows 9
Two pr. Iron traces to each 18
Old Bridles for ditto 18
N.B. These Traces serve the
Waggon
Hilling Hoes helved 20
unhelved pretty g. 3
indifferent 2
At the Smith Shop 2 27

Mattocks but indifft. 6
Ditto said to have come
to the Home Ho. 7 13

Grubbing Hoes indifft. 3
Axes 7
Ditto at Smith's Shop 1
Ditto old Iron 1 9

Iron Wedges—pairs 3
Open Iron Wire Sieve 1
Sand Sieve 1 2

Note these to be sent to the Home
Ho.
Harvest Rakes 5 only gd. 13
Pitch forks 1
Half Bushels—new 1
Old—Do. 1 2

Plantation Gun 1 . . .

"*Wednesday, 16th.* . . . Went early in the Morning to take an acct of my Stocks, etca. at Doeg Run and Muddy hole Plantns.

"At the first

Horses

	height	age	
Dabster, a grey..	14¼..	8	
Buck, Bay......	14 ..	6	Workers 2
Nancy, Bay.....	14 ..	old	
From Camp, Ditto	14¼..		
Fly, Ditto......	13 ..	8	
Brandy, Ditto...	13½		
Fancy, Black....	13 ..	old	
——, Sorrel..	13 ..	old	
——, Ditto....	13 ..		
Bonny Bay very old	—........	8	
Englh. Hunter Brown	15 ..	old	
Grey mare bot. at Bristol	Do.		
Dray..Black Camp......	Do.	3	

Bay likely in foal 14 6
Bay Roan white
face.. 14 5
Sorrel 14½
Black Snip on ye
Nose .... 13 ..
Iron grey—dark.. 14 .. 3
Black from Huster...... 2
Black Star and snip likely. 2
Bay—white face........ 1
Black—long star........ 1
Bay near hind foot wh.. 1
Bay—small star......... 1
Bay (blood near hind f.
We 1
Bay—star and snip...... 1 13

A Grey..Snip... 14 .. 3
Bay Roan—wh. face..... 1
Sorrell..Snip 1
Dark Grey............. 1
Grey Colt frm. Bristl. M.
Sps.
It is not certain whether
these are horses or Mares
not having distinguished
them on the Spot at the
time — 5

In all............ 31

Cattle

Working Oxen.................... 7
Fatting Steers in Meadow........... 2
Cows 15
Heifers ....4 yrs. old.... 5
3 yrs. old.... 3
2 yrs. old.... 6
1 yr. old.... 2
Spring Calves.........6 22

Steers ....full grown.... 7
3 years old.... 1
2 yrs. old.... 2
1 yr. old.... 7
Spring Calves.........5 22

Bulls 1

Total 69

Sheep

Rams 7
Ewes 32
Weathers 7
Do. in Meadow fatg.......... 7 14

Total 53
Old Cows in ye Mead........ 2

"N. B. The Tools not being got up no acct. was taken of them at this time.

"Muddy hole Plantation

	height	age	
Jockey—a black......	13½....	14	
Diamond—Ditto	14	10....	2
Rankins	14	10	
Fly—a Grey.........	14¼ ...	8	
Jenny—Brown	13¼ ...	8	
Fenwick—Dun Sorrel.	13½	7	
Fancy—Grey	13¼ ...	9	5

White 13 7
Bay—Small Star &ca. 13 5
Bay—long blaze...... 13 5
Bay—very small Star.. 13 5
Dark Bay sml. Star and
Snp........13
Dark Brown—Simpson. 13½ 3
Bay—midlg. likely............ 1
Bay—Small Star Spring........
Black—sml. Star Spring...... — 9
Brown Boy—crooked blaze
13 hands high.... ..5 yrs. old
Grey unlikely............. 2
Bay—sml. Star unlikely
Grey—natural pacer—spg........ 4

Total 20

Cattle

Working Oxen 4
Cows 10
Heifers......1 yr. old 1
Cow Calves...this Spring 1
Steers—full grown 8
2 years old...... 2
1 year old...... 1 11

Male Calves 4

Total 31

Sheep

Rams 5
Ewes 39
Lambs 11

Total 50

Tools and Implements

A good Oxe Cart—2 Oxe yokes
& Iron Rings—Compleat...... 1
Oxe Chain 1
Bar shear plows 3
Iron Traces—pairs 6
Haims. Collars, Bridles &ca. Compt.
2 spare colters 2
Mattoxs 5

Axes—includg. 1 at the Home Ho.   4
Iron Wedges—pairs   1
Hilling Hoes   11
Pitch fork   1
A Wheat Fan   1
Half Bushel   1

"The Hogs at all the plantations running in the woods after the most, no acct. could be taken of them."

FARM BUILDINGS (1789)

"*Saturday* [October] 10*th*. . . .On our return we stopped at the seats of General and Mr. Gouvernr. Morris, and viewed a barn, of which I had heard the latter speak much, belonging to his farm—but it was not of a construction to strike my fancy—nor did the conveniences of it at all answer their cost. From hence we proceeded to Harlaem, where we were met by Mrs. Washington, Mrs. Adams and Mrs. Smith. Dined at the tavern kept by a Capt. Mariner, and came home in the evening."

A THRESHING MACHINE (JANUARY, 1790)

"*Friday*, 22*d*. Exercised on horseback in the forenoon.

"Called in my ride on the Baron de Polnitz, to see the operation of his (Winlaw's) threshing machine. The effect was, the heads of the wheat being seperated from the straw, as much of the first run through the mill in 15 minutes as made half a bushel of clean wheat—allowing 8 working hours in the 24, this would yield 16 bushels pr. day. Two boys are sufficient to turn the wheel, feed the mill, and remove the threshed grain after it has passed through it. Two men were unable, by winnowing, to clean the wheat as it passed through the mill, but a common Dutch fan, with the usual attendance, would be *more* than sufficient to do it. The grain passes through without bruising and is well separated from the chaff. Women, or boys of 12 or 14 years of age, are fully adequate to the management of the mill or threshing machine. Upon the whole, it appears to be an easier, more expeditious, and much cleaner way of getting out grain than by the usual mode of threshing; and vastly to be preferred to treading, which is hurtful to horses, filthy to the wheat, and not more expeditious, considering the numbers that are employed in the process from the time the head is begun to be formed until the grain has passed finally through the fan."

FARM INSPECTION (1791)

"*Sunday*, [June] 12*th*. About Sunrise we were off—breakfasted at Dumfries and arrived at Mt. Vn. to Dinr. From Monday 13th until Monday the 27th (being the day I had appointed to meet the Commissioners under the residence act, at Georgetown) I remained at home; and spent my time in daily rides to my severl. farms and in receiving many visits."

SCIENTIFIC AGRICULTURE (1794)

"I know of no pursuit in which more real and important services can be rendered to any country, than by improving its agriculture,—its breed of useful animals—and other branches of a husbandman's cares:—nor can I conceive any plan more conducive to this end than the one you have introduced for bringing to view the actual state of them in all parts of the Kingdom."

"For the sake of humanity, it is devoutly to be wished, that the manly employment of Agriculture, and the humanizing benefit of Commerce, would supersede the waste of war, and the rage of conquest; that the swords might be turned into ploughshares, the spears into pruning-hooks, and, as the Scriptures express it, 'the Nations learn war' no more."

SPECIAL INTERESTS (1796)

"It must be obvious to every man, who considers the agriculture of this country, (even in the best improved parts of it) and compares the produce of our lands with those of other countries, no ways superior to them in *natural fertility*, how miserably defective we are in the management of them; and that if we do not fall on a better mode of treating them, how ruinous it will prove to the landed interest. Ages will not produce a systematic change without public attention and encouragement; but a few years more of increased sterility will drive the Inhabitants of the Atlantic States westwardly for support; whereas if they were taught how to improve the old, instead of going in pursuit of new and productive soil, they would make those acres which now scarcely yield them any thing, turn out beneficial to themselves—to the Mechanics, by supplying them with the staff of life on much cheaper terms—to the Merchants, by encreasing their Commerce and exportation—and to the Community generally, by the influx of Wealth resulting therefrom."

BOARD OF AGRICULTURE (1797)

"I have endeavored both in a public and private character to encourage the establishment of Boards of Agriculture in this Country, but hitherto in vain; . . . Since the first Establishment of the National Board of Agriculture in Great Britain, I have considered it as one of the most valuable Institutions of modern times, and conducted with so much ability and zeal as it appears to be under the auspices of Sir John Sinclair, must be productive of great advantages to the Nation and to Mankind in General."

Selected Authorities

BALLAGH, JAMES CURTIS — *History of Slavery in Virginia*. Baltimore, Johns Hopkins Press, 1902.

BALLAGH, JAMES CURTIS—*White Servitude in the Colony of Virginia*. Baltimore, Johns Hopkins Press, 1895.

BASSETT, JOHN SPENCER—"Relation between the Virginia Planter and the London Merchant"; in American Historical Association, *Report* for *1901*, Vol. I, p. 551.

BEARD, CHARLES AUSTIN—*Economic Interpretation of the Constitution of the United States*. New York, Macmillan, 1913.

BEER, GEORGE LOUIS—*Old Colonial System, 1660-1754*. 2 vols. New York, Macmillan, 1912.

BROOKE, WALTER E., ED.—*Agricultural Papers of George Washington*. Boston, Badger, 1912.

CONWAY, MONCURE DANIEL, ED.—*George Washington and Mount Vernon*. Brooklyn, Long Island Historical Society, 1889.

CRAVEN, AVERY ODELLE—*Soil Exhaustion as a Factor in the Agricultural History of Virginia and Maryland*. Urbana, University of Illinois, 1926.

CUSTIS, GEORGE WASHINGTON PARKE—*Recollections and Private Memoirs of Washington*. Philadelphia, Flint, 1859. (Other eds.)

FORD, PAUL LEICESTER — *True George Washington*. Philadelphia, Lippincott, 1896. (Especially chs. v, vi.)

FORD, WORTHINGTON CHAUNCEY—*George Washington*. 2 vols. New York, Scribner, 1900. (Especially Vol. I, ch. vii, Vol. II, chs. vi, xv.)

FORD, WORTHINGTON CHAUNCEY—*Washington as an Employer and Importer of Labor*. Brooklyn, 1889.

HAWORTH, PAUL LELAND—*George Washington, Country Gentleman*. Indianapolis, Bobbs-Merrill, 1925.

JEFFERSON, THOMAS—*Notes on the State of Virginia*. Philadelphia. Prichard and Hall, 1788. (First Am. ed.; later eds.)

MEADE, WILLIAM—*Old Churches, Minis-*

ters and Families of Virginia. 2 vols. Philadelphia, Lippincott, 1857. (Later eds.)

MOORE, CHARLES—*Family Life of George Washington.* Boston, Houghton Mifflin, 1926.

PARKINSON, RICHARD—*George Washington.* Baltimore, Lord Baltimore Press, 1909. (A reprint from *Tour in America,* 2 vols., London, 1805, of portion on Washington.)

PRUSSING, EUGENE E.—*Estate of George Washington, Deceased.* Boston, Little Brown, 1927.

WASHINGTON, GEORGE — *Diaries, 1748-1799.* Ed. by John C. Fitzpatrick. 4 vols. Boston, Houghton Mifflin, 1925.

WASHINGTON, GEORGE—*Letters . . . to Arthur Young . . . and Sir John Sinclair.* Alexandria, Cotton and Stewart, 1803. (Other eds., including separate ones of letters to Young and to Sinclair.)

WASHINGTON, GEORGE—*Writings.* Ed. by Worthington Chauncey Ford. 14 vols. New York, Putnam, 1889-93.

WERTENBAKER, THOMAS J.—*Planters of Colonial Virginia.* Princeton, Princeton University Press, 1922.

WILSTACH, PAUL—*Mount Vernon, Washington's Home and the Nation's Shrine.* Garden City, Doubleday-Page, 1916.

MOUNT VERNON

From a rare aquatint, engraved by Francis Jukes after Alexander Robertson, 1800, in the William L. Clements Library, Ann Arbor, Michigan.

Washington as a Religious Man
By John C. Fitzpatrick
Part I
George Washington and Religion

GEORGE WASHINGTON
From a contemporary silhouette

YOUTHFUL EXPERIENCES

AN examination of the religion of George Washington should be unhampered by any allegiance to traditional reminiscences. While speculation in relation to certain controversal questions may be interesting, it is at best of doubtful value in arriving at definite historical conclusions and exerts an inevitable temptation to wander far afield in the realm of mere conjecture. The safe course in so important an investigation lies in consulting the incontestable evidences of religious faith left by George Washington himself. Therefore, in these pages the writer has carefully adhered to those references in relation to Washington's religion of established documentary authenticity.

George Washington was born on February 11, 1731 (old style calendar), or February 22, 1732 (new style calendar), and on April 5, a little less than two months later, was baptized in the orthodox Episcopalian manner; two god-fathers and one god-mother being recorded as standing for him.

After his baptism, George, in a religious way, disappears from view for a number of years, and when he again emerges he does so in a purely boyish character, for he scrawls his youthful signature over the title-page of his father's copy of the Sermons of the Bishop of Exeter. In this assault upon the title, or title-page, of a dignitary of the Established Church may be found, perhaps, the germ of the cherry tree and the I-cannot-tell-a-lie fable. Perhaps the cherry tree was really this book of sermons in arboreal disguise and the pen was the hatchet.

A man's religious ideas are peculiarly personal and to attempt an analysis of them after the man himself has passed off the stage of life is a difficult matter at best; but it does not solve the difficulty to present merely the laudatory opinions of his contemporaries. We cannot rest content with this in Washington's case and will try, therefore, to form an opinion by examining Washington's own self-record for: His personal record of church attendance; his estimate of the value of religious practices among the people at large; his desire and effort to encourage a recognition of God's goodness and to inculcate in the people a spirit of gratitude towards the Deity; and, lastly, his own expressions of opinion respecting God. An examination of these evidences as they develop in Washington's own writings will give a fairly balanced and accurate picture of Washington's religious attitude.

ON THE FRONTIER (1756)

The scanty material of his youthful days is relatively unimportant and the record practically starts with the time when he was commanding the Virginia troops on the western frontier, after Braddock's defeat. At Fort Loudoun, Winchester, at the age of twenty-four, this colonel of Virginia militia, on Saturday, Septeember 18, 1756, ordered that "The men parade tomorrow morning at beating the long roll, with their arms and ammunition clean and in good order, and to be marched by the Sergeants of the respective companies to the Fort, there to remain until prayers are over." It is plain that the danger of an Indian surprise attack was a factor, as the men were sent to prayers under arms; also it is plain that Washington took it for granted that the officers would display some interest and was annoyed that they did not, for the next Saturday came a more pointed order: "The men are to parade at beating the long roll tomorrow morning at 10 o'clock; and to march as usual to the Fort to attend Divine Service. The officers are to be present at calling the roll, and see that the men do appear in the most decent manner they can." Every Sunday thereafter the men were marched to prayers and in the middle of November the Sunday service was made a standing order for the future.

CHURCH GOING (1759-1799)

We have no means of judging the effect of these rough, hard, and brutal years upon Washington's religious views, for there is nothing of value for this purpose in the record until after his marriage with Mrs. Custis and his settling down to a normal life at Mount Vernon. We cannot state positively that Washington became a church-goer, or a more consistent church-goer, after his marriage with Mrs. Custis, but scrutiny of the records induces the opinion that she was an influence in this respect. I have checked up, as closely as possible, his record of church attendance, from the earliest available date to the end of his life, and though there are unfortunate gaps which can never be filled, some interesting results are obtainable from the eighteen years for which data has survived.

After his marriage Washington attended church at Pohick, and, later, Christ Church, Alexandria, on an average of once a month. Both churches were distant from Mount Vernon so that it was something of a journey to reach them by coach and we find many entries in Washington's diaries of his being prevented from attending by the carriage being away from Mount Vernon, by his starting for church and having the carriage break down on the way (a commentary upon the state of the Virginia roads in colonial times), or of his nearly reaching Pohick, only to be met by a message that the minister was too sick to conduct the services. There are a few instances of Washington's illness and once he was held at home by the toothache.

A particularly interesting diary entry is that of May 4, 1760: "Set out for Fredk. to see my negroes that lay ill of the Small Pox. Took Church in my way to Coleman's." Most of us have forgotten that Washington rode post-haste, from Mount Vernon across the Blue Ridge, into the Shenandoah Valley to see that his slaves received proper care and attention. He collected doctors, nurses, medicines, and blankets and did everything humanly possible to aid. Of course the misanthrope will say that he was only interested in saving his property and that he ran no personal risk as he was immune from the disease; but if we grant this privilege to as-

sign motives for actions, we are entitled to the same privilege ourselves and, in this case, we prefer to think that a decent humanity was an element of weight. If material welfare, the saving of slave property, was the main motive of this hurried journey, would it have risked an hour's delay? It seems reasonable to look upon this stop for church as a natural act of faith and trust in the Almighty.

The important point established by a close check up of Washington's church attendance is that throughout his public life, in times of political stress and strain, George Washington went to church oftener than he did in times of national calm and quiet. After the Stamp Act flurry subsided, Washington relapsed again into his once a month church attendance. On August 19, 1765, we have record of his taking the oath to conform to the doctrine and discipline of the Church of England "as by Law established" and during the year 1774, when political relations with the Mother Country were becoming dangerously strained and no one in the colonies was able to foresee the outcome, he went to church twice, and sometimes three times a month. It was on June 1, 1774, the day the Boston Port Bill went into effect, that he "went to Church and fasted all day." A very little knowledge of the times makes it plain that the outlook was dark and gloomy for the colonies and nowhere could they see ways and means of saving themselves from what they felt was tyranny. The political situation seemed to Washington beyond the power of man to control, but he was far from being "the bewildered giant" a recent biographer calls him; rather we incline to the opinion that Washington's more frequent attendance at church at this time shows the direct opposite of bewilderment.

REVOLUTIONARY PERIOD
(1775-1783)

In the hectic days of the outbreak of the Revolutionary War, George Washington and religion do not appear together, so far as documentary evidence goes, beyond a statement in his letter to Martha, that he relied confidently "on that Providence which has heretofore preserved and been bountiful to me." In the manly speech with which he accepted the appointment of commander-in-chief of the army he made no reference to God or to heaven; but one month after taking command of the army reference to prayers and church service again appears in the general orders for August 5, 1775, at Cambridge. These orders directed that "the Church be cleared tomorrow and the Revd. Mr. Doyles will perform Divine Service therein at ten o'clock."

But it is the expedition against Canada, undertaken shortly thereafter, that first reveals the broadmindedness of Washington toward religion. It is difficult to see the path by which the commander-in-chief reached this attitude of mind, singular in its contrast to that of the majority of the pa-

triots of 1775, both in the army and in the Continental Congress; but it reveals George Washington, even at this early date, as the remarkable man of the Revolution. The first article of the instructions which the commander-in-chief drew up for the guidance of Colonel Benedict Arnold reads: "You are immediately, on their march from Cambridge, to take command of the detachment of the Continental Army against Quebec and use all possible expedition as the winter season is now advancing and the Success of this Enterprise (under God) depends Wholly upon the Spirit with which it is pushed; and the favourable Disposition of the Canadians and Indians." And the 14th instruction is in these remarkable words: "As the Contempt of the Religion of a Country by ridiculing any of its Ceremonies or affronting its Ministers or Votaries has ever been deeply resented You are to be particularly careful to restrain every Officer and Soldier from such Imprudence and Folly and to punish every Instance of it. On the other hand as far as lays in your Power you are to protect and support the free Exercise of the Religion of the Country and the undisturbed Enjoyments of the Rights of Conscience in religious Matters with your utmost Influence and Authority." The letter to Arnold enclosing these instructions emphasized the point: "I also give it in charge to you to avoid all Disrespect or Contempt of the Religion of the Country and its Ceremonies. Prudence, policy and a true Christian Spirit will lead us to look with compassion upon their Errors without insulting them. While we are contending for our own Liberty, we should be very cautious of violating the Rights of Conscience in others, ever considering that God alone is the judge of the Hearts of men and to him only in this case, they are answerable." The delightful human egoism in that compassion for error is readily forgiven and more than canceled by the rights of conscience principle that follows it.

RELATIONS TO CANADA CAMPAIGN
(1775)

A dominant reason for the emphatic warnings may be found in Washington's recognition of the prejudices against "popery" existing in New England in 1775, which had so valiantly assisted in ruining all chance of a Canadian alliance in the Congress of 1774. This same, militant Protestantism, two months after Arnold's instructions were drafted, drew from Washington a blast of anger which shows that the Virginia Episcopalian was a better man, a better patriot, and a better politician than the native sons of the colony that had started the rebellion. On November 5, the general orders announced that "The Commander in chief has been apprized of a design form'd for the observance of the ridiculous and childish custom of burning the Effigy of the pope. He cannot help expressing his surprise that there should be Officers and Soldiers in this army so void of common sense as not to see the impropriety of such a step at this juncture; at a time when we are solliciting and have really obtained the friendship of the people of Canada, whom we ought to consider as Brethren embarked in the same Cause: the defence of the general Liberty of America. At such a juncture and in such circumstances, to be insulting their Religion, is so monstrous, as not to be suffered or excused; indeed instead of offering the most remote insult, it is our duty to address public thanks to these our Brethren for every late happy Success over the common enemy in Canada." Needless to say Pope's Night was not celebrated in the army in 1775, nor at any time thereafter.

Just ten days later we find the announcement of the victory at St. John's, Canada, in these words: "The Commander in chief is confident the army under his immediate direction will show their gratitude to Providence for thus favoring the cause of Freedom and America by their thankfulness to God, and by their zeal and perseverance in this righteous cause, continue to deserve his future blessings." Next came the news, two weeks later, of the capture of Montreal and the orders announced that "The General hopes such frequent favours from divine Providence will animate every American to continue to exert his utmost in the defence of the Liberties of his Country, as it would now be the basest ingratitude to the Almighty and to their Country to shew any the least backwardness in the public cause."

The naiveté of this reasoning is of value as indicative of George Washington's mental attitude towards the Supreme Being and, regardless of other conclusions, there is in it a simple, childlike faith which commands respect. Was there ever a war since the Christian era when it was not claimed by both combatants that God was on their side? But George Washington has given the idea a distinctly American flavor by calling on the Continental soldier to help God.

RELIANCE ON PROVIDENCE (1776)

Then comes a personal note of soul humility in his letter to Joseph Reed in January, 1776: "I have scarcely," wrote Washington, "emerged from one difficulty before I have plunged into another. How it will end, God in his great goodness will direct. I am thankful for his protection to this time." One thing that speedily became clear to the mind of George Washington was that the military and governmental difficulties of America were not, and could not, be properly met without the help of God. They were too great and America was too feeble, in Washington's judgment, to admit of their successful solution without help from on high, and certainly the verdict of history as to the magnitude of these difficulties has confirmed Washington's judgment, though the muse is still too profane to admit the accuracy of his religious belief. Also, instead of becoming opinionated, instead of developing

an ego, instead of becoming confident of his abilities as he succeeded in surmounting one difficulty after another, George Washington became more and more convinced that the hand of God was in those triumphs and greater and greater became his spiritual humility, although weak dependence on his Creator was no part of his character. This humility in success and willingness to accept failure without complaint is exemplified at the end of the siege of Boston. You recall the seizure and fortification of Dorchester Heights and how the British prepared for another Bunker Hill. They attempted to cross the bay and storm the works, and Bunker Hill would have been child's play compared to the slaughter that would have ensued. You recall also, that the red-coats were prevented from crossing the water by a sudden and violent storm which lasted so long that by the time it was over Howe felt that the works had become too strong for him, gave over the attempt and evacuated the town. Here is Washington's comment to his brother John on the occurrence: "That this remarkable interposition of Providence is for some wise purpose, I have not a doubt." And this was rather an extraordinary thing to say. With all preparations made, all contingencies provided for, and with a sufficiency of ammunition in the hands of the Americans conditions were different from those prevailing at Bunker Hill, and it is quite reasonable to assume that Howe's attempt would have resulted in the complete annihilation of the British army.

WORSHIP IN THE ARMY (1776-1777)

The setting up of the actual machinery of religion in the Continental Army affords some evidence of value for our purpose. The Congress authorized the employment of chaplains, after Washington had urged it, and the general orders of July 9, 1776, when the Army was in New York City, directed that: "The Colonels or commanding officers of each regiment are directed to procure for Chaplains accordingly, persons of good character and exemplary lives. To see that all inferior officers and soldiers pay them a suitable respect and attend carefully upon religious exercises. The blessing and protection of Heaven are at all times necessary but especially so in times of public distress and danger. The General hopes and trusts, that every officer and man will endeavor so to live and act as becomes a Christian Soldier defending the dearest rights and Liberties of his country." And in the announcement, in these same orders, of the Declaration of Independence, the commander-in-chief hoped that "this important Event will serve as a fresh incentive to every officer and Soldier to act with Fidelity and Courage as knowing that now the peace and safety of his Country depends (under God) solely on the success of our arms." Here again we have the phrase "under God" which was so important an impromptu addition to Abraham Lincoln's Gettysburg Address. Was Lincoln guilty of

plagiarism? Or was it that the simple religious fervor of our two greatest Americans was closely akin?

In January, 1777, the Continental Army for the first time since the siege of Boston, established a permanent encampment base. This was at Morristown, New Jersey, and among the early things attended to was the practice of regular Sunday worship for the troops. On April 12, a Saturday, it was ordered that "All the troops in Morristown except the guards, are to attend divine worship tomorrow at the second Bell; the Officers commanding the Corps, are to take special care to have their men clean and decent, and that they are to march in proper order to the place of worship." For the next week, "All the troops in town (not on duty) to attend divine service tomorrow agreeable to the orders of the 12th instant." The convenience of a church building was an element in Morristown and the army paid due observance to Sunday. It may be noted, however, that only the troops in the town itself were ordered to church, for no building would have been large enough to hold the army encamped in the vicinity. When the encampment was shifted to Middlebrook the well-known order against profanity was issued on May 31. Washington characterized it as the "foolish and scandulous practice of *profane swearing*" and "As a means to abolish this and every other species of immorality Brigadiers are enjoyned to take effectual care, to have divine service duly performed in their respective brigades." At Middlebrook, also, on June 28, the orders were "That all Chaplains are to perfom divine service tomorrow and on every succeeding Sunday, with their respective brigades and regiments, where the situation will possibly admit of it. And the Commanding officers of corps are to see that they attend themselves with officers of all ranks setting the example. The Commander in chief expects an exact compliance with this order, and that it be observed in the future as an invariable rule of practice. And every neglect will be considered not only as a breach of orders, but a disregard to decency, virtue and religion."

THANKSGIVING (1777)

The announcement (at Peter Wentz's, Worcester Township, Pennsylvania, October 18, 1777) of the surrender of Burgoyne, concluded with the words: "Let every face brighten and every heart expand with grateful joy and praise to the supreme disposer of all Events, who has granted to us this signal success. The Chaplains of the army are to prepare short discourses, suit'd to the joyful occasion and to deliver them to their several corps and brigades at 5 o'clock this afternoon." Perhaps Washington's information as to the events in the north was such as convinced him that only God could have gained a victory for General Horatio Gates!

After the wearing campaign of 1777, when the battlescarred troops were on their march to Valley Forge for the winter, the commander-in-chief issued orders on December 17, for the observance of a thanksgiving day: "Tomorrow being the day set apart by the Honorable Congress for public Thanksgiving and Praise; and duty calling us devoutly to express our grateful acknowledgments to God for the manifold blessings he has granted us. The General directs that the Army remain in its present quarters and that the Chaplains perform divine service with their several corps and brigades. And earnestly exhorts all officers and soldiers whose absence is not indispensably necessary, to attend with reverence the solemnities of the day."

The suffering at Valley Forge, the terrible weather, and the activities needful to secure enough food for the troops explain, to some extent, why church services were not mentioned during that winter. Also many of the chaplains were absent from camp and there were a number of vacancies among them, as shown by the orders of May 2, 1778: "The Commander in chief directs that divine services be performed every Sunday at 11 o'clock in those brigades to which there are chaplains—those which have none to attend the places of worship nearest to them. It is expected that Officers of all Ranks will by their attendance set the example to their men. While we are zealously performing the duties of good citizens and Soldiers we certainly ought not to be inattentive to the higher duties of religion. To the distinguished character of Patriot it should be our highest glory to add the more distinguished character of Christian. The Signal instances of providential Goodness which we have experienced and which have now almost crowned our labours with complete success, demand from us in a peculiar manner the warmest returns of Gratitude and Piety to the Supreme Author of all Good."

GRATITUDE FOR THE FRENCH ALLIANCE (1778)

The statement that the cause of independence was almost crowned with complete success on May 2, 1778, may be considered slightly optimistic; but it raises the interesting question as to what were the rumors in the army, on that day, as to aid from France, for three days later the French alliance was announced: "It having pleased the Almighty Ruler of the Universe to defend the cause of the United American States, and finally to raise up a powerful friend among the princes of the Earth, to establish our liberty and independence upon a lasting foundation; it becomes us to set apart a day for gratefully acknowledging the divine goodness and celebrating the important event which we owe to his divine interposition." An echo of this feeling is found in Washington's letter to Governor Nelson, of Virginia, August 20, 1778. Writing from White Plains, New York, he said: "It is not a little pleasing, nor less wonderful to contemplate, that after two years manoeuvering and

undergoing the strangest vicissitudes, that perhaps ever attended any one contest since creation, both armies are brought back to the very point they set out from and that the offending party at the beginning [the British] is now reduced to the use of the spade and pickaxe for defence. The hand of Providence has been so conspicuous in all this that he must be worse than an infidel that lacks faith, and more than wicked who has not gratitude enough to acknowledge his obligations." When we find touches of romance like this in Washington's writing it raises the question as to the accuracy of the prevailing concept of the man. Though the romance of this appealed to him, even as he wrote he added a little touch of human feeling that brings him nearer to us, in this deprecatory gesture: "But it will be time enough for me to turn preacher when my present appointment ceases." And in addition to this romance and human feeling we can see also a touch of dry humor which has been persistently denied to Washington, but which he had in measure.

SAINT PATRICK (1776-1780)

Twice during the Revolution the Continental Army honored Saint Patrick's Day by order of the commander-in-chief. The first time was immediately after the evacuation of Boston, when the countersign for March 17, 1776, was "Saint Patrick." And the second time was in 1780, when on March 16 the orders read: "The General congratulates the Army on the very interesting proceedings of the Parliament of Ireland and of the Inhabitants of that Country which have been lately communicated; not only as they appear calculated to remove those heavy and tyrannical oppressions on their trade but to restore to a brave and Generous People the ancient Rights and Freedom and by their operation to promote the cause of America— Desirous of impressing on the minds of the Army, transactions so important in their nature the General directs that all fatigue and working parties cease for tomorrow the 17th —a day held in particular regard by the People of that Nation. At the same time he orders this he persuades himself that the celebration of the day will not be attended by the least rioting or disorder. The Officers to be at their quarters in camp and the troops of each state line are to keep within their own encampment." The next day, March 17, the parole was "Saints" and the countersigns "Patrick" and "Shela."

Washington was well aware of the healthy recklessness of many of his stalwarts and knew the Irish liking for a good rough and tumble. There is in these orders also, a recognition of the existence of that feeling which had prompted the attempted celebration of Pope's Night in 1775, so it was wise caution that guarded against a possible Donnybrook Fair in camp.

Two more general orders should be noted. On the day after the surrender of Cornwallis, October 20, 1781, Washington's greatest

military triumph of the war, he directed that "Divine Service is to be performed tomorrow in the several Brigades and Divisions. The Commander in chief earnestly recommends that the troops not on duty should universally attend with that seriousness of Deportment and gratitude of Heart which the recognition of such reiterated and astonishing interpositions of Providence demands of us."

THANKS FOR VICTORY (1783)

In the midst of this overwhelming victory George Washington's mind reverted to the repeated and astonishing interposition of Providence in behalf of America, though he can, by no means, be classed as a religious enthusiast. General George Washington ordered that the cessation of hostility should begin on April 19, 1783, eight years to the day from the commencement of hostilities at Lexington. It would have been just as easy for him to have ordered hostilities to cease on April 17, or April 18, or April 20, for that matter, but Washington, the cold, the austere, suddenly displays a sense of the poetic, in deliberately planning for this precise date. The orders for ceasing hostilities display some of those traits which have been ignored: "The Commander in chief orders the Cessation of Hostilities between the United States and the King of Great Britain to be publickly proclaimed tomorrow at the New Building and that the Proclamation which will be communicated herewith, be read tomorrow evening at the head of every regiment and corps of the army. After which the Chaplains with the several brigades will render thanks to Almighty God for all his mercies, particularly for his overruling the wrath of Man to his own glory and causing the rage of war to cease amongst the nations." After warning that no disorder or "licentiousness" will be tolerated he directed "An extra ration of liquor to be issued to *every* man tomorrow, to drink Perpetual Peace, Independence and Happiness to the United States of America."

WASHINGTON'S FAITH

No man knew better than Washington the frightfully thin ice over which the United States of America had skated to victory. Every weakness of the governmental and military machine had been laid bare before him at one time or another. Time after time he had seen the cause dragged back from the brink of ruin by an unexpected event, or an unforeseen happening, when he was well aware that no human effort could save it. That he himself had tried his utmost did not blind his eyes to the fact that this utmost, of itself, was not sufficient. The situation has its puzzle for us. Washington was the essence of practicality; but the instincts of his old horse-racing and fox-hunting days made him ever ready to take the sporting chance.

And sporting chances he took. Long Island was one. Trenton was another, Germantown another, and even Yorktown itself was largely a sporting chance. All of these chances, however, were backed by the most painstaking efforts. Yet the man declined to grant anything to the heathen god of Luck and, when the seemingly impossible became a success, when the weak spot in his plan, of which he was well aware, became strong through no apparent human arrangement, George Washington's firm belief in the righteousness of human liberty, drew from him frank acknowledgment of God's aid. Many times his plans failed; but when they did he merely assumed that Providence, for some inscrutable reason, had intervened. He accepted failure with calmness and began at once to build again for success. There is no trace of superstion in Washington; his faith was too strong and simple for that and it is this simplicity that makes analysis difficult. Napoleon's cynical remark that "Heaven is on the side of the heaviest artillery," and the claim that he was the man of destiny shrink to mere flippancies in comparison with George Washington's steadfast faith in God's aid to liberty. If ever there was a man who could rightfully claim to be a man of destiny it was George Washington; but he was the last man to entertain such a thought.

RELIGION IN WASHINGTON'S REPLIES TO ADDRESSES

There is a final group of papers among the Washington manuscripts which should be drawn upon in an effort to analyze Washington's religious ideas. Probably no President of the United States, certainly no American of lesser rank, ever received so many complimentary addresses as did Washington. He was scrupulous in answering them and in these answers we find much that is valuable for our purpose. We have seen Washington's mental attitude toward things religious during the colonial period; the General Orders of the Revolutionary War and the diaries give his attitude during the Revolution. But the replies to these addresses contain what may be considered as Washington's mature convictions, coming as they do in the last years of his life. I shall not quote many. The first is the clear, succinct statement in the reply to the General Committee of the United Baptist Churches in Virginia, in May, 1789: "I have often," he wrote, "expressed my sentiments that every man conducting himself as a good citizen, and being accountable to God alone for his religious opinions, ought to be protected in worshipping the Deity according to the dictates of his own conscience. . . . If I could have entertained the slightest apprehension that the Constitution framed in the Convention, where I had the honor to preside, might possibly endanger the religious rights of any ecclesiastical Society, certainly I would never have placed my signature to it; if I could now conceive that the general Government

might ever be so administered as to render liberty of conscience insecure, I beg you will be persuaded that no one would be more zealous than myself to establish effectual barriers against the horrors of spiritual tyranny, and every species of religious persecution . . . be assured, Gentlemen, that I entertain a proper sense of your fervent supplications to God for my temporal and eternal happiness." This acknowledgment of appreciation of the value of prayer in obtaining temporal and eternal happiness is worth something in generalizing upon Washington's belief in an hereafter.

RELATION TO THE DENOMINATIONS

A note of interest is the diary entry for May 27, 1787, in Philadelphia: "Went to the Romish Church to high mass." This was old St. Mary's and Washington was then attending the sessions of the Constitutional Convention. Could there have been a little of the Greek idea here, the same that we find in St. Paul's address to the Athenians? Two years later, when President, Washington made the delightful entry at Pomfret, Connecticut (November 8, 1789), while touring the eastern states: "It being contrary to law and disagreeable to the People of this State (Connecticut) to travel on the Sabbath Day—and my horses, after passing through such intolerable roads, wanting rest, I stayed at Perkins' tavern (which, by-the-bye is not a good one,) all day—and a meeting house being within a few rods of the door, I attended morning and evening service, and heard very lame discourses from a Mr. Pond." The layman's hearty understanding and sympathy goes out to Washington in this experience and the recollection of it may help us, in the future, to bear similar ills with fortitude.

A month later, in New York City, we find a perfect example of the sense of duty: "November 26, Thursday: Being the day appointed for a thanksgiving, I went to St. Paul's Chapel, though it was most inclement and stormy—but few people at Church." This was the first national Thanksgiving Day under our present government and, as he had summoned the nation to give thanks, Washington felt that he had to brave the elements and appear in church in compliance with his own proclamation. It is difficult to disentangle Washington's strong sense of duty in this from his religious feeling; but the two things are properly interchangeable in this case and it is doubtful if Washington himself could have analyzed them.

The diary entry for July 3, 1791, at York, Pennsylvania, has a bit of dry humor in it from our viewpoint: "There being no Episcopal Minister resident in the place, I went to hear morning Service performed in the Dutch reformed Church—which, being in that language not a word of which I understood I was in no danger of becoming a proselyte to its religion by the eloquence of the Preacher."

THE QUAKERS

To the address of the Pennsylvania Quakers, Washington's reply was particularly plain and outspoken: "We have reason to rejoice in the prospect that the present national Government, which by the favour of Divine Providence, was formed by the common counsels and peaceably established with the common consent of the People will prove a blessing to every denomination of them. . . . The liberty enjoyed by the People of these States, of worshipping Almighty God agreeable to their consciences is not only among the choicest of their *blessings* but also of their *rights*. While men perform their social duties faithfully, they do all that Society or the State can with propriety demand or expect; and remain responsible only to their Maker for the religion or modes of faith which they may prefer to profess. Your principles and conduct are well known to me, and it is doing the people called Quakers no more than justice to say that (excepting their declining to share with others the burthen of the common defence) there is no denomination among us who are more exemplary or useful citizens. I assure you very explicitly that in my opinion the conscientious scruples of all men should be treated with delicacy and tenderness, and it is my wish and desire that the laws may always be as extensively accommodated to them, as a due regard to the Protection and essential interests of the Nation may justify and permit."

Here is the willingness of the broad-minded statesman to admit the rights of conscience in religious matters, but the practical administrator pointing out with inexorable logic that unless the government which guarantees those rights is supported, there can be neither rights nor government.

ADVICE TO CHURCHES

To this may be joined Washington's reply to the Ministers and Ruling Elders of the Churches of the Massachusetts and New Hampshire Presbyteries: "I am persuaded you will permit me to observe that the path of true piety is so plain as to require but little political direction. To this consideration we ought to ascribe the absence of any regulation respecting religion from the Magna Charta of our country. To the guidance of the ministers of the gospel this important object is perhaps, more properly committed. It will be your care to instruct the ignorant and to reclaim the devious and in the progress of morality and science, to which our government will give every furtherance, we may confidently expect the advancement of true religion and the completion of our happiness." This from an Episcopalian to Presbyterians of the 18th century may certainly be taken as indicative of Washington's belief in the value of religion in education. In this reply he also touches upon a point made sensitive by our recent experiences with the so-called "Fundamentalists," so it is perhaps tactful to leave the idea as Washington puts it, merely remembering that he believed that science as well as religion contributes a share to human happiness.

Catholics are interested naturally in Washington's reply to the address made to him in December, 1789. In that reply Washington expresses the hope "ever to see America among the foremost nations in examples of justice and liberality. And I presume," he wrote, "that your fellow citizens will not forget the patriotic part which you took in the accomplishment of their revolution and the establishment of their government; or the important assistance which they received from a nation in which the roman catholic religion is professed." Washington never completely mastered the personal pronouns and the tangle here should be ascribed properly to a weakness of the head rather than of the heart.

Washington's reply to the address of the Members of the New Church in Baltimore has more than passing interest: "We have abundant reason to rejoice that in this Land the light of truth and reason has triumphed over the power of bigotry and superstition and that every person may here worship God according to the dictates of his own heart. In this enlightened age and in this land of equal liberty it is our boast that a man's religious tenets will not forfeit the protection of the law, nor deprive him of the right of attaining and holding the highest offices that are known in the United States."

There will be noted throughout these extracts a consistent uniformity of expression, such an uniformity as could only be based upon a habit of mind. There is no evidence that Washington thought like the Virginian who is credited with saying that while he was quite willing to admit there were many different ways to heaven, he was quite sure that no gentleman would choose any other than the Episcopalian way; for we may recall Washington's letter to Lafayette, August 15, 1787: "I am not less ardent in my wish that you may succeed in your plan of toleration in religious matters. Being no bigot myself, I am disposed to indulge the professors of Christianity in the church with that road to Heaven, which to them shall seem most direct, plainest, easiest and least liable to exception."

ESSENTIALS OF WASHINGTON'S RELIGION

As a young man Washington probably thought as little about religion as any healthy, normal youth. There are indications that his half-brother Lawrence was of a religious turn of mind and George had a great deal of affection and admiration for Lawrence. At the age of twenty-three he counted the bullet-holes in his coat after Braddock's defeat and acknowledged, with commonsense practicality, that a power higher than man had saved him; the Revolutionary War taught him lessons he was too honest to deny and, as a result, Washington's belief in God became the simple faith of a child, confirmed and strengthened by the actual, living experience of a man. Beyond this point of a firm belief in God, of belief in his absolute justice and his "interposition" in the affairs of man there is little of a tangible nature; but is not this enough? We know that Washington's concepts of truth, honor, and justice were founded upon and woven into this belief in God, and we can find slight fault with George Washington's truth, honor, and justice. Can we, as individuals, demand that the religion of our neighbor do more than make that neighbor an honorable man and an upright citizen? Is it worth while to insist on knowing more than this about George Washington's religion? It is plain that the two great commandments were well obeyed by him, and his reply to the address of the Hebrew Congregation of Newport, Rhode Island, in August, 1790, is one of the best: "It is now no more that toleration is spoken of, as if it was by the indulgence of one class of people that another enjoyed the exercise of their inherent natural rights. For happily the Government of the United States, which gives to bigotry no sanction, to persecution no assistance, requires only that those who live under its protection should demean themselves as good citizens, in giving it, on all occasions, their effectual support. . . . May the Father of Mercies scatter light and not darkness on our paths, and make us all, in our several vocations useful here, and in his own due time and way everlastingly happy."

And now as a last quotation read this from the Farewell Address: "Morality is a necessary spring of popular government . . . let us with caution indulge the supposition that morality can be maintained without religion. Whatever may be conceded to the influence of refined education on minds of peculiar structure, reason and experience both forbid us to expect that national morality can prevail in exclusion of religious principle." Is not this satisfying? "The influence of refined education upon minds of peculiar structure" might almost refer to our Haeckels and our Spencers. And Washington knew that the Haeckels and the Spencers do not influence the mass of the people to any extent and he was sure, from his own experience with men, that refined education without religion could not produce the sterling virtue of rugged and uncompromising honesty.

On his deathbed, after nearly twenty-four hours of struggle for breath, he placed the final seal of courageous manhood upon his life and went to his Maker with his brave faith unshaken: "I felt from the first," he whispered, "that the disorder would prove fatal . . . but I am not afraid to go." These last half-dozen words tell the worth of his religion to George Washington.

Part II

Washington's Own Words on Religion

QUESTION OF A BISHOP (1769)

"After a tiresome, and in my opinion, a very unimportant Session, I returned home about the middle of last Month. . . . The expediency of an American Episcopate was long & warmly debated, and at length rejected. As a substitute, the House attempted to frame an Ecclesiastical Jurisdiction, to be composed of a President and four other clergymen, who were to have full power and authority to hear and determine all matters and causes relative to the clergy, and to be vested with the [power] of Suspension, deprivation, & visitation. From this Jurisdiction an Appeal was to be had to a Court of Delegates, to consist of an equal number of Clergymen and Laymen; but this Bill, after much canvassing, was put to Sleep, from an opinion that the subject was of too much Importance to be hastily entered into at the end of a Session."

A YEAR OF WASHINGTON'S SUNDAYS (1773)

January—*Sunday, 3rd*—"In the Afternoon Mr. Ben Dulany came here; the other Gentleman continued all day here."

Sunday, 10th—"At home all day. Mr. Geo. Digges, Messrs. David and Chas. Stewart, Mr. Danl. Carrol Junr., and Mr. Richmond, dind and lodged here."

Sunday, 17th—"At home all day alone. Mrs. Barnes went up to Alexandria."

Sunday 24th—"At home all day alone."

Sunday 31st—"At home all day alone."

February—*Sunday, 7th*—"At home all day alone."

Sunday, 14th—"At home all day—alone."

Sunday, 21st—"At home all day. Mr. Hoops and a Mr. Warton calld here, but would not stay [to] dinner, taking a Cut before it."

Sunday, 28th—"At home all day. About Noon, Mr. Francis Willis, Mr. Warnr. Washington, and my Brothr. Saml came here."

March—Sunday 7th—"Dined at the Governor's and Spent the Evening at Mrs. Campbell's."

Sunday, 14th—"Set off about 10 Oclock. Dind at King William Court and lodgd at Todd's Bridge."

Sunday, 21st—"At Home all day alone."

Sunday, 28th—"Went with Mr. Dulany and Mr. Digges, &ca., to Dine with Mr. Benj. Dulany at Mrs. French's. Returnd again in the afternoon."

April—Sunday, 4th—"Mrs. Fairfax and Polly Brazier Dined here, as did Majr. Wagener. The latter stayd all Night. Mr. Jno. Baylor came in the afternoon."

Sunday, 11th—"Went to Pohick Church with Mrs. Washington and Mr. Custis, and returnd to Dinner."

Sunday, 18th—"Reachd home to Dinner after passing through Piscataway Town."

Sunday, 25th—"At home all day with the above Company."

May—Sunday, 2nd—"Went to Belvoir and dined. Returned in the Afternoon."

Sunday, 9th—"At home all day, Messrs. Ramsay, Rumney and Herbert dind here; the last of whom went away, the others stayd all Night."

Sunday, 16th—"Breakfasted at Chester and Dined at Govr. Penn's in Philadelphia."

Sunday, 23rd—"Set out for New York with Lord Sterling, Majr. Bayard and Mr. Custis, after Breakfasting with Govr. Penn. Dined with Govr. Franklin at Burlington and lodgd at Trenton."

Sunday, 30th—"Dined with Genl. Gage and Spent the Evening in my own Room writing."

June—Sunday, 6th—"Breakfasted at Slade's, 10 Miles from Sutton's, and dind and lodgd at Baltimore Town."

Sunday, 13th—"Went up with Miss Reed, etca., to Alexa. Church. Returnd to Dinner with Mr. Willis. Doctr. Rumney w[en]t away."

Sunday, 20th—"Colo. Fairfax and Lady, as also Mr. Massey dined here, Patcy Custis being buried. The first went away, Mr. Massey stayd."

Sunday, 27th—"The two Miss Calverts went up to Church. Mr. Calvert came over to Dinner and stayd all Night, as did Mr. Tilghman from Alexa."

July—Sunday 4th—"At home all day. Mrs. Peake and her daughter dind here."

Sunday, 11th—"Old Mr. Digges came over in the Forenoon; also Mr. Willis and Polly Brazier. Willis returnd in the afternoon."

Sunday, 18th—"Mr. Tilghman returned to Alexa. Miss Calvert and Mrs. Washington and self went to Pohick Church. In the Afternoon Mr. B. Fairfax came."

Sunday, 25th—"Went up to Alexandria Church and returnd to Dinner."

August—Sunday, 1st—"At Mr. Calvert's all day."

Sunday, 8th—"Went up to Alexa. Church and returnd to Dinner. Captn. Posey and Son Price here, the last of whom went away after Dinner."

Sunday, 15th—"At home all day—alone."

Sunday, 22nd—"Went up to Church at Alexandria and returnd to Dinner. Found Doctr. Craik here, who stayd all Night."

Sunday, 29th—"Govr. Eden and the other Gentn. went away after breakfast. I continued at home all day."

September—Sunday, 5th—"Went up with him and Miss Nelly Calvert to Alexa. Church. Returnd to Dinner."

Sunday, 12th—"Govr. Eden, Captn. Ellis, Mr. Dulany, Mr. Lee and Mr. Fendal came to Dinner and stayd all Night, as did Mr. F. Willis, Junr."

Sunday, 19th—"The two Mr. Alexanders went away after breakfast. My Brother Sam, his Wife and two children, came to Dinner."

Sunday, 26th—"I set of for Annapolis Races. Dined at Rollin's and got into Annapolis between five and six Oclock. Spent the Evening and lodged at the Governor's."

October—Sunday, 3rd—"At home all day, alone."

Sunday, 10th—"Mr. Herbert went away before Breakfast. Mr. Tilghman went with Mrs. Washington and I to Pohick Church and returnd with us."

Sunday, 17th—"At home all day—Captn. Conway Breakfasting here from the Maderias. Mr. Willis and my Brother went up to Church."

Sunday, 24th—"At Colo. Bassett's all [day.]"

Sunday, 31st—"At Colo. Bassett's all day."

November—Sunday, 7th—"Dined at Mrs. Dangerfield's and returnd to Colo. Bassett's in the afternoon."

Sunday, 14th—"Returnd to Colo. Bassett's to Dinner."

Sunday, 21st—"Dined at the Speaker's and spent the Evening in my own Room."

Sunday, 28th—"At Colo. Bassett's all day."

December—Sunday, 5th—"At Colo. Bassett's all day."

Sunday, 12th—"At home all day the above Company here. Mrs. Washington and Miss Brown going to Chh. and returng. to Dinner."

Sunday, 19th—"At home all day alone. After Dinner Mrs. Barnes went to Mrs. French's."

Sunday, 26th—"At home all day. Mr. Ben Dulany, and Mr. Peale dined here."

PRESBYTERIAN MEETING AND CATHOLIC SERVICE (1774)

"Went to the Presbyterian Meeting [at Philadelphia] in the forenoon and Romish Church in the afternoon. Dind at Bevan's."

MORALS (1776)

"The unhappy Fate of Thomas Hickey, executed this day for Mutiny, Sedition and Treachery, the General hopes will be a warning to every Soldier, in the Army, to avoid those crimes, and all others, so disgraceful to the character of a Soldier, and pernicious to his country, whose pay he receives and Bread he eats.—And in order to avoid those Crimes the most certain method is to keep out of temptation of them, and particularly to avoid lewd Women, who, by the dying Confession of this poor Criminal, first led him into practices which ended in an untimely and ignominious Death."

"The General is sorry to be informed that the foolish and wicked practice of profane cursing and swearing (a Vice heretofore little known in an American Army,) is growing into fashion; he hopes the officers will by example as well as influence endeavor to check it, and that both they and the men will reflect, that we can have little hopes of the Blessing of Heaven on our Arms if we insult it by our impiety and folly; added to this it is a vice so mean and low, without any temptation, that every man of sense and character, detests and despises it."

PROVIDENCE (1778)

"The violent gale . . . and the withdrawing of the Count d'Estaing to Boston, . . . I consider storms and victory under the direction of a wise providence who no doubt directs them for the best of purposes, and to bring round the greatest degree of happiness to the greatest number of his people."

PROTECTION OF THE ALMIGHTY (1783)

"I consider it an indispensable duty to close this last solemn act of my official life, by commending the Interests of our dearest country to the protection of Almighty God, and those who have the superintendence of them to his holy keeping."

TO THE GOVERNORS OF THE STATES (1783)

"The free cultivation of letters, the unbounded extension of commerce, the progressive refinement of manners, the growing liberality of sentiment, and above all, the pure and benign light of Revelation, have had a meliorating influence on mankind and increase the blessings of society. . . .

"I now make my earnest prayer, that God would have you and the States over which you preside, in his holy protection; that he would incline the hearts of the citizens to cultivate the spirit of subordination and obedience to government; to entertain a brotherly affection and love for one another, for their fellow citizens of the United States at large, and particularly for their brethren who have served in the field; and finally, that he would most graciously be pleased to dispose us all to do justice, to love mercy, and to demean ourselves with that charity, humility, and pacific temper of mind which were the characteristics of the Divine Author of our blessed religion, and without an humble imitation of whose example in these things we can never hope to be a happy nation."

SUNDAYS (1784, 1785)

September, 1784—Sunday, 19th—"Being Sunday, and the People living on my Land, *apparently* very religious, it was thought best to postpone going among them till tomorrow."

October, 1785—Sunday, 2d—"Went with Fanny Bassett, Burwell Bassett, Doctr. Stuart, G. A. Washington, Mr. Shaw and Nelly Custis to Pohick Church; to hear a Mr. Thompson preach, who returned home with us to Dinner, where I found the Revd. Mr. Jones, formerly a Chaplin in one of the Pennsylvania Regiments.

"After we were in Bed (about eleven Oclock in the Evening) Mr. Houdon, sent from Paris by Doctr. Franklin and Mr. Jefferson to take my Bust, in behalf of the State of Virginia, with three young men assistants, introduced by a Mr. Perin a French Gentleman of Alexandria, arrived here by Water from the latter place."

RELIGIOUS FREEDOM (1785)

"Although no man's sentiments are more opposed to *any kind* of restraint upon religious principles than mine are, yet I must confess, that I am not amongst the number of those, who are so much alarmed at the thoughts of making people pay towards the support of that which they profess, if of the denomination of Christians, or declare themselves Jews, Mahometans, or otherwise, and thereby obtain proper relief. As the matter now stands, I wish an assessment had never been agitated, and as it has gone so far, that the bill could not die an easy death; because I think it will be productive of more quiet to the State, than by enacting it into a law, which in my opinion would be impolitic, admitting there is a decided majority for it, to the disquiet of a respectable minority. In the former case, the matter will soon subside; in the latter, it will rankle and perhaps convulse the State."

THANKSGIVING TO GOD IN THE INAUGURAL (1789)

"Such being the impressions under which I have, in obedience to the public summons, repaired to the present station, it would be peculiarly improper to omit, in this first official act, my fervent supplications to that Almighty Being, who rules over the universe, who presides in the councils of nations, and whose providential aids can supply every human defect, that his benediction may consecrate to the liberties and happiness of the people of the United States a government instituted by themselves for

these essential purposes, and may enable every instrument employed in its administration to execute with success the functions allotted to his charge.

"In tendering this homage to the great Author of every public and private good, I assure myself that it expresses your sentiments not less than my own; nor those of my fellow-citizens at large, less than either. No people can be bound to acknowledge and adore the invisible hand, which conducts the affairs of men, more than the people of the United States. Every step, by which they have advanced to the character of an independent nation, seems to have been distinguished by some token of providential agency.

"And, in the important revolution just accomplished in the system of their united government, the tranquil deliberations and voluntary consent of so many distinct communities, from which the event has resulted, cannot be compared with the means by which most governments have been established, without some return of pious gratitude along with an humble anticipation of the future blessings which the past seem to presage. These reflections, arising out of the present crisis, have forced themselves too strongly on my mind to be suppressed. You will join with me, I trust, in thinking that there are none, under the influence of which the proceedings of a new and free government can more auspiciously commence.

* * *

"Having thus imparted to you my sentiments, as they have been awakened by the occasion that brings us together, I shall take my present leave; but not without resorting once more to the benign Parent of the human race, in humble supplication, that, since he has been pleased to favor the American people with opportunities for deliberating in perfect tranquillity, and dispositions for deciding with unparalleled unanimity on a form of government for the security of their union and the advancement of their happiness, so his divine blessing may be equally *conspicuous* in the enlarged views, the temperate consultations, and the wise measures, on which the success of this government must depend."

SUPPORT OF THE ALMIGHTY (1789)

"GENTLEMEN, I thank you for your address, in which the most affectionate sentiments are expressed in the most obliging terms. The coincidence of circumstances, which led to this auspicious crisis, the confidence reposed in me by my fellow-citizens, and the assistance I may expect from counsels, which will be dictated by an enlarged and liberal policy, seem to presage a more prosperous issue to my administration, than a diffidence of my abilities had taught me to anticipate. I now feel myself inexpressibly happy in a belief, that Heaven, which has done so much for our infant nation, will not withdraw its providential influence before our political felicity shall have been

completed; and in a conviction that the Senate will at all times co-operate in every measure which may tend to promote the welfare of this confederated republic.

"Thus supported by a firm trust in the great Arbiter of the universe, aided by the collected wisdom of the Union, and imploring the divine benediction on our joint exertions in the service of our country, I readily engage with you in the arduous but pleasing task of attempting to make a nation happy."

CHRISTIANITY (1789)

"It affords edifying prospects indeed to see Christians of every denomination dwell together in more charity, and conduct themselves in respect to each other with a more Christian-like spirit than ever they have done in any former age or in any other nation."

SUNDAY VISITS TO STRANGERS (1789)

"On the seventh, now called the first day, for want of a place of Worship (within less than nine miles) such letters as do not require immediate acknowledgment I give answer to. . . . But it hath so happened, that on the two last Sundays—call them the first or the seventh as you please, I have been unable to perform the latter duty on account of visits from Strangers, with whom I could not use the freedom to leave alone, or recommend to the care of each other, for their amusement."

THANKSGIVING PROCLAMATION (1789)

"It is the duty of all nations to acknowledge the providence of Almighty God, to obey His will, to be grateful for His benefits, and humbly to implore His protection and favor, . . . that great and glorious Being who is the beneficent Author of all the good that was, and is, and is to come."

TO BALTIMORE (1789)

"I know the delicate nature of the duties incident to the part I am called to perform. I feel my incompetence without the singular assistance of Providence to discharge them in a satisfactory manner."

TO PHILADELPHIA (1789)

"When I contemplate the interposition of Providence as it was manifested in guiding us through the Revolution, in preparing us for the reception of a general government, and in conciliating the good-will of the people of America towards one another after its adoption, I feel myself oppressed and almost overwhelmed with a sense of the divine munificence."

TO THE GENERAL ASSEMBLY OF THE PRESBYTERIAN CHURCH (1789)

"It is not necessary for me to conceal the satisfaction I have felt upon finding that my compliance with the call of my country, and my dependence upon the assistance of Heaven to support me in my arduous undertakings, have, so far as I can learn, met the universal approbation of my countrymen. I reiterate the profession of my dependence upon Heaven as the source of all public and private blessings."

TO THE BISHOPS OF THE METHODIST CHURCH (1789)

"It always affords me satisfaction when I find a concurring sentiment and practice between all conscientious men in acknowledgment of homage to the great Governor of the universe, and in professions of support to a just civil government. . . . I shall always strive to be a faithful and impartial patron of genuine vital religion. . . . I take in the kindest part the promise you make of presenting your prayers at the throne of grace for me, and I likewise implore the divine benediction on yourselves and your religious community."

TO MASSACHUSETTS (1789)

"For the benedictions you have been pleased to implore of the Parent of the universe on my person and family, I have a grateful heart, and the most ardent wish that we may all, by rectitude of conduct and a perfect reliance on His beneficence, draw the smiles of Heaven on ourselves and posterity to the latest generation."

TO THE SYNOD OF THE REFORMED DUTCH CHURCH (1789)

"If such talents as I possess have been called into action by great events, and those events have terminated happily for our country, the glory should be ascribed to the manifest interposition of an overruling Providence. . . . You, gentlemen, act the part of pious Christians and good citizens by your prayers and exertions, etc. I beseech the Almighty to take you and yours under His special care."

TO CONNECTICUT (1789)

"I was but the humble agent of favoring Heaven, whose benign interference was so often manifested in our behalf, and to whom the praise of victory alone is due."

TO THE ROMAN CATHOLICS OF THE UNITED STATES (1789)

"May the members of your society in America, animated alone by the pure spirit of Christianity, and still conducting themselves as the faithful subjects of our free government, enjoy every temporal and spiritual felicity."

TO VIRGINIA (1790)

"In looking forward to that awful moment when I must bid adieu to sublunary scenes, I anticipate the consolation of leaving our country in a prosperous condition; and while the curtain of separation shall be drawing, my last breath will, I trust, expire in a prayer for the temporal and eternal felicity of those who have not only endeavored to gild the evening of my days with unclouded serenity, but extended their desires to my happiness hereafter in a brighter world."

TO THE HEBREW CONGREGATION OF SAVANNAH (1790)

"May the same wonder-working Deity who long since delivered the Hebrews from their Egyptian oppressors, and planted them in the promised land, whose providential agency has lately been conspicuous in establishing these United States as an independent nation, still continue to water them with the dews of heaven, and to make the inhabitants of every denomination participate in the temporal and spiritual blessings of that people whose God is Jehovah."

CHURCH UNIVERSAL

"Of all the animosities which have existed among mankind, those which are caused by difference of sentiments in religion appear to be the most inveterate and distressing, and ought most to be deprecated. I was in hopes, that the lightened and liberal policy, which has marked the present age, would at least have reconciled *Christians* of every denomination so far, that we should never again see their religious disputes carried to such a pitch as to endanger the peace of society."

DIVINE INTERPOSITION (1792)

"There never was a people, who had more reason to acknowledge a divine interposition in their affairs, than those of the United States; and I should be pained to believe that they have forgotten that agency, which was so often manifested during our revolution, or that they failed to consider the omnipotence of that God who is alone able to protect them."

TO CONGRESS (1793)

"I humbly implore that Being on whose will the fate of nations depends to crown with success our mutual endeavors for the general happiness."

TO CONGRESS (1794)

"Let us unite, therefore, in imploring the Supreme Ruler of nations to spread His holy protection over these United States: . . . to perpetuate to our country that prosperity which His goodness has already conferred, and to verify the anticipations of this government being a safeguard to human rights."

TO CONGRESS (1795)

"I derive peculiar satisfaction from your concurrence with me in the expression of gratitude to Almighty God which a review of the auspicious circumstances that distinguish our happy country have excited. . . . The sentiments we have mutually expressed of profound gratitude to the Source of those numerous blessings, the Author of all good, and pledges of our obligations to unite our sincere and zealous endeavors, as the instruments of divine Providence, to preserve and perpetuate them."

THANKSGIVING PROCLAMATION (1795)

"It is in an especial manner our duty as a people with devout reverence and affectionate gratitude to acknowledge our many and great obligations to Almighty God, and to implore Him to continue and confirm the blessings we experience, . . . at the same time humbly and fervently to beseech the kind Author of those blessings graciously to prolong them to us, and to imprint upon our hearts a deep and solemn sense of our obligations to Him for them."

TO CONGRESS (1796)

"I find ample reason for a renewal of that gratitude to the Ruler of the universe which a continued series of prosperity has so often and so justly called forth. . . .

"I cannot omit the occasion now to repeat my fervent supplication to the Supreme Ruler of the universe and Sovereign Arbiter of nations, that His providential care may still be extended to the United States."

TO THE CLERGY OF DIFFERENT DENOMINATIONS, PHILADELPHIA (1797)

"Believing as I do that religion and morality are the essential pillars of civil society, I view with unspeakable pleasure that harmony and brotherly love which characterize the clergy of different denominations, as well in this as in other parts of the United States, exhibiting to the world a new and interesting spectacle, at once the pride of our country and the surest basis of universal harmony.

"That your labors for the good of mankind may be crowned with success, that your temporal enjoyments may be commensurate with your merits, and that the future reward of good and faithful servants may be yours, I shall not cease to supplicate the divine Author of life and felicity."

Selected Authorities

ANDREWS, CHARLES M.—*Colonial Folkways* (*Chronicles of America*, Vol. IX). New Haven, Yale University Press, 1919. (Especially ch. vii.)

GREENE, EVARTS BOUTELL — *Provincial America* (*American Nation*, Vol. VI). New York, Harper, 1905. (Especially ch. xviii.)

HART, ALBERT BUSHNELL, ED.—*American History told by Contemporaries*, Vol. II. New York, Macmillan, 1898. (Especially ch. xv.)

HUMPHREYS, EDWARD FRANK—*Nationalism and Religion in America, 1774-1789.*

Boston, Chipman Law Publishing Co., 1924.

JERNEGAN, MARCUS WILSON—*American Colonies, 1492-1750* (*Epochs of American History*, Vol. I). New York, Longmans Green, 1929. (Especially ch. xv.)

JOHNSTONE, WILLIAM J.—*George Washington the Christian.* New York, Abingdon Press, 1919.

M'GUIRE, EDWARD C.—*Religious Opinions and Character of Washington.* 2d ed. New York, Harper, 1847.

MEADE, WILLIAM—*Old Churches, Ministers and Families of Virginia.* 2 vols. Philadelphia. Lippincott, 1857.

SLAUGHTER, PHILIP—*Christianity the Key to the Character and Career of Washington.* New York, Whittaker, 1886.

WASHINGTON, GEORGE — *Diaries, 1748-1799.* Ed. by John C. Fitzpatrick. 4 vols. Boston, Houghton Mifflin, 1925.

WASHINGTON, GEORGE—*Writings.* Ed. by Worthington Chauncey Ford. 14 vols. New York, Putnam, 1889-93.

Washington's Addresses to the Churches (*Old South Leaflets*, No. 65). Boston, 1896.

THE DAY'S BEGINNING
From a painting by J. L. G. Ferris

Washington the Colonial and National Statesman

By David M. Matteson

Part I

Washington in Colonial Politics (1755-1775)

GEORGE WASHINGTON

This portrait, known as the "Gibbs-Channing portrait," was painted in 1795 by Gilbert Stuart

WASHINGTON AS A CANDIDATE
(1755-1758)

WASHINGTON'S experience as a politician began in 1755. That year he became a candidate for election as Burgess for Frederick County, at that time covering the northern half of Virginia, west of the Blue Ridge, with Winchester as the county seat. He was defeated, partly, it is said, because he would not resort to the usual method of canvassing and his opposition to tippling houses in the garrison town. There is evidence, however, that at the same time he stood or had ideas of standing for Fairfax County within which were both Alexandria and Mount Vernon. He wrote his brother: "I should be glad if you could discover [their] . . . real sentiments on this head; . . . without disclosing much of mine, . . . If they seem inclinable to promote my interest, and things should be drawing to a crisis, you then may declare my intention, and beg their assistance. If, on the contrary, you find them more inclined to favour some other, I would have the affair entirely dropped. . . . sound their pulse . . . with an air of indifference and unconcern; after that, you may regulate your conduct according to circumstances." Evidently, though, the sounding, if attempted, was not favorable. In July, 1758, while himself absent with the Forbes expedition he was again a candidate for Frederick and this time successful, his agent being chaired through the street with much enthusiasm, the reason for which is made somewhat evident by Washington's bill for election expenses. This in a gross of £39.6s included 118 gallons of liquor in various forms, besides one hogshead, one barrel, and ten bowls of punch, and £3 for a "dinner for your Friends." He wrote his thanks to the agent, including a promise to the constituents such as nowadays would be made before the election: "If thanks flowing from a heart replete with joy and Gratitude can in any Measure compensate for the fatigue, anxiety and Pain you had at my Election, be assured you have them; 'tis a poor, but I am convinced, welcome tribute to a generous Mind. Such, I believe yours to be. How shall I . . . acknowledge my sense of obligations to the People in general for their choice of me, I am at a loss to resolve on. But why? Can I do it more effectually than by making their Interest (as it really is) my own, and doing everything that lyes in my little Power for the Honor and welfare of the Country? I think not; and my best endeavors they may always command. I promise this now, when promises may be regarded, before they might pass as words of course."

WASHINGTON ON THE STAMP ACT
(1765)

His attendance began on February 22, 1759, and he continued to be a member of the House until 1775 through several re-elections, first for Frederick County and then for Fairfax. Our interest in this service is its relation to his later political policies, especially as in it originated the principles for which he fought during the Revolution.

The Stamp Act agitation was the first influence. September 20, 1765, Washington wrote: "The Stamp Act, imposed on the colonies by the Parliament of Great Britain, engrosses the conversations of the speculative part of the colonists, who look upon this unconstitutional method of taxation, as a direful attack upon their liberties and loudly exclaim against the violation. What may be the result of this, and of some other (I think I may add) ill-judged measures, I will not undertake to determine; but this I may venture to affirm, that the advantage accruing to the mother country will fall greatly short of the expectations of the ministry; for certain it is, that our whole substance does already in a manner flow to Great Britain, and that whatsoever contributes to lessen our importations must be hurtful to their manufacturers. And the eyes of our people, already beginning to open, will perceive, that many luxuries, which we lavish our substance in Great Britain for, can well be dispensed with, whilst the necessaries of life are (mostly) to be had within ourselves. This, consequently, will introduce frugality, and be a necessary stimulation to industry. If Great Britain, therefore, loads her manufactures with heavy taxes, will it not facilitate these measures? They will not compel us, I think, to give our money for their exports, whether we will or not; and certain, I am, none of their traders will part from them without a valuable consideration. Where, then, is the utility of these restrictions? As to the Stamp Act, taken in a single view, one and the first bad consequence attending it, I take to be this, our courts of judicature must inevitably be shut up; for it is impossible (or next of kin to it), under our present circumstances, that the act of Parliament can be complied with, were we ever so willing to enforce the execution; for, not to say, which alone would be sufficient, that we have not money to pay the stamps, there are many cogent reasons to prevent it; and if a stop be put to our judicial proceedings, I fancy the merchants of Great Britain, trading to the colonies, will not be among the last to wish for a repeal of it." July 25, 1767, he added: "Those . . . who . . . were instrumental in securing the repeal . . . are . . . deservedly entitled to the thanks of the well-wishers to Britain and her colonies, . . . Mine they accordingly have, and always shall have for their opposition to any act of oppression; and that act could be looked upon in no other light by every person, who would view it in its proper colors."

WASHINGTON ON NON-IMPORTATION (1769-1770)

Four years later after the Townshend Acts had become law he had a correspondence with his neighbor George Mason in April, 1769, the outgrowth of which was the Virginia Non-importation Association of May 18, adopted at a meeting of Burgesses just after they had been dissolved by the governor for voting the Virginia Resolves. The Association was drafted by Mason; Washington was a member of the committee. Washington in his letter of April 5, wrote: "At a time, when our lordly masters in Great Britain will be satisfied with nothing less than the deprivation of American freedom, it seems highly necessary that something should be done to avert the stroke, and maintain the liberty, which we have derived from our ancestors. But the manner of doing it, to answer the purpose effectually, is the point in question. That no man should scruple, or hesitate a moment, to use a-ms in defence of so valuable a blessing, on which all the good and evil of life depends, is clearly my opinion. Yet a-ms, I would beg leave to add, should be the last resource, the dernier resort. Addresses to the throne, and remonstrances to Parliament, we have already, it is said, proved the inefficacy of. How far, then, their attention to our rights and privileges is to be awakened or alarmed, by starving their trade and manufactures, remains to be tried.
. . .

"The more I consider a scheme of this sort, the more ardently I wish success to it, because I think there are private as well as public advantages to result from it,—the former certain, however precarious the other may prove. For in respect to the latter, I have always thought, that by virtue of the same power, (for here alone the authority derives) which assumes the right of taxation, they may attempt at least to restrain our manufactories, especially those of a public nature, the same equity and justice prevailing in the one case as the other, it being no greater hardship to forbid my manufacturing, than it is to order me to buy goods of them loaded with duties, for the express purpose of raising a revenue. But as a measure of this sort would be an exertion of arbitrary power, we cannot be worsted, I think, but by putting it to the test."

His deeds lived up to his words and in his orders to his English agents he was careful to specify in August, 1770, that: "You will perceive, in looking over the several invoices, that some of the goods there required, are upon condition, that the act of Parliament imposing a duty on tea, paper, &c. for the purpose of raising a revenue in America, is totally repealed; and I beg the favor of you to be governed strictly thereby, as it will not be in my power to receive any articles contrary to our non-importation agreement, which I have subscribed, and shall religiously adhere to, and should, if it were, as I could wish it to be, ten times as strict."

WASHINGTON ON THE BOSTON PORT BILL (1774)

Excellent authorities assure us that but for the insistent agitation by certain of the American radicals and the wrong-headedness of certain English leaders, particularly the King, affairs might have resumed the normal condition, Parliament being satisfied with placing on record its right to control the colonies while the latter continued virtually to govern themselves. However, the attempt to force taxed tea through the colonial ports, the general resistance of this, and the subsequent coercive acts against Massachusetts, because she had been most active in the decade of resistance, precipitated the conflict. When the news reached Williamsburg of the enactment of the Boston Port Bill the Burgesses voted on May 24, 1774, that June 1, when the act became operative, should be a day of fasting and prayer in Virginia. Lord Dunmore, the governor, dissolved the House in order to prevent more drastic resolves, which Richard Henry Lee intended to introduce. Once more the Burgesses resorted to a private meeting, May 25, drew up another Association and recommended an intercolonial congress. Several days later twenty-five of them met again, and not considering that so few of them should take the further action deemed essential, proposed that the Burgesses meet in convention on August 1. Washington was one of these twenty-five. He was becoming weary of half measures, of ignored addresses, petitions, and humble approaches to the Throne.

The letter he wrote his loyalist friend, Bryan Fairfax, July 4, 1774, shows this: "As to your political sentiments, I would heartily join you in them, so far as relates to a humble and dutiful petition to the throne, provided there was the most distant hope of success. But have we not tried this already? Have we not addressed the Lords, and remonstrated to the Commons? And to what end? Did they deign to look at our petitions? Does it not appear, as clear as the sun in its meridian brightness, that there is a regular, systematic plan formed to fix the right and practice of taxation upon us? Does not the uniform conduct of Parliament for some years past confirm this? Do not all the debates, especially those just brought to us, in the House of Commons on the side of government, expressly declare that America must be taxed in aid of the British funds, and that she has no longer resources within herself? Is there any thing to be expected from petitioning after this? Is not the attack upon the liberty and property of the people of Boston, before restitution of the loss to the India Company was demanded, a plain and self-evident proof of what they are aiming at? Do not the subsequent bills (now I dare say acts), for depriving the Massachusetts Bay of its charter, and transporting offenders into other colonies or to Great Britain for trial, where it is impossible from the nature of the thing that justice can be obtained, convince us that the administration is determined to stick at nothing to carry its point? Ought we not, then, to put our virtue and fortitude to the severest test?"

Before the meeting of the Convention there were various conferences with his neighbor, George Mason, which resulted in meetings of the citizens of the county on July 5 and 18, when Washington presided and Mason's famous Fairfax County Resolves, which undoubtedly had been moulded into shape at the discussions between the two leaders, were adopted, but considered as Mason's work.

WASHINGTON IN THE FIRST VIRGINIA CONVENTION (1774)

The first Virginia Convention met at Williamsburg, August 1-6. Washington attended not only as a Burgess but as a delegate appointed at the Fairfax County meeting to present that meeting's resolves. The journals of the Convention show no special activity by him; but John Adams, in his diary, at second or third hand, accredits him with making the most eloquent speech in the gathering: "I will raise one thousand men, subsist them at my own expense, and march myself at their head for the relief of Boston." Silas Deane makes a somewhat similar statement, so it was evidently one of the current stories among the delegates of the Continental Congress that autumn. On the fifth Washington was elected a delegate to the Continental Congress, and this was the beginning of his intercolonial and later political career. Continuing his correspondence with Fairfax, he exposed the attitude with which he approached the larger meeting, writing August 24: "I have no new lights to throw upon the subject, or any other arguments to offer in support of my own doctrine, than what you have seen; and could only in general add, that an innate spirit of freedom first told me, that the measures, which administration hath for some time been and now are most violently pursuing, are repugnant to every principle of natural justice; whilst much abler heads than my own hath fully convinced me, that it is not only repugnant to natural rights, but subversive of the laws and constitution of Great Britain itself, in the establishment of which some of the best blood in the kingdom hath been spilt. . . . For my own part, I shall not undertake to say where the line between Great Britain and the colonies should be drawn; but I am clearly of opinion, that one ought to be drawn, and our rights clearly ascertained. I could wish, I own, that the dispute had been left to posterity to determine, but the crisis is arrived when we must assert our rights, or submit to every imposition that can be heaped upon us, till custom and use shall make us as tame and abject slaves, as the blacks we rule over with such arbitrary sway. . . . if you disavow the right of Parliament to tax us, (unrepresented as we are) we only differ in respect to the mode of opposition, and this difference principally arises from your belief, that they—the Parliament, I mean,—want a decent opportunity to repeal the acts; whilst I am as fully convinced, as I am of my own existence, there has been a regular, systematic plan formed to enforce them, and that nothing but unanimity in the colonies (a stroke they did not expect) and firmness, can prevent it. . . . P. S. Pray what do you think of the Canada Bill?"

He was giving much thought, evidently, to the approaching session, for he asked for authentic lists of exports and imports annually, more especially to and from Great Britain, and there were further conferences. The night before he started for Philadelphia, Henry and Pendleton, fellow delegates, as well as Mason, were with him over night.

WASHINGTON IN THE FIRST CONTINENTAL CONGRESS (1774)

The meetings of what is usually called the "First" Continental Congress began on September 5 and ended on October 26. Washington was not a member of any committee. His position in the gathering is best known through Henry's tribute: "If you speak of eloquence, Mr. Rutledge of South Carolina is by far the greatest orator, but if you speak of solid information and sound judgment, Colonel Washington is unquestionably the greatest man on that floor." Silas Deane wrote that he "speaks very modestly and in cool but determined style and accent."

The published letters of members of Congress make but slight reference to him. He was, however, profiting by the intercourse with leaders from other colonies, weighing their desires with those of his own region, and solidifying his principles. When a former companion of the French War, now an officer of the British troops in Boston, made accusations against the Massachusetts leaders, Washington "Spent the afternn. with the Boston Gentn.," and then made a warm reply to Mackenzie on October 9: "I conceive, when you condemn the conduct of the Massachusetts people, you reason from effects, not causes; otherwise you would not wonder at a people, who are every day receiving fresh proofs of a systematic assertion of an arbitrary power, deeply planned to overturn the laws and constitution of their country, and to violate the most essential and valuable rights of mankind, being irritated, and with difficulty restrained from acts of the greatest violence and intemperance. For my own part, I confess to you candidly, that I view things in a very different point of light from the one in which you seem to consider them; and though you are led to believe by venal men,—for such I must take the liberty of calling those new-fangled counsellors, who fly to and surround you, and all others, who, for honors or pecuniary gratifications, will lend their aid to overturn the constitution, and introduce a system of arbitrary government,—although you are taught, I say, by discoursing with such men, to believe, that the people of Massachusetts are rebellious, setting up for independency, and what not, give me leave, my good friend, to tell you, that you are abused, grossly abused. This I advance with a degree of confidence and boldness, which may claim your belief, having better opportunities of knowing the real sentiments of the people you are among, from the leaders of them, in opposition to the present measures of the administration, than you have from those whose business it is, not to disclose truths, but to misrepresent facts in order to justify as much as possible to the world their own conduct. Give me leave to add, and I think I can announce it as a fact, that it is not the wish or interest of that government, or any other upon this continent, separatively or collectively, to set up for independence; but this you may at the same time rely on, that none of them will ever submit to the loss of those valuable rights and privileges, which are essential to the happiness of every free state, and without which, life, liberty, and property are rendered totally insecure. These, Sir, being certain consequences, which must naturally result from the late acts of Parliament relative to America in general, and the government of Massachusetts Bay in particular, is it to be wondered at, I repeat, that men, who wish to avert the impending blow, should attempt to oppose it in its progress, or prepare for their defence, if it cannot be averted? Surely I may be allowed to answer in the negative; and again give me leave to add as my opinion, that more blood will be spilled on this occasion, if the ministry are determined to push matters to extremity, than history has ever yet furnished instances of in the annals of North America, and such a vital wound will be given to the peace of this great country, as time itself cannot cure, or eradicate the remembrance of."

WASHINGTON'S FINAL ACTIONS AS A VIRGINIAN (1775)

Washington's final public actions as a Virginia colonial gentleman were reviews of various independent companies. He wrote his brother, March 25, 1775, promising to review the latter's company in Shenandoah Valley: "I . . . shall very cheerfully accept the honor of commanding it, if occasion requires it to be drawn out, as it is my full intention to devote my life and fortune in the cause we are engaged in, if needful." He attended the second Virginia Provincial Convention at Richmond on March 20-27, and was reelected to the Continental Congress. Again at Mount Vernon, the conferences went on. Mason, the Lees, and others with whom he undoubtedly discussed the situation were his guests, and it is significant that he also entertained Charles Lee and Horatio Gates, both of whom were soon to be generals in the Continental Army. He left his home, which he was not to see again for more than six strenuous years, on May 4, 1775. The second session of Congress began at Philadelphia on May 10, and he was appointed to the committees on fortifying New York, ammunition, army rules, and raising money. Before this, however, the news of the battle of Lexington and Concord was received; and on May 3 he had written his friend George William Fairfax, then in England: "Unhappy it is, though, to reflect, that a brother's sword has been sheathed in a brother's breast, and that the once happy and peaceful plains of America are either to be drenched with blood or inhabited by slaves. Sad alternative! But can a virtuous man hesitate in his choice?"

There could be no more hesitation, the issues were finally joined; and with his mind made up he saw that it was his duty to accept the command of the army when on June 15 Congress offered it to him. This did not withdraw him from politics; rather it made it sharply needful to bear in mind both political and military necessity and to strive to reconcile the two opposing elements. It became his task to make an often reluctant Congress, jealous of its own entirely self-ordained rights, realize facts; a task of wise and patient statecraft. This phase of his career during the Revolution is often lost sight of; but its importance was scarcely less than success on the field; indeed, the latter was dependent upon the other.

This relationship with Congress began with his commission and instructions. Although he was "vested with full power and authority to act as you shall think for the good and welfare of the service," he was also "punctually to observe and follow such orders and directions, from time to time, as you shall receive from this, or a future Congress." Congress intended to hold the strings.

Part II

Washington's Relation to Congress

(1775-1786)

WASHINGTON ON UNITY OF MILITARY AUTHORITY

Washington's military relations with Congress have been summed up by Van Tyne as "handicapped by the most unwieldly superior council that ever hampered a military chieftain." Yet Washington considered from the first that the power of Congress was paramount within the colonies, at least in military affairs. He wrote Governor Trumbull, July 18, 1775: "As the army is upon a general establishment, their right, to supersede and control a Provincial one, must be unquestionable." At the same time he began the incessant effort to induce Congress to put the army upon a unified and secure basis; the first problem being the right of the colonies to appoint all the officers under generals for the troops raised in each. "I submit," he wrote Rodney, August 30, "that as the whole troops are now taken into the pay of the United Colonies, the Congress . . . ought to reserve the filling up of all vacancies themselves, in order that volunteers from every government may have an equal chance of preferment, instead of confining all officers to a few governments to the total exclusion of the rest." At that time almost all the troops before Boston were from New England. This desire for a strong, active, central government runs through all his wartime correspondence; he did not need the evidence of the weakness of the later Confederation to form his mind; that merely strengthened his position.

INEFFICIENCY OF CONGRESS

The realization that Congress was not the instrument for such a government must have come to him early. September 21, 1775, it gave him "great pain to be obliged to solicit the attention of the honorable Congress to the state of this army, in terms which imply the slightest apprehension of being neglected. But my situation is inexpressibly distressing." Nonetheless he welcomed the first committee from Congress, consisting of Franklin, Lynch of South Carolina, and his friend Harrison from Virginia, who were at camp in October, sent there as President Hancock wrote Washington, that "Congress, before they come to a final Determination," might have the "Advantage of your experience and Knowledge." Congress might show much lack of strength, but it was the chosen instrument, and since he could not alter it, Washington at all times was ready to consult with it and its committees and to do the best he could with its decisions— or lack of them. However severe the trials, the rule that he made for his subordinates applied equally to himself. "The retirement of a General Officer . . . appears to me to be big with fatal consequences both to the public cause and his own reputation, . . . in such a cause as this, when the object is neither glory nor extent of territory, but a defence of all that is dear and valuable in private and public life, surely every post ought to be deemed honorable in which a man can serve his country."

There were too many divergencies, social and economic, among the colonial regions, as well as among the individual colonies, for Congress ever to become a harmonious body. Lynch wrote Washington in December: "One of our members of Congress [John Adams] set out today for New England. Whether his intents are wicked or not, I doubt much; he should be watched." Adams himself wrote: "It is almost impossible to move anything, but you instantly see private friendships and enmities, and provincial views and prejudices intermingle in the consultation." This was early in the contest, while enthusiasm was yet high and there had been no military reverses, and while the men in Congress were more distinctly the leaders than later. Washington was aware of the difficulty, and this intercolonial and interstate jealousy in and out of Congress was one of his problems, one that helped materially to broaden his own lookout and to prepare him for his later high civil authority. He wrote that his chief wish was "to make my conduct coincide with the wishes of mankind, as far as I can consistently; I mean, without departing from that great line of duty, which, though hid under a cloud for some time, from a peculiarity of circumstances, may nevertheless bear a scrutiny." This was a large order, especially when there was a lack of accord in the wishes of mankind of his world; and not being phlegmatic, he was severely tried at times.

POLICY OF ENLISTMENTS

One of the main problems of the army and one upon which he never succeeded in getting Congress to agree with him was that of the term of enlistments. The matter, so far as it affected military operations belongs to another article, but as it was a cardinal element in his relations with Congress, an early statement of his position in the matter, while the army was yet before Boston, and after the troubles accompanying the first reenlistment, is of value here. "The evils arising from short, or even any limited inlistment of the troops, are greater, and more extensively hurtful than any person (not an eye-witness to them) can form an idea of. It takes you two or three months to bring new men in any tolerable degree acquainted with their duty; it takes a longer time to bring a people of the temper and genius of these into such a subordinate way of thinking as is necessary for a soldier. Before this is accomplished, the time approaches for their dismissal, and you are beginning to make interest with them for their continuance for another limited period; in the doing of which you are obliged to relax in your discipline, in order as it were to curry favor with them, by which means the latter part of your time is employed in undoing what the first was accomplishing, and instead of having men always ready to take advantage of circumstances, you must govern your movements by the circumstances of your Inlistments. This is not all; by the time you have got men arm'd and equip'd, the difficulty of doing which is beyond description, and with every new sett you have the same trouble to encounter, without the means of doing it.—In short, the disadvantages are so great and apparent to me, that I am convinced, uncertain as the continuance of the war is, that Congress had better determine to give a bounty of 20, 30, or even 40 Dollars to every man who will Inlist for the whole time, be it long or short."

INDEPENDENCE AND UNION

The successful termination of the siege of Boston transferred the theater of war to New York. Meanwhile the question of independence was in agitation. As early as February 10, 1776, Washington showed his own change of view, writing Reed: "I have never entertained an idea of an accommodation, since I heard of the measures, which were adopted in consequence of the Bunker's Hill fight. . . . I would tell them . . . that we had done every thing which could be expected from the best of subjects, that the spirit of freedom beat too high in us to submit to slavery, and that, if nothing else could satisfy a tyrant and his diabolical ministry, we are determined to shake off all connexions with a state so unjust and unnatural. This I would tell them, not under covert, but in words as clear as the sun in its meridian brightness."

He advanced the "liberty and union" thought in a letter to Adams, April 15: "I have ever thought, and am still of opinion, that no terms of accommodation will be offered by the British ministry, but such as cannot be accepted by America. We have nothing, my dear Sir, to depend upon but the protection of a kind Providence, and unanimity among ourselves." Again, he wrote Reed, April 23: "Your letter . . . descriptive of the jealousies and uneasinesses which exist among the Members of Congress is really alarming—if the House is divided, the fabrick must fall, and a few Individuals perish in the Ruins." At the end of May he was "very glad to find that

the Virginia Convention have passed so noble a vote [for independence], and with so much unanimity;" but his comment to the President of Congress on the Declaration itself is rather trite: "I perceive that Congress have been employed in deliberating on measures of the most interesting nature. It is certain, that it is not with us to determine in many instances what consequences will flow from our counsels; but yet it behoves us to adopt such, as, under the smiles of a gracious and all-kind Providence, will be most likely to promote our happiness. I trust the late decisive part they have taken is calculated for that end, and will secure us that freedom and those privileges, which have been and are refused us, contrary to the voice of nature and the British constitution." There is, however, more spirit and hope in the general order of July 9, announcing the Declaration to the army: "The General hopes this important Event will serve as a fresh incentive to every officer and soldier, to act with Fidelity and Courage, as knowing that now the peace and safety of his Country, depends (under God) solely on the success of our Arms: And that he is now in the service of a State, possessed of sufficient power to reward his merit, and advance him to the highest Honors of a free Country." Here, as in many other cases, Washington's public utterances were more optimistic than his private reasoning; he did not lack the political sense.

NEW YORK AND NEW JERSEY CAMPAIGNS (1776)

The latter half of 1776, the period of the New York and New Jersey campaigns, was one that "tried men's souls." For Congress and the General it began when President Hancock wrote Washington, May 16, the request "that you will repair to Philada. as soon as you can conveniently, in order to consult with Congress, upon such Measures as may be necessary for the carrying on the ensuing Campaign;" which, being done, Hancock, June 3, bestowed "the Thanks of that Body to you, for the unremitted Attention you have paid to your important Trust; and in particular for the Assistance they have derived from your military Knowledge and Experience, in adopting the best Plans for the Defence of the United Colonies." It ended with Congress in flight from Philadelphia and Washington in possession of temporary dictatorial military power, "vested with full, ample and complete powers . . . for and during the term of six months . . . unless sooner determined by Congress."

With the retirement of the American army to Harlem Heights and the general demoralization that ensued, both Congress and the General went on record to shift responsibility. John Adams, noticing the general condition, procured from Congress on September 19 a resolution: "That the commander in chief of the forces of these

states in the several departments, be directed to give positive orders to the brigadier generals and colonels, and all other officers in their several armies, that the troops, under their command, may, every day, be called together, and trained in arms, in order that officers and men may be perfected in the manual exercise and manœuvers, and inured to the most exemplary discipline, and that all officers be assured, that the Congress will consider activity and success, in introducing discipline into the army, among the best recommendations for promotion." It was this same Adams who in debate the next winter is credited by a fellow delegate with saying: "I have been distressed to see some members of this house disposed to idolise an image which thier own hands have molten. I speak here of the superstitious veneration that is sometimes paid to General Washington. Altho' I honour him for his good qualities, yet in this house I feel myself his Superior." One of the delegates at this time wrote, "to the Grief of Congress the Genl has wrote several (they think) too gloomy Letters. some speak with great Resolution."

CONGRESS AND THE ARMY (1776)

Washington probably had received the above resolution before he wrote one of these "gloomy" letters on September 24: "We are now, as it were, upon the eve of another dissolution of our army. The remembrance of the difficulties, which happened upon that occasion last year, and the consequences, which might have followed the change if proper advantages had been taken by the enemy, added to a knowledge of the present temper and situation of the troops, reflect but a very gloomy prospect in the appearances of things now, and satisfy me beyond the possibility of a doubt, that, unless some speedy and effectual measures are adopted by Congress, our cause will be lost. It is in vain to expect, that any more than a trifling part of this army will again engage in the service on the encouragement offered by Congress."

He was far milder than some of his generals considered that the occasion justified. Greene wrote: "The policy of Congress has been the most absurd and ridiculous imaginable, pouring in militia—men who come and go every month. A military force established on such principles defeats itself." While Lee, who had no love for or exalted opinion of Washington, wrote: "Inter nos Congress seems to stumble at every step. I have been very free in delivering my opinion of them. General Washington is much to blame in not menacing them with resignation, unless they refrain from unhinging the army by their absurd interference."

The letter however had its effect. Congress *tried* to make reforms; it planned a new army, directed the states to furnish their quotas to serve during the war, but was powerless to make the states do so. New articles of war were also adopted.

WASHINGTON AND POSTERITY

Washington did not intend that posterity should be ignorant of his case. He wrote Lund Washington, September 30: "In short, such is my situation that if I were to wish the bitterest curse to an enemy on this side of the grave, I should put him in my stead with my feelings; and yet I do not know what plan of conduct to pursue. I see the impossibility of serving with reputation, or doing any essential service to the cause by continuing in command, and yet I am told that if I quit the command inevitable ruin will follow from the distraction that will ensue. In confidence I tell you that I never was in such an unhappy, divided state since I was born. To lose all comfort and happiness on the one hand, whilst I am fully persuaded that under such a system of management as has been adopted, I cannot have the least chance for reputation, nor those allowances made which the nature of the case requires; and to be told, on the other, that if I leave the service all will be lost, is, at the same time that I am bereft of every peaceful moment, distressing to a degree. But I will be done with the subject, with the precaution to you that it is not a fit one to be publicly known or discussed. If I fall, it may not be amiss that these circumstances be known, and declaration made in credit to the justice of my character."

The retreat across New Jersey began November 20, the army dwindling with every march, until, December 8, it finally stood on the western bank of the Delaware River a mere skeleton, and that made up of men whose term of enlistment was already expired or about to expire, and with the general's letters continuing his unremittent urgings upon Congress, and nearer despair than at any other time during the war. He voiced this to Lund Washington on December 17: "Our only dependence now is upon the speedy enlistment of a new army. If this fails, I think the game will be pretty well up." Yet, "under the full persuasion of the justice of our cause, I cannot entertain an Idea, that it will finally sink, tho' it may remain for some time under a cloud." But that cloud, and without a new army, he removed by the brilliant operations at Trenton and Princeton, making winter quarters at Morristown, New Jersey, with that state recovered and the British again confined to the immediate vicinity of New York City and Long Island.

IMPRACTICABLE CONGRESSIONAL ORDERS

Congress meanwhile, somewhat recovered from its scare, but not yet returned to Philadelphia from Baltimore because of the fear of a new British movement against the Quaker city, was energetic—in debate, and took the field—on paper, in spite of the dictatorial power which was, presumably, still active. It resolved that it would be "agreeable to Congress," if the troops under Heath were called over to the main army, that the general-in-chief "order all the continental troops that are at Providence, immediately to join him," that troops enlisted march immediately to join the army, and that the authorities of New Jersey and Pennsylvania order their militia to the same front; since it was the "earnest desire of Congress to make the army under the immediate command of General Washington, sufficiently strong, not only to curb and confine the enemy within their present quarters, and prevent them from drawing support of any kind from the country, but by the divine blessing, totally to subdue them before they can be reinforced." Burke of North Carolina in his notes on this debate wrote: "This [last] pompous Paragraph was very much Condemned by some gentlemen as an unworthy Gasconade, and it was warmly debated. North Caroli[na] observed that Threats were unbecoming a Private Gentleman, and much more unbecoming a Political Body. That this pompous boast if not realised would render the Congress exceedingly ridiculous, and there was great reason to fear it would not, that our vigor ought to appear by Efforts, not Words, that at best it was an useless superfluity and ought to be expunged. the Question was put and Jersey Pensylvania North Carolina and South Carolina voted for expunging, the rest for retaining. . . . there appeared upon the whole debate a great desire in the Delegates of the Eastern States, and in one of New Jersey to insult the General."

Washington's comment, March 14, on the resolutions is pathetic: "Could I accomplish the important objects so eagerly wished by Congress, . . . I should be happy indeed. But what prospect or hope can there be of my effecting so desirable a work at this time? The enclosed return, to which I solicit the most serious attention of Congress, comprehends the whole force I have in Jersey. It is but a handful, and bears no proportion, in the scale of numbers, to that of the enemy. Added to this, the major part is made up of militia. The most sanguine in speculation cannot deem it more than adequate to the least valuable purposes of war. The reinforcements mentioned to be drawn from General Heath were merely ideal; nearly the whole of the eastern troops, who were with him, being here before. They were only engaged till to-day; and to-day they leave the camp. . . . What prospect there may be of immediate succors from other quarters, I know not; . . . I confess, Sir, I feel the most painful anxiety when I reflect on our situation and that of the enemy. Unless the levies arrive soon, we must before long experience some interesting and melancholy events. . . . On recurring to the last promotions of brigadiers, I find the number appointed to be short of what I took the liberty to recommend, and not competent to the exigencies of the service. supposing the whole in office before, and those lately created, consent to act, which I have reason to believe will not be the case."

PROBLEM OF GENERAL OFFICERS

Congress retaining the power to appoint general officers, even under the resolves giving the virtual—if temporary—dictatorship, its action in this matter was a fertile cause of discontent on the part of officers who did not receive the rewards their merits—on their own estimation of the same—deserved; and it was, of course, to Washington that the complaints and threats of resignation were made. Sullivan was piqued because he did not have a "separate" command. Arnold was passed over in the appointment of major-generals—the beginning of the discontent that ended in treason—and on April 3, 1777, Washington acknowledged his surprise but advised against "any hasty step," adding: "General Greene . . . was informed, that the members from each State seemed to insist upon having a proportion of general officers, adequate to the number of men which they furnish, and that, as Connecticut had already two major-generals, it was their full share. I confess this is a strange mode of reasoning; but it may serve to show you, that a promotion, which was due to your seniority, was not overlooked for want of Merit in you."

The attitude of Congress was consistent with that expressed by John Adams: "I will vote upon the general principles of a republic for a new election of General Officers annually." He had "no fear from the resignation of Officers if junior Officers are preferred to them. If they have virtue they will continue with us. If not, their resignation will not hurt us."

PHILADELPHIA CAMPAIGN (1777)

Howe's campaign of 1777 having finally disclosed its objective as Philadelphia, Congress again went into retirement. On August 22 it voted that it wished "the General . . . to proceed in such manner, as shall appear to him most conducive to the general interest," and on the next day, that the President should "inform General Washington, that Congress never intended by any commission hitherto granted by them, or by the establishment of any department whatever, to supersede or circumscribe the power of General Washington as the commander in chief of all the continental land force within the United States." On September 17, after the battle of Brandywine and when the fall of Philadelphia impended, it again bestowed high powers on the general for sixty days, and later continued them to March 1. Congress adjourned to Lancaster, met there one day, September 27, and then crossed the Susquehanna to York. Having neglected once more to make adequate preparations, partly, indeed, because it was without the power to move the states into action even when convinced of the need, it left the commander and the fragmentary army to bear the consequences, which in this particular case included the winter cantonment at Valley Forge, with the breakdown of both the commissary and quartermaster departments. Congress, December 10, reproved Washington for not making requisitions, being able to "impute his forbearance . . . to a delicacy in exerting military authority on the citizens of the states; a delicacy, which though highly laudable in general, may, on critical exigencies, prove destructive to the army and prejudicial to the general liberties of America." This was what Lovell, Massachusetts delegate, called rapping "a Demi G - - over the Knuckles." Washington confessed that he felt "greatly embarrassed with respect to a vigorous exercise of military power," because the people at large "have ever looked with a jealous and suspicious eye" on the acts of military authority.

CONGRESSIONAL INTRIGUE
(1777-1778)

Between Washington and Congress, however, the most important matter as respects its possible effect on American history was the intrigues, and especially the Conway Cabal. Congressional opposition to Washington had been growing during 1777. Henry Laurens writing to his son John, who was on Washington's staff, reported on these growlings as early as October, and his later letters throw new light on the matter. The Cabal itself, which according to Burnett, is still partly a mystery, was only one phase of the opposition, of what Burnett terms the "whines and whiffling criticisms, the nagging tactics, the snaps and snarls of small-fry politicians in Congress." Washington, perhaps not unconscious that he was a chosen instrument, kept silent until he was able to demolish the conspiracy with a single phrase.

That ended the only attempt to displace him as the head of the army, since the Cabal could not stand exposure. Yet the backbiting, in which Lovell was prominent, went on. Lovell complained of the "privy Councellors of one great Man whom no citizen *shall* dare even to talk about, say Gentlemen of the Blade." In the end the caviling died down. This was inevitable, for it lacked public support. Burnett says: "In viewing this episode of our history in which a severe indictment stands against many members of Congress, sometimes indeed against a majority of them, it should not be forgotten that there remained nevertheless in Congress many hearts that were right and heads with wisdom to perceive that with Washington they might win, without him they must lose. . . . And this conviction not only took deeper and deeper hold upon the minds of Congress, it speedily gripped the mind and heart of the nation. It does to this day."

WASHINGTON ON THE INTRIGUE

Washington, besides his effective stifling of the Cabal, made other references that showed his scorn of the whole affair and of the wider opposition. He wrote Laurens privately, January 31: "I was not unapprized, that a malignant faction had been for some time forming to my prejudice; which, conscious as I am of having ever done all in my power to answer the important purposes of the trust reposed in me, could not but give me some pain on a personal account. But my chief concern arises from an apprehension of the dangerous consequences, which intestine dissensions may produce to the common cause. As I have no other view than to promote the public good, and am unambitious of honors not founded in the approbation of my country, I would not desire in the least degree to suppress a free spirit of inquiry into any part of my conduct, that even faction itself may deem reprehensible. . . . My enemies take an ungenerous advantage of me. They know the delicacy of my situation, and that motives of policy deprive me of the defence I might otherwise make against their insidious attacks. They know I cannot combat their insinuations, however injurious, without disclosing secrets, which it is of the utmost moment to conceal."

CARTEL INCIDENT (1778)

One of the affronts put upon him by the prevailing spirit of Congress was in connection with a general cartel. This had been a serious and long standing problem, which seemed about to be solved. Washington's letters to the President of Congress tell the story. March 7, 1778, he wrote: "I was about to send commissioners to meet those appointed by General Howe . . . but, yesterday morning, . . . I found that a resolution had been made on the 26th of February, calling for all accounts against prisoners in our hands, and declaring that no exchange should take place, till the balance due thereon to the United States is discharged. . . . This resolution I cannot consider as an intended infraction of my engagements with General Howe; yet its operation is diametrically opposite both to the spirit and letter of the propositions made on my part, and acceded to on his. I supposed myself fully authorized 'by the instructions and intentions' of Congress to act as I did; and I now conceive, that the public as well as my own personal honor and faith are pledged for the performance. . . . it is much to be feared, if the exchange should be deferred till the terms of the last resolve were fulfilled, that it would be difficult to prevent our being generally accused of a breach of good faith." He wrote again, April 4: "It gives me pain to observe they appear to contain several implications by which my sensibility is not a little wounded."

This letter caused a furore in Congress. Burke of North Carolina in his account of it declared that an important phase was the exchange of Lee, which might not be effected by the military agreement but upon which Congress was determined. It is a valid presumption that the malcontents expected to find in him a new leader against Washington. Burke wrote that Washington "recommends that the Laws be suffered to sleep . . . and that a rule of practice be adopted directly contrary to them; but this proposal met with very great and almost general opposition and indignation in Congress." The proposed letter to the General and the debate on it were so virulent that Laurens wrote his son, April 9: "I am greatly distressed by circumstances now in agitation respecting your friend. I think I once said 'I hope he will never afford him or them his own consent to hurt him,'" meaning, thereby, forcing him to resign. The letter as reported bore these statements: "by strictly attending to their Resolutions you will find they are founded in Humanity as well as Policy, and invariably regard the Dignity, Safety and Independence of these States. . . . It is the unalterable Determination of Congress, that unless this Point [the preliminary exchange of Lee] is acceded to, all further Negotiations . . . should cease, it being in their Opinion more eligible that no Cartel should take Place, than that the honor of these States should be sullied, and their Wisdom impeached, . . . I am further directed, Sir, by Congress to inform you, that in their opinion, the late Conduct and Correspondence of General Howe, render a strict Attention to the Support of the Dignity of these Free and Independent States, at this time peculiarly necessary; and that they esteem that Dignity Injured by permitting the Enemy's Officers . . . to go on Parole, before ours are sent out: a Practice admitting an Imputation of a want of good Faith on our Part, and a Perfect Confidence in an enemy whom we cannot trust: . . . they therefore doubt not from your Zeal for the Honor of these States, that you will pay a strict Attention to this Matter, as nothing can tend to sink us both in our Estimation and in that of all the World, than a patient Submission to that Insolent Superiority, which our Enemies affect in carrying on this War."

This, however, was too much for Burke who, by absenting himself, prevented a quorum, and the obnoxious matter was later cut out of the letter. The letter as sent, contained the following expression: "Congress with great Concern perceive that your Sensibility is wounded by their Resolutions. Placing the finest Confidence in your Prudence, Abilities and Integrity, they wish to preserve that Harmony with you, which is essential to the general Weal: you may be assured that far from any Intention to give you Pain, their Resolutions have no other Motive or End, but the public Good; they, therefore hope that you will not in future be distrest by Apprehensions, as injurious to their Honor, as they are to your own Feelings."

WASHINGTON AND THE FRENCH ALLIANCE (1778)

North's proposals for reconciliation were under consideration during 1778. Washington urged that Congress be not misled by them, since "nothing short of independence, it appears to me, can possibly do," taking the initiative in a manner that is suggestive not only of the real leadership but also of a realization of it on his part; but Congress was in complete harmony with the general's view and the affair had no influence upon their mutual relations. The same is true as to the French alliance, though he gave warning early of the danger of a letdown from too great expectations and dependence on it. It is questionable, however, whether he realized how great that danger was, though he was aware of the possible political effect. In the matter of the Canadian expedition which Congress had voted, he wrote November 11, 1778: "I am sorry to say that the plan proposed . . . does not appear to me to be eligible under our present circumstances," giving military reasons for it. But three days later he wrote Laurens privately: "The question of the Canadian expedition, in the form it now stands, appears to me one of the most interesting that has hitherto agitated our national deliberations. I have one objection to it, untouched in my public letter, which is, in my estimation, insurmountable, and alarms all my feelings for the true and permanent interests of my country. This is the introduction of a large body of French troops into Canada, and putting them in possession of the capital of that Province, attached to them by all the ties of blood, habits, manners, religion, and former connexion of Government. I fear this would be too great a temptation to be resisted by any power actuated by the common maxims of national policy." Under such circumstances he welcomed the direction of Congress to repair to Philadelphia in order to confer on the next campaign and military problems in general. The Canadian expedition was dropped; but by 1781 Washington himself was ready, in his instructions to John Laurens who was being sent to France, to implore for a liberal financial aid and more troops, as "indespensable" to the safety of the United States.

ATTEMPTED ARMY REFORMS (1780)

The clash over the necessity of an adequate army continued. In the summer of 1780 he went over the whole ground with the Congressional Committee of Co-operation, evidently with conviction. He also once more admonished Congress, "we are again relapsing into the same Chaos." But the committee on its return to Philadelphia met with such a reception as gave Washington "much pain," as he wrote Delegate Mathews, who had been a member of the committee, October 4: "At a time when public harmony was so essential, when we should aid and assist each other with all our abilities, when our hearts should be open to information and our hands ready to administer relief, to find distrusts and jealousies

taking possession of the mind, and a party spirit prevailing, is a most melancholy reflection, and forbodes no good."

And to Delegate Duane, the same day: "I should have been happy in the information you give me, that some progress had been made in the business of raising a permanent army, had it not been intimated to me, through other channels, that in the resolutions framed on this article, the fatal alternative of *for one year* has been admitted. . . . The present juncture is, in my opinion, peculiarly favorable to a permanent army, and I regret that an opening is given for a temporary one. It also gives me pain to find, that the pernicious State system is still adhered to, by leaving the reduction and incorporation, &c., of the regiments to the particular States. This is one of the greatest evils of our affairs. . . . The history of the war is a history of false hopes and temporary expedients. Would to God they were to end here!"

But Congress as well as the General had begun to realize their relative positions, so the military plan as adopted was referred to Washington. He replied, courteously as always, October 11: "I am much obliged to Congress for the honor they do me by the fresh mark of their attention and confidence, conferred upon me in the reference they have been pleased to make. My wish to concur in sentiment with them, and a conviction that there is no time to be lost in carrying the measures relative to the army into execution, make me reluctantly offer any objections to the plan, that has been adopted; but a sense of what I owe to Congress, and a regard to consistency, will not permit me to suppress the difference of opinion, which happens to exist upon the present occasion, on points that appear to me far from unessential. In expressing it, I can only repeat the ideas, which I have more than once taken the liberty to urge."

WASHINGTON AND POLITICAL REFORM (1778)

Thereupon, as Steuben reported October 23, "the plan of arrangement for the army, which your Excellency sent to Congress, has been agreed to without any alteration." Not that it was carried out; the political situation did not permit, and by the end of 1778, Washington had begun to express freely the realization that he must have had much earlier, of the necessity of political amendment. He wrote Harrison, December 18: "What may be the effect of such large and frequent emissions, of the dissentions,—parties,—extravagance, and a general lax of public virtue, Heaven alone can tell! I am afraid even to think of It. But it appears as clear to me as ever the Sun did in its meridian brightness, that America never stood in more eminent need of the wise, patriotic, and spirited exertions of her Sons than at this period; and if it is not a sufficient cause for genl. lamentation, my misconception of the matter impresses it too

strongly upon me, that the States, separately, are too much engaged in their local concerns, and have too many of their ablest men withdrawn from the general council, for the good of the common weal. In a word, I think our political system may be compared to the mechanism of a clock, and that our conduct should derive a lesson from it; for it answers no good purpose to keep the smaller wheels in order, if the greater one, which is the support and prime mover of the whole, is neglected. . . .

"I have seen nothing since I came here [Philadelphia] . . . to change my opinion of Men or Measrs., but abundant reason to be convinced that our affairs are in a more distressed, ruinous, and deplorable condition than they have been in since the commencement of the War. . . . If I was to be called upon to draw a picture of the times and of Men, from what I have seen, and heard, and in part know, I should in one word say that idleness, dissipation & extravagance seems to have laid fast hold of most of them.—That speculation—peculation—and an insatiable thirst for riches seems to have got the better of every other consideration and almost of every order of Men.—That party disputes and personal quarels are the great business of the day whilst the momentous concerns of an empire—a great and accumulated debt—ruined finances—depreciated money—and want of credit (which in their consequences is the want of everything) are but secondary considerations and postponed from day to day—from week to week as if our affairs wear the most promising aspect—after drawing this picture, which from my Soul I believe to be a true one, I need not repeat to you that I am alarmed and wish to see my Countrymen aroused."

WASHINGTON AND POLITICAL AFFAIRS (1779)

He wrote Jay, President of Congress, March 1, 1779: "I have been a little surprised, that the several important pieces of intelligence lately received from Europe . . . have not been given to the public in a manner calculated to attract the attention and impress the minds of the people. . . . I have taken the liberty to trouble you with this hint, as sometimes things the most obvious escape attention." Again, April 23: "In one of your former letters you intimate, that a free communication of sentiments will not be displeasing to you. If, under this sanction, I should step beyond the line you would wish to draw, and suggest ideas, and ask questions, which are improper to be answered, you have only to pass them by in silence. I wish you to be convinced, that I do not desire to pry into measures, the knowledge of which is not necessary for my government as an executive officer [he does not say military!], or the premature discovery of which might be prejudicial to the plans in contemplation." Then he proceeds to make suggestions about the navy, Bermudian trade, and state of the currency. These were scarcely military matters. On September 7 he gave Jay his opinions on the European situation. Another indication was the greater frequency with which he wrote directly to the state authorities, ignoring Congress, the self-chosen medium for such communications. He had even appealed directly to the inhabitants of the middle states on February 18, 1778, though he might have justified that by his then existing enlarged direct powers. He corresponded directly with the French ministers; he issued circular letters to the states; he wrote to the commissioners at Paris. He may not have been conscious of the change, but it was there; the instinct of leadership was arousing and preparing to move into larger quarters.

WASHINGTON ON STATE RESPONSIBILITY (1780)

By 1780 the experience with a Congress that had no power to uphold its decrees, which could order by what Washington called "a timid kind of recommendations" but never enforce obedience upon the states, which had indeed no legal position other than that of wartime acceptance, showed clearly in Washington's writings. In a letter to Duane, May 13, 1780, he welcomed the "endeavors to accomplish the Confederation;" and wrote Joseph Jones, another delegate, that same month: "Certain I am, unless Congress speak in a more decisive tone, unless they are vested with powers by the several States competent to the great purposes of war, or assume them as matter of right, and they and the States respectively act with more energy than they hitherto have done, that our cause is lost. We can no longer drudge on in the old way. By ill timing the adoption of measures, by delays in the execution of them, or by unwarrantable jealousies, we incur enormous expenses and derive no benefit from them. One State will comply with a requisition of Congress; another neglects to do it; a third executes it by halves; and all differ either in the manner, the matter, or so much in point of time, that we are always working up hill, and ever shall be; and, while such a system as the present one or rather want of one prevails, we shall ever be unable to apply our strength or resources to any advantage. This, my dear Sir, is plain language to a member of Congress; but it is the language of truth and friendship. It is the result of long thinking, close application, and strict observation. I see one head gradually changing into thirteen. I see one army branching into thirteen, which, instead of looking up to Congress as the supreme controlling power of the United States, are considering themselves as dependent on their respective States. In a word, I see the powers of Congress declining too fast for the consideration and respect, which are due to them as the great representative body of America, and I am fearful of the consequences."

And in his circular to the states on the new army plan, October 18, he was very explicit in his condemnation of their recalcitrant attitude. "Every motive which can arise from a consideration of our circumstances, either in a domestic or foreign point of view, calls upon us to abandon temporary expedients and substitute something durable, systematic, and substantial. This applies as well to our civil administration as to our military establishment. It is as necessary to give Congress, the common head, sufficient powers to direct the common forces, as it is to raise an army for the war; but I should go out of my province to expatiate on civil affairs."

WASHINGTON'S CONSTRUCTIVE CRITICISM (1781)

His constructive criticism of Congress became even more direct, as in a letter to Sullivan, then a delegate, November 20: "This leads me to a remark, which I could wish never to make, and which is, that the multiplicity of business, in which Congress are engaged, will not let them extend that seasonable and provident care to many matters, which private convenience and public œconomy indispensably call for, and proves, in my opinion, the evident necessity of committing more of the executive business to small boards or responsible characters, than is practised at present; for I am very well convinced, that, for want of system in the execution of business, and a proper timing of things, that our public expenditures are inconceivably greater than they ought to be."

This was probably merely an expression of a general opinion; nevertheless it is interesting to note that on February 7, 1781, which was before the consent of Maryland made the Articles of Confederation active, a plan for executive departments—finance, war, and marine—was agreed to, a department of foreign affairs having been previously established. Washington welcomed these departments: "Proper Powers to and a judicious choice of men to fill these departments, will soon lead us to system, order, & œconomy—without which our affairs, already on the brink of ruin, would soon have passed redemption." And he remonstrated against the delay in making the appointments.

INADEQUACY OF THE CONFEDERATION

It is significant, however, that his comment on the Articles of Confederation going into operation was merely that it would "undoubtedly enable Congress to speak with more decision in their requisitions on the respective States." Evidently he did not consider the Articles as effecting the political reforms he desired; he wrote Custis just before they became active on March 1, 1781, of the necessity of vesting Congress with competent powers. "A nominal head which at present is but another name for Congress, will no longer do. That

honorable body, after hearing the interests and views of the several States fairly discussed and explained by their respective representatives, must dictate, and not merely recommend and leave it to the States afterwards to do as they please, which, as I have observed before, is in many cases to do nothing at all."

To Harrison, March 4, 1783, he was even more vehement: "What, my dear Sir, could induce the State of Virginia to rescind their assent to the Impost Law? . . . The Alarm Bell which has been rung with such tremendous sound of the danger of entrusting Congress with the money is too selfish & futile to require a serious answer—Who are Congress, but the People?—do they not return to them at certain short periods?—Are they not amenable at all times to them for their Conduct—& subject to recall?—What interests therefore can a man have under these circumstances distinct from his Constituents?—Can it be supposed, that with *design*, he would form a junto—or dangerous Aristocracy that would operate against himself in less than a Month perhaps after it should be established?—I can have no conception of it. But from the observations I have made in the course of this war—and my intercourse with the States both in their united and seperate capacities have afforded ample opportunities of judging—I am decidedly of opinion that if the Powers of Congress are not enlarged, and made competent to all *general purposes* that the blood that has been spilt—the Expences which have been incurred—and the distresses which we have undergone will avail us nothing—and that the band which at present holds us together, by a very feeble thread, will soon be broken when anarchy & confusion must ensue."

NEWBURGH ADDRESSES (1783)

After Yorktown victory was in the air, though he wrote in June, 1782, that the "end of our warfare is not to be obtained but by vigorous exertions"; and the concern turned from how to get and use an army to what to do with the army already on hand. With approaching peace and the inevitable result to discipline of inaction, the troops began to think more than ever of their past hardships, present prospects, and future rewards, and threatened not to disband until they had received justice.

The discontent of the officers culminated in the Newburgh Addresses; the principal one was later claimed by Armstrong, Gates's aide, but possibly Hamilton and Gouverneur Morris engineered the movement. Hamilton had urged Washington to take the lead in the army's plan for redress, but under cover, and even suggested Knox as a proper dummy. Washington's reply to the Addresses, March 15, 1783, prevented the crisis. Madison wrote: "The steps taken by the General to evert the gathering storm, and his professions of inflexible adherence to his duty to Congress and to his country, excited the most affectionate sentiments towards him." In that reply, the general gave the expression of his final public opinion of the wartime Congress: "I cannot, in justice to my own belief, and what I have great reason to conceive is the intention of Congress, conclude this address without giving it as my decided opinion, that that honorable body entertain exalted sentiments of the services of the army, and, from a full conviction of its merits and sufferings, will do it complete justice. That their endeavors to discover, and establish funds for this purpose have been unwearied, and will not cease, till they have succeeded, I have no doubt; but, like all other large bodies, where there is a variety of different interests to reconcile, their deliberations are slow. Why then should we distrust them; and, in consequence of that distrust, adopt measures, which may cast a shade over that glory, which has been so justly acquired, and tarnish the reputation of an army, which is celebrated through all Europe for its fortitude and patriotism? And for what is this done? To bring the object we seek nearer? No! Most certainly, in my opinion, it will cast it at a greater distance. For myself . . . I . . . declare in this public and solemn manner, that, in the attainment of complete justice for all your toils and dangers, and in the gratification of every wish, so far as may be done consistently with the great duty I owe to my country, and those powers we are bound to respect, you may freely command my services to the utmost extent of my abilities."

But his private letters to Jones and Harrison show his realization that even if Congress were willing nothing would result from his efforts unless the states did their duty by providing the funds. It was much of a grandstand play after all, which only his great prestige made successful, for a letter written soon after to Hamilton showed clearly that he had no expectation of progress until there had been a radical change in the basis of the union.

OFFER OF KINGSHIP (1782)

So it happened that when he surrendered his commission to Congress at Annapolis at the end of the year, the army had already dispersed. An earlier episode is worthy of notice and it is interesting to speculate whether it would not have been much more important if he had not used his great influence to soothe the officers. This was the suggestion of kingship. Col. Lewis Nicola, who was the medium of the suggestion, had been in 1782 selected by the officers to confer with Washington about their grievances; he addressed to the general, possibly at the instigation of others, possibly not, a paper in which he spoke of the weakness of republics and ended, "I believe strong arguments might be produced for admitting the title of King, which I conceive would be attended with some material advantages." Washington's reaction was immediate and

explicit. His reply to the colonel was written on May 22, and he deemed it so important that he had Humphreys and Trumbull, aide and secretary, certify to the exactness of the copy he kept. "With a mixture of great surprise and astonishment, I have read with attention the sentiments you have submitted to my perusal. Be assured, Sir, no occurence in the course of the war has given me more painful sensations, than your information of there being such ideas existing in the army, as you have expressed, and I must view with abhorrence and reprehend with severity. For the present the communicatn. of them will rest in my own bosom, unless some further agitation of the matter shall make a disclosure necessary. I am much at a loss to conceive what part of my conduct could have given encouragement to an address, which to me seems big with the greatest mischiefs, that can befall my Country. If I am not deceived in the knowledge of myself, you could not have found a person to whom your schemes are more disagreeable. . . . Let me conjure you, then, if you have any regard for your Country, concern for yourself or posterity, or respect for me, to banish these thoughts from your mind, and never communicate, as from yourself or any one else, a sentiment of the like nature."

SURRENDER OF COMMISSION (1783)

The surrender of the commission to Congress was the occasion of mutual felicitations as well as much natural emotion. Washington might well have passed in review in his mind his repeated admonitions and prophecies of irretrievable ruin unless certain reforms were made, which never were made. How did it happen that in spite of all his forebodings the army kept the field, the obvious weakness of Congress was not fatal, the recalcitrancy of the states did not utterly destroy, and a successful war brought independence? Washington does not attempt an explanation unless a characteristic statement in his farewell to the army may be so considered: "The singular interpositions of Providence in our feeble condition were such, as could scarcely escape the attention of the most unobserving; while the unparalleled perseverance of the armies of the United States, through almost every possible suffering and discouragement for the space of eight long years, was little short of a standing miracle." The proper summing up of the reasons has yet to be made, and in the recent death of Professor Van Tyne history has been deprived of the scholar probably best equipped to make it. Many factors entered into it: foreign aid and European conditions were a fundamental element; a greater determination on the part of the people than Washington suspected was probably there and it rose to meet crises; British mistakes; development of American generalship; the Allies' temporary control of the sea; even the militia did its appreciable part in such emergencies as the

Burgoyne and Yorktown campaigns, and in the harrowing of the British army in the South; above all, Washington probably did not realize the power of his own great example and influence.

One change which he made in his farewell address to Congress is of interest. Originally he wrote, "Happy in the confirmation of our Independence and Sovereignty, as well as in the contemplation of our prospects of national happiness," but as delivered the second phrase had become, "and pleased with the opportunity afforded the United States of becoming a respectable nation." He had written Hamilton on March 31 that he had a great inclination "to contribute my mite to pointing out all the defects of the present constitution"; and to Greene, Theodorick Bland, William Gordon, and others he continued to show the need of the reforms; as he expressed it, "all my private letters have teemed with these sentiments," and they continued to do so after his retirement.

CIRCULAR LETTER TO THE STATES
(1783)

In his last circular letter to the states, June 8, 1783, he summed up his public utterances: "There are four things, which, I humbly conceive, are essential to the wellbeing, I may even venture to say, to the existence of the United States, as an independent power.

"First. An indissoluble union of the States under one federal head.

"Secondly. A sacred regard to public justice.

"Thirdly. The adoption of a proper peace establishment; and

"Fourthly. The prevalence of that pacific and friendly disposition among the people of the United States, which will induce them to forget their local prejudices and policies; to make those mutual concessions, which are requisite to the general prosperity; and, in some instances, to sacrifice their individual advantages to the interest of the community. . . .

"Under the first head, . . . That, unless the States will suffer Congress to exercise those prerogatives they are undoubtedly invested with by the constitution, every thing must very rapidly tend to anarchy and confusion. That it is indispensable to the happiness of the individual States, that there should be lodged somewhere a supreme power to regulate and govern the general concerns of the confederated republic, without which the Union cannot be of long duration. That there must be a faithful and pointed compliance, on the part of every State, with the late proposals and demands of Congress, or the most fatal consequences will ensue. . . . It is only in our united character, as an empire, that our independence is acknowledged, that our power can be regarded, or our credit supported, among foreign nations. The treaties of the European powers with the United States of America will have no validity on a dissolution of the Union.

. . .

"If, after all, a spirit of disunion, or a temper of obstinacy and perverseness should manifest itself in any of the States; if such an ungracious disposition should attempt to frustrate all the happy effects that might be expected to flow from the Union; if there should be a refusal to comply with the requisition for funds to discharge the annual interest of the public debts; and if that refusal should revive again all those jealousies, and produce all those evils, which are now happily removed, Congress, who have, in all their transactions, shown a great degree of magnanimity and justice, will stand justified in the sight of God and man; and the State alone, which puts itself in opposition to the aggregate wisdom of the continent, and follows such mistaken and pernicious counsels, will be responsible for all the consequences."

REFORM THROUGH EXPERIENCE ONLY

In a letter to Lafayette, April 5, 1783, he makes the interesting statement that the reforms would probably be brought about only through the experience of their need: "We stand, now, an Independent People, and have yet to learn political Tactics. We are placed among the nations of the Earth, and have a character to establish; but how we shall acquit ourselves, time must discover. The probability (at least I fear it), is that local or State politics will interfere too much with the more liberal and extensive plan of government, which wisdom and foresight, freed from the mist of prejudice, would dictate; and that we shall be guilty of many blunders in treading this boundless theatre, before we shall have arrived at any perfection in this art; in a word, that the experience, which is purchased at the price of difficulties and distress, will alone

convince us that the honor, power, and true Interest of this Country must be measured by a Continental scale, and that every departure therefrom weakens the Union, and may ultimately break the band which holds us together." Certainly the first years of peace furnished sufficient experience.

POPULAR RESPONSIBILITY (1786)

He not only continued to see the danger, but now he began to fear that the necessary reforms would not take place. He wrote Jay, who was then Foreign Secretary, May 18, 1786: "I shall find myself happily mistaken if the remedies are at hand. We are certainly in a delicate situation; but my fear is, that the people are not yet sufficiently *misled* to retract from error. To be plainer, I think there is more wickedness than ignorance mixed in our councils. Under this impression I scarcely know what opinion to entertain of a general convention. That it is necessary to revise and amend the articles of confederation, I entertain no doubt; but what may be the consequences of such an attempt is doubtful. Yet something must be done, or the fabric must fall, for it certainly is tottering . . . From the high ground we stood upon, from the plain path which invited our footsteps, to be so fallen! so lost! it is really mortifying. But virtue, I fear, has in a great degree taken its departure from our land, and the want of a disposition to do justice is the source of the national embarrassments; . . ."

It is noticeable here that his reference has turned from the states to the people; and this idea is also in a letter to Lafayette, May 10, 1786, which, in addition shows that he did not entirely despair: "It is one of the evils of democratical government, that the people, not always seeing and frequently misled, must often feel before they can act right; but then evils of this nature seldom fail to work their own cure."

SHAYS REBELLION (1786)

He was to have his patience yet further tried, however, as in the final failure of the impost amendment and in the popular tumults, of which the most serious was the Shays Rebellion in Massachusetts. His comments on this are almost the last of those caused by, or at least under, the weak Confederation. He expressed his mind to Henry Lee, October 31, 1786: "You talk, my good Sir, of employing influence to appease the present tumults in Massachusetts. I know not where that influence is to be found, or, if attainable, that it would be a proper remedy for the disorders. *Influence* is no *government*. Let us have one by which our lives, liberties, and property will be secured, or let us know the worst at once. Under these impressions, my humble opinion is, that there is a call for decision. Know precisely what the insurgents aim at. If they have *real* grievances, redress them if possible; or acknowledge the justice of them, and your inability to do it in the present moment. If they have not, employ the force of government against them at once. If this is inadequate, *all* will be convinced, that the superstructure is bad, or wants support."

Also to Knox, December 26: "I feel, my dear General Knox, infinitely more than I can express to you, for the disorders, which have arisen in these States. Good God! Who, besides a Tory, could have foreseen, or a Briton predicted them? Were these people wiser than others, or did they judge of us from the corruption and depravity of their own hearts?" But even in this letter there is mention of the new interest, of the proposed Federal Convention, which was to turn the speculations upon evils, the need of remedies, and the bewailing of the failure of inadequate, half-spirited, piecemeal efforts at reform, to the consideration of an active, general attempt to sweep away the old hampered government in favor of an entirely new plan. His interest and promotion of this is the subject of another article.

Selected Authorities

AMES, WILLIAM HOMER—*Select List of Books dealing with the American Colonial and Revolutionary Periods.* Philadelphia, 1926.

BECKER, CARL—*Eve of the Revolution* (*Chronicles of America*, Vol. XI). New Haven, Yale University Press, 1918.

BURNETT, EDMUND C., ED.—*Letters of Members of the Continental Congress.* 5 vols. pub., into 1781. Washington, Carnegie Institution, 1921—.

CHANNING, EDWARD—*History of the United States.* Vol. III. New York, Macmillan, 1912.

CHANNING, HART AND TURNER—*Guide to the Study and Reading of American History.* Rev. ed. Boston, Ginn, 1912. (Especially §§ 149-153, 157-159, 166-172.)

CONTINENTAL CONGRESS—*Journals.* Ed. by Division of Manuscripts, Library of Congress. 29 vols. pub., through 1785. Washington, Government Printing Office, 1904—.

FISHER, SYDNEY GEORGE—*Struggle for American Independence.* 2 vols. Philadelphia, Lippincott, 1908.

HART, ALBERT BUSHNELL, ED.—*American History told by Contemporaries.* 5 vols. New York, Macmillan, 1897-1929. (Especially Vol. II, pts. vi-viii, Vol. III, pt. iii.)

JAMESON, J. FRANKLIN—*American Revolution considered as a Social Movement.* Princeton, Princeton University Press, 1926.

LODGE, HENRY CABOT—*George Washington* (*American Statesman*, Library ed.). 2 vols. Boston, Houghton Mifflin, 1898. (Especially Vol. I, chs. vi-x.)

McMASTER, JOHN BACH—*History of the People of the United States.* Vol. I. New York, Appleton, 1883.

NEVINS, ALLAN—*American States during and after the Revolution.* New York, Macmillan, 1924.

OGG, FREDERICK A.—*Builders of the Republic* (*Pageant of America*, Vol. VIII).

New Haven, Yale University Press, 1927. (Especially chs. ii-vi.)

OSBORN, LUCRETIA PERRY, ED.—*Washington speaks for Himself.* New York, Scribner, 1927. (Especially chs. iii-vi.)

SANDERS, JENNINGS B.—*Presidency of the Continental Congress.* Decatur, Ga., 1930.

SAWYER, JOSEPH DILLAWAY—*Washington.* 2 vols. New York, Macmillan, 1927. (Especially chs. xv-xxxii.)

SCHLESINGER, ARTHUR MEIER—*Colonial Merchants and the American Revolution, 1763-1776.* New York, Columbia, University, 1918.

THAYER, WILLIAM ROSCOE—*George Washington.* Boston, Houghton Mifflin, 1922. (Especially chs. iii-vii.)

TREVELYAN, SIR GEORGE OTTO—*American Revolution.* New ed. 4 vols. New York, Longmans Green, 1905-12. (Continued by next title.)

TREVELYAN, SIR GEORGE OTTO—*George the Third and Charles Fox, the Concluding Part of the American Revolution.* 2 vols. New York, Longmans Green, 1912-14.

VAN TYNE, CLAUDE H.—*Founding of the American Republic.* Vols. I-II. Boston, Houghton Mifflin, 1922-29.

WASHINGTON, GEORGE—*Writings.* Ed. by Worthington Chauncey Ford. 14 vols. New York, Putnam, 1889-93.

WILSON, WOODROW—*George Washington.* New York, Harper, 1896. (Especially chs. v, vi, viii, ix.)

WASHINGTON RESIGNING HIS COMMISSION
From a painting by John Trumbull

Washington and the Constitution
By David M. Matteson
Part I
Preliminaries of the Convention

GEORGE WASHINGTON
From the Gilbert Stuart "Athenaeum" Portrait

INFLUENCE OF POTOMAC NAVIGATION (1772-1785)

ASHINGTON'S first link in the chain of the Federal Convention was his interest in the improvement of the Potomac River navigation. Development of a route into the West had long been under consideration. It was a concern of the original Ohio Company, in which the Washington family was active; and George's early surveying and western journeys and campaigns, with the attendant acquirement of land, gave him both information and reason to advance the project. This improvement as a commercial and engineering matter is treated elsewhere in this series; here the concern is with its political relation. Through Washington's efforts Virginia in 1772 passed an act "empowering Trustees . . . to raise money . . . for the purpose of opening and extending the Navigation of Potowmack from the Tide water to Fort Cumberland." Nothing was accomplished, however, until the close of the Revolution, when the general's enthusiasm for the project became great; and his western trip in 1784 was in part an inspection of possible water routes or of combined water and land routes over the mountains.

His concern was not entirely economic. He realized that the developing West had a natural trade outlet down the Mississippi, and in order to counteract this tendency and to keep that distant region loyal to the yet fragile Union such an eastern route as he proposed was essential. He wrote Humphreys, July 25, 1785: "My attention is more immediately engaged in a project, which I think big with great political, as well as commercial consequences to these States, especially the middle ones; it is by removing the obstructions and extending the inland navigation of our rivers, to bring the States on the Atlantic in close connexion with those forming to the westward, by a short and easy transportation. Without this, I can easily conceive they will have different views, separate interests, and other connexions. I may be singular in my ideas, but they are these; that, to open a door to, and make easy the way for, those settlers to the westward (which ought to progress regularly and compactly) before we make any stir about the navigation of the Mississippi, and before our settlements are far advanced towards that river, would be our true line of policy.

"It can, I think, be demonstrated, that the produce of the western territory, (if the navigations which are now in hand succeed, and of which I have no doubt,) as low down the Ohio as the Great Kanhawa, I believe to the Falls, and between the parts above and the Lakes, may be brought either to the highest shipping port on this or James river, at a less expense, with more ease, (including the return,) and in a much shorter time, than it can be carried to New Orleans, if the Spaniards, instead of restricting, were to throw open their ports and invite our trade. But if the commerce of that country should embrace this channel, and connexions be formed, experience has taught us, and there is a very recent proof with great Britain, how next to impracticable it is to divert it; and, if that should be the case, the Atlantic States, (especially as those to the westward will in a great degree fill with foreigners,) will be no more to the present Union, except to excite perhaps very justly our fears, than the country of California, which is still more to the westward, and belonging to another power."

RIVALRY OF VIRGINIA AND MARYLAND (1784-1785)

The Potomac was the boundary between Virginia and Maryland; indeed the waters were in the jurisdiction of the latter, Virginia had only reserved her right of navigation; so that an agreement between the two states was essential. Jefferson shared in Washington's desire for the development, and so did Thomas Johnson, formerly Governor of Maryland. Washington wrote Jefferson, who was then in Congress at Annapolis, March 29, 1784: "The plan, however, was in a tolerably good train, when I set out for Cambridge in 1775, and would have been in an excellent way, had it not been for the difficulties, which were met with in the Maryland Assembly from the opposition which was given (according to report) by the Baltimore merchants, who were alarmed, and perhaps not without cause, at the consequence of water transportation to Georgetown of the produce, which usually came to their market by land. The local interest of that place, joined to the short-sighted politics or contracted views of another part of that Assembly, gave Mr. Thomas Johnson, who was a warm promoter of the scheme on the north side of the Potomac, a great deal of trouble. . . . It appears to me, that the interest and policy of Maryland are proportionably concerned with those of Virginia, to remove obstructions, and to invite the trade of the western country into the channel you have mentioned. You will have frequent opportunities of learning the sentiments of the principle characters of that State, respecting this matter; and I wish, if it should fall in your way, that you would discourse with Mr. Thomas Johnson, formerly Governor of Maryland, on this subject."

At this same time Madison was writing to Jefferson concerning methods of an agreement with Maryland on the use of the river; suggesting as best "a mutual appointment of Commissioners for the general purpose of preserving a harmony and efficacy in the regulations on both sides." Accordingly, he carried through a resolution in the Virginia Assembly, June 28, 1784, for such a joint commission to "frame such liberal and equitable regulations concerning said river as may be mutually advantageous." Maryland agreed and the meeting was to take place in March, 1785.

Meanwhile Washington took his last trip over the mountains and returned more than ever persuaded of the need and possibility of the communication. He wrote Governor Harrison, October 10, a long letter on the subject, pointing out the efforts which Pennsylvania and New York were making, and the political consideration, "which is of still greater importance," since the "western settlers (I speak now from my own observation) stand as it were upon a pivot. . . . A combination of circumstances makes the present conjuncture more favorable for Virginia, than for any other State in the Union, to fix these matters. . . . One thing more remains, . . . the supposed difficulty of obtaining a passage through the State of Pennsylvania. How an application to its legislature would be relished, in the first instance, I will not undertake to decide."

After his return from this journey a mass meeting was held in Alexandria, November 15, 1784, attended by gentlemen from both Maryland and Virginia. It is to be presumed that Washington was there. The newspaper report on the meeting contains this interesting sentence: "This is perhaps a work of more political than commercial consequence, and it will be one of the grandest chains for preserving the Federal Union."

ARRANGEMENTS FOR A CONFERENCE (1784-1785)

Here then was a commercial project in active contemplation, which would involve the interests of at least three of the states. Washington sent to Richmond and also to Annapolis a bill to incorporate the company he desired, which passed both legislatures; but a conference was necessary to iron out differences. Washington headed the Virginia delegation. He wrote Knox, January 5, 1785: "I am just returned from Annapolis to which place I was requested to go by our Assembly (with my bosom friend Genl. G-tes, who being at Richmond contrived to edge himself into the commission) for the purpose of arranging matters, and forming a Law which should be similar in both States, so far as it respected the river Potomack, which seperates them. I met the most perfect accordance in that legislature; and the matter is now reported to ours, for its concurrence."

The recommendations made were later approved by the two legislatures. Madison in commenting on the matter wrote, December 25, 1784, that there would probably be provision made "for a survey of the different routes for a communication between the waters of Elizabeth River and those of North Carolina." The Virginia Legislature adopted a resolution directing the commissioners who were to meet those from Maryland the next summer to join "in a representation to Pennsylvania on the subject of the waters of the Ohio within her limits." Also it was well known that Maryland desired a canal connecting the waters of the Chesapeake and Delaware, which would involve yet one more state in the commercial agitation.

The Maryland-Virginia joint commission on the navigation of the Potomac met in Alexandria on March 20, 1785, and continued its meeting at Mount Vernon where the compact was signed, March 28. Madison on July 26 spoke of the "urgency of General Washington in the late negociation

with Maryland." The outcome is a part of national history. Both legislatures ratified the compact, but Maryland, November 21, on the motion of Stone, who had been a signer of the document, asked for a further conference and proposed the inclusion of Pennsylvania and Delaware. Both these states accepted and Maryland appointed new commissioners.

PROPOSAL OF A GENERAL CONVENTION (1786)

Meanwhile, a resolution went very quickly through the Virginia Legislature, January 21, 1786, which ignored Congress and appointed commissioners to meet with such other commissioners as should be appointed by any of the states to consider the trade of the Union. These Virginia delegates, of whom Madison was the leader, issued invitations which were generally accepted; but delegates from only five states met at Annapolis in September, 1786. A report was prepared by Hamilton and a new convention was proposed to meet in Philadelphia the next May. This call was addressed directly to the states, but a copy was sent to Congress; that body in the end ignored the particular summons but issued an invitation of its own for the same place and time. Thus the Federal Convention of 1787 is linked up with the question of transportation to the West.

Washington had no public share in any of these preliminary matters, but his interest was active. Madison was a frequent visitor at Mount Vernon at this time, staying over night or several days at a time. Mason and Edmund Randolph, as well as prominent men of other colonies, were also Washington's guests. The comments in his letters begin with one to Lafayette, May 10, 1786: ". . . whilst a measure, in which this State has taken the lead at its last session, will, it is to be hoped, give efficient powers to that body for all commercial purposes. This is a nomination of some of its first characters to meet other commissioners from the several States, in order to consider of and decide upon such powers, as shall be necessary for the sovereign power of them to act under; which are to be reported to the respective legislatures at their autumnal sessions, for, it is to be hoped, final adoption; thereby avoiding those tedious and futile deliberations, which result from recommendations and partial concurrences, at the same time that it places it at once in the power of Congress to meet European nations upon decisive and equal ground. All the legislatures, which I have heard from, have come into the proposition, and have made very judicious appointments. Much good is expected from this measure, and it is regretted by many, that more objects were not embraced by the meeting. A general convention is talked of by many for the purpose of revising and correcting the defects of the federal government; but whilst this is the wish of some, it is the dread of others, from an opinion that matters are not yet sufficiently ripe for such an event."

After the Annapolis Convention had adjourned and its recommendation was before the Virginia Legislature, Washington wrote Madison, November 5: "No morn ever dawned more favorably than ours did; and no day was ever more clouded than the present. Wisdom and good examples are necessary at this time to rescue the political machine from the impending storm. Virginia has now an opportunity to set the latter, and has enough of the former, I hope, to take the lead in promoting this great and arduous work."

WOULD WASHINGTON ATTEND THE CONVENTION (1786)?

Madison, in his reply, brought directly to the general the problem of breaking his retirement once more. He wrote, November 8: "The expediency of complying with the recommendation from Annapolis in favor of a general revision of the federal system, was *unanimously* agreed to. A bill for the purpose is now depending, and in a form which attests the most federal spirit. As no opposition has been yet made, and it is ready for the third reading, I expect it will soon be before the public. It has been thought advisable to give this subject a very solemn dress, and all the weight which could be derived from a single State. This idea will also be pursued in the selection of characters to represent Virginia in the federal convention. You will infer our earnestness on this point from the liberty, which will be used, of placing your name at the head of them. How far this liberty may correspond with the ideas, by which you ought to be governed, will be best decided when it must ultimately be determined. In every event, it will assist powerfully in marking the zeal of our legislature, and its opinion of the magnitude of the occasion."

For the next few months the struggle between Washington's wishes and his sense of public responsibility engrossed his correspondence. He wrote Madison, December 16, stating that he had already refused to attend the meeting of the Cincinnati, also called for Philadelphia in May, and this alone would seem to preclude his attending the other convention; but adding: "That the present moment is pregnant of great and strange events, none who will cast their eyes around them can deny. What may be brought forth between this and the first of May, to remove the difficulties, which at present labor in my mind against the acceptance of the honor, which has lately been conferred on me by the Assembly, is not for me to predict; but I should think it incompatible with that candor, which ought to characterize an honest mind, not to declare, that, under my present view of the matter, I should be too much embarrassed by the meeting of these two bodies in the same place at the same moment, after what I have written to be easy in my situation, and

therefore that it would be improper to let my appointment stand in the way of another. Of this, you, who have had the whole matter before you, will judge; for, having received no other than private intimation of my election, and unacquainted with the formalities, which are or ought to be used on these occasions, silence may be deceptious, or considered as disrespectful. This imputation of both or either I would wish to avoid."

ADVICE OF FRIENDS (1786)

Madison persisted in his urging: "But I am still inclined to think, that the posture of our affairs, if it should continue, would prevent any criticism on the situation, which the contemporary meetings would place you in; and wish that at least a door could be left open for your acceptance hereafter, in case the gathering clouds should become so dark and menacing, as to supersede every consideration but that of our national existence or safety.'

The retired warrior, anxious to know his duty, appealed then to Humphreys, his former aide, December 26: "That the federal government is nearly if not quite at a stand, none will deny. The first question then is, shall it be annihilated or supported? If the latter, the proposed convention is an object of the first magnitude, and should be sustained by all the friends of the present constitution. In the other case, if, on a full and dispassionate revision, the continuance shall be adjudged impracticable or unwise, as only delaying an event which must ere long take place, would it not be better for such a meeting to suggest some other, to avoid if possible civil disorder or other impending evils? I must candidly confess, as we could not remain quiet more than three or four years in time of peace, under the constitutions of our own choosing, which it was believed, in many States at least, were formed with deliberation and wisdom, I see little prospect either of our agreeing upon any other, or that we should remain long satisfied under it if we could. Yet I would wish any thing and every thing essayed to prevent the effusion of blood, and to avert the humiliating and contemptible figure we are about to make in the annals of mankind.

"If this second attempt to convene the States, for the purposes proposed by the report of the partial representation at Annapolis in September, should also prove abortive, it may be considered as an unequivocal evidence, that the States are not likely to agree on any general measure, which is to pervade the Union, and of course that there is an end of federal government. The States, therefore, which make the last dying essay to avoid these misfortunes, would be mortified at the issue, and their deputies would return home chagrined at their ill success and disappointment. This would be a disagreeable circumstance for any one of them to be in, but more particularly so for a person in my situation."

WASHINGTON ADVOCATES THE CONVENTION (1787)

Knox, too, was taken into his confidence; he wrote February 3, 1787: "Thus the matter stands, which is the reason of my saying to you *in confidence*, that at present I retain my first intention not to go. In the mean while, as I have the fullest conviction of your friendship for and attachment to me, know your abilities to judge, and your means of information, I shall receive any communication from you on this subject with thankfulness. My first wish is to do for the best, and to act with propriety. You know me too well to believe, that reserve or concealment of any opinion or circumstance would be at all agreeable to me. The legality of this convention I do not mean to discuss, nor how problematical the issue of it may be. That powers are wanting none can deny. Through what medium they are to be derived will, like other matters, engage the attention of the wise. That, which takes the shortest course to obtain them, in my opinion will, under present circumstances, be found best; otherwise, like a house on fire, whilst the most regular mode of extinguishing the flames is contended for, the building is reduced to ashes. My opinion of the energetic wants of the federal government are well known. My public annunciations and private declarations have uniformly expressed these sentiments; and, however constitutional it may be for Congress to point out the defects of the federal system, I am strongly inclined to believe, that it would not be found the most efficacious channel for the recommendations, more especially the alterations, to flow, for reasons too obvious to enumerate."

WASHINGTON'S ESTIMATE OF THE DIFFICULTIES

Given the advisability of the convention, he was not inclined to stress the question of unconstitutionality: "I would fain try what the wisdom of the proposed convention will suggest, and what can be effected by their counsels. It may be the last peaceable mode of essaying the practicability of the present form, without a greater lapse of time, than the exigency of our affairs will allow. In strict propriety, a convention so holden may not be legal. Congress, however, may give it a coloring by recommendation, which would fit it more to the taste, without proceeding to a definition of the powers. This, however constitutionally it might be done, would not in my opinion be expedient."

Still, as he wrote Humphreys again, March 8, the action of Congress in the matter somewhat eased his troubles: "I am still indirectly and delicately pressed by many to attend this meeting; and a thought has run thro' my mind of late attended with more embarrassment than any former one. It is whether my not doing it will not be considered as an implied dereliction to Republicanism—nay more, whether (however injurious the imputation) it may not be ascribed to other motives. My wish is I confess to see this Convention tied [tried?]; after which, if the present form is not made efficient, conviction of the propriety of a change will pervate all ranks, and many [may] be effected by peace. Till then, however necessary it may appear to the more discerning part of the community, my opinion is, that it cannot be accomplished without great contention and much confusion for reasons too obvious to enumerate. It is one of the evils, perhaps not the smallest, of democratical governments that they must feel before they will see or act under this view of matters, and not doubting but you have heard the sentiments of many respectable characters since the date of your letter of the 20th of January on this subject, and perhaps since the business has been moved in Congress of the propriety or impropriety of my attendance, let me pray you, my dear Sir, to give me confidentially the public opinion and expectation as far as it has come to your knowledge of what it is supposed, I will or ought to do on this occasion."

QUESTION OF MONARCHY

The letter of March 31 to Madison is of unusual interest, because therein he spoke directly of the monarchical possibility at which he merely hinted in the letters to Humphreys: "I think the reasons in favor have the preponderancy over those against it. It is idle in my opinion to suppose that the Sovereign can be insensible to the inadequacy of the powers under which they act, and that, seeing it, they should not recommend a revision of the federal system; especially when it is considered by many as the only constitutional mode by which the defects can be remedied. Had Congress proceeded to a delineation of the powers, it might have sounded an alarm; but, as the case is, I do not conceive that it will have that effect. . . .

"I am fully of opinion that those, who lean to a monarchical government, have either not consulted the public mind, or that they live in a region, which (the levelling principles in which they were bred being entirely eradicated) is much more productive of monarchical ideas, than are to be found in the southern States, where, from the habitual distinctions which have always existed among the people, one would have expected the first generation and the most rapid growth of them. I am also clear, that, even admitting the utility, nay, necessity of the form, yet that the period is not arrived for adopting the change without shaking the peace of this country to its foundation. That a thorough reform of the present system is indispensable, none, who have capacities to judge, will deny; and with hand [and heart] I hope the business will be essayed in a full convention.

"After which, if more powers and more decision is not found in the existing form, if it still wants energy and that secrecy and

despatch (either from the nonattendance or the local views of its members), which is characteristic of good government, and if it shall be found (the contrary of which, however, I have always been more afraid of than of the abuse of them), that Congress will, upon all proper occasions, exert the powers which are given, with a firm and steady hand, instead of frittering them back to the States, where the members, in place of viewing themselves in their national character, are too apt to be looking,—I say, after this essay is made, if the system proves inefficient, conviction of the necessity of a change will be disseminated among all classes of the people. Then, and not till then, in my opinion, can it be attempted without involving all the evils of civil discord.

"I confess, however, that my opinion of public virtue, is so far changed, that I have my doubts whether any system, without the means of coercion in the sovereign, will enforce due obedience to the ordinances of a general government; without which every thing else fails. Laws or ordinances unobserved, or partially attended to, had better never have been made; because the first is a mere nihil, and the second is productive of much jealousy and discontent. But what kind of coercion, you may ask. This indeed will require thought, though the non-compliance of the States with the late requisition is an evidence of the necessity."

Of interest in the light of the proceedings of the Federal Convention, in this insistence on the power of coercion in the central government, though there is no indication that he had in mind at this time at least the eventual solution of direct action of the federal government upon the people. It is interesting, too, to contrast the above statement with his indignant rejection of Nicola's suggestion of kingship in 1782.

COUNSELS ON ATTENDING THE CONVENTION (1787)

These and other letters produced replies that in general urged his attendance. Knox had no doubts, and was almost prophetic in his reply: "I imagine that your own satisfaction, or chagrin, and that of your friends, will depend entirely on the result of the convention. For I take it for granted, that, however reluctantly you may acquiesce, you will be constrained to accept of the president's chair. Hence the proceedings of the convention will more immediately be appropriated to you than to any other person. Were the convention to propose only amendments and patchwork to the present defective confederation, your reputation would in a degree suffer. But, were an energetic and judicious system to be proposed with your signature, it would be a circumstance highly honorable to your fame, in the judgment of the present and future ages; and doubly entitle you to the glorious republican epithet, *The Father of your Country*.

"But, the men generally chosen being of the first information, great reliance may be placed on the wisdom and vigor of their counsels and judgment, and therefore the balance of my opinion preponderates greatly in favor of your attendance. I am persuaded, that your name has had already great influence to induce the States to come into the measure, that you attendance will be grateful, that your presence would confer on the assembly a national complexion, and that it would more than any other circumstance induce a compliance with the propositions of the convention."

Humphreys personally thought Washington's attendance unwise. He wrote his General, January 20, 1787: "The personal character of yourself and some other Gentlemen would have a weight on individuals—but on democratic Assemblies & the bulk of the People, your opinions & your eloquence would be 'triffles light as air.' After the abominable neglects, with which your recommendations of the Army have been treated; he must indeed have faith to remove mountains, who can believe in the good dispositions of the Country." However, he later acknowledged that Gouverneur Morris and others had wished him to use whatever influence he might have to induce Washington to attend. "I could not have promised this without counteracting my own judgment. I will not, however, hesitate to say, that I do not conceive your attendance can hazard such personal ill consequences, as were to be apprehended before the proposed meeting had been legitimated by the sanction of Congress."

WASHINGTON AGREES TO ATTEND (1787)

In the end Washington decided to attend the Convention, writing Governor Randolph March 28: "I apprehend, too much cause to arraign my conduct with inconsistency in again appearing on a public theatre, after a public declaration to the contrary, and because it will, I fear, have a tendency to sweep me back into the tide of public affairs, when retirement and ease is so essentially necessary for and is so much desired by me. However, as my friends, with a degree of solicitude which is unusual, seem to wish for my attendance on this occasion, I have come to a resolution to go, if my health will permit."

The spirit with which he looked forward to the Convention was not very hopeful. To Madison he wrote in the letter above quoted, March 31: "It gives me great pleasure to hear, that there is a probability of a full representation of the States in convention; but if the delegates come to it under fetters, the salutary ends proposed will in my opinion be greatly embarrassed and retarded, if not altogether defeated. I am desirous of knowing how this matter is, as my wish is that the convention may adopt no temporizing expedients, but probe the defects of the constitution to the bottom, and provide a radical cure, whether they are agreed to or not. A conduct of this kind will stamp wisdom and dignity on their proceedings, and hold up a light which sooner or later will have its influence."

To Randolph he sounded the more personal note, April 9: "I very much fear that all the States will not appear in convention, and that some of them will come fettered so as to impede rather than accelerate the great object of their convening; which,

under the peculiar circumstances of my case, would place me in a more disagreeable situation than any other member would stand in. As I have yielded, however, to what appeared to be the earnest wishes of my friends, I will hope for the best."

Part II
Results of the Convention

OPENING OF THE CONVENTION
(MAY, 1787)

Washington set out for the Convention on May 9; on the 13th was met at Chester by Generals Knox, Mifflin, and Varnum, Humphreys, Major Jackson, who was to become secretary of the Convention, and other former army officers. "At Gray's Ferry the city light horse . . . met me, and escorted me in by the artillery officers who stood arranged and saluted as I passed. . . . kindly pressed by Mr. and Mrs. Robert Morris to lodge with them, I did so. . . . Waited on the President, Doctr. Franklin, as soon as I got to Town. On my arrival, the Bells were chimed." For lack of a quorum the Convention did not meet until May 25, "when by a unanimous vote I was called up to the chair as President." Meetings were secret; Washington respected this so thoroughly that "nothing being suffered to transpire, no minutes of the proceedings has been, or will be inserted in this diary." There is an anecdote that when one member happened to drop his copy of the proceedings, luckily found by another member and given to the president, Washington's criticism was so scathing that the papers were never reclaimed.

VOTES AND ATTITUDE IN CONVENTION (1787)

Since Washington followed his usual habit of making no use of his diary as a record of consultations or arguments, purposely confining the entries in this crisis to very brief notes on social engagements, we are dependent upon fellow members for knowledge of the participation and personal influence of the president of the Convention. So far as known he made but one speech in the Convention; Madison's notes give this as a plea, in the final hours of the meeting, in favor of a more liberal ratio of representation. The eloquent brief speech with which he is accredited during the early dark days is apocryphal. It appears first in Gouverneur Morris's funeral oration on Washington, and must be classed with the address on independence put in Adams's mouth by Webster, and Lincoln's tariff speech as imagined by Robert Ingersoll. His

only known votes were: (1) in favor of a single executive; (2) against the election of the executive by Congress; (3) in favor of an export tax requiring a two-thirds vote; (4) ratification by seven states; (5) and against overruling the veto by a two-thirds vote. He was originally opposed to restricting the introduction of money bills to the lower house, but receded from that stand for the sake of harmony, not deeming it important. Luther Martin declared that in committee of the whole he advocated a strong centralized government, which is very likely.

In the pamphlet on his earlier politics an attempt has been made in the quotations from his letters to give his thoughts on the proper form of government; and a study of these and other utterances in the present article will show points that throw light on his probable attitude toward the various problems in the Convention. Certain points deserve special attention. John Corbin, in a recent study of Washington's constitutional influence, points out that the basic principle of his polity was republican and not democratic: that is, government of the people, for the people, but by the constituted authorities. Washington believed in representative government. When his nephew Bushrod informed him of the formation of a local patriotic society to keep a check on its legislator, a sort of early local substitute for the initiative and referendum, Washington replied, September 30, 1786: "I am no friend to institutions, except in local matters, which are wholly or in a great measure confined to the county of the delegates. To me it appears much wiser and more politic to choose able and honest representatives, and leave them, in all national questions to determine from the evidence of reason, and the facts which shall be adduced, when internal and external information is given to them in a collective state. What certainty is there that societies in a corner or remote part of a State can possess that knowledge which is necessary for them to decide on many important questions which may come before an Assembly? . . . What figure then must a delegate make, who comes there with his hands tied, and his judgment forestalled?"

BASIS OF SOUND GOVERNMENT
(1785-1787)

Washington believed in the absolute necessity of the federal government possessing coercive power, although he was uncertain of the form that power should take. This appears in his letter to Madison, March 31, 1786, previously quoted; and in various other places, such as a letter to Jay, August 1, 1786. On May 20 and again on November 5, 1785, Noah Webster was a visitor at Mount Vernon and remained over night in both cases. In this year Webster published his *Plan for the Union of the American States* which, though it probably made little impression at the time, contains thoughts on the need of coercion and direct application of the federal government—ideas upon which he and Washington undoubtedly exchanged opinions. Knox wrote Washington, January 4, 1787, offering some suggestions on government, including a separation of powers and also: "All national objects, to be designed and executed by the general government, without any reference to the local governments." Washington replied, February 3: "The system on which you seem disposed to build a national government, is certainly . . . in every point of view more desirable than the present, which . . . having the legislative, executive, and judiciary branches concentred, is exceptionable." This shows not only that he had placed before him ideas from which the Law-of-the-Land principle might have originated, but this last quotation shows also his belief in the separation of powers.

Washington believed in a bicameral Congress. In the letter to his nephew he commented upon the Shays movement in Massachusetts, declaring as some evidences of its evil: "Why, they have declared the senate useless, many other parts of the constitution unnecessary, salaries of public officers burthensome, &c." He believed in a federal court. As early as 1775 he was urging the necessity of establishing without loss of time proper courts for the decision of property rights and the legality of seizures. As a result of this and other promptings, Congress first established a prize committee and later a fixed Court of Appeals in Cases of Capture, which Dr. Jameson considers "may be justly regarded not simply as the predecessor, but as one of the origins of the Supreme Court of the United States."

The Massachusetts Constitution of 1780 was nearer a model of the Federal Constitution than any other of the early constitutional documents. John Adams, who was the chief author of it, wrote a *Defence of the Constitutions of the Government of the United States*, which was originally published in London, but the first part of which was available in Philadelphia during the Federal Convention. Washington possessed a copy of it but we do not know from his accounts whether or not it came into his hands during the Convention.

WASHINGTON'S INFLUENCE IN THE CONVENTION

We know that he was acquainted with the Virginia Plan in advance. Madison wrote, April 16: "Having been lately led to resolve the subject which is to undergo the discussion of the Convention, and formed *some* outlines of a new system, I take the liberty of submitting them without apology to your eye." Undoubtedly, too, he attended the preliminary meetings of the Virginia delegation which discussed the plan.

Of his great influence in the Convention we get a few sidelights from other correspondence, especially on the subject of the presidency. Pierce Butler, who was a delegate, wrote, May 5, 1788: "Nor, Entre Nous, do I believe they would have been so great had not many of the members cast their eyes towards General Washington as President; and shaped their Ideas of the Powers to be given to a President by their opinions of his Virtue. So that the Man, who by his Patriotism and Virtue, Contributed largely to the Emancipation of his Country, may be the Innocent means of its being, when He is lay'd low, oppressed." This clearly indicates a belief in a presidential life tenure; and Jefferson wrote, August 12, 1788: "Another defect, the perpetual reeligibility of the same President, will probably not be cured during the life of General Washington. His merit has blinded our countrymen to the danger of making so important an office re-eligible. I presume there will not be a vote against him in the United States." An unknown writer, October 11, 1787, probably addressing Jefferson, supports this view: "I may pronounce that it will be adopted. General Washington lives; and as he will be appointed President, jealousy on this head vanishes."

Monroe wrote Jefferson, July 27, 1787, expressing a common opinion: "The convention is an expedient that will produce a decisive effect. It will either recover us from our present embarrassments or complete our ruin; for I do suspect that if what they recommend shod. be rejected this wod. be the case. But I trust that the presence of Genl. Washington will have great weight in the body itself so as to overawe and keep under the demon of party, & that the signature of his name to whatever act shall be the result of their deliberations will secure its passage thro' the union."

WASHINGTON ON THE COMPROMISES OF THE CONSTITUTION
(1787)

Through our present knowledge of the proceedings we can read between the lines of Washington's letters during the Convention. Thus he undoubtedly had the compromises in mind when he wrote Stuart, July 1: "I have had no wish more ardent, through the whole process of this business, than that of knowing what kind of government is best calculated for us to live under. No doubt there will be a diversity of sentiments on this important subject; and, to inform the judgment, it is necessary to hear all arguments that can be advanced. To please all is impossible, and to attempt it would be vain. The only way, therefore, is, under all the views in which it can be placed, and with a due consideration to circumstances, habits, &c., &c., to form such a government as will bear the scrutinizing eye of criticism, and trust it to the good sense and patriotism of the people to carry it into effect."

Hamilton, who was a New York delegate, had at this time withdrawn temporarily, because his colleagues had left in protest. When Washington wrote him, July 10, the Convention was in a critical state, having then under special consideration the proposition of the grand committee in favor of an equal state vote in the Senate, with the House to control the origin of money bills. This, which was being debated, seemed to involve a setback for the big states and for the advocates of a strong central government, men like King, Hamilton, Wilson, Madison, and Washington. The great Law-of-the-Land solution, by which the federal government was to operate directly on the people, had not yet been wrought out. Washington wrote: "When I refer you to the state of the counsels, which prevailed at the period you left this city, and add that they are now if possible in a worse train than ever, you will find but little ground on which the hope of a good establishment can be formed. In a word, I almost despair of seeing a favorable issue to the proceedings of our convention, and do therefore repent having had any agency in the business. The men who oppose a strong and energetic government, are in my opinion narrow-minded politicians, or are under the influence of local views. The apprehension expressed by them, that the *people* will not accede to the form proposed, is the *ostensible*, not the *real* cause of opposition. But, admitting that present sentiment is as they prognosticate, the proper question ought nevertheless to be, Is it, or is it not, the best form that such a country as this can adopt? If it be the best, recommend it, and it will assuredly obtain, maugre opposition. I am sorry you went away. I wish you were back. The crisis is equally important and alarming, and

no opposition, under such circumstances, should discourage exertions till the signature is offered."

CLOSE OF THE CONVENTION
(SEPTEMBER, 1787)

These doubts vanished with the successful accomplishment of the task. As Alexander wrote to Jefferson in November: "I never saw him so keen for anything in my life as he is for the adoption of the new scheme of government." Happy he was in being able to agree with Franklin that the device on the back of the president's chair was a rising and not a setting sun. Washington's Diary records the final session: *"Monday [Sept.] 17th.* Met in Convention, when the Constitution received the unanimous assent of 11 States and Colo. Hamilton's from New York (the only delegate from thence in Convention), and was subscribed to by every Member present except Govr. Randolph and Colo. Mason from Virginia, and Mr. Gerry from Massachusetts.

"The business being thus closed, the Members adjourned to the City Tavern, dined together and took a cordial leave of each other; after which I returned to my lodgings, did some business with, and received the papers from the Secretary of the Convention, and retired to meditate on the momentous w[or]k which had been executed, after not less than five, for a large part of the time Six, and sometimes 7 hours sitting every day, [except] sundays and the ten days adjournment to give a comee. opportunity and time to arrange the business, for more than four months."

WASHINGTON'S INFLUENCE ON THE RATIFICATION CONTEST
(1787-1788)

Washington took no public part in the agitation for ratification, but from Mount Vernon there proceeded a stream of private support and advice that filtered through various channels to public information. The mere knowledge that this venerated character had presided over the Convention and signed the drafted Constitution was one of the most powerful reasons in public opinion why it was worthy of acceptance. He was provoked because some "hasty and indigested sentiments" in a letter from him to Charles Carter got into the newspapers in a distorted form, even though Madison thought that on the whole "it may have been of service, notwithstanding the scandalous misinterpretations of it which have been attempted."

Never before, not even during the pre-revolutionary excitement, had there been so extensive and virulent use of newsletters and pamphlets. Washington's opinions, even rumors of them, were too good copy to be passed over even at his desire. Hamilton in some conjectures about the prospects of ratification wrote soon after the Convention adjourned: "The new Constitution has in favour of its success these circumstances—a very great weight of influence of the persons who framed it, particularly in the universal popularity of General Washington."

This was a valuable factor, but actual expressions from the mouth or pen of the great hero would be of still greater value; so much so that after ratification had been secured Washington wrote: "I did not incline to appear as a partisan in the interesting subject, that has agitated the public mind since the date of my last letter to you. For it was my sincere wish, that the constitution, which had been submitted to the people, might, after a fair and dispassionate investigation, stand or fall according to its merits or demerits. Besides, I found from disagreeable experience, that almost all the sentiments extracted from me in answer to private letters, or communicated orally, by some means or another found their way into the public gazettes, as well as some other sentiments ascribed to me, which never had an existence in my imagination."

SUPPORT OF WASHINGTON AND FRANKLIN (1787)

Even the objectors considered it necessary to explain away the fact that Washington and Franklin had endorsed the constitutional plan. Thus an "Officer in the Late Continental Army," in a newsletter, November 3, 1787, wrote: "The great names of Washington and Franklin have been taken in vain and shockingly prostituted to effect the most infamous purposes. What! because our august chieftain has subscribed his name in his capacity of president of the convention . . . will any one infer from this that it has met with . . . [his] entire approbation, and that . . . [he considers] it as a masterpiece of human wisdom? I am apt to think the contrary, as I have good reason to ground my opinion on."

"Centinel," who was probably Samuel Bryan, explained at greater length: "I would be very far from insinuating that the two illustrious personages alluded to, have not the welfare of their country at heart; but that the unsuspecting goodness and zeal of the one has been imposed upon, in a subject of which he must be necessarily inexperienced, from his other arduous engagements; and that the weakness and indecision attendant on old age, has been practiced on the other. . . . Is it derogating from the character of the illustrious and highly revered Washington, to suppose him fallible on a subject that must be in a great measure novel to him? As a patriotic hero, he stands unequalled in the annals of time, . . . In despair they are weakly endeavoring to screen their criminality by interposing the shield of the virtues of a Washington, in representing his concurrence in the proposed system of government as evidence of the purity of their intentions; but this impotent attempt to degrade the brightest ornament of his country to a base level with themselves will be considered as an aggravation of their treason, who have too much discern-

ment not to make a just discrimination between the honest mistaken zeal of the patriot and the flagitious machinations of an ambitious junto, and will resent the imposition that Machiavelian arts and consummate cunning have practiced upon our illustrious chief."

WASHINGTON'S ANALYSIS OF THE SITUATION (1788)

Washington did not consider the plan flawless but, as he wrote Mrs. Macauly-Graham, November 16, 1787: "I think it is much to be wondered at that any thing could be produced with such unanimity as the Constitution proposed."

To Lafayette he wrote with more freedom, February 7, 1788: "It appears to me, then, little short of a miracle, that the delegates from so many different States (which States you know are also different from each other), in their manners, circumstances, and prejudices, should unite in forming a system of national government, so little liable to well-founded objections. . . . With regard to the two great points (the pivots upon which the whole machine must move) my creed is simply,

"1st. That the general government is not invested with more powers, than are indispensably necessary to perform the functions of a good government; and consequently, that no objection ought to be made against the quantity of power delegated to it.

"2ly. That these powers, (as the appointment of all rulers will for ever arise from, and at short, stated intervals recur to, the free suffrage of the people,) are so distributed among the legislative, executive, and judicial branches, into which the general government is arranged, that it can never be in danger of degenerating into a monarchy, an oligarchy, an aristocracy, or any other despotic or oppressive form, so long as there shall remain any virtue in the body of the people.

"I would not be understood, my dear Marquis, to speak of consequences, which may be produced in the revolution of ages, by corruption of morals, profligacy of manners, and listlessness for the preservation of the natural and unalienable rights of mankind, nor of the successful usurpations, that may be established at such an unpropitious juncture upon the ruins of liberty, however providently guarded and secured; as these are contingencies against which no human prudence can effectually provide. It will at least be a recommendation to the proposed constitution, that it is provided with more checks and barriers against the introduction of tyranny, and those of a nature less liable to be surmounted, than any government hitherto instituted among mortals hath possessed. We are not to expect perfection in this world; but mankind, in modern times, have apparently made some progress in the science of government. Should that, which is now offered to the

people of America, be found on experiment less perfect than it can be made, a constitutional door is left open for its amelioration."

His idea of the probable opposition and the proper answer to the candid portion of it he gives in a letter to Knox, October, 1787: "The constitution is now before the judgment-seat. It has, as was expected, its adversaries and supporters. Which will preponderate is yet to be decided. The former more than probably will be most active, as the major part of them will, it is to be feared, be governed by sinister and self-important motives, to which every thing in their breasts must yield. The opposition from another class of them may perhaps, (if they should be men of reflection, candor, and information,) subside in the solution of the following simple questions. 1. Is the constitution, which is submitted by the convention, preferable to the government, (if it can be called one,) under which we now live? 2. Is it probable that more confidence would at the time be placed in another convention, provided the experiment should be tried, than was placed in the last one, and is it likely that a better agreement would take place therein? What would be the consequences if these should not happen, or even from the delay, which must inevitably follow such an experiment? Is there not a constitutional door open for alterations or amendments? and is it not likely that real defects will be as readily discovered after as before trial? and will not our successors be as ready to apply the remedy as ourselves, if occasion should require it? To think otherwise will, in my judgment, be ascribing more of the *amor patriae*, more wisdom and more virtue to ourselves, than I think we deserve."

WASHINGTON'S OPPOSITION TO A SECOND CONVENTION (1788)

Later when the movement for a second convention was actively advanced, especially by Patrick Henry, Washington was quick to point out the weakness of the proposition in a letter to Randolph, January 8, 1788: "The various passions and *motives*, by which men are influenced, are concomitants of fallibility, engrafted into our nature for the purposes of unerring wisdom; but, had I entertained a latent hope, (at the time you moved to have the constitution submitted to a second convention,) that a more perfect form would be agreed to, in a word, that any constitution would be adopted under the impressions and instructions of the members, the publications, which have taken place since, would have eradicated every form of it. How do the sentiments of the influential characters in this State, who are opposed to the constitution, and have favored the public with their opinions, quadrate with each other? Are they not at variance on some of the most important points? If the opponents in the *same* State

WASHINGTON AND THE CONSTITUTION

79

cannot agree in their principles, what prospect is there of a coalescence with the advocates of the measure, when the different views and jarring interests of so wide and extended an empire are to be brought forward or combated? To my judgment it is more clear than ever, that an attempt to amend the constitution, which is submitted, would be productive of more heat and greater confusion than can well be conceived."

Being not at all fearful of the result of a thorough public discussion into the merits of the Plan, he wrote Humphreys, October 10, 1787: "Much will depend however upon literary abilities, and the recommendation of it by good pens should be *openly*, I mean, publickly afforded in the Gazettes." This was after Congress had submitted the draft to the states, which action received the General's comment in a letter to Madison, who was in Congress: "I am better pleased that the proceedings of the convention are submitted from Congress by a unanimous vote, feeble as it is, than if they had appeared under strong marks of approbation without it. This apparent unanimity will have its effect. Not every one has opportunities to peep behind the curtain; and, as the multitude are often deceived by externals, the appearance of unanimity in that body on this occasion will be of great importance."

WASHINGTON ON THE FEDERALIST (1788)

He followed carefully the course of the public discussion, writing Stuart, who later was elected a delegate to the Virginia Convention, November 30: "I have seen no publication yet, that ought in my judgment to shake the proposed constitution in the mind of an impartial and candid public. In fine, I have hardly seen one, that is not addressed to the passions of the people, and obviously calculated to alarm their fears. Every attempt to amend the constitution at this time is in my opinion idle and vain. . . . That there are some writers, and others perhaps who may not have written, that wish to see this union divided into several confederacies, is pretty evident.

"As an antidote to these opinions, and in order to investigate the ground of objections to the constitution which is submitted, the *Federalist*, under the signature of PUBLIUS, is written. . . . They are, I think I may venture to say, written by able men; and before they are finished will, or I am mistaken, place matters in a true point of light. Although I am acquainted with the writers, who have a hand in this work, I am not at liberty to mention names, nor would I have it known, that they are sent by *me* to *you* for promulgation."

Later, when the battle had been won, he expressed again, this time to Hamilton, the chief author, his opinion on the merits of *The Federalist*: "As the perusal of the political papers under the signature of PUBLIUS has afforded me great satisfaction, I shall certainly consider them as claiming a most distinguished place in my library. I have read every performance, which has been printed on one side and the other of the great question lately agitated (so far as I have been able to obtain them); and, without an unmeaning compliment, I will say, that I have seen no other so well calculated, in my judgment, to produce conviction on an unbiased mind as the *production* of your *triumvirate*. When the transient circumstances and fugitive performances, which attended this *crisis*, shall have disappeared, that work will merit the notice of posterity, because in it are candidly and ably discussed the principles of freedom and the topics of government, which will be always interesting to mankind, so long as they shall be connected in civil society."

PERSONAL DISCUSSIONS ON RATIFICATION (1788)

Washington seems to have been optimistic during most of the ratification contest. Throughout the whole period of ratification his residence continued to be "a well resorted tavern," and with such men as Madison, the Lees, Robert and Gouverneur Morris, Carrington, Dulany, Humphreys, Harrison of Maryland, Powell of Pennsylvania, Jones of North Carolina, and many other visitors, there must have been lively discussions over the dinner table. These visitors not only carried home but later voiced the general's impressions. Henry Lee wrote, December 7, 1787: "Genl. Washington . . . continues firm as a rock." Washington himself wrote Carter at this time, "My decided opinion of the matter is that there is no alternative between the adoption of it and anarchy"; and to Jay, March 3, 1788, "for myself I have never entertained much doubt of its adoption." This last statement was after the plan had successfully passed its first real test, in the Massachusetts Convention. The only large state which had previously ratified had been Pennsylvania, and there a species of dragoonage had checked the opposition.

Washington did not approve of the Massachusetts "concomitants" — the proposed amendments; but nevertheless he wrote Lincoln, February 28, 1788: "The full and fair discussion, which you gave the subject in your convention, was attended with the happiest consequences. It afforded complete information to all those, who went thither with dispositions to be informed, and at the same time gave an opportunity to confute and point out the fallacy of those specious arguments, which were offered in opposition to the proposed government. Nor is this all. The conciliating behavior of the minority will strike a damp on the hopes, which opponents in other States might otherwise have formed from the smallness of the majority, and must be greatly influential in obtaining a favorable determination in those States, which have not yet decided upon it."

DANGER IN ADJOURNMENTS (1788)

The ratification by Massachusetts was the sixth. The New Hampshire convention convened but adjourned. Though this action was really a measure to prevent rejection, since a majority of the convention were instructed against acceptance, it alarmed Washington. He wrote Knox, March 30: "The conduct of the State of New Hampshire has baffled all calculation, and has come extremely *malapropos* for a favorable decision on the proposed constitution in this State; for, be the real cause of the late adjournment what it may, the anti-federal party with us do not scruple to pronounce, that it was done to await the issue of this convention before it would decide, and add, that, if this State should reject it, all those who are to follow will do the same, and consequently that it cannot obtain, as there will be only eight States in favor of the measure."

When later the Maryland convention met he warned Thomas Johnson: "I take the liberty of expressing a single sentiment on the occasion. It is, that an adjournment, if attempted, of your convention, to a later period than the decision of the question in this State, will be tantamount to the rejection of the constitution. I have good reasons for this opinion, and am told it is the blow which the leading characters of the opposition in the next State [to meet in convention] have meditated, if it shall be found that a direct attack is not likely to succeed in yours. If this be true it cannot be too much deprecated and guarded against. The postponement in New Hampshire, (although it made no reference to the convention of this State, but proceeded altogether from the local circumstances of its own,) is ascribed by the opposition here to complaisance towards Virginia, and great use is made of it. An event similar to this in Maryland would have the worst tendency imaginable; for indecision there would certainly have considerable influence upon South Carolina, the only other State, which is to precede Virginia, and submits the question almost wholly to the determination of the latter. The pride of the State is already touched upon this string, and will be raised much higher if there is fresh cause."

INFLUENCE OF WASHINGTON ON THE VIRGINIA CONVENTION (1788)

Success or failure would turn probably on the action of Virginia, where the opposition was led by the Lees, Patrick Henry, Mason, Grayson, and Harrison. Washington wrote James Wilson, April 4, "It is impossible to say, with any degree of certainty, what will be the determination of the convention in this State upon the proposed plan of government." When the Virginia Convention met, eight states had acceded; if that state ratified, the Constitution could go into operation. To Washington's

Federalistic mind there could be no question of the duty of the Convention. He wrote Madison, who, with Randolph and Marshall, was to be a leading proponent in the Convention: "The decision of Maryland and South Carolina by so large majorities, and the almost certain adoption of the proposed constitution by New Hampshire, will make *all*, except desperate men, look before they leap into the dark consequences of rejection. The ratification by eight States without a negative, by three of them unanimously, by six against one in another, by three to one in another, by two to one in two more, and by *all* the weight of *abilities* and *property* in the other, is enough, one would think, to produce a cessation of opposition. I do not mean, that this alone is sufficient to produce conviction in the mind, but I think it ought to produce some change in the conduct of any man, who distrusted his infallibility."

The effects of rejection must also be considered, as he had written his nephew in the previous November: "Let the opponents of the proposed constitution in this State be asked, and it is a question they certainly ought to have asked themselves, what line of conduct they would advise to adopt, if nine other States, of which I think there is little doubt, should accede to the constitution. Would they recommend, that it should stand single? Will they connect it with Rhode Island? Or even with two others checkerwise, and remain with them, as outcasts from the society, to shift for themselves? Or will they return to their dependence on Great Britain? Or, lastly, have the mortification to come in when they will be allowed no credit for doing so?"

CRITICAL ACTION OF VIRGINIA
(1788)

Maryland had been the seventh state to ratify. The procession at Baltimore in celebration included a miniature ship fifteen feet long, fully rigged. Later, June 9, this was navigated down the Chesapeake and up the Potomac to Mount Vernon by Capt. Joshua Barney and presented to Washington. On July 24 it sank in a gale; but the event could no longer be taken as an omen, for by that time South Carolina, New Hampshire, and Virginia had ratified. Even if, as then seemed likely, rejection by New York should separate New England from the rest of the states, that difficulty probably would not prevent the new government going into operation.

The Virginia Convention met on June 2, 1788. Washington followed with great interest the reports of the proceedings by which Madison and others kept him informed. By a small majority ratification was accomplished. Alexandria celebrated with a dinner, June 28. Washington wrote C. C. Pinckney the same day: "Thus the citizens of Alexandria, when convened, constituted the first public company in America,

which had the pleasure of pouring libation to the prosperity of the ten States, that had actually adopted the general government. The day itself is memorable for more reasons than one. It was recollected, that this day is the anniversary of the battles of Sullivan's Island and Monmouth. I have just returned from assisting at the entertainment, and mention these details, unimportant as they are in themselves, the rather because I think we may rationally indulge the pleasing hope, that the Union will now be established upon a durable basis, and that Providence seeems still disposed to favor the members of it with unequalled opportunities for political happiness."

PROSPECTS IN THE LAST THREE STATES (1788)

As to prospects in North Carolina, New York, and Rhode Island, he continued in the letter to Pinckney: "From the local situation, as well as the other circumstances of North Carolina, I should be truly astonished if that State should withdraw itself from the Union. On the contrary, I flatter myself with a confident expectation, that more salutary counsels will certainly prevail. At present there is more doubt how the question will be immediately disposed of in New York; for it seems to be understood, that there is a majority in the convention opposed to the adoption of the new federal system. Yet it is hardly to be supposed, (or rather in my judgment it is irrational to suppose,) they will reject a government, which, from an unorganized embryo ready to be stifled with a breath, has now in the maturity of its birth assumed a confirmed bodily existence. Or, to drop the metaphor, the point in debate has at least shifted its ground from policy to expediency. The decision of ten States cannot be without its operation. Perhaps the wisest way in this crisis will be not to attempt to accept or reject, but to adjourn until the people in some parts of the State can consider the magnitude of the question, and of the consequences involved in it, more coolly and deliberately. After New York shall have acted, then only one little State will remain. Suffice it to say, *it is universally believed, that the scales are ready to drop from the eyes, and the infatuation to be removed from the heart, of Rhode Island.* May this be the case before that inconsiderate people shall have filled up the measure of iniquity, before it shall be too late."

WASHINGTON SUGGESTED FOR PRESIDENT (1788)

After New York ratified he expressed his thankfulness and praise with characteristic gallantry to Mrs. Stockton, August 31: "I can never trace the concatenation of causes, which led to these events, without acknowledging the mystery and admiring the goodness of Providence. To that Superintending Power alone is our retraction from the brink of ruin to be attributed. A spirit of ac-

comodation was happily infused into the leading characters of the Continent and the minds of men were gradually prepared, by disappointment, for the reception of a good government. Nor would I rob the fairer sex of their share in the glory of a revolution so honorably to human nature, for, indeed, I think you ladies are in the number of the best Patriots America can boast."

Even before any of the States had ratified, Washington was being informed of the necessity, the inevitableness, of his being President. Among the characteristic predictions was that of Hamilton: "If the government be adopted, it is probable General Washington will be President of the United States—This will insure a wise choice of men to administer the government and a good administration." Humphreys wrote his former chief, September 28, 1787: "Your good Angel, I am persuaded will not desert you. What will tend, perhaps, more than any thing to the adoption of the new System, will be an universal opinion of your being elected President of the United States, and an expectation that you will accept it for a while." Gouverneur Morris a month later added his plea: "I have observed that your Name to the new Constitution has been of infinite Service. Indeed I am convinced that if you had not attended the Convention, and the same Paper had been handed out to the World, it would have met with a colder Reception. . . . As it is, should the Idea prevail that you would not accept of the Presidency it would prove fatal in many Parts. . . . Your cool steady Temper is indispensibly necessary to give a firm and manly Tone to the new Government. . . . The Horses once trained may be managed by a Woman or a Child; not so when they first feel the Bit. . . . You therefore must I say *must* mount the Seat."

At that time Washington seems to have ignored the matter, at least so far as his published correspondence shows; though Alexander Donald's letter to Jefferson in November shows that the subject was also one of discussion by visitors: "As the eyes of all America are turned towards this truly Great and Good man, for the First President, I took the liberty of sounding him upon it, He appears to be greatly against going into Publick Life again, . . . but . . . I am fully of opinion he may be induced to appear once more on the Publick Stage of Life —I form my opinion from what passed between us in a very long & serious conversation, as well as from what I could gather from Mrs. Washington on the same subject."

After Virginia had ratified, Monroe wrote Jefferson, July 12: "The conduct of Genl. Washington upon this occasion has no doubt been right and meritorious. . . . To forsake the honorable retreat to which he had retired & risque the reputation he had so deservedly acquir'd, manifested a zeal for the publick interest, that could after so many and illustrious services, & at this stage of his life, scarcely have been expected from him.

. . . Be assured his influence carried this Government." And, as he had so successfully emerged from his retreat at the call of public duty, so this same call would not permit him to retire again.

PRESSURE TO ACCEPT THE PRESIDENCY (1788)

After ratification was accomplished, the burden of letters from all over the Union was that Washington must be President. Such men as Knox, Lincoln, Trumbull, Morris, Hamilton, Thomas Johnson, Henry Lee, Madison, and Lafayette united in their plea. Hamilton's urgency and Henry Lee's are characteristic. It will be noticed that in them not only duty but the effect of refusal upon the general's own reputation are stressed. The former wrote: "I should be deeply pained, my dear Sir, if your scruples in regard to a certain station should be matured into a resolution to decline it; though I am neither surprised at their existence, nor can I but agree in opinion that the caution you observe in deferring the ultimate determination is prudent. I have, however, reflected maturely on the subject, and have come to a conclusion (in which I feel no hesitation), that every public and personal consideration will demand from you an asquiescence in what will *certainly* be the unanimous wish of your country.

"First; in a matter so essential to the well being of society as the prosperity of a newly instituted government, a citizen of so much consequence as yourself to its success has no option but to lend his services if called for. Permit me to say, it would be inglorious, in such a situation, not to hazard the glory, however great, which he might have previously acquired.

"Secondly; your signature to the proposed system pledges your judgment for its being such an one as upon the whole was worthy of the public approbation. If it should miscarry, (as men commonly decide from success or the want of it) the blame will in all probability be laid on the system itself. And the framers of it will have to encounter the disrepute of having brought about a revolution in government, without substituting any thing that was worthy of the effort; they pulled down one Utopia, it will be said, to build up another. This view of the subject, if I mistake not, my dear Sir, will suggest to your mind greater hazard to that fame, which must be and ought to be dear to you, in refusing your future aid to the system, than in affording it. I will only add, that in my estimate of the matter, that aid is indispensable."

Henry Lee declared, September 13: "Solicitous for our common happiness as a people, and convicted as I continue to be, that our peace and prosperity depends on the proper improvement of the present period, my anxiety is extreme, that the new govt. may have an auspicious beginning—To effect this & perpetuate a nation formed under your auspices, it is certain that again you will be called forth—"

WASHINGTON ON THE PRESIDENCY (1788)

Washington's reluctance was not assumed. To Hamilton he wrote, August 28: "On the delicate subject with which you conclude your letter, I can say nothing, because the event alluded to may never happen, and because, in case it should occur, it would be a point of prudence to defer forming one's ultimate and irrevocable decision, so long as new data might be afforded for one to act with the greater wisdom and propriety. I would not wish to conceal my prevailing sentiment from you; for you know me well enough, my good Sir, to be persuaded, that I am not guilty of affectation when I tell you, that it is my great and sole desire to live and die in peace and retirement on my own farm."

As the pressure increased, he enlarged on his reasons to Henry Lee, September 22: "The principal topic of your letter is to me a point of great delicacy indeed, insomuch that I can scarcely without some impropriety touch upon it. In the first place, the event to which you allude may never happen; among other reasons, because, if the partiality of my fellow citizens conceive it to be a means by which the sinews of the new government would be strengthened, it will of consequence be obnoxious to those, who are in opposition to it, many of whom unquestionably will be placed among the electors.

"This consideration alone would supersede the expediency of announcing any definite and irrevocable resolution. You are among the small number of those, who know my invincible attachment to domestic life, and that my sincerest wish is to continue in the enjoyment of it solely until my final hour. But the world would be neither so well instructed, nor so candidly disposed, as to believe me uninfluenced by sinister motives, in case any circumstance should render a deviation from the line of conduct I had prescribed to myself indispensable.

"Should the contingency you suggest take place, and (for argument's sake alone let me say it) should my unfeigned reluctance to accept the office be overcome by a deference for the reasons and opinions of my friends, might I not, after the declarations I have made (and Heaven knows they were made in the sincerity of my heart), in the judgment of the impartial world and of posterity, be chargeable with levity and inconsistency, if not with rashness and ambition? Nay farther, would there not even be some apparent foundation for the two former charges? Now justice to myself and tranquility of conscience require, that I should act a part, if not above imputation, at least capable of vindication. Nor will you conceive me to be too solicitous for reputation. Though I prize as I ought the good opinion of my fellow citizens, yet, if I know myself, I would not seek or retain popularity at the expense of one social duty or moral virtue.

"While doing what my conscience informed me was right, as it respected my God, my country, and myself, I could despise all the party clamor and unjust censure, which must be expected from some, whose personal enmity might be occasioned by their hostility to the government. I am conscious, that I fear alone to give any real occasion for obloquy, and that I do not dread to meet with unmerited reproach. And certain I am, whensoever I shall be convinced the good of my country requires my reputation to be put in risk, regard for my own fame will not come in competition with an object of so much magnitude. If I declined the task, it would lie upon quite another principle. Notwithstanding my advanced season of life, my increasing fondness for agricultural amusements, and my growing love of retirement, augment and confirm my decided predilection for the character of a private citizen, yet it would be no one of these motives, nor the hazard to which my former reputation might be exposed, nor the terror of encountering new fatigues and troubles, that would deter me from an acceptance; but a belief, that some other person, who had less pretence and less inclination to be excused, could execute all the duties full as satisfactorily as myself."

To Hamilton he acknowledged, October 3, that: "I will not suppress the acknowledgment, my dear Sir, that I have always felt a kind of gloom upon my mind, as often as I have been taught to expect I might, and perhaps must, ere long, be called to make a decision. You will, I am well assured, believe the assertion, (though I have little expectation it would gain credit from those who are less acquainted with me,) that, if I should receive the appointment, and if I should be prevailed upon to accept it, the acceptance would be attended with more diffidence and reluctance than I ever experienced before in my life. It would be, however, with a fixed and sole determination of lending whatever assistance might be in my power to promote the public weal, in hopes that at a convenient and early period my services might be dispensed with, and that I might be permitted once more to retire, to pass an unclouded evening after the stormy day of life, in the bosom of domestic tranquillity."

WASHINGTON ACCEPTS THE PRESIDENCY (1789)

Duty won. Although not legally informed of his unanimous election until April 14, 1789, when Charles Thomson, who had been Secretary of the Continental Congress throughout almost the whole of its life, reached Mount Vernon with the notification, it was a foregone conclusion long before. His preparation for the new dignity included borrowing some money: "Under this statement, I am inclined to do what I never expected to be driven to, that is, to borrow money on Interest. Five hundred pounds would enable me to discharge what I owe in Alexandria, &c., and to leave the State (if it shall not be in my power to remain at home in retirement) without doing this, would be exceedingly disagreeable to me." Also he had a foretaste of the bitter cup of politics, in finding it necessary to refuse applicants for offices while still awaiting his election. To one of these requests from Benjamin Harrison, destined to be the ancestor of two Presidents, and who had opposed ratification, he replied: "I will go to the chair under no pre-engagement of any kind or nature whatsoever. But, when in it, I will, to the best of my judgment, discharge the duties of the office with that impartiality and zeal for the public good, which ought never to suffer connections of blood or friendship to intermingle so as to have the least sway on de-

cisions of a public nature. I may err, notwithstanding my most strenuous efforts to execute the difficult trust with fidelity and unexceptionably; but my errors shall be of the head, not of the heart. For all recommendations and appointments, so far as they may depend upon or come from me, a due regard shall be had to the fitness of characters, the pretensions of different candidates, and, so far as is proper, to political consideration. These shall be invariably my governing motives."

INAUGURATION OF WASHINGTON (1789)

April 16, 1789, with feelings, as he wrote Knox, April 1, "not unlike those of a culprit, who is going to the place of his execution," he left Mount Vernon for New York, the temporary capital. The journey was

one long triumphal procession; but according to an entry in a diary which Irving used but which is now lost, he remarked, after describing the crossing to New York and the reception there: "The display . . . filled my mind with sensations as painful (considering the reverse of this scene, which may be the case after all my labor to do good) as they are pleasing." On April 30, on the balcony of the New York City Hall, where now a statue stands before the sub-treasury, at the acme of his popularity though not of his fame, he took the oath: "I will faithfully execute the Office of President of the United States, and will to the best of my Ability, preserve, protect and defend the Constitution of the United States." And the multitude shouted, "Long live George Washington, President of the United States."

Selected Authorities

Birth of the Nation (Old South Leaflets, 5th Series.) Boston, 1887.

CORBIN, JOHN — *Unknown Washington; Biographic Origins of the Republic.* New York, Scribner, 1930.

DELAPLAINE, EDWARD S.—*Life of Thomas Johnson.* New York, Hitchcock, 1927. (Especially chs. xxv-xxvii.)

ELLIOT, JONATHAN, ED.—*Debates in the Several State Conventions on the Adoption of the Federal Constitution.* 2d ed. 5 vols. Philadelphia, Lippincott, 1836-59. (Especially Vols. I, II; debates in Massachusetts, New York, and Virginia.)

FARRAND, MAX—*Framing of the Constitution of the United States.* New Haven, Yale University Press, 1913.

FARRAND, MAX, ED.—*Records of the Federal Convention of 1787.* 3 vols. New Haven, Yale University Press, 1911.

Federalist: a Collection of Essays written in Favour of the New Constitution. 2 vols. New York, 1788. (Various later and specially edited eds.)

FISKE, JOHN—*Critical Period of American History, 1783-1789.* Boston, Houghton Mifflin, 1888.

FORD, PAUL LEICESTER, ED.—*Essays on the Constitution . . . published during its Discussion by the People, 1787-1788.* Brooklyn, 1892.

FORD, PAUL LEICESTER, ED.—*Pamphlets on the Constitution . . . published during its Discussion by the People, 1787-1788.* Brooklyn, 1888.

HARDING, SAMUEL BANNISTER—*Contest over the Ratification of the Federal Constitution in the State of Massachusetts.* New York, Longmans Green, 1896.

HART, ALBERT BUSHNELL, ED.—*American History told by Contemporaries.* Vol. III. New York, Macmillan, 1901. (Especially pt. iv.)

HUNT, GAILLARD—*Life of James Madison.* New York, Doubleday Page, 1902. (Especially chs. x-xvii.)

JAMESON, J. FRANKLIN—"Studies in the History of the Federal Convention of 1787"; in American Historical Association, *Report for 1902*, Vol. I, p. 87.

LODGE, HENRY CABOT—*Alexander Hamilton* (American Statesmen, Library ed.). Boston, Houghton Mifflin, 1898. (Especially ch. iv.)

LODGE, HENRY CABOT—*George Washington* (American Statesmen, Library ed.). 2 vols. Boston, Houghton Mifflin, 1898. (Especially Vol. II, ch. i.)

MCLAUGHLIN, ANDREW CUNNINGHAM—*Confederation and the Constitution*

(American Nation, Vol. X). New York, Harper, 1905.

MINER, CLARENCE EUGENE—*Ratification of the Federal Constitution by the State of New York.* New York, Columbia University, 1921.

OSBORN, LUCRETIA PERRY, ED.—*Washington speaks for Himself.* New York, Scribner, 1927. (Especially chs. vii-viii.)

ROOSEVELT, THEODORE—*Gouverneur Morris* (American Statesmen, Library ed.). Boston, Houghton Mifflin, 1898. (Especially ch. vi.)

SCOTT, JAMES BROWN—*United States of America: a Study in International Organization.* New York, Oxford University Press, 1920. (Especially chs. vii-xv.)

UNITED STATES DEPARTMENT OF STATE, BUREAU OF ROLLS AND LIBRARY, ED.—*Documentary History of the Constitution of the United States.* Vols. IV-V. Washington, Department of State, 1905. (Letters relating to framing of Constitution; also Bibliography.)

WASHINGTON, GEORGE—*Writings.* Ed. by Worthington Chauncey Ford. 14 vols. New York, Putnam, 1889-93. (Especially Vol. XI.)

Washington as President

By Albert Bushnell Hart

Part I

Washington's Domestic Policy (1789-1797)

GEORGE WASHINGTON
From the Edward Savage Portrait

TRADITIONS OF GOVERNMENT

THE colonial tradition of the relation of the executive to the legislative branch was that of opposition and friction; but the royal governors were always between two fires: the British government (which appointed governors for all the colonies except Rhode Island, Connecticut, and the three proprietary colonies), and the colonial legislatures, which were frequently at odds. The whole trend of colonial effort for fifty years before the Revolution was to hedge the governor in as much as possible and to weaken his prestige. From the early charters to the outbreak of the Revolution there was a running fight between the colonial assemblies and the colonial governors.

Hence Washington had little to learn about executive government from the pre-revolutionary experience of the Americans. On the other hand, in all the colonies there was a system of legislative committees exercising or seizing upon executive power.

Upon those committees the organization of the first revolutionary governments was based. The Continental Congress started with a system of standing committees. Later there was a postmaster general and also boards, such as those of war and treasury, with outside officials. Finally, just before the Articles of Confederation became active, departments with single executive heads were provided for the management of foreign, finance, war, and marine affairs, but no secretary for marine was even appointed. This system was not changed by the Articles of Confederation, which merely gave to Congress a general power to "appoint such . . . committees and civil officers as may be necessary for managing the general affairs of the United States under their direction."

The basis of that government in 1789 was modest. The total population was only four millions, of whom 700,000 were negro slaves. The arguments and influence of the leading statesmen, of whom Washington was the chief, brought about the adoption of the Federal Constitution. Up to the going into effect of that Constitution in 1789 there had been no national system of taxation or of commerce or regulation of interstate affairs.

The energies of the new nation were divided between two fields, military and financial. Most of the promising and active young men had gone into the military service and had left their plantations and their businesses behind them. When peace made efforts for private economic recuperation possible, public conditions under the feeble Confederation hampered recovery greatly. The colonies had enjoyed the protection and privileges of the British Acts of Trade, as well as been subjected to the annoyances; but the war had dislocated this normal trend of commerce, and as independent states the colonies were now, under the prevailing mercantile system, cut off from what had previously been their main market. Such great questions as the settlement of the national debt, the provision of a national revenue, the regulation of interstate and foreign commerce, had to be faced and settled after the Constitution went into effect.

FIRST ELECTION OF PRESIDENT
(1788-1789)

In this critical period the whole country turned to George Washington as the most sagacious, most experienced, and ablest man. His views on public questions and the methods of government which he favored, quickly became a part of the history of the United States. During the eight years of his presidency no serious national question arose in which Washington's convictions and decisions were not essential. He was the center of all the great legislation during his presidency; and he had the opportunity to lay down the principles of such vital questions as public revenue, public debt, the civil and criminal law of the federation, the admission of new states, the treatment of the Indians, the system of taxation, the protection of life and property. Though he vetoed but two bills as President, his influence was felt on every important act of Congress. The first of the vetoes, in 1792, was of a bill for the apportionment of representatives, because not in harmony with the constitutional requirement. The second one, at the end of his administration, related to the provision for cavalry in the military establishment. Neither bill was passed over the veto.

As has been shown in the preceding pamphlet, Washington had at first strongly deprecated the idea that he should become the first President; but, as ever, he recognized the call of duty, and when forced to the realization that it was necessary that he should once more emerge from private life, he bent all his energies to his new task. His election was unanimous, and his journey from Mount Vernon to New York was a triumphal tour.

The first inauguration of Washington, April 30, 1789, took place on the portico of the New York City Hall of that period. An official eyewitness of this scene was Senator Maclay, of Pennsylvania, who felt it to be his duty to criticise anything that seemed to him undemocratic.

"The President advanced between the Senate and Representatives, bowing to each. He was placed in the chair by the Vice-President; the Senate with their president on the right, the Speaker and the Representatives on his left. The Vice-President rose and addressed a short sentence to him. The import of it was that he should now take the oath of office as President. He seemed to have forgot half what he was to say, for he made a dead pause and stood for some time, to appearance, in a vacant mood. He finished with a formal bow, and the President was conducted out of the middle window into the gallery, and the oath was administered by the Chancellor. . . .

"As the company returned into the Senate chamber, the President took the chair and the Senators and Representatives their seats. He rose, and all arose also, and addressed them. This great man was agitated and embarrassed more than ever he was by the leveled cannon or pointed musket. He trembled, and several times could scarce make out to read, though it must be supposed he had often read it before. . . . When he came to the words *all the world*, he made a flourish with his right hand, which left rather an ungainly impression. . . . He was dressed in deep brown, with metal buttons, with an eagle on them, white stockings, a bag, and sword."

PRESIDENT WASHINGTON'S SOCIAL LIFE

Washington was a grand gentleman. He had a large property; and though at times short for ready money, as was often the case with landed proprietors, he had a salary which was certainly the largest amount then paid to any man in America for personal services. First in New York and then in Philadelphia he lived in a handsome house (at his own expense) and held formal receptions open to members of Congress and senators, to executive officials, to foreign representatives and to substantial citizens and accredited visitors from overseas. To be a guest at the state dinners was an event to remember and record, as did Senator Maclay as follows:

"Senate adjourned early. At a little after four I called on Mr. Bassett, of the Delaware State. We went to the President's to dinner. . . . The President and Mrs. Washington sat opposite each other in the middle of the table; the two secretaries, one at each end. It was a great dinner, and the best of the kind I ever was at. The room, however, was disagreeably warm. . . .

"It was the most solemn dinner ever I sat at. Not a health drank; scarce a word said until the cloth was taken away. Then the President, filling a glass of wine, with great formality drank to the health of every individual by name round the table. Everybody imitated him, charged glasses, and such a buzz of 'health, sir,' and 'health, madam,' and 'thank you, sir,' and 'thank you, madam,' never had I heard before. Indeed, I had liked to have been thrown out in the hurry; but I got a little wine in my glass, and passed the ceremony. The ladies sat a good while, and the bottles passed about; but there was a dead silence almost. Mrs. Washington at last withdrew with the ladies.

"I expected the men would now begin, but the same stillness remained. The President told of a New England clergyman who had lost a hat and wig in passing a river called the Brunks. He smiled, and everybody else laughed. He now and then said a sentence or two on some common subject, and what he said was not amiss. . . . The President kept a fork in his hand, when the cloth was taken away, I thought for the purpose of picking nuts. He ate no nuts, however, but played with the fork, striking on the edge of the table with it. We did not sit long after the ladies retired. The President rose, went up-stairs to drink coffee; the company followed. I took my hat and came home."

PROBLEMS OF ORGANIZATION
(1789-1793)

Looking back a hundred and forty years the process of putting the machinery of the federal government into action looks simple and easy. We have no verbatim debates of Congress; but the accounts below the surface of the proceedings in both houses of Congress show exceedingly lively discussions. Regular political parties did not develop till after 1793. The necessary machinery of government was easily set in motion. Some of the states had two-house legislatures; and the general principles of parliamentary law and procedure were developed in colonial times. No colony or state, however, ever had formed a legislature of two about equally powerful houses. Deadlocks would have occurred in the new Federal Congress, but for the balance wheel—the President.

One of the most efficient men in Congress, and at first a cordial supporter and friend of the President, was James Madison of Virginia. Congress contained many men of experience. In a few months acts for the executive departments were passed and Washington began not only to require the written opinions of the principal officers, as permitted by the Constitution, but to hold meetings with them in cabinet, which was the origin of this extra-constitutional body. The executive post of most importance was the headship of the department of foreign affairs, which Washington filled with a great Virginian, Thomas Jefferson. Another Virginian, Edmund Randolph, was appointed Attorney General. The important office of Secretary of the Treasury was filled by Alexander Hamilton, a young man, allied by marriage to the wealthy Schuyler family in New York, and a believer in a strong financial system. The War Department was under Henry Knox of Massachusetts, and the Post Office continued under Samuel Osgood of the same state.

Washington's fortunes had suffered much from his eight years' absence as head of the national army. He accepted the salary of $25,000 a year voted by Congress, but appears to have expended more than the amount in maintaining the expenditures incident to the office. Appointments to office included men from every section of the Union, with special pains to search out and bring into the public service men whose qualities he had learned while they were fellow members of the Continental Army. He was responsible for filling up the new Supreme Court, the first important tribunal ruling on the constitutionality of acts of the legislative body in the history of human government.

DEVELOPMENT OF PARTIES
(1793-1797)

No political parties in the modern sense existed in the states during the Revolutionary War. Hence there was no opportunity in the Continental Congress or the Congress of the Confederation to build up an opposition to the body of adherents to the Revolution who were carrying on the war. Washington in his first administration was the only President of the United States who did not have behind him a political party extending through most of the Union.

That inevitable division began to show itself in national affairs about 1793, when there was a deep split between those who wished the United States to take a strong part in favor of France and against Great Britain in the European war that then broke out, and a conservative party which included those who were not willing to go to war on behalf of Great Britain or to break with the French, who a few years earlier had made possible the success of the Revolution. Coincident with this surface manifestation, and antedating it among the leaders, was the division over whether the Constitution should be interpreted along broad or restricted lines.

Two champions appeared as the leading spirits in this party division. Thomas Jefferson of Virginia, Secretary of State in Washington's first Cabinet, was the most talented member in what speedily became the Republican Party, that is, republican in the sense of opposition to aristocracy and royalty. It was nearly forty years later that that party took up the name of Democrat. This was also the party of strict construction. The opposite great party chieftain was Alexander Hamilton, Secretary of the Treasury, recognized as representing what we should now call the financial and commercial interests of the country; and which advocated liberal construction through the doctrine of implied powers. Washington believed in both men. Nevertheless Washington's mind naturally took the same side as Hamilton's on the great questions of giving the nation power over a sufficient revenue to carry on national affairs, and sufficient military and naval power at least to protect itself from invasion. The name adopted by this group was the Federalist Party, the main principles of which were years later taken over by the Whig Party and subsequently by the Republican Party, founded in 1854. Washington strove hard to maintain a neutral attitude between the two early parties; but in the difficulties brought about by the European wars Washington definitely sided with the Federalists. The financial phase of Washington's administration is considered in a later pamphlet of this series.

STABILITY OF THE GOVERNMENT
(1793-1797)

Nothing in Washington's whole life is a stronger evidence of his character and his abilities as a statesman than the serene judgment of men and affairs which he showed in the first political crisis. His reelection as President was an evidence of the confidence of the people; and he needed such confidence inasmuch as the crisis in foreign relations caused by the European war of 1793 tested his popularity and his statesmanship. The French revolutionary government and its diplomatic representative, Citizen Genêt, expected, if not an alliance, at least a strong preference for the French, particularly with regard to French commerce and French captures of British ships by cruisers and privateers. Genêt was not simply a very high tempered diplomat; he was an apostle of a democratic type of government far more extreme and aggressive than any democracy ever known in the United States. He began at once to found and to consult with the so-called democratic clubs formed in various parts of the Union on the model of the French Jacobins. President Washington found a hostile feeling in Philadelphia, although a remark of John Adams to the effect that there was some danger of personal violence to the President is not borne out by the real conditions. Certainly nothing in Washington's own writings indicates that he was afraid of the American people in the streets of an American city. Washington held steadily on his course and his friends and supporters chose John Adams, Vice-President and sharer in Washington's political fortunes, as President from 1797.

Nevertheless the political ordeal was severe and but for the courage and steadfastness of President Washington the federal government could not have been successfully organized. It could not have lived through the excitement of the French Revolution. It could not have weathered the storm and maintained neutrality in the midst of the European War. Or rather it was the confidence of the majority of the voters in the United States that President Washington was an upright, truthful, able, and courageous man that enabled the Republic to weather the storm.

A LIVELY CABINET MEETING (1793)

Jefferson has left an account of a Cabinet episode that brought out the passionate division of opinion within the Cabinet and outside, and indicated his own growing opposition to Washington.

"The President manifestly inclined to the appeal to the people. Knox, in a foolish, incoherent sort of a speech, introduced the pasquinade lately printed, called the funeral of George W-n, and James Wilson, King and Judge, &c., where the President was placed on a guillotine. The President was much inflamed; got into one of those passions when he cannot command himself; ran on much on the personal abuse which had been bestowed on him; defied any man on earth to produce one single act of his since he had been in the government, which was not done on the purest motives; that he had never repented but once the having slipped the moment of resigning his office, and that was every moment since; that *by God* he had rather be in his grave than in his present situation; that he had rather be on his farm than to be made *Emperor of the world;* and yet that they were charging him with wanting to be a King. That that *rascal Freneau* sent him three of his papers every day, as if he thought he would become the distributor of his papers; that he could see in this, nothing but an impudent design to insult him. He ended in this high tone. There was a pause. Some difficulty in resuming our question; it was, however, after a little while, presented again, and he said there seemed to be no necessity for deciding it now; the propositions before agreed on might be put into a train of execution, and perhaps events would show whether the appeal would be necessary or not. He desired we would meet at my office the next day, to consider what should be done with the vessels armed in our ports by Mr. Genet, and their prizes."

THE INDIAN QUESTION (1793-1797)

No statesman of his time had so deep an interest in the problem of the native Indian tribes as Washington. He had been a great figure in the relations of the settlers with the Indians for forty years. He had a name given by the Indians, "Conoctocarius"—destroyer of villages. He was in the thick of the frontier wars from 1754 to 1758. He had some Indians under his command in the Revolution. Washington had large personal holdings of frontier lands which depended for their value on clearing them of Indian claims. Above all, Washington's unflagging interest in the West as the future home of immigrants from the existing eastern states was bound up with the Indian country.

The practice of colonial times, affecting the federal government, was to treat each tribe of Indians as an independent political power capable of making treaties and land cessions that could not be revoked. The new federal government, through the regulation of "common treaties" with the Indian tribes, acclaimed itself the only government that could negotiate boundary treaties with Indians. On the other hand, the federal government had a permanent armed force—though for a long time only a few hundred soldiers—which was the only military protection of the settlers, except their own trained militia.

THE WHISKEY REBELLION (1794)

The western settlements in the states were troublesome and difficult to manage. Pennsylvania beyond the mountains had a crude, Indian fighting, frontier community, acknowledging the supremacy of the state of Pennsylvania—but not much interested in the government of the United States of America. Among the formal measures urged in Congress by Washington and Hamilton was a moderate tax on the manufacture of whiskey; and distilling was a western industry.

In protest an armed body in 1794 around Pittsburgh interrupted the collection of the tax. Washington looked upon this outburst as a direct defiance of the government of the United States. Therefore he called upon the militia of neighboring states to suppress the insurrection, and at the rendezvous at Bedford, Pennsylvania, he gave orders to the 15,000 troops which marched into the disturbed region.

This spirited action broke up the insurrection—there was no fighting, though some men were prosecuted in the civil courts. Washington's own comment on the affair, in a speech to Congress, November 19, 1794, runs as follows: "It has demonstrated, that our prosperity rests on solid foundations; by furnishing an additional proof, that my fellow-citizens understand the true principles of government and liberty; that they feel their inseparable union; that, notwithstanding all the devices, which have been used to sway them from their interest and duty, they are now as ready to maintain the authority of the laws against licentious invasions, as they were to defend their rights. Let them persevere in their affectionate vigilance over that precious depository of American happiness, the Constitution of the United States. Let them cherish it, too, for the sake of those, who, from every clime, are daily seeking a dwelling in our land."

HARMONY OF THE SECTIONS (1796)

Many times during his service as President, and particularly in the Farewell Address of 1796, Washington dwelt upon the reciprocal interest of the sections. For example: "The *North* in an unrestrained intercourse with the *South*, protected by the equal Laws of a common government, finds in the productions of the latter great additional resources of maritime and commercial

enterprise—and precious materials of manufacturing industry. The *South* in the same intercourse, benefiting by the agency of the *North*, sees its agriculture grow and its commerce expand. Turning partly into its own channels the seamen of the *North*, it finds its particular navigation envigorated;—and, while it contributes, in different ways, to nourish and increase the general mass of the national navigation, it looks forward to the protection of a maritime strength to which itself is unequally adapted.—The *East*, in a like intercourse with the *West*, already finds, and in the progressive improvement of interior communications, by land and water, will more and more find, a valuable vent for the commodities which it brings from abroad, or manufactures at home.—The *West* derives from the *East* supplies requisite to its growth and comfort,—and what is perhaps of still greater consequence, it must of necessity owe the *secure* enjoyment of indispensable *outlets* for its own productions to the weight, influence, and the future maritime strength of the Atlantic side of the Union, directed by an indissoluble community of interest, as *one Nation*."

OPENING OF THE WEST (1791-1799)

So long and so bitter was the struggle between the radical and the conservative elements in Congress, in the Cabinet, and in the country at large that it seemed for a time as though the government would break down. Questions arose as to the admission of new states. Besides the thirteen political units previously represented in the Continental Congress and the Congress of the Confederation, several other areas asked admission. Rhode Island completed "the old thirteen" by ratifying the new Constitution in 1790, after which Washington took pains to make a visit to the new member of the Federal Union. The people of the so-called New Hampshire Grants, next west of the state of New Hampshire, were admitted as the state of Vermont in 1791. Virginia consented that the part of Virginia west of

the mountains should be allowed separate organization; and in 1792 the commonwealth of Kentucky was admitted. The West again made a loud call and Tennessee, which until its cession to the federal government in 1790 had been a part of North Carolina, came into the Union in 1796. Thus the number of states was raised to sixteen, each with its two senators and at least one representative in Congress. Among the early western senators was Andrew Jackson of Tennessee, then a backwoodsman who came to be the sixth man to follow Washington into the presidency.

Before 1789 various states had ceded their claims to the region north of the Ohio River, and this had been formed in 1787 into the Northwest Territory. At the time of Washington's death in 1799, the eastern portion of the territory was almost ready to enter the Union as the state of Ohio, thus creating a block of three states which extended from the British possessions of the north to near the Spanish colonies on the south.

These admissions carried out a principle which Washington had long had in his mind, namely, that the West must be a part of the Union on equal terms with the New England, middle, and southern states. Washington, though born and brought up in the oldest English community on the continent of North America, was always a western man, looking toward the Great Lakes and the Mississippi and their control as elements of a great western empire. The rapid development of the Union exactly fitted in with the hopes and expectations of his whole life. It was part of Washington's character that, though naturally interested in trade and commerce across the Atlantic, he believed more than any other statesman of his time in the policy of pushing the frontier, as it had been pushed ever since the earliest colonization. No man of his time had so great an influence as Washington in the expansion of population and of political and social ideas into the West.

Part II

Washington's Foreign Policy (1789-1797)

BASIS OF A NATIONAL POLICY

As in domestic matters, so in the external relations of the United States, the foundations of a national diplomatic policy were laid in the colonial and revolutionary eras. For a century and a half the English colonies were occupied in settling wild North America. They even made some local treaties with neighboring French and Dutch colo-

nies, set on foot military and naval expeditions of their own, and sent envoys to the capitals of non-English colonies. Nevertheless all permanent decisions as to lands, harbors, fisheries, boundaries, and wars by land and sea were made in England by Englishmen.

The one field of local diplomacy was with the Indian tribes, who were fierce enemies, but understood treaties and alliances.

George Washington in 1753 was an early colonial representative sent by the English in America to the Western Indians, as an incidental duty of his mission to the French commandant on the Ohio River, and he gained a knowledge of their character and their customs which was of great use to him during his presidency.

The Revolution gave the first practical experiences to American diplomats—Jay,

Deane, Jefferson, John Adams, and others; but Franklin had been abroad for many years, and the others probably already knew as much so-called international law as most European statesmen. They gained an acquaintance with foreign courts and with the methods of diplomatic intercourse which made possible the treaties of that period. The United States found its strongest friend in France; and through the French officers Washington was brought into close contact with the French point of view.

The two British questions of the debts and the boundary between the United States and Canada were adjusted for the time being while Washington was President. The relations with France resulted from the Revolution of 1789 which in a few years made France a conquering and aggressive power under Napoleon. Spain was an unwelcome neighbor in Louisiana and Florida during Washington's administration; and he was much disturbed by the practice of the North African pirates of capturing and enslaving American sailors. Most of these difficulties were postponed for adjustment by his successors.

PRIMARY OBJECTS OF DIPLOMACY

In the thick of the difficulties caused by the diplomatic representatives of France, in 1793, using the ports of the United States as a basis for naval operations against England, Washington wrote: "I believe it is the sincere wish of United America to have nothing to do with the political intrigues, or the squabbles, of European nations; but, on the contrary, to exchange commodities and live in peace and amity with all the inhabitants of the earth. And this I am persuaded they will do, if rightly it can be done. To administer justice to, and receive it from, every power with whom they are connected will, I hope, be always found the most prominent feature in the administration of this country; and I flatter myself that nothing short of imperious necessity can occasion a breach with any of them. Under such a system, if we are allowed to pursue it, the agriculture and mechanical arts, the wealth and population of these States will increase with that degree of rapidity as to baffle all calculation, and must surpass any idea your Lordship can hitherto have entertained on the occasion."

Again he wrote: "What is to be done in the case of the *Little Sarah* now at Chester? Is the minister of the French Republic to set the acts of this government at defiance *with impunity?* And then threaten the executive with an appeal to the people? What must the world think of such conduct, and of the government of the United States in submitting to it?"

AVOIDING OFFENSE TO OTHER NATIONS (1794)

The coming to the United States of visitors from Europe gave rise to protests from the legations of their home countries which led Washington to express himself on this type of immigration in 1794, as follows: "My wish is, and it is not less my duty as an officer of the republic, to avoid offence to powers with which we are in friendship, by conduct towards their proscribed citizens, which would be disagreeable to them; whilst at the same time these emigrants, if people of a good character, ought to understand, that they will be protected in their persons and property, and will be entitled to all the benefits of our laws. For the rest, they must depend upon their own behavior and the civilities of the citizens at large, who are less restrained by political considerations, than the officers of the government must be."

In 1797, he warned against expecting "disinterested favors of friendship from any nation whatever." Again: "My policy has been and will continue to be . . . friendly terms with but independent of all the nations of the earth; to share in the broils of none; to fulfill our own engagements; to supply the wants and be carrier for them all."

FOREIGN POLICY IN THE FAREWELL ADDRESS (1796)

These principles are carefully stated in the familiar Farewell Address of September 17, 1796: "Observe good faith and justice toward all Nations. Cultivate peace and harmony with all.—Religion and Morality enjoin this conduct; and can it be that good policy does not equally enjoin it?—It will be worthy of a free, enlightened, and, at no distant period, a great nation, to give to mankind the magnanimous and too novel example of a People always guided by an exalted justice and benevolence.—Who can doubt that in the course of time and things, the fruits of such a plan would richly repay any temporary advantages, which might be lost by a steady adherence to it? . . .

"Europe has a set of primary interests, which to us have none, or a very remote relation.—Hence she must be engaged in frequent controversies, the causes of which are essentially foreign to our concerns.—Hence, therefore, it must be unwise in us to implicate ourselves, by artificial ties in the ordinary vicissitudes of her politics, or the ordinary combinations and collisions of her friendships, or enmities.

"Our detached and distant situation invites and enables us to pursue a different course.—If we remain one People, under an efficient government, the period is not far off, when we may defy material injury from external annoyance; when we may take such an attitude as will cause the neutrality we may at any time resolve upon to be scrupulously respected. When beligerent nations, under the impossibility of making acquisitions upon us, will not lightly hazard the giving us provocation; when we may choose peace or war, as our interest guided by our justice shall counsel."

"So, likewise, a passionate attachment of one Nation for another produces a variety of evils.—Sympathy for the favourite nation, facilitating the illusion of an imaginary common interest in cases where no real common interest exists, and infusing into one the enmities of the other, betrays the former into a participation in the quarrels and wars of the latter, without adequate inducement or justification: it leads also to concessions to the favourite Nation of privileges denied to others, which is apt doubly to injure the Nation making the concessions; by unnecessarily parting with what ought to have been retained, and by exciting jealousy, ill will, and a disposition to retaliate, in the parties from whom equal privileges are withheld."

PLACE IN THE FAMILY OF NATIONS (1789-1790)

Much more serious even than the selection of the group of American diplomats, most of whom had seen previous service at foreign courts, was the question of the reception of foreign representatives. The government of the United States was organized just as the government of France was plunged into a crisis by the French Revolution. One of the most difficult episodes in the diplomatic history of the United States was the mission of Genêt, a fiery and uncontrollable representative of the new French Republic, who assumed that the United States was bound by gratitude to take up arms against Great Britain. Nowhere in his whole life was the hardheaded Washington more needed than in the quenching of this firebrand, who was backed up by a broad popular movement and, to some degree, by Thomas Jefferson, Secretary of State. Washington held that the United States of America had become a part of a family of nations and could not ally itself with any of the European powers, and was in no condition to risk its existence by ranging itself along fiery France or eager Great Britain. Washington thus laid the corner stone of the American diplomacy of the succeeding century and a half, under which the United States refused to be a party to European wars until it felt itself attacked in 1917. Washington's appeal to his countrymen, particularly in his Farewell Address of 1796, was to keep out of disputes between other nations and to preserve their own republic if attacked.

AUTHORITY OF THE PRESIDENT

The Federal Constitution for the first time established a definite and continuous authority over foreign relations through the express power of the President to appoint diplomatic representatives and to instruct them as to the bases of treaties, subject to ratification of the eventual document by a two-thirds vote of the Senate. Several of the American diplomats of the war period entered the new public service, Thomas Jefferson, John Adams, John Jay, and others; and the treaties already made with England, France, Holland, and Prussia continued in force. Otherwise it was necessary for Washington to build up a diplomatic service; and still more important to decide what should be the attitude of the United States towards foreign nations.

JAY TREATY (1794)

One of the great services of Washington was to extend the diplomatic intercourse with other nations; and to settle, by means of the Jay Treaty, most of the vexatious questions left open with Great Britain by the treaty of peace of 1783. The Jay Treaty provided for the relinquishment of the western posts which the British continued to occupy, for an arbitration of the British debts, and also for a settlement of the disputed northeastern boundary of the United States. The treaty, the first commercial one with Great Britain, was not very satisfactory to the Americans, especially as regards neutral trade and trade with the British West Indies; but it was all that England was willing to grant, and it gave to the United States the peace with honor which was at that time so necessary to its own secure establishment.

Washington diagnosed clearly from the beginning that the trade and good will of England was essential to the prosperity of his country. He was strong for settling the debts with English merchants which were outstanding at the beginning of the Revolution, and therefore remarked: "With respect to British debts, I would feign hope, let the eloquence or abilities of any man or set of men be what they may, that the good sense and justice of this State will never suffer a violation of the treaty or pass acts of injustice to individuals. Honesty in States, as well as individuals, will ever be found the soundest policy."

NAVIGATION OF THE MISSISSIPPI RIVER

Washington felt a keen interest in the control of the mouth of the Mississippi. In the years immediately following the war, when he was especially interested in the development of the Potomac River navigation as a means of directing western commerce to the Atlantic shore, he had considered that while Spain's policy in closing the navigation of the river was impolitic, it gave a favorable opportunity for attaching the West to the Union by commercial ties. As President, however, he had come to realize that the free navigation of the Mississippi was of primary importance. It was during his second administration that the United States, taking advantage of the conditions in Europe which led Spain to desire peace in the New World, was able in 1795 to negotiate the treaty of San Lorenzo, by which Spain agreed to the northern boundary of West Florida which the United States claimed, opened the navigation of the lower portion of the Mississippi, where Spain controlled both sides of the river, and also granted a place of deposit at New Orleans.

The British and Spanish treaties strengthened the Union in the West.

QUALIFICATIONS OF A FOREIGN MINISTER

Washington records very early in his first administration a discussion of a confidential character on several persons available for foreign appointments. "Mr. Madison took his leave to-day. He saw no impropriety in my trip to the eastward; but with respect to the private agent to ascertain the disposition of the British Court with respect to the Western Posts and a Commercial treaty, he thought if the necessity did not press, it would be better to wait the arrival of Mr. Jefferson, who might be able to give the information wanted on this head—and with me thought that if Mr. Gouv'r Morris was employed in this business, it would be a commitment for his appointment as Minister, if one should be sent to that Court, or wanted at Versailles in place of Mr. Jefferson, and moreover if either of these was his wish, whether his representations might not be made with an eye to it. He thought with Colo. Hamilton, and as Mr. Jay also does, that Mr. Morris is a man of superior talents—but with the latter that his imagination sometimes runs ahead of his judgment—that his manners before he is known, and where known, had created opinions of himself that were not favourable to him, and which he did not merit."

COURTESIES TO DIPLOMATS (1790)

One of the amusing features of the new diplomatic corps was the solemn conferences between the President of the United States and his advisors over a presentation medal to retiring diplomatic representatives accredited to the United States. Washington's diary thus states the issue: "Fixed with the Secretary of State on the present which (according to the custom of other Nations) should be made to Diplomatic characters when they return from that employment in this Country—and this was a gold Medal, suspended to a gold Chain—in ordinary to be of the value of about 120 or 130 Guineas—Upon enquiry into the practice of other Countries, it was found, that France generally gave a gold Snuff-box set with diamonds; and of differt. costs; to the amount, *generally*, to a Minister Plenipotentiary of 500 Louisdores—That England usually gave to the same grade 300 guineas in *Specie*—and Holld. a Medal and Chain of the value of in common, 150 or 180 guineas the value of which to be encreased by an additional weight in the chain when they wished to mark a distinguished character. The Reason why a Medal and Chain was fixed upon for the American present, is, that the die being once made the Medals could at any time be struck at very little cost and the chain made by our artisans, which (while the first should be retained as a memento) might be converted into Cash."

TREATY MAKING AND THE SENATE (1789)

In 1789 Washington, in the consideration of an Indian treaty, presented to the Senate the problem of the "advice and consent," which the Constitution enjoined upon that body: "It doubtless is important that all treaties and compacts formed by the United States with other nations, whether civilized or not, should be made with caution and executed with fidelity.

"It is said to be the general understanding and practice of nations, as a check on the mistakes and indiscretions of ministers or commissioners, not to consider any treaty negotiated and signed by such officers as final and conclusive until ratified by the sovereign or government from whom they derive their powers. This practice has been adopted by the United States respecting their treaties with European nations, and I am inclined to think it would be advisable to observe it in the conduct of our treaties with the Indians; . . . It strikes me that this point should be well considered and settled, so that our national proceedings in this respect may become uniform and be directed by fixed and stable principles. . . .

"You have, indeed, advised me 'to execute and enjoin an observance of' the treaty with the Wyandottes, etc. You, gentlemen, doubtless intended to be clear and explicit, and yet, without further explanation, I fear I may misunderstand your meaning, for if by my executing that treaty you mean that I should make it (in a more particular and immediate manner than it now is) the act of Government, then it follows that I am to ratify it. If you mean by my executing it that I am to see that it be carried into effect and operation, then I am led to conclude either that you consider it as being perfect and obligatory in its present state, and therefore to be executed and observed, or that you consider it as to derive its completion and obligation from the silent approbation and ratification which my proclamation may be construed to imply."

RELATION OF THE HOUSE OF REPRESENTATIVES TO TREATIES (1796)

On the important question of the ultimate treaty power, Washington had very clear views which he thus expressed:

"Having been a member of the General Convention, and knowing the principles on which the Constitution was formed, I have ever entertained but one opinion on this subject; and from the first establishment of the Government to this moment my conduct has exemplified that opinion—that the power of making treaties is exclusively vested in the President, by and with the advice and consent of the Senate, provided two-thirds of the Senators present concur; and that every treaty so made and promulgated thenceforward became the law of the land.

It is thus that the treaty-making power has been understood by foreign nations, and in all the treaties made with them we have declared and they have believed that, when ratified by the President, with the advice and consent of the Senate, they became obligatory. In this construction of the Constitution every House of Representatives has heretofore acquiesced, and until the present time not a doubt or suspicion has appeared, to my knowledge, that this construction was not the true one. Nay, they have more than acquiesced; for till now, without controverting the obligation of such treaties they have made all the requisite provisions for carrying them into effect."

BOUNDARY DIFFICULTIES
(1783-1789)

To most foreign powers—which then meant only European powers—the United States of America in 1789 stood on about the footing of the present South African Free State toward Europe. It was a vigorous small country with great resources, a small population, far distant from the world centers of power and military might. The only neighboring possessions of European settlers at that time were English Canada, Spanish Louisiana, Spanish Florida, and the various West Indian Islands. It is hard now to realize this isolation from civilization of the American people back of the coast.

Nevertheless many forces were at work to draw the new little federal republic into the circles of European interests. The first of these was the transfer of Canada and the French colonies on the Atlantic coast to Great Britain in 1763. The "habitans" of French race and speech had no mind to be incorporated in the Protestant United States of America. The Great Lakes boundary as drawn by the treaty of peace in 1783 was very easy to lay out. Washington divined the significance of that line and also foresaw the establishment of a western center of trade for the United States. His engineer's eye saw the future importance of the Lakes; and he actually sketched an overland route from Virginia to the present Cleveland, and thence by water to Detroit.

The treaty of 1783 dealt also with a northeastern frontier little known in detail, and very soon after the Revolution a serious difficulty came to the front regarding the boundary line between Maine (till 1820 a part of Massachusetts) and New Brunswick—a province said to be named for New Brunswick, New Jersey. That line caused an international difficulty which was not settled till 1842, and which kept alive a resentful feeling toward Great Britain, though, as stated above, the solving of the problem was begun under the Jay Treaty.

EFFECT OF WAR IN EUROPE
(1793-1797)

Just as Washington was stepping into the presidency came the appalling French Revolution which did its best to draw the United States into war with England. Speedily followed the Terror, the destruction of royal government in France—the excesses of the Terror and the Jacobins. In 1794 the forces of order rallied and in a street fight in Paris in 1795 a young artillery officer named Bonaparte stood by the established government. Neither Washington nor anybody else in America foresaw the establishment of a French Empire.

The outbreak of the European war brought Washington face to face with the issue of neutrality. France claimed special international privileges under the treaty of alliance of 1778. President Washington took the safe and reasonable ground that the United States was the ally of neither party in the European wars.

PRINCIPLES OF NEUTRALITY
(1793-1796)

On all these great questions of international responsibility Washington was in council with such men as John Adams and John Jay and Thomas Jefferson, skilled diplomats and experts in international law. Upon such councils was based his message of December 3, 1793. "As soon as the war in Europe had embraced those powers with whom the United States have the most extensive relations there was reason to apprehend that our intercourse with them might be interrupted and our disposition for peace drawn into question by the suspicions too often entertained by belligerent nations. It seems, therefore, to be my duty to admonish our citizens of the consequences of a contraband trade and of hostile acts to any of the parties, and to obtain by a declaration of the existing legal state of things an easier admission of our right to the immunities belonging to our situation. Under these impressions the proclamation which will be laid before you was issued.

"In this posture of affairs, both new and delicate, I resolved to adopt general rules which should conform to the treaties and assert the privileges of the United States. These were reduced into a system, which will be communicated to you. Although I have not thought myself at liberty to forbid the sale of the prizes permitted by our treaty of commerce with France to be brought into our ports, I have not refused to cause them to be restored when they were taken within the protection of our territory, or by vessels commissioned or equipped in a warlike form within the limits of the United States. It rests with the wisdom of Congress to correct, improve, or enforce this plan of procedure.

"Where individuals shall, within the United States, array themselves in hostility against any of the powers at war, or enter upon military expeditions or enterprises within the jurisdiction of the United States, or usurp and exercise judicial authority within the United States, or where the penalties on violations of the law of nations may have been indistinctly marked, or are inadequate—these offenses can not receive too early and close an attention, and require prompt and decisive remedies."

WASHINGTON'S QUERIES ON NEUTRALITY (1793)

On this basis Washington stood firm in refusing the demand of Genêt that not only should the prizes captured by French vessels be brought into United States ports, which Washington acknowledged was a right under the treaty with France, but also that United States should become a place for fitting out expeditions against the British, and that captures made by such expeditions or those made within territorial waters of the United States should also be brought within the treaty privilege. Even Jefferson, who was far more sympathetic than Washington with the French, considered Genet's demands excessive.

The significance of the issue well appears in a list of questions which Washington sent to his Cabinet. The whole theory and practice of modern neutrality is involved.

"I. Shall a proclamation issue for the purpose of preventing interferences of the citizens of the United States in the war between France and Great Britain, &c.? Shall it contain a declaration of neutrality or not? What shall it contain?

"II. Shall a minister from the Republic of France be received?

"III. If received, shall it be absolutely or with qualifications; and, if with qualifications, of what kind?

"IV. Are the United States obliged by good faith to consider the treaties heretofore made with France as applying to the present situation of the parties? May they either renounce them, or hold them suspended till the government of France shall be *established*?

"V. If they have the right, is it expedient to do either, and which?

"VI. If they have an option, would it be a breach of neutrality to consider the treaties still in operation?

"VII. If the treaties are to be considered as now in operation, is the guarantee in the treaties of alliance applicable to a defensive war only, or to war either offensive or defensive?

"VIII. Does the war in which France is engaged appear to be offensive or defensive on her part? Or of a mixed and equivocal character?

"IX. If of a mixed and equivocal character, does the guarantee in any event apply to such a war?

"X. What is the effect of a guarantee such as that to be found in the treaty of alliance between the United States and France?

"XI. Does any particle in either of the treaties prevent ships of war, other than privateers, of the powers opposed to France from coming into the ports of the United States to act as convoys of their own merchantmen. Or does it lay any other restraint upon them more than would apply to the ships of war of France?

"XII. Should the future regent of France send a minister to the United States, ought he to be received?

"XIII. Is it necessary or advisable to call together the two houses of Congress, with a view to the present posture of European affairs? If it is, what should be the *particular* object of such a call?"

POLICY OF NEUTRALITY (1793)

The outcome proved how wise Washington was in this policy of insisting upon our rights as an independent nation, of standing by our treaties, for preventing aggressions by Americans on the territorial rights of other nations. His policy of neutrality saved his country from being tangled in the Napoleonic Wars and eventually perhaps from suffering invasion. He always advocated good temper and moderation in our diplomacy, and stood by his constitutional right as a President to direct the diplomacy of the country, subject to the right of the Senate to ratify treaties by a two-thirds vote. His foreign policy is summed up in a letter to his Secretary of State, Randolph, in 1794:

"My objects are, to prevent a war, if justice can be obtained by fair and strong representations (to be made by a special envoy) of the injuries which this country has sustained from Great Britain in various ways, to put it into a complete state of military defence, and to provide *eventually* for such measures, as seem to be now pending in Congress for execution, if negotiation in a reasonable time proves unsuccessful."

Also in 1796 he wrote James Monroe, whom he was about to supersede because of Francophilism: "I have always given it as my decided opinion, that no nation had a right to intermeddle in the internal concerns of another; that every one had a right to form and adopt whatever government they liked best to live under themselves; and that, if this country could, consistently with its engagements, maintain a strict neutrality and thereby preserve peace, it was bound to do so by motives of policy, interest, and every other consideration, that ought to actuate a people situated and circumstanced as we are, already deeply in debt, and in a convalescent state from the struggle we have been engaged in ourselves."

FRIENDLY TERMS WITH ALL NATIONS (1796)

Similarly in 1795 he wrote Gouverneur Morris, Monroe's predecessor: ". . . sure I am, if this country is preserved in tranquillity twenty years longer, it may bid defiance in a just cause to any power whatever; such in that time will be its population, wealth, and resources. . . . a liberal [British] policy will be one of the most effectual means of deriving advantages to their trade and manufactures from the people of the United States, and will contribute, more than any-

thing else, to obliterate the impressions, which have been made by their late conduct towards us."

The same sentiment is in his Farewell Address in 1796: "In the execution of such a plan nothing is more essential than that permanent, inveterate antipathies against particular nations and passionate attachments for others should be excluded; and that in place of them just and amicable feelings toward all should be cultivated.— The Nation, which indulges toward another an habitual hatred or an habitual fondness, is in some degree a slave. It is a slave to its animosity or to its affection, either of which is sufficient to lead it astray from its duty and its interest. Antipathy in one nation against another disposes each more readily to offer insult and injury, to lay hold of slight causes of umbrage, and to be haughty and intractable, when accidental or trifling occasions of dispute occur."

NO PERMANENT ALLIANCES (1796)

Washington's treaty of arbitration with Great Britain led him into a settlement of the boundary between Maine and Canada. He was greatly interested in the Mississippi question which was settled within four years after his death by the annexation of Louisiana. He had a hand in the construction of the first ships of war built by the United States under the Constitution. He began a long and heartbreaking negotiation with the Barbary powers for the freedom of Americans who had been made slaves by those pirate countries.

Washington's ideas as to foreign relations were the same from the beginning of the Revolution to the end of his life twenty-four years later. As general of the armies he urged that temporary alliance with France which made independence possible. As President he declined to consider that the alliance of 1778 with France bound the United States to make war on Great Britain. As head of the diplomatic service he obtained commercial treaties and agreements with Great Britain and Spain, and opened the way for the later development of American commercial relations.

In his Farewell Address of 1796 he laid down the basis of the relation of the United States and foreign countries in unforgettable phrases: "Against the insidious wiles of foreign influence, I conjure you to believe me, fellow-citizens, the jealousy of a free people ought to be *constantly* awake, since history and experience prove that foreign influence is one of the most baneful foes of republican Government. . . .

"The great rule of conduct for us, in regard to foreign Nations, is, in extending our commercial relations, to have with them as little *Political* connection as possible.—So far as we have already formed engagements, let them be fulfilled with perfect good faith.—Here let us stop."

PREPAREDNESS (1782, 1793)

Preparedness was always an essential part of Washington's foreign policy. His attitude is shown by a letter written to McHenry in 1782, when it was a question whether peace would come without further fighting: "If we are wise, let us prepare for the worst. There is nothing, which will so soon produce a speedy and honorable peace, as a state of preparation for war; and we must either do this, or lay our account for a patched up inglorious peace, after all the toil, blood, and treasure we have spent."

Being criticised for insisting upon a well-organized militia, Washington defined his policy as follows: "Nor can such arrangements, with such objects, be exposed to the censure or jealousy of the warmest friends of republican government. They are incapable of abuse in the hands of the militia, who ought to possess a pride in being the depository of the force of the Republic, and may be trained to a degree of energy equal to every military exigency of the United States. But it is an inquiry which can not be too solemnly pursued, whether the act 'more effectually to provide for the national defense by establishing an uniform militia throughout the United States' has organized them so as to produce their full effect."

Upon national defense Washington said in 1793: "I can not recommend to your notice measures for the fulfillment of our duties to the rest of the world without again pressing upon you the necessity of placing ourselves in a condition of complete defense and of exacting from them the fulfillment of their duties toward us. The United States ought not to indulge a persuasion that, contrary to the order of human events, they will forever keep at a distance those painful appeals to arms with which the history of every other nation abounds. There is a rank due to the United States among nations which will be withheld, if not absolutely lost, by the reputation of weakness. If we desire to avoid insult, we must be able to repel it; if we desire to secure peace, one of the most powerful instruments of our rising prosperity, it must be known, that we are at all times ready for war."

MILITARY ACADEMY (1796)

Military preparation included the intensive training of officers for the small standing army, and in his last annual address to Congress Washington said: "The institution of a military academy is also recommended by cogent reasons. However pacific the general policy of a nation may be, it ought never to be without an adequate stock of military knowledge for emergencies. The first would impair the energy of its character, and both would hazard its safety, or expose it to greater evils when war could not be avoided. Besides that war might often not depend upon its own choice. In proportion as the observance of pacific maxims might exempt a nation from the necessity of practising the rules of the military art, ought to be its care in preserving and transmitting, by proper establishments, the knowledge of that art. . . . [We know] that the art of war is at once comprehensive and complicated; that it demands much previous study; and that the possession of it, in its most improved and perfect state, is always of great moment to the security of a nation. This, therefore, ought to be a serious care of every government; and for this purpose, an academy, where a regular course of instruction is given, is an obvious expedient, which different nations have successfully employed."

COMBINATIONS OF NATIONS

Since the World War of 1914-1918 and the formation of a League of Nations in 1919, some efforts have been made to show that President Washington had in his mind something resembling that form of international organizations. Though alliances and military leagues abounded throughout the eighteenth century, nothing approaching a league of nations to act in time of peace was put into effect.

His unwillingness to venture the future of the United States on any combination of states is shown by a remark in 1793: "All our late accounts from Europe hold up the expectation of a general war in that quarter. . . . I ardently wish we may not be forced into it by the conduct of other nations. If we are permitted to improve without interruption the great advantages, which nature and circumstances have placed within our reach, many years will not revolve before we may be ranked not only among the most respectable, but among the happiest people on this globe."

After retirement from the presidency he wrote to a friend: "No policy, in my opinion, can be more clearly demonstrated, than that we should do justice to all, and have no political connexion with any of the European powers beyond those, which result from and serve to regulate our commerce with them. Our own experience, if it has not already had this effect, will soon convince us, that the idea of disinterested favors or friendship from any nation whatever is too novel to be calculated on, and there will always be found a wide difference between the words and actions of any of them."

PERMANENT WORLD PEACE

Washington's most striking remark on permanent world peace was made in 1786 to Lafayette: "Although I pretend to no peculiar information respecting commercial affairs, nor any foresight into the scenes of futurity, yet, as the member of an infant empire, as a philanthropist by character, and, (if I may be allowed the expression,) as a citizen of the great republic of humanity at large, I cannot help turning my attention sometimes to this subject. I would be understood to mean, I cannot avoid reflecting with pleasure on the probable influence, that commerce may hereafter have on human manners and society in general. On these occasions I consider how mankind may be connected like one great family in fraternal ties. I indulge a fond, perhaps an enthusiastic idea, that, as the world is evidently much less barbarous than it has been, its melioration must still be progressive; that nations are becoming more humanized in their policy, that the subjects of ambition and causes for hostility are daily diminishing; and, in fine, that the period is not very remote, when the benefits of a liberal and free commerce will pretty generally succeed to the devastations and horrors of war."

Valiantly he strove in the succeeding years of his presidency for peace abroad as well as progress at home, for "a General Peace" which he did not live to witness. He laid deeply and broadly the foundations of domestic and foreign policy upon which his country has become a world power which, more than any other great nation, stands for permanent peace.

Part III

Significant Events in the Public Life of George Washington
(1749-1799)

1749, July 20—Official surveyor of Culpeper County, Va., through examination and commission of William and Mary College.

1752, November 6—Appointed an Adjutant General of Virginia with rank of major; assigned to northern district November, 1753.

1753, October 31-1754, January 16—Takes Governor Dinwiddie's letter demanding that the French withdraw from the Ohio country, to Le Gardeur de St. Pierre, French commandant "on the Ohio," at Fort Le Boeuf (near Waterford, Pa.), and returns with reply. Perilous frontier journey.

1754, April 2—Begins march as Lieutenant Colonel of Virginia Regiment to reinforce and complete the fort at Forks of the Ohio (Pittsburgh).

May 28—Attacks French detachment under Jumonville; kills leader; beginning of French and Indian War.

May 30—Throws up a rude fort, Fort Necessity, in Great Meadow, Fayette Co., Pa.

June 4—Notice of appointment as Colonel on death of Colonel Fry, his superior officer.

July 3—Surrenders to French detachment at Fort Necessity, and under terms of capitulation begins march back to Virginia the next day.

October—Resigns his commission as Colonel of Virginia Regiment; question of rank involved.

1755, April 23—Leaves Mount Vernon to join General Braddock's forces at Fort Cumberland, as volunteer aide on general's staff; appointment announced on May 10.

July 9—Defeat of Braddock's army at the Monongahela; Washington active in withdrawing the remnant to Fort Cumberland.

August 14 — Commissioned Colonel and Commander-in-Chief of the Virginia forces for protection of the frontier against Indians and French.

1756, February 4-March 23—Trip to Boston to have Shirley decide question of rank in relation to a captain of Maryland militia who has a minor royal commission.

1757, February 13-April 1—Trip to Philadelphia to attend conference Loudoun has called of governors of southern colonies.

1758, June 24—Begins his march from Fort Loudoun (Winchester) to join the Forbes expedition against Fort Duquesne.

July 24—Elected to House of Burgesses (in his absence) from Frederick County.

November 25—Forbes's army occupies site of Fort Duquesne, French having destroyed the fort and retreated the day before. Washington resigns militray commission soon after.

1759, January 6—Married to Martha (Dandridge) Custis, a wealthy widow.

February 22—Attends House of Burgesses as representative of Frederick County. Continues as Burgess from Frederick County, and after 1765 from Fairfax County, until he goes to the Continental Congress in 1774.

1769, May 16—Votes with other Burgesses in unanimous adoption of Virginia Resolves; Governor dissolves them.

May 17.—Meets with other Burgesses at Raleigh Tavern, Williamsburg, to formulate the Virginia Non-importation Association, which he signs next day.

1770, October 5-December 1—Trip to and down the Ohio, and up the Great Kanawha, to select land for the grant to the officers of the First Virginia Regiment for their service in 1754.

1772, April 11—Virginia act for the improvement of the Potomac. Washington active in the promotion, but the Revolution interrupts all plans.

1773, March 12—The Burgesses appoint an intercolonial committee of correspondence.

May 10-June 8—Trip to New York to place stepson Custis in King's College. Dines with several governors and has intercourse with other prominent men along the way.

1774, May 24—Burgesses appoint a day of fasting because of the Boston Port Bill, and on being dissolved next day meet at Raleign Tavern and renew the Non-importation Association, and suggest the calling of an intercolonial congress.

May 31—Attends a further deliberation of twenty-five Burgesses that results in a call for Burgesses to meet in a Provincial Convention on August 1.

July 18—Presides over Fairfax County mass meeting, which adopts the Fairfax County Resolves; member of Committee of Safety.

August 1-6—Attends the Virginia Provincial Convention at Williamsburg; elected a delegate to the (First) Continental Congress.

September 5-October 26 — Attends Continental Congress at Philadelphia.

1775, March 20-27—Attends at Richmond the Second Provincial Convention; is again elected to Continental Congress.

May 10-June 22—Attends (Second) Continental Congress at Philadelphia; appointed to various military and financial committees.

June 15—Elected by Congress as General and Commander-in-Chief of the Army of the United Colonies;

accepts June 16; commissioned June 19.

June 23-July 2—Journey to the army before Boston. Battle of Bunker Hill has occurred June 17.

July 3—Takes command at Cambridge.

1776, January 18—Arrival of Knox at camp with train of artillery from Fort Ticonderoga.

March 4—Dorchester Heights fortified.

March 17—British evacuate Boston.

April 4-13—Journey to New York, where a British attack is expected; adequate preparations not possible, but defense of the city required for political reasons.

May 23-June 5—At Philadelphia in consultation with Congress on plan of campaign.

June 29—British forces arrive before New York.

August 27—Battle of Long Island; followed by American retreat to New York City.

September 13—Skirmish at Kips Bay and evacuation of New York City.

October 21 — Headquarters moved from Harlem Heights to Westchester County; White Plains, October 23.

October 28—Battle of White Plains.

November 16—Surrender of Fort Washington, followed November 21 by abandonment of Fort Lee on western side of the Hudson, and beginning of the retreat across New Jersey.

December 8—Army crosses into Pennsylvania.

December 25-26—Recrossing of Delaware River and Battle of Trenton.

1777, January 2—Battle of the Assanpink.

January 3—Battle of Princeton, followed by advance across New Jersey and establishment of winter quarters at Morristown, January 6.

May 29-July 3—Headquarters at Middlebrook, N. J.

July 3—Army prepares to follow Howe either northward or southward.

July 31—Army crosses into Pennsylvania as Howe has gone southward.

August 2-4—At Philadelphia in consultation with Congress.

August 25—British army begins to debark at Head of Elk, Chesapeake Bay.

September 11—Battle of Brandywine.

September 26—British occupy Philadelphia.

October 4—Battle of Germantown.

October 17—Surrender of Burgoyne to Gates at Saratoga.

November 9—Letter to Conway on the Cabal.

December 19—Army goes into winter quarters at Valley Forge.

1778, May 6—Announces French alliance to army.

June 18—British evacuate Philadelphia, retire across New Jersey, Washington in pursuit.

June 28—Battle of Monmouth.

July 20—British and American armies in about the same position as before the battle of White Plains. No major movements by either army until 1781.

December 11-June 3, 1779—Winter quarters at Middlebrook.

December 22 to February 2, 1779—Washington in Philadelphia.

1780, July 10—French fleet and army under Rochambeau arrive off Newport, R. I.

September 21 - 22 — Conference at Hartford, Conn., with Rochambeau and Admiral de Ternay.

December 6 to June 25, 1781—Winter quarters at New Windsor, N. Y.

1781, March 6-13—At Newport in consultation with the French.

May 19-24—At Weathersfield, Conn., in consultation with Rochambeau, planning ostensible attack against New York.

July 6—Junction of American and French armies at Phillipsburg, N. Y., but plan to attack New York not carried out.

August — Cornwallis's British army following a Virginia campaign with Lafayette and Steuben, takes post at Yorktown.

August 14 — Washington receives word of Comte de Grasse's fleet being intended for Chesapeake Bay.

August 19—Washington's and Rochambeau's armies begin the march to Virginia.

September 5—De Grasse prevents the British fleet under Graves from relieving Cornwallis.

September 28—Siege of Yorktown begins.

October 19—Surrender of Yorktown; American army returns to the Hudson, but the French remain in Virginia until the latter part of 1782, when most of them march to Boston and embark.

November 26-1782, March 22—At Philadelphia.

1782, May 22—Washington rejects a suggestion of kingship.

July 14-24—At Philadelphia, with Rochambeau.

July 27-1783, August 18—Headquarters at Newburgh, N. Y.

1783, March 15—Reply to the Newburgh Addresses; blocks direct action on grievances.

April 19—Cessation of hostilities.

May 8—Dines on a British warship with Carleton, after a conference; saluted with seventeen guns on departure, as high official of an independent nation.

June 8—Circular letter to the governors of the states on political situation.

June 19—Elected President General of the newly organized military Society of the Cincinnati.

July 18-August 5—Makes a tour with Gov. Clinton through the Lake Champlain and Mohawk regions.

August 25-November 9—Headquarters at Rocky Hill, N. J.; to be near Congress, then at Princeton.

November 2—Farewell Orders to the armies.

November 25—Reoccupies New York City on British evacuation.

December 4—Takes leave of his officers at Fraunces' Tavern, New York City.

December 23—Surrenders his commission of Commander-in-Chief to Congress at Annapolis.

December 24—Reaches Mount Vernon to resume private life.

1784, May 4-18—Attends first general meeting of the Cincinnati at Philadelphia.

September 1-October 4—Tour of his lands beyond the Alleghanies. Because of Indian conditions does not go down the Ohio; makes inquiries and observations respecting the interlocking of branch headwaters of Potomac and Ohio and the possibility of improvements and uniting roads.

December 20-29 — Conference with committee of the Maryland Legislature as Virginia representative at Annapolis on Potomac improvement agreement.

1785, January 5—Virginia act to incorporate the Potomac Company; organization effected May 17 with Washington as president; operations begin soon after and Washington makes many inspections.

October 6—Washington has first sitting for Houdon bust.

1787, May 25—Federal Convention meets at Philadelphia; Washington, a Virginia delegate, elected president.

September 17 — Draft Constitution signed; Convention adjourns.

1788, June 26—Constitution ratified by Virginia; strong influence of Washington.

1789, February 4—Electoral vote for President; Washington the unanimous choice; notified of election April 14.

April 16-23—Triumphal journey to New York; on arrival occupies executive mansion already prepared for him.

April 30—Inauguration as President.

June 1—Signs first act of Congress.

August 25—Death of mother at Fredericksburg, Va.

September 26—Appointment of head executive officers completed, forming what came to be the Cabinet; but Jefferson as Secretary of State does not assume office until March, 1790.

October 15-November 13—Tour of New England states (except Rhode Island and Vermont, neither being yet a member of the new federal government).

1790, February 23—Moves to second executive mansion in New York.

April 20-24—Tour of Long Island.

July 16—Signs act for the permanent federal capital on the Potomac; Washington to appoint commissioners and have an oversight in deciding on exact location of district, laying out of city, and selection of sites of public buildings. He is active in this work during his two administrations.

August 15-22—Visits Rhode Island via Long Island Sound, that state having finally ratified the Constitution.

August 30—Leaves New York for Philadelphia, the new temporary capital.

1791, March 28-30—At Georgetown; examines surveys and L'Enfant's plans on location of federal capital.

March 30—Proclaims the boundary lines of the District.

April 7-June 12—Tour of the Southern States.

1792, April 5—First of Washington's two vetoes of acts of Congress; on apportionment of representation.

December 5—Electoral votes cast; Washington unanimously reëlected President.

1793, March 4—Second inauguration.

April 22—Proclamation of neutrality in war between France and Great Britain.

May 18—Receives Genêt as French Minister.

August 1—Cabinet meeting; decision to request Genêt's recall.

September 18—Lays cornerstone of Federal Capitol at city of Washington.

December 31—Jefferson resigns and becomes leader of opposition to the administration.

1794, April 16—Nominates Jay as special minister to negotiate treaty with England; final attempt to avoid war over neutral rights and frontier posts.

August 7—Proclamation on insurrection in western Pennsylvania against excise tax; so-called Whiskey Rebellion.

September 2—Calls out the militia of several states against the insurgents.

September 30-October 27—Journey to Bedford, Pa.; rendezvous of the militia; orders the advance over the mountains to begin on October 23.

November 19—Annual message, in which he denounces the Democratic "self-created" societies.

1795, June 8—Submits Jay Treaty to the Senate in special session.

July 10—Proclamation of amnesty for Western insurgents.

August 18—Ratifies Jay Treaty.

1796, March 3—Ratifies Spanish treaty of San Lorenzo.

March 30—Refuses House request for Jay Treaty papers.

September 17—Issues Farewell Address to people of the United States; it first appeared in Claypoole's (Philadelphia) *American Daily Advertiser*, September 19.

1797, February 28 — Washington's second veto; on military establishment.

March 4—Attends inauguration of John Adams, his successor.

March 9-15—Journey to Mount Vernon where he resumes life of active farmer.

1798, July 4—Appointed Lieutenant General and Commander-in-Chief of the armies for threatened French war; accepts, July 13, with a reservation as to field service.

November 5-December 19—Trip to Philadelphia for consultation on military matters; his last extensive journey from Mount Vernon.

1799, December 12—Takes last ride out to his farms; catches cold, develops quinsy.

December 14—Dies in his room at Mount Vernon.

December 18—Buried in the family vault.

Selected Authorities

BAKER, WILLIAM SPOHN — *Washington after the Revolution.* Philadelphia, Lippincott, 1898.

BASSETT, JOHN SPENCER—*Federalist System, 1789-1801 (American Nation,* Vol. XI). New York, Harper, 1906.

BEARD, CHARLES A.—*Economic Origins of Jeffersonian Democracy.* New York, Macmillan, 1915.

BEMIS, SAMUEL FLAGG, ED.—*American Secretaries of State and their Diplomacy.* Vol. II. New York, Knopf, 1927.

BEMIS, SAMUEL FLAGG—*Jay's Treaty; a Study of Commerce and Diplomacy.* New York, Macmillan, 1923.

BEVERIDGE, ALBERT J.—*Life of John Marshall.* Vol. II. Boston, Houghton Mifflin, 1916. (Especially chs. ii-iv.)

BOWERS, CLAUDE G.—*Jefferson and Hamilton; the Struggle for Democracy in America.* Boston, Houghton Mifflin, 1925.

CHANNING, EDWARD — *History of the United States.* Vol. IV. New York, Macmillan, 1917. (Especially chs. ii-vi.)

CHANNING, HART AND TURNER—*Guide to the Study and Reading of American History.* Rev. ed. Boston, Ginn, 1912. (Especially §§ 176-182.)

FORD, HENRY JONES—*Washington and his Colleagues (Chronicles of America,* Vol. XIV.) New Haven, Yale University Press, 1918.

FORD, WORTHINGTON CHAUNCEY—*George Washington.* 2 vols. New York, Scribner, 1900. (Especially Vol. II, chs. ix-xiv.)

LODGE, HENRY CABOT—*George Washington (American Statesmen,* Library ed.). 2 vols. Boston, Houghton Mifflin, 1898. (Especially Vol. II, chs. ii-v.)

LODGE, HENRY CABOT—*Alexander Hamilton (American Statesman,* Library ed.). 2 vols. Boston, Houghton Mifflin, 1898. (Especially chs. v-ix.)

MACLAY, WILLIAM — *Journal . . . 1789-1791.* New York, Boni, 1927. (Earlier eds.)

MORSE, JOHN T., JR.—*Thomas Jefferson (American Statesman,* Library ed.). Boston, Houghton Mifflin, 1898. (Especially chs. viii-xi.)

OSBORN, LUCRETIA PERRY, ED.—*Washington speaks for Himself.* New York, Scribner, 1927. (Especially chs. ix, x.)

RICHARDSON, JAMES D., ED.—*Compilation of the Messages and Papers of the Presidents.* Vol. I. Washington, Government Printing Office, 1896.

VAN DYKE, HENRY — *Americanism of Washington.* New York, Harper, 1906.

WASHINGTON, GEORGE — *Diaries, 1748-1799.* Ed. by John C. Fitzpatrick. Vol. IV. Boston, Houghton Mifflin, 1925.

WASHINGTON, GEORGE—*Farewell Address to the People of the United States.* (First printed in the *American Daily Advertiser* of Philadelphia, September 19, 1796; many reprints.)

WASHINGTON, GEORGE—*Writings.* Ed. by Worthington Chauncey Ford. 14 vols. New York, Putnam, 1889-93. (Especially Vols. XI-XIII.)

FIRST IN PEACE
From a painting by Henry Hintermeister

Washington Proprietor of Mount Vernon
By James Hosmer Penniman
Part I
The Estate

GEORGE WASHINGTON

From the bust by Joseph Nollekens, modeled in London about 1805, and here reproduced by permission of the Honorable Sol Bloom, of New York

A NATIONAL SHRINE

N the Potomac, a few miles below the city of Washington, has been standing for nearly two centuries a mansion which is a shrine of humanity, for Mount Vernon is more than a national memorial. Distinguished pilgrims of many races lay wreaths at the tomb of him who devoted all he was and all he had to making freedom secure for mankind.

Mount Vernon is the most famous home in the world. Nowhere else do we get so close to such an illustrious man. It is at Mount Vernon alone that Washington comes down from his heroic pedestal and reveals himself to us in the majestic simplicity of the Virginia farmer, the Cincinnatus of the West. Washington was not common clay, nor is Mount Vernon common earth. He could not have been such a patriot if he had not loved the place so much, because affection for the actual ground and wood and stone of the home is the most natural foundation of love of country.

The Mount Vernon Ladies' Association, incorporated in 1856, is the oldest patriotic organization of women in the United States. Wisely directed energy, unselfish devotion, and reverent patriotism—these conspicuous qualities of Washington have been manifested in an eminent degree by the Ladies of Mount Vernon in making permanent for us his hallowed shrine. Reassembling the original furniture and relics is the most wonderful of all the things that the Ladies of Mount Vernon have done. They have made the mansion a museum of priceless treasures, and it is the duty of patriotic Americans to see to it that everything that used to be at Mount Vernon is returned there.

THE HISTORIC MANSION

To know Mount Vernon one must visit it in rain and in sunshine, in winter and in summer, in the morning and with the lengthening shadows of the afternoon. The mansion is kept in such perfect condition that it gives no indication of having endured the storms of so many years. Yet you are surrounded by the atmosphere of the eighteenth century, that age of silk stockings, lace cuffs, powdered hair, and stately manners, so that one almost expects to see Lady Washington drive up with her coach and four. Life at Mount Vernon, though simple, was in the grand style; and the mansion, too, is simple, but with an air of elegance to a certain extent its own, for it is not entirely derived from its association with its illustrious proprietor.

Though rich in memories, they are all noble; there is no skeleton in the closet and no ghost. Listen to what the old house has to tell you, for it is silently eloquent. As you walk through these rooms you are turning the pages of history. No other private residence in the world is so permeated with the annals of a great nation, and its associations are all the result of the life work of one great man. Here the ablest men came to confer with Washington. In the library he drafted historic documents and wrote hundreds of letters of the utmost importance to our country. It adds interest to the reading of a letter of Washington to be able to picture him as he wrote it in his library.

We must visit Mount Vernon to know the real Washington; and, to know him as we ought, we should visit it many times and read and re-read his works, for the more we know of Washington the more we appreciate his home. There have been hundreds of books written about Washington, but the best will always be those he wrote himself. We should hear less about the hatchet and the cherry tree and other myths, and we should be better Americans if we read as much as we can of what Washington himself has written; for, in so doing, we not only become acquainted with the first American but we also learn how our country was made a nation.

ORIGIN OF MOUNT VERNON

The Vestry Book of Pohick Church recorded November 18, 1735, that Augustine Washington, father of George, was sworn in as vestryman and attended meetings August 18, 1736, August 13, 1737, and October 3, 1737, after which his name does not appear. By a deed recorded in October, 1740, Augustine Washington conveyed to his son Lawrence the 2500 acres of land at Hunting Creek, which was later called Mount Vernon. From Jamaica, May 30, 1741, Lawrence wrote his father, "I hope my lotts are secured, which, if I return, shall make use of as my dwelling." He did not return until the spring of 1743, and on the 19th of July was married to Anne Fairfax. It is difficult to understand how Lawrence could have given attention to the building of the original central part of the mansion at this time, and it seems more reasonable to attribute its construction to the loving care of Augustine for his son, who was to be married as soon as his military service was over, and to suppose that Augustine alluded to these facts when he had cut on the corner stone the initials L. W. with the heart and military axes. Augustine's will, executed April 11, 1743, gives Lawrence the "Land at Hunting Creek . . . with the water mill adjoyning thereto . . . And all the slaves, Cattle & Stocke . . . and all the household Furnature whatsoever now in & upon or which have been Commonly possessed by my said son."

Lawrence called his estate Mount Vernon, thus showing his affection for his old chief, Admiral Vernon. The construction of the Great House went on at intervals during most of George Washington's life, nor did he consider it finished when he died. Augustine, Lawrence, and George were probably its only architects. You may restore the house to its condition in Lawrence's time, in your imagination, by removing the portico, the colonnades, the third story, the banquet hall, the library, and replacing with a few cabins all the outbuildings except the barn. The mansion will be left about one-third of its present size, with two stories and a garret with gable roof and dormer windows. There were four rooms on each floor, a small porch at the front door, and chimneys at each end. Lawrence died at Mount Vernon, July 26, 1752, aged thirty-four.

At the death of Lawrence's daughter and only surviving child, George inherited Mount Vernon, subject to a life interest in favor of the widow of Lawrence, who died in 1761. In October, 1754, George Washington resigned his military command of the Virginia forces and retired to Mount Vernon, where he stayed till he set out with General Braddock in 1755; after that campaign he returned to Mount Vernon, where he remained in a weak and feeble condition. August 14 he was commissioned commander-in-chief of the Virginia forces, and he was for four years busy on the frontier, returning to Mount Vernon from time to time.

In 1756, Washington wrote from Winchester asking for leave of absence to attend a meeting of executors of the estate of Lawrence in September at Alexandria, "as I am very deeply interested, not only as an executor and heir of part of his estate, but also in a very important dispute, subsisting between Colonel Lee, who married the widow, and my brothers and self, concerning advice in the will, which brings the whole personal estate in question." In September, 1757, Washington came to Mount Vernon to the funeral of William Fairfax, of Belvoir, the father of Anne. In November, Washington returned to Mount Vernon in bad health and was attended by his physician, Charles Green, who was also rector of Pohick Church.

THE FAMILY MANSION (1759)

When Washington's approaching marriage made it necessary to enlarge his mansion, John Patterson wrote him, June 17, 1758, that he would take the roof off the house as soon as the carpenters got the laths to shingle on. July 13, Patterson wrote, "The Great House was rais'd six days ago; sixteen thousand bricks have been burnt for the underpinning." July 14, Colonel John Carlyle wrote Washington that his house was now uncovered. August 13, Patterson reported that the outside of the house was finished. Humphrey Knight wrote Washington, August 24, "The great house goes on as brisk as possible. The painter has been painting 3 days. Our carpenter is now getting laths to sheath ye great house." The repairs included new weather boards, closets, floors, and a stairway to the attic. It is not necessary to go into the extensive alterations and additions which were made at various times later, as they have been fully described by other writers.

In December, 1758, Washington resigned his commission. In January, 1759, he was married to Mrs. Martha Custis and stayed at his bride's estate, White House, in New Kent on the Pamunkey, and at Williamsburg, until the close of the session of the House of Burgesses in May, when the couple came to live at Mount Vernon. Washington wrote September 20, 1759: "I am now I believe fixd at this seat with an agreable Consort for Life. And hope to find more happiness in retirement than I ever experienced amidst a wide and bustling World." Both the White House and Mrs. Washington's other residence, the Six Chimney House in Williamsburg, were finer mansions than Mount Vernon was at that time, but she cheerfully made her home in the remote "and humble" dwelling of Colonel Washington.

CHANGES AND FURNITURE

From then until 1775 it was truly his home, and he proceeded at once to develop and enlarge the estate, adding many acres to the original property, but not at that time altering the main house, though he adjoined various outhouses in immediate connection, and improved the grounds. For instance, the diaries under date of March 27, 1760, record: "Agreed to give Mr. William Triplet £18 to build the two houses in the Front of my House [this means the side away from the river] (plastering them also), and running walls for Pallisades to them from the Great house, and from the Great House to the Wash House and Kitchen also." January 9, 1769, he was "At home all day, opening the Avenue to the House, and for bringing the Road along." The interior was largely refurnished, partly with Mrs. Washington's goods, partly with supplies from England; though it must always be remembered that the fact that he ordered such and such articles did not prove that he ever received them.

For instance, the invoices show that for his painstaking order of busts of Alexander the Great, Julius Caesar, Charles XII of Sweden, and the King of Prussia (Frederick the Great), Prince Eugene, and the Duke of Marlborough, together with "Wild Beasts" and "Sundry Small Ornaments for chimy piece," he received, with the agent's explanation, "A Groupe of Aeneas carrying his Father out of Troy, with four statues, viz. his Father Anchises, his wife Cresusa and his son, Ascanius, neatly finisht and bronzed with copper . . . Two Groupes, with two statues each of Bacchus & Flora, . . . T w o ornamented vases . . . T w o Lyons." Nevertheless he probably received the "1 Tester Bedstead 7½ feet pitch with fashionable bleu or bleu and White Curtains to suit a Room lind w't the Ireld. paper." The English traveler Burnaby, writing in 1760, says of Mount Vernon at this time: "This place is the property of colonel Washington, and truly deserving of its owner. The house is most beautifully situated upon a high hill on the banks of the Potowmac; and commands a noble prospect of water, of cliffs, of woods, and plantations."

PRIDE IN MOUNT VERNON

Washington described Mount Vernon as follows: "No estate in United America, is more pleasantly situated than this. It lies in a high, dry and healthy country, 300 miles by water from the sea, and, as you will see by the plan, on one of the finest rivers in the world. Its margin is washed by more than ten miles of tide water; . . . This river, which encompasses the land the distance above-mentioned, is well supplied with various kinds of fish, at all seasons of the year; and, in the spring, with the greatest profusion of shad, herrings, bass, carp, perch, sturgeon, &c. Several valuable fisheries appertain to the estate; the whole shore, in short, is one entire fishery." The estate was divided into Mansion House Farm, River Farm, Union Farm, Muddy Hole Farm, Dogue Run Farm. There were some thirty buildings at Mount Vernon, among which were the kitchen, connected with the mansion by an arcade, servants' quarters, butler's house, gardener's house, store house, smoke house, wash house, stable, coach house, barns, salt house, carpenter shop, spinning house, where sixteen wheels were kept going, green house, spring house, milk house, and an ice house which in mild winters was filled with snow.

Washington was never really happy away from Mount Vernon. After the Revolution he wrote: "Agriculture has ever been the most favorite amusement of my life." In 1785 a visitor to Mount Vernon stated that Washington's greatest pride was to be thought the first farmer in America. That combination of accurate knowledge of human nature and untiring industry which made him a great commander made him also a great farmer. He was master of the art of turning his circumstances to the best account. At Mount Vernon there was no want, because there was no waste when the master was there.

It is extraordinary how much Washington, who was the busiest man in America, did for his estate in a lifetime, during large portions of which he was absent in the service of his country. With the art of a skillful landscape gardener, he improved the natural beauties of the place. He wrote General Knox that, in the course of the conversation at Boston, he "was most interested by something which was said respecting the composition for a public walk." Washington remarked that the Mount Vernon land has "an understratum of hard clay impervious to water, which, penetrating that far and unable to descend lower, sweeps off the upper soil." Washington was anxious about the possibility of fire at Mount Vernon, and that his fears were not without cause is shown by an entry in his diary, January 5, 1788: "About Eight oclock in the evening we were alarmed, and the house a good deal a dangered, by the soot of one of the Chimneys taking fire and burning furiously, discharging great flakes of fire on the Roof, but happily by having aid at hand and proper exertion no damage ensued." He wrote his manager: "I beg you will make my people (about the Mansion house) be careful of the fire; for it is no uncommon thing for them to be running from one house to another in cold, windy nights with sparks of fire flying and dropping as they go along, without paying the least attention to the consequences."

SCIENTIFIC IMPROVEMENTS

In what he called his Botanical Garden, between the flower-garden and the spinner's house, Washington carried on much of his investigation. The nurseries, gardens, and greenhouse were filled with choice collections of rare plants, fruit trees, vegetables, and flowers. To do this was not easy at a time when means of communication and transportation were almost primitive, but admirers in all parts of the world knew that the best way to please the most distinguished man in the world was to send him a choice plant or animal for his estate. Washington's favorite Bible quotation about the shade of his own vine and fig-tree was not entirely a figure of speech, for fig-trees were trained on the warm side of the north garden wall, and he paid much attention to the cultivation of grapes. It is not in accordance with his character that the story by which Washington is most widely known represents him as wantonly destroying a cherry tree. In later years he wrote: "It is always in one's power to cut a tree down, but time only can place them where one would have them." The passages in Washington's letters and diaries, in which he spoke of his trees, would make a book of considerable size. The last time he left the house, which was the afternoon of the day before he died, he walked out through the snow to mark some trees to be cut down between mansion and river. One of his last letters was to his manager about the care of Mount Vernon. At his death he left written plans for the rotation of crops up to the end of 1803.

THE LIBRARY

Washington took great pains to secure the most exact information on subjects which interested him. All his life he was buying books. His library of more than a thousand volumes, mostly on agriculture, government, and military affairs, was a large one for that time. An interesting date is Friday, June 16, 1786, when Washington recorded: "Began about 10 Oclock to put up the Book press in my study." This was probably a press for copying letters. Washington had at Mount Vernon more than two hundred folio volumes of his documents, and these formed only a part of his manuscripts. His diary noted entire days spent in writing. In 1797, he stated that he intends to erect a building at Mount Vernon for the security of his papers. How restful it was for him to turn aside from weighty and perplexing matters of state and the selfish designs of politicians, and to write: "I have a high opinion of beans." "Of all the improving and ameliorating crops, none in my opinion is equal to potatoes."

It was in his library that Washington made those painstaking studies of republican forms of government, the notes of which still exist in his writing. He made good use of them when he presided at the

Constitutional Convention, which convened in 1787. We form a better idea of his sacrifices for our country as we picture him before the convention, going around Mount Vernon for ten days with his arm in a sling because of rheumatism. Few Americans understand that if we had had no Washington we should not have had our Constitution; not only because of his powerful agency in framing it and his great influence in securing its adoption, but because the certainty that Washington would be first President made the people sure that the provisions of the Constitution would be interpreted with wisdom and executed with justice. Not until Washington was elected was the chief power in America vested in a single person, and in Washington the highest power was entrusted to the most worthy, which is the greatest assurance of good government. Respect for Washington among the nations of Europe gave dignity to our new government.

POLITICS (1774)

George Mason, who drafted the first Constitution of Virginia, lived at Gunston Hall, a few miles down the river. Among Washington's papers are the Fairfax Resolves, in the writing of Mason, adopted by a county meeting of which Washington was chairman, July 18, 1774. There were twenty-four of these resolutions, forming one of the most important documents in our early history. They may be summed up in the statement—we will religiously maintain and inviolably adhere to such measures as shall be concerted by the general Congress for the preservation of our lives, liberties, and fortunes. There can be little doubt that Washington and Mason did a large part of the work on these resolutions at Mount Vernon. Two weeks later these resolves were in effect adopted by the Virginia Convention, where Washington represented Fairfax County, and they formed the basis of Virginia's instructions to her delegates to the First Continental Congress. Before that Congress Washington entered in his diary: "August 30—Colo. Pendleton, Mr. Henry, Colo. Mason and Mr. Thos. Triplet came in the Eveng. and stayd all Night. 31. All the above Gentlemen dined here, after which, with Colo. Pendleton and Mr. Henry, I set out on my journey to Phila." Horatio Gates, Richard Henry Lee, and others had an important conference at Mount Vernon, May 3, 1775, and the next day Washington set out for the Second Congress at Philadelphia.

A VISITOR'S JUDGMENT (1785)

Several of the many visitors to what Washington called his "well resorted tavern" have left descriptions of the house in these days of its prime. John Hunter, an English merchant, who was there in November, 1785, wrote that he "rose early and took a walk about the General's grounds—which are really beautifully laid out. . . . The style of his house is very elegant, something

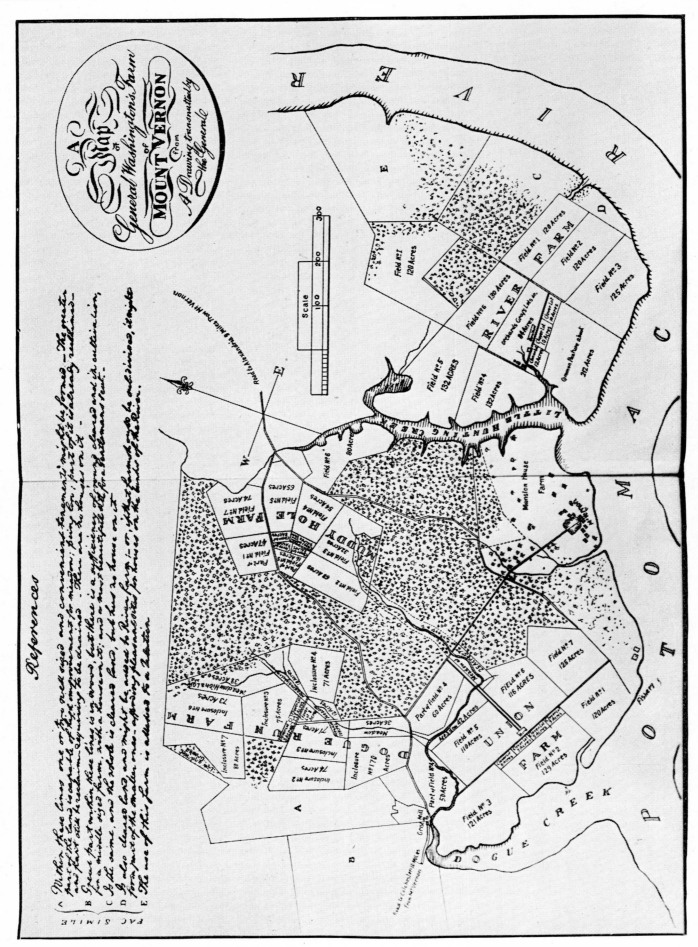

MAP OF MOUNT VERNON

Sent by George Washington to Arthur Young in England, 1793

like the Prince de Conde's at Chantille, near Paris, only not quite so large; but it's a pity he did not build a new one at once, as it has cost him nearly as much repairing his old one. His improvements I'm told are very great within the last year. He is making a most delightful bowling green before the house and cutting a new road thro' the woods to Alexandria. It would be endless to attempt describing his house and grounds—I must content myself with having seen them. The situation is a heavenly one, upon one of the finest rivers in the world."

Brissot de Warville gives his impressions in 1788: "You discover a country house of an elegant and majestic simplicity. It is preceded by grass plats; on one side of the avenue are the stables, on the other a greenhouse, and houses for a number of negro mechanics. . . . This house overlooks the Potowmack, enjoys an extensive prospect, has a vast and elevated portico on the front next the river, and a convenient distribution of the apartments within. . . . Every thing has an air of simplicity in his house; his table is good, but not ostentatious; and no deviation is seen from regularity and domestic economy."

Amariah Frost in 1797 "viewed the garden and walks, which are very elegant, abounding with many curiosities, Fig trees, raisins, limes, oranges, etc., large English mulberries, artichokes, etc. . . . There are beautiful groves arranged in proper order back of both the gardens and rows of trees exactly corrisponding with each other, between which and the two gardens is the great green and circular walk fronting northerly from the house and seen at a great distance. The southern part of the house fronts the river. The house is long but not high, with a cupola in the center of the roof. The chamber windows are small, being only 12 lights, 8 or 10, or less, to a window. The lower windows are larger. Two wings and other buildings corresponding to each other on either side, also, a large piazza in the front, add much to the beauty of the house."

ABSENCES FROM MOUNT VERNON (1789-1797)

When it became probable that Washington would be chosen first President of the United States, he wrote John Armstrong: "I well remember the observation you made in your letter to me of last year, 'that my domestic retirement must suffer an interruption.' This took place, notwithstanding it was utterly repugnant to my feelings, my interests, and my wishes. I sacrificed every private consideration, and personal enjoyment, to the earnest and pressing solicitations of those, who saw and knew the alarming situation of our public concerns, and had no other end in view but to promote the interests of their country; conceiving, that under those circumstances, and at so critical a moment, an absolute refusal to act might

on my part be construed as a total disregard of my country, if imputed to no worse motives. . . . I am so wedded to a state of retirement, and find the occupations of a rural life so congenial with my feelings, that to be drawn into public at my advanced age would be a sacrifice, that would admit of no compensation."

When he was leaving to be inaugurated at New York, Washington wrote, April 16, 1789: "I bade adieu to Mount Vernon, to private life and to domestic felicity." That Mrs. Washington shared her husband's regret at leaving Mount Vernon is clear from the following letter written in December, 1789: "I little thought when the war was finished that any circumstances could possibly happen which would call the General into public life again. I had anticipated that, from that moment, we should be suffered to grow old together, in solitude and tranquility. That was the first and dearest wish of my heart. I will not, however, contemplate with too much regret disappointments that were inevitable; though his feelings and my own were in perfect unison with respect to our predelictions for private life, yet I cannot blame him for having acted according to his ideas of duty in obeying the voice of his country. It is owing to the kindness of our numerous friends, in all quarters, that my new and unwished for situation is not, indeed, a burden to me. When I was much younger I should probably have enjoyed the innocent gayeties of life as much as most persons of my age; but I had long since placed all the prospects of my future worldly happiness in the still enjoyments of the fireside at Mount Vernon."

LAST RESIDENCE AT MOUNT VERNON (1797-1799)

Washington lived but two years and nine months after he retired from the Presidency, March 4, 1797. He wrote General Knox: "The remainder of my life, (which in the course of nature cannot be long,) will be occupied in rural amusements; and, though I shall seclude myself as much as possible from the noisy and bustling crowd, none more than myself would be regaled by the company of those I esteem, at Mount Vernon; more than twenty miles from which, after I arrive there, it is not likely that I shall ever be." Washington wrote in October, 1797: "An eight years absence from home (excepting short occasional visits) had so deranged my private affairs;—had so despoiled my buildings;—and in a word had thrown my domestic concerns into such disorder,—as at no period of my life have I been more engaged than in the last six months to recover and put them in some tolerable train again." September 28, 1799, he wrote Lawrence Lewis: "It is my wish to place my estate in this country on a new establishment, thereby bringing it into so narrow a compass as not only to supersede the necessity of a manager, but to make the management of what I retain in my own

hands a healthy and agreeable amusement to look after myself, if I should not be again called to the public service of the country." Who does not sympathize with Washington when he writes McHenry: "Although I have not houses to build (except one, which I must erect for the accommodation and security of my Military, Civil and private Papers, which are voluminous and may be interesting), yet I have not one, or scarcely anything else about me that does not require considerable repairs. In a word, I am already surrounded by Joiners, Masons, Painters, &c.; and such is my anxiety to get out of their hands, that I have scarcely a room to put a friend into, or to sit in myself, without the music of hammers, or the odoriferous smell of paint."

AMUSEMENTS AND DIVERSIONS

When you cross the threshold of the mansion, you step into the home life of the Washingtons. George and Martha made their house a beautiful home, filled with handsome furniture of a period when furniture was noted for its substantial elegance. They were both of them particular about the appointments of the table, and Washington goes with minute care into details of wine-glasses, finger-bowls, decanters, butter-boats, tureens, and other dishes. It is possible here to mention but a few of the priceless relics of Washington with which the Ladies of Mount Vernon have filled the mansion. His surveyor's tripod is in the library. At sixteen he was earning his living by surveying, and he worked at it in later years, sometimes making surveys of Hunting Creek and other streams on the ice. As late as April 21, 1785, he records that he went to Abingdon in his barge, "Took my Instruments, with intent to Survey the Land I hold by purchase on 4 Mile Run," three miles above Alexandria, but the surveying ended abruptly, because Billy Lee, who was carrying the chain, fell and broke his knee pan, so that he had to be carried to Abingdon on a sled, as he could neither walk, stand, nor ride.

In the hall of Mount Vernon are the swords with which he directed his troops. In leaving them to his nephews he told them not to unsheath them for the purpose of shedding blood, except for self-defense or in defense of their country and its rights, and in the latter case to keep them unsheathed, and to prefer falling with them in their hands to the relinquishment thereof. Washington's spyglasses are poor things compared with modern binoculars, but he was the best observer in either army, and always wished to do his reconnoitering with his own eyes. He strained his eyes, so that he had to use spectacles, and remarked that he had not only grown old but blind in the service. There is a flute in the music room, though Washington wrote Francis Hopkinson that he could neither sing one of his songs nor raise a single note on any instrument. In his earliest account-book there is an entry when Washington was sixteen "to cash pd ye Musick Master for my Entrance 3/9." Thirty windsor chairs were provided for the porch. The large number of chairs indicates that the Washingtons had to be prepared to receive many friends.

Elkanah Watson, in January, 1785, spent at Mount Vernon what he called "two of the richest days of my life." He said: "I found him [Washington] kind and benignant in the domestic circle, revered and beloved by all around him; agreeably social, without ostentation; delighting in anecdote and adventures, without assumption; his domestic arrangements harmonious and systematic. His servants seemed to watch his eye, and to anticipate his every wish; hence a look was equivalent to a command. His servant, Billy, the faithful companion of his military career, was always at his side, smiling content, animated and beamed on every countenance in his presence." Watson had a severe cough, and he said that some time after he had retired, "the door of my room was gently opened and on drawing my bed-curtains, to my utter astonishment, I beheld Washington himself, standing at my bed-side with a bowl of hot tea in his hand."

PORTRAITURE

In the hall hangs the original deed of 1674 by which John Washington, the emigrant, great grandfather of George, derived from Lord Culpeper his title to Mount Vernon. The Houdon bust, which Stuart called the only representation of Washington better than his own portraits, was made at Mount Vernon. Houdon, the most celebrated sculptor of that time, came from France at the request of the General Assembly of Virginia in order to model Washington from life. With his three assistants he arrived from Alexandria by water at eleven o'clock at night. He remained about three weeks, and made a cast of the face, head, and shoulders, and took minute measurements of the body. Amid so much that is vague and legendary, the Houdon statue stands forth clear in its artistic and historic accuracy. No work of art exists that is more authentic. It is historically marked by a chronological record of facts, resolutions, correspondence, and inscriptions. Lafayette said that it is a "fac-simile of Washington's Person."

Other representations of Washington had been executed at Mount Vernon before the arrival of Houdon. In May, 1772, Charles Willson Peale painted Washington in the blue and red uniform of a colonel of Virginia militia, and he made also miniatures of Mrs. Washington and her two children. Peale returned in January, 1774, and painted the portrait of John Parke Custis. April 28, 1784, Robert Edge Pine came and remained three weeks, painting Washington and the two grandchildren, George Washington Parke Custis and Nelly Custis.

CONSIDERATION FOR THE POOR

Washington paid his debts promptly, and no man was more liberal to the poor or more ready to give his time and money to the public service. When he took command of the Army, in 1775, he wrote Lund Washington, who had charge of his affairs at Mount Vernon: "Let the hospitality of the house, with respect to the poor, be kept up. Let no one go hungry away. If any of this kind of people should be in want of corn, supply their necessities, provided it does not encourage them in idleness; and I have no objection to your giving my money in charity, to the amount of forty or fifty pounds a year, when you think it well bestowed. What I mean by having no objection is, that it is my desire that it should be done." "I wish that my horses and stock of every kind should be fed with judicious plenty and economy, but without the least profusion or waste."

One of the overseers wrote: "I had orders from General Washington to fill a corn-house every year, for the sole use of the poor in my neighborhood, to whom it was a most seasonable and precious relief, saving numbers of poor women and children from extreme want, and blessing them with plenty. . . . He owned several fishing stations on the Potomac, at which excellent herring were caught, and which, when salted, proved an important article of food to the poor. For their accommodation he appropriated a station—one of the best he had—and furnished it with all the necessary apparatus for taking herring. Here the honest poor might fish free of expense, at any time, by only an application to the overseer; and if at any time unequal to the labor of hauling the seine, assistance was rendered by order of the General."

VISITORS

In 1794, Washington gave his overseer definite instructions with regard to the entertainment of visitors at Mount Vernon. There were, he said, three classes of persons to whom should be given: "first, my *particular* and intimate acquaintance, in case business should call them there, such for instance as Doctor Craik. 2dly, some of the *most* respectable foreigners who may, perchance, be in Alexandria or the federal city; and be either brought down, or introduced by letter, from some of my particular acquaintance as before mentioned; or thirdly, to persons of some distinction (such as members of Congress, &c.) who may be travelling through the country from North to South, or from South to North. . . . I have no objection to any sober, or orderly person's gratifying their curiosity in viewing the buildings, gardens, &c., about Mt. Vernon; but it is only to such persons as I have described that I ought to be run to any expence on account of these visits of curiosity, beyond common civility and hospitality. No gentleman who has a proper respect for his own character (except relations

and intimates) would use the house in my absence for the sake of conveniency (as it is far removed from the public roads), unless invited to do so by me or some friend; nor do I suppose any of this description would go there without a personal, or written introduction."

Washington's ability to express a proposition clearly and to refuse a request gracefully is exemplified in the following letter, which he wrote October 30, 1787: "My fixed determination is, that no person whatever shall hunt upon my grounds or waters. —To grant leave to one, and refuse another, would not only be drawing a line of discrimination which would be offensive, but would subject one to great inconvenience— for my strict and positive orders to all my people are if they hear a gun fired upon my Land to go immediately in pursuit of it.— Permission therefore to any one would keep them either always in pursuit—or make them inattentive to my orders under the supposition of its belonging to a licensed person by which means I should be obtruded upon by others who to my cost I find had other objects in view. Besides, as I have not lost my relish for this sport when I can find time to indulge myself in it, and Gentlemen who come to the House are pleased with it, it is my wish not to have the game within my jurisdiction disturbed. For these reasons I beg you will not take my refusal amiss, because I would give the same to my brother if he lived off my land."

DISTINGUISHED VISITORS
(1780-1789)

A letter of General Greene, November 13, 1780, tells of a hurried visit paid to Mount Vernon by Generals Greene and Steuben during the Southern Campaign, and was written to Washington:

"*Sir:* I arrived here yesterday about noon, and met with a kind and hospitable reception by Mrs. Washington and all the family. Mrs. Washington, Mr. and Mrs. Custis (who are here) and Mr. Lund Washington and his Lady are all well.

"We set out this morning for Richmond, and it is now so early that I am obliged to write by candlelight. Nothing but the absolute necessity of my being with my command as soon as possible should induce me to make my stay so short at your Excellency's seat, where there is everything that nature and art can afford to render my stay happy and agreeable. Mount Vernon is one of the most pleasant places I ever saw; and I don't wonder that you languish so often to return to the pleasures of domestic life. Nothing but the glory of being Commander in Chief, and the happiness of being universally admired could compensate a person for such a sacrifice as you make. Baron Steuben is delighted with the place, and charmed with the reception we met with. Mrs. Washington sets out for camp about the middle of this week."

In March, 1781, Lafayette, who was carrying on operations in Virginia which resulted in the penning up of Cornwallis at Yorktown, came to Mount Vernon, but he was not entertained there by the General until he returned to America in 1784. Mrs. General Knox visited Mrs. Washington at Mount Vernon in October, 1781, while the siege of Yorktown was in progress.

April 12, 1784, Luzerne, the French minister, who was spending several days at Mount Vernon, wrote of Washington: "He dresses in a gray coat like a Virginia farmer, and nothing about him recalls the recollection of the important part which he has played, except the great number of foreigners who come to see him." Lafayette arrived in New York from France August 4, 1784, and reached Mount Vernon August 17, where he remained twelve days. November 14 Washington went to Richmond, met Lafayette there, and the Marquis returned to Mount Vernon for a second visit of a week. November 29 Washington and Lafayette went to Annapolis, where he bade a final farewell to the Marquis.

The years from 1784 to 1789 Washington called his furlough. Brissot de Warville, who visited Mount Vernon in 1788, wrote: "Mrs. Washington superintends the whole, and joins to the qualities of an excellent house-wife the simple dignity which ought to characterize a woman, whose husband has acted the greatest part on the theater of human affairs; while she possesses that amenity, and manifests that attention to strangers which renders hospitality so charming." Thomas Lee Shippen wrote from Mount Vernon: "Mrs. Washington is the very essence of kindness. Her soul seems to overflow with it like the most abundant fountain and her happiness is in exact proportion to the number of objects upon which she can dispense her benefits."

During the Revolution Washington was always looking forward to the time when he could return to his beloved home. He wrote his wife: "I should enjoy more real happiness in one month with you at home, than I have the most distant prospect of finding abroad, if my stay were to be seven times seven years."

RETURN TO MOUNT VERNON (1783)

Washington resigned his commission at Annapolis, December 23, 1783, and, once more a private citizen, reached Mount Vernon with Mrs. Washington on Christmas eve. Relatives and friends had gathered to welcome them, and the servants made the night gay with bonfires, fiddling, and dancing. February 1, 1784, Washington wrote Lafayette: "At length, my dear Marquis, I am become a private citizen on the banks of the Potomac; and under the shadow of my own vine and my own fig-tree, free from the bustle of a camp, and the busy scenes of public life, I am solacing myself with those tranquil enjoyments, of which the soldier,

who is ever in pursuit of fame, the statesman, whose watchful days and sleepless nights are spent in devising schemes to promote the welfare of his own, perhaps the ruin of other countries, as if this globe was insufficient for us all, and the courtier, who is always watching the countenance of his prince, in hopes of catching a gracious smile, can have very little conception."

OUTDOOR SPORTS

All his life Washington was an outdoor man. He was conceded to be the best horseman in Virginia. Before the Revolution he rode a hunting two or three times a week with neighbors and guests, and the mellow baying of the long-eared hounds, the distant horn, and the view halloo, resounded from field and wood as the hunt swept on. When after foxes, sometimes the hounds would start a deer. Bears were seen near Mount Vernon as late as 1772. The wild turkeys sometimes weighed thirty or forty pounds. Before the Revolution we find Washington ordering for himself "1 pr. of best Buck Breeches pr. Mea'e sent last y'r, to J. Coleman, to have a side Pocket, and a Buckle behind A Gentleman's Hunt'g Cap, Coverd with Black Velvet, to fit a pretty large head, cushioned round or stuffd to make it sit easy thereon. A Silk Band, and handsome Silv'r Buckle to it. 1 pr. of Silver Spur's of the New'r Fashn. . . . 1 Best whole hunting Whip, pretty stout and strong, cap'd with Silver and my name and the y'r engraved thereon" "A Riding Frock of a handsome Drab colour'd broad Cloth with plain dble gilt Button's A Riding Waistcoat of Superfine Scarlet Cloth, and gold Lace with Button's like those of the Coat." "1 large loud Hunting Horn, lap'd and secur'd in the strongest manner."

Washington went to many horse races, and on one occasion to a boat race on the Potomac. He made a fishing trip on his schooner that lasted for several days. Washington and his neighbors on the Potomac had barges manned by negroes in uniform. Among his orders from England were "a whale boat, long narrow sharp at both ends"; also "1 doz'n Neat and light 18 Feet oars for a Light Whale Boat, the Blades scoop'd &ca. and Painted." Mr. Digges was a wealthy planter, whose estate, Warburton, could be seen across the Potomac in Maryland. At a signal his barge and that of Washington would meet in the middle of the river and transfer passengers. Washington had also a ferry boat in which carriages and horses were "put over" the Potomac. In Washington's time hundreds of shad and thousands of herring were taken at Mount Vernon by means of seines drawn in by a windlass turned by horses.

TREE CULTURE

On each side of the east lawn a grove of locusts extended to the river. Trees and shrubs were carefully trimmed to make a frame to the view of the Potomac, and care

was taken to keep vistas open in every direction. The level lawn on the west front, with the wide serpentine walk shaded by weeping willows, the oval grass plot, the flower garden on one side and the kitchen garden on the other, were all laid out according to a plan drawn by Washington himself and still unchanged. He paid great attention to his lawns, and the first order sent to England after his marriage includes "a large assortment of grass seed." Carefully trimmed box borders outline the paths today exactly as in Washington's time, their dark green making the flower beds flame like stained-glass windows. Roses named by Washington for his mother and for Nelly Custis still bloom, together with yellow, damask, tea, and guilder roses. Old-fashioned flowers and plants are cherished—iris, sweetwilliams, spice pinks, ivy, honeysuckle, lilacs, and jasmine. Mrs. Washington's active interest in the garden is indicated by this extract from a letter of her husband: "I have, too, Mrs. Washington's particular thanks to offer you for the flower roots and seeds."

No other living things bring us so close to Washington as some of the trees of Mount Vernon, for they were planted by him, and on them his eyes have rested with long and loving gaze. Washington studied as well as he could the economic value of forests and the ornamental properties of trees, but the technical aspects of forestry, such as reforestration, the relation of forests to moisture and rain fall, water supply, climate, and public health were not so well understood in his time as they are now. The magnolia planted by Washington is the most famous tree at Mount Vernon. Three hemlocks planted by him still remain. Three box trees probably planted by him are among the handsomest and most interesting trees. Washington wished to have perfect specimens of every tree that would grow at Mount Vernon. He personally superintended the selection of the most beautiful from the neighboring woods, and watched them with care until it was clear that the transplanting was successful. He arranged them symmetrically, and mingled forest trees, flowering shrubs, and evergreens so as to produce the most agreeable effect.

Washington wrote January 27, 1785: "I went to Belvoir and viewed the ruined Buildings of that place. In doing this I passed along the side of Dogue Creek and the River to the White Ho. in search of Elm and other Trees for my Shrubberies, etca. Found none of the former, but discovered one fringe Tree and a few Crab trees in the first field beyond my line, and in returning home (which I did to Dinner) by the way of Accatinck Creek I found several young Holly trees." The next day he wrote: "Road to day to my Plantations in the Neck, partly with a view to search for Trees; for which purpose I passed through the Woods and in the first drain beyond the Bars in my lower pasture, I discovered in tracing it upwards, many small and thriving plants of the Magnolio, and about and within the Fence, not far distant, some young Maple Trees; and the red berry of the Swamp. I also, along the Branch within Colo. Mason's field, . . . came across a mere nursery of young Crab trees of all sizes and handsome and thriving, and along the same branch on the outer side of the fence I discovered several young Holly Trees. But whether from the real scarcity, or difficulty of distinguishing, I could find none of the fringe tree."

RELIGIOUS OBSERVANCES

At Mount Vernon the cultivation of no part of Washington's nature was neglected. He found abundant exercise for his body in hard work on his farms, in the long rides which it was necessary for him to take, in hunting with his horses and hounds, and he was a stately and graceful dancer. Books, letters, pondering on important matters and converse with intellectual neighbors like George Mason and Lord Fairfax, exercised his mind. He found uplift for his soul in reading his Bible, in communion with his good wife, who was a woman of eminent piety, and in the church services at Pohick and Alexandria. On Sundays, when the Washingtons were stormbound, he read the Bible and sermons to his family with distinct and precise enunciation. There is a pocket note-book in which Washington has entered Bible references. His answers to the many congratulatory addresses from religious societies are models of their kind. In 1794 he wrote Charles Thomson that he had finished reading the first part of his translation of the Septuagint.

Washington often quoted the Scriptures, his favorite reference being to the verse in Micah about reposing under his own vine and fig-tree. He expresses a wish that the swords might be turned to plough shares, the spears into pruning-hooks, and as the Scripture expresses it, "the nations learn war no more." He regretted that Noah allowed the tobacco worms to get into the ark.

His nephew, Robert Lewis, said that he had accidentally witnessed Washington's private devotions in his library both morning and evening, and had seen him kneeling with an open Bible before him, and that this was his daily habit. Washington went to his library at four in the morning, and, after his devotions, spent the time till breakfast in writing and study. He also spent an hour in his library before retiring at night, and he wrote: "It is my intention to retire (and unless prevented by very particular company, I always do retire) either to bed or to my study soon after candlelight."

In 1789, acknowledging a sermon on the text "But ye shall die like men," Washington not only said that he has read the sermon, but also that he approved the doctrine inculcated. August 14, 1797, Washington wrote the Reverend Zachariah Lewis, thanking him for the sermons he had sent, and saying that the doctrine in them was sound and did credit to the author.

CHURCH GOING

Nelly Custis wrote Jared Sparks with regard to Washington: "He attended the church at Alexandria when the weather and roads permitted, a ride of ten miles. In New York and Philadelphia he never omitted attendance at church in the morning, unless detained by indisposition. The afternoon was spent in his own room at home; the evening with his family, and without company. Sometimes an old and intimate friend called to see us for an hour or two; but visiting and visitors were prohibited for that day. No one in church attended to the services with more reverential respect. My grandmother, who was eminently pious, never deviated from her early habits. She always knelt. The General, as was then the custom, stood during the devotional parts of the service." Bishop White stated that Washington's manner at church was always serious and attentive. A foreign house guest at Mount Vernon observed that on Sabbath evening there was no secular music and not even a game of chess.

Throughout his campaigns Washington was always careful about religious services. William Fairfax wrote him in 1754 that he had no doubt that his having public prayers in camp would have great influence with the Indians. Washington persisted in his efforts for the welfare of his frontier troops and frequently read prayers and the Scriptures to his men. During the French and Indian War Colonel Temple "more than once found him on his knees at his devotions." In his diary at Williamsburg, June 1, 1774, Washington recorded: "went to Church and fasted all day." Unless a clergyman was present Washington always asked a blessing at his table. The Pohick vestry book shows that from 1763 to 1774 George Washington attended twenty-three of the thirty-one meetings of Pohick vestry, once he was sick in bed, twice he was in attendance on the House of Burgesses, and three times he is known to have been out of the county, and the other two times he was probably out of the county. Rev. Charles Green, who was rector of Pohick, 1738-65, was also the family physician and a valued friend. His successor, Rev. Lee Massey, wrote: "I never knew so constant an attendant in church as Washington, and his behavior in the house of God was ever so deeply reverential that it produced the happiest effect on my congregation and greatly assisted me in my pulpit labors."

SOCIAL LIFE

In a letter to his neighbor, George Mason, written in 1769, Washington spoke of those "who live genteely and hospitably on clear estates," and this is an exact description in eight words of the life at Mount Vernon. Though Washington said, "We live in a state of peaceful tranquillity," Mount Vernon was by no means quiet. The original brass knocker hangs on the central door, but it was rarely used, for long before reaching the door the arrival of company was announced by the barking of the dogs. Martha Washington wrote that when she had gone on a visit and left her small son at home, every time the dogs barked she thought it was a messenger for her. If a day passed without company at Mount Vernon, Washington mentioned it in his diary. It has been figured out that in two months in 1768, Washington had company to dinner or to spend the night on twenty-nine days, and dined away or visited on seven.

People whose very names their host did not know were entertained there. Mount Vernon stands back a mile from the road to Colchester. Though the house can be seen from a considerable distance, people did not arrive there by accident. In 1787 Washington wrote that his house "may be compared to a well resorted tavern, as scarcely any strangers who are going from north to south, or from south to north, do not spend a day or two at it." "Those who resort here are strangers and people of the first distinction." Washington had so many letters to write and so much company that he was deprived of exercise. Persons who had been connected with the army wished certificates in order to prove claims against the government; these made it necessary to spend much time consulting his records. For more than two years after the war he had no secretary.

Though he lived simply and kept early hours, George Washington always paid great attention to the manner of doing things, and the grand air which he learned in his youth from Lord Fairfax he always retained. Distinguished guests were lighted to their rooms by the general himself. The broad piazza overlooking the river was the usual meeting place when the weather permitted. The amount of entertaining which the Washingtons expected to do may be inferred from the fact that six carving knives and forks were in the first order from England after their marriage. They were both of them particular about their clothes, china, furniture, and equipages. When at Mount Vernon Mrs. Washington dressed plainly. When she drove to Alexandria or Annapolis or Williamsburg with her coach and four, with the negro postillions and coachman in white and scarlet, she dressed as was fitting. In December, 1755, Washington ordered from London two complete livery suits for servants. "I wou'd have you choose the livery by our Arms; only, as the Field of the Arms is white. I think the Cloaths had better not be quite so but nearly like the inclos'd. The Trimmings and Facings of Scarlet and a Scarlet Waistcoat . . . If livery Lace is not quite disus'd I shou'd be glad to have these cloaths laced. I like that fashion best; also two Silver lac'd hatts to the above Livery's." August 10, 1764, he ordered: "A Livery suit to be made of worsted Shagg of the Inclosed colour and fineness lined with red shalloon; and made as follows: The Coat and Breeches alike with a plain white washed button; the Button holes worked with Mohair of the same col'r. A collar of red shagg to the Coat with a narrow lace like the Inclosed round it; a narrow Cuff of the same colour of the Coat turn'd up to the bent of the Arm and laced round at that part; the waistcoat made of red Shagg (worsted Shagg also) and laced with the same lace as that upon the Collar and Sleeves." No doubt it was that the white flowers of the dogwood and the red of the red bud might reproduce his colors that, March 1, 1785, Washington planted "a circle of Dogwood with a red bud in the Middle, close to the old Cherry tree near the South Garden Ho[use]."

MARTHA WASHINGTON IN THE MANSION

While the sweet influences of Mount Vernon are sinking into our souls, let us not forget the gracious lady who inspired and comforted her husband throughout so many anxious years. Martha Washington preferred to remain in the background, so that her services to our country have never been understood and appreciated. She always encouraged the general to patriotic effort at the sacrifice of that domestic life to which both were devoted. At the very beginning of the Revolution she wrote: "My mind is made up; my heart is in the cause." For that cause, which was our cause, the Washingtons placed at stake their lives and all their earthly possessions.

Edmund Pendleton left a charming description of their hostess at Mount Vernon at the critical period of 1774: "I was much pleased with Mrs. Washington and her spirit. She seemed ready to make any sacrifice, and was cheerful, though I know she felt anxious. She talked like a Spartan mother to her son on going to battle. 'I hope you will all stand firm. I know George will,' she said. The dear little woman was busy from morning until night with domestic duties, but she gave us much time in conversation and affording us entertainment. When we set off in the morning, she stood in the door and cheered us with the good words, 'God be with you gentlemen.'"

Martha Washington little thought, when she said good-bye to her husband in May, 1775, that it would be more than six years before he returned to Mount Vernon, and that when she saw him next he would be five hundred miles away from home, at the head of the American army. Till she went to Cambridge she had never been farther north than Annapolis. She traveled in state in the family coach, attended by liveried servants and accompanied by her son and his wife. She filled her difficult position at headquarters in the Longfellow House with tact and courtesy, for she was equal to every situation in which her husband's exalted station placed her.

The uniform testimony of those who knew Martha Washington is that she combined, in an extraordinary degree, dignity and affability. You will realize her delicacy of feeling and elevation of character when you read this exquisite letter which Martha Washington wrote in 1773 to the girl bride of her only son:

"*My dear Nelly:* God took from Me a Daughter when June Roses were blooming. He has now given me another daughter about her Age when Winter winds are blowing, to warm my Heart again. I am as Happy as One so Afflicted and so Blest can be. Pray receive my Benediction and a wish that you may long live the Loving Wife of my Happy Son, and a Loving Daughter of

"Your Affectionate Mother,

"M. WASHINGTON."

WASHINGTON'S FONDNESS FOR MARTHA

One of the three letters to his wife that has been preserved is the following:

"PHILADELPHIA, *June 23, 1775.*

"*My Dearest:* As I am within a few minutes of leaving this city, I would not think of departing from it with out dropping you a line, especially as I do not know whether it may be in my power to write again till I get to the camp at Boston. I go fully trusting in that providence, which has been more bountiful to me than I deserve and in full confidence of a happy meeting with you some time in the fall. I have no time to add more as I am surrounded with company to take leave of me. I return an unalterable affection for you which neither time or distance can change my best love to Jack and Nelly and regard for the rest of the family; conclude me with the utmost truth and Sincerity,

"Yr. entire,

"G. WASHINGTON."

On his appointment to command of the army, Washington wrote his brother, John Augustine: "I shall hope that my friends will visit and endeavor to keep up the spirits of my wife, as much as they can, as my departure will, I know, be a cutting stroke upon her; and on this account alone I have many disagreeable sensations." The general also wrote Jack Custis that he thought it absolutely necessary for the peace and satisfaction of his mother that he and his wife should live at Mount Vernon during his own absence.

MARTHA WASHINGTON DURING THE WAR

Mrs. Washington described herself as being "a kind of walking perambulator" during the war. She spent every winter with the general at headquarters, and said that she heard the first and last guns every season, and "marched home when the campaign was about to open." Lord Dunmore came up the Potomac to capture her, but the Virginia militia assembled in such numbers that he did not dare to attempt it. When her friends advised her to move back into the interior of the country, she said: "No, I will not desert my post." Valuables and important papers were kept in trunks, so that they could be moved at a moment's notice. In those times, when there were no telegraphs and telephones, what anxious days Martha Washington must have spent when important operations were in progress! For instance, when the British army was landing at the head of Elk, about to fight a battle which they expected would destroy her husband's army. Late in August, 1777, while reconnoitering before the battle of the Brandywine, Washington spent the night near the Head of Elk. This was the nearest that he came to Mount Vernon during the war, until, as he entered in his diary on Sunday, September 9, 1781: "I reached my own Seat at Mount Vernon (distant 120 Miles from the Hd. of Elk) where I staid till the 12th." The 10th, Washington wrote Lafayette: "We are thus far on our way to you. The Count de Rochambeau has just arrived. General Chastellux will be here, and we propose, after resting to-morrow, to be at Fredericksburg on the night of the 12th."

THE CUSTISES

No man loved his home more than Washington, and yet no man was so ready to leave it at his country's call. His accepting the command of the army in 1798 was the most patriotic act of all his patriotic life. His fame was bright and secure; he was comfortably established at Mount Vernon, where the infirmities of age were creeping upon him; he had everything to lose and nothing to gain; no man would be shrewder than Washington in understanding this; yet he was ready to sacrifice reputation and comfort, because he thought that he might serve his country. He wrote: "As my whole life has been dedicated to my country in one shape or another, for the poor remains of it, it is not an object to contend for ease and quiet, when all that is valuable in it is at stake, further than to be satisfied that the sacrifice I should make of these is acceptable and desired by my Country."

John Parke Custis, Mrs. Washington's son, left four children, the two youngest of whom were brought up by Washington. When in 1824 Lafayette last visited America, he told G. W. P. Custis that he had seen him first on the portico at Mount Vernon in 1784. "A very little gentleman, with a feather in his hat, holding fast to one finger of the good general's remarkable hand, which (so large that hand!) was all, my dear sir, you could well do at that time." Nelly, the sister of George Washington Parke Custis, used to stand on tiptoe to hold the button of the General's coat while she charmed him with her girlish confidences. Nelly Custis was married to Lawrence Lewis at Mount Vernon on Washington's last birthday. At the wedding the General wore his old continental uniform of blue and buff, and this was probably the last time he had it on. The first child of Nelly Custis was born a few days before Washington's death at Mount Vernon.

Washington would have been touched by the important part which school children have borne in the restoration of Mount Vernon. He took an affectionate interest in the bringing up of youth, and there was no philanthropy for which he opened his purse more freely than education. Though God left him childless in order that he might be the Father of his Country, fondness for children was a charming characteristic, and the beautiful children and grandchildren of Mrs. Washington added joy to their life at Mount Vernon. Mrs. Fitzhugh, who, as a child, was a frequent visitor to Mount Vernon, said that often, when at their games in the drawing room at night —perhaps romping, dancing and noisy— they would see the general watching their movements at some side door, enjoying their sport; and if at any time his presence seemed to check them, he would beg them not to mind him, but go on just as before, encouraging them in every possible way to continue their amusements to their hearts' content.

When, in 1773, Mrs. Washington's only daughter, beautiful Patsy Custis, was fatally stricken, Washington stated in his diary, June 19: "At home all day. About five oclock poor Patcy Custis Died Suddenly." The next day Washington wrote: "It is an easier matter to conceive, than to describe the distress of this Family; . . . the Sweet Innocent Girl Entered into a more happy & peaceful abode than any she has met with in the afflicted Path she hitherto has trod. She . . . expired in . . . less than two minutes without uttering a word, a groan, or scarce a sigh.—This sudden and unexpected blow, I scarce need add has almost reduced my poor Wife to the lowest ebb of Misery; which is encreas'd by the absence of her son, (whom I have just fixed at the College in New York . . .)." Patsy was laid to rest in the old tomb on the twentieth. The diary states

the nineteenth as very warm and clear, with a south wind. The day of the funeral it was still very warm, with thunder and appearances of rain, but none fell at Mount Vernon. The custom of placing the tomb near the mansion caused the departed to continue in a peculiar and intimate manner members of the household.

THE END OF LIFE AT MOUNT VERNON

In spite of the fact that his mother was vigorous to an advanced age, Washington wrote: "I am of a short-lived family and cannot expect to remain very long upon the earth." A few days before his death he pointed out to his nephew, Major Lewis, the spot where he intended to build the new family vault, saying: "This change I shall make the first of all for I may require it before the rest." The last entries in his diary are as follows: December 12, 1799, "Morning Cloudy. Wind at No. Et. and Mer. 33. A large circle round the Moon last Night. About 10 o'clock it began to snow, soon after to Hail, and then to a settled cold Rain. Mer. 28 at Night. 13. Morning Snowing and abt. 3 inches deep. Wind at No. Et., and Mer. at 30, contg. Snowing till 1 O'clock, and abt. 4 it became perfectly clear. Wind in the same place but not hard. Mer. 28 at Night." These are no doubt the last words Washington wrote.

The passing of this great soul has been described by Tobias Lear, who says that, although Washington himself had been in the saddle in the storm most of Thursday the twelfth, on the evening of which he was stricken with his last illness, he considered the weather too bad to send his servant to the post office. "Between 2 and 3 o'clk on Saturday morning he awoke Mrs. Washington and told her he was very unwell, and had had an ague. She would . . . have got up to call a servant; but he would not permit her lest she should take cold." He lay nearly four hours in a chill in a cold bedroom before anything was done or a fire lighted. When on his death bed, Washington said to Mr. Lear:

"I am afraid I shall fatigue you too much; . . . it is a debt we must pay to each other,

and I hope, when you want aid of this kind you will find it." He motioned to his attendant, Christopher, who had been standing, to take a seat by his bedside. Washington's patience, fortitude, and resignation never forsook him for a moment. He said: "I am not afraid to die, and therefore can bear the worst." The clock which was in the death chamber marked the hour 10.20 P. M.

MOUNT VERNON A NATIONAL POSSESSION (1799-1932)

The history of the Mount Vernon Estate, including the tomb of George Washington and Martha Washington, is long and complicated. George Washington left the central part of the estate, including the mansion, to his nephew, Bushrod Washington, who had not the means to keep up such a property and properly to receive the numerous visitors. Twenty years after Washington's death the house and the tomb were falling into decay. Bushrod Washington, in 1829, left the mansion and the surroundings to his nephew, John Augustine Washington, a son of Corbin Washington. Thence it passed to John Augustine's widow and to her son, the second John Augustine Washington.

This story of neglect and decay would be sad enough if it did not lead up to the saving of Mount Vernon by the insistence of one woman, Ann Pamela Cunningham, of South Carolina. In 1853 she began to agitate for a federal society of women to take over and preserve the estate as a national shrine. What was then the immense sum of $200,000 was raised for the purchase of the mansion and the two hundred acres surrounding it. February 22, 1860, the Mount Vernon Ladies' Association, which became the Mount Vernon Ladies' Association of the Union, took possession of the estate. The history of that Association and its skillful and patriotic management of the Mount Vernon estate is a part of the long story of the association of the Washingtons with that estate. From 1674 to the present day, more than two hundred and fifty years, Mount Vernon has been a part of the history of the Washington family and hence of the history of the nation.

Part II
Ownership of Mount Vernon

1607-1932 (325 YEARS)

1607—Occupied by Indian tribes; politically unorganized.

1607—Colony of Virginia; asserts jurisdiction by first charter of 1606.

1649—Grant of Northern Neck by Charles II to a body of his adherents. Patent renewed August 3, 1663,

and new patent granted May 8, 1669, of which Lord Culpeper became managing partner.

1674-5, March 1—Joint grant by Culpeper to Nicholas Spencer and John Washington of 5,000 acres on the Potomac River.

1677—Confirmation by Virginia Council of

the grant to Spencer and Washington.

1677-8, January 11—Will proved by which John Washington left his half of the grant to his son, Lawrence.

1690—Tract divided, Lawrence Washington taking 2,500 acres next to Little Hunting Creek.

1698, March 30—Will proved by which Lawrence Washington left the tract to his daughter, Mildred (Gregory).

1726, May—Mildred Gregory and her husband deed the property to her brother, Augustine.

1740, October — Augustine Washington transfers the property to his son, Lawrence. Confirmed by will, April 11, 1743, with reversion to George if Lawrence died without issue.

1752, September 26—Will of Lawrence Washington proved, by which he leaves the property of 2,700 acres now called Mount Vernon to his infant daughter, Sarah, subject to his wife's life interest, and with reversion to his brother, George, for life only failing lawful issue.

1752—Death of the child, Sarah. George

Washington inherits Mount Vernon.

1754, December 16—Widow of Lawrence Washington sells her life interest to George Washington.

1754-1799—Complete and undisputed ownership of Mount Vernon by George Washington.

1802-1829—By will of George Washington proved on January 20, 1800, and following Martha Washington's life occupancy, his nephew, Bushrod Washington, occupies the Mount Vernon mansion and some 3,500 acres of surrounding land, the lawful heirs accepting other bequests in lieu.

1829-1832—Mansion and 1,225 acres of land held by John Augustine Washington, nephew of Bushrod Washington.

1832-1850—Property held by Jane C.

Washington, widow of John Augustine.

1850-1858—By deed of his mother, confirmed by will in 1855, John Augustine Washington is owner of the property.

1858, April 6—Contract to transfer Mount Vernon mansion, the tomb, and some 200 acres of land to the Mount Vernon Ladies' Association of the Union.

1860, February 22—The Association takes formal possession of the property; but legal title does not pass until November 12, 1868.

1860-1932—Property held and enlarged by the Association.

1932—The Mount Vernon Memorial Highway opened from the Arlington Memorial Bridge along the Potomac, to Mount Vernon by the United States George Washington Bicentennial Commission.

Selected Authorities

BAKER, WILLIAM SPOHN—*Washington after the Revolution*. Philadelphia, Lippincott, 1898.

CONWAY, MONCURE DANIEL—*Barons of the Potomack and the Rappahannock*. New York, Grolier Club, 1892.

CONWAY, MONCURE DANIEL, ED.—*George Washington and Mount Vernon*. Brooklyn, Long Island Historical Society, 1889.

CUSTIS, GEORGE WASHINGTON PARKE—*Recollections and Private Memoirs of Washington*. Philadelphia, Flint, 1859. (Other eds.)

FORD, PAUL LEICESTER—*True George Washington*. Philadelphia, Lippincott, 1896. (Especially chs. vii, viii.)

FORD, WORTHINGTON CHAUNCEY—*George Washington*. 2 vols. New York, Scribner, 1900. (Especially Vol. I, ch. vii; Vol. II, ch. vi.)

HARLAN, MARIAN—*Colonial Homesteads and their Stories*. New York, Putnam, 1897.

HAWORTH, PAUL L.—*George Washington, Country Gentleman*. Indianapolis, Bobbs-Merrill, 1925.

HERBERT, LEILA — *First American; his Homes and his Households*. New York, Harper, 1900.

KING, GRACE—*Mount Vernon on the Potomac*. New York, Macmillan, 1929.

LEAR, TOBIAS—*Letters and Recollections of George Washington*. New York, Doubleday Page, 1906.

LOSSING, BENSON J.—*Home of Washington*. New York, Virtue & Yorston, 1871. (Other eds.; title varies.)

LOWTHER, MINNIE KENDALL—*Mount Vernon, its Children, its Romances, its Allied Families and Mansions*. Philadephia, Winston, 1930.

MOORE, CHARLES—*Family Life of George Washington*. Boston, Houghton Mifflin, 1926.

MOUNT VERNON LADIES' ASSOCIATION OF THE UNION—*Annual Reports*.

OSBORN, LUCRETIA PERRY, ED.—*Washington speaks for Himself*. New York, Scribner, 1927. (Especially ch. i.)

PRUSSING, EUGENE E.—*Estate of George Washington, deceased*. Boston, Little Brown, 1927.

RUSH, RICHARD—*Washington in Domestic Life*. Philadelphia, Lippincott, 1857.

SAWYER, JOSEPH D.—*Washington*. 2 vols. New York, Macmillan, 1927.

SIPE, C. HALE—*Mount Vernon and the Washington Family; a Concise Handbook on the Ancestry, Youth and Family of George Washington, and History of his Home*. Butler, Pa., the Author, 1927.

WASHINGTON, GEORGE — *Diaries, 1748-1799*. Ed. by John C. Fitzpatrick. 4 vols. Boston, Houghton Mifflin, 1925.

WASHINGTON, GEORGE—*Writings*. Ed. by Worthington Chauncey Ford. 14 vols. New York, Putnam, 1889-93.

WILSTACH, PAUL—*Mount Vernon, Washington's Home and the Nation's Shrine*. Garden City, Doubleday Page, 1916.

Washington the Military Man
By Col. Samuel C. Vestal
Part I
Preparation for Command

GEORGE WASHINGTON
From a portrait by Charles Willson Peale

EARLY TRAINING

WASHINGTON is one of the most venerated men in history. His grave is a hallowed shrine for people of every race and nation. In his lifetime friends and foes alike joined in acclaiming his greatness; and, when he died, European nations, at war with each other, paid homage to his memory. He ranks so high in the esteem of mankind that he seems to stand above conflict and malice. The basis of his reputation in history is his career as a military man.

As a boy, Washington learned much from Lord Fairfax, an English nobleman, a contributor to the *Spectator,* and an accomplished gentleman, who had come to America to look after his vast estates beyond the Blue Ridge Mountains. They became fast friends. From Lord Fairfax, Washington gained a knowledge of men and manners that no school could give.

He was always an earnest student of the art of war. His elder brother, Lawrence Washington, brought military instructors to Mount Vernon to teach him all that was necessary to qualify young British officers for their positions. Washington, like Wellington, was never drilled as a soldier in a company. Nor did he ever drill a company. In the British service, the instruction of the men was done by drill sergeants. Not until Baron von Steuben came to the American army at Valley Forge did American officers drill their companies.

Few officers, who have come to high command at the beginning of a war, ever had as good and thorough training in command as Washington, when Congress selected him to lead the American forces. From his sixteenth to his twenty-seventh year, he passed his life on the frontier, surveying, exploring, and fighting the Indians and the French, with occasional returns to civilization. When he was sixteen, Lord Fairfax employed him to survey his estate. At twenty-one, he went on a march through the wilderness to a French military post that challenged control in the West. At twenty-two he commanded an expedition against the French. When he was twenty-three, Braddock took him on his personal staff for his ill-fated expedition; and then, for more than two years, he was stationed, in command, upon the frontier. In his twenty-seventh year, he led the advance guard of General Forbes' army through the wilderness and captured Fort Duquesne, now Pittsburgh. Thus, by turns, he led the hardy life of the frontiersman in contact with the Indians, and a cultivated, refined life in touch with the most important people in Virginia.

In October, 1753, on the eve of the French and Indian War, he was chosen by Governor Dinwiddie, of Virginia, as an agent to warn the French away from the Ohio Valley. Dinwiddie wrote to the governor of Pennsylvania that he was sending "a person of distinction." Washington delivered Dinwiddie's letter to the French commandant at Fort le Boeuf, about twenty miles south of Lake Erie, and, after many hardships and perilous adventures, returned to Williamsburg, the capital of Virginia, in January, 1754.

FRONTIER CAMPAIGN OF 1754

On March 15, 1754, he was commissioned lieutenant colonel of the Virginia regiment, whose colonel, Joshua Fry, was ordered to march to the fort of the Ohio Company at the place where the Monongahela and Allegheny unite to form the Ohio River. Washington himself was to advance, with two companies, and clear a road, wide enough for artillery and baggage, from Wills Creek to Red Stone Creek on the Monongahela. At Red Stone Creek, he was to fortify a position and hold it until reinforcements came. Washington learned, at Wills Creek, that the French had taken the fort, on the site of the present Pittsburgh. Although there was no bloodshed, this was the opening act of the Seven Years' War. The French strengthened the fort and named it Fort Duquesne.

Washington began his advance through the wilderness, and, at Great Meadows, forti-

ginians should march out with their arms, on condition that they would not return to the Ohio for one year. As Washington was short of ammunition, he agreed to these terms, and returned to Virginia with his troops.

For his services, he received the thanks of the House of Burgesses. Governor Din-

ness. The youthful Washington learned a principle at Fort Necessity, which was of decisive importance in the Revolution—he never again allowed himself to be surrounded and besieged.

FRONTIER CAMPAIGN OF 1755

The qualities which account for the ascendancy of Washington over the Virginia authorities caused General Braddock to select him as a volunteer aide, when he arrived at Alexandria in February, 1755. There is no better measure of the character of Washington than the impression he made upon the stern English general. To the Englishman of that day, the colonists were beings of an inferior order. There was something, however, about Washington which made the English treat him with the utmost courtesy and gained for him the respect and affection of the general. In wilderness warfare, Washington was a veteran; Braddock was a novice.

On May 29, the advance guard of Braddock's army began to move from Fort Cumberland upon Fort Duquesne. Its progress was slow, as it had to build a road through the wilderness. When Braddock was setting out on his march, Washington made one of the astounding rides for which he was noted, from Fort Cumberland to Williamsburg, borrowed four thousand pounds for Braddock, and rejoined the army.

The column crossed the Monongahela on July 9, seven miles from Fort Duquesne, and was almost immediately attacked by a force of French and Indians, within the present city limits of Pittsburgh. There was no ambush. It was a meeting engagement, in the forest, between 1,300 British and 900 French and Indians. The British fired first and, at the third volley, killed Captain Beaujeu, the French leader. One hundred of his men fled, but the rest, under Captain Dumas, quickly deployed into a formation resembling a two-tined fork, and enveloped the British flanks. The British remained in the narrow road and fired at an unseen foe. Had they, as Washington expressed it, filed off to the right and left, and taken to trees, gaining the enemy's flanks, as a party of Virginians actually did on the right flank, under Washington's direction, there would have been no such overwhelming disaster. On the contrary, the British would probably have won an easy victory.

The day before the battle, Washington, who was suffering from a fever, joined the main body, in a covered wagon. The sound of firing seems to have cured him. He mounted a horse and rode everywhere, carrying the orders of his general. Braddock, after having four horses killed under him, was mortally wounded. When the fallen Braddock gave the order to retreat, the men rushed to the rear and could be no more stopped, as Washington said, than "the wild bears of the mountains." Three hundred

WASHINGTON'S JOURNEY TO FORT LE BOEUF 1753

fied a position, which he named Fort Necessity. Presently, he learned that the French were advancing against him. He did not await attack. He "set out in a heavy rain, and, in a night as dark as pitch," attacked a party of French and Indians, killed ten, including the French commander, Jumonville, and captured twenty-one. Washington continued his advance until he learned that a large force was moving against him. He returned to Great Meadows, and resumed work on Fort Necessity. Meanwhile, Colonel Fry had died at Wills Creek; and thus Washington came to the command of the Virginia Regiment. The enemy appeared on July 3. After fighting all day, the French called out for a parley. They proposed that the Vir-

widdie refused to be bound by the condition in the capitulation on the ground that, after signature, the French took eight British subjects, exposed them for sale, "and, missing thereof, sent them prisoners to Canada."

Throughout the campaign Washington had shown great boldness. With one hundred and fifty raw recruits he had advanced to meet a force, which, to his knowledge, numbered a thousand men. His fearlessness and the consequent timidity of the French went far to offset his inferiority in numbers. The selection of Fort Necessity as a defensive position has been severely criticized, but without full account being taken of the firearms of the time, the need of water, and conditions in the dense wilder-

French and six hundred Indians killed or wounded seven hundred British troops. Seventy-two of the officers were casualties. Washington aided in carrying his wounded chief from the field. There was no pursuit. Washington had four bullet holes through his clothes, and he had two horses shot under him. Four days after the battle Braddock died. He bequeathed to Washington, as tokens of his gratitude and affection, his servant and his favorite horse.

FRONTIER SERVICE (1755-1757)

Washington emerged from the campaign the heroic redeemer of colonial honor. On August 14, 1755, he was commissioned colonel and commander in chief of the forces raised for the defense of Virginia, and given full power to carry on offensive and defensive action. He was not yet twenty-four years of age. Washington's plan was to establish a central fort at Winchester and a few smaller posts as points of support for moving columns. He built Fort Loudoun at Winchester; but he got no further with his plan. The Assembly insisted upon a cordon system and voted to erect a chain of small forts; whereas Washington, with good reason, desired to have few forts and larger garrisons, so that more men would be available to seek out the savages in their fastnesses.

He established his headquarters at Winchester, and for more than two years defended 350 miles of frontier with 700 men, a task made difficult by the insubordination and irregular service of the soldiers and a lack of supplies. This situation was a precursor of his experience in the Revolution. Virginia, like the Continental Congress, selected him for a most difficult service and then failed to support him adequately; each let him carry the burden almost unaided. In April, 1757, he wrote: "I have been posted . . . for twenty months past upon our cold and barren frontiers, to perform, I think I may say, impossibilities; that is, to protect from the cruel incursions of a crafty, savage enemy a line of inhabitants, of more than three hundred and fifty miles in extent, with a force inadequate to the task."

FRONTIER SERVICE (1758)

From this irksome duty Washington was relieved by Pitt's energetic military program for 1758, which called for an expedition against Fort Duquesne. Washington had urged the futility of defensive war, and the necessity of attacking the enemy. He joined the expedition. The new commander, General Forbes, decided to cut a new road and move from Pennsylvania, instead of Vir-

ginia, as a base. Washington insisted, in vain, that much time would be saved by following Braddock's route. The new road was shorter; but the work of construction delayed the expedition until the bad weather approached.

A detachment of 813 men, under Major James Grant, of the Highlanders, sent forward contrary to Washington's views, met the fate of Braddock's army. Grant himself and Major Andrew Lewis were captured. The garrison of Fort Duquesne did not await the attack of the main army, but retreated in the night; and, on November 25, 1758,

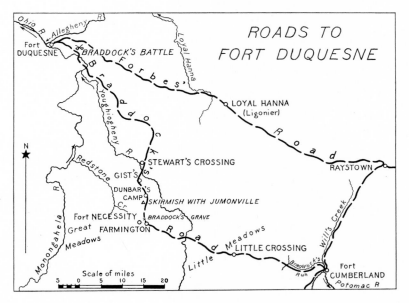

ROADS TO FORT DUQUESNE

the advanced troops under Washington took possession of the smoking ruins of Fort Duquesne. They had passed through the field where the frozen bodies of Grant's men lay scattered. To these and the skeletons of Braddock's men they gave honorable burial.

Scarcity of provisions compelled the army to flee from its conquest. A small garrison was left to rebuild the fort, which was christened Fort Pitt, in honor of the British Prime Minister; and the colonial troops returned to their homes.

MILITARY EDUCATION

Here ended Washington's military service prior to the Revolution. He retired from the army and resumed his peaceful and industrious life at Mount Vernon. He had entered the French and Indian War as a mere youth, and he came out the most distinguished soldier of the British North American Colonies.

Washington was not an unlettered man, in spite of the fact that he left school at an early age; like Wellington, he read whenever he had an opportunity and he read

always to good purpose. In early life he read carefully the history of England and the essays of the *Spectator;* and in later life, in writing to his step-grandson, he quoted Shakespeare from memory. His correspondence and his books deposited in the Boston Athenaeum give unmistakable evidence that for more than forty years he bought and read practically every technical military work upon which he could lay his hands. His report in 1753 upon Fort le Boeuf, and his solution of a tactical problem submitted to him by General Forbes in 1758 for marching the command through forty miles of forested country, are the work of an officer with good training in technique. In his correspondence of 1776-1777, dealing with his second reconstruction of his army, the views expressed, especially as to cavalry and artillery, are decidedly such as could have been formulated only by a man of broad military reading and culture; and we know enough of his military household at that time to be sure that the views were his own. He had that rare combination of education, intuition, and common sense that go to make a man great. When asked by the Marquis de Chastellux, in later life, what professional military books he read with greatest pleasure, he replied, "*The King of Prussia's Instructions to His Generals,* and *The Tactics of M. de Guibert.*" In regard to his reading, he was silent, as on everything concerning himself. But no one has ever pointed to an instance where he showed himself to be ignorant of history or literature. Washington's writings are a monument to his greatness. He employed secretaries and he signed papers prepared for him by his subordinates, but his writings were essentially his own.

Part II
The Revolution to Valley Forge

EVE OF THE REVOLUTION
(1774-1775)

Washington was a member of the Virginia Convention of 1774. All eyes were fixed on Boston, which had been closed as a port on June 1, by General Gage, commandant of the British garrison of 5,000 men.

nental Congress, which was to meet in Philadelphia on September 5, 1774.

In the Continental Congress, Washington's polish, graciousness, practical knowledge, and reputation for personal intrepidity, showed their effect upon his fellow members. "If you speak of solid information and sound judgment," said Patrick Henry,

Washington was called to command independent companies, by the popular will and the demand of the troops themselves.

He was a member of the Second Continental Congress, which met in Philadelphia on May 10, 1775; and he attended, in his uniform of blue and buff, as commander of the Virginia militia.

The battle of Lexington had been fought on April 19, and on the next day General Artemas Ward had assumed command of the patriot forces assembling around Boston. In May, the British garrison was reinforced to 10,000 men. In the same month Ethan Allen and Seth Warner captured Ticonderoga and Crown Point.

COMMANDER IN CHIEF (1775)

On June 15, 1775, on a suggestion made by John Adams and seconded by Samuel Adams, both of Massachusetts, George Washington, of Virginia, then in his forty-fourth year, was unanimously chosen Commander in Chief of the Army of the United Colonies. It was the most important act of the Continental Congress. On that date the Army of the United States was born. It consisted of one man.

Washington's selection was due to the reputation which he had gained in the French and Indian War, and to the deep impression which he had made upon the members of Congress. Washington's commission and the instructions of Congress to him were drawn up by a committee consisting of Richard Harry Lee, Edward Rutledge, and John Adams.

Never was a mightier task given to a human being. "I have launched into a wide and extensive field," wrote he, "too boundless for my abilities, and far, very far, beyond my experience."

Washington knew that he had behind him a brave and patriotic people; but one unskilled, untrained, unprepared for war, without arms, allies, money, or credit. He knew that he faced, almost inevitably, a repetition of his experience at Winchester; summer campaigns with unskilled forces and long winter vigils with an ever-diminishing number of famishing soldiers. His great struggle, as at Winchester, was not with the enemy, but with indifference and inefficiency at the seat of government. Washington's commission as "General and Commander in Chief of the Army of the United Colonies" was dated June 19, 1775. He set out with General Lee and his aides on the 23rd for Boston. When the people of Philadelphia saw the heroic figure of Washington riding northward to assume command of the army, they took new courage. He had not gone twenty miles when he met a hard-riding

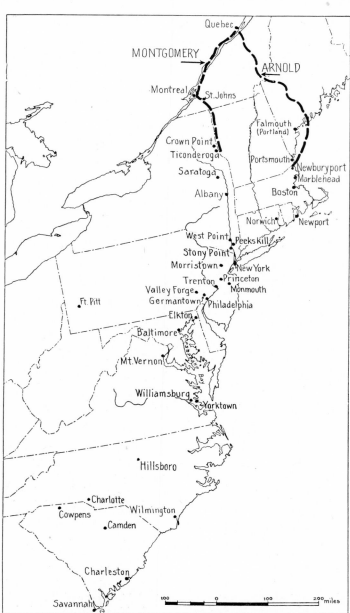

Colonel Washington made the most eloquent speech in this colonial convention. "I will raise one thousand men," said he, "subsist them at my own expense, and march myself at their head for the relief of Boston." His national career began with his appointment by the convention as one of Virginia's seven delegates to the First Continental Congress.

"Colonel Washington is unquestionably the greatest man on the floor."

When Washington returned home after the adjournment of Congress, Virginia was arming for war. Although he had long been out of the service, and Virginia had officers, like Andrew Lewis, who had won victories in recent conflicts with the Indians,

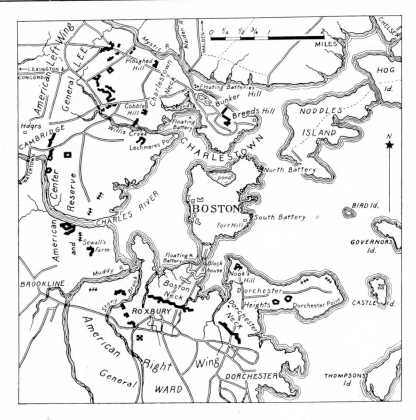

courier bringing news of the Battle of Bunker Hill, then six days old. The Colonists had lost 495, including 30 prisoners, while the British had lost 1,054.

On Monday morning, July 3, General Ward turned over his command to Washington. "His excellency," wrote Surgeon Thacher in his journal on seeing him later in the same month, "was on horseback, in company with several military gentlemen. It was not difficult to distinguish him from all others; his personal appearance is truly noble and majestic, being tall and well proportioned." Mrs. John Adams, who saw him about the time he assumed command, wrote to her husband: Dignity with ease and complacency, the gentleman and soldier, look agreeably blended in him. Modesty marks every line and feature of his face."

Washington found Boston enclosed, on a 10-mile front, by American trenches and redoubts, manned by about 14,000 soldiers. One of his first acts was to order a raid on the British lines, in order to get information by capturing a prisoner, or as he himself said: "Having some Reason to suspect they were extending their Lines at Charles Town, I last Saturday Evening, ordered some of the Riffle Men down to make a Discovery, or to bring off a Prisoner. . . . They brought in two Prisoners whose Acct confirmed by some other Circumstances removed my Suspicions in part."

After the battle of Bunker Hill, the British did not again attack American troops in intrenched lines. That battle taught them to respect the American marksman in a prepared position. The Americans were expert with the spade, and they astonished

the British by their ability to construct field fortifications. Washington knew that, if his men were sheltered behind parapets, breastworks, or stone walls, they would give a good account of themselves; but he was convinced that they would not march boldly up to a work or stand exposed on a plain.

WAR POWERS OF THE COMMANDER IN CHIEF (1775-1776)

From the first, Washington laid down the principle, for himself and for all other commanders, that Congress was the absolute master. He himself was its executive. Thus, he established the principle that the civil government is supreme.

Washington's authority as commander in chief was not limited to the land forces. His control extended over the naval forces, as the President's power as commander in chief extends over our navy to-day; and he devoted much time and thought to creating a navy. He established a force of armed ships; commissioned ship commanders; and organized crews from soldiers. His naval personnel came from Colonel Glover's Marblehead regiment. This was the beginning of the United States Navy. Later, on October 5, 1775, Congress instructed Washington to fit out armed vessels. He commissioned John Manley, of Marblehead, commodore of the fleet.

The origin of the war powers of the President of the United States, as Commander in Chief of the Army and Navy, is to be found in the acts of George Washington, the General and Commander in Chief of the Continental Forces. The action of Washington in creating a navy, to meet an

immediate necessity, without previous authority from Congress, is one of the first and best illustrations of the exercise of the war powers of the Commander in Chief of the Land and Naval Forces. The difficulty of reconciling the constitutional war powers of the President and the constitutional powers of Congress, more apparent than real, may be traced back to the relations between Washington and the Continental Congress.

MILITARY VIGOR

Lack of powder was the great obstacle to offensive operations. Washington had only enough powder to supply 25 rounds per man and one day's artillery fire, while the British had large reserves and their soldiers carried 60 rounds. It is said that, when the battle of Lexington was fought, there was not enough powder in America, outside of the British magazines, to last for a week's fighting. Washington sent an expedition to Ticonderoga and Crown Point, under Colonel Knox, who secured for him artillery and ammunition so necessary for his siege operations against the city of Boston. The Americans also owed much to captures by Washington's naval forces. The British supply ship *Nancy*, captured during the siege, alone yielded 2,000 British muskets, 30,000 round shot, 100,000 flints, and a 2,700-pound 13-inch mortar.

Washington showed his characteristic boldness in the first year of his command, by sending an expedition, under Montgomery, against Montreal and another, under Arnold, against Quebec. These expeditions failed, but they had their compensations, because the British accumulated in Canada troops which could have been used more effectively in the insurgent colonies. In 1776, their armed forces in Canada numbered 13,000 men. Washington's instructions to Arnold, in regard to his treatment of the Canadians, their property, and their religion, are models of wisdom from a political and military point of view.

Welcome reinforcements arrived from the South; but, as the leaves fell and the wild fowl flew southward, Washington found himself face to face with the first of eight dreary winters, which he was to pass in cantonments, beleaguering British troops comfortably quartered in American cities.

CAPTURE OF BOSTON (1776)

Washington gained possession of Boston in March, 1776, by a manoeuvre similar to that by which Napoleon Bonaparte forced the evacuation of Toulon, in 1793. He seized high ground on Dorchester Heights, overlooking the city and the harbor, from which he could bring artillery fire upon the British shipping. The British withdrew hastily, leaving much valuable property.

They burnt or blew up their harbor defenses and attempted to destroy or spike their cannon, with little success, or threw them into the sea. The Americans found, or recovered, 250 cannon of various calibers,

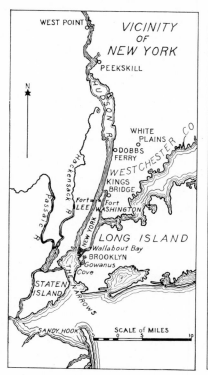

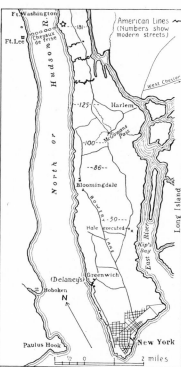

doned the city without a struggle, however, would have been fatal politically to the American cause. Washington reached New York on April 13. British men-of-war soon began to arrive in the harbor, and a large force, under General Sir William Howe, debarked on Staten Island. Admiral Lord Howe arrived with a fleet and more troops on July 12. Thither came Lord Dunmore, from Virginia, and Clinton and Cornwallis, from South Carolina, after the British naval repulse on June 28, at Fort Moultrie. With 15,000 ragged troops fit for duty, Washington faced 30,000 of the best European troops, aided by the best navy in the world.

PREPARATION TO MEET BRITISH ATTACK

To defend New York it was necessary to defend Brooklyn; and the measures for the defense of Brooklyn had been taken by Lee before Washington's arrival. The extent of the British effort exceeded Washington's expectations. He was in a quandary as to whether they intended to attack New York or Brooklyn.

On August 22, 1776, the British landed, according to information received by Washington, about eight thousand men on Long Island. He immediately sent six regiments over to Brooklyn, where the Americans held lines behind the village. He was playing a dangerous but skillful game with the British naval and military commanders, in which he was taking full account of winds, tides, fogs, and the movements of the enemy. On August 23, he wrote, "The flood tide will begin to make about eleven o'clock, at which time, if the detachment ordered yesterday were to move to the high and open grounds about Mr. Delancey's and Bloomingdale,

by the aid of which they reconstituted the old harbor defenses and built new ones. Thanks to these defenses, Boston was the only important American port that was not taken or burnt by the British during the remainder of the war.

The capture of Boston was a great achievement. Washington had maintained his army for six months without powder, and had virtually disbanded one army and recruited another within musket shot of twenty British regiments. For taking the city he received a gold medal and a vote of thanks from Congress. This was the first of eight occasions when Congress passed a vote of thanks in honor of its illustrious general.

A reported conversation of Washington with a little girl in Boston, the day his forces occupied the city, March 17, 1776, gives a graphic picture of the Revolutionary Army. He asked her which she liked better, the Redcoats or the Provincials. "The Redcoats," said the child. "Ah, my dear," said Washington, "they look better, but they don't fight. The ragged fellows are the best for fighting."

DEFENSE OF NEW YORK (1776)

The British retired to Halifax; but Washington anticipated that their next move would be against New York. He left a garrison of five regiments in Boston, and hurried away with the rest of the forces to New York.

While the British were still in Boston, Washington had sent General Charles Lee to New York to prepare its defense. As early as March 14, 1776, Washington pointed out, in a letter to Lord Stirling, the strategic value of New York and the Hudson as a

means for the British to "stop the intercourse between the northern and southern colonies, upon which depends the safety of America."

The shore of Manhattan Island was girdled with small forts, erected by General Lee, but unfortunately the range of the guns was not sufficient to prevent British vessels from passing through the wide channel. Owing to the lack of heavy guns in the harbor defenses, New York was indefensible against the combined attack of the British military and naval forces. To have aban-

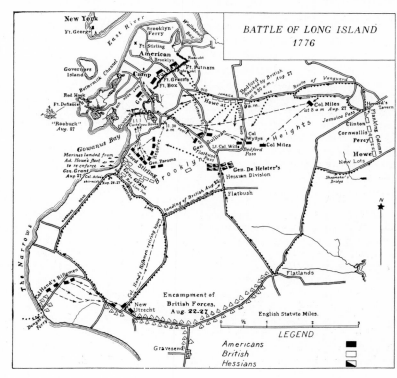

they would be ready to come forward, or turn back, as occasion should require."

On the same day Washington visited Long Island, and, as a result of his inspection, sent over four more regiments, with boats, ready to reinforce the Brooklyn lines or to return to New York, in case the British ships should stand in toward the city, a thing they had been unable to do, as the wind had been ahead, or too light, when the tide served. During the next three days the British ships fell down to the Narrows; and, from this fact and the disappearance of their tents from Staten Island, Washington concluded that their main effort would be made on Long Island. He therefore ordered considerable reinforcements from New York, and informed Congress that he would continue to do so, as circumstances might require.

BATTLE OF LONG ISLAND (1776)

General Greene had been in command on Long Island. He fell sick; and his illness caused oversights unknown to Washington, which led to a tactical reverse. The American position, nearly a mile long, faced southeast, and ran from Gowanus Cove to Wallabout Bay. It was strongly fortified. Two or three miles in advance, along Brooklyn Heights, the Americans had strong outposts. On August 27, General Howe made a skillful turning movement around the left of the American outpost line, and routed it. The American loss was about 1,000. But here the success ended. Howe has been severely criticised for not making a general assault upon the main American lines; but, having commanded the assaulting troops at Bunker Hill, he doubtless remembered how the British had twice fallen back from its bloody slopes.

Washington committed no error in defending Long Island; but his temerity was not as great as it appears to us to-day. New York Harbor was not the deep basin that it is now; tidal currents, shallows, uncharted rocks, fogs, and adverse winds made it difficult to handle sailing ships; and the American soldier, in an intrenched position, had a prestige, after Bunker Hill, that has not been sufficiently recognized. These things were given due weight in the mind of Washington, and they had their effect upon General Howe, who, after his unexpected success on August 27, settled down to the slow operations of a siege.

RETURN TO NEW YORK (1776)

General Putnam was in command on Long Island. Washington was not present at the beginning, but he crossed over from Manhattan Island, during the battle, and did much to reorganize the American position. The next day he brought over more troops; but, early on the morning of the 29th, he made up his mind that the troops must be removed from their exposed position. His skill in withdrawing an army by water from immediate contact with a powerful enemy has never been surpassed—not

even by the British at Gallipoli, in 1915-1916.

Washington collected boats under the pretense of sending battalions to Long Island, and he issued a general order for the relief of a "proportionate number of regiments," and a change of positions. Everything was in readiness for this movement; each regiment thought it was one of the chosen regiments; and, in the night of August 29, Washington crossed to New York. A few heavy guns were left in position. The British wounded four men in one of the last boats to leave the shore.

On September 15, Clinton's division, covered by the fire of British war vessels at musket range from the shore, crossed the East River in barges and landed at Kip's Bay (34th Street), well above the New York City of that day. The garrison made a precipitate retreat to Washington's main position in the upper part of the island. On the 16th, in a four-hour action, known as the Battle of Harlem Heights, the Americans drove the British a mile and a quarter from what is now 130th Street to 105th Street. This was a happy interlude in a long series of tragic reverses and retreats.

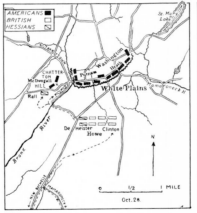
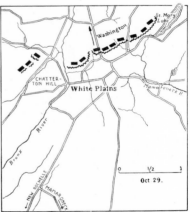

WHITE PLAINS ENGAGEMENT (1776)

At the northern end of Manhattan Island, the ascent of the Hudson was guarded, on the east, by Fort Washington, and, on the west, by Fort Lee, on the New Jersey shore. On October 9, two British frigates demonstrated the uselessness of the forts by running between them.

On October 12, Howe landed in Westchester County, New York. Washington evacuated his lines on Harlem Heights and moved to White Plains, where, on October 22, he began to dig in with 13,000 men. On October 28, Howe came up to Washington's position, at White Plains, and found the Americans intrenched, awaiting attack. He stormed a detached post at Chatterton Hill. The Americans, after inflicting a loss more than double their own, retreated to the main position. Howe remained several days before the American lines, and, finding no weak spot, declined to assault, and returned to Manhattan Island. Many reasons, other

than the true one—the futility of attacking American marksmen in intrenched positions—have been assigned for Howe's failure to bring the war to a conclusion at White Plains.

FALL OF FORT WASHINGTON (1776)

On Halloween, Washington fell back upon Northcastle, where he took a position so strong it was useless to think of assailing him. Howe moved to Dobbs Ferry, on the east bank of the Hudson, where he could either attack Fort Washington, or cross into New Jersey and advance upon Philadelphia. To checkmate Howe, Washington moved 5,000 men, under Putnam, to the vicinity of Hackensack, west of the Hudson; he sent General Heath, with 3,000 men, to Peekskill, where the narrowness of the Hudson would enable batteries to guard the entrance to the Highlands; and he left Lee at Northcastle, east of the Hudson, with 7,000 men, where he could cooperate with either Heath or Putnam.

He wrote to General Greene, "I am . . . inclined to think, that it will not be prudent to hazard the Men and Stores at Mount Washington; but, as you are on the spot, leave it to you to give such orders, as to evacuating Mount Washington, as you may judge best." He himself repaired to Peekskill, to make sure that the British should not ascend the Hudson. Instead of evacuating, Greene threw useless reinforcements into the doomed fort. When Washington returned, it was too late to save the garrison. On November 16, Howe captured Fort Washington, with nearly 3,000 prisoners and immense stores, inflicting on the Americans their greatest disaster in the war.

THE DANGER POINT OF THE REVOLUTION (1776-1777)

The Commander in Chief still had 6,000 men on the Jersey side of the river; on November 17, he ordered Lee to join him. Washington evacuated Fort Lee and began to retreat, followed by the British, who advanced as rapidly as bad roads and lack of transportation permitted. On his retreat across New Jersey, Washington's army

RETREAT ACROSS NEW JERSEY
1776

LEGEND
Washington ....
Sullivan — — —
Lee —+—+—+—

melted away rapidly. The state troops, whose time had expired, marched off in solid bodies. General Lee loitered and neglected frequent orders from Washington to rejoin. Not until December 2-3 did he cross the Hudson. On the 2nd, Washington, with 3,000 ragged men, was at Princeton, with the British close upon his heels. As he retreated toward the Delaware, his detachments gathered all boats for seventy miles along the river, for his own service and to deprive the enemy of their use. The little army crossed the Delaware on December 8.

Congress voted not to leave Philadelphia, and then fled to Baltimore, on December 12, leaving Washington "full power to order and direct all things relative to the Department and to the operations of war." This was the first of several occasions when Congress conferred dictatorial powers upon the general. In the confident belief that Washington was no longer dangerous, Howe sent Clinton, with 6,000 men, to seize Newport. Howe and Cornwallis returned to New York, a fact which Washington promptly learned from his secret service. Cornwallis prepared to go to England for the winter season. General James Grant promised to keep peace in New Jersey with "a corporal's guard."

Howe had pushed back Washington's force, but he had not defeated Washington. Throughout the retreat, Washington was seeking an opportunity to strike the enemy, whose forces were much scattered and living in fancied security. With 4,000 men, he was confronting 25,000. Fortunately for the American cause, the British captured the incompetent and insubordinate General Lee; and, on December 20, General Sullivan

joined Washington with Lee's troops. Two days later a trusted spy, John Honeyman, brought information that enabled Washington to plan a decisive blow.

Washington was his own chief of secret service. He was adept in penetrating the enemy's designs and in concealing his own. He had several cipher codes; wrote letters with a view to their falling into the enemy's hands; gave out misleading information; and closely superintended his spy service. Never was he surprised; while surprise was an important element in all his offensive operations. He had not studied the ways of the fox and of the Indian in vain; and the British aptly called him the "Old Fox."

Five days before Christmas, he wrote, "I

have labored, ever since I have been in the service, to discourage all kinds of local attachments and distinctions of country, denominating the whole by the greater name of AMERICAN." This was the keynote of his life. He was now to do things that would give that name a meaning. In a chance remark two years later he revealed his state of mind at this time, in what he called the "dark days of America." He stated that he was not despondent. His actions showed it. He had an unfathomable faith which was never daunted and which bore him up amidst manifold discouragements and difficulties.

BATTLE OF TRENTON (1776)

Contempt for the Americans had now reached the point where the enemy dispersed his troops, in order to take advantage of billeting facilities, and neglected to throw up intrenchments. East of the Delaware, Hessian commands were quartered in Trenton, Mount Holly, Black Horse, Burlington, and Bordentown. Washington planned to attack all these troops in their winter quarters the morning after Christmas. Five bodies of Americans were to take part, and three columns were to cross the Delaware and converge on Trenton. Washington accompanied the column that had the longest march, after it crossed the river. Timepieces were set by Washington's watch, and a zero hour fixed in the modern way. The surface of the Delaware was a mass of floating ice, and two of the column commanders concluded it would be impossible to cross. The night was bitter cold and a storm of sleet assailed the troops. All division commanders failed except those who were with Washington; and one of these would have given up, if Washington had not been present. This commander sent word to Washington that the firearms of the men were wet. "Tell General Sullivan," said Washington, "to use the bayonet. I am resolved to take Trenton."

More than ten hours were consumed in

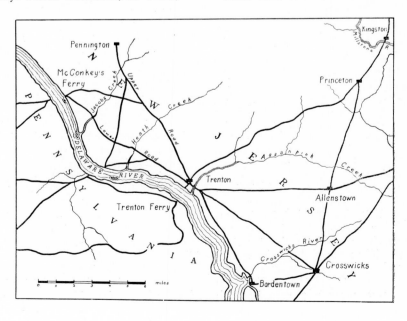

crossing the river, and the troops had to march nine miles, into a blinding storm of sleet and snow. An aide of General Gates, with a message of explanation and excuse from his chief, found his way to Washington by following the bloody tracks of the soldiers. About 8 o'clock in the morning, a huge officer galloped up to a farmer chopping wood near Trenton, and inquired: "Can you tell me where the Hessian picket is?" The man hesitated. "You need not be frightened," said an aide, "it is General Washington who asks the question."

The action was soon over. Twenty-two Hessians were killed. Washington reported "the number that submitted . . . was twenty-three officers and eight hundred and eighty-six men. . . . Our own loss is very trifling indeed, only two officers and one or two privates wounded." Lieutenant James Monroe, later President of the United States, and Captain William Washington were the wounded officers. Later reports increased the number of prisoners to about one thousand.

BATTLE OF PRINCETON (1777)

Washington recrossed the Delaware with his prisoners. The troops at Burlington and Bordentown abandoned their sick and their heavy baggage and retreated to Princeton. Cornwallis was sent from New York to retrieve the disaster. Washington's army again crossed the Delaware into New Jersey on December 31, 1776. To retain his troops in service, he and his officers pledged their personal funds. On the evening of January 2, 1777, with about 5,000 men, in a selected position on high ground outside of Trenton, on the southeast side of the Assanpink Creek, he confronted Cornwallis, who had an equal or greater force. Washington's object was to strike quick blows at the British detachments and supplies, while avoiding battle with their main forces.

The situation was "most critical," as Washington himself said. Leaving his camp-fires burning, he slipped away to Princeton. About sunrise the next morning, Washington met a British detachment. In two sharp, quick actions, he defeated the enemy, and captured 230 prisoners. When Washington looked about after the fight, most of his men were lying on the ground, fast asleep. He gave up his original purpose of capturing British treasure and stores at New Brunswick, because of the sheer exhaustion of his men. He had ordered all available troops to move toward Morristown to cooperate with his own forces. Thither he marched with his exhausted men.

Before the end of the month he had recovered all of New Jersey except three British posts at Paulus (Powles) Hook, Amboy, and New Brunswick. Trenton and Princeton mark an epoch in the American Revolution. They revealed to the British the spirit and genius of the man with whom they had to deal. On Christmas Day, the Revolution was apparently near its end;

within less than two weeks, the British were concentrating and preparing to defend themselves in their winter quarters.

EFFECT OF THE WINTER CAMPAIGN (1777)

By his victories and the spirit which they infused into the despairing people, Washington saved the Revolution in its darkest hour. There were still many anxious days before the final triumph, but the tide of American disasters had passed its lowest ebb. Von Moltke, the great modern German strategist, says, "No finer movement was ever executed than the retreat across the Jerseys, the return across the Delaware a first time, and then a second, so as to draw out the enemy in a long thin line." Horace Walpole pronounced Washington's march through the British lines "a prodigy of generalship." In London, the youthful Lafayette heard of Trenton and Princeton, and hastened his preparations to sail for America.

Washington remained at Morristown from January 7 to May 28, 1777. Congress had already passed a law authorizing an army of 66,000 men, to be raised by quotas among the states. It had also authorized Washington to raise, in the name of the United States, 12,000 infantry, 3,000 artillery, some light cavalry, and engineers. Under this authority Washington raised and organized a new Continental Army, while at Morristown.

DIFFICULTIES OF THE COMMANDER IN CHIEF

Washington's difficulty in maintaining his army arose from the weakness of the government behind him. Congress could fix the needed amount of revenue; but had to depend upon the states to collect the revenue. It could recognize a state of war; but had no power to enlist, arm, and support an army. It could give good advice; but could compel no one to accept that advice. Washington fought the Revolution with an unpaid, half naked, starving army, which was disbanded at the close of the war and has never to this day been paid. Many of its members became a charge upon the community. The bane of the service was short enlistments. The nation never fully overcame this defect until the World War, when troops were taken into the service for the duration of the war.

The personal qualities of Washington made up for the weakness of the government behind him. No man could have been better formed for command. He was a well-proportioned, handsome man, six feet three and one-half inches in height. His shoulders were large, his chest was broad; and he possessed great physical strength, which, upon occasions, he did not hesitate to use. His mental qualities were in keeping with his physical perfection. In the larger affairs of statesmanship and strategy his vision was clear and unerring. He accepted responsi-

bility with the equanimity of transcendent genius.

WASHINGTON'S RELATIONS TO THE BURGOYNE CAMPAIGN (1777)

The plan of the British Ministry for 1777 contemplated an invasion of New York, from Canada, by an army under Burgoyne, and the movement of Howe's forces up the Hudson to form a junction with him. Through an oversight, Howe received no instructions to this effect. He himself desired to capture Philadelphia; and, in the absence of instructions, he pursued a course quite at variance with the British plan.

Washington's problem was to prevent Howe both from taking possession of the Highlands of the Hudson and from capturing Philadelphia. On May 28, he took up a strong position with 8,000 men on the heights of Middlebrook, seven miles from the British position at New Brunswick. Howe, with 18,000 men, began his march on Philadelphia on June 12, 1777. Washington's position was close to the flank of Howe's line of march. A campaign of 18 days followed. Howe could find no opening to attack Washington. Since he was unwilling to continue his march and leave Washington in his rear, he abandoned his plan on June 30, and retired to Staten Island.

AID TO THE NORTHERN ARMY (1777)

News came of Burgoyne's advance, and Washington wrote, "If this proves to be any thing more than a diversion, there is no doubt General Howe will proceed up Hudsons River; for if they have any rational end in view, it must be a junction of the two armies to intercept the communication between the Eastern and Southern States, and will make it necessary for Howe and Carleton [Governor of Canada] to cooperate." He knew from his campaigns in the wilderness that Burgoyne's task was most difficult; he predicted its failure, and never lost faith in his prediction. He sent two of his best officers, Arnold and Morgan, to the Northern Army; and the capture of Burgoyne was made possible by the organized forces and the supplies which he provided.

Washington took a position for a quick movement to oppose Howe's advance to aid Burgoyne. On July 23, Howe put to sea with 18,000 men, while he left 7,000 in New York, under General Clinton. Washington set out for the Delaware, but moved with great circumspection, lest Howe should suddenly return and sail up the Hudson. On July 31, Washington learned that Howe's fleet had been seen the day before off the Delaware Capes, and had sailed away into the unknown. Early in August, Lafayette joined Washington's headquarters as a major general without a command.

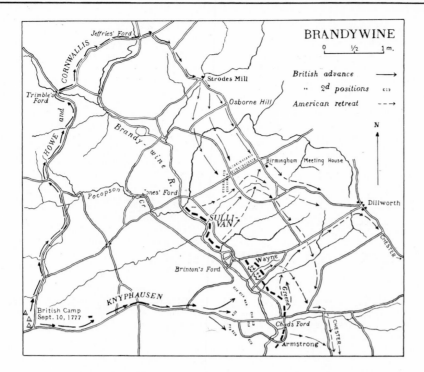

BRANDYWINE

0   ½   1 m.

British advance ⟶
  "   2d positions ⟷
American retreat ---→

BRANDYWINE CAMPAIGN (1777)

Washington had about decided to march against Burgoyne, when news came that Howe had entered the Chesapeake; and Washington marched toward Philadelphia. Howe landed at Elkton, on August 23. Washington took up a strong defensive position at the Brandywine. Howe had a superiority in numbers of about three to two; but both friends and foes believed that Washington's army was greater than Howe's. Washington encouraged this belief, "because," he said, "next to being strong, it is best to be thought so by the enemy." In going over the ground he pointed out to Greene a good second position near Dilworth, if the Americans should be obliged to fall back.

Howe drove back the American right flank on September 11. Washington ordered Greene to occupy the Dilworth position, where he held the enemy until nightfall. To Congress, which suggested that Washington send continental soldiers to work on batteries to prevent British ships from ascending the Delaware River to Philadelphia, he replied, "If we should be able to oppose General Howe with success in the Field, the works will be unnecessary; If not, and he should force us from hence, he will certainly possess himself of 'em." Like Napoleon, he would not permit himself to be besieged. He had not forgotten Fort Necessity. When he could not hold a place without being shut up in it, he retreated; and never was he more dangerous than when his case seemed most desperate. He had abandoned New York; and, when it was impossible to hold Philadelphia, he allowed Howe to take possession on September 25, 1777.

After the battle of the Brandywine, the British never again took the offensive against Washington. Hard battles were fought; but

he was always the attacker. He had a sure eye for ground. He occupied strong defensive positions, which confined the British to the cities that they held. The British would come out, reconnoiter his position, and then retire. When it suited him, he attacked.

BATTLE OF GERMANTOWN (1777)

Washington now prepared to make his first attack on the main body of the enemy, with all his forces. At the Brandywine he had kept a reserve, for an emergency, as is necessary in defensive battles; but when he took the offensive, he attacked with every available man. He aimed to capture or destroy the British army. On October 4, Washington attacked the British in Germantown, after a 14-mile night march. An element of surprise came from the fact that the British did not dream his army could possibly take the offensive.

It was a bold, well-planned effort to destroy the British army, which all but succeeded. When the attack failed, Washington slowly retired to Pennibecker's Mill, twenty miles from Germantown. The American loss was 672; the British 537. With good reason, Congress thanked Washington for his "wise and well concerted at-

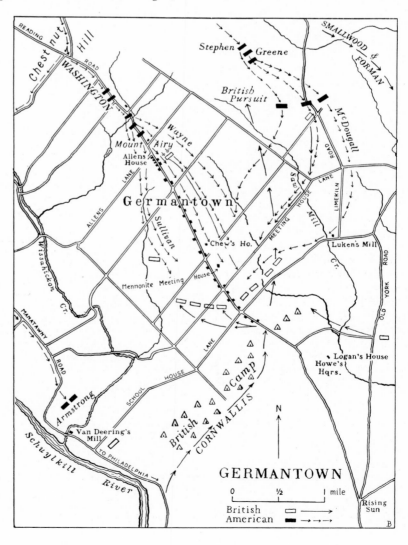

GERMANTOWN

0   ½   1 mile

British ⟞⟝
American ■ ⟶

tack." The quick recovery of his army after its defeat at the Brandywine, and its spirited attack at Germantown, also impressed the French Cabinet that there was good fighting material in the American Army, and bold and skillful leadership. Hence, the Battle of Germantown was not less influential than the surrender of Burgoyne at Saratoga (October 17) in bringing on the French alliance in 1778.

Early in December, Howe spent three days in examining Washington's position at Whitemarsh, 14 miles from Philadelphia. He then put his troops into winter quarters in Philadelphia, and Washington moved into winter quarters at Valley Forge, 23 miles northwest of Philadelphia.

At the close of the year 1777, the British held only the seaports of New York, Phila-

delphia, and Newport. The patriots controlled the rest of the country. For the British it was a fatal error to adopt a policy of capturing and holding the important cities. Every city thus captured weakened their army by the strength of its garrison. When Dr. Franklin was told in Paris that Howe had taken Philadelphia, he replied that Philadelphia had taken Howe.

Part III
Valley Forge and Afterward

DARK HOURS OF THE REVOLUTION
(1778)

If Washington could have used his discretion about calling upon the Northern Army for reinforcements after the surrender of Burgoyne, Howe's position in Philadelphia would have been very precarious; but Congress voted that Washington could not recall more than 2,500 men, including Morgan's corps. Congress had begun to fear its popular general. Congress feared not only Washington, but the army itself. It was the critical season of the Conway Cabal, of the French Alliance, of the coming of Baron Steuben, and of Valley Forge.

The term "Conway Cabal" refers to a scheme for superseding Washington by General Gates, to whom Burgoyne had surrendered. The conspirators employed the lowest form of anonymous slander. Conway was a soldier of fortune from the French service. At the first breath of exposure the conspirators fled to cover, leaving Conway the scapegoat. They had succeeded in having Congress interfere with the system of control of the army; and the supply department, as a result, broke down. Hence Valley Forge became the supreme test of fortitude of the American Army.

No better description of the miseries of that winter can be found than the words of Washington himself. "To see men," said he, "without clothes to cover their nakedness, without blankets to lie on, without shoes, by which their marches might be traced by the blood from their feet, and almost as often without provisions as with them, marching through the frost and snow, and at Christmas taking up their winter quarters within a day's march of the enemy, without a house or hut to cover them till they could be built, and submitting to it without a murmur, is a proof of patience and obedience which, in my opinion, can scarcely be paralleled." Yet Washington was always hopeful. In the midst of the Conway Cabal, he wrote to Lafayette: "I

have no doubt that everything happens for the best, that we shall triumph over all our misfortunes and in the end be happy; when, my dear Marquis, if you will give me your company in Virginia, we will laugh at our present difficulties and the folly of others."

STEUBEN TO THE FORE (1778)

Whilst Washington, in his camp at Valley Forge, watched the British army in Philadelphia, two things happened which had a powerful effect in aiding the Americans to achieve their liberty: the signing of a treaty of alliance with France, and the arrival of Baron von Steuben at Washington's headquarters.

Steuben had formerly served on the personal staff of Frederick the Great, and, encouraged by the French Minister of War, had come to America to offer his services to the American Army. He turned the desolate camp into a training school and taught the troops what they had never known before, precision in the technique of war, the use of the bayonet, the mastery of the charge. Neither Washington nor any of his officers, native or foreign, had known how to give this kind of training. Following the English custom, American officers did not instruct their men. They thought their duty consisted in mounting guard and leading their commands when going into action. The English system depended upon the existence of a permanent corps of noncommissioned officers. Washington had been unable to build up such a corps out of the rapidly changing personnel of his army.

The successes of the army prior to Valley Forge were due, not to the superiority of the troops, but to the skill of the general. The cause of the reverses had been the lack of discipline and training. Washington was thoroughly alive to the situation and he was on the lookout for competent instructors. At this time, the state of discipline, training, organization, and equipment in the American Army was deplorable.

PLAN OF MILITARY TRAINING
(1778)

Washington asked Steuben to make plans to correct the manifold abuses in the army. Steuben had the aid of three officers of great ability, General Greene and Lieutenant Colonels John Laurens and Alexander Hamilton. It was difficult to form a plan which would not excite so much opposition amongst the officers and men as to frustrate it before its merits became manifest to all. Steuben proposed that an inspector general be appointed, who should establish uniform formations, manoeuvres, and exercises, a regular system of accounting for money and property, and uniform records for all units, and who should define the duties of every officer.

Washington approved the plan and requested Steuben to assume the duties of inspector general and carry the reforms into effect. Steuben began operation by drafting 120 men from the line, whom he formed into a guard for the general in chief. He made this guard his military school. He drilled it twice a day; and, to remove the English and American prejudice that to drill the troops was a sergeant's duty, beneath the station of an officer, he took a musket and showed the men the manual of arms.

His example was contagious; and Valley Forge became a great training camp, where the American officers, for the first time, became the instructors of their men. He appointed inspectors for each division, and all his inspectors were present at each drill. In two weeks, his company had a military air and knew how to bear arms, to form column, deploy, and execute small manoeuvres and exercises. The men were well dressed, their arms were clean and in good order, and their general appearance was quite respectable. He paraded them before all the officers and gave them an opportunity to exhibit what they knew. Having demonstrated his method of drill, Steuben dispersed the inspectors, and his doctrines were adopted throughout the army. He applied his system to battalions, to brigades, and, in a short time, he manoeuvred entire divisions in the presence of the commander in chief.

When the officers grasped the importance of Steuben's work and realized that their earlier defeats had been due to their inability to match themselves with the well-trained British, a remarkable change came over the army. A generous but spirited rivalry set in between organizations to make the best appearance and exhibit the greatest efficiency; and the spirit of military discipline soon pervaded the entire force. By April, 1778, the general officers were writing their friends in the other armies, recounting the wonderful transformation wrought by Steuben.

QUALITY OF THE AMERICAN SOLDIER

It was truly a great accomplishment. Steuben had arrived at headquarters at the end of February, knowing almost no English. Acting at first largely through interpreters, and then speaking a jargon of English, German, and French, which greatly amused the officers and men, he had introduced a strict form of discipline amongst men who had extreme ideas about freedom and personal liberty. While the soldiers laughed at the funny incidents, they did their best to obey orders. Steuben soon found he had to deal with a type of man entirely different from that which he had known in Europe. "You say to your soldier, 'do this,' and he doeth it," Steuben wrote to an old comrade in Prussia; "I am obliged to say to mine, 'this is the reason why you ought to do it,' and then he doeth it."

The Revolution may be divided into two sharply contrasting periods: that which preceded the coming of Steuben, and that which followed. Faithful histories of the Revolution are filled with tirades upon the cowardice and utter worthlessness of the men that filled the ranks of our revolutionary armies. But the source material for these estimates comes from the period prior to the coming of Steuben. When Clinton landed at Kip's Bay, in 1776, and the Americans ran, Washington belabored the panicky soldiers, and even a brigadier general, with his sword. Now, when these same men had learned to act together and could depend upon one another, they became heroes; and nothing more was heard about the "pusillanimous wretches." As a result of Steuben's training, they were, man for man, a match for the best British troops.

On May 6, 1778, when "May breezes had begun to blow through the lovely groves in which the army was encamped," the entire force was turned out to celebrate the news of the French Alliance, which had been signed on February 6, 1778. War between England and France resulted from the alliance, but there was no formal declaration.

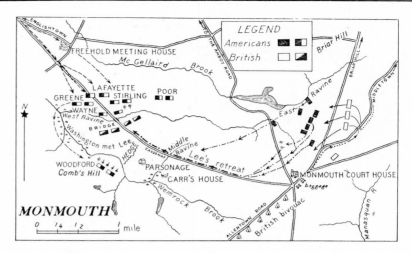

MONMOUTH CAMPAIGN (1778)

It was a valiant, well-drilled, and highly disciplined army that issued from Valley Forge when good weather made campaigning practicable. In June, 1778, the Americans broke camp and pursued the British, who had evacuated Philadelphia and were retreating across New Jersey. Then, for the first time, Washington had a real army in the field. He appreciated the change that had been wrought in the army. He had attained what was probably the greatest hope of his life. He now had an army that was more than equal to the enemy in a pitched battle. Unfortunately, few of his general officers had been able to cast off the feeling of inferiority. They were still unwilling to come to grips with the British army in the open field. Councils of officers urged that the army should avoid a general engagement.

Washington was determined to fight. His army numbered 15,000 men, all trained by Steuben and all anxious to show their efficiency. Washington therefore attacked the British on June 28, at Monmouth Court House; but, in the midst of the battle, General Charles Lee, through treachery or cowardice, gave orders which confused the Americans and caused them to retreat. Washington rebuked Lee, sent him to the rear, and ordered Steuben to rally the fleeing troops. When Steuben rode up to the fugitives and shouted out a few commands, they "wheeled in the line with as much precision as on an ordinary parade." Alexander Hamilton, as witness of these events, declared that for the first time he appreciated the overwhelming importance of military training and discipline. Washington took charge of the troops himself and rode his great white charger until it collapsed and died. He then mounted his "chestnut blood mare with long mane and tail." Lafayette said of Washington at Monmouth, "I never beheld so superb a man."

Late in the day, Clinton yielded the field and fell back to a strong position where his flanks were protected by natural obstacles. Washington prepared to attack, but before the troops were ready, night had fallen.

Clinton stole away at night, leaving Washington to bury his dead.

The Americans had now learned how to fight in the open, to manoeuvre under fire, and to display the heroism *en masse* which discipline alone can give. Henceforth Washington no longer feared to meet the British in the open field; and they recognized his superior strength and his superior military genius, for they never again gave him the opportunity.

In July, Washington established his army, for the second time, at White Plains, ready for a combined sea and land assault on New York. With just pride, he noted that "after two years manoeuvring and undergoing the strangest vicissitudes, that perhaps ever attended any one contest since the creation, both armies are brought back to the very point they first set out from, and that which was the offending party in the beginning is now reduced to the use of the spade and pickaxe for defense."

RHODE ISLAND CAMPAIGN (1778)

A French fleet, under Count d'Estaing, arrived on July 8, bringing M. Gérard, the first minister from France to the United States, and a landing force of 4,000 men. Washington was anxious to attack New York in concert with the French fleet, but the draft of the large French vessels was too great for them to pass over the bar into the harbor.

In August, the French fleet, in conjunction with an American force under Sullivan, moved against Newport. Sullivan had established himself on Rhode Island (the island of that name) when a British fleet, under Admiral Howe, appeared in the offing. The two fleets had manoeuvred two days for advantage of position, when a West Indian hurricane, coming up the coast, scattered them. D'Estaing sailed for Boston to refit; and the expedition against Newport was abandoned by the Americans in disgust. Much bitter criticism followed. It required all of Washington's tact to preserve harmony between the allies.

Henceforth, Washington's most difficult task was to control the criticising tongues and pens of his own people. He had long since emancipated himself from the feeling of inferiority to Europeans then prevalent among Americans; but he never lost sight of the value of the French alliance to America. In his relations with the French, Lafayette was always a most helpful and loyal coadjutor. The French heard the clamorous voice of the multitude; but they listened only to the wise and conciliatory words of Washington.

After the Rhode Island campaign, no further operations took place in the north which can properly be called a campaign. Henceforth, the British were confined in that region to predatory operations. At the end of the year all that they held in the territory of the new United States was New York, Newport, and Savannah. Washington disposed his troops for winter in lines extending from Danbury, Connecticut, to New Jersey. His headquarters were near Middlebrook. Early in the war, Washington saw that, if the British could establish themselves upon the Hudson River by seizing New York and the Highlands about Peekskill, they would be able to sever communications between New England, the great center of wealth, industry, population, and resistance, and the southern colonies, and bring the Revolution to a close. He never lost sight of the necessity of holding the Highlands and of watching the British in New York. He was ready to go elsewhere, if some great opportunity should offer; but, until then, he hovered around the main British force in New York.

STONY POINT AND PAULUS HOOK
(1779)

The British had seized and fortified Stony Point, on the west bank of the Hudson, below West Point; and Washington determined to retake it. "Secrecy," wrote Washington to Wayne, to whom he had entrusted the task, "is so much more essential . . . than numbers, that I should not think it advisable to employ any other than the light troops. If a surprize takes place, they are fully competent to the business; if it does not, numbers will avail little." On the night of July 15, 1779, Wayne's command stormed the works at Stony Point, with unloaded muskets, and took them at the point of the bayonet. The British lost 63 killed and 542 prisoners.

Not long after, Major Henry Lee executed a similar exploit against Paulus (Powles) Hook, within cannon shot of New York City. "The usual time for exploits of this kind," wrote Washington to Lee, "is a little before day, for which reason a vigilant officer is then more on the watch. I therefore recommend a midnight hour." Early in the morning of August 19, Lee stormed Paulus Hook. The alarm guns were booming in New York and dawn was breaking when he escaped with his prisoners. Washington's menacing attitude toward New York caused Clinton to evacuate Rhode Island in order to strengthen the garrison in New York. At the close of 1779, the British held nothing in the United States except New York and Savannah.

Washington's army spent the winter of 1779-80 at Morristown. The hardships endured by the troops far exceeded those at Valley Forge; but Washington now commanded a disciplined army; and history has little to say of the sufferings at Morristown. Amidst all the suffering, there was a tone of gayety. Never was there any enforced sadness about the American camps. Washington remained constantly with his troops. "To share the common lot," said he, "and participate in the inconveniences, which the army, from the peculiarity of our circumstances, are obliged to undergo, has with me been a fundamental ideal."

SOUTHERN CAMPAIGNS PRELIMINARY TO YORKTOWN
(1779-1781)

In December, 1779, Sir Henry Clinton and Lord Cornwallis sailed for Savannah. Early in 1780, they advanced with an overwhelming force upon Charleston. The government of South Carolina demanded that Charleston be defended. Washington learned with dismay that General Lincoln was collecting his whole force, for the defense of

Charleston. "I have the greatest reliance on General Lincoln's prudence," said he, "but I cannot forbear dreading the event." Lincoln allowed himself to be trapped in the city, instead of evacuating it when he could no longer defend it. He surrendered Charleston, May 12, 1780, with 6,000 men. The continental troops, 3,000 in number, were held as prisoners, while the militia was allowed to go home on parole. Clinton returned to New York, leaving Cornwallis, with 5,000 men, to maintain and extend the British conquest.

Congress appointed General Gates to command the Southern Army, without consulting Washington, and made Gates independent of the commander in chief. With

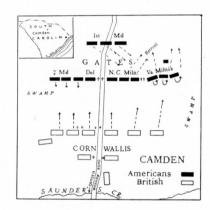

3,000 men, Gates marched toward Camden, South Carolina, where, on August 16, 1780, he was utterly defeated by Cornwallis. This was the second American army wiped out of existence in the southern states within three months. It was the most complete defeat ever inflicted upon an American army.

When news came of the disaster at Camden, Congress allowed Washington to choose a successor to Gates. Washington selected Greene and Steuben to go south. Steuben remained in Virginia to collect men and

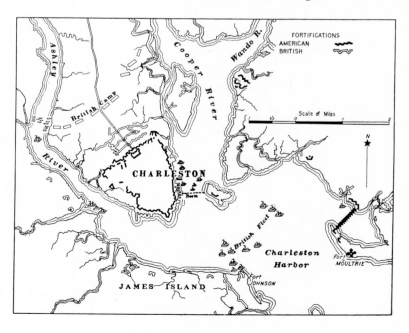

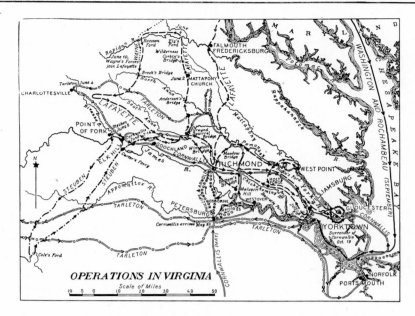

OPERATIONS IN VIRGINIA
Scale of Miles

means and send them to Greene in the Carolinas. Congress wisely made Greene subject to the control of the commander in chief. Greene took command at Charlotte, December 2, 1780. Preceding this, the frontier battle of Kings Mountain had checked Cornwallis's advance.

On January 17, 1781, General Daniel Morgan practically destroyed Tarleton's British corps, at the Cowpens, in South Carolina, near the North Carolina line. Morgan joined Greene, who retreated across North Carolina, closely pursued by Cornwallis. Greene escaped across the Dan River into Virginia. The moment Cornwallis ceased the pursuit and turned away, Greene recrossed the Dan and hovered about the rear of Cornwallis. On March 15, the two armies met at Guilford Court House. Cornwallis was tactically victorious; but his losses were so severe that he retired to Hillsboro and then to Wilmington, to refit and prepare to carry the war into Virginia. Greene boldly moved southward towards Camden and Charleston.

Late in April, Cornwallis left Wilmington and, on May 20, reached Petersburg, Virginia, where he joined 2,000 British troops, that had been sent from New York to establish a British base in that state. He overran Virginia as far north as Fredericksburg; but he was harassed by an American force under Lafayette, whom he was unable to bring to battle. Early in August, 1781, he retired to Yorktown to refit his forces and await developments. Fate was preparing a dramatic ending to his campaigns in America. He had been lured into Virginia, where he was within reach of superior French and American forces under the personal command of Washington.

Early in May, 1780, Rochambeau had sailed from Brest with 5,500 men. On July 10, he arrived off Rhode Island. "My Master's orders," wrote he to Washington, "place me at the disposal of your Excellency. I have arrived full of submission and zeal and of veneration for yourself and for the talents you have shown in sustaining a war that will be forever memorable."

OPERATIONS WITH THE FRENCH
(1780-1781)

Whilst the French were subject to his orders, Washington knew, as he wrote to Lafayette, that his authority was nominal; and that he must exercise it with discretion. Almost a year elapsed before the French army took part in the war. Washington wished to use it for some decisive stroke that would end the conflict; and he had no desire to impose any losses upon it except for this purpose.

Washington's army spent the summer of 1780 in camp at Orangetown (Tappan). He planned a surprise assault on New York for the night of November 24, 1780, while en route to winter quarters, for which he had boats on wheels for a quick embarkation. British ships accidentally blocked the way, and he moved into winter quarters at New Windsor, near West Point.

On March 9, 1781, news arrived that a fleet, under the Comte de Grasse, was ordered to the West Indies, with instructions to sail to the coast of North America later in the year for joint operations against the British. Six million francs were promised, not as a loan, but as a gift, to be placed at Washington's disposal. Later in the year, the French government guaranteed an American loan of ten million francs from Holland. This financial aid enabled Washington's army to undertake the Yorktown campaign.

On May 22, 1781, Washington had an interview with Rochambeau at Weathersfield, and it was agreed that the French army should join Washington for combined operations, depending upon the presence of the French fleet. On June 10, the French broke camp at Newport. The army was taken by water to Providence, and then marched westward. Rochambeau joined Washington at White Plains and the two armies were united for the campaign of 1781. The French were astonished at the manner in which the Americans marched. Perfect order and perfect silence reigned. An American regiment was sent to capture a redoubt. It marched under the fire of cannon in admirable style.

A plan determined by Washington, "nearly twelve months before," contemplated an attack upon the British forces in Virginia or in South Carolina, as circumstances should dictate, in the summer of 1781. To deceive the enemy, it was necessary for Washington to delude his own army, the people, the state governments, and even Congress itself, which asked no questions. Extensive preparations were actually made to attack New York; and Washington's correspondence in the year 1781 has misled historians to the present day into the belief that he was obstinate in his desire to make this attack. His real intentions are disclosed in a letter to Noah Webster, dated July 31, 1788.

On August 14, he received a letter from Barras, stating that on the 13th of August de Grasse would sail for the Chesapeake with 3,000 soldiers, borrowed from the French general commanding in Santo Domingo. On October 15, he must start back to the West Indies, in order to return the borrowed soldiers. "Employ me promptly and usefully that time may be turned to profit," said de Grasse. There was no time to lose. De Grasse would probably reach the Chesapeake before the allied army from New York.

JOINT PLANS OF CAMPAIGN (1781)

History teaches that every allied army should have a commander subject to the orders of a commander in chief, who, himself, should not be an army commander. But Washington commanded his own army and, at the same time, secured the most loyal support and obedience from Rochambeau, who commanded the French army, and the loyal cooperation of two admirals commanding French fleets. Nothing is more difficult in war than to command allied forces in joint operations. Washington did it so well that we often overlook the fact that he furnishes the most successful instance in history of the exercise of such a command.

Washington's first marches were designed to impress friend and foe alike that he intended to attack New York. The task of deceiving Clinton was facilitated by the fact that the British had captured several of Washington's letters, in which his desire to attack New York was convincingly disclosed. The sheer audacity of the movement served to screen its true meaning. The skill with which the Roman Consul Nero left the presence of Hannibal in south Italy, to join the forces confronting Hasdrubal in central Italy, and the deftness with which Robert E. Lee slipped away from McClellan's army, near Richmond, to fight Pope, near Washington, in 1862, did not exceed the address displayed by Washington in deceiving Sir Henry Clinton.

Washington and Rochambeau took southward 2,000 Continentals and 4,000 Frenchmen. The army crossed the Hudson at King's Ferry and began its march on August 19. The weather was fine and the sight most inspiring and impressive. The column was nearly two miles long. First came the Americans, in their ragged regimentals that told the story of extreme poverty and many campaigns; then followed the French in gorgeous new uniforms. On August 27, the French officers were still debating

and Rochambeau came with an allied army from New York. De Grasse was the first to arrive, on August 28. He entered the James River and landed his military forces on Jamestown Island. A British fleet appeared. There was a naval battle in which the French gained the advantage; and the British sailed away. On September 9, Barras appeared with his fleet, which assured French naval superiority. On the 14th, Washington and Rochambeau arrived, and a royal salute was fired as the generals approached. They visited de Grasse on his flagship at Cape Henry, and concerted plans for combined operations. De Grasse took station with the main fleet in Lynnhaven Bay.

had not yet developed leaders equal to the task of carrying out his ideas. If he had been successful at Germantown, his victory, taken in connection with Burgoyne's surrender, would undoubtedly have brought the war to an early close. At Monmouth, he failed to get decisive results because of the treachery or cowardice of the officer second in rank in the army. Complete success came at last to crown his efforts at Yorktown.

RESPONSIBILITY OF GENERAL WASHINGTON

In its consequences, the defeat at Yorktown was the most momentous ever suffered by an army of Imperial Britain. It put an end to the Revolutionary War. Away up in the mountains of Virginia, the aged Lord Fairfax, now in his ninetieth year, heard the news of the surrender. "It is time for me to die," said he; and he took to his bed. Few victories in history have had the far-reaching and enduring effect of Yorktown. The battle of Actium, which settled the form of the Roman State for five centuries, can, perhaps, alone be compared with it. The assurance of all that America stands for can be traced to the physical and moral forces operating at Yorktown. There General George Washington was the guiding genius. His greatness as a general is beyond dispute.

Washington desired to follow up the capture of Cornwallis by a combined movement of the allied forces against Charleston; but de Grasse had to return to the West Indies, and Washington's army went back to its old camps on the Hudson. After the surrender, Rochambeau went into winter quarters near Williamsburg. In June, 1782, he started northward on a leisurely march. He reached the Hudson in September and arrived in Rhode Island in November. On December 24, 1782, the French army sailed from Boston for the West Indies, except the legion of Lauzun, which remained in America until May, 1783.

In his relations with the French military and naval commanders, Washington showed himself to be a diplomatist of the highest order. In his correspondence, he displayed a courtesy, a simple dignity, and an incomparable ability to turn a sentence in such a way as to secure the end in view.

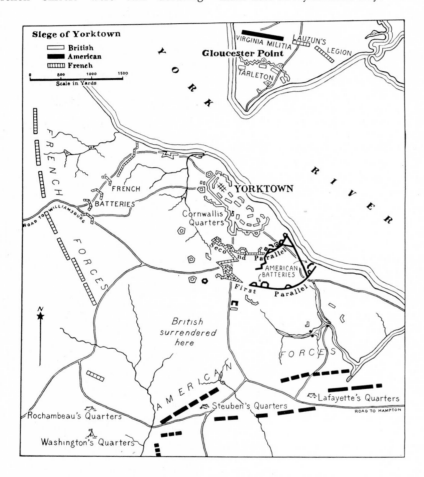

whether Staten Island were the objective. However, the army left Trenton on September 1, and arrived at the head of the Chesapeake on the 5th, whence it was conveyed in ships to the vicinity of Yorktown. Washington and Rochambeau rode through Virginia, making 60 miles a day, and paid a visit to Mount Vernon, which Washington had not seen since 1775.

FINAL VICTORY AT YORKTOWN
(1781)

It was remarkable concentration. Lafayette, with 5,000 American soldiers, was already facing Cornwallis. De Grasse came with one fleet and 3,000 soldiers from the West Indies. Barras came from Rhode Island with another fleet; and Washington

On October 19, 1781, after a siege of 21 days, Cornwallis surrendered his forces, which numbered 7,157 men, to the allied army of 15,000, approximately half French and half American. Without the aid of the French fleet and the French army, the capture of Cornwallis would have been impossible. On board the French fleet there were, in addition, 24,000 seamen, but this force was matched potentially against British naval forces, which were operating in near-by waters, and is scarcely to be reckoned as part of the besieging force.

Whenever Washington took the offensive, he aimed at a victory that would end the war. At Trenton his success was dazzling. That he did not attain all that he had planned came from the fact that the war

Preliminary articles of peace were signed on November 30, 1782; but there was no armistice, and Washington passed one more winter with his army on the Hudson. A definitive treaty of peace was signed on September 3, 1783. The British evacuated New York on November 25. Washington returned his commission to Congress in a memorable scene in the State House in Annapolis on December 23, and retired once more into private life at Mount Vernon, where he arrived on Christmas eve.

RENEWED MILITARY SERVICE
(1794-1799)

Washington's military service did not end with the Revolution. In 1794, in his second administration as President, the so-called Whiskey Rebellion occurred in western Pennsylvania. Seven thousand rebels gathered in arms. Washington assembled an army of 15,000 militia under the command of General Henry Lee. The existence of the national government was at stake. The President accompanied the army, ready to assume command, if necessary, until all possibility of a serious conflict vanished. It lies with the President, as constitutional commander in chief, whether he shall command in person any part of the land or naval forces. Washington set a precedent which has not been followed by any later President.

In 1798, when we were at war with the French on the sea and our navy was making prizes of French men-of-war, Washington was called once more to command the army. Congress created the rank of lieutenant general for him, and he was duly commissioned. Later, Congress revived the rank of general, which he had held throughout the Revolution; but his death came before he was again commissioned as general.

DEATH OF WASHINGTON (1799)

On December 21, 1799, the New York newspapers announced the death of Lieutenant General George Washington. One of them truly prophesied "that in every quarter of the globe, where a free government is ranked amongst the choicest blessings of Providence, and virtue, morality, religion, and patriotism are respected, the name of Washington will be held in veneration." When the news reached Europe, the white ensigns of the British fleet, blockading the port of Brest, were lowered to half-mast, the armies of France wore badges of mourning, and Bonaparte, First Consul of France, attended a service in memory of Washington.

He had the infinite respect of friends and enemies. In all the voluminous correspondence of the aristocratic French officers in Rochambeau's army, no word of criticism of Washington can be found, only respect and love and admiration. Many years after the war, when Lord Cornwallis was Governor General of India, he sent a verbal message to his old antagonist, General Washington, wishing him "a long enjoyment of tranquillity and happiness," but adding that, for himself, he "continued in troubled waters."

His popularity in the villages and in the country was touching to behold. On a journey through Connecticut, returning from a conference with Rochambeau, he arrived at a village after nightfall. The people turned out in mass, the children bearing torches; the men and women pressed about him to touch his garments. Turning to young Count Dumas, who has left an account of the journey, he said: "We may be beaten by the English; it is the chance of war; but there is the army they will never conquer."

He was fond of cards, dancing, and plays. He was an agreeable companion and delighted in anecdotes and tales of adventure; but he was always silent about his personal exploits, though few men have ever led a more adventurous life than he. He was jocular in the presence of danger. On the memorable night at Trenton, in crossing the icy waters of the Delaware, whilst the fate of the nation depended upon his success or failure, he turned to General Knox with a joke that relieved the tension and put all about him in good humor.

WASHINGTON THE MAN

The United States was made independent by the military genius of Washington. His greatest problem was to maintain an army in the field. He succeeded, in spite of the greatest difficulties and under the most discouraging circumstances, and thereby approved himself worthy to be ranked among the great commanders.

Washington, like Napoleon, never allowed himself to be besieged in any city, town, or village. His cardinal doctrine was that the Revolution depended upon the existence of his army, not upon the possession of any particular geographical spot. A nation's capital and many of its important cities may fall; but, if its forces remain in the field, they may be victorious in the end. This was the guiding principle which Washington followed in his conduct of the War of the Revolution.

A compilation of military maxims as profound, incisive, and trenchant as those of Napoleon could be produced by selecting passages from the orders and writings of Washington. We think of him as wise and prudent; but he was also daring and could strike quick and hard, as he demonstrated at Trenton, Princeton, Germantown, Monmouth, and Yorktown. His military fame has been overshadowed by his eminence in other fields. Had he died at the close of the Revolution, with his military achievements standing alone in bold relief, he would to-day be honored as one of the world's greatest captains, as he is honored as one of the world's greatest statesmen. He was bolder than Alexander, more crafty than Hannibal, wiser than Caesar, more prudent than Gustavus Adolphus, more resourceful than Frederick, more sagacious than Napoleon, and more successful than Scipio; and his star will not pale by the side of theirs.

Selected Authorities

AVERY, ELROY McKENDREE—*History of the United States and its People.* Vols. IV-VI. Cleveland, Burrows, 1908-09. (Especially the maps and illustrations.)

CARRINGTON, HENRY B.—*Washington the Soldier.* New York, Scribner, 1899.

CARTER, GEORGE H.—*Proceedings upon the Unveiling of the Statue of Baron von Steuben.* Washington, Government Printing Office, 1914.

CRONAU, RUDOLF—*Army of the American Revolution.* New York, Cronau, 1923.

DUMAS, MATHIEU, COUNT—*Memoirs of his Own Times.* 2 vols. Philadelphia, Lea & Blanchard, 1839.

FISKE, JOHN—*American Revolution.* 2 vols. Boston, Houghton Mifflin, 1891.

FITZPATRICK, JOHN C.—*Spirit of the Revolution.* Boston, Houghton Mifflin, 1924.

FORD, PAUL LEICESTER—*True George Washington.* Philadelphia, Lippincott, 1896. (Especially ch. xi.)

FORTESCUE, SIR JOHN WILLIAM—*History of the British Army.* Vols. II, III. New York, Macmillan, 1899-1902.

FROTHINGHAM, THOMAS G.—*Washington, Commander in Chief.* Boston, Houghton Mifflin, 1930.

GANOE, WILLIAM ADDLEMAN—*History of the United States Army.* New York, Appleton, 1924. (Especially chs. i-iv.)

HART, ALBERT BUSHNELL, ED.—*American History told by Contemporaries.* Vol. II. New York, Macmillan, 1898.

JOHNSON, BRADLEY T.—*General Washington.* New York, Appleton, 1894.

JOHNSTON, HENRY P.—*Yorktown Campaign.* New York, Harper, 1881.

KAPP, FRIEDRICH—*Life of Frederick William von Steuben.* New York, Mason, 1859.

LECKY, WILLIAM EDWARD HARTPOLE—*American Revolution, 1763-1783.* New York, Appleton, 1898.

LEE, HENRY—*Memoirs of the War in the Southern Department.* Rev. ed. New York, University Publishing Co., 1869. (First pub. in 1812.)

LODGE, HENRY CABOT—*George Washington* (*American Statesmen,* Library ed.). 2 vols. Boston, Houghton Mifflin, 1898.

PARKMAN, FRANCIS—*Montcalm and Wolfe.* 2 vols. Boston, Little Brown, 1884.

PERKINS, JAMES BRECK—*France in the American Revolution.* Boston, Houghton Mifflin, 1911.

SIMCOE, JOHN G.—*Simcoe's Military Journal.* New York, Bartlett & Welford, 1844. (First pub. in 1787.)

STEDMAN, CHARLES—*History of the Origin, Progress, and Termination of the American War.* 2 vols. London, Murray, 1794.

STRYKER, WILLIAM S.—*Battle of Monmouth.* Princeton, Princeton University Press, 1927.

STRYKER, WILLIAM S.—*Battles of Trenton and Princeton.* Boston, Houghton Mifflin, 1898.

THACHER, JAMES—*Military Journal during the American Revolutionary War.* Rev. ed. Boston, Cottons & Barnard, 1827.

THAYER, WILLIAM ROSCOE—*George Washington.* Boston, Houghton Mifflin, 1922. (Especially chs. iii-vii.)

TREVELYAN, SIR GEORGE OTTO—*American Revolution.* New ed. 4 vols. New York, Longmans Green, 1905-12. (Continued by next title.)

TREVELYAN, SIR GEORGE OTTO—*George the Third and Charles Fox.* 2 vols. New York, Longmans Green, 1912-14.

VAN TYNE, CLAUDE H.—*Founding of the American Republic.* Vol. II. Boston, Houghton Mifflin, 1929.

WASHINGTON, GEORGE—*Writings.* Ed. by Jared Sparks. 12 vols. Boston, American Stationers' Co., 1834-1837.

WASHINGTON, GEORGE—*Writings.* Ed. by Worthington Chauncey Ford. 14 vols. New York, Putnam, 1889-93.

WILSON, WOODROW—*George Washington.* New York, Harper, 1903. (Especially chs. vii, viii.)

WISTER, OWEN—*Seven Ages of Washington.* New York, Macmillan, 1907. (Especially ch. v.)

A PRIVATE IN THE CONTINENTAL ARMY

Washington the Traveler

By Prof. Archibald Henderson

Part I

Western Journeys

GEORGE WASHINGTON
From a portrait by John Trumbull in the City Hall at Charleston, S. C.

THE TRAVEL RECORDS

WASHINGTON was one of those singular prophetic historical characters who conducted himself as if aware that his doings were to become the material of history. Posterity profits by Washington's methodical habits, his factual viewpoint, his patience and persistence in recording, even under the most trying circumstances, the events of his daily life, of his surveying expeditions, his embassies, his journeys into the West for the inspection of lands, his tours through all the original thirteen states after he became President.

If these diaries are to be taken as evidence, Washington was an extravert. He never unpacked his soul in a journal and committed to the revealing pages of a diary a record of his thoughts and emotions. Many of these records must have been jotted down when Washington, for all his strength and endurance, was weary, even to exhaustion. So he carefully husbands space, and meticulously records only the most interesting of external events. Occasionally he indulges in observations, which are usually those of a surveyor, an agriculturist, or a captain of industry.

Washington was endowed with a mind of great practicality and a literalness which proceeded in great measure from natural clarity of thought. His diaries contain no poetic descriptions of mountains, rivers, forests, or landscapes. He assessed the country through which he passed in terms of its value, actual or potential, for cultivation, water power, canals, mill sites, development as farms, residential sites, or sources of mineral deposit. The greatest man of his age never saw Great Britain, against which he headed a revolt; France, America's friend and ally; or any foreign soil, save the Barbados.

Washington was no ordinary tourist, reveling in travel for its own sake, but a traveler with a purpose. He always had an objective; and concerned himself very largely with recording the events of the journey or describing the country with reference to that objective. Washington had a single-track mind for the mission in hand; yet with prophetic vision, he was looking ahead, planning for the future of the American Republic, which lay so near his heart.

PURPOSE OF WASHINGTON'S TRAVELS

An inkling of some of the hardships and penances of pioneer life is conveyed by extracts printed in Pamphlet No. 1 as well as here. Throughout his life Washington, who lived at home as handsomely as any gentleman in the colonies, accepted the difficulties and hardships of travel as a matter of course. And during the Revolutionary War he many times occupied rough and narrow quarters.

Washington was no mere tourist, no dilettante traveler. He saw things in the large, with the eye of the engineer, the promoter, the paternalistic head of a great state. It is worthy of remembrance today that on his last western journey Washington gave his profoundest thought and attention to a great national problem of incalculable significance in the country's transportation and internal navigation future. Never to be forgotten are the words entered in this diary, pointing clearly the way to cement East and West in close sympathy and union:

"It is to open a wide door, and make a smooth way for the produce of that Country [the West] to pass to our Markets before the trade may get into another channel . . ."

OVER THE BLUE RIDGE (1748)

Like many of the active, vigorous men of that day—George Rogers Clark, William Preston, Daniel Boone, for example—Washington was trained as a surveyor. It was the type of work which suited the hardy young Washington, with its physical exercise out of doors, its accuracy in sighting, measurement, calculation, and record, and its practical utility. Washington soon became adept in the use of compass, transit, and rod, and spent much of his time in a profession which was both pleasant and reasonably lucrative. Many of his surveys are preserved; and they are models for the accuracy of the plot, the clearness of the description, and the neatness of the chirography. Some of them and maps of his travels are here reproduced in the *George Washington Atlas,* which is the cartographical counterpart of these pamphlets.

In 1747 Lord Fairfax, who owned a proprietary in Virginia known as the Northern Neck, came to this country and visited his cousin and agent, William Fairfax, at Belvoir on the Potomac. George Washington's elder brother, Lawrence, had married William Fairfax's eldest daughter, Ann, four years earlier. The year following Lord Fairfax's arrival in Virginia, George, though but sixteen years old, was chosen as a surveyor of Lord Fairfax's holdings beyond the Blue Ridge. He accompanied George William Fairfax, son of the Honorable William Fairfax and of his second wife, Sarah Walker, on this surveying party, James Genn, county surveyor, being the leader. George Fairfax had already served arduously as surveyor the two preceding years, in running out lines for Lord Fairfax, and was a competent mentor for the as yet inexperienced young Washington.

On this journey they surveyed some large tracts, one of 500 acres, and many small lots, killed wild turkeys, ate their food off chips, and at one place a "great Company" of German immigrants, men, women, and children, who spoke no English "attended us through ye. Woods as we went showing there Antick tricks." The most interesting event of the journey occurred on March 23. By the tender of "some Liquor" the surveyors had put a party of thirty-odd Indians returning from war "in y. Humour of Dauncing," thus described by Washington: "They clear a Large Circle and make a Great Fire in y. middle then seats themselves around it y. Speaker makes a grand speech telling them in what Manner they are to Daunce after he has finished y. best Dauncer jumps up as one awaked out of a Sleep and runs and Jumps about y. Ring in a most comical Manner he is followed by y. Rest then begins there Musicians to Play ye.

Musick is a Pot half [full] of Water with a Deerskin Stretched over it as tight as it can and a goard with some Shott in it to Rattle and a Piece of an horses Tail tied to it to make it look fine y. one keeps Rattling and y. other Drumming all y. while y. others is Dauncing."

WESTERN LAND GRANTS AND CLAIMS (1753-1754)

During the middle years of the eighteenth century, with a vast and rich country at her back, Virginia vigorously promoted western colonization. Between the years 1743 and 1760, the Virginia Council made forty-three grants, many of them of vast tracts of land, to individuals and groups of individuals, totaling slightly more than 3,000,000 acres. One of these grants, for 200,000 acres, was made to the Ohio Company on July 12, 1749. Washington's older brothers, Lawrence and Augustine, were prominent members of the company, Lawrence becoming its head on the death of Thomas Lee; and after Lawrence Washington's death, Governor Dinwiddie of Virginia became the company's leader. The original grant of 200,000 acres was to be increased by 300,000 acres if a hundred families were settled within seven years and a fort built and maintained.

On the strength of La Salle's explorations, the French claimed the region about the Forks of the Ohio, where the Ohio Company grant was laid. So Dinwiddie, who represented in his own person the combination of governor and speculator, decided to send the energetic younger brother of two partners in the Ohio Company on a difficult mission to the commander of the French garrison at Fort Le Boeuf. Dinwiddie regarded Washington with favor, and had a year earlier appointed this inexperienced man of twenty to be district adjutant general, with the rank of major. Washington was dispatched to warn the French that they were encroaching upon private property granted by the English king. Washington was also instructed to take careful note of all he saw, especially of the French forts, and to select a site for the Ohio Company's fort.

Government thus allied itself with speculation in precipitating the mighty contest between England and France for the possession of America. The speculator on the grand scale was the advance guard of civilization, the avant courier of empire. "The historic muse," says Alvord, "has always delighted in singing of the daring deeds of the explorer wandering through the dark forest, or paddling his canoe on unknown rivers; and even the homesteader, with family goods packed in his prairie schooner, has had his exploits chanted in majestic measures; but few have noted the fact that both explorer and homesteader were frequently only the advance agents of the speculator who dreamed of large enterprises in land exploitation—that the Daniel Boones of the

wilderness were only the pawns of some Richard Henderson." Washington began as the pawn of Dinwiddie and the Ohio Company; in time he changed sides and fought, as leader, with the French against the English.

ACCOUNT OF THE WILDERNESS (1753)

The ambitious young Washington, competent, prudent, and diplomatic, was ideally fitted for this delicate mission. With its political aspects we are here not concerned, but only with Washington's experiences as traveler. Washington set out from Williamsburg on the last day of October, 1753, and at Cumberland, Maryland, engaged the services as guide of the famous frontiersman, Christopher Gist, who had made a memorable tour of Kentucky two years earlier on behalf of the Ohio Company. On the outward journey, there were no memorable happenings, Washington being a splendid horseman and capable of great exertion.

On the return journey, however, there were hardships and excitements in plenty. "[December] 16th . . . We had a tedious and very fatiguing Passage down the Creek. Several Times we were like to have been staved against Rocks; and many Times were obliged all Hands to get out and remain in the Water Half an Hour or more, getting over the Shoals. At one Place the Ice had lodged and made it impassable by Water; therefore we were obliged to carry our Canoe across a Neck of Land, a quarter of a Mile over."

The horses became so fatigued on the overland journey that Washington donned "Indian walking Dress"—long leggins and belted shirt—and set out across country with Gist on December 26, walking eighteen miles that day. The following day, after passing a settlement appropriately named "Murdering-Town," they were fired on by a French Indian, who missed his aim. The most desperate experience which came near robbing America of the present celebration, was on the return journey above Shanapins, a town of the Six Nations above later Fort Duquesne on the Allegheny River, where the ice was "driving in vast Quantities." Washington's description is vivid:

"There was no way for getting over but on a Raft; Which we set about with but one poor Hatchet, and finished just after Sun-setting. This was a whole Day's Work. Then set off; But before we were Half Way over, we were jammed in the Ice, in such a Manner that we expected every Moment our Raft to sink, and ourselves to perish. I put-out my setting Pole to try to stop the Raft, that the Ice might pass by; when the Rapidity of the Stream threw it with so much Violence against the Pole, that it jerked me out into ten Feet Water; but I fortunately saved myself by catching hold of one of the Raft Logs. Notwithstanding all our efforts we could not get the Raft to either Shore; but were obliged, as we were near an Island to quit our Raft and make to it.

"The Cold was so extremely severe, that Mr. *Gist* had all his Fingers, and some of his Toes frozen; but the water was shut up so hard, that we found no Difficulty in getting-off the Island, on the Ice, in the Morning, . . ."

FRONTIER CAMPAIGNS (1755-1758)

This was not the last of Washington's journeys beyond the mountains. In 1754 he headed a military expedition which fell in with the French on Great Meadows and Jumonville, commander of the French detachment, was killed. A few weeks later Washington was captured at Fort Necessity, the site of which is well known. In 1755 he was a member of the Braddock Expedition. In 1758 he was turned aside from the road he had helped to make and compelled to advance with Forbes on a rival road, coming west from Raystown (Bedford), but leading at last to Fort Duquesne, which a few weeks later became an English stronghold called Fort Pitt, from which Pittsburgh has sprung.

And there were later more peaceful journeys upon which we have diaries revealing how that impetuous spirit played with the wilderness, using the water highway of the Ohio, explored the lower Kanawha Valley. Washington reveled in the wilderness—and yet looked forward to seeing it peopled. He lived to see Kentucky and Tennessee come into the Union, and Ohio on the skids of statehood.

LAND INTERESTS ON THE OHIO (1754-1770)

Washington throughout his life was interested in the West as the seat of future communities attached to the East, and also as a field for investment. Although handicapped by the lack of ready money, he was constantly intent upon investing in enterprises for the development of the natural resources of virgin America. For him the West, ever after his trip to Fort Le Boeuf, had a singular and powerful allure. Like the leading Virginians of his day, Washington looked upon the vast back country, of literally fabulous richness and unknown extent, lying within the ancient charter limits of Virginia, as the potential field of great fortune. Under Governor Dinwiddie's proclamation of 1754, promising land to those who would enlist for the Fort Necessity expedition, Washington was entitled to a tract of 15,000 acres; and the total amount allocated for the soldiers was 200,000 acres.

Washington was eager to engross lands in the Ohio country for himself, in addition to the bounty land promised under the proclamation of 1754. Undeterred by the royal proclamation of 1763, prohibiting any land grants west of the heads of the rivers flowing into the Allegheny, which he thought would in a few years prove a dead letter, owing to the inexorable westward

advance of the ruthless pioneers, as early as 1767 Washington engaged an agent, Captain William Crawford, living at present Connellsville, Pennsylvania, to look out secretly a rich tract of land for him, of 2,000 acres, more or less.

Impatient over the delay in securing the land for the soldiers under the proclamation of 1754, Washington volunteered to take the matter in hand and perfect the grants for his old comrades in arms. He engaged in voluminous correspondence, made representations, and personally appeared before the Governor and Council. Finally, through a conference with the officers of the troops held at Fredericksburg in August, 1770, he was authorized to act as their representative in pushing their claims and perfecting their grants to the lands on the Ohio.

In this matter, Washington was not animated by wholly unselfish motives; for knowing the carelessness and inefficiency of old soldiers, he sought to purchase at low figures, personally and through his brother Charles and others, some of the officers' claims. The 200,000 acres was to be taken up in not more than twenty surveys; and Washington, as he himself says, "rather than be at the trouble and expense of dividing with others bought and exchanged until I got entire tracts to myself." For the greater part of the expense incurred in the management of this affair and the trip to the Ohio, Washington was never reimbursed.

JOURNEY ON THE OHIO RIVER (1770)

Washington's interests in the West brought out some of his most characteristic writings. His journal of his long trip to the Ohio in 1770 and down that river to the mouth of the Great Kanawha is full of the frontier experience.

Accompanied by Dr. Craik, his physician and friend, his two negro boys, Billy and Giles, and Craik's servant, with a lead horse and baggage, Washington set off on October 5, 1770, for the "Settlement on Redstone." During the journey he encountered and talked at length with two striking characters, Col. George Croghan, one of the greatest land speculators of the day, and the ingenious Dr. John Connolly, later as Gov. Dunmore's agent to provoke the outbreak of the Shawnee war in 1774, and to suffer arrest on the eve of the Revolution.

Prophetic of impending trouble was the attitude of the Indians who, despite the grant of the Six Nations to the Crown at Fort Stanwix two years earlier, were still grumbling, declaring, as Crawford said, that they "shall not Run any farther till they are paid for the Land." Washington's observation, November 17, 1770, of their attitude, is significant: "The Indians who live upon the Ohio (the upper parts of it at least) are composed of Shawnas, Delawares, and some of the Mingos, who getting but little paid of the consideration that was given for the Lands Eastward of the Ohio,

view the Settlement of the People upon this River with an uneasy and jealous Eye, and do not scruple to say that they must be compensated for their Right if the People settle thereon, notwithstanding the Cession of the Six Nation's thereto. On the other hand, the People from Virginia and elsewhere, are exploring and Marking all the Lands that are valuable not only on Redstone and other waters of Monongahela but along down the Ohio as low as the little Kanhawa; . . ."

STAKING OUT CLAIMS (1770-1772)

On this journey Washington reveals that "eye for ground" which is at once the distinguishing feature of the engineer, the agriculturist, and the land speculator. He shot buffalos, was entertained by his old friend, the Indian Kiashuta; and measured a giant sycamore "(3 feet from the Gd.) 45 feet round, lacking two Inches." On November 3, he marked out at the mouth of the Great Kanawha River some corners of the "Soldiers Ld. (if we can get it)."

On November 5, 1772, Washington wrote to Lord Dunmore and the Council that the entire 200,000 acres had at last been obtained, and most of the certificates deposited. "After the Patents were granted and the Land thereby secured," wrote Washington a quarter of a century later, "I concerned myself no further with any part thereof excepting my own." Under the later much more liberal allowance for the soldiers, as well as by individual purchases made for a "trifle," Washington eventually secured some 32,373 acres, fronting for sixteen miles on the Ohio, for forty miles on the Great Kanawha.

LAST JOURNEY TO THE WEST (1784)

After the Revolution was over, and well over, and Washington had returned to Mount Vernon, it was not long before he resolved to make a tour to the westward, to inspect his land holdings. For his military services throughout the Revolution, Washington refused to receive anything but his expenses. Owing to long absence from home, his business affairs had of necessity been much neglected. To the Chevalier de la Luzerne, who invited him to visit France, Washington made clear why he could not consider a foreign tour: his financial affairs compelled the closest attention and his presence at home.

In 1784 Washington was not intent upon any journey of exploration for new lands; he merely wished to establish his rights to those he had. Accompanied by his devoted friend, Dr. Craik, he set off on September 1, 1784, for Bath, now Berkeley Springs, West Virginia, where he arrived on September 5. Three days later, with accessions of Dr. Craik's son, William, and Washington's nephew, Bushrod Washington, the party pushed on to Washington's old mill, some twelve miles from present New Haven, Pennsylvania. Here he transacted the business he had in hand, in connection with the mill, and some land he owned in partnership with one Gilbert Simpson, land now overrun by squatters.

IMPROVEMENT OF RIVER NAVIGATION (1784-1785)

Washington did not accomplish one of the main purposes of his journey, namely to visit his land holdings on the Ohio and the Great Kanawha, and rescue them "from the hands of Land Jobbers and Speculators." But in the course of the journey, mental speculation he had long indulged in occupied him, one might almost say obsessed him. It concerned a water route from Virginia to the West, in particular the navigation of the Potomac River. The conclusion of the diary, in which he summarises the results of the journey, reveals Washington as an able engineer, a man with a large vision for the future development of transportation. His conclusions were reached after elaborate inquiries from many people whom he encountered or visited upon this tour.

Almost immediately upon his return home he wrote an extended letter to Gov. Harrison of Virginia, urging the opening of communications with the Great Lakes and the interior. The direct outcome was the passage of a law by both Maryland and Virginia the following year (1785), for the formation of a navigation company to connect East and West. Washington himself was elected president of the company thus established, known as the Potomac Company, an organization elsewhere described in these pamphlets.

At the same session of the Virginia Assembly an act was passed for clearing and improving the navigation of the James River. On October 20, 1785, Washington was elected president of the James River Navigation Company, the active duties of which he declined. These progressive steps toward the development of inland navigation and communication with the interior stimulated corresponding movements in other states, and gave impetus to a national program of internal improvements.

Part II
New England Journeys

REVOLUTIONARY TRANSITS

No officer and no soldier in the Continental Army traveled so many miles and visited so many places as Washington. During the period of hostilities from 1775 to 1780, he never was able to visit Mount Vernon; but he stopped there on his way to and from the Yorktown campaign in 1781. Except for this, the theater of his movements after the siege of Boston was from the Connecticut border to the Head of Elk. These journeys can hardly be considered travels; they are part of the military experience of Washington. He did visit New York and Philadelphia and the numerous towns strung along that narrow and extended field of war; but that was simply a part of his profession of arms. A hundred places can now be identified as having seen the general ride past in the midst of his ragged army of patriots.

FIRST EXPERIENCES IN NEW ENGLAND (1756-1776)

Washington's first trip to New England resulted from a question of rank between himself as a provincial colonel and a captain of Maryland troops who also held a minor royal commission. The Maryland captain refused to receive orders from his nominal superior. After other means had been exhausted, Washington with the permission of Governor Dinwiddie undertook a trip to Boston in 1756 in order to place the matter before Governor William Shirley, who was also commander-in-chief of the British forces in America. Accompanied by his aide and servants in livery, Washington left Virginia on February 4 and returned to his command on March 28. During the journey he stopped at Philadelphia and New York, where, as well as in Boston, he was entertained socially and met prominent men. This was the beginning of Washington's acquaintance with such men outside his own colony, which was an interesting phase of his career, for the knowledge of leaders throughout the colonies and later states was one element of his primacy.

Washington's second visit to New England was nearly twenty years after his first. Appointed General and Commander in Chief of the Army of the United Colonies on June 15, 1775, on June 23 he was on the road northward. On the road he received the news of the battle of Bunker Hill. He took the southern route and at New Haven reviewed a military company of good character composed of students. At Springfield he was met by a committee of the Massachusetts Provincial Congress, at Watertown was greeted by the Congress itself, and arrived at Cambridge on July 2.

Washington's stay in Cambridge lasted till after the evacuation of Boston by the British on March 17, 1776. In April he started on his return journey via Providence, New London, and New Haven; and on the 13th reached New York.

NEW ENGLAND JOURNEYS DURING THE FRENCH ALLIANCE

An interesting and important series of journeys were the three trips to New England during 1780 and 1781, without any military accompaniment except an escort. The first of these was a six-day journey from headquarters at the "Hopper House" in New Jersey to Hartford and return to West Point, to confer with Rochambeau, commander of the French forces then in Narragansett Bay. Count Fersen, the gallant Swede who was on Rochambeau's staff, thus reports his experiences:

"I was at Hartford . . . with M. de Rochambeau. We were only six, the Admiral [Ternay], his Chief of Engineers [Desandrouins], his son, the Viscomte de Rochambeau, and two aids-de-camp. . . . M. de R—sent me in advance . . . I had time to see this man, illustrious, if not unique in our century. . . . His suite was more numerous than ours. The Marquis de Lafayette, General Knox . . . M. de Gouvion, . . . and six aids-de-camp. . . . He had besides an escort of 22 dragoons."

The second journey was from New Windsor, N. Y., March 1, 1781, to Newport and Providence, with the purpose of a further conference with the French, returning to New Windsor March 20.

The third New England journey was made at the request of Rochambeau to meet him at Wethersfield, Connecticut, starting from New Windsor May 18, 1781, and returning on May 25. It was at this meeting that the final plans were made for joint action by the two armies, which, while ostensibly aimed at New York City, eventuated before Yorktown, Virginia.

PRESIDENTIAL TOURS

The most important and extended travels in which Washington engaged, aside from the military campaigns of the Revolution, were the three separate tours he made as President of the United States, visiting all the thirteen original states. Although Andrew Johnson invented the phrase, Washington was the first American President to go "swinging round the circle." No strong bond of national feeling yet united the states. In making these tours Washington was actuated by the desire to win the good-will, the support, of the people for the general government. By his dignified and gracious presence, which evoked the love and enthusiastic loyalty of the people, Washington could accomplish far more than by innumerable messages and state papers. The purpose of these tours was to become acquainted with the country and the people as a whole, and to learn "the temper and disposition of the inhabitants towards the new government."

EASTERN JOURNEY (1789)

The first of these presidential tours was Washington's sixth New England journey and extended as far north as Kittery, Maine, then a part of Massachusetts. This trip was to have one momentous incident in establishing permanently and fixing in the public mind the supremacy of the President over the Governor of a state.

October 15, 1789, Washington set out from New York on his "tour through the Eastern States." His diary is a model of circumspection, strongly objective, and reminiscences of his own past experiences are conspicuously absent. His mention of persons is unaccompanied by personalities, and it is characteristic of Washington that one of his chief concerns was the welfare of the horses. With paternal interest, he gives particular attention to the geographical and agricultural features of the country, the quality of the houses and places of entertainment, the general welfare of the people, and a description of promising industries indicative of future development and prosperity.

CONDITIONS OF THE TOUR (1789)

The tour was marked by democratic simplicity. Although Washington was regarded with a reverence amounting to awe, and was thought of in monarchical rather than in republican terms by a people still largely rural and provincial, he carefully avoided aristocratic pretentiousness. In the minds of the people Washington was the great soldier, the saviour of his country as the military leader of a revolution. In these piping times of peace Washington sought to divert the minds of the people from martial preoccupations towards peaceful pursuits. As far as he was able he declined military escorts; and in his utterances or addresses omitted allusions to the Revolution, looking always to the future rather than to the past.

On this tour Washington drove in a hired coach, or "chariot" as it was called, and was accompanied by Major William Jackson, his aide-de-camp, and Tobias Lear, his private secretary. In addition, there were six servants, nine horses, and a luggage wagon. It was Washington's habit to retire not later than nine o'clock; and one cannot but wonder when he found time to make entries in his diary. His hour of rising was four o'clock and he was often some miles on his journey before breakfasting. By making an

early start each day he often avoided the attendance of large cavalcades which for all the compliment implied, nevertheless kicked up a lot of dust. The attitude of the people along the way is quaintly expressed in this quotation from a contemporary newspaper: "At his approach party disappears, and everyone runs a race in endeavoring who shall be foremost in paying him the tribute of grateful respect. Old and young—men and women,—all, all are alike affected and all alike endeavor to express their feelings by the most lively testimonials."

FROM NEW YORK TO BOSTON (1789)

Passing through Rye, Horse Neck, Stamford, Fairfield, Stratford, and Milford, the party arrived at New Haven, Connecticut, a town of about four thousand inhabitants, on October 17. Yale and its president, Dr. Ezra Stiles, Washington mentions as "a College, in which there are at this time 120 Students under the auspices of Dr. Styles." After receiving courteous attentions from the governor, state officials, and Revolutionary veterans, Washington resumed his journey; Wallingford, Middletown, Wethersfield, Hartford, Springfield, Palmer, Brookfield, Leicester, Worcester. Unwilling to establish a precedent, Washington declined to review the militia drawn up to receive him at Cambridge "otherwise than as a private man."

THE HANCOCK INCIDENT (1789)

The awkward incident occurred on leaving Cambridge, where Washington and party arrived at ten on the morning of Saturday, October 24. It was occasioned by the assurance of Governor Hancock, who unduly magnified his own office. At Cambridge, Washington was met, not by the governor, but by the lieutenant governor—this being a detail of Hancock's plan to force the President of the United States to pay the first call upon the Governor of Massachusetts. The selectmen of Boston, who had made elaborate preparations to receive the President, resolutely refused to give way to the state officials, and the latter, with reluctance, yielded and the selectmen had their way.

Prior to reaching Boston, Washington had declined, according to rule, to lodge at Governor Hancock's house; but had accepted his invitation to an informal dinner. After elaborate greetings, chiefly a sort of pageant of the occupations, and passing through a handsome memorial arch, Washington finally arrived at his lodgings, at the home of the widow of Joseph Ingersoll. As soon as Washington realized that Hancock was seeking to demonstrate that a state's executive should take precedence within the state over the President of the nation, he acted instantly and appropriately, as indicated by the entry in his diary: *"Saturday, 24th. . . .* Having engaged yesterday to take an informal dinner with the Govr. to-day, but under a full persuasion that he would have waited upon me so soon as I should have

arrived—I excused myself upon his not doing it, and informing me thro' his Secretary that he was too much indisposed to do it, being resolved to receive the visit."

GOVERNOR HANCOCK YIELDS

Governor Hancock, a man of no little vanity and a great lover of display, now realized that he had committed a grave breach of etiquette, which was a matter less of social than of national importance, affecting the relative stations of Governor and President. Availing himself of the very transparent excuse of suffering from the gout, he dispatched two members of the Council to Washington, with this explanation. Washington, with grave frankness, informed the bearers of Hancock's explanation that he did not feel himself at liberty to waive the matter or respect due to his office and that he would not see the governor save at his own lodgings. On Sunday, 25th, Hancock sent Washington a note, at 12:30 o'clock, proposing, if agreeable to the President, to call in half an hour to pay his respects. The note contains the comically self-important phrase, as if his life were at stake, "He now hazards every thing, as it respects his health, for the desirable purpose." Washington's reply is stern and ironical:

"25 October, one o'clock.

"The President of the United States presents his best respects to the Governor, and has the honor to inform him that he shall be at home till two o'clock.

"The President needs not express the pleasure it will give him to see the Governor; but at the same time, he most earnestly begs that the Governor will not hazard his health on the occasion."

The climax of the affair was lower than high comedy: it was *opera bouffe*. Hancock, staging the scene with dramatic effectiveness, drove to Washington's unpretentious lodgings in his gorgeous coach, with liveried attendants; and had himself, swathed in red baize, borne into Washington's presence in the arms of his servants. Washington notes in his diary Hancock's plea in extenuation of his conduct: "*Sunday, 25th.* . . . I received a visit from the Gov'r, who assured me that indisposition alone prevented his doing it yesterday, and that he was still indisposed; but as it had been suggested that he expected to *receive* the visit from the President, which he knew was improper, he was resolved at all haz'ds to pay his Compliments to-day."

Hancock's personal dislike for Washington doubtless dated from that humiliating moment in Congress when John Adams proposed as commander in chief of the armies of the American colonies not the egotistic Hancock, who expected to be nominated, but the self-effacing Washington. The Boston incident marks the first defeat in American history of state rights in conflict with national sovereignty.

BOSTON TO PORTSMOUTH AND RETURN JOURNEY (1789)

The remainder of Washington's tour was marked by no especially noteworthy incidents. Everywhere he encountered the most respectful, even enthusiastic receptions, with speeches and addresses, parades and salutes. He visited Harvard College, and displayed much interest in the fishing industry at Marblehead, the shoe emporium at Lynn, the "Cotton Manufactory," conducted by John and George Cabot, near Beverly, and the duck manufactories at Stratford and Haverhill. Comments on these industries are in Pamphlet No. 12. At Portsmouth, New Hampshire, he received every courtesy from state officials, and sat for his portrait to a Danish artist, Christian Gülager, at the request of Mr. Samuel Breck of Boston "who wrote Majr. Jackson that it was an earnest desire of many of the Inhabitants of that Town that he might be indulged." The return journey to New York was swift, and he happily arrived, in refutation of superstition, on Friday, November 13.

LONG ISLAND AND RHODE ISLAND TOURS (1791)

In April, 1790, Washington made a tour of observation through the western half of Long Island, particularly to notice agricultural conditions. It was, probably, the first time he had been on the island since the retreat after the battle of 1776. An extract showing with what a keen eye he viewed the land will be found in a later part of this pamphlet.

At the time of making the "tour to the eastward," Rhode Island had not yet become a part of the Union. In consequence Washington did not pass through that state in 1789. Following the ratification of the Constitution by Rhode Island on May 29, 1790, Washington visited that state in August, 1790, being absent from the 14th until the 24th and "everywhere cordially welcomed by the inhabitants."

He traveled by water from New York in a packet boat and landed first at Newport. Of this trip we have no diary, but Congress having just adjourned, he was accompanied by various statesmen, one of whom, Congressman Smith of South Carolina, wrote an account of the journey, extracts from which are in the final portion of this pamphlet. As was the case in Boston the President had the memory of a wartime visit to contrast with the circumstances of the present reception. The French forces were no longer there, the nation was now at peace, and the last of the pillars to support the Federal Dome had been erected.

After an over-night stop at Newport the water trip was resumed to Providence. Here the same sort of a general welcome awaited the party; similar dinners, addresses, and promenades of the town, a visit to the college that is now Brown University, and an inspection of the shipyard of the family after whom the college is named. The return to New York was also by packet boat.

Part III
Southern Journeys

VOYAGE TO BARBADOS (1751)

The only open ocean journey made by Washington was as companion and amateur nurse to his brother, Lawrence, a sufferer from tuberculosis, who sought benefit in the climate of Barbados. In earlier years George had studied navigation; and so now he kept a journal with paper ruled in the usual logbook form, with appropriate entries regarding the weather, direction of prevailing winds, hours, and the speed and course, thickly sprinkled with nautical terms. Though destined to be the father of his country, Washington proved not immune to sea sickness; but he was much impressed by the violent seas and winds blowing big guns. "[October] 19th. Hard Squals of Wind and Rain with a f[o]mented [?] Sea jostling in heaps occasion[ed] by Wavering wind . . . the Compass not remaining 2 hours in any point. The Seamen seemed disheartned confessing they never had seen such weather before. . . . A prodigy in ye West appear'd towards ye suns setting abt. 6 P. M., remarkable for its extraordinary redness."

EXPERIENCES IN BARBADOS
(1751-1752)

With youthful enthusiasm George says of a drive into the country in the cool of the evening of November 4 that he "was perfectly rav[ished with delight by?] the beautiful prospects which on every side presented to our view The fields of Cain, Corn, Fruit Trees, &c in a delightful Green." He makes many comments on the island and its inhabi-

tants, praises the fruit, notably the "Pine Apple China Orange" and the "Avagado pair," but of the fair sex can only say: "The Ladys Generally are very agreeable but by ill custom or wt. [not?] affect the Negro Style." The brothers were frequently entertained by the leading families on the island, and George, who later became such a lover of drama and devotee of the theater, was "treated with a play ticket by Mr. [James] Carter to see the Tragedy of George Barnwell," to which "was Musick a Dapted."

The most interesting comment of the journal, revealing Washington's early predilection for agriculture, concerns a practice of the Barbados, thus described: "[December] 22d. . . . Their dung they are very careful in saving, and curious in makg. which they do by throughing up large heaps of Earth and a number of Stakes drove there in Sufficient for Sixten head of Cattle to Stand separately tied too which they are three months together tramplg. all the trash &ca. than . . . and then its fit to manu[re?] the Ground."

George was so unfortunate as to contract the smallpox, which kept him confined from November 17 until December 12, but fortunately left no grave disfigurement. Lawrence died July 26, 1752, following his return in despair to Virginia.

THE GREAT DISMAL SWAMP
(1763-1768)

Wilderness could be found hundreds of miles to the eastward of the mountains. Not far from Williamsburg lay a kind of un-

drained plateau, commonly called the Dismal Swamp. Washington had doubtless read Colonel William Byrd's earlier writings concerning the region, especially with reference to making it available. He was active in organizing a stock company for the purpose, of which he was president and general manager. In the preamble of the original act, which was passed by the Virginia Assembly January 18, 1764, it is stated that "a number of gentlemen have recently formed themselves into a company of adventurers for the purpose of draining, and rendering fit for cultivation, a large tract of marshy ground, known by the name of the Great Dismal Swamp." The "adventurers" associated with Washington were Col. Fielding Lewis, Burwell Bassett, Dr. John Walker, John Robinson, and perhaps John Washington.

The object was to reclaim the land, not only for agriculture, but for the timber. In the early operations of the Dismal Swamp Canal Company, much attention was paid to getting out material for shingles. One item in Washington's ledger is an account of 70,300 shingles. Small canals were built by "Colonel Washington and Company," as the organization was popularly called, for lightering the timber out from Lake Drummond, at the center of the great swamp. One of the canals, a lovely little waterway, is derisively but unjustly called Washington's Ditch.

Washington was an engineer and a big business man; had he lived today he would have been called a captain of industry. He was so interested in the project of draining the canal that he visited it repeatedly, notably in May and October, 1763, July, 1764, November, 1766, April and October, 1767, and October, 1768. In the course of these visits he went entirely around Lake Drummond and penetrated far into the interior of the Swamp. As the result of Washington's discovery that the current of Lake Drummond flowed into one of the rivers of Albermarle Sound, and the advocacy of the project by Hugh Williamson, North Carolina and Virginia nearly sixty years later united to cut the Dismal Swamp Canal, which was opened in 1822.

ADVENTURES IN THE SWAMP

During his examination and survey of the Dismal Swamp in North Carolina, Washington usually stopped at the homes of Gen. Joseph Reddick and Gen. Kedar Ballard, the plantation of the latter adjoining lands owned by Washington. Washington's concise record of his survey in May, 1763, stands as evidence of his vigor as traveler and surveyor.

One entry is especially of interest: ". . . we crossed from Elias Stallens (one Mile above the upper bridge on Pequemin) across to a set of People which Inhabit a small slipe of Land between the said River Pequemen [Perquimans] and the Dismal Swamp, and from thence along a new cut path through the Main Swamp a Northerly Course for 5 Miles, to the Inhabitants of what they call new found land, which is thick settled, very rich Land, and about 6 Miles from the aforesaid River Bridge of Paspetank [Pasquotank]. The Arm of the Dismal which we passed through to get to this New land (as it is called) is 3 1/4 Miles Measured little or no timber in it, but veryfull of Reeds and excessive rich. Thro this we carried horses without any great difficulty.

"The Land was formerly esteemed part of the Dismal, but being higher, tho' full of Reeds, People ventured to settle upon it and as it became more open, it became more dry and is now prodigeous fine land, but subject to wets and unhealthiness."

Washington still possessed some of this land at his death; and the investment appears to have been one of his few wild-land ventures which paid dividends.

PREPARATIONS FOR A SOUTHERN TOUR (1791)

Before making the inspection tour of the southern states, Washington waited for North Carolina to ratify the Constitution, which took place on November 21, 1789. He made elaborate preparations for the tour, which was to last three and a half months. His coach was thoroughly overhauled, and in its new coat of gleaming white put up a brave appearance: painted designs of the four seasons on doors and front and back, and the Washington arms on the four quarter panels, gilded framework for the coach,

and brass buckles for the harness. On this tour Major Jackson was his companion, secretary, and aide. Besides the four horses to the "Charriot," and two horses to the baggage wagon, there were four saddle horses and a led one for Washington; and five attendants: "Valet de Chambre, two footmen, Coachmen [sic] and postilion." The outriders in their bright livery of red and white gave a touch of gallantry and distinction to the equipage and cavalcade.

VIRGINIA (1791)

Washington left Philadelphia on March 21 for Mount Vernon, breaking the journey by a pleasant stop at Annapolis where he was graciously received, and at Georgetown, where he transacted important business concerning the laying out of the Federal City.

After a full week sojourn at Mount Vernon, the party set off on April 7 for the long southern tour. At Fredericksburg where he had spent his youth he was warmly received by the citizenry; at Richmond he "viewed the Canal, Sluces, Locks, and other works" in company with the governor and officials of the James River Navigation Company, which had been established six years earlier. At Petersburg he was suitably entertained and attended a large ball at the Mason's Hall. As was his custom, he mentioned that there were present "between 60 and 70 ladies," but was evidently wholly uninterested in the number of men present, as he does not mention it. Here and at other points on this tour Washington was described in public addresses as the "father of your country;" but the term had been used before.

THE CAROLINAS (1791)

In North Carolina, entertainments and receptions greeted him at Halifax, Tarborough, and Greenville; and New Berne received him with unusual demonstrations of pleasure. At the latter place, he was twice entertained at the Palace, built by the royal governor, William Tryon; and by one of those singular reverses of destiny in which history is so rich, Tryon's office served as a stable for Washington's horses. A notable reception greeted Washington at Wilmington and the address of the citizens was doubtless very agreeable to Washington, in predicting "the effectual operation of the new constitution."

The reception at Georgetown was marked by heartiness and fervor. But the climax of the tour—and of all Washington's tours—was reached at Charleston, where he was elaborately entertained for a solid week. This is the most lavish and prolonged entertainment ever accorded any American President. The masses vied with the aristocrats in doing homage to the truly beloved Washington. Noteworthy features of the entertainment at Charleston were: the banquet to Washington by the members of the Society of the Cincinnati, which had been organized only eight years earlier; and the concert of the famous St. Cecilia Society, inaugurated

as early as 1737. Even the imperturbable Washington, a great admirer of feminine charms, was dazzled by the sparkling scene and the beautiful gentlewomen of Charleston, at the St. Cecilia Society concert: "*Thursday*, [May] 5*th* . . . in the evening went to a Concert at the Exchange at wch. there were at least 400 ladies the number and appearance of wch. exceeded anything of the kind I had ever seen."

There hangs today in the Charleston City Hall a full length portrait of Washington painted by Trumbull, according to a resolution of the City Council of May 7, 1791—one of the most signal tributes paid to Washington on his tour. A reproduction of it is the frontispiece of this pamphlet. When the Charleston Battalion of Artillery offered to serve as his body guard, Washington politely declined, declaring that he felt himself perfectly safe in "the affection and amicable attachment of the people."

GEORGIA AND RETURN JOURNEY (1791)

Savannah, Augusta, Columbia, and Camden vied with one another in paying tribute to Washington. At Mulberry Grove Washington called upon the sprightly and witty widow of the ablest American general in the Revolution after Washington, Nathanael Greene, and as he inadequately describes the visit, "asked her how she did." At Charlotte, where he was hospitably entertained, Washington refers to Queen's College, with an attendance sometimes reaching sixty boys; and here he was told of the famous and much disputed Mecklenburg Declaration of Independence.

At Salisbury Washington was welcomed by, among others, Judge Spruce Macay, the law preceptor of another great President of the United States, Andrew Jackson, and by John Steele, afterwards comptroller of the treasury under Washington, Adams, and Jefferson. Washington is said to have visited the tavern of Elizabeth Maxwell Steele, who aided General Greene in the darkest hour of his career with the gift of her savings of years, two bags of specie; and to have seen there the picture of George III on the back of which Green exultantly wrote with a dead coal taken from the fireplace, after receiving Mrs. Steele's gift: "O George! Hide thy face and mourn." The reception given Washington by the Moravians at Salem was particularly pleasing to him; and he considered Salem a model community.

Washington performed this tour of 1887 miles in record time, arriving at each place on the day scheduled. In a letter to David Humphreys, July 20, 1791, he said: "The country appears to be in a very improving state, and industry and frugality are becoming much more fashionable than they have hitherto been there. Tranquillity reigns among the people, with that disposition towards the general government, which is likely to preserve it."

Part IV
Incidents of Travel

ORDERING A CHARIOT (1768)

"Gentn: My old Chariot havg. run its race, and gone through as many stages as I could conveniently make it travel, is now renderd incapable of any further Service; The intent of this Letter therefore is to desire you will bespeak me a New one, time enough to come out with the Goods (I shall hereafter write for) by Captn. Johnstown, or some other Ship.

"As these are kind of Articles, that last with care agst. number of years, I woud willingly have the Chariot you may now send me made in the newest taste, handsome, genteel and light; yet not slight and consequently unserviceable. To be made of the best Seasond Wood, and by a celebrated Workman. The last Importation which I have seen, besides the customary steel springs have others that play in a Brass barrel, and contribute at one and the same time to the ease and Ornament of the Carriage; One of this kind therefore woud be my choice; and Green being a colour little apt, as I apprehend to fade, and grateful to the Eye, I would give it the preference, unless any other colour more in vogue and equally lasting is entitled to precedency, in that case I woud be governd by fashion. A light gilding on the mouldings that is, round the Pannels) and any other Ornaments that may not have a heavy and tawdry look (together with my Arms agreeable to the Impression here sent) might be added, by way of decoration. A lining of a handsome, lively cold. leather of good quality, I sh'd also prefer; such as green, blew, or &ca., as may best suit the col'r of the outside, Let the box that slips under Seat, be as large as it conveniently can be made (for the benefit of Storage upon a journey), and to have a Pole (not shafts) for the Wheel Horses to draw by; together with a handsome sett of Harness for four middle sized Horses orderd in such a manner as to suit either two Postilions (without a box) or a box and one Postilion. The box being made to fix on, and take off occasionally, with a hammel Cloth &ca., suitable to the lining. On the Harness let my Crest be engravd.

"If such a Chariot as I have here describd cd. be got at 2d. hand little or nothg. the worse of wear, but at the same time a good deal under the first cost of a new one (and sometimes tho perhaps rarely it happens so), it wd. be very desirable; but if I am obligd to go near to the origl. cost I wd. even have one made; and have been thus particular, in hopes of gettg. a handsome Chart. through your direction, good taste, and managt.; not of Copper however, for these do not stand the powerful heat of our sun."

JOURNEY IN THE CENTRAL COLONIES (1773)

"[May] 9. At home all day, Messrs. Ramsay, Rumney, and Herbert dind here; the last of whom went away, the others stayd all Night.

"10. Those two Gentlemen stayd to Dinner; after which I set out on my journey for New York. Lodgd at Mr. Calvert's.

"11. Breakfasted at Mr. Igns. Digge's. Dind at the Coffee Ho. in Annapolis and lodgd at the Govr's.

"12. Dined, Supped and lodgd at the Governor's.

"13. After Breakfast and abt. 8 Oclock, set out for Rockhall where we arrived in two hours and 25 Minutes. Dind on Board the Annapolis at Chester Town, and Supped and lodged at Ringold's.

"14. Stopd at George Town on Sassafras, and dind and lodgd at Mr. Dl. Heath's.

"15. Dined at Newcastle and lodged at Wilmington.

"16. Breakfasted at Chester and Dined at Govr. Penn's in Philadelphia.

"17. Dined again at Govr. Penn's and spent the Evening at the Jocky Club.

"18. Dined with sevl. Gentlemen at our own lodgings and went to the Assembly in the Evening.

"19. Dined at the Govr's. and spent the Evening at Allan's.

"20. Dined with Mr. Cadwalader and went to the Ball.

"21. Dined with Mr. Merideth and Spent the Evening at Mr. Mease's.

"22. Dined at Mr. Morris's and Spent the Evening at the Club.

"23. Set out for New York with Lord Sterling, Majr. Bayard and Mr. Custis, after Breakfasting with Govr. Penn. Dind with Govr. Franklin at Burlington and lodgd at Trenton.

"24. Breakfasted at Princeton. Dined at Bound Brooke, and Reachd Lord Sterling's at Basking Bridge in the Afternoon.

"25. Din'd and Lodg'd at Lord Sterling's. Drank Tea at Mr. Kimble's.

"26. Din'd at Elizabeth Town, and reach'd New York in the Evening wch. I spent at Hull's Tavern. Lodgd at a Mr. Farmer's.

"27. Din'd at the Entertainment given by the Citizens of New York to Genl' Gage.

"28. Dined with Mr. James Dillancey and went to the Play and Hull's Tavern in the Evening.

"29. Dined with Majr. Bayard and Spent the Evening with the Old Club at Hull's.

"30. Dined with Genl. Gage and Spent the Evening in my own Room writing.

"31. Set out on my return home."

ALLURE OF THE FRONTIER (1783)

October 12. "I have lately made a tour through the Lakes George and Champlain, as far as Crown Point. Then returning to Schenectady, I proceeded up the Mohawk River to Fort Schuyler (formerly Fort Stanwix), and crossed over to the Wood Creek, which empties into the Oneida Lake, and affords the water communication with Ontario. I then traversed the country to the head of the eastern branch of the Susquehanna, and viewed the Lake Otsego, and the portage between that Lake and the Mohawk River at Canajoharie. Prompted by these actual observations, I could not help taking a more contemplative and extensive view of the vast inland navigation of these United States, from maps and the information of others; and could not help but be struck with the immense diffusion and importance of it, and with the goodness of that Providence, which has dealt her favors to us with so profuse a hand. Would to God we may have wisdom enough to improve them. I shall not rest contented, till I have explored the western country, and traversed those lines, or great part of them, which have given bounds to a new empire."

"I have it in contemplation to make a tour thro' all the Eastern States, thence into Canada, thence up the St. Laurence and thro' the lakes to Detroit, thence to Lake Michigan by land or water, thence through the Western Country, by the river Illinois to the river Mississippi, and down the same to New Orleans, thence into Georgia by the way of Pensacola, and then thro' the two Carolinas home. A great tour this, you will say. Probably it may take place nowhere but in imagination, tho' it is my *wish* to begin it in the latter end of April of next year."

ADVICE ON THE TOURS (1789)

October 5, 1789. "Had conversation with Colo. Hamilton on the propriety of making a tour through the Eastern States during the recess of Congress, to acquire knowledge of the face of the Country, the growth and agriculture thereof—and the temper and disposition of the inhabitants towards the new government, who thought it a very desirable plan, and advised it accordingly."

October 6. "Conversed with Gen. Knox, Secretary at War, on the above tour, who also recommended it accordingly."

October 7. "Upon consulting Mr. Jay on the propriety of my intended tour into the Eastern States, he highly approved of it, but observed, a similar visit w'd be expected by those of the Southern."

October 8. "Mr. Madison took his leave today. He saw no impropriety in my trip to the eastward; . . ."

IMPRESSION OF A FUTURE PRESIDENT (1789)

John Quincy Adams to his mother, Newburyport, December 5: "I was not one of the choir who welcomed the President to New England's shore, upon his arrival here by land. I was, however, in the procession, which was formed here to receive him, in humble imitation of the capital. And, when he left us, I was one of the respectable citizens (as our newspapers term them) who escorted him on horseback to the lines of New-Hampshire. . . .

"I had the honour of paying my respects to the President upon his arrival in this town, and he did me the honour to recollect that he had seen me a short time at New York. I had the honour of spending part of the evening in his presence at Mr. Jackson's. I had the honour of breakfasting in the same room with him the next morning at Mr. Dalton's. I had the honour of writing the billet which the major general of the county sent him to inform him of the military arrangements he had made for his reception. And I had the honour of draughting an address which, with many alterations and additions, commonly called amendments), was presented to him by the town of Newbury-Port. So you see

'I bear my blushing honours thick upon me.'

"But as half the truth is oftentimes a great falsehood I am constrained to account for these distinctions in a manner which I must honestly confess defalcates considerably from the quantum of my importance. To the peculiar civility of Mr. Jackson and Mr. Dalton, I am indebted for having been thus admitted into the company of the President. One of the major general's aid de camps is my fellow student; he was then much hurried with other business relating to the same occasion, and, at his request, I wrote the billet. Mr. Parsons was chosen by the town to draught the address; and his indolence was accomodated in shifting a part of the burthen upon his clerk, so that all my dignities have not been sufficient to elevate me above the insignificant station of a school-boy; in which character I still remain, your dutiful son."

A GIFT AND AN ACKNOWLEDGMENT AT UXBRIDGE (1789)

Washington spent the night of November 6 at the house of Samuel Taft in Uxbridge, and later the following correspondence took place:

"Sir, Being informed that you have given my name to one of your sons and called another after Mrs. Washington's family, and being, moreover, very much pleased with the modest and innocent looks of your two daughters Patty and Polly, I do for these reasons send each of these girls a piece of chintz; and to Patty, who bears the name of Mrs. Washington and who waited more upon us than Polly did, I send five guineas, with which she may buy herself any little ornaments she may want, or she may dispose of them in any other manner more agreeable to herself. As I do not give these things with a view to have it talked of, or even to its being known, the less there is said about the matter the better you will please me; but that I may be sure that the chintz and money have got safe to hand, let Patty, who, I dare say, is equal to it, write me a line informing me thereof, directed to 'The President of the United States at New York.' I wish you and your family well, and am

"Your humble Servant,
"GEO. WASHINGTON."

UXBRIDGE, Dec. 28, 1789

"May it please your Highness

"Agreeable to your commands, I, with pleasure, inform the President, that, on the 25th inst, I received the very valuable present, by the hand of the Revd. Mr. Pond of Ashford, you, Sir, were pleased to send me and my Sister, accompanied with a letter from your benevolent hand, of 8th ult.

"The articles mentioned in the letter, viz, two pieces of chintz, containing 30 yds, and five Guineas, same safely to hand, well seeled.

"As it was far beyond my deserving, to receive such a distinguished mark of your approbation, so it wholly exceeded my expectations.

"And I want words to express my gratitude to you, Great Sir, for the extraordinary favour & honour, conferred on me and our family, both, at this time, and while your Highness was pleased to honour my Papa's house with your presence. I shall endeavour to comply with your desires expressed in the letter. And, as I have great reason, I shall ever esteem and revere the name of him whose noble deeds and Patriotism, has laid a permanent obligation on all the Sons and Daughters of the American Empire ever to adore their unequal Benefactor.

"And my ardent desires are that the best of heavens blessings may, both in this and in the future world ever rest on the head of him who stands at the head of our United Empire. My Sister joins with me in the unfeigned acknowladgment I've made, likewise hon'd Papa and Mama with sincere thank and duty desired to be remembered to your Highness. I conclude, resting assured that it's wholly unnecessary [to] apologize for the incorrectness of the above to him whose candour will paliate the want of ability and Education in her, who is unacquainted with epistolary correspondence, with one of the first characters on the Globe—and shall take the libity to subscribe myself, May it please your Highness,

"Your sincere & Most ob't most humble sev't
"MERCY TAFT.

"G. Washington, Esq.,

"Pray pardon me sir if I mention the mistake in my name you se, sir, it is not Patty."

AGRICULTURAL OBSERVATIONS ON LONG ISLAND (1790)

April. 24. "This Island (as far as I went) from West to East seems to be equally divided between flat and Hilly land, the former on the South next the Seaboard, and the latter on the No. next the Sound. The highland they say is best and most productive, but the other is the pleasantest to work, except in wet seasons when from the levelness of them they are sometimes, (but not frequently having a considerable portion of Sand) incommoded by heavy and continual rains. From a comparative view of their crops they may be averaged as follows:—Indian Corn 25 bushels—Wheat 15—Rye 12—Oats 15 bushels to the acre. According to their accts. from Lands highly manured they sometimes get 50 of the first, 25 of the 2d and 3d, and more of the latter.

"Their general mode of Cropping is,—first Indian Corn upon a lay, manured in the hill, half a shovel full in each hole—(some scatter the dung over the field equally)—2d. Oats and Flax—3d. Wheat with what manure they can spare from the Indian Corn land—with the Wheat, or on it, towards close of the Snows, they sow Clover from 4 to 6 lb; and a quart of Timothy Seed. This lays from 3 to 6 years according as the grass remains, or as the condition of the ground is, for so soon as they find it beginning to bind, they plow. Their first plowing (with the Patent tho' they call it the Dutch plow) is well executed at the depth of about 3 or at most 4 inches—the cut being 9 or 10 Inches and the sod neatly and very evenly turned. With Oxen they plough mostly. They do no more than turn the ground in this manner for Indian Corn before it is planted; making the holes in which it is placed with hoes the rows being marked off by a stick—two or three workings afterwards with the Harrows or Plough is all the cultivation it receives *generally*. Their fences, where there is no Stone, are very indifferent; frequently of plashd trees of *any* and *every* kind which have grown by chance; but it exhibits an evidence that very good fences may be made in this manner either of white Oak or Dogwood which from this mode of treatment grows thickest, and most stubborn.—This however, would be no defence against Hogs."

JOURNAL OF A TRAVELING COMPANION IN RHODE ISLAND (1790)

Congressman William Loughton Smith of South Carolina: "The day after we adjourned, viz., Friday, the 13th [of August], the President of the United States, General Washington, who had on that morning resolved to pay a visit to the State of Rhode Island in consequence of its accession to the Union, did me the honor to invite me to be of his party; I could not decline so acceptable an invitation, and accordingly sat off with his company on Sunday morning, the 15th, on board a Rhode Island packet. We arrived at Newport Tuesday morning, after an agreeable passage. As we entered the harbour, a salute was fired from the fort and some pieces on the wharves; at our landing we were received by the principal inhabitants of the town, and the clergy, who, forming a procession, escorted us through a considerable concurse of citizens to the lodgings which had been prepared for us; the most respectable inhabitants were there severally presented to the President by Mr. Merchant, Judge of the District Court.

"The President then took a walk around the town and the heights above it, accompanied by the gentlemen of the party and a large number of gentlemen of Newport. We returned to our lodgings, and at four o'clerk the gentlemen waited again on the President, and we all marched in procession to the Town Hall or State House, where, while dinner was serving up, a number of gentlemen were presented. The dinner was well dished, and conducted with great regularity and decency; the company consisted of about eighty persons; after dinner some good toasts were drank; among others, following: 'May the last be first,' in allusion to Rhode Island being the last State which ratified the Constitution. The President gave the 'Town of Newport,' and as soon as he withdrew, Judge Merchant gave 'The man we love,' which the company drank standing. The company then followed the President in another walk which he took around the Town: He passed by Judge Merchant's and drank a glass of wine, and then went to his lodgings, which closed the business of the day. I slept in the room with Governor Clinton. . . .

"We have a tedious passage to Providence, being seven hours in performing it. The same salute took place as at Newport, but the procession up to the Tavern was more solemn and conducted with much greater formality, having troops and music. The Governor of the State was so zealous in his respects that he jumped aboard the packet as soon as she got to the wharf to welcome the President to Providence. The President with the Governor of the State on his right hand and Mr. Forster, a Senator in Congress, from Rhode Island, on his left moved in the front ranks; then followed Governor Clinton, Mr. Jefferson (the Secretary of State for the United States), Mr. Blair (a judge of the Supreme Federal Courts), myself, and the three gentlemen of the President's family, viz., Col. Humphreys, Maj. Jackson, and Mr. Nelson—who formed the party—afterwards followed the principal inhabitants of Providence and some from Newport, and other citizens making a long file, preceded by some troops and music; the doors and windows for the length of a mile, were crowded with ladies and spectators. When we arrived at the tavern (Dagget's) the President stood at the door, and the troops and the procession passed and saluted. In the procession were three negro scrapers making a horrible noise. We then sat down to a family dinner. After tea, just as the President was taking leave to go to bed, he was informed by Col. Peck (Marshall of the District, who had sailed with us from New York) that the students of the College had illuminated it, and would be highly flattered at the President's going to see it, which he politely agreed to do, though he never goes out at night and it then rained a little, and was a disagreeable night. We made a nocturnal procession to the College, which indeed was worth seeing, being very splendidly illuminated. . . .

"Thursday morning began with heavy rain and cold easterly wind. It cleared at nine o'clock, and then the President, accompanied as before, began a walk which continued until one o'clock and which completely fatigued the company which formed his escort. We walked all around the Town, visited all the apartments of the College, went on the roof to view the beautiful and extensive prospect, walked to a place where a large Indiaman of 900 tons was on the stocks, went on board her, returned to town, stopped and drank wine and punch at Mr. Clarke's, Mr. Brown's, Gov. Turner's, and Gov. Bowen's, and then returned home. As soon as the President was rested he received the addresses of the Cincinnati, the Rhode Island College, and the Town of Providence, and then went immediately to dinner to the Town Hall. The dinner consisted of 200 persons, and an immense crowd surrounded the hall. . . .

"Cannon was fired at each toast; at the conclusion of the toasts, the President rose, and the whole company, with a considerable crowd of citiens, walked down to the wharf, where he and his suite embarked for New York."

UNCERTAINTIES OF FERRY TRAVEL (1791)

"*Wednesday*, [March] 23*d*. Set off at 6 o'clock—breakfasted at Warwick [Maryland]—bated with hay 9 miles miles farther, and dined and lodged at the House of one Worrell's in Chester; from whence I sent an Express to Rock Hall to have Boats ready for me by 9 o'clock to morrow morning; after doing which Captn. Nicholson obligingly set out for that place to see that every thing should be prepared against my arrival. . . .

"*Thursday*, 24*th*. Left Chestertown about 6 oclock; before nine I arrived at Rock-Hall where we breakfasted and immediately; after which we began to embark. The doing of which employed us (for want of contrivance) until near 3 o'clock,—and then one of my Servants (Paris) and two horses were left, nothwithstanding two Boats in aid of the two Ferry Boats were procured. Unluckily, embarking on board of a borrowed Boat because she was the largest, I was in imminent danger, from the unskillfulness of the hands, and the dulness of her sailing, added to the drakness and storminess of the night—for two hours after we hoisted sail the wind was light and ahead—the next hour was a stark calm—after which the wind sprung up at So. Et. and increased until it blew a gale—about which time, and after 8 o'clock P. M. we made the Mouth of Severn River (leading up to Annapolis) but the ignorance of the People on board, with respect to the navigation of it run us a ground. . . .

"*Friday*, 25*th*. Having lain all night in my Great Coat and Boots, in a birth not long enough for me by the head, and much cramped; we found ourselves in the morning within about one mile of Annapolis, and still fast aground. Whilst we were preparing our small Boat in order to land in it, a sailing Boat came of to our assistance in wch. with the Baggage I had on board I landed, and requested Mr. Man at whose Inn I intended lodging, to send off a Boat to take off two of my Horses and Chariot which I had left on board and with it my Coachman to see that it was properly done; but by mistake the latter not having notice of this order and attempting to get on board afterwards in a small sailing Boat was overset and narrowly escaped drowning."

PROVISION FOR PUBLIC EMERGENCIES (1791)

To the Cabinet, April 4: "As the public service may require, that communications should be made to me during my absence from the seat of government by the most direct conveyances, and as, in the event of any very extraordinary occurrence, it will be necessary to know at what time I may be found in any particular place, I have to inform you, that, unless the progress of my journey to Savannah is retarded by unforeseen interruptions, it will be regulated, including days of halt, in the following manner: . . .

After thus explaining to you, as far as I am able at present, the direction and probable progress of my journey, I have to express my wish, if any serious and important cases (of which the probability is but too strong) should arise during my absence, that the Secretaries for the Departments of State, Treasury, and War, may hold consultations thereon, to determine whether they are of such a nature as to demand my personal attendance at the seat of government; and, should they be so considered, I will return immediately from any place at which the information may reach me. Or should they determine, that measures, relevant to the case, may be legally and properly pursued without the immediate agency of the President, I will approve and ratify the measures, which may be conformed to such determination.

"Presuming that the Vice-President will have left the seat of government for Boston, I have not requested his opinion to be taken on the supposed emergency; should it be otherwise, I wish *him* also to be consulted."

AN ACCIDENT ON THE ROAD (1791)

"*Thursday*, [April] 7*th*. . . . In attempting to cross the ferry at Colchester with the four horses hitched to the Chariot by the neglect of the person who stood before them, one of the leaders got overboard when the boat was in swimming water and 50 yards from the shore—with much difficulty he escaped drowning before he could be disengaged. His struggling frightened the others in such a manner that one after another and in quick succession they all got overboard harnessed and fastened as they were and with the utmost difficult they were saved and the Carriage escaped been dragged after them, as the whole of it happened in swimming water and at a distance from the shore. Providentially—indeed miraculously—by the exertions of people who went off in Boats and jumped into the River as soon as the Batteau was forced into wading water—no damage was sustained by the horses, Carriage or harness."

SOUNDING THE PUBLIC PULSE IN THE SOUTH (1791)

Richmond, April 12. "In the course of my enquiries, chiefly from Colo. Carrington, I cannot discover that any discontents prevail among the people at large, at the proceedings of Congress. The conduct of the Assembly respecting the assumption he thinks is condemned by them as intemperate and unwise; and he seems to have no doubt but that the Excise law, as it is called, may be executed without difficulty—nay more, that it will become popular in a little time. His duty as Marshall having carried him through all parts of the State lately, and of course given him the best means of ascertaining the temper and disposition of its Inhabitants, he thinks them favorable towards the General Government, and that they only require to have matters explained to them in order to obtain their full assent to the measures adopted by it."

OFFICIAL BUSINESS BY THE WAY (1791)

"*Wednesday*, 13*th*. Fixed with Colo. Carrington (the supervisor of the district) the surveys of Inspection for the District of this State and named the characters for them, an acct. of which was transmitted to the Secretary of the Treasury."

ESCAPE FROM AN ESCORT (1791)

"*Friday*, [April] 15*th*. Having suffered very much by the dust yesterday, and finding that parties of Horse, and a number of other Gentlemen were intending to attend me part of the way to day, I caused their

enquiries respecting the time of my setting out, to be answered that, I should endeavor to do it before eight o'clock; but I did it a little after five, by which means I avoided the inconveniences above mentioned."

COMMENT ON SOUTHERN COMMERCE (1791)

"*Sunday*, [April] 24*th*. . . . Wilmington is situated on the Cape Fear River, about 30 miles *by water* from its mouth, but much less by land. It has some good houses pretty compactly built. The whole under a hill; which is formed entirely of sand. The number of Souls in it amount by the enumeration to about 1000, but it is agreed on all hands that the Census in this State has been very inaccurately and Shamefully taken by the Marshall's deputies; . . . Wilmington, unfortunately for it, has a Mud bank—miles below, over which not more than 10 feet of water can be brought at common tides, yet it is said vessels of 250 Tons have come up. The qu'ty. of Shipping, which load here annually, amounts to about 1200 Tonns. The exports consist chiefly of Naval Stores and lumber. Some Tobacco, Corn, Rice, and flax seed with Porke. It is at the head of the tide navigation, but inland navigation may be extended 115 miles farther to and above Fayettesville which is from Wilmington 90 miles by land, and 115 by Water as above. Fayettesville is a thriving place containing near (   ) Souls. 6000 Hhds. of Tobacco and 3000 Hhds. of Flax Seed have been recd. at it in the course of the year."

A POETIC GREETING BY AN ADMIRER (1791)

"Now let some Shakespear sweep the sounding lyre

Or some brave Milton with prophetic fire

And soar aloft with some new strain sublime,

Beyond the reach of each dull creeping line.

From High Olympus let the gods descend,
And to this poet their assistance lend
While he in strains heroic sings the fame
Of Washington and gilds his noble name.
O let the sacred nine their aid diffuse
In strains sublime t' inspire his chanting muse
And may his song the sleeping echoes raise
From their soft slumber to resound his praise.

Till his glorious theme reaches every soul
From the arctic to the antarctic pole
But if a genius with such matchless strain
Cannot be found to sing our Hero's fame
The *Sons of Freedom* will I hope excuse
This imperfect strain from a willing muse . . .

But, to do this, requires a wiser hand,
And higher strains, than I can now command.

O, may no trifling bard, with creeping lays
Ever attempt to sing his matchless praise;

But may some Milton full of lyric sound⎫
Whose matchless strain whole nations will⎬
astound   ⎭
To sing his praises speedily be found!
He comes!—He comes!—methinks I see him near;
Now Columbians raise the joyful cheer!
Ye sons of Freedom who revere his name,
Beat loud your drums, and sound the trump of fame!"

A LOYAL ADDRESS (1791)

"Sir, The Mayor and Aldermen of the City of Savannah do unanimously concur in presenting their most affectionate congratulations to you on your arrival in this city. Impressed with a just sense of your great and eminent services to America, permit us, the Representatives of the City, to assure you of the high opinion the citizens entertain of your elevated virtues.

"We respect you as one of the richest and most valuable blessings divine goodness has bestowed on the People of these United States; your presence is an evidence of the watchful care you have for every part of the extended empire over which you preside. If we cannot, by external shew, demonstrate that respect for you which is in the power of the more wealthy of our sister states to display, yet none estimate your merits higher than the People of Georgia. The historic page bears record of our sufferings in the late Revolution, and the vestiges of war remain within view of our capital; and although peace was, in 1783, restored to America, yet Georgia continued to suffer under the destructive ravages of an Indian war, and it has been reserved for the efficiency of the present Government to give peace to our state.

"May the blessings of the Government long continue under your administration, and may it please the Great Ruler of Events to grant you long residence on earth, and to length of days add the blessings of uninterrupted health, that the advantages of the present Government may be permanently established.

"TH. GIBBONS, Mayor.
"Council Chamber, May 13, 1791."

MILITARY RENDEZVOUS IN WESTERN PENNSYLVANIA (1794)

"*Tuesday*, [September] 30*th*. Having determined from the Report of the Commissioners, who were appointed to meet the Insurgents in the Western Counties in the State of Pennsylvania, and from other circumstances—to repair to the place appointed for the Rendezvous of the Militia of New Jersey Pennsylvania Maryland and Virginia; I left the City of Philadelphia about half past ten oclock this forenoon accompanied by Colo. Hamilton (Secretary of the Treasury) and my private Secretary. . . .

"[October] 4*th*. Forded the Susquehanna; . . . On the Cumberland side I found a detachment of the Philadelphia light horse was ready to receive, and escort me to Carlisle 17 miles; where I arrived about 11 Oclock. Two miles short of it, I met the Governors of Pennsylvania and New Jersey with all the Cavalry that had rendezvoused at that time drawn up passed them and the Infantry of Pennsylvania before I alighted at my quarters. . . .

"*6th* to the *12th.* Employed in Organizing the several detachments, which had come in from different Counties of this State, in a very disjointed and loose manner; or rather I ought to have said in urging and assisting Genl. Mifflin to do it; as I no otherwise took the command of the Troops than to press them forward, and to provide them with necessaries for their March, as well, and as far, as our means would admit. . . .

"*16th.* After an early breakfast we set out for Cumberland—and about 11 Oclock arrived there.

"Three Miles from the Town I was met by a party of Horse under the command of Major Lewis (my Nephew) and by Brigr. Genl. Smith of the Maryland line, who Escorted me to the Camp; where, finding all the Troops under Arms I passed along the line of the Army; was conducted to a house the residence of Major Lynn of the Maryland line (an old Continental Officer) where I was well lodged, and civily entertained.

"*17th* and *18th.* Remained at Cumberland, in order to acquire a true knowledge of the strength—condition—&ca. of the Troops; and to see how they were provided, and when they could be got in readiness to proceed. . . .

"*19th.* In company with Genl. Lee, who I requested to attend me, that all the arrangements necessary for the Army's crossing the Mountns. in two columns might be made;—Their routs, and days Marches fixed, that the whole might move in unison—and accompanied by the Adjutant General and my own family we set out, abt eight oclock, for Bedford, and making one halt at the distance of 12 Miles, reached it a little after 4 Oclock in the afternoon being met a little out of the Encampment by Govr. Mifflin—Govr. Howell—and several other Officers of distinction. . . .

"The Road from Cumberld. to this place is, in places, stoney but in other respects not bad. It passes through a valley the whole way; and was opened by Troops under my command in the Autumn of 1758. The whole Valley consists of good farming land, and part of it—next Cumberland—is tolerably well improved in its culture but not much so in Houses.

"*20th.* Called the Quarter Master General, Adjutant General, Contractor, and others of the Staff departmt. before me, and the Commander in chief, at 9 Oclock this morning, in order to fix on the Routs of the two Columns and their stages; and to know what the situation of matters were in their respective departments and when they wd. be able to put the Army in motion. Also to obtain a correct return of the strength and to press the commanding Officers of Corps to prepare with all the Celerity in their power for a forward movement.

"Upon comparing accts., it was found that the army could be put in motion 23d—and it was so ordered, by the Routs which will be mentioned hereafter.

"Matters being thus arranged I wrote a farewell address to the Army through the Commander in Chief—Govr. Lee—to be published in orders—and having prepared his Instructions and made every arrangement that occurred, as necessary I prepared for my return to Philadelphia in order to meet Congress, and to attend to the Civil duties of my Office."

Selected Authorities

ALVORD, CLARENCE WALWORTH—*Mississippi Valley in British Politics.* 2 vols. Cleveland, Clark, 1917.

BAKER, WILLIAM S.—*Itinerary of General Washington from June 15, 1775, to December 23, 1783.* Philadelphia, Lippincott, 1892.

BAKER, WILLIAM S.—*Washington after the Revolution.* Philadelphia, Lippincott, 1898.

BEVERIDGE, ALBERT J.—*Life of John Marshall.* Vol. I. Boston, Houghton Mifflin, 1919. (Especially ch. vii.)

BRISSOT DE WARVILLE, JACQUES PIERRE—*New Travels in the United States, performed in 1788.* 2 vols. London, Jordan, 1794. (Other eds.)

BURNABY, ANDREW—*Travels through the Middle Settlements . . . 1759 and 1760.* London, Payne, 1775. (Other eds.)

CHADWICK, MRS. FRENCH E.—*Visit of General Washington to Newport in 1781* (Newport Historical Society, *Bulletin,* No. 6). Newport, 1913.

CHASTELLUX, FRANÇOIS JEAN, MARQUIS DE —*Travels in North America, in the Years 1780, 1781, and 1782.* Translated by J. Kent. 2 vols. London, Robinson, 1787. (Other eds.)

DUNBAR, SEYMOUR—*History of Travel in America.* Vol. I. Indianapolis, Bobbs-Merrill, 1915. (Especially chs. i-xiii.)

EARLE, ALICE MORSE—*Stage Coach and Tavern Days.* New York, Macmillan, 1900.

FITZPATRICK, JOHN C.—*George Washington, Colonial Traveller, 1732-1775.* Indianapolis, Bobbs-Merrill, 1927.

FORD, WORTHINGTON CHAUNCEY—*George Washington.* 2 vols. New York, Scribner, 1900.

GIST, CHRISTOPHER—*Journals.* Ed. by William M. Darlington. Pittsburgh, Weldin, 1893. (Other eds.)

HENDERSON, ARCHIBALD—*Conquest of the Old Southwest.* New York, Century, 1920.

HENDERSON, ARCHIBALD — *Washington's Southern Tour.* Boston, Houghton Mifflin, 1923.

HULBERT, ARCHER BUTLER, ED.—*Washington and the West.* New York, Century, 1905.

KEIR, MALCOLM — *March of Commerce* (*Pageant of America,* Vol. IV). New Haven, Yale University Press, 1927. (Especially ch. iii.)

KALM, PETER—*Travels into North America.* Translated by J. R. Forster. 2d ed. 2 vols. London, Lowndes, 1772. (Original ed. in Swedish of journey in 1748-49.)

LA ROCHEFOUCAULD-LIANCOURT, FRANÇOIS A. F., DUC DE—*Travels through the United States of North America in the Years 1795, 1796, and 1797.* Translated by H. Neuman. 2d ed. 4 vols. London, Phillips, 1800.

MAY, JOHN—*Journal and Letters, relative to Two Journeys to the Ohio Country in 1788 and '89.* Cincinnati, Clarke, 1873.

THOMPSON, WINFIELD M.—"When Washington toured New England, 1789"; in *Magazine of History,* Vols.XXIII-XXV. (Unfinished.)

TWINING, THOMAS—*Travels in America One Hundred Years Ago.* New York, Harper, 1894. (Tour in 1795-96.)

WASHINGTON, GEORGE — *Diaries, 1748-1799.* Ed. by John C. Fitzpatrick. 4 vols. Boston, Houghton Mifflin, 1925. (Contains the journals of the journeys of 1748, 1751, 1753, 1754, 1770, 1784, 1789, 1791, 1794, and many of the minor ones.)

WASHINGTON, GEORGE—*Writings.* Ed. by Worthington Chauncey Ford. 14 vols. New York, Putnam, 1889-93.

WELD, ISAAC, JR.—*Travel through the States of North America . . . during the Years 1795, 1796, and 1797.* 3d ed. 2 vols. London, Stockdale, 1800.

Washington the Business Man
By Hon. Sol Bloom
Part I
Conditions of Colonial Business

GEORGE WASHINGTON
From a painting by Gilbert Stuart

THE BUSINESS MIND

EVIDENCE accumulated in this set of Washington Pamphlets confirms the national belief that George Washington was the most successful American of his century. General testimony proves that he was so held, and posterity calls him a great man of the world. Nearly all of these favorable judgments, however, relate either to Washington as a soldier, or to Washington as a statesman. Americans are only now beginning to realize that the same qualities that made him indispensable as head of the Continental Army and the necessary choice as first President of the United States of America, made him also a remarkable man of affairs in the colonies and the federal republic. A study of his interest in many lines of business and his success in most of them, will therefore bring out his unusual abilities as a practical modern spirit without diminishing his greatness as a public man.

COLONIAL ECONOMICS

The circumstances of practical life in America in the eighteenth century were very different from those of later times. It might be said that Washington crossed an economic bridge; for business conditions radically changed in his half century of active life; and at the time of his death the modern era of commerce and manufacturing was beginning.

In the South, and in considerable areas of occupied territory in other parts of the colonies in Washington's time, no roads existed in the modern sense. The usual highways were beaten tracks with many fords and few bridges. Washington lived to see the beginnings of the planked or surfaced turnpikes, which were the predecessors of our modern highways. Navigation in that period was confined to sailing craft, which for ocean travel averaged less than 200 tons late in Washington's life. Washington was one of the first men to realize the possibilities of power boats. Down to the Revolution, in America as in Europe, nearly all manufactured goods were made by hand in private houses or small shops. Such manufactures were carried on at Mount Vernon. About the time of Washington's death began the period of factories using water power on a considerable scale to move machines.

Washington was in early life accustomed to very primitive methods of finance, which consisted chiefly in the accounts kept by his agents in England, and the bills of exchange drawn on them, with an occasional local loan. We shall see that he lived to be head of a joint stock enterprise and a stockholder in banks, and helped to inaugurate the first national banking system. His success as a business man, therefore, must be placed against the background of his own times and the business methods of an early community. He began life as a cadet of a planter family; began to accumulate property before he was of age; and made himself a successful business man by sterling honesty, by force of character, by forward-looking judgment, by capacity to grasp facts and control conditions.

Down to 1775 the business element in most of the colonies, especially in the South, was overshadowed by the landholder. In New England and the middle colonies merchants or shipowners, such as John Hancock, might aspire to enter a high social class of recognized families, and to be a power in the government of their colonies. Some of them founded permanent hereditary fortunes. In Washington's part of the country there were few wealthy men except the large landowners into whose fellowship Washington was born. To be sure a small class of wealthy merchants and shipowners was growing up even in some of the southern ports, particularly Charleston and Savannah, but most of the holders of large wealth owned inherited acres and formed a landed aristocracy. One reason for the success of the great Revolutionary movement was that the Virginia planters mostly joined the democratic movement for independence. In the Revolution, therefore, Washington was politically on the same side as his immediate friends and neighbors. Yet he had the force to win the confidence of the canny merchant classes of New England and the middle colonies.

DESCENT FROM BUSINESS MEN

According to modern doctrines of heredity the business sagacity of Washington was presumably in part a matter of descent. In his direct line, father to son, seven generations back, appeared Lawrence Washington, mayor of Northampton, England. Lawrence Washington's father had married Margaret Kitson, sister of the great Sir Thomas Kitson, who was a kind of Henry Ford of his time. Kitson developed a great and profitable business in fish; and hence his arms bear three fish. He also developed a large business in wool, with the intention of furnishing the raw material on English soil and encouraging its weaving into cloth of English style.

Kitson's nephew, Lawrence, mayor of Northampton, acquired in 1538 by royal grant (not without payment of smart fees) a portion of the recently confiscated landed estates of the Priory of St. Andrew in Northampton, which were sequestrated by Henry VIII. Among them was the estate of Sulgrave, which for some years was the seat of George Washington's direct ancestors. His great-grandfather, the immigrant John, also showed remarkable ability, became a sailor and a trader and made voyages to the West Indies and eventually Virginia. His sons and grandsons acquired considerable estates and George, through the early death of his halfbrother, Lawrence, came into possession of a handsome portion of his father's landed property. From his youth up therefore Washington associated with men who had wealth, increased it, and transmitted it. Fortune favored George Washington. It placed in his hands large opportunities of testing his talents of organization, supervision, record, and willingness to try new methods.

CUSTIS WEALTH

Washington's business capacity was evident long before the Revolution and in the first stages of the accumulation that made him one of the wealthiest Americans of his time, at least in land values, he was aided by his marriage. When nearly 27 years old he married a wealthy woman, heir, with her two children, to the property of the deceased Daniel Parke Custis, embracing plantations, a town house, slaves, livestock, and household and farm equipment, besides more liquid resources. The Custis wealth has per- haps been overestimated, but the portion of it in funds which came to Washington as part of his wife's dower, was evidently the means by which he began to enlarge his land holdings at Mount Vernon and elsewhere. Throughout his life his income came chiefly from the returns of his farms and interest on bonds which constituted a large part of the financial business of Virginia at that time. These returns were the basic capital of his other business ventures.

The records of the Custis estate are no longer available, but according to an entry under probable date of 1759, each of the two children had about $33,000, and it has been supposed that Mrs. Washington's share was the same. Evidently this did not include the landed property. Washington's letters to his agents in England refer to the division of the estate. He informed an agent in 1762 that the Bank of England stock of a par value of £1,650 had been allocated to Patsy. There is no evidence in the writings of any investment abroad except this bank stock, or of any tobacco being shipped on Patsy's account. In the absence of exact figures it seems likely that there was no division of the estate into equal thirds of personal and real property, but it has been estimated that Washington's eventual share, as his wife's third in the estate, was about $100,000 measured by the specie standard of the time. He was a prudent administrator and the value of his wards' estates, as well as his own, increased in his hands.

Part II
Washington's Business Records

BOOKKEEPING SYSTEM

Washington had a neat and methodical mind; he was an early example of economic efficiency. He recognized the value of records, and to that recognition we owe the great body of material available upon his career and its share in the history of the country. This bent of mind was shown as early as 1748, when he began to keep an expense account and in the early establishment of the diary habit. Washington's account books are valuable not only as a personal record, but also as source material for economic study.

Rigorous commercial bookkeeping, like that of today, was not one of the accomplishments of the colonial Americans. Even heavy merchants like John Hancock were satisfied with direct records. The so-called Italian system of double-entry bookkeeping appears to have been little known in the colonies. There were no banks, few insurance companies, very few commercial corporations; and, notwithstanding a very extensive credit system, both wholesale and retail, the usual books of account were simple.

Washington's strong sense of system enabled him to summarize his yearly financial condition, though it does not appear that he classified his minor expenses with absolute exactness. He kept an elaborate system of classified accounts for his farm activities; and tobacco, weaving, fishing, and other definite industries were debited and credited in separate accounts, as illustrated by the table given below.

Washington carried out a simple but effective system of records of all cash transactions and was very careful to obtain legal documents for payments made by him. He never "kept books" in the modern sense, but throughout his life, besides many financial entries in his diaries, he kept a series of little books of original entry of cash transactions, later transferred to the ledgers, which reveal his habits of life. He was a generous man and his books abound in such entries as the following:

"By Cash gave a Soldiers wife 5/;" "Gave a man who had his House Burnt £1. ;" "By a begging woman /5;" "By Charity to an invalid wounded Soldier who came from Redston with a petition for Charity 18/;" "Delivd to the President to send to two distress'd french women at Newcastle $25;" "By Madame de Seguer a french Lady in distress gave her $50;" "By subscription paid to Mr. Jas. Blythe towards erecting and Supporting an Academy in the State of Kentucky $100;" "By Charity sent Genl Charles Pinckney in Columbus Bank Notes, for the sufferers by the fire in Charleston So. Carolina $300;" "By an annual Donation to the Academy at Alexandria pd. Dr. Cook $166.67;" "By Charity to the poor of Alexandria deld. to the revd. Dr. Muir $100."

He was particularly regardful of the members of his own family, and he recorded various loans to his kindred, which were eventually transferred into gifts. The diary accounts of his visits to his mother at Fredericksburg are often paralleled by an expense account showing that he presented her with money. He never denied a loan to a friend if he had the cash on hand. There is no end to these minor entries of occasional expense for a multitude of purposes, which bring into relief a daily life of great variety of interests and amusements.

ILLUSTRATIVE ENTRIES

This variety of Washington's payments and the minuteness of his accounts may be illustrated by a few extracts from his ledgers and diaries. For example: "By a year's and 3 Months Ferriage at ye lower Ferry on Rappaoppe [Rappahanock], my Mothers. 12s. 6d." "To my Burgesses Wages untill the adjournment in Octr. Sessions—viz 54 days @ 15/ £40.10." "To 12 traveling days—to and from Do, @ ....Do. £9." "To Ferriages going and coming over Occoquan, Rappahannock and Pamunky £1.17.9." "Dancing Master—Mackay for Childn. £1." "To washing while Quartered in Alexandria £1.13.3." "To gave away at Edward Thompson's 3/9."

"By a Chr. [chariot] bot. of Mr. P. Claiborne Mr. Braxton's £50." "Surgn. Dentist £4.0.0.:" "By Dinners & Clubs thereat, at Mrs. Campbell's during my stay in Willmsburg £7.7.6." "By Mrs. Charltons Acct. against Miss Custis 16s. 3d. By Ditto for Mrs. Washington. 16s. 0d. By Ditto for my board there since the 1st of March.. £11.0.0." "Mr. Robinson's Servants £1.4.0." "By Ditto for a Ticket to ye Assembly 7/6." "By Cash to my Nurse £1.0.0." This last was the soldier who attended him in the illness just before Braddock's defeat.

Almost the only knowledge that we have of his journey to Boston in 1756 comes from his account books, which disclose the route as well as evidence of his social activities.

February 15-20. New York City.

"By Cash for my Club at Tavn. 5/1. for treatg. Ladies to ye Mi[crocos]m £1.8.0. At Mrs. Baron's Rout 6/ Club at Willets 4/2 . . . treating Ladies to ye Microcosm £1.4.0 . . . Mr. Robinson's Servts. £1.8.6 . . . lost at cards 8/. Gave to Servants on ye Rd. 10/."

His election expenses in 1771 at Alexandria are also enlightening:

"Went up to the Election and the Ball I had given at Alexa. Mr. Crawford and Jno. P. Custis with me. Stayd all Night."

"Dec. 19 By Mr. Arroll Balle.
of Acct. to this date   £ 15 12—
By Mr. Lomax getting a Supper at My Ball the Night
of Election   4. 7. 8
By Mr. William Shaw providg. Sundries &ca. for ye
Election & Ball & his own
Trouble   4. 1. 9
By Mr. Piper's Charles playg.
Fiddle   12.
1772, May 18. 'By Mrs. Young
for cakes at ye last Electn. £ 1. 9. 8.' "

Lotteries were a regular occurrence in those days, many of them for religious and educational purposes. Washington took his share of such chances and records the result, often with dry humor. In 1766 he "invested" in the York Lottery; and in 1775 two of the six tickets he held in the land lottery in Ulster County, New York, were "fortunate." He recorded another transaction as "By profit & loss in two chances in raffling for encyclopadia Bretannica, which I did not win, 1£ 4 shillings."

His diaries and cash books are full of entertaining out-goes. "To ye Club of a bottle of Rhenish at Mitchells 1£ 3 shillings." —"By Ball[ance] I never expected 2. 5. 2." "I got Nation's Estate Apprais'd by Messrs. McCarty, Barry and Triplet,—as follows, viz.

One old Gun and Lock 7–6
1 Small Bell.............. 2–6
1 Suit of Cloaths, viz.
   a Coat Waist't Breechs
   Shirt, Hat, Shoes &   } 10
   Garters ....
A Small Parcel of Leather ...   1

On the last day of 1769 he noted: "By Cash lost, Stolen, or paid away without charging £143.15.2." What looks like a very unhumanitarian entry refers not to a man but to a weapon: "To Cash paid Mr. Lewis for a Baby and 2 doz. Gun Flints 5/."

A class of expenditures of which there were several during his life, is the following in 1772:

"By Mr. P e a l e Painter,
   Drawg. my Picte.   £18.4.0
Miniature Do. for
   Mrs. Washingtn.   £13.
Ditto Do. for Miss
   Custis   13.
Ditto Do. for Mr.
   Custis   13.   £57.4.0"

ANALYTICAL ACCOUNTS

These simple records enabled him to judge whether a particular commercial transaction or product was profitable. Hence he was one of the earliest Virginia planters to realize that tobacco was an exhausting and, therefore, an unprofitable crop. He finally abandoned it entirely at the Mount Vernon farms and substituted the cultivation of other crops, particularly wheat. An example of the accounts of the special industries already mentioned are pictured in a general statement for the whole Mount Vernon estate, as in the form, item by item, shown in the following extract from his books:

"BALANCE OF GAIN AND LOSS,
1798.

Dr. gained.

Dogue Run Farm 397.11. 2
Union Farm 529.10.11½
River Farm 234. 4.11
Smith's Shop 34.12. 9½
Distillery 83.13. 1

Jacks 56. 1
Traveller (stud horse)...... 9.17
Shoemaker 28.17. 1
Fishery 165.12. 0¾
Dairy .... 30.12.

Cr. lost.

Mansion House 466.18.2½
Muddy Hole Farm.......... 60. 1.3½
Spinning 51. 2.0
Hire of head overseer....... 140. 0.0
By Clear gain on the Estate..£898.16.4¼"

Thus in one direction Washington adopted a method of financial records little practiced then on a large scale even among prosperous merchants. He developed an analytic bookkeeping system with regard to his great landed estate. His habit (not carried out every year) of keeping his accounts so that he could distinguish payments and receipts from each of the farms that together constituted Mount Vernon, enabled him to record the crops that were planted in each of these subdivisions and to follow out the results for each crop on each of the associated farms. This practice gave him a control possessed by few planters over the causes of loss on a particular crop, or on a particular plantation, and recorded gains on another. Hence he knew where to stop and where to go forward. He substituted a rational, understandable record for the guesses and repetitions of unprofitable methods which were often the bases of farm methods of planters.

BUSINESS INCOME

In provincial days at least, his financial system was essentially one of English accounts, long credit, orders against his presumed balance, and bills of exchange. Even after he ceased shipping tobacco to Europe and sent flour and fish to the West Indies instead, payment was in orders or bills on England. It is not easy under such conditions to suppose that he possessed much ready money, yet the items given above from his accounts suggest the presence of an adequate cash balance, and a very characteristic entry of 1772 reproduced in facsimile on the next page shows that he sometimes had considerable amounts of cash on hand, including a variety of colonial paper money.

Naturally the question arises as to what were the sources of supply for the payment of his bills and for his ready cash? First in importance came his farms. No summary has been found of his total investments in land purchases or buildings or betterments of the property previous to his will of 1799. Even as late as that date it is probable that, in spite of large holdings, almost all the income came from Mount Vernon and a few other places east of the Alleghenies. The York River dower property had been sold; but there were some 8,000 other acres in Virginia and Maryland, a portion of which was under cultivation. He had an uncertain income from his fisheries adjacent to his property and from a ferry. The Dismal

Swamp drainage enterprise seems to have brought him a profit in his lifetime; and some unsold lands in that property were a part of his estate at his death. He sold land from time to time and a portion of the proceeds paid debts or current expenses.

He held some bonds though evidently none at the end of his life, except the federal issue mentioned below. Occasionally he

Besides this federal stock at the end of his life he held shares in the Potomac Company, in the James River Company, and in the Columbia and Alexandria banks. The river-improvement stock brought him personally no income, that of the Potomac was a dead loss to the estate. The bank holdings were small, and belonged to the late period of his life.

Pocket...day..Book
or
Cash..Memorandums
began.
9th of Augt.. 1772

Cash on hand this 9th of Augta
In Gold   1772
66 half Joes Weigh £148.17.6
7 Guineas..a 26/......9.2 -
10 Pistoles Weighg.....10.18
Other Peces.........2.9 -191.6.6
Silver
Dollars & Parts a 5/9..87.8
Cut half Bitts a...NS 36 -
Other Silver........5.5 128.13.0
Paper
Virginia Money..16 -
Maryld Dollars a 5/9 62.7.9
Pensa.£7.10.9.29 Do - 5.13.1 84.0.10
Total amount.............£404.0.4

made loans on mortgages or otherwise, but if one may judge correctly from his writings these were more fruitful of trouble than income, resulting in some cases in his taking over the land or chattel. His loans were never those of a professional money lender, but he could be sharp when he considered that the condition justified it. Thus in 1799 he wrote a debtor: "I am in extreme want of the money which you gave me a solemn promise I should receive the first of January last; and secondly—that however you may have succeeded in imposing upon, and deceiving others, you shall not practice the like game with me with impunity."

Like all moneyed men of his time, he suffered very severe losses through the depreciation of paper, so that a nominal $50,-000 of loans made in Virginia colonial currency when realized sank to a capital of about $6,000 in federal bonds.

BANK OF ENGLAND STOCK

His most interesting investment was the £1650 in stock of the Bank of England. As we have seen this was a portion of the Custis estate, allocated to Patsy. On her death in 1773 it was equally divided between her brother and mother; Washington's share of the dividend during the next two years was collected by his English agent and made a portion of the general accounts, of which the balance was usually against Washington. After the Revolution broke out, and the guardianship of young Custis terminated, Washington took over the rest of the bank stock in order that all of the loss due to the rebellion might fall upon himself. It is a striking tribute to the Governor and Company of the Bank of England that they continued to pay dividends after Washington had become a public enemy of the British

Government, perhaps because, as Prussing suggests, he was not an alien enemy but only a rebel, probably because the stock was not in his name on the books of the bank, but in that of his wife as administratrix. The English agents collected the dividends during the war, placed them to Washington's account and charged against them the interest due through Washington's unfavorable balance, but also credited interest on the assets in their hands, which were chiefly Custis items. After the war Washington sold the stock and paid his "British debt."

OTHER PEOPLE'S AFFAIRS

Washington's business acumen was not limited in its practice to his own affairs, nor to the guardianship of his wife's children. He gave freely of his time and knowledge to his neighbors and friends; and before the Revolution shared as executor in the management of various estates, and served also as arbitrator in property disputes. In stating the difficulties in granting the request that he undertake the guardianship of John West's son, Washington wrote in 1775: ". . . two things are essentially necessary in the Man to whom this charge is committed. A Capacity of judging with propriety, of Measures proper to be taken in the Government of a youth; and leizure sufficient to attend the Execution of these Measures. That you are pleased to think favorably of me, in respect to the first, I shall take for granted, from the request you have made, but to shew my incapacity of attending to the latter with that good faith which I think every man ought to do, who undertakes a trust of this Interesting nature, I can solemnly declare to you, that for this year or two past, there has been scarce a Moment that I can properly call my own: For what with my own business, my present Wards, My Mothers (which is wholely in my hands), Colo. Colvills, Mrs. Savages, Col. Fairfax's, Colo. Mercers (for Colo. Tayloe though he accepted of the Trust jointly with myself, seems no ways inclined to take any part of the Execution of it), and the little Assistance I have undertaken to give in the management of my Brother Augustines Affairs (for I have absolutely refused to qualify as an Executor) keeps me, together with the share I take in publick Affairs, constantly engaged in writing Letters, Settling Accts., and Negotiating one piece of business or another in behalf of one or other of these Concerns; by which means I have really been deprivd of every kind of enjoyment, and had almost fully resolved, to engage in no fresh matter. till I had entirely wound up the old."

On January 25, 1771, he spoke of being at Dumfries "in a very disagreeable arbitration which I suppose will keep me till sometime in next week." These affairs gave him much trouble, but he considered them with the same care that he did his own business. An evidence of this is in an entry in his diary, January 8, 1772, respecting his joint executorship in the Savage matter:

"Engaged to advance by, or at the April General Court for the use of Mr. Bryan Fairfax £150, or thereabouts, to discharge the Balle of his Bond to Doctr. Savage. Also promised, if I could, to take up a Bill of Excha. of about £160 Sterg. with Intt. thereon at the same time; In consideration of which he has given me a Memm. at the prices there Stipulated in case I like them, or either of them upon examination thereof within   Months from this day. If not, he is then to become my Debtor for these two Accts."

Part III
The Promoter and Planter

FAMILY EXPERIENCE

The first established permanent business of the Washington family was that of clearing Virginia land until sufficient soil could be exposed to make crops possible, particularly tobacco, the great export crop for many years. After tobacco culture was prohibited in England in 1652, it became almost a monopoly product in the southern colonies.

John Washington and his sons, grandsons, and great-grandsons undertook the never-ending process of clearing the land. That meant the destruction of vast and noble forests, little or no part of which could be exported. Some of this was used in building houses, fences, and shelters for stock. Eventually the native timber furnished part of the material of spacious mansions, suggested by the "great houses" in England.

Down to the time of Washington's birth, there were no cities in the South and few towns. The commercial towns as they arose were on waters which could be navigated from the sea. For the small planters, especially on tidewater, the store was the sales agency for surplus products, and the nearest approach to a bank, through its credit facilities. The towns of these local stores grew up around the tobacco warehouses built under the colonial inspection act, which regulated the export of the staple. Alexandria and Dumfries originated in this manner. Washington's letters refer to the inspection: "I have got 4 more inspected and all on Float ready to deliver at the Ships side"; and again, "It will appear by our Inspectors that my Tobacco was delivered in good order."

Washington bought from local stores, sometimes paying cash, and also bought on book accounts, settled from time to time. In a letter to Matthew Campbell, a merchant at Alexandria, August 7, 1772, Washington showed his attitude on patronizing his neighbor: "I was not lead to enquire into the price of the Goods I had purchased of you already, and might hearafter take from any thing that passed between us at the time I offered to discontinue my own Importations (upon Condition I could get my Goods at nearly what they would cost to Import them myself). I very well remember that nothing conclusive passd between you and me on that occasion; . . . If . . . you still think proper to let me have the Goods I may find occasion to buy in the Country at 25 pr. Ct. Sterling advance upon the genuine Cost dischargeable at the Curr'y exchange I will confine my whole Country dealings to your Store and will endeavour to thro the Wages which I pay to hirelings into your hands also; provided you will let me know upon what certain reasonable advance they can have their Goods (upon the strength of my Credit) for unless they can deal with you upon better terms than with others I should not think myself justifyable in attempting to influence their choice, and this knowledge I must come at in order that I may convince them (if satisfied myself) of the propriety of the Measure."

BUSINESS OF PLANTATION MANAGEMENT

As a man of affairs, Washington's immediate and continuous business was that of managing a plantation. Once settled in Mount Vernon he gradually increased the property so that he had a group of five farms under his ownership and management. The evidence with regard to his management of that large estate is abundant. Upon no agricultural enterprise of the time have we such detailed information as to the plans and the results of Washington's agricultural management. We have his accounts and a correspondence which included many letters on farm affairs.

Probably no agricultural proprietor in the English colonies and the later United States made such efforts to avail himself of the scientific knowledge of his time. He bought numerous English works on agriculture. He was long in correspondence with Arthur Young, the English agricultural reformer. He invented a plow and was not much disturbed when it failed to meet his expectations. He contrived something closely approaching our modern seed drills.

He appears to have been the most important large proprietor to practice scientific diversification of crops. He raised wheat when the land would no longer carry good crops of tobacco, and the marketing of that staple became uneconomic. Then he ran a mill to grind his wheat, and accepted customs grinding. Later he built a distillery to make available his raw materials. In fact, the Mount Vernon property was a sort of confederation of farms with their appurtenances of orchards and farm buildings, farm roads, quarters for the slaves, and houses for the hired white men and the redemptioners or indentured servants bound to serve a stipulated number of years in payment of their passage money from Europe. Besides his main estate he had some outside farm properties, especially the Bullskin Plantation, and during ante-bellum days the dower estate on York River.

But Mount Vernon was his home, his main source of revenue, and his chief delight. There, also, his engineering instincts had full opportunity of action, for he was frequently out with his surveying instruments estimating drainage possibilities, running his boundary lines over again, or checking up those of newly acquired land. On the border line between one of his plantations and that of Thomson Mason can still be seen two parallel lines of ditching about fifteen yards apart. These—referred to in his will—are said to mark an amicable controversy between the two neighbors. By mutual agreement each dug a ditch five feet wide on what he supposed to be the proper line. The space between remained a "no man's land," left to be adjusted by the heirs of the parties.

When the Revolutionary War broke out, Washington had brought the Mount Vernon estate into a productive and profitable condition. But from 1775 to 1783, and again from 1789 to 1797, he spent most of his time away from his estates and was obliged to depend upon overseers and estate managers. His experience of those men is summed up in a paragraph written in 1793 in one of the many letters of instruction which he wrote during his presidency to the successive managers of his estate:

"To treat them civilly is no more than what all men are entitled to, but, my advice to you is, to keep them at a proper distance; for they will grow upon familiarity, in proportion as you will sink in authority, if you do not.—Pass by no faults or neglects (especially at first) for overlooking one only serves to generate another, and it is more than probably that some of them (one in particular) will try, at first, what lengths he may go.—A steady and firm conduct, with an inquisitive inspection into, and a proper arrangement of everything on your part, will, though it may give trouble at first, save a great deal in the end . . ."

One of the main items in the cost of the

plantation was the amount of the proprietor's time and attention when he was managing the property himself and the losses due to the stupidity and disobedience of orders by the overseers. The story of the round barn is a comment upon the difficulties of managing overseers. The round barn, which appears to have been actually twelve or possibly sixteen sided, had a threshing floor indoors, and great was Washington's wrath on one occasion to find that the grain had been thrown out of the barn onto the ground and was being trodden out by horses in the old wasteful manner. He wrote his stepson in 1776: "I have no doubt myself, but that middling land under a man's own eye, is more profitable than rich land at a distance."

WASHINGTON AS A BUSINESS FARMER

Washington's agricultural system was in advance of his age though it is questionable whether he had much direct or contemporary influence. The German farmers of Pennsylvania and the Valley followed many of his principles and probably Washington was acquainted with their methods. Land was still too cheap for extensive farming. Jefferson's belief that it was better to exhaust the land and then move on was more in the spirit of the age. But considered in its relation to agricultural history, the Mount Vernon estate was an important project, and even more important as illustrating the character of its cultivator.

The five farms were all under cultivation. He also exercised a remarkable business sagacity in the well-organized system which is emphasized in this pamphlet. He applied to the estate of Mount Vernon the principles of division of labor, of the use of export laborers, of caring for the sick, and in general of making the laborers on the estate comfortable and contented, which are a part of the best factory practice of our own time.

The farsightedness of Farmer Washington was shown by his establishment of what was in effect an agricultural experiment station, perhaps the only one in the United States at his time, as has been shown in the pamphlet on Washington the Farmer; while his system of accounting made it possible to keep track of the financial results of his experiments.

ENGLISH SUPERINTENDENT

One of the most interesting episodes in Washington's relations with labor was his employment of James Bloxham as head farmer of the Mount Vernon complex—a transaction described in another pamphlet of this series. Through Arthur Young, he secured this real English bailiff, and in 1786 brought him over "to live with and superintend my farming business" under the title "Farmer and Manager." In a letter of 1787 Washington complained of Bloxham that: "in a word he seems rather to have expected to have found well organized farms, than that the end and design of my employing him was to make them so." Bloxham, however, was much respected by his employer, who kept him on for several years.

Bloxham's side of the relation appears in a letter much less widely known. A portion of this is given in the earlier pamphlet; in addition he complained: "things are verey Desagreable to Do Bisness it is impossable for any man to Do Bisness in any form the Genral have a Bout 25 hundrd akers of Clear Land under is on ocyping. Ther is nothing agreble about on the plase which I can not Do no Bisnss form nor no Credet but I have you send the plow And the Seeds which the Genearel will send for to you and send half a Dosen of Good Clean made Shupicks [spades] for they have nothing but woodon forks I have got one or two made but in a very bad manner that I should be glad if you would not for this Contey is verey pore and there is no chance for any Body to Do any god and I should be glad if you and my Brother Thomas would See if these velins would Com to any terms [Bloxham left debts in England] or I would go to any part of Englun to be out of thare way But this Countruy will not Do for me but to Be Shore what the General have offered in wages is quite Well he Gives for this year we have a Gred for 50 English ginnes per yeare and Bord and washing and Lodging and if I Would send for my wife and famly he would alow me ten Ginnes towards thare Coming to this Contry an if I would Stay and to alow me 8 hundard weight of flower and 6 hundred Wait of pork and Bef and to alow me two milche Cows for the youse of my family and to low me a Sow to Bree[d] Som pigs for my own yous but Not to Sell and to alow me a Comfortable house to Live in. . . . But my wife may youse ore one will A Bout Comming over. . . . I hope that the Sun will Shine upon me wonce more the general have some very [good?] laynd But badly manedge and he never well have them no better for he have a Sett About him which I nor you would be troubled with But the General is goot them and he must keep them but they are a verey Desagreable People and I will leave the Contey But I Should be glad of answer Immedatly to know how afares Stand and then I sall be a better Judge of the matter . . . I have whent thro a greatt Dele Since I laft England."

LABOR PROBLEMS

Throughout his life, Washington was the head of large organizations which made use of human strength of body and mind. The owner of a plantation was in much the same situation as the captain of a ship at sea. The object of the sailor driver and of the plantation driver alike was to get as much as possible of muscular exertion out of the workers at the least cost of support. The shipmaster had to pay wages besides feeding and keeping up his men. The plantation owner nominally got his labor without paying wages; but after he had fed and clothed the slaves, provided for their housing, and suffered from deaths and illness, immaturity and age, malingering and runaways, his labor was really costly. A profit came to the slave owners through the growing up of young slaves to the point where they could be worked or marketed; but much of that gain was offset.

Washington hired employees for various tasks on the farm. His numerous building operations and repairs brought in skilled white workmen. In his diary he notes that "Three Carpenters belonging to the Estate of Colo. Steptoe (hired of Jas. Hardige Lane) at £7 pr. Month) come to work here." He had a succession of overseers or managers on the York River farms and those on the Rappahannock. In 1773 he wrote: "This day agreed with my Overseer [William] Powell, at the lower Plantation on Rappah., to continue another year on the same lay as the last, provided the number of hands are not Increasd; but, if I should add a hand or two more, and let him (as I am to do at any rate) choose 5 of the best Horses at that Quarter and the upper one, he is in that case to receive only the 8th of what Corn, Wheat, and Tobo. he makes on the Plantation."

WHITE REDEMPTIONERS

Throughout the eighteenth century a traffic in what was practically white slavery went on, especially in the middle colonies and Virginia. Normally the immigrants agreed that for their passage over from Europe they were liable to give service for seven years to anyone who would pay their passage money. Those who survived the horrors of the voyage and the chattel service, founded families. Washington had such white servants among his laborers, mostly artisans. In 1775 he offered a reward of forty dollars for the return of a joiner and brickmaker who had run away.

With regard to an importation from Germany, he wrote in 1784: "I am informed that a ship with Palatines is gone up to Baltimore, among whom are a number of tradesmen. I am a good deal in want of a house joiner and brick-layer who really understand their profession, and you would do me a favor by purchasing one of each for me, if to be had, I would not confine you to Palatines; if they are good workmen, they may be from Asia, Africa or Europe; they may be Mahometans, Jews or Christians of any sect, or they may be Atheists. I would, however, prefer middle aged to young men, and those who have good countenances, and good characters on ship board, to others who have neither of these to recommend them; altho' after all, I well know, the proof of the pudding must be in the eating. I do not limit you to a price, but will pay the purchase money on demand."

SLAVE LABOR

Washington was born into a slave-owning family and early became the owner of slaves, who were the "Desagreable People" of Bloxham's letter. Slave holding began with the enslavement of Indian captives by the various colonies, was shortly simplified by the bringing over of African slaves, and was legal in Virginia for more than sixty years after Washington's death.

The profits of Mount Vernon, never very large, were due chiefly to slave labor; but Washington was one of the small number of southern slave holders at that time who felt that slavery was an unnatural institution. There were few antislavery men and women in the United States in 1799; but that one who lived in Mount Vernon tested his convictions in his will by ordering that the slaves held in his own right should be set free after Mrs. Washington's death. The dower slaves were on a different footing. He left money for annuities to slaves who could not support themselves, some of which continued for nearly forty years. George Washington and John Randolph were among the few blueblood Virginians holding large numbers of slaves who at any epoch hated slavery sufficiently to free their own slaves, by will or otherwise.

We possess no account of a large slave-holding plantation of the period which compares in completeness with our knowledge of Washington's slaves. His diaries and accounts contain a vast amount of detail, both with regard to particular slaves and to the general condition of his slaves. The total number on the five Mount Vernon farms seem never to have exceeded about two hundred and fifty, man, woman, and child, though William Loughton Smith in his journal of a visit to Mount Vernon in 1791 wrote: "he owns 300 slaves, about 150 or 160 workers"; and since Washington was not in the habit of selling slaves in order to raise money, the number of children, old people, and poor workers proportionately increased. On few plantations were the hands so well treated as on the Mount Vernon property. They were as well fed as any slaves of the time. There is next to nothing in the diaries about the punishment of slaves and much about the expense of medical attendance.

OPINION ON EMANCIPATION

Washington was early aware that slave labor was costly and otherwise questionable, and he did not later alter his opinion. In 1767 he wrote: "God knows I have losses enough in Negroes to require something where with to supply their places." Also in 1794 he wrote to Alexander Spotswood: "Were it not then, that I am principled against selling negroes, as you would do cattle at a market, I would not in twelve months from this date, be possessed of one as a slave. I shall be happily mistaken, if they are not found to be very troublesome

species of property ere many years pass over our heads—(but this by the bye)." Yet whatever profit there was out of Mount Vernon was the outcome, under efficient management, of slave labor; and as Washington's possession of funds depended chiefly upon successful agriculture it is probable that even during his absences, when his oversight was indirect, the balance was not usually unfavorable.

Washington in 1790 recorded a conversation with "a Mr. Warner Miflin, one of the People called Quakers; active in pursuit of the Measures laid before Congress for emancipating the Slaves: . . . he used arguments to show the immorality—injustice—and impolicy of keeping these people in a state of Slavery; with declarations, however, that he did not wish for more than a gradual abolition, or to see any infraction of the Constitution to effect it. To these I replied, that as it was a matter which might come before me for official decision I was not inclined to express any sentimts. on the merits of the question before this should happen." This reply was probably the caution of the official rather than the sentiments of the man, though the only legislation during his administrations upon slavery was the fugitive law of 1793, and the act of 1794 to prohibit the export of slaves.

PRINCIPLES AS EMPLOYER

His labor questions were not confined to farming. They occurred in connection with the engineering projects, and were not absent from the problems of higher class employees. In reference to the workmen of the Potomac Navigation Company, Washington wrote: "We are endeavoring to engage our miners to bore by the foot; rather than by the day; but as yet have not agreed with any in this way:—they ask a shilling, which we think is too much—to common labourers we pay 40/ per month; and we find paying the workmen every fortnight, rather troublesome—once a month would do better:—as they will be frequently moving, we have provided Tents as most convenient & least expensive, for their accommodation."

Washington was precise in his statements of the needed qualifications of his secretary as shown in his letter to Tench Tilghman on June 2, 1785, and in informing General Lincoln on February 6, 1786, as to the duties of Tobias Lear. He wrote in 1776 concerning the merits of a possible military secretary: "What kind of a hand he writes, I know not. I believe but a cramped one; latterly none at all, as he has either the gout, or rheumatism, or both. He is a man fond of company and gayety, and is of a tender constitution. Whether, therefore, such a person would answer your purpose as well as a plodding, methodical person, whose sole business should be to arrange his papers in such order as to produce any one at any instant it is called for, and capable at the same time of composing a letter, is what you have to consider."

As President he was called upon to fill all the newly created offices in accordance with his avowal that "three things, in my opinion, ought principally to be regarded, namely, the fitness of characters to fill offices, the comparative claims from the former merits and sufferings in service of the different candidates, and the distribution of appointments in as equal a proportion as might be to persons belonging to the different States in the Union. . . . Besides, I thought, whatever the effect might be in pleasing or displeasing any individuals at the present moment, a due concern for my own reputation, not less decisively than a sacred regard to the interests of the community, required, that I should hold myself absolutely at liberty to act, while in office, with a sole reference to justice and the public good."

THE PLANTER AND THE ENGLISH AGENTS

In Washington's early life there was a lively commerce with the mother country and a system of credit business into which the Washington family entered. This trade system had a political side. It was one of the means of keeping the colonists aware of their dependence upon the mother country. The new republic, when formed and at peace with the world, resumed relations with England, but the latter stood now upon an equal political footing with the rival commercial interests of France and Holland and Spain, and the commercial readjustment was one of the first serious problems of Washington's administration as first President.

Washington's main commercial and business relation with England was with the firm which had previously served the Custis family. These "factors" for many years were the firm of Robert Cary & Company in London, later transformed into Wakelin Welch. He also did business occasionally with other English firms. He practiced the Virginia method of shipping produce to them, sometimes in vessels direct from his wharf to England, as payment for goods of various kinds shipped or to be shipped to Virginia. Naturally shrewd and hard-headed, Washington more than his neighbors chafed under this arrangement, the result of which seemed to be that the debits against him were always overrunning the credits, though the normal factor of percentage was not unreasonable. After the Revolution, Washington's direct purchases in England were only incidental, though some of his luxuries must still have been of foreign production.

OVERSEAS TRADE RELATIONS

Reading the letters Washington wrote his agents before the Revolution makes it evident that the chief responsibility for poor results in this system lay upon the agents and the shipmasters. Washington soon after his marriage wrote Cary the following warning: "I shall be candid in telling you that duty to the Charge with which I am entrusted as well as self Interest will incline me to abide by those who gives the greatest proof of their Abilities in selling my own and the Estates Tobo. and purchasing Our Goods which I can no otherwise judge of than by the Accts. that will be render'd."

Throughout the succeeding years there were many complaints of captains who failed to appear and were otherwise very erratic, of tobacco damaged in transit, of unaccountable low prices for the staple and unreasonably high prices for goods sent in return. These goods, not seldom landed at inconvenient ports or delayed beyond excuse, were often poor in quality, incomplete, misfits, unfit for their purpose, or downright dishonest.

He also complained of lack of reciprocity on the part of the agents, writing in 1764: "I did not expect that a corrispondant so steady, and constant as I have proved, and was willing to have continued to your House while the advantages were in any degree reciprocal would be reminded in the Instant it was discovered how necessary it was for him to be expeditous in his payments." A further hurt was recorded in 1768: ". . . unless the Sales with you are high, we shall be a considerable looser by adhering to our usual custom of assisting your Ships here, this we hope you will endeavour to avoid, and make the advantages reciprocal; at least that we do not suffer by our Attachment to your House."

In the case of a minor agent such conduct caused, in 1774, a quick discharge. "I came to the knowledge of your having noted the Bills . . . for Protest although it since appears by your Acct. that you did afterwards pay them. Your Motives for this piece of conduct surprizing as they seem to me I do not mean to give you the trouble of Accounting for. I was going however upon the first notice of it, to recall my order to Captn. Eston; but, as my word was out to him, I did, upon Second thoughts forbare to do this, but now desire that the proceeds of these twelve Hhds of Tobacco so soon as sold, together with the Ballance of Mr. Custis's Acct. be it more or less paid into the hands of Robt. Cary Esq. & Co. who shall be impowered to receive them."

INVOICES AND SHIPMENTS

Washington's letters are full of interesting orders for goods to be sent from England, all the way from babies' dolls to coaches. A few quotations will make clear the nature and extent of this overseas business. When possible Washington was exact and specific in ordering his goods, as is shown by this detailed extract from his early accounts:

"Memorandom: To have my Coat made by the following Directions to be made a Frock with a Lapel Breast the Lapel to Contain on each side six Button Holes, and to be about 5 or 6 Inches wide all the way equal and to turn as the Breast of the Coat does to have it made very long Waisted and in Length to come down to or below the Bent of the knee the Waist from the armpit to the Fold to be exactly as long or Longer than from thence to the Bottom not to have more than one fold in the Skirt and the top to be made just to turn in and three Button Holes the Lapel at the top to turn as the Cape of the Coat, and Bottom to Come Parrallel with the Button Holes the Last Button hole in the Breast to be right opposite to the Button on the Hip."

Later in writing for an invoice of clothes, he said: "I want neither Lace nor Embroidery; plain Cloathes with a gold or Silver Button (if worn in genteel Dress) is all I desire."

However, he was an ocean's length from the shops and necessarily many of his orders were left to the decision and taste, and sometimes the honesty, of the dealers. In 1758 he wrote: "I have receiv'd my Goods from the Recovery, and cant help again complaining of the little care taken in the purchase: Besides leaving out one half and the most material half too! of the Articles I sent for, I find the Sein is without Leads, Corks and Ropes which renders it useless; the Crate of Stone ware don't contain a third of the Pieces I am charg'd with, and only two things broke, and everything very high Charg'd."

Various writers have noted the result of his order for busts of Alexander the Great, Julius Caesar, Charles XII of Sweden, Frederick the Great, Prince Eugene, and the Duke of Marlborough; also of two wild beasts. In due time he received a group showing Aeneas bearing his father from Troy, two groups with two statues of Bacchus and Flora, two ornamental vases, and two "Lyons."

His resentment over the quality and fashion of the goods sometimes sent caused some years later the following burst: "It is needless for me to particularise the sorts, quality, or taste I woud choose to have them in unless it is observd; and you may believe me when I tell you that instead of getting things good and fashionable in their several kinds we often have Articles sent Us that coud only have been usd by our Forefathers in the days of yore. 'Tis a custom, I have some Reason to believe, with many Shop keepers, and Tradesmen in London when they know Goods are bespoke for Exportation to palm sometimes old, and sometimes very slight and indifferent Goods upon Us taking care at the same time to advance 10, 15 or perhaps 20 pr. Ct. upon them. My Packages fr. the Polly Captn. Hooper are not yet come to hand, and the Lord only knows when they will without more trouble than they are worth."

These invoices listed many household, personal, and plantation requirements, including clothing for himself and Mrs. Washington—such articles as stays, cloves, and "a very handsome and fashl. Woman's Hg. Saddle with Bridle, and everythg. Comp." After the political clouds began to gather he notified Cary & Co. in 1770 that enclosed orders for merchandise were to be filled if "the Act imposing a Duty upon the Tea, Paper &ca, shoud be totally repeald before the above Goods are Shipd." This was in accordance with the requirements of the Virginia nonimportation agreement of which he was a signer.

MARITIME INTERESTS

Washington was born within a few yards of salt water, and lived most of his life on the Potomac estuary, an artery of overseas trade. About 1746 there may have been a plan (probably upset by the good counsel of an uncle in England) for Washington to go to sea, in the merchant service, or in the navy, presumably as a midshipman. One has only to read the maritime novels of Captain Marryat, born a few years before Washington's death, to learn how miserable was the training and how small the opportunity in the navy. The practical uncle set forth the hardships and slight chances of advancement in the freighters. Washington's only open sea voyage was his early trip to Barbados with his brother Lawrence, in 1751.

Nevertheless Washington was a shipbuilder to the extent of constructing a schooner in 1765, at a spot still identifiable at Mount Vernon, to be used for cargoes on the Potomac, and throughout the Chesapeake Bay region. A consignment to the West Indies having been diverted by the shipmaster, Washington found it necessary in the settlement of the matter to buy the seagoing vessel itself: "much against my Inclination, as I had no desire of being Concerned in Shipping; but I was obliged to make the best of a bad Matter." This was in March, 1774, but the later history of the brigantine is not known.

Washington's interest in transportation by water is evident from the earlier section on his exports and his imports. His letters contain the following examples of his shipments and interest in maritime affairs: "Went to Alexandria to see Captn. Littledale's Ship Launched, wch. went of extremely well." "Before I left home I shipd 18 Hhds. of my Potomak Tobacco on Board the Bland Captn. Hugh Wylie now lying in the Rappahannock River on which please to Insure £140 only."

"Since mine of the 27th. Ulto. Capt. McGachin who will do me the favour to deliver this, and who for several years past has commanded a Convict Ship into this River (a service neither consistent with his Inclinations or Health to perserve in) has expressed a desire of being recommended to the Command of the Ship which you have given us Reasons to expect into Potomack. A Request I do most readily comply with, because a personal acquaintance with Mr. McGachin added to his general good Character enables me to introduce him to you as a Gentleman of known skill, deligence and Integrety." "By Mr. Campbell of Norfolk for sales and Rigg. for my schooner pr. Rect. &ca. £59.4.8." "Imbarkd on board my Schooner for Nomony. Lay of Captn. Laidler's." "Set out from Nomony in my return to Chotanck. Ldgd on board the vessel between Swan Point and Ced[ar] P[oint]." "Came up as high as Hoes ferry and Walk[ed] to my Brother Sam's." "Went to Alexandria after an early dinner to see a ship (the Jenny) Launched, but was disappointed and came home." "Went up again, saw the Ship Launchd; stayd all night to a Ball and set up all Night."

THE FISHERMAN

One of the great advantages of the frontage on the great rivers of Virginia and Maryland was the water privileges. Hunting wild fowl was one of the most obvious pastimes and means of replenishing the larder. Washington made a special drive at the fisheries and built and acquired landings connected with that business. The product helped feed his laborers and he also shipped it salted to the West Indies. An illustration is a diary entry for February, 1770:

"3. Agreed with Mr. Robt. Adam for the Fish catchd at the Fishing Landing I bought of Posey, on the following terms, to wit:

"He is obligd to take all I catch at the place, provided the quantity does not exceed 500 Barls; and will take more than this qty. if he can get cask to put them in. He is to take them as fast as they are catchd, without giving any interruption to my people; and is to have the use of the Fish House for his Salt, fish, &ca., taking care to have the House clear at least before the next Fishing Season.

"In consideration of which he is to pay me Ten pounds for the use of the House; give 3/ a thousd. for the Herrings (Virg. Money) and 8/4 a hundred (Maryland curry.) for the white fish.

"Mr. Piper and Lund Washington present."

THE FERRYMAN

Washington owned a ferry privilege from Dogue Run to Maryland which proved to be an old man of the sea, for being public it had to be operated as required, and it dragged his laborers from their work at inconvenient times. Other reasons for its discontinuance appear in a petition to the General Assembly dated October 10, 1790. Some extracts from this may serve as an example of Washington's habit of setting down exact details:

"That in the year 1753 a Ferry from the land of John Posey of Fairfax County to the land of Thomas Marshall of Maryland, was established by law.— That the land of the said Posey and the Ferry thereunto belonging hath since become the property of the said George Washington, and the latter being exceedingly inconvenient to him the said George Washington, the discontinuance of it is earnestly prayed for.

"As evidence of the reasonableness of this petition, it is humbly and truly stated, that, however convenient this Ferry may have been to travellers and however productive to the owner in the early stages of its existence it is far from being the case at present: the income of it having decreased from more than a hundred (which your Petitioner is informed it has yielded) to less than thirty five pounds per Annum . . . That the said Ferry being more than a mile wide, and much exposed to the NE. and So. W. winds, it requires large and expensive Boats to render the passage safe; and a tender (the landing being shoal) to avoid wading in the cold weather.—That the N. W. winds blowing at this place directly from the Virginia to the Maryland shore, and the banks of the former being high, Passengers are often deceived by the apparent smoothness of the water on the hither side, and will cross contrary to the remonstrances of the ferryman. . . .

"But the greatest grievance of all and which will be most severely felt by the proprietor is the public Roads which this Ferry occasions through a Neck of upwards of 6000 acres of land; the whole of which now being the property of the said George Washington will this fall (on the land side) be under a five feet ditch with a strong Post and Rail fence of six miles in length as may be seen by the plan annexed; laid down from actual Survey and exhibited to show how inadequate the emoluments of the Ferry is to the injury that will be sustained by Roads, which must if continued make the land a common."

THE LUMBERMAN

Every Virginia planter was confronted by the wearing out of lands and the consequent necessity of clearing new areas of virgin forest in order to keep up tillage. A good part of the timber involved was simply rolled up and burned where it lay. Washington had timber on his Mount Vernon plantation, some of which he used in his building operations. There is no distinct record of a sawmill on the place, although there is frequent reference to timber and shingles and other building materials which appear to have come from the place.

Extensive lumber operations chiefly in shingles were a part of the Dismal Swamp development, discussed in their engineering aspects in the pamphlet on Washington as an Engineer and City Builder. The enterprise hung fire; but Washington's interest in it was shown in his will. It appears to have been one of the capital investments in which Washington was the head of the business for other people. His other lands gained value without application of capital. The Dismal Swamp Company was at once a first-class company proposition and a joint stock venture with several participants and Washington as leader.

DOMESTIC MANUFACTURE

More cotton was imported than exported before the Revolution, and though the sizable import was for the most part made into cloth, this was a domestic process until after the war. Washington's technical interest extended to the manufacture of cloth, and in his journeys, especially the New England one in 1789, he visited the newly established factories, and recorded his impressions in the diaries as noticed later. That he made no recorded attempt to build up a cotton factory interest in the South is not strange. It was not till a century after he died that the South developed cotton mills with native white labor.

On his own plantation he made some cloths, producing in 1768 about 1,300 yards of linen, woolen, and cotton goods. He mentions as this product "striped woollen, woolen plaided, cotton striped, linen, wool-birdseye, cotton filled with wool, linsey, M's and O.'s, cotton-India dimity, cotton jump stripe, linen filled with tow, cotton striped with silk, Roman M., Janes twilled, huccabac, broadcloth, counterpain, birdseye, diaper, Kirsey wool, barragon, fustian, bedticking, herringbox, and shalloon." The estate also had its own shoemaker, though there are many items for fine shoes for the family in his antebellum invoices. Cloth as well as clothing was ordered from abroad for domestic making for the family, and there are orders for cloth and clothing for slaves; probably most of these were for the house servants or else for the slaves on the York River plantation. The same is true of hosiery.

Part IV
The Business Organizer

THE LANDED PROPRIETOR

No part of Washington's abundant business life is more interesting than his acquirement of real estate, the taste for which began while he was a lad surveying Lord Fairfax's land, and lasted to a short time before his death. Washington always had the landed proprietor's restless desire to buy the next farm alongside and thus round out his property. At the time of his death, besides the Mount Vernon estate he held about 6,500 acres within the settled portion of Virginia, and 1,100 acres in Maryland, and also 234 acres in the Great Meadows of Pennsylvania, at that time remote from the frontier line. Various other pieces of property, such as that on the Rappahannock which he inherited and the York River estate which his wife brought him, had been disposed of.

Washington had a small interest in city real estate, particularly the rest house that he erected in Alexandria and the two brick dwellings that he constructed in the new city of Washington. Also he built a small house at Bath as a kind of summer place.

WASHINGTON AND THE WEST

Some of the fellow pioneers of George Washington went out into the West to make their homes and to grow up with the country. John Sevier and George Rogers Clark and General Rufus Putnam were members of groups of eastern men of means and of power who preferred to be western. In Washington's mind there were always two motives working side by side with respect to the western lands, occupied till 1754 almost entirely by wild Indian tribes, except for a few French settlements on the Lakes, the Wabash, and the Mississippi River.

Washington took a businesslike view of the West, first of all in a nationalistic sense. Only two great national statesmen of the period adequately foresaw the possibilities of the West as the future home of millions of settlers of the English and related stocks. These two were Benjamin Franklin and George Washington. Franklin was interested in the West as an outgrowth of Pennsylvania; and within that state, as its boundary was finally fixed, was Pittsburgh, the leading gateway to the West. Maryland was cut off by an unfortunately worded charter. Even before the Revolution pioneers from Pennsylvania, Virginia, and North Carolina had begun to carry civilization west of the Alleghenies and to create a new section of the coming American Union. In that process Washington was one of the active and effective spirits.

In speaking of this phase of George Washington's career, Calvin Coolidge has said: "That he should have been responsible in large measure for the opening of the West and for calling attention to the commercial advantages the country might derive therefrom is by no means the least of his benefactions to the Nation. He demonstrated that those who develop our resources, whether along agricultural, commercial, and industrial lines or in any other field of endeavor, are entitled to the approval, rather than the censure, of their countrymen.

"Washington was a builder—a creator. He had a national mind. He was constantly warning his countrymen of the danger of settling problems in accordance with sectional interests. His ideas in regard to the opening of our western territory were thought out primarily for the benefit of the Nation. It has been said that he would have been 'the greatest man in America had there been no Revolutionary War.'"

BUSINESS OF COLONIZATION

Considering Washington's success as the manager of a great plantation and as an acquirer of western land, it is remarkable that he had no success as a colonizer. As a landed proprietor probably Robert Morris and his associates were the only men in America who could compete with Washington in the size of their holdings. Washington began early to acquire western lands and in 1784 remarked that it was not to be supposed that those who were first on the ground failed to take advantage of the situation. Besides his own lands, he bought the land bounty warrants from those French and Indian War soldiers who were willing to dispose of these almost worthless certificates for ready cash. These purchases were, as he himself described them, mere lotteries which acquired value only by being joined into one large tract.

His western lands beyond the mountains footed up at the time of his death to about 45,000 acres, including a stretch of many miles on the fertile bottoms of the Great Kanawha, other tracts in present West Virginia on the Ohio, on the Little Miami near Cincinnati, in Kentucky, and on the Mohawk River in New York. At one time he tried to locate a tract in West Florida. The eventual sales of such lands were the chief cash value of his estate.

That personal holdings in the West created a motive in his efforts to bring about a canal system which would reach at least to the foot of the western mountains was but natural, but from his first experience as

a surveyor in the wilderness to his death, he looked forward to the West as a region which must be retained by the United States. There is some evidence to show that he had New Orleans in his mind as an essential part of the American Republic.

Washington clearly expected to lease his western lands as fast as settlers came who could pay for them. In 1773 he advertised western lands for lease and settlement, and in his western journey of 1784 he found squatters on his valuable tracts but could come to no agreement with them. He offered terms of sale or to give 99-year leases; but they decided to "stand suit," hopeful evidently of getting a title for nothing.

FOUNDER OF THE NATIONAL CAPITAL

While George Washington was primarily interested in the development of lands for agricultural purposes, he, nevertheless, was a keen observer of urban life and needs. Upon him was laid the chief responsibility for selecting the site of the National Capital. We find him in the unique role of a city planner, largely instrumental in the selection of the exact location on the Potomac River, in which is now the District of Columbia, and in the development of the site.

In further comment upon the business phase of George Washington's activity, Calvin Coolidge said: "It included his plan of the waterway to the West, through the Potomac, the Monongahela, and the Ohio Rivers, which he used to speak of as 'the channel of commerce to the extensive and valuable trade of a rising empire.' He, of course, could not foresee the development of railway transportation and the great ocean-going vessels, because of which the seat of our Government became separated from active contact with commerce and was left to develop as the cultural and intellectual center of the Nation. Due to the genius of L'Enfant, the great engineer, this city from the first has had a magnificent plan of development. Its adoption was due in no small degree to the engineering foresight and executive ability of Washington. By 1932 we shall have made much progress toward perfecting the ideal city planned by him in the closing days of the eighteenth century." This topic is developed in the next pamphlet.

MINING

The mineral wealth of the present states of Virginia and West Virginia was little developed until after the Revolution, partly because the deposits were difficult of access, still more because they were almost unexplored. George Washington's father possessed an iron mine not far from Fredericksburg which furnished ore for a smelter nearer the river. The title of the mining and smelting operation, first formed in 1715, was the Principio Company of Maryland and Virginia. Washington had no direct connection with it. The father's interest was willed to Lawrence who in his own will bequeathed it to his brother Augustine. The business was gradually closed up after 1753.

It is an interesting fact that Washington wrote in his diary, on October 13, 1770: "Went to see a Coal Mine not far from his house on the Banks of the River; the Coal seemd to be of the very best kind, burning freely and abundance of it." This was on the Youghiogheny in the center of the great bituminous region; but the later immense commercial significance of that coal never came home to his mind, for steam power produced from coal was an unknown energy to him.

His nearest approach to interest in the making of iron seems to have been in 1760 in the lower Shenandoah Valley: "*Friday* [May] 9th. . . . Calld at the Bloomery and got Mr. Wm. Crawford to show me the place that has been so often talkd of for erecting an Iron Work upon.

"The Convenience of Water is great. First it may be taken out of the River into a Canal and a considerable Fall obtaind, and then a Run comes from the Mountain on which the largest fall may be got with Small Labour and expence. But of the constancy of this Stream I know nothing, nor coud Crawford tell me. I saw none of the Ore, but all People agree that there is an inexhaustable fund of that that is rich. But wood seems an obstacle; not but that there is enough of it, but the G[roun]d is so hilly and rugged as not to admit of making Coal or transporting it."

In 1786 he recorded: "A Captn. Hite came here between breakfast and dinner to see if I would join him in an Iron work on the So. Branch, wch. proposition I rejected."

THE LEGAL MIND

One of the remarkable aspects of the American Revolution is the legal knowledge displayed by the great leaders and their ability to draw up laws and constitutions which were adapted to the new dispensation of independence. Some ideas of government and international law came from courses or reading in college by the rising generation, such as John Adams and John Hancock and Thomas Jefferson. Alexander Hamilton's education was largely private. The main training in political philosophy was in hot debates in the colonial legislatures.

George Washington was an outstanding example of a self-taught man. His schooling amounted to little more than acquiring the rudiments of what would now be considered a grade-school course. By purchase, but probably more extensively through gifts, he acquired a large and miscellaneous library, particularly bearing on agricultural and military matters, but also with some standard literary, historical, and political works. However, it was his contact with men, and his studious attention to the moving drama of public affairs, that rounded out his mental character and gave him high standing among the most intelligent men and women of his time.

Washington was for years a member of the legislative assembly in which Patrick Henry was such a motive force; but Washington is not recorded as having made a single political speech there, though reputed to have been an excellent committee man. Nor was he much of a student. As a justice of the peace he ordered a copy of Burn's treatise on the subject in 1771; but his legal mind was mainly developed by practical experience in connection with his own estate and the other properties under his care, as described earlier in this pamphlet. His experience in Congress was brief; but his experience with Congress was long and troublesome, and it taught him many things about government. Also at home he enjoyed the privilege during the "Critical Period of American History" of intellectual intercourse with many men of many minds.

His power to think in legal terms and to draw up a legal document of the highest importance is brought out by his will. Such a tour de force is hardly to be found in the annals of America. A man without legal education had the courage to sit down and with his own hand, unaided by the counsel of any person, to write out a will in 29 sheets providing for the distribution, with intimate details, of a fortune that has been estimated at more than half a million dollars. In that will he introduced a principle of dividing an estate into shares which was thought to be a discovery when practiced by an American financial magnate a hundred and twenty years later. That will stood without modification by court decree. It is a crowning example of the fairness of mind of the maker and at the same time of his power to grasp and improve upon the fiduciary principles of his time.

CORPORATIONS

Washington's experience with corporations began early. In the Ohio Company, organized in 1747, both his half brothers, Lawrence and Augustine, were interested and Lawrence became the president. The history of this company and its connection with Washington's journey to the Ohio in 1753 and the Fort Necessity expedition of the next year are explained in Pamphlets Nos. 11 and 13. Washington, however, held no stock in the company, Lawrence's share being sold at his early death, and the French and Indian War virtually ended the enterprise. Nor was Washington directly concerned with the later Grand Ohio Company or Walpole Grant, though he did have an idea of acquiring shares in it if possible.

Washington's first company was the Dismal Swamp one, of which he was the leader and which began operations in 1763 and was still in being at the time of Washington's death. It was a successful engineering operation and it was the only one from which he appears to have derived a reasonable profit.

Washington's chief company, however, was that for improving the navigation of the Potomac River, which was carried to the operating point under his direction, though the most important part of its unfortunate history came after his death. It was in 1772 that the Virginia Assembly gave the original authorization, and Washington later wrote that the plan "was in a tolerably good train," when the Revolution began. As soon as the war was over his mind reverted to the project and a new company, sanctioned by both Virginia and Maryland, was formed. Details of the development are given in Pamphlet No. 13 of this series. With what was in a measure a rival concern, the James River Company, he had only a nominal connection, though he became honorary president of it.

These organizations bear witness to the constructive mind of the moving spirit and also to his remarkable ability to bring other minds to connect with his in a commercial and engineering organization. He had the type of mind useful to the later canal and railroad builders both east and west of the mountains.

In 1763 Washington was the active organizer of the Mississippi Company, of which he wrote the articles of incorporation. The purpose was to get a royal grant on the Mississippi and across the Wabash, Ohio, and Tennessee. Washington devoted time to the matter until 1772, and considerable expense was incurred by the associates, but the grant was never made.

THE SOCIAL PROMOTER

One of the evidences of modern business organization is the growth of the service clubs and other associations of business men for mutual acquaintance and the furtherance of common ends. Despite the massiveness of his character, Washington was a natural "joiner." His personal records tell us of hundreds of agreeable parties, going to the extent of playing cards all night. As we have seen in the account of Washington's earlier life, he was very fond of a good time, liked to go to shows, danced, dined, and played with the children. He was also a man who made the warmest and most attached friends and he was particularly gracious to young and rising men like Alexander Hamilton. The majesty of Washington in uniform at the head of his troops and in the full dress of the time as President of the United States causes us to forget his extreme interest in his fellow men, and in that interest lay much of his success as a business man, of his ability to handle men.

He joined the Masons as a very young man and was later for a time master of the Alexandria Lodge and admitted to honorary fellowship with other lodges. He accepted the five academic honors that were bestowed upon him and he deserved them in spite of the rather envious criticism of men like Senator Maclay. He was a gracious host and was even known to tell a funny story about a parson who lost his wig crossing a river called the Brunx—a standing warning to northward bound clergy of New York City.

THE TRAVELING MAN

If Washington possessed no sample case, he went through all the manoeuvers of the proficient traveling man of nowadays. He made journeys to meetings of the boards of which he was a member. He was constantly going back and forth from Mount Vernon to places near and far that he frequented. He also had the official traveling man's intimate knowledge of inns and taverns and their relative merits. In the pamphlet on Washington as a Traveler appear relations of his journeys and stopping places; and his diaries contain intimate ac-

counts of his many travels back and forth between Mount Vernon and Philadelphia and New York. He made seven journeys into New England, including four in connection with his military command. His journey from Mount Vernon south in 1791 extended to Augusta, Georgia, and back by a different route. He was an adept in travel by horseback or by coach. One of the many agreeable attributes of the man was his care for the animal motive power. Probably no man of his time had such an intimate knowledge of the roads, the inns, the hospitable houses, and the food and drink of his country.

Part V
Washington and Public Business

ASSOCIATE SPIRIT

So far this pamphlet has dealt chiefly with Washington as an individual business man, or as a man associated with friends and neighbors in land, colonizing, and other corporations. The full story of his influence in business affairs must include the effect of his great experience in lines of business previous to the Federal Constitution upon public affairs later. Washington's part in the creation of the United States of America seems a miracle, not so much because there was a General Washington and then a President Washington, as that the planter George Washington, born in a community almost entirely agricultural, should have throughout his life interested himself in so many methods of production of national wealth, through that combination of forces for economic, social, and political purposes which we call business; and that the strongest personal force for a union of the states which would centralize commerce and create vast business organizations within the federal government came from a Virginia planter in an agricultural area. Throughout the Revolution, Washington was urging the states to come closer together for promotion of their joint interests.

No records were preserved either by Washington or his friends of the conversations which must have taken place during the Constitutional Convention regarding the authority of the proposed national government in commercial and business affairs. One hundred years elapsed after the Revolution before the interstate commerce powers of the federal government were developed. Nevertheless foreign commerce and public finance were from the first workings of the Constitution regulated by statutes and backed up by a system of national officials. Whatever the unrecorded influence of Washington on the many clauses of the

Constitution relating to regulations for recognizing or centralizing business, there can be no doubt of his very strong influence upon the early financial and commercial legislation which established federal authority and limited the powers of the states.

THE BUSINESS OF WAR

Mention has been made of the influence of the Revolution in developing Washington's legal or political mind. The maritime efforts of government in business were also enlightening. It was fundamental in all of Washington's connections with the wartime Congress that the legislature ruled and he was its military servant, and his concern was with the operation of the army. But the army could not be recruited or trained or moved or armed or clothed or even subsisted without the sinews of war, and the funds raised put to proper uses. That the economic problems as well as the economic origins of the American Revolution were fundamental has been accepted by historians. It was even realized at the time. Samuel Huntington, president of the Congress, wrote on September 4, 1780: "The situation of our finances yet remains distressing, and seems the true cause to which every other difficulty and embarrassment may be traced up." Still another delegate insisted that the British were successful because the war had become a financial one.

Though Washington did not attempt to advise Congress on financial affairs, he was fully aware that the causes of the trouble lay in the lack of power of Congress over the sources of income, proper machinery of credit, effective promotion of production, and fit instruments of distribution; and he again and again emphasized in his private letters, especially to delegates in Congress, the need of a stronger central government capable in its own action of remedying these defects. Thus he wrote Joseph Jones on May 31, 1780: "Certain I am, unless Congress

speak in a more decisive tone, unless they are vested with powers by the several States competent to the great purposes of war, or assume them as matter of right, and they and the States respectively act with more energy than they hitherto have done, that our cause is lost." The expression is typical. This matter has been developed in Pamphlet No. 6.

Perhaps it was impossible that a body made up as Congress was, and in which lawyers were perhaps the most numerous, should accept financial advice from the few men who were accustomed to business affairs on a large scale. No specific and definite plan for raising money by general taxation was ever carried out until the Federal Constitution went into effect. Every state as well as the Continental Congress had recourse to paper money; and much of this was eventually repudiated, although a small portion figures in Hamilton's funding operations. In the end this commercial as well as political bankruptcy brought good though entirely unintentional results; for had there been better economic action under Congress and the Confederation, it is doubtful whether the people would have sanctioned the entirely new system of the Federal Constitution.

THE STAFF AND LINE

The Continental Army was never an efficient machine, but its worst portion was the staff—its business section, which was least directly under Washington's control. Congress was desirous enough of making the various departments efficient, but it was not itself sufficiently efficient to do this; or, having made proper provisions, to see that they were carried out. Incompetent and occasionally dishonest officials; refusal or neglect of the states to cooperate; the disinclination of the people to exchange their goods for the paper money, loan certificates, or staff certificates that were offered; the breakdown of transportation; and, even when matters were at their worst and the disintegration or mutiny of the army threatened daily, the fear to use direct action—the lesson of all this was not forgotten by the commander-in-chief when, later, he helped to frame a document which would give economic powers to the federal government.

In one respect Washington had a better opportunity to bring business principles into the army. He used his utmost influence to secure the appointment and promotion of competent men as officers; and yet to the end of the war the army roll bore the names of men of no marked military ability. The thing that held the army together was not so much the business sagacity of Washington, which had little opportunity to make itself felt, as the confidence which most men who approached him felt in his unselfishness, his character, and his unyielding grit.

FEDERAL FINANCE

Although George Washington was the most conspicuous man in the national councils from the end of the Revolutionary War to his retirement from the presidency in 1797, it was not till recent years that the people of the United States have begun to realize that his experience in business affairs made it possible for him to render an immense service to his country. Washington was the inevitable first President, though not because the American people realized his business sagacity and experience. He was the first President because he was the successful general and a national character, known and admired in every state. Once entered on the presidency, however, his judgment in such matters as taxes and tariffs and salary scales and military expenses and encouragement of commerce proved extraordinarily sound and timely.

He was much influenced by Hamilton in such matters because he recognized Hamilton's brillancy and because he shared Hamilton's belief that interests of business must be considered in founding and carrying on the Republic. The four great questions of funding the public debt, incorporating the state debts incurred in aid of the Revolution, protection to American shipping, and the United States Bank, were settled along lines publicly approved and urged by President George Washington.

After a brief era of over-expansion, a new banking system was set up in the states and nation. It was at first conservative and lasted for many years. Washington himself became a stockholder in two banks; one at Alexandria and the other, the Columbia, at Georgetown in the new District of Columbia. He understood the importance of bank notes that would circulate at par in gold. He recognized the necessity for sound private and public finance for the perpetuity of the nation. He signed the first national tariff, which gave both revenue and protection, and signed acts for excise duties. His presence as head of the government, his backing up

of Hamilton who represented the moneyed circles of the country, made possible the foundation of sound and enduring federal finance. His influence was especially strong in the chartering of the United States Bank which proved to be an important force in the political union of the state. It was not so much his acquaintance with the details of commercial and banking transactions as his sound and vigorous judgment upon economic questions that gave weight to his convictions.

FOUNDATIONS OF THE NAVY

Washington's leadership included valuable service in the founding of the American navy. When he was appointed commander in chief of the American forces in 1775, nothing was said in terms about sea fighting or sea forces, and this landsman was the first responsible military man in the Revolutionary War to discern the importance of sea warfaring as an element in the struggle.

In September, 1775, he issued instructions to Nicholson Broughton: "1st. You being appointed a Captain in the Army of the United Colonies of North America, are hereby directed to take the Command of a Detachment of said Army and proceed on Board the *Schooner Hannah*, at Beverly lately fitted out & equipp'd with Arms, Ammunition and Provisions at the Continental Expence. 2nd. You are to proceed as Commander of *Sd. Schooner*, immediately on a Cruize against such Vessels as may be found on the High Seas or elsewhere, bound inward and outward to or from Boston, in the Service of the ministerial Army, and to take and seize all such Vessels, laden with Soldiers, Arms, Ammunition, or Provisions for or from sd. Army, or which you shall have good Reason to susspect are in such Service."

Similar commissions were given to John Manly of the *Lee* and to others. These vessels, constituting what was known as "Washington's Fleet," did good service in intercepting vessels loaded with military stores for the British army in Boston and furnishing the besieging army with much needed war material.

This marks the beginning of the little American navy which served with spirit and effect during the Revolution. Also President Washington in 1794 participated in ordering the construction of the first frigates of the federal navy, the *Constitution, President, Constellation, Congress, United States,* and *Chesapeake,* intended to deal with the Barbary Pirates, and which later—in Washington's lifetime—began their exploits in the brief and informal French War of 1798.

INTERNATIONAL TRADE

As has been shown elsewhere in this pamphlet, Washington throughout his life was interested in foreign trade, as an outlet for American raw products. In 1784 he stated his convictions on this subject as follows: "Without going into the investigation of a question, which has employed the pens

of able politicians, namely, whether trade with foreigners is an advantage or disadvantage to a country, this State, as a part of the confederated States, all of whom have the spirit of it very strongly working within them, must adopt it, or submit to the evils arising therefrom without receiving its benefits. Common policy, therefore, points clearly and strongly to the propriety of our enjoying all the advantages, which nature and our local situation afford us; and evinces clearly, that, unless this spirit could be totally eradicated in other States as well as in this, and every man be made to become either a cultivator of the land or a manufacturer of such articles as are prompted by necessity, such stimulus should be employed as will *force* this spirit, by showing to our countrymen the superior advantages we possess beyond others, and the importance of being upon a footing with our neighbors."

He even foresaw the export value of western products: "If this is fair reasoning, it ought to follow as a consequence, that we should do our part towards opening the communication with the fur and peltry trade of the Lakes, and for the produce of the country which lies within, and which will, so soon as matters are settled with the Indians, and the terms on which Congress mean to dispose of the land, found to be favorable, are announced, be settled faster than any other ever did, or any one would imagine. This, then, when considered in an interested point of view, is alone sufficient to excite our endeavors. But in my opinion there is a political consideration for so doing, which is of still greater importance."

The regulations for this foreign commerce were one of his tasks as first President. Both legislation and treaties were necessary. Congress passed laws for coastwise and overseas navigation, the government of seamen in the merchant service, lighthouses and buoys, port rules, tonnage duties, and consuls; all of which received his approval, and in the framing of which he and Hamilton undoubtedly had a hand. Commercial treaties already existed with France, Holland, and Prussia; but the far more important one with Great Britain was made during his second administration, and also one with Spain. This gave the new federal government working arrangements with the chief maritime nations. It was at this time, too, that American trade with the Orient had its inception.

INTERSTATE COMMERCE

The regulation of interstate commerce was also a federal function. There were laws for trade with the Indians, for a mint and the regulation of coins, and for the post-office and post roads; but direct aid through internal improvements did not develop during Washington's control. As engineer, business man, and head of a developing nation Washington was observant of measures for the improvement of communication and transportation, and active in promoting them. During his travels he commented upon commercial affairs and upon the condition of roads and ferries, and mentioned with pleasure the new bridges he crossed in Massachusetts—those across the Charles and Mystic and the one between Salem and Beverly, "built for about £4500 lawful money—a price inconceivably low in my estimation." His interest in the Potomac River improvement continued unabated, though his active participation in its progress was no longer possible. When in Richmond on his southern tour he inspected the works on the James River; and in 1793, he took a little-known journey through Reading, Pennsylvania, to Lancaster, which undoubtedly included an inspection of the Union Canal then being built. Various of his commercial observations are given in Pamphlet No. 11.

His messages to Congress displayed his policy. In the first annual one he said: "The advancement of agriculture, commerce, and manufactures by all proper means will not, I trust, need recommendation; but I can not forbear intimating to you the expediency of giving effectual encouragement as well to the introduction of new and useful inventions from abroad as to the exertions of skill and genius in producing them at home, and of facilitating the intercourse between the distant parts of our country by a due attention to the post-office and post-roads."

Also in his third message he advised: "The importance of the post-office and post-roads on a plan sufficiently liberal and comprehensive, as they respect the expedition, safety, and facility of communication, is increased by their instrumentality in diffusing a knowledge of the laws and proceedings of the Government, which, while it contributes to the security of the people, serves also to guard them against the effects of misrepresentation and misconception. . . . The disorders in the existing currency, and especially the scarcity of small change, a scarcity so peculiarly distressing to the poorer classes, strongly recommend the carrying into immediate effect the resolution already entered into concerning the establishment of a mint. . . . An uniformity in the weights and measures of the country is among the important objects submitted to you by the Constitution, and if it can be derived from a standard at once invariable and universal, must be no less honorable to the public councils than conducive to the public convenience."

FEDERAL RELATION TO INDUSTRY

The connection of the federal government with industry was less direct than with trade; but, as said above, a tariff act was passed which gave some protection, and one of Hamilton's monumental reports was on Manufacturing, while Congress passed a law on "patents for useful inventions." There was also an act on the government of fisheries. Washington's own interest in the growth of industrialism has already been shown. This was particularly the case during his presidency, and furnished material for interesting entries in his diary during his journeys.

"*Tuesday* [October] *20th* [1789]. After breakfast, accompanied by Colo. Wadsworth, Mr. Ellsworth and Colo. Jesse Root, I viewed the Wollen Manufactory at this place, which seems to be going on with spirit. Their Broad-cloths are not of the first quality, as yet, but they are good; as are their Coatings, Cassimeres, Serges and Everlastings; of the first, that is, broad-cloth, I ordered a suit to be sent to me at New York—and of the latter a whole piece, to make breeches for my servants. All the parts of this business are performed at the Manufactory except the spinning—this is done by the Country people, who are paid by the cut.

"Hartford is more compactly built than Middletown, and contains more souls; the computed number of which amount to about dble. The number of Houses in Middletown are said to be 250 or 60—these reckoning eight persons to a house, would make two thousand at least. The depth of water which Vessels can bring to the last place, is about ten feet; and is as much as there is over Saybrook bar. From Middletown to Hartford there is not more than 6 feet water."

"*Wednesday, 28th.* Went after breakfast, to visit the duck manufacture [at Boston], which appeared to be carrying on with spirit, and is in a prosperous way. They have manufactured 32 pieces of Duck 30 or 40 yds. each in a week; and expect in a short time to increase it to [ ]. They have 28 looms at work, and 14 Girls spinning with Both hands, (the flax being fastened to their waste.) Children (girls) turn the wheels for them, and with this assistance each spinner can turn out 14 lbs. of Thread pr. day when they stick to it, but as they are pd. by the piece, or work they do, there is no other restraint upon them but to come at 8 o'clock in the morning, and return at 6 in the evening. They are the daughters of decayed families, and are girls of Character—none others are admitted."

SERVICE TO THE NATION'S BUSINESS

In the enormous development of American business since Washington's time the little mills and small banks and restricted commerce of the eighteenth century seem trifling; for the resources and aggregate annual business of the whole United States in 1799 were less than the output of a single present state, such as Ohio or Illinois. The best evidence of extraordinary business ability is Washington's persistent interest in the discoveries and advances of his own time. He was the leading spirit in developing the canal system which was at that time the most scientific type of inland transportation. No other public man was so interested in the application of power to the propulsion of vessels which Fulton was to make practical after the experiments of Rumsey and Fitch. He said somewhere "I hope, some day, that we will become a storehouse and granary for the world."

The greatest business thought of George Washington, however, was his conception of the United States as a commercial unit. Whoever may have been responsible for the broad powers over foreign and interstate commerce conferred by the Constitution, it accorded with Washington's lifelong insistence on the common interest and common policy of the colonies which in due time became states in a Union. Washington was at the same time an Eastern man and a Western man. In the writings of his later life, he insisted that the West should be held by the United States against Great Britain, France, and Spain. He predicted that Detroit would become a trade center. He had his eye upon the commercial importance of the head of Lake Michigan. He went so far as to plan a journey down the Illinois and Mississippi Rivers to New Orleans.

To sum up Washington as a business man, he was unusually capable and successful in many lines of private affairs. Inflexibly honest in his private dealings, his immense influence as President was directed toward a settlement of just debts, the establishment of a sound currency, the fostering of foreign commerce, a proper system of public accounts, the equitable distribution of taxation, and the creation of a feeling of joint national responsibility for the business affairs of the government. Also he saw the necessity of encouragement of both shipping and domestic manufactures, provision for future needs, the establishment of substantial means of transportation, the building up of banks and other commercial corporations, and the protection of public interests against local pressure and against extravagance. To him the government of business and the business of government were combined for the welfare of the American people.

Selected Authorities

ADAMS, HERBERT B.—*Maryland's Influence upon Land Cessions to the United States.* Baltimore, Johns Hopkins University, 1885.

ALVORD, CLARENCE WALWORTH—*Mississippi Valley in British Politics.* 2 vols. Cleveland, Clark, 1917.

BALLAGH, JAMES CURTIS—*White Servitude in the Colony of Virginia.* Baltimore, Johns Hopkins Press, 1895.

BASSETT, JOHN SPENCER—"Relation between the Virginia Planter and the London Merchant"; in American Historical Association, *Report for 1901,* Vol. I, p. 551.

BEARD, CHARLES AUSTIN—*Economic Interpretation of the Constitution of the United States.* New York, Macmillan, 1913.

BEER, GEORGE LOUIS—*Old Colonial System, 1660-1754.* 2 vols. New York, Macmillan, 1912.

BEER, GEORGE LOUIS—*British Colonial Policy, 1754-1756.* New York, Macmillan, 1907.

BROOKE, WALTER E., ED.—*Agricultural Papers of George Washington.* Boston, Badger, 1912.

BURRITT, ELIHU, ED.—*Washington's Words to Intending English Emigrants to America.* London, Low & Marston, 1870.

BUTTERFIELD, CONSUL W., ED.—*Washington-Crawford Letters.* Cincinnati, Clarke, 1877.

CONWAY, MONCURE DANIEL, ED.—*George Washington and Mount Vernon.* Brooklyn, Long Island Historical Society, 1889.

COOK, ROY BIRD—*Washington's Western Lands.* Strasburg, Va., Shenandoah Publishing House, 1930.

FORD, AMELIA CLEWLEY—*Colonial Precedents of our National Land System as it existed in 1800.* Madison, University of Wisconsin, 1910.

FORD, WORTHINGTON CHAUNCEY, ED.—*Washington as an Employer and Importer of Labor.* Brooklyn, 1889.

HATCH, LOUIS CLINTON—*Administration of the American Revolutionary Army.* New York, Longmans Green, 1904.

HAWORTH, PAUL LELAND—*George Washington, Country Gentleman.* Indianapolis, Bobbs-Merrill, 1925.

HULBERT, ARCHER BUTLER, ED.—*Washington and the West.* New York, Century, 1905.

JENNINGS, WALTER W.—*History of Economic Progress in the United States.* New York, Crowell, 1926. (Especially pts. i, ii.)

JERNEGAN, MARCUS WILSON—*American Colonies, 1492-1750.* New York, Longmans Green, 1929.

JOHNSON, EMORY R., AND OTHERS—*History of Domestic and Foreign Commerce of the United States.* 2 vols. Washington, Carnegie Institution, 1915.

KEIR, MALCOLM—*Epic of Industry* (*Pageant of America,* Vol. V). New Haven, Yale University Press, 1926. (Especially chs. i, ii.)

KEIR, MALCOLM — *March of Commerce* (*Pageant of America,* Vol. IV). New Haven, Yale University Press, 1927. (Especially chs. i-iii, xiv, xv.)

"Letters of George Washington bearing on the Negro"; in *Journal of Negro History,* Vol. II, p. 411.

PRUSSING, EUGENE E.—*Estate of George Washington, deceased.* Boston, Little Brown, 1927.

PRUSSING, EUGENE E.—*George Washington in Love and Otherwise.* Chicago, Covici, 1925. (Chs. iv, v.)

RIPLEY, WILLIAM ZEBINA—*Financial History of Virginia, 1609-1776.* New York, Columbia College, 1893.

RITTER, HALSTED L.—*George Washington as a Business Man.* New York, Sears, 1931.

TONER, JOSEPH M.—*George Washington as an Inventor and Promoter of the Useful Arts.* Washington, Gedney & Roberts, 1892.

WASHINGTON, GEORGE — *Diaries, 1748-1799.* Ed. by John C. Fitzpatrick. 4 vols. Boston, Houghton Mifflin, 1925.

WASHINGTON, GEORGE—*Writings.* Ed. by Worthington Chauncey Ford. 14 vols. New York, Putnam, 1889-93.

Washington as Engineer and City Builder
By Lieut. Col. U. S. Grant, 3d
Part I
George Washington, Engineer

GEORGE WASHINGTON
*From a painting by Charles Willson Peale in the
New York Historical Society*

CHOICE OF A PROFESSION

EORGE WASHINGTON, the greatest citizen of his time, a successful military leader and the founder of a new form of government, based on the application of principles never before tried, started life as an engineer with the practice of surveying. This fact is interesting because throughout his life, even though he was soon diverted by the urgent calls of public duty from the practice of this profession, he showed in a marked degree those characteristics which are recognized as most essential to the practical engineer: an insistence upon knowing all ascertainable facts before adopting a theory or reaching a conclusion; a refusal to be carried away by emotion or even an accepted and fondly held theory beyond the limits of practical accomplishment; instinctive skill in utilizing moral and natural forces for the accomplishment of useful ends; regard for ultimate results rather than immediate effects; meticulous accuracy as to facts and unusual intellectual as well as social honesty.

To be sure, few engineers attain these characteristics to the same degree, as few intellectuals have attained the same well balanced combination of mental gifts which went to make up his unusually well rounded wisdom. Nevertheless, it is evident that to the recognition of his possessing these *engineer characteristics,* with breadth of vision and an exalted personality, was largely due the public confidence which he earned as a mere youth and held throughout his life, and without which he could not have wielded the great personal influence and leadership that made his successes possible. To what extent his achievements can be attributed to these characteristics is an elusive problem in psychology, but there can be no doubt that the lack of them prevented any one of the brilliant galaxy of patriots by whom he was surrounded from successfully rivalling him or contesting his individual leadership.

When George Washington's father died in 1743 he was but a lad of eleven, and the question of his education and career became a family problem of difficulty and importance. Naturally full of curiosity, impulsive and adventurous, he was not satisfied to stop with the education of a colonial country school, although from the teacher, Mr. Williams, he appears to have acquired that knowledge of geometry and trigonometry and of the rudiments of surveying which later enabled him to establish his status as a certified surveyor. He early showed an interest in "the art military" and probably longed for the romance of a life at sea as so many boys did and still do. His elder half brother, Lawrence, had served in the British service at the siege of Cartagena under Admiral Vernon; and there was a plan for young George to go to sea. His mother's brother in England in 1747 wrote against a trial of the merchant service, and pointed out that posts in the navy could be secured only by political influence which the family did not possess.

Deprived of this outlet for his energies, he apparently set himself to work cheerfully and with determination to achieve the next most interesting career near at hand and to seek adventure in the wilderness of the continental frontier, which concealed in its depths nearly as much mystery and as many possibilities as the sea. He learned what he could of surveying from his "Young Man's Companion," from his friend George William Fairfax, and from the Westmoreland County surveyor, James Genn. There is still existing an old plat by him of a five acre

"Turnip Field" dated "This 27 Day of February—1747/8."

When still only sixteen he was employed on surveying work by Lord Fairfax and in 1748 participated with George William Fairfax under Genn in an adventurous journey into the Blue Ridge Mountains to explore and map the less known frontier of the Fairfax estate. This journey has already been treated quite fully in previous pamphlets of this series, but some extracts from the lad's Diary may be quoted here to indicate the vicissitudes of frontier surveys and the sort of experience by which young George attained that practical knowledge of the wilderness and of his country's topography which later stood him in such good stead.

They started on March 11, 1748, on horseback, traversed the mountains and the Shenandoah Valley to Harper's Ferry, and examined the branches of the Potomac. It was excellent frontier experience. The following quotations describe some of these experiences:

"Began my Journey in Company with George Fairfax, Esqr., we travell'd this day 40 Miles to Mr. George Neavels in Prince William County . . . This Morning Mr. James Genn ye. surveyor came to us we travell'd over ye. Blue Ridge to Capt. Ashbys on Shannondoah River, Nothing remarkable happen'd . . . Rode to his Lordships Quarter about 4 Miles higher up y. River we went through most beautiful Groves of Sugar Trees and spent ye. best part of y. Day in admiring ye. Trees and richness of ye Land . . . We . . . went ourselves down ye River about 16 Miles to Capt. Isaac Penningtons (the Land exceeding Rich and Fertile all ye. way produces abundance of Grain Hemp Tobacco &ca.) in order to lay of some Lands on Cates Marsh and Long Marsh . . .

"We set out early with Intent to Run round ye sd. Land but being taken in a Rain and it Increasing very fast obliged us to return it clearing about one oClock and our time being too Precious to Loose we a second time ventur'd out and Worked hard till Night and then return'd to Penningtons we got our Supper and was lighted into a Room and I not being so good a Woodsman as ye rest of my Company striped myself very orderly and went in to ye Bed as they called it when to my Surprize I found it to be nothing but a Little Straw-Matted together without Sheets or any thing else but only one thread Bear blanket with double its Weight of Vermin such as Lice Fleas &c I was glad to get up (as soon as y. Light was carried from us) I put on my Cloths and Lay as my Companions. Had we not been very tired I am sure we should not have slep'd much that night I made a Promise not to Sleep so from that time forward chusing rather to sleep in y. open Air before a fire as will appear hereafter. . . .

"Survey'd for George Fairfax Esqr. a Tract of Land lying on Cates Marsh and Long Marsh. . . . We set out early and finish'd about one oClock and then Travell'd up to Frederick Town [Winchester] where our Baggage came to us we cleaned ourselves (to get Rid of y. Game we had catched y. Night before) and took a Review of y. Town and thence return'd to our Lodgings where we had a good Dinner prepar'd for us Wine and Rum Punch in Plenty and a good Feather Bed with clean Sheets which was a very agreeable regale . . .

"We Travell'd up about 35 Miles to Thomas Barwicks on Potomack where we found y. River so excessively high by Reason of y. Great Rains that had fallen up about y. Alleghany Mountains as they told us which was then bringing down y. melted Snow and that it would not be fordable for severall Days it was then above Six foot Higher than usual and was rising we agreed to stay till Monday we this day call'd to see y. Fam'd Warm Springs we camped out in y. field . . .

"finding y. River not much abated we in y. Evening Swam our horses over and carried them to Charles Polks in Maryland for Pasturage till y. next Morning . . . We went over in a Canoe and travell'd up Maryland side all y. Day in a Continued Rain to Collo Cresaps right against y. Mouth of y. South Branch about 40 Miles from Polks I believe y. worst Road that ever was trod by Man or Beast . . .

"Rain'd till about two oClock and Clear'd when we were agreeably surpris'd at y. sight of thirty odd Indians coming from War with only one Scalp We had some Liquor with us of which we gave them Part it elevating their Spirits put them in y. Humour of Daucing of whom we had a War Daunce there manner of Daucing is as follows Viz They clear a Large Circle and make a Great Fire in y. middle then seats themselves around it y. Speaker makes a grand speech telling them in what Manner they are to Daunce after he has finished y. best Dauncer jumps up as one awaked out of a Sleep and runs and Jumps about y. Ring in a most comical Manner he is followed by y. Rest then begins there Musicians to Play ye. Musick is a Pot half [full] of Water with a Deerskin Streched over it as tight as it can and a goard with some Shott in it to Rattle and a Piece of an horses Tail tied to it to make it look fine y. one keeps Rattling and y. other Drumming all y. while y. others is Daucing . . .

"This Morning went out and Survey'd five Hundred Acres of Land and went down to one Michael Stumps on ye. So Fork of ye. Branch on our way Shot two Wild Turkies. . . . Survey'd for Mr. James Rutlidge ye following a piece of Land . . .

"Last Night was a blowing and Rainy night Our Straw catch'd a Fire yt. we were laying upon and was luckily Preserv'd by one of our Mens awaking when it was in a [blaze] . . .

"Last Night was a much more blostering night then ye, former we had our Tent Carried Quite of with ye. Wind and was obliged to Lie ye. Latter part of ye. night without covering . . .

"Last Night was so Intolerable smoky that we were obliged all hands to leave ye Tent to ye. Mercy of ye Wind and Fire this day was attended by our afored Company untill about 12 oClock when we finish'd we travell'd down ye Branch to Henry Vanmetris's on our Journey was catched in a very heavy Rain we got under a Straw House untill ye Worst of it was over and then continued our Journey . . .

"Rain'd Successively all Last night this Morning one of our men Killed a Wild Turkie that weight 20 Pounds we went and Survey'd 15 Hundred Acres of Land and Return'd to Vanmetris's about 1 oClock about two I heard that Mr. Fairfax was come up and at 1 Peter Casseys about 2 Miles of in ye. same Old Field I then took my Horse and went up to see him . . .

"we breakfasted at Casseys and Rode down to Vanmetris's to get all our Company together which when we had accomplished we Rode down below ye. Trough in order to Lay of Lots there we laid of one this day The Trough is [a] couple of Ledges of Mountain Impassable running side and side together for above 7 or 8 Miles and ye River down between them you must Ride Round ye back of ye. Mountain for to get below them we Camped this Night in ye Woods near a Wild Meadow where was a Large Stack of Hay after we had Pitched our Tent and made a very Large Fire we pull'd out our Knapsack in order to Recruit ourselves every [one] was his own Cook our Spits was Forked Sticks our Plates was a Large Chip as for Dishes we had none"

Next year he wrote the following letter: "Since you received my letter in October last, I have not sleep'd above three nights or four in a bed, but, after walking a good deal all the day, I lay down before the fire upon a little hay, straw, fodder, or bearskin, which ever is to be had, with man, wife, and children, like a parcel of dogs and cats; and happy is he, who gets the berth nearest the fire. There's nothing would make it pass off tolerably but a good reward. A doubloon [$7.20] is my constant gain every day that the weather will permit my going out, and sometimes six pistoles [a pistole is $3.60]. The coldness of the weather will not allow of my making a long stay, as the lodging is rather too cold for the time of year. I have never had my clothes off, but lay and sleep in them, except the few nights I have lay'n in Frederic Town."

In 1749 after the bulk of the field exploration had been completed, he used a small brick house near Greenway Court, about twelve miles from present Winchester, as an office to work up and plat his notes. Although but seventeen years old, he was earning his own living and probably assisting materially in the support of his mother and her four small children.

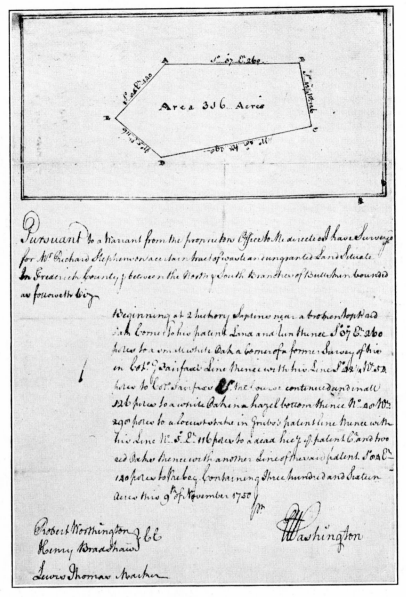

A SURVEY BY GEORGE WASHINGTON IN 1750
From the original in the Boston Public Library

TECHNICAL EDUCATION

At that time no scientific school existed in the American colonies and a scientific education could be obtained only by home study or by a voyage abroad and a course at one of the European universities. No distinguished American of that period received such a professional training. It far exceeded the means of George Washington. Hence he had recourse to the former. We know him always to have been an omnivorous reader and may suppose that he supplemented the instruction he received from **Mr. Genn**.

However ill-equipped the colonies were with technical schools, the importance of competent surveyors was recognized. Reconciliation of the grants of land by the Crown with the actual topography on this side of the Atlantic, the ease with which settlers could establish themselves on other people's land and remain there for years without discovery, and the division of the family ownership among the rapidly increasing numbers of each generation, created conditions under which a surveyor's competence, accuracy, and honesty were of unusual and special importance.

By its charter the College of William and Mary was given the office of Surveyor General of Virginia, including the privilege of appointing county surveyors, one-sixth of whose fees reverted to the college. Under this authority county surveyors seem to have been selected by the college faculty after examination and test. Unfortunately there is a gap in the minutes of the faculty from 1747 to 1752, but we have evidence of Washington's qualification in the following record in Culpeper County for July 20, 1749: "George Washington, Gent. produced a Commission from the President and Masters of William and Mary College, appointing him to be surveyor of this county, which was read and thereupon he took the usual oaths to his majesty's person and government and took and subscribed the adjuration oath and test, and then took the oath of surveyor, he became an officer of the colony."

Thus at the age of seventeen George Washington was inducted into the public service in a position of trust, and had placed his foot firmly on the first step of the ladder of the engineering profession. This position of county surveyor was not a sinecure. His diaries bear ample testimony to the activity and hard work involved, requiring travel over "y. worst Road that ever was trod by Man or Beast." Mistakes occurred at times and the work had to be done over. Incompetent assistants occasionally added their bit to the surveyor's troubles, and one rodman "either stupidly or maliciously, cut his pole only fifteen feet long, instead of sixteen and a half feet, as required by law," causing confusing results until the error was discovered.

EARLY MILITARY TRAINING

However, the young Washington did not allow his duties as county surveyor to engross his thought and efforts entirely. His interest in military affairs was sufficient to command some serious attention and he probably received instruction in the rudiments of drill and tactics from some unrecorded source; perhaps Van Braam who taught him fencing, or from some of his half brother's soldier friends. His interest and progress in this avocation were sufficient to secure for him in 1752 a commission as major and adjutant-general for one of the province's militia districts.

Although but twenty-one years old, by 1753 the young major had already gained such a reputation for good sense, faithfulness, and zeal, and as a consummate frontiersman, that Governor Dinwiddie selected him to bear a message to the French commander on the Ohio to inquire the latter's authority for invading King George's dominions, and to ascertain as far as practicable his further designs.

THE YOUNG SURVEYOR'S MISSION TO THE FRENCH

He accepted this perilous and delicate international mission at once and started from Williamsburg October 31, 1753, without military escort on this 600-mile trip over the mountains and into the little-known wilderness. On January 16, 1754, he was back again at Williamsburg to deliver his report and the French commander's reply to Governor Dinwiddie, together with a manuscript map which is reproduced on the next page.

His report was a sensible, concise, and clear statement of desired information, although hastily thrown together. Of it he himself said: "There is nothing can recommend it to the Public, but this. Those

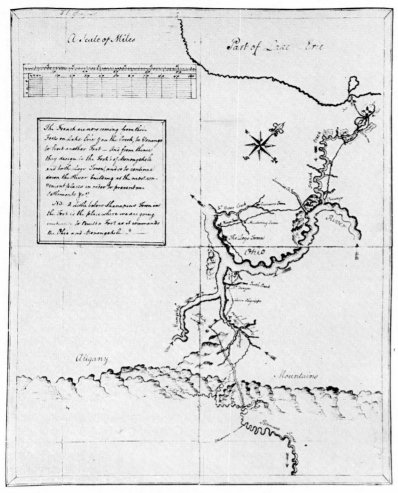

GEORGE WASHINGTON'S MAP
Accompanying his "Journey to the Ohio," 1753

Things which came under the Notice of my own Observation, I have been explicit and just in a Recital of:—Those which I have gathered from Report, I have been particularly cautious not to augment, but collected the Opinions of the several Intelligencers, and selected from the whole, the most probable and consistent Account."

This report was thought sufficiently important and interesting to be sent without Washington's knowledge by the governor to the printer at Williamsburg without the map, however, and to be reprinted in 1754 by T. Jefferys in London with a different map. The knowledge acquired on this trip must have been of inestimable value, not only to Washington himself, but also to other colonial authorities in the French and Indian War that followed almost immediately. Without his knowledge of the wilderness, his powers of observation, and his facility in map making acquired as a surveyor, the feat would not have been of any real practical value.

THE MILITARY ENGINEER

The success of George Washington the military commander was here initiated and continued to rest on the special competence of Washington the engineer. In 1754 he planned and built Fort Necessity, the first of many fortifications planned by him, carefully placing it so as to utilize a running stream as the essential water supply.

The history of George Washington from this time until the end of the Revolution belongs to history as a military chieftain; but throughout his military service his characteristics as an engineer continued an essential element of his career. During the French and Indian War he showed special skill and aptitude in the use of field fortification and in the ingenuity with which he found expedients for overcoming practical difficulties. Yet he did not permit his appreciation of the value of the protection afforded by fortification to usurp mastery over his realization of the greater effectiveness of the offensive, as has been the case with some other engineers who attained high command. This is amply shown by the following, written in 1756 about the defense of the western frontier: "As defensive measures are evidently insufficient for the security and safety of the country, I hope no arguments are requisite to convince of the necessity of altering them to a vigorous offensive war, in order to remove the cause."

Again, in 1757, he urged an invasion of the enemy's country and the attack on Fort Duquesne in adequate force: "This method will strike terror to the heart of the red man and be a more effective defence than all the fortifications and troops on the border."

Like Napoleon at Toulon, Washington at the siege of Boston in 1775 saw the military value of Dorchester Heights because of its command over the British position. The spirited defense of Bunker Hill had proved to be a tactical success, since it prevented the British from breaking up the siege begun by the raw militia and continued under Washington. Doubtless it had great moral value in convincing the untrained colonials that, behind fortifications, they could withstand an attack *en regle* by British regulars; but the subsequent occupation of Dorchester Heights forced the British to abandon Boston without further bloodshed. The crude map drawn by Washington's own hand, which is still in existence, shows his understanding of the envelopment which caused the British to evacuate Boston.

During the Revolution, George Washington showed great and unusual aptitude as a strategist—one who utilizes his military forces and resources so as to secure from a successful combat the greatest possible results and to make a defeat or repulse render the least effective return to the enemy. But strategic judgment alone would not have secured ultimate success with an army so untrained for united action, without his organizing gifts and his capacity for overcoming practical difficulties, his engineer's capacity for measuring physical obstacles and completely thinking out each job before beginning it.

Doubtless Washington would have been a great commander whatever his previous education and experience; but his early training and the engineer's point of view helped him immeasurably, so that the facts justify the statement of Prussing: "Outstanding throughout that dreadful time is the constant, faithful foresight, planning, providing and protecting mind of the engineer. The very drafts and plans of the camps and battlefields are often in his own hand. The thoroughness of preparation which enabled him to force the evacuation of Boston, to cross and recross the Hudson about New York and the Delaware River at Trenton, and later, to send his army from New York to Yorktown without arousing the suspicion of the British, all of these are the work of a great engineer."

If any commander ever appreciated more fully the possible use of engineers in war, surely none ever suffered from a greater lack of them. In one of his letters as early as 1756, during the French and Indian War, he noted as necessary "engineers to conduct the affairs, if we hope to approach Fort Duquesne." In the course of the Revolution Duportail, Kosciuszko, and L'Enfant came from abroad to supply this need, and ever after enjoyed his special confidence. They constantly turned to him for the sympathetic understanding they could not find among the politicians, nor with many of the Continental officers.

The lesson learned from his experience as commander-in-chief prompted many suggestions in 1776, which were followed up by earnest recommendations while he was President, that a military academy should be established as a school for engineers and artillery officers. This last recommendation was finally carried out in 1802 after his death, and the graduates of this military academy, for so many years the only scientific school in the country, in peace times have built canals and railroads, and explored and mapped the vast West, carrying on his great work of winning a continent for civilization. They have continued to take a tremendously important part in just those great national works upon which George Washington himself placed such emphasis as essential to the development and uniting of the country he had founded.

THE ENGINEER AT HOME

When hardly yet of age the young George had become interested in the western expansion of the colonies and in the various ways of facilitating the occupation and settlement of that region. The construction of roads and improvement of waterways naturally commanded his eager attention. As a land owner on a large scale he was ever alert to any new devices or methods to improve agriculture or make life on the farm more agreeable. Of the many items of this kind which commanded his personal attention, we find scattered references throughout his diaries and writings, such as in the letter of February 13, 1764: "We have been curiously entertained of late with the description of an Engine lately constructed (I believe in Switzerland, and undergone some Improvements since in England) for taking up Trees by the Roots; among other things it is related that Trees of considerable Diameter are forced up by this Engine, . . ."

His interest in machinery is shown by an entry of September 3, 1787: "Visited a Machine at Doctr. Franklin's (called a Mangle) for pressing, in place of Ironing, clothes from the wash. Which Machine from the facility with which it dispatches business is well calculated for Table cloths and such articles as have not pleats and irregular foldings and would be very useful in all large families."

A similar entry on January 22, 1790, describes his inspection and the working of Winlaw's threshing machine. The construction and operation of mills and iron foundries also received his attention. Another entry, March 19, 1760, speaks of "several efforts to make a plow after a new model— partly of my own contriving," which on trial he found "answered very well in the Field in the lower Pasture."

WASHINGTON'S EXPERIMENTAL BARN

In the same spirit of scientific experiment he wrote, December 1, 1785: "In order to try the difference between burning Spermaciti and Tallow Candles I took one of each, the 1st weighing 3 oz. 10 p.w. 6 g., and the 2d 5 oz. 2 p.w., and lighted them at the same instant. The first burnt 8 hours and 21 Minutes; when, of the latter, their remained 14 pennyweight; which continued to burn one hour and a quarter longer, making in all 9 hours and 36 Minutes, By which it appears (as both burnt without flairing) that, estimating Spermaceti Candles at 3/ pr. lb., the former is dearer than the latter as 30 is to nearly 13, in other words more than 2¼ dearer."

INTEREST IN POWER BOATS

Always convinced of the special value of inland water transportation, Washington was naturally deeply interested in the various attempts to discover a practical means of mechanically propelling ships and boats, as is shown by the following extract from his journal, September 6, 1784: "Remained at Bath all day and was showed the Model of a Boat constructed by the ingenious Mr. Rumsey, for ascending rapid currents by mechanism; the principles of this were not only shown, and fully explained to me, but to my very great satisfaction, exhibited in practice in private under the injunction of Secresy, untill he saw the effect of an application he was about to Make to the Assembly of this State, for a reward.

"The Model, and its operation upon the water, which had been made to run pretty swift, not only convinced me of what I before thought next to, if not quite im-

practicable, but that it might be turned to the greatest possible utility in inland Navigation; and in rapid currents; that are shallow—and what adds vastly to the value of the discovery, is the simplicity of its works; as they may be made by a common boat builder or carpenter, and kept in order as easy as a plow, or any common impliment of husbandry on a farm."

The next day he gave Rumsey the following certificate: "I have seen the model of Mr. Rumsey's Boats constructed to work against stream; have examined the power upon which it acts;—have been an eye witness to an actual experiment in running water of some rapidity; & do give it as my opinion (altho' I had little faith before) that he has discovered the Art of propelling Boats, by mechanism & small manual assistance, against rapid currents;—that the discovery is of vast importance—may be of the greatest usefulness in our inland navigation—&, if it succeeds, of which I have no doubt, that the value of it is greatly enhanced by the simplicity of the works, which when seen & explained to, might be executed by the most common mechanics."

He also wrote Governor Harrison a month later: "I consider Rumsey's discovery for working boats against stream, by mechanical powers (principally), as not only a very fortunate invention for these States in general, but as one of those circumstances, which have combined to render the present epocha favorable above all others for fixing, if we are disposed to avail ourselves of them, a large portion of the trade of the western country in the bosom of this State irrevocably."

Washington was an intelligent witness of the first attempts at steam navigation: "In the Evening [November 4, 1785] a Mr. Jno. Fitch came in, to propose a draft and model of a Machine for promoting Navigation, by means of a steam [boat]."

INTEREST IN AERONAUTICS

A still wider interest in the possibilities of transportation was shown by the assistance he gave to the French aeronaut Jean Pierre Blanchard for his first balloon ascension in this country in 1793, as recorded by Blanchard. "I hastened to take leave of the President, and of Mr. Ternan[t], Minister Plenipotentiary of France to the United States. I then received from the President the most flattering mark of his good will in the passport which he was pleased to deliver to me with his own hand. I never felt the value of glory so much as I did in that moment, in the presence of a Hero, whom she had constantly attended at the head of armies, and with whom she still presided over the councils of his country. . . .

"I landed at last and set my foot on ground . . . my passport served me instead of an interpeter. In the midst of a profound silence was it read with loud and audible voice. How dear the name of Washington is to this people! With what eagerness they gave me all possible assistance, in consequence of his recommendation! . . . My first care was to go and present my respects to President Washington, and to inform him of the happy effects of the passport he had been pleased to grant me. I had the honor to offer him my colours, which he politely accepted, and thereby acquired a fresh claim to my gratitude."

The text of the remarkable document which Blanchard called a "passport" has been preserved and is as follows:

"George Washington, President of the United States of America.

"To all to whom these presents shall come.

"The bearer hereof, Mr. Blanchard a citizen of France proposing to ascend in a balloon from the city of Philadelphia, at 10 o'clock, A. M. this day, to pass in such direction and to descend in such place as circumstances may render most convenient—These are therefore to recommend to all citizens of the United States, and others, that in his passage, descent, return or journeying elsewhere, they oppose no hindrance or molestation to the said Mr. Blanchard; and, that on the contrary, they receive and aid him with that humanity and good will, which may render honor to their country, and justice to an individual so distinguished by his efforts to establish and advance an art, in order to make it useful to mankind in general.

"Given under my hand and seal at the city of Philadelphia, this ninth day of January, one thousand seven hundred and ninety three, and of the independence of America the seventeenth.

(Seal) Signed GEORGE WASHINGTON"

In a private letter nine years earlier Washington jokingly suggested the most recent modern development of aerostation: "I have only newspaper accounts of air balloons, to which I do not know what credence to give; as the tales relating to them are marvellous and lead us to expect that our friends at Paris in a little time will come flying through the air instead of ploughing the ocean to get to America."

INTEREST IN SUBMARINES

Another proof of Washington's sustained interest in new devices was shown in 1776 when his attention was directed to the earliest known type of submarine, graphically outlined a hundred and forty-eight years later by Commander Bemis, U. S. N.: "Washington wrote Thomas Jefferson to the effect that a Mr. Bushnell had contrived a machine that could carry itself under water at any given depth, and for a considerable distance, by means of an appendage, charged with powder, which, when striking an anchored ship, would destroy it. The craft was a small, one-man affair, possessing several features that are recognized in these days, as essential for submarine navigation—buoyancy among them. The vessel was lighter than the water displaced when submerged, had a fixed center of gravity, and arrangements for compensating with water ballast for weight expended. It was forced under the surface by a vertical propeller, and driven forward by a horizontal one. Both were operated, through a crank system, by one man.

"Admiral Howe's flagship, the *Eagle*, narrowly escaped destruction in 1776 by this first submarine in New York harbor. Ezra Lee, who was operating the boat, attached a bomb to the ship's keel, but it failed to hold. In order to escape capture he put on speed. The bomb exploded at a distance of about one hundred feet from the ship. Washington, who spent the night on the dock, heard the explosion, and saw the half-drowned patriot finally reach shore."

Washington's actual comment on the invention was written to Jefferson in 1785: "I am sorry I cannot give you full information respecting Bushnell's project for the destruction of ships. No interesting experiments having been made, and my memory being bad, I may in some measure be mistaken in what I am about to relate. Bushnell is a man of great mechanical powers, fertile of invention and master of execution. He came to me in 1776, recommended by Governor Trumbull and other respectable characters, who were converts to his plan. Although I wanted faith myself, I furnished him with money and other aids to carry his plan into execution. He labored for some time ineffectually; and, though the advocates of his scheme continued sanguine, he never did succeed. One accident or another always intervened. I then thought, and still think, that it was an effort of genius, but that too many things were necessary to be

combined, to expect much from the issue against an enemy, who are always upon guard."

PIONEER DRAINAGE ENGINEER

In a country where agriculture was the basis of all wealth and where the main crop, tobacco, soon exhausted the fertility of the soil, as was the case in the southern colonies, a constant supply of additional arable land was a necessary condition to progress. But the colonists could push their farms westward only by dint of reclaiming more land from the wilderness, laboriously clearing it of trees and underbrush by hand labor. To a man so practical as Washington, and so interested as an engineer in finding the most effective way of accomplishing practical results, the reclamation of rich lands by draining swamps had a real appeal. Hence his interest in the reclamation of the Dismal Swamp, which he first visited in 1763, starting from Williamsburg the end of May.

He appears to have entered the swamp from Colonel Edward Reddick's, Nansemond County. ". . . we crossed from Elias Stallens (one Mile above the upper bridge on Pequemin) across to . . . a small slipe of Land between the said River Pequemen and the Dismal Swamp, and from thence along a new cut path through the Main Swamp a Northerly course for 5 Miles, to the Inhabitants of what they call new found land, which is thick settled, very rich Land, and about 6 Miles from the aforesaid River Bridge of Paspetank." From here Washington swung round to the Great Bridge, Roberts's, and Colonel Reddick's again.

There were several later visits in 1764, 1766, 1767, and 1768. He helped to organize a company for draining the Dismal Swamp and attended meetings of the Board of Directors as late as 1786.

Another drainage project nearer home and which he could carry out on his own property was that of the Mill Swamp on the "Muddy hole Plantation." The following entry will show the personal attention he gave to such problems and how the old surveyor naturally went back to his trade when the Revolution was over.

August 8, 1786. "Rid by Muddy hole Plantation to my meadow in the Mill Swamp; and leveled from the old dam, just below Wade's Houses, to the head of the Old race by the stooping red oak; stepping 27½ yds. or as near as I could judge 5 rods between each stake, which are drove in as follows: 1st, at the Water edge where I begun, and levl. with the Surface thereof; two, in the old race (appearances of which still remain); and a fourth, by a parcel of small Persimon bushes after having just passed the Bars leading into the Meadows. The others at the distance above mentioned from each other to the stooping red oak. . . .

"By this [a list of survey observations] it appears that the ground from the level of the water at the old dam by Wade's Houses to the Race by the Stooping red oak, is higher by two feet (wanting half an Inch) than the bottom of the race in its present filled up State, is; and that the ditch, or old race must be considerably sunk. The old dam considerably raised, and strengthned in order to throw the Water into the New ditch, or a dam made higher up the run, so as to gain a greater fall, which of the three may be most eligable as it will, without any great additional expence drain a good deal more of the Swamp; but if it should be thought more eligable, deepning the race and raising the dam will carry of the Water from the Meadow below, but then it may drown the land above."

THE OHIO COMPANY (1747-1754)

Among the many interests and responsibilities of the Washington family was the Ohio Company, shares in which were held by Lawrence and Augustine, the half brothers of George. This enterprise, undertaken in 1747 by some prominent Virginians and London merchants, received a royal grant in 1749. Their petition, the original of which is preserved in the British Museum, has been summarized as follows: "They promised to build a fort and settle 200 families in the region within seven years, the result of which would be, they said, to protect the frontiers of the older Colonies from Indian raids. Its second effect would be to cut the line of communications between the two great French colonies, one in the valley of the St. Lawrence River and the other at the mouth of the Mississippi; and, as a third consideration, they would gain for the English Colonies the rich fur trade of the country between the Ohio River and the Great Lakes."

King George II or his councilors readily saw the advantage of a British settlement in the Ohio country and the importance to their foreign policy of thus cutting the line of French communications; it was also easy enough for the King to give his consent to the grant of land, but not so easy for the colonists to capture the land from the French and Indians already in possession and carve out of the wilderness new farms and homes for themselves. A station fort at Piqua, established north of the Ohio, was destroyed by the French late in October, 1750. Christopher Gist, a well-known pioneer and explorer, undertook a preliminary journey of exploration for the company, crossing the mountains to the Ohio River and beyond to the Muskingum, thence south into Kentucky and returning to Virginia in the spring of 1751 by a southerly route, probably that later used by Boone and the early settlers of Kentucky. Seventeen years later the company's claims were not extinguished, inasmuch as George Washington then wrote: "I will inquire particularly concerning the Ohio Company's that one may know what to apprehend from them."

In July, 1751, Gist received further instructions for constructing a pack trail from

the company's storehouse at Wills Creek (the Cumberland of today) to the Monongahela. Another storehouse was built on that river at the mouth of Redstone Creek where Brownsville, Pennsylvania, now stands; and Washington, on his famous trip with the message from Governor Dinwiddie along with Gist, proceeded down to the confluence of the Monongahela with the Allegheny and thence northward to the Indian town of Venango, where Franklin now stands, and to Fort Le Boeuf, at present Waterford.

In 1754 the French pushed farther, disregarding Governor Dinwiddie's warning, and with their 600 men and artillery dislodged Trent with his 60 Virginians from the point where the Monongahela and Allegheny converge to form the Ohio. The French completed his unfinished fort, calling it Fort Duquesne. Meanwhile coming up the trail from Wills Creek was George Washington with a battalion of Virginians. The campaign which followed is part of his military history, but the fact of importance here is that on this march he had to widen Gist's trail and make it practicable for wagon transportation so that the beginnings of the Cumberland Road, later called the National Pike, can be traced back to its first engineer, George Washington.

THE PROPOSED MISSISSIPPI COMPANY (1763)

The Ohio Company having suffered practical extinction by the French and Indian War, Washington in 1763 attempted to organize a successor to be called the Mississippi Company, and petitioned the King for a grant of a million acres in the newly conquered territory *beyond* the Ohio. The company maintained an agent for some time in London without success, and the events leading up to the Revolution necessitated abandonment of the project in 1772. The project bears testimony to Washington's early vision of what the development of the vast Southwest, as well as the Northwest, might be if connected with the Atlantic coast region by adequate transportation lines.

SEARCH FOR A TRANSMONTANE WATER ROUTE

The deep interest which this connection between his own Virginia coast settlements and the great interior of the continent forever after commanded in Washington's mind is easy to understand. However, in this as in all else, he did not let even such early acquired and passionately held beliefs make him unmindful of other possibilities and facts. In 1783 he made a trip to visit properties in the Mohawk Valley near present Utica, which he purchased, and doubtless to satisfy himself in person as to the likelihood of a rival to his Potomac Canal project. The Erie Canal was later built very much along this line, as had been suggested by Cadwallader Colden in 1724 as giving New

York an advantageous route for interior trade.

Soon after this trip he wrote to his friend the Chevalier de Chastellux: "I have lately made a tour through the Lakes George and Champlain, as far as Crown Point. Then returning to Schenectady, I proceeded up the Mohawk River to Fort Schuyler (formerly Fort Stanwix), and crossed over to the Wood Creek, which empties into the Oneida Lake, and affords the water communication with Ontario. I then traversed the country to the head of the eastern branch of the Susquehanna, and viewed the Lake Otsego, and the portage between that Lake and the Mohawk River at Canajoharie. Prompted by these actual observations, I could not help taking a more contemplative and extensive view of the vast inland navigation of these United States, from maps and the information of others; and could not but be struck with the immense diffusion and importance of it, and with the goodness of that Providence, which has dealt her favors to us with so profuse a hand. Would to God we may have wisdom enough to improve them."

Washington's engineering eye had drawn on the tablets of his mind in 1784 a waterways map of the western country, and the possibility of uniting the Ohio and the Lakes by continuous water routes—a forecast of the canal network later built in the States of Ohio, Indiana, and Illinois.

"The Ohio River embraces this Commonwealth from its Northern, almost to its Southern limits. It is now, our western boardary and lyes nearly parallel to our exterior, and thickest settled Country.

"Into this River French Creek, big bever Creek, Muskingham, Hockhocking, Scioto, and the two Miames (in its upper Region) and many others (in the lower) pour themselves from the westward through one of the most fertile Countries of the Globe; by a long island navigation; which, in its present state, is passable for Canoes and such other small craft as has, hitherto, been made use of for the Indian trade.

"French Creek, down which I have myself come to Venango, from a lake near its source, is 15 Miles from Prisque Isle on lake Erie; and the Country betwn. quite level. Both big bever creek and Muskingham, communicates very nearly with Cayahoga; which runs into lake Erie; the portage with the latter (I mean Muskingham) as appears by the Maps, is only one mile; and by many other accts. a very little further; and so level between, that the Indians and Traders, as is affirmed, always drag their Canoes from one River to the other when they go to War—to hunt—or trade. The great Miame, which runs into the Ohio, communicates with a River of the same name, as also with Sandusky, which empty themselves into Lake Erie, by short and east [? easy] Portages. And all of these are so many channels through which not only the produce of the

New States contemplated by Congress, but the trade of *all* the lakes, quite to that of the Wood, may be conducted according to my information, and judgment—at least by one of the Routs—thro' a shorter, easier, and less expensive communication than either of those which are now, or have been used with Canada, New Yk. or New Orleans."

Washington was aware of the rival overland route to Pittsburgh, through Carlisle and Bedford, since he vigorously opposed the plan of General Forbes, who succeeded Braddock, for building a road along the established trail through Pennsylvania. But Washington was full of the importance of Virginia as the great centrally located colony on the Atlantic seaboard, confirmed later by the selection there of the site of the new National Capital, and he prophetically realized the primacy of water transportation in his day. While it is seen from the foregoing quotation that he appreciated the possibilities of the Mohawk Valley as a great thoroughfare of future commerce between the Great Lakes and New York, his imagination was stirred by the potential value of a commercial route, at least mostly by water, from Chesapeake Bay to the Ohio River, thence to the Great Lakes and to the lower Mississippi Valley. Moreover, it was one of his strongest inherent traits to do what could be done where he was. Hence his expenditure of energy and his persistence in carrying out his project for joining the waters of the Chesapeake Bay with the Ohio.

THE POTOMAC CANAL PROJECT

As early as August, 1754, in a letter to Thomas Lee, he gives an account of a trip down the Potomac River by canoe "to discover the Navigation of the Potomack." As early as 1772, when a member of the Virginia Assembly, he secured the first legislation authorizing a canal to connect the tidewater of the Potomac with the Ohio River.

When John Ballendine in 1774 proposed a scheme for the navigation of the Potomac and James Rivers, Washington was one of the subscribers to form a company to execute the plan. This plan was held up by the Revolution. That Washington's interest in the enterprise was not equaled by that of his co-adventurers is shown by such entries in his diaries as the following: November 12, 1774. "I went up to George Town to an intended meeting of Trustees for openg. Potomack River. None met. Returnd home at Night." January 26, 1775. "Went up to Alexandria to an intended meeting of the Trustees for opening the Rivr. Potomack. None met."

On March 15, 1784, Jefferson wrote to him: "The union of this navigation [Ohio] with that of the Patowmac is a subject on which I mentioned that I would take the liberty of writing to you. . . . This is the moment however for seizing it if we ever mean to have it. All the world is becoming commercial. . . . For the trade of the Ohio or that which shall come into it from it's own waters or the Missisipi, it is nearer to Alexandria than to New York by 730 miles, and is interrupted by one portage only. Nature then has declared in favour of the Potowmac, and through that channel offers to pour into our lap the whole commerce of the Western world."

In reply, Washington wrote on March 29, 1784: "More than ten years ago I was struck with the importance of it; and, despairing of any aids from the public, I became the principal mover of a bill to empower a number of subscribers to undertake at their own expense, on conditions which were expressed, the extension of the navigation from tide water to Will's Creek, about one hundred and fifty miles; and I devoutly wish that this may not be the only expedient by which it can be effected now. To get this business in motion, I was obliged even upon that ground to comprehend James River, in order to remove the jealousies, which arose from the attempt to extend the navigation of the Potomac. The plan, however, was in a tolerably good train, when I set out for Cambridge in 1775, and would have been in an excellent way, had it not been for the difficulties, which were met with in the Maryland Assembly from the opposition which was given (according to report) by the Baltimore merchants, who were alarmed, and perhaps not without cause, at the consequence of water transportation to Georgetown of the produce, which usually came to their market by land."

Six months later on a journey over the mountains to settle some disputes on his lands near Fort Pitt, he wrote in his diary on September 3: ". . . one object of my journey being to obtain information of the nearest and best communication between the Eastern and Western Waters; and to facilitate as much as in me lay the Inland Navigation of the Potomack; . . ." This trip lasted six weeks over a journey of 680 miles, including a search for a possible good portage from the Potomac to the Little Kanawha, so as to avoid Pennsylvania territory. His views and expectations were set forth

REMAINS OF WASHINGTON'S POTOMAC CANAL

in a letter to General Knox dated January 5, 1785: "In my last I informed you that I was endeavoring to stimulate my Countrymen to the extension of the inland Navigation of our Rivers; and to the opening of the best and easiest communication for Land transportation between them and the Western Waters. I am just returned from Annapolis to which place I was requested to go by our Assembly (with my bosom friend Genl. G—tes, who being at Richmond contrived to edge himself into the commission) for the purpose of arranging matters, and forming a Law which should be similar in both States, so far as it respected the river Potomack, which seperates them. I met the most perfect accordance in that legislature; and the matter is now reported to ours, for its concurrence.

"The two Assemblies (not being in circumstances to undertake this business *wholly* at the public expense) propose to incorporate such private Adventures as shall associate for the purpose of extending the navigation of the River from tide water as far up as it will admit craft of ten tons burthen, and to allow them a perpetual toll and other emoluments to induce them to subscribe freely to a work of such magnitude; whilst they have agreed (or, I should rather say, probably will agree, as the matter is not yet concluded in the Virginia Assembly) to open at the public expence, the communication with the Western territory. To do this will be a great political work—may be immensely extensive in a commercial point; and beyond all question, will be exceedingly beneficial for those who advance the money for the purpose of extending the Navigation of the river, as the tolls arising therefrom are to be held in perpetuity, and will increase every year."

The necessary legislation was finally secured from the Maryland Assembly during the following winter, and on May 17, 1785, the Potomac Company was officially organized with Washington as its first president. It is noteworthy that the difficulties Washington had experienced in securing from the two states concurrent authorization for this important commercial and engineering enterprise must have had great weight in convincing him of the inadequacy of the Articles of Confederation and of the urgent need for a more effective federal government, with powers to regulate interstate commerce.

CONSTRUCTION OF THE POTOMAC CANAL

Washington took a very active part in the affairs and work of the new company and spent a great deal of time on inspection trips along the river in August, 1785. In February, 1786, work was actually begun on the locks on the Virginia side at Great Falls with James Rumsey in charge. Meetings with Washington on the spot are reported for three days in March, for two days in October, and at other times, and the first annual report of the company, in

Washington's own hand, was written on August 17, 1786. At this time over 200 men were employed.

During the following years progress was slow, due to lack of funds, labor difficulties, and lack of engineering experience. This was a novel work in this country and all pioneer engineering. By 1795, "the locks and works at Little Falls were reported as completed and all impediments removed between that place and Great Falls. £10 ster. was called on the new shares. Renewed vigor was infused into the directory and two of them made a close inspection of the river from Cumberland down. Workmen were employed at many places, but still an experienced engineer was badly needed at Great Falls in the erection of the large locks. . . .

"In July, 1796, a market house, thirty by fourteen feet, was built in Matildaville [a town laid out at Great Falls]. There was another call for twenty per cent. on new shares. The breadth of the locks at Great Falls was extended to fourteen from twelve feet. More Irish laborers [possibly redemptioners] were bought in Baltimore on a credit of sixty days. Tobias Lear [Washington's secretary] was in August elected president, with Keith, Templeman, Fendall, and John Mason directors. A settlement was had with General Darke, who had furnished supplies to the company from its organization."

"The three locks at the Little Falls of the Potomac were the first constructed, they were made 18 feet wide and of wood, the next which was finished was the upper lock at the Great Falls—this was made 14 feet wide. A little farther experience satisfied the Directors of the Company that the width

of 12 feet was sufficient for any vessel that would navigate the river, and so were formed all that followed. The remedy in this case as to the upper lock at Great Falls, was soon applied, its greater capacity aided by an adjoining basin, was made to serve to fill more readily the lower locks. At Little Falls . . . it is proposed when the wood decays to rebuild of granite (of which there is a quarry of excellent quality on the canal just above, belonging to the Company, reserved for the purpose) and then to contract them to 12 feet in width.

"In the next instance it is now thought that in the labor applied to the bed of the river too much has been done in removing rocks and that obstructions to the passing off of the water have sometimes been mistaken for obstructions to navigation. . . .

"On the Potomac at the lower extremity of the canals at the Great Falls are five locks: Dimensions—one, length 100 feet, width 14 feet, lift 10 feet, contents 18,200 cubic feet—construction, rectangular, walled with hewn free stone, sluice gates discharge thro' the larger gates,—one, length 100 feet, width 12 feet, lift 16 feet, contents 22,800 cubic feet, construction rectangular of hewn stone, sluice gates as before described,—one, length 100 feet, width 12 feet, lift 14 feet, contents 20,400 cubic feet, construction as the last,—two, length 100 feet, width 12 feet, lift 18 feet, contents 25,200 cubic feet each, construction rectangular, blown out of the solid rock, the natural rock worked tolerably smooth forming the sides, some mason work being used where the fixtures are inserted for supporting the gates, the sluice gates in these locks as in several of the others that are deep, do not lift but are made of cast iron

REMAINS OF ONE OF THE POTOMAC CANAL LOCKS

and turn on a pivot fixed in the center, so that when the sluice is open this little gate or stopper is turned edgewise to the stream, they work very easy and are managed in deep locks much more readily than those of the ordinary construction.

"At tide water, at the canal at the Little Falls, three—dimensions, length 100 feet, width 18 feet, lift 11 feet, contents 23,400 cubic feet each, construction of wood, rectangular—sluice gates discharge as described for those at Great Falls."

Ample evidence of the interest Washington took in the enterprise and the personal supervision he gave the work of construction is contained in many entries in his diaries, too long to quote here. He put into the enterprise more than $10,000 of his own, a material indication of confidence in its economic soundness, and he never accepted any pay for his services.

THE JAMES RIVER CANAL PROJECT

Washington's interest in the James River project was never equal to that in the Potomac and he does not seem to have given it the same personal attention, though both had the same all-important purpose. He wrote Edmund Randolph, August 13, 1785: "The great object, for the accomplishment of which I wish to see the inland navigation of the rivers Potomac & James improved & extended, is to connect the Western Territory with the Atlantic States; all others with me, are secondary. Tho' I am clearly of opinion that it will greatly increase our commerce, & be an immense saving, in the articles of transportation, & draft cattle, to the Planters & Farmers who are in a situation to have the produce of their labor water borne."

It is, therefore, not without justification that Whitford, in his *History of the Canal System of New York*, wrote: "The immortal Washington was the original father and promoter of these canals and improvements, and well did he deserve that admirable motto,—'Twice the saviour of his country.' After conducting her to liberty, he opened her the way to prosperity by new roads and canals, and varying the produce of agriculture." Part of the Potomac canal trench and the ruins of the locks remain to this day near the Great Falls of the Potomac to bear witness to George Washington's practical work as an engineer—a monument to amaze future generations by its difficulties overcome with such scant means—and to the importance he set upon improved lines of communication between the Atlantic seaboard and the great undeveloped West as the permanent and most effectual way of achieving "a more perfect union."

WATER ROUTES AND A MORE PERFECT UNION

The political significance of Washington's engineering plans was vast. He had in mind not merely a profitable investment but a means of keeping the eastern slope of the Mississippi Valley loyal. That this result was uppermost in his mind is evident from his comment on his trip to the Ohio in 1784: "Hitherto, the people of the Western Country have had no excitements to Industry, labour very little;—the luxuriency of the Soil, with very little culture, produces provisions in abundance—these supplies the wants of the encreasing population—and the Spaniards when pressed by want have given high prices for flour—other articles they reject; and at times, (contrary I think to sound policy) shut their ports against them altogether—but let us open a good communication with the Settlements west of us—extend the inland Navigation as far as it can be done with convenience—and shew them by this means, how easy it is to bring the produce of their Lands to our Markets, and see how astonishingly our exports will be increased; and these States benefitted in a commercial point of view—wch. alone is an object of such Magnitude as to claim our closest attention—but when the subject is considered in a political point of view, it appears of much greater importance."

This interest extended far; in fact, Washington had a plan for a journey to the head of the Lake Michigan and thence down by river to New Orleans. Hence he wrote: "The Western Settlers—from my own observation—stand as it were on a pivot—the touch of a feather would almost incline them any way—they looked down the Mississippi until the Spaniards (very impoliticly I think for themselves) threw difficulties in the way, and for no other reason that I can conceive than because they glided gently down the stream, without considering perhaps the tediousness of the voyage back, and the time necessary to perform it in; and because they have no other means of coming to us but by a long land transportation and unimproved Roads. . . .

"The way to avoid both, happily for us, is easy, and dictated by our clearest interest. It is to open a wide door, and make a smooth way for the produce of that Country to pass to our Markets before the trade may get into another channel—this, in my judgment, would dry up the other Sources; or if any part should flow down the Mississippi, from the Falls of the Ohio, in Vessels which may be built—fitted for Sea—and sold with their Cargoes, the proceeds I have no manner of doubt, will return this way; and that it is better to prevent an evil than to rectify a mistake none can deny—commercial connections of all others, are most difficult to dissolve—if we wanted proof of this, look to the avidity with which we are renewing, after a *total* suspension of Eight years, our corrispondence with Great Britain;—So, if we are supine, and suffer without a struggle the Settlers of the Western Country to form commercial connections with the Spaniards, Britons, or with any of the States in the Union we shall find it a difficult matter to dissolve them altho' a better communication should thereafter, be presented to them—time only could effect it; such is the force of habit!"

Again in a letter of August 22, 1785, to Richard Henry Lee he said: "However singular the opinion may be, I cannot divest myself of it, that the navigation of the Mississippi, *at this time*, ought to be no object with us. On the contrary, until we have a little time allowed to open and make easy the ways between the Atlantic States and the western territory, the obstruction had better remain. There is nothing which binds one country or one State to another, but interest. Without this cement the western inhabitants, who more than probably will be composed in a great degree of foreigners, can have no predilection for us, and a commercial connexion is the only tie we can have upon them."

His anxiety about the allegiance of the West was not so devoid of foundation as might be thought now. Some restless spirits were already nibbling at the thought of a new western state, or a connection with Spain. General Wilkinson may already have been in the pay of Madrid; and only a few years later Aaron Burr started on his adventure, in which he undoubtedly had an idea of founding a community not subject to the United States, and not a colony of Spain.

THE ENGINEER AS A NATION BUILDER

The enthusiastic engineer was not to be allowed to indulge himself in the congenial pursuits of doing his share as a private citizen in developing the natural resources of the new country he had liberated. If the United States of America was to be established on a permanent foundation, Washington must again leave his home and privacy *pro bono publico* and become a master builder indeed. A new government had to be designed, on original lines, in order to realize the promises of the Declaration of Independence and to meet the heretofore unsolved problem of a more perfect union of independent sovereign states, with an almost unlimited territory to be settled, from which new states might be formed. It was distinctly a problem for an engineer, needing a design strong enough and stiff enough to secure future unity and ensure permanence, but with such elasticity as to take up the internal stresses of political faction and local pride and to permit immeasurable expansion without disruption.

Hence the successful engineer in private affairs and in corporate projects was called upon to preside at that great Constitutional Convention of 1787, taking practically no part in the eloquent debates on legal tradition and theories of government, and little account of them except as showing him the materials from which the new structure was to be built and developed, the kind of stresses and strains that it must withstand.

We have no record in the Diary or elsewhere of the conflicts and adjustments of Washington's mind and other great minds. Yet it is certain that at the conclusion of each day's forensic battle he was interviewing individual members, persuading each in his quiet, wise way to give a little here or accept a little there, thus one by one fashioning and chiseling the blocks of which the structure of the Constitution was to be built.

What a solid construction that engineer mind helped to erect, a structure strong and adapted to its purpose beyond any expectations he could have had, with a factor of safety able to withstand stresses unforeseen and immeasurable! How fortunate for us that he was the master builder and that his handiwork was strengthened by his collaborators and successors, and that he had able assistants from the start. We now realize that Chief Justice Marshall, his one time intimate friend, later added by his decisions the girders that were needed to support added loads discovered during the first test period; but it was George Washington himself who wisely and firmly made the new Constitution function as he had intended it should, and established the practical methods, the technique so essential to success.

As Prussing says: "it was still an engineer's job. And an engineer took hold and for eight years he kept his grip on the works. He brought together the men needed to construct the Government. He was neither a lawyer nor a statesman, but he knew who and what would work. He studied with them what departments should first and what should next be built up; what was necessary to be done to pay the debts, raise the taxes and protect the frontier; how to deal with France, England, Spain, and the Indians; where the capital city should be located and how it should be laid out. These were practical questions for an engineering mind. The great treaties and acts of Congress soon followed and one piece of timber after another was put into that structure of which the Constitution was but the plan, and which men now call the Government of the United States."

Part II
George Washington, City Builder

CONSTITUTIONAL PROVISION FOR THE NATIONAL CAPITAL

As though determined that Washington should not lack any of the means by which warriors and statesmen of the past had impressed themselves upon posterity, Providence vouchsafed him the opportunity to found a great city, a capital among capitals, the federal capital of a union of sovereign states. It bears his name and, if it continues to develop, as it has of late, in accordance with the plan he adopted for it, we may expect it to stand for centuries a living monument to the wisdom, foresight, and energy of George Washington in later years.

The Continental Congress had much experience, not all pleasant, of a national government holding its sessions and trying to transact its business as a guest in some one of the cities of sovereign states, and had as early as 1784 passed a vote for a federal district. This experience led the Constitutional Convention to include in the instrument it was drafting, provision for a capital over which the federal government was to have full authority. So we find in Article I, Section 8: "The Congress shall have power . . . To exercise exclusive legislation in all Cases whatsoever, over such District (not exceeding ten Miles square) as may, by Cession of particular States, and the Acceptance of Congress, become the Seat of the Government of the United States."

This provision stands out by its especially emphatic terminology in a document otherwise subdued and unusually laconic. In keeping with the economy of words used elsewhere, we would have expected merely "The Congress shall have power to exercise jurisdiction over such District, etc."; but no, the Constitution provided for *exclusive* jurisdiction, so that the intention might be clear that there was to be no concurrent jurisdiction of state or municipality, no limitation on the power of Congress except the other articles of the Constitution itself; and then, lest there be any possibility of mistake or misinterpretaion, here was added "in all Cases whatsoever." Truly there seems to have been nothing about which the Convention was more decided and emphatic than this matter of exclusive federal jurisdiction over the Capital of the Nation.

SELECTION OF A SITE FOR THE CAPITAL

After the adoption of the Constitution, it was not easy for the newly formed government to decide upon the exact location for the capital. To have the federal city within its boundaries would naturally confer upon any state certain anticipated advantages of population, commerce, and special interest from the national government. For the members of the government itself, a central location would have a special advantage and convenience, much more important then than now. The site actually chosen had this great advantage in Washington's judgment, as well as that of being on the Potomac River which, as we have already seen, he expected would be the main highway of commerce between the Atlantic seaboard and the West.

However, he seems to have held aloof from the squabble and to have let his two great Cabinet officers, Hamilton and Jefferson, settle it between them. Suffice it to say here that "An act establishing the temporary and permanent seat of government" was passed by Congress and approved by Washington on July 16, 1790. This required it "to be located . . . on the river Potomac, at some place between the mouths of the Eastern Branch and Conococheaque"; authorized the President to appoint three commissioners to survey and define the district under his supervision, "to purchase or accept such quantity of land on the eastern side of said river within the said district as the President shall deem proper for the use of the United States, and . . . provide suitable buildings for the accommodation of Congress and of the President and for the public offices of the Government." In lieu of appropriations for the cost of land and buildings the President was "authorized and requested to accept grants of money." The first Monday in December, 1800, was fixed as the date for establishing the government in the new capital.

In selecting the site, Washington decided to include the hills on the southerly shore of the Eastern Branch (now the Anacostia River) and the town of Alexandria in Virginia. The law was accordingly amended to permit this. The new city was thus located in the center of a panorama of hills within the boundary of the federal district. Virginia had already offered to cede territory for the district on December 3, 1789, and later gave $120,000, while Maryland took the necessary action on December 19, 1791, and appropriated $72,000.

QUALIFICATIONS FOR THE JOB OF CITY BUILDER

Although he had never visited any of the great foreign cities, Washington was not without the experience, supplemented by much careful thought, requisite to perform well the duties imposed upon him by Congress in relation to founding the new Federal

City. He had had a hand in the development of various towns, some of which eventually came to be cities; and was one of the earliest men to recognize the commercial significance of Wills Creek (Cumberland, Maryland), as the point of departure of a transmontane route to what is now the vast city of Pittsburgh. At Fredericksburg and at Mount Vernon, Washington had lived outside a commercial town. Throughout his life he was much interested in Alexandria, where he built a house as a stopping place for Mrs. Washington and himself and had his business headquarters, practically at the foot of the Potomac Canal system in which he was so much interested as engineer and stockholder. He had a sort of summer place which he used very little at Warm Springs, now Berkeley Springs, West Virginia.

In the course of his life he visited every place that was then of note in the United States from Kittery, in the present state of Maine, to Portsmouth, Newburyport, Ipswich, Salem, Marblehead, Lynn, Boston, Worcester, Springfield, Hartford, New Haven, Providence, Newport, New York, the Long Island towns, Albany, New Brunswick, Princeton, Trenton, Philadelphia, Easton, York, Lancaster, Baltimore, Annapolis, Richmond, Wilmington, Charleston, Savannah, Augusta, and many other places. He was received in most of the state capitals of the period. No man of his time was so well acquainted with the principal places and the principal buildings. As President he lived in two rented houses in New York and one in Philadelphia, though not one of the three was adapted to his conception of what a President's Mansion ought to be.

This wide acquaintance with the country and its public buildings proved to be of immense advantage to the United States, because it caused slowly to grow up in his mind a great conception of a national capital situated in a federal district not subject to the governmental control of any state, conveniently near the center of what was then the inhabited United States, a seaport of easy access, and at the foot of the Potomac Valley which cleaved the mountains with, what was for a long time, the most practicable route from the seaboard to the Ohio Valley.

Washington also had a great experience in building and in buildings. He lived in five or six different houses, from the hunting lodge of Lord Fairfax to the little town house in Alexandria. He rebuilt Mount Vernon twice and made of it the most renowned American gentleman's residence of his time. It is still remarkable for its plan and its proportions. He had a natural sense for disposing groups of buildings and parts of buildings so as to secure an architectural effect. Without ever having seen any of the great European buildings, without ever entering the Houses of Parliament, without any but a knowledge gained by reading and conversation of the great parks, squares, and places of other countries, Washington had a

conception of the future magnificence of a federal capital city which was heightened by his official influence and authority as President. To the knowledge and experience so acquired, supplemented by his innate wisdom and the advice of those whom he selected to assist him, we owe it that the new federal city was so planned and started as to become one of the most magnificent capitals of the world.

BEGINNING THE NEW CAPITAL
(1791)

As the three commissioners Washington promptly appointed Daniel Carroll, a Maryland representative in the expiring Congress; Thomas Johnson, formerly governor of Maryland; and David Stuart, of Virginia, to serve without compensation, thus inaugurating a long list of patriotic and competent commissioners and administrators who have given their services to make the capital the best example of America's ability in city building. He ordered Major Andrew Ellicott, later surveyor general of the United States, "to proceed by the first stage to the federal territory on the Potomac for the purpose of making a survey of it." He selected Major Charles Pierre L'Enfant, a French engineer who had served with distinction during the Revolution and had already rendered services in civil life which bore evidence of his good taste and judgment in design, to "prepare a plan of the city." In the letter of instructions written by Jefferson, Major L'Enfant was told: "The special object of asking your aid is to have drawings of the particular grounds most likely to be approved for the site of the Federal town and buildings." Thus, with the services of these two engineer officers, began the contributions to the city's proper growth and development under direction of officers of the Corps of Engineers of the Army which have continued to this day.

No one understood better than Washington that, as Goethe said, if you would have a thing done well, you will assign the best man you can find for the job; but if you would have it done exactly right, you will go and do it yourself. So, having made his selection of technical assistants to do the work, very wisely as events proved, Washington proceeded to the spot himself.

With long experience as a landowner and real estate developer on a large scale, Washington was quick to realize the land speculation possibilities opened by the selection of a site for the capital. On February 3, 1791, he wrote to two merchants of Georgetown, a settlement within the newly selected district, whom he knew and trusted: "The federal territory being located, the competition for the location of the town now rests between the mouth of the Eastern branch and the lands on the river below and adjacent to Georgetown. . . . The object of this letter is to ask you to endeavor to purchase these grounds for the public, particularly the second parcel, but as if for yourselves,

and to conduct your proposition so as to excite no suspicion that they are on behalf of the public."

Ellicott had been instructed to place his first corner stone of the district at the most southerly point near Alexandria and run his boundary lines from there to the easterly and westerly corners, thence back to meet at the north point. According to Washington, L'Enfant was to keep "within the Eastern branch, the Potomac and the Tyber and the road leading from Georgetown to the ferry on the Eastern Branch"; while in Jefferson's letter of instructions he was "to begin on the Eastern branch and proceed from thence upwards, laying down the hills, valleys, morasses and waters between that and the Potomac, the Tyber, and the road leading from Georgetown to the Eastern branch and connecting the whole with certain fixed points on the map Mr. Ellicott is preparing." Evidently the work of his various agents was to be so dispersed, pending Washington's arrival in person, as to give no clue to the particular area to be acquired by the government, or at least not to allow any special display of interest to indicate the locality.

In a postscript to a letter to L'Enfant, dated March 19, 1791, in which he had asked for preparation of "a drawing . . . of the ground between Rock Creek and the Tyber," Jefferson added: "There are certainly considerable advantages on the Eastern branch; but there are very strong reasons also in favor of the position between Rock Creek and Tyber, independent of the face of the ground. It is desired that the proper amount should be in equilibrio between the two places till the President arrives, and we shall be obliged to you to endeavor to poise their expectations."

On March 28, 1791, Washington arrived. His diaries for this day and the following tell the story in his own words: "Left Bladensburgh at half after six, and breakfasted at George Town about 8; where, having appointed the Commissioners under the Residence Law to meet me, I found Mr. Johnson one of them (and who is Chief Justice of the State) in waiting—and soon after came in David Stuart, and Dan'l Carroll, Esqrs. the other two. A few miles out of Town I was met by the principal Citizens of the place and escorted in by them; and dined at Suter's tavern (where I also lodged) at a public dinner given by the Mayor and Corporation—previous to which I examined the Surveys of Mr. Ellicot who had been sent on to lay out the district of ten miles square for the federal seat; and also the works of Majr. L'Enfant who had been engaged to examine and make a draught of the grds. in the vicinity of George Town and Carrollsburg on the Eastern branch making arrangements for examining the ground myself to morrow with the Commissioners.

"*Tuesday, 29th.* . . . Finding the interests of the Landholders about George Town and those about Carrollsburg much at variance and that their fears and jealousies of each were counteracting the public purposes and might prove injurious to its best interests, whilst if properly managed they might be made to subserve it, I requested them to meet me at six o'clock this afternoon at my lodgings, which they accordingly did.

"To this meeting I represented that the contention in which they seemed engaged, did not in my opinion comport either with the public interest or that of their own; that while each party was aiming to obtain the public buildings, they might by placing the matter on a contracted scale, defeat the measure altogether; not only by procrastination but for want of the means necessary to effect the work; That neither the offer from George-town or Carrollsburgh, seperately, was adequate to the end of insuring the object. That both together did not comprehend more ground nor would afford greater means than was required for the federal City; and that, instead of contending which of the two should have it they had better, by combining more offers make a common cause of it, and thereby secure it to the district; other arguments were used to show the danger which might result from delay and the good effects that might proceed from a Union."

The difficulty as to the existing holdings was adjusted March 30, 1791, by agreement. "The parties to whom I addressed myself yesterday evening, having taken the matter into consideration saw the propriety of my observations; and that whilst they were contending for the shadow they might loose the substance; and therefore mutually agreed and entered into articles to surrender for public purposes, one half of the land they severally possessed within bounds which were designated as necessary for the City to stand with some other stipulations, which were inserted in the instrument which they respectively subscribed.

"This business being thus happily finished and some directions given to the Commissioners, the Surveyor and Engineer with respect to the mode of laying out the district—Surveying the grounds for the City and forming them into lots, I left George-town, dined in Alexandria and reached Mount Vernon in the evening."

THE L'ENFANT PLAN (1791)

Of this visit L'Enfant wrote Jefferson on April 4. After expressing regret that in spite of his utmost endeavors he had been able to present to the President only a rough drawing in pencil (a very interesting preliminary report is still preserved which was probably submitted at the same time, and sets forth most of the basic ideas later elaborated into the L'Enfant plan), he continued: ". . . nevertheless the President indulgent disposition making him account for the difficulties encountered, I had the satisfaction to see the little I had done agreeable to his wish—and the confidence with which he has been pleased since to Honor me in ordering the survey to be continued and the

delineation of a grand plan for the local distribution of the city, to be done in principle conformable to the ideas which I took the liberty to hold before him as the proper for the Establishment being to highly flatering to my Embition to fail exerting the best of my hability." This is important because it is the first direct recognition L'Enfant got as a city planner for the capital, instead of a mere surveyor; and seems to have been enough to encourage him to perfect his great plan.

In the same letter he said: "I would be very much obliged to you in the mean time if you could procure for me whatever map may fall within your reach—of any of the differents grand city now Existing such as— for example—as london—madry [Madrid]— paris—Amsterdam—naples—venice—genoa —florence together with particular maps of any such sea-ports or dock-yards and arsenals as you may know to be the most compleat in their Improvement, for, notwithstanding, I would reprobate the Idea of Imitating and that contrary of Having this Intention it is my wish and shall be my endeavor to delineate on a new and original way the plan the contrivance of which the President has left to me without any restriction soever—yet the contemplation of what exists of well improved situation iven the parallel of these with deffective ones, may serve to suggest a variety of new Ideas and is necessary to refine and strengthen the Judgment particularly in the present instance when having to unite the useful with the comodious and agreeable viewing these will by offering means of comparing enable me the better to determine with a certainty the propriety of a local which offer an Extensive field for combinations." This letter is especially interesting as showing L'Enfant's search for an original plan, and the perfectly proper and sensible use he was prepared to make of the experience and successful work of those who had wrought before him. There is ample internal evidence in the plan of L'Enfant to show its originality; and his succession of letters and reports show how he arrived at it, step by step, finding the best treatment for each particular feature of the local topography.

This letter excited Jefferson's interest and received a full and cordial response from that amateur of architecture. Unfortunately this state of mutual confidence gradually changed. The correspondence indicates that Jefferson's impatience with the Frenchman's peculiarities, particularly his insistence on looking upon Washington as his immediate chief and on paying too little attention to the instructions of others, fostered the breach between L'Enfant and the commissioners which finally led to his dismissal.

ACQUISITION OF THE NEEDED LAND

The commissioners seem to have been primarily interested in the proper form of conveyance for the land and in matters of organization. They did not enter into the plan

of the city of which L'Enfant was so full. Subsequently the latter carried a more finished drawing and project report, dated June 22, 1791, to Washington now back at Mount Vernon after a southern tour.

The next step was to execute his agreement with the landowners. "*Monday* [June] *27th.* Left Mount Vernon for Georgetown before Six oclock;—and according to appointment met the Commissioners at that place by 9—then calling together the Proprietors of those Lands on which the federal City was proposed to be built who had agreed to cede them on certain conditions at the last meeting I had with them at this place but from some misconception with respect to the extension of their grants had refused to make conveyances and recapitulating the principles upon which my comns. to them at the former meeting were made and giving some explanation of the present State of matters and the consequences of delay in this business they readily waved their objections and agd. to convey to the utmost extent of what was required.

"*Tuesday, 28th.* Whilst the Commissioners were engaged in preparing the Deeds to be signed by the Subscribers this afternoon, I went out with Majr. L'Enfant and Mr. Ellicot to take a more perfect view of the ground, in order to decide finally on the spots on which to place the public buildings and to direct how a line which was to leave out a Spring (commonly known by the name of the Cool Spring) belonging to Majr. Stoddart should be run.

"*Wednesday, 29th.* The Deeds which remained unexecuted yesterday were signed to day and the Dowers of their respective wives acknowledged according to Law.

"This being accomplished, I called the several subscribers together and made known to them the spots on which I meant to place the buildings for the P: and Executive departments of the Government—and for the Legislature of Do.—A Plat was also laid before them of the City in order to convey to them general ideas of the City but they were told that some deviation from it would take place—particularly in the diagonal streets or avenues, which would not be so numerous; and in the removal of the Presidents house more westerly for the advantage of higher ground—they were also told that a Town house, or exchange wd be placed on some convenient ground between the spots designated for the public buildings, before mentioned.—and it was with much pleasure that a general approbation of the measure seemed to pervade the whole."

AN EXAMPLE OF UNUSUAL FORESIGHT

The agreement which George Washington thus persuaded the landowners to sign furnishes not only a concrete example of his powers as a bargainer, but also exceptional proof of his foresight and wisdom. He secured by this voluntary contract "sole power of directing the Federal City to be laid off in what manner he pleases," that is city-plan control, and the right to prescribe "for regulating the materials and manner of the buildings and improvements generally in the said city, or in particular streets or parts thereof for convenience, safety, and order," that is architectural and zoning control. After years of effort, American cities are only now recovering these two classes of jurisdiction over private enterprise, which Washington secured for his city by voluntary agreement and were forfeited by later presidents who did not appreciate their importance.

DISMISSAL OF L'ENFANT (1792)

With characteristic energy, Major L'Enfant had set about his task and in the incredibly short time of twenty days, he had a preliminary report and outline plan ready to present. He worked on perfecting this plan as rapidly as the survey of the territory covered by it progressed and submitted the final plan and report to Washington at Philadelphia on August 27, 1791. Three months thereafter an incident occurred which engendered such bad feeling between him and the three commissioners appointed under the Act of 1790, that it may be considered the initial cause of his subsequent dismissal at the end of February, 1792, and of his separation from the work in which he was so tremendously interested. This dismissal practically wrecked his life, but from the incident city officials may today draw some comfort and consolation, since it shows that even "in the good old days" of our Revolutionary forefathers the way of the city planner was hard.

Daniel Carroll of Duddington (not the commissioner), one of the original owners of land in the area selected for the city, had started a handsome residence which was found to be located in the middle of one of Major L'Enfant's main avenues (since named New Jersey Avenue) south of the site chosen for the Capitol. The major insisted that construction should be stopped immediately and that the work already begun should be demolished. Since Carroll did not comply with this demand, the fiery Frenchman gathered together some workmen and saw to the job of demolition himself.

Although the law of 1790 provided for three commissioners to have charge of the work on the Federal City under direction of the President, Major L'Enfant never fully acknowledged their authority and persistently reported directly to his chief, General Washington. Seeing that L'Enfant had the engineer qualifications in a high degree, that he had taste and vision, and inspiration derived from a great conception and plan, Washington must have felt deep satisfaction in his work. But the commissioners did not appreciate the major's plan, did not always comprehend his reasons. He had not been appointed by them and would not fully subject himself to their orders, feeling that he

was really the representative of the great President who understood him and that he was there in some measure to see that the commissioners did not spoil things.

It was perhaps not unnatural, therefore, that the commissioners should take advantage of the complaint of Carroll to make a case against L'Enfant. Then they kept interfering with his work and finally with evident true regret, President Washington dismissed him on their recommendation. But L'Enfant had completed his plan, and the city was laid out and the new public buildings were built in substantial conformity with it, so that it is to him that the nation chiefly owes the original and convenient arrangement of streets, avenues, squares, and reserved lands, which have made possible the magnificent city of Washington.

Appreciating the weakness of a three-man commission as an executive, especially when the members were frequently absent, and recognizing its greater safety and soundness in establishing policies, Washington wrote to Benjamin Stoddert, November 14, 1792: ". . . the administration of the affairs of the Federal City ought to be under the immediate direction of a judicious and skilful superintendent, appointed by and subject to the orders of the commissioners (who in the eye of the law, are the responsible characters), one in whom is united knowledge of men and things, industry, integrity, impartiality, and firmness; and that this person should reside on the spot." We may imagine how deeply he regretted the loss of L'Enfant's services.

INTEREST IN PUBLIC BUILDINGS

Thus far we have followed Washington's participation in founding the new federal city step by step. This, and the multitude of his other letters on the subject are sufficient proof of the deep personal interest he took in this child of his old age. He continued to lend his support to L'Enfant's plan, to suggest changes and improvements from time to time, to advise and prod the commissioners to further work, personally to examine and criticize the plans for the public buildings, and in every way to see to it that the work was done and done to his satisfaction. He even bought property in the new city and left an item in his will to help found in it a national university.

When Jefferson had proposed selecting a much smaller area for the city—even in the L'Enfant plan it covered but a small fraction of the District and this was adequate for the population until the Civil War—and so avoid paying so much for land, Washington wrote to the commissioners, May 7, 1791: "Will they not recollect my observation that Philadelphia stood upon an area of three by two miles, and if the metropolis of *one State* occupied so much ground, what ought that of the United States to occupy?"

THE WHITE HOUSE

In a letter to Tobias Lear, July 30, 1792, he said: "I found at George Town many well conceived, & ingenious plans for the Public buildings in the New City: it was a pleasure, indeed, to find in an infant Country such a display of Architectural abilities. —The Plan of Mr. Hoben, who was introduced to me by Doctr Tucker, from Charleston, & who appears to be a very judicious Man, was made choice of for the President's House; and the Commissioners have agreed with him to superintend the building of it— & that of the Capitol also,—if they should, hereafter, be disposed to put both under one management." The "Mr. Hoben" mentioned is James Hoban, the architect of the White House and subsequently in charge of work at the Capitol, as Washington foresaw might be the case.

Of the two public buildings then projected Washington wrote in a letter to David Stuart, one of the commissioners, March 8, 1792: ". . . the plan ought to be prosecuted with all the despatch the nature of the case will admit, and that the public buildings in size, form and elegance, should look beyond the present day. I would not have it understood from hence that I lean to extravagance.—A chaste plan sufficiently capacious and convenient for a period not *too* remote, but one to which we may reasonably look forward, would meet my idea in the Capitol. For the President's House I would design a building which should also look forward but execute no more of it at present than might suit the circumstances of this country, when it shall be first wanted. A Plan comprehending more may be executed at a future period when the wealth, population, and importance of it shall stand upon much higher ground than they do at present."

The reference to the size of the White House is particularly interesting, as the commissioners were about to have Hoban's plans reduced one fifth in size, so as to reduce the cost of carrying them out. How fortunate that this gem of American architecture was originally built on a scale sufficient to remain adequate and in use to the present day!

LAYING THE CORNERSTONE OF THE CAPITOL (1793)

The dismissal of L'Enfant must have been a real blow to Washington and redoubled his sense of responsibility for the progress of affairs at the Capital. On September 18, 1793, he personally laid the cornerstone of the Capitol with due ceremony. The procession, consisting of the dignitaries, Virginia Artillery, Masonic lodges, two bands, etc., formed at the President's Square and marched to the site of the Capitol, for which Dr. William Thornton's design had been selected. Tiber Creek the dignitaries and their escort had to cross in single file on logs and stepping stones, reforming on the eastern bank. What a humble precursor to the gorgeous succession of parades that have since marched with all "the glorious pomp and circumstances of war" from the Capitol to the White House! It is interesting and fitting that the extension of the Capitol Grounds now in course of development should include lot 16 in Square 634 which Washington selected in 1798, after a personal examination "to build on."

THE NATION'S MONUMENT TO WASHINGTON

The commissioners had early decided upon naming the new city "Washington" in honor of its founder. He usually referred to it modestly as the Federal City and but rarely as the city of Washington. It remains an enduring and living monument to his wisdom, energy, enterprise, and achievements as a city builder.

Where the line drawn west from the center of the Capitol intersected that drawn directly south from the President's house, L'Enfant proposed an equestrian statue of George Washington. Nearly half a century later the National Washington Monument Association, under the presidency of his old friend and biographer, Chief Justice Marshall, started to raise subscriptions to carry out this idea in accordance with the design of Robert Mills. The obelisk, which was an essential and the most prominent part of the design selected, was started in 1848, and societies, lodges, states, and even nations sent stones to be incorporated in it. Because the site suggested by L'Enfant was under water in the estuary of the Tiber, the structure was placed on a natural elevation nearby.

However, the funds raised proved insufficient, settlement of the shaft became noticeable, and the unfinished structure was covered with a temporary roof and allowed to stand as an unsightly stump until 1874.

During President Grant's administration there was a great revival of interest in the National Capital. The enormous amount of work done towards turning the neglected village into a modern city and carrying out the plans of L'Enfant and Washington naturally led to an effort to complete the monument to the First President and Founder of the city. For a time the engineers faced difficulties of a tremendously concentrated load and inadequate foundation, difficulties which seemed insurmountable. But a military engineer was found to finish the job. The shaft was completed in 1884 under the direction of Lieut. Col. Thomas Lincoln Casey with some very ad-

vantageous changes in the shape as well as structural design, notably the elimination of the incongruous Greek colonnade and gigantic figure of Washington in classic costume driving a chariot. The recent statement of a noted architect is, therefore, substantially justified: "There is in Washington a construction designed by engineers. The wind piles up masses of sculptural clouds

behind it. The rising sun paints it silver, and the setting sun paints it gold, and it is, I venture to think, the most beautiful single object in the world today, . . ."—and so, it may be added, it stands a fitting and unique monument to

GEORGE WASHINGTON, ENGINEER AND NATION BUILDER

Base of Pantheon, 250 feet diameter; height 100 feet; height of Obelisk 500 feet

DESIGN OF THE

NATIONAL WASHINGTON MONUMENT

IN THE

CITY OF WASHINGTON

MILLS' DESIGN FOR THE WASHINGTON MONUMENT

THE WASHINGTON MONUMENT TODAY

Selected Authorities

(See also Authorities on p. 145.)

BACON-FOSTER, CORRA—*Early Chapters in the Development of the Potomac Route to the West*. Washington, Columbia Historical Society, 1912. (Also, in part, in the Society's *Records*, Vol. XV.)

BRYAN, WILHELMUS BOGART—*History of the National Capital*. 2 vols. New York, Macmilan, 1914-16. (Especially Vol. I, chs. i-ix.)

CORBIN, JOHN—*Unknown Washington*. New York, Scribner, 1930.

JUSSERAND, JEAN J.—*Brothers in Arms*. New York, Chautauqua Press, 1919. (No. 2.)

KITE, ELIZABETH S., ED.—*L'Enfant and Washington, 1791-1792*. Baltimore, Johns Hopkins Press, 1929.

LATIMER, LOUISE PAYSON—*Your Washington and Mine*. New York, Scribner, 1924.

LEFFMAN, HENRY—"George Washington as an Engineer"; in Engineer Club of Philadelphia, *Proceedings*, Vol. XXI, p. 277. (Also separate, Philadelphia, 1904.)

OSBORNE, JOHN B.—"First President's Interest in Washington as told by Himself"; in Columbia Historical Society, *Records*, Vol. IV.

PHILLIPS, PHILIP LEE—"Washington as a Surveyor and Map-Maker"; in *Daughters of the American Revolution Magazine*, Vol. LIV, p. 115.

PICKELL, JOHN—*New Chapter in the Early Life of Washington in Connection with the Narrative History of the Potomac Company*. New York, Appleton, 1856.

PRUSSING, EUGENE E.—*Estate of George Washington, deceased*. Boston, Little Brown, 1927.

PRUSSING, EUGENE E.—*George Washington in Love and Otherwise*. Chicago, Covici, 1925. (Chs. ii, iii.)

TINDALL, WILLIAM—*Standard History of the City of Washington*. Knoxville, H. W. Crew, 1914. (Especially chs. i-iv.)

TONER, JOSEPH M.—*Washington as an Inventor and Promoter of the Useful Arts*. Washington, 1892.

WASHINGTON, GEORGE — *Diaries, 1748-1799*. Ed. by John C. Fitzpatrick. 4 vols. Boston, Houghton Mifflin, 1925.

WASHINGTON, GEORGE—*Writings*. Ed. by Worthington Chauncey Ford. 14 vols. New York, Putnam, 1889-93.

WASHINGTON, GEORGE — "Writings of George Washington relating to the National Capital"; in Columbia Historical Society, *Records*, Vol. XVII.

"Washington and the Potomac: Manuscripts"; in *American Historical Review*, Vol. XXVIII, pp. 497, 705.

Washington's Home and Fraternal Life
By Carl H. Claudy
Part I
Family Life and Friends

THE WILLIAMS MASONIC PORTRAIT

From the portrait painted from life by William Williams; now in possession of Alexandria-Washington Lodge No. 22, Alexandria, Va.

EDUCATION

Washington's schooling was a haphazard affair and of it we lack definite information. He possibly attended a field school kept by one Hobby, a sexton, before his father died, and for some months after that event lived with Augustine at Wakefield and attended the school of Henry Williams who is credited with developing George's inclination toward mathematics. When he went to live with his mother his schooling was perhaps in Fredericksburg under the rector there, Rev. James Marye, on and off, until probably 1747. He may have received, but quickly forgot, a smattering of Latin, continued his interest in mathematics, left school with a power of literary expression which he never lost, and a clear chirography. His largest education was outside. Vigorous outdoor activity combined with great strength prepared his body for the demands of the later strenuous life, and made him a superb horseman. His visits to the homes of his elder brothers brought him into contact with colonial polite society, taught him manners, and developed his character, while also starting him on his career.

BROTHERS AND SISTER

From 1747 on, the main influences upon the youth were his half brother Lawrence and the latter's friends and relatives by marriage, the Fairfax family. His time was spent chiefly at Mount Vernon. Interest in mathematics undoubtedly began the tendency toward accuracy and method which remained a chief characteristic throughout Washington's life. It may also have turned his attention to surveying as a career, but the choice may have been made because it was the best possible business opening. Lord Fairfax, a great promoter, far from the indifferent nobleman of the period, was the youth's patron and if he did not encourage him to become a surveyor, at least gave him the opportunity of practical experience in the laying out of his Lordship's frontier lands in Shenandoah Valley and elsewhere. At the end of 1751 George went with Lawrence, then a pulmonary invalid, to Barbados, where he had smallpox himself. His brother made no gain in health, and returned some months later to Mount Vernon to die.

EARLY YEARS

EORGE WASHINGTON was born on the Bridges Creek estate on Friday, February 11, 1731/32, o. s. (February 22, 1732, N. S.). The plantation was later called Wakefield. A building has been erected on the estate, reproducing as far as possible the birthplace. When George Washington was about three years of age the family moved up the Potomac to the estate which later became Mount Vernon, and from there about 1739 to a farm on the Rappahannock opposite Fredericksburg, possibly because of Augustine Washington's mining interests. There, on April 12, 1743, the father died. He devised the Mount Vernon estate to his oldest son, Lawrence, the Bridges Creek estate to Augustine, and the Rappahannock farm to George, but subject to his mother's control during his minority. The will made no mention of property other than the land and its adjuncts, including slaves, and the interest in the iron works. The estate was considerable and Mary Ball was left what profit she could make from the Bridges Creek plantation for five years. All the estates were left in Mary's hands until the sons came respectively of age. She had property in her own right, including another farm on the Rappahannock.

With Augustine, the other half brother, George Washington's later relations are uncertain. Augustine died before the outbreak of the Revolution and George, who thus became head of the family and who survived his sister and all his brothers, declined to qualify as an executor of the estate, but evidently because of the stress of other duties. This brother's children were remembered with the rest of the nephews and nieces in the General's will.

Elizabeth ("Betty"), George Washington's sister, married Fielding Lewis, lived at Fredericksburg, and is said to have resembled the General. John Augustine was his favorite brother and the younger man had charge of Mount Vernon, to which George fell heir in 1752, during the French and Indian War campaigns. Samuel, the second of Mary Washington's sons, died in 1781, widowing his fifth wife. His will showed a considerable estate but his brother George's correspondence indicates that it was involved and not productive for some years at least. The General assumed the education of two of his brother's sons and the care of a daughter, Harriot, his brotherly affection being indicated in his will by the statement that the charges for these and other accounts "shall stand balanced," while in addition these collateral descendants shared equally with the others in the general division of the estate. The other brother, Charles, predeceased George so closely that he was mentioned in the latter's will. A son of George Washington's sister and of each of his brothers were executors of the General's estate.

MARRIAGE

On the traditional love affairs of Washington—of the "Lowland Beauty," of his interest in Sally Cary, the wife of George William Fairfax, of his visit to Mary Philipse in New York (there is no evidence of either engagement or proposal), and the rest—it is not essential to dwell. He met his future wife, Martha Dandridge, widow of Daniel Parke Custis, early in 1758. She was a few months older than Washington. The marriage took place on January 6, 1759, as soon as he had resigned his military commission. It is not known whether the ceremony took place at her house or at the church. His attitude toward life at that time is indicated by a letter written soon after this happy event to an English correspondent of his own name whom he supposed to be a distant relative: "I am now I believe fixd at this seat with an agreable Consort for Life. And hope to find more happiness in retirement than I ever experienced amidst a wide and bustling World."

THE LADY OF THE MANOR

Martha Washington in her forty-one years as consort to "the General" revealed a person of breeding, dignified in society, and adequate as First Lady. She was very fond of her husband, who reciprocated her affec-

tion, and domestic in her tastes, always active in the care of the Mount Vernon household when she was at home. She had little influence on her husband's public career, except so far as her wealth enabled him to engage in it. She brought him a large estate and he took from her agents the management not only of her share but that of her two minor children, John Parke and Martha (or "Patsy"). All the world knows of the tender care he took of her all his life and of her children and grandchildren. Evidences of this care, of her solicitude, and its relation to his public duties is well shown in a letter he wrote Tobias Lear in 1793 at the time of the yellow fever epidemic in Philadelphia: "It was my wish to have continued there longer; but as Mrs. Washington was unwilling to leave me surrounded by the malignant fever which prevailed, I could not think of hazarding her, and the Children any longer by *my* continuance in the City, . . . I therefore came off with them."

A reserved man even in his diary, and formal even in the most friendly letters, Washington was not the type to fling his heart on paper for all the world to read. But his references to his home life in general and to Mrs. Washington in particular show him as a devoted husband who loved his home not only for what it was—a place of peace and sanctuary to which he returned again and again from the arduous duties to which his country called him—but as the setting for the jewel which was the honored wife.

When his country called him he wrote her, June 18, 1775: "I should enjoy more real happiness in one month with you at home, than I have the most distant prospect of finding abroad, if my stay were to be seven times seven years. . . . It was utterly out of my power to refuse this appointment, without exposing my character to such censures, as would have reflected dishonor upon myself, and given pain to my friends. This, I am sure, could not, and ought not, to be pleasing to you, and must have lessened me considerably in my own esteem."

No pen picture of Martha Washington packs more into less space than that written by Brissot de Warville, a young Frenchman who visited Washington with a letter of introduction from Lafayette. He said: "Every thing has an air of simplicity in his house; his table is good, but not ostentatious; and no deviation is seen from regularity and domestic economy. Mrs. Washington superintends the whole, and joins to the qualities of an excellent house-wife, the simple dignity which ought to characterize a woman, whose husband has acted the greatest part on the theater of human affairs; while she possesses that amenity, and manifests that attention to strangers which render hospitality so charming."

EARLY FRIENDS

Washington loved his friends and was as happy in entertaining them as in visiting them. His diaries and his letters prove his interest in and his dependence upon his chosen comrades; if indeed a man is known by the company he keeps, then is Washington known as the peer of his day and age, for his friends were the leaders in the political, social, and economic life of his time.

His near neighbors, the Ramsays, the Johnsons, the Fairfaxes, the McCartys, the Diggeses across the Potomac, Dr. Craik, the Masons, his wife's relatives, the Bassetts of York Peninsula, and many others were often at Mount Vernon and Washington and his wife visited them to dine or sup or spend the night. Craik, Mercer, Wagener, and other comrades of early days in the border wars were often around his fireside, living over again the brave days of youth and daring, adventure and danger.

Few if any of his immediate neighbors held the place in Washington's heart which was occupied by George Mason, of Gunston Hall. The two men were singularly alike in certain ways; both were enthusiastic planters, both proprietors of great estates, both intensely interested in public affairs. The famous author of the Virginia Bill of Rights had five hundred people on his plantation, and Gunston Hall vied with Mount Vernon in both beauty and hospitality. Here the likeness between the friends ceased. Washington was a public character; Mason was a semi-recluse, who very unwillingly permitted himself to be thrust into active participation in civic affairs. He was a profound student, a sagacious leader who possessed a thoughtful, well balanced mind, but he preferred to work quietly through friends, rather than publicly through personal influence; later he abandoned the seclusion of home to enter public life. Close association and constant correspondence with Mason had a profound effect upon Washington, who turned to the owner of Gunston Hall for counsel and a fresh viewpoint as he turned to no one else. Hence it was but natural that the social intercourse between the two "great houses" should be so constant in the antebellum days, or that we find Washington so often at Gunston, and Mason so often at Mount Vernon. After the Revolution they differed politically and the intimacy was evidently much lessened.

AT MOUNT VERNON

With his marriage began the real home life of George Washington. The American home has always been one of the foundation stones of the Republic. Luckily for all in whom love of home is next to love of country, we have a picture of Washington's home life which is well rounded. His diary, his letters, the accounts left to us by the friends who visited him, the happiness and relief with which he returned to Mount Vernon whenever the cares of public life permitted, all limn the details so that the visitor to Mount Vernon has small difficulty in peopling it with the gracious figures of colonial days, seeing it as a center of culture and hospitality, a focus of those ideals of home which make Washington a living, breathing personality.

Washington's diaries are an expression of a singularly direct nature. They neither minimize nor magnify. He was sparing of words and packed into a few sentences events which to him were of paramount importance. Reading them as a whole, perhaps nothing stands out with greater clearness than that George Washington was essentially a home lover. He left Mount Vernon reluctantly to go to war, to be President, to explore, to visit his property in distant places. Always he returned as to a haven; his home meant to him peace and comfort and surcease from care. He loved the earth and all that sprang from it; he loved the woods and the wild game; he loved his friends much and was never happier than when with them, in their homes, or, preferably, at Mount Vernon. He loved his wife and her children, and later the grandchildren; he gave them home and love and a father's care—and when Patsy died, a deep grief.

Across the years we see a vivid picture of Washington not only the revered leader but a Washington content to be a simple planter, a home body, a man whose affections included not only wife and children but overpoured to other relatives and friends, slaves and servants, dogs, horses, cattle, and the insensate but beloved acres of his estate.

STYLE OF LIVING

If Washington lived in a style which in these days might be considered above the average, it was far more for his family and his guests than for himself. We have his own words for his love of simplicity. He wrote: "My manner of living is plain and I do not mean to be put out of it; a glass of wine and a bit of mutton are always ready, and such as will be content to take of them, are always welcome. Those who expect more will be disappointed."

Repeatedly he referred to "the shadow of my own vine and my own fig tree." He called Mount Vernon "a small villa" and again "my cottage." He liked "the simplicity of rural life."

Washington lived in a state befitting the man. It was luxurious, but luxury was the fashion of the times. Especially did he wish his wife to enjoy those comforts and luxuries to which his position and his means entitled her. Mrs. Washington never had reason to complain of her wardrobe. She had silks and satins of the finest. When occasion required Washington traveled on horseback, but when time was available he used a coach and four, and his outriders dressed in livery. His home was furnished with the best and his entertainments if not actually lavish were at least more than ample. The best

was none too good for all those he loved, as befitted a wealthy man, the President of the nation, the general of its armies, beloved by his countrymen.

DAILY LIFE AT MOUNT VERNON

An English writer, Charles Varlo, who toured America in 1784, left us this charming word picture of General Washington's domestic hearth: "I crossed the river from Maryland into Virginia, near to the renowned General Washington's where I had the honour to spend some time, and was kindly entertained with that worthy family. As to the General, if we may judge by the countenance, he is what the world says of him, a shrewd, good-natured, plain, humane man, about fifty-five years of age, and seems to wear well, being healthful and active, straight, well made, and about six feet high.

"He keeps a good table, which is always open to those of a genteel appearance. He does not use many Frenchified *congees,* or flattering useless words without meaning, which savours more of deceit than an honest heart; but on the contrary, his words seem to point at truth and reason, and to spring from the fountain of a heart, which, being good of itself, cannot be suspicious of others, . . .

"The General's house is rather warm, snug, convenient, and useful, than ornamental. The size is what ought to suit a man of about two or three thousand a year in England. The out-offices are good, and seem to be not long built; and he was making more offices at each wing to the front of the house, which added more to ornament than real use.

"The situation is high, and commands a beautiful prospect of the river which parts Virginia and Maryland, but in other respects the situation seems to be out of the world, being chiefly surrounded by woods, and far from any great road or thoroughfare, and nine miles from Alexandria in Virginia.

"The General's lady is a hearty, comely, discreet, affable woman, some few years older than himself; she was a widow when he married her. He has no children by her.

"The General's house is open to poor travelers as well as rich; he gives diet and lodging to all that come that way, which indeed cannot be many, without they go out of their way on purpose. . . .

"I have travelled and seen a great deal of the world, have conversed with all degrees of people, and have remarked that there are only two persons in the world which have every one's good word, and those are—the Queen of England and General Washington, which I never heard friend or foe speak slightly of."

The Reverend Jedidiah Morse, the geographer, visited Mount Vernon in 1786, and left this delightful sketch of the General's home:

"He rises, in winter as well as summer, at the dawn of day; and generally reads or writes some time before breakfast. He

breakfasts about seven o'clock on three small Indian hoe-cakes and as many dishes of tea. He rides immediately to his different farms, and remains with his labourers until a little past two o'clock, when he retires and dresses. At three he dines, . . . Whether there be company or not, the table is always prepared, by its elegance and exuberance for their reception; and the General remains at it for an hour after dinner, in familiar conversation and convivial hilarity. It is then that every one present is called upon to give some absent friend as a toast; the name not unfrequently awakens a pleasing remembrance of past events, and gives a new turn to the animated colloquy. General Washington is more chearful than he was in the army. Although his temper is rather of a serious cast, and his countenance commonly carries the impression of thoughtfulness, yet he perfectly relishes a pleasant story, an unaffected sally of wit, or a burlesque description which surprises by its suddenness and incongruity with the ordinary appearance of the object described. After this social and innocent relaxation, he applies himself to business, and about nine o'clock retires to rest. This is the rotine, and this the hour he observes, when no one but his family is present; at other times he attends politely upon his company until they wish to withdraw."

HOSPITALITY

The hospitality of Mount Vernon left nothing to be desired; the high and the low, the rich and the poor, the politician and the small farmer, the soldier and the civilian were often present—sometimes with their ladies, sometimes with whole families—to break bread and spend the night or longer with the beloved host.

Washington inherited the original estate of Mount Vernon which he increased from time to time until he owned eight thousand acres of land, one of the finest plantations in Virginia. He introduced advanced methods of preparing the soil; he selected his seed with great care. He built slave quarters in many places, so that he could divide his holdings into five sections and put an overseer in charge of each. As far as possible, he paid daily visits to the various sections, making his agriculture almost a science, as well as a business. But it was distinctly a home business and one which did not interfere with hospitality; rather, plantation life encouraged the practice of hospitality. Washington wrote in his diary, June 30, 1785: "dined with only Mrs. Washington, which I believe is the first instance of it since my retirement from public life." Later he said that his house "may be compared to a well resorted tavern." To make the "tavern" accommodate its guests, he added wings to the old house, until it grew to be ninety-six feet in length.

It was a great house in Washington's day; indeed, its beautiful proportions and its architectural excellence excite the admiration of artists of the present day. The curved colonades at each end, the noble porch, the formal landscaping of the grounds, with the trees planted by Washington and others, were all according to the General's own plans.

The house was roomy after its enlargement, as it had to be when so many came to visit the man whom all knew to be at once the maker and the savior of the new Republic. The Virginia planters inherited their ideas of lavish hospitality from the Motherland. Inns were few and incommodious, hence great estates were as naturally the focus of constant streams of visitors, as were Virginia gentlemen themselves patterned on the centuries of tradition. A planter's home was not only always open to his friends, but in days when travel was difficult and hostelries far apart, was a stopping place for travelers who often claimed a night's lodging and a seat at the family board by the right of a common background and common interests.

DANCING

It is delightful to read that Washington was very fond of dancing! This grave man, so filled with the cares of state, so self sacrificing of all that he held dearest in life—home, plantation, friends, association with a loved wife—enjoyed to the full all varieties of the social intercourse of his age. Colonial days were a mixture of social formality and unceremonious hospitality. Dancing was a social grace in which both men and women were schooled as an essential part of a well rounded education. The stately minuet and the jolly Virginia reel were both performed according to ceremonial forms, and beautiful must both have been in the colonial silken knee breeches and ruffled shirts and powdered wigs of the men, the long full skirts and low cut evening gowns of the women.

Not only was dancing a home pleasure at Mount Vernon, but also at social affairs in Fredericksburg and Williamsburg. The General and his lady went often to grace a ball even as far as Annapolis. Of one of these, at Alexandria, where the refreshments were not to his liking, being mostly bread and butter and coffee which "the Drinkers of coud not Distinguish from Hot water sweetned," he wrote in his diary, "I shall therefore distinguish this Ball by the Stile and title of the Bread and Butter Ball."

Washington gave up dancing with regret. In 1799 he wrote to the committee on arrangements of the balls to be held by the Washington Society of Alexandria: "Mrs. Washington and myself have been honored with your polite invitation to the assemblies of Alexandria this winter, and thank you for this mark of your attention. But, alas! our dancing days are no more. We wish, however, all those who have a relish for so agreeable and innocent an amusement all the pleasure the season will afford them."

SPORTS

Washington's home life was interrupted time after time; but when he could enjoy Mount Vernon, his home life was not all work. He built, he farmed, he improved and conserved his holdings, but he also lived the life of a gentleman of the period and hunted and fished and rode to hounds.

Mount Vernon had miles of water front, and the Potomac was—and still is—filled with fish. Washington was extremely fond of fishing but he regarded his water rights as more than mere adjuncts to sport. The spring run of shad and herring was an important source of food and wealth for the owner of Mount Vernon.

He knew the woods within miles of his home from boyhood days and frequently hunted the abundant game of the Virginia hills and vales: Virginia deer, hares, squirrels, gray fox, and 'possum, many species of birds and of course the ruffed grouse, the wild turkey, and quail.

His diaries show that he loved fox hunting more than any other sport, during the season often coursing three or four times a week. It was the sport of the community; he and his neighbors kept kennels and the bay of the hound was often heard in the land.

Of his numerous mentions of fox hunts one will suffice, especially as it shows that Washington hunted for sport and not for the mere killing of the quarry. He wrote December 22, 1785: "Went a Fox hunting with the Gentlemen who came here yesterday [Daniel Dulany, Jr., Benjamin Dulany, Samuel Hanson, Thomas Hanson, Philip Alexander], together with Ferdinando Washington and Mr. Shaw, after a very early breakfast. Found a Fox just back of Muddy hole Plantation, and after a Chase of an hour and a quarter with my Dogs, and eight couple of Doctor Smith's (brought by Mr. Phil Alexander) we put him into a hollow tree, in which we fastened him; and in the Pincushion put up another Fox which in an hour and 13 Minutes was killed. We then after allowing the Fox in the hole half an hour, put the Dogs upon his Track and in half a Mile he took to another hollow tree and was again put out of it, but he did not go 600 yards before he had recourse to the same shift. Finding therefore that he was a conquered Fox we took the Dogs off and all came home to Dinner."

THE PLANTER

Washington loved the earth; he was a planter from inclination as well as from necessity. To watch the brown mould being plowed, to see his crops sprout and grow, to count them as harvested, satisfied an inner spiritual need of the man whose whole life was a succession of planting and sowing and reaping; planting effort, sowing ideas, and reaping independence and good government.

A husbandman as well as farmer, live

stock was a hobby with Washington. The several estuaries which indented his estate made marshes suitable for hogs and his average annual hog kill mounted to two hundred and fifty head, largely used in feeding his slaves and servants, although the best of the ham and bacon would be for the home table and the guests.

In his diary and letters are many references to matters which pertain to farming and planting, stock and slaves, the work of the plantation. He wrote in 1788: "The more I am acquainted with agricultural affairs, the better I am pleased with them; insomuch that I can no where find so great satisfaction as in those innocent and useful pursuits. In indulging these feelings, I am led to reflect how much more delightful to an undebauched mind, is the task of making improvements on the earth, than all the vain glory which can be acquired from ravaging it, by the most uninterrupted career of conquest.'

CHILDREN AT MOUNT VERNON

George Washington and Mrs. Washington missed the gift of children of their own. Washington's paternal affections were lavished upon his wife's children, Martha and John Custis, and the grandchildren (son and daughters of John Custis), Eliza, Martha, Eleanor, and George Washington Parke Custis.

Martha Washington's two children grew up at Mount Vernon, to which beautiful home George Washington took his new wife and her babies in 1759. Both Martha and John Custis were dearly loved by the General; we may believe, too, that the shouts and the laughter, the play and the merriment which youth brought to Mount Vernon made it the sweeter in the eyes of the owner.

Then came grief. Just rounding into womanhood, the young Martha, after suffering one of what Washington referred to as "her usual fits," died very suddenly in 1773. She left a broken-hearted mother, and a stepfather who was overcome with sorrow at the loss of a girl whom he could not have loved more had she been of his own blood.

John Custis lived long enough to marry, establish a home, and father four children, but he was very young when his call came—twenty-seven. He was a volunteer aide to General Washington; during the siege of Yorktown, exposure led to a camp fever which was fatal.

Two of his children, George Washington Parke and Nellie (Eleanor) Custis, taken into their home by the Washingtons, brought youth again to Mount Vernon and young blood and laughter to lawns and halls that had too long been serious. The young grandchildren seem to have been of the greatest comfort and joy to their grandmother and General Washington. Nellie Custis was married at Mount Vernon on Washington's last birthday, to which he devoted a scant entry in his diary: "The Revd. Mr. Davis and Mr. Geo. Calvert came to dinner and Miss Custis was married abt. Candle light to Mr. Lawe. Lewis."

HOME LIFE AWAY FROM MOUNT VERNON

Washington was away from Mount Vernon for almost seventeen of the forty-one years of his married life, though during the last six years of his presidency he was able to spend much of his time there. Mrs. Washington was with him whenever possible during these periods of public service. During the war army headquarters were perhaps a poor excuse for a home; but it will be recalled that except for the Yorktown campaign Washington's army engaged in no decisive operations after the summer of 1778; and that the first winter before Boston was spent by him in the commodious quarters of the Cragie (Longfellow) House at Cambridge, and the winter of 1781-82 at Philadelphia. Mrs. Washington joined him sooner or later each winter, and was with him continuously after the Yorktown campaign until just before the final scene of the occupation of New York City, so that even during the stress and misery of the war home life was not entirely denied to him.

At New York and Philadelphia the mansions Washington occupied as President were evidently both office and home. The social obligations the position imposed would have required the presence of Mrs. Washington even if there could have been any thought of separation. Also the children, Nellie and George Washington Parke, were with them there. However, the home relations were circumscribed by the official requirements, so that the family was glad to journey from Philadelphia to Mount Vernon whenever circumstances permitted.

CHURCH RELATIONS

The fifth pamphlet in this series is devoted to the story of Washington as a religious man, and sets forth his interest in the church and his services to it. In this land of freedom of faith, from the very beginning home and church have been intertwined and related.

As a side light on Washington's habit of piety, the following comments are interesting, though traditional: "It was her [Washington's mother's] life long habit to rise at dawn and spend the first hour of the day in silent thought to prepare herself for the family worship and the day's events. Her eldest son, George, was only eleven when his father died but upon him she placed the old patriarchal duty of saying grace at table and prayers at night and morning. From this early age his mother expected him to assume and carry such responsibility as the circumstances of life brought him. Under her pious guidance he could not have evaded any service that she deemed her duty."

Washington's interest in the church was deep and sincere. He not only attended divine services frequently both at home and abroad, but he worked for the church. The church building at Pohick (Truro), a beautiful structure still standing and in use, was the result of the labors of Washington and Mason. George Washington was a member of the vestry of the Truro for eleven years. That body held thirty-one meetings during that interval of which Washington attended twenty-three. He was absent only because of sickness, attendance at the General Assembly, or distance beyond reach.

In Washington's day going to church was not the simple matter it is today. Distances were great if measured in time of travel. Roads were often little more than mud wallows. Washington was thoughtful of animals, and would not urge his horses over or through impossible roads. His diaries record many journeys to Pohick and Alexandria to attend divine services.

LATER FRIENDS

When Washington in 1774 stepped into the wider arena and became the most conspicuous personage in it, he was brought in contact with men not only from all portions of the colonies and the United States into which they grew, but with characters from Europe as well. From this resulted not only that general reverence which he could not help realizing and appreciating even while deprecating, but cherished personal associations which continued throughout his life. Most of these had their birth in the army, and with the younger comrades in arms. Among his generals, Greene and Knox were favorites of his heart as well as approved of by his mind. He sincerely mourned the untimely death of the former, and was happy in having the latter as a member of his Cabinet in later years. His greatest attachment, however, was for Lafayette, the young French nobleman who offered his services in aid of the Republic, who was dearer perhaps than any other person outside Washington's immediate family. He had his chief's trust and confidence without limit, and was addressed in the most intimate terms. Washington gave his affection to certain members of his military family, especially Hamilton, David Humphreys, Robert Hanson Harrison, Tench Tilghman, and John Laurens. Hamilton did not appreciate the regard while Washington's aide as much as the others did. Laurens, with the high chivalry of his Huguenot blood, knew no bounds in his attachment to the General. Henry Lee, Light Horse Harry, though never on Washington's staff, was also a favorite, but in his case there had been a family familiarity for many years. John Cadwalader, though a somewhat older man, and a member of the Philadelphia aristocracy, showed his regard by challenging General Conway as John Laurens did General Charles Lee because they had been false to their commander-in-chief. Among the civilians, sage Benjamin Franklin, Gouverneur Morris, John Jay, Robert Morris, and Henry Laurens, the father of John, had Washington's regard as well as appreciation; but to none of them did he display the warmth of heart which he had for some of his military friends.

CHRISTMAS

In colonial Virginia, as in the Motherland, the social season held no more precious joys than those of the Christmas holidays. For a week before and after, the planters devoted much of their time to the round of balls, dances, dinners, house parties, week-end guests, hunting, and sleighing. The climax, of course, was Christmas Eve and Christmas Day.

Mansion and humble home were garlanded with greens. The tables groaned with the fat of the land; turkeys fattened for weeks for the date, hams cured as only Virginia can cure them, wild fowl hung until highly flavored, ducks from the marshes, and breads, pastries, vegetables, and the preserved fruits which were the pride of housewives high and low, provided a fare which, if different, was none the less in keeping with the traditions of Yule in England.

Of all the Christmases at Mount Vernon, none could have been happier for the General than that of 1783, and perhaps it was typical of all. On December 23 Congress assembled in the State House at Annapolis, where Washington had arrived four days before and where Mrs. Washington had met him, to receive the general's resignation as commander-in-chief of the Continental Army. He left Annapolis the day following the short ceremony which marked the close of the last act of the great drama of the Revolution, departing as a private citizen for the beloved home on the Potomac.

Washington reached Mount Vernon on Christmas Eve. He had left his home merely a man—a strong man, a man believed in by his country, a man untried in any such fire as was to scorch the world with its heat during the heartbreaking days of the war. He returned to it the victorious general, the savior of his country, the man to whom not only the states but the world paid tribute. As he approached the home he loved, after the prolonged absence, its hospitable doors flung wide, fires burning, song and joy that the Master was home filling the air, did he think of that other Christmas time when he crossed the Delaware or the terrible Christmas spent at Valley Forge?

Men write least of their happiest hours. Little has come down to us of that joyous Christmas, but a young girl guest at Mount Vernon in a letter to friends in Fredericksburg told in the briefest form the story of that home-coming: "The servants were in great glee. They came from all quarters to get a glimpse of their idol. The General, much affected, received them on the front veranda; some (the old ones) were in tears, others were in raptures of mirth."

LAST DAYS

To a friend in Philadelphia, Nellie Custis wrote after Washington retired from the Presidency in 1797: "We arrived here on Wednesday, March 15, without any accidents after a tedious and fatiguing journey of seven days. Grandpa is very well and much pleased with being once more farmer Washington."

Washington was, indeed, happy to be once more "farmer Washington." There was much to do. Farm buildings had fallen into disrepair. The old plantation system which had run so smoothly had gradually become disorganized. Shortly after his return to the beloved home he wrote to his friend, Secretary of War McHenry, "I find myself in the situation nearly of a young beginner; for, although I have not houses to build (except one, which I must erect for the accommodation and security of my Military, Civil, and private Papers, which are voluminous and may be interesting), yet I have not one, or scarcely anything else about me that does not require considerable repairs. In a word, I am already surrounded by Joiners, Masons, Painters, &c., &c.; and such is my anxiety to get out of their hands, that I have scarcely a room to put a friend into, or to sit in myself, without the music of hammers, or the odoriferous smell of paint."

Not until the repairs were completed could Washington settle down for his last placid years. He looked forward to them with pleasure, and with a sense of duty well done. He said in a letter to Oliver Wolcott: "To make and sell a little flour annually, to repair houses (going fast to ruin), to build one for the security of my papers of a public nature, and to amuse myself in agricultural and rural pursuits, will constitute employment for the few years I have to remain on this terrestrial globe. If, to these, I could now and then meet the friends I esteem, it would fill the measure and add zest to my enjoyments; but if ever this happens, it must be under my own vine and fig-tree, as I do not think it probable that I shall go beyond twenty miles from them."

Again he wrote to James McHenry: "I begin my diurnal course with the sun; . . . if my hirelings are not in their places at that time I send them messages expressive of my sorrow for their indisposition; . . . having put these wheels into motion, I examine the state of things further; and the more they are probed, the deeper I find the wounds are which my buildings have sustained by an absence and neglect of eight years; by the time I have accomplished these

matters, breakfast . . . is ready; . . . this being over, I mount my horse and ride round my farms, which employs me until it is time to dress for dinner, at which I rarely miss seeing strange faces, . . ."

To his nephew Lawrence Lewis, son of his sister Betty, he wrote: "Whenever it is convenient to you to make this place your home I shall be glad to see you. . . . As both your aunt and I are in the decline of life and regular in our habits, especially in our hours of rising and going to bed, I require some person (fit and proper) to ease me of the trouble of entertaining company, particularly of nights, as it is my inclination to retire (unless prevented by very particular company, I always do retire) either to bed or to my study soon after candle light. In taking these duties (which hospitality obliges one to bestow on company) off my hands, it would render me a very acceptable service."

LAST VISITORS

Even in those last days he was not freed from public cares, for the threat of French War had again drawn him into his country's service as lieutenant-general of the armies. However, though he gave much thought and correspondence to matters of organization and offices, he was not obliged to leave his home except for a visit to Philadelphia in the latter part of 1798 to consult the President and Secretary of War. So that in the main those last years were tranquil ones, occupied with the affairs of his beloved estate, and the intimacies of home life. If his fame followed him into his retreat, and imposed upon his hospitality the demands of strangers, there were compensations in the visits of the real and tried friends. The letter which Mrs. Edward Carrington wrote from Mount Vernon on November 22, 1799, less than a month before General Washington died, makes a fitting, final record of this:

"We arrived at this remarkable mansion in perfect safety, where we experienced every mark of hospitality and kindness that the good old General's continued friendship to Col. C. could lead us to expect; his reception of my husband was that of a Brother; he took us each by the hand, and with a warmth of expression not to be described, pressed mine, and told me that I had conferred a favor never to be forgotten in bringing his old friend to see him, then bidding a servant to call the ladies, entertained us most facetiously till they appeared.

"It is wonderful after a life spent as these good people have necessarily spent theirs to see them in retirement assume domestic manners that prevail in our country, when, but a year since they were forced to forego all these innocent delights which are so congenial to their years and tastes, to sacrifice to the parade of the drawing-room and levee. The recollection of these lost days as Mrs. W. calls them seems to fill her with regret, but the extensive knowledge she has gained in this general intercourse with persons from all parts of the world, has made her a most interesting companion, and having a vastly retentive memory, she presents an entire history of half a century. . . .

"Even friends who make a point of visiting him are left much to themselves, indeed scarcely see him from breakfast to dinner, unless he engages them in a ride, which is very agreeable to him; but from dinner till tea our time is most charmingly spent. Indeed one evening the General was so fascinating and drew my husband out into so many old stories relating to several campaigns where they had been much together."

Thus, at home in the beloved estate, surrounded by friends, the wife of his youth by his side, engaged in the small but to him important tasks of looking after buildings, the farm, the stock, arranging his papers, talking to visitors, receiving the adulation of an admiring world, Washington, at last at peace, passed the remaining days of his life; days not to be long, but a period filled with the quiet happiness of knowing he had measured up to one of the greatest responsibilities ever put on the shoulders of mortal man.

Washington's home life shows him as a lover of the fireside; a domestic-minded householder; a man careful of his property, but generous with his servants; a devoted husband; a father whose loving kindness was no less that the relationship was not of blood; a man who loved the outdoors, the earth, the growing grain, the wild game; a hospitable man who offered the best he had in happiness that there were many who enjoyed breaking bread with him; a man to whom church and divine worship were a part of life. His home was refuge and a haven of peace and joy; he left it with regret, he returned to it as to a heaven on earth. No glimpses we have of the great warrior and statesman across the years are more intimate, none more charming, than those of Washington the husband, the devoted father of children not his own, the host, the home lover.

Part II
Fraternal Life

FREEMASONRY

So obviously a man's man, a soldier, a statesman, a planter, a diplomat, a thinker of great thoughts of government and his people, it is no wonder that the fraternal side of life made to Washington a powerful appeal; no wonder that the Ancient Craft of Freemasonry should have become so interwoven with his life. But particularly is it natural that a man who so loved his home, and whose religious feeling was so strong, should turn to the lodge for this particular variety of spiritual strength, which, to many, comes from no other place.

The effect upon character produced by a man's religion and church affiliations can only be measured by the yard stick of a man's reputation; few great men have set down in black and white those things of the spirit which, intimate and personal, are the very man himself. The same may be said of a man's Freemasonry. What it is "in his heart" can only be judged by the externals. Judging by this standard Washington frequently expressed his love and veneration for his Masonry and his lodge; many of his closest friends and associates, his generals and military aides in the Revolution were of the Ancient Craft, and his whole life of consecration and service to his fellowmen carried out the ideals which radiate from the Masonic Altar.

Members of the Ancient Craft understand why Freemasonry made so great an appeal to the great leader but anyone who will read even a little of the history of Freemasonry will readily comprehend why this body of truth, this organization of great teaching and high endeavor, this crystallization of moral ideals, was at once a magnet and a comfort to Washington.

MOTHER GRAND LODGE

Seventeen Hundred and Seventeen is the dividing line between before and after; the old Freemasonry and the new; an operative Craft slowly expiring and one which began to grow with a new vitality; between the last lingering remains of operative Freemasonry and a Craft wholly speculative.

No man knows the events which led up to the formation of the first Grand Lodge in London. No minutes were kept during its first six years. The Constitutions, first published in 1723, were republished fifteen years after. In this second edition of 1738 is only a meager record of the first meetings of the Grand Lodge.

In modern perspective a Grand Lodge is as much a part of the existing order of things as a state or federal government. In 1717 it was a new idea, accompanied by many other new ideas. When Washington became a Mason, Virginia had no Grand Lodge. Some men, some set of men, saw that if the ancient Order were not to die it must be given a new life through a new organization. Doubtless they were influenced by Mother Kilwinning Lodge of Scotland, which had assumed and exercised certain functions in regard to her daughter lodges, all of which had Kilwinning as a part of their name and apparently of their obedience.

The newly formed Grand Lodge in London went the whole way. It proposed to and did take command of its lodges. It branched out beyond the jurisdiction originally proposed "within ten miles of London" and invaded the Provinces. It gave enormous powers to the Grand Master. It prohibited the working of the "Master's Part" in private lodges, thus throwing back to the ancient Annual Assemblies. It divided the Craft into Entered Apprentices and Fellowcrafts. It resolved "against all Politicks as what never yet conduced to the welfare of the Lodge and never will." This was a highly important declaration at the time when every organization in England was taking part in politics, especially in the Jacobite struggle against the House of Hanover.

This prohibition of "politicks" in the lodge had much to do with making Freemasonry a refuge to men like Washington, Marshall, Lafayette, Revere, Warren, Franklin—statesmen and soldiers who had enough of politics in daily life and must have looked with great pleasure on meetings of their lodges where politics were not discussed. What a relief it must have been to the great leader to mingle "on the level" with men of all political faiths, secure in the knowledge that here was one place where neither religious nor political opinions could divide mind from mind!

THE RELIGION OF FREEMASONRY

Finally, Grand Lodge erased the ancient Charge "to be true to God and Holy Church" and substituted this Charge:

"A Mason is oblig'd, by his Tenure to obey the moral Law; and if he rightly understands the Art, he will never be a stupid Atheist, nor an irreligious Libertine. But though in ancient Times Masons were charg'd in every Country to be of the Religion of that Country or Nation; whatever it was, yet 'tis now thought more expedient only to oblige them to that Religion in which all Men agree, leaving their particular Opinions to themselves; that is to be *good Men and true*, or Men of Honour and Honesty, by whatever Denominations or Persuasions they may be distinguish'd; whereby Masonry becomes the *Center* of *Union,* and the Means of conciliating true Friendship among Persons that must have remain'd at a perpetual Distance."

This Charge was of unparalleled importance; it founded modern Speculative Freemasonry on the rock of non-sectarianism and the brotherhood of all men who believe in a common Father, regardless of His name, or the way in which He is worshipped.

Here again the Mother Grand Lodge did something which was profoundly to affect the First President. That Washington was deeply and sincerely religious is doubted by none who read his diaries and letters. When he could not go to one church, he went to another, and worshipped apparently with equal satisfaction, no matter at what altar he kneeled. It seems obvious, then, that the Craft which offered only the doctrine of a universal Father, leaving to men to name Him as they would, a place where each brother might worship as he would, must have made mighty appeal to Washington by this very tolerant and broad-minded attitude. All Washington's life was a demonstration of his belief in the equality and the brotherhood of men under one common Father. The wonder would have been if he had not appreciated the Order of which those principles are foundation stones.

Between 1717 and 1751 the Craft spread rapidly, not only in England but on the continent and in the colonies, especially colonial America, where both time and people, conditions and social life provided fallow ground for the seeds of Freemasonry. But in spite of a new life and the wise counsels of brethren who restricted the acts if not the power of the new Grand Lodge, all was not plain sailing. Dissensions appeared. Causes of friction, if not numerous, were important and went deep. In 1751 a rival Grand Lodge was formed. It came into being with a brilliant stroke, for it chose the name "The Most Antient and Honorable Fraternity of Free and Accepted Masons." Calling itself "Antient" and the other body "Modern" at once enlisted the support of hundreds of brethren who did not go beneath the surface to learn which was really which. Then arose this peculiar and confused terminology; the original, the older, the most ancient Grand Lodge, was called the "Modern" Grand Lodge, and the newer body was called "Antient."

The new Grand Lodge kept the religious issue alive; by implication it made the "Moderns" seem anti-religious. The "Antients" were a Christian body and its Constitutions and its documents contained many distinctly Christian sentiments and references.

The benefits which came from this schism seem today to be greater than the evils. When one Grand Lodge established lodges on war ships, the other formed army lodges which carried Freemasonry to far places; when one body started a school for girls, the other organized a school for boys—both still in existence, by the way!—as one Grand Lodge reached out to the Provinces the other cultivated Scotland and Ireland. Both worked indefatigably in the American colonies.

The final reconciliation took place in Freemasons' Hall in London, on St. John's Day, December 27, 1813. The two Grand Lodges filed together into the Hall; the articles of Union were read, the Duke of Kent retired as Grand Master in favor of the Duke of Sussex, who was elected Grand Master of the United Grand Lodge.

A united Freemasonry agreed that forever more it would have no religious tests and would "welcome to her doors and admit to her privileges worthy men of all creeds and of every race." The "Antient" Grand Lodge, which had been so aggressively Christian, made no difficulties over this significant and important ground of difference.

In 1815 a new Book of Constitutions proclaimed to all the world forever the non-sectarian character of Freemasonry in this Charge concerning God and religion:

"Let a man's religion or mode of worship be what it may, he is not excluded from the Order, provided he believes in the glorious Architect of heaven and earth, and practice the sacred duties of morality."

IN THE NEW WORLD

Freemasonry came to America just before Washington was born, as an organization in which no religious tests were involved, except the fundamental belief in the Great Architect of the Universe. It taught morality, brotherly love, mutual help. It inculcated patriotism. It selected its members most carefully for character, reliability, manhood. It speedily became a meeting ground for men of diverse minds, characters, ideals, who found then, as men have always found, that in the lodge where all meet "on the level" the necessary social, monetary, and other distinctions of civil life could drop away and allow mind to meet with mind and man with man, untroubled by artificial barriers.

Naturally this appeal to Washington was great; Washington, who proved so well how democratic an aristocrat may be, how the qualities of heart and mind transcend those of influence and wealth.

FREEMASONRY IN WASHINGTON'S DAY

With the present Grand Lodges in every state, with Masonic Temples of beauty and permanency dotting the land everywhere, with a great body of Masonic literature, Masonic libraries, historians and research workers, with jurisdictional lines tightly drawn and a Fraternity organized, governed, and conducted the world over in unity in essentials, it is rather difficult to picture the Fraternity as it was in Washington's day. The brethren of the colonies necessarily conducted their affairs with due regard to the physical, governmental, and economic conditions which surrounded them. Travel was difficult. Roads were few, poor, and often dangerous. Railroads, telegraph, the telephone were unknown, and mail slow and often unreliable. The ties which bound the colonies to the mother country, strong in fraternal feeling and social intercourse, economically grew weaker as the eighteenth century passed its half way mark. Freemasonry was then far less democratic and all-inclusive than it is today; common dangers, the need of an intimate and select association of leaders, and the usage of the times, added to the schism in the Mother Grand Lodge of England, combined to make secrecy in non-essentials seem as important as in the real *aporhetta* of the Craft. The result is a paucity of Masonic record of early days which is more or less the despair of the historian.

Unquestionably the conduct of the Craft when Washington was raised, as an organization, was far less formal than today. Meetings were often called by word of mouth. Expenses were born as much by fines and by contributions from those present at the meeting as from fixed dues. Meeting places were often in taverns and inns (following the early custom of English lodges). During the Revolution lodge meetings were often held in tents, in private homes, even in barns.

During the late colonial days (1750 to 1760) the colonies of Maryland and Virginia flowered to their full growth as the homes of aristocrats who carried into colonial life the principles and practice of the better classes of English society from which they sprang. *Noblesse oblige* was a watchword. Dignity, hospitality, mutual respect, and personal independence were considered of the highest importance.

The Freemasonry of the times naturally partook of the general character of the life surrounding it. Brethren lived well; Masonic brethren were convivial and Masonic banquets frequent. Society was exclusive and bound with the obligations of class and caste; the Freemasonry of Washington's time was small and select. Travel was difficult; the personal independence of planters was highly esteemed. Hence Lodges met infrequently, and often with no better authority than the mutual desire of brethren living in the same neighborhood to foregather together about the Three Great Lights.

Jacob Hugo Tatsch (*Freemasonry in the Thirteen Colonies*) says:

"American Freemasonry, like its progenitor in old England, is the outgrowth of the times in which it had its roots. It was not superimposed upon the New World as a finished and perfect institution; rather, it was the survival of principles which men had learned in their association as builders, both literally and figuratively. Never, in the history of the Craft, have Freemasons been found assembled in questionable places. The inns and taverns which we may now regard askance are dubious locations only in the light of the present day standards; the free and convivial habits of early Freemasons are only a reflection of the times as a whole. Forced to meet in public houses, because there were no other places, the brethren withdrew to upper chambers by themselves, and carried on their labors safe from the eyes and ears of the curious. The excellent reputation which Freemasons of all ages have enjoyed is proof of the worth of the institution, for the prestige of the Craft is only the sum total of that possessed by the individual members. Friendship, morality and brotherly love have always been fostered where Freemasons fore-gathered. The story of the Craft in America furnishes no exceptions."

E. A.—F. C.—M. M.

It was against this background that George Washington, aged twenty, became an Entered Apprentice, a Fellow Craft, and a Master Mason in 1752 and 1753.

From the minutes of "The Lodge at Fredericksburg" (Now Fredericksburg Lodge, No. 4) the following is quoted verbatim:

4th Novbr. Charles Lewis
     George Washington
3rd March George Washington pass'd fellow Craft.

4th August 5753 Which Day the Lodge being Assembled present

R. Wpl. Daniel Campbell,	Transactions of the
I. Neilson, S.W.	Evening are——
Rot. Halkerston, J.W.	
George Washinton, (Sic)	George Washington rais'd
James Strakan	Master Mason
Alex'r Wodrow, Secretary pro. Temp.	
Thoms. Robertson,	Thomas James Entd. an Apprentice
William McWilliams, Treasr.	

(The date, "5753," is "1753" according to the Masonic chronology which adds four thousand years to the Christian era.)

"THE LODGE AT FREDERICKSBURG"

The first meeting of the Lodge at Fredericksburg was held September 1, 1752 (o. s.) Modern lodges record in their minutes full information of their first meetings but, as has been noted, the practice in the early days of Freemasonry in the colonies was to record only the barest essentials, and not always even these. Hence the first minutes show only a list of names of officers and members.

We do not know by what authority the Lodge at Fredericksburg held its first meetings. Hayden, *Washington and His Masonic Compeers,* states that the lodge was organized "under authority from Thomas Oxnard, Provincial Grand Master at Boston." Thomas Oxnard was Provincial Grand Master at Boston when the Lodge at Fredericksburg first met, and an oral tradition has been handed down from generation to generation that the Lodge at Fredericksburg worked under a dispensation from the Grand Lodge of Massachusetts.

Whether the tradition reflects a fact, or whether the brethren in Fredericksburg met and formed a lodge by mutual consent, under what was then "immemorial usage," they did meet and did Masonic work for nearly five years before they felt the need for "an ample charter."

On April 4, 1757, the Lodge of Fredericksburg appropriated seven pounds to pay the expenses of obtaining this instrument, and on July 21 of the following year, the Grand Lodge of Scotland issued that historic instrument which is now so dearly prized by Fredericksburg Lodge, No. 4. The charter is signed by "Geo. Frayser, Dep'ty G Master. Rich'd Tod, Sub. G.M. David Ross, S.G.W. Will'm McGhie, J.G.W." The charter provides, among other things, that the brethren:

"Record in their Books this Charter, with their own Private Regulations and By-laws and their whole acts and proceedings from time to time as they occur and not to desert their said Lodge hereby Constituted or form themselves into separate meetings without the Consent and Approbation of their Master and Wardens for the time being."

In spite of his mandatory language, the secretary failed to record the charter in his minutes! Luckily, the charter itself is in an excellent state of preservation despite its one hundred and seventy-five years of existence and its danger of destruction through the wars of 1776, 1812, and 1861-65.

BY-LAWS

The quaint by-laws (adopted 1769) reflect the character of the Masonry of Washington's time. They are short enough to quote in full:

Rules and Regulations for Fredericksburg Lodge

"1. That the meetings in course be the first Friday of every month, from March to September at 6 o'clock in the evening, and from September to March at 5 o'clock in the afternoon.

"2. Every member of the Lodge shall pay three Shillings Quarterly for expenses thereof, Vist, at lady day, Midsummer, Michaelmas, and Christmas—Extra Expenses to be defrayed by such members as are present on these Occasions.

"3. Every new made Brother shall pay the Fee of three Pistoles for being admitted to the first degree, The Fee of one Pistole for being passed to the Second and the same sum on being raised to the third. These Fees must be received the night of his admission, passing, or raising, or the Brothers who recommend to be responsible for them.

"4. Any Brother not made in this Lodge, Petitioning to become a member thereof, shall upon his being received as such (after due examination) pay the Fee of one Pistole. But Brethren made here may become members without further Fee than that of their admission.

"5. No visiting Brother is to be admitted without due Examination, unless vouched for by a Brother present; nor more than once without paying One Shilling and Three Pence.

"6. No person to be admitted to become a Mason in this Lodge under the age of Twenty One years on any account whatever, being Contrary to the Constitutions of Masonry, nor without the unanimous Consent of the Lodge by Ballot.

"7. All Fees and Quarterages to be paid to the Treasurer for the time being. His Acc't to be Annually examined and Balanced on the Night his Office expires."

It is particularly interesting to note by-law Number 6, which provides that no one is "to be admitted to become a Mason" in the Lodge under twenty-one years of age. Washington was only twenty when he received the degrees, sixteen years before these By-laws were adopted.

MASONIC LIFE

Any condensed history of Washington's fraternal life must necessarily omit most of his Masonic correspondence and many occasions which have Masonic significance, even if of minor importance.

Not much is known of Washington's Masonic life during the quarter century following his raising. Tradition puts him in various English Army Lodges during this time, but the paucity of early records prevents definite statements. While living at Mount Vernon he was miles from the nearest lodge, and travel was difficult in those days. Nevertheless his presence at a number of lodge meetings in Fredericksburg is recorded, and he attended a number of public Masonic functions, such as the Festival of St. John the Baptist, June 24, 1779, with American Union Lodge at the Robinson House on the Hudson, New York; the Festival of St. John the Evangelist, December 27, 1779, with American Union Lodge at Morris Hotel, Morristown, New Jersey; the Festival of St. John the Evangelist, December 27, 1782, with King Solomon's Lodge at Poughkeepsie, New York; the Festival of St. John the Baptist, June 24, 1784, with Lodge No. 39 at Alexandria, Virginia, and the Masonic funeral of Brother William Ramsay, February 12, 1785, at Alexandria.

Most important Masonically is his acceptance of the Charter Mastership of the Lodge at Alexandria.

For Alexandria, Virginia, was the background for much of Washington's private life. Christ Church, one of the many in which he showed devotional interest, was (and is) there. In 1766 Washington was elected one of the trustees of the town; here lived many of his personal friends. Here, too, was organized Alexandria Lodge No. 39 (later to become Alexandria-Washington Lodge No. 22.)

In 1782 six brethren of Alexandria petitioned the Provincial Grand Lodge of Pennsylvania for a charter; in spite of the fact that the Grand Lodge of Virginia was organized in 1777-8, the Provincial Grand Lodge of Pennsylvania, under the Grand Lodge of England, granted the charter.

According to the *Proceedings, Grand Lodge of Pennsylvania,* February 3, 1783:

"A petition being preferred to this Grand Lodge on the 2nd Sept. last, from several brethren of Alexandria, in Virginia, for a warrant to hold a Lodge there, which was ordered to lie over to the next communication, in consequence of Bro. Adam, the proposed Master thereof, being found to possess his knowledge of Masonry in a clandestine manner, since which the said Bro. Adams, having gone through the several steps of Ancient Masonry in Lodge No. 2, under the Jurisdiction of this R. W. Grand Lodge, further prays that a warrant may now be granted for the purposes mentioned in said petition.

"Ordered, That the prayer of said petition be complied with, and that the Secretary present Brother Adams with a warrant to hold a Lodge of Ancient Masons in Alexandria, in Virginia, to be numbered 39.

"Bro. Robert Adam was then duly recommended, and presented in form to the R. W. Grand Master in the chair, for installation as Master of Lodge No. 39, to be held in the borough of Alexandria, in Fairfax County, Virginia, and was accordingly installed as such."

The word "clandestine" falls with unhappy significance upon modern Masonic ears, but it did not in those days mean quite the same thing as it does to Masons of this age. Prior to the "Lodge of Reconciliation" and the formation of the United Grand Lodge of England in 1813, the two Grand Bodies of England, the "Moderns" (who were the older) and the "Antients" (who were the younger, schismatic body) each considered the other "clandestine." Brother Adam's Mother Lodge is not known, but as he lived for a time in Annapolis, where a "Modern" lodge worked, it is probable it was here that he received the degrees which the Grand Lodge of Pennsylvania ("Antients") considered "clandestine." Transition of Masons from lodges of one obedience to those of the other was neither infrequent nor difficult, so that "clandestine" could not then have had the connotation of irregularity and disgrace which it has with Freemasons of today.

ALEXANDRIA LODGE CHARTERED BY PENNSYLVANIA

The Lodge at Alexandria was chartered in 1783 and met for the first time on February 25, when four of the petitioners and two members of the Grand Lodge of Pennsylvania opened on the Entered Apprentice's Degree, read the charter giving them life and the number 39, and proceeded to exercise jurisdiction "in the borough of Alexandria or within four miles of the same."

In a very few years the brethren of Alexandria Lodge No. 39 were informed that the Provincial Grand Lodge of Pennsylvania was initiating steps to become sovereign and independent of the Grand Lodge of England. Alexandria Lodge was intensely interested in the proposal, but somewhat doubtful as to its Masonic propriety. The Grand Lodge of Pennsylvania stated, as one reason for the proposed step, that as this country was independent of all other countries, Masonic lodges should also be independent, in order that Masonic obligations might never conflict with those owed to the mother country. To this Alexandria Lodge No. 39 returned this fine and spirited answer:

"That we are as separate and independent of Great Britain, as of Denmark, is politically true, and as we owe them no subjection as a State or Nation, how can the subjects of the one owe any of the subjects of the other? If it is answered, none; then, query, how this political truth may, with propriety be applied to the Masonic Order, who, as they do not intermeddle with State matters, ought not to draw arguments from thence to dismember themselves from the jurisdiction of those they hold under, except from similar burdens, or impositions exacted inconsistent with Masonry. But those, no doubt, are the matters to be discussed. We have only to request, (In case we should stand unrepresented,) that you will inform us of the result of your deliberations."

The Grand Lodge of Pennsylvania dissolved and reformed, a Sovereign and Independent Jurisdiction (1786). The new Grand Lodge required all charters issued by its predecessor turned in, that new ones might be issued. This did not suit Alexandria Lodge, No. 39. The Grand Lodge of Virginia had been formed shortly before (1778). At first holding aloof from the new Virginia Grand Lodge (many lodges in Virginia did the same, to satisfy themselves that the Virginia Grand Lodge would live and grow) but now faced with the parting of the ways, Alexandria Lodge decided to petition the Grand Lodge of its own state for a charter, rather than receive a new one at the hands of Pennsylvania.

CHARTER WORSHIPFUL MASTER

Right here occurred that step in the affairs of Masonry which was to have so far-reaching an effect upon the Fraternity. Desiring to honor the man and brother Mason who had delivered the nation from bondage and become the foremost citizen of the new country, the brethren of Alexandria asked Washington's consent to name him as their first Worshipful Master under the new Charter.

The Masonic world knows the result. On April 28, 1788, Edmund Randolph, "Governor of the Commonwealth aforesaid and Grand Master of the Most Ancient and Honorable Society of Freemasons within the same, by and with the consent of the Grand Lodge of Virginia," issued a charter to the petitioning brethren, constituting them a lodge of Freemasons "by the name, title and designation of Alexandria Lodge, No. 22." George Washington was named as the Worshipful Master and was unanimously elected Worshipful Master to succeed himself December 20, 1788, serving in all about twenty months. He was inaugurated as President April 30, 1789, thus becoming the first and so far the only brother to be President of the Nation and Master of his Lodge at the same time.

After Washington's death, the brethren desired to change the name to Alexandria-Washington Lodge, No. 22. The Grand Lodge of Virginia consented, and asked for the old charter, in which was named George Washington, "late General and Commander in chief of the forces of the United States of America" as the first Master, so that a new charter might be issued.

Alexandria Lodge, No. 22, did not wish to give up this historic instrument, nor did the plea it made fall upon unsympathetic ears. The Grand Lodge of Virginia permitted the Lodge to retain the old charter, and yet change its name; the Grand Lodge Resolution effecting this unusual act reads:

"Resolved, That the said Lodge be permitted to assume the said name, and that it be henceforth denominated the Alexandria-Washington Lodge, No. 22, and that an authenticated copy of this resolution be attached to their said Charter." And Alexandria-Washington Lodge No. 22, it has remained from that day to this.

LAYING THE CAPITOL CORNER STONE

George Washington was always a busily occupied man. The cares of the Presidency, the duties of his military service, the direction of his personal fortune and his estate at Mount Vernon, his large correspondence, his home life and church associations left him little leisure. The wonder is not that he attended Masonic functions so seldom, but that his complicated and much-engaged life permitted him to foregather so much with his brethren, write so many Masonic letters, consider his Freemasonry so important.

That it was vital in his eyes has been shown in a hundred ways, but perhaps never more than on that occasion which links together Washington, the Mason, and Washington, the President, the laying of the corner stone of the United States Capitol, September 18, 1793.

This ceremony, so important both historically and Masonically, was conducted by the Grand Lodge of Maryland, which body invited President Washington to act as Grand Master *pro tem*. It was reported in the *Columbian Mirror and Alexandria Gazette* of September 23, 1793, as follows:

"On Wednesday, one of the grandest Masonic processions took place, for the purpose of laying the cornerstone of the Capitol of the United States, which, perhaps, was ever exhibited on the like important occasion. About ten o'clock, Lodge No. 9 was visited by that congregation so graceful to the craft, Lodge No. 22, of Virginia, with all their officers and regalia; and directly afterwards appeared on the southern banks of the grand river Potomac, one of the finest companies of Volunteer Artillery that has been lately seen, parading to receive the President of the United States, who shortly came in sight with his suite, to whom the artillery paid their military honors, and his Excellency and suite crossed the river and was received in Maryland by the officers and brethren of No. 22, Virginia, and No. 9, Maryland, whom the President headed, preceeded by a band of music; the rear brought up by the Alexandria Volunteer Artillery, with grand solemnity of march, proceeded to the President's Square, in the city of Washington, where they were met and saluted by No. 15, of the city of Washington, in all their elegant badges and clothing, headed by Brother Joseph Clarke, Rt. Wor. G. M. p. t., and conducted to a large lodge prepared for the purpose of their reception. After a short space of time, by the vigilance of Brother Clotworthy Stephenson, Grand Marshall p. t., the brotherhood and other bodies were disposed in a second order of procession, which took place amidst a brilliant crowd of spectators of both sexes, according to the following arrangement, viz.:

The Surveying Department of the city of Washington.
Mayor and Corporation of Georgetown.
Virginia Artillery.
Commissioners of the city of Washington, and their Attendants.
Stone-cutters—Mechanics.
Masons of the first degree.
Bible, etc., on grand cushions.
Deacons, with staffs of office.
Masons of the second degree.
Stewards, with wands.
Masons of the third degree.
Wardens, with truncheons.
Secretaries, with tools of office.
Past Masters, with their regalia.

MASONIC PROCESSION

At the laying of the corner stone of the National Capitol (1793)

Treasurers, with their jewels.
Band of music.
Lodge No. 22, Virginia, disposed in their own order.
Corn, wine, and oil.
Grand Master pro tem. Brother George Washington, and Worshipful Master of No. 22, of Virginia.
Grand Sword Bearer.

"The procession marched two abreast, in the greatest solemn dignity, with music playing, drums beating, colors flying, and spectators rejoicing, from the President's Square to the Capitol, in the city of Washington, where the Grand Marshal ordered a halt, and directed each file in the procession to incline two steps, one to the right and one to the left, and face each other, which formed a hollow oblong square, through which the Grand Sword-Bearer led the van; followed by the Grand Master *pro tem.* on the left, the President of the United States in the center, and the Worshipful Master of No. 22, Virginia, on the right; all the other orders that composed the procession advanced in the reverse of their order of march from the President's Square to the southeast corner of the Capitol, and the artillery filed off to a destined ground to display their maneuvers and discharge their cannon. The President of the United States, the Grand Master *pro tem.*, and the Worshipful Master of No. 22, taking their stand to the east of a large stone, and all the Craft forming a circle westward, stood a short time in solemn order.

"The artillery discharged a volley. The Grand Marshal delivered the Commissioners

a large silver plate, with an inscription thereon, which the Commissioners ordered to be read, and was as follows:

" 'This southeast corner-stone of the Capitol of the United States of America in the city of Washington, was laid on the 18th day of September, 1793, in the thirteenth year of American Independence, in the first year of the second term of the presidency of George Washington, whose virtues in the civil administration of his country have been as conspicuous and beneficial as his military valor and prudence have been useful in establishing her liberties, and in the year of Masonry 5793, by the President of the United States, in concert with the Grand Lodge of Maryland, several Lodges under its jurisdiction, and Lodge No. 22, from Alexandria, Virginia. Thomas Johnson, David Steuart and Daniel Carroll, Commissioners. Joseph Clark, R.W.G.M. *pro tem.*, and James Hoban and Stephen Hallate, Architects. Colin Williamson, Master Mason.'

"The artillery discharged a volley. The plate was then delivered to the President, who, attended by the Grand Master *pro tem.* and three Most Worshipful Masters, descended to the cavazion trench and deposited the plate, and laid it on the corner-stone of the Capitol of the United States of America, on which were deposited corn, wine and oil, when the whole congregation joined in reverential prayer, which was succeeded by Masonic chanting honors, and a volley from the artillery.

"The President of the United States, and his attendant brethren, ascended from the

cavazion to the east of the corner-stone, and there the Grand Master *pro tem.*, elevated on a triple rostrum, delivered an oration fitting the occasion, which was received with brotherly love and commendation. At intervals during the delivery of the oration, several volleys were discharged by the artillery. The ceremony ended in prayer, Masonic chanting honors, and a 15-volley from the artillery.

"The whole company retired to an extensive booth, where an ox of five hundred pounds weight was barbecued, of which the company generally partook, with every abundance of other recreation. The festival concluded with fifteen successive volleys from the artillery, whose military discipline and maneuvers merit every commendation. Before dark the whole company departed with joyful hopes of the production of their labor."

Some confusion has resulted in the minds of many Masonic students at the apparent contradictions in this account of just who acted as Grand Master *pro tem.* But there need be none. George Washington, President of the United States, and Past Master of Alexandria Lodge No. 22, was invited by the Grand Master *pro tem.* of Maryland to act as Grand Master and lay the corner stone of the capitol.

The Grand Lodge of Maryland was represented by R.W. Brother Joseph Clark, as Grand Master *pro tem.*, and he delegated his authority during the actual corner-stone laying ceremonies to Worshipful Brother George Washington, who thus became Grand Master of Maryland, *pro tem.*

The confusion has resulted from the last line but one in the list of those "in the second order of procession," which some have taken to mean that George Washington was the *only* representative of the Grand Lodge of Maryland at the corner stone laying. It would have been most unusual, and most discourteous to the President, had this been so. It was not so. R.W. Brother Joseph Clark acted as Grand Master *pro tem* for the Grand Lodge of Maryland, until the actual ceremony of corner stone laying commenced, when, as we read, "the plate was then delivered to the President, who, attended by the Grand Master P.T. and three most Worshipful Masters, descended to the cavazion trench and deposited the plate, and laid it on the corner stone of the Capitol of the United States, etc."

HISTORIC GAVEL

The marble gavel used by Washington on this occasion was presented by him to Brother Valentine Reintzel, then Worshipful Master of Lodge No. 9 of Georgetown (now Potomac Lodge No. 5) who later became the first Grand Master of the District of Columbia. The gavel is the most treasured possession of Potomac Lodge, as are the silver trowel, the square and level made for the purpose by John Daffey with which the corner stone was laid and the Watson Apron and also the sash, worn by Washington at this ceremony, the chief jewels in the collection of Masonic treasures of Washington, in the possession of the Alexandria-Washington Lodge No. 22.

WASHINGTON'S MASONIC LETTERS

Washington wrote many Masonic letters to lodges, Grand Lodges and brother Masons, on Masonic matters. Many of these documents are the priceless possessions of the nation, housed with loving care in the Library of Congress.

Brother Julius F. Sachse, as Librarian of the Grand Lodge of Pennsylvania, under the auspices of that Grand Lodge and with the assistance of the Library of Congress, published these in a volume under the title of *Washington's Masonic Correspondence.*

From it the following list is taken of those Masonic letters and documents from the hand of the First President in the Library:

Draft of Letter to Watson and Cassoul, Nantes, France, August 10, 1782.

Letter to Alexandria Lodge, No. 39, Virginia, December 28, 1783.

Address from King David's Lodge, No. 1, Rhode Island, August 17, 1790, and Washington's reply.

Address from St. John's Lodge, No. 2, Newbern, North Carolina, April 20, 1791, and his reply.

Address from Prince George's Lodge (Moderns), Georgetown, South Carolina, April 30, 1791, and his reply.

Draft of reply to Grand Lodge of South Carolina, May 5, 1791.

Address from Grand Lodge of Georgia, May 14, 1791, and his reply.

Address from Grand Lodge of Pennsylvania, March, 1792, and his reply.

Address of Grand Lodge of Massachusetts, December 27, 1792, and his reply.

Address from Grand Lodge of Pennsylvania, December 27, 1796, and his reply.

Address from Alexandria Lodge, No. 22, Virginia, April 4, 1797, and his reply.

Letter to Paul Revere and Grand Officers, April 24, 1797.

Draft of Letter to Grand Lodge of Massachusetts in reply to an address, April, 1797.

Draft of a reply to an address from the Grand Lodge of Maryland, November 8, 1798.

Letter from G. W. Snyder to Washington, August 22, 1798.

Washington's reply to Snyder, September 25, 1798.

Washington's reply to Snyder's letter of October 17, 1798.

Other letters are treasured possessions of other depositories such as the Washington letter in the archives of the Grand Lodge of New York, which is the original letter to Watson and Cassoul.

Space forbids lengthy quotations from these letters, which breathe a spirit of love, admiration, and respect for the Craft he honored, and which honored him. A few expressions, however, may serve to show the general tenor of the whole.

On December 28, 1783, he wrote to Alexandria Lodge No. 39:

"I shall always feel pleasure when it may be in my power to render service to Lodge No. 39, and in every act of brotherly kindness to the Members of it."

On June 19, 1784, he wrote again:

"With pleasure, I received the invitation of the master and members of Lodge No. 39, to dine with them on the approaching anniversary of St. John the Baptist. If nothing unforeseen at present interferes, I shall have the honor of doing it."

Washington did attend this dinner at Wise's Tavern, and, returning to the lodge room was elected an Honorary Member of the lodge over which he was later to preside as its Master under a new charter from the Grand Lodge of Virginia.

In a letter of August 22nd, 1790, to King David's Lodge, Newport, Rhode Island, Washington wrote:

"Being persuaded that a just application of the principles, on which the Masonic Fraternity is founded, must be promotive of private virtue and public prosperity, I shall always be happy to advance the interests of the Society, and to be considered by them as a deserving brother."

To St. John's Lodge, Newbern, N. C., he wrote (1791):

"My best ambition having ever aimed at the unbiassed approbation of my fellow citizens, it is peculiarly pleasing to find my conduct so affectionately approved by a fraternity whose association is founded in justice and benevolence."

Prince George's Lodge No. 16, Georgetown, South Carolina, received the following expression in a letter in 1791:

"I am much obliged by your good wishes and reciprocate them with sincerity, assuring the fraternity of my esteem, I request them to believe that I shall always be ambitious of being considered a deserving Brother."

Washington responded to an address of Charleston, South Carolina, Masons in these terms:

"The fabric of our freedom is placed on the enduring basis of public virtue, and will, I fondly hope, long continue to protect the prosperity of the architects who raised it. I shall be happy on every occasion, to evince my regard for the Fraternity."

The Grand Lodge of Pennsylvania was the recipient of a choice Masonic sentiment in 1792:

"At the same time I request you will be assured of my best wishes and earnest prayers for your happiness while you remain in this terrestial Mansion, and that we may thereafter meet as brethren in the Eternal Temple of the Supreme Architect."

Washington responded in part to the dedication of the Constitutions of the Grand Lodge of Massachusetts in these words:

"It is most fervently to be wished, that the conduct of every member of the fraternity, as well as those publications that discover the principles which actuate them; may tend to convince mankind that the grand object of Masonry is to promote the happiness of the human race."

Washington wrote in his Diary, February 12, 1785:

"Received an Invitation to the Funeral of Willm. Ramsay, Esqr. of Alexandria, the oldest Inhabitt. of the Town; and went up. Walked in a procession as a free mason, Mr. Ramsay in his life being one, and now buried with the ceremonies and honors due to one."

WASHINGTON MASONIC PORTRAITS

Many artists and engravers have given to the world their conceptions of Washington the Freemason, and with the same right possessed by any painter to limn the features of any historic character. Only one of these, so far as we know, was painted from life, the august subject wearing the Masonic clothing of apron, sash, collar, and jewel. But many of our most cherished paintings, not only of Washington, but of other characters and events dear to our national history, are wholly imaginative; Washington Crossing the Delaware, Washington at Valley Forge, the Signing of the Declaration of Independence, the Spirit of '76, to mention but a few, are not actual records, but portrayals of facts as seen through the eyes of the artists.

The portrait of Washington in Masonic regalia is the Williams painting, now the

WASHINGTON THE PRESIDENT-MASON
From the painting by Hattie Burdette

most valuable and most cherished possession of Alexandria-Washington Lodge No. 22 of Alexandria, Va. This work of art is inscribed on the back "His Excellency George Washington Esquire President of the United States, aged 64—Williams Pinxit ad vivum in Philadelphia, September 18, 1794."

The portrait is not a flattering likeness, compared to the general conception of the First President. But it was undoubtedly a true portrait of the General in his old age. It was ordered by the lodge and accepted by it; in other words, by Washington's Masonic brethren, his friends, men who knew him well. It is not thinkable that men who venerated, revered, almost worshipped the great Washington should have accepted a portrait which was not a faithful transcript of his features as he then appeared.

If this is the only Masonic portrait for which Washington actually sat, it is but one of a large number which were made by adaptation or imagination. Among these, one of the most often printed and best known is the Kearny print, which is nothing more nor less than a rank plagiarism of what is known as the Stothard-Bartolozzi engraving, dated 1802. The original shows the Chevalier Bartholomew Ruspini leading two little girls from the Freemasons' Charity for Female Children, as the Royal Masonic Institution for Girls was then called, in a procession in Freemasons' Hall, London. The engraver substituted Washington for Rus-

pini, and put portrait heads of noted Americans on the bodies of many men in the background. The picture is supposed to typify Masonic charity and was dedicated to the Grand Lodges of the United States.

A portrait of "Washington the President-Mason" has been painted by Miss Hattie Burdette of Washington, D. C., one of America's foremost painters of colonial subjects. Charles H. Callahan, Past Grand Master of Virginia, and an authority on the Masonic activities of George Washington, made the following comments on this painting:

". . . the painting representing General George Washington as a Mason, executed by Miss Hattie Burdette, has been completed and so far as I am able to judge is a faithful and striking representation of Washington as Worshipful Master of the Alexandria Lodge in 1787-1788.

"Miss Burdette has pictured the great Mason standing in the old Lodge Room in Alexandria, Virginia, wearing the Cassoul apron, the jewel and the regalia which were the personal possessions of the renowned patriot and which are now cherished heirlooms of the Lodge. The General is represented as having just called the Lodge to prayer and is standing in front of the old chair which he presented to the Lodge upon his election, with his right hand holding the gavel and resting on the original pedestal. . . .

"The painting represents Washington in the full vigor of his middle age and bears out in its environment and execution the richest of our local Masonic traditions. It is Washington the Mason true to life."

This full-length Masonic portrait has been approved by many leaders of the Craft and may be considered today as an authentic representation of George Washington as a Master Mason and the Master of his Lodge.

WASHINGTON MASONIC LEGENDS

The Masonic Fraternity has not been immune from tradition and mythology in which Washington has been a central figure. He has been said to have been a member of various lodges, other than Fredericksburg and Alexandria, but these are in all probability apocryphal—at least we have no evidence of such memberships. Thus, in 1851, the *Freemasons' Monthly Magazine* of Boston credits him with having "united" with a lodge in "one of the Royal Regiments quartered at Jamestown" (Va.). He was said by Grand Master Robert C. Scott of Virginia, in 1850, to have met in Yorktown Lodge No. 9 at Yorktown, with Lafayette, Marshall and Nelson, but the Grand Secretary of Virginia has no records to prove the statement. A certain Captain Hugh Malloy, of Ohio, is "said to have been" initiated in 1782 in General Washington's markee, Washington presiding in person and performing the ceremonies! But again there is no evidence to sustain the contention that

Washington held lodge meetings in his tent and conferred degrees.

Among the most cherished of these legendary Masonic happenings is that of the "Washington Masonic Cave," and enthusiastic believers in the facts point triumphantly to the cave to those who doubt. There is a cave, and it is called "Washington's Masonic Cave." It is near Charles Town, West Va. Henry Howe published *Historical Collections of Virginia* in 1849; from it is quoted:

"Washington's Masonic Cave is two and a half miles southeast of Charlestown. It is divided into several apartments, one of which is called the lodge-room. Tradition informs us that Washington, with others of the Masonic fraternity, held meetings in this cavern. In the spring of 1844 the Masons in this vicinity had a celebration there."

Still further "evidence" is presented to doubters by natives who show a signature "G. Washington" on the roof of the cavern. If it is objected that the printing bears no relationship to Washington's signature, the objectors are told that Washington was only sixteen when he "signed his name on the cave" and anyway, one cannot write well on a ceiling!

Washington is alleged by the historian Lossing to have received his degrees in the Morris Hotel, at Morristown, N. J., while the General had his headquarters at Freeman's Tavern, but in the face of absolute evidence that his degrees were given him in Fredericksburg years before, the story falls to the ground.

It would be pleasant to chronicle as truth the pretty story of Washington having received, if not "the degrees," at least "a degree" (Royal Arch?) in the Irish Military Lodge No. 227, "Lodge of Social and Military Virtues." Robertson's *History of Freemasonry in Canada* tells with some detail of a Bible this lodge possessed, on which Washington is supposed to have put his hands while receiving this "degree." The Bible is said to have been twice taken by the "enemy" and "returned to the regiment with all the honors of war."

Another Washington tradition, which has appeared in more than one form, is of his return, under a guard of honor, of Masonic property captured by his soldiers in battle. *The Freemasons' Quarterly Review*, London, 1834, printed the following story of this return of a lodge chest supposedly lost by British soldiers in an American engagement in 1777:

"The surprise, the feeling of both officers and men may be imagined, when they perceived the flag of truce that announced this elegant compliment from their noble opponent, but still more noble brother. It was a scene of moral beauty; a triumphant vindication of the purity of Masonic principles. The guard of honor with their flutes playing a sacred march—the chest containing the constitution and the implements of the Craft borne aloft, like another ark of the covenant, equally by Englishmen and Americans, who, lately engaged in the strife of war, now marched through the enfiladed ranks of the gallant regiment, that with presented arms and colors hailed the glorious act by cheers, which the sentiment rendered sacred as the hallelujahs of an angel's song."

It must not be forgotten that the early records of Freemasonry are few and far between; that much that was history was not recorded; that our brethren of colonial days regarded much that we think may be published with propriety, of such a secret character that it must go unwritten. It is possible that these stories of Washington are not myths, but legends, begun in fact, yet carried down the years by that "word of mouth" which is at once the method of teaching the secrets of Freemasonry, and the preserver of a thousand stories of history dear to us all, of which the cold evidence of black and white is missing.

Many well-informed brethren believe that the weight of such evidence as there is, is preponderantly on the side of Washington's having received the Mark Master's Degree in the Irish Military Lodge No. 227 and that the stories of the return of the captured Bible and the lodge chest are actual facts, even though the accounts which we have were written long after they are said to have occurred.

Into such matters this little history cannot attempt to go; it is at least safe to say that in the absence of real evidence to the contrary, there is nothing out of keeping with these stories and what is known of Washington's Masonry and his sterling character as a man and a Freemason. Not from these pages shall any reader have taken from him that faith in the truth of these legends of what Washington did in Masonry, merely because there is no cold type, official document, or contemporary record to substantiate them.

WASHINGTON MASONIC BIBLES

Freemasons revere the Holy Bible—"The Great Light in Masonry"—not only for its religious but for its Masonic significance. American Freemasons especially venerate two bibles intimately associated with Washington; that on which he received his degrees, and that on which he took the oath of office as President.

Fredericksburg Lodge has carefully preserved the original Bible on which Washington was obligated as a Freemason. It has traveled much, always with a guard of honor from the Lodge; perhaps its most significant journey was to the Grand Lodge of New York, November 4, 1920, when, on Washington's Masonic birthday, the historic old volume (printed in 1668) lay side by side on the Altar with the Bible of St. John's Lodge, on which Washington took the oath of office as President.

This ceremony took place in New York City, April 30, 1789. Chancellor Robert R. Livingston, then Grand Master of Masons in New York, administered the oath. General Jacob Morton, Worshipful Master of St. John's Lodge, No. 1, brought the Bible from his Lodge to Federal Hall, where Washington, his hand upon the Holy Book, obligated himself as First President of the United States. On the fly leaf of the old volume (printed 1767) is recorded the story of the Great Leader's oath to support the Constitution of the United States.

WASHINGTON'S MASONIC APRONS

That his brethren delighted to pay honor to their distinguished brother in Masonic as well as political, social and military ways, is evidenced by many documents, addresses, dedications, and gifts. Among the latter, the two Masonic aprons which have such Masonic historical importance are particularly to be noted.

The first of these (chronologically) was the gift of Brothers Elkanah Watson and M. Cassoul, of Nantes, France. These men were confidential agents of the American government during the Revolution. Watson was an American and personal friend and admirer of Washington. This apron (now in possession of Alexandria-Washington Lodge, No. 22) reached General Washington when in camp at Newburgh, New York, accompanied by the following letter:

"To His Excellency, General Washington,
    "America.
"*Most Illustrious and Respected Brother:*

"In the moment when all Europe admire and feel the effects of your glorious efforts in support of American liberty, we hasten to offer for your acceptance a small pledge of our homage. Zealous lovers of liberty and its institutions, we have experienced the most refined joy in seeing our chief and brother stand forth in its defence, and in defence of a new-born nation of Republicans.

"Your glorious career will not be confined to the protection of American liberty, but its ultimate effect will extend to the whole human family, since Providence has evidently selected you as an instrument in his hands, to fulfill his eternal decrees.

"It is to you, therefore, the glorious orb of America, we presume to offer Masonic ornaments, as an emblem of your virtues. May the Grand Architect of the Universe be the Guardian of your precious days, for the glory of the Western Hemisphere and the entire universe. Such are the vows of those who have the favor to be by all the known numbers.

    "Your affectionate brothers,
            "Watson & Cassoul.
"East of Nantes, 23d 1st Month, 5782."

To this Washington wrote the following reply:

"State of New York Augt 10th, 1782.
"Gentn.

"The Masonick Ornamts which accompanied your Brotherly Address of the 23d of Jany last, tho' elegant in themselves, were rendered more valuable by the flattering sentiments, and affectionate manner, in which they were presented.—

"If my endeavours to avert the evil, with which this Country was threatned, by a deliberate plan of Tyranny, should be crowned with the success that is wished— The praise is due to the *Grand Architect* of the Universe; who did not see fit to suffer his superstructures and justice, to be subjected to the Ambition of the Princes of this World, or to the rod of oppression, in the hands of any power upon Earth.—

"For your affectionate Vows, permit me to be grateful;—and offer mine for true Brothers in all parts of the world; and to assure you of the sincerity with which I am

"Yrs

"G. Washington

"Messrs. Watson & Cosson
"East of Nantes."

Julius F. Sachse in *Washington's Masonic Correspondence*, says:

"This autograph letter . . . is now in the possession of the Grand Lodge of New York, . . . It is written upon two pages of an ordinary letter sheet, and was a copy of one written by Washington, with which he was not entirely satisfied, as shown by the changes made in the text before it was sent to France. The first copy Washington retained, and is now in the Library of Congress."

Washington wore this apron as Master of his Lodge, and also at the laying of the corner stone of the National Capitol.

The Lafayette Masonic Apron is now a treasured possession of the Grand Lodge of Pennsylvania. It was embroidered by Madame Lafayette and presented by her distinguished husband, Washington's brother Mason, in August, 1784, when he visited Mount Vernon. Masonically, the Lafayette Apron is the more interesting of the two, as its embroideries picture many familiar Masonic emblems, among them the Sprig of Acacia, Four Pillars surmounted by globes, the Square and the Compasses, the All Seeing Eye, the Anchor, held by a figure of Hope, a Cable Tow, a Setting Maul, the Pentalpha, the Mosaic Pavement, a Flight of Five Steps, the Trowel, the Forty-seventh Problem, and, most interesting of all, a Beehive in a circle on the rounded flap of the apron, surrounded by the letters H T W S S T K S, familiar to all Masons of the Royal Arch.

The Royal Arch Degree was conferred in Fredericksburg Lodge as early as December 23, 1753, and in other lodges in America prior to the formation of the General Grand Chapter of Capitular Masonry in this country in 1797-8. Washington would hardly have been a Mason of the Royal Arch without informing his friend and brother Lafayette of the fact; it does not seem probable that General Lafayette would have presented an apron with the circle and letters inclosing a Beehive (which would have been most appropriate for Washington to have chosen as his "mark") unless he had known that Washington was at least a Mark Mason. However, no documentary evidence exists that Washington was a Royal Arch Mason, and the difficult research involved in this question is not yet complete.

MASONIC DEDICATIONS TO WASHINGTON

To dedicate a book to a friend is a pretty custom by which an author honors him whose name thus begins a volume, but it is by no means an uncommon occurrence. Official volumes of Grand Lodges are inscribed to individuals but seldom, yet Washington received the honor from several sovereign Grand Lodges, four of which are here set forth to show the exalted esteem in which Washington was held by his brethren.

The Pennsylvania *Ahiman Rezon* of 1783 is thus inscribed:

"To his Excellency, GEORGE WASHINGTON, Esq., General and Commander in Chief of the Armies of the United States of America: In *Testimony*, as well of his exalted Services to his Country, as of that noble Philanthropy which distinguishes Him among Masons, the following Constitutions of the most ancient and honourable Fraternity of *Free and Accepted Masons*, by Order and in Behalf of the Grand Lodge of *Pennsylvania*, &c. is dedicated, By his Excellency's Most humble Servant, and faithful Brother, William Smith, G. Secretary."

The New York *Constitutions* of 1785 is dedicated as follows:

"To His Excellency, GEORGE WASHINGTON, Esq. In testimony, as well of his exalted Services to his Country, as of his distinguished Character as a MASON, the following BOOK of CONSTITUTIONS of the most antient and honourable Fraternity of *Free and Accepted Masons*, by order and in behalf of the GRAND LODGE of the State of New-York, is dedicated, By his most Humble Servant, JAMES WILES, G. Secretary. A. L. 5785."

In 1791 Virginia brought out her own *New Ahiman Rezon* which is inscribed:

"To George Washington, Esq. President of the United States of America. The Following Work is Most Respectfully Dedicated by His Obedient, and Devoted Servant, THE EDITOR."

In 1792 Isaiah Thomas, then Grand Mas-

THE LAFAYETTE MASONIC APRON

Presented to Brother George Washington by Brother Lafayette. Now in the possession of the Grand Lodge of Pennsylvania

ter of Masons in Massachusetts, brought out the *Constitutions of the Honourable Fraternity of Free and Accepted Masons*, dedicated to Washington as follows:

"In *Testimony* of His Exalted Merit, And of Our inalienable Regard, THIS WORK IS *Inscribed and Dedicated* To our Illustrious BROTHER GEORGE WASHINGTON: The Friend *of Masonry*, Of his COUNTRY, and *Of Man*."

PROPOSED AS GRAND MASTER

Washington was proposed as the Grand Master of the Grand Lodge of Virginia, on June 23, 1777. He declined on the dual grounds that as he had not served as a Master he was not eligible and that his military duties were too arduous for him to consider added responsibilities.

Washington was thrice proposed as General Grand Master of Masons in the United States, first by American Union (Military) Lodge, at Morristown, Pennsylvania, December 15, 1779; next by the Grand Lodge of Pennsylvania, on December 20, 1779, and again by the same body on January 13, 1780.

In 1782 Washington rejected the suggestion that he become King. The same inherent modesty, sound sense and democratic principles of the Great Citizen, led him to refuse this highest of Masonic honors—as it would have been had it ever become an actuality. Had General Washington not declined, it is possible that several Grand Lodges, favorable to this action, might have joined with Pennsylvania in a further effort to form a central Masonic body with Washington as its General Grand Master. Masons know now that neither Craft nor nation were then old enough to give healthy growth to a General Grand Lodge; in face of the health and the vigor of the Craft in the United States today under its forty-nine Grand Lodges, the Fraternity can but be profoundly grateful to the First President for his Masonic modesty and wisdom in declining to foster an untried experiment which was as potent for disaster as for good.

SPRIG OF ACACIA

Brother George Washington passed to the Celestial Lodge Above at twenty minutes past ten o'clock P. M. on Saturday, December 14, 1799, in his sixty-eighth year.

He was buried with full Masonic honors, Alexandria Lodge, No. 22 officiating, Brooke Lodge, No. 47, of Alexandria, assisting. Of the six pall bearers, Col. Charles Simms, Col. Dennis Ramsey, Col. William Payne, Col. George Gilpin, Col. Phillip Marsteller, and Col. Charles Little, all officers who had served in the Revolution, all were Masons and members of Alexandria Lodge, No. 22, except Col. Marsteller, whose son, Phillip G., was a member and attended the funeral.

The sermon at the tomb was preached by Reverend Thomas Davis, of Christ Church—Washington's own church—Alexandria, and the Masonic services were conducted by Dr. Elisha Cullen Dick, Worshipful Master of Alexandria Lodge No. 22, and the Reverend James Muir, D.D., Chaplain of the Lodge. Dr. Dick retired from the East of the Lodge when it was rechartered, to allow Washington to be named as the Charter Master, remaining again a year out of the East when Washington was unanimously reelected and again became Master after Washington retired as a Past Master. To Dr. Dick fell the solemn duty of interring the distinguished dead with the Lambskin Apron of the fraternity and its Sprig of Acacia of immortal hope.

WASHINGTON'S MASONIC HISTORY

The following chronology of the major events in Washington's Masonic life is taken from Boyden's *Masonic Presidents, Vice Presidents and Signers*:

Fredericksburg Lodge, No. 4, Fredericksburg, Virginia:
    Initiated November 4, 1752.
    Passed March 3, 1753.
    Raised August 4, 1753.
    Remained a member until time of his death (1799).

Alexandria-Washington Lodge No. 22, Alexandria, Virginia:
    First chartered as Alexandria Lodge No. 39, under the Grand Lodge of Pennsylvania, 1783.
    Became Alexandria Lodge, No. 22, under the Grand Lodge of Virginia in 1788.
    After Washington's death was named Alexandria-Washington Lodge, No. 22, in 1805.
    Washington was made an Honorary Member of Lodge No. 39 of Alexandria, June 24, 1784.
    Became Charter Master of Alexandria Lodge No. 22 when a Charter was issued to it by the Grand Lodge of Virginia, April 28, 1788.
    Unanimously reelected Master December 20, 1788.

Holland Lodge No. 8, New York City, New York:
    Elected Washington an Honorary Member, 1789.

1753, September 1—Visited his Lodge at Fredericksburg shortly before leaving for the western country.

1755, January 4—Again visited his Lodge.

1777, June 23—Proposed as Grand Master of the Grand Lodge of Virginia.

1778, December 28—Marched in procession in Philadelphia, Pennsylvania, at the Masonic celebration in honor of St. John the Evangelist.

1779, June 24—Celebrated with American Union (Military) Lodge, the festival of St. John the Baptist, at West Point, New York.

1779, October 6—Washington (Military) Lodge was instituted by the Grand Lodge of Massachusetts. Washington visited this Lodge.

1779, December 15—Proposed by American Union (Military) Lodge at Morristown, New Jersey, as General Grand Master of the United States.

1779, December 20—Proposed by the Grand Lodge of Pennsylvania as General Grand Master of the United States.

1779, December 27—Celebrated with American Union (Military) Lodge, the festival of St. John the Evangelist, at Morristown, New Jersey.

1780, January 13—Again proposed by the Grand Lodge of Pennsylvania as General Grand Master of the United States.

1781, October—Said to have visited with General Lafayette, Lodge No. 9 at Yorktown, Virginia, after the surrender of Cornwallis there.

1782—Presented with a Masonic apron, and other Masonic regalia, by Brothers Watson and Cassoul, of Nantes, France. Acknowledged the gifts August 10, 1782.

1782, June 24—Celebrated with American Union (Military) Lodge the festival of St. John the Baptist, at West Point, New York.

1782, December 27—Solomon's Lodge, No. 1, Poughkeepsie, New York, records: "Visitors. Bro. George Washington, Comdr. in Chief." Celebrated with them on this date the festival of St. John the Evangelist.

1784, June 24—Celebrated with Alexandria Lodge, Alexandria, Virginia, the festival of St. John the Baptist.

1784, August—Was presented by General Lafayette with a Masonic apron made by Madame Lafayette.

1785, February 12—Walked in the Masonic procession at the funeral of Brother William Ramsay, at Alexandria, Virginia.

1789, April 30—Inaugurated as President of the United States, and took the oath of office on the Bible belonging to St. John's Lodge, No. 1, New York City, New York.

1791, April 15—Visited Newbern, North Carolina, and was welcomed by the Freemasons of St. John's Lodge, No. 2, "with the mystic numbers," and attended a ball in the evening.

1791, May—While on a visit to Charleston, South Carolina, was greeted by General Mordecai Gist, Grand Master of the Grand Lodge of South Carolina, who extended the greetings of that Grand Lodge.

1793, September 18—Acting as Grand Master laid the corner stone of the United States Capitol, at Washington, D. C.

1794—Late in this year Alexandria Lodge received and accepted the Masonic portrait of Washington, painted by Williams of Philadelphia, Pennsylvania, on order of the Lodge, and for which Washington sat while in that city some time in the latter part of 1793 or early part of 1794.

1797, March 28 — Received a delegation from Alexandria Lodge and accepted an invitation to be present in Alexandria, April 1st.

1797, April 1—Attended Alexandria Lodge, and, at the banquet, proposed a toast.

Buried Masonically, at Mount Vernon, December 18, 1799, by Alexandria Lodge No. 22.

Throughout his life his Masonic brethren delighted in honoring Washington; that he took pleasure in his brotherhood with his fellow Masons none can doubt who read his letters. Washington's feeling for the Ancient Craft he summed up himself in one toast which he gave at an Alexandria Lodge dinner, Saturday, April 1, 1797:

"To the Lodge of Alexandria, and all Masons throughout the world."

Among the thousands of Masonic tributes paid Brother Washington these beautiful words from the pen of Dr. Joseph Fort Newton, foremost among modern Masonic writers, epitomize at once the veneration of his brethren for his character and his achievements, and the fraternal love of all the gentle Craft wheresoever dispersed:

"*A great and simple man—modest, quiet, gentle, wise—in whom patriotism was a passion and a prophecy, Freemasonry a fragrance, a fellowship and a philosophy; great enough to refuse a crown and live a life of private nobility and public service; picking his way where no path was, amid wild passions and perils; leading his people to victory, peace and ordered honor; leaving his labor as a legacy of inspiration to mankind, and his character as a consecration to his country.*"

Part III
Genealogical Table

ENGLISH FAMILY

George Washington in early life seemed to feel little interested in his ancestry. When he became a wealthy land-owner, he was interested in the coat of arms of the family, which was perfectly well known to the Virginia Washingtons; and he used several forms slightly different from each other for his tableware, his carriages, his seal, and his bookplate, all of them bearing the three mullets which heraldically were the spurs of a knight, and the two bars.

In 1791 Sir Isaac Heard, Garter King of Arms in England, and therefore an official authority, wrote to Washington asking about his ancestry. Washington replied: "Our ancestors who first settled in this Country came from some one of the Northern Countries of England, but whether from Lancashire Yorkshire or one still more northerly I do not precisely remember."

This tradition is powerfully supported by a memorial tablet in Maidstone Church, England, evidently written by Lawrence Washington, son of Lawrence of Sulgrave, before his death in 1619. It runs as follows: "Here resteth the body of Lawrence Washington Esquire of the Family of the Washingtons antientlie of Washington in the Countie Palatine of Durham." This is absolute proof that in 1619, a century before George Washington was born, the Palatinate of Durham was recognized as the original home of the Washingtons.

Soon after Washington's death investigations began into his family history. Washington Irving visited Durham and was the first American to take account of the fact that in 1183 a manuscript volume was drawn up called the Bolden Buke in which was an entry to the effect that William de

Hertburn held certain lands in the town of Wessyngton (a few miles north of Durham), which he had received by exchange for lands in Hertburn; and that he thereby held the title of Sir William de Wessyngton. Hertburn was an outlying district of what is now the city of Stockton on Tees. The site of the ancient manor house at the village of Washington can still be traced.

In the neighborhood of that town is Hilton Castle, upon the front of which are displayed the arms of the Washington family, perhaps derived from a female descendant of William de Wessyngton—namely the Lady Dionysia de Tempest.

For several generations the descendants of William de Wessyngton can be traced in Durham and the nearby countries. They took advantage of the widespread practice of marrying heiresses. After three or four generations the direct descent becomes less clear. A writer named Plantagenet Harrison was sure that the cradle of the race was the present insignificant village of Washton (perhaps derived from Washington), near Richmond. An ingenious but highly imaginative author not many years ago made up a genealogy which completely satisfied him, leading straight back from George Washington of Mount Vernon to the God Odin of supernal regions.

About the year 1300 members of the family are found sixty or seventy miles west in what are now the counties of Lancaster and Westmoreland. The first very distinct western Washington is Sir Robert, Lord of Milburne, which is probably the Milbourne in Westmoreland not far from Appleby. At Appleby George Washington's father and his two half brothers went to school several centuries later. The neighboring castle of Howgill was very likely one of the cradles of the Washington race. The Washingtons

were landed people and at least thirty places in that region can be identified as having been owned by members of the family, particularly in the neighborhood of Kendall and the present Carnforth, then called Kernford.

A few miles from Kernford lies the present town of Warton, which is very near the coast of Morecambe Bay. Here the arms of the Washington family such as George Washington bore, have been discovered on the church wall.

Several English writers have attempted to find the missing link between the eastern and western Washingtons of England. More important are Mr. T. Pape, the Rev. Isham Longden, and Canon John Solloway of Selby Abbey, a church in which an American flag floats alongside a magnificent glass escutcheon of the Washington arms, which has been there probably five hundred years. Canon Solloway, whose work is yet unpublished, comes nearer to bridging the chasm between eastern and western English Washingtons than any previous writer.

At present the first safely identified direct ancestor of Washington is Robert de Wessyngton (possibly Robert of Milburne). A century later we find John Washington of Tewitfield (named from the tewit, a bird) near Warton on the west coast, and Warton may be a shorter form of Washington. From Robert, who married Joan of Strickland, the genealogical line is probably as follows:

I. ROBERT DE WESSYNGTON (1). (Died, 1324.) Married Joan de Strickland.

II. ROBERT DE WASHINGTON (2). (Died about 1348.) Married Agnes de Gentyl.

III. JOHN DE WASHINGTON (1). (Died about 1380.) Married Alianora de Warton.

IV. JOHN WASHINGTON (2). (Died about 1408.) Married Joan Croft.

V. JOHN WASHINGTON (3), of Whitfield. Wounded at the battle of Agincourt with King Henry V (1415).

VI. ROBERT WASHINGTON (3), of Intwhytefeld. (Died, 1483.)

VII. ROBERT WASHINGTON (4), of Warton. (Died about 1520.) Married Elizabeth Westfield.

VIII. JOHN WASHINGTON (4), of Warton. (Died about 1560.) Married Margaret Kytson.

IX. LAWRENCE WASHINGTON (1), of Northampton, Gray's Inn, and Sulgrave. (1538-1584.) Married Amy Pargiter.

X. ROBERT WASHINGTON (5), of Sulgrave. (1544 - 1619.) Married Elizabeth Light.

XI. LAWRENCE WASHINGTON (2), of Sulgrave, Brington, and Wicken. (Died, 1616.) Married Margaret Butler.

XII. REV. LAWRENCE WASHINGTON (3), of Oxford, Purleigh, and Maldon. (1602-1654-5.) Married Annphillis Twigden.

XIII. JOHN WASHINGTON (5), immigrant to Virginia. (1634-1675.) Married Ann Pope.

XIV. LAWRENCE WASHINGTON (4), of Virginia. (Died, 1697.) Married Mildred Warner.

XV. AUGUSTINE WASHINGTON, of Virginia. (1694-1743.) Married Mary Ball.

XVI. PRESIDENT GEORGE WASHINGTON. (1732-1799.) Married Martha (Dandridge) Custis. No children.

VIRGINIA FAMILY

John Washington, great-grandfather of George, settled in Virginia about 1657, and became a planter at Bridges Creek on the Potomac in Westmoreland County. On this estate were born his son Lawrence and Lawrence's son Augustine, father of George Washington. Augustine Washington, born in 1694, was well to do, a man of energy, a good planter, and interested in the development of Virginia iron mines. He also followed the sea for a while. He was married twice. His first wife, Jane Butler, bore him several children of whom only Lawrence and Augustine survived the father. In March, 1731, he married Mary Ball, who became the mother of six children, George, Elizabeth (Betty), Samuel, John Augustine, Charles, and Mildred. The last died young.

Tradition has been very kind to Mary Ball, the mother of George Washington, but the established facts concerning her are not numerous. She passed the last years of her life in a house in Fredericksburg, given to her by her son George. He seems to have resembled her in looks and owed to her strong elements of character. He was a dutiful son and throughout her life had his careful consideration. She was perhaps over fond of him while he was still a boy. After he had attained manhood he paid much attention to the management of her affairs.

Details as to the genealogical descent of George Washington are to be found in the publications of Pape, Isham Longden, Worthington C. Ford's edition of the *Writings* of *George Washington*, and in the forthcoming volumes by Canon Solloway, and by Washington Lee, descended from a collateral of George Washington.

Though Washington left no descendants, his brothers and uncles and great-uncles founded families of which there are many descendants. No list has been published of the living persons bearing the name of Washington and descended from Washington's ancestors, but there are probably not fewer than two hundred in the United States.

Selected Authorities

BOYDEN, WILLIAM L.—*Masonic Presidents, Vice-Presidents and Signers.* Washington, 1927.

BROCKETT, FRANKLIN L.—*Lodge of Washington: a History of the Alexandria-Washington Lodge.* Alexandria, G. E. French, 1876. (Later eds.)

CALLAHAN, CHARLES H.—*Washington, the Man and Mason.* Washington, 1913.

CUSTIS, GEORGE WASHINGTON PARKE—*Recollections and Private Memoirs of Washington.* Philadelphia, Flint, 1859. (Other eds.; to be used with caution.)

EVANS, HENRY R.—"Washington's Masonic Apron"; in *Master Mason*, June, 1925.

FORD, PAUL LEICESTER—*True George Washington.* Philadelphia, Lippincott, 1896.

GRAND LODGE OF IOWA—*Grand Lodge Bulletin.* October, 1925.

GRAND LODGE OF PENNSYLVANIA—*Proceedings . . . of the Sesqui-Centennial Anniversary of the Initiation of Brother George Washington.* Philadelphia, Grand Lodge of Pennsylvania, 1902.

HARPER, KENTON N.—*History of the Grand Lodge and of Freemasonry in the District of Columbia.* Washington, Grand Lodge of District of Columbia, 1911.

HAYDEN, SIDNEY—*Washington and his Masonic Compeers.* 8th ed. New York, Macoy, 1905.

HERBERT, LEILA—*First American; his Homes and his Households.* New York, Harper, 1900.

IRVING, WASHINGTON—*Life of George Washington.* 5 vols. New York, Putnam, 1855-59. (Later eds.)

MITCHELL, SILAS WEIR—*Youth of Washington, told in the Form of an Autobiography.* New York, Century, 1904.

MOORE, CHARLES—*Family Life of George Washington.* Boston, Houghton Mifflin, 1926.

MORSE, SIDNEY—*Freemasonry in the American Revolution.* Washington, Masonic Service Association, 1924.

OSBORN, LUCRETIA PERRY, ED.—*Washington speaks for Himself.* New York, Scribner, 1927. (Especially ch. i.)

PAPE, T.—*Warton and George Washington's Ancestors.* (An English pamphlet.)

RUSH, RICHARD—*Washington in Domestic Life.* Philadelphia, Lippincott, 1857.

SIPE, C. HALE—*Mount Vernon and the Washington Family; a Concise Handbook on the Ancestry, Youth and Family of George Washington, and History of his Home.* Butler, Pa., the Author, 1927.

SOLLOWAY, JOHN—*English Washingtons.* (Not yet published.)

TATSCH, J. HUGO—*Facts about George Washington as a Freemason.* 2d ed. New York, Macoy, 1931.

TATSCH, J. HUGO—*Freemasonry in the Thirteen Colonies.* New York, Macoy, 1929.

WASHINGTON, GEORGE — *Diaries, 1748-1799.* Ed. by John C. Fitzpatrick. 4 vols. Boston, Houghton Mifflin, 1925.

WASHINGTON, GEORGE—*Washington's Masonic Correspondence.* Ed. by Julius F. Sachse. Philadelphia, Grand Lodge of Pennsylvania, 1915.

WASHINGTON, GEORGE—*Writings.* Ed. by Worthington Chauncey Ford. 14 vols. New York, Putnam, 1889-93. (Vol. XIV contains a genealogical table and memoirs on the Washington Family.)

WASHINGTON, S. E. LEE—*Enquiry into the Origin and Early History of the Washington Family.* (Not yet published.)

WATERS, HENRY E.—*Examination of the English Ancestry of George Washington.* Boston, 1889.

Classified Washington Bibliography
By Committee of American Library Association
Introduction

By
ALBERT BUSHNELL HART
Historian
UNITED STATES GEORGE WASHINGTON
BICENTENNIAL COMMISSION

IN the "Act to e n a b l e the George Washington Bicentennial Commission to carry out and give effect to certain approved plans" approved February 21, 1930, provision is made for "one hundred thousand copies of the pamphlet entitled 'Reading about George Washington.'" From the first it was the intention of the Commission to secure the collaboration of the American Library Association in the preparation of a select bibliography. By vote of the American Library Association a special committee was duly appointed as follows:

Chairman, Augustus H. Shearer, Grosvenor Library, Buffalo, N. Y.

Mary E. Eastwood, New York State Library, Albany, N. Y.

Joseph D. Ibbotson, Librarian, Hamilton College Library, Clinton, N. Y.

Paul M. Paine, Librarian, Public Library, Syracuse, N. Y.

Helmar L. Webb, Librarian, Tulane University Library, New Orleans, La.

The chairman came to Washington several times to consult with the authorities responsible for the publishing and editing of the various works provided for by the act of Congress. The work was subdivided among the members of his committee named above. It was an arduous task inasmuch as it would have been possible to find at least three times as many titles of published works bearing upon Washington and the background of his times. The first principle adopted by the committee was that in most cases specific reference should be made only to volumes separately published, many of which are in print, and most of the others can still be obtained at second-hand. It was impossible to list the immense Washington

literature in the proceedings of historical and other learned societies, or in periodicals devoted to history and particularly to American history, or in the general literary periodicals some of which contain very valuable Washington material. The committee had in its mind the duty of furnishing aid to libraries, ranging from small school collections up to the immense public, university, and society libraries throughout the country. It must therefore be borne in mind by those who use this pamphlet that one of its main purposes is to assist the buyers of books for both public and private libraries in building up their Washington collections. The precise citations of place and date of publication and the exact titles will be found very helpful for this purpose. It will also enable private libraries in their purchases of Washington books in general or in the special lines into which the committee has divided its list, to fill up gaps and complete their series.

The committee has taken especial account of the needs of school libraries by its three lists of select books for small public schools, elementary schools, and high schools; a field in which the United States George Washington Bicentennial Commission is particularly interested. These lists will enable schools to prepare for the essay and debate competitions and for the general reading about Washington which has been pushed by several departments of the Commission. In most cases libraries, schools, and other public institutions should be able to purchase at a discount the books here listed.

The pamphlet will aid the numerous public libraries in satisfying the great public demand for interesting and authentic books on Washington for their millions of readers. Most titles throughout the work are flanked by a note on the value and authenticity of that particular book, quoted from the criticisms by authorities appended to each title, or expressing the judgment of the committee. The system of consecutive numbers with cross-references from one to

another makes it possible to increase the number of titles printed without diminishing the critical apparatus.

Part IV of the pamphlet, "Extended List for Study and Research," has in mind particularly research possibilities, and the opportunity of comparison of the views of thoughtful writers. For historical writers and teachers Part IV is an avenue to special books upon the many fields of interest and public service in which Washington was interested. Such topics as his travels, his relations with the other great men of his time, his home life, his interest in agriculture, and his large experience in business of various kinds, can thus be followed to the sources.

The editorial force of the Commission has taken a deep interest in the report of the Committee and has made some additions and changes of classification so as to make possible type reduction to the space required for the pamphlet; but it has not undertaken to exercise any control over the findings of the American Library Association Committee as to what should be retained and what should be omitted in the list of books. The appreciations of the different volumes for the most part stand as made up by the Committee, even in cases where the judgment of the editor of the George Washington Pamphlets does not precisely correspond with that of the Committee.

The Commission hereby expresses its thanks to the American Library Association and to the Special Committee for their interest and service in producing this bibliographical work of national importance. The titles have been checked and the classifications have been examined by Mr. David M. Matteson, as an historical expert of the Commission, who has added a few titles, but has not substituted his own judgment as to the value of any work herein mentioned against that of the Committee, which is responsible for the work and whose gratuitous service has made possible this excellent and highly serviceable bibliography.

Part I
Books for the Home Library

GEORGE WASHINGTON

*From a portrait by Rembrandt Peale, known as the Porthole Portrait, in the
New York Historical Society*

BIOGRAPHY

1. FORD, PAUL LEICESTER—*George Washington.* Philadelphia, Lippincott, 1926 (c.1896), $3.50; 1926 ed. same as *True George Washington,* pub. 1896.

"Few writers have used more abundant historical resources, or made better use of them," says Larned's *Literature of American History.* Hart in *Publisher's Weekly* for Feb. 14, 1931, adds: "He was one of the first Washington biographers to make use of his invaluable diaries. His book remains one of the most readable, and truest to nature that has ever been written about Washington."

1-A. FROTHINGHAM, THOMAS GODDARD —*Washington, Commander in Chief.* Boston, Houghton Mifflin, 1930, $5.00.

The most remarkable and most authentic book about Washington published for many years. Solves the problem of the military success of the Virginia planter and colonial soldier who defeated the best trained gen-

erals that England knew to send into the Revolutionary war. (A. B. Hart in *Publisher's Weekly,* Feb. 14, 1931, p. 823.)

2. HART, ALBERT BUSHNELL—*George Washington (Reading with a Purpose,* No. 42). Chicago, American Library Association, 1927, $.50, paper, $.35.

This contains a list of books recommended. It is a brief introduction to the many-sided Washington and a guide to a few very readable books about him.

3. MOORE, CHARLES — *Family Life of George Washington . . . with an introduction by Mrs. Theodore Roosevelt.* Boston, Houghton Mifflin, 1926, $5.00.

Not only an account of Washington's family life but of his direct ancestry and of the connections and descendants of his beloved step-children, Martha Parke and John Parke Custis. This genealogical matter is enlivened with occasional extracts from letters and some gossipy anecdotes. (Cleveland Public Library, *Open Shelf.*)

4. OSBORN, LUCRETIA PERRY, ED. — *Washington speaks for Himself.* New York, Scribner, 1927, $2.50.

This is made up of extracts from his "letters, journals, diaries, addresses, messages, etc.," but the text has not been compared with the originals. "It is a highly interesting collection of source material for the matters upon which it touches, and these of course include the most important incidents of his career," says W. E. Garrison in *Christian Century,* March 1, 1928.

5. WASHINGTON, GEORGE—*Rules of Civility and Decent Behaviour in Company and Conversation.* Ed. with an introduction by Charles Moore. Boston, Houghton Mifflin, 1926, $2.00.

Here are the one hundred and ten rules of etiquette from the youthful Washington's copy book, illustrated with facsimile pages of neat lines and flourishes and in a following section compared with an early English version of the very early French original of the rules. Washington's maxims are condensed from this English version. (*Book Review Digest,* 1926.)

5-A. WILSTACH, PAUL—*Mount Vernon, Washington's Home and the Nation's Shrine.* New ed. Indianapolis, Bobbs-Merrill, 1930, $5.00.

First published in 1916. The history of the estate from earliest title deeds to the present. A pleasant picture of Washington's home life is given and the later vicissitudes of the house.

6. WISTER, OWEN — *Seven Ages of Washington; a Biography.* New York, Macmillan, 1907; new ed. 1917, $2.00.

A truly delightful biography giving a finished portrait, broad and vigorous in treatment, not overlaid with commonplace or labored details. The author concerns himself with the man, only incidently with the soldier or the statesman, but does not neglect background or the final impress upon history. (*A. L. A. Booklist,* Feb., 1908.)

GENERAL WORKS ON THE REVOLUTION AND FOLLOWING PERIOD

7. BASSETT, JOHN SPENCER—*Federalist System, 1789-1801 (American Nation).* New York, Harper, 1906, $2.25.

The volume in a standard cooperative history which brings to both the student and general reader a succinct account of Washington's administrations and of social and economic conditions of the times.

8. BECKER, CARL—*Eve of the Revolution; a Chronicle of the Breach with England (Chronicles of America).* New Haven, Yale University Press, 1918, $1.50.

There is no book . . . which shows a more profound knowledge of the essential historical problems of the decade preceding the Declaration of Independence than does this small, unpretentious volume. (C. H. Van Tyne, in *American Historical Review*, 24: 734.)

9. CHANNING, EDWARD—*History of the United States*. Vols. II-IV. New York, Macmillan, 1912-1917, $12.00 for the three volumes.

These volumes cover the period 1761-1815. The result of life-long study of American history, they show a great scholar's unbiased and fresh view on social as well as political and military history. Provided with critical bibliographical notes.

10. FISKE, JOHN—*American Revolution*. 2 vols. Boston, Houghton Mifflin, 1894, $3.00 each.

A popular military and personal history of the war, broad in view, often inaccurate in detail, and neglectful of important phases of the struggle. Its charming style makes it the most generally read of all accounts. (C. H. Van Tyne in *American Revolution*, p. 335.)

11. FISKE, JOHN—*Critical Period of American History, 1783-1789*. Boston, Houghton Mifflin, 1888, $3.00.

Study of the characters of the two contrasted originators of policies, Washington and Jefferson, of the economic problems of the times, of the way in which the Tories or Loyalists were dealt with at the close of the war, and of the course of events in Great Britain upon the close of the Revolution. (*Reader's Digest of Books*.)

12. MCLAUGHLIN, ANDREW CUNNINGHAM—*Confederation and the Constitution, 1783-1789* (*American Nation*). New York, Harper, 1906, $2.25.

This volume in the series edited by Albert Bushnell Hart treats of the period between the end of the Revolution and the inauguration of Washington. The account of the development of the Constitution in the Convention is especially good.

13. TREVELYAN, SIR GEORGE OTTO—*American Revolution*. New ed. 4 vols. New York, Longmans Green, 1912, $2.50 each.

13a. TREVELYAN, SIR GEORGE OTTO—*George the Third and Charles Fox, the Concluding Part of the American Revolution*. 2 vols. New York, Longmans Green, 1912-14, $2.50 each.

These two works of Trevelyan cover the Revolution to the fall of Lord North's ministry. They are clear and readable, just to both England and America. (*A. L. A. Catalog*, 1926.)

14. VAN TYNE, CLAUDE HALSTEAD—*History of the Founding of the American Republic*. 2 vols. Boston, Houghton Mifflin, 1922-29, $5.00 each.

Unfinished, extends to the French alliance. A very scholarly and well-written work by a recognized authority on the period, and based on an exhaustive use of printed and manuscript sources, it presents the origins and elements of the contest in the light of modern research.

FICTION

15. ATHERTON, GERTRUDE FRANKLIN—*The Conqueror; a Dramatized Biography of Alexander Hamilton*. New York, Stokes, 1916, $2.50.

This is a "novelized biography" and brings in Washington frequently.

16. FORD, PAUL LEICESTER—*Janice Meredith*. New York, Mead, 1899, $2.50; reprint, New York, Grosset & Dunlap, 1924, $.75.

A fair-minded picture of events and conditions at the time of the American Revolution, bringing in Washington in a correct setting.

17. MITCHELL, SILAS WEIR — *Hugh Wynne, Free Quaker, sometime Brevet Lieutenant-Colonel on the Staff of His Excellency General Washington*. New York, Century, 1897, $2.00; school ed., 1922, $1.00.

Most of the action takes place in Philadelphia with Washington and other important men as characters.

18. MITCHELL, SILAS WEIR—*Youth of Washington, told in the Form of an Autobiography*. New York, Century, 1904, $2.00.

The narrative extends to the year 1758. This mixture of history and fiction tells the story of Washington's life to the close of the French and Indian War. It is based upon a wide study of the sources and traditions and follows them closely.

19. THACKERY, WILLIAM MAKEPEACE—*Virginians; a Tale of the Eighteenth Century*. Home Library, New York, Burt, 1923, $1.25; Everyman's Library, 2 vols., New York, Dutton, 1911, $.90 each. Others available.

This novel, first published in 1859, includes the early career of George Washington, Braddock's defeat, and the American Revolution.

Part II
Books for School Libraries

SMALL PUBLIC SCHOOLS

20. BROOKS, ELBRIDGE STREETER—*True Story of George Washington*. Boston, Lothrop, Lee and Shepard, 1895, $2.00.

A simple and popular biography, abundantly illustrated. (*A. L. A. Catalog*, 1926.)

21. GERWIG, GEORGE WILLIAM—*Washington, the Young Leader*. New York, Scribner, 1923, $1.25; school ed. $.88.

Readable biography of the boyhood and young manhood of Washington; ends with the fall of Fort Duquesne.

22. HILL, FREDERICK TREVOR—*On the Trail of Washington*. New York, Appleton, 1910, $2.50.

A direct and entertaining biography in which only admitted facts are used.

22a. LODGE, HENRY CABOT — *George Washington, the Man*. Boston, Houghton Mifflin, 1921, clo. $.44, board $.28.

The author's final characterization of

Washington, taken from his biography (see No. 44).

23. MACE, WILLIAM HARRISON—*Washington, a Virginia Cavalier* (*Little Lives of Great Men*). New York, Rand McNally, 1916, $.65.

Intimate biography that pictures Washington as the man loved by his neighbors, relatives, and friends.

24. SCHAUFFLER, ROBERT HAVEN, ED.—*Washington's Birthday* (*Our American Holidays*). New York, Dodd Mead, 1910, $2.00.

Glimpses of Washington's life, with selections from his writings as well as tributes and other poems about him; designed to aid in the celebration of Washington's birthday.

25. SCUDDER, HORACE ELISHA—*George Washington; an Historical Biography* (*Riverside Literature Series*). Boston, Houghton Mifflin, c. 1889, reset 1920, clo. $.56.

Among the best one volume lives of Washington for readers of any age.

26. WASHINGTON, GEORGE — *Rules of Conduct, Diary of Adventure, Letters, and Farewell Addresses* (*Riverside Literature Series*). Boston, Houghton Mifflin, 1887, paper $.28.

A brief compilation of typical writings, with an introduction and notes.

27. WISTER, OWEN—*Seven Ages of Washington* (see No. 6).

ELEMENTARY SCHOOLS

28. BROOKS, ELBRIDGE STREETER—*True Story of George Washington* (see No. 20).

29. FISKE, JOHN—*War of Independence* (*Riverside Literature Series*). Boston, Houghton Mifflin, 1889, $.56.

Covers the field to 1789. Very readable, and while not a condensation of his larger books on the period (see Nos. 10, 11), it possesses the same qualities.

30. GERWIG, GEORGE WILLIAM—*Washington* (see No. 21).

31. HILL, FREDERICK TREVOR—*On the Trail of Washington* (see No. 22).
32. MITCHELL, SILAS WEIR—*Youth of Washington* (see No. 18).
33. RIDEING, WILLIAM HENRY — *George Washington.* New ed. New York, Macmillan, 1916, $1.00.

Compact and interesting book with passages quoted from his diary and from different biographies.

34. SCHAUFFLER, ROBERT HAVEN, ED.— *Washington's Birthday* (see No. 24).
35. SCUDDER, HORACE ELISHA—*George Washington* (see No. 25).
36. TURNER, NANCY BYRD—*In the Days of Young Washington.* Boston, Houghton Mifflin, 1931, $2.00; educational ed. $.92.

This is a lively story of child life in colonial Virginia, in which George Washington is a minor character.

HIGH SCHOOLS

37. ATHERTON, GERTRUDE FRANKLIN— *The Conqueror* (see No. 15).
38. FISKE, JOHN—*American Revolution* (see No. 10).
39. FORD, HENRY JONES — *Washington and his Colleagues: a Chronicle of the Rise and Fall of Federalism* (*Chronicles of America*). New Haven, Yale University Press, 1918, $1.50.

His view seems to be that Washington,

while careful and methodical, was not overburdened with brains. Perhaps the most interesting part is the account of Washington's carriages and horses, his barge, his costumes, his levees. (*American Historical Review,* 24: 735.)

40. FORD, PAUL LEICESTER — *George Washington* (see No. 1).
41. FORD, WORTHINGTON CHAUNCEY— *George Washington* (*Beacon Biographies*). Boston, Small Maynard, 1910, $.75.

Small, compact biography, considering the political and military career of Washington rather than his personality. (*A. L. A. Catalog.*)

42. HART, ALBERT BUSHNELL — *George Washington* (see No. 2).
43. LITTLE, SHELBY—*George Washington.* New York, Minton Balch, 1929, $5.00.

A biography which might almost be called autobiography from its extensive though legitimate use of Washington's letters, public papers and diary. (Cleveland Public Library, *Open Shelf.*)

44. LODGE, HENRY CABOT—*George Washington* (*American Leaders*). 2 vols. Boston, Houghton Mifflin, 1930, $.75 each. A reprint of the volumes in the *American Statesmen Series,* rev. ed., 1898, $2.50 each.

Written from abundant knowledge, it embodies excellent judgment and temper and a strong desire to be accurate.

45. MITCHELL, SILAS WEIR — *Hugh Wynne* (see No. 17).

46. MITCHELL, SILAS WEIR—*Youth of Washington* (see No. 18).
47. OSBORN, LUCRETIA PERRY, ED. — *Washington speaks for Himself* (see No. 4).
48. SCHAUFFLER, ROBERT HAVEN, ED.— *Washington's Birthday* (see No. 24).
49. SCUDDER, HORACE ELISHA—*George Washington* (see No. 25).
50. TREVELYAN, SIR GEORGE OTTO — *American Revolution* (see Nos. 13, 13a).
51. VAN TYNE, CLAUDE HALSTEAD — *Founding of the Republic* (see No. 14).
52. WASHINGTON, GEORGE — *Rules of Civility* (see No. 5).
53. WILSON, WOODROW—*George Washington.* New York, Harper, 1903, $3.00.

Distinctive diction, clear characterization, and smoothly moving narrative makes this a pleasant and informing life of Washington, the man, the soldier, and the statesman. Well illustrated.

54. WILSTACH, PAUL — *Mount Vernon, Washington's Home and the Nation's Shrine.* New ed. Indianapolis, Bobbs-Merrill, 1930, $5.00.

First published in 1916. The history of the estate from earliest title deeds to the present. A pleasant picture of Washington's home life is given and the later vicissitudes of the house.

55. WISTER, OWEN — *Seven Ages of Washington* (see No. 6).

Part III

Books For Public Libraries

This list includes a considerable number of biographies, general works about Washington and his times, fiction, and drama.

BIOGRAPHIES

Including books covering special phases of Washington's life
56. FORD, PAUL LEICESTER — *George Washington* (see No. 1).
57. FROTHINGHAM, THOMAS GODDARD— *Washington, Commander in Chief.* Boston, Houghton Mifflin, 1930, $5.00.

The most remarkable and most authentic book about Washington published for many years. Solves the problem of the military success of the Virginia planter and colonial soldier who defeated the best trained generals that England knew to send into the Revolutionary war. (A. B. Hart in *Publisher's Weekly,* Feb. 14, 1931, p. 823.)

58. HART, ALBERT BUSHNELL — *George Washington* (see No. 2).
59. HAWORTH, PAUL LELAND — *George Washington, Country Gentleman.* Indianapolis, Bobbs-Merrill, 1925, $3.00. Pub. 1915 under title: *George Washington, Farmer.*

"Washington as a private citizen, with some special account of his farming," might in more precise and spacious days have been the title. A brief, popular book, yet packed with recondite information, assiduously compiled from the diary (beginning January 1785), and other first-hand sources. (*Nation,* 101:575.) "Mr. Haworth claims that Washington was one of the first experimental agriculturists, always alert for better methods. He believes that Washington was a successful farmer."

60. HILL, FREDERICK TREVOR—*On the Trail of Washington* (see No. 22).
61. HUGHES, RUPERT—*George Washington.* 3 vols. New York, Morrow, 1926-30, $5.00 each.

The three volumes appear with different titles: *George Washington, the Human Being and the Hero, 1732-1762; George Washington, the Rebel and the Patriot, 1762-1777; George Washington, the Savior of the States, 1777-1781.* The appearance of Hughes's first volume brought about considerable criticism, some very severe, some amused, some very favorable. The later volumes have given due credit to Washington's achievements. The collection of facts is full. The opinions are often calculated to stir up readers. (Reviews in Cleveland Public Library, *Open Shelf; Political Science Quarterly,* 12:481.)

62. LITTLE, SHELBY—*George Washington* (see No. 43).
63. LODGE, HENRY CABOT—*George Washington* (see No. 44).
64. MOORE, CHARLES — *Family Life of George Washington* (see No. 3).
65. OSBORN, LUCRETIA PERRY, ED. — *Washington speaks for Himself* (see No. 4).
66. THAYER, WILLIAM ROSCOE — *George Washington* (*Riverside Library*). Boston, Houghton Mifflin, 1922, $1.00.

A well written, fairly proportioned and thoroughly orthodox history among the better short biographies of Washington. (Cleveland Public Library, *Open Shelf.*)

67. WISTER, OWEN—*Seven Ages of Washington* (see No. 6).
68. WILSON, WOODROW — *George Washington* (see No. 53).

JUVENILES

69. BROOKS, ELBRIDGE STREETER—*True Story of George Washington* (see No. 20).

70. GERWIG, GEORGE WILLIAM—*Washington* (see No. 21).

71. MACE, WILLIAM HARRISON—*Washington* (see No. 23).

72. SCUDDER, HORACE ELISHA—*George Washington* (see No. 25).

BOOKS ABOUT THE TIMES

73. BASSETT, JOHN SPENCER — *Federalist System* (see No. 7).

74. BECKER, CARL—*Eve of the Revolution* (see No. 8).

75. BOWERS, CLAUDE GERNADE—*Jefferson and Hamilton: the Struggle for Democracy in America.* Boston, Houghton Mifflin, 1925, $5.00.

This book is the most readable and the most interesting which there is on the subject. . . . Any Jeffersonophil penchant which appears in these pages serves as a good antidote to the several recent studies extolling the marvels of Federalism and glorifying too exclusively the genius of Hamilton. (S. F. Bemis in *American Historical Review,* 31: 543.)

76. CHANNING, EDWARD—*United States* (see No. 9).

77. FISKE, JOHN—*American Revolution* (see No. 10).

78. FISKE, JOHN—*Critical Period* (see No. 11).

79. HART, ALBERT BUSHNELL—*Formation of the Union, 1750-1829 (Epochs of American History).* Rev. ed. New York, Longmans Green, 1925, $1.40.

An admirably constructed book, well provided with maps and classified list of books for further reading. The narrative is confined mainly to political history, only brief attention being given to the military events. The treatment is scientific and devoid of partisan bias, and in choice and presentation of the subject matter is abreast of the best scholarship of the day. (Larned, *Literature of American History.*)

80. JAMESON, JOHN FRANKLIN—*American Revolution considered as a Social Movement.* P r i n c e t o n, Princeton University Press, 1926, $1.50.

Dr. Jameson addresses himself to a much neglected aspect of the Revolution, its social implications and consequences, . . . It need not be said that the scholarship is impeccable, . . . and that, above all, the outlook is broad and thoughtful . . . concerns himself almost wholly with the beneficial

changes, and passes rapidly over the . . . shocks to social health which the six years of active war inevitably produced. (Allan Nevins in *American Historical Review,* 32: 167.)

81. JERNEGAN, MARCUS WILSON — *The American Colonies, 1492-1750 (Epochs of American History).* New York, Longmans Green, 1929, $1.60.

Strong on the social side of the development of the colonies, with elaborate bibliography.

82. MCLAUGHLIN, ANDREW CUNNINGHAM—*Confederation and the Constitution* (see No. 12).

83. MORISON, SAMUEL ELIOT—*Sources and Documents illustrating the American Revolution, 1764-1788, and the Formation of the Federal Constitution.* New York, Oxford University Press, 1923, $3.50.

An admirable introduction analyzes with particular care pertinent phases of scholarly opinion concerning the origins of the Revolution and gives a proper historical setting for the collection as a whole. (W. K. Boyd in *American Historical Review,* 29:805.)

84. NEVINS, ALLAN — *American States during and after the Revolution, 1775-1789.* New York, Macmillan, 1924, $4.50.

There are several subjects untouched by the book, upon which light is much more wanted than upon state politics . . . Yet after all is said, the fact remains that Mr. Nevins's book is a valuable one, crammed full of useful facts that were not readily accessible heretofore. (S. E. Morison in *American Historical Review,* 30:611.)

85. TREVELYAN, SIR GEORGE OTTO — *American Revolution* (see Nos. 13, 13a).

86. VAN TYNE, CLAUDE HALSTEAD — *Formation of the Republic* (see No. 14).

87. WHARTON, ANNE HOLLINGSWORTH— *English Ancestral Homes of Noted Americans.* Philadelphia, Lippincott, 1915, $2.50.

Beginning with Plymouth, the author describes in readable fashion her visits to towns and neighborhoods associated with the Washingtons, Franklins, Penns, and many less distinguished early settlers in the United States. Index and many good illustrations. (New York State Library, *Best Books of 1915,* 30.)

FICTION AND DRAMA

88. ATHERTON, GERTRUDE FRANKLIN— *The Conqueror* (see No. 15).

89. BLOEM, WALTER—*Son of his Country.* New York, Harper, 1928, $2.50.

90. COOPER, JAMES FENIMORE—*The Spy: a Tale of the Neutral Ground.* Home Library, New York, Burt, $1.25. Many other eds. at various prices.

First pub. in 1821. On the armies in New York.

91. FORD, PAUL LEICESTER—*Janice Meredith* (see No. 16).

92. MACKAYE, PERCY—*Washington, the Man who made Us.* New York, Knopf, 1918, $2.00.

Washington, Hamilton, Monroe, Lord Fairfax, Patrick Henry, Martha Washington, Lafayette, Betsy Ross, and others are portrayed in a series of effective scenes. A ballad play, consisting of a prologue, three acts and an epilogue, intended for community acting. The historic scenes are connected by contemporary ballads sung by a wandering minstrel. There is an abridged version for the theater. The ballads with their music are separately published. (A. L. A. Booklist, April, 1919.)

93. MITCHELL, SILAS WEIR — *H u g h Wynne* (see No. 17).

94. MITCHELL, SILAS WEIR—*Red City; a Novel of the Second Administration of President Washington.* New York, Century, 1908, $2.00.

Concerns the fortunes in love, business and revenge of a young vicomte who escaped to Philadelphia from the Reign of Terror. Local coloring, historical accuracy, and characterization take precedence over plot in a leisurely story in which Hugh Wynne, . . . Washington, Hamilton, Jefferson and Randolph appear. (New York State Library, *Best Books of 1908,* 35.)

95. MITCHELL, SILAS WEIR—*Youth of Washington* (see No. 18).

96. SCHAUFFLER, ROBERT HAVEN, ED.— *Washington's Birthday* (see No. 24).

97. THACKERY, WILLIAM MAKEPEACE — *Virginians* (see No. 19).

98. TURNER, NANCY BYRD—*In the Days of Young Washington* (see No. 36).

99. SEAWELL, MOLLY ELLIOT—*Virginia Cavalier.* New York, Harper, 1903, $1.75.

Period of the French and Indian War.

Part IV

Extended List For Study and Research

This list includes most of the source material available, the productions of scholars who have delved into special features of Washington's life and achievements, and other writings which throw light upon Washington. Many libraries have already much of the material, and some will have additional titles. Colleges and universities ought to have strong collections, and it is still possible to acquire some of the out-of-print material at no excessive price. On the other hand, some titles are given for reference purposes even though they cannot be bought at the present time. The large collections in the country, such as the Library of Congress, Pennsylvania Historical Society, New York Public Library, Boston Athenaeum, Harvard College Library, Boston Public Library, American Antiquarian Society, possess a considerable portion of this material. The holdings of the seven above and nine other libraries make a composite list containing about 2,600 titles, from which the following titles compose a selection of the most representative and most available.

The list is divided into groups for convenience in locating material, and annotations have been made whenever it seemed advisable. Prices have not been given, as many titles are out of print, and are to be picked up only at second hand sales or auctions. The place and date of publication are given. The publisher can readily be identified if desired.

BIBLIOGRAPHIES

A great many books about Washington contain bibliographies, some with comments, Baker, in his enthusiasm for Washington, prepared in 1889 a bibliography arranged by the year of publication, and this is a very valuable repository of information. A set of Library of Congress cards on Washington would make a much larger bibliography. The Boston Anthenaeum is the only library holding a large Washington collection which has printed a bibliography. This is still valuable, although published in 1897. Among the recent biographers who have appended bibliographical information to their works are Corbin, Hughes, Little, Sears, and Woodward.

100. BAKER, WILLIAM SPOHN—*Bibliotheca Washingtoniana; a Descriptive List of the Biographies and Biographical Sketches of George Washington.* Philadelphia, 1889.

Descriptive list of biographies and biographical sketches of Washington in order of their publication. 502 titles. Most exhaustive yet made. (Larned, *Literature of American History.*)

101. BOSTON ATHENAEUM—*Catalogue of the Washington Collection in the Boston Athenaeum; compiled and annotated by Appleton P. C. Griffin. With an Appendix, The Inventory of Washington's Books drawn up by the Appraisers of his Estate; with Notes in regard to the Full Titles of the Several Books and the Later History and Present Ownership of those not in the Athenaeum Collection, by William Coolidge Lane.* Cambridge, 1897.

In four parts: I. Books from the library of General George Washington. II. Other books from Mount Vernon. III. The Writings of Washington. IV. Washingtoniana. Index by F. O. Poole, Cambridge, 1900.

A considerable portion of these books was left to George C. Washington. Sold by him to Henry Stevens in 1847 or 1848, and by the latter to the Boston Athenaeum in 1849.

102. CHANNING, E., HART, A. B., TURNER, F. J.—*Guide to the Study and Reading of American History.* Rev. ed. Boston, 1912. Chs. xix-xxii.

103. HART, ALBERT BUSHNELL—*George Washington* (see No. 2).

BIOGRAPHIES

From the days of John Marshal and Wash-ington Irving efforts have been made to write authoritative comprehensive biographies of Washington. Some of the great number of briefer works are of value, and others are wholly worthless. Some are written by those who have been enthused by reading and contemplation on Washington and his times, and others with a particular object in view. A number are in foreign languages and some of these are given as examples. A few which were prepared for juvenile use are included.

104. BAKER, WILLIAM SPOHN—*Itinerary of General Washington from June 15, 1775, to December 23, 1783.* Philadelphia, 1892.

Reprinted with additions, from *Pennsylvania Magazine of History and Biography,* Vols. 14-15. A remarkably complete picture of the daily movements of Washington. Notes clear and full. Invaluable for students.

105. BAKER, WILLIAM SPOHN—*Washington after the Revolution, MDCCLXXXIV–MDCCXCIX.* Philadelphia, 1898.

A calendar, showing the whereabouts and occupation of Washington each day, as gathered from his writings, correspondence, and the newspapers. (Larned, *Literature of American History.*)

106. BAKER, WILLIAM SPOHN, ED.—*Early Sketches of George Washington, reprinted with Biographical and Bibliographical Notes.* Philadelphia, 1894.

Fifteen biographical sketches, by various writers, dating from 1760 to 1795. They gratify curiosity to see the early opinions concerning Washington rather than serve any historic purpose. (Larned, *Literature of American History.*)

107. BROOKS, ELBRIDGE STREETER—*True Story of George Washington* (see No. 20).

108. CLARK, JONATHAN—*Life of General Washington, late President of the United States; together with his Farewell Address, and a Short Account of the American Revolutionary War.* Albany, 1813.

The laudatory character is evident from the admonitory quotation of the title-page: "Begin with the infant in the cradle: let the first word he lisps be Washington."

109. CONDIE, THOMAS—*Memoirs of George Washington, Esq., late President of the United States.* Philadelphia, 1798. Reprinted as: *Biographical Memoirs of the Illustrious George Washington, late President of the United States of America, &c. Containing a History of the Principal Events of his Life, with Extracts from his Journals, Speeches to Congress and Public Addresses. Also, a Sketch of his Private Life.* Brattleborough, 1814.

Compiled from earlier sketches by John Bell and Jedidiah Morse, with some documents included. It was reprinted with some changes under the reputed authorship of James Trumbull, in 1829.

110. CORBIN, JOHN—*Unknown Washington: Biographic Origins of the Republic.* New York, 1930.

A hitherto neglected phase of Washington's career is made the background of this new portrait, his contribution to the Constitution. His love for Sally Fairfax and her influence upon his Republicanism are made the topic of an interesting chapter. In Washington's personality the author sees a nature "at once richer and more complicated than that of any of the brilliant and versatile group with whom he surrounded himself." The book makes drastic criticisms of most historians' accounts of Washington and the Constitutional period. (*Booklist,* Dec., 1930.)

111. CORRY, JOHN—*Life of George Washington, late President and Commander in Chief of the Armies of the United States of America; interspersed with Biographical Anecdotes of the most Eminent Men who effected the American Revolution.* London, 1800.

The author was an Irishman, a topographer, and miscellaneous writer. One of the earliest English lives, repeatedly reprinted.

112. CUSTIS, GEORGE WASHINGTON PARKE—*Recollections and Private Memoirs of Washington.* Philadelphia, 1859. Other eds.

Contributed for most part to newspapers at various times for twenty years. A storehouse for the usual traditions about Washington, accepted but largely unproven. Topical rather than chronological. (Larned, *Literature of American History.*)

113. EVERETT, EDWARD—*Life of George Washington.* New York, 1860.

Originally prepared for and published (without the appendix) in the Encyclopaedia Britannica, 8th ed., 1860. It avowedly follows Spark's like, is well proportioned, but has no special merit. (Larned, *Literature of American History.*)

114. FORD, HENRY JONES—*Washington* (see No. 39).

115. FORD, PAUL LEICESTER—*George Washington* (see No. 1).

116. FORD, WORTHINGTON CHAUNCEY—*George Washington.* 2 vols. New York, 1900.

Mr. Ford spent many years in the study and presentation of material on Washington and his period, and in these volumes he records the impressions which are the result of that study.

117. FROST, JOHN—*Pictorial Life of George Washington: embracing a Complete History of the Seven Years' War, the Revolutionary War, the Formation of the Federal Constitution, and the Administration of Washington. With upwards of One Hundred Engravings, by Croome & Devereux.* Philadelphia, 1847.

A popular work by an author who developed the pictorial idea for selling books. Not worth much historically. Reprinted various times.

118. GERWIG, GEORGE WILLIAM—*Washington* (see No. 21).

119. GLASS, FRANCIS—*Life of George Wash-

ington in Latin Prose. New York, 1835.

LANCE, WILLIAM—*Georgii Washington vita.* Carolopoli [Charleston], 1836.

> Of course there is no historical value, but there is a considerable interest in the two Latin lives appearing almost simultaneously. Glass' work was highly recommended for its Latin prose.

120. GUIZOT, FRANCOIS PIERRE GUILLAUME—*Washington.* Tr. by Henry Reeve. London, 1840.

> A translation of the introduction to Jared Sparks, *Vie, Correspondance et Ecrits de Washington.* Paris, 1840. The introduction is a eulogistic essay by the eminent French historian and statesman.

121. HALE, EDWARD EVERETT—*Life of George Washington, studied anew.* New York, 1888.

> Emphasizing the domestic rather than the public side of his life; judicious selection of materials, vivacious style. (Larned, *Literature of American History.*)

122. HAPGOOD, NORMAN—*George Washington.* New York, 1901.

> Shows Washington's practical and matter-of-fact mind, his mingled modesty and self-confidence, his human side, which, while at times somewhat painful to hero-worshipers, happily avoids the belittling manner into which this style of biography easily falls. (*Nation,* 74:112.)

123. HILL, FREDERICK TREVOR—*On the Trail of Washington* (see No. 22).

124. HILL, FREDERICK TREVOR—*Washington, the Man of Action.* Illustrated by Comte J. Onfroy de Breville (Job). New York, 1914.

> For a boy old enough to take an intelligent interest in his country's history, nothing more suitable. (*Nation,* 99:666.)

125. HUBBARD, ELBERT—"George Washington"; in his *Little Journeys to the Homes of American Statesmen,* pp. 1–40. New York, 1898.

> Included mainly because of the author, whose trenchant pen described other little journeys for numerous readers.

126. HUGHES, RUPERT—*George Washington* (see No. 61).

127. IRVING, WASHINGTON—*Life of George Washington.* 5 vols. New York, 1855–1859.

> There are many later editions, with some variations in number of volumes, plates, and portraits in the different sets. This admirable biography at once took its place among the three standard biographies. Though Mr. Irving's mental equipment for historical investigation would not now be called an ideal one, his work is expressed with fair judgment and temper, and much care, though compiled in too much haste. It is preeminent in its literary style. (Larned, *Literature of American History.*)

128. IRVING, WASHINGTON—*Washington and his Country; being Irving's Life of Washington abridged for the Use of Schools, with Introduction and Continuation, giving a Brief Outline of United States History from the Discovery of America to the End of the Civil War,* by John Fiske. Boston, 1887.

> Fiske's part shows competent knowledge, judgment, fairness. (Larned, *Literature of American History.*)

129. JOHNSTON, ELIZABETH BRYANT—*George Washington Day by Day.* New York, 1895.

> Brief extracts from Washington's writings and other sources and accounts of events of his life arranged in the form of a calendar. Several fine and accurate illustrations of historic places.

130. KING, COOPER—*George Washington.* London, 1894.

> By an officer in the English army. Interesting from its point of view. Style clear, simple and cogent. (Larned, *Literature of American History.*)

131. LITTLE, SHELBY—*George Washington* (see No. 43).

132. LODGE, HENRY CABOT—*George Washington* (see No. 44).

133. LOSSING, BENSON JOHN—*Life of Washington; a Biography Personal, Military, and Political.* 3 vols. New York, 1860.

> This was planned by Rufus W. Griswold, who wrote the first part, but it was finished by Lossing. It was reissued in 1870 as *Washington and the American Republic,* 3 vols.

134. LOSSING, BENSON JOHN—*Mary and Martha, the Mother and Wife of George Washington.* New York, 1886.

> Belongs to the better class of popular writing. Remarkably free from the gushing style. (Larned, *Literature of American History.*)

135. MACE, WILLIAM HARRISON—*Washington* (see No. 23).

136. MARSHALL, JOHN—*Life of George Washington, Commander in Chief of the American Forces during the War which established the Independence of his Country, and First President of the United States. Compiled under the Inspection of the Hon. Bushrod Washington from Original Papers . . . to which is prefixed an Introduction, containing a Compendious View of the Colonies planted by the English on the Continent of North America.* 5 vols. and atlas. Philadelphia, 1804–07. There is a recent reprint; 5 vols., Fredericksburg, Va., 1926.

> Written by an eminent Virginian contemporary of Washington, and based on the Bushrod Washington manuscripts. The first three volumes appeared within five years after Washington's death; and, though the haste with which it was prepared is deprecated in the author's preface, its nearness to the events together with several other notable qualities, make it one of the three most famous lives of Washington. Marshall carried his eminently judicial temper into the composition of this book; yet he did not wholly avoid giving it a bias which has caused it to be regarded as a "Federalist narrative." (Larned, *Literature of American History.*) Numerous editions, including translations into French, German, Dutch.

137. MINNEGERODE, MEADE — "Martha Washington"; in his *Some American Ladies,* pp. 3–46. New York, 1926.

> The author has written of various subjects, and "makes a picture rather than a portrait" of each.

138. MOORE, CHARLES—*Family Life of George Washington* (see No. 3).

139. OSBORN, LUCRETIA PERRY, ED.—*Washington speaks for Himself* (see No. 4).

140. PARKER, THEODORE—"Washington"; in his *Historic Americans,* pp. 73–146. Boston, 1870.

> Treats of the life, labors, and characteristics of Washington. Shows the fruits of extensive investigation, and a spirit of caustic criticism.

141. PARKINSON, RICHARD—*George Washington.* Baltimore, 1909.

> The author, a Lincolnshire farmer, came to Virginia at Washington's invitation with a view to running one of his farms. His *Tour in America,* 2 vols., London, 1805, gives a very interesting account of his visits to Mount Vernon. This small volume reprints the statements about Washington.

142. PAULDING, JAMES KIRKE—*Life of Washington.* 2 vols. New York, 1836.

> Written for children; many anecdotes from contemporaries of his subject. Its delightful style gives it a lasting charm. The sketch of Washington in the last chapter is generally accepted as unexcelled. (Larned, *Literature of American History.*)

143. RAMSAY, DAVID—*Life of George Washington, Commander in Chief of the Armies of the United States in the War which established their Independence; and First President of the United States.* New York, 1807.

> Between 1807 and 1832, five editions were printed in English, one in French and two in Spanish. (Larned, *Literature of American History.*)

144. RIDEING, WILLIAM HENRY—*George Washington* (see No. 33).

145. SAINT-GEORGE, MRS. A.—*Sketch of the Life of the Illustrious Washington, First President of the United States of America.* New York, 1834.

> A straightforward, non-effusive account, by an English lady, drawn from documents in the British Museum.

146. SAWYER, JOSEPH DILLAWAY—*George Washington.* 2 vols. New York, 1927.

> "Mr. Sawyer has assailed the problem with unbounded, honest enthusiasm and a wealth of illustration." There are over 1,500 illustrations, including 250 portraits. The biography is conventional.

147. SCHROEDER, JOHN FREDERICK—*Life and Times of Washington, containing a Particular Account of National Principles and Events, and of the Illustrious Men of the Revolution. Illustrated with highly-finished Steel Engravings . . . by Alonzo Chappel.* 2 vols. New York, 1857; rev. and enl. ed., Albany, 1903.

> Not completed at Schroeder's death, finished by others. A mid-century pretentious work, full of documentary material.

148. SCUDDER, HORACE ELISHA—*George Washington* (see No. 25).

148a. SEARS, LOUIS MARTIN—*George Washington*. New York, 1932.
With maps and a comparative chronology. A new study based on Washington's published writings, with the narrative following their sequence. The consideration of Washington's actions, motives, and character is excellent.

149. SEELYE, ELIZABETH (EGGLESTON)—*Story of Washington (Delights of History)*. Ed. with an introduction by Edward Eggleston; illustrated by Allegra Eggleston. New York, 1893.
Juvenile. Gives many personal anecdotes and details, with popular summary of public life.

150. SPARKS, JARED—*Life of George Washington*. Boston, 1839. First pub. Boston, 1837, as Vol. 1 of Sparks' ed. of *Writings of Washington*.
Sparks was admittedly a hero-worshipper of his subject. The life was reprinted in various editions, and translated into other languages.

151. THAYER, WILLIAM ROSCOE—*George Washington* (see No. 66).

152. TRENT, WILLIAM PETERFIELD—"George Washington"; in his *Southern Statesmen of the Old Regime*, pp. 3–45. New York, 1897.
Pleasantly written and useful as popular account. (Larned, *Literature of American History*.)

153. TURNER, NANCY BYRD—*Mother of Washington*. New York, 1930.
The author "fills in the background with understanding and insight." The book has been done with especial fidelity. (*New York Times*, Dec. 28, 1930; *A. L. A. Booklist*, May, 1931.) Adheres to the traditional view.

154. UPHAM, CHARLES WENTWORTH, ED.—*Life of General Washington, First President of the United States, written by himself, comprising his Memoirs and Correspondence, as prepared by him for Publication, including several Original Letters now first printed*. 2 vols. London, 1851.
A work derived from Sparks, by the antiquarian and author of *Salem Witchcraft*. The edition of 1840 (Boston) was suppressed by the Circuit Court as infringing on Sparks.

155. WEEMS, MASON LOCKE—*History of the Life and Death, Virtues and Exploits of General George Washington*. New York, 1927.
First published at Georgetown, D. C., in 1800. Ran through perhaps seventy editions. The 1927 text is taken from one of the later editions. Larned says: "This 'Life,' from which the letter f might be justly omitted, achieved its early success from the announcement on its title page that its author was 'formerly Rector of Mt. Vernon Parish' . . . For the fifth edition (Augusta, 1806) the hatchet and other stories were invented, and it became a standard book for Sunday schools."

156. WHIPPLE, WAYNE, ED.—*Story Life of Washington*. 2 vols. Philadelphia, 1911.

A collection of 500 anecdotes and descriptions from various writers, chronologically arranged, giving a kaleidoscopic view of Washington's career. A few extracts from Washington's journals, letters, and state papers are also included and a considerable number of historical pictures are reproduced. (Carnegie Library of Pittsburgh, *Monthly Bulletin*, 17:152.)

157. WILSON, WOODROW—*George Washington* (see No. 53).

158. WISTER, OWEN—*Seven Ages of Washington* (see No. 6).

159. WOODWARD, WILLIAM E. — *George Washington, the Image and the Man*. New York, 1926.
The author chose rather to play the iconoclast and produce a biography out of the usual order, which dispels illusions by portraying the failings or the mistakes of his hero. . . . The book will be useful in correcting unintelligent adulation, and it is one that American hero-worshipers need to read. It will not, however, affect the place in history of this greatest and most sagacious of the early Americans. (J. A. Woodburn in *American Historical Review*, 32:614.)

WASHINGTON'S WRITINGS

Washington was a prolific writer, and some of his productions have been frequently published. Among these especially his Farewell Address, Will, and Rules of Civility. His diaries, letters, and military orders, make up an immense amount of material. Jared Sparks first collected his writings in anything like a complete edition, later Worthington C. Ford edited a very satisfactory edition, and now the United States George Washington Bicentennial Commission is preparing a definitive edition under the editorship of John C. Fitzpatrick. This publication will not include the Diaries but will include the General Orders, of which up to this time only a few excerpts have been printed. Included in this list are the titles of works to be found in many libraries, some of the complete editions mentioned above, other collections of separate writings.

Many letters by Washington as well as to him are included in the Contemporary Authorities of this Part.

A. EXTENDED EDITIONS

160. WASHINGTON, GEORGE—*Writings of George Washington; being his Correspondence, Addresses, Messages, and Other Papers, Official and Private, selected and published from the Original Manuscripts; with a Life of the Author, Notes and Illustrations*. Ed. by Jared Sparks. 12 vols. Boston, 1834-37.
This was for years the standard set of Washington's works, but it has to a certain extent been superseded by Ford's edition. Sparks followed the copies of Washington's letters as they were found in his letter book. Discrepancies between the copies and the originals as preserved caused charges that the editor had made wilful alterations in addition to "editing" the letters. He explains his method in the preface to the second volume. On the ensuing controversy, see pamphlets by Sparks, Lord Mahon, and

Wm. B. Reed. (Larned, *Literature of American History*.)

161. WASHINGTON, GEORGE—*Writings of George Washington*. Ed. by Worthington Chauncey Ford. 14 vols. New York, 1889–93.
Should supersede that of Sparks, as being a rigidly accurate reproduction of the text. Mr. Ford's editorial work has been done on the basis of long familiarity with the subject, as well as of fullest knowledge, exceptional judgment and critical discernment, and a fair-minded spirit; and it is marked by painstaking accuracy and lucidity of language. (Larned, *Literature of American History*.)

B. BUSINESS ACCOUNTS

162. WASHINGTON, GEORGE — *George Washington's Accounts of Expenses while Commander-in-Chief of the Continental Army, 1775–1783, reproduced in Facsimile, with Annotations by John C. Fitzpatrick*. Boston, 1917.

163. WASHINGTON, GEORGE — *Monuments of Washington's Patriotism: containing a Facsimile of his Publick Accounts kept during the Revolutionary War; and some of the most Interesting Documents connected with his Military Command and Civil Administration*. Washington, 1838.

C. DIARIES

164. WASHINGTON, GEORGE — *Diaries of George Washington, 1748–1799*. Ed. by John C. Fitzpatrick. 4 vols. Boston, 1925.
The Mount Vernon Ladies' Association of the Union here issues all the available diaries of George Washington in four well-bound volumes, putting them in an accessible form. Most of the material comes from the archives in the Library of Congress. The figure presented is that of a country gentleman rather than a statesman. (*A. L. A. Booklist*, Feb., 1926.)

165. WASHINGTON, GEORGE—*Daily Journal of Major George Washington, in 1751–2, kept while on a Tour from Virginia to the Island of Barbados, with his Invalid Brother, Maj. Lawrence Washington*. Ed. with notes by J. M. Toner. Albany, 1892.
It contains valuable information and supplies links in the chain of the history of the early life of Washington.

166. WASHINGTON, GEORGE — *Diary of George Washington from 1789 to 1791; embracing the Opening of the First Congress, and his Tours through New England, Long Island, and the Southern States. Together with his Journal of a Tour to the Ohio, in 1753*. Ed. by Benson J. Lossing. New York, 1860.
The original of a portion of this is now missing.

167. WASHINGTON, GEORGE—*Journal of my Journey over the Mountains; by George Washington, while surveying*

for Lord Thomas Fairfax, Baron of Cameron, in the Northern Neck of Virginia, beyond the Blue Ridge, in 1747–8. Ed. with notes by J. M. Toner. Albany, 1892.

Its chief interest centers in the fact that it is the earliest known composition of Washington. The major part surveying notes and records. (Larned, *Literature of American History*.)

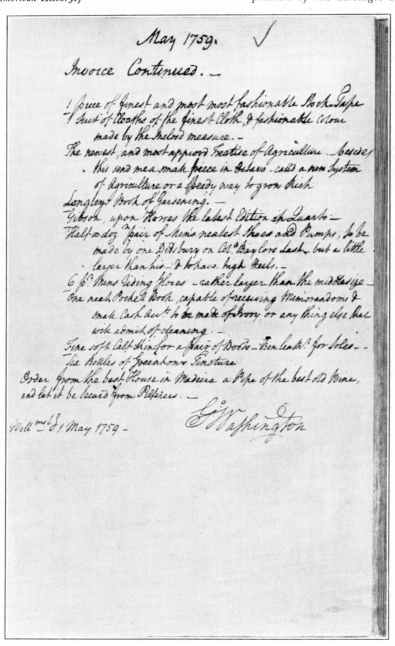

ORDER FOR BOOKS BY GEORGE WASHINGTON

168. WASHINGTON, GEORGE—*Washington and the West; being George Washington's Diary of September, 1784, kept during his Journey into the Ohio Basin*. Ed. by Archer Butler Hulbert. New York, 1905.

D. LETTERS AND DOCUMENTS

169. FITZPATRICK, JOHN C., ED.—*Calendar of the Correspondence of George Washington, Commander in Chief of the Continental Army*. 5 vols. Washington, 1906–15.

This calendar, well indexed, is of the original manuscripts in the Library of Congress, and summarizes the official correspondence of Washington with Congress and the army officers.

170. RICHARDSON, JAMES D., ED.—*Compilation of the Messages and Papers of the Presidents*. Vol. I. Washington, 1896.

Contains Washington's inaugural addresses and messages to Congress, and proclamations.

171. WASHINGTON, GEORGE—*Agricultural Papers of George Washington*. Ed. by Walter E. Brooke. Boston, 1912.

Washington's correspondence on this topic, especially with Sir John Sinclair and Arthur Young, appeared in various earlier editions.

172. WASHINGTON, GEORGE—*Correspondence of General Washington and Comte de Grasse, 1781*. Washington, 1931.

This is a congressional publication; Senate Document 211, 71st Congress, 2nd Session. The correspondence relates to the siege of Yorktown and includes letters to and from other officers.

173. WASHINGTON, GEORGE — *George Washington and Mount Vernon; a Collection of Washington's unpublished Agricultural and Personal Letters*. Ed. with historical and genealogical introduction by M. D. Conway. Brooklyn, 1889.

174. WASHINGTON, GEORGE—*Letters and Recollections of George Washington; being Letters to Tobias Lear and Others between 1790 and 1799, showing the First American in the Management of his Estate and Domestic Affairs. With a Diary of Washington's Last Days, kept by Mr. Lear. Illustrated from Rare Old Portraits, Photographs, and Engravings*. New York, 1906.

This collection has been variously printed and entered, sometimes under the name of Tobias Lear, this edition under Mrs. Louisa L. Eyre's name (she was granddaughter of Tobias Lear), and in 1857 under the title *Washington in Domestic Life*, by Richard Rush. Washington is portrayed in the light of a domestic man managing his own affairs; as a planter looking over crops, cattle and overseers; and as a business man driving bargains, suing for bad debts, collecting rents, and making investments. (*Book Review Digest*, 1906.)

175. WASHINGTON, GEORGE—*Official Letters to the Honorable American Congress, written during the War between the United Colonies and Great Britain, by His Excellency, George Washington*. 2 vols. London, 1795.

The letters, "copied by special permission from the original papers in the office of the Secretary of State," cover the period from June 24, 1775, to December 31, 1778. Other volumes, to include the later correspondence of Washington, were projected by the editor, John Carey, but no more were published.

176. WASHINGTON, GEORGE—*Spurious Letters attributed to Washington*. Brooklyn, 1889.

With a bibliographical note by Worthington Chauncey Ford.

177. WASHINGTON, GEORGE—*Washington-Crawford Letters. Being the Correspondence between George Washington and William Crawford, from 1767 to 1781, concerning Western Lands*. Ed. by C. W. Butterfield. Cincinnati, 1877.

Valuable information concerning Washington's business habits. (Larned, *Literature of American History*.)

178. WASHINGTON, GEORGE—*Washington-Duché Letters*. Ed. with an introduction by Worthington Chauncey Ford. Brooklyn, 1890.

179. WASHINGTON, GEORGE—*Washington-Irvine Correspondence. The Official Letters which passed between Washington and Brig.-Gen. William Irvine and between Irvine and Others concerning Military Affairs in the West from 1781 to 1783.* Ed. with an introduction by C. W. Butterfield. Madison, 1882.

180. WASHINGTON, GEORGE—*Writings of George Washington (Writings of American Statesmen).* Ed. by L. B. Evans. New York, 1908.

A handy selective edition of 150 characteristic writings, including the Farewell Address.

E. RULES OF CIVILITY

181. WASHINGTON, GEORGE — *George Washington's Rules of Civility, traced to their Sources and restored.* Ed. by M. D. Conway. New York, 1890.

182. WASHINGTON, GEORGE — *Rules of Civility* (see No. 5).

F. WILL

183. PRUSSING, EUGENE ERNST—*Estate of George Washington, deceased.* Boston, 1927.

Includes a page by page copy of the will, and a statement as to the acquirement and eventual disposal of each item. He is a trained lawyer and a patient investigator. His is a book for archives and collections, and an interesting, rational and unexpectedly readable piece of work. (*Boston Transcript*, Dec. 17, 1927.)

184. WASHINGTON, GEORGE—*Last Will and Testament of George Washington of Mount Vernon. The only Authenticated Copy, full and complete, embracing a Schedule of his Real Estate, and Explanatory Notes thereto by the Testator; to which is added important Historical Notes, Biographical Sketches, and Anecdotes.* Washington, 1911.

This is a congressional publication; Senate Document No. 86, 62nd Congress, 1st Session. It is a reprint of an issue in 1876; the transcription is poor and the notes obsolete and erroneous.

185. WASHINGTON, GEORGE—*Will of General George Washington: to which is annexed a Schedule of his Property, directed to be sold.* Alexandria, Printed from the record of the County Court of Fairfax, 1800.

This, the earliest printing, was reprinted this same year in Baltimore, Boston, London, New York, Philadelphia, and Worcester.

186. WASHINGTON, GEORGE — "*Will of George Washington*"; in *Writings* (Ford ed.), Vol. 14, p. 271.

BACKGROUND OF WASHINGTON'S CAREER

This includes books on the general history of the times, on the country or the region, or on social or political conditions. It naturally includes some of the best histories written about the United States, colonial days, the Revolution, the republic, or about Virginia or parts of it. Of course many more could be added; this is a selection only.

187. ADAMS, JAMES TRUSLOW—*Revolutionary New England, 1691–1776.* Boston, 1923.

He has skillfully developed the social and economic background of the Revolution and helped us to see more clearly than before the varied and complex situations which, in one locality and another, tended to produce a revolutionary state of mind. (E. B. Greene in *American Historical Review*, 29: 343.)

188. ALVORD, CLARENCE WALWORTH—*Mississippi Valley in British Politics: a Study of the Trade, Land Speculation and Experiments in Imperialism Culminating in the American Revolution.* 2 vols. Cleveland, 1916.

What was the connection between "British muddling in the West" and the Revolution? . . . while it had a bearing, and at times an important bearing, upon the conflict over taxation and legislative independence, it was in fact largely obscured by this conflict, and must for that very reason occupy, in any explanation of the causes of the Revolution, a strictly subordinate place. That place, however, cannot henceforth be denied it, thanks to Professor Alvord's book. (Carl Becker in *American Historical Review*, 22: 671.)

189. ANDREWS, CHARLES MCLEAN—*Colonial Background of the American Revolution: Four Essays in American Colonial History.* Rev. ed. New Haven, 1931.

It is the purpose of Professor Andrews . . . to show that "these years from 1607 to 1783 were colonial before they were American or national" and that to leave out of the reckoning the interactions and interrelations of colonies and mother country is to leave our understanding of colonial history "imperfect and incomplete." (W. T. Root in *American Historical Review*, 30: 832.)

190. ANDREWS, CHARLES MCLEAN—*Colonial Folkways: a Chronicle of American Life in the Reign of the Georges (Chronicles of America).* New Haven, 1919.

There is probably no other presentation of the subject which enables the reader to visualize so clearly the American society of the later colonial era. (*American Historical Review*, 25:298.)

191. AVERY, ELROY MCKENDREE—*History of the United States and its People from their Earliest Records to the Present Time.* 7 vols. Cleveland, 1904–10.

The work has been severely criticised because of some mistakes and because the author was not a historical scholar, but it is magnificent in its conception. Vols. IV-VII deal with Washington's period and are provided with unusually good illustrations and maps. The remainder of the history remains in manuscript.

192. BAYARD, FERDINAND MARIE—*Voyage dans l'intérieur des États-Unis, à Bath, Winchester, dans la Vallée de Shenandoah, etc., etc., pendant l'Été de 1791.* 2 ed., augm. de descriptions et d'anecdotes sur la vie militaire et politique de Georges Washington.* Paris, An VIe (1798).

A French writer and traveler, 1763-1818. The first edition, 1797, did not contain the Washington references.

193. BECKER, CARL—*Eve of the Revolution* (see No. 8).

194. BEER, GEORGE LOUIS—*British Colonial Policy, 1754–1765.* New York, 1907.

A well-reasoned, and in the main, convincing study of eighteenth-century imperial problems. The book shows throughout unusual mastery of printed and manuscript sources. (*Political Science Quarterly*, 23: 326.)

195. BELCHER, HENRY—*First American Civil War; First Period, 1775–1778, with Chapters on the Continental or Revolutionary Army and on the Forces of the Crown.* 2 vols. London, 1911.

Belcher wrote as a British Tory, but makes Washington stand out as a commanding figure.

196. CAMPBELL, CHARLES—*History of the Colony and Ancient Dominion of Virginia.* Philadelphia, 1860.

Early portion based on the now discredited publications of Capt. John Smith. Otherwise the work is sufficiently accurate. (Larned, *Literature of American History*.)

197. CHANNING, EDWARD—*United States* (see No. 9).

198. CONWAY, MONCURE DANIEL—*Barons of the Potomack and the Rappahannock.* New York, 1892.

Privately printed book dealing with Washington's region.

199. CORWIN, EDWARD SAMUEL—*French Policy and the American Alliance of 1778.* Princeton, 1916.

We are now able to comprehend the aims of the French government, the peculiar limitations of its freedom of action on account of the relations with Spain, and the substantial loyalty of the king and his ministers to their engagements with the colonies. (D. J. Hill in *American Historical Review*, 22:393.)

200. EARLE, ALICE MORSE—*Home Life in Colonial Days.* New York, 1899.

Written for the general reader, but of value also for the scholar.

201. EARLE, ALICE MORSE—*Stage-Coach and Tavern Days.* New York, 1900.

There is not one of her books that may not be cordially recommended for its accuracy and readableness. (Larned, *Literature of American History*.)

202. FARIS, JOHN THOMSON—*When America was Young.* New York, 1925.

"It is the author's hope that the chapters . . . will give some assistance to those who turn to records of the past as they seek inspiration for the present and hope for the future."—Foreword. Ch. vi is "George Washington as revealed by his Correspondence," and there are other references to Washington.

203. FISHER, SYDNEY GEORGE—*Struggle for American Independence.* 2 vols. Philadelphia, 1908.

Criticisms vary from highest praise because of readableness, of perception, and luminous understanding to objection because of his viewpoint. "Can not be overlooked by any who wish to be well informed upon the origins and fundamentals of our nation."

204. FISKE, JOHN—*American Revolution* (see No. 10).

205. FISKE, JOHN—*Critical Period* (see No. 11).

206. FITZPATRICK, JOHN CLEMENT—*Spirit of the Revolution.* Boston, 1924.

Whoever reads these vibrant chapters will not fail to get a better understanding of the times that tried men's souls. (*Review of Reviews*, 70:670.)

207. GRAYDON, ALEXANDER—*Memoirs of his Own Time.* Philadelphia, 1846.

A Pennsylvanian, an officer in the Revolution. The memoirs are mainly concerned with Pennsylvania.

208. GRISWOLD, RUFUS WILMOT—*Republican Court; or, Society in the Days of Washington.* New York, 1854.

A social history of the period, full of interesting matter from numerous memoirs and biographies, illustrated by portraits. (Duyckinck.)

209. HART, ALBERT BUSHNELL—*Formation of the Union* (see No. 79).

210. HOWARD, GEORGE ELLIOTT—*Preliminaries of the Revolution, 1763–1775 (American Nation).* New York, 1905.

Its causes were not social, but political and economic, the primary cause in the old colonial system. His attitude is strongly partisan. (G. L. Beer in *Political-Science Quarterly*, 21:129.)

211. JAMESON, JOHN FRANKLIN—*American Revolution* (see No. 80).

212. JERNEGAN, MARCUS WILSON—*American Colonies* (see No. 81).

213. MCILWAIN, CHARLES HOWARD—*American Revolution; a Constitutional Interpretation.* New York, 1925.

A study of the constitutional relations of the colonies to the king and especially to parliamentary supremacy in the light of precedents. Washington does not appear; but the treatment is a setting for his activity.

214. MCLAUGHLIN, ANDREW CUNNINGHAM—*Confederation and the Constitution* (see No. 12).

215. MCMASTER, JOHN BACH—*History of the People of the United States from the Revolution to the Civil War.* 8 vols. New York, 1883–1913.

A most useful and valuable work which does not attempt to give a connected narrative of the broader political movements of the time, but pictures economic and social conditions in a series of essays based on newspapers, journals, and other contemporary sources. (*A. L. A. Catalog*, 1926.) Vol. I gives the main references to Washington.

216. MEADE, WILLIAM — *Old Churches, Ministers and Families of Virginia.* 2 vols. Philadelphia, 1857.

The author collected the material by means of personal investigations and searches especially made for him in this country and in England. Numerous woodcuts. In recent years much additional material has been found, some of which varies considerably from Meade.

217. NEVINS, ALLAN — *American States* (see No. 84).

218. NICKERSON, HOFFMAN — *Turning Point of the Revolution or Burgoyne in America.* Boston, 1928.

This is the most complete study yet made of the campaign of 1777. . . . In many respects particularly as far as the American sources are concerned, it almost might be called the final word on the subject. (R. G. Adams in *American Historical Review*, 34:352.)

219. PAULLIN, CHARLES OSCAR—*Navy of the American Revolution; its Administration, its Policy, and its Achievements.* Cleveland, 1906.

As Dr. Paullin says, the book is written from the point of view of the naval administrators, and not from that of the naval officers . . . with a description of the various classes of naval movements showing the total results, with details only in the case of a few typical cruises and fights. (C. H. Van Tyne in *American Historical Review*, 12:666.)

220. ROOSEVELT, THEODORE—*Winning of the West.* 4 vols. New York, 1889–96. Various reprints, including eds. of collected works.

It treats what may be called the sequel of the Revolution; a period of American advance, the interest and significance of which are very little understood. Washington himself prophesied, and almost planned, the future of the great region beyond the Ohio. It is in many ways a fascinating narrative, and in every way a most instructive history. (*Reader's Digest of Books*.)

221. SCHLESINGER, ARTHUR MEIER—*Colonial Merchants and the American Revolution, 1763–1776.* New York, 1918.

The story that Professor Schlesinger tells us is not the whole story of the years before the Revolution, but it is a very important part of that story and one that has hitherto been strangely ignored . . . what Professor Schlesinger has written will stand as a landmark in our progress toward a better understanding of the causes of the Revolution. (C. M. Andrews in *American Historical Review*, 24:104.)

222. SMITH, HELEN EVERTSON—*Colonial Days & Ways as gathered from Family Papers.* Decorations by T. Guernsey Moore. New York, 1900.

It would be difficult to find another volume relating to the period comprising so much of personal, general and public interest. (*Nation*, 71:450.)

223. STANNARD, MARY NEWTON—*Colonial Virginia.* Philadelphia, 1917.

This work, important in content and spirited in style, has facts drawn largely from unpublished manuscripts of various kinds. (R. H. Dabney in *American Historical Review*, 23:655.)

224. TOWER, CHARLEMAGNE—*Marquis de la Fayette in the American Revolution.* 2 vols. Philadelphia, 1895.

For its accounts of the battles of Brandywine, Monmouth, and the campaign in 1781 in Virginia, it is unequaled; and scarcely less good is its outline of the French services to the United States during the Revolution. Mr. Tower writes clearly and interestingly, and has the additional advantage of being an admirable linguist; so his translations can be absolutely relied upon. (Larned, *Literature of American History*.)

225. TREVELYAN, SIR GEORGE OTTO—*American Revolution* (see Nos. 13, 13a).

226. VAN TYNE, CLAUDE HALSTEAD—*Founding of the Republic* (see No. 14).

227. WHARTON, ANNE HOLLINGSWORTH—*Social Life in the Early Republic.* Philadelphia, 1902.

Extracts from old letters and papers, connected by comments, and deductions. (Larned, *Literature of American History*.)

228. WINSOR, JUSTIN, ED.—*Narrative and Critical History of America.* 8 vols. Boston, 1889.

Critical essays by different writers covering American history in detail. Most valuable are the critical essays on sources and Mr. Winsor's notes. Vols. V–VII especially deal with the period of Washington.

CONTEMPORARY AUTHORITIES

As would naturally be expected, there is a mass of material in the lives and writings of contemporaries of Washington. The period of the Revolution and the beginning of the Republic was marked by numerous statesmen of first rank. Their works have been collected, and their lives have been written. This list is confined mainly to contemporary writings and documents. Biographies to 1912 of Washington's contemporaries will be found listed in Channing, Hart and Turner, *Guide to American History*, §39 (see No. 102). A few books of travel that shed light on Washington are also included. The number of references to Washington as noted in the indexes of these books, is given in some cases, but as indexes are made up differently, these do not always indicate the relative wealth of material.

229. ADAMS, JOHN — *Works . . . with a Life of the Author.* Ed. by his grandson, Charles Francis Adams. 10 vols. Boston, 1850–56.

Indexed references to Washington, 123.

230. ADAMS, JOHN QUINCY — *Writings.* Ed. by W. C. Ford. 7 vols. pub., extending to 1823. New York, 1913–17.

Unfinished; no index.

231. ADAMS, SAMUEL—*Writings.* Ed. by H. A. Cushing. 4 vols. New York, 1904–06.

Indexed references to Washington, 39.

232. *American State Papers: Documents Legislative and Executive.* 38 vols. Washington, 1832–61.

The first portion of each of the subject divisions of this compilation gives important documents of Washington's administrations.

233. BURNETT, EDMUND CODY, ED.—*Letters of Members of the Continental Congress.* 5 vols. pub., to 1781. Washington, 1921—.

This is an admirably edited and indispensable book for any serious study of the civil history of the period from 1774 to 1789, and Washington's connection with Congress. A large portion of the letters are to him, many others concern him.

234. CHASTELLUX, FRANCOIS JEAN, MARQUIS DE—*Travels in North-America, in the Years 1780, 1781, and 1782.* Tr. by J. Kent. 2 vols. London, 1787. Other eds.

Includes meetings with Washington and estimates of his character; interestingly written; warm sentiment with worldly wisdom. Chastellux was a member of the French Academy and came to America with Rochambeau.

235. *Documents illustrative of the Formation of the Union of the American States.* Washington, 1927.

A congressional publication; House Document No. 398, 69th Congress, 1st Session. Includes the great state papers from 1774 to 1789, the notes and plans in the Constitutional Convention, and the state ratifications. Does not include the correspondence in Farrand (No. 237) and the *Documentary History* (No. 261).

236. ELLIOT, JONATHAN, ED.—*Debates in the several State Conventions on the Adoption of the Federal Constitution.* 4 vols. Washington, 1836.

Incomplete, but the only compilation; especially on Massachusetts, Virginia, and New York.

237. FARRAND, MAX, ED.—*Records of the Federal Convention of 1787.* 3 vols. New Haven, 1911.

Includes the journal, notes made by various delegates, and letters and other illustrative material. Madison's notes have been issued in various editions.

238. *Federalist: a Collection of Essays written in Favour of the New Constitution.* 2 vols. New York, 1788.

These famous essays by Hamilton, Jay, and Madison, which appeared in the newspapers during the ratification struggle, and were most important on the Federalist side, have been repeatedly republished.

239. FORCE, PETER, ED.—*American Archives.* 9 vols. Washington, 1837–53.

This great project for the publication of practically all the contemporary material on the American Revolution from 1774 remains unfinished, extending only into 1776.

240. FORD, PAUL LEICESTER, ED.—*Essays on the Constitution.* Brooklyn, 1892.

241. FORD, PAUL LEICESTER, ED.—*Pamphlets on the Constitution.* Brooklyn, 1888.

These two volumes show the character of popular discussion of the Federal Constitution during the period of ratification.

242. FRANKLIN, BENJAMIN—*Writings.* Ed. by A. H. Smyth. 10 vols. New York, 1905–07.

Indexed references to Washington, 50.

243. HAMILTON, ALEXANDER—*Works.* Ed. by H. C. Lodge. 9 vols. New York, 1885–86.

Indexed references to Washington, 32. In John C. Hamilton's edition of Hamilton's writings, 60.

244. HAMILTON, STANISLAUS MURRAY, ED.—*Letters to Washington and Accompanying Papers.* 5 vols. Boston, 1898–1902.

These volumes cover the pre-revolutionary period.

245. JAY, JOHN—*Correspondence and Public Papers.* Ed. by H. P. Johnston. 4 vols. New York, 1890–93.

Indexed references to Washington, 39.

246. JEFFERSON, THOMAS—*Writings.* Issued under the auspices of the Thomas Jefferson Memorial Association. 20 vols. Washington, 1904–05.

This collection aiming at completeness, was issued in several "editions." Indexed references to Washington, 200; many letters to Washington. The edition by P. L. Ford, 10 vols., New York, 1892-99, is selective.

247. *Journals of Continental Congress.* Complete ed., 29 vols. pub., through 1785. Washington, 1904—.

This definitive edition of the Journals, with Burnett's *Letters* and the *Calendar of the Washington Correspondence*, furnishes the student with necessary source material on the period of the Revolution and the Confederation.

248. KING, RUFUS—*Life and Correspondence.* Ed. by C. R. King. 6 vols. New York, 1894–1900.

Indexed references to Washington, 34.

249. LEE, CHARLES—*Lee Papers, 1754–1811.* 4 vols. New York, 1872–75.

In the *Collections* of the New York Historical Society. The basis of the whole collection has been the mass of original papers left by General Lee to William Goddard, and still preserved in his family. Indexed references to Washington, 245.

250. LEE, RICHARD HENRY—*Letters.* Ed. by J. C. Ballagh. 2 vols. New York, 1911–14.

These letters of one of the most prominent of the Revolutionary characters from Virginia are intimately connected with Washington's career, and especially with his relations with Congress. Indexed references to Washington, 46; various letters to him.

251. MACLAY, WILLIAM—*Journal . . . 1789–1791.* With introduction by C. A. Beard. New York, 1927; earlier eds.

Senator Maclay's acerb comments on conditions and personnel during the first Congress are valuable sidelights.

252. MADISON, JAMES—*Writings . . . comprising Public Papers and Private Correspondence, including Letters and Documents now for the first time printed.* Ed. by Gaillard Hunt. 9 vols. New York, 1900–10.

Indexed references to Washington, 55.

253. MONROE, JAMES—*Writings.* Ed. by S. M. Hamilton. 7 vols. New York, 1898–1903.

Monroe's somewhat unhappy relations with Washington are mainly of the post-bellum period. Indexed references to Washington, 30.

254. MORISON, SAMUEL ELIOT, ED.—*Sources and Documents* (see No. 83).

255. REED, JOSEPH—*Life and Correspondence.* Ed. by W. B. Reed. Philadelphia, 1847.

Reed was military secretary to Washington, adjutant general, and volunteer aide, 1775-77, before becoming president of Pennsylvania. Indexed references to Washington, 124.

256. ROWLAND, KATE MASON—*Life of George Mason . . . including his Speeches, Public Papers and Correspondence; with an introduction by General Fitzhugh Lee.* 2 vols. New York, 1892.

The work is the result of great industry, constant efforts to secure accuracy, but is not so strong in judicious selection and sense of proportion. (Larned, *Literature of American History*.) Indexed references to Washington, 205.

257. SMITH, WILLAM HENRY, ED.—*St. Clair Papers. The Life and Public Services of Arthur St. Clair.* 2 vols. Cincinnati, 1882.

St. Clair was an advisor of Washington during the Revolution, the pioneer of law and institutions in the North West. (*Nation*, 34:383.)

258. SPARKS, JARED, ED.—*Correspondence of the American Revolution; being Letters of Eminent Men to George Washington, from his taking Command of the Army to the End of his Presidency.* 4 vols. Boston, 1853.

The collection is not exhaustive. About three-fourths of the collection relates to the Revolution, and the rest to the later events of Washington's career. (Larned, *Literature of American History*.)

259. TRUMBULL, JONATHAN—*Trumbull Papers.* 4 vols. Boston, 1885-1902.

The correspondence of the wartime governor of Connecticut, Washington's "Brother Jonathan," printed in the *Collections* of the Massachusetts Historical Society, is the best illustration of the commander-in-chief's relations with the states. The correspondence with Washington is in the second volume.

260. TWINING, THOMAS—*Travels in America One Hundred Years Ago.* New York, 1894.

This little book is of particular interest on Philadelphia during Washington's second administration. No index.

261. UNITED STATES DEPARTMENT OF STATE, BUREAU OF ROLLS AND LIBRARY, ED.—*Documentary History of the Constitution of the United States.* Vols. IV-V. Washington, 1905.

These volumes include the letters relating to the adoption of the Constitution, and a bibliography. The other volumes of the work contain matter accessible in the later official compilation (see No. 235).

262. WANSEY, HENRY—*Excursion to the United States of North America in the Summer of 1794.* 2 ed. with additions. Salisbury, Eng., 1798.

He had "the honor of an interview with the President of the United States. I confess I was struck with awe and veneration."

MILITARY ACTIVITIES

Many earlier writers were interested in the military side of Washington's life, and in the general biographies and accounts of the times that side prevailed. Also special battles and campaigns were studied and written about by those interested. In more recent years, although the military emphasis has been lessened, there have been some good treatments of Washington as a general.

263. ADAMS, CHARLES FRANCIS—*Studies Military and Diplomatic, 1775–1865.* New York, 1911.

> Contains several pungent criticisms on Washington as a military man.

264. BEAN, THEODORE WEBER—*Washington at Valley Forge One Hundred Years Ago; or the Foot-Prints of the Revolution.* Norristown, Pa., 1876.

> Handbook of the Pennsylvania campaign of 1777-78. Supplied with maps. Carefully written. (Larned, *Literature of American History.*)

265. BOLTON, CHARLES KNOWLES—*Private Soldier under Washington.* New York, 1902.

> The material has been collected with great care, and seems to be used with discretion and judgment. A view of the war as a real episode in human affairs, not the basis for a patriotic epic. (*American Historical Review*, 8:386.)

266. CARRINGTON, HENRY BEEBE—*Battles of the American Revolution, 1775–1781; Historical and Military Criticism, with Topographical Illustration.* New York, 1876.

> Based on careful study of leading sources. An admirable book. Detailed index of Washington's military career. (Larned, *Literature of American History.*)

267. CARRINGTON, HENRY BEEBE—*Washington the Soldier.* New York, 1899.

> In the main, an abridgment of the valuable work by the same author, *Battles of the Revolution.* (*Nation*, 68:126.)

268. CRAIG, NEVILLE BENJAMIN—*Washington's First Campaign, Death of Jumonville, and Taking of Fort Necessity; also Braddock's Defeat and the March of the Unfortunate General explained by a Civil Engineer.* Pittsburgh, 1849.

> Made up of papers from Mr. Craig's monthly publication, *Olden Time.*

269. FROTHINGHAM, RICHARD—*History of the Siege of Boston, and the Battles of Lexington and Concord, and Bunker Hill; also, an Account of the Bunker Hill Monument.* 3d ed. Boston, 1872.

> Well illustrated with plans. Well written though often dry. The standard work on the subject.

270. FROTHINGHAM, THOMAS GODDARD—*Washington* (see No. 57).

271. GIST, CHRISTOPHER — *Christopher Gist's Journal.* Ed. by W. M. Darlington. Pittsburgh, 1893.

> Gist was the explorer for the Ohio Com-

pany, and also Washington's guide on the journey to the French commandant in 1753. His journal of the trip supplements Washington's.

272. GREENE, FRANCIS VINTON—*The Revolutionary War and the Military Policy of the United States.* New York, Scribner, 1911.

> The chief merits of the book . . . are its compactness, its excision of all extraneous information, and its plain and clear statement of the essential facts of the war, . . . well supplied with maps. (C. O. Paullin in *American Historical Review*, 17:622.)

273. HATCH, LOUIS CLINTON—*Administration of the American Revolutionary Army.* New York, 1904.

> A thorough study of the sources, well proportioned and well written, especially valuable for the appointment and promotion of officers, the pay and half-pay controversies, the mismanagement of the supplies and the Newburgh plot. (*A. L. A. Booklist*, Feb., 1906.)

274. HEATH, WILLIAM—*Memoirs of Major-General Heath, containing Anecdotes, Details of Skirmishes, Battles, and other Military Events, during the American War.* Boston, 1798.

> Valuable for accounts of the British from Lexington, Bunker Hill, and around New York. Also concerns the prisoners after Burgoyne's surrender, and the cooperation of the French forces. (Larned, *Literature of American History.*)

275. HULBERT, ARCHER BUTLER—*Historic Highways of America.* 16 vols. Cleveland, 1902–13.

> Vols. III-V deal with Washington's frontier campaigns in connection with his own 1754 road, and those of the Braddock and Forbes campaigns.

276. JOHNSON, BRADLEY TYLER—*General Washington* (Great Commanders). New York, 1881.

> Few of the lives of Washington exceed this in serviceableness to the military student, written as it is by one of the most eminent of the Confederate generals in the Civil War; and yet it is to be regretted that the few and inadequate maps in the book had not been replaced by a more liberal equipment. The book shows intelligent acquaintance with the subject, and a fair temper. (Larned, *Literature of American History.*)

277. JOHNSTON, HENRY PHELPS—*Yorktown Campaign and the Surrender of Cornwallis, 1781.* New York, 1881.

> Standard history of the campaign, well documented.

278. KNOX, DUDLEY WRIGHT — *Naval Genius of Washington.* Boston, 1932.

> A study based on the sources, showing how Washington's military fortunes were affected by sea power and how he developed a keen impression of this influence and made it fundamental in his strategy.

279. SPAULDING, OLIVER LYMAN—*Military Studies of George Washington.* New York, 1924.

> An article first published in the *American Historical Review* by a colonel of Field Artillery, U. S. A.

280. STRYKER, WILLIAM SCUDDER—*Battles*

of Trenton and Princeton. Boston, 1898.

> The author uses many documents never before laid under contribution, especially German records of the Hessian soldiers. (Larned, *Literature of American History.*)

281. STRYKER, WILLIAM SCUDDER—*Battle of Monmouth.* Ed. by W. S. Myers. Princeton, 1927.

> A companion volume to the above.

282. THACHER, JAMES—*Military Journal during the American Revolutionary War, from 1775 to 1783; . . . To which is added an Appendix, containing Biographical Sketches of several General Officers.* 2d ed., rev. and cor. Boston, 1827; also reprints.

> Dr. Thacher served as surgeon in the American army, and his journal has the great value of first-hand knowledge of the events. The work of a fair-minded man. (Larned, *Literature of American History.*)

283. WRONG, GEORGE McKINNON—*Washington and his Comrades in Arms: a Chronicle of the War of Independence* (Chronicles of America). New Haven, 1921.

> It is a great boon to have them soberly, judiciously, capably handled by a distinguished scholar. (C. H. Van Tyne in *American Historical Review*, 28:164.)

THE STATESMAN

This phase of Washington's activities is presented in every biography and history of the times, but there are some books especially dealing with the Constitution and Washington's presidency.

284. BASSETT, JOHN SPENCER—*Federalist System* (see No. 7).

285. BEMIS, SAMUEL FLAGG—*Jay's Treaty; a Study in Commerce and Diplomacy.* New York, 1923.

> "A notable contribution to American history." . . . More than half the book is devoted to a reexamination of the grievances on both sides. . . . The general conclusion of the author, that Jay's Treaty might more aptly be called Hamilton's Treaty . . . is . . . certainly not heterodox. (*American Historical Review*, 26:345.)

286. BEMIS, SAMUEL FLAGG—*Pinckney's Treaty; a Study of America's Advantage from Europe's Distress, 1783–1800.* Baltimore, 1926.

> The author of *Jay's Treaty* has produced a companion volume that maintains his reputation for scholarly research, mastery of technique, and sprightly writing. Together the two books present a readable, well documented, logical review of our early national diplomacy. (*American Historical Review*, 32:616.)

287. BOWERS, CLAUDE GERNADE—*Jefferson and Hamilton* (see No. 75).

288. BRACKENRIDGE, HENRY MARIE—*History of the Western Insurrection in Western Pennsylvania, commonly called the Whiskey Insurrection, 1794.* Pittsburgh, 1859.

> Drawn mainly from contemporary accounts by Findley and H. H. Brackenridge.

289. CORBIN, JOHN—*Unknown Washington* (see No. 110).

290. FORD, HENRY JONES—*Washington* (see No. 39).

290a. FARRAND, MAX—"George Washington in the Federal Convention"; in *Yale Review*, 1907.
   A consideration of his influence and the way in which it was probably exerted.

291. GIBBS, GEORGE, ED.—*Memoirs of the Administrations of Washington and John Adams, from the Papers of Oliver Wolcott, Secretary of the Treasury.* 2 vols. New York, 1846.
   A source of primary importance for the history of the Federalist party. The editor's narrative is clear and accurate, but his judgments are strongly biased against the Republicans. (Larned, *Literature of American History.*)

292. OGG, FREDERIC AUSTIN—*Opening of the Mississippi.* New York, 1904.
   It is a book to inform and entertain the reader and to stimulate in him an interest in the sources and more elaborate studies. (F. W. Moore in *American Historical Review*, 10:154.)

293. TRESCOT, WILLIAM HENRY—*Diplomatic History of the Administration of Washington and Adams.* Boston, 1857.
   A clear, well-proportioned narrative. The author exceptionally temperate and fairminded. (Larned, *Literature of American History.*)

PHASES OF WASHINGTON'S LIFE

There are numerous books each developing some one phase of Washington's life or career. Usually these are careful and detailed studies and must be used by anyone studying or writing about Washington. The various headings will indicate the multiplicity of phases. Some books are frankly propaganda, but others are serious and well-executed productions. For some subjects there is much better treatment in the general biographies.

294. MERRIAM, GEORGE ERNEST, ED.—*More precious than Fine Gold; Washington Commonplace Book.* New York, 1931.
   A collection of over 1,500 classified estimates of Washington in his various spheres of action.

A. ANCESTRY

295. CONWAY, MONCURE DANIEL—"English Ancestry of Washington"; in *Harper's Magazine*, vol. 84, 1891.

296. FORD, WORTHINGTON CHAUNCEY, ED.—*Wills of George Washington and his Immediate Ancestors.* Brooklyn, 1891.

297. FORD, WORTHINGTON CHAUNCEY—"Washington Family"; in his ed. of the *Writings* (see No. 161), vol. 14, p. 317.

B. BUSINESS

298. COOK, ROY BIRD — *Washington's Western Lands.* Strasburg, Va., 1930.

299. FORD, WORTHINGTON CHAUNCEY, ED.—*Washington as an Employer and Importer of Labor.* Brooklyn, 1889.

300. HERZBERG, M. J.—*George Washington, Man of Affairs.* Newark, 1929.

301. HULBERT, ARCHER BUTLER—*Colonel Washington.* Marietta, Ohio, 1903.

302. PRUSSING, EUGENE ERNST—*George Washington in Love and Otherwise.* Chicago, 1925.
   Essays on various phases of Washington's life; chs. ii-v deal cogently with the engineer and business man.

303. RITTER, HALSTED L.—*Washington as a Business Man.* New York, 1931.
   A careful study from the sources of a phase of Washington's career hitherto much neglected.

C. DEATH

304. HOUGH, FRANKLIN BENJAMIN, ED.—*Washingtoniana; or Memorials of the Death of George Washington.* 2d ed. Roxbury, Mass., 1865.
   A reprint with changes from *Washingtoniana*, Baltimore, 1800. Descriptions of Washington's death and funeral, the proceedings of the various public bodies, and the eulogies and poems. The collection is not confined to America. (Larned, *Literature of American History.*)

D. EDUCATION AND LITERATURE

See also the section on Washington's Writings.

305. LIPPINCOTT, HORACE WALKER — *George Washington and the University of Pennsylvania.* Philadelphia, 1916.

306. MITCHELL, SILAS WEIR—*Washington in his Letters.* Philadelphia, 1903.

307. MOORE, GEORGE HENRY—*Washington as an Author, with Extracts from his Diaries, 1787-89.* New York, 1778; reprinted, 1907.

308. PENNIMAN, JAMES HOSMER—*Washington as a Man of Letters.* Philadelphia, 1918.

309. POTTER, ELIPHALET NOTT—*Washington a Model in his Library and Life.* New York, 1895.

310. PRUSSING, EUGENE ERNST—*Estate of George Washington, deceased* (see No. 183).
   In the appendix is a list of the books in Washington's library.

311. TONER, JOSEPH MEREDITH—"Some Account of George Washington's Library and Manuscript Records"; in American Historical Association, *Annual Report for 1892*, p. 73.

E. ENGINEER

312. KITE, ELIZABETH S., ED.—*L'Enfant and Washington, 1791-1792.* Introduction by J. J. Jusserand; foreword by Charles Moore, Baltimore, 1929.
   Contains documents by L'Enfant, Washington, Jefferson, and others, concerning L'Enfant's plan and laying out of the city of Washington; also a copy of the plan.

313. LEFFMAN, HENRY—*George Washington as an Engineer.* Philadelphia, 1904.

314. PICKELL, JOHN—*New Chapter in the Early Life of Washington in Connection with the Narrative History of the Potomac Company.* New York, 1856.
   The records of the company and Washington's letters are drawn upon for material.

F. FARMER

315. ABBOTT, WILBUR CORTEZ—"James Bloxham, Farmer"; in Massachusetts Historical Society, *Proceedings*, 59:177.
   Bloxham was Washington's farm manager, brought over from England.

316. HAWORTH, PAUL LELAND—*George Washington* (see No. 59).

317. PARKINSON, RICHARD—*George Washington* (see No. 141).

G. INAUGURATION

318. BOWEN, CLARENCE WINTHROP — "Inauguration of George Washington"; in *History of the Centennial Celebration of the Inauguration of George Washington.* New York, 1892.
   Many valuable portraits and other illustrations. See also Mr. Bowen's article in *Century Magazine*, vol. 37.

H. INVENTOR

319. TONER, JOSEPH MEREDITH—*George Washington as an Inventor and Promoter of the Useful Arts.* Washington, 1892.

I. LANDS

320. ADAMS, HERBERT BAXTER — *Maryland's Influence upon Land Cessions to the United States. With Minor Papers on George Washington's Interest in Western Lands, the Potomac Company, and a National University.* Baltimore, 1885.

321. COOK, ROY BIRD — *Washington's Western Lands* (see No. 298).

322. RANDALL, EMILIUS OVIATT—"Washington's Ohio Lands"; in *Ohio Archaeological and Historical Quarterly*, 1910.

323. VOLWILER, ALBERT TANGEMAN—*George Croghan and the Westward Movement, 1741-1782.* Cleveland, 1926.
   Washington references scattered through the book.

J. LIBELS

324. FITZPATRICK, JOHN CLEMENT — *George Washington Scandals.* Alexandria, Va., 1929.
   Republished with some additions, from

Scribner's Magazine, April, 1927. Shows the original of some of the spurious letters.

325. MOORE, GEORGE HENRY—*Libels on Washington, with a Critical Examination thereof.* New York, 1889.

K. MASONIC CONNECTION

326. CALLAHAN, CHARLES H.—*Washington, the Man and the Mason.* Washington, 1913.

327. HAYDEN, SIDNEY—*Washington and His Masonic Compeers.* New York, 1866; later eds.

328. LAMBERTON, JAMES McCORMICK—*Washington as a Freemason.* Philadelphia, 1902.

329. LANIER, JOHN JABEZ—*Washington, the Great American Mason.* New York, 1922.

330. RITNER, JOSEPH—*Vindication of General Washington from the Stigma of Adherence to Secret Societies . . . Communicated by Request of the House of Representatives [of Pennsylvania] . . . with the Proceedings which took place on its Reception.* Harrisburg, 1837. Later eds. with varying titles.

This was during the Antimasonic agitation and illustrates how proponents of every cause have brought proof to show that Washington believed as they did.

331. SACHSE, JULIUS FRIEDRICH, ED.—*Washington's Masonic Correspondence as found among the Washington Papers in the Library of Congress.* Philadelphia, 1915.

L. RELIGION

332. JOHNSTONE, WILLIAM JACKSON — *George Washington the Christian.* New York, 1919.

333. LITTELL, JOHN STOCKTON—*Washington; Christian.* Keene, N. H., 1913.

334. MANGASARIAN, MANGASAR MURGURDITCH—*Religion of Washington, Jefferson and Franklin.* Chicago, 1907.

335. REMBURG, JOHN ELEAZER—*Six Historic Americans; Paine, Jefferson, Washington, Franklin, Lincoln, Grant, the Fathers and Saviors of Our Republic, Freethinkers.* New York, 1906.

The above are samples of reading into Washington's life the author's opinions. Better treatment generally in the good biographies.

M. THEATER

336. FORD, PAUL LEICESTER—*Washington and the Theater.* New York, 1899.

N. TRAVEL

337. BAKER, WILLIAM SPOHN—*Itinerary* (see No. 104).

338. BAKER, WILLIAM SPOHN—*Washington after the Revolution* (see No. 105).

339. FITZPATRICK, JOHN CLEMENT — *George Washington, Colonial Traveller, 1732–1775.* Indianapolis, 1927.

A very interesting book showing how widely acquainted Washington was with the colonies before he became their leader.

340. HENDERSON, ARCHIBALD — *Washington's Southern Tour, 1791.* Boston, 1923.

Events given with much detail and many illustrations.

O. WAR AND PEACE

341. MEAD, EDWIN DOAK—*Washington, Jefferson, and Franklin on War.* Boston, 1913.

LITERATURE RELATING TO WASHINGTON

Washington has become a theme for poets, dramatists, and fiction writers. In poetry the beginning was made with Alsop's eulogy, which is well known in libraries and to collectors; but the quality of the poetical contributions has not been high. In drama there has been an increase in production on Washington in recent years with the revival of interest in pageantry, and there are in existence at least 260 plays or pageants bearing on Washington or Washington's time. In fiction there have been numerous efforts but the real successes have been few, except the incessant efforts, following Parson Weems, to make Washington a character in fiction.

As to addresses, eulogies, and essays about Washington, they are very numerous. In 1916 the New York Public Library made a list of Washington eulogies, which numbered 440 up to that date. It included as far as possible every separately printed item and some others in collections. A great number were delivered in 1800 immediately after Washington's death, especially on February 22, 1800. But the number increases annually and early scarce and out-of-the-way items are being found, so that the Washington eulogies extant in 1932 must be greatly increased over the list of 1916. Only a few are given here, together with some essays by well known writers. Delvers in various libraries large and small will always find a number of eulogies, and the material in them might well give subjects for essays.

A. ADDRESSES, EULOGIES, ESSAYS

342. BANCROFT, GEORGE — "Washington's Birthday; his Monument"; in his *History of the Battle of Lake Erie, and Miscellaneous Papers.* New York, 1860.

A good example of the extremely laudatory eulogy, and included because of Bancroft's prominent position as statesman and historian.

343. ELIOT, CHARLES WILLIAM—"George Washington"; in his *Four American Leaders.* Boston, 1908.

344. HARRISON, FREDERIC—"George Washington and the Republican Ideal"; in *George Washington and other American Addresses.* New York, 1901.

This was written by one of the great English historical critics, and emphasizes Washington's statesmanship without militarism.

345. JUSSERAND, JEAN ADRIEN ANTOINE JULES — "Washington and the French"; in his *With Americans of Past and Present Days.* New York, 1916.

Jusserand always wrote well and was very sympathetic with America and Americans as was apparent during his long ambassadorship at Washington. You read with enjoyment and you remember what you have read. The French estimate of Washington is brought out. (*American Historical Review*, 22:669.)

346. LARNED, JOSEPHUS NELSON—"Washington: Impressive in Greatness"; in his *Study of Greatness in Men.* Boston, 1911.

This series of lectures by Larned was one of his ablest pieces of historical work. He found in Washington a fit subject for his theme.

347. LIEBER, FRANCIS—"Washington and Napoleon"; in his *Miscellaneous Writings*, Vol. I. Philadelphia, 1881.

The treatment discloses the great qualities of the author as publicist, thinker and citizen. Lieber's style, though not brilliant, is good. (Larned, *Literature of American History.*)

348. McLAUGHLIN, ROBERT WILLIAM—*Washington and Lincoln, Leaders of the Nation in the Constitutional Eras of American History.* New York, 1912.

This is a comparative study, more of the times, than of the personalities, of the men named in the title. The book is obviously designed for the general reader. (*American Historical Review*, 18:404.)

349. PALMER, JOHN McAULEY—*Washington, Lincoln, Wilson; Three War Statesmen.* With an introduction by Gen. John J. Pershing. Garden City, N. Y., 1930.

An interesting, instructive, and well-argued tract in favor of preparedness along the lines of Washington's citizen army. It is based upon the soundest historical research. (*Bookman*, 71:563.)

350. SCHLESINGER, ARTHUR MEIER—*New Viewpoints in American History.* New York, 1922.

The main parts about Washington are in ch. vii. The author considers Washington as one of the greatest Presidents.

B. DRAMA

351. ALLEN, ETHAN—*Washington; or, The Revolution; a Drama founded upon the Historic Events of the War for American Independence.* 2 vols. in 1. Chicago, 1899.

Contents.—pt. 1. From the Boston Massacre to the surrender of Burgoyne.—pt. 2. From Valley Forge to Washington's inauguration as President of the United States.

352. ARCHER, WILLIAM—*Three Plays by William Archer, with Foreword by George Bernard Shaw.* New York, 1927.

"Martha Washington" is the first play, and part of it is Washington's wedding.

353. MACKAYE, PERCY — *Washington* (see No. 92).

C. FICTION

See Nos. 88–99.

D. POEMS

354. ALSOP, RICHARD—*A Poem; sacred to the Memory of George Washington, Late President of the United States, and Commander in Chief of the Armies of the United States.* Hartford, 1800.

One of the earliest poetical eulogies, well known to libraries and collectors.

355. LOWELL, JAMES RUSSELL—"Under the Old Elm"; in *Three Memorial Poems.* Boston, 1877.

Included in the collections of his works.

356. NORTHMORE, THOMAS—*Washington; or, Liberty Restored; a Poem in Ten Books.* Baltimore, 1809.

256a. OLCOTT, FRANCES JENKINS, ED.—*Stories and Poems about George Washington.* Boston, 1932.

Includes a group of short poems on Washington.

357. PIERPONT, JOHN—*The Portrait.* Boston, 1812.

PLACES ASSOCIATED WITH WASHINGTON

Washington as surveyor, soldier, and statesman, visited a great number of places in the eastern states. In some places, as Philadelphia, he spent long periods of time. The result has been that through local pride, antiquarian interest, and historical research, books have been written about many of these places. Included here are some of the best of these, for different sections of the country, a mere selection from a large number. Of course Mount Vernon holds a first place in these accounts.

358. ANDREWS, MARIETTA MINNIGERODE—*George Washington's Country.* New York, 1931.

Travel and descriptions with gossip about places and people.

359. BURK, WILLIAM HEBERT—*Historical and Topographical Guide to Valley Forge.* 7th ed., rev. and enl., illustrated with photographs. North Wales, Pa., 1928.

By the enthusiastic and well-informed rector of the memorial church.

360. DILLER, THEODORE—*Place of Washington in the History of Western Pennsylvania.* Pittsburgh, 1916.

Deals with six journeys in the region and

Washington's interest in commerce and real estate.

361. EARLE, SWEPSON — *Chesapeake Bay Country.* Baltimore, 1923.

The author an engineer interested in writing. Over two hundred illustrations of the country and its historic homes and churches. It is a region Washington knew fairly well.

362. HEUSSER, ALBERT HENRY—*In the Footsteps of Washington; Popes Creek to Princeton.* Paterson, 1921.

A fully illustrated book covering places identified with Washington to 1777.

363. HULBERT, ARCHER BUTLER—*Historic Highways* (see No. 275).

364. JENKINS, CHARLES FRANCIS—*Washington in Germantown.* Philadelphia, 1905.

365. KING, GRACE—*Mount Vernon on the Potomac: History of the Mount Vernon Ladies' Association of the Union.* New York, 1929.

The story of the preservation and restoration of Mount Vernon has been told many times. . . . The tale has not been told more gracefully or with more fervor than Grace King has done it. . . . Quite incidentally this book is the complete and convincing answer to the recurring agitation to have Congress take the management of Mount Vernon away from the Ladies' Association. (Charles Moore in *American Historical Review*, 34:888.)

366. LOSSING, BENSON JOHN—*Mount Vernon and its Associations.* New York, 1859.

Amply illustrated. Later editions called *Home of Washington.*

367. PRESTON, HOWARD WILLIS—*Washington's Visits to Providence, gathered from Contemporary Accounts.* Providence, 1926.

368. RIDDLE, JAMES WHITFORD—*Valley Forge Guide and Handbook.* Philadelphia, 1910.

369. SINGLETON, ESTHER—*Story of the White House.* New York, 1907.

She has confined herself strictly to the social life, devotes a chapter to each administration and extra ones to the building. Washington's administration included, although he did not live in the White House. (*Dial*, 43:431.)

370. SIPE, CHESTER HALE—*Mount Vernon and the Washington Family; a Concise Handbook on the Ancestry, Youth and Family of George Washington, and History of his Home.* Butler, Pa., 1929.

371. WASHINGTON CROSSING PARK COMMISSION OF PENNSYLVANIA—*Brief Itinerary of a Trip from Philadelphia to Washington Crossing and Other*

Points of Historic Interest in Bucks County, Pennsylvania. Philadelphia, 1926.

372. WHARTON, ANNE HOLLINGSWORTH—*English Ancestral Homes of Noted Americans* (see No. 87).

373. WILSTACH, PAUL—*Mount Vernon* (see No. 54).

ICONOGRAPHY

This subject has not been completely dealt with, but the books listed here will give a rather comprehensive treatment sufficient to satisfy all but the most exacting expert.

374. BAKER, WILLIAM SPOHN—*Engraved Portraits of Washington, with Notices of the Originals and brief Biographical Sketches of the Painters.* Philadelphia, 1880.

375. BAKER, WILLIAM SPOHN — *Medallic Portraits of Washington, with Historical and Critical Notes and a Descriptive Catalogue of the Coins, Medals, Tokens and Cards.* Philadelphia, 1885.

376. BELOTE, THEODORE THOMAS—"Descriptive Catalogue of the Washington Relics in the United States National Museum"; in U. S. National Museum, *Proceedings*, 49: 1–24. 27 plates. Washington, 1916.

377. FIELDING, MANTLE—*Gilbert Stuart's Portraits of George Washington.* Philadelphia, 1923.

Reproduction of the portraits, with descriptions and names of owners. Includes the life of Gilbert Stuart.

378. HART, CHARLES HENRY—*Catalogue of the Engraved Portraits of Washington.* New York, 1904.

A carefully compiled, handsomely printed book.

379. HART, CHARLES HENRY, and BIDDLE, EDWARD—*Jean Antoine Houdon.* Philadelphia, 1911.

Account of Houdon's modeling of Washington; very thorough.

380. JOHNSTON, ELIZABETH BRYANT—*Original Portraits of Washington.* Boston, 1882.

381. MORGAN, JOHN HILL, and FIELDING, MANTLE—*Life Portraits of George Washington, with a Catalogue of the Original Paintings, their Replicas, and Biographies of the Artists.* Philadelphia, 1931.

382. PARK, LAWRENCE—*Gilbert Stuart; an Illustrated Descriptive List of his Works.* 4 vols. New York, 1926.

The Washington list is in vol. 2, with plates in vol. 4.

GEORGE WASHINGTON

(As painted by different artists)

Top, left: BY CHARLES WILLSON PEALE (probably painted at Valley Forge, 1778). *Top, right:* BY ROBERT EDGE PINE (painted in 1785 at Mount Vernon.) *Bottom, left:* BY JAMES PEALE (Miniature). *Bottom, right:* BY JAMES SHARPLES

PROGRAMS AND PAPERS

PORTRAYING

THE

PERSONALITY, CHARACTER, AND
ACHIEVEMENTS

OF

GEORGE WASHINGTON

Originated by and Prepared Under the Direction of

MRS. JOHN DICKINSON SHERMAN

PROGRAMS

FAMILY RELATIONSHIPS OF GEORGE WASHINGTON

HOMES OF GEORGE WASHINGTON

YOUTH AND MANHOOD OF GEORGE WASHINGTON

THE MOTHER OF GEORGE WASHINGTON

GEORGE WASHINGTON THE MAN OF SENTIMENT

GEORGE WASHINGTON THE MAN OF ACTION
    IN MILITARY AND CIVIL LIFE

GEORGE WASHINGTON THE CHRISTIAN

GEORGE WASHINGTON THE LEADER OF MEN

THE SOCIAL LIFE OF GEORGE WASHINGTON

GEORGE WASHINGTON THE BUILDER OF THE NATION

GEORGE WASHINGTON THE PRESIDENT (1789-1797)

THE HOMEMAKING OF GEORGE AND MARTHA WASHINGTON

INTRODUCTION

THE twelve George Washington Programs are divided into forty-eight subjects. On each of these subjects a paper has been prepared. These papers portray the personality, character and achievements of George Washington, and are interesting, informative and accurate.

For thousands who have prepared their own papers and addresses and who have engaged in research, study, or general reading, the papers were of distinct assistance. Each paper is complete in itself.

A list of selected books relating to George Washington appears at the end of this section, and at the end of each program will be found reference numbers to books bearing upon the subject of the paper to that program.

These papers and programs were issued by the Commission especially for patriotic societies, clubs and schools.

PLEDGE TO THE FLAG

I PLEDGE ALLEGIANCE TO THE FLAG OF THE UNITED STATES OF AMERICA AND TO THE REPUBLIC FOR WHICH IT STANDS; ONE NATION INDIVISIBLE, WITH LIBERTY AND JUSTICE FOR ALL.

THE AMERICAN'S CREED

I BELIEVE IN THE UNITED STATES OF AMERICA AS A GOVERNMENT OF THE PEOPLE, BY THE PEOPLE, FOR THE PEOPLE; WHOSE JUST POWERS ARE DERIVED FROM THE CONSENT OF THE GOVERNED; A DEMOCRACY IN A REPUBLIC; A SOVEREIGN NATION OF MANY SOVEREIGN STATES; A PERFECT UNION, ONE AND INSEPARABLE; ESTABLISHED UPON THOSE PRINCIPLES OF FREEDOM, EQUALITY, JUSTICE, AND HUMANITY FOR WHICH AMERICAN PATRIOTS SACRIFICED THEIR LIVES AND FORTUNES. ¶I THEREFORE BELIEVE IT IS MY DUTY TO MY COUNTRY TO LOVE IT; TO SUPPORT ITS CONSTITUTION; TO OBEY ITS LAWS; TO RESPECT ITS FLAG; AND TO DEFEND IT AGAINST ALL ENEMIES.

—William Tyler Page

IT WAS SUGGESTED THAT THE PROGRAMS BE OPENED WITH PATRIOTIC MUSIC, FOLLOWED BY THE "PLEDGE TO THE FLAG" AND "THE AMERICAN'S CREED," AND CLOSED WITH THE SINGING OF "THE STAR SPANGLED BANNER"

DESCRIPTION OF PROGRAM PAPERS

GEORGE WASHINGTON THE BUSINESS MAN AND ENGINEER—Visioning the greatness of his country, he advocated enterprises that developed transportation and communication, commerce and colonization. (Paper No. 5.)

GEORGE WASHINGTON THE CITIZEN—As burgess, Freemason, vestryman, justice, and trustee, he gave long, faithful, and constructive service. (Paper No. 6.)

For this program see numbers 6, 7, 32, 34, 45, 53, 78 in list of selected books on pages 300A and 300B.

PROGRAM SEVEN

GEORGE WASHINGTON THE CHRISTIAN

INHERITED RELIGIOUS ATTITUDE—Born of Christian parents, christened in the Episcopalian service, reared in deeply religious training, he gave reverence to God and respect to religious matters. (Paper No. 1.)

GEORGE WASHINGTON AS A CHRISTIAN: IN MILITARY EXPERIENCES—Knowing the need of his men for religious support, he provided a place for services in his commands, appealed for chaplains for the Army, and attended church services whenever possible. (Paper No. 2.)

GEORGE WASHINGTON AS A CHRISTIAN: REVEALED RELIGIOUS CONVICTIONS—Through his diaries and his letters his abiding faith in God is revealed. For his escapes and for his victories he gave grateful thanks to the Divine Power. (Paper No. 3.)

For this program see numbers 23, 99, 103 in list of selected books on pages 300A and 300B.

PROGRAM EIGHT

GEORGE WASHINGTON THE LEADER OF MEN

GEORGE WASHINGTON: PATRON OF EDUCATION—Through life a patron of education, he instituted the first free schooling in Alexandria, Virginia, and by his will left funds for an American university. (Paper No. 1.)

GEORGE WASHINGTON: LEADER IN ADVANCEMENT OF CIVILIZATION—In every period, position, and occupation, in industry and statecraft, public or private, he stood for progress. (Paper No. 2.)

GEORGE WASHINGTON: LEADER IN PHILANTHROPY—The number and extent of his charities were not matters of record. He helped people to help themselves by the most practical measures. Relatives and strangers found him responsive to need. (Paper No. 3.)

For this program see numbers 33, 40, 62, 92, 104 in list of selected books on pages 300A and 300B.

PROGRAM NINE

THE SOCIAL LIFE OF GEORGE WASHINGTON

SOCIAL LIFE OF CHILDHOOD HOME—From his parents, especially his mother, came his strict attention to social amenities. Through the social activities in the homes of his friends he gained additional social graces. (Paper No. 1.)

SOCIAL LIFE BEFORE THE REVOLUTION: AT WILLIAMSBURG AND MOUNT VERNON—After his marriage his duties as a burgess kept them in the midst of the elegant and formal social life of Williamsburg. The same type of conventional social routine was the rule at Mount Vernon. (Paper No. 2.)

SOCIAL LIFE IN LATER YEARS—The long adherence to conventional usages, the great dignity and the constant formality of the military headquarters, also characterized the etiquette of the presidential mansion. (Paper No. 3.)

For this program see numbers 23, 72, 81, 85, 102 in list of selected books on pages 300A and 300B.

PROGRAM TEN

GEORGE WASHINGTON THE BUILDER OF THE NATION

MILITARY EXPERIENCES UNDER BRITISH RULE—Through his mission to the French, his command of the frontier, and the expeditions against Fort Duquesne, he gave loyal service and gained valuable knowledge. (Paper No. 1.)

CHANGING VIEWS ON BRITISH CONTROL—Under the English policy of taxation his views changed, and from a loyal subject he turned to a radical Colonial who offered to go to the aid of Boston at the head of a thousand men. (Paper No. 2.)

CREATION AND ORGANIZATION OF A NEW NATION—A leader in the War for Independence, he was also a leader in stabilizing the Government and aided in framing the Constitution under which he became the first President. (Paper No. 3.)

For this program see numbers 18, 22, 33, 96, 98 in list of selected books on pages 300A and 300B.

PROGRAM ELEVEN

GEORGE WASHINGTON THE PRESIDENT
(1789-1797)

TRIUMPHANT JOURNEY AS PRESIDENT ELECT—Notified of his election, he bade his mother farewell and rode to New York through a continuous ovation. (Paper No. 1.)

FIRST TERM OF THE FIRST PRESIDENT—Epoch making were the events of the first administration, when an infant Nation was set upon its feet and its precedents and policies defined and established. (Paper No. 2.)

THE FIRST PRESIDENTIAL TOURS: NEW ENGLAND, LONG ISLAND, AND RHODE ISLAND—Seeking for himself a knowledge of his land in peace, President Washington established the precedent for presidential tours, first visiting the New England States. (Paper No. 3.)

THE SOUTHERN TOUR—His tour of the South covered 1,887 miles and occupied 66 days and never deviated from schedule. (Paper No. 4.)

SECOND TERM OF PRESIDENT WASHINGTON—At the Philadelphia presidential residence during his second term the social and official life was most formal. A third term was refused. (Paper No. 5.)

For this program see numbers 11, 12, 13, 33, 47, 98 in list of selected books on pages 300A and 300B.

PROGRAM TWELVE

THE HOME MAKING OF GEORGE AND MARTHA WASHINGTON

COLONEL AND MRS. WASHINGTON IN RESIDENCE BEFORE THE REVOLUTION—As one of the wealthiest couples of Virginia, the lavish life and hospitality of the prosperous planter prevailed until the approach of the Revolution. (Paper No. 1.)

WAR-TIME HOUSEHOLDS—The Mount Vernon household early banned all imported luxuries. Mrs. Washington spent almost every winter in the military headquarters, ministering to the welfare of the soldiers. (Paper No. 2.)

PRESIDENTIAL HOUSEHOLDS—President and Mrs. Washington planned every detail of their official residences so that their régime should inspire respect for the chief office of the new Nation. (Paper No. 3.)

LAST YEARS AT MOUNT VERNON—After General Washington's retirement to private life he was the magnet that drew throngs to Mount Vernon. He held first place in the hearts of his people and his home became America's first shrine. (Paper No. 4.)

For this program see numbers 21, 23, 41, 63, 72, 105 in list of selected books on pages 300A and 300B.

Family Relationships of George Washington

<small>THE WASHINGTON FAMILY AT HOME</small>

FAMILY NAME OF WASHINGTON: DERIVATIONS AND CHANGES

OR EIGHT HUNDRED YEARS, through successive generations, the name of Washington or de Wessyngton has been known for the valor, chivalry, high code of honor, and military distinction of those who bore it. Knights and gentlemen of the Old World and citizens of the New, each in their turn, through service and achievement have given to it a notable place in history.

In the process of evolution this name, like many others known to fame, has had many variations from the modern spelling. It is apparently of Saxon origin and is known to have existed in the twelfth century. Early records refer to the village of Warton in Lancashire and of Wessyngton in the Palatine Durham. It was from this latter village that the name of de Wessyngton was derived by the progenitor of the Washington family.

In those days, back in the twelfth century, it was the custom for families high in the social scale to take their surnames from their native towns and to change them for that of another town when they took up residence in a different territory, or for the name of an estate when promoted to more extensive holdings.

The village and estate of Wessyngton, Palatine Durham, was in the territory conquered by William the first and apportioned by him to his Norman or Saxon followers. Among the descendants of these Norman knights was William de Hertburn who, by 1183 "exchanged his village of Hertburn for the manor and village of Wessyngton, . . . changing his surname with the estate."

Tribute is paid to the bravery of William de Wessyngton in the fact that he was transferred to these new possessions which were on the border of northern England, a section subjected to constant warfare, where the most worthy of the King's followers were stationed.

As years went by the prefix *de*, pertaining to the lord of the manor, gradually fell into disuse, and finally disappeared from before the family name. Meanwhile changes of fortune caused members of the Wessyngton family to become scattered throughout England. Some distinguished themselves in religious fields, some in the professions, and others were knighted for public service. In different sections the name was spelled in divers ways; one form, Vysington, had a significance of its own, for *vyse* is also spelled *viss* and is defined as *wise*. Other forms appearing in important records are Weschington, Wassington, and Washington.

In the standardized form of the present day this name is widely mentioned in early county records of England and is engraved on time-worn monuments in churches and cathedrals. A parish in the County of Durham bears the name of Washington; there is another parish of that name in the County of Sussex, which has no historical connection with the George Washington family, and in our own country we have Washington Parish in Westmoreland County, Virginia, which was named for the great-grandfather of George Washington. The places and the people named for George Washington himself are legion. Each place and each person so named is thereby linked with a character that is glorified for all time, and all have had an opportunity to shine in reflected glory by doing their part in putting over the nation-wide celebration, in 1932, of the two hundredth anniversary of the birth of the illustrious man whose name they bear.

The family name which has come down through the ages to George Washington has carried with it the characteristics of his forbears; the bravery and gallantry of the de Hertburns who became de Wessyngtons; the support of parish churches analogous to that of Bondo de Wessyngton and William, his son, whose names appeared in 1257 on charters granting lands to religious houses; the loyalty of William Weshington, of Weshington, who fought for his country in the disastrous Battle of Lewes; the sportsmanship of Sir Stephen de Wessyngton, one of the noble chevaliers who was listed to tilt at a tournament in Dunstable, and the spirit of justice exhibited by John de Wessyngton, who "fought divers good fights for the honor of his priory." In later years there were sacrifices for King and country, patient endurance for a time of domination and oppression, and courage that led to protest, culminating in this country in the war for independence of which Bacon's Rebellion was the forerunner, when John Washington, fearless pioneer, who had gained renown as an Indian fighter, became a Virginia colonel in the service of his sovereign.

Each generation has brought added glory to the name of Washington, and this glory is manifested in resplendent form in the person of George Washington, to whom Webster has paid tribute in a masterly oration in which he claims that—

"America has furnished to the world the character of Washington. . . . Born upon our soil, of parents also born upon it, never for a moment having had a sight of the Old World; instructed according to the modes of his time, only the spare, plain, but wholesome elementary knowledge which our institutions provide for the children of the people; growing up beneath and penetrated by the influence of American society—growing up amidst our expanding but not luxurious civilization—partaking in our great destiny of labor, our long contest with unreclaimed nature and uncivilized man; our agony of glory, the War of Independence—our great victory of peace, the formation of the Union, and the establishment of the Constitution—he is all, all our own!"

And yet we must concede that "blood will tell," and that the blood and the inherent qualities of the long line of Washingtons in the mother country had their influence upon the character of that great mind which unfolded in the open spaces and developed under the pioneer spirit of a new country.

As Jared Sparks has said in his *Life of Washington:* "It is a happy combination of rare talents and qualities, the harmonious union of the intellectual and moral powers, rather than the dazzling splendor of any one trait, which constitute the grandeur of his character." A character indeed in which culminates the honor and glory of the family name of Washington.

Paternal Ancestry

"George Washington was great to a great extent because of what his ancestors were before him."

Though a true illustration of this doctrine of heredity, George Washington was quite unaware of the achievements of his ancestors beyond his great-grandfather, John Washington, who came to these shores about the middle of the seventeenth century and settled in Westmoreland County, Virginia,

on the very plantation where, in later years, George Washington was born.

It was a matter of common knowledge that John Washington emigrated from England, but from what section long remained a mystery. His great-grandson did not know from which branch of the English Washingtons he was descended. When an inquiry came to George Washington from an eminent London genealogist about his English ancestry he wrote: "It is a subject to which I have paid but little attention."

But others did pay attention, for no sooner did the head and shoulders of George Washington rise above the great and near great about him than his contemporaries across the sea commenced to ask, "Who is this superman who has defied our sovereign and wrested our American possessions from our grasp? From which branch of our Washingtons is he descended?"

So the queries were set afoot, and since that time many genealogists have devoted much study and research to this subject. The wealth of material that has been assembled is quite amazing. Only a judicial mind, accustomed to weighing evidence and eliminating that which can not be substantiated, could arrive at any definite conclusion as to what is and what is not authentic.

Many years were consumed in searching for documentary evidence which would establish the English pedigree of John Washington and of his great-grandson who had risen from the ranks to the head of a new nation. Elusive clues were followed without definite results until, through the persistent efforts of Henry F. Waters, the connecting links between the American and the English ancestry were eventually discovered.

The last bit of necessary evidence, which bridged the gap across the seas, was found on a little slip of paper folded on itself which, when opened out, was only about 3 inches long by 2 inches wide. It was a memorandum written in Latin and signed "Laurentia Washington" and was attached to a document connected with a bequest to his son, "Lawrence the younger," and others of his children.

Further research demonstrated that this Laurentia (or Lawrence) Washington was a fellow of Brasenose College, Oxford, and later a rector of Purleigh, and that he and his wife, Amphillis Roades, stepdaughter of Andrew Knowling, were the parents of six children—John, William, Lawrence, Elizabeth, Margaret, and Martha Washington. These names appear in the parish register of Tring and also in the will of Andrew Knowling which contained generous bequests to Amphillis Washington and her children.

Three of the children of the rector of Purleigh and his wife, Amphillis, emigrated to Virginia; John about 1657, and Lawrence, and later their sister Martha. To this sister who became Martha Hayward, John Washington bequeathed "ten pounds out of the money I have in England and whatsoever

she may be owing me for transporting her into this country and a year's accommodation after coming in."

Having established the connecting link, it was then possible to trace the English ancestry of George Washington back, through the rector of Purleigh, to the Sulgrave branch of the family, and on back for seven generations to John Washington, of Tewhitfield, County Lancashire, whose great-grandson, Lawrence Washington, of Grays Inn, was Mayor of Northampton and grantee of the Sulgrave estate, which remained in the direct family for two generations.

In commemoration of this Lawrence Washington and his second wife, Amee, daughter of Robert Pargiter, of Gretworth, there is still a memorial stone in St. James Church, Sulgrave. One of the brass plates on this stone bears the Washington coat of arms. There were also effigies of Lawrence and Amee Washington and of their eleven children, with an inscription relating to the worthy husband and wife.

Robert Washington, one of the eleven children, inherited Sulgrave Manor. He, with the consent of his son Lawrence, who married Margaret Butler, had the entail broken and the estate was sold to a nephew in 1610.

Lawrence Washington, rector of Purleigh, was next in line. His mother, Margaret Butler Washington, was a daughter of Margaret Sutton, through whom a strain of royal blood descended into the veins of George Washington, the man who, above all others, was instrumental in bringing to a successful termination the revolt of the Colonies against the oppressive rule of England's royalty.

George Washington was unaware of his claims to royal pedigree and came to disapprove of the monarchial form of government. Though fitted in every way to serve as a wise and considerate sovereign had he permitted the people to proclaim him King of the United States of America, he most emphatically declined that honor, preferring to be called the President.

He was true to his ancestry, however, in recognizing that most human beings "dearly love a lord," and while he would have no high-sounding title for himself he forebore from condemnation of the title "Lady Washington" which was applied to his wife during and following the Revolution. When elected to the Presidency of the United States he saw fit to adopt a ceremonious course befitting the dignity of his position and likewise the dignity of a descendant of knights and nobles of England and of a member of the "First Families of Virginia."

In his Farewell Address, upon retiring from the Presidency, he stressed his belief that "a government of as much vigor as is consistent with the perfect security of liberty is indispensable," and claimed for himself the liberty to take up again his peaceful agricultural pursuits which had been so frequently interrupted by his patriotic service. In this, too, he exemplified an instinct which had been inherited from his forbears, one which has been but lightly touched upon in history.

Some of the arms of the families allied with the Washingtons are still in existence in a set of six stained-glass panels formerly in Sulgrave, reproductions of which are in the White House in Washington. Another evidence of the high regard in which the Washingtons were held is a magnificent carved stone shield of many quarterings, containing the arms of the Washingtons and Standish arms—the Myles Standish branch. The various modifications show that the English Washingtons have been prominent cultivators of the land, eminent divines, magistrates, belted knights, and navigators. Truly they were versatile and worthy ancestors of a versatile and worthy offspring who is universally recognized as a great and good citizen, an incomparable General and President.

MATERNAL ANCESTRY

The ancients had a saying that the mother always gave the tone to the character of the child. The laws of heredity likewise affirm that it is the mother who inherits her father's greatness and hands it down to her children.

George Washington is said to have resembled his mother physically, and he recognized that the mental and spiritual debt due to her for training, if not through inheritance, was a great one. He gave public tribute to her as his "revered mother, by whose Maternal hand, (early deprived of a Father) I was led from Childhood."

Back of this mother, whose maiden name was Mary Ball, there were many generations of free-thinking and free-speaking people who fought bravely for equality and liberty. It has been stated that there are "weighty reasons for believing that Mary Ball, mother of George Washington, was a lineal descendant from John Ball, the medieval champion of the rights of man," who was known as the "Mad Preacher of Kent." Because of his "irrepressible preachments" that all men are free and equal he helped to promote a rebellion against the rule of royalty. This resulted in the sacrifice of his life in behalf of his chosen cause of equality and liberty.

Who can say but that it was from that period of the fourteenth century, and from that ancestor, that George Washington derived the characteristics which made it possible for him, some four centuries later, to lead an army of rebellion against the oppressions of royalty and to carve out a new and independent nation which sounded the same keynote, "That all men are created equal; that they are endowed by their Creator with certain inalienable rights; that among these are life, liberty, and the pursuit of happiness."

The more immediate ancestry of Mary Ball is traced back to Col. William Ball, who emigrated to Virginia about 1650 and settled in Lancaster County on a plantation called Millenbeck, on the Rappahannock River.

This Col. William Ball was the father of Col. Joseph Ball, of Epping Forest. The latter was the father of Mary Ball by his second wife, who was known as the "widow Johnson" but whose maiden name was probably Mary Montague, a descendant of the extinct Earls of Salisbury.

From these ancestors Mary Ball inherited many of the qualities which, through her, descended to her son and strengthened similar inherent traits that had come also from his paternal forbears.

Though little heed was paid by George Washington to either his paternal or maternal ancestry, it is worthy of note that skilled genealogists have devoted years of study and research to the task of uncovering documentary evidence that would definitely establish his pedigree.

Both of Mary Ball's parents passed away during her early girlhood, and she was left to the guardianship of George Eskridge, an eminent lawyer of Virginia, in whose honor, tradition says, she gave her eldest son the name of George.

Little is known of the education and domestic influence by which the remarkable character of Mary Ball was developed and matured. There was little provision made at that period for systematic education. Mary Ball is said to have written to her brother, Joseph, "We have not had a schoolmaster in our neighborhood until now (January 14, 1723) in nearly four years." It is apparent, however, that she received adequate training in domestic routine and religious observance and that she was "gifted with great firmness and constancy of purpose, as well as with a clear judgment and remarkable mental independence." By contemporary testimony and tradition she is credited with the noblest qualities of mind and heart. Tradition also says that the character of George Washington was strengthened, if not formed, by the care and precepts of his mother, and that his mother taught him the duties of obedience the better to prepare him for those of command; that she held a firm hand in the enforcement of discipline, but it was never otherwise than kindly in its operations. Such was her dignity and majestic mien that a youthful playmate of her children said of her in later years, "She awed me in the midst of her kindness."

The escutcheon of Mary Ball's family bears upon it a black lion on a silver shield with a crest having a lion rampant, holding a golden ball in his paws. The motto, *Coelumque Tueri* (And Look to Heaven), suggests a striking characteristic of Mary Ball, displayed in her earnest supplications for guidance from above and her calmness and self-control under most trying circumstances even though the spirit of the "lion rampant" was within her.

Through his maternal ancestor there came to George Washington the strength of a philosopher and the truthfulness of a Christian; he was taught to love God supremely, his kind tenderly, and to be good and generous to all living creatures. And above all he was always considerate of his mother's wishes and ever addressed her as "Honored Madam," thus paying a courtly tribute to her and through her to her distinguished forbears.

BROTHERS, SISTERS, NIECES, AND NEPHEWS

The youth of today can scarcely realize the close family ties and the home influence that existed two centuries ago, when George Washington grew up from a country lad to become a leader among men and to fill the highest position in a land which largely owed to him its liberty and freedom.

With none of the modern means of transportation and amusement, and with neighbors few and far between, the bonds of relationship had a deep significance and the experience of each member of the family circle helped to shape the lives and character of the whole.

The greatest influence upon the life of young George Washington, aside from that of his mother, is credited to his half brother Lawrence, the oldest son of his father by his first wife. Lawrence and his brother Augustine had the advantage of being sent to England for a broader education than was afforded in this country at that early period. George was denied this opportunity due to the death of his father when he was but 11 years old, which resulted in a division of the estate and a consequent curtailment of resources.

Lawrence, according to the feudal custom that the oldest son should inherit the major portion of the patrimonial estate, was bequeathed large holdings on the Potomac and Little Hunting Creek, which he named Mount Vernon. He received also his father's interest in iron mines from which had come a portion of the family income. The family estate at Bridges Creek, reaching to Pope's Creek, went to the second son of Augustine Washington's first wife, who was his father's namesake. To the widow and his second family went the later home, on the Rappahannock near Fredericksburg, together with various nonproductive lands.

Both Lawrence and Augustine intermarried with the gentry—or "first families"—of Virginia, and, being gentlemen and educated men, they became of considerable consequence in the Colony.

George was at all times a welcome visitor in the homes of both his half brothers. He lived for a time with his brother Augustine at the old family home at Bridges Creek, in Westmoreland County, for the purpose of attending a private school conducted on the plantation. It is recorded that he was most proficient in mathematics and that while there he received his first instruction in surveying, which later he adopted as a profession, a profession which one of his maternal uncles was following.

Meanwhile, however, his brother Lawrence had other plans for him and arranged for him to go to sea, but these plans were frustrated by his mother, who was influenced by the advice of her brother Joseph against such a calling. Though sorely disappointed, young George was dutifully obedient to the dictates of his mother, and solaced himself by experimental surveys on his visits to Mount Vernon. This activity and his superb horsemanship brought him to the attention of Thomas, Lord Fairfax, then a neighbor and close friend of his brother Lawrence, who had married a Fairfax. Through such acquaintanceship as this, and the opportunity afforded him to mingle with other important men of the day who visited Mount Vernon and who were helping to mold the political interest of the Colonies, George Washington early acquired a wide interest in colonial affairs.

During his frequent visits to Mount Vernon, George was welcomed into close companionship with his brother Lawrence, and with him shared a dream for the development of the then almost unknown region of the West, which was largely an unbroken forest. Lawrence, with his interest in the iron mines, saw the necessity of seeking commercial connection with the western country and realized that such connection would naturally be by water. This aroused in George Washington "an ambition that remained an aspiration of a lifetime" which led, finally, to the development of the Potomac River and the Chesapeake and Ohio Canal.

It was during these visits also that the young lad first became interested in the breeding of livestock and other plantation procedure which served as a foundation for his later activity in agricultural pursuits. Thus he was fitted to become the heir and successor of his elder brother, who apparently foresaw the grim shadow of the Great Reaper approaching. During his military service in the West Indies Lawrence had contracted lung trouble, to which he later succumbed. Shortly before his death George accompanied him, as nurse and companion, to the Barbadoes, which proved to be the only occasion on which George Washington traveled beyond the shores of his native land.

After the death of Lawrence, in 1752, George returned for a time to the family home near Fredericksburg. While there he made a survey of a tract of land which his friend and brother-in-law, Fielding Lewis, had recently purchased to build a home for his young bride, Betty Washington, who was next younger than George and had been his favorite playmate. She grew up to be so much like him both in features and stature that she might have donned his military cloak and chapeau and passed herself off as her distinguished brother.

In later years, Fielding Lewis having suffered reverses in his fortune during the Revolution, George Washington frequently provided his sister Betty with funds and helped her in other ways. Three of her sons—Robert, Lawrence, and Howell—were each in turn taken into his home and were employed as secretaries and rent collectors. With Lawrence Lewis his Uncle George was especially pleased, and he appointed the lad as an officer in the Light Dragoons in 1798.

For his brother Samuel, though nearer his own age, George Washington did not seem to hold the same affection or regard that he expressed for his two younger brothers, especially John Augustine. Apparently Samuel's tendencies toward extravagance proved an irritant to the more prudent elder brother. Samuel was married five times, and though his will disclosed a considerable estate, apparently it was not in a condition to support the heirs properly. For a number of years thereafter George Washington's correspondence contains references to the involved condition and litigation of his late brother's affairs. Even some eleven years after Samuel's death he spoke of the education of two of Samuel's sons as part of his own burden, "their father's estate being unable to discharge the executions as fast as they are issued against it." Also in his will George Washington mentioned obligations due from Samuel's estate, which he declared "shall stand balanced."

For Samuel's eldest son, Thornton, General Washington obtained an ensigncy and entrusted him, during the Revolutionary War, with the conveyance of important dispatches and large sums of money. He also assumed the care of Samuel's daughter, Harriot, who was a member of his household, with but slight intervals, for more than a decade. She was, it seems, a true child of her father and must have taxed her uncle's patience, for he wrote of her to his sister Betty, "She has no disposition to be careful with her clothes, . . . her best things always in use, . . . she costs me enough."

To his favorite brother, John Augustine, George Washington refers as "the intimate companion of my youth and the friend of my ripened years." It was to him that he entrusted all of his affairs, including the management of Mount Vernon, during his early military service in the British Army. Throughout their entire lifetime visits between them were frequent, and one of John Augustine's sons, Bushrod, was a favorite nephew. Through the influence of his Uncle George this nephew was admitted to study law with James Wilson, of Philadelphia, became proficient in his profession, and was appointed by President Adams a Justice of the Supreme Court. Though proud of Bushrod's achievements, George Washington, as was his custom, withheld official influence in obtaining a coveted appointment and wrote him frankly: "Your standing at the bar would not justify my nomination of you as attorney to the Federal District Court in preference to some of the oldest and most esteemed general court lawyers in your State who are desirous of the appointment."

At all times George Washington refrained from seeking political preference for his kinfolk, and especially so while he was serving as President of the United States. In a letter addressed to Thomas Jefferson he wrote: "The public will never be made to believe that an appointment of a relative is made on the ground of merit alone, uninfluenced by family views."

He was cautious also in suggesting or approving military appointments for his relatives, and invariably stationed them where they would have their full share of danger and responsibility. Thus he impressed upon them that they must stand upon their own merit and courage, and demonstrated his own stand against partiality. The precedent he set, both as a general and as President of the United States, in avoiding undue preferment and in unerringly picking for each place the man best fitted to fill it, is a noteworthy one and a good one to follow.

Little can be learned of George Washington's relations with his youngest brother, Charles. In his will there is a bequest of "the gold-headed cane left me by Doctor Franklin," with the comment, "I add nothing else because of the ample provision I have made for his issue." Charles did not live to receive this bequest, his death occurring prior to that of his illustrious brother.

This and other bequests and comments in the will of George Washington make of it a most human document, which testifies to the fatherly interest he felt for all his nieces and nephews. It records not only his affection for them but his appreciation for the loyal services that have been rendered by them in various capacities, and above all it bears messages which were surely cherished as much or more than the monetary value of the item bequeathed.

To the acquaintances and friends of juvenile years, Lawrence Washington and Robert Washington, of Chotank, he left two gold-headed canes with the Washington arms engraved thereon. Among others who received special mention were five nephews— William Augustine Washington, George Lewis, George Steptoe Washington, Bushrod Washington, and Samuel Washington—each of whom was to be the recipient of—

"one of the swords or cutteaux of which I die possessed, and they to chuse in the order they are named.—These swords are accompanied with an injunction not to unsheath them for the purpose of shedding blood except it be for self-defence, or in defence of their country and its rights, and in the latter case to keep them unsheathed and prefer falling with them in their hands to the relinquishment thereof."

To one of the above-mentioned nephews, Bushrod, who was a prime favorite, he bequeathed a considerable portion of the Mount Vernon estate, including the mansion. But the bequest was not due to favoritism alone, for a careful explanation is given that it was "partly in consideration of an intimation to his deceased father while we were bachelors, and he had kindly undertaken to superintend my estate during my military service in the former war between Great Britain and France, that if I should fall therein, Mount Vernon (then less extensive in domain than at present) should become his property." To Bushrod he bequeathed also important papers and stipulated that he was to receive his library after the death of his widow, Martha Washington. Perhaps this bequest recalled to his nephew, to whom George Washington had appealed in legal matters, a sort of promissory statement: "You may think me an unprofitable applicant in asking opinions and requiring services of you without dousing my money, but pay day may come."

Another nephew of whom George Washington was particularly fond, a namesake, George Augustine Washington, son of his youngest brother, Charles, had been amply provided for during his lifetime, and after his early decease the two fatherless children and their mother had been taken into the home at Mount Vernon and were left a portion of the Mount Vernon estate.

After the special bequests the rest and residue of George Washington's estate was left to Martha Washington, his widow, during her lifetime, with the provision that it be apportioned, ultimately, into 23 *equal* parts. This, his last act, emphasized his impartiality and sense of equality.

In the final settlement of the estate many of the younger men, nephews and great-nephews, chose land that was situated in what was still considered as "the wilds," and to this day their descendants are to be found on both sides of the Ohio, while later generations, venturing farther afield, settled on the banks of the Mississippi and helped to people the Middle West. Still others are now living in the great "Lone Star" State and on the Pacific coast, in sections quite remote from the Old Dominion.

So have the descendants of the brothers and the sister of George Washington become scattered through this great Nation; so have they, through his influence and through their family relationship and consequent inheritances, impregnated this entire country with the high type of men and women who can ever be counted upon to stand for high ideals and good citizenship as did their illustrious kinsman, George Washington.

STEPCHILDREN AND STEPGRANDCHILDREN

When George Washington brought his bride to Mount Vernon he simultaneously took into his home and heart her two children by a former husband. To these little ones, Jackey and Patsey Custis, he became a true and affectionate father and a careful and conscientious guardian. To them and to their affairs he gave the most circumspect attention, fully realizing, as he wrote to a friend, "there is greater circumspection to be observed by a guardian than by a natural parent." Save for the ties of blood, he was a real parent to them. He lavished as much care and love upon them as if they had actually been his own, and his filial tenderness and generosity won from them a strong and lasting devotion. He was ever thoughtful of their needs and their pleasure, as is shown by the things he ordered for them from his London merchant.

Shortly after he assumed the responsibilities of stepfatherhood he included in an order "one pair of handsome silver shoe and knee buckles," also ten shillings' worth of toys, and six little books for children beginning to read. For Miss Custis, 4 years old, two caps, two pairs of ruffles, two tuckers, bibs and aprons, if fashionable, a fashionably dressed baby (10 shillings), and other toys. Later on he ordered "A Bible and Prayer Book neatly bound in Turkey, with names in gilt letters on the inside of the cover," also a spinet and other items of a cultural character.

The best instructors and dancing masters obtainable were provided, and the fond foster father took a personal interest in their studies and their games. It is recounted that "often, when at their games in the drawing room at night—perhaps romping and dancing and noisey—they (the children) would see him watching their movements at some side door, enjoying their sport, and if at any time his presence seemed to check them, he would beg them not to mind him, but to go on just as before, encouraging them in every possible way to continue their amusement to their heart's content."

Little Martha Custis, or Patsey, as she was called, was very delicate in health from early childhood, and everything that affection and ample means could afford for the preservation of her health was provided. A record appears in George Washington's own handwriting of a journey to the Frederick Springs (now Berkeley Springs, W. Va.) in August, 1769, undertaken solely on her account to try (by the advice of her physician) the effect of the waters on her complaint. This was one of the few instances in which George Washington charged extra expense incurred in behalf of his stepchildren to their estate. Their own father had left them well provided for, and their property was judiciously managed by their stepfather, who "never charged them one farthing for all the trouble."

The death of the "dark lady," as Patsey was called because of her deeply brunette complexion, brought deepest sorrow to the little family at Mount Vernon. In a letter to her uncle, Burwell Bassett, George Washington wrote: "She rose from dinner about 4 o'clock in better health and spirits than she appeared to have been for some time, soon after which she was seized with one of her usual fits, and expired in less than two minutes without uttering a word, a groan, or scarcely a sigh."

His grief and that of his wife caused him to cancel arrangements he had made for a trip to the western country with the Governor of Virginia, that he might remain with the bereaved mother, whose grief was so increased by the absence of her son at King's College, in New York, that he was recalled to solace her.

Young Jack Custis did not take kindly to the restraints of the classroom and welcomed an opportunity to return to Mount Vernon, for he was very much in love with young Eleanor Calvert, "a slip of a girl and a budding beauty." Though saddened by his sister's death, he was ever a high-spirited youth, fond of horses, dogs, and guns, and of outdoor activity. In Eleanor Calvert he found a kindred spirit, and with the ardency of extreme youth he wooed and won her. When George Washington discovered the matrimonial engagement he met the issue squarely and wrote frankly to the girl's father that he considered the youth, inexperience, and unripened education of the suitor "insuperable obstacles." While he did not wish to break off the match, he sought to have it postponed until his stepson could be "carried through a regular course of education."

It had been agreed that Jack Curtis was to pass two years at college, but fate willed it otherwise, and Eleanor Calvert Custis came into the family to help fill the vacancy left by the death of Patsey. For a year or more they lived at Mount Vernon. Then came the War for Independence, and they accompanied Martha Washington on the long journey to join the General at his first military headquarters, in Cambridge. Later they settled at Abingdon, where their third child, Nellie Custis, was born. She and a younger brother were informally adopted by George Washington as his own at the death-bed of their father, who had served as aide-de-camp to the General at the siege of Yorktown and there contracted a violent camp fever to which he quickly succumbed.

Thus Eleanor Parke Custis, at the age of 3, and her younger brother, George Washington Parke Custis, became the wards of George Washington and grew up at Mount Vernon, where they were surrounded by the same care and love that had been given to their father and his sister before them. The ever-increasing demands upon their stepgrandfather's time and his call to public duties did not prevent him, even while President of the United States, from giving to his wards the personal guidance and friendly advice of a fond father. To Eleanor, when she was 16 and had just attended her first ball, he wrote playfully and yet seriously about her prospective beaux, teasingly suggesting that she "retain the resolution to love with moderation, . . . at least until you have secured your game." Having "entered upon the chapter of advices," he proceeded with a lecture drawn from the text, "Love is said to be an involuntary passion, and it is, therefore, contended that it can not be resisted." He took the stand that this is true only in part, and pointed out that it is rapid in progress only when nourished, but let this be withdrawn and "it may be stifled in its birth or much stinted in its growth." He then advises:

"When the fire is beginning to kindle, and your heart growing warm, propound these questions to it: Who is this invader? Have I a competent knowledge of him? Is he a man of good character; a man of sense? For, be assured, a sensible woman can never be happy with a fool. What has been his walk in life? ? Is he a gambler, a spendthrift, or drunkard? Is his fortune sufficient to maintain me in the manner I have been accustomed to live, and my sisters do live, and is he one to whom my friends can have no reasonable objection? If these interrogatories can be satisfactorily answered, there will remain but one more to be asked, that, however is an important one. Have I sufficient ground to conclude that his affections are engaged by me?"

Apparently this "sprightly ward" profited by this kindly advice, and when she did "secure her game" the General was especially pleased with her choice of one of his favorite nephews, Lawrence Lewis. They were married on the 22d of February, the last birthday George Washington lived to see. In September of that year (1799) he wrote to the young bridegroom: "From the moment Mrs. Washington and myself adopted the two youngest children of Mr. Custis, it became my intention (if they survived me and conducted themselves to my satisfaction) to consider them in my will when I was about to make a distribution of my property. This determination has undergone no diminution, but is strengthened by the connection one of them has formed with my family." To them he left a portion of the Mount Vernon tract and other valuable holdings.

George Washington Parke Custis was also remembered in the will of George Washington, though from the General's letters to him while he was away at school one might be led to suppose that there were times when the youth did not "conduct himself to the satisfaction" of his guardian and stepgrandfather. His chief failing seemed to be "indolence in everything that did not tend to his amusements." But the General was lenient and wrote to him in the most friendly and parental manner, urging him to devote his mind to useful pursuits. Following some "error," which is not explained, the young man wrote: "My very soul, tortured with the stings of conscience, at length called reason to its aid, and happily for me triumphed." To this the General replied most graciously with the assurance that "Your endeavors to fulfill these reasonable wishes of ours can not fail of restoring all the attentions, protection, and affection of one who has ever been, and will continue to be, your sincere friend." In a later letter he is told "no innocent amusement or reasonable expenditure will ever be withheld from you."

The relationship of George Washington with his stepchildren and stepgrandchildren might be summed up by amending the quotation, "God left him childless that he might be a father to his country" by adding to it, "and a fond parent and guardian to the children of others."

(FOR THIS PROGRAM SEE NUMBERS 19, 23, 32, 54, 101 IN LIST OF SELECTED BOOKS ON PAGES 300-A AND 300-B)

STANDISH PEW IN CHORLEY PARISH CHURCH, ENGLAND
Showing quarterings of Washington, Butler, Laurence, Standish and other allied families

Homes of George Washington

MOUNT VERNON, VIRGINIA—RIVER FRONT

EARLY HISTORY OF WAKEFIELD, THE BIRTHPLACE, AND MOUNT VERNON

TWO SACRED SHRINES, most dear to the heart of every American, were the objects of many pilgrimages in 1932, in commemoration of the Two Hundredth Anniversary of the Birth of George Washington.

One is the hallowed birthplace of the "Father of his Country"—the other, his last resting place. Both are within easy motor distance from the Nation's Capital and are connected with it and with each other by scenic highways that traverse a section steeped in romance and historic lore. There will be facilities also for those who wish to view the intervening landscape from the air, while those who prefer a more leisurely mode of travel can enjoy the shore line from excursion steamers.

There were pilgrimages, also, to the boyhood home of George Washington on the Rappahannock River and to various temporary homes, or the sites where they once stood; to the scenes of his various military headquarters; to famous battlefields, and to other places closely associated with his notable achievements.

But first of all, interest centers in the birthplace of the foremost American of all times, for that is the focal point of the entire celebration. It is situated in Washington Parish, named for John Washington, who emigrated from England about 1657 and settled in Westmoreland County, Virginia. There, on a large plantation between Bridges Creek and Popes Creek, overlooking the "River of Swans"—the lower Potomac—three generations of the Washington family had made their home prior to the birth of the boy whose name has become so famous as to lend fame to all things and places connected with his active life and remarkable career.

In selecting the acres in Westmoreland County as his family seat, John Washington had the same wisdom and foresight which he later displayed when (in 1674), in company with Nicholas Spencer, he secured a land grant of 5,000 acres on the west bank of the upper Potomac between Dogues Run and Little Hunting Creek.

Until long after the birth date of George Washington the Westmoreland County plantation was known as Bridges Creek or Popes Creek, but has since become known as Wakefield. The later acquisition, on the upper Potomac, was known as Epsewasson or Hunting Creek, also as the Washington plantation, until it was christened Mount Vernon, in 1743, by Lawrence Washington, an elder half brother of George Washington and, like him, a great-grandson of the original owner.

The chief reason for the selection of these two sites by John Washington must have been based upon the facilities afforded for wharfage and navigation. This was a necessary precaution, for the early settlers depended almost entirely upon the Old World for their manufactured supplies, paying for them with the products of their fields, which consisted chiefly of tobacco. Second to the navigable opportunities which nature had provided in each of these locations, were the advantages which each of these beautiful sites offered for a home. Scarcely could any two points on the Potomac be more adaptable, with ground sloping back from the river and overlooking the broad expanse of water in the foreground.

The stretch of country between these two important holdings of John Washington and his descendants, which had previously been infested with savages and wild beasts, gradually became populated with representatives of the best families of England; for by 1670 cavaliers and "women of gallant heritage" had settled permanently in Virginia. The founder of these two ancestral homes of George Washington, which were destined to become the most noted and revered spots in America, was prominent among the early settlers and had much to do with the making of the early history of Virginia.

While the far-famed "First Families of Virginia" were loyal to their sovereign across the seas, they were not blind to the injustice and oppression of the colonial governors, and it is recorded that John Washington was among those who joined Nathaniel Bacon in "hurling defiance at loot-saturated Governor Berkeley, of hated memory, who knowingly allowed the Indians to sell him pelts with one hand while they tomahawked Virginians with the other."

It is also believed that "from the site of the future Mount Vernon estate 2,500 savages were driven over the hills into the Shenandoah Valley in that early Indian war by that first American Washington, who gained the name of 'Conotocarius' (Devourer of Villages) through his prowess as an Indian fighter." These exploits of John Washington were so indelibly impressed upon the "race that never forgets" that some three generations later, when our own George Washington, then a young Virginia colonel, came into prominence as an Indian fighter, this same title was bestowed upon him.

Though Governor Berkeley "thanked God there were no printing presses nor free schools in Virginia and hoped there would not be for a hundred years," the dissemination of news and the opportunities for acquiring education could not be entirely suppressed as the population and the number of the early homes increased.

Keeping step with the march of civiliza-

tion came the early churches, and though there was a scarcity of ministers they did double duty by teaching the young as well as preaching to them and to their elders.

The faith and piety of the early settlers is especially emphasized in contemporary records. That John Washington was pious is shown by the first paragraph of his will, in which he expresses trust and belief that he will "assuredly be saved" and that his soul and body "at the general resurrection shall rise again with joy."

John Washington had been a resident of the British Colonies in the New World scarcely more than two decades when death claimed him, yet he had laid a solid foundation for those who came after him. In commercial, military, and political affairs he ranked far above the average, representing his country in the House of Burgesses, bearing the military rank of lieutenant colonel, and standing on a par socially with the gentry of that period.

There has been much conjecture about the original rooftree of the Washington family in Westmoreland County. It is logical to assume that the first structure stood near Bridges Creek, for it is there that the family burying ground was located. Some traces have been found, moreover, of buildings in that vicinity. Half a mile distant, on the banks of Popes Creek, there are indications of a pretentious mansion with the customary outbuildings. It would seem, therefore, that the first home on Bridges Creek was eventually abandoned and a new home site selected. It is probable, also, that the new home was later called Popes Creek, as many historians give it that name.

There is a supposition that the actual house in which George Washington was born burned in 1735, but this statement has been thoroughly discredited by a member of the Washington family and by others who contend that the veritable birthplace stood until Christmas eve of 1780, when a fire took place which wiped out the mansion then standing upon the foundations which have been so carefully uncovered in recent years.

Upon these foundations, where George Washington Parke Custis, stepgrandson of George Washington, placed a memorial tablet in 1815 and where, later, the United States Government erected a monument to mark the spot, a structure has arisen, phœnixlike, which is typical of the one consumed by fire and will represent as nearly as is humanly possible the birthplace of George Washington. The monument erected by the United States Government has meanwhile been shifted to a near-by spot to make possible the erection of the new building upon the original foundations.

This work and the restoration of the family tomb and preservation of the burial ground is being carried on by the Wakefield National Memorial Association, Incorporated, an organization created especially for this purpose. It raised a goodly sum through individual contributions and also enlisted

some support from the National and State Governments. This Association also by prolonged and painstaking efforts procured authentic data upon which to base its work of restoration and preservation; and acquired priceless heirlooms, furniture, letters, and other documents for the completed mansion.

By the dawn of 1932, the year of the Bicentennial Celebration of the Birth of George Washington, the work was accomplished, and Wakefield became a place of pilgrimage and will be forever linked with Mount Vernon in the minds and hearts of all people as the cradle is linked to the grave; the scenes of the beginning and of the end of an illustrious life—these two sacred national shrines.

MOUNT VERNON

Relics of the Doeg Indians of the Algonquin race, unearthed in the vicinity of the private deer park and the fisheries established at Mount Vernon by George Washington, bring to the imagination picturesque scenes of the intervening generations of hunters and fishermen who roamed over that territory in days gone by. Wigwams and camp fires fade into the background and give place to substantial colonial mansions with all the comforts and luxuries of the early American homes; red-skinned savages stalking game are succeeded by red-coated huntsmen following the hounds; and proprietorship by virtue of possession is superseded by land grants issued to the favorites of ruling monarchs.

One of the large Virginia grants was issued by Charles II to several of his adherents in 1649, and he renewed it in 1663. Lord Culpeper gained control of the grant and in 1674 conveyed title covering a certain tract of 5,000 acres along the west bank of the Potomac from Dogues Run to Little Hunting Creek, to Lieut. Col. John Washington and Col. Nicholas Spencer.

A dozen years prior to this, John Washington had established a home on the lower Potomac, which expanded to include Popes Creek and Bridges Creek, in Westmoreland County, where, three generations later, his greatgrandson, George Washington, was born. Nicholas Spencer, the cograntee, was doubtless a descendant or relative of Lord Spencer, neighbor and friend of Lawrence Washington, of Little Brington, England. Thus the representatives of two Old World families were linked together by business interests in the New World to which they had emigrated.

Following down the chain of title we find in the will of John Washington that he bequeathed his half of the 5,000-acre tract to his son, Lawrence. Thirteen years later, in 1690, the tract was divided, Lawrence Washington taking the eastern half, facing Little Hunting Creek, leaving the western half, facing Dogues Run, for the Spencer family.

Lawrence Washington bequeathed to his daughter, Mildred, the 2,500 acres which constituted the original site of what was later named Mount Vernon, and in 1726 Mildred's brother, Augustine, purchased it from her, as shown by deed of transfer from Mildred and her husband, Roger Gregory. This Mildred Washington Gregory was the aunt and godmother of George Washington, who later inherited the property.

The first residence of the future "Father of His Country" at Little Hunting Creek was when he was between the ages of 3 and 7, his father having removed to the property from the family home at Bridges Creek. This removal resulted in the establishment of a country seat which he gave to his eldest son, Lawrence, in 1740, and confirmed the gift in his will, but with the proviso that, if Lawrence should die without issue, it was to go to George, the eldest son of his second wife. The home where George was born in Westmoreland County, which is now known as Wakefield, was bequeathed by Augustine Washington to his second son by his first wife. This son, Augustine, was his namesake but was frequently called Austin.

There is much conjecture as to just where the first residence was erected on Little Hunting Creek; one theory is that it stood on or near the present site of Mount Vernon Mansion, another is that it was on the site now occupied by the greenhouses. There are indications that the original structure burned to the ground in 1739. About this time Augustine Washington removed his family to his third and last residence, on the Rappahannock River across from Fredericksburg.

The Little Hunting Creek estate, a few years later, became the home of Lawrence Washington and his bride, Anne Fairfax. Meanwhile a commodious mansion had been erected upon what is literally a mount, which Lawrence named Mount Vernon in compliment to the British admiral under whom he served in the West Indies. Whether Lawrence built this mansion, which forms the central portion of the present Mount Vernon Mansion, or whether it was erected for him by his father, can not now be established.

The original mansion is described as a plain structure of two stories and a gable, with a porch in front and a large substantial chimney at either end of the house. It had a most commanding view and was ideally situated, lending itself admirably to later additions and development.

During his ten years of residence in this delightful home Lawrence Washington developed into one of the important men of the colony. Through his marriage to Anne Fairfax, a cousin of Thomas Lord Fairfax, he was united with one of the greatest families of Virginia, and through his military service he had merited and received an appointment by the royal governor as adjutant of his military district with the rank of major. He also represented his county in the House of Burgesses at Williamsburg, and in 1750 was made president of the Ohio Company, which, largely at his instigation, had been formed in 1747 to colonize the great wilderness of the Ohio Valley.

Into this congenial atmosphere George Washington frequently came to pay extended visits. About 1747 he came to make his permanent home at Mount Vernon. His association here with men of prominence and position doubtless had much to do with the cultivation of the taste he acquired for the sedate and sober acquaintanceship of his elders.

When George Washington was but 20 he came into control and active management of Mount Vernon through the death of his brother, Lawrence, which was followed within a few weeks by that of Lawrence's only surviving child. While he was engaged in the settlement of his brother's affairs he turned his attention to agricultural pursuits, in which he was extremely interested. These activities were interrupted when he was called into service by Governor Dinwiddie. This resulted in a military and public career which frequently called him away from Mount Vernon during the 46 years of his ownership. And yet he invariably gave his personal attention and supervision to the improvement and development of both the house and grounds.

His stepgrandson, George Washington Parke Custis, in his *Recollections and Private Memoirs of Washington,* comments:

"When Colonel Washington first resided at Mount Vernon, both the mansion and the estate were inconsiderable. All of the embellishments of the house and grounds are owing to his creative hand."

Perhaps the first extensive improvements made by him were during the summer of 1758, when he put Mount Vernon in order, to receive his bride, though the wedding did not occur until January of the following year.

Some years later, when he found the mansion totally inadequate in size properly to entertain the many notables and other guests who came to pay him honor, he drew plans for additions to the house and for the surrounding buildings, also for the arrangement of the grounds, including the beautiful flower garden and kitchen garden.

At each end of the house he built a considerable extension, conforming to the architecture of the original building, which made the dwelling about three times its former size. As altered, the mansion was rather long for its height. This was remedied by an artistic balustrade over the portico, which George Washington had built, and by an addition to the observatory tower, thus raising the skyline considerably.

The exterior of the mansion is wood and is painted white. It has been restored in comparatively recent years to appear as nearly as possible as it did a century or more ago, when it and the surrounding buildings sheltered the family and retainers of the noble, kindly-hearted man who was "first in war, first in peace, and first in the hearts of his countrymen."

During the ownership and intermittent residence of George Washington at Mount Vernon his inheritance of 2,700 acres was increased to approximately 8,000 acres, with a consequent diversity of activities. It has been described as a "bustling village with multifarious employments and products." Amongst the 250 or more slaves and white servants to be fed and clothed, there were weavers, carpenters, brickmakers, charcoal burners, shoemakers, blacksmiths, millers, and a cooper to make the barrels in which to ship the famous Mount Vernon flour ground at the water mill on Dogues Run. The latter site, formerly belonging to the Spencer family, had meanwhile been acquired by the Washingtons.

Besides the wheat, which was grown in quantities, the crops included flax, hay, clover, buckwheat, rye, maize, turnips, and potatoes. There were also sheep of the best stock to provide wool for the weavers and mutton for the table; hogs, blooded horses and cattle, for which good pasturage was provided, and valuable fisheries. So from necessity, as well as from choice, "this warrior-statesman-farmer" became a past master in agricultural economics.

The devotion of George Washington to "that duty which lies nearest" was perhaps the primary cause of his sudden death, between 10 and 11 p. m. on Saturday, the 14th day of December, 1799. His stepgrandson tells us that "on the morning of the 13th, the General was engaged in making some improvements in the front of Mount Vernon. As usual with him, he carried his own compass, noted his observations and marked out the ground."

His long exposure to the inclemency of the weather was followed by extreme chilliness and nausea, and yet having changed his clothes and partaken of a single cup of tea, he sat down to his indoor work, "there being no moment for which he had not provided an appropriate employment." To this indoor work he devoted himself until late into the night, and, when chided by Mrs. Washington for remaining up so late when he was unwell, George Washington made this memorable reply: "I came as soon as my business was accomplished. You well know that through a long life it has been my unvaried rule never to put off till the morrow the duties which should be performed to-day."

It was by this rule, not only at Mount Vernon but elsewhere, that George Washington accomplished the results for which he is honored and revered, and it was something of this same principle which impelled Ann Pamela Cunningham, founder and first regent of the Mount Vernon Ladies' Association of the Union, to rally around her the group of women who have made possible the acquisition, restoration, and preservation of Mount Vernon as a national shrine.

WASHINGTON HOMESTEAD ON THE RAPPAHANNOCK RIVER

Generations of children throughout the past century and the present have heard the traditional stories of George Washington's youthful days. Every youth in the land must have a desire to visit the scene where the tale of the hatchet and the cherry tree is laid; where the stone is reputed to have been thrown across the Rappahannock River by the young lad whose physical strength was supported by strength of mind and morals; where he galloped over fields and meadows on unbroken colts; and where he and his schoolmates played at Indian warfare.

These tales bring a thrill to the grownups as well as to the boys and girls, for, though they may be largely imaginative, they depict the life of the colonial period when history was in the making. They help us to realize what we owe to those brave boys and men and to their sisters, wives, and mothers, who were then laying the corner stone for the structure of liberty and freedom which we now enjoy.

Until recently very little has been really known about the boyhood home of George Washington, where he spent the formative years of his life, and yet this home is of especial interest, for it was bequeathed to him by his father, Augustine Washington, who died when George was but 11 years old. Within the past decade, however, old records have been carefully searched, the boundaries of the property have been painstakingly traced and verified, and a group of patriotic and public-spirited people have contributed to its purchase with a view to saving this historic site and restoring it as nearly as possible to the condition in which it was during the period of George Washington's residence there.

It is their purpose to dedicate it to the youth of America in commemoration of the Two Hundredth Anniversary of the Birth of George Washington, and by so doing to give to the boys and girls of our country a tangible proof that we as a people honor that honesty of word, thought, and deed which characterized the "Father of His Country" as a boy and man.

The State of Virginia has placed a marker at the entrance to the property, which is across the Rappahannock River from Fredericksburg and on the direct route from the National Capital to the birthplace of George Washington, in Westmoreland County.

The marker reads:

WASHINGTON'S
BOYHOOD HOME
At This Place, George Washington Lived Most of the Time From 1739 to 1747. Here, According to Tradition, He Cut Down the Cherry Tree. Washington's Father Died Here in 1743; the Farm Was His Share of the Paternal Estate. His Mother Lived Here Until 1771.

Here the happy, care-free days of George Washington's childhood were suddenly overshadowed by the sorrow of bereavement, and all too soon he was forced to face and realize the stern necessities of an undeveloped new world. After his father's death he was, for a time, left largely to his own resources, though his mother's watchful care and guiding hand had much to do with his development and proved to be a strong influence upon his afterlife. Many years afterward, in a public address in Fredericksburg, he speaks of this home as "the place of my growing infancy," and of his mother, "by whose maternal hand, early deprived of a father, I was led to manhood."

An interesting item in connection with the purchase of the Rappahannock River property by the father of George Washington is an advertisement which appeared in April, 1738, in the *Virginia Gazette*, published in Williamsburg, then the capital of the State. A copy of the original *Gazette* containing the advertisement is still extant. It reads, in part:

TO BE SOLD FOR CASH

On the 25th of October, next, by the way of auction, to the highest bidder, several Tracts of Land, . . .
One Tract containing 100 acres, lying about 2 miles below the Falls of the Rappahannock close on the River side, with a handsome Dwelling House, 3 storehouses, several other convenient Outhouses and a Ferry, belonging to it, being the place where Mr. Strother lived. It is a very beautiful Situation and very commodious for Trade.
One other tract of 160 acres, of very good land, adjoining thereto. The Plantation Houses, Fences, etc., in good order. . . .

Augustine Washington was apparently "the highest bidder" for these two pieces of property, for a deed, dated November 3, 1738, covering them, in his favor, appears on the records of King George County, the boundaries of which then included this section, which later became a part of Stafford County.

The "handsome Dwelling House" referred to in the advertisement, which the deed mentions as "the Mansion House where the said William Strother lately Dwelt," has long since ceased to exist, and there seems to be no authenticated picture of it, regardless of the fact that several biographers use an illustration which they believed to be a sketch of the original dwelling, while others believe that this same sketch represents the family home in Westmoreland County where George Washington was born.

There is, however, a little shedlike structure still standing which, accorded to accredited biographers, was used by George Washington as a workroom. One writer ventures to state it is "the only structure now in existence which is positively known to have been in constant use by him during his boyhood," and cites a tradition that some of his earliest surveying problems were worked out in this lean-to workshop. The author com-

ments that "this hallowed shrine of courageous youth . . . is overshadowed by the two-and-a-half-story building placed against it some years ago," and expresses the opinion that the new buildings occupy practically the same sites as those in George Washington's day.

Another authority, who writes of the rooftree of the Washington family on the Rappahannock River, described the residence as "a two-story house on a rise of ground, with a fertile meadow sloping gently to the river." This brings to mind descriptions that have been given of the two other country seats which were owned and occupied by Augustine Washington and his family when George was but a child. Either they must have been similarly situated or the descriptions are largely conjecture. At any rate, each one may well have been "on a rise of ground" and certainly each "overlooked the river." The first home, where George Washington was born, now known as Wakefield, was on the lower Potomac between Popes and Bridges Creeks, in Westmoreland County, and the second, later christened Mount Vernon, was on the upper Potomac between Little Hunting Creek and Dogues Run. The latter descended indirectly to George Washington and became his permanent home after he had reached manhood.

It is not improbable that the removal of Augustine Washington and his family to this third home on the Rappahannock River was for the purpose of enabling him to give closer supervision to the iron mines in which he was financially interested and to the hauling of the ore to a convenient smelting point. At that period ships from many ports entered the Rappahannock and moored at its wharves, and for a time the commerce of Fredericksburg is said to have exceeded that of New York of the same epoch. A scholarly gentleman still living recounts that "one who may be called 'the oldest inhabitant' has assured the author that he has seen the river so filled with craft that a crossing could be made from Fredericksburg to the Washington farm by leaping from one ship to another."

It is not difficult to visualize the lads of those early days, in their colonial style of attire, taking advantage of such an opportunity, and it is safe to assume that young George Washington would take the lead in such a venture. Doubtless he indulged in dreams of the outside world with which these vessels plied their trade and welcomed the suggestion of his brother, Lawrence, that he choose seamanship as his life work. Fortunately for this Nation, fate, in the form of his mother, intervened, and he was deflected from the roving life of a sailor lad.

This disappointment, together with the realization that he was not to have the opportunity of attending the school in England where his father and his two half brothers had been educated, served to develop an early self-reliance, and it was not long until he had so perfected himself in mathematics and surveying that an avenue of self-support was opened to him. This he doubtless welcomed, for his patrimony had been left to the management of his mother until he attained the age of 21. At the age of 16 he mentions his earnings as a doubloon every day the weather will permit going out, and sometimes six pistoles. With a pistole valued at $3.60 this seems a rather princely sum.

From this time on the young surveyor journeyed to and from the family home on the Rappahannock River, the last reference found to his work in that vicinity being the survey in 1752 of land purchased by his brother-in-law, Fielding Lewis, where the beautiful home, now known as Kenmore, was erected for George Washington's only sister, Betty, and where his mother later also had a little home adjoining that of his sister and connected by a private walk bordered with boxwood.

Pilgrims to the Washington homestead on the Rappahannock River will find pleasure in crossing over to see Kenmore, which is a perfect example of colonial architecture and decoration, and will also wish to visit the site of the Masonic lodge in Fredericksburg to which George Washington belonged, having joined it before reaching his majority; also to St. George's Church, where he worshiped, for both the lodge and the church played their part in shaping and rounding out his character and preparing him for his career.

MIGRATORY ABIDING PLACES

The comings and goings of George Washington to and from Mount Vernon have been carefully chronicled, and his life and work while there is an open book. Few historians, however, have paid more than passing comment upon the various temporary domiciles that were very dear to George and Martha Washington. Though places of transitory residence, they were real homes, for—

"Home is where affection calls,
Filled with shrines the heart hath builded."

They were no more, those homes of migratory abode, but the brief record to be found of them is a hallowed bit of history that touches the most intimate family life of that hospitable couple whose doors were ever open to all comers.

Their first home together was in the "White House" owned by Martha Dandridge Custis, in New Kent County, near Williamsburg, Virginia. There George Washington wooed and won its mistress, the charming widow Custis, and it was there that the bride and groom spent their honeymoon.

The original White House is mentioned as a colonial mansion, on the right bank of the Pamunkey, "a spacious and picturesquely environed residence of the familiar Virginia type." No description of the house is available, but it is believed that the new White House which stands on the site of the original mansion is a reproduction of its predecessor, which was burned during the Civil War, despite the placard affixed to its door:

"In this house George Washington and Martha Dandridge [Custis] were united in marriage. Whether you be friend or foe, spare it from the depredations of war."

It is inconceivable that the historic landmark should have been deliberately and maliciously destroyed. The theory is advanced that the torch must have been applied after dark or possibly by some isolated band of ruffians or inebriated soldiers.

Though we can not picture that very first home of the bride and groom together, with the 4,000 surrounding acres, we can visualize the wedding party that gathered there to do them honor. Included among the guests were His Excellency, Lieutenant Governor Fauquier, in official regalia, and his lady; Speaker Robinson of the House of Burgesses, and other officials; and of course the socially élite in colorful costumes of the day.

The bride wore heavy satin, threaded with silver, a quilted petticoat, pointed lace and pearls, and the little satin slippers decorated with silver lace which are now a prized possession of her descendants. She was a tiny figure beside the tall and stately bridegroom, who was arrayed in a striking but stylish costume in which the predominating colors were those later embodied in our National Flag; blue cloth coat lined with red silk, white satin waistcoat elaborately embroidered, knee breeches, gold knee and shoe buckles, and dress sword.

The marriage was solemnized on January 6, 1759, and on February 22 of that same year, on his twenty-seventh birthday, George Washington commenced his legislative career as a member of the House of Burgesses.

For four months George and Martha Washington tarried at the White House in New Kent County, dividing their time between it and the "House of Six Chimneys" in Williamsburg, where the newly married couple resided during the sessions of the Assembly.

It is to be assumed that the "House of Six Chimneys" stood in close proximity to the capitol and the governor's palace, as one historian mentions those two structures, "together with Mrs. Washington's home," as having disappeared. It must have commanded a pleasing view, and surely its environs were inspiring. We, as a Nation, should be grateful for the influence of the surroundings of this second temporary home of George and Martha Washington, for that influence has been handed down to us and will live for all time in the plan of our Nation's Capital. Charles Moore, an authority on city planning, tells us in *The Family Life of Washington* that "Williamsburg was laid out on a generous scale for those days. The main features of its design were used in 1792 for the location of the Congress House and the President's House in the Federal City, when Washington was charged with planning the National Capital."

When the Assembly at Williamsburg adjourned, the new member of the House of Burgesses and his bride, with her two children, journeyed to Mount Vernon, where the mansion had been put in readiness to receive the happy family.

There, relieved for a time from his official duties, George Washington devoted himself to his family and to the care of their permanent home and to the administration of the Custis estate, which had been inherited by his wife and stepchildren. These and other duties often took him to Alexandria for days at a time, and, though the distance from Mount Vernon was not great, the weather, the condition of the roads, and the slow means of transportation were not conducive to daily travel. George Washington therefore built a small home in Alexandria that he might have his family with him when detained overnight on business or when he and his wife had social engagements which kept them in town until after dark.

They were attached to this little home, which was perched on an eminence at the southwest corner of Pitt and Cameron Streets. Next to Mount Vernon it was dearest to them, and in his will it was this one piece of real property which George Washington left unreservedly to his dearly beloved wife, Martha Washington, and her heirs forever. For three generations this little house was occupied by members of the family, but all traces of it have long since vanished.

One other temporary home known to have been erected by George Washington for his occupancy was in the Town of Bath, in the northern neck of Virginia, historically known as Warm Springs and Frederick Springs, now Berkeley Springs, West Virginia.

He records in his diary September 6, 1784, the following:

"Having obtained a Plan of this Town (Bath) and ascertained the situation of my Lots therein, which I examined; it appears that the disposition of a Dwelling House, Kitchen, and Stable cannot be more advantageously placed than they are marked in the copy I have taken from the plan of the Town; to which I refer for recollection of my design; and Mr. Rumsey being willing to undertake these Buildings, I have agreed with him to have them finished by the 10th of next July."

Then follows a specific description of each building—dimensions, number of rooms, location of chimneys, stairways, cellar, and so on.

In this same entry George Washington includes an item on James Rumsey's mechanical boat, a forerunner of the steamboat, of which Rumsey was also one of the inventors. The entry reads:

"Remained at Bath all day and was showed the Model of a Boat constructed by the ingenious Mr. Rumsey, for ascending rapid currents by mechanism; the principles of this were not only shown, and fully explained to me, but to my very great satisfaction, exhibited in practice in private under the injunction of Secresy, untill he saw the effect of an application he was about to Make to the Assembly of the State, for a reward. The Model, and its operation upon the water, which had been made to run pretty swift, not only convinced me of what I thought before next to, if not quite impracticable, but that it might be turned to the greatest posible utility in inland Navigation; and in rapid currents; that are shallow— and what adds vastly to the value of the discovery, is the simplicity of its work; as they may be made by a common boat builder or carpenter, and kept in order as easy as a plow, or any common implement of husbandry on a farm."

Perhaps it was on this same occasion that George Washington planted the American elm in the corner of Bath Square, on Washington Avenue, which to-day measures more than 20 feet in circumference and casts the shade of its projecting limbs over the nearby millstone monument to the memory of James Rumsey. This stone was brought from Rumsey's mill at the mouth of Sir Johns Run, where the model of his boat was successfully operated in the presence of George Washington and other distinguished gentlemen who have testified as to its value.

Whether or not this home, erected in the Town of Bath in 1784, was actually occupied by George and Martha Washington does not seem to be recorded. Presumably it was, as tradition says, a summer residence. That the dwelling house and kitchen were built as planned has been definitely determined. Within the memory of men and women yet living, both buildings stood upon the half block of ground which was deeded to George Washington, Generalissimo, in 1777, when some 130 half-acre lots were sold at auction with the proviso that houses must be built thereon within a limited period to accommodate ill and wounded Revolutionary soldiers and other infirm persons. A faded photograph of the dwelling has recently been discovered, and complete floor plans of the dwelling house and log kitchen have been sketched and filed at the Library of Congress.

Prior to the purchase of this ground George Washington occupied other quarters at the Town of Bath. His first visit there was before the town was created, when, as a youth, he was on a surveying tour. He entered in his journal, March 18, 1748, "call'd to see y. Fam'd Warm Springs, we camped out in y. field this Night." His next visit, apparently, was during his bachelor days while recuperating from illness brought on by his early military service.

An interesting page in Washington's account book records "the Expense of a journey to the Fred'k Springs in Aug. 1769— undertaken solely on her [Patsey Custis] acct. to try (by the advice of her physicians) the effect of the waters on her complaint."

Paul Wilstach in his *Mount Vernon* records that George Washington "occasionally took his family to the Bath Warm Springs. The trips were made partly in the hopes of benefiting Patsy Custis, and partly to counteract the malaria imbibed at Mount Vernon. . . . On one occasion, in 1769, he wrote: 'Lodgings can be had on no terms but building them. Had we not succeeded in getting a tent and marquee from Winchester, we should have been in a most miserable station here.' " Washington's answer to a desire by Dulany to rent a house in 1771 shows that Washington had none at the Springs then, and his diary clearly established the building of a new house, kitchen, and stable there in 1784.

There are other migratory abiding places occupied by George and Martha Washington, but they belong in a separate classification, as they were more of a public character, particularly the homes which they occupied while he was filling the high office of the President of the United States. These and the quarters occupied by General Washington during the Revolution, which, whenever possible, were shared by his wife, were the extreme opposite of their peaceful and happy retreats from their semipublic domiciles.

MILITARY HEADQUARTERS

The ability to transform temporary quarters at a military camp into a home is a gift which was possessed by both George and Martha Washington. By their very presence they seemed to create a homey atmosphere even in the most cramped and inconvenient quarters.

An incident is recounted (as follows) of one occasion when Martha Washington came to spend an unusually cold season with her husband at his winter quarters:

"There were but two frame houses in the settlement [geographical location omitted] and neither had a furnished upper story. The General was contented with the rough dwelling but wished to prepare for his wife a more retired and comfortable apartment. One of the mechanics who was called in to fit up a room in the upper story for 'Lady Washington' tells of her arrival before the work was even commenced and of her comments to the workmen: 'Now, young men, I care for nothing but comfort here; I should like you to fit me up a beauffet on one side of the room and some shelves and places for hanging things on the other.'

"When the work was completed, the men in charge of it said to her, 'Madam, we have endeavored to do the best we could; I hope we have satisfied you.'

"With a gracious smile, she replied, 'I am astonished. Your work would do honor to an old master, and you are mere lads. I am not only satisfied but highly gratified with what you have done for my comfort.' "

Lady Washington, as the wife of the Commander in Chief was usually designated in the Army, was noted for keeping a warm place in her motherly heart for all the young men of the Army, and whenever she was at headquarters the home of the commanding officer, whether colonial mansion or crude dwelling, was always a favorite resort.

The residence in which General Washington established his headquarters after taking command of the Continental Army in Cambridge, Mass., on July 3, 1775, afforded every comfort and convenience. It had belonged to a Tory leader who had vacated it to join his associates in Boston. The Provisional Congress confiscated it and furnished the mansion for General Washington's personal use. It later became known as Craigie House and bore that name until it passed into the hands of Henry W. Longfellow, whose descendant still lives there.

Ascending the five stone steps which lead from the terraces to the broad porch, the visitors approach reverently and peer through the windows to the right of the front door into the room where the beloved poet penned many an immortal line. In a room above George Washington wrote his dispatches and half a century later Jared Sparks, during his residence in this house, edited much of the Washington correspondence.

The General's Lady, after a long and tiresome journey in the family coach, accompanied by her son, Jack Custis, and his wife, was heartily welcomed to this fine colonial mansion, with its wide hall and spacious rooms, which offered ample accommodation. Here, as elsewhere in later and less pretentious surroundings, "her sweetness and charm made the house the center of much pleasant sociability."

Soon after her arrival in Cambridge (December 11, 1775) she proposed keeping "Twelfth Night" in due style, as the anniversary of her wedding. The General, though at first negatively inclined, apparently realized after thoughtful consideration that a little amusement would cheer both officers and men, gave his consent, and so "the sixth of January was duly celebrated with cake, candles, and rejoicing."

While domiciled in this Cambridge home Martha Washington formed a lasting friendship for Mercy Warren, wife of Dr. James Warren, president of the Provisional Council of Massachusetts. Mrs. Warren, in a letter to Mrs. John Adams, says of Martha Washington: "Her affability, candor, and gentleness qualify her to soften the hours of private life, or to sweeten the cares of the Hero, and smooth the rugged paths of war."

The home life of General and Mrs. Washington at the Cambridge headquarters continued until April 4, 1776, when the General set out for New York, where he was joined by Mrs. Washington, who, with her son and daughter-in-law, drove to New York, where she took up her abode at the General's headquarters on Pearl Street, the young folks continuing their journey to Virginia. Within a few weeks Mrs. Washington went on to Philadelphia, so there was neither time nor opportunity for real home life in New York City.

In the winter and spring of 1777 General Washington had his headquarters at Morristown, N. J., occupying the Arnold Tavern on the west side of the "Green," where Benjamin Lossing tells us "the accommodations were so limited and the movements of the troops so uncertain that he (the General) thought it not prudent for Mrs. Washington to come to camp." Besides, "there was danger from marauding armies of the enemy," also "an alarm of smallpox." During the previous summer, while in Philadelphia, Mrs. Washington had been inoculated and "had the smallpox so favorably" that she had no dread of the disease. Regardless of this, and of danger from the enemy, she could not have been persuaded to remain away had she known the General was suffering so severely from quinsy sore throat that his life was despaired of, and he was asked whom he considered the most competent man to succeed him in case of death. According to tradition, he pointed out General Greene as that man.

When rumor of the General's illness reached Mrs. Washington she hastened to join him, arriving at Morristown on the 15th of March to find him "perfectly recovered."

The Arnold Tavern is described as a two-story house, the first floor divided into four rooms and a hall, running from the front door to the rear. The two rooms on the south side of the hall were occupied by Washington, who used the front room as a general office and the back room for a sleeping apartment. What provisions were made for Mrs. Washington is not mentioned, but that she established a home is evidenced by the statement that "a delightful social circle gathered and under its influence, despite the discouragements and hardships of the campaign, the face of war sometimes took on a cheerful aspect."

Anne Hollingsworth Wharton, in her *Martha Washington*, quotes from a letter written from Morristown by a Virginia matron, "The General's worthy lady seems in perfect felicity by the side of her 'old man,' as she calls him." In the same letter "horseback parties" are mentioned, in which the younger ladies joined the General and Mrs. Washington.

But social pleasures were of secondary consideration, as some of the Morristown ladies discovered when they donned their "best bibs and bands" to call on Mrs. Washington and found her "knitting and with a specked (check) apron on." "And that was not all," they commented to their friends, "in the afternoon her ladyship took occasion to say, in a way that we could not be offended at, that at this time it was very important that American ladies should be patterns of industry to their countrywomen, because the separation from the mother country will dry up the sources whence many of our comforts have been derived."

As an illustration of her forethought, Martha Washington had garments made for herself out of homespun cotton striped with the ravelings of brown silk stockings and of red damask.

It was said of Mrs. Washington that "as soon as breakfast was over she would bring out her fathomless mending basket from which she was content to mend 'from morn to noon, from noon to dewy eve.'"

The following winter General Washington's headquarters were at Valley Forge, and there, in February, 1778, Mrs. Washington joined him. In a letter to her New England friend, Mrs. Mercy Warren, Mrs. Washington writes: "The General's apartment is very small; he has had a log cabin built to dine in, which has made our headquarters much more desirable than they were at first."

When Mrs. Washington's grandson, George Washington Parke Custis, visited this house years later he was shown a cavity in the deep east window, formed with a lid, in which the Commander in Chief kept his papers when he resided there.

During that dreadful winter at Valley Forge, George and Martha Washington unquestionably experienced the most gruesome home life of their many years together. The conditions are too well known to require further comment. We can picture the General going forth to rally and hearten his tattered troops, hungry and half frozen, and the General's wife and those she gathered around her in the sitting room of the Potts home, "knitting socks, patching garments, and making shirts for the poor soldiers, when material could be procured."

December 11, 1778, General George Washington went into winter quarters at Middlebrook, N. J., and the establishment was not broken up until June 3, 1779. The General, however, was in Philadelphia from December 22 to February 2 and Mrs. Washington joined him there, coming in February to Middlebrook for the rest of the winter. The chief social event was probably the entertainment at the artillery camp at Pluckamin by General Knox and his officers to celebrate the first anniversary of the French alliance. There was a dinner, fireworks, and a ball at which the General distinguished himself with Mrs. Knox as his partner. Mrs. Washington returned to Mount Vernon late in May.

In December, 1779, Mrs. Washington was again with the General at Morristown, "an excellent observation post as well as a sheltered winter home for the Army." Again there were horseback rides and a congenial social circle, intermingled with even greater devotion to industry. During this second winter at Morristown the Washingtons occupied the home of Mrs. Theodosia Ford, "quite a spacious mansion, pleasantly situated near the highway," but overcrowded with Mrs. Ford and her attendants and the General's military family, until two log cabins were added for kitchen and offices. Occasionally there would be an enemy alarm when the Life Guards "would at once take possession of the headquarters, barricade the entrances, five men being placed at each window, where, with guns loaded and cocked, they would remain until troops from camp surrounded the house." Meanwhile Mrs. Ford and Mrs. Washington would "shiver under all the cover they could get, while the winter winds swept through the open windows of their sleeping rooms."

But there were many happy occasions, for Mrs. Wharton pictures the great American generals, governors of States, and Members of Congress "passing under the arch of the most beautiful colonial doorway, coming to call on the Commander in Chief," also the New Jersey patriots, "bringing their wives and daughters with them to pay respects to Lady Washington."

To describe the home life of General and Mrs. Washington at other headquarters would be largely repetition. In 1780-81 they occupied a plain Dutch house at New Windsor. The winter of 1781-82 was spent by the General and Mrs. Washington in Philadelphia, but the first of April headquarters were resumed at Newburgh, about 2½ miles distant from New Windsor, where they lived in a not very commodious one-story dwelling containing seven rooms. Mrs. Washington remained here until the summer of 1783. Here the General and Mrs. Washington entertained many famous guests, and here also, "Mrs. Washington indulged her taste for gardening. The slope in front of the headquarters, under her skillful hands, bloomed like the desert of the Scriptures."

During these last days of camp life, Mrs. Washington suffered an attack of fever which caused the General much concern. Late in August she was able to leave Newburgh and journey to the headquarters at Rocky Hill, Princeton, where she remained until November, thus rounding out a wide and varied experience as homemaker and helpmate at the military camps. She always remained at headquarters until the opening of the succeeding campaign, and she herself was accustomed to say that it had been her fortune to hear the first cannon at the opening and the last at the close of all of the campaigns of the Revolutionary War.

Presidential Mansions

A tablet on Brooklyn Bridge, New York City, marks the site of the Executive Mansion first occupied by the First President of the United States of America. This structure, known as the Franklin House, was situated on the corner of Franklin and Cherry Streets, now Franklin Square, which was once the somewhat modish residence section. It was considered one of the handsomest houses in town. Quakers called it the Palace. The French minister spoke of it as "a humble dwelling."

In this first presidential home many precedents were established. Much thought was given by the President and Mrs. Washington to the proper adjustment of both social and political etiquette; others meanwhile speculating as to the proper manner of addressing the former General in his new office.

There was much discussion whether court functions were in order, or simple customs befitting a new Republic. Simplicity prevailed, for the President and the *first* First Lady carried out their own well-balanced ideas of dignified formality without pomp and ceremony. The accepted titles were The President of the United States and Lady Washington.

They were so besieged with callers, officials, ex-soldiers, and with both high and low in social and private life that it became necessary to set aside certain days for the President to receive. On Tuesdays from 3 to 4 o'clock he was "at home" exclusively to men, including especially foreign ministers and other distinguished callers who sought an introduction. State dinners were given on Thursdays, at 4 in the afternoon, and on Friday evenings, from 7 to 9 o'clock, Mrs. Washington held her drawing rooms which the President attended in an unofficial capacity. At these evening receptions light refreshments were served, but the guests were not permitted to linger overlong, for Mrs. Washington is said to have reminded them: "The General retires at 9, and I usually precede him."

During his residence in the Franklin House, President Washington was dangerously ill. Much anxiety was felt, and he demanded to know the worst, saying, "Do not flatter me with vain hopes. I am not afraid to die."

Demands upon the hospitality of the first Presidential Mansion were constantly increasing, and at best space was lacking for the comfortable accommodation of the family and entourage of the President. So, after 10 months' residence in the Franklin House, a larger Executive Mansion was secured. The Macomb House, recently vacated by the French minister, was secured and became known as the Mansion House. This was the finest house in the city and in the most fashionable quarter, located at 39 Broadway, a short distance from Trinity Church. The rear windows commanded an extended view of the Hudson River and the Jersey shore.

The President personally supervised a great part of the moving and the putting up of furniture, which he supplemented by purchasing from the French minister the large mirrors in the drawing room "and other things particularly suited to the rooms in which he found them." A stable was built at the President's personal expense, to accommodate his favorite horses and cream-colored coach, which was embellished with his coat of arms and the "Four Seasons."

While living in this house the President received the Key of the Bastille, which afterwards hung in a glass case on the wall, and which is now at Mount Vernon. It was sent by Lafayette with the message: "That the principles of America opened the Bastille is not to be doubted, therefore the Key comes to the right place."

Six months after the removal of the President's family to the Mansion House another move became imminent, due to the transfer of the Capital to Philadelphia. The New York Assembly was building a Presidential Mansion but, with the loss of the Capital, it was, of course, doomed to disuse as such.

The city of Philadelphia, upon securing the temporary Capital, proudly erected a Presidential Mansion there, but it was so large that the President refused to occupy it, and it became the early home of the University of Pennsylvania. It was located on the spot where the post office now stands.

When Congress adjourned in New York the President's family repaired to Mount Vernon for a time, leaving Mr. Lear, "secretary, tutor, and right-hand man, to superintend the removal of the household effects from New York to Philadelphia."

Of the Executive Mansion in Philadelphia, opinions differ. It was smaller than the Macomb Mansion in New York, but larger than the Franklin House. One writer describes it as "a large double house, its whole external aspect marking it as the abode of opulence and respectability." A visitor from abroad, accustomed as was the French minister in New York, to Old World mansions, described it as "a small red brick house on the left side of High Street—nothing in the exterior of the house that denoted the rank of its possessor."

It was, however, the largest and most suitable house to be had, and its owners, the Morrises, moved into a similar home next door, which they also owned, voluntarily vacating the more commodious mansion to let the President have it. Back of the house was a walled garden extending to the stables on Minor Street. The President planned a new bow window to project into the garden and "directed that the back yard be kept as clean as a drawing-room, since the view into it was uninterrupted from the state dining room where he was to hold his levees and from Mrs. Washington's best drawing-room above."

Many of the surrounding houses were occupied by former friends and Army officers. These neighbors and the frequent presence of the eldest two of Mrs. Washington's granddaughters, in addition to Nellie Custis, also some of their nieces and other young folk, added much to the gayety of home and social life. But, as a rule, there was a cessation of gayety at 9 o'clock, for Mrs. Washington was accustomed to retiring to her room at that hour, attended by her favorite granddaughter, Nellie Custis. One of the young ladies of that day, who was a frequent guest, gives a very homelike picture of the scene she witnessed when invited one evening by Nellie Custis to accompany her to grandmother's room:

"Then, after some little chat, Mrs. Washington apologized to me for pursuing her usual preparations for the night, and Nellie entered upon her accustomed duty by reading a chapter and a psalm from the old family Bible, after which all present knelt in evening prayer; Mrs. Washington's faithful maid then assisted her to disrobe and lay her head upon the pillows. Nellie then sang a verse of some sweetly soothing hymn, and then, leaning down, received the parting blessing for the night, with some emphatic remarks on her duties, improvements, etc."

And the witness of this scene adds: "The effect of these judicious habits and teachings appeared in the granddaughter's character through life."

Opinions differ also respecting the interior and fittings of the Morris Mansion while occupied by the Chief Executive. Some commented upon "the magnificent table ornaments," and so on; others admired the good taste and simplicity. The Secretary of the Treasury, Mr. Walcott, wrote to his wife: "The example of the President and his family will render parade and expense improper and disreputable." The President inspected the domestic accounts every week and directed that expenses must be "reasonable."

In the summer of 1793 "the gayety that had marked the presence of Government officials" was summarily terminated by yellow fever. There was a general flight from the pestilence. The President and the Government departments removed to Germantown. There, for a month or so, a furnished house belonging to Col. Isaac Franks, a Revolutionary officer, became the temporary Executive Mansion.

The following description of the house is given by Leila Herbert in *The First American:*

"With a front of about 40 feet, it is of stone, two stories in height, an attic with dormer windows above. On the first floor great solid wooden blinds barred, when closed, the many-paned windows. A heavy wrought-iron latch a foot and a half long dropped into a stout hasp on the quaint old door. Sweet dappled shadows played under an arbor of green grape vines running far down the garden, which surrounded the house on three sides. Crisp, trim hedges of box and shading trees hid the back buildings that gave commodiousness unsuspected from the front."

Miss Herbert also writes vividly of the last days of the President in the Morris House. "They were not particularly happy days," she says, the President by signing the Jay treaty having "stirred up a storm of indignation"; and the President was also disquieted by the misfortunes of Lafayette, repudiated by his own country, thrown into prison, while his wife and daughter were confined in another prison, and his young son sought refuge in America but, for the sake of diplomacy, could not be taken into the bosom of the President's family.

With the termination of President Washington's second term of office, as at the beginning of his first, it remained for him to establish a precedent, a custom that has since generally prevailed, that the outgoing President shall entertain the incoming Chief Executive. The final function, therefore, given by the Washingtons in the Morris Mansion was a dinner, on the 3d of March, 1797, to the President-elect and Mrs. Adams. President Washington chaffed his successor upon "entering servitude" and in an especially good humor raised his glass and said: "Ladies and gentlemen, this is the last time I shall drink your health as a public man; I do it with sincerity and wishing you all possible happiness."

President Washington also set the precedent of accompanying the President-elect to the inauguration ceremonies, which with but one or two exceptions has been observed by his successors. The inauguration of President Adams automatically marked the termination of George Washington's occupancy of the Presidential Mansion.

(FOR THIS PROGRAM SEE NUMBERS 48, 72, 81, 98, 105 IN LIST OF SELECTED BOOKS ON PAGES 300-A AND 300-B)

MOUNT VERNON, VIRGINIA—HOME OF GEORGE WASHINGTON
Airplane view showing north side of mansion and Potomac River

Youth and Manhood of George Washington

Rules of Civility & Decent Behaviour In Company and Conversation

[The first page of the Rules of Civility, reproduced in George Washington's handwriting]

FIRST PAGE OF THE RULES OF CIVILITY

THE BOYHOOD OF GEORGE WASHINGTON AND HIS RULES OF CIVILITY

THE BOYHOOD of George Washington—his education, his sports, his adventures, and his ambitions, so interesting to all Americans—forms one of the least-known chapters in the life of the Founder of our Country, about whose life and achievements as a man more than twenty-five hundred books have been written and published. In his day children were "seen and not heard"; and for many years very little was known about this boy outside of a collection of fables, legends, and historical fiction with which writers and biographers have chosen to surround him in their efforts to give him the background for the heroic figure he is in our national history.

George Washington was born at Bridges Creek plantation, Westmoreland County, Virginia, at 10 o'clock on the morning of Friday, February 22, 1732 (old-style calendar February 11, 1731).

This plantation as purchased by George Washington's great-grandfather and added to by his grandfather was bounded by Popes Creek on one side and Bridges Creek on the other, and was an extensive triangle of fine fertile land. The estate continued in the family, and the grandfather and George's father, Capt. Augustine Washington, were born on the same plantation. The house of his birth faced Popes Creek.

His mother, second wife of Captain Augustine, was Mary Ball, a descendant of Capt. William Ball of Lancaster County, who came to Virginia about 1650. From both parents he came of fine ancestry, branches of both the Washingtons and Balls being recorded in English records for centuries.

The baby George was christened, in the April following his birth, with the solemn formality of the Episcopal baptismal service. It is believed that the Rev. Lawrence de Butts officiated. For the occasion the infant wore a soft white brocade christening robe lined with rose silk. This robe is carefully treasured in the National Museum at Washington, D. C. He had for godfathers Mr. Beverly Whiting and Capt. Christopher Brooks, while his father's sister, Mrs. Mildred Gregory, served as his godmother. The silver bowl used as a font is also preserved and may be seen at the National Museum.

At the time of his birth little George was already richly supplied with relatives. His two half brothers and half sister by his father's first wife, Jane Butler, were Lawrence, aged 14; Augustine or Austin, as he was frequently called, 12; and the little girl Jane, 10, who died when George was 2 years old. Besides these half brothers and half sister, there was a large group of cousins in the two families most closely related. John Washington (his father's brother) had a large family, and his aunt, Mildred Gregory, had three girls.

When George was 3 years old Capt. Augustine Washington moved his family to another plantation of his, called by the Indians "Epsewasson," in what was then Prince William County, which estate afterwards came to be called Mount Vernon.

Here the family lived until George was 7 years old, and here his education by his father and mother was begun. The two half brothers, Lawrence and Augustine, had been sent to England to the famous "Appleby Charter School," where it is believed their father had also attended.

Just about the time Augustine Washington decided to move his family to a farm he had purchased in 1738 on the Rappahannock River, opposite Fredericksburg, he made another trip to England. He brought back a shipload of convicts. Among them was one William Grove, a man of education, probably a political prisoner, as were so many of the early exiles to the Colonies. To this man, nicknamed Hobby, was entrusted the first schooling of George. He was made sexton of the church at Falmouth, 2 miles from the Washington farm. To his farm on the Rappahannock River, Captain Augustine moved his family about 1740. Possibly this move was due to his interest in the Principio Iron Company, for whom he worked a mine on his property.

Rev. Jonathan Boucher, an English clergyman, who was employed by General

Washington as a tutor for his stepson, John Parke Custis, said of Washington: "George, like most people thereabouts at the time, had no other education than reading, writing, and accounts, which he was taught by a convict servant whom his father bought for a schoolmaster."

Despite the plentiful myths, which make him a little prig, George Washington was a natural, normal lad. He possessed a strong, vigorous body. His father taught him to set his pony and sent him to school in care of a servant until he learned to manage it, and impressed upon him the importance of exercise and developed in him a strong love of sports and the desire to play every game to win. He loved all games.

We can picture the soldier play and many sham battles staged by the boys of Hobby's school due to the traditions of Indian warfare, and the recent participation of colonial forces in the Cartagena expedition, with part as pioneer settlers and part as Indian raiders. In these war games, legend places little George Washington always as the commander.

It was at the farm on the Rappahannock that Captain Washington died at the age of 49, when George was 11 years old. This farm of 280 acres by his will was left to George in his mother's hands until he was of age. Epsewasson went to Lawrence, and the Bridges Creek plantation to the other half brother, Augustine.

The death of his father was the first tragedy of George Washington's life. A family conference on the question of his education resulted in the decision that he be sent to live with Augustine at Bridges Creek, because the best school available was within easy distance of the old home. Augustine Washington had married a wealthy girl and was living in the comfortable fashion of the prosperous planter. He had a library, 30 horses in his stable, and close by were many young folks of George's age, so George found the change to William's school very pleasant. Here he was a leader in all games and sports—vaulting, running, jumping, pitching quoits, throwing the bar—and he excelled in horsemanship.

Here he became interested in surveying. Possibly because he realized that his education would be limited at best, owing to restricted means, George Washington applied himself seriously to his studies, although the life at Wakefield was delightful, with its hunting and fishing and the gay parties of visitors always coming and going. Despite his rather remarkable absorption in his books, adventure lured him. There is evidence that when the boy was 14 or 15 there was a plan for him to go to sea either as a midshipman or in the merchant service. The exact facts are not known; but according to the tradition, his mother gave a reluctant consent, but later, after preparations had been made, and the lad even ready to embark, she reversed her decision. When the sea service had been proposed, Mrs. Washington wrote

to her brother, Joseph, in England, for his advice. He replied, disapproving the plan, and this strengthened her decision. His reply read as follows:

"STRATFORD-BY-BOW,
19th of May, 1747.

"I understand that you are advised and have some thoughts of putting your son George to sea. I think he had better be put a prentice to a tinker, for a common sailor before the mast has by no means the common liberty of the subject; for they will press him from a ship where he has 50 shillings a month and make him take 23, and cut and slash and use him like a negro, or rather like a dog. And, as to any considerable preferment in the navy, it is not to be expected, as there are always so many gaping for it here who have interest, and he has none. And if he should get to be master of a Virginia ship (which it is very difficult to do), a planter that has three or four hundred acres of land and three or four slaves, if he be industrious, may live more comfortably, and leave his family in better bread, than such a master of a ship can. . . . He must not be too hasty to be rich, but go on gently and with patience, as things will naturally go. This method, without aiming at being a fine gentleman before his time, will carry a man more comfortably and surely through the world than going to sea, unless it be a great chance indeed. "I pray God keep you and yours.
"Your loving brother,
"JOSEPH BALL."

George possibly went back to his studies, now under the Reverend Marye at Fredericksburg, and at that time copied into his notebook the 110 Rules of Civility and Decent Behavior which it is believed he took from the work by Hawkins, and which were well known in France and England. But if the uncle's letter is correctly dated George had little opportunity for further study between its receipt and the time when he went to live at Mount Vernon.

He had also realized that he must obtain for himself the education needed along all lines by which he hoped to advance himself. Realizing the importance of finished manners, and habits of the socially elite, he resolved to educate himself. This desire for self-education became a passion with him and caused him to give concentrated and absorbed study to the information he sought to acquire. It was this quality that impressed all people he met.

About the time he was 15 he went to live at Mount Vernon with Lawrence, and his predilection to become a surveyor became his objective, as surveyors in a new country were few and their earnings were exceptionally good.

Having met Lord Fairfax, who was much impressed with the good sense, courtly manners, fine horsemanship, and manly, fear-

less sportsmanship of this boy of 16, he was engaged by him as an assistant to his instructor, James Genn, county surveyor, to aid in the surveys of the Fairfax holdings in the Shenandoah Valley, which consisted of thousands of acres.

Lord Fairfax loved this boy who was so entirely a kindred spirit of his own though half a century younger. He is said to have summed up his estimate of this favorite in a letter to Mrs. Mary Washington in which he said:

"BELVOIR.

"HONOURED MADAM: You are so good as to ask what I think of a temporary residence for your son George in England. It is a country for which I myself have no inclination, and the gentlemen you mention are certainly renowned gamblers and rakes, which I should be sorry your son were exposed to, even if his means easily admitted of a residence in England. He is strong and hardy, and as good a master of a horse as any could desire. His education might have been bettered, but what he has is accurate and inclines him to much life out of doors. He is very grave for one of his age, and reserved in his intercourse; not a great talker at any time. His mind appears to me to act slowly, but, on the whole, to reach just conclusions, and he has an ardent wish to see the right of questions—what my friend, Mr. Addison, was pleased to call 'the intellectual conscience.' Method and exactness seem to be natural to George. He is, I suspect, beginning to feel the sap rising, being in the spring of life, and is getting ready to be the prey of your sex, wherefore may the Lord help him, and deliver him from the nets those spiders, called women, will cast for his ruin. I presume him to be truthful because he is exact. I wish I could say that he governs his temper. He is subject to attacks of anger on provocation, and sometimes without just cause; but as he is a reasonable person, time will cure him of this vice of nature, and in fact he is, in my judgment, a man who will go to school all his life and profit thereby.

"I hope, madam, that you will find pleasure in what I have written, and will rest assured that I shall continue to interest myself in his fortunes.

"Much honoured by your appeal to my judgment, I am, my dear madam, your obedient humble servant,

"FAIRFAX."

Thus did his great friend, his patron through early life, estimate this boy. He was strong of body, grave of spirit, with a full sense of responsibility, a seeker of knowledge always, and an abiding love of the great outdoors.

His boyhood was a budding promise of the man he was to become—true to the standards and ideals his parents implanted in him; true to the quaintly worded precepts he copied as the guide and rule of his school days and by which he measured his actions; and always true to himself.

Rules of Civility and Decent Behavior in Company and Conversation

[From a paper found among the early writings of George Washington copied from the original with literal exactness and edited with notes by J. M. Toner, M.D.—1888.

[The text following is an exact copy from the original manuscript, having been carefully compared with the corrected therefrom, even when errors or omissions are obvious.

[This book has been knawed by mice—Rule 12—and all at bottom of any of the pages had been nearly destroyed. Every word and letter remaining has been copied and are here given:]

1. Every Action done in Company, ought to be with Some Sign of Respect, to those that are present.

2. When in Company, put not your Hands to any Part of the Body, not usually Discovered.

3. Shew Nothing to your Friend that may affright him.

4. In the Presence of Others sing not to yourself with a humming Noise, nor Drum, with your Fingers or Feet.

5. If you Cough, Sneeze, Sigh, or Yawn, do it not Loud, but Privately; and Speak not in your Yawning, but put Your handkerchief or Hand before your face and turn aside.

6. Sleep not when others Speak, Sit not when others stand, Speak not when you Should hold your Peace, walk not on when others Stop.

7. Put not off your Cloths in the presence of Others, nor go out your Chamber half Drest.

8. At play and at Fire its Good manners to give Place to the last Commer, and affect not to Speak Louder than ordenary.

9. Spit not in the Fire, nor Stoop low before it neither Put your Hands into the Flames to warm them, nor Set your Feet upon the Fire especially if there be meat before it.

10. When you Sit down, Keep your Feet firm and Even, without putting one on the other or Crossing them.

11. Shift not your self in the Sight of others nor Gnaw your nails.

12. Shake not the head, Feet, or Legs, rowl not the Eys, lift not one eyebrow higher than the other, wry not the mouth, and bedew no mans face with your Spittle, by appr . . . r him . . . you Speak.

13. Kill no Vermin as Fleas, lice ticks &c in the Sight of Others, if you See any filth or thick Spittle put your foot Dexteriously upon it, if it be upon the Cloths of your Companions, Put it off privately, and if it be upon your own Cloths return Thanks to him who puts it off.

14. Turn not your Back to others especially in Speaking, Jog not the Table or Desk on which Another reads or writes, lean not upon any one.

15. Keep your Nails clean and Short, also your Hands and Teeth Clean, yet without Shewing any great Concern for them.

16. Do not Puff up the Cheeks, Loll not out the tongue rub the Hands, or beard, thrust out the lips, or bite them or keep the Lips too open or too Close.

17. Be no Flatterer, neither Play with any that delights not to be Play'd Withal.

18. Read no Letters, Books, or Papers in Company but when there is a Necessity for the doing of it you must ask leave: come not near the Books or Writings of Another so as to read them unless desired or give your opinion of them unask'd also look not nigh when another is writing a Letter.

19. let your Countenance be pleasant but in Serious Matters Somewhat grave

20. The Gestures of the Body must be Suited to the discourse you are upon

21. Reproach none for the Infirmities of Nature, nor Delight to Put them that have in mind thereof.

22. Shew not yourself glad at the Misfortune of another though he were your enemy.

23. When you see a Crime punished, you may be inwardly Pleased; but always shew Pity to the Suffering Offender.

. . . too much at any Publick . . .

25. Superfluous Complements and all Affectation of Ceremonie are to be avoided yet where due they are not to be Neglected.

26. In pulling off your Hat to Persons of Distinction, as Noblemen, Justices, Churchmen &c make a Reverence, bowing more or less according to the Custom of the Better Bred, and Quality of the Persons Amongst your equals expect not always that they Should begin with you first, but to Pull off the Hat when there is no need is Affectation, in the Manner of Saluting and resaluting in words keep to the most usual Custom.

27. Tis ill manners to bid one more eminent than yourself be covered as well as not to do it to whom it's due Likewise he that makes too much haste to Put on his hat does not well, yet he ought to Put it on at the first, or at most the Second time of being ask'd; now what is herein Spoken, of Qualification in behaviour in Saluting, ought also to be observed in taking of Place, and Sitting down for ceremonies without Bounds is troublesome.

28. If any one comes to Speak to you while you are Sitting Stand up tho he be your Inferiour, and when you Present Seats let it be to every one according to his Degree.

29. When you meet with one of Greater Quality than yourself, Stop, and retire especially if it be at a Door or any Straight place to give way for him to Pass

30. In walking the highest Place in most Countrys Seems to be on the right hand therefore Place yourself on the left of him whom you desire to Honour; but if three walk together the middle Place is the most Honourable the wall is usually given to the most worthy if two walk together.

31. If any one far Surpasses others, either in age, Estate, or Merit, . . . would give Place to a meaner than himself . . . the one ought not to except it, So . . . it above once or twice.

32. To one that is your equal, or not much inferior you are to give the chief Place in your Lodging and he to who 'tis offered ought at the first to refuse it but at the Second to accept though not without acknowledging his own unworthiness

33. They that are in Dignity or in office have in all places Preceedency but whilst they are Young they ought to respect those that are their equals in Birth or other Qualitys, though they have no Publick charge.

34. It is good Manners to prefer them to whom we speak before ourselves especially if they be above us with whom in no Sort we ought to begin.

35. Let your Discourse with Men of Business be Short and Comprehensive.

36. Artificers & Persons of low Degree ought not to use many ceremonies to Lords, or Others of high Degree but Respect and highly Honour them, and those of high Degree ought to treat them with affibility & Courtesie, without Arrogancy.

37. In Speaking to men of Quality do not lean nor Look them full in the Face, nor approach too near them at lest Keep a full Pace from them.

38. In visiting the Sick, do not Presently play the Physician if you be not Knowing therein.

39. In writing or Speaking, give to every Person his due Title According to his Degree & the Custom of the Place.

40. Strive not with your Superiors in argument, but always Submit your Judgment to others with Modesty.

41. Undertake not to Teach your equal in the art himself Professes; it flavours of arrogancy.

. . . courtesie be proper to the . . . Dignity of his place . . . t yr. same with a . . .Clown and a Prince.

43. Do not express Joy before one sick or in pain for that contrary Passion will aggravate his Misery.

44. When a man does all he can though it Succeeds not well blame not him that did it.

45. Being to advise or reprehend any one, consider whether it ought to be in Publick or in Private; presently, or at Some other time in what terms to do it & in reproving Shew no Signs of Cholar but do it with all Sweetness and Mildness.

46. Take all Admonitions thankfully in what Time or Place Soever given but after-

wards not being culpable take a Time or Place Convenient to let him know it that gave them.

47. MOCK not nor Jest at anything of Importance break no Jest that are Sharp Biting and if you Deliver anything witty and Pleasent abstain from Laughing thereat yourself.

48. WHEREIN Wherein you reprove Another be unblameable yourself; for example is more prevalent than Precepts

49. USE no Reproachfull Language against any one neither Curse nor Revile.

50. BE not hasty to believe flying Reports to the Disparagement of any.

51. WEAR not your Cloths, foul, unript or Dusty but See they be Brush'd once every day at least and take heed that you approach not to any Uncleaness.

52. IN your Apparel be Modest and endeavour to accomodate Nature, rather than to procure Admiration keep to the Fashion of your equals, Such as are Civil and orderly with respect to Times and Places.

53. RUN not in the Streets, neither go too slowly nor with Mouth open go not Shaking Yr. Arms. . . . not upon the toes, nor in a Dancing . . .

54. PLAY not the Peacock, looking everywhere about you, to See if you be well Deck't, if your Shoes fit well if your Stockings Sit neatly, and Cloths handsomely.

55. EAT not in the Streets, nor in ye House, out of Season.

56. ASSOCIATE yourself with Men of good Quality if you Esteem your own Reputation; for 'tis better to be alone than in bad Company.

57. IN walking up and Down in a House, only with One in Company if he be Greater than yourself, at the first give him the Right hand and Stop not till he does and be not the first that turns, and when you do turn let it be with your face towards him, if he be a Man of Great Quality, walk not with him Cheek by Jowl but Somewhat behind him; but yet in Such a Manner that he may easily Speak to you.

58. LET your Conversation be without Malice or Envy, for 'tis a Sign of a Tractable and Commendable Nature, & in all Causes of Passion admit Reason to Govern.

59. NEVER express anything unbecoming, nor Act ag'tt ye Rules of Moral before your inferiours

60. BE not immodest in urging your Friends to Discover a Secret.

61. UTTER not base and frivilous things amongst grave and Learn'd Men nor very Difficult Questions or Subjects, among the Ignorant or things hard to be believed, Stuff not your Discourse with Sentences amongst your Betters nor Equals.

62. SPEAK not of doleful Things in a Time of Mirth or at the Table; Speak not of Melancholy Things as Death and Wounds, and if others Mention them Change if you can the Discourse tell not your Dreams, but to your intimate Friend.

63. A MAN ought not to value himself of his Atchievements or rare Qual . . . les Virtue or Kindred . . .

64. BREAK not a Jest where none take pleasure in mirth Laugh not aloud, nor at all without Occasion, deride no man's Misfortune, tho' there seem to be Some cause.

65. SPEAK not injurious Words neither in Jest nor Earnest Scoff at none although they give Occasion

66. BE not forward but friendly and Courteous; the first to Salute hear and answer & be not Pensive when It's a time to converse.

67. DETRACT not from others neither be excessive in Commanding.

68. GO not thither, where you know not, whether you Shall be Welcome or not. Give not Advice whth being Ask'd & when desired do it briefly.

69. IF two contend together take not the part of either unconstrained, and be not obstinate in your Opinion, in Things indiferent be of the Major side.

70. REPREHEND not the imperfections of others for that belongs to Parents Masters and Superiours.

71. GAZE not on the marks or blemishes of Others and ask not how they came. What you may Speak in Secret to your Friend deliver not before others.

72. SPEAK not in an unknown Tongue in Company but in your own Language and that as those of Quality do and not as ye Vulgar; Sublime matters treat Seriously.

73. THINK before you Speak pronounce not imperfectly nor bring out your Words too hastily but orderly and Distinctly.

74. WHEN Another Speaks be attentive your Self and disturb not the Audience if any hesitate in his Words help him not nor Prompt him without desired, Interrupt him not, nor Answer him till his Speech be ended

75. IN the midst of Discourse ask . . . but if you Perceive any Stop because of . . . to Proceed: If a Person of Quality comes in while your Conversing its handsome to Repeat what was said before.

76. WHILE you are talking, Point not with your Finger at him of Whom you Discourse nor Approach too near him to whom you talk especially to his face.

77. TREAT with men at fit Times about Business & Whisper not in the Company of Others.

78. MAKE no Comparisons and if any of the Company be Commended for any brave act of Virtue, commend not another for the Same.

79. BE not apt to relate News, if you know not the truth thereof. In Discoursing of things you Have heard Name not your Author always A Secret Discover not.

80. BE not Tedius in Discourse or in reading unless you find the Company pleased therewith.

81. BE not Curious to Know the Affairs of Others neither approach to those that Speak in Private

82. UNDERTAKE not what you cannot Perform but be Carefull to keep your Promise

83. WHEN you deliver a matter do it without Passion & with Discretion, however mean ye Person be you do it too

84. WHEN your Superiours talk to any Body hearken not neither Speak nor Laugh

85. IN Company of these Higher Quality than yourself Speak not till you are ask'd a Question then Stand upright put of your Hat & Answer in few words

86. IN Disputes, be not so Desirous to Overcome as not to give Liberty to each one to deliver his Opinion and Submit to ye Judgment of ye Major Part especially if they are Judges of the Dispute.

87. . . . . as becomes a Man Grave . . . Settled and attentive . . . dict not at every turn what others Say.

88. BE not tedius in Discourse, make not many Digressions, nor repeat often the Same manner of Discourse

89. SPEAK not Evil of the absent for it is unjust

90. BEING Set at meat Scratch not neither Spit Cough or blow your Nose except there's a Necessity for it.

91. MAKE no Shew of taking great Delight in your Victuals, Feed not With Greediness; cut your Bread with a Knife, lean not on the Table neither find fault with what you Eat

92. TAKE no Salt or cut Bread with your Knife Greasy.

93. ENTERTAINING any one at table it is decent to present him wt meat. Undertake not to help others undesired by ye Master.

94. IF you Soak bread in the Sauce let it be no more than what you put in your Mouth at a time and blow not your broth at Table but Stay till Cools of it Self

95. PUT not your meat to your Mouth with your Knife in your hand neither Spit forth the Stones of any fruit Pye upon a Dish nor cast anything under the table

96. IT's unbecoming to Stoop much to ones Meat Keep your Fingers clean & when foul wipe them on a Corner of your Table Napkin.

...7. PUT not another bit into your Mouth til the former be Swallowed let not your Morsels be too big for the jowls

98. DRINK not nor talk with your mouth full neither Gaze about you while you are a Drinking

99. DRINK not too leisurely nor yet too hastily. Before and after Drinking wipe your Lips breath not then or Ever with too Great a Noise, for its uncivil

100. CLEANSE not your teeth with the Table Cloth Napkin Fork or Knife but if Others do it let it be done wt a Pick Tooth

101. RINCE not your Mouth in the Presence of Others

102. IT is out of use to call upon the Company often to Eat nor need you Drink to others every Time you Drink

103. IN Company of your Betters be not . . . than they are lay not your Arm but ar..

104. IT belongs to ye Chiefest in Com-

pany to unfold his Napkin and fall to Meat first, But he ought then to Begin in time and to Dispatch with Dexterity that ye Slowest may have time allowed him

105. BE not Angry at Table whatever happens & if you have reason to be so, Shew it not but on a Chearfull Countenance especially if there be Strangers for good Humour makes one Dish of Meat a Feast

106. SET not yourself at ye upper . . . of ye Table but if it be your Due or that ye Master of ye house will have it so, Contend not lest you Should Trouble ye company.

107. IF others talk at Table be attentive but talk not with Meat in your Mouth

108. WHEN you Speak of God or his Atributes, let it be Seriously & . . . Reverence. Honour & obey your Natural Parents altho they be Poor

109. LET your Recreations be Manfull not Sinfull.

110. LABOUR to keep alive in your Breast that Little Spark of Celestial fire called Conscience.

TRAVELS, PURSUITS, AND IDEALS

(Pre-Revolutionary Period)

The imaginative powers of George Washington, his natural disposition to do all things well, and the influence around him in his youth which encouraged him to strive toward the high standard of perfection, were important factors in shaping his career.

How nearly he attained that high standard in his first occupation as a surveyor is attested by the more recent surveys of the same territory with modern instruments, which show that the lines George Washington helped to mark out when but a lad of sixteen years are decidedly exact.

This first experience of George Washington as a surveyor in the service of Thomas Lord Fairfax was the best training he could have had to bring out and develop his inherent qualities and fit him for the future responsibilities awaiting him. His trip "through most beautiful Groves of Sugar Trees . . . admiring ye Trees and richness of ye Land," thence onward through the Allegheny foothills, is concisely described in his surveying journal.

When he set out upon this journey, "not being so good a Woodsman as ye rest," according to his own account, he had much to learn about the hardships of pioneering and the customs of the frontier. The manner in which he records some of his experiences shows a keen sense of humor, and his comments interspersed between surveying data indicate that he was a most observant youth.

Being detained by heavy rains and unfordable rivers, the surveying party "call'd to se y. Fam'd Warm Springs," in the Allegheny foothills (now Berkeley Springs, West Virginia). A few days later he records being "agreeably surpris'd at y. sight of thirty odd Indians coming from War," and describes a "War Daunce" to the music of an improvised drum and a "goard with some Shott in it to Rattle."

The spring rains were apparently almost incessant. Tents were blown down by violent winds, which at times necessitated sleeping in the open or "under a Straw House," while delayed provisions resulted in exhausted stores. Wild turkeys were plentiful, however, and other game available. Each man served as his own cook, using forked sticks for spits and large chips for plates.

Thus did this first journey prepare George Washington for future travel of a similar nature, when sent upon an important mission by Governor Dinwiddie. This, in turn, fitted him for the part he was called upon to take when serving under General Braddock and later as Commander in Chief of the Virginia forces. It also helped to fit him for an appointment as public surveyor, which was officially made.

Meanwhile, however, he had escorted his half brother, Lawrence, on a journey to the Barbadoes, where the latter went in search of health. This was the only occasion upon which George Washington found opportunity to travel beyond his native shores. It was while in the Barbadoes that he contracted smallpox, which is said to have left permanent marks upon his face. His diary of this journey also records stormy weather, with occasional mention of a smooth sea, and of catching a dolphin, also a shark and one of his pilot fish.

It was in the following year (1753) that George Washington was commissioned by Governor Dinwiddie to deliver a letter to the commandant of the French forces on the Ohio, protesting against their erecting defenses and making settlements within territory known to be the property of the Crown of Great Britain. The initiative, diplomacy, and dispatch with which he accomplished the undertaking were most commendatory, and led to the honor of a commission as lieutenant colonel in command of troops sent by Virginia to aid in building forts and in defending the British possessions against the hostilities of the French. This march ended disastrously in the surrender and retirement from Fort Necessity. The capitulation, written in French and signed by George Washington upon the imperfect translation of one of his trusted lieutenants, was so worded as to form an acknowledgment of the so-called "murder" of Jumonville, though other evidence shows that Jumonville's reconnoiter was hostile and that he fell in a justifiable attack by Washington.

Upon the sudden death of Colonel Fry, the chief command of the troops fell upon George Washington. Independent companies arrived at the fort and still others were en route. When George Washington was apprised of the approach of Captain Mackay he wrote to Governor Dinwiddie, saying: "I should have been particularly obliged if you had declared whether he was under my command or independent of it." The experience of the young commander had taught him that officers commissioned by the Crown sought precedence over those commissioned by colonial governors.

This question of rank came up again the next year when George Washington, having resigned his commission and returned to agricultural pursuits, was invited by General Braddock, through one of his aides, to join the general's official family as a volunteer, which would remove "any disagreeableness which might arise from regulations of command."

In the Braddock campaign the experience and knowledge of Indian warfare which George Washington had previously gained proved invaluable. With the honorable distinction he won at Monongahela and with the assurances of General Braddock, George Washington was led to expect a royal commission. He had steadily refused to serve under any commander whose titular dignity was inferior to his own, and in this attitude he was upheld by his companions in arms.

When the question of rank at Fort Cumberland between himself and the commander of a Maryland company who had previously held a royal commission could not be otherwise settled, George Washington asked permission to go to Boston to get Governor Shirley, commander in chief of the King's forces in America, to decide the matter.

Governor Dinwiddie readily granted George Washington leave of absence for this memorable journey to Boston on which he took occasion to maintain an appearance "suitable for a Virginia gentleman of fortune, possessing an eminent position in society," and to visit the leading cities of the country en route from Williamsburg to Boston, including Philadelphia and New York. At the latter place he spent several days both going and returning and, according to tradition, was deeply impressed with Miss Mary Philipse, a young sister-in-law of Mr. Robinson, at whose home he stopped.

Governor Shirley did not have the power to grant commissions in the standing Army, but he complied so far with the application presented to him as to give an order that Washington should command when he and the captain should join at Fort Cumberland.

Upon the return of George Washington from the North he was called almost immediately to his headquarters at Winchester to take steps against the French and Indians who were raiding the frontier. While serving as Commander in Chief of the Virginia forces he found it necessary to travel up and down the entire frontier of Virginia, including the region now known as West Virginia.

With the close of this campaign came two important events in the life of George Washington. His marriage to Martha Dandridge Custis and the taking of his seat in the Virginia House of Burgesses, to which he had been elected while he himself was absent on military duty. Then came the happy journey when he conducted his bride from Williamsburg to his home at Mount Vernon, which had been placed in readiness to receive her. With his usual forethought George Washington planned every detail of the itinerary. The great coach halted at Fredericksburg that the bride might rest at the home of his sister, Betty, and go across the Rappahannock River to meet his mother at the family farm. Another stop was made at Belle Aire, then onward, across the head of Belmont Bay on Colchester Ferry, past the old parish church, through the valleys and over the hills, to their own domain on the banks of the Potomac.

Here, for a period of sixteen years, George Washington followed peaceful pursuits upon his plantation, punctuated by occasional short journeys; to Williamsburg for the sessions of the House of Burgesses, to the Warm Springs seeking a cure for his young stepdaughter, to New York City to place his stepson in King's College, and one long trip into the West, in 1770, extending over a period of nine weeks.

This journey was undertaken to inspect and locate land granted by Governor Dinwiddie to the regiment as a reward for their services in the French War. There were many obstacles to be overcome, but their colonel, which was George Washington's title at that period, did not remit his efforts until every officer and private soldier had received his due proportion.

While on this tour he traveled through the Shenandoah Valley and on to Fort Cumberland (Maryland) by way of Romney (Now West Virginia), stopping at Little Meadows on the old Braddock Road and at Great Meadows across the Youghiogheny River, which flows northwest and joins the Monongahela about twelve miles above Pittsburgh. From the latter point George Washington, who was accompanied by Doctor Craik, together with several settlers who had joined them, embarked in canoes for a journey down the Ohio River, stopping at many points along the way to explore inland, and making a detour up the Kanawha River, where they "incamped and went a Hunting, killd 5 Buffaloes . . . three deer, etca."

The character and quality of the land, the variety of trees, and comparisons between different sections are all carefully noted in the diary which George Washington kept of this journey.

Returning to Pittsburgh (November 21, 1770), after giving a dinner for "the Officers and some other Gentlemen," George Washington and Doctor Craik set off for home, encountering snow, impassable rivers, and other obstacles en route, but arriving safely at their destination on the 1st day of December.

Of this and other efforts to obtain possession of the lands granted to the officers and soldiers of the First Virginia Regiment, George Washington wrote:

"The burthen of obtaining the Grants . . . indeed the greater part of the expence attending this business from the first move that was made therein until the issuing of the Patents, were thrown upon me nor has the latter been reimbursed to this day."

By the time the matter was entirely settled and the deserving men received their lands, the Revolutionary War was close at hand.

The Man Himself

Contemporaries of George Washington have commented that none of his portraits accurately resembled him, and a member of his immediate family is quoted as having said that pictures of him, painted by various artists, all look very much alike but are not really like the General himself. This is attributed to the fact that the expression of George Washington's face varied, according to circumstances, and the painter saw it only in repose.

A great similarity exists, also, in the word pictures penned by those who met George Washington at different periods of his life and under varying circumstances. One of the earliest of these depicts a handsome youth of nineteen, "full height of 6 feet 2 inches, slender, . . . blue eyes, an abundance of brown hair and a clear ruddy complexion. His manner self controlled, his speech well considered." But his personality is not revealed.

One of the most comprehensive delineations of the physical appearance of George Washington was written by a friend and companion in arms, George Mercer, in 1760, not long after the young Colonel had become, almost simultaneously, a benedict and a member of the House of Burgesses. He is described as being—

"as straight as an Indian, measuring six feet two inches in his stockings and weighing 175 pounds. . . . His frame is padded with well-developed muscles, indicating great strength, His bones and joints are large, . . . He is wide shouldered, . . . is neat waisted, but is broad across the hips, and has rather long arms and legs. His head is well shaped though not large, but is gracefully poised on a superb neck. A large and straight rather than a prominent nose; blue-gray penetrating eyes, which are widely separated, and overhung by a heavy brow. His face is long rather than broad, with high, round cheek bones, and terminates in a good firm chin. He has a clear though rather a colorless pale skin, which burns with the sun. A pleasing, benevolent, though a commanding countenance, dark brown hair, which he wears in a cue. His mouth is large and generally firmly closed. . . . His features are regular and placid, with all the muscles of his face under perfect control, though flexible and expressive of deep feeling when moved by emotion. In con-

versation he looks you full in the face, is deliberate, deferential and engaging. His voice is agreeable rather than strong. His demeanor at all times composed and dignified. His movements and gestures are graceful, his walk majestic, and he is a splendid horseman."

From a physical standpoint in the descriptions given from time to time covering a period of nearly forty years, there is very little variation. Invariably, however, as the years go by, comments upon his physique are submerged by a somewhat futile attempt to read his countenance and interpret the deep thought and feeling therein detected.

When George Washington was nearing his fiftieth milestone one writer described him as "remarkably tall, full 6 feet, erect and well proportioned." Then, without further detail as to form and features he goes on to say, "The strength and proportion of his joints and muscles appear to be commensurate with the preeminent powers of his mind." After eulogizing his peculiar charactertistics, "The serenity of his countenance, and majestic gracefulness of his deportment," he adds, "no one can stand in his presence without feeling the ascendancy of his mind, and associating with his countenance the idea of wisdom, magnanimity, philanthropy, and patriotism."

In later years, "The President in his person" is portrayed as "tall and thin, but erect." Jefferson said of him, "His person, you know, was fine, his stature exactly what one would wish, his deportment easy, erect and noble." One writer sees in the countenance of the first President of the United States "a settled aspect of melancholy," another describes it as having "a serious cast," while still another observes, "His pensive eyes are more attentive than sparkling, but their expression is benevolent, noble, and self possessed."

"The languor of the General's eye," is mentioned in the criticism of a miniature painting which brought forth from one of the General's aides an explanation that the artist was not altogether mistaken, saying, "his countenance when affected either by joy or anger, is full of expression, yet when the muscles are in a state of repose, his eye certainly wants animation."

George Washington himself realized the effect of varying moods upon his countenance. He touched upon this subject in a letter written to a friend at the time one of the earliest sketches of him was made, saying, "I fancy the skill of Gentleman's Pencil will be put to it, in describing to the World what manner of a man I am." On a later occasion he writes, "I am so hackneyed to the touches of the painter's pencil that I am now altogether at their beck; and sit, 'like Patience on a monument,' whilst they are delineating the lines of my face."

To those who had the privilege of close association with George Washington, particularly those who served under him in the American Revolution, he is considered as "a perfect whole" with a "physiognomy mild and agreeable, but such as to render it impossible to speak particularly of any of his features, so that in quitting him you have only the recollection of a fine face."

It is somewhat strange that writers as well as artists have almost invariably disregarded the pox marks with which the face of George Washington was slightly marred. Apparently they were minimized by the awe-inspiring air and manner and the superior character of the man himself.

The personality of George Washington, his dignified bearing and thoughtful consideration, not only endeared him to his friends but commanded the admiration and respect of his opponents and avowed enemies and even his false friends—for with such all public men are burdened. He was always remarkable for his firmness and directness, yet at all times courteous and, in every sense of the word, a true gentleman. Perhaps one of the greatest tributes to this great man was the interpolation of the following lines in a topical song rendered in a play witnessed by George Washington during his Presidency of the United States:

. . . "With one accord
He's called to be a kind of—not a lord—
I don't know what, he's not a *great man*, sure,
For poor men love him just as he were poor.
They love him like a father or a brother
As we poor Irishmen love one another."

In the same play one of the actors was asked to describe the President, to which he responded that he "had *not seen him*, because he had mistaken a man 'all lace and glitter, botherum, and shine' for him until the show had passed." This brought a hearty laugh from the President, but it was more than a mere joke, for it bore out the old adage that "clothes do not make the man."

In his attire, as in all other matters, George Washington was most circumspect. He always chose garments that were especially fitting for the occasion on which they were to be worn, in the fashion of the day, yet not so extreme as to be conspicuous. In this respect, as in others, his personality was so commanding that all else practically sank into oblivion.

That he was early observant of the current style is evident from a "Memorandum to have my Coat made by the following Directions" which appears in his journal when he was about sixteen, and which reads:

"To be made a Frock with a Lapel Breast the Lapel to Contain on each side six Button Holes and to be about five or six inches wide all the way equal and to turn as the Breast on the Coat does to have it made very long waisted and in length to come down to or below the bent of the knee, the Waist from the armpit to the Fold to be exactly as long or Longer than from thence to the Bottom not to have more than one fold in the Skirt and the top to be made just to turn in and three Button Holes the Lapel at the top

to turn as the Cape of the Coat and Bottom to come Parallel with the Button Holes the last Button Hole in the Breast to be right opposite to the Button on the Hip."

This description shows a sense of proportion and balance, while later "Memorandums" and instructions to his tailors reveal his knowledge of fine fabrics and trimmings, also his desire to have well-fitting garments. In this he experienced great difficulty and wrote on one occasion, "whether it be the fault of the tailor, or of the measure sent, I can't say, but certain it is, my clothes have never fitted me well."

It was at that time the custom to import from England almost every manufactured article for domestic use and, as a rule, the garments of the gentry were made by London tailors. One of the orders sent by George Washington during his bachelor days at Mount Vernon, included "As much of the best superfine blue Cotton Velvet as will make a Coat, Waistcoat, and Breeches for a Tall Man, with a fine silk button to suit it, and all other necessary trimmings and linings, together with garters for the Breeches."

While in the service of his country, first with the British Army and later as Commander in Chief of the American Army, George Washington was a striking figure in his colorful uniform, but did not hesitate to meet emergencies by laying aside his regimentals and "proceeding as light as any Indian in the woods" when occasion demanded. He urged the British commander to allow him and his men to adopt Indian dress, adding, "'Tis an unbecoming dress, I confess, for an officer; but convenience rather than shew, I think should be consulted." The General gave him leave, and it was done.

When the uniform for the American Army was under consideration George Washington personally gave it thoughtful attention, and chose buff and blue for the colors, but provided also for field officers a less conspicuous brown coat, more in tone with the tints of the woods and fields, guided again by "convenience rather than shew" and by the necessity for blending with the landscape.

After the separation of the Colonies from the Mother Country, George Washington became an ardent advocate of having his garments "made in America," both as to material and tailoring. His taste in clothes became softened and more sober. In 1784 he instructed his Philadelphia agent: "If there be any homespun Cloths in Philadelphia which are tolerably fine, that you can come reasonably at, I would be obliged to you to send me patterns of some of the best kinds— I should prefer that mixed in the grain, because it will not so readily discover its quality as a plain cloth." Just before his inauguration as President he wrote to General Knox asking him "to procure me homespun broadcloth of the Hartford fabric, to make a suit of clothes for myself," adding, "I hope it will not be a great while before it will be unfash-

ionable for a gentleman to appear in any other dress."

But the market in America did not afford the materials required for such garments as must be included in the wardrobe of the President of the United States, so from necessity rather than choice London merchants were again patronized. But the specifications were prefaced by the instructions, "I want neither lace nor embroidery. Plain clothes with a gold or silver button (if worn in genteel dress) are all I desire."

During his later years at Mount Vernon he is described as he came in from the farm, "dressed in a plain blue coat, white cassimer waistcoat and black breeches, and boots. . . . He came in again with his hair neatly powdered, a clean shirt on, new plain drab coat, white waistcoat, and white silk stockings."

In his younger days, when the principal sport was fox hunting, he donned the colorful and attractive riding garments of the period, which became him well. This was his favorite diversion, but next to his fondness for horses, dogs, and the chase, he found amusement in dancing, and enjoyment in surveying, the latter being in the nature of sport as well as a profession. In later life he enjoyed the theater, but his chief interest was centered in home life, with the companionship of old friends and new, and with his well-chosen library, the current publications, and the general supervision of his estates. The latter he termed, "The most favorite amusement of my life."

GEORGE WASHINGTON: HIS FRIENDS AND ENEMIES

The lives of some great men occasionally remind one of a kaleidoscope made up of many loose pieces. A cynic once said that we go through life with only one true friend, and that person is his or her mother. This certainly was not the case of George Washington. He possessed his mother's deep affection, and he also had the devotion of the majority who crossed his pathway. As he ascended step by step until he reached the pinnacle of fame, his old friends, even those of boyhood's day, stood shoulder to shoulder by his side.

Very few lives have been laid bare in the same manner as that of George Washington and stood the test of time as well as critics. The new historical facts concerning his boyhood have been distorted, his private life has been discussed from every angle, and his official life, which rightly belongs to the public, stands out in bold relief as a shining example to the world. No man's career, and especially that of no great leader, is ever entirely self-determined, and it may be of interest to hear how George Washington was aided by his friends and affected by his enemies.

Turning back, therefore, the pages of history to the early life of George Washington, we find him the central figure of boyish groups, his early friends, many of whom looked to him as their leader. The friendship of some of these youthful chums he carried to the end of his life. All that is necessary to prove this assertion is to read George Washington's will. It reads, "I leave to the acquaintances and friends of my juvenile years, Lawrence and Robert Washington . . ." The latter presumedly was the "dear Robin" of his earliest letters. Both of them were distant kinsmen and boy friends of his young life.

Nothing in George Washington's life gave him more real pleasure than his intimacy with the Fairfaxes and Carlisles. These friendships began during a visit made early in life to his half brother, Lawrence, and, like the above boyish association, only ended with death. The Fairfax family lived only four miles from Mount Vernon at Belvoir, and their kinsfolk, the Carlisle family, lived in near-by Alexandria. Lawrence Washington had married Anne Fairfax, and it was undoubtedly through his influence that his brother, George, was taken into the employ of Lord Fairfax as surveyor of his great tract of land located in the Northern Neck of Virginia. Lord Fairfax had become heir to this vast estate through his mother, who was a daughter of Lord Culpeper. In proof of his lasting gratitude and friendship for the Fairfax family, George Washington told one of his brothers in 1755 "to that family I am under many obligations, particularly the old gentleman," but as it will be clearly seen as time passed he more than paid the debt. During the Revolution the Fairfaxes were loyalists. But notwithstanding this fact George Washington assured them that the friendship "which I ever professed and felt for you met no diminution from the differences in our political sentiments." In 1778 he was able to secure the safety of Lord Fairfax from persecution at the hands of the Whigs, and in acknowledgment of his kindness his lordship wrote the following words:

"There are times when favors conferred make a greater impression than at others, for, though I have received many, I hope that I have not been unmindful of them; yet that, at a time your popularity was at the highest and mine at the lowest, and when it is so common for men's resentments to run up high against those who differ from them in opinion, you should act with your wonted kindness towards me, has affected me more than any favor I have received; and could not be believed by some New Yorkers, it being above the run of common minds."

To another member of this same family, George William Fairfax, Washington wrote:

"I shall please myself with the hope of hearing from you frequently; and till you forbid me to indulge the wish, I shall not despair of seeing you and Mrs. Fairfax once more the inhabitants of Belvoir, and greeting you both there the intimate companions of our old age as you have been of our younger years."

Across the Potomac from Mount Vernon, where now is located Fort Washington, was the estate of William Digges, called Warburton Manor. A great intimacy existed between Washington and this well-known Maryland family. A code of signals was arranged between the two families of a decidedly unique character and intercourse was maintained by barges gayly manned by liveried black men.

Possibly the dearest friendship formed by George Washington was with Dr. James Craik, who was an Army surgeon and attended him in two serious illnesses. He had served originally with General Washington through the Fort Necessity expedition and the Braddock campaign and he continued to serve in later operations to be near his friend. His home was not far from Mount Vernon, at Port Tobacco, farther down the Potomac on the Maryland side. As friend as well as physician, he continued to be a comrade throughout life. General Washington's faith in Craik was unlimited, and he had unbounded confidence in him as a physician. In writing of Dr. Craik he said: "If I should ever have occasion for a Physician or Surgeon, I should prefer my old Surgeon, Dr. Craik, who, from forty years experience, is better qualified than a Dozen of them put together." Craik was the first physician to reach his bedside during his last illness, and in George Washington's will he left "to my compatriot in arms and old and intimate friend Doct'r Craik . . . my Bureau . . . and the circular chair, an appendage of my study."

The arrival of Braddock and his army at Alexandria was instrumental in bringing a new set of military friends into George Washington's life. The general saw great possibilities in the Virginia youth, and took him into his military family as an extra aide. He and George Washington, it is said, had frequent disputes. It is, however, generally known of Braddock that though his "enmities were strong" his "attachments" were warm, and he grew to like and admire the young volunteer. It was George Washington who, when Braddock was wounded in the lung, lifted him into a covered wagon and brought him to a place of safety. Around his waist at the time he wore a red sash of woven silk and he was carried from the field in it. This sash now occupies an important place in one of the cases at Mount Vernon, and is stained with Braddock's blood. Three days later Braddock died of his wounds, bequeathing to Colonel Washington his favorite horse and his body servant as tokens of eternal gratitude.

Even before his public life had made him conspicuous George Washington was the friend and guest of many of the leading families of Virginia. Between 1747 and 1754 he visited the Carters of Shirley, the Byrds of Westover, and the Lewises of Warner Hall. The Lees of Stratford were among his earliest friends. He also counted among his acquaintances the Spotswoods, Fauntleroys, Corbins, Masons, Randolphs, Robinsons, Nicholases, and other distinguished families of Virginia.

Again, the command of the Continental Army brought another element into George Washington's life, that of a younger set of officers of decidedly inspiring character. And it might well be said to his credit he never lost the opportunity of advancing those who served under him. John Laurens, an aide in 1777, quickly endeared himself to the Commander in Chief, and he always displayed the keenest affection for General Washington. Of another aide, Tench Tilghman, General Washington spoke in the most exalted terms. He said, "He has been a zealous servant and slave to the public, and a faithful assistant to me for five years, part of which time he refused to receive pay. Honor and gratitude interest me in his favor." As an illustration of his keen sense of justice, General Washington gave to Tilghman the distinction of bearing to Congress the news of the surrender of Cornwallis, with the request to that body that he be honored in some way.

To another aide, David Humphreys, he gave the honor of carrying to Congress the standards captured at Yorktown, and at the same time he recommended Humphreys for "attention, fidelity, and good service." It was this aide who escorted General Washington at the close of the Revolution to Mount Vernon, and was the last officer connected with the army to part with the Commander in Chief. Humphreys was devoted to his chief all through life, and on one especial occasion we find General Washington bemoaning the fact that Humphreys was not at Mount Vernon, "which has deprived us of your aid in attacking Christmas pies." When General Washington was notified of his election to the Presidency, Humphreys was visiting him, and he was the only person outside of servants to accompany the President-elect on his journey to New York to be inaugurated, except Charles Thomson, who carried the official announcement to Mount Vernon from Congress and made the return journey with him.

Gen. Henry Knox, who subsequently became Secretary of War in President Washington's first Cabinet, was the earliest army friend of those who rose to the rank of general and was honored by Washington with absolute trust. Perhaps, however, no one was closer to him than Gen. Nathanael Greene, an officer of unusual military talent. It fell to Greene to sign the death sentence of the unfortunate André, and it is said he did it with tears in his eyes.

Undoubtedly one of the longest and closest friendships formed by General Washington among his younger officers was with Alexander Hamilton. When he first came into the life of the Commander in Chief he was not only young but obscure. However, in the campaign of 1776 he attracted the attention of General Washington, and the following year he became a member of his staff. General Washington was deeply attached to him, and it is known he frequently spoke of him affectionately as "my boy." Alexander Hamilton was never exactly true to his chief, General Washington, as history shows. After four years of staff service he resigned under circumstances he pledged himself to General Washington never to disclose, and then in evident irritation he told the cause. In a long epistle to a friend he wrote in regard to his chief as follows:

"I believe you know the place I held in the General's confidence and councils, which will make more extraordinary to you to learn that for three years past I have felt no friendship for him and have professed none. The truth is, our dispositions are the opposite of each other, and the pride of my temper would not suffer me to profess what I did not feel. Indeed, when advances of this kind have been made to me on his part, they were received in a manner that showed at least that I had no desire to court them, and that I desired to stand rather on a footing of military confidence than of private attachment."

Queer words for a man to express in regard to a benefactor! George Washington's magnanimity to Hamilton was remarkable all through their long intercourse. However, some of General Washington's friends realized Hamilton's lack of loyalty. In after years James Madison stated "that Hamilton often spoke disparagingly of Washington's talents, particularly after the Revolution, and the first part of the Presidency." Benjamin Rush confirmed Hamilton's antagonistic attitude toward the Commander in Chief. He said, "Hamilton often spoke with contempt of General Washington."

When General Washington became first President of the United States he appointed Alexander Hamilton his Secretary of the Treasury, and apparently the two men were more in accord. From this time on Hamilton became probably the President's most trusted friend. In 1792 President Washington wrote him from Mount Vernon a decidedly cordial letter, welcoming him there as a guest, and signing himself "always and affectionately yours."

Another close intimacy of General Washington's was with "Light Horse Harry" Lee, who kept him closely informed in regard to politics in Virginia. Lee was in Congress when the death of this great American was announced, and to him is given the credit of coining the famous words, "First in war, first in peace, and first in the hearts of his countrymen."

It seems almost needless to say that another strong affection of George Washington's life was for General Lafayette. The latter's services were deeply appreciated and the Commander in Chief realized his extreme loyalty. It was undoubtedly out of gratitude that General Washington gave him the command of the attacking party of one of the sectors at Yorktown. The story is related that after Monmouth battle the two officers passed the night together, lying on the same mantle talking over the happenings of the day. In 1797, after the French Revolution, when General Lafayette was confined in the Austrian prison at Olmutz, George Washington Lafayette, the General's only son, lived at Mount Vernon as a member of the family.

The intimacy with Robert Morris, the financier of the Revolution, was close, and General Washington and his family were several times inmates of his home in Philadelphia. Gouverneur Morris was one of his trusted advisers, and Charles Carroll of Carrollton was a decided partisan of the General's. Edward Rutledge, of South Carolina, was another friend. To the latter he wrote: "I can but love and thank you, and I do it sincerely for your polite and friendly letter."

There is an old saying that no person is without enemies, certainly not those who possess character. George Washington had his friends and also his enemies. No better illustration of this fact can be given than a brief history of the Conway Cabal, a conspiracy to deprive General Washington of his command of the Army. The plot developed in 1777, and received the support of a strong faction in Congress, most of whom were misguided, but their loyalty to the country was never for a moment doubted. Gen. Horatio Gates, an Englishman by birth, was in command at the victorious battle of Saratoga, and he received the surrender of General Burgoyne's army, although historians of today feel that the laurels for this American victory should have gone to Schuyler and Arnold. However, Congress in the first flush of gratitude passed a vote of thanks to General Gates and gave him a gold medal. Gates had wider military experience than General Washington, and the whole country was carried away by the brilliancy of the Saratoga achievement. John Adams, in one of his unfortunate moods of bitterness and jealously toward General Washington, exclaimed, "I am weary of so much insipidity." Another time he asked the question, "Would Washington have been commander of the Revolutionary Army or President of the United States if he had not married the rich widow of Custis?" In asking this question John Adams lost sight of the fact that some of his military fame had been attained before his marriage.

Through the influence of this division of opinion in Congress, Gates was made president of the Board of War, and a Canadian campaign was suggested. Lafayette was asked to lead this expedition and it was proposed to make Conway his assistant. It is pleasing to know that this offer was promptly declined by this loyal Frenchman, unless approved by General Washington. The story is also told that he was daring enough to meet the whole cabal party, and on this same occasion he made them drink to the health of the Commander in Chief. Meanwhile Conway was busy. He wrote anonymous letters to various men of distinction, asserting General Washington's accountability for certain military disasters, and it is even said he went further by forging the name of the Commander in Chief. It is interesting to hear that at such a critical moment how staunch were General Washington's friends. It is said that his devoted friend, Dr. James Craik, was one of the persons instrumental in warning him of the cabal.

It is generally conceded that James Wilkinson, who was serving on the staff of General Gates, and who was deep in the Conway Cabal, confessed the plot in a convivial moment to an aide of Lord Stirling, who passed it to his chief. But George Washington never lacked friends. All through these troublesome cabal days they seemed to spring up on every side, even to the point of actually fighting his battles. For an illustration, Gen. John Cadwalader, when he fully realized that a conspiracy was forming against his Commander, challenged the chief plotter, Thomas Conway, and shot him in the mouth.

Fortunately for the glory of America, the plot of relieving General Washington of the Army never materialized. Gates rushed down from the North and tried to convince Congress that the plot was absolutely unknown to him. Few persons believed him, however, and the man who was responsible for the whole plot, Thomas Conway, became an object of scorn and spent the remainder of his life in obscurity. Thus "right was might," and the peerless Washington triumphed over his enemies.

A formidable enemy of General Washington's was Charles Lee, who had been an officer in the English Army and a military adventurer, and was second in command during the early part of the Revolution. In the beginning Lee extolled the virtues of the Commander, but barely four months had passed before he was lamenting over the General's "fatal indecision" and was also calling him a "blunderer." While fighting in the American Army, Lee was captured by the British and is suspected of treasonable intimacy while a prisoner. In time he was exchanged, and he led the troops at the Battle of Monmouth, and it was while in command of the battlefield he apparently aided the British in other ways. After barely engaging the enemy he led a retreat, which was developing into a rout when General Washington personally saved the day. Lee was subsequently court-martialed and found guilty. He ended his days in Virginia, surrounded by dogs, always contending that he preferred them to human beings.

For personal as well as party reasons certain newspapers during President Washington's second administration began actively to attack him. Jefferson reported that the President was "extremely affected by these attacks made and kept up on him by the public papers. I think he feels these things more than any person I have ever met." At a Cabinet meeting Jefferson said, "the Presdt was much inflamed, got into one of those passions . . . ran on much on the personal abuse which had been bestowed upon him, defied any man on earth to produce a single act of his since he had been in the govmt which has not been done on the purest motives." President Washington's political course was the cause of his estrangement with several statesmen with whom he had been closely associated; of these Jefferson was the most prominent.

One of the abusive editors was Philip Freneau, well known as a poet, who held a Government position under Jefferson but continued his misrepresentation of the Washington administration just the same. Many persons were convinced at the time that he was sustained in his line of conduct by Jefferson; it should, however, be taken into consideration that this was a period when party feeling ran high. President Washington could not at first be convinced that Thomas Jefferson was not truly his friend, but once convinced all relations were severed.

Benjamin Franklin Bache, Franklin's grandson, was also exceedingly abusive of the President in his newspaper, *The General Advertiser and Aurora,* and, as can be readily understood, it was bitterly resented. The President expressed his condemnation of such an attempt to injure him, by saying that the Bache's publication was an "outrage on all decency." The third of these editors was James Thomson Callender, whose publications were numerous. At one time he ended a tirade of abuse of President Washington with the following remark: "The extravagant popularity possessed by this citizen reflects the utmost ridicule on the discernment of the American people!"

The bitterest attack, however, was penned by Thomas Paine. For many years there was good feeling between these two strong characters, and in 1782, when Paine was in great financial distress, it was through General Washington's influence he obtained a position. In other well-known instances he was also helped. In subsequent years he went to France, where he was too outspoken in his utterances during the French Revolution. For nearly a year he languished in

the Luxembourg prison. He was finally rescued by the second minister to France, James Monroe. It was his belief that a word from President Washington would rescue him, but it was decided that governmental interference was not proper. Some years subsequent to the Revolution, Paine was asked his view on General Washington. Rising to his feet, he uttered the following lines:

"Take from the rock the roughest and
    rudest stone,
It needs no sculptor, it is Washington;
But if you chisel, let the strokes be rude,
And on his bosom write ingratitude."

It is a well-known fact that persons of unusual force of character are apt to have enemies as well as friends. This was certainly true in the case of George Washington. Later in life, moreover, those who had posed as enemies went out of their way to deny all antagonism, and they even went further; many of them took especial pains to destroy all proofs of ill feeling. George Washington was triumphant in the end, and has ever since lived "first in the hearts of his countrymen."

(FOR THIS PROGRAM SEE NUMBERS 15, 31, 32, 71, 105 IN LIST OF SELECTED BOOKS ON PAGES 300-A AND 300-B)

GEORGE WASHINGTON CROSSING THE ALLEGHENY RIVER—1753

The Mother of George Washington

AN APOCRYPHAL PORTRAIT OF MARY BALL WASHINGTON
(No authentic portrait of her is known)

MARY BALL IN EARLY LIFE

WHILE historians and biographers have searched far and wide for documents and data relating to George Washington, and over 2,500 books have been written based upon his character and achievements, but few have felt the urge to devote a comparable study to the life of his mother. Because she lived in a day when a woman's life was merged in that of her family and the careers of the men of her household her paramount concern, little attention was given to women individually, and much that has found expression in books and writings about Mary Ball Washington must be attributed to legend and tradition, particularly of her childhood and girlhood.

Mary Ball has been fitted with ancestry of almost mythological antiquity. Some writers have claimed for her a direct descent from the martyred apostle of liberty, John Ball, called the Mad Preacher of Kent, who stirred up riot and rebellion in certain sections of England by riding up and down the highways and through the villages preaching that all men were created free and equal. For this he was imprisoned by the orders of the Archbishop of Canterbury, and met death on the scaffold in 1387 because of his teachings.

The Balls belonged to the landed gentry of England, with the right to call themselves gentlemen, though their lands were not extensive.

The facts about her birth and her family that have been substantiated show that her first American ancestor was Col. William Ball. Colonel Ball came to Virginia in 1650 and established himself in Lancaster County, on the Rappahannock River. This estate he named Millenbeck. Very soon he became prominent in the community and was appointed a colonel in the militia by Governor Spotswood in 1710. He married a belle of Williamsburg. They had two sons, William and Joseph. To the former he left the plantation of Millenbeck, while Joseph received Epping Forest, named for a notable hunting park near the English homestead of the Balls.

Bishop William Meade has written of the Ball family in Virginia and of the coat of arms brought to this country by Col. William Ball, the first of the family in Virginia. The crest shows a lion rampant, with a ball in his paws. The motto is a Latin inscription, *Coelumque tueri,* which translated means "And look to Heaven," or "Seek the things which are above."

When Joseph sought a second wife his choice fell upon a widow, Mrs. Mary Montague Johnson. Their marriage took place in 1707, and in 1708 Mary Ball was born. When she was but 3 years old her father died, and in his will, dated June 25, 1711, he bequeathed to his little girl, later called the Rose of Epping Forest, 400 acres lying in the freshes of the Rappahannock, part of his patent of 1,600 acres.

Under her mother's careful training, Mary Ball was undoubtedly given all of the educational advantages available to girls of her day, when colleges were not open to women and skill in housewifery was always placed far above book learning. She was taught all the arts of the gentlewoman of her time— to dance the minuet, curtsy, to know the catecism, embroider, paint, sew a fine seam, be a fine horsewoman, and handle her slaves. Shortly after the death of Mary's father, her mother married for the third time, becoming the wife of Capt. Richard Hewes, a vestryman of St. Stephen's parish, Northumberland, whose home was at Sandy Point. Then Mary Ball left Epping Forest to live in her stepfather's home. Captain Hewes lived but a short time, as his death occurred in 1713, and his wife did not long survive him, and Mary Ball found herself an orphan at the age of 13. From the provisions of her mother's will, dated December 17, 1720, it will be seen that Mary Ball had always lived in comfortable circumstances and that she had possessions such as were only found among people of affluence and social standing. This will was discovered recently in the archives of Northumberland County, by the Rev. G. W. Beale, who thus commented upon its contents in an article in a Virginia historical magazine:

"It is seldom that in a document of this kind—maternal affection, having other and older children to share its bequest—concentrates itself upon a youngest daughter, and she a child of thirteen summers. Perhaps of all of the tributes laid at the feet of Mary Washington, none has been more heartfelt or significant of her than legacies of her mother's last will and testament, written, as they were, all unconsciously of her future distinction."

Mrs. Mary Montague Johnson Ball Hewes's will is as follows:

"IN THE NAME OF GOD, AMEN, the seventeenth Day of December in this year of our Lord one thousand seven hundred and twenty.

"I Mary Hewes of St. Stephen's parish, Northumberland County, widow, being sick and weak in body but of sound and perfect memory, thanks be to Almighty God for the same & calling to mind the uncertain state of this transitory life & that the flesh must yield unto death, when it shall please God to call, do make & ordain this my last will and testament.

"First, I give and bequeath my soul (to God) that gave it me, & my body to the Earth to be buried in Decent Christian burial at the discretion of my executors in these presents nominated. And as touching such worldly estate which it hath pleased God to bestow upon me, I give, devise & dispose of in the following manner & form.

"Imprimis, I give & devise unto my Daughter Mary Ball one young likely negro woman to be purchased for her out of my Estate by my executors & to be delivered unto her and said Mary Ball at the age of eighteen years, but my will is that if the said Mary Ball should dye without issue lawfully begotten of her body that the said negro woman with her increase shall return to my loving son John Johnson to him, his heirs & assigns forever.

"Item I give & bequeath unto said Daughter Mary Ball two gold rings, the one being a large hoop & the other a stoned ring.

"Item I give unto my said Daughter Mary Ball one young mare & her increase which said mare I formerly gave her by word of mouth.

"Item I give & bequeath unto my said Daughter Mary Ball sufficient furniture for the bed her father, Joseph Ball, left her, vizt: One suit of Good curtains and fullens, One Rugg, One Quilt, one pair Blankets.

"Item I give & bequeath unto my said Daughter Mary Ball two Diaper Table Clothes marked M. B. with inck, & one Dozen of Diaper napkins, two towels, six plates, two pewter dishes, two basins, one large iron pott, one Frying pan, one old trunk.

"Item I give & bequeath unto my said Daughter Mary Ball, one good young pacing horse together with a good silk plush side saddle to be purchased by my executors out of my estate.

"Item I give & bequeath unto my Daughter Elizabeth Bonum one suit of white & black callico, being part of my own wearing apparel.

"Item All the rest of my wearing apparel, agent for the securing of my said Daughter Mary Ball & I do hereby appoint her (to) be under the Tutilage & government of Capt. George Eskridge during her minority.

"Item My will is I do hereby oblige my executors to pay to the proprietor or his agent for the securing of my said Daughter Mary Ball her land Twelve pounds if so much (be) due.

"Item All the rest of my Estate real & personal whatsoever & wheresoever I give & devise unto my son John Johnson & to his heirs lawfully to be begotten of his body & for default of such issue I give & devise the said Estate unto my Daughter Elizabeth Bonum, her heirs & assigns forever.

"Item I do hereby appoint my son John Johnson & my trusty and well beloved friend George Eskridge Executors of this my last Will & Testament & also revoke & Disannul all other former Wills & Testaments by me heretofore made or caused to be made either by word or writing, ratifying & confirming this to be my last Will & Testament & no other.

"In witness whereof I have hereunto set my hand & seal the Day & Date at first above written.

"The mark & seal of Mary III Hewes
"Sig.   (Seal)
"Signed, Sealed & Published & Declared by Mary Hewes to be her last Will & Testament in presence of us.
"The Mark of Robert X Bradley
"The Mark of Ralph X Smithurst
"David Stranghan."

Little Mary Ball must have indeed been a winsome lass. Her stepbrother John Johnson, named as joint executor in his mother's will, died very soon after her death; the first bequest in his will reveals his affection for this little half-sister, and to the legacies of this child's father and of her mother were added his own, thus expressed:

"Imprimis. I give & bequeath unto my sister Mary Ball all my land in Stafford which my father-in-law Richard Hewes gave me to the said Mary Ball and her heirs lawfully begotten of her body forever."

He also left her some money.

Still another "in-law" had an affection for the Rose of Epping Forest and left her a legacy. This came to her through the will of Samuel Bonum, husband of the "Elizabeth" named in Mrs. Hewes's will, which was probated in Westmoreland County February 22, 1726, and which contained an item bequeathing "to my sister-in-law, Mary Ball, my young dapple gray riding horse."

Thus Mary Ball at 18 years of age, while not rich according to the standard of her day or of this, was well endowed with Virginia land, had several good riding horses, a handsome saddle, her own maid, some jewels, and enough proper household equipment for any young lady of her social standing. George Eskridge, her guardian, who lived at Sandy Point, Westmoreland County, just a short distance from the home of Mary's mother and also of her sister Mrs. Bonum, was a man of education and one of the leading legal lights of Virginia. He had a daughter within a year of Mary's age and, owing to this fact, it is believed that her time was well divided between the Eskridge home and that of her sister Mrs. Bonum, who had been married seven years when her mother died. In both her sister's home and at that of the Eskridges her associations were of the best of the colony's residents.

With young ladyhood came, it is said, a blossoming out of beauty which gave her another complimentary title, "the Belle of the Northern Neck." With youth, beauty, and a goodly inheritance of land, suitors were numerous, but Mary Ball was interested in none until she was past 22 years of age and her relatives had begun to predict spinsterhood as her lot.

By some writers it is asserted that her brother, Joseph Ball, after living in Virginia for a while, returned to England, taking Mary along, after aiding her to close her mother's house and set her affairs in order; and that while in England she met in most romantic fashion the stalwart, genial Capt. Augustine Washington, a widower from Virginia and an old neighbor, who had come to England to place his boys in the well-known Appleby School and also to settle up some matters relative to his father's estate. There is just as much reason to believe they met in England as to believe that they met in Virginia. There is no authoritative document to prove either, but the fact remains that they met and developed a romance that culminated in a speedy marriage, and Mary Ball was taken to her husband's home at Bridges Creek, which he had built or enlarged for his first wife, Jane Butler, whose death two years before had been preceded by the death of one of their children. There Mary Ball Washington quickly fitted herself into her new life and made a real home for her husband and her stepchildren.

It is alleged that, although so courageous and poised, Mary Ball had one weakness that neither age nor experience changed. She had a fear of lightning so great that the approach of a storm sent her to her room in such terror as to be distressing to witness. This was due to a harrowing girlhood experience, in which a companion seated at table with her was instantly killed, the knife and fork in her hands being melted by the current.

Mary Ball has been described as a fearless and expert horsewoman, as from the time she was 13 she had owned her own horses, always used a stylish saddle, and when 20 tradition claims that she made a brave and handsome picture in "habit, hat, and feather," at home on her own dapple gray pacing through roads and lanes in an English habit of scarlet cloth, long and flowing as to skirt and tightly fitted as to bodice. Her hat was of beaver and black with a long handsome black plume, and she was a handsome and distinguished figure.

MARY BALL WASHINGTON AS WIFE AND MOTHER

As the mother of George Washington, America's greatest hero, Mary Ball Washington should be enshrined in the hearts of the people of the United States and every bit of fact, legend, tradition, and gossip that throws light upon this remarkable woman, who typifies the highest type of American motherhood, is eagerly read and welcomed.

The young bride of Capt. Augustine Washington must have been delighted with her new home to which her husband took her immediately after their marriage on March 6, 1730. Bridges Creek (Wakefield), a lovely spot for a homestead, had been chosen by John Washington, soon after he came to America, for his home plantation. It was situated on the point of a triangle formed by two creeks and the Potomac River, with its lawns sloping down to the river's edge and great stretches of forest for a background. She found a commodious, comfortable house of the type used by well-to-do planters. Around the great fireplace in the parlor was a border of square Dutch tiles in blue, their enameled surfaces reflecting the faces of the family circle in the firelight and offering awe-inspiring biblical scenes, to form the basis of many a bedtime story for the children of the Washington family. Here, too, was a staff of slaves to be kept busy and many domestic matters to direct. She could gratify her natural curiosity as to her predecessor, Jane Butler Washington, and her possessions as mistress of Augustine Washington's home for 13 years. In inventorying the contents of closets, storeroom, and shelves she came across some books, among them a copy of Matthew Hale's Contemplations, Moral and Divine. On the flyleaf she read the name of the first wife, "Jane Washington," and at once wrote beneath it "and Mary Washington." This book she put among her own treasures, read it and studied it while life lasted. From it she continued the teachings of her stepsons that their mother had begun, and when her children came along they, too, were trained in its precepts. No woman of ignorance could have found pleasure and benefit in Matthew Hale's *Contemplations*. Her constant use of this book is a proof of the high type of mentality and culture of the woman Augustine Washington selected to be his second wife and to help him rear his children.

It was at Bridges Creek that little George Washington, blue-eyed and sandy haired, first saw the light of day on February 22, 1732. Within a few weeks after his birth his proud parents took him, in April, 1732, to visit some relatives, during which visit he was christened according to the observances of the Episcopal Church, of which his parents were members. For this important ceremony his mother had prepared a lovely christening robe of creamy brocade, silk lined with a soft rose pink of finest quality. He was well supplied with godparents, his father's sister, Mrs. Mildred Gregory, being his godmother, and Mr. Beverly Whiting and Capt. Christopher Brooks his godfathers. It is said that all three presented the babe with silver cups. None of them dreamed of the fame that was one day to crown the life work of the

chubby babe they had sponsored, who was named for his mother's beloved guardian, George Eskridge. The robe and the silver bowl used as a font are still in existence and may be seen in the National Museum at Washington.

Midst the busy life of a plantation with its frequent visitors, in a family of many relatives, some of them close neighbors, the first three years of George Washington's life was spent. Meanwhile, George's sister Betty was born, in 1733, and Captain Washington, believing the location to be unhealthful, decided to move his family to the Epsewasson plantation, also known as Little Hunting Creek farm. This was part of the tract of 5,000 acres granted to Col. John Washington, the immigrant, and his friend Nicholas Spencer, by Lord Culpeper, for their efforts in colonization. It is believed that Captain Augustine built his house on the site now occupied by the Mount Vernon Mansion. On this plantation George and Betty romped and grew sturdy and strong, with their mother giving some time each day to their education. Finally their father became concerned about their schooling, and on one of his trips to England he brought back, among a batch of servants, a white man of education, believed to be a political exile. Upon his shoulders was placed the duty of the first real schooling of the Washington children. This man's name was William Grove, which later was lost in the nickname "Hobby." As neither the big genial Captain Washington nor his wife kept any diaries or journals of their daily lives, and as but few letters were written, much of the detail of the life of this family which has come to be so important to people of the United States has been lost to record. However, parish records have helped to fix the time of the migrations of the Washington family. These show that Captain Washington was interested in the appointment of a rector and that he attended vestry meetings in Truro parish during 1736 and 1737, and that he did not do so after the latter year. Through old letters come faint glimpses of the proud young mother riding beside her little son on his pony, and her great pride when he became old enough to ride without her hand on his bridle.

Meanwhile, Augustine Washington had purchased a farm on the Rappahannock opposite Fredericksburg, in Stafford County, about a mile below Falmouth. Here the family moved when George was about 7 years of age. Here Augustine Washington died in 1743, when George Washington, the eldest of a group of five, was but 11 years old, and Mary Washington was left to rear five children with much more land than cash. These were the days when Mary Washington, still under 36, found strength and great solace in her lifetime habit of rising at dawn to spend the first hour of her day in silent thought and prayer to prepare herself for the family worship and the day's events. With the death of the father, she required George to conduct fam-

ily prayers and say grace at the table. George Washington Parke Custis, although too young to have remembered very much of her or to have formed his own opinion of her high character, lived in the home of the General from infancy and was fully acquainted with her life.

Of her, he has written:

"Bred in those domestic and independent habits which graced the Virginia Matrons in the old days, this lady by the death of her husband, became involved in the cares of a young family, at a period when these responsibilities seem more especially to claim the aid and control of the stronger sex; and it was left for this remarkable woman, by a method most rare, by an education and discipline the most peculiar and imposing, to form in the youth time of her son those great and essential qualities which led him on to the glories of his after life. If the school savored more of the Spartan than the Persian character, it was a fitter one in which to form a hero, destined to be the ornament of the time in which he flourished, and a standard of excellence for ages yet to come.

"The Home of Mrs. Washington, of which she was always mistress, was a pattern of order. There the levity and indulgence common to youth, was tempered by a deference and a well regulated restraint which, while it neither suppressed nor condemned any rational enjoyment usual in the spring time of life, prescribed those enjoyments within the bounds of moderation and propriety. Thus the chief was taught the duty of obedience, which prepared him to command. The matron held in reserve an authority, which never departed from her, not even when her son had become the most illustrious of men. It seemed to say, 'I am your mother, the being who gave you life, the guide who directed your steps when they needed the guidance of age and wisdom.' Nor did the chief dissent from the truths, but to the last moments of his venerable parent, yielded to her will the most dutiful and implicit obedience."

"A lady of high breeding, and high courage, Mary Washington, according to Custis was just exactly the type of woman one would expect the mother of the great First President to be—plain, dignified, sincere, strong in the possession of the homely and home-like virtues, absolutely devoid of vanity and ostentation without frivolity of feminine captiousness, reticent to a degree and so free from self-consciousness, she was a thorough-bred lady in her unpretentious homespun and as much at ease as though it were the purple and ermine of royalty. No hysterical excitement ever carried her out of the bounds of her reserves. Though apparently endowed with equability of temperament, Mary Washington's nature glowed with a suppressed fervor which transmitted itself to her son and in him became power for endurance, passion for command, ambition to do and to dare in the Colonial wars, spontaneous assumption of leadership and the natural and easy command of men. This suppressed fire, force or energy or whatever it may be termed was felt by everybody who contacted either George Washington or his stately mother.

"Such, were the domestic influences under which the mind of Washington was formed; and that he not only profited by, but fully appreciated, their excellence and the character of his mother, his behavior toward her at all times testified."

He inherited from his mother not only her features but strong self-reliance, a courage that could endure long continued suspense, bear the weight of great responsibility, and endure unpopularity and misrepresentation without shrinking. She had great executive ability, supreme power of awing and governing others.

So strong was the influence of her training that all of her children respected her decisions and obeyed her commands. Against her veto there was no appeal. When she changed her original decision and vetoed the plan for George to go to sea, he accepted her right to order his life and settled himself back into his study routine. Thereby he was prevented from entering a calling in which the opportunity of distinction was very small.

Under the heavy responsibility of her young family, the duty of training them, getting them educated, and managing their resources to furnish an income for their support developed in Mrs. Washington a certain reserve dignity and an austerity of manner that frequently awed those of her own family. This is expressed in the words of Lawrence Washington, of Chotank, who said:

"I was often there [at the Washington home] with George, his playmate, schoolmate, and young man's companion. Of the mother I was ten times more afraid than I ever was of my own parents. She awed me in the midst of her kindness, for she was, indeed, truly kind. I have often been present with her sons, proper tall fellows too, and we were all as mute as mice; and even now, when time has whitened my locks, and I am the grandparent of a second generation, I could not behold that remarkable woman without feelings it is impossible to describe. Whoever has seen that awe-inspiring air and manner so characteristic in the Father of his Country, will remember the matron as she appeared when the presiding genius of her well-ordered household, commanding and being obeyed."

Mary Washington's family consisted of six children, four sons and two daughters— George, Elizabeth, Samuel, John Augustine, Charles, and Mildred, the last of whom lived only 14 months. These children addressed her as "Honored Madam," after the formal fashion of the times.

However, beneath her austerity of manner Mary Washington was a loving and true mother. She devoted her life to her family. Both history and tradition have recorded little stories of boyish pranks of George Washington, chiefly in pursuit of adventure such as might be true of any boy of high spirits and love of the open. In these matters Mary Washington seemed unusually wise and farseeing, for she put aside her mother impulse to forget the incident and secured from her boy his own story. She invariably forgave the act because he told her the straightforward truth. Thus she fostered the code of honor which his father first instilled in his children.

Brought up under such high principles, it was but natural that he should rise through positions of importance to the highest leadership. This his mother accepted as a matter of course and simply a part of his duty. He had been earning his living since he was 16, but he continued to defer to his mother's judgment and wishes regarding his affairs until they came to an issue on his military service. Mrs. Washington was opposed to George's joining the Braddock expedition. She was not anxious for him to be in the military service.

Her anxiety over his safety was very keen when he went with Braddock; distances were great, means of communication difficult, so that it was with deep thankfulness that she received a letter from him telling her of his safety and miraculous escapes. She hoped this would be the end of his war service and when she learned that her son was about to go on another expedition she drove to Mount Vernon to try to induce him to give up the idea altogether. Through her visit he did not give her his answer. He deliberated for several days and after her return to her home she received a letter saying:

"Honored Madam: If it is within my power to avoid going to the Ohio again, I shall; but if the command is pressed upon me, by the general *voice* of the country, and offered upon such terms as cannot be objected against, it would reflect dishonor upon me to refuse; and *that*, I am sure, must or *ought* to give you greater uneasiness; than my going in an honorable command, for upon no other terms I will accept of it."

Very human in her reactions, she was delighted over his marriage, and according to family legends sent gifts and good wishes to Martha and was happy when the bridal pair stopped to visit her and Mrs. Fielding Lewis en route to establish themselves at Mount Vernon. In mother fashion she felt sure that a wife would "keep George at home."

MARY BALL WASHINGTON IN LATER LIFE

Before the opening of the Revolutionary War Mrs. Mary Washington enjoyed living upon her farm on the Rappahannock. Her son George had given her a comfortable low-swung carriage or open chaise with good horses and the best of trappings. According to family tradition, her one man servant, neatly liveried, served as coachman and sat stiffly in his place. This outfit she used on daily drives to see her property, give directions about her crops, and to visit her relatives and friends. For the charity and church work with which she filled her time she wore in summer a dark straw hat with broad brim and low crown, tied beneath her chin with black strings. In the winter she wore a warm hood and wrapped herself in the handsome purple cloth cloak lined with silk shag, also a gift from her son, George. (This is mentioned in the bequests in her will.) From the farm she always brought a jug of the good water from her well.

Her brother was a well-to-do lawyer in London and sent her good advice and doubtless handsome presents.

Washington wrote in 1781: "A year or two before I left Virginia (to make her latter days comfortable and free from care) I did, at her request, but at my own expense, purchase a commodious house, garden and Lotts (of her own choosing) in Fredericksburg, . . ." This house was near that of her son-in-law, Fielding Lewis, which as well as her house is still standing and known as Kenmore. This statement contradicts the tradition that she was persuaded to move on the outbreak of war.

She was in the midst of all the social activity of the little place. She was godmother to most of Betty Lewis' 11 children, 6 of whom survived childhood, as well as so sponsoring other grandchildren and the infants of various relatives and close friends. Her handsome black brocade silk was worn over a satin petticoat on all such important occasions, and this was rather frequently, between the weddings, christenings, church attendance, sick visiting, charity, and relief work, in all of which she took an active part. She kept herself from the pangs of loneliness by being always busy at something. The frequent visits of children and grandchildren helped to liven the days for her.

After her son entered the great struggle for independence she spent more and more time on the big boulder close to her little cottage, in silent meditation and prayer, with her Bible and Matthew Hale's Contemplations.

When the news came of the successful crossing of the Delaware and the victory of December 26, 1776, her friends and neighbors rushed to felicitate her. She received them with placid calmness and expressed her pleasure at the brightening prospects of her native land and received the praises of the Commander, her son, with due maternal pride.

During the troubled war days Mrs. Mary Washington knitted constantly, making garments for the soldiers. When the news was bad, to keep her own faith strong she would often say (according to family legends): "The mothers and wives of brave men must be grave women." One day when the tidings brought a cry of despair from Mrs. Lewis with four sons in the service of their country, it is said her mother murmured: "The sister of the Commanding General must be an example of fortitude and faith."

Whatever news the messengers brought, good or bad, Mary Washington held fast to her calmness and serenity and often was said to have quietly asserted: "George is apt to succeed in anything he undertakes. He was always a good boy."

She did not see her son during the war until 1781. As he, accompanied by Rochambeau, passed through Fredericksburg on the way to the Yorktown campaign, presumably she saw him then. After the surrender of Cornwallis, which his mother is said to have welcomed reverently as a harbinger of peace and independence, General George Washington went to Eltham and stood in sorrow at the deathbed of his stepson, John Parke Custis, and then hastened northward to Philadelphia by way of Fredericksburg and Mount Vernon. According to the traditional account of the stay at the home of his mother and sister, Betty Lewis, the Yorktown victor was accompanied by various American and French officers whom he had the honor of presenting to his mother at a reception given by the town to celebrate the great event.

Who the officers were with the General, especially the French ones, is not known. Lafayette, De Grasse, and Rochambeau are all mentioned in this tradition but none of them could have been there. This event has become mixed with a later one. After General Washington's surrender of his commission at Annapolis, he reached Mount Vernon in time for Christmas and was stormbound there until February. According to the newspaper accounts he arrived at Fredericksburg February 12, 1784, "on a visit to his ancient and amiable parent," when "with every mark of heart-felt gladness, the Body Corporate, the next day waited on his Excellency" with an address to which he replied. On the 14th a "public dinner was provided" at the coffee house, and "on the evening, an elegant ball was given at the Town Hall, . . . at twelve o'clock the General withdrew; and the next day left this place for Chatham, on his return to Mount Vernon." This was Fredericksburg's "peace ball," which coincided closely with General Washington's birthday according to the old style, not entirely superseded.

Traditional accounts are given of Lafayette's visit in 1784 to Fredericksburg expressly to pay his respects to the mother of his beloved chief. Piloted by one of her grandchildren, he found her in her garden busily working. Without embarrassment at being caught unawares, she greeted him, and, turning toward the house, said: "I can make you welcome to my poor home without the parade of changing my dress." 'Tis said

her maid served spiced gingerbread and home-made wine. The marquis asked her blessing on his departure, and with a sweet graciousness she gave it.

An accidental blow in the breast, unnoticed at the time, developed into a cancer, considered incurable in her day, when surgery was crude. For several years she suffered greatly. When General Washington received the notification of his election to the Presidency he at once went to Fredericksburg on horseback to see his mother, as he had to leave at once for New York. He found her greatly altered by the suffering and progress of her affliction. In telling her of his plans of hastening back to Virginia as soon as his new duties would permit, she told him he would see her no more; that through age and disease she could not be long for this world. She urged him to hasten on to fulfill the high destinies which heaven appeared to have intended for him, and gave him her blessing.

Memories and the sorrow, of what he knew to be their farewell, for a moment submerged all other thoughts. She died on August 25, 1789, at the age of 81. President Washington was unable to attend her funeral. Over her simple grave, many years later, a public monument was erected in grateful remembrance. It bears the inscription, "Mary the Mother of Washington." Her greatest tribute lies in the immortal fame of her son, who never failed to honor and revere the maternal hand that led him to manhood.

Mary Ball Washington's will, in its methodical brevity, is worthy of study. None will doubt that with many other of his mother's qualities and characteristics, General Washington also inherited his mother's love of order and system.

The following is a copy of the will of the mother of George Washington, as registered in the clerk's office at Fredericksburg, Va.:

"In the name of God, Amen. I, Mary Washington, of Fredericksburg, in the county of Spotsylvania, being in good health, but calling to mind the uncertainty of this life, and willing to dispose of my worldly estate, do make and publish this, my last will, recommending my soul into the hands of my Creator, hoping for a remission of all my sins through the merits and mediation of Jesus Christ, the Saviour of mankind; I dispose of my worldly estate as follows:—

"Imprimis. I give, to my son, General George Washington, all my land in Accokeek Run, in the county of Stafford, and also my negro boy, George, to him and his heirs forever. Also my best bed, bedstead and Virginia cloth curtains (the same that stands in my best bedroom) my quilted blue-and-white quilt, and my best dressing-glass.

"Item. I give and devise to my son, Charles Washington, my negro man, Tom, to him and his assigns forever.

"Item. I give and devise to my daughter, Betty Lewis, my phaeton, and my bay horse.

"Item. I give and devise to my daughter-in-law, Hannah Washington, my purple cloth coat lined with shag.

"Item. I give and devise to my grandson, Corbin Washington, my negro wench, old Bet, my riding chair and two black horses, to him and his assigns forever.

"Item. I give and devise to my grandson, Fielding Lewis, my negro man, Frederick, to him and his assigns forever; also eight silver tablespoons, half of my crockery ware and the blue-and-white tea china with bookcase, oval table, one bedstead, one pair sheets, one pair blankets and white cotton counterpane, two table cloths, six red leather chairs, half my pewter and one half of my iron kitchen furniture.

"Item. I give and devise to my grandson, Lawrence Lewis, my negro wench, Lydia, to him and his assigns forever.

"Item. I give and devise to my granddaughter, Bettie Carter, my negro woman, little Bet, and her future increase, to her and her assigns forever; also my largest looking glass, my walnut writing desk, with drawers, a square dining table, one bed, bedstead, bolster, one pillow, one blanket and pair of sheets, white Virginia cloth counterpane and purple curtains, my red-and-white tea china, teaspoons, and the other half of my pewter, crockery ware, and the remainder of my iron kitchen furniture.

"Item. I give to my grandson George Washington, my next best dressing glass, one bed, bedstead, bolster, one pillow, one pair sheets, one blanket and counterpane.

"Item. I devise all my wearing apparel to be equally divided between my granddaughters, Bettie Carter, Fannie Ball, and Milly Washington, but should my daughter, Betty Lewis, fancy any one or two or three articles, she is to have them before a division thereof.

"Lastly. I nominate and appoint my said son, General George Washington, executor of this my will, and as I owe few or no debts, I direct my executor to give no security nor to appraise my estate, but desire the same may be allotted my devisees, with as little trouble and delay as may be, desiring their acceptance thereof as all the token I now have to give them of my love for them.

"In Witness whereof, I have hereunto set my hand and seal this 20th day of May, 1788.

"MARY WASHINGTON.

"Witness: John Ferneyhough.

"Signed, sealed and published in our presence, and signed by us in the presence of the said Mary Washington, and at her desire.

"J. MERCER

"JOSEPH WALKER."

(FOR THIS PROGRAM SEE NUMBERS 23, 32, 65, 72, 81 IN LIST OF SELECTED BOOKS ON PAGES 300-A AND 300-B)

George Washington the Man of Sentiment

NELLIE CUSTIS'S WEDDING ON GEORGE WASHINGTON'S LAST BIRTHDAY
After a painting by H. A. Ogden

GEORGE WASHINGTON THE SON

IN AN ADDRESS at Fredericksburg in 1784 General George Washington made what is probably the only public reference to his mother. He voiced his gratitude for the "congratulatory smiles . . . from the respectable inhabitants of the place of my growing Infancy and the honorable mention wch is made of my revered mother; by whose Maternal hand, (early deprived of a Father) I was led from Childhood."

This tribute, coming from so great a man as George Washington, indicates that his mother was a most remarkable character, a character who inspired loyalty and devotion, who commanded obedience to the demands of duty, but "submitted to the Divine Will with the strength of a philosopher and the trustfulness of a Christian."

The deference which her son paid to her while under her jurisdiction was equaled by the consideration he gave to her expressed desire in later years. Early he learned that his mother religiously adhered to the same principle of equity and justice which she firmly but lovingly instilled into her children and that her guidance and judgment were exercised with a view to his best interests. As a child he was deeply impressed with the lessons in religion and morality which she daily taught and practiced and with the maxims that she read aloud from Matthew Hale's *Meditations and Contemplations, Moral and Divine,* a book which the dutiful son treasured in after years and which is still preserved at Mount Vernon. In it his mother's name appears in her own handwriting.

Many of these maxims are exemplified in the honor and respect he paid to his mother.

According to tradition, in the first real crisis of his young life a vehement veto from his mother shattered the plans that had been made for a career on the sea.

On one occasion (July 18, 1755) George Washington wrote to his mother: "Honour'd Mad'm: As I doubt not but you have heard of our defeat, and perhaps have it represented in a worse light (if possible) than it deserves; I have taken this earliest oppertunity to give you some acct. of the Engagement." He tells her that "The Virginia Troops shew'd a good deal of Bravery, and were near all kill'd. . . . The Genl. [Braddock] was wounded; of w'ch he died 3 Days after." He recounts how he luckily escaped, and mentions that he was the only person left to distribute the General's orders, which he was scarcely able to do as he had only half recovered from a violent illness that had confined him to bed and "waggon" for about ten days. He might well have added to this communication one of the familiar maxims of his childhood days: "When a man does all he can, though it succeeds not well, blame not him that did it."

There is a tradition that before setting out upon his first journey into the wilderness, as the bearer of dispatches from Governor Dinwiddie to the French commander on the frontier, George Washington paid a parting visit to his mother, who bade him farewell with the admonition, "Remember that God only is our sure trust. To Him I commend you." Tradition also brings down the story that subsequently, when George Washington was offered a higher commission his mother journeyed hurriedly to Mount Vernon, hoping to dissuade him from risking his life in so dangerous an expedition. Not alone because his life was so dear to her did she make this plea, but she pointed out that it was too valuable to his country and that the colony required his services as one who was among the largest landholders in that region. She felt that her son was making a great sacrifice through a mistaken sense of duty.

For two days, according to the story, he considered her point of view. Recalling with what composure she had sent him forth on an earlier occasion, bidding him "Remember that God alone is our sure trust," he met and overcame her objections by first convincing her that he was keenly alive to his country's need of him but felt that need to be on the frontier rather than in peaceful pursuits at home; and then, adroitly but with all seriousness, reverence, and honor, he concluded his remarks by assuring his mother that he was placing his trust in God, saying to her, "The God to whom you commended me, Madam, when I set out upon a more perilous errand, defended me from all harm, and I trust He will do so now. Do not you?" Thus did he exemplify the maxim learned long ago: "When you speak of God or His attributes, let it be seriously . . ."

Upon a later occasion he wrote his mother a considerate letter, apparently in response to an expressed desire that he avoid further military duty. He addressed her, as was his custom, "Honored Madam," and wrote:

"If it is in my power to avoid going to the Ohio again, I shall; but if the command is pressed upon me, by the general *voice* of the country, and offered upon such terms as cannot be objected against, it would reflect dishonor upon me to refuse; and *that*, I am sure must or *ought* to give you greater uneasiness, than my going in an honorable command, for upon no other terms I will accept of it."

Here, unconsciously perhaps, he stressed the maxim, "They that are in dignity or in office have in all places preceedency; . . ." for he had previously had occasion to combat and determine a question of precedence, due to the dignity of his rank.

Under no circumstances, however pressing his public duties, was George Washington unmindful of his mother's comfort and interests. She looked to him, her eldest son, for such counsel as she might require in the conduct of her affairs. She wrote to him during the American Revolution of the knavery of one of her overseers and requested him to see to the plantation that was being mismanaged. From his military headquarters he wrote promptly to a younger brother, asking him to look into the matter and reminding him to inquire into his mother's real wants to see that she had everything to make her comfortable.

After the war was over and he was again domiciled at Mount Vernon, he wrote direct to his mother: "I take the (first safe) conveyance by Mr. John Dandridge to send you 15 guineas." And then, with almost childlike confidence and longing for understanding, he opens his heart to her in a manner in which it would have been perhaps impossible for him to confide in any other human being. He tells her of the pressing demands upon him, that for the past two years he has made no crops, and those who owe him money can not or will not pay it without suits, and of the constant drain upon him. He assures her, however, "I do not mean by this declaration to withhold any aid or support I can give from you; for whilst I have a shilling left you shall have part, if it is wanted, whatever my own distress may be." He painstakingly explains:

"My expences, not from any extravagance, or an inclination on my part to live splendidly, but for the absolute support of my family and the visitors who are constantly here, are exceedingly high; higher indeed than I can support without selling part of my estate, which I am disposed to do, rather than run in debt, or continue to be so; but this I cannot do, without taking much less than the lands I have offered for sale are worth. This is really and truely my situation."

He then urges his mother to break up housekeeping and live with one of her children, that she may be relieved of the burden of keeping up a separate household. He speaks of his brother John and mentions that "it was determined he should endeavor to get you to live with him. He, alas, is no more, and three, only of us remain." While he assures her that "My house is at your service," he feels it incumbent upon him to add—

"And would press you most sincerely and most devoutly to accept it but I am sure, and candor requires me to say it, will never answer your purpose in any shape whatsoever. For in truth it may be compared to a well resorted tavern, as scarcely any strangers who are going from north to south, or from south to north, do not spend a day or two at it. This would, were you to be an inhabitant of it, oblige

you to do one of 3 things: 1st, to be always dressed to appear in company, 2d, to come into [the room] in a dishabille, or 3d, to be as it were a prisoner in your own chamber. The first you'ld not like; indeed for a person at your time of life it would be too fatiguing. The 2d, I should not like, because those who resort here are, as I observed before, strangers and people of the first distinction. And the 3d, more than probably, would not be pleasing to either of us. Nor indeed could you be retired in any room in my house; . . . you would not be able to enjoy that calmness and serenity of mind, which in my opinion you ought now to prefer to every other consideration in life."

Some have read into it a supposition that the mother of George Washington was not a woman who could adapt herself to the entertaining of a cultured home. It must be remembered that Mary Washington had then (in 1787) reached the advanced age of almost fourscore years; and it was therefore most logical and considerate of her son to shield her from the experiences that she must have faced in such "a well resorted tavern" as Mount Vernon had come to be.

That both she and he were pressed for ready funds following the War for Independence was not surprising, for George Washington and his family had sacrificed much, financially and otherwise, in the service of a well-loved country.

One of the most pleasant of the many traditions about Mary Ball Washington is that of the reception or "ball" at Fredericksburg after the surrender of Cornwallis, when her illustrious son presented to his mother the officers who were accompanying him northward. Unfortunately, the story seems based only on reminiscences at second or third hand. It is an excellent example of such accounts, the reliability of which is questionable. There was great rejoicing over the surrender of Cornwallis. George Washington was the hero of the hour, but his first duty on arriving was to his mother. The meeting between them was characteristic of their temperaments, so much alike. They were not given to many words or to dramatics. The scene as described, from family hearsay, by the General's stepgrandson, depicts the venerable mother bidding welcome to her hero son by a warm embrace, with an anxious inquiry as to his health. It is recorded that she spoke to him of old times and old friends, "but of his glory not one word." And this was as the General would have it, for he had a proverbial dislike of spoken praise, while the Spartan mother held to an invariable rule that praise of one's offspring was in bad taste.

The scene at the hall, when Mary Washington arrived on the arm of her son, has been minutely described, in flowery language:

"The superb son . . . led her into the room with the respectful courtesy due a queen. A path was opened from the foot to the top of the hall as they appeared in the doorway, and 'every head was bowed in reverence.' It must have been the proudest moment of her life, but she bore herself with perfect composure then, and after her son, seating her in an armchair upon the dais reserved for distinguished guests, faced the crowd in prideful expectancy that all his friends would seek to know his mother. She had entered the hall at eight o'clock, and for two hours held court, the most distinguished people there pressing eagerly forward to be presented to her. She received them with placid dignity, as little excited, to all appearances, as when entertaining her Fredericksburg neighbors. . . . From her slightly elevated position she could, without rising, overlook the floor, and watched with quiet pleasure the dancers, among them the kingly figure of the Commander in Chief. . . . At 10 o'clock she signed to him to approach, and rose to take his arm, saying in her clear, soft voice: 'Come, George, it is time for old folk to be at home!'

"Smiling a good night to all, she walked down the room, as erect in form and as stately in gait as any dancer there.

"One of the French officers . . . exclaimed aloud, as she disappeared: 'If such are the matrons of America, she may well boast of her illustrious sons!'"

Another touching scene, "Washington's Farewell to his Mother," has been ably depicted by pen and by brush as well. The painting by Ferris shows the General on his knees beside his mother's chair. It was on the eve of his departure for his inauguration as President of the United States of America. The pen picture follows:

"He must leave for New York on the morrow. He had galloped up from Mount Vernon to snatch an hour with the woman he revered in weakness and old age as when her will had overruled the boy's plans of a career. He found her in 'the chamber,' alert in mind and serene of spirit, but so altered in appearance that his heart misgave him. Concealing his dreads, he began to speak cheerfully of his intention, as soon as public business could be disposed of, to return to Virginia and see her again. She stayed him there with steady voice and feeble hand. This would be their last meeting in this life, she said. She was old, . . . she would not be long for this world. She trusted in God that she was somewhat prepared for a better. Then, laying the wasted hand upon the head bowed to her shoulder, she told him that Heaven's and his mother's blessing would always be with him. . . . As he stooped for a parting embrace, she felt him slip a purse into her hand. She put it back, raising her head with the old-time pride.

'I don't need it!' she said, . . . 'My wants are few' . . . Time passed, but he lingered to plead tenderly, 'Whether you think you need it or not,—for *my* sake, mother!'"

His loving care was shown in many ways. Some time before the war, at her request, he bought for her the house she selected in Fredericksburg, near Millbrook, now called Kenmore, the home of her daughter, Betty Lewis, to which she moved from her farm. Washington also took over the farm at an unprofitable rentage.

It was to this only sister that George Washington wrote quite fully upon receiving word of his mother's death. His own state of health and the impassable roads made it impossible for them to summon him, and the funeral was over before the sad news reached him. He wrote, in part:

"Awful and affecting as the death of a parent is, there is consolation in knowing, that heaven has spared ours to an age beyond which few attain, and favored her with the full enjoyment of her mental faculties, and as much bodily strength as usually falls to the lot of fourscore. Under these considerations, and the hope that she is translated to a happier place, it is the duty of her relatives to yield due submission to the decrees of the Creator."

While writing this letter his thoughts must have turned backward to review all that his mother had meant to him, all that he owed to her whose "maternal hand" had, as he himself stated, led him to manhood; whose rules and maxims had meant so much to him. They helped to guide him throughout his life, and they, together with the principles set forth in the Rules of Conduct that he copied in his exercise books at school, were in a considerable part responsible for his well-known grace and courtesy of bearing and of his consideration for others. Of the oft-quoted Rules of Conduct an early biographer has said:

"In studying the character of Washington it is obvious that this code of rules had an influence upon his whole life. His temperament was ardent, his passions strong, and, amidst the multiplied scenes of temptation and excitement through which he passed, it was his constant effort to check the one and subdue the other. His intercourse with men, public and private, in every walk and station, was marked with a consistency, a fitness to occasions, a dignity, decorum, condescension and mildness, a respect for the claim of others, and a delicate perception of the nicer shades of civility, which were not more the dictates of his native good sense and incomparable judgment than the fruits of long and unwearied discipline."

These rules merely supplemented the influence of his mother, as shown by George Washington in his appreciative phrase and filial conduct.

GEORGE WASHINGTON THE COUNTRY SQUIRE

In a new country, with the problems of the frontier to face and with many responsibilities upon his young shoulders, George Washington, at the age of 20, emerged from a well-developed youth into a country squire. At the death of his father, when he was but 11 years old, he had inherited the family's residential farm on the Rappahannock River across from Fredericksburg, Va., which was subject to his mother's control until he became 21. Nine years later, before he became of legal age, he was serving as executor of the Mount Vernon estate, which he was soon to inherit, as his late brother's infant daughter survived him for a few months only. A life interest in this estate, however, went to his brother's widow, so that the young squire did not come into full ownership until some years later. Perhaps it was because there were others depending upon both the estates bequeathed to him that George Washington did not earlier select a life companion; or possibly for this very reason he was not looked upon with especial favor as a suitor either by the parents or by the young ladies of the community. Or perhaps it was his natural reserve and his diffidence in personally pressing his suit that permitted others to outstrip him in winning the favor of the fair ones to whom he may have been drawn by the sentiment of youth.

It is a well-known fact that George Washington was really shy and that throughout his entire lifetime he found it much easier to put his thoughts and sentiments on paper than to express them orally. This may account for his committing to paper several youthful "affairs of the heart" rather than attempting an ardent courtship. Or it may be what is considered the love affairs of his youth were merely an awakening of the muse of poetry within his soul and demanding an expression. At any rate, in numbers there is safety, and it is quite conceivable that the several objects of his poetic effusions meant less to him than did the urge for self-expression.

A frequently quoted letter from George Washington to a boyhod friend which has been taken quite seriously, as a rule, might be readily construed as presiflage. In it he refers to "a very agreeable young lady" with whom he might pass the time very agreeably "was my heart disengaged," and rambles on about a "Low Land Beauty" and "burying that chast and troublesome Passion in the grave of oblivion," mentioning also "a second assault from a different quarter."

Some years later young George Washington addressed a letter to William Fauntleroy expressing his desire to "wait on Miss Betsy in hopes of a revocation of the former cruel sentence." This indicates a real desire on his part to win that young lady, who evidently did not respond.

Seekers after romance have woven a plausible story of unrequited love out of the brief acquaintance of George Washington with Mary Philipse, whom he met in New York while en route to and from Boston, in 1756. Had this really been the case he would surely have endeavored to carry the acquaintance further, as he did not easily relinquish anything he desired to attain or readily accept defeat.

Much ado has also been made over the few poems penned by George Washington which are still extant, but they are such as any young man might write at a time when youth is emerging into manhood and experiencing a new realization and rhythm in life itself.

An unfinished poem in acrostic form, which was apparently an exercise, trailed off beyond the bounds of imagination. This would hardly have been the case had the author really been inspired by love. Possibly it was the letter "X" in "A-L-E-X-A" that broke the rythm, for after floundering over—

"Xerxes the Great, wasn't free from Cupid's dart,
And all the greatest Heroes felt the smart"—

the poem abruptly ended, as, no doubt also, did the love affair, if it ever existed.

Bearing out the belief that such a serious-minded man as George Washington would not lightly mention any matter which aroused in him so deep a feeling as real love, we have an extract from one of his letters to the woman with whom his troth was pledged and who shortly was to become his wife. When military duties made it impossible for him to see her, he wrote:

"Since that happy hour when we made our pledges to each other my thoughts have been continually going to you as another self. That an all-powerful Providence may keep us both in safety is the prayer of your ever faithful and affectionate friend."

It was characteristic of him that he did not permit the public to witness his inner feelings. This, too, is borne out by an extract from one of his letters which was written to a very dear friend of his who was also apparently a friend of his bride to be. He tells her: "The world has no business to know the object of my Love," which, to the logical mind, clearly means that he was speaking of the woman to whom he was soon engaged, and not addressing a veiled declaration to the lady to whom the lines were written, as some authors have indicated.

Certainly George Washington was not a laggard in love after having once met and admired the charming widow Custis. With the same promptness with which he followed up all important matters throughout his entire life, he stormed the citadel and won an almost immediate surrender.

Both Martha Dandridge Custis and George Washington were to be congratulated upon the outcome of their whirlwind courtship, which was consummated by the plighting of their troth on an early visit to her home in Kent County after their chance meeting at the mansion of a mutual friend.

Circumstances which necessitated his absence on military duty for many months delayed the wedding but did not prevent him, meanwhile, from refitting his bachelor home at Mount Vernon and having it in readiness to receive his bride, where he welcomed her the following year, and where "they lived happily ever after," save when his presence was required elsewhere by the repeated demands upon him to render patriotic and public service for his country.

GEORGE WASHINGTON THE HUSBAND

From the pen of a society reporter of the eighteenth century comes a picturesque description of the wedding of Col. George Washington and Martha Dandridge Custis, which establishes it as a very "smart" affair:

"They came in bridal state, coach-and-four and the train of wedding guests. . . . The bride was attired in heavy brocade silk, interwoven with silver thread; embroidered satin petticoat, high-heeled satin shoes, with buckles of brilliants, point lace and ruffles. Her ornaments were a pearl necklace, earrings and a bracelet. The bridegroom appeared in a citizen's dress of blue cloth, . . . his shoe and knee buckles were of gold. His hair was powdered and at his side hung a dress sword."

Other writers mention that his coat was blue and silver, trimmed with scarlet. His stepgrandson, George Washington Parke Custis, writes:

"Much hath the biographer heard of that marriage, . . . and rare and high was the revelry, at that palmy period of Virginia's festal age; for many were gathered to that marriage, of the good, the great, the gifted and the gay, while Virginia, with joyous acclamation hailed in her youthful hero a prosperous and a happy bridegroom."

Whether the wedding was solemnized in St. Peter's Church at New Kent, or in the home of the bride, known as the White House, in New Kent County, is a matter impossible to determine, but it is definitely known that the bride's home was the scene of the wedding reception and the honeymoon.

The bride and the bridegroom were described as a well-matched pair, both "dowered with those fine but somewhat elusive attributes which make marriage a success." Both were generously endowed with this world's goods, for the young colonel had the holdings which he inherited, and the widow Custis had come into possession of a goodly fortune from her late husband in the form of houses and lands, negro slaves, and pounds sterling. They were of the same social sphere and favorites in the exclusive society of that period.

From the White House in New Kent County the bride and groom repaired to another home of the bride, "The House of the Six Chimneys," in Williamsburg, where they resided during the assembly of the House of Burgesses, to which George Washington had been recently elected.

When the session of the assembly closed he took his wife and her two children to his home at Mount Vernon, which had been especially enlarged and refitted to receive them. There they settled down to the enjoyment of domestic life and the peaceful pursuits which were most acceptable to the young colonel after having experienced the hardships of his early military career.

To a friend he wrote: "I am now, I believe, fixed in this seat, with an agreeable partner for life and I hope to find more happiness in retirement than I ever experienced in the wide and bustling world."

Though so frequently called from his retirement to render public service, there is every evidence to show that he had truly found "an agreeable partner for life," a woman of straightforward character, charming and sympathetic, yet quite as practical and capable as her sedate husband could wish.

His unbounded affection for her, for her children and, later, for her grandchildren is evidenced by the care and courteous consideration which he invariably found time to give them, no matter how overburdened he might be with the responsibilities of warfare or the affairs of state.

It was ever the desire of the husband and wife to be together and to surround themselves with the atmosphere of home wherever duty led them. Many a long journey did she make, under escort which he provided for her, that she might join him in Army headquarters or elsewhere when circumstances demanded his absence from Mount Vernon. On shorter journeys she traveled with him, en route to attend the meetings of the House of Burgesses at Williamsburg, where they maintained a home for use on those occasions. Even the few miles between Mount Vernon and Alexandria did not separate them from each other and from the atmosphere of home life, for he erected a small town house there for occupancy when business or social engagements kept them in town from one day to another.

His stepchildren and stepgrandchildren he considered as his very own, and scarce could a real parent have bestowed upon his own offspring a greater affection and more prudent guidance than George Washington gave to the two generations of Custis children who were reared by him. So attached was he to young Martha, or "Patsey," Custis that when she died at 16 he wrote of the "Sweet Innocent Girl Entered into a more happy and peaceful abode than any she had met with in the afflicted Path she hitherto has trod."

The bonds of affection that existed between George and Martha Washington were tightened by their mutual grief over the death of this beloved child. For a long period he remained beside his wife at Mount Vernon to console her and help alleviate her sorrow, setting aside important engagements rather than leave her to bear the bereavement alone. In this same letter Washington added: "This sudden, and unexpected blow, I scarce need add has almost reduced my poor Wife to the lowest ebb of Misery; which is encreas'd by the absence of her son, . . . and want of the balmy consolation of her Relations; . . ."

For his stepson, Jack Custis, George Washington also evinced a great fondness, but this did not prevent him, when necessary, from exercising a wholesome restraint when the somewhat wayward boy neglected his studies to engage in fox hunting and other amusements at Mount Vernon, and when, as a mere youth, he became engaged to Eleanor Calvert, of Mount Airy, Md. The views of his stepfather are frankly expressed in a letter to the father of the young lady in which he stated "an alliance with your family will be pleasing to his," but mentions the boy's youth, inexperience, and unripened education as insuperable obstacles, and adds: "As his guardian, I conceive it my indispensable duty to endeavor to carry

him through a regular course of education . . . and to guard his youth to a more advanced age before an event, on which his own peace and the happiness of another are to depend, takes place."

It was mutually agreed that the youth was to pass two years at college before the marriage should take place, but "love and learning did not move in harmony," and after a few months in King's College (now Columbia University), New York City, the young couple took matters into their own hands and were married when the bridegroom was nineteen and the bride "sweet sixteen."

The four children of this union were cherished by the stepgrandfather as their father and his deceased sister had been before them. The two younger he took into his home and reared them from infancy, following the untimely death of their father, Jack Custis, from camp fever, with which he was stricken during the siege of Yorktown, where he had served the General as aide-de-camp. As the story goes, when informed by the physician that all was over, "the Chief bowed his head and gave vent to his deep sorrow, then, turning to the weeping mother, he said, 'I adopt the two younger children as my own.'"

Touching evidence of the affection between George and Martha Washington is

shown in a reference to her way of attracting his attention when he was deep in thought or especially occupied. At no time did she hesitate to approach him, firmly grasp a button of his coat, look up into his face and state the purpose which impelled her to seek his opinion or advice. When thus brought to a realization of her immediate presence and her need of his counsel, he would promptly put aside whatever occupied him and, smiling down into her upturned face, give his undivided attention to her problem or project.

Never did this very considerate head of the family permit the most important position which a public man could hold to alienate his thoughts from the private affairs that concerned the comfort and happiness of his loved ones. While he was President of the United States he personally attended to the removal of his family from the first Presidential Mansion to a more commodious one, thus relieving the First Lady of the Land from every exertion.

At times when she was ill or indisposed he arranged his affairs to make it possible for him to be near her. Thus in his every action did he express his devotion to the "agreeable partner for life" with whom he journeyed through four decades of his notable career.

(FOR THIS PROGRAM SEE NUMBERS 23, 71, 78, 81, 103 IN LIST OF SELECTED BOOKS ON PAGES 300-A AND 300-B)

GEORGE WASHINGTON'S FIRST MEETING WITH MARTHA CUSTIS

George Washington the Man of Action in Military and Civil Life

WASHINGTON AS A SOLDIER
From a portrait by Rembrandt Peale

GEORGE WASHINGTON THE SURVEYOR

IT IS DOUBTFUL if George Washington could have chosen any career that would have provided him with a finer training for the course he was destined to follow than that of a surveyor. A study of this early experience leaves the conviction that every part of his life was a very definite preparation for that which was to follow. Yet to neither his parents, half brothers, nor the boy himself was surveying the first choice of a vocation.

When the untimely death of Augustine Washington placed an English education for George beyond the restricted family finances, it was decided to send him to school to the best teacher available. The consensus of family opinion selected Henry Williams, in the vicinity of the old home at Bridges Creek (Wakefield); so George went to live at the home where he had been born 11 years pre-viously, now occupied by his half brother Augustine.

Through his affectionate relations with both his half brothers, 14 and 12 years his senior, George Washington learned much and benefited greatly. Both men were edu-cated, traveled, cultured, of high esteem in the affairs of Virginia. Both had charming wives from wealthy families, and each home was a center of a delightful circle of the most interesting people of the colony. At Augustine's, with a library and a stable of 30 horses, young companions among neigh-bors who knew him since birth, George was very happy. Under Mr. Williams his natural aptitude for figures was developed, until he excelled in mathematics and also made a beginning in practical surveying.

He visited his mother from time to time at the Rappahannock River home, perhaps going to school in Fredericksburg from there,

with his sister Betty, when their instructor was the Reverend Marye, first rector of St. George's Church, of Hugenot descent, from whom it is supposed that George received the original set of the Rules of Civility and Decent Behavior which he copied so pains-takingly in his copybook at the age of 13 and which are said to have influenced his life materially. A number of these rules were drawn from translation of a foreign publication.

He liked best of all to stay at Mount Vernon with Lawrence, who had married Anne Fairfax. To the serious-minded, am-bitious lad, Lawrence's experiences in the Cartagena campaign in the West Indies under General Wentworth, and with the fleet under Admiral Vernon, must have been subjects of unabating interest. Then, too, the Lawrence Washingtons were hospitable, socially popular, and the frequent gay com-pany, with the visits from Lawrence's for-mer comrades in arms, or visitors from some naval or merchant ship that happened to anchor in the Potomac, all tended to create an atmosphere of absorbing delight to a lad longing for adventure and eager to follow his brother's military example.

Washington Irving recounts that when George was 14, Lawrence, and his father-in-law, William Fairfax, who had also been a soldier, noting the boy's keen desire for mili-tary experience or adventure, secured for him a warrant as a midshipman in the Navy. His mother's reluctant consent was with-drawn when the hour of departure came. Between her first consent and the completion of the plans, she had received a letter from her brother Joseph, in England, in which he advised her against letting her boy go to sea. This is the only surviving document on the matter, and it does not confirm the tradition further than as to a plan to send George to sea. The letter, dated May 19, 1747, says:

"I understand that you are advised and have some thoughts of putting your son George to sea. I think he had better be put a prentice to a tinker, for a common sailor before the mast has by no means the common liberty of the subject; for they will press him from a ship where he has 50 shillings a month and make him take 23, and cut, and slash, and use him like a negro, or rather like a dog. And, as to any considerable preferment in the navy, it is not to be expected, as there are always so many gaping for it here who have interest, and he has none. And if he should get to be master of a Virginia ship (which it is very difficult to do), a planter that has three or four hundred acres of land and three or four slaves, if he be industrious, may live more comfortably, and leave his family in better bread, than such a master of a ship can."

Her decision made it impossible for George to seek success either as a sailor or midshipman or to seek his fortune as a prosperous merchantman. He returned to school, devoting his energies with marked concentration to mathematics and surveying. Irving says "he schooled himself in the branches to fit him either for civil or military service." He made surveys about the neighborhood, and kept regular field books in which the boundaries and measurements were carefully entered and diagrams made with a neatness and exactness as if the whole were actual records of land transactions instead of school exercises.

When it was decided in family conference that he should become a surveyor, it is said that his mother at first felt this was not suitable employment for a gentleman's son, but her objections were overcome by the great demand for surveyors in the new land under colonization in so many sections. George took up his chain and other surveying implements and followed Mr. Genn in his work as county surveyor. He made his first surveys around the age of 14, as is proved by the fact that at Cornell University there is a manuscript volume of his "Book of Surveys 1746," while the Library of Congress "Copy Book 1745" contains, with other mathematical data, definitions and simple exercises in the "Art of Measuring Land." In his own journal at 15, it is recorded that he bought a "gunter"—a Gunter's chain being used in land measurement. He also made a "Plan of Major Law. Washington's Turnip Field as Surveyed by me This 27 Day of February 1747/8 G W." He acquired all his schooling before he was 16 and had a very thorough and complete knowledge of mathematics.

Among the many notable friends of Lawrence Washington that young George met in his brother's home at Mount Vernon was Lord Fairfax, who came to America first in 1743 to look over the vast dominion of land in the Northern Neck, which he had inherited through his mother from her father, Lord Culpeper, which embraced over 5,000,-000 acres of land between the Potomac and Rappahannock Rivers, extending from Chesapeake Bay to the headwaters of the Potomac.

For several years Lord Fairfax lived with his cousin, William Fairfax, at Belvoir, the estate adjoining Mount Vernon, while his own mansion in the Shenandoah Valley was under construction. This mansion was never finished. Lord Fairfax constructed his hunting lodge, Greenway Court, on such a spacious scale and furnished it so elegantly as to be content with it for his home during the remainder of his life. William had acted as agent in care of his estate. Lawrence Washington had married Anne Fairfax, daughter of the master of Belvoir, and established close social relations between the two neighboring plantations. This was of particular pleasure and advantage to young George, whose dignity and courtesy won for him the regard of older people. Lord Fairfax was attracted to the shy lad who was such a fearless and expert horseman and who possessed the poise of courage and efficiency, and whose gallant deferential manners were so winning.

The result was that between these two kindred spirits, though so far apart in age, a strong friendship was formed which lasted through life; and whenever possible young George Washington was the hunting companion of the English nobleman, who became one of the strongest influences in the life of the future Father of His Country. Through the visits at Greenway Court, where he was urged to make use of the rather unusual library, his taste for good literature was developed. There from the books, periodicals, and newspapers of the day he also learned much of English thoroughness in farming and agriculture that was useful to him later on.

Lord Fairfax was so favorably impressed with the young man's surveying knowledge that he appointed him to aid in the surveys of his extensive holdings beyond the Blue Ridge. The first expedition started out in the spring of 1748. The party included James Genn, the licensed surveyor of Prince William County, a man of great experience in wilderness surveying, and George William Fairfax, son of William Fairfax, who was about seven years the senior of George Washington. He had already put in two seasons in surveying the Fairfax lands.

The entries in George Washington's diary tell of the events of the trip and his varied experiences during the first five weeks of the job of surveying in a most interesting manner, as follows:

"Fryday March 11th 1747/8. Began my Journey in Company with George Fairfax, Esqr., we travell'd this day 40 Miles to Mr. George Neavels in Prince William County.

"Saturday March 12th This Morning Mr. James Genn ye. surveyor came to us we travell'd over ye. Blue Ridge to Capt. Ashbys on Shannondoah River, Nothing remarkable happen'd

"Sunday March 13 Rode to his Lordships Quarter about 4 Miles higher up y. River we went through most beautiful Groves of Sugar Trees and spent ye. best part of y. Day in admiring ye. Trees and richness of ye Land

"Monday 14th We sent our Baggage to Capt. Hites (near Frederick Town) went ourselves down ye River about 16 Miles to Capt. Isaac Penningtons (the Land exceeding Rich and Fertile all ye. way produces abundance of Grain Hemp Tobacco &ca.) in order to lay of some Lands on Cates Marsh and Long Marsh

"Tuesday 15th We set out early with Intent to Run round ye sd. Land but being taken in a Rain and it Increasing very fast obliged us to return and it clearing about one oClock and our time being too Precious to Loose we a second time ventur'd out and Worked hard till Night and then return'd to Penningtons we got our Supper and was lighted into a Room and I not being so good a Woodsman as ye rest of my Company striped myself very orderly and went in to ye Bed as they called it when to my Surprize I found it to be nothing but a Little Straw-Matted together without Sheets or anything else but only one thread Bear blanket with double its Weight of Vermin such as Lice Fleas &c I was glad to get up (as soon as y. Light was carried from us) I put on my Cloths and Lay as my Companions. Had we not been very tired I am sure we should not have slep'd much that night I made a Promise not to Sleep so from that time forward chusing rather to sleep in y. open Air before a fire as will appear hereafter. . . .

"Wednesday 16th We set out early and finish'd about one oClock and then Travell'd up to Frederick Town where our Baggage came to us we cleaned ourselves (to get Rid of y. Game we had catched y. Night before) and took a Review of y. Town and thence return'd to our Lodgings where we had a good Dinner prepar'd for us. . . . and a good Feather Bed with clean Sheets which was a very agreeable regale . . .

"Wednesday 23d Rain'd till about two oClock and Clear'd when we were agreeably surpris'd at y. sight of thirty odd Indians coming from War with only one Scalp . . . of whom we had a War Daunce there manner of Dauncing is as follows Viz They clear a Large Circle and make a Great Fire in y. middle then seats themselves around it y. Speaker makes a grand speech telling them in what Manner they are to Daunce after he has finished y. best Dauncer jumps up as one awaked out of a Sleep and runs and Jumps about y. Ring in a most comical Manner he is followed by y. Rest then begins their Musicians to Play ye. Musick is a Pot half [full] of Water with a Deerskin Stretched over it as tight as it can and a goard with some Shott in it to Rattle and a Piece of an horses Tail tied to it to make it look fine y. one keeps Rattling and y. other Drumming all y. while y. others is Dauncing . . .

"Saterday [April] 2d Last Night was a blowing and Rainy night Our Straw catch'd a Fire yt. we were laying upon and was luckily Preserv'd by one of our Mens awaking when it was in a [blaze] we run of four Lots this Day which Reached below Stumps. . . .

"Monday 4th this morning Mr. Fairfax left us with Intent to go down to ye. Mouth of ye Branch we did two Lots and was attended by a great Company of People Men Women and Children that attended us through ye. Woods as we went showing there Anticks tricks I really think they seemed to be as Ignorant a Set of People as the Indians they would never speak English but when spoken to they speak all Dutch this day our Tent was blown down by ye. Violentness of ye. Wind"

The first expedition covered about five weeks, as is noted by the final entry: "Wednesday ye. 13th of April 1748 Mr. Fairfax got safe home and I myself safe to my Brothers which concludes my Journal."

Difficult, dangerous, and beset with adventures to try the spirit of a seasoned wilderness pioneer, this was a period of pleasure and satisfaction to George Washington. The knowledge he gained in the work gave him unusual advantages in his later land purchases. The dangers met his love of adventure and the hardships and privations but hardened his frame and sharpened his perception for greater difficulties to come.

Like any lad earning his first salary, this first pay was very important. In a letter to a friend he said, "A doubloon is my constant gain every day that the weather will permit my going out, and sometimes six pistoles." Seven dollars per day and some days over 20 was not a poor remuneration for his day, although it has been said that the hardships and dangers combated in surveying a virgin forest wilderness of swamps, rivers, and mountains were comparable to a journey in our day to the heart of Africa, the ice wastes of Alaska, or the uncertainties of the Arctic.

George Washington's painstaking work—his carefully prepared surveys—brought him his induction into his first public office in Culpeper, Virginia, as is shown by the record in the county court for July 20, 1749:

"George Washington, Gentleman, produced a commission from the President and Master of William and Mary College appointing him to be surveyor of this County, which was read, and thereupon he took the usual oaths to His Majesty's person and government, and took and subscribed to the adjuration oath and test, and then took the oath of surveyor."

By this oath taking he became a servant of the Government, an officer of the colony, before he was 21 years of age. His salary as a county surveyor was about 50 pounds per year.

Through its charter the College of William and Mary possessed the office of surveyor general of Virginia. The privileges of this office included the appointment of county surveyors and had as a perquisite one-sixth of all fees received by county surveyors in laying off new grants. A county surveyor was appointed by the faculty of the college usually after some preliminary examination to see that the applicant was equipped in a practical way to do the work.

Following the receipt of his commission he became busily occupied with laying off more tracts in the Shenandoah Valley and elsewhere.

Along with all of this activity came another commission from Williamsburg. This second one made him district adjutant of militia, and with it his work as a military engineer began to unfold. Because of the constant disputes with the French over the frontier, all campaigns required considerable engineering in the building of roads through the forests and fields, and the construction of bridges, forts, and fortifications.

His surveying for the county was interrupted when he was ordered to the frontier in 1754, and the road which his advance guard hacked and hewed from the underbrush west of Cumberland is still called Washington's road. Once again his surveying knowledge and engineering abilities were called into use at Great Meadows, where he built his first fort, calling it in a moment of grim humor Fort Necessity.

He kept a little one-story shop or workroom on the home farm on the Rappahannock for his maps and implements. It is said to be the only structure standing today positively known to have been used by him as a youth. He had another small building on the grounds of Greenway Court built just for his use and convenience in handling the surveys of the Fairfax estates and later a building in Winchester, Virginia, where he placed his surveys and drawings for safekeeping and ready reference.

Some idea of the confidence reposed in this youth is shown by the fact that two years after the building of Fort Necessity the Virginia Assembly voted an appropriation of $20,000 to construct and equip a chain of frontier forts covering a distance of about 400 miles. Twenty-three forts were planned—one to about every 18 miles. Upon the shoulders of the 24-year-old engineer and surveyor as commander of the Virginia forces guarding the frontier rested the responsibility of securing the necessary tools, materials, and workmen, as well as the selecting of locations and the making of the plans for the forts.

In the Library of Congress may be found a few of these drawings, in all seven sketches with explanatory notes, rough plans of Fort Loudoun, Winchester, and Fort Cumberland, or Wills Creek. Because of its position commanding the Shenandoah Valley, he made Winchester his preferred headquarters, though the authorities required him to change them to Fort Cumberland for a while.

Throughout his work as a public surveyor George Washington was efficient and methodical. His Book of Surveys shows his extreme care and considerable skill. It represents many surveys still existing and unquestioned by the expert surveyors and title searchers of the present day. From the time he was placed in command of the forces in Virginia the necessities of the hour dominated the situation, and George Washington

had to be military leader as well as surveyor, engineer, and architect in order to achieve the needed results. Tradition claims that to hasten the construction of Fort Loudoun he brought his own blacksmith from Mount Vernon, placed him in a shop on a lot of his own in the vicinity to get out the iron-work required. The last fort on which he did construction work was that of Fort Duquesne, located on the site now occupied by Pittsburgh, which had been partially destroyed when the French abandoned it.

It was also due to his own surveying and engineering knowledge that he managed to impress upon the Continental Congress during the War of the Revolution the great disadvantage under which the Army labored through lack of accurate maps. He had "to make shift" with such sketches as he could trace out from observation and finally secured the appointment of Robert Erskine as the first geographer of the Army.

In promoting and encouraging activities such as the founding of development companies, the Dismal Swamp Company, the Potomac Company, and the James River Improvement, his experience as a surveyor was of great usefulness. With L'Enfant and the commissioners he went over the plans, surveys, and grounds of the Federal City, placing streets and avenues and locating the sites of public buildings, determining boundary lines of a city beautiful that should last until the end of time and serve the Nation adequately as the seat of government.

In his plea for ample territory for the site of the Federal City he said:

"Will they not recollect my observation that Philadelphia stood upon an area of three by two miles, and that if the metropolis of one State occupied so much ground, what ought that of the United States to occupy?"

In his home at Mount Vernon his grounds, farm, and gardens were all surveyed by himself and all improvements and changes made with a careful attention to every detail.

The homes of his brothers, like beautiful Milbrook, the home of his sister, Betty Washington Lewis (now called Kenmore, but for the forty-five years it belonged to the Lewises its name was Milbrook), had the benefit of his surveying skill in the placement of their houses and buildings.

Although he was engaged in surveying exclusively for but five years—1747-1751—all through life he found the knowledge of this profession useful in measuring and plotting his own property. His diary has records of surveying work done by him on his own lands a number of times during the last year of his life. In April, 1799, in spite of a bitter cold and a high wind, he spent three days surveying his land at Four Mile Run, near Arlington. In June, in the midst of summer heat, he surveyed three fields on his Dogue Run Farm because a former survey did not satisfy him; and as close to his death as the end of November, 1799, he made a survey of his lands on Difficult Run, south of the Potomac Falls. On this expedition he took his own notes and transcribed them with the same care that he gave to this work in the days when trudging over the mountains on the Fairfax estate.

GEORGE WASHINGTON THE SOLDIER THROUGH FRENCH AND INDIAN WAR

George Washington's military career presents the most outstanding illustrations of a characteristic peculiarly his own, that he did not mark time in any of the important positions of his life. His passion for education caused him to concentrate upon hard study, to acquire the necessary knowledge to excel, whether it was surveying, farming, building forts, shipping produce, or leading armies.

One of the many legends woven around the life of George Washington claims that his father discovered the child's military bent when he was quite a small boy and gave him a toy sword which delighted him greatly. While there is no more documentary evidence to prove the truth of this story than there is of the original cherry tree tale and the highly-colored romances attributed to his young manhood, it is definitely shown that he inherited the military tendency of the Washingtons and that this received decided impetus by the military atmosphere created through the activities prevailing in the colony of Virginia in the raising of the troops to be sent to the West Indies to combat the Spaniards.

Lawrence Washington, the elder of George's two half brothers, 14 years his senior, had offered his services and had been commissioned captain in the contingent that sailed in 1740 to join the combined expeditions of Admiral Vernon and General Wentworth. Little 8-year-old George may well have experienced all of a small boy's thrilling excitement and admiration over watching the drilling and preparations for departure of Lawrence and his comrades for the scene of war.

The love of military affairs did not abate and pass as most boyish enthusiasms do, but developed into a fixed interest which was strengthened when the loved elder brother returned two years later and continued his own military associations by becoming adjutant of his own district in Virginia with the rank of major.

Having inherited the plantation on the Potomac which he renamed Mount Vernon and taken to himself Miss Anne Fairfax as wife, Lawrence Washington drew about him an exclusive circle of the best people of the colony, and retained his interest in both military and naval matters. Association with these men of society and affairs was of the greatest benefit and advantage to young George during the impressionable period of his life and enhanced and encouraged what was probably a natural military predilection.

The determination of both France and England to secure and hold the supremacy of the Mississippi Valley, and the growing indications of an impending contest between them, brought about a revival of the military spirit in the colony of Virginia, and through it came active preparations for any part she might be called upon to take in consequence. This matter vitally interested Lawrence Washington, who was associated with the Ohio Company recently organized to develop the region over the mountains, and while there is a lack of record on the fact, it seems evident that, with the aid of former army companions, such as Van Braam and George Muse, he had his young brother not only instructed in fencing but also in the elements of military science. From the beginning of George Washington's writings upon his military experiences there are evidences of great natural ability and also of training. Hence, when in 1752 Governor Dinwiddie appointed him a district adjutant of militia, with the rank of major, there was probably in it a recognition that, in spite of youth, Washington possessed the requirements for the task.

To this military training he undoubtedly gave the same concentrated study that distinguished his school life and the study of surveying. He seemed to have been possessed of a passion to acquire all available knowledge on matters of paramount interest to him. His exercise books before he was 16, which have been preserved, show an unusual grasp of mathematics. Regarding his knowledge of this science as manifested in these books, Charles Moore wrote:

"The one devoted to Mathematics exhibits a wide range of subjects combined with sureness and accuracy in working and clearness and neatness of presentation. Few graduates of colleges today, unless they specialize in mathematics, become as well trained in that subject."

When it became necessary to take some action in regard to what was considered French encroachments upon English territory on the Ohio, Governor Dinwiddie followed the example of Lord Fairfax and selected Major Washington for the job. This was the second instance of the effect of George Washington's personality upon older people. The impression of efficiency, dependability, and high courage, which from boyhood had radiated from him, made an extraordinary impression upon those with whom he came in contact. The quality never left him, and it has never been disputed. It carried with it an unspoken assurance that he was fitted by some remarkable combination of talents for tasks he was willing to undertake, and that he would carry them through to successful completion if that were possible. While in others of his extreme youth the years may have implied limitations in the expectations focused upon his endeavors, this never seemed to be considered in respect to the tasks put upon his shoulders.

This quality was first recognized by Lord Fairfax, who marked by his confidence and comradeship the fitting of a man's tasks to the square young shoulders of a boy without cutting those tasks to a boy's measure. Just as George Washington stepped into a man-sized job as a surveyor, so when he accepted Governor Dinwiddie's mission to the Ohio he stepped not only into a man-sized task but into a path which led, as we now are able to trace it, directly to the American independence, of which he was the chosen instrument.

His training, whether theoretical in military elements or practical in surveying and frontier life, had fitted him for the duty. Through his knowledge of the rugged, hazardous life of the scattered, isolated pioneers beyond the settlements and the extreme hardships and emergencies of dangers to be met and combated in transportation, afoot, on horseback, or by canoe, he was not only grounded in self-reliance and resourcefulness but what was a marvelous advantage for the man destined to lead a nation through eight years of war to victory was that he was wholly fearless. Never was George Washington known to feel or exhibit any fear in any situation. He is credited with saying that fear was absent from his make-up, and he could not tolerate cowardice in others.

By 1753 the situation on the Ohio region had become so serious through the French occupation, and their efforts to attach the Indians to them against the English, that Governor Dinwiddie, under orders from England, prepared a letter for the French commander which he intrusted to Major Washington for delivery, as it was a mission of greatest difficulty and danger, and of utmost importance not only that the letter be gotten to the French commandant but that a full report of the situation, the location of the forts, etc., be brought back. One messenger had already returned, beaten and baffled by the dangers, before making any real headway, and the colonial governor pinned all of his faith to the young officer whose fearlessness, masterfulness, and good judgment had already made for him a place of distinction among his fellows.

Major Washington began his journey on October 31, 1753; and though beset with the greatest difficulties, extreme hardships, and actual endangerment of life, he completed this mission January 16, 1754, when he brought to Governor Dinwiddie the important reply and his own report with a map. This report, which, although hastily written in a few hours from his daily journal, demonstrated George Washington's ability clearly and forcefully to express his thoughts in writing, the governor had printed immediately, and it helped to arouse the Colonies and British Government to the importance and difficulties of the problem.

Pending Washington's report, preparations had already been begun by the Ohio Company to build a fort at the junction of the Allegheny and the Monongahela Rivers, and to complete and defend this a regiment of Virginia volunteers was ordered recruited. Washington was commissioned on March 15, 1754, lieutenant colonel as second in command under Col. Joshua Fry, and ordered to the site of the new fort, with his available force—then fewer than 150 men—though he was to be reinforced by Colonel Fry with the main body of the regiment later. But before the small detachment got over the mountains the French ejected the little group of about 40 engaged upon the fort, took possession, and renamed it Fort Duquesne.

Washington continued his march and held parleys with the Indians. On May 28 he attacked and captured a reconnoitering French force, and in doing so started the French and Indian War. Not succeeding in attaching the Indians to the English side and finding his advanced position otherwise untenable, he started to retire, but on July 3 surrendered to the French his hastily constructed works, called Fort Necessity. He had put up a valiant fight and was permitted to continue his march back to the Potomac. This was the only time he ever surrendered.

The news of this skirmish aroused both French and English to the imminence of conflict between them. However chagrined Colonel Washington may have felt over his first baptism of war, his position was so entirely all that could be expected that he received the thanks of the House of Burgesses.

The next turn in the wheel of fate brought General Braddock to America at the head of 1,000 smart British Regulars. He was a gallant officer of distinguished record, but he was totally unfitted to cope with the Indian warfare, although convinced that he and the British Regulars would be impervious to any mishap, an opinion in which Washington and other colonists who were familiar with Indian warfare may not have agreed, in spite of the traditional respect for the professional. An equal force of colonies troops joined Braddock's army.

Considerable dissatisfaction had been aroused by the King's order that all provincial commissions were inferior in rank to the royal ones. General Braddock, having heard of Colonel Washington's exploits, invited him to become a special aid "in his family, by which all inconvenience of that kind will be obviated." To this invitation Colonel Washington replied, acknowledging frankly—

"an inclination to serve the ensuing campaign as a volunteer; and this inclination is not a little increased, since it is likely to be conducted by a gentleman of the General's experience. But, besides this, and the laudable desire I may have to serve, with my best abilities, my King and country, I must be ingenuous enough

to confess, that I am not a little biassed by selfish considerations. To explain, Sir, I wish earnestly to attain some knowledge in the military profession, and, believing a more favorable opportunity cannot offer, than to serve under a gentleman of General Braddock's abilities and experience, it does, as may reasonably suppose, not a little contribute to influence my choice."

The catastrophe which followed, bringing to young Colonel Washington much bitter disillusionment and great responsibility, is best gathered from his letter to Governor Dinwiddie, giving his first account of the defeat of Braddock and his forces on July 9, 1755:

"We continued our march from Fort Cumberland to Frazier's (which is within 7 miles of Duquesne) without meeting any extraordinary event, having only a straggler or two picked up by the French Indians. When we came to this place, we were attacked (very unexpectedly) by about three hundred French and Indians. Our numbers consisted of about thirteen hundred well armed men, chiefly Regulars, who were immediately struck with such an inconceivable panick, that nothing but confusion and disobedience of orders prevailed among them. The officers, in general, behaved with incomparable bravery, for which they greatly suffered, there being near 60 killed and wounded—a large proportion, out of the number we had! The Virginia companies behaved like men and died like soldiers; for I believe out of three companies that were on the ground that day scarce thirty were left alive. Capt. Peroney and all his officers, down to a corporal, were killed; Captn. Polson had almost as hard a fate, for only one of his escaped. In short, the dastardly behaviour of the Regular troops (so-called) exposed those who were inclined to do their duty to almost certain death; and, at length, in spite of every effort to the contrary, broke and ran as sheep before hounds, leaving the artillery, ammunition, provisions, baggage, and in short, everything a prey to the enemy. And when we endeavoured to rally them, in hopes of regaining the ground and what we had left upon it, it was with as little success as if we had attempted to have stopped the wild bears of the mountains, or rivulets with our feet; for they would break by, in despite of every effort that could be made to prevent it."

In another letter George Washington expressed his utter disgust at the debacle, so contrary to the valor and record of the British Regular troops. He wrote:

"It is true, we have been beaten, shamefully beaten, by a handful of men, who only intended to molest and disturb our march. Victory was their smallest

expectation . . . had I not been witness to the fact on that fatal day, I should scarce have given credit to it even now."

The British Regulars would have acquitted themselves with credit on a formal battle ground of Europe, but in the wilds of the American forests with Indians fighting from ambush they were helpless and terrified. George Washington had been so ill that on the march he had had to ride in one of the wagons, but was beside General Braddock at the time of the attack. As the other aides had soon been wounded, the carrying of the General's orders fell upon him. In constant danger, two horses were shot from under him, and four bullets went through his clothes. Although reported killed, he attributed his preservation to the all-powerful dispensations of Providence. Out of 1,370 noncommissioned officers and men, only 550 came off unharmed. Washington, however, underestimated considerably the French and Indian force.

The immediate effect of the defeat of Braddock's forces was disastrous; for Colonel Dunbar, who commanded the rear of Braddock's Army that had not participated in the battle, refused, after receiving the fugitives, to advance or even to stand his ground, but retreated to Fort Cumberland and then decided to place himself and his troops out of reach of such border warfare and withdrew his men to Philadelphia, leaving the entire border at the mercy of the raids of French and Indians.

This emergency brought forth the convening of the House of Burgesses of the colony of Virginia by Governor Dinwiddie, which voted 40,000 pounds and authorized the raising of a regiment of 1,000 men. The governor gave George Washington a commission as colonel and commander in chief of all of the forces raised in Virginia for the protection of the frontier. This commission was the answer to the general demand for the services of George Washington, whose actions under all emergencies had been an unusual tribute to the qualities of a 23-year-old officer. To him it meant a constant struggle to organize forces for the defense of the border without the necessary means with which to do so. He made sound and practical plans, but was not permitted to get them beyond the beginning of the central Fort Loudoun at Winchester. His own desire was for offensive operations, but he was overruled and forced to abide by the policy of a chain of small fortified posts, so poorly provided with men for their defense that they were helpless to defend their surrounding territory against Indian raids, which were growing steadily in frequency and in atrocity.

George Washington was gravely disturbed over the situation, and he wrote many letters in his efforts to induce the authorities to provide him with adequate means to protect the border settlers. One of these shows how deeply he was stirred by the conditions:

"I see their situation, know their danger, and participate in their sufferings, without having it in my power to give them further relief, than uncertain promises. In short, I see inevitable destruction in so clear a light, that, unless vigorous measures are taken by the Assembly, and speedy assistance sent from below, the poor inhabitants that are now in forts, must unavoidably fall while the remainder of the country are flying before the barbarous foe. . . . The supplicating tears of women, and moving petitions from the men, melt me into such deadly sorrow, that I solemnly declare, if I know my own mind, I could offer myself a willing sacrifice to the butchering enemy, provided that would contribute to the people's ease."

The Virginia authorities made some efforts to remedy these troubles, but there was a lack of intercolonial cooperation, and under the commanding generalship of Lord Loudoun, Virginia was not only left to its own defense but required to send troops to South Carolina. Recruiting was slow. Men were not willing to leave their homes and families, and George Washington had a most arduous service in trying to defend 350 miles of frontier with less than a thousand men. This condition continued through 1756-57. For two years there was nothing but a series of failures under Lord Loudoun until he was recalled. Then, when William Pitt became Prime Minister, the tide of war turned in America. Under his able administration the British actually began to send substantial military forces into America, with a strong naval force to supplement them. France did not match these moves, and the French forces in America were abandoned to their fate. It was not until 1758 that the change of affairs brought relief to George Washington. He had always urged that an expedition be sent to Fort Duquesne, a center of border depredations, to destroy it. At last, in 1758, the expedition was made a part of the energetic program for the year. The expedition was to be under Brigadier General Forbes, and George Washington was to lead the Virginia troops, which had then been augmented to about 2,000. There were many long delays owing to the difficulty of preparations. This was the time when, owing to the shortage of regimental clothing, George Washington decided to fit out his command in the light Indian hunting garb. This was a first departure from the cumbersome uniforms of the period. George Washington pointed out the advantages in comfort and the great reduction of impedimenta to be transported. The serviceability of this Indian costume soon proved its utility, and George Washington was responsible for introducing an equipment which was to be of great value to Americans later in the Revolution.

George Washington was anxious to move forward in short order, following the road made under such difficulty by Braddock. However, while these matters were being settled, he met, loved, and wooed Martha Custis, and when he did start his march to Fort Duquesne they were betrothed. Another honor came to him while on military duty. This was his election to the House of Burgesses of Virginia as representative for Frederick County. Military duty kept him from the polls, but he was elected by a large majority.

A notable contrast to General Braddock's disregard of George Washington's advice was the respect tendered his military opinions by General Forbes, who asked the young officer to make for him a plan of march, a tactical scheme for the conduct of an expeditionary force of 4,000 men. It was also astonishing to find the young officer fully prepared to offer the right solution to the problem with tactics so flexible as to change quickly a line of march into a battle line in the event of an attack. The value of this plan was so apparent that it was adopted and followed.

The above proves that George Washington had a grasp of military matters that was extraordinary. General Forbes's expedition advanced with painful slowness. Colonel Bouquet, who had advocated the new route, was energetic, but the making of the new road through the wilderness was very difficult, and the approach to Fort Duquesne was delayed until in danger of being halted by the winter weather. However, it was all settled by the capture of Fort Frontenac. After the defeat of General Abercromby in his attack on Fort Ticonderoga, July 8, 1758, Fort Frontenac had been left with only a little over a hundred men to garrison it and was therefore easily captured in August by a brilliant dash of Colonel Bradstreet across Lake Ontario with a force of 2,500 colonial troops. The loss of this valuable French post cut the French line of communications, and by the time the Forbes expedition appeared the weakened forces at Fort Duquesne abandoned their isolated position. They had routed a rash advance force under Grant but, abandoned by their Indian allies, they could not withstand the main body and after burning their fort retreated on November 24. It saved the situation, for General Forbes was then fatally ill. The fort was made defensible and renamed by him Fort Pitt (afterwards Pittsburgh). Two hundred of Washington's Virginians were left as a garrison, and the expedition returned to Virginia. The downfall of Fort Duquesne ended the border troubles, just as George Washington had predicted it would, as it had been the base of all the Indian raiding activities. The restoration of order on the border ended the war for Virginia; the French being driven away, the end of 1758 was the end of George Washington's military service in the French and Indian War.

GEORGE WASHINGTON THE COMMANDER IN CHIEF

As the Commander in Chief of the Continental Army the services and achievements of George Washington are unique in the world's history. He was much more than the Commander in Chief. He was the one necessary person, whose calm, unswerving, determined sense of patriotic duty to country, and ability put real backbone into the Revolution and kept it from collapsing or merging into a civil conflict, under the hardships and unexpected privations encountered during the eight years of war. Without General Washington at its head it could never have succeeded. His faith in the cause and his devotion to the ideals it embodied made him the symbol of America—the spirit of the Revolution.

From boyhood on George Washington lived in a military atmosphere much of his time. Under his brother's influence and direction he was trained in fencing, also probably in the manual of arms. He assumed service and responsibility in the Virginia militia; and by the time he was serving as aide to General Braddock he made the assertion, "My inclinations are strongly bent to arms."

Each of the different tasks that fell to his hand seemed to contribute to the store of knowledge useful to him in the next one to follow. His experience as a surveyor was a fine preparation for the dangerous mission to the Ohio with Governor Dinwiddie's letter to the French commander. These gave him a real insight into pioneer settlement conditions, the wary methods of Indian warfare, and the difficulties of travel through unbroken forests in midwinter. The Braddock campaign taught him many of the weaknesses in the military system of training British Regular officers and men. He also had tragic evidence of the uselessness and folly of the pomp and display, and the paraphernalia of the formal English movements and practices, and learned some vastly important facts of the helplessness of the British soldier in unfamiliar environment where his formal European battlefield training could not be employed.

Witnessing all of the horrors of Braddock's defeat, more of a massacre than a battle, George Washington's personal courage had its baptism of fire and bore the acid test of every experience with honor. With two horses shot beneath him and four bullets through his coat, he not only continued his duties as aide but when General Braddock was mortally wounded and most of the other officers either killed or wounded, it was the young provincial colonel who was most active in directing the retreat of the remnant of the brilliant British Army.

Following this, his experiences of the French and Indian War gave him additional knowledge of border warfare, invaluable experience in training, disciplining, and subsisting his men far from their base of supplies, meeting every emergency and through resourcefulness and initiative creating out of every emergency opportunity to turn to the advantage of his forces. In these early days it is said that fear had no part in his make-up.

Through his 15 years in the House of Burgesses his opinions were solidifying into fixed standards and settled convictions that were to hold him fast and keep him true to the defense of the principles of representative government for the Colonies. He had felt the spell of Patrick Henry's ringing challenge to the spirit of free-born Englishmen: "If this be treason, make the most of it—Give me liberty or give me death."

He had absorbed the ideals that prompted the protests, petitions, debates, discussions, had a voice in the Resolves, in the denunciation of the Stamp Act and the Port Bill and the call for a General Congress of the American Colonies to which he was a delegate. George Washington's power and personality must have been marked in this Congress, since Patrick Henry on being asked to name the greatest man in the Congress replied, "If you speak of eloquence, Mr. Rutledge of South Carolina is by far the greatest orator; but if you speak of solid information and sound judgment, Colonel Washington is unquestionably the greatest man on the floor."

In the Virginia Convention some time before he had expressed his stand on the closing of the port of Boston, thus: "I will raise one thousand men, subsist them at my own expense and march myself at their head for the relief of Boston."

Then came the news of April 19, 1775, that Major Pitcairn, of the British Army, had fired upon the American militia, assembled on Lexington Common, shouting, "Disperse, ye rebels!" and thereby started the American Revolution. Washington, at the second meeting of the Continental Congress, May 10, 1775, like his colleagues, realized that settling matters without conflict became impossible with the news of the bloodshed at Lexington and Concord. Americans from 23 towns were found among the dead and wounded, and as the word spread the almost hourly appearance of more companies of armed men from far and near soon resulted in the assemblage of a determined army around Boston. This siege of Boston by its suddenness and the overwhelming numbers put a changed aspect upon the entire situation. A royal governor was hemmed in, apparently with abundant naval and military forces to enforce his orders, but was unable to command a single bit of aid outside of Boston, where he was regarded merely as a military commander of a besieged town.

One of the first steps of the new Congress was to adopt the army gathered about Boston, calling it the Continental Army to distinguish it from that of England, which they called the Ministerial Army. It then became necessary to give that body a leader—a commander in chief to handle it. Opinions varied; several were ambitious for the post. George Washington, who, it is alleged, arrived clad in his old uniform as a colonel of Virginia forces, was named, but was opposed by some of the delegates. However, John Adams, of Massachusetts, proposed him, recording in his diary afterward much of his comments:

"I had no hesitation to declare that I had but one gentleman in my mind for that important command and that was a gentleman from Virginia, who was among us and very well known to all of us; a gentleman, whose skill and experience as an officer, whose independent fortune, great talents and excellent universal character would command the approbation of all America, and unite the cordial exertions of all of the colonies better than any other person in the Union."

George Washington was elected Commander in Chief on June 15, 1775. The following day, from his place in the assembly, he accepted the appointment in a brief speech, in which he said:

"I beg they will accept my cordial thanks for this distinguished testimony of their approbation. But lest some unlucky event should happen, unfavorable to my reputation, I beg it may be remembered by every gentleman in the room that I this day declare with the utmost sincerity I do not think myself equal to the command I am honored with. As to pay, Sir, I beg leave to assure the Congress that as no pecuniary consideration could have tempted me to accept this arduous employment at the expense of my domestic ease and happiness, I do not wish to make any profit from it. I will keep an exact account of my expenses. Those I doubt not they will discharge, and that is all I desire."

General Washington, with his instructions and a packet of commissions for his staff of officers, made preparations to leave for Boston. Those to serve under him were Maj. Gens. Artemas Ward, Charles Lee, Phillip Schuyler, and Israel Putnam. Eight brigadier generals were also commissioned. These were Seth Pomeroy, Richard Montgomery, David Wooster, William Heath, Joseph Spencer, John Thomas, John Sullivan, Nathanael Greene. At the General's request, Horatio Gates was appointed adjutant general and given the rank of brigadier.

Before departing he wrote to Mrs. Washington, and among other things he said:

"You may believe me, my dear Patsy, when I assure you, in the most solemn manner, that, so far from seeking this appointment, I have used every endeavor in my power to avoid it, not only from my unwillingness to part with you and the family, but from a consciousness of its being a trust too great for my capacity, and that I should enjoy more happiness in one month with you at home than I have the most distant prospect of finding abroad."

His anxiety for her was great. He was worried and anxious over her loneliness and uneasiness. He wrote to his stepson and desired that he and Nellie would stay at Mount Vernon with their mother. He wrote to his wife's relatives and friends asking them to visit her and keep up her spirits. "My departure, will, I know be a cutting stroke upon her; and on this account alone I have many very disagreeable sensations."

This done, he set out for Boston, and en route the new Commander in Chief heard of the Battle of Bunker Hill, which acquainted him with the spirit of his new force, and also with its problems. Twenty thousand minutemen and militia had gathered, made up of the farmers, fishermen, sailors, mechanics, artisans of New England, with very little discipline and much confusion.

In taking over the command on July 3, 1775, from the temporary directions of Gen. Artemas Ward, the Commander in Chief endeavored to infuse into his new Army something of the spirit of the task before them. He said:

"The Continental Congress having now taken all the Troops of the several Colonies, which have been raised, or which may be hereafter raised, for the support and defence of the Liberties of America; into their Pay and Service: They are now the Troops of the United Provinces of North America; and it is hoped that all Distinctions of Colonies will be laid aside; so that one and the same spirit may animate the whole, and the only contest be, who shall render, on this great and trying occasion, the most essential Service to the great and common cause in which we are all engaged."

To his utter dismay, he found that withal the imposing numbers of men before him there was not enough powder among them or available to put up even the feeblest resistance to an attack; and had the English not been so thoroughly astonished at the results of Lexington and Concord and Bunker Hill, they probably could have driven the provincial army from Boston, since they had abundant military and naval forces at their command. However, they did not know the weaknesses of the colonial troops, and one of George Washington's greatest policies of military strategy grew out of this crisis when he managed to keep his enemy in ignorance of his real strength by being apparently constantly preparing to attack.

Sending Col. Henry Knox in midwinter to bring on 42 oxen-drawn sleds the 59 cannon from Ticonderoga, Washington fortified Dorchester Heights, which compelled General Howe to evacuate Boston, embarking his force for Halifax. Howe left a supply of cannon, small arms, powder, and other important military stores to the value of forty to fifty thousand pounds, very welcome to an army that had been watchfully waiting for weary months without sufficient powder for each soldier. This first score for the Americans in putting the enemy to flight was a bitter blow to British pride and a great encouragement to the Americans, and it placed the war on a different basis.

Never has New York seen a more brilliant military pageant than assembled off Gravesend during July and August, 1776, when General Howe with his forces arrived from Halifax and was joined by his brother, Lord Howe, admiral of the British fleet, with between three and four hundred ships, with the Germans hired to aid the British in subduing the colonists. Sir Henry Clinton also arrived with troops from the south, and fully 30,000 veteran soldiers stood ready to annihilate the American Army, which never attained greater numbers than 18,000 men. The English planned to seize New York and then the rest of the country, quickly subdue the Colonials, and bring the war to a speedy end. As they landed and established themselves in and around New York, General Washington kept close watch upon their movements. He had 9,000 men in a fortified camp at Brooklyn, and on August 22, when he learned that the enemy had landed 10,000 men and 40 cannon at the lower end of Long Island, he endeavored to encourage his men in the following brief address:

"The enemy have now landed on Long Island and the hour is fast approaching on which the honor and success of this army and the safety of our bleeding country depend. Remember, officers and soldiers, that you are freemen fighting for the blessings of liberty—that slavery will be your portion and that of your posterity if you do not acquit yourselves like men."

Despite his instructions and watchfulness, a road or pass was left unguarded, and the British discovering this, overwhelmed and defeated the Americans, driving them to their entrenchments before General Washington arrived on the scene. However, it cost the British such heavy losses that General Howe delayed following his advantage. This Battle of Long Island, one of the most spectacular of the engagements of the Revolution, although a defeat for the American Army, was also a defeat of the main object of General Howe's plans—to get the entire American Army in combat at one time after the methods of European warfare, in which event he felt assured of a complete victory that would at once settle the status of the rebellious Americans. This purpose General Washington had divined and thwarted. While General Howe was deliberating his next move General Washington quietly secured all available boats of every kind and had them sent to him at Brooklyn, where

he personally directed the removal of the soldiers with their arms, ammunition, baggage, supplies, horses, carts, etc., out of reach of the enemy during the hours of one night, and put a river between them before morning, without the loss of a man or their departure being prematurely discovered.

By the time General Washington had withdrawn his forces from Manhattan Island and established them at White Plains, he had learned enough of the British methods of fighting to realize thoroughly that unless the British soldiers could fight according to their long and rigid European training, after the method of Frederick the Great, they were at great disadvantage. He, therefore, endeavored at all times to defeat the attempts to get his Army as a whole in a battle line. He also early learned the value of camouflage. The breastworks thrown up over night and covered with hastily pulled cornstalks with the earth clinging to their roots would not have offered much resistance to an attacking enemy, but this deception helped to rob the British victory at White Plains, on October 28, of the full measure of advantage by inspiring General Howe with such a dread of the possible American strength that he deliberated two days before following up his advantage and awoke to find that General Washington had again slipped his entire Army from beneath his grasp. But shortly after this the loss of Forts Washington and Lee, which guarded the Hudson, compelled Washington to retreat across New Jersey, and on December 8, 1776, he crossed the Delaware into Pennsylvania, with Cornwallis close upon his heels. The American General avoided pursuit only by securing all of the boats on the river. Cornwallis regarded the Continental Army with such contempt that he did not feel the necessity of putting forth any extra effort to catch up with the Americans or to push on to take Philadelphia, and after stationing his troops in various places in New Jersey he returned to New York. At Trenton he had left a body of Hessians under Colonel Rahl. When this officer asked General Grant for reinforcements the latter replied, "I will undertake to keep the peace in New Jersey with a corporal's guard."

General Washington, feeling the importance of some decisive activity on the part of his army so soon to be depleted by the termination of the short time enlistments, staged a desperate venture at a time when the tide of public opinion and the morale of the Army was at its lowest ebb, and when he knew the British least expected it. He resolved to surprise the Hessians and seize Trenton while they were lulled to security and absorbed in Christmas festivities. The story of the crossing of the ice-filled Delaware on a dark and stormy night is familiar history. So also the gallant courage of his men, marching 9 miles in the teeth of a sleet and snowstorm which disabled their muskets. Under the bitter cold two men died, but the surprise and the com-

plete victory all came to pass just as General Washington planned and expected. Hope was revived, and under the inspiration of the hour money and men materialized.

Cornwallis, appalled at the American victory of Trenton, returned to resume charge of New Jersey activities. On January 2, 1777, General Washington awaited him across the Assunpink River with 5,000 troops and repulsed his attempts to cross. Arriving in the afternoon, he decided to await making the attack until morning, saying, "We may easily bag the fox in the morning." During the night General Washington executed another of his brilliant moves and made his way to Princeton and engaged the troops left there. In the conflict that followed General Washington, by his example and presence, inspired his men to victory and then marched them to Morristown, where they went into winter quarters. During this period he pledged his own private fortune for the pay of the soldiers, and his example was followed by some of his officers.

The result of this short campaign of only three weeks has been expressed by a modern British historian:

"As things fell out, the whole cause of the revolution in America was saved by Washington's bold and skilful action. The spirits of the revolutionary party revived; and an advance of 5,000 militia upon Kingsbridge showed Howe that enemies were ready to swarm upon him from every side at the first sign of a British reverse . . . the whole of the work excepting the capture of New York required to be done again."

The struggle to keep and increase the American Army during the winter at Morristown is expressed forcefully by this British writer:

"The military force which Washington brought into shape at Morristown— waxing or waning in numbers but constantly improving in quality—followed him obediently, resolutely, and devotedly as long as their country had occasion for a general and an Army."

During the months of anxious watching of Howe he kept his army ready to proceed northward or to Philadelphia. The British forces outnumbered his own three to two and were equipped to the highest efficiency, while the Americans were but poorly supplied. When Howe finally made his approach to Philadelphia through Chesapeake Bay, Washington confronted him at Brandywine Creek, September 11, but was defeated through the frustration of General Sullivan's part of the plan.

General Howe took possession of Philadelphia, and General Washington watched for the opportune moment to make an attack upon the troops. This he did near Germantown on October 5, 1777, and there was early promise of a victory, but the whole plan was spoiled by the confusion due to a thick fog, which prevented coordination. The Americans even made the mistake of attacking each other. It is said that General Washington always believed that the Americans had retreated at the instant when victory was near. Although unsuccessful, the battle showed that the Americans possessed a spirit that the defeat at Brandywine had not impaired, and its general effect was favorable.

October 17, 1777, Burgoyne surrendered at Saratoga to the army under Gates; and this fact, aided by the influence of Lafayette and Benjamin Franklin eventually secured the French alliance with the aid of money, men, and ships. Meanwhile General Howe went into winter quarters in Philadelphia, and General Washington and his army went to Valley Forge, December 19, 1777, where he could watch Howe's army and guard the country about Philadelphia. Howe's admission that he had no hope of ending the war without 10,000 more troops proved that the Americans had scored beyond their hopes in 1777.

The rigor and hardships of Valley Forge would have vanquished any other man than General Washington. Owing to the inefficiency of the commissary departments fully 2,898 soldiers in camp at Valley Forge were unfit for duty because they were barefoot and destitute of clothing. At times there were not three days' provisions for men or horses in camp, and often not sufficient for one day. It was in the midst of this poverty and privation that Baron von Steuben began his work of drill and discipline. He aroused the enthusiasm of the officers, and they imbibed his zeal, with a result in morale and efficiency that was astonishing and which continued in spite of Washington's failure to convince Congress and the States of the futility of short-term enlistments. Within a few months Von Steuben was a witness to the effect of his training in the turning of the tide at Monmouth.

The year 1778 brought the departure of Howe, and Sir Henry Clinton succeeded him. Clinton soon decided to evacuate Philadelphia and move his forces to New York. This they did by such slow marches that the Americans came upon them at Monmouth on June 28, led by Major General Lee, who for no cause whatever ordered a retreat, to the astonishment of Wayne and Lafayette. However, General Washington came riding out to meet Lee and, seeing his men in retreat, severely reprimanded Lee, took command of the situation, and turned the tide against the enemy so strongly that after nightfall they slipped away to New York. After two years of war the British were again confined to the city, and Washington was again at White Plains. There was no further attempt to conquer the Northern States; and the military situation was such as to be proof positive that General Washington had accomplished his entire object against the British, whose attempt to overrun the country he had entirely de-

feated; baffling and outwitting a superior army still huddled on the coast.

The British then attempted to subjugate the South, while continuing to hold New York against Washington's immediate army. Watching the ebb and flow of conflict in the South, minor engagements along the Hudson, the problem of cooperative movement with the French Army and fleet, the ever-present financial deficiency, the treason of Arnold, with many lesser vicissitudes, kept the Commander in Chief of the American Army constantly alert and watchful of the next move in the conflict, until the exciting close of hostilities at Yorktown in 1781.

When the Revolution began General Washington, unlike the British generals against whom he was fighting and the French generals with whom he became associated, had no powerful, organized, central government back of him to keep him supplied with the sinews and munitions of war, with its bureaus and departments to facilitate the conduct of military campaigns. Instead, only an elective committee represented all the Colonies. To secure supplies became the all-important issue and the never-ending struggle. Jealousies between States north and south and the personal jealousy not only of ambitious officers but of Congress, lest General Washington become too popular, brought upon his head petty slights and indifference from the very agencies that should have given him the utmost support in their power. Criticism of every act also hampered him, and his military skill was even disputed and belittled. He was criticised for inactivity, though in most cases when a council of officers was called to decide upon an attack the General's opinion was outvoted. However, it is noticeable that when he did decide to follow his own judgment for action brilliant victories were usually the result.

He was a past master at strategy and planned strategy for each campaign and for the war as a whole. He had to be commander, chief engineer, chief of intelligence, soldier, judge, statesman, quartermaster, commissary head, sanitary head, and not only take orders from Congress but also to advise with Congress on legislative matters. He had to pledge his own fortune to keep soldiers in the service, which the short-time enlistment policy of Congress kept in a constantly moving procession of partly trained men going through the ranks, many of them remaining less than three months.

Incapable of fear, the same indifference to his own personal safety which characterized his actions through the Braddock Expedition and the French and Indian War, was the source of great uneasiness to his men. One of his officers wrote:

"Our army love their General very much, but they have one thing against him which is the little care he takes of himself in any action. His personal bravery and the desire he has of animat-

ing his troops by example, make him fearless of danger. This occasions much uneasiness."

Although considered stern, cold, and remote, commanding the respect of the rank and file and the public by the forcefulness of his personality and his high character, he was not a hard man nor a martinet. He suffered in sympathy for his ragged, half-starved, poorly fed soldiers and shared every privation with them. For more than six years, although often within a couple of hundred miles of his own home of ease and plenty, he did not visit it. Despite his formal and austere manner, every man in the ranks knew that he had the complete sympathy of his Commander and rested in the assurance of his justice.

Through the long struggle when every victory seemed to be checked by a defeat, when disloyalty, indifference, and treason in his own official family added to the burden of that which he carried, he never faltered at the rigors imposed nor for a moment let go of the conviction that ultimate victory was to come. Washington's constant retreating before the British Army brought upon him much severe criticism, but in the end those who so bitterly assailed him for this seeming lack of success were forced to admit that an open fight would have crushed the Continental Army.

General Washington considered the Revolution as a war of posts. He urged against the danger of dividing and subdividing forces, so that no one would be sufficiently guarded, saying "it is a military observation strongly supported by experience that a superior force may fall a sacrifice to an inferior by an injudicious division." General Washington, observing this weakness in operation of the English forces, said before the Revolution was even a third of its way, "I am well convinced myself, that the enemy long ere this, are perfectly satisfied that the possession of our towns while we have an army in the field will avail them little."

The English had not been able to keep to the field against the Americans. They seemed unable to occupy American territory away from the sea. At the end of the year 1778 they were held on the defensive in New York and in Newport where they could be supplied by the navy. Although they had unlimited resources, they conceded themselves defeated in their effort to subdue the Northern States. This very fact is the greatest praise of General Washington's military skill—he outgeneraled them—and is the incontestable proof of General Washington's greatness as a military leader.

The greatest task that fell so heavily on the Commander was that of keeping his army actually in existence. Here his great business training and ability showed itself. The British could and did repeatedly beat the Continental Army, but they could not beat General Washington. Neither abuse, attack, defeat, nor discontentment could make him resign, and as long as he was in the field he was the rallying point for whatever fighting spirit could still be aroused.

General Washington had early formulated a set of six rules for his military guidance, by which he measured and directed the actions of his Army and followed to the letter himself. They are:

"1. Never attack a position in front which you can gain by turning.

"2. Charges of cavalry should be made if possible on the flanks of infantry.

"3. The first qualification of a soldier is fortitude under fatigue and privation. Courage is only the second. Hardship, poverty, and actual want are the soldier's best school.

"4. Nothing is so important in war as an undivided command.

"5. Never do what the enemy wishes you to do.

"6. A General of ordinary talent, occupying a bad position and surprised by superior force, seeks safety in retreat; but a great captain supplies all deficiencies by his courage and marches boldly to meet the attack."

While the Conway Cabal was exercising its spell over Congress the Commander in Chief, stung to retort by the criticism of lack of activity of the military under such conditions, wrote that body:

"I am informed that it is a matter of amazement and that reflections have been thrown out against this army for not being more active and enterprising. In the opinion of some they ought to have been. If the charge is just, the best way to account for it will be to refer you to the returns of our strength and those I can produce of the enemy and to the enclosed abstract of the clothing now actually wanting for the army."

"I can assure these gentlemen [he said in reply to political criticism] that it is a much easier and less distressing thing to draw remonstrances in a comfortable room by a good fireside, than to occupy a cold, bleak hill, and sleep under frost and snow, without clothes or blankets."

The soldiers felt perfect confidence in the wise leadership of the Commander in Chief, and his splendid courage, foresight, and marvelous ability to endure won the final liberty of the long-suffering Colonies. He held the Army together and through his letters to Congress prevented that body from doing too many unwise things that would have spoiled completely his carefully laid plans. The end of the long struggle for liberty came on October 19, 1781, with the surrender of Cornwallis at Yorktown. On November 20, 1782, Great Britain acknowledged the independence of the United States, and on September 3, 1783, a treaty of peace was signed at Versailles in France, and America was free.

General Washington, wise and unselfish Commander of a tattered citizen soldiery, wrung victory from the seasoned legions of Europe under discouragements that would have crushed any save an indomitable spirit. Of his leadership and skill Von Moltke is quoted as saying in Berlin in 1874:

"You have in American history one of the great captains of all time. It might be said of him, as it was of William the Silent, that he seldom won a battle but he never lost a campaign."

George Washington the Farmer

George Washington was first, last, and always a farmer. In addition, he was a surveyor, soldier, statesman, commander, and President; but through all of the demands made by these different positions upon his time and attention, he kept in touch with his estate and was always keenly interested in the cultivation of his farms. This was even true during the Revolutionary War, when he did not visit Mount Vernon for a space of over six years.

His correspondence and various letters on subjects relating to agriculture and farming operations show his deep interest and his own wide knowledge in the management of his farms and in all details concerning them.

While absent he required written reports from the manager of his estate, and in return laid out explicit detailed instructions as to what should be done and when. During his long absence while leading the Continental Army to victory and during the Presidency, he constantly anticipated with deep pleasure and satisfaction the time when he could lay down all civic and patriotic burdens, return to his beloved Mount Vernon, and resume his farming.

In 1788 he wrote to Arthur Young, the leading scientific farmer and then the editor of the Annals of Agriculture, and the author of a number of books:

"The more I am acquainted with agricultural affairs, the better I am pleased with them; insomuch that I can no where find so great satisfaction as in those innocent and useful pursuits. In indulging these feelings, I am led to reflect how much more delightful to an undebauched mind, is the task of making improvements on the earth than all the vain glory that can be acquired from ravaging it, by the most uninterrupted career of conquests."

To the same person he again wrote:

"I think with you that the life of a husbandman is the most delectable. It is honorable, it is amusing and with judicious management, it is profitable. To see the plants rise from the earth and flourish by the superior skill and bounty of the laborer fills a contemplative mind with ideas which are more easy to be conceived than expressed."

George Washington's English ancestors held manorial lands and in Virginia agriculture was fundamental in both economic and political conditions. To this necessary basis General Washington added a real enthusiasm. When he had his bookplate engraved he added to the ornamentation around the coat of arms some spears of wheat to indicate what he once called "The most favorite Amusement of my life."

Although the work of the surveyor interested him and inspired him to such painstaking careful work that some of it still stands the tests, and the adventure and duties of a soldier and commander of the armies enthused him and aroused military ambitions, the soul-trying experiences of the man high in authority and power, the target for so much that was unpleasant, caused him to look forward with longing eyes toward that quiet and lovely home on the Potomac, of which he wrote to an English friend soon after his marriage, "I am now I believe fixd at this seat with an agreeable Consort for Life. And hope to find more happiness in retirement than I ever experienced amidst a wide and bustling World."

After his marriage it was noted that he always quitted his home and its quiet life with real reluctance. And it was assuredly with deep content and satisfaction that soon after the national independence was assured he wrote his comrade in arms, the Marquis de Chastellux:

"I am at length become a private citizen on the banks of the Potomac, where under my own vine and fig tree free from the bustle of a camp and the intrigues of a court, I shall view the busy world with calm indifference, and with serenity of mind, which the soldier in pursuit of glory, and the statesman of a name, have not the leisure to enjoy."

George Washington inherited his English forbears' love of land. Owning land and lots of it became his joy and ambition. To him it was the solid basis for all advancement in life. During his lifetime he acquired 63,000 acres of land in various sections of the country, that are now in seven States, and also in the District of Columbia. But of all of this vast estate, his deepest interest and real affection was centered in the five farms that made up the 8,000 acres of the Mount Vernon plantation. These were called the Mansion House Farm, on which the residence stood and quarters for slaves; Union Farm, 928 acres arable with ferry and fishery; Muddy Hole Farm; River Farm; and Dogue Run Farm. This last he considered the best of all of his farms and willed to Lawrence Lewis and Nellie Custis Lewis, on which they built Woodlawn.

George Washington was a progressive farmer. He was one of the first American agriculturists, for he was always seeking newer, better methods of doing everything on his farms. He was willing to expend any amount of effort, time, and money to find the best fertilizer, the best seeds, roots, cuttings, or bulbs and always on the alert for new discoveries that would aid in avoiding or checking plant disease, or for newer ways of cultivating. He is said to have once declared that he had little patience with those content to tread the ruts their fathers trod. Like other colonial Virginia planters, he tried specializing in tobacco. From his accounts we find that in 1759 he made 34,160 pounds of tobacco, the next year 65,037 pounds, and in 1763, 89,079 pounds, which seems to have been his largest crop. He soon came to a realization that the soil at Mount Vernon was not rich and that tobacco as his chief crop was depleting the soil of what fertility it had, making it too poor for other uses. He, therefore, turned his attention to the planting and cultivating of other crops, particularly wheat, and to the enrichment of his land. This was not an easy matter. Had he lived today, this would have been simple, for he could have written to our Department of Agriculture, to farm journals, attended State agricultural college or experiment stations, or consulted the local county agent, had the soil tested and been advised regarding all matters of concern relating to the management and development of his farms. This, of course, he could not do, as but few Americans were then interested in agriculture as deeply as he was, so he turned to England and entered into correspondence with Sir Arthur Young, who was heading a small group of people experimenting and writing on the improved methods of agriculture. George Washington left copious notes which prove how deeply interested he was in the work of these men.

Much of the time he spent at Mount Vernon was given over to various experiments of his own by which he sought methods to improve farming on his own land, and which when established as practicable and feasible he would pass on for general use. From his diaries, which are interspersed so frequently with notations on his plantings and farm operations, it is learned that as early as 1760 he sowed luzerne, now called alfalfa.

His great interest in clover, rye, hop, trefoil, timothy, and other grasses lay in his belief that they would conserve and enrich his indifferent type of soil. He also had in mind the value of winter feed for the improvement of his livestock. He made many experiments with different kinds of fertilizers and had muck from the bed of the river for some of his fields. He did not altogether agree with Thomas Jefferson that "we can buy a new acre of land cheaper than we can manure an old one," because he was a conservationist interested in intensive cultivation. Finding a plow not to his satisfaction, he proceeded to work over its construction until he made it better suited to his work. He also invented what he called a barrel plow, which was not a real plow but more like a seed drill. He treated his seed wheat to prevent smut. He also struggled with experiments to protect his grain from rust and from the Hessian fly. Through these careful experiments he came to raise very good wheat and was proud of

the flour from his grist mill, which he shipped to the West Indies. This he is said to have claimed to be as good in quality as any made in America.

His farming operations embraced an extensive interest and development in stock raising. He was the first American to try his hand at the raising of mules and received with great satisfaction the gift of the King of Spain, Charles III, in 1785, of two jacks. One of the jacks died on the journey, and the one that reached Mount Vernon safely was named Royal Gift and was later taken on a tour of the South. The following year the Marquis de Lafayette sent General Washington another jack and two jennies, and the master of Mount Vernon raised mules and used them most advantageously as work animals. At the time of his death he had about 50 mules. In 1783 he had 13 yoke of oxen. These animals did all the heavy farm work on the Mount Vernon estate.

Always an expert horseman, he broke his own horses and took special pride in his old war horses and those he purchased for his own use and for the other members of the family and for his carriages. In 1785 his writings show that he had distributed over his farms 130 horses. Twenty-one of these were kept in the stables of the mansion house.

Very few Virginia farmers kept sheep. But in 1758 George Washington's overseer reported 65 old sheep and 48 lambs. To his sheep the master of Mount Vernon gave deep study, and as a result of his investigations he was able by selection so to improve the breed that he was able to secure an average of 5½ pounds of wool, while his neighbors seldom managed to average 2 pounds to the sheep. Seven years later the count of sheep was 156, and in 1793 his flock had grown to over 600.

He seems not to have been as greatly interested in cattle as he was in other kinds of stock, although in 1793 he had over 300 black cattle of all sorts. He was accustomed to brand his cattle with the letters G. W., and the location on the body indicated the farm on which the animal was raised. In spite of owning 101 cows, he had to buy butter for his family.

George Washington worked hard as a farmer. He struggled with droughts, oversupply of rains, storms, and freezes, causing failure of crops and consequent money losses. He tried his luck with various kinds of wheat. He had experimental plots on all of his plantations and made a regular round of inspections to note the progress of the plants. He also tried new methods of potato planting and adopted the Pennsylvania method of cultivating buckwheat.

Each plantation was operated separately with an overseer to manage it, and a general superintendent over all, especially during the owner's absence and last years. On Saturday of each week reports were made and turned in by all the overseers. These were placed in books for the purpose and so arranged as to show how each negro's and

laborer's time had been occupied during the week, what crops planted or harvested, increase or loss of stock, and every detail of the work of each of the farms.

At the time George Washington started his farming there was but one system of agriculture in use in Virginia. This he later described as follows:

"A piece of land is cut down, and kept under constant cultivation, first in tobacco, and then in Indian corn (two very exhausting plants), until it will yield scarcely anything; a second piece is cleared, and treated in the same manner; then a third, and so on, until probably, there is but little more to clear. When this happens, the owner finds himself reduced to the choice of one of three things—either to recover perhaps the land which he has ruined, to accomplish which, he has perhaps neither the skill, the industry, or the means; or to retire beyond the mountains; or to substitute quantity for quality in order to raise something. The latter has been generally adopted, and, with the assistance of horses, he scratches over much ground, and seeds it, to very little purpose."

Having no better plan he followed the above, even to buying corn and hogs to feed his slaves and servants. Not finding this method satisfactory to his ideas of progress, he cast about for better methods, and he was soon convinced that the Virginia method was wrong. He early became a convert to the rotation of crops and made out elaborate schedules extending over a period of five years for his own use. Thus he kept his fields in constant change. All of this was on a large scale, as an example, in one year he planted over 300 bushels of potatoes and sowed over 27 bushels of flaxseed.

The lack of rains and the overabundance of it in 1785 and 1786 caused him much loss in crops, and he was so hard up he was anxious to sell some lands to meet his bills. In February, 1787, in sending his mother 15 guineas, he wrote her:

"I have now demands upon me for more than 500£, three hundred and forty odd of which is due for the tax of 1786; and I know not where or when, I shall receive one shilling with which to pay it. In the last two years I made no crops. In the first I was obliged to buy corn and this year have none to sell, and my wheat is so bad, I can neither eat it myself nor sell it to others; and Tobacco I make none. Those who owe me money cannot or will not pay it without suits, and to sue is to do nothing; whilst my expenses, not from any extravagance, or an inclination on my part to live splendidly, but for the absolute support of my family and the visitors who are constantly here, are exceedingly high."

After he had gotten the Government in running order following his inauguration as

President he made a trip through New England, and whenever opportunity permitted between social festivities he studied the farm land and methods. Every feature of the methods of New England life interested him, and he took many notes on the horses, fences, and cattle. On the first day out from New York he recorded seeing good crops of corn mixed with pumpkin and met four droves of beef cattle, some of which were very fine, and a flock of sheep. The houses also interested him with their shingle roofs, stone and brick chimneys, as did the fences and cider making. His own farms were equipped with every kind of improved tool and implement calculated to do better work. At his death he had not only threshing machines and a Dutch fan, but a wheat drill, a corn drill, a machine for gathering clover seed, and another for raking up wheat.

General Washington had a dream of an empire of farms west of the Alleghenies and made himself the leader in the efforts to improve transportation facilities between the headwaters of the Ohio and those of the Potomac in order that western farmers could have a market for their crops.

While President, George Washington was most anxious to improve the general state of agriculture, and in his last annual message to Congress he recommended the establishment of a board of agriculture to collect and diffuse information and by premiums and small pecuniary aids to encourage and assist a spirit of discovery and improvement. He did not live to see this far-sighted policy materialize.

GEORGE WASHINGTON THE BUSINESS MAN AND ENGINEER

George Washington was one of the leading business men of his day. From early boyhood he gave evidences of unusual commercial understanding and planned his habits with an attention to system and detail that provided a solid basis for the building of his life's diversified activities and insured his financial success. He has, however, been so constantly presented to the world in his great patriotic roles—as gallant soldier, farsighted statesman, famous first President, and Father of His Country—that his commercial achievements have been overshadowed by his prominence.

George Washington, as a leading business man, the successful farmer, the builder of canals, promoter of commercial projects, land investor on a large scale, was comparable to the founders of great fortunes based upon the development of our vast natural resources. If alive today, he would be perfectly at home in the midst of any group of modern business barons, developing plans for large undertakings of national or even international scope.

Convincing evidence of his business acumen, which amounted to genius, is to be found in the fact that although he gave practically a third of his life, and this at the best productive period, to the most exacting public service, which gave him little or no time to devote to his own affairs, yet he left one of the largest estates of his day and a record of business achievements that placed him in the class of pioneers of American finance.

Inheriting the thrift and business energy of his father, and trained by his mother in methodical detail, in avoidance of waste, and in ways of forethought and conservation, George Washington learned as a little boy to make out bills of sale, transfers, deeds, and various other documents of commercial usage. He was also taught to keep careful account of all of his moneys, his income, and his expenditures. This habit he followed through life, to regard the smallest item worthy of record, and tried to implant such systematic budget keeping in the minds of his stepson and his step grandson.

Possessing the Englishman's love of land and appreciating early in life that to the large landowner came the honors of life in the southern colonies, George Washington began acquiring land with the earnings from his first job as surveyor's assistant. Realizing also the importance of being possessed of an objective, he devised the plan of paying for some of his land by surveying. Although he had inherited at his father's death 10 slaves and the Rappahannock River homestead and farm and several other small pieces of land, these were subject to his mother's control until he was of age, and he seems never to have had any returns from this during her lifetime. By the time Mount Vernon came to him with its 2,700 acres he had already begun through his own efforts a foundation upon which to build his fortune.

During his surveying experience he learned to judge land, knew where the best acres lay, how to select lands that would prove good investments, and also how to plan for future roads and lines of transportation. He became imbued with a love of the beautiful Shenandoah Valley, in which so much of Lord Fairfax's great dominion of 5,000,000 acres was located. He also early caught a vision of the future course of settlement and was one of the earliest of our public men to plan for the extension of westward frontiers. Hence, during his long, dangerous trip to the Ohio for Governor Dinwiddie, he was taking notes of land conditions, appraising, and deciding upon the values of certain sections. During the French and Indian War he was authorized to raise a body of troops. Because practically all colonial residents were primarily farmers drawing their living from their farms, it was very difficult to get the quota of 800 men, and George Washington persuaded the governor to offer a bonus in western lands to those who would volunteer. Governor Dinwiddie consented, and offered 200,000 acres on the Ohio and its tributaries. Before these lands were allotted, Dinwiddie had been re-

called and his successors were not inclined to regard the deal as binding, and it looked as though the land bonus was to be lost. However, George Washington kept busy with correspondence, and as leader of the Virginia forces his word had much weight; and, keeping after the matter until 1772, he finally succeeded in getting the land assigned according to the old promise. In this his own share was 15,000 acres. Since the region was wild, remote, unsettled, and more or less dangerous through Indian depredations from time to time, many of the soldiers and officers preferred ready cash to their faraway acres. Here George Washington stepped in with his land hunger and bought up many of their allotments, thus adding materially to his own holdings. His faith in the western lands was steadfast. He eventually owned 63,000 acres of land, much of it bottom land on the Ohio, Great Kanawha, and Little Miami Rivers, besides land in Maryland, western Pennsylvania, New York, and Kentucky, and holdings scattered through Virginia.

It is noticeable that Washington, always a methodical person, was careful about exacting value and in giving it. He performed his contracts and kept his promises both in spirit and in letter, and this too when so doing involved him in losses.

He hated shiftiness and all appearance of deception. He formed his judgment of men by their sense of honor in carrying out a bargain. During the Revolution, being unable to look after his own affairs, he suffered serious losses. He wrote to a relative that he made no money from his estate during the nine years he was absent from it, "and brought none home with me. Those who owed me, for the most part, took advantage of the depreciation, and paid me off with sixpence on the pound" [2½ cents on the dollar]. He paid his debts, which then were not small, at 20 shillings on the pound with interest. He did it promptly, and with pride, and to do so he had to sell valued land and one of his best investments, a block of stock in the Bank of England.

Like many business men engaged in promoting expanding enterprises, Washington knew what it was at times to be in need of ready cash. He did borrow money at various times for various projects, and it is well known that at the time he was called to the Presidency he had to borrow several hundred pounds to finance himself in proper style. These obligations were always paid as promptly as possible. He avoided being drawn into schemes when he felt uncertain in their prospects of profit. He was persuaded to undertake as a patriotic venture the building of two houses in the National Capital to help provide quarters for Members of Congress when the seat of government should be moved thither. These cost him considerably more than he had expected, and he was obliged to borrow money from the bank at Alexandria to pay the contractor. Part of this was unpaid at the time of his death a few months later and was paid by his executors.

George Washington early learned the knack of getting along with people, and this was no small factor in his successes. He knew that one can not carve out a successful career alone but must have cooperation. He made a practice of choosing his associates or subordinates with greatest care, then he trusted them but also checked their performances. He early became a good judge of men and had a wide knowledge of them, rarely selecting a helper who failed him. He always kept close tab on the details of his important affairs even when they were intrusted to some one else. He not only spent a great deal of time in personally inspecting his farms, but he also required written reports from his superintendent in his absence.

George Washington would never have been caught in any spectacular investments. When he was ready to put his money into a project it was invariably something of which he was fully informed—some venture close at hand or of a nature that he could investigate and watch carefully. He found most of his investment opportunities immediately about him. He could therefore rely upon his personal knowledge. His purchases of lands were nearly all made after he had personally inspected them and made personal surveys, even those located far beyond the mountains.

Through his marriage with Mrs. Custis, George Washington came into control of a fortune great for those days, that added much to his resources. He enlarged his Mount Vernon estate by purchasing neighboring farms. His estate there grew from 2,700 acres to more than 8,000 acres at the time of his death. This home was always his most cherished possession. Upon it he lavished unremitting labor, care, expense, and affection. Always interested deeply in matters agricultural, he read and studied the well-known books on the subject. While free to oversee his farming activities, it is said that he averaged in profits between ten and fifteen thousand dollars annually.

Living as he did in the days before the machinery age, his home plantation was like a little empire where a great diversity of enterprises were in constant operation, as the place had to maintain itself and supply the wants of the family and the large number of servants and slaves who had to be provided with their food, shelter, clothing, fuel, medicines, etc. So in addition to crops of tobacco, wheat, corn, etc., George Washington maintained a gristmill at Dogue's Run. He also conducted fisheries on a wholesale scale along his almost 10 miles of water front. He sent his flour and his salted shad and herring to the West Indies, in large quantities. He maintained a ferry across the Potomac, profitable at first but later a great nuisance. For the operation of these projects or industries he had a large number of slaves and indentured servants under the direction of overseers.

The earliest enterprise that had the benefit of George Washington's keen knowledge and for five years his best energies and considerable of his money was the Dismal Swamp project. The promotion of this arose from a grant from the Commonwealth of Virginia dated November 1, 1763, when by an order in council, William Nelson, Thomas Nelson, Robert Burwell, John Robinson, George Washington, Thomas Walker, Fielding Lewis, Anthony Bacon & Co., J. Syme, Samuel Gist, Robert Tucker, and William Walters, as the original proprietors of the Dismal Swamp, were authorized to undertake the reclamation of this swamp. This group of men were leaders in politics and business in the period between the French and Indian War and the Revolution. Their plan was to drain and make fit for cultivation the large tract of spongy land in southeastern Virginia below the James River, extending from the Nansemond River east and south to the North Carolina boundary, and far into that State. The original proposition embraced more than 40,000 acres.

George Washington was chosen the manager of the enterprise. Irving describes his interest thus:

"With his usual zeal and hardihood, he explored it on horseback and on foot. In the center of the morass he came to a great piece of water, six miles long and three broad, called Drummond's Pond, but more poetically celebrated as the Lake of the Dismal Swamp. Having made the circuit of it and noted all of its characteristics, he encamped for the night up on the firm land which bordered it and finished his explorations on the following day."

In his diary in 1768 he mentions the Dismal Swamp:

"Oct. 26 Breakfasted in Suffolk; dined and lodgd in the Dismal Swamp at Jno. Washington's.

"Oct. 27 Went up to our Plantation at Norfleet's in Carolina and returnd in the aftern.

"Oct. 28 Went into the Pond with Colo. Lewis, Majr. Reddick Jno. Washington, and at Night went to ye Majrs.

"Oct. 29 Got to Smithfield in return to Wmsburg.

"Oct. 30 Set out early; breakfasted at Hog Island and dined in Wms."

This is the last entry found regarding his presence at the site. The accounts in his ledger show expenses incurred in seven trips, of which the last one noted is the one in October, 1768.

The plan of the company to build one or more canals on the east side of the Lake of the Dismal Swamp to carry off the surplus water to the sound and the sea was not realized in George Washington's lifetime. The timber, however, was cut and transported by the short canals on the north and west side of the lake to Suffolk and in merchantable forms to the markets of the upper country. Sawmills were established in

Suffolk, and there were docks on the Nansemond River, whence the passage to the James River and the Chesapeake was easy.

Colonel Washington after 1768 left the management of the property to others. After the close of the Revolutionary War he again took up the matter in connection with others he was promoting. Soon, however, the demands upon him leading to the Presidency put such enterprises into the background. In 1793, midway in his service as President of the United States, he sought to relieve his financial burdens by selling some of his western lands and his Dismal Swamp share. When he learned that Gen. Henry Lee was interested in the property, he prepared for him an explicit letter of information regarding the Dismal Swamp, which may be found in his writings.

He sold his interest in the Dismal Swamp Company in November, 1796, by written agreement to Gen. Henry Lee, received a part payment and the promise of $20,000 more in money payable in three equal annual installments with 6 per cent interest. General Washington retained the title to the Dismal Swamp land as security. While General Washington considered the matter settled, and so informed the members of the Dismal Swamp Company, he was mistaken. General Lee forfeited the payment he had made, and the share owned by General Washington in the Dismal Swamp Company was finally sold at auction for $12,000 by his estate in 1828.

Another great project in which George Washington was a prime mover was the Potomac River Company, which was his first public engineering enterprise after the Revolution. He had tried from 1769 to 1773 to interest the people of Virginia and Maryland in improving the navigation of the Potomac River to its northern branch and in the attempt to join it to the headwaters of the Ohio, either by road and portage or canal connection, in the hope of securing the fur trade and other commerce of the great valleys beyond. He had secured the enactment of a bill in 1772 in the Virginia Assembly for the organizing of a stock company to clear the Potomac. This was the beginning of the Potomac Company.

In October, 1774, George Washington and John Ballandyne had circulated a subscription paper to raise at least £30,000 of capital to make a beginning of the work, but troubles with England intervened, so nothing came of the deal. However, he did not forget his hopes and plans to clear the Potomac of rocky obstructions, build canals and locks around its several falls, and find a way to bring Pittsburgh and the tidewater towns into connection, so shortly after his return to Mount Vernon after the Revolution he resumed his active interest in the enterprise.

In September, 1784, he set out to make his sixth and last trip across the Alleghenies. He made the tour on horseback across the 10 ranges of mountains which formed the headwaters of the Potomac, the Cheat, and

Monongahela Rivers. Much of the time he was sleeping out of doors. He returned to Mount Vernon on October 4, having traveled 681 miles. The result of his tour was the incorporation of the Potomac Company, the first great interstate commerce corporation of the United States, by the States of Virginia and Maryland. The company organized in 1785 with Washington as president.

For almost four years he devoted time, energy, and money to the development of this project. He planned the work, traveled up and down the river to mark its location, employed the superintendents, attended meetings of directors and stockholders, and was the active executive of this great undertaking.

Washington's original superintendent on the Potomac Company job was James Rumsey, who made the first successful experiments with mechanical propulsion of boats. Washington was so impressed with the practical features of Rumsey's plans that he did all in his power to forward the movement many years before Robert Fulton's *Clermont* made its notable journey up the Hudson.

Washington's example gave an impetus to internal improvements in the form of canals in Pennsylvania and New York and in roads to connect them across the mountains with the Ohio Valley. He not only gave time and tireless effort, but invested $10,000 of his own money. The State of Virginia sought to give him over $20,000 worth of Potomac Company stock and in addition a block of James River Company stock as an evidence of its appreciation. He declined both as private gifts, but accepted if permitted to devote them to public purposes. Accordingly he left the Potomac stock to his projected National University and the James River stock to what became Washington and Lee University.

His hopes and the purposes in the Potomac Company had been only to clear the Potomac River channel of rocks, dredge the shallow places, and to build a few miles of canal around the Great Falls and the rapids called Little Falls, which was accomplished. He had further intentions of building a road from headwaters of the Potomac across mountains to headwaters of the Ohio, which should permit of easy transportation of goods to and from the western waters and plains, but the Potomac improvement was not a financial success and these further projects fell through. It was not until after the War of 1812 and during the administration of Monroe and John Quincy Adams that the policy of which George Washington was the sponsor and the Potomac Company the example again found favor and support in the establishment of the Chesapeake & Ohio Canal Company, under the Acts of Virginia, Maryland, and the Congress of the United States. Out of these not only grew the canal completed to Cumberland but also the Baltimore & Ohio Railroad, one of the first railroads to bind the plains to the coastal regions, as Washington had planned when he predicted the rising empire.

George Washington's deep interest in land investment prompted him to purchase 3,000 acres in the Mohawk Valley of New York. This with the interest cost him £1,875. By 1793 he had sold about two-thirds of it and valued the balance at $6,000.

He was also interested from boyhood in the Ohio Company, which was chartered in 1749 to establish settlements of white people west of the Allegheny Mountains and to develop and manage trade with the Ohio Indians. The stockholders included Governor Dinwiddie and some of the most important men of Virginia, including both of Washington's half brothers. The company erected a storehouse near the mouth of Red Stone Creek and Col. James Byrd built a fort there in 1758. This is where the town of Brownsville is now situated. Also the company began the fort at the forks of the Ohio at the site of Pittsburgh, which the French captured and completed as Fort Duquesne. The activity of the Ohio Company was one of the causes of the French and Indian War.

George Washington was an investor in bank stock. He came into a goodly holding in the Bank of England in connection with the Custis properties. The shares that came to him by law were sold for him by his agent after the Revolution. As a result of his efforts toward making Alexandria a large commercial city a bank was chartered for that city by the Virginia Assembly after the first subtreasury and customhouse had been established there. In this, as in the bank of Columbia, George Washington was a stockholder.

In summing up Washington's activities as a business man and promoter and engineer, it is easy to see that he had some very definite principles upon which he based his actions. It is clear that while still a boy, George Washington determined upon an objective—a worthy, creditable, and profitable line of activity and bent all of his efforts toward fitting himself to attain success in it.

By the time he was 21, when he crossed the Alleghenies in midwinter to warn the French to leave the Ohio Valley, he formed the idea that the colonies, towns, and cities of the coast must be connected by mutual interests in commerce to sections of the country beyond the mountains. For 40 years he worked for this development. He built roads, bought lands, fought wars, organized companies, encouraged settlements, planned canals, in order to tie the Potomac to the Ohio and the James with the Kanawha, and to tie the commerce of the west with the seacoast. Far-sighted beyond his contemporaries, he visioned the growth and settlement of the land and the development of its rich resources.

GEORGE WASHINGTON THE CITIZEN

George Washington was fulfilling the duties of a citizen as a surveyor before he had attained his majority. He became a servant of the government in 1749 at the age of 17, when he received, after qualifying before William and Mary College, the appointment as official surveyor of Culpeper County, Virginia, at the salary of £50 a year. That this was not a lucrative or particularly easy berth may be gathered from excerpts from his own writings. In following this vocation he had to live in a frontier country and to travel, as he wrote—

over "y. worst Roads that ever was trod by Man or Beast"; and to camp out where one night "Our Straw catch'd Fire . . . and was luckily Preserv'd by one of our Mens awaking." The next night "we had our Tent Carried Quite of with ye. Wind and was obliged to Lie ye. Latter part of ye. night without covering."

And at other times they were driven from the tent by smoke.

By the time he was 20 years of age, through the example and interest of his brother Lawrence, he became an adjutant of one of the military districts of Virginia, with a salary of about £100. This was followed by regular military service, which began in 1754 and in which he continued for five years until he resigned from the service.

Next to being a member of the Virginia Council, a seat in the House of Burgesses, the lower branch of the legislature, was most sought by Virginia landowners. As George Washington's great grandfather, Col. John Washington, the emigrant who came to Virginia about 1657, had been a member of the House of Burgesses and his father and brothers also, it was quite natural that he, too, should desire this distinction when he became the head of his family. This ambition took definite form in 1755, while he was on the frontier. He wrote to his brother, who was taking charge of Mount Vernon for him, to ask him to find out whether or not Colonel Fairfax intended to be a candidate, saying "If he does not, I should be glad to take a poll, if I thought my chance tolerably good." He also wished his brother to ascertain the real sentiments of Major Carlyle regarding him as a candidate, as Major Carlyle had bantered him about it. His brother was also to find out the sentiments of the prominent men of the country, and especially of the clergymen—

"Sound their pulse, without disclosing much of mine. If they seem inclinable to promote my interests, and things should be drawing to a crisis, you may declare my intention and beg their assistance. If on the contrary you find them more inclined to favor someone else I would have the affair entirely dropped."

It was evident that he did not have the support of the important men of Fairfax County, for he did not stand.

He did, however, stand for Frederick County, on the frontier. Although he had saved Winchester and the surrounding country from being overrun by murdering Indians, he was not altogether popular. He was held responsible for the massacres of outlying inhabitants, whom it was impossible to protect, but in this very defense he had given cause for ill feeling. He admitted that he had several times given rise to resentment, as he had been forced to impress the horsemen and wagons of the district and had in other ways so angered some of the people that they had threatened "to blow out my brains." Moreover, he had committed a far more serious crime in a political sense. Virginia elections were usually "wet" and he pointed out "the great nuisance the number of tippling houses in Winchester are to the soldiers who by this means, in spite of the utmost care and vigilance, are, so long as their pay holds, incessantly drunk, and unfit for service." And he wished that the new commission for the country may have the intended effect, "for the number of tippling houses kept here is a great grievance." However admirable this procedure may have been, it was not particularly good politics for an ambitious young man, for as soon as he offered himself as a candidate the saloon element headed by one Lindsay, whose family were tavern keepers for many years in Winchester, decided to oppose him. His opponent, Capt. Thomas Swearingen, was elected by 270 votes and Washington defeated with but 40 ballots.

With this defeat Colonel Washington learned a lesson in politics, in campaigning, and vote getting that brought him victory in the election in 1758. From this time until the Revolution, George Washington was a member of the House of Burgesses, a period of about 15 years. Twice he was elected from Frederick and then in 1765 he stood for Fairfax, in which Mount Vernon was located. He spent between £40 and £75 at each of these and usually gave a ball to the voters on the night he was chosen.

The first duty that fell to the new burgess was service on a committee to draft a law to prevent hogs from running at large in Winchester. He held this position seriously and was regular in attendance. He took little part in proceedings, yet he made his influence felt, so that when the time came to elect deputies to the First Continental Congress he stood third in order among the seven appointed to attend that body. A year later in the delegation to the Second Continental Congress he stood second, Peyton Randolph receiving one more vote only, and all of the others fewer. This distinction was due to the sound judgment of the man rather than to those qualities that are considered senatorial.

Throughout all of his life George Washington was no speech maker. Thomas Jefferson said of him:

"I served with General Washington in the legislature of Virginia before the revolution and during it with Dr. Franklin in Congress. I never heard either of them speak ten minutes at a time nor to any but the main point which was to decide the question. They had their shoulders to the great points knowing that the little ones would follow of themselves."

The extreme diffidence which he felt and exhibited in 1759 never entirely left him. At that time Speaker Robinson, by an order of the assembly, was directed to return its thanks to Colonel Washington on behalf of the colony for the distinguished military services which he had rendered to the country. As soon as he took his seat in the House the Speaker performed this duty in such glowing terms as quite overwhelmed him. Colonel Washington rose to express his acknowledgment for the honor but was so disconcerted as to be unable to articulate a word distinctly. He blushed and faltered for a moment, when the Speaker relieved him from his embarrassment by saying: "Sit down Mr. Washington, your modesty equals your valor and that surpasses the power of any language that I possess."

When Adams was proposing him for Commander in Chief in complimentary terms he left the room. At his inauguration as President it was noted that this great man was agitated. His reluctance to speaking in public was characteristic throughout his life, and was believed to have been as much from principle as from natural modesty. From 1749 until 1784, and from 1789 until 1799, a period of over 40 years, he held offices of various kinds, and there were really but 6 years, outside of his boyhood, when he was not in public service.

One of George Washington's earliest affiliations was his induction into the Masonic order, which transpired at the Fredericksburg Lodge in 1752, before he was of age. He completed his Master Mason degree in August, 1753. From then little is known of his Masonic record until the beginning of the Revolutionary War, as the records of that lodge were either lost or destroyed.

Before his marriage he was engaged in surveying and in military activities, in which capacities he was moving about or on the frontier, and after marriage, with the exception of his attendance on the sessions of the Assembly in Williamsburg, his time was chiefly spent at Mount Vernon, which was 50 miles from his mother lodge at Fredericksburg. As he thus had so little opportunity for Masonic association it is believed that he took advantage of his visits to his mother and sister also to keep in close touch with his lodge, as many of his intimate friends and associates were among its members.

That he was well known in Masonic circles and that he must have been most zealous and faithful in his interest in its matters is indicated by his active participation in important functions of the craft and the numerous distinguished attentions paid to him by the fraternity from the opening of the Revolutionary struggle.

The first of the many honors conferred upon him by this body was his choice for the post of Grand Master of the Grand Lodge of Virginia in 1778, although he was with the Army in the north. He declined the honor, as he had held no official Masonic position.

Records of Masonic functions of importance during the following years show that Gen. George Washington's name was always presented in connection with some honor or distinction. Lodges were named for him, Masonic literature was dedicated to him, and in many ways the Masonic fraternity acknowledged and saluted him as their most honored and distinguished member not only in America but abroad. The honor of receiving a dedication of Masonic publication had not been given to any American previous to its being conferred three times upon George Washington.

When he was inaugurated first President of the United States, Gen. Jacob Morton, Worshipful Grand Master of St. John's Lodge, the oldest lodge in the city of New York, and also the Grand Secretary of the Grand Lodge of New York, was Marshal of the Day. General Morton brought from the altar of his lodge the Bible on its cushion of red velvet upon which Robert R. Livingston, Chancellor of the State of New York and also Grand Master of its Grand Lodge, administered to George Washington the oath of office as President of the United States.

During his travels, whenever possible, President Washington accepted the invitations of the Masonic groups in the cities he visited.

One of the earliest and most notable events of his second administration as President was the laying of the corner stone of the United States Capitol with Masonic services, on September 18, 1793. These were arranged under the supervision of the Grand Lodge of Maryland and the Alexandria Lodge, No. 22, of which George Washington became the Charter Master under Virginia jurisdiction, April 28, 1788, and served as such about 20 months, called meanwhile to fill the Presidency. His association with this lodge was also peculiarly pleasant to him, especially in his last years, as its membership included many of his lifelong friends, those who had joined him in the chase before the Revolution, served with him through it, and were with him in all associations of public and private life until his earthly career closed. Naturally his association brought this lodge into prominence, as there were few important ceremonies in the locality in which the Masonic body participated without General Washington as the conspicuous figure.

When the lodge decided to have a portrait painted of their Distinguished Master for their lodge rooms, they employed William Williams, an artist of Philadelphia, to execute this commission, following upon a resolution passed in 1793. President Washington sat for the artist in Philadelphia, and in 1794 it was finished and brought to the lodge at Alexandria, after being approved by the President and his family. It is the only painting from life showing General Washington in Masonic regalia. Entirely different from any other portrait of the General, it somewhat resembles in cast and features the famous original Houdon statue in Richmond.

It was ordered, received, and accepted by the group of men who had known the General intimately. They were satisfied that they had preserved for posterity a true, unidealized likeness of their friend, patron, and companion, as the artist followed instructions literally, "Paint him as he is!" These men loved him as he was, and the smallpox scars and black mole under the right ear were faithfully reproduced in the portrait, as were the heavy lines produced by age, and the faulty fit of false teeth incompletely eliminated by Stuart by stuffing the General's lips and cheeks with cotton. So highly do the Masons of the Alexandria Lodge, No. 22, value this faithful likeness of the great Washington that none of the many flattering offers to purchase the picture have received consideration. This lodge also proudly possesses a collection of Washington relics, which they call "The Washingtonia."

These carefully treasured letters, documents, and articles will find a permanent place of high honor when the new memorial to Washington the Mason, now arising on Shooters Hill on the edge of Alexandria, is completed, which is to be for all time the mecca for Masons of the world to do honor to Washington as a man and a Mason.

With the evacuation of Boston by the British, Harvard College conferred upon him the honorary degree of LL.D., the diploma being dated April 3, 1776. Yale followed suit with a similar honor. When William and Mary College made him chancellor in 1788, he was highly gratified and expressed himself in the following letter (February 20) to Samuel Griffin:

"I have been duly honored and greatly affected with the receipt of the resolution of the visitors and governors of William and Mary College, appointing me chancellor of the same, and have to thank you for your polite attention in the transmission. Not knowing particularly what duties, or whether any active services, are immediately expected from the person holding the office of chancellor, I have been greatly embarrassed in deciding upon the public answer proper to be given. It is for that reason I have chosen to explain in this private communication my situation and feelings, and to defer an ultimate decision until I shall have been favored with farther information on the subject.

"My difficulties are briefly these. On the one hand, nothing in this world could be farther from my heart, than a want of respect for the worthy gentlemen in question, or a refusal of the appointment with which they have honored me, provided its duties are not incompatible with the mode of life to which I have entirely

addicted myself; and, on the other hand, I would not for any consideration disappoint the just expectations of the convocation by accepting an office, whose functions I previously knew, (from my pre-engagements and occupations), I should be absolutely unable to perform.

"Although as I observed before, I know not specifically what those functions are, yet, Sir, I have conceived that a principal duty required of the chancellor might be a regular and indispensable visitation once, or perhaps twice, a year. Should this be expected, I must decline accepting the office. For, notwithstanding I most sincerely and ardently wish to afford whatever little influence I may possess, in patronizing the cause of science, I cannot, at my time of life and in my actual state of retirement, persuade myself to engage in new and extensive avocations.

"Such being the sentiments of a heart unaccustomed to disguise, I flatter myself the candid manner in which I have explained them, cannot be displeasing to the convocation; and that the intervening delay between the present, and the moment in which I shall have the pleasure of receiving such ulterior explanations as may enable me to give a definite answer, will not prove very detrimental to the college interests."

Griffin sent him an extract from the statute respecting the duties of the chancellor, which disclosed the fact that neither oath nor personal attendance was obligatory. The Bishop of London had been the last chancellor. Upon receipt of this information, General Washington replied:

"Influenced by a heartfelt desire to promote the cause of science in general, and the prosperity of the College of William and Mary in particular, I accept the office of chancellor in the same; and request you will be pleased to give official notice thereof to the learned body, who have thought proper to honor me with the appointment. I confide fully in their strenuous endeavors for placing the system of education on such a basis, as will render it most beneficial to the State and the republic of letters, as well as to the more extensive interests of humanity and religion. In return, they will do me the justice to believe, that I shall not be tardy in giving my cheerful concurrence to such measures, as may be best calculated for the attainment of those desirable and important objects."

Between the time of his induction into Masonry as a lad of 20 and his death in 1799 he received many honors from academic, municipal, and fraternal organizations. The most important of which a record exists are as follows:

1752, November 4. Fredericksburg Lodge of Freemasons, enters; master of Alexandria Lodge, December, 1788; honorary member

of Holland Lodge, New York City, March 7, 1789.

1776, April 3. Harvard Degree of LL.D.

1780, January 19. American Philosophical Society at Philadelphia, elected member; accepted, February 15; certificate is dated March 22.

1781, January 31. American Academy of Arts and Sciences at Boston, elected honorary member.

April 26. Yale, Degree of LL.D.; diploma is dated September 12.

December 17. Society of the Friendly Sons of St. Patrick at Philadelphia, adopted member.

1782, June 27. Freedom of the City of Albany, N. Y.

1783, June 19. President-General of the Society of the Cincinnati; continued in office through reelection rest of life.

July 4. University of Pennsylvania Degree of LL.D.

November 27. Marine Society of New York, honorary member; certificate is dated November 28.

1784, January 13. Charleston (S. C.) Library Society, honorary member.

December 2. Freedom of the City of New York.

1785, July 4. Philadelphia Society for the Promotion of Agriculture; honorary member.

November. S. C. Society for promoting and improving Agriculture and other Rural Concerns; honorary member.

December 17. Trustees of proposed Alexandria Academy, attends meeting. Academy incorporated in 1786, with Washington named as a trustee until the first annual election by the supporters of the Academy.

1788, January 18. Chancellor of William and Mary College, date of vote of Visitors and Governors in convocation; honorary life position.

1789, June 24. Washington College Degree of LL.D.

1790, September 2. Brown Degree of LL.D.

1795, March 25. Board of Agriculture of Great Britain, foreign honorary member.

In his private life as a plain citizen, George Washington's life was an expression of his ideals of honesty, truth, justice, and charity. He attended every civic duty with the same careful attention he gave to those of his military life and his career as a statesman, even to riding 10 miles to the polling town to vote in the elections because he believed it his duty to do so. Of the many tributes to his character which came alike from friends and enemies, the words of Thomas Jefferson seem most fitting:

"His integrity was most pure, his justice the most inflexible I have ever known, no motives of interest or consanguinity or friendship or hatred, being able to bias his decision. He was indeed in every sense of the word, a wise, a good, and a great man."

(FOR THIS PROGRAM SEE NUMBERS 6, 7, 32, 34, 45, 53, 78 IN LIST OF SELECTED BOOKS ON PAGES 300-A AND 300-B)

George Washington the Christian

COLONEL GEORGE WASHINGTON READING PRAYERS IN CAMP ON THE FRONTIER

INHERITED RELIGIOUS ATTITUDE

USTICE TO MAN and faith in God are two of the most outstanding attributes of George Washington and of his forbears. His recorded lineage and the family history of the Washingtons and the Balls indicate that there were devout Christians in both his paternal and maternal lines.

Dating back to 1426, an account is given of a learned treatise maintaining the rights of his priory written by John de Wessyngton, who was prior of the Benedictine Convent connected with the Durham Cathedral, in northern England. Genealogical records show that it was most probably from these de Wessyngtons of Durham that the Washingtons descended. Two centuries later, comprehensive records show that an immediate progenitor of George Washington served as rector of Purleigh in Essex. This reverend gentleman, Lawrence Washington, was of the Sulgrave branch of the family and the father of John and Lawrence Washington, who emigrated to America about 1657. The elder brother, John, located in Westmoreland County, Virginia. The parish in which he lived was named for him, and in his will he provided that a tablet containing the Ten Commandments be set up as his memorial stone. These facts and the pious phraseology of his will indicate that the great-grandfather of George Washington adhered to the faith of his fathers and handed down that faith through successive generations to his great-grandson.

The motto of the Ball coat of arms, *Coelumque Tueri* (and look to Heaven) is also significant of reverence of a Supreme Being. There is a tradition extant that George Washington is a lineal descendant of John Ball, the "Mad Preacher of Kent," so called because of his "irrepressible preachments" that all men are free and equal.

It is assumed that the religious attitude of this supposed ancestor had its influence, four centuries later, on the son of Mary Ball Washington, inspiring within him that valiant spirit which enabled him to carry the Starry Banner of liberty and freedom to the heights of success. A banner which stood for religious freedom; for George Washington, though christened according to the rites of the English Church, at all times respected the religious convictions of others.

The piety of the American branch of the Ball family is attested to by church and county records. Prominent among the vestrymen of St. Mary's White Chapel, Lancaster County, Virginia, the name of Ball appears for more than 100 years, including that of Col. Joseph Ball, the grandfather of George Washington. It is recorded that he asked for and obtained leave to construct a gallery in White Chapel for his family pew; also that he subscribed £5 (equal then to ten times that sum in our day) toward the salary of the rector of Christ Church, located in the same parish. His son, also named Joseph, half brother of Mary Ball, who became Mrs. Augustine Washington and the mother of George, showed his concern for the future of the clergy in America by

"directing to the Honorable the General Assembly of Virginia a proposition in behalf of himself and the rest of the inhabitants of Virginia, concerning the instructing a certain number of young gentlemen, Virginians born, in the study of divinity, at the county's charge."

He thus signified his willingness to be taxed that the ranks of the native clergy might be filled.

Comment has been made that on the bookshelves in the home where George Washington was born were devotional works. When Augustine Washington brought his second wife to the family home at Bridges Creek she found there a volume bearing the name of his first wife, beneath which she inscribed her own; a volume which she used in her daily devotions, in training her stepsons, and later in teaching her own children; a volume which in still later years George Washington treasured at Mount Vernon and which may still be seen there—Sir Matthew Hale's *Meditations and Contemplations, Moral and Divine.* Another volume to which young George Washington had access was *Sermons of the Bishop of Exeter,* in which his youthful signature appears upon the title page.

There is something soothing in the thought of this little family, so isolated in that little home on the lower Potomac River, between Bridges Creek and Popes Creek, the birthplace of George Washington, now known as Wakefield, and in their later homes on the upper Potomac and on the Rappahannock; finding comfort and companionship in the messages conveyed to them from the printed page; finding spiritual uplift in the family prayers led by Augustine Washington, and in the scriptural lessons, supplemented by such passages as that mentioned by a noted writer of the nineteenth century, who says:

"We note with respect, not unmixed with awe, that the essay *The Great Audit,*—the solemn searching of heart and summing up of and for himself of England's great and good chief justice,— was used by the mother as a lesson to be committed to memory by her children. What pious prescience dictated for her eldest boy a study that closes with these words:

" 'When Thy honor, or the good of my country was concerned, I then thought it was a seasonable time to lay out my reputation for the advantage of either, and to act with it, and by it, to the highest, in the use of all lawful means. And upon such an occasion the counsel of Mordecai to Esther was my encouragement: *'Who knoweth whether God hath not given thee this reputation and esteem for such a time as this.'* "

Contrast with this summing up the words of George Washington in after years, which mayhap were a restatement and personal application of this particular lesson which he mastered so thoroughly under his mother's tutelage. When the notice of his appointment as Commander in Chief of the Continental Army was officially communicated to him, George Washington said:

". . . as the Congress desire it, I will enter upon the momentous duty and exert every power I possess in the service and for support of the glorious cause. . . . But lest unlucky event should happen unfavorable to my reputation. I beg it may be remembered by every gentleman in the room, that I did this day declare with the utmost sincerity I do not think myself equal to the command I am honored with."

Shortly thereafter he wrote to his wife assuring her that the appointment was not of his seeking and of his unwillingness to part with her and the family, adding, "But as it has been a kind of destiny that has thrown me upon this service, I shall hope that my undertaking is destined to answer some good purpose."

So, in keeping with the teachings which sank deep into his consciousness as a young lad, and with his inherited religious attitude, did George Washington solemnly search his heart and lay out his reputation for the honor and good of his country, thereby demonstrating the cardinal virtues of patriotism, courage, justice to man, and faith in God.

GEORGE WASHINGTON AS A CHRISTIAN: IN MILITARY EXPERIENCES

Throughout his military career, from the time he was placed in command of Virginia troops in 1754 to his Farewell Address to the Armies of the United States, George Washington by his own example and by his military orders sought to direct the minds and hearts of his men toward religion and morality and to impress upon them the importance of the proverb that "cleanliness is next to Godliness,"—cleanliness of body, mind, and spirit. His severe chastisement of those who indulged in immoralities and profane language tended to discourage such indulgence, while his commendatory appreciation of deeds well done endeared him to those who were under his command.

Early training had prepared George Washington to fit into unexpected situations and to meet and master emergency duties. After the death of his father, when he was but 11 years old, according to a creditable authority, he was called upon as the eldest son of the family circle to lead the family prayers, while shortly after he had reached the age of majority traditional accounts indicate that he personally read the impressive funeral service of the Church of England at the burial of General Braddock, who had received a mortal wound on the field of battle; the momentous battle where his army was defeated, and where George Washington repeatedly risked his own life endeavoring to rally the soldiers and bring the wounded general off the field. Of this occasion the young warrior wrote to his brother attributing his own escape to "the miraculous care of Providence."

When placed in command of the Virginia Regiment, George Washington earnestly endeavored to have chaplains provided for his little army on the frontier and while stationed at or near Winchester, Va., he required the troops to attend religious service.

There seems to have been some laxity in obeying one of the early military orders of George Washington, that—

"The men parade tomorrow morning at beating the long roll, with their arms and ammunition clean and in good order, and to be marched by the Sergeants of the respective companies to the Fort, there to remain until prayers are over."

The orders for the following Sunday were similar, but doubtless more effective, as they were supplemented by instructions to the officers "to be present at calling the roll, and see that the men so appear in the most decent manner they can." For several Sundays thereafter the men were marched to prayers and within a few weeks the Sunday service was made a standing order for the future. He thereby established a custom which must have proved to be a beneficial influence; if nothing more, it helped the men under his command to form a commendable habit. Perhaps also some of them grasped that "broader view of the influence of religion which comprehends the public good as well as individual well-being" with which George Washington was gifted and which he so ably expressed in after years when he wrote, "Of all the dispositions and habits which lead to political prosperity, religion and morality are indispensible supports."

From the diaries of George Washington and from other sources a close check-up has been made upon the regularity of his church attendance. This establishes a noteworthy fact, that throughout his public life and in times of stress and strain there are more frequent records of his church going than in times of national quiet. On June 1, 1774, he records, "Went to church and fasted all day." This was in conformity with a resolution adopted by the Virginia Burgesses that the day on which the Boston Port Bill went into effect be made a day of fasting and prayer, a resolution to which he religiously adhered, as he did to all such acts of patriotism which were intended for the best interests of the Colonies as a whole.

Shortly after assuming command of the Continental Army at Cambridge, George Washington issued general orders for August 5, 1775, directing that "the Church be cleared tomorrow, and the Revd. Mr. Doyles will perform Divine Service therein at ten o'clock." A later general order provided:

"That the troops may have an opportunity of attending public worship, as well as take some rest, after the great fatigue they have gone through, the General in future, excuses them from fatigue duty on Sunday (except at Ship Yards, or special occasions) until further orders."

The General himself made it a point to attend divine service whenever possible, no matter by what denomination the service was conducted. He was unusually tolerant and broadminded in his religious views and severely condemned the refractory attitude of some of his officers and soldiers who were inclined to mock at certain religious ceremonies. In his instructions to Benedict Arnold, who was given command of the detachment of the Continental Army against Quebec, George Washington specifically stated that—

"the Success of this Enterprise (under God) depends Wholly upon the Spirit with which it is pushed; and the favourable Disposition of the Canadians and Indians. . . . As the Contempt of the Religion of a Country by ridiculing any of its Ceremonies or affronting its Ministers or Votaries has ever been deeply resented You are to be particularly careful to restrain every Officer and Soldier from such Imprudence and Folly and to punish every Instance of it."

In the letter which accompanied these instructions, George Washington again charged Major Arnold to "avoid all Disrespect or Contempt of the Religion of the Country and its Ceremonies."

He further wrote:

"While we are contending for our own Liberty, we should be very cautious of violating the Rights of Conscience in others, ever considering that God alone is the judge of the Hearts of men and to Him only in this case, they are answerable."

There were repeated occasions during the Revolution when George Washington demonstrated his faith in the guidance and protection of the Supreme Being and expressed his belief that "God in His great goodness will direct" the course of the conflict. One incident is cited where, according to the interpretation of a present-day writer, George Washington apparently reversed his usual custom and gave "a distinctly American flavor" to the idea that God was on the side of the American Army by "calling upon the Continental soldier to help God." This interpretation refers to a message sent by George Washington shortly after the capture of Montreal and other victories, in which he wrote:

"The General hopes such frequent favours from divine Providence will animate every American to continue to exert his utmost in the defence of the Liberties of his Country, as it would now be the basest ingratitude to the Almighty and to their Country to shew any the least backwardness in the public cause."

But this same writer concedes with all due reverence that "George Washington became more and more convinced that the hand of God was in those triumphs and greater and greater became his spiritual humility, but not weak dependence on his Creator." An incident is then cited which bears out this point of view. A sudden and violent storm had prevented the British forces from crossing the water to attack the American fortifications at Dorchester Heights. The following quotation is given from a letter written by George Washington to his brother: "That this remarkable interposition of Providence is for some wise purpose, I have not a doubt." This "willingness to accept failure without complaint" the writer considers an exemplification of humility, and adds, "This was rather an extraordinary thing to say, for with the preparations made, all contingencies provided for, and with a sufficiency of ammunition . . . it is quite reasonable to assume that Howe's attempt would have resulted in the complete annihilation of the British Army."

Extraordinary as it may seem to consider the storm which defeated his well-laid plans as an "interposition of Providence," yet it displays the true Christian spirit.

Complying with the urgent request of General Washington, Congress authorized the employment of chaplains for the Army, and the general orders of July 9, 1776, directed that—

"The Colonels or commanding officers of each regiment are directed to procure for Chaplains accordingly, persons of good character and exemplary lives. To see that all inferior officers and soldiers pay them a suitable respect and attend carefully upon religious exercises. The blessing and protection of Heaven are at all times necessary but especially so in times of public distress and danger. The General hopes and trusts, that every officer and man will endeavor so to live and act as becomes a Christian Soldier defending the dearest rights and Liberties of his country."

These same general orders contain an announcement of the Declaration of Independence and express the hope that—

"this important Event will serve as a fresh incentive to every officer and Soldier to act with Fidelity and Courage as knowing that now the peace and safety of his Country depends (under God) solely on the success of our arms."

The custom established two decades before at Winchester was revived during the encampment at Morristown, N. J., where a convenient church edifice was located. It was ordered that—

"All the troops in Morristown except the guards, are to attend divine worship tomorrow at the second Bell; the Officers commanding the Corps are to take special care to have their men clean and decent, and that they are to march in proper order to the place of worship."

Similar orders applied to succeeding Sundays, while the orders for the encampment at Middlebrook were—

"That all Chaplains are to perform divine service . . . with their respective brigades and regiments, where the situation will possibly admit of it."

In announcing (October 18, 1777) the surrender of Burgoyne, George Washington exhorted his troops to "Let every face brighten and every heart expand with grateful joy and praise to the supreme disposer of all Events, who has granted to us this signal success." On this occasion, and also upon December 18, 1777, the day "set apart by the Honorable Congress for public Thanksgiving and Praise," the chaplains were directed to hold divine service with their several corps and brigades.

It was while the army was encamped at Valley Forge that a messenger arrived from Congress bearing the official intelligence that France, through entering into a treaty providing for recognition and alliance, regarded the Confederation as an independent nation. In celebration of this occasion George Washington set apart a special day early in May for military and religious observance. The following orders were issued:

"It having pleased the Almighty Ruler of the Universe to defend the cause of the United American States, and finally to raise us up a powerful friend among the princes of the earth, to establish our liberty and independence upon a lasting foundation; it becomes us to set apart a day for gratefully acknowledging the divine goodness, and celebrating the important event, which we owe to His divine interposition."

Then follows specific instructions to the chaplains to "deliver a discourse suitable to the occasion" and to the commanders of brigades relative to the military formation and procedure, culminating in three huzzas, "Long live the King of France!" "Long live the friendly European Powers!" and finally, "The American States!" Each to be accompanied by specific discharge of musketry and 13 rounds of artillery.

But the third huzza did not prove to be final, for when the General took leave of the scene "there was universal huzzaing 'Long live General Washington!'" Nor was this the final occasion for celebrating special occasions, for the conflict was far from finished. On the day following the surrender of Cornwallis, General Washington directed that "Divine Service is to be performed" and recommended that "the troops not on duty should universally attend with that seriousness of Deportment and gratitude of Heart which the recognition of such reiterated and astonishing interpositions of Providence demands of us."

Eight years to the day (April 19, 1783) from the commencement of hostilities at Lexington, the Commander in Chief ordered "The Cessation of Hostilities between the United States and the King of Great Britain to be publickly proclaimed." After directing the chaplains with the several brigades "to render thanks to Almighty God for all his mercies, particularly for his overruling the wrath of Man to his own glory and causing the rage of war to cease amongst the nations," he provided that every man should be furnished with the means "to drink Perpetual Peace, Independence and Happiness to the United States of America."

The spirit of Christianity and brotherly love was truly manifested in the Farewell Orders of George Washington to the Armies of the United States. Out of the fullness of his heart he spoke to his men as a father might speak to his beloved children. The entire document is well worthy of a careful perusal, but lack of space forbids more than a brief quotation:

"But before the Commander-in-chief takes his final leave of those he holds most dear, he wishes to indulge himself a few moments in calling to mind a slight review of the past. He will then take the liberty of exploring with his military friends their future prospects, of advising the general line of conduct, which, in his opinion, ought to be pursued; and he will conclude the address by expressing the obligations he feels himself under for the spirited and able assistance he has experienced from them, in the performance of an arduous office. . . . May ample justice be done them here, and may the choicest of Heaven's favors, both here and hereafter, attend those, who, under the Divine auspices, have secured innumerable blessings for others."

George Washington as a Christian: Revealed Religious Convictions

In one short sentence George Washington reveals and affirms his deep religious convictions: "It is impossible to reason without arriving at a Supreme Being." In another sentence, still more brief: " 'Tis well," he passes from this world into the presence of that Supreme Being upon whom he so frequently called for aid and guidance in times of stress and turmoil and to whom he so earnestly gave thanks for miraculous protection and successive blessings.

But in the profession of religion it was characteristic of George Washington that his actions spoke louder than his words. Cryptic entries in his diaries afford abundant opportunities for reading between the lines something of far greater import than the terse facts therein set forth; something that revealed his faith, which was invariably supported by his works.

As an able writer of the present day has said, "It was not Washington's habit to picture his own conduct in odes or sonnets," nor do we have documentary evidence that reveal his views at any great extent from a specific standpoint, save in such comments as this: "I shall always strive to prove a faithful and impartial patron of genuine, vital religion." Though he was an Episcopalian, he did not confine his religion to any one denomination. While in Philadelphia, during the four months he presided over the Constitutional Convention, he records in his diary, May 27, 1787: "Went to the Romish Church to high mass." A few Sundays later, at his own church, he "heard Bishop White preach," the first Protestant Episcopal Bishop of Pennsylvania, who was also chaplain of the Continental Congress.

While on a presidential tour through New England (1789) his diary shows that he attended the Episcopal Church in the forenoon and the Congregational in the afternoon, and two Sundays later, "It being contrary to the law and disagreeable to the People of this State (Connecticut) to travel on the Sabbath day . . . I stayed at Perkins' tavern . . . and a meeting house being within a few rods of the door, I attended morning and evening service." The following Sunday he was back in New York and attended service at St. Paul's Chapel, his usual place of worship while at the first Capital.

Upon his election to the Presidency he received many letters of congratulations from the different religious organizations, and his addresses in response thereto are said to "constitute one of the most salutory features of his life and influence, . . . especially memorable for their revelation of his broad spirit of toleration and sympathy and their inculcation of the duty of fraternity and mutual respect which should always govern the various religious bodies living together in the free republic."

To each of the denominations—German Lutheran, Presbyterian, Methodist Episcopal, Reformed Dutch, Quakers, United Baptist, German Reformed, United Brethren, Protestant Episcopal, Roman Catholics, Hebrews, Universal, Congregational, and the New Church in Baltimore—he conveyed assurances of the common protection of the National Government, which knows no differences of creeds but holds all alike before the law. He also touched upon their common duties as citizens. In his letter to the Quakers he pressed this point home by a parenthetical reservation "(except their declining to share with others the burthen of the common defence) there is no denomination among us, who are more exemplary and useful citizens."

In one form or another President Washington reiterates "professions of my dependence upon Heaven as the source of all public and private blessings." To the bishops of the Methodist Church he wrote:

"I take in the kindest part the promise you make of presenting your prayers at the throne of grace for me, and I likewise implore the divine benediction on yourselves and your religious community."

To the United Baptist Churches:

"Every man conducting himself as a good citizen and being accountable to God alone for his religious opinions, ought to be protected in worshiping the Deity according to the dictates of his own conscience."

"Accountable to God alone for his religious opinions." That one phrase speaks volumes. To the Roman Catholics he wrote in similar vein:

"As mankind become more liberal, they will be more apt to allow that all those, who conduct themselves as worthy members of the community, are equally entitled to the protection of civil government."

To the Hebrews:

"I rejoice, that a spirit of liberality and philanthropy is much more prevalent than it formerly was among the enlightened nations of the earth, and that your brethren will benefit thereby in proportion as it shall become still more extensive."

To the New Church in Baltimore:

"In this enlightened age, and in this land of equal liberty, it is our boast that a man's religious tenets will not forfeit the protection of the laws, nor deprive him of the right of attaining and holding the highest offices that are known in the United States."

And to his own denomination, through the bishops, clergy, and laity of the Protestant Episcopal Church, he wrote even more fully:

"On this occasion it would ill become me to conceal the joy I have felt in perceiving the fraternal affection, which appears to increase every day among the friends of genuine religion. It affords edifying prospects, indeed, to see Christians of different denominations dwell together in more charity and conduct themselves in respect to each other with a more

Christian-like spirit than ever they have done in any former age or in any other nation."

To these officials of his own church he also extended—

"cordial thanks for your devout supplications to the Supreme ruler of the Universe in behalf of me. May you and the people whom you represent be the happy subjects of the divine benedictions both here and hereafter."

In his first Thanksgiving Proclamation as President of the United States of America, George Washington declared:

"It is the duty of all nations to acknowledge the providence of the Almighty God, to obey His will, to be grateful for His benefits, and humbly to implore His protection and favor, . . . that great and glorious Being, who is the beneficent Author of all the good that is, or that will be."

Upon retiring from the Presidency he reviewed the incidents of his administration and stated:

"I may have committed errors. Whatever they may be I fervently beseech the Almighty to avert or mitigate the evils to which they may attend."

As in all things, George Washington shrank from any ostentatious display in the practice of his religion. This point is well illustrated in a story that presumably emanated from the minister of Christ Church, in Philadelphia, which emphasized the reticence of the President in publicly expressing his religious views and yet showed his faithful adherence to his own convictions. The President and Mrs. Washington were accustomed to attend regular morning service at Christ Church, while in Philadelphia.

John Marshall, Chief Justice of the United States, said of him, "Without making ostentatious profession of religion, he was a sincere believer in the Christian faith and a truly devout man." It has also been said of him that "His hopes for his country were always founded on the righteousness of the cause, and the blessing of Heaven.

His was the belief of reason and revelation; and that belief was illustrated and exemplified in all his actions."

His own words on various occasions bear out these tributes. He frequently referred to "the all-powerful dispensation of Providence"; the "Benign Parent of the human race"; the "Supreme Ruler of Nations"; and the "Great Author of every public and private good." In reiterating his professions of dependence upon Heaven as the source of all public and private blessings, he observed, "that the general prevalence of piety, philanthropy, honesty, industry, and economy seems, in the ordinary course of human affairs, particularly necessary for advancing and confirming the happiness of our country."

Continuing, he said, "While all men within our territories are protected in worshiping the Deity according to the dictates of their consciences, it is rationally to be expected from them, in return, that they will all be emulous of evincing the sancity of their professions, by the innocence of their lives, and the beneficence of their actions; for no man who is a profligate in his morals, or a bad member of the civil community, can possibly be a true Christian, or a credit to his own religious society."

In his Farewell Address upon retiring from the Presidency of the United States, he expressed a belief that "Morality is a necessary spring of popular government" and that "reason and experience both forbid us to expect that national morality can prevail in exclusion of religious principle." Upon another occasion he asserted, "Of all the dispositions and habits, which lead to political prosperity, religion and morality are indispensable supports," and asked, "Where is the security for property, for reputation, for life, if the sense of religious obligation *desert* the oaths which are the instruments of investigation in the Courts of Justice?"

In his private as well as in his public life, George Washington revealed his religious convictions by his participation in the affairs of the church and by his attendance. He was a vestryman of Truro Parish (which

included the Mount Vernon estate) and warden of Pohick Church. His diary contains repeated entries showing that he and the family "Went to Pohick Church," or "Went up to Church at Alexandria." The latter refers to Christ Church, which is still standing and is still a mecca. There are other entries showing that the condition of the roads prevented travel, and on one occasion there is mention of the carriage breaking down while en route to church. One of the members of his family, George Washington Parke Custis, his step-grandson, recounts that the General "frequently read to his family extracts from the new publications of the day; and, on Sunday, sermons and other sacred writings."

The library of Mount Vernon was well supplied with volumes of sermons and with other religious books, some of them written by old English divines, one of which was especially treasured because of its association with his youth. This volume, Sir Matthew Hale's *Meditations and Contemplations, Moral and Divine,* which bears his mother's autograph on the flyleaf, is still treasured in the Mount Vernon library.

On numerous occasions when George Washington was exposed to unusual danger and was seemingly face to face with the grim reaper, he attributed the preservation of his life to Providence. Once while in camp, during the Revolution, his life was endangered by a severe attack of quinzy sore throat, so serious was his illness that he was asked to indicate a suitable successor. Calmly he pointed out General Greene. Could he have spoken he doubtless would have said, as he did on two later occasions, that he was not afraid to go. Once, while in the first year of his Presidency, when he was prostrated by a malignant carbuncle, he demanded of his physician to know the worst, saying, "Do not flatter me with vain hopes; I am not afraid to die. . . . Whether to-night or twenty years hence makes no difference—I know that I am in the hands of a good Providence." Again, in his last illness, his faith was once more manifested in the words, "I am not afraid to go."

(FOR THIS PROGRAM SEE NUMBERS 23, 99, 103 IN LIST OF SELECTED BOOKS ON PAGES 300-A AND 300-B)

George Washington the Leader of Men

GEORGE WASHINGTON, COMMANDER IN CHIEF, AND HIS GENERALS
After an engraving by A. H. Ritchie

GEORGE WASHINGTON: PATRON OF EDUCATION

GEORGE WASHINGTON was denied the opportunity of supplementing his limited schooling by finishing his education in England as his two half brothers and their father before them had done. He was also not able to attend William and Mary College, where many sons of well-to-do Virginians received their diplomas. Although his youth came to an end with a mere smattering of scholastic culture, yet, as was proven in later years, he had developed a keen appreciation of the value of knowledge. The instruction he received at school was extremely limited, being confined to reading and writing of the English language, a little geography, and a somewhat general knowledge of arithmetic, until he studied under Henry Williams, who taught him surveying. The handicaps that the financial conditions imposed, by preventing him from having the advantages given his brothers, developed in him a strong desire for knowledge.

Education had long been defective or neglected in the Colonies. It fared badly in Virginia for a time. Governor Berkeley, during the seventeenth century, wrote:

"I thank God there are no free schools or printing in Virginia and I hope we shall not have them these hundred years, for learning has brought disturbance and heresy and sects into the world, and printing has divulged them and libels on the best governments. God keep us from both."

The lad George Washington was fortunate in having a cultured father who had a keen desire to see his children educated. And the education of the boy George at a tender age was begun at Epsewasson (Mount Vernon), where his father had moved the family when George was 3 years old. Some idea of the scope of the early schools may be gathered from Rev. Jonathan Boucher, an English clergyman, who came to America

in 1759 and who was later a tutor of John Parke Custis. He wrote of George Washington:

"George, like most people thereabouts at the time, had no other education than reading, writing, and accounts, which he was taught by a convict servant whom his father brought for a schoolmaster."

To have given his son a convict for a teacher was no reflection on Augustine Washington, as many of the transported exiles were educated gentlemen; and, further, it indicates that, in the absence of a school, he was determined to start his son on the road to learning. His first schoolmaster was a convict. His name was William Grove, nicknamed "Hobby," and he was sexton at Falmouth Church, 2 miles from the Washington farm on the Rappahannock, to which George Washington's father moved with his family from Mount

Vernon to be near Fredericksburg about 1739. George was then 7 years old.

In the early schools in Virginia coeducation early appeared in the attendance of both sexes, and George had as schoolmates the girls of the community also.

Most writers have strangely overlooked the preeminent educational and literary influence on Washington of Augustine Washington, his father. The study of Washington's relation to books and the growth of his literary accomplishments, the classical allusions in his writings, as well as the clear, distinct style of the competent man of business, must arouse some recognition of his genial father's influence on the boy's character, which was strengthened by the example and influence of the two half brothers.

The father's death when George was but 11 years old, which left the widowed mother with an estate yielding comparatively little, changed the entire plan of the boy's life. The Virginia gentry had instruction for their daughters at home and sought to have their sons finish abroad or at William and Mary College; but the early death of George's father made this course impossible and a family council decided that he should be trained to earn his living and help his mother.

Soon after the death of his father, George went to visit his brother Augustine at Wakefield. Here he attended the school of Williams, from whom he received his first instruction in surveying and his first inspiration to make it his vocation.

George was especially determined to write a good hand, and eventually acquired a clarity of penmanship that makes his manuscripts remarkably legible. Later in his written regulations for copyists of Government records he directed that there be employed "only those who write a fair hand, that there may be similarity and beauty in the whole execution."

Returning to his mother's home on the Rappahannock, he possibly then entered the school of Rev. James Marye at Fredericksburg. It was then that his earliest manuscript, his school copybook, was written. In addition to documents of business and accounting, it contains the 110 "Rules of Civility" that no doubt were an influence in molding his remarkable character.

George Washington enjoyed surveying. He devoted to it a passionate enthusiasm that never abated and to his last days he surveyed his lands and made his maps and drawings. When he was 15 he went to live with his brother at Mount Vernon and his schooling ended at this time. He was faced with the necessity of earning a living. A short time later he was given a surveying position with Lord Fairfax and then secured a post as public surveyor, receiving his license from William and Mary College as surveyor, and appointment as official surveyor of Culpeper through Lord Fairfax's influence.

Washington, although not a university-trained or a college-bred man, was a reading man, who reflected and deliberated on his reading. Thus he grew intellectually as well as in every other way. He early acquired a habit of seeking all available information upon the subject of the moment. Lord Fairfax said of him: "His education might have been bettered but he is a man who will go to school all his life and profit thereby."

Although Washington had only the common-school education of the day and some engineering and surveying, he made mental and written notes on what he saw and heard and read. In minute and important matters, Washington, from the influence of books, came to be a man of culture.

George Washington acquired a remarkable library of books covering a large variety of subjects. The keynote of his conception of the acquirement of knowledge he expressed in his writings. He said: "I conceive a knowledge of books is the basis upon which other knowledge is to be built."

A strong realization of the deficiencies of his own education and knowledge of its neglect and defectiveness in this country perhaps influenced Washington in the strong attitude he assumed toward the acquirement of knowledge for the youth of the land. Not only was education among the topics in his library and conspicuous among his subjects of research and conference, but his aid to educational institutions and to individuals desiring education was so discriminating and timely as to indicate a standing incentive to thoughtful liberality.

He contributed to the education of many boys in addition to his stepchildren. His interest in the education of youth led Washington to undertake the expense of Bushrod Washington's law studies; of placing two other nephews in school at Georgetown; of the offer of a substantial sum toward the training of George Washington Craik, the son of his friend and physician, Dr. James Craik; and to pay for the education of young John V. Weylie, a lad entirely unknown to him, simply because he had been recommended as a boy of unusual promise. He also paid for the education of Thomas Posey, son of Capt. John Posey, who served under him in the Forbes campaign in 1758 and was a neighbor with a plantation near Mount Vernon.

Washington's continued efforts in the interest of universal education show that his mind was always on the general welfare of the Nation and that he sought practical achievement through the instruction of its youth. During his life he did his utmost to aid and insure education, and when he wrote his will he devoted six pages to the subject.

In the will he made provision for schools, colleges, and universities. The first was a fund for the free education of orphaned and poor children at the Alexandria Academy. A substantial gift was made to Liberty Hall Academy, now Washington and Lee University. In a letter to the trustees of the academy, Washington said:

"To promote literature in this rising empire and to encourage the arts have ever been among the warmest wishes of my heart."

The chief object of Washington's interest in public education was the establishment of a national university in Washington. During his Presidency he persistently urged Congress to heed his suggestions of the need of such an institution. Hopeful to the last, he left for the university a bequest which he considered worth £5,000 sterling, believing that this sum would induce the Federal Government sooner or later to find the means to carry out his plan. This bequest was in the form of 50 shares in the Potomac Company, which he had accepted as a gift from the State of Virginia only on the condition that he should apply it to public purposes. Congress did nothing to take over the bequest and the company failed, so that Washington's design was doubly nullified. But the idea that Washington so fondly cherished still persists and patriotic men and women continue to foster the hope that in some form it may be nobly embodied, a fitting tribute and an added monument to "The Father of His Country."

George Washington: Leader in Advancement of Civilization

It was most fortunate for the United States that its first President was a pioneer in every effort to advance its progress in civilization.

The first two years after the Revolution, the new Government, struggling through its infantile disorders, was literally limping and tottering in its feeble efforts to find a solid footing. Having led his country to victory in the struggle for freedom, Washington still had to lend a hand to the shaping of future policy. In expansion lay the hope of the future. If the United States was to be a living nation it must first of all be an expanding one. Washington was our first expansionist.

He was a practical business man, a careful investor, engineer, builder, explorer, organizer of vast developments, a creator with a vision that leaped ahead of all obstacles and handicaps, bridged a century, as in his mind's eye the completed projects unfolded in the full magnitude of their possibilities; and he did not overlook the detail of operation.

It was thus he visioned an empire from ocean to the Mississippi, as he planned the first steps to unite the country beyond the mountains with the coastal towns by inland waterways, the highways of commerce. No one was a more consistent promoter of colonization than George Washington, in which he was following in the footsteps of his American forbears, whose first large landed holdings came as the reward of their colonizing efforts. But George Washington realized that in order to get the colonists to go to a distant wilderness, to remain there and cultivate the land, to develop the natural resources to a profitable commercial status, they must be provided with means of transport to market their products and means of communication with the centers of population and trade.

To these views Washington's first youthful surveying experiences contributed largely by giving him an unusually keen understanding of the difficulties, dangers, and handicaps of frontier life. He also learned to judge land from various standpoints of value, as farm land, land suitable for grazing stock, locations for mills, and sites for towns. In these matters research shows that George Washington was never actuated by any motives but those of broadest justice, that the benefits might stretch over the largest number of people. His surveys were so true and so skilfully done that they bear the test of modern times.

Back in 1763 he had organized the Mississippi Company. Though it never reached operation, the articles of association in his own handwriting, signed by himself, Francis Lightfoot Lee, John Augustine Washington, Richard Henry Lee, Thomas Bullett (who later founded Louisville), is preserved in the Library of Congress and is a monument to the foresight of these contemporaries of his who followed his leadership. He saw and made them see boundless opportunities in western settlement in the rich country of the Mississippi and of the Great Lakes and never did he regard the vast stretches of western land as waste or incumbrance.

With such ideas he began in 1784 to forge links of trade and commerce that should unite the East and West. So strongly was he convinced of the importance of expansion that even before the close of the Revolution he left his Newburgh camp and made a three weeks' tour up the Mohawk River into the heart of New York State to view for himself that avenue of communication to the West and the Lakes. His letters show the impressions gathered on that journey. The later settlement of the West as far as the Mississippi did not go beyond his vision of a western empire.

His love for his soldiers and his strong sense of justice kept him patiently struggling to secure for them the long-promised bounty lands by which many profited substantially. He proved his own faith in the future value of these lands by adding to his own holdings purchases of tracts of lands in

territory that is now embraced in seven States.

The promotion of canal building, the development of inland waterways to advance settlement, also found practical expression through the various development companies in which he was member, stockholder, and director—the Potomac Company, Dismal Swamp Company, and James River Company—show his abiding interest in the promotion and development of the land to prepare for the settlement which he knew the future would bring.

As a farmer George Washington did his best, in the fragments of time between public services, to attain his ambition of being the leading farmer of America. This was not for personal gratification. He knew the prevailing methods of farming were poor, and that the American farmer lacked the knowledge to raise the best crops from his farms. He made a study of agricultural matters and entered into correspondence with English agricultural experts. He conducted many experiments at Mount Vernon with seeds and soils, fertilizers, cuttings, etc., hoping to make discoveries that would be of value to farmers.

He early abandoned tobacco raising for wheat, and took steps to rejuvenate the land exhausted by tobacco so that other crops would flourish. He made his farming operations intensive rather than extensive, and hoped that his neighbors would follow his methods rather than follow the wasteful practice implied in Jefferson's suggestion that it cost more to fertilize one old acre than to buy a new one. Though land was both cheap and plentiful, so that most of the planters were land poor, cash was so scarce that George Washington did not consider the buying of new land as the answer to the farmer's problem; for he believed the solution lay less in acreage than in induced fertility. He followed the same lines of reasoning in stock raising, in which he also was a leader. He hoped through his own trials, disappointments, and successes to promote methods and practices that would result in a better, finer grade of horses, cattle, sheep, hogs, and poultry. His experiment in mule raising was most successful. He sent his first jack, "Royal Gift," on a tour through the South that the farmers and stock raisers might see the animal, then unknown in America. He hoped by raising a sturdier, less expensive animal to make them popular for both carriage use and as work animals.

In his grounds George Washington was always on the alert for new plans of improvement. He experimented with plants, shrubs, and trees from all parts of the world and was a lover of trees. He planned to have a specimen of every kind of tree indigenous to the climate growing at Mount Vernon. He set out thousands of seeds and cuttings of trees brought from many places

during his various tours and marches. With Thomas Jefferson, George Washington was a pioneer in the planting and culture of pecan trees (sent to him by his correspondents overseas), now such a profitable industry.

George Washington was keenly interested in every new invention and mechanical discovery that promised progress in methods and advancement in productivity. His own plantation boasted possession of new farming implements and labor savers. He went to Bath (Berkeley Springs), W. Va., en route to his western lands in 1784 and watched with great interest the demonstration at the mouth of Sir John's Run of James Rumsey's early experiment in a mechanically propelled boat planned to take the place of the heavy keel boats that required from four to ten men to propel them upstream. Rumsey's boat was intended to save living expenses and wages, as it required but two or three boatmen, and also saved time. General Washington was deeply interested in the demonstration. He encouraged Rumsey and felt that he was on the right track, though he would have to make improvements in his model. Two years later Rumsey successfully propelled a boat by steam on the Potomac River, and in 1792 he successfully operated a steamboat on the Thames. Through the patronage of George Washington he was enabled to get public attention for his models and was undoubtedly a factor in the arousing of America to new possibilities of transportation.

Another most interesting statement showing the foresight of our first President and his faith that anything might be possible to invention is his comment found in his writings under date of April 4, 1784, in which he said that he had only—

"newspaper accounts of air-balloons, to which I do not know what credence to give; as the tales related of them are marvellous, and lead us to expect, that our friends at Paris in a little time will come flying through the air, instead of ploughing the ocean to get to America."

Nearly 10 years later Blanchard made the first balloon ascension in America at Philadelphia, January 9, 1793, which was witnessed by President Washington and his Cabinet. The President presented M. Blanchard with the first aerial passport written in America, which reads:

"To all to whom these presents shall come:

"The bearer hereof, Mr. Blanchard, a citizen of France, proposing to ascend in a ballon from the city of Philadelphia, at 10 o'clock A. M. this day, to pass in such direction and to descend in such place as circumstances may render most convenient — These are therefore to recommend to all citizens of the United States, and others, that in his passage, descent, return or journeying elsewhere, they oppose no hindrance or molestation to the said Mr. Blanchard; and, that on the contrary, they receive and aid him with that humanity and good will, which may render honor to their country, and justice to an individual so distinguished by his efforts to establish and advance an art, in order to make it useful to mankind in general.

"Given under my hand and seal at the city of Philadelphia, this ninth day of January, one thousand seven hundred and ninety-three, and of the independence of America the seventeenth.

"[SEAL]

"(Signed)   George Washington."

Too little attention has been given to George Washington's library, where he gathered his inspiration and his vast fund of information. His cultural growth must have increased greatly in the last years of his life. He was rated by Patrick Henry as the best-informed man in Congress in the days before the Revolution. Among the few private libraries that existed among the early homes of America was that of Lord Fairfax of Greenway Court, and here the young surveyor's choice of books was directed by his patron. When George Washington was the head of his household, he quickly acquired a library of nearly 2,000 volumes that must ever command the respect of American people.

George Washington's high regard for books and his appreciation of education has never been thoroughly understood, probably because he has always been associated in the public mind with military affairs; and when not engaged in military pursuits he is remembered chiefly as the first President of the United States and the hospitable host of Mount Vernon. His achievements as a man of letters and of affairs have been overlooked.

To gaze upon the 400 volumes of carefully written documents, reports, and letters to friends and associates upon every conceivable subject bearing upon the diversified interest that made up this man's public and private life is to feel a respect for him that verges upon awe. Thousands of handwritten sheets came from his hand before the period when there were mechanical devices to substitute for the patient labors of the hand with its quill pen. These volumes of his writings, like his will, suggest a portrait of far more importance than the limning of his physical features. Through them America and the world may read the truest, most perfect biography of George Washington without roseate background of homage or the flourish of ostentation. He stamped his own personality upon his leisure-time reading. His appreciation of books he expressed in these words:

"I conceive a knowledge of books is the basis upon which other knowledge is to be built."

"To promote literature in this rising empire and to encourage the arts have ever been amongst the warmest wishes of my heart."

To be convinced of his personal use of the worn, much-used volumes in his library one has but to study his own writings. It is easy to see that he read for a purpose and that he used his books constantly as a master.

His masterly conception of statecraft, when called to fill the office of first President of the United States, with all precedents to make and none to follow, points clearly to his study of a large number of books on matters historical, governmental, political, educational, military and nautical.

He found serviceable many volumes bearing upon his activities at Mount Vernon relating to building, farming, rotation of crops, road building, horticulture, care of cattle, forestry, shrubbery, flowers, horses, and horsemanship.

Owing to the fact that his library at Mount Vernon became so widely scattered, it is not possible to state positively which were his favorite books and his system of reading. It is evident that he most frequently consulted books that would supply him quickly with the information he sought. He also bought books constantly on the subjects that most absorbed his interest.

His library was augmented by many gifts of books, both in sets and single volumes, in the selection of which he had no part. William Evarts Benjamin has been quoted as saying that in examining 200 of Washington's letters, fully a fourth related to books.

No greater tribute to George Washington's efforts to advance the status of his own country exists than the beautiful Capital City which owes its location so largely to his efforts. To prove his faith in the new Federal city, which was given his name, he also purchased lots and built two houses, although at the time his finances were in a state of depletion. He laid the corner stone of the Capitol Building on September 18, 1793, and before his death he had the satisfaction of walking through the White House, then nearly completed.

The best guide to an understanding of the dreams and the calm faith of the Father of His Country in the high destiny of the Nation he brought into being is to study some of his own words, which reveal the type of government he felt that he and his compatriots had set in motion and under which he believed the United States would one day lead the world. Among them one of the most significant is his circular letter to the governors of the States dated June 8, 1783, preparatory to resigning his commission, in which he says:

"There are four things, which, I humbly conceive, are essential to the well-being, I may even venture to say, to the existence of the United States, as an independent power.

"First. An indissoluble union of the States under one federal head.

"Secondly. A sacred regard to public justice.

"Thirdly. The adoption of a proper peace establishment; and,

"Fourthly. The prevalence of that pacific and friendly disposition among the people of the United States, which will induce them to forget their local prejudices and policies; to make those mutual concessions, which are requisite to the general prosperity; and, in some instances, to sacrifice their individual advantages to the interest of the community.

"These are the pillars on which the glorious fabric of our independency and national character must be supported. Liberty is the basis; and whoever would dare to sap the foundation, or overturn the structure, under whatever specious pretext he may attempt it, will merit the bitterest execration, and the severest punishment, which can be inflicted by his injured country."

George Washington: Leader in Philanthropy

It is a somewhat difficult task to define clearly the meaning of the word philanthropy. Usually the idea given is of an individual who gives large sums of money for charitable purposes or who endows in some substantial manner educational institutions, hospitals, etc. The true meaning is quite different, and in its literal sense it signifies a great love of mankind. In looking back over the pages of American history can a more shining example of a great philanthropist be found than George Washington, who all through his long life showed the strongest disposition to promote happiness or to elevate socially his fellow beings?

To this illustrious Virginian, the welfare of his family was always his dearest interest. His mother was an unfailing source of solicitude to him from his earliest manhood, and it was the strong desire of his heart to make her always comfortable. To the end of his existence he aided his sister and brothers, nieces and nephews in a financial way. Their troubles and disappointments were his, and at times he made great personal sacrifices in his desire to give them a helping hand.

George Washington's sister, Betty, who was said to resemble him in appearance, had married a wealthy man, Fielding Lewis, and for a time their home was beautiful Kenmore, in Fredericksburg. Fielding Lewis manufactured rifles used in the Revolution, and in this manner, by advancing large sums of money, became impoverished. George Washington lent him money from time to time, and he died very much in debt. After her husband's death General Washington continued to give his sister money at different times, and in many other ways he helped her. One of the Lewis boys especially pleased him so well that he appointed him in the Army. Of another General Washington when President wrote to his sister:

"If your son Howell is living with you, and not usefully employed in your own affairs and should incline to spend a few months with me, as a writer in my office (if he is fit for it) I will allow him at the rate of three hundred dollars a year, provided he is diligent in discharging the duties of it from breakfast until dinner— Sundays excepted."

Another son, Lawrence, was advanced by George Washington in every way possible. He was also employed as one of his uncle's secretaries. He eventually lived at Mount Vernon, and most likely through propinquity his life there led to his marriage to Mrs. Washington's granddaughter, Nellie Custis. This marriage so pleased the Washington family that the General made arrangements for Lawrence to build a house on the Mount Vernon estate. He was also made one of the executors of George Washington's will, and he was handsomely remembered in this document.

Another source of heavy weight and great responsibility to George Washington were his brothers. His brother Samuel, who was Mary Ball Washington's third child, was the first of her grown children to die. He had married five times, left a considerable family and a sufficient estate. The property, however, was incumbered. In 1783, two years after his brother's death, George Washington inquired of another brother how Samuel managed "to get himself so enormously in debt?" For years thereafter George Washington's correspondence makes occasional reference to his dead brother's affairs. He undertook the education of two of Samuel's sons, and in his will directed that the accounts between his brother's estate and himself should stand balanced.

Samuel's sons and also his daughter Harriot, also shared in George Washington's estate. He had assumed the care of Harriot on her father's death, and she was an inmate at Mount Vernon until her marriage 11 years later. She was evidently a trial to the Washington household. One of her chief failings was "no disposition . . . to be careful of her cloaths" which were "dabbed about in every hole and corner and her best things always in use," so much so that her uncle said, "She costs me enough."

General Washington was particularly devoted to his brother, John Augustine, who was most helpful to him at times by managing his estate when he was absent from home, and it was to his brother's son, Bushrod, that Mount Vernon was left. George Washington's nephews seem to have been

legion, and in his kind, generous way he carried them all. Another nephew, George Augustine Washington, a son of his brother Charles, he helped in every way, and when he was threatened with consumption it was his uncle's purse which supplied him with funds. When George Augustine died, he wrote to the young widow and invited her and her children "to return to your old habitation at Mount Vernon. You can go no place where you are more welcome, nor to any where you can live at less expense and trouble," an offer he added, "made with my whole heart."

To his wife's kith and kin he was equally generous. General Washington several times urged his mother-in-law, Mrs. Dandridge, to make Mount Vernon her home. He invited Colonel Bassett, who had married his sister-in-law, with his whole family, to be his guests for an indefinite period at the Warm Springs. To a brother-in-law, Bartholomew Dandridge, he lent money and forgave the debt to his widow in his will. He also gave her the use for life of a number of slaves, bid in by him at the bankruptcy sale of her husband's property. At different times George Washington had as wards or assumed the expenses of nine children belonging to his immediate family.

It might be well said of George Washington that although he was generous to a fault he tried hard not to be imposed upon. Realizing his generous nature he received constant applications for aid, most of which he investigated. One fact which stands out in bold relief is that he never forgot a friend. The truthfulness of this statement is shown in his friendship for Ramsey, Craik, Greene, and Lafayette. In George Washington's ledger a special act of kindness is shown to Dr. James Craik, who was his friend and physician all through his life. He helped materially to educate his young son, and on his graduation the youth for a time was in his employ. George Washington Lafayette was the son of Marquis de Lafayette, who was one of General Washington's commanders during the Revolution. At the time of the French Revolution General Lafayette languished for several years in the Austrian prison at Olmutz. His wife, Madam Lafayette, was also in prison, but husband and wife were separated. She was confined in the prison La Force in Paris. Upon hearing about the predicament of this French woman, realizing at such times money is one's best friend, George Washington, through the American Minister, James Monroe, deposited 200 guineas at a bank in Paris subject to her order. Upon Madame Lafayette's release from prison her first act was to engage passage for her son George for America, where he remained until his father's release. George Washington took a lively interest in the young man. In returning to France all of young Lafayette's traveling expenses were defrayed

by General Washington, and he was also generously provided with pocket money.

Another instance of the philanthropy of the first President is the family of Gen. Nathanael Greene, a devoted friend of the great General. After General Greene's death George Washington learned that his widow was left in embarrassed circumstances, and in his usual compassionate manner offered to give his namesake, George Washington Greene, if entrusted to his care, "as good an education as this country (I mean the United States) will afford, and will bring him up to either of the genteel professions that his frds. may chuse, or his inclination shall lead to pursue at my cost & expense."

General Washington was a kind master, and many striking illustrations are given of his kindness to his slaves. In 1791 there were about 250 "hands" at Mount Vernon, not counting house servants. It can be readily understood that with so many mouths to feed and individuals to be clothed it was a case of literally eating one "out of house and home." It was a serious predicament and apparently there seemed no remedy. General Washington was unwilling to sell the overplus, thereby often separating families, because as he so humanely said, "I am principaled against this kind of traffic in the human species." Continuing he said, "it would really be to my interest to set them free, rather than give them victuals and cloaths." When the great State of South Carolina refused to pass an act to end the slave trade he expressed the "wish from my soul that the legislature of that state would see the policy of a gradual Abolition of Slavery, it would prevent much further mischief." What vision! Could it be possible that he was accorded the privilege of looking through the vistas of time? To the end of life George Washington never changed his views on this momentous question. A clause in his will directed that "upon the decease of my wife it is my will and desire that all slaves which I hold shall receive their freedom."

For his long and arduous services during the Revolutionary War General Washington took no compensation. He kept a correct book of his business transactions and produced a written voucher for every disbursement he made of public funds.

During his lifetime General Washington had been generous to the cause of education. He had voluntarily assisted many of his young relatives to educate their young sons and had annually subscribed 50 pounds a year for the education of the children of Alexandria. He carried this thought of the education of the poor to the framing of his will, bequeathing canal shares as part of the endowment of a proposed university in the District of Columbia and to Liberty Hall, now Washington and Lee University. From day to day his account books show strong evidence of his numerous charities.

During his absence from Mount Vernon in Revolutionary days he left orders behind that all poor persons applying for food or shelter should have ample care.

All through his long life George Washington was deeply affected by physical suffering in others. On one of his many visits to Bath, now Berkeley Springs, West Virginia, where the waters were reputed to help persons suffering from rheumatism, he found many gathered there hoping to be relieved from distress. Some were poverty-stricken who could ill afford to pay all expenses attendant on such an expedition. After viewing this suffering George Washington, tradition tells, went to a near-by baker shop and left an order that all patients at the Springs who applied for bread were to be given as much as they could consume at his expense.

Many other instances of the philanthropy of George Washington could be cited. Much has been related of this great man's fame as well as his fortune. In ages to come George Washington will stand out as America's most humane citizen. Philanthropists are born, not made.

(FOR THIS PROGRAM SEE NUMBERS 33, 40, 62, 92, 104 IN LIST OF SELECTED BOOKS ON PAGES 300-A AND 300-B)

GEORGE WASHINGTON THE LEADER OF MEN

Top, left: SURVEYOR—STARTING ON THE 1748 EXPEDITION. *Top, right:* FARMER—THE HARVEST AT MOUNT VERNON.
Bottom, left: STATESMAN—ON THE WAY TO THE CONTINENTAL CONGRESS. *Bottom, right:* SOLDIER—BATTLE OF PRINCETON

The Social Life of George Washington

A RECEPTION BY MRS. WASHINGTON
From a painting by Henry A. Ogden

SOCIAL LIFE OF CHILDHOOD HOME

HISTORY tells us less than we should like to know about the childhood days of George Washington. Unfortunately for posterity, he wrote little about his own recreations and boyish experiences. Using a hackneyed quotation, however, "boys will be boys," leads one to believe that he was just a normal, fun-loving youngster. About the time George was 3 years old his father, Augustine Washington, removed from the Bridges Creek home, taking his family to the Little Hunting Creek (Mount Vernon) property. The second move to a plantation on the Rappahannock River opposite Fredericksburg was in order to be near his iron business. This farm, then in King George County, is now within the boundary of Stafford.

Augustine Washington did not tarry long on earth after his removal to the farm on the Rappahannock, but, like many of his early known forbears, died at a comparatively early age, being only 49. Thus widowed at the early age of 35, Mary Ball Washington gathered her little brood closer around her knee and started off in life alone with but one thought in mind, making them sober-minded and industrious, as well as God-fearing citizens. Her means were narrow; for although Augustine Washington was able to leave what was called a landed estate to each son, it was little more than

idle capital, and the income in ready money was by no means as evident as the acres. Social life in the home under these circumstances must have been decidedly restricted.

It is not difficult to place Mary Ball Washington in her home on the Rappahannock River. She was the central figure there, gifted with strong sense and the power of conducting business matters providently and exactly. It was therefore from this abode on the banks of the picturesque Rappahannock that George Washington went forth to attend his first school in Falmouth, just across the river from Fredericksburg, kept by Sexton "Hobby." It is apparent that he learned the rudiments readily, the alphabet and pothooks, as George Washington was a studious lad. Work and play at this stage of life must have been much intermingled in his case, as it is with every red-blooded child.

School life in these days was an all-day affair. Each pupil, as the distances were so long, carried his lunch basket or dinner along, and under these circumstances the boys must have enjoyed fine frolics around the primitive log-cabin schoolhouse in the Virginia hills. "Hop Scotch," "bandy," and marbles were played, and still more wonderful to relate, each youngster could produce a jackknife. What boy from the beginning of creation has not been the proud possessor of a jackknife? With its aid endless toys were fashioned, popguns, willow whistles, windmills, box traps, etc., and best of all, George could whittle to his heart's content.

It was at this farm, it is traditionally said, that George Washington performed the miraculous task of throwing a coin across the Rappahannock. Possibly it might not be inappropriate to state apropos of this great feat that a well-known wit over 25 years ago was escorting a distinguished party of foreigners to Mount Vernon. One of them asked whether it was really true that General Washington in his youth had thrown a shilling clear across a certain river. The loyal American replied that every word of it was gospel truth, but that in after years he had done still better—he had tossed a sovereign across the Atlantic. Little remains of the Washington home on the Rappahannock River. The house was replaced long ago by a more modern structure. The visitor, however, may drink from the same spring from which George Washington drank and see the old ferryhouse where he is said to have crossed the river.

The home Mary Washington made for her five children was one of great simplicity, fitting the quiet surroundings, of unquestionable order, and of the highest moral tone. There was an active outdoor life there, too, and nothing could have been more wholesome for manly boys. There were always horses to ride. There was plenty of game in the forest or in the surrounding hills, which supplemented other abundant supplies of the times. At the foot of the eminence was the Rappahannock, where seagoing ships were often anchored and where a fishing rod could be obtained. The youths of the neighborhood during the long, hot summer days generally met at the old ferryhouse and went in swimming together. Hobbs' Hole was said to be the deepest place in the river. It was reputed to be four fathoms deep, and here George Washington and his companions became past masters in aquatic sports. Apropos of swimming, it is a matter of court record that upon one occasion when George had been in for a long swim, when coming ashore he discovered that his clothes had been stolen. The thief chanced to be a colored woman who was subsequently punished for the act. Another source of pleasure for the boys of the county was an old race course which ran back to Chatham and was another general meeting ground for the growing lads of the region.

The quiet hour of the day came early for the little Washingtons, the hour known to every boy and girl of long ago when the mother of the family gathered her little ones around her. Can you see the picture? George and his brothers close up, while small Betty Washington has the seat of honor, her mother's lap. The candles are lighted, and shadows fall here and there in the old bedroom. Think of restless boys called in from their sports to sit in silence! But hark, what is Mary Washington saying? She is telling them, perhaps, to "Remember thy Creator in the days of thy youth," of self-denial, forebearance, or of the vexations and vanities which arise from earthly hopes, and perchance of moderation in every form. Pretty stern talk for tired children. But this Virginia mother was sowing seed and laying a foundation for a life to follow, which the world feels was a hallowed one.

At the precocious age of 11 George Washington was sent back to the Bridges Creek estate (which later became known as Wakefield), to be under the care of his half brother, Augustine Washington, who had inherited the plantation from his father. In family council it was decided that Mary Washington, though quite capable of rearing her family, should be relieved of some of the many great responsibilities which surrounded her. In this manner the youngster, George, found himself again back at his birthplace, in a section of the country often called the Athens of America. Augustine Washington had married a Virginia heiress, Anne Aylett, and George soon found plenty to do, not only advancing himself in his studies but also playing with the children of the vicinity. Meanwhile he was learning to be decidedly expert in mathematics. He also studied hard to be a skilled penman, training himself at this juncture to produce the handwriting which so distinguished all of his letters throughout his life.

Popes Creek, a shallow inlet, touched the bluff below the plantation. Here the companions of George Washington congregated, fished, swam, and perchance watched the fish, whole schools of them, as they flashed their silver sides in open defiance of the boys on the banks of the stream. Westmoreland County has always been a great country for sheltering pines and cedar trees, and where cedar berries grow birds are always to be found both winter and summer. Here, too, the bobwhite whistles in the upland fields, and the redbirds in the briars down among the branches. Waterfowls fed in the creek or passed honking overhead. Every youth was a "crack shot," and young George Washington was no exception to the rule.

The neighborhood was a social one. Apart from the large family connection gathered there, some of the near-by neighbors were especially congenial. This certainly was the case of the Lee family of Stratford, only 2 miles away. Thomas Lee, at this time the owner of Stratford, had six sons, and his third son, "Dickey," as he was then called, and George Washington were born only a month apart. They were bosom friends, and we hear of "Dickey" and George spinning tops and doubtless swapping marbles. If these two youngsters playing so heartily together then and there could have looked through the vistas of time they might have marveled. Future greatness awaited them both. "Dickey," or Richard Henry Lee, became one of the Signers of the Declaration of Independence. His pathway and George Washington's frequently converged. When President-elect Washington arrived in New York to be inaugurated first President of the United States, "Dickey" Lee, his companion of childhood days, was among the first to greet him. He was one of the five Members of Congress appointed to welcome the President-elect. Other early playmates of George Washington later found a place in history.

In Westmoreland County, as elsewhere, George Washington was particularly active in athletic sports. He was always a faithful student, but at the same time he was always a leader in all boyish games. It is said above all else he dearly loved to play soldier, and tradition states that he was the boy generally selected by popular vote to be the captain. The same source of tradition is responsible for the story that it was at the Rappahannock River Farm as a much younger child he organized his first small company of soldiers with the help of his first cousin, Lewis Willis, who lived in the nearby hills. This certainly was the age of soldiery, conforming to the modern newspaper cap and broomstick once so well known to every little boy.

When George Washington was about 15 he went to live with his brother Lawrence at Mount Vernon, which was destined ever afterwards to be his home. Lawrence, who had married a Fairfax of Belvoir, had established himself at Mount Vernon. Life now opened to our youthful hero a broader and gayer horizon. The Washington and Fairfax families resided near each other and, socially speaking, the two families were one. It was in this exhilarating environment that George Washington spent the formative years of his social life. Suddenly to find himself placed in a decidedly more lively neighborhood must have been at first a trifle disconcerting. However, the young lad appears to have been quite equal to the emergency, as he soon appears riding to the hounds, drinking tea in Mrs. Fairfax's drawing room, and even making up to several young girls, guests of his hostess, who touched his boyish fancy. The English style of living prevailed in this part of Virginia, and Mrs. Lawrence Washington and the Fairfax family entertained each other at dinner parties in the most conventional style. With his new, gay friends and companions George Washington drank in moderation from the fountain of pleasure, learning from them many things. These happy, early days spent at Mount Vernon brought to the growing youth a knowledge not obtained from books. Unthinking and young, the pleasure of life must have seemed almost made for him. As the years passed, however, honors were thrust upon him; but it can be truthfully said of George Washington that he never for a single moment lost his poise, and to the end of life was the same unobtrusive, sympathetic, enduring American citizen.

The question has been asked, what did the grown-up people in Virginia in colonial days do for amusement? The New England women gave quilting parties and apple-paring "bees" were enjoyed, but it was not so in the Old Dominion. Most of the pleasures centered around the church. Spending the whole day with a friend was a form of sociability much in vogue in Virginia, when both dinner and supper were served, and the table would fairly groan with good things to eat. Transient guests were offered eggnog or wine and cake.

It is told of colonial Virginia that neighbors literally vied with each other in keeping the hearth fires burning. Matches at this time were not invented; the flint and steel alone was used in making a fire. Often the housewife in her extremity found the easiest way out was to send to the nearest neighbor for live coals. Distances were frequently great and oftentimes these coals were carried a mile. Occasionally these hot-coal carriers are to be found in antique shops.

"The lady of the house," as she was usually called in colonial days, carried heavy responsibilities. Everything possible was produced on the plantation. Cloth to be made into garments was spun by the women slaves, there was a shoemaker, and a blacksmith, among the bond servants, and usually a feed mill was part of the equipment of every farm. Candles were molded in the kitchen. Preserves were cooked out-of-doors in a kettle hanging from a tripod over a wood fire. During fruit-drying times everybody worked hard, as canning was unknown, and sun-dried apples, peaches, and cherries gave variety to the winter's fare. Each mistress of the establishment weighed and measured every day from locked storerooms the food for the household as well as for the slaves. Delicious food was cooked in an outdoor kitchen, having the facilities of a great open fireplace with various cooking utensils. Abundant hospitality prevailed all through Virginia, and it is reasonable to believe Mary Ball Washington's happiness and pleasure were in keeping a well-regulated home.

SOCIAL LIFE BEFORE THE REVOLUTION: AT WILLIAMSBURG AND MOUNT VERNON

It is quite apparent in turning over the pages of musty books of the past that George Washington did not consider himself as a citizen of any especial section of his native State but of the whole of Virginia. To illustrate this fact some of his commissions are on file in various counties. A copy of his commission as Commander and Chief of the Continental Army is to be seen in the records of Spotsylvania County. Strange to say, there is nothing in the archives in the ancient college of William and Mary at Williamsburg of a surveyor's commission being granted him. The present officials of the college firmly believe that it was obtained there, but in some unfortunate way it was not noted. However, this record has not been entirely lost. In the clerk's office of the ancient courthouse of Culpeper County there is on file the following entry:

"20th of July 1749 [o. s.] George Washington, Gentleman, produced a commission from the President and Masters of William and Mary College, appointing him to be surveyor of this county, which was read, and thereupon he took the usual oath to His Majesty's person and government, and took and subscribed to the abjuration oath and test, and then took the oath of surveyor."

The date of the foregoing copy of George Washington's commission as a surveyor establishes him in or around Williamsburg at an earlier period than generally given. The world considers a boy of 17 decidedly immature, but, socially speaking, a lad of this age in colonial days and also in society nowadays plays a man's rôle. As is so well known, Williamsburg was the seat of the colonial government, which in Virginia resembled a little royal court. During the months when the House of Burgesses met it was filled with government officials and with the families of the lowland grandees. Naturally, it was regarded by the young people as a place to have a thoroughly good time. Possibly in some of these hurried trips to Williamsburg Washington met charming young women who especially struck his fancy. The Cary family lived on a plantation on the James River, and Mary Cary, Lucy Grimes, and Mary Bland were among the lively, handsome girls who in boyhood's day seem to have made an impression upon him.

George Washington was always a prime favorite, and it may be well said it was not without reason. Even in boyhood his appearance was engaging. His face, though a trifle sober, always beamed with intelligence, but best of all with a happy, hopeful spirit. His figure was particularly fine; he was a dashing rider and he was devoted to manly sports. He loved to dance and he did it well and gracefully. Indeed, he so thoroughly enjoyed the rhythm that he kept it up until quite late in life. These were the days of the Virginia reel, the stately minuet, and probably some square dances. The round dances—waltz, polka, polonaise, mazurka, and schottish—came into Europe and America much later.

But his occasional trips to the gay capital, Williamsburg, did not keep George Washington from his books. Habits formed in early life had made him a student, and his application was unusual. It was some years after he had received his commission as a surveyor from William and Mary College that he made the acquaintance of the colonial Governor of Virginia, Robert Dinwiddie, who started him out on his first military career by sending him on a mission to the French on the Ohio River. He left Williamsburg without any military escort in 1753, on a journey out and back of nearly 600 miles. No more signal test could have been given George Washington's characteristics and talents than this expedition. The following year he commanded an advance force against the French; but in the end, after a valiant defense of the rude works in Great Meadows, which he called Fort Necessity, surrendered to a superior French force, and marched back over the mountains to Virginia again. There is a parchment deed in the possession of Mrs. Lorenzo Lewis, of Berryville, Virginia, the wife of a direct descendant of Nellie Custis Lewis, in which King George gives George Washington many acres of land. This deed bears the signature of the Earl of Dunmore and the royal seal, and was given to Washington as his share of the Fort Necessity expedition bounty.

There is every evidence to suppose that the youthful George Washington while on his short trips to Williamsburg was included in the parties at the Palace, as the residence of the royal Governor was called. Also, he was often at the Raleigh Tavern, which stood next to the capitol and the college, and where all of the routs, barbecues, and splashes were held. In this same tavern the great and mighty met for their discussions; in fact, it was one of the most popular meeting places in George Washington's time.

Ten years after George Washington had received his commission as a surveyor he returned again to Williamsburg. He had been elected to the House of Burgesses, a position at one time held by both of his half brothers and naturally a place to which every Virginia gentleman aspired. He had tried before in 1755 to be elected, but without success, in both Frederick and Fairfax Counties. At the time of his election both seats from Fairfax County were filled, but George Washington showed at this youthful age a characteristic which he possessed to an unlimited degree; he was undaunted. He made the application again in Frederick

County, where he had the courage to try his luck for the second time. He took the poll at Winchester and was duly elected. In selecting Frederick County he had been strongly influenced by the fact that his friend, Lord Fairfax, was there and could throw much influence toward his election. Washington's headquarters had also been at Winchester for several years. Naturally his Lordship materially aided him; he was always interested in his young protégé, but it must have been decidedly discouraging, a real wet blanket as it were, to be told in the beginning of his campaign by Fairfax "that he would be very hard pushed." Possibly this remark in the end was quite justified.

These were still the days of Williamsburg's glory. The town had been originally laid out on a generous scale. The tavern keepers then were often the big men of the place, and at this period the Raleigh Tavern was still flourishing, kept by Anthony Hay. The House of Burgesses met in the Apollo Room of this inn for unofficial action, and within these same walls most of the social festivities were held. Fine orchestras were then unknown. Happy youth danced to the music of the fiddle, and often these musicians belonged to the colored race. It is tradition that the best music was played in the "wee sma' hours." The gayety was often kept up until morning light, when the fair maidens were conducted to their doors by manly escorts. These were happy, rollicking days of colonial life in Virginia, and doubtless young George Washington and his bride were among the gayest of the gay.

A true story of social life before the Revolution could not be told without dwelling briefly upon the horse racing of the period. Large sums of money changed hands at such times, and the race course was a favorite meeting place for the old-fashioned Virginia gentlemen. Cards were played for high stakes, and lotteries added thrills and excitement to the everyday life. In his diary George Washington frequently speaks of lotteries; indeed, William and Mary, Princeton, and some of the other colleges held lotteries from time to time.

In 1765 George Washington was again elected to the House of Burgesses. He had previously been reelected in 1761 from Frederick County. This time he had the gratification of being selected for this high office from his own county, Fairfax. Six years before he had married the widow Custis, and it was in a house owned by her they resided when at Williamsburg. The house was always called the House of the Six Chimneys. Unfortunately, with a number of other historic buildings, including Raleigh Tavern, it has disappeared. During one of these sessions attended by George Washington, called by Lord Botetourt, 89 laws were enacted. It seems almost like current history to hear the titles of some of them—"suppressing private lotteries," "laying the duties on liquor," etc. One of these sessions was a particularly gay one, judging from George Washington's diary of that date. Every evening for one week a dinner party was given, and during this period a ball at the Capital is especially noted. Late dinners are noticed, an innovation which did not exist outside of the capital city.

Social life at Mount Vernon before the Revolution is an inspiring theme. In 1758 Mount Vernon was put in fine condition to receive its new mistress. Repairs were supervised by George William Fairfax, who was asked by George Washington to have an eye to the job. The roof was raised and the mansion generally freshened, and it was during the following year the bride was brought to her new home on the banks of the Potomac. In fact, everything had been put in order for the home-coming of George and Mrs. Washington, and the new wife soon settled down to the routine of everyday life. The rôle played by a mistress of an establishment of this size must have been a somewhat difficult one. In Martha Washington's case she had two young children, and there were numerous servants whose duties required constant supervision. Then there were many guests to be entertained. Mount Vernon had always had a great reputation for hospitality, and undoubtedly she tried to the best of her ability and strength to live up to its former record.

George Washington, as is generally known, was a man of action and when he came in from inspecting the farm from one of his long horseback rides his wife would always have ready for him some refreshments—sugar cakes, thin biscuits, chocolate cakes, etc., and hot mulled chocolate. Mrs. Washington was a notable housekeeper and attended personally to everything which was for the comfort of her husband.

George and Mrs. Washington drove from Mount Vernon to attend the "bread and butter" ball in Alexandria. The proprietors of this ball were Messrs. Carlyle, Laurie, and Robert Wilson. In George Washington's diary he tells of this entertainment in not too flattering terms. Music and dancing seem to have been the chief diversion, and in a detached room provided for the purpose abounded plenty of bread and butter, some biscuits, and tea and coffee. The latter, it is said, the guests could not distinguish from sweetened water. Pocket handkerchiefs served for tablecloths and napkins, and no apologies were made for this informality. George Washington did not regard this ball as a pleasing episode. To him it was a humiliation to take his new wife to such an ill-arranged and meager affair, especially as she was accustomed to the formality and state attending many of the Williamsburg parties.

A few days after this unfortunate entertainment the Washingtons gave a dinner at Mount Vernon for Lord Fairfax, who was visiting at Belvoir. The party was a most congenial one. Among those attending were Col. and Mrs. George William Fairfax, Col. Thomas Bryan Martin, and Rev. Doctor Charles Green, the rector of Pohick Church, who was accompanied by his wife.

And so the days passed at Mount Vernon before the Revolution. The guest rooms were always filled, and even the attic was furnished to accommodate the overflow. All the principal food was furnished by the plantation. Vegetables were raised in profusion in the garden. The butter was made in the dairy, and with milk and cream was kept in the cool spring house near by. Turkeys and chickens were raised on the farm, barrels of sugar were in the pantry, brown sugar to be used by the slaves and for cooking, and lump sugar for the mistress's table. Desserts were all made in the kitchen and consisted principally of pies, puddings, jellies, whips, floating island, sweetmeats, etc. Yeast powders were not in vogue at this period, and stiffly beaten eggs were principally used to lighten cake dough. For what was known as "light bread" a combination was used made of hops and potatoes, which was allowed to ferment. The beaten biscuits, so well known below Mason and Dixon's line, and corn cakes, or batter cakes, were the breakfast breads used. The biscuit ingredients were of the simplest kind—flour, water, and a little shortening—but the dough was beaten half an hour with a flatiron to lighten it.

At Mount Vernon the latchstring was always out to George and Mrs. Washington's relatives and friends, and here the man of destiny, George Washington, lived. The doors of the threshold of the Revolution were ajar. From this home he went forth to fight for American liberty, and a few years later to fill the exalted office of the first President of the United States.

SOCIAL LIFE IN LATER YEARS

When George Washington rode forth from Mount Vernon on the 4th day of May, 1775, accompanied by two other Delegates bound for the Second Continental Congress, he could not foresee that he was leaving behind for so long a period the pleasures of social enjoyment and domestic repose beneath his own hospitable roof. He was deeply attached to his wife, his friends, and his home, but when the call of his country came he went forth to take command of the troops at Cambridge without turning back to bid his loved ones farewell, "not doubting," as he wrote to Mrs. Washington, "but I shall return safe to you in the fall."

But the fall came and went, and it became apparent that his return was indefinite indeed, so he sent for Mrs. Washington to join him at his military headquarters in Cambridge. Meanwhile, realizing as he did the need of social diversion at Mount Vernon to offset war-time worries, he had written to his brother, "I shall hope that my friends will visit and endeavor to keep up the spirits of my wife as much as they can."

The journey of George Washington to Cambridge was somewhat interrupted by receptions which awaited him along the route. On the last stretch of 100 miles, from Springfield, Mass, to Cambridge, the cavalcade was greeted by a continuous ovation.

A stately colonial mansion, Craigie House, had been fitted up, by order of the Provincial Congress, for the permanent headquarters of the Commander in Chief, a mansion which later became the home of Henry Wadsworth Longfellow. During its occupancy by General Washington, as well as before and since, highly cultured society gathered there. Mrs. John Adams and Mrs. Mercy Warren were among the patriotic women who helped to make life more homelike for the General and his staff. Mrs. Warren was a sister of James Otis (one of the earliest advocates of the cause of colonial freedom).

Writing of Washington, Lee, and Gates, Mercy Warren said: "The first of them I think one of the most amiable and accomplished gentlemen, both in person, mind and manners, I have ever met with." Of Maj. Gen. Charles Lee, second in command, she made mention as—"careless . . . his garb ordinary, his voice rough, his manners rather morose, yet sensible, learned, judicious and penetrating, a considerable traveller, agreeable in his narrations, and a zealous, indefatigable friend of the American cause."

It was sad that he should later merit his dismissal by insubordination and even treasonable intrigues. Adjutant General Gates was described as "a gentleman in manners, thoroughly acquainted with the arts and blandishments of good society; social, pliant, obseqious and vain, . . . his deportment extremely winning."

General Greene, who commanded a Rhode Island corps, which he had drilled himself and which, because of exceptional military bearing, formed the elite of the Army, welcomed General Washington on behalf of himself and his fellow officers. Every day these and other cultured officers dined at the table of the Commander in Chief, who, though always social, was not convivial, being a stranger to excess in eating and drinking. These dinners were more in the way of military conferences than social diversion, for there were many problems to solve and many handicaps to overcome.

Amidst his absorbing cares and military duties George Washington found time to give consideration to affairs at home. He arranged for Mrs. Washington to join him in Cambridge, but wrote to his manager to "let the hospitality of the house with respect to the poor be kept up." On the journey to Cambridge Mrs. Washington was accompanied by her son, John Parke Custis,

and his wife, also by a retinue of servants. They traveled by chariot, as was the custom of that period. Their military escort was supplemented by guards of gentry made up from the country and villages through which they passed. They received unremitting attentions, and in Philadelphia a ball had been arranged in Mrs. Washington's honor, which she was to have attended with Mrs. Hancock, wife of the President of the Continental Congress. For diplomatic reasons it was deemed advisable at the last moment to cancel the arrangements, "such an assembly being in violation of the eighth article of the American Association, adopted by Congress a year before." She was constantly entertained, however, in a more private manner during the few days she spent in Philadelphia. All through New Jersey, New York, and New England she received delicate attentions, and arrived in Cambridge December 11, 1775.

Her advent has been described as "a joyous occasion, not only for the commander-in-chief, but for the whole army. . . . The presence of Mrs. Washington seemed to shed a genial light upon the rough visage of war."

Wives of other officers came to help make the Christmas holidays more homelike and there were many social gatherings at headquarters and among the inhabitants. Cares were lightened by the presence of joyous and beautiful femininity mingling with the gayly attired military forces.

The friendships which Mrs. Washington formed at Cambridge and at other military headquarters with the socially elect of that period were treasured by her throughout the remainder of her lifetime, as is shown by existing correspondence. She treasured also the friendly and cordial relationship with those less versed in social amenities, but no less true patriots, and made them feel at home with her and with those whom she received. She became known at military headquarters as the General's Lady, and as Lady Washington, by which name she was ever after called.

What may be considered the final social event of the Revolution or perhaps the first of the next period was the "peace ball" at Fredericksburg, which took place on February 14, 1784, when General George Washington, as a private citizen, had come from Mount Vernon to the town to visit his mother. Mrs. Washington evidently did not accompany him. There was a corporate address and reply, a public dinner, and then the ball at the Town Hall, into the pleasure of which, according to the reminiscences, the General entered heartily. If his mother graced the festivities with her presence it was probably one of the few and doubtless the last of their public appearances together.

During the five years after the Revolution, which the General and his Lady spent at Mount Vernon, they sought once more the quiet and repose of a country planter's

life, of which they both were very fond. But they were too well known and loved to be privileged to retire into seclusion. On their first Christmas at Mount Vernon, after eight years of absence, the scene was indeed a festive one. They reached home on Christmas eve of 1783, the General having resigned his commission as Commander in Chief, two days before at Annapolis, which was then the meeting place of the Congress.

Within the mansion, near relatives were gathered to make merry for the occasion. One of the Lewis children, who was there from Fredericksburg, wrote to a friend:

"I must tell you what a charming day I spent at Mount Vernon with Mama and Sally. The General and Madame came home on Christmas Eve, and such a racket as the servants made! They were glad of their coming. Three handsome young officers came with them. All Christmas afternoon people came to pay their respects and duty. Among these were stately dames and gay young women. The General seemed very happy and Mrs. Washington was up before daybreak making everything as agreeable as possible for everybody."

That last phrase so adequately describes the estimable hostess, who was always bent upon "making everything as agreeable as possible for everybody."

Both the General and Lady Washington were fond of their respective nieces and nephews. There were many of these in each of their families. They were frequent guests at Mount Vernon, and it is said the General was glad especially to have the girls come and meet the distinguished visitors, with an eye to desirable husbands for them. One of the results of this propinquity was the wedding at Mount Vernon, in 1785, of the General's nephew, George Augustine Washington (son of his youngest brother, Charles), and Frances Bassett, a niece of Mrs. Washington. This was apparently a quiet event, and is recorded in quite a casual way in the Diary of George Washington:

"Saturday, 15th. The Reverend Mr. Grayson, and Doctr. Griffith; Lund Washington and his Wife and Miss Steuart came to Dinner—all of whom remained the Evening, except L. W. After the Candles were lighted George Auge. Washington and Frances Bassett were married by Mr. Grayson."

To close personal friends the General wrote of retiring from public life and retiring also within himself, but his diaries show that he was not to be unmolested in his wish "to view the solitary walk, and tread the paths of private life, with heartfelt satisfaction." He records a visit to his mother in Fredericksburg, in February, and in May a trip to Philadelphia to attend a meeting of the Society of the Cincinnati. He went also on a long horseback journey to inspect possible means of transportation over the mountains in connection with improvement of the Potomac. On this journey he was entertained by the settlers in true frontier fashion. But for these journeys and an occasional trip to Richmond or an overnight stay in Alexandria for the theater or other entertainment he rarely traveled far from his own hearthstone. But he was seldom as "solitary" as he had hoped, for practically every traveler from the North to the South and vice versa stopped to pay his respects and discuss the needs of the new Nation. It followed, of course, that they were guests for the night, and frequently near-by neighbors came to spend the day or evening. Then came the four months spent in Philadelphia in 1787, during the framing of the new Constitution, which was punctuated with tea or dinner with various friends, and an occasional dinner with organizations, one club "consisting of several associated families of the City, the Gentlemen of which met every Saturday accompanied by the females of the families every other Saturday." There was also an "excursion with a party for Tea to Gray's Ferry" and long rides or drives into the country on Sunday, sometimes for breakfast and again for dinner with the Morrises and other friends.

With the election of George Washington to the Presidency of the United States of America and his triumphant journey to New York for the inauguration came the very apex of the social life of the period. Each village and hamlet along the route seemed to vie with all others in paying social tribute to the illustrious first President of the young Republic. There were triumphal arches at many points, and in New York a flattering reception awaited the President-elect and his party. On the last stage of the journey they were borne in a state barge manned by masters of vessels in port who had proudly volunteered for such distinguished service. All the vessels were gaily decorated and on many there were bands and vocal music. The crowd which gathered at Murray's Wharf, where the barge landed, comprised all classes, including many from the ranks of the Revolutionary Army. Governor Clinton and General Knox served as escorts to the mansion on Cherry Street, which had been prepared for the President's occupancy.

The inauguration ceremony on April 30, 1789, has been described as "simplicity itself," but the first inaugural ball, however, is said to have been a dazzling affair. It was postponed at first, awaiting the arrival of Mrs. Washington, but as the date seemed indefinite the ball was held on the 7th of May, in the DeLancey mansion on the Bouwerie, then a fashionable residence section, in a setting of beautiful gardens and majestic trees. An account of the ball states that the collection of ladies in attendance was numerous and brilliant, richly attired, with consummate taste and elegance,

but hardly more splendid than the gentlemen—"the officers in their gorgeous uniforms, the civilians in their picturesque evening clothes of velvet or satin; all being further adorned with elaborately dressed and powdered hair, fine lace ruffles, silken hose, and buckles of precious metal or diamonds at knees and instep."

One week later the French minister, Count de Moustier, gave a splendid ball in honor of the President. The French minister was then residing in the McComb house on Broadway, which later became the Presidential Mansion. Marchioness de Brienne, a sister of Count de Moustier, directed the arrangements. She was an amateur artist of considerable distinction and was heard to declare by one of the guests that she had exhausted every resource to produce an entertainment worthy of France.

Although Lady Washington did not arrive in time for either of these two balls, she was a participant in many other gala occasions. A contemporary artist, Lundgren, has admirably depicted her, in an oil painting at one of the capital balls, and another artist, Daniel Huntington, has left to posterity an attractive painting of one of Lady Washington's receptions.

It fell to the lot of the President and the first First Lady to determine to what extent the official functions should partake of pomp and ceremony. Fortunately they chose a happy medium and set a precedent in keeping with the dignity of the Nation but free from ostentatiousness, a precedent that has come down through succeeding administrations to the present time. Despite the entire absence of pomp and parade at Mrs. Washington's Friday evening receptions, which always closed precisely at 9 o'clock, they were sometimes ill-naturedly referred to as "court levees" and "queenly drawing-rooms." Perhaps this was because, as a frequent guest commented, "There was no place for the vulgar electioneerer or imprudent place-hunter." Mrs. Washington is said to have been "proud of her husband's fame and jealous of the honors due, not only to his own lofty character, but to the dignified station to which a grateful country had called him," and was therefore "careful in her drawing-rooms to exact those courtesies to which she knew he was entitled, as well on account of personal merit as of official consideration."

The President set aside Tuesday, from 2 to 3 o'clock, to receive his visitors, and is said to have "conversed with them freely after introduction, if opportunities were afforded; and in every respect, while maintaining perfect dignity, he made all feel that he was their fellow-citizen."

The well-regulated economy with which the presidential household was governed is reputed to have had a salutary effect toward restraining extravagant living in New York,

toward which there was a strong tendency at that period.

The receptions that were later held at the Presidential Mansion in Philadelphia are described at length by Mrs. Washington's grandson, George Washington Parke Custis:

"When Mrs. Washington received company it was on Friday, commencing about seven, and ending about nine o'clock. Two rooms were thrown open. The furniture that was thought handsome in those days would be considered barely decent in modern times. The principal ornament was a glass chandelier in the largest room, burning wax lights. The chair of the lady of the President was a plain armchair lined with green morocco leather.

"The ladies visiting the drawing-room were always attended by gentlemen. It was not the habit for very young girls to be present at the drawing-room, but only those of the age when it is proper for ladies to go into company. Upon the ladies being introduced they were seated, and the President, who always attended the drawing-room, passed round the circle, paying his respects to each in succession. . . .

"Refreshments were handed round by servants in livery; and about that period first appeared the luxury, now so universal, of ice crem. Introductions to eminent personages and conversation formed the entertainments for the drawing-room. Cards were altogether unknown.

"But the leading and most imposing feature of the drawing-room was the men of mark, the 'Revolutionaries,' both civil and military, who were to be seen there. The old officers delighted to pay their respects to the wife of Washington, and to call up the reminiscences of the headquarters, and of the 'times that tried men's souls.' These glorious old chevaliers were the greatest beaux of the age, and the recollections of their gallant achievements, together with their elegant manners, made them acceptble to the ladies everywhere. They formed the elite of the drawing-room. General Wayne— the renowned 'Mad Anthony'—with his aides-de-camp, Lewis and De Butts, frequently attended, with Mifflin, Walter Stewart, Colonel Hartley, and many others. Indeed, there was often to be met with at the mansion of the first President an assemblage of intellect and honor, public virtue and private worth, exalted merit and illustrious services, such as the world will never see again."

Young Custis was but a lad during the two terms of President Washington's incumbency in office, but apparently an observant one. His sisters, Nellie and the two elder ones, were doubtless somewhat privileged characters, for according to accounts they were among those present at the receptions in Philadelphia. Both Nellie and her young brother became charges of General Washington at the deathbed of their father, shortly after the surrender of Cornwallis, and were permanently at home with their grandmother and stepgrandfather, but the two elder girls were but temporarily ensconced as members of the household.

The last official function over which President and Lady Washington presided was a dinner on March 3, 1797, in honor of the President-elect, John Adams, and a leave-taking of the foreign ministers, heads of departments, and other high officials. Bishop White, one of the guests, wrote of this dinner:

"Much hilarity prevailed but on the removal of the cloth, it was put an end to by the President,—certainly without design. Having filled his glass, he addressed the company, with a smile on his countenance, saying, 'Ladies and gentlemen, this is the last time I shall drink your health as a public man. I do it with sincerity, and wishing you all possible happiness.' There was an end to the hilarity, and the cheeks of Mrs. Liston, wife of the British minister, were wet with tears."

The following evening, after George Washington had stepped down from officialdom, he was tendered a splendid farewell banquet by the merchants of Philadelphia in testimony of their love and fellowship. The amphitheater where the banquet and the entertainment took place had been appropriately decorated. The scene, fully described by a newspaper of the day, was symbolic, America being represented by a female figure, large as life, seated on an elevation composed of 16 marble steps.

"At her left side stood the federal shield and eagle, and at her feet lay the *cornucopia*; in her right hand she held the Indian calumet of peace supporting the cap of liberty; in the perspective appeared the temple of fame; and, on her left hand, an altar dedicated to public gratitude, upon which incense was burning. In her left hand she held a scroll inscribed 'Valedictory'; and at the foot of the altar lay a plumed helmet and sword, from which the figure of General Washington, large as life, appeared retiring down the steps, pointing with his right hand to the emblems of power which he had resigned, and with his left to a beautiful landscape representing Mount Vernon, in front of which oxen were seen harnessed to the plough. Over the General appeared a *Genius*, placing a wreath of laurels on his head."

This "display of taste, fashion, gayety, and refinement," of which the heads of departments, foreign ministers and distinguished guests formed a part, ended the public life of Washington. Though he departed from Philadelphia a private citizen, his journey to Mount Vernon was marked by attentions so flattering as to be embarrassing. In writing of them to a friend, George Washington commented that "by some whose minds are differently formed from my own, would have been highly relished; but I avoided in every instance, when I had previous knowledge of the intention, and could by earnest entreaties prevail, all parade and escorts."

Again, his return to Mount Vernon brought joy to the household and all over the estate; again "the servants flocked around him like children come to greet a returning father, . . . The master fairly revelled in the luxury of private life and the repose of domestic enjoyment." He was not unsocial; he loved his friends and enjoyed having them around him, but he was relieved at being spared the tumult of public life. But even his home ceased to be private; strangers having no claim whatever to friendship or patronage continually called upon him until he described Mount Vernon as "a well resorted tavern." Finally he evolved a plan by which he could be somewhat relieved from intrusion and yet have genuine hospitality extended to passing guests. One of his favorite nephews, Lawrence Lewis, son of his sister Betty, was engaged as secretary, one of his duties being to serve as host when the master should desire repose. The young man welcomed this duty, for he loved the society he met at Mount Vernon, and particularly did he love Nellie Custis, granddaughter of Mrs. Washington and beloved by the General. He was not the only claimant for Miss Nellie's favor, but in due season he triumphed over all his rivals, and once again the two families of the General and his Lady were linked together in the wedding of this young couple, which took place at Mount Vernon on the last anniversary of the birth of George Washington that he lived to see. The occasion has been described as a "red-letter day in the history of the mansion." The bride had been the idol of the household from the time she became a member of it at 3 years of age, and as she grew in years she had acquired many accomplishments and much personal charm. One admirer said of her, "Her sweetness equals her beauty, and that is perfect." Another said, "She was as witty as she was beautiful"; and still another, speaking of her bridal eve, "She was the center of all eyes, the theme of all praise."

In his usual concise manner, George Washington made mention of this event in his diary, "The Rev. Mr. Davis and Mr. George Calvert came to dinner, and Miss Custis was married about candlelight to Mr. Lawrence Lewis." Other pens have ventured to describe the event more fluently and in a colorful manner, making mention of a brilliant assemblage, though family tradition indicates that the wedding was a quiet one, the General giving the bride away.

The young couple continued to reside at Mount Vernon and to do the honors socially whenever the General and Mrs. Washington wished to be relieved. Here little Frances, her first child, was born shortly before the beloved Father of His Country passed away.

(FOR THIS PROGRAM SEE NUMBERS 23, 72, 81, 85, 102 IN LIST OF SELECTED BOOKS ON PAGES 300-A AND 300-B)

George Washington the Builder of the Nation

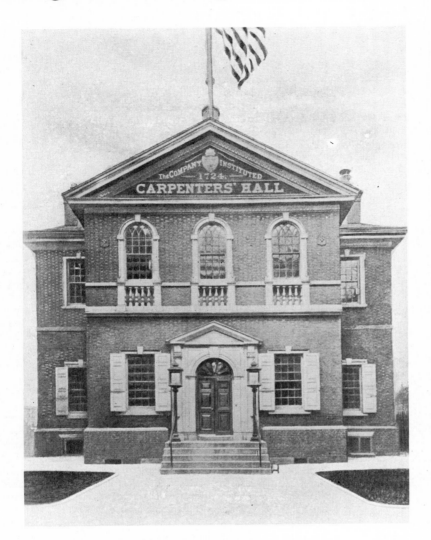

CARPENTER'S HALL, PHILADELPHIA
Where Washington attended the First Continental Congress

MILITARY EXPERIENCE UNDER BRITISH RULE

SYMBOLIC DREAMS and prophetic visions, from time immemorial, have been given credence, notably in the period covered by the Holy Scriptures. According to tradition the mother of George Washington saw in a dream, when he was but a child, the measure of his future greatness. Another tradition states that an aged Indian chieftain pronounced a divine inspiration when he said of George Washington:

"There is a something bids me speak in the voice of prophecy. Listen! The Great Spirit protects that man, and guides his destinies. He will become the chief of nations, and a people yet unborn will hail him as the founder of a mighty empire!"

According to the legend, this prophecy was prefaced by an impressive speech in which the aged Indian stated that he had beheld the Great White Chief in battle and had called to his own young men saying, "Mark yon tall and daring warrior, he is not of the red-coat tribe—he hath an Indian's wisdom and his warriors fight as we do—himself alone is exposed. Quick, let your rifle aim be certain and he dies." The narrator recounted also that their rifles "but for him, knew not how to miss." In describing this same battle (under General Braddock), Doctor Craik is quoted as having stated: "I expected every moment to see him [George Washington] fall. Nothing but the superintending care of Providence could have saved him from the fate all

around him." Doctor Craik is credited also with having often commented, during the American Revolution, upon this early experience of George Washington and upon the Indian chieftain's prophecy when, in so many dangerous situations, the life of the General was so miraculously spared.

In a letter to his brother, John Augustine (June 18, 1755), George Washington wrote somewhat facetiously, yet seriously, about his escape at the battle of Monongahela, commenting upon a "circumstantial account" of his death and dying speech, as follows:

"I take this early opportunity of contradicting the first, and assuring you, that I have not as yet composed the latter. But, by the all-powerful dispensations of Providence, I have been protected beyond all human probability and expectation; for I had four bullets through my coat, and two horses shot under me, yet escaped unhurt, altho' death was levelling my companions on every side of me!"

Of an earlier experience, after a skirmish in which he was reputed to have been wounded, George Washington wrote to this same brother, May 31, 1754:

"I fortunately escaped without any wound, for the right wing, where I stood, was exposed to and received all the enemy's fire, and it was the part where the man was killed, and the rest wounded."

Looking back upon the outstanding events in the life of George Washington another Great White Chief, Woodrow Wilson, has given a most comprehensive summary of the situation as it existed in this country during that period. In his facile manner he writes:

"George Washington was bred a gentleman and a man of honor in the free school of Virginia society. . . . He was born in a season of quiet peace, when the plot of colonial history was thickening noiselessly and without observation. He came to his first manhood upon the first stir of revolutionary events; caught in their movement, he served a rough apprenticeship in arms at the thick of the French and Indian War; the Revolution found him a leader and veteran in affairs at 44; every turn of fortune confirmed him in his executive habit of foresight and mastery; death spared him, stalwart and commanding, until, his rising career rounded and complete, no man doubted him the first character of the age."

Commencing with his experience as a surveyor George Washington advanced gradually and steadily. It was during these years that he devoted to that profession, while still in his minority, that he first carried the responsibilities of directing important projects and commanding the movements of other men. This experience also afforded him his first opportunity to become acquainted with the habits and feelings of the frontier settlers and to study the character and temper of the Indians whose uncertain dispositions made them a continual terror and menace.

Of prime importance also was the "education of the eye" acquired in his surveying practice, which enabled him accurately to measure distances, ranges, and elevations, and to estimate with astonishing rapidity and certainty the features and capacities of any field within his vision. This gave him, in after years, a singular advantage in directing the movements of his forces upon the field of battle.

Preparation for the fathering of a new nation included his experiences as an emissary of Governor Dinwiddie to bear a message to the French who were encroaching upon the British frontier; his subsequent part in the French and Indian War and his services in the House of Burgesses. His first election was a significant event. It was the custom at that period for the candidate to be at the polls during the voting, but he was at the time engaged elsewhere with military duties, and no force of personal consideration could draw him away from his post of duty. The election was carried through without his presence, and he was chosen by a large majority over all his competitors, not only upon this occasion but at later elections during the 15 years he continued as a member of the Assembly.

Throughout his entire lifetime this principle of devotion to duty was observed by George Washington, and he was at all times clear visioned as to the course of his duty. How well he fulfilled the first mission entrusted to him by Governor Dinwiddie is shown by the fact that the journal he kept of the journey was published and distributed throughout the Colonies and reprinted in London under the auspices of the British Government. It was considered a document of great importance, covering, as it did, the first proof of hostile acts by the French along the Ohio River and its tributaries. In commendation of the capacity and foresight he exhibited on this occasion, George Washington was appointed as lieutenant colonel and placed in charge of the troops that were at once enlisted to build a fort at the strategic point he had selected and to disperse interlopers who were attempting to establish settlements in the disputed area.

As George Washington and his forces advanced toward Fort Duquesne an expedition was sent out to meet him. It was commanded by M. de Jumonville, who met his death in the resulting conflict. Through trusty Indians, George Washington learned that the French forces at Fort Duquesne had been strengthened by a considerable reenforcement from Canada and that the enemy, which was rapidly approaching, was "as numerous as the pigeons in the woods." Washington's forces, limited in number and nearly destitute of provisions, had few advantages for defense. Perforce they fell back to Fort Necessity at Great Meadows and took immediate steps to strengthen the fortification. Many of the Indians deserted when the hour of peril arrived, giving credence to the suspicion that they were emissaries from tribes secretly engaged in the French interests. When the French troops arrived, after desultory firing from a distance, they requested a parley. After twice rejecting inadmissible terms of capitulation, the third revision of the French phraseology, orally translated by Van Braam, a Dutchman not well versed in either the French or English language, George Washington signed the terms of capitulation as drawn up in French quite unaware that the killing of Jumonville would later be misinterpreted to mean a treacherous killing.

The records which George Washington kept of this expedition fell into the hands of the French (apparently through pilfering) when Fort Necessity was surrendered to them. Of the version published and used by France as an argument to justify her in the seizure of the Ohio region, George Washington wrote (March 27, 1757):

"In regard to the journal, I can only observe in general, that I kept no regular one during that expedition; rough minutes of occurrences I certainly took, and find them as certainly and strangely metamorphosed; some parts left out, which I remember were entered, and many things added that never were thought of; the names of men and things egregiously miscalled; and the whole of what I saw Englished is very incorrect and nonsensical."

The statement as retranslated into English, "We killed Mr. de Jumonville, the Commander of the party," was given much notoriety throughout Europe, and George Washington was considered a murderer, since war had not then been declared between France and Great Britain, which elicited a statement from George Washington:

"That we were wilfully, or ignorantly, deceived by our interpreter in regard to the word assassination, I do aver, and will to my dying moment; so will every officer that was present."

Official communications which George Washington addressed to Governor Dinwiddie and which were by him conveyed to higher officials in London served effectively to refute the charge. They made it clear that Jumonville had precipitated the encounter in which he met his death, that George Washington had acted in strict conformity with his orders and military usage, and that his conduct in this affair met with unqualified approbation of the Governor and Legislature of Virginia and of the British Ministry. A vote of thanks was passed by the House of Burgesses to Colonel Washington and his officers "for their bravery and gallant defence of their country."

Governor Dinwiddie, unfamiliar with military affairs, made futile attempts to organize a larger army for an immediate march over the mountains, which were impassable at that season of the year. Orders from England, impossible to carry out, and other arbitrary regulations reduced the highest officers of the Virginia regiment to the rank of captain and made them inferior to less experienced officers of the same rank who were holding King's commissions. Hence George Washington resigned his commission and retired from the regiment.

After spending the winter in retirement at Mount Vernon, meanwhile declining to serve under Governor Sharpe, of Maryland, who had received an appointment from the King as commander in chief of the British forces employed against the French, he accepted an invitation from General Braddock to join his official family as volunteer aide-de-camp. Having previously referred to an empty commission, "holding neither rank nor emolument," George Washington took occasion to explain to his friends, upon consenting to serve under Braddock, that his sole motive was a laudable desire to serve his country, that he was "going as a volunteer without expectations of reward" and stated that he expected to be a considerable loser in his private affairs by going. He might well have added that he was risking his life as well for, as has been shown, his escape was considered a miracle.

His conduct during this campaign served to enhance his reputation in the colonies. An eloquent divine, Rev. Samuel Davies, afterwards president of Princeton College, after praising the zeal and courage shown by the Virginia troops, thus eulogized their leader:

"As a remarkable instance . . . I may point out to the public that heroic youth, Colonel Washington, whom I cannot but hope that Providence has hitherto preserved in so signal a manner for some important service to his country."

With the passage of a bill by the General Assembly at Williamsburg, providing for funds for a larger Army, came intimations to George Washington from his friends that he might be appointed to the command of the Army under its new organization, stressing the advantage he might gain by coming at once to the capital. His answer was that he would not seek what he did not covet nor be thought to solicit what he would receive only as voluntarily bestowed by his countrymen. He mentioned also several conditions as essential; among others, a voice in choosing his officers, a better system of military regulations, more promptness in payment of the troops, and a better method of procuring supplies. His demands were conceded, his appointment was confirmed, and he was given the additional privilege of an aide-de-camp and secretary.

For so young a commander George Washington displayed remarkable ability and sagacity in handling the intricate situations which arose. The army regulations had been somewhat reformed but were still deficient with no powers provided to prevent desertions, punish offenses, and secure obedience. Repeatedly yet diplomatically he urged the necessity of putting the troops under better regulations, commenting upon the regularity observed by other nations and asking, "Why then should it be expected from us, (who are all young and inexperienced,) to govern and keep up a proper spirit without laws, when the best and most experienced can scarcely do it with [them]?" He urged also the need of a train of artillery and engineers, stating that defensive measures were evidently insufficient and proposed altering them to a vigorous offensive war. He made repeated pleas, also, for Indian auxiliaries and for an assortment of Indian goods to give them for their services. He recommended the appointment of an Indian agent to study their dispositions, the art of pleasing them, and the authority to treat with them and reward them properly for every piece of service. Captain Gist, he stated, was held in great esteem by them and was especially fitted for such an appointment.

The dangers encountered by the settlers upon the frontier were a matter of much concern; on every hand there were cries of distress and alarm from the unceasing incursions from the savages. But the campaign continued to be a defensive one, and the Governor, hampered by his Assembly and instructions from the home office across the ocean, did not receive kindly the overzealous epistles of the young Colonel who, engrossed with his own difficulties and insistent upon his closer observation and knowledge of frontier conditions, was overlooking the Governor's own difficulties.

There were skirmishes with the Indians; old forts were repaired and new ones built. Though of the opinion that three or four strong garrisons would constitute a better defense than a chain of forts, George Washington, in conformity with his instructions, drew up a plan for 22 forts, fixing their respective positions and required garrisons. He visited these from time to time while the work was in progress, exposing himself to imminent danger from the savages. Danger also threatened the stores at Fort Cumberland, an outpost accessible to the enemy,

not defensible against cannon and no real hindrance to the Indian forays. Fearing the stores and the guard of 150 men might be suddenly cut off, Colonel Washington advocated their removal to a safer position. Moreover, the post was in Maryland; and if kept up at all, he advised that it should be done at the expense of that colony. But the Virginia governor considered it a King's fort and ordered that it be strengthened by calling in smaller garrisons. The patience and equanimity of the Commander were sorely tried, but he wrote to the Speaker of the House of Burgesses:

"I am determined to bear up under all the embarrassments some time longer in hope of better regulation on the arrival of Lord Loudoun, to whom I look for the future fate of Virginia."

Lord Loudoun's plans to visit Virginia suffered a change. Instead he called a conference of governors and principal officers at Philadelphia, which Colonel Washington attended. There his views were given serious consideration, but his hopes were only partially fulfilled. Fort Cumberland was left to the charge of Maryland, but his recommendation that an expedition be promptly sent against Fort Duquesne was not seasonably heeded.

Upon his return to headquarters at Winchester George Washington continued with routine duties until forced, through extreme fatigue, which settled into a fever, to take a furlough. After four months of confinement at Mount Vernon he resumed his command on the 1st of March, 1758. Governor Dinwiddie had meanwhile sailed for England. Under the new governor, Francis Fauquier, the prospects seemed brighter. At last Colonel Washington's wish for an aggressive expedition to the Ohio bade fair to be realized. Plans for the campaign of 1758 were soon under way; previous mistakes were recognized and avoided, yet there was cause for anxiety over the unanticipated delays and the apprehensions of failure due to misspent time and misguided effort. That the campaign terminated successfully was due largely to a fortunate circumstance through which the weak state of Fort Duquesne was discovered. This encouraged a forced march toward final victory, though the British forces found only an abandoned site where the fort had stood.

Two hundred of the Virginia troops were stationed there to retain possession of the post and to keep the Indians in check. Colonel Washington, after arranging with the frontier inhabitants to keep the detachment supplied with provisions, returned with the rest of his troops to Winchester, where they went into winter quarters. This left Colonel Washington free to carry out his determination, if the campaign should prove successful, to retire from military service. For five years he had been actively and almost uninterruptedly engaged in the serv-

ice of his country, and the resignation of his commission was marked by many expressions of appreciation and wide recognition of his military talents, his patriotism, and private virtues. During these five years he acquired the "habit of authority" which had been attributed, by a learned group of character analysts, to be the chief cause of his greatness, and which helped to fit him to become "the father of a mighty empire," as the Indian chieftain had predicted.

CHANGING VIEWS ON BRITISH CONTROL

Reasoning from cause to effect, it may be permissible to suppose that the thought of independent government became implanted in the subconscious mind of George Washington during his military experience under British rule. The handicaps which he encountered, the partiality displayed toward army officers commissioned by the King, the unnecessary sacrifice of lives due to vexatious delays, and the arbitrary attitude of British generals and colonial governors surely proved sufficient cause for a man of his great vision to foresee the need of greater liberty and freedom.

But if such subconscious thoughts existed, they were buried deeply and germinated slowly. Any disillusionment that might have lingered to nourish such tentative thoughts into active being became dissipated by the happy anticipation of claiming a bride and by his approaching induction as a member of the House of Burgesses at Williamsburg, to which he had been elected while still absent on military duty.

These two events marked a complete change in his life; from the hardships of camp life to the comforts of a settled home surrounded by family and friends and in the midst of scenes he loved; from the position of a suppliant for better laws to that of a lawmaker; and from the standpoint of serving his country with sword and rifle to the more tranquil yet patriotic service with voice and pen and ploughshare.

Through his continuous service in the House of Burgesses for the next 15 years George Washington kept closely in touch with public sentiment. He came to realize more clearly than did the majority of his contemporaries the trend of the growing controversies between Great Britain and the Colonies. The latter, long accustomed to self-government to a considerable degree, felt justified in remonstrating against the ministerial policies. Due to the power of patronage, even the government of the mother country had never been truly representative and that of the Colonies continually became less independent. In seeking to protect their own rights and privileges, the thinking men of the Colonies were, in reality, upholding the liberty of English-speaking people as a whole.

No one among those thinking men took a more early or a more decided part in asserting and defending the rights of the colonies than did George Washington, though he was by no means biased in his judgment. His convictions were based upon a deliberate and thorough study of the conditions from every standpoint. Not being a ready speaker, he seldom voiced his views while the Burgesses were in session. In the heat of argument he calmly sat apart, concerned and thoughtful, and seldom absent from his place. In quiet conversations with his friends and neighbors and with his fellow-members of the House of Burgesses he expressed his views cautiously, but in such a manner as to influence the actions of those whose voices were most frequently heard in the discussions on the floor. Through his correspondence he also helped to direct public sentiment and action. In writing of the Stamp Act, he pronounced it an "unconstitutional method of taxation" and "a direful attack" upon the liberties of the colonists. He realized also that it was inimical to the best interests of Great Britain, and so stated in a letter addressed to a family connection in London, affirming that "the advantage accruing to the mother country will fall greatly short of the expectations of the ministry; . . . whatsoever contributes to lessen our importations must be hurtful to her manufacturers. . . . I fancy the merchants of Great Britain trading to the Colonies will not be among the last to wish for a repeal of it."

This point of view was concurred in by a few of the best thinkers in the British Parliament; Pitt boldly proclaimed, "I rejoice that America has resisted." Charles Fox declared, "The resistance of the Americans to the oppressions of the mother-country has undoubtedly preserved the liberties of mankind."

Whether George Washington supported Patrick Henry in his bold stand and in the resolutions he presented in the Virginia House of Burgesses (in 1765), is not a matter of record; but the fact of his reelection by the people soon after the assembly had been dissolved for passing these Virginia resolves, is offered as strong presumptive evidence that he was in complete accord with his popular colleague.

The repeal of the Stamp Act did not end the attempted taxation. Charles Townshend proposed a plan to draw a revenue from the Colonies which, presumably, "would not give offence." Parliament accordingly proceeded to enact a law fixing a tax upon trade, with a view to collecting revenue upon important imports into the Colonies, for the use of the Government. Furthermore, provisions were made for emphasizing the control of the British Board of Trade over the Colonies by creating resident commissioners to enforce the Acts of Trade and Navigation.

In the spring of 1769 George Washington addressed a letter to his friend and neighbor, George Mason, in which he stated, "our lordly masters in Great Britain will be satisfied with nothing less than the deprivation of American freedom," and declared, "it seems highly necessary that something should be done to avert the stroke, and maintain the liberty which we have derived from our ancestors." He advocated nonimportation as a weapon with a possible future resort to arms as a last resource "in defence of so valuable a blessing" as liberty and freedom. This letter, together with George Mason's reply, formed the groundwork for a draft of articles of association which they drew up for presentation at the coming assembly in Williamsburg. They were held in abeyance pending action on other important resolutions, the passage of which caused the assembly to be dissolved. On the following morning, May 17, the members assembled in Raleigh Tavern, formed themselves into a voluntary convention; the articles creating the Non Importation Association of Virginia were signed by every person present and copies were sent throughout the country for the signatures of the people. George Washington religiously adhered to the agreement while it remained in force and stated that he would do so "if it were as I could wish it to be, ten times as strict."

During these unsettled times no action had been taken to locate and give actual possession of the lands promised in 1754 to the soldiers and officers who would enlist and participate in what became the Fort Necessity expedition. Early in 1770 it was discovered that an immediate danger threatened this promised bounty land through a grant solicited by an English company which would include its boundaries. George Washington pressed the adjustment of the soldiers' claims, making an extensive trip throughout the territory involved at his personal expense and eventually succeeded in securing for each officer and soldier the quota of land allotted to him.

This experience must have impressed George Washington as one more evidence that the Ministry of the mother country either did not understand or did not intend to recognize the just dues of the King's subjects overseas. The attitude of Parliament in seeking to control and harrass the Colonies brought about a climax in 1774. The taxes on trade had been repealed with the exception of a duty on tea, but the feeling of injury remained uppermost in the minds of the colonists. So bitterly did they resent the remaining tax and the presence of troops in Boston that riots resulted there, and large consignments of tea were destroyed there and elsewhere. Massachusetts, being the most active in the agitation and brought into prominence through the Boston Tea Party, was selected as a target for retaliation. The port of Boston was closed, which

took its commerce away; the charter of Massachusetts was changed so as to deprive it of self-government; the trial of any soldier or Crown officer accused of a capital crime in the colony was transferred to England, and British soldiers were billeted upon the inhabitants, thus facilitating the establishment of a temporary military government in Massachusetts. The Quebec Act gave further cause for apprehension over the annexation of outlying territory and the question of religious freedom.

The Colonies arose as one to the support of Massachusetts. The Virginia House of Burgesses, then in session, upon receiving word that the act closing the Boston port was to become operative on June 1 (1774), set aside that day for fasting and prayer. To forestall action upon more drastic resolutions the royal governor promptly dissolved the assembly. As on the previous occasion, the members forthwith held a meeting in Raleigh Tavern. The outcome of this and of a successive meeting, a few days later, was a recommendation for an intercolonial congress and a call for a convention of the Burgesses on August 1.

The diary of George Washington shows that on June 1, 1774, he "went to Church and fasted all day." This was in fulfillment of the resolution the Burgesses had adopted. Returning to Mount Vernon he conferred with the citizens of the county, and a local meeting was called for July 18, 1774, which was held in the Fairfax County courthouse. At this meeting, presided over by George Washington, the famous Fairfax County Resolves were adopted. They had been framed by George Mason, in consultation with George Washington, and represented their mutual views concerning the late acts of Parliament, the rights of the Colonies, and the proper course to be pursued by them. These resolves, 24 in number, clearly and forcibly set forth the whole question at issue and indicated most fairly the existing conditions. An early biographer has stated that they form "a lucid exposition of the matured political feelings and opinions of Washington."

At the Virginia Convention, called for August 1, 1774, George Washington presented the Fairfax County Resolves. A recorded statement "by one who was present" comments that George Washington spoke upon these resolutions in "a strain of uncommon eloquence, which shows that his latent ardor had been excited on the occasion, as eloquence was not in general among his attributes." It is also recorded that he declared his readiness to raise 1,000 men, subsist them at his own expense, and march at their head to the relief of Boston. In substance and in spirit these resolves were adopted at the Williamsburg convention and excited much favorable comment. The reaction of John Adams is shown in his diary (August 23, 1774): "Went to the coffee-house [New York], and saw the Virginia paper; the spirit of the people is prodigious; their resolutions are really grand."

Just prior to the First Continental Congress, which assembled in Philadelphia on September 5, 1774, a meeting of great minds in preliminary deliberation occurred at Mount Vernon. Patrick Henry and Edmund Pendleton had joined George Washington there, and the three journeyed together to Philadelphia. Richard Henry Lee was to have been one of the party but was detained. He arrived, however, in time to take his seat in the Congress and take a prominent part in the proceedings.

There is no record of the part that George Washington may have taken in the debates of the Continental Congress, but from the standpoint of "solid information and sound judgment" he was pronounced "the greatest man on the floor." The measures that were adopted were so completely in accord with the Virginia resolution that originated in the Fairfax County courthouse as to create historical comment later upon their similarity.

Though the name of George Washington does not appear as a member of any of the committees of the First Continental Congress, it is to be surmised that his "solid information and sound judgment" were sought and welcomed, thus enabling him to wield a greater influence than had he been absorbed in the work of any one committee. Doubtless he took the stand, as he had recently done in a letter addressed to Bryan Fairfax—

"that the measures, which administration hath for sometime been and now are most violently pursuing, are repugnant to every principle of natural justice; . . . not only repugnant to natural right, but subversive of the laws and constitution of Great Britain itself, . . . the crisis is arrived when we must assert our rights, or submit to every imposition that can be heaped upon us, till custom and use shall make us . . . tame and abject slaves."

In the interim between the First and Second Continental Congresses George Washington attended the Second Virginia Provincial Convention, held at Richmond, in March, 1775, and continued to hold conferences with his colleagues and other leading thinkers who visited him at Mount Vernon. Two of those who were with him shortly after word was received of bloodshed in New England—Horatio Gates and Bryan Fairfax—were extreme opposites in disposition and convictions; the one eager for military action, the other distressed over the trend of events but retaining allegiance to Great Britain. To the elder brother of Bryan Fairfax, George William, who was then in England, George Washington expressed his views and explained his position:

"Unhappy it is, though [he wrote], to reflect, that a brother's sword has been sheathed in a brother's breast, and that the once happy and peaceful plains of America are either to be drenched with blood or inhabited by slaves. Sad alternative! But can a virtuous man hesitate in his choice?"

In the Second Continental Congress George Washington served on several important committees, fortifying New York, ammunition, Army rules, and raising money. He was suggested by John Adams and nominated by Thomas Johnson as Commander in Chief. Adams said:

"A gentleman whose skill and experience as an officer, whose independent fortune, great talents and excellent universal character, would command the approbation of all America, and unite the cordial exertions of all the colonies better than any other person in the Union."

The resolution was seconded by Samuel Adams. In the ensuing debate there were a few dissenting voices; not on account of personal objections to George Washington but because the army at Boston was made up of New Englanders who had their own general, with whom they appeared to be satisfied and to whom they owed the bottling up of the British troops in Boston.

During a recess which was taken prior to the vote the prime movers, John and Samuel Adams, readily convinced their colleagues that the appointment of so able and so well known a military leader from Virginia would serve a double purpose—that of impressing upon Great Britain the fact that the conflict was not sectional but of a national nature, and, on the other hand, of winning the unqualified support of the Colonies. So, when the meeting was again called together and the vote taken each and every ballot bore the name of George Washington—a further recognition of his "solid information and sound judgment."

When the notice of his appointment was officially conveyed to George Washington he modestly expressed his thanks and declared, "I do not think myself equal to the command I am honored with." He also assured Congress that he desired only payment of his expenses, "as no pecuniary consideration could have tempted me to accept the arduous employment at the expense of my domestic ease and happiness."

In commemoration of this act, Lord Byron wrote:

"Great men have always scorn'd great recompenses; . . .
George Washington had thanks, and naught beside,
Except the all cloudless glory . . .
To free his country."

Though he was "vested with full power and authority to act . . . for the good and welfare of the service," he was hampered by the lack of a stable central government and the lack of power on the part of the Continental Congress to furnish sorely needed supplies and to compel the States to keep up an adequate army. But it was given to him, despite hardships and deprivations, to uphold the principles of liberty and freedom for which he so firmly stood and which had been so severely threatened through the altering changes in Great Britain. These led to a gradual changing of views on the part of the colonists toward British control and resulted in changing them from subjects of a Monarch into citizens of an independent Nation—a Nation long since proud to proclaim that George Washington was "First in war, first in peace, and first in the hearts of his countrymen."

CREATION AND ORGANIZATION OF A NEW NATION

The crystallized utterances of George Washington, the sincerity of which is attested by his momentous acts, became the foundation upon which a new nation was builded. His influence, from pre-Revolutionary days to the adoption and ratification of the Constitution, was continually predominant. This influence was exerted in a quiet but effective manner. He was too modest to proclaim publicly, or privately to harbor, preconceived opinions. By diligent inquiry and study he sought to ascertain real conditions. He conducted a voluminous correspondence and conferred with small groups here and there—his neighbors, his fellow Burgesses between assembly meetings, his fellow colonists between sessions of the Continental Congress. From far and near his compatriots journeyed to Mount Vernon to confer with him on the problems of the period.

A Virginian, in a recent patriotic address, proudly asserted: "It is not inaccurate to say that the Federal Constitution had its origin at Mount Vernon." True it is, as the diaries of George Washington show, that both before and after the American Revolution, Mount Vernon was practically besieged with visitors who came to discuss the trend of events and topics of both national and international import. From that historic spot the influence of George Washington swept far and wide. He was "a man endowed with what has been called uncommon common sense, with tireless industry, with a talent for taking infinite pains, and with a mind able to understand the universal and eternal problems of mankind."

On the same program with this Virginian, another speaker emphasized a point which is too seldom considered. He said:

"We must remember that Washington, while the leader of what was called the Revolutionary Army, was himself no 'revolutionist.' The American Revolution was not to overthrow a whole order of society and bring in a new system; rather it was to restore the ancient rights of British freemen which an irresponsible and autocratic British King and ministry had deprived us of. It was a war for independence in defense of fundamental rights."

Had those fundamental rights remained unmolested, there would have been no occasion for any thought of severance from the mother country. Could these rights have been restored without a complete severance from Great Britain, the new nation, the United States of America, might never have been created. The Continental or Union Flag was first hoisted by the army at the Siege of Boston on January 1, 1776. Its origin is still unexplained; but the purpose of the design has been interpreted to be an expression of a half hope that the differences might be adjusted without a complete separation. It bore the crosses of Saint George and Saint Andrew combined, like the British flag, as the Union in the canton or upper left-hand corner. The rest of the flag differed from the British emblem by having six white stripes drawn across the red field, making 13 alternate red and white stripes, typifying the 13 Colonies. On June 14, 1777, a year after independence was declared, Congress resolved that "the Union be thirteen stars, white in a blue field, representing a new constellation." Thus the Stars and Stripes came into being, a flag flying not only for independence, but also for the liberty which the Declaration of Independence demanded.

Liberty! That was the battle cry of the colonists. Liberty and freedom! It was to insure liberty and freedom that George Washington consented to serve as Commander in Chief of the Continental Army. It was for liberty and freedom and unity, while overwhelmed with rigorous military affairs, that he importuned the shifting body of representatives comprising the Continental Congress for better coordination and for quicker and more efficient action upon military matters of great moment.

Unfortunately the Congress had no real legal status and no actual enforcing powers. The Colonies did not consider themselves "answerable to Congress for not agreeing with its recommendations." There was no settled national government.

Simultaneously with the preparation and signing of the Declaration of Independence a committee was engaged in framing Articles of Confederation. When these were submitted for consideration, July 12, 1776, the discussion revealed innumerable differences of opinion. Chief among the problems were methods of representation, raising of revenue, disposition of the western territory, national or central power versus the rights of the individual States, and how disputes within the Union should be settled. It was not until March 1, 1781, that the Articles of Confederation became operative. Maryland had held up their adoption for several years until satisfied that the various

States would cede their western land claims to the Union. In October of 1781 Cornwallis surrendered. Thus it will be seen that throughout practically the entire period of aggressive warfare George Washington experienced many difficulties through lack of an efficient central government. While he had been given certain powers, almost equivalent to dictatorship, he was hampered by jealousies and treachery both in Congress and in camp and grieved by tendered resignations of his most dependable generals due to the trying conditions and unjust treatment they were experiencing. To one he wrote, appealing to his patriotism and stating that he, himself, had been called upon to endure all and more trials and calumnies than had been heaped upon his generals.

From a distance, under authority conferred upon him by Congress, as Commander in Chief, George Washington endeavored to exert what influence he could upon the political situation, which naturally affected military affairs. He inquired into the state of the currency, trade conditions, and the European situation. He communicated direct with officials in France and issued circular letters to the 13 States in which he urged that temporary expedients be abandoned and something durable, systematic, and substantial be substituted both as to civil administration and military establishment.

While the treaty of peace was pending, following the surrender of Cornwallis, George Washington was constantly alert and ready to meet any situation that might arise. Apparently the Members of Congress were somewhat indifferent as to its consummation. The provisional treaty, signed November 30, 1782, was definitely completed September 3, 1783. It was with great difficulty that a quorum of Congress could be gotten together to ratify it. But this was accomplished on January 14, 1784, and the treaty was considered "a triumph for American diplomacy."

Meanwhile George Washington had resigned as Commander in Chief and had surrendered his commission at Annapolis, where the seat of government was temporarily located.

Some time previously a suggestion had been conveyed to General Washington touching upon the weakness of republics and stating that "strong arguments might be produced for admitting the title of King." To this George Washington indignantly responded:

"No occurrence in the course of the war has given me more painful sensations . . . you could not have found a person to whom your schemes are more disagreeable. . . . Let me conjure you, then, if you have any regard for your Country, concern for yourself or posterity, or respect for me, to banish these thoughts from your mind, and never communicate,

as from yourself to any one else, a sentiment of the like nature."

Though he decried the idea of kingship, he was not unaware of the defects of the Articles of Confederation which governed the young Republic. In his last circular letter to the States, June 8, 1783, he stressed the points he had repeatedly touched upon in his public utterances:

"There are four things [he wrote] which, I humbly conceive, are essential to the well-being, I may even venture to say, to the existence of the United States, as an independent power.

"First. An indissoluble union of the States under one federal head.

"Secondly. A sacred regard to public justice.

"Thirdly. The adoption of a proper peace establishment; and,

"Fourthly. The prevalence of that pacific and friendly disposition among the people of the United States, which will induce them to forget their local prejudices and policies; to make those mutual concessions, which are requisite to the general prosperity; and, in some instances, to sacrifice their individual advantages to the interest of the community."

The first admonition he amplified in the following phraseology:

"That, unless the States will suffer Congress to exercise those prerogatives they are undoubtedly invested with by the constitution, every thing must very rapidly tend to anarchy and confusion. . . . It is only in our united character, as an empire, that our independence is acknowledged, that our power can be regarded, or our credit supported, among foreign nations."

Under the heading of the second article he wrote:

"The ability . . . to discharge the debts, which have been incurred in its defence, is not to be doubted; . . . The path of our duty is plain before us; honesty will be found, on every experiment, to be the best and only true policy."

As to the third and fourth articles, bearing upon "a proper peace establishment" and "mutual concessions," his views on these also proved to be prophetic.

In a letter to Lafayette, April 5, 1783, George Washington wrote:

"We stand now, an Independent People and have yet to learn political Tactics. We are placed among the nations of the earth and have a character to establish, but how we shall acquit ourselves, time must discover."

To John Jay, Foreign Secretary, he wrote in May, 1786:

"We are certainly in a delicate situation: . . . I scarcely know what opinion to entertain of a general convention. That it is necessary to revise and amend the articles of confederation I entertain no doubt, . . . something must be done, or the fabric must fall, for it certainly is tottering . . . the want of a disposition to do justice is the source of the national embarrassments."

The weakness of the Articles of Confederation, the inefficiency of Congress, and the disintegration of the Union became so apparent that 1786 marked the culmination of threatened crises. The constitutional duties of the States were neglected, ignored, and resented; Rhode Island recalled her delegates and refused to appoint new members to attend sessions of Congress; New Jersey felt injured by a New York tariff and sought means of retaliation; Massachusetts, Pennsylvania, North Carolina, and Georgia raised troops on their own account and for their own purposes, in violation of the Articles of Confederation. It was imperative that "Congress must be invested with more powers or the Federal Government must fall."

During Shays's Rebellion in Massachusetts, George Washington, on October 31, 1786, expressed his sentiments to Henry Lee, as follows:

"You talk, my good Sir, of employing influence to appease the present tumults in Massachusetts. . . . *Influence* is no *government.* Let us have one by which our lives, liberties, and properties will be secured, or let us know the worst at once. . . . If they have *real* grievances, redress them if possible; . . . If they have not, employ the force of government against them at once. If this is inadequate *all* will be convinced, that the superstructure is bad, or wants support."

This disintegration of the Union led to the Federal Convention (1787), over which George Washington was called to preside. In this convention the principles for which he had long stood took permanent form. The identical principles which, some 12 years previously, were incorporated in the Fairfax County Resolves, are conceded to have been the veritable inception of the Constitution itself.

It is reasonable to assume that the presence and guidance of George Washington during and following the Constitutional Convention, and his sponsorship of the articles adopted as a whole, influenced public opinion in their favor, and that his signature, leading all the rest that appeared upon the document, had a great deal to do with its being ratified. And when it became assured that the Constitution would be the accepted form of Government there was no question but that George Washington must be the first President of the United States and take the lead in the organization as he had done in the creation of the new nation.

The office was not of his seeking. Nothing but patriotic ardor could have induced him to sacrifice the tranquillity of domestic life at Mount Vernon to again respond to his country's call. To General Knox, George Washington wrote:

"In confidence I tell you (with the *world* it would obtain little credit) that my movements to the chair of government will be accompanied by feelings not unlike those of a culprit who is going to his place of execution; so unwilling am I, in the evening of a life nearly consumed in public cares, to quit a peaceful abode for an ocean of difficulties, without that competency of political skill, abilities, and inclination, which are necessary to manage the helm. . . . Integrity and firmness are all I can promise."

Though he discounted his own competency of political skill and abilities, he was an able judge of such qualifications in others, as shown by the selection of his Cabinet; while his integrity and firmness are repeatedly illustrated.

Much has been written of the triumphal journey of the President-elect to New York for the inauguration, and the scenes of enthusiastic welcoming along the way. The Vice President, John Adams, notes in his diary that the arrival of George Washington "arrested the public attention beyond all powers of description." One of the vast throng who witnessed the administering of the Oath of Office, wrote of the occasion: "The scene was solemn and aweful beyond description." The gracious and sincere welcome everywhere accorded to him apparently lulled his apprehension of serious trials in store for him. He seemed to have gathered confidence for in his response to the Members of the Senate who waited upon him and addressed him at the President's mansion, he said:

"Thus supported by a firm trust in the Great Arbiter of the Universe, aided by the collective wisdom of the Union, and imploring the Divine benediction on our joint exertions in the service of our country, I readily engage with you in the arduous but pleasing task of attempting to make a nation happy."

The task was indeed arduous, but scarcely a pleasing one save for the pleasure one derives from work well done. The spirit of the States as to their respective rights had to be coped with; the pretext of Great Britain that debts due to British subjects was justification for holding certain frontier forts, an act in violation of the peace treaty; the deplorable state of finances, with an empty treasury and credit prostrated; the foreign commerce situation and the piratical marauding upon American merchant vessels; the conciliation of hostile Indians; all of these serious prebloms, and others as well, presented themselves for solution.

In dealing with these situations the President "had few precedents as an executive officer to guide him, and no experience as the chief of civil affairs." He, himself, said, "I walk, as it were, upon untrodden ground." He called into counsel the men on whose judgment he could rely: Vice President Adams; the newly selected Chief Justice, John Jay, former Secretary of Foreign Affairs; General Knox, who was made Secretary of War; Alexander Hamilton, Secretary of the Treasury; Thomas Jefferson, Secretary of State; Edmund Randolph, Attorney General; and Samuel Osgood, Postmaster General, the latter office not then being included in the Cabinet.

It was in keeping with the custom of George Washington that he should draw into his official family the best minds on various questions and weigh carefully the conflicting opinions that might arise, as in the differences which arose between Hamilton and Jefferson. He welcomed those whose opinions differed from his own. His Attorney General, Edmund Randolph, for instance, had held such pronounced objections to certain phases of the Constitution that he had refused to sign it, though later in the ratification contest a lively supporter of it. Through all these discussions they had remained warm friends, and doubtless each had profited and the Constitution strengthened because of their respective arguments, for and against the points at issue.

It was the genius of George Washington in drawing out and reconciling or discarding the opinions of the best minds among his compatriots that made possible the perfection of an efficient organization to carry on the activities of the new Nation. His practice of seeking competent advice, sifting and choosing, enabled him to establish a system of intercourse with the public, both official and social, that set most of the precedents that are now followed and still recognized as most satisfactory.

With his usual painstaking care to secure first-hand information, the better to fit himself for the duties of his office, his first thought was to make himself thoroughly acquainted with the exact conditions of the country. He inspected, personally, all of the most important official documents issued since the establishment of the Confederacy and called for written reports respecting operations of the bureaus of the several departments.

There were a number of serious controversies over State boundaries as well as the annoying presence of British garrisons at Fort Niagara, Detroit, and other points within the territory of the United States. There was the question of slavery, some of the States having been conceded to be permanently slaveholding, while others were antislavery in both principle and practice. The educational and economic conditions were far from satisfactory. The Constitution itself, although ratified without arbitrary demand for amendments, was subjected to a battery of proposed amendments which constituted, practically, a bill of rights. Of the 147 submitted to the first Congress, 12 were reported upon favorably to the States and 10 were ratified and became operative.

It is worthy of note that the general forms adopted by the first Congress for the transaction of its business, as well as the parliamentary procedure, still continue very much the same as in that early period. The Federal judicial system was also organized substantially as it now stands.

During the first year of the first administration, on July 4, the thirteenth anniversary of Independence Day, an act "for the encouragement and protection of manufactures" was passed. Thus a protective tariff was introduced. Shortly thereafter Hamilton developed and proposed a general financial system, which the President supported. This proved to be the chief cause for a parting of the ways which resulted in the retirement of Jefferson from the Cabinet and the consequent organization of an opposing political party upholding Jeffersonian democracy as against the administration or Federalist policy. Federal politics along these lines have since continued to exist, with the Democrats and Republicans as the main constructive parties, through which the weak spots of opposing points of view have been weighed and corrected. In this manner the methods of George Washington in bringing out and adopting the best views and most logical course of procedure is being perpetuated.

Other momentous questions arose in connection with the Hamiltonian system of finance. A federal tax upon distilled spirits led to the Whisky Rebellion in Pennsylvania, the quelling of which involved the calling out of troops and dispatching them toward the scene of the insurrection. Fortunately the disturbance died down while the troops were en route, and the situation was adjusted without actual battle. The event served to prove the power of the Central Government in meeting and overcoming such a crisis.

On the other hand, a momentous question was settled in connection with the adoption of the financial policy of Hamilton. Perhaps it was the first and most far reaching of all the "trades" then made in Congress. Hamilton was shrewd enough to insure a vote in favor of the adoption of his policy by winning additional support from the Southern and Middle States, giving to them in return his influence in the selection of a site for the National Capital which would meet with their approval.

With the close of George Washington's first term as President of the United States the new Government was well organized and its success was assured. The Union was complete and two new States, Vermont and Kentucky, had been admitted. The country was prosperous; its shipping increased, and foreign trade was also growing steadily. He felt that he could consistently retire. This he was not permitted to do, as the people unanimously demanded his reelection.

War between France and England cast a threatening cloud over the new Nation, which to a certain extent owed its very existence to the support of France during the American Revolution. Should America repay her debt to France by going to her aid, or should a neutral policy be adopted? The Government of France, meanwhile, had changed, and Hamilton considered that previously existing treaties had been abrogated; Jefferson insisted that they were binding. Both, however, supported the President in his neutrality proclamation and in his determination to avoid entangling alliances.

The arrival of Genet as Minister from France, popularly known as "Citizen Genet," and his activities which culminated in an attempt to override the President of the United States, and in offering an insult to the Nation, served to turn the trend of public sentiment away from France toward England. America continued neutral but suffered from the violation of neutral rights by both France and England through their aggressions upon American commerce.

Public feeling reached such a state that it was deemed advisable to cut off commercial intercourse with Great Britain, and a temporary embargo was laid. The President appointed John Jay, Chief Justice of the United States, as special envoy to England, in a last effort to adjust the existing conditions. The resulting treaty, as submitted by Jay, though it removed some of the old grievances, caused great excitement in the United States. Jay was burned in effigy; Hamilton, who favored the adoption of the treaty, was stoned in a public meeting; George Washington was submitted to villainous attacks in language that he himself condemned as such that "could scarcely be applied to Nero, to a notorious defaulter, or even to a common pickpocket."

The great personal popularity of the President offset these attacks, and he was able to secure the ratification by the Senate of the Jay Treaty, which accomplished its purpose of leaving the Nation at honorable peace, with the much-needed opportunity to get safely established financially and otherwise. The framing of the treaty was accomplished under difficulties that "frequently had the appearance of being insurmountable." Jay wrote to the President, "To do more was impossible," and added, "I ought not to conceal from you that the confidence reposed in your personal character was visible and useful throughout the negotiations."

The Treaty with Spain, which Thomas Pinckney had meantime negotiated, helped to offset the "paroxysm of fever." Together with a satisfactory arrangement for trade with Spain, the treaty settled the boundary line of West Florida in accordance with the American claims, and, by opening the navigation of the Mississippi at its lower end where Spain controlled both banks, and giving a place of free deposit at New Orleans, quieted agitation in the West and promoted its settlement.

While attention was being given to the adjustment of external affairs, numerous internal problems were brewing. Changes in the Cabinet resulted, the minister plenipotentiary at Paris was recalled, and political jealousies were in the air and serving to arouse animosities. The time for another presidential election was approaching. The President was urged to accept a third term of office. This he was not disposed to entertain. The Nation had been created and organized, the site for its permanent capital had been determined, and was being laid out, affairs had reached a point where they did not actually require his further fostering care, and he felt the time had come when he could consistently retire. His Farewell Address, "the noblest production of Washington's mind and heart," has been pronounced by an eminent British historian to be "unequaled by any composition of uninspired wisdom," and one of our biographers says: "It is a political legacy which not only the countrymen of Washington but the inhabitants of the civilized world ought to value as one of the most precious gifts ever bestowed by man upon his race. It is permeated with the immortal spirit of a true MAN, a true PATRIOT, and a true CHRISTIAN."

(FOR THIS PROGRAM SEE NUMBERS 18, 22, 33, 96, 98 IN LIST OF SELECTED BOOKS ON PAGES 300-A AND 300-B)

George Washington the President (1789-1797)

PRESIDENT WASHINGTON AND THE FIRST CABINET

TRIUMPHANT JOURNEY AS PRESIDENT-ELECT

THE CONVENTION that formed the Constitution of the United States terminated in Philadelphia, September 17, 1787, and three days later a copy of the new Constitution was laid before the Continental Congress holding sessions in New York for its approval. The request was made that it should be submitted for ratification to the States, and that when it received the approval of nine States Congress should name a day on which presidential electors should be chosen by the States, and a later day when the electors should meet to vote for a President.

The majority of the members of the Constitutional Convention felt that they had a just right to be well satisfied with their work. At the same time they had reasons for believing that the ratification would not be easily accomplished. But to some of them it must have been a surprise to discover, at a later period, how uncompromising and bitter was the contest which remained to be fought out before a President could be elected.

A battle at once commenced in the Continental Congress when an attempt was made to alter essentially the Constitution as submitted. After eight days of heated argument it was voted to submit the Constitution to the States. A few months later, in December, 1787, Delaware, Pennsylvania, and New Jersey adopted the Constitution, and Georgia and Connecticut followed the next month. After a lively discussion Massachusetts ratified, suggesting amendments; Maryland and South Carolina continued the progress; and to New Hampshire belongs the glory of being the ninth State to ratify and complete the conditions necessary for starting the new Government.

The country had divided into two parties, the Federalists and the anti-Federalists, according to their approval or disapproval of the Constitution, and the contest between the factions in Virginia and New York was long and acute. It was realized that in spite of the completion of requirements without them, these two great States were essential to any real union. Both, however, came into line with the other States before the machinery was put into operation for the first Federal election, though New York did not share in the electoral vote for President.

Meanwhile Congress reported a resolution for putting the new Government into operation. At sunset March 3, 1789, the death of the old Confederation of States was announced by the guns of the fort opposite Bowling Green, in New York. The next day the new era was ushered in by the firing of a salute of 11 guns in honor of the

11 States that had adopted the Constitution. On April 6, 1789, George Washington, of Virginia, was declared President, having received the total number of votes cast.

Great public events were now scheduled in rapid succession. Charles Thomson, an Irishman by birth, who had acted as secretary of the Continental Congress for 13 years was selected to convey to George Washington the tidings of the great honor conferred upon him. In these days of fast travel it is certainly interesting to know the amount of time consumed in this journey from New York to Mount Vernon. Secretary Thomson left New York Tuesday morning, April 7, and on the following Thursday evening he was in Philadelphia. Friday morning he continued his journey, passing through Wilmington the same day. He reached Baltimore Sunday evening. Monday, April 13, he left Baltimore and arrived at Mount Vernon at half past 12 o'clock Tuesday afternoon. He was more than a week making a journey now made in six hours.

After the formal presentation by Thomson to the President-elect of his certificate of election, General Washington replied in a solemn, convincing manner:

"Upon considering how long a time some of the gentlemen of both Houses of Congress have been in New York, how anxiously desirous they must be to proceed to business, and how deeply the public mind seems to be impressed with the necessity of doing it speedily, I can not find myself at liberty to delay my journey. I shall, therefore, be in readiness to set out the day after tomorrow, and shall be happy in the pleasure of your company; if you will permit me to say that it is a peculiar gratification to have received this communication from you."

Just before leaving Mount Vernon the President-elect wrote in his diary the following words:

"I bade adieu to Mount Vernon, to private life, and to domestic felicity; and with a mind oppressed with more anxious and painful sensations than I have words to express, set out for New York in company with Mr. Thomson and Colo. Humphreys, with the best disposition to render service to my country in obedience to its calls, but with less hope of answering its expectations."

President-elect Washington was met by his friends and neighbors and escorted into Alexandria, where he was given an early dinner at Mr. Wise's tavern. The toasts which were drunk at this meal told the story of the times: "The King of France"; "The Federal Constitution—may it be fairly tried"; "The memory of those martyrs who fell in vindication of the rights of America"; "American manufacturers"; "American ladies, may their manners accord with the spirit of the government."

At the conclusion of the dinner the mayor of Alexandria addressed General Washington. In his concluding remarks he said, "Go and make a grateful people happy—a people who will be doubly happy when they contemplate this recent sacrifice for their interests." General Washington's emotions were concealed with difficulty. He was leaving behind many of "the ties that bind," his neighbors and friends who fairly adored him, and his beloved home. His reply was brief. "Unutterable sensations," he said, "must be left to more expressive silence while from an aching heart I bid you all, my affectionate friends and kind neighbors, farewell."

On the journey from Alexandria to Georgetown General Washington was accompanied by some of his friends and neighbors and a company of children who in this manner paid tribute to their hero. Meanwhile some of the most distinguished citizens of Georgetown met General Washington on the banks of the Potomac and acted as an escort on his journey toward Baltimore. At this juncture of the journey the presidential party was met by a committee specially appointed to welcome them to Maryland. Amid the firing of cannon General Washington was conducted through crowds of spectators to Grant's Tavern, where he received an address of welcome and was accorded a public reception. A supper was served in lieu of a dinner, as the time was too short to prepare a more elaborate entertainment. Can a Maryland supper be visualized? Cold fried chicken, Maryland ham, Maryland beaten biscuits, and perchance terrapin, cooked only as a Marylander knew how in days gone by.

After leaving Baltimore the next morning, to the firing of artillery salutes, General Washington was conducted by a train of admirers 7 miles on his journey northward. He was met on the border of Delaware on Sunday by a large group from Wilmington. Out of deference to the day, in place of illuminating the houses as many desired, the decoration of a vessel on the Delaware was substituted. Before leaving Wilmington, however, the next morning the President-elect received an address from the burgesses and the common council of the city. Delaware accompanied her guest to the Pennsylvania line. In the meanwhile Philadelphia had been preparing a royal welcome for this feted individual. The State authorities had appropriated $1,000 to defray the expense of a military escort; and Thomas Mifflin, of the supreme executive council of the State; Richard Peters, a speaker of the legislature, accompanied by the old City Troop, went forth to greet the President-elect. Other troops followed, and after receiving the customary salute and congratulations, General Washington was escorted into Chester for breakfast and a rest.

On leaving Chester, General Washington ordered his carriage to the rear of the line, mounting a beautiful white horse. Thomson and Humphreys were also mounted. As the procession advanced, many distinguished Philadelphians fell into line. At Gray's Ferry Bridge, the next point reached, the scene was indeed imposing. The most elaborate preparations had been made. Triumphal arches decorated with laurel and evergreens appeared on every side. On one of them 11 flags swung in the breezes with the names of the 11 States that had adopted the Constitution. All the boats on the river were decorated. All was in holiday attire, and the cheering as the President-elect approached the bridge, with thousands on every side to bid him welcome, made an occasion never to be forgotten. A beautiful scene was then enacted. When General Washington passed under one of the arches a wreath of laurel was lowered upon his brow by Angelica Peale, daughter of Charles Willson Peale. Everywhere was heard the spirited cry, "Long live George Washington; Long live the father of his people."

As the procession neared the Quaker City it grew larger. Salutes were fired from a beautifully decorated ship, the *Alliance*, and also from a Spanish merchant ship moored on the river. As the procession moved down Market Street the church bells of Philadelphia joined in the celebration. General Washington was conducted to the historic City Tavern, on Second and Walnut Streets, where a great banquet was given. It was in this same tavern that the Members of the First Continental Congress had gathered some 15 years before and several of them now came again to add cheer to the occasion. All the clergy of the city and the high officials vied with each other to honor the man they had learned to love. Two hundred and fifty guests sat down to this elegant entertainment. A band of music played throughout the dinner, and general good cheer prevailed. The toasts proposed were to "Louis the Sixteenth of France," "Charles the Fourth of Spain," and the "United Netherlands," these being the countries which had legations here. A discharge of artillery followed each toast.

Before leaving Philadelphia, President-elect Washington wrote to John Langdon, of New Hampshire, who was then in New York, and who had been one of the delegates from his native State to the Convention which framed the Constitution, and was President pro tempore of the Senate. The letter, dated April 20, 1789, follows:

"Upon alighting in this city I received your communication of the 17th with the resolution of the two Houses which accompanied it and in answer thereto beg leave to inform you that knowing how anxious both Houses must be to proceed to business I shall certainly journey with as much dispatch as possible. Tomorrow night I purpose to be at Trenton—the night following at Brunswick, and hope to have the pleasure of meeting you at Elizabethtown port on Thursday morning."

The City Troop of Philadelphia fully intended escorting General Washington to Trenton, but as the morning of his departure was rainy, the President-elect insisted upon their abandoning the trip. He was unwilling to drive under the protection of a carriage while the troop on horseback was exposed to the elements. The clouds, however, broke about noon, and the presidential party was taken across the Delaware by a distinguished number of citizens, a troop of horse, and a company of infantry, amid the booming of cannon and the huzzas of the people of Trenton village. An ever-memorable sight greeted them when the procession crossed Assunpink Creek, the same water where Washington had in 1777 first checked Cornwallis and then eluded him to fall upon the British at Princeton. A triumphal arch, 20 feet high, supported by 13 columns, all entwined with evergreens, was raised over the bridge. Upon it was inscribed in large gilt letters the words, "The Defender of the Mothers will be the Protector of the Daughters." Towering over this inscription, on a square ornamented with flowers and evergreens, were these historic dates, "December 26, 1776-January 2, 1777." On the summit of the arch was a large sunflower, designed to express the motto, "To you alone."

On the other side of the bridge stood the ladies of Trenton who had planned this tribute of their admiration for the first American. Maj. Richard Howell wrote the verses sung by the young girls who strewed flowers in General Washington's pathway. These verses are as follows:

"Welcome mighty chief, once more,
Welcome to this grateful shore!
Now no mercenary foe
Aims again the fatal blow—
Aims at thee the fatal blow.

Virgins fair and matrons grave,
Those thy conquering arms did save,
Build for thee triumphal bowers!
Strew, ye fair his way with flowers—
Strew your hero's way with flowers."

These young girls were all uniformly dressed in white, and as the beautiful scene was enacted General Washington stopped his horse and many of those who witnessed this unusual scene were affected to tears. That evening General Washington spent at the City Tavern, kept by Henry Drake. The night was also spent in Trenton at Vandigrift's tavern.

One phase of General Washington's character was that he was exceedingly punctilious in connection with the amenities of social life. He was peculiarly affected by the reception accorded him by the gracious women of Trenton, and that same day he addressed a note of thanks to the ladies and young girls who had taken part in the beautiful ceremonies which is given verbatim:

"General Washington can not leave this place without expressing his acknowledgments, to the Matrons and young ladies who received him in so novel and grateful a manner at the Triumphal Arch at Trenton, for the exquisite sensation he experienced in that affecting moment—the astonishing contrast between his former and actual situation on the spot—the elegant taste it was adorned for the present occasion—the innocent appearance of the *white robed choir* who met him with gratulatory song, have made such an impression on his remembrance as he assures them will never be effaced."

President-elect Washington was nearing the end of his long journey when he reached Elizabethtown, where he received a Federal salute. He stopped at the public house of Samuel Smith and breakfasted at the home of his old friend, Elias Boudinot. The march was again taken up under a large civic and military escort, which included companies from Newark and other near-by places. At Elizabethport a surprise awaited him. He learned that his journey was to be considerably shortened. A magnificent barge awaited him, especially constructed for the occasion to convey him up the bay to New York. James Nicholson was its commander and Thomas Randall acted as coxswain. Aboard the President-elect's barge, which was rowed by 13 masters of vessels, dressed in white uniforms and black caps ornamented with fringe, and the 6 others which accompanied it, were members of the committee appointed to meet General Washington and the presidential party. It was composed of John Langdon, Charles Carroll, and William Samuel Johnson for the Senate; Elias Boudinot, Theoderic Bland, Thomas Tudor Tucker, Egbert Benson, and John Laurance for the House; Chancellor Livingston; John Jay, at the time Secretary for Foreign Affairs; Samuel Osgood, Arthur Lee, and Walter Livingston, Commissioners of the Treasury; General Knox, head of the War Department; Ebenezer Hazard, Postmaster General; Col. Nicholas Fish, the adjutant general of the forces of New York State; Richard Varick; and other dignitaries.

The final arrival of President-elect Washington at his destination, New York City, was so magnificent that it is somewhat difficult to describe. The French and Spanish ministers wrote accounts to their home governments, which glow with interest, of the brilliancy of General Washington's reception in New York.

The presidential barge at length arrived at Murray's Wharf, and President-elect Washington was greeted by the firing of cannon, the ringing of bells, and the blowing of whistles, as the honored guest ascended the carpeted stairway of the ferry. He was simply dressed in a plain suit consisting of a blue coat, buff waistcoat, and breeches. His whole style and manner was as unassuming as his quiet clothes.

The New York procession was headed by Col. Lewis Morgan. It consisted of music, a troop of horse, artillery officers off duty, a company of grenadiers who served as a guard of honor to the President-elect, the governor and officers of the State, the congressional committee, the mayor of New York, James Duane, the corporation council of the city, the clergy, the French and Spanish diplomatic representatives, and many private citizens. The whole parade passed by Governor Clinton's house and finally stopped at the mansion, which had been fitted up for the President-elect's accommodation. After a brief reception General Washington drove to the governor's house for dinner. From 7 until 9 that evening the whole city was exquisitely illuminated. The day had indeed been a glorious one, and in the crowded streets on all sides were heard words that almost became stereotyped, "He deserves it all." Some were even more extravagant in their remarks, they asserted that they should now die content as there was nothing more to add to their happiness now that they had seen the "Saviour of the Country." It had been a happy day for all, and President-elect Washington must have been pleased over the reception accorded him by his countrymen. The Nation had risen up as one man to say "Well done."

First Term of the First President

On the first day of April, 1789, in New York City, the House of Representatives formed a quorum and immediately proceeded to the transaction of business. The most important immediate business was the counting of the electoral vote for President and Vice President of the United States. It was not until five days later that the Senate was sufficiently organized to meet with the House, consequently it was not until April 6, in the presence of both Houses of Congress, that the vote for the two highest offices in the land was proclaimed. George Washington, of Virginia, was the unanimous choice for President, having received 69 votes, or the total number of votes cast. John Adams, of Massachusetts, was elected Vice President.

Twenty-four days later, on a date never to be forgotten in the annals of American history, April 30, 1789, George Washington was inaugurated first President of the United States in New York City. This ceremony took place in Federal Hall. This building had recently been transformed from the City Hall, the money for the purchase being advanced by several wealthy men, Maj. Pierre Charles L'Enfant, who later engineered the plan for the National Capital, planning the alterations. The spot where General Washington stood is now marked, as nearly as possible, by a colossal statue of the first President.

The patriotic public felt that the top-stone was to be placed on a structure, the foundation of which had been laid in 1776, 13 years before.

The great day dawned bright and clear and the ceremonies for the event were ushered in at sunrise by the firing of cannon from old Fort George, near Bowling Green. At 9 the bells of all the churches rang for half an hour, congregations gathered in their prospective places of worship "to implore the blessing of Heaven on the new Government, its favor and protection to the President and success and acceptance to his administration." In the meanwhile all the military that New York and that general region could muster was preparing to march to a house on Cherry Street, the Franklin House, a home especially fitted up as the presidential residence.

The contrast of an inauguration of nearly 150 years ago with the present time is so great that it may be of interest to hear about the line of march on this particular auspicious occasion. The procession was led by Col. Morgan Lewis as grand marshal, attended by Maj. Van Horne and Maj. Jacob Morton as aides-de-camp. A troop of mounted officers led the way, followed by the artillery, two companies of grenadiers, a company of light infantry led by Major Bricker and Major Chrystie, followed by a regiment of Scotch Highlanders in full uniform, playing their national airs on bagpipes. The sheriff of New York, Robert Boyd, rode alone in state on horseback, and in line with him came the Senate committee, John Langdon, Charles Carroll, and William Samuel Johnson. Following closely in the footsteps of the Senators in the line of march came a number of men of distinction known as the "assistants": Gen. Samuel Blatchley Webb, at one time aide-de-camp to General Washington; Col. William S. Smith, active in the campaign against Yorktown; Lieut. Col. Nicholas Fish, major and inspector of the Second New York Regiment during the Revolution; Lieutenant Colonel Franks; Maj. Leonard Bleecher, who served under Lafayette and was a great friend of General Washington; and Mr. John R. Livingston, a New York merchant and a brother of Chancellor Livingston.

The President-elect came next in a coach of state, drawn by four white horses, and by his side rode Col. David Humphreys, who had been one of the General's aides and later a member of the family at Mount Vernon, and Tobias Lear, his private secretary. Following the presidential coach was the committee from the House of Representatives—Richard Henry Lee, a near neighbor and former playmate of the great Washington, and a signer of the Declaration of Independence; Ralph Izard, grandson of one of the founders of the State of South Carolina, also an intimate friend of Washington; and Tristram Dalton, of Massachusetts. Great interest centered around two diplomats, both of whom rode in their own private carriages—His Excellency the French Minister, Comte de Moustier, and His Excellency the Spanish Minister, Don Diego Gardoqui. The procession came finally to an end with a following of distinguished citizens, who walked along the line of march to express thus openly their admiration for their hero, George Washington.

When the prosession, or, as it is called now, the inaugural parade, arrived within 200 yards of Federal Hall about 1 o'clock, a line was drawn up on either side, and President-elect Washington, accompanied by those especially invited, passed through, walking to the Senate Chamber. This building, the windows of all the houses in the vicinity, and the roof tops all around had been crowded since early morning.

Meanwhile the Senate had met about 11 o'clock and all was excitement. In the most solemn manner Vice President Adams addressed those present. "Gentlemen," he said, "I wish for the directions of this body. The President, I suppose, will address Congress. How shall I behave? How shall I receive him? Shall it be standing or sitting?" A long discussion followed. Some of the Senators had attended meetings of the British Parliament, and they thought the method of procedure should be somewhat similar. A day or two before another great discussion had arisen, how to address the President, and the question seemed so momentous a committee had been appointed to decide it. It was settled by them that the title should be 'His Highness the President of the United States and Protector of their Liberties." The House, however, objected to such a long prefix and rejected it, and the question was never settled.

An hour later great confusion reigned, when the Members of the House of Representatives arrived at the Senate door with the view of receiving the President-elect. Accompanied by the joint committee of both Houses, General Washington arrived. He was introduced by the chairman of the Senate committee, and, bowing as he passed along, he was conducted to the chair next to Vice President Adams. On the right was the Vice President and the Senators, while on the left was the Speaker and Members of the House of Representatives.

After a few minutes' interval the President was formally conducted to an open gallery in front of the Senate Chamber looking out on Wall Street. His appearance was the signal for the wildest applause—bands played, flags waved, and the multitude gathered and shouted until exhausted. Over this balcony hung a canopy from which were suspended red curtains. A table stood near covered with a rich cloth of crimson velvet, on the center of which was a red cushion especially placed for a large and elegant Bible. Acknowledging the shouts of joy and this hilarious welcome, George Washington advanced to the front of the balcony, laid his hand upon his heart and bowed several times, returning immediately to an armchair near the table. Then for a moment all was hushed.

Chancellor Robert R. Livingston read the oath of office prescribed by the Constitution. "You do solemnly swear," said Livingston, "that you will faithfully execute the office of President of the United States, and will to the best of your ability, preserve, protect, and defend the Constitution of the United States." With bowed head George Washington repeated these solemn words, adding "so help me God." The Chancellor raised the Bible to the lips of the newly elected President, who stooped and kissed it. At this stage a signal was given for the raising of a flag upon Federal Hall; there was a tremendous discharge of artillery at the Battery, and all the bells of the city rang out their peals of joy. The multitude by this time had gotten their second wind, sending forth such huzzas and shouts as almost to rend the skies. The newly inaugurated President waived his hand and bowed again, retiring from a scene such as the proudest monarch might have enjoyed.

President Washington was dressed in a full suit of dark brown cloth manufactured at Hartford, with metal buttons with an eagle on them, white stockings, and plain silver shoe buckles. He carried a dress sword with a steel hilt, and his hair was dressed and powdered in the fashion of the day. Chancellor Livingston, who, by the way, was one of the committee of five (13 years before) to draft the Declaration of Independence, wore plain black clothes and the robe of his office.

It is amusing to hear so many years later that just before the oath was administered it was discovered that there was no Bible in Federal Hall. Happily, Chancellor Livingston remembered that there was one at St. John's Masonic Lodge in the neighborhood, and a messenger was dispatched in great haste to secure it. The Bible is now in the possession of this well-known lodge and is most highly prized.

President Washington, followed by the distinguished company on the balcony, now returned to Senate Chamber, where he took his seat. When he began to speak all arose and listened with eager and marked attention to his inaugural address. As he stood with his hand resting on a near-by table it was generally conceded that he was agitated and embarrassed more than he ever was by the leveled cannon and pointed muskets. In his address are to be found the following words which may prove an inspiration to many: "It would be peculiarly improper to omit," said he, "in this first official act, my fervent supplication to the Almighty Being, who rules the universe, who presides in the councils of nations, and whose providential aids can supply every human defect, that his benediction may consecrate to the liberties and happiness of the people of the United States a government instituted by themselves for these essential purposes."

At the close of the inaugural address the newly elected President, accompanied by the Vice President, the Speaker, and the two Houses of Congress, proceeded on foot to St. Paul's Chapel, followed by the military escort which amounted to about 500 men. The services in the church were conducted by the Right Rev. Dr. Samuel Provoost, of the Episcopal Church of New York. There was no sermon preached, prayers were offered, and the Te Deum sung, after which the President entered the state coach and was escorted to his newly established home.

The evening of this same day was a gala one for the citizens of New York. Through private subscription of several wealthy men gorgeous fireworks were provided, private homes were illuminated by the placing of tallow candles in the windows, often surrounding the portrait of the great national hero, and in most public buildings transparencies were displayed. Perhaps the finest of them all was one exhibited at a theater on St. John's Street, and another one at the old Fly market at the foot of Maiden Lane.

President Washington watched the fireworks from Chancellor Livingston's home, and nothing seemed to interest him more than the beginning and end of the display, which was composed of the flight of 13 skyrockets and the discharge of 13 cannon in honor of the original States.

At 10 o'clock President Washington returned to his home on foot, the crowd being so great as not to permit a carriage to pass through it. That evening as he reviewed the happenings of the eventful day his thoughts no doubt turned to what the future held for the nation, and perchance he may have remembered his own inspiring words, "Integrity and firmness are all I can promise."

The record of his administration is conclusive evidence that he lived up to this promise. His first duties were concerned with the details of transition from the old form of Government to the new. He stated in a letter to Edward Rutledge, "I anticipate that one of the most difficult and delicate parts of the duty of my office will be that which relates to nominations for appointments."

Realizing the necessity for the adoption by the President of some plan for his mode of living, and that as first incumbent of the office he must set a precedent, George Washington propounded a number of queries as to the official and social relations of a President of the United States, which he submitted to James Madison and others to obtain their point of view. These queries related in part to a method of procedure that would allow the President time for all the official duties of his station and yet avoid as much as possible the charge of superciliousness, and seclusion from information. He aimed to avoid "too much reserve and too great a withdraw of himself from company, on the one hand, and the inconveniences, as well as a reduction of respectibility, from too free intercourse and too much familiarity, on the other."

One of these queries related to the tours which he later made, and which he was apparently considering during the first fortnight of his administration. He asked of his advisers—

"Whether, during the recess of Congress, it would not be advantageous to the interests of the Union for the President to make the tour of the United States, in order to become better acquainted with their principal characters and internal circumstances, as well as to be more accessible to numbers of well-informed persons, who might give him useful information and advice on political subjects."

Following the custom which he had long since established, George Washington sought "useful information and advice" from every reliable channel, seeking the counsel of those who held opposite views that he might arrive at a general consensus of opinion. One of the most noteworthy examples of this frame of mind was his appointment of Thomas Jefferson as Secretary of State and Alexander Hamilton as Secretary of the Treasury, holding them both in his Cabinet throughout his first term of office and drawing from each of them firm statements respecting their opposing points of view which helped him to shape his own course of action.

Seeking and receiving information, as he did, from so many reliable sources, yet George Washington was not unaware of the fact that persons most concerned are often the last to hear adverse comments. This is brought out in a letter to Gouverneur Morris, dated New York, October 13, 1789:

". . . the national government is organized, and, as far as *my* information goes, to the satisfaction of all parties; that opposition to it is either no more, or hides its head; that it is hoped and expected it will take strong root; and that the nonacceding States will very soon become members of the Union."

In the same letter President Washington comments, "The revolution, which has been effected in France is of so wonderful a nature, that the mind can hardly realize the fact," and adds, "in the commencement of any work one rarely sees the progress or the end of it." This phrase has a double significance, for he applies it to his letter, which, he says, "is an evidence, though of a trifling sort." He then proceeds to ask of Gouverneur Morris, who was then in Europe, the favor to select for the presidential mansion some mirrors and plated ware of a style which he describes in minute detail, and impresses upon him one idea, "to avoid extravagance. For extravagance would not comport with my own inclination, nor with the example which ought to be set."

At the time this letter was written George Washington had but recently recovered from a serious illness and was preparing for his departure on the first of his tours of the States, the itineraries of which are covered quite comprehensively in accompanying papers of this series.

On two or three occasions the President sought to confer direct with the Senate as a body, visiting the Senate Chamber personally, with a secretary, for that purpose. The result was so unsatisfactory that he abandoned this method of gaining advance information on matters pending, but he continued to advise in his own mansion or at social functions with leading thinkers of the period, including individual Senators and Representatives as well as with the members of the executive branch of the Government. He ceased, however, to consult the Senate in advance as to his measures as he had at first considered advisable.

Through this early recognition on the part of President Washington of the difficulties attendant upon such a personal relation with the Senate and the House he was able to direct his own course more directly and effectively than would otherwise have been possible.

The President was especially gratified when the last of the 13 States, Rhode Island, ratified the Constitution and came into the Union. In acknowledgment of this ratification he wrote:

"Since the bond of Union is now complete, and we once more consider ourselves as one family, it is much to be hoped that reproaches will cease and prejudices be done away; . . . if we mean to support the liberty and independence, which it has cost us so much blood and treasure to establish, we must drive far away the demon of party spirit and local reproach."

But the "demon of party spirit" continued to hover near, and in his address to both Houses of Congress in 1790 the President called for "cool and deliberate exertion of your patriotism, firmness, and wisdom." He dwelt upon "many interesting objects which will engage your attention," referring particularly to—

". . . that of providing for the common defence . . . intercourse with other nations . . . a competent fund designated for defraying the expenses incident to the conduct of our foreign affairs . . . the terms on which foreigners may be admitted to the rights of citizens. . . . Uniformity in the currency, weights and measures of the United States, . . . the advancement of agriculture, commerce, and manufactures, . . . the promotion of science and literature."

On this occasion he voiced his thought in relation to the need of a national university, for which project he later left a bequest in his will to be used according to the discretion of Congress. This bequest was in accord with the views here expressed, namely:

"Whether this desirable object will be the best promoted by affording aids to seminaries of learning already established, by the institution of a national university, or by other expedients, will be well worthy of a place in the deliberations of the legislature."

The following year an "Act for the Encouragement of Arts" was passed, which in effect became the first patent law.

In the second year of his administration, on July 16, 1790, "An Act establishing the temporary and permanent seat of government of the United States" was passed by Congress and signed by President Washington. It provided for "a district of territory not exceeding ten miles square, to be located as hereafter directed on the river Potomac, at some place between the mouths of the Eastern Branch and Conococheague," thus giving a range of 105 miles in length from which to choose.

The selection of this general location was particularly gratifying to the President and had been made possible through a trade proposed to Thomas Jefferson by Alexander Hamilton, who promised the aid of his "organization" in support of the Potomac River location for the capital in return for Jefferson's support of the plan which Hamilton had devised for funding the State and National debts of the new Union. The Hamilton plan appealed to President Washington, as he wished to arrange the National debt and stabilize the credit of the country. Although Jefferson had strongly opposed this funding scheme, including the State debts incurred in support of the Revolution, he agreed to the compromise, influenced no doubt by his recognition of the weight of measures supported by the President.

The President was authorized, by the act providing for the establishment of the seat of government, to appoint three commissioners to survey, under his direction, the territory indicated along the Potomac River and by proper metes and bounds to define and limit the district selected for the seat of government. He did not take this responsibility lightly. Although he knew the country well, he rode over the entire territory, receiving deputations, urging the superiority of their respective localities, and weighing carefully the advantages of each possible situation. Finally,, with the aid of Jefferson and Madison, he chose the exact site for the Capital City and Capitol Building. Later, he accompanied Major L'Enfant and Mr. Ellicott, "to take a more perfect view of the ground, in order to decide finally on the spots on which to place the public buildings." He also cooperated with the three commissioners he had appointed, in negotiating for the purchase of the desired property from its respective owners.

During his first term of office the President dealt with the very difficult question of the rights and claims of the Indians in a manner that further demonstrated his sagacity. He also supported the movement toward limitation of the slave trade, which he had long advocated. It was his privilege to welcome two new States into the Union, Vermont and Kentucky, the former a free State. He initiated the framing of the judiciary system and was largely instrumental in making provisions for the reduction of the public debt and effecting new loans abroad at low rates of interest, and under such circumstances as to confirm the high state of credit accorded to the young Republic. In reporting upon these loans, upon the provisions for requisite buildings, and upon other matters connected with finance the President mentioned "the prosperous state of our revenue" and recommended that provision be made for the reimbursement of a loan from the Bank of the United States. He also recommended particular notice of various temporary laws about to expire, and in closing an address to both Houses of Congress he urged once again "the careful cultivation of harmony, combined with a due regard to stability in the public councils."

It was his wish to retire from office at the close of his first term, but he was brought to realize that he could not well be spared. His patriotism, which had stood first throughout his entire lifetime, outweighed his personal desire to retire to his own vine and fig tree, and he suffered himself to be reelected and to serve an additional four years as the Chief Executive.

THE FIRST PRESIDENTIAL TOURS: NEW ENGLAND, LONG ISLAND, AND RHODE ISLAND

When General Washington became President of the young Republic he had brought into being, he decided to make a complete tour of the entire territory comprising the United States. In the autumn of his first year he started this plan by visiting New England, between October 15 and November 13, 1789, omitting Rhode Island, as she had not yet ratified the Constitution. However, he did visit the smallest of the States between August 15 and 22 the following year, after she had fallen into line with her sister States.

President Washington and his family were established in the Presidential Home in New York City, and this trip, as all others while he was President, was made in his state coach with outriders in livery and mounted aides. He also took along his own saddle horses, so that he could ride horseback if the road and weather conditions made it advisable. He had felt from the time of his inauguration that it would only be through this personal visitation to the different parts of the new Nation that he could get a clear idea of the peace-time conditions under which the people were living and working. He wanted to view their industries, their farms, their homes, the progress of manufactures, and the development of all natural resources that were slowly but surely bringing national prosperity. He also desired to get into personal touch with the people of the country to make his own appeal for their support of their new Government.

In his diary he recorded in detail all of the places he visited, even the straggling hamlets he passed through and all of the matters of interest to him in each place. He noted the condition of houses, outhouses, public buildings, the population in each town, the churches, the business interests, the crops, and the state of livestock. Wherever he stopped long enough to receive addresses and ovations he recorded his impressions of the social life. Thus posterity owes to its first President an excellent picture of the life and progress in the United States during his first administration. One can but wonder at his energy and his devotion to his country and his high sense of responsibility as Chief Executive voluntarily to undergo the fatigue and discomforts of such journeys under such strenuous conditions of travel as the roads and highways of the period must have imposed upon a man no longer young and in the case of the first tour just recovering from a painful and serious illness.

His start from New York is thus described in his own diary:

"Thursday 15th (October 1789) Commenced my Journey about 9 o'clock for Boston and a tour through the Eastern States. The Chief Justice, Mr. Jay—and the Secretaries of the Treasury and War Departments accompanied me some distance out of the city. About 10 o'clock it began to Rain, and continued to do so till 11, when we arrived at the house of one Hoyatt who keeps a Tavern at Kingsbridge, where we, that is, Major Jackson, Mr. Lear and myself with six servants, which composed my Retinue, dined. After dinner through frequent light showers we proceed'd to the Tavern of a Mrs. Haviland at Rye; who keeps a very neat and decent Inn."

Some idea of the close observation and the careful detail with which President Washington kept a record of his journeys may be gathered from this first day's record in his diary:

"The Road for the greater part, indeed the whole way, was very rough and stoney, but the Land strong, well covered with grass and a luxuriant crop of Indian Corn intermixed with Pompions [pumpkins] (which were yet ungathered) in the fields. We met four droves of Beef

Cattle for the New York Market (about 30 in a drove) some of which were very fine—also a flock of Sheep for the same place. We scarcely passed a farm house that did not abd. in Geese. Their Cattle seemed to be of a good quality, their hogs large but rather long legged."

They visited Norwalk and Fairfield, which still showed the marks of the British foray in 1779. All of the way into New Haven the little party received in every town and hamlet salutes and greetings showing the honor and reverence felt for their President. "Light your bonfires, the white chariot is coming over the hill," seemed to be a clarion call to which the housewives, farmers, mechanics, and clerks all left their tools and their tasks to rush to the roadsides to see the President go by in his handsome state coach, with its white and gold elegance, its leather cushions and silk curtains, and the Washington coat of arms and mottoes on its door panels. Addresses of welcome, bell ringing, triumphal arches, cannon salutes, banquets, and every honor that the people could devise was paid to their leader, to whom each town was just as important as its predecessor on his itinerary and received from him the closest inspection.

In these places he also visited the plants that were manufacturing duck, linen, and woolens, and noted the cider making, the cultivation of the white mulberry for silk worms, the making of lutestring from the silk. At Hartford, after participating in the ceremonies prepared in his honor, he viewed the woolen manufactory and ordered some broadcloth for a suit for himself and a piece or bolt of other material for breeches for his servants. Of the people of Connecticut he recorded:

"There is a great equality in the People of this State. Few or no opulent men—and no poor—great similitude in their buildings—the general fashion of which is a Chimney (always of Stone or brick) and door in the middle, with a stair case fronting the latter, running up by the side of the former—two flush stories with a very good show of sash and glass windows—the size generally is from 30 to 50 feet in length, and from 20 to 30 in width, exclusive of a back shed, which seems to be added as the family encreases."

At Spencer the President received the messenger with Governor Hancock's invitation to be his guest, which he declined, as he did all such on his journeys. At Worcester he rode through the town on horseback at the request of some of his old soldiers, who desired to see their former chief in the manner they best knew and loved him.

Before reaching the city of Boston he was met by a company of the Middlesex Militia, who saluted him with 13 guns, and who desired to make arrangements for the ceremonies planned for Boston and Cambridge. Although the President desired to avoid these elaborate ceremonies, the people would not be denied.

They arrived at Cambridge at 10 o'clock, where the militia made a brave showing, and there Lieut. Gov. Samuel Adams met him with the executive council to escort him into the city, where the selectmen and townspeople had arranged a parade. The school children of Cambridge were accorded the privilege of escorting the President to the Boston line.

At the Statehouse he appeared in the balcony to receive the applause of the people and listen to an ode composed in his honor. Memory must have carried George Washington back to the days of his youth in 1756, when in spruce and handsome uniform he came to Boston to demand of Governor Shirley proper recognition of provincial officers by commission of the Virginia Governor in relation to those appointed by the King. Once again it must have recast the stage and the setting for the events of his taking command of the Army at Cambridge, of his anxious waiting for Colonel Knox and the Ticonderoga cannon to make the Dorchester Heights feat possible, and in his mind he must have contrasted the peaceful scenes in Boston Harbor with those of the evacuation of the British troops and ships.

John Adams, Vice President, accompanied him to his lodgings and dined with him, Governor Hancock having sent word of an attack of gout that made it impossible to present himself to the President. Upon the receipt of this the President excused himself from dining with the governor, feeling that he was but trying to evade making the first call, and President Washington resolved once for all to make it very plain that the office of the President of the United States was above that of the governors of the States. Many honors filled the day, and the next day Governor Hancock managed to present himself at the President's lodgings after being made to realize that unless he did so he would not see his Chief Executive. According to legend he was bundled in red flannel to emphasize his illness.

Of the duck manufactory, which greatly interested him, the President's diary records:

"They have manufactured 32 pieces of Duck, of 30 or 40 yds. each in a week; ... They have 28 looms at work, and 14 Girls spinning with Both hands, (the flax being tied to their waste.) Children (girls) turn the wheels for them, and with this assistance each spinner can turn out 14 lbs. of Thread pr. day when they stick to it, but as they are pd. by the piece, or work they do, there is no other restraint upon them but to come at 8 o'clock in the morning and return at 6 in the evening. They are daughters of decayed families, and are girls of Character—none others are admitted."

Visits to other factories were followed by a tour of French warships and his attendance of an assembly in the evening, where there were upwards of 100 ladies, whose appearance was recorded as "elegant," and many of them very handsome.

The President visited Harvard College at Cambridge accompanied by the Vice President and Mr. Bowdoin. At Beverly he was much interested in the cotton manufactory, for he realized the importance of domestic cotton manufacture. In his diary he recorded all of the processes, which he watched with deepest interest.

At the New Hampshire State line he was met by the President of the State, the Vice President, and some of the council, with troops of horse in handsome uniforms. This State rivaled Massachusetts and Connecticut in its efforts to do honor to the distinguished visitor, and on November 2, 1789, the President, accompanied by State officials, went sight-seeing by boat in the harbor of Portsmouth, stopping at Kittery, Maine. They viewed the old fort at the entrance of the harbor, which had been the scene of one of the first exploits of the Revolution, and which saluted him with 13 guns; and then proceeded to give the jaunt a real holiday touch by trying their luck at cod fishing. The President recorded the results: "But it not being proper time of tide, we only caught two."

This practically ended the trip, and the return journey was made as rapidly as possible. Out of regard for the law of Connecticut against traveling on Sunday, the President wrote under the date of November 8, 1789:

"It being contrary to law and disagreeable to the people of this State (Connecticut) to travel on the Sabbath day—and my horses after passing through such intolerable roads, wanting rest, I stayed at Perkins Tavern (which by the way, is not a good one) all day—and a meeting house being within a few rods of the door, I attended morning and evening service, and heard very lame discourses from a Mr. Pond."

He reached New York on November 13, just in time to put in an appearance at one of Mrs. Washington's receptions.

President Washington started on his 5-day tour of Long Island on April 20, 1790. He traversed the territory as fully as conditions would permit and wrote observations in his diary which indicate his invariable interest in agricultural matters.

"This Island (as far as I went) from West to East seems to be equally divided between flat and Hilly land, the former on the South next the Seaboard, and the latter on the No. next the Sound. The highland they say is best and most productive, but the other is the pleasantest to work, except in wet seasons when from the levelness of them they are sometimes.

(but not frequently having a considerable portion of Sand) incommoded by heavy and continual rains. From a comparative view of their crops they may be averaged as follows:—Indian Corn 25 bushels—Wheat 15—Rye 12—Oats 15 bushels to the acre. According to their accts. from Lands highly manured they sometimes get 50 of the first, 25 of the 2d and 3d, and more of the latter. . . . Towards close of the Snows, they sow Clover from 4 to 6 lb; and a quart of Timothy seed. This lays from 3 to 6 years according as the grass remains, or as the conditions of the ground is, for so soon as they find it beginning to bind, they plow. Their first plowing (with the Patent tho' they call it the Dutch plow) is well executed at the depth of about 3 or at most 4 Inches—the cut being 9 or 10 Inches and the sod neatly and very evenly turned. With Oxen they plough mostly. They do no more than turn the ground in this manner for Indian Corn before it is planted; making the holes in which it is placed with hoes the rows being marked off by a stick—two or three workings afterward with the Harrows or Plough is all the cultivation it receives generally. Their fences, where there is no Stone, are very indifferent; frequently of plashed trees of any and every kind which have grown by chance; but it exhibits an evidence that very good fences may be made in this manner either of white Oak or Dogwood which from this mode of treatment grows thickest, and most stubborn.—This however, would be no defence against Hogs."

Upon the adjournment of Congress, August 12, 1790, General Washington decided to visit Rhode Island, as it had ratified the Constitution the past May. His party started August 15 in a Rhode Island packet, making the trip by sea—the only sea voyage recorded by Washington in his life except the Barbadoes experience in his youth. At Newport, on the 17th, he was received with enthusiasm, with salutes and a long procession awaiting at the wharf to greet him. A walk about the town was followed by a dinner at the Statehouse.

The next day, after the addresses of the morning, the President departed for Providence. The passage to this place was tedious, consuming seven hours. A more formal procession headed by the Governor of the State, with troops and bands, greeted him on arrival. After tea at Dagget's Tavern the President was prevailed upon to view the illumination of the college to please the students. The next day the President decided to walk about the town, in the course of which he visited the college, inspected it minutely, went aboard a large Indianman of 900 tons which was on the stocks, received the addresses of the Cincinnati, the College of Rhode Island, and the city of Providence.

He then attended a public dinner with the citizens to the number of 200 at the Town Hall, after which he embarked for New York. On September 2 Brown College conferred the degree of Doctor of Laws upon General Washington.

The Southern Tour

Having thus seen with his own eyes the thrift and progress of the Northern States, he balanced matters by a similar tour through the South, noting the economic conditions, giving himself the pleasure of visiting the battlefields and forts, and tracing the routes of the armies of the great Revolutionary struggle that had climaxed at Yorktown under his own direction; and appealing directly to the people for a national spirit of unity that would put an end to the provincial prejudices retarding national progress. With these ideas in mind, and in spite of his almost 60 years, he completed this extensive itinerary in his huge and elegant chariot, lumbering over unbroken country, along roads which in those days were little more than crooked trails.

Being perhaps the most experienced traveler of his day in his own land, and knowing what he might expect to encounter, yet he let no thought of fatigue or hardship deter him in planning this journey of three months, in which, according to his own diary, he traveled 1,887 miles, using the same horses. So carefully and systematically did he make his schedule of arrivals and departures and places to stay in varying periods that not a single mishap or accident occurred throughout the journey to delay his program or upset the routine he so punctiliously followed. He not only attended to all of the details himself but he prepared a copy of his itinerary with its full complement of dates for the guidance of his Cabinet, with full instructions covering all possible contingencies, which he sent to them before he left Mount Vernon.

This double swing around the circle by our first President established the precedent for all of the journeys and junkets of his successors in the presidential chair; and made journeys of observation, investigation, and promotion of good feeling and participation in leading local events a very real and necessary part of the presidential job. So much a part of the presidential obligation has it become that Congress has for a number of years past provided a substantial sum for the traveling expenses of the President of the United States.

The first President, however, not only paid his own house rent and maintained his presidential household, but he also paid the expenses of his journeys, manifesting a pronounced reluctance to accept private hospitality thrust upon him at every hand. By his personal visits to every State, his presence in their midst, his democratic attitude to-

ward both public and private organizations and individuals, he satisfied the pride of his fellow countrymen in him as their chosen leader, which was then not far removed from that accorded to royalty. He thereby secured anew their trust and their allegiance to his plans for solidifying the new Government and making acceptable its new laws and conditions. In turn, from his contact with the masses as well as classes, limited though both were in numbers, he secured for himself, and through his carefully kept and voluminous diary for posterity, a true and revealing picture of America of his day.

Feeling the necessity of reflecting at all times the prestige of his high office in order to command public respect, the first President traveled in imposing fashion, and in his diary notes his departure for Mount Vernon:

"Monday, 21st. Left Philadelphia about 11 o'clock to make a tour through the Southern States. Reached Chester about 3 o'clock—dined and lodged at Mr. Wythes. Roads exceedingly deep, heavy and cut in places by the Carriages which used them.

"In this tour I was accompanied by Majr. Jackson—my equipage and attendance consisted of a Charriot and four hourses drove in hand—a light baggage Waggon and two horses—four saddle horses besides a led one for myself—and five—to wit;—my valet de Chambre, two footmen, Coachman and postilion."

In Maj. William Jackson the President had the benefit of an aide or secretary who was both a writer and fluent speaker, also a gallant soldier and possessed of much tact and diplomacy. He had been secretary to the Federal Convention.

After about a week spent at Mount Vernon completing preparations, in course of which, because of the hardships of the impending trip and the likelihood of frequent upsets of habits of sleep, meals, and rest, the President vetoed Mrs. Washington's accompanying him, they resumed their journey on April 7, 1791, heading for Richmond by way of Fredericksburg. There General Washington stopped for a little visit with his sister Betty and her family, renewed old friendships, and revisited the scenes of his boyhood, between the various functions arranged in his honor.

While in Richmond he made a trip of inspection to the James River Canal with the governor and the director of the company. He had urged the construction of this transportation project in 1784. The Legislature of Virginia voted George Washington 100 shares of this stock in 1785. This he accepted only to hold in trust for some public philanthropy and eventually gave them to the Liberty Hall Academy, which grew into the Washington and Lee University.

By the time the President had participated in the main functions of Richmond, Manchester, and Petersburgh, the latter so replete with memories of his beloved Lafayette and reminders of his own anxieties over the activities of Cornwallis, Tarleton, and Arnold, he felt the need of escaping some of the insistent attentions of large parties of escort, especially on his early morning departures. His own words describe his thoroughly human subterfuge by which he secured for himself at least a temporary relief. He wrote:

"Friday [April] 15th. Having suffered very much by the dust yesterday, and finding that parties of Horse, and a number of other Gentlemen were intending to attend me part of the way to day, I caused their enquiries respecting the time of my setting out, to be answered that, I should endeavor to do it before eight o'clock; but I did it a little after five, by which means I avoided the inconveniences above mentioned."

The spontaneous enthusiasm and real affection, not unmixed with awe, with which the people through the country along the little-frequented byways and in the remote settlements greeted their President must have given him a sense of great pleasure and satisfaction, especially as he had never before traveled southward. The prayers for his safety, health, and success as fervently made as the huzzas of praise and shouts of welcome must indeed have been gratifying, and compensated for the long stretches of rough travel, hard upon man and horses. Here and there in most of the larger centers, the distinguished traveler was congenially entertained by the various lodges of the Masonic fraternity, of which he had been a member since he was 20 years old.

The ovations at Newbern were elaborate and extensive; the President attended a brilliant ball at the Palace, where in years gone by the royal Governor Tryon and his lady had presided over so many handsome balls, while the President's horses were stabled in the former office of the Tory governor.

On approaching Wilmington the President was met by a large committee of important men, and after greeting them left his coach and joined them on horseback to be escorted into the city, where he received a Federal salute and was conducted to the "very good lodgings" prepared for him. There the President invited the committee to dine with him. Through two crowded days there were addresses from the citizens, with his responses, a banquet by the gentlemen of the town, a procession and grand ball at the Assembly Hall, of which the General noted in his diary the presence of "sixty-two ladies," bonfires, and illuminations. Having sent his carriage on the day previous, the President was escorted by the committee aboard the "elegantly decorated revenue barge manned by six American Captains of ships, attended by boats from the harbor, and proceded to the firing of cannon to

'Belvidere' the plantation of Colonel Benjamin Smith in Brunswick County." Tradition claims that at the river landing at Brunswick he was met by 13 young girls in white, representing the 13 States, who preceded him up the avenue of old trees from the landing to the mansion, scattering flowers in his path.

On April 27 the party crossed the line between the Carolinas and on the 29th they arrived at the home of Capt. William Alston, where the President met General Moultrie, hero of Sullivans Island and twice Governor of South Carolina.

The President was particularly impressed with Captain Alston's rice fields. He wrote of him:

"Captain Alston is a Gentleman of large fortune and esteemed one of the neatest Rice planters in the State of So. Carolina and a proprietor of the most valuable ground for the culture of this article. His house which is large, new and elegantly furnished stands on a sand hill, high for the Country, with his Rice fields below; the contrast of which with the lands back of it, and the Sand and piney barrens through which we had passed is scarcely to be conceived."

They left in boats the next morning for Georgetown. Two days later they reached the plantation of Governor Pinckney, and from there on to a ferry at Haddrels Point, where another boat, a 12-oared barge, awaited him. Here was a most festive gathering; more than 40 boats had assembled loaded with important citizens. Two boats, provided with music, led the procession across the Santee River to Charleston. At the wharf the governor, lieutenant governor, and a large number of city officials awaited the distinguished guest, and escorted him to his lodgings, where he dined with them. At Charleston the President was entertained at every meal. He breakfasted with Mrs. Rutledge, the wife of the Chief Justice, then away on the circuit, and dined with the citizens at the Exchange. In the afternoon he received a call from a delegation of women of the city. He recorded their visit thus:

"Was visited about 2 o'clock by a great number most respectable ladies of Charleston—the first honor of the kind I had ever experienced and it was as flattering as it was singular."

The next day, Wednesday, May 4, after inspecting the lines of the siege of 1780, he dined with members of the Cincinnati and attended an elegant dancing assembly, at which were 256 elegantly dressed and handsome ladies. After visiting the forts of the harbor on May 5, he went to another evening function, where there were 400 ladies. Next day he viewed the town by horseback and went to a ball, and on the 7th visited an orphan asylum.

The President won all hearts by his democratic and gracious manner, and this was accentuated by his polite refusal of the offer of the Charleston Battalion of Artillery of their attendance upon him during his stay and to mount guard regularly for the purpose. He declared that he considered himself perfectly safe in "the affection and amicable attachment of the people." To enumerate all of the ceremonies, honors, and celebrations of Charleston is prohibitive in a limited paper, but all organizations vied with each other in making his visit an event of unsurpassed brilliance, a civic entertainment which was without parallel in the city for duration, variety, elegance, and universal cordiality.

Leaving Charleston on May 9, he next stopped 28 miles away at the home of Col. William Washington, called Sandy Hill. This Washington who had been called "the sword of the army," was a cousin of the President. At this place the President broke his rule of not accepting private hospitality, remaining over night. Next day he parted with all of his escort, and on May 12 at Purysburg (where for a time General Lincoln had his headquarters) he was met by five patriots of the Revolution, comprising a committee from Savannah. They were Noble Wymberly Jones, Joseph Habbersham, John Houston, Lachlen McIntosh, and Joseph Clay. They escorted the President and his party aboard a bedecked barge and were rowed down the Savannah River by nine captains of ships in gay uniforms. Two miles below Purysburg the President called upon Mrs. Greene, widow of Gen. Nathanael Greene, at her home, Mulberry Grove, the estate presented to her husband by the State of Georgia in appreciation of his Revolutionary services.

At Savannah he was escorted by the mayor and city officials to a public dinner with the citizens at the Coffee Room; next day he had dinner with the members of the Cincinnati, and attended a dancing assembly, where he observed 100 ladies, "well dressed and handsome."

On May 14, accompanied by General McIntosh, Gen. Anthony Wayne, the mayor, and many other important gentlemen of the State, he visited the old military lines and went over the history of the attack on the British in the year 1779 by the forces of the United States and France commanded by Maj. Gen. Benjamin Lincoln and Count d'Estaing.

A banquet or dinner was served the party in a bower on the river bank and there was a display of fireworks in the evening. After more calls the President left for Augusta, Georgia, May 15, dining with Mrs. Greene at Mulberry Grove en route. The journey for the next few days was uneventful. At Augusta, Thursday, May 19, the program was but a repetition of those of previously visited places, including a notable dinner at the private residence of Governor and Mrs. Telfair, and a ball at the Academy.

A visit to the ruins of the forts erected by the British during the war and captured by Henry Lee and Andrew Pickens in 1781, and a trip to the Falls, concluded the President's most pleasurable visit to Augusta. On August 21 he started his homeward journey; making the first stop at Columbia, South Carolina. This had been the State capital since 1786, chosen because of its many natural advantages as an inland center; but in 1791 the Statehouse was still unfinished.

To greet the people of neighboring places, the President held a huge midday reception to the assemblage that represented Columbia, Granby, Winnisborough, Camden, Statesburgh, Bellville, Orangeborough, and their vicinity. Following this he was presented individually to 60 ladies, and they and their partners, comprising a party of 153, sat down to a farmer's dinner in the Senate chamber. After this came a ball.

The President's diary records the necessity for delaying his visit through another day, owing to the condition of his foundered horse, which time he devoted to viewing the town and writing responses to the various addresses made to him.

While at Camden, General Washington responded to the tributes to himself and Baron de Kalb, who fell at Camden, and paid a visit to the site of the action of General Greene and Lord Rawdon.

Passing into North Carolina, the President next visited Salisbury, May 30, and the Moravian settlement of Salem the next day, where he awaited the arrival of Governor Martin. His diary records his visiting the shops and listening to their music. On the arrival of the Governor the party set out for Guilford to examine the site of the action between Greene and Cornwallis. Here the President prevailed upon Governor Martin to dismiss the assembled soldiery and countermand all of his orders for further military escort and attendance.

Without further events of importance President Washington reached Mount Vernon at dinner time on Sunday, June 12, a few days ahead of his schedule, in which he made a week's allowance for delays. The most complete résumé of President Washington's visit to the Southern States and the impressions of the South which he gathered on the trip is preserved to posterity in his own writing in a letter, July 20, to his friend, aide, and former secretary, David Humphrey, who was then United States minister to Portugal. In this he said:

". . . In my last I mentioned my intention of visiting the southern States, which I have since accomplished, and have the pleasure to inform you, that I performed a journey of 1887 miles without meeting with any interruption by sickness, bad weather, or any untoward accident—Indeed, so highly were we favored, that we arrived at each place, where I proposed to make any halt, on the very day I fixed upon before we set out. The same horses performed the whole tour; and, although much reduced in flesh, kept up their full spirits to the last day.

"I am much pleased that I have taken this journey, as it has enabled me to see with my own eyes the situation of the country through which we travelled, and to learn more accurately the disposition of the people than I could have done by any information.

"The country appears to be in a very improving state, and industry and frugality are becoming much more fashionable than they have hitherto been there. Tranquility reigns among the people, with that disposition towards the general government, which is likely to preserve it. They begin to feel the good effects of equal laws and equal protection. The farmer finds a ready market for his produce, and the merchant calculates with more certainty on his payments. Manufactures have as yet made but little progress in that part of the country, and it will probably be a long time before they are brought to that state, to which they have already arrived in the middle and eastern parts of the Union.

"Each day's experience of the government of the United States seems to confirm its establishment, and to render it more popular. A ready acquiescence in the laws made under it shows in a strong light the confidence, which the people have in their representatives, and in the upright views of those, who administer the government."

SECOND TERM OF PRESIDENT WASHINGTON

The second inauguration of General Washington was the first of the March inaugurals and was quite an impressive occasion. This occurred in Philadelphia and was attended with great display.

The President's own appearance was much more elegant than at the first ceremony, for this time he was garbed in a handsome suit of black velvet, with an abundance of silver lace, diamond-studded knee and shoe buckles, a delicate white satin vest, yellow kid gloves, cocked hat, and a long sword with glittering steel belt and scabbard of polished white leather.

He was driven to Hall of Congress in splendid style. His great state coach had been repaired and done over in very elaborate fashion. In the Senate Chamber Justice Cushing administered the oath of office. The reelected President made a brief but impressive address before as large an audience of officials as could find space within the Senate Chamber. He spoke of his gratitude and pleasure at the demonstration of faith and loyalty of the people as expressed in his reelection.

On December 3, 1793, he addressed both Houses of Congress. He said in part:

"But influenced by the belief, that my conduct would be estimated according to its real motives, and that the people, and the authorities derived from them, would support exertions having nothing personal for their object, I have obeyed the suffrage, which commanded me to resume the executive power; and I humbly implore that Being, on whose will the fate of nations depends, to crown with success our mutual endeavors for the general happiness."

One of the interesting events in the first year of the second term, September 18, 1793, was the laying of the corner stone of the United States Capitol—at Washington, D. C.—by President Washington with Masonic ceremonies. The *Maryland Gazette* of September 26, 1793, published a detailed account of the imposing Masonic ceremonial which attended the laying of that stone:

"General Washington had long been a member of the Masonic fraternity, and it was but natural in his difficult rôle of the first President to an infant nation, when among other duties it fell to him to dedicate buildings and the like, that his mind turned to the solemn rites of this order as the most suitable with which to conduct the official dedication of new landmarks in the nation's life and history."

Dearly as Washington was loved and highly as he was trusted and respected, many decisions in his second administration were bitterly attacked by the group that made up the Anti-Federalist or Republican Party. The principles of this party were similar to those of the present Democratic Party. With part of his tiny Cabinet advocating the concentration of power in the National Government and part of it clinging to State sovereignty, Washington could not fail of meeting grave problems. Alexander Hamilton, Secretary of the Treasury, was the leader of the Federalists, while Thomas Jefferson, Secretary of State, was the head of the Republican contingent. The division of political adherence in the Cabinet was bad enough, but along came Freneau, recently made translator of French by Secretary Jefferson, to add to the disruption with his radical Republican doctrines, which he kept constantly circulating through the columns of the *National Gazette*. Wielding a vitriolic pen, he was a disturbing element, for in Philadelphia he kept his paper bristling with anathemas and arraignments of the President and his advisers, and the most lavish praise of Jefferson's acts and theories. Freneau's publication was the forerunner of the "party organ," which, in lauding its friends and villifying its foes, became the greatest weapon of the respective parties.

Along with the vexing situations in our national affairs, another great storm cloud gathered and rolled itself across the world's horizon, threatening to embroil the United States as well as England in the maelstrom of war and disaster. France was in the throes of a revolution. Its monarchy had been destroyed, and its king and queen and all that belonged to their régime had met the violent death of the guillotine, or become exiles.

All America was fired to the highest pitch of sympathy for her former ally in the attempt of her people to erect above the funeral pyre of its hapless rulers a new republic, similar to our own, in the cause of which so many Frenchmen had served. Especially difficult was the task of the Executive when the interest and enthusiasm of the American people carried them to the point of demanding that all of our resources be used in aid of the hysterical element in France that daily kept the world gasping with horror over the orgies of murder and destruction in Paris, where 1,800 were slain in one night.

Despite his love for the country of his friend and comrade, Lafayette, and the gratitude which Washington always felt toward France for her timely assistance, he felt it his duty to turn a deaf ear to all pleas that would involve the United States in any war. Upon the declaration of war between France and England, M. Genet, the first minister of the new French Republic, arrived in the United States, prepared to obtain recognition for his Government, and money and men from our people. Without waiting until he should be presented to the President, and his credentials accepted, he started propagandist operations among the French sympathizers, and afterwards so annoyed the President that his recall was requested.

President Washington never wavered in his determination to avoid being drawn into the French-British quarrel; for with a marvelous vision of the future he saw that the hope of American progress and power lay in a policy of strict neutrality in all European entanglements. Hence, on April 22, 1793, he issued his proclamation of neutrality. This established the policy of the United States. Regarding his attitude in this matter, in which his friendship for Lafayette, and his anxiety over his plight, caused him such real, personal suffering, he wrote to Patrick Henry October 9, 1795:

"I persuade myself, Sir, it has not escaped your observation, that a crisis is approaching, that must, if it cannot be arrested, soon decide whether order and good government shall be preserved, or anarchy and confusion ensue. I can most religiously aver that I have no wish, that

is incompatible with dignity, happiness, and true interest of the people of this country. My ardent desire is, and my aim has been, (as far as depended upon the executive department,) to comply strictly with *all* our engagements, foreign and domestic, but to keep the United States free from political connexions with *every* other country, to see them independent of *all* and under the influence of *none*. In a word, I want an *American* character, that the powers of Europe may be convinced we act for *ourselves,* and not for *others*. This, in my judgment, is the only way to be respected abroad and happy at home; . . ."

Under the influence of French agitators the proclamation aroused greater virulence in the opposition than had ever before existed. For his determined stand to hold to this policy against all argument, President Washington and his followers were abused intensely and called monarchists and accused of intriguing to set up a despotic kingdom. Other causes contributing to the national unrest were the dissatisfaction over the state of the treaty of 1783 with England, and the tax imposed upon domestic distilled liquors, which produced the Whisky Rebellion among the farmer-distillers in the vicinity of Pittsburgh. This was successfully quashed by the appearance of Gen. Henry Lee with his body of militia ordered out by the President.

England still molested our sea trade, impressed our seamen into her service, and kept some of her troops in forts within our boundary. She in turn had grievances against the United States, and in the general turmoil it looked as though war was again imminent. However, President Washington's calm statesmanship averted trouble, as he sent John Jay to England in April, 1794, to discuss the disputed points and upon his shoulders was placed the task of preventing the two nations from drifting into war. He was courteously received and the troublesome matters on both sides were carefully considered. After much deliberation and discussion England agreed to surrender the frontier forts; the debts were to be referred to a claims commission. The British claim that their loyalists had not been indemnified for their losses was offset by the American grievance that the British during the war had carried off many valuable slaves. East Indian trade was opened to American vessels, but the much-desired trade with the West Indies was hedged with restrictions. By the November following his arrival Jay had succeeded in bringing about a treaty upon these terms, by which both nations made compromises; and while it was far from being for the Americans what had been desired in such a document, it was better than a continuance of the harassments or a recourse to war.

The President received the treaty in March, 1795, but as the Senate did not meet until June the provisions were kept within the secrecy of the Cabinet circles until that time. Just as the Senate, after a bitter debate, was about to ratify the treaty, one of the Senators violated this secrecy and gave the provisions of the treaty to the papers, though by so doing he barely anticipated Washington's desire to ascertain public opinion by this means. Publicity resulted in vicious attacks upon the treaty. These attacks were not confined to scathing editorials, as Alexander Hamilton was stoned in a public meeting and John Jay was burned in effigy in several cities. The British minister was insulted, copies of the treaty provisions were burned in front of the British minister's house, and great excitement ensued. So strongly did the feeling run that later some Members of the House threatened to impeach President Washington for standing upon his constitutional rights, in refusing to lay before it the correspondence relating to the ratification of the treaty when only the assent of the Senate was needed.

When the news of the Jay treaty reached the Spanish Premier, Godoy, at Madrid in 1794, it alarmed him lest England and America form an alliance. As William Pinckney, wearied with his long and fruitless efforts to get negotiations completed, asked for his passports and announced London as his destination, the Spanish Premier suddenly decided to agree to the treaty of San Lorenzo (1795). By this the boundary between the United States and Florida was fixed, and the Mississippi was thrown open to American navigation with the privilege of using New Orleans as a port.

On August 19, 1795, in the presence of the rest of the Cabinet, President Washington gave to Secretary of State Randolph a dispatch of the French Minister which the British had intercepted and turned over to the American Government. In this Minister Fauchet hinted that Randolph had solicited money from him. Randolph requested an opportunity to throw his ideas on paper, but instead of doing so he resigned his position that evening. At the end of the year he issued a vindication in which he criticized the President sharply, accusing him of rank partisanship. The matter has never been cleared up; Randolph was indiscreet and his vindication is not convincing. The episode was connected with the Whisky Rebellion and also with the Jay treaty negotiation, to which naturally the French objected.

The relations between President Washington and Thomas Jefferson came to an end in 1796 when the President sent the following letter to his former Secretary of State:

"Until within the last year or two, I had no conception that parties would or even could go the length I have been witness to; nor did I believe until lately, that it was within the bounds of probability, hardly within those of possibility, that while I was using my utmost exertions to establish a national character of our own, independent, as far as our obligations and justice would permit, of every nation of the earth, and wished, by steering a steady course, to preserve this country from the horrors of a desolating war, I should be accused of being the enemy of one nation, and subject to the influence of another; and, to prove it, that every act of my administration would be tortured, and the grossest and most insidious misrepresentations of them be made, by giving one side *only* of a subject, and that too in such exaggerated and indecent terms as could scarcely be applied to a Nero, a notorious defaulter, or even to a common pickpocket. But enough of this, I have already gone farther in the expression of my feelings than I intended."

A few months later President Washington, about six months before the actual end of his last term, issued his Farewell Address to the People of the United States, which is regarded as not only a marvel of political sagacity and statesmanship but a classic in American patriotic literature; and in his last annual message to Congress, December 7, 1796, in conclusion he said:

"The situation in which I now stand, for the last time, in the midst of the representatives of the people of the United States, naturally recalls the period when the administration of the present form of government commenced; and I cannot omit the occasion to congratulate you and my country, on the success of the experiment, nor to repeat my fervent supplications to the Supreme Ruler of the Universe and Sovereign Arbiter of Nations, that his providential care may still be extended to the United States; that the virtue and happiness of the people may be preserved; and that the government, which they have instituted for the protection of their liberties, may be perpetual."

President Washington persistently refused to consider a third term, despite the pressure brought to bear upon him, thereby setting an example which no successor of his has ever set aside.

The final formal levees were packed with admiring friends and eminent men who seemed loath to lose a moment of his society, and a few days after the inauguration of John Adams he and Mrs. Washington took their departure for Mount Vernon, a boon long desired. His administration was remarkable for the wisdom and skill with which he handled the problems that presented themselves in a perpetual stream for solution.

(FOR THIS PROGRAM SEE NUMBERS 11, 12, 13, 33, 47, 98 IN LIST OF SELECTED BOOKS ON PAGES 300-A AND 300-B)

RECEPTION OF PRESIDENT-ELECT WASHINGTON AT THE BRIDGE AT TRENTON

The Homemaking of George and Martha Washington

THE WASHINGTON FAMILY
After a painting by Edward Savage

COLONEL AND MRS. WASHINGTON IN RESIDENCE BEFORE THE REVOLUTION

FAIRFAX COUNTY, VIRGINIA, was formed in 1742 from Prince William County and named in honor of Lord Fairfax, the proprietor of what is generally called the Northern Neck of Virginia. In this picturesque, fertile county of the Old Dominion State is situated Mount Vernon, the home for 40 years of President and Mrs. Washington. The historic Potomac River washes the foot of the lawn of this old-time Virginia mansion.

It was in 1759 that Col. George Washington married the Widow Custis, and before them both apparently were years of married life and happiness. Martha was regarded as the richest woman in the colony, and George had already won his military spurs and was about to become a member of the House of Burgesses. For a time the bride and groom remained at Williamsburg, where the assemblies were held, and then the young couple went home to Mount Vernon, the estate inherited by George from his half brother, Lawrence. Naturally they were accompanied on the journey to the new home by the bride's two children of a former marriage, John Parke and Martha Custis, who all through their lives were treated by their childless stepfather just as if they were

his own. Unfortunately, both Jackey and Patsey, as they were called, were delicate children, which caused their mother great anxiety. Soon after her marriage Martha Washington wrote to one of her sisters:

"I have the pleasure to receive you kind letter . . . just as I was setting out on a visit to Mr. Washington in Westmoreland, whare I spent a week most agreeabley. I carried my little patt [Patsey] with me and left Jackey at home for a trial to see how well I coud stay without him; though we were gon but one fortnight I was quite impatient to get home. . . . We all enjoy pretty good health at preasant. I think patsey seems quite well now, Jackey is very thin but in good health, and learns thaire books very fast. . . . If I could leave my children in as good case as you can I would never let Mr. W——n come down without me."

This last sentence meant that she would have always accompanied her husband to the sessions of the House of Burgesses in Williamsburg. It is apparent from this letter that the mother love was one of Martha Washington's strongest emotions.

For 15 years Colonel and Mrs. Washington

lived at Mount Vernon in the happiest possible manner, and undoubtedly if both of them could have been consulted they would have continued to live on, as private citizens, in the same manner. The Colonel assumed the duties of an enthusiastic gentleman farmer, while Martha Washington was content to be the farmer's wife, living from day to day immersed in her household. She busied herself with her needlework, her charities, and, last but by no means least, with her housekeeping, which at this time was no easy task. For these 15 years it is more than apparent that both Colonel and Mrs. Washington were ideally happy as they drifted along entertaining many guests, each looking out for his or her self-imposed tasks. The hospitality all through the Virginia colony was unceasing, and George and Martha Washington loved to gather around their board their many friends and neighbors. Colonel Washington not only raised crops, but he rode to the hounds with his gay neighbors, the Fairfaxes, the Digges family on the other side of the Potomac, and the Carlyles in what was then far-away Alexandria.

The Washington family owned a coach and four, and Martha Washington often entertained her guests with long drives as they sat behind the white and scarlet liveried postilions. In this happy manner both Colonel and Mrs. Washington led well-ordered lives, elegantly clothed because the Colonel would not have it otherwise, well fed from the best raised on the plantation and from the finest food obtainable elsewhere.

No life is without its shadows even in this case, but they were not, however, serious ones. As Jackey approached manhood Colonel and Mrs. Washington found him difficult to manage. He paid little attention to his studies in the school at Annapolis, and was somewhat urgent in his demands that he be sent to Europe. When finally his stepfather decided to send him to King's College in New York he was far from content. The real reason for all of this discontent was he had fallen in love with a beautiful Maryland girl, Eleanor Calvert, of Mount Airy. After some opposition on account of his extreme youth, in February, 1774, the young couple were married, and went to live at Abingdon on the Potomac. It was a trial to Martha Washington just at that time, as Patsey had died some months before at the age of 16, and she was too grief-stricken still to attend even the wedding. However, she wrote her prospective daughter-in-law an affectionate letter. She said:

"God took from Me a Daughter when June Roses were blooming. He has now given me another daughter, about her Age, when winter winds are blowing to warm my heart again. I am Happy as One so afflicted and one so Blest can be. Pray receive my benediction and a wish that you may long be the Loving wife of my happy Son, and a loving Daughter to your Affectionate Mother, M. Washington."

In looking back through so many years the impression such a letter is apt to make upon the average mind is of the great dignity of Martha Washington, and this attribute is largely tempered by sweetness and grace.

From the beginning of their married life Colonel and Mrs. Washington lived in great style and with great regularity. Breakfast was served promptly at 7 o'clock, dinner at 3, tea at 7, and supper at 9. The last meal was most simple and seldom varied, principally fruit and cream and cake and wine. Ten o'clock was the retiring hour, when each individual took a lighted candle with him or her and retired for the night to an upper chamber.

Dinner was the principal meal at Mount Vernon and was decidedly formal, everything being served on the most liberal scale. The dining-room table was always spread with a double cloth, and after the first course, which varied from time to time, but which on one special occasion consisted of oyster soup, beef, mutton, and a number of vegetables, the upper cloth was removed, and the one underneath was quickly loaded with pies, puddings, tarts, jellies, whips, floating island, sweet-meats, etc. In time the second cloth was also removed, and the black walnut table top exposed. Fresh glasses were brought and a light wine was served with fruit, raisins, and almonds. Coffee was served at a later hour in the parlor. During the evening the guests were generally entertained by instrumental music, Martha Washington herself being a good deal of a musician.

The delightful domesticity for Colonel and Mrs. Washington at Mount Vernon was destined not to continue. There was already trouble brewing in the Colonies, indeed a decided undercurrent was apparent. About this time in 1774 Edmund Pendleton and Patrick Henry stopped at Mount Vernon to join George Washington, and the three friends journeyed together from there to the Congress in Philadelphia. In speaking of his short stay at Mount Vernon, Pendleton said:

"The dear little woman was busy from morning until night with domestic duties, and she gave us much time in conversation and afforded us entertainment. When we set off in the morning she stood at the door and cheered us with good words, 'God be with you gentlemen.'"

It was in June of the following year that Martha Washington received a letter from her Colonel. He wrote:

"My dearest, I am now set down to write to you on a subject, which fills me with inexpressible concern, and this concern is greatly aggravated and increased, when I reflect upon the uneasiness I know it will give you. It has been determined in Congress, that the whole army raised for the defence of the American cause shall be under my care, . . . You may believe me, my dear Patsy, when I assure you . . . that . . . I have used every endeavor in my power to avoid it, . . . I shall feel no pain from the toil or the danger of the campaign, my unhappiness will flow from the uneasiness I know you will feel from being left alone. I therefore beg, that you will summon your whole fortitude, and pass your time as agreeably as possible."

Fortitude was given this distinguished Virginia woman, Martha Washington. If affairs went wrong, if there was a war with all of its horrors, and dangers of pillage and confiscation, she felt that she had more to lose than any woman in the country. According to tradition, although many friends and relatives gathered around her and suggested that she select an inland retreat, Martha Washington never faltered in what she regarded as her duty, and to them all she said, "No, I shall not desert my post."

War-Time Households

During the winter of 1774-75 Mount Vernon was the scene of continual conferences of the leaders of action in the Virginia Colony and the country at large. They came from far and near to consult George Washington. At this time George Washington was a member of the House of Burgesses. Reelected, he attended the Virginia Convention in the old church in Richmond in 1775 and brought home with him his appointment to represent his native State in the Second Continental Congress. He had heard Patrick Henry's thrilling address in which he uttered, "I know not what course others may take, but as for me give me liberty or give me death."

George Washington had scarcely reached Mount Vernon before rumors followed him that the Royal Governor had confiscated the powder stores in Williamsburg. Washington at once rode to Fredericksburg to calm the 600 men who had rushed to arms. Meanwhile he was receiving daily messages from the militia of various counties in Virginia offering to serve under his command. A little later, unconsciously bidding Mount Vernon farewell for many years, he departed to attend the Congress in Philadelphia. When he said good-bye to his wife at this time probably neither of them understood what that separation meant. It was the impression of both George and Martha that they would meet again in a few weeks, at most at the close of the Continental Congress, but under tremendous pressure George Washington accepted the office of Commander in Chief of the Army of the Colonies, and he did not see Mount Vernon again for six years.

Mount Vernon was now indeed desolate for Martha Washington. She must have felt keenly the responsibilities of her husband, and to a great extent she realized that the destiny was in his hands. She was deeply in sympathy with the cause, and brave woman as she was, she at once recognized that her part was to "carry on" to the extent of her strength and ability during his absence. This required courage of an unusual type. Within two years she had seen the most painful changes. Her only daughter had died, her son had married, and now her husband had been called into the service of his country; a less resolute woman would have fallen by the way.

After receiving his commission, General Washington evidently realized how dreary life must be for Martha at this juncture. Accordingly, he wrote to certain friends and relatives urging them to go to Mount Vernon and "comfort his lonely wife." To be sure Jack Custis and his wife made frequent visits from Abingdon, and as the years passed by Martha Washington found solace, comfort, and happiness in welcoming Jack's little family. The children soothed her loneliness and helped make life worth while again.

During these dreary months Mrs. Washington's brothers and sisters, the Dandridges and Bassetts, journeyed from New Kent County to see her, and her friends and neighbors vied with one another in their desire to alleviate the loneliness of her life. In this manner the old mansion was seldom without company, and it is not a difficult task to see this brave, proud little woman reading to those around her the latest news from headquarters.

A distant connection of General Washington, Lund Washington, was in charge of the Mount Vernon estate at this time, and Bishop, the old-time servant, who had accompanied the General on so many of his former expeditions, now too old for active service, and who was living in a small house on the plantation, was occasionally called upon for minor duties. Meanwhile the mistress of the establishment, Martha Washington, busied herself as never before about her household, trying by force of example as well as the practical viewpoint to help the cause of freedom with all of her might. She personally superintended the making of the cotton dresses striped with silk from the ravelings of old silk stockings and faded damask chair covers, while 16 spinning wheels were kept in constant motion with the view to replacing the English goods. As much as Martha Washington loved fine clothes, her attire was now of the simplest, and she ceased to serve luxuries on her table. In her strong desire to help the cause of freedom she was busy from morning until night, and best of all she was in perfect sympathy with her husband's patriotic aims. As can be readily understood at this remote period there was no postal system to speak of. The mails in consequence were in private hands, and it was not considered safe to intrust these carriers with large sums of money or letters of great importance. Fortunately for Martha Washington, her husband had express riders to Congress, and undoubtedly utilzed them to get his letters to her. Therefore her opportunity of hearing from the General was better possibly than that of the general neighborhood.

Not long after the commencement of war an alarm was spread through tidewater Virginia that several English ships were in the Potomac River on their way to Mount Vernon to lay waste to towns en route and finally to capture Mrs. Washington and burn Mount Vernon. In writing to the General, however, Lund Washington was decidedly reassuring in his desire to calm his fears. In a letter he wrote about this time he said that she did not believe in the danger, neither did he. "Without they attempt to take her in the dead of night, they would fail, for ten minutes notice would be sufficient for her to get out of the way." A few days later he again wrote to General Washington: "Mrs. Washington was under no apprehension of Lord Dunmore doing her an injury until you mentioned it in several letters."

Nevertheless it is interesting to relate of this brave woman that while she went straight ahead with her life in the usual channel, packing the General's papers, the silver and other valuables, she held herself in readiness for instant departure inland. About this time George Mason, who was living in the neighborhood at Gunston Hall, wrote General Washington as follows:

"Dunmore has come and gone, and left us untouched except by some alarms. I sent my family many miles back in the country, and advised Mrs. Washington to do likewise as a prudential measure. At first she said, 'No I will not desert my post,' but finally she did so with reluctance, and rode only a few miles, and, plucky little woman as she is, stayed away one night."

All through the Revolution rumors of the destruction of Mount Vernon were renewed, but fortunately for the country and posterity it was never touched. It was in 1777 that Mrs. Washington was at the General's headquarters, and Lund Washington must have in a measure lost his nerve, as in writing his monthly report he says:

"I am about packing your China and glass in barrels, and other things in chests, trunks, and bundles, and I shall be able at the shortest notice to remove them out of the way. I fear that the destruction will be great, although the best of care has been taken. Everybody I see tells me that if the people could have notice they would immediately come and defend your property as long as they have life, from Loudon, Prince William, Fauquier, and this county."

Of the eight years and eight months General Washington was absent from Mount Vernon during the war, Mrs. Washington spent half of the time with him. Its mistress gone, Mount Vernon was indeed deserted It was upon the invitation of the Commander in Chief that Mrs. Washington visited headquarters at Cambridge. Her presence was immediately felt, as already the question of social etiquette was bothering General Washington, and she ironed out in a highly satisfactory manner all difficulties. She immediately gave a number of parties for the younger officers, and made two lifelong friends, Mrs. Knox and Mrs. Warren. The latter in speaking of Mrs. Washington said:

"I think the complacency of her manner speaks at once the benevolence of her heart, and her affability, Candor and gentleness qualify her to soften the hours of private life, or to sweeten the cares of the Hero, and smooth the rugged paths of war."

From this time on Martha Washington was almost always in camp with the Army when in winter quarters. She usually re-

turned to Mount Vernon when the spring brought a resumption of warfare. Occasionally she made visits to Philadelphia. In 1776 she was invited by the Hancock family, who were temporarily living in this city, to visit them and be inoculated for smallpox. To use their own language, they asked her to come and "take smallpox with them." Only twice in over eight years did General Washington visit his beloved Mount Vernon, while going to and returning from the Yorktown campaign, and he remained only a few days.

In reading over the pages of history of the various winter encampments where Martha Washington spent so much of her time, what impresses one is the amount of real fun going on in these camps. There was always a great deal of society, such as dinners, parties, horseback riding, and dancing. An interesting illustration of this fact is that General Washington on a memorable occasion is said to have danced with Mrs. Henry Knox for three consecutive hours. But it was by no means all play for the women. There was a vast amount of knitting and mending to be done for the soldiers, in which Martha Washington took the lead. She also enjoyed long rides with the General, and occasionally there were receptions at the various headquarters, "all according to certain ceremonials."

At Morristown and Valley Forge where the officers and men were obliged to live in huts or tents, where they were only "tolerably comfortable," and where Mrs. Knox, Mrs. Biddle, and Lady Stirling shared the hardships of what might have been otherwise a most dreary and gloomy winter, the gayeties were still continued.

In 1781 a deep sorrow came into the life of Martha Washington. Word was received that her son, Jack Custis, was desperately ill at Eltham of a fever caught in camp. She hastened to his bedside, and only reached her destination in time to see him die. Alas, these were days when there was no time for private sorrows. The country was at war, and a few weeks later broken-hearted Martha Washington was with the General again, this time in Philadelphia at the home of Robert Chew, and the whole city was glittering with illumination and uproarious with festivals and public functions.

It was in March, 1782, surrounded by the City Troop, that General and Mrs. Washington left for Newburgh, and the gayety continued notwithstanding confused and crowded conditions. Martha Washington was now only a small part of all of this merriment, and she devoted herself to her garden, trying in this simple manner to be diverted from her great sorrow. There was a great affair at West Point in May in honor of the birth of the Dauphin of France. They were especially invited to see fireworks, for which occasion the General and a distinguished party of guests went down the Hudson to this great military station in a laurel-decorated barge. A banquet attended by many ladies and gentlemen followed the fireworks.

It was in December, 1783, that President Washington journeyed to Annapolis. Mrs. Washington was at Mount Vernon, and she joined him there. Here again the festivities were on a magnificent scale, and a ball for rejoicing was given. The next day in the presence of many ladies, who had gathered around Martha Washington in the gallery of the Senate Chamber at the Statehouse, General Washington placed his commission in the hands of Mr. Mifflin, the President of the Congress.

The Washingtons reached Mount Vernon just in time to celebrate Christmas in their own home. The war was over, and they were at home again to stay. "All Christmas afternoon people came from far and near to pay their respects and duty. Among them were stately dames and gay young women. The General seemed very happy, and Mrs. Washington had been from daybreak making everything as agreeable as possible for everybody." A long vista of domesticity stretched out before this distinguished couple, and their pathway seemed flooded with sunshine.

PRESIDENTIAL HOUSEHOLDS

A concrete history of President Washington's two administrations in New York and Philadelphia must necessarily be a medley of business and social life. The Republic was too new to have set forms on any subject. To be sure, the Constitution had been ratified, but there were no precedents for etiquette to guide the President and Mrs. Washington except the great courts of Europe and colonial customs. There were also difficulties besetting the presidential pathway through another channel. There certainly must have been members of both the Senate and House of Representatives still unconvinced of the feasibility of the Constitution and the new Government. President Washington's correspondence at the beginning of his administration showed how strong were his convictions of duty and how great were the obstacles surrounding him. Arthur Lee, in writing to a kinsman in Alexandria a short time after the inaugural ceremonies, says:

"I do not know that it is possible for any human happiness to be greater than his must be in feeling the genuine heartfelt affection of all men and the good opinion universally entertained of him. But there is no human happiness without its alloy, his, I am afraid, will not be exempt."

Comte de Moustier, the French Minister at New York during the first administration, in writing to his home government under date of June 5, 1789, says in speaking of George Washington's inauguration: "The

President resumed his seat, and, after allowing time for the two Chambers to gain theirs, he arose and pronounced a very pathetic speech on the political situation, and on the position in which he personally found himself." General Washington had always suffered from a certain amount of diffidence, and as is so generally known accepted the high office thrust upon him with reluctance. It is rather sad to read his words written after his election, "My movements to the chair of government will be accompanied by feelings not unlike those of a culprit, who is going to the place of his execution." Such a statement is enough to make each individual who makes a study of this great statesman "pause and ponder" over the sacrifices made in accepting the high office. Undoubtedly President Washington realized the complex situation that confronted him, but he possessed certain qualities, justice, modesty, fidelity, and patriotism, a combination of virtues seldom excelled."

One week after President Washington was installed in the highest office in the gift of the land an inaugural ball was given in the city assembly rooms, a large ballroom on the east side of Broadway just above Wall Street. It was a brilliant affair. It had been the general plan of the committee in charge to give the ball on the evening of the day of the President's inauguration, but it was postponed to give Mrs. Washington the opportunity of attending. It was, however, learned that she would not arrive at the seat of Government until late in May, consequently it was decided to hold the ball without her. The committee for the arrangements of this festive occasion was composed of Col. David Humphreys, Col. W. S. Smith, and Mrs. Henry Knox, wife of President Washington's Secretary of War. The following unsympathetic and unauthentic description is given of this first inaugural ball in Jefferson's Anas, giving an idea of the ceremonials employed on the occasion of this great historical function:

"Mr. Brown gave me the following specimen of the frenzy which prevailed in New York on the opening of the new government. The first public ball which took place after the President's arrival. . . . The arrangements were as follows: A sofa at the head of the room, raised on several steps whereon President Washington was to be seated. The gentlemen were to dance in swords. Each one on going to dance was to lead his partner to the foot of the sofa, make a low obeisance to the President, then go and dance, and, when done, bring his partner again to the foot of the sofa for new obeisances and then retire to their chairs. It was understood to, that the gentlemen were to be dressed in bags."

The word "bag" is used in connection with dressing of the hair of men. The "bag

wigs" were well known and were popular during the colonial period.

About 300 persons attended this first inaugural ball; and it is related that President Washington, who had danced repeatedly while Commander in Chief, entered into the pleasures of the evening by dancing a number of times. He opened the ball with the wife of the mayor, Mrs. James Duane. The cotillion he led with Mrs. Peter Van Brugh Livingston and Mrs. James Homer Maxwell in turn. The festivities closed with a minuet, the President dancing with Miss Van Zandt, Mrs. Maxwell's sister. With Mrs. Maxwell he had frequently danced before her marriage, when his headquarters were at Morristown, her father being Jacobus Van Zandt, a member of the Committee of One Hundred appointed in New York in 1775, who had also served with General Washington in the campaign of the Jerseys. The company retired about 2 o'clock, after having spent an enjoyable evening. Joy, satisfaction, and vivacity were expressed on every countenance, the pleasure of the evening being considerably heightened by the democratic condition prevailing, the President mingling with all of the guests.

Among the distinguished persons attending this ball, besides Vice President Adams, Gov. and Mrs. George Clinton, and many of the Members of both Houses of Congress, were the foreign ministers wearing their court dresses; Chancellor and Mrs. Robert R. Livingston; Col. and Mrs. Alexander Hamilton; Senator and Mrs. John Langdon, of New Hampshire; Mrs. Peter Van Brugh Livingston (sister-in-law of Lord Stirling); Mr. and Mrs. James Homer Maxwell; Mrs. James Thompson and her daughter, Mrs. Elbridge Gerry; Mrs. Montgomery, widow of General Montgomery; Sir John and Lady Temple; Mrs. Macomb; Lord and Lady Stirling, and their two daughters, Lady Kitty Duer, the wife of Col. William Duer, and Lady Mary Watts; Madame de Brehan, sister-in-law of the French Minister, Comte de Moustier; Col. and Mrs. William S. Smith; Mr. and Mrs. Dominick Lynch; Mr. and Mrs. John Houston, of Georgia; Bishop and Mrs. Provoost, the former the first Episcopal Bishop of New York; and Col. and Mrs. Beverly Robinson.

Soon after his inauguration, the President appointed Tuesday afternoon, between the hours of 2 and 3 o'clock, to receive formal visits. When the question of levees was brought before him for his approval, President Washington openly opposed them for almost a month, but at length he yielded and left to Colonel Humphreys the arrangements for these levees, the name applied to presidential receptions of miscellaneous guests from the earliest days of the Republic. According an antechamber and a "presence room" were provided in the presidential mansion. When those who had arrived to pay their respects to the Chief Magistrate had assembled, the President walked into the antechamber accompanied by Humphreys. An amusing anecdote is told about President Washington the first time he formally received guests. After passing through the first room he paused for a moment when the door of the inner room was thrown wide open. Colonel Humphreys entered first, calling out in a loud voice, "The President of the United States." The President was so disconcerted by this act that he did not recover from it during the whole time of the levee. When the company had departed he said in vigorous terms not to be mistaken, "Humphreys, you have taken me in once but you will never take me in the second time."

A contemporary of that period, in writing of the early days of the Washington administration, says that the cares and labors of the President were incessant. "Exhortations, example, and authority were the methods employed to excite zeal and activity for the advancement of the Government." An able Cabinet was selected entirely upon merit, and, as is well known, they distinguished themselves by their successful management of public affairs.

One of the few sources of discontent and unhappiness of the early days of President Washington's administration was the great army of office seekers looking for positions under the new Government. Nineteen out of twenty of these the President was obliged to turn down, and occasionally much dissatisfaction was expressed. He never showed the slightest partiality, but at the earliest moment he adopted principles on this subject which might well be followed by Presidents of later days. He evidently felt the unpleasantness of the situation most deeply, as less than six weeks after his inauguration he wrote to a friend, James Bowdoin, as follows: "No part of my duty will be more delicate and in many instances more unpleasant than that of appointing persons to office."

A shining example of President Washington's lack of favoritism is told by a present member of the Washington family in regard to his distinguished kinsman, never before related. Robert Lewis, one of the sons of Betty Washington Lewis, President Washington's only sister, was appointed at an early date secretarial aide to the new President. He came direct from his beautiful home, Milbrook, now known as Kenmore, in Fredericksburg, Va., to serve under him. He had just commenced his term of office when by chance he took several keys out of his pocket tied with a string. In rather stern tones his Uncle George said, "Robert, if that is the way you keep your keys together I will give you a key ring." Suiting his words to action, he took his own keys off a ring which held them, adding, "I have another in my room." Robert found the great man in such a receptive frame of mind that he seized the opportunity to announce an interesting piece of news, his engagement of marriage. After a few congratulatory words, to the youth's

dismay President Washington remarked, "I am sorry to tell you that you must look around for another position, you are my nephew and under these circumstances I can show no favors." The key ring given to Robert is still owned by his descendants and is one of their treasured possessions.

With the people's hero, George Washington, at the helm the country was gradually, step by step, settling down—the farmer to his plow, the mechanic plying his trade, the merchant in his store. Peace prevailed. Prosperity was returning throughout the land, when in 1790 Congress decided to move the seat of the Federal Government from New York to Philadelphia.

Congress reassembled on the first Monday in December, 1790, in Philadelphia, which for a time was to be the seat of government. A house belonging to Robert Morris, the financier of the Revolution, had been engaged some time in advance by President Washington for his residence, and at his request had undergone additions and alterations in a not at all extravagant way. Indeed, the house was very limited in accommodations, so much so that all three of the private secretaries were obliged to occupy the same room. The President had left it to his secretary, Tobias Lear, to make the preparations for the arrival of the family, and in a measure both cities were gainers by the change of capital. The Quaker City had the satisfaction of having the National Government meet within its limits, and busy, bustling New York could now settle down to routine life without giving so much time to politics.

The first year of capital life in Philadelphia was marked by a division of the people into parties on account of two members of the Cabinet, Jefferson and Hamilton, distrusting each other. Each man had his followers. The Members of Congress soon began to take sides, the people of Philadelphia followed in their train, and even the general public began to be partisan. But fortunately there were other matters to discuss during Cabinet meetings. This was at a time when the Indians were troublesome on the border, and expeditions were being sent against them that cost heavily in human life and money, and, generally speaking, the white man met with disaster. Newspapers, too, were very aggressive politically, and they said pretty much what they pleased, never letting the truth stand in the way of a cutting paragraph.

Mrs. Washington continued her drawing-rooms and President Washington his levees in Philadelphia. At his wife's receptions apparently the President did not view himself as a host but "conversed without restraint, generally with women, who rarely had other opportunities of seeing him." It is said that the young ladies would gather around him and engage him in conversation. These occasions were the only opportunities when the young people had the satisfaction of seeing

their hero, and they apparently made the most of the occasion. In a southern trip made by President Washington in 1791, he speaks with pleasure of a visit made to him by a number of the most respectable ladies of Charleston. "The first honor of the kind I had ever experienced and it was as flattering as it was singular."

It is related that the expenses of the Presidential Mansion were paid weekly, and often when the bills were presented by the steward, President Washington would scold him for his extravagance, saying that while he wanted to live comfortably he abhored waste. Senator Maclay gives a very interesting account of a dinner he attended at the President's house in Philadelphia. He writes:

"The President and Mrs. Washington sat opposite each other in the middle of the table; the two secretaries one at each end. It was a great dinner, and the best of the kind I ever was at. The room, however; was disagreeably warm. First the soup; fish roasted and boiled, meats, sammon [sic], fowls, etc. . . . The middle of the table was garnished in the usual tasty way, with small images, flowers (artificial), etc. The desserts were apple pie, puddings, etc.; then ice creams, jellies, etc.; then water melons, musk melons, apples, peaches, nuts. It was the most solemn dinner I ever was at. Not a health drank, scarcely a word was said until the cloth was taken away. . . . Mrs. Washington at last withdrew with the ladies. I thought that the men would now begin but the same stillness remained. . . . The President rose, went up stairs to drink coffee; the company followed."

It is related that President Washington was exceedingly fond of fish and that it was frequently served on his table. It was while living in Philadelphia that some New England women prepared codfish in some very appetizing manner, and sent it weekly carefully wrapped in cloths, arranging to have it arrive in time for the President's Saturday dinner, he making it a rule always to eat codfish on that day in compliment to his happy New England recollections.

It was after a long consideration that President Washington consented to be a candidate for reelection to the Presidency. Fortunately there was no opposition of any kind, and the vote for him in the Electoral College was unanimous. Again much discussion arose in regard to the form of ceremonies for this second inauguration. After a consultation of a number of high officials it was found that there was a difference of opinion regarding how exactly the oath of office should be administered. Finally, on March 4, 1793, the oath of office was administered to President Washington by Mr. Justice Cushing, in the Senate Chamber, in the presence of the heads of the various departments, foreign ministers, and such Senators and Members of Congress as chanced to be in the city.

It may be interesting to hear how President Washington was dressed on the occasion of his second inauguration. He wore a full suit of the richest black velvet, with diamond knee buckles, and square silver shoe buckles. His shirt was ruffled at the breast and waist, and he carried a light dress sword. His hair was profusely powdered, gathered behind and tied with black ribbon, forming a rose. In his hand he carried a cocked hat, which he laid on a table as he read his inaugural address.

In later years a writer, who chanced to be a schoolboy in Philadelphia at the time of President Washington's inauguration, speaks of the impressiveness of the occasion. He writes:

"I stood before the door of the Hall of Congress in Philadelphia when the carriage of the President drew up. It was a white coach or rather of light cream color, painted on the panels with beautiful groups representing the four seasons. As Washington alighted and ascended the steps, pausing on the platform, he was preceded by two gentlemen bearing large white wands, who kept back the eager crowd that pressed on every side."

Four years later, on the 4th of March, 1797, President Washington attended the inauguration of his successor, John Adams. He and Mrs. Washington were now released to return to his beloved home, Mount Vernon. He must have felt a new life running through his veins; he was free again. In writing from Mount Vernon shortly after his long absence, he says: "I do not think it probable that I shall go beyond twenty miles from there."

LAST YEARS AT MOUNT VERNON

Although George Washington became the possessor of Mount Vernon at the end of 1752, it was only during the years 1759-1774 and 1784-1788, twenty-one years in all, that he was in real residence there until after his retirement from the Presidency. War and statecraft kept him away. Yet the home, after all, is the hub around which the wheels revolve, and George Washington going forth from his dwelling place to fill the numerous high offices thrust upon him must have generally departed with a quiet mind, with the assurance that for him there would always be a haven of rest—Mount Vernon. In 1797 President Washington completed his second term as Chief Executive of the land, and the Washington family came home to stay.

When the Washingtons returned to Mount Vernon many changes had taken place. The General was now one of the last of his generation. The interior of the mansion immediately assumed a more elaborate appearance by reason of the addition of much of the fine furniture, silver, glass, and china which President and Mrs. Washington had accumulated at the Presidential Mansion in Philadelphia. To these were added the numerous curios and presents sent to the President by admiring well-wishers. Friends and strangers alike were welcomed to the Mount Vernon fireside. It was at this time that "Lady Washington," as she was frequently called, extended an invitation to a young girl from Philadelphia to visit her. One can readily imagine with what eagerness this invitation was accepted. Fortunately for posterity this young woman wrote to her mother an account of this visit, and still more fortunately the letter has been preserved. It gives an account of the daily life at Mount Vernon, which from a historical point of view can not be excelled. The letter is given verbatim:

"I have just returned from a visit to Mount Vernon and have been really quite delighted with the place and its inhabitants. I stayed there but three days and two nights but in that time received so much attention from President and Mrs. Washington that I never can forget. I have promised to stay some time with them before I return to Philadelphia, which I shall most readily do as I never in my life felt more perfectly at home than with them. They live in great style and with the utmost regularity. Breakfast is on the table at seven o'clock, dinner at three, tea at seven and supper at nine. The hours before breakfast are spent in any manner most agreeable to the individual. After breakfast we work, read or attend to Miss Custis who plays most charmingly on the piano, until about twelve o'clock when we dress for dinner. This is only the females of the family. The male part never make their appearance from the time of breakfast until dinner. The President employs his mornings in riding over the farm. He gave me an invitation to get up behind him which I very unexpectedly accepted and he was under the necessity of offering some excuse to get off, which however, he did not fairly do until he promised I should accompany him at another time. He is one of the most charming men in the world, always in good spirits, and makes it his chief duty to render all around him as happy as possible. His attentions to young Lafayette are exactly those he would pay to his own son and are received as they should be by him. He is one of the most pleasing young men that I have ever known, indeed the situation of his family would alone render him interesting, no part of which is ever spoken of without his shedding tears. But to conclude with the amusements of the day—after the ladies left the drawing-room we spend the hours until tea time in conversation, reading or writing as is most agreeable to us, when we resort to a large and magnificent portico at the back of the house where the tea equipage was paraded in order. After tea we walked until the dew began to fall, when we again turned our steps to the portico which commands a most extensive view of the Potomac and the adjacent country. The prospect is most noble indeed and at the same time beautifully romantic. We sit in this delightful place admiring the scenery around rendered more beautiful from the serenity of the evening and the moon which shone most sweetly and appeared to greater advantage as it played upon the water together with the most beautiful music from Miss Curtis and Mr. Fayette, and I can't say to what length my fancy would have led me if I had been suffered to remain uninterrupted much longer. Precisely at nine o'clock my reveries were disturbed by the servants calling us to supper which consisted of fruit and cream, cake and wine, etc: We sat at the table until ten o'clock when we retired to our respective apartments, though not to bed, at least I did not, preferring the contemplation of the beauties around me (of which I had a full view from my chamber window) to spend my time in sleep. You don't know what a reformation has taken place as to my rising of a morning. I am not seldom in bed after five and all the time I was at Mount Vernon I was up at four to see the sun rise which I am sure is not so beautiful in any other place. Mrs. Washington was quite surprised to hear that I had been out before breakfast and when the President told her he saw me out a little after four she scolded."

Nellie Custis, in a letter to Mrs. Oliver Wolcott, spoke of her "grandpa," as she always called him, as "Farmer Washington." It is traditionally told of this young girl that she was decidedly fond of walking alone in the woods in the moonlight. Her grandmother, thinking that this was unwise, exacted a promise of her that she would never do it again. Once Mrs. Washington was seated in her favorite armchair in the drawing-room when Nellie entered. She had learned that the lass had broken her promise. At once she began to reprove her in General Washington's presence. The girl was reminded of her promise and taxed with delinquency. She frankly admitted her fault but offered no excuse, moving as she talked toward the door, when she heard her beloved adopted father trying to intercede for her. Addressing his wife in low tones he said, "I would say no more about it, perhaps she was not alone." General Washington possibly meant, as is usual with young people, she was accompanied by a male companion. His intercession stopped the culprit in her retreat. She vigorously opened the door, advanced to the General, holding her head very high, and said, "Sir, you brought me up to speak the truth. When I told grandmamma I was alone, I was alone. I hope that you believe me." In reply, George Washington, deeply impressed by the earnestness of the girl, made one of his profound bows, and in an humble manner said, "I beg your pardon."

Nellie Custis was married at Mount Vernon. The occasion was made a festive one. She paid General Washington the high compliment of being married on his birthday, which chanced to be the last one spent on earth. There is a card of invitation written in General Washington's well-known handwriting on the day of the wedding, February 22, 1799, in which he invites Mr. and Mrs. Andrew Ramsey to dine at Mount Vernon on Tuesday next "with the young couple just married." Apparently no bridal tour was taken by Mr. and Mrs. Lawrence Lewis, as it was not the fashion of the period. After General Washington's death his bereaved widow could not live in the big mansion alone, and it was Nellie Custis Lewis and her husband who lived with her until her death.

General and Mrs. Washington spent 40 years of married life together. These years were marked by great tenderness and devotion on both sides. It is said that often, especially during the eight years he served as President, his mind was often burdened with the cares of state and the perplexities of his many private interests and he would appear abstracted and inattentive. Then it was, according to tradition, that Mrs. Washington would reach up, seize a button of his coat, and give it a vigorous pull. Thus brought down to earth again, the great man would smile and be quite his normal self.

These latter days at Mount Vernon passed very pleasantly for General and Mrs. Washington. Agricultural pursuits had always been the former's great hobby, and he now gave up his time principally to managing his vast estates. On one occasion when one of George Washington's comrades-in-arms called at Mount Vernon to see his old Chief he was told that the General was making his daily inspection of the plantations. The visitor decided to go out to meet him, and was directed to look for "an old gentleman with a white hat and umbrella riding alone on horseback." Hospitality now as well as in former years was the dominating spirit at Mount Vernon. In writing to a friend about this period General Washington said that the night previous he and Mrs. Washington had dined alone, and it was the first time in many years. This mansion on the banks of the Potomac was certainly a typical southern home. Thither flocked the many officers who had served under the Commander, old Revolutionary soldiers of the ranks, Members of Congress, diplomats, planters, and friends and admirers from every section of the country and from abroad.

In the early autumn of 1799 General Washington learned that the last of his brothers, Charles Washington, had passed away. His sister, Betty, Mrs. Fielding Lewis, had died the year before. The great man was deeply affected. He immediately wrote to a relative, Col. Burgess Ball, who had informed him of his brother's death, a letter in which is the following paragraph:

"I was the *first* and am now the *last*, of my father's children by the second marriage who remain. When I shall be called up to follow them, is known only to the giver of life. When the summons comes, I shall endeavor to obey it with good grace."

His brother's death certainly sobered considerably his life, but it was typical of him to go about his affairs just as usual. Winter had now set in; and although it was not more severe than usual, it seemed to make an impression on General Washington. On the 12th of December, 1799, he wrote in his diary:

"Morning cloudy. Wind at No. Et., and Mer. 33. A large circle around the Moon last Night. About 10 o'clock it began to snow, and soon after to Hail, and then to a settled cold Rain. Mer. 28 at Night."

The following day he made the customary entry in his diary without referring to any indisposition, undoubtedly the last words ever penned by him. It was midnight this same day before he retired to his room. Apparently he was not feeling well, and in replying to his wife's anxious comments he said:

"I came as soon as my business was accomplished. You well know that all through a long life it has been my unvaried rule never to put off until tomorrow the duties which should be performed today."

This same night General Washington was taken very ill, but in his unselfish way would not allow his wife to summon aid, fearing that she would suffer if she got up in the cold. During the next day, as he was gradually growing weaker, he turned to Doctor Craik, saying, "I am dying, Sir, but I am not afraid to die." He died that night at 20 minutes past 10 o'clock.

Life at Mount Vernon after General Washington's death was quiet indeed. The room in which he passed away was by Mrs. Washington's orders closed; nothing was touched, and the sorrowful widow retired to an upper chamber, where unmolested she watched the sacred spot where he was buried. Just before she died she destroyed almost her entire correspondence with George Washington and only three of his letters to her are now known to exist, thus, according to her own argument, proving her undying love for him. These letters to her were sacred, and she was unwilling to share them with others.

(For this program see numbers 21, 23, 41, 63, 72, 105 in list of selected books on pages 300a and 300-b)

Selected Books Relating To
George Washington

Out of the hundreds of volumes relating to George Washington and his service to his country the following will be especially accurate, interesting, and generally available:

1. ADAMS, JOHN. *Works.* Vols. II, III, IX. (Boston, Little Brown, 1850-1854.)

2. ANDREWS, CHARLES M. *Colonial Folkways* (*Chronicles of America*, Vol. IX). (New Haven, Yale University Press, 1921.)

3. ANDREWS, CHARLES M. *Colonial Period.* (N. Y., Holt, 1912.)

4. AVERY, ELROY M. *History of the United States and Its People.* Vols. V-VII. (Cleveland, Burrows, 1908-1910.)

5. BAKER, WILLIAM, S., ed. *Early Sketches of George Washington.* (Philadelphia, Lippincott, 1893.)

6. BAKER, WILLIAM S. *Itinerary of General Washington from June 15, 1775, to December 23, 1783.* (Philadelphia, Lippincott, 1892.)

7. BAKER, WILLIAM S. *Washington After the Revolution.* (Philadelphia, Lippincott, 1898.)

8. BEER, GEORGE L. *British Colonial Policy, 1754-1765.* (New York, Macmillan, 1907.)

9. BELCHER, HENRY. *First American Civil War.* 2 vols. (New York, Macmillan, 1911.)

10. BEMIS, SAMUEL F. *Jay's Treaty.* (New York, Macmillan, 1923.)

11. BEVERIDGE, ALBERT J. *Life of John Marshall.* Vol. II. (Boston, Houghton Mifflin, 1916.)

12. BOWEN, CLARENCE W. "Inauguration of Washington." (*Century Magazine*, vol. 37, 1889.)

13. BOWERS, CLAUDE G. *Jefferson and Hamilton.* (Boston, Houghton Mifflin, 1925.)

14. BRACKENRIDGE, HENRY M. *History of the Western Insurrection in Western Pennsylvania.* (Pittsburgh, W. S. Haven, 1859.)

15. BROOKS, ELBRIDGE S. *True Story of George Washington.* (Boston, Lothrop, 1895.)

16. BRYAN, WILHELMUS B. *History of the National Capital.* Vol. I. (New York, Macmillan, 1914.)

17. CALLAHAN, CHARLES H. *Washington the Man and the Mason.* (Washington, 1913.)

18. CHANNING, EDWARD. *History of the United States.* Vols. III, IV. (New York, Macmillan, 1912-1917.)

19. CONWAY, MONCURE D. *Barons of the Potomack and the Rappahannock.* (New York, Grolier Club, 1892.)

20. CONWAY, MONCURE D. "English Ancestry of Washington." (*Harper's Magazine*, vol. 84, 1891.)

21. CONWAY, MONCURE D., ed. *George Washington and Mount Vernon.* (Brooklyn, Long Island Historical Society, 1889.)

22. CORBIN, JOHN. *Unknown Washington.* (New York, Scribner, 1930.)

23. CUSTIS, GEORGE W. P. *Recollections and Private Memoirs of Washington.* (Philadelphia, William Flint, 1859, other eds.)

24. EARLE, ALICE M. *Child Life in Colonial Days.* (New York, Macmillan, 1899.)

25. EARLE, ALICE M. *Home Life in Colonial Days.* (New York, Macmillan, 1898.)

26. EARLE, ALICE M. *Old Time Gardens.* (New York, Macmillan, 1901.)

27. EARLE, ALICE M. *Stage-Coach and Tavern Days.* (New York, Macmillan, 1900.)

28. EARLE, ALICE M. *Two Centuries of Costume in America.* 2 vols. (New York, Macmillan, 1903.)

29. EARLE, SWEPSON, *Chesapeake Bay Country.* (Baltimore, Thomsen-Ellis, 1923.)

30. FISHER, SYDNEY G. *Struggle for American Independence.* 2 vols. (Philadelphia, Lippincott, 1908.)

31. FITZPATRICK, JOHN C. *George Washington, Colonial Traveller, 1732-1775.* (Indianapolis, Bobbs-Merrill, 1927); also *George Washington Himself*, to be published early in 1932.

32. FORD, PAUL L. *True George Washington.* (Philadelphia, Lippincott, 1896.)

33. FORD, WORTHINGTON C. *George Washington.* 2 vols. (New York, Scribner, 1900.)

34. FROTHINGHAM, THOMAS G. *Washington, Commander in Chief.* (Boston, Houghton Mifflin, 1930.)

35. GERWIG, GEORGE W. *Washington, the Young Leader.* (New York, Scribner, 1923.)

36. GIBBS, GEORGE. *Memoirs of the Administrations of Washington and John Adams.* Vol. I. (New York, Van Norden, 1846.)

37. GIST, CHRISTOPHER. *Journals.* (Pittsburgh, Weldin, 1893.)

38. HAMILTON, JOHN C. *History of the Republic of the United States of America as traced in the Writings of Alexander Hamilton and his Contemporaries.* 7 vols. (New York, Appleton, 1857-1864.)

39. HAMILTON, STANISLAUS M., ed. *Letters to Washington.* 5 vols. (Boston, Houghton Mifflin, 1898-1902.)

40. HAPGOOD, NORMAN. *George Washington.* (New York, Macmillan, 1901.)

41. HARLAND, MARION. *Some Colonial Homesteads and their Stories.* (New York, Putnam, 1897.)

42. HART, ALBERT B. *Formation of the Union, 1750-1829.* Rev. ed. (New York, Longmans Green, 1925.)

43. HART, ALBERT B. *George Washington: Reading with a Purpose.* (Chicago American Library Association, 1930.)

44. HATCH, LOUIS C. *Administration of the American Revolutionary Army.* (New York, Longmans Green, 1904.)

45. HAWORTH, PAUL L. *George Washington, Country Gentleman.* (Indianapolis, Bobbs-Merrill, 1925.)

46. HEATH, WILLIAM, *Memoirs.* (Boston, Thomas & Andrews, 1798; later eds.)

47. HENDERSON, ARCHIBALD. *Washington's Southern Tour, 1791.* (Boston, Houghton, Mifflin, 1923.)

48. HERBERT, LEILA. *First American, His Homes and His Households.* (New York, Harper, 1900.)

49. HILL, FREDERICK T. *On the Trail of Washington.* (New York, Appleton, 1910.)

50. HOWARD, GEORGE E. *Preliminaries of the Revolution.* (*American Nation*, Vol. VIII.) (New York, Harper, 1905.)

51. HULBERT, ARCHER B. *Colonel Washington.* (Marietta, Ohio, Western Reserve University, 1903.)

52. HULBERT, ARCHER B. *Historic Highways of America.* Vols. II-V. (Cleveland, Clark, 1902-3.)

53. HULBERT, ARCHER B. *Washington and the West.* (New York, Century, 1905.)

54. IRVING, WASHINGTON. *Life of George Washington.* 5 vols. (New York, Putnam, 1855-1859; later eds.)

55. JERNEGAN, MARCUS B. *American Colonies, 1492-1750.* (New York, Longmans Green, 1929.)

56. JOHNSON, BRADLEY T. *General Washington.* (New York, Appleton, 1894.)

57. KITE, ELIZABETH S. *L'Enfant and Washington, 1791-1792.* (Baltimore, Johns Hopkins Press, 1929.)

58. LEAR, TOBIAS. *Letters and Recollections of George Washington.* (New York, Doubleday Page, 1906.)

59. LECKY, WILLIAM E. H. *American Revolution.* (New York, Appleton, 1898.)

60. LEE, CHARLES. *Lee Papers.* 4 vols. (New York Historical Society, *Collections,* 1871-1874.)

61. LITTLE, SHELBY. *George Washington.* (New York, Minton Balch, 1929.)

62. LODGE, HENRY C. *George Washington.* 2 vols. (*American Statesmen.*) Rev. ed. (Boston, Houghton Mifflin, 1898.)

63. LOSSING, BENSON J. *Home of Washington.* (New York, Virtue & Yorston, 1871; earlier eds.)

64. LOSSING, BENSON J. *Life of Washington.* 3 vols. (New York, Virtue, 1860; later eds.)

65. LOSSING, BENSON J. *Mary and Martha, the Mother and Wife of George Washington.* (New York, Harper, 1886.)

66. MACE, WILLIAM H. *Washington, a Virginia Cavalier.* (Chicago, Rand McNally, 1916.)

67. MACKAYE, PERCY. *Washington, the Man Who Made Us.* (New York, Knopf, 1919.)

68. McMASTER, JOHN B. *History of the People of the United States.* Vols. I, II. (New York, Appleton, 1883-1885.)

69. MARSHALL, JOHN. *Life of George Washington.* 5 vols. (Fredericksburg, Va., 1926; first pub. 1804-1807.)

70. MEADE, WILLIAM. *Old Churches, Ministers, and Families of Virginia.* 2 vols. (Philadelphia, Lippincott, 1857.)

71. MITCHELL, S. WEIR. *Youth of Washington.* (New York, Century, 1904.)

72. MOORE, CHARLES. *Family Life of George Washington.* (Boston, Houghton Mifflin, 1926.)

73. NELSON, WILLIAM. "American Newspapers of the Eighteenth Century as Sources of History." (American Historical Association, *Report for 1908,* Vol. I.)

74. OGG, FREDERIC A. *Opening of the Mississippi.* (New York, Macmillan, 1904.)

75. OSBORN, LUCRETIA P., ed. *Washington Speaks for Himself.* (New York, Scribner, 1927.)

76. PITT, WILLIAM. *Correspondence with Colonial Governors,* Edited by Gertrude S. Kimball. 2 vols. (New York, Macmillan, 1906.)

77. PRUSSING, EUGENE E. *Estate of George Washington, Deceased.* (Boston, Little Brown. 1927.)

78. PRUSSING, EUGENE E. *George Washington in Love and Otherwise.* (Chicago, Covici. 1925.)

79. ROOSEVELT, THEODORE. *Winning of the West.* 4 vols. (New York, Putnam, 1889-1896.)

80. ROWLAND, KATE M. *Life of George Mason.* (New York, Putnam, 1892.)

81. SAWYER, JOSEPH D. *Washington.* 2 vols. (New York, Macmillan, 1927.)

82. SCHAUFFLER, ROBERT H., ed. *Washington's Birthday.* (New York, Moffat Yard, 1910.)

83. SCHLESINGER, ARTHUR M. *Colonial Merchants and the American Revolution.* (New York, Columbia University, 1917.)

84. SEELYE, ELIZABETH. *Story of Washington.* (New York, Appleton, 1893.)

85. SMITH, HELEN E. *Colonial Days & Ways.* (New York, Century, 1900.)

86. SMITH, WILLIAM H. *St. Clair Papers.* 2 vols. (Cincinnati, Clarke, 1882.)

87. SPARKS, JARED. *Life of George Washington.* (Boston, Tappan & Dennet, 1842.)

88. STANARD, MARY N. *Colonial Virginia.* (Philadelphia, Lippincott, 1917.)

89. STRYKER, WILLIAM S. *Battles of Trenton and Princeton.* (Boston, Houghton Mifflin, 1898.)

90. STRYKER, WILLIAM S. *Battle of Monmouth.* (Princeton, Princeton University Press, 1927.)

91. THACHER, JAMES. *Military Journal During the American Revolutionary War.* 2d ed., rev. (Boston, Cotton & Barnard, 1827.)

92. THAYER, WILLIAM R. *George Washington.* (Boston, Houghton Mifflin, 1922.)

93. TOWER, CHARLEMAGNE. *Marquis de La Fayette in the American Revolution.* 2 vols. (Philadelphia, Lippincott, 1895.)

94. TREVELYAN, SIR GEORGE OTTO. *American Revolution.* New ed. 4 vols. (New York, Longmans Green, 1905-1912.)

95. TREVELYAN, SIR GEORGE OTTO. *George the Third and Charles Fox.* 2 vols. (New York, Longmans Green, 1912-1914.)

96. VAN TYNE, CLAUDE H. *Founding of the American Republic.* Vols. I, II. (Boston, Houghton Mifflin, 1922-1929.)

97. VOLWILLER, ALBERT T. *George Croghan and the Westward Movement.* (Cleveland, Clark, 1926.)

98. WASHINGTON, GEORGE. *Diaries.* Edited by John C. Fitzpatrick. 4 vols. (Boston, Houghton Mifflin, 1925.)

99. WASHINGTON, GEORGE. *Rules of Civility.* Edited by Charles Moore. (Boston, Houghton Mifflin, 1926.)

100. WASHINGTON, GEORGE. *Writings.* Edited by Worthington C. Ford. 14 vols. (New York, Putnam, 1889-1893.)

101. WATERS, HENRY F. *Examination of the English Ancestry of George Washington.* (Boston, New England Historic Genealogical Society, 1889.)

102. WHARTON, ANNE H. *Social Life in the Early Republic.* (Philadelphia, Lippincott, 1902.)

103. WHIPPLE, WAYNE, ed. *Story-Life of Washington.* (Philadelphia, Winston, 1911.)

104. WILSON, WOODROW. *George Washington.* (New York, Harper, 1896.)

105. WILSTACH, PAUL. *Mount Vernon.* (Garden City, N. Y., Doubleday Page, 1916.)

106. WINSOR, JUSTIN. *Narrative and Critical History of America.* Vols. VI, VII. (Boston, Houghton Mifflin, 1887-1888.)

107. WISTER, OWEN. *Seven Ages of Washington.* (New York, Macmillan, 1907.)

HANDBOOK

OF THE

GEORGE WASHINGTON APPRECIATION COURSE

FOR THE

CELEBRATION
OF THE
TWO HUNDREDTH ANNIVERSARY
OF THE
BIRTH OF GEORGE WASHINGTON

By

HAZEL B. NIELSON

Director of Educational Activities

WASHINGTON AND OUR SCHOOLS AND COLLEGES

By CHARLES W. ELIOT
President of Harvard University in 1889

And what shall I say in behalf of the three hundred thousand teachers of the United States? They deserve some mention to-day. None of them are rich or famous; most of them are poor, retiring, and unnoticed; but it is they who are building a perennial monument to Washington. It is they who give him a million-tongued fame. They make him live again in the young hearts of successive generations, and fix his image there as the American ideal of a public servant.

It is through the schools and colleges of the country and the national literature that the heroes of any people win lasting renown; and it is through the same agencies that a nation is molded into the likeness of its heroes. This local commemoration of one great event in the life of Washington and of the United States is well; but it is as nothing compared with the incessant memorial of him which the schools and colleges of the country maintained from generation to generation. I have mentioned only the pupils and teachers now in school and college; but all the generations for a hundred years past have sounded the praise of this Virginia country gentleman, and countless generations to come will swell the loud acclaim. What a reward is Washington's! What an influence is his, and will be! One mind and will transfused by sympathetic instruction into millions; one character, a standard for millions; one life a pattern for all public men, teaching what greatness is, and what the pathway to undying fame.

"Our Schools and Colleges"; in *Centennial Celebration of the Inauguration of George Washington*, p. 379 (Response to toast, April 30, 1889, New York).

THE HANDBOOK

Purpose.—The United States George Washington Bicentennial Commission planned to celebrate in 1932 the Two Hundredth Anniversary of the Birth of George Washington in keeping with the motive expressed by Congress, "that future generations of American citizens may live according to the example and precepts of his exalted life and character and thus perpetuate the American Republic."

To aid the teachers of the United States in their participation in the Nation-Wide Celebration this *Appreciation Course* of the life, history, and achievements of George Washington and the period in which he lived has been prepared in Handbook form.

It has been truly said: "You can not compel good American citizenship. If anything must be compulsory let it be the furnishing of proper educational opportunities." With this thought in mind, the United States George Washington Bicentennial Commission issued this Handbook for the teachers of the Nation.

Contents.—This Handbook points out the outstanding events and achievements in the life of George Washington, the period in which he lived, and the heritage he left to our Nation. Emphasis is also placed upon the city of Washington, D. C., the Nation's Capital, and the inspiration to be gained from a study of it. It furnishes authentic material regarding "The Father of His Country."

Material.—The two main sources of information prepared by the Commission to be used with this Handbook are:

1. Forty-eight Papers in a series of 12 *George Washington Programs.* The list of *Selected Books Relating to George Washington* used as authority for these Papers is included.
2. Fifteen Pamphlets of the series *Honor to George Washington and Reading About George Washington.* Selected authorities are listed in each Pamphlet.

Reference is made also to many current histories and biographies. Many quotations are included, as it may be difficult in some schools to supply reference books in sufficient numbers for all students. It will be found, however, that much can be supplied by the instructor and student, for, as Calvin Coolidge says, "the subject [of Washington] never seems to be exhausted." As the course is pursued, many opportunities will appear in which to enrich the study through the creative results of further research by the teacher and the class.

Name.—This publication is called a Handbook, as it is more than a syllabus or a course of study. It is hoped that it may serve as a suggestive guide to those who carry on the work outlined in the George Washington Appreciation Course.

GENERAL OBJECTIVES AND AIMS

General Objectives

Development of an American consciousness of the George Washington Bicentennial.

Focusing of an active Nation-wide interest in the life and achievements of George Washington.

Proper interpretation and application of a higher conception of American citizenship.

Specific Aims

1. To present the historical facts in the life of George Washington.
2. To give a knowledge of the vision, power, and leadership of George Washington and of his ideals of faith, loyalty, and courage.
3. To assist students to acquire an understanding of the problems that confronted our national growth and the active participation of George Washington in solving those problems.
4. To interpret the history of Washington's time in such a way that the student-teachers may be inspired to develop the spirit of George Washington in their pupils so as to enable them to apply his principles to situations as they arise.
5. To instill in the hearts of the students an appreciation of the contributions made by George Washington to his own period and to posterity.
6. To stimulate a desire in the student-teachers to serve the Community, State, and Nation as an expression of their gratitude for the services rendered by George Washington, the Father of His Country.
7. To increase and perpetuate a living *George Washington Americanism* in the hearts of the American people.
8. To emphasize the significance of the Federal Constitution, respect for the Flag of the United States of America, and a love of our Country.
9. To inspire the students with a desire to visit the shrines of George Washington.
10. To encourage a continuation of the study of George Washington and his writings.

SUGGESTED COURSES

Residence

This course includes a study of the outlined work for credit toward graduation.

Correspondence

This course is for those who can not be in residence at teacher-training institutions but desire the knowledge and credit. This may be carried on individually or in study groups.

Historic Travel

This course includes trips to Washington, the Nation's Capital, to be arranged by the school authorities. It may be a continuation of the residence or correspondence, or offered as a separate unit of work. Neither residence nor correspondence course is necessarily a prerequisite.

Radio

George Washington School of the Air. This course may be conducted by extension divisions of institutions of learning wherever broadcasting facilities permit. It may include the formation in communities of study groups who can not do residence work, or may be carried on through educational and patriotic societies. It is not designed for school credit. The Commission will furnish to schools and extension divisions certificates of recognition to be given to those who take the radio work.

SUGGESTED TIME REQUIREMENT

The outlined course, *George Washington Appreciation,* was suggested for study beginning the school year 1931-32. It was urged that the course be offered in every quarter or semester of 1932 commemorating the Two Hundredth Anniversary of the Birth of George Washington, and then be established as a part of the curriculum. The *Course* is outlined for a period of twelve weeks, but may be given in six or eight weeks with intensive study and double periods.

The amount of time which should be given during the twelve weeks to the various units will be determined by the individual educational institutions.

GEORGE WASHINGTON

Photograph of the Famous Bust of George Washington, made from life at Mount Vernon by the great French Sculptor, Jean Antoine Houdon, in 1785. It was selected as the official picture of the Father of His Country, for the Bicentennial Celebration of His Birth

Unit I
The Setting for the Course

SULGRAVE MANOR, ENGLAND
Home of George Washington's Ancestors, which is now preserved as an International Shrine

Brief Outline

I. BACKGROUND—Knowledge of the Historical and Geographical Conditions Relating to the Colonies at the Birth of George Washington, 1732.

A. Relation of Geography and History.

B. Colonial America at the End of Period of New Colonization with the Founding of Georgia in 1732.

1. Effect of Geographic Conditions on the Settlement of the Colonies.

a. New England.
b. Middle Section.
c. South.

2. Population.

a. Race Conditions in the Colonies.

3. Industrial Development.

a. *Conditions of Colonial Business.*

4. Political Development.

5. Social Development.

6. Intercolonial Relations.

7. Virginia a Typical Southern Colony.

a. Comparison of Virginia with Colonies of the Other Sections.

b. Causes of Its Prominence.

II. STUDY OF MAPS OF THIS PERIOD.

NOTE: *Topics in italics are titles of 48 papers in a series of 12 George Washington Programs and the parts of the Honor to George Washington series of 15 pamphlets issued by the United States George Washington Bicentennial Commission.*

Development

I. BACKGROUND—Knowledge of the Historical and Geographical Conditions Relating to the Colonies at the Birth of George Washington, 1732.

To know George Washington, we must first of all know the society in which he was born and brought up. (Lodge, Henry C.—*George Washington (American Statesmen)*, Vol. I, p. 15.)

A. Relation of Geography and History.

The most important geographical fact in the past history of the United States has been their location on the Atlantic opposite Europe; and the most important geographical fact in lending a distinctive character to their future history will probably be their location on the Pacific opposite Asia. . . .

History shows us by repeated instances that the geographical conditions most favorable for the early development of a people are such as secure to it a certain amount of isolation. . . .

Of the three leading colonizing nations which came to North America from Europe, one appropriated the only part of this continent which could afford geographic isolation in any way approximating that which it had enjoyed in Europe. That people were the English. At the end of the first century of permanent settlement they found themselves in possession of a narrow strip of coast, shut off from the interior of the country by an almost unbroken mountain wall. Sea and watershed drew their boundary lines and constituted at the same time their frontier defenses. Only one border was really open, that to the south along the Spanish possessions in Florida. The English were therefore in a naturally defined area, isolated enough to lend them the protection and cohesion which colonial life so much needs, affording the long line of coast which could give to this maritime people its most favorable environment, large enough for growth and strength, but small enough to secure concentration and to guard against the evils of excessive expansion. (Semple, Ellen Churchill—*American History and Its Geographic Conditions*, pp. 1, 36-37.)

B. Colonial America at the End of Period of New Colonization with the Founding of Georgia in 1732.

> The English colonies in America lay very tranquil in 1732, the year in which Washington was born. It fell in a season betweentimes, when affairs lingered, as if awaiting a chance. (Wilson, Woodrow—*George Washington*, p. 4.)

> Each of the English colonies that lay along the Atlantic coast in the middle of the eighteenth century had its own individuality and its own peculiarities. (McLaughlin, Andrew C.—*History of the American Nation*, p. 112.)

1. **Effect of Geographic Conditions on the Settlement of the Colonies.**
    - a. New England.
    - b. Middle Section.
    - c. South.

    > Hemmed in thus by the mountains, for the first one hundred and fifty years of their occupancy the English settlers were limited to the tide-water region of the Atlantic coast. This seaboard country presented in its different portions different aspects, which had a corresponding effect upon the colonists. In New England the lowland belt is only from fifty to eighty miles wide; but it gradually broadens as it continues southward, till in the Carolinas the mountains are two hundred and fifty miles back from the sea. The area adapted to settlement was therefore more extensive in the South than in the North. (Semple, Ellen Churchill—*American History and Its Geographic Conditions*, pp. 42-43.)

    - d. References.
        Brigham, Albert P.—*Geographic Influences in American History*, chs. i-iii.
        Semple, Ellen Churchill—*American History and Its Geographic Conditions*, ch. iii (The Influence of the Appalachian Barrier upon Colonial History).

2. **Population.**

    > The population of 1,370,000 people [in 1750] occupied a space which in 1920 furnished homes for more than 40,000,000. (Hart, Albert B.—*Formation of the Union*, p. 5.)

    > The population, amounting to about 1,500,000 in 1760, was heterogeneous, though mainly English in New England and New Jersey. In Pennsylvania the Germans and Scotch-Irish were especially numerous, and they pushed to the frontier and then spread south through Shenandoah Valley into the back country of the Carolinas, where they were separated from the lower settlements geographically, socially, and economically. This frontier element existed in all the colonies and was of importance in colonial development. It stood usually for natural rights as superior to vested ones, and towards the more settled portion of each colony as the colony as a whole did towards English control. (Matteson, David M.—*Epitome of United States History*, p. 351.)

    > The builders of new worlds are usually men of courage, enterprise and independence, with a spirit of conquest in their veins which craves an outlet, and the English colonials were largely recruited from this class. (Hill, Frederick T.—*Washington—The Man of Action*, p. 4.)

    - a. Race Conditions in the Colonies.
    - b. References.
        Channing, Edward—*A History of the United States*, Vol. II, ch. xiv (The Coming of the Foreigners).
        Jernegan, Marcus W.—*The American Colonies,*
        ch. xii (Population and Immigration Problems, 1689-1750).
        Wilson, Woodrow—*George Washington*, ch. i (In Washington's Day).

3. **Industrial Development.**

    > We live in a period of great cities, rapid communication, vast and varied business interests, enormous diversity of occupation, great industries. . . . We transport ourselves to the Virginia of Washington's boyhood, and find a people without cities or towns, with no means of communication except what was afforded by rivers and wood roads; . . . Once a fortnight a mail crawled down from the North, and once a month another crept on to the South. (Lodge, Henry C.—*George Washington (American Statesmen)*, Vol. I, pp. 16, 18.)

    - a. Conditions of Colonial Business—*Honor to George Washington*, No. 12 (*Washington the Business Man*), Part I.
    - b. References.
        Coman, Katherine—*Industrial History of the United States*, ch. iii (Industrial Development under British Control).
        Hart, Albert B.—*American History Told by Contemporaries*, Vol. II, ch. xiii (Commerce and Currency).
        Jernegan, Marcus W.—*The American Colonies*, ch. x (Political and Commercial Policy of England towards the Colonies).

4. **Political Development.**

    > In essence, all the colonies of all three groups had the same form of government. In each there was an elective legislature; in each the suffrage was very limited; . . . The legislative branch was composed in almost all cases of two houses; the lower house was elective, and by its control over money bills it frequently forced the passage of measures unacceptable to the co-ordinate house. This latter, except in a few cases, was a small body appointed by the governor, and had the functions of an executive council as well as of an upper house. The governor was a third part of the legislature in so far as he chose to exercise his veto power. The only other limitation on the legislative power of the assemblies was the general proviso that no act "was to be contrary to the law of England, but agreeable thereto," which could be enforced by a veto by the British government. . . . The governor's chief power was that of appointment, although the assemblies strove to deprive them of it by electing treasurers and other executive officers. He had also the prestige of his little court, and was able to form at least a small party of adherents. As a representative of the home government he was the object of suspicion and defiance. As the receiver and dispenser of annoying fees, he was likely to be unpopular; and wherever it could do so, the assembly made him feel his dependence upon it for his salary. (Hart, Albert B.—*Formation of the Union*, pp. 15-16.)

    - a. Reference.
        Jernegan, Marcus W.—*The American Colonies*, ch. xi (Constitutional and Political Development of the Colonies, 1689-1750).

5. **Social Development.**

    > The New England colonies differed somewhat from one another in their social, industrial, and political makeup; but on the whole they were much alike,

while they presented many sharp contrasts to the colonists of the South. (McLaughlin, Andrew C.—*History of the American Nation*, p. 118.)

The only professional men were the clergy, for the lawyers were few, . . . while the physicians were still fewer. . . . The great planters were the men who owned, ruled, and guided Virginia. (Lodge, Henry C.—*George Washington* (*American Statesmen*), Vol. I, p. 21.)

a. Reference.
    Jernegan, Marcus W.—*The American Colonies*, ch. xv (Social Development).

6. Intercolonial Relations.

Intercolonial relations were mainly controversial, boundaries being the chief dispute. Social and economic differences were many: spirit of settlement in the various colonies and local pride; general democratic tendency in the North and the growth of a plantation aristocracy in the South; diversity of interests in the North and lack of it in the South; causes and results of local government; social diversity; the Puritan social survivals in New England and the lighter ethical attitude elsewhere. The common sentiment was the result of dangers from without and the inheritance of rights as Englishmen. (Matteson, David M.—*Epitome of United States History*, p. 352.)

a. Reference.
    Greene, E. B.—*Provincial America* (*American Nation*, Vol. VI), chs. xvi-xviii.

7. Virginia a Typical Southern Colony.

No single influence molded the life of the colony of Virginia. The beginnings in a wilderness are never easy. But this was no such land to struggle with as the Puritan found. Its climate was genial, its virgin soils were rich, and the battle with the winter's cold did not consume the energies that were sorely needed in other ways. (Brigham, Albert P.—*Geographic Influences in American History*, p. 75.)

There was but one center of social life in Virginia: at Williamsburg, the village capital, where

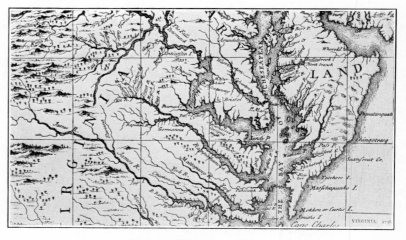

MAP OF VIRGINIA, 1738

the Governor had his "palace," . . . (Wilson, Woodrow—*George Washington*, p. 6.)

The large Virginia plantation was a small community almost sufficient unto itself. (McLaughlin, Andrew C.—*History of the American Nation*, p. 116.)

Virginians stayed at home, and sought and welcomed the rare stranger at their gates as if they were well aware that they were entertaining angels. (Lodge, Henry C.—*George Washington* (*American Statesmen*), Vol. I, p. 20.)

a. Comparison of Virginia with Colonies of the Other Sections.
    (1) Size.
    (2) Population.
    (3) Government.
    (4) Commerce.
    (5) Social Life.
b. Causes of Its Prominence.

II. STUDY OF MAPS OF THIS PERIOD.
    A. Reference.
        Fox, Dixon R.—*Harper's Atlas of American History*.

"EPPING FOREST," VIRGINIA
Birthplace of Mary Ball Washington, Mother of George Washington, which is still standing

Unit II
Early Life of George Washington

BIRTHPLACE OF GEORGE WASHINGTON, WAKEFIELD, VIRGINIA
As rebuilt by The Wakefield National Memorial Association and dedicated in 1932

Brief Outline

I. BIRTH—Time and Place.
A. 1732, February 22 new style (February 11 old style) —George Washington was born at the estate between Bridges Creek and Popes Creek, then known as Bridges Creek Estate, later called "Wakefield."

II. FAMILY.
A. Parents.
1. His Father, Augustine.
a. *Paternal Ancestry.*
b. *Family Name of Washington.*
c. *Genealogical Table.*
2. His Mother, Mary Ball.
a. *Maternal Ancestry.*
b. *Mary Ball in Early Life.*
B. Relatives.
1. *Brothers, Sisters, Nieces, and Nephews.*
2. *Stepchildren and Stepgrandchildren.*

III. BOYHOOD.
A. Activities.
1. Home.
a. Location of the Homes.
b. *Early History of Wakefield, the Birthplace, and Mount Vernon.*
c. *Mount Vernon.*
d. *Washington Homestead on the Rappahannock River.*
e. *Mary Ball Washington as Wife and Mother.*
2. School.
a. *The Boyhood of George Washington.*
b. *Washington's Rules of Civility.*
3. Social and Religious.
a. *Social Life of Childhood Home.*
b. Religious Life of Childhood Home.
1. *Inherited Religious Attitude.*
2. *George Washington the Son.*

IV. SIGNIFICANT DATES.
NOTE: *Topics in italics are titles of 48 papers in a series of 12 George Washington Programs and the parts of the Honor to George Washington series of 15 pamphlets issued by the United States George Washington Bicentennial Commission.*

Development

I. BIRTH—Time and Place.
A. 1732, February 22 new style (February 11 old style) —George Washington was born at the estate between Bridges Creek and Popes Creek, then known as Bridges Creek Estate, later called "Wakefield."
Washington stands at the commencement of a new era, as well as at the head of the New World. (Webster, Daniel—"The Character of Washington," *Works* (1853 ed.), Vol. I, p. 221.) (Speech, Washington, D. C., February 22, 1832.)

II. FAMILY.
A. Parents.
1. His Father, Augustine.
a. Paternal Ancestry—Program One (*Family Relationships of George Washington*), No. 2.
The story of the ancestors of George Washington tells of their descent from about 1183 and of the positions of the English family at various periods.
b. Family Name of Washington: Derivations and Changes—Program One (*Family Relationships of George Washington*), No. 1.
George Washington's name is found in English records as early as seven and a half centuries ago. It is of Saxon origin and came from the name of a village. After many changes it became the Washington we know.
c. Genealogical Table—*Honor to George Washington*, No. 14 (*Washington's Home and Fraternal Life*), Part III.

2. His Mother, Mary Ball.

   a. Maternal Ancestry—Program One (*Family Relationships of George Washington*), No. 3.

      George Washington's maternal ancestry is almost as historic as the Washingtons. The Ball family is represented in England by many branches. His mother's forebears were democratic in principle and of strong religious bent.

   b. Mary Ball in Early Life—Program Four (*The Mother of George Washington*), No. 1.

      Mary Ball was of honorable ancestry. Early orphaned, her mother's will placed her and her property in the care of George Eskridge as guardian. She was known as the "Rose of Epping Forest" and the "Belle of the Northern Neck."

B. Relatives.

   1. Brothers, Sisters, Nieces, and Nephews—Program One (*Family Relationships of George Washington*), No. 4.

      George Washington was well supplied with relatives. He had two stepbrothers, three brothers, one sister, at least twenty-two nephews and nieces, two stepchildren, four stepgrandchildren. The story of his relations with them makes interesting reading.

   2. Stepchildren and Stepgrandchildren—Program One (*Family Relationships of George Washington*), No. 5.

      Washington cannot really be understood by one who is unfamiliar with his family relations, with the hospitable habits of Virginia—visiting back and forth, hunting (of which Washington was very fond), horse racing, plays of a traveling theatrical troupe, drives to church and church services, weddings and merry-makings, state dinners at Mount Vernon, and visits of hosts of friends from America and Europe who were hospitably received. (Hart, Albert B.—*George Washington (Reading with a Purpose*, No. 42), p. 13.)

III. BOYHOOD.

A. Activities.

   1. Home.

      a. Location of the Homes.

         On Popes Creek in Bridges Creek Estate, now Wakefield.

         At Epsewasson, the Estate later called Mount Vernon, on the Potomac near Little Hunting Creek.

         Washington Homestead on the Rappahannock River.

      b. Early History of Wakefield, the Birthplace, and Mount Vernon—Program Two (*Homes of George Washington*), No. 1.

         George Washington was born at Bridges Creek estate, later called Wakefield, February 22, 1732. Three years later the family moved away.

      c. Mount Vernon—Program Two (*Homes of George Washington*), No. 2.

         At Epsewasson, renamed Mount Vernon, George Washington lived in childhood. It became his property after his brother's death. There he lived for over 50 years. It was the first home in America in his lifetime as it is the first shrine in the United States today.

      d. Washington Homestead on the Rappahannock River—Program Two (*Homes of George Washington*), No. 3.

         The Rappahannock River homestead was the one home purchased by George Washington's father. There he died in 1743. George's mother resided there until the Revolution.

      e. Mary Ball Washington as Wife and Mother—Program Four (*The Mother of George Washington*), No. 2.

         The care-free, hospitable life of the Virginia planters prevailed at the homes of the Washingtons at Popes Creek, at Little Hunting Creek, and on the Rappahannock during the life of Augustine Washington, but this changed at his death.

   2. School.

      a. The Boyhood of George Washington—Program Three (*Youth and Manhood of George Washington*), No. 1.

         Strong, zestful, and ambitious, Washington was a leader of his mates. An expert surveyor, largely self-educated, he secured the patronage of Lord Fairfax.

      b. Washington's Rules of Civility—Program Three (*Youth and Manhood of George Washington*), No. 1.

         Among the hundreds of volumes of Washington Manuscripts in the Library of Congress, two contain the school exercises of George Washington, written before he had reached the age of sixteen years. . . . The second book begins with legal forms, . . . The remaining ten pages of the second book are occupied by one hundred and ten "Rules of Civility and Decent Behaviour in Company and Conversation," about which much has been written and little is known. These maxims were so fully exemplified in George Washington's life that biographers have regarded them as formative influences in the development of his character.

         During the days before mere hero worship had given place to understanding and comprehension of the fineness of Washington's character, of his powerful influence among men, and of the epoch-making nature of the issues he so largely shaped, it was assumed that Washington himself composed the maxims, or at least that he compiled them. It is a satisfaction to find that his consideration for others, his respect for and deference to those deserving such treatment, his care of his own body and tongue, and even his reverence for his Maker, all were early inculcated in him by precepts which were the common practice in decent society the world over. These very maxims had been in use in France for a century and a half, and in England for a century, before they were set as a task for the schoolboy Washington. . . .

         A comparison of texts furnishes proof positive that the Maxims copied by George Washington came from the Hawkins version, and not from the French. The doubts thrown on the Hawkins work because of the author's youth are unfounded. . . .

         The open questions are: who condensed, and arranged as exercises in writing, the Hawkins Maxims; and, second, who taught George Washington penmanship by the use of them?

         In any event, and whoever the teacher, it was the Hawkins English version and not the French version that was the source of the rules Washington copied. Is it not probable that the Hawkins book was one of those compilations that "no gentleman's library could be without," notwithstanding the fact that no such title appears in the catalogue of the library of William Byrd, of Westover, reputed to have been the finest in the Colonies? Is it not possible that either Washington's father or one of his half-brothers, all three of whom were educated in England, brought back a copy of one of the Hawkins editions? . . .

Here, then, is the conclusion of the whole matter as it now stands: The Rules of Civility were composed originally, or compiled, and published in France, by the Jesuits, about 1595; they were translated into English by Francis Hawkins about 1640, and passed through no fewer than eleven editions down to 1672. From the Hawkins book the one hundred and ten Rules written by Washington were selected, simplified and arranged by some person at present unknown. One copy came into the hands of George Washington, who from it wrote out the manuscript that is among the Washington Papers purchased from the family by Congress in 1834 and 1849, and held in the Department of State until 1903, when they were transferred to the Library of Congress. (Moore, Charles—*George Washington's Rules of Civility and Decent Behaviour In Company and Conversation*, pp. ix-xiv.)

3. Social and Religious.
   a. Social Life of Childhood Home—Program Nine (*Social Life of George Washington*), No. 1.

   Grounded in social amenities by his mother in the simplicity of her widow's farm house, George Washington gained additional social training in the hospitable social activities of the homes of his married brothers and their neighbors.

   b. Religious Life of Childhood Home.
      (1) Inherited Religious Attitude—Program Seven (*George Washington The Christian*), No. 1.

      George Washington's Christian parents had him christened according to the rites of the Episcopal Church. The Bible and Sir Matthew Hale's Contemplation were part of his training, for he was reared to reverence God and give due respect to religious matters.

      (2) George Washington the Son—Program Five (*George Washington The Man of Sentiment*), No. 1.

      George Washington, loving, dutiful, and thoughtful, gave his parents obedience as a boy. As a young man he gave his mother's wishes respectful attention, and at the pinnacle of his fame paid tribute to the maternal hand that led him to manhood.

IV. SIGNIFICANT DATES SELECTED FROM *George Washington Year by Year*.

1183—William de Wessyngton is found in English records as occupying an estate in the Palatine Durham, which he received in exchange for lands in Hertburn. As families took the names of estates or villages, the de Hertburn gave place to de Wessyngton. Then the "de" was dropped and the name passed through changes in spelling, being recorded as Wessyngton, Wassington, until it came to Washington.

1264, May 14—A William de Wessyngton fought for his King in the Battle of the Lewes.

1300 (about)—Robert de Washington, Lord of Milbourne (near Warton).

1450—John Washington at Tewhitfield, Lancashire; Robert Washington, his son, at Warton.

1538—Lawrence Washington, son of John Washington of Warton, and his wife, Margaret Kitson, sister to Sir Thomas Kitson of London. This Lawrence Washington was listed in the Visitation of the Heralds of Northamptonshire in

1618, which traced the ancestry for seven generations. He was twice Mayor of Northampton. In 1538-39 he obtained from King Henry VIII a grant of the lands previously belonging to the Priory of St. Andrew in Northampton, and other monastic property of the region, including the small estate of Sulgrave Manor. He died in 1584.

1543-44—Robert Washington, son of Mayor Lawrence, born. He married Elizabeth Light and died in January, 1620.

1588, Aug. 3—Lawrence, son of Robert and Elizabeth Light Washington, married Margaret Butler, daughter of William Butler of Tees or Tighes Essex, at Aston-le-Walls, Northamptonshire. Lawrence and Margaret Butler Washington were the grandparents of the three emigrants to the colony of Virginia.

1610—Robert Washington, with the consent of his son Lawrence, cut off the entail and sold the Manor of Sulgrave to his nephew, Lawrence Makepeace.

1616—Lawrence Washington, husband of Margaret Butler, died before his father. In St. Mary's Church, Brington, England, where he is buried, may be seen a memorial slab with epitaph and the Washington arms emblazoned with those of his wife, Margaret Butler, impaled.

1621—Lawrence Washington, the son of Lawrence and Margaret Butler Washington, matriculated at Brasenose College, Oxford. He received the degree of bachelor of arts in 1623.

1631—Lawrence Washington became proctor of the university.

1632—Lawrence Washington became the rector of Purleigh in Essex. After being thus established he married Amphilis Roades. His rectory was taken from him for political reasons. He received the small living of Little Braxted.

1646—When Cromwell's forces were besieging the city of Worcester, England, the attacking general was Sir Thomas Fairfax and the defender of the city was Sir Henry Washington, an uncle of the emigrants. He refused to surrender.

1652—The rector of Purleigh died and was buried in All Saints' Church, Maldon. He and Amphilis Roades Washington were the parents of a large family. Among their children were the two sons, John and Lawrence, who came to Virginia after visiting the West Indies, and the daughter, Martha, who followed her brothers to the new land.

1657—John, son of the rector of Purleigh, settled in Virginia about this time. He was about 23 years of age then and was the great grandfather of George Washington. He settled on a plantation, previously occupied, at Bridges Creek. His wife and two children died, and he married Ann Pope, daughter of Col. Nathaniel Pope, of Popes Creek, adjacent to Bridges Creek. Of this second marriage there were three children.

Date uncertain—Lawrence Washington, eldest son of John and Ann Pope Washington, was born at the Bridges Creek home. He married Mildred Warner, by whom he had three children. He was the grandfather of George Washington. He died in 1698.

1694—Augustine Washington, son of Lawrence and Mildred Warner Washington, was born at the Bridges Creek plantation. He accompanied his mother and her other children to England after the death of their father. In England she married George Gale, who brought his stepchildren back to Virginia 12 years later and after their mother's death.

1716—Augustine Washington married Jane Butler, by whom he had four children, two of whom died in infancy. Jane Butler died in 1729.

1730, March 6—Augustine Washington married, as second wife, Mary Ball, of Epping Forest, born in 1708. They had six children; the eldest was George Washington, 10 generations removed from John Washington, of Tewhitfield.

1732, February 11 o. s. (n. s. 22)—George Washington was born at Bridges Creek estate (later called "Wakefield"), which extended to Popes Creek.

1743, April 12—Augustine Washington, father of George Washington, died at the age of 49. He was buried in the family vault at the Bridges Creek plantation.

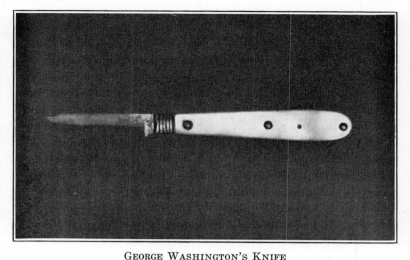

GEORGE WASHINGTON'S KNIFE

Given to him by his mother and now in possession of the Alexandria-Washington Lodge, Alexandria, Virginia

1746—George Washington, when about 15 years old, made preparation for a career at sea, but his mother vetoed the plan.

THE HOME AND GARDEN OF MARY BALL WASHINGTON IN FREDERICKSBURG, VIRGINIA

Unit III
The Young Manhood of George Washington

NOTE: *Topics in italics are titles of 48 papers in a series of 12 George Washington Programs and the parts of the Honor to George Washington series of 15 pamphlets issued by the United States George Washington Bicentennial Commission.*

Development

I. THE YOUTH HIMSELF.

A. Physique and Personality.

1. Personal Appearance.

He had just passed his sixteenth birthday. He was tall and muscular, approaching the stature of more than six feet which he afterwards attained. He was not yet filled out to manly proportions, but was rather spare, after the fashion of youth. He had a well-shaped, active figure, symmetrical except for the unusual length of the arms, indicating

GEORGE WASHINGTON

The first known portrait, painted at Mount Vernon in 1772, the first of many by Charles Willson Peale. Now in the Lee Memorial Chapel, Washington and Lee University, Lexington, Va.

uncommon strength. . . . "Fair and florid," big and strong, he was, take him for all in all, as fine a specimen of his race as could be found in the English colonies. (Lodge, Henry C.—*George Washington (American Statesmen)*, Vol. I, pp. 54-55.)

In person Washington was unique: he looked like no one else. To a stature lofty and commanding, he united a form of the manliest proportions, limbs cast in Nature's finest mould, and a carriage the most dignified, graceful, and imposing. No one ever approached the Pater Patriae that did not feel his presence. (Custis, George Washington Parke—*Recollections and Private Memoirs of Washington*, p. 39.)

2. The Man Himself—Program Three (*Youth and Manhood of George Washington*), No. 3.

> At man's estate Washington was of heroic mold, poised, dignified, intuitively sensing his destiny, and acquitting himself accordingly.
>
> At twenty he was physically a young giant capable of enduring any hardship and of meeting any foe. (Thayer, William R.—*George Washington*, pp. 254-255.)
>
> The physical strength mentioned by nearly every one who described Washington is so undoubted that the traditions of his climbing the walls of the Natural Bridge, throwing a stone across the Rappahannock at Fredericksburg, and another into the Hudson from the top of the Palisades, pass current more from the supposed muscular power of the man than from any direct evidence. In addition to this, Washington in 1755 claimed to have "one of the best constitutions," and again he wrote, "for my own part I can answer, I have a constitution hardy enough to encounter and undergo the most severe trials." (Ford, Paul L.—*George Washington*, p. 47) (1896 ed.—*True George Washington*.)

B. Activities.
  1. Home.
    a. In the Home of Lawrence Washington.

> The place of father was taken by his half-brother Lawrence, his elder by fourteen years, who had the merchant-planter character of the Washingtons and added new graces. . . . When he was sixteen, Lawrence took him in at Mount Vernon, making him neighbor and friend of the kinsmen of Lord Fairfax, who was the only nobleman then resident in the colonies. (Corbin, John—*The Unknown Washington*, p. 33.)
>
> Lawrence Washington, . . . proved himself such an elder brother as it could but better and elevate a boy to have. (Wilson, Woodrow—*George Washington*, p. 47.)

    b. In the Home of the Fairfaxes.

> From him [Lord Fairfax] the boy could gain that knowledge of men and manners which no school can give and which is as important in its way as any that a teacher can impart. . . . Lord Fairfax and Washington became fast friends. (Lodge, Henry C.—*George Washington* (*American Statesmen*), Vol. I, pp. 53-54.)

  2. Outside.
    a. Sports and Athletics.

> Though myths of which he is the hero are plentiful, and facts are few, these facts are strong in vividness and go far to drawing a distinct picture of him, and to giving it definite color as well. We had best not make too much, separately, of the rather uncertain legends concerning his deeds of strength, his taming of wild colts, his long throws, his high climbs; he was evidently well muscled from the first—though somewhat lank and hollow chested, and with no ruddiness of face—and the value of the legends is not their individual authenticity, but their united testimony. . . . and it is sure that Washington as a boy possessed a body strong and energetic beyond the common, and that he gave much attention to its exercise. . . . He had seen his half-brother Lawrence making ready for real wars; to imitate was inevitable, and military sports have been frequent among generations of children who never came to fame either as soldiers or civilians. (Wister, Owen—*The Seven Ages of Washington*, pp. 23-24.)

    (1) Horseback Riding.

> . . . he loved and understood horses from the time when he rode bareback in the pasture to those later days when he acted as judge at a horse-race. (Lodge, Henry C.—*George Washington* (*American Statesmen*), Vol. I, p. 95.)
>
> Washington . . . broke his own horses, and, in consequence, could judge intelligently their weak and strong points, their mentality and psychology. Blueskin, Nelson and Magnolia were some of the stable "stars." Blueskin was for years his favorite hunter; Nelson was the charger that carried him through much of the Revolutionary War, afterward being relieved of all duty to spend his last days in ease and comfort on the farm.
>
> Kindness to animals was always a pronounced trait in Washington's character, and thoroughness in training them one of his strongest points. He bred and trained his own hunting dogs, . . . (Sawyer, Joseph D.—*Washington*, Vol. I, pp. 233-234.)

    (2) Fox Hunting.

> They [with Lord Fairfax] hunted the fox together, and hunted him hard. They engaged in all the rough sports and perilous excitements that Virginia winter life could afford, and the boy's bold and skilful riding, his love of sports and his fine temper, commended him to the warm and affectionate interest of the old nobleman. (Lodge, Henry C.—*George Washington* (*American Statesmen*), Vol. I, p. 54.)
>
> Prior to the war of Independence, he was much attached to the pleasures of the chase, and is described as a bold and fearless rider. He kept hounds for a short time after the Revolution, but declined hunting altogether about 1787 or '88. (Custis, George Washington Parke—*Recollections and Private Memoirs of Washington*, pp. 11-12.)
>
> Although Washington was a thorough-going sportsman, he did not greatly care for shooting. Fishing was a frequent source of enjoyment, . . . but the fox hunt, . . . was his favorite form of outdoor sport. It is an open question whether it was not the horsemanship, rather than the hunt, that most appealed to him. Washington was completely at his ease when he was in the saddle. (Sawyer, Joseph D.—*Washington*, Vol. I, p. 235.)

II. EARLY OCCUPATIONS.
  A. Surveyor.

> The effect of his experience as surveyor lasted throughout George Washington's life. (Thayer, William R.—*George Washington*, p. 5.)
>
> Into this region [west and northwest] young George Washington was sent, first as a surveyor, then as a soldier, in repeated campaigns against the western Indians. His journey . . . to warn the French to keep out of the Ohio Valley is one of the bold adventures of human history. (Hart, Albert B.—*George Washington* (*Reading with a Purpose*, No. 42), p. 14.)

  1. Period of Washington's Youth—*Honor to George Washington*, No. 1 (*Frontier Background of Washington's Career*), Part I.
  2. George Washington, Engineer—*Honor to George Washington*, No. 13 (*Washington as Engineer and City Builder*), Part I.
  3. George Washington the Surveyor—Program Six (*George Washington the Man of Action in Military and Civil Life*), No. 1.

> Temperament, training, and circumstance always made George Washington a man of action. As a sur-

veyor, soldier, commander in chief, farmer, and builder of canals, his life was diversified, and to each of his many vocations he gave the utmost of knowledge and effort for success.

4. Travels.
   a. Western Journeys—*Honor to George Washington*, No. 11 (*Washington the Traveler*), Part I.
   b. Travels, Pursuits, and Ideals (Pre-Revolutionary Period)—Program Three (*Youth and Manhood of George Washington*), No. 2.

   > Surveyor, soldier, and legislator, Washington's frontier experience, wide travel, and social position gave him a complete view of Colonial life.

   > For Washington in person, the lasting effect of the early training and fighting in western Pennsylvania was that it gave him direct knowledge of the Indian and his ways, and that it turned his imagination to thinking out the problems of developing the Middle West, and of keeping the connections between the East and the West strong and open. (Thayer, William R.—*George Washington*, pp. 255-256.)

B. Military.
   1. Expeditions into the Ohio Valley.

   > The opening act of the contest for the Ohio Valley is of special interest as introducing George Washington on the stage of American history. (Muzzey, David S.—*The American People*, p. 99.)

   > Robert Dinwiddie, the governor of Virginia, sent George Washington, the young adjutant-general of the Virginia militia, to remonstrate with the French against occupying territory which was "so notoriously known to be the property of the Crown of Great Britain." (Forman, Samuel E.—*Advanced American History*, p. 92.)

   > The governor intrusted it [the message of warning] to a young land surveyor, only twenty-one years of age, but already familiar with Indians and with woodcraft, and already noted for courage and sound judgment. The name of this young man was George Washington. (Fiske, John—*History of the United States*, pp. 168-169.)

   a. Washington's Contact with the Indians—*Honor to George Washington*, No. 1 (*Frontier Background of Washington's Career*), Part II.
   2. Participation in the French and Indian War as Preparation for the American Revolution.

   > He was also the bravest spirit at the frightful defeat of Braddock in 1755, when a bullet . . . came within a few inches of depriving a future country of its future father. (Hart, Albert B.—*George Washington* (*Reading with a Purpose*, No. 42), p. 15.)

   a. Preparation for Command—*Honor to George Washington*, No. 10 (*Washington the Military Man*), Part I.
   b. George Washington the Soldier Through French and Indian War—Program Six (*George Washington The Man of Action in Military and Civil Life*), No. 2.
   c. Military Experience Under British Rule—Program Ten (*George Washington The Builder of The Nation*), No. 1.

   > As messenger to warn away the French, as colonial officer in the expeditions against Fort Duquesne, and as guardian of the frontier, George Washington gave loyal service and acquired valuable experience.

   d. Maps.
      (1) References.

   > Map in *Honor to George Washington*, No. 1

(*Frontier Background of Washington's Career*).
   Maps—*The George Washington Atlas* (See Unit XI—Geography).
   Maps—*Honor to George Washington*, No. 10 (*Washington the Military Man*).
   e. Reference.
      Coman, Katherine—*Industrial History of the United States*, ch. xiii (The French and Indian War).

C. Political.
   1. Office Holder in the House of Burgesses.
   a. Washington in Colonial Politics (1755-1775)—*Honor to George Washington*, No. 6 (*Washington the Colonial and National Statesman*), Part I.

   > In the House of Burgesses Washington was a taciturn member, yet he seemed to have got a great deal of political knowledge and wisdom so that his colleagues thought of him as the solid man of the House . . . (Thayer, William R.—*George Washington*, p. 256.)

D. Farmer at Mount Vernon.

   > George Washington is commonly spoken of as a surveyor, a general, a statesman; but first of all he was a farmer. (Stine, O. C., Principal Agricultural Economist, Dept. of Agriculture.—*Address*, February 22, 1929.)

   1. Ownership of the Estate.
   a. The Estate—*Honor to George Washington*, No. 9 (*Washington Proprietor of Mount Vernon*), Part I.

   > The Mount Vernon estate, amounting in the end to over eight thousand acres, was, with the exception of a few outlying tracts, subdivided into five farms, namely, The Mansion House Farm, the Union Farm, the Dogue Run Farm, Muddy Hole Farm and the River Farm. (Haworth, Paul L.—*George Washington, Country Gentleman*, p. 61.)

   b. Ownership of Mount Vernon—*Honor to George Washington*, No. 9 (*Washington Proprietor of Mount Vernon*), Part II.

   > To have thrust upon him, at the age of twenty, the management of a large estate might seem a heavy burden for any young man; but George Washington was equal to the task, and it seems as if much of his career up to that time was a direct preparation for it. He knew every foot of its fields and meadows, of its woodlands and streams; he knew where each crop grew, and its rotation; he had taken great interest in horses and cattle, and in the methods for maintaining and improving their breed; and now, of course being master, his power of choosing good men to do the work was put to the test. But he had not been long at these new occupations before public duties drew him away from them. (Thayer, William R.—*George Washington*, p. 12.)

   2. Agricultural Development.

   > From a very early time Washington had been a careful student of such books on agriculture as he could obtain, even preparing lengthy abstracts of them, and the knowledge he thus obtained, combined with his own practical experience, soon convinced him that the Virginia system was wrong. . . .

   > In connection with this change of system, Washington became an early convert to the rotation of crops, and drew up elaborate tables sometimes covering periods of five years, so that the quantity of each crop should not vary, yet by which his fields should have constant change. This system nat-

urally very much diversified the product of his estate, and flax, hay, clover, buckwheat, turnips, and potatoes became large crops. . . .

In all things he was an experimentalist, carefully trying different kinds of tobacco and wheat, various kinds of plants for hedges, and various kinds of manure for fertilizers; he had tests made to see whether he could sell his wheat to best advantage in the grain or when made into flour, and he bred from selected horses, cattle, and sheep. (Ford, Paul L.—*George Washington*, pp. 117, 119, 120.)

. . . he was the best and most prosperous planter of Virginia. (Lodge, Henry C.—*George Washington* (*American Statesmen*), Vol. I, p. 100.)

3. Map of Mount Vernon—*Honor to George Washington*, No. 9 (*Washington Proprietor of Mount Vernon*).

III. SOCIAL LIFE.

A. George Washington the Country Squire—Program Five (*George Washington the Man of Sentiment*), No. 2.

Washington was much like other young men of his day. A most eligible young bachelor of Virginia, with his estate and position. His attractions and attachments were part of his youth. His courtship of Mrs. Custis is one of the cherished stories of his life.

B. George Washington the Husband—Program Five (*George Washington the Man of Sentiment*), No. 3.

To his wife Washington gave the chivalrous tender care and devotion of forty years of married life. He wrote her letters for her, made up her accounts, her orders, and kept her with him wherever possible, even at military headquarters.

C. Migratory Abiding Places—Program Two (*Homes of George Washington*), No. 4.

Life in the White House in New Kent County and in the "House of Six Chimneys," in Williamsburg; at Alexandria and Berkeley Springs, W. Va.

D. Social Life Before the Revolution: At Williamsburg and Mount Vernon—Program Nine (*The Social Life of George Washington*), No. 2.

With his marriage to Mrs. Custis, a belle at the viceregal court of Williamsburg, his official part of colonial society was formal and elegant. Such social life was likewise established in the Mount Vernon household and maintained until the Revolution.

E. Colonel and Mrs. Washington in Residence Before the Revolution—Program Twelve (*The Homemaking of George and Martha Washington*), No. 1.

Colonel and Mrs. Washington established their home at Mount Vernon on a luxurious scale. The plantation, with its many slaves and servants, was like a small empire. The wealthiest couple of their community, they lived accordingly.

IV. SIGNIFICANT DATES Selected from *George Washington Year by Year*.

1748—George Washington, when 16 years old, made a surveying trip to the Shenandoah Valley and the South Branch of the Potomac to assist in surveying the estate of Thomas, Lord Fairfax.

1749—George Washington received a surveyor's commission from William and Mary College, and was appointed surveyor of Culpeper County.

1751, Sept. 28—George Washington accompanied his halfbrother Lawrence Washington, to Barbadoes, where the brother went in search of health. While there the young man contracted smallpox and was ill four weeks.

1752, March 6—George Washington arrived at Mount

MARTHA WASHINGTON AS A YOUNG WOMAN
Painted by John Woolaston in 1757

Vernon with letters and messages for Lawrence's wife.

1752, July 26—Lawrence Washington returned to Virginia and died at Mount Vernon. His death was followed a few months later by that of his last remaining child.

1752, Nov. 4—George Washington was admitted to Fredericksburg Lodge of Masons, though a minor.

1752, Nov. 6—George Washington, then 20 years old, was appointed as district adjutant general of the Virginia Militia with the rank of major. His pay was £150 per year.

1752, Dec.—George Washington came into possession of Mount Vernon by the terms of the will of of his halfbrother Lawrence.

1753, Oct. 31—Major Washington was chosen to carry Governor Dinwiddie's expostulatory letter to Le Gardeur de St. Pierre, French commandant on the Ohio at Fort Le Boeuf (near Waterford, Pa.), and on January 16, 1754, returned with the reply. The Governor had his journal printed and widely distributed.

1754, March 15—Major Washington was commissioned lieutenant colonel of the Virginia Regiment and began (April 2) the march with two companies to complete the fort at the forks of the Ohio (now the site of Pittsburgh).

1754, May 28—First battle with French detachment under Jumonville, beginning of French and Indian War; Jumonville killed.

1754, June 4—Became Colonel Washington on death of Colonel Fry; date of the announcement.

1754, July 3—Colonel Washington surrendered to a French detachment at Fort Necessity, Great Meadows, Fayette County, Pa., which he had thrown up on May 30, and under the terms of the capitulation he began to march back to Virginia the next day.

1754, Oct.—Colonel Washington resigned commission.

1755, Apr. 23—George Washington left Mount Vernon to join General Braddock's forces at Fort Cumberland as aide on the General's staff. This was a volunteer service.

1755, July 9—General Braddock's army was defeated by the French and Indians on the Monongahela River. The General was mortally wounded. Washington was active in effecting the withdrawal of the remnant. He had two horses killed under him and four bullets through his coat.

1755, Aug. 14—Washington was made colonel and commander in chief of the Virginia forces for the protection of the frontier.

1756, Feb. 4-Mar. 23—Colonel Washington made a trip to Boston to have Governor Shirley, the commander of the British troops in America, decide the question of rank between Colonial officers and subordinate officers claiming a royal commission.

1757, Feb. 13-Apr. 1—Colonel Washington went to Philadelphia to attend a conference called by the Earl of Loudoun of the governors of several colonies.

1758—Colonel Washington became engaged to Martha Dandridge Custis.

1758, June 24—Colonel Washington began his march from Fort Loudoun (Winchester) to join General Forbes' campaign against Fort Duquesne.

1758, July 24—Colonel Washington was elected burgess for Frederick County, first election.

1758, Nov. 25—General Forbes occupied the site of Fort Duquesne; the French, after having destroyed the fort, retreated the day before.

1758, Dec.—Colonel Washington resigned his commission and retired from the army.

1759, Jan. 6—Colonel George Washington and Mrs. Martha Dandridge Custis were married. She was the widow of John Parke Custis, who left her with two children and a large fortune in money and lands.

1759, Feb. 22—Colonel Washington took his seat as a burgess in the Virginia Assembly as a representative of Frederick County, having been elected while on the Forbes campaign. He continued as a burgess from Frederick County and later from Fairfax County until he went to the Continental Congress.

1759, May—Colonel Washington and Mrs. Washington took up their residence at Mount Vernon at the close of the session of Assembly, living in Williamsburg from the time of their marriage until going to Mount Vernon to stay.

1761, May 18—Colonel Washington was reelected to the House of Burgesses.

1762, Oct. 25—Colonel Washington became vestryman of Truro Parish in Fairfax County.

1763, Oct. 3—Colonel Washington became warden of Pohick Church of Truro Parish for one year. Served other terms later.

1765, July 16—Colonel Washington's first election as burgess for Fairfax County.

1768, Dec. 1—Colonel Washington was reelected burgess for Fairfax County.

1769, May 16—Virginia burgesses adopt Virginia Resolves; Governor Botetourt dissolves House.

1769, May 17—Colonel Washington met with other burgesses at the Raleigh Tavern, Williamsburg, where was presented the Non-Importation Agreement prepared by George Mason. It was signed the next day by each member and then printed and circulated.

© *William and Mary College*

William and Mary College in 1774

1769, Sept. 14—Colonel Washington was reelected burgess for Fairfax County.

1770, Oct. 5—Colonel Washington, accompanied by Doctor Craik, set out on a trip to and down the Ohio River as far as the Great Kanawha, a distance of 265 miles, to inspect and select lands for the grant to soldiers of Virginia for their war service. This trip consumed nine weeks.

1771, Dec. 4—Colonel Washington was reelected burgess for Fairfax County.

1772, Apr. 11—Colonel Washington, interested in the promotion of the improvement of the Potomac for commercial navigation, secured an act from the Virginia Assembly incorporating a company. Nothing was done, however, until after the Revolution.

1773, Mar. 12—The House of Burgesses, every member of whom had been reelected after the dissolution by Governor Botetourt, appointed an intercolonial committee of correspondence.

1773, May 10-June 8—Colonel Washington made a trip to New York, dining with several governors and meeting prominent men in the course of his journey.

1774, May 24—The burgesses appointed a day of fasting because of the Boston Port Bill. Governor Dunmore dissolved the assembly next day, but it met at Raleigh Tavern to renew the Non-Importation Association, also to discuss the calling of an intercolonial congress.

1774, May 31—Colonel Washington attended a deliberation of burgesses that resulted in a call for a Virginia convention on August 1.

1774, July 5—Colonel Washington was a member of Fairfax County meeting.

1774, July 18—Colonel Washington presided over a county convention which adopted the Fairfax County Resolves.

1774, Aug. 1-6—Colonel Washington was made a member of the First Virginia Provincial Convention at Williamsburg, where he is reported to have said: "I will raise one thousand men, subsist them at my own expense, and march at their head to the relief of Boston." He was elected one of the Delegates to represent Virginia at the First Continental Congress.

1774, Sept. 5-Oct. 26—Colonel Washington attended the Continental Congress in Philadelphia. It was held in Carpenters' Hall. Peyton Randolph, of Virginia, was elected president.

Unit IV
George Washington a Leader of Men During the Struggle for Independence

Brief Outline

I. AMERICAN REVOLUTION.
  A. Historical Background.
    1. Causes of the Separation.
      a. Political.
      b. Economic—Acts of Trade and Navigation.
      c. Geographical.
  B. Political Activity of George Washington Prior to Military Command.
    1. *Washington in Colonial Politics.*
      a. In the House of Burgesses of Virginia.
      b. In the First and Second Continental Congresses.
    2. *Changing Views on British Control.*
  C. Campaigns.
    1. Northern—New England Area; Siege of Boston. June 15, 1775, George Washington chosen General and Commander in Chief of the Army of the United Colonies.
    2. Central—Hudson Valley and Philadelphia Area.
    3. Southern—Georgia, Carolinas, and Virginia.
    4. Western.
    5. Naval.
    6. Maps of Principal Campaigns.
  D. Results.
    1. Treaty of Peace, 1783.
      a. Terms of Treaty.
    2. Need for a Stronger Union.
      a. Articles of Confederation, 1781-1789.
  E. Race Contributions to the American Revolution.
  F. The Contributions Made by Women During the Revolution.
    1. Service of Martha Washington.
    2. *Mary Ball Washington in Later Life.*
    3. The Origin of the Flag—The Betsy Ross Fiction.
    4. Abigail Adams—Her Service to the Cause.
II. GEORGE WASHINGTON IN THE REVOLUTION.
  A. *George Washington the Commander in Chief.*
  B. *Washington's Relations to Congress* (1775-1786).
  C. *The Revolution to Valley Forge.*
  D. *Valley Forge and Afterwards.*
    1. The French Alliance.
  E. Military Homes.
    1. *Military Headquarters.*
    2. *War-Time Households.*
    3. *Social Life in Later Years.*
  F. Resignation of Commission to Congress.
  G. Recognitions for Services.
  H. Characteristics of George Washington Displayed in This Period.
    1. Faith.
      a. *George Washington as a Christian: In Military Experiences.*
    2. Courage.
      Physical and Moral.
    3. Fortitude.
    4. Loyalty.
      To an Ideal and Purpose.
    5. Determination.
      Surmounting All Difficulties to Reach the Goal.
    6. Magnanimity.
    7. Humility.
      Cause Before Personal Ambition.
    8. Self-Control.
      Master of Himself.

GEORGE WASHINGTON

Painted in 1792 by John Trumbull. Now in Yale University

    9. Leadership.
      Ability to Handle Men.
III. SIGNIFICANT DATES.

NOTE: *Topics in italics are titles of 48 papers in a series of 12 George Washington Programs and the parts of the Honor to George Washington series of 15 pamphlets issued by the United States George Washington Bicentennial Commission.*

Development

I. AMERICAN REVOLUTION.
  A. Historical Background.
    1. Causes of the Separation.
      a. Political.
        (1) Theory of Colonial System of George III and His Tory Ministry.
        (2) Development of Self-government in America.

317

(3) Difference in Idea of Representation.

b. Economic—Acts of Trade and Navigation.
  (1) Commercial Policies of Walpole and Grenville.
  (2) Development of Colonial Trade.
    Growth of Illegal Trade—Smuggling.
  (3) Enforcement of Laws Regulating Trade.

c. Geographical.
  (1) Lack of Understanding Due to Distance between America and Great Britain.

> In revolting against England the American colonies followed a recognized law of political geography. They constituted the remote western frontier of Europe; and a tendency towards defection manifests itself in all peripheral holdings. History is full of examples. The causes are deep-seated. Differences of geographical conditions, of climate, soil, economic methods, and therefore of political and social ideas, rapidly differentiate colonists from the parent nation. (Semple, Ellen Churchill—*American History and Its Geographic Conditions*, p. 47.)

B. Political Activity of George Washington Prior to Military Command.

1. Washington in Colonial Politics, 1755-1775—*Honor to George Washington*, No. 6 (*Washington the Colonial and National Statesman*), Part I (See Unit III).

a. In the House of Burgesses of Virginia.

b. In the First and Second Continental Congresses.

> Before the war could be fought, some kind of civil organization had to be formed. May 10, 1775, three weeks after the battle of Lexington, the Second Continental Congress assembled in Philadelphia, and continued, with occasional adjournments, till March 1, 1781. . . .
>
> In a word, the Continental Congress constituted a government exercising great sovereign powers. It began with no authority; it never received specific authority until 1781. (Hart, Albert B.—*Formation of the Union*, pp. 81, 84.)

2. Changing Views on British Control—Program Ten (*George Washington the Builder of the Nation*), No. 2.

> As the struggle between the English demands and the Colonial rights developed toward armed conflict, his views changed. He advocated nonimportation of British products. When Parliament sought to coerce Massachusetts he is reported to have stated he would raise and equip a thousand men and lead them to the relief of Boston.

C. Campaigns.

1. Northern—New England Area; Siege of Boston.

a. Plan of the British to break up the Revolution at the Beginning.

b. June 15, 1775, George Washington was chosen General and Commander in Chief of the Army of the United Colonies.

> Washington was selected commander-in-chief of the "Continental Army." Preparations were made for the support of the troops. Washington was then in the very prime of life—forty-three years of age, tall, stalwart, and strong. His experience in the French and Indian War, his undoubted military talents, the unqualified respect which all felt who knew him, coupled with the fact that the choice of a Southern general was the imperative demand of common sense, made his selection the only possible one. It was a fateful moment when the question was under consideration. From that time the Revolution rested on Washington's shoulders. Had the task fallen to

> any other man the war would probably have been a failure; for he was not simply a great man, he was a great general, possessed of wonderful judgment and self-control, and yet capable of bold, quick, decisive action. The campaigns of the Revolution, which can be given here only in outline, prove that, in a century which boasted of some of the greatest commanders in history, Washington won deserved renown as one of the ablest of them all. (McLaughlin, Andrew C.—*History of the American Nation*, p. 155.)

c. Lexington and Concord; Bunker Hill; Dorchester Heights, and Evacuation of Boston.

> Although this has not been appreciated by military critics, yet it is undoubtedly true that the siege of Boston had already developed the military situation that was destined to control the American Revolution. The outstanding feature of this military situation was its demonstration of a state of affairs, differing from anything that could exist in the Europe of the times, which actually precluded the possibility of a war waged in the European meaning of the word. A European war in the eighteenth century implied, as a matter of course, campaigns and battles fought by regular armies, trained in the formal tactics of the day and equipped to conform to a high standard of requirements. . . . There could be no such war between the British and the Americans, because only one side could meet the demands of the game. The British were able to put well-equipped armies into the field. The Americans could not. (Frothingham, Thomas G.—*Washington: Commander in Chief*, p. 104.)

2. Central—Hudson Valley and Philadelphia Area.

a. Plan of British to gain control of the Hudson, and to isolate New England from Virginia and use the loyalists of the central section.

b. New York; Trenton and Princeton; Philadelphia and Valley Forge; Saratoga.

> . . . this assured British superiority was limited to the areas where the British armies could be supplied by sea. Inland the British were unable to maintain themselves, much less conquer the countryside. Whenever a British force marched out into the country, it met disaster, and, sooner or later, was either chased back or overwhelmed. Saratoga was only the Lexington and Concord Fight on a large scale. Burgoyne was a victim of the same conditions that had disconcerted the Regulars on the first day of the Revolution. (Frothingham, Thomas G.—*Washington: Commander in Chief*, p. 107.)

3. Southern—Georgia, Carolinas, and Virginia.

> The war was over in Massachusetts before it was begun in New York and it was not begun in the South until it was finished in the middle colonies. (Muzzey, David S.—*History of the American People*, p. 130.)

a. Plan of British to save the South for their control.

b. Savannah; Charleston; Yorktown.
  (1) French Army and Navy.

4. Western.

> Clark conceived and executed a plan of campaign which entitles him to be called the Washington of the West. (Muzzey, David S.—*History of the American People*, p. 145.)
>
> No account of the Revolution—no matter how brief it may be—can omit the trials of the frontiersmen and the part they played in the conflict;

. . . (McLaughlin, Andrew C.—*History of the American Nation*, p. 171.)

a. Reference.

Roosevelt and Lodge—*Hero Tales from American History*, pp. 29-41.

5. Naval.

The injury to British commerce was sufficiently serious to aid materially in rendering the war unpopular in England; insurance rates rose to an unprecedented figure, and the available sources from which revenue might be derived by taxation were nearly exhausted. The shores of the British Isles were harassed as never before or since by the repeated visits of American naval cruisers and privateers, and the seacoast population alarmed. An active and regular commerce was carried on between the United States and continental Europe, providing the latter with American products and furnishing the new nation with much-needed money and supplies. . . .

Their [French and Spanish] naval supremacy, therefore, was most of the time potential only, although by no means for that reason without effect. It finally became actual and decisive at one critical juncture, when a fortunate train of circumstances secured the control of Chesapeake Bay. Fortunate, indeed, was this event for the American cause, for whose success the temporary possession of sea power was indispensable.

To revert, in conclusion, to the maritime achievements of the Revolutionists, it would appear that keeping open the intercourse with Continental Europe, especially France, and the diversion of supplies from the British to the American army, were the most valuable services performed by the American armed forces afloat, public and private, during the war; the injury done to the British navy being almost negligible, and to British commerce far from disabling, to say the least, although not without effect in the general result. It is certain that the Revolution would have failed without its sailors. (Allen, Gardner W.—*Naval History of the American Revolution*, Vol. II, pp. 665, 667-668.)

6. Maps of Principal Campaigns.

Maps in *Honor to George Washington*, No. 10 (*Washington the Military Man*).

The George Washington Atlas (See Unit XI—Geography).

7. References.

Allen, Gardner W.—*Naval History of the American Revolution*.

Avery, Elroy—*A History of the United States*, Vols. V-VI (Maps and Illustrations).

Frothingham, Thomas G.—*Washington: Commander in Chief*.

Mahan, A. T.—*Major Operations of Navies in War of American Independence*.

Van Tyne, Claude H.—*The Founding of the American Republic*, Vols. I-II.

D. Results.

1. Treaty of Peace, 1783.

On April 19, 1783, the eighth anniversary of the first fighting at Concord, a proclamation was issued [by Washington's general orders] to the American army announcing the official end of all hostilities. In June Washington issued a circular letter to the Governors of the States, bidding them farewell and urging them to guard their precious country. (Thayer, William R.—*George Washington*, p. 135.)

a. Terms of Treaty.

(1) Recognition of Independence of the Colonies.

(2) Boundaries.

(3) Fisheries.

(4) Debts.

(5) Loyalists.

2. Need for a Stronger Union.

a. Articles of Confederation, 1781-1789.

The United States were now independent, but the problems which confronted the American people were no less arduous of solution than the securing of their independence had been. (Channing, Edward—*Student's History of the United States*, rev. ed., p. 211.)

Now they had their freedom, but what a freedom! There were thirteen unrelated political communities bound together now only by the fact of having been united in their common struggle against England. Each had adopted a separate constitution, and the constitutions were not uniform nor was there any central unifying power to which they all looked up and obeyed. . . . What principle could be found to knit them together? (Thayer, William R.—*George Washington*, p. 127.)

E. Race Contributions to the American Revolution.

1. Reference.

Massachusetts George Washington Bicentennial Commission, Pamphlet No. 3 (Selected Authorities).

F. The Contributions Made by Women During the Revolution.

1. Service of Martha Washington.

. . . we know that at Valley Forge she worked day and night knitting socks, patching garments and making shirts for the loyal band of winter patriots who stood by their leader and their cause in the darkest hour of the Revolution. (Haworth, Paul L.—*George Washington, Country Gentleman*, pp. 221-222.)

And proud and happy were these veterans in again beholding their own good *Lady Washington*. Greatly was she beloved in the army—her many intercessions with the Chief for the pardon of offenders; her kindness to the sick and wounded—all of which caused her annual arrival in camp to be hailed as an event that would serve to dissipate the gloom of winter quarters. (Custis, George Washington Parke—*Recollections and Private Memoirs of Washington*, p. 63.)

2. Mary Ball Washington in Later Life—Program Four (*The Mother of George Washington*), No. 3.

With a restricted income, the first years of widowhood were spent on the farm, devoted to the care and training of her five children. Later she lived in Fredericksburg, honored by her son and honored as his mother.

3. The Origin of the Flag—The Betsy Ross Fiction.

a. References.

Johnson, Willis Fletcher—*The National Flag: a History*.

Preble, George Henry—*Origin and History of the American Flag*, Part III.

4. Abigail Adams—Her Service to the Cause.

5. References.

Adams, Charles F.—*Letters of Mrs. Adams, the Wife of John Adams*, Vols. I-II.

Ellet, Mrs. Elizabeth F.—*The Women of the American Revolution*, Vols. I-II.

Hart, Albert B.—*American History Told by Contemporaries*, Vol. II, pp. 467-468, Mrs. Esther Reed, "Woman's Work for the Soldiers."
Pryor, Mrs. Roger A.—*The Mother of Washington and Her Times.*

II. GEORGE WASHINGTON IN THE REVOLUTION.

With little genius, and not much natural aptitude for war, it was courage, noble character, the gift of inspiring confidence, and the ability to learn by experience which were, before the war's end, to place him [Washington] in the forefront among the leaders of men, safe and competent as a commander-in-chief. Even in the midst of his worst errors, his greatness, his magnanimity surmounts everything. (Van Tyne, Claude H.—*The War of Independence* (*The Founding of the American Republic*, Vol. II), p. 251.)

We should not overlook the fact that Washington declined all gifts, including a donation from Virginia, for his services as General during the war. He had refused to take any pay, merely keeping a strict account of what he spent for the Government from 1775 to . . . [1783]. This amounted to over . . . [£20,000] and covered only sums actually disbursed by him for the army. Unlike . . . foreign chieftains on whom grateful countrymen conferred fortunes and high titles, Washington remains as the one great state-founder who literally *gave* his services to his country. (Thayer, William R.—*George Washington*, p. 146.)

A. George Washington The Commander in Chief—Program Six (*George Washington The Man of Action in Military and Civil Life*), No. 3.

B. Washington's Relations to Congress (1775-1786)—*Honor to George Washington*, No. 6 (*Washington the Colonial and National Statesman*), Part II.

C. The Revolution to Valley Forge—*Honor to George Washington*, No. 10 (*Washington the Military Man*), Part II.

D. Valley Forge and Afterward—*Honor to George Washington*, No. 10 (*Washington the Military Man*), Part III.

1. The French Alliance.

E. Military Homes.

1. Military Headquarters—Program Two (*Homes of George Washington*), No. 5.

During the Revolution the many military headquarters in seven States were his homes.

2. War-Time Households—Program Twelve (*The Homemaking of George and Martha Washington*), No. 2.

Patriotism banned imported luxuries from Mount Vernon with the approach of the Revolution. Mrs. Washington's regular winter visits brightened the meager life of military households during the war.

3. Social Life in Later Years—Program Nine (*The Social Life of George Washington*), No. 3 (In Part—See Unit VII).

F. Resignation of Commission to Congress.

Congress was then in session at Annapolis, in Maryland, to which place General Washington repaired, for the purpose of resigning into their hands the authority with which they had invested him. . . .

To give more dignity to the act, they determined that it should be offered at a public audience on the following Tuesday, at twelve.

When the hour arrived for performing a ceremony so well calculated to recall the various interesting scenes which had passed since the commission now to be returned was granted, the gallery was crowded with spectators, and several persons of distinction were admitted on the floor of congress. The members remained seated and covered. The spectators were standing, and uncovered. The general was introduced by the secretary, and conducted to a chair. After a short pause, the president [General Mifflin] informed him that "The United States in congress assembled, were prepared to receive his communications." (Marshall, John—*The Life of George Washington*, Vol. IV, pp. 106-107.)

G. Recognitions for Services.

1. By the Government.

After advancing to the chair and delivering his commission to the president, he [Washington] returned to his place, and received standing the following answer of congress, which was delivered by the president:

"Sir,

"The United States in congress assembled, receive with emotions too affecting for utterance, the solemn resignation of the authorities under which you have led their troops with success through a perilous and a doubtful war. Called upon by your country to defend its invaded rights, you accepted the sacred charge, before it had formed alliances, and whilst it was without funds or a government to support you. You have conducted the great military contest with wisdom and fortitude, invariably regarding the rights of the civil power, through all disasters and changes. You have by the love and confidence of your fellow citizens, enabled them to display their martial genius, and transmit their fame to posterity. You have persevered until these United States, aided by a magnanimous king and nation, have been enabled under a just Providence, to close the war in freedom, safety, and independence; on which happy event we sincerely join you in congratulations.

"Having defended the standard of liberty in this new world, having taught a lesson useful to those who inflict and to those who feel oppression, you retire from the great theatre of action with the blessings of your fellow citizens. But the glory of your virtues will not terminate with your military command; it will continue to animate remotest ages.

"We feel with you our obligations to the army in general, and will particularly charge ourselves with the interests of those confidential officers who have attended your person to this affecting moment.

"We join you in commending the interests of our dearest country to the protection of Almighty God, beseeching him to dispose the hearts and minds of its citizens, to improve the opportunity afforded them of becoming a happy and respectable nation. And for you, we address to him our earnest prayers that a life so beloved, may be fostered with all his care; that your days may be as happy as they have been illustrious; and that he will finally give you that reward which this world cannot give." (Marshall, John—*The Life of George Washington*, Vol. IV, pp. 109-110.)

It was not by addresses alone that this country manifested its attachment to him. Soon after peace was proclaimed, congress unanimously passed a resolution for the erection of an equestrian statue of their general, at the place which should be established for the residence of the government. (Marshall, John—*The Life of George Washington*, Vol. IV, pp. 115-116.)

2. By the State of Virginia.

The legislature of Virginia too, at its first session after his resignation, passed the following resolution.

"Resolved, that the executive be requested to take measures for procuring a statue of General Washington, to be of the finest marble and best workmanship, with the following inscription on its pedestal:

"The general assembly of the commonwealth of Virginia have caused this statue to be erected as a monument of affection and gratitude to GEORGE WASHINGTON, who, uniting to the endowments of the HERO, the virtues of the PATRIOT, and exerting both in establishing the liberties of his country, has rendered his name dear to his fellow citizens, and given the world an immortal example of true glory." (Marshall, John—*The Life of George Washington*, Vol. IV, p. 116.)

H. Characteristics of George Washington Displayed in This Period.

1. Faith.

a. George Washington as a Christian: In Military Experiences—Program Seven (*George Washington the Christian*), No. 2.

As a military officer, George Washington gave to religious services their place in his commands. Realizing that through the stress and suffering of war men needed the support of their religious faith, he appealed for chaplains for the army. He attended church whenever war movements permitted.

But if you would know the depth and the intensity of the divine fire that burned within his breast you must go back to the dark and icy days of Valley Forge, . . . (Van Dyke, Henry—*The Americanism of Washington*, pp. 41-42.)

The Commander-in-Chief of the national armies was well aware that some of the cleverest, and all the least estimable, Congressmen were plotting his downfall with adroit and unscrupulous assiduity. They calumniated his motives. They disparaged his abilities. They deliberately withheld from him absolute necessities, while demanding of him utter impossibilities. Depressed and anxious, he was not perturbed out of measure, inasmuch as he believed himself to be in direct relations with an authority which was superior to Congress. (Trevelyan, Sir George O.—*The American Revolution*, Vol. IV, p. 301.)

2. Courage.

Physical and Moral.

Courage, physical and moral, was a part of his nature; and, whether in battle or in the midst of popular excitement, he was fearless of danger and regardless of consequences to himself. (Sparks, Jared—*The Life of George Washington*, p. 458.)

At all times and amid all conditions Washington rang true to the note of a splendid manhood. Hypocrisy and a trafficking in expedients for popular applause no more match with his life than the crime of murder. He had little of the captivating style of speech or manner; but regard for the nobility of his character, rather than any rhetorical art or charm of personal address on his part, kept wavering lines from retreat in battle and from mutiny amid privation and suffering to which our neglect had exposed the soldiers of the Revolution. (Underwood, Oscar—*The Career and the Words of Washington*, p. 12.) (State Society of Cincinnati, Philadelphia, Pa., February 22, 1912.)

Then came the horrors of Valley Forge and of the winters in Morris County. Those were the days when desertions were many and enlistments were few, when Washington dared not give open battle and there was hardly left to him a place for retreat. Then came the Conway conspiracy, and the ambition of Gates, and the cowardice of Lee and the treason of Arnold, and a series of persecutions so petty, so bitter, so malignant, that it is amazing how Washington survived them. Then, too, came defeats like that at Brandywine, and battles of uncertain meaning like that at Monmouth. . . .

It is easy for us as we read these events in the light of the issue to keep up our courage and understand the triumph that finally came, but it was a very different thing for Washington. Congress was weak, meddlesome, and vacillating. The soldiers were raw, undisciplined and sometimes mutinous. There were jealousies and libels and forgeries and slanders almost beyond our present ability to believe. . . . When I recall Washington's calmness in the midst of exasperating annoyances, his unselfish loyalty when surrounded by cupidity and jealousy and hatred, his faith that put courage into the hearts of men who marched hungry and left bloody footprints in the snow; when I remember how after eight years of this and more he emerged victorious, as calm in victory as he had been serene in defeat, I do not wonder that Frederick the Great is said to have pronounced George Washington's campaign in the Jerseys the most brilliant in military annals, . . . (Barton, William E.—*George Washington*.) (Address, Oak Park, Ill., February 22, 1920.)

Washington did not leave his men and go home to live in luxury, but stayed to endure privation with them. Only he who reads his letters written during these trying times can appreciate his troubles and anxieties. (McLaughlin, Andrew C.—*History of the American Nation*, p. 168.)

The personal courage of the man was very great. . . . The same carelessness of personal danger was shown all through the Revolution. At the battle of Brooklyn, on New York Island, at Trenton, Germantown, and Monmouth, he exposed himself to the enemy's fire, and at the siege of Yorktown an eyewitness relates that "during the assault, the British kept up an incessant firing of cannon and musketry from their whole line." (Ford, Paul L.—*George Washington*, pp. 269-270.)

3. Fortitude.

Behold him [George Washington] in 1775 taking leave of his family and his home, and hastening to the relief of a distant and then unknown part of America. See him transforming and cementing a band of rustics into an army. Follow him to the field of battle, and see him first in danger and last out of it. Go with him into Valley Forge, and see him sharing the hunger, the cold, the fatigue of every soldier in the camp. Was there ever such fortitude in adversity? Was there ever such moderation in the hour of victory? (McMaster, John B.—*History of the People of the United States*, Vol. I, p. 465.)

The national character is best represented by Washington. His patience and endurance, his ability to hold in check large forces with small armies imperfectly equipped, his power to keep the country up to the support of the war, mark him as one of the world's great military commanders. (Hart, Albert B.—*Formation of the Union*, p. 98.)

On only one point did there seem to be unanimity and accord. That was that the dogged prosecution of the war and the ultimate victory must be credited to George Washington. Others had fought valiantly and endured hardships and fatigues and gnawing suspense, but without him, who never wavered, they could not have gone on. (Thayer, William R.—*George Washington*, p. 128.)

The American Revolution from a military point of view was a group of little wars rather than a single war. The one integrating force was the person of the great commander, but George Washington held the army and the cause together by his exhaustless patience and courage rather than by any comprehensive plan of war. (Muzzey, David S.—*History of the American People*, p. 130.)

To Washington no duty, however obscure, was unimportant, and no deviation from duty, however trifling, was possible. (Hoar, George F.—*Washington*, p. 31.) (Chicago, February 23, 1903.)

4. Loyalty.
To an Ideal and Purpose.

Washington was an incorruptible patriot. He was one of the few rich men who was not a Tory. A very large proportion of men of large means sided with the British crown; nor must we too hastily condemn them. But Washington, who had more to lose than almost any other man in the thirteen colonies, was not blinded by vested interests, nor bound to conservative action by his wealth and station.

For the sake of the country which he loved he suffered innumerable hardships, was stung by ingratitude and hurt by slander, but he stood firm in his loyalty to the cause he had espoused, and was faithful to the end. (Barton, William E.—*George Washington*.) (Address, Oak Park, Ill., February 22, 1920.)

There is a life that is worth living now, as it was worth living in the former days, and that is the honest life, the useful life, the unselfish life, cleansed by devotion to an ideal. There is a battle that is worth fighting now, as it was worth fighting then, and that is the battle for justice and equality. To make our city and our State free in fact as well as in name; to break the rings that strangle real liberty, and to keep them broken; to cleanse, so far as in our power lies, the foundations of our national life from political, commercial, and social corruption; to teach our sons and daughters, by precept and example, the honor of serving such a country as America—that is work worthy of the finest manhood and womanhood. . . . The well educated are those who see deepest into the meaning and the necessity of that work. Nor shall their labor be for naught, nor the reward of their sacrifice fail them. For high in the firmament of human destiny are set the stars of faith in mankind, and unselfish courage, and loyalty to the ideal; and while they shine, the Americanism of Washington and the men who stood with him shall never, never die. (Van Dyke, Henry—*The Americanism of Washington*, pp. 70-72.)

5. Determination.
Surmounting All Difficulties to Reach the Goal.

The colonies, with their wealth and population, could have raised and equipped an army ten times as large as the force that Washington had at any time in the war. That he and his faithful comrades in arms achieved the victory in the face of these discouraging facts only entitles him to the greater glory. (Muzzey, David S.—*History of the American People*, pp. 130-131.)

Washington never delayed the announcements of his views to determine whether he was in the majority or minority. In this particular he was far from modern. Washington endeavored to secure the adoption of his convictions after a careful reflection on their sense, morals and patriotism. Having announced his opinions and conclusions, he set out to put them into concrete results. Washington spent

no time in proclaiming his own virtues; he was too busy being virtuous. (Hedges, Job E.—*Washington a Living Force*, p. 16.) (At Washington's Headquarters, Morristown, N. J., February 23, 1914.)

6. Magnanimity.

There are a hundred other points in Washington's career in which the same supremacy of character, magnanimity focussed on service to an ideal, is revealed in conduct. . . . I see it in the generosity with which he praised the achievements of his associates, disregarding jealous rivalries, and ever willing to share the credit of victory as he was to bear the burden of defeat. I see it in the patience with which he suffered his fame to be imperiled for the moment by reverses and retreats, if only he might the more surely guard the frail hope of ultimate victory for his country. I see it in the quiet dignity with which he faced the Conway Cabal, not anxious to defend his own reputation and secure his own power, but nobly resolute to save the army from being crippled and the cause of liberty from being wrecked. I see it in the splendid self-forgetfulness which cleansed his mind of all temptation to take personal revenge upon those who had sought to injure him in that base intrigue. I read it in his letter of consolation and encouragement to the wretched Gates after the defeat at Camden. I hear the prolonged reechoing music of it in his letter to General Knox in 1798, in regard to military appointments, declaring his wish to "avoid feuds with those who are embarked in the same general enterprise with myself."

Listen to the same spirit as it speaks in his circular address to the governors of the different States, urging them to "forget their prejudices and policies; to make those mutual concessions which are requisite to the general prosperity, and in some instances to sacrifice their individual advantages to the interest of the community." Watch how it guides him unerringly through the critical period of American History which lies between the success of the Revolution and the establishment of the nation, enabling him to avoid the pitfalls of sectional and partisan strife, and to use his great influence with the people in leading them out of the confusion of a weak confederacy into the strength of an indissoluble union of sovereign states. (Van Dyke, Henry—*The Americanism of Washington*, pp. 34-38.)

Washington never worried about whether other men appreciated him. He tried to have them appreciate the Republic and do their duty toward it in the light of their conscience, as he was trying to do. There is no difficulty about being a hero when the band is playing. There is no trouble about being good when your best friends are looking on. (Hedges, Job E.—*Washington a Living Force*, p. 20.) (At Washington's Headquarters, Morristown, N. J., February 23, 1914.)

7. Humility.
Cause Before Personal Ambition.

What was it that secured for them a long, unbroken opportunity of development in the activities of leadership, until they reached the summit of their perfection? It was a moral quality. It was the evident magnanimity of the man, which assured the people that he was no self-seeker who would betray their interests for his own glory or rob them for his own gain. It was the supreme magnanimity of the man, which made the best spirits of the time trust him implicitly, in war and peace, as one who would never forget his duty or his integrity in the sense of his own greatness.

From the first, Washington appears not as a man aiming at prominence or power, but rather as one under obligation to serve a cause. Necessity was laid upon him, and he met it willingly. After Washington's marvelous escape from death in his first campaign for the defense of the colonies, the Rev. Samuel Davies, fourth president of Princeton College, spoke of him in a sermon as "that heroic youth, Colonel Washington, whom I can but hope Providence has hitherto preserved in so signal a manner for some important service to his country." It was a prophetic voice, and Washington was not disobedient to the message. Chosen to command the Army of the Revolution in 1775, he confessed to his wife his deep reluctance to surrender the joys of home, acknowledged publicly his feeling that he was not equal to the great trust committed to him, and then, accepting it as thrown upon him "by a kind of destiny," he gave himself body and soul to its fulfilment, refusing all pay beyond the mere discharge of his expenses, of which he kept a strict account, and asking no other reward than the success of the cause which he served. . . .

I am sick of the shallow judgment that ranks the worth of a man by his poverty or by his wealth at death. Many a selfish speculator dies poor. Many an unselfish patriot dies prosperous. It is not the possession of the dollar that cankers the soul, it is the worship of it. The true test of a man is this: Has he labored for his own interest, or for the general welfare? Has he earned his money fairly or unfairly? Does he use it greedily or generously? What does it mean to him, a personal advantage over his fellow-men, or a personal opportunity of serving them? (Van Dyke, Henry—*The Americanism of Washington*, pp. 24-27, 33-34.)

Little happens in this country wrongly that does not happen by default. If something transpires, the advantage of which is not confirmed in the mind of the community as beneficial, it takes but a moment's reflection to see that it could have been prevented in the beginning, had the community been alert to existing conditions. The result is that we are prone to dodge responsibility and place it upon others. The further result of this tendency is that we frequently become more dedicated to personalities than to issues. The life of Washington can well be studied in this respect. He never shifted responsibility. He never made the conduct of others an excuse for a change in his own. He did criticise. He did comment adversely. He did endeavor to hold others up to their full share of responsibility, but while doing so never rested for a moment in his own endeavor to accomplish what he thought was for the best interest of the young republic. I have never read a single line whereby he shifted in taking responsibility for an act done by a subordinate. He may have explained, but he never side-stepped. Washington never lost his nerve. He never lost his courage. He was downcast at times; he was depressed, but he never lost control of himself and never failed to be resilient. With all his greatness fundamentally he was "just like folks." If he had not been "just like folks" the Republic might not have succeeded. (Hedges, Job E.—*Washington a Living Force*, pp. 13-14.) (At Washington's Headquarters, Morristown, N. J., February 23, 1914.)

8. Self-Control.
Master of Himself.

The chief thought that runs through all the say-

ings is to practice self-control, and no man ever displayed that most difficult of virtues to such a degree as George Washington. (Lodge, Henry C.— *George Washington (American Statesmen)*, Vol. I, p. 51.)

Solitude, indeed, is the last quality that an intelligent student of his career would ascribe to him. Dignified and reserved he was, undoubtedly; and as this manner was natural to him, he won more true friends by using it than if he had disguised himself in a forced familiarity and worn his heart upon his sleeve. But from first to last he was a man who did his work in the bonds of companionship, who trusted his comrades in the great enterprise even though they were not his intimates, and who neither sought nor occupied a lonely eminence of unshared glory. (Van Dyke, Henry—*The Americanism of Washington*, pp. 4-5.)

His passions were strong, and sometimes they broke out with vehemence, but he had the power of checking them in an instant. Perhaps self-control was the most remarkable trait of his character. It was in part the effect of his discipline; yet he seems by nature to have possessed the power to a degree which has been denied to other men. (Sparks, Jared—*The Life of George Washington*, p. 460.)

9. Leadership.
Ability to Handle Men.

More familiar is his extraordinary work in keeping the little army of the infant Republic together in the seven years of the war, and under circumstances such as never before tried any military leader. He was obliged to be at once its civil administrator as well as its Commander-in-Chief, and only Washington could ever have brought the epic struggle to a successful issue. (Beck, James M.— *The Washington Tradition and Our Foreign Policy*, p. 8.)

Was it in any sense a misfortune for the people of America, even the poorest among them, that there was a man able to advance sixty-four thousand dollars out of his own purse, with no other security but his own faith in their cause, to pay his daily expenses while he was leading their armies? This unsecured loan was one of the very things, I doubt not, that helped to inspire general confidence. (Van Dyke, Henry—*The Americanism of Washington*, pp. 28-29.)

Soldiering is not all fighting nor all marching. It begins with the people at home who furnish the recruits and the arms, the food, the clothing, and hospital supplies (little enough in the Revolution). It is not too much to say that the Revolutionary War was virtually won by the weak and ill-provided American force at Valley Forge in 1778, three years before the surrender of Cornwallis; because that experience proved that enough men believed in Washington and stood by him to keep the British inactive in Philadelphia until the colonial force could get its breath again and take the offensive. The American victory is a proof that Washington was a great soldier, for without him the victory would have gone the other way. (Hart, Albert B.— *George Washington (Reading with a Purpose*, No. 42), p. 16.)

The problem of the Revolution was not one of military strategy, but of keeping an army in existence, and it was in this that the commander-in-chief's great ability showed itself. The British could and did repeatedly beat the Continental army, but they could not beat the General, and so long as he was in the field there was a rallying ground for whatever fighting spirit there was. (Ford, Paul L.—*George Washington*, p. 279.)

III. SIGNIFICANT DATES Selected from *George Washington Year by Year*.

1775—Colonel Washington was field officer of the Independent Companies in several counties in Virginia.

1775, Feb. 20—Colonel Washington was elected member of Second Provincial Convention for Fairfax County.

1775, Mar. 20-27—Colonel Washington attended the Virginia convention assembled in St. John's Church, Richmond. Colonel Washington was elected to the Second Continental Congress.

1775, May 10—The Second Continental Congress assembled in the State House (Independence Hall), Philadelphia; John Hancock was elected president on Randolph's departure. June 15, on John Adams' nomination, Colonel George Washington, of Virginia, was elected "General and Commander in Chief of the Army of the United Colonies"; accepted June 16; commissioned June 19.

1775, June 23-July 2—General Washington made the journey to Cambridge.

1775, July 3—The new commander in chief took command of the Continental forces besieging Boston.

1776, Jan. 18—Colonel Henry Knox completed the task of bringing 59 cannon weighing 124,000 pounds on 42 sleds over the mountains from Ticonderoga to the Cambridge lines.

1776, Mar. 4—General Washington fortified Dorchester Heights, which made the British position in Boston untenable.

1776, Mar. 17—General Washington occupied Boston on its evacuation by the British the same day.

1776, Apr. 3—General Washington received degree of LL. D., which Harvard College conferred.

1776, Apr. 4-13—General Washington journeyed to New York to start plans to strengthen the place before the anticipated British attack.

1776, June 29—The long-expected arrival of the British forces began. Within a week General Howe, the British commander, established headquarters on Staten Island.

1776, July 9—General Washington received from Congress the Declaration of Independence, and at 6 o'clock that evening the regiments were paraded and the document read to them.

1776, Aug. 27—The Battle of Long Island took place; the Americans were defeated. General Washington then led the retreat across the East River. He transported 9,000 men and military stores to New York by boats without the enemy discovering the retreat.

1776, Sept. 12—The American evacuation of New York City was decided upon. Afterward General Washington established headquarters on Harlem Heights, moving later to White Plains.

1776, Oct. 28—The Battle of White Plains was fought. The English effected a lodgment in one American position, but were not able to follow it up.

1776, Nov. 16—The surrender of Fort Washington, followed by the abandonment of Fort Lee November 21, on the western side of the Hudson River, was followed by the retreat of the Americans across New Jersey.

1776, Dec. 8—General Washington crossed the Delaware River into Pennsylvania with his decimated force, securing all the boats.

1776, Dec. 25-26—On Christmas night General Washington led his army across the Delaware River amid the ice, surprised the British, and secured the victory of Trenton.

1777, Jan. 3—General Washington's sudden attack on Princeton resulted in another victory, followed by an advance across New Jersey and establishment of winter quarters at Morristown.

1777, Aug. 2—General Washington was at Philadelphia, his army in the neighborhood awaiting news of Howe's landing place, which was made at the Head of the Elk.

1777, Sept. 11—The Battle of Brandywine took place following Howe's advance from the Chesapeake. The Americans were forced to retreat.

1777, Sept. 26—General Howe entered Philadelphia and established his winter quarters.

1777, Oct. 4—The battle of Germantown took place. Washington's plan of attack was frustrated by fog and mistakes, and the Americans were repulsed.

1777, Oct. 17—Surrender of Burgoyne's army at Saratoga, made possible by Washington's position on the flank of Clinton's army.

1777, Dec. 19—General Washington established the army in winter quarters at Valley Forge, where great suffering was experienced. General Steuben introduced new drill and organization into the army.

1778, May 6—General Washington announced the French alliance to the army.

1778, June 18—The British, under Sir Henry Clinton, Howe's successor, evacuated Philadelphia. They retired across New Jersey, with General Washington's forces in pursuit.

1778, June 28—The battle of Monmouth took place. General Washington turned retreat into victory by personally leading his men. General Lee was rebuked in the field by General Washington.

1778, Dec. 11—General Washington established winter quarters at Middlebrook, N. J., on the Raritan.

1779—General Washington's headquarters during the summer and fall were at New Windsor and West Point, N. Y. In December they were moved to Morristown, N. J., for six months.

1780, Jan. 19—General Washington was elected member of the American Philosophical Society at Philadelphia. He accepted on February 15 and his membership certificate was dated March 22.

1780, July—French fleet and army under Rochambeau arrived at Newport, R. I.

1780, Sept. 21—General Washington and Count de Rochambeau met in conference at Hartford, Conn., to make preliminary arrangements for the future campaign.

1780, Dec. 6—Winter headquarters were established at New Windsor, N. Y.

1781, Mar. 2-20—General Washington made a trip to Newport to have a consultation with the French.

1781, Apr. 26—General Washington was given degree of LL. D., by Yale College; diploma dated September 12.

1781, May 22—Conference with Rochambeau at Wethersfield, Conn.; attack on New York planned. Armies joined July 6, but plan abandoned.

1781, Aug.—Cornwallis's British army, following a Virginia campaign with Lafayette and Steuben, established its base at Yorktown.

1781, Aug. 14—General Washington learned of the intention of Count de Grasse to bring his fleet to the Chesapeake.

1781, Aug. 19—General Washington and Rochambeau began their joint march to Virginia.

1781, Sept. 5—De Grasse prevented the British fleet under Admiral Graves from aiding Cornwallis.

1781, Sept. 9-12—General Washington on the march stopped at Mount Vernon for the first time since May 4, 1775.

1781, Sept. 28—The siege of Yorktown began.

1781, Oct. 19—Cornwallis surrendered his whole army. The American Army returned to the Hudson River, but the French remained in Virginia until the latter part of 1782, when they marched to Boston and embarked. Washington spent the winter at Philadelphia.

1782, May 22—General Washington emphatically rejected a proposal of Kingship.

1782, Aug. 18—Washington College at Chestertown, Md., named the college for General Washington. He accepted the honor.

1783, Mar. 15—General Washington made a stirring reply to the Newburgh address, quieting the officers' demand for redress before the army was disbanded.

1783, Apr. 19—Cessation of hostilities proclaimed.

1783, May 8—General Washington dined on board a British warship with General Carleton; saluted with seventeen guns as high official of an independent nation.

1783, June 8—General Washington sent a circular letter to the States, pointing out the dangers and needs of the country with the return of peace.

1783, June 19—General Washington was elected President General of the newly organized Society of the Cincinnati.

1783, July 4—General Washington received degree of LL. D. from University of Pennsylvania.

1783, July 18-Aug. 5—General Washington made a tour through the Hudson and Mohawk regions with Governor George Clinton, observing the possibilities of the Mohawk navigation—the future Erie Canal route.

1783, Aug. 25-Nov. 9—General Washington had his headquarters near Princeton so as to be able to confer with Congress on "arrangements for peace and public concerns."

1783, Nov. 2—General Washington made his Farewell Address to the army.

1783, Nov. 25—General Washington reentered New York. This was a gala day as the British troops evacuated the city and embarked for England.

1783, Nov. 27—General Washington was made honorary member of Marine Society of New York; certificate dated November 28.

1783, Dec. 4—General Washington, at Fraunces's Tavern, New York City, bade his officers farewell.

1783, Dec. 23—General Washington resigned his commission to Congress assembled in the statehouse at Annapolis.

WASHINGTON CROSSING THE DELAWARE
From a painting by George Harding

Unit V
George Washington a Private Citizen Immediately Following the Revolution

WASHINGTON FAMILY
Painting by Thomas P. Rossiter (1817-1871)

Brief Outline

I. RETIREMENT TO MOUNT VERNON FOLLOWING RESIGNATION OF COMMISSION TO CONGRESS.

II. ACTIVITIES.

  A. As a Farmer.

    1. *George Washington the Farmer.*

    2. *Land and Crops and Stock.*

    3. *Organization and Labor.*

  B. As a Business Man.

    1. *George Washington, the Business Man and Engineer.*

    2. *George Washington, Engineer.*

    3. *The Promoter and Planter.*

    4. *The Business Organizer.*

  C. *George Washington, the Citizen.*

III. SOCIAL LIFE AT MOUNT VERNON.

  A. Week Days.

  B. Sundays.

    1. *George Washington as a Christian.*

    2. *George Washington and Religion.*

    3. *Washington's Own Words on Religion*

IV. FRATERNAL RELATIONS.

  A. *Fraternal Life.*

  B. *Academic, Municipal, and Fraternal Honors Held by George Washington.*

V. MAN OF LETTERS.

  A. Personal Writings.

    1. Diaries.

    2. *Literary Records.*

    3. *Washington Sayings.*

    4. Correspondence.

    5. Business Books.

      a. *Washington's Business Records.*

    6. The Writings of George Washington—Edited by John C. Fitzpatrick.

  B. Scientific Writings.

    1. Engineering.

      a. *George Washington, Engineer.*

      b. *George Washington: Leader in Advancement of of Civilization.*

    2. Agriculture.

      a. *Washington's Scientific Farm Methods.*

    3. Education.

      a. *Practical Education.*

      b. *George Washington: Patron of Education.*

      c. Washington's Words on a National University as Found in His Will.

VI. SIGNIFICANT DATES.

NOTE: *Topics in italics are titles of 48 papers in a series of 12 George Washington Programs and the parts of the Honor to George Washington series of 15 pamphlets issued by the United States George Washington Bicentennial Commission.*

Development

I. RETIREMENT TO MOUNT VERNON FOLLOWING RESIGNATION OF COMMISSION.

He returned from the Revolution with a strong desire to beautify his estate, a desire in part due no doubt to seeing beautiful homes elsewhere and to contact with cultured people, both Americans and foreigners. One of his first tasks was to rebuild and enlarge his house. From a small house of eight rooms he transformed Mount Vernon into the present large mansion, ninety-six feet and four inches long by thirty-two feet in depth, with two floors and an attic, an immense cellar and the magnificent portico overlooking the Potomac. The plans and specifications he drew with his own hands, . . . The flagstones for the floor of the portico he imported from

Whitehaven, England, and these still remain in place, though many are cracked or broken. (Haworth, Paul L.—*George Washington, Country Gentleman*, pp. 151-152.)

Though invited to visit France, the demands of his private affairs would not permit his absence. He returned to Mount Vernon at Christmas time. By March he was making his plans, and the day after the departure of Lafayette, September 1st, he was off for the West. It was ostensibly to look after his Western lands, of which he had then 40,000 acres, but he was only three days out when he wrote in his diary that the one object of his journey was to obtain information of the nearest and best communication—I am quoting his language—"to obtain information of the nearest and best communication between the Eastern and Western waters and to facilitate, as much as in him [me] lay, the inland navigation of the Potomac; . . ." (Finley, John H.—*Washington and the West*, p. 11.) (Address, Morristown, N. J., February 22, 1925.)

II. ACTIVITIES.

After all, the most fascinating facts about Washington are not those concerned with his public achievements but with the man himself—"the many-sided Washington." His versatility challenges us, for he was an exceptional farmer, a good business man, explorer, engineer, a founder of corporations, an organizer of armies, a great commander, a great president, and a great statesman. (Hart, Albert B.—*George Washington* (*Reading with a Purpose*, No. 42), p. 11.)

A. As a Farmer.

Nor was his enthusiasm for agriculture the evanescent enthusiasm of the man who in middle age buys a farm as a plaything and tries for the first time the costly experiment of cultivating the soil. He was born on a plantation, was brought up in the country and until manhood he had never even seen a town of five thousand people. . . . he was one of the first American experimental agriculturists, always alert for better methods, willing to take any amount of pains to find the best fertilizer, the best way to avoid plant diseases, the best methods of cultivation, and he once declared that he had little patience with those content to tread the ruts their fathers trod. If he were alive to-day, we may be sure that he would be an active worker in farmers' institutes, an eager visitor to agricultural colleges, a reader of scientific reports and an enthusiastic promoter of anything tending to better American farming and farm life. (Haworth, Paul L.—*George Washington, Country Gentleman*, pp. 3, 6-7.)

1. George Washington the Farmer—Program Six (*George Washington the Man of Action in Military and Civil Life*), No. 4.
2. Land and Crops and Stock—*Honor to George Washington*, No. 4 (*Washington the Farmer*), Part I.
3. Organization and Labor—*Honor to George Washington*, No. 4 (*Washington the Farmer*), Part II.

The bent of our Farmer's mind was to the practical, yet he took pride in the appearance of his estate. "I shall begrudge no reasonable expense that will contribute to the improvement and neatness of my farms," he wrote one of his managers, "for nothing pleases me better than to see them in good order, and everything trim, handsome, and thriving about them; nor nothing hurts me more than to find them otherwise." (Haworth, Paul L.—*George Washington, Country Gentleman*, pp. 161-162.)

B. As a Business Man.

Washington was the most methodical man that ever lived. He had a place for everything and insisted that everything should be kept in its place. There was nothing haphazard about his methods of business. He kept exact accounts of financial dealings.

His habit of setting things down on paper was one that developed early. (Haworth, Paul L.—*George Washington, Country Gentleman*, p. 76.)

1. George Washington the Business Man and Engineer—Program Six (*George Washington the Man of Action in Military and Civil Life*), No. 5.

With a vision far beyond his day George Washington sought to promote all enterprises that developed transportation and communication between the seaboard and the frontiers. Every business project for the advancement of commerce and colonization had his support.

2. George Washington, Engineer—*Honor to George Washington*, No. 13 (*Washington as Engineer and City Builder*), Part I.

. . . but Washington was, in a sense, the first great American, because, having freed the Colonies, he was the first to realize the importance of tying that Great Valley of the Western waters to the East and making a unity of what might have become two nations divided by the lateral range, or perhaps three, with the Rocky Mountain barrier for another boundary, as in Europe; or, perchance a group of little American Balkans. He was the original expansionist; not only the father of his country, but the "prophet of the West." (Finley, John H.—*Washington and the West*, p. 8.) (Address, Morristown, N. J., February 22, 1925.)

3. The Promoter and Planter—*Honor to George Washington*, No. 12 (*Washington the Business Man*), Part III.
4. The Business Organizer—*Honor to George Washington*, No. 12 (*Washington the Business Man*), Part IV.

He was a man of private enterprise, the equal of our greatest business magnates in his vision and capacity. He built the first grist mill the other side of the mountains. (Finley, John H.—*Washington and the West*, p. 12.) (Address, Morristown, N. J., February 22, 1925.)

A few years later, when his large sagacity perceived that the development of internal commerce was one of the first needs of the new country, at a time when he held no public office, he became president of a company for the extension of navigation on the . . . Potomac. The Legislature of Virginia proposed to give him a hundred and fifty shares of stock. Washington refused this, or any other kind of pay, saying that he could serve the people better in the enterprise if he were known to have no selfish interest in it. He was not the kind of a man to reconcile himself to a gratuity (which is the Latinized word for a "tip" offered to a person not in livery), and if the modern methods of "coming in on the ground-floor" and "taking a rake-off" had been explained and suggested to him, I suspect that he would have described them in language more notable for its force than for its elegance. (Van Dyke, Henry—*The Americanism of Washington*, pp. 31-32.)

The situation confronting "Farmer Washington" was this: He had a great abundance of land, but most of it on his home estate was mediocre in quality. Some of that lying at a distance was more fertile, but much of it was uncleared and that on the Ohio was hopelessly distant from a market. With the exception of Mount Vernon even those plantations in Virginia east of the Blue Ridge could not be looked after in person. He must either rent them, trust them to a manager, or allow them to lie idle. Even the Mount Vernon land was distant from a good market, and the cost of transportation was so great that he must produce for selling purposes articles of little bulk compared with value. Finally, he had an increasing number of slaves for whom food and clothing must be provided. (Haworth, Paul L.—*George Washington, Country Gentleman*, p. 67.)

C. George Washington the Citizen—Program Six (*George Washington the Man of Action in Military and Civil Life*, No. 6.

> As a citizen George Washington had many interests and affiliations. He gave long and constructive service as a burgess, became a Freemason before he was of age, and was pleased and proud of his chancellorship of William and Mary. Education with him was more than a hobby—it was a passion.

III. SOCIAL LIFE AT MOUNT VERNON.
A. Week Days.

> About sunrise, General Washington invariably visited and inspected his stables. He was very fond of horses, and his equipages were always of a superior order. The horses which he rode, in the war of Independence, were said to be superb. . . . The library, and a visit to the stables, occupied the morning till the hour of breakfast: this meal was without change to him, whose habits were regular, even to matters which others are so apt to indulge themselves in, to endless variety. Indian cakes, honey and tea, formed this temperate repast. On rising from table, if there were guests, and it was seldom otherwise, books and paper were offered for their amusement; they were requested to take good care of themselves, and the illustrious farmer proceeded to the daily tour of his agricultural concerns. He rode upon his farms entirely unattended, opening his gates, pulling down and putting up his fences, as he passed, visiting his laborers at their work, inspecting all the operations of his extensive agricultural establishments with a careful eye, directing useful improvements, and superintending them in their progress. . . . The tour of the farms might average from ten to fifteen miles per day. . . .
>
> The afternoon was usually devoted to the library. At night, his labors o'er, the venerable citizen would join his family and friends at the tea-table, and enjoy their society for several hours—took no supper, and about nine o'clock retired to bed. When without company, he frequently read to his family extracts from the new publications of the day, and, on Sunday, sermons and other sacred writings. He read with distinctness and precision, though with a voice, the tones of which had been considerably broken by a pulmonary affection in early life, and which, when greatly excited, produced a laboring of the chest. He would frequently, when sitting with his family, appear absent; his lips would move, his hand be raised, and he would evidently seem under the influence of thoughts, which had nothing to do with the quiescent scene around him. This peculiarity is readily accounted for, since it must be no very easy matter for one who so long had borne the cares of public life, at once to lay aside all thought for others, and become content with individual concerns.

MUSIC ROOM, MOUNT VERNON, VA.

> In winter, when stress of weather prevented his taking his usual exercise, he was in the habit of walking for an hour in the portico, before retiring to rest. As the eastern portico of the Mansion House is more than ninety feet in length, his walk would comprise several miles. (Custis, George Washington Parke—*Recollections and Private Memoirs of Washington*, pp. 6-9.)
>
> For several months after arriving at Mount Vernon, almost every day brought him the addresses of an affectionate and grateful people. The glow of expression in which the high sense universally entertained of his services was conveyed, manifested the warmth of feeling which animated the American bosom. This unexampled tribute of voluntary applause, paid by a whole people, to an individual no longer in power, made no impression on the unassuming modesty of his character and deportment. . . . The same firmness of mind, the same steady and well tempered judgment, which had guided him through the most perilous seasons of the war, still regulated his conduct; . . . (Marshall, John—*The Life of George Washington*, Vol. IV, pp. 114-115.)

B. Sundays.

> General Washington was always a strict and decorous observer of the Sabbath. . . . His respect to the clergy, as a body, was shown by public entertainments to them, the same as to the Corps Legislative and Diplomatic, and among his bosom friends were the venerable Bishop of Pennsylvania and the late excellent prelate and ardent friend of American liberty, Dr. Carroll, Archbishop of Baltimore. (Custis, George Washington Parke—*Recollections and Private Memoirs of Washington*, p. 9.)

1. George Washington as a Christian: Revealed Religious Convictions—Program Seven (*George Washington the Christian*), No. 3.

> No one can read the diaries or writings of George Washington without being impressed with his unfailing faith in Divine guidance and care. For his escapes he gave thanks to God, and for his victories and successes he gave the tribute of gratitude to Divine dispensation.

2. George Washington and Religion—*Honor to George Washington*, No. 5 (*Washington as a Religious Man*), Part I.

3. Washington's Own Words on Religion—*Honor to George Washington*, No. 5 (*Washington as a Religious Man*), Part II.

IV. FRATERNAL RELATIONS.

A. Fraternal Life—*Honor to George Washington*, No. 14 (*Washington's Home and Fraternal Life*), Part II.

B. Academic, Municipal, and Fraternal Honors Held by George Washington—*Honor to George Washington*, No. 2 (*Washington The Man of Mind*), Part IV.

V. MAN OF LETTERS.

We are accustomed to leave out of account one of the most important phases of Washington's service to this country. Though he had very little schooling, he probably wrote more than any other man of his time in America (not even excepting Franklin). Much of this has been published and is now open to the world. He kept his papers carefully so that we have his earliest letters and documents, well spelled for the time, though some modern detractors, who call themselves biographers, would like to send him back to the primary grades.

We may truly say that if by "literary" man we mean a man who has great thoughts and expresses them in a clear, lucid, broad, and intellectual way, then Washington deserves a high place in the academy of American literary men. (Hart, Albert B.— *George Washington* (*Reading with a Purpose*, No. 42), pp. 19-20.)

A. Personal Writings.

All told, according to Mr. Gaillard Hunt, who has them in charge, the Washington manuscripts in the Library of Congress is the largest collection of papers of one person in the world. The collection contains . . . [eight or ten thousand] papers in his own hand, press copies, or drafts in the writing of his secretaries, and many times that number of others. (Haworth, Paul L.—*George Washington, Country Gentleman*, p. 87.)

1. Diaries.

At present there are forty original diaries known to be in existence; thirty-six of these came into the possession of the Government when the Washington Papers were purchased from the family in 1834 and 1849, and are now, with those Papers, in the Library of Congress. . . .

It seems unlikely that the diary habit became confirmed until Washington was nearly forty years old, and it is altogether probable that his early diaries were kept only as records of special and unusual times, such as the trip to Barbadoes in 1751-52. . . . The inference is strong that no personal diaries were kept during the years 1755-59. . . .

There is abundant evidence that Washington's method in keeping his diary was to make rough memoranda of the day's occurrences upon loose slips, or improvised notebooks of a few leaves stitched together, and, later, sometimes some days later to copy out these rough notes into a permanent diary record. . . .

Ruled paper was unknown in America during Washington's lifetime and his invariable regularity of line spacing was obtained by means of a heavily ruled guide-sheet (which he made himself) beneath his writing-paper; he followed this plan in copying out his diaries. . . .

The value of the diaries as an historical record is such that it is greatly to be regretted that any

of them should be missing, or unavailable. As a whole they constitute a most remarkable record of a remarkable man. (*The Diaries of George Washington, 1748-1799*, ed. by John C. Fitzpatrick, Vol. I, Introduction, pp. vii-x.)

2. Literary Records—*Honor to George Washington*, No. 2 (*Washington The Man of Mind*), Part II.

3. Washington Sayings—*Honor to George Washington*, No. 2 (*Washington The Man of Mind*), Part III.

4. Correspondence.

a. Facsimile of a George Washington Letter—*Honor to George Washington*, No. 2 (*Washington The Man of Mind*).

Washington soon found the greatest of his burdens—letter-writing. His correspondence increased rapidly and to an enormous extent. (Thayer, William R.—*George Washington*, p. 147.)

5. Business Books.

Washington also kept cash memorandum books, general account books, mill books, and a special book in which he recorded his accounts with the estate of the Custis children. These old books, written in his neat, legible hand, are not only one of our chief sources of information concerning his agricultural and financial affairs but contain many sidelights upon historical events. (Haworth, Paul L.—*George Washington, Country Gentleman*, p. 81.)

a. Washington's Business Records—*Honor to George Washington*, No. 12 (*Washington The Business Man*), Part II.

6. The Writings of George Washington—Edited by John C. Fitzpatrick.

B. Scientific Writings.

1. Engineering.

a. George Washington, Engineer—*Honor to George Washington*, No. 13 (*Washington as Engineer and City Builder*), Part I.

b. George Washington: Leader in Advancement of Civilization—Program Eight (*George Washington The Leader of Men*), No. 2.

In occupations, exact surveys, rotation of crops, diversified industry; in public affairs, a self-controlling central government and the development of the West through it; in life, exact justice for himself and others, temperance, wide reading, rational pleasure—these were elements in Washington's stand for progress.

2. Agriculture.

Throughout his entire life Washington kept a record of the weather as an aid, apparently, to his agricultural activities; . . . (*The Diaries of George Washington*, ed. by John C. Fitzpatrick, Vol. I, Introduction, p. xi.)

Washington's correspondence on agricultural matters with Arthur Young and Sir John Sinclair, eminent English agriculturists, was collected soon after his death in a volume that is now rare. In it are a number of letters written by other American farmers, including Thomas Jefferson, relative to agriculture in their localities. These letters were the result of inquiries made of Washington by Young in 1791. In order to obtain the facts desired Washington sent out a circular letter to some of the most intelligent farmers in the Middle States, and the replies form perhaps our best source of information regarding agricultural conditions in that period. . .

Some of Washington's other agricultural papers have been printed in one form and another, but a great number, and some the most interesting, can still be consulted only in manuscript. (Haworth, Paul L.—*George Washington, Country Gentleman,* pp. 83-84.)

a. Washington's Scientific Farm Methods—*Honor to George Washington,* No. 4 (*Washington the Farmer*), Part III.

3. Education.

Washington was the firm friend of American education. (Barton, William E.—*George Washington.*) (Address, Oak Park, Ill., February 22, 1920.)

a. Practical Education—*Honor to George Washington,* No. 2 (*Washington The Man of Mind*), Part I.

b. George Washington: Patron of Education—Program Eight (*George Washington The Leader of Men*), No. 1.

George Washington, always regretful of his own lack of formal training, throughout his life advocated education and by his will sought to establish for our country such a university as he thought would develop good Americans.

Washington bequeathed his books and papers, along with his Mansion House, to his nephew, Bushrod Washington, an associate justice of the Federal Supreme Court. . . .

Bushrod Washington died in 1829 and left the papers and letter books for the most part to his nephew, . . . [George] Corbin Washington. In 1834 the Nation purchased of this gentleman the papers of a public character, paying twenty-five thousand dollars. The owner reserved the private papers, including invoices, ciphering book, rules of civility, etc., but in 1849 sold these also to the same purchaser for twenty thousand dollars. The papers were kept for many years in the Department of State, but in the administration of Theodore Roose-

velt most of them were transferred to the Library of Congress, where they could be better cared for and would be more accessible. (Haworth, Paul L.—*George Washington, Country Gentleman,* pp. 84-85.)

c. Washington's Words on a National University as Found in His Will (Unit VIII).

VI. SIGNIFICANT DATES Selected from *George Washington Year by Year*—(See Dates given in Unit VI).

1783, Dec. 25—General and Mrs. Washington celebrated Christmas Day at Mount Vernon for the first time in seven years.

1784, Jan. 13—General Washington was made honorary member of Charleston (S. C.) Library Society.

1784, Sept. 1-Oct. 4—General Washington made a tour of his lands beyond the Alleghenies. He investigated the interlocking of Potomac and Ohio branch headwaters with a view to the establishment of an extensive navigation system.

1784, Dec. 2—General Washington was given freedom of City of New York.

1784, Dec. 20-29—General Washington attended the conference at Annapolis as the Virginia representative on the interstate control of Potomac River navigation.

1785, May 17—The Potomac Navigation Company was organized, with General Washington as president; operations began shortly after. This called for many trips of inspection.

1785, Dec. 17—General Washington, a trustee of the proposed Alexandria Academy, attended meeting. Academy was incorporated in 1786, with George Washington named as trustee until first annual election by supporters of the academy.

THE GARDENS AT MOUNT VERNON LAID OUT BY GEORGE WASHINGTON

Unit VI
George Washington a Leader in the "Critical Period" of American History (1783-1789)

INDEPENDENCE HALL, PHILADELPHIA

Brief Outline

I. ANTECEDENTS OF THE CONSTITUTION.
  A. Plans for Union Prior to the Revolution.
    1. New England Confederation.
    2. Albany Plan of Union.
    3. Stamp Act Congress.
    4. Intercolonial Committees of Correspondence.
    5. First Continental Congress.
  B. Plans for Union During and After the Revolution.
    1. Second Continental Congress.
    2. Declaration of Independence.
    3. Articles of Confederation.
      a. Origin and Nature.
      b. Adoption.
      c. Value.
      d. Defects.
      e. Results from Operation.
II. THE CONSTITUTIONAL CONVENTION.
  A. *Preliminaries of the Convention.*
    1. Commercial Conferences.
      a. Alexandria-Mount Vernon, 1785.
      b. Annapolis Convention, September, 1786.
  B. Meeting at Philadelphia.
  C. Organization and Membership.
    1. Representation of States.
    2. Delegates.
      a. Number.
      b. Character of Men.
    3. George Washington as Delegate and Presiding Officer.
    4. *Creation and Organization of a New Nation.*
  D. Work of the Convention.
    1. Debates in the Federal Convention as Reported by James Madison.
    2. The Great Compromises.
    3. Notes of Alexander Hamilton and Others in the Federal Convention of 1787.

4. *Results of the Convention.*
5. The Leading Features of the Constitution.
6. The Six Fundamental Principles of the Constitution —James M. Beck.
III. RATIFICATION OF THE CONSTITUTION (1787-1790).
  A. Difficulties Encountered.
  B. Public Discussion.
  C. The Federalist.
  D. Conventions and Ratification of the Constitution by the Several States.
IV. SIGNIFICANT DATES.

NOTE: *Topics in italics are titles of 48 papers in a series of 12 George Washington Programs and the parts of the Honor to George Washington series of 15 pamphlets issued by the United States George Washington Bicentennial Commission.*

Development

I. ANTECEDENTS OF THE CONSTITUTION.

The doubt, the drifting, the incongruities and inconsistencies, the mistakes and follies which marked the five years after 1783 form what has been well called "The Critical Period of American History." . . . Who should be the builders of the Ship of State? Those who had courage and clear vision, who loved justice, who were patient and humble and unflagging, and who believed with an ineluctable conviction that righteousness exalteth a nation; . . . (Thayer, William R.—*George Washington*, p. 151.)

A. Plans for Union Prior to the Revolution.
  1. New England Confederation, 1643.

In 1643, the four colonies of Massachusetts, Plymouth, Connecticut, and New Haven formed a confederation for purposes of defense in case of attacks or depredations by the Dutch on the Hudson, or the Indians. The name of the confederation was

"The United Colonies of New England." (Fiske, John—*History of the United States*, p. 107.)

2. Albany Plan of Union, 1754.

The long series of wars which came to an end in 1763 had tended to bring the several English colonies together. Frequently, it had been necessary to take combined action against the French and their Indian allies, and conferences had been held from time to time from 1684 onwards. The most famous of these meetings was the one held at Albany in 1754, and known as the Albany Congress; but the word "congress," as now used in America, is inapplicable; it was rather a conference or convention, in our political language. (Channing, Edward—*Student's History of the United States*, rev. ed., p. 119.)

In 1754, when the war with France was breaking out, several colonies sent delegates to a Congress at Albany, to insure the friendly aid of the Six Nations. Franklin was present at this Congress, and proposed a Plan of Union for the colonies. (Fiske, John—*History of the United States*, p. 187.)

A plan of union drafted by Benjamin Franklin . . . was adopted, providing for an appointed president-general and a council of elected representatives, with power over Indian affairs, military and naval affairs, public lands, and new settlements, and the right to make laws and levy taxes for these purposes. The colonies all rejected the plan because it limited their independent action, and the home government disapproved because it infringed too much on the royal prerogative. (Matteson, David M.—*Epitome of United States History*, p. 352.)

a. Reference.

Hart, Albert B.—*American History Told by Contemporaries*, Vol. II, pp. 357-360, Chief Justice Stephen Hopkins, "The Albany Plan of Union" (1754).

3. Stamp Act Congress, 1765.

On the 7th of October [1765], the proposed congress assembled at New York, comprising delegates from Massachusetts, South Carolina, Pennsylvania, Rhode Island, Connecticut, Delaware, Maryland, New Jersey, and New York, in all nine colonies, which are here mentioned in the order of the dates at which they chose their delegates. In Virginia, the governor succeeded in preventing the meeting of the legislature, so that this great colony did not send delegates; and for various reasons, New Hampshire, North Carolina, and Georgia were likewise unrepresented at the congress. (Fiske, John—*American Revolution*, p. 21.)

It was the first unmistakable evidence that the colonies would make common cause. After a session of two weeks the congress adjourned, having drawn up petitions to the English government, and a "Declaration of Rights and Grievances of the Colonists in America." (Hart, Albert B.—*Formation of the Union*, p. 58.)

The Declaration of Rights is important, because it is the first utterance of any considerable number of the colonies on the questions which were soon to be of supreme importance. (Channing, Edward—*Student's History of the United States*, rev. ed., p. 146.)

The Stamp Act Congress, as the meeting was called, claimed for Americans the same inherent rights as were enjoyed by Englishmen, and declared that since the colonists were not represented in Parliament—and from the circumstances they could not be—their only lawful representatives were those chosen as members of the colonial legislatures.

(Forman, Samuel E.—*Advanced American History*, pp. 112-113.)

a. Reference.

Hart, Albert B.—*American History Told by Contemporaries*, Vol. II, pp. 402-404, The Stamp Act Congress, "Declaration of the Rights and Grievances of the Colonists" (1765).

4. Intercolonial Committees of Correspondence, 1772.

Under the leadership of Patrick Henry and Thomas Jefferson, a permanent Committee of Correspondence was appointed . . . "to maintain a correspondence with our sister colonies." Massachusetts, Rhode Island, Connecticut, New Hampshire, and South Carolina appointed similar committees. (Channing, Edward—*Student's History of the United States*, rev. ed., p. 159.)

When the Continental Congress met, there is good reason to believe that it was looked upon as a meeting of the committees of correspondence of the several colonies; indeed, its members were in most cases the members of the committees of correspondence in the respective provinces. In later generations, when States and sections quarreled as to whom the honor belonged of having been the first to rebel, Virginia or Massachusetts, North or South, there was much ado over the origin of the committees of correspondence. The truth seems to be that Samuel Adams, inspired perhaps by Otis or Mayhew, established the first system of local committees. . . . It was Virginia, however, imitating at first standing legislative committees already existing in England, which set up various like committees in the House of Burgesses, . . .

Out of this experience Virginia was inspired on the eve of the Revolution (1773) to establish and to urge other colonies to set up legislative committees of correspondence which would keep each other informed as to the state of the public mind and strive to preserve unity. From this committee now came the first invitation of one colony to others to meet in an all-American Congress, though many town gatherings here and there in America had already proposed that plan. Indeed, the time was ripe and the logic of events put the idea in every fertile mind. (Van Tyne, Claude H.—*The Causes of the War of Independence* (*The Founding of the American Republic*, Vol. I), pp. 427-429.)

a. Reference.

Howard, G. E.—*Preliminaries of the Revolution* (*American Nation*, Vol. VIII), ch. xiv (Royal Orders and Committees of Correspondence).

5. First Continental Congress, 1774.

By September, 1774, all the colonies (except Georgia) had sent delegates to Philadelphia to meet in a body that became known as the First Continental Congress. . . . The congress of 1774 provided for the holding of another congress in May, 1775, at Philadelphia, . . . (Forman, Samuel E.—*Advanced American History*, p. 122.)

They drew up a declaration of rights specifying a dozen vexatious laws passed since the Grenville administration to which they "could not submit." (Muzzey, David S.—*History of the American People*, p. 118.)

a. Reference.

Hart, Albert B.—*American History Told by Contemporaries*, Vol. II, pp. 434-439, John Adams, "The First Continental Congress" (1774).

B. Plans for Union During and After the Revolution.

1. Second Continental Congress, 1775-1781.

> This Congress, like the first, was only a kind of committee of advice. It had no power to make laws binding the people of America like the present Congress of the United States. (Muzzey, David S.—*History of the American People*, p. 122.)

a. Work of the Congress.
Managed the War.
Declaration of Independence.
Produced Articles of Confederation.

2. Declaration of Independence, July 4, 1776.

a. Resolution Introduced in the Continental Congress by Richard Henry Lee (Va.), June 7, 1776.

> *Resolved*, That these United Colonies are, and of right ought to be, free and independent States, that they are absolved from all allegiance to the British Crown, and that all political connection between them and the State of Great Britain is, and ought to be, totally dissolved.
>
> That it is expedient forthwith to take the most effectual measures for forming foreign Alliances.
>
> That a plan of confederation be prepared and transmitted to the respective Colonies for their consideration and approbation. (Quoted from *Journals of the Continental Congress*, Library of Congress edition, Vol. V, p. 425.) (Reprint—*Documents Illustrative of the Formation of the Union of the American States*, p. 21. Government Printing Office, 1927.)
>
> The second day of July, 1776, will be the most memorable epocha in the history of America. I am apt to believe that it will be celebrated by succeeding generations as the great anniversary festival. It ought to be commemorated, as a day of deliverance, by solemn acts of devotion to God Almighty. It ought to be solemnized with pomp and parade, with shows, games, sports, guns, bells, bonfires, and illuminations, from one end of this continent to the other, from this time forward, forevermore.
>
> You will think me transported with enthusiasm, but I am not. I am well aware of the toil, and blood, and treasure, that it will cost us to maintain this declaration, and support and defend these States. Yet, through all the gloom, I can see the rays of ravishing light and glory. I can see that the end is more than worth all the means, and that posterity will triumph in that day's transaction, even although we should rue it, which I trust in God we shall not. (Adams, John—*Works*, Vol. IX, p. 420.) (Letter to Mrs. Adams, July 3, 1776.)
>
> The Declaration was yesterday published and proclaimed from that awful stage in the State-house yard; by whom, do you think? By the Committee of Safety, the Committee of Inspection, and a great crowd of people. Three cheers rended the welkin. The battalions paraded on the Common, and gave us the *feu de joie*, notwithstanding the scarcity of powder. The bells rang all day and almost all night. Even the chimers chimed away. (Adams, John—*Works*, Vol. IX, pp. 420-421.) (Letter to Samuel Chase, Philadelphia, July 9, 1776.)

b. References.

> In Congress, July 4, 1776—The Unanimous Declaration of the Thirteen United States of America; *Documents Illustrative of the Formation of the Union of the American States*, p. 22. Government Printing Office.
>
> Hart, Albert B.—*American History Told by Contemporaries*, Vol. II, pp. 537-539, Thomas

LIBERTY BELL

Jefferson, "Drafting of the Declaration of Independence."

3. Articles of Confederation, 1781-1789.

a. Origin and Nature.

> One cause of the weakness of Congress and the disorders in the States was the want of a settled national government. The Continental Congress understood that it was but a makeshift, and on the day when a committee was formed to frame a Declaration of Independence, another committee was appointed to draw up Articles of Confederation. (Hart, Albert B.—*Formation of the Union*, p. 103.)

(1) References.

> Hart, Albert B.—*American History Told by Contemporaries*, Vol. II, pp. 539-543, John Adams, "Difficulties in Framing Articles of Confederation" (1776).
>
> Hart, Albert B.—*American History Told by Contemporaries*, Vol. III, chs. vi, vii.

b. Adoption.

(1) Second Continental Congress Becomes the Congress of the Confederation.

> Congress spent a year and a half in forming the Articles of Confederation. The States took three and a half years in ratifying them. . . .
>
> March 1, 1781, it was announced that Maryland had ratified the Articles of Confederation, and they were duly put into force. From that date the Congress, though little changed in personnel or in powers, was acting under a written constitution, and the States had bound themselves to abide by it. (Hart, Albert B.—*Formation of the Union*, pp. 104-105.)

(2) Articles of Confederation, March 1, 1781; *Documents Illustrative of the Formation of the Union of the American States*, pp. 27-37. Government Printing Office.

c. Value.

(1) Preservation of the Idea of Unity.
(2) Payment of Soldiers for Service during the Revolution. Influence of George Washington in securing Settlement.

> The lands were unsurveyed and the form of government undetermined, and the soldiers who had received grants in this wilderness thought them about as valuable as "quarter sections of the moon." The bringing order out of this chaos was the last work of the congress of the confederation. (Coman, Katherine—*Industrial History of the United States*, p. 158.)

(3) Northwest Ordinance, 1787.
   Provisions for territorial government.

> The ordinance established a territorial government, with a governor, secretary, and judges. A General Assembly was authorized as soon as there should be five thousand free male inhabitants in the district. The lower house was elective, the upper house, or council, was appointive. The Legislature was to elect a territorial delegate to Congress. . . .
>
> In truth, the Ordinance of 1787 was so wide-reaching in its effects, was drawn in accordance with so lofty a morality and such far-seeing statesmanship, and was fraught with such weal for the nation, that it will ever rank among the foremost of American state papers, coming in that little group which includes the Declaration of Independence, the Constitution, Washington's Farewell Address, and Lincoln's Emancipation Proclamation and Second Inaugural. It marked out a definite line of orderly freedom along which the new States were to advance. (Roosevelt, Theodore—*The Winning of the West*, Vol. V (1930 ed.), pp. 31, 33.)

d. Defects.
   (1) No provision for executive branch.
   (2) Importance of legislative branch—one House.
   (3) Authority left in States.
   (4) Lacked power to enforce laws, raise revenue or regulate commerce.

e. Results from Operation—Critical Condition due to Weak Government.
   (1) Jealousy between the States over Commerce and Boundaries.

> During the war the sense of a common danger had lent the Congress a not easily defined but quite real coherence, which vanished when peace came, and the local ideals of the States took precedence. (Thayer, William R.—*George Washington*, p. 154.)
>
> Between the Congress thus constituted and the several state governments the attributes of sovereignty were shared in such a way as to produce a minimum of result with a maximum of effort. . . .
>
> They [the Articles] show that political action was at no time based on the view of the states as absolutely sovereign, but they also show that a share of sovereignty accorded to Congress was very inadequate even to the purposes of an effective confederation. The position in which they left Congress was hardly more than that of the deliberative head of a league. For the most fundamental of all the attributes of sovereignty—the power of taxation—was not given to Congress. It could neither raise taxes through an excise nor through custom-house duties; it could only make requisitions upon the thirteen members of the confederacy in proportion to the assessed value of their real estate, and it was not provided with any means of enforcing these requisitions. (Fiske, John—*The Critical Period of American History, 1783-1789*, pp. 96-98.)

II. The Constitutional Convention.
A. Preliminaries of the Convention—*Honor to George Washington*, No. 7 (*Washington and the Constitution*), Part I.
   1. Commercial Conferences.
      a. Alexandria-Mount Vernon, 1785.

> Again Washington was to save the cause. On March 28, 1785, joint commissioners of Virginia and Maryland were invited to Washington's home at Mount Vernon to arrange an agreement between the two States regarding rights of navigation in Chesapeake Bay and the Potomac. . . . Washington pointed out clearly the necessity of a Union, in fact as well as in name. (Atwood, Harry—*The Constitution Explained*, p. 13.)

      b. Annapolis Convention, September, 1786.

> In 1786 representatives from five States met in a convention at Annapolis to consider the hard times and the troubles in trade. Washington, Hamilton, and Madison were thought to be behind the convention, which accomplished little, but made it clear that a large general convention ought to meet and discuss the way of securing a strong central government. (Thayer, William R.—*George Washington*, p. 158.)

      (1) Reference.
> Proceedings of Commissioners to remedy defects of the Federal Government, Annapolis, Md., 1786; *Documents Illustrative of the Formation of the Union of the American States*, pp. 39-43. Government Printing Office.

B. Meeting at Philadelphia.
C. Organization and Membership.
   1. Representation of States.
   2. Delegates.
      a. Number.

> When taking up the all-important work of the convention in framing the constitution of the United States, it is well to keep certain facts and conditions continually in mind. In the first place while there were fifty-five delegates who attended the convention at one time or another, that is not the number of those who were usually present. Some delegates were late in arriving in Philadelphia, some left early, and many were irregular in their attendance. From a careful study of all available data, supported by a single contemporary statement, it would seem that the average attendance was little if any more than thirty. (Farrand, Max—*The Framing of the Constitution of the United States*, p. 61.)

      (1) Reference.
> *Documents Illustrative of the Formation of the Union of the American States*, pp. 85-86. Government Printing Office.

      b. Character of Men.
      (1) Reference.
> Atwood, Harry—*The Constitution Explained*, pp. 166-177 (The Men Who Wrote the Constitution).

   3. George Washington as Delegate and Presiding Officer.

> Gen. Washington is well known as the Commander in chief of the late American Army. Having conducted these States to independence and peace, he now appears to assist in framing a Government to

make the People happy. Like Gustavus Vasa, he may be said to be the deliverer of his Country;—like Peter the Great he appears as the politician and the Statesman; and like Cincinnatus he returned to his farm perfectly contented with being only a plain Citizen, after enjoying the highest honor of the Confederacy,—and now only seeks for the approbation of his Country-men by being virtuous and useful. The General was conducted to the Chair as President of the Convention by the unanimous vote of its Members. He is in the 52d year of his age. (Notes of Major William Pierce (Ga.) in the Federal Convention of 1787; in *Documents Illustrative of the Formation of the Union of American States*, p. 104.) Government Printing Office.

It is a difficult, if not a dangerous thing, to attempt to ascribe controlling importance or influence to any particular men where the evidence is so scanty. The parts which were taken by various men in the debates of the convention will be partially brought out in describing the proceedings, but it seems worth while to notice one man who took no part in the discussions but whose influence is believed to have been important. That man was George Washington, the presiding officer of the convention. His commanding presence and the respect amounting almost to awe which he inspired must have carried weight, especially in so small a gathering in the "long room" with the president sitting on a raised platform. (Farrand, Max—*The Framing of the Constitution of the United States*, p. 64.)

To his initiative in connecting the States by water routes and his strong counsel that the conflicting commercial regulations of the States should give way to a common control over commerce, we owe first the Annapolis Convention and then the Philadelphia Convention of 1787; and while Washington, in the four months of that Convention, sat silent as its presiding officer, without his masterful influence and sagacious counsel that masterpiece of statecraft, the Constitution of the United States, would never have been. (Beck, James—*The Washington Tradition and Our Foreign Policy*, p. 8.)

Washington had more to do with the formation of the constitution than our enthusiasm for other phases of the great work he did for his country usually makes prominent. He fought the battles which cleared the way for it. He best knew the need of consolidating under one government the colonies he had made free, and he best knew that without this consolidation, a wasting war, the long and severe privations and sufferings his countrymen had undergone and his own devoted labor in the cause of freedom were practically in vain. The beginning of anything like a public sentiment looking to the formation of our nation is traceable to his efforts. The circular letter he sent to the governors of the States, as early as the close of the War of the Revolution, contained the germ of the constitution; and all this was recognized by his unanimous choice to preside over the convention that framed it. His spirit was in and through it all. (Cleveland, Grover—*Writings and Speeches* (ed. by George F. Parker), "Sentiment in Our National Life," p. 353.) (Address, University of Michigan, Ann Arbor, February 22, 1892.)

4. Creation and Organization of a New Nation—Program Ten (*George Washington The Builder of the Nation*), No. 3 (In Part, See Unit VII).

As first in war he created nationality; as first in peace he advocated and helped frame an efficient and endurable Constitution; and because first in the hearts of his countrymen he was unanimously elected President.

D. Work of the Convention.

The builders of this Republic were the busiest and hardest working people of history, which is one of the chief causes why within a century this country became the leading nation of the world, . . .

The Constitution provided for a representative government, and the founders called it a Republic. . . .

The greatest heritage that has fallen to any single people in history is our Federal Constitution. (Atwood, Harry—*Safeguarding American Ideals*, pp. 15, 30, 43.)

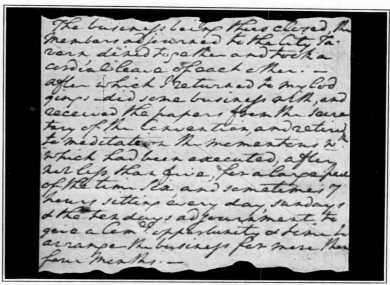

WASHINGTON'S DIARY OF SEPTEMBER 17, 1787, ON CLOSE OF FEDERAL CONVENTION

1. Debates in the Federal Convention of 1787 as reported by James Madison—*Documents Illustrative of the Formation of the Union of the American States*, pp. 109-745. Government Printing Office.

There was one man, however, who recognized the importance of this gathering, and appreciated the interest that in all probability would attach to its proceedings, and who determined to leave as complete a record as was possible of all that took place. That man was Madison, and he set about his self-imposed task in his usual methodical way, . . . But every student of the subject is under the deepest obligation to him. From his Debates, as supplemented by the other very irregular notes, one is able to obtain a fairly accurate and complete account of the proceedings. (Farrand, Max—*The Framing of the Constitution of the United States*, pp. 59-60.)

2. The Great Compromises.
   a. Upon Representation of Small and Large States.
   b. Upon Representation of Slaves.
   c. Upon Control Over Commerce.
   d. Reference.
      Farrand, Max—*The Framing of The Constitution of the United States*, chs. vii-x.

3. Notes of Alexander Hamilton and others in the Federal Convention of 1787; *Documents Illustrative of the Formation of the Union of the American States*, pp. 87-108, 746-952. Government Printing Office.

4. Results of the Convention—*Honor to George Washington*, No. 7 (*Washington and the Constitution*), Part II.
5. The Leading Features of the Constitution.
   The Basic Supreme Law of the Land.
   a. Reference
      McLaughlin, Andrew C.—*The Confederation and the Constitution* (*The American Nation*, Vol. X), ch. xv (The Law of the Land).
6. The Six Fundamental Principles of the Constitution—James M. Beck.
   a. Representative Government.
   b. Our Dual Form of Government—Division of Powers.
   c. Guaranty of Individual Liberty through Constitutional Limitations.
   d. Independent Judiciary—Separation of Powers.
   e. Governmental Checks and Balances.
   f. Concurrent Power of the Senate and the Executive Over the Foreign Relations of the Government (and Appointive Power).
7. Letter of the President [George Washington] of the Federal Convention, September 17, 1787; *Documents Illustrative of the Formation of the Union of the American States*, pp. 1003-1004. Government Printing Office.
8. Reference.
   McLaughlin, Andrew C.—*The Confederation and the Constitution* (*The American Nation*, Vol. X), ch. xix (Critical Essay on Authorities).

III. RATIFICATION OF THE CONSTITUTION (1787-1790).
   A. Difficulties Encountered.
   B. Public Discussion.
   C. The Federalist.
   D. Conventions and Ratification of the Constitution by the Several States, arranged in the order of their ratification; *Documents Illustrative of the Formation of the Union of the American States*, pp. 1009-1059. Government Printing Office.

By June 21 [1788] nine States had ratified, and it was certain that the new Federal Government would come into power. Accordingly, on July 2, 1788, the President of the old Congress of the Confederation announced that the necessary States required had ratified the Constitution and that steps should be taken to put the new government into operation. With this purpose in view the Congress ordered that the States should choose Presidential electors on the first Wednesday in January, 1789; that the electors should vote for President and Vice-President on the first Wednesday in February; and the Senate and House of Representatives should meet in New York on the first Wednesday in March, which happened to be March 4. Thus the old Government passed quietly out of existence, and thus the way was prepared for the installation of the new Government. (Forman, Samuel E.—*Advanced American History*, pp. 184-185.)

E. Reference.
   Hart, Albert B.—*American History Told by Contemporaries*, Vol. III, ch. xi (Ratification of the Constitution).

IV. SIGNIFICANT DATES Selected from *George Washington Year by Year*—(See Dates given in Units IV and V).

1787, May 25—The Federal Convention met in Philadelphia. General Washington attended as a Virginia delegate. He was elected president.

1787, Sept. 17—The draft of the Constitution was signed and the convention adjourned.

1788, Jan. 18—General Washington was elected chancellor of William and Mary College by Visitors and Governors in Convocation (honorary life position).

1788, Apr.—General Washington became charter member and also first master of new Alexandria Lodge of Freemasons.

THE FEDERAL BUILDING, NEW YORK CITY
Inauguration of George Washington as First President took place here

Unit VII
George Washington the Executive

Brief Outline

I. THE FIRST PRESIDENT OF THE UNITED STATES.
  A. Election.
    1. *Triumphant Journey as President-Elect.*
    2. Inauguration.
      a. *First Term of the First President.*
  B. Organization of the New Republic.
    1. Formation of Cabinet and Judiciary.
      a. *Creation and Organization of a New Nation.*
  C. Problems of the Administration.
    1. *Washington's Domestic Policy.*
    2. *Washington's Foreign Policy.*
    3. *Washington and Public Business.*
    4. Development of Political Parties.
      a. *George Washington: His Friends and Enemies.*
    5. Second Administration.
      a. Election.
      b. Inauguration.
      c. Events—*Second Term of President Washington.*
  D. Washington's Farewell Address.
  E. Social Life.
    1. Travels.
      a. *New England Journeys.*
      b. *The First Presidential Tours.*
      c. *Southern Journeys.*
      d. *The Southern Tour.*
      e. Map of the Principal Routes.
    2. *Presidential Mansions.*
    3. Official Society.
      a. *Presidential Households.*
      b. *Social Life in Later Years.*

II. CHARACTERISTICS PORTRAYED.
  A. Judgment.
  B. Balance.
  C. Wisdom.
  D. Vision.
  E. Integrity.
  F. Justice.

III. SIGNIFICANT DATES.
  NOTE: *Topics in italics are titles of 48 papers in a series of 12 George Washington Programs and the parts of the Honor to George Washington series of 15 pamphlets issued by the United States George Washington Bicentennial Commission.*

Development

I. THE FIRST PRESIDENT OF THE UNITED STATES.
  A. Election.
    1. Triumphant Journey as President-Elect—Program Eleven (*George Washington The President: 1789-1797*), No. 1.
        Washington's popularity received its greatest expression during this journey. Everyone acclaimed the hero of war who was now called upon to be the leader in peace.
    2. Inauguration.
    a. First Term of the First President (1789-1793)— Program Eleven (*George Washington The President: 1789-1797*), No. 2.
        Great rejoicing, honor, and responsibility marked Washington's first administration. Precedents were made and the world shown that a wise man was in control.
  B. Organization of the New Republic.
    1. Formation of Cabinet and Judiciary.
        The government being completely organized, and a system of revenue established, the important duty of filling the offices which had been created remained

From an engraving by Amos Doolittle, after a portrait by Joseph Wright

to be performed. In the execution of this delicate trust, the purest virtue and the most impartial judgment were exercised in selecting the best talents, and the greatest weight of character, which the United States could furnish. (Marshall, John—*Life of George Washington*, Vol. IV, pp. 319-320.)

    a. Creation and Organization of a New Nation— Program Ten (*George Washington The Builder of The Nation*), No. 3 (In Part—See Unit VI).
  C. Problems of the Administration.
    1. Washington's Domestic Policy (1789-1797)—*Honor to George Washington*, No. 8 (*Washington as President*), Part I.
    2. Washington's Foreign Policy (1789-1797)—*Honor to George Washington*, No. 8 (*Washington as President*), Part II (Includes First and Second Terms).
      a. Difficulties with England.
      b. Difficulties with France.
    3. Washington and Public Business—*Honor to George Washington*, No. 12 (*Washington the Business Man*), Part V.
    4. Development of Political Parties.
      a. George Washington: His Friends and Enemies— Program Three (*Youth and Manhood of George Washington*), No. 4.
        Broadminded, Washington attached understanding minds. Eminence brought the antagonism of those jealous or incapable of sharing in his wide outlook.

5. Second Administration.

a. Election.

b. Inauguration.

Washington, though he never courted popularity, was attentive to the signs of public opinion, and disposed to be guided by them when right. The time for entering upon his second term of Presidency was at hand. There had been much cavilling at the parade attending his first installation. Jefferson especially had pronounced it "not at all in character with the simplicity of republican government, and looking, as if wishfully, to those of European courts."

To guide him on the coming occasion, Washington called the heads of departments together, and desired they would consult with one another, and agree on any changes they might consider for the better, assuring them he would willingly conform to whatever they should advise.

c. Events—Second Term of President Washington (1793-1797)—Program Eleven (George Washington The President: 1789-1797), No. 5.

D. Washington's Farewell Address.

The "Farewell Address" belongs among the few supreme utterances on human government. . . . During the late World War we heard it revived, and a great many persons who had never read the "Farewell Address" gravely reminded us of Washington's warning against "entangling alliances." As a matter of fact, that phrase does not appear in the "Farewell Address" at all. It was first used by Thomas Jefferson in his first Inaugural Address, March 4, 1801, sixteen months after Washington was dead and buried. No doubt the meaning could be deducted from what Washington said in more than one passage of his "Farewell." (Thayer, William R.—George Washington, pp. 224-225, 227.)

If the latter [Washington] had written nothing more than the "farewell address," his fame would

George Washington   General Henry Knox,   Alexander Hamilton,   Thomas Jefferson,   Edmund Randolph,
                          Sec'y of War   Sec'y of Treasury   Sec'y of State   Attorney General
The First Cabinet of President Washington

They held such consultation, and ultimately gave their individual opinions in writing, with regard to the time, manner, and place of the President's taking the oath of office. As they were divided in opinion, and gave no positive advice as to any change, no change was made. On the 4th of March, the oath was publicly administered to Washington by Mr. Justice Cushing, in the Senate Chamber, in presence of the heads of departments, foreign ministers, such members of the House of Representatives as were in town, and as many other spectators as could be accommodated. (Irving, Washington—Life of George Washington, Vol. V, pp. 144-145.)

be secure, for no leader of men ever gave to a people a wiser or a nobler political testament. . . . It was in the Farewell Address that he framed in the most deliberate and precise manner his views as to the foreign policy of the government. I need not remind you of the care and deliberation with which this immortal valedictory was prepared. He first planned it at the end of his first term, and it evidently occupied his thoughts during the whole of his second term. He submitted drafts of it to Madison, discussed it with Jefferson and Knox, and finally engaged the acute mind and eloquent pen of Hamilton in its final preparation. Thus the Farewell Address, possibly the noblest state document in the history of the world, represents the mature wisdom and deliberate political philosophy of Washington, not only for his own day but for the future of his nation. (Beck, James—*The Washington Tradition and Our Foreign Policy*, pp. 6, 18-19.)

E. Social Life.

1. Travels.

a. New England Journeys—*Honor to George Washington*, No. 11 (*Washington the Traveler*), Part II.

b. The First Presidential Tours: New England, Long Island, and Rhode Island—Program Eleven (*George Washington the President: 1789-1797*), No. 3.

Washington set the precedent for presidential tours. Desiring to see the States under peace, he visited each section, traveling in his great state coach with proper display.

c. Southern Journeys—*Honor to George Washington*, No. 11 (*Washington the Traveler*), Part III.

d. The Southern Tour: Program Eleven (*George Washington the President: 1789-1797*), No. 4.

e. Map of the Principal Routes.
(1) Reference.
The George Washington Atlas.

2. Presidential Mansions—Program Two (*Homes of George Washington*), No. 6.

The Presidential Mansions were in New York and Philadelphia.

3. Official Society.

a. Presidential Households—Program Twelve (*The Homemaking of George and Martha Washington*), No. 3.

To the Executive Mansions of New York and Philadelphia, President and Mrs. Washington devoted careful thought. Every detail was planned with regard for the dignity of the chief office of an independent nation.

b. Social Life in Later Years—Program Nine (*The Social Life of George Washington*), No. 3 (In Part, See Unit IV).

The First President established a code of official etiquette which is the basis of that at the White House to-day.

II. CHARACTERISTICS PORTRAYED.

A. Judgment.

Washington, with his remarkable judgment of men, had selected an able staff of officers, representing all the sections of the country. (Hart, Albert B.—*Formation of the Union*, p. 167.)

The end of Washington's administration saw the country free from many perils and on the high road to prosperity. The new Government had weathered severe storms and had proven itself efficient. Much of its success was due to the President's good judgment, sound sense, and firmness. . . .

One can hardly overestimate the importance of Washington's personal character upon the life of his country. His wisdom and courage, his simple integrity, his tact and forbearance, his dignity and manliness, his purity and magnanimity of soul, exalted the Nation. Without him it is difficult to see how the Revolution could have succeeded or the new Government have been established. (McLaughlin, Andrew C.—*History of the American Nation*, p. 214.)

I think Washington was the most impersonal man of intense personality whom I have ever studied.

He grasped with intense rapidity the significance of a general proposition and was able instinctively to tell where was the real kernel of the difficulty, and then dedicate himself to the task immediately before him with an intensity of application, . . . (Hedges, Job E.—*Washington a Living Force*, p. 11.) (Address, Morristown, N. J., February 23, 1914.)

No man ever stood for so much to his country and mankind as George Washington. Hamilton, Jefferson and Adams, Madison and Jay, each represented some of the elements which formed the Union. Washington embodied them all. They fell at times under popular disapproval, were burned in effigy, were stoned, but he with unerring judgment was always the leader of the people. Milton said of Cromwell that "war made him great, peace greater." (Depew, Chauncey M.—*The Centennial Oration*, pp. 43-44.) (One Hundredth Anniversary of the Inauguration of George Washington as President of the United States, at Sub-Treasury, New York.)

The reflex action of the French Revolution upon the American people was so great that the infant Republic would have been strangled in its very birth if it had not been for the patience and sagacity of Washington. He selected for his cabinet the leaders of the two great parties which were then in process of formation. (Beck, James—*The Washington Tradition and Our Foreign Policy*, p. 13.)

[George Washington] read and understood men, and had that power of choosing among them which is essential in its highest form to the great soldier or statesman. . . . Even more remarkable than the ability to recognize great talent was his capacity to weigh and value with a nice exactness the worth of men who did not rise to the level of greatness. . . . He did not expect to discover genius everywhere, or to find a marshal's baton in every knapsack, but he used men according to their value and possibilities, which is quite as essential as the preliminary work of selection. . . . It seems little to say, but if we stop to think of it, this power to read men aright and see the truth in them and about them is a power more precious than any other bestowed by the kindest of fairy godmothers. . . . He was slow, when he had plenty of time, in adopting a policy or plan, or in settling a public question, but he read men very quickly. (Lodge, Henry C.—*George Washington* (*American Statesmen*), Vol. II, pp. 329-331.)

No man ever saw more clearly the relative importance of things and actions, or divested himself more entirely of the bias of personal interest, partiality, and prejudice, in discriminating between the true and false, the right and the wrong, in all questions and subjects that were presented to him. (Sparks, Jared—*The Life of George Washington*, p. 458.)

Elsewhere he wrote, "In a word, if a man cannot act in all respects as he would wish, he must do what appears best, under the circumstances he is in." (Ford, Paul L.—*George Washington*, p. 305.)

B. Balance.

He stood like the rock-ribbed coast of a continent between the surging billows of fanaticism and the child of his love. Order is Heaven's first law, and the mind of Washington was order. (Depew, Chauncey M.—*The Centennial Oration*, p. 43.) (One Hundredth Anniversary of the Inauguration of George Washington as President of the United States, New York.)

With scant co-operation, even from his immediate

Cabinet advisers, of whom Knox and Hamilton were avowed in their sympathies for England, and Jefferson and Randolph were equally ardent for France, Washington, with extraordinary sagacity, kept the ship on an even keel, for he saw that nothing could be more fatal than to steer the infant Republic into the then seething maelstrom of European politics. (Beck, James—*The Washington Tradition and Our Foreign Policy*, p. 16.)

Washington was opinionated, full of just pride, with profound confidence in himself. I say, in himself, for the reason that his cause embraced himself. With all his striking personality and with all of his intense devotion to the duty before him, he was respectful and considerate of the opinions of others and only in rare moments presented his thoughts in other than gracious and kindly phrase.

It is difficult to understand why the encomiums passed on Washington should be so universal, unless it be that he was so intensely genuine and played the game of life so undemonstratively without seeking spectacular effect for personal exploitation. He was void of passion for head-lines, and yet he knew full well the dramatic value to popular imagination of clever stage-setting. He expressed his own position on every topic with such openness and frankness that it was impossible to impeach his motives. His judgment might be questioned, as it was, but no one dared to assail his motives, and no one, being purer in motive than was he, was in a position consistently to question that feature of his life. (Hedges, Job E.—*Washington a Living Force*, p. 11.) (Address, Morristown, N. J., February 23, 1914.)

His devotion to the "balance of orders and interests" is evidenced in his whole life—a government that unites to their common advantage the humble and wise, agriculture and commerce. . . . His regard for rival "interests" was equally catholic. A Virginian passionately devoted to farm life, he felt no less deeply the importance of manufactures and commerce, labored devotedly to promote them. Many surpassed him in constitutional learning and disquisition, but no one had a wider knowledge of the nation as a whole, a warmer attachment to it, or a purer desire to give justice to each and every group in it. (Corbin, John—*Unknown Washington*, pp. 315-316.)

He had a weighing and balancing mind. His intellect was like a pair of accurately adjusted scales. He did not often, especially in civil affairs, originate the policies upon which he acted. But he listened carefully and patiently to every counsel from which he could get instruction, and then brought it in the end to the sure test of his own unerring judgment. He weighed the advice of his great counsellors, the claims of contending parties, and of Jefferson and Hamilton and Adams and Pickering, in a balance as infallible as the golden scales which the Eternal hung forth in Heaven. (Hoar, George F.—*Washington*, p. 23.) (Chicago, February 23, 1903.)

Washington, no doubt, was pre-eminent among his contemporaries in natural endowments. Less brilliant in his mental gifts than some, less eloquent and accomplished than others, he had a rare balance of large powers which justified Lowell's phrase of "an imperial man." His athletic vigor and skill, his steadiness of nerve restraining an intensity of passion, his undaunted courage which refused no necessary risks and his prudence which took no unnecessary ones, the quiet sureness with which he grasped large ideas and the pressing energy with which he executed small details, the breadth of his intelligence, the depth of his convictions, his power to apply great thoughts and principles to everyday affairs, and his singular superiority to current prejudices and illusions—these were gifts in combination which would have made him distinguished in any company, in any age. (Van Dyke, Henry—*The Americanism of Washington*, pp. 22-24.)

C. Wisdom—Guidance of "Ship of State" on Uncharted Seas.

But with all our pride in Washington we not infrequently fail to give him credit for his marvelous genius as a constructive statesman. We are constantly in danger of losing sight of the sweep and clearness of his comprehension, which accurately grasped the problems of the remote future and knew how to formulate the best means for their solution. It was committed to Washington to launch our ship of state. He had neither precedent nor predecessor to help him. He welded the scattered and at times antagonistic colonies into an indestructible Union, and inculcated the lessons of mutual forbearance and fraternity which have cemented the States into still closer bonds of interest and sympathy. (McKinley, William—*Address*, pp. 14-15.) (University of Pennsylvania, February 22, 1898.)

His contemporaries never questioned his intellectual qualifications. (Beck, James—*The Washington Tradition and Our Foreign Policy*, p. 6.)

The light elicited from the rise and fall of ancient empires, and beaming from the advanced political knowledge and intellect of the age, enabled him to grasp the destinies of the States, and wield their energies with monarchical facilities and republican simplicity. In fine, such was the wisdom of his policy, and the philanthropy of his counsels, and the comprehensiveness of his views, that with the aid of the co-ordinate branches of the government, and the co-operation of his patriotic compeers, he extricated the country from the want of credit in which it was entangled: he laid the foundations of the national character in the staid principles of private morality; and exhibited, to the confusion and tyranny of despotism the pre-eminence of institutions based on equality of rights, and illustrated by every attractive attribute which can command the support of the citizen, and claim the admiration of the enlightened friends of freedom. (Collier, Robert R.—*Oration*, p. 8.) (Petersburg, February 22, 1832.)

To appreciate the bold outlines of his personality and at the same time the patriarchal attitude he was entitled to assume toward the Republic, which was so much of his own making, we have only to read his Farewell Address—that wonderful product of affection and intelligence and insight. We can not think of it as written by any one of his contemporaries. The tone of it forbids this. Not one of them could have made use of its language without being open to the charge of affectation or arrogance. The words of dignity and injunction and warning came naturally from him, for they were the words of the guardian of the Nation as his ward, or, as he said, of an old and affectionate friend. He was the Gamaliel at whose feet the people sought wisdom. He was, in truth, the Father of his Country, as he enjoined upon us all those virtues and practices which can keep us strong and just and prosperous at home and respected in the councils of the world. (Underwood, Oscar W.—*The Career and the Words of Washington*, p. 7.) (State Society of Cincinnati, Philadelphia, Pa., February 22, 1912.)

D. Vision—Commercial and Industrial Policy of the Nation.

It is one of the qualities of great men that they seem to belong not to their own time alone but to all ages. Few characters surpass that of Washington in this regard. The symmetry of his life was remarkable. He was a man of his own age, but he exhibited rare foresight and had a broad outlook for the future. He was a Southerner, but his interests were national. He lived close to tidewater on the Atlantic seaboard, but he was a prophetic believer in the whole great country. He was a slave holder, yet an Abolitionist and a friend of freedom. He was born in the East and lived and died near his birthplace; but no man in his generation realized more fully the prophecy of the great West, or cherished more highly the vision of a country stretching far beyond the mountains toward the sunset. (Barton, William E.—*George Washington*.) (Address, Oak Park, Ill., February 22, 1920.)

For many years Washington had a fixed idea that if the new country could live for twenty years without a conflict with its chief neighbors, its future would be safe; for he felt that at the end of that time it would have grown so strong by the natural increase in population and by the strength that comes from developing its resources, that it need not fear the attack of any people in the world. The Jay Treaty helped toward this end; it prevented war for sixteen years only; but even that delay was of great service to the Americans and made them more ready to face it than they would have been in 1795. . . . In every act he looked far forward into the future. (Thayer, William R.—*George Washington*, pp. 213, 258.)

Among these men whose union in purpose and action made the strength and stability of the republic, Washington was first, not only in the largeness of his nature, the loftiness of his desires, and the vigor of his will, but also in that representative quality which makes a man able to stand as the true hero of a great people. He had an instinctive power to divine, amid the confusions of rival interests and the cries of factional strife, the new aims and hopes, the vital needs and aspirations, which were the common inspiration of the people's cause and the creative forces of the American nation. The power to understand this, the faith to believe in it, and the unselfish courage to live for it, was the central factor of Washington's life, the heart and fountain of his splendid Americanism. (Van Dyke, Henry—*The Americanism of Washington*, pp. 7-8.)

E. Integrity.

He was, in the modest enterprises of his time, which were the precursors of the great businesses of today, scrupulously careful to keep his public service free of any taint of private interest. There is no public man in all our history whose shining example needs more, perhaps, to be held before our eyes today, when the great problem of government is to give individual enterprise all possible freedom and incentive without harm to the many. (Finley, John H.—*Washington and the West*, p. 14.) (Morristown, N. J., February 22, 1925.)

Twice during Washington's terms he was forced to act counter to the public sentiment. The first time was when a strenuous attempt was made by the French minister to break through the neutrality that had been proclaimed, when, according to John Adams, "ten thousand people in the streets of Philadelphia, day after day, threatened to drag Washington out of his house, and effect a revolution in the government, or compel it to declare in favor of the French revolution and against England." The second time was when he signed the treaty of 1795 with Great Britain, which produced a popular outburst from one end of the country to the other. In neither case did Washington swerve an iota from what he thought right, writing, "these are unpleasant things, but they must be met with firmness." Eventually the people always came back to their leader, and Jefferson sighed over the fact that "such is the popularity of the President that the people will support him in whatever he will do or will not do, without appealing to their own reason or to anything but their feelings toward him." (Ford, Paul L.—*George Washington*, pp. 304-305.)

Both his enemies and his friends bore evidence to his honesty. Jefferson said, "his integrity was most pure, his justice the most inflexible I have ever known, no motives of interest or consanguinity or friendship or hatred, being able to bias his decision. He was indeed in every sense of the words, a wise, a good, and a great man." Pickering wrote that "to the excellency of his virtues I am not disposed to set any limits. All his views were upright, all his actions just." Hamilton asserted that "the General is a very honest Man;" and Tilghman spoke of him as "the honestest man that I believe ever adorned human nature." (Ford, Paul L.—*George Washington*, p. 310.)

F. Justice.

If Washington's foreign policy be in part limited to his times and the then prevailing conditions, yet in part it is intended to be our guide for all time. Thus he says:

"Observe good faith and justice toward all nations, cultivate peace and harmony with all. Religion and morality enjoin this conduct, and can it be that good policy does not equally enjoin it? It will be worthy of a free, enlightened, and, at no distant period, a great nation to give to mankind the magnanimous and too novel example of a people always guided by an exalted justice and benevolence."

Thus spoke and still speaks the world's noblest citizen, and to that ideal of peace mankind is steadily marching. At its head is still the great soldier, who, if "first in war," was also "first in peace." (Beck, James—*The Washington Tradition and Our Foreign Policy*, p. 29.)

The Society of the Cincinnati, of which he was president, had aroused much odium in the country among those who were jealous or envious that such a special privileged class should exist, and among those who really believed that it had the secret design of establishing an aristocracy if not actually a monarchy. Washington held that its original avowed purpose, to keep the officers who had served in the Revolution together, would perpetuate the patriotic spirit which enabled them to win, and might be a source of strength in case of further ordeals. But when he found that public sentiment ran so strongly against the Cincinnati, . . . he told Madison that he would vote to have the Society disbanded if it were not that it counted a minority of foreign members. . . .

Stronger than a desire for a private life and for the ease of Mount Vernon was his sense of duty as a patriot; so that when this was strongly urged upon him he gave way and consented. (Thayer William R.—*George Washington*, p. 159.)

III. SIGNIFICANT DATES Selected from *George Washington Year by Year.*

1789, Feb. 4—The electoral vote for first President of the United States showed General Washington the unanimous choice.

1789, Mar. 7—General Washington was made honorary member of Holland Lodge of Freemasons, New York City.

1789, Apr. 14—General Washington received official notification of his election as President at his home, from Charles Thomson, Secretary of Congress.

1789, Apr. 15—Paid farewell visit to his mother at Fredericksburg, Va.

1789, Apr. 16—General Washington started his triumphal journey to New York accompanied by Charles Thomson and Colonel Humphreys.

1789, Apr. 30—General Washington was inaugurated President of the United States at Federal Hall, New York City. Robert R. Livingston, Chancellor of the State of New York, administered the oath.

1789, June 1—General Washington signed the first act of Congress.

1789, June 24—General Washington was given degree of LL. D. by Washington College, Chestertown, Md.

1789, Aug. 25—Mary Washington, the President's mother, died at her home in Fredericksburg, Va.

1789, Sept. 26—The appointments of Cabinet completed. Four were appointed. Thomas Jefferson was made Secretary of State, but did not assume office until the spring. There was also a Postmaster General, who during the early years was not considered a member of the Cabinet.

1789, Oct. 15-Nov. 13—President Washington during a recess of Congress made a tour of the New England States, excepting Rhode Island.

1790, July 16—President Washington signed the act providing for the location of the permanent Federal Capital on the Potomac.

1790, Aug. 15-22—President Washington visited Rhode Island, which had in the interval since his New England visit ratified the Constitution, thus completing the Union.

1790, Aug. 30—President Washington left New York for Philadelphia, where the new temporary capital was established.

1790, Sept. 2—General Washington was given degree of LL. D. by Brown College.

1791, Mar. 28-30—President Washington met at Georgetown, Md., with the commissioners he had appointed to establish the new Federal district. L'Enfant's plans for the capital were inspected, the boundaries of the district settled and proclaimed.

1791, Apr. 7-June 12—President Washington made a

tour from Mount Vernon of the Southern States. He covered 1,887 miles in his coach, and kept to the schedule he published before leaving.

1792, Apr. 5—President Washington exercised his veto, the first of two.

1792, Dec. 5—When the electoral votes were cast, President Washington was found to be unanimously elected for a second term.

1793, Mar. 4—The second inauguration of George Washington took place in Philadelphia, in Independence Hall. Justice William Cushing administered the oath.

1793, Apr. 22—President Washington issued the Proclamation of Neutrality, which established the policy of avoiding complications with European affairs.

1793, Aug. 1—President Washington called a Cabinet meeting to request officially the recall of Genet, diplomatic representative of France, whose conduct had been at variance with the policy of neutrality.

1793, Sept. 18—President Washington laid the cornerstone of the Federal Capitol with Masonic ceremonies.

1793, Dec. 31—Thomas Jefferson resigned his portfolio in the Washington Cabinet and was thereafter leader of the opposition to the administration.

1794, Apr. 16—President Washington nominated John Jay as special minister to negotiate a treaty with England. This was the final attempt to avoid war over neutral rights and frontier posts.

1794, Aug. 7—President Washington issued a proclamation against the western insurgents, who were engaged in the so-called Whisky Rebellion.

1794, Sept. 2—President Washington called out the militia of several States against the insurgents.

1794, Sept. 30-Oct. 27—President Washington journeyed in Pennsylvania, Maryland, and Virginia during the gathering of the militia, and at the rendezvous at Bedford, Pa., ordered an advance over the mountains to begin October 23. The insurrection ended without conflict.

1795, June 8—President Washington submitted the Jay Treaty with England to the Senate in special session.

1795, July 10—President Washington issued a proclamation of amnesty for the western insurgents.

1795, Aug. 18—The Jay Treaty ratified by Washington.

1796, Mar. 30—The President refused the request of the House of Representatives for the papers of the Jay Treaty.

1796, Sept. 17—President Washington, having emphatically refused to consider a third presidential term, issued his Farewell Address.

Unit VIII
George Washington a Private Citizen Following the Presidency

MOUNT VERNON—NATIONAL SHRINE
(*Airplane view*)

Brief Outline

I. LIFE AT MOUNT VERNON.
  A. Activities.
    1. Business on the Farm and in the Home.
    2. Public.
      a. July 4, 1798, General Washington was appointed Lieutenant General and Commander in Chief of the Armies.
      b. *George Washington: Leader in Philanthropy.*
      c. *Significant Events in the Public Life of George Washington.*
      d. *Principal Official Appointments.*
    3. Home and Social.
      a. *Personal Appearance.*
      b. *Family Life and Friends.*
      c. *Last Years at Mount Vernon.*

II. DEATH AND WILL.
  A. December 14, 1799, Death of George Washington.
  B. December 18, 1799, Funeral of George Washington.
  C. Washington's Fortune and Will.

III. MOUNT VERNON A NATIONAL SHRINE.

IV. SIGNIFICANT DATES.

NOTE: *Topics in italics are titles of 48 papers in a series of 12 George Washington Programs and the parts of the Honor to George Washington series of 15 pamphlets issued by the United States George Washington Bicentennial Commission.*

Development

I. LIFE AT MOUNT VERNON.

His official career being terminated, Washington set off for Mount Vernon accompanied by Mrs. Washington, her grand-daughter Miss Nelly Custis, and George Washington Lafayette, with his preceptors. (Irving, Washington—*The Life of George Washington*, Vol. V, p. 272.)

A. Activities.
  1. Business on the Farm and in the Home.

He is at length at Mount Vernon, that haven of repose to which he had so often turned a wishful eye, throughout his agitated and anxious life, and where he trusted to pass quietly and serenely the remainder of his days. He finds himself, however, "in the situation of a new beginner; almost everything about him required considerable repairs, and a house is immediately to be built for the reception and safe keeping of his military, civil, and private papers." "In a word," writes he, "I am already surrounded by joiners, masons, and painters, and such is my anxiety to be out of their hands, that I have scarcely a room to put a friend into, or to sit in myself, without the music of hammers and the odoriferous scent of paint." (Irving, Washington—*The Life of George Washington*, Vol. V, pp. 272-273.)

He rode from one farm to another and reacquainted himself with the localities where the various crops were either already springing or would soon be. Indoors there was an immense volume of correspondence to be attended to with the aid of Tobias Lear, the faithful secretary who had lived with the President during the New York and Philadelphia periods. . . . On December 10, 1799, Washington sent a long letter to James Anderson in regard to agricultural plans for his farm during the year 1800. . . . December 12th, he wrote a short note to Alexander Hamilton, in regard to the organization of a National Military Academy, a matter in which the President had long been deeply interested. (Thayer, William R.—*George Washington*, pp. 232, 240, 241.)

After his retirement from public life, all the time

which he could spare from his library, was devoted to the improvement of his estates, and the elegant and tasteful arrangement of his house and grounds. He was his own surveyor; and the disposition and appearance of his farms, gave evident proofs that the genius of useful improvement had directed its energies with beneficial as well as ornamental effects. (Custis, George Washington Parke—*Recollections and Private Memoirs of Washington*, p. 12.)

No one would ever think of characterizing George Washington as frivolous minded, but from youth to old age he was a believer in the adage that all work and no play makes Jack a dull boy—a saying that many an overworked farmer of our own day would do well to take to heart. (Haworth, Paul L.—*George Washington, Country Gentleman*, p. 239.)

General Washington, during the whole of both his public and private life, was a very early riser; indeed, the Maternal Mansion, at which his first habits were formed, abhorred the character of a sluggard, as much as nature does a vacuum. Whether as Chief Magistrate or the retired Citizen, we find this man of method and labor seated in his library from one to two hours before day, in winter, and at day-break in summer. We wonder at the amazing deal of work which he performed. Nothing but a method the most remarkable and exemplary could have enabled him to accomplish an amount of labor, which might have given pretty full employment to the lives of half a dozen ordinary, and not idle men. When we consider the volume of his official papers—his vast foreign, public, and private correspondence—we are scarcely able to believe that the space of one man's life should have comprehended the doing so many things, and doing them so well. (Custis, George Washington Parke—*Recollections and Private Memoirs of Washington*, p. 5.)

2. Public.
   a. **July 4, 1798, General Washington was appointed Lieutenant General and Commander in Chief of the Armies.**

The highly prized retirement to Mount Vernon did not now, more than at any previous time, separate Washington from the affairs of the country. He continued to take a keen interest in all that went on, to correspond with his friends, and to use his influence for what he thought wisest and best for the general welfare. . . .

To any other appeal to come forward Washington would have been deaf, but he could never refuse a call to arms. (Lodge, Henry C.—*George Washington* (American Statesmen), Vol. II, pp. 279-280.)

He declined all public undertakings except that which President Adams begged him to assume—the supreme command of the army in case of the expected war with France. That new duty was good for him, for it proved to him that at least all his official relations with the Government had not ceased, and it also served to cheer the people of the country to know that in case of military trouble their old commander would lead them once more. (Thayer, William R.—*George Washington*, p. 240.)

From 1749 till 1784, and from 1789 till 1797, or a period of forty years, Washington filled offices of one kind or another, and when he died he still held a commission. Thus, excluding his boyhood, there were but seven years of his life in which he was not engaged in the public service. Even after his retirement from the Presidency he served on a grand jury, and before this he had several times acted as petit juror. In another way he was a good citizen, for when at Mount Vernon he invariably attended the election, rain or shine, though it was a

MARTHA WASHINGTON
From the Gilbert Stuart painting

ride of ten miles to the polling town. (Ford, Paul L.—*George Washington*, p. 309.)

   b. George Washington: Leader in Philanthropy—Program Eight (*George Washington The Leader of Men*), No. 3.

George Washington's many charities will probably never be known. His idea seemed always to help people to help themselves, but he fed them, clothed and housed them, paid their debts, and gave a real start to many with no claim of kinship.

   c. Significant Events in the Public Life of George Washington—*Honor to George Washington*, No. 8 (*Washington as President*), Part III.

   d. Principal Official Appointments — *Honor to George Washington*, No. 3 (*Tributes to Washington*), Part IV.

3. Home and Social.
   a. Personal Appearance—*Honor to George Washington*, No. 3 (*Tributes to Washington*), Part I.

   b. Family Life and Friends—*Honor to George Washington*, No. 14 (*Washington's Home and Fraternal Life*), Part I.

On Saturdays he rested somewhat from his labors, by either riding into the country, attended by a groom, or with his family in his coach drawn by six horses. (Custis, George Washington Parke—*Recollections and Private Memoirs of Washington* p. 59.)

   c. Last Years at Mount Vernon—Program Twelve (*The Homemaking of George and Martha Washington*), No. 4.

Mount Vernon drew people of every class and kind. General Washington held first place in the hearts of the people.

The influx of strange faces . . . soon became overwhelming, and Washington felt the necessity of having some one at hand to relieve him from a part of the self-imposed duties of Virginia hospitality.

With this view he bethought him of his nephew, Lawrence Lewis, the same who had gained favor with him by volunteering in the Western expedition, . . . He accordingly addressed a letter to him in which he writes: "Whenever it is convenient to you to make this place your home, I shall be glad to see you. . . . As both your aunt and I are in the decline of life, and regular in our habits, especially in our hours of rising and going to bed, I require some person (fit and proper) to ease me of the trouble of entertaining company, particularly of nights, as it is my inclination to retire (and unless prevented by very particular company, I always do retire,) either to bed or to my study soon after candle light. In taking those duties (which hospitality obliges one to bestow on company) off my hands, it would render me a very acceptable service." (Irving, Washington—*The Life of George Washington*, Vol. V, pp. 275-276.)

His great employment, and a constant stream of company, gave the General but little time to go abroad; still he occasionally visited his old and long-remembered friends in Alexandria. He attended a martial exhibition, representing an invasion by the French, which ended in an old-fashioned sham battle and the capture of the invaders; it was handsomely gotten up, Alexandria at that time possessing a numerous and well-appointed military, and the whole went off with great eclat. (Custis, George Washington Parke—*Recollections and Private Memoirs of Washington*, pp. 75-76.)

He was constantly thinking of others; and the education of his nephews, the care of young Lafayette until he should return to France, as well as the happy love-match of Nellie Custis and his nephew, supplied the human interest without which he was never happy. (Lodge, Henry C.—*George Washington (American Statesmen)*, Vol. II, pp. 275-276.)

An event occurred on the 22d February, 1799, that, while it created an unusual bustle in the ancient halls, shed a bright gleam of sunshine on the "Last Days at Mount Vernon." It was the marriage of Major Lewis, a favorite nephew, with the adopted daughter of the Chief. It was the wish of the young bride that the General of the Armies of the United States should appear in the splendidly embroidered uniform (the costume assigned him by the board of general officers) in honor of the bridal; but alas, even the idea of wearing a costume bedizzened with gold embroidery, had never entered the mind of the Chief, he being content with the old Continental blue and buff, while the magnificent white plumes presented to him by Major General Pinckney he gave to the young bride, preferring the old Continental cocked hat, with the plain black riband cockade, a type of the brave old days of '76. (Custis, George Washington Parke—*Recollections and Private Memoirs of Washington*, p. 74.)

I. DEATH AND WILL.

A. December 14, 1799—George Washington died in his room at Mount Vernon about 11 o'clock in the evening.

B. December 18, 1799—The funeral of George Washington was held at his home, Mount Vernon, and he was buried in the family vault on the estate within sight of the house.

The news of Washington's death did not reach the capital until Wednesday, December 18th. The House immediately adjourned. On the following day, when it reassembled, John Marshall delivered a brief tribute and resolutions were passed to attend the funeral and to pay honor " . . . [to the man] first in war, first in peace, and first in the hearts of his countrymen." The immortal phrase was by Colonel Henry Lee, the father of General Robert E. Lee. President Adams, in response to a letter from the Senate of the United States, used the less happy phrase, "If a Trajan found a Pliny, a Marcus Aurelius can never want biographers, eulogies, or historians." (Thayer, William R.—*George Washington*, p. 251.)

The whole American nation was plunged into grief by the death of Washington. Funeral services were held in the large cities; . . . Upon the recommendation of Congress, the President of the United States (John Adams) issued a special Proclamation, setting apart Washington's Birthday, February 22, 1800, as a day of public grief, prayer and eulogy. . . .

General "Light Horse Harry" Lee was chosen to give Washington's eulogy in Congress; . . . [On Dec. 26, 1799] This eulogy was given in the German Lutheran Church, Philadelphia, to which Congress walked in a body from Independence Hall. (Sawyer, Joseph D.—*Washington*, Vol. II, pp. 363, 366, 369.)

C. Washington's Fortune and Will.
 1. Facsimile of Washington's Will.
 2. References.
  Callahan, Charles H.—*Washington: the Man and the Mason* (Appendix).
  Prussing, Eugene E.—*Estate of George Washington, Deceased*.

III. MOUNT VERNON A NATIONAL SHRINE.

Go, when the day is fine, down the river to Mount Vernon. There, following the path up from the shore among the trees, you will slowly come to where his tomb is, the simple vault half up the hill, which vines partly cover, built according to his directions. From this you will still ascend among grass and trees, and pass up by old buildings, old barns, an old coach-house with the coach in it, and so come to the level green upon which the house gives with its connecting side offices at either flank. Inside the house, all through the rooms of bygone comfort so comfortable still, so mellowed with the long sense of home, you will feel the memory of his presence strangely, and how much his house is like him. He seems to come from his battles and his austere fame, and to be here by the fireplace. Here are some of his very books on the shelves, here the stairs he went up and down, here in the hall his swords, and the key of the Bastille that Lafayette sent to him. Upstairs is the room he died in, and the bed; still above this chamber, the little room where Martha Washington lived her last years after his death, with its window looking out upon the tomb where he was first laid. Everything, every object, every corner and step, seems to bring him close, not in the way of speaking of him or breathing of him, as some memorial places seem to speak and breathe their significance; a silence fills these passages and rooms, a particular motionlessness, that is not changed or disturbed by the constant moving back and forth of the visitors. What they do, their voices, their stopping and bending to look at this or that, does not seem to affect, or even to reach, the strange influence that surrounds them. It is an exquisite and friendly serenity which bathes one's sense, that brings him so near, that seems to be charged all through with some meaning or message of beneficence and reassurance, but nothing that could be put into words.

auguration of John Adams, who thus became second President of the United States.

1797, Mar. 9-15—Ex-President Washington journeyed to his home at Mount Vernon, where he resumed the life of an active farmer. The throngs that followed him there forced him to keep open house.

THE MANSION AT MOUNT VERNON, OVERLOOKING THE POTOMAC RIVER

And then, not staying too long in the house, stroll out upon the grounds. Look away to the woods and fields, whence he rode home from hunting. . . . Turn into his garden and look at the walls and the walks he planned, the box hedges, the trees, the flower-beds, the great order and the great sweetness everywhere. And among all this, still the visitors are moving, looking, speaking, the men, women, and children from every corner of the country, some plain and rustic enough, some laughing and talking louder than need be, but all drawn here to see it, to remember it, to take it home with them, . . . and no more disturbing the lovely peace of it than they disturbed the house. For again, as in the house, only if possible more marvellously still, there comes from the trees, the box hedges, the glimpses of the river, that serenity with its message of beneficence and reassurance, that cannot be put into words. It seems to lay a hand upon all and make them, for a moment, one. . . .

Then go down the hill again, past the old buildings, past the tomb, among the trees to the shore. As you recede from the shore, you watch the place grow into the compactness of distance, and then it seems to speak: "I am still here, my countrymen, to do you what good I can." (Wister, Owen—*The Seven Ages of Washington*, pp. 249-253.)

IV. SIGNIFICANT DATES SELECTED FROM *George Washington Year by Year*.

1797, Mar. 4—President Washington attended the in-

1798, July 4—General Washington was appointed Lieutenant General and Commander in Chief of the Armies; war with France threatened.

1798, July 13—General Washington accepted the command with a reserve as to field service.

1798, Nov. 5-Dec. 19—General Washington made a trip to Philadelphia for a consultation on military matters. This was his last journey.

1799, Feb. 22—The wedding of Nellie Custis and Lawrence Lewis took place on the General's last birthday.

1799, Dec. 12—General Washington made a circuit of his farms, where he caught a severe cold and developed quinsy.

1799, Dec. 14—George Washington died in his room at Mount Vernon about 11 o'clock in the evening.

1799, Dec. 18—The funeral of General Washington was held at his home, Mount Vernon, and he was buried in the family vault on the estate within sight of the house.

1802, May 22—Martha Washington died and was buried in the family vault.

1831—The bodies of George and Martha Washington were reinterred in the new vault at Mount Vernon.

Unit IX
Selected Tributes to George Washington

Brief Outline

I. PRIOR TO THE CENTENNIAL OF HIS BIRTH (1832).

  A. By contemporaries.
    1. *Character and Service.*
    2. *World Status.*

II. AT THE CENTENNIAL (1832).

III. BETWEEN THE CENTENNIAL AND BICENTENNIAL.

NOTE: *Topics in italics are titles of 48 papers in a series of 12 George Washington Programs and the parts of the Honor to George Washington series of 15 pamphlets issued by the United States George Washington Bicentennial Commission.*

Development

I. PRIOR TO THE CENTENNIAL OF HIS BIRTH (1832).

  A. By Contemporaries.
    1. Character and Service—*Honor to George Washington, No. 3 (Tributes to Washington), Part II.*
    2. World Status—*Honor to George Washington, No. 3 (Tributes to Washington), Part III.*

> He was, like the Sun, shining in his strength, dissipating, to an endless remove, the mists of prejudice and passion. There was no spot, on the broad disk of his private, and public life, to obscure the lustre of the one, or, obstruct the shedding and effulgent glories of the other. He suffered no eclipse. Nothing earthly, ever interposed between him and his country. He was a patriot "full orbed," brightening the sphere, in which he moved; not shining to bewilder and delude; but diffusing light, and life, and splendor; clothing the earth, with richer verdure, and awakening a universal carol, throughout the region, on which he rose. (Bates, Isaac C.—*George Washington*, pp. 13-14.) (Benevolent Society of Hampshire County, 1812.)

> It is not merely for some temporary purpose and only for the benefit of the age in which he lives, that Heaven in compassion to the necessities of a people vouchsafes to raise up a great and favored man in their defence. The good as well as "the evil men do, live after them"—and never was richer inheritance bequeathed by expiring Patriot to his country than we have received from ours. Lasting as his name will be the blessings achieved for us by his life if we are not wanting to ourselves—in that name alone he has left us a defence and a perpetual excitement to the highest efforts of patriotism. (Key, Francis Scott—*Oration*, p. 4.) (Washington Society, Alexandria, Va., February 22, 1814.)

NATIONAL MONUMENT TO WASHINGTON

I. AT THE CENTENNIAL (1832).

> We are assembled to unite, in sentiment, with millions of our fellow-citizens, in a festive act, which the nation honors, and all enlightened freemen will learn to revere. We are pledged to perform our part, however humble, with suitable feelings, and in such fitness of style and manner as we can attain, in the great Jubilee of the first Centennial Anniversary of the Birth-day of Washington. In its own nature, as well as from the object of it, the festival is peculiarly interesting, and calculated to recommend itself to our choicest affections. But there is a consideration connected with it, which should doubly endear it to us, and enhance, in an equal degree, our devotedness in observing it. None of us can hope to join in it again. . . . As we shall partake of the festival but once, let us do it in a spirit of gladness and gratulation, worthy of the boon, for which it is instituted. While we do homage to the occasion, with sentiments of gratitude and veneration, it is our duty to enliven it with libations of joy. . . . In this tribute to the Father of his country, it is my wish to be liberal and discriminating, as well as correct. Applause is substantial and lasting, only when tempered with justice and truth. It is therefore that I make the following admissions.

> Many individuals may have surpassed Washington in extent of knowledge, depth of wisdom, and brilliancy of genius. Chieftains superior to him in war may have lead armies to victory. Statesmen of greater attainment and sagacity, and of more vigorous intellects and a wider reach of mind, may have figured in the councils and cabinets of nations. Patriots of equal purity may have devoted their lives to the service of their country; and some men may

have exhibited a moral and social example as free from blemish. But, in no one known to fame have all these elements been at once so abundantly and happily blended. In no one has the aggregate been so great, and the balance so complete. . . . Hence, if it is not now, it will be received hereafter, as a conceded truth, that, as a monument of moral sublimity, individual grandeur, and unsullied worth, the Leader of our revolution, and the Chief Founder of our present Government, is without a rival. The catalogue of human greatness, extending through modern and ancient times, contains no other name so elevated and spotless. (Caldwell, Charles—*A Discourse*, pp. 6-7, 9-10.) (On the First Centennial Celebration of the Birth-Day of Washington, delivered by request to the Citizens of Lexington, Ky., February 22, 1832.)

Yet he had not done enough; and in the fulness of his patriotism and philanthropy, he gave that *last legacy* to posterity. Follow its light, my countrymen; it is the blended light of virtue and wisdom, and, in moral sublimity, rivals the mild glory and mingled beauties of the rainbow. It issues, as it were, from the tomb of him who was the Epaminondas of your fathers in elevating the glory of his country; who was the refuge of their hope in the dark hour of adversity; their pilot in the storm, and the pillar of their strength, amid the rumbling vibrations of the convulsion. The dearest hopes of the human race, bid you follow its monitions; bid you eschew the strife of party spirit; bid you recollect that interest is a rock, and the fervor of transient sentiments is stubble; and, therefore, be just and firm with all nations, and partial to none. Forget not that fair national reputation is as valuable and important as independence itself: that it carries along with it a charm which wins upon the world; which claims respect from all, and extorts it even from obstinate hostility. Rejoice that this fair character has been preserved inviolate; and

"While one great clime, in full and free defiance,

Yet rears her crest, unconquer'd and sublime;"

while the lustre of our Fathers' glorious deeds yet illumines our onward march, and this day's associations kindle afresh our gratitude; let us assume the solemnities of "their pledge of life, of fortune, and of sacred honor," and re-assert the firm and holy resolve to transmit their rich gifts to posterity, with the sign, and seal, and attestations of an honorable conveyance. (Collier, Robert R.—*An Oration*, pp. 9-10.) (Petersburg, Va., February 22, 1832.)

. . . standing at last, all alone in his pre-eminence, fixed forever in the solitude of his glory, as the Miracle of Men, the greatest earthly Benefactor of mankind, . . . (Gray, Francis C.—*Washington*, p. 77.) (Oration, Legislature of Mass., One Hundredth Anniversary of Birth of George Washington.)

It has been justly remarked that the character of Washington belongs not to a country or a people. Bright as is his example to us, instructive as are his lessons of wisdom, the light of them is upon the world. We see it—we feel it—we rejoice at it. We know that it was he who first administered a government which is now a model for imitation. . . .

It was he, who, when amid contending prejudices and passions, our political bark was launched upon the ocean of experiment, stood at the helm, and conducted her steadily over its breaking waves, amid the tempest and the storm, guided and cheered by that light alone which sparkled from the heavens at his birth, and whose benignant rays had illumined his path through all his perilous warfare with civilized or savage man.

Fortunate was it for the country, fortunate for posterity, fortunate for the cause of liberty, fortunate for his own fame, that it was entrusted to him to carry into effect the provisions of our Constitution. He infused into it his own, and its true spirit, and he accomplished more to perpetuate our civil rights and privileges by his sagacity, his prudence and decision, as the chief executive officer of the Union, than he had done by all his military achievements—more towards placing this nation above the

CENTENNIAL BADGE, 1832

reach of those influences which undermined the foundation of the ancient republics, and buried their magnificent fabrics in ruins. (Lincoln, Solomon—*Oration*, pp. 18-19.) (Pronounced at Plymouth, on the Centennial Anniversary of the Birth of George Washington.)

I need not recur to the principles by which he was governed, and the policy he pursued. When he was about to resign his civil authority, as he had before resigned his military power, he left to us, his political legacy . . . and we shall best honor his memory by a reverential regard for the principles it contains. In every line of it we read the language of a father's heart, solicitous for the welfare of his children—the wisdom of a statesman, who embraced within his comprehension the widest interests of his country and of man—the friend of equal and just laws—the lover of the Union as the ark of safety which must not be approached with unhallowed purposes—the advocate of civil liberty throughout the world. It is a precious legacy—and if, on that height of prosperity on which we stand, we will but listen to its warnings, in our aspirations of ambition . . . in the mad strugglings of party strife, we shall act wisely for ourselves—safely for our country and justly to his fame, which forms so fair a portion of our rich inheritance. We need not fear that we shall elevate him too highly in our praises; or copy too closely his bright example. It is the deliberate judgment, pronounced not by this country alone but by all countries, that in purity, as well as splendor of character and magnitude of service to the happiness of his fellow creatures, he stands without an equal. . . . Washington alone, rose above every selfish consideration, and lived for his country and mankind. (Southard, Samuel L.—*Centennial Ad dress*, pp. 19-21.) (Trenton, N. J., February 22, 1832.)

A true friend of his country loves her friends and benefactors, and thinks it no degradation to commend and commemorate them. The voluntary outpouring of the public feeling, made to-day, from the North to the South, and from the East to the West, proves this sentiment to be both just and natural. In the cities and in the villages, in the public temples and in the family circles, among all ages and sexes, gladdened voices to-day bespeak grateful hearts and a freshened recollection of the virtues of the Father of his Country. And it will be so, in all time to come, so long as public virtue is itself an object of regard. The ingenuous youth of America will hold up to themselves the bright model of Washington's example, and study to be what they behold; they will contemplate his character till all its virtues spread out and display themselves to their delighted vision; as the earliest astronomers, the shepherds on the plains of Babylon gazed at the stars till they saw them form into clusters and constellations, overpowering at length the eyes of the beholders with the united blaze of a thousand lights. (Webster, Daniel—"The Character of Washington," *Works* (1853 ed.), Vol. I, pp. 220-221.) (Speech, Washington, D. C., February 22, 1832.)

III. BETWEEN THE CENTENNIAL AND BICENTENNIAL.

We are today the nation that we are because George Washington was the man that he was. . . .

It is wholly unjust to an historical character to demand that he be judged by any other standard than that of the age in which he lived. We have no moral right to ask how Washington would have handled Grant's army at Lookout Mountain, or that of Foch at the Battle of the Marne, or how he would have dealt with the diplomatic questions that beset John Hay in protecting the integrity of China, or Woodrow Wilson in dealing with the League of Nations. We do not know, and it is idle to ask, unless we also ask with what different preparation and experience and equipment Washington would probably have approached these hypothetical situations. The real question to ask is: How did George Washington face the problems of his own age? How did he handle the forces that rallied about him when he unsheathed his sword under the Cambridge elm? How did he behave in the battles which he actually fought? How did he address himself to the political situation attending the organization of a new republic? Washington at Lookout Mountain or at Chateau Thierry would have been an historic absurdity, but Washington at Dorchester Heights, at Trenton, at Princeton, was very far from being absurd. He was indeed a close approach to the sublime. Washington facing the problems of Grant or of Roosevelt or Wilson would have been an anachronism, but Washington presiding over the Continental Congress, bringing order out of chaos in a new and untried government, holding together the discordant elements in a strong but heterogeneous cabinet, and creating out of raw material a nation, that Washington was no anachronism. He was a Saul among his contemporaries—standing head and shoulders above them. He was the man for the time and the place—the man called of God to create a nation, and bequeath to posterity a new and noble ideal of national heroism and national character.

It is well that we honor the father of our country. No other modern nation begins its history with such a character, so commanding, so symmetrical, so fit to belong to the ages. . . .

We cannot afford to forget the past nor to renounce our heritage of great names. Least of all among our American heroes can we afford to forget him of whom an eminent British statesman (Lord Brougham) has said, "Until time shall be no more will a test of the progress which our race has made in wisdom and virtue be derived from the veneration paid to the immortal name of Washington." (Barton, Rev. William E.—*George Washington*.) (Oak Park, Ill., February 22, 1920.)

We need in our public and private life such pure and chastened sentiments as result from the sincere and heartfelt observance of days like this, and we need such quickening of our patriotism as the sedate contemplation of the life and character of Washington creates. . . .

Washington was the most thorough American that ever lived. His sword was drawn to carve out American citizenship, and his every act and public service was directed to its establishment. . . . Let us thank God that he has lived, and that he has given to us the highest and best example of American citizenship. (Cleveland, Grover—*Writings and Speeches*, ed. by George F. Parker, pp. 350-352.) (Address, "The Character of Washington," Southern Society, New York, February 22, 1890.)

It is doubtful if anyone outside of certain great religious teachers ever so thoroughly impressed himself on the heart of humanity as has George Washington. No figure in America has been the subject of more memorial tributes and more unstinted praise. And yet the subject never seems to be exhausted and the public interest never seems to be decreased. The larger our experience with affairs of the world, the more familiar we become with his life and teachings, the more our admiration enlarges, and the greater grows our estimation of his wisdom. He represented the marvelous combination of the soldier, the patriot, and the statesman. In the character of each he stands supreme. (Coolidge, Calvin—"Washington and Education"; in National Education Association, *Proceedings*, 1926, p. 706.)

Grand and manifold as were its phases, there is yet no difficulty in understanding the character of Washington. He was no Veiled Prophet. He never acted a part. Simple, natural and unaffected, his life lies before us—a fair and open manuscript. He disdained the arts which wrap power and mystery in order to magnify it. He practiced the profound diplomacy of truthful speech—the consummate tact of direct attention. Looking ever to the All-Wise Disposer of events, he relied on that Providence which helps men by giving them high hearts and hopes to help themselves with the means which their Creator has put at their service. There was no infirmity in his conduct over which Charity must fling its veil; no taint of selfishness from which Purity averts her gaze; no dark recess of intrigue that must be lit up with colored panegyric; no subterranean passage to be trod in trembling lest there be stirred the ghost of a buried crime. (Daniel, John Warwick—"Washington and the Nation"; in *Congressional Record*, Vol. 73, pp. 2000-2001.) (Oration, dedication of Washington Monument, House of Representatives, February 21, 1885.)

Blot out from the page of history the names of all the great actors of his time in the drama of nations, and preserve the name of Washington, and the century would be renowned. (Depew, Chauncey M.—*The Centennial Oration*, pp. 46-47.) (The One Hundredth Anniversary of the Inauguration of

George Washington as President of the United States, at Sub-Treasury, New York.)

Yet, with all the humanizing, he is still the austere, rugged, inaccessible mountain, its fiery passions hidden; its head above the forests; and so he will stand in history the justest of men, a man of highest purity of purpose and of greatest practical wisdom; but if he is as a mountain, then, as one that hides somewhere in its slopes, a portage path, which he himself sought between the eastern and the western waters. (Finley, John H.—*Washington and the West*, p. 17.) (Address, Morristown, N. J., February 22, 1925.)

I will then say that if, among all the pedestals supplied by history for public characters of extraordinary nobility and purity, I saw one higher than all the rest, and if I were required at a moment's notice to name the fittest occupant for it, I think my choice, at any time during the last forty-five years would have lighted, and it would now light, upon Washington. (Gladstone, William E.—"Letter," October 4, 1884; in George W. Smalley, *London Letters*, Vol. II, p. 299.)

We are upon the eve of the celebration of the two hundredth anniversary of the birth of George Washington. It is, therefore, appropriate that our observance of Memorial Day should this year be at this place, so intimately associated with the moral grandeur of the Father of Our Country. . . .

Here Washington and his little band of hungry and almost naked patriots kept alive the spark of liberty in the lowest hours of the Revolution. They met the crisis with steadfast fortitude; they conserved their strength; they husbanded their resources; they seized the opportunity, which, with the turn and the tide of war, led on to victory. It was a triumph of character and idealism and high intelligence over the counsels of despair, of prudence, and material comfort. This was one of those moral victories that are the glory of the race. Without such victories the life of man would descend to a sheer materialism for "where there is no vision the people perish." Lacking these high inspirations mankind could claim no distinction higher than the beasts of the field, that sing no songs, dream no dreams, inspire no hope, and grasp no faith. . . . God grant that we may prove worthy of George Washington and his men of Valley Forge. (Hoover, Herbert—*Address*, pp. 1-2, 5.) (Valley Forge, Pa., May 30, 1931.)

There is one unerring test of true greatness, whether in literature, or in science, or thought, or action, or character. This is, that it seems to be contemporaneous with all the generations. . . . That is conspicuously true of Washington. If you were to read of him in Plutarch there would be no sense that he was out of place. . . . So I believe there never will be a period in all coming time when a character like that of Washington will excite a sense of incongruity, or of antiquity, but only the natural feeling that a character of supreme excellence has been bestowed by God upon man. (Hoar, George F.—*Washington*, p. 6.) (Chicago, February 23, 1903.)

Washington is the mightiest name of earth—long since mightiest in the cause of civil liberty, still mightiest in moral reformation. On that name no eulogy is expected. It can not be. To add brightness to the sun, or glory to the name of Washington is alike impossible. Let none attempt it. In solemn awe we pronounce the name, and in its naked deathless splendor leave it shining on. (Lincoln, Abraham—*Complete Works*, ed. (1894) by John G. Nico-

lay and John Hay, Vol. I, pp. 63-64.) (Address, Springfield, Ill., February 22, 1842.)

I see in Washington a great soldier who fought a trying war to a successful end impossible without him; a great statesman who did more than all other men to lay the foundations of a republic which has endured in prosperity for more than a century. I find in him a marvellous judgment which was never at fault, a penetrating vision which beheld the future of America when it was dim to other eyes, a great intellectual force, a will of iron, an unyielding grasp of facts, and an unequalled strength of patriotic purpose. I see in him too a pure and high-minded gentleman of dauntless courage and stainless honor, simple and stately of manner, kind and generous of heart. Such he was in truth. The historian and the biographer may fail to do him justice, but the instinct of mankind will not fail. The real hero needs not books to give him worshippers. George Washington will always receive the love and reverence of men because they see embodied in him the noblest possibilities of humanity. (Lodge, Henry Cabot—*George Washington* (*American Statesmen*), Vol. II, p. 388.)

This is not a newly established Anniversary, but the return of an old one; and although always hitherto celebrated by the American people with pride and joy, there must be some cause for this unusual display of popular interest and enthusiasm. It is found in the present condition of our National affairs, in which the hearts and minds of the people are turned to contemplate the character, services and teachings of Washington, in order to draw from the contemplation, lessons of wisdom to guide their action in the present fearful emergency. . . . He who does not recognize in Washington the chosen instrument of a Divine Power for the accomplishment of great and benign purposes in behalf of mankind, takes but an Atheistic view of the subject. (Palmer, Robert—*Washington and the Union*, pp. 3-4, 7.) (Oration, Harrisburg, Pa., February 22, 1861.)

In the Revolution and in the period of constructive statesmanship immediately following it, for our good fortune it befell us that the highest military and the highest civic attributes were embodied in Washington, and so in him we have one of the undying men of history—a great soldier, if possible an even greater statesman, and above all a public servant whose lofty and disinterested patriotism rendered his power and ability—alike on fought fields and in council chambers—of the most far-reaching service to the Republic. (Roosevelt, Theodore—*Presidential Addresses and State Papers*, Vol. I, p. 232.)

But Washington, it seems to me, though high-statured even beyond the other giants of his day, bore in his mien and stature the marks of the race to which he belonged. In him we may discern the "brief chronicle and abstract" of a time and a nation. . . . Washington was neither an accident nor a miracle. Neither chance nor a special Providence need be assumed to account for him. It was God, indeed, who gave him to us; but God had been preparing him ever since English constitutional history began. He was of the same breed with Hampden and Pym and Cromwell. Burke and Chatham both recognized him as a brother so soon as they saw opened before them the credentials of his deeds. He was of such heroic stuff as God had for centuries been so graciously and so lavishly weaving into the character of the race. (Wilson, Woodrow—*The Public Papers of Woodrow Wilson—College and State*, ed. by Ray Stannard Baker and William E.

Dodd, Vol. 1, pp. 180-181.) (Address, April 30, 1889, place not given.)

In the whole history of the world it may be doubted whether any man can be found, who has exerted a more controlling influence over men and over events than George Washington. To what did he owe that influence? How did he win, how did he wield, that magic power, that majestic authority, over the minds and hearts of his countrymen and of mankind? In what did the power of Washington consist? . . . I hazard nothing in saying that it was the high moral element of his character which imparted it to its preponderating force. His incorruptible honesty, his uncompromising truth, his devout reliance on God, the purity of his life, the scrupulousness of his conscience, the disinterestedness of his purposes, his humanity, generosity, and justice,—these were the ingredients which, blending harmoniously with solid information and sound judgment and a valor only equalled by his modesty, made up a character to which the world may be fearlessly challenged for a parallel. (Winthrop, Robert C.—*Addresses and Speeches*, Vol. I, pp. 80-81.) (Oration, Laying the Corner-Stone of the National Monument to Washington, July 4, 1848.)

Reference: Coolidge, Calvin—*Birth of George Washington* (Address, February 22, 1927).

STATUE OF GEORGE WASHINGTON

By Lorado Taft. At the University of Washington, Seattle, Wash.

Unit X
Washington the Nation's Capital

THE UNITED STATES CAPITOL

Brief Outline

I. WASHINGTON THE CITY BEAUTIFUL.
  A. History.
    1. Participation of President Washington in Creation.
      a. Selection of Site.
      b. Early Plans.
      c. *George Washington, City Builder.*
    2. Occupation by Federal Government.
    3. Growth.
    4. Present-Day Plans.
      a. McMillan Plan (1901) and Its Development.
      b. The National Commission of Fine Arts.
      c. The National Capital Park and Planning Commission.
    5. Early Maps of District of Columbia.
    6. General References.
II. THE FEDERAL GOVERNMENT AND ITS BUILDINGS.
  A. Legislative.
    1. The Capitol.
      a. Rotunda and Dome.
      b. Senate Chamber.
      c. Hall of Representatives.
      d. Art of the Capitol—Correlate with "Art" in Unit XI.
    2. Office Buildings.
      a. Senate.
      b. House.
    3. The Government Printing Office.
  B. Executive.
    1. The White House.
      a. The Home of the President.
      b. The Executive Office of the President.
    2. Departments of the Executive, and Buildings.
      a. State.
      b. Treasury.
      c. War.
      d. Post Office.
      e. Navy.
      f. Interior.
      g. Justice.
      h. Agriculture.
      i. Commerce.
      j. Labor.
  C. Judicial.
    1. Supreme Court.
    2. The United States Court of Claims.
    3. United States Court of Customs and Patent Appeals.
  D. Boards and Commissions.
III. THE MUNICIPAL GOVERNMENT AND ITS BUILDINGS.
  A. The District Building.
  B. District of Columbia Municipal Center.
  C. Courthouse.
  D. Court of Appeals.
  E. Washington City Post Office.
  F. Transportation.
    1. Union Station.
    2. Recent Highway Plan.
  G. Public School Buildings.
  H. Public Library.
  I. Recent Building Regulations.
    1. Zoning Law.
    2. Shipstead-Luce Act.
IV. FOREIGN DIPLOMATIC ESTABLISHMENTS.
V. EDUCATIONAL INSTITUTIONS.
  A. Library of Congress.
  B. Smithsonian Institution.
  C. National Academy of Science.
  D. Pan American Union.
  E. Carnegie Institution of Washington.
  F. Universities and Colleges.
    1. American University.
    2. Catholic University.
    3. Columbian Institution for the Deaf.
    4. Georgetown University.
    5. George Washington University.
    6. Howard University.
    7. National University.

G. National Associations.
   1. National Education Association.
   2. National Congress of Parents and Teachers.
   3. National Geographic Society.
   4. Other National Headquarters.
H. Centers of Art—Correlate with "Art" in Unit XI.
   1. Old National Museum, Arts and Industries Building.
     a. Relics of George Washington and Family.
     b. Costumes of the Mistresses of the White House.
   2. New National Museum, Natural History Building.
     a. National Gallery of Art.
   3. Freer Gallery of Art.
   4. Corcoran Gallery of Art.
   5. Phillips Memorial Gallery.
I. Churches of Washington.

VI. SHRINES AND MEMORIALS IN WASHINGTON—Correlate
    with "Art" in Unit XI.
A. Washington Monument.
B. Lincoln Memorial.
C. Lincoln Museum.
D. Memorial Continental Hall.
E. Constitution Hall.
F. American Red Cross.

VII. HISTORIC HOMES.
A. Reference.

VIII. PARKS AND PARKWAYS.
A. National Capital Park System.
B. Monuments and Statues in the Public Grounds.
C. The Historic Potomac River.

IX. ENVIRONS RELATED TO THE LIFE OF GEORGE WASHING-
    TON AND NATIONAL HISTORY.
A. Mount Vernon.
B. Alexandria.
   1. Alexandria Academy.
   2. Alexandria-Washington Lodge, A. F. and A. M.
   3. Christ Church.
   4. Gadsby's Tavern.
   5. George Washington National Masonic Memorial.
   6. Home of John Carlyle.
C. Great Falls.
D. Arlington.
   1. Restoration of the Arlington Mansion (Custis-Lee
     House).
   2. Arlington National Cemetery.
     a. The Tomb of the Unknown Soldier.
     b. Memorial Amphitheater.
E. Fort Washington.
F. Civil War Forts and Battlefields.

X. PROJECTS IN CONNECTION WITH THE GEORGE WASHING-
    TON BICENTENNIAL.
A. The Restoration of Wakefield—George Washington's
    Birthplace.
B. Mount Vernon Highway.
C. Arlington Memorial Bridge.
D. George Washington Memorial Parkway.

NOTE: *Topics in italics are titles of 48 papers in a series of 12
George Washington Programs and the parts of the Honor to George
Washington series of 15 pamphlets issued by the United States George
Washington Bicentennial Commission.*

Development

I. WASHINGTON THE CITY BEAUTIFUL.
A. History.
   1. Participation of President Washington in Creation.
     a. Selection of Site.

> Washington picked a site for the thousands of
> years which we hope will be the measure of our na-
> tional destiny. The capital of no other nation ap-
> proaches it in the beauty of its situation, and no-
> where else does nature so admirably lend itself to
> the embellishing touch of art. (Taft, William H.—
> "Washington: Its Beginning, Its Growth, and Its

Future"; in *The National Geographic Magazine,*
March, 1915, p. 223.)

Indeed, L'Enfant, on making application to President Washington to be appointed to design the city
contemplated by Congress, anticipated just such conditions as now prevail. In his letter of September
11, 1789, he writes:

> "No nation had ever before the opportunity offered
> them of deliberately deciding on the spot where their
> capital city should be fixed, or of combining every
> necessary consideration in the choice of situation,
> and although the means now within the power of
> the country are not such as to pursue the design to
> any great extent, it will be obvious that the plan
> should be drawn on such a scale as to leave room
> for that aggrandizement and embellishment which
> the increase of the wealth of the Nation will permit
> it to pursue at any period however remote." (The
> National Commission of Fine Arts—*Eleventh Re-
> port,* ch. ii (The Public Buildings Program), p. 23.)

The only man who seems to have foreseen the
greatness of this city, so far as I can learn, was
George Washington himself. . . . he appears to have
realized that this was going to be an enormous country and ought to have a grand capital, and you
ought to go back to his ideals and render the greatest tribute you can render to his immortal memory.
What you have got to do is to make the nation
feel that it has a real living interest in Washington. Make the man from Maine and from Minnesota and from Florida feel that Washington belongs to him. (Bryce, James—"The Nation's Capital"; in The National Geographic Society, *The Capital of Our Country,* pp. 106-107.)

     b. Early Plans.

> Washington's appointment of L'Enfant, an edu-
> cated French army engineer, to lay out the Capi-
> tal City was a most lucky circumstance in our his-
> tory. L'Enfant's plan in a way resembles the Fed-
> eral Constitution. That great instrument of gov-
> ernment has proven itself adaptable to a change of
> conditions that even the most clear-sighted man of
> affairs could not have anticipated. The simple com-
> prehensiveness of its broad lines under the states-
> manlike interpretation of Marshall has proved equal
> to the greatest emergencies and the most radical
> crises that could possibly confront a nation.
> So Washington and L'Enfant and Jefferson in
> their planning for Washington have left a frame-
> work for its development that the ablest architects
> and artists now more than 100 years after the plan
> was drawn and its execution begun have confessed
> themselves unable to improve. (Taft, William H.—
> "Washington: Its Beginning, Its Growth, and Its
> Future"; in *The National Geographic Magazine,*
> March, 1915, p. 226.)

> According to the plan of L'Enfant the city of
> Washington had two dominant features—the Capitol
> as the seat of the legislative branch of the Govern-
> ment and the White House as the seat of the execu-
> tive. From the Capitol and the White House the
> great avenues radiate, and on them these avenues
> converge. (National Commission of Fine Arts—
> *The Plan of The National Capital,* p. 9.)

     c. George Washington, City Builder — *Honor to
      George Washington,* No. 13 (*Washington as En-
      gineer and City Builder*), Part II.
   2. Occupation by Federal Government.

> President Adams, in the course of his message,
> called attention to the clause in the law of 1790
> which directed that the sessions of that body should
> begin in the new city on the first Monday of De-

cember, 1800, and then added that the commissioners of the city report that the removal at that time of the seat of government to the new location will be practicable and the accommodations satisfactory. . . .

On May 13, 1800, the day before congress adjourned, a resolution was adopted directing that the next session be held in Washington, beginning the third Monday in November, 1800. . . .

The afternoon of June 4 [1800] the president continued his journey and passed over the Rock Creek Bridge at K Street into the new city. . . .

On the morning of June 13 he left the city, . . . The president had the satisfaction of seeing the executive departments of the government established in the new city before he left. (Bryan, Wilhelmus B.—*A History of the National Capital*, Vol. I, pp. 339, 341, 348, 350.)

3. Growth.

The plan has been departed from in two or more notable instances through the obstinacy of men in power who could not appreciate its admirable qualities. Instead, however, of manifesting regret at these we should be grateful that they are so few in number, and that we are still able to carry out the plan and to make what its complete execution will make of Washington—the most beautiful city in the world. The reason why this is possible is because it has never been a center for business or manufacture, because its raison d'etre is only to provide a seat for government activities and a home for public servants who carry them on. It thus is singularly free in its opportunity to devote its energies to enhancing its own stateliness and acquiring a dignity appropriate to the heart of our national sovereignty. (Taft, William H.—"Washington: Its Beginning, Its Growth, and Its Future"; in *The National Geographic Magazine*, March, 1915, p. 226.)

The National Capital developed slowly and with small regard for the L'Enfant Plan until the period following the Civil War, when Alexander Shepherd, supported by President Grant, succeeded in reinstating the ideals of the city founders.

4. Present-Day Plans.
a. McMillan Plan (1901) and Its Development.

Senator James McMillan reported to the Senate from the Committee on the District of Columbia a plan for the development of the park system of the District and for the location of Government buildings. . . . it was simply a project for the development of the Capital along lines of convenience, good order, and beauty. (The National Commission of Fine Arts—*The Plan of the National Capital*, p. 5. Government Printing Office, 1923.)

For years he [James A. McMillan] was at the head of the Committee on the District of Columbia in the Senate. To him is due the revival of interest in the proper development of our country's capital. . . . By the time of the centennial of the removal of the seat of government to Washington he had his ideal clearly in mind, and before the architects were called in, he had planned to make Washington a model capital. (Taft, William H.—"Washington: Its Beginning, Its Growth, and Its Future"; in *The National Geographic Magazine*, March, 1915, p. 277.)

I am glad that the opportunity has come to me as President to contribute to impulse and leadership in the improvement of the National Capital. This is more than merely the making of a beautiful city. Washington is not only the Nation's Capital; it is the symbol of America. By its dignity and archi-

tectural inspiration we stimulate pride in our country, we encourage that elevation of thought and character which comes from great architecture. (Hoover, Herbert—"Washington, The City Beautiful"; in *Development of the United States Capital*, p. 19, Government Printing Office, 1930.) (Address, Washington, D. C., April 25, 1929.)

b. The National Commission of Fine Arts.
Created by Act of Congress, May 17, 1910.
Duties

The duties of the commission, . . . now embrace advising upon the location of statues, fountains, and monuments in the public squares, streets, and parks in the District of Columbia; upon the selection of models for statues, fountains, and monuments erected under the authority of the United States, and the selection of the artists for their execution; also for medals, insignia, and coins; upon the plans and designs for public structures and parks in the District of Columbia, as well as upon all questions involving matters of art with which the Federal Government is concerned. (*Congressional Directory*, 71st Congress, 3d Session, p. 449. Government Printing Office, 1931.)

c. The National Capital Park and Planning Commission.
Created by Act of Congress, June 6, 1924 (Name of Commission changed April 30, 1926).

The new commission retained all the powers of the park commission and was given further important advisory powers. It was charged with the duty of preparing, developing, and maintaining a comprehensive, consistent, and coordinated plan for the National Capital and its environs, . . . (*Congressional Directory*, 71st Congress, 3d Session, p. 449. Government Printing Office, 1931.)

5. Early Maps of District of Columbia.
a. Reference.
National Fine Arts Commission—*Washington the National Capital*.

6. General References
Bryan, Wilhelmus B.—*History of the National Capital*, Vols. I, II.
Congressional Directory—71st Congress, 3d Session, Government Printing Office.
Development of the United States Capital—Government Printing Office.
Director of Public Buildings and Public Parks of the National Capital Commission, *Annual Reports* (1929, 1930), Government Printing Office.
Grant, Lieut. Col. U. S., 3d—"Washington Looks Ahead"; in *American Civic Annual*, Vol. I, pp. 69-75.
Kite, Elizabeth S.—*L'Enfant and Washington*.
Moore, Charles—*Washington Past and Present*.
National Capital Park and Planning Commission—*Reports*, Government Printing Office.
National Commission of Fine Arts—*The Plan of the National Capital; also The Central Composition of The National Capital and The Public Buildings Program* (excerpts from Ninth and Eleventh Reports), Government Printing Office.
National Commission of Fine Arts—*Washington the National Capital*, Government Printing Office, 1931.
National Geographic Society—*The Capital of Our Country*.

Nicolay, Helen—*Our Capital on the Potomac.*

Papers Relating to Improvement of Washington, D. C., 56th Congress, 2d Session, S. Doc. 94, Government Printing Office.

Points of Historic Interest in National Capital. Reprint 1929, 71st Congress, 1st Session, S. Doc. 10, Government Printing Office.

Public Buildings Commission—*Annual Reports* (1929, 1930), Government Printing Office.

Proctor, John C.—*Washington, Past and Present,* Vols. I, II.

Taft, William H.—"Washington: Its Beginning, Its Growth, and Its Future"; in *The National Geographic Magazine,* March, 1915.

United States Office of Education—*Helps for Schools.* Government Printing Office, 1931.

NOTE: *Washington, the National Capital* (National Commission of Fine Arts) contains information on all items mentioned in this unit and may be used as reference for outlined study.

Write Superintendent of Documents, Washington, D. C., for List of Publications Relating to Washington, D. C.

II. THE FEDERAL GOVERNMENT AND ITS BUILDINGS.
A. Legislative.
1. The Capitol.

The Capitol is the Nation's most significant building. From the laying of its corner stone by President Washington [1793] it has represented in its construction and extensions work of the best architects, sculptors, and painters in the country during the times when they worked. To-day, judged by the world standards, it stands the peer architecturally of any house of a national legislature. (National Commission of Fine Arts—*The Central Composition of The National Capital and The Public Buildings Program,* p. 5.)

a. Rotunda and Dome.
 The Central Building contains the Rotunda with the historic paintings.
 The imposing dome is the crowning glory of the Capitol.
b. Senate Chamber.
c. Hall of Representatives.
d. Art of the Capitol—Correlate with "Art" in Unit XI.
 (1) Architecture.
 (2) Painting.
 (3) Sculpture
  Statuary Hall—Set apart for two statues from each State.
 (4) References
  Fairman, Charles E.—*Works of Art in the United States Capitol Building,* Government Printing Office, 1913.
  Fairman, Charles E.—*Art and Artists in the Capitol of the United States of America,* Government Printing Office, 1927.

2. Office Buildings—These buildings form a part of the "Frame" on Capitol Hill.

The report of the Park Commission lays down the axiom that the Capitol should be surrounded by buildings related to the work of Congress, forming the legislative group. (The National Commission of Fine Arts—*The Central Composition of The National Capital and The Public Buildings Program,* p. 11.)

a. Senate.
b. House.
3. The Government Printing Office.

Here all of the Government printing is done, including the bills of Congress, *Congressional Record,* also Department Reports and Publications.

B. Executive.
1. White House.
a. The Home of the President.

It was built for the Presidential residence, but was not completed at the time of Washington's death. John Adams was the first President to occupy it. (Sawyer, Joseph D.—*Washington,* Vol. II, p. 561.)

The river, which runs up to Alexandria, is in full view of my window, and I see the vessels as they pass and repass. The house is upon a grand and superb scale, requiring about thirty servants to attend and keep the apartments in proper order, and perform the ordinary business of the house and stables; an establishment very well proportioned to the President's salary. . . . It is a beautiful spot, capable of every improvement, and, the more I view it, the more I am delighted with it. (Adams, Abigail—*Letters,* pp. 382-383.) (Letter to Mrs. Smith [her daughter], Washington, November 21, 1800.)

Through a wise provision of the Congress at its last session the White House, which had become disfigured by incongruous additions and changes, has now been restored to what it was planned to be by Washington. In making the restorations the utmost care has been exercised to come as near as possible to the early plans . . . The White House is the property of the Nation, and so far as is compatible with living therein it should be kept as it originally was, for the same reasons that we keep Mount Vernon as it originally was. The stately simplicity of its architecture is an expression of the character of the period in which it was built, and is in accord with the purposes it was designed to serve. It is a good thing to preserve such buildings as historic monuments which keep alive our sense of continuity with the Nation's past. (Roosevelt, Theodore—"Annual Message," 1902; in *Congressional Record,* Vol. 36, p. 12.)

b. The Executive Office of the President.
2. Departments of the Executive, and Buildings.
 Each Department has numerous activities. Those listed are of particular interest to students and teachers.
a. State.
 Here are found the Great Seal of the United States; also famous documents, treaties, and state papers which have shaped world affairs.
b. Treasury.
 "Uncle Sam's Money Chest"; Bureau of Engraving and Printing; Bureau of Public Health Service.
c. War.
 General Staff College; Citizens' Military Training Camps; Service in times of peace as well as war—Engineer Corps.
d. Post Office.
 Here is supervised the Postal System. Railway Mail Service; Air Mail Service; Division of Rural Mails; Division of Dead Letters and Dead Parcel Post; Money Orders; Stamps; Parcel Post; Postal Savings.
e. Navy.
 Naval Observatory; Navy Yards; Marine Corps and Marine Barracks; Service in times of peace as well as war.

f. Interior.
United States Office of Education; Indian Affairs; National Parks.
g. Justice.
The fountain head of national law and order.
h. Agriculture.
Where Uncle Sam makes things grow and stimulates others to do the same. Varied types of scientific investigation; Extension Service; Bureau of Home Economics; 4-H Clubs; Weather Bureau; Bureau of Public Roads.
i. Commerce.
Bureau of Foreign and Domestic Commerce; Bureau of Census; Radio Division; Bureau of Standards; Bureau of Fisheries; Bureau of Mines; Patent Office.
j. Labor.
Children's Bureau; Bureau of Immigration; Bureau of Naturalization; Women's Bureau.
Note: Information on divisions and duties of each Department found in *Congressional Directory*.
Explanation of Buildings given in *Washington, the National Capital* (See References).
Annual Reports issued by each Department. Secure price list from Superintendent of Documents, Washington, D. C.

C. Judicial.
1. Supreme Court.
This high tribunal now occupying the former Senate Chamber in the Capitol will be located in a new building now in process of erection.
2. The United States Court of Claims.
3. United States Court of Customs and Patent Appeals.
D. Boards and Commissions.
Created by Congress—Duties and Personnel given in Congressional Directory.
. . . "the Farm Board dealing with the well-being of 40,000,000 of our citizens; the Commerce Commission whose rulings affect our gigantic rail system; the Shipping Board, to supervise our merchant marine; the Federal Trade Commission, the Tariff Commission, and a hundred other bureaus and commissions passing in review as they make economic and social history." (Thorpe, Merle—"Making Washington Known to the American People"; in *Greater Washington*, p. 9, February, 1931.)

III. The Municipal Government and Its Buildings.
Know Your "Federal City" (as George Washington called it), Its Government, and Development.
A. The District Building.
B. District of Columbia Municipal Center.
C. Court House.
D. Court of Appeals.
E. Washington City Post Office.
F. Transportation.
1. Union Station.
A union station has been constructed in accordance with the Commission plans. To-day it forms the gateway to Washington. In its architecture, in its landscape setting, and in its subordinate but vital relation to the buildings on Capitol Hill the Union Station is unsurpassed among the railroad terminals of the world. (The National Commission of Fine Arts—*The Plan of the National Capital*, p. 11. Government Printing Office.)
2. Recent Highway Plan.
G. Public School Buildings.
H. Public Library.
I. Recent Building Regulations.
1. Zoning Law.
2. Shipstead-Luce Act.

IV. Foreign Diplomatic Establishments.
V. Educational Institutions.
A. Library of Congress.
The Declaration of Independence and the Constitution of the United States are preserved in a shrine of bronze and marble in the Library.
Contains over four million books, included among the numerous special collections is the Toner Collection of Washingtoniana.
B. Smithsonian Institution.
Created by Act of Congress in 1846, for the "increase and diffusion of knowledge among men" in accordance with the will of James Smithson of England.
C. National Academy of Science.
Interesting exhibits show recent progress in scientific research.
D. Pan American Union.
Composed of twenty-one republics of North and South America, it is promoting international harmony.
Exhibits of the American republics and the beautiful gardens attract thousands of visitors.
E. Carnegie Institution of Washington.
Founded "to encourage in the broadest and most liberal manner investigation, research, and discovery, and the application of knowledge to the improvement of mankind." Includes a Division of Historical Research.
F. Universities and Colleges.
George Washington's interest in education is shown in many ways. His will is unique in the vision he possessed of the part education must play in a republic. He made provision for the creation of a national university.
1. American University.
2. Catholic University.
3. Columbian Institution for the Deaf.
4. Georgetown University.
5. George Washington University.
6. Howard University.
7. National University.
8. Reference.
Proctor, John C.—*Washington Past and Present*, Vol. I, ch. xl (Higher Education in the District of Columbia).
G. National Associations.
1. National Education Association.
This association stands today as the greatest educational body in the world. Organized in 1857 and later incorporated by Congress, its activities now embrace the needs and interests of the teachers of the Nation and its influence is far-reaching. Teachers from every state and from every branch of service shape the policies of this national association.
2. National Congress of Parents and Teachers.
This organization, numbering a million and a half people interested in the promotion of child welfare through the partnership of the home and school, is in close touch with the great educational movements of the day. The National Headquarters are located in the new building of the National Education Association.
3. National Geographic Society.
The purpose of this society is "to promote the interest and diffusion of geographic knowledge." Since its organization in 1888, the Society has aroused a wide-spread interest in geography, both in schools and among the general public.
4. Other National Headquarters.
H. Centers of Art—Correlate with "Art" in Unit XI.
1. Old National Museum, Arts and Industries Building.

a. Relics of George Washington and Family.
b. Costumes of the Mistresses of the White House.
2. New National Museum of Natural History Building.
   a. National Gallery of Art.
3. Freer Gallery of Art.
   a. Whistler's Peacock room.
4. Corcoran Gallery of Art.
5. Phillips Memorial Gallery.

I. Churches of Washington.
   The churches attended by the Presidents, the Washington Cathedral, National Shrine, and Monastery are of great interest to visitors.

VI. SHRINES AND MEMORIALS IN WASHINGTON—Correlate with "Art" in Unit XI.

> All experience evinces that human sentiments are strongly influenced by associations. The recurrence of anniversaries, or of longer periods of time, naturally freshens the recollection, and deepens the impression, of events with which they are historically connected. Renowned places, also, have a power to awaken feeling, which all acknowledge. No American can pass by the fields of Bunker Hill, Monmouth, and Camden, as if they were ordinary spots on the earth's surface. Whoever visits them feels the sentiment of love of country kindling anew, as if the spirit that belonged to the transactions which have rendered these places distinguished still hovered round, with power to move and excite all who in future time may approach them. (Webster, Daniel—"The Character of Washington," *Works* (1853 ed.), Vol. I, p. 220.) (Speech, Washington, D. C., February 22, 1832.)

A. Washington Monument.

> One tribute to his memory is left to be rendered. One monument remains to be reared. A monument which shall bespeak the gratitude, not of States, or of cities, or of governments; not of separate communities, or of official bodies; but of the people, the whole people of the nation;—a National Monument, erected by the citizens of the United States of America. (Winthrop, Robert C.—*Addresses and Speeches*, Vol. I, p. 71.) (Oration, Laying the Corner-Stone of the National Monument to Washington, July 4, 1848.)

> Henceforth and forever it shall be lovingly associated, not only with the memory of him in whose honor it has been erected, but with an era of assured peace, unity, and concord, which would have been dearer to his heart than the costliest personal memorial which the toil and treasure of his countrymen could have constructed. (Winthrop, Robert C.—*The National Monument to Washington*, p. 9.) (Oration on the completion of the National Monument, February 21, 1885.)

B. Lincoln Memorial.

> In this Temple as in the hearts of the people for whom he saved the union the memory of Abraham Lincoln is enshrined forever. (Inscription in Memorial.)

C. Lincoln Museum.
D. Memorial Continental Hall.
E. Constitution Hall.
F. American Red Cross.
   Memorial to Women of the Civil War.
   Memorial to Women of the World War.
G. Reference
   Proctor, John C.—*Washington Past and Present*, Vol. II, ch. xlvi (Memorials and Monuments).

VII. HISTORIC HOMES.
   The National Capital has many homes of outstanding historic interest, homes of the Presidents, statesmen, and diplomats.
   A. Reference
      Moore, Charles—*Washington Past and Present*, ch. xii (Historic Homes of Washington).

VIII. PARKS AND PARKWAYS.
   A. National Capital Park System.

   The system of Public Parks and Squares is one of the most attractive features of Washington, and unique among the cities of the Nation. Some of the outstanding ones are:

   The Mall.

   The central axis of the L'Enfant Plan, stretching from the Capitol to the Potomac River, includes the Grant Statue, Washington Monument, Lincoln Memorial, the Smithsonian Grounds, and the Agricultural Grounds.

   Potomac Park.

   Each spring thousands of visitors enjoy the Japanese flowering cherry trees which adorn Tidal Basin and the Potomac River. Three thousand cherry trees were presented to the City of Washington by the City of Tokyo. Two bronze tablets mark the first two cherry trees officially planted on March 27, 1912, by Mrs. Taft, then the First Lady of the Land, and Viscountess Chinda.

   Rock Creek Park.

   > To Rock Creek [Park] there is nothing comparable in any capital city of Europe. (Bryce, James—"The Nation's Capital"; in The National Geographic Society, *The Capital of Our Country*, p. 101.)

   The National Zoological Park, situated in Rock Creek Park, quarters a large collection of living animals. This park is maintained as part of the Smithsonian Institution.

   B. Monuments and Statues in the Public Grounds.

   > Here, too, should be erected those national memorials and monuments which not only commemorate great men and events but also teach the history of this country to the successive generations about to take their turn in the administration of government. (The National Commission of Fine Arts—*The Plan of the National Capital*, p. 9, Government Printing Office.)

   C. The Historic Potomac River.

   > Next to the fundamental plan in a capital city comes the treatment of the river. . . . Some day the Potomac River will flow between thirty miles of parks, from the cascades at the Great Falls, through the Palisades at the Little Falls, under the Memorial Bridge, and along the Mount Vernon Highway to the American Shrine. It is the history of all great rivers flowing through cities that in time the people seize upon their banks, expel or subordinate commercial uses, and develop them to purposes of adornment. Such is the manifest destiny of the Potomac, unless indeed the power trust shall accomplish its design of seizing it. Already the work is so well begun that the pattern can be traced. (Moore, Charles—*Washington Past and Present*, pp. 6-7.)

IX. ENVIRONS RELATED TO THE LIFE OF GEORGE WASHINGTON AND NATIONAL HISTORY.
   A. Mount Vernon.

   > Not far distant from the city of Washington is Mount Vernon, the beloved home of George Wash-

ington. It is, unquestionably, the most deeply venerated private home in America, if not in the world; a shrine to which admiring pilgrims, from every quarter of the globe, throng in larger and larger numbers every year. Few there are who do not carry away with them something of the inspiration of George Washington's life and achievements; for Mount Vernon, after many vicissitudes, presents to twentieth-century eyes a rare and charming picture of the orderliness and dignity of its Colonial days; still breathes the unquenchable spirit of the man who, though a great soldier and a great statesman, spent the happiest hours of his life as Master of Mount Vernon. (Sawyer, Joseph D.—*Washington*, Vol. II, p. 405.)

I cannot get away from the memory of Mount Vernon, as a farm-house, a farm home, which may carry its humanizing lesson to every American farmer. While I pause and wonder, I find myself saying, "Yes, the Washington farm-house can be a pattern for every farm home, even as Washington himself is a pattern for every American." (Galpin, Charles J.—*Rural Social Problems*, p. 250.)

1. References
   Honor to George Washington, No. 9 (*Washington Proprietor of Mount Vernon*).
   Wilstach, Paul—*Mount Vernon, Washington's Home and the Nation's Shrine.*

B. Alexandria—The Home Town of George Washington.
  1. Alexandria Academy—Endowed in Washington's Will.
  2. Alexandria-Washington Lodge A. F. and A. M.— Located in City Hall. General Washington served as Worshipful Master. Contains collection of Washington heirlooms and paintings.
  3. Christ Church—George Washington was an attendant and vestryman. Washington family pew preserved.
  4. Gadsby's Tavern.

    Gadsby's Tavern, . . . was—in the eighteenth century—the scene of most of Alexandria's important social gatherings; . . . Gadsby's Tavern was a rare old Virginia hostelry, . . .

    From the steps of Gadsby's Tavern Washington announced to the assembled Alexandrians the adoption of the Federal Constitution by the Richmond Convention, in . . . [1788]; . . . Again, in 1789, from those same steps Washington bade farewell to his Virginia friends before leaving his native State for his Inauguration as First President; . . . (Sawyer, Joseph D.—*Washington*, Vol. II, pp. 256, 262.)

  5. George Washington National Masonic Memorial— Erected by Masons from every section of the United States.
  6. Home of John Carlyle—Used as headquarters by General Braddock.
  7. References.
   Callahan, Charles—*Washington The Man and The Mason.*
   George Washington Bicentennial News — Published by the Alexandria Gazette in cooperation with the United States George Washington Bicentennial Commission.

C. Great Falls.
  Remains of the canal and locks surveyed and built by Washington.
D. Arlington.
  1. Restoration of the Arlington Mansion (Custis-Lee House).

. . . the project calls for its restoration as a southern home representing the first half century of the Republic. It was built about 1803, during the earliest years of the nineteenth century by George Washington Parke Custis, who, with his sister Nelly Custis, was adopted by Gen. George Washington. From the death of Mrs. Washington until his own death in 1857, Mr. Custis maintained at Arlington Mansion a proverbial hospitality. (The National Commission of Fine Arts—*Eleventh Report*, p. 127. Government Printing Office, 1930.)

  a. Reference.
   Moore, Charles—*Washington Past and Present*, ch. xxi (Arlington and Memorial Bridge).
  2. Arlington National Cemetery—The most historic and beautiful burial ground of the Nation.
   a. The Tomb of the Unknown Soldier—Body of the Unknown Soldier was brought from France and was buried with impressive ceremonies, November 11, 1921.
   b. Memorial Amphitheater — Dedicated May 15, 1920.
  3. Reference.
   The National Commission of Fine Arts—*Eleventh Report*, ch. ix (Arlington National Cemetery), Government Printing Office, 1930.

E. Fort Washington.
  Located on the Maryland side of the Potomac opposite Mount Vernon. Significance of its site pointed out by Washington. Fort planned by L'Enfant for the defense of the capital.
F. Civil War Forts and Battlefields.
  Fort Drive, designed as a parkway following the hills around the city, connects the Civil War forts.

X. PROJECTS IN CONNECTION WITH THE GEORGE WASHINGTON BICENTENNIAL.
A. The Restoration of Wakefield—George Washington's Birthplace.

    The project for the recovery and restoration of the birthplace of George Washington, now known as Wakefield, was begun before the creation of the Bicentennial Commission. The Wakefield National Memorial Association, incorporated under the laws of Virginia in 1924, began by raising the money necessary to purchase 64 acres of land immediately adjoining the 11 acres owned by the Government, on which stood the house (built by Augustine Washington) in which George Washington was born. . . . the association obtained from Congress (act approved June 7, 1926) authority to build on the Government property a replica of the house in which George Washington was born, together with outbuildings and gardens, the aim being to reproduce not so much the actual dwelling (all traces of which have disappeared) as the atmosphere of the birthplace, to which the boy Washington returned, after his father's death, to live with his half-brother, Augustine, . . . The original house was burned in 1780 and was never rebuilt. (The National Commission of Fine Arts—*Eleventh Report*, pp. 118-119. Government Printing Office, 1930.)

  1. Reference.
   Moore, Charles, "Wakefield, the Birthplace of Washington"; in *American Civic Annual*, Vol. II, pp. 30-33.
B. Mount Vernon Highway.
    Congress, May 23, 1928, passed an act authorizing and directing the survey, construction, and maintenance of a memorial highway to connect Mount Vernon with the Arlington Memorial Bridge, . . .

(The National Commission of Fine Arts—*Eleventh Report*, p. 115. Government Printing Office, 1930.)

C. Arlington Memorial Bridge.

The great Arlington Memorial Bridge across the Potomac River connects the Mall with the beautiful Arlington National Cemetery, the historic Arlington Mansion, once the property of George Washington Parke Custis, the Amphitheater, and the Tomb of the Unknown Soldier.

The project for a monumental bridge across the Potomac—a bridge monumental in spirit as well as in design—first found expression in an address delivered by Daniel Webster on the occasion of laying the cornerstone of the extension of the United States Capitol, on the Fourth of July, 1851. In the course of pleadings for the preservation of the Union, the dissolution of which even at that date seemed imminent, the orator exclaimed: "Before us is the broad and beautiful river, separating two of the original thirteen States, which a late President, a man of determined purpose and inflexible will, but patriotic heart, desired to span with arches of everenduring granite, symbolical of the firmly established union of the North and the South. The President was General Jackson." (Moore, Charles—*Washington Past and Present*, p. 295.)

D. George Washington Memorial Parkway.

By the passage of the Capper-Cramton bill, Congress provided for the preservation of the unique natural beauties of the Potomac River as a most important element of the park system of the National Capital region. Since this park will extend from Mount Vernon, where Washington lived most of his unofficial life, by the Capital City which he founded and which bears his name, to above the Great Falls of the Potomac, including the remains of the old Patowmack Canal, which he organized and the construction of which he supervised, it seems most appropriate that it should be designated by law as the Washington Memorial Parkway.

THE ARLINGTON MEMORIAL BRIDGE
Looking across the Potomac toward the hills of Virginia

Unit XI
Correlation of This Course With Other Subjects of the Curriculum

Brief Outline

I. AGRICULTURE.
  A. George Washington Up-to-Date in Methods.
    1. Conducted Experiments to Improve Agriculture.
    2. Promoted Stock Raising.
    3. Kept Farm Records.
    4. Sought New Ideas Through Correspondence.
    5. Owned Flour Mills.
    6. Interested in Commerce and Transportation Facilities.
    7. Recommended Board of Agriculture.

II. ART.
  A. Paintings and Pictures of George Washington.
  B. Sculpture.
    1. Statues of George Washington (partial list).
    2. Memorials (partial list).
  C. Landscapes.
    1. Mount Vernon.
    2. The Capital City.
  D. In the City of Washington.
    1. Paintings—Unit X.
    2. Monuments—Unit X.
    3. Architecture—Unit X.
  E. Museums—Unit X.

III. BUSINESS.
  A. Discussion Brought Out in Unit V.
    1. Methods of Business.
    2. Business Man and Engineer.
    3. Vision Displayed by George Washington in His Policy Regarding the Commerce and Industry of the United States.

IV. CIVICS.
  A. Origin and Growth of Representative Government in the United States—Unit IV.
  B. Background of the Constitution—Unit VI.
  C. Essentials of American Constitutional Government—Unit VI.
  D. Creation of a Nation—Units VI and VII.
  E. Functions of the Government.
    1. Divisions—Correlated with Units VI, VII, and X.
  F. Flag of the United States—Units IV and VII.
  G. Character Education.
    1. Discussions Centered Around Characteristics Set Forth in Units IV and VII.
    2. George Washington an Exponent of Patriotism and Citizenship.

V. GEOGRAPHY.
  A. Travel Trails.
    1. Correlated with Units III, VII, and X.
     a. Pre-Presidential Journeys.
     b. Presidential Tours.
     c. *Incidents of Travel.*
  B. Places Named for George Washington.
    1. State.
    2. Counties.
    3. Townships.
    4. Cities.
    5. Mountains and Other Physical Features.
    6. Schools and Other Civic Institutions.
  C. Study of Maps.
    1. Maps in *Honor to George Washington and Reading about George Washington Series* in Units III, IV, and X.
    2. The George Washington Atlas.
    3. Maps and Articles; in The National Geographic Magazines.

ALEXANDRIA ACADEMY, ALEXANDRIA, VIRGINIA,
To which Washington bequeathed a fund for the instruction of poor children

VI. HEALTH EDUCATION.
  A. Physical.
    1. Health Habits of George Washington.
    2. Opportunity to Revive Dances of Colonial Days.
    3. Games of Colonial Days.
  B. Mental.
    1. Link Up with Discussions Produced in Study of Washington's Characteristics Enumerated in Units IV and VII.

VII. HOME ECONOMICS.
  A. Life in the Home—See Units II, III, V, VII, and VIII.
  1. Manner of Living.

VIII. LITERATURE.
  A. By George Washington.
    1. The Writings of George Washington—Edited by John C. Fitzpatrick.
    2. *Highlights of the Writings;* also *George Washington's Words on Religion.*
    3. Man of Letters—See Unit V.
  B. About George Washington.
    1. *Classified Washington Bibliography* (by American Library Association), *Honor to George Washington,* No. 15.

2. Tributes—See Unit IX.
3. Poems, Stories, and Books.
   a. *Washington the Nation-Builder*, Bicentennial Poem by Edwin Markham.
C. Political Documents of This Period.
   1. Declaration of Independence.
   2. Articles of Confederation.
   3. Constitution of the United States.

IX. MUSIC.
A. Songs of This Period (partial list).
   1. Yankee Doodle.
   2. The Battle of the Kegs.
   3. Other Revolutionary Ballads of Francis Hopkinson.
   4. Hail Columbia.
   5. Other Ballads.
B. Musical Instruments Used in Colonial Days.
C. Marches—In Honor of George Washington.
   1. President's March.
   2. George Washington Bicentennial March by John Philip Sousa.
D. Colonial Dances.
E. Patriotic Songs and Their Historical Background.
   1. America.
   2. Star-Spangled Banner.
   3. Columbia, the Gem of the Ocean.
   4. America the Beautiful.
F. *Father of the Land We Love*, Bicentennial Song by George M. Cohan.
G. *Song of Faith*, Choral Ode by John A. Carpenter.

X. OUTSIDE ACTIVITIES—EXTRA CURRICULAR.
A. Plays.
B. Pageants.
C. Educational Contests.
   1. Declamatory Contests in Elementary Schools.
   2. Essay Contests in High Schools.
   3. Oratorical Contests in Colleges.
D. George Washington Bicentennial Tree and Garden Planting.

NOTE: *Topics in italics are titles of 48 papers in a series of 12 George Washington Programs and the parts of the Honor to George Washington series of 15 pamphlets and other publications issued by the United States George Washington Bicentennial Commission.*

Development

I. AGRICULTURE.
A. George Washington, Up-to-Date in Methods.
   1. Conducted Experiments to Improve Agriculture.
      a. Testing and Selecting of Seed Wheat.
      b. Protection from Rust.
      c. Conserving and Improving the Soil.
         (1) Discontinued Specializing in Raising Tobacco Which Impoverished the Soil.
         (2) Planted Other Crops.
         (3) Improved Soil by Fertilization.
      d. Sought the Best Implements.
      e. Planted Fruit and Nut Trees.

      A detailed account of all of Washington's agricultural experiments would require several hundred pages. (Haworth, Paul L.—*George Washington, Country Gentleman*, p. 90.)

   2. Promoted Stock Raising.
      a. First American to Raise Mules.
      b. Improved Flock of Sheep.
      c. Owned Herds of Cattle.
   3. Kept Farm Records.
      a. Weather Record—Provided Information as to Best Time for Planting.
      b. Agricultural Experiments.
      c. Cash Accounts and Millbooks.
      d. Reports Required from Farm Managers.
      e. Reports Required during Absence while in the Revolution.

4. Sought New Ideas through Correspondence.
   a. Learned from English Agricultural Authorities.
5. Owned Flour Mills.
   a. Ground Wheat and Sold Flour.

   Washington divided his flour into superfine, fine, middlings and ship stuff. (Haworth, Paul L.—*George Washington, Country Gentleman*, p. 98.)

6. Interested in Commerce and Transportation Facilities.
   a. Vision of opening Highways to the West so that Western Farmers might have a Market for their Crops.
7. Recommended Board of Agriculture.
   a. In Last Message to Congress the Creation of a Board of Agriculture.

II. ART.
A. Paintings and Pictures of George Washington.
   1. Discussion of the Portraits of Washington by the following Artists:
      Guiseppe Ceracchi, Thomas Crawford, Jean Antoine Houdon, Charles Willson Peale, James Peale, Rembrandt Peale, Robert Edge Pine, Archibald Robertson, John Ramage, Charles Saint Mémin, Edward Savage, James Sharples, Pierre Eugene du Simitiere, Gilbert Stuart, John Trumbull, Adolph Wertmueller, William Williams, John Woolaston, and Joseph Wright.
      a. References.
         Irving, Washington—*Life of Washington*, Vol. V, Appendix.
         Morgan, John Hill and Fielding, Mantle—*The Life Portraits of Washington and Their Replicas.*
         Sawyer, Joseph D.—*Washington*, Vol. II, pp. 421-557.

         Probably no public man has ever lived whose features have been so frequently immortalized on canvass as those of George Washington. Of portraits alone, some painted from life and others copied or adapted from life portraits, there are—collected herein—some two hundred and fifty; while in groups and historical scenes are hundreds more. . . .
         It was during the Presidency that he began to listen with more tolerance to the importunities of admirers who desired his portrait and painters who were eager to paint it. . . .
         Besides John Wollaston, twelve prominent artists and some eighteen others portrayed Washington from life; Gilbert Stuart, Jean Antoine Houdon; the three Peales—Charles Willson Peale, his son Rembrandt, and his brother James; Charles B. J. F. de St. Memin; John Trumbull, Washington's former aide de camp, son of Jonathan Trumbull, Connecticut's war governor; Edward Savage; James Sharples; Archibald Robertson; Robert Edge Pine, and Joseph Wright. George Washington Parke Custis, the General's adopted son, who was often present at sittings, in later years summarized the special gifts of three of these painters thus:
         "Stuart for head, Trumbull for figure, Sharples for expression." (Sawyer, Joseph D.—*Washington*, Vol. II, pp. 421, 422-423.)
         Of the many painted portraits of Washington, those of Gilbert Stuart have come to be accepted as authentic; especially the head in the painting which hung in the Boston Athenaeum as a pendant to that of Martha Washington, and is now in the Boston Museum of Fine Arts. But as I remarked earlier, the fact that none of the painters indicate the very strong marks of smallpox (which he took on his trip

to Barbados) on Washington's face creates a natural suspicion as to accuracy in detail of any of the portraits. (Thayer, William R.—*George Washington*, p. 149.)

Of the portraits of Washington, the most of them give to his person a fulness that it did not possess, together with an abdominal enlargement greater than in the life, while his matchless limbs have in but two instances been faithfully portrayed—in the equestrian portrait by Trumbull of 1790, a copy of which is in the City Hall of New York, and in an engraving by Losier, from a painting by Coginet, French artists of distinguished merit. The latter is not an original painting, the head being from Stuart, but the delineation of the limbs is the most perfect extant. (Custis, George Washington Parke—*Recollections and Private Memoirs of Washington*, p. 42.)

3. Illustrations—*Honor to George Washington* Series.
   a. Portrait—C. W. Peale (Virginia Colonial Portrait), *Honor to George Washington, No. 1 (Frontier Background of Washington's Career).*
   b. Portrait—Gilbert Stuart-Vaughan—*Honor to George Washington, No. 2 (Washington the Man of Mind).*
   c. Portrait—Wertmueller—*Honor to George Washington, No. 3 (Tributes to Washington).*
   d. Portrait—Wright—*Honor to George Washington, No. 4 (Washington the Farmer).*
   e. Portrait—Silhouette; Contemporary—*Honor to George Washington, No. 5 (Washington as a Religious Man).*
   f. Portrait—Gibbs-Channing—*Honor to George Washington, No. 6 (Washington the Colonial and National Statesman).*
   g. Portrait—Gilbert Stuart, Athenaeum—*Honor to George Washington, No. 7 (Washington and the Constitution).*
   h. Portrait—Edward Savage—*Honor to George Washington, No. 8 (Washington as President).*
   i. Portrait—Nollekens Bust Profile—*Honor to George Washington, No. 9 (Washington Proprietor of Mount Vernon).*
   j. Portrait—C. W. Peale—*Honor to George Washington, No. 10 (Washington the Military Man).*
   k. Portrait—John Trumbull, City Hall, Charleston, S. C.—*Honor to George Washington, No. 11 (Washington the Traveler).*
   l. Portrait—Gilbert Stuart, New York Public Library—*Honor to George Washington, No. 12 (Washington the Business Man).*
   m. Portrait—C. W. Peale, New York Historical Society—*Honor to George Washington, No. 13 (Washington as Engineer and City Builder).*
   n. Portrait—William Williams, Masonic Lodge, Alexandria, Va.—*Honor to George Washington, No. 14 (Washington's Home and Fraternal Life).*
   o. Portrait—Rembrandt Peale, N. Y. Historical Society—*Honor to George Washington, No. 15 (Classified Washington Bibliography).*
   p. Portrait—St. Mémin—*Honor to George Washington* (Frontispiece).

B. Sculpture.
   1. Statues of George Washington (partial list).
      a. In Washington, D. C.
         (1) Statue of George Washington by Horatio Greenough in Old National Museum.
         (2) Statue of George Washington in Statuary Hall—Modeled after the Statue by Houdon in the State Capitol, Richmond, Va.
         (3) Bust of George Washington by David d'Angers.
         (4) Equestrian Statue of George Washington in Washington Circle by Clark Mills.
         (5) Bust of George Washington by Nollekens.
      b. Outside of Washington, D. C.
         (1) Mount Vernon, Va.—Bust of George Washington by Jean Antoine Houdon.
         (2) Allegheny City, Pa.—Washington Statue in Granite by Edward Pausch.
         (3) Boston, Mass.—Ball's Statue of Washington.
         (4) Newark, N. J.—Statue of Washington by J. Massey Rhind.
         (5) New York City—Statue of Washington in Front of the Sub-Treasury Building, Wall Street.
         Replica of Houdon's Statue, Metropolitan Museum of Art.
         Bust of George Washington by Ceracchi, Metropolitan Museum of Art.
         Statue of Washington in Union Square, Henry Kirke Brown (First Equestrian Statue in United States).
         (6) Philadelphia, Pa.—Statue of Washington.
         (7) Richmond, Va.—Marble Statue in State Capitol, by Jean Antoine Houdon.
         Equestrian Statue of Washington, Capital Square—Thomas Crawford, Sculptor; Robert Mills, Designer of Monument.
      c. References.
         Fairman, Charles E.—*Art and Artists of the Capitol of the United States of America.* Government Printing Office, 1927.
         Fairman, Charles E.—*Works of Art in the United States Capitol Building.* Government Printing Office, 1913.
         Sawyer, Joseph D.—*Washington*, Vol. II (The Washington Portraits, also Sculptures and Monuments).
   2. Memorials (partial list).
      a. Washington, D. C.—Washington National Monument—See Unit X.
      b. Alexandria, Va.—The George Washington National Masonic Memorial.
      c. Baltimore, Md.—Washington Monument, Mount Vernon Place. First Outdoor Memorial to Washington.
      d. Brooklyn, N. Y.—Washington Monument at the Williamsburg Bridge, Edward F. Shrady.
      e. Keystone, S. Dak.—Mt. Rushmore National Memorial, Gutzon Borglum, Sculptor—Washington, Jefferson, Lincoln, and Roosevelt in relief.
      f. Methuen, Mass.—Washington Monument.
      g. New York City—The Washington Arch, Washington Square, H. H. MacNeill, Sculptor.
      h. Philadelphia, Pa.—Washington Memorial, Fairmount Park.
      i. Seattle, Wash.—Statue of George Washington, at University of Washington, Lorado Taft, Sculptor.
      j. Valley Forge, Pa.—Statue of George Washington, Franklin Simmons, Sculptor.

C. Landscapes.
   1. Mount Vernon.

One of the sights to-day at Mount Vernon is the formal garden, which all who have visited the place will remember. (Haworth, Paul L.—*George Washington, Country Gentleman*, p. 160.)

But while he gave close attention to the business management of his large estate, Washington did not neglect the artistic side of its development. On the contrary, under his experienced direction and unremitting care the private grounds about the residence at Mount Vernon were gradually transformed into a veritable paradise. In course of time they were extended to include a bowling green, a botanical garden, conservatories, grouped and scattered shrubbery and a deer park. (Sawyer, Joseph D.—*Washington*, Vol. I, p. 233.)

To the average country person, a visit to Mount Vernon, the home of George Washington, is a revelation. . . . the charm of his home is not so much due to his wealth, as to his loving thought for the beautiful effect of his home surroundings. He was a student of landscape gardening, and we are told that he spent many hours planning what kind of trees to set out and just where to set them to give the harmonious groups about the grounds, and where to cut down others to open delightful vistas to the hills beyond or to the broad bend of the Potomac. And now Mount Vernon is a shrine to the American people because everything about the place speaks of the great patriot-farmer. (Atkeson, Mary Meek—*The Woman on the Farm*, p. 59.)

2. The Capital City.
   a. Early Plans Made by George Washington—Unit X.
   b. Present Day Plans—Unit X.
D. In the City of Washington.
  1. Paintings—Unit X.
    a. Discussion of the Portraits of George Washington, Individually and with Groups, in the Capitol, by the Following Artists: Charles Willson Peale, Gilbert Stuart, Rembrandt Peale, John Trumbull.
    b. Description of Other Paintings in the Capitol Building.
    c. Paintings of George Washington and Martha Washington in the White House.
    d. Paintings of George Washington in Corcoran Gallery of Art and Other Galleries in the National Capital.
    e. Paintings of the Colonial Period in the Galleries of Washington, D. C.
  2. Monuments—Correlate with Unit X, Washington the Nation's Capital.
    a. Located in the Mall.
    b. Located in the Circles.
    c. Located in the Parks.
  3. Architecture—Correlate with Unit X, Washington the Nation's Capital.
    a. Reference.
      Bennett, Edward H.—"The Architecture of the Capital" (Address, in *Development of the United States Capital*. Government Printing Office, 1930).
E. Museums—Correlate with "Art" in Unit X.
  1. Smithsonian Institution.
  2. Old National Museum.
    a. Relics of George Washington and Martha Washington.
      At the death of Mrs. Lawrence Lewis (Nellie Custis) her heirs sold this collection to the United States Government. It was purchased by an Act of Congress approved June 20, 1878, and was first placed on exhibition in the United States Patent Office. In 1883 this collection was transferred to the United States National Museum.
    b. Costumes of the Mistresses of the White House.
      In the Costume Exhibition the dress of every mistress of this historic mansion is exhibited from Martha Washington down through the Hoover administration. Most of the dresses are inaugural gowns or dresses that have been worn at some important function. These dresses are draped on plaster cast figures, no

likenesses having been attempted, but the hair arrangement represents the fashion of the period when the dress was worn. They show the changes in the fashions of women for nearly 150 years. This collection was commenced in 1912 and is now regarded as one of the most important historical government exhibitions.
     (1) Reference.
        Hoes, Rose Gouverneur—*The Costumes of the Mistresses of the White House as Shown in the United States National Museum*.
    c. Statue of George Washington by Horatio Greenough.
    d. Replica—Statue of Freedom on Dome of Capitol.
  3. New National Museum.
  4. Continental Memorial Hall—National Headquarters, Daughters of American Revolution.
    a. Relics of George Washington.
    b. Relics of Revolutionary Days.

F. References.
    Fairman, Charles E.—*Works of Art in the United States Capitol Building*. Government Printing Office (1913).
    Fairman, Charles E.—*Art and Artists of the Capitol of the United States of America*. Government Printing Office, 1927.
    Moore, Charles—*Washington Past and Present*.
    National Capital Park and Planning Commission—*Annual Report*, 1927-1930. Government Printing Office.
    National Commission of Fine Arts—*Reports*. Government Printing Office.
    National Commission of Fine Arts—*Washington the National Capital*. Government Printing Office.
    National Galleries of History and Art, Aggrandizement of Washington. Government Printing Office, 1900.
    National Geographic Society—*The Capital of Our Country*.
    Proctor, John C.—*Washington Past and Present*, Vol. II, ch. xli (History of Architecture in Washington), ch. xlii (Art in Washington).
    Small, Herbert—*Handbook of the New Library of Congress*.
    United States Office of Education.—*Helps for Schools*. Government Printing Office, 1931.

III. BUSINESS.
  A. Discussion Brought Out in Unit V.
    1. Methods of Business.
    a. Accurate Records.
    2. Business Man and Engineer.
    3. Vision Displayed by George Washington in His Policy Regarding the Commerce and Industry of the United States.

IV. CIVICS.
  A. Origin and Growth of Representative Government in the United States—Unit IV.
  B. Background of the Constitution—Unit VI.
  C. Essentials of American Constitutional Government—Unit VI.
    1. Advantages the Citizens of the United States of America have in Living in a Land Governed by the Principles Set Forth in the Federal Constitution.
    2. What the Constitution Means to Our Country and to Each Individual.
    3. Services Rendered by Citizens for the Benefits Received by the Constitution.

4. Significance and Stability of the Federal Constitution.

  The Basic Supreme Law of the Land.
  Obedience Due the Constitution.

D. Creation of a Nation—Units VI and VII.

 1. Part Played by George Washington in the Creation of the Federal Constitution.
 2. George Washington an Exponent of Service to Country.

  It was said by Washington that wherever the Constitution guarantees a right, it also imposes a duty.

E. Functions of the Government.

 1. Divisions—Correlate with Units VI, VII, and X.
  a. Legislative.
  b. Executive.
   Departments of the Cabinet.
   Comparison with Washington's Administration.
  c. Judicial.
 2. Study of the Pictures of Government Buildings.
 3. Visitation to Government Buildings.

F. Flag of the United States—Units IV and VII.

 1. Origin—See Unit IV.
 2. History.
 3. Sacrifices Made for It.
 4. Pledge to the Flag and the Correct Salute.

PLEDGE TO THE FLAG

I pledge allegiance to the Flag of the United States of America and to the Republic for which it stands; one Nation indivisible, with Liberty and Justice for all.

THE AMERICAN'S CREED

I believe in the United States of America as a government of the people, by the people, for the people, whose just powers are derived from the consent of the governed; a democracy in a Republic; a sovereign Nation of many sovereign States; a perfect Union, one and inseparable; established upon those principles of freedom, equality, justice, and humanity for which American patriots sacrificed their lives and fortunes.

I therefore believe it is my duty to my country to love it, to support its Constitution, to obey its laws, to respect its flag, and to defend it against all enemies.

       WILLIAM TYLER PAGE.

The complete proceedings in regard to the official acceptance of THE AMERICAN'S CREED, on April 6, 1918, may be found in the *Congressional Record*, 65th Congress, 2nd Session (April 13, 1918), from which is taken the following explanation of the doctrinal origin of THE CREED:

 "I am asked to make this explanation, that the first clause—
 "I believe in the United States of America"—
 "is from the preamble to the Constitution of the United States; that the second clause—
 "A government of the people, by the people, for the people"—
 "is from the preamble to the Constitution of the United States, Daniel Webster's speech in the Senate of January 26, 1830, and Abraham Lincoln's Gettysburg speech.
 "Whose just powers are derived from the consent of the governed"—
 "is from the Declaration of Independence.
 "A democracy in a republic"—
 "is in substance from No. 10 of the Federalist, by Madison, and Article X of the amendments to the Constitution of the United States.
 "A sovereign Nation of many sovereign States"—
 "from 'E pluribus unum,' the great seal of the United States, and Article IV of the Constitution of the United States.

 "A perfect Union"—
 "goes back to the preamble to the Constitution.
 "One and inseparable"—
 "Webster's speech in the Senate of January 26, 1830.
 "Established upon those principles of freedom, equality, justice, and humanity"—
 "from the Declaration of Independence.
 "For which American patriots sacrificed their lives and fortunes"—
 "from the Declaration of Independence, and Lincoln's Gettysburg Address.
 "I therefore believe it is my duty to my country to love it"—
 "in substance from Edward Everett Hale, The Man Without a Country.
 "To support its Constitution"—
 "from the oath of allegiance, section 1757 of the Revised Statutes of the United States.
 "To obey its laws"—
 "from Washington's Farewell Address and from Article VI of the Constitution of the United States.
 "To respect its flag"—
 "the national anthem, the Star-Spangled Banner; Army and Navy Regulations; War Department circular on Flag Etiquette, April 14, 1917.
 "And to defend it against all enemies"—
 "from the oath of allegiance, section 1757 of the Revised Statutes of the United States.

    —*Congressional Record*, Vol. 56, Appendix, p. 287.

GEORGE WASHINGTON BICENTENNIAL PLEDGE

As an American, I will follow the example of George Washington in upright living, integrity and in loyalty and service to my country. I will strive "Never to say anything about a man that I have the slightest scruple of saying to him," and "Never to forfeit my word, nor break my promise made to anyone." In heart and mind, in word and deed, I will keep faith with Washington.

     MRS. JOHN DICKINSON SHERMAN.

NOTE: Words quoted are George Washington's thoughts.

G. Character Education.

  I believe thoroughly in the sound and vigorous body. I believe still more in the vigorous mind. And I believe most of all in what counts for more than body, for more than mind, and that is character. That is the sum of the forces that make the man or woman worth knowing, worth revering, worth holding to. (Roosevelt, Theodore—*Presidential Addresses and State Papers*, Vol. I, pp. 293-294) (Speech, Minneapolis, Minn., April 4, 1903.)

  From all our citizens we have a right to expect good citizenship; but most of all from those who have received most; most of all from those who have had the training of body, of mind, of soul, which comes from association in and with a great university. (Roosevelt, Theodore—*Presidential Addresses and State Papers*, Vol. II, pp. 406-407.) (Speech, San Francisco, Calif., May 14, 1903.)

 1. Discussions Centered Around Characteristics Set Forth in Units IV and VII.

  a. Characteristics.
   Faith, Courage, Fortitude, Loyalty, Determination, Magnanimity, Humility, Self-Control, Leadership, Judgment, Balance, Wisdom, Vision, Integrity, and Justice.

  b. Compare Washington's Rules of Civility—See Unit II, with the following Creeds:
   The Roosevelt Creed.
   Code of Morals, Dr. William J. Hutchins.

Young America's Creed; in Baylor, Adelaide S. and Colbert, Emma—*Young America's First Book*, p. 166.

Other Codes for Right Living.

> The future of the republic depends upon the character of its citizenship. We are not building permanently unless the youth of the land are made fully acquainted with the meaning of American citizenship. We must give patriotism a vitality which will find expression in service. The spirit of democracy must be in the minds of the people, and this means that they must understand the basic principles of democratic government. (Marshall, Thomas R.—*Speech*, Mooseheart, Ill., July 27, 1913.)

2. George Washington an Exponent of Patriotism and Citizenship.

V. GEOGRAPHY.
  A. Travel Trails.
     1. Correlate with Units III, VII, and X.
        a. Pre-Presidential Journeys.
        b. Presidential Tours.
        c. Incidents of Travel—*Honor to George Washington*, No. 11 (*Washington the Traveler*), Part IV.
  B. Places Named for George Washington.
     1. State.
     2. Counties.
     3. Townships.
     4. Cities.
     5. Mountains and Other Physical Features.
     6. Schools and Other Civic Institutions.
  C. Study of Maps.
     1. Maps in *Honor to George Washington and Reading about George Washington* Series in Units III, IV, and X.
     2. The George Washington Atlas. Forty-eight Map Plates Including the Following:
        a. General Itinerary Map.
        b. Facsimiles of more than 25 Maps drawn by George Washington.
        c. State Maps and Combinations. Names of places visited by George Washington are on these State Maps.
        d. Five Campaign Maps.
        e. Three Battle Maps.
        f. Land Ownership Maps.
        g. Residences and Some Army General Headquarters.
        h. Location of Land and City Surveying by George Washington.
        i. Places and Things Named after George Washington. No name except that of *Washington* is on this Map.
     3. National Geographic Society—Special Articles and Maps Dealing with the Travels of George Washington.
     4. References.
        Baker, William S.—*Itinerary of General Washington*.
        Baker, William S.—*Washington after the Revolution*.
        Fitzpatrick, John C.—*George Washington, Colonial Traveller*.

VI. HEALTH EDUCATION.
  A. Physical.
     1. Health Habits of George Washington.
        a. Systematic Method of Living. Exemplified Franklin's Maxim "Early to bed, early to rise makes a man healthy, wealthy, and wise."
           > ... he had a "time for all things." (Custis, George Washington Parke—*Recollections and Private Memoirs of Washington*, p. 66.)
           > ... so remarkable was the punctuality of Wash-

ington in all his engagements, whether for business or pleasure, that he was never waited for a moment in appointments for either. (Custis, George Washington Parke—*Recollections and Private Memoirs of Washington*, p. 20.)

> He did not spring into life a perfect and impossible man, as is so often represented. On the contrary, he was educated by circumstances; but the metal came out of the furnace of experience finely tempered, because it was by nature of the best and with but little dross to be purged away. (Lodge, Henry C.—*George Washington (American Statesmen)*, Vol. I, p. 76.)

     2. Opportunity to Revive Dances of Colonial Days.
        Minuet, March, Reels, and Jigs may be used with pleasure and profit in physical education classes.
     3. Games of Colonial Days.
        a. Reference.
           United States Office of Education—*Helps for Schools*. Government Printing Office, 1931.
  B. Mental.
     > For as he thinketh in his heart, so is he. Prov. 23:7.
     1. Link up with Discussions Produced in Study of Washington's Characteristics Enumerated in Units IV and VII.

VII. HOME ECONOMICS.
  A. Life in the Home—See Units II, III, V, VII, and VIII.
     1. Manner of Living.
        a. Food.
        b. Clothing.
        c. Customs—Hospitality.
           Suggestions may be obtained for this correlation from Miss Adelaide Baylor, Chief of the Division of Home Economics, Federal Board for Vocational Education, Washington, D. C.

VIII. LITERATURE.
  A. By George Washington.
     1. The Writings of George Washington—Edited by John C. Fitzpatrick.
     2. United States George Washington Bicentennial Commission—*Highlights of the Writings of General George Washington;* also *George Washington's Words on Religion*.
     3. Man of Letters—See Unit V.
  B. About George Washington.
     1. *Classified Washington Bibliography* (By American Library Association), *Honor to George Washington*, No. 15.
        a. Books for the Home Library, Part I.
        b. Books for School Libraries, Part II.
        c. Books for Public Libraries, Part III.
        d. Extended List for Study and Research, Part IV.
     2. Tributes in Prose—See Unit IX.
     3. Poems, Stories, and Books.
        a. *Washington the Nation-Builder*, Bicentennial Poem by Edwin Markham.
        b. References.
           United States George Washington Bicentennial Commission — *Selections for Declamatory Contests*.
           United States Office of Education—*Helps for Schools*. Government Printing Office, 1931.
           United States George Washington Bicentennial Commission—*Special News Releases;* also *The United States Congress on George Washington* (Library of Congress, 1932).
  C. Political Documents of This Period.
     1. Declaration of Independence.
     2. Articles of Confederation.

3. Constitution of the United States.
   a. Reference.
     Documents Illustrative of the Formation of the Union of the American States. Government Printing Office, 1927.

IX. Music.

A. Songs of This Period (partial list).

    The great epic struggle for freedom furnished an astonishing abundance of songs and ballads. Several volumes of them gathered from newspapers and broadsides have been issued and there is material for volumes more. (Pattee, Fred L.—*Century Readings for a Course in American Literature*, p. 69.)

    In the beginning, when our plucky Thirteen Colonies decided to break away from the Mother Country, and start out on life as a separate Nation, we had no Song,—and no Flag,—that we could call our own. Yet, at this date, to tell the Story of Our National Songs, is to put the history of our country in a nutshell. For every period of that history has brought its own individual music with it; consequently, the annals of America are embodied in her patriotic ballads to a far greater degree than those of any other land seem to be. (Browne, C. A.— *The Story of Our National Ballads*, p. 4.)

1. Yankee Doodle.

    During the Revolution, we acquired "Yankee Doodle." In fact, it is our one song legacy from the Revolutionary War; and while it may not be a treasure of the highest value, it absolutely belongs to us,—is public property, and has its peculiar place. For its quaint, incisive character redeems it from vulgarity; and its historic associations are woven and interwoven with the establishment of American Independence. . . .

    Strange to say, "Yankee Doodle" changed sides during the conflict. From being a British tune at the beginning of the struggle, it emerged as a severely American melody, at the close. The earlier history of the air is shrouded in mystery; many countries having laid claim to all, or to fragments of it. The tune of "Yankee Doodle," like the story of the flood, appears to flourish in the myths of every nation. The word "Yankee" is probably an Indian corruption of the word English; though the term is still a bone of contention among the etymologists. But they agree that "Doodle" means a trifling, half-witted fellow. During Revolutionary times, the word "Yankee" was used as an especially insulting term. During the Boston Massacre, the British commanding officer took great pains to shout it at the crowd of citizens,—this and various other choice epithets. And the song itself was distinctly against the Americans, at first. (Browne, C. A.— *The Story of Our National Ballads*, pp. 4-6.)

2. The Battle of the Kegs.

    Then, on March 4 [1778], Hopkinson published in the *Pennsylvania Packet* his famous ballad, "The Battle of the Kegs." . . .

    This ballad became one of the most popular songs of the Revolution. It was set to music—possibly by Hopkinson himself—and was sung by the soldiers at the front. It was republished as a pamphlet and as a broadside. (Footnote—Dr. James Thatcher, . . . has this entry for July 10, 1780: "Our drums and fifes afforded us a favorite amusement till evening, when we were delighted with the song composed by Mr. Hopkinson called the 'Battle of the Kegs' sung in the best style by a number of gentlemen.") (Hastings, George E.—*The Life and Works of Francis Hopkinson*, pp. 292, 295.)

3. Other Revolutionary Ballads of Francis Hopkinson.

    Hopkinson next wrote two songs for the encouragement of the Americans. . . . "A Camp Ballad" first appeared in the *Pennsylvania Gazette* of April 4, 1778, over the signature of "Bob Jingle." . . . That it was sung to a popular air is indicated by the fact that in the *Post* it bears the title, "A Song to the Tune of Peperell and Pumpkinville People."

    In the *Packet* of April 8 appeared also the second song, entitled "The Toast." [Given to Washington's health.] . . .

    The last of Hopkinson's Revolutionary ballads is a group of four songs entitled *A Tory Medley*, which he published as a broadside in 1780. The "Medley" begins with a song of four stanzas set to the tune of "The World Is a Well Furnish'd Table." (Hastings, George E.—*The Life and Works of Francis Hopkinson*, pp. 298-299, 305.)

4. Hail Columbia.

   a. The Air—The President's March.
    Until recently the musical origin of "Hail Columbia" was as obscure as its literary history was clear. . . . A methodical analysis of the contradictory accounts left the problem open, and it became probable that merely an accidental find would enable us to solve it. . . . That it was popular about 1794 is clear, . . . We must not forget that . . . had the air been really popular during the years immediately following 1789, at least one of the innumerable political and patriotic songs . . . would show the indication: "Tune—President's March." Such is not the case, . . . recently the hoped-for accident helped to clear the situation . . . the Library of Congress acquired a lot of miscellaneous early American musical publications. Among the fragments appears an unnumbered page, evidently torn from an engraved music collection for the pianoforte, bearing two marches, one, THE PRESIDENTS MARCH, BY PHEIL, the other, fortunately, "March, by Moller." Fortunately, because the reference to the name of John Christopher Moller proves that the page can not have been printed before his arrival in America in 1790, and that it most probably forms part of one of the publications issued . . . in 1793. . . . Consequently this probably earliest edition of the march . . . though it does not assist us in dating and locating the origin of "The President's March," removes all reasonable doubt from the tradition that the music of "Hail Columbia" was composed by Philip Phile. (Sonneck, O. G.—*Report on [National Songs]*, 1909, pp. 49, 68, 69.)

   b. The Words, by Joseph Hopkinson.
    It was during this summer of 1798, while the violence of dissension was at its height, that the words of "Hail Columbia" were written, by Joseph Hopkinson, a Philadelphia lawyer, son of that other Philadelphia lawyer, Francis Hopkinson, author, statesman, eminent judge, wit, musician, writer of many dainty songs, clever artist with brush and pencil, who was one of the signers of the Declaration of Independence, and a distinguished patriot of Revolutionary times. He is remembered now chiefly by a satirical little poem called the "Battle of the Kegs," based upon an amusing incident of those early war times. . . .

    Luckily, in a letter to the Reverend Rufus W. Griswold, a short time before his own death, Dr. Hopkinson tells how the words of "Hail Columbia" came to be penned. In speaking of the troublous times spoken of above, he explains that "Amidst all the political turmoil the theatre was then open in our city." He goes on to say that "a young actor belonging to it, Mr. Gilbert Fox, called upon me one Saturday afternoon. I had known him when he was at school." The young man, it seems, was about to have a benefit performance on the following Monday, and he came to Hopkinson in despair, saying, "that as twenty boxes still remained unsold, it looked as though the proposed benefit would prove to be a failure." His prospects were very disheartening, but he told his former schoolmate that if he could only get a patriotic song, adapted to the then popular "President's March," he was quite sure it would win the day for him. He said that the poets of the theatrical corps had been trying in vain to accomplish this.

"I told him," goes on the letter, "I would try what I could do for him. He came the next afternoon, and the song, such as it is, was ready for him. The object of the song was to get up an American spirit, which should be independent of, and above the interests, passions and policy of both of the foreign powers. And at the same time, no allusion is made either to France or England, or to the quarrel between them."

It was duly advertised, that after the play,—"The Italian Monk,"—an entirely new song, written by a citizen of Philadelphia, would be performed, to the tune of "The President's March," and accompanied by a full band as well as a grand chorus.

The house was packed. The song found favor, of course, with both parties, as both were American. And it was encored and re-encored, in wild enthusiasm, more than half a dozen times. Before its seventh repetition, the audience, already familiar with the tune, had also learned the words of the refrain, and finally all rose and joined with Mr. Fox in the chorus, "Firm united let us be."

At first it was known as "The Favorite New Federal Song." Afterward, the song took as its title the first two words of the opening stanza. It is pleasing to note that Mr. Fox, at this benefit performance, is said to have reaped a golden harvest through the courtesy and patriotism of his poetic friend, who did not cease to be a friend because the other man was in need of help.

The fourth stanza, which begins, "Behold the Chief," refers to the President, John Adams. (Browne, C. A.—*The Story of Our National Ballads*, pp. 37-40.)

5. Other Ballads.

a. "The Liberty Song," by John Dickinson.
b. "Chester," by William Billings.
c. "The Toast," by Francis Hopkinson.
d. References.
  Eggleston, George Cary—*American War Ballads and Lyrics*.
  Holland, Rupert—*Historic Poems and Ballads*.
  Moore, Frank—*Songs and Ballads of the American Revolution*.
  Pattee, Fred L.—*Century Readings for a Course in American Literature*, pp. 69-80 (Songs and Ballads of the Colonial and Revolutionary Periods).
  United States George Washington Bicentennial Commission—*The Music of George Washington's Time; also Music from the Days of George Washington*.

B. Musical Instruments Used in Colonial Days.

Music of a simple and social kind—principally sentimental songs, ballads, containing a story, tuneful airs and dances—entered largely into Colonial Virginia life. In the seventeenth century young women played on Queen Elizabeth's instrument, the virginal, and in the eighteenth on the spinet and harpsichord. Men, from the planter to his Negro slave, scraped tunes from the violin—or the fiddle, as it was more often called—and everybody sang. . . .

Musical instruments—especially violins—figure in wills and inventories throughout the Colonial period. . . .

[The Virginia Gazette] in 1752: "Just imported from London. A very neat hand organ in a mahogany case with gilt front, which plays sixteen tunes on two barrels; it has four stops and everything in the best order." . . .

Gay little Williamsburg was a music-loving town, and the diary of President John Blair (1751) makes frequent mention of the musical instruments at William and Mary College and in private houses. Mr. Blair himself had a spinet on which the ladies of his family played, and when he had friends to dine with him, or when he dined out with friends, he took pains to record "We had fine music." (Stanard, Mary N.—*Colonial Virginia, Its People and Customs*, pp. 308-311.)

C. Marches—In Honor of George Washington.

1. Washington's March.
2. President's March—(Note: Hail Columbia, Air).
3. *George Washington Bicentennial March*, by John Philip Sousa—Written in commemoration of the Two Hundredth Anniversary of the Birth of George Washington.

D. Colonial Dances.

NOTE: Health Education of this Unit—Opportunity for revival of the Dances of Colonial Days.

The Minuet (now obsolete), for the graceful and elegant dancing of which Washington was conspicuous, in the vice regal days of Lord Botetourt in Virginia, declined down after the Revolution. The Commander-in-Chief danced, for his last time, a minuet, in 1781, at the ball given in Fredericksburg, in honor of the French and American officers on their return from the triumphs of York-Town. (Custis, George Washington Parke—*Recollections and Private Memoirs of Washington*, p. 20.)

John Kello, in a letter to London from Hampton, Va., in 1755, declared, "Dancing is the chief diversion here, and hunting and racing," and the English traveller Burnaby said of the women, "They are inordinately fond of dancing, and indeed it is almost their only amusement." . . .

There is abundant evidence that dancing was by far the most generally popular amusement in the colony. Wherever there was "company" there was dancing. Everybody danced. Girls and boys, men and women capered fantastically in jigs and reels, stepped forward and back and turned their partners in the picturesque country dances —later known as square dances, or quadrilles—tripped through the rollicking and immensely popular Sir Roger de Coverley—which under the name of the "Virginia reel" was the last dance at every ball until long after the War between the States—or courtsied low to each other in the rhythmic minuet. . . .

Burnaby thought that the jigs were borrowed from the negroes, but he was mistaken. The negroes had, and still have, grotesque dances of their own, but it is much more likely that they got their quaint jigs from the white people whose forefathers had danced them time out of mind in the old country. (Stanard, Mary N.—*Colonial Virginia, Its People and Customs*, pp. 140-141.)

E. Patriotic Songs and Their Historical Background.
  1. America.
  2. Star-Spangled Banner.
  3. Columbia, the Gem of the Ocean.
  4. America the Beautiful.

F. *Father of the Land We Love*, Bicentennial Song—Written for the American People by George M. Cohan.

G. *Song of Faith*, A Choral Ode by John Alden Carpenter.

H. General References.
  Browne, C. H.—*The Story of Our National Ballads.*
  Howard, John H.—*Our American Music.*
  Sonneck, O. G.—*Report on [National Songs]*, 1909.
  United States George Washington Bicentennial Commission—*George Washington: As a Friend and Patron of Music.*
  United States Office of Education—*Helps for Schools.* Government Printing Office, 1931.

X. OUTSIDE ACTIVITIES—EXTRA CURRICULAR.

A. Plays.
  1. Presentation in Schools—Upper Grades, High Schools, and Colleges.
    a. One Act Plays.
      Subjects cover Whole Range of George Washington's Life from Boyhood to Manhood.
    b. Full Length Plays.
      Subjects portray the True Character of Our First President.
  2. Presentation in Community Activities—Little Theaters, and Dramatic Organizations.
  3. Catalog of Plays About George Washington.
    NOTE: Furnished Upon Request.

B. Pageants.
  1. School.
    Adaptable to Different Grades.
  2. Community.
    Adaptable to Local Needs.
  3. Reference List of Pageants.
    Contains Lists of All Pageants written on the Theme of George Washington.
    NOTE: Furnished to Teachers Upon Request.

C. Educational Contests.
  1. Declamatory Contests in all Grades of the Elementary Schools.
  2. Essay Contests in High Schools.
  3. Oratorical Contests in Colleges.
  4. References.
    United States George Washington Bicentennial Commission—*Organization and Regulations of Contests;* also *Selections for Declamatory Contests.*

D. George Washington Bicentennial Tree and Colonial Garden Planting.
  1. Tree Planting. Conducted by The American Tree Association Cooperating with the George Washington Bicentennial Commission.
    NOTE: Information Furnished by The American Tree Association, Washington, D. C.
  2. Colonial Gardens.
    NOTE: Upon request suggestions will be sent out by the United States George Washington Bicentennial Commission.

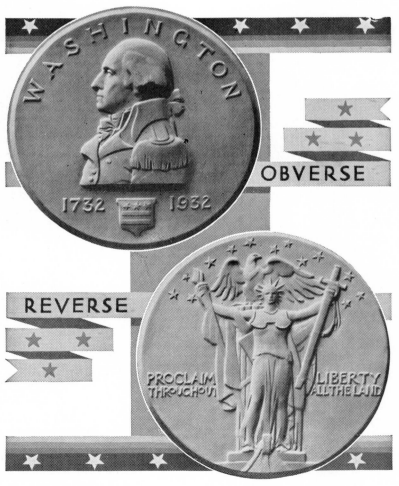

GEORGE WASHINGTON COMMEMMORATIVE MEDAL
Awarded to the Winners in the National and State Bicentennial Declamatory, Essay, and Oratorical Contests

Unit XII
Contributions of George Washington to Civilization

Brief Outline

I. ELEMENTS OF GEORGE WASHINGTON'S CONTRIBUTIONS WORTHY OF EMPHASIS.

II. PROMOTION OF STUDENT'S ORIGINAL PRODUCTIONS.

Development

I. ELEMENTS OF GEORGE WASHINGTON'S CONTRIBUTIONS WORTHY OF EMPHASIS.

A. Administrator, Launching a New Nation.

B. Business Man, Originating New Enterprises.

C. Farmer, Developing New Methods of Agriculture.

D. Moral Leader, Demonstrating Honesty and Truth.

E. National Guide, Steering the New Republic Away from Dangerous Entanglements.

F. Patriot, Exemplifying Unselfish Devotion to his Country.

G. Political Leader, Aiding in the Establishment of a National Government, instead of a Confederacy.

H. Soldier and Commander, Bringing Independence to America.

I. Statesman, Determining a Republican Form of Government for the United States of America.

J. Surveyor and Engineer, Encouraging Western Expansion.

> If we work upon marble, it will perish; if we work on brass, time will efface it. If we rear temples, they will crumble to dust. But if we work on men's immortal minds, if we impress on them high principles, the just fear of God, and love for their fellow-men, we engrave on those tablets something which no time can efface, and which will brighten and brighten to all eternity. (Webster, Daniel—*Writings and Speeches* (National Ed.), Vol. XIII, pp. 518-519.) (Address, Faneuil Hall, Boston, Mass., May 22, 1852.)

The contributions which George Washington made to civilization are without number. They are still being enjoyed by this generation and will continue to be enjoyed by humanity for all time.

The suggestions given in this Unit are purposely few, as it is felt the opportunity should not be taken from the student to work out his own contribution of appreciation.

II. PROMOTION OF STUDENT'S ORIGINAL PRODUCTIONS.

Upon completion of the study of the first 11 units of this George Washington Appreciation Course the student is ready to make some deductions for himself. The value of the study of this Course to the student will be found through the deductions he makes.

Intensive original work should be done by the student to express his own ideas as to the "Contributions of George Washington to Civilization." Such a topic is a Challenge to any American.

From this Bicentennial Celebration of the Birth of George Washington it is hoped many lasting and

GEORGE WASHINGTON
Houdon Statue, Capitol, Richmond, Va

far reaching contributions may be forthcoming from the students and teachers as evidence of their appreciation of the life work of George Washington, contributions which may be used in the future study of George Washington and for the benefit of society in general.

The opportunities are abundant for the student *to develop his creative powers* in working out ideas through his pen, pencil, pallette, or other mediums of expression.

The United States George Washington Bicentennial Commission will appreciate receiving copies of any creation, made by a student of this George Washington Appreciation Course, which his instructor deems worthy of preservation for future use in doing honor to George Washington.

1732   1932

GEORGE WASHINGTON BICENTENNIAL

𝔓𝔩𝔢𝔡𝔤𝔢

AS AN AMERICAN, I WILL FOLLOW THE EXAMPLE OF GEORGE WASHINGTON IN UPRIGHT LIVING, INTEGRITY AND IN LOYALTY AND SERVICE TO MY COUNTRY. I WILL STRIVE "NEVER TO SAY ANYTHING ABOUT A MAN THAT I HAVE THE SLIGHTEST SCRUPLE OF SAYING TO HIM," AND "NEVER TO FORFEIT MY WORD, NOR BREAK MY PROMISE MADE TO ANYONE." IN HEART AND MIND, IN WORD AND DEED, I WILL KEEP FAITH WITH WASHINGTON.

NOTE—Words quoted paraphrase the thoughts of George Washington.

MRS. JOHN DICKINSON SHERMAN IS THE AUTHOR OF THE GEORGE WASHINGTON BICENTENNIAL PLEDGE APPEARING ON THIS PAGE. THE PLEDGE WAS WIDELY DISTRIBUTED AMONG ORGANIZATIONS, SCHOOLS, AND COLLEGES.

The
George Washington
Atlas

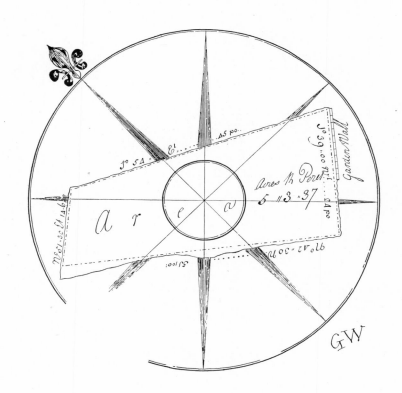

UNITED STATES
GEORGE WASHINGTON BICENTENNIAL COMMISSION

UNITED STATES
GEORGE WASHINGTON BICENTENNIAL
COMMISSION

Commissioners
THE PRESIDENT OF THE UNITED STATES, Chairman
THE VICE PRESIDENT OF THE UNITED STATES
THE SPEAKER OF THE HOUSE OF REPRESENTATIVES

United States Senate		House of Representatives	
SIMEON D. FESS, Vice Chairman	Ohio	WILLIS C. HAWLEY	Oregon
ARTHUR CAPPER	Kansas	JOHN Q. TILSON	Connecticut
CARTER GLASS	Virginia	JOSEPH W. BYRNS	Tennessee
MILLARD E. TYDINGS	Maryland	R. WALTON MOORE	Virginia

Presidential Commissioners

MRS. ANTHONY WAYNE COOK	Pennsylvania	C. BASCOM SLEMP	Virginia
MRS. JOHN DICKINSON SHERMAN	Colorado	WALLACE McCAMANT	Oregon
HENRY FORD	Michigan	ALBERT BUSHNELL HART	Massachusetts
	JOSEPH SCOTT	California	

Executive Committee
THE SENATE AND HOUSE COMMISSIONERS
MRS. ANTHONY WAYNE COOK
C. BASCOM SLEMP

Associate Director
REPRESENTATIVE SOL BLOOM

General Geographical Committee

ALBERT PERRY BRIGHAM *
Honorary Consultant in Geography, Library of Congress

JOHN C. FITZPATRICK
Editor of "The Writings of George Washington"

GILBERT GROSVENOR
President, National Geographic Society, Editor of "A Map of the Travels of George Washington"

LAWRENCE MARTIN, Chairman
Chief, Division of Maps, Library of Congress

EDWARD B. MATHEWS
Johns Hopkins University, Baltimore, Maryland

WILLIAM TYLER PAGE, Secretary
Former Clerk of the House of Representatives

CHARLES O. PAULLIN
Historical Division Carnegie Institution of Washington

ROBERT R. RALSTON
Chairman, Board of Surveys and Maps of the Federal Government

EARL G. SWEM
Librarian, College of William and Mary; Williamsburg, Virginia

JOHN K. WRIGHT
Librarian, American Geographical Society of New York

Regional Committee for New England

WALTER G. DAVIS
President, Maine Historical Society, Portland, Maine

OTIS G. HAMMOND
Director, New Hampshire Historical Society, Concord, New Hampshire

KIRTLEY F. MATHER, Chairman
Division of Geology and Geography, Harvard University, Cambridge, Massachusetts

LAWRENCE C. WROTH
Librarian, John Carter Brown Library, Providence, Rhode Island

GEORGE S. GODARD
State Librarian, Hartford, Connecticut

Regional Committee for the States Between New England and the Potomac

H. M. LYDENBERG, Chairman
Assistant Director, New York Public Library

GEORGE A. OSBORN
Librarian, Rutgers University, New Brunswick, New Jersey

FRANK E. WILLIAMS
University of Pennsylvania, Philadelphia

GEORGE H. RYDEN
State Archivist, Newark, Delaware

LOUIS H. DIELMAN
Librarian, Peabody Institute, Baltimore, Maryland

Regional Committee for the District of Columbia and Area to the South and West

H. R. McILWAINE, Chairman
State Librarian, Richmond, Virginia

THEODORE W. NOYES
Editor-in-chief, Washington Evening Star, Washington, D. C.

ARCHIBALD HENDERSON
University of North Carolina, Chapel Hill, North Carolina

A. S. SALLEY, JR.
Secretary, State Historical Commission, Columbia, South Carolina

S. W. McCALLIE
State Geologist, Atlanta, Georgia

CLIFFORD R. MYERS
State Historian and Archivist, Charleston, West Virginia

GUY-HAROLD SMITH
Department of Geography, Ohio State University, Columbus, Ohio

ELLEN CHURCHILL SEMPLE *
Louisville, Kentucky

WILLIAM W. BRUNSWICK
American Consul, Bridgetown, Barbados

The publication of this quarto edition of The George Washington Atlas is authorized by the Congress of the United States. The folio edition of The George Washington Atlas, 14 by 18 inches, bound, and with forty of the fifty plates in color, may be purchased at cost by prepayment of $2.00 to the Superintendent of Documents. Government Printing Office, Washington, D. C.

* *Deceased*

THE
GEORGE WASHINGTON
ATLAS

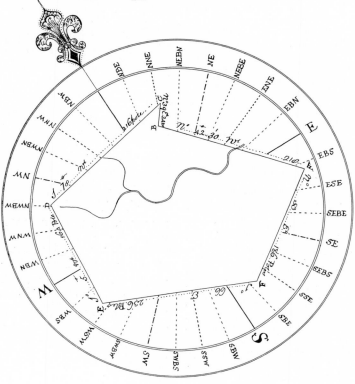

A collection of eighty-six maps on fifty plates
including twenty-eight maps made by George Washington
seven used and annotated by him
eight made at his direction, or for his use
or otherwise associated with him
and forty-three new maps concerning his activities in peace and war
and his place in history

EDITED BY
LAWRENCE MARTIN
CHIEF, DIVISION OF MAPS
LIBRARY OF CONGRESS

UNITED STATES
GEORGE WASHINGTON BICENTENNIAL COMMISSION
WASHINGTON, D. C.
1932

PREFACE

Half of this atlas is devoted to George Washington's maps. This is appropriate because his maps are as significant as his writings. The intention of establishing Pittsburgh, for example, is expressed in a note upon the face of Plate 11 and nowhere else. The remarks upon Plate 22 with respect to navigation upon the Potomac are important to economists. Moreover, many of Washington's maps are unfamiliar and have never been used by historians. This is true of the map of Boston and Cambridge (Plate 12), the map of part of the Susquehanna valley in New York (Plate 18), and many others.

George Washington surveyed in the course of his life more than 226 tracts, containing upwards of 84,028 acres of land (Plate 18). Most of this was in addition to the surveys of his own property at Mount Vernon and elsewhere. He owned at one time or another some 69,615 acres of land in thirty-seven localities, to say nothing of twenty-four city lots and one whole square (Plate 48). By the end of his second term as President of the United States he had himself seen more of the national domain of that day than any other American. The extent of his journeys included the territory from Kittery, Maine, and Crown Point, New York, on the north, to Point Pleasant, West Virginia, on the west, and Savannah, Georgia, on the south (Plate 1). In addition he had been to the island of Barbados in the Lesser Antilles near South America. The number of miles he travelled from youth to old age has never been computed. Washington thought that his wilderness journey of 1784, in Pennsylvania, West Virginia, Maryland, and Virginia, covered 680 miles. He estimated 1,887 miles as the length of his tour from Philadelphia to Savannah and back in 1791. He went repeatedly over many of the roads from Mount Vernon southward to Williamsburg, Virginia, westward to Cumberland, Maryland, and northward to Boston, Massachusetts. Thus he took ten journeys in New England, one hundred and thirty-six in Maryland, and a still greater number in Virginia.

Washington made his first map in 1747 and his last one in 1799, so that he made maps for a period of over half a century. At least one hundred and thirty-six of his maps and related drawings are preserved and twenty-eight of these have been reproduced in this atlas (Plates 2-8, 11-13, 18-24), to say nothing of those on the half-title, title-page, and the last page of the index. It will be observed that, contrary to popular impression, these maps of George Washington's are related to landscape gardening, city planning, exploration, transportation, and the arts of war, as well as to the surveying of land in connection with the acquisition of property, and that he made a plan of a church as well as several plans of forts. The atlas also includes facsimiles of seven of the nineteen maps known to have been used and annotated by George Washington (Plates 14-17, 22, 25), one of the many maps made at his direction (Plate 40), and one of the several maps dedicated to him (Plate 41). Among the annotated maps, that on Plate 25 has for a hundred years been considered to have been made by George Washington, but the annotation shows that it was made by another man.

Three maps in the atlas bear unusual relations to the personal life of George Washington. One of the fourteen maps of Mount Vernon here reproduced is Washington's own map of the whole estate (Plate 2). It has never been published before and its fortunate possessor, the Huntington Library, has been generous enough to permit the Bicentennial Commission to include it in this atlas, although its presentation in facsimile by the Huntington Library itself, as a special publication of the bicentennial year, had already been determined upon. A second map (Plate 8) has been in the Division of Manuscripts at the Library of Congress for many years. It has never been associated till now, however, with the farm at Bridges Creek (Wakefield) where George Washington was born. This is one of the earliest of his maps which is preserved. A third map (Plate 9) is unusual in several respects. It represents Washington's boyhood home on the Rappahannock, the scene of the legends of the cutting down of the cherry tree and of the throwing of the coin across the river. Washington surveyed the cultivated portion of the Rappahannock Farm in 1771 but seems never to have reduced his survey notes to the form of a map. The notes are preserved in a record of similar surveys which A. S. W. Rosenbach of Philadelphia has been good enough to permit us to use. Washington's survey notes were platted into a map in 1932. The river bluffs, hills, gullies, roads, and other features described in the notes so precisely fit the features on the ground at the site of the traditional Washington farm southeast of Fredericksburg that the resulting map settles for all time the controversy as to whether Washington's boyhood home was there rather than at a supposed site northeast of Fredericksburg. Incidentally this map fully confirms the general evidence that Washington was a good surveyor.

The copies of Washington's maps which are included in this atlas have been reproduced as faithfully as modern printing methods permit. The sizes of the original maps vary greatly, and the facsimiles are reduced in scale and lack the colors of the originals. The annotations upon the backs of several of the manuscript maps have been made to appear as if they were upon the faces of the maps.

All the decorations on pages near the front and

back of the atlas were made by Washington himself in his youth. The corners of the title-page are ornamented with George Washington's coat of arms.

The other half of this atlas consists of forty-three maps relating to George Washington, each of them newly compiled for *The George Washington Atlas*. These maps (Plates 1, 26-39, 42-48) are based upon Washington's diaries, his accounts, and his letters and other writings. The diary entries used are (a) those in the four volumes published by the Mount Vernon Ladies Association; (b) amplifications from the originals where geographical descriptions have been abbreviated; (c) in the case of Washington's journey to Barbados, the latitude and longitude of the vessel's position each noon as published in the edition of the Barbados diary which was edited by John M. Toner; and (d) those in the unpublished survey diaries and survey notes which are preserved in the Library of Congress, the Huntington Library, the private library of A. S. W. Rosenbach, and the library of Cornell University. The letters and other writings which have been utilized in making the modern maps of this atlas include those published in the series of volumes which were edited by Jared Sparks and by Worthington C. Ford, respectively, as well as the first volumes of the edition which is being edited by John C. Fitzpatrick and printed by the Bicentennial Commission. The bulk of the geographical materials in these publications has been conveniently summarized in three books, —John C. Fitzpatrick's "George Washington, Colonial Traveller, 1732-1775," William S. Baker's "Itinerary of General Washington from June 15, 1775 to December 23, 1783," and the same author's work entitled "Washington After the Revolution." The editor of the atlas has gleaned additional information from diaries of Washington's contemporaries, certain colonial gazettes, and statements in a number of books, to say nothing of articles in county histories, periodicals, etc.

An attempt has been made to show upon these maps the locations of all the places visited by Washington which can now be identified. One symbol is used for precise localities, another for approximate localities, but it has not been feasible to make this distinction upon the city maps. A small number of places specifically mentioned cannot be identified on modern maps at present. Most of these are houses in the country.

It should be recognized that traditions have arisen that Washington went to places which it cannot be demonstrated that he ever did visit. In making this atlas an attempt has been made to eliminate all such places. There is, for example, no compelling proof that Washington ever visited the Natural Bridge of Virginia, the city of Ben-

nington in Vermont, or the stone house on M Street in Georgetown, District of Columbia, which some persons have considered to have been the office of Pierre Charles L'Enfant.

Two maps at the end of the atlas (Plates 49 and 50) are indicative of the extent to which George Washington is known and revered not only in all parts of continental United States, including those which he never visited, but also in our outlying possessions, and in foreign countries.

Plate 49, the world map showing more than one hundred and fifty instances of the use of Washington's name in Alaska, the Philippine Islands, and foreign countries, includes streets and monuments, as well as rivers, mountains, islands, capes, straits, gulfs, etc. Its making resulted from the suggestion of a seven-year-old school-girl in Washington, D. C. An interesting and wholly unexpected outcome of the inquiries as to where there are foreign statues of George Washington or streets named after George Washington was the announcement in several countries that they proposed to celebrate Washington's bicentennial year by naming additional streets or plazas for him.

Every State and commonwealth in the United States of America except two has named a county, township, city, village, mountain, river, creek, lake, island, bay, or cape after George Washington. In some States there are many such names. Plate 50 is not large enough to show all the places where there are American monuments to Washington's memory, or streets, buildings, parks, bridges, schools, and colleges in the United States which bear Washington's name. Of other features there are nearly four hundred and fifty in this country, and the list is by no means complete. Nor does the map indicate all instances where Washington's name was used and then discontinued, as in the cases of Washington County, D. C., and "Washington District," an early designation for the State of Tennessee. It would be instructive to learn why the name Washington is less frequently used in Illinois than on either side, in Indiana and Iowa, and why it happens to be absent in Delaware and Wyoming except for streets and buildings. Plate 50 is unusual in containing no other name than that of Washington.

In the series of State maps, Washington's chief routes are shown in Maine, New Hampshire, Vermont, Massachusetts, Rhode Island, Connecticut, northern New York, western Pennsylvania, parts of Maryland, Ohio, and West Virginia, and in North Carolina, South Carolina, and Georgia, but not in southeastern New York, New Jersey, eastern Pennsylvania, Delaware, eastern Maryland, or Virginia. In these States, however, they are shown on Plate 1. Curiously enough, it is in the places where Washington travelled the most that it is hardest to show his routes clearly and accurately on maps as small as the State maps in this atlas. Accordingly it seemed best to leave all routes off the map of New Jersey, for example, and to show Washington's important routes of travel in that State on Plates 1, 36, 37, 38, and 39. The same thing is true of Virginia where Washington's routes of travel are represented on Plates 1, 34, 35, and 39. The State boundaries drawn are those of 1932.

The limitations of space also made it impossible to indicate the specific dates at which Washington visited places. There was plenty of space to show the dates when he went to relatively unimportant outlying localities but no room to show when he made his repeated visits to such cities as Williamsburg, Philadelphia, and New York. It would have been necessary to have given thirty-six dates at Baltimore and a still greater number at Alexandria. Except on Plate 1, however, the routes have all been dated.

The editor of the atlas is indebted to many persons and institutions for assistance in the identification and selection of the maps of Washington's which are here reproduced, for permission to reproduce manuscript maps which Washington made or annotated, and for aid in the compilation of the other maps in this atlas. Particular acknowledgment is due to Representative Sol Bloom, Associate Director of the Bicentennial Commission, to Albert Bushnell Hart, historian of the commission, to John C. Fitzpatrick, editor of the forthcoming edition of the writings of George Washington, to the members of the four geographical committees whose names are printed upon a preceding page, and to the persons and institutions whose names appear in the Table of Contents of this atlas, and in the list of Washington's maps at the end. The editor is also under obligations to the Secretary of State, the Secretary of Commerce, and the members of the American Foreign Service for contributing much of the data upon which Plate 49 is based. Valuable advice respecting the campaign maps and battle maps was given by Gen. Peyton C. March, Gen. James G. Harbord, Gen. George Van Horn Moseley, Gen. Frank McCoy, Col. S. C. Vestal, Col. Sherman Miles, Col. Girard L. McEntee, and Col. Charles H. Mason, of the United States Army. The officers of other federal departments and independent offices in Washington have contributed substantially to the making of the atlas, as have Herbert Putnam, the Librarian of Congress, and Charles Moore, the Chairman of the Fine Arts Commission.

The editor is greatly obliged to Samuel Flagg Bemis, George Washington University; S. W. Boggs, Department of State; Frank Bond, United States Geographic Board; G. F. Bowerman, District of Columbia Public Library; Solon J. Buck, Minnesota Historical Society; Arthur H. Buffington, Williams College; Albert H. Bumstead, Chief Cartographer, National Geographic Society; F. A. Carlson, Ohio State University; Allen C. Clark, Washington, D. C.; Allen P. Cubbage, Leitchfield, Ky.; Harrison H. Dodge, Mount Vernon, Va.; Max Farrand, Huntington Library; Worthington C. Ford, European Representative, Library of Congress; C. W. French, George Washington Foundation; Ralph A. Graves, Assistant Editor, National Geographic Magazine; Fairfax Harrison, Washington, D. C.; C. F. Heartman, Metuchen, N. J.; W. W. Husband, Assistant Secretary of Labor; W. R. Jillson, State Geologist of Kentucky; John K. Lacock, Boston, Mass.; Byron McCandless, United States Navy; Arthur Martin, Cheshire, Mass.; George C. Martin, Washington, D. C.; David M. Matteson, of the Bicentennial Commission; Albert Cook Myers, Pennsylvania Historical Society; Charles J. Palmer, Lanesborough, Mass.; Walter G. Peter, Washington, D. C.; W. H. Richardson, Jersey City, N. J.; Miss Helen M. Strong, Department of Commerce; R. C. B. Thruston, Louisville, Ky.; Mrs. Bertha T. Voorhorst, Berkeley Springs, W. Va.; W. K. Watkins, Boston, Mass.; and Samuel M. Wilson, Lexington, Ky.

Emphatic acknowledgment is due to A. F. Hassan and A. H. Linsenmeyer, of the United States Geological Survey, and to Miss Clara Egli and Miss Edna S. Banks, of the Library of Congress, each of whom has contributed substantially to the drafting, photographing, compilation, arrangement, and verification of the materials in the atlas.

The making of the folio edition of *The George Washington Atlas* was accomplished in a period of less than a year. This quarto edition represents a slight revision. The excellence of its reproduction is a testimonial to the high standards of work performed by the Topographic Branch and the Engraving Division of the United States Geological Survey and the lithographers and printers who made the printing plates and printed the atlas.

At the end of the atlas is a list of all the maps made or annotated by George Washington which can now be identified. It is hoped that the publication of this list will result in the finding of still other maps which are somewhere preserved. We know definitely that there are such maps. Only about two-fifths of two hundred and fourteen maps of tracts laid out by Washington as a public surveyor have been located and identified. We also have references to Washington's lost maps of other types.

October 26, 1932   Lawrence Martin, *Editor.*

Drawn by George Washington in 1750

DETAILED TABLE OF CONTENTS, WITH ACKNOWLEDGMENTS

Washington's maps (continued)

Kanawha Rivers. Map drawn by George Washington in 1787. Reproduced by permission of Montagu Hankin of Morristown, New Jersey.

Plate 25. Parts of Maryland, Pennsylvania, and West Virginia, to illustrate plans for water transportation from the Atlantic seaboard to the Mississippi valley. The upper map, erroneously attributed to George Washington in 1826 (House Rept. 228, 19th Congress, 1st Session, page 24) is here proved by his own annotation of the lower map to have been drawn by Normand Bruce in 1784. The lower map is reproduced by permission of the Minnesota Historical Society.

State maps

Plate 26. New England, showing George Washington's ten journeys. Map compiled by Dr. Laura H. Martin, of Washington, D. C. The United States Coast and Geodetic Survey supplied the supposed routes of the sea voyages south of Long Island.

27. New York State, showing the localities visited by George Washington and the routes of his northern journeys in 1782 and 1783. Routes compiled by the late Albert Perry Brigham, emeritus professor of geology at Colgate University, Hamilton, N. Y., honorary consultant in geography at the Library of Congress.

28. New Jersey, showing the localities visited by George Washington. George de B. Keim of the New Jersey Commission on Historic Sites, and Miss Marion Cushman of the Rutgers University Library identified a number of the localities.

29. Pennsylvania, showing the localities visited by George Washington and the routes of his journeys to Fort Le Boeuf in 1753-54, with Braddock in 1755, and with Forbes in 1758. Frank E. Williams of the University of Pennsylvania identified a number of the localities.

30. Maryland and Delaware, showing the localities visited by George Washington. J. Alexis Shriver of Bel Air, Maryland, and George H. Ryden, State Archivist of Delaware, identified a number of the localities.

31. West Virginia and Ohio, showing the localities visited by George Washington and the routes of his Ohio River journey in 1770, and his journey across West Virginia in 1784. The localities on the Ohio River were identified by Guy-Harold Smith of the Ohio State University and Roy Bird Cook of the West Virginia Board of Pharmacy. Some of those elsewhere in West Virginia were identified by Clifford R. Myers, State Historian and Archivist of West Virginia.

32. The region of the lower Potomac, showing Mount Vernon and the localities visited by George Washington.

33. Virginia, showing the localities visited by George Washington. See also Plate 32. A number of the localities were identified by H. J. Ekenrode and Bryan Conrad of the Virginia Commission of Conservation and Development and William Joseph Showalter, Chief of the Research Division of the National Geographic Society.

34. North Carolina, South Carolina, and Georgia, showing the localities visited by George Washington; the insert map gives the route of his whole southern tour in 1791. Some of the localities were identified by A. S. Salley, Secretary of the South Carolina Historical Commission, and by S. W. McCallie, State Geologist of Georgia.

Campaign maps

Plate 35. Washington's campaign with Braddock in 1755.

36. Washington's campaign in 1776 from Brooklyn to Morristown, via White Plains, Trenton, and Princeton. Numbers indicate the order in which places were visited or revisited.

37. Washington's campaign in 1777 from Morristown to Valley Forge, via Middlebrook, Quibbletown, the highlands of the Hudson, the Brandywine, and Germantown. Numbers indicate the order in which places were visited or revisited.

38. Washington's campaign in 1778 from Valley Forge to the Hudson via Monmouth Court House, with insert map showing winter quarters, 1778-9.

39. Washington's campaign in 1781 from the Hudson to Yorktown.

Battle maps

Plate 40. Map of the siege of Boston, made at Washington's direction, in 1775, by John Trumbull, the painter, and transmitted to Congress (upper); a French map of the battle of Monmouth in 1778, preserved in the French Ministry of War, L. I. D. 105 (lower).

Plate 41. Sebastian Bauman's map of the siege of Yorktown, published at Philadelphia in 1782 and dedicated to Washington.

City maps

Plate 42. Cambridge and Boston, Massachusetts, showing localities associated with George Washington. Map compiled by Laurence La Forge of the Division of Geology and Geography of Harvard University.

43. New York City, showing localities on Manhattan Island, associated with George Washington.

44. Newburgh and New Windsor, New York (upper right), Morristown, New Jersey (upper left), Philadelphia (lower), showing localities associated with George Washington. A number of the localities in Morristown and in Philadelphia were identified by Montagu Hankin of Morristown and Frank E. Williams of the University of Pennsylvania, respectively.

45. Annapolis, Maryland (upper), and Alexandria, Virginia (lower), showing localities associated with George Washington. The upper map was compiled by J. Alexis Shriver of Bel Air, Maryland. Several of the localities in Alexandria were identified by Miss Margaret Germond of the Washington Evening Star.

46. Washington, D. C., showing localities associated with George Washington; insert map on right shows the Patowmack Company's canal and locks at Great Falls, Virginia, parts of which were constructed during the period when George Washington was president of the company. The main map was compiled by the Board of Surveys and Maps of the Federal Government.

47. Fredericksburg, Virginia (upper), and Williamsburg, Virginia (lower), showing localities associated with George Washington. The lower map was compiled by E. G. Swem, Librarian of the College of William and Mary, in collaboration with the Research Bureau of the Williamsburg Holding Corporation.

Washington's lands

Plate 48. The localities in New York, Pennsylvania, Ohio, Kentucky, West Virginia, the District of Columbia, Maryland, and Virginia where George Washington owned land. Part of the data for this map was compiled by the General Land Office.

See also Plates 2, 3, 4, 5, 6, 7, 9, 10, 21, 22, 23, and 24.

Recognition of Washington

Plate 49. The world showing over 150 features named for and statues of George Washington outside of continental United States. There are 23 mountains, rivers, islands, capes, and arms of the sea, 18 statues and monuments, more than 100 streets and plazas, and 11 villages and miscellaneous features.

50. The United States of America, showing nearly 450 features named for George Washington, other than streets, buildings, schools, colleges, monuments, &c., and including 2 States, 33 counties, 257 townships, 121 cities, towns, and villages, 10 lakes, 8 streams, and 7 mountains, besides miscellaneous features. Map compiled by the United States Geographic Board.

List of maps made by George Washington and of maps made by others but used and annotated by him. A note describes 135 of Washington's lost maps. The chain, compasses, and scale at the end of the list were drawn by George Washington when he was 14 years old.

Index; the tail piece is a decorated map made by George Washington in 1749.

George Washington's letter to one of his geographers, Simeon De Witt, written August 29, 1781, in connection with the making of maps for the march to Yorktown. Reproduced by permission of the Rutgers University Library.

Portrait of the Washington family at Mount Vernon, with the L'Enfant Plan of Washington, D. C., upon the table. Painted by Edward Savage between 1789 and 1796.

PLATE 1

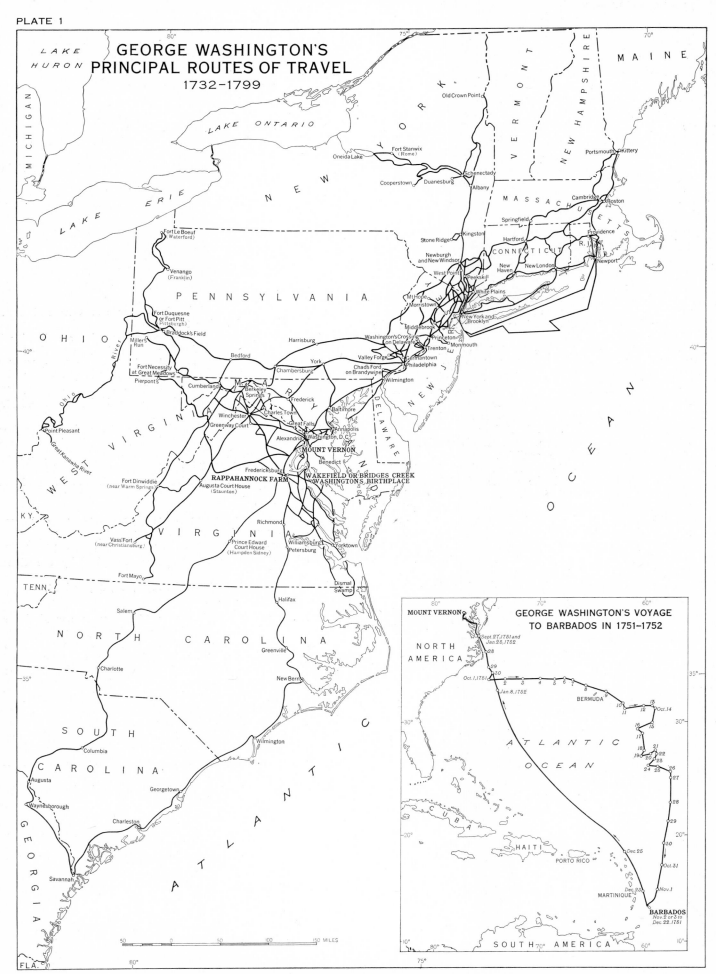

GEORGE WASHINGTON'S
PRINCIPAL ROUTES OF TRAVEL
1732-1799

GEORGE WASHINGTON'S VOYAGE
TO BARBADOS IN 1751-1752

General map of George Washington's principal routes of travel, with insert map of his sea voyage to Barbados in 1751-2.

PLATE 2

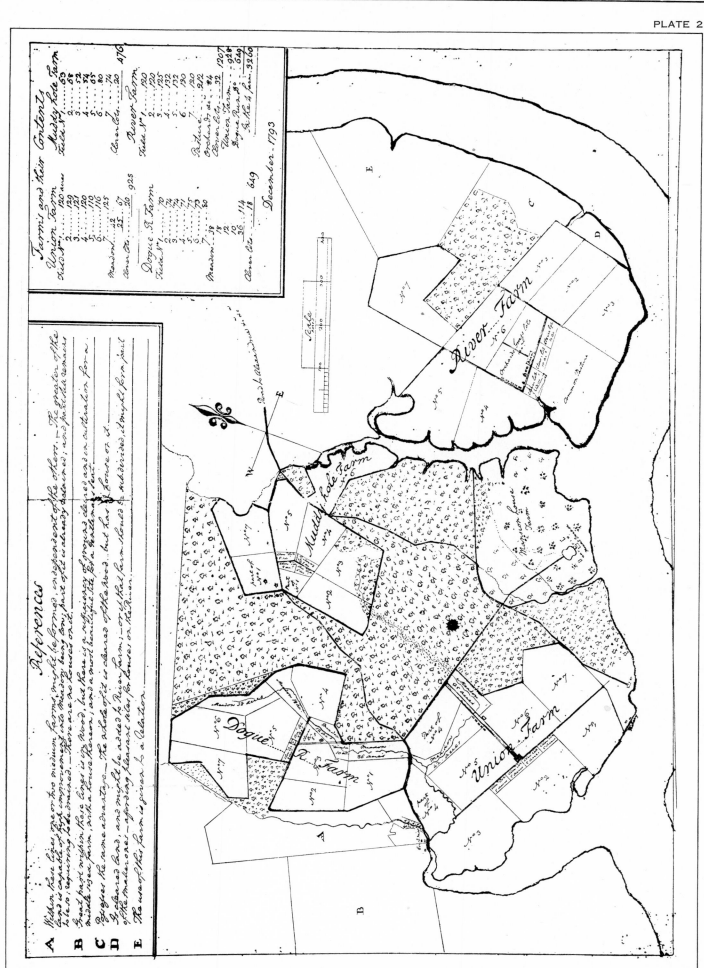

Mount Vernon. George Washington's own map of all his farms, drawn in 1793. Copyright, 1931, by the Huntington Library.

PLATE 3

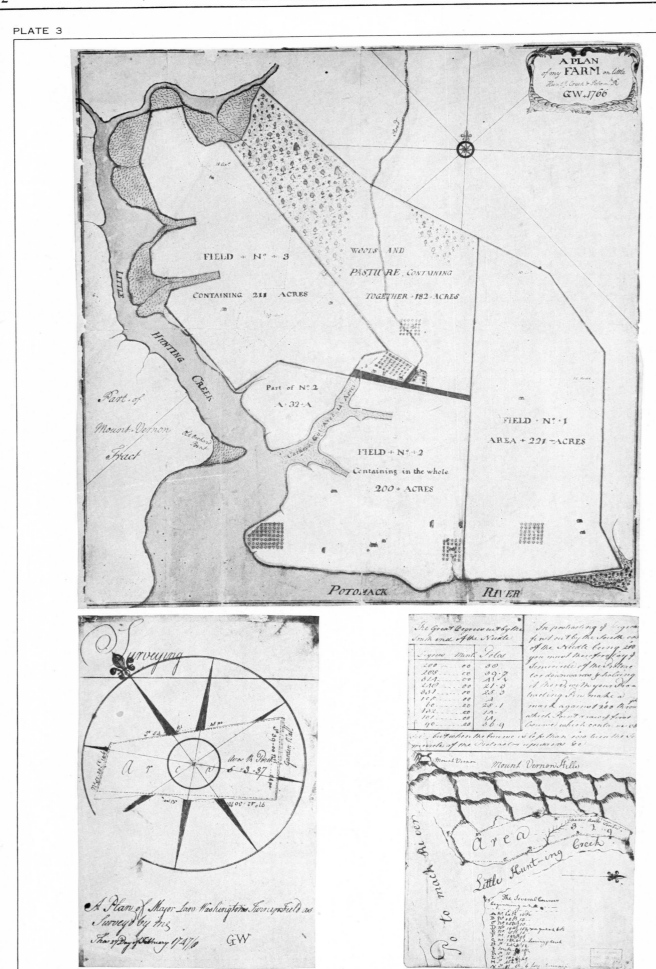

Mount Vernon.   The River Farm in 1766 (upper); plan of Lawrence Washington's turnip field in 1748 (lower left); sketch of part of the estate near the
Mansion House and Little Hunting Creek about 1747 (lower right).   All three maps were made by George Washington.

PLATE 4

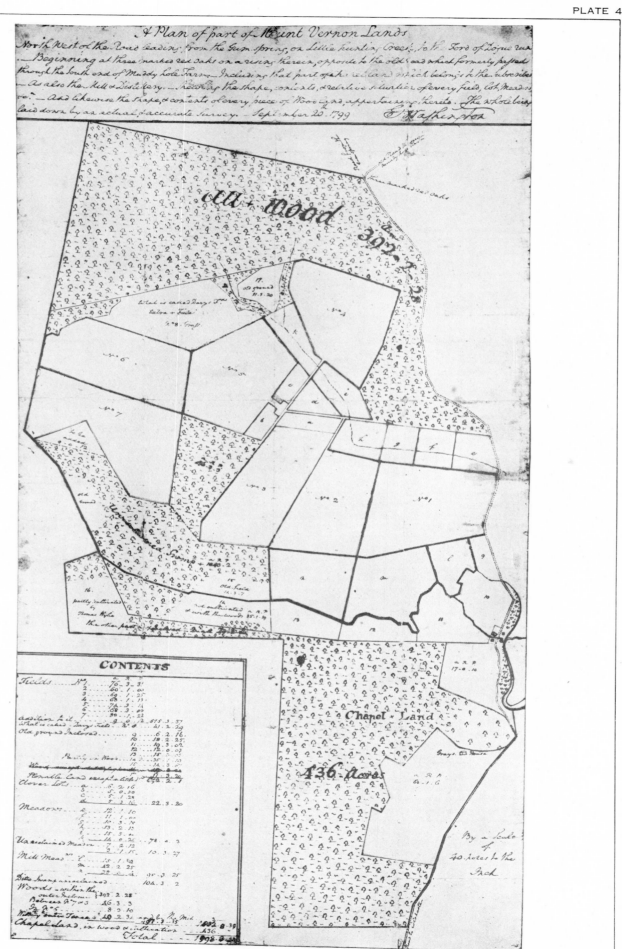

Mount Vernon.   The Dogue Run Farm as mapped by George Washington in 1799.

PLATE 5

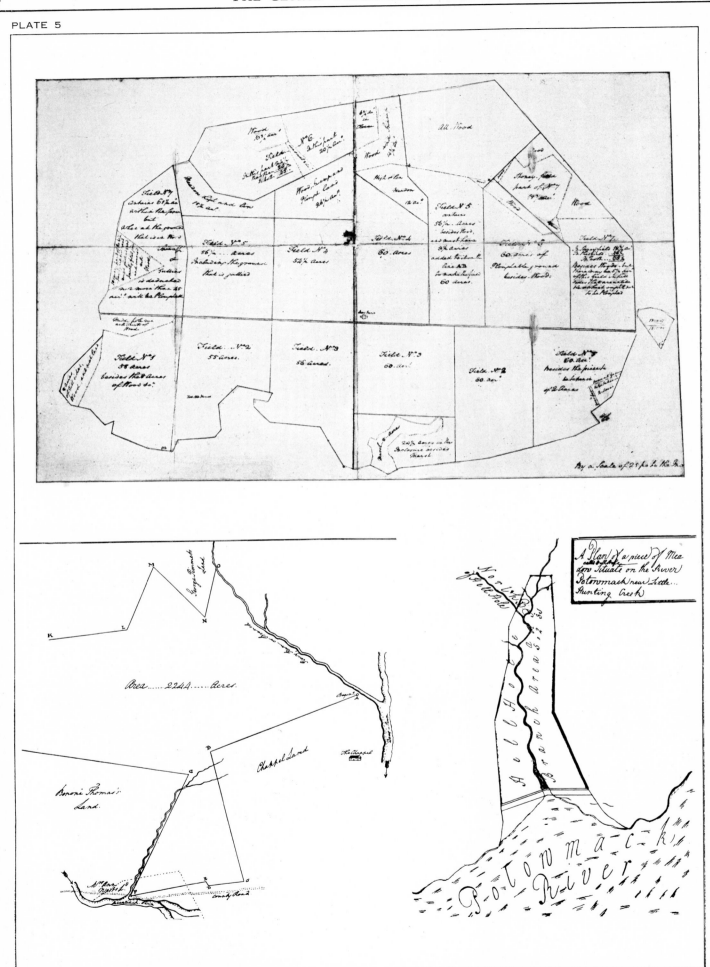

Mount Vernon. The Union Farm about 1787 (upper); the "Chappel Land" west of Dogue Run (lower left); a field and stream at "Hell Hole" between
the Potomac River and Little Hunting Creek about 1747 (lower right). All three maps were made by George Washington.

PLATE 6

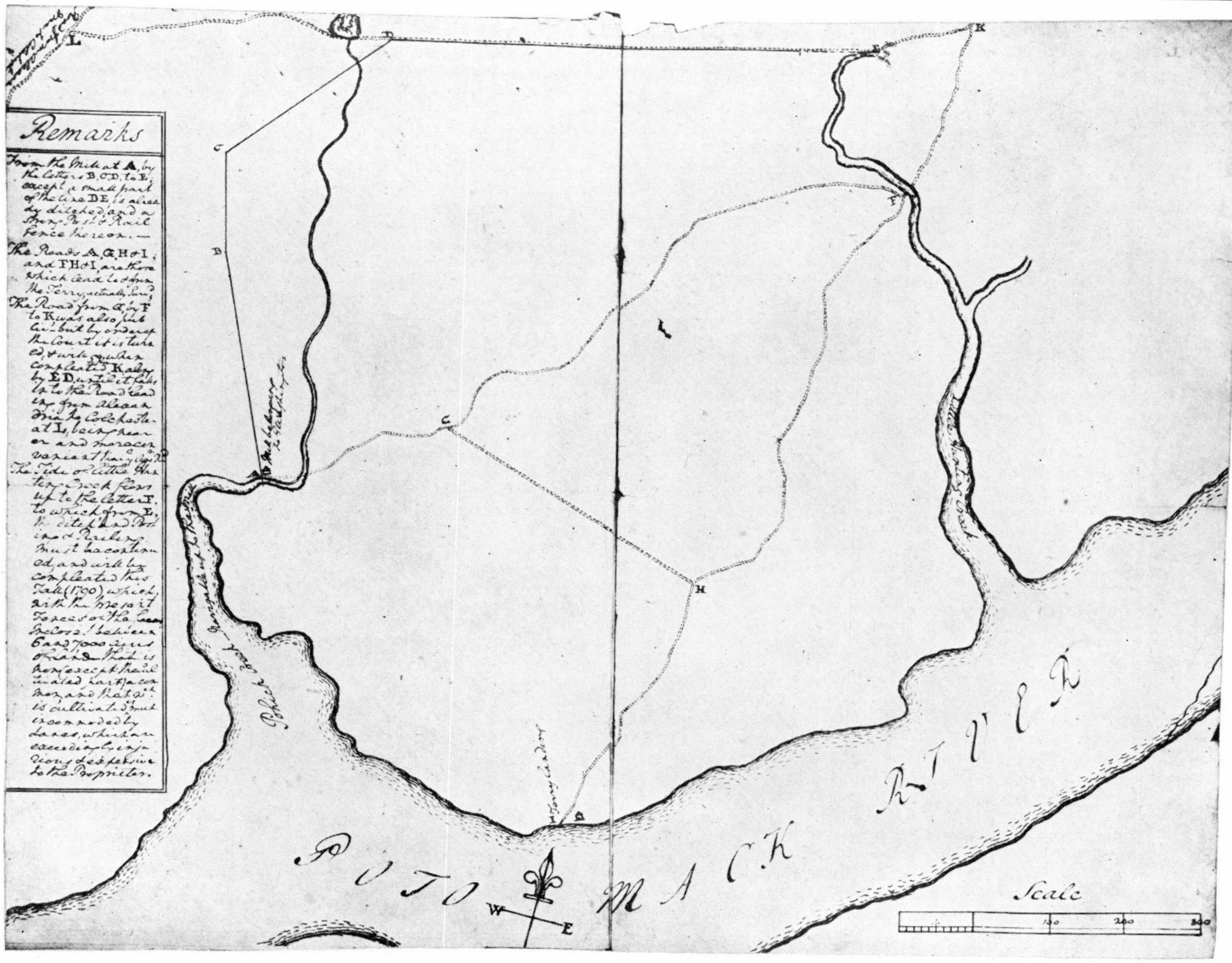

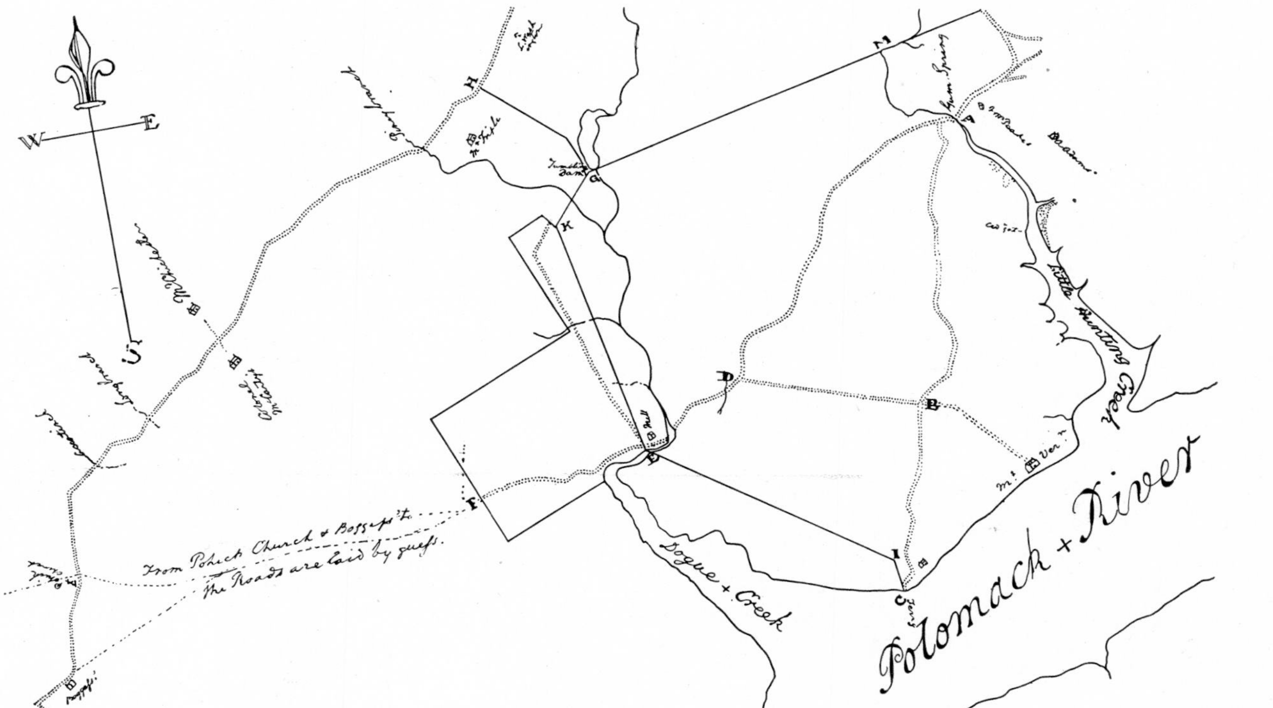

Mount Vernon. Roads leading to Ferry Landing in 1790 (upper): part of the map of the roads from Mount Vernon to Pohick Church and to Cameron, surveyed Nov. 13–15, 1788, with sketch of the Mansion House (lower). Both maps were made by George Washington.

PLATE 7

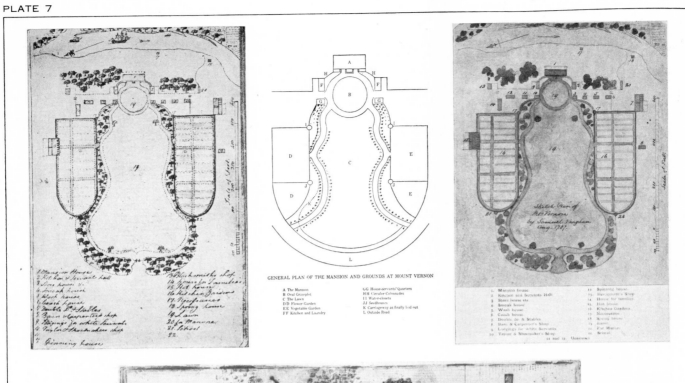

GENERAL PLAN OF THE MANSION AND GROUNDS AT MOUNT VERNON

A   The Mansion
B   Oval Grassplot
C   The Lawn
DD   Flower Garden
EE   Vegetable Garden
FF   Kitchen and Laundry

GG   House-servants' Quarters
HH   Circular Colonnades
II   Water-closets
JJ   Seedhouses
K   Carriageway as finally laid out
L   Outside Road

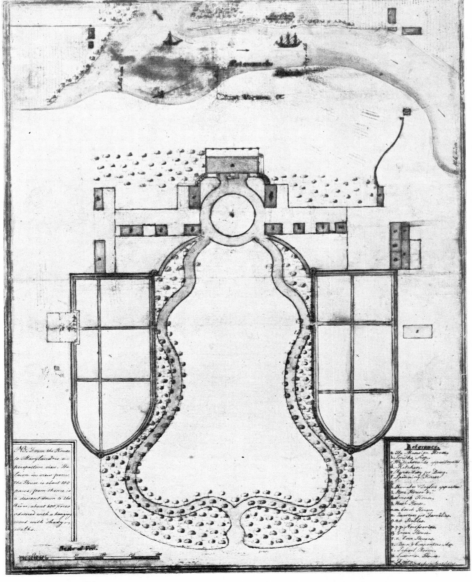

Mount Vernon. The Mansion House grounds. The upper middle map is a rough facsimile of one made by George Washington about 1784. The other three maps were made by Samuel Vaughan in 1787, when he was corresponding with Washington about the landscape gardening of the place. Lower map copyright, 1931, by Walter G. Peter.

PLATE 8

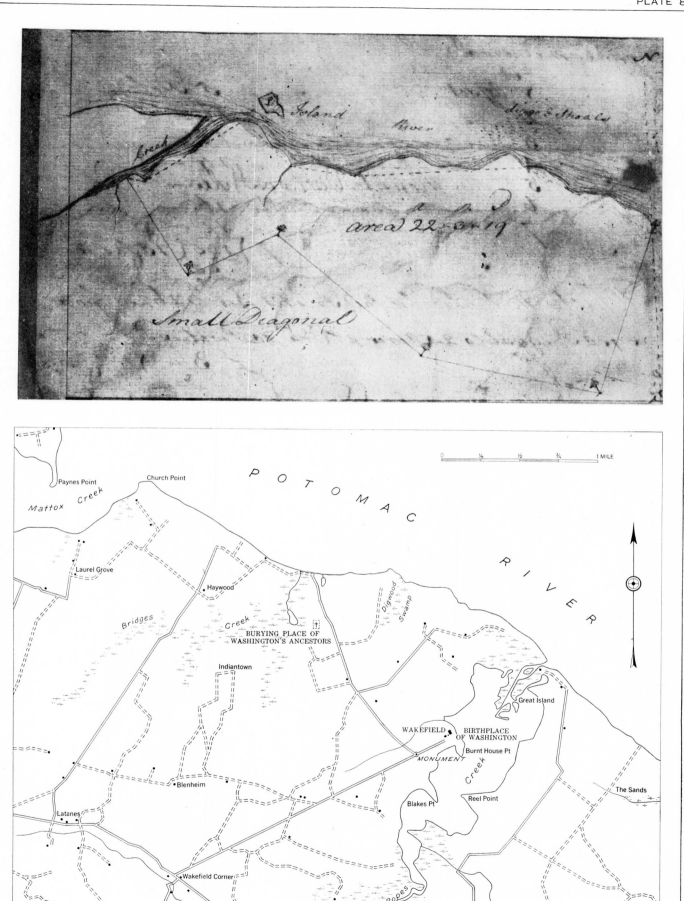

Wakefield or Bridges Creek, Westmoreland County, Virginia, where George Washington was born.   The upper map was made by George Washington
in 1747 and appears to represent the northern part of the estate.   The lower map is a modern one showing the locations of the birthplace of
George Washington and the burial place of his ancestors in relation to Pope's Creek, Bridges Creek, and the Potomac River.

PLATE 9

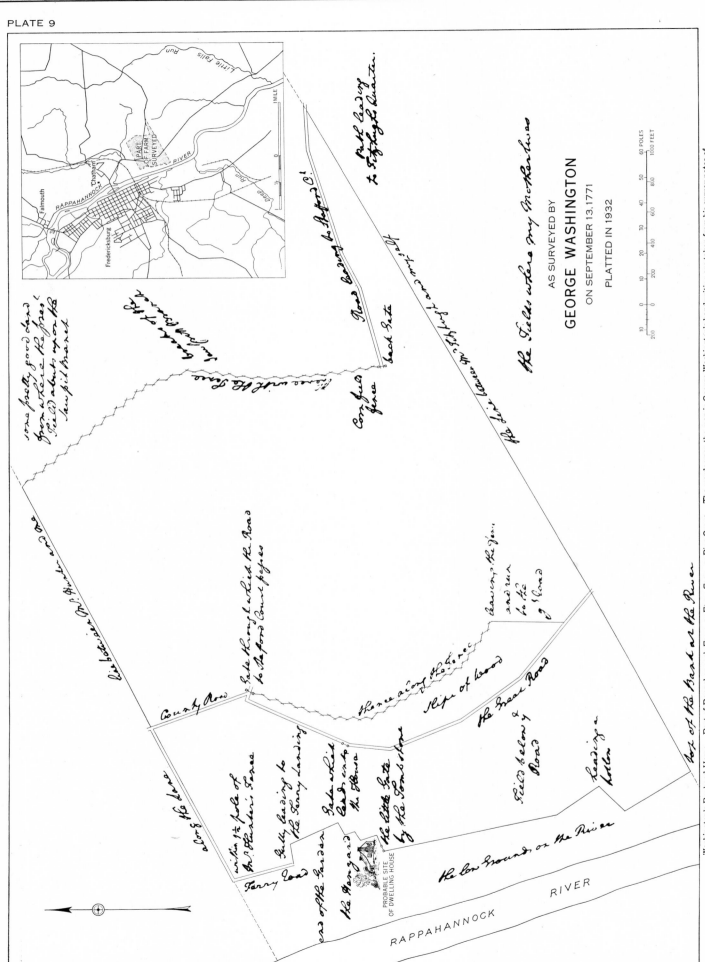

AS SURVEYED BY

GEORGE WASHINGTON

ON SEPTEMBER 13, 1771

PLATTED IN 1932

Washington's Boyhood Home.   Part of Rappahannock Farm, or Ferry Farm, or Pine Grove.   The words upon the map in George Washington's handwriting are taken from his survey notes of September 13, 1771.   The insert map shows the relation of the land mapped by Washington to Fredericksburg, Falmouth, Deep Run, and Little Falls Run.

PLATE 10

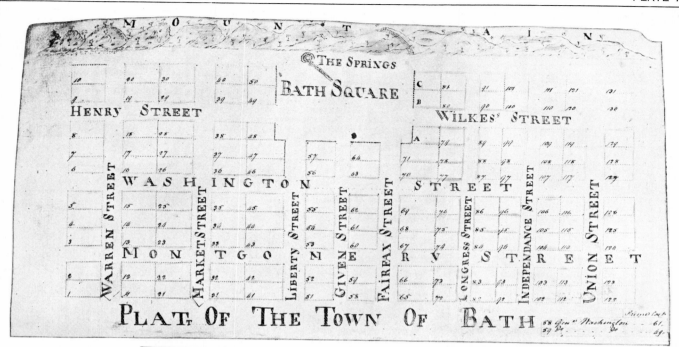

Bath or Warm Springs, now Berkeley Springs, West Virginia, showing lots 58 and 59 upon which George Washington built a house; the indenture under which he bought the land. The map was not drawn by Washington.

PLATE 11

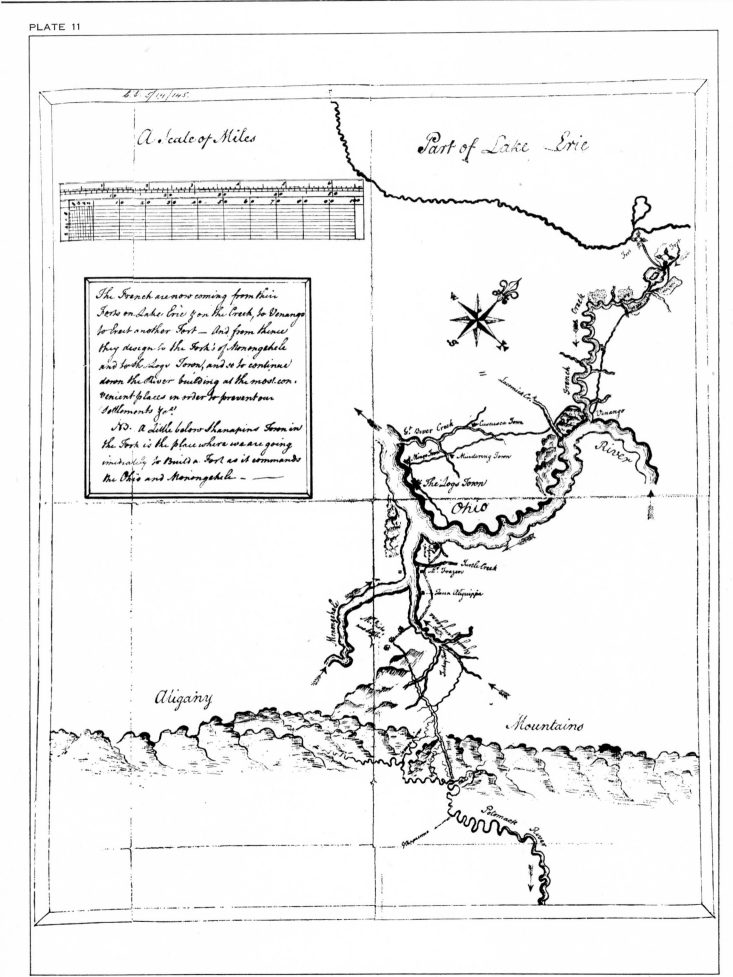

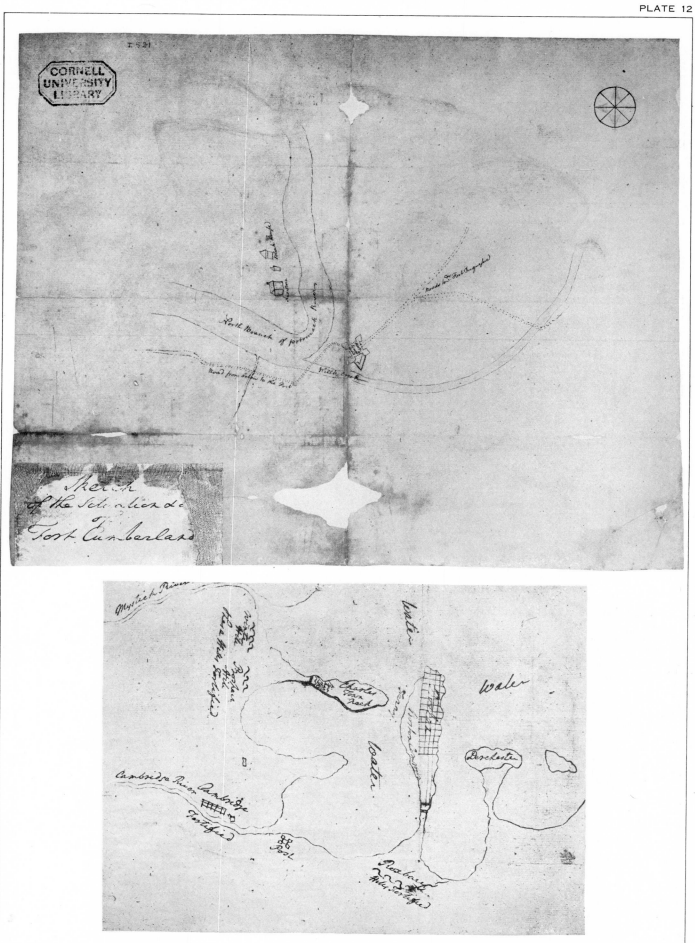

George Washington's own maps of Fort Cumberland, now Cumberland, Maryland, made about 1758 (upper), and of Boston
and Cambridge, Massachusetts, made about 1775 (lower).

PLATE 13

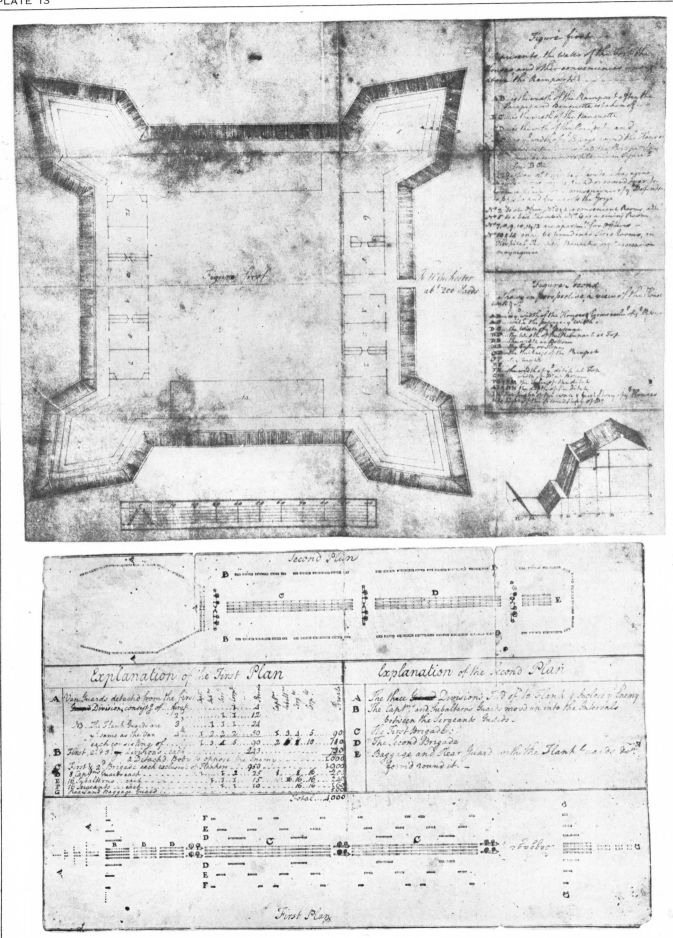

Fort Loudoun at Winchester, Virginia, drawn by George Washington about 1756 (upper); his plan for a line of march
in a forest country in 1758 (lower).

PLATE 14

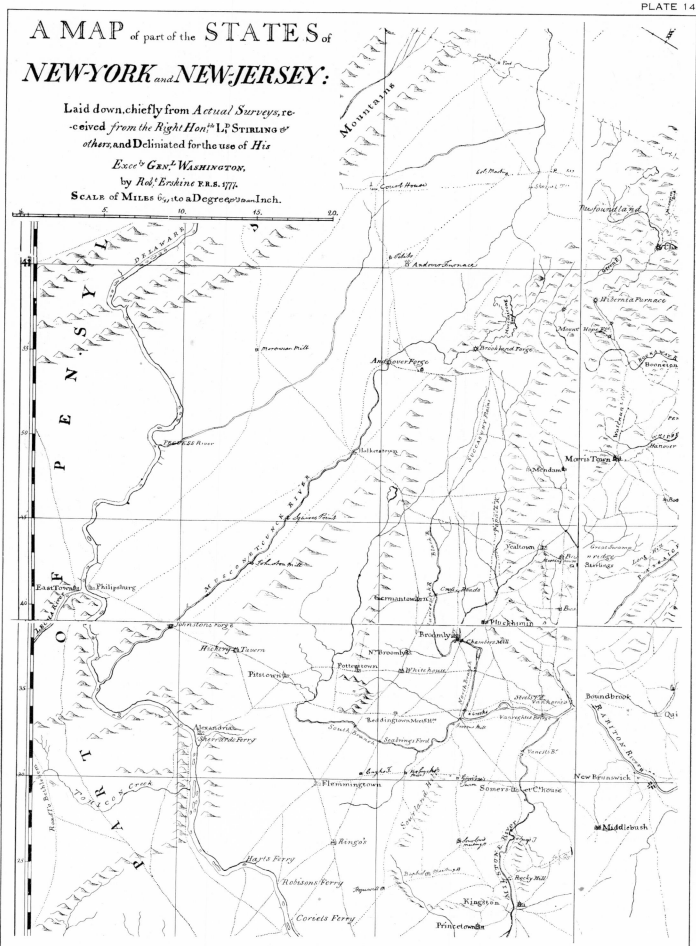

A MAP of part of the STATES of

NEW-YORK and NEW-JERSEY:

Laid down, chiefly from *Actual Surveys*, re-
-ceived *from the Right Hon.ble Lp Stirling &
others*, and Deliniated for the use of *His*

Excely Genl Washington,
by *Robt Erskine* F.R.S. 1777.
Scale of Miles 69¼ to a Degree ⅓ ¾ of an Inch.

Part of Robert Erskine's map of New Jersey in 1777, delineated for the use of George Washington and annotated by him.
The annotations include 17 place names, 4 symbols for unnamed localities, and a number of roads and streams.

PLATE 15

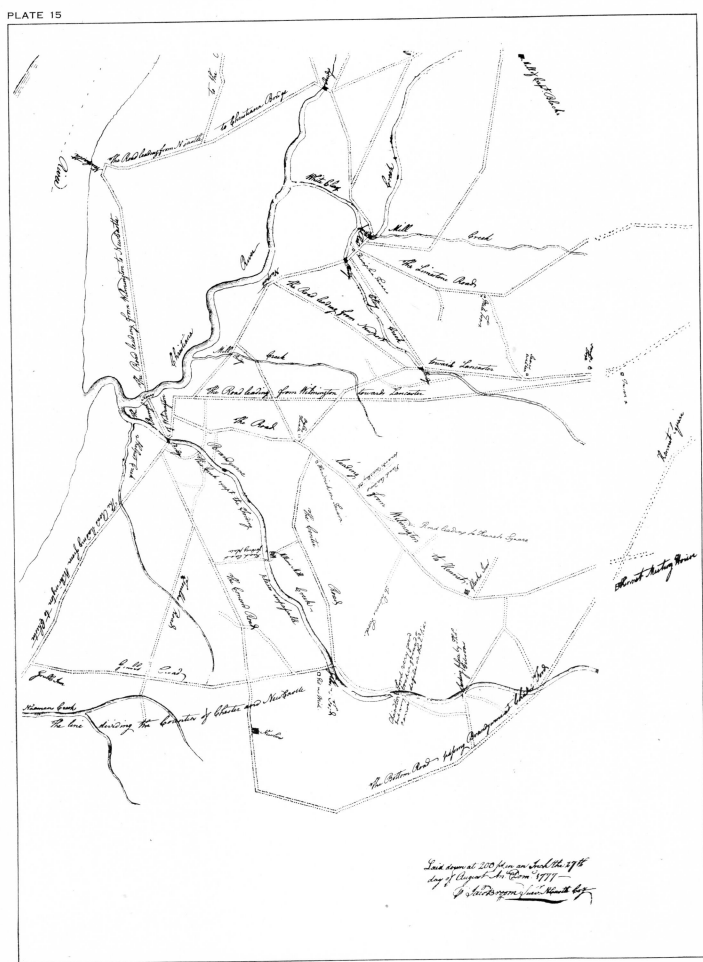

Part of Jacob Broom's map of a portion of the battlefield of the Brandywine, made in 1777
and annotated by George Washington in fourteen places.

PLATE 16

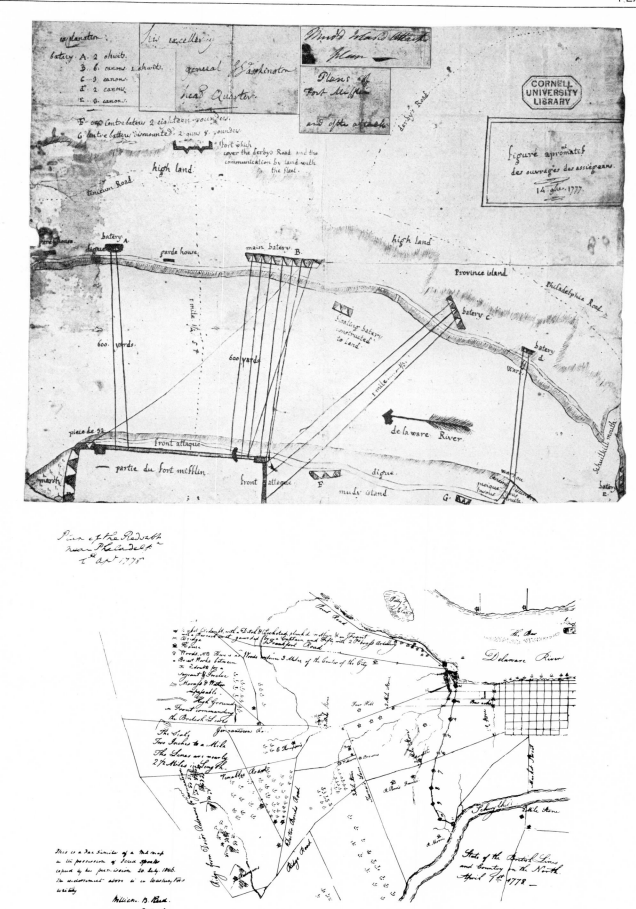

The attack upon Fort Mifflin on the Delaware River, November 14, 1777 (upper); the redoubts near Philadelphia
in 1778 (lower); both maps annotated by George Washington.

PLATE 17

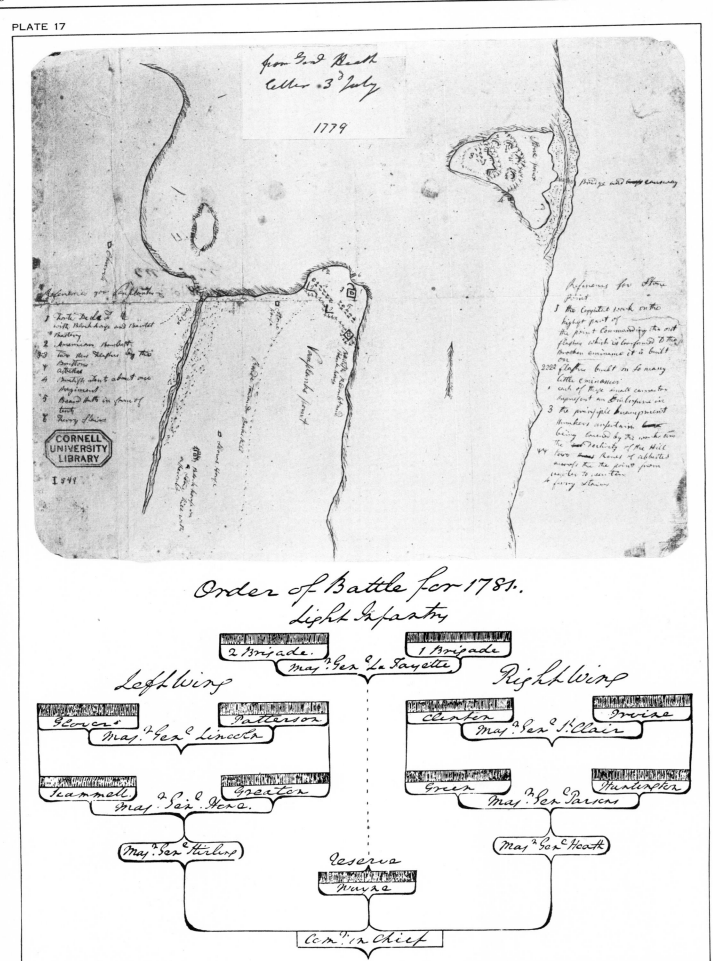

Stony Point and Verplanck's Point, New York, in 1779, annotated by George Washington (upper); Washington's plan of the order of battle for 1781 (lower).

PLATE 18

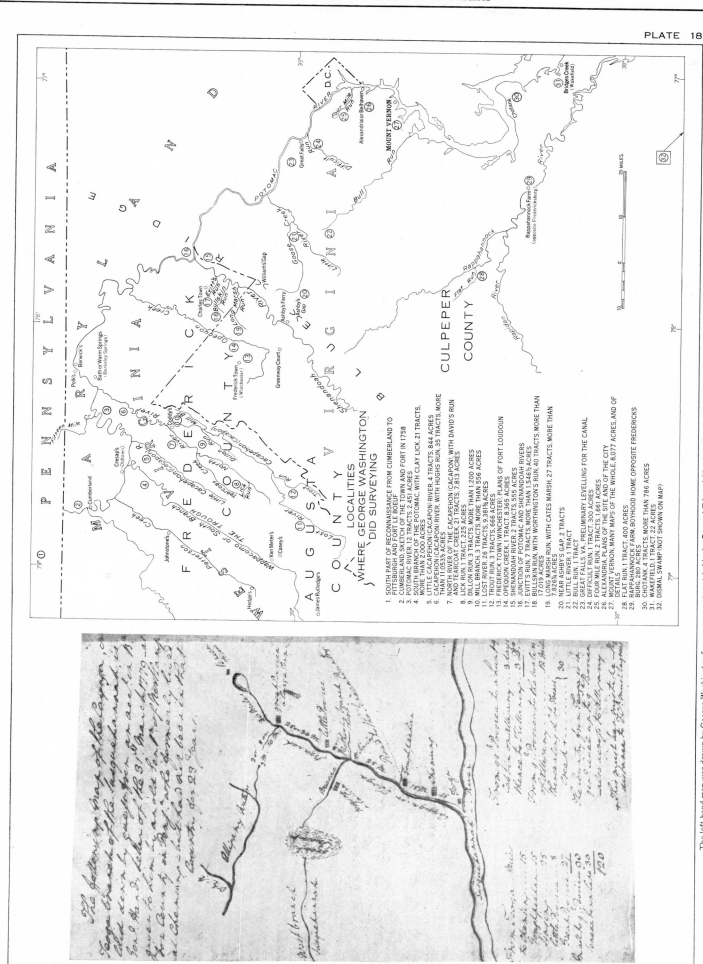

LOCALITIES
WHERE GEORGE WASHINGTON
DID SURVEYING

1. SOUTH PART OF RECONNAISSANCE FROM CUMBERLAND TO PITTSBURGH AND FORT LE BOEUF
2. CUMBERLAND, SKETCH OF THE TOWN AND FORT IN 1758
3. POTOMAC RIVER, 12 TRACTS, 2,451 ACRES
4. SOUTH BRANCH OF THE POTOMAC, WITH CLAY LICK, 21 TRACTS, MORE THAN 2,000 ACRES
5. LITTLE CACAPEHON (CACAPON) RIVER, 4 TRACTS, 844 ACRES
6. CACAPEHON (CACAPON) RIVER, WITH HUGHS RUN, 35 TRACTS, MORE THAN 11,053½ ACRES
7. NORTH RIVER OF THE CACAPEHON (CACAPON), WITH DAVID'S RUN AND TEARCOAT CREEK, 21 TRACTS, 7,813 ACRES
8. LICK RUN, 1 TRACT, 225 ACRES
9. DILLON RUN, 3 TRACTS, MORE THAN 1,200 ACRES
10. MILL BRANCH, 3 TRACTS, MORE THAN 556 ACRES
11. LOST RIVER, 26 TRACTS, 9,381¾ ACRES
12. TROUT RUN, 3 TRACTS, 666 ACRES
13. FREDERICK TOWN (WINCHESTER); PLANS OF FORT LOUDOUN
14. OPEQUON CREEK, 1 TRACT, 8,365 ACRES
15. SHENANDOAH RIVER, 2 TRACTS, 555 ACRES
16. JUNCTION OF POTOMAC AND SHENANDOAH RIVERS
17. EVITT'S RUN, 7 TRACTS, MORE THAN 1,546½ ACRES
18. BULLSKIN RUN, WITH WORTHINGTON'S RUN, 40 TRACTS, MORE THAN 17,019 ACRES
19. LONG MARSH RUN, WITH CATES MARSH, 27 TRACTS, MORE THAN 7,826¼ ACRES
20. NEAR ASHBY'S GAP, 2 TRACTS
21. LITTLE RIVER, 1 TRACT
22. BULL RUN, 1 TRACT
23. GREAT FALLS, VA. PRELIMINARY LEVELLING FOR THE CANAL
24. DIFFICULT RUN, 1 TRACT, 300 ACRES
25. FOUR MILE RUN, 2 TRACTS, 1,661 ACRES
26. ALEXANDRIA, PLANS OF THE SITE AND OF THE CITY
27. MOUNT VERNON, MANY MAPS OF THE WHOLE, 8,077 ACRES, AND OF DETAILS
28. FLAT RUN, 1 TRACT, 400 ACRES
29. RAPPAHANNOCK FARM, BOYHOOD HOME OPPOSITE FREDERICKSBURG, 280 ACRES
30. CHOTANK, 4 TRACTS, MORE THAN 786 ACRES
31. WAKEFIELD, 1 TRACT, 22 ACRES
32. DISMAL SWAMP (NOT SHOWN ON MAP)

The left hand map was drawn by George Washington from an account sent to him by General Edward Hand on March 31, 1779, and shows an area on the Susquehanna River in southern New York and northern Pennsylvania. The right-hand map is a modern one, showing localities where George Washington did surveying.

PLATE 19

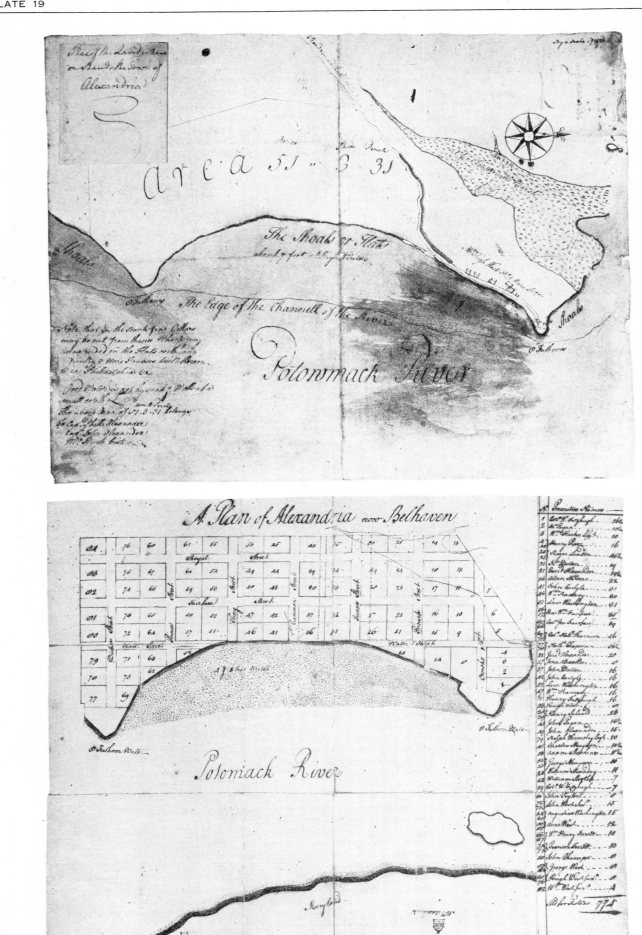

George Washington's survey of the site of Belhaven (Alexandria), Virginia, about 1748 (upper); his plan of the town,
believed to have been drawn a year later (lower).

PLATE 20

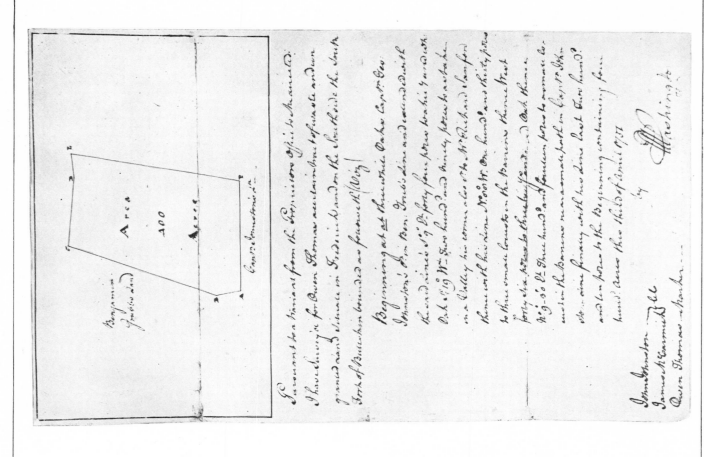

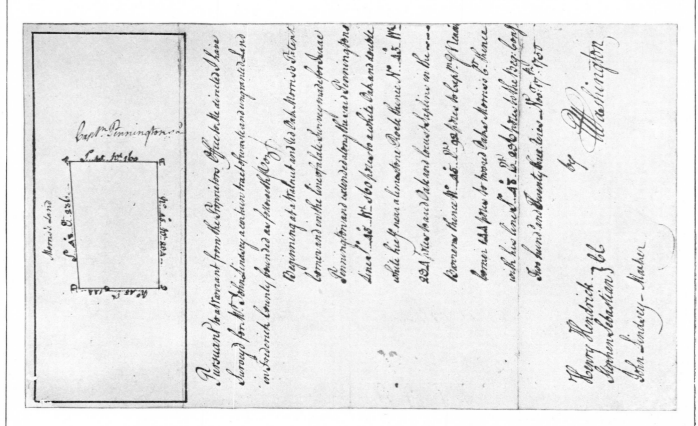

Two simple land surveys made by George Washington on November 17, 1750 (left). and April 3, 1751 (right).

PLATE 21

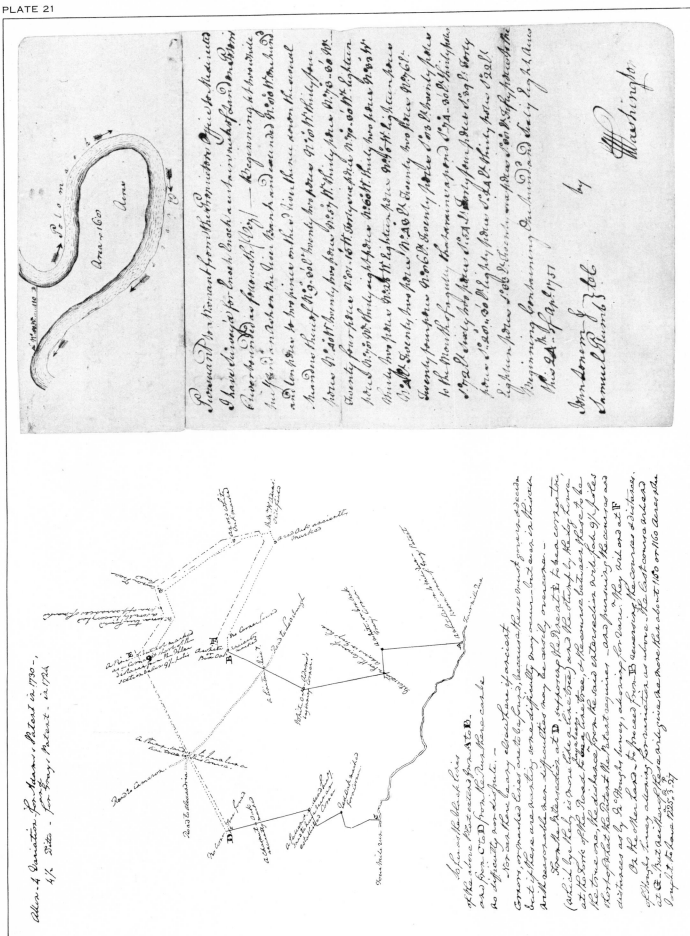

Two complex surveys. George Washington's land on Four Mile Run, Virginia, surveyed in April, 1799 (left); a tract on the Potomac near Pawpaw, West Virginia, surveyed in April, 1751 (right).

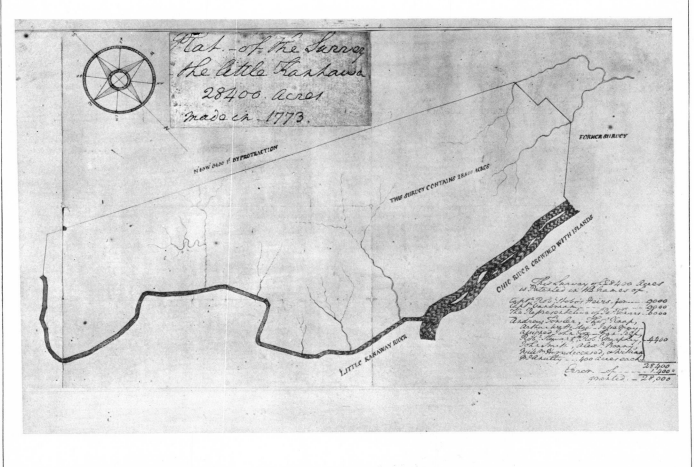

The Potomac River near Harpers Ferry with George Washington's comments on its navigability, 1754 (upper); a tract at the mouth of the Little Kanawha,
West Virginia, 1773 (lower).   Washington made the upper map and annotated the lower one.

PLATE 23

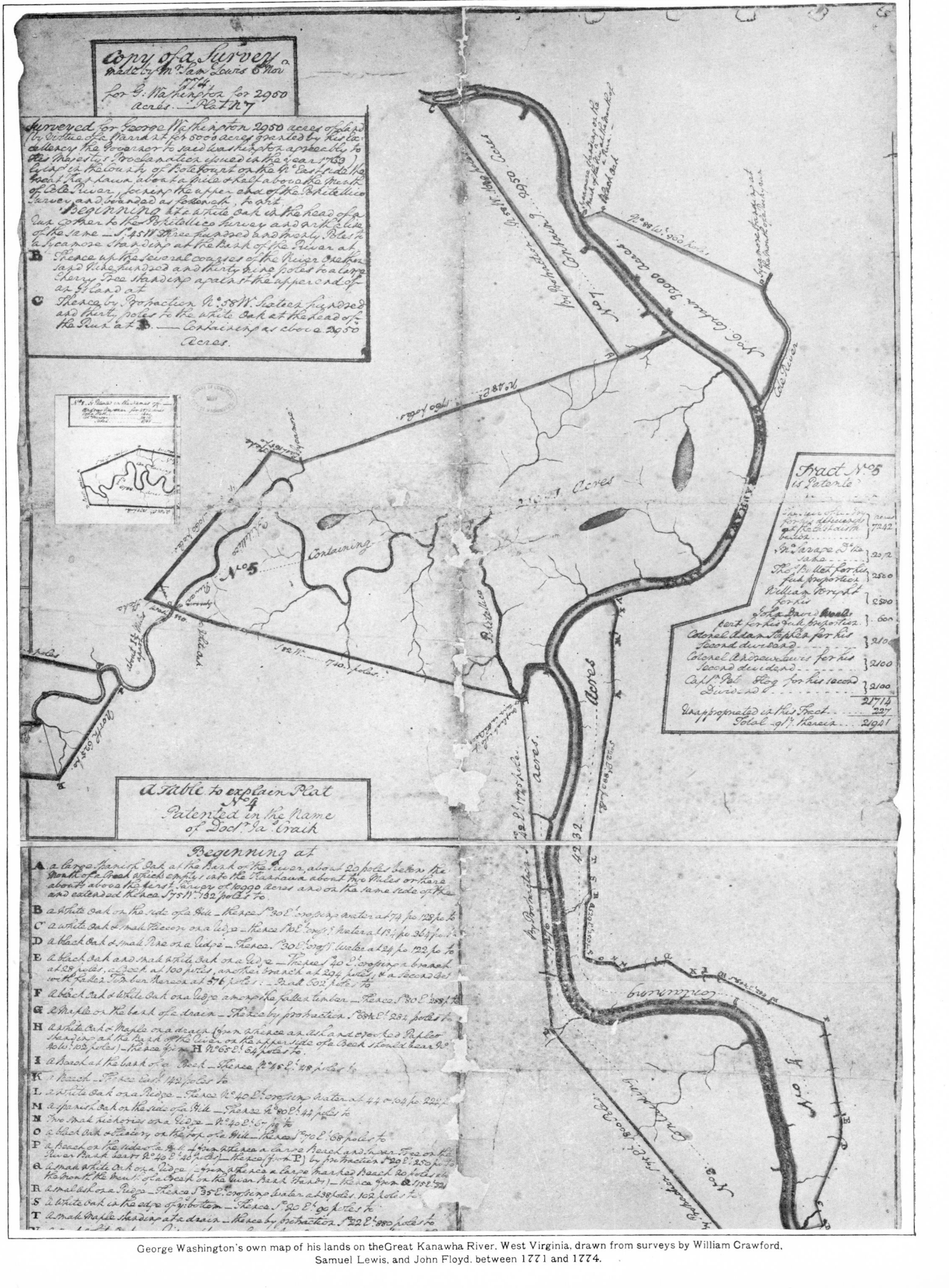

George Washington's own map of his lands on the Great Kanawha River, West Virginia, drawn from surveys by William Crawford,
Samuel Lewis, and John Floyd, between 1771 and 1774.

PLATE 23 (continued)

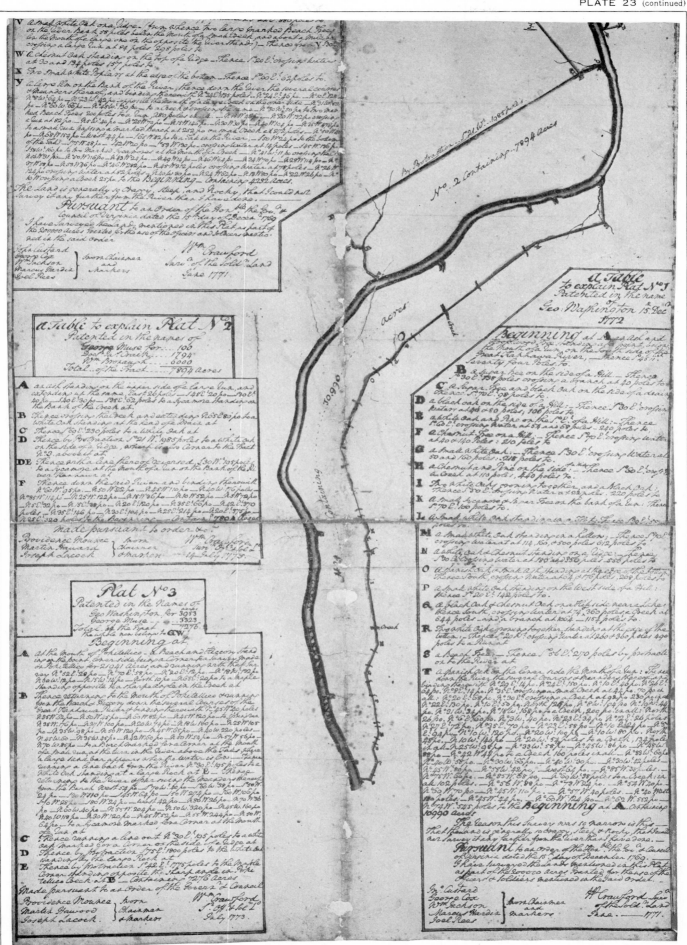

George Washington's own map of his lands on the Great Kanawha River, West Virginia, drawn from surveys by William Crawford, Samuel Lewis, and John Floyd, between 1771 and 1774.

PLATE 24

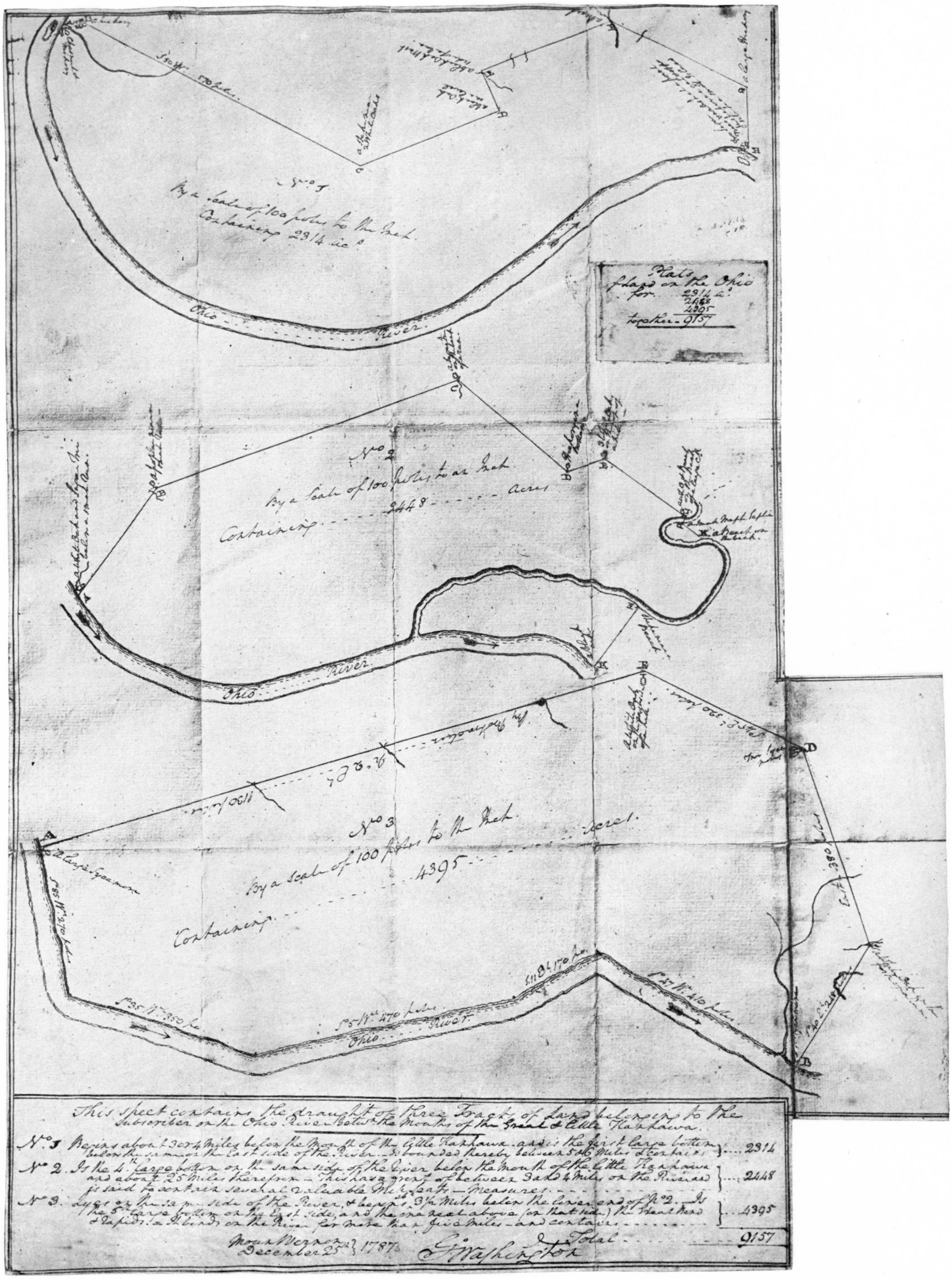

Three tracts of Washington's land on the Ohio River in West Virginia between the mouths of the Great and Little Kanawha Rivers.
Map drawn by George Washington in 1787.

PLATE 25

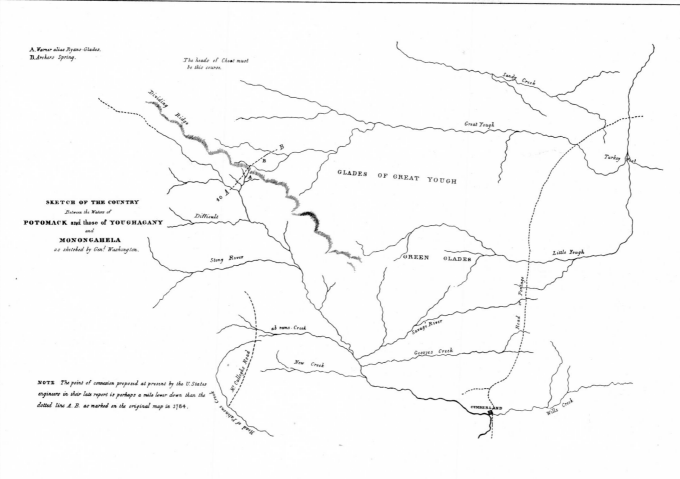

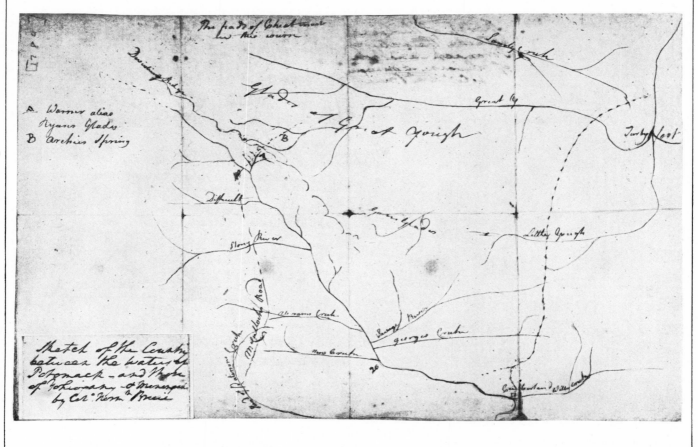

Parts of Maryland, Pennsylvania, and West Virginia, to illustrate plans for water transportation from the Atlantic seaboard to the Mississippi valley
The upper map, attributed to George Washington, is here proved by his own annotation of the lower map
to have been drawn by Normand Bruce in 1784.

PLATE 26

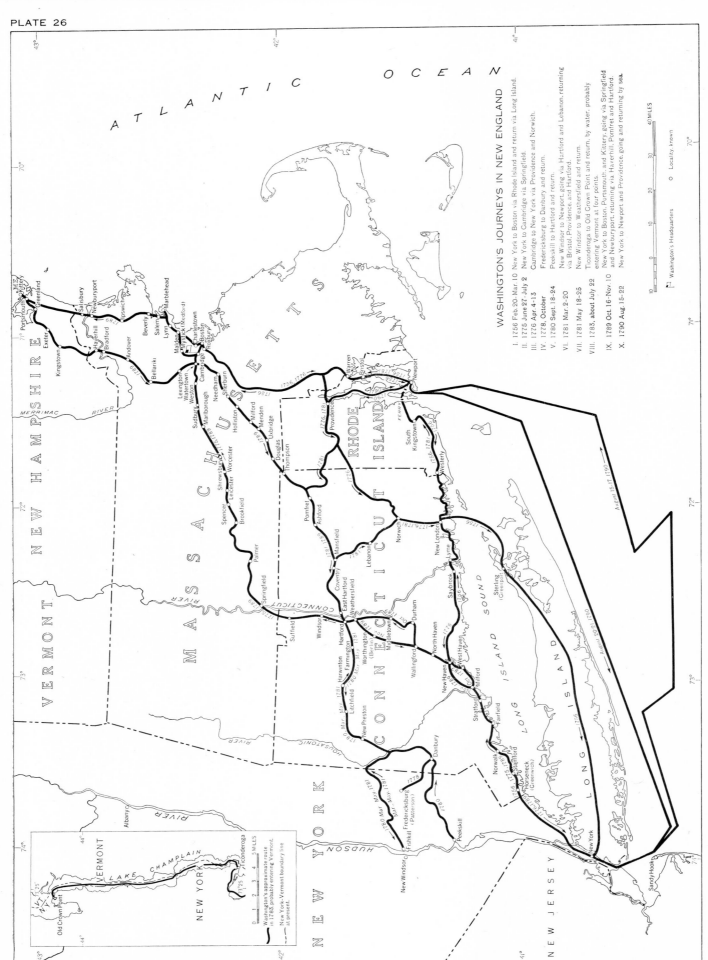

WASHINGTON'S JOURNEYS IN NEW ENGLAND

I. 1756 Feb. 20-Mar. 10   New York to Boston via Rhode Island and return via Long Island.
II. 1775 June 27-July 2   New York to Cambridge via Springfield.
III. 1776 Apr. 4-13   Cambridge to New York via Providence and Norwich.
IV. 1778, October   Fredericksburg to Danbury and return.
V. 1780 Sept. 18-24   Peekskill to Hartford and return.
VI. 1781 Mar. 2-20   New Windsor to Newport, going via Hartford and Lebanon, returning via Bristol, Providence, and Hartford.
VII. 1781 May 18-25   New Windsor to Weathersfield and return.
VIII. 1783, about July 22   Ticonderoga to Old Crown Point and return, by water, probably entering Vermont at four points.
IX. 1789 Oct. 16-Nov. 10   New York to Boston. Portsmouth: and Kittery, going via Springfield and Newburyport, returning via Haverhill, Pomfret and Hartford.
X. 1790 Aug. 15-22   New York to Newport and Providence, going and returning by sea.

New England, showing George Washington's ten journeys.

PLATE 27

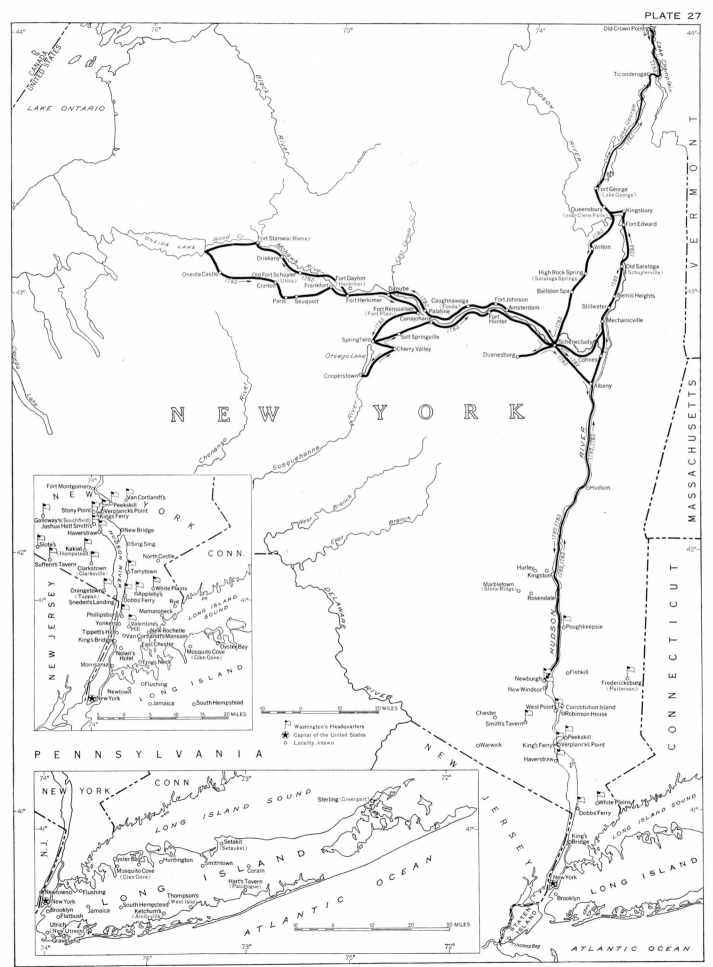

New York State, showing the localities visited by George Washington and the routes of his northern journeys in 1782 and 1783.

PLATE 28

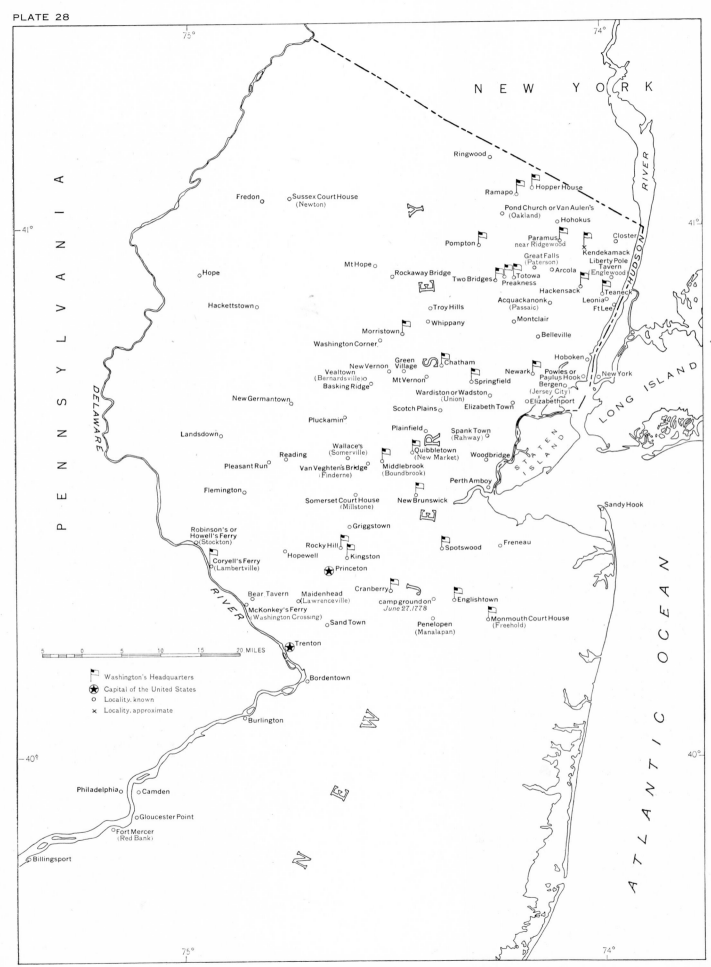

New Jersey, showing the localities visited by George Washington.

PLATE 29

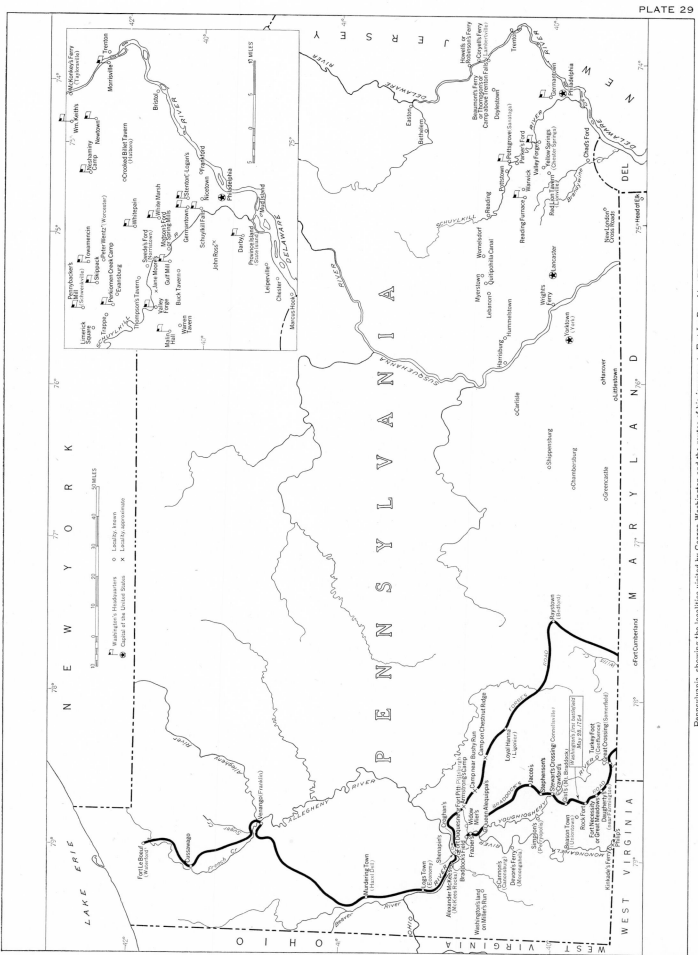

Pennsylvania, showing the localities visited by George Washington and the routes of his journeys to Fort Le Boeuf in 1753-54 with Braddock in 1755, and with Forbes in 1758.

PLATE 30

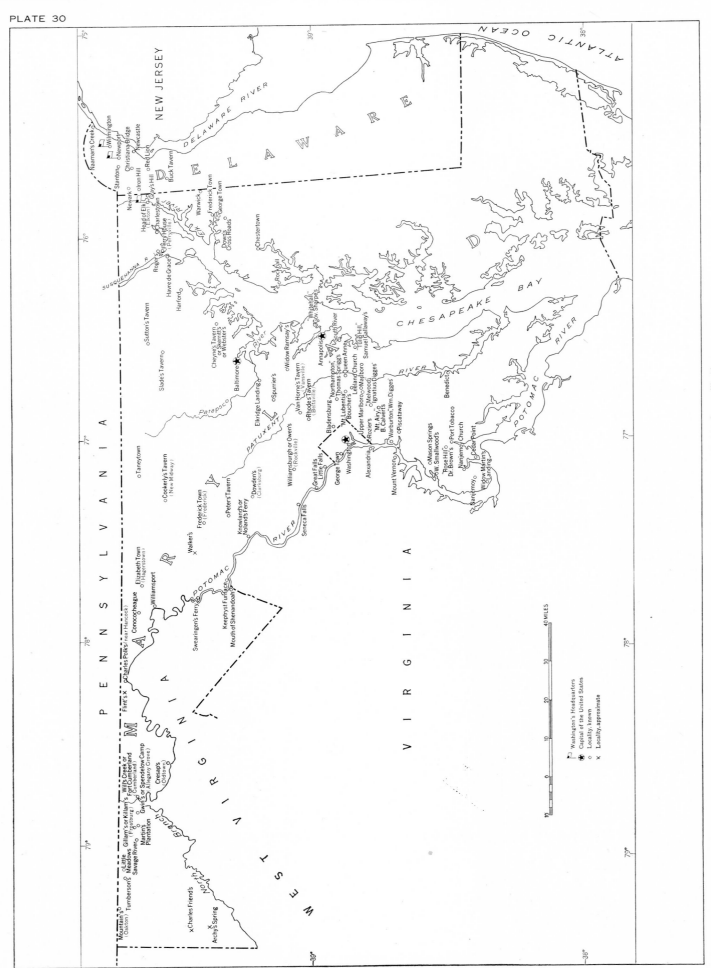

Maryland and Delaware, showing the localities visited by George Washington.

PLATE 31

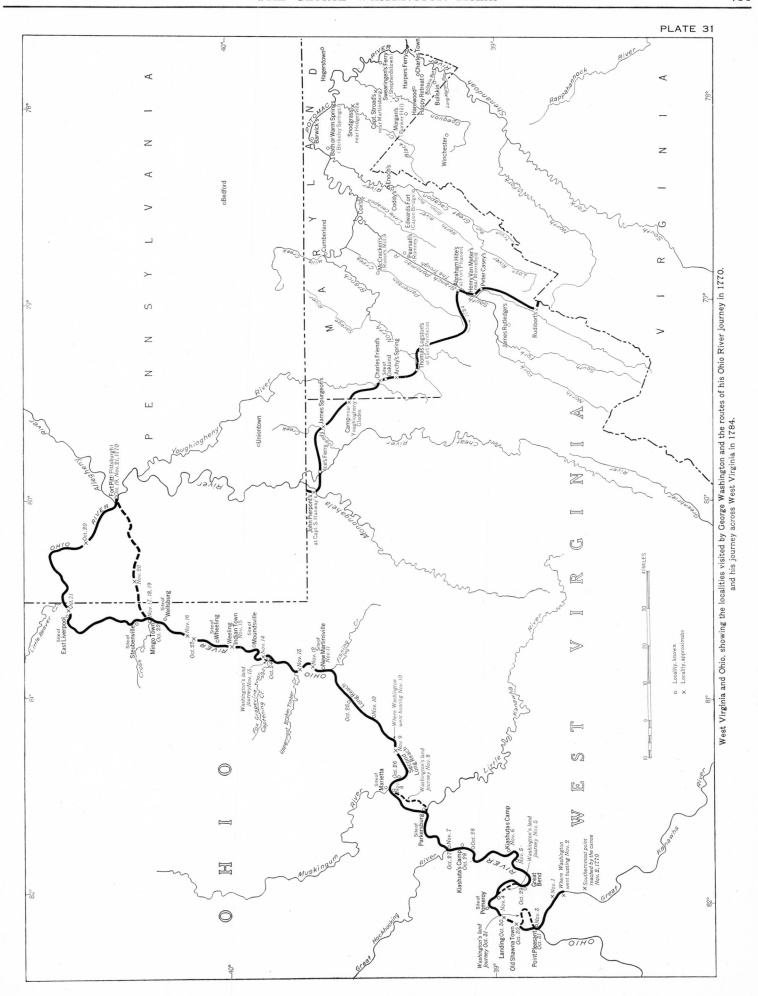

West Virginia and Ohio, showing the localities visited by George Washington and the routes of his Ohio River journey in 1770,
and his journey across West Virginia in 1784.

PLATE 32

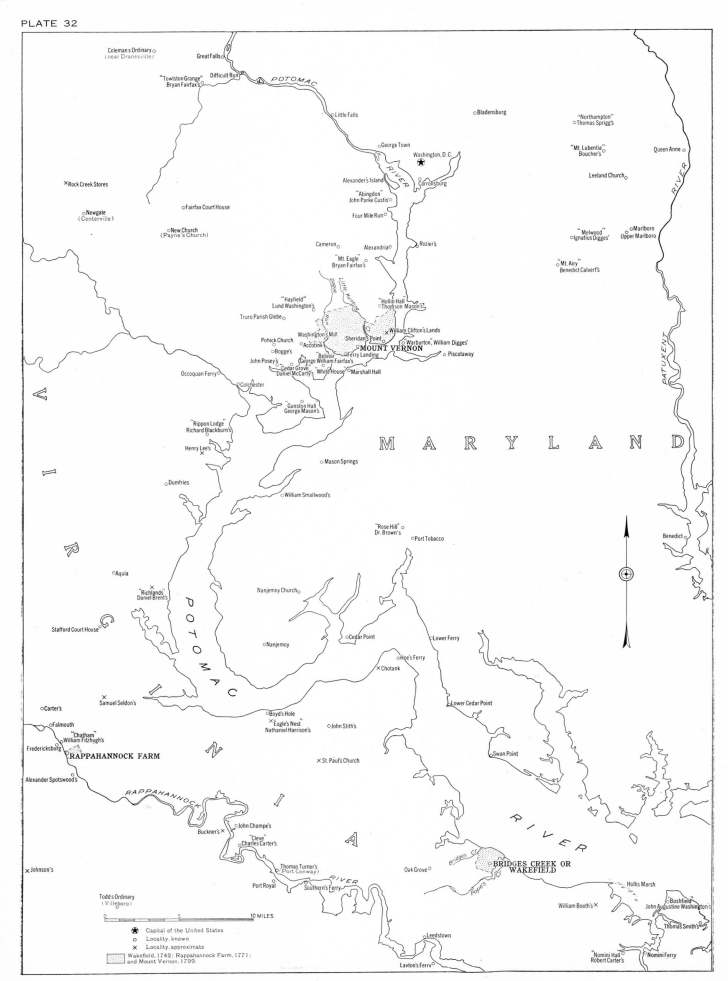

Coleman's Ordinary
(near Dranesville)

Great Falls

"Towlston Grange"
Bryan Fairfax's   Difficult Run   POTOMAC

Little Falls   Bladensburg   "Northampton"
                                                                                   Thomas Sprigg's

                                                                                   "Mt. Lubentia"   Queen Anne
                                          George Town   Boucher's

Rock Creek Stores   Washington, D.C.   Leeland Church

                                          Alexander's Island   Carrollsburg

Newgate   Fairfax Court House   "Abingdon"
(Centerville)   John Parke Custis

New Church   Four Mile Run   "Melwood"   Marlboro
(Payne's Church)   Ignatius Digges' Upper Marlboro

                                    Cameron   Alexandria   "Mt. Airy"
                                                              Rozier's   Benedict Calvert's
                                          "Mt. Eagle"
                                          Bryan Fairfax's

                                    "Hayfield"   "Hollin Hall"
                                    Lund Washington's   Thomson Mason's

                        Truro Parish Glebe   William Clifton's Lands

                        Pohick Church   Washington's Mill   Sheridan's Point   "Warburton", William Digges'
                           Bogge's   Accotink   MOUNT VERNON
                        John Posey's   Belvoir   Piscataway
                                    Cedar Grove George William Fairfax's
                        Occoquan Ferry   Daniel McCarty's White House   Marshall Hall   Ferry Landing
                              Colchester

                                    Gunston Hall
                                    George Mason's

                        "Rippon Lodge"
                        Richard Blackburn's

                        Henry Lee's ×   M A R Y L A N D

                                          Mason Springs
V   Dumfries
  I
    R   William Smallwood's
      G
                                                         "Rose Hill"
        I   Dr. Brown's
          N   Aquia   Port Tobacco   Benedict
            I
              A   "Richlands"   Nanjemoy Church
                         Daniel Brent's
                                                                                        ↑
              Stafford Court House   (compass)
                                          Nanjemoy   Cedar Point
                                                                    Lower Ferry
                                          Hoe's Ferry
            Carter's   Samuel Seldon's ×   × Chotank
          Falmouth   Lower Cedar Point
  "Chatham"   Boyd's Hole
  William Fitzhugh's   × Eagle's Nest
Fredericksburg   Nathaniel Harrison's   John Stith's
                                                                    Swan Point
RAPPAHANNOCK FARM
                        P   × St. Paul's Church
Alexander Spotswood's   O
                        T   R
              RAPPAHANNOCK   O
                             M
× Johnson's   A   Buckner's × John Champe's   Hollis Marsh
                           C   "Cleve"
                                        Charles Carter's   BRIDGES CREEK OR
                                                                            WAKEFIELD   Bushfield
            Todd's Ordinary   Thomas Turner's   John Augustine Washington's
            (Villeboro)   (Port Conway)   Oak Grove   Pope's Cr
                      Port Royal   Southern's Ferry   William Booth's ×   Thomas Smith's
                                                                                        "Nomini Hall"
                                    Leedstown   Robert Carter's   Nomini Ferry
                                    Layton's Ferry

10 MILES

★ Capital of the United States
○ Locality, known
× Locality, approximate
░ Wakefield, 1742; Rappahannock Farm, 1771;
   and Mount Vernon, 1799.

The region of the lower Potomac, showing Mount Vernon and the localities visited by George Washington.

PLATE 33

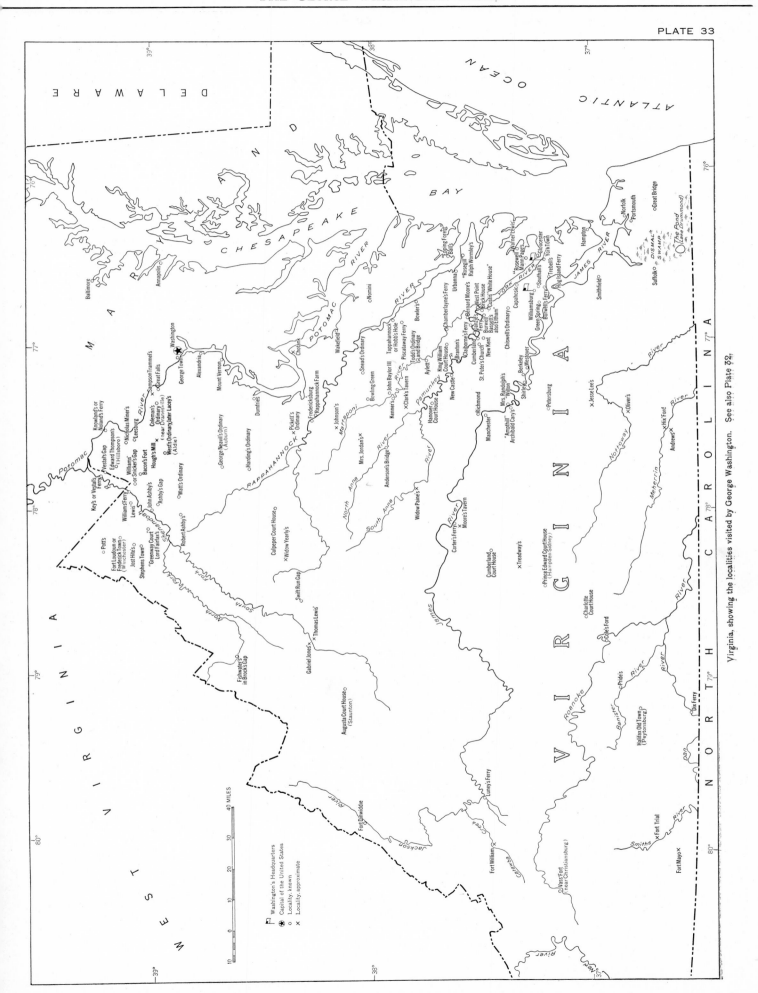

Virginia, showing the localities visited by George Washington.   See also Plate 32.

PLATE 34

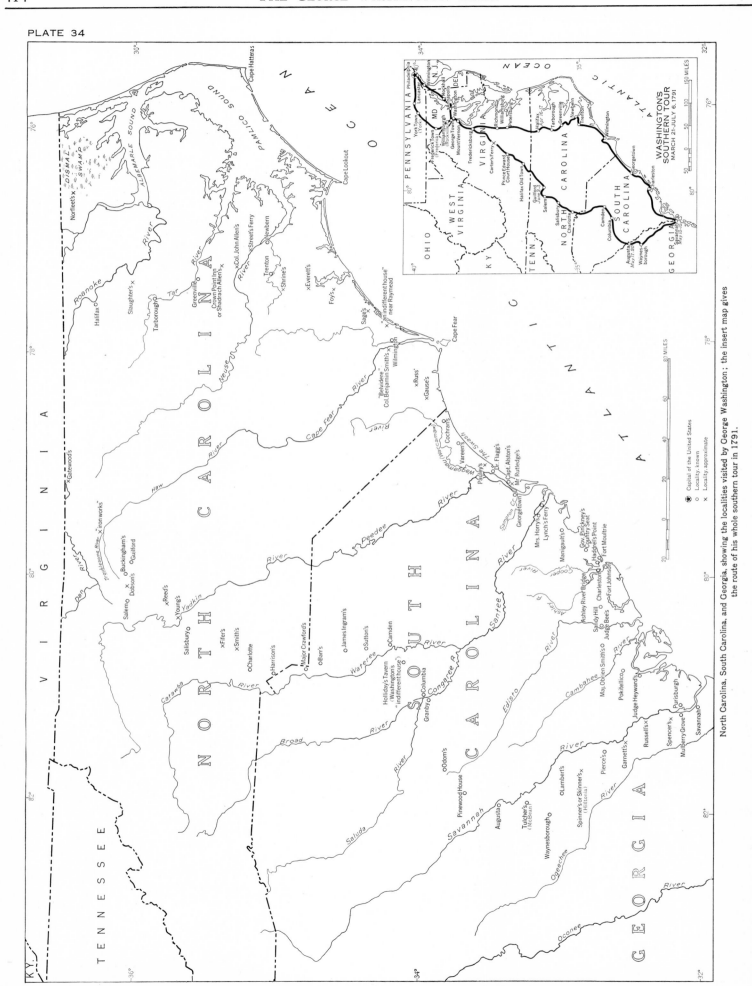

North Carolina, South Carolina, and Georgia, showing the localities visited by George Washington; the insert map gives the route of his whole southern tour in 1791.

PLATE 35

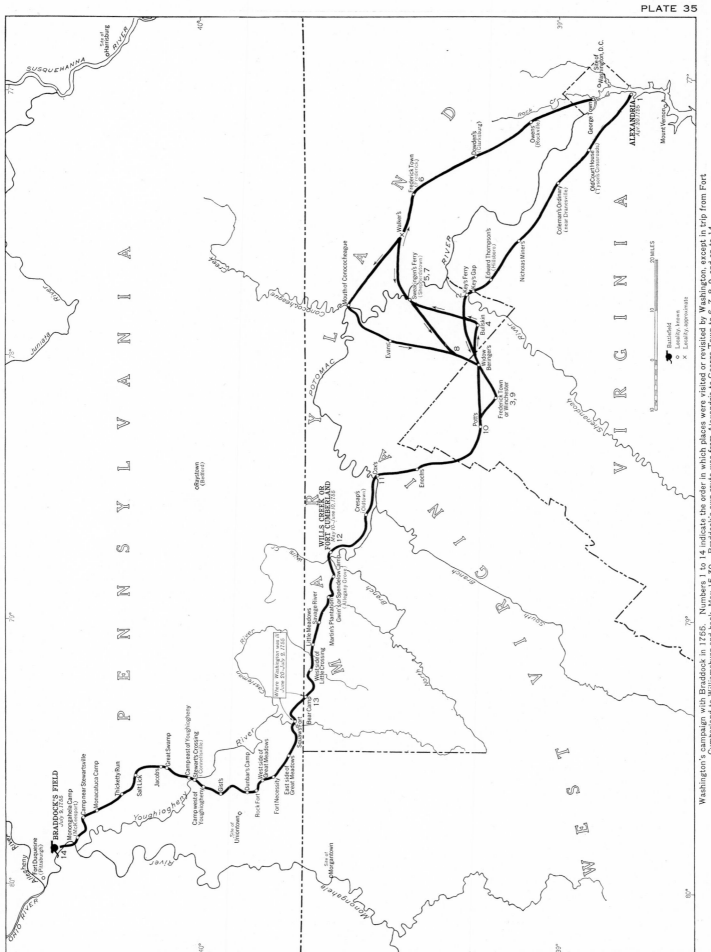

Washington's campaign with Braddock in 1755. Numbers 1 to 14 indicate the order in which places were visited or revisited by Washington, except in trip from Fort Cumberland to Williamsburg and back, May 15–30. Braddock's own route was from Alexandria to George Town to 6, 7, 8, 9, and on to 14.

PLATE 36

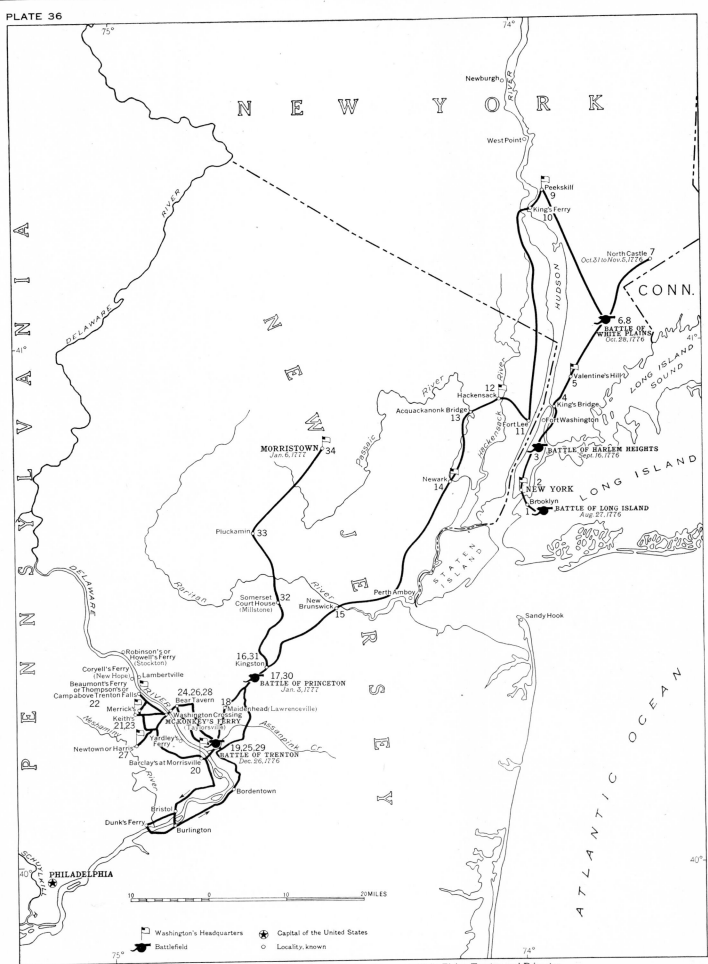

Washington's campaign in 1776 from Brooklyn to Morristown, via White Plains, Trenton, and Princeton.
Numbers indicate the order in which places were visited or revisited.

PLATE 37

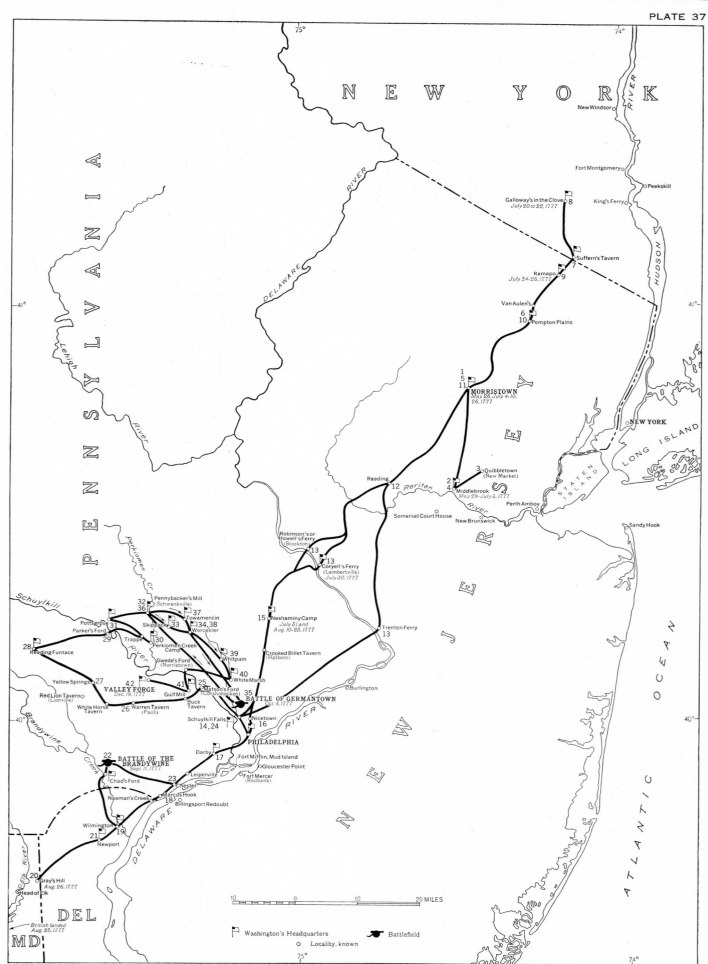

Washington's campaign in 1777 from Morristown to Valley Forge, via Middlebrook, Quibbletown, the highlands of the
Hudson, the Brandywine, and Germantown.   Numbers indicate the order in which places were visited or revisited.

PLATE 38

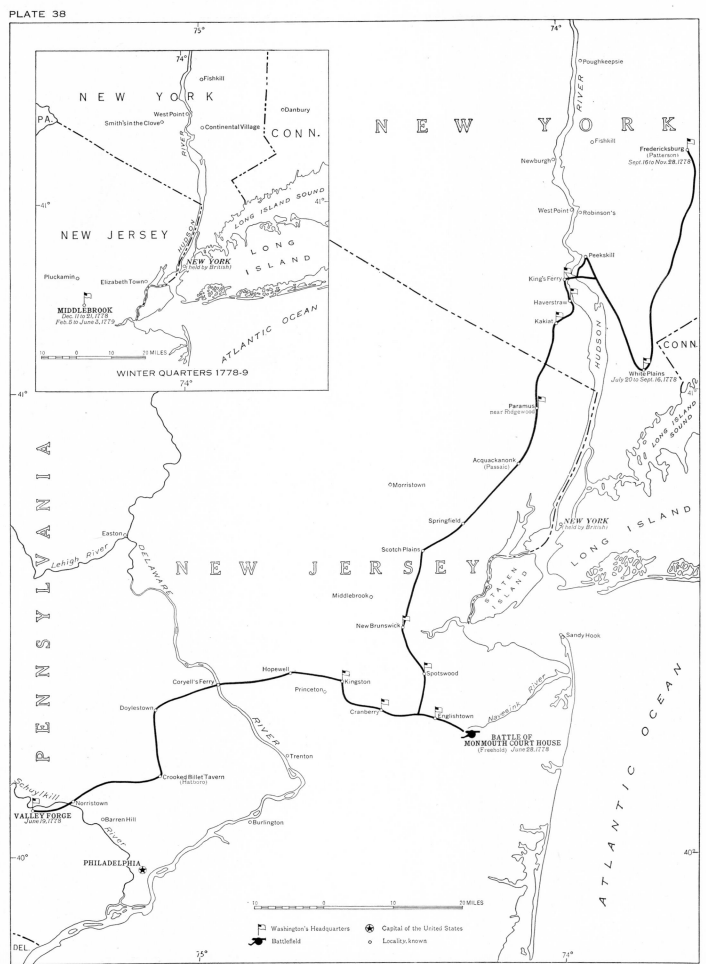

Washington's campaign in 1778 from Valley Forge to the Hudson via Monmouth Court House, with insert map
showing Winter Quarters, 1778-9.

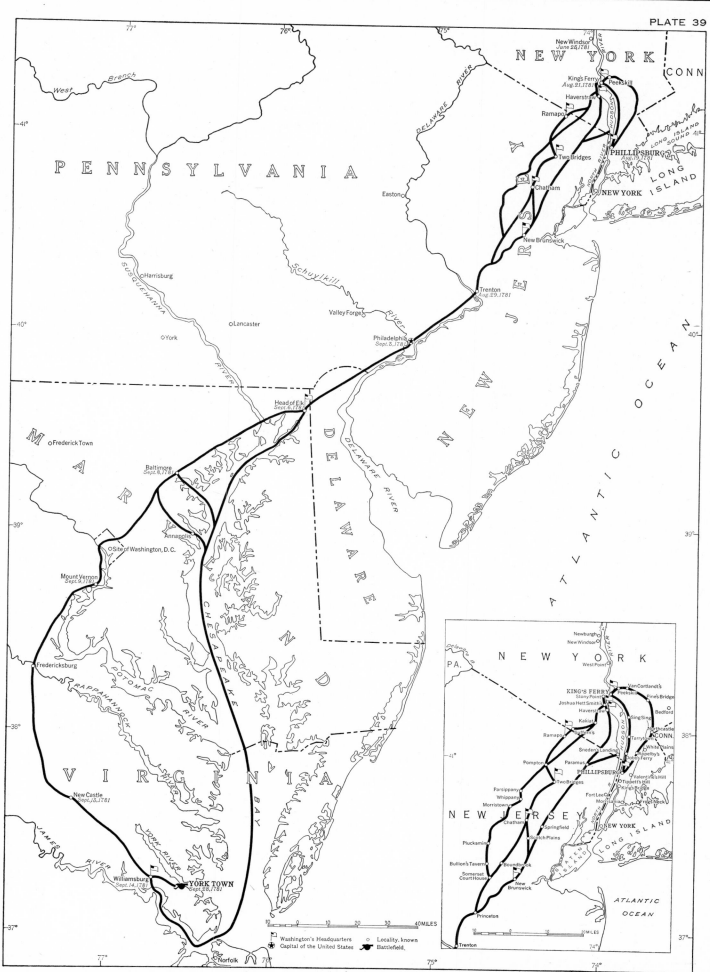

Washington's campaign in 1781 from the Hudson to Yorktown.

PLATE 40

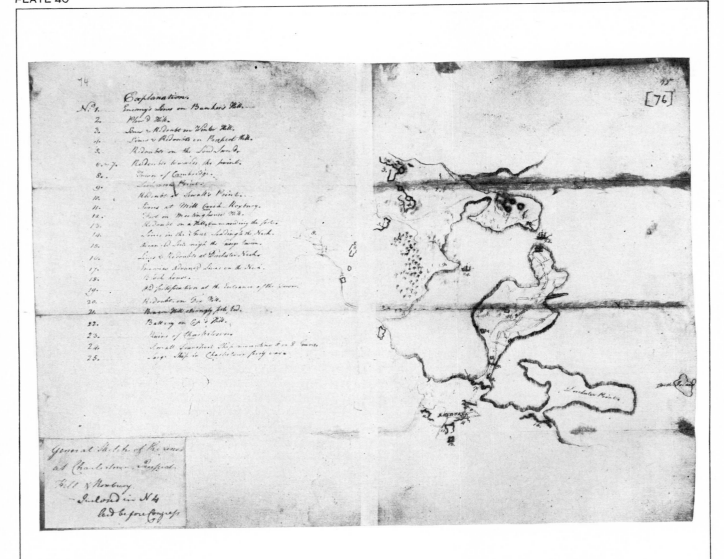

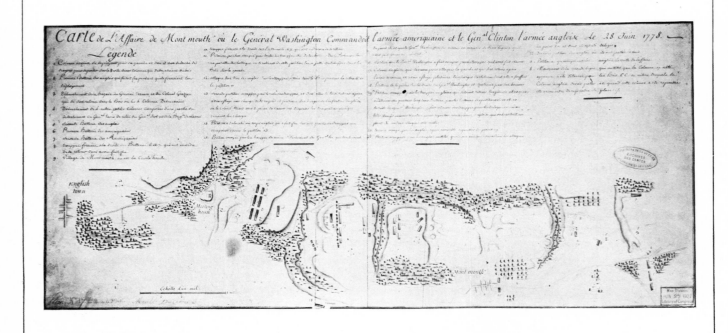

Map of the siege of Boston, made by John Trumbull, the painter, at Washington's direction and sent by him to Congress August 4, 1775 (upper);
a French map of the battle of Monmouth (lower).

PLATE 41

Sebastian Bauman's map of the siege of Yorktown, dedicated to Washington.

PLATE 42

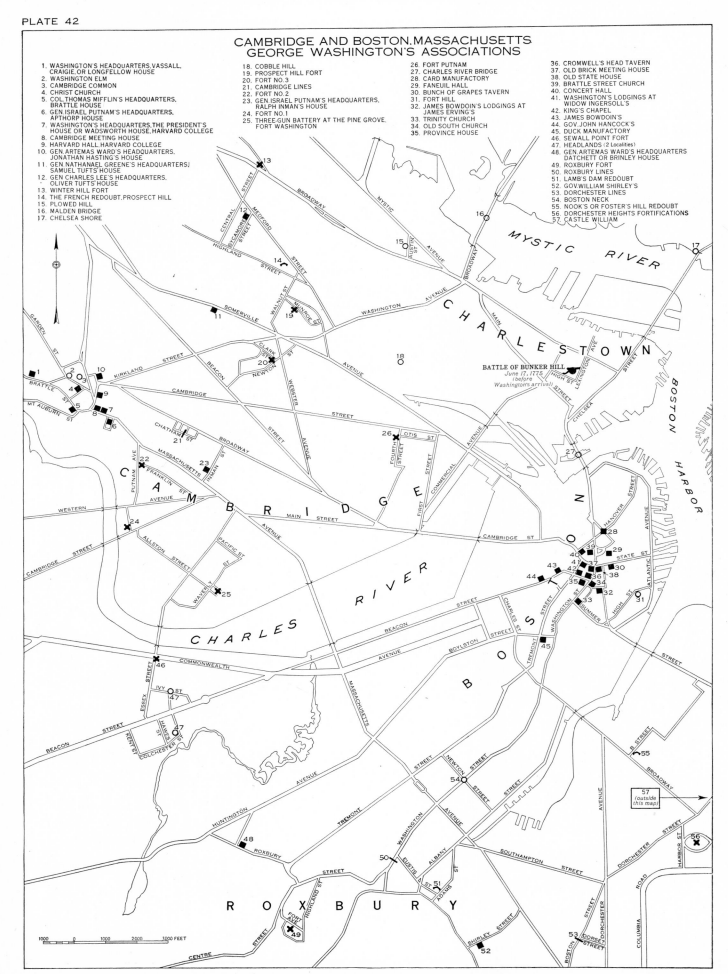

CAMBRIDGE AND BOSTON, MASSACHUSETTS
GEORGE WASHINGTON'S ASSOCIATIONS

1. WASHINGTON'S HEADQUARTERS, VASSALL, CRAIGIE, OR LONGFELLOW HOUSE
2. WASHINGTON ELM
3. CAMBRIDGE COMMON
4. CHRIST CHURCH
5. COL. THOMAS MIFFLIN'S HEADQUARTERS, BRATTLE HOUSE
6. GEN. ISRAEL PUTNAM'S HEADQUARTERS, APTHORP HOUSE
7. WASHINGTON'S HEADQUARTERS, THE PRESIDENT'S HOUSE OR WADSWORTH HOUSE, HARVARD COLLEGE
8. CAMBRIDGE MEETING HOUSE
9. HARVARD HALL, HARVARD COLLEGE
10. GEN. ARTEMAS WARD'S HEADQUARTERS, JONATHAN HASTING'S HOUSE
11. GEN. NATHANAEL GREENE'S HEADQUARTERS, SAMUEL TUFTS' HOUSE
12. GEN. CHARLES LEE'S HEADQUARTERS, OLIVER TUFTS' HOUSE
13. WINTER HILL FORT
14. THE FRENCH REDOUBT, PROSPECT HILL
15. PLOWED HILL
16. MALDEN BRIDGE
17. CHELSEA SHORE

18. COBBLE HILL
19. PROSPECT HILL FORT
20. FORT NO. 3
21. CAMBRIDGE LINES
22. FORT NO. 2
23. GEN. ISRAEL PUTNAM'S HEADQUARTERS, RALPH INMAN'S HOUSE
24. FORT NO. 1
25. THREE-GUN BATTERY AT THE PINE GROVE, FORT WASHINGTON

26. FORT PUTNAM
27. CHARLES RIVER BRIDGE
28. CARD MANUFACTORY
29. FANEUIL HALL
30. BUNCH OF GRAPES TAVERN
31. FORT HILL
32. JAMES BOWDOIN'S LODGINGS AT JAMES ERVING'S
33. TRINITY CHURCH
34. OLD SOUTH CHURCH
35. PROVINCE HOUSE

36. CROMWELL'S HEAD TAVERN
37. OLD BRICK MEETING HOUSE
38. OLD STATE HOUSE
39. BRATTLE STREET CHURCH
40. CONCERT HALL
41. WASHINGTON'S LODGINGS AT WIDOW INGERSOLL'S
42. KING'S CHAPEL
43. JAMES BOWDOIN'S
44. GOV. JOHN HANCOCK'S
45. DUCK MANUFACTORY
46. SEWALL POINT FORT
47. HEADLANDS (2 Localities)
48. GEN. ARTEMAS WARD'S HEADQUARTERS, DATCHETT OR BRINLEY HOUSE
49. ROXBURY FORT
50. ROXBURY LINES
51. LAMB'S DAM REDOUBT
52. GOV. WILLIAM SHIRLEY'S
53. DORCHESTER LINES
54. BOSTON NECK
55. NOOK'S OR FOSTER'S HILL REDOUBT
56. DORCHESTER HEIGHTS FORTIFICATIONS
57. CASTLE WILLIAM

BATTLE OF BUNKER HILL
June 17, 1775
(before Washington's arrival)

Cambridge and Boston, Massachusetts, showing localities associated with George Washington.

PLATE 43

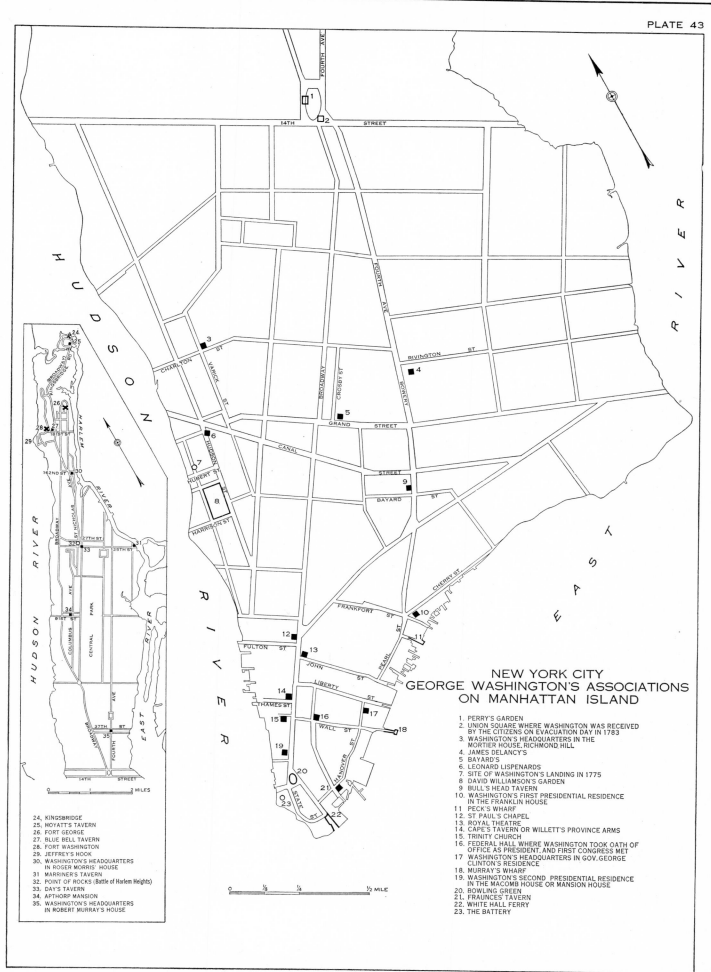

NEW YORK CITY
GEORGE WASHINGTON'S ASSOCIATIONS
ON MANHATTAN ISLAND

1. PERRY'S GARDEN
2. UNION SQUARE WHERE WASHINGTON WAS RECEIVED
   BY THE CITIZENS ON EVACUATION DAY IN 1783
3. WASHINGTON'S HEADQUARTERS IN THE
   MORTIER HOUSE, RICHMOND HILL
4. JAMES DELANCY'S
5. BAYARD'S
6. LEONARD LISPENARDS
7. SITE OF WASHINGTON'S LANDING IN 1775
8. DAVID WILLIAMSON'S GARDEN
9. BULL'S HEAD TAVERN
10. WASHINGTON'S FIRST PRESIDENTIAL RESIDENCE
    IN THE FRANKLIN HOUSE
11. PECK'S WHARF
12. ST PAUL'S CHAPEL
13. ROYAL THEATRE
14. CAPE'S TAVERN OR WILLETT'S PROVINCE ARMS
15. TRINITY CHURCH
16. FEDERAL HALL WHERE WASHINGTON TOOK OATH OF
    OFFICE AS PRESIDENT, AND FIRST CONGRESS MET
17. WASHINGTON'S HEADQUARTERS IN GOV.GEORGE
    CLINTON'S RESIDENCE
18. MURRAY'S WHARF
19. WASHINGTON'S SECOND PRESIDENTIAL RESIDENCE
    IN THE MACOMB HOUSE OR MANSION HOUSE
20. BOWLING GREEN
21. FRAUNCES' TAVERN
22. WHITE HALL FERRY
23. THE BATTERY

24. KINGSBRIDGE
25. HOYATT'S TAVERN
26. FORT GEORGE
27. BLUE BELL TAVERN
28. FORT WASHINGTON
29. JEFFREY'S HOOK
30. WASHINGTON'S HEADQUARTERS
    IN ROGER MORRIS' HOUSE
31. MARRINER'S TAVERN
32. POINT OF ROCKS (Battle of Harlem Heights)
33. DAY'S TAVERN
34. APTHORP MANSION
35. WASHINGTON'S HEADQUARTERS
    IN ROBERT MURRAY'S HOUSE

New York City, showing localities associated with George Washington.

PLATE 44

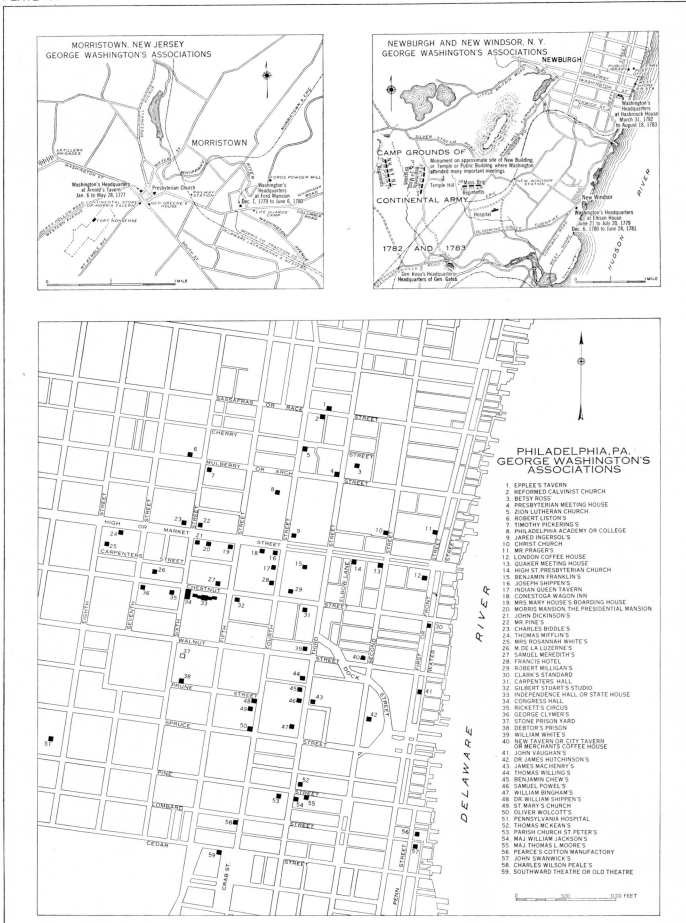

MORRISTOWN, NEW JERSEY
GEORGE WASHINGTON'S ASSOCIATIONS

MORRISTOWN

Washington's Headquarters
at Arnold's Tavern
Jan. 6 to May 28, 1777

Presbyterian Church

Washington's
Headquarters
at Ford Mansion
Dec. 1, 1779 to June 6, 1780

ARTILLERY
BRIGADES

CONTINENTAL STORE
OR MORRIS TAVERN

Gen Greene's
House

FORT NONSENSE

"LIFE GUARDS'
CAMP"

FORDS POWDER MILL

0   1 MILE

NEWBURGH AND NEW WINDSOR, N. Y.
GEORGE WASHINGTON'S ASSOCIATIONS

NEWBURGH

Washington's Headquarters
at Hasbrouck House
March 31, 1782
to August 18, 1783

CAMP GROUNDS OF

Monument on approximate site of New Building,
or Temple or Public Building where Washington
attended many important meetings.

Temple Hill

2nd Mass. Brig.

CONTINENTAL ARMY

NEW WINDSOR
STATION

New Windsor

Washington's Headquarters
at Ellison House
June 21 to July 20, 1779
Dec. 6, 1780 to June 24, 1781

1782   AND   1783

Hospital

HUDSON RIVER

Gen. Knox's Headquarters
Headquarters of Gen. Gates

0   1 MILE

PHILADELPHIA, PA.
GEORGE WASHINGTON'S
ASSOCIATIONS

1. EPPLEE'S TAVERN
2. REFORMED CALVINIST CHURCH
3. BETSY ROSS'
4. PRESBYTERIAN MEETING HOUSE
5. ZION LUTHERAN CHURCH
6. ROBERT LISTON'S
7. TIMOTHY PICKERING'S
8. PHILADELPHIA ACADEMY OR COLLEGE
9. JARED INGERSOL'S
10. CHRIST CHURCH
11. MR. PRAGER'S
12. LONDON COFFEE HOUSE
13. QUAKER MEETING HOUSE
14. HIGH ST. PRESBYTERIAN CHURCH
15. BENJAMIN FRANKLIN'S
16. JOSEPH SHIPPEN'S
17. INDIAN QUEEN TAVERN
18. CONESTOGA WAGON INN
19. MRS. MARY HOUSE'S BOARDING HOUSE
20. MORRIS MANSION, THE PRESIDENTIAL MANSION
21. JOHN DICKINSON'S
22. MR. PINE'S
23. CHARLES BIDDLE'S
24. THOMAS MIFFLIN'S
25. MRS ROSANNAH WHITE'S
26. M. DE LA LUZERNE'S
27. SAMUEL MEREDITH'S
28. FRANCIS HOTEL
29. ROBERT MILLIGAN'S
30. CLARK'S STANDARD
31. CARPENTERS' HALL
32. GILBERT STUART'S STUDIO
33. INDEPENDENCE HALL OR STATE HOUSE
34. CONGRESS HALL
35. RICKETT'S CIRCUS
36. GEORGE CLYMER'S
37. STONE PRISON YARD
38. DEBTOR'S PRISON
39. WILLIAM WHITE'S
40. NEW TAVERN OR CITY TAVERN
    OR MERCHANTS COFFEE HOUSE
41. JOHN VAUGHAN'S
42. DR. JAMES HUTCHINSON'S
43. JAMES MACHENRY'S
44. THOMAS WILLING'S
45. BENJAMIN CHEW'S
46. SAMUEL POWEL'S
47. WILLIAM BINGHAM'S
48. DR. WILLIAM SHIPPEN'S
49. ST. MARY'S CHURCH
50. OLIVER WOLCOTT'S
51. PENNSYLVANIA HOSPITAL
52. THOMAS MCKEAN'S
53. PARISH CHURCH, ST. PETER'S
54. MAJ. WILLIAM JACKSON'S
55. MAJ. THOMAS L. MOORE'S
56. PEARCE'S COTTON MANUFACTORY
57. JOHN SWANWICK'S
58. CHARLES WILSON PEALE'S
59. SOUTHWARD THEATRE OR OLD THEATRE

DELAWARE RIVER

0   500   1000 FEET

Newburgh and New Windsor, New York (upper right), Morristown, New Jersey (upper left), Philadelphia (lower),
showing localities associated with George Washington.

PLATE 45

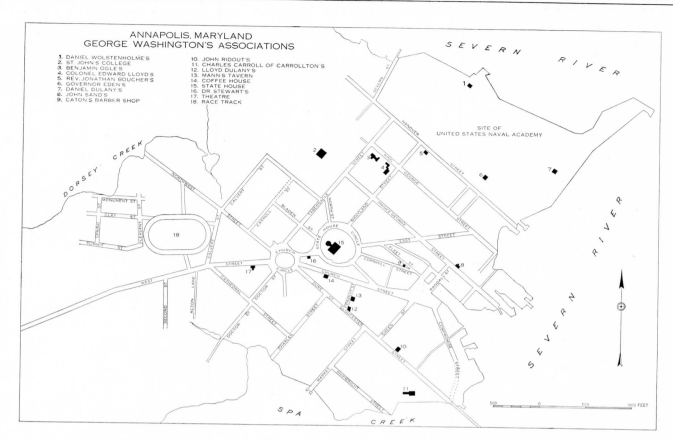

ANNAPOLIS, MARYLAND
GEORGE WASHINGTON'S ASSOCIATIONS

1. DANIEL WOLSTENHOLME'S
2. ST. JOHN'S COLLEGE
3. BENJAMIN OGLE'S
4. COLONEL EDWARD LLOYD'S
5. REV. JONATHAN BOUCHER'S
6. GOVERNOR EDEN'S
7. DANIEL DULANY'S
8. JOHN SAND'S
9. CATON'S BARBER SHOP
10. JOHN RIDOUT'S
11. CHARLES CARROLL OF CARROLLTON'S
12. LLOYD DULANY'S
13. MANN'S TAVERN
14. COFFEE HOUSE
15. STATE HOUSE
16. DR. STEWART'S
17. THEATRE
18. RACE TRACK

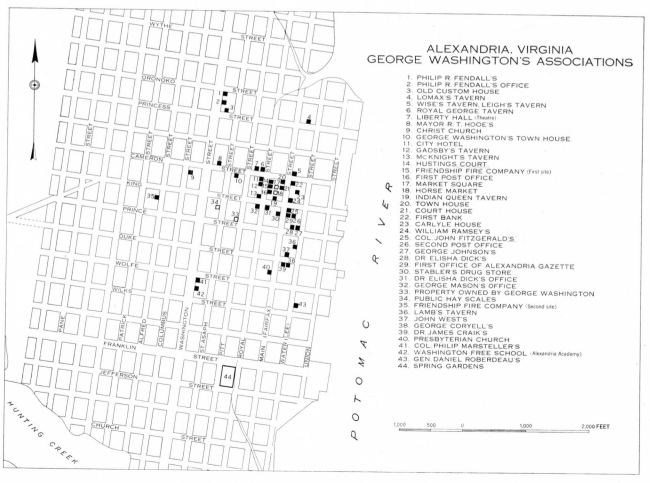

ALEXANDRIA, VIRGINIA
GEORGE WASHINGTON'S ASSOCIATIONS

1. PHILIP R. FENDALL'S
2. PHILIP R. FENDALL'S OFFICE
3. OLD CUSTOM HOUSE
4. LOMAX'S TAVERN
5. WISE'S TAVERN, LEIGH'S TAVERN
6. ROYAL GEORGE TAVERN
7. LIBERTY HALL (Theatre)
8. MAYOR R. T. HOOE'S
9. CHRIST CHURCH
10. GEORGE WASHINGTON'S TOWN HOUSE
11. CITY HOTEL
12. GADSBY'S TAVERN
13. McKNIGHT'S TAVERN
14. HUSTINGS COURT
15. FRIENDSHIP FIRE COMPANY (First site)
16. FIRST POST OFFICE
17. MARKET SQUARE
18. HORSE MARKET
19. INDIAN QUEEN TAVERN
20. TOWN HOUSE
21. COURT HOUSE
22. FIRST BANK
23. CARLYLE HOUSE
24. WILLIAM RAMSEY'S
25. COL. JOHN FITZGERALD'S
26. SECOND POST OFFICE
27. GEORGE JOHNSON'S
28. DR. ELISHA DICK'S
29. FIRST OFFICE OF ALEXANDRIA GAZETTE
30. STABLER'S DRUG STORE
31. DR. ELISHA DICK'S OFFICE
32. GEORGE MASON'S OFFICE
33. PROPERTY OWNED BY GEORGE WASHINGTON
34. PUBLIC HAY SCALES
35. FRIENDSHIP FIRE COMPANY (Second site)
36. LAMB'S TAVERN
37. JOHN WEST'S
38. GEORGE CORYELL'S
39. DR. JAMES CRAIK'S
40. PRESBYTERIAN CHURCH
41. COL. PHILIP MARSTELLER'S
42. WASHINGTON FREE SCHOOL (Alexandria Academy)
43. GEN. DANIEL ROBERDEAU'S
44. SPRING GARDENS

Annapolis, Maryland (upper), and Alexandria, Virginia, (lower), showing localities associated with George Washington.

PLATE 46

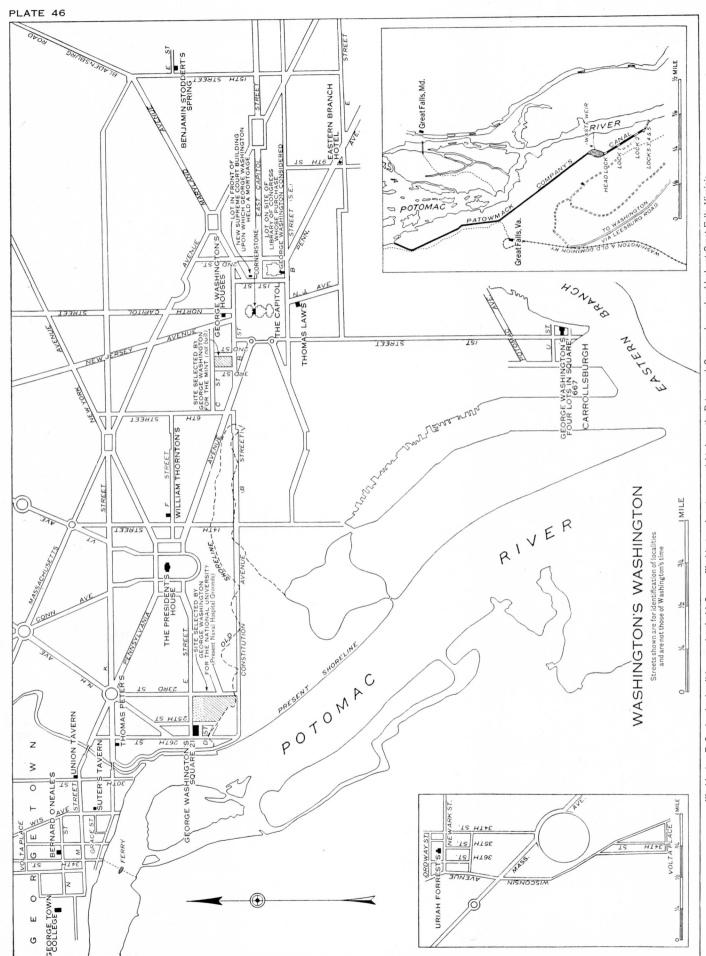

WASHINGTON'S WASHINGTON

Streets shown are for identification of localities
and are not those of Washington's time

Washington, D. C., showing localities associated with George Washington; insert map on right shows the Patowmack Company's canal and locks at Great Falls, Virginia.
parts of which were constructed during the period when Washington was president of the company.

PLATE 47

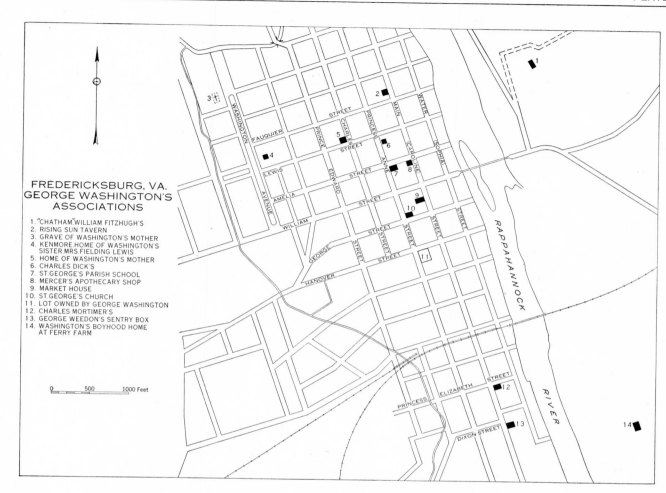

FREDERICKSBURG, VA.
GEORGE WASHINGTON'S
ASSOCIATIONS

1. "CHATHAM," WILLIAM FITZHUGH'S
2. RISING SUN TAVERN
3. GRAVE OF WASHINGTON'S MOTHER
4. KENMORE, HOME OF WASHINGTON'S
   SISTER, MRS. FIELDING LEWIS
5. HOME OF WASHINGTON'S MOTHER
6. CHARLES DICK'S
7. ST. GEORGE'S PARISH SCHOOL
8. MERCER'S APOTHECARY SHOP
9. MARKET HOUSE
10. ST. GEORGE'S CHURCH
11. LOT OWNED BY GEORGE WASHINGTON
12. CHARLES MORTIMER'S
13. GEORGE WEEDON'S SENTRY BOX
14. WASHINGTON'S BOYHOOD HOME
    AT FERRY FARM

0   500   1000 Feet

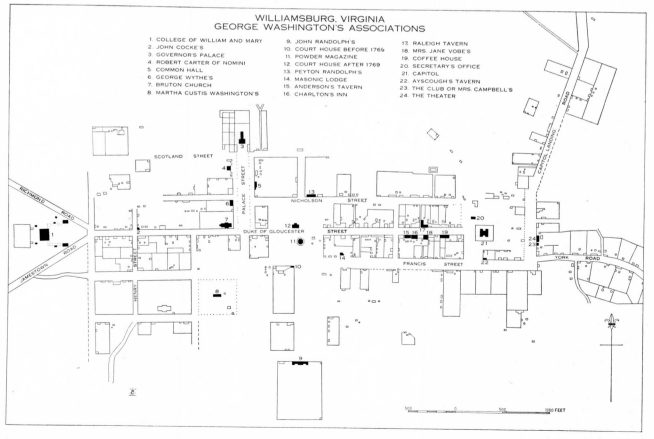

WILLIAMSBURG, VIRGINIA
GEORGE WASHINGTON'S ASSOCIATIONS

1. COLLEGE OF WILLIAM AND MARY	9. JOHN RANDOLPH'S	17. RALEIGH TAVERN
2. JOHN COCKE'S	10. COURT HOUSE BEFORE 1769	18. MRS. JANE VOBE'S
3. GOVERNOR'S PALACE	11. POWDER MAGAZINE	19. COFFEE HOUSE
4. ROBERT CARTER OF NOMINI	12. COURT HOUSE AFTER 1769	20. SECRETARY'S OFFICE
5. COMMON HALL	13. PEYTON RANDOLPH'S	21. CAPITOL
6. GEORGE WYTHE'S	14. MASONIC LODGE	22. AYSCOUGH'S TAVERN
7. BRUTON CHURCH	15. ANDERSON'S TAVERN	23. THE CLUB OR MRS. CAMPBELL'S
8. MARTHA CUSTIS WASHINGTON'S	16. CHARLTON'S INN	24. THE THEATER

500   0   500   1000 FEET

Fredericksburg, Virginia (upper), and Williamsburg, Virginia (lower), showing localities associated with George Washington.

PLATE 48

GEORGE WASHINGTON'S LANDS

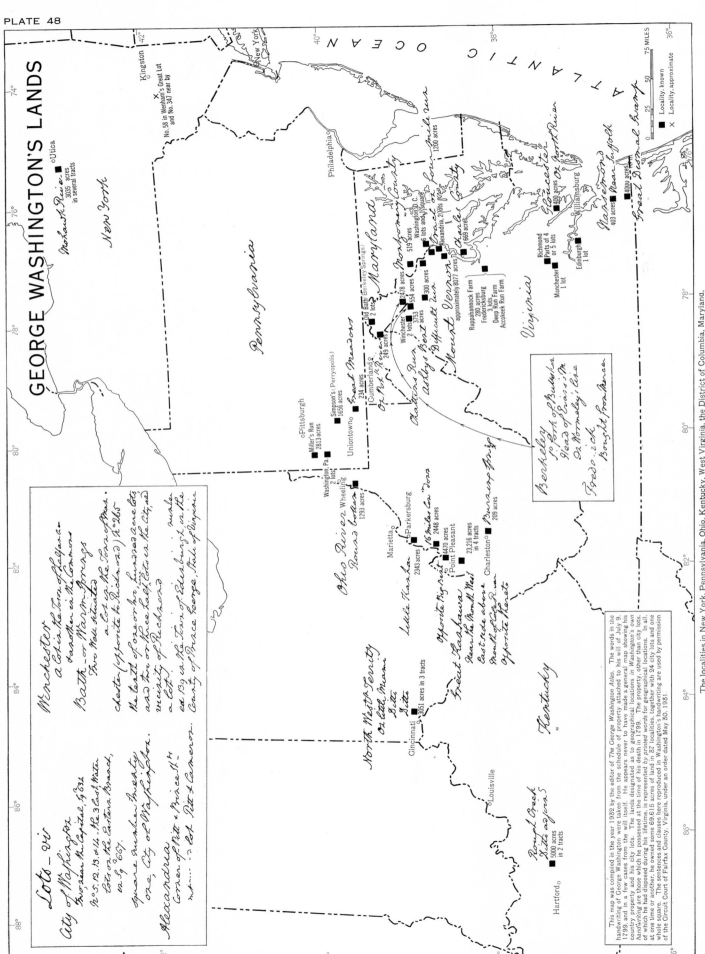

The localities in New York, Pennsylvania, Ohio, Kentucky, West Virginia, the District of Columbia, Maryland, and Virginia where George Washington owned land.

PLATE 49

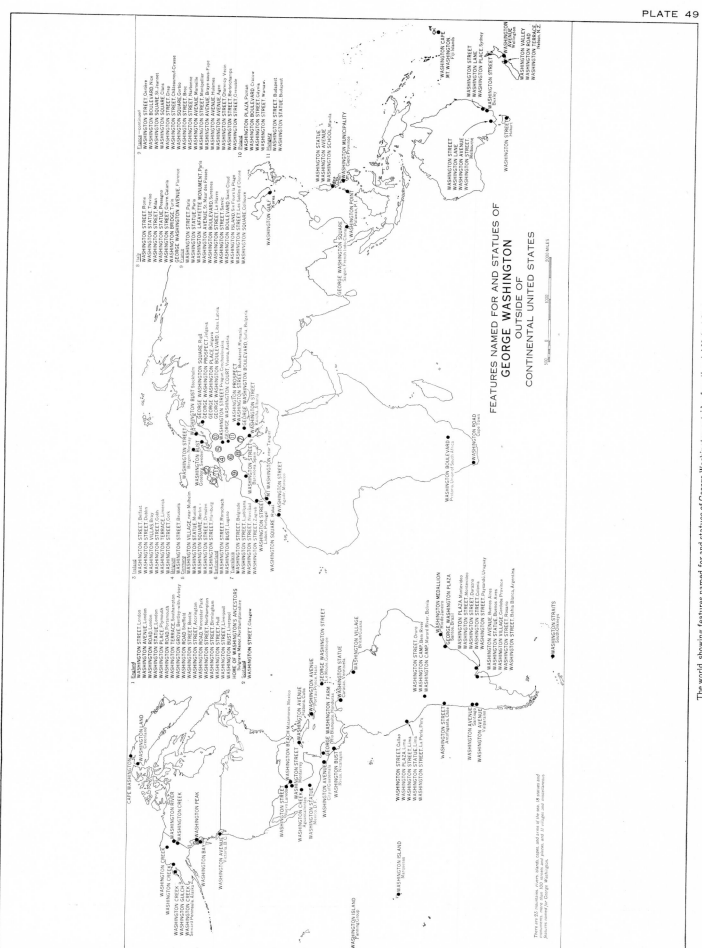

FEATURES NAMED FOR AND STATUES OF
GEORGE WASHINGTON
OUTSIDE OF
CONTINENTAL UNITED STATES

The world, showing features named for and statues of George Washington outside of continental United States.

PLATE 50

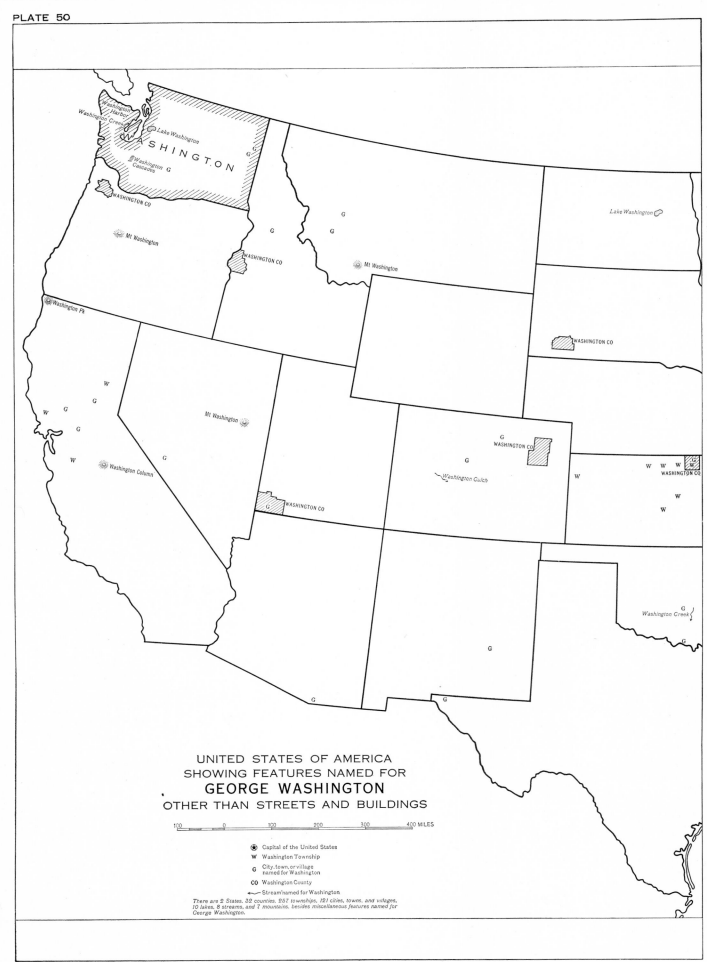

UNITED STATES OF AMERICA
SHOWING FEATURES NAMED FOR
GEORGE WASHINGTON
OTHER THAN STREETS AND BUILDINGS

100   0   100   200   300   400 MILES

⊛   Capital of the United States

W   Washington Township

G   City, town, or village
named for Washington

CO   Washington County

←   Stream named for Washington

*There are 2 States, 32 counties, 257 townships, 121 cities, towns, and villages,
10 lakes, 8 streams, and 7 mountains, besides miscellaneous features named for
George Washington.*

The United States of America, showing nearly 450 features named for George Washington,
other than streets, buildings, schools, colleges, monuments, etc

PLATE 50 (continued)

Capital of the United States
W   Washington Township
G   City, town, or village
    named for Washington
CO Washington County
↞ Stream named for Washington

There are 2 States, 32 counties, 257 townships, 121 cities, towns, and villages, 10 lakes, 8 streams, and 7 mountains, besides miscellaneous features named for George Washington.

The United States of America, showing nearly 450 features named for George Washington, other than streets, buildings, schools, colleges, monuments, etc.

LIST OF MAPS MADE BY GEORGE WASHINGTON

The italicised words show where the maps were in 1932

(a) 1747, September 29. Plat of a survey for Caleb Butler of 25 acres, 0 roods, 21 perches, probably in Westmoreland County, Va. *Pennsylvania Historical Society.*

(b) 1747, September 30. Plat of a survey for John Watts of 761 acres, 0 roods, 21 perches, probably in Westmoreland County, Va. *Pennsylvania Historical Society.*

(1) 1747, October 1. Plat of a survey of 22 acres, 3 roods, 19 perches, probably at Bridges Creek (Wakefield), Westmoreland County, Va. *Library of Congress,* Div. of MSS., Washington Papers, School Copy Book No. 2, page 103. Reproduced on Plate 8 of this atlas.

(2) [1747] Plat of a survey of 3 acres, 1 rood, 19 perches on the west side of Little Hunting Creek, at its mouth, showing the "Mount Vernon Hills" and the Mount Vernon Mansion House. *Library of Congress,* Div. of MSS., Washington Papers, School Copy Book No. 2, page 107. Reproduced on Plate 3 of this atlas.

(2a) [1747] "A Plan of a piece of Meadow situate on Little Hunting Creek", [Mount Vernon, Va.], containing 3 acres, 1 rood, 19 perches. *Dr. A. S. W. Rosenbach, Philadelphia.*

(3) [1747] "A Plan of a piece of Meadow called Hell Hole, Situate on the River Potowmack near Little Hunting Creek", [Mount Vernon, Va.], containing 5 acres, 2 roods, 31 perches. *Library of Congress,* Div. of MSS., Washington Papers, School Copy Book No. 2, page 106. Reproduced on Plate 5 of this atlas.

(4) 1748, February 27. "A Plan of Major Law: Washingtons Turnip Field . . .", [Mount Vernon, Va.] Drawn within an ornamental compass. *Library of Congress,* Div. of MSS., Washington Papers, School Copy Book No. 2, page 104, reverse side. Reproduced on Plate 3 of this atlas, and on the half-title.

(5) [1748] "Plat of the Land where on Stands the Town of Alexandria", scale 1 inch to 15 poles. *Library of Congress,* Div. of Maps. Reproduced on Plate 19 of this atlas.

(6) [1749, July 22] Plat of a survey for Richard Barnes of 400 acres in Culpeper County, Va., on Flat Run, near Mount Poney. Drawn within an ornamental compass. *Library of Congress,* Div. of MSS., Washington Papers, Survey Note Book, page 8. Reproduced on the title-page of this atlas.

(7) 1749, July 22. Another plat of the same survey for Richard Barnes of 400 acres in Culpeper County, Va., on Flat Run, near Mount Poney, showing a road, the profile of Mount Poney, and the names of adjacent property owners. *Cornell University Library,* title-page of "A Book of Survey's Began July 22d. 1749". Reproduced at the end of the index of this atlas.

(8) 1749, November 3. Plat of a survey for William McBride of 386¼ acres in Augusta County, Va. [Hardy County, W. Va.] on the Lost River. *Virginia State Library.*

(8a) 1749, November 4. Plat of a survey for Ann Dunbarr of 212 acres in Augusta County, Va. [Hardy County, W. Va.] on the Lost River. Facsimile in C. F. Heartman's Catalogue No. 195, 1927, page 81. *The location of the original is not known.*

(8b) 1749, November 5. Plat of a survey for John Ellswick of 406 acres in Augusta County, Va. [Hardy County, W. Va.] on the Lost River. *Mr. H. P. McCullough, North Bennington, Vt.*

(9) 1749, November 7. Plat of a survey for Joseph How of 386¼ acres in Augusta County, Va. [Hardy County, W. Va.] on the Lost River. *Library of Congress,* Div. of MSS., Washington Papers, Survey Note Book, page 20.

(9a) 1749, November 8. Plat of a survey for Andrew Viney of 386¼ acres in Augusta County, Va. [Hardy County, W. Va.] on the Lost River. *Mr. H. P. McCullough, North Bennington, Vt.*

(9b) 1749, November 10. Plat of a survey for Samuel Baker of 396 acres in Augusta County, Va. [Hardy County, W. Va.] on the Lost River. *Mr. H. P. McCullough, North Bennington, Vt.*

(10) 1749, November 11. Plat of a survey for William Warden of 400 acres in Augusta County, Va. [Hardy County, W. Va.] on the Lost River. *Huntington Library,* HM 5500.

(11) [1749] "A Plan of Alexandria Now Belhaven", scale 1 inch to about 247 feet. *Library of Congress,* Div. of Maps. Reproduced on Plate 19 of this atlas.

(12) 1750, March 30. Plat of a survey for David Edwards of 412 acres in Frederick County, Va. [Hampshire or Morgan County, W. Va.] on the Cacapon River. Facsimile in Maggs Catalogue No. 510, 1928, Plate 32. *The location of the original is not known.*

(13) 1750, March 30. Plat of a survey for Thomas Edwards of 400 acres in Frederick County, Va. [Hampshire or Morgan County, W. Va.] on the Cacapon River. *Judge E. A. Armstrong, Princeton, N. J.*

(13a) 1750, March 31. Plat of a survey for George Hyatt of 272 acres in Frederick County, Va. [Hampshire County, W. Va.] on Davids Run. *Mr. Alwin J. Scheuer, New York City.*

(13b) 1750, March 31. Plat of a survey for John Parke, Jr., of 250 acres in Frederick County, Va. [Hampshire County, W. Va.] on a branch of the Cacapon River. *Mr. Frank C. Deering, Biddeford, Me.*

(14) 1750, April 2. Plat of a survey for Evan Pugh, Sr., of 226 acres in Frederick County, Va. [Hampshire or Morgan County, W. Va.] on Trout Run. *Mr. Forest G. Sweet, Battle Creek, Mich.*

(14a) 1750, April 4. Plat of a survey for William Hughes, Jr., of 460 acres in Frederick County, Va. [Hampshire or Morgan County, W. Va.] on the Cacapon River. *Mr. Albert E. Lownes, Providence, R. I.*

(15) 1750, April 5. Plat of a survey for Edward Kinnison, Jr., of 400 acres in Frederick County, Va. [Hampshire or Morgan County, W. Va.] on the Cacapon River. *Mr. Thomas F. Madigan, New York City.*

(16) 1750, April 10. Plat of a survey for Darby McKeaver, Jr., of 412½ acres in Frederick County, Va. [Hampshire or Morgan County, W. Va.] on the Cacapon River. *Washington Association of New Jersey, Morristown, N. J.*

(17) 1750, April 11. Plat of a survey for John Parke, Sr., of 400 acres in Frederick County, Va. [Hampshire or Morgan County, W. Va.] on the Cacapon River. *Mr. Alwin J. Scheuer, New York City.*

(17a) 1750, April 11. Plat of a survey for Joseph Edwards of 400 acres in Frederick County, Va. [Hampshire or Morgan County, W. Va.] on the Cacapon River. *E. F. Bonaventure, Inc., New York City.*

(17b) 1750, April 12. Plat of a survey for James Caudy of 98 acres in Frederick County, Va. [Hampshire or Morgan County, W. Va.] on the Cacapon River. *Mr. J. Percy Sabin, Summit, N. J.*

(18) 1750, April 12. Plat of a survey for Thomas Parker, Sr., of 237 acres in Frederick County, Va. [Hampshire County, W. Va.] on the North River. *New York Historical Society,* C. A. Munn Collection.

(18a) 1750, April 13. Plat of a survey for Evan Pugh, Jr., of 160 acres in Frederick County, Va. [Hampshire or Morgan County, W. Va.] on a small branch that runs into the Cacapon River. *Mr. J. Percy Sabin, Summit, N. J.*

(18b) 1750, April 13. Plat of a survey for Benjamin Phipps of 400 acres in Frederick County, Va. [Hampshire County, W. Va.] on the North River. *Mr. Alwin J. Scheuer, New York City.*

(18c) 1750, April 14. Plat of a survey for Josiah Arnold of 400 acres in Frederick County, Va. [Hampshire County, W. Va.] on the North River. *Mr. J. Percy Sabin, Summit, N. J.*

(19) 1750, April 14. Plat of a survey for James Smith of 400 acres in Frederick County, Va. [Hampshire County, W. Va.] on the North River. *Massachusetts Historical Society.*

(19a) 1750, April 16. Plat of a survey for John Stackhouse of 400 acres in Frederick County, Va. [Hampshire County,

W. Va.] on the North River. *Mr. J. Percy Sabin, Summit, N. J.*

(19b) 1750, April 18. Plat of a survey for David Dunbar of 425 acres in Augusta County, Va. [Hardy County, W. Va.] on the Lost River. *Mr. J. Percy Sabin, Summit, N. J.*

(19c) 1750, April 20. Plat of a survey for James Dilouza of 400 acres in Frederick County, Va. [Hampshire County, W. Va.] on a branch of the North River. *Mr. J. Percy Sabin, Summit, N. J.*

(19d) 1750, April 20. Plat of a survey for David Wood of 400 acres in Frederick County, Va. [Hampshire County, W. Va.] on the North River. *Mr. J. Percy Sabin, Summit, N. J.*

(19e) 1750, April 23. Plat of a survey for Henry Enoch of 388 acres in Frederick County, Va. [Hampshire County, W. Va.] at the fork of the Cacapon and North Rivers. *Mr. J. Percy Sabin, Summit, N. J.*

(19f) 1750, April 24. Plat of a survey for Isaac Dawson of 270 acres in Frederick County, Va. [Morgan County, W. Va.] in the neck between the Potomac and Cacapon Rivers. *Mr. J. Percy Sabin, Summit, N. J.*

(20) 1750, April 24. Plat of a survey for Thomas Williams of 95 acres in Frederick County, Va. [Morgan County, W. Va.] on the Potomac River, east of the mouth of the Cacapon River. *Chicago Historical Society.*

(20a) 1750, April 26. Plat of a survey for John Parker of 400 acres in Frederick County, Va. [Hampshire County, W. Va.] on Little Cacapon River about ½ mile above Buffalo Lick. *Mr. J. Percy Sabin, Summit, N. J.*

(20b) 1750, April 28. Plat of a survey for James McCay of 400 acres in Frederick County, Va. [Hampshire or Hardy County, W. Va.] on the Great Wagon Road that leads to the South Branch. *Mr. J. Percy Sabin, Summit, N. J.*

(21) 1750, June 14. Plat of a survey for George Nickson of 400 acres in Frederick County, Va. [Hampshire County, W. Va.] on the North River. *Mr. Albert F. Madlener, Chicago, Ill.*

(21a) 1750, June 16. Plat of a survey for James Warden of 330 acres in Augusta County, Va. [Hardy County, W. Va.] on the Lost River. *Mr. J. Percy Sabin, Summit, N. J.*

(21b) 1750, August 21. Plat of a survey for Lawrence Washington of 209 acres in Frederick County, Va. [Jefferson County, W. Va.] on Worthington's Run. *Mr. J. Percy Sabin, Summit, N. J.*

(21c) 1750, August 22. Plat of a survey for Lawrence Washington of 595 acres in Frederick County, Va. [Jefferson County, W. Va?]. *Mr. J. Percy Sabin, Summit, N. J.*

(21d) 1750, August 23. Plat of a survey for Lawrence Washington of 613 acres in Frederick County, Va. [Jefferson County, W. Va?]. *Pennsylvania Historical Society.*

(22) 1750, August 23. Plat of a survey for Lawrence Washington of 613 acres in Frederick County, Va. [Jefferson County, W. Va?). *Huntington Library, HM 5498.*

(22a) 1750, August 24. Plat of a survey for Lawrence Washington of 1,106 acres in Frederick County, Va. [Jefferson County, W. Va?] on Worthington's Run. *Mr. J. Percy Sabin, Summit, N. J.*

(22b) 1750, August 25. Plat of a survey for Augustine Washington of 500 acres in Frederick County, Va. [Jefferson County, W. Va?]. *Mr. J. Percy Sabin, Summit, N. J.*

(23) 1750, August 25. Plat of a survey for Lawrence Washington of 554 acres in Frederick County, Va. [Jefferson County, W. Va?]. *Huntington Library, HM 5497.*

(23a) 1750, August 28. Plat of a survey for George Johnston of 552 acres in Frederick County, Va. [Jefferson County, W. Va.] on the south side of the south fork of Bullskin Run. *Mr. J. Percy Sabin, Summit, N. J.*

(24) 1750, October 17. Plat of a survey for Thomas Loftan of 265¼ acres in Frederick County, Va. [Jefferson County, W. Va.] on Long Marsh Run. *Huntington Library, HM 5339.*

(24a) 1750, October 18. Plat of a survey for John Cuszine of 455 acres in Frederick County, Va. [Jefferson County, W. Va?]. *Pennsylvania Historical Society.*

(24b) 1750, October 19. Plat of a survey for John Vance of 353 acres in Frederick County, Va. [Jefferson County, W. Va?]. *Mr. J. Percy Sabin, Summit, N. J.*

(24c) 1750, October 22. Plat of a survey for Samuel Isaac of 415 acres in Frederick County, Va. [Jefferson County, W. Va?]. *Mr. H. P. McCullough, North Bennington, Vt.*

(25) 1750, October 24. Plat of a survey for John Madden of 400 acres in Frederick County, Va. [Jefferson County, W. Va?] at Joes Hole. *Huntington Library, HM 5340.*

(26) 1750, October 24. Plat of a survey for Jeremiah Wood of 292 acres in Frederick County, Va. [Jefferson County, W. Va?]. *Judge E. A. Armstrong, Princeton, N. J.*

(27) 1750, October 29. Plat of a survey for Hannah Southerd of 311 acres in Frederick County, Va. [Jefferson County, W. Va?]. *Huntington Library, HM 5342.*

(28) 1750, November 9. Plat of a survey for Richard Stephenson of 316 acres in Frederick County, Va. [Jefferson County, W. Va.] between the north and south forks of Bullskin Run. *Boston Public Library.*

(29) 1750, November 12. Plat of a survey for Lawrence Washington of 507 acres in Frederick County, Va., joining Worthington's Patent and at the head of Smith's Glade. *Huntington Library, HM 5492.*

(30) 1750, November 17. Plat of a survey for John Lindsey of 223 acres in Frederick County, Va. *Library of Congress, Div. of Maps.* Reproduced on Plate 20 of this atlas.

(31) 1750, November 20. Plat of a survey for John Lindsey of 660 acres in Frederick County, Va. [Jefferson County, W. Va.] on Long Marsh Run. *New York Public Library.*

(32) 1751, March 19. Plat of a survey for George Martin of 385 acres of land in Frederick County, Va. *Mr. Alwin J. Scheuer, New York City.*

(33) 1751, March 25. Plat of a survey for Lawrence Washington of 570 acres in Frederick County, Va. [Jefferson County, W. Va.] at the mouth of the south fork of Bullskin Run. *Huntington Library, HM 5493.*

(34) 1751, April 3. Plat of a survey for Owen Thomas of 400 acres in Frederick County, Va. [Jefferson County, W. Va.] on the south side of the south fork of Bullskin Run. *New York Public Library.* Reproduced on Plate 20 of this atlas.

(34a) 1751, April 15. Plat of a survey for John Waite of 225 acres in Frederick County, Va. [Hampshire County, W. Va.] on the south fork of Bullskin Run. *Chapin Library, Williams College.*

(35) 1751, April 17. Plat of a survey for John Ashbrook of 400 acres in Frederick County, Va. [Hampshire County, W. Va.] on the North River. *Canon Anson Phelps Stokes, Washington, D. C.*

(36) 1751, April 18. Plat of a survey for William Horner of 292 acres in Frederick County, Va. [Hampshire County, W. Va.] on the North River. *Huntington Library, Brock Collection.*

(37) 1751, April 24. Plat of a survey for Enoch Enoch of 168 acres in Frederick County, Va. [Morgan County, W. Va.] on the Potomac River near Pawpaw. *Mr. Walter Hunnewell, Wellesley, Mass.* Reproduced on Plate 21 of this atlas.

(38) 1751, April 27. Plat of a survey for Owen Rogers of 260 acres [in Morgan, Hampshire, or Hardy County, W. Va.] on a branch of the Cacapon River. Printed facsimile in the Boston Athenaeum. *The location of the original is not known.*

(39) 1752, March 11. Plat of a survey for Gersham Keyes of 420 acres in Frederick County, Va. [Jefferson County, W. Va.] on the Shenandoah River near its mouth. *Pierpont Morgan Library.*

(40) 1752, March 13. Plat of a survey for John Maccarmick of 157 acres in Frederick County, Va. [Jefferson County, W. Va.] on Bullskin Run. *Williamsburg Holding Corporation, Williamsburg, Va.*

(41) 1752, March 19. Plat of a survey for George Fout of 800

acres in Frederick County, Va. [Hampshire County, W. Va.] on Dillon Run. *Mr. Lloyd W. Smith, Madison, N. J.*

(42) 1752, March 21. Plat of a survey for John Donbarr of a tract of land in Frederick County, Va. [Hampshire or Morgan County, W. Va.] on the Cacapon River. *Cornell University Library.*

(42a) 1752, March 23. Plat of a survey for James Baker of 220 acres in Frederick County, Va. [Hardy County, W. Va.] on the Lost River. *Mr. George A. Ball, Muncie, Ind.*

(42b) 1752, March 27. Plat of a survey for Henry Enoch of 271½ acres in Frederick County, Va. [Hampshire County, W. Va.] on Little Cacapon River. *Mr. George A. Ball, Muncie, Ind.*

(42c) 1752, March 30. Plat of a survey for George Washington of King George of 240 acres in Frederick County, Va. [Morgan County, W. Va.] on the Potomac River about 2 miles above the mouth of Fifteen Mile Creek in Maryland. *Mr. George A. Ball, Muncie, Ind.*

(42d) 1752, March 30. Plat of a survey for Daniel Osborne of 270 acres in Frederick County, Va. [Morgan County, W. Va.] on the Potomac River. *Mr. George A. Ball, Muncie, Ind.*

(42e) 1752, March 30. Plat of a survey for William Williams of 121 acres in Frederick County [Morgan County, W. Va.] on the Potomac River, just below the mouth of Fifteen Mile Run. *Mr. George A. Ball, Muncie, Ind.*

(42f) 1752, March 30. Plat of a survey for Daniel Osborne of 220 acres in Frederick County, Va. [Morgan County, W. Va.] on the Potomac River. *Mr. George A. Ball, Muncie, Ind.*

(42g) 1752, March 31. Plat of a survey for William Demose of 320 acres in Frederick County, Va. [Hampshire or Morgan County, W. Va.] on the Cacapon River. *Mr. George A. Ball, Muncie, Ind.*

(42h) 1752, April 2. Plat of a survey for David Edwards of 200 acres in Frederick County, Va. [Hampshire or Morgan County, W. Va.] on the Cacapon River. *Mr. George A. Ball, Muncie, Ind.*

(42i) 1752, April 3. Plat of a survey for John Parke, Jr., of 135 acres in Frederick County, Va. [Hampshire or Morgan County, W. Va.] on Mill Run, a branch of the Cacapon. *Mr. George A. Ball, Muncie, Ind.*

(42j) 1752, May 6. Plat of a survey for Major Marquis Calmes of 1,110 acres in Frederick County, Va. [Jefferson County, W. Va.] on the south side of Bullskin Run. *Mr. George A. Ball, Muncie, Ind.*

(42k) 1752, October 23. Plat of a survey for Mr. Christopher Beiler of 67 acres [in Frederick County, Va?] deducted from John Hardin's survey. *Mr. George A. Ball, Muncie, Ind.*

(43) 1752, October 25. Plat of a survey for Robert Johnston of 239 acres in Frederick County, Va. [Jefferson County, W. Va.] on the south fork of Bullskin Run. *Huntington Library, HM 5341.*

(43a) 1752, October 25. Plat of a survey for Robert Johnston of 239 acres in Frederick County, Va. [Jefferson County, W. Va.] on the south fork of Bullskin Run. *Chapin Library, Williams College.*

(44) 1754. Sketch map of the country traversed by Washington on his journey in 1753-54 from Cumberland, Maryland, to the site of Pittsburgh, Pa., and Fort Le Boeuf near Lake Erie, scale 1 inch to about 17 miles. *Public Record Office, London,* M. G. P. 118. Reproduced on Plate 11 of this atlas.

(45) 1754. Map of part of the Potomac River near Harpers Ferry. *Minnesota Historical Society.* Reproduced on Plate 22 of this atlas.

(46) [1756] Plan of a fortification, probably Fort Loudoun, Winchester, Va. *Library of Congress,* Div. of MSS., Washington Papers, Vol. 5, folio 566. Annotated on reverse side with the words: "Rough Plans of Fort Loudoun near Winchester and Cumberland . . . Wills Creek".

(47) [1756] Plan of Fort Loudoun, Winchester, Va. *Library of Congress,* Div. of MSS., Washington Papers, Vol. 5, folio 567.

(48) [1756] Preliminary sketch of the proportions of a fortification. *Library of Congress,* Div. of MSS., Washington Papers, Vol. 5, folio 568.

(49) [1756] Plan of a fortification, probably Fort Loudoun, Winchester, Va. *Library of Congress,* Div. of MSS., Washington Papers, Vol. 5, folio 569.

(50) [1756] Plan of Fort Loudoun, Winchester, Va. *Library of Congress,* Div. of MSS., Washington Papers, Vol. 5, folio 570. Reproduced on Plate 13 of this atlas.

(51) [1756] Plan of Fort Loudoun, Winchester, Va. *Library of Congress,* Div. of MSS., Washington Papers, Vol. 5, folio 571.

(52) [1756] Ground plan of a fortification. *Library of Congress,* Div. of MSS., Washington Papers, Vol. 5, folio 572.

(53) [1758] "Sketch of the Situation &c. of Fort Cumberland", Md. *Cornell University Library,* Sparks Collection, L 521. Reproduced on Plate 12 of this atlas.

(54) 1758. Plan of a line of march in a forest country. *Pierpont Morgan Library.* Reproduced on Plate 13 of this atlas.

(55) 1760, April 7. Plat of a survey of 183 acres of land patented by George Washington, March 31, 1760, in Frederick County, Va. *Huntington Library,* HM 5496.

(56) 1766. "A Plan of my Farm on little Hunt'g Creek & Potom'k R" [This is the River Farm of the Mount Vernon estate]. *Library of Congress,* Div. of Maps. Reproduced on Plate 3 of this atlas.

(57) 1766. "A Plan of my Farm on little Hunt'g Creek & Potom'k R" [This is another map of the River Farm of the Mount Vernon estate]. *Dr. A. S. W. Rosenbach, Philadelphia.*

(57a) 1769, March. "Plat of Land belonging to Geo. Carter Esq'r. on Opeckon Riv 8,365 Ac'r." [Jefferson County, W. Va?]. *Pennsylvania Historical Society.*

(57b) 1771, February 25. Plat of a survey of 20½ acres of land on Dogue Run and Piney Run, a portion of the Mount Vernon estate. *Mr. Gabriel Wells, New York City.*

(58) 1771. "Plat of the Survey for 4,232 Acres upon the Great Kanhawa above the Survey of 10,990 Acres granted to Doct'r Craik". *Library of Congress,* Div. of MSS., Washington Papers, Vol. 12, folio 1534.

(59) 1771. "Survey of 51,302 acres of land in the Fork of Ohio & Kanhawa . . . patented to Muse & others, 15th Dec'r 1772". *Library of Congress,* Div. of MSS., Washington Papers, Vol. 12, folios 1542-43.

(60) [1771] Plat of a survey of 2,314 acres of land, being the first large bottom on the east side of the Ohio River, 3 or 4 miles below the mouth of the Little Kanawha River, a portion of which is divided into 17 lots. Scale 1 inch to about 100 poles. *Library of Congress,* Div. of MSS., Washington Papers, Vol. 12, folio 1548.

(61) [1771] Plat of a survey of 2,448 acres of land being the fourth large bottom on the east side of the Ohio River about sixteen miles below the Little Kanawha River, a portion of which is divided into 7 lots. Scale 1 inch to about 100 poles. *Library of Congress,* Div. of MSS., Washington Papers, Vol. 12, folio 1549.

(62) [1771] Plat of a survey of 4,395 acres of land being the fifth large bottom below the Little Kanawha; and the bottom just below the great bend in the Ohio, a portion of which is divided into 19 lots. Scale 1 inch to 100 poles. *Library of Congress,* Div. of MSS., Washington Papers, Vol. 12, folio 1547.

(63) [1771] Plat of a survey of 4,149 acres on the Ohio between the Long Bottom and Sandy Creek, patented in the name of John Fry. *Library of Congress,* Div. of MSS., Washington Papers, Vol. 12, folio 1590.

(63a) [1771] Plat of a survey of 13,532 acres of land being the first long bottom on the east side of the Ohio River just below the Great Kanawha River [in Mason County, W. Va.], patented in the name of George Mercer. *Mr. Eugene H. Kahn, Philadelphia.*

(64) [1772] Plan of the tenements on the South Fork of Bullskin

Run [Jefferson County, W. Va.] *Huntington Library*, HM 5508.

(65) 1772. Plat of a survey of 2,084 acres of land on Big Sandy Creek, 30 miles from its confluence with the Ohio [in Lawrence County, Ky., and Wayne County, W. Va.], patented in the name of John Fry, heir of Col. Joshua Fry. *Library of Congress*, Div. of MSS., Washington Papers, Vol. 13, folio 1654.

(66) 1772. Plat of a survey of 1,525 acres of land on Little Sandy Creek, 2 miles above the survey on Sandy Creek [in Lawrence County, Ky.], patented in the name of John Fry, heir of Col. Joshua Fry. *Library of Congress*, Div. of MSS., Washington Papers, Vol. 13, folio 1655.

(67) [1772] Plat of a survey of 28,627 acres of land on the Ohio River and on Sandy Creek, patented to John Savage & others. *Library of Congress*, Div. of MSS., Washington Papers, Vol. 13, folio 1661.

(68) [1773] Ground plan and elevation of Pohick Church, Pohick, Va. Reproduced in B. J. Lossing's "Mount Vernon and its Associations", New York, 1859, page 74. *The location of the original is not known*. This is, of course, an architectural drawing rather than a map. It is convenient to have it referred to here and to record that Washington also drew a plan of the tomb at Mount Vernon, which is preserved in the State Library at Hartford, Connecticut, and made a drawing of one of the barns at Mount Vernon, which is preserved in the Division of Manuscripts at the Library of Congress.

(69) [1774] Map of eight tracts of George Washington's own land on the Great Kanawha and Pocatellico Rivers in West Virginia, made from surveys by William Crawford, Samuel Lewis, and John Floyd, 1771-74. *Library of Congress*, Div. of Maps. Reproduced on Plate 23 of this atlas.

(70) [1775, July 27] "the Situation of Boston, and Bay on this side [Cambridge, Mass.]; as also of the Post they have Taken in Charles Town Neck, Bunker's Hill and our Posts". *Library of Congress*, Div. of MSS., Washington Papers, Vol. 16, folio 2069. Reproduced on Plate 12 of this atlas.

(71) [1778] Plat to show the manner of affecting exchange of land with William Triplett. *Huntington Library*, HM 5507.

(72) 1779. ". . . Map of the Cayuga, or Teoga branch [Chemung River] of the Susquehannah . . ." [Includes portions of southern New York and northern Pennsylvania]. *Library of Congress*, Div. of MSS., Washington Papers, Vol. 109, folio 14,496. Reproduced on Plate 18 of this atlas.

(73) [1781] Plan of the "Order of Battle for 1781". *Cornell University Library*. Reproduced on Plate 17 of this atlas.

(74) [1784] Plan of the Mansion House grounds, gardens, and walks at Mount Vernon. Reproduced in B. J. Lossing's "Mount Vernon and its Associations", New York, 1859, page 141. *The location of the original is not known*. Reproduced on Plate 7 of this atlas.

(75) [1784] A portion of a shaded carriage-way at Mount Vernon, indicating the kinds of trees planted. Reproduced in *Harper's New Monthly Magazine*, Vol. 18, 1859, page 442. *The location of the original is not known*.

(76) 1787, December 25. "Draught of three Tracts of Land belonging to the Subscriber [George Washington] on the Ohio River betw'n the mouths of the Great & little Kanhawa". *Mr. Montagu Hankin, Morristown, N. J.* Reproduced on Plate 24 of this atlas.

(77) 1787, December 25. "Draught of four Tracts of Land belonging to the Subscriber [George Washington] on the Great Kanhawa". *New York Historical Society*.

(78) [1787] Map of the Union Farm at Mount Vernon. Scale 1 inch to 25 poles. *Mount Vernon Ladies Association*. Reproduced on Plate 5 of this atlas.

(79) [1788] Map of Washington's lands on Rough Creek, Kentucky. *Mr. Forest G. Sweet, Battle Creek, Mich.*

(80) [1788, Nov. 13-15] Map of roads from Mount Vernon to Pohick Church, and to Cameron, Va. *Mount Vernon Ladies Association*. Reproduced in part on Plate 6 of this atlas.

(81) 1790. Map of the Mount Vernon lands between Little Hunting Creek and Dogue Run, showing the roads leading to the Ferry Landing. *Virginia State Library*. Reproduced on Plate 6 of this atlas.

(82) 1793, December. George Washington's own map of all his farms at Mount Vernon. Scale 1 inch to about 100 poles. *Huntington Library*. Reproduced on Plate 2 of this atlas.

(83) 1793, December 12. "A Map of General Washington's Farm of Mount Vernon from a Drawing transmitted by the General". This map differs slightly from the one at the Huntington Library and was reproduced in "Letters from his Excellency General George Washington to Arthur Young", London, 1801, facing page vi. *The location of the original is not known*.

(83a) [1799] George Washington's final map of all his farms at Mount Vernon. This map differs slightly from the two maps made in December, 1793, and shows the whole western extension of the estate. It was reproduced upon W. Gillingham's "Map of George Washington's Land at Mount Vernon, Fairfax Co'y Virginia. As it was & As it is. Laid down from old Maps made by G. Washington, and from actual surveys by W. Gillingham", scale 1 inch to 120 poles, published in 1859. *The location of the original is not known*.

(84) 1799, April. Plat of a survey of 1,225 acres, 3 roods, 27 perches of George Washington's own land on Four Mile Run, Va. Facsimile in G. W. P. Custis' "Recollections and Private Memoirs of Washington", New York, 1860, facing page 445. *The location of the original is not known.* Reproduced on Plate 21 of this atlas.

(85) 1799, April 29. Plat of a survey of 436 acres of land on Four Mile Run in Arlington County, Va., bought from Mr. C. West. *Dr. A. S. W. Rosenbach of Philadelphia*, a Washington survey note book, page 30.

(86) 1799, September 20. "A Plan of part of Mount Vernon lands North West of the Road leading from the Gum Spring, on Little Hunting Creek to the Ford of Dogue Run . . ." This is the Dogue Run Farm, containing 1,998 acres, 3 roods, 39 perches, and including "Woodlawn". Scale 1 inch to 40 poles. *Huntington Library*. Reproduced on Plate 4 of this atlas.

(86a) [1799] Outline of a survey of part of the Mount Vernon estate, west of Dogue Run. *Pennsylvania Historical Society*.

(86b) Survey of 4 fields, probably at Mount Vernon, Va. *Pennsylvania Historical Society*.

(87) Plat of a survey of two tracts of land on Dogue Run attached to the deed of Margaret Lady Culpeper to Thomas Derrick and Samuel Wells, dated October 5, 1694. *Washington Association of New Jersey, Morristown, N. J.* The dates of Washington's copying of this and the following six items have not been established.

(87a) Plat of a survey of Harrison's Patent according to the courses of the original deed, Dec. 4, 1706, near Piney Run. *Pennsylvania Historical Society*.

(88) Plat of a survey of 2,244 acres of land between Piney Run and Accotink Creek, adjoining the "Chappel Land" and Benoni Thomas' land, granted to Mason and Herriford, January 4, 1715. *Huntington Library*, HM 5509. Reproduced on Plate 5 of this atlas.

(89) Plat of a survey made for John Brown of 601 acres on Dogue Run which had been granted to Wells and Derrick, dated August 29, 1742. *Chicago Historical Society*.

(90) Plat of a survey of 7,108 acres in Frederick County, Va., made by John Baylis. *Mr. Thomas F. Madigan, New York City*.

(91) Plat of a survey of Col. Mann Page's patent on the Shenandoah being Ralph Wormley's land, made from Lord Fairfax's copy. *Huntington Library*, HM 5494.

(92) Plat of a survey of 3,023 acres on Long Marsh in Frederick County, Va. [Jefferson County, W. Va.], surveyed by James Genn. *Library of Congress*, Div. of MSS., Washington Papers, School Copy Book No. 2, page 105.

MAPS MADE BY OTHERS BUT USED AND ANNOTATED
BY GEORGE WASHINGTON

(93) [1690] Map of Mount Vernon, showing a possible site of the original dwelling house ["D. Mr. Williams his House"]. Photostat in the Library of Congress, Div. of Maps. *The location of the original is not known.* Annotated on the reverse side with the words: "Survey & Division between Spencer & Washington Sept'r & December 1690".

(94) 1769. Map of Frederick County, Virginia, "drawn by J. Moffett Sur'r 20th April 1769", scale 1 inch to 20 miles. *Library of Congress,* Div. of Maps. Annotated on the reverse side with the words: "Map of the County of Frederick 1769".

(95) [1771] Plat of a survey of land in West Virginia on the Ohio River. *Library of Congress,* Div. of MSS., Washington Papers, Vol. 13, folio 1589. Annotated on reverse side with the words: "Plat of the Land above Capteening opposite Pipe C'k 1771".

(96) 1771, June. Plat of a survey of land on the east side of the Great Kanawha River, by William Crawford, scale 1 inch to 200 poles. *Library of Congress,* Div. of MSS., Washington Papers, Vol. 12, folio 1544. Annotated with the words: "Patented in the name of George Washington", and, on the reverse side, "Survey of 10,990 Acres, on the Kanhawa made in 1771".

(97) 1771, June. Plat of a survey of land "being the third large Bottom below the Little Kanhawa on the Ohio River", by William Crawford, scale 1 inch to 100 poles. *Library of Congress,* Div. of MSS., Washington Papers, Vol. 12, folio 1536. Annotated with the words: "Patented in the name of George Muse", and, on the reverse side, "Survey of 927 acres, 3d. Bottom—Ohio, made in 1771".

(98) 1771, June. Plat of a survey of land "Being the fourth large Bottom on the East side of the Ohio River about Sixteen Miles below the Little Kanhawa", by William Crawford, scale 1 inch to 100 poles. *Library of Congress,* Div. of MSS., Washington Papers, Vol. 12, folio 1540. Annotated with the words: "Patented in the name of Geo. Washington", and, on the reverse side, "Survey of 2,448 Acres, 4th Bottom—made 1771".

(99) 1771, June. Plat of a survey of land "being the Fifth large Bottom below the Little Kanhawa; and the Bottom just above the great Bend in the Ohio", by William Crawford, scale 1 inch to 100 poles. *Library of Congress,* Div. of MSS., Washington Papers, Vol. 12, folio 1529. Annotated with the words: "Patented in the name of George Washington," and, on the reverse side, "Survey of 4,395 Acres 5th Bottom—Ohio made in 1771".

(100) 1771, June. Plat of a survey of land "being the Sixth large Bottom on the East side of the Ohio, below the Little Kanahwa, the next below the great Bend," by William Crawford, scale 1 inch to 200 poles. *Library of Congress,* Div. of MSS., Washington Papers, Vol. 12, folio 1538. Annotated on the reverse side with the words: "Survey of 3,373 Acres, 6th Bottom Ohio made in 1771".

(101) 1771, June. Plat of a survey of land "being the Seventh large Bottom on the East side of the Ohio below the Little Kanhawa and the Second below the great Bend in the Ohio", by William Crawford, scale 1 inch to 100 poles. *Library of Congress,* Div. of MSS., Washington Papers, Vol. 12, folio 1545. Annotated on the reverse side with the words: "Survey of 1,990 Acres. 7th Bottom—Ohio made in 1771".

(102) 1771, June. Plat of a survey of land in the fork between the Ohio and the Kanawha Rivers, by William Crawford, scale 1 inch to 200 poles. *Library of Congress,* Div. of MSS., Washington Papers, Vol. 12, folio 1531. Annotated on the reverse side with the words: "Survey of 29,753 Acres, 8th Bottom—Ohio, made in 1771".

(103) 1773. Plat of a survey of land at the mouth of the Little Kanawha River. *Johns Hopkins University Library.* Annotated on the face of the map with 15 lines of notes, and, on the reverse side, with the words: "Plat of the Survey on the little Kanhawa, 28,400 Acres made in 1773". Reproduced on Plate 22 of this atlas.

(104) [1774] Plan for a city at the confluence of the Ohio and Great Kanawha Rivers, on the site of Point Pleasant, W. Va. *Mr. Forest G. Sweet, Battle Creek, Mich.* Annotated with the words: "Plan of the Town at the confluence of the Ohio and G. Kanhawa".

(105) 1777. Part of the battlefield of the Brandywine in Pennsylvania. "Laid down at 200 p's in an Inch, the 27th day of August, An. Domi. 1777. Pr. Jaco'b Broom, Surv'r N. Castle Co'y". *Pennsylvania Historical Society.* Annotated by George Washington in 14 places. Reproduced in part on Plate 15 of this atlas.

(106) 1777. "figure aproximatif des ouvrages des assiegeans, 14. 9bre 1777", [Fort Mifflin near Philadelphia]. *Cornell University Library,* Sparks Collection, L 537. Annotated on the reverse side with the words: "Mudd Island Attack plan". Reproduced on Plate 16 of this atlas.

(107) 1777. "A Map of part of the States of New-York and New-Jersey . . . Deliniated for the use of His Exce'ly Gen'l Washington, by Rob't Erskine F. R. S. 1777", scale 1 inch to 3 miles. *Pierpont Morgan Library.* Annotated by George Washington with 17 place-names, 4 symbols for unnamed localities, and a number of roads and streams. Reproduced in part on Plate 14 of this atlas.

(108) 1778. "State of the British Lines and Country on the North [of Philadelphia] April 1st 1778". Manuscript tracing in New York Public Library. *The location of the original is not known.* Annotated with the words: "Plan of the Redoubts near Philadelp'a 1st April 1778". Reproduced on Plate 16 of this atlas.

(109) 1779. Map of Stony Point and Verplanck's Point, N. Y. *Cornell University Library,* Sparks Collection, L 549. Annotated on the reverse side with the words: "from Genl Heath letter 3d July 1779". Reproduced on Plate 17 of this atlas.

(109a) [1780] A map of the region in southwestern Pennsylvania and northwestern West Virginia lying south of the Ohio River. *Library of Congress,* Div. of Maps. Annotated by George Washington 7 times on the face of the map, and on the reverse side with the words: "A Map of the Lands ab't. Red Stone and Fort Pitt given to me by Cap. Crawf'd".

(110) 1784. Parts of Maryland, Pennsylvania, and West Virginia, to illustrate plans for water transportation from the Atlantic seaboard to the Mississippi valley, drawn by Normand Bruce in 1784. *Minnesota Historical Society.* Annotated on the reverse side with the words: "Sketch of the Country between the Waters of Potomack—and those of Yohiogany—& Monongahe[la], by Colo. Norm'n Bruce". Reproduced on Plate 25 of this atlas.

NOTE. When *The George Washington Atlas* was first planned the Library of Congress was familiar with less than two dozen Washington map items. In February, 1932, we had identified nearly five times that number. Accordingly, since the investigation of so short a time rendered it possible for us to list eighty-two maps made by George Washington, two military plans, seven plans of forts, and one plan of a church, as well as eighteen maps used and annotated by George Washington, or 110 items in all, to say nothing of a plan of a tomb, a drawing of a barn, &c., it appeared certain that still other Washington maps exist.

From February to October, 1932, we found fifty-three additional maps by George Washington and one annotated by him, making a total of 164 items.

Persons possessing or knowing of the whereabouts of other items of the types listed above are urged to write the Library of Congress about them.

Washington's lost maps include those referred to below: (a) In 1753 he made a map of a French fort, Fort Le Boeuf, near Lake Erie, and Governor Dinwiddie sent it to England (Sparks' "Writings of George Washington", Vol. 1, 1837, pp. 29-30; *ibid.*, Vol. 2, 1834, page 431; Ford's edition, Vol. 1, 1889, pp. 19, 30; Fitzpatrick's edition, Vol. 1, 1931, page 27). (b) In 1755 Washington sent General Braddock "a small Chart of the back Country" which he had evidently made himself (Ford, *op. cit.*, Vol. 1, 1889, page 145; Fitzpatrick, *op. cit.*, Vol. 1, page 111). (c) During the seventeen fifties he is said to have made a plan for or else to have laid out the streets of the present city of Perryopolis in southwestern Pennsylvania (Moore's "Daniel H. Burnham, Architect, Planner of Cities", Vol. 1, Boston, 1921, page 216). (d) In 1764 Washington is believed to have made a map, showing the distribution of the homes of the parishoners of Pohick Church, which was used in determining where the new church was to be built (Lossing's "Mount Vernon and its Associations", New York, 1859, page 73). (e) In 1776 he made "a rough sketch of the Country in wch. we have been Manourvreing [near New York City]", referring to it as one "which I had taken off to carry in my pocket" (Fitzpatrick, *op. cit.*, Vol. 5, 1932, page 243). (f) In 1779 Washington directed Robert Erskine, his geographer, to add certain roads in New Jersey near Morristown to his "pocket Map" (Heusser's "Forgotten General", Paterson, N. J., 1928, page 154). (g) In 1784 he copied a plan of the city of Bath, now Berkeley Springs, W. Va., to show the location of his own lots (Washington's diary, Sept. 6, 1784). (h) In 1789 he sent Thomas Jefferson a sketch of "the country between the sources of the Potomac and those navigable waters that fall into the Ohio" (Sparks, *op. cit.*, Vol. 9, 1835, page 471). (i) Between August 18, 1747, and October 25, 1752, Washington surveyed at least two hundred and fourteen tracts of land for persons other than himself; we lack knowledge of the whereabouts of one hundred and twenty-seven of the plats of these surveys. (j) Items 8a, 12, 38, 68, 74, 75, 83, 83a, 84, 93, and 108 in the foregoing list represent maps made or annotated by Washington; we know what these eleven maps looked like, but the locations of the originals are not known.

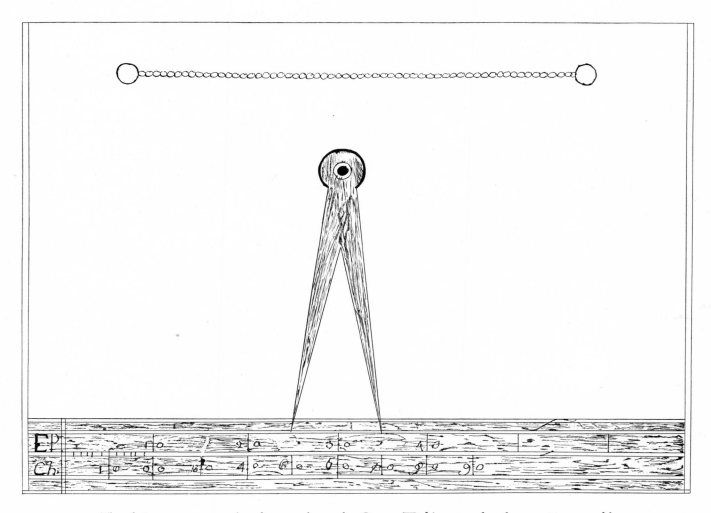

The chain, compasses and scale were drawn by George Washington when he was 14 years old

INDEX OF THE GEORGE WASHINGTON ATLAS

Numbers refer to plates

INDEX OF THE GEORGE WASHINGTON ATLAS (Continued)

INDEX OF THE GEORGE WASHINGTON ATLAS (Continued)

INDEX OF THE GEORGE WASHINGTON ATLAS (Continued)

INDEX OF THE GEORGE WASHINGTON ATLAS (Continued)

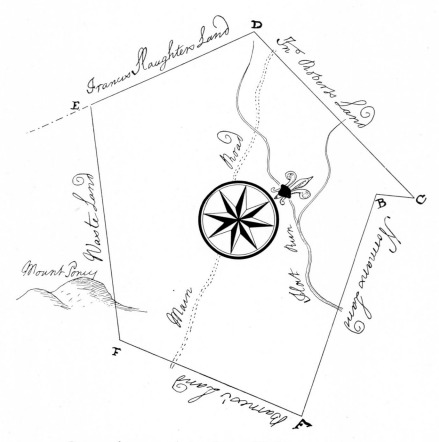

Decorated map made by George Washington in 1749

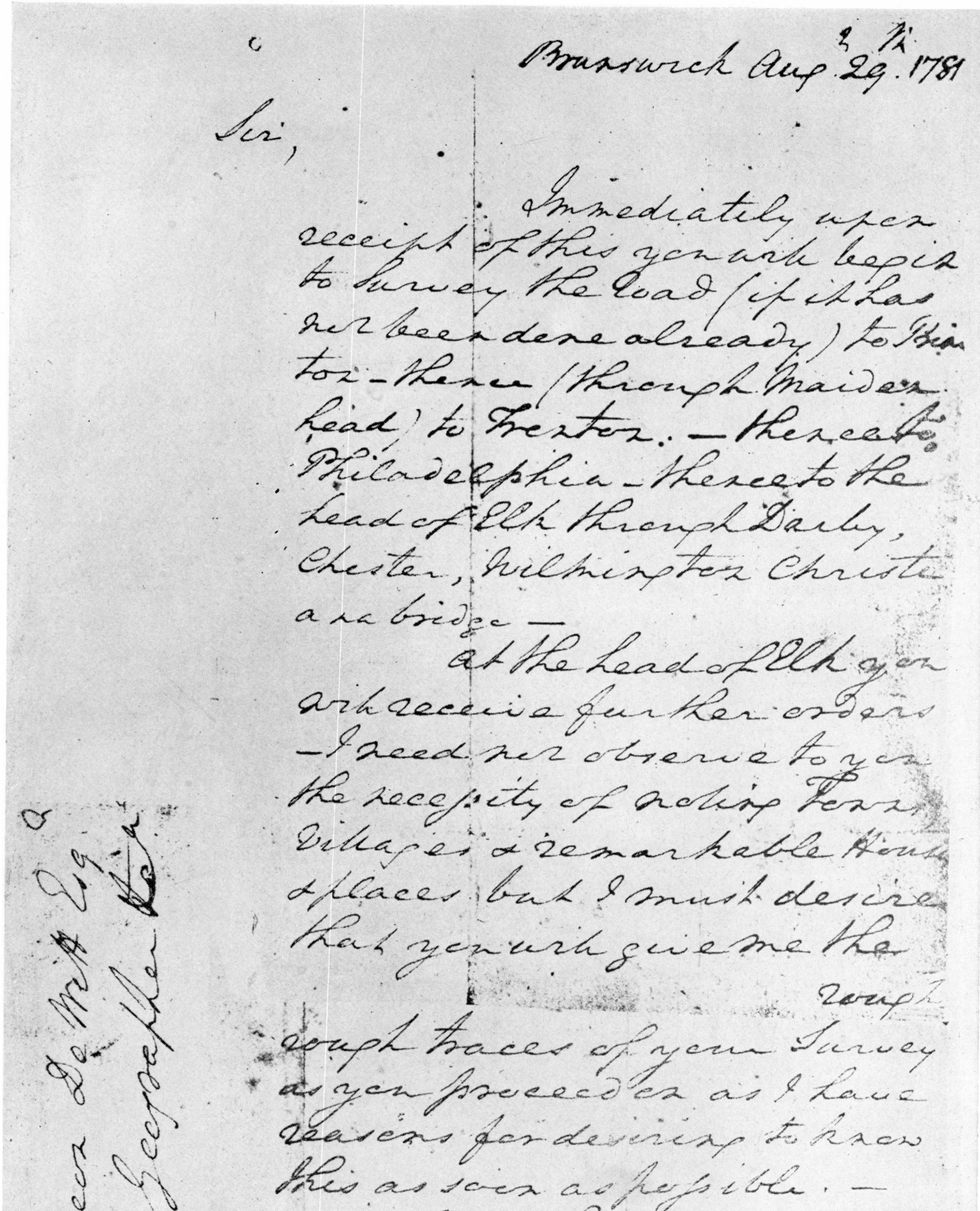

Brunswick Aug. 29. 1781

Sir,

Immediately upon
receipt of this you will begin
to survey the road (if it has
not been done already) to Prin-
ton – thence (through Maiden
head) to Trenton. – thence to
Philadelphia – thence to the
head of Elk through Darby,
Chester, Wilmington Christen
a na bridge –

At the head of Elk you
will receive further orders
– I need not observe to you
the necessity of noting Towns,
Villages & remarkable Houses
& places but I must desire
that you will give me the
rough
rough traces of your Survey
as you proceed on as I have
reasons for desiring to know
this as soon as possible. –
I am Sir
Yr. very Hble Servt.
G. Washington.

Simeon De Witt Esq.
Geographer &c.

George Washington's letter to one of his geographers, Simeon De Witt, written August 29, 1781,
in connection with the making of maps for the march to Yorktown.

Portrait of the Washington family at Mount Vernon, with the L'Enfant Plan of Washington, D. C. upon the table.
Painted by Edward Savage between 1789 and 1796.

HIGHLIGHTS

OF THE

WRITINGS

OF

GENERAL GEORGE WASHINGTON

Compiled by

DAVID M. MATTESON

Assistant Historian

INTRODUCTION

D ANIEL WEBSTER, in his speech at a public dinner in Washington in 1832, at the Centennial Celebration of the birth of George Washington, said:

"A hundred years hence, other disciples of Washington will celebrate his birth, with no less of sincere admiration than we now commemorate it. When they shall meet, as we now meet, to do themselves and him that honor, so surely as they shall see the blue summits of his native mountains rise in the horizon, so surely as they shall behold the river on whose banks he lived, and on whose banks he rests, still flowing on toward the sea, so surely may they see, as we now see, the flag of the Union floating on the top of the Capitol; and then, as now, may the sun in his course visit no land more free, more happy, more lovely, than this our own country!"

That "hundred years hence" has now become history, and in its passing has verified Webster's prophesy. He did not, however, venture upon a prediction of the manner of the Bicentennial Celebration. In 1832 a day of glorification passed and all was done; no records were left except of such speeches as that by Webster. In 1932 a greater permanence was sought, and an earnest endeavor made to make the career and character of Washington alive to all the people of the country. No other great man of history shows forth so spotless in the glare of complete investigation. No other world character has left a self-record so vivid, so revealing of the man himself. To select from this record examples which stand out as best illustrating Washington's character and his expression of it is not easy. Certain of his papers must always be in such a compilation; others here show his dauntless spirit, his modesty, his courtesy and consideration, his determined stand for Americanism and a republican form of government, and his firmness for what he considered good policy, however unpopular. All show his greatness. Throughout these volumes of historical material will be found many more of his utterances, some on special topics, others extracts covering a wider range. In *George Washington Every Day,* in another volume of the series, events and sayings that cover the whole life of George Washington are shown in calendar arrangement, with a topical index.

Letter of George Washington to His Mother after Braddock's Defeat

FORT CUMBERLAND, JULY 18, 1755.

Honour'd Mad'm,

As I doubt not but you have heard of our defeat, and perhaps have had it represented in a worse light (if possible) than it deserves; I have taken this earliest oppertunity to give you some acct. of the Engagement, as it happen'd within 7 miles of the French Fort, on Wednesday the 9th. Inst.

We March'd on to that place with't any considerable loss, having only now and then a stragler pick'd up by the French Scoutg. Ind'nd. When we came there, we were attack'd by a Body of French and Indns. whose number, (I am certain) did not exceed 300 Men; our's consisted of abt. 1,300 well arm'd Troops; chiefly of the English Soldiers, who were struck with such a panick, that they behav'd with more cowardice than it is possible to conceive; The Officers behav'd Gallantly in order to encourage their Men, for which they suffer'd greatly; there being near 60 kill'd and wounded; a large proportion out of the number we had! The Virginia Troops shew'd a good deal of Bravery, and were near all kill'd; for I believe out of 3 Companys that were there, there is scarce 30 Men left alive; Capt. Peyrouny and all his Officer's down to a Corporal was kill'd; Capt. Polson shar'd near as hard a Fate; for only one of his was left: In short the dastardly behaviour of those they call regular's expos'd all others that were inclin'd to do their duty to almost certain death; and at last, in dispight of all the efforts of the Officer's to the Contrary, they broke and run as sheep pursued by dogs; and it was impossible to rally them.

The Genl. was wounded; of w'ch he died 3 Days after; Sir Peter Halket was kill'd in the Field; where died many other brave Officer's; I luckily escap'd with't a wound, tho' I had four Bullets through my Coat, and two Horses shot under me; Capts. Orme and Morris two of the Genls. Aids de Camp, were wounded early in the Engagem't. which render'd the duty hard upon me, as I was the only person then left to distribute the Genl's. Orders which I was scarcely able to do, as I was not half recover'd from a violent illness, that confin'd me to my Bed, and a Waggon, for above 10 Days; I am still in a weak and Feeble cond'n; which induces me to halt here, 2 or 3 Days in hopes of recov'g. a little Strength, to enable me to proceed homewards; from whence, I fear I shall not be able to stir till towards Sept., so that I shall not have the pleasure of seeing you till then, unless it be in Fairfax; please to give my love to Mr. Lewis and my Sister, and Compts. to Mr. Jackson and all other Fds. that enquire after me. I am, Hon'd Madam Yr. most dutiful Son

G. Washington

P. S. You may acqt. Priscilla Mullican that her Son Charles is very well, hav'g only rec'd a slight w'd in his Foot, w'ch will be cur'd with't detrimt. to him, in a very small time.

We had abt. 300 Men kill'd and as many, and more, wounded.

Letter to Bryan Fairfax on Resistance to Great Britain

MOUNT VERNON, 20 JULY, 1774

Dear Sir,

Your letter of the 17th was not presented to me till after the resolutions, (which were adjudged advisable for this county to come to), had been revised, altered, and corrected in the committee; nor till we had gone into a general meeting in the court-house, and my attention necessarily called every moment to the business that was before it. I did, however, upon receipt of it, (in that hurry and bustle,) hastily run it over, and handed it round to the gentlemen on the bench of which there were many; but, as no person present seemed in the least disposed to adopt your sentiments, as there appeared a perfect satisfaction and acquiescence in the measures proposed (except from a Mr. Williamson, who was for adopting your advice literally, without obtaining a second voice on his side), and as the gentlemen, to whom the letter was shown, advised me not to have it read, as it was not like to make a convert, and repugnant, (some of them thought,) to the very principle we were contending for, I forbore to offer it otherwise than in the manner above mentioned; which I shall be sorry for, if it gives you any dissatisfaction in not having your sentiments read to the county at large, instead of communicating them to the first people in it, by offering them the letter in the manner I did.

That I differ very widely from you, in respect to the mode of obtaining a defeat [repeal] of the acts so much and so justly complained of, I shall not hesitate to acknowledge; and that this difference in opinion may probably proceed from the different construction we put upon the conduct and intention of the ministry may also be true; but, as I see nothing on the one hand, to induce a belief that the Parliament would embrace a favorable opportunity of repealing acts, which they go on with great rapidity to pass, and in order to enforce their tyrannical system; and, on the other, I observe, or think I observe, that government is pursuing a regular plan at the expense of law and justice to overthrow our constitutional rights and liberties, how can I expect any redress from a measure, which has been ineffectually tried already? For, Sir, what is it we are contending against? Is it against paying the duty of three pence per pound on tea because burthensome? No, it is the right only, we have all along disputed, and to this end we have already petitioned his Majesty in as humble and dutiful manner as subjects could do. Nay, more, we applied to the House of Lords and House of Commons in their different legislative capacities, setting forth, that, as Englishmen, we could not be deprived of this essential and valuable part of a constitution. If, then, as the fact really is, it is against the right of taxation that we now do, and, (as I before said), all along have contended, why should they suppose an exertion of this power would be less obnoxious now than formerly? And what reasons have we to believe, that they would make a second attempt, while the same sentiments filled the breast of every American, if they did not intend to enforce it if possible?

The conduct of the Boston people could not justify the rigor of their measures, unless there had been a requisition of payment and refusal of it; nor did that measure require an act to deprive the government of Massachusetts Bay of their charter, or to exempt offenders from trial in the place where offences were committed, as there was not, nor could not be, a single instance produced to manifest the necessity of it. Are not all these things self evident proofs of a fixed and uniform plan to tax us? If we want further proofs, do not all the debates in the House of Commons serve to confirm this? And has not General Gage's

conduct since his arrival, (in stopping the address of his Council, and publishing a proclamation more becoming a Turkish bashaw, than an English governor, declaring it treason to associate in any manner by which the commerce of Great Britain is to be affected,) exhibited an unexampled testimony of the most despotic system of tyranny, that ever was practised in a free government? In short, what further proofs are wanted to satisfy one of the designs of the ministry, than their own acts, which are uniform and plainly tending to the same point, nay, if I mistake not, avowedly to fix the right of taxation? What hope then from petitioning, when they tell us, that now or never is the time to fix the matter? Shall we, after this, whine and cry for relief, when we have already tried it in vain? Or shall we supinely sit and see one province after another fall a prey to despotism? If I was in any doubt, as to the right which the Parliament of Great Britain had to tax us without our consent, I should most heartily coincide with you in opinion, that to petition, and petition only, is the proper method to apply for relief; because we should then be asking a favor, and not claiming a right, which, by the law of nature and our constitution, we are, in my opinion, indubitably entitled to. I should even think it criminal to go further than this, under such an idea; but none such I have. I think the Parliament of Great Britain hath no more right to put their hands into my pocket, without my consent, than I have to put my hands into yours for money; and this being already urged to them in a firm, but decent manner, by all the colonies, what reason is there to expect any thing from their justice?

As to the resolution for addressing the throne, I own to you, Sir, I think the whole might as well have been expunged. I ex-

pect nothing from the measure, nor should my voice have accompanied it, if the non-importation scheme was intended to be retarded by it; for I am convinced, as much as I am of my existence, that there is no relief but in their distress; and I think, at least I hope, that there is public virtue enough left among us to deny ourselves every thing but the bare necessaries of life to accomplish this end. This we have a right to do, and no power upon earth can compel us to do otherwise, till they have first reduced us to the most abject state of slavery that ever was designed for mankind. The stopping our exports would, no doubt, be a shorter cut than the other to effect this purpose; but if we owe money to Great Britain, nothing but the last necessity can justify the non-payment of it; and, therefore, I have great doubts upon this head, and wish to see the other method first tried, which is legal and will facilitate these payments.

I cannot conclude without expressing some concern, that I should differ so widely in sentiment from you, in a matter of such great moment and general import; and should much distrust my own judgment upon the occasion, if my nature did not recoil at the thought of submitting to measures, which I think subversive of every thing that I ought to hold dear and valuable, and did I not find, at the same time, that the voice of mankind is with me.

I must apologize for sending you so rough a sketch of my thoughts upon your letter. When I looked back, and saw the length of my own, I could not, as I am also a good deal hurried at this time, bear the thoughts of making off a fair copy. I am, &c.

G Washington

Acceptance of Appointment as Commander in Chief

IN CONGRESS AT PHILADELPHIA, 16 JUNE, 1775.

Mr. President,

Though I am truly sensible of the high honor done me in this appointment, yet I feel great distress from a consciousness that my abilities and military experience may not be equal to the extensive and important trust. However, as the Congress desire it, I will enter upon the momentous duty and exert every power I possess in the service

and for support of the glorious cause. I beg they will accept my most cordial thanks for this distinguished testimony of their approbation. But lest some unlucky event should happen unfavourable to my reputation, I beg it may be remembered by every gentleman in the room, that I this day declare with the utmost sincerity I do not think myself equal to the command I am honored with.

As to pay, Sir, I beg leave to assure the Congress, that as no pecuniary consideration could have tempted me to accept this arduous employment at the expense of my domestic ease and happiness, I do not wish to make any profit from it. I will keep an exact account of my expenses. Those I doubt not they will discharge, and that is all I desire.

Address to the New York Provincial Congress
on Civil and Military Power

NEW YORK, 26 JUNE, 1775.

Gentlemen,

At the same time that with you I deplore the unhappy necessity of such an appointment, as that with which I am now honored, I cannot but feel sentiments of the highest gratitude for this affecting instance of distinction and regard.

May your warmest wishes be realized in the success of America, at this important and interesting period; and be assured, that every exertion of my worthy colleagues and myself will be equally extended to the re-establishment of peace and harmony between the mother country and these colonies, as to the fatal but necessary operations of war. When we assumed the soldier, we did not lay aside the citizen; and we shall most sincerely rejoice with you in that happy hour, when the establishment of American liberty, on the most firm and solid foundations, shall enable us to return to our private stations in the bosom of a free, peaceful, and happy country. I am, &c.

G. Washington

Letter to Lieutenant-General Gage
on Rebellion

HEADQUARTERS, CAMBRIDGE, 20 AUGUST, 1775.

Sir,

I addressed you, on the 11th instant, in terms which gave the fairest scope for that humanity and politeness, which were supposed to form a part of your character. I remonstrated with you on the unworthy treatment shown to the officers and citizens of America, whom the fortune of war, chance, or a mistaken confidence had thrown into your hands.

Whether British or American mercy, fortitude, and patience are most pre-eminent; whether our virtuous citizens, whom the hand of tyranny has forced into arms to defend their wives, their children, and their property, or the mercenary instruments of lawless domination, avarice, and revenge, best deserve the appellation of rebels, and the punishment of that cord, which your affected clemency has forborne to inflict; whether the authority under which I act is usurped, or founded upon the genuine principles of liberty, were altogether foreign to the subject. I purposely avoided all political disquisition; nor shall I now avail myself of those advantages, which the sacred cause of my country, of liberty, and of human nature, give me over you; much less shall I stoop to retort and invective; but the intelligence you say you have received from our army requires a reply. I have taken time, Sir, to make a strict inquiry, and find it has not the least foundation in truth. Not only your officers and soldiers have been treated with a tenderness due to fellow citizens and brethren, but even those execrable parricides, whose counsels and aid have deluged their country with blood, have been protected from the fury of a justly enraged people. Far from compelling or permitting their assistance, I am embarrassed with the numbers, who crowd to our camp, animated with the purest principles of virtue and love to their country. You advise me to give free operation to truth, to punish misrepresentation and falsehood. If experience stamps value upon counsel, yours must have a weight, which few can claim. You best can tell how far the convulsion, which has brought such ruin on both countries, and shaken the mighty empire of Britain to its foundation, may be traced to these malignant causes.

You affect, Sir, to despise all rank not derived from the same source with your own. I cannot conceive one more honorable, than that which flows from the uncorrupted choice of a brave and free people, the purest source and original fountain of all power. Far from making it a plea for cruelty, a mind of true magnanimity and enlarged ideas would comprehend and respect it.

What may have been the ministerial views, which have precipitated the present crisis, Lexington, Concord, and Charlestown can best declare. May that God, to whom you then appealed, judge between America and you. Under his providence, those who influence the councils of America, and all the other inhabitants of the United Colonies, at the hazard of their lives, are determined to hand down to posterity those just and invaluable privileges, which they received from their ancestors.

I shall now, Sir, close my correspondence with you, perhaps for ever. If your officers, our prisoners, receive a treatment from me different from that, which I wished to show them, they and you will remember the occasion of it. I am, Sir, your very humble servant.

G. Washington

General Orders before the Battle of Long Island

HEAD-QUARTERS, NEW YORK, AUGUST 23, 1776.

Parole Charleston—Countersign Lee

* * * * * * *

The Enemy have now landed on Long Island, and the hour is fast approaching, on which the Honor and Success of this army, and the safety of our bleeding Country depend. Remember officers and Soldiers, that you are Freemen, fighting for the blessings of Liberty—that slavery will be your portion, and that of your posterity, if you do not acquit yourselves like men: Remember how your Courage and Spirit have been dis-

pised, and traduced by your cruel invaders; though they have found by dear experience at Boston, Charlestown and other places, what a few brave men contending in their own land, and in the best of causes can do, against base hirelings and mercenaries—Be cool, but determined; do not fire at a distance, but wait for orders from your officers—It is the Generals express orders that if any man attempt to skulk, lay down, or retreat without Orders he be instantly shot down as an example, he hopes no such Scoundrel will be found in this army; but

on the contrary, every one for himself resolving to conquer, or die, and trusting to the smiles of heaven upon so just a cause, will behave with Bravery and Resolution: Those who are distinguished for their Gallantry, and good Conduct, may depend upon being honorably noticed, and suitably rewarded: And if this Army will but emulate, and imitate their brave Countrymen, in other parts of America, he has no doubt they will, by a glorious Victory, save their Country, and acquire to themselves immortal Honor.

Letter to the President of Congress
on Dependence on Militia

CAMP, ABOVE TRENTON FALLS, 20 DECEMBER, 1776.

Sir,

* * * * * * *

In short, the present exigency of our affairs will not admit of delay, either in council or the field; for well convinced I am, that, if the enemy go into quarters at all, it will be for a short season. But I rather think the design of General Howe is to possess himself of Philadelphia this winter, if possible; and in truth I do not see what is to prevent him, as ten days more will put an end to the existence of our army. That one great point is to keep us as much harassed as possible, with a view to injure the recruiting service and hinder a collection of stores and other necessaries for the next campaign, I am as clear in, as I am of my existence. If, therefore, we have to provide in the short interval and make these great and arduous preparations, every matter that in its nature is self-evident is to be referred to Congress, at the distance of a hundred and thirty or forty miles, so much time must necessary elapse, as to defeat the end in view.

In may be said, that this is an application for powers that are too dangerous to be entrusted. I can only add, that desperate diseases require desperate remedies; and I with truth declare, that I have no lust after power, but I wish with as much fervency as any man upon this wide-extended continent for an opportunity of turning the sword into the ploughshare. But my feelings, as an

officer and a man, have been such as to force me to say, that no person ever had a greater choice of difficulties to contend with than I have. It is needless to add, that short enlistments, and a mistaken dependence upon militia, have been the origin of all our misfortunes, and the great accumulation of our debt. We find, Sir, that the enemy are daily gathering strength from the disaffected. This strength, like a snow-ball by rolling, will increase, unless some means can be devised to check effectually the progress of the enemy's arms. Militia may possibly do it for a little while; but in a little while, also, and the militia of those States, which have been frequently called upon, will not turn out at all; or, if they do, it will be with so much reluctance and sloth, as to amount to the same thing. Instance New Jersey! Witness Pennsylvania! Could any thing but the river Delaware have saved Philadelphia? Can any thing (the exigency of the case indeed may justify it) be more destructive to the recruiting service, than giving ten dollars' bounty for six weeks' service of the militia, who come in, you cannot tell how, go, you cannot tell when, and act, you cannot tell where, consume your provisions, exhaust your stores, and leave you at last at a critical moment?

These, Sir, are the men I am to depend upon, ten days hence; this is the basis, on which your cause will and must for ever depend, till you get a large standing army sufficient of itself to oppose the enemy. I

therefore beg leave to give it as my humble opinion, that eighty-eight battalions are by no means equal to the opposition you are to make, and that a moment's time is not to be lost in raising a greater number, not less, in my opinion and the opinion of my officers, than a hundred and ten. It may be urged that it will be found difficult enough to complete the first number. This may be true, and yet the officers of a hundred and ten battalions will recruit many more men, than those of eighty-eight. In my judgment this is not a time to stand upon expense; our funds are not the only object of consideration. The State of New York have added one battalion (I wish they had made it two) to their quota. If any good officers will offer to raise men upon Continental pay and establishment in this quarter, I shall encourage them to do so, and regiment them when they have done it. If Congress disapprove of this proceeding, they will please to signify it, as I mean it for the best. It may be thought that I am going a good deal out of the line of my duty, to adopt these measures, or to advise thus freely. A character to lose, an estate to forfeit, the inestimable blessing of liberty at stake, and a life devoted, must be my excuse. . . .

I have the Honor to be with great respect Sir Your Most Obedt. Servt.

G Washington

Letter to the President of Congress
on Army Conditions

VALLEY FORGE, 23 DECEMBER, 1777.

Sir,

Full as I was in my representation of the matters in the commissary's department yesterday, fresh and more powerful reasons oblige me to add, that I am now convinced beyond a doubt, that, unless some great and capital change suddenly takes in that line, this army must inevitably be reduced to one or other of these three things; starve, dissolve, or disperse in order to obtain subsistence in the best manner they can. Rest assured, Sir, this is not an exaggerated picture, and that I have abundant reason to suppose what I say.

Yesterday afternoon, receiving information that the enemy in force had left the city, and were advancing towards Derby with the apparent design to forage, and draw subsistence from that part of the country, I ordered the troops to be in readiness, that I might give every opposition in my power; when behold, to my great mortification, I was not only informed, but convinced, that the men were unable to stir on account of provision, and that a dangerous mutiny, begun the night before, and which with difficulty was suppressed by the spirited exertions of some officers, was still much to be apprehended for want of this article. This brought forth the only commissary in the purchasing line in this camp; and, with him, this melancholy and alarming truth, that he had not a single hoof of any kind to slaughter, and not more than twenty-five barrels of flour! From hence form an opinion of our situation when I add, that he could not tell when to expect any.

All I could do under these circumstances, was to send out a few light parties to watch and harass the enemy, whilst other parties were instantly detached different ways to collect, if possible, as much provision as would satisfy the present pressing wants of the soldiery. But will this answer? No, Sir; three or four days of bad weather would prove our destruction. What then is to become of the army this winter? And if we are so often without provisions now, what is to become of us in the spring, when our force will be collected, with the aid perhaps of militia to take advantage of an early campaign, before the enemy can be reinforced? These are considerations of great magnitude, meriting the closest attention; and they will, when my own reputation is so intimately connected with the event and to be affected by it, justify my

saying, that the present commissaries are by no means equal to the execution of the office, or that the disaffection of the people is past all belief. The misfortune, however, does in my opinion proceed from both causes; and, though I have been tender heretofore of giving any opinion, or lodging complaints, as the change in that department took place contrary to my judgment, and the consequences thereof were predicted; yet, finding that the inactivity of the army, whether for want of provisions, clothes, or other essentials, is charged to my account, not only by the common vulgar but by those in power, it is time to speak plain in exculpation of myself. With truth, then, I can declare, that no man in my opinion ever had his measures more impeded than I have, by every department of the army.

Since the month of July we have had no assistance from the quartermaster-general, and to want of assistance from this department the commissary-general charges great part of his deficiency. To this I am to add, that, notwithstanding it is a standing order, and often repeated, that the troops shall always have two days' provisions by them, that they might be ready at any sudden call; yet an opportunity has scarcely ever offered, of taking an advantage of the enemy, that has not been either totally obstructed, or greatly impeded, on this account. And this, the great and crying evil, is not all. The soap, vinegar, and other articles allowed by Congress, we see none of, nor have we seen them, I believe, since the battle of Brandywine. The first, indeed, we have now little occasion for; few men having more than one shirt, many only the moiety of one, and some none at all. In addition to which, as a proof of the little benefit received from a clothier-general, and as a further proof of the inability of an army, under the circumstances of this, to perform the common duties of soldiers, (besides a number of men confined to hospitals for want of shoes, and others in farmers' houses on the same account,) we have, by a field-return this day made, no less than two thousand eight hundred and ninety-eight men now in camp unfit for duty, because they are barefoot and otherwise naked. By the same return it appears, that our whole strength in Continental troops, including the eastern brigades, which have joined us since the surrender of General Burgoyne, exclusive of the Maryland troops sent to Wilmington, amounts to no more than eight

thousand two hundred in camp fit for duty; notwithstanding which, and that since the 4th instant, our numbers fit for duty, from the hardships and exposures they have undergone, particularly on account of blankets (numbers having been obliged, and still are, to sit up all night by fires, instead of taking comfortable rest in a natural and common way) have decreased near two thousand men.

We find gentlemen, without knowing whether the army was really going into winter-quarters or not (for I am sure no resolution of mine would warrant the Remonstrance), reprobating the measure as much as if they thought the soldiers were made of stocks or stones, and equally insensible of frost and snow; and moreover, as if they conceived it easily practicable for an inferior army, under the disadvantages I have described ours to be, which are by no means exaggerated, to confine a superior one, in all respects well-appointed and provided for a winter's campaign, within the city of Philadelphia, and to cover from depredation and waste the States of Pennsylvania and Jersey. But what makes this matter still more extraordinary in my eye is, that these very gentlemen,—who were well apprized of the nakedness of the troops from ocular demonstration, who thought their own soldiers worse clad than others, and who advised me near a month ago to postpone the execution of a plan I was about to adopt, in consequence of a resolve of Congress for seizing clothes, under strong assurances that an ample supply would be collected in ten days agreeably to a decree of the State (not one article of which, by the by, is yet come to hand),—should think a winter's campaign and the covering of these States from the invasion of an enemy so easy and practicable a business. I can assure those gentlemen, that it is a much easier and less distressing thing to draw remonstrances in a comfortable room by a good fireside, than to occupy a cold, bleak hill, and sleep under frost and snow, without clothes or blankets. However, although they seem to have little feeling for the naked and distressed soldiers, I feel superabundantly for them, and, from my soul, I pity those miseries, which it is neither in my power to relieve or prevent.

It is for these reasons, therefore, that I have dwelt upon the subject; and it adds not a little to my other difficulties and distress to find, that much more is expected of me than is possible to be performed, and that upon the ground of safety and policy I am obliged to conceal the true state of the army from public view, and thereby expose myself to detraction and calumny. The honorable committe of Congress went from camp fully possessed of my sentiments respecting the establishment of this army, the necessity of auditors of accounts, the appointment of officers, and new arrangements. I have no need, therefore, to be prolix upon these subjects, but I refer to the committee. I shall add a word or two to show, first, the necessity of some better provision for binding the officers by the tie of interest to the service, as no day nor scarce an hour passes without the offer of a resigned commission; (otherwise I much doubt the practicability of holding the army together much longer, and in this I shall probably be thought the more sincere, when I freely declare, that I do not myself expect to derive the smallest benefit from any establishment that Congress may adopt, otherwise than as a member of the community at large in the good, which I am persuaded will result from the measure, by making better officers and better troops;) and, secondly, to point out the necessity of making the appointments and arrangements without loss of time. We have not more than three months, in which to prepare a great deal of business. If we let these slip or waste, we shall be laboring under the same difficulties all next campaign, as we have been this, to rectify mistakes and bring things to order.

Military arrangement, and movements in consequence, like the mechanism of a clock, will be imperfect and disordered by the want of a part. In a very sensible degree have I experienced this, in the course of the last summer, several brigades having no brigadiers appointed to them till late, and some not at all; by which means it follows, that an additional weight is thrown upon the shoulders of the Commander-in-chief, to withdraw his attention from the great line of his duty. The gentlemen of the committee, when they were at camp, talked of an expedient for adjusting these matters, which I highly approved and wish to see adopted; namely, that two or three members of the Board of War, or a committee of Congress, should repair immediately to camp, where the best aid can be had, and with the commanding officer, or a committee of his appointment, prepare and digest the most perfect plan, that can be devised, for correcting all abuses and making new arrangements; considering what is to be done with the weak and debilitated regiments, if the States to which they belong will not draft men to fill them, for as to enlisting soldiers it seems to me to be totally out of the question; together with many other things, that would occur in the course of such a conference; and, after digesting matters in the best manner they can, to submit the whole to the ultimate determination of Congress.

If this measure is approved, I would earnestly advise the immediate execution of it, and that the commissary-general of purchases, whom I rarely see, may be directed to form magazines without a moment's delay in the neighbourhood of this camp, in order to secure provision for us in case of bad weather. The quartermaster-general ought also to be busy in his department. In short, there is as much to be done in preparing for a campaign, as in the active part of it. Every thing depends upon the preparation that is made in the several departments, and the success or misfortunes of the next campaign will more than probably originate with our activity or supineness during this winter. I have the honor to be, &c.

G Washington

Letter of Courtesy to Lieutenant-General Burgoyne

HEAD-QUARTERS, 11 MARCH, 1778.

Sir,

I was only two days since honored with your very obliging letter of the 11th of February. Your indulgent opinion of my character, and the polite terms in which you are pleased to express it, are peculiarly flattering; and I take pleasure in the opportunity you have afforded me, of assuring you, that, far from suffering the views of national opposition to be embittered and debased by personal animosity, I am ever ready to do justice to the merit of the man and soldier, and to esteem where esteem is due, however the idea of a public enemy may interpose. You will not think it the language of unmeaning ceremony, if I add, that sentiments of personal respect, in the present instance, are reciprocal.

Viewing you in the light of an officer, contending against what I conceive to be the rights of my country, the reverses of fortune you experienced in the field cannot be unacceptable to me; but, abstracted from considerations of national advantage, I can sincerely sympathize with your feelings as a soldier, the unavoidable difficulties of whose situation forbid his success; and as a man, whose lot combines the calamity of ill health, the anxieties of captivity, and the painful sensibility for a reputation exposed, where he most values it, to the assaults of malice and detraction.

As your aid-de-camp went directly to Congress, the business of your letter to me had been decided before it came to hand. I am happy that their cheerful acquiescence with your request prevented the necessity of my intervention; and wishing you a safe and agreeable passage, with a perfect restoration of your health, I have the honor to be, very respectfully, &c.

G Washington

Letter to Major-General Sullivan
on Criticism of French Allies

HEAD-QRS., WHITE PLAINS, 1st SEPT., 1778.

Dear Sir,

I have not received any letter from you since the 23d Ulto., which I attribute to some mishap of the messengers with whom they were sent. I was anxious to learn the determination and designs of the Council of Officers, that so I might be prepared for eventual measures.—the success or misfortune of your army will have great influence in directing the movement and fortune of this.

The disagreement between the army under your command and the fleet has given me very singular uneasiness. The Continent at large is concerned in our cordiality, and it should be kept up by all possible means, consistent with our honor and policy. First impressions you know are generally longest remembered, and will serve to fix in a great degree our national character among the french. In our conduct towards them we should remember, that they are a people old in war, very strict in military etiquette, and apt to take fire, where others scarcely seem warmed. Permit me to recommend, in the most particular manner, the cultivation of harmony and good agreement, and your endeavors to destroy that ill humor, which may have got into the officers. It is of the greatest importance also, that the minds of the soldiers and the people should know nothing of the misunderstanding, or, if it has reached them, that ways may be used to stop its progress and prevent its effects.

I have received from Congress the enclosed, by which you will perceive their opinions with regard to keeping secret the protest of the general officers. I need add nothing on this head. I have one thing however more to say. I make no doubt but you will do all in your power to forward the repair of the Count's fleet, and rendering it fit for service, by your recommendations for that purpose to those, who can be immediately instrumental. I am, dear Sir, &c.

G Washington

Letter to Count d'Estaing
on Rhode Island Affair

HEAD-QUARTERS, 11TH SEPTEM., 1778.

Sir,

I have had the honor of receiving your Letter of the 5th inst., accompanied by a Copy of two Letters to Congress and Genl. Sullivan. The confidence, which you have been pleased to show in communicating these papers, engages my sincere thanks. If the deepest regret, that the best concerted enterprise and bravest exertions should have been rendered fruitless by a disaster, which human prudence is incapable of foreseeing or preventing, can alleviate disappointment, you may be assured, that the whole Continent sympathizes with you. It will be a consolation to you to reflect, that the thinking part of mankind do not form their judgment from events; and that their equity will ever attach equal glory to those actions, which deserve success, as to those which have been crowned with it. It is in the trying circumstances to which Your Excellency has been exposed, that the virtues of a great mind are displayed in their brightest lustre, and that the General's Character is better known, than in the moment of Victory. It was yours, by every title which can give it; and the adverse element, which robbed you of your prize, can never deprive you of the Glory due to you. Tho' your success has not been equal to your expectations, yet you have the satisfaction of reflecting, that you have rendered essential services to the common cause.

I exceedingly lament, that, in addition to our misfortunes, there has been the least suspension of harmony and good understanding between the generals of allied nations, whose views must, like their interests, be the same. On the first intimation of it, I employed my influence in restoring what I regard as essential to the permanence of an Union founded on mutual inclination, and the strongest ties of reciprocal advantage. Your Excellency's offer to the Council of Boston had a powerful tendency to promote the same end, and was a distinguished proof of your zeal and magnanimity. . . .

I have, &c.

G Washington

Letter to Henry Laurens
on French Allies and Canada

FRED[ERICKSBUR]G, [N. Y.,] 14TH NOVR., 1778.

Dr. Sir,

This will be accompanied by an official letter on the subject of the proposed expedition against Canada. You will perceive I have only considered it in a military light; indeed I was not authorized to consider it in any other; and I am not without apprehensions, that I may be thought, in what I have done, to have exceeded the limits intended by Congress. But my solicitude for the public welfare, which I think deeply interested in this affair, will, I hope, justify me in the eyes of all those, who view things through that just medium. I do not know, Sir, what may be your sentiments in the present case; but, whatever they are, I am sure I can confide in your honor and friendship, and shall not hesitate to unbosom myself to you on a point of the most delicate and important nature.

The question of the Canadian expedition, in the form it now stands, appears to me one of the most interesting that has hitherto agitated our national deliberations. I have one objection to it, untouched in my public letter, which is, in my estimation, insurmountable, and alarms all my feelings for the true and permanent interests of my country. This is the introduction of a large body of French troops into Canada, and putting them in possession of the capital of that Province, attached to them by all the ties of blood, habits, manners, religion, and former connexion of government. I fear this would be too great a temptation to be resisted by any power actuated by the common maxims of national policy. Let us realize for a moment the striking advantages France would derive from the possession of Canada; the acquisition of an extensive territory, abounding in supplies for the use of her Islands; the opening a vast source of the most beneficial commerce with the Indian nations, which she might then monopolize; the having ports of her own on this continent independent of the precarious good will of an ally; the engrossing of the whole trade of Newfoundland whenever she pleased, the finest nursery of seamen in the world; the security afforded to her Islands; and, finally, the facility of awing and controlling these States, the natural and most

formidable rival of every maritime power in Europe. Canada would be a solid acquisition to France on all these accounts, and because of the numerous inhabitants, subjects to her by inclination, who would aid in preserving it under her power against the attempt of every other.

France, acknowledged for some time past the most powerful monarchy in Europe by land, able now to dispute the empire of the sea with Britain, and if joined with Spain, I may say, certainly superior, possessed of New Orleans on our right, Canada on our left, and seconded by the numerous tribes of indians in our rear from one extremity to the other, a people so generally friendly to her, and whom she knows so well to conciliate, would, it is much to be apprehended, have it in her power to give law to these States.

Let us suppose, that, when the five thousant french troops (and under the idea of that number twice as many might be introduced) were entered the city of Quebec, they should declare an intention to hold Canada, as a pledge and surety for the debts due to France from the United States, or, under other specious pretences, hold the place till they can find a bone of contention, and, in the mean while, should excite the Canadians to engage in supporting their pretences & claims; what should we be able to say, with only four or five thousand men to carry on the dispute? It may be supposed, that France would not choose to renounce our friendship by a step of this kind, as the consequence would be a reunion with England on some terms or other, and the loss of what she had acquired in so violent and unjustifiable a manner, with all the advantages of an alliance with us. This, in my opinion, is too slender a security against the measure, to be relied on. The truth of the position will entirely depend on naval events. If France and Spain should unite, and obtain a decided superiority by Sea, a reunion with England would avail very little, and might be set at defiance. France, with a numerous army at command, might throw in what number of land forces she thought proper, to support her pretensions; and England, without men, without money, and inferior on her favorite element, could give no effectual aid

to oppose them. Resentment, reproaches, and submission seem to be all that would be left to us. Men are very apt to run into extremes. Hatred to England may carry some into an excess of Confidence in France, especially when motives of gratitude are thrown into the scale. Men of this description would be unwilling to suppose France capable of acting so ungenerous a part. I am heartily disposed to entertain the most favorable sentiments of our new ally, and to cherish them in others to a reasonable degree. But it is maxim, founded on the universal experience of mankind, that no nation is to be trusted farther than it is bound by its interest; and no prudent statesman or politician will venture to depart from it. In our circumstances we ought to be particularly cautious; for we have not yet attained sufficient vigor and maturity to recover from the shock of any false step, into which we may unwarily fall.

If France should even engage in the scheme, in the first instance, with the purest intentions, there is the greatest danger that, in the progress of the business, invited to it by circumstances, and perhaps urged on by the solicitations and wishes of the Canadians, she would alter her views.

As the Marquis clothed his proposition, when he spoke it to me, it would seem to originate wholly with himself; but, it is far from impossible, that it had its birth in the Cabinet of France, and was put into this artful dress to give it the readier currency. I fancy that I read in the countenances of some people, on this occasion, more than the disinterested zeal of allies. I hope I am mistaken, and that my fears of mischief make me refine too much, and awaken jealousies that have no sufficient foundation. But upon the whole, Sir, to wave every other consideration, I do not like to add to the number of our national obligations. I would wish, as much as possible, to avoid giving a foreign power new claims of merit for services performed to the United States, and would ask no assistance that is not indispensable. I am, with the truest attachment and most perfect confidence, dear Sir, &c.

GWashington

Letter to Count de Rochambeau
welcoming Him to America

HEAD-QUARTERS, NEW JERSEY, 16 JULY, 1780.

Sir,

I hasten to impart to you the happiness I feel at the welcome news of your arrival; and, as well in the name of the American army, as in my own, to present you with an assurance of our warmest sentiments for allies, who have so generously come to our aid. As a citizen of the United States, and as a soldier in the cause of liberty, I thankfully acknowledge this new mark of friendship from his Most Christian Majesty, and I feel a most grateful sensibility for the flattering confidence he has been pleased to honor me with on this occasion.

Among the obligations we are under to your Prince, I esteem it one of the first, that he has made choice, for the command of his troops, of a Gentleman whose high reputation and happy union of social qualities and military abilities promise me every public advantage and private satisfaction. I beg, Sir, that you will be the interpreter of my sentiments to the Gentlemen under your command. Be pleased to assure them, that, to the pleasure I anticipate of an acquaintance with them, I join the warmest desire to do every thing that may be agreeable to them and to the soldiers under their command. But in the midst of a war, the nature and difficulties of which are peculiar and uncommon, I cannot flatter myself in any way to recompense the sacrifices they have made, but by giving them such opportunities in the field of glory, as will enable them to display that gallantry and those talents, which we shall be always happy to acknowledge with applause.

The Marquis de Lafayette has been by me desired from time to time to communicate such intelligence, and make such propositions, as circumstances dictated. I think it so important, immediately to fix our plan of operations, and with as much secrecy as possible, that I have requested him to go himself to New London, where he will probably meet you. As a General officer, I have the greatest confidence in him; as a friend, he is perfectly acquainted with my sentiments and opinions. He knows all the circumstances of our army and the country at large. All the information he gives, and all the propositions he makes, I entreat you will consider as coming from me. I request you will settle all arrangements whatsoever with him; and I shall only add, that I shall exactly conform to the intentions of his Most Christian Majesty, as explained in the several papers put into my hands by his order, and signed by his ministers.

Permit me to refer you to the Marquis de Lafayette for more particular assurances of what I feel on this occasion, which I the more readily do, from a knowledge of his peculiar affection and regard for you. Impatiently waiting for the time when our operations will afford me the pleasure of a personal acquaintance with you, I have the honor to be, with the most perfect consideration, &c.

G. Washington

Letter to Lord Cornwallis
giving Terms of Surrender

HEAD QUARTERS, BEFORE YORK, 18 OCTOBER, 1781.

My Lord,

To avoid unnecessary discussion and delays I shall at once, in answer to your Lordships letters of yesterday, declare the general basis upon which a definitive treaty and capitulation must take place. The garrisons of York and Gloucester, including the seamen, as you propose, will be received Prisoners of War. The condition annexed, of sending the British and German troops to the parts of Europe to which they respectively belong, is inadmissible. Instead of this they will be marched to such parts of the Country as can most conveniently provide for their subsistence, and the benevolent treatment of Prisoners, which is invariably observed by the Americans, will be extended to them. The same honors will be granted to the surrendering Army as were granted to the Garrison of Charlestown. The shipping and boats in the two harbors, with all their Guns, Stores, Tackling, furniture and apparel, shall be delivered in their present state to an officer of the Navy, appointed to take possession of them.

The Artillery, Arms, Accoutrements, Military Chest, and public stores of every denomination, shall be delivered, unimpaired to the heads of departments to which they respectively belong.

The officers will be indulged in retaining their side arms, and the officers and soldiers may preserve their baggage and effects, with this reserve, that property taken in the Country will be reclaimed.

With regard to the individuals in civil capacities whose interests, your Lordship wishes may be attended to; until they are more particularly described, nothing definitive can be settled.

I have to add that I expect the sick and wounded will be supplied with their own Hospital Stores, and be attended by British Surgeons, particularly charged with the care of them.

Your Lordship will be pleased to signify your determination either to accept or reject the proposals now offered in the course of two hours from the delivery of this letter that Commissioners may be appointed to digest the articles of capitulation, or a renewal of hostilities may take place. I have the honor, &c.

G. Washington

General Orders
on the Surrender of Yorktown
HEAD-QUARTERS, BEFORE YORK, SATURDAY OCTOBER 20TH, 1781.

Parole Congress—Countersigns York
Gloucester

*   *   *   *   *   *   *

After Orders

The General congratulates the Army upon the glorious event of yesterday

The generous proofs which his most Christian Majesty has given of his attachment to the Cause of America must force conviction on the minds of the most deceived among the Enemy: relatively to the decisive good consequences of the Alliance and inspire every citzen of these States with sentiments of the most unalterable Gratitude

His Fleet the most numerous and powerful that ever appeared in these seas commanded by an Admiral whose Fortune and Talents ensure great Events

An Army of the most admirable composition both in officers and men are the Pledges of his friendship to the United States and their co-operation has secured us the present signal success

The General upon this occasion entreats his Excellency Count de Rochambeau to accept his most grateful acknowledgements for his Counsels and assistance at all times He presents his warmest thanks to the Generals Baron Viomenil Chevalier Chastellux Marquis de S. Simond and Count Viomenil

and to Brigadier General de Choissy (who had a seperate command) for the illustrious manner in which they have advanced the interest of the common cause.

He requests that Count de Rochambeau will be pleased to communicate to the Army under his immediate command the high sense he entertains of the distinguished merits of the officers and soldiers of every corps and that he will present in his name to the regiments of Gattinois and Deuxponts the two Pieces of Brass Ordnance captured by them; as a testimony of their Gallantry in storming the Enemy's Redoubt on the Night of the 14th instant, when officers and men so universally vied with each other in the exercise of every soldierly virtue

The General's Thanks to each individual of Merit would comprehend the whole Army But he thinks himself bound however by Affection Duty and Gratitude to express his obligations to Major Generals Lincoln de La Fayette and Steuben for their dispositions in the Trenches

To General Du Portail and Colonel Carney for the Vigor and Knowledge which were conspicuous in their Conduct of the Attacks and to General Knox and Colonel D'Aberville for their great care and attention and fatigue in bringing forward the Artillery and stores and for their judicious

and spirited management of them in the Parallels.

He requests the Gentlemen abovementioned to communicate his thanks to the officers and soldiers of their respective commands

Ingratitude which the General hopes never to be guilty of would be conspicuous in him was he to omit thanking in the warmest terms His Excellency Governor Nelson for the Aid he has derived from him and from the Militia under his Command to whose Activity Emulation and Courage much Applause is due the Greatness of the Acquisition will be an ample Compensation for the Hardships and Hazards which they encountered with so much patriotism and firmness

In order to diffuse the general Joy through every Breast the General orders that those men belonging to the Army who may now be in confinement shall be pardoned, released and join their respective corps.

Divine Service is to be performed tomorrow in the several Brigades or Divisions.

The Commander in Chief earnestly recommends that the troops not on duty should universally attend with that Seriousness of Deportment and gratitude of Heart which the recognition of such reiterated and astonishing interpositions of Providence demand of us.

Letter to Colonel Lewis Nicola
refusing to be made King
NEWBURG, 22 MAY, 1782.

Sir,

With a mixture of great surprise and astonishment, I have read with attention the sentiments you have submitted to my perusal. Be assured, Sir, no occurrence in the course of the war has given me more painful sensations, than your information of there being such ideas existing in the army, as you have expressed, and I must view with abhorrence and reprehend with severity. For the present the communicatn. of them will rest in my own bosom, unless some further agitation of the matter shall make a disclosure necessary.

I am much at a loss to conceive what part of my conduct could have given encouragement to an address, which to me seems big with the greatest mischiefs, that can befall my Country. If I am not deceived in the knowledge of myself, you could not have found a person to whom your schemes are more disagreeable. At the same time, in justice to my own feelings, I must add, that no man possesses a more sincere wish to see ample justice done to the army than I do; and, as far as my powers and influence, in a constitutional way, extend, they shall be employed to the utmost of

my abilities to effect it, should there be any occasion. Let me conjure you, then, if you have any regard for your Country, concern for yourself or posterity, or respect for me, to banish these thoughts from your mind, and never communicate, as from yourself or any one else, a sentiment of the like nature. I am, Sir, your most obedient servant.

G. Washington

Circular Letter addressed to the Governors of all the States on disbanding the Army

HEAD-QUARTERS, NEWBURG, 8 JUNE, 1783.

Sir,

The great object, for which I had the honor to hold an appointment in the service of my country, being accomplished, I am now preparing to resign it into the hands of Congress, and to return to that domestic retirement, which, it is well known, I left with the greatest reluctance; a retirement for which I have never ceased to sigh, through a long and painful absence, and in which (remote from the noise and trouble of the world) I meditate to pass the remainder of life, in a state of undisturbed repose. But before I carry this resolution into effect, I think it a duty incumbent on me to make this my last official communication; to congratulate you on the glorious events which Heaven has been pleased to produce in our favor; to offer my sentiments respecting some important subjects, which appear to me to be intimately connected with the tranquillity of the United States; to take my leave of your Excellency as a public character; and to give my final blessing to that country, in whose service I have spent the prime of my life, for whose sake I have consumed so many anxious days and watchful nights, and whose happiness, being extremely dear to me, will always constitute no inconsiderable part of my own.

Impressed with the liveliest sensibility on this pleasing occasion, I will claim the indulgence of dilating the more copiously on the subjects of our mutual felicitation. When we consider the magnitude of the prize we contended for, the doubtful nature of the contest, and the favorable manner in which it has terminated, we shall find the greatest possible reason for gratitude and rejoicing. This is a theme that will afford infinite delight to every benevolent and liberal mind, whether the event in contemplation be considered as the source of present enjoyment, or the parent of future happiness; and we shall have equal occasion to felicitate ourselves on the lot which Providence has assigned us, whether we view it in a natural, a political, or moral point of light.

The citizens of America, placed in the most enviable condition, as the sole lords and proprietors of a vast tract of continent, comprehending all the various soils and climates of the world, and abounding with all the necessaries and conveniences of life, are now, by the late satisfactory pacification, acknowledged to be possessed of absolute freedom and independency. They are, from this period, to be considered as the actors on a most conspicuous theatre, which seems to be peculiarly designated by Providence for the display of human greatness and felicity. Here they are not only surrounded with every thing, which can contribute to the completion of private and domestic enjoyment; but Heaven has crowned all its other blessings, by giving a fairer opportunity for political happiness, than any other nation has ever been favored with. Nothing can illustrate these observations more forcibly, than a recollection of the happy conjuncture of times and circumstances, under which our republic assumed its rank among the nations. The foundation of our empire was not laid in the gloomy age of ignorance and superstition; but at an epocha when the rights of mankind were better understood and more clearly defined, than at any former period. The researches of the human mind after social happiness have been carried to a great extent; the treasures of knowledge, acquired by the labors of philosophers, sages, and legislators, through a long succession of years, are laid open for our use, and their collected wisdom may be happily applied in the establishment of our forms of government. The free cultivation of letters, the unbounded extension of commerce, the progressive refinement of manners, the growing liberality of sentiment, and, above all, the pure and benign light of Revelation, have had a meliorating influence on mankind and increased the blessings of society. At this auspicious period, the United States came into existence as a nation; and, if their citizens should not be completely free and happy, the fault will be entirely their own.

Such is our situation, and such are our prospects; but notwithstanding the cup of blessing is thus reached out to us; notwithstanding happiness is ours, if we have a disposition to seize the occasion and make it our own; yet it appears to me there is an option still left to the United States of America, that it is in their choice, and depends upon their conduct, whether they will be respectable and prosperous, or contemptible and miserable, as a nation. This is the time of their political probation; this is the moment when the eyes of the whole world are turned upon them; this is the moment to establish or ruin their national character for ever; this is the favorable moment to give such a tone to our federal government, as will enable it to answer the ends of its institution, or this may be the ill-fated moment for relaxing the powers of the Union, annihilating the cement of the confederation, and exposing us to become the sport of European politics, which may play one State against another, to prevent their growing importance, and to serve their own interested purposes. For, according to the system of policy the States shall adopt at this moment, they will stand or fall; and by their confirmation or lapse it is yet to be decided, whether the revolution must ultimately be considered as a blessing or a curse; a blessing or a curse, not to the present age alone, for with our fate will the destiny of unborn millions be involved.

With this conviction of the importance of the present crisis, silence in me would be a crime. I will therefore speak to your Excellency the language of freedom and of sincerity without disguise. I am aware, however, that those who differ from me in political sentiment, may perhaps remark, I am stepping out of the proper line of my duty, and may possibly ascribe to arrogance or ostentation, what I know is alone the result of the purest intention. But the rectitude of my own heart, which disdains such unworthy motives, the part I have hitherto acted in life; the determination I have formed, of not taking any share in public business hereafter; the ardent desire I feel, and shall continue to manifest, of quietly enjoying, in private life, after all the toils of war, the benefits of a wise and liberal government, will, I flatter myself, sooner or later convince my countrymen, that I could have no sinister views in delivering, with so little reserve, the opinions contained in this address.

There are four things, which, I humbly conceive, are essential to the well-being, I may even venture to say, to the existence of the United States, as an independent power.

First. An indissoluble union of the States under one federal head.

Secondly. A sacred regard to public justice.

Thirdly. The adoption of a proper peace establishment; and,

Fourthly. The prevalence of that pacific and friendly disposition among the people of the United States, which will induce them to forget their local prejudices and policies; to make those mutual concessions, which are requisite to the general prosperity;

and, in some instances, to sacrifice their individual advantages to the interest of the community.

These are the pillars on which the glorious fabric of our independency and national character must be supported. Liberty is the basis; and whoever would dare to sap the foundation, or overturn the structure, under whatever specious pretext he may attempt it, will merit the bitterest execration, and the severest punishment, which can be inflicted by his injured country.

On the three first articles I will make a few observations, leaving the last to the good sense and serious consideration of those immediately concerned.

Under the first head, although it may not be necessary or proper for me, in this place, to enter into a particular disquisition on the principles of the Union, and to take up the great question which has been frequently agitated, whether it be expedient and requisite for the States to delegate a larger proportion of power to Congress, or not; yet it will be a part of my duty, and that of every true patriot, to assert without reserve, and to insist upon, the following positions. That, unless the States will suffer Congress to exercise those prerogatives they are undoubtedly invested with by the constitution, every thing must very rapidly tend to anarchy and confusion. That it is indispensable to the happiness of the individual States, that there should be lodged somewhere a supreme power to regulate and govern the general concerns of the confederated republic, without which the Union cannot be of long duration. That there must be a faithful and pointed compliance, on the part of every State, with the late proposals and demands of Congress, or the most fatal consequences will ensue. That whatever measures have a tendency to dissolve the Union, or contribute to violate or lessen the sovereign authority, ought to be considered as hostile to the liberty and independency of America, and the authors of them treated accordingly. And lastly, that unless we can be enabled, by the concurrence of the States, to participate of the fruits of the revolution, and enjoy the essential benefits of civil society, under a form of government so free and uncorrupted, so happily guarded against the danger of oppression, as has been devised and adopted by the articles of confederation, it will be a subject of regret, that so much blood and treasure have been lavished for no purpose, that so many sufferings have been encountered without a compensation, and that so many sacrifices have been made in vain.

Many other considerations might here be adduced to prove, that, without an entire conformity to the spirit of the Union, we cannot exist as an independent power. It will be sufficient for my purpose to mention but one or two, which seem to me of the greatest importance. It is only in our united character, as an empire, that our independence is acknowledged, that our power can be regarded, or our credit supported, among foreign nations. The treaties of the European powers with the United States of America will have no validity on a dissolution of the Union. We shall be left nearly in a state of nature; or we may find, by our own unhappy experience, that there is a natural and necessary progression from the extreme of anarchy to the extreme of tyranny, and that arbitrary power is most easily established on the ruins of liberty, abused to licentiousness.

As to the second article, which respects the performance of public justice, Congress have, in their late address to the United States, almost exhausted the subject; they have explained their ideas so fully, and have enforced the obligations the States are under, to render complete justice to all the public creditors, with so much dignity and energy, that, in my opinion, no real friend to the honor of independency of America can hesitate a single moment, respecting the propriety of complying with the just and honorable measures proposed. If their arguments do not produce conviction, I know of nothing that will have greater influence: especially when we recollect, that the system referred to, being the result of the collected wisdom of the continent, must be esteemed, if not perfect, certainly the least objectionable of any that could be devised; and that, if it shall not be carried into immediate execution, a national bankruptcy, with all its deplorable consequences, will take place, before any different plan can possibly be proposed and adopted. So pressing are the present circumstances, and such is the alternative now offered to the States.

The ability of the country to discharge the debts, which have been incurred in its defence, is not to be doubted; and inclination, I flatter myself, will not be wanting. The path of our duty is plain before us; honesty will be found, on every experiment, to be the best and only true policy. Let us then, as a nation, be just; let us fulfil the public contracts, which Congress had undoubtedly a right to make for the purpose of carrying on the war, with the same good faith we suppose ourselves bound to perform our private engagements. In the mean time, let an attention to the cheerful performance of their proper business, as individuals and as members of society, be earnestly inculcated on the citizens of America; then will they strengthen the hands of government, and be happy under its protection; every one will reap the fruit of his labors, every one will enjoy his own acquisitions, without molestation and without danger.

In this state of absolute freedom and perfect security, who will grudge to yield a very little of his property to support the common interest of society, and insure the protection of government? Who does not remember the frequent declarations, at the commencement of the war, that we should be completely satisfied, if, at the expense of one half, we could defend the remainder of our possessions? Where is the man to be found, who wishes to remain indebted for the defence of his own person and property to the exertions, the bravery, and the blood of others, without making one generous effort to repay the debt of honor and gratitude? In what part of the continent shall we find any man, or body of men, who would not blush to stand up and propose measures purposely calculated to rob the soldier of his stipend, and the public creditor of his due? And were it possible, that such a flagrant instance of injustice could ever happen, would it not excite the general indignation, and tend to bring down upon the authors of such measures the aggravated vengeance of Heaven? If, after all, a spirit of disunion, or a temper of obstinacy and perverseness should manifest itself in any of the States; if such an ungracious disposition should attempt to frustrate all the happy effects that might be expected to flow from the Union; if there should be a refusal to comply with the requisition for funds to discharge the annual interest of the public debts; and if that refusal should revive all those jealousies, and produce all those evils, which are now happily removed, Congress, who have, in all their transactions, shown a great degree of magnanimity and justice, will stand justified in the sight of God and man; and the State alone, which puts itself in opposition to the aggregate wisdom of the continent, and follows such mistaken and pernicious counsels, will be responsible for all the consequences.

For my own part, conscious of having acted, while a servant of the public, in the manner I conceived best suited to promote the real interests of my country; having, in consequence of my fixed belief, in some measure pledged myself to the army, that their country would finally do them complete and ample justice; and not wishing to conceal any instance of my official conduct from the eyes of the world, I have thought proper to transmit to your Excellency the enclosed collection of papers, relative to the half-pay and commutation granted by Congress to the officers of the army. From these communications, my decided sentiments will be clearly comprehended, together with the conclusive reasons which induced me, at an early period, to recommend the adoption of this measure, in the most earnest and serious manner. As the proceedings of Congress, the army, and myself, are open to all, and contain, in my opinion, sufficient information to remove the prejudices and errors, which may have been entertained by any, I think it unnecessary to say any thing more than just to observe, that the resolutions of Congress, now alluded to, are undoubtedly as absolutely binding upon the United States, as the most solemn acts of confederation or legislation.

As to the idea, which, I am informed, has in some instances prevailed, that the half-pay and commutation are to be regarded merely in the odious light of a pension, it ought to be exploded for ever. That provision should be viewed, as it really was, a reasonable compensation offered by Congress, at a time when they had nothing else to give to the officers of the army for services then to be performed. It was the only means to prevent a total dereliction of the service. It was a part of their hire. I may be allowed to say, it was the price of their blood, and of your independency; it is therefore more than a common debt, it is a debt of honor; it can never be considered as a pension or gratuity, nor be cancelled until it is fairly discharged.

With regard to a distinction between officers and soldiers, it is sufficient that the uniform experience of every nation of the world, combined with our own, proves the utility and propriety of the discrimination. Rewards, in proportion to the aids the public derives from them, are unquestionably due to all its servants. In some lines, the soldiers have perhaps generally had as ample a compensation for their services, by the large bounties which have been paid to them, as their officers will receive in the proposed commutation; in others, if, besides the donation of lands, the payment of arrearages of clothing and wages (in which articles all the component parts of the army must be put upon the same footing), we take into the estimate the douceurs many of the soldiers have received, and the gratuity of one year's full pay, which is promised to all, possibly their situation (every circumstance being duly considered) will not be deemed less eligible than that of the officers. Should a further reward, however, be judged equitable, I will venture to assert no one will enjoy greater satisfaction than myself, on seeing an exemption from taxes for a limited time, (which has been petitioned for in some instances,) or any other adequate immunity or compensation granted to the brave defenders of their country's cause; but neither the adoption or rejection of this proposition will in any manner affect, much less militate against, the act of Congress, by which they have offered five years' full pay, in lieu of the half-pay for life, which had been before promised to the officers of the army.

Before I conclude the subject of public justice, I cannot omit to mention the obligations this country is under to that meritorious class of veteran non-commissioned officers and privates, who have been discharged for inability, in consequence of the resolution of Congress of the 23d of April, 1782, on an annual pension for life. Their peculiar sufferings, their singular merits, and claims to that provision, need only be known, to interest all the feelings of humanity in their behalf. Nothing but a punctual payment of their annual allowance can rescue them from the most complicated misery; and nothing could be a more melancholy and distressing sight, than to behold those, who have shed their blood or lost their limbs in the service of their country, without a shelter, without a friend, and without the means of obtaining any of the necessaries or comforts of life, compelled to beg their daily bread from door to door. Suffer me to recommend those of this description, belonging to your State, to the warmest patronage of your Excellency and your legislature.

It is necessary to say but a few words on the third topic which was proposed, and which regards particularly the defence of the republic; as there can be little doubt but Congress will recommend a proper peace establishment for the United States, in which a due attention will be paid to the importance of placing the militia of the Union upon a regular and respectable footing. If this should be the case, I would beg leave to urge the great advantage of it in the strongest terms. The militia of this country must be considered as the palladium of our security, and the first effectual resort in case of hostility. It is essential, therefore, that the same system should pervade the whole; that the formation and discipline of the militia of the continent should be absolutely uniform, and that the same species of arms, accoutrements, and military apparatus, should be introduced in every part of the United States. No one, who has not learned it from experience, can conceive the difficulty, expense, and confusion, which result from a contrary system, or the vague arrangements which have hitherto prevailed.

If, in treating of political points, a greater latitude than usual has been taken in the course of this address, the importance of the crisis, and the magnitude of the objects in discussion, must be my apology. It is, however, neither my wish or expectation, that the preceding observations should claim any regard, except so far as they shall appear to be dictated by a good intention, consonant to the immutable rules of justice, calculated to produce a liberal system of policy, and founded on whatever experience may have been acquired by a long and close attention to public business. Here I might speak with the more confidence, from my actual observations; and, if it would not swell this letter (already too prolix) beyond the bounds I had prescribed to myself, I could demonstrate to every mind open to conviction, that in less time, and with much less expense, than has been incurred, the war might have been brought to the same happy conclusion, if the resources of the continent could have been properly drawn forth; that the distresses and disappointments, which have very often occurred, have, in too many instances, resulted more from a want of energy in the Continental government, than a deficiency of means in the particular States; that the inefficacy of measures arising from the want of an adequate authority in the supreme power, from a partial compliance with the requisitions of Congress in some of the States, and from a failure of punctuality in others, while it tended to damp the zeal of those, which were more willing to exert themselves, served also to accumulate the expenses of the war, and to frustrate the best concerted plans; and that the discouragement occasioned by the complicated difficulties and embarrassments, in which our affairs were by this means involved, would have long ago produced the dissolution of any army, less patient, less virtuous, and less persevering, than that which I have had the honor to command. But, while I mention these things, which are notorious facts, as the defects of our federal constitution, particularly in the prosecution of a war, I beg it may be understood, that, as I have ever taken a pleasure in gratefully acknowledging the assistance and support I have derived from every class of citizens, so shall I always be happy to do justice to the unparalleled exertions of the individual States on many interesting occasions.

I have thus freely disclosed what I wished to make known, before I surrendered up my public trust to those who committed it to me. The task is now accomplished. I now bid adieu to your Excellency as the chief magistrate of your State, at the same time I bid a last farewell to the cares of office, and all the employments of public life.

It remains, then, to be my final and only request, that your Excellency will communicate these sentiments to your legislature at their next meeting, and that they may be considered as the legacy of one, who has ardently wished, on all occasions, to be useful to his country, and who, even in the shade of retirement, will not fail to implore the Divine benediction upon it.

I now make it my earnest prayer, that God would have you, and the State over which you preside, in his holy protection; that he would incline the hearts of the citizens to cultivate a spirit of subordination and obedience to government; to entertain a brotherly affection and love for one another, for their fellow citizens of the United States at large, and particularly for their brethren who have served in the field; and finally, that he would most graciously be pleased to dispose us all to do justice, to love mercy, and to demean ourselves with that charity, humility, and pacific temper of mind, which were the characteristics of the Divine Author of our blessed religion, and without an humble imitation of whose example in these things, we can never hope to be a happy nation.

I have the honor to be, with much esteem and respect, Sir, your Excellency's most obedient and most humble servant.

G. Washington

Farewell Orders
to the Armies of the United States

ROCKY HILL, NEAR PRINCETON,
[SUNDAY] 2 NOVEMBER, 1783.

The United States in Congress assembled, after giving the most honorable testimony to the merits of the federal armies, and presenting them with the thanks of their country for their long, eminent and faithful services, having thought proper, by their proclamation bearing date the 18th day of October last, to discharge such part of the troops as were engaged for the war, and to permit the officers on furlough to retire from service from and after tomorrow; which proclamation having been communicated in the public papers for the information and government of all concerned, it only remains for the Commander-in-chief to address himself once more, and that for the last time, to the armies of the United States (however widely dispersed the individuals who compose them may be), and to bid them an affectionate, a long farewell.

But before the Commander-in-Chief takes his final leave of those he holds most dear, he wishes to indulge himself a few moments in calling to mind a slight review of the past. He will then take the liberty of exploring with his military friends their future prospects, of advising the general line of conduct, which, in his opinion, ought to be pursued; and he will conclude the address by expressing the obligations he feels himself under for the spirited and able assistance he has experienced from them, in the performance of an arduous office.

A contemplation of the complete attainment (at a period earlier than could have been expected) of the object, for which we contended against so formidable a power, cannot but inspire us with astonishment and gratitude. The disadvantageous circumstances on our part, under which the war was undertaken, can never be forgotten. The singular interpositions of Providence in our feeble condition were such, as could scarcely escape the attention of the most unobserving; while the unparalleled perseverance of the armies of the United States, through almost every possible suffering and discouragement for the space of eight long years, was little short of a standing miracle.

It is not the meaning nor within the compass of this address, to detail the hardships peculiarly incident to our service, or to describe the distresses, which in several instances have resulted from the extremes of hunger and nakedness, combined with the rigors of an inclement season; nor is it necessary to dwell on the dark side of our past affairs. Every American officer and soldier must now console himself for any unpleasant circumstances, which may have occurred, by a recollection of the uncommon scenes in which he has been called to act no inglorious part, and the astonishing events of which he has been a witness; events which have seldom, if ever before, taken place on the stage of human action; nor can they probably ever happen again. For who has before seen a disciplined army formed at once from such raw materials? Who, that was not a witness, could imagine, that the most violent local prejudices would cease so soon; and that men, who came from the different parts of the continent, strongly disposed by the habits of education to despise and quarrel with each other, would instantly become but one patriotic band of brothers? Or who, that was not on the spot, can trace the steps by which such a wonderful revolution has been effected, and such a glorious period put to all our warlike toils?

It is universally acknowledged, that the enlarged prospects of happiness, opened by the confirmation of our independence and sovereignty, almost exceeds the power of description. And shall not the brave men, who have contributed so essentially to these inestimable acquisitions, retiring victorious from the field of war to the field of agriculture, participate in all the blessings, which have been obtained? In such a republic, who will exclude them from the rights of citizens, and the fruits of their labors? In such a country, so happily circumstanced, the pursuits of commerce and the cultivation of the soil will unfold to industry the certain road to competence. To those hardy soldiers, who are actuated by the spirit of adventure, the fisheries will afford ample and profitable employment; and the extensive and fertile regions of the West will yield a most happy asylum to those, who, fond of domestic enjoyment, are seeking for personal independence. Nor is it possible to conceive, that any one of the United States will prefer a national bankruptcy, and a dissolution of the Union, to a compliance with the requisitions of Congress, and the payment of its just debts; so that the officers and soldiers may expect considerable assistance, in recommencing their civil occupations, from the sums due to them from the public, which must and will most inevitably be paid.

In order to effect this desirable purpose, and to remove the prejudices, which may have taken possession of the minds of any of the good people of the States, it is earnestly recommended to all the troops, that, with strong attachments to the Union, they should carry with them into civil society the most conciliating dispositions, and that they should prove themselves not less virtuous and useful as citizens, than they have been persevering and victorious as soldiers. What though there should be some envious individuals, who are unwilling to pay the debt the public has contracted, or to yield the tribute due to merit; yet let such unworthy treatment produce no invective, or any instance of intemperate conduct. Let it be remembered, that the unbiassed voice of the free citizens of the United States has promised the just reward and given the merited applause. Let it be known and remembered, that the reputation of the federal armies is established beyond the reach of malevolence; and let a consciousness of their achievements and fame still incite the men, who composed them, to honorable actions; under the persuasion that the private virtues of economy, prudence, and industry, will not be less amiable in civil life, than the more splendid qualities of valor, perserverance and enterprise were in the field. Every one may rest assured, that much, very much, of the future happiness of the officers and men, will depend upon the wise and manly conduct, which shall be adopted by them when they are mingled with the great body of the community. And, although the General has so frequently given it as his opinion in the most public and explicit manner, that, unless the principles of the Federal Government were properly supported, and the powers of the Union increased, the honor, dignity, and justice of the nation would be lost forever; yet he cannot help repeating, on this occasion, so interesting a sentiment, and leaving it as his last injunction to every officer and every soldier, who may view the subject in the same serious point of light, to add his best endeavors to those of his worthy fellow citizens towards effecting these great and valuable purposes, on which our very existence as a nation so materially depends.

The Commander-in-chief conceives little is now wanting, to enable the soldier, to change the military character into that of the citizen, but that steady and decent tenor of behavior, which has generally distinguished, not only the army under his immediate command, but the different detachments and separate armies, through the course of the war. From their good sense and prudence he anticipates the happiest consequences; and, while he congratulates them on the glorious occasion, which renders their services in the field no longer necessary, he wishes to express the strong obligations he feels himself under for the assistance he has received from every class and in every instance. He presents his thanks in the most serious and affectionate manner to the general officers, as well for their counsel on many interesting occasions, as for their ardor in promoting the success of the plans he had adopted; to the commandants of regiments and corps, and to the other officers, for their great zeal and attention in carrying his orders promptly into execution; to the staff, for their alacrity and exactness in performing the duties of their several departments; and to the non-commissioned officers and private soldiers, for their extraordinary patience and suffering, as well as their invincible fortitude in action. To the various branches of the army, the General takes this last and solemn opportunity of professing his inviolable attachment and friendship. He wishes more than bare professions were in his power; that he were really able to be useful to them all in future life. He flatters himself, however, they will do him the justice to believe, that whatever could with propriety be attempted by him has been done.

And being now to conclude these his last public orders, to take his ultimate leave in a short time of the military character, and to bid a final adieu to the armies he has so long had the honor to command, he can only again offer in their behalf his recommendations to their grateful country, and his prayers to the God of armies. May ample justice be done them here, and may the choicest of Heaven's favors, both here and hereafter, attend those, who, under the Divine auspices, have secured innumerable blessings for others. With these wishes and this benediction, the Commander-in-chief is about to retire from service. The curtain of separation will soon be drawn, and the military scene to him will be closed for ever.

Address to Congress
on resigning his Commission

ANNAPOLIS, 23 DECEMBER, 1783.

Mr. President,

The great events, on which my resignation depended, having at length taken place, I have now the honor of offering my sincere congratulations to Congress, and of presenting myself before them, to surrender into their hands the trust committed to me, and to claim the indulgence of retiring from the Service of my Country.

Happy in the confirmation of our Independence and Sovereignty, and pleased with the opportunity afforded the United States of becoming a respectable nation, I resign with satisfaction the appointment I accepted with diffidence; a diffidence in my abilities to accomplish so arduous a task, which, however, was superseded by a confidence in the rectitude of our cause, the support of the supreme Power of the Union, and the patronage of Heaven.

The successful termination of the war has verified the most sanguine expectations; and my gratitude for the interposition of Providence, and the assistance I have received from my Countrymen, encreases with every review of the momentous contest.

While I repeat my obligations to the Army in general, I should do injustice to my own feelings not to acknowledge, in this place, the peculiar services and distinguished merits of the Gentlemen, who have been attached to my person during the war. It was impossible that the choice of confidential officers to compose my family should have been more fortunate. Permit me, Sir, to recommend in particular those, who have continued in Service to the present moment, as worthy of the favorable notice and patronage of Congress.

I consider it an indispensable duty to close this last solemn act of my official life, by commending the Interests of our dearest country to the protection of Almighty God, and those who have the superintendence of them to his holy keeping.

Having now finished the work assigned me, I retire from the great theatre of action; and, bidding an affectionate farewell to this august body, under whose orders I have so long acted, I here offer my commission, and take my leave of all the employments of public life.

Diary on Communication with the West

OCTOBER 4, 1784.

Hitherto, the people of the Western Country having had no excitements to Industry, labour very little;—the luxuriency of the Soil, with very little culture, produces provisions in abundance—these supplies the wants of the encreasing population—and the Spaniards when pressed by want have given high prices for flour—other articles they reject; and at times, (contrary I think to sound policy) shut their ports against them altogether—but let us open a good communication with the Settlements west of us—extend the inland Navigation as far as it can be done with convenience—and shew them by this means, how easy it is to bring the produce of their Lands to our Markets, and see how astonishingly our exports will be increased; and these States benefitted in a commercial point of view—wch. alone is an object of such Magnitude as to claim our closest attention—but when the subject is considered in a political point of view, it appears of much greater importance.

No well informed Mind need be told, that the flanks and rear of the United territory are possessed by other powers, and formidable ones too—nor how necessary it is to apply the cement of interest to bind all parts of it together, by one indissoluble band—particularly the middle States with the Country immediately back of them—for what ties let me ask, should we have upon those people; and how entirely unconnected shod. we be with them if the Spaniards on their right or great Britain on their left, instead of throwing stumbling blocks in their way as they now do; should invite their trade and seek alliances with them? What, when they get strength, which will be sooner than is generally imagined (from the emigration of Foreigners who can have no predeliction for us, as well as from the removal of our own Citizens) may be the consequence of their having formed such connections and alliances; requires no uncommon foresight to predict.

The Western Settlers—from my own observation—stand as it were on a pivot—the touch of a feather would almost incline them any way—they looked down the Mississippi until the Spaniards (very impoliticly I think for themselves) threw difficulties in the way, and for no other reason that I can conceive than because they glided gently down the stream, without considering perhaps the tediousness of the voyage back, and the time necessary to perform it in; and because they have no other means of coming to us but by a long land transportation and unimproved Roads.

A combination of circumstances make the present conjuncture more favorable than any other to fix the trade of the Western Country to our Markets. The jealous and untoward disposition of the Spaniards on one side, and the private views of some individuals coinciding with the policy of the Court of G. Britain on the other, to retain the Posts of Oswego, Niagara, Detroit, &ca. (which tho' done under the letter of the treaty is certainly an infraction of the Spirit of it, and injurious to the Union) may be improved to the greatest advantage by this State if she would open her arms, and embrace the means which are necessary to establish it. The way is plain, and the expence, comparitively speaking deserves not a thought, so great would be the prize. The Western Inhabitants would do their part towards accomplishing it, weak as they now are, they would, I am persuaded meet us half way rather than be *driven* into the arms of, or be in any wise dependent upon, foreigners; the consequence of which would be, a seperation, or a War.

The way to avoid both, happily for us, is easy, and dictated by our clearest interest. It is to open a wide door, and make a smooth way for the produce of that Country to pass to our Markets before the trade may get into another channel—this, in my judgment, would dry up the other Sources; or if any part should flow down the Mississippi, from the Falls of the Ohio, in Vessels which may be built—fitted for Sea—and sold with their Cargoes, the proceeds I have no manner of doubt, will return this way; and that it is better to prevent an evil than to rectify a mistake none can deny—commercial connections of all others, are most difficult to dissolve—if we wanted proof of this, look to the avidity with which we are renewing, after a *total* suspension of Eight years, our corrispondence with Great Britain;—So, if we are supine, and suffer without a struggle the Settlers of the Western Country to form commercial connections with the Spaniards, Britons, or with any of the States in the Union we shall find it a difficult matter to dissolve them altho' a better communication should thereafter, be presented to them—time only could effect it; such is the force of habit!

Rumseys discovery of working Boats against stream, by mechanical powers principally, may not only be considered as a fortunate invention for these States in general but as one of those circumstances which have combined to render the present epoche favorable above all others for securing (if we are disposed to avail ourselves of them) a large portion of the produce of the Western Settlements, and of the Fur and Peltry of the Lakes, also—the importation of which alone, if there were no political considerations in the way, is immense.

It may be said perhaps, that as the most direct Routs from the Lakes to the Navigation of Potomack are through the State of Pennsylvania—and the intert. of that State opposed to the extension of the Waters of Monongahela, that a communication cannot be had either by the Yohiogany or Cheat River;—but herein I differ—an application to this purpose would in my opinion, place the Legislature of that Commonwealth in a very delicate situation. That it would not be pleasing I can readily conceive, but that they would refuse their assent, I am by no means clear in. There is in that State, at least 100,000 Souls West of the Laurel hill, who are groaning under the inconveniences of a long land transportation. They are wishing, indeed looking, for the extension of inland Navigation; and if this can not be made easy for them to Philadelphia—at any rate it must be lengthy—they will seek a Mart elsewhere; and none is so convenient as that which offers itself through Yohiogany or Cheat River—the certain consequence therefore of an attempt to restrain the extension of the Navigation of these Rivers, (so consonant with the interest of these people) or to impose any extra duties upon the exports, or imports, to or from another State, would be a seperation of the Western Settlers from the old and more interior government; towards which there is not wanting a disposition at this moment in the former.

Letter to Henry Lee, in Congress,
on Shays Rebellion

MOUNT VERNON, 31 OCTOBER, 1786.

My dear Sir,

I am indebted to you for your several favors of the 1st, 11th, and 17th of this instant, and shall reply to them in the order of their dates. But first let me thank you for the interesting communications imparted by them.

The picture which you have exhibited, and the accounts which are published of the commotions and temper of numerous bodies in the eastern States, are equally to be lamented and deprecated. They exhibit a melancholy proof of what our transatlantic foe has predicted; and of another thing perhaps, which is still more to be regretted, and is yet more unaccountable, that mankind, when left to themselves, are unfit for their own government. I am mortified beyond expression when I view the clouds, that have spread over the brightest morn that ever dawned upon any country. In a word, I am lost in amazement when I behold what intrigue, the interested views of desperate characters, ignorance, and jealousy of the minor part, are capable of effecting, as a scourge on the major part of our fellow citizens of the Union; for it is hardly to be supposed, that the great body of the people, though they will not act, can be so shortsighted or enveloped in darkness, as not to see rays of a distant sun through all this mist of intoxication and folly.

You talk, my good Sir, of employing influence to appease the present tumults in Massachusetts. I know not where that influence is to be found, or, if attainable, that it would be a proper remedy for the disorders. *Influence* is no *government*. Let us have one by which our lives, liberties, and properties will be secured or let us know the worst at once. Under these impressions, my humble opinion is, that there is a call for decision. Know precisely what the insurgents aim at. If they have *real* grievances, redress them if possible; or acknowledge the justice of them, and your inability to do it in the present moment. If they have not, employ the force of government against them at once. If this is inadequate, *all* will be convinced, that the superstructure is bad, or wants support. To be more exposed in the eyes of the world, and more contemptible than we already are, is hardly possible. To delay one or the other of these, is to exasperate on the one hand, or to give confidence on the other, and will add to their numbers; for, like snow-balls, such bodies increase by every movement, unless there is something in the way to obstruct and crumble them before the weight is too great and irresistible.

These are my sentiments. Precedents are dangerous things. Let the reins of government then be braced and held with a steady hand, and every violation of the constitution be reprehended. If defective, let it be amended, but not suffered to be trampled upon whilst it has an existence.

With respect to the navigation of the Mississippi, you already know my sentiments thereon. They have been uniformly the same, and, as I have observed to you in a former letter, are controverted by one consideration, only of weight, and that is, the operation which the conclusion of it may have on the minds of the western settlers, who will not consider the subject in a relative point of view, or on a comprehensive scale, and may be influenced by the demagogues of the country to acts of extravagance and desperation, under a popular declamation, that their interests are sacrificed. Colonel Mason at present is in a fit of the gout. What [his] sentiments on the subject are, I know not, nor whether he will be able to attend the Assembly during the present session. For some reasons, however, (which need not be mentioned,) I am inclined to believe he will advocate the navigation of that river. But in all matters of great national moment, the only true line of conduct, in my opinion, is dispassionately to compare the advantages and disadvantages of the measure proposed, and decide from the balance. The lesser evil, where there is a choice of them, should always yield to the greater. What benefits, more than we now enjoy, are to be obtained by such a treaty as you have delineated with Spain, I am not enough of a commercial man to give any opinion on. The china came to hand without much damage & I thank you for your attention in the procuring & forwarding it. Mrs. Washington joins me in best wishes for Mrs. Lee and yourself and I am very affectionately, Dear Sir Yr. Most Obedt. & Obliged Hble. Servant.

G Washington

Letter to Henry Knox
on Crisis in the Confederation

MOUNT VERNON, 26 DECEMBER, 1786.

My dear Sir,

. . . I feel, my dear General Knox, infinitely more than I can express to you, for the disorders, which have arisen in these States. Good God! Who, besides a Tory, could have foreseen, or a Briton predicted them? Were these people wiser than others, or did they judge of us from the corruption and depravity of their own hearts? The latter I am persuaded was the case and that notwithstanding the boasted virtue of America we are very little if anything behind them in dispositions to every thing that is bad.

I do assure you, that even at this moment, when I reflect upon the present prospect of our affairs, it seems to me to be like the vision of a dream. My mind can scarcely realize it as a thing in actual existence; so strange, so wonderful does it appear to me. In this, as in most other matters, we are too slow. When this spirit first dawned, probably it might have been easily checked; but it is scarcely within the reach of human ken, at this moment, to say when, where, or how it will terminate. There are combustibles in every State, which a spark might set fire to. In this a perfect calm prevails at present; and a prompt disposition to support and give energy to the federal system is discovered, if the unlucky stirring of the dispute respecting the navigation of the Mississippi does not become a leaven that will ferment and sour the mind of it.

The resolutions of the present session respecting a paper emission, military certificates, &c., have stamped justice and liberality on the proceedings of the Assembly. By a late act, it seems very desirous of a general convention to revise and amend the federal constitution. *Apropos;* what prevented the eastern States from attending the September meeting at Annapolis? Of all the States in the Union it should have seemed to me, that a measure of this sort, (distracted as they were with internal commotions and experiencing the want of energy in the government,) would have been most pleasing to them. What are the prevailing sentiments of the one now proposed to be held in Philadelphia in May next? and how will it be attended? You are at the fountain of intelligence, where the wisdom of the nation, it is to be presumed, is concentred; consequently better able, (as I have had sufficient experience of your intelligence, confidence, and candor,) to solve these questions.

The Maryland Assembly has been violently agitated by the question for a paper emission. It has been carried in the House of Delegates; but what has been or may be the fate of the bill in the Senate, I have not yet heard. The partisans in favor of the measure in the lower House threaten, *it is said,* a secession, if it is rejected by that branch of the legislature. Thus are we advancing. In regretting, which I have often done with the keenest sorrow, the death of our much lamented friend General Greene, I have accompanied it of late with a query, whether he would not have preferred such an exit to the scenes, which, it is more than probable, many of his compatriots may live to bemoan.

In both your letters you intimate, that the men of reflection, principle, and property in New England, feeling the inefficacy of their present government, are contemplating a change; but you are not explicit with respect to its nature. It has been supposed, that the constitution of the State of Massachusetts was amongst the most energetic in the Union. May not these disorders then be ascribed to an indulgent exercise of the powers of administration? If your laws authorized, and your powers are equal to the suppression of these tumults in the first instance, delay and unnecessary expedients were improper. These are rarely well applied; and the same causes would produce similar effects in any form of government, if the powers of it are not exercised. I ask this question for information. I know nothing of the facts.

That Great Britain will be an unconcerned spectator of the present insurrections, if they continue, is not to be expected. That she is at this moment sowing the seeds of jealousy and discontent among the various tribes of Indians on our frontiers, admits of no doubt in my mind; and that she will improve every opportunity to foment the spirit of turbulence within the bowels of the United States, with a view of distracting our governments and promoting divisions, is with me not less certain. Her first manoeuvres in this will no doubt be covert, and may remain so till the period shall arrive when a decided line of conduct may avail her. Charges of violating the treaty, and other pretexts, will then not be wanting to color overt acts, tending to effect the great objects of which she has long been in labor. A man is now at the head of their American affairs, well calculated to conduct measures of this kind, and more than probably was selected for the purpose. We ought not therefore to sleep nor to slumber. Vigilance in watching and vigor in acting is become in my opinion indispensably necessary. If the powers are inadequate, amend or alter them; but do not let us sink into the lowest state of humiliation and contempt, and become a by-word in all the earth. I think with you, that the spring will unfold important and distressing scenes, unless much wisdom and good management is displayed in the interim. Adieu. Be assured no man has a higher esteem and regard for you, than I have; none more sincerely your friend and more affectly. yr. hble. Servt.

G Washington

Letter to Alexander Hamilton
on The Federalist and Presidency
MOUNT VERNON, 28 AUGUST, 1788.

Dear Sir,

    *   *   *   *   *   *   *

As the perusal of the political papers under the signature of PUBLIUS has afforded me great satisfaction, I shall certainly consider them as claiming a most distinguished place in my library. I have read every performance, which has been printed on one side and the other of the great question lately agitated (so far as I have been able to obtain them); and, without an unmeaning compliment, I will say, that I have seen no other so well calculated, in my judgment, to produce conviction on an unbiassed mind as the *production* of your *triumvirate.* When the transient circumstances and fugitive performances, which attended this *crisis,* shall have disappeared, that work will merit the notice of posterity, because in it are candidly and ably discussed the principles of freedom and the topics of government, which will be always interesting to mankind, so long as they shall be connected in civil society.

The circular letter from your convention I presume was the equivalent, by which you obtained an acquiescence in the proposed constitution. Notwithstanding I am not very well satisfied with the tendency of it, yet the federal affairs had proceeded, with few exceptions, in so good a train, that I hope the political machine may be put in motion, without much effort or hazard of miscarrying.

On the delicate subject with which you conclude your letter, I can say nothing, because the event alluded to may never happen, and because, in case it should occur, it would be a point of prudence to defer forming one's ultimate and irrevocable decision, so long as new data might be afforded for one to act with the greater wisdom and propriety. I would not wish to conceal my prevailing sentiment from you; for you know me well enough, my good Sir, to be persuaded, that I am not guilty of affectation when I tell you, that it is my great and sole desire to live and die in peace and retirement on my own farm. Were it even indispensable, a different line of conduct should be adopted, while you and some others who are acquainted with my heart would acquit, the world and posterity might possibly accuse me [of] inconsistence and ambition. Still I hope I shall always possess firmness and virtue enough to maintain (what I consider the most enviable of all titles), the character of *an honest man,* as well as prove, what I desire to be considered in reality, that

I am, with great sincerity and esteem, Dear Sir, &c.

G Washington

Inaugural Address
to Both Houses of Congress

APRIL 30, 1789.

*Fellow-Citizens of the Senate
and House of Representatives,*

Among the vicissitudes incident to life, no event could have filled me with greater anxieties, than that of which the notification was transmitted by your order, and received on the 14th day of the present month. On the one hand, I was summoned by my country, whose voice I can never hear but with veneration and love, from a retreat which I had chosen with the fondest predilection, and, in my flattering hopes, with an immutable decision, as the asylum of my declining years; a retreat which was rendered every day more necessary as well as more dear to me, by the addition of habit to inclination, and of frequent interruptions in my health to the gradual waste committed on it by time. On the other hand, the magnitude and difficulty of the trust, to which the voice of my country called me, being sufficient to awaken in the wisest and most experienced of her citizens a distrustful scrutiny into his qualifications, could not but overwhelm with despondence one, who, inheriting inferior indowments from nature, and unpractised in the duties of civil administration, ought to be peculiarly conscious of his own deficiencies. In this conflict of emotions, all I dare aver is, that it has been my faithful study to collect my duty from a just appreciation of every circumstance by which it might be affected. All I dare hope is, that, if in executing this task, I have been too much swayed by a grateful remembrance of former instances, or by an affectionate sensibility to this transcendent proof of the confidence of my fellow-citizens; and have thence too little consulted my incapacity as well as disinclination for the weighty and untried cares before me; my error will be palliated by the motives which misled me, and its consequences be judged by my country with some share of the partiality in which they originated.

Such being the impressions under which I have, in obedience to the public summons, repaired to the present station, it would be peculiarly improper to omit, in this first official act, my fervent supplications to that Almighty Being, who rules over the universe, who presides in the councils of nations, and whose providential aids can supply every human defect, that his benediction may consecrate to the liberties and happiness of the people of the United States a government instituted by themselves for these essential purposes, and may enable every instrument employed in its administration to execute with success the functions allotted to his charge. In tendering this homage to the great Author of every public and private good, I assure myself that it expresses your sentiments not less than my own; nor those of my fellow-citizens at large, less than either. No people can be bound to acknowledge and adore the invisible hand, which conducts the affairs of men, more than the people of the United States. Every step, by which they have advanced to the character of an independent nation, seems to have been distinguished by some token of providential agency. And, in the important revolution just accomplished in the system of their united government, the tranquil deliberations and voluntary consent of so many distinct communities, from which the event has resulted, cannot be compared with the means by which most governments have been established, without some return of pious gratitude along with an humble anticipation of the future blessings which the past seem to presage. These reflections, arising out of the present crisis, have forced themselves too strongly on my mind to be suppressed. You will join with me, I trust, in thinking that there are none, under the influence of which the proceedings of a new and free government can more auspiciously commence.

By the article establishing the executive department, it is made the duty of the President "to recommend to your consideration such measures as he shall judge necessary and expedient." The circumstances, under which I now meet you, will acquit me from entering into that subject farther than to refer you to the great constitutional charter under which we are assembled; and which, in defining your powers, designates the objects to which your attention is to be given. It will be more consistent with those circumstances, and far more congenial with the feelings which actuate me, to substitute, in place of a recommendation of particular measures, the tribute that is due to the talents, the rectitude, and the patriotism, which adorn the characters selected to devise and adopt them. In these honorable qualifications I behold the surest pledges, that as, on one side, no local prejudices or attachments, no separate views or party animosities, will misdirect the comprehensive and equal eye, which ought to watch over this great assemblage of communities and interests; so, on another, that the foundations of our national policy will be laid in the pure and immutable principles of private morality, and the pre-eminence of a free government be exemplified by all the attributes, which can win the affections of its citizens, and command the respect of the world.

I dwell on this prospect with every satisfaction, which an ardent love for my country can inspire; since there is no truth more thoroughly established, than that there exists in the economy and course of nature an indissoluble union between virtue and happiness, between duty and advantage, between the genuine maxims of an honest and magnanimous policy, and the solid rewards of public prosperity and felicity; since we ought to be no less persuaded that the propitious smiles of Heaven can never be expected on a nation that disregards the eternal rules of order and right, which Heaven itself has ordained; and since the preservation of the sacred fire of liberty, and the destiny of the republican model of government, are justly considered as *deeply*, perhaps as *finally* staked, on the experiment intrusted to the hands of the American people.

Besides the ordinary objects submitted to your care, it will remain with your judgment to decide, how far an exercise of the occasional power delegated by the fifth article of the Constitution is rendered expedient at the present juncture by the nature of objections which have been urged against the system, or by the degree of inquietude which has given birth to them. Instead of undertaking particular recommendations on this subject, in which I could be guided by no lights derived from official opportunities, I shall again give way to my entire confidence in your discernment and pursuit of the public good; for I assure myself, that, whilst you carefully avoid every alteration, which might endanger the benefits of a united and effective government, or which ought to await the future lessons of experience; a reverence for the characteristic rights of freemen, and a regard for the public harmony, will sufficiently influence your deliberations on the question, how far the former can be more impregnably fortified, or the latter be safely and advantageously promoted.

To the preceding observations I have one to add, which will be most properly addressed to the House of Representatives. It concerns myself, and will therefore be as brief as possible. When I was first honored with a call into the service of my country, then on the eve of an arduous struggle for its liberties, the light in which I contemplated my duty required, that I should renounce every pecuniary compensation. From this resolution I have in no instance departed. And being still under the impression which produced it, I must decline as inapplicable to myself any share in the personal emoluments, which may be indispensably included in a permanent provision for the executive department; and must accordingly pray, that the pecuniary estimates for the station in which I am placed may, during my continuance in it, be limited to such actual expenditures as the public good may be thought to require.

Having thus imparted to you my sentiments, as they have been awakened by the occasion which brings us together, I shall take my present leave; but not without resorting once more to the benign Parent of the human race, in humble supplication, that, since he has been pleased to favor the American people with opportunities for deliberating in perfect tranquillity, and dispositions for deciding with unparalleled unanimity on a form of government for the security of their union and the advancement of their happiness; so his divine blessing may be equally *conspicuous* in the enlarged views, the temperate consultations, and the wise measures, on which the success of this government must depend.

Letter to John Jay
on Democratic Societies and Whiskey Insurrection
PHILADELPHIA, 1 NOVEMBER, 1794.

My dear Sir,

On Tuesday last I returned from my tour to the westward. On Monday Congress by adjournment are to meet, and on the day following Mr. Bayard, according to his present expectation, is to leave this city for London. . . .

As you have been, and will continue to be, fully informed by the Secretary of State of all transactions of a public nature, which relate to, or may have an influence on, the points of your mission, it would be unnecessary for me to touch upon any of them in this letter, was it not for the presumption that the insurrection in the western counties of this State has excited much speculation, and a variety of opinions abroad, and will be represented differently according to the wishes of some and the prejudices of others, who may exhibit it as an evidence of what has been predicted, "that we are unable to govern ourselves." Under this view of the subject, I am happy in giving it to you as the general opinion, that this event having happened at the time it did was fortunate, although it will be attended with considerable expense.

That the self-created societies, which have spread themselves over this country, have been laboring incessantly to sow the seeds of distrust, jealousy, and of course discontent, thereby hoping to effect some revolution in the government, is not unknown to you. That they have been the fomenters of the western disturbances admits of no doubt in the mind of any one, who will examine their conduct; but fortunately they have precipitated a crisis for which they were not prepared, and thereby have unfolded views, which will, I trust, effectuate their annihilation sooner than it might otherwise have happened; at the same time that it has afforded an occasion for the people of this country to show their abhorrence of the result, and their attachment to the constitution and the laws; for I believe that five times the number of militia, that was required, would have come forward, if it had been necessary, in support of them.

The spirit, which blazed out on this occasion, as soon as the object was fully understood, and the lenient measures of the government were made known to the people, deserves to be communicated. There are instances of general officers going at the head of a single troop, and of light companies; of field-officers, when they came to the places of rendezvous, and found no command for them in that grade, turning into the ranks and proceeding as private soldiers, under their own captains; and of numbers, possessing the first fortunes in the country, standing in the ranks as private men, and marching day by day with their knapsacks and haversacks at their backs, sleeping on straw with a single blanket in a soldier's tent, during the frosty nights, which we have had, by way of example to others— nay more, many young Quakers, not discouraged by the elders, of the first families, character, and property, having turned into the ranks and are marching with the troops.

These things have terrified the insurgents, who had no conception that such a spirit prevailed, but, while the thunder only rumbled at a distance, were boasting of their strength, and wishing for and threatening the militia by turns; intimating that the arms they should take from them would soon become a magazine in their hands. Their language is much changed indeed, but their principles want correction.

I shall be more prolix in my speech to Congress on the commencement and progress of this insurrection, than is usual in such an instrument, or than I should have been on any other occasion; but, as numbers at home and abroad will hear of the insurrection, and will read the speech, that may know nothing of the documents to which it might refer, I conceived it would be better to encounter the charge of prolixity by giving a cursory detail of facts, that would show the prominent features of the thing, than to let it go naked into the world, to be dressed up according to the fancy or inclination of the readers, or the policy of our enemies.

I write nothing in answer to the letter of Mr. Wangenheim, enclosed by you to me. Were I to enter into correspondences of that sort, admitting there was no impropriety in the measure, I should be unable to attend to my ordinary duties. I have established it as a maxim neither to invite nor to discourage emigrants. My opinion is, that they will come hither as fast as the true interest and policy of the United States will be benefited by foreign population. I believe many of these, as Mr. Wangenheim relates, have been, and I fear will continue to be, imposed on by speculators in land and other things; but I know of no prevention but caution, nor any remedy except the laws. Nor is military or other employment so easily obtained as foreigners conceive, in a country where offices bear no proportion to the seekers of them.

With sincere esteem, & very grt. regd. I am Dr. Sir Yr. Affe. Sert.

G. Washington

Letter to Secretary Randolph on Jay Treaty

MOUNT VERNON, 31 JULY, 1795.

My dear Sir,

*   *   *   *   *   *   *

To be wise and temperate, as well as firm, the present crisis most eminently calls for. There is too much reason to believe, from the pains which have been taken before, at, and since the advice of the Senate respecting the treaty, that the prejudices against it are more extensive than is generally imagined. This I have lately understood to be the case in this quarter, from men, who are of no party, but well-disposed to the present administration. How should it be otherwise, when no stone has been left unturned, that could impress on the minds of the people the most arrant misrepresentation of facts; that their rights have not only been *neglected*, but absolutely *sold;* that there are no reciprocal advantages in the treaty; that the benefits are all on the side of Great Britain; and, what seems to have had more weight with them than all the rest, and most pressed, that the treaty is made with the design to oppress the French, in open violation of our treaty wtih that nation, and contrary, too, to every principle of gratitude and sound policy? In time, when passion shall have yielded to sober reason, the current may possibly turn; but, in the mean while, this government in relation to France and England may be compared to a ship between the rocks of Scylla and Charybdis. If the treaty is ratified, the partisans of the French, (or rather of war and confusion,) will excite them to hostile measures, or at least to unfriendly sentiments; if it is not, there is no foreseeing *all* the consequences, which may follow, as it respects Great Britain.

It is not to be inferred from hence, that I am or shall be disposed to quit the ground I have taken, unless circumstances more imperious than have yet come to my knowledge should compel it; for there is but one straight course, and that is to seek truth and pursue it steadily. But these things are mentioned to show, that a close investigation of the subject is more than ever necessary, and that they are strong evidences of the necessity of the most circumspect conduct in carrying the determination of government into effect, with prudence as it respects our own people, and with every exertion to produce a change for the better from Great Britain.

The memorial seems well designed to answer the end proposed; and by the time it is revised and newdressed, you will probably (either in the resolutions, which are or will be handed to me, or in the newspaper publications, which you promised to be attentive to,) have seen all the objections against the treaty, which have any real force in them, and which may be fit subjects for representation in the memorial, or in the instructions, or both. But how much longer the presentative of the memorial can be delayed without exciting unpleasant sensations here, or involving serious evils elsewhere, you, who are at the scene of information and action, can decide better than I. In a matter, however, so interesting and pregnant of consequences as this treaty, there ought to be no precipitation; but, on the contrary, every step should be explored before it is taken, and every word weighed before it is uttered or delivered in writing.

The form of the ratification requires more diplomatic experience and legal knowledge than I possess, or have the means of acquiring at this place, and therefore I shall say nothing about it. I am, &c., &c.

G Washington

George Washington's Farewell Address to the People of the United States

SEPTEMBER 17TH, 1796.

WASHINGTON'S *Farewell Address to the people of the United States was issued September 17, 1796, primarily for the purpose of eliminating himself as a Presidential candidate for a third term. It was never read by the President in public, but was given to the people through the medium of David Claypoole's AMERICAN DAILY ADVERTISER, Philadelphia, in its issue of September 19, 1796.*

The address may be analyzed as consisting of two parts: The first, the definite declination to serve a third term as President, and an explanation of Washington's reason therefor, together with the acknowledgment of his debt of gratitude to the country for the honors conferred upon him and the confidence with which the people had supported him.

The second, and more important part of the address, presents, as a last legacy of advice, Washington's thoughts upon the government of the United States, the result of his experience.

Friends, and Fellow-Citizens,

The period for a new election of a Citizen, to administer the Executive Government of the United States, being not far distant, and the time actually arrived, when your thoughts must be employed in designating the person, who is to be clothed with that important trust, it appears to me proper, especially as it may conduce to a more distinct expression of the public voice, that I should now apprise you of the resolution I have formed, to decline being considered among the number of those, out of whom a choice is to be made.

I beg you, at the same time, to do me the justice to be assured, that this resolution has not been taken, without a strict regard to all the considerations appertaining to the relation, which binds a dutiful citizen to his country—and that, in withdrawing the tender of service which silence in my situation might imply, I am influenced by no diminution of zeal for your future interest, no deficiency of grateful respect for your past kindness; but act under and supported by a full conviction that the step is compatible with both.

The acceptance of, and continuance hitherto in, the office to which your suffrages have twice called me, have been a uniform sacrifice of inclination to the opinion of duty, and to a deference for what appeared to be your desire.—I constantly hoped, that it would have been much earlier in my power, consistently with motive, which I was not at liberty to disregard, to return to that retirement, from which I had been reluctantly drawn.—The strength of my inclination to do this, previous to the last election, had even led to the preparation of an address to declare it to you; but mature reflection on the then perplexed and critical posture of our affairs with foreign Nations, and the unanimous advice of persons entitled to my confidence, impelled me to abandon the idea.—

I rejoice that the state of your concerns, external as well as internal, no longer renders the pursuit of inclination incompatible with the sentiment of duty, or propriety; and am persuaded, whatever partiality may be retained for my services, that in the present circumstances of our country, you will not disapprove my determination to retire.

The impressions, with which I first undertook the arduous trust, were explained on the proper occasion.—In the discharge of this trust, I will only say, that I have, with good intentions, contributed towards the organization and administration of the government, the best exertions of which a very fallible judgment was capable.—Not unconscious, in the outset, of the inferiority of my qualifications, experience in my own eyes, perhaps still more in the eyes of others, has strengthened the motives to diffidence of myself; and every day the increasing weight of years admonishes me more and more, that the shade of retirement is as necessary to me as it will be welcome.—Satisfied, that if any circumstances have given peculiar value to my services, they were temporary, I have the consolation to believe, that, while choice and prudence invited me to quit the political scene, patriotism does not forbid it.

In looking forward to the moment, which is intended to terminate the career of my public life, my feelings do not permit me to suspend the deep acknowledgment of that debt of gratitude, which I owe to my beloved country,—for the many honors it has conferred upon me; still more for the stedfast confidence with which it has supported me; and for the opportunities I have thence enjoyed of manifesting my inviolable attachment, by services faithful and persevering, though in usefulness unequal to my zeal.—If benefits have resulted to our country from these services, let it always be remembered to your praise, and as an instructive example in our annals, that under circumstances in which the Passions agitated in every direction were liable to mislead, amidst appearances sometimes dubious, vicissitudes of fortune often discouraging, in situations in which not unfrequently want of success has countenanced the spirit of criticism, the constancy of your support was the essential prop of the efforts, and a guar-

antee of the plans by which they were effected.—Profoundly penetrated with this idea, I shall carry it with me to the grave, as a strong incitement to unceasing vows that Heaven may continue to you the choicest tokens of its beneficence—that your union and brotherly affection may be perpetual—that the free constitution, which is the work of your hands, may be sacredly maintained—that its administration in every department may be stamped with wisdom and virtue—that, in fine, the happiness of the people of these States, under the auspices of liberty, may be made complete, by so careful a preservation and so prudent a use of this blessing as will acquire to them the glory of recommending it to the applause, the affection, and adoption of every nation, which is yet a stranger to it.

Here, perhaps, I ought to stop.—But a solicitude for your welfare, which cannot end but with my life, and the apprehension of danger, natural to that solicitude, urge me on an occasion like the present, to offer to your solemn contemplation, and to recommend to your frequent review, some sentiments; which are the result of much reflection, of no inconsiderable observation and which appear to me all important to the permanency of your felicity as a People.—These will be offered to you with the more freedom, as you can only see in them the disinterested warnings of a parting friend, who can possibly have no personal motive to bias his counsels.—Nor can I forget, as an encouragement to it your indulgent reception of my sentiments on a former and not dissimilar occasion.

Interwoven as is the love of liberty with every ligament of your hearts, no recommendation of mine is necessary to fortify or confirm the attachment.—

The Unity of Government which constitutes you one people, is also now dear to you.—It is justly so; for it is a main Pillar in the Edifice of your real independence; the support of your tranquillity at home; your peace abroad; of your safety; of your prosperity in every shape; of that very Liberty, which you so highly prize.—But as it is easy to foresee, that, from different causes, and from different quarters, much pains will be taken, many artifices employed, to weaken in your minds the conviction of this truth;—as this is the point in your political fortress against which the batteries of internal and external enemies will be most constantly and actively (though often covertly and insidiously) directed, it is of infinite moment, that you should properly estimate the immense value of your national Union to your collective and individual happiness;—that you should cherish a cordial, habitual, and immoveable attachment to it; accustoming yourselves to think and speak of it as of the Palladium of your political safety and prosperity; watching for its preservation with jealous anxiety; discountenancing whatever may suggest even a suspicion that it can in any event be abandoned, and indignantly

frowning upon the first dawning of every attempt to alienate any portion of our Country from the rest, or to enfeeble the sacred ties which now link together the various parts.

For this you have every inducement of sympathy and interest.—Citizens by birth or choice of a common country, that country has a right to concentrate your affections.— The name of AMERICAN, which belongs to you, in your national capacity, must always exalt the just pride of Patriotism, more than any appellation derived from local discriminations.—With slight shades of difference, you have the same Religion, Manners, Habits, and political Principles.—You have in a common cause fought and triumphed together. The Independence and Liberty you possess are the work of joint councils, and joint efforts—of common dangers, sufferings and successes.—

But these considerations, however powerfully they address themselves to your sensibility, are greatly outweighed by those, which apply more immediately to your Interest.—Here every portion of our country finds the most commanding motives for carefully guarding and preserving the Union of the whole.

The *North* in an unrestrained intercourse with the *South*, protected by the equal Laws of a common government, finds in the productions of the latter great additional resources of maritime and commercial enterprise—and precious materials of manufacturing industry.—The *South* in the same intercourse, benefiting by the agency of the *North*, sees its agriculture grow and its commerce expand. Turning partly into its own channels the seamen of the *North*, it finds its particular navigation envigorated;—and, while it contributes, in different ways, to nourish and increase the general mass of the national navigation, it looks forward to the protection of a maritime strength to which itself is unequally adapted.—The *East*, in a like intercourse with the *West*, already finds, in the progressive improvement of interior communications, by land and water, will more and more find, a valuable vent for the commodities which it brings from abroad, or manufactures at home.—The *West* derives from the *East* supplies requisite to its growth and comfort,—and what is perhaps of still greater consequence, it must of necessity owe the *secure* enjoyment of indispensable *outlets* for its own productions to the weight, influence, and the future maritime strength of the Atlantic side of the Union, directed by an indissoluble community of interest, as *one Nation*.—Any other tenure by which the *West* can hold this essential advantage, whether derived from its own separate strength, or from an apostate and unnatural connexion with any foreign Power, must be intrinsically precarious.

While then every part of our Country thus feels an immediate and particular interest in Union, all the parts combined in the united mass of means and efforts cannot fail to find greater strength, greater resource, proportionably greater security from external danger, a less frequent interruption of their Peace by foreign Nations; and, what is of inestimable value! they must derive from Union an exemption from those broils and wars between themselves, which so frequently afflict neighboring countries, not tied together by the same government; which their own rivalships alone would be sufficient to produce; but which opposite foreign alliances, attachments, and intrigues would stimulate and embitter.—Hence likewise they will avoid the necessity of those overgrown Military establishments, which under any form of government, are inauspicious to liberty, and which are to be regarded as particularly hostile to Republican Liberty: In this sense it is, that your Union ought to be considered as a main prop of your liberty, and that the love of the one ought to endear to you the preservation of the other.

These considerations speak a persuasive language to every reflecting and virtuous mind,—and exhibit the continuance of the UNION as a primary object of Patriotic desire.—Is there a doubt, whether a common government can embrace so large a sphere? —Let experience solve it.—To listen to mere speculation in such a case were criminal. We are authorized to hope that a proper organization of the whole, with the auxiliary agency of governments for the respective subdivisions, will afford a happy issue to the experiment. 'Tis well worth a fair and full experiment. With such powerful and obvious motives to Union, affecting all parts of our country, while experience shall not have demonstrated its impracticability, there will always be reason to distrust the patriotism of those, who in any quarter may endeavor to weaken its bands.—

In contemplating the causes which may disturb our Union, it occurs as a matter of serious concern, that any ground should have been furnished for characterizing parties by *Geographical* discriminations—*Northern* and *Southern*—*Atlantic* and *Western*; whence designing men may endeavor to excite a belief, that there is a real difference of local interests and views. One of the expedients of Party to acquire influence, within particular districts, is to misrepresent the opinions and aims of other districts. —You cannot shield yourselves too much against the jealousies and heart burnings which spring from these misrepresentations; —They tend to render alien to each other those who ought to be bound together by fraternal affection.—The inhabitants of our Western country have lately had a useful lesson on this head.—They have seen, in the negotiation by the Executive, and in the unanimous ratification by the Senate, of the treaty with Spain, and in the universal satisfaction at that event, throughout the United States, a decisive proof how unfounded were the suspicions propagated among them of a policy in the General Government and in the Atlantic States unfriendly to their interests in regard to the MISSISSIPPI.—They have been witnesses to the formation of two Treaties, that with G. Britain, and that with Spain, which secure to them every thing they could desire, in respect to our Foreign Relations, towards confirming their prosperity.—Will it not be their wisdon to rely for the preservation of these advantages on the UNION by which they were procured?—Will they not henceforth be deaf to those advisers, if such there are, who would sever them from from their Brethren, and connect them with Aliens?—

To the efficacy and permanency of your Union, a Government for the whole is indispensable.—No alliances however strict between the parts can be an adequate substitute.—They must inevitably experience the infractions and interruptions which all alliances in all times have experienced.—Sensible of this momentous truth, you have improved upon your first essay, by the adoption of a Constitution of Government, better calculated than your former for an intimate Union, and for the efficacious management of your common concerns.—This government, the offspring of your own choice uninfluenced and unawed, adopted upon full investigation and mature deliberation, completely free in its principles, in the distribution of its powers, uniting security with energy, and containing within itself a provision for its own amendment, has a just claim to your confidence and your support. —Respect for its authority, compliance with its Laws, acquiescence in its measures, are duties enjoined by the fundamental maxims of true Liberty.—The basis of our political systems is the right of the people to make and to alter their Constitutions of Government.—But the Constitution which at any time exists, 'till changed by an explicit and authentic act of the whole People, is sacredly obligatory upon all.—The very idea of the power and the right of the People to establish Government, presupposes the duty of every individual to obey the established Government.

All obstructions to the execution of the Laws, all combinations and associations, under whatever plausible character, with the real design to direct, controul, counteract, or awe the regular deliberation and action of the constituted authorities, are destructive of this fundamental principle, and of fatal tendency.—They serve to organize faction, to give it an artificial and extraordinary force—to put in the place of the delegated will of the Nation, the will of a party;— often a small but artful and enterprizing minority of the community;—and, according to the alternate triumphs of different parties, to make the public administration the mirror of the ill-concerted and incongruous projects of faction, rather than the organ of consistent and wholesome plans digested by common councils, and modified by mutual interests.—However combinations or associations of the above description may now and then answer popular ends, they are likely, in the course of time and things, to become potent engines, by which cunning, ambitious, and unprincipled men will be enabled to subvert the Power of the People and to usurp for themselves the reins of Government; destroying afterwards the very engines, which have lifted them to unjust dominion.—

Towards the preservation of your Government and the permanency of your present happy state, it is requisite, not only that you steadily discountenance irregular oppositions to its acknowledged authority, but also that you resist with care the spirit of innovation upon its principles, however specious the pretexts.—One method of assault may be to effect, in the forms of the Constitution, alterations which will impair the energy of the system, and thus to undermine what cannot be directly overthrown.—In all the changes to which you may be invited, remember that time and habit are at least as necessary to fix the true character of Governments, as of other human institutions—that experience is the surest standard, by which to test the real tendency of the existing Constitution of a Country— that facility in changes upon the credit of mere hypothesis and opinion exposes to perpetual change, from the endless variety of hypothesis and opinion:—and remember, specially, that, for the efficient management of your common interests, in a country so extensive as ours, a Government of as much vigor as is consistent with the perfect security of Liberty is indispensable.—Liberty itself will find in such a Government, with powers properly distributed and adjusted, its surest Guardian.—It is, indeed, little else than a name, where the Government is too feeble to withstand the enterprises of faction, to confine each member of the society within the limits prescribed by the laws, and to maintain all in the secure and tranquil enjoyment of the rights of persons and property.

I have already intimated to you the danger of Parties in the State, with particular reference to the founding of them on Geographical discriminations.—Let me now take a more comprehensive view, and warn you in the most solemn manner against the baneful effects of the Spirit of Party, generally.

This Spirit, unfortunately, is inseparable from our nature, having its root in the strongest passions of the human mind.—It exists under different shapes in all Governments, more or less stifled, controuled, or repressed; but, in those of the popular form, it is seen in its greatest rankness, and is truly their worst enemy.—

The alternate domination of one faction over another, sharpened by the spirit of revenge natural to party dissension, which in different ages and countries has perpetrated the most horrid enormities, is itself a frightful despotism.—But this leads at length to a more formal and permanent despotism.—The disorders and miseries, which result, gradually incline the minds of men to seek security and repose in the absolute power of an Individual: and sooner or later the chief of some prevailing faction, more able of more fortunate than his competitors, turns this disposition to the purposes of his own elevation, on the ruins of Public Liberty.

Without looking forward to an extremity of this kind, (which nevertheless ought not to be entirely out of sight), the common and continual mischiefs of the spirit of Party are sufficient to make it the interest and duty of a wise People to discourage and restrain it.—

It serves always to distract the Public Councils, and enfeeble the Public administration.—It agitates the community with ill founded jealousies and false alarms, kindles the animosity of one part against another, foments occasionally riot and insurrection. —It opens the doors to foreign influence and corruption, which find a facilitated access to the Government itself through the channels of party passion. Thus the policy and the will of one country, are subjected to the policy and will of another.

There is an opinion that parties in free countries are useful checks upon the Administration of the Government, and serve to keep alive the Spirit of Liberty.—This within certain limits is probably true—and in Governments of a Monarchical cast, Patriotism may look with indulgence, if not with favour, upon the spirit of party.— But in those of the popular character, in Governments purely elective, it is a spirit not to be encouraged.—From their natural tendency, it is certain there will always be enough of that spirit for every salutary purpose,—and there being constant danger of excess, the effort ought to be, by force of public opinion, to mitigate and assuage it.—A fire not to be quenched; it demands a uniform vigilance to prevent its bursting into a flame, lest, instead of warming, it should consume.

It is important, likewise, that the habits of thinking in a free country should inspire caution in those entrusted with its administration, to confine themselves within their respective constitutional spheres; avoiding in the exercise of the powers of one department to encroach upon another.—The spirit of encroachment tends to consolidate the powers of all the departments in one, and thus to create, whatever the form of government, a real despotism.—A just estimate of that love of power, and proneness to abuse it, which predominates in the human heart, is sufficient to satisfy us of the truth of this position.—The necessity of reciprocal checks in the exercise of political power, by dividing and distributing it into different depositories, and constituting each the Guardian of the Public Weal against invasions by the others, has been evinced by experiments ancient and modern; some of them in our country and under our own eyes.—To preserve them must be as necessary as to institute them. If in the opinion of the People, the distribution or modification of the Constitutional powers be in any particular wrong, let it be corrected by an amendment in the way which the Constitution designates.—But let there be no change by usurpation; for though this, in one instance, may be the instrument of good, it is the customary weapon by which free governments are destroyed.—The precedent must always greatly overbalance in permanent evil any partial or transient benefit which the use can at any time yield.—

Of all the dispositions and habits, which lead to political prosperity, Religion and morality are indispensable supports.—In vain would that man claim the tribute of Patriotism, who should labour to subvert these great Pillars of human happiness, these firmest props of the duties of Men and Citizens.—The mere Politician, equally with the pious man, ought to respect and to cherish them.—A volume could not trace all their connexions with private and public felicity.—Let it simply be asked where is the security for property, for reputation, for life, if the sense of religious obligation *desert* the oaths, which are the instruments of investigation in Courts of Justice? And let us with caution indulge the supposition, that morality can be maintained without religion.—Whatever may be conceded to the influence of refined education on minds of peculiar structure—reason and experience both forbid us to expect, that national morality can prevail in exclusion of religious principle.—

'Tis substantially true, that virtue or morality is a necessary spring of popular government.—The rule indeed extends with more or less force to every species of Free Government.—Who that is a sincere friend to it can look with indifference upon attempts to shake the foundation of the fabric?—

Promote, then, as an object of primary importance, institutions for the general diffusion of knowledge. In proportion as the structure of a government gives force to public opinion, it is essential that public opinion should be enlightened.—

As a very important source of strength and security, cherish public credit.—One method of preserving it is, to use it as sparingly as possible:—avoiding occasions of expense by cultivating peace, but remembering also that timely disbursements to prepare for danger frequently prevent much greater disbursements to repel it—avoiding likewise the accumulation of debt, not only by shunning occasions of expense, but by vigorous exertions in time of Peace to discharge the debts which unavoidable wars may have occasioned, not ungenerously throwing upon posterity the burthen which we ourselves ought to bear. The execution of these maxims belongs to your Representatives, but it is necessary that public opinion should cooperate.—To facilitate to them the performance of their duty, it is essential that you should practically bear in mind, that towards the payment of debts there must be Revenue—that to have Revenue there must be taxes—that no taxes can be devised which are not more or less inconvenient and unpleasant—that the intrinsic embarrassment inseparable from the selection of the proper objects (which is always a choice of difficulties) ought to be a decisive motive for a candid construction of the conduct of the Government in making it, and for a spirit of acquiescence in the measures for obtaining Revenue which the public exigencies may at any time dictate.—

Observe good faith and justice towards all Nations. Cultivate peace and harmony with all.—Religion and Morality enjoin this conduct; and can it be that good policy does not equally enjoin it? It will be worthy of a free, enlightened, and, at no distant period, a great nation, to give to mankind the magnanimous and too novel example of a People always guided by an exalted justice and benevolence.—Who can doubt that in the course of time and things, the fruits of such a plan would richly repay any temporary advantages, which might be lost by a steady adherence to it? Can it be that Providence has not connected the permanent felicity of a Nation with its virtue? The experiment, at least, is recommended by every sentiment which ennobles human nature.—Alas! is it rendered impossible by its vices?

In the execution of such a plan nothing is more essential than that permanent, inveterate antipathies against particular nations and passionate attachments for others should be excluded; and that in place of them just and amicable feelings towards all should be cultivated.—The Nation, which indulges towards another an habitual hatred or an habitual fondness, is in some degree a slave. It is a slave to its animosity or to its affection, either of which is sufficient to lead it astray from its duty and its interest.—Antipathy in one nation against another disposes each more readily to offer insult and injury, to lay hold of slight causes of umbrage, and to be haughty and intractable, when accidental or trifling occasions of dispute occur.—Hence frequent collisions, obstinate, envenomed and bloody contests.—The Nation prompted by ill-will and resentment sometimes impels to War the Government, contrary to the best calculations of policy.—The Government sometimes participates in the national propensity, and adopts through passion what reason would reject;—at other times, it makes the animosity of the Nation subservient to projects of hostility instigated by pride, ambition, and other sinister and pernicious motives.—The peace often, sometimes perhaps the Liberty, of Nations has been the victim.—

So likewise a passionate attachment of one Nation for another produces a variety of evils.—Sympathy for the favourite nation, facilitating the illusion of an imaginary common interest in cases where no real common interest exists, and infusing into one the enmities of the other, betrays the former into a participation in the quarrels and wars of the latter, without adequate inducement or justification: It leads also to concessions to the favourite Nation of privileges denied to others, which is apt doubly to injure the Nation making the concessions; by unnecessarily parting with what ought to have been retained, and by exciting jealousy, ill-will, and a disposition to retaliate, in the parties from whom equal privileges are withheld; and it gives to ambitious, corrupted, or deluded citizens, (who devote themselves to the favourite Nation) facility to betray, or sacrifice the interests of their own country, without odium, sometimes even with popularity:—gilding with the apearances of a virtuous sense of obligation, a commendable deference for public opinion, or a laudable zeal for public good, the base or foolish compliances of ambition, corruption or infatuation.—

As avenues to foreign influence in innumerable ways, such attachments are particularly alarming to the truly enlightened and independent Patriot.—How many opportunities do they afford to tamper with domestic factions, to practise the arts of seduction, to mislead public opinion, to influence or awe the public councils! Such an attachment of a small or weak, towards a great and powerful nation, dooms the former to be the satellite of the latter.

Against the insidious wiles of foreign influence, I conjure you to believe me, fellow-citizens, the jealousy of a free people ought to be *constantly* awake, since history and experience prove that foreign influence is one of the most baneful foes of republican Government.—But that jealousy, to be useful, must be impartial; else it becomes the instrument of the very influence to be avoided, instead of a defence against it.—Excessive partiality for one foreign nation and excessive dislike of another, cause those whom they actuate to see danger only on one side, and serve to veil and even second the arts of influence on the other.—Real Patriots, who may resist the intrigues of the favourite, are liable to become suspected and odious; while its tools and dupes usurp the applause and confidence of the people, to surrender their interests.—

The great rule of conduct for us, in regard to foreign Nations, is, in extending our commercial relations, to have with them as little *Political* connection as possible.—So far as we have already formed engagements, let them be fulfilled with perfect good faith. Here let us stop.—

Europe has a set of primary interests, which to us have none, or a very remote relation.—Hence she must be engaged in frequent controversies, the causes of which are essentially foreign to our concerns.—Hence therefore it must be unwise in us to implicate ourselves, by artificial ties in the ordinary vicissitudes of her politics, or the ordinary combinations and collisions of her friendships, or enmities.

Our detached and distant situation invites and enables us to pursue a different course.—If we remain one People, under an efficient government, the period is not far off, when we may defy material injury from external annoyance; when we may take such an attitude as will cause the neutrality we may at any time resolve upon to be scrupulously respected. When belligerent nations, under the impossibility of making acquisitions upon us, will not lightly hazard the giving us provocation; when we may choose peace or war, as our interest guided by our justice shall counsel.

Why forego the advantages of so peculiar a situation?—Why quit our own to stand upon foreign ground?—Why, by interweaving our destiny with that of any part of Europe, entangle our peace and prosperity in the toils of European ambition, rivalship, interest, humour, or caprice?—

'Tis our true policy to steer clear of permanent alliances, with any portion of the foreign world;—so far, I mean, as we are now at liberty to do it—for let me not be understood as capable of patronizing infidelity to existing engagements, (I hold the maxim no less applicable to public than to private affairs, that honesty is always the best policy).—I repeat it therefore let those engagements be observed in their genuine sense.—But in my opinion it is unnecessary and would be unwise to extend them.—

Taking care always to keep ourselves, by suitable establishments, on a respectably defensive posture, we may safely trust to temporary alliances for extraordinary emergencies.—

Harmony, liberal intercourse with all nations, are recommended by policy, humanity, and interest. But even our commercial policy should hold an equal and impartial hand:—neither seeking nor granting exclusive favours or preferences;—consulting the natural course of things; — diffusing and diversifying by gentle means the streams of commerce, but forcing nothing;—establishing with Powers so disposed—in order to give trade a stable course, to define the rights of our Merchants, and to enable the Government to support them—conventional rules of intercourse, the best that present circumstances and mutual opinion will permit; but temporary, and liable to be from time to time abandoned or varied, as experience and circumstances shall dictate; constantly keeping in view that 't is folly in one nation to look for disinterested favors from another,—that it must pay with a portion of its independence for whatever it may accept under that character—that by such acceptance, it may place itself in the condition of having given equivalents for nominal favours and yet of being reproached with ingratitude for not giving more.—There can be no greater error than to expect, or calculate upon real favours from Nation to Nation.—'T is an illusion which experience must cure, which a just pride ought to discard.

In offering to you, my Countrymen, these counsels of an old and affectionate friend, I dare not hope they will make the strong and lasting impression, I could wish,—that they will controul the usual current of the passions, or prevent our Nation from running the course which has hitherto marked the destiny of Nations.—But if I may even flatter myself, that they may be productive of some partial benefit; some occasional good; that they may now and then recur to moderate the fury of party spirit, to warn against the mischiefs of foreign intrigue, to guard against the impostures of pretended patriotism, this hope will be a full recompense for the solicitude for your welfare, by which they have been dictated.—

How far in the discharge of my official duties, I have been guided by the principles which have been delineated, the public Records and other evidences of my conduct must witness to You, and to the world.—To myself the assurance of my own conscience is, that I have at least believed myself to be guided by them.

In relation to the still subsisting War in Europe, my Proclamation of the 22d of April 1793 is the index to my plan.—Sanctioned by your approving voice and by that of Your Representatives in both Houses of Congress, the spirit of that measure has continually governed me:—uninfluenced by any attempts to deter or divert me from it.

After deliberate examination with the aid of the best lights I could obtain, I was well satisfied that our country, under all the circumstances of the case, had a right to take, and was bound in duty and interest, to take a Neutral position.—Having taken it, I determined, as far as should depend upon me, to maintain it, with moderation, perseverance, and firmness.—

The considerations which respect the right to hold this conduct, it is not necessary on this occasion to detail. I will only observe, that, according to my understanding of the matter, that right, so far from being denied by any of the Belligerent Powers, has been virtually admitted by all.—

The duty of holding a neutral conduct may be inferred without anything more, from the obligation which justice and humanity impose on every Nation, in cases in which it is free to act, to maintain inviolate the relations of Peace and Amity towards other Nations.—

The inducements of interest for observing that conduct will best be referred to your own reflections and experience.—With me, a predominant motive has been to endeavour to gain time to our country to settle and mature its yet recent institutions, and to progress without interruption to that degree of strength and consistency, which is necessary to give it, humanly speaking, the command of its own fortune.

Though, in reviewing the incidents of my Administration, I am unconscious of intentional error—I am nevertheless too sensible of my defects not to think it probable that I may have committed many errors.—Whatever they may be, I fervently beseech the Almighty to avert or mitigate the evils to which they may tend.—I shall also carry with me the hope that my country will never cease to view them with indulgence; and that after forty-five years of my life dedicated to its service, with an upright zeal, the faults of incompetent abilities will be consigned to oblivion, as myself must soon be to the mansions of rest.

Relying on its kindness in this as in other things, and actuated by that fervent love towards it, which is so natural to a man, who views in it the native soil of himself and his progenitors for several generations;—I anticipate with pleasing expectation that retreat, in which I promise myself to realize, without alloy, the sweet enjoyment of partaking, in the midst of my fellow-citizens, the benign influence of good Laws under a free Government,—the ever favourite object of my heart, and the happy reward, as I trust, of our mutual cares, labours, and dangers.

Letter to General Lafayette
on Trouble with France
MOUNT VERNON, 25 DECEMBER, 1798.

My dear Sir,

❊   ❊   ❊   ❊   ❊   ❊   ❊   ❊

To give you a complete view of the politics and situation of things in this country would far exceed the limits of a letter, and to trace effects to their causes would be a work of time. But the sum of them may be given in a few words, and amounts to this. That a party exists in the United States, formed by a combination of causes, which oppose the government in all its measures, and are determined (as all their conduct evinces) by clogging its wheels indirectly to change the nature of it, and to subvert the constitution. To effect this, no means which have a tendency to accomplish their purposes are left unessayed. The friends of government, who are anxious to maintain neutrality, and to preserve the country in peace, and adopt measures to secure these are charged by them as being monarchists, aristocrats, and infractors of the constitution, which, according to their interpretation of it, would be a mere cipher. While they arrogated to themselves (until the eyes of the people began to discover how outrageously they had been treated in their commercial concerns by the Directory of France, and that that was a ground on which they could no longer tread) the sole merit of being the friends of France, when in fact they had no more regard for that nation than for the Grand Turk, further than their own views were promoted by it; denouncing those who differed in opinion, (whose principles are purely American, and whose sole view was to observe a strict neutrality) with acting under British influence, and being directed by her counsels, now with being her pensioners.

This is but a short sketch of what requires much time to illustrate; and is given with no other view, than to show you what would be your situation here at this crisis under such circumstances as it unfolds.

You have expressed a wish, worthy of the benevolence of your heart, that I would exert all my endeavors to avert the calamitous effects of a rupture between our countries. Believe me, my dear friend, that no man can deprecate an event of this sort with more horror than I should, and that no one, during the whole of my administration, labored more incessantly, and with more sincerity and zeal, than I did, to avoid this, and to render every justice, nay favor, to France, consistent with the neutrality, which had been proclaimed, sanctioned by Congress, approved by the State legislatures, and the people at large in their town and county meetings. But neutrality was not the point at which France was aiming; for, whilst it was crying *Peace, Peace,* and pretending that they did not wish us to be embroiled in their quarrel with Great Britain, they were pursuing measures in *this country* so repugnant to its sovereignty, and so incompatible with every principle of neutrality, as must inevitably have produced a war with the latter. And when they found, that the government *here* was resolved to adhere steadily to its plan of neutrality, their next step was to destroy the confidence of the people in and to separate them from it; for which purpose their diplomatic agents were specially instructed, and in the attempt were aided by inimical characters among ourselves, not, as I observed before, because they loved France more than any other nation, but because it was an instrument to facilitate the destruction of their own government.

Hence proceeded those charges, which I have already enumerated, against the friends to peace and order. No doubt remains on this side of the water, that to the representations of, and encouragement given by, these people is to be ascribed, in a great measure, the infractions of our treaty with France; her violation of the laws of nations, disregard of justice, and even of sound policy. But herein they have not only deceived France, but were deceived themselves, as the event has proved; for, no sooner did the yeomanry of this country come to a right understanding of the nature of the dispute, than they rose as one man with a tender of their services, their lives, and their fortunes to support the government of their choice, and to defend their country. This has produced a declaration from them (how sincere let others judge), that, if the French should attempt to invade this country, they themselves would be amongst the foremost to repel the attack.

You add in another place, that the Executive Directory are disposed to accommodation of all differences. If they are sincere in this declaration, let them evidence it by actions; for words unaccompanied therewith will not be much regarded now. I would pledge myself, that the government and people of the United States will meet them heart and hand at *fair* negotiations; having no wish more ardent, than to live in peace with all the world, provided they are suffered to remain undisturbed in their just rights. Of this, their patience, forbearance, and repeated solicitations under accumulated injuries and insults, are incontestable proofs; but it is not to be inferred from hence, that they suffer any nation under the sun, (while they retain a proper sense of virtue and independence,) to trample upon their rights with impunity, or to direct or influence the internal concerns of their country.

It has been the policy of France, and that of the opposition party among ourselves, to inculcate a belief that all those, who have exerted themselves to keep this country in peace, did it from an overweening attachment to Great Britain. But it is a solemn truth, and you may count upon it, that it is void of foundation, and propagated for no other purpose, than to excite popular clamor against those, whose aim was peace, and whom they wished out of the way.

That there are many among us, who wish to see this country embroiled on the side of Great Britain, and others, who are anxious that we should take part with France against her, admits of no doubt. But it is a fact, on which you may entirely and absolutely rely, that the governing powers of the country and a large part of the people are truly Americans in principle, attached to the interest of it, and unwilling under any circumstances whatsoever to participate in the politics or contests of Europe; much less, since they have found that France, having forsaken the ground she first took, is interfering in the internal concerns of all nations, neutral as well as belligerent, and setting the world in an uproar.

After my Valedictory Address to the people of the United States, you would no doubt be somewhat surprised to hear, that I had again consented to gird on the sword. But, having struggled eight or nine years against the invasion of our rights by one power, and to establish our independence of it, I could not remain an unconcerned spectator of the attempt of another power to accomplish the same object, though in a different way, with less pretensions; indeed, without any at all.

On the politics of Europe I shall express no opinion, nor make any inquiry who is right or who is wrong. I wish well to all nations and to all men. My politics are plain and simple. I think every nation has a right to establish that form of government, under which it conceives it shall live most happy; provided it infracts no right, or is not dangerous to others; and that no governments ought to interfere with the internal concerns of another, except for the security of what is due to themselves.

I sincerely hope, that Madame de Lafayette will accomplish all her wishes in France, and return safe to you with renovated health. I congratulate you on the marriage of your eldest daughter, and beg to be presented to them both and to Virginia in the most respectful and affectionate terms. To George I have written. In all these things Mrs. Washington, as the rest of the family would do if they were at home, most cordially joins me; as she does in wishing you and them every felicity, which this life can afford, as some consolation for your long, cruel, and painful confinement and sufferings.

I shall now only add, what you knew well before, that, with the most sincere friendship and affectionate regard, I am always yours,

G Washington

P. S. Your old aid de camp—and my worthy nephew George A. Washington; died about five years ago of a pulmonary complaint. He left 3 fine children, a daughter & two sons, the eldest of the boys was called after you.

The letters herewith enclosed and directed one to yourself, another to George and the third to Mr. Frestel, have been some time in my possession and detained to be delivered to you here upon the same principle that prevented me from writing to you at an earlier period.

The Will of George Washington

In the name of God amen.

I George Washington of Mount Vernon, a citizen of the United States, and lately President of the same, do make, ordain, and declare this Instrument, which is written with my own hand and every page thereof subscribed with my name, to be my last Will & Testament, revoking all others.

Imprimus. All my debts, of which there are but few, and none of magnitude, are to be punctually and speedily paid—and the Legacies hereinafter bequeathed, are to be discharged as soon as circumstances will permit, and in the manner directed.

Item. To my dearly loved wife Martha Washington I give and bequeath the use, profit and benefit of my whole Estate, real and personal, for the term of her natural life, except such parts thereof as are specifically disposed of hereafter:—My improved lot in the Town of Alexandria, situated on Pitt & Cameron Streets, I give to her & her heirs forever, as I also do my household & kitchen furniture of every sort & kind, with the liquors and groceries which may be on hand at the time of my decease; to be used & disposed of as she may think proper.

Item Upon the decease of my wife, it is my Will & desire that all the Slaves which I hold in *my own right*, shall receive their freedom.—To emancipate them during her life, would, tho' earnestly wished by me, be attended with such insuperable difficulties on account of their intermixture by Marriages with the Dower Negroes, as to excite the most painful sensations, if not disagreeable consequences from the latter, while both descriptions are in the occupancy of the same proprietor; it not being in my power, under the tenure by which the dower Negros are held, to manumit them.—And whereas among those who will receive freedom according to this devise, there may be some, who from old age or bodily infirmities, and others who on account of their infancy, that will be unable to support themselves; it is my Will and desire that all who come under the first & second description shall be comfortably cloathed & fed by my heirs while they live;—and that such of the latter description as have no parents living, or if living are unable, or unwilling to provide for them, shall be bound by the Court until they shall arrive at the age of twenty five years;—and in cases where no record can be produced, whereby their ages can be ascertained, the judgment of the Court, upon its own view of the subject, shall be adequate and final.— The Negros thus bound, are (by their Masters or Mistresses) to be taught to read & write; and to be brought up to some useful occupation, agreeably to the Laws of the Commonwealth of Virginia, providing for the support of Orphans and other poor Children.—and I do hereby expressly forbid the sale, or transportation out of the said Commonwealth, of any slave I may die possessed of, under any pretence whatsoever.— And I do moreover most pointedly, and most solemnly enjoin it upon my Executors hereafter named, or the Survivors of them, to see that *this* clause respecting Slaves; and every part hereof be religiously fulfilled at the Epoch at which it is directed to take place; without evasion, neglect or delay, after the Crops which may then be on the ground are harvested, particularly as it respects the aged and infirm;—seeing that a regular and permanent fund be established for their support so long as there are subjects requiring it;—not trusting to the uncertain provision to be made by individuals.—And to my Mulatto man William (calling himself William Lee) I give immediate freedom; or if he should prefer it (on account of the accidents which have befallen him, and which have rendered him incapable of walking or of any active employment) to remain in the situation he now is, it shall be optional in him to do so: In either case however, I allow him an annuity of thirty dollars during his natural life, which shall be independent of the victuals & cloaths he has been accustomed to receive, if he chuses the last alternative; but in full with his freedom, if he prefers the first;—& this I give him as a testimony of my sense of his attachment to me, and for his faithful services during the Revolutionary War.—

Item. To the Trustees (Governors, or by whatsoever other name they may be designated) of the Academy in the Town of Alexandria, I give and bequeath, in Trust, four thousand dollars, or in other words twenty of the shares which I hold in the Bank of Alexandria, towards the support of a Free school established at, and annexed to, the said Academy; for the purpose of Educating such orphan children, or the children of such other poor and indigent persons as are unable to accomplish it with their own means; and who, in the judgment of the Trustees of the said Seminary, are best entitled to the benefit of this donation.—The aforesaid twenty shares I give & bequeath in perpetuity;—the dividends only of which are to be drawn for, and applied by the said Trustees for the time being, for the uses above mentioned;—the stock to remain entire and untouched; unless indications of a failure of the said Bank should be so apparent, or a discontinuance thereof should render a removal of this fund necessary;—in either of these cases, the amount of the stock here devised, is to be vested in some other Bank or public Institution, whereby the interest may with regularity & certainty be drawn, and applied as above.—And to prevent misconception, my meaning is, and is hereby declared to be, that these twenty shares are in lieu of, and not in addition to, the thousand pounds given by a missive letter some years ago; in consequence whereof an annuity of fifty pounds has since been paid towards the support of this Institution

Item. Whereas by a Law of the Commonwealth of Virginia, enacted in the year 1785, the Legislature thereof was pleased (as an evidence of Its approbation of the services I had rendered the Public during the Revolution—and partly, I believe, in consideration of my having suggested the vast advantages which the Community would derive from the extension of its Inland Navigation, under Legislative patronage) to present me with one hundred shares of one hundred dollars—each, in the incorporated company established for the purpose of extending the Navigation of James River from tide water to the Mountains:—and also with fifty shares of one hundred pounds sterling each, in the Corporation of another Company, likewise established for the similar purpose of opening the Navigation of the River Potomac from tide water to Fort Cumberland; the acceptance of which, although the offer was highly honourable, and grateful to my feelings, was refused, as inconsistent with a principle which I had adopted, and had never departed from, namely—not to receive pecuniary compensation for any services I could render my country in its arduous struggle with great Britain, for its Rights, and because I had evaded similar propositions from other States in the Union;—adding to this refusal, however, an intimation that, if it should be the pleasure of the Legislature to permit me to appropriate the said shares to *public uses,* I would receive them on those terms with due sensibility;—and this it having consented to, in flattering terms, as will appear by a subsequent Law and sundry resolutions, in the most ample and honourable manner, I proceed after this recital, for the more correct understanding of the case, to declare—

That as it has always been a source of serious regret with me to see the youth of these United States sent to foreign countries for the purpose of Education, often before their minds were formed, or they had inbibed any adequate ideas of the happiness of their own;—contracting, too frequently, not only habits of dissipation & extravagance, but principles unfriendly to Republican Governmt. and to the true &

genuine liberties of mankind; which, thereafter are rarely overcome.—For these reasons, it has been my ardent wish to see a plan devised on a liberal scale which would have a tendency to sprd. systematic ideas through all parts of this rising Empire, thereby to do away local attachments and State prejudices, as far as the nature of things wound, or indeed ought to admit, from our National Councils.—Looking anxiously forward to the accomplishment of so desirable an object as this is, (in my estimation) my mind has not been able to contemplate any plan more likely to effect the measure than the establishment of a UNIVERSITY in a central part of the United States, to which the youth of fortune and talents from all parts thereof might be sent for the completion of their Education in all the branches of polite literature;—in arts and Sciences,—in acquiring knowledge in the principles of Politics & good Government;—and (as a matter of infinite Importance in my judgment) by associating with each other, and forming friendships in Juvenile years, be enabled to free themselves in a proper degree from those local prejudices & habitual jealousies which have just been mentioned; and which, when carried to excess, are never failing sources of disquietude to the Public Mind, and pregnant of mischievous consequences to this country:—Under these impressions, so fully dilated,

Item I give and bequeath in perpetuity the fifty shares which I hold in the Potomac Company (under the aforesaid Acts of the Legislature of Virginia) towards the endowment of a UNIVERSITY to be established within the limits of the District of Columbia, under the auspices of the General Government, if that government should incline to extend a fostering hand towards it;—and until such Seminary is established, and the funds arising on these shares shall be required for its support, my further Will & desire is that the profit accruing therefrom shall, whenever the dividends are made, be laid out in purchasing stock in the Bank of Columbia, or some other Bank, at the discretion of my Executors; or by the Treasurer of the United States for the timebeing under the direction of Congress; provided that Honourable body should Patronize the measure, and the Dividends proceeding from the purchase of such Stock is to be vested in more stock, and so on, until a sum adequate to the accomplishment of the object is obtained, of which I have not the smallest doubt, before many years passes away; even if no aid or encouraged is given by Legislative authority, or from any other source

Item. The hundred shares which I held in the James River Company, I have given, and now confirm in perpetuity to, and for the use & benefit of Liberty Hall Academy, in the County of Rockbridge, in the Commonwealth of Virga.

Item. I release exonerate and discharge,

the Estate of my deceased brother Samuel Washington, from the payment of the money which is due to me for the Land I sold to Philip Pendleton (lying in the County of Berkeley) who assigned the same to him the said Samuel; who, by agreement was to pay me therefor.—And whereas by some contract (the purport of which was never communicated to me) between the said Samuel and his son Thornton Washington, the latter became possessed of the aforesaid Land, without any conveyance having passed from me, either to the said Pendleton, the said Samuel, or the said Thornton, and without any consideration having been made, by which neglect neither the legal nor equitable title has been alienated;—it rests therefore with me to declare my intentions concerning the Premises—and these are, to give & bequeath the said land to whomsoever the said Thornton Washington (who is also dead) devised the same; or to his heirs forever if he died Intestate:—Exonerating the estate of the said Thornton, equally with that of the said Samuel from payment of the purchase money; which, with Interest; agreeably to the original contract with the said Pendleton, would amount to more than a thousand pounds.—And whereas two other Sons of my said deceased brother Samuel—namely, George Steptoe Washington and Lawrence Augustine Washington, were, by the decease of those to whose care they were committed, brought under my protection, and in conseqe. have occasioned advances on my part for their Education at College, and other Schools, for their board—cloathing—and other incidental expences, to the amount of near five thousand dollars over and above the sums furnished by their Estate, wch sum may be inconvenient for them, or their fathers Estate to refund.—I do for these reasons acquit them, and the said estate from the payment thereof.—My intention being that all accounts between them and me, and their fathers estate and me shall stand balanced.—

Item The balance due to me from the Estate of Bartholomew Dandridge deceased (my wife's brother) and which amounted on the first day of October 1795 to four hundred and twenty five pounds (as will appear by an account rendered by his deceased son John Dandridge, who was the acting Exr. of his fathers Will) I release & acquit from the payment thereof.—And the Negroes, then thirty three in number) formerly belonging to the said estate, who were taken in execution—sold—and purchased in on my account in the year and ever since have remained in the possession, and to the use of Mary, Widow of the said Bartholomew Dandridge with their increase, it is my Will & desire shall continue & be in her possession, without paying hire, or making compensation for the same for the time past or to come, during her natural life; at the expiration of which, I direct that all of them who are forty years old & upwards, shall receive their freedom; all under that age and above sixteen, shall serve seven years and no longer;—and all under sixteen years, shall serve until they are twenty five years of age, and then be free.—And to avoid disputes resspecting the ages of any of these Negros, they are to be taken to the Court of the County in which they reside, and the judgment thereof, in this relation shall be final; and a record thereof made; which may be adduced as evidence at any time thereafter, if disputes should arise concerning the same—And I further direct that the heirs of the said Bartholomew Dandridge shall, equally, share the benefits arising from the services of the said negros according to the tenor of this devise, upon the decease of their Mother.—

Item   If Charles Carter who intermarried with my niece Betty Lewis is not sufficiently secured in the title to the lots he had of me in the town of Fredericksburgh, it is my Will & desire that my Executors shall make such conveyances of them at the Law requires, to render it perfect.—

Item   To my Nephew William Augustine Washington and his heirs (if he should conceive them to be objects worth prosecuting) and to his heirs,—a lot in the Town of Manchester (opposite to Richmond) No. 265—drawn on my sole account, and also the tenth of one or two, hundred acre lots, and two or three half acre lots in the City, and vicinity of Richmond, drawn in partnership with nine others, all in the lottery of the deceased William Byrd are given—as is also a lot which I purchased of John Hood, conveyed by William Willie and Samuel Gordon Trustees of the said John Hood, numbered 139 in the Town of Edenburgh, in the County of Prince George, State of Virginia

Item   To my Nephew Bushrod Washington, I give and bequeath all the Papers in my possession, which relate to my Civil and Military Administration of the affairs of this County;—I leave to him also, such of my private Papers as are worth preserving;—and at the decease of wife, and before if she is not inclined to retain them, I give and bequeath my library of Books, and Pamphlets of every kind.—

Item   Having sold Lands which I possessed in the State of Pennsylvania, and part of a tract held in equal right with George Clinton, late Governor of New York, in the State of New York;—my share of land, & interest, in the Great Dismal Swamp, and a tract of land which I owned in the County of Gloucester;—withholding the legal titles thereto, until the consideration money should be paid.—And having moreover leased, & conditionally sold (as will appear by the tenor of the said leases) all my lands upon the Great Kanhawa, and a tract upon Difficult Run, in the County of Loudoun, it is my Will and direction, that whensoever the Contracts are fully, & respectively complied with, according to the spirit; true intent & meaning thereof, on

the part of the purchasers, their heirs or assigns, that then, and in that case, Conveyances are to be made; agreeably to the terms of the said Contracts; and the money arising therefrom, when paid, to be vested in Bank stock; the dividends whereof, as of that also wch is already vested therein, is to inure to my said wife during her life but the Stock itself is to remain, & be subject to the general distribution hereafter directed.—

Item   To the Earl of Buchan I recommit "the Box made of the Oak that sheltered the Great Sir William Wallace after the battle of Falkirk"—presented to me by his Lordship, in terms too flattering for me to repeat,—with a request "to pass it, on the event of my decease, to the man in my country, who should appear to merit it best, upon the same conditions that have induced him to send it to me." Whether easy, or not, to select *the man* who might comport with his Lordships opinion in this respect, is not for me to say; but conceiving that no disposition of this valuable curiosity can be more eligable than the re-commitment of it to his own Cabinet, agreeably to the original design of the Goldsmiths Company of Edenburgh, who presented it to him, and at his request, consented that it should be transfered to me; I do give & bequeath the same to his Lordship, and in case of his decease, to his heir with my grateful thanks for the distinguished honour of presenting it to me; and more especially for the favourable sentiments with which he accompanied it.—

Item   To my brother Charles Washington I give & bequeath the gold headed Cane left me by Doctr. Franklin in his Will—I add nothing to it, because of the ample provision I have made for his Issue.—To the acquaintances and friends of my Juvenile years, Lawrence Washington & Robert Washington of Chotanck, I give my other two gold headed Canes, having my Arms engraved on them; and to each (as they will be useful where they live) I leave one of the Spy-glasses which constituted part of my equipage during the late War.—To my compatriot in arms, and old & intimate friend Doctr. Craik, I give my Bureau (or as the Cabinet makers call it, Tambour Secretary) and the circular chair—an appendage of my Study.—To Doctor David Stuart I give my large shaving & dressing-Table, and my Telescope.—To the Reverend, now Bryan, Lord Fairfax, I give a Bible in three large folio volumes, with notes, presented to me by the Right Reverend Thomas Wilson, Bishop of Sodor & Man —To General de la Fayette I give a pair finely wrought steel Pistols, taken from the enemy in the Revolutionary War.—To my Sisters in law Hannah Washington & Mildred Washington;—to my friends Eleanor Stuart, Hannah Washington of Fairfield, and Elizabeth Washington of Hayfield, I give, each, a mourning Ring of the value of one hundred dollars.—These bequests are

not made for the intrinsic value of them, but as mementos of my esteem & regard.— To Tobias Lear, I give the use of the Farm which he now holds, in virtue of a Lease from me to him and his deceased wife (for and during their natural lives) free from Rent, during his life;—at the expiration of which, it is to be disposed as is hereinafter directed.—To Sally B. Haynie (a distant relation of mine) I give and bequeath three hundred dollars—To Sarah Green daughter of the deceased Thomas Bishop, & to Ann Walker daughter of Jno. Alton, also deceased, I give, each one hundred dollars, in consideration of the attachment of their fathers to me, each of whom having lived nearly forty years in my family.—To each of my Nephews, William Augustine Washington, George Lewis, George Steptoe Washington, Bushrod Washington and Samuel Washington, I give one of the Swords or Cutteaux of which I may die possessed; and they are to chuse in the order they are named.—These Swords are accompanied with an injunction not to unsheath them for the purpose of shedding blood, except it be for self defence, or in defence of their Country and its rights; and in the latter case, to keep them unsheathed, and prefer falling with them in their hands, to the relinquishment thereof.

And now

Having gone through these specific devises, with explanations for the more correct understanding of the meaning and design of them; I proceed to the distribution of the more important parts of my Estate, in manner following—

First   To my Nephew Bushrod Washington and his heirs (partly in consideration of an intimation to his deceased father while we were Bachelors, & he had kindly undertaken to superintend my Estate during my Military Services in the former War between Great Britain & France, that if I should fall therein, Mount Vernon (then less extensive in domain than at present) should become his property) I give and bequeath all that part thereof which is comprehended within the following limits—viz—Beginning at the ford of Dogue run, near my Mill, and extending along the road, and bounded thereby as it now goes, & ever has gone since my recollection of it, to the ford of little hunting Creek at the Gum spring until it comes to a knowl, opposite to an old road which formerly passed through the lower field of Muddy hole Farm; at which, on the north side of the said road are three red, or spanish oaks marked as a corner, and a stone placed—thence by a line of trees to be marked, rectangular to the back line, or outer boundary of the tract between Thomson Mason & myself.—thence with that line Easterly (now double ditching with a Post & Rail fence thereon) to the run of little hunting Creek.—thence with that run which is the boundary between the Lands of the late Humphrey Peake and me, to the tide water of the said Creek; thence by that water to Potomac River.—thence with the River to the mouth of Dogue Creek.—and thence with the said Dogue Creek to the place of beginning at the aforesaid ford; containing upwards of four thousand acres, be the same more or less—together with the Mansion house and all other buildings and improvemts. thereon.—

Second In consideration of the consanguinity between them and my wife, being as nearly related to her as to myself, as on account of the affection I had for, and the obligation I was under to, their father when living, who from his youth had attached himself to my person, and followed my fortunes through the viscissitudes of the late Revolution—afterwards devoting his time to the Superintendence of my private concerns for many years, whilst my public employments rendered it impracticable for me to do it myself, thereby affording me essential services, and always performing them in a manner the most felial and respectful—for these reasons I say, I give and bequeath to George Fayette Washington, and Lawrence [Charles] Augustine Washington and their heirs, my Estate East of little hunting Creek, lying on the River Potomac,—including the farm of 360 acres, Leased to Tobias Lear as noticed before, and containing in the whole, by Deeds, Two thousand and seventy seven acres—be it more or less.—which said Estate it is my Will & desire should be equitably, & advantageously divided between them, according to quantity, quality & other circumstances when the youngest shall have arrived at the age of twenty one years, by three judicious and disinterested men;—one to be chosen by each of the brothers, and the third by these two.—In the meantime, if the termination of my wife's interest therein should have ceased, the profits, arising therefrom are to be applied for their joint uses and benefit.—

Third. And whereas it has always been my intention, since my expectation of having Issue has ceased, to consider the Grand children of my wife in the same light as I do my own relations, and to act a friendly part by them; more especially by the two whom we have reared from their earliest infancy—namely—Eleanor Parke Custis, & George Washington Parke Custis.—And whereas the former of these hath lately intermarried with Lawrence Lewis, a son of my deceased Sister Betty Lewis, by which union the inducement to provide for them both has been increased;—Wherefore, I give & bequeath to the said Lawrence Lewis & Eleanor Parke Lewis, his wife, and their heirs, the residue of my Mount Vernon Estate, not already devised to my Nephew Bushrod Washington,—comprehended within the following description.—viz—All the land North of the Road leading from the ford of Dogue run to the Gum spring as described in the devise of the other part of the tract to Bushrod Washington, until it comes to the stone & three red or Span-

ish Oaks on the knowl.—thence with the rectangular line to the back line (between Mr. Mason & me)—thence with that line westerly, along the new double ditch to Dogue run, by the tumbling Dam of my Mill;—thence with the said run to the ford aforementioned;—to which I add all the Land I possess West of the said Dogue run, & Dogue Crk bounded Easterly & Southerly thereby;—together with the Mill, Distillery, and all other houses & improvements on the premises, making together about two thousand acres—be it more or less

Fourth Actuated by the principal already mentioned, I give and bequeath to George Washington Parke Custis, the Grandson of my wife, and my ward, and to his heirs, the tract I hold on four mile run in the vicinity of Alexandria, containing one thoud two hundred acres, more or less,—& my entire Square, number twenty one, in the City of Washington.—

Fifth   All the rest and residue of my Estate, real & personal—not disposed of in manner aforesaid—In whatsoever consisting—wheresoever lying—and whensoever found—a schedule of which, as far as is recollected, with a reasonable estimate of its value, is hereunto annexed—I desire may be sold by my Executors at such times—in such manner—and on such credits (if an equal, valid, and satisfactory distribution of the specific property cannot be made without)—as, in their judgment shall be most conducive to the interest of the parties concerned; and the monies arising therefrom to be divided into twenty three equal parts, and applied as follow—viz—

To William Augustine Washington, Elizabeth Spotswood, Jane Thornton, and the heirs of Ann Ashton; son and daughters of my deceased brother Augustine Washington, I give and bequeath four parts;—that is—one to each of them

To Fielding Lewis, George Lewis, Robert Lewis, Howell Lewis & Betty Carter, sons & daughter of my deceased sister Betty Lewis, I give & bequeath five other parts—one to each of them

To George Steptoe Washington, Lawrence Augustine Washington, Harriot Parks, and the heirs of Thornton Washington, sons & daughter of my deceased brother Samuel Washington, I give and bequeath other four parts, one part to each of them.—

To Corbin Washington, and the heirs of Jane Washington, son & daughter of my deceased Brother John Augustine Washington, I give & bequeath two parts;—one part to each of them.—

To Samuel Washington, Francis Ball & Mildred Hammond, son & daughters of my Brother Charles Washington, I give & bequeath three parts;—one part to each of them.—And to George Fayette Washington Charles Augustine Washington & Maria I give one other part,—that is—to each a Washington, sons and daughter of my deceased nephew Geo: Augustine Washington, third of that part.

To Elizabeth Parke Law, Martha Parke Peter, and Eleanor Parke Lewis, I give and bequeath three other parts,—that is a part to each of them.—

And to my nephews Bushrod Washington & Lawrence Lewis,—and to my ward, the grandson of my wife, I give and bequeath one other part;—that is, a third thereof to each of them.—And if it should so happen that any of the persons whose names are here ennumerated (unknown to be) should now be deceased—or should die before me, that in either of these cases, the heirs of such deceased person shall, notwithstanding, derive all the benefits of the bequest; in the same manner as if he, or she, was actually living at the time

And by way of advice, I recommend it to my Executors not to be precipitate in disposing of the landed property (herein directed to be sold) if from temporary causes the sale thereof should be dull; experience having fully evinced, that the price of land (especially above the Falls of the Rivers, & on the Western Waters) have been progressively rising, and cannot be long checked in its increasing value.—And I particularly recommend it to such of the Legatees (under this clause of my Will) as can make it convenient, to take each a share of my stock in the Potomac Company in preference to the amount of what it might sell for; being thoroughly convinced myself, that no uses to which the money can be applied will be so productive as the Tolls arising from this Navigation when in full operation (and this from the nature of things it must be 'ere long) and more especially if that of the Shanondoah is added thereto.—

The family Vault at Mount Vernon requiring repairs, and being improperly situated besides, I desire that a new one of Brick, and upon a larger Scale, may be built at the foot of what is commonly called the Vineyard Inclosure,—on the ground which is marked out.—In which my remains, with those of my deceased relatives (now in the old Vault) and such others of my family as may chuse to be entombed there, may be deposited.—And it is my express desire that my Corpse may be Interred in a private manner, without parade or funeral oration.—

Lastly I constitute and appoint my dearly beloved wife Martha Washington, My Nephews William Augustine Washington, Bushrod Washington, George Steptoe Washington, Samuel Washington, & Lawrence Lewis, & my ward George Washington Parke Custis (when he shall have arrived at the age of twenty years) Executrix & Executors of this Will & testament,—In the construction of which it will readily be perceived that no professional character has been consulted or has had any agency in the draught—and that, although it has occupied many of my leisure hours to digest; & to through it into its present form, it may, notwithstanding, appear crude and incorrect.—But having endeavoured to be plain, and explicit in all the Devises—even at the expence of prolixity, perhaps of tautology, I hope, and trust, that no disputes will arise concerning them; but if, contrary to expectation, the case should be otherwise from the want of legal expression, or the usual technical terms, or because too much or too little has been said on any of the Devises to be consonant with law, my Will and direction expressly is, that all disputes (if unhappily any should arise) shall be decided by three impartial and intelligent men, known for their probity and good understanding;—two to be chosen by the disputants—each having the choice of one—and the third by those two.—Which three men thus chosen, shall, unfettered by Law, or legal constructions, declare their sense of the Testators intention;—and such decision is, to all intents and purposes to be as binding on the Parties as if it had been given in the Supreme Court of the United States.—

In witness of all, and of each of the things herein contained, I have set my hand and seal, this ninth day of July, in the year one thousand seven hundred and ninety and of the Independence of the United States the twenty fourth.

Gₒ Washington

Notes

(a) This tract for the size of it is valuable,—more for its situation than the quality of its soil, though that is good for Farming; with a considerable portion of grd. that might, very easily, be improved into Meadow.—It lyes on the great road from the City of Washington, Alexandria and George Town, to Leesburgh & Winchester; at Difficult bridge,—nineteen miles from Alexandria,—less from the City & George Town, and not more than three from Matildaville at the Great Falls of Potomac.—There is a valuable seat on the Premises—and the whole is conditionally sold—for the sum annexed in the Schedule

(b) What the selling prices of lands in the vicinity of these two tracts are, I know not; but compared with those above the ridge, and others below them, the value annexed will appear moderate——a less one would not obtain them from me.—

(c) The surrounding land, not superior in soil, situation or properties of any sort, sells currently at from twenty to thirty dollars an acre.—The lowest price is affixed to these—

(d) The observations made in the last note applies equally to this tract tract: being in the vicinity of them, and of similar quality, altho' it lyes in another County

(e) This tract, though small, is extremely valuable.—It lyes on Potomac River about 12 miles above the Town of Bath (or Warm springs) and is in the shape of a horse Shoe; —the river running almost around it.—Two hundred Acres of it is rich low grounds; with a great abundance of the largest & finest Walnut trees; which, with

[Continued on page 478]

Schedule of property comprehended in the foregoing Will, which is directed to be sold, and some of it, conditionally is sold; with description, and explanatory notes relative thereto.—

In Virginia

	acres	price	dollars.	
Loudoun County				
Difficult run	300		6,666	(a)
Loudoun & Fauquier				
Ashbys Bent	2481	$10	24,810	(b)
Chattins Run	885	8	7,080	
Berkeley				
So. fork of Bullskin	1600			
Head of Evans's M	453			
In Wormeley's line	183			
	2236	20	44,720	(c)
Frederick				
Bought from Mercer	571	20	11,420	(d)
Hampshire				
On Potk. River above B	240	15	3,600	(e)
Gloucester				
On North River	400	abt.	3,600	(f)
Nansemond				
Near Suffolk 1/3 of 1119 acres	373	8	2,984	(g)
Great Dismal Swamp				
My dividend thereof		abt.	20,000	(h)
Ohio River				
Round bottom	587			
Little Kanhawa	2314			
	2901		124,880	

			Dollars	
Amount brot. ovr.	2901		124,880	
16 Miles lowr. down	2448			
Opposite Big Bent	4395	dol:		
	9744	10	97,440	(i)
Great Kanhawa				
Near the Mouth West	10990			
East side above	7276			
Mouth of Cole River	2000			
Opposite thereto	2950			
Burning Spring	125			
	23341		200,000	(k)
Maryland				
Charles County	600	6	3,600	(l)
Montgomery Do.	519	12	6,228	(m)
Pennsylvania				
Great Meadows	234	6	1,404	(n)
New York				
Mohawk River .... abt.	1000	6	6,000	(o)
North Westn. Territy.				
On little Miami	839			
Ditto	977			
Ditto	1235			
	3051	5	15,251	(p)
Kentucky				
Rough Creek	3000			
Ditto adjoining	2000			
	5000	2	10,000	(q)

Lots—viz

City of Washington
Two near the Capital, Sqr. 634.......... }
cost $963—and with Buildgs............ }   15,000   (r)

Carried over...................... 479,803

Amt. brot. over...................   Dollars
                                         479,803
Lots—City of Washington
No. 5. 12. 13. & 14—the 3 last, Water lots on the Eastern Branch, }
in Sqr. 667. containing together 34.438 Sqr. feet a 12 Cts. }   4,132   (s)
Alexandria
Corner of Pitt & Prince Strs. half an Acre—laid out into buildgs. }
3 or 4 of wch. are let on grd. Rent at $3 pr. foot }   4,000   (t)
Winchester
A lot in the Town of half an Acr. & another in the Commons }
of about 6 Acs.—supposed }   400   (u)
Bath—or Warm Springs
Two Well situated, & had buildings to the amt. of £150........   800   (w)

Stock

United States 6 pr. Cts.............................. 3746
   Do defered .... 1873 } 2500
   3 pr. Cts................................ 2946 }   ____   6,246   (x)
Potomack Company
   24 Shares—cost ea. £100 Sterg.................   10,666   (y)
James River Company
   5 Shares—each cost $100......................   500   (z)
Bank of Columbia
   170 Shares—$40 each..........................   6,800 }
Bank of Alexandria—besides 20 to the Free School 5 .... 1,000 }   (&)

                                                               514,347

Amount brot. over...............................   dollars
                                                       514,347
Stock—living—viz.—
   1 Covering horse, 5 Coh. Horses—4 Riding do. six brood Mares |
   —20 working horses & Mares.—2 Covering Jacks & 3 young |
   ones—10 she asses, 42 working Mules—15 younger ones 329 |
   head of horned Cattle 640 head of Sheep—and a large Stock } 15,653
   of Hogs—the precise number unknown My Manager has |
   estimated this live Stock at £7,000 but I shall set it down in |
   order to make rd. sum at |

Agregate amt. $530,000

[Continued from page 477]

the produce of the Soil, might (by means of the improved Navigation of the Potomac) be brought to a shipping port with more ease, and at a smaller expence, than that which is transported 30 miles only by land.—

(f) This tract is of second rate Gloucester low grounds.—It has no Improvements thereon, but lyes on navigable water, abounding in Fish and Oysters.—It was received in payment of a debt (carrying interest) and valued in the year 1789 by an impartial Gentleman to £800.—NB. it has lately been sold, and there is due thereon, a balance equal to what is annexed the Schedule.

(g) These 373 acres are the third part of undivided purchases made by the deceased Fielding Lewis Thomas Walker and myself; on full conviction that they would become valuable.—The land lyes on the Road from Suffolk to Norfolk—touches (if I am not mistaken) some part of the Navigable water of Nansemond River—borders on, and comprehends part of the rich Dismal Swamp;—is capable of great improvement; —and from its situation must become extremely valuable.

(h) This is an undivided Interest wch. I held in the Great Dismal Swamp Company—containing about 4000 acres, with my part of the Plantation & Stock thereon belonging to the Company in the sd. Swamp.

(i) These several tracts of land are of the first quality on the Ohio River, in the parts where they are situated;—being almost if not altogether River bottoms.—The smallest of these tracts is actually sold at ten dollars an Acre but the consideration therefor, not received—the rest are equally valuable & will sell as high—especially that which lyes just below the little Kanhawa and is opposite to a thick settlement on the West side the Rivr.—The four tracts have an aggregate breadth upon the River of Sixteen miles and is bounded there by that distance.—

(k) These tracts are situated on the Great Kanhawa River, and the first four are bounded thereby for more than forty Miles.—It is acknowledged by all who have seen them (and of the tract containing 10990 acres which I have been on myself, I can assert) that there is no richer, or more valuable land in all that Region;— They are conditionally sold for the sum mentioned in the Schedule—that is $200,000 and if the terms of that Sale are not complied with they will command considerably more. —The tract of which the 125 acres is a Moiety, was taken up by General Andrew Lewis and myself for, and on account of a bituminous Spring which it contains, of so inflamable a nature as to burn as freely as spirits, and is nearly as difficult to extinguish

(l) I am but little acquainted with this land, although I have once been on it.—It was received (many years since) in discharge of a debt due to me from Daniel Janifer Adams at the value annexed thereto —and must be worth more.—It is very level, lyes near the River Potomac

(m) This tract lyes about 30 miles above the City of Washington, not far from Kittoctan.—It is good farming Land, and by those who are well acquainted with it I am informed that it would sell at twelve or $15 pr. acre.—

(n) This land is valuable on account of its local situation, and other properties.— It affords an exceeding good stand on Braddocks road from Fort Cumberland to Pittsburgh—and besides a fertile soil, possesses a large quantity of natural Meadow, fit for the scythe.—It is distinguished by the appellation of the Great Meadows—where the first action with the French in the year 1754 was fought.—

(o) This is the moiety of about 2000 Acs. which remains unsold of 6071. Acres on the Mohawk River (Montgomery Cty.) in a Patent granted to Daniel Coxe in the Township of Coxeborough & Carolana—as will appear by Deed from Marinus Willet & wife to George Clinton (late Governor of New York) and myself.—The latter sales have been Six dollars an acr; and what remains unsold will fetch that or more

(p) The quality of these lands & their Situation, may be known by the Survayers Certificates—which are filed along with the Patents.—They lye in the vicinity of Cincinnati;—one tract near the mouth of the little Miami—another seven & the third ten miles up the same—I have been informed that they will readily command more than they are estimated at.—

(q) For the description of these tracts in detail, see General Spotswoods letters filed with the other papers relating to them.— Besides the General good quality of the Land there is a valuable Bank of Iron Ore thereon:—which, when the settlement becomes more populous (and settlers are moving that way very fast) will be found very valuable; as the rough Creek, a branch of Green River affords ample water for Furnaces & forges.—

Lots—viz.—

City of Washington

(r) The two lots near the Capital, in square 634, cost me 963 $ only; but in this price I was favoured, on condition that I should build two Brick houses three Story high each:—without this reduction, the selling prices of those Lots would have cost me about $1350.—These lots, with the buildings thereon, when completed will stand me in $15000 at least.

(s) Lots No. 5. 12. 13. & 14 on the Eastn. branch, are advantageously situated on the water—and although many lots much less convenient have sold a great deal higher I will rate these at 12 Cts. the square foot only.—

Alexandria

(t) For this lot, though unimproved, I have refused $3500.—It has since been laid off into proper sized lots for building on—three or 4 of which are let on ground Rent —forever—at three dollars a foot on the Street.—and this price is asked for both fronts on Pitt & Princes Street.—

Winchester

(u) As neither the lot in the Town or Comon have any improvements on them, it is not easy to fix a price, but as both are well situated, it is presumed the price annexed to them in the Schedule, is a reasonable valun.

Bath

(w) The Lots in Bath (two adjoining) cost me, to the best of my recollection, betwn. fifty & sixty pounds 20 years ago; —and the buildings thereon £150 more.— Whether property there has increased or decreased. in its value, and in what condition the houses are I am ignorant.—but suppose they are not valued too high

Stocks

(x) These are the sums which are actually funded.—and though no more in the aggregate than $7,566—stand me in at least ten thousand pounds Virginia money.—besides the amount of bonded and other debts due to me, & discharged during the War when money had depreciated in that ratio—and was so settled by public authory.

(y) The value annexed to these shrs. is what they have actually cost me, and is the price affixed by Law:—and although

the present selling price is under par, my advice to the Legatees (for whose benefit they are intended, especially those who can afford to lye out of the Money is that each should take and hold one;—there being a Moral certainty of a great and increasing profit arising from them in the course of a few years

(z) It is supposed that the Shares in the James River Company must also be productive.—But of this I can give no decided opinion for want of more accurate informtn.

(&) These are nominal prices of the Shares of the Banks of Alexandria & Columbia, the selling prices vary according to circumstances. But as the Stock usually divided from eight to ten per cent per annum, they must be worth the former, at least, so long as the Banks are conceived to be Secure, although circumstances may, sometimes [be] below it.—

The value of the live stock depends more upon the quality than quantity of the different species of it, and this again upon the demand, and judgment or fancy of purchasers

Mount Vernon
9th July 1799.

G. Washington

Washington and the Constitution of the United States

*T*HE correct text of the Federal Constitution and the first ten amendments finds a place in the Highlights of the Writings of General George Washington because, though he had little to do with the wording of them, he did have much to do with the formation of them. Washington's Unionism dates back to the French and Indian War, and his insistence upon this is a prominent feature in his writings during the Revolution. He experienced more than any other man the evils of a Congress generally desirous of furnishing him with sufficient men and adequate means to carry on the war efficiently and in accordance with his plans, but with no power to carry out the measures and with no authority to compel the states to do so. Bitterly did Washington see his strategy brought to naught by failure of soldiers and supplies, and bitingly did he sum up the reasons for this when he exclaimed, "One nation to-day and thirteen to-morrow."

With peace came further elements of disintegration; and as in retirement he continued by word, pen, and action to combat this, the practicable character of his statesmanship is admirably illustrated by the fact that he recognized that the issue was primarily an economic one. He promoted commercial conferences between Virginia and Maryland, and recognized that the interstate interests of Delaware and Pennsylvania should be considered. The next step was the Annapolis Convention for a nation-wide conference on commercial welfare, of which he approved. Finally, when this convention, not sufficiently attended to produce results, suggested a more comprehensive gathering, Washington with great reluctance consented to be a delegate from Virginia; and his choice as president of this Federal Convention, which met at Philadelphia on May 25, 1787, was merely the formal recognition of his right of leadership.

We do not know precisely in what manner this leadership was exerted in the Convention. His diary is silent on the subject, and the journal and private notes of debates do not show direct participation in the proceedings, though Luther Martin declared that in committee of the whole Washington advocated a strong centralized government. We do know that the immortal document which the Convention framed was in harmony with his avowed principles and met with his approval, and that his approval was, more than any other fact, the cause of its ratification by the states.

Washington did not consider the document perfect, but pointed out that there was a "constitutional door open for alterations or amendments" if experience should show the need of such changes. He did not approve of amendment as a condition of ratification; but when many of the states made recommendations intended to prevent Congress from usurping power or adopting tyrannous measures, Washington in his inaugural address said: "It will remain with your judgment to decide, how far an exercise of the occasional power delegated by the fifth article of the Constitution is rendered expedient at the present juncture by the nature of objections which have been urged against the system, or by the degree of inquietude which has given birth to them. Instead of undertaking particular recom-

mendations on this subject, in which I could be guided by no lights derived from official opportunities, I shall again give way to my entire confidence in your discernment and pursuit of the public good; for I assure myself, that, whilst you carefully avoid every alteration, which might endanger the benefits of a united and effective government, or which ought to await the future lessons of experience; a reverence for the characteristic rights of freemen, and a regard for the public harmony, will sufficiently influence your deliberations on the question, how far the former can be more impregnably fortified, or the latter be safely and advantageously promoted." Following this suggestion, the first ten amendments, which became a part of the Constitution on November 3, 1791, are merely a bill of rights that does not diminish the powers granted to Congress.

This copy of the Federal Constitution has been carefully compared with the original manuscript in order to assure accuracy. As it is included here as a Washington document, the amendments after he ceased to be President of the United States are omitted.

The Constitution of the United States

We the People of the United States, in Order to form a more perfect Union, establish Justice, insure domestic Tranquility, provide for the common defence, promote the general Welfare, and secure the Blessings of Liberty to ourselves and our Posterity, do ordain and establish this Constitution for the United States of America.

Article. I.

Section. 1. All legislative Powers herein granted shall be vested in a Congress of the United States, which shall consist of a Senate and House of Representatives.

Section. 2. The House of Representatives shall be composed of Members chosen every second Year by the People of the several States, and the Electors in each State shall have the Qualifications requisite for Electors of the most numerous Branch of the State Legislature.

No Person shall be a Representative who shall not have attained to the Age of twenty five Years, and been seven Years a Citizen of the United States, and who shall not, when elected, be an Inhabitant of that State in which he shall be chosen.

Representatives and direct Taxes shall be apportioned among the several States which may be included within this Union, according to their respective Numbers, which shall be determined by adding to the whole Number of free Persons, including those bound to Service for a Term of Years, and excluding Indians not taxed, three fifths of all other Persons. The actual Enumeration shall be made within three Years after the first Meeting of the Congress of the United States, and within every subsequent Term of ten Years, in such Manner as they shall by Law direct. The Number of Representatives shall not exceed one for every thirty Thousand, but each State shall have at Least one Representative; and until such enumeration shall be made, the State of New Hampshire shall be entitled to chuse three, Massachusetts eight, Rhode-Island and Providence Plantations one, Connecticut five, New-York six, New Jersey four, Pennsylvania eight, Delaware one, Maryland six, Virginia ten, North Carolina five, South Carolina five, and Georgia three.

When vacancies happen in the Representation from any State, the Executive Authority thereof shall issue Writs of Election to fill such Vacancies.

The House of Representatives shall chuse their Speaker and other Officers; and shall have the sole Power of Impeachment.

Section. 3. The Senate of the United States shall be composed of two Senators from each State, chosen by the Legislature thereof, for six Years; and each Senator shall have one Vote.

Immediately after they shall be assembled in Consequence of the first Election, they shall be divided as equally as may be into three Classes. The Seats of the Senators of the first Class shall be vacated at the Expiration of the second Year, of the second Class at the Expiration of the fourth Year, and of the third Class at the Expiration of the sixth Year, so that one third may be chosen every second Year; and if Vacancies happen by Resignation, or otherwise, during the Recess of the Legislature of any State, the Executive thereof may make temporary Appointments until the next Meeting of the Legislature, which shall then fill such Vacancies.

No Person shall be a Senator who shall not have attained to the Age of thirty Years, and been nine Years a Citizen of the United States, and who shall not, when elected, be an Inhabitant of that State for which he shall be chosen.

The Vice President of the United States shall be President of the Senate, but shall have no Vote, unless they be equally divided.

The Senate shall chuse their other Officers, and also a President pro tempore, in the Absence of the Vice President, or when he shall exercise the Office of President of the United States.

The Senate shall have the sole Power to try all Impeachments. When sitting for that Purpose, they shall be on Oath or Affirmation. When the President of the United States is tried, the Chief Justice shall preside: And no Person shall be convicted without the Concurrence of two thirds of the Members present.

Judgment in Cases of Impeachment shall not extend further than to removal from Office, and disqualification to hold and enjoy any Office of honor, Trust or Profit under the United States: but the Party convicted shall nevertheless be liable and subject to Indictment, Trial, Judgment and Punishment, according to Law.

Section. 4. The Times, Places and Manner of holding Elections for Senators and Representatives, shall be prescribed in each State by the Legislature thereof; but the Congress may at any time by Law make or alter such Regulations, except as to the Places of chusing Senators.

The Congress shall assemble at least once in every Year, and such Meeting shall be on the first Monday in December, unless they shall by Law appoint a different Day.

Section. 5. Each House shall be the Judge of the Elections, Returns and Qualifications of its own Members, and a Majority of each shall constitute a Quorum to do Business; but a smaller Number may adjourn from day to day, and may be authorized to compel the Attendance of absent Members, in such Manner, and under such Penalties as each House may provide.

Each House may determine the Rules of its Proceedings, punish its Members for disorderly Behaviour, and, with the Concurrence of two thirds, expel a Member.

Each House shall keep a Journal of its Proceedings, and from time to time publish the same, excepting such Parts as may in their Judgment require Secrecy; and the Yeas and Nays of the Members of either House on any question shall, at the Desire of one fifth of those Present, be entered on the Journal.

Neither House, during the Session of Congress, shall, without the Consent of the other, adjourn for more than three days, nor to any other Place than that in which the two Houses shall be sitting.

Section. 6. The Senators and Representatives shall receive a Compensation for their Services, to be ascertained by Law, and paid out of the Treasury of the United States. They shall in all Cases, except Treason, Felony and Breach of the Peace, be privileged from Arrest during their Attendance at the Session of their respective Houses, and in going to and returning from the same; and for any Speech or Debate in either House, they shall not be questioned in any other Place.

No Senator or Representative shall, during the Time for which he was elected, be appointed to any civil Office under the Authority of the United States, which shall have been created, or the Emoluments whereof shall have been encreased during such time; and no Person holding any Office under the United States, shall be a Member of either House during his Continuance in Office.

Section. 7. All Bills for raising Revenue shall originate in the House of Representatives; but the Senate may propose or concur with Amendments as on other Bills.

Every Bill which shall have passed the House of Representatives and the Senate, shall, before it become a Law, be presented to the President of the United States; If he approve he shall sign it, but if not he shall return it, with his Objections to that House in which it shall have originated, who shall enter the Objections at large on their Journal, and proceed to reconsider it. If after such Reconsideration two thirds of that House shall agree to pass the Bill, it shall be sent, together with the Objections, to the other House, by which it shall likewise be reconsidered, and if approved by two thirds of that House, it shall become a Law. But in all such Cases the Votes of both Houses shall be determined by yeas and Nays, and the Names of the Persons voting for and against the Bill shall be entered on the Journal of each House respectively. If any Bill shall not be returned by the President within ten Days (Sundays excepted) after it shall have been presented to him, the Same shall be a Law, in like Manner as if he had signed it, unless the Congress by their Adjournment prevent its Return, in which Case it shall not be a Law.

Every Order, Resolution, or Vote to which the Concurrence of the Senate and House of Representatives may be necessary (except on a question of Adjournment) shall be presented to the President of the United States; and before the Same shall take Effect, shall be approved by him, or being disapproved by him, shall be repassed by two thirds of the Senate and House of Representatives, according to the Rules and Limitations prescribed in the Case of a Bill.

Section. 8. The Congress shall have Power To lay and collect Taxes, Duties, Imposts and Excises, to pay the Debts and provide for the common Defence and general Welfare of the United States; but all Duties, Imposts and Excises shall be uniform throughout the United States;

To borrow Money on the credit of the United States;

To regulate Commerce with foreign Nations, and among the several States, and with the Indian Tribes;

To establish an uniform Rule of Naturalization, and uniform Laws on the subject of Bankruptcies throughout the United States;

To coin Money, regulate the Value thereof, and of foreign Coin, and fix the Standard of Weights and Measures;

To provide for the Punishment of counterfeiting the Securities and current Coin of the United States;

To establish Post Offices and post Roads;

To promote the Progress of Science and useful Arts, by securing for limited Times to Authors and Inventors the exclusive Right to their respective Writings and Discoveries;

To constitute Tribunals inferior to the supreme Court;

To define and punish Piracies and Felonies committed on the high Seas, and Offences against the Law of Nations;

To declare War, grant Letters of Marque and Reprisal, and make Rules concerning Captures on Land and Water;

To raise and support Armies, but no Appropriation of Money to that Use shall be for a longer Term than two Years;

To provide and maintain a Navy;

To make Rules for the Government and Regulation of the land and naval Forces;

To provide for calling forth the Militia to execute the Laws of the Union, suppress Insurrections and repel Invasions;

To provide for organizing, arming, and disciplining, the Militia, and for governing such Part of them as may be employed in the Service of the United States, reserving to the States respectively, the Appointment of the Officers, and the Authority of training the Militia according to the discipline prescribed by Congress;

To exercise exclusive Legislation in all Cases whatsoever, over such District (not exceeding ten Miles square) as may, by Cession of particular States, and the Acceptance of Congress, become the Seat of the Government of the United States, and to exercise like Authority over all Places purchased by the Consent of the Legislature of the State in which the Same shall be, for the Erection of Forts, Magazines, Arsenals, dock-Yards, and other needful Buildings;—And

To make all Laws which shall be necessary and proper for carrying into Execution the foregoing Powers, and all other Powers vested by this Constitution in the Government of the United States, or in any Department or Officer thereof.

Section. 9. The Migration or Importation of such Persons as any of the States now existing shall think proper to admit, shall not be prohibited by the Congress prior to the Year one thousand eight hundred and eight, but a Tax or duty may be imposed on such Importation, not exceeding ten dollars for each Person.

The Privilege of the Writ of Habeas Corpus shall not be suspended, unless when in Cases of Rebellion or Invasion the public Safety may require it.

No Bill of Attainder or ex post facto Law shall be passed.

No Capitation, or other direct, Tax shall be laid, unless in Proportion to the Census or Enumeration herein before directed to be taken.

No Tax or Duty shall be laid on Articles exported from any State.

No Preference shall be given by any Regulation of Commerce or Revenue to the Ports of one State over those of another: nor shall Vessels bound to, or from, one State, be obliged to enter, clear, or pay Duties in another.

No Money shall be drawn from the Treasury, but in Consequence of Appropriations made by Law; and a regular Statement and Account of the Receipts and Expenditures of all public Money shall be published from time to time.

No Title of Nobility shall be granted by the United States: And no Person holding any Office of Profit or Trust under them, shall, without the Consent of the Congress, accept of any present, Emolument, Office, or Title, of any kind whatever, from any King, Prince, or foreign State.

Section. 10. No State shall enter into any Treaty, Alliance, or Confederation; grant Letters of Marque and Reprisal; coin Money; emit Bills of Credit; make any Thing but gold and silver Coin a Tender in Payment of Debts; pass any Bill of Attainder, ex post facto Law, or Law impairing the Obligation of Contracts, or grant any Title of Nobility.

No State shall, without the Consent of the Congress, lay any Imposts or Duties on Imports or Exports, except what may be absolutely necessary for executing it's inspection Laws: and the net Produce of all Duties and Imposts, laid by any State on Imports or Exports, shall be for the Use of the Treasury of the United States; and all such Laws shall be subject to the Revision and Controul of the Congress.

No State shall, without the Consent of Congress, lay any Duty of Tonnage, keep Troops, or Ships of War in time of Peace, enter into any Agreement or Compact with another State, or with a foreign Power, or engage in War, unless actually invaded, or in such imminent Danger as will not admit of delay.

Article. II.

Section. 1. The executive Power shall be vested in a President of the United States of America. He shall hold his Office during the Term of four Years, and, together with the Vice President, chosen for the same Term, be elected as follows

Each State shall appoint, in such Manner as the Legislature thereof may direct, a Number of Electors, equal to the whole Number of Senators and Representatives to which the State may be entitled in the Congress: but no Senator or Representative, or Person holding an Office of Trust or Profit under the United States, shall be appointed an Elector.

The Electors shall meet in their respective States, and vote by Ballot for two Persons, of whom one at least shall not be an Inhabitant of the same State with themselves. And they shall make a List of all the Persons voted for, and of the Number of Votes for each; which List they shall sign and certify, and transmit sealed to the Seat of the Government of the United States, directed to the President of the Senate. The President of the Senate shall, in the Presence of the Senate and House of Representatives, open all the Certificates, and the Votes shall then be counted. The Person having the greatest Number of Votes shall be the President, if such Number be a Majority of the whole Number of Electors appointed; and if there be more than one who have such Majority, and have an equal Number of Votes, then the House of Representatives shall immediately chuse by Ballot one of them for President; and if no Person have a Majority, then from the five highest on the List the said House shall in like Manner chuse the President. But in chusing the President, the Votes shall be taken by States, the Representation from each State having one Vote; A quorum for this Purpose shall consist of a Member or Members from two thirds of the States, and a Majority of all the States shall be necessary to a Choice. In every Case, after the Choice of the President, the Person having the greatest Number of Votes of the Electors shall be the Vice President. But if there should remain two or more who have equal Votes, the Senate shall chuse from them by Ballot the Vice President.

The Congress may determine the Time of chusing the Electors, and the Day on which they shall give their Votes; which Day shall be the same throughout the United States.

No Person except a natural born Citizen, or a Citizen of the United States, at the time of the Adoption of this Constitution, shall be eligible to the Office of President; neither shall any Person be eligible to that Office who shall not have attained to the Age of thirty five Years, and been fourteen Years a Resident within the United States.

In Case of the Removal of the President from Office, or of his Death, Resignation, or Inability to discharge the Powers and Duties of the said Office, the Same shall devolve on the Vice President, and the Congress may by Law provide for the Case of Removal, Death, Resignation or Inability, both of the President and Vice President, declaring what Officer shall then act as President, and such Officer shall act accordingly, until the Disability be removed, or a President shall be elected.

The President shall, at stated Times, receive for his Services, a Compensation, which shall neither be encreased nor diminished during the Period for which he shall have been elected, and he shall not receive within that Period any other Emolument from the United States, or any of them.

Before he enter on the Execution of his Office, he shall take the following Oath or Affirmation:—"I do solemnly swear (or affirm) that I will faithfully execute the Office of President of the United States, and will to the best of my Ability, preserve, protect and defend the Constitution of the United States."

Section. 2. The President shall be Commander in Chief of the Army and Navy of the United States, and of the Militia of the several States, when called into the actual Service of the United States; he may require the Opinion, in writing, of the principal Officer in each of the executive Departments, upon any Subject relating to the Duties of their respective Offices, and he shall have Power to grant Reprieves and Pardons for Offences against the United States, except in Cases of Impeachment.

He shall have Power, by and with the Advice and Consent of the Senate, to make Treaties, provided two thirds of the Senators present concur; and he shall nominate, and by and with the Advice and Consent of the Senate, shall appoint Ambassadors, other public Ministers and Consuls, Judges of the supreme Court, and all other Officers of the United States whose Appointments are not herein otherwise provided for, and which shall be established by Law: but the Congress may by Law vest the Appointment of such inferior Officers, as they think proper, in the President alone, in the Courts of Law, or in the Heads of Departments.

The President shall have Power to fill up all Vacancies that may happen during the Recess of the Senate, by granting Commissions which shall expire at the End of their next Session.

Section. 3. He shall from time to time give to the Congress Information of the State of the Union, and recommend to their Consideration such Measures as he shall judge necessary and expedient; he may, on extraordinary Occasions, convene both Houses, or either of them, and in Case of Disagreement between them, with Respect to the Time of Adjournment, he may adjourn them to such Time as he shall think proper; he shall receive Ambassadors and other public Ministers; he shall take Care that the Laws be faithfully executed, and shall Commission all the Officers of the United States.

Section. 4. The President, Vice President and all civil Officers of the United States, shall be removed from Office on Impeachment for, and Conviction of, Treason, Bribery, or other high Crimes and Misdemeanors.

Article III.

Section. 1. The judicial Power of the United States, shall be vested in one supreme Court, and in such inferior Courts as the Congress may from time to time ordain and establish. The Judges, both of the supreme and inferior Courts, shall hold their Offices during good Behaviour, and shall, at stated Times, receive for their Services, a Compensation, which shall not be diminished during their Continuance in Office.

Section. 2. The judicial Power shall extend to all Cases, in Law and Equity, arising under this Constitution, the Laws of the United States, and Treaties made, or which shall be made, under their Authority;—to all Cases affecting Ambassadors, other public Ministers and Consuls,—to all Cases of admiralty and maritime Jurisdiction;—to Controversies to which the United States shall be a Party;—to Controversies between two or more States;—between a State and Citizens of another State;—between Citizens of different States,—between Citizens of the same State claiming Lands under Grants of different States, and between a State, or the Citizens thereof, and foreign States, Citizens or Subjects.

In all Cases affecting Ambassadors, other public Ministers and Consuls, and those in which a State shall be Party, the supreme Court shall have original Jurisdiction. In all the other Cases before mentioned, the supreme Court shall have appellate Jurisdiction, both as to Law and Fact, with such Exceptions, and under such Regulations as the Congress shall make.

The Trial of all Crimes, except in Cases of Impeachment, shall be by Jury; and such Trial shall be held in the State where the said Crimes shall have been committed; but when not committed within any State, the Trial shall be at such Place or Places as the Congress may by Law have directed.

Section. 3. Treason against the United States, shall consist only in levying War against them, or in adhering to their Enemies, giving them Aid and Comfort. No Person shall be convicted of Treason unless on the Testimony of two Witnesses to the same overt Act, or on Confession in open Court.

The Congress shall have Power to declare the Punishment of Treason, but no Attainder of Treason shall work Corruption of Blood, or Forfeiture except during the Life of the Person attainted.

Article. IV.

Section. 1. Full Faith and Credit shall be given in each State to the public Acts, Records, and judicial Proceedings of every other State. And the Congress may by general Laws prescribe the Manner in which such Acts, Records and Proceedings shall be proved, and the Effect thereof.

Section. 2. The Citizens of each State shall be entitled to all Privileges and Immunities of Citizens in the several States.

A Person charged in any State with Treason, Felony, or other Crime, who shall flee from Justice, and be found in another State, shall on Demand of the executive Authority of the State from which he fled, be delivered up, to be removed to the State having Jurisdiction of the Crime.

No Person held to Service or Labour in one State, under the Laws thereof, escaping into another, shall, in Consequence of any Law or Regulation therein, be discharged from such Service or Labour, but shall be delivered up on Claim of the Party to whom such Service or Labour may be due.

Section. 3. New States may be admitted by the Congress into this Union; but no new State shall be formed or erected within the Jurisdiction of any other State; nor any State be formed by the Junction of two or more States, or Parts of States, without the Consent of the Legislatures of the States concerned as well as of the Congress.

The Congress shall have Power to dispose of and make all needful Rules and Regulations respecting the Territory or other Property belonging to the United States; and nothing in this Constitution shall be so construed as to Prejudice any Claims of the United States, or of any particular State.

Section. 4. The United States shall guarantee to every State in this Union a Republican Form of Government, and shall protect each of them against Invasion; and on Application of the Legislature, or of the Executive (when the Legislature cannot be convened) against domestic Violence.

Article. V.

The Congress, whenever two thirds of both Houses shall deem it necessary, shall propose Amendments to this Constitution, or, on the Application of the Legislatures of two thirds of the several States, shall call a Convention for proposing Amendments, which, in either Case, shall be valid to all Intents and Purposes, as Part of this Constitution, when ratified by the Legislatures of three fourths of the several States, or by Conventions in three fourths thereof, as the one or the other Mode of Ratification may be proposed by the Congress; Provided that no Amendment which may be made prior to the Year One thousand eight hundred and eight shall in any Manner affect the first and fourth Clauses in the Ninth Section of the first Article; and that no State, without its Consent, shall be deprived of it's equal Suffrage in the Senate.

Article. VI.

All Debts contracted and Engagements entered into, before the Adoption of this Constitution, shall be as valid against the United States under this Constitution, as under the Confederation.

This Constitution, and the Laws of the United States which shall be made in Pursuance thereof; and all Treaties made, or which shall be made, under the Authority of the United States, shall be the supreme Law of the Land; and the Judges in every State shall be bound thereby, any Thing in the Constitution or Laws of any State to the Contrary notwithstanding.

The Senators and Representatives before mentioned, and the Members of the several State Legislatures, and all executive and judicial Officers, both of the United States and of the several States, shall be bound by Oath or Affirmation, to support this Constitution; but no religious Test shall ever be required as a Qualification to any Office or public Trust under the United States.

Article. VII.

The Ratification of the Conventions of nine States, shall be sufficient for the Establishment of this Constitution between the States so ratifying the Same.

done in Convention by the Unanimous Consent of the States present the Seventeenth Day of September in the Year of our Lord one thousand seven hundred and Eighty seven and of the Independance of the United States of America the Twelfth In witness whereof We have hereunto subscribed our Names,

G͞ Washington - - - Presidt.
and deputy from Virginia

Attest William Jackson Secretary

Delaware	Geo: Read Gunning Bedford jun John Dickinson Richard Bassett Jaco: Broom
Maryland	James McHenry Dan of St Thos. Jenifer Danl Carroll
Virginia	John Blair— James Madison Jr.
North Carolina	Wm. Blount Richd. Dobbs Spaight. Hu Williamson
South Carolina	J. Rutledge Charles Cotesworth Pinckney Charles Pinckney Pierce Butler.
Georgia	William Few Abr Baldwin
New Hampshire	John Langdon Nicholas Gilman
Massachusetts	Nathaniel Gorham Rufus King
Connecticut	Wm. Saml. Johnson Roger Sherman
New York	Alexander Hamilton
New Jersey	Wil: Livingston David Brearley. Wm. Paterson Jona: Dayton
Pennsylvania	B Franklin Thomas Mifflin Robt Morris Geo. Clymer Thos. FitzSimons Jared Ingersoll James Wilson Gouv Morris

THE FIRST TEN AMENDMENTS
TO THE CONSTITUTION

Article I

Congress shall make no law respecting an establishment of religion, or prohibiting the free exercise thereof; or abridging the freedom of speech, or of the press; or the right of the people peaceably to assemble, and to petition the Government for a redress of grievances.

Article II

A well regulated Militia, being necessary to the security of a free State, the right of the people to keep and bear Arms, shall not be infringed.

Article III

No Soldier shall, in time of peace be quartered in any house, without the consent of the Owner, nor in time of war, but in a manner to be prescribed by law.

Article IV

The right of the people to be secure in their persons, houses, papers, and effects, against unreasonable searches and seizures, shall not be violated, and no Warrants shall issue, but upon probable cause, supported by Oath or affirmation, and particularly describing the place to be searched, and the persons or things to be seized.

Article V

No person shall be held to answer for a capital, or otherwise infamous crime, unless on a presentment or indictment of a Grand Jury, except in cases arising in the land or naval forces, or in the Militia, when in actual service in time of War or public danger; nor shall any person be subject for the same offence to be twice put in jeopardy of life or limb; nor shall be compelled in any criminal case to be a witness against himself, nor be deprived of life, liberty, or property, without due process of law; nor shall private property be taken for public use, without just compensation.

Article VI

In all criminal prosecutions, the accused shall enjoy the right to a speedy and public trial, by an impartial jury of the State and district wherein the crime shall have been committed, which district shall have been previously ascertained by law, and to be informed of the nature and cause of the accusation; to be confronted with the witnesses against him; to have compulsory process for obtaining witnesses in his favor, and to have the Assistance of Counsel for his defence.

Article VII

In Suits at common law, where the value in controversy shall exceed twenty dollars, the right of trial by jury shall be preserved, and no fact tried by a jury, shall be otherwise re-examined in any Court of the United States, than according to the rules of the common law.

Article VIII

Excessive bail shall not be required, nor excessive fines imposed, nor cruel and unusual punishments inflicted.

Article IX

The enumeration in the Constitution, of certain rights, shall not be construed to deny or disparage others retained by the people.

Article X

The powers not delegated to the United States by the Constitution, nor prohibited by it to the States, are reserved to the States respectively, or to the people.

CONSTITUTION OF THE UNITED STATES
Facsimile of the beginning, from the original in the Library of Congress, Washington, D. C.

THE
"OLIVE BRANCH" PETITION
TO
KING GEORGE III

FROM THE

SECOND CONTINENTAL CONGRESS

JULY 8, 1775

INTRODUCTION

THE "Olive Branch" Petition sent by the Continental Congress to King George III in July, 1775, is a valuable historic document. It was sent to England because of the feeling in the colonies that unless some final effort was made at reconciliation with the Mother Country, the middle colonies could not be aroused to action.

While it is couched in most respectful, even humble, language, it yet shows the determination of the people of the colonies to uphold their rights. By some it was considered as the final gesture of the people of this country to avoid war, which even then was considered by others as inevitable.

The document belongs with the other petitions and addresses of the early Congress, the failure of which left the way clear for the Declaration of Independence—an essential preliminary of that great state paper and referred to in it. This signed duplicate of the original petition has recently come to light, and was brought to the United States, the original petition being still preserved in the Public Record Office in London. It is certified by comparison with the original and is now presented as properly belonging to the history of our country. It has been duly authenticated by the historians of the United States George Washington Bicentennial Commission as a genuine document; and though it is not one of Washington's writings or unknown, the rediscovery of this duplicate makes opportune its inclusion in the historical material issued by this Commission.

SOL BLOOM.

A Study of the "Olive Branch" Petition

The "Olive Branch" petition, manuscript document, seven pages, folio, undated, but July 8, 1775, signed by John Hancock and forty-five other Members of the Second Continental Congress. To the King's Most excellent Majesty. Stitched with old blue tape and enclosed in a polished Cambridge calf box, silk-lined, with protecting moiré silk covers. On the front cover of the box are the Fitzwilliam Arms.

This is practically the last official effort of the United Colonies to head off the American Revolution. Lexington, Concord, and Bunker Hill had already been fought. The second Continental Congress had assembled in Philadelphia, to decide what should be done next. On June 10, 1775, John Adams, of Massachusetts, delegate to Congress wrote his friend, Moses Gill, in Cambridge:

"I find the general sense abroad is, to prepare for a vigorous defensive war, but at the same time to keep open the door of reconciliation; to hold the sword in one hand and the olive branch in the other."

Here is the "Olive Branch"—autographed by forty-six Members of Congress. Twenty-five of these forty-six also signed the Declaration of Independence a year later. Moreover, many of the "Olive Branch" signers who did not sign the Declaration are as important as those who affixed their autographs to the independence document. Patrick Henry, the orator of the Revolution; John Jay, first Chief Justice of the United States; Silas Deane, the first American diplomat; Robert R. Livingston, who officiated at the first inaugural of George Washington as President—all signed the "Olive Branch" but not the Declaration.

But what was the "Olive Branch?" The First Continental Congress met in 1774, and adopted a petition to the King, wherein it blamed all the trouble on the ministers of George III, and begged His Majesty to call them off before it was too late. The King gave little heed—and the result was seen at Lexington on the 19th of April, 1775. The Second Continental Congress met at Philadelphia on May 10, 1775, and adopted a "Declaration of the Causes of taking up Arms," which it addressed to the people of Great Britain. Yet the colonies were not ripe for independence. Only nine months before, George Washington himself had said that no thinking man in all North America desired independence. It was not yet assured that the colony of Georgia would join in the general revolt. The conservative business men of two leading commercial cities, New York and Philadelphia, were by no means sure they wanted to make the final decision of war. Therefore, the Second Continental Congress drew up a second petition to the King, again requesting him to call off his minions.

Such a paper has far more significance than its importance in the history of the United States. The supreme problem of politics for a thousand years has been how to mediate between the claim of complete independence and the obvious fact that no nation can live unto itself alone. The lack of a political formula which will allow a nation political autonomy, yet prevent it from hurting its neighbors, underlies most of the wars of modern times—and many of the revolutions. Ireland, Poland, Manchuria, South Africa, India, and the Philippines are but a few of the states involved in this problem. In all truth it is the same problem which confronts the greater states. France and her "honor;" Italy and her "fascismo;" Russia and her "communism;" Germany and her "Deutschtum"—all the way down to California and her "immigration problem"—all these ought to be "internal problems," if they did not constantly involve external difficulties. It is becoming increasingly difficult to draw any line between dependence and independence.

Now, among the most effective political thinkers who saw that problem as a problem were our Revolutionary ancestors. They did not want to break up the British Empire. They wanted political and economic autonomy within the British Empire. Lord Chatham spoke better than he knew, when he said that in ability and sagacity the Congress at Philadelphia was the equal of any similar assembly in history. These Americans were boldly attacking the supreme problem of politics, and in their many writings they made a contribution to the subject, the significance of which we are only just beginning to appreciate. The "Olive Branch" was the last effort of those who said, as they had said before, that what they wanted for America was dominion self government. Because they could not make the King of England understand that they would be loyal to him but wanted no truck with his Parliament, they cut the Gordian knot, and finally declared independence. But the Declaration of Independence was a confession of failure—failure to solve the great problem of politics. Therefore, this "Olive Branch" may be presented as a document of equal, if not greater, historical importance than the great Declaration of a year later.

Who wrote the "Olive Branch?" The first petition to the King of 1774, the Declaration of the Causes of taking up Arms, and the second petition to the King (the "Olive Branch") were all three the products of that "penman of the Revolution," John Dickinson, of Pennsylvania, author of the famous "Farmer's Letters." Two historians have attempted to disprove this general statement, because Jefferson had some hand in the Declaration of the Causes of taking up Arms. Both historians burned their fingers. It is of considerable interest that John Marshall and George Bancroft had publicly to retract their doubts about Dickinson's claim to the authorship. As to the "Olive Branch"—we have Jefferson's own evidence that Dickinson was solely responsible for writing it, and that an indulgent Congress adopted it very largely because of the respect they had for Dickinson's opinions.

What is the history of the document? The Journals of Congress record that it was ordered engrossed and signed on July 8, 1775. John Adams records on July 10, "A petition was sent yesterday by Mr. Richard Penn in one ship and a Duplicate goes in another Ship this day." When Penn reached London, he associated with him Arthur Lee, and the two waited on Lord Dartmouth, at the Colonial Office. His Lordship was down in the country. On August 21, Penn and Lee sent Dartmouth a "copy" by post, saying that they retained the "original" to present to the King. This "copy" was probably not the one which came over in John Adams' "another Ship," but that which is still in Lord Dartmouth's family archives at Patshull. From the description given by the Historical Manuscripts Commission, it is apparently unsigned. It was not until September 1 that Penn and Lee were able to hand the "original" to Dartmouth, by whom they were told that "as His Majesty did not receive it upon the throne, no answer would be given." George III is on record as giving a general refusal to receive any communications from any congress in America. Moreover, he may have been a little embarrassed by this one, because Penn and Lee appeared with it at the same time that he was delivering his own bloodthirsty proclamation on rebellion.

Of course, the "Olive Branch" was good American propaganda, as demonstrating the intense sincerity of the colonists. Many contemporary unsigned manuscript copies were made, which is the reason one finds them in the Archives des Affaires Etrangeres at Paris, in the Rijks-Archiv at The Hague, and in the Archives at both Madrid and Simancas. The "original" signed copy delivered to Dartmouth is probably that in the Public Record Office, Chancery Lane, London. An excellent facsimile of the Record Office copy has been prepared by Mr. B. F. Stevens in his famous series, "Facsimiles of Manuscripts in European Archives relating to America, 1773 to 1783," and is now in the Library of Congress.

Up to the present time one might have been justified in assuming that the only surviving signed copy of the "Olive Branch" was that preserved in the Public Record Office. Whence, then, this second signed copy? John Adams' remark doubtless supplies the answer. In those days it was often necessary to prepare more than one copy of an important document, forwarding the duplicate or triplicate by different carriers to avoid loss at sea or in war. When Major Henry Gladwin was being besieged by Pontiac at Detroit, he sometimes sent the same letter by three different carriers, and there are instances where only the third signed copy reached its destination.

The present signed copy of the "Olive Branch" has recently been discovered at Milton, near Peterborough, in England. Milton was the country seat of the second Earl Fitzwilliam, a nephew of the second Marquis of Rockingham. Rockingham was a well-known Whig leader and an advocate of conciliation with America. When Cornwallis surrendered at Yorktown, it was Rockingham whom the King called to succeed Lord North and save the British Empire. Rockingham might well have had this paper given to him. He had no direct heirs, and his estates went to Earl Fitzwilliam. Later, the Earls Fitzwilliam moved, with most of their papers, to Rockingham's country estate in Yorkshire. This paper may have been left for the branch of the family which retained Milton.

There is another possibility. Edmund Burke was also a great friend of the colonies and at the time was acting as agent for New York. When Congress sent Richard Penn to England, it instructed him to associate with him the other colonial agents —hence Arthur Lee's participation. Burke was asked to be present with Penn and Lee when they presented the petition, but he declined on the ground that he had no definite instructions from the colony of New York. It is, however, altogether possible that Penn and Lee turned this second signed copy over to Burke. At all events, Burke was at this time closely associated with both Rockingham and the second Earl Fitzwilliam—so intimate was he with the latter that at Burke's death, Mrs. Burke turned most of Burke's papers over to Earl Fitzwilliam. Which of these explanations is correct, or whether some third story of the

document's provenance will yet be worked out, it is at present difficult to say. At all events the signed copy of the "Olive Branch" was found at Milton, by its present owner, Mr. George C. W. Fitzwilliam.

That there is nothing unusual about this copy's having found its way to private hands may be seen by the fact that Benjamin Franklin himself kept the second signed copy of the *first* Petition to the King of 1774. It was found among the Franklin papers by Henry Stevens of Vermont. This copy of the 1774 petition is now in the Library of Congress, but only because the Library bought it from Mr. Stevens.

Who signed the "Olive Branch"? This question is best answered in the following tabulated form. Because of the variety of terms then used to designate the various colonial assemblies, the word "legislature" is here used to mean the supreme legislative body of both colonies and states. The modern name of colleges and universities is employed. All these men were, of course, members of the Second Continental Congress. Those marked with the asterisk (*) also signed the Declaration of Independence.

*JOHN HANCOCK (1737-1793) of Massachusetts. Harvard. Merchant. Member of Massachusetts legislature; President of the Continental Congress; Major General of Massachusetts militia; Governor of Massachusetts; signer of the Articles of Confederation.

JOHN LANGDON (1741-1819) of New Hampshire. Seaman and soldier. Speaker in New Hampshire legislature; three times Governor of New Hampshire; present at battle of Bennington and surrender at Saratoga; President *pro tem.* of the U. S. Senate which counted the votes and announced the first election of Washington as President; signer of the Federal Constitution.

THOMAS CUSHING (1725-1788) of Massachusetts. Harvard. Merchant. Speaker of Massachusetts legislature; acting Governor of Massachusetts.

*SAMUEL ADAMS (1722-1803) of Massachusetts. Harvard. Merchant. Politician. Author of the Massachusetts Circular Letter of 1768; one of the instigators of the Boston Tea-Party; member of the Massachusetts constitutional convention of 1779 and the Massachusetts convention to ratify the Federal Constitution; signer of Articles of Confederation; Governor of Massachusetts.

*JOHN ADAMS (1735-1826) of Massachusetts. Harvard. Lawyer. U. S. Minister to Holland; commissioner to negotiate peace of 1782-3; Vice-President of the U. S.; President of the U. S.

*ROBERT TREAT PAINE (1731-1814) of Massachusetts. Harvard. Lawyer. Prose-

cuted the British soldiers in the *cause celebre* of the Boston Massacre; Speaker of Massachusetts legislature; Attorney General of Massachusetts; member of Massachusetts constitutional convention of 1779; Justice of the Supreme Court of Massachusetts.

*STEPHEN HOPKINS (1707-1785) of Rhode Island. Merchant and pamphleteer. Speaker in Rhode Island legislature; Chief Justice of Rhode Island; Governor of Rhode Island.

SAMUEL WARD (1725-1776) of Rhode Island. Member of Rhode Island legislature; Chief Justice of Rhode Island; Governor of Rhode Island; one of the founders of Brown University.

ELIPHALET DYER (1721-1807) of Connecticut. Yale. Lawyer. Regiment in French and Indian War; member of Connecticut legislature; agent of the Susquehanna Company; delegate to Stamp Act Congress; Chief Justice of Connecticut.

*ROGER SHERMAN (1721-1793) of Connecticut. Lawyer. Justice of Supreme Court of Connecticut; signer of Articles of Confederation; signer of Constitution of the United States; member of U. S. House of Representatives; U. S. Senator.

SILAS DEANE (1737-1789) of Connecticut. Yale. Lawyer. U. S. envoy to France, who helped negotiate treaty of alliance of 1778; spent large sums of his own money to advance cause of independence, which Congress would not repay. His heirs were paid by Congress 53 years after his death.

*PHILIP LIVINGSTON (1716-1778) of New York. Yale. Merchant and philanthropist. Member of New York legislature; co-founder of Columbia University.

JAMES DUANE (1733-1797) of New York. Lawyer. State Senator; Mayor of New York City; signer of Articles of Confederation; member of New York convention to ratify Federal Constitution; U. S. judge.

JOHN ALSOP (———-1794) of New York. Merchant. Member of First Continental Congress.

JOHN JAY (1745-1829) of New York. Columbia. Lawyer. Chief Justice of Supreme Court of New York; President of Continental Congress; U. S. envoy to Spain; commissioner to negotiate treaty of peace 1782-3; Secretary for Foreign Affairs; co-author of *The Federalist;* Chief Justice of the Supreme Court of the U. S.; commissioner to negotiate treaty with England in 1794; Governor of New York.

*FRANCIS LEWIS (1713-1803) of New York. Merchant. Contractor for supplying troops in French and Indian War, and Revolution; signer of Articles of Confederation.

*WILLIAM FLOYD (1734-1821) of New York. State Senator; member of U. S. House of Representatives; member of New York constitutional convention of 1801.

HENRY WISNER (1725-1790) of New York. Member of New York legislature; member of New York constitutional conventions of 1777 and 1788; State Senator.

*LEWIS MORRIS (1726-1798) of New York. Yale. Farmer. Member of New York legislature; Major-General of New York militia.

ROBERT R. LIVINGSTON, JR. (1747-1813), of New York. Columbia. Lawyer. Member of New York legislature; member of committee to draft Declaration of Independence; Secretary for Foreign Affairs; chairman of New York convention to ratify Federal Constitution; Chancellor of New York before whom Washington took oath of office as first President of the United States; envoy to France who negotiated Louisiana purchase; shared Robert Fulton's steamboat experiments on the Seine and on the Hudson (Fulton's "Clermont" was named for Livingston's country seat); patron of arts and sciences.

WILLIAM LIVINGSTON (1723-1790) of New Jersey. Yale. Lawyer and author. Brigadier General of New Jersey militia; Governor of New Jersey; signer of Federal Constitution.

*JOHN DE HART (or HART) (1708-1780) of New Jersey. Farmer. Member of New Jersey legislature; best remembered by the extreme fortitude with which he endured the depredations of the British forces during the campaigns in his state.

RICHARD SMITH (1735-1803) of New Jersey. Best known for the correspondence he conducted with Tobias Smollett.

*BENJAMIN FRANKLIN (1706-1790) of Pennsylvania. Printer; author; newspaper man; scientist; philosopher. Postmaster-General; colonial agent in England; envoy to France who negotiated treaty of alliance of 1778; commissioner to negotiate treaty of peace of 1782-3; signer of Federal Constitution.

*GEORGE ROSS (1750-1779) of Pennsylvania. Lawyer. Member of Pennsylvania legislature; chairman of committee that framed the organization of the state government; judge of Court of Admiralty.

*JAMES WILSON (1742-1798) of Pennsylvania. Lawyer. Director of Bank of North America; signer of Federal Con-

stitution; founder of University of Pennsylvania Law School; Justice of Supreme Court of the U. S. Next to Madison, he was the greatest single influence in the formation of the Federal Constitution.

EDWARD BIDDLE (1739-1779) of Pennsylvania. Lawyer. Speaker in Pennsylvania legislature.

JOHN DICKINSON (1732-1808) of Pennsylvania and Delaware. Lawyer. Member of Delaware and Pennsylvania legislatures; author of the "Olive Branch"; signer of the Articles of Confederation and Federal Constitution.

*CAESAR RODNEY (1728-1783) of Delaware. Speaker in Delaware legislature; delegate to Stamp Act Congress; Judge of Court of Admiralty; President of Delaware; General of militia.

*THOMAS MCKEAN (1734-1817) of Delaware and Pennsylvania. Lawyer. Member of Delaware legislature; delegate to Stamp Act Congress; Chief Justice of Pennsylvania; signer of Articles of Confederation; author of first constitution of Delaware; member of Pennsylvania constitutional convention of 1790; President of Congress; Governor of Pennsylvania.

*GEORGE READ (1733-1798) of Delaware. Lawyer. Attorney-General of Delaware; member of first Delaware constitutional convention; member of Delaware convention to ratify Federal Constitution; U. S. Senator; Chief Justice of Delaware.

MATTHEW TILGHMAN (1718-1790) of Maryland. Lawyer. Speaker in Maryland legislature; president of Maryland constitutional convention of 1776; State Senator.

THOMAS JOHNSON, JR. (1732-1819), of Maryland. Lawyer. Governor of Maryland; U. S. Judge; Justice of Supreme Court of the U. S. He nominated George Washington Commander-in-Chief of Army of the United Colonies.

*WILLIAM PACA (1740-1799) of Maryland. Lawyer. Member of Maryland legislature; State Senator; Chief Justice of Maryland; Governor of Maryland; member of Maryland convention to ratify Federal Constitution; U. S. District Judge.

*SAMUEL CHASE (1741-1811) of Maryland. Lawyer. Justice of Supreme Court of the U. S.

*THOMAS STONE (1743-1787) of Maryland. Lawyer. Member of Maryland legislature; elected to Federal Constitutional Convention of 1787, but died in that year.

PATRICK HENRY (1736-1799) of Virginia. Lawyer. Member of Virginia legislature; Governor of Virginia; member

of Virginia convention to ratify the Federal Constitution.

*RICHARD HENRY LEE (1732-1794) of Virginia. Lawyer. Member of Virginia legislature; moved resolution for Declaration of Independence; signer of Articles of Confederation; effective advocate of first ten amendments to Federal Constitution; U. S. Senator; President pro tem, of U. S. Senate; committeeman extraordinary.

EDMUND PENDLETON (1721-1803) of Virginia. Lawyer. Member of Virginia legislature; Speaker; president of Virginia conventions of 1775-6 offering the instruction to the Virginia delegates for independence; president of Virginia convention to ratify Federal Constitution.

*BENJAMIN HARRISON (1726-1791) of Virginia. College of William and Mary. Lawyer. Member of Virginia convention of 1774; Speaker in Virginia legislature; Governor of Virginia; member of Virginia convention to ratify Federal Constitution.

*THOMAS JEFFERSON (1743-1826) of Virginia. College of William and Mary. Lawyer. Member of Virginia legislature; author of Declaration of Independence; Governor of Virginia; U. S. Minister to France; Secretary of State; President of the U. S.

*WILLIAM HOOPER (1742-1790) of North Carolina. Harvard. Lawyer. Member of North Carolina legislature; opposed the "Regulators."

*JOSEPH HEWES (1730-1779) of North Carolina. Merchant. Member of North Carolina legislature; first de facto Secretary of the Navy.

THOMAS LYNCH (1720-1776) of South Carolina. Planter. His son, Thomas Lynch, Jr., signed the Declaration of Independence.

CHRISTOPHER GADSDEN (1724-1805) of South Carolina. Delegate to Stamp Act Congress; Brigadier General of the Continental Army; elected Governor of South Carolina but could not serve; member of South Carolina convention to ratify Federal Constitution; member of South Carolina constitutional convention of 1790.

JOHN RUTLEDGE (1739-1800) of South Carolina. Lawyer. President of South Carolina and Commander-in-Chief of South Carolina militia; signer of the Federal Constitution; member of U. S. House of Representatives; Chief Justice of South Carolina; Chief Justice of the Supreme Court of the U. S.

At least seventeen members of the Congress did not sign the "Olive Branch"—and for a variety of reasons. General George Washington of Virginia had already gone to take command of the army at Cambridge, and with him went Thomas Mifflin of Pennsylvania as a member of his staff. General John Sullivan of New Hampshire was commanding his brigade outside of Boston. George Clinton and General Philip Schuyler of New York were busy organizing the defences of the state. Richard Caswell and Robert Goldsborough were absent on official business connected with the new constitutional organization of their respective states of North Carolina and Maryland. Peyton Randolph of Virginia was ill. Lyman Hall of the Parish of St. Johns, in Georgia, could not sign, as his state had not yet properly accredited its delegation to Congress.

Charles Humphrey of Pennsylvania, Henry Middleton and Edward Rutledge of South Carolina signed the Public Record Office copy of the "Olive Branch" but not this copy.

A word should be said about John Dickinson, whose reputation at this time was so great as to compel the adoption of the "Olive Branch." A year later he suffered an eclipse by declining to vote for independence—but when most of the Signers of the Declaration affixed their autographs, Colonel John Dickinson was absent from Congress because he was commanding his regiment of Pennsylvania troops against Sir William Howe near Elizabeth, New Jersey.

That was not exactly timidity, at any rate.

Yet the "Olive Branch" ought not to be considered merely because of the Signers it contains. Its historic importance should in no way be subordinated to that of the Declaration of Independence. Since George III would not receive what John Adams called the olive branch, there was no alternative for the people of America but to take up the sword which Adams noted was being carried in the other hand. Years later, in 1807, John Dickinson wrote: "After the rejection [of this petition], not a syllable, to my recollection, was ever uttered in favor of reconciliation with Great Britain."

RANDOLPH G. ADAMS.
Director, William L. Clements Library, University of Michigan.

THE CONTINENTAL CONGRESS IN SESSION
After a painting by Robert Edge Pine and Edward Savage. Now in Independence Hall, Philadelphia.

To the Kings most excellent Majesty

Most gracious Sovereign,

We your Majesty's faithful Subjects of the colonies of New-hampshire, Massachusetts-bay, Rhode-island and Providence plantations, Connecticut, New-York, New Jersey, Pennsylvania, the counties of New Castle Kent & Sussex on Delaware, Maryland, Virginia, North-Carolina and South Carolina in behalf of ourselves and the inhabitants of these colonies, who have de--puted us to represent them in general Congress, en--treat your Majesty's gracious attention to this our humble petition.

The Union between our Mother country and these colonies, and the energy of mild and just govern--ment, produced benefits so remarkably important. and afforded such an assurance of their permanency and increase, that the wonder and envy of other nations were excited, while they beheld Great Britain rising to a power the most extraordinary the world had ever known.

Her rivals observing, that there was no probability of this happy connection being broken by civil dissentions, and apprehending its future effects if left any longer undisturbed, resolved to pre--vent her receiving such continual and formidable accessions of wealth and strength, by checking the

growth

growth of those settlements from which they were to be derived

In the prosecution of this attempt, events so unfavourable to the design took place, that every friend to the interests of Great Britain and these colonies entertained pleasing and reasonable expectations of seeing an additional force and extention immediately given to the operations of the union hitherto experienced, by an enlargement of the dominions of the crown, and the removal of ancient and warlike enemies to a greater distance

At the conclusion therefore of the late war, the most glorious and advantageous that ever had been carried on by British arms, your loyal colonists having contributed to its success, by such repeated and strenuous exertions, as frequently procured them the distinguished approbation of your Majesty, of the late king, and of Parliament doubted not, but that they should be permitted with the rest of the empire, to share in the blessings of peace and the emoluments of victory and conquest.

While these recent and honorable acknowledgments of their merits remained on record in the journals and acts of that august legislature the parliament, undefaced by the imputation or even the suspicion of any offence; they were alarmed by a new system of statutes and regulations adopted for the administration of the colonies, that filled their minds with the most painful fears & jealousies; and to their inexpressible astonishment, perceived the dangers of a foreign quarrel quickly succeeded by domestick dangers, in their judgment of a more dreadful kind.

Nor were their anxieties alleviated by any tendency in this system to promote the welfare of their Mother country:

For

For 'tho its effects were more immediately felt by them, yet its influence appeared to be injurious to the commerce and prosperity of Great Britain .

We shall decline the ungrateful task of describing the irksome variety of artifices practised by many of your Majestys ministers, the delusive pretences, fruitless terrors, and unavailing severities, that have from time to time been dealt out by them in their attempts to execute this impolitic plan, or of tracing thro' a series of years past the progress of the unhappy differences between Great Britain and these colonies, that have flowed from this fatal source .

Your Majesty's ministers, persevering in their measures and proceeding to open hostilities for enforcing them, have compelled us to arm in our own defence, and have engaged us in a controversy so peculiarly abhorrent to the affections of your still faithful colonists, that when we consider whom we must oppose in this contest, and if it continues what may be the consequences, our own particular misfortunes are accounted by us, only as parts of our distress .

Knowing, to what violent resentments and incurable animosities, civil discords are apt to exasperate and inflame the contending parties, we think ourselves required by indispensable obligations to Almighty God, to your Majesty, to our fellow subjects, and to ourselves, immediately to use all the means in our power not incompatible with our safety, for stopping the further effusion of blood, and for averting the impending calamities that threaten the British empire .

Thus

Thus called upon to address your Majesty on af-
-fairs of such moment to America, and probably to
all your dominions, We are earnestly desirous of per
-forming this office with the utmost deference for your
Majesty; and we therefore pray, that your royal mag-
-nanimity and benevolence may make the most favourable
construction of our expressions on so uncommon an oc-
-casion . Could we represent in their full force the
sentiments that agitate the minds of us your dutiful
subjects, we are persuaded, your Majesty would ascribe
any seeming deviation from reverence, in our lan -
-guage, and even in our conduct, not to any reprehen
-sible intention, but to the impossibility of reconciling
the usual appearances of respect with a just attenti-
-on to our own preservation against those artful
and cruel enemies, who abuse your royal confidence
and authority for the purpose of effecting our destruc-
-tion .

Attached to your Majestys person, family
and government with all the devotion that principle
and affection can inspire; connected with Great Bri-
-tain by the strongest ties that can unite societies, and
deploring every event that tends in any degree to weak-
-en them, we solemnly assure your Majesty, that we
not only most ardently desire the former harmony
between her and these colonies may be restored, but that
a concord may be established between them upon so
firm a basis, as to perpetuate its blessings uninterrupted
by any future dissentions to succeeding generations in
both countries, and to transmit your Majestys name
to posterity adorned with that signal and lasting glory
that has attended the memory of those illustrious person
-ages, whose virtues and abilities have extricated states
from dangerous convulsions, and by securing happiness to others have erected the most noble and durable
monuments to their own fame .

We

We beg leave further to assure your Majesty, that not-withstanding the sufferings of your loyal colonists during the course of the present controversy, our breasts retain too tender a regard for the kingdom from which we derive our origin, to request such a reconciliation, as might in any manner be inconsistent with her dignity or her welfare. These, related as we are to her, honor & duty, as well as inclination induce us to support and advance; and the apprehensions that now oppress our hearts with unspeakable grief, being once removed, your Majesty will find your faithful subjects on this continent, ready and willing at all times, as they ever have been, with their lives and fortunes to assert and maintain the rights and interests of your Majesty and of our Mother country.

We therefore beseech your Majesty, that your royal authority and influence may be graciously interposed to procure us relief from our afflicting fears and jealousies occasioned by the System before menti-oned, and to settle peace thro' every part of your domi-nions, with all humility submitting to Your Majesty's wise consideration, whether it may not be expedient for facilitating those important purposes, that your Ma-jesty be pleased to direct some mode by which the unit-ed applications of your faithful colonists to the throne, in pursuance of their common councils may be improv-ed into a happy and permanent reconciliation; and that in the mean time, measures be taken for prevent-ing the further destruction of the lives of your Ma-jestys subjects; and that such statutes as more imme-diately distress any of your Majestys colonies be repeal-ed: For by such arrangements as your Majestys wisdom can form, for collecting the united sense of your American people, we are convinced, your Majesty would receive such satisfactory proofs of the disposi-tion of the colonists towards their sovereign and the

parent

parent State, that the wished for opportunity would be restored to them, of evincing the sincerity of their professions by every testimony of devotion becoming the most dutiful subjects and the most affectionate colonists

That your Majesty may enjoy a long & prosperous reign, and that your descendants may govern Your dominions with honor to themselves and happiness to their subjects is our sincere and fervent prayer .

John Hancock

Colony of New hampshire
John Langdon

Massachusetts-bay
Thomas Cushing
Sam¹ Adams
John Adams
Rob Treat Paine

Rhodeisland & providenceplantations
Step Hopkins
Sam: Ward

Connecticutt
Eliph¹ Dyer
Roger Sherman
Silas Deane

New York
Phil Livingston
Jas. Duane
John Alsop
John Jay
Fran⁸ Lewis
W⁸ Floyd
Henry Wisner
Lewis Morris
Rob¹ R. Livingston Jun

New Jersey
Wil. Livingston
John DeHart
Rich⁸ Smith

Pennsylvania
B Franklin
Geo: Ross
James Wilson
Edw: Biddle
John Dickinson

Newcastle Kent & Sussex on delaware
Cæsar Rodney
Tho⁸ M:Kean
Geo Read

Maryland
Mat. Tilghman
Th⁸ Johnson Jun⁸
W⁸ Paca
Samuel Chase
Tho⁸ Stone

Virginia

P. Henry Jr.

Richard Henry Lee

Edmund Pendleton

Benj: Harrison

Th Jefferson

North Carolina

Will Hooper

Joseph Hewes

South Carolina

Tho: Lynch

Christ Gadsden

E. Rutledge

WASHINGTON THE NATION-BUILDER

BICENTENNIAL POEM

Written especially for the
CELEBRATION OF THE TWO HUNDREDTH ANNIVERSARY
OF THE BIRTH OF GEORGE WASHINGTON

By

EDWIN MARKHAM

Author of "The Man With the Hoe"

A Spartan mother called him into Time,
And kindled duty in him as a flame;
While he was schooled by the primeval hills
Of old Virginia—schooled by her mighty woods,
Where Indians war-whooped and the wild beast prowled.
His name was written on no college scroll;
But he drank wisdom from the wilderness.
The mountains poured into his soul their strength,
The rocks their fortitude, the stars their calm.

He grew a silent man;
Yet carried on all roads
The lofty courtesies, the high reserves.
He seemed to know, even in this noise of time,
The solemn quiets of Eternity.
But fiery energy, a live crater, slept
Under that mountain calm; yet never blazed
Into a passion, save in some black hour
When craven souls betrayed the people. Then
He was all sword and flame, a god in arms.

With the heart of a child, the wisdom of a sage,
He toiled with no self to serve.
He grew in greatness, year by luminous year
Until he carried empire in his brain.
Yet if no Cause, no high commanding Cause,
Had called him to the hazard of the deed,
None would have guessed his power
To build a nation out of chaos, give
To her the wings of soaring destinies.
But at the Hour, the People knew their Man,
The one ordained of Heaven, ordained to stand
In the deadly breach and hold the gate for God.

And when the Scroll was signed and the glad Bell
Of Independence echoed round the world,
He led his tattered host on stubborn fields,
Barefoot and hungry, thru the ice and mire—
Thru dolors, valors, desperations, dreams—
Thru Valley Forge on to world-startling hours
When proud Cornwallis yielded up his sword.
And all the way, down to the road's last bend,
Cool Judgment whispered to his listening mind.
Where there was faltering, he was there as faith;
Where there was weakness, he was there as strength;
Where there was discord, he was there as peace.

His trust was in the Ruler of Events—
In Him who watches. He could say, "The ends
Are in God's hands. I trust,
But while I trust I battle." In this creed,
His soul took refuge and his heart found rest.
When, after Yorktown, all the guns were husht,
Still was our Chieftain on a battle line,
Fighting old laws, old manners, old beliefs.
He fought the outworn old,
And lit new torches for the march ahead.

Life tried his soul by all the tests of time——
By hardship, treachery, ingratitude;
Yes, even by victory and the loud applause.
When fortune flung to him a crown, he flung
The bauble back and followed the People's dream.
He turned from all the tempters,
Stood firm above the perils of success——
Stood like Monadnock high above the clouds.

He did the day's work that was given him:
He toiled for men until he flamed with God.
Now in his greatness, ever superbly lone,
He moves in his serene eternity,
Like far Polaris wheeling on the North.

RELIGIOUS REFERENCES

IN THE

WRITINGS, ADDRESSES, AND MILITARY ORDERS

OF

GEORGE WASHINGTON

Compiled by
DAVID M. MATTESON,
Assistant Historian

INTRODUCTION

FROM the searching inquiry into every phase of the life and character of George Washington conducted by the distinguished historians of the United States George Washington Bicentennial Commission, no fact has been more definitely luminous than the fundamental religious nature of the Father of Our Country. It is for this reason that the Commission has stressed a phase of George Washington's career which seems to have distinctly influenced every thought and act of his public and private life. While these religious references are scattered throughout George Washington's biographies and his writings, it seemed desirable that the more important documental quotations be collected and presented as a separate pamphlet. This is done not only as a convenience to students, but also to focus attention upon the moral concepts of George Washington and to emphasize his constant dependence upon Divine Guidance.

It cannot fail to be noticed by even the most casual reader of this pamphlet, that George Washington possessed none of the narrow or bigoted ideas of religious feeling. He was essentially a liberal, not with regard to the expansion of the rules of moral conduct, but liberal in his attitude toward all men of all religious convictions. He was a respecter of conscience, a courteous and tolerant believer in that All-Wise Providence which makes men truly brothers. He did not stress creeds or formulas, but always found solid comfort and consolation in the belief in a Divine Being guiding the affairs of mankind. We find these attributes not alone in his personal conduct, but also and more especially in his military orders, his letters and his speeches.

These writings are presented with historic fidelity and without extraneous comment, save occasional short explanatory notes. They reveal George Washington as a man so far above the influence of prejudice and doctrinal tradition that we find in him a great and sublime exemplar of an all-embracing religious benevolence.

The extracts here given follow the exact editions of Washington's Writings, by Dr. W. C. Ford and Dr. J. C. Fitzpatrick, or else, except in a single instance, have been copied from original manuscripts.

A short article has been added, entitled "Washington's Religious Life."

RELIGIOUS REFERENCES

IN THE

WRITINGS, ADDRESSES, AND MILITARY ORDERS

OF

GEORGE WASHINGTON

Military Orders

Winchester, September 25, 1756.

Parole Falkirk.

The men are to parade at beating the long roll tomorrow morning at 10 o'clock; and be marched as usual to the Fort, to attend Divine Service. The Officers to be present at calling the roll, and see that the men do appear in the most decent manner they can.

Writings (Fitzpatrick ed.), I. 473.

Letter to Acting Governor John Blair

Fort Loudoun, April 17, 1758.

Honble. Sir: . . .

The last Assembly, in their Supply Bill, provided for a chaplain to our regiment, for whom I had often very unsuccessfully applied to Governor Dinwiddie. I now flatter myself, that your Honor will be pleased to appoint a sober, serious man for this duty. Common decency, Sir, in a camp calls for the services of a divine, and which ought not to be dispensed with, altho' the world should be so uncharitable as to think us void of religion, and incapable of good instructions. . . .

[signature: G Washington]

Writings (Fitzpatrick ed.), II. 177.

Letter and Instructions to Col. Benedict Arnold on Canadian Expedition

Camp at Cambridge, September 14, 1775.

Sir: . . .

I also give it in Charge to you to avoid all Disrespect to or Contempt of the Religion of the Country and its Ceremonies. Prudence, Policy, and a true Christian Spirit, will lead us to look with Compassion upon their Errors without insulting them. While we are contending for our own Liberty, we should be very cautious of violating the Rights of Conscience in others, ever considering that God alone is the Judge of the Hearts of Men, and to Him only in this Case, they are answerable. . . .

14th. As the Contempt of the Religion of a Country by ridiculing any of its Ceremonies or affronting its Ministers or Votaries has ever been deeply resented, you are to be particularly careful to restrain every Officer and Soldier from such Imprudence and Folly and to punish every Instance of it. On the other Hand, as far as lays in your Power, you are to protect and support the free Exercise of the Religion of the Country and the undisturbed Enjoyment of the rights of Conscience in religious Matters, with your utmost Influence and Authority. . . .

[signature: G Washington]

Writings (Fitzpatrick ed.), III. 491-496.

Military Orders

Head Quarters, Cambridge, November 5, 1775.

Parole Montgomery. Countersign Chamblee. . . .

As the Commander in Chief has been apprized of a design form'd for the observance of that ridiculous and childish custom of burning the Effigy of the pope—He cannot help expressing his surprise that there should be Officers and Soldiers in this army so void of common sense, as not to see the impropriety of such a step at this Juncture; at a Time when we are solliciting, and have really obtain'd, the friendship and alliance of the People of Canada, whom we ought to consider as Brethren embarked in the same Cause. The defence of the general Liberty of America: At such a juncture, and in such Circumstances, to be insulting their Religion, is so monstrous, as not to be suffered or excused; indeed instead of offering the most remote insult, it is our duty to address public thanks to these our Brethren, as to them we are so much indebted for every late happy Success over the common Enemy in Canada.

Writings (Fitzpatrick ed.), IV. 64, 65.

Letter to Joseph Reed

Cambridge, January 14, 1776.

Dear Sir: . . .

The reflection on my situation, and that of this army, produces many an uneasy hour when all around me are wrapped in sleep. Few people know the predicament we are in, on a thousand accounts; fewer still will believe, if any disaster happens to these lines, from what cause it flows. I have often thought how much happier I should have been, if, instead of accepting of a command under such circumstances, I had taken my musket on my shoulder and entered the ranks, or, if I could have justified the measure to posterity and my own conscience, had retired to the back country, and lived in a wigwam. If I shall be able to rise superior to these and many other difficulties, which might be enumerated, I shall most religiously believe, that the finger of Providence is in it, to blind the eyes of our enemies; for surely if we get well through this month, it must be for want of their knowing disadvantages we labour under.

[signature: G Washington]

Writings (Fitzpatrick ed.), IV. 240, 243.

Answer to an Address from the Massachusetts Legislature

[March 28, 1776.]

. . . That the metropolis of your colony is now relieved from the cruel and oppressive invasions of those, who were sent to erect the standard of lawless domination, and to trample on the rights of humanity, and is again open and free for its rightful possessors, must give pleasure to every virtuous and sympathetic heart; and its being effected without the blood of our soldiers and fellow-citizens must be ascribed to the interposition of that Providence, which has manifestly appeared in our behalf through the whole of this important struggle, as well as to the measures pursued for bringing about the happy event.

May that being, who is powerful to save, and in whose hands is the fate of nations, look down with an eye of tender pity and compassion upon the whole of the United Colonies; may He continue to smile upon their counsels and arms, and crown them with success, whilst employed in the cause of virtue and mankind. May this distressed colony and its capital, and every part of this wide extended continent, through His divine favor, be restored to more than their former lustre and once happy state, and have peace, liberty, and safety secured upon a solid, permanent, and lasting foundation.

Writings (Fitzpatrick ed.), IV. 440-442.

Military Orders

Head Quarters, New York, May 15, 1776.

Parole Barre. Countersign Dublin.

The Continental Congress having ordered, Friday the 17th. Instant to be observed as a day of "fasting, humiliation and prayer, humbly to supplicate the mercy of Almighty God, that it would please him to pardon all our manifold sins and transgressions, and to prosper the Arms of the United Colonies, and finally, establish the peace and freedom of America, upon a solid and lasting foundation"—The General commands all officers, and soldiers, to pay strict obedience to the Orders of the Continental Congress, and by their unfeigned, and pious observance of their religious duties, incline the Lord and Giver of Victory, to prosper our arms. . . .

Writings (Fitzpatrick ed.), V. 43.

Military Orders

Head Quarters, New York, July 9, 1776.

Parole Manchester. Countersign Norfolk. . . .

The Hon. Continental Congress having been pleased to allow a Chaplain to each Regiment, with the pay of Thirty-three Dollars and one third pr month—The Colonels or commanding officers of each regiment are directed to procure Chaplains accordingly; persons of good Characters and exemplary lives—To see that all inferior officers and soldiers pay them a suitable respect and attend carefully upon religious exercises. The blessing and protection of Heaven are at all times necessary but especially so in times of public distress and danger—The General hopes and trusts, that every officer and man, will endeavour so to live, and act, as becomes a Christian Soldier defending the dearest Rights and Liberties of his country. . . .

Writings (Fitzpatrick ed.), V. 244.

Military Orders

Head Quarters, New York, August 3, 1776.

Parole Uxbridge. Countersign Virginia.

That the Troops may have an opportunity of attending public worship, as well as take some rest after the great fatigue they have gone through; The General in future excuses them from fatigue duty on Sundays (except at the Ship Yards, or special occasions) until further orders. The General is sorry to be informed that the foolish, and wicked practice, of profane cursing and swearing (a Vice heretofore little known in an American Army) is growing into fashion; he hopes the officers will, by example, as well as influence, endeavour to check it, and that both they, and the men will reflect, that we can have little hopes of the blessing of Heaven on our Arms, if we insult it by our impiety, and folly; added to this, it is a vice so mean and low, without any temptation, that every man of sense, and character, detests and despises it. . . .

Writings (Fitzpatrick ed.), V. 367.

Military Orders

Head Quarters, New York, August 25, 1776.

Parole Marlborough. Countersign Newtown. . . .

The General Order against working on Sunday is revoked the time not admitting of any delay. . . .

Writings (Fitzpatrick ed.), V. 489.

Letter to Landon Carter

Morristown in New Jersey, April 15, 1777.

Dear Sir: . . .

Your friendly and affectionate wishes for my health and success has a claim to my most grateful acknowledgements. That the God of Armies may Incline the Hearts of my American Brethren to support, and bestow sufficient abilities on me to bring the present contest to a speedy and happy conclusion, thereby enabling me to sink into sweet retirement, and the full enjoyment of that Peace and happiness which will accompany a domestick Life, is the first wish, and most fervent prayer of my Soul. . . .

Writings (Fitzpatrick ed.), VII. 413, 414.

Letter to Gen. Samuel Holden Parsons

Morris Town, April 23, 1777.

Dear Sir. . . .

The Languor and Supineness that have taken place, but too generally, of late, are truly mortifying, and are difficult to be accounted for. All agree our claims are righteous and must be supported; Yet all, or at least, too great a part among us, withhold the means, as if Providence, who has already done much for us, would continue his gracious interposition and work miracles for our deliverance, without troubling ourselves about the matter. . . .

Writings (Fitzpatrick ed.), VII. 455, 456.

Military Orders

Head Quarters, at Wentz's, Worcester Township,

October 18, 1777.

Parole Reading. Countersigns Rochester, Ridgefield.

The General has his happiness completed relative to the successes of our northern Army. On the 14th [sic] instant, General Burgoyne, and his whole Army, surrendered themselves prisoners of war. Let every face brighten, and every heart expand with grateful Joy and praise to the supreme disposer of all events, who has granted us this signal success. The Chaplains of the army are to prepare short discourses, suited to the joyful occasion to deliver to their several corps and brigades at 5 O'clock this afternoon—immediately after which, *Thirteen* pieces of cannon are to be discharged at the part of artillery, to be followed by a *feu-de-joy*. . . .

Writings (Fitzpatrick ed.), IX. 390.

Military Orders

Head-Quarters V. Forge Saturday May 2nd 78.

Parole Bavaria—C Signs Bristol—Burlington.

The Commander in Chief directs that divine Service be performed every Sunday at 11 oclock in those Brigades to which there are Chaplains, those which have none to attend the places of worship nearest to them. It is expected that officers of all Ranks will by their attendence set an Example to their men.

While we are zealously performing the duties of good Citizens and soldiers we certainly ought not to be inattentive to the higher duties of Religion. To the distinguished Character of Patriot, it should be our highest Glory to add the more distinguished Character of Christian. The signal Instances of providential Goodness which we have experienced and which have now almost crowned our labours with complete Success, demand from us in a peculiar manner the warmest returns of Gratitude & Piety to the Supreme Author of all Good. . . .

Varick Transcripts, General Orders, III. 180.

Military Orders

Head-Quarters V. Forge Tuesday May 5th 1778.

Parole Europe—CSigns Exeter—Eltham. . . .

After Orders May 5th 1778.

It having pleased the Almighty ruler of the Universe propitiously to defend the Cause of the United American-States and finally by raising us up a powerful Friend among the Princes of the Earth to establish our liberty and Independence upon lasting foundations, it becomes us to set apart a day for gratefully acknowledging the divine Goodness & celebrating the important Event which we owe to his divine Interposition.

The several Brigades are to be assembled for this Purpose at nine o'clock tomorrow morning when their Chaplains will communicate the Intelligence contain'd in the Postscript to the Pennsylvania Gazette of the 2nd instant and offer up a thanksgiving and deliver a discourse suitable to the Occasion. . . .

Varick Transcripts, General Orders, III. 184-186.

Letter to Gen. Thomas Nelson

Camp, at the White Plains, 20 August, 1778.

My dear Sir, . . .

It is not a little pleasing, nor less wonderful to contemplate, that after two years' manoeuvring and undergoing the strangest vicissitudes, that perhaps ever attended any one contest since the creation, both armies are brought back to the very point they set out from, and that which was the offending party in the beginning is now reduced to the use of the spade and pickaxe for defence. The hand of Providence has been so conspicuous in all this, that he must be worse than an infidel that lacks faith, and more than wicked, that has not gratitude enough to acknowledge his obligations. But it will be time enough for me to turn preacher, when my present appointment ceases; and therefore I shall add no more on the doctrine of Providence; . . .

G Washington

Writings (Ford ed.), VII. 159, 161.

Military Orders after Yorktown

Head-Quarters Before York Saturday October 20th 1781

Parole Congress Countersigns York Gloucester . . .

Divine Service is to be performed tomorrow in the several Brigades or Divisions.

The Commander in Chief earnestly recommends that the troops not on duty should universally attend with that seriousness of Deportment and gratitude of Heart which the recognition of such reiterated and astonishing interpositions of Providence demand of us.

Varick Transcripts, General Orders, VI. 58, 61.

To the Reverend the Minister, the Elders & Deacons of the reformed Protestant Dutch Church in the City of Albany

[Albany, June 28, 1782.]

Gentlemen

I am extreamly happy in this opportunity of blending my public duty with my private satisfaction, by paying a due attention to the Frontiers, & advanced Posts of this State, and at the same time visiting the antient & respectable City of Albany.

While I consider the approbation of the Wise & the Virtuous as the highest possible reward for my services, I beg you will be assured, Gentlemen, that I now experience the most sensible pleasure from the favorable sentiments you are pleased to express of my Conduct

Your benevolent wishes & fervent prayers for my personal welfare & felicity, demand all my gratitude.

May the preservation of your civil & religious Liberties still be the care of an indulgent Providence; and may the rapid increase & universal extension of knowledge virtue & true Religion be the consequence of a speedly & honorable Peace.

G Washington

Washington Papers, CCI.

To the Minester Elders and Deacons of the Reformed Prodistant Dutch Churtch of the Town of Schenectady

[Schenectady, June 30, 1782.]

Gentlemen,

I sincearly thank you for your Congratulations on my arrival in this place

Whilst I join you in adoring that supreem being to whome alone can be attrebuted the signel successes of our Arms I can not but Express gratitude to you Gentlemen for so distinguished a testemony of your Regard.

May the same providence that has hitherto in so Remarkable a manner Evinced the Justice of our Cause lead us to a speady and honourable peace and may I'ts attendant blessings soon Restore this your Florishing place to its former prosperity.

Magazine of American History, XIX. 257.

To the Dutch Church at Kingston, N. Y.

Gentlemen,

I am happy in receiving this public mark of the esteem of the Minister, Elders and Deacons of the Reformed Protestant Dutch Church in Kingston.

Convinced that our religious Liberties were as essential as our Civil, my endeavors have never been wanting to encourage & promote the one, while I have been contending for the other; and I am highly flattered by finding that my efforts have met the approbation of so respectable a body.

In return for your kind concern for my temporal & eternal happiness, permit me to assure you that my wishes are reciprocal, and that you may be enabled to hand down your Religion pure & undefiled to a Posterity worthy of their Ancestors is the fervent prayer of

Gentln.
Yr. Most Obedt. Ser.

Kingston
16th Novr. } 1782

G Washington

Facsimile in *Christian Intelligencer*, CIII. No. 23.

Military Orders

[Head Quarters, Newburgh] Friday April 18th 1783

Parole Kinalal.   Countersigns Litchfield—Montreal. . . .

The Commander in Chief orders the Cessation of Hostilities between the United States of America and the King of Great Britain to be publickly proclaimed tomorrow at 12 o'clock at the New building, and that the Proclamation which will be communicated herewith, be read tomorrow evening at the head of every regiment & corps of the army. After which the Chaplains with the several Brigades will render thanks to almighty God for all his mercies, particularly for his over ruling the wrath of man to his own glory, and causing the rage of war to cease amongst the nations. . . .

Varick Transcripts, General Orders, VII. 126.

Circular Letter addressed to the Governors of all the States on Disbanding the Army

Head-Quarters, Newburg, 8 June, 1783.

Sir, . . .

The citizens of America, placed in the most enviable condition, as the sole lords and proprietors of a vast tract of continent, comprehending all the various soils and climates of the world, and abounding with all the necessaries and conveniences of life, are now, by the late satisfactory pacification, acknowledged to be possessed of absolute freedom and independency. They are, from this period, to be considered as the actors on a most conspicuous theatre, which seems to be peculiarly designated by Providence for the display of human greatness and felicity. Here they are not only surrounded with every thing, which can contribute to the completion of private and domestic enjoyment; but Heaven has crowned all its other blessings, by giving a fairer opportunity for political happiness, than any other nation has ever been favored with. Nothing can illustrate these observations more forcibly, than a recollection of the happy conjuncture of times and circumstances, under which our republic assumed its rank among the nations. The foundation of our empire was not laid in the gloomy age of ignorance and superstition; but at an epocha when the rights of mankind were better understood and more clearly defined, than at any former period. The researches of the human mind after social happiness have been carried to a great extent; the treasures of knowledge, acquired by the labors of philosophers, sages, and legislators, through a long succession of years, are laid open for our use, and their collected wisdom may be happily applied in the establishment of our forms of government. The free cultivation of letters, the unbounded extension of commerce, the progressive refinement of manners, the growing liberality of sentiment, and, above all, the pure and benign light of Revelation, have had a meliorating influence on mankind and increased the blessings of society. At this auspicious period, the United States came into existence as a nation; and, if their citizens should not be completely free and happy, the fault will be entirely their own. . . .

It remains, then, to be my final and only request, that your Excellency will communicate these sentiments to your legislature at their next meeting, and that they may be considered as the legacy of one, who has ardently wished, on all occasions, to be useful to his country, and who, even in the shade of retirement, will not fail to implore the Divine benediction upon it.

I now make it my earnest prayer, that God would have you, and the State over which you preside, in his holy protection; that he would incline the hearts of the citizens to cultivate a spirit of subordination and obedience to government; to entertain a brotherly affection and love for one another, for their fellow citizens of the United States at large, and particularly for their brethren who have served in the field; and finally, that he would most graciously be pleased to dispose us all to do justice, to love mercy, and to demean ourselves with that charity, humility, and pacific temper of mind, which were the characteristics of the Divine Author of our blessed religion, and without an humble imitation of whose example in these things, we can never hope to be a happy nation. . . .

G Washington

Writings (Ford ed.), X. 254-256, 264.

[The last paragraph of the above letter has in recent times been paraphrased into the so-called Washington's Prayer, as follows:

Almighty God: We make our earnest prayer that thou wilt keep the United States in thy holy protection; that thou wilt incline the hearts of the citizens to cultivate a spirit of subordination and obedience to government; and entertain a brotherly affection and love for one another and for their fellow citizens of the United States at large. And finally that thou wilt most graciously be pleased to dispose us all to do justice, to love mercy and to demean ourselves with that charity, humility and pacific temper of mind which were the characteristics of the divine author of our blessed religion, and without a humble imitation of whose example in these things we can never hope to be a happy nation. Grant our supplication, we beseech thee, through Jesus Christ our Lord. Amen.]

To the Magistrates & Inhabitants of the Borough of Elizabeth

Gentlemen,

It gives me the most pleasing sensations to find so cordial a wellcome on my return in peace to this pleasant Town, after the vicissitudes of so long and obstinate a Contest.

On this happy occasion, suffer me, Gentlemen, to join you in grateful adoration of that divine Providence, which hath rescued our Country from the Brink of destruction, which hath crown'd our exertions with the fairest fruits of success, and which now (instead of the anxiety and distress occasioned by perpetual Alarms) permits you to enjoy, without molestation, the sweets of Peace and Domestic happiness. May a Spirit of Wisdom and rectitude preside over all our Councils and Actions, and dispose us, as a Nation, to avail ourselves of the Blessings which are placed before us, then shall we be happy indeed, and as a just reward for your liberal and virtuous sentiments, may the felicity of the Magistracy and Inhabitants of this Corporation, be only limited by the duration of time, and exceeded by the fruition of a Glorious immortality.

Elizabeth Town Augt. 21st 1783.

Varick Transcripts, C. V. 51.

Farewell Orders to the Armies of the United States

Rocky Hill, near Princeton, 2 November 1783.

. . . A contemplation of the complete attainment (at a period earlier than could have been expected) of the object, for which we contended against so formidable a power, cannot but inspire us with astonishment and gratitude. The disadvantageous circumstances on our part, under which the war was undertaken, can never be forgotten. The singular interpositions of Providence in our feeble condition were such, as could scarcely escape the attention of the most unobserving; while the unparalleled perseverance of the armies of the United States, through almost every possible suffering and discouragement for the space of eight long years, was little short of a standing miracle. . . .

And being now to conclude these his last public orders, to take his ultimate leave in a short time of the military character, and to bid a final adieu to the armies he has so long had the honor to command, he can only again offer in their behalf his recommendations to their grateful country, and his prayers to the God of armies. May ample justice be done them here, and may the choicest of Heaven's favors, both here and hereafter, attend those, who, under the Divine auspices, have secured innumerable blessings for others. With these wishes and this benediction, the Commander-in-chief is about to retire from service. The curtain of separation will soon be drawn, and the military scene to him will be closed for ever.

Writings (Ford ed.), X. 330-334.

To the Minister Elders, Deacons & Members of the reformed German Congregation in the City of New York

Gentlemen,

The illustrious and happy event on which you are pleased to congratulate and wellcome me to this City, demands all our gratitude; while the favourable sentiments you have thought proper to express of my conduct, intitles you to my warmest acknowledgements.

Disposed, at every suitable opportunity to acknowledge publicly our infinite obligations to the Supreme Ruler of the Universe for rescuing our Country from the brink of destruction; I cannot fail at time to ascribe all the honor of our late successes to the same glorious Being. And if my humble exertions have been made in any degree subservient to the execution of the divine purposes, a contemplation of the benediction of Heaven on our righteous Cause, the approbation of my virtuous Countrymen, & the testimony of my own Conscience, will be a sufficient reward and augment my felicity beyond any thing which the world can bestow.

The establishment of Civil and Religious Liberty was the Motive which induced me to the Field; the object is attained and it now remains to be my earnest wish & prayer, that the Citizens of the United States would make a wise and virtuous use of the blessings, placed before them; and that the reformed german Congregation in New York; may not only be conspicious for their religious character, but as examplary, in support of our inestimable acquisitions, as their reverend Minister has been in the attainment of them.

New York Novr. 29 1783

Varick Transcripts, C. V. 88.

To the Members of the Volunteer Association and other Inhabitants of the Kingdom of Ireland who have lately arrived in the City of New York

Gentlemen, . . .

The bosom of America is open to receive not only the Opulent and respectable Stranger, but the oppressed & persecuted of all Nations and Religions; whom we shall wellcome to a participation of all our rights and privileges, if by decency and propriety of conduct they appear to merit the enjoyment.

New York December 2 1783

Varick Transcripts, C. V. 92.

To the Learned Professions of Philadelphia

Gentlemen, . . .

Conscious of no impropriety in wishing to merit the esteem of my fellow Citizens in general; I cannot hesitate to acknowledge that I feel a certain pleasing sensation in obtaining the good opinion of men eminent for their Virtue, knowledge and humanity; but I am sensible at the same time, it becomes me to receive with humility the warm commendations you are pleased to bestow on my conduct; for if I have been led to detest the folly and madness of unbounded Ambition, if I have been induced from other motives to draw my sword and regulate my public behaviour, or if the management of the War has been conducted upon purer principles: let me not arrogate the merit to human imbecility, but rather ascribe whatever glory may result from our successful struggle to a higher and more efficient Cause. For the re-establishment of our once violated rights; for the confirmation of our Independence; for the protection of Virtue, Philosophy and Literature; for the present flourishing state of the Sciences, and for the enlarged prospect of human happiness, it is our common duty to pay the tribute of gratitude to the greatest and best of Beings. . . .

December 13th 1783 Philadelphia.

Varick Transcripts, C. V. 124.

To the Mayor Recorder Aldermen and Common Council of the City of Annapolis

Permit me, Gentlemen, to offer to you my sincere thanks for your Congratulations on the happy events, of Peace and the Establishment of our Independence.

If my Conduct throughout the War has merited the confidence of my fellow Citizens, and has been instrumental in obtaining for my Country the blessings of Peace and Freedom, I owe it to that supreme being who guides the hearts of all, who has so signally interposed his aid in every Stage of the Contest and who had graciously been pleased to bestow on me the greatest of Earthly Rewards—*the approbation and affections of a free people.*

Tho' I retire from the employments of public life I shall never cease to entertain the most anxious care for the welfare of my Country. May the Almighty dispose the heart of every Citizen of the United States to improve the great prospect of happiness before us; and may you, Gentlemen, and the Inhabitants of this City long enjoy every felicity, this world can afford.

Annapolis Decr. 22d 1783

Varick Transcripts, C. V. 149.

Letter to George Mason

Mount Vernon, 3 October, 1785.

Dear Sir,

I have this moment received yours of yesterday's date, enclosing a memorial and remonstrance against the Assessment Bill, which I will read with attention. At *present* I am unable to do it, on account of company. The bill itself I do not recollect ever to have read; with attention I am certain I never did, but will compare them together.

Although no man's sentiments are more opposed to *any kind* of restraint upon religious principles than mine are, yet I must confess, that I am not amongst the number of those, who are so much alarmed at the thoughts of making people pay towards the support of that which they profess, if of the denomination of Christians, or declare themselves Jews, Mahometans, or otherwise, and thereby obtain proper relief. As the matter now stands, I wish an assessment had never been agitated, and as it has gone so far, that the bill could not die an easy death; because I think it will be productive of more quiet to the State, than by enacting it into a law, which in my opinion would be impolitic, admitting there is a decided majority for it, to the disquiet of a respectable minority. In the former case, the matter will soon subside; in the latter, it will rankle and perhaps convulse the State. . . .

Writings (Ford ed.), X. 506.

Letter to the Marquis de Lafayette

[Philadelphia, August 15, 1787.]

My dear Marqs., . . .

News paper acct. inform us that the Session of the Assembly of Notables is ended, . . . I am not less ardent in my wish that you may succeed in your plan of toleration in religious matters. Being no bigot myself to any mode of worship, I am disposed to endulge the professors of Christianity in the church, that road to heaven which to them shall seem the most direct plainest easiest and least liable to exception. . . .

Washington's Letter Books, VI B. 131.

To the Mayor, Corporation, and Citizens of Alexandria

[April 1789.]

Gentlemen, . . .

All that now remains for me is to commit myself and you to the protection of that beneficent Being, who on a former occasion hath happily brought us together, after a long and distressing separation. Perhaps the same gracious Providence will again indulge us with the same heartfelt felicity. But words, my fellow-citizens, fail me: unutterable sensations must then be left for more expressive silence: while, from an aching heart, I bid you all, my affectionate friends, and kind neighbours, farewell!

Washington's Letter Books, XXIX. 2.

To the Mayor, Recorder, Aldermen, and Common Council of the City of Philadelphia

[April 1789.]

. . . When I contemplate the interposition of Providence, as it was visibly manifested, in guiding us through the Revolution, in preparing us for the reception of a general government, and in conciliating the good will of the People of America towards one another after it's adoption, I feel myself oppressed and almost overwhelmed with a sense of the divine munificence. I feel that nothing is due to my personal agency in all these complicated and wonderful events, except what can simply be attributed to the exertions of an honest zeal for the good of my country.

If I have distressing apprehensions that I shall not be able to justify the too exalted expectations of my countrymen: I am supported under the pressure of such uneasy reflections by a confidence that the most gracious Being, who hath hitherto watched over the interests, and averted the perils, of the United States will never suffer so fair an inheritance to become a prey to anarchy, despotism, or any other species of oppression. . . .

Washington's Letter Books, XXIX. 14.

First Inaugural Address

April 30, 1789.

Fellow-Citizens of the Senate and House of Representatives, . . .

Such being the impression under which I have, in obedience to the public summons, repaired to the present station, it would be peculiarly improper to omit, in this first official act, my fervent supplications to that Almighty Being, who rules over the universe, who presides in the councils of nations, and whose providential aids can supply every human defect, that his benediction may consecrate to the liberties and happiness of the people of the United States a government instituted by themselves for these essential purposes, and may enable every instrument employed in its administration to execute with success the functions allotted to his charge. In tendering this homage to the great Author of every public and private good, I assure myself that it expresses your sentiments not less than my own; nor those of my fellow-citizens at large, less than either. No people can be bound to acknowledge and adore the invisible hand, which conducts the affairs of men, more than the people of the United States. Every step, by which they have advanced to the character of an independent nation, seems to have been distinguished by some token of providential agency. And, in the important revolution just accomplished in the system of their united government, the tranquil deliberations and voluntary consent of so many distinct communities, from which the event has resulted, cannot be compared with the means by which most governments have been established, without some return of pious gratitude along with an humble anticipation of the future blessings which the past seem to presage. These reflections, arising out of the present crisis, have forced themselves too strongly on my mind to be suppressed. You will join with me, I trust, in thinking that there are none, under the influence of which the proceedings of a new and free government can more auspiciously commence. . . .

Having thus imparted to you my sentiments, as they have been awakened by the occasion which brings us together, I shall take my present leave; but not without resorting once more to the benign Parent of the human race, in humble supplication, that, since he has been pleased to favor the American people with opportunities for deliberating in perfect tranquillity, and dispositions for deciding with unparalleled unanimity on a form of government for the security of their union and the advancement of their happiness; so his divine blessing may be equally *conspicuous* in the enlarged views, the temperate consultations, and the wise measures, on which the success of this government must depend.

Writings (Ford ed.), XI. 381-386.

To the Ministers, Church-Wardens, and Vestry-men of the German Lutheran Congregation in and near Philadelphia

[New York, May 1789.]

Gentlemen,

While I request you to accept my thanks for your kind address, I must profess myself highly gratified by the sentiments of esteem and consideration contained in it. The approbation my past conduct has received from so worthy a body of citizens, as that whose joy for my appointment you announce, is a proof of the indulgence with which my future transactions will be judged by them.

I could not, however, avoid apprehending that the partiality of my countrymen in favor of the measures now pursued has led them to expect too much from the present government; did not the same providence which has been visible in every stage of our progress to this interesting crisis, from a combination of circumstances, give us cause to hope for the accomplishment of all our reasonable desires.

Thus partaking with you in the pleasing anticipation of the blessings of a wise and efficient government; I flatter myself opportunities will not be wanting for me to shew my disposition to encourage the domestic and public virtues of industry, economy, patriotism, philanthropy, and that righteousness which exalteth a nation.

I rejoice in having so suitable an occasion to testify the reciprocity of my esteem for the numerous people whom you represent. From the excellent character for diligence, sobriety, and virtue, which the Germans in general, who are settled in America, have ever maintained; I cannot forbear felicitating myself on receiving from so respectable a number of them such strong assurances of their affection for my person, confidence in my integrity, and zeal to support me in my endeavors for promoting the welfare of our common country.

So long as my conduct shall merit the approbation of the *wise* and the *good*, I hope to hold the same place in your affections, which your friendly declarations induce me to believe I possess at present; and amidst all the vicissitudes that may await me in this mutable state of existence, I shall earnestly desire the continuation of an interest in your intercessions at the Throne of Grace.

Washington's Letter Books, XXIX. 24.

To the General Committee, representing the United Baptist Churches in Virginia

[New York, May 1789.]

Gentlemen,

I request that you will accept my best acknowledgements for your congratulation on my appointment to the first office in the nation. The kind manner in which you mention my past conduct equally claims the expression of my gratitude.

After we had, by the smiles of Heaven on our exertions, obtained the object for which we contended, I retired at the conclusion of the war, with an idea that my country could have no farther occasion for my services, and with the intention of never entering again into public life. But when the exigence of my country seemed to require me once more to engage in public affairs, an honest conviction of duty superseded my former resolution, and became my apology for deviating from the happy plan which I had adopted.

If I could have entertained the slightest apprehension that the constitution framed in the convention, where I had the honor to preside, might possibly endanger the religious rights of any ecclesiastical Society, certainly I would never have placed my signature to it; and if I could now conceive that the general Government might ever be so administered as to render the liberty of conscience insecure, I beg you will be persuaded that no one would be more zealous than myself to establish effectual barriers against the horrors of spiritual tyranny, and every species of religious persecution. For you, doubtless, remember that I have often expressed my sentiment, that every man, conducting himself as a good citizen, and being accountable to God alone for his religious opinions, ought to be protected in worshipping the Deity according to the dictates of his own conscience.

While I recollect with satisfaction that the religious Society of which you are members, have been, throughout America, uniformly, and almost unanimously, the firm friends to civil liberty, and the preserving Promoters of our glorious revolution; I cannot hesitate to believe that they will be the faithful supporters of a free, yet efficient general Government. Under this pleasing expectation I rejoice to assure them that they may rely on my best wishes and endeavors to advance their prosperity.

In the meantime be assured, Gentlemen, that I entertain a proper sense of your fervent supplications to God for my temporal and eternal happiness.

Washington's Letter Books, XXIX. 84.

[The address contains this statement: "When the constitution first made its appearance in Virginia, we, as a Society, had unusual strugglings of mind; fearing that *the liberty of conscience,* dearer to us than property or life, was not sufficiently secured."]

To the General Assembly of the Presbyterian Church in the United States of America

[New York, May, 1789.]

Gentlemen,

I receive with great sensibility the testimonial, given by the General Assembly of the Presbyterian Church in the United States of America, of the lively and unfeigned pleasure experienced by them on my appointment to the first office in the nation.

Although it will be my endeavor to avoid being elated by the too favorable opinion which your kindness for me may have induced you to express of the importance of my former conduct, and the effort of my future services: yet, conscious of the disinterestedness of my motives, it is not necessary for me to conceal the satisfaction I have felt upon finding, that my compliance with the call of my country, and my dependence on the assistance of Heaven to support me in my arduous undertakings, have, so far as I can learn, met the universal approbation of my countrymen.

While I reiterate the profession of my dependence upon Heaven as the source of all public and private blessings; I will observe that the general prevalence of piety, philanthropy, honesty, industry and economy seems, in the ordinary course of human affairs, particularly necessary for advancing and confirming the happiness of our country. While all men within our territories are protected in worshipping the Deity according to the dictates of their consciences; it is rationally to be expected from them in return, that they will all be emulous of evincing the sincerity of their professions by the innocence of their lives, and the beneficence of their actions: For no man, who is profligate in his morals, or a bad member of the civil community, can possibly be a true Christian, or a credit to his own religious society.

I desire you to accept my acknowledgements for your laudable endeavors to render men sober, honest, and good citizens, and the obedient subjects of a lawful government; as well as for your prayers to Almighty God for his blessing on our common country and the humble instrument, which he has been pleased to make use of in the administration of it's government.

G. Washington

Washington's Letter Books, XXIX. 28.

To the Bishops of the Methodist Episcopal Church in the United States of America

[New York, May 1789.]

Gentlemen,

I return to you individually, and (through you) to your Society collectively in the United States my thanks for the demonstrations of affection, and the expressions of joy, offered in their behalf, on my late appointment. It shall still be my endeavor to manifest, by overt acts, the purity of my inclinations for promoting the happiness of mankind, as well as the sincerity of my desires to contribute whatever may be in my power towards the preservation of the civil and religious liberties of the American People. In pursuing this line of conduct, I hope, by the assistance of divine providence, not altogether to disappoint the confidence which you have been pleased to repose in me.

It always affords me satisfaction, when I find a concurrence in sentiment and practice between all conscientious men in acknowledgements of homage to the great Governor of the Universe, and in professions of support to a just civil government. After mentioning that I trust the people of every denomination, who demean themselves as good citizens, will have occasion to be convinced that I shall always strive to prove a faithful and impartial Patron of genuine, vital religion: I must assure you in particular that I take in the kindest part the promise you make of presenting your prayers at the Throne of Grace for me, and that I likewise implore the divine benedictions on yourselves and your religious community.

G. Washington

Washington's Letter Books, XXIX. 26.

To the Ministers and Elders of the German Reformed Congregations in the United States

[New York, June 1789.]

Gentlemen,

I am happy in concurring with you in the sentiments of gratitude and piety towards Almighty God, which are expressed with such fervency of devotion in your address; and in believing, that I shall always find in you, and the German Reformed Congregations in the United States a conduct correspondent to such worthy and pious expressions.

At the same time, I return you my thanks for the manifestation of your firm purpose to support in your persons a government founded in justice and equity, and for the promise that it will be your constant study to impress the minds of the People entrusted to your care with a due sense of the necessity of uniting reverence to such a government and obedience to it's laws with the duties and exercises of Religion.

Be assured, Gentlemen, it is, by such conduct, very much in the power of the virtuous members of the community to alleviate the burden of the important office which I have accepted; and to give me Occasion to rejoice, in this world, for having followed therein the dictates of my conscience.

Be pleased also to accept my acknowledgements for the interest you so kindly take in the prosperity of my person, family, and administration.

May your devotions before the Throne of Grace be prevalent in calling down the blessings of Heaven upon yourselves and your country.

G. Washington

Washington's Letter Books, XXIX. 30.

To the Governor and Council of the State of North-Carolina

Gentlemen, . . .

Gratified by the favorable sentiments which are evinced in your address to me, and impressed with an idea that the citizens of your State are sincerely attached to the Interest, the Prosperity, and the Glory of America; I most earnestly implore the divine benediction and guidance in the Counsels, which are shortly to be taken by their Delegates on a subject of the most momentous consequence, I mean the political relation which is to subsist hereafter between the State of North Carolina, and the States now in union under the new general government.

Done at New York, this 15th day of June 1789.

G. Washington

Washington's Letter Books, XXIX. 36.

To the Senate and House of Representatives of the State of Massachusetts

Gentlemen, . . .

For the benedictions you have been pleased to implore the Parent of the Universe on my person and family I have a grateful heart—and the most ardent wish that we may all, by rectitude of conduct and a perfect reliance on his beneficence, draw the smiles of Heaven on ourselves and posterity to the latest generation.

New York July 9th 1789.

G Washington

Washington's Letter Books, XXIX. 32.

To the Directors of the Society of the United Brethren for Propagating the Gospel among the Heathen
[New York, July 1789.]

Gentlemen,

I receive with satisfaction the congratulations of your Society and of the Brethren's Congregations in the United States of America. For you may be persuaded that the approbation and good wishes of such a peaceable and virtuous Community cannot be indifferent to me.

You will also be pleased to accept my thanks for the Treatise which you presented; and be assured of my patronage in your laudable undertakings.

In proportion as the general Government of the United States shall acquire strength by duration, it is probable they may have it in their power to extend a salutary influence to the Aborigines in the extremities of their territory. In the meantime, it will be a desireable thing for the protection of the Union to co-operate, as far as the circumstances may conveniently admit, with the disinterested endeavors of your Society to civilise and christianise the Savages of the Wilderness.

Under these impressions I pray Almighty God to have you always in his holy keeping.

G Washington

Washington's Letter Books, XXIX. 34.

To the Bishops, Clergy, and Laity of the Protestant Episcopal Church in the States of New York, New Jersey, Pennsylvania, Delaware, Maryland, Virginia, and South Carolina, in general Convention assembled

[New York, August 19, 1789.]

Gentlemen,

I sincerely thank you for your affectionate congratulations on my election to the chief magistracy of the United States.

After having received from my fellow-citizens in general the most liberal treatment, after having found them disposed to contemplate in the most flattering point of view, the performance of my military services, and the manner of my retirement at the close of the war, I feel that I have a right to console myself in my present arduous undertakings, with a hope that they will still be inclined to put the most favorable construction on the motives which may influence me in my future public transactions.

The satisfaction arising from the indulgent opinion entertained by the American People of my conduct, will, I trust, be some security for preventing me from doing any thing, which might justly incur the forfeiture of that opinion. And the consideration that human happiness and moral duty are inseparably connected, will always continue to prompt me to promote the progress of the former, by inculcating the practice of the latter.

On this occasion it would ill become me to conceal the joy I have felt in perceiving the fraternal affection which appears to encrease every day among the friends of genuine religion. It affords edifying prospects indeed to see Christians of different denominations dwell together in more charity, and conduct themselves in respect to each other with a more christian-like spirit than ever they have done in any former age, or in any other nation.

I receive with the greater satisfaction your congratulations on the establishment of the new constitution of government; because I believe it's mild, yet efficient, operations will tend to remove every remaining apprehension of those with whose opinions it may not entirely coincide, as well as to confirm the hopes of it's numerous friends; and because the moderation, patriotism, and wisdom of the present federal Legislature, seem to promise the restoration of order, and our ancient virtues; the extension of genuine religion, and the consequent advancement of our respectability abroad, and of our substantial happiness at home.

I request most reverend and respected Gentlemen that you will accept my cordial thanks for your devout supplications to the Supreme Ruler of the Universe in behalf of me. May you, and the People whom you represent be the happy subjects of the divine benedictions both here and hereafter.

G Washington

Washington's Letter Books, XXIX. 42.

By the President of the United States of America A Proclamation

Whereas it is the duty of all Nations to acknowledge the providence of Almighty God, to obey his will, to be grateful for his benefits, and humbly to implore his protection and favor. And whereas both Houses of Congress have, by their joint Committee requested me "to recommend to the People of the United States a day of public thanksgiving and prayer to be observed by acknowledging with grateful hearts the many signal favors of Almighty God, especially by affording them an opportunity peaceably to establish a form of government for their safety and happiness."

Now therefore I do recommend and assign Thursday the 26th day of November next to be devoted by the People of these States to the service of that great and glorious Being, who is the beneficent Author of all the good that was, that is, or that will be. That we may then all unite in rendering unto him our sincere and humble thanks, for his kind care and protection of the People of this country previous to their becoming a Nation; for the signal and manifold mercies, and the favorable interpositions of his providence, which we experienced in the course and conclusion of the late war; for the great degree of tranquillity, union, and plenty, which we have since enjoyed; for the peaceable and rational manner in which we have been enabled to establish constitutions of government for our safety and happiness, and particularly the national One now lately instituted; for the civil and religious liberty with which we are blessed, and the means we have of acquiring and diffusing useful knowledge; and in general for all the great and various favors which he hath been pleased to confer upon us.

And also that we may then unite in most humbly offering our prayers and supplications to the great Lord and Ruler of Nations and beseech him to pardon our national and other transgressions; to enable us all, whether in public or private stations, to perform our several and relative duties properly and punctually; to render our national government a blessing to all the People, by constantly being a government of wise, just, and constitutional laws, discreetly and faithfully executed and obeyed; to protect and guide all Sovereigns and nations (especially such as have shown kindness unto us) and to bless them with good government, peace, and concord; To promote the knowledge and practice of true religion and virtue, and the encrease of science among them and Us; and generally to grant unto all mankind such a degree of temporal prosperity as he alone knows to be best.

Given under my hand at the City of New York the third day of October in the year of our Lord 1789.

G Washington

Washington Papers, CCXLIV.

To the Religious Society Called Quakers, from their yearly meeting for Pennsylvania, New Jersey, Delaware, and the Western Part of Maryland and Virginia

[New York, October 1789.]

Gentlemen,

I receive with pleasure your affectionate address, and thank you for the friendly sentiments and good wishes which you express for the success of my administration, and for my personal happiness.

We have reason to rejoice in the prospect that the present national Government, which by the favor of Divine Providence, was formed by the common counsels and peaceably established with the common consent of the People, will prove a blessing to every denomination of them. To render it such my best endeavors shall not be wanting.

Government being, among other purposes, instituted to protect the persons and consciences of men from oppression, it certainly is the duty of Rulers, not only to abstain from it themselves, but according to their stations, to prevent it in others.

The liberty enjoyed by the People of these States of worshipping Almighty God agreeable to their consciences is not only among the choicest of their *blessings*, but also of their *rights*. While men perform their social duties faithfully, they do all that Society or the State can with propriety demand or expect; and remain responsible only to their Maker for the religion or modes of faith which they may prefer or profess.

Your principles and conduct are well known to me, and it is doing the People called Quakers no more than justice to say, that (except their declining to share with others the burthen of the common defence) there is no denomination among us, who are more exemplary and useful citizens.

I assure you very explicitly that in my opinion the conscientious scruples of all men should be treated with great delicacy and tenderness, and it is my wish and desire that the laws may always be as extensively accommodated to them, as a due regard to the Protection and essential interests of the nation may justify and permit.

G Washington

Washington's Letter Books, XXIX. 52.

To the Synod of the Reformed Dutch Church in North America

[New York, October 1789.]

Gentlemen,

I receive with a grateful heart your pious and affectionate address, and with truth declare to you that no circumstance of my life has affected me more sensibly or produced more pleasing emotions than the friendly congratulations, and strong assurances of support which I have received from my fellow-citizens of all descriptions upon my election to the Presidency of these United States.

I fear, Gentlemen, your goodness has led you to form too exalted an opinion of my virtues and merits. If such talents as I possess have been called into action by great events, and those events have terminated happily for our country, the glory should be ascribed to the manifest interposition of an over-ruling Providence. My military services have been abundantly recompensed by the flattering approbation of a grateful people; and, if a faithful discharge of my civil duties can ensure a like reward, I shall feel myself richly compensated for any personal sacrifice I may have made by engaging again in public life.

The Citizens of the United States of America have given as signal a proof of their wisdom and virtue in framing and adopting a constitution of government, without bloodshed or the intervention of force, as they, upon a former occasion, exhibited to the world of their valor, fortitude, and perseverance; and it must be a pleasing circumstance to every friend of good order and social happiness to find that our new government is gaining strength and respectability among the citizens of this country in proportion as it's operations are known, and its effects felt.

You, Gentlemen, act the part of pious Christians and good citizens by your prayers and exertions to preserve that harmony and good will towards men which must be the basis of every political establishment; and I readily join with you that, "while just government protects all in their religious rights, true religion affords to government its surest support."

I am deeply impressed with your good wishes for my present and future happiness, and I beseech the Almighty to take you and yours under his special care.

G Washington

Washington's Letter Books, XXIX. 50.

To the Congregational Ministers of the City of New Haven

[October 1789.]

Gentlemen,

The kind congratulations contained in your address claim and receive my grateful and affectionate thanks. Respecting, as I do, the favorable opinions of men distinguished for science and piety, it would be false delicacy to disavow the satisfaction, which I derive from their approbation of my public services and private conduct.

Regarding that deportment, which consists with true religion, as to the best security of temporal peace, and the sure mean of attaining eternal felicity, it will be my earnest endeavor (as far as human frailty may resolve) to inculcate the belief and practice of opinions which lead to the consummation of those desireable objects.

The tender interest which you have taken in my personal happiness, and the obliging manner in which you express yourselves on the restoration of my health are so forcibly impressed on my mind as to render language inadequate to the utterance of my feelings.

If it shall please the great Disposer of Events to listen to the pious supplications which you have preferred in my behalf, I trust that the remainder of my days will evince the gratitude of a heart devoted to the advancement of those objects, which receive the approbation of Heaven, and promote the happiness of our fellow-men.

My best prayers are offered to the Throne of God for your happiness and that of the Congregations committed to your care.

Washington's Letter Books, XXIX. 56.

To the Ministers and Ruling Elders delegated to represent the Churches in Massachusetts and New Hampshire, which compose the first Presbytery of the Eastward

[Portsmouth, N. H., November 2, 1789.]

Gentlemen,

The affectionate welcome, which you are pleased to give me to the eastern part of the union, would leave me without excuse, did I fail to acknowledge the sensibility, which it awakens, and to express the most sincere return that a grateful sense of your goodness can suggest.

To be approved by the praise-worthy is a wish as natural to becoming ambition, as its consequence is flattering to our self-love. I am, indeed, much indebted to the favorable sentiments which you entertain towards me, and it will be my study to deserve them.

The tribute of thanksgiving which you offer to "the gracious Father of lights" for his inspiration of our public-councils with wisdom and firmness to complete the national Constitution, is worthy of men, who, devoted to the pious purposes of religion, desire their accomplishment by such means as advance the temporal happiness of their fellow men. And, here, I am persuaded, you will permit me to observe that the path of true piety is so plain as to require but little political direction. To this consideration we ought to ascribe the absence of any regulation, respecting religion, from the Magna-Charta of our country.

To the guidance of the ministers of the gospel this important object is, perhaps, more properly committed. It will be your care to instruct the ignorant, and to reclaim the devious; and, in the progress of morality and science, to which our government will give every furtherance, we may confidently expect the advancement of true religion, and the completion of our happiness.

I pray the munificent Rewarder of virtue that your agency in this good work may receive its compensation here and hereafter.

Washington's Letter Books, XXIX. 80.

[Diary, Nov. 2. ". . . returned an answer in the Evening to one . . . from the Presbyterian Clergy of the State of Massachusetts and New Hampshire, delivered at Newbury Port; . . . which I had been unable to answer before."

In the long address of the Presbytery appears the following, which explains a portion of Washington's reply: "Whatever any may have supposed wanting in the original plan, we are happy to find so wisely providing [sic] in its amendments; and it is with peculiar satisfaction we behold how easily the entire confidence of the people, in the man who sits at the helm of Government, has eradicated every remaining objection to its form. Among these we never considered the want of *a religious test,* that grand engine of persecution in every tyrant's hand: But we shall not have been alone in rejoicing to have seen some explicit acknowledgement of the *only true God and Jesus Christ, whom he hath sent* inserted somewhere in the Magna Charta of our country."]

To the Roman Catholics in the United States of America

[New York, December 1789.]

Gentlemen,

While I now receive with much satisfaction your congratulations on my being called, by a unanimous vote, to the first station in my country; I cannot but duly notice your politeness in offering an apology for the unavoidable delay. As that delay has given you an opportunity of realizing, instead of anticipating, the benefits of the general government; you will do me the justice to believe that your testimony to the encrease of the public prosperity enhances the pleasure which I should otherwise have experienced from your affectionate address.

I feel, that my conduct in war and in peace has met with more general approbation than could reasonably have been expected; and I find myself disposed to consider that fortunate circumstance, in a great degree, resulting from the able support, and extraordinary candor of my fellow-citizens of all denominations.

The prospect of national prosperity now before us is truly animating, and ought to excite the exertions of all good men to establish and secure the happiness of their country, in the permanent duration of its freedom and independence. America, under the smiles of a divine Providence, the protection of a good government, the cultivation of manners, morals, and piety, can hardly fail of attaining an uncommon degree of eminence in literature, commerce, agriculture, improvements at home, and respectability abroad.

As mankind become more liberal, they will be more apt to allow, that all those who conduct themselves as worthy members of the community are equally entitled to the protection of civil government. I hope ever to see America among the foremost nations in examples of justice and liberality. And I presume that your fellow-citizens will not forget the patriotic part which you took in the accomplishment of their revolution, and the establishment of their government; or the important assistance which they received from a nation in which the roman catholic religion is professed.

I thank you, Gentlemen, for your kind concern for me. While my life and my health shall continue, in whatever situation I may be, it shall be my constant endeavor to justify the favorable sentiments you are pleased to express of my conduct. And may the members of your Society in America, animated alone by the pure spirit of christianity, and still conducting themselves as the faithful subjects of our free government, enjoy every temporal and spiritual felicity.

Washington's Letter Books, XXIX. 100.

To the Convention of the Universal Church lately assembled in Philadelphia

[New York (?), 1790.]

Gentlemen,

I thank you cordially for the congratulations which you offer on my appointment to the office I have the honor to hold in the government of the United States.

It gives me the most sensible pleasure to find, that, in our nation, however different are the sentiments of citizens on religious doctrines, they generally concur in one thing, for their political professions and practices are almost universally friendly to the order and happiness of our civil institutions. I am also happy in finding this disposition particularly evinced by your society. It is moreover my earnest desire, that all the members of every association or community, throughout the United States, may make such use of the auspicious years of Peace, Liberty, and free enquiry, with which they are now favored, as they shall hereafter find occasion to rejoice for having done.

With great satisfaction I embrace this opportunity to express by acknowledgements for the interest my affectionate fellow-citizens have taken in my recovery from a late dangerous indisposition, and I assure you, Gentlemen, that in mentioning my obligations for the effusions of your benevolent wishes on my behalf, I feel animated with new zeal, that my conduct may ever be worthy of your favorable opinion, as well as such as shall in every respect best comport with the character of an intelligent and accountable Being.

G Washington

Washington's Letter Books, XXX. 15.

To the Hebrew Congregations in the Cities of Philadelphia, New York, Charleston and Richmond

[New York, 1790 (?).]

Gentlemen,

The liberal sentiment toward each other which marks every political and religious denomination of men in this country stands unrivalled in the history of nations. The affection of such a people is a treasure beyond the reach of calculation; and the repeated proofs which my fellow citizens have given of their attachment to me, and approbation of my doings form the purest source of my temporal felicity. The affectionate expressions of your address again excite my gratitude, and receive my warmest acknowledgements.

The power and goodness of the Almighty were strongly manifested in the events of our late glorious revolution, and his kind interposition in our behalf has been no less visible in the establishment of our present equal government. In war he directed the sword and in peace he has ruled in our councils—my agency in both has been guided by the best intentions, and a sense of the duty which I owe my country: and as my exertions hitherto have been amply rewarded by the approbation of my fellow citizens, I shall endeavor to deserve a continuance of it by my future conduct.

May the same temporal and eternal blessings which you implore for me, rest upon your congregations.

G Washington

Washington's Letter Books, XXX. 32.

To the Members of the religious Society of free Quakers

[New York, March 1790.]

Gentlemen,

I desire to assure you of the sensibility with which I receive your congratulations on my appointment to the highest office and most extended trust which can be confided by a free People, and I thank you with sincerity for the obliging terms in which you express yourselves in my behalf. Ever happy in being favored with the approbation of my fellow-citizens, the time at which yours is declared does not diminish my sense of the obligation it confers.

Having always considered the conscientious scruples of religious belief as resting entirely with the sects that profess, or the individuals who entertain them, I cannot, consistent with this uniform sentiment, otherwise notice the circumstances referred to in your address, than by adding the tribute of my acknowledgement, to that of our country, for those services which the members of your particular community rendered to the common cause in the course of our revolution. And by assuring you that, as our present government was instituted with an express view to general happiness, it will be my earnest endeavor, in discharging the duties confided to me with faithful impartiality, to realize the hope of common protection which you expect from the measures of that government.

Impressed with gratitude for your supplications to the Supreme Being in my favor, I entreat his gracious beneficence in your behalf.

G Washington

Washington's Letter Books, XXIX. 116.

[The passage to which Washington refers in the above is as follows: "They indeed saw that by discharging the great duty they were called upon to perform, in support of their own civil rights and those of our country and posterity, they would, probably, be disowned by that people [the regular Quakers]; and there was no means of retaining or recovering their rights among them; but by neglecting that duty, or by publickly condemning their conduct in the discharge of it: A treachery to the cause of liberty and truth, of which they feel themselves utterly incapable. They were not unaware of the alienation of friendship, and many other injurious effects on temporal affairs, which too commonly attend offence given by individuals to a body so numerous as the Quakers are, and of such weight in civil society; but in the course of divine providence they were called to make so great a sacrifice, and they obeyed."]

To the Hebrew Congregation of the City of Savannah

[New York, May 1790.]

Gentlemen,

I thank you with great sincerity for your congratulations on my appointment to the office, which I have the honor to hold by the unanimous choice of my fellow-citizens: and especially for the expressions which you are pleased to use in testifying the confidence that is reposed in me by your congregation.

As the delay which has naturally intervened between my election and your address has afforded an opportunity for appreciating the merits of the federal-government, and for communicating your sentiments of its administration, I have rather to express my satisfaction than regret at a circumstance, which demonstrates (upon experiment) your attachment to the former as well as approbation of the latter.

I rejoice that a spirit of liberality and philanthropy is much more prevalent than it formerly was among the enlightened nations of the earth; and that your brethren will benefit thereby in proportion as it shall become still more extensive. Happily the people of the United States of America have, in many instances, exhibited examples worthy of imitation. The salutary influence of which will doubtless extend much farther, if gratefully enjoying those blessings of peace which (under favor of Heaven) have been obtained by fortitude in war, they shall conduct themselves with reverence to the Deity, and charity towards their fellow-creatures.

May the same wonder-working Deity, who long since delivered the Hebrews from their Egyptian Oppressors planted them in the promised land, whose providential agency has lately been conspicuous in establishing these United States as an independent nation, still continue to water them with the dews of Heaven and to make the inhabitants of every denomination participate in the temporal and spiritual blessings of that people whose God is Jehovah.

G Washington

Washington's Letter Books, XXIX. 131.

To the Clergy of the Town of Newport in the State of Rhode Island

[Newport (?), August 1790.]

Gentlemen,

The salutations of the Clergy of the Town of Newport on my arrival in the State of Rhode Island are rendered the more acceptable on account of the liberal sentiments and just ideas which they are known to entertain respecting civil and religious liberty.

I am inexpressibly happy that by the smiles of divine Providence, my weak but honest endeavors to serve my country have hitherto been crowned with so much success, and apparently given such satisfaction to those in whose cause they were exerted. The same benignant influence, together with the concurrent support of all real friends to their country will still be necessary to enable me to be in any degree useful to this numerous and free People over whom I am called to preside.

Wherefore I return you, Gentlemen, my hearty thanks for your solemn invocation of Almighty God that every temporal and spiritual blessing may be dispensed to me, and that, under my administration, the families of these States may enjoy peace and prosperity, with all the blessings attendant on civil and religious liberty. In the participation of which blessings may you have an ample share.

G Washington

Washington's Letter Books, XXIX. 149.

To the Hebrew Congregation in New Port, Rhode Island

[Newport (?), August 1790.]

Gentlemen,

While I receive with much satisfaction your address replete with expressions of affection and esteem; I rejoice in the opportunity of assuring you that I shall always retain a grateful remembrance of the cordial welcome I experienced in my visit to New Port from all classes of Citizens.

The reflection on the days of difficulty and danger which are past is rendered the more sweet from a consciousness that they are

succeeded by days of uncommon prosperity and security. If we have wisdom to make the best use of the advantages with which we are now favored, we cannot fail, under the just administration of a good government to become a great and a happy people.

The Citizens of the United States of America have a right to applaud themselves for having given to mankind examples of an enlarged and liberal policy, a policy worthy of imitation. All possess alike liberty of conscience and immunities of citizenship. It is now no more that toleration is spoken of, as if it was by the indulgence of one class of people, that another enjoyed the exercise of their inherent natural rights. For happily the government of the United States, which gives to bigotry no sanction, to persecution no assistance, requires only that they who live under its protection should demean themselves as good citizens, in giving it on all occasions their effectual support.

It would be inconsistent with the frankness of my character not to avow that I am pleased with your favorable opinion of my administration, and fervent wishes for my felicity.

May the children of the Stock of Abraham, who dwell in this land, continue to merit and enjoy the good will of the other inhabitants, while every one shall sit in safety under his own vine and fig-tree, and there shall be none to make him afraid. May the Father of all mercies scatter light and not darkness in our paths, and make us all in our several vocations useful here, and in his own due time and way everlastingly happy.

G Washington

Washington's Letter Books, XXX. 19.

To the congregational Church and Society at Medway (formerly St. John's Parish) State of Georgia

[Savannah, May 1791.]

Gentlemen,

I learn, with gratitude proportioned to the occasion your attachment to my person, and the pleasure you express on my election to the Presidency of the United States.

Your sentiments on the happy influence of our equal government impress me with the most sensible satisfaction; they vindicate the great interests of humanity, they reflect honor on the liberal minds that entertain them, and they promise the continuance and improvement of that tranquility, which is essential to the welfare of nations, and the happiness of men.

You over-rate my best exertions when you ascribe to them the blessings which our country so eminently enjoys. From the gallantry and fortitude of her citizens, under the auspices of heaven, America has derived her independence. To their industry and the natural advantages of the country she is indebted for her prosperous situation. From their virtue she may expect long to share the protection of a free and equal government, which their wisdom has established, and which experience justifies, as admirably adapted to our social wants and individual felicity.

Continue, my fellow-citizens, to cultivate the peace and harmony which now subsist between you, and your indian-neighbours —the happy consequence is immediate, the reflection, which arises on justice and benevolence, will be lastingly grateful. A knowledge of your happiness will lighten the cares of my station, and be among the most pleasing of their rewards.

G Washington

Washington's Letter Books, XXX. 81.

To the United Brethren in Wachovia

[Salem, N. C., May 31, 1791.]

Gentlemen,

I am gratefully indebted to your respectful and affectionate expressions of personal regard, and I am not less obliged by the patriotic sentiments contained in your address.

From a Society, whose governing principles are industry and the love of order, much may be expected towards the improvement and prosperity of the country in which their settlements are formed, and experience authorizes the belief that much will be obtained.

Thanking you with grateful sincerity for your prayers in my behalf I desire to assure you of my best wishes for your social and individual happiness.

G Washington

Washington's Letter Books, XXX. 95.

Letter to Sir Edward Newenham

Philada. 20, Octo. 1792.

Dear Sir, . . .

I was sorry to see the gloomy picture which you drew of the affairs of your Country [Ireland] in your letter of December; but I hope events have not turned out so badly as you then apprehended. Of all the animosities which have existed among mankind, those which are caused by a difference of sentiment in religion, appear to be the most inveterate and distressing, and ought most to be deprecated. I was in hopes that the enlightened & liberal policy which has marked the present age, would at least have reconciled *Christians* of every denomination so far, that we should never again see their religious disputes carried to such a pitch as to endanger the peace of Society. . . .

G Washington

Washington's Letter Books, XIII. 282.

To the members of the New [Swedenborgian] Church at Baltimore

[Philadelphia, January 1793.]

Gentlemen,

It has ever been my pride to merit the approbation of my fellow citizens by a faithful and honest discharge of the duties annexed to those stations in which they have been pleased to place me; and the dearest rewards of my services have been those testimonies of esteem & confidence with which they have honored me. But to the manifest interposition of an over-ruling Providence, & to the patriotic exertions of united America are to be ascribed those events which have given us a respectable rank among the nations of the Earth.

We have abundant reason to rejoice that in this Land the light of truth & reason has triumphed over the power of bigotry and superstion [sic], and that every person may here worship God according to the dictates of his own heart. In this enlightened Age & in this Land of equal liberty it is our boast, that a man's religious tenets will not forfeit the protection of the Laws, nor deprive him of the right of attaining & holding the highest offices that are known in the United States.

Your prayers for my present & future felicity are received with gratitude; and I sincerely wish, Gentlemen, that you may in your social & individual capacities taste those blessings which a gracious God bestows upon the Righteous.

G Washington

Washington's Letter Books, XXX. 110.

Letter to George Augustine Washington

Philadelphia, 27 January, 1793.

My dear George, . . .

It has given your friends much pain to find that change of air has not been productive of that favorable change in your health which was the wish of them all. But the will of Heaven is not to be controverted or scrutinized by the children of this world. It therefore becometh the creatures of it to submit to the will of the Creator, whether it be to prolong or to shorten the number of our days, to bless them with health, or afflict them with pain. . . .

G Washington

Writings (Ford ed.), XII. 259.

To the Inhabitants of the City of Hartford

[Philadelphia, August 1793.]

Fellow Citizens,

The Address of the Inhabitants of the City of Hartford contains sentiments too favorable to the public weal, too partial to myself not to claim & receive my affectionate acknowledgments.

It, at the same time, affords a new proof of that characteristic love of order and peace, of that virtuous & enlightened zeal, for the public good, which distinguishes the Inhabitants of Connecticut.

'Tis from dispositions like these that we may hope to avoid an interruption of the numerous blessings, which demand our gratitude to Heaven; or that we may be encouraged to meet with firmness, confiding in the protection of a just Providence, any attempts to disturb them, which intemperance or injustice, from whatever quarter, may at any time make it our duty to encounter.

G Washington

Washington's Letter Books, XXX. 126.

[This and the following illustrate replies to addresses on the Proclamation of Neutrality.]

To the Inhabitants of Richmond, and its Vicinity

[Philadelphia, August 28, 1793.]

Fellow Citizens, . . .

True to our duties and interests as Americans, firm to our purpose as lovers of peace, let us unite our fervent prayers to the great ruler of the Universe, that the justice & moderation of all concerned may permit us to continue in the uninterrupted enjoyment of a blessing, which we so greatly prize, & of which we ardently wish them a speedy & permanent participation.

G Washington

Washington's Letter Books, XXX. 135.

Sixth Annual Address to Congress

Philadelphia, November 19, 1794.

Fellow-Citizens of the Senate and House of Representatives:

When we call to mind the gracious indulgence of Heaven, by which the American people became a nation; when we survey the general prosperity of our country, and look forward to the riches, power, and happiness to which it seems destined; with the deepest regret do I announce to you, that, during your recess, some of the citizens of the United States have been found capable of an insurrection. . . .

Let us unite, therefore, in imploring the Supreme Ruler of nations, to spread his holy protection over these United States; to turn the machinations of the wicked to the confirming of our constitution; to enable us at all times to root out internal sedition, and put invasion to flight; to perpetuate to our country that prosperity, which his goodness has already conferred; and to verify the anticipations of this government being a safeguard to human rights.

Writings (Ford ed.), XII. 491, 498.

Farewell Address to the People of the United States

Philadelphia, September 17, 1796.

Friends, and Fellow-Citizens, . . .

Of all the dispositions and habits, which lead to political prosperity, Religion and morality are indispensable supports.—In vain would that man claim the tribute of Patriotism, who should labour to subvert these great Pillars of human happiness, these firmest props of the duties of Men and Citizens.—The mere Politician, equally with the pious man, ought to respect and to cherish them.—A volume could not trace all their connexions with private and public felicity.—Let it simply be asked where is the security for property, for reputation, for life, if the sense of religious obligation *desert* the oaths, which are the instruments of investigation in Courts of Justice? And let us with caution indulge the supposition, that morality can be maintained without religion.—Whatever may be conceded to the influence of refined education on minds of peculiar structure—reason and experience both forbid us to expect, that national morality can prevail in exclusion of religious principle. . . .

Writings (Ford ed.), XIII. 277, 307.

Eighth Annual Address to Congress

Philadelphia, December 7, 1796.

Fellow-Citizens of the Senate and House of Representatives,

In recurring to the internal situation of our country, since I had last the pleasure to address you, I find ample reason for a renewed expression of that gratitude to the Ruler of the Universe, which a continued series of prosperity has so often and so justly called forth. . . .

The situation in which I now stand, for the last time, in the midst of the representatives of the people of the United States, naturally recalls the period when the administration of the present form of government commenced; and I cannot omit the occasion to congratulate you and my country, on the success of the experiment, nor to repeat my fervent supplications to the Supreme Ruler of the Universe and Sovereign Arbiter of Nations, that his providential care may still be extended to the United States; that the virtue and happiness of the people may be preserved; and that the government, which they have instituted for the protection of their liberties, may be perpetuated.

Writings (Ford ed.), XIII. 344, 351.

Reply to a Masonic Address

[Philadelphia, December 1796.]

Fellow Citizens and Brothers, of the Grand Lodge of Pennsylvania.

I have received your address, with all feelings of Brotherly affection, mingled with those sentiments, for the society, which it was calculated to excite.

To have been in any degree, an instrument in the hands of Providence, to promote order and union, and erect upon a solid foundation the true principles of Government, is only to have shared with many others in a labor, the result of which, let us hope, will prove through all ages, a sanctuary for Brothers and a lodge for the virtuous.

Permit me to reciprocate your prayers for my temporal happiness, and to supplicate that we may all meet thereafter in that eternal temple, whose builder is the great architect of the universe.

G Washington

Washington's Letter Books, XXXI. 245.

To the Rector, Church Wardens, & Vestrymen of the United Episcopal churches of Christ Church and St. Peters

[Philadelphia, March 1797.]

Gentlemen,

To the public testimony of your approbation of my conduct and affection for my person I am not insensible, and your prayers for my present and future happiness merit my warmest acknowledgments. It is with peculiar satisfaction I can say, that, prompted by a high sense of duty in my attendance on public worship, I have been gratified, during my residence among you, by the liberal and interesting discourses which have been delivered in your Churches. Believing that that Government alone can be approved by Heaven, which promotes peace and secures protection to its Citizens in every thing that is dear and interesting to them, it has been the great object of my administration to insure those invaluable ends; and when, to the consciousness of the purity of my intentions, is added the approbation of my fellow Citizens, I shall experience in my retirement that heartfelt satisfaction which can only be exceeded by the hope of future happiness.

G Washington

Washington's Letter Books, XXXI. 279.

To the Clergy of different Denominations, residing in and near the City of Philadelphia

[Philadelphia, March 1797.]

Gentlemen,

Not to acknowledge with gratitude and sensibility the affectionate addresses and benevolent wishes of my fellow Citizens on my retiring from public life, would prove that I have been unworthy of the confidence which they have been pleased to repose in me.

And, among those public testimonies of attachment and approbation, none can be more grateful than that of so respectable a body as your's.

Believing, as I do, that *Religion* and *Morality* are the essential pillars of civil society, I view, with unspeakable pleasure, that harmony and Brotherly Love which characterizes the clergy of different denominations, as well in this, as in other parts of the United States; exhibiting to the world a new and interesting spectacle, at once the pride of our Country and the surest basis of universal Harmony.

That your Labours for the good of Mankind may be crowned with success, that your temporal enjoyments may be commensurate with your merits, and that the future reward of good and faithful servants may be your's, I shall not cease to supplicate the Divine Author of life and felicity.

Washington's Letter Books, XXXI. 282.

To the General Assembly of the State of Rhode Island &ca.

[Mount Vernon, 1797.]

Gentlemen, . . .

Although guided by our excellent constitution, in the discharge of official duties, and actuated, through the whole course of my public life, solely by a wish to promote the best interests of our Country; yet, without the beneficent interposition of the Supreme Ruler of the Universe we could not have reached the distinguished situation which we have attained with each unprecedented rapidity. To him, therefore, should we bow with gratitude and reverence, and endeavour to merit a continuance of his special favors.

Deeply and gratefully impressed by your affectionate address and benevolent wishes, I shall not fail to supplicate the throne of grace, that the best of Heavens blessings may rest upon your state and upon yourselves individually.

Washington's Letter Books, XXXI. 286.

THE FIRST PRAYER IN CONGRESS

WASHINGTON'S RELIGIOUS LIFE

THE FACTS pertaining to Washington's religious life have not been handed down in satisfactory detail, and the attempts to fill the lacuna by means of reminiscences, traditions, and even less historical means have not improved matters. We know much more of his fundamental religious principles than we do of his religious observances. The former have been summarized in the Introduction of this collection, and are shown in the extracts. Here an attempt will be made to bring together the real facts of the latter.

In Colonial Virginia the Church of England was established and dissent was under legal restriction; church and state were united, and officials were required to subscribe to the "adjuration oath and test," as Washington did when commissioned surveyor of Culpeper County and at sundry other times. But after the Great Awakening dissenting sects, especially active on the frontier, made great progress in the colony and wrung more or less practical toleration from the governing conservative class. The Germans and Scotch-Irish who settled the Shenandoah Valley were almost all nonconformists, and the religious life of these dissenters was much more vital to them than religion was to the adherents of the established church.

Local government in colonial Virginia was on the county basis and the chief instrument was the county court composed of justices of the peace. Each county was also divided into parishes, the units of the established church, ruled by vestries. The vestries acquired much civil power also; had the care of the poor, and of roads and ferries, as well as the levy to support the minister and church, and actual control over the appointment of the ministers, though the governor was supposed to have the right of induction, and there was a commissary, usually the president of William and Mary, who was, as representative of the bishop of London, head of the church in the colony. The vestrymen, chosen from the prominent Anglicans of the parish, were of wealth and social position, likely also to include among their number the members of the county court and the burgesses. The planter aristocracy of colonial Virginia, the class which governed the colony, was, formally at at least, completely Anglican.

This was the ecclesiastical background of Washington's youth and early manhood. His family were, of course, members of the established church. His father was, during the few years of residence at what later became Mount Vernon, a vestryman of the parish. What little is known of his mother indicates that her conformity was real, that her religious belief was fervent, and that, widowed when George, her oldest child, was eleven, she brought up her children in active observance of the tenets of her creed.

An entry in a Washington family Bible, states that he was baptized in April of the year of his birth. There is no record of his confirmation. There was no bishop in colonial America, and it is probable that the requirement of confirmation was generally ignored, and that many partook of the Lord's Supper who never had been confirmed.

While still in the plastic age Washington's surveying took him to the frontier, and then and during military experience a few years later he was brought into active relation with the nonconformists of the Valley; people who themselves or through their immediate ancestry had felt the horrors of religious persecution, and had emigrated to America in order to worship God according to their own desires. Many of them were perhaps at heart as illiberal as their persecutors had been; but the earnestness of their various convictions, when contrasted with the somewhat decadent character of the established church in Virginia at that period, may well have had strong influence in developing the liberalism which so greatly characterized Washington's later life.

During five years, 1754-1758, Washington had, on and off, command of the Virginia forces on the frontier and his orders and letters show his wish that the troops should possess the moral and spiritual benefits of religious instruction; he reiterated his desire for a chaplain at headquarters at least, and ordered attendance at services upon both officers and rank and file. In 1759 Washington married a woman of his own aristocratic class, one whose religious habits seem to have been similar to those of his mother; and in their home at Mount Vernon they held their proper position as a first family of the aristocracy of the county. Washington became a burgess, and a justice of the peace; he also became a vestryman of

POHICK CHURCH, POHICK, VIRGINIA
Where General Washington worshipped

Truro Parish, with the main church at Pohick, and a church warden. The vestry records show that he was chosen a member on October 25, 1762, and as such he signed the declaration: "I will be conformable to the Doctrine and discipline of the Church of England as by Law established." This still existing document has been called his "confession of faith;" there is no reason for supposing, however, that it meant any more in his case than in that of the hundreds of other colonial Virginia officials who were required to make it. As in all other things which he undertook, Washington's service as vestryman for many years was an active one. In 1762 besides the main church there were chapels of ease at Alexandria and Falls Church. In 1765 the parish was divided and Fairfax Parish erected, within which the Alexandria and Falls Church portions were included. The original boundaries of Fairfax Parish embraced Mount Vernon, and on March 28, 1765, Washington was voted a vestryman of the new parish. However, the boundaries were speedily changed and Mount Vernon restored to Truro Parish and Washington re-elected to that vestry. There seems to have been no meeting of the Fairfax vestry between the dates, and there is no other evidence that he was ever officially connected with Fairfax Parish, of which Christ Church at Alexandria became the main seat.

On October 3, 1763, Washington became a church warden, the principal administrator of parish affairs, some of its duties being that of overseer of the poor, the levy and sale of the tobacco rate, offenses against decency and morality, and keeping of accounts. He served one year, also in 1767, and was again elected in November, 1774, though absence soon prevented his rounding out this third period of executive duties. Pohick Church was ordered rebuilt in 1767 and it was finished in 1773. This, third, church is still standing. It and Christ Church and the building at Falls Church are all on the same general plan, the tower at Alexandria being added after Washington's death. The present Falls Church was ordered in 1763 before the parish was divided and Christ Church was contemporary with the new Pohick. While there is no direct evidence that the plan for any of them is Washington's, he was on the building committee for the Pohick Church and undoubtedly had a hand in the final shaping of the plans, which were common to other such edifices of the period. February 24, 1774, was Washington's last vestry, although he was nomi-

nally a member until 1782 or 1784. In his eleven years of active service he was present at 23 of the 31 vestries, and was out of the county at the time of meeting of most of the others.

Colonial parishes were large and the members of it lived far apart upon their plantations. Church attendance was often a serious undertaking; on the other hand, the weekly assemblage was a social as well as a religious occasion, serving for the parish much the same function as court day did for the county as a whole. Beginning in 1760 we have, though with many unfortunate gaps, Washington's diaries as a main source on his religious life; in fact, almost the only dependable source. Because of the gaps it is not possible to make any estimation of the regularity of his attendance at church. There are earlier records of attendance at the vestry meetings, but it is not until April 3, 1768, that we have the first of the characteristic entries "Went to Pohick Church and returnd to Dinner," although this is not the first evidence of church attendance. In the Barbados journal of November 11, 1751, he recorded that he "Dressed in order for Church but got to town too Late"; on January 6, 1760, we read "The Chariot not returng. time enough from Colo. Fairfax's we were prevented from Church"; on February 3, 1760, "we to Church at Alexandria"; and on February 17, "Went to Church," which probably meant Pohick. The next item is that of attendance, on April 27, 1760, at Bruton Church in Williamsburg, he being then at the capital as a burgess. On May 4, 1760, he "set out [from Mount Vernon] for Frederick [Winchester] to see my Negroes that lay ill of the Small Pox. Took Church in my way to Coleman's." The items from 1768 on down to the Revolution are fairly frequent, interspersed with Sundays when presumably he did not go; sometimes he was "at home," sometimes he was traveling, occasionally at work when necessity required. On August 20, 1769, while at the Warm Springs (Berkeley Springs) he "Went to Church in the fore and afternoon," and did likewise two weeks later. On October 8 he was again "home all day" and had company; in fact, he did not go to church at all that month, unless he merely failed to record it. On December 10 at Williamsburg he "Dined at the Speaker's," and the next Sunday "at the Palace and went in the afternoon to Colo. Bassett's"; but he "went to prayers" on the day before Christmas, being at Fredericksburg. On May 13, 1770, he "Went to Church with all the

CHRIST CHURCH, ALEXANDRIA, VIRGINIA
Where George Washington attended services

Compy. here. Dind at Belvoir and returnd in the afternoon"; while on December 23 he "Rid to the Mill before Dinner; at home afterwards alone." Church is mentioned only six times in 1771, including Christmas, which was on Wednesday that year; in 1772 nine times, including a week day Christmas service again. In 1773 he went to church at Alexandria five times in eight Sundays, just after the death of Patsy Custis. Dr. Fitzpatrick has called attention to the fact that in times of stress Washington's church attendance became more regular, so that we are prepared to find that he is recorded as attending 13 times in 1774, including the week day service of prayer and fast on June 1 when the Boston Port Bill went into operation. Most of his pre-revolutionary church-going from Mount Vernon was at Pohick, but after 1772 oftener at Alexandria, where he had purchased a pew in Christ Church. It should be borne in mind that failure to mention church does not necessarily preclude attendance.

There seems to be no record of Washington attending any Church in Virginia except the Anglican. Outside that colony he was less regular. Religious liberty was an element of the spirit of the Revolution, and it was the Congregationalist Samuel Adams who proposed the Episcopalian Duche as chaplain of the first Continental Congress. While attending this Congress Washington went to Christ Church, but also on September 25 "to the Quaker Meeting" and on October 9 "to the Presbeterian Meeting in the forenoon and Romish Church in the afternoon."

Spiritual matters in the army of the Revolution were in the main merely a much larger edition of those experienced by Washington when in command of the Virginia frontier. His orders and correspondence show his determination that the men should be as fit as possible morally as well as physically, and the reiteration shows that it continued to be a problem. His second general orders, July 4, 1775, directed "a punctual attendance on divine Service, to implore the blessings of heaven upon the means used for our safety and defence." It is in connection with the Revolutionary service that most of the apocryphal accounts of Washington's own religious actions have originated. Except for a portion of 1781 he evidently kept no diaries during the war, at least no other has survived, and there is little in other contemporary accounts on this subject; but he was not a man to preach one thing and do another, so that there is every

reason to believe that his example to the troops was as high as the precepts indicated by the extracts in this pamphlet.

Again at Mount Vernon during the years 1784-1788, Washington evidently resumed his former habits of church attendance, going mainly to Christ Church in Alexandria, for Pohick had no regular minister. There was an occasional supply at Pohick and Washington mentions attendance there a few times, during which perhaps he sat under Parson Weems. The references on the subject are few, Sunday being often omitted entirely from the entries. While in attendance on the Federal Convention at Philadelphia in 1787 he again went to high mass at the Catholic Church.

As President, Washington attended St. Paul's Chapel in New York. Trinity had been burned during the war and on its restoration the President seems to have changed to that church; at least after its reconsecration on March 25, 1790, which Washington attended and where there was a special Presidential pew, there is no record of further attendance at St. Paul's. The temporary federal capital was moved to Philadelphia in 1790 and during the rest of his administrations Christ Church, and possibly occasionally St. Peter's, received the President and his family. Bishop William White was the leading divine here and a personal friend.

More interest attaches to the President's church-going during his tours. During the New England one in 1789 there were four Sundays; on three of them Washington went to the Episcopal Church in the morning and to the Congregational Church in the afternoon, at New Haven, Boston, and Portsmouth. The fourth Sunday found him at Ashford, Conn., where "It being contrary to law and disagreeable to the People of this State (Connecticut) to travel on the Sabbath day—and my horses, after passing through such intolerable roads, wanting rest, I stayed at Perkins' tavern (which, by the bye, is not a good one,) all day—and a meeting-house being within a few rods of the door, I attended morning and evening service, and heard very lame discourses from a Mr. Pond."

In the Southern tour of 1791 he traveled on seven of the ten Sundays; was at Halifax with no mention of church on one, attended St. Philip's and St. Michael's at Charleston on another, and at Savannah, before traveling, on a third. During this trip he was with the Moravians at Salem, N. C., on two week days and was interested in their community,

FALLS CHURCH, AT FALLS CHURCH, VIRGINIA
Where George Washington was a vestryman

especially in the church music. He had visited the chief settlement at Bethlehem, Pa., during the war, and attended the evening service.

From Mount Vernon on his return from the Southern tour he proceeded to Philadelphia by the inland route through York and Lancaster, Pa., and being at York on Sunday, July 3, he records in his diary: "there being no Episcopal Minister present in the place, I went to hear morning Service performed in the Dutch [German] reformed Church—which, being in that language not a word of which I understood I was in no danger of becoming a proselyte to its religion by the eloquence of the Preacher."

During his last extensive trip, in 1794, in connection with the rendezvous of militia to suppress the Whiskey Insurrection, he was at Carlisle, Pa., on October 5. "Went to the Presbiterian meeting and heard Doctr. Davidson Preach a political Sermon, recommendations of order and good government; and the excellence of

that of the United States." Evidently, he traveled the other three Sundays.

Of Washington's daily religious habits we get occasional glimpses. He said grace at table, sometimes at least, and we have a nephew's later record of private devotions. He read the Bible; and there are biblical references in his writings, and in his notebook. On March 5, 1794, he wrote Charles Thomson that he had finished reading the first part of Thomson's translation of the Septuagint. Undoubtedly Washington's religious activities varied in character and regularity from time to time, according to circumstances and surroundings. He was more regular in church attendance during his Presidency than at any other time. In his war-time and peace-time journeys over the wide stretch of his country he attended over forty churches—Congregational, Presbyterian, German Reformed, Roman Catholic, Quaker, Moravian, and probably others, including those of the sect of which he was a member.

IN THE HOUR OF TRIAL
From a painting by Percy Moran

Facsimile of the Original First Thanksgiving Proclamation, Issued by President George Washington on October 3, 1789

By the President of the United States of America. —

a Proclamation

Whereas it is the duty of all Nations to acknowledge the providence of Almighty God, to obey his will to be grateful for his benefits, and humbly to implore his protection and favor — and whereas both Houses of Congress have by their joint Committee requested me "to recommend to the People of the United States a day of public thanksgiving and prayer to be observed by acknowledging with grateful hearts the many signal favors of Almighty God especially by affording them an opportunity peaceably to establish a form of government for their safety and happiness."

Now therefore I do recommend and assign Thursday the 26th day of November next to be devoted by the People of these States to the service of that great and glorious Being who is the beneficent Author of all the good that was, that is, or that will be — That we may then all unite in rendering unto him our sincere and humble thanks — for his kind care and protection of the People of this country previous to their becoming a Nation — for the signal and manifold mercies, and the favorable interpositions of his providence, which we experienced in the course and conclusion of the late war — for the great degree of tranquility, union, and plenty, which we have since enjoyed — for the peaceable and rational manner in which we have been enabled to establish constitutions of government for our safety and happiness, and particularly the national One now lately instituted — for the civil and religious liberty with which we are blessed, and the means we have of acquiring and diffusing useful knowledge and in general for all the great and various favors which he hath been pleased to confer upon us.

And also that we may then unite in most humbly offering our prayers and supplications to the great Lord and Ruler of Nations and beseech him to pardon our national and other transgressions — to enable us all, whether in public or private stations to perform our several and relative duties properly and punctually — to render our national government a blessing to all the People, by constantly being a government of wise, just and constitutional laws, discreetly and faithfully executed and obeyed — to protect and guide all Sovereigns and Nations (especially such as have shown kindness unto us) and to bless them with good government, peace, and concord — To promote the knowledge and practice of true religion and virtue, and the increase of science among them and Us — and generally to grant unto all Mankind such a degree of temporal prosperity as he alone knows to be best.

Given under my hand at the City of New York the third day of October in the year of our Lord 1789.

Go. Washington

(Text of the Proclamation is on page 522)

By the President of the United States of America

A Proclamation

WHEREAS it is the duty of all Nations to acknowledge the providence of Almighty God, to obey his will, to be grateful for his benefits, and humbly to implore his protection and favor. And whereas both Houses of Congress have, by their joint Committee requested me "to recommend to the People of the United States a day of public thanksgiving and prayer to be observed by acknowledging with grateful hearts the many signal favors of Almighty God, especially by affording them an opportunity peaceably to establish a form of government for their safety and happiness."

Now therefore I do recommend and assign Thursday the 26th day of November next to be devoted by the People of these States to the service of that great and glorious Being, who is the beneficent Author of all the good that was, that is, or that will be. That we may then all unite in rendering unto him our sincere and humble thanks, for his kind care and protection of the People of this country previous to their becoming a Nation; for the signal and manifold mercies, and the favorable interpositions of his providence, which we experienced in the course and conclusion of the late war; for the great degree of tranquillity, union, and plenty, which we have since enjoyed; for the peaceable and rational manner in which we have been enabled to establish constitutions of government for our safety and happiness, and particularly the national One now lately instituted; for the civil and religious liberty with which we are blessed, and the means we have of acquiring and diffusing useful knowledge; and in general for all the great and various favors which he hath been pleased to confer upon us.

And also that we may then unite in most humbly offering our prayers and supplications to the great Lord and Ruler of Nations and beseech him to pardon our national and other transgressions; to enable us all, whether in public or private station, to perform our several and relative duties properly and punctually; to render our national government a blessing to all the People, by constantly being a government of wise, just, and constitutional laws, discreetly and faithfully executed and obeyed; to protect and guide all Sovereigns and nations (especially such as have shown kindness unto us) and to bless them with good government, peace, and concord; to promote the knowledge and practice of true religion and virtue, and the encrease of science among them and Us; and generally to grant unto all mankind such a degree of temporal prosperity as he alone knows to be best.

Given under my hand at the City of New York the third day of October in the year of our Lord 1789.

G Washington

THE EDUCATIONAL VIEWS OF GEORGE WASHINGTON

BASED ON HIS LETTERS, DIARIES, AND ADDRESSES

By

WALTON C. JOHN
Senior Specialist in Higher Education
United States Office of Education

and

ALMA H. PREINKERT
Assistant Registrar, University of Maryland

INTRODUCTION

THE MORE one studies the career of George Washington, the more one is surprised at the many fields of his amazing activity. He was surveyor, soldier, farmer, statesman, business man, and engineer; but there is nothing in all these practical demonstrations of his ability to prepare one for the fact that he was also, for his time, a farsighted educator. The proof of it, however, is to be found in his writings. An important phase of the work of the United States George Washington Bicentennial Commission has been that of emphasizing through its publications the various aspects of this many-sidedness of George Washington's character, and it is, therefore, gratified to include among these publications one prepared by Dr. Walton C. John, of the United States Office of Education, and Miss Alma H. Preinkert, in the Graduate School of the American University. In a way this Office of Education itself is foreshadowed in George Washington's interests, for he did not consider that the state alone should promote public instruction; his liberal interpretation of the Federal Constitution embraced participation in the social advancement of the people, including the proper development of future citizens. In his first annual address to Congress he dwelt upon the promotion of science and literature, the advancement of knowledge as the surest basis of public happiness, and the teaching of the people that was the best security of a free constitution; and to these sentiments he returned repeatedly in his public utterances.

George Washington's own education was fragmentary, and evidently he considered this as a severe handicap; his innate modesty perhaps prevented him from realizing that rules do not apply to genius, but at least he realized that his experience could not be made the basis for rules. His self-instruction, to make up for the early deficiency, continued throughout his life; and probably had much to do with turning his attention to educational conditions and needs, making it a fixed policy that the younger members of his own family and kin should have proper advantages, and that by word and deed he should himself promote general education. The results of this policy are fully shown in the statements and extracts in this paper and need not be revealed here.

George Washington was first called the Father of his Country during the American Revolution, and evidently the term became well established during his lifetime. In no way is the justness of it better shown than in his interest in children and their right to the development of the ability with which nature had severally endowed them, an equality of opportunity which is fundamental in American democracy. Deprived of children himself that he might father a nation, how clearly he saw that the hope of the future resides from generation to generation in the training of the youths for the leadership which they must assume in later years.

Foreword

THIS pamphlet represents the views of George Washington on education and other matters in which children and the youth of America are concerned. The United States George Washington Bicentennial Commission has authorized the collection of George Washington's expressions of opinion on education from which it is compiled. The fact that he thoroughly believed in educating children is well known and his disappointments over the progress of his nephew, George Steptoe Washington, and his step-grandson, G. W. P. Custis, are set forth in this pamphlet in his own words. But Washington's view of education was not limited; he was deeply interested in a plan of universal education for this country in addition to his well known interest in higher education. The Office of Education feels that this is one of the important booklets of a series issued by the United States George Washington Bicentennial Commission and urges that it be read by educators all over the country.

WM. JOHN COOPER,
United States Commissioner of Education.

THE ALEXANDRIA ACADEMY, ALEXANDRIA, VIRGINIA

George Washington was always interested in education, despite, or probably because, of the fact that he had had but little formal schooling himself. Of his many contributions to the education of others, none is more interesting than his endowment of this school in his home town. The Alexandria Academy was a private, pay school, there being no public free school system in Virginia at that time, though free schools were not unknown. Washington knew that many children whose fathers had been killed in the Revolutionary War were deserving of the education they could not obtain. He notified the trustees of the Academy that he intended to invest £1,000 with them, "the interest only of which [is] to be applied . . . for the purpose of educating orphan children, who have no other source, or the children of such indigent parents as are unable to give it." This bequest Washington confirmed in his will, conferring a block of his stock in the Bank of Alexandria to the Academy, as may be seen in the extract from that document, which appears on page 554. Through Washington's beneficence the Alexandria Academy became one of the first schools in Virginia to provide free instruction. The building which housed it still stands facing the new Mount Vernon Memorial Boulevard, on ground which now belongs to the public schools of Alexandria, and overflow classes from the modern building next to it are held in its classrooms. On it the Washington Society of Alexandria placed a memorial plaque on December 14, 1932. United States Commissioner William John Cooper on that occasion urged that this Academy be made a national shrine commemorating Washington's interest in free education.

THE EDUCATIONAL VIEWS OF GEORGE WASHINGTON

CHAPTER I

HIS EARLY EDUCATION

AS FAR as we can learn, Washington began to receive some form of elementary education after he had been taken from his early home at Bridges Creek, in Westmoreland County. When George was about three years old his family moved to the estate now known as Mount Vernon. About 1749 he went to the new estate on the Rappahanock, near Fredericksburg. The home environment was of such a nature as to provide an excellent foundation for George's moral character. He enjoyed until his twelfth year the example of a kind father. And at the same time, and long after his father's death, he was strengthened and inspired by the dignified yet vigorous character of his mother. It is also probable that he went to school to the sexton of the parish named William Grove, who was also known as Hobby, of whom he learned the elements of reading and writing. After his father's death in 1743 it is believed that he went back to Bridges Creek where, under the protection of his half-brother Augustine, he obtained the rudiments of a common school education under a Mr. Henry Williams, who encouraged George in his study of mathematics; but after a time it is said he returned to his mother's home and attended the school kept by the Rev. James Mayre in Fredericksburg. He became an expert penman, and the clear and precise script which makes his papers and letters so easy to read, was cultivated in his youth. His teachers had grounded him sufficiently in mathematics to enable him to study surveying. In the autumn of 1747, before reaching the age of 16, his formal education ended. During his youth George perhaps enjoyed a very popular English book entitled *The Young Man's Companion.* Washington apparently studied this book very carefully. It not only taught how to read, write, and figure, but gave instruction in the writing of letters, wills, deeds, and legal forms. It also taught measures, surveying, navigation, housebuilding, planting, how to treat the sick, and how to conduct one's self in company. He also copied a body of rules of etiquette from a French source which numbered over one hundred. Primarily this was probably copy-book exercise; but it is possible to give it a wider significance.

It is not known exactly how Washington obtained his knowledge of military affairs; however, his interest and ability in these matters were sufficient to obtain for him a commission as major and adjutant general for one of the military districts of Virginia by the time he was 20 years old.

But what Washington lacked in formal study was supplied in part by an excellent social environment. His close and affectionate relationship with his two half-brothers, fourteen and twelve years his senior, was of great benefit to him, as both had been educated in England and had traveled extensively. Friendship with Lord Fairfax gave the opportunity for the exercise of his profession as a surveyor for three years, and the association with a man of wide English culture. It was during the administration of President Dawson that Washington was granted by William and Mary College upon examination the commission of Official Surveyor of Culpeper County, and he took the oath as such on July 20, 1749.

It was Washington's good fortune to have as a growing youth personal association with the men who were the leaders in business as well as in public affairs. Perhaps no clearer evaluation of Washington's character as related to education has been made than the one by Woodrow Wilson:

He was, above all things else, a capable, executive boy. He loved mastery, and he relished acquiring the most effective means of mastery in all practical affairs. His very exercise-books used at school gave proof of it. They were filled, not only with the rules, formulae, diagrams, and exercises of surveying, which he was taking special pains to learn, at the advice of his friends, but also with careful copies of legal and mercantile papers, bills of exchange, bills of sale, bonds, indentures, land warrants, leases, deeds, and wills, as if he meant to be a lawyer's or a merchant's clerk. It would seem that, passionate and full of warm blood as he was, he conned these things as he studied the use and structure of his fowling-piece, the bridle he used for his colts, his saddle-girth, and the best ways of mounting. He copied these forms of business as he might have copied Beverley's account of the way fox, or 'possum or beaver was to be taken or the wild turkeys trapped. The men he most admired—his elder brothers, Mr. Fairfax, and the gentlemen planters who were so much at their houses—were most of them sound men of business, who valued good surveying as much as they admired good horsemanship and skill in sport. They were their own merchants, and looked upon forms of business paper as quite as useful as ploughs and hogsheads. Careful exercise in such matters might well accompany practice in the equally formal minuet in Virginia. And so the boy learned to show in almost everything he did the careful precision of the perfect marksman.

Other deficiencies in Washington's formal education were largely overcome by his continuous struggle from the beginning to conquer his physical environment. This challenged his utmost powers, and gave a permanent stimulus to his acquisition of knowledge and information, not only through books but through the manifold experiences of everyday life. President Lowell of Harvard University has often emphasized the fact that all education is self education. Accepting that definition, there can be no question as to the adequacy of Washington's training. His education, dominated by the highest ideals, was nevertheless developed on a pragmatic basis. The motto on his bookplate, *Exitus Acta Probat,* which signifies that the result proves (or tests) the act, is a recognition of this, though it is not known whether Washington chose the motto or inherited it.

Washington's habits of study and reflection are worthy of attention. Having, in his boyhood days, received a thorough training in the Bible under the inspiration of his mother, he continued the practice of Bible study throughout his life. Penniman calls attention to Bible references which George entered in his pocket notebook. "With the exception of an interlined note, all the entries in the family Bible are in his writing." Penniman adds:

March 5, 1794, Washington wrote Charles Thomson that he had finished reading the first part of his translation of the Septuagint. Washington spent many hours of his life in church, where he was an attentive listener and where he obtained a great deal of knowledge of the Bible. His nephew, Robert Lewis, said that he had accidentally witnessed Washington's private devotions in his library both morning and evening, and had seen him kneeling with an open Bible before him, and that this was his daily habit. Washington went to his library at four in the morning, and, after his devotions, spent the time till breakfast in writing and study. He also spent an hour in his library before retiring at night.

EDUCATIONAL ACTIVITIES

When George Washington brought his bride to Mount Vernon with her two children by a former marriage, he began his efforts in behalf of the education of youth which he continued throughout his life. A schoolhouse was built on the estate and the children were taught to read and write. Later he became interested in the education of his nephews, of the grandchildren of Mrs. Washington, and of the children of some of his friends. He believed in sending the boys away to school rather than having tutors for them in the home. He was very careful in the selection of their schools, their instructors, and in their courses of study. He did not consider that the schooling of the boys was finished until a college or university education had been completed. For the girls, tutors in the home seemed to be sufficient, with a visit now and then from a music teacher or a dancing master. However, even for girls he felt that education had some importance, for in writing to one of his nieces, he told her that a well cultivated mind was important, especially since she was lacking in worldly goods.

Washington encountered the same difficulties with the education of the boys in his family as do some modern parents. His stepson was sent to a preparatory school in Annapolis and then entered King's College, now Columbia University, in New York. Here he remained only three months, coming home, in spite of the objections of his stepfather, and getting married. His nephews, the sons of his brother Samuel, for whose education he assumed the responsibility, changed from one school to another, and were finally brought to Philadelphia where Washington was living and entered in college.

He arranged for his nephew Bushrod to come to Philadelphia to study law, and urged him to become eminent in the profession. He selected as his teacher James Wilson, who later became one of the Justices of the Supreme Court of the United States. The grandson of Mrs. Washington, George Washington Parke Custis, was sent to three colleges, Pennsylvania, Princeton, and St. John's, in Annapolis. At none of these schools did he remain long or make a very satisfactory record. From his busy life Washington took time to write to these young people repeatedly, admonishing or praising them, pleading with them to apply themselves and urging their instructors to keep the boys at their studies. He constantly reminded them that it was of utmost importance for them to receive a thorough education in order to fit themselves for the greatest enjoyment of life, and in order to be of the most service to their country.

Not only was Washington concerned about the education of the members of his own family but there were other young people who were able to attend schools and colleges because of his interest and financial assistance. Some of these were the children of his friends for whose education he paid directly. Others were some of the poor children of Alexandria who up to that time had found no opportunity to procure a schooling. By financial arrangements which he made with Alexandria Academy it became possible for them to receive an elementary education, including reading, writing, and arithmetic. Washington was an original member of the Board of Trustees of Alexandria Academy, and was vitally concerned with the work of the school. These efforts in behalf of the education of the poor, by a man of such standing and influence in his community, had far-reaching effects and anticipated a free public school system. Another institution which received financial assistance was Washington College in Chestertown, Maryland. In acknowledging the honor of having the school named after him, Washington wrote to the trustees as follows:

"To promote literature in this rising empire and to encourage the arts have ever been amongst the warmest wishes of my heart."

An expression of this sentiment recurs in his gifts to Liberty Hall Academy, now Washington and Lee University, and in his letters accepting the chancellorship of William and Mary College.

But Washington was not satisfied with the assistance he could give to the education of youth by his interest in and financial support of the colleges and schools already in existence. His most ambitious project was a national university to be located in the Federal Capital. In his first address to Congress we find a national university mentioned, and with the succeeding years, the idea grew and expanded. In his last address to Congress he made a final and eloquent appeal for such an institution.

There is a lengthy correspondence with the Commissioners of the Federal District concerning plans for a university. He writes to them that "it has always been a source of serious reflection and sincere regret with me, that the youth of the United States should be sent to foreign countries for the purpose of education." He had in mind a great educational center for all the professions and sciences from which knowledge could be diffused throughout the land. He realized the unusual opportunity which study in the capital city would afford. No action was taken by Congress or the Commissioners of the Federal District, even though Washington offered to assist in financing the undertaking. A large bequest of stock was made in Washington's will to endow such an institution. Throughout the Congresses of the years following Washington's appeal, the successive presidents, Adams, Jefferson, and Madison, each reminded with eloquent words of Washington's request and of the country's obligation to its youth. Nothing came of these efforts, however, and the stock which at the time of Washington's death was valued at $22,200 became worthless by the failure of the company.

Not only was Washington interested in the establishment of a national university but he also advocated a military academy. Probably his last letter was the one written two days before his death, to Alexander Hamilton, stressing the importance of establishing such an institution. Six years earlier he had first suggested to Congress that an opportunity should be afforded "for the study of those branches of the military art which can scarcely ever be attained by practice alone," and in the last annual address he made a final public appeal for an academy with a regular course of instruction in military science.

Washington had a thorough knowledge of the Indians through his service in the French and Indian War and when as President he was confronted with Indian difficulties he proposed articles to the Senate which included the sending of agents among the Indians to teach them the arts of civilization. This action probably marks the beginning of a Federal program of education for the Indian.

One of the most significant contributions of Washington to education is included in a provision in his will whereby he granted freedom to his slaves. This provision directed that slaves who were minors should be bound by the court until they were 25 years of age and that during this time they should be "taught to read and write and to be brought up to some useful occupation." Here is a definite provision for the teaching of a group of people who received but scant consideration in that day. George Washington was convinced that education was essential for all classes.

George Washington's foresight and clear thinking are perhaps nowhere more definitely shown than in his attitude toward education. Realizing the important part it must play in a republic, he was a pioneer in advocating universal education from the primary school through the college and university. Educational matters engaged his attention and thought throughout his life and fully six pages of his will are devoted to setting forth his ideas concerning them. Here, as in other fields, Washington made a great contribution to American life which had far-reaching effects.

EDUCATIONAL HONORS

George Washington, in view of his great services to the country, was the recipient of the highest educational honors. The honorary degree of Doctor of Laws was conferred upon him by the following institutions:

Harvard College, April 3, 1776.
Yale College, April 26, 1781.
Pennsylvania College, July 4, 1783.
Washington College, Chestertown, Md., June 24, 1789.
Brown College, September 2, 1790.

He was elected a member of the American Philosophical Society of Philadelphia January 19, 1780. He was elected an honorary member of the American Academy of Arts and Sciences at Boston January 31, 1781; he was also elected an honorary member of the Marine Society of New York November 27, 1783. He became an honorary member of the Charleston (S. C.) Library Association January 13, 1784. He also accepted honorary membership of the Philadelphia Society for the Promoting of Agriculture July 4, 1785, of the South Carolina Society for the Promoting and Improving Agriculture and other Rural Concerns, and he became a foreign honorary member of the Board of Agriculture of Great Britain March 25, 1795.

In 1782 the corporation of Kent County, Maryland, Public School, having raised it to collegiate rank, obtained permission from Washington to call the new college by his name. This is the first school and the only college to bear his name with his personal consent. He also accepted a position on the Board of Visitors and Governors and is known to have attended at least one board meeting at Chestertown.

Washington also accepted on April 30, 1788, the office of chancellor of the College of William and Mary, a position of honor corresponding to a patron or adviser.

In 1790, when Washington was president, he attended the introductory lecture of the professor of law, Judge Wilson, at College Hall, University of Pennsylvania. Later, on Washington's birthday in 1794, at noon the Faculty waited upon him in person to present their felicitations which he graciously acknowledged.

In August, 1783, Washington moved his household to Princeton, making his headquarters at Rocky Hill, three miles from Princeton, and became a familiar figure in the neighborhood. In the prayer-hall he received at a formal audience with Congress the thanks of the nation for his conduct of the war. At the commencement he was, of course, the marked guest, and with Congress sat on the platform, and is said to have showed some embarrassment at the complimentary language of Ashbel Green, valedictorian of the day.

As evidence of his esteem, he presented 50 guineas to the College, a gift which the trustees did not sink into the bottomless pit of repairs, but spent it in commissioning Charles Willson Peale to paint the General's portrait.

Washington also attended the commencement of King's (Columbia) College in 1789. It is of interest to learn that Washington borrowed a telescope belonging to the laboratory of King's College.

The institution most favored in the Washington family, however, was the far-off Phillips Academy at Andover, Massachusetts, which numbers among its former students no fewer than nine nephews and grandnephews of General Washington, and their descendants even to these days. The General was partial to the brand of education supplied at Andover, and he was particularly fond of Judge Samuel Phillips, Jr., whom he came to know well in Boston during the earliest days of the Revolution. The acquaintance was renewed in 1789, when President Washington was the guest of Judge Phillips, and thus had an opportunity to observe the progress the school had made in the fifteen years since it had been started through the benefactions of the Phillips family. Howell Lewis, the first of the nine to climb Andover Hill, came in 1785, at the age of thirteen. He was the fourth child of Betty Washington Lewis.

The most striking event of Pemberton's administration (Pemberton was the second principal of Phillips Academy) was probably the visit of General Washington to Andover during his tour of the Eastern States in the autumn of 1789. Leaving Haverhill on the morning of Thursday, November 5, he drove to Andover, where he breakfasted at Deacon Isaac Abbot's tavern, a building still standing on Elm Street. From there, escorted by Judge Phillips and other prominent citizens on horseback, he passed near the Old South Church and up to the turnpike (now known as School Street) to the Phillips Mansion House, then a comparatively new residence. Here he was entertained by Madame Phoebe Phillips and her husband, who had been intimately associated with Washington in 1775, while Boston was under siege. Later the President held an informal reception on horseback on the training-field, the open lawn in front of the present Treasurer's house. When the ceremony was over, he and his party rode down the lane now called Phillips Street, over the Wilmington Road to the battlefield of Lexington. The moment General Washington left that southeast room in the Mansion House Madame Phillips tied a strip of ribbon on the chair which he had occupied and there it remained until the day of his death, when she substituted for it a band of crepe. This chair is now in the possession of Andover Theological Seminary.

Copy and translation of the honorary degree of Doctor of Laws conferred by Harvard College on George Washington April 3, 1776.

Latin Text

Senatus Academiae Cantabrigiensis in Novanglia, omnibus in Christo Fidelibus ad quos Literae presentes pervenerint, Salutem in Domino semperternam.

Cum cum in finem Gradus Academici instituti fuerint, ut viri Scientia, sapientia, et virtute insignes, qui de re literaria et de Republica optime meruerunt, Honoribus hisce laureatis remunerarentur—Maxime decet ut honore tali afficiatur vir illustrissimus *Georgius Washington,* Armiger, Exercitus Coloniarum in America federatarum Imperator praeclarus, cujus Scientia et Amor Patriae unduque patent; qui, propter eximias Virtutes, tam civiles quam militares, primum, Civibus suis legatus electus, in Congressu celeberrimo Americano de Libertate ad extremum periclitata, et de salute Publica fideliter et peritissime consuluit; deinde postulante Patria, Sedem in Virginia amoenissimam et Res proprias perlubenter reliquit, ut per omnes Castrorum Labores et Pericula, nulla mercede accepta, Nov-Angliam ab armis Britannorum iniquis et crudelibus reliberaret, et Colonias caeteras tueretur; et qui, sub auspiciis Divinis maxime spectandis, ab urbe Bostonia per undecim Menses clausa, munita, et plusquam septem millium. Militum Praesidio firmata, naves et Copias Hostium in fugam praecipitem et probosam deturbavit; adeo ut Cives, plurimus duritiis et Saevitiis oppressi, tandem salvi laetentur, Villa vicinae quiescant, atque sedibus suis Academia nostra restituator.

Sciatis igitur quod nos Praeses, et Socii Colegii Harvardini in Cantabridgia Nov-Anglorum (consentientibus honorandis abmodum et reverendis Academiae nostrae inspectoribus) Dominum supradictum summo honore dignum, *Georgium Washington*, Doctorem utriusque Juris, tum Naturae et Gentium, tum Civilis statuimus et creavimus, eique simul dedimus et concessimus, ommia Jura Privilegia et Honores, ad istum Gradum Pertinentia.

In cujus Rei Testimonium nos communi Sigillo Universitatis in hisce Literis affixo Chirographa apposiumus, Die Tertio Aprilis, Anno salutis millesimo Septingentesimo Septuagesimo sexto.
Sigillium
Communui.

Samuel Langdon, S.T.D. Praeses
Nathanael Appleton, S.T.D.
Johannes Winthrop, Mat. et Phi. P.   Socii
Andraes Eliot, S.T.C. (Hol. L. L. D.)   Thesaurarius.
Saml. Cooper, S.T.C.
Johannes Wadsworth, Log. et Eth. Pre.

Translation

The Corporation of Harvard College in Cambridge, in New-England, to all the Faithful in Christ, to whom these Presents shall come, Greeting.

Whereas Academical Degrees were originally instituted for this Purpose, That Men, eminent for Knowledge, Wisdom and Virtue, who have highly merited of the Republick of Letters and the Common-Wealth, should be rewarded with the Honor of these Laurels; there is the greatest Propriety in conferring such Honor on that very illustrious Gentleman, GEORGE WASHINGTON, Esq.; the accomplished General of the confederated Colonies of America; whose Knowledge and patriotic Ardor are manifest to all: Who, for his distinguished Virtue, both Civil and Military, in the first Place being elected by the Suffrages of the Virginians, one of their Delegates, exerted himself with Fidelity and singular wisdom in the celebrated Congress of America, for the Defence of Liberty, when in the utmost Danger of being for ever lost, and for the Salvation of his Country; and then, at the earnest Request of that Grand Council of Patriots, without Hesitation, left all the Pleasures of his delightful Seat in Virginia, and the Affairs of his own Estate, that through all the Fatigues and Dangers of a Camp, without accepting any Reward, he might deliver New-England from the unjust and cruel Arms of Britain, and defend the other Colonies; and Who, by the most signal Smiles of Divine Providence

on his Military Operations, drove the Fleet and Troops of the Enemy with disgraceful Precipitation from the Town of Boston, which for eleven Months had been shut up, fortified, and defended by a Garrison of about seven Thousand Regulars; so that the Inhabitants, who suffered a great Variety of Hardships and Cruelties while under the Power of their Oppressors, now rejoice in their Deliverance, the neighbouring Towns are freed from the Tumults of Arms, and our University has the agreeable Prospect of being restored to its ancient Seat.

Know you therefore, that We, the President and Fellows of Harvard-College in Cambridge, (with the Consent of the Honored and Reverend Overseers of our Academy) have constituted and created the aforesaid Gentleman, GEORGE WASHINGTON, who merits the highest Honor, Doctor of Laws, the Law of Nature and Nations, and the Civil Law; and have given and granted him at the same Time all Rights, Privileges, and Honors to the said Degree pertaining.

In Testimony whereof, We have affixed the common Seal of our University to these Letters, and subscribed them with our Hand writing this Third Day of April in the Year of our Lord one Thousand seven Hundred Seventy-six.

WASHINGTON'S LIBRARY

Washington's interest in books was practical. His library at Mount Vernon contained at the time of his death at least 884 volumes besides many other publications and documents, many of which were gifts to him.

His collection included works in the fields of literature, religion, geography and travel, history, politics and political economy, law, legislation, military science, agriculture and other useful arts, science, education, miscellaneous works, pamphlets, maps and charts, periodicals, and dictionaries and encyclopedias.

Among the 73 titles in the field of literature may be mentioned Homer's Iliad and Odyssey, Butler's Hudibras, Chesterfield's Letters, Poems of M. Grecourt (in French), Adventures of Telemachus, Fielding's The Foundling, Tom Jones (now known as Tom Jones), Pope's Works, Smollett's Peregrine Pickle, Shakespeare's Works, Swift's Works, Voltaire's Letters, and Don Quixote.

The 44 works on religion included Bishop Wilson's Bible in three volumes, Cruttwell's Concordance, Priestley's Evidences, and Winchester's Lectures on the Prophecies, in 4 volumes.

The 34 works on geography and travel included Warville's Voyage (in French), 3 volumes, Carver's Travels, Morse's Geography, Guthrie's Geography, and "The World Displayed."

The 53 historical books included Adam's Rome, Belknap's History of New Hampshire, Gibbon's Roman Empire, Gordon's History of America, Hume's History of England, Smollett's History of England, and Lord North's Administration.

The 71 works on politics and political economy included the Federalist, Flower's French Constitution, Principles of Taxation by Andrew Hamilton, Tom Paine's Rights of Man, Sharp on the People's Rights, Sharp on Limitation of Slavery, and Adam Smith's Wealth of Nations.

The 48 works on law and legislation included Martin's Law of Nations, An Essay on Property, Dallas' Reports on Pennsylvania, and in addition a number of reports of different States, also the Laws of New York, Parliamentary Debates by Chandler, and the Debates of Congress.

The 46 works on military affairs included a Treatise on Military

Discipline by Bland, a Treatise on Cavalry by Drummond de Melfort, Muller on Fortification, the Art of War by Turpin de Crisse, Guibert on Tactics, Saxe's Memoirs, and Prussian Evolutions by Thomas Hanson.

The 57 works on agriculture and the useful arts included a four volume set on Agriculture by Anderson, Bradley on Husbandry, the Complete Farmer, Gibson's Diseases of Horses, Higgins on Cements, Miller's Gardener's Calendar, Young's Annals of Agriculture, and Elements of Rigging by Steel.

The 23 works on science include Buffon's Natural History, Principles of Hydraulics by Du Buat, Goldsmith's Natural History in 8 volumes, and Mair's Bookkeeping.

Among other books we find a number of works on Education including Locke on the Understanding.

WORKS ON EDUCATION

Washington's interest in educational matters is shown by the following list of 21 publications which are given in bibliographic form:

1. ————. The Rise and Progress of the Young Ladies' Academy of Philadelphia, containing an account of a number of public examinations and commencements, the Charter and Bye-Laws, etc. Phila. 1794. 119 pp. 8°.

2. Advice to a son directing him how to demean himself in the most important passages of life. 4th edition. London. 1716. 24°. Inscribed to "Jno. Custis."

3. Chapman, George, LL.D. Chapman on Education. 1 vol. A treatise on education, with a sketch of the author's methods. Edinburgh. 1773. 12°. See letter by Washington to Chapman, p. 12.

4. Coke, Thomas and Asbury, Francis. An address to the annual subscribers for the support of Cokesbury College and to the members of the Methodist Society, to which are added the Rules and Regulations of the College. New York: Printed by W. Ross. M.DCC.LXXXVII. 12 pp. 12°.

5. Dearborn, Benjamin. Teacher and inventor, 1755-1738. The Columbian Grammar: or, an essay for reducing a grammatical knowledge of the English language to a degree of simplicity, which will render it easy for the instructor to teach and for the pupil to learn. Boston: printed by Samuel Hall, 1795.

6. Dossie, Robert. The Handmaid to the Arts. London: printed for J. Hourse.

7. Graham, Mrs. Catherine Macaulay. Graham on Education. Letters on education with observations on religious and metaphysical subjects. London. 1790. 8°.

8. Home, Henry. Loose hints upon education, chiefly concerning the culture of the heart. Edinburgh. 1782. 8°.

9. Jay, Sir James, M.D. A Letter to the Governors of the College of New York; respecting the Collection that was made in this Kingdom in 1762 and 1763, for the Colleges of Philadelphia and New York. London: printed for G. Kearsly. 1771.

10. Knox, Rev. Samuel. President of the Frederick Academy. An Essay on the best System of liberal Education, adapted to the Genius of the Government of the United States. Comprehending also, an uniform, general Plan for instituting and conducting public Schools, in this country on Principles of the most extensive Utility. To which is pre-

fixed, an Address to the Legislature of Maryland on that Subject. 1799, 173 pp. 8°. Published by Warner and Hanna, Baltimore.

11. Lowell, John, LL.D. Statesman, 1743-1802. An Eulogy, on the Honorable James Bowdoin, Esq. LL.D. late President of the American Academy of Arts and Sciences.

12. Neal, J. A. An essay on the education & genius of the female sex. Phila. 1795. V (3). 37 pp. 12°.

13. Nicolls, Samuel, LL.D. Prebendary of St. Pauls, died 1763. A Sermon preach'd before the Society corresponding with the Incorporated Society for Dublin, for promoting English protestant Working Schools in Ireland, at their General Meeting in the Parish-Church of St. Mary le Bow April 4, 1749. 94 pp. Published by J. Oliver, London.

14. Nisbet, Charles, D.D. Scottish educator in America, 1736-1804. The Usefulness & Importance of human Learning, a Sermon preached before the Trustees of Dickinson College. Met at Carlisle, May 11, 1786, and published at their desire.

15. Patrick, Samuel. Clavis Homerica sive Lexicon vocabulorum omnium quae continentur in Homeri Illiade et potissima parte Odyssaeae. Londini 1742. 8°.

   On a fly-leaf is written,—

   "Hunc mihi quaeso (bone Vir) Libellum Redde, si forsan tenues repertum. Ut scias qui sum sine fraude scriptum.

   Est mihi nomen
   Georgio Washington
   George Washington
   Fredericksburg
   Virginia"

   On inside of cover is written
   "Bushrod Washington's Book, given him by
   G. Washing."

16. Priestley, Joseph. English divine and scientist, 1733-1804. The proper Objects of Education in the present State of the World; represented in a Discourse, delivered on Wednesday, the 27th of April 1791 at the Meeting House in the Old-Jewry London; to the Supporters of the New College at Hackney.

17. Rush, Benjamin. Thoughts upon female education, accommodated to the present state of society, manners, and government. Addressed to the visitors of the Young Ladies' Academy in Philadelphia, 28 July, 1787. Phila. 1787. 32 pp. 8°.

18. Seneca's Morals, by way of abstract. To which is added, A Discourse under the Title of an After-Thought, by Sir Roger L. 'Estrange, Kent. London: printed for G. Strahan. MDCCXLVI, 406 pp. 12°.

19. Smith, William, D.D. Provost of the College and Academy of Philadelphia, 1727-1803. An Account of Washington College in the State of Maryland. Philadelphia: printed by Joseph Crukshank, MDCCLXXXIV. 50 pp.

20. Wheelock, Eleazar, D.D. President of Dartmouth College. 1711-1799. A Continuation of the Narrative of the Indian Charity-School, in Lebanon in Connecticut from the Year 1768, to the Incorporation of it with Dartmouth College, and Removal and Settlement of it in Hanover, in the Province of New Hampshire. 1771. Hartford: printed by Ebenezer Watson in 1771. 61 pp. 8°. Followed by three additional narratives, published in 1773 and 1775.

The foregoing works are listed in A Catalogue of the Washington Collection in the Boston Athenaeum. Compiled and annotated by Appleton P. C. Griffin. With an Appendix "The Inventory of Washington's Books" Drawn up by the Appraisers of His Estate. By William Coolidge Lane. The Boston Athenaeum, 1897.

This random selection of books can be duplicated by other selections equally as interesting. However, many of the books in Washington's library show considerable care in selection or interests which are indicative of the real use to which they were put in keeping him abreast of all contemporary as well as historical literature published at that time which had any bearing upon his manifold activities.

Lodge reports "that when Washington was at Newburgh at the close of the war, he wrote to Colonel Smith in New York to send him the following books:—

"Charles the XIIth of Sweden
Lewis the XVth, 2 vols.,
History of the Life and Reign of the Czar, Peter the Great
Campaigns of Marshal Turenne
Locke on the Human Understanding
Robertson's History of America, 2 vols.
Robertson's History of Charles V.
Voltaire's Letters
Life of Gustavus Adolphus
Sully's Memoirs
Goldsmith's Natural History
Mildman on Trees
Vertot's Revolution of Rome, 3 vols.   ⌠ If they are in
Vertot's Revolution of Portugal, 3 vols. ⌡ estimation.

"If there is a good Bookseller's shop in the City, I would thank you for sending me a catalogue of the Books and their prices that I may choose such as I want."

This order is typical of his larger interests. While at Mount Vernon he gave a large share of his time to the reading of his books and pamphlets on agriculture. It is said that his table was always covered with agricultural literature.

It is also worthy of note that Washington had a clear sense of his early lack of training, as is shown by his revision in later life of the old letterbooks which contained copies of his correspondence while commander of the Virginia regiment between 1754 and 1759. He went through these volumes and made changes giving the letters improved literary form.

EDUCATIONAL SUBJECTS INCLUDED IN HIS WRITINGS

The scope of Washington's educational thought is shown by the different subjects which were covered in his writings. These subjects are listed below with the page references.

Agriculture: 9, 15, 26, 28.
Arithmetic: 12, 13, 18, 19.
Bookkeeping: 16, 29.

Books on Education: 8, 9, 14.
Books, School: 11.
Books, Other: 14, 18, 29.
Classics: 12, 13, 16.
Composition: 16, 19.
Corporal Punishment: 18.
Dancing: 11.
Discipline in Studies: 12, 18, 19, 20, 25, 27, 28, 29.
French: 12, 13, 16, 29.
Geometry: 12.
Greek: 12, 13.
Importance of Education: 14, 16, 18, 19, 20, 21, 24, 25, 26.
Indian Education: 20, 21, 28.
Latin: 13.
Law: 14.
Leisure, Use of: 14, 19, 21, 28.
Mathematics: 12, 13, 18, 19, 29.
Mechanical Education: 16.
Military Education: 14, 22, 26, 30.
Music: 29.
Objectives of Education: 13.
Philosophy, Natural and Moral: 12.
Poor, Education of: 15, 30.
Promotion of Science and Literature: 14, 17, 20, 29.
Reading-Writing-Arithmetic: 16.
Science of Government, Education in: 14, 24, 26, 31.
Slaves, Education of: 30.
Student Conduct: 18, 25, 26.
Surveying: 13, 29.
Travel, Educational Value of: 12, 13.
Universal Education: 23, 29.
University and College Education: 17, 19, 20, 24, 31.
University, National: 20, 22, 23, 24, 26.

ARRANGEMENT OF WRITINGS ON EDUCATION

The writings pertaining to education are those found in Worthington C. Ford's 14 volume edition of the writings of George Washington; in the Diaries of George Washington, 4 volumes, edited by John C. Fitzpatrick; from the Addresses and Messages of the President's edited by James D. Richardson, and from the Catalogue of the Washington Collection in the Boston Athenaeum compiled by A. P. C. Griffin. A few letters are from other sources, as indicated.

Beginning with Washington's letter to William Ramsay, January 29, 1769, the letters continue in chronological order to his letter to Alexander Hamilton dated December 12, 1799, or two days before his death. The diaries begin with July 25, 1769, and are interspersed chronologically with the letters and other data, closing with the entry on February 28, 1799. The parts of his addresses and other matters concerned with education are likewise interspersed chronologically with the letters and diaries.

CHAPTER II

LETTERS, DIARIES, AND ADDRESSES HAVING REFERENCES TO EDUCATION

Washington Encourages William Ramsay to Send His Son to Jersey College (Rutgers) and Offers a Substantial Sum toward Completion of His Education

Mount Vernon, 29 January, 1769.

Dear Sir: . . .

Having once or twice of late heard you speak highly in praise of the Jersey College, as if you had a desire of sending your son William there (who, I am told, is a youth fond of study and instruction, and disposed to a sedentary studious life, in following of which he may not only promote his own happiness, but the future welfare of others), I should be glad, if you have no other objection to it than what may arise from the expense, if you would send him there as soon as it is convenient, and depend on me for twenty-five pounds this currency a year for his support, so long as it may be necessary for the completion of his education. If I live to see the accomplishment of this term, the sum here stipulated shall be annually paid; and if I die in the mean while, this letter shall be obligatory upon my heirs, or executors, to do it according to the true intent and meaning hereof. No other return is expected, or wished, for this offer, than that you will accept it with the same freedom and good will, with which it is made, and that you may not even consider it in the light of an obligation, or mention it as such; for, be assured, that from me it will never be known.

Ford, II. 262.

Washington had recommended Ramsay to Governor Dinwiddie in 1756 and he became a contractor to supply the troops.

Washington Orders Books for His Stepson

[July] 25, [1769]. At home all day writing Letters and Invoices for England.

Diary, I. 336.

Among these invoices was a rather formidable list of books for Master Custis, then 14 years of age, which included Greek and Latin classics as well as textbooks of geography, mathematics, and history. The books were ordered at the request of young Custis's tutor, Rev. Jonathan Boucher, who probably found more use for many of them than his pupil ever did. The list, which follows, is taken from the new edition of Washington's Writings (now being edited by John C. Fitzpatrick), II. 515.

Pub: Terent Apri Comod:, Editio Ricard: Bentleii, Cantab
Am Edi'n of Horace
All Ciceros Works; a very neat Editn. by the Forlis's of Glasgow in 20 12 mo. Vol.
Titi Livii Patavin: Historian Libri Edit Rudimanni 4 vols.
M Valin: Martialis, and Aliorum Epigrammate.
Hugo Grotius de veritate Xtiana Religionis
Graecae Grammatices Rudiments, in Unum Scholie Westmonasterensis
Gr. Test an elegant Edn. printed for R Urie in Glasgow
Dawson's Lexicon to the Gr'k Test't
Graecae Gramatices Rudimenta &ca. by Thoms. Stackhouse AM 8vo.
Origin, and structure of the Greek Tongue by Gregory Sharpe L.L.D.
De Verbis Mediis L. Kusteri I Clerici, I Clarkii, and E Schmidii Commentationes Auxit Suamg adjicit Christ: Wolfe to be sold by Vaillant
Clavis Homerica, Editis recentissima
Harwoods liberal Translation of the N: T: with his Introductory Observ'ns to the Study of the Scriptures
Blackwells Sacred Classics, 2 vols.
Sharpes Arguments in defence of Christianity 2 vols.
Gerards Dissertations on subjects relatg. to the Evidens. of Xtianity
Oswalds Appeal to Common Sense in behalf of Religion
Squire on Indifference for Religion
Ferguson on the Histy. of Civil Society
Beccerias Essay on Crimes and Punishmts.
Dodsleys Collection of English Poetry
Vision's in Verse by Doctr. Cotton
The Amuranth, or a Collection of Religious Poems
Thompson Works
Milton's Works the Editn. by Baskerville
A Genl. History of the World by Grey and Guthrie
Baron Hombergs Introduction to Genl. Histry. translated by Dr. Sharpe
Humes History of England the 4th Edtn.
Mrs. McCauley's Do
Hookes Roman History, 10 vol.
Kennets Roman Antiquities
Potters Greek Antiquities
A good Collection of Voyages and Travels
Matho, or Cosmotheoria Puerilis
Burgs Dignity of Human Nature
Watts's Logick
Fishers Arithmetick
Rolling Method of Studying the Belles Lettres
Steels Christian Hero
Burgs Art of Speaking
History of England in a Series of Letters from a Nobleman to his Son.
Martins Philsopl. Grammer
Robertson's History of Scotland
Tookes Pantheon
Wells Geographia Classica
Recueil des Auteurs Francois

Dancing Lessons for the Children

[March] 13, [1770] . . . Returnd abt. 5 O'clock and found Colo. Mason and Mr. Christian here.

Diary, I. 368.

Christian was the dancing master who taught the young people of Fairfax. His classes met at the different houses. On April 18, 1770, Washington entered in his ledger: "By Mr. Christian Entrance for P. Custis and Milly Posey £2."

Washington Questions Dr. Boucher as to Opportuneness for the Plan to Travel Abroad Suggested for Jack Custis

Mount Vernon, 13 May, 1770.

Sir,

Your favor of the 9th came to hand last night, but I do not think myself prepared at this time to give any conclusive answer to the question you propounded, respecting Mr. Custis's traveling to perfect his Education.

It is a matter of very great consequence and well deserving of the most serious consideration, especially [by] one who stands in the degree of affinity to him that I do. A natural parent has only two things principally to consider, the improvement of his son, and the finances to do it with: if he fails in the first (not through his own neglect) he laments it as a misfortune; if exceeded in the Second, he endeavors to correct it as an abuse unaccountable to any, and regardless of what the world may say, who do not, cannot suspect him of acting upon any other motive than the good of the party; he is to satisfy himself only. But this is not the case with respect to guardians: they are not only to be actuated by the same motives which govern in the other case, but are to consider in what light their conduct may be viewed by those whom the constitution hath placed as a controulling power over them; because a faupas committed by them often incurs the severest censure, and sometimes punishment; when the intention may be strictly laudable.

Thus much, Sir, I have taken the liberty of saying to shew you in what light I consider myself, (generally) as the guardian of this youth. But before I could adopt the measure finally upon the extensive plan you seem to propose, and give a definite answer, it would be incumbent on me (as the person who is to account for his worldly concerns, as well as personal accomplishments,) to have some regular System proposed; that it may be seen at one view how the expence and his income are proportioned to each other; for tho' I am far, very far, from harboring any distrust of your being influenced by any similar views, or that you would be unreasonable in your expectations as his governor, yet some plan should be pointed out, some estimate formed, by which I am to be guided; otherwise were I hastily to determine that a year or two hence (or as his education and judgment ripened) he was to travel and when that period arrived it was found to be upon a plan too enlarged for his fortune and a stop thereby put to it, it might be a disappointment to you which I should be sorry for, as I make it a point, at least endeavor to do so, not to deceive any one.

From what I have said, you may possibly conceive that I am averse to his travelling, for the completion of his education; but be assured, Sir, I am not; there is nothing, in my opinion more desirable to form the manners and encrease the knowledge of observant youth than such a plan as you have sketched out; and I beg of you to believe, that there is no gentleman under whose care Mrs. Washington and myself would so soon entrust Mr. Custis as yourself (after he is sufficiently instructed in classical knowledge here). It may be depended on therefore, that the gratification of this passion in him, will never meet with any interruption from me, and I think I may venture to add, from his mother, provided he is disposed to set out upon such a plan of improvement as your good sense is capable of dictating to him; and provided also that you will undertake to accompany and guide him in the pursuit of it. Add to this, that he will be content with such an allowance as his income can afford; . . .

Ford, II. 277-280.

Washington Urges Dr. Boucher to Keep a Watchful Eye on Jacky Custis and to Keep Him at His Studies

Mount Vernon, Decr 16th, 1770.

According to appointment Jacky Custis now returns to Annapolis. His mind [is] a good deal released from Study, & more than ever turned to Dogs Horses and Guns; indeed upon Dress and equipage, which till of late, he has discovered little Inclination of

giving into. I must beg the favor of you, therefore, to keep him close to those useful branches of Learning which he ought now to be acquainted with, and as much as possible under your own Eye. Without these, I fear he will too soon think himself above controul, and be not much the better for the extraordinary expence attending his living in Annapolis; which I should be exceeding sorry for, as nothing but a hasty progress towards the completion of his Education, can Justify my keeping him there as such an expence as his Estate will now become chargeable with. . . .

Ford, II. 316.

Washington Consults with Dr. Boucher on the Possible Advantages to Jack Custis in Studying Greek, French, Mathematics, and Philosophy

Mount Vernon, Jan 2nd, 1771.

Jack's return has been delayed, as well from a belief that you might not be well settled, as from a desire of gratifying him in his favourite amusement of Hunting, these Hollidays. He returns now he says, with a determination of applying close to his Studies; and I confide entirely in your promise of making him do so, as time slips of[f] a pace, and other Idea's & pursuits, will soon render it more difficult to keep him confined to them, than at present. In respect to the kinds, & manner of his Studying, I leave it wholely to your better Judgment—had he begun, or rather pursued his study of the Greek Language, I should have thought it no bad acquisition; but whether [if] he acquire this now, he may not forego some more useful branches of learning, is a matter worthy of consideration. To be acquainted with the French Tongue is become a part of polite Education; and to a man who has [the prospect] of mixing in a large Circle absolutely [necessary. Without] Arithmetick, the common [affairs of] Life are not to be managed [with success. The study of Geo]metry, and the Mathe-[matics (with due regard to the li]mites of it) is equally [advantageous. The principles] of Philosophy Moral, Natural, &c. I should think a very desirable knowledge for a Gentleman; but as I said before, I leave the whole to your direction; with this earnest request, that, in whatever kind of Study you think proper to engage him, he may be kept diligently to it, for he really has no time to loose. . . .

Ford, II. 318-320.

Washington Writes to Dr. Boucher that He Doubts the Value of a Trip to England for Jack. He Fears that Jack Lacks the Essential Foundation in His Studies

Mount Vernon, June 5th, 1771.

I should have set Mr. Custis off for Annapolis as soon as I heard of your passing by (being very unwilling that he should loose any time from School that [is] possible to be avoided) but it was thought necessary to [keep] him till his cloaths could be Washd & got in readiness [to] take with him, which has detained him till now. . . .

In respect to the other matters contained in your Letter of the 9th Ulto I shall endeavour to be as explicit as I can. And first in regard to Mr. Custis going to England.—My own Inclinations have always been strong in favour of his prosecuting the plan you formerly laid down for him—his Friends a good deal divided in theirs—some on acct of the expence; others, as being almost the last of a Family, thinks he shoud run no risks that are to be avoided—These opinions tho they are insufficient to bias my own Judgment in this matter (as I think the more conspicuous the point of view a man is to appear in, the more pains should be taken to enlarge his mind and qualify him for a useful Member of Society) yet they determined me in some measure not to appear sollicitous or forward in promoting it; but leave things a little more to their own workings, and to the turn and disposition of the Youth himself, after his Genius is a little more unfolded and he better able to have an opinion of his own.—In this state of mind I was, when your prospects of a change, & doubts [about] accompanying him, were communicated to me; which will have no small weight in turning the Scale; for, however desirable it may be to see him travel (if his Income shoud be thought by Genl Court sufficient to admit of the expence) under the care of a Gentleman who would endeavour to guard, & steer him clear of those follies & vices which youth almost imperceptably falls into, at the same time that he was Instilling into him taste for useful knowledge and Improvement, Yet I must own I should never wish to see him set out for England, at his time of Life recommended to the care of a merchant only—or to Embark on a Tour of the kind you proposed without a Conductor; as pleasure and dissipation without a kirb, would leave little room for study, & more than probably end in his Ruin: I am therefore more perplex'd than ever I was, & find the difficulty of giving a defenitive answer encreased by your doubts; and [can only] add, that when the period arrives at which you [think] it eligible for him to set out on a Tour of this [kind, it will] if it appears to be his own desire, upon a pro[bability of your intention] & your inclination to accompany him, meet [with my] hearty concurrence, notwithstanding the ex-[pense. . . .

This opinion of mine is not known to my Ward—He believes, for anything I know to the contrary, that his Trip to England is resolved on—& I should be glad if his time was devoted to the Study of those useful Branches of Learning as will render him fit for it. . . .

I cannot conclude, without requesting [in the] most Importunate manner that all due attention [and considera]tion may be given to Jack's Education—I fear [the progress] he has made in Classical knowledge has of la[te been] trifling; as I cannot discover that he is much [farther] in Latten than when he left Mr. Magowan, know[s little] Arithmetick, and is quite ignorant of the Greek Language, which he has begun under the Tuition of that Gentleman; & therefore, as well as from some enquiries which I [have] lately made, apprehend, that he lacks that Attention which is necessary to advance him in his Studies—the Information which I have but Just come to the knowledge of has filled me with a sincere concern, not because of the expence attendg his Living in Annapolis were it 4 times as great; but on acct of the lost time which is never to be regained.—Duty & Inclination both prompt me to mention this matter to you, as I have his Improvement much at heart, and wd wittingly leave nothing unattempted on my part to see this accomplished. . . .

Ford, II. 320-324.

Washington Again Tells Dr. Boucher that Jack Lacks Sufficient Intellectual Preparation for a Tour. He Further Criticizes Jack's Lack of Attainment

Mount Vernon, 9 July, 1771.

Dear Sir, . . .

In my last I informed you, (as well as I can recollect the contents of the letter) that the friends (I do not confine myself to the relations) of Mr. Curtis, were divided in their opinions, of the propriety of his travelling, not on account of the advantages which might result from it, but on account of the expense, as he would set out with so heavy a charge, as you thought sufficient to induce you to accompany him, which would at once anticipate half his income. . . .

These are the reasons why I said in my last, that my own inclinations were still as strong as ever for Mr. Custis's pursuing his travelling scheme, but that it was necessary the Court should approve of the expense, (I did not want their opinion of the utility of travelling) and provided, that it should appear, when his judgment is a little more matured, that he is desirous of undertaking this tour upon a plan of improvement, rather than a vague desire of gratifying an idle curiosity, or spending his money wantonly. For by the bye, if his mother does not speak her sentiments, rather than his, he is abundantly lukewarm in the scheme; and I cannot help giving it as my opinion, that his education, from what I have understood of his improvements, (however advanced it may be for a youth of his age,) is by no means ripe enough for a tour of travelling; not that I think his becoming a mere scholar is a desirable education for a gentleman, but I conceive a knowledge of books is the basis upon which other knowledge is to be built, and that it is men and things more than books he is to be acquainted with by travelling. At present, however, well versed he may be in the principles of the Latin language (which is not to be wondered at, as he began the study of it as soon as he could speak), he is unacquainted with several of their classical authors, which might be useful to him to read. He is ignorant of the Greek, (which the advantages of understanding I do not pretend to judge), knows nothing of French, which is absolutely necessary to him as a traveller; little or nothing acquainted with arithmetic, and totally ignorant of the mathematics, than which, so much of it at least as relates to surveying, nothing can be more essentially necessary to any person possessed of a large landed estate, the bounds of some part of other of which is always in controversy.

Now, whether he has time between this and next spring to acquire a sufficient knowledge of these, or so much of them as are requisite, I leave you to judge of; and whether a boy of seventeen years old, which will be his age the last of November next, can have any just notions of the end and design of travelling? I have already given it as my opinion, that it would be precipitating this event, unless he was to go immediately to the university for a couple of years, and in this case he could see nothing of America; which might be a disadvantage to him, as it is to be expected that every man, who travels with a view of observing the laws and customs of other countries, should be able to give some description of the situation and government of his own. . . .

Ford, II. 329-331.

Washington Expresses to Dr. Cooper (King's) His Great Satisfaction with Mr. Custis' Conduct at College, but Deeply Regrets that Custis is to Return Home against His Wishes for the Purpose of Marriage

December 15, 1773.

The favorable account, which you were pleased to transmit to me, of Mr. Custis's conduct at college, gave me very great satisfaction. I hoped to have felt an increase of it by his continuance at that place, under a gentleman so capable of instructing him in every branch of useful knowledge. But this hope is at an end;

and it has been against my wishes, that he should quit college, in order that he may enter soon into a new scene of life, which I think he would be much fitter for some years hence, than now. But having his own inclination, the desires of his mother, and the acquiescence of almost all his relatives to encounter, I did not care, as he is the last of the family, to push my opposition too far, and I have therefore submitted to a kind of necessity. . . .

Ford, II. 397n.

Washington Sends Draft to Dr. Cooper to Pay Custis' Expenses for Three Months' Residence at King's College (Columbia) and Regrets the Necessity of His Return Home

15 April, 1774.

You will now receive a Draft . . . against Mr. Custis; whose residence at Kings College, I little expected would have been of such short duration; otherwise, I shou'd not (as his guardian) have thought myself justified in incurring so great an expense; not that I think he could have got conveniently & agreeably fixed in the College for less than what is charged on that account, but then, for the benefit of only three months residence there, this might have been avoided.—however, as his discontinuance at it, is an act of his own, & much against my judgment, he can only blame me (if he blames at all) for yielding too easily to his importunities, supported by the concurrence of his relations. . . .

Ford, II. 403n.

Educational Society

[June] 15, [1774]. Dined at Mrs. Dawson's and spent the Evening at the Capitol at a Meeting of the Society for promoting useful Kn[owledge].

Diary, II. 154.

On November 3, 1773, Washington subscribed ten shillings to this society and on this date, June 15, 1774, he subscribed 1 pound. This was the second meeting of the society. John Page was then its president and James Madison one of its secretaries.

College Commencement

[May] 17, [1775]. Went to Commencement at the College [Philadelphia], and dind at Mr. Saml. Griffin's.

Diary, II. 195.

Washington Recommends that Officers in Their Vacant Moments Make a Study of Military Authors

Orderly Book, 8 May, 1777.

Officers attentive to their duty, will find abundant employment in training and disciplining their men, providing for them, and seeing that they appear neat, clean and soldier-like. Nor will any thing redound more to their honor—afford them more solid amusement, or better answer the end of their appointment, than to devote the vacant moments, they may have, to the study of military authors.

Ford, V. 357n.

Washington Acknowledges to Pres. William Smith, D.D., the Honor of Having Washington College in Chestertown Named after Him, and Sends a Gift of Money to the Institution

Headquarters, Newburgh, 18th August, 1782.

I have had the honor to receive your favor of the 8th ult. by Colonel Tilghman, who arrived here about ten days ago, and to whom I have committed the charge of forwarding this answer. To the gentlemen who moved the matter, and to the Assembly

for adopting it, I am much indebted for the honor conferred on me, by giving my name to the College at Chester. At the same time I acknowledge the honor, I feel a grateful sensibility for the manner of bestowing it; which, as it will remain a monument of their esteem, cannot but make a deep impression on my mind, only to be exceeded by the flattering assurance of the lasting and estensive usefulness of the Seminary.

If the trifling sum of Fifty Guineas will be considered as an Earnest of my wishes for the prosperity of the Seminary, I shall be ready to pay that sum to the order of the Visitors, whenever it is their pleasure to call for it—it is too trifling to stand in any other point of view—nor would I wish it to do so. . . .

When that period shall arrive, when we can hail the blest return of peace, it will add to my pleasure to see this infant seat of learning rising into consistency and proficiency in the sciences, under the nurturing hands of its founders.

Washington College, *Catalogue*, VIII (1930).

Washington Urges His Nephew, Bushrod Washington, in His Study of the Law to Seek Eminence in the Profession

Newburgh, 15 January, 1783.

. . . Let the object, which carried you to Philadelphia, be always before your Eyes. Remember, that it is not the mere study of the Law, but to become eminent in the profession it, which is to yield honor and profit. The first was your choice; let the second be your ambition, . . .

Ford, X. 133.

Washington Writes to John Augustine Washington Giving a Favorable Opinion of the Character of His Son

Nuburgh, 16 January, 1783.

My Dear Brother, . . .

I have heard a favorable account of Bushrod, and doubt not but his prudence will direct him to a proper line of conduct; I have given him my sentiments on his head, and persuade myself that with the advice of Mr. Wilson, to whose friendship, as well as instruction in his profession, I recommended him; and the admonition of others: he will stand as good a chance as most youth of his age, to avoid the vices of large cities, which have their advantages and disadvantages in fitting a man for the great theater of public life. . . .

Ford, X. 136.

Washington Addresses Governors on the Enlightened Foundation of Our Empire, and Praises the Advantages of Culture to Society

Circular Letter Addressed to the Governors of all the States on Disbanding the Army

Head-Quarters, Newburg, 8 June, 1783.

. . . The foundation of our empire was not laid in the gloomy age of ignorance and superstition; but at an epocha when the rights of mankind were better understood and more clearly defined, than at any former period. The researches of the human mind after social happiness have been carried to a great extent; the treasures of knowledge, acquired by the labors of philosophers, sages, and legislators, through a long succession of years, are laid open for our use, and their collected wisdom may be happily applied in the establishment of our forms of government. The free cultivation of letters, the unbounded extension of commerce, the progressive refinement of manners, the growing liberality of sentiment, and, above all, the pure and benign light of Revelation, have had a meliorating influence on mankind and increased the blessings of society. At this auspicious period, the United States came into existence as a nation; and, if their citizens should not be completely free and happy, the fault will be entirely their own. . . .

Ford, X. 256.

Washington Writes to George Chapman, the Author, on the Importance of Education on Receiving a Copy of "Chapman on Education"

December 15, 1784.
Mount Vernon.

Not until within a few days have I been honor'd with your favor of the 27th of Septr. 1783 accompanying your treatise on education.

My sentiments are perfectly in unison with yours Sir, that the best means of forming a manly, virtuous and happy people, will be found in the right education of youth. Without this foundation, every other means, in my opinion, must fail; & it gives me pleasure to find that Gentlemen of your abilities are devoting their time & attention in pointing out the way. For your lucubrations on this Subject which you have been so obliging as to send me, I pray you to accept my thanks, & an expression of the pleasure I felt at the declaration of your intention to devote a further portion of your time to so useful a study. Of the importance of education our Assemblies, happily, seem fully impressed; they establishing new & giving further endowments to the old Seminaries of learning, and I persuade myself—will leave nothing unessayed to cultivate literature & useful knowledge, for the purpose of qualifying the rising generation for patrons of good government, virtue & happiness.

Boston Athenaeum, *Catalogue of the Washington Collection*, 552.

Education of Nephews

[February] 21st. [1785]. George Steptoe Washington returned this morning to the Academy at George Town, and in the Evening the Manager of his and [his] Brother's Estate came here with some money for their use—sent by my Brother Charles.

Diary, II. 344.

Washington Writes to Tench Tilghman as to a Suitable Secretary for Himself and a Tutor for Mr. Custis' Children

Mount Vernon,
2 June, 1785.

Dear Sir, . . .

I had been in hopes, that a young man of no great expectations might have begun the world with me for about fifty or sixty pounds—, but for one qualified in all respects to answer my purposes, I would have gone as far as seventy-five—more would rather distress me.

My purposes are these—To write letters agreeably to what shall be dictated. Do all other writing which shall be entrusted to him. Keep Accts.—examine, arrange, and properly methodize my Papers, which are in great disorder.—Ride, at my expence, to such other States, if I should find it more convenient to send, than attend myself, to the execution thereof. And, which was not hinted at in my last, to initiate two little children (a girl of six and a boy

of 4 years of age, descendants of the deceased Mr. Custis, who lived with me and are very promising) in the first rudiments of education. This to both parties, would be mere amusement, because it is not my wish that the children should be confined. If Mr. Falconer should incline to accept the above stipend in addition to his board, washing and mending.—and *you* (for I would rather have *your opinion* of the gentleman than the *report* of a thousand others in his favor) upon a close investigation of his character, Temper and moderate political tenets (for supposing him an English man, he may come with prejudices, and doctrines of his Country) the sooner he comes, the better my purpose would be promoted.

Ford, X. 457, 458.

Washington Writes to George William Fairfax in England as to Improvement of Farming Procedure and His Desire to Follow a Complete Course of Husbandry as Practiced There

Mount Vernon, 30 June, 1785.

My Dear Sir, . . .

Our course of Husbandry in this country, & more especially in this State, is not only exceedingly unprofitable, but so destructive to our Lands, that it is my earnest wish to adopt a better; & as I believe no country has carried the improvement of Land & the benefits of Agriculture to greater perfection than England, I have asked myself frequently of late, whether a thorough bred practical English Farmer from a part of England where husbandry seems to be best understood & is most advantageously practised could not obtain'd and upon what terms? . . .

It may not in this place be amiss to observe to you that I still decline the growth of Tobacco, and to add, that it is my intention to raise as little Indian Corn as may be:—in a word, that I am desirous of entering upon a compleat course of husbandry as practiced in the best Farming countries of England.— . . .

Ford, X. 466, 468-470.

Washington Pleads a Defective Education in Letter to David Humphreys Regarding the Writing of Some Commentaries

Mount Vernon, 25 July, 1785.

My dear Humphreys, . . .

In a former letter I informed you, my dear Humphreys, that if I had *talents* for it, I have not *leisure* to turn my thoughts to Commentaries. A consciousness of a defective education, and a certainty of the want of time, unfit me for such an undertaking. What with company, letters, and other matters, many of them quite extraneous, I have not been able to arrange my own private concerns so as to rescue them from that disordered state into which they have been thrown by the war, and to do which is become absolutely necessary for my support whilst I remain on this stage of human action. The sentiments of your last letter on this subject gave me great pleasure. I should be pleased indeed to see you undertake this business. Your abilities as a writer, your discernment respecting the principles which led to the decision by arms, your personal knowledge of many facts as they occurred in the progress of the war, your disposition to justice, candor, and impartiality, and your diligence in investigating truth, combining, fit you, when joined with the vigor of life, for this task; and I should with great pleasure, not only give you the perusal of all my papers, but any oral information of circumstances, which can-

not be obtained from the former, that my memory will furnish;
. . .

Ford, X. 472-474.

*Washington Writes to Edmund Randolph Telling Him that His
Presented Shares in the Potomac Company are to
be Used for Education*

Mount Vernon, 30 July, 1785.

Dear Sir,

Although it is not my intention to derive any pecuniary advantage from the generous vote of the Assembly of this State,
consequent of its gratuitous gift of shares in the navigation of each
of the rivers Potomac and James; yet, as I consider these undertakings as of vast political and commercial importance to the States
on the Atlantic, especially to those nearest the centre of the Union,
and adjoining the western territory, I can let no act of mine impede the progress of the work. I have therefore come to the
determination to hold the shares, which the treasurer was directed
to subscribe on my account, in trust for the use and benefit of the
public; unless I should be able to discover, before the meeting of
the Assembly, that it would be agreeable to it to have the product
of the tolls arising from these shares applied as a fund, on which
to establish two charity schools, one on each river, for the education and support of the children of the poor and indigent of this
country, who cannot afford to give it, particularly the children of
those men of this description, who have fallen in defence of the
rights and liberties of it. If the plan succeed, of which I have no
doubt, I am sure it will be a very productive and increasing fund,
and the moneys thus applied will be a beneficial institution.

Ford, X. 481.

Education of Friend's Son

[August] 31st. [1785]. . . . This day I told Doctr. Craik that I
would contribute one hundred dollars pr. ann. as long as it
was necessary, towards the Education of His Son, George
Washington, either in this Country or in Scotland.

Diary, II. 410, 411.

Washington contributed to the education of several children of his various
friends. Thomas Posey, son of his neighbor, Captain John Posey, was one of
these. George Washington Craik later acted as secretary to Washington for a
short time.

*Washington also Writes to Thomas Jefferson Regarding His Plans
for Two Charity Schools*

Mount Vernon, 26 September, 1785.

Dear Sir, . . .

I am very happy to find, that your sentiments respecting the interest the Assembly was pleased to give me in the two navigations
of the Potomac and James Rivers coincide with my own. I never
for a moment entertained an idea of accepting it. The difficulty,
which labored in my mind was how to refuse without giving
offence. Ultimately I have it in contemplation to apply the profits
arising from the tolls to some public use. In this, if I know how, I
would meet the wishes of the Assembly; but, if I am not able to
come at these, my own inclination leads me to apply them to the
establishment of two charity schools, one on each river, for the
education and support of poor children, especially the descendants
of those, who have fallen in defence of their country. . . .

Ford, X. 501, 503.

*Washington Asks Fairfax to Help Him Obtain a Preceptor for
G. W. P. Custis, One who can also be His Private Secretary*

Mount Vernon, 10 November, 1785.

My Dear Sir, . . .

The two youngest children of Mr. Custis—the oldest a girl of
six years—the other a boy a little turned of four live with me.
They are both promising children; but the latter is a remarkable
fine one—and my intention is to give him a liberal education;
the rudiments of which shall, if I live, be in my own family.—
Having promised this, let me next, my good Sir, ask if it is in your
power conveniently, to engage a proper preceptor for him?—at
present, and for a year or two to come, much confinement would
be improper for him; but this being the period in which I should
derive more aid from a man of Letters and an accomptant than at
any other, to assist me in my numerous correspondences, and to
extricate the latter from the disordered state into which they have
been thrown by the war, I could usefully employ him in this
manner until his attention should be more immediately required
for his pupil. . . .

To answer *my* purposes, the Gentleman must be a master of
composition, and a good accomptant:—to answer his pupil's, he
must be a classical scholar, and capable of teaching the French
language grammatically:—the more universal his knowledge is, the
better. . . .

To you my Dr. Sr, I have offered this my first address; but if you
should think my purposes cannot be subserved in your circle, upon
the terms here mentioned; I beg, in that case, that you will be so
obliging as to forward the enclosed letter as it is directed.—This
gentleman has written to me upon another subject, & favored me
with his lucubrations upon Education, which mark him a man of
abilities, at the same time that he is highly spoken of as a teacher,
and a person of good character. In Scotland we all know that
Education is cheap, and wages not so high as in England:—but I
would prefer, on account of the dialect, an Englishman to a Scotchman, for all the purposes I want.

Ford, XI. 6, 7.

Education of Nephews

[November] 23d [1785]. . . . Sent Mr. Shaw through Alexandria,
to agree for the Schooling and Board of My Nephews, George
Steptoe and Lawrence Washington now at the Academy at
George Town, and thence to the latter place to conduct them
to the former for the purpose of going to School at the
Alexandria Academy.

Diary, II. 446.

*Washington Writes to the Trustees of the Alexandria Academy as
to His Plan to Institute a School in Alexandria for
Children of the Poor and Orphans*

17 December, 1785.

Gentlemen,

That I may be perspicuous and avoid misconception, the proposition which I wish to lay before you is committed to writing,
and is as follows:

It has long been my intention to invest, at my death, one thousand pounds current money of this State in the hands of trustees,
the interest only of which to be applied in instituting a school in
the town of Alexandria, for the purpose of educating orphan
children, who have no other resource, or the children of such

indigent parents, as are unable to give it; the objects to be considered of and determined by the trustees for the time being, when applied to by the parents or friends of the children, who have pretensions to this provision. It is not in my power at this time to advance the above sum; but that a measure, that may be productive of good, may not be delayed, I will until my death, or until it shall be more convenient for my estate to advance the principal, pay the interest thereof, to wit, fifty pounds annually.

Under this state of the matter, I submit to your consideration the practicability and propriety of blending the two institutions together, so as to make one seminary under the direction of the president, visitors, or such other establishment as to you shall seem best calculated to promote the objects in view, and for preserving order, regularity, and good conduct in the academy. My intention, as I have before intimated, is, that the principal sum shall never be broken in upon; the interest only to be applied for the purposes above-mentioned. It was also my intention to apply the latter to the sole purpose of education, and of that kind of education, which would be most extensively useful to people of the lower class of citizens, namely, reading, writing, and arithmetic, so as to fit them for mechanical purposes.

The fund, if confined to this, would comprehend more subjects; but, if you shall be of opinion, that the proposition I now offer can be made to comport with the institution of the school which is already established, and approve of an incorporation of them in the manner before mentioned, and thereafter, upon a full consideration of the matter, should conceive that this fund would be more advantageously applied towards clothing and schooling, than solely to the latter, I will acquiesce in it most cheerfully; and shall be ready, (as soon as the trustees are established upon a permanent footing,) by deed or other instrument of writing, to vest the aforesaid sum of one thousand pounds in them and their successors for ever, with powers to direct and manage the same agreeably to these my declared intentions.

Ford, XI. 16-18.

Alexandria Academy

[December] 17th [1785]. Went to Alexandria to meet the Trustees of the Academy in that place, and offered to vest in the hands of the said Trustees, when they are permanently established by Charter, the Sum of One thousand pounds, the Interest of which only, to be applied towards the establishment of a charity School for the education of Orphan and other poor Children, which offer was accepted.

Diary, II. 457.

Country School

[February] 21 [1786]. A Mr. McPherson of Alexandria came and returned before dinner. His business was, to communicate the desires of a Neighbourhood in Berkeley County, to build a School and Meeting House on some Land of mine there, leased to one [   ]. My answer was, that if the tenant's consent could be obtained, and the spot chosen was upon the exterior of my Land, so as that no damage would result from Roads, etca., to it, mine should not be wanting.

Diary, III. 22.

Washington Writes to John Jay on Ill Effects of Ignorance on Republican Governments

Mount Vernon, 18 May, 1786.

Dear Sir, . . .

Ignorance and design are difficult to combat. Out of these proceed illiberal sentiments, improper jealousies, and a train of evils which oftentimes in republican governments must be sorely felt before they can be removed. The former, that is ignorance, being a fit soil for the latter to work in, tools are employed by them which a generous mind would disdain to use; and which nothing but time, and their own puerile or wicked productions, can show the inefficacy and dangerous tendency of. . . .

Ford, XI. 30-32.

Secretary and Tutor

[May] 29th [1786]. About 9 Oclock, Mr. Tobias Lear, who had been previously engaged on a Salary of 200 dollars, to live with me as a private Secretary and precepter for Washington Custis, a year came here from New Hampshire, at which place his friends reside.

Diary, III. 66.

Copy Press

[June] 16th [1786]. . . . Began about 10 Oclock to put up the Book press in my study.

Diary, III. 76.

This probably was the press for copying letters. Washington appears to have been among the earliest American users of this method of copying his letters. Few, if any, of the press copies of his letters, prior to 1790, however, seem to have survived.

Academy Commencement

[September] 30th [1786]. . . . Mr. McQuir came here to Dinner and to invite me to the Academical commencement in Alexandria on Thursday next.

Diary, III. 121.

Washington Writes to Jeremiah Wadsworth, Offering an Education to the Son of General Greene

October 22, 1786.

. . . I would fain hope however that the case may, ultimately, be otherwise; and that upon a final settlement of his affairs there will be a handsome competence for Mrs. Greene and the children,— But should the case be otherwise, and Mrs. Greene, yourself, and Mr. Rutledge would think proper to entrust my namesake G. Washington Greene to my care, I will give him as good an education as this country (I means the United States) will afford, and will bring him up to either of the genteel professions that his frds. may chuse, or his own inclination shall lead him to pursue, at my own cost & expence. . . .

Ford, XI. 52n.

Schoolhouse

[November] 13th [1786]. . . . Agreed to let the Widow Alton have the House used for a School by my Mill, if the School should be discontinued; . . .

Diary, III. 137.

Agricultural Society

[July] 3d [1787]. . . . Dined at Mr. Morris's and drank Tea at Mr. Powell's. After which in Company with him, I attended the Agricultural Society at Carpenter's Hall.

Diary, III. 226.

Washington was at Philadelphia as president of the Federal Convention.

School Exhibition

[November] 1st [1787]. Rid by the way of Muddy hole . . . to Alexandria to attend a Meeting of the Directors of the Potomack Company, and the Exhibition of the Boys at the Alexandria Academy.

Diary, III. 263.

Washington Tells Samuel Griffin of His Sense of Responsibility in Considering and Finally Accepting the Chancellorship of William and Mary College

Mount Vernon, 20 February, 1788.

Sir,

I have been duly honored and greatly affected with the receipt of the resolution of the visitors and governors of William and Mary College, appointing me chancellor of the same, and have to thank you for your polite attention in the transmission. Not knowing particularly what duties, or whether any active services, are immediately expected from the person holding the office of chancellor, I have been greatly embarrassed in deciding upon the public answer proper to be given. It is for that reason I have chosen to explain in this private communication my situation and feelings, and to defer an ultimate decision until I shall have been favored with farther information on this subject.

My difficulties are briefly these. On the one hand, nothing in this world could be farther from my heart, than a want of respect for the worthy gentlemen in question, or a refusal of the appointment with which they have honored me, provided its duties are not incompatible with the mode of life to which I have entirely addicted myself; and, on the other hand, I would not for any consideration disappoint the just expectations of the convocation by accepting an office, whose functions I previously knew, (from my preengagements and occupations,) I should be absolutely unable to perform.

Although as I observed before, I know not specifically what those functions are, yet, Sir, I have conceived that a principal duty required of the chancellor might be a regular and indispensable visitation once, or perhaps twice, a year. Should this be expected, I must decline accepting the office. For, notwithstanding I most sincerely and ardently wish to afford whatever little influence I may possess, in patronizing the cause of science, I cannot, at my time of life and in my actual state of retirement, persuade myself to engage in new and extensive avocations.

Such being the *sentiments* of a heart unaccustomed to disguise, I flatter myself the candid manner in which I have explained them, cannot be displeasing to the convocation; and that the intervening delay between the *present*, and the *moment* in which I shall have the pleasure of receiving such ulterior explanations as may enable me to give a *definitive* answer, will not prove very detrimental to the collegiate interests.

Ford, XI. 226.

Mr. Griffin sent to him an extract from the statute respecting the duties of the Chancellor, which runs thus: "The Chancellor is to be the Maecenas, or patron of the college, such a one as by his favor with the King, and by his interest with all other persons in England, may be enabled to help on all the college affairs. His advice is to be taken, especially in all such arduous and momentous affairs, as the college shall have to do in England. If the college has any petitions at any time to the King, let them be presented by their Chancellor. If the college wants a new president, or pro-

fessor, or master, let the college senate rely chiefly on his assistance, advice, and recommendation."

Mr. Griffin added, that neither an oath nor personal attendance was necessary. The Bishop of London had been the last Chancellor. Upon these facts Washington wrote to Mr. Griffin, 30 April, 1788:

"Influenced by a heartfelt desire to promote the cause of science in general, and the prosperity of the College of William and Mary in particular, I accept the office of chancellor in the same; and request you will be pleased to give official notice thereof to the learned body, who have thought proper to honor me with the appointment. I confide fully in their strenuous endeavors for placing the system of education on such a basis, as will render it most beneficial to the State and the republic of letters, as well as to the more extensive interests of humanity and religion. In return, they will do me the justice to believe, that I shall not be tardy in giving my cheerful concurrence to such measures, as may be best calculated for the attainment of those desirable and important objects."

Ford, XI. 227n, 228n.

Washington Writes to John Armstrong Regretting the Financial Difficulties at Dickinson College and Urges Remedies

Mount Vernon, 25 April, 1788.

Dear Sir, . . .

I am sorry to hear, that the college in your neighborhood [Dickinson College, Carlyle, Pa.] is in so declining a state as you represent it, and that it is likely to suffer a further injury by the loss of Dr. Nisbet, whom you are afraid you shall not be able to support in a proper manner, on account of the scarcity of cash, which prevents parents from sending their children thither. This is one of the numerous evils, which arise from the want of a general regulating power; for in a country like this, where equal liberty is enjoyed, where every man may reap his own harvest, which by proper attention will afford him much more than is necessary for his own consumption, and where there is so ample a field for every merchantile and mechanical exertion, if there cannot be money found to answer the common purposes of education, not to mention the necessary commercial circulation, it is evident that there is something amiss in the ruling political power, which requires a steady, regulating, and energetic hand to correct and control it. . . .

Ford, XI. 249, 253.

Washington Writes to Nicholas Pike, on the Receipt of a Copy of His "New and Complete System of Arithmetic Composed for the Use of Citizens of the United States"

Mt. Vernon, June 20, 1788.

Sir:

I request you will accept my best thanks for your polite letter of the 1st of January (which did not get to my hand till yesterday)—and also for the copy of your "System of Arithmetic" which you were pleased to send me.

The handsome manner in which the work is printed, and the elegant manner in which it is bound, are pleasing proofs of the progress which the arts are making in this country. But I should do violence to my own feelings, if I suppressed an acknowledgement of the belief that the work itself is calculated to be equally useful & honourable to the United States.—

It is but right, however, to appraise you, that, diffident of my own decision, the favourable opinion I entertain of your performance is founded rather on the explicit & ample testimonies of Gentlemen confessedly possessed of great mathematical knowledge, than on the partial and incompetent attention I have been able to pay it myself.—But I must be permitted to remark that the subject, in my estimation, holds a higher rank in the literary scale than you are disposed to allow.—The science of figures, to a certain degree, is not only indispensably requisite in every walk of civilized life, but the investigation of mathematical rules accustoms the mind to method and correctness in reasoning, and is an employment peculiarly worthy of rational beings. In a cloudy state of existence, where so many things appear precarious to the bewildered research, it is here that the rational faculties find a firm foundation to rest upon.—From the high ground of Mathematical & Philosophical demonstration, we are insensibly led to far nobler speculations & sublime meditations.

I hope & trust that the work will ultimately prove not less profitable than reputable to yourself.—It seems to have been conceded, on all hands, that such a system was much wanted.—Its merits being established by the approbation of competent Judges, I flatter myself that the idea of its being an American production and the first of the kind which has appeared; will induce every patriotic and liberal character to give it all the countenance & patronage in his power.—In all events, you may rest assured, that, as no person takes more interest in the encouragement of American genius, so no one will be more highly gratified with the success of your ingenious, arduous & useful undertaking than he, who has the unfeigned pleasure to subscribe himself with esteem & regard.

Boston Athenaeum, *Catalogue of the Washington Collection*, 165.

Washington Writes to His Nephew, George Steptoe Washington, Giving Strong Advice as to His Conduct and that of His Nephew's Brother

Mount Vernon, 6 August, 1788.

Dear George, . . .

It is as much my wish and intention to see justice done to you and your brother, as it is to punish either when it is merited; but there are proper modes by which this is to be obtained, and it is to be sought by a fair and candid representation of facts which can be supported, and not by vague complaints, disobedience, perverseness, or disobliging conduct, which make enemies without producing the smallest good. So often and strenuously have I endeavored to inculcate this advice, and to show you the advantages, which are to be expected from close application to your studies, that it is unnecessary to repeat it. If the admonitions of friendships are lost, other methods must be tried, which cannot be more disagreeable to you, than it would be to one, who wishes to avoid it, who is solicitous to see you and your brother (the only remaining sons of your father) turn out well, and who is very desirous of continuing your affectionate uncle, . . .

Ford, XI. 298.

Washington Writes to Samuel Hanson Suggesting, with Respect to His Nephews at Their Particular Ages, Better Means of Discipline than Corporal Punishment

6 August, 1788.

The letter, which I have written to his brother on the subject, is under this cover, and open for your perusal. He is arrived at that *age* and *size* now, as to be a fitter subject to be reasoned with than to receive corporal punishment; and my primary object

in placing these boys with you *last* was, that they, at least George, should be treated more on the footing of friendship and as companions, than as *mere* schoolboys. This I hoped would draw George's attention to objects and conversations, that would improve and might contribute in a degree to wean him from boyish amusements, the influence of which would extend to Lawrence.

Ford, XI. 298*n*.

Washington in a Strong Letter Urges George Steptoe Washington to Take His Educational Development Seriously

Mount Vernon, 23 March, 1789.

Dear George, . . .

You have now arrived to that age when you must quit the trifling amusements of a boy, and assume the more dignified manners of a man.

At this crisis your conduct will attract the notice of those who are about you; and as the first impressions are generally the most lasting; your doings now may mark the leading traits of your character through life. It is therefore, absolutely necessary, if you mean to make any figure upon the stage, that you should take the first steps right. What these steps are and what general line is to be pursued to lay the foundation of an honorable and happy progress, is the part of age and experience to point out. This I shall do, as far as in my power with the utmost chearfulness; and, I trust, that your own good sense will shew you the necessity of following it. The first and great object with you at present is to acquire, by industry and application, such knowledge as your situation enables you to obtain, as will be useful to you in life. In doing this two other important objects will be gained besides the acquisiton of knowledge—namely a habit of industry, and a disrelish of that profusion of money and dissipation of time which are ever attendant upon idleness. I do not mean by a close application to your studies that you should never enter into those amusements which are suited to your age and station. They may be made to go hand in hand with each other, and used in their proper seasons, will ever be found to be a mutual assistance to each other. But what amusements are to be taken, and when, is the great matter to be attended to—your own judgment, with the advice of your real friends who may have an opportunity of a personal intercourse with you can point out the particular manner in which you may *best* spend your moments of relaxation, much better than I can at a distance.—One thing, however, I would strongly impress upon you, viz: that when you have leisure, to go into company; that it should always be of the best kind that the place you are in will afford; by this means you will be constantly improving your manners and cultivating your mind while you are relaxing from your books; and good company will always be found much less expensive than bad. . . .

If you comply with the advice herein given, to pay a diligent attention to your studies, and employ your time of relaxation in proper company, you will find but few opportunities and little inclination, while you continue at an Acadimy, to enter into those scenes of vice and dissipation which too often present themselves to youth in every place, and particularly in towns. If you are determined to neglect your books, and plunge into extravagance and dissipation nothing that I can now say would prevent it,—for you must be employed, and if it is not in pursuit of those things profitable, it must be in pursuit of those which are———. . . .

Ford, XI. 369-373.

Washington Receives an Honorary Degree from Washington Col-
lege and Discusses the Importance of Colleges and
Seminaries of Learning

New York, July 11, 1789.

Your very affectionate Address, and the honorary Testimony to your regard which accompanied it, call forth my grateful acknowledgment.

A recollection of past events, and the happy termination of our glorious struggle for the establishment of the rights of Man cannot fail to inspire every feeling heart with veneration and gratitude toward the Great Ruler of Events, who has so manifestly interposed in our behalf.

Among the numerous blessings which are attendant upon Peace, and as one whose consequences are of the most important and extensive kind, may be reckoned the prosperity of Colleges and Seminaries of Learning.

As, in civilized societies, the welfare of the State and happiness of the people are advanced or retarded, in proportion as the morals and education of the youth are attended to; I cannot forbear, on this occasion to express the satisfaction which I feel on seeing the increase of our seminaries of learning through this extensive country, and the general wish which seems to prevail for establishing and maintaining these valuable institutions.

It affords me peculiar pleasure to know that the Seat of Learning under your direction hath attained to such proficiency in the Sciences since the Peace; and I sincerely pray the great Author of the Universe may smile upon the Institution, and make it an extensive blessing to this country.

Washington College, *Catalogue*, VIII (1930).

Washington Expresses to James Craik His Pleasure in Learning of
the Attentive Attitude of His Nephews George and
Lawrence to Their Studies

New York, 8 September, 1789.

Dear Sir, . . .

It gives me pleasure to hear, and I wish you to express it to them, that my nephews George and Lawrence Washington are attentive to their studies, and obedient to your orders and admonition. That kind of learning, which is to fit them for the most useful and necessary purposes of life, among which writing well, arithmetic, and the less abstruse branches of the mathematics are certainly to be comprehended, ought to be particularly attended to, and it is my earnest wish that it should be so. . . .

Ford, XI. 424, 425.

Washington Proclaims a National Day of Thanksgiving and Men-
tions the Blessings of Acquiring and Diffusing Useful Knowledge

New York, October 3, 1789.

Whereas it is the duty of all nations to acknowledge the providence of Almighty God, . . .

Now, therefore, I do recommend and assign Thursday, the 26th day of November next, to be devoted by the people of these States to the service of that great and glorious Being who is the beneficent author of all the good that was, that is, or that will be; that we may then all unite in rendering unto Him our sincere and humble thanks for His kind care and protection of the people of this country previous to their becoming a nation; for the signal and manifold mercies . . . for the peaceable and rational manner in which we have been enabled to establish constitutions of govern-

ment for our safety and happiness, and particularly the national one now lately instituted; for the civil and religious liberty with which we are blessed, and the means we have of acquiring and diffusing useful knowledge; and, in general, for all the great and various favors which He has been pleased to confer upon us.

And also that we may then unite in most humbly offering our prayers and supplications to the great Lord and Ruler of Nations, and beseech Him to pardon . . . to render our National Government a blessing to all the people by constantly being a Government of wise, just, and constitutional laws, discreetly and faithfully executed and obeyed; to protect and guide all sovereigns and nations (especially such as have shown kindness to us), and to bless them with good governments, peace, and concord; to promote the knowledge and practice of true religion and virtue, and the increase of science among them and us; and, generally, to grant unto all mankind such a degree of temporal prosperity as He alone knows to be best.

Richardson, I. 64.

Visit to Harvard College

[October] 29th [1789]. Left Boston about 8 o'clock. Passed over the Bridge at Charles-Town, and went to see that at Malden, but proceeded to the College at Cambridge, attended by the Vice-President, Mr. Bowdoin, and a great number of Gentlemen.

At this place I was shown by Mr. Willard, the President, the Philosophical apparatus, and amongst others Pope's Orary (a curious piece of Mechanism for shewing the revolutions of the Sun, Earth, and many other of the Planets), the library, (containing 13,000 volumes,) and a Museum.

Diary, IV. 39.
President Washington was on his tour of the New England States.

College Address

[November] 14th [1789]. . . . At 4 o'clock received and answered an Address from the President and Corporation of Dartmouth College.

Diary, IV. 52.
This was after his return to New York from the Tour.

Portrait

[December] 21st [1789]. . . . Sat from ten to one o'clock for a Mr. Savage, to draw my Portrait for the University of Cambridge, in the State of Massachusetts, at the request of the President and Governors of the said University.

Diary, IV. 60.

Washington Addresses Both Houses of Congress and Urges the
Promotion of Science and Literature

January 8th, 1790.

. . . The advancement of agriculture, commerce, and manufactures, by all proper means, will not, I trust, need recommendation. But I cannot forbear intimating to you the expediency of giving effectual encouragement, as well to the introduction of new and useful inventions from abroad, as to the exertions of skill and genius in producing them at home; and of facilitating the intercourse between the distant parts of our country by a due attention to the post-office and post-roads.

Nor am I less persuaded, that you will agree with me in opinion, that there is nothing which can better deserve your patronage than the promotion of science and literature. Knowledge is in every country the surest basis of public happiness. In one, in which the measures of government receive their impression so immediately from the sense of the community, as in ours, it is proportionably essential. To the security of a free constitution it contributes in various ways; by convincing those who are intrusted with the public administration, that every valuable end of government is best answered by the enlightened confidence of the people; and by teaching the people themselves to know, and to value their own rights; to discern and provide against invasions of them; to distinguish between oppression and the necessary exercise of lawful authority, between burthens proceeding from a disregard to their convenience and those resulting from the inevitable exigencies of society; to discriminate the spirit of liberty from that of licentiousness, cherishing the first, avoiding the last, and uniting a speedy but temperate vigilance against encroachments, with an inviolable respect to the laws.

Whether this desirable object will be the best promoted by affording aids to seminaries of learning already established, by the institution of a national university, or by any other expedients, will be well worthy of a place in the deliberations of the legislature.

Ford. XI. 457, 458.

Note on Washington's Interesting Visit to Brown University from Journal of William Smith, M.C., a Member of the Party

Congress adjourned on the 12th of August [1790], and Washington took the opportunity to visit Rhode Island, . . . "Wednesday, 18th. . . . We had a tedious passage to Providence, . . . After tea, just as the President was taking leave to go to bed, he was informed by Col. Peck . . . that the students of the college had illuminated it, and would be highly flattered at the President's going to see it, which he politely agreed to do, . . . We now made a nocturnal procession to the college, which indeed was worth seeing, being very splendidly illuminated. . . . Thursday morning . . . We walked all around the Town, visited all the apartments of the college, went on the roof to view the beautiful and extensive prospect, . . .

Ford, XI. 500-u, 502n.

Washington Writes to His Nephew George Giving Strong Advice as to the Serious Attitude He Expects His Nephews to Take if They Pursue Their College Studies in Philadelphia

Philadelphia, 5 December, 1790.

Dear George,

Agreeably to the promise, which I gave to you in Virginia, I have made the necessary inquiries respecting the course of studies and expenses, which would enable you and your brother Lawrence to finish your education at the college in this place, provided you are masters of those books and studies, which you informed me you had passed through.

The enclosed account of studies and expenses, which I wish you to return to me, you will see is under the hand of the Reverend Dr. Smith, provost of the college, and may therefore be relied upon for its accuracy. After you and Lawrence have carefully perused and well considered the enclosed statement, I wish you to determine whether you will come or not. If your determination should be in favor of coming on, I must impress this upon you both in the strongest manner, namely, that you come with good dispositions, and full resolution to pursue your studies closely, conform to the

established rules and customs of the college, and to conduct yourselves on all occasions with decency and propriety.

To you, George, I would more particularly address myself at this time, as from your advanced age it may be presumed, that such advice, as I am about to give, will make a deeper impression upon you, than upon your brother, and your conduct may very probably mark the line of his; but, at the same time, Lawrence must remember, that this is equally applicable to him.

Should you enter upon the course of studies here marked out, you must consider it as the finishing of your education, and, therefore, as the time is limited, that every hour misspent is lost for ever, and that future *years* cannot compensate for lost *days* at this period of your life. This reflection must show the necessity of an unremitting application to your studies. To point out the importance of circumspection in your conduct, it may be proper to observe, that a good moral character is the first essential in a man, and that the habits contracted at your age are generally indelible, and your conduct here may stamp your character through life. It is therefore highly important, that you should endeavor not only to be learned, but virtuous. Much more might be said to show the necessity of application and regularity; but when you must know, that without them you can never be qualified to render service to your country, assistance to your friends, or consolation to your retired moments, nothing further need be said to prove their utility.

As to your clothing, it will, I presume, cost much the same here as in Alexandria. I shall always wish to see you clothed decently and becoming your stations; but I shall ever discountenance extravagance or foppishness in your dress. At all times, and upon all occasions, I shall be happy to give you both such marks of my approbation, as your progress and good conduct merit.

If you determine to come on, you had better do it immediately, and Major Washington will furnish you with such money as may be necessary for the stage and expenses from Alexandria to this place. But I must repeat what I have before enjoined, that you come with good dispositions and determined resolutions to conform to establishments and pursue your studies. . . .

Ford, XI. 508-510.

Washington Addresses Seneca Indian Chiefs and Expresses Desire to Aid Them and Teach Them Practical Arts

Philadelphia, January 19, 1791.

Brothers, . . .

You may, when you return from this city to your own country, mention to your nation my desire to promote their prosperity, by teaching the use of domestic animals, and the manner that the white people plough and raise so much corn; and if, upon consideration, it would be agreeable to the nation at large to learn these arts, I will find some means of teaching them at such places within their country as shall be agreed upon. . . .

Ford, XII. 10-12.

Washington Discusses with Timothy Pickering the Advantages of a more Practical Type of Education for the Indians

Philadelphia, 20 January, 1791.

Sir,

I have had the pleasure to receive your letters of the 8th and 15th of this month. I feel myself much obliged by the trouble you have taken, in the former, to detail your ideas with respect to introducing the art of husbandry and civilization among the

Indians. I confess that your plan, or something like it, strikes me as the most probable means of effecting this desirable end; and I am fully of opinion with you, that the mode of education, which has hitherto been pursued with respect to those young Indians, who have been sent to our colleges, is not such as can be productive of any good to their nations. Reason might have shown it, and experience clearly proves it to have been the case. It is perhaps productive of evil. Humanity and good policy must make it the wish of every good citizen of the United States, that husbandry, and consequently civilization, should be introduced among the Indians. So strongly am I impressed with the beneficial effects, which our country would receive from such a thing, that I shall always take a singular pleasure in promoting, as far as may be in my power, every measure which may tend to ensure it.

I should have been very glad, if it had comported with your interest and inclination to superintend the northern Indians, as I am persuaded that nothing would have been wanting on your part to attach them to the United States, and to cultivate that spirit for civilization, which now begins to dawn among them. Whoever undertakes this business must be actuated by more enlarged views, than his individual interest, or he can never accomplish the wished for end.

Ford, XII. 12, 13.

Washington in an Address to Congress Emphasizes Value of Improved Communication in Relation to the Advancement of the People

October 25, 1791.

. . . The importance of the post-office and post-roads on a plan sufficiently liberal and comprehensive, as they respect the expedition, safety, and facility of communication, is increased by the instrumentality in diffusing a knowledge of the laws and proceedings of the government; which, while it contributes to the security of the people, serves also to guard them against the effects of misrepresentation and misconception. . . .

Ford, XII. 83.

Washington Gives Sound Educational Advice to His Niece Harriot

Philadelphia, 30 October, 1791.

Dear Harriot, . . .

You are not to learn, I am certain, that your fortune is small. Supply the want of it, then, with a well cultivated mind, with dispositions to industry and frugality, with gentleness of manners, obliging temper, and such qualifications as will attract notice, and recommend you to a happy establishment for life.

Ford, XII. 84, 86.

Washington Thanks Eliphalet Pearson for Sending Him the Eulogy of Bowdoin and a Catalogue of Harvard College

Philadelphia, November 14, 1791.

I have received your letter of the 10th of September enclosing by order of the American Academy of Arts & Sciences, Judge Lowell's Eulogy on the late Governor Bowdoin. I must beg, Sir, you will transmit my proper acknowledgments to the Academy for this mark of attention, and at the same time receive yourself my thanks for the polite manner in which you have transmitted to me the Eulogy on that worthy Character, and for the catalogue of Harvard College which accompanied it.

From original in the Library of the American Academy.

Washington Proposes among Other Things that Useful Artificers Reside with Indians to Promote Their Happiness

March 23, 1792.

Gentlemen of the Senate:

At the conferences which Colonel Pickering had with the Five Nations at the Painted Post the last year ideas were then held out of introducing among them some of the primary principles of civilization, in consequence of which, as well as more firmly to attach them to the interests of the United States, they have been invited to the seat of the General Government. . . .

I therefore request the advice of the Senate whether an article shall be stipulated with the Five Nations to the following purport, to wit:

The United States, in order to promote the happiness of the Five Nations of Indians, will cause to be expended annually the amount of $1,500 in purchasing for them clothing, domestic animals, and implements of husbandry, and for encouraging useful artificers to reside in their villages.

Richardson, I. 122.

Washington Considers Bishop John Carroll's Plan of Giving Instruction to the Indians in the Principles and Duties of Christianity

Philadelphia, 10 April, 1792.

Sir,

I have received and duly considered your memorial of the 20th ultimo, on the subject of instructing the Indians, within and contiguous to the United States, in the principles and duties of Christianity. . . .

Impressed as I am with an opinion, that the most effectual means of securing the permanent attachment of our savage neighbors is to convince them that we are just, and to show them that a proper and friendly intercourse with us would be for our mutual advantage, I cannot conclude without giving you my thanks for your pious and benevolent wishes to effect this desirable end, upon the mild principles of religion and philanthropy. And, when a proper occasion shall offer, I have no doubt but such measures will be pursued, as may seem best calculated to communicate liberal instruction, and the blessings of society, to their untutored minds.

Ford, XII. 116-118.

Carroll was the head of the Roman Catholic Church in the United States.

Washington Writes to His Sister, Betty Lewis, About His Heavy Expenditures for the Education of Two Nephews

Mount Vernon, 7 October [1792].

My dear Sister: . . .

I have had both her brothers upon my hands and I have been obliged to pay several hundred pounds out of my own pocket for their board, schooling, and cloathing, &c., for more than the period aforementioned, their father's estate being unable to discharge the executions as fast as they are issued against it. . . .

Ford, XII. 200.

Washington Urges Congress to Lay Plans for Promoting Civilization among Friendly Indians

November 7, 1792.

. . . I cannot dismiss the subject of Indian affairs, without again recommending to your consideration the expediency of more adequate provision for giving energy to the laws throughout our interior frontier, and for restraining the commission of outrages upon the Indians; without which all pacific plans must prove nugatory. To enable, by competent rewards, the employment of qualified and trusty persons to reside among them as agents, would also contribute to the preservation of peace and good neighborhood. If, in addition to these expedients, an eligible plan could be devised for promoting civilization among the friendly tribes, and for carrying on trade with them upon a scale equal to their wants, and under regulations calculated to protect them from imposition and extortion, its influence in cementing their interests with ours could not but be considerable. . . .

Ford, XII. 207.

Washington Offers to Provide for the Education of a Grand Nephew

Philadelphia, 17 March, 1793.

My dear Fanny: . . .

The offer of a residence at Mount Vernon was made to you with my whole heart; but it is with you, nevertheless, to consider whether any other plan will comport better with the views, which my nephew had, or with such as you may have entertained for your own ease, for the education of your children, or for the interest of the estate. . . . and I shall, when I see you, request that Fayette may be given up to me, either at that time, or as soon after as he is old enough to go to school. This will relieve you of that portion of attention, which his education would otherwise call for.

Ford, XII. 271.

Frances Washington was the widow of the President's nephew, George Augustine, and a niece of Mrs. Washington. Later she married Tobias Lear.

Washington Urges Upon Congress the Value of Military Education and Newspapers

December 31, 1793.

. . . But it is an inquiry, which cannot be too solemnly pursued, whether the act "more effectually to provide for the national defence by establishing a uniform militia throughout the United States," has organized them so as to produce their full effect; whether your own experience in the several States has not detected some imperfections in the scheme; and whether a material feature, in an improvment of it, ought not to be to afford an opportunity for the study of those branches of the military art which can scarcely ever be attained by practice alone. . . .

But here I cannot forbear to recommend a repeal of the tax on the transportation of public prints. There is no resource so firm for the government of the United States, as the affections of the people, guided by an enlightened policy; and to this primary good, nothing can conduce more than a faithful representation of public proceedings, diffused without restraint throughout the United States. . . .

Ford, XII. 353, 355.

Washington Writes to John Adams Questioning the Expediency of Importing the Staff of the University of Geneva as Part of Plan for a National University

Saturday, 15 November, 1794.

Dear Sir, . . .

The picture drawn in them, of the Genevese, is really interesting and affecting. The proposition of transplanting the members, entire, of the University of that place to America, with the requisition of means to establish the same, and to be accompanied by a

considerable emigration is important; requiring more consideration, than, under the circumstances of the moment I am able to bestow on it.

That a National University in *this* country is a thing to be desired, has always been my decided opinion; and the appropriation of ground and funds for it in the Federal Ctiy, have long been contemplated and talked of; but how far matured, or how far the transplanting of an *entire* Seminary of *Foreigners*, who may not understand our Language, can be assimilated therein is more than I am prepared to give an opinion upon—or indeed how far funds in either case are attainable. . . .

Ford, XII. 489-490.

Washington Praises Handwriting and Style of Letter of Eleanor Parke Custis and Makes Some Suggestions

Philadelphia, 16 January, 1795.

Your letter, the receipt of which I am now acknowledging, is written correctly and in fair characters, which is an evidence that you command, when you please, a fair hand. Possessed of these advantages, it will be your own fault if you do not avail yourself of them, and attention being paid to the choice of your subjects, you can have nothing to fear from the malignancy of criticism, as your ideas are lively, and your descriptions agreeable. . . .

Ford, XIII. 29.

Washington Expounds to the Commissioners of the Federal District His Plans for a University in the Federal City

Philadelphia, 28 January, 1795.

Gentlemen,

A plan for the establishment of an university in the Federal City has frequently been the subject of conversation; but, in what manner it is proposed to commence this important institution, on how extensive a scale, the means by which it is to be effected, how it is to be supported, or what progress is made in it, are matters altogether unknown to me.

It has always been a source of serious reflection and sincere regret with me, that the Youth of the United States should be sent to foreign countries for the purpose of education. Although there are doubtless many, under these circumstances, who escape the danger of contracting principles unfavorable to republican government, yet we ought to deprecate the hazard attending ardent and susceptible minds, from being too strongly and too early prepossessed in favor of other political systems, before they are capable of appreciating their own.

For this reason I have greatly wished to see a plan adopted, by which the arts, sciences, and belles-lettres could be taught in their *fullest* extent, thereby embracing *all* the advantages of European tuition, with the means of acquiring the liberal knowledge, which is necessary to qualify our citizens for the exigencies of public as well as private life; and (which with me is a consideration of great magnitude) by assembling the youth from the different parts of this rising republic, contributing from their intercourse and interchange of information to the removal of prejudices, which might perhaps sometimes arise from local circumstances.

The Federal City, from its centrality and the advantages, which in other respects it must have over any other place in the United States, ought to be preferred, as a proper site for such an university. And if a plan can be adopted upon a scale as *extensive* as I have described, and the execution of it should commence under favorable auspices in a reasonable time, with a fair prospect of success, I will grant in perpetuity fifty shares in the navigation of Potomac River towards the endowment of it.

What annuity will arise from these fifty shares, when the navigation is in full operation, can at this time be only conjectured; and those, who are acquainted with the nature of it, can form as good a judgment as myself.

As the design of this university has assumed no form with which I am acquainted, and as I am equally ignorant who the persons are, that have taken or are disposed to take the maturation of the plan upon themselves, I have been at a loss to whom I should make this communication of my intentions. If the Commissioners of the Federal City have any particular agency in bringing the matter forward, then the information, I now give to them, is in its proper course. If, on the other hand, they have no more to do in it than others, who may be desirous of seeing so important a measure carried into effect, they will be so good as to excuse my using them as the medium for disclosing these intentions; because it appears necessary, that the funds for the establishment and support of the institution should be known to the promoters of it; and I see no mode more eligible for announcing my purpose.

Ford, XIII. 36-38.

Washington Explains to Thomas Jefferson His Plans and Theories Respecting the Establishment of a University in the Federal City

Philadelphia, 15 March, 1795.

Dear Sir,

I received your letter of the 23d ultimo [this was respecting a plan of several professors of Geneva for migrating to the United States]; but not at so early a period as might have been expected from the date of it. My mind has always been more disposed to apply the shares in the inland navigation of Potomac and James Rivers, which were left to my disposal by the legislature of Virginia, towards the endowment of an university in the United States, than to any other object it had contemplated. In pursuance of this idea, and understanding that other means are in embryo for establishing so useful a seminary in the Federal City, I did, on the 28th of January last, announce to the commissioners thereof my intention of vesting in perpetuity the fifty shares I hold under that act in the navigation of Potomac, as an additional mean of carrying the plan into effect, provided it should be adopted upon a scale so liberal as to extend to and embrace a *complete* system of education.

I had little hesitation in giving the Federal City a preference of all other places for the institution, for the following reasons. 1st, on account of its being the permanent seat of the government of this Union, and where the laws and policy of it must be better understood than in any local part thereof. 2d, because of its centrality. 3d, because one half (or near it) of the District of Columbia is within the Commonwealth of Virginia, and the whole of the State not inconvenient thereto. 4th, because, as a *part* of the endowment, it would be useful, but *alone* would be inadequate to the end. 5th, because many advantages, I conceive, would result from the jurisdiction, which the general government will have over it, which no other spot would possess. And, lastly, as this seminary is contemplated for the completion of education and study of the sciences, (not for boys in their rudiments,) it will afford the students an opportunity of attending the debates in Congress, and thereby becoming more liberally and better acquainted with the principles of law and government.

My judgment and my wishes point equally strong to the application of the James River shares to the same object at the same place; but, considering the source from whence they were derived, I have, in a letter I am writing to the executive of Virginia on this subject, left the application of them to a seminary *within the State,* to be located by the legislature.

Hence you will perceive, that I have in a degree anticipated your proposition. I was restrained from going the whole length of the suggestion by the following considerations. 1st, I did not know to what extent or when any plan would be so matured for the establishment of an university, as would enable any assurances to be given to the application of M. D'Ivernois. 2d, the propriety of transplanting the professors *in a body* might be questioned for several reasons; among others, because they might not be all good characters, nor all sufficiently acquainted with our language. And again, having been at variance with the levelling party of their own country, the measure might be considered as an aristocratical movement by more than those, who, without any just cause that I can discover, are continually sounding the bell of aristocracy. And, 3d, because it might preclude some of the first professors in other countries from a participation, among whom some of the most celebrated characters in Scotland, in this line, might be obtained.

Something, but of what nature I am unable to inform you, has been written by Mr. Adams to M. D'Ivernois. Never having viewed my intended donation as more than a part of the means, that were to set this establishment afloat, I did not incline to go too far in the encouragement of professors, before the plan should assume a more formal shape, much less to induce an entire college to migrate. The enclosed is the answer I have received from the commissioners; from which, and the ideas I have here expressed, you will be enabled to decide on the best communication to be made to M. D'Ivernois.

My letter to the commissioners has bound me to the fulfillment of what is therein engaged; and if the legislature of Virginia, in considering the subject, should view it in the same light I do, the James River shares will be added thereto; for I think one good institution of this sort is to be preferred to two imperfect ones, which, without other aid than the shares in *both* navigations, is more likely to fall through, than to succeed upon the plan I contemplate; which, in a few words, is to supersede the necessity of sending the youth of this country abroad for the purpose of education, (where too often principles and habits unfriendly to republican government are imbibed, and not easily discarded,) by instituting such an one of our own, as will answer the end, and associating them in the same seminary, will contribute to wear off those prejudices and unreasonable jealousies, which prevent or weaken friendships and impair the harmony of the Union.

P. S. Mr. Adams *laid* before me the communications of M. D'Ivernois; but I said nothing to him of my intended donation towards the establishment of an university in the Federal District. My wishes would be to fix this on the Virginia side of the Potomac River; but this would not embrace or accord with those other means, which are proposed for the establishment.

Ford, XIII. 48-52.

Washington Urges the Importance of a Plan of Universal Education for United States in Letter to Gov. Robert Brooke of Virginia and Discusses His Plan for a Seminary in Virginia

Philadelphia, 16 March, 1795.

Sir,

Ever since the General Assembly of Virginia were pleased to submit to my disposal fifty shares in the Potomac, and one hundred in the James River Company, it has been my anxious desire to appropriate them to an object most worthy of public regard.

It is with indescribable regret, that I have seen the youth of the United States migrating to foreign countries, in order to acquire the higher branches of erudition, and to obtain a knowledge of the sciences. Although it would be injustice to many to pronounce the certainty of their imbibing maxims not congenial with republicanism, it must nevertheless be admitted, that a serious danger is encountered by sending abroad among other political systems those, who have not well learned the value of their own.

The time is therefore come, when a plan of universal education ought to be adopted in the United States. Not only do the exigencies of public and private life demand it, but, if it should ever be apprehended, that prejudice would be entertained in one part of the Union against another, an efficacious remedy will be, to assemble the youth of every part under such circumstances as will, by the freedom of intercourse and collision of sentiment, give to their minds the direction of truth, philanthropy, and mutual conciliation.

It has been represented, that a university corresponding with these ideas is contemplated to be built in the Federal City, and that it will receive considerable endowments. This position is so eligible from its centrality, so convenient to Virginia, by whose legislature the shares were granted and in which part of the Federal District stands, and combines so many other conveniences, that I have determined to vest the Potomac shares in that university.

Presuming it to be more agreeable to the General Assembly of Virginia, that the shares in the James River Company should be reserved for a similar object in some part of that State, I intend to allot them for a seminary to be erected at such place as they shall deem most proper. I am disposed to believe, that a seminary of learning upon an enlarged plan, but yet not coming up to the full idea of an university, is an institution to be preferred for the position which is to be chosen. The students who wish to pursue the whole range of science, may pass with advantage from the seminary to the university, and the former by a due relation may be rendered cooperative with the latter.

I cannot however dissemble my opinion, that if all the shares were conferred on an university, it would become far more important, than when they are divided; and I have been constrained from concentring them in the same place, merely by my anxiety to reconcile a particular attention to Virginia with a great good, in which she will abundantly share in common with the rest of the United States.

I must beg the favor of your Excellency to lay this letter before that honorable body, at their next session, in order that I may appropriate the James River shares to the place which they may prefer. They will at the same time again accept my acknowledgments for the opportunity, with which they have favored me, of attempting to supplement so important a desideratum in the United States as an university adequate to our necessity, and a preparatory seminary. . . .

Ford, XIII. 52-54.

Gov. Brooke referred the letter to the Virginia Assembly, which on December 1 took the following action:

"Resolved, therefore, that the appropriation by the said George Washington of the aforesaid shares in the Potomac Company to the university, intended to be erected in the Federal City, is made in a manner most worthy of public regard, and of the approbation of this commonwealth.

"Resolved, also, that he be requested to appropriate the aforesaid shares in the James River Company to a seminary at such place in the upper country, as he may deem most convenient to a majority of the inhabitants thereof."

Ford, XIII. 54n, 55n.

Washington Confides to George Cabot His Desire to Befriend Lafayette's Son, and Offers to Pay For His Education at Harvard University

Philadelphia, 7 September, 1795.

Dear Sir,

The enclosed letters, which, after reading, be so good as to return to me, will be the best apology I can offer for the liberty I am about to take, and for the trouble, which, if you comply with my request, it must necessarily give.

To express all the sensibility, which has been excited in my breast by the receipt of young Lafayette's letter, from the recollection of his father's merits, services, and sufferings, from my friendship for him, and from my wishes to become a friend and father to his son is unnecessary. Let me in a few words declare, that I will be his friend; but the manner of becoming so, considering the obnoxious light in which his father is viewed by the French government, and my own situation as the executive of the United States, requires more time to consider in all its relations, than I can bestow on it at present, the letters not having been in my hands more than an hour, and I myself on the point of setting out for Virginia to fetch my family back, whom I left there about the 1st of August.

The mode, which at the first view strikes me as the most eligible to answer his purposes and to save appearances, is, first to administer all the consolation to the young gentleman, that he can derive from the most unequivocal assurances of my standing in the place of and becoming to him a father, friend, protector, and supporter. But, secondly, for prudential motives, as they may relate to himself, his mother and friends, whom he has left behind, and to my official character, it would be best not to make these sentiments public; and of course it would be ineligible, that he should come to the seat of the general government, where all the foreign characters (particularly that of his own nation) are residents, until it is seen what opinions will be excited by his arrival; especially, too, as I shall be necessarily absent five or six weeks from it on business in several places. Thirdly, considering how important it is to avoid idleness and dissipation, to improve his mind, and to give him all the advantages, which education can bestow, my opinion and my advice to him are, if he is qualified for admission, that he should enter as a student at the university in Cambridge, although it should be for a short time only; the expense of which, as also of every other means for his support, I will pay. And I now authorize you, my dear Sir, to draw upon me accordingly;

and, if it is in any degree necessary or desired, that M. Frestel, his tutor, should accompany him to the university in that character, any arrangements which you shall make for the purpose, and any expense thereby incurred for the same, shall be borne by me in like manner.

Ford, XIII. 100-102.

George Washington Lafayette with M. Frestel, his tutor, had recently arrived in Boston from France, and had written to Washington giving notice of their arrival. He did not go to Harvard, but continued with his tutor at New York and Philadelphia, and after Washington retired from the presidency was at Mount Vernon until in October, 1797, news of his father's release caused his return to France.

Washington Writes to Alexander Hamilton on the Importance of a High Type of Training on the University Level for Youth From All Parts of the Country

Philadelphia, 1 September, 1796.

My dear Sir,

About the middle of last week I wrote you; . . .

Since then, revolving on the paper that was inclosed therein, on the various matters it contained, and on the first expression of the advice or recommendation which was given in it, I have regretted that another subject (which in my estimation is of interesting concern to the well-being of this country) was not touched upon also;—I mean education generally, as one of the surest means of enlightening and giving just ways of thinking to our citizens, but particularly the establishment of a university; where the youth from all parts of the United States might receive the polish of erudition in the arts, sciences, and belles-lettres; and where those who were disposed to run a political course might not only be instructed in the theory and principles, but (this seminary being at the seat of the general government) where the legislature would be in session half the year, and the interests and politics of the nation of course would be discussed, they would lay the surest foundation for the practical part also.

But that which would render it of the highest importance, in my opinion, is, that the juvenal period of life, when friendships are formed, and habits established, that will stick by one; the youth or young men from different parts of the United States would be assembled together, and would by degrees discover that there was not that cause for those jealousies and prejudices which one part of the Union had imbibed against another part:—of course, sentiments of more liberality in the general policy of the country would result from it. What but the mixing of people from different parts of the United States during the war rubbed off these impressions? A century, in the ordinary intercourse, would not have accomplished what the seven years' association in arms did; but that ceasing, prejudices are beginning to revive again, and never will be eradicated so effectually by any other means as the intimate intercourse of characters in early life,—who, in all probability, will be at the head of the counsels of this country in a more advanced stage of it.

To show that this is no new idea of mine, I may appeal to my early communications to Congress; and to prove how seriously I have reflected on it since, and how well disposed I have been, and still am, to contribute my aid towards carrying the measure into effect, I inclose you the extract of a letter from me to the governor of Virginia on this subject, and a copy of the resolves of the legislature of that State in consequence thereof.

I have not the smallest doubt that this donation (when the navigation is in complete operation, which it certainly will be in less than two years), will amount to £1200 to £1500 sterling a year, and become a rapidly increasing fund. The proprietors of the federal city have talked of doing something handsome towards it likewise; and if Congress would appropriate some of the western lands to the same uses, funds sufficient, and of the most permanent and increasing sort, might be so established as to invite the ablest professors in Europe to conduct it.

Let me pray you, therefore to introduce a section in the address expressive of these sentiments, and recommendatory of the measure, without any mention, however, of my proposed personal contribution to the plan.

Such a section would come in very properly after the one which relates to our religious obligations, or in a preceding part, as one of the recommendatory measures to counteract the evils arising from geographical discriminations.

Ford, XIII. 266-269.

Washington in the Farewell Address Urges Promotion of Institutions of Knowledge

September 17, 1796.

. . . 'Tis substantially true, that virtue or morality is a necessary spring of popular government.—The rule indeed extends with more or less force to every species of Free Government.—Who that is a sincere friend to it can look with indifference upon attempts to shake the foundation of the fabric?—

Promote, then, as an object of primary importance, institutions for the general diffusion of knowledge. In proportion as the structure of a government gives force to public opinion, it is essential that public opinion should be enlightened. . . .

Ford, XIII. 308, 309.

Washington Sends George Washington Parke Custis Money for an Academic Gown and Gives Him Excellent Advice as to His Conduct at Princeton

Philadelphia, 15 November, 1796.

Dear Washington:

Yesterday's mail brought me your letter of the 12th instant, and under cover of this letter you will receive a ten-dollar bill, to purchase a gown, &c., if proper. But as the classes may be distinguished by a different insignia, I advise you not to provide these without first obtaining the approbation of your tutors; otherwise you may be distinguished more by folly, than by the dress.

It affords me pleasure to hear that you are agreeably fixed; and I receive still more from the assurance you give of attending closely to your studies. It is you yourself who is to derive immediate benefit from these. Your country may do it hereafter. The more knowledge you acquire, the greater will be the probability of your succeeding in both, and the greater will be your thirst for more.

I rejoice to hear you went through your examination with propriety, and have no doubt but that the president has placed you in the class which he conceived best adapted to the present state of your improvement. The more there are above you, the greater your exertions should be to ascend; but let your promotion result from your own application, and from intrinsic merit, not from the labors of others. The last would prove fallacious, and expose you to the reproach of the daw in borrowed feathers. This would be inexcusable in you, because there is no occasion for it; forasmuch, as you need nothing but the exertion of the talents you possess, with proper directions, to acquire all that is necessary; and the hours allotted for study, if properly improved, will enable you to do this. Although the confinement may feel irksome at first, the advantages resulting from it, to a reflecting mind, will soon overcome it.

Endeavor to conciliate the good will of *all* your fellow-students, rendering them every act of kindness in your power. Be particularly obliging and attentive to your chamber-mate, Mr. Forsyth; who, from the account I have of him, is an admirable young man, and strongly impressed with the importance of a liberal and finished education. But above all, be obedient to your tutors, and in a particular manner respect the president of the seminary who is both learned and good.

For any particular advantage you may derive from the attention and aid of Mr. Forsyth, I shall have a disposition to reward. One thing more and I will close this letter. Never let an indigent person ask, without receiving *something*, if you have the means; always recollecting in what light the widow's mite was viewed.

Your grandmother, sister, and all here are well, and feeling a strong interest in your welfare, join most cordially with me in every good wish for it.

Ford, XIII. 335-337.

Washington Writes Expressing Pleasure at the Diligence in Study of George Washington Parke Custis. He emphasizes the Need for the Formation of Good Habits

Philadelphia, 28th November, 1796.

Dear Washington: . . .

The assurances you give me of applying diligently to your studies, and fulfilling those obligations which are enjoined by your Creator and due to his creatures, are highly pleasing and satisfactory to me. I rejoice in it on two accounts; first, as it is the sure means of laying the foundation of your own happiness, and rendering you, if it should please God to spare your life, a useful member of society hereafter; and secondly, that I may, if I live to enjoy the pleasure, reflect that I have been, in some degree, instrumental in effecting these purposes.

You are now extending into that stage of life when good or bad habits are formed. When the mind will be turned to things useful and praiseworthy, or to dissipation and vice. Fix on whichever it may, it will stick by you; for you know it has been said, and truly, "that as the twig is bent so it will grow." This, in a strong point of view, shows the propriety of letting your inexperience be directed by maturer advice, and in placing guard upon the avenues which lead to idleness and vice. The latter will approach like a thief, working upon your passions; encouraged, perhaps, by bad examples; the propensity to which will increase in proportion to the practice of it and your yielding. This admonition proceeds from the purest affection for you; but I do not mean by it, that you are to become a stoic, or to deprive yourself in the intervals of study of any recreations or manly exercise which reason approves.

'Tis well to be on good terms with all your fellow-students, and I am pleased to hear you are so, but while a courteous behavior is due to all, select the most deserving only for your friendships, and before this becomes intimate, weigh their dispositions and character *well*. True friendship is a plant of slow growth; to be sincere, there must be a congeniality of temper and pursuits. Virtue and

vice can not be allied; nor can idleness and industry; of course, if you resolve to adhere to the two former of these extremes, an intimacy with those who incline to the latter of them, would be extremely embarrassing to you; it would be a stumbling block in your way; and act like a millstone hung to your neck, for it is the nature of idleness and vice to obtain as many votaries as they can.

I would guard you, too, against imbibing hasty and unfavorable impressions of any one. Let your judgment always balance well before you decide; and even then, where there is no occasion for expressing an opinion, it is best to be silent, for there is nothing more certain than that it is at all times more easy to make enemies than friends. And besides, to speak evil of any one, unless there is unequivocal proofs of their deserving it, is an injury for which there is no adequate reparation. For, as Shakespeare says, "He that robs me of my good name enriches not himself, but renders me poor indeed," or words to that effect. Keep in mind that scarcely any change would be agreeable to you at first from the sudden transition, and from never having been accustomed to shift or rough it. And, moreover, that if you meet with collegiate fare, it will be unmanly to complain. . . .

Ford, XIII. 339-341.

Washington Writes to the Commissioners of the Federal City on the Question of a Site for the University

Philadelphia, 1 December, 1796.

Gentlemen, . . .

In the case however before us, I conceive Mr. Corachichi might have received a definitive answer, without referring the matter to the Executive. On what part of the Contract with Greenleaf he has founded an opinion that a site was designated for a University, and has built his complaints—or how it came to pass, that any allusion to such a measure should have found its way into that contract, I have no more recollection than I have a conception, of what could have induced it;—for your clerk has omitted sending the Extract.

It is a well known fact, or to say the least, it has been always understood by me, that the establishment of a University in the Federal City depended upon several contingencies;—one of which, and a material one too—was donations for the purpose. Until lately, this business could scarcely be said to have advanced beyond the *wishes* of its advocates, although these wishes were accompanied generally with expressions of what might be expected; and whenever the names of Mr. Blodget and the proprietors of that vicinity; were mentioned in relation to this business the idea (expressed or implied) always was—that they meant to give the ground.

Is this the intention of Mr. Corachichi relative to the object he is now contending for? if it is, and a sufficient space of ground, on these terms, can be obtained there for this purpose, without interfering with the property of Orphans, my opinion is, that the University ought to be placed there.—But, if this is *not* the design, can that Gentleman, or any other expect that the public will buy (for an exchange is a purchase, and may be of the most troublesome kind) when it has unappropriated ground nearly as convenient?—and why do this?—because a site has been loosely talked of, because a proprietor to enhance the sale of his property has colored the advantages of it as highly as he could,—and because the purchaser, omitting to investigate matters beforehand, wants the public to encounter an expence—it is unable to bear—by way of redress for his own incaution.—For what would have been the answer of the Commissioners, if he had previously applied to them, to know if a University would be placed where he is now contending for?—Certainly, that he ought not to calculate upon it.—If that would have been the answer then (and unless there are facts which have escaped my recollection) I can conceive no other could have been given, it is not inapplicable at present.

A University was not even contemplated by Major L'Enfant in the plan of the city which was laid before Congress; taking its origin from another source. . . .

Ford, XIII. 341-343.

Washington in Address to Congress Urges the Support of Institutions for the Promotion of Agriculture and Calls Attention to the Need for a National University and a Military Academy

December 7, 1796.

. . . It will not be doubted, that, with reference either to individual or national welfare, agriculture is of primary importance. In proportion as nations advance in population and other circumstances of maturity, this truth becomes more apparent, and renders the cultivation of the soil more and more an object of public patronage. Institutions for promoting it grow up, supported by the public purse; and to what object can it be dedicated with greater propriety? Among the means, which have been employed to this end, none have been attended with greater success than the establishment of boards, composed of proper characters, charged with collecting and diffusing information, and enabled by premiums, and small pecuniary aids, to encourage and assist a spirit of discovery and improvement. This species of establishment contributes doubly to the increase of improvement, by stimulating to enterprise and experiment, and by drawing to a common centre the results everywhere of individual skill and observation, and spreading them thence over the whole nation. Experience accordingly has shown, that they are very cheap instruments of immense national benefits.

I have heretofore proposed to the consideration of Congress, the expediency of establishing a national university, and also a military academy. The desirableness of both these institutions has so constantly increased with every new view I have taken of the subject, that I cannot omit the opportunity of once for all recalling your attention to them.

The assembly to which I address myself, is too enlightened not to be fully sensible how much a flourishing state of the arts and sciences contributes to national prosperity and reputation.

True it is, that our country, much to its honor, contains many seminaries of learning highly respectable and useful; but the funds upon which they rest are too narrow to command the ablest professors, in the different departments of liberal knowledge, for the institution contemplated, though they would be excellent auxiliaries.

Amongst the motives to such an institution, the assimilation of the principles, opinions, and manners of our countrymen, by the common education of a portion of our youth from every quarter, well deserves attention. The more homogeneous our citizens can be made in these particulars, the greater will be our prospect of permanent union; and a primary object of such a national institution should be, the education of our youth in the science of gov-

ernment. In a republic, what species of knowledge can be equally important, and what duty more pressing on its legislature, than to patronize a plan for communicating it to those, who are to be the future guardians of the liberties of the country?

The institution of a military academy is also recommended by cogent reasons. However pacific the general policy of a nation may be, it ought never to be without an adequate stock of military knowledge for emergencies. The first would impair the energy of its character, and both would hazard its safety, or expose it to greater evils when war could not be avoided. Besides that war might often not depend upon its own choice. In proportion as the observance of pacific maxims might exempt a nation from the necessity of practising the rules of the military art, ought to be its care in preserving and transmitting, by proper establishments, the knowledge of that art. Whatever argument may be drawn from particular examples, superficially viewed, a thorough examination of the subject will evince, that the art of war is at once comprehensive and complicated; that it demands much previous study; and that the possession of it, in its most improved and perfect state, is always of great moment to the security of a nation. This, therefore, ought to be a serious care of every government; and for this purpose, an academy, where a regular course of instruction is given, is an obvious expedient, which different nations have successfully employed. . . .

Ford, XIII. 348-350.

Washington Approves the Course of Reading for George W. P. Custis Under Dr. Smith of Princeton

Philadelphia, 19 December, 1796.

Dear Washington: . . .

The pleasure of hearing you were well, in good spirits, and progressing as we could wish in your studies, was communicated by your letter of the fourteenth instant, to your grandmamma; but what gave me particular satisfaction, was to find that you were going to commence a course of reading with Doctor Smith, of such books as he had chosen for the purpose. The first is very desirable, and the other indispensable; for, besides the duty enjoined upon you by the instructions of your preceptors, while your own judgment is locked up in immaturity; you now have a peculiar advantage in the attentions of Doctor Smith to you, who, being a man of learning and taste himself, will select such authors and subjects, as will lay the foundation of useful knowledge; let me impress it upon you, therefore, again and again, not only to yield implicit obedience to his choice and instructions in this respect, but to the course of studies also, and that you would pursue both with zeal and steadiness. Light reading (by this, I mean books of little importance) may amuse for the moment, but leaves nothing solid behind.

The same consequences would follow from inconstancy and want of steadiness—for 'tis to close application and constant perseverance, men of letters and science are indebted for their knowledge and usefulness; and you are now at that period of life (as I have observed to you in a former letter) when these are to be acquired, or lost forever. But as you are well acquainted with my sentiments on this subject, and know how anxious all your friends are to see you enter upon the grand theatre of life, with the advantages of a finished education, a highly cultivated mind, and a proper sense of your duties to God and man, I shall only add one sentiment more before I close this letter (which, as I have others to write, will hardly be in time for the mail), and that is, to pay due respect and obedience to your tutors, and affectionate reverence for the president of the college, whose character merits your highest regards. Let no bad example, for such is to be met in all seminaries, have an improper influence upon your conduct. Let this be such, and let it be your pride, to demean yourself in such a manner to obtain the goodwill of your superiors, and the love of your fellow-students. . . .

Ford, XIII. 354, 355.

Washington Tells Custis Not to Spend Too much Time in Writing Letters Home, and to Spend More Time on Study

Philadelphia, 11 January, 1797.

Dear Washington: . . .

As you have the best and most unequivocal evidence the case is susceptible of, that I have no other object in view by extending my cares and advice to you than what will redound to your own respectability, honor, and future happiness in life, so be assured, that while you give me reasons to expect a ready submission to my counsels, and while I hear that you are diligent in pursuing the means which are to acquire these advantages, it will afford me infinite gratification. Your last letter is replete with assurances of this nature—I place entire confidence in them. They have removed all the doubts which were expressed in my last letter to you, and let me repeat it again, have conveyed very pleasing sensations to my mind.

It was not my wish to check your correspondences—very far from it; for with proper characters (and none can be more desirable than with your papa and Mr. Lear) and on proper subjects, it will give you a habit of expressing your ideas upon all occasions with facility and correctness. I meant no more, by telling you we should be content with hearing from you once a week, than that these correspondences were not to be considered as an injunction or an imposition, thereby interfering with your studies or concerns of a more important nature. So far am I from discountenancing writing of any kind (except upon the principle above mentioned) that I should be pleased to hear, and you yourself might derive advantages from a short diary, . . .

Ford, XIII. 363, 364.

Washington Writes to Pres. Samuel Stanhope Smith, of Princeton Regarding the Weakness of Young Custis, and Hopes that the President's Efforts in Behalf of Custis May Succeed

Mount Vernon, 24 May, 1797.

Reverend and Dear Sir, . . .

Your favor of the 18th instant was received by the last post, the contents of which, relative to Mr. Custis, filled my mind (as you naturally supposed it would) with extreme disquietude. From his infancy I have discovered an almost unconquerable disposition to indolence in everything that did not tend to his amusements; and have exhorted him in the most parental and friendly manner often, to devote his time to more useful pursuits. His pride has been stimulated, and his family expectations and wishes have been urged as inducements thereto. In short, I could say nothing to him now by way of admonition, encouragement, or advice, that has not been repeated over and over again.

It is my earnest desire to keep him to his studies as long as I am able, as well on account of the benefits he will derive from them, as for the purpose of excluding him from the company of idle and dissipated young men until his judgment is more matured.

I am to thank you, sir, for your exertions to remove the error of his present thoughts, and I shall hope for your further endeavor to effect it. If you find, however, that the attempt will be in vain, I shall rely on your judgment to employ his time in such studies as you conceive will be most advantageous to him during his continuance with you, and I know of none more likely to prove so than those you have suggested, if his term at college will close with the next vacation.

Ford, XIII. 388.

Washington Stresses the Importance of Studying to Custis

Mount Vernon, 4 June, 1797.

. . . To insure permanency, think seriously of the advantages which are to be derived, on the one hand, from the steady pursuit of a course of study to be marked out by your preceptor, whose judgment, experience, and acknowledged abilities, enables him to direct them; and, on the other hand, revolve as seriously on the consequences which would inevitably result from an indisposition to this measure, or from an idle habit of hankering after unprofitable amusements at your time of life, before you have acquired that knowledge which would be found beneficial in every situation; I say *before,* because it is not my wish that, having gone through the essentials, you should be deprived of any rational amusement *afterward;* or, lastly, from dissipation in such company as you would most likely meet under such circumstances, who but too often, mistake ribaldry for wit, and rioting, swearing, intoxication, and gambling for manliness.

These things are not without momentary charms to young minds susceptible of any impression, before the judgment in some measure is formed, and reason begins to preponderate. It is on this ground, as well as on account of the intrinsic advantages that you yourself would experience hereafter from it, that I am desirous of keeping you to your studies. And if such characters as I have described should be found instrumental, either by their advice or example, in giving your mind a wrong bias, shun them as you would a pestilence; for, be assured, it is not with such qualities as these you ought to be allied, or with those who possess them to have any friendship.

These sentiments are dictated by the purest regard for your welfare, and from an earnest desire to promote your true happiness, in which all your friends feel an interest, and would be much gratified to see accomplished, while it would contribute in an eminent degree to your respectability in the eyes of others.

Your endeavors to fulfill these reasonable wishes of ours can not fail of restoring all the attentions, protection, and affection of one who has ever been, and will continue to be, your sincere friend.

Ford, XIII. 394, 395.

Washington Writes to William Strickland in England on the Value of Boards of Agriculture

Mount Vernon, 15 July, 1797.

Sir, . . .

Your strictures on the Agriculture of this country are but too just—it is indeed wretched—but a leading, if not the primary, cause of its being so is that, instead of improving a little ground well, we attempt much and do it ill.—A half a third or even a fourth of what we mangle, well wrought and properly dressed, wou'd produce more than the whole under our system (if it deserves that epithet) of management. Yet, such is the force of habit, that we cannot depart from it. The consequence of which is that we ruin the lands that are already cleared and either cut down more wood if we have it, or emigrate into the Western Country.—I have endeavored both in a public and private character to encourage the establishment of Boards of Agriculture in this Country, but hitherto in vain; . . . Since the first Establishment of the National Board of Agriculture in Great Britain, I have considered it as one of the most valuable Institutions of modern times, and conducted with so much ability and zeal as it appears to be under the auspices of Sir John Sinclair, must be productive of great advantages to the Nation and to Mankind in General. . . .

For the detailed account of your observations on the Husbandry of these United States, and your reflection thereon, I feel myself much obliged; and shall at all times be thankful for any suggestions on agricultural subjects, you may find leizure and inclination to favor me with, as the remainder of my life (which in the common course of things Now in my 66th year, cannot be of long continuance) will be devoted wholly to rural and agricultural pursuits. . . .

Ford, XIII. 404-407, 411.

Washington Urges Custis to Continue His Studies after His Vacation

Mount Vernon, 29 August, 1797.

Dear Washington:

Your letter of the 21st instant, came to hand by the last post, and as usual, gave us pleasure to hear that you enjoyed good health, were progressing well in your studies, and that you were in the road to promotion.

The senior class having left, or being on the point of leaving college, some of them with great eclat, ought to provoke strong stimulus to those who remain, to acquire equal reputation, which is not otherwise to be done than by perseverance and close application; in neither of which I hope you will be found deficient. . . . Although I persuade myself that there is no occasion for the admonition, yet I exhort you to come with a mind steadfastly resolved to return precisely at the time alloted, that it may be guarded against those ideas and allurements which unbend it from study, and cause reluctance to return to it again. Better remain where you are than suffer impressions of this sort to be imbibed from a visit, however desirous that visit may be to you, and pleasing to your friends, who will prefer infinitely your permanent good, to temporary gratifications; but I shall make all fears of this sort yield to a firm persuasion, that every day convinces you more and more of the propriety and necessity of devoting your youthful days in the requirement of that knowledge which will be advantageous, grateful, and pleasing to you in maturer years, and may be the foundation of your usefulness here, and happiness hereafter.

Ford, XIII. 417-419.

Washington Budgets Time for Custis

7 January, 1798.

System in all things should be aimed at; for in execution it renders everything more easy.

If now and then, of a morning before breakfast, you are inclined by way of change, to go out with a gun, I shall not object to it; provided you return by the hour we usually set down to that meal.

From breakfast, until about an hour before dinner (allowed for dressing and preparing for it, that you may appear decent) I shall expect you will confine yourself to your studies, and diligently attend to them; endeavoring to make yourself master of whatever is recommended to, or required of you.

While the afternoons are short, and but little interval between rising from dinner and assemblying for tea, you may employ that time in walking, or any other recreation.

After tea, if the studies you are engaged in require it, you will no doubt perceive the propriety and advantage of returning to them, until the hour of rest.

Rise early, that by habit it may become familiar, agreeable, healthy, and profitable. It may, for a while, be irksome to do this, but that will wear off; and the practice will produce a rich harvest forever thereafter; whether in public, or private walks of life. . . .

Ford, XIII. 436, 437.

Washington, in a Letter to His Nephew William Augustine, Compares Advantages of Schooling in the Home with Sending a Boy to a Public Seminary

Mount Vernon, 27 February, 1798.

My dear Sir, . . .

The reason which you assign for giving the rudiments of education to your sons at home is a weighty and conclusive one; —but much will depend upon the qualifications and fitness of the preceptor you employ, to render it more or less beneficial. To a certain point tuition under the eye of Parents or Guardian of youth, is much to be preferred, because the presumption is: that the properties and passions will be watched with more solicitude and attention by them, than by their Tutors:—but when the direction of these are unfolded and can be counteracted by the discipline of Public schools and the precepts of the professors. Especially too when the judgment is beginning to form; when pride becomes a stimulus; and the knowledge of men, as well as of Books are to be learnt, I should give the preference to a public Seminary. . . .

Ford, XIII. 442-444.

Education of Stepgrandson

[March] 5, [1798]. Doctr. Stuart left this, to accompany Washington Custis to St. Johns College at Annapolis.

Diary, IV. 272.

Washington Exhorts Custis to Study

Mount Vernon, 10 May, 1798.

Dear Washington: . . .

And let me exhort you, in solemn terms, to keep steadily in mind the purposes and the end for which you were sent to the seminary you are now placed at, and not disappoint the hopes which have been entertained from your going thither, by doing which you will ensure the friendship, &c. of.

Ford, XIII. 496.

Music Lessons

[June] 11 [1798]. Mr. Tracy came in the evening.

Diary IV. 278.

Tracy was Nelly Custis's music master.

Washington, in Acknowledging the Honor of Having "Liberty Hall Academy" Named "Washington Academy" Voices His Interest in Education and Contributes a Gift to the Institution

Mount Vernon, 17th June, 1798.

Unaccountable as it may seem, it is nevertheless true that the address with which you were pleased to honor me, dated the 12th of April, never came to my hands until the 14th inst.

To promote literature in this rising empire and to encourage the arts have ever been amongst the warmest wishes of my heart, and if the donation which the generosity of the Legislature of the Commonwealth of Virginia has enabled me to bestow on Liberty Hall—now by your politeness called Washington Academy—is likely to prove a means to accomplish these ends, it will contribute to the gratification of my desires.

Sentiments like those which have flowed from your pen excite my gratitude, whilst I offer my best vows for the prosperity of the Academy and for the honor and happiness of those under whose auspices it is conducted.

Washington and Lee University, *Catalogue* (1931-32).

Robert Alexander, educated in Trinity College, Dublin, founded this institution about 1749. It was first called Augusta Academy, and during the revolution was named Liberty Hall, and was chartered in 1782. In 1785 it was moved to near Lexington, and in 1803 to its present location. In 1813 it became Washington College. After the Civil War Robert E. Lee was president of it, and following his death it became Washington and Lee University.

Washington Suggests to Pres. McDowell the Course of Study for Custis at St. John's College, which he Feels should Include French, Mathematics, Surveying, and Bookkeeping

Mount Vernon, 2 September, 1798.

Sir: . . .

It was my intention to have written fully to you by the return of this young gentleman to college, but the debilitated state into which I have been thrown by a fever, with which I was seized on the 18th, and could procure no remission of until the 25th past, renders writing equally irksome and improper.

Were the case otherwise, I should, I confess, be at a loss to point out any precise course of study for Mr. Custis. My views, with respect to him, have already been made known to you, and, therefore, it is not necessary to repeat them on this occasion. It is not merely the best course for him to pursue that requires a consideration, but such an one as he can be induced to pursue, and will contribute to his improvement and the object in view. In directing the first of these objects, a gentleman of your literary discernment and knowledge of the world, would be at no loss, without any suggestions of mine, if there was as good a disposition to receive, as there are talents to acquire knowledge; but as there seems to be in this youth an unconquerable indolence of temper, and a dereliction, in fact to all study, it must rest with you to lead him in the best manner, and by the easiest modes you can devise, to the study of such useful acquirements as may be serviceable to himself, and eventually beneficial to his country.

French, from having become in a manner the universal language, I wish him to be master of, but I do not find from inquiry, that he has made much progress in the study yet. Some of the branches of mathematics, particularly surveying, he ought, possessor as he is of large landed property, to be well acquainted with, as he may have frequent occasion for the exercise of that study.

I have already exceeded the limit I had prescribed to myself when I began this letter, but I will trespass yet a little more, while I earnestly entreat that you will examine him, as often as you can make it convenient, yourself; and admonish him seriously of his omissions and defects; and prevent, as much as it can be done, without too rigid a restraint, a devotion of his time to visitations of the families in Annapolis; which, when carried to excess, or beyond a certain point, can not but tend to divert his mind from study, and lead his thoughts to very different objects. Above all, let me request, if you should perceive any appearance of his attaching himself, by visit or otherwise, to any young lady of that place, that you would admonish him against any such step, on account of his youth and incapability of appreciating all the requisites for a connection which, in the common course of things, can terminate with the death of one of the parties only; and, if done without effect, to advise me thereof. If, in his reading, he was to make common-place notes, as is usual, copy them fair and show them to you, two good purposes would be answered by it. You would see with what judgment they were done, and it might tend much to improve his handwriting, which requires nothing but care and attention to render it good. At present, all of his writing that I have seen is a hurried scrawl, as if to get to the end speedily, was the sole object of writing. . . .

P.S. Knowledge of book-keeping is essential to all who are under the necessity of keeping accounts.

Ford, XIV. 76-79.

Washington Writes to Rev. Samuel Knox M.A., President of the Frederick Academy, Declining the Dedication of Knox's "Essay on the Best System of Liberal Education Adapted to the Genius of the Government of the United States"

Mount Vernon, 14 October, 1798.

Your favor of the 16th instant has been duly received and I feel grateful for the honor of your proposed Dedication of your [work?] on Uniform System of Education adapted to the United States to me.

Had I not declined similar honors in all cases where previous applications have been made, I certainly should, with much pleasure have yielded to one on so important a subject as you have written.—But this being the case I am compelled for the sake of consistency to decline accepting the compliment of yours. I certainly wish success to your production and shall very cheerfully subscribe to the work.

From the Washington Letter Books in the Library of Congress.

Washington Writes David Stuart, Custis's Stepfather, in Distress Concerning the Education of Custis. He Considers the Advisability of Sending Him to Harvard or to William and Mary College

Mount Vernon, 22 January, 1799.

Dear Sir,

Washington leaves this day on a visit to Hope Park, which will afford you an opportunity to examine the progress he has made in the studies he was directed to pursue.

I can, and believe I do, keep him in his room a certain portion of the twenty-four hours, but it will be impossible for me to make him attend to his books, if inclination on his part is wanting; nor while I am out if he chooses to be so, is it in my power to prevent it. I will not say this is the case, nor will I run the hazard of doing him injustice, by saying he does not apply as he ought to what has been prescribed, but no risk will be run, and candor requires I should declare it as my opinion, that he will not derive much benefit in any course which can be marked out for him at this place, without an able preceptor always with him.

What is best to be done with him I know not. My opinion always has been, that the university in Massachusetts would have been the most eligible seminary to have sent him to; first, because it is on a larger scale than any other; and secondly, because I believe that the habits of youth there, whether from the discipline of the school, or the greater attention of the people generally to morals, and a more regular course of life, are less prone to dissipation and excess than they are at the colleges south of it. It may be asked, if this was my opinion, why did I not send him there?

The answer is as short as to me it was weighty; being the only male of his line, and knowing (although it would have been submitted to) that it would have proved a heart-rending stroke to have him at that distance, I was disposed to try a nearer seminary, of good repute, which, from some cause, or combination of causes, has not, after the experiment of a year, been found to answer the end that was contemplated. Whether to send him there now, or, indeed, to any other public school, is, indeed, problematical, and to misspend his time at this place would be disgraceful to himself and to me.

If I were to propose to him to go to the university at Cambridge, in Massachusetts, he might, as has been usual for him on like occasions, say, he would go wherever I chose to send him, but if he should go, contrary to his inclination, and without a disposition to apply himself properly, an expense without any benefit would result from the measure. Knowing how much I have been disappointed, and my time disturbed by his conduct, he would not, I am sure, make a candid disclosure of his sentiments to me on this or any other plan I might propose for the completion of his education, for which reason, I would pray that you (or perhaps Mrs. Stuart could succeed better than any one) would draw from him a frank and explicit disclosure of what his own wishes and views are; for, if they are absolutely fixed, an attempt to counteract them by absolute control would be as idle as the endeavor to stop a rivulet that is constantly running. Its progress, while mound upon mound, is erected, may be arrested, but this must have an end, and everything will be swept away by the torrent. The more I think of his entering William and Mary, unless he could be placed in the bishop's [James Madison] family, the more I am convinced of its inutility on many accounts, which had better be the subject of oral communication than by letter. I shall wish to hear from you on the subject of this letter. I believe Washington means well, but has not resolution to act well. . . .

Ford, XIV. 146-148.

Washington Writes Alexander Hamilton Concerning His Efforts in Behalf of the Establishment of a Military Academy

Mount Vernon, 12 December, 1799.

Sir,

I have duly received your letter of the 28th ultimo, enclosing a copy of what you had written to the Secretary of War, on the subject of a Military Academy.

The establishment of an Institution of this kind, upon a respectable and extensive Basis, has ever been considered by me as an object of primary importance to this Country; and while I was in the Chair of Government, I omitted no proper opportunity of recommending it, in my public speeches and other ways, to the attention of the Legislature. But I never undertook to go into a *detail* of the Organization of such an Academy; leaving this task to others whose pursuits in the paths of Science, and attention to the arrangements of such Institutions, had better qualified them for the execution of it. For the same reason I must now decline making any observations on the details of your plan; and as it has already been submitted to the Secretary of War, through whom it would naturally be laid before Congress, it might be too late for alterations if any should be suggested.

I sincerely hope that the subject will meet with due attention, and that the reasons for its establishment which you have so clearly pointed out in your letter to the Secretary, will prevail upon the Legislature to place it upon a permanent and respectable footing.

Ford, XIV. 241.

SELECTIONS FROM GEORGE WASHINGTON'S WILL

Washington Provides in His Will that such Slaves as are Minors at the Time of His Death shall be Taught to Read and Write and to be Brought up to Some Useful Occupation

. . . Upon the decease of wife it is my will and desire, that all the slaves which I hold in *my own right* shall receive their freedom— . . . And whereas among those who will receive freedom according to this devise there may be some who from old age, or bodily infirmities & others who on account of their infancy, that will be unable to support themselves, it is my will and desire that all who come under the first and second description shall be comfortably clothed and fed by my heirs while they live and that such of the latter description as have no parents living, or if living are unable, or unwilling to provide for them, shall be bound by the Court until they shall arrive at the age of twenty five years, and in cases where no record can be produced whereby their ages can be ascertained, the Judgment of the Court upon it's own view of the subject shall be adequate and final.—The negroes thus bound are (by their masters and mistresses) to be taught to read and write and to be brought up to some useful occupation, agreeably to the laws of the commonwealth of Virginia, providing for the support of orphans and other poor children— . . .

Ford, XIV. 272.

Washington Makes a Bequest in His Will to Alexandria Academy for the Education of Poor and Orphan Children

. . . To the Trustees, (Governors or by whatsoever other name they may be designated) of the academy in the Town of Alexandria, I give and bequeath, in Trust, Four thousand dollars or in other words twenty of the shares which I hold in the Bank of Alexandria towards the support of a Free School, established at, and annexed to the said academy for the purpose of educating such orphan children, or the children of such other poor and indigent persons as are unable to accomplish it with their own means, and who in the judgment of the trustees of the said Seminary, are best entitled to the benefit of this donation—The aforesaid twenty shares I give and bequeath in perpetuity—the dividends only of which are to be drawn for and applied by the said Trustees for the time being, for the uses above mentioned, the stock to remain entire and untouched unless indications of a failure of the said Bank should be so apparent or discontinuance thereof should render a removal of this fund necessary, in either of these cases the amount of the stock here devised is to be vested in some other bank or public institution whereby the interest may with regularity and certainty be drawn and applied as above.—And to prevent misconception, my meaning is, and is hereby declared to be that, these twenty shares are in lieu of and not in addition to the Thousand pounds given by a missive letter some years ago in consequence whereof an annuity of fifty pounds has since been paid towards the support of this institution. . . .

Ford, XIV. 275.

Washington States His Views on Higher Education and Makes Bequests Towards an Endowment of a National University and to Liberty Hall Academy

. . . Whereas by a law of the Commonwealth of Virginia, enacted in the year 1785, the Legislature thereof was pleased (as an evidence of it's approbation of the services I had rendered the public, during the Revolution—and partly, I believe in consideration of my having suggested the vast advantages which the community would derive from the extension of its Inland navigation under legislative patronage) to present me with one hundred shares, of one hundred dollars each, in the incorporated company established for the purpose of extending the navigation of James River from tide water to the mountains; and also with fifty shares of one hundred pounds sterling each in the corporation of another company likewise established for the similar purpose of opening the navigation of the River Potomac from tide water to Fort Cumberland; the acceptance of which, although the offer was highly honorable and grateful to my feelings, was refused, as inconsistent with a principle which I had adopted, and had never departed from, namely not to receive pecuniary compensation for any services I could render my country in its arduous struggle with Great Britain for it's Rights; and because I had evaded similar propositions from other States in the Union—adding to this refusal however an intimation, that, if it should be the pleasure of the Legislature to permit me to appropriate the said shares to *public uses,* I would receive them on those terms with due sensibility—and this it having consented to in flattering terms, as will appear by a subsequent law and sundry resolutions, in the most ample and honorable manner, I proceed after this recital for the more correct understanding of the case to declare—

That as it has always been a source of serious regret with me to see the youth of these United States sent to foreign countries for the purpose of education, often before their minds were formed or they had imbibed any adequate ideas of the happiness of their own, contracting too frequently not only habits of dissipation and *extravagance,* but principles unfriendly to Republican Governm't and to the true and genuine liberties of mankind, which thereafter are rarely overcome.—For these reasons it has been my ardent wish to see a plan devised on a liberal scale which would have a tendency to spread systamatic ideas through all parts of this rising Empire thereby to do away local attachments and state prejudices as far as the nature of things would, or indeed ought to admit, from our national councils—Looking anxiously forward to the accom-

plishment of so desirable an object as this is, (in my estimation) my mind has not been able to contemplate any plan more likely to effect the measure than the establishment of a University in a central part of the United States to which the youth of fortune and talents from all parts thereof might be sent for the completion of their education in all the branches of polite literature in arts and sciences—in acquiring knowledge in the principles of Politics and good Government and (as a matter of infinite importance in my judgment) by associating with each other and forming friendships in Juvenile years, be enabled to free themselves in a proper degree from those local prejudices and habitual jealousies which have just been mentioned and which when carried to excess are never failing sources of disquietude to the Public mind and pregnant of mischievous consequences to this country:—under these impressions so fully dilated,—

Item—I give and bequeath in perpetuity the fifty shares which I hold in the Potomac Company (under the aforesaid Acts of the Legislature of Virginia) towards the endowment of a University to be established within the limits of the District of Columbia, under the auspices of the General Government, if that Government should incline to extend a fostering hand towards it, —and until such seminary is established, and the funds arising on these shares shall be required for its support, my further will and desire is that the profit accruing therefrom shall whenever the dividends are made be laid out in purchasing stock in the Bank of Columbia or some other Bank at the discretion of my Executors, or by the Treasurer of the United States for the time being under the direction of Congress, provided that Honorable body should *patronize* the measure. And the dividends proceeding from the purchase of such Stock is to be vested in more Stock and so on until a sum adequate to the accomplishment of the object is obtained, of which I have not the smallest doubt before many years pass away, even if no aid or *encouraged* is given by Legislative authority or from any other source.

Item—The hundred shares which I held in the James River Company I have given and now confirm in perpetuity to and for the use and benefit of Liberty Hall Academy in the County of Rockbridge, in the Commonwealth of *Virga.* . . .

Ford, XIV. 276-279.

Washington in His Will Acquits His Nephews of Their Indebtedness to Him on Account of the Sums He had Advanced to Them for Their Education

. . . —and whereas two other sons of my said deceased brother Samuel,—namely, George Steptoe Washington and Lawrence Augustine Washington were by the decease of those to whose care they were committed, brought under my protection and in consequence have occasioned advances on my part for their education at college and other schools for their board *cloathing* and other incidental expenses to the amount of near five thousand dollars over and above the sums furnished by these estate, *wch* sum may be inconvenient for them or their father's Estate to refund—I do for these reasons acquit them and the said Estate from the payment thereof.—My intention being that all accounts between them and me and their father's Estate and me shall stand balanced.

Ford, XIV. 280.

ASHINGTON IS THE MIGHTIEST NAME OF EARTH—LONG SINCE MIGHTIEST IN THE CAUSE OF CIVIL LIBERTY, STILL MIGHTIEST IN MORAL REFORMATION. ON THAT NAME NO EULOGY IS EXPECTED. IT CAN NOT BE. TO ADD BRIGHTNESS TO THE SUN, OR GLORY TO THE NAME OF WASHINGTON IS ALIKE IMPOSSIBLE. LET NONE ATTEMPT IT. IN SOLEMN AWE WE PRONOUNCE THE NAME, AND IN ITS NAKED DEATHLESS SPLENDOR LEAVE IT SHINING ON.

ABRAHAM LINCOLN

CATALOGUE OF
PAGEANTS and PLAYS

DEPICTING THE LIFE OF

GEORGE WASHINGTON
AND HIS TIME

FOR THE

CELEBRATION OF THE TWO HUNDREDTH ANNIVERSARY
OF THE BIRTH OF GEORGE WASHINGTON

Compiled by
JAMES K. KNUDSON

INTRODUCTION

THE George Washington Bicentennial Celebration in 1932 afforded an opportunity for child and adult, student and teacher, for clubs, colleges, and churches, for civic, fraternal, cultural, and patriotic bodies, for both the American and foreign-born in our midst, to give wide use to the play and pageant.

It was the purpose of the Commission in issuing this booklet to acquaint those who are interested in George Washington dramatic presentations with a list of available plays and pageants, together with certain data pertaining thereto, centering around the theme of George Washington and his time.

It was hoped that this would enable the reader to select that form of drama most suitable or adaptable to the given need as related to the auspices and the places of production.

The reader will find two main divisions of dramatic material in the Catalogue:

        (1) That issued by the Commission.

        (2) That available from publishers.

The Commission expressed its thanks to the publishers and others who supplied information in reference to their dramatic publications. It was not thought to be within the province of the Commission to evaluate their respective merits, but only to list the various George Washington plays and pageants with the data furnished.

Additional information in respect to the plays and pageants on the publishers' list can be secured by communicating directly with the publishers, whose names and addresses are given on page 570, and a list of whose books containing George Washington dramatic material appears on page 571.

HOW TO SELECT PAGEANTS AND PLAYS

GUIDE TO THE REFERENCE INDEX

This index is to assist the reader in making an intelligent choice of dramatic material suitable for use in celebrating a George Washington anniversary. Pageants and plays especially prepared for and issued by the Commission are numbered as follows:

PAGEANTS 1 to 13. PLAYS 20 to 38.
Dramatic material issued by publishers:
PAGEANTS 50 to 75. PLAYS 100 to 217.

Organizations that are listed in Reference Index are lettered from A to L for cross-reference purposes. As a play or pageant may be adapted to more than one type of organization, several numerals in some instances are cited opposite the name of the organization.

If you are interested in securing a George Washington play or pageant for presentation by a certain type of organization, refer to the Reference Index and, having noted the number or numbers applying, locate such numbers on the following pages and read the data. A Special Reference Index for schools appears on pages 559, 560 and 561.

The plays and pageants issued by publishers are alphabetically listed. The full list of addresses of publishers to whom communications should be sent if further information is desired will be found on page 570.

REFERENCE INDEX

(For instruction as to use see Guide above)

Organizations — **Pageant and Play Numbers**

A. KINDERGARTEN: 3, 9, 69, 102, 103, 124, 125, 136, 148, 151, 155, 172, 182, 198, 201.

B. GRAMMAR GRADE: 2, 3, 6, 7, 9, 11, 12, 13, 20, 61, 62, 63, 64, 65, 69, 70, 71, 101, 102, 103, 104, 106, 107, 108, 113, 114, 115, 123, 124, 125, 126, 127, 128, 131, 132, 134, 136, 140, 141, 142, 143, 145, 146, 147, 148, 150, 151, 152, 153, 154, 155, 156, 157, 158, 159, 160, 162, 164, 165, 172, 173, 174, 175, 176, 177, 178, 179, 181, 182, 183, 186, 187, 188, 189, 191, 193, 197, 198, 199, 201, 207, 209.

C. JUNIOR HIGH SCHOOLS: 2, 3, 6, 7, 9, 12, 13, 20, 21, 27, 51, 55, 58, 59, 60, 61, 62, 63, 64, 65, 66, 68, 70, 71, 101, 106, 108, 109, 110, 112, 113, 114, 115, 120, 121, 123, 126, 127, 128, 130, 131, 132, 134, 135, 137, 138, 144, 145, 146, 147, 150, 153, 158, 160, 162, 164, 165, 168, 170, 174, 180, 181, 183, 185, 186, 189, 193, 195, 207, 208.

D. HIGH SCHOOLS: 4, 7, 10, 12, 13, 21, 22, 24, 27, 34, 35, 36, 37, 38, 50, 51, 52, 53, 54, 55, 56, 57, 58, 59, 60, 61, 65, 68, 70, 100, 105, 109, 110, 112, 116, 117, 118, 120, 121, 122, 131, 135, 137, 138, 139, 144, 158, 161, 163, 166, 167, 168, 169, 170, 171, 180, 183, 192, 195, 196, 200, 206, 208, 211.

E. COLLEGES: 1, 4, 5, 7, 10, 22, 23, 24, 25, 26, 27, 28, 29, 30, 31, 32, 33, 34, 35, 36, 37, 38, 50, 52, 53, 54, 56, 57, 60, 70, 72, 73, 74, 100, 105, 111, 117, 119, 122, 129, 130, 133, 139, 144, 149, 161, 166, 167, 169, 171, 184, 190, 192, 194, 195, 200, 202, 203, 204, 205, 206, 210, 212, 213, 214, 215, 216, 217.

F. JUNIOR ORGANIZATIONS: 2, 3, 6, 7, 9, 11, 12, 13, 20, 21, 27, 55, 58, 61, 62, 63, 64, 65, 66, 69, 70, 71, 101, 102, 103, 104, 105, 107, 108, 109, 110, 112, 113, 114, 115, 116, 118, 120, 121, 123, 124, 126, 127, 128, 132, 134, 135, 137, 138, 140, 141, 143, 145, 146, 147, 148, 150, 151, 152, 153, 154, 155, 156, 157, 158, 159, 160, 162, 164, 165, 170, 172, 173, 174, 175, 176, 177, 178, 179, 180, 181, 182, 183, 185, 186, 187, 188, 189, 191, 193, 196, 197, 198, 199, 201, 207, 208, 209, 211.

G. PATRIOTIC AND CIVIC: 1, 2, 4, 5, 6, 7, 10, 12, 13, 20, 21, 22, 23, 24, 25, 26, 27, 28, 29, 30, 31, 32, 33, 34, 35, 36, 37, 38, 50, 51, 52, 53, 54, 55, 56, 57, 58, 59, 60, 61, 62, 63, 64, 65, 66, 68, 69, 70, 71, 72, 73, 74, 75, 100, 101, 104, 105, 106, 107, 109, 111, 112, 113, 116, 117, 118, 119, 122, 129, 131, 133, 135, 139, 144, 149, 156, 160, 163, 166, 167, 168, 169, 170, 171, 180, 183, 184, 190, 192, 194, 195, 196, 200, 202, 203, 204, 205, 206, 208, 210, 211, 212, 213, 214, 215, 216, 217.

H. RELIGIOUS: 1, 2, 4, 5, 6, 7, 10, 12, 13, 20, 21, 22, 24, 26, 27, 28, 29, 30, 31, 32, 33, 50, 52, 53, 54, 55, 56, 57, 58, 59, 60, 61, 62, 63, 64, 65, 66, 68, 69, 70, 71, 72, 73, 74, 100, 101, 102, 103, 106, 107, 108, 111, 113, 116, 119, 124, 129, 132, 133, 134, 135, 139, 156, 160, 161, 163, 166, 167, 168, 169, 171, 183, 184, 194, 195, 196, 200, 202, 203, 204, 205, 206, 213.

I. SOCIAL: 4, 5, 6, 22, 23, 24, 25, 26, 27, 28, 29, 30, 31, 32, 33, 34, 35, 36, 37, 38, 50, 51, 53, 54, 56, 57, 71, 72, 105, 113, 117, 121, 122, 129, 134, 139, 144, 149, 167, 171, 184, 190, 192, 194, 196, 200, 202, 210, 215, 216, 217.

J. WOMEN'S CLUBS: 4, 5, 8, 20, 33, 36, 37, 38, 41, 70, 71, 75, 106, 130, 137, 139, 163, 164, 167, 183, 184.

K. DRAMATIC CLUBS: 4, 21, 22, 23, 24, 25, 26, 27, 28, 29, 30, 31, 32, 33, 34, 35, 36, 37, 38, 50, 56, 72, 73, 74, 105, 118, 122, 129, 133, 144, 149, 161, 163, 166, 167, 169, 184, 190, 192, 194, 200, 202, 206, 210, 211, 212, 214, 215, 216, 217.

L. MISCELLANEOUS: 1, 2, 4, 5, 6, 7, 8, 10, 11, 12, 13, 20, 21, 22, 23, 24, 25, 26, 27, 28, 29, 30, 31, 32, 33, 34, 35, 36, 37, 38, 50, 51, 52, 53, 54, 55, 56, 57, 58, 59, 60, 61, 62, 63, 64, 65, 66, 67, 68, 69, 70, 71, 72, 73, 74, 75, 100, 101, 102, 103, 104, 105, 106, 107, 109, 110, 111, 112, 113, 114, 116, 118, 120, 121, 122, 123, 124, 126, 127, 128, 129, 130, 131, 132, 133, 135, 137, 138, 139, 144, 145, 147, 149, 150, 151, 153, 156, 158, 160, 161, 163, 164, 165, 166, 167, 168, 169, 170, 171, 177, 178, 180, 183, 184, 185, 186, 190, 194, 195, 200, 203, 204, 205, 206, 207, 208, 210, 211, 212, 213, 214, 215, 216, 217.

REFERENCE INDEX FOR SCHOOLS

(The Plays and Pageants listed under this heading were published by the United States George Washington Bicentennial Commission)

KINDERGARTEN

Catalogue Number — **Plays**

20 MOTHER AND SON—Depicts young George Washington's early inheritance of manhood and his deep respect for his mother.

Catalogue Number

3 FROM PICTURE BOOK TOWNE—Scenes from days of Washington introduced by a Sprite from Radioland.

9 THE REDBUD TREE—A pageant-play for children written in the spirit of fantasy and set at Mount Vernon.

GRAMMAR GRADES (1 to 6)
Plays

20 MOTHER AND SON—Depicts young George Washington's early inheritance of manhood and his deep respect for his mother.

21 THE LURE OF THE SEA—Based on incident of George Washington giving up a fond desire—the career of a midshipman.

27 THE INDIAN'S PROPHECY—On the shores of the Great Kanawha an Indian Sachem foretells a great future for George Washington.

Pageants

2 CHILDHOOD DAYS IN WASHINGTON'S TIME—A pageant in five episodes—wherein we see Washington defend an unfortunate schoolmaster, rescue a little bond girl from an indenture, repent of anger toward a plantation pickaninny, beg leniency for a poor boy sentenced to the pillory and deal mercifully with an Indian boy.

3 FROM PICTURE BOOK TOWNE—Scenes from days of Washington introduced by a Sprite from Radioland.

6 THE BOY'S GEORGE WASHINGTON—A pageant-play for juveniles depicting Washington as a boy; as a Virginia Colonel; as Commander-in-Chief; crossing the Delaware; as President; and refusing a third term.

9 THE REDBUD TREE—A pageant-play for children written in the spirit of fantasy and set at Mount Vernon.

11 THROUGH THE CALENDAR TO MOUNT VERNON—An historical fantasy that transports modern children to a colonial age.

12 WASHINGTON RETURNS—Four episodes: "The Youth and Adventure"; "The Man and Home"; "The General and Fame"; and "The Statesman."

13 WHO'S WHO IN FEBRUARY—A pageant-play for children in which Miss February Twenty-Second plays a leading role.

JUNIOR HIGH SCHOOL
Plays

20 MOTHER AND SON—Depicts young George Washington's early inheritance of manhood and his deep respect for his mother.

21 THE LURE OF THE SEA—Based on incident of George Washington giving up a fond desire—the career of a midshipman.

27 THE INDIAN'S PROPHECY—On the shores of the Great Kanawha an Indian Sachem foretells a great future for George Washington.

Pageants

2 CHILDHOOD DAYS IN WASHINGTON'S TIME—A pageant in five episodes—wherein we see Washington defend an unfortunate schoolmaster, rescue a little bond girl from an indenture, repent of anger toward a plantation pickaninny, beg leniency for a poor boy sentenced to the pillory and deal mercifully with an Indian boy.

3 FROM PICTURE BOOK TOWNE—Scenes from days of Washington introduced by a Sprite from Radioland.

6 THE BOY'S GEORGE WASHINGTON—A pageant-play for juveniles depicting Washington as a boy; as a Virginia Colonel; as Commander-in-Chief; crossing the Delaware; as President; and refusing a third term.

9 THE REDBUD TREE—A pageant-play for children written in the spirit of fantasy and set at Mount Vernon.

12 WASHINGTON RETURNS—Four episodes: "The Youth and Adventure"; "The Man and Home"; "The General and Fame"; and "The Statesman."

13 WHO'S WHO IN FEBRUARY—A pageant-play for children in which Miss February Twenty-Second plays a leading role.

HIGH SCHOOLS
Plays

21 THE LURE OF THE SEA—Based on incident of George Washington giving up a fond desire—the career of a midshipman.

22 A YOUTH OF THE FRONTIER—Portrays George Washington in the role of a young surveyor among the "squatters" on the frontier.

24 VINDICATED—Though certain aristocrats accuse Washington of cowardice for withdrawing from Fort Necessity, he is fully vindicated.

27 THE INDIAN'S PROPHECY—On the shores of the Great Kanawha an Indian Sachem foretells a great future for George Washington.

34 THE BLUE GOBLET—George and his brother, Lawrence, attend a meeting of the "Beefsteak and Tripe Club" in the Barbados, where George frustrates a plot to poison the host.

35 THE VIEW FROM THE WINDOW—A short three-act play wherein Washington escapes betrayal by a supposed friend into British hands.

36 WASHINGTON DANCED—Wherein the Commander-in-Chief employs the dance as a medium of strategy in time of war.

37 THE WASHINGTONS AT HOME—A play set at Mount Vernon in which the Minuet and Colonial music are featured.

Pageants

4 LIVING PAGES FROM WASHINGTON'S DIARY—A candle-time reverie. Washington tableaux interspersed with dialogue and song.

7 THE GREAT AMERICAN—A community pageant-drama in six actions, portraying Washington as Surveyor, Frontiersman, Legislator, Commander-in-Chief, Statesman, and the Man.

10 THE FATHER OF HIS COUNTRY—Thirteen important events in the life of George Washington for adult presentation.

12 WASHINGTON RETURNS—Four episodes: "The Youth and Adventure"; "The Man and Home"; "The General and Fame"; and "The Statesman."

13 WHO'S WHO IN FEBRUARY—A pageant-play for children in which Miss February Twenty-Second plays a leading role.

COLLEGES AND UNIVERSITIES
Plays

22 A YOUTH OF THE FRONTIER—Portrays George Washington in the role of a young surveyor among the "squatters" on the frontier.

23 MATCHING WITS—Revolves about Major Washington's trip to Fort Le Boeuf to warn the French to leave the territory.

24 VINDICATED—Though certain aristocrats accuse Washington of cowardice for withdrawing from Fort Necessity, he is fully vindicated.

25 I FOLLOW WASHINGTON—A dramatic page from history dealing with General Braddock's disastrous march on Fort Duquesne.

26 THAT IS MY ANSWER—Reveals how Washington defeats an intrigue set afoot to make him a Tory leader.

27 THE INDIAN'S PROPHECY—On the shores of the Great Kanawha an Indian Sachem foretells a great future for George Washington.

28 WASHINGTON GOES IN—Washington's mastery and influence make possible the sending of Virginia delegates to the Continental Congress.

29 WASHINGTON TAKES THE RISK—Despite the warning coun-

sel of Lord Fairfax, Washington determines to serve the Colonial cause.

30 THE CRISIS AT YORKTOWN—Victory—a dreadful uncertainty, until the flag of truce is seen waving over the besieged British camp.

31 THE DOMINANT FORCE—Certain foreign agents are thwarted in their efforts to align President Washington with the large States.

32 BUILDING A NATION—A popular and frenzied demand for another war against England is quelled by President Washington.

33 HAPPINESS DAY—An atmosphere play concerning Martha Washington's observance of her wedding anniversary after the death of the President.

34 THE BLUE GOBLET—George and his brother, Lawrence, attend a meeting of the "Beefsteak and Tripe Club" in the Barbados, where George frustrates a plot to poison the host.

35 THE VIEW FROM THE WINDOW—A short three-act play wherein Washington escapes betrayal by a supposed friend into British hands.

36 WASHINGTON DANCED—Wherein the Commander-in-Chief employs the dance as a medium of strategy in time of war.

37 THE WASHINGTONS AT HOME—A play set at Mount Vernon in which the Minuet and Colonial music are featured.

Pageants

4 LIVING PAGES FROM WASHINGTON'S DIARY—A candle-time reverie. Washington tableaux interspersed with dialogue and song.

5 MANY WATERS—A pageant in thirteen scenes. The action carries one to the shores of rivers that Washington frequented—beginning and ending on the Potomac at Mount Vernon. Musical interludes.

7 THE GREAT AMERICAN—A community pageant-drama in six actions, portraying Washington as Surveyor, Frontiersman, Legislator, Commander-in-Chief, Statesman, and the Man.

10 THE FATHER OF HIS COUNTRY—Thirteen important events in the life of George Washington for adult presentation.

12 WASHINGTON RETURNS—Four episodes: "The Youth and Adventure"; "The Man and Home"; "The General and Fame"; and "The Statesman."

1 WAKEFIELD—A folk masque of America, being a Midwinter Night's Dream of the Birth of Washington. Illustrated. In two parts: consisting of choruses, processionals, folk songs, dances, pantomime, and tableaux. Participants: 100 to 1,000 children and adults.

I. PAGEANTS AND PLAYS

PUBLISHED BY THE UNITED STATES GEORGE WASHINGTON BICENTENNIAL COMMISSION

Note: Under this General Heading are listed Pageant, Masque, Fantasy, and Playlet. The scenes portrayed in the pageants and plays reflect the spirit of George Washington and his time. Whatever departure is made from strict historical accuracy is done by the authors with the idea of enhancing the dramatic effectiveness of the production.

A. *Pageants*

1. WAKEFIELD. *Percy MacKaye.* A folk masque of America, being a Midwinter Night's Dream of the Birth of Washington. Illustrated with designs by *Arvia MacKaye.*

In two parts: One setting, adapted to both indoor and outdoor presentation. The action, lasting about one hour and a half, is developed by choruses, processionals, folk songs, the speech of poetry, rhythmic movement, the dance, pantomime, and tableaux.

The participants, 100 to 1,000 children and adults, comprise 14 speaking persons (8 men, 4 women, 2 boys), 9 symbolic groups, 13 or more racial groups, and 7 tableau groups. The costumes are of three kinds: symbolic, folk, historic.

Adapted to: E, G, H, L, and community participation.

The masque is a tribute to the spiritual will power of Washington—his deep-rooted goodness, stability, and vision, as "the cedar, rock, and polar star" of his country. It is a modern parable play, dedicated to "The Children of America," both young and grown, in the naive spirit of the mystery play of old. One of its aims is to suggest fresh meanings in the old, familiar song, "The Star-Spangled Banner."

Its dramatic conflict is between WILL and VACILLATION. It sets forth the victorious power of Washington's self-mastery to overcome the chaotic powers of DRIFT. Part 1 pictures the early folk circle of America, menaced by these powers. Part 2 reveals to the same circle (widened to include all world races) how Washington met and averted that menace.

The story tells how the SPIRIT OF WASHINGTON, being free and brave itself, set us free.

2. CHILDHOOD DAYS IN WASHINGTON'S TIME. *Florence C. Fox.* Five episodes, one and a half hours (may be divided into selected episodes, each playing from 15 to 20 minutes). From 30 to 300 characters, equal number of parts for boys and girls, 8 or 10 principal parts for each episode. Two interior, five exterior sets. Adaptable to both indoor and outdoor performance.

Adapted to: B, C, F, G, H, L.

The pageant presents George Washington during the ages of 9 to 16 and his interesting and varied association with the boys and girls of the neighborhood. Five dramatic episodes of that early time are accompanied by appropriate dancing and singing. In them we see Washington defend an unfortunate schoolmaster, rescue a little bond girl from indenture, repent of his anger toward a plantation pickaninny, beg leniency for a poor boy sentenced to the pillory, and deal mercifully with an Indian boy. As we follow him we understand more clearly the influences that shaped his character and appreciate the lessons he learned of courage, forbearance, and fortitude. Finally, we see the boys and girls paying tribute to the flag of today.

3. FROM PICTURE BOOK TOWNE. *Olive M. Price.* One interior scene. About 40 minutes. Boys, 4; girls, 6. Three groups of boys and girls; number in each group optional. They are GUESTS AT MOUNT VERNON, the MINUET DANCERS, and GEORGE WASHINGTON'S SERVANTS.

Adapted to A, B, C, F.

Designed to present to young children interesting scenes from the life of George Washington and days at Mount Vernon. A little schoolgirl is transported from the present to colonial times. The PICTURE-BOOK MAN appears in the room of a charming old house before her and Mammy. He brings a huge picture book, and as each page is turned a quaint scene from George Washington's life is revealed. The closing scene provides for dancing at the first inaugural ball.

4. LIVING PAGES FROM WASHINGTON'S DAIRY—A Candlelight Reverie. *Kathleen Read Coontz.* A series of 10 tableaux interspersed with speaking, acting, songs, and music of the period. Plays about one hour and fifteen minutes. Twenty or more women, or women and men, for tableaux. Several singers, five children (boys or girls, or both). One interior. Written with particular reference to women's clubs.

Adapted to: D, E, G, H, I, J, K, L.

This pageant, written in poetic form, illustrates the following scenes suggested by entries from George Washington's famous Diary: *The Queen's Birthday Ball, The Mother and Her Son, After the*

Hunt, The Committee Meeting, The Return to Mount Vernon, Christmas at Mount Vernon, The President's Levee, Thanksgiving Day, Music Hour with Nellie Custis, Independence Day with Washington. A large reproduction of the Diary itself has an important position upon the stage.

THE ARCHIVIST, brooding over his books by candlelight, comes upon Washington's Diary and is fired with a longing to see the life and love which once inspired the old pages. He invokes THE SPIRIT OF BYGONE YEARS, who answers his call from out of the CURTAIN OF THE PAST. THE QUILLS bring in the DIARY, the little DATES pop out, and the CURTAIN OF THE PAST is drawn aside on the tableaux.

Old pictures suggesting the grouping of the tableaux and the titles of the songs rendered by the SINGERS OF OLDEN SONGS throughout the pageant are included in the text.

5. MANY WATERS. *Marietta Minnigerode Andrews.* Thirteen episodes, about two hours. Men, 13; women, 5; boys, 5; girl, 1. Provides for either large or small groups. A single episode or a series of episodes may be used. Six interior, seven exterior sets.

Adapted to: E, G, H, I, J, L.

The pageant begins and ends as the life of George Washington began and ended—to the sound of waters—and the action carries one to the shores of Popes Creek, the Potomac, the Shenandoah, the Allegheny, the Pamunkey, the Severn, the Charles, the Hudson, the Delaware, the Schuylkill, and the York.

The Music Story for the pageant is arranged by Lyman McCrary and the main motif is suggested by Handel's "Water Music Suite." Other music used is of George Washington's time and consists of various folk tunes, and both chamber and martial music.

In the words of the late author, "The pageant seeks to present the personal character, fortitude, patriotism, humanity, and resourcefulness of the man George Washington; to emphasize the idea of the thirteen Colonies; to portray the tact, sympathy, sound sense, and good breeding of Martha Washington, and George Washington's thoughts on engineering, farming and education, as revealed in confidential discourse with her; the attitude of the great colonial landholders and slaveholders upon the matter of a race in bondage; to show the music of the slave as an integral part of American life; it shows country life in the old South; introduces some of the great foreigners who made our cause their own; it touches upon George Washington's lifelong interest in Free Masonry; it takes us into the studio of Gilbert Stuart; it reaches the founding of the city of Washington—the Federal City—and shows the charming Major L'Enfant who designed the same. The pageant ends where it begins—on the Potomac; the last scene completes the cycle, the elderly couple in the warmth of Mount Vernon, little Nellie Custis tracing in silhouette their shadows cast upon the wall by the candlelight."

6. THE BOYS' GEORGE WASHINGTON. *M. Elizabeth Salois.* Six episodes, one hour. Groups of boys varying from few to many in number. Four exterior, two interior.

Adapted to: B, C, F, G, H, L.

This pageant reveals an American boy explaining to a foreign boy who George Washington was and what he did. The episodes show Washington as a young boy, as a Virginia colonel under General Braddock, his selection as Commander-in-Chief, crossing the Delaware, the First Inauguration, and his refusal of a third term as President.

7. THE GREAT AMERICAN. *Ethel Claire Randall* and *James K. Knudson.* A pageant-drama of George Washington, with prologue, three actions, two interludes, fourteen scenes, and epilogue. Participants include both adults and children of both sexes, and may vary in number from several hundred to several thousand. While it may be adapted to indoor presentation, the pageant as a whole is designed for outdoor production and may be given in its entirety or in part.

Adapted especially to community presentation, although any of the episodes can be presented by schools and organizations in general.

The prologue: *The Call of 1732,* in which the VOICE OF AMERICA summons TRUTH, COURAGE, and DEVOTION, and incarnates them

in the YOUTH GEORGE WASHINGTON. The drama, THE GREAT AMERICAN, in which the three virtues inherent in the youth flower into manhood is revealed in words of wisdom and prophecy, and by acts of leadership and sacrifice.

Epilogue: *The Answer of 1932,* in which the VOICE OF AMERICA summons the United States—a Nation that George Washington founded and bequeathed to the people thereof, and who in this day would so honor and emulate him as to insure the weal and perpetuity of their common country.

The three actions (containing 14 scenes) show George Washington as the Surveyor, the Frontiersman, the Legislator, the Commander-in-Chief, the Statesman, and the Man.

The pageant provides for the use of chorus, band or orchestra, dramatic and lyric rhythmic movement and dance, tableaux, and for the military and mounted figures. The music is of Washington's time, as well as adapted music of other periods.

8. THE MAGIC SQUARE. *Belva Cuzzort.* One episode, 30 minutes. Men, 1; women, 1; boys, 7 or 14; girls, 7 or 13. One interior.

Adapted to 4-H Clubs.

Members of a 4-H Club have attended an exhibit of their products where many of them have won blue ribbons. One 4-H Club member, whom Congress has chosen to represent these farm boys and girls, has never won a first prize. This girl, Mary, is chagrined, as are the other club members. The boy leader alone gives her encouragement. He tells the girl, who must go before Congress to represent the 4-H Clubs, of a magic square he has and which may help her. He adds that possibly George Washington knew of it. Hopefully, Mary takes from him the small paper upon which 25 little squares compose the large square. She sees no sense to it and says so. Later, however, in her sleep, George Washington appears and shows her the magic of the square, a magic that she finds to be a key both to the achievement of George Washington and the 4-H Clubs. In her dream, George and Martha Washington, while viewing the 4-H Club exhibit, apply the magic to the articles displayed until Mary finally catches its significance and, with Martha's encouragement, Mary makes a fine loaf of prize-winning bread and recovers her own and the others confidence in her ability prior to her appearance before Congress as representative of the 4-H Clubs. The pageant stirs interest in Washington and gives rise to a practical plan for applying the magic of the Square to 4-H projects.

9. THE RED-BUD TREE. *Olive M. Price.* One outdoor and one indoor scene, about 40 minutes. Boys, 6; girls, 4. Nine groups of boys and girls; number in each group optional. Suitable for both indoor and outdoor performance.

Adapted to: A, B, C, F.

A pageant-play for children written in the spirit of fantasy. A little school girl and boy meet the RED-BUD SPIRIT, who shows them the heart of Mount Vernon. They see the WATER SPRITES that dwell in the Potomac and the DRYADS who live in the trees on the lawn. The SANDMAN visits them, too, and the HOURS that stay in the GRANDFATHER CLOCK on the stairs. THE GREAT-GREAT-GRANDFATHER SPIDER who hung his cobwebs in the west parlor when George Washington lived tells them old stories, and the VERY OLD LIGHTNING BUG speaks of George Washington's time. MARTHA WASHINGTON'S KITTENS are frightened away by the big FRENCH HOUND sent by Lafayette to Mount Vernon. NELLIE CUSTIS appears in the heart of a rose surrounded by a court of bright BUTTERFLIES, and GENERAL WASHINGTON escorts LADY MARTHA down the wide stairs.

10. THE FATHER OF HIS COUNTRY. *Esther C. and Lawrence A. Averill.* Prologue, five episodes, four interludes, epilogue, full length (may be divided into selected episodes). From 50 to 300 characters, men, women, and children. Adaptable to indoor or outdoor performance.

Adapted to: D, G, H, L.

The pageant is introduced by the MUSE OF HISTORY, a symbolic figure, who recites the Prologue. THE NARRATOR enters to preface each scene with a brief word of explanation giving continuity to the various episodes. Beginning with Washington in the wilderness, we see him encountering the British ideas of warfare; courting the Widow Custis; taking command of the army at Cambridge; authorizing the reading of the Declaration of Independence; about to cross the Delaware; wintering at Valley Forge; welcoming volunteers from beyond the sea; viewing the surrender at Yorktown; refusing a crown; at home at Mount Vernon; taking the oath of office as first President; co-designer and founder of the Federal City; and lastly before the MUSE OF HISTORY pronounces the Finale, "Memorials to Washington."

11. THROUGH THE CALENDAR TO MOUNT VERNON. An historical fantasy or playlet. *Edna M. Dubois.* One act, 35 minutes. Boys, 10; girls, 4, in principal parts; small group of boys and girls. One interior, one inset.

Adapted to: B, L.

A group of children are amusing themselves on Washington's Birthday by reading the great man's "Rules For His Own Guidance in His Fourteenth Year." The boys wish they had lived in Washington's time, but one of the girls longs for Alice-in-Wonderland adventures and suggests their trying to turn back the calendar. Having gone through the calendar, back into George Washington's time, they learn from a group of little negroes that they are at Mount Vernon. Jack and Patsy Custis come looking for Mr. Washington, and the children discover life to be very different in 1932 and 1784. When the Washingtons appear, General Washington questions the newcomers as to the United States in 1932. Guests arrive, the flag is talked of, the minuet danced by the company, and, satisfied, the modern children return through the calendar to 1932.

12. WASHINGTON RETURNS. *Kathleen Read Coontz.* Four episodes of two scenes each—two hours (may be divided into four half-hour performances). 100 or 500 characters; equal number of boys and girls, about 50 speaking parts. Three interior, five exterior sets. Adaptable to both indoor and outdoor performance.

Adapted to: B, C, D, F, G, H, L.

The title suggests the theme of the pageant, which opens with a prelude in which a tiny girl falls asleep in a schoolroom where the pupils are studying history lessons. In dream vision she sees George Washington, glorious in his Continental buff and blue, step forth from behind the Star-Spangled Banner. HISTORY, a character from the past, appears and, calling to the child, whom she names POSTERITY, takes her by the hand and leads her (and the audience), with the aid of the other allegorical characters—ADVENTURE, YOUTH, and HOME—through scenes depicting epochs in the life of George Washington.

First episode—*The Youth and Adventure*—contains two scenes: *Sea Dreams*, which deals with his boyhood ambition for a sea life and his mother's final denial of his plans; and *The Courier*, which pictures his early adventures among the Indians.

Second episode—*The Man and Home*—consists of: Scene 1: *Courtship*, the incident of his meeting with Martha Dandridge Custis; and scene 2: *Mount Vernon*, at home with his family.

Third episode—*The General and Fame*—depicts *The Glory of the Revolution*, in which scene Washington is revealed as Commander-in-Chief of the Continental Army; and *The Gloom of the Revolution*, the darkest days of the war, Valley Forge.

Fourth episode—*The Statesman and Immortality*—pictures in *A Nation's Homage*, Washington's triumphal journey to the Presidency; and in *Friendship's Tribute* reveals the closing scenes of his great life, his last birthday, when friends gather to voice his immortality.

13. WHO'S WHO IN FEBRUARY. An historical fantasy or playlet. *Edna M. Dubois.* One act, 25 minutes. Boys, 3; girls, 5. One interior, one inset.

Adapted to: B, F, L.

Bill and Jane, a boy and girl of grammar-school age, sit lamenting that it is February rather than March or April, when they could be out at their games. In the midst of their grumblings they are startled by the voice of MRS. FEBRUARY, who appears to them, introduces herself, tells them of her family, and finally goes out to

return with her most famous child, FEBRUARY TWENTY-SECOND. Of course, they know whose birthday FEBRUARY TWENTY-SECOND is, and are delighted when she promises to show them what Washington did. Then in three little scenes the story of Our First Flag is told. At the end the children are quite reconciled to its being February rather than March or April, and with MRS. FEBRUARY and FEBRUARY TWENTY-SECOND sing "The Meaning of the Colors" in honor of the flag.

B. *Plays*

The scenes portrayed in the following plays reflect the spirit of George Washington and his time. Whatever departure is made from strict historical accuracy is done by the authors with the idea of enhancing the dramatic effectiveness of the production.

20. MOTHER AND SON. *Major R. B. Lawrence.* One act, 25 minutes. Men, 1; women, 3; boys, 4; girls, 2. One interior.

Adapted to: B, C, F, G, H, J, L.

George Washington's mother, Mary Ball Washington, is discovered grieving over the death of her husband, Augustine Washington. A kindly neighbor brings a loaf of gingerbread and offers assistance. Young George prevents a quarrel among the smaller Washington children over the gingerbread, which they have taken from the pantry on the sly. He censures his younger brothers and sisters. The death of his father leaves George, age 11, next to his mother, since his half brothers had left home, the head of the household. He feels this responsibility deeply, and the final scene reveals him as stepping over the threshold of youth into manhood.

21. THE LURE OF THE SEA. *Maj. R. B. Lawrence.* One act, 40 minutes. Men, 5; women, 1; boys, 3; girls, 1. One interior.

Adapted to: C, D, F, G, H, K, L.

At the age of 15 a passionate longing to go to sea burns within Washington. Encouraged by his half brother, Lawrence, and despite the misgivings of his mother, he makes up his mind to sail. A letter arrives from his uncle, Joseph Ball, of England, warning Mrs. Washington of the folly of allowing George to follow his inclination. This, together with the tearful pleas of his mother, finally prevail over the boy's consuming desire, and George abandons a promising career as a sailor.

22. A YOUTH OF THE FRONTIER. *Maj. R. B. Lawrence.* One act, 45 minutes. Men, 6; women, 1; boys, 2; girls, 2. One exterior.

Adapted to: D, E, G, H, I, K, L.

Washington is sent with a party to the Shenandoah Valley to survey Crown grants owned by Lord Fairfax. "Squatters" have settled on these lands, and Washington comes in contact with a family who protest Lord Fairfax's claim to the property. Washington recognizes the injustice that must result if such pioneers are expelled from the land they have spent years in clearing, and as a consequence he makes it possible for them to acquire the tract by legitimate means. Incidentally, he furthers a pretty love affair between two young mountaineers.

23. MATCHING WITS. *Maj. R. B. Lawrence.* One act, 40 minutes. Men, 7; women, 1. One interior.

Adapted to: E, G, I, K, L.

Washington goes to Fort Le Boeuf with Governor Dinwiddie's summons to the French to leave the country of the Ohio. St. Pierre, French commandant of the fort, receives Washington and his party courteously, but tries to overcome the young Virginian with an excess of entertainment and to win over the "Half King" to the French cause. He finds Washington more than a match for him strategically and is foiled in his attempt upon the Indian's allegiance.

24. VINDICATED. *Maj. R. B. Lawrence.* One act, 40 minutes. Men, 10; women, 5. One interior.

Adapted to: D, E, G, H, I, K, L.

Washington's withdrawal from Fort Necessity was not a surrender, as was thought by Governor Dinwiddie and his coterie. This play is based on recently discovered evidence which proves that the French were as eager for withdrawal as Washington, who only agreed to leave Fort Necessity when his food and ammunition became exhausted. Although he was allowed to leave the fort with honors of war, a clause inserted in the articles of surrender by the French commandant nearly proved his undoing. Owing to culpable oversight on the part of Washington's interpreter, the clause branded Washington—over his own signature—as the assassin in a previous skirmish of a French officer. Governor Dinwiddie and certain of his aristocratic friends slur Washington because of his supposed cowardice. Washington's friends, however, stand by him, and in the end Washington is "vindicated."

25. I Follow Washington. *Maj. R. B. Lawrence.* One act, 35 minutes. Men, 14; women, 1. One interior.

Adapted to: E, G, I, K, L.

General Braddock's march on Fort Duquesne, the perils of the journey, the overbearing character of Braddock and his subordinates, and the part played by the Indians and Colonists are delineated, and Washington is shown as a central figure. His grim fortitude in withstanding the slurs and rebuffs of Braddock, his influence over the disgruntled Indians, and his final decision to serve the King despite the lack of consideration he receives from the British officers make up the warp of the play pattern. The woof is supplied by the other characters—in a love scene, a challenge, and finally in the determination of Captain Croghan and his Colonist van to "follow Washington."

26. That Is My Answer. *Maj. R. B. Lawrence.* One act, 40 minutes. Men, 7; women, 2. One interior.

Adapted to: E, G, H, I, K, L.

A group of Virginia Royalists opposed all moves on the part of the Colonies toward greater representation, lower taxes, and increased liberty. Patrick Henry, with his doctrines of freedom, is pronounced anathema and treasonable. An intrigue is set afoot to enlist Washington, a member of the Virginia House of Burgesses, to lead the Royalists. In the final scene, the voice of Patrick Henry is heard above the furore of the assembly, crying: "If this be treason, make the most of it!" To this declaration of patriotism Washington refers those who would bribe him into position and power in the King's cause, saying: "Gentlemen, that is my answer."

27. The Indian's Prophecy. *Maj. R. B. Lawrence.* One act, 25 minutes. Men, 7; total, optional. One exterior.

Adapted to: C, D, E, F, G, H, I, K, L.

In the summer of 1770 Washington made an expedition to the Ohio to claim certain lands that had been apportioned to Colonial soldiers. The voyagers encamped at the mouth of the Great Kanawha River. Here Washington is approached with great reverence by an old Sachem, who makes it known that he was himself one of the warriors who lay in ambush on the Monongahela and wrought such havoc in Braddock's army. He also declares the Indians had repeatedly singled out Washington in the battle and fired upon him without success. Whence they concluded that he is under the protection of the Great Spirit and can not be slain in battle. Said the Sachem: "Washington will become the chief of many nations, and a people yet unborn will hail him as the founder of a mighty empire."

28. Washington Goes In. *Maj. R. B. Lawrence.* One act, 30 minutes. Men, 8; women, 2. One interior.

Adapted to: E, G, H, I, K, L.

Whether to join the other Colonies and send delegates to the first Continental Congress is the issue before the Virginia convention in August, 1774. Patrick Henry, Peyton Randolph, and Richard Henry Lee realize that if the silent Washington would speak the other Conservatives would fall in line and a majority for the measure would result. The action of the play is based on the circumstances and conditions that finally arouse Washington to a statement which settles the point at issue. The subplot shows how the son of a Tory household turns Whig. The scene is laid in the famous Raleigh Tavern at Williamsburg, Va., with students of *William and Mary College* having a part in the denouement.

29. Washington Takes the Risk. *Maj. R. B. Lawrence.* One act, 35 minutes. Men, 14; women, 6; girls, 1. One interior.

Adapted to: E, G, H, I, K, L.

Washington and his old friend and patron, Lord Fairfax, together with members of the Washington household and friends, are dining at Mount Vernon when startled by the "momentous news from the North" that the King's forces and New England Minute Men have clashed at Lexington in a bloody encounter. War is considered inevitable. Lord Fairfax, realizing that George Washington is the most likely choice of Congress as a leader for the "rebel" army, endeavors to dissuade his protege from aligning himself with the Colonial cause. "Failure," exclaims Lord Fairfax, "would mean forfeiture of your estates, confiscation of your revenues—a traitor's hideous doom!" To which Washington replies that he is ready and willing, if his country calls, to "take the risk," since he "stands against all who stand against liberty."

30. The Crisis at Yorktown. *Maj. R. B. Lawrence.* One act, 45 minutes. Men, 15; women, 2; total, optional. One exterior.

Adapted to: E, G, H, I, K. L.

Yorktown—besieged by Colonial and French forces, the river approach guarded by Count de Grasse and a French fleet; Cornwallis "bottled up," on the verge of capitulation—and victory certain, Count de Grasse receives orders from his French superiors to withdraw his men from General Rochambeau's land forces, thus leaving the issue a dreadful uncertainty. To add to the ill news, Clinton, the British General who held New York, is reported arriving at the Capes to strengthen Cornwallis. Immediate action is imperative. Washington is about to issue an order commanding the storming of the bulwarks of Yorktown en masse, himself leading the van, when the white flag of truce is seen flying over the British camp. Victory and peace!

31. The Dominant Force. *Maj. R. B. Lawrence.* One act, 35 minutes. Men, 13; women, 2. One interior.

Adapted to: E, G, H, I, K, L.

Mistress Bingham entertains. She has as house guests a Madam Blauvelt, of New Orleans, and this evening members of the Committee of Compromise are met in secret at her house. Madam Blauvelt, however, makes it her business to overhear and report the findings to a Mr. Darnell. Employed by foreign governments, the pair search for a means of preventing the hoped for reconciliation between the large and small States which will make possible a strong Federal Government in America. Darnell goes to General Washington with plans for financing the canal that Washington hopes to build—the plans, of course, to depend upon the establishment of a republic. In this way they hope to line up Washington with the large States and prevent the reconciliation. But Washington senses the intrigue and adroitly but forcefully suggests the sailing of the foreign agents on the good ship *Bonaventura*, now in port; whereupon a compromise is effected.

32. Building a Nation. *Maj. R. B. Lawrence.* One act, 38 minutes. Men, 9; women, 3. One interior.

Adapted to: E, G, H, I, K, L.

There was a demand for war against England; mobs of French sympathizers formed on the Philadelphia streets; popular feeling in sections ran so strongly in favor of French republicanism that many good men were greatly incensed against President Washington for his refusal to break the neutrality treaty. To aggravate matters, "Citizen" Edmond Genet, the French minister plenipotentiary, sought to turn the already restive Nation against its President by publicly excoriating Hamilton and his Federalist doctrines, and the President's seeming sympathy therefor. Washington was faced with the problem of rescuing the Nation from this maelstrom and bringing order from chaos. How he achieved this is set forth in the play "Building a Nation."

33. Happiness Day. *Maj. R. B. Lawrence.* One act, 20 minutes. Four women, 1 baby. One interior.

Adapted to: E, G, H, I, J, K, L.

The forty-second anniversary of Washington's betrothal to Martha Custis fell upon May 24, 1800, five months after the death of Washington. The scene opens with Martha seated in her little rocking chair before the dormer window which looks out on the tomb of her husband. The theme deals with the future disposal of

Washington's letters to his wife. Nellie Custis Lewis makes a touching appeal that the letters be saved for her infant daughter and posterity. Martha, grieving over the loss of her husband, torn by conflicting emotions, aroused by the significance of the day, faithful to the last, makes her decision.

34. THE BLUE GOBLET. *James K. Knudson.* One act, one hour and ten minutes. Men, 9 or 13. One interior.

Adapted to: D, E, G, I, K, L.

Relatively little is known concerning George Washington's first and only journey beyond the shores of America—his trip to the Barbados with his elder half-brother, Lawrence. It is recorded in George's diary, however, that during his sojourn in the Barbados he attended dinner meetings of the "Beefsteak and Tripe Club"—a society no doubt composed of many of the prominent men of the island. It is safe to assume, for the sake of a dramatic plot, that Washington, a keen and perceptive youth at the time, must have noticed, together with other things, the deplorable conditions existing among the slaves and indentures on the island. This play is set in the tropical home of one of the members of the "Beefsteak and Tripe Club." Washington accidentally discovers a plot to poison the host, but also hears from the slave plotters such harrowing tales of hunger and privation that he is instilled with a definite sympathy for them. Hence his problem is twofold—to prevent the master from discovering the plot and to keep him from drinking the contents of the blue goblet, and also to save the slaves from the gibbet. Clever and quick headwork enables him to achieve this end.

35. THE VIEW FROM THE WINDOW. *Kathleen Read Coontz.* Three short acts, 1 hour 30 minutes. Men, 8; women, 1; small group of soldiers. Two interiors.

Adapted to: D, E, G, I, K, L.

The play is based upon a traditional incident when Washington maintained headquarters near West Point, a nest for Tory sympathizers. The Commander-in-Chief believes his friends of long standing, Colonel and Mrs. Morris, to be loyal to the cause of liberty. The colonel's friendship, however, cloaks his pro-British activities, unbeknown even to his wife. The colonel "jollies" Washington about coming to the home of a friend guarded, and the general promises to come to River Manor unattended the following Thursday as a token of his entire confidence in his friend. In the second act, Pat, the Irish peg-legged butler at the manor, turns up

at Washington's headquarters with a letter retrieved from a British sergeant leaving Morris's study. The letter reveals the colonel's perfidious plot to deliver Washington into British hands. George Washington comes to River Manor unattended. British soldiers enter. The traitorous host orders these soldiers to seize the general, but fortunately they are Washington's own soldiers in disguise, ordered by him to carry out the colonel's evil designs and thus reveal his true colors.

36. WASHINGTON DANCED. *France Goldwater.* One-act play, 45 minutes. Men, 8; women, 2. One exterior.

Adapted to: D, E, G, I, J, K, L.

The play is based on tradition and introduces such noted figures as General and Mrs. Washington and Nathan Hale. The scene is laid at the home of Robert Morris in New York. Even during the days of war General Washington is shown as employing the dance as a medium of strategy.

37. THE WASHINGTONS AT HOME. *Dwight Marfield.* A one-act play with music. About one hour. Men, 7; women, 6. One interior set.

Adapted to: D, E, G, I, J, K, L.

The scene is laid at Mount Vernon February 22, 1799. It is a festive occasion with animated dialogue, in which music plays a leading part. The music is of George Washington's time, and is tendered in the form of solos, duet, quartet, violin and spinet, harpsichord or piano. The minuet is danced.

38. 'TWIXT CUP AND LIP. *Pauline Hopkins and Ellen Garrigues.* The prize-winning play of the Daughters of the American Revolution Bicentennial Play Contest. Forty minutes. Men, 9; women, 1. One interior.

Adapted to: D, E, G, I, K, L.

General Washington and his generals meet under the roof of the Sam Fraunces—a tavern in New York City—on June 20, 1776. The atmosphere is tense with the approaching and inevitable struggle for the possession of New York. Hints of a Tory plot to burn the town and assassinate General Washington are rife. The plot of the play centralizes around one Hickey, a traitorous body guard of General Washington who almost succeeds in poisoning the Commander and is only foiled in his wicked scheme by the timely action of Phoebe, the innkeeper's patriotic daughter who loved Hickey, and Billy, Washington's faithful Negro body servant.

II. PUBLISHERS' PAGEANTS AND PLAYS

[The asterisk (*) indicates that the pageant is contained in a collection. See page 571. The letters refer to the Reference Index on page 559. For publishers' addresses, see page 570.]

A. Pageants

50. AMERICA TRIUMPHANT. *Constance D'Arcy Mackay.* Six episodes, full length. Approximation: Men, 25; women, 11; extras: boys and girls; total cast, optional. Six exterior sets. $1.25. Royalty, $25 per performance. Two episodes show Washington. Publisher: D. Appleton & Co.

Adapted to: D, E, G, H, I, K, L.

51. ANOTHER WASHINGTON. *Julian Lee.* Forty-five minutes. Approximation: 26 boys, 36 girls; total cast, optional. One exterior. 35 cents. Publisher: The Dramatic Publishing Co.

Adapted to: C, D, G, I, L.

52. BICENTENNIAL PAGEANT IN HONOR OF GEORGE WASHINGTON. *Beatrice Gaule.* Fourteen episodes, full length. Total cast optional, figures 50 to 500 men, women, and children. Cyclorama for exteriors and interiors. 25 cents. Royalty, $5. Publisher: Dramatic Publishers, Briggsville, Wis.

Adapted to: D, E, G, H, L.

53. A COLONIAL GARDEN PARTY. *Walter Ben Hare.* One episode, 30 minutes. Men, 8; women, 7; boys and girls optional. One exterior. 35 cents. Publisher: Walter H. Baker Co.

Adapted to: D, E, G, H, I, L.

54. A COLONIAL DAY PROGRAM: THE SPIRIT OF WASHINGTON.

Kathryn de Luhery. Two scenes, 30 minutes. Characters, 7. One interior. Publisher: The Progress Publishing Co.

Adapted to: D, E, G, H, I, L.

55. *IN DAYS OF WASHINGTON. *Effa E. Preston.* One episode, 25 minutes. Men, 10; women, 5; boys, 2; girls, 2; total cast, optional. One interior. 40 cents. Publisher: F. A. Owen Publishing Co.

Adapted to: C, D, F, G, H, L.

56. THE DRAMA OF AMERICAN INDEPENDENCE. *J. L. McBrien.* Ten episodes; full length. Men, 85; women, 25; boys, 20; girls, 20; total cast, optional. Eight interior, two exterior. 50 cents. Publisher: National Education Association.

Adapted to: D, E, G, H, I, K, L.

57. *GEORGE WASHINGTON, THE SPIRIT OF AMERICANIZATION. *Phyllis Marschall.* Four episodes, full length. Cast includes men, women, and children; total cast, optional. One exterior. $2.50. Royalty, $30. Publisher: Dodd, Mead & Co.

Adapted to: D, E, G, H, I, L.

58. IN THE HEARTS OF HIS COUNTRYMEN. *Marion Holbrook.* Five episodes, one hour. Men, women, and children—200 to 500. 25 cents. Publisher: National Recreation Association, Community Drama Service.

Adapted to: C, D, F, G, H, L.

59. PILGRIM'S PRIDE. *Elizabeth Hines Hanley.* One episode, full length. 50 to 150 men, women, and children, optional. One exterior. $1. Publisher: Ivan Bloom Hardin Co.
Adapted to: D, E, G, H, L.

60. *PAGEANT OF INAUGURATION OF PRESIDENT GEORGE WASHINGTON. *May Pashley Harris.* Five episodes, 1 hour. Sixty men, 20 women, 20 boys, 30 girls. Two interior, four exterior. 25 cents. Publishers: Walter H. Baker Co., National Recreation Association.
Adapted to: C, D, E, G, H, L.

61. *PANORAMIC DIALOGUES AND SCENES OF THE REVOLUTION. *Willis N. Bugbee.* Nine episodes, 45 minutes. Boys, 125; girls, 21. Three interior, six exterior sets. 40 cents. Publisher: The Penn Publishing Co.
Adapted to: B, C, D, F, G, H, L.

62. PATRIOTIC PAGEANT FOR WASHINGTON DAY. *Miss L. B. Duncan.* Six episodes, 30 minutes. Cast, optional. One exterior. 50 cents. Publisher: The Bruce Publishing Co.
Adapted to: B, C, F, G, H, L.

63. POLLY AND THE PAGES. *Karin Sundelof-Asbrand.* One episode, 30 minutes. Boys, 5; girls, 10; total, optional. One interior set. 35 cents. Publisher: Eldridge Entertainment House.
Adapted to: B, C, F, G, H, L.

64. *ROSES OF LOVE FOR ALTAR OF SERVICE. *Margaret Emma McNinch.* One episode, 25 minutes. 28 boys or girls or both. One interior. 79 cents. Publisher: Means & McLean.
Adapted to: B, C, F, G, H, L.

65. *THE SEVEN AGES OF WASHINGTON. *Maude Stewart Beagle.* Seven episodes, 30 minutes. Men, 20; women, 12; boys, 3; total, optional. Two interior, five exterior sets. $2.50. Royalty, $5 per performance. Publisher: Dodd, Mead & Co.
Adapted to: B, C, D, F, G, H, L.

66. THE SPIRIT OF INDEPENDENCE. *Mabel Mason Carlton and Henry Fisk Carlton.* Eight episodes, 45 minutes. Boys, 45; girls, 11; extras, optional. 80 cents. Publisher: Charles Scribner's Sons.
Adapted to: B, F, G, H, L.

67. UNIFIED BY THE SPIRIT OF PRAYER. THE LIFE OF GEORGE WASHINGTON. *Sister M. Agatha O'Neill.* Fourteen episodes, two hours. Total cast optional, 50 to 500, either mixed or all women. Cyclorama for all scenes. Royalty, $5. Publisher: Catholic Dramatic Movement.
Adapted to: Catholic schools and organizations.

68. *A WASHINGTON'S BIRTHDAY PAGEANT. *Marguerite Merington.* Three episodes, 25 minutes. Men, 12; women, 4; boys, 2; girls, 1. Three interior sets. $1.50. Royalty, $10. Publisher: Duffield & Green.
Adapted to: C, D, G, H, L.

69. *WASHINGTON'S BIRTHDAY. *Marion Kennedy and Katharine Bemis.* One episode, 15 minutes. Nine boys or girls. $1.50. Publisher: A. S. Barnes & Co.
Adapted to: A, B, F, G, H, L.

70. GEORGE WASHINGTON OF YOUNG AMERICA. *Esther Willard Bates.* Complete presentation of the pageant requires from two to two and one-half hours. Men, 43; women, 7; symbolic figures, 20 men and women. Large or small groups of Indians, soldiers, colonial men and women and children. Members of Congress, wedding guests, 48 States. Provision is made for music of the time of George Washington and appropriate adapted selections. Publisher: Walter H. Baker Co.
Adapted to: D, E, G, L.

71. THE WASHINGTON PAGEANT-REVUE. *Willis N. Bugbee.* Six episodes, 40 minutes. 12 men, 8 women, 1 boy; total, optional. One interior, one exterior set. 35 cents. Publisher: The Willis N. Bugbee Co.
Adapted to: B, C, F, G, H, I, J, L.

72. WASHINGTON PREEMINENT. *Alice Hunt Bartlett.* Thirty-

[The asterisk (*) indicates that the play is contained in a collection. See page 571. The letters refer to the Reference Index on page 559.]

five scenes of varied length. Cast varies in size with scenes. $4. Publisher: Brentano's.
Adapted to: E, G, H, I, K, L.

73. WASHINGTON MARCHES ON. *Olive M. Price.* Three parts, fifteen scenes, full length, musical background. Men, 35; women, 15; total cast, optional. Seven interior, eight exterior (simple sets). $1. Royalty, $10. Publisher: Samuel French.
Adapted to: E, G, H, I, K, L.

74. *THE YORK PAGEANT. *Lilian White Spencer.* Action V, Valley Forge, suitable. Eight speaking parts; total cast, optional. 35 minutes. One exterior. $2.50. Royalty to be arranged with author. Publisher: Dodd, Mead & Co.
Adapted to: E, G, H, I, K, L.

75. THE SPIRIT OF WASHINGTON. *Emma McNinch.* One episode. Characters, 50 men and women. One interior. 25 cents. Royalty, $5. Publisher: W. S. Peterson.
Adapted to: G, J, L.

B. *Plays*

100. ABOUT CANDLE-LIGHT TIMES. *Dorothy C. Allan.* One act, 40 minutes. Men, 34; women, 4. One interior. Publishers: Walter H. Baker Co.
Adapted to: D, E, G, H, L.

101. *ALL ABOUT WASHINGTON. *Julian Lee.* One act, 15 minutes. Boys, 6; girls, 3. One interior set. Publisher: Dramatic Publishing Co.
Adapted to: B, C, F, G, H, L.

102. ALL BECAUSE HE COULD NOT TELL A LIE. *Harry C. Eldridge.* One act, 10 minutes. Boys, 3; girls, 1. One interior. 40 cents. Publisher: Eldridge Entertainment House.
Adapted to: A, B, F, H, L.

103. AMERICANS ALL. *Fannie Barnett Linsky.* One act, 30 minutes. Boys, 13; girls, 5. One interior, one exterior. 25 cents. Publisher: Eldridge Entertainment House.
Adapted to: A, B, F, H, L.

104. *BACKWOODS. *Marion Holbrook.* One act, 15 minutes. Boys, 4; extras, optional. One exterior. Publishers: Walter H. Baker Co., Dodd, Mead & Co.
Adapted to: B, F, G, L.

105. *BEFORE FORT DUQUESNE. *Anna Jane Harnwell.* One act, 30 minutes. Men, 7; women, 1. One exterior. $2.50. Royalty, $5. Publisher: Dodd, Mead & Co.
Adapted to: D, E, G, I, K, L.

106. *BEING LIKE WASHINGTON. *Ruth L. Jenkins.* One act, 10 minutes. Women, 2; boys and girls, optional. One interior, one exterior. In Margaret A. Whiting's *Plays and Pageants for Children*, vol. 1, obtainable at libraries.
Adapted to: B, C, F, G, H, J, L.

107. BETSY ROSS MAKING THE FLAG. *Evelyn Hoxie.* Two acts, 20 minutes. Men, 3; women, 3. One exterior. 50 cents. Publisher: Walter H. Baker Co.
Adapted to: B, F, G, H, L.

108. *BRANDYWINE. *Marion Holbrook.* One act, 15 minutes. Men, 5. One exterior. $2.50. Publishers: Walter H. Baker Co., Dodd, Mead & Co.
Adapted to: B, C, F, H, L.

109. A BRAVE LITTLE TOMBOY. *Elizabeth F. Guptell.* Four scenes, 35 minutes. Men, 4; boys, 4; girls, 5. 35 cents. Publisher: Eldridge Entertainment House.
Adapted to: C, D, F, G, L.

110. *CAPTAIN WASHINGTON. *Olive White Garvey.* One act, 40 minutes. Men, 5. One exterior. $2.50. Royalty, $5. Publisher: Dodd, Mead & Co.
Adapted to: C, D, F, L.

111. *CAVALIER. *Olive M. Price.* One act, 20 minutes. Men, 4; women, 2. One interior. $1.75. Publisher: Walter H. Baker Co.
Adapted to: E, G, H, L.

112. *THE CHOICE. *Jerry Emerson.* One act, 12 minutes.

Men, 2; women, 2. One interior. $2.50. Permission from Geraldine B. Emerson, Winnetka, Ill. Publisher: Dodd, Mead & Co.
Adapted to: C, D, F, G, L.

113. *CLOSING SCENE OF CONSTITUTIONAL CONVENTION. From *Help-U Washington, Lincoln Collection.* One act, 15 minutes. Fifteen to 50 men, optional. One interior. 40 cents. Publisher: Eldridge Entertainment House.
Adapted to: B, C, F, G, H, I, L.

114. *COLONIAL TIMES. *Margaret E. Whiting.* Five short acts, 15 minutes. Men, 21; women, 17; girls, 1. Three interior, three exterior. In *Plays and Pageants for Children,* vol. 1, obtainable at libraries.
Adapted to: B, C, F, L.

115. *COMMANDER-IN-CHIEF. *Mary Ellen Whitney.* One act, 15 minutes. Men, 7; women, 2; girls, 1; total, optional. Two interior. 90 cents. Publisher: Beckley-Cardy Co.
Adapted to: B, C, F.

116. *THE CRITICAL UTTERANCE. *Julia M. Martin.* One act, 15 minutes. Men, 10 or more. One interior. 40 cents. Publisher: Eldridge Entertainment House.
Adapted to: D, F, G, H, L.

117. CRINOLINE AND CANDLELIGHT. *Jean Lee Latham.* One act, 25 minutes. Boys, 7; girls, 7. One interior. 35 cents. Publisher: Dramatic Publishing Co.
Adapted to: D, E, G, I.

118. *THE DOLL THAT SAVED AN ARMY. *Edyth M. Wormwood.* One act, 1 hour. Men, 12; women, 6. One interior, two exterior. Publisher: Walter H. Baker Co.
Adapted to: D, F, G, J, L.

119. THE DRAMA OF AMERICAN INDEPENDENCE. *Ethan Allen.* Five acts, full length. One hundred and fifty mixed characters. Eighteen interior, 20 exterior—only scenes in which Washington appears producible. Obtainable at libraries.
Adapted to: E, G, H.

120. *EAGLESFEATHER. *Madalene D. Barnum.* Three acts, 30 minutes. Men, 14. Three exterior. $1.25. Publisher: Barse & Co.
Adapted to: C, D, F, L.

121. *THE EVACUATION OF BOSTON. *Esther Willard Bates.* One act, 30 minutes. Men, 7; women, 6; extras, optional. One interior. Publisher: Walter H. Baker Co.
Adapted to: C, D, F, I, L.

122. *THE FALL OF BRITISH TYRANNY. *John Leacock.* Scenes 3 and 4 of Act V only applicable. Twenty minutes. Men, 7. One interior. $3. Publisher: E. P. Dutton & Co.
Adapted to: D, E, G, I, K, L.

123. *THE FIRST AMERICAN FLAG. *Goffrey F. Morgan.* Two acts. Boys, 3; girls, 1. One interior. 50 cents. Obtainable in libraries in collection *The First Flag and Other Patriotic Plays.*
Adapted to: B, C, F, L.

124. *THE FIRST FLAG. *Marguerite Merington.* One act, 20 minutes. Men, 3; women, 3; boys, 1. One interior. $1.50. Royalty, $10. Publisher: Duffield & Green.
Adapted to: A, B, F, H, L.

125. *THE FIRST IN WAR. *Eleanor Hubbard.* One act, 5 minutes. Boys, 4. 84 cents. Publisher: Benj. H. Sanborn & Co.
Adapted to: A, B.

126. FOLLOWING THE FLAG. *Willis N. Bugbee.* One act, 12 minutes. Men, 7; women, 2; any number of boys and girls. One interior, one exterior. 40 cents. Publisher: F. A. Owen Publishing Co.
Adapted to: B, C, F, L.

127. *FOR HIS COUNTRY. *Rea Woodman.* One act, 10 minutes. Men, 4. One interior. $2.50. Permission of author. Publisher: Dodd, Mead & Co.
Adapted to: B, C, D, F, L.

128. *FRIENDS IN NEED. *Constance Cottin Cooke.* Two acts, 30 minutes. Men, 16; women, 3; boys, 1; extras optional. Two exterior. 60 cents. Publisher: Walter H. Baker Co.
Adapted to: B, C, F, L.

129. *GENERAL GEORGE WASHINGTON. *Perry Boyer Corneau.* One act, 20 minutes. Men, 11. One interior. $2.50. Royalty, $5 per performance. Publisher: Dodd, Mead & Co.
Adapted to: E, G, H, I, K, L.

130. *THE GENERAL GOES HOME. *Lucy Barton.* One act, 30 minutes. Girls, 11. One exterior. $2.50. Publisher: Dodd, Mead & Co.
Adapted to: C, D, E, J, L (especially for all women groups).

131. GEORGE WASHINGTON. *Mary Hazleton Wade.* Nine acts (short), 1 hour. Men, 13; women, 11; boys, 7; girls, 5. Three interior, seven exterior. Publisher: Richard G. Badger.
Adapted to: B, C, G, L.

132. GEORGE WASHINGTON. *T. B. Weaver.* One act, 15 minutes. Number of characters optional. One interior. 50 cents. Publisher: The Bruce Publishing Co.
Adapted to: B, C, F, H, L.

133. *GEORGE WASHINGTON AT THE DELAWARE. *Percy MacKaye.* One act, 20 minutes. Men, 6; boys, 1; girls, 1. One exterior. $2.50. Permission from author. Publishers: Dodd, Mead & Co., D. Appleton & Co., Samuel French.
Adapted to: E, G, H, K, L.

134. *GEORGE WASHINGTON AT THE HELM OF STATE. *Minnie A. Niemeier.* One act, 30 minutes. Boys, 6; girls, 6. One interior. $2. Publisher: Noble & Noble.
Adapted to: B, C, F, H, L.

135. *GEORGE WASHINGTON DOES NOT GO TO SEA. *Clara M. Love.* One act, 15 minutes. Men, 5; boys, 11. One interior. Royalty, $2.50. Publisher: Ginn & Co.
Adapted to: C, D, F, G, H, L.

136. GEORGE WASHINGTON'S DREAM. *Minet Blackwell Moore.* One act, 15 minutes. Boys, 2; girls, 12. One interior. 25 cents. Publisher: The Grade Teacher.
Adapted to: A, B.

137. *GEORGE WASHINGTON'S FORTUNE. *Constance D'Arcy Mackay.* One act, 30 minutes. Men, 5; women, 1. One exterior. $1.75. Publisher: Henry Holt & Co.
Adapted to: C, D, F, J, L.

138. *GEORGE WASHINGTON, MIDSHIPMAN. *Alta E. Thompson.* One act, 45 minutes. Boys, 4; girls, 5. One interior. $2.50. Royalty, $5. Publisher: Dodd, Mead & Co.
Adapted to: C, D, F, L.

139. *GEORGE WASHINGTON'S WEDDING. *William Archer.* One act, 15 minutes. Men, 10; women, 5. One interior. $2.50. Publisher: Dodd, Mead & Co.
Adapted to: D, E, G, H, I, J, L.

140. GOOD GEORGE WASHINGTON. *Mayme R. Bitney.* One act, 15 minutes. Boys, 5; girls, 6. One interior. 40 cents. Publisher: Paine Publishing Co.
Adapted to: B, F.

141. *THE GREAT GENERAL'S LESSON TO THE LITTLE CORPORAL. *Eleanore Hubbard.* One act, 5 minutes. Boys, 6. One exterior. 84 cents. Publisher: Benj. H. Sanborn & Co.
Adapted to: B, F.

142. A HALF HOUR WITH WASHINGTON. *Harriette Wilbur.* One act, 20 minutes. Men, 1; boys, 8; girls, 9; total, optional. One interior. 25 cents. Publisher: Eldridge Entertainment House.
Adapted to: B.

143. *HARDSHIPS AT VALLEY FORGE. *F. Ursula Payne.* One act, 10 minutes. Boys, 4. One exterior. $1.50. Royalty, 10 per cent. Publisher: Harper & Brothers.
Adapted to: B, F.

144. THE HEIR OF MOUNT VERNON. *Effie Louise Koogle.* Four scenes, 1 hour and a half. Boys, 8; girls, 8; total, optional. Two exterior, 2 interior. 35 cents. Publisher: Edgar S. Werner, March Brothers.
Adapted to: C, D, E, G, I, K, L.

145. HIS FIRST COMMISSION. *Rea Woodman.* One act, 15 minutes. Boys, 4. One interior. 25 cents. Publisher: Old Tower Press.
Adapted to: B, C, F, L.

146. HISTORY'S PATRIOTIC PLAY. *Lillian H. Campbell.* One act, 20 minutes. Men, 12; women, 2; any number boys and girls. One interior. 40 cents. Publisher: F. A. Owen Publishing Co.
    Adapted to: B, C, F.

147. LAFAYETTE REMEMBERS. *Perry Boyer Corneau.* One act, 20 minutes. Men, 3; boys, 6; total, optional. One exterior. 25 cents. Publisher: Old Tower Press.
    Adapted to: B, C, F, L.

148. *LAFAYETTE, THE FRIEND OF AMERICA. *Eleanore Hubbard.* Three short acts, 15 minutes. Boys, 4; total, optional. One interior. 84 cents. Publisher: Benj. H. Sanborn & Co.
    Adapted to: A, B, F.

149. LIKE AS A FATHER. *Lidian Moore.* One act, 30 minutes. Men, 5; women, 2. One interior. Publisher: Address author, 680 Harwood Drive, Des Moines, Iowa.
    Adapted to: E, G, I, K, L.

150. *THE LITTLE GENERAL. *Marion Holbrook.* One act, 10 minutes. Boys, 4; girls, 3. One exterior. $2.50. Publisher: Dodd, Mead & Co.
    Adapted to: B, C, F, L.

151. *LITTLE GEORGE WASHINGTON'S VALENTINE. *Patten Beard.* One act, 20 minutes. Boys, 5; girls, 1. One exterior. $2.50. Publishers: Dodd, Mead & Co., Beckley-Cardy Co.
    Adapted to: A, B, F, L.

152. *LITTLE LADY DRESDEN. *Olive M. Price.* One act, 20 minutes. Boys, 4; girls, 5. One interior. $1.25. Publisher: Samuel French.
    Adapted to: B, F.

153. THE LITTLE PATRIOT. *Margaret Getchell Parsons.* Three acts, 45 minutes. Boys, 4; girls, 1. One interior. 50 cents. Publisher: The Woman's Press.
    Adapted to: B, C, F, L.

154. MADAME CHERRY TREE SPILLS THE BEANS. *Peggy Reece.* One Act, 25 minutes. Boys, 7; girls, 9. One interior. 37 cents. Publisher: Means & McLean.
    Adapted to: B, F.

155. *MAKING OUR FLAG. *Margaret C. Fairlie.* Two short acts, 15 minutes. Boys, 5; girls, 4; total, optional. One interior, one exterior. 40 cents. Publisher: F. A. Owen Publishing Co.
    Adapted to: A, B, F.

156. *THE MAKING OF THE CONSTITUTION. *Hague and Chalmers.* Five acts, 1 hour. Boys, 55. One interior. $1.16. Publisher: University Publishing Co.
    Adapted to: B, F, G, H, L.

157. *MAKING A FLAG. *Bertha E. Bush.* One act, 20 minutes. Boys, 2; girls, 3. One interior. 50 cents. Obtainable at libraries in collection *The First Flag and Other Patriotic Plays.*
    Adapted to: B, F.

158. *THE MAKING OF THE FLAG. *Rosamond Kimball.* One act, 15 minutes. Boys, 10; girls, 4. Two interior. $2.50. Publisher: Dodd, Mead & Co.
    Adapted to: B, C, D, F, L.

159. MAKING THE FIRST AMERICAN FLAG. *Florence M. Miller.* Three acts. Boys, 1; girls, 1. One interior. 50 cents. Publisher: The Educational Publishing Co. Obtainable at libraries in collection *The First Flag and Other Patriotic Plays.*
    Adapted to: B, F.

160. MAKING THE FLAG. *Anna May Kimball.* One act, 20 minutes. Men, 2; women, 1; or boys, 2; girls, 1. One interior. 50 cents. Publisher: The Bruce Publishing Co.
    Adapted to: B, C, F, H, L.

161. *THE MAN WHO BORE THE BURDEN. *Augusta Stevenson.* Three acts, 1 hour and a half. Men, 47; women, 7; boys, 6; total, optional. Four interior, one exterior. $1. Publisher: Houghton Mifflin Co.
    Adapted to: D, E, G, H, K, L.

162. MARSE GAWGE, DE LUBINES' MAN. *May L. Treadwell.* One act, 10 minutes. Boys, 2; girls, 9. One interior. 40 cents. Publisher: F. A. Owen Publishing Co.
    Adapted to: B, C, F.

163. MARTHA WASHINGTON. *William Archer.* Eight scenes, full length. Men, 31; women, 16; total, optional. Three interior, one exterior. Publisher: Constable & Co. (Ltd.). Obtainable only at libraries.
    Adapted to: D, G, H, J, K, L.

164. MASSA WASHUMTON AT HOME. *Fannie E. Price-Wilson.* One act, 20 minutes. Men, 2; women, 3; girls, 1; total, optional. One interior, one exterior. 25 cents. From *Normal Instructor and Primary Plans,* February, 1923.
    Adapted to: B, C, F, J, L.

165. MASTER GEORGE WASHINGTON. *Effie Louise Koogle.* Three short acts, 30 minutes. Boys, 8; girls, 4. One interior. One exterior. 60 cents. Publisher: March Brothers Publishing Co.
    Adapted to: B, C, F, L.

166. THE MASTER WASHINGTON MARCHES ON. *Olive M. Price.* Three acts, two hours. Men, 36; women, 10; boys, 3; girls, 3; total, optional. Four interior, seven exterior. 50 cents. Royalty, $10. Publisher: Samuel French.
    Adapted to: D, E, G, H, K, L.

167. THE MOTHER OF WASHINGTON. *Le Roy Phillips.* One act, 40 minutes. Men, 4; women, 3. One interior. Royalty, $5. Publisher: Walter H. Baker Co.
    Adapted to: D, E, G, H, I, J, K, L.

168. *MOUNT VERNON. *Marion Holbrook.* One act, 10 minutes. Men, 2; women, 1. One exterior. $2.50. Publishers: Dodd, Mead & Co., Walter H. Baker Co.
    Adapted to: C, D, G, H, L.

169. NATHAN HALE. *Clyde Fitch.* Act 3, one hour. Men, 14; women, 4; boys, 1; total, optional. One interior. 75 cents. Royalty, $10. Publishers: Walter H. Baker Co., Dodd, Mead & Co.
    Adapted to: D, E, G, H, K, L.

170. *NATHAN HALE. *Elizabeth F. Hague* and *Mary Chalmers.* Five acts, full length. Men, 16; women, 1; boys, 3; girls, 2. Three interior, two exterior. $1.16. The University Publishing Co. Obtainable at libraries.
    Adapted to: C, D, F, G, L.

171. *OUR FIRST FLAG. *Karl B. Pauly.* Two acts, 20 minutes. Men, 6; women, 2. One interior. 60 cents. Publisher: March Bros.
    Adapted to: D, E, G, H, I, L.

172. *OUR FIRST FLAG. *Eleanor Hubbard.* Two short acts, 5 minutes. Boys, 3; girls, 2. 84 cents. Publisher: Benj. H. Sanborn & Co.
    Adapted to: A, B, F.

173. *OUR FLAG. *Margaret C. Fairlie.* One act, one hour. Total cast, optional. One interior. 50 cents. In *Catholic School Journal,* May, 1912.
    Adapted to: B. F.

174. *PANORAMIC DIALOGUES AND SCENES OF THE REVOLUTION. *Willis N. Bugbee.* Nine scenes, 30 minutes. Number of characters, optional. Three interior, four exterior. 40 cents. Publisher: The Penn Publishing Co.
    Adapted to: B, C, F.

175. *A PATRIOTIC FINANCIER. *Eleanore Hubbard.* Two short acts, 15 minutes. Boys, 4. Two interiors. Publisher: Benj. H. Sanborn & Co.
    Adapted to: B, F.

176. *THE PINE TREE SHILLINGS. *John Merrill.* Two short acts, 15 minutes. Boys, 7; girls, 3. Two interior. $2.60. Publisher: The Macmillan Co.
    Adapted to: B, F.

177. POLLY IN HISTORY LAND. *Edith F. A. U. Painton.* Four short acts, 1 hour. Boys, 8; girls, 6; total, optional. Three interior, four exterior. 25 cents. Publisher: Beckley-Cardy Co.
    Adapted to: B, F, L.

178. *A PRECARIOUS SITUATION IN BOSTON'S HISTORY. *Francis O'Ryan* and *Anna Wynne O'Ryan.* One act, 15 minutes. Boys, 12. One interior, 84 cents. Publishers: Hinds, Hayden & Eldridge.
    Adapted to: B, F, L.

179. *THE PRICE OF LIBERTY. *Eleanore Hubbard.* One act, 10

minutes. Boys, 5. One interior. $1. Publisher: Benj. H. Sanborn & Co.

Adapted to: B, F.

180. *THE PROPHECY. *Margaret Getchell Parsons.* One act, 12 minutes. Men or boys, 9. One exterior. 40 cents. Publishers: Dodd, Mead & Co., Walter H. Baker Co.

Adapted to: C, D, F, G, L.

181. *A REVOLUTIONARY MASQUERADE. *Willis N. Bugbee.* Two acts, 20 minutes. Boys, 9; girls, 5. One interior, one exterior. 40 cents. Publisher: The Penn Publishing Co.

Adapted to: B, C, F.

182. THE SANDMAN'S PACK O' DREAMS. *Olive M. Price.* One act, 35 minutes. Boys, 8; girls, 7. One interior, one exterior. 25 cents. Publisher: Walter H. Baker Co.

Adapted to: A, B, F.

183. *THE SEVEN AGES OF WASHINGTON. *Maude Stewart Beagle.* Seven short acts, 30 minutes. Men, 20; women, 12; boys, 3; total, optional. Two interior, five exterior. $2.50. Royalty, $5 each performance. Publisher: Dodd, Mead & Co.

Adapted to: B, C, D, F, G, J, H, L.

184. *SHE WHO WILL NOT WHEN SHE MAY. *Anna Jane Harnwell.* One act, 15 minutes. Men, 2; women, 4. One exterior. $2.50. Royalty, $5 per performance. Publisher: Dodd, Mead & Co.

Adapted to: E, G, I, J, K, L.

185. *THE SPIRIT OF '76. *Lettie C. Van Derveer.* One act, 20 minutes. Men, 4; women, 1. One interior. $1.50. Publisher: Walter H. Baker Co.

Adapted to: C, F, L.

186. *THAT BOY GEORGE. *Mabel L. Eaton.* One act, 10 minutes. Boys, 2; girls, 2. One interior. 60 cents. Publisher: March Bros. Publishing Co.

Adapted to: B, C, F, L.

187. THREE COMPROMISES OF THE CONSTITUTION. *Blanche W. Shoemaker.* One act, 15 minutes. Men, 11. One interior. 75 cents. Publisher: The Grade Teacher.

Adapted to: B, F.

188. THE THREE GEORGES. *Clara J. Denton.* One act, 12 minutes. Men, 6. One exterior. 40 cents. Publisher: Means & McLean.

Adapted to: B, F.

189. THE TRUTH ALWAYS. *Clara Childs.* One act, 15 minutes. Women, 2; boys, 3. One interior. 25 cents. Publisher: *Normal Instructor and Primary Plans.*

Adapted to: B, C, F.

190. *AT VALLEY FORGE. *Jean Lee Latham.* One act, 20 minutes. Men, 8. One exterior. 50 cents. Publisher: Dramatic Publishing Co.

Adapted to: E, G, I, K, L.

191. VALLEY FORGE. *W. Linwood Chase.* Three short acts, 45 minutes. Boys, 11; girls, 5. Two interior, one exterior. 25 cents. Publisher: The Grade Teacher.

Adapted to: B, F.

192. VALLEY FORGE. *Edward S. Lovejoy.* One act, 30 minutes. Men, 8; girls, 1. One exterior. 25 cents. Publisher: Edgar S. Werner Co.

Adapted to: D, E, G, I, K.

193. *THE VISION. *Clara J. Denton.* Two short acts, 15 minutes. Boys, 3; girls, 3. One exterior. 40 cents. Publisher: Means & McLean.

Adapted to: B, C, F.

194. WASHINGTON AND BETSY ROSS. *Percy MacKaye.* One act, 35 minutes. Men, 10; women, 2; boys, 1; girls, 1. One interior, one exterior. 50 cents. Publisher: Samuel French.

Adapted to: E, G, H, I, K, L.

195. WASHINGTON AT VALLEY FORGE. *Mayme R. Bitney.* One act, 20 minutes. Men, 6; women, 2. One interior. 40 cents. Publisher: Paine Publishing Co.

Adapted to: C, D, E, G, H, L.

196. WASHINGTON AT VALLEY FORGE. *Esther Willard Bates.* One act, 25 minutes. Men, 8; women, 1. One exterior. 30 cents. Royalty, $2.50 for every performance after first. Publisher: Walter H. Baker Co.

Adapted to: D, F, G, H, I.

197. WASHINGTON AT VALLEY FORGE. *Connecticut School Children.* Five episodes, 20 minutes. Boys, 8; total cast, optional. One interior, two exterior. 25 cents. Publisher: Milton Bradley Co. From *American Childhood Magazine,* February, 1928.

Adapted to: B, F.

198. WASHINGTON'S BIRTHDAY. *Marion I. Noyes* and *Blanche H. Ray.* One act, 15 minutes. Women, 1; boys, 2; girls, 2. One interior. Publisher: Ginn & Co.

Adapted to: A, B, F.

199. WASHINGTON'S BIRTHDAY. *E. E. Preston.* One act, 1 hour. Boys, 4 to 20; girls, 4 to 20. One interior. 50 cents. Publisher: The Bruce Publishing Co.

Adapted to: B, F.

200. WASHINGTON'S FIRST DEFEAT. *Charles F. Nirdlinger.* One act. Men, 1; women, 2. One interior. 30 cents. Publisher: Samuel French.

Adapted to: D, E, G, H, I, K, L.

201. *WASHINGTON'S MESSAGE TO ANY CHILD. *F. Ursula Payne.* One act, 20 minutes. Boys, 4; girls, 4. One interior. $1.25. Publisher: Harper & Bros.

Adapted to: A, B, F.

202. WASHINGTON THE MAN WHO MADE US. *Percy MacKaye.* Prologue, three acts, epilogue, full length. Twenty-five to one hundred mixed characters. Four interiors, seven exteriors. $2. Publisher: Alfred A. Knopf.

Adapted to: E, G, H, I, K.

203. *WASHINGTON THE PIONEER. *Belle Willey Gue.* Four acts, two hours. Men, 32; women, 1. One interior, 11 exteriors. $1.50. Publisher: The Canterbury Co.

Adapted to: E, G, H, L.

204. WASHINGTON THE STATESMAN. *Belle Willey Gue.* Four acts, two hours. Men, 13; women, 7; girls, 5. Six interiors, two exteriors. $1.50. Publisher: The Canterbury Co.

Adapted to: E, G, H, L.

205. WASHINGTON THE WARRIOR. *Belle Willey Gue.* Three acts, two hours. Men, 20; women, 1. Three interiors, one exterior. $1.50. Publisher: The Canterbury Co.

Adapted to: E, G, H, L.

206. WHEN COURAGE WAS NEEDED. *Augusta Stevenson.* Three acts, one hour and a half. Men, 27; women, 4. Three interiors. $1. Publisher: Houghton Mifflin Co.

Adapted to: D, E, G, H, K, L.

207. WHEN DUTY CALLS. *Clara J. Denton.* One act, 12 minutes. Men, 4; women, 2. One interior. 40 cents. Publisher: Eldridge Entertainment House.

Adapted to: B, C, F, L.

208. *YOUNG HALE OF CONNECTICUT. *Olive M. Price.* Two acts, one hour. Men, 6; women, 6. One interior, one exterior. $1.85. Publisher: Samuel French Co.

Adapted to: C, D, F, G, L.

209. THE YOUNG PATRIOT'S LEAGUE. *Willis B. Bugbee.* Two acts, 30 minutes. Boys, 5; girls, 5. Two interiors. 25 cents. Publisher: Eldridge Entertainment House.

Adapted to: B, F.

210. YOUNG WASHINGTON AT MOUNT VERNON. *Percy MacKaye.* One act, 35 minutes. Men, 12; women, 6. One interior. 50 cents. Royalty, $10. Publishers: Samuel French, D. Appleton & Co., Dodd, Mead & Co.

Adapted to: E, G, I, K, L.

211. THE SPY. *Joseph P. Brentano.* Three acts, full length. Men, 13; women, 3, boys, 2; total, optional. Three interiors, two exteriors. 50 cents. Royalty, $10. Publisher: Catholic Dramatic Movement.

Adapted to: D, E, G, K, L.

212. THAT CRUCIAL AFFAIR. *Edna Drake Scudder.* Four acts, full length. Men, 20; women, 6. One exterior, seven interiors. $1.50. Publisher: The Christopher Publishing House.

213. GENERAL WASHINGTON. *Frederick Schneider.* Three acts, full length. Men, 26; women, 4; total, optional. One exterior, four interiors. Permission from publisher: Frederick Schneider.

Adapted to: E, G, H, L.

214. HIS SUPERIOR IN COMMAND. *Walter L. Bissell.* One act, one hour. Men, 9; women, 4. One interior. 50 cents. Royalty, $5. Publisher: Walter L. Bissell.

Adapted to: E, G, K, L.

215. COLONEL GEORGE OF MOUNT VERNON. *Augustus Thomas.* Four acts, full length. Men, 11; women, 4; total, optional. One exterior, two interiors. 75 cents. Royalty, $25. Publisher: Samuel French.

Adapted to: E, G, I, K, L.

216. CAPTAIN BARRINGTON. *Victor Mapes.* Four acts, full length. Men, 25; women, 5; total, optional. One exterior, three interiors. 75 cents. Royalty, $25. Publisher: Samuel French.

Adapted to: E, G, I, K, L.

217. PATRIOTS. *Sara King Wiley.* One act, 45 minutes. Men, 3; women, 2. One interior. 30 cents. Permission from publisher: Samuel French.

Adapted to: E, G, I, K, L.

218. WHEN WASHINGTON CAME TO NEWPORT. *Maud L. Stevens* and *Elizabeth G. Covell.* Three scenes, 20 minutes. Men, 10; women, 7; boys, 5; girls, optional. One interior. Publisher: Authors, Newport, R. I.

Adapted to: C. D. F. I.

219. THE TURNING POINT OF THE REVOLUTION. *Laura Anderson Fritz.* One act, 25 minutes. Men, 6; women, 3; boys, 1; total, optional. Two exteriors. Price, 35 cents. Publisher: Author, 1614 Spruce Street, Philadelphia, Pa.

Adapted to: E. G. I. K. L.

PUBLISHERS' INDEX

D. APPLETON CO., 25 WEST 32D ST., NEW YORK, N. Y.

RICHARD G. BADGER (THE GORHAM PRESS), BOSTON, MASS.

WALTER H. BAKER CO., 41 WINTER ST., BOSTON, MASS.

A. S. BARNES & CO., 67 WEST 44TH ST., NEW YORK, N. Y.

BARSE & CO., 21-39 DIVISION ST., NEWARK, N. J.

BECKLEY-CARDY CO., 17 EAST 23D ST., CHICAGO, ILL.

WALTER L. BISSELL, 3397 BRADFORD RD., CLEVELAND, OHIO.

BRENTANO'S, 5TH AVENUE AT 27TH, NEW YORK, N. Y.

THE CATHOLIC DRAMATIC MOVEMENT, BRIGGSVILLE, WIS.

THE CHRISTOPHER PUBLISHING HOUSE, 1140 COLUMBUS AVE., BOSTON, MASS.

THE BRUCE PUBLISHING CO., 524 NORTH MILWAUKEE ST., MILWAUKEE, WIS.

WILLIS N. BUGBEE CO., 1401 NORTH SALINA ST., SYRACUSE, N. Y.

THE CANTERBURY CO., 4804 DEL MAR AVE., SAN DIEGO, CALIF.

DODD, MEAD & CO., 449 FOURTH AVE., NEW YORK, N. Y.

THE DRAMATIC PUBLISHING CO., 542 SOUTH DEARBORN ST., CHICAGO, ILL.

DUFFIELD & GREEN, 200 MADISON AVE., NEW YORK, N. Y.

E. P. DUTTON & CO., 286 FOURTH AVE., NEW YORK, N. Y.

ELDRIDGE ENTERTAINMENT HOUSE, DENVER, COLO., OR FRANKLIN, OHIO.

A. FLANAGAN & CO., 920 NORTH FRANKLIN ST., CHICAGO, ILL.

SAMUEL FRENCH, 25 WEST 45TH ST., NEW YORK, N. Y.

GINN & CO., 15 ASHBURTON PLACE, BOSTON, MASS.

THE GRADE TEACHER, 425 FOURTH AVE., NEW YORK, N. Y.

IVAN BLOOM HARDIN CO., 3806 COTTAGE GROVE, DES MOINES, IOWA.

HARPER & BROS., 49 EAST 33D ST., NEW YORK, N. Y.

HENRY HOLT & CO., 1 PARK AVE., NEW YORK, N. Y.

HINDS, HAYDEN & ELDRIDGE (INC.), 5 UNION SQUARE WEST, NEW YORK, N. Y.

HOUGHTON, MIFFLIN CO., 2 PARK ST., BOSTON, MASS.

ALFRED A. KNOPF, 730 FIFTH AVE., NEW YORK, N. Y.

MARCH BROS. PUBLISHING CO., 208 WRIGHT AVE., LEBANON, OHIO.

THE MACMILLAN CO., 60 FIFTH AVE., NEW YORK, N. Y.

MEANS & McLEAN, 525 ARLINGTON PLACE, CHICAGO, ILL.

NATIONAL EDUCATION ASSOCIATION, 1201 16TH ST., WASHINGTON, D. C.

NATIONAL RECREATION ASSOCIATION, 315 FOURTH AVE., NEW YORK, N. Y.

NOBLE & NOBLE, 76 FIFTH AVE., NEW YORK, N. Y.

OLD TOWER PRESS, LOCKPORT, ILL.

F. A. OWEN PUBLISHING CO., DANSVILLE, N. Y.

PAINE PUBLISHING CO., 40 EAST FIRST ST., DAYTON, OHIO.

THE PENN PUBLISHING CO., 925 FILBERT ST., PHILADELPHIA, PA.

THE PROGRESS PUBLISHING CO., GRINNELL, IOWA.

BENJAMIN H. SANBORN & CO., 131 CLARENDON ST., BOSTON, MASS.

FREDERICK SCHNEIDER, 21 CLINTON AVE., CLIFTON, N. Y.

CHARLES SCRIBNER'S SONS, 597 FIFTH AVE., NEW YORK, N. Y.

UNIVERSITY PUBLISHING CO., 239 FOURTH AVENUE, NEW YORK, N. Y.

THE WOMAN'S PRESS, 600 LEXINGTON AVE., NEW YORK, N. Y.

EDGAR S. WERNER, 701 SEVENTH AVE., BELMAR, N. J.

Dramatic Collections

Each of the following collections includes one or more plays or pageants dealing with George Washington and his time.

Title	Author or Compiler	Publisher
Acting Plays for Boys and Girls. .	Patten Beard.	Beckley-Cardy Co.
American History in Masque and Wig.	Olive M. Price.	Walter H. Baker Co.
The American Patriot Collection. .	Julia M. Martin.	Eldridge Entertainment House.
Citizenship Plays	Eleanore Hubbard.	Benj. H. Sanborn & Co.
Dramatic Adventures in History. .	Clara M. Love.	Ginn & Co.
Dramatic Moments in American History.	Hague and Chalmers. . .	University Publishing Co.
Dramatized Scenes from American History.	Augusta Stevenson.	Houghton Mifflin Co.
English Class Plays for New Americans.	Emily M. Gibson.	The Woman's Press.
Entertainments for All the Year. .	Clara J. Denton.	The Penn Publishing Co.
George Washington Anniversary Plays.	Theodore Johnson.	Walter H. Baker Co.
George Washington Plays.	A. P. Sanford.	Dodd, Mead & Co.
A Half Hour With Washington. . .	Hariette Wilbur.	Eldridge Entertainment House.
The Help-U Washington-Lincoln Collection.	. . . .	Edgar S. Werner & Co.
Holidays and In-Between Times. . .	L. C. VanDerveer.	Walter H. Baker Co.
Holiday Plays	Marguerite Merington. . .	Duffield & Green.
Jolly Dialogues	W. N. Bugbee.	The Penn Publishing Co.
Little Plays for Little People.	A. P. Sanford.	Dodd, Mead & Co.
Little American History Plays.	Eleanore Hubbard.	Benj. Sanborn & Co.
New Plays for Everyday Schools Celebrate.	Minnie A. Niemeier. . . .	Noble & Noble.
Outdoor Plays for Boys and Girls. .	A. P. Sanford.	Dodd, Mead & Co.
Pageants and Plays for Holidays. .	Mayme R. Bitney.	Paine Publishing Co.
Pageants of Our Nation.	A. P. Sanford.	Dodd, Meade & Co.
A Patriot in the Making.	Beatrice Guinnet.	Dramatic Publishing Co.
Patriotic Plays and Pageants.	Constance D. Mackay. .	Henry Holt & Co.
Patriotic Programs for Patriotic Days.	Evelyn Hoxie.	Walter H. Baker Co.
Pieces and Plays for Washington's Birthday.	Grace B. Faxon.	F. A. Owen Publishing Co
Plays and Pageants for Democracy	F. Ursula Payne.	Harper & Brothers.
Plays for School Days.	Florence R. Signor.	F. A. Owen Publishing Co.
Plays for American Holidays.	A. P. Sanford.	Dodd, Mead & Co.
Plays for Any Child.	F. Ursula Payne.	Harper & Brothers.
Plays from American History.	F. and Anna W. O'Ryan	Hinds, Hayden & Eldredge.
Plays About George Washington. . .	Theodore Johnson.	Walter H. Baker Co.
Playmaking and Plays.	Merrill and Fleming. . . .	The Macmillan Co.
Representative Plays.	Montrose J. Moses.	E. P. Dutton & Co.
School Plays for All Occasions. . . .	Madalene D. Barnum. . .	Barse & Co.
Short Plays from American History	Olive M. Price.	Samuel French.
Some Little Plays.	Mary E. Whitney.	Beckley-Cardy Co.
Special Day Pageants for Little People.	Bemis and Kennedy.	A. S. Barnes Co.
Successful Entertainments	Willis N. Bugbee.	The Penn Publishing Co.
George Washington Anniversary Plays.	Theodore Johnson.	Walter H. Baker Co.
Unusual Plays and Poems.	. . . .	Means & McLean.
Washington Day Entertainments. . .	Jos. C. Sindelar.	A. Flanagan Co.
Washington for All.	Julian Lee.	Dramatic Publishing Co.
Washington Preeminent	Alice Hunt Bartlett. . . .	Brentano's.

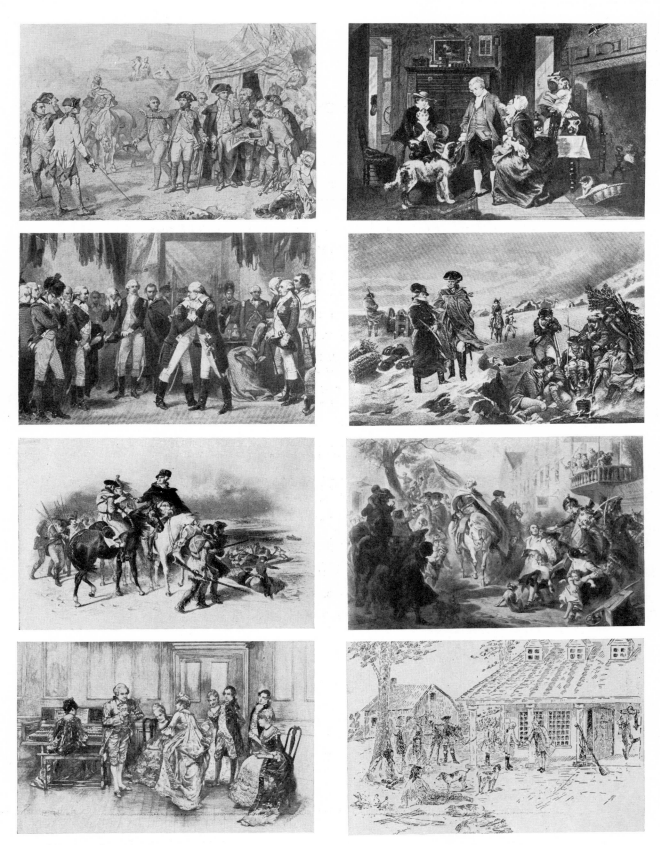

Left, top to bottom—THE ALLIED GENERALS AT THE SIEGE OF YORKTOWN. (After an engraving by A. M. Fontaine, of a painting by Conder.) WASHINGTON'S FAREWELL TO HIS OFFICERS. (After an engraving by Thomas Phillibrown, of a painting by Alonzo Chappel.) WASHINGTON CROSSING THE DELAWARE. (An engraving by James Duthrie, of a drawing by F. O. C. Darly.) WASHINGTON DANCING THE MINUET. *Right, top to bottom*—MRS. WASHINGTON PLEADING WITH GEORGE TO GIVE UP THE PLAN TO GO TO SEA. (After a painting by Alonzo Chappel.) WASHINGTON AT VALLEY FORGE. (After a painting by Alonzo Chappel.) WASHINGTON'S ENTRY INTO NEW YORK, 1783. (After an engraving by A. H. Ritchie.) WASHINGTON AT LORD FAIRFAX'S HUNTING CAMP.

George Washington Play and Pageant Costume Book

Part I
Costume in the Time of George Washington
By Edith Porter Lapish

Part II
Military Uniforms and Stage Properties
By Major R. B. Lawrence

ORIGINAL DRESS OF MARTHA WASHINGTON
AS SEEN IN THE UNITED STATES NATIONAL MUSEUM
CITY OF WASHINGTON

This heavy corded salmon-pink silk dress was worn by Martha Washington in
Colonial days. The skirt is made of many straight widths, gathered on a bodice,
pointed both back and front. The sleeves are to the elbow. The whole surface
of the silk dress is painted in a blue scroll design, caught up here and there by
green jewels. In the large spaces are all the wild flowers of nature—the arbutus,
daisy, buttercup, violet, etc., while in the small spaces are the insects of North
America—the grasshopper, butterfly, caterpillar, wasp, bee, etc.

INTRODUCTION

D URING the year 1932 the United States and four score foreign
countries participated in the Celebration of the Two Hundredth
Anniversary of the Birth of the greatest of our National heroes, General
George Washington.

The United States George Washington Bicentennial Commission
prepared a series of booklets for the guidance of those in charge of programs for the celebration. In addition to those dealing with the historical facts of George Washington's life and outlining a series of programs for the nation-wide celebration, this book was prepared, from
authentic and historical sources, to provide information regarding costumes of every variety suitable for the pageants, plays and playlets, social
gatherings, costume balls and similar entertainments, which the various
local committees organized. It was of manifest importance that the
costumes worn in the various celebrations be authentic and historically
correct.

The Commission was in no way interested in the sale of the costumes described; its sole aim was a patriotic one, and its only desire was
to make sure that directors of George Washington pageants and plays
had full information in regard to authentic costumes, in order to insure
the success of their programs. The Commission, upon request, furnished
the names of pattern-makers and firms which make, rent or sell costumes.

FRONT VIEW OF ORIGINAL DRESS WORN BY ELIZABETH MONROE, AS SHOWN IN THE UNITED STATES NATIONAL MUSEUM, CITY OF WASHINGTON

This dress of Mrs. James Monroe is a fine example of the Washington period. It was worn originally at one of the great Courts of Europe. In fashion parlance, it is known as the "Sacque" dress. The skirt is long and full and made with a wide ruffle around the hem. The material is of the heaviest brocade, and the pattern of the material is unusual—brocaded all over the dress are great bunches of poppies in brilliant color. The over-skirt is attached to the basque, with a great deal of fullness. The sleeves reach the elbow and are very full, and the basque is cut square both back and front.

ORIGINAL DRESS WORN BY DOLLY MADISON (MRS. JAMES MADISON), AS SHOWN IN THE UNITED STATES NATIONAL MUSEUM, CITY OF WASHINGTON

This dress of Mrs. Madison is one of great beauty. It is said that it was worn while she was acting as Mistress of the White House. The skirt is made of plain white satin, and is elaborately embroidered in forget-me-nots, cherry blossoms and green leaves. Over this is draped an over-skirt or panier, reaching almost to the hem of the skirt, of yellow satin, brocaded in silver. The over-skirt is fastened to a basque of similar material, and the long flowing over-skirt in the back which trails on the ground begins in a Watteau pleat at the shoulders. The over-skirt is trimmed with Valenciennes lace. The basque is low neck and the sleeves are to the elbow.

Part I

COSTUME IN THE
TIME OF GEORGE WASHINGTON

OLD costumes, like old letters and old diaries, bring us closer to an understanding of those who have lived before us. So, in celebrating the Two Hundredth Anniversary of the Birth of George Washington, this story of the costumes of the period is written to give a keener insight into the time when America's greatest hero lived.

In 1732, the year of Washington's birth, much of the ruggedness of the early colonial days had passed. Virginia and the southern Colonies were shipping tobacco to England; the central Colonies were sending foodstuffs and furs; and New England was building ships and exporting lumber, fish and rum. The Colonies were flourishing. Philadelphia had grown to more than two hundred houses; New York had a population of about five thousand; while Boston, then the largest city in America, had some seven thousand residents.

With the growth and wealth of the Colonies, fashion became a conspicuous element in early American life. Until the time of the Revolution, London was the fashion dictator of America. To illustrate the latest fashions, jointed dolls, dressed in the latest mode, were sent to the Colonies at regular intervals. These fashion "babies" were dressed by mantua-makers of Paris and sent to fashionable patrons in London. From England they continued their journey to the Colonies to stimulate feminine taste. When they were no longer of use, the Colonial children were permitted to play with them.

Dress of Colonial Ladies

The most fashionable dress a woman could wear at this period, 1732, was the "sacque." This garment, a loose overdress, hung from the shoulders above a large hooped petticoat. It was open in front to reveal a stomacher and petticoat of either the same or a contrasting material. The "sacque" was worn by fashionable women from 1720 until 1777 and underwent several changes.

Women who were not quite so fashion-conscious were wearing a dress with a long-waisted bodice which came to a point in front and bared the neck in a square or round decolletage. Both the dress and the sacque had short sleeves, either elbow length or ending midway between the shoulder and the elbow. Often ruffles of lace, shorter at the front of the arm and longer at the back, were used to finish the short sleeves.

About 1740, it became the fashion to pleat the fullness at the back of the sacque into a series of box pleats. This is generally spoken of as the "Watteau gown" and the pleats as "Watteau pleats." Sometimes the body of the gown was made to fit the figure and the two box pleats attached at the neck hung free until they merged into the fullness of the hooped skirt. As time went on, the box pleating was brought into the bodice and sewed down flat.

Then came a new gown called the "polonaise." The bodice, which was fitted and laced tightly over a stomacher, came down to a point in front. The full skirt was either looped with ribbons to form three festoons or hung in rippling fullness over a hooped petticoat. The polonaise was somewhat shorter than the Watteau gown which had touched the floor all the way around. The fashionable new length was just above the ankle. Fichus of lace, or shawls, were often worn over the low-cut polonaise gown.

Styles of Hair Dressing

Shortly after 1700, the roll, or pompadour, as we call it, came into vogue. With few variations it remained the fashion for more than fifty years. A portrait of Martha Washington, when she was still Martha Custis, shows how the hair was arranged over a roll and allowed to fall in loose curls upon the shoulders.

At first pompadours were not much in evidence, but as time went on the hair was dressed higher and higher over immense, artificial rolls. In 1760, it was the fashion to entwine the hair with pearls and wear symmetrical clusters of curls on either side of the head. Perhaps a curl or two would hang over the shoulder from the back of the head.

In Europe women were already powdering their hair. This, however, did not become a general fashion in America until 1750. After that time, fashionable dames powdered their hair for dress occasions. The vogue disappeared in 1785.

One coiffure which was all the rage in America and France about 1778, consisted of thirteen set rows of curls. It was called "a l'Independence" in honor of the thirteen new States. A few years later, fashion decreed a long lock of hair looped low at the back of the neck, then brought up to the crown of the head and caught with a comb. This mode was followed by the "Titus" hairdress. Locks were clipped close in the back and only a few straggling curls allowed to fall over the forehead. By 1800, since women's hair was obviously suffering from much frizzing and burning, the universal reign of wigs began.

577

1. THE FULL, BROCADED SKIRT OF THIS COSTUME IS TRIMMED WITH CIRCULAR RUFFLES OF CONTRASTING MATERIAL. SMALL RUFFLES ON THE POINTED BODICE AND THE NECK AND SLEEVES.

Hoods, Hats and Bonnets

Until 1690 women wore only hoods and 'kerchiefs to cover their hair. Then by a strange accident the "Fontange" came into fashion. It was named after Mademoiselle de Fontange. One day when she was hunting with King Louis XIV, her hair became disarranged and fell down her back. She quickly took off one of her garters and tied it up. The King was so pleased with the effect that all the women of the court began to wear ribbons tied around their heads with bows in front.

Later fashions grew more elaborate. Lace and lawn caps were made with frills and ribbons on the front. This combination of ribbon and lace or lawn was known as the "commode-Fontange." The little caps which women in America wore in the early 1700's were inspired by these. Frequently they were finished by an addition of streamers or lappets which hung down in the back or at the sides. As it became the fashion to dress the hair higher, the caps grew in size. One of Martha Washington's favorite caps was called "the Queen's Night Cap." A diary of the time describes this magnificent cap of ruffles and ribbon: "If the material it is made of were more substantial than gauze it might serve occasionally to hold anything measured by one-fourth peck."

Straw hats, broad of brim and with low crown, appeared soon after 1730. They were frequently held in place by ribbons that went over the crown and tied under the chin. From this time on, it would be impossible to describe the many styles of hats. And they were worn at every conceivable angle or perched at the top of the tower of hair. Feathers, flowers, fruit, and ribbons were used as trimming. During the time of the Revolution there were even "kitchen garden" styles of hats with vegetable trimmings; "rural" styles with windmills; and the famous "peal of bells," which was a steeple head-dress of ringing bells.

Bonnets also were worn during this period. Slat sunbonnets were popular in the country and the calash, or bashful bonnet, was worn as early as 1765. This headcovering was usually made from green or brown silk, shirred over whalebones placed about two inches apart. It resembled a miniature hood or top to an old chaise or calash. The calash bonnet was extensible and could be worn either standing up at the back of the head or extended over the face.

2. THIS UNUSUALLY BEAUTIFUL COLONIAL COSTUME, FOR EVENING WEAR, HAS ITS PANNIER AND SKIRT FINISHED IN A RUFFLE OF FINE PLEATING.

Clothes for Travel

The most popular means of travel during the eighteenth century was by horseback. Women did not ride alone as they do now, they rode seated *apillion*. This pillion was a wooden seat strapped to the horse's back behind the saddle. It usually had a padded cushion and stirrup. There was a metal handle to which the rider might cling for safety, if she preferred not to put one arm around her escort or cling to a specially designed leather belt which he wore.

Riding habits generally consisted of a coat and a "safeguard," donned over the regular bodice and skirt to protect them against flying dust or mud. The safeguard, or riding petticoat as it was sometimes called, was made out of a sturdy linen or similar material. The coat was long (to the knee at first; in 1790, longer) and full-skirted, made to fit closely into the waist and fastened with buttons. At the throat the feminine rider favored a frill of lace or tailored cravat. Feathered cocked hats were the fashion. Later, an extremely impractical broad-brimmed hat was worn for all except long distance traveling. While

4. A SIMPLE HOME DRESS FOR INDOOR WEAR OF FLOWERED MATERIAL, MADE VERY PLAIN WITH FULL SKIRT.

riding, a fan or parasol was often carried as a protection from the sun.

Cloaks and Other Wraps

Cloaks were in use with few changes from the time of the first settlements in America until the end of the nineteenth century. The most popular color for them during the time of Washington was scarlet, probably because this color did not fade as did many of the home-made dyes. Some garments were three-quarters length and some even longer. They were made both with and without attached hoods. The most fashionable style by 1730 was the "Roquelaure," named after the Duke of Roquelaure, a short, hoodless cape made of bright colored silk or camlet. The style called the "Cardinal" was a very warm cloak made of cardinal wool. The "Capuchins" were patterned after the habit of the Capuchin friars, with two long points in front and a hood attached. A most fashionable style in the later eighteenth century was the pelisse, a garment made with or without sleeves, but when made with slits for the arms termed a cloak. Sometimes a pelisse had a broad collar, at other times a hood. Costly pelisses were trimmed with fur.

3. THIS EXAMPLE OF CALICO OR DIMITY WAS A FAVORITE MORNING DRESS. THE APRON WAS ALWAYS PART OF THE COSTUME AND WAS WORN BY BOTH WOMEN AND CHILDREN.

5. THIS EXAMPLE IS MADE WITH A FULL PLAIN EFFECT WITH LACE-EDGED PANNIER. SOFT SILK RUFFLES OF GRADUATING SIZE TRIM THE BOTTOM OF THE SKIRT AND THE BODICE.

Various Vanities

Accessories varied according to the wealth of the Colonial ladies. Gloves were considered a necessity. Long ones of black, white, or purple, in either kid or silk, were decidedly fashionable. In the summer many women wore fingerless gloves, or mitts, of lace or silk.

Aprons, in various shapes and sizes, were considered not only a necessity but a fashionable accessory as well.

An *etui,* "an ornamental case, hanging from the waist, intended to hold thimble, scissors, and scent bottle," was popular. The pomander was another accessory of vanity. It was a silver ball with perforations used to hold perfumed wax.

Patch boxes of ivory, silver and tortoise shell were carried. They contained patches of every shape and a little mirror to assist my lady in placing the beauty mark most advantageously.

On dress occasions it was the rule for ladies to appear with a bouquet of real or artificial flowers upon her gown.

If the flowers were real, she placed them in a slim glass tube filled with water, which she tucked into the stomacher of her gown.

Every lady of fashion carried a fan. These were made of painted kid, silver filigree, carved ivory, shell, satin, and feathers.

The beautiful laces of this period deserve special mention. Every one wore lace—it trimmed gowns, made caps, appeared as mitts, and was put to many other uses.

Muffs were an accessory throughout the eighteenth century. At first they were narrow and long but later became wider.

Footwear

The fashion of wearing red heeled shoes started in 1710. American women enthusiastically sponsored the vogue.

6. WATTEAU PLEATED GOWN, WORN BY WOMEN OF THE COLONIAL PERIOD AT COURT FUNCTIONS. THIS GRACEFUL PLEAT ALWAYS ENDED IN A VERY FULL TRAIN.

By 1751 high heels were indispensable to well-dressed ladies. Various materials were used in making the shoes—"fine silk," "flowered russet," "white calamanco," "black shammy," "black velvet," "red morocco," etc. Most of the footwear bore the maker's name inside and the phrase, "Rips mended free." In 1790 heels disappeared completely and women wore sandal-like foot covering. The buckles of paste jewels were replaced by tiny bows or ribbon edging. But whatever else women's shoes were at this time, they were thin soled and quite unfit for wet weather. On such occasions, as well as for rough walking, women wore pattens or clogs, which raised the wearer clumsily from the ground.

8. ANOTHER DAINTY FIGURED BROCADE GOWN OF THE PERIOD. THE EDGING OF THE PANNIER AND THE 'KERCHIEF, ENDING IN A SOFT BOW AT THE NECK, WERE OFTEN OF A CONTRASTING PLAIN COLOR.

Stays, Stomachers and Such

Underneath the sacques of Colonial times it was necessary to wear stays that laced tightly. Sometimes whaleboned stomachers added to the discomfort of the fashionably dressed.

The Colonial Bride

It was not the accepted custom for brides to wear white as it is today. They chose any color they wished. Pale blue was very popular. Brocade was the most fashionable fabric and the bride selected as costly a gown as she could afford. Bridal veils were the exception rather than the rule. It was not until after 1800 that the convention of the white bridal gown and veil was established fully. One very lovely gown designed for a bride is described as being

7. ANOTHER EXAMPLE OF THE MORNING DRESS OF THE COLONIAL PERIOD. THE APRON, AN EVERYDAY ACCESSORY FOR MORNING WEAR, IS MORE CLEARLY OUTLINED IN THIS PICTURE. THE 'KERCHIEF WAS FASTENED TO THE BODICE AND THE SLEEVES WERE WORN HALF WAY TO THE ELBOW.

of a golden yellow, brocaded in flowers of various colors. This was looped or draped over a petticoat of yellow satin veiled in white gauze shot with silver. The slippers were lavender satin.

Brides in Colonial times as well as today liked to have an extensive trousseau of finery. Clothes had a definite place in the quaint old custom of "coming out bride." Throughout the Colonies, except where churchly segregation made it impossible, the bride and groom in their finest clothes attended service the first Sunday after their marriage. In some communities the newly married couple were given the front seat and at an appointed time in the service they arose and turned slowly about. Often-times the bridal pair were supposed to wear bridal finery to church on each Sunday of the honeymoon month, and since these Sunday shows made the bride very conscious of her finery or lack of it, it was a proud bride who could don a new costume each Sunday.

Men's Apparel in Washington's Time

Coats were made fitted in at the waist, with full, square-cut, stiffened skirts and sleeves with very wide cuffs that fell over the wrist. The hilt of the sword protruded from beneath the coat, for wide sword belts had been laid aside. Full-gathered breeches of the knickerbocker style were in general wear. Blue and scarlet silk stockings often adorned with silver or gold clocks were the fashion. Velvet garters, caught on one side with a sparkling buckle, were fastened over the stockings just below the knee. Practically all gentlemen of the eighteenth century wore periwigs and cocked hats.

Periwigs

Because periwigs were one of the most characteristic features of men's dress from 1660 to 1770 they deserve special mention. Frequently they were made of human hair combined with horsehair in the parts that did not show. There was no pretense at making periwigs look real. Just why wigs were so generally popular is hard to understand, as they were cumbersome affairs of corkscrew curls, heavy, hot, and far from comfortable.

Until 1735 the periwig seems to have grown larger and larger. When it became impractical for wear in hunting, traveling, or, indeed, for everyday routine, a lighter wig, called the peruke, became fashionable for active affairs. Whereas the curls of the periwig surrounded the face, in the peruke they were brought back from the face, the side locks were turned up and tied with ribbons in a bob or knot.

In 1706 the "Ramillies" wig came into fashion. It had a long, plaited queue with a large bow at the top and a small one at the bottom. The story goes that this is the manner in which the soldiers fixed their hair during the Battle of Ramillies in order to escape the burden of a full wig.

Other queue wigs followed in fashion. Those imported from France were popular. One of the most attractive styles was the Tie-Wig. It had a low toupe, full sides and back curls tied in a bunch with a black ribbon. Bag-Wigs were also fashionable. In these, the back hair was gathered into a little bag which protected gentlemen's coats from the powder of the flowing locks. But it would be impossible to name all the wig styles. From the advertisements of the day it seems that wigs were given different names by different barbers. The "Beau-peruke," "Fox-tail," "Feather-top," "Full-bottom," and "Grecian Fly Wig" name only a few varieties.

Wigs were not only uncomfortable but costly as well. They demanded a great deal of care, the curls having to be retightened and powdered. Consequently, about 1770 it became fashionable to wear one's own hair again. It was, however, dressed with puffs and queues in the manner of wigs. Gentlemen continued to powder their hair until the last decade of the eighteenth century.

Coats and Waistcoats

From 1700 to 1750 there were few changes in the general appearance of gentlemen's coats and waistcoats. The fashionable coat reached the knees or just below, and the waistcoat varied from just a few inches to several shorter. As a general rule neither garment had a collar. At first the skirts of the coats were only moderately full. Then it became the fashion to gather them into fan-shaped pleats, and after a while, to stiffen them with buckram until they stood out as though hooped. Around 1750, plain, close-fitting, skirted coats took the place of the exaggerated stiffened styles. As time went on, the front of the coats was left more and more open. Large, turned-back cuffs with ruffles of lace showing below them were in fashion until 1760. Gradually cuffs became smaller and tight. The great pocket flaps, likewise, became smaller and less conspicuous.

In discussing men's coats, the question is sure to arise as to why two buttons are placed at the b a c k . Various reasons have been advanced. One is that the buttons were placed there in order to attach a protective garment when horseback riding. Another theory is that they were used for looping back the skirts of the coat and that cord loops were sewn under the corners of the skirts. In the days when dress swords were the rule, the sash of the sword was held in place by a cord or strap fastened to the coat by these buttons.

A favorite material for gentlemen's coats w a s velvet or other fine cloth.

9.   A COLONIAL GENTLEMAN.

Black was worn, although the two most fashionable shades were the far from somber claret and green. Waistcoats were frequently made of rich silks flowered in large patterns and ornamented with gold or silver laces.

Knee Breeches

Knee breeches, which at the opening of the century had been full, like knickerbockers, were now tailored tightly over the legs and brought in snugly at the knee, or were full in the seat and gathered into a tight fitting waistband. Buckles and buttons at the knee served for embellishment.

Odd breeches may have been worn on some occasions, usually, however, they matched the color and material of the coat. Little or no change was made in the cut of breeches after they were made to fit the leg.

Banyans and Turbans

Admire as you will the picturesque and charming costumes of Colonial days, it is obvious that they were not comfortable. It was only natural that the Colonial gentleman should have donned a more comfortable garment in the privacy of his own home. The "banyan," which became widely popular, was just such an article of apparel. By 1730, the banyan was being worn both in America and Europe. It was a loose robe made as handsome or as simple as the wearer could afford: soft china silk banyans for summer; heavy damasks for winter; striped or figured cotton also served. In the southern Colonies, the masters wore the banyan in travelling over their plantations. Not infrequently lawyers and merchants wore it at work. Some gentlemen had their portraits painted in banyans.

With the banyan was worn a turban-like headdress. With the wig removed for comfort, some covering was necessary for the shaven head. The most approved manner of wearing the turban was at a jaunty angle.

Cocked Hats

When the brims of hats had increased in width to seven or eight inches they lost their stiffness and dropped down about the face. Then the wearer began rolling up the brim, sometimes at one side, sometimes at another. Soon it became the style to cock the hat. By 1700 the three-cornered, cocked hat was general and it retained its popularity until after the Revolution. There was a great difference in three-cornered, cocked hats, however. Fairholt writes:

10. A COLONIAL TRAVELLING COSTUME.

"By the cock of the hat, the man who wore it was known; and they varied from the modest broad brim of the clergy and country gentleman or citizen, to the more decidedly fashionable cock worn by merchantmen and would-be-fashionable Londoners; while a very pronounced *a la militaire* cock was affected by the gallant."

As the brim was caught up by loops to a button on the top, in case of rain one or all of the flaps of the hat could be let down. Soldiers were penalized during the Revolutionary War for wearing their hats uncocked, because this careless unlooping gave them a "hang-dog look." The edge of the brim of the cocked hat was bound with braid or lace.

In the '70s a new style in hats appeared—a round-crowned, broad brimmed hat of felt or beaver. Next came the top hat with narrow brim and tapering crown, an obvious predecessor of the hats men wear today.

Overcoats

By the beginning of the eighteenth century cloaks and capes were no longer fashionable. They were still worn occasionally in severe weather or for travelling. Great loose overcoats, double-breasted and belted, were much in favor. Wide cuffs and large collars distinguished them. As time went on, shoulder capes were added. Fur coats and leather coats, in simple, practical styles, were also worn.

Shirts, Cravats and Solitaires

Under his coat and waistcoat the Colonial gentleman wore a beautiful shirt. If he were of wealth and position, it was more than likely to be of the finest Holland linen; if he could not afford that, of cotton or calico. Some of the young men of this period insisted upon wearing no waistcoat at all and letting their long, full shirts fall in blouse style over the waistbands of their breeches; or, the waistcoat was left unbuttoned a short way down to show the meticulously arranged cravat. Of course the ruffles of the shirt sleeves appeared from beneath the cuffs of the coat.

Ruffs and bands were the neckwear of the early Colonists. By 1700 cravats, said to be named for the Cravates of the French military service who adopted such neckwear, were in general use in the Colonies. The cravat was worn whenever and wherever a wig was worn. The first cravats were like long scarfs. Usually made of sheer linen and about two yards long, they were wrapped several times about the throat and looped under the chin. The shorter, upper end of the scarf was often embroidered or trimmed with lace and allowed to hang free; the longer end was tucked in between the buttons of the waistcoat well below the waist.

The "Steinkirk" cravat was a favorite with young dandies. It was a nonchalant twist of the scarf rather than the exact tie. The folds were loose and the ends tucked through button holes. The fashion of lace frills supplanted cravats in the early eighteenth century. Gentlemen had lace frills attached to their shirts under the stock or neckband. These frills, generally termed "jabots," gained rapidly in popularity. Plain stocks buckled at the neck were worn with jabots.

The "solitaire" was a black silk ribbon worn about the neck. In the back, it was attached to the wig-bag of the back hair and in front lost itself in the frills of the jabot or was caught by a broach. Sometimes the solitaire was tied in a bow knot under the chin. It added to the great charm of the Colonial gentleman's costume—ruffled jabot at the throat, jeweled stock buckle, powdered wig with bag and solitaire—these were very becoming fashions.

Shoes and Boots

Square shoe buckles are often spoken of in this country as "George Washington buckles," though as a fact they had been worn many years before. At the time of his birth, it was an accepted custom to wear pointed shoes with high tongues fastened on the instep by a square buckle.

Boots were worn for travelling and hunting, jack-boots most frequently. These were made of stiff leather. Just below the knee they swelled out in an immense cuff to give freedom of movement to the wearer. In stormy weather leggings, called spatterdashes, were worn to protect the stockings.

Stockings

Russet and green silk stockings, for dress occasion, adorned with gold or silver clocks, were the acme of perfection in dress in 1732. By Revolutionary times white stockings had supplanted them in the popular taste and this style prevailed until 1790 when stripes held sway. Those who could not afford silk stockings wore "good knit worsted stockings," cloth stockings, leather stockings or homespun stockings.

Cost of Clothes

Many people are of the opinion that clothes cost very little in Colonial times. This is a mistake. It was not exceptional for a gentleman to pay two guineas for his embroidered silk stockings (a guinea was worth five dollars). Handsome wigs cost from thirty to fifty guineas.

It was no wonder sneak thieves considered them a rich prize. Aside from the original cost of the wig, gentlemen had to pay large sums to have them kept in shape. Ten pounds a year is what it usually cost to have a barber call for one wig. A coat might cost only a guinea and breeches no more, but stock buckles and shoe buckles were as costly as the wearer could afford.

Muffs, Earrings and Snuff Boxes

It was the custom throughout this period for men to carry muffs; not only the dandies, but the clergy and lawyers likewise. At first muffs were made of cloth and richly embroidered. Later feathers and furs were used. In 1725 a Boston paper carried Dr. Prince's advertisement that he had lost his "black bearskin muff." Muffs varied in size, from ones that reached from waist to knee to "a decent smallish muff that you may put in your pocket, and it cost but fourteen shillings."

Earrings, usually a pearl or gold, were likewise considered masculine accessories during the eighteenth century. It was more customary for sea-going men to pierce their ears, however, as there was a superstition that ear-piercing prevented and cured sore eyes. It was a safe guess during the 1700's that the man with pierced ears had seen the world and sailed around the Horn.

Almost every gentleman carried a snuff box. It was as important to him as a fan was to a lady. The material and workmanship of the little box depended upon the owner's wealth and fancy. Another interesting masculine vanity was the great comb to put the periwig in order—which the gentleman often did in public.

Dress of Colonial Children

Colonial babies were clad in the softest linen. Little linen shirts, perhaps embroidered with the motto, "God bless the Babe," linen mitts, and little linen petticoats and sacques made up the usual dress of the baby of the eighteenth century. Mrs. Alice Morse Earle writes, "I think infants wore no woolen petticoats; their shirts, petticoats, and gowns were of linen or some cotton stuff like dimity." Warmth was supplied by little shawls which were pinned around the shoulders, or perhaps the baby was wrapped in a blanket or quilt.

Baby dresses were usually shapeless garments gathered in at the neck. Some, however, were made in a very grown-up fashion with straight lines and square necks. All were made by hand with painstaking care. In the country sections homespun was used if linen or dimity was not procurable. It was not out of the way to have a baby's dress as long as his mother's when she held him on her arm, although during the eighteenth century the "three-quarters" dress was more generally in use.

Bands and bibs have changed little. But the lace mitts, cuffs, and caps have been put aside. Babies wore caps in bed and when they were taken out a heavier cap, perhaps of velvet, was slipped over the lace one. Few people today have ever heard of the "puddings" children used to wear. A pudding, or pudding-cap, was a huge, cushion-like headgear put on a child when he was learning to walk to prevent his bumping his head. But the most striking difference in the dress of children of Colonial times and today is the way in which their mothers changed them to grown-up clothes. Today, there is no marked change in costume to correspond to the "coating" and "leaving off of coats" of years ago. The little Colonial boy was "coated" when he

left off baby cloth. When coated, he wore a short frock and petticoats. Next came the donning of breeches or "leaving off coats," which usually took place when the child was about six.

"Pinners" were another characteristic of Colonial children's dress. Even boys wore aprons until they left off coats. These were little aprons with bibs. The kind that covered skirt and sleeves were known as "tiers." For dress-up occasion there were dainty aprons of starched lawn or lace.

Even corsets were made for children. Mrs. Earle writes that she has seen "a pair of stays labelled as having been made for a boy of five." They were made of board, sewed into a buckram waist and reenforced with steel, a veritable straight jacket.

Nankeen was a material popular for children's clothes as well as for adults' apparel. Nothing could be more fashionable for a boy than nankeen breeches with silver knee-buckles. In winter, on the very coldest days, some children wore woolens. Strange to say, it was yellow flannel and not the proverbial red flannel.

For party occasions little girls wore dresses of lawn or cambric. They were cut in the same styles as their mother's sacques. From Colonial portraits we learn that children wore, also, the powdered, uncomfortable wigs which were such a source of pride to their parents. Likewise the mask, which women wore to keep the rays of the sun from marring their complexions, was worn by little girls. Nellie Custis had one, as had Mrs. Washington. Children seem to have been miniatures of grown-ups, most of the costumes of adults being adopted for them.

11. EVERY DAY CLOTHES FOR OUT-OF-DOOR WEAR,
OF THE COLONIAL PERIOD.

12. SIMPLE PLAY DRESS FOR BOYS AND GIRLS OF
THE COLONIAL PERIOD.

Washington's Attention to Dress

Although George Washington's advice on dress was given two centuries ago it is just as sound wisdom today as it was then:

"Decency and cleanliness will always be the first object in the dress of a judicious and sensible man. A conformity to the prevailing fashion in a certain degree is necessary— but it does not follow from thence that a man should always get a new coat, or other clothes, upon every trifling change in the mode, when, perhaps he has two or three very good ones by him. A person who is anxious to be a leader of the fashion, or one of the first to follow it, will certainly appear in the eyes of judicious men, to have nothing better than a frequent change of dress to recommend him to notice."

This, and Washington's further admonition: "Do not conceive that fine clothes make fine men any more than fine feathers make fine birds," show that Washington was far from being a dandy, although he had a reputation for always being "very neat and genteel" in dress.

Before the Revolution he sent frequent orders to his agent in London. Here are a few of the most interesting. They give a vivid insight into Colonial costume.

Orders Sent to England

Soon after Washington became master of Mount Vernon he wrote for:

A riding waistcoat of superfine scarlet cloth and gold lace with buttons like those of the coat.

A very neat and fashionable New Market saddle cloth.

6 pairs of the very neatest shoes, viz: 2 pr. double channelled pumps; two pair turned ditto and two pair stitched shoes, to be made on Colonel Baylor's last but to be a little wider over the insteps.

6 prs. gloves, 3 pairs of which to be proper for riding and not to have stiff tops; the whole larger than middle size.

My Lady at Home and Abroad

Note how the gesture of the little girl, as well as her dress, imitates that of her mother. In Colonial Days children were imitations of their elders, Not only were their party clothes of the rich materials affected by their parents, with every accessory of wig and stays, patch and fan or muff, but even their play dresses of dimity or nankeen were cut from the same patterns.

13. THE PLAIN FULL SKIRT IS TRIMMED WITH A BAND OF FLOWERED MATERIAL, EDGED WITH A TINY RUFFLE. SPECIAL ATTENTION IS CALLED TO THE TABBED BODICE OR WAIST, MADE OF FLOWERED MATERIAL AND LACED UP THE FRONT.

14. THIS WAS A PERIOD WHEN WOMEN WORE STAYS, AND THE ABOVE COSTUME GIVES A FINE EXAMPLE OF THE SMALL WAIST PERIOD. THE PANNIER IS EDGED WITH A VERY FULL RUFFLE OF A DIFFERENT COLOR.

An Order for Martha Washington

The following order has been preserved in Washington's own handwriting. It is one sent in 1759 for his wife:

Two fine flowered lawn aprons.
One pair women's white silk hose.
Four pairs thread hose.

Six pairs women's fine cotton hose.
One pair black satin shoes.
One pair white satin shoes of smallest 5's.
Four pairs calamanco shoes.
One fashionable hat or bonnet.

Six pairs women's best kid gloves.

Six pairs women's best mitts.

One dozen round silk laces.

One black mask.

One dozen most fashionable pocket handkerchiefs.

One piece of narrow white satin ribbon with pearl edge.

Four pieces of binding tape.

Six thousand miniken pins.

Six thousand short whites.

Six thousand corking pins.

One thousand hair pins.

16. THE PANNIER EFFECT IN THIS FIGURE IS LONG AND FULL, GENERALLY ENDING IN A TRAIN. THE 'KERCHIEF EFFECT AROUND THE POINTED BODICE WAS POPULAR.

15. A PLAIN SATIN SKIRT MADE VERY FULL OVER A HOOP SKIRT; PANNIERS OF FLOWERED BROCADE, LOOPED HIGH OVER THE HIPS. BODICE, ALSO OF BROCADE, POINTED BOTH BACK AND FRONT, WITH ELBOW SLEEVES.

An Order for "Miss Custis"

When his stepdaughter was six years old he sent the following order to England to provide for her needs. This was in 1761:

1 stiffened coat made of fashionable silk.

A fashionable cap or fillet, with bib apron, ruffles and tuckes, to be laced.

4 fashionable dresses made of long lawn.

2 fine cambrick frocks.

A satin capuchin hat and neckatees.

A Persian quilted coat.

1 p. pack thread stays.

4 p. calamanco shoes.

17. A FINE EXAMPLE OF OUTDOOR DRESS FOR GIRLS, WITH THE LOOSE WRAPS OF THE PERIOD.

6 p. leather shoes.

2 p. satin shoes with flat heels.

6 p. fine cotton stockings.

4 p. white worsted stockings.

12 p. mitts.

6 p. white kid gloves.

1 p. silver shoe buckles.

1 p. neat sleeve buttons.

6 handsome egrets different sorts.

6 yards ribbon different sorts.

12 yards coarse green calamanco.

Costumes of the Mt. Vernon Servants

An order sent to England in 1759 tells exactly what the Washington servants wore:

2 doz. pairs of plaid hose sorted.

2 doz. Monmouth caps.

25 yds. broadcloth to cost about 7 s. 6d.

15 yds. coarse double thick broadcloth.

6 yds. scarlet broadcloth.

30 yds. red shallon.

12 doz. white washed waistcoat buttons.

20 doz. white washed coat buttons.

40 yds. coarse jean or fustian for summer frocks for negro servants.

1½ doz. pairs strong coarse thread hose.

1 doz. pairs coarse shoes and knee buckles.

1 postillion cap.

6 castor hats.

Troubles of Colonial Customers

From letters of Washington, written in 1760, we learn that English merchants were not always careful to send Colonial customers the best goods at the best prices:

"And here Gentn. I cannot forbear ushering in a Complaint of the exorbitant prices of my Goods this year all of which are to come to hand. . . . For many Years I have Imported Goods from London as well as other Ports of Britain and can truely say I never had such a penny worth before. It woud be a needless Task to innumerate every Article that I have cause to except against, let it suffice to say that Woolens, Linnens, Nails &ca. era mean in quality but not in price, for in this they excel indeed, far above any I have ever had."

18. BOYS' HUNTING DRESS.

"Let me beseech you Gentn. to give the necessary directions for purchasing of them upon the best Terms. It is needless for me to particularise the sorts, quality, or taste I woud choose to have them in unless it is observd; and you may believe me when I tell you that instead of getting things good and fashionable in their several kinds we often have Articles sent Us that coud only have been used by our Forefathers in the days of yore. Tis a custom, I have some Reason to believe, with many Shop Keepers, and Tradesmen in London when they know Goods are bespoke for Exportation to palm sometimes old, and sometimes very slight and indifferent Goods upon Us taking care at the same time to advance 10, 15 or perhaps 20 pr. Ct. upon them."

After the Revolution

Orders were not so commonly sent to England after the war as they had been before the conflict. Washington set a patriotic example by sometimes wearing native-made clothes fashioned of American-made cloth. Mrs. Washington followed his example, but the war-time use of domestic-made cloth was probably discontinued.

The Inaugural Ball

A vivid and often quoted description of the first Inaugural Ball in New York in 1789 is given by Colonel Stone:

"Few jewels were then worn in the United States, but in other respect their dresses were rich and beautiful, according to the fashions of the day. We are not quite sure that we can describe the full dress of a lady of rank in the period under consideration so as to render it intelligible. But we will make the attempt. One favorite dress was a plain celestial blue satin gown, with a white satin petticoat. On the neck was worn a large Italian gauze handkerchief, with border stripes of satin. The head-dress was a *pouf* of gauze, in the form of a globe, the *creneaux* or head-piece of which was composed of white satin, having a double wing, in large plaits, and trimmed with a wreath of artificial roses falling from the left at the top to the right at the bottom in front, and the reverse be-

19. WASHINGTON'S UNIFORM.

20. PARTY COSTUMES FOR BOYS, EDGED WITH EMBROIDERY. THIS WAS A PERIOD WHEN BOTH MEN AND BOYS WORE KNEE BREECHES FOR FULL DRESS.

hind. The hair was dressed all over in detached curls, four of which, in two ranks, fell on each side of the neck, and was relieved behind by a floating *chignon*. Another beautiful dress was a perriot, made of gray Indian taffeta, with dark stripes of the same color, having two collars, the one yellow, and the other white, both trimmed with a blue silk fringe, and a reverse trimmed in the same manner. Under the perriot they wore a yellow corset or boddice, with large cross stripes of blue. Some of the ladies with this dress wore hats *a l'Espagnole* of white satin, with a band of the same material placed on the crown, like the wreath of flowers on the head-dress above-mentioned. This hat, which, with a plume, was a very popular article of dress, was relieved on the left side, having two handsome cockades, one of which was at the top and the other at the bottom. On the neck was worn a very large plain gauze handkerchief, the ends of which were hid under the bodice."

At Washington's second inauguration, in Philadelphia, 1793, we learn that he wore: "a full suit of black velvet, his hair powdered and in a bag; diamond knee buckles, and a light sword with gray scabbard." Jefferson was dressed in a blue suit with red vest. Mr. Adams wore a suit of fine gray cloth.

Part II
MILITARY UNIFORMS AND STAGE PROPERTIES

To those patriotic citizens, who in 1932 will celebrate the Bicentennial of General George Washington's birth by pageant or play, the uniforms worn by American, French, Hessian and British soldiers during the Revolution are of signal interest and as important a matter for dramatic consideration as the costumes of the citizenry.

The costumer of a production is interested: first, in the materials and design of the garments; second, in the decorations and appurtenances.

From the records of the French, Hessian and British regiments, which served in America during the Revolution, authentic descriptions are available as to the type of uniforms, their color and decorations. It is regrettable that more complete records are not accessible concerning the clothing worn by American soldiers during the Revolution. Only from the patient research of Colony, State and Continental records, diaries, orderly books, and descriptions of deserters have writers been able to collect the knowledge on this subject from which the information for this chapter has been derived.

Uniforms of American Army

Soldiers in the American Army, prior to 1780, wore many varieties of uniforms. Each Colony, each regiment, and at times each company dressed its men as it desired. This wide variation in uniforms worn by the Continental Army was due to the fact that the obtaining of clothing was a major problem confronting American leaders. The color and cut of the uniform was of secondary importance and consideration. Throughout the war the source of supply was limited. There were practically no manufactories in the Colonies for production of clothing materials. Each family grew its own flax and wool, which was prepared and woven in the home, and the quantity of this home-made material was necessarily limited during the war. Welcome were the stores of British uniforms captured at St. Johns, Saratoga, or at sea by privateers fitted out by General Washington's order, although expedients to disguise them in order to prevent confusion on the battlefield had to be devised. Even before the consummation of the French alliance, some materials were secured abroad.

At the outbreak of the Revolution, little thought was given to military dress by the American farmers and townsmen who first formed themselves into companies of Minute Men, or even by those who organized the active militia. Both officers and men wore their most serviceable civilian clothing. They supplied their own arms and equipment. Some had shoulder belts and cartridge boxes made of leather or canvas, although the usual method of carrying powder and ammunition was by way of the familiar powder-horn and bullet pouches. Most of the officers were armed as were their men, with musket or rifle, which they always carried while on duty. As a designation of rank, officers carried a short sword of no regular design.

Uniforms for Americans are not mentioned in the accounts of Lexington and Concord, though it is possible there were present veterans of the French and Indian Wars, who wore their old uniforms of red or blue faced with red as prescribed for Colonial troops in British service. At the battle of Bunker Hill, the only uniformed organization was the Wethersfield Company of Connecticut, commanded by Captain John Chester, which company wore blue uniforms faced with red. However, the men of this company, not desiring to expose themselves to danger because of their unusual dress, donned hunting frocks and trousers over their uniforms.

Materials Used in Continental Uniforms

Almost every kind of material was used in the making of the early uniforms, from broadcloth to canvas. The coats were of coarse, home-woven, woolen materials. Commissioned and non-commissioned officers' coats were often made of a finer grade of woolen than those of the privates. Waistcoats and breeches were fashioned from a variety of materials—

21.   AMERICAN OFFICER.   22.   AMERICAN PRIVATE.

drilling, linen, woolen, leather and buckskin. In warm weather, breeches and waistcoats of coarse linen were generally worn; for winter wear, those garments were made of woolen material when such was obtainable.

The Indian hunting shirt and leggings, which were more often seen than any other type of uniforms, were made of doeskin, buckskin, and linen.

Variety of materials was used also in the manufacture of the hats and caps. Many of the hats were made of felt. The caps were fashioned from cloth, different skins, or heavy leather. The coonskin cap of the frontiersman was popular head-dress. Straw hats were worn in summer by some regiments.

The Rifle Dress or Hunting Shirt

The settlers on the outskirts of Colonial civilization were quick to note the advantages of certain Indian raiment and adopted a costume that was variously called the rifle dress, hunting frock or Indian hunting shirt. It was the picturesque garb worn by the expert rifleman of the Carolinas, Maryland, Virginia, and Pennsylvania. Washington was particularly familiar with this type of garment, having donned it himself during his frontier experiences. He appreciated its advantages for field service and early in the war expressed the desire that the army be uniformed in this attire. In fact, it became the field dress of almost the entire army.

The hunting shirt was made of deerskin, linen or homespun. The pattern was cut very simply on the lines of an ordinary shirt to be pulled on over the head and gathered in at the waist by a belt. The length varied from just below the hips to knee length—the most popular design. Different regiments adopted different color schemes and the hunting shirts were dyed various colors, such as tan, green, blue, yellow, purple, black or white. Some had capes and cuffs only of different colors. With the hunting shirts were worn long leggings or overalls, also preferred by Washington to breeches and stockings. These were made of linen or duck, undyed, or of deer leather, and later in the war were furnished in wool for winter wear. They were shaped to the leg, fastened at the ankle with four buttons, and had a strap under the shoe.

In his General Orders of July 24, 1776, General Washington pointed out several advantages of the rifle dress: "No Dress can be had cheaper, nor more convenient, as the Wearer may be cool in warm weather, and warm in cool weather by putting on under Cloaths which will not change the outward dress, Winter or Summer—Besides which it is a dress justly supposed to carry no small terror to the enemy, who think every such person a complete Marksman."

Hunting shirts were not considered uniforms but were a substitute when coats could not be procured. Their general use was such, however, that they were practically service uniforms or field dress. Early in the war, they were required to be worn by both officers and men of the regular Virginia troops in Continental service, all dyed the same color in each regiment. The hunting shirts of at least the 6th. Virginia Regiment, in 1775 and 1776, were differentiated to show rank, with small white cuffs on the sergeant's shirts, dark cuffs on the drummers', and fringe on the officers', while the men's were plain.

The Design of the Uniform Coat

Since the introduction of firearms, the uniforms of most armies have been much the same in line and cut. Aside from the decorations and a few individual features, such as the collar and cuffs, the same pattern could have been used for the American, French, British and Hessian forces. The coat was cut with a rather tight sleeve and full skirt, knee length, a trifle short of the knee, or half-way between waist and knee. The longer length predominated.

The linings of the coat were of various colors and when the tails were turned back and buttoned, as was the custom, the lining was prominently displayed. Practically all coats were double-breasted with lapels to the waist, having colored facings which showed as a decorative feature when buttoned back. A variety of collars and cuffs were used, the general favorite being a collar of generous proportions which could be turned up high for protection in cold weather or worn folded over. Later in the war, because of French influence, both American and British armies adopted the straight standing collar. The coats were provided with ample pockets, the opening at the waist line protected by a flap fashioned with buttonholes.

The Waistcoat

The waistcoats were designed without sleeves and cut on the same gen-

23. BRITISH PRIVATE   24. BRITISH OFFICER

eral lines as those worn today, with the exception of the length and neck opening; that of the Colonial uniform being longer and having a higher cut at the neck. The pockets of the vest were provided with flaps which could be buttoned down the same as those on the coat.

The breeches were tight-fitting, cut to end below the knee. From the bottom of the leg to a point three or four inches above the knee, the outside seam was left open and held snug to the knee with buttons or straps and buckles.

Both the waistcoat and breeches were of the same design in the American, French, British and Hessian forces.

Washington Introduces Trousers

General Washington wrought an innovation in military uniforms of that period and perhaps was responsible for the introduction of the long trousers worn today. The superiority of the long trousers over breeches and stockings for field service became apparent early in the war. After the campaign of 1776, General Washington prescribed this type of garment for general field wear. Like the leggings of the hunting costume, these were slashed to the leg and fastened with four buttons at the ankle and a strap under the shoe.

The British soon saw the advantages of this garment in campaigning a country like America and adopted it for their troops. On the return of British troops to England after peace was declared, they took this style with them and later it was generally adopted by the British army and Englishmen influenced by the army, until soon long trousers became the prevalent fashion for male civilian wear.

25. A MINUTEMAN.

26. A FRONTIERSMAN

Color of Uniforms

The first official color for Continental uniforms was brown, it being adopted by the Continental Congress on November 4, 1775, after consulting with General Washington and the New England Governors. Regiments were to be distinguished by facings of different colors. This action by Congress was not much more than a recommendation, as the troops were never all in brown. The majority of the Connecticut troops, throughout the war, wore uniform coats of brown faced with buff, white, or red. The first Pennsylvania Battalion also wore a brown coat, as did many of the first Continental regiments.

Early in the war, blue was the favorite color for officers' dress, and by the end of 1778, blue was the color preferred by the men. On March 23, 1779, the Continental Congress, in an ordinance regulating the clothing department, authorized Washington to prescribe the colors and cut of the uniforms of the respective states and regiments. Washington complied in the General Order of October 2, 1779, which fixed blue as the color for all branches of the service and for all the State regiments in the Continental line, with distinctive differences in linings and facings. For artillery and artillery artificer regiments, the uniform was ordered to be blue, faced and lined with scarlet, with yellow buttons, the coats to be edged, and the buttonholes to be bound, with narrow lace or tape. The light dragoons were to wear blue, faced and lined with white and with white buttons. The blue coats of the infantry regiments were all to be lined with white and to have white buttons, and States were distinguished by different colored facings, as follows: the New England States—New Hampshire, Massachusetts, Rhode Island, and Connecticut—white facings; New York and New Jersey—buff facings; Pennsylvania, Delaware, Maryland, and Virginia—red facings; North Carolina, South Carolina and Georgia—blue facings and buttonholes edged with narrow white tape.

All Continental troops were not at once clothed according to this order, and some of them probably never were, but officers were requested to conform to it, and the men were furnished the standard uniform in so far as supplies would permit. Thus, eventually, after the Revolutionary War had progressed for several years, blue became the prescribed color for the coats of the American Army. The reason for its adoption as the distinctive color was undoubtedly because it had been the insignia, with the addition of buff, of the Whigs of Great Britain in their struggle for constitutional liberty, and naturally blue and buff became the colors of the Whig party in America.

There prevails, in the minds of most Americans, the erroneous belief that the blue coat faced or trimmed with buff was the regulation uniform coat of the Continental Armies. Red was the color most popular and was more generally in use for facings and the trimming of collars, cuffs and edgings. It is plain that but few troops ever wore the "blue and buff," and after General Washington's "uniform" order of 1779, it was worn only by general officers, unattached aides, the First and Second New York Continental Infantry, First and Second New Jersey Continental Infantry of the Line, Corps of Engineers, Sappers and Miners, and Washington's bodyguards, who were selected men from the Infantry arm—altogether numerically few.

Trimmings of Uniforms and Insignia of Rank

As the uniform coats were all double-breasted and the custom was to turn back the lapels from collar to waistline and button them to show the brighter facings, many buttons were used, often a dozen, necessarily set close together. The corresponding button holes were worked with silk or edged with braid of the regimental colors.

The collars were of the same color as the facings and usually had a button-hole at the angle of the wing so that they could be buttoned to the coat, close to the neck, thus insuring an upright position. The cuffs were made to turn back at the wrist, displaying the colored facings; button-holes in the cuffs permitting them to be buttoned to the sleeve and so held in place. In cold weather the cuffs could be turned down over the hand.

The lining of the coat was usually of a different color from the facings. Occasionally the edges of the coat were trimmed with a braid of a different color. The waistcoat was without decoration, beyond button-holes on the flaps of the pockets and now and then an edging of braid.

The hat was generally untrimmed, though some regiments had the edge of the brims finished in a bright colored braid.

Up to 1780 the insignia of rank was as varied as the types and colors of the uniforms. On the Sabbath Day, from his Headquarters, Short Hills, New Jersey, 18th June, 1780, Washington issued a General Order, prescribing, apparently for the first time, the uniform of general officers and of the staff generally. The order was as follows:

"As it is at all times of great importance, both for the sake of appearance and for the regularity of service, that the different military ranks should be distinguished from each other, and more especially at the present, the Com-

27. FRENCH PRIVATE.　28. FRENCH OFFICER.

mander-in-Chief has thought proper to establish the following distinctions, and strongly recommends it to all officers to endeavor to conform to them as speedily as possible. The Major Generals to wear blue coats, with buff facings and lining, yellow buttons, white or buff underclothes, two epaulettes, with two stars upon each, and a black and white feather in the hat. The stars will be furnished at Headquarters. The Brigadier Generals, the same uniform as the Major Generals, with the difference of one star in the place of two, and a white feather. The Colonels, Lieut. Colonels and Majors, the uniform of their regiments and two epaulettes. The captains, the uniforms of their regiments and an epaulette on the right shoulder. The Subalterns, the uniform of their regiments and an epaulette on the left shoulder. The Aides-de-Camp, the uniform of their General officers. Those of the Major Generals and brigadier Generals to have a green feather in the hat. Those of the Commander-in-Chief, a white and green. The Inspectors, as well Sub. as Brigade, the uniforms of their ranks and Corps, with a blue feather in the hat. The Corps of Engineers and that of Sappers and Miners, a blue coat with buff facings, red lining, buff underclothes, and the epaulettes of their respective ranks. Such of the Staff as have military rank to wear the uniform of their ranks, and of the Corps to which they belong in the line. Such as have no military rank to wear plain coats, with a cockade and sword. All officers, as well warrant as commissioned, to wear a cockade and side arms—either a sword or genteel bayonet. The General recommends it to the officers, as far as practicable, to provide themselves with the uniforms prescribed for their respective Corps by the regulations of Congress, published in General Orders, the 2d of October last."

Soon after, General Washington forbade officers to make any alteration in the prescribed uniform. He also directed that the feathers to be worn by Major-Generals should have white below and black above, and recommended to the officers to have white and black cockades, a black ground with a white relief, emblematic of the expected union of the two armies, American and French—the French uniform for the Infantry of the line was then white.

Suggested Uniforms for Pageants and Plays

The farmers of Lexington and Concord and the Minute Men should be dressed in civilian costumes—smallclothes (breeches and waistcoat) of almost any color. The breeches tight fitting and buttoned at the knee; the waistcoat cut long with flaps on the pockets. The character may wear a coat or not as desired. The coats were of a wide range of colors.

The shirts were generally made of white material cut with very full sleeves and having a wide collar open at the throat, or a stock. The stockings should be of a plain color, white, gray or blue. Figured stockings were never worn. Low shoes with large buckles are the prescribed footwear.

The hats of the three-cornered variety, usually termed tricorne, should be of felt. For equipment, a long rifle of the muzzle-loading type and a powder-horn slung across the shoulder by a leather string. Plate No. 25, page 592, illustrates the dress of these characters.

The Frontiersman

This character is best represented when dressed in the Indian hunting shirt, preferably cut with a cape. It should be fringed at the bottom of the skirt, the outside seams of the sleeves and the bottom of the cape.

The leggings or trousers should be close-fitting and follow closely the shape of the leg. At the bottom they should extend over the instep, the outside seam should be fringed. For material use soft leather or khaki.

Moccasins should be used for footwear with this costume.

A coonskin cap was usually worn both in summer and winter; however, any fur cap with a tail fastened pendant to the back is appropriate.

The hunting shirt should be brought together at the waist with a wide leather belt; attached to it, a sheath for a hunting knife. Tomahawks, part of the frontiersman's equipment, were as a rule carried thrust through the belt. A muzzle-loading rifle with a powder-horn slung about shoulder.

Plate No. 26, on page 592, gives an excellent illustration of the frontiersman's dress.

As it is impossible to fea-

ture the many different uniforms of the various organizations in the Colonial Army, it is well to select one authentic type. And it is suggested that the uniform illustrated in Plate No. 22, page 590, be used, as it was the most popular uniform of the American Army.

The Colonial Private Soldier

The coat is of blue faced with red and lined with white, the waistcoat and breeches of a buff colored material. White or gray stockings should be worn, with black half gaiters or spatterdashes covering the ankles and reaching to the calf of the leg. The gaiters can be made of duck or linen. A dark blue or black stock should be worn, the ends inside the vest.

The hat of felt is the familiar tricorne, with a rosette or pompon of red, white and blue.

French Uniforms

For the private of the French Army, in the full dress uniform of a corporal of a grenadier company, Plate 27, page 593, furnishes an illustration that it would be advisable to follow.

The coat, breeches, waistcoat and long leggings are of a white material. The facing of the coat is cut differently from the American and British uniforms with a standing collar in place of the roll collar. Violet or green was used in facings and trimmings. In the field, the troops usually wore long black leggings in place of the white.

No striking distinction in dress was made between the officers and men beyond the fact that the officers' uniforms were of finer cloth. Plate No. 28, page 593, illustrates a captain of Infantry on parade.

White coat, waistcoat, breeches and leggings, with facings and trimmings of green. Note the high standing collar and the gorget at the throat. This latter decoration was a quarter moon, shaped and made in gilt with the Royal Arms superimposed in silver. The officers were distinguished by a white pompon on the hat.

The officers on campaign wore black leggings and in cold weather cloak of white

29. DETAILS OF COLONIAL UNIFORM.

cloth with a cape six or seven inches wide on the shoulders. No jabots or cuffs of lace, and no sashes were allowed at this period. The coat collars and lapels were always worn hooked.

British Uniforms

There is said to have been sixty-six different British Regiments in America between 1775 and 1783. As each of these regiments had its own distinctive uniforms, space does not permit of a description of each. Red was the color most used for the coats of all branches of the service—infantry, artillery and cavalry—though some few regiments wore other colors for full dress.

As a typical example of the uniform worn by the majority of British soldiers in America during the Revolution, we have selected a grenadier of the Fifth Regiment of Foot. See Plate No. 23, on page 591.

A red coat, faced with green, is of the usual military cut of the period, white waistcoat and breeches, white stockings, black half gaiters.

The tall bearskin cap with the coat of arms of Great Britain on the tall visor can be used; or, if this type of cap is not obtainable, a black felt tricorne hat is appropriate, for many British regiments used that type of head-dress,—such as the 43rd Regiment of Foot, which had the misfortune to lose its colors at Yorktown when captured with Cornwallis.

Plate No. 24, page 591, illustrates a general officer of the British Army. The same uniform, with the exception of the star on the coat and the ribbon across the waistcoat—which are both insignia of the Order of the Bath—can be worn by a regimental line officer.

A faithful reproduction of this uniform for all British officers is recommended to costumers. Top-boots or long leggings were worn when in the field.

The coat is red with blue velvet facings. Gold braid is used to edge button-holes and for the decorations. Waistcoat and breeches of white, white stockings. The brim of the hat is trimmed with gold braid.

A crimson sash was worn by all general officers.

Accoutrements

SWORDS.—There was a wide variety of swords used by American officers, from the heavy cavalry saber to the dress sword. Those worn by the Infantry officers were not as long as those used later by our Army. Washington's sword is a fine example of the sword used at that time.

The scabbard was made of leather and the sword hung from a waist belt and often by a belt worn across the shoulder. The belt or shoulder belt was never worn outside the coat, both types being worn over the vest, beneath the coat.

RIFLES AND BAYONETS.—The rifles and muskets used at that time were all of the muzzle-loading variety and longer than the service rifle of today. The bayonet was the same type as that used during the Civil War, more like a rapier than the knife type used now. The bayonet was worn in a leather scabbard attached to a white shoulder or cross belt.

CARTRIDGE BOXES AND CROSS BELTS.—The bayonet shoulder belt worn over the right shoulder and the cartridge-box belt worn over the left shoulder were known as cross-belts. In color, white, made of leather or canvas, they stood out in sharp contrast against the dark color of the coat. The cartridge box, which held powder and shot, was usually of black leather.

HAVERSACKS.—The haversack was a bag, closed by a flap and provided with a wide sling so it could be carried slung across the shoulder. The haversack was used by the soldier to carry his spare clothing and personal effects and was more often used than the knapsack. As it is extremely difficult to secure the Colonial type of knapsack, it is advisable for the costumer to provide his soldier characters, when in heavy marching order, with the haversack.

BOOTS, SHOES.—The private soldier wore a heavy, square-toed, low-cut black shoe, fastened with a large buckle of brass. Costumers can provide this type of shoe or a low, modern oxford with square toes can be used with a buckle, cut out of tin and gilded, fastened about the instep with a wide elastic. Boots were worn by general officers, staff and mounted officers of the American, French and British Armies, in the field and practically on all occasions. Boots were even correct for social functions, though as a rule were discarded for stockings and buckled shoes at dances and evening social affairs. The top-boot, as it was called, was made on the same general lines as the riding boot or officers' dress boot of today, except the top, from which it derives its name. The fox-hunting clubs still use the top-boot, which can be purchased at almost any large shoe store or can be supplied by costumers. An expedient often used, and one that is very satisfactory, is to use a black riding boot, of the type worn today, with a false top made from a piece of thin brown leather about four or five inches wide and long enough to encircle the boot. Sew the ends together and draw the false top over the boot leg, bringing the top edges together and fastening them to prevent the false top from slipping.

The cavalry soldier of all the armies wore the high jack-boot.

LEGGINGS AND GAITERS.—When in the field, to protect their stockings, infantry officers and privates of all armies wore some form of gaiter or legging. The American Army adopted the half-gaiters, or spatterdashes, as they were then called. These were made in the same form as modern gaiters or spats, except that they extended farther up the leg to the swell of the calf. They were buttoned on the outside and made of canvas and painted black. The majority of the British infantry wore the spatterdashes while the others wore a long, buttoned legging, reaching above the knee and gaitered below the knee. This type of legging was made of a black woolen material. The French and Hessian troops also wore the long legging. That of the French was white, of the Hessian, black.

GLOSSARY

AIGRET (egret)—Cluster of feathers to be worn on the head.

ALAMODE—Plain, glossy silk used throughout the eighteenth century.

ALLAPINE, ALLPINE, ELLOPINE, ALPINE—A woolen used for men's clothing in the early 1700's.

AMAZEEN—Corded silk popular in the Colonies and on the Continent until late eighteenth century.

APRON—An article of utility and also of fashion. First worn for protection and later for style. In 1744, most fashionable if very long.

ARTOIS—A many caped cloak worn by men and women in the late eighteenth century.

BAND—Kind of collar. Made of lace or linen.

BAND BOX—A box made to hold bands.

BANDILEERS—Cases in which soldiers carried charges of powder.

BANYAN—Lounging gown worn by both men and women.

BARRY, BARRIE—A petticoat.

BARNELL—Leather apron worn by working men.

BATTS—Low shoes with lacings.

BELL-HOOPS—Petticoats stiffened to have the shape of a bell. Fashionable in 1731.

BINDER—A baby band.

BIRDET—Silk from the Orient.

BOLE-WIG—The wig worn upon ordinary occasions from 1725 to 1780. It was cut short with the hair closely dressed.

BONE-LACE—So called because it was made with bone bobbins. Usually a linen lace.

BONNET—Headgear popular throughout the eighteenth century. Silk bonnets worn as early as 1725.

BONNET-PAPER—Pasteboard put in bonnets to give them their shape.

BOSOM BOTTLE—Tiny glass bottle worn in the lady's stomacher to hold water for flowers.

BREAST KNOT—A knot of colored ribbon which came into fashion in 1730. George Washington ordered ones from England for his wife and stepdaughter.

BREECHES—Worn by men during the Colonial and early national period. At first baggy affairs drawn tight at the waist and knees; later skin tight.

BREECHES HOOKS—A man writing of life in Alexandria, Va., in Washington's time, said that breeches were hung upon hooks and the gentleman donned them by going up several steps and lowering himself into them.

BUFFONTS—A puffed-out fichu. Worn over the bodice and above the breast to give a pouter pigeon effect. Usually made of gauze or net. Worn in the later eighteenth century—1771 and on.

BUTTONS—Buttons and buttonholes were very ornate. George Washington had several sets of fine shell buttons. Covered buttons, semi-precious stone buttons, steel buttons, shell buttons and paste buttons were all in style.

CALAMANCO—A popular patterned material, a glossy woolen satin-twilled stuff. The design was only on one side of the fabric. Used for shoes as well as dresses.

CALASH—A bonnet which was extensible and could be brought down over the face or pushed back; in shape resembling the top of a chaise or calash.

CALICO—Cotton fabric in general wear at the time of the Revolution. Originally a material imported from Calicut, India—hence the name.

CALKS—Spiked soles to help the wearer walk on ice.

CAMPAIGN WIG—A wig for undress wear, fashionable in the late seventeenth and early eighteenth century. Not as elaborate as the peruke but made full and curled to the front.

CAPUCHIN—A fashionable cloak of the eighteenth century patterned after the garb of a Capuchin friar—short silk cloak with hood attached.

CARDINAL—A cloak patterned after that of cardinals. Worn in red and other bright colors.

CASKET GIRLS—Girls sent by the French government to Louisiana. So called because each had an allotment of clothing in a trunk or casket as part payment for emigration.

CANSHETS—Corsets worn by children.

CHICKEN SKIN—Used for gloves—and worn at night—to keep hands white.

CHINTS—A cotton print—chintz.

CHIN-CLOUT—A lace cravat for women.

CLOGS—Wooden shoe tipped and shod with iron. Worn as overshoes in bad weather. Eighteenth century.

COMING OUT BRIDE—Quaint custom of the bride showing off her smart apparel at church on Sunday.

Commode—Women's head-dress arranged upon a frame of wire and draped with thin silk.

Curli Wurlis—Fancy curls.

Dag Wain—Coarse material for utilitarian purposes.

Damask—An elaborately patterned fabric, in silk, wool, or linen.

Drawers—Breeches for summer wear.

Engagements—Lace elbow ruffles.

Eschelles—A ladder-laced stomacher.

Fontange—Ribbon bow worn on the head. Named after Mlle. Fontange who introduced it at the French Court.

Furbelow—A gathered flounce for trimming a dress.

Glove Tightens—Hair- or ribbon-bands worn to keep gloves in place.

Goloe-shoes—Goloshes or overshoes, worn in bad weather.

Hair—Was used for many purposes during the eighteenth century—lace and jewelry of hair were frequently worn.

Hoops—Worn in various shapes and sizes—from 1712 to 1778.

Lappets—Lace pendants which hung from a woman's head-dress or cap.

Lawn—Lovely sheer fabric.

Loo-masks, Masks—Masks, covering only half the face, worn for protection against the sun.

Mantua—A type of sacque worn out of doors. Also the name of a silk.

Mitts—Fingerless gloves made of kid, lace, linen, and silk.

Modesty-piece—Strip of lace placed across the top of the stays.

Muffs—Carried by men and women from the early seventeenth century. First of wool, later of feathers or fur.

Nightrail—A dressing-gown adopted by women for morning wear.

None-So-Prettys—Trimming tapes in fancy patterns.

Palisade—A wire used in hairdressing. Part of the commode head-dress.

Panniers—Series of hoops fastened together by tapes.

Patches—Beauty marks of court-plaster, various shapes and sizes, stuck on the face.

Pattens—Shoes with wooden sole and iron bands that raised the feet of the wearer out of the mud or dust.

Petty-cote—A petticoat. Quilted ones were in fashion in the eighteenth century.

Pillion—Platform behind the saddle upon which women rode.

Pinner—Child's bib or apron. George Washington ordered pinners for little Nelly Custis.

Pomander—Perforated ball for perfume.

Ramillies—Style of wig—which came in vogue about 1708—had a braided tail in back with a large bow at the top and little one at the bottom.

Safeguard—An outside petticoat pulled on over the dress for protection. Worn when riding.

Smock—Workman's shirt of heavy linen.

Snuff Boxes—Used for carrying snuff. In general use in 1702.

Solitaire—A black ribbon worn around the neck. Men usually tied it to the back of the wig, brought it around in front and tucked it in their shirt ruffle.

Steinkirk—A cravat looped around the neck in a nonchalant manner.

Stock—Stiff neckwear fastened in back with a stock buckle.

Turban—Head-dress worn with the banyan when the wig was removed.

COSTUMES WORN IN THE AMERICAN
COLONIES 1740-1800

Early Indians —— —— Early Settlers —— Frontiersmen —— Early Soldiers ——

Townspeople —— ·British· —— Morgan Phila· Colonial
Infantry ·Militia· ·Line Officer· ·Rifleman· 1ˢᵗ City Troop· Infantry ·Artillery· Cavalry· Clergy· Townspeople ——

Schoolboy   Surveyor — Officer with Braddock — Commander-in-Chief   President
GEORGE WASHINGTON

Authorities Consulted

Collection at the National Museum, Washington, D. C., prepared by Mrs. Rose G. Hoes.

Two Centuries of Costume in America—Alice Morse Earle.

Child Life in Colonial Days—Alice Morse Earle.

Historic Dress in America—Elizabeth McClellan.

The Psychology of Dress—Frank Alvah Parsons.
Early American Costume—Edward Warwick and Henry Pitz.
Short History of the English Colonies in America—Henry Cabot Lodge.
Uniforms of the United States Army, published by U. S. Government.

George Washington

PLAYS

WRITTEN FOR THE

CELEBRATION OF THE TWO HUNDREDTH ANNIVERSARY

OF THE

BIRTH OF GEORGE WASHINGTON

LIST OF
GEORGE WASHINGTON PLAYS

The following plays were written by Major R. B. Lawrence of the Play and Pageant Department of the United States George Washington Bicentennial Commission, with the exception of "The Blue Goblet," which was written by Mr. James K. Knudson, of the same Department:

MOTHER AND SON—Depicts young George Washington's early inheritance of manhood and his deep respect for his mother.

THE LURE OF THE SEA—Based on incident of George Washington giving up a fond desire—the career of a midshipman.

A YOUTH OF THE FRONTIER—Portrays George Washington in the role of a young surveyor among the "squatters" on the frontier.

THE BLUE GOBLET—George and his brother Lawrence attend a meeting of the "Beefsteak and Tripe Club" in the Barbados, where George frustrates a plot to poison the host.

MATCHING WITS—Revolves about Major Washington's trip to Fort Le Boeuf to warn the French to leave the territory.

VINDICATED—Though certain aristocrats accuse Washington of cowardice for withdrawing from Fort Necessity, he is fully vindicated.

I FOLLOW WASHINGTON—A dramatic page from history dealing with General Braddock's disastrous march on Fort Duquesne.

THAT IS MY ANSWER—Reveals how Washington defeats an intrigue set afoot to make him a Tory leader.

THE INDIAN'S PROPHECY—On the shores of the Great Kanawha an Indian Sachem foretells a great future for George Washington.

WASHINGTON GOES IN—Washington's mastery and influence make possible the sending of Virginia delegates to the Continental Congress.

WASHINGTON TAKES THE RISK—Despite the warning counsel of Lord Fairfax, Washington determines to serve the Colonial cause.

THE CRISIS AT YORKTOWN—Victory—a dreadful uncertainty, until the flag of truce is seen waving over the besieged British camp.

THE DOMINANT FORCE—Certain foreign agents are thwarted in their efforts to align President Washington with the large States.

BUILDING A NATION—A popular and frenzied demand for another war against England is quelled by President Washington.

HAPPINESS DAY—An atmosphere play concerning Martha Washington's observance of her wedding anniversary after the death of the President.

The following plays were contributed by the playwrights indicated:

'TWIXT CUP AND LIP, by *Pauline Hopkins* and *Ellen Garrigues*—A plot to assassinate the Commander-in-Chief is foiled. D. A. R. prize one-act play.

WASHINGTON DANCED, by *France Goldwater*—Wherein the Commander-in-Chief employs the dance as a medium of strategy in time of war.

THE VIEW FROM THE WINDOW, by *Kathleen Read Coontz*—A short three-act play wherein Washington escapes betrayal by a supposed friend into British hands.

THE WASHINGTONS AT HOME, by *Dwight Marfield*—A play set at Mount Vernon in which the Minuet and Colonial music are featured.

FOREWORD

The George Washington Bicentennial Celebration in 1932 afforded an opportunity for child and adult, student and teacher; for clubs, schools, and churches; for civic, fraternal, cultural, patriotic, and dramatic organizations; for both the American and the foreign-born in our midst, to give wide expression to forms of dramatic entertainment and enlightenment concerning the life of George Washington.

To satisfy the great demand for authentic historical and effective dramatic material about General Washington and his time, the Commission published a series of nineteen George Washington plays, fifteen of which were written in the Play and Pageant Department of the Commission, and the remaining four by playwrights whose interest was aroused by the dramatic possibilities of the Bicentennial Celebration.

The object of the plays was to portray the true character of George Washington as the writer conceived it to be. In the main, the characters and the scenes are faithful pictures of persons, events, and crises. Whatever departure was made from strict historical accuracy was done with the idea of enhancing the dramatic effectiveness of the play.

The actual production of the play must, of course, be left to the discretion and skill of the director and to the enthusiasm of the actors in portraying the roles which represent many of the greatest characters in American history.

The United States George Washington Bicentennial Commission offered a wide variety of historical material, to aid in the production of the plays under given needs and auspices, and every one was invited, whether professional or amateur, to participate in reliving and re-enacting the life of THE FATHER OF HIS COUNTRY.

GEORGE WASHINGTON AND THE THEATRE

EXCERPTS FROM AN ADDRESS OF HON. SOL BLOOM, ASSOCIATE DIRECTOR, UNITED STATES GEORGE WASHINGTON BICENTENNIAL COMMISSION, BEFORE THE NATIONAL MOTION PICTURE THEATRE OWNERS CONVENTION IN WASHINGTON, MARCH 14, 1932

. . . George Washington was all his life a devoted lover and a pioneer promoter of the theatre in America. . . .

From his boyhood days onward, and especially during his two terms as President of the United States, he visited the theatre whenever opportunity permitted. This country had no more devoted upholder of the stage. It was at a time when the theatre was not popular. There were comparatively few theatres in America and the acting profession was not upon the high and dignified plane that it is today. But George Washington through his personal prestige and the influence of his high station as President, did a vast amount to foster and develop the theatre in our country.

Perhaps if the full truth were known George Washington did more than any other one person to bring the legitimate stage to an honorable recognition among the public. . . . If he had chosen to regard the theatre unfavorably he might have retarded its development for years. The great majority of Americans in his day would have followed his example and turned their backs upon it. . . . But he set his stamp on the theatre, and that stamp was a guarantee that the plays presented were of a high order.

The details of George Washington's delight in plays and entertainment of any kind make one of the brightest pages in his life story.

In all this love of drama and spectacle and music he was of the broadest gauge. He visited the circus. He attended that form of entertainment that we call vaudeville today. He took guests to see a mechanical marvel known as the "Microcosm." He liked light opera—what we now call musical comedy. Yet he enjoyed Shakespeare and Moliere and Addison as much as he did light comedy and farce. . . .

George Washington saw his first play when he went with his brother Lawrence to the Barbados. We find it recorded in his diaries that the play he saw was "George Barnwell," written by a George Lillo. This experience so impressed him that as soon as he got back to Fredericksburg, Va., the home of his mother, he went to see another play. . . .

So strong was the passion for the theatre in George Washington that even on one of his military expeditions during the French and Indian War in 1757, we find him attending an amateur performance at Fort Cumberland, in the heart of the Maryland wilderness.

After his marriage and while he was a member of the Virginia legislature, Col. Washington and his bride attended theatrical performances, concerts and even a sleight of hand performance. During his early married life at Mount Vernon he rode up to Alexandria to see a distinguished company produce "The Tragedy of Douglass." And he thought so well of the good influence of the theatre that he took his stepson Jackie Custis along.

In 1771, when Washington was on one of his visits to Annapolis, we find such entries in his diaries as "Dinner and the theatre," or "Dined at the club and went to the play"—precisely as we do today.

In 1773, Washington took his stepson Jackie Custis to place him as a student in what is now Columbia University. While in New York on that errand, he made a point of seeing "Hamlet" performed. . . .

While the Revolutionary War was still on, we find George Washington enjoying a play written by a French sympathizer who did so much to bring his country to the aid of the struggling colonies. As Commander-in-Chief he witnessed a performance of Shakespeare's "Tempest," and he even unbent to attend a comic opera, as well as concerts.

So it was that on the very night of his inauguration day, President Washington visited the theatre and lent his great influence in its development. . . . Spectators noted that he went to the theater not as a matter of form, but because he enjoyed it.

. . . Finally it fell to Washington's beloved enjoyment, the theatre, to stage one of the most dramatic incidents connected with his own passing from the great stage on which he himself had played so grand a part—the great stage of world affairs.

On January 14, 1800, a play called "The Robbery" was to be given in the leading theatre of New York. The audience had assembled, but the curtain failed to go up. The assembly became impatient with the delay and demanded action. At last, an hour late, the house was darkened and very slowly the curtain rose. But all there was to be seen on the stage was a placard bearing the word: "Mourn, For Washington Is Dead."

The news had just reached New York, and the theatre that Washington loved was among the first agencies to spread the tidings that plunged a nation into sorrow.

So, even in death, George Washington figured in the theatre which he had respected all his life, and which thus loved and honored him in return. . . .

MOTHER AND SON

A GEORGE WASHINGTON PLAY IN ONE ACT

DRAMATIS PERSONAE

(IN ORDER OF THEIR APPEARANCE)

MARY BALL WASHINGTON, *Mother of George Washington.*

JASPER, *an old Negro servant.*

MRS. LITTLETON, *a neighbor.*

BETTY WASHINGTON, *sister to George.*

SALLY, *a young Negress.*

SAMUEL WASHINGTON, *brother to George.*

GEORGE WASHINGTON.

JESSIE, *a Negro nurse.*

JOHN WASHINGTON
CHARLES WASHINGTON } *Brothers to George.*

TIME: *Six days after the death of George Washington's father. Just before dusk, April 18th, 1743.*

PLACE: *Living room of Washington's house near Fredericksburg, Virginia.*

DESCRIPTION OF CHARACTERS

MARY BALL WASHINGTON:

A handsome woman, thirty-five years of age. She has an austere countenance, a dignified bearing, possessed of a certain reserve but outspoken. She is dressed in a black brocade gown over a black satin petticoat made in the style of the period. Her dark hair is arranged high on her head.

JASPER:

An old Negro servant, is dressed in very plain homespun livery, with white stock and stockings. Wears buckled shoes.

MRS. LITTLETON:

A middle-aged woman, dressed in a polonaise gown, reaching just above the ankles, the bodice laced. On her head, a frilled linen bonnet relieved by a spray of flowers. On her hand, lace, fingerless mits.

BETTY WASHINGTON:

Sister of George. Large for her ten years of age and has a blond complexion. She wears clothes of a dark hue fashioned in the style worn by children of that period. She is impulsive, headstrong, mischievous, a bit of a hoyden.

SALLY:

A young Negress about thirteen years of age, barefooted and wearing a slip of some colorful material.

SAMUEL WASHINGTON:

Aged eight, a greedy little fellow dressed in plain clothes of the period.

GEORGE WASHINGTON:

Eleven years old, very tall for his age, light brown hair worn in a queue. Wears dark brown clothes of the period.

JESSIE:

A Negro nurse of about middle age, buxom, wears a plain homespun dress with no adornment except a plain white kerchief crossed over her ample bosom. On her head a gay bandanna.

JOHN WASHINGTON AND CHARLES WASHINGTON:

Aged seven and five. Both dressed plainly in clothes worn by children of the period.

SCENE: *Just before dusk. The living room of the Washington farm on the Rappahannock. Centering the right wall, a large fireplace with its appurtenances—poker, tongs, and brush—beside it. Hanging on the wall above the fireplace, Augustine Washington's musket, powder-horn and sword. On the walls flanking the fireplace a sampler or prints of the colonial period. A window in the direct center of the rear wall overlooking a garden plot with the Rappahannock River and the hills beyond where the sun is setting. During the action dusk gathers and candles are brought in. A little to the rear of center in the left wall, a door that opens into a small hall. Against the rear wall, between the window and left wall, an early American or Old English highboy, the most beautiful piece of furniture in the room. Near the fireplace a straight-back chair, with a footstool before it and beside it a small table on which rests a work-basket plentifully filled with mending. Opposite the chair, toward the audience, but near the fireplace, a low bench about three feet long. To the left of center a large table with a chair beside it. On the table, the family Bible and Prayer Book. Two or three other chairs are placed about the room. All the furnishings should be of the type used in colonial homes.*

Seated in the chair near the fireplace is MARY BALL WASHINGTON. Her head is bowed as she slowly takes a few stitches; laying aside her mending, she takes a handkerchief and wipes away a tear, then with her face in her hands gives way to grief. There is the sound of an—"Ahem"! and shuffling footsteps in the hall. She hurriedly wipes her eyes, seizes her mending and sits bolt upright as JASPER, an old Negro servant, enters from the door at left.

JASPER: Ma'am Washington, Mis'tis Littleton has done called an' wants foh to pay her re-spe'ce.

MRS. WASHINGTON: Tell Mistress Littleton I will be pleased to see her.

[*JASPER shuffles out. MRS. WASHINGTON wipes away any traces of her grief and resumes her mending. JASPER opens the door and steps aside as MRS. LITTLETON enters. JASPER is holding a covered dish in his hand.*]

MRS. WASHINGTON: [*Standing.*] Good evening, Sarah.

MRS. LITTLETON: Good evening, Madam Washington. Tom, my husband, told me you had just got back from Bridges Creek, so I came right over.

MRS. WASHINGTON: I am glad you came, Sarah.

MRS. LITTLETON: I brought some gingerbread for you and the children. [*With a gesture toward JASPER and the dish he holds.*]

MRS. WASHINGTON: Won't you be seated? [*MRS. WASH-*

INGTON *resumes her seat by the fireplace and MRS. LITTLETON takes the chair by the table.*]

MRS. LITTLETON: [*Not quite at ease.*] It's from the recipe you wanted. I writ it and brought it along. [*Fumbles in her bag and brings out a paper and gives it to MRS. WASHINGTON and returns to her chair.*]

MRS. WASHINGTON: Oh, yes, the gingerbread. 'Tis famous all about Fredericksburg. Thanks, Sarah. It's so kind of you; I always wanted that recipe. [*To JASPER still standing by the door with the dish.*] Take the gingerbread to the springhouse, Jasper, and have Mrs. Littleton's dish ready to take with her.

MRS. LITTLETON: You must be about spent, ma'am.

MRS. WASHINGTON: The hardest journey a woman can take is the first from the grave of her husband.

MRS. LITTLETON: [*Impulsively.*] Oh, Mrs. Washington, our hearts ache for you.

MRS. WASHINGTON: I appreciate your sympathy, Sarah.

MRS. LITTLETON: Tom was a-saying only last evening, he wondered how I'd make out if he was taken sudden like. Faith, he was in a dark mood all the evening from thinking on it.

MRS. WASHINGTON: When such misfortune o'ertakes us and we must needs face the dark future alone—and yet not alone—[*Raises her eyes to One above.*] Well [*shrugs*], I can only do my best.

MRS. LITTLETON: And you will do your best, as I and everybody else knows.

MRS. WASHINGTON: 'Twill not be easy, Sarah.

MRS. LITTLETON: 'Tis well that Captain Lawrence Washington is back home. He and Mr. Augustine will be a help to you.

MRS. WASHINGTON: Captain Washington is not robust; his health was nigh ruined in the Cartagena campaign.

MRS. LITTLETON: I apprehend many of our young men will never recover from that wild goose chase.

MRS. WASHINGTON: Lawrence has, of a necessity, delayed for three months his marriage to Miss Anne Fairfax. He has plenty on his mind without being troubled by my affairs.

MRS. LITTLETON: Aye.

MRS. WASHINGTON: I do not desire assistance from my stepsons.

MRS. LITTLETON: In your own son, George, you will have comfort and a ready helper, I vow. He's such a wholesome youth.

MRS. WASHINGTON: George. I doubt if he fully realizes what his father's loss means.

MRS. LITTLETON: Faith, indeed he does, Madam. As I drove in, I saw him standing alone by the river and he hastily wiped his eyes as he beheld my carriage and bowed to me.

MRS. WASHINGTON: Weeping, my boy?

MRS. LITTLETON: How old is he now, Madam?

MRS. WASHINGTON: He has only passed his eleventh natal day.

MRS. LITTLETON: He seems much older.

MRS. WASHINGTON: He is large for his age.

MRS. LITTLETON: He rides a spirited horse as well as a grown man. My Tom says he will make much of himself. Tom says he is much like you.

MRS. WASHINGTON: Mayhap he is, but he has his father's calm, determined way. George is a good boy as boys go. Though he has a hot temper and can get into mischief aplenty, I assure you.

MRS. LITTLETON: He wouldn't be the manly boy he is, if he didn't get into mischief.

MRS. WASHINGTON: Aye, boys will. He will have but little time for pranks from now on. He must learn to be thrifty.

MRS. LITTLETON: Well, ah—now your last word brings to my mind a matter that Tom wished me to speak on—Ah—[*clears her throat*].

MRS. WASHINGTON: [*Waiting.*] Aye. What is it, Sarah?

MRS. LITTLETON: [*Flustered and embarrassed.*] I—I hope you will understand, Madam Washington, that Tom—that I—that we——

MRS. WASHINGTON: [*A trifle impatiently.*] What is it you're trying to say, Sarah? Speak up.

MRS. LITTLETON: Well, Tom wanted me to tell you that if—if——

MRS. WASHINGTON: If what?

MRS. LITTLETON: If you needed anything—that is for the time being—money, for instance—he could loan you——

MRS. WASHINGTON: Thanks, Sarah; that won't be necessary.

MRS. LITTLETON: [*A trifle hurt.*] Tom is only a trying to be neighborly, Madam. Some of our most forehanded planters are often in want of cash, goodness knows! It's scarce enough in the Colonies!

MRS. WASHINGTON: Sarah Littleton, don't you mistake me. I have the greatest respect and admiration for Thomas Littleton, and you, too.

MRS. LITTLETON: Oh, thanks, ma'am.

MRS. WASHINGTON: I am grateful for your kind offer. But, I hate debt. 'Tis true I will needs be careful and exercise due thrift to provide for my children. But my husband left me plenty of land, and——

MRS. LITTLETON: We all have plenty of land.

MRS. WASHINGTON: There is sufficient help, though the Negroes are a shiftless, trifling lot.

MRS. LITTLETON: Aye, we all have our troubles with 'em. [*She rises.*] I must be on my way before darkness is upon us. Now, if at any time——

MRS. WASHINGTON: [*Also rising.*] If by some extremity I must ask for assistance, I would first turn to Thomas and Sarah Littleton.

MRS. LITTLETON: If we could only help you——

MRS. WASHINGTON: Tell your husband for me, Sarah, that I say in all Virginia there is no kinder or more thoughtful man or better neighbor.

MRS. LITTLETON: 'Tis not seeming that I, his wife, should say so but I must agree with you, Madam.

MRS. WASHINGTON: Right you should, Sarah. And thanks for the gingerbread and recipe; 'twas kind of you to fetch them.

MRS. LITTLETON: 'Twas only fitting a neighbor should. Good night, Madam Washington.

[MRS. WASHINGTON *places the recipe in the Bible and is about to resume her mending when* JASPER *enters.*]

JASPER: Pahdon, Ma'am.

MRS. WASHINGTON: What is it?

JASPER: Tanger, dat Wes' Injun nigger, done got de mis'ry 'in an' he's took pow'ful bad, Ma'am.

MRS. WASHINGTON: I will go to the quarters at once. Have 'rry fetch my medicine chest.

JASPER: Yes-um, yes-um, Ma'am.

[MRS. WASHINGTON *leaves at left, followed by* JASPER. *As they go,* BETTY *sticks her head in the door at the right, enters and beckons to* SALLY.]

BETTY: They've gone. Come on in.

SALLY: [*Entering.*] I'se scat to deff, Miss Betty.

BETTY: Huh, scart! Mother's gone to the quatahs; Tanger's wn with the mis'ry.

SALLY: Iffen Mist'is' cotches us—ooh! [*Rolls her eyes.*]

BETTY: Did you get some?

SALLY: Uh huh.

BETTY: Give it to me. [*Holds out her hand.*]

SALLY: Yes-um. [*Takes some gingerbread, wrapped in a nap-n, from out of her waist.*]

BETTY: Three pieces only? [*Unwrapping gingerbread.*]

SALLY: Ah di'nt dast——

BETTY: 'Fraid cat.

SAMUEL: [*Enters.*] What y'a got? Gimme some.

BETTY: [*Tries to hide gingerbread behind her.*] You go right out of here, Sam.

SAMUEL: I know what 'tis. Mist'is' Littleton's gingerbread; I w Sally snitch it from the spring-house. Gimme some er I'll tell other.

BETTY: [*Breaking off a piece.*] Here. Now go!

SAMUEL: I want a big piece er I'll tell.

BETTY: You won't get any if you tell.

SAMUEL: I'll go tell mother.

BETTY: Tattle-tale! Tattle-tale!

SALLY: Ooh, heah come Massy Geo'ge!

[GEORGE WASHINGTON *enters quietly, on his face are signs of recent tears.*]

SAMUEL: Geo'ge, Sally stole gingerbread from the spring-use!

BETTY: She did not.

SAMUEL: She did so, whilst I watched.

BETTY: You mean little tattle-tale.

SAMUEL: Gimme some er I'll tell mo——

GEORGE: [*Interrupting.*] You won't tell, Samuel Wash-gton.

SAMUEL: I'll get a whole piece er I'll tell.

GEORGE: And be a sneaking tale-bearer.

BETTY: Tattle-tale! Tattle-tale!

GEORGE: Be still, Betty! Sam, we Washingtons do not carry les.

SAMUEL: [*About to cry.*] But——but, I want gingerbread.

GEORGE: That you won't have. [*To* BETTY.] We Washingtons don't take what is not our own.

BETTY: Hoity-toity, Master George. You took some melons from the Todd garden last summer.

GEORGE: Aye, Jacky Willing told on me. For it I was birched aplenty.

BETTY: [*Astonished but interested.*] Were you?

GEORGE: The beating, I didn't mind. But when father talked to me after—Oh, Betty, father will never talk to us again! [*He is close to breaking, but manfully recovers himself.*]

BETTY: [*Suddenly thoughtful.*] He never will.

GEORGE: Father said 'twas sneaking to take things and Washingtons have never been sneaky. And, said he, 'twas equally contemptuous to tell tales and Washingtons don't do such.

BETTY: [*To* SALLY, *giving her the gingerbread.*] Take it back to the spring-house quick. [*On second thought snatches it back.*] No, I'll take it back my own self. [BETTY *runs off stage, at right, with* SALLY *following her.* SAMUEL *runs off after them.* GEORGE *goes to the window, gazes at the sunset for a moment, then returns to the center and stands gazing at his father's sword and musket hanging over the mantel. A spasm of grief passes over his countenance, he is near to tears.* MRS. WASHINGTON *enters from the left, watches* GEORGE *for a moment.*]

MRS. WASHINGTON: [*Very kindly.*] Your eyes are ever turned to the instruments of war and the chase, my son. [GEORGE *turns, gazes at her, then drops his head as though in assent; she crosses to her chair by the fireplace.*] God directs our lives. Mayhap some day you will be called upon to assume the soldier, though I would have it otherwise——

GEORGE: I would be a soldier, mother.

MRS. WASHINGTON: ——should such a time arise, remember the Washingtons have never drawn their swords except in a just cause and have ever been loyal to their king.

GEORGE: I shall remember.

MRS. WASHINGTON: Divine Providence has seen fit to change the course of our lives, my son, and some of your most cherished hopes and ambitions must needs be put aside.

GEORGE: Yes, ma'am.

MRS. WASHINGTON: Your father willed the greater portion of his fortune to Captain Lawrence Washington and to Augustine Washington.

GEORGE: It was right they should have the two farms.

MRS. WASHINGTON: Of a certainty it was, but we shall have a hard struggle.

GEORGE: Will not I be sent to Appleby, as were Lawrence and Austin?

MR. WASHINGTON: I fear not; but I apprehend that while men's manners are finished in England, so, too, are some of their virtues.

GEORGE: I must keep on going to school.

MRS. WASHINGTON: That you shall, my son; to the best schools I can afford to send you.

GEORGE: [*Sorrowfully.*] I had hoped to go to school in England.

MRS. WASHINGTON: Such thoughts you must put aside.

GEORGE: Yes, ma'am.

MRS. WASHINGTON: You are the only one I have to lean on now.

GEORGE: There's Lawrence and Augustine, surely they—

MRS. WASHINGTON: They have their own affairs to attend. You are my son, my eldest. George?

GEORGE: Yes, mother.

MRS. WASHINGTON: You are now the natural head of this family, my son. [GEORGE is at first bewildered; he begins to realize the meaning of her words and again he gazes at his father's sword, squares his shoulders; a look of pride and resolution is on his countenance. MRS. WASHINGTON watches him intently.]

MRS. WASHINGTON: God has seen fit to put this responsibility upon you. Will you be worthy? Will you do as your father would have you do?

GEORGE: [Much affected, his eyes on the sword.] I'll try, mother.

MRS. WASHINGTON: [JASPER enters with candles.] Then 'tis time you started. 'Tis the hour of evening worship. Jasper!

JASPER: Yes-um, ma'am.

MRS. WASHINGTON: Have Jessie fetch the children.

JASPER: Yes-um, ma'am. [Speaking to JESSIE who is in the hall.] De ma'am done wants de chiluns, Jessie.

JESSIE: [In the hall.] Yes-um. I'se comin', we all's comin'.

[BETTY, SAMUEL, JOHN AUGUSTINE enter, followed by JESSIE leading CHARLES by the hand. BETTY curtsies, SAMUEL and JOHN bow ceremoniously to their mother, cross and sit bolt upright on the bench by the fireplace. CHARLES goes to his mother, she takes him on her lap. JASPER and JESSIE stand by the door.]

MRS. WASHINGTON: Children, give heed to the reading of the "Word." George, as head of this family, it is your duty to read the lesson. I have marked the place.

[GEORGE crosses to the table and opens the Prayer Book, his eyes are near to filling; for some time he stands vainly trying to make out the words.]

MRS. WASHINGTON: You may now begin, son.

GEORGE: [Swallowing.] Mother, I—I just can't see the—the words. Please, I can't tonight, mother.

MRS. WASHINGTON: Then just a short prayer in your ow[n] words, my son.

GEORGE: Oh, mother, I just can't.

BETTY: He can, too, mother; he can pray right hard. I hear[d] him pray when father was sick.

SAMUEL: I heard him, too.

MRS. WASHINGTON: [Kindly but firmly.] George, th[e] Washingtons never say can't; they always try.

GEORGE: I'll try. [He clasps his hands before him and bou[ws] his head, the others follow his example. In a broken voice.] Oh, God, make me like my father—make Betty and Samuel and John an[d] Charles like him, too—bless my mother and Captain Lawrence an[d] Austin and all our dear friends—Amen.

JESSIE: [Softly.] Come, chillun.

[The children kiss their mother, say their good-nights, bow ceremoniously as they reach the door and pass out. JESSIE and JASPER following. GEORGE stands with bowed head as the children pass him with awed glances.]

GEORGE: Mother,—I—I——?

MRS. WASHINGTON: Yes, George.

GEORGE: Mayhap father is looking on us from up above?

MRS. WASHINGTON: Mayhap he is, my son.

GEORGE: [Almost in tears.] "Be good to your mother" wer[e] the last words father said to me.

MRS. WASHINGTON: That he did say, George.

GEORGE: And often he said: "Americans always look afte[r] their women."

MRS. WASHINGTON: Americans do.

GEORGE: I guess you're my woman now.

MRS. WASHINGTON: Aye, I hope I will so be for a long tim[e.]

GEORGE: I hope you will so be forever, and, mother, I'll a[l]ways take care of you.

MRS. WASHINGTON: I believe you will, George.

GEORGE: I want to be like father. Oh—[He suddenly drop[s] on his knees beside his mother, buries his head in her lap, and sobs.]

MRS. WASHINGTON: Fie! Fie! George, you are too big [a] boy to give way to grief.

GEORGE: Oh, let me be a little boy just this once. I fear I'[ll] never be a little boy again.

CURTAIN

THE LURE OF THE SEA

A GEORGE WASHINGTON PLAY IN ONE ACT

DRAMATIS PERSONAE
(IN ORDER OF THEIR APPEARANCE)

GEORGE WASHINGTON.
MADAM WASHINGTON.
THE SAILOR.
CAPTAIN LAWRENCE WASHINGTON.

PETER.
RICHARD HENRY LEE.
BETTY WASHINGTON.
SAMUEL WASHINGTON.
JOHN WASHINGTON.
CHARLES WASHINGTON.

TIME: *A late summer morning in 1747.*

SCENE: *The Washington home near Fredericksburg.*

DESCRIPTION OF CHARACTERS AND COSTUMES

GEORGE WASHINGTON:

Fifteen years old, very tall for his age, light brown hair worn in a queue. Wears the uniform of a Midshipman of the British Navy—tight-fitting breeches of light yellow, with white stockings drawn over them to above the knees, garters with gold buckles below the knees; a vest, of same material as the breeches, buttoned high; a blue coat, without collar, is open, showing vest; the sleeves are turned back just below the elbow, the cuffs buttoned to the sleeves half-way between shoulder and elbow; a row of closely set gold buttons two inches from each edge of coat; at waist a wide crimson sash of silk, tied on left side; a tricorne hat of black felt.

MADAM WASHINGTON:

Thirty-nine years of age; handsome, austere countenance, dignified bearing, possessed of a certain reserve but outspoken. Wears a full gown of rich material, a fichu of lace, with lace in ruffles on the elbow sleeves; cap also of lace.

CAPTAIN LAWRENCE WASHINGTON:

Twenty-nine years of age, half-brother of GEORGE. A tall, slender, graceful figure. Wears breeches and riding boots, vest and coat of fine material decorated with braid and buttons, lace at his cuffs and throat. Hair worn in a queue and powdered. Tricorne hat. Carries a riding crop.

SAILOR:

An old sailor of the British frigate "Bellona." Wears a fringe of beard commonly called galloway, has hair in a long queue bound with black silk. A red silk handkerchief tight about his head, and worn beneath his hat. Wears tight-hipped, bell-bottomed trousers of light blue, short navy jacket of dark blue and a sailor cap of the period, shirt with red and blue stripes crosswise.

BETTY WASHINGTON:

Fourteen years of age; like her brother, GEORGE, large for her age; well developed, vivacious, a bit of a hoyden; outspoken, like her mother. Wears a long, full frock, with very short sleeves and low neck; her hair in curls.

SAMUEL, JOHN AND CHARLES, WASHINGTON:

Aged twelve, eleven and nine. Dressed in knee-breeches, white hose, buckled shoes, frilled shirts, vests and coats of rich material trimmed with braid and buttons.

RICHARD HENRY LEE:

Aged fifteen years, companion and friend of GEORGE WASHINGTON; dressed as the other boys.

PETER:

An old, colored servant. Wears white hose, breeches, coat and vest of homespun. A severe white stock.

SET: *A typical colonial room with fireplace centered on rear wall; left wall, an open window, entrance to room, left wall. Furniture of the period.*

On chairs and table are a boy's wearing apparel. MADAM WASHINGTON sits by the table looking over some of her son's clothes. GEORGE is standing by the window at left looking out.

GEORGE: [*With controlled eagerness.*] Mother, the sailor is fetching it. [*He strides to the door at left.*]

MRS. WASHINGTON: George!

GEORGE: [*Stops at the door.*] Yes, mother.

MRS. WASHINGTON: Control thy impatience, Peter will admit him.

GEORGE: But Peter ever moves like unto a snail.

MRS. WASHINGTON: And time moves on swift wings. It seems but yesterday that——[*Quickly she wipes away a tear.*]

GEORGE: [*Goes to his mother and touches her arm.*] Don't—mother—please!

MRS. WASHINGTON: ——you were a baby in my arms—my first-born.

GEORGE: Almost am I a man, now.

MRS. WASHINGTON: Manly, yes. [*Looks up at him, smiles piteously.*] Oh, my son. But a child to me.

GEORGE: [*A trifle impatiently.*] Oh, mother! Surely not a child.

[*PETER enters followed by the SAILOR with a sea chest on his shoulders. The chest is very new, carved on the front is the name "G. Washington."*]

PETER: [*Bowing.*] Ma'am Washin'n, de sea-farin' man done fetched Massa George's chess.

MRS. WASHINGTON: [*Rising and speaking to SAILOR.*] Place it here. [*Indicates a place in the center of the stage, where it is placed by the SAILOR. GEORGE kneels beside it, rubs his hand over the polished surface.*]

GEORGE: Lawrence had it made for me. Is it not a splendid chest, mother?

MRS. WASHINGTON: Splendid, yes. [*To sailor.*] 'Tis not overly large?

SAILOR: [*Bowing and pulling a forelock.*] Plenty large, ma'am. 'Tis not a great house he goeth to, but one of the King's frigates.

GEORGE: Like father's ships, there is but scant space for a crew.

SAILOR: Aye, ships of war are packed to the gunnals wi' men and cannon.

MRS. WASHINGTON: But my son will have a cabin of his own.

SAILOR: Cabin! law, ma'am! [*Notes MRS. WASHINGTON'S haughty stare.*] I axes yer pardon, ma'am—'Tis only captains and highups as gets cabins.

GEORGE: We midshipmen room together, mother.

SAILOR: Not room, me young sir, bunk together.

GEORGE: [*Quickly hiding his confusion.*] 'Tis time my chest was packed. [*Goes to chair and picks up an armful of clothes.*] Peter, you will assist.

MRS. WASHINGTON: No, [*Takes clothes from GEORGE'S arms.*] 'tis my choice, to do it for you, son. Peter may go.

PETER: Yes'sum, ma'am. [*Bows and leaves.*]

MRS. WASHINGTON: [*Kneels by chest, offers pair of stockings for SAILOR'S inspection.*] Think you these are of sufficient weight? [*GEORGE brings more clothes.*]

SAILOR: [*Feels of hose.*] They are none too heavy. He'll need 'em, ma'am.

GEORGE: [*With clothes in arms.*] But see these underclothes.

SAILOR: [*Feels of them.*] Aye, me hearty, times there has been, I'd hae given many a muckle for such.

GEORGE: [*With controlled eagerness.*] Mayhap, you were once shipwrecked?

SAILOR: Faith, that I hae—on the north Atlantic 'twas.

GEORGE: I would know of it. [*Puts down bundle.*]

SAILOR: 'Twas on the good ship *Camperdoon.*

GEORGE: A King's ship?

SAILOR: Nay, 'twas a cargo ship. Come ten weeks out of Southampton bound for Portsmouth.

GEORGE: In the Colony of New Hampshire?

SAILOR: Aye, the same. Heavy weather we made o' it—head winds fra cross the ice fields o' the north.

GEORGE: Icebergs were about? [*MADAM WASHINGTON ceases her packing and listens to the sailor.*]

SAILOR: A plenty. An' cold, whah! Freeze ye ter the marrer o' yer bones. Off the rocky coast we was hit by a gale that veered round ter the northeast quarter. The mizzen mast went o'er side snappin' the main stays, down came the main, afollowed by the fore.

GEORGE: No masts. No sails.

SAILOR: Then the good ship struck——

GEORGE: Went aground?

SAILOR: ——on one o' the reefs o' that God-forsaken coast.

GEORGE: But you got safe to shore.

SAILOR: Aye, me an' four ithers, wi' our feet an' 'ands freezed.
[*MRS. WASHINGTON shudders.*]

GEORGE: [*Notices his mother's agitation.*] In the seas to the south, 'tis calmer.

SAILOR: Aye, me young sir, betimes 'tis. But there be monsoons an' hurricanes to be reckoned wi'.

GEORGE: [*Attempting to head him off.*] When you were at Cartagena with Admiral Vernon, did you know of Captain Lawrence Washington?

SAILOR: Aye, as brave an officer as ever drew a cutlass.

GEORGE: Lawrence would be such.

SAILOR: But the likes o' that campaign!

GEORGE: [*Hastily.*] I know all of it; Captain Washington told me.

SAILOR: Told ye o' the fever an' the fightin', eh——?

MRS. WASHINGTON: What a life of deprivation and hardship for a man! How must it be for a child?

SAILOR: Toughens the fiber, ma'am; aye, toughens the fiber and makes men.

MRS. WASHINGTON: George, I would you were not to be of this life a sea. I feel—I feel——!

GEORGE: Oh, mother, 'tis not all shipwrecks and fevers and fighting. [*Appeals to SAILOR.*] Is't?

SAILOR: 'Tis a merry life all ta'en together ma'am. There be a plenty o' glory in a sailor's life. An' this likely lad ul be an Admiral some day, that he will.

GEORGE: And mayhap, I will come a-sailing up the Rappahannock, fire a salute in your honor, mother. Step ashore, grand in a cocked hat and gold lace, bringing you presents from—places round about the China seas—silks and ivory fans and——

MRS. WASHINGTON: [*Interrupting.*] Rather would I have you stay with me, than have you Lord High Admiral of the King's Navy.

GEORGE: I ever longed to be a sailor. A man must sometime start his career.

MRS. WASHINGTON: [*Shakes her head.*] A man——?

GEORGE: Methinks, in any adventure I will acquit myself like a man.

LAWRENCE WASHINGTON: [*Hears GEORGE'S words as he enters.*] Spoken like a true Washington, eh Madam. [*He bows to MRS. WASHINGTON. The SAILOR salutes LAWRENCE.*]

MRS. WASHINGTON: He is enchanted by your tales, but I—I have heard other stories of the sea.

LAWRENCE WASHINGTON: [*With a suspicious glance at the SAILOR.*] The yarns of an old salt.

GEORGE: [*Goes to LAWRENCE.*] Never can I thank you enough for this fine uniform, brother.

LAWRENCE WASHINGTON: It becomes you. Faith, it does indeed.

GEORGE: And the chest, 'tis more than I expected.

LAWRENCE WASHINGTON: Glad I am, it pleaseth you. Now let me not delay the packing.

MRS. WASHINGTON: [*Returns to packing.*] 'Tis nearly done.

LAWRENCE WASHINGTON: Good. The frigate *Bellona* is apt to drop anchor at Choptank within the hour. And he must be ready to go aboard.

MRS. WASHINGTON: Peter, go you for the gingerbread and baked ham.

PETER: Yes'sum, ma'am. [*Leaves.*]

GEORGE: [*To LAWRENCE.*] Think you gingerbread and ham proper for placement in a sailor's chest?

LAWRENCE: Of a surety. 'Twill be a welcome change from sailors' fare.

MRS. WASHINGTON: [*To SAILOR.*] Do you fare well aboard ship?

SAILOR: Well now, ma'am. I am not saying as how—[*He receives a warning look from LAWRENCE.*]—but no ship has a better mess than that o' the *Bellona*, ma'am.
[*PETER enters with ham and gingerbread in packages.*]

PETER: Ma'am, William don jest came from meeting the post, wid de letter you'se spectin'. [*Gives letter to MRS. WASHINGTON.*]

MRS. WASHINGTON: [*Takes it and breaks seal.*] From London—from my brother Joseph Ball! [*To PETER.*] Take the seaman to the kitchen; see that food is provided him.

PETER: Yes'sum, ma'am.

SAILOR: Thank ye, ma'am.

MRS. WASHINGTON: [*At door.*] I go to consider my brother's advisement. [*PETER and the SAILOR follow her out.*]

GEORGE: Mayhap Uncle Joseph disapproves of my venture, Lawrence.

LAWRENCE: 'Twould not affect your going, lad.

GEORGE: [*Trying to throw off his apprehension.*] No, of a certainty, I have my warrant from Admiral Vernon, my chest packed and—

LAWRENCE: [*Interrupting.*] Think no more of it. Your mother hath given her consent, reluctantly enough, 'tis true.

GEORGE: I would she put a braver face on it.

LAWRENCE: 'Tis ever the way with mothers, lad.

GEORGE: Aye, 'tis so. But it saddens me. I——

LAWRENCE: 'Twill pass when you are once at sea—faring forth to behold the world's wonders—the West Indies, the Thames—London, the ports of the Mediterranean, Egypt, India, Cathay. 'Tis not beseeming in me, I know, none the less I feel an envy of your future, George.

GEORGE: You do, Lawrence?

LAWRENCE: Who would not? Though I must be content with the stolid life of a planter, ever anon my thought will go to you, there proudly treading the quarter deck—

GEORGE: Of my own ship. [He strides up and down the room, laughs.] Mayhap, some day.

LAWRENCE: An admiral you will be. Commanding a fleet—winning victories over the French and Spaniards.

GEORGE: [Thoughtfully.] Dreams do sometimes come true.

LAWRENCE: After a fashion, yes.

GEORGE: If anything should happen to stop my going, I would—I could not bear it.

LAWRENCE: Tut, tut! Nothing will happen! Lock you the chest.

GEORGE: [With the key in the lock, looks up.] You are certain?

LAWRENCE: Aye. Come, give me your hand, lad, the hour is passing.

GEORGE: [Turns key, goes to brother.] I have writ Lord Fairfax thanking him for his favors. You have done for me far more than he; I know not how to thank you, brother—

LAWRENCE: Don't try it.

GEORGE: —unless by striving to be a credit to you and all the Washingtons.

LAWRENCE: You will ever be that, lad.

GEORGE: Is there any admonition—any advice to give me?

LAWRENCE: None—Be what you have always been—do what you have always done, and the next time I lay eyes on you, I vow, you will be of higher rank than midshipman. [They grasp hands and embrace. MRS. WASHINGTON enters. She stops in her tracks.]

MRS. WASHINGTON: You are leaving, Captain Washington? [Gazes at them for a moment, her countenance takes on a look of decision, when LAWRENCE WASHINGTON does not answer, she approaches them.] My brother hath writ, strongly advising against the venture.

LAWRENCE: I regret, Madam, he is not in accord with us.

MRS. WASHINGTON: He says, 'twere better that George be apprenticed to a tinker than be a common sailor——

GEORGE: Common sailor? 'Tis a midshipman I am!

MRS. WASHINGTON: —that they will cut and slash and use him like unto a negro, or rather a dog.

LAWRENCE: Fiddlesticks!

MRS. WASHINGTON: That there are too many gaping for preferment in the Navy for him to rise—

LAWRENCE: [Interrupting.] With the influence of My Lord Fairfax—my connections—his own worth—?

MRS. WASHINGTON: His own worth! Methinks 'twill show better in another career.

GEORGE: But, Mother, what other career is open to me?

MRS. WASHINGTON: Your Uncle Joseph saith better you should be a planter.

GEORGE: A planter without lands? Lawrence has Mount Vernon, Augustine has Wakefield, and this farm must needs be for you and the children.

LAWRENCE: Methinks, honored Madam, your brother has writ with more feeling than fact. [MRS. WASHINGTON stiffens.] Due no doubt to misinformation.

MRS. WASHINGTON: My brother is a man of large affairs.

LAWRENCE: One of narrow vision. Pardon my plain speech, Madam.

MRS. WASHINGTON: Verging on rudeness.

GEORGE: [Quickly.] Lawrence does not so mean it.

LAWRENCE: Madam, the occasion warrants plain speech. Consider well—Britannia rules the waves and 'tis ever at sea Englishmen win fame and fortune.

MRS. WASHINGTON: Ever you speak of fame and fortune. I——

LAWRENCE: 'Tis a man's right to strive for both.

MRS. WASHINGTON: Aye, a man, but a mere child——

LAWRENCE: George is more of a man than many twice his age. Have you not found him such?

MRS. WASHINGTON: And 'tis a man I need to lean on, now.

LAWRENCE: Augustine and myself, we will always be near, your other children are coming on. George must have his chance—the chance every man merits—to choose his own pathway in life.

MRS. WASHINGTON: Mayhap, 'twould be the wrong choice.

LAWRENCE: You do but hinder him. Forget not that Lord Fairfax and I have been to some pains to secure this cadetship for George.

MRS. WASHINGTON: Perchance, I should feel grateful to you as well as my Lord Fairfax.

LAWRENCE: To him at least. 'Twill not set well with my Lord Fairfax to have his best efforts so lightly considered.

MRS. WASHINGTON: A man's feelings! I am a mother—something tells me—[Her hand at her heart.]—'twere best he does not go to sea.

LAWRENCE: 'Tis but an idle fancy. Come, give the lad your blessing, and speed him on his way.

[PETER and the SAILOR enter and stop just inside the door.]

GEORGE: Do, Mother. The hour is late.

SAILOR: Shall I be on wi' the chest?

MRS. WASHINGTON: No! He shall not go!

LAWRENCE: How could you be so cruel, Madam? Your own son—would you blast his whole career by your—pardon me!—obstinancy?

[MRS. WASHINGTON gives him a haughty look, turns, and goes out the door. GEORGE is dazed, stunned. LAWRENCE, angry.]

SAILOR: Mayhap, I better be on——?

LAWRENCE: Wait by the landing, where you be within call. [GEORGE drops onto the chest, his head bowed, a hand stroking its surface.]

SAILOR: Aye, Aye, Sir. [He leaves, followed by PETER.]

LAWRENCE: [With a hand on GEORGE'S shoulder.] My lad, we were sired by the same father. Had you been born of the same mother as I, my regard for you would be no stronger, I could not have your welfare more at heart.

GEORGE: [Holding back a sob.] I know—I know—

LAWRENCE: My advice is to go.

GEORGE: Without mother's consent?

LAWRENCE: With or without it. A man can not forever be ruled by his mother.

GEORGE: 'Tis so.

LAWRENCE: For the past four years you have been the virtual head of this family.

GEORGE: I have so acted.

LAWRENCE: You have occupied a man's station, methinks 'tis your privilege to think like one—act like one.

[BETTY opens the door.]

BETTY: [Speaks to those following.] He has not as yet gone. Come on! [She enters room followed by SAMUEL, JOHN and CHARLES, last comes RICHARD HENRY LEE.]

LAWRENCE: [As GEORGE rises.] The sailor is by the riverside, call him when you are ready. [He strides out the door. GEORGE stands gazing after him.]

BETTY: Such disrespect, why Lawrence never noticed us! [To GEORGE.] What is amiss? [GEORGE shakes his head.] Here is Dicky Lee come to give you good-bye.

RICHARD: [Goes to GEORGE.] Greetings, friend George, how becoming is your splendid uniform! [GEORGE takes his hand, tries to speak, drops on the chest. Dicky sits beside him.] What is amiss, George?

[The others crowd around awaiting his reply.]

GEORGE: [Almost in tears.] Mother hath withdrawn her consent to my venture.

BETTY: She has! 'Tis a shame!

SAM: Then you are not going?

BETTY: Of course he is to go!

SAM: Huh! Not if mother saith not.

BETTY: [Shrewdly, to GEORGE.] Nevertheless, our brother, Lawrence, would have you go? [GEORGE nods his head.] Then go I would.

SAM: Disobey mother, who would do that?

BETTY: I would, were I a man. Fancy me staying here on a plantation when I could go to see the world—London, Paris, Rome.

RICHARD: Would Captain Lawrence really have you go?

GEORGE: He is of a mind that I am old enough to decide for myself.

RICHARD: He would have you disobey your mother?

BETTY: Lawrence is right!

CHARLES: 'Tis twenty-one you must be before you dare disobey.

BETTY: Hush, child. [Sits beside GEORGE, her arm about him.] 'Tis true you are old enough to decide, George.

JOHN: [Withdrawn a bit from the others has been watching GEORGE and thinking deeply.] George, is your chest packed—ready?

GEORGE: Yes, I was about to go when Uncle Joseph's letter came.

BETTY: Oh—! So our Uncle Joseph hath a finger in the pie.

JOHN: Lawrence said the sailor was waiting, he could take you to the ship.

BETTY: Of course he could! Call him, George.

SAM: You would have him sneak off?

BETTY: [With heat.] Sneak! [Rises and goes to SAMUEL.] We Washingtons sneak!

JOHN: George, go to mother and tell her good-bye—then go to the ship.

SAM: I think mother is right, not to let him go.

BETTY: Oh, you do! [With scorn.] You would not be a sailor!

SAM: No, would you, Dicky Lee?

RICHARD: I am to be a soldier.

JOHN: [Who has gone to the window.] The sailor still waits, George. Shall I call him?

BETTY: Aye, do so! George will go in his fine uniform and come home an admiral!

SAM: [Scornfully.] He, an admiral!

BETTY: At least a captain; as we walk the streets of Fredericksburg, people will ask, who is the handsome Naval Officer with Betty Washington?

SAM: Were I a captain, I would not walk with you. [PETER enters and stands at the door.]

BETTY: You! You would not get the chance!

JOHN: I can see the top masts of the Bellona, George. She is making the harbor. [GEORGE rises.]

BETTY: [To GEORGE.] Give him leave, George. [GEORGE paces the floor then goes toward the window. To RICHARD, in a breathless whisper.] He's going to call him. [On GEORGE'S face a look of decision. He leans out the window.]

PETER: Massa George!

GEORGE: [Looks to PETER.] What is it?

PETER: Ma'am Washin'n don comin' to speak you. [For a long moment they are all speechless. GEORGE leaves window, slowly walks to center.]

RICHARD: I must be on my way. [To GEORGE.] My friend, would I could be of service. If you go, I wish you much happiness and may you succeed in all your adventures. If you stay—I

BETTY: I hear mother's step. George, be firm.

JOHN: I will stand by, brother. [He leaps through the window.]

GEORGE: It's good-bye, Dickey. [Takes RICHARD'S hand.]

BETTY: [With a grimace at SAMUEL.] There! [SAMUEL disdains to reply and followed by CHARLES goes toward the door.]

RICHARD: [Gives GEORGE'S hand a final squeeze, goes to door.] Good luck, George.

MRS. WASHINGTON: [Enters, hears RICHARD'S words, looks searchingly at GEORGE.] Must you go, Master Richard?

RICHARD: Aye, Madam. [He bows ceremoniously and leaves. BETTY behind her mother signals to GEORGE to stand fast. SAMUEL gives BETTY a contemptuous glance. BETTY, SAMUEL, CHARLES and PETER, leave. GEORGE looks steadfastly at his mother as she comes toward him and stops.]

MRS. WASHINGTON: [Calmly.] You would disobey me, my Son?

GEORGE: [Agitated.] Force me not to do it, Mother!

MRS. WASHINGTON: Then my wishes merit no consideration?

GEORGE: Is not my honor engaged to my brother, My Lord Fairfax and Admiral Vernon?

MRS. WASHINGTON: Your brother, doubtless, means kindly to you, for that I shall ever be grateful. There be others who think of your welfare, Son.

GEORGE: Forgive me, Mother, but I think my Uncle Joseph a very ignorant man——

MRS. WASHINGTON: [*Reproachfully.*] George!

GEORGE: —especially of my affairs.

MRS. WASHINGTON: My brother is a man of the world. He knows much more than I—much more than a youth like you, George.

GEORGE: He knows not better than my brother.

MRS. WASHINGTON: Then you intend to disobey me?

GEORGE: Oh, Mother, please—give me your consent.

MRS. WASHINGTON: Never shall I give it.

GEORGE: I am sorry to hear you say that, Mother, more sorry than I know how to say, but you can not choose my life for me.

MRS. WASHINGTON: [*In jealous anger.*] You would have others choose it for you?

GEORGE: I choose for myself—providing my choice is respectable and I ever live honestly, none shall gainsay me.

MRS. WASHINGTON: [*Astonished at his defiance.*] You do refuse to obey me?

GEORGE: I promise never to discredit you; but I can not—I can not obey you in this.

[*For a long moment she stares at him, unbelievingly. He faces her with respectful determination. Suddenly she sobs piteously, takes a faltering step toward him, touches his arm.*]

MRS. WASHINGTON: George, you are breaking my heart.

GEORGE: [*Astonished that his iron-willed mother has lost self-control.*] Mother!

MRS. WASHINGTON: Do not leave me! [*He turns away to hide his emotion. She drops on her knees beside him with a heart-breaking sob, grasps his hand, kisses it.*] Oh—my Son—I never knew until this moment how much I loved you!—my first born—my best beloved child!

GEORGE: Mother—this is not like you.

MRS. WASHINGTON: [*With tears and sobs.*] Oh, Son, what know you of a mother's heart?—I beg you give up the sea—I implore you—

GEORGE: [*Breaking.*] Mother, you make it—hard.

MRS. WASHINGTON: [*Piteously.*] My Son—my dearest Son —you belong to me—to Virginia—to America!—oh— [*Sobs.*]

GEORGE: Mother, don't! Please don't!

MRS. WASHINGTON: I am on my knees to you—will you abandon me?—or will you abandon your will?—just this once!

[*GEORGE gently removes her hand, she throws herself across the chest in an agony of tears and sobs. He goes to the window. JOHN'S head appears above the sill.*]

JOHN: Do I call him?

[*GEORGE shakes his head, closes the window, goes back to his mother, stands for a moment watching her, then sits on the chest and gathers her in his arms.*]

CURTAIN

A YOUTH OF THE FRONTIER

A GEORGE WASHINGTON PLAY IN ONE ACT

DRAMATIS PERSONAE

(IN ORDER OF THEIR APPEARANCE)

TOM JENKINS, *an old settler.*

MOLLY JENKINS, *his daughter-in-law.*

EDDIE, *aged nine.*

SALLY, *aged six.*

JIM, *aged twelve.*

BESS JENKINS, *aged sixteen, step-daughter to* MOLLY.

COLIN ROBERT.

GEORGE WASHINGTON.

THUNDER BIRD, *an Indian.*

TOBIAS GRAHAM.

JEREMIAH JENKINS, *son of* TOM.

TIME: *Late afternoon, early Summer, 1748.*

PLACE: *The Jenkins' cabin by the Shenandoah Valley.*

DESCRIPTION OF CHARACTERS

TOM JENKINS:

An old settler, white of hair, his face wrinkled and weather-beaten, he wears buckskin breeches and leggings of Indian fashion, a

homespun shirt open at the throat, a waistcoat that has seen better days. On his head a coonskin cap. He is a dreamer, visionary.

MOLLY JENKINS:

A shrewish woman of middle age, hair unkempt. Wears plain homespun clothes, heavy shoes. She is an unlettered, uncultured woman of the settlements.

EDDIE:

A boy of nine years, wears breeches of nondescript cut, much worn, a homespun shirt; barefoot, and without a hat.

SALLY:

A little six-year-old girl, dressed in a homespun slip; barefooted, with hair unkempt.

JIM:

A bright lad of twelve years, wears an Indian buckskin hunting shirt, with leggings and moccasins, without a cap. Carries a rifle and powder horn.

BESS JENKINS:

A pretty sixteen-year-old girl with an innate air of refinement. Her hair is neatly but plainly arranged. She wears a faded homespun ankle-length dress, with coarse shoes and heavy stockings.

COLIN ROBERT:

A young man about twenty-two years of age. A fine, upstanding type of the early American woodsman. He wears Indian hunting shirt and leggings and moccasins of buckskin and coonskin cap, at his belt a knife and tomahawk. His rifle is always in his hands, a powder-born on leather thong about his shoulder.

GEORGE WASHINGTON:

Sixteen and a half years of age, but appears much older. He is about six feet in height, slender, athletic. Wears buckskin Indian hunting shirt, leggings and moccasins, a coonskin cap. Carries a rifle, powder horn slung across his shoulders. His hair is light brown, worn in a queue. He is of serious though alert mien, bashful in the presence of women.

THUNDER BIRD:

An Indian, wears leggings of buckskin and moccasins, about his shoulders a blanket. His hair, hanging over his chest, braided with strips of red cloth. About his brow, a red cloth with one eagle's feather standing erect at back of his head. He is armed with rifle, knife and a tomahawk, which also serves as a pipe. A powder-horn swung about his shoulder. Wears necklace of bears' claws or beads and arm bands.

TOBIAS GRAHAM:

About forty-five or fifty. The coarse, crude type of frontiersman. Wears Indian hunting shirt and leggings, and attempts a bit of style by wearing a tri-cornered hat at a rakish angle. Carries rifle, powder horn and wears a knife at his belt.

JEREMIAH JENKINS:

An uncouth, surly man of middle-age. Wears the same type of dress as Colin. On his entrance carries a pack of supplies. He is armed with knife, rifle and powder-horn.

SET: *A log cabin in a forest of the Alleghanies, overlooking the Shenandoah Valley. Projecting diagonally onto the stage from the right back, the rude log cabin, the corner of one end showing. A heavy oaken door at the front, just beyond the corner, and toward back a window. Tall trees and foliage at end of cabin near back. At the left, trees and dense foliage with a clump of bushes left front set out from wings. At the back, an open space gives a view of the valley and hills beyond. A rude bench beside the cabin door. At left center, a log with an axe head half buried in the wood, the handle projecting upward; wood split for a fireplace is scattered about the log.*

TOM JENKINS *sits on the bench, with pipe in mouth, scraping a skin, his rifle is leaning against the cabin wall near at hand.*

TOM: [*Taking pipe from mouth, calls.*] Molly! Oh, Molly!

MOLLY: [*From within cabin.*] Aye, what be thee wantin' now, Pa?

TOM: Come you here.

MOLLY: [*Stands in doorway.*] Well?

TOM: Sit thee down.

MOLLY: 'Tis no time I have for restin'.

TOM: I would talk with ye, whilst we're alone. Sit ye down. [*MOLLY sits beside him. He takes a puff or two.*] There be a party o' white men in these hills, near at hand.

MOLLY: Freenchies?

TOM: English.

MOLLY: What be they doin' hereabouts?

TOM: Surveyin'.

MOLLY: Surveyin'?

TOM: A way o' measurin' lands.

MOLLY: Why would they be a doin' o' that?

TOM: 'Tis what I'm wonderin'.

MOLLY: That may a be all ye have to do, Pa Jenkins [*she rises*], but I have aplenty more'n that to tax me. [*As she steps into the cabin.*] Wonderin'—allus wonderin'.

TOM: Yer never git anywhere without wonderin'—thinkin'——

MOLLY: Ye never git any place without work; what good's thinkin' do? Iffen you'd done more work like unto yer son, Jeremiah, an' less wonderin' we ud all been ferther along today.

TOM: How mean ye, ferther along? Knowin' helps ye get on. 'Tis why I learned Bess and Jim tu read and figger.

MOLLY: A lot of good that does 'em. Readin' don't raise crops, nor figgerin' don't bring meat in the door.

TOM: It will some day.

MOLLY: You'll not be alive to see it.

TOM: I'm wonderin'—the surveyors now—

MOLLY: That all ye got to talk about? [*Goes into cabin, disgusted. TOM returns to scraping the skin. A young woman's voice in heard off stage at left. "Y-o-u-h-oo-o!" TOM listens and smiles; again the call "Y-o-u-h-o-o!"*]

TOM: [*Cups his hands to mouth.*] Y-o-u-h-o-o!

MOLLY: [*Comes to cabin door.*] 'Tis time they be comin'.

TOM: They went but a step.

MOLLY: [*Contemptuously.*] What's a step with red varmints about?

TOM: They're peaceable enow, when left alone. You worryin'? —Jim's along.

MOLLY: A twelve-year-old.

TOM: A capital shot.

[*Voices are heard at left, and EDDIE enters on the run, with SALLY following, they carry gourds filled with berries.*]

EDDIE: Look, ma! Look, ain't they fine! [*Shows her the gourd. SALLY runs to her Grandfather's outstretched arms and sits on his knee.*]

MOLLY: Where ye bin so long?

EDDIE: We saw some men, ma—white men!

TOM: [*Thoughtfully.*] The surveyors.

EDDIE: Aye. They be campin' nearby.

[*BESS and JIM enter from left, carrying gourds of berries. JIM carries a musket. They come forward as the others are talking.*]

MOLLY: [*Suspiciously, to BESS.*] You bin talkin' to them white folks?

BESS: The leader was gentry, ma.

MOLLY: [*Sneeringly.*] Gentry! What have you to do with the likes o' them! Keep you clear of gentry.

JIM: They be well spoken, ma.

MOLLY: Aye. Well spoken, and mean no good to the likes o' us. [*As BESS turns away.*] Now, none o' yer high and mighty airs, darter.

TOM: Don't be hard on the girl, Molly.

MOLLY: Trapsin' around talkin' to gentry—a promised woman.

BESS: [*Turns quickly.*] I'm not promised, ma!

MOLLY: Ye are!

BESS: [*Scornfully.*] Tobias Graham, I can't marry him—I won't!

MOLLY: Don't ye dast say ye won't. Was yer pa here now—!

BESS: He would make me—?

MOLLY: Tobias has ten acres o' cleared land an' three cows.

BESS: I don't like him! I don't care how many acres or cows he has. I don't want to marry anyone [*Under her breath*]—yet.

MOLLY: Well, ye'll marry him. Jim, get me some wood. [*She goes into the cabin. JIM goes to wood pile, gathers an armful of wood, takes it in cabin. TOM rises, touches BESS' arm, she follows him to log at left. TOM sits.*]

TOM: Sit ye down and tell me o' the surveyors, lass.

BESS: [*Brightens and sits beside him.*] The leader was gentry, Grandpa. A Mister Washington.

TOM: Never hern tell o' him. The others?

BESS: Two called chain men, one the marker and one the pilot.

TOM: This Washington now.

BESS: A shy young man, he talked not with me but with Jim.

TOM: Jim larned sumpin'?

BESS: How they measure land, with instruments.

TOM: He could understand?

BESS: 'Cause you learned us to read and figger, Grandpa.

TOM: This young lad say who he's surveyin' fer?

BESS: Nay. But he's comin' here.

TOM: Comin' here?

BESS: Told Jim he would. [*Suddenly thoughtful.*] Grandpa, think you, when dad comes back he'll make me marry Tobias?

TOM: 'Twouldn't surprise me.

BESS: He's old—old as pa————

TOM: 'Tween forty and fifty.

BESS: ————and ugly and mean.

TOM: Mean?

BESS: To animals—he'd be mean to me.

TOM: [*Clenches a fist.*] He wouldn't dast with me livin'.

BESS: I won't marry him, I'll go away from here.

TOM: Ye don't love us no more, lass?

BESS: I love you, and Eddie and Sally and Jim.

TOM: Where would ye go, lass?

BESS: To the settlements, where I could work—learn—be free of all this.

TOM: Free! Free to marry Colin Robert.

BESS: [*She shyly hangs her head.*] He's not mean!

TOM: Oh, Colin Robert's a good lad.

BESS: What sets pa and ma again him? Everybody knows he's the best trapper and woodsman in these parts.

TOM: He has no home to take a wife to.

BESS: But he aims to have a house and plenty of land.

TOM: He'll git on. He'll make a good husband.

BESS: Ma says he won't settle down. He will, won't he, Grandpa?

TOM: Men like him most genally do.

[*From the forest at left comes the coo of a wood dove.*

BESS *starts then listens.* TOM *cocks an ear, smiles knowingly without* BESS *noticing it.*]

TOM: Guess I'll get to working on my skins. [*He leisurely rises, goes to bench by cabin, picks up skin and walks around back of cabin.* BESS *is agitated, looks first to* TOM, *then the clump of bushes near the trail, as* TOM *disappears she glances at the cabin door, then steals behind the clump of bushes.* COLIN ROBERTS *meets her. She goes to his arms. As they embrace,* WASHINGTON *steps into view beside them.* BESS *is abashed,* COLIN *surprised, signals silence with a finger to lips.* COLIN *and* WASHINGTON *shake hands.* WASHINGTON *bows to* BESS, *smiles and goes into the clearing, stands near the log, looks about.* TOM *comes from behind the cabin.* BESS *and* Colin *exit, left.*]

WASHINGTON: Good evening, sir. My name is George Washington.

TOM: [*Looking up.*] Evenin', Mister Washington.

WASHINGTON: Is this the home of Jeremiah Jenkins?

TOM: Aye, 'tis that.

WASHINGTON: I met his son, Jim—a likely lad.

TOM: He's that. Sit ye down. [*TOM takes a seat on the log,* WASHINGTON *beside him.*]

WASHINGTON: Mister Jenkins is not at home?

TOM: My son. He's gone to the settlement. Be you the surveyor?

WASHINGTON: Aye, sir.

TOM: Kinda hard work, ain't it?

WASHINGTON: At times, but I take pleasure in it.

TOM: Surveyin' the lands, hereabouts?

WASHINGTON: Aye, sir.

TOM: Doin' it fer the Colony? ?

WASHINGTON: Nay, sir.

TOM: Oh, just t' git yer hand in?

WASHINGTON: Why no, sir. I am surveying for my Lord Fairfax.

TOM: Lord Fairfax, I've hern tell o' him. Lives he hereabouts?

WASHINGTON: Twelve miles southeast of Winchester, at Greenway Court.

TOM: Greenway Court—purty name, ain't it?

WASHINGTON: 'Tis his hunting lodge.

TOM: Yer surveyin' a long way from this Greenway Court.

WASHINGTON: He owns all the lands in these regions, Sir.

TOM: All the lands?

[*From the forest at left,* THUNDER BIRD *steps from behind a tree in view of* TOM *and* WASHINGTON, *who look steadfastly at the Indian.*]

THUNDER BIRD: How!

TOM: What do ye here?

THUNDER BIRD: Thunder Bird weary. Thunder Bird rest. [*He sits on log beside* TOM. TOM *looks at* WASHINGTON *inquiringly, and tilts head toward the Indian.*]

WASHINGTON: Methinks he was one of a war-party of Delawares who did a war dance at our camp near Cresaps.

THUNDER BIRD: Young chief got sharp eyes.

TOM: Ye come in peace Thunder Bird?

THUNDER BIRD: Tobacco.

TOM: [*Gives Indian some tobacco from his pouch.*] You were sayin' Lord Fairfax owns all the lands hereabouts.

WASHINGTON: For many miles.

THUNDER BIRD: [*Who has filled pipe.*] Indian owns lands.

TOM: [*Paying no attention to THUNDER BIRD.*] Lord Fairfax owns not these lands of ours.

WASHINGTON: I am sorry, Sir, but he does.

TOM: How come he by them?

WASHINGTON: He inherited a Royal grant, 'twas from King Charles II.

TOM: [*Thinks for a time as THUNDER BIRD lights pipe with flint.*] How got King Charles these lands—buy 'em from Injins?

THUNDER BIRD: No buy Indian's lands.

WASHINGTON: They were crown lands, Sir.

TOM: Crown lands? What may crown lands be.

WASHINGTON: Lands owned by the Crown.

TOM: By what right doth ye Crown own these lands?

WASHINGTON: By right of discovery—conquest.

TOM: Humph! Methinks 'tis most odd.

WASHINGTON: How so?

TOM: Some one discovers this broad land, takes it in the name of the Crown. The King gives it away to his friends.

WASHINGTON: They come to settle it.

TOM: 'Tis the likes o' us that settle it, clear the forest, conquer it. Then yer King's friend, with a royal grant, takes it from the likes o' us.

WASHINGTON: [*Meditates.*] Some of the King's friends brought settlers.

TOM: Mayhap, but that was long ago.

WASHINGTON: Have you been here long?

TOM: Up the Potomac from St. Mary's, twenty-five years ago.

WASHINGTON: You came alone?

TOM: Aye, struck out fer myself into the free forest.

WASHINGTON: You wanted land?

TOM: Aye, land and a home.

WASHINGTON: You knew not My Lord Fairfax was the owner?

TOM: Nay. Lord Fairfax pays nothin'. Come twenty-five years ago I settled here, built yon cabin, cleared land in the valley. Along comes my son, Jeremiah, a follerin' me, with Bess' mother—she died here. Jeremiah cleared more land, we've been livin' here fer a right good spell. Aint we got some rights for our labor, lad?

WASHINGTON: On that side of it I never looked.

TOM: The Crown pays nothin' fer the land.

THUNDER BIRD: No pay Indian.

WASHINGTON: [*Thoughtful.*] It does seem you have a claim.

TOM: Ain't we the real settlers—the real conquerers?

WASHINGTON: Aye, 'tis true, but the law—the English law.

TOM: Neither just there nor here.

WASHINGTON: There I know not—but here———

TOM: Is it just of Lord Fairfax to drive us off our lands?

WASHINGTON: My Lord Fairfax is a most generous man.

TOM: Is he a just man?

WASHINGTON: I have always found him so.

TOM: Then mayhap he'll let us stay on here.

WASHINGTON: I would think it, if brought to satisfactory usage.

TOM: If not—ejection!

WASHINGTON: Mayhap for a small sum?

TOM: What settler has even a small sum o' money?

WASHINGTON: Even so, arrangements may be effected. Say two hundred acres from a nearby stake on into the valley.

TOM: [*Sententiously.*] Master and man. Lord and varlet. I'm wonderin' now—

WASHINGTON: What may you be wondering, Sir?

TOM: "When Adam delved and Eve span, who then was the gentleman?"

WASHINGTON: [*Meditates.*] "Who then was the gentleman?"—I have heard that before.

TOM: The words of John Ball.

WASHINGTON: My mother was a Ball.

TOM: He preached: Equality o' man.

WASHINGTON: He was hanged, drawn and quartered.

TOM: Fer tryin' to make things a bit better fer the under dog.

WASHINGTON: Some have said he was an ancestor of my mother's.

TOM: Well, son, if ye think o' things from two sides—the under as well as the top side—if ye would have justice fer all men—mayhap 'tis old John Ball's blood a stirrin' in yer veins.

WASHINGTON: I would ever be just to all men.

[*As they talk, JIM and SALLY enter from front cabin. JIM goes eagerly to WASHINGTON, SALLY follows. JIM suddenly stops abashed. SALLY runs on. WASHINGTON stretches his arms toward her, she glances uncertainly at her grandfather, then springs to WASHINGTON'S arms and sits on his lap.*]

TOM: Jim, yer a bustin' with queries.

WASHINGTON: [*Looks up with a smile at JIM*] You were interested in my work. Perchance you, too, would be a surveyor?

JIM: That I would! Could I? I can figger, can't I, Grandpa?

TOM: He's right good at figgerin', Jim is.

JIM: You went to school, Mister?

WASHINGTON: [*Regretfully.*] Only for a time.

JIM. Costs many a pound, don't it?

WASHINGTON: Quite a sum.

JIM: [*Sadly.*] Then I reckon I never'll get to school.

TOM: Some day in these here colonies, schoolin' ul be free.

WASHINGTON: [*Looking at TOM speculatively.*] You believe that?

TOM: Folks that come out here set store by larnin'. Larnin' helps them to know what they want and to get it. Some time there'll be free land and free school.

[*THUNDER BIRD suddenly rises, glances at left, grunts and quickly disappears in forest at left.*]

MOLLY: [*At cabin door.*] What did the Injin want?

TOM: [*With a nod toward the disappearing Indian.*] They come an' go like shadders.

JIM: Learnin' would git me what I want.

WASHINGTON: And what may it be?

JIM: To be a surveyor. If I could but gather together a few pounds.

[*TOBIAS GRAHAM enters from right at corner of cabin, peers around the cabin at the group by the log. Then goes toward them.*]

TOBIAS: Evenin'. [*Looks at WASHINGTON inquiringly.*]

TOM: Evenin', Tobias. Mister Washington, this here's Tobias Graham.

WASHINGTON: Good evening, Mister Graham.

TOBIAS: [*Suspiciously.*] What ye doin' in these parts?

WASHINGTON: Surveying.

TOM: A way o' measurin' Lord Fairfax's lands.

TOBIAS: Where are his lands?

WASHINGTON: All about. [*SALLY has fallen asleep in WASHINGTON'S arms.*]

TOBIAS: Sure yer not here fer sumpin' else?

WASHINGTON: I do not understand you, Mister Graham.

[*MOLLY comes out of the cabin, goes to them.*]

MOLLY: Evenin', Tobias.

TOBIAS: Evenin', Mistress Jenkins.

MOLLY: [*Goes to WASHINGTON.*] I'll have my child.

WASHINGTON: Could not I carry her for you?

MOLLY: No. Time she was abed. [*She takes SALLY in her arms.*]

TOM: Molly, this is Mister Washington, a—[*She turns toward cabin.*]

MOLLY: [*Over her shoulder.*] Tobias, Bess is somewhere about. [*TOBIAS grins. Then his face hardens as he looks at WASHINGTON.*]

TOBIAS: [*Shouts.*] Ho, Bess! Ho, Bess! [*Looks sneeringly at WASHINGTON.*] Ain't yer feared o' bein' in the woods at dark? [*WASHINGTON gazes calmly at him without speaking.*] Better be gettin' on afore the sun sets.

TOM: I reckon Mister Washington ull leave when he's of a mind to, Tobias, and not afore.

TOBIAS: Mayhap afore he's a mind to. [*He turns as BESS comes out of the forest and strolls toward them.*]

BESS: You wantin' to see me, Tobias?

TOBIAS: Aye, 'tis why I'm here. Let us walk on a piece.

BESS: I don't want to walk, I'll sit. [*She sits down on the log.*]

TOBIAS: I got sumptin' t' tell thee.

BESS: Tell it, then.

TOBIAS: Not afore folks.

BESS: Then 'twill keep.

TOBIAS: [*In anger.*] Ye'll not walk with me?

BESS: No.

[*TOBIAS gives her a hard look, goes to and enters the cabin.*]

TOM: I want to talk to Tobias, ye young folks might go fer a look where that stake would start the two hundred acres. He'll tell ye about it, Bess.

BESS: [*Rises and smiles at WASHINGTON.*] I would like to go, will you—?

WASHINGTON: Why, I—[*Hesitates, then bows.*] Why, I shall be honored. [*He offers his arm, she takes it, they stroll down the path to the right.*]

JIM: Bess will catch it.

TOM: Mayhap.

MOLLY: [*Coming from cabin followed by TOBIAS.*] Where she gone?

TOM: Fer a walk.

MOLLY: Fer a walk? With that surveyer feller?

TOM: Aye. [*MOLLY gasps in indignation.*]

TOBIAS: [*In anger lifts his rifle.*] I'll give him a taste o' lead. [*Starts for path.*]

TOM: Hold, Tobias. I'de have a word with ye. [*TOBIAS stops.*]

MOLLY: Go fetch her, Tobias. [*TOBIAS starts.*]

TOM: [*Voice of authority.*] Hold, Tobias. Come ye here. [*To MOLLY.*] Bess is no kith or kin o' yourn—

MOLLY. If her pa was here now. She wouldn't be—

TOM: Hold yer tongue, woman. [*In a huff she enters the cabin. TOM turns to TOBIAS.*] So—ye'd take a shot at this young Washington?

TOBIAS: 'Tis no right she has to go walkin' with him—she's a marryin' me.

TOM: Not if she don't want ter.

TOBIAS: Jeremiah promised her to me.

TOM: How come he to do that?

TOBIAS: 'Tis our affair.

TOM: What's about Bess is my affair too.

TOBIAS: He's her pa.

TOM: I'm her Grandpa.

TOBIAS: Think I'm not good enow fer her, eh?

TOM: No, yer not, Tobias. Nor none like thee.

TOBIAS: If thee have nothin' more to talk of than Bess and me, I'd have thee mind your own affairs.

JIM: [*Running in from right.*] Grandpa! Grandpa! Pa's comin'. [*TOM for a moment is shaken, then becomes resolute.*]

TOBIAS: [*With a leer.*] Guess someun else ull have sump'n' to say bout that now. [*They look to the right, as JEREMIAH enters. He throws down his pack by the cabin door, gives TOM and TOBIAS a surly glance. Leans his rifle against the cabin.*] Evenin', Jeremiah.

MOLLY: [*Coming to the door.*] 'Tis time thee came, with Bess—

JEREMIAH: What o' Bess?

MOLLY: Trapsin' about with gentry. And her a promised woman.

TOBIAS: [*Who has drawn near.*] I was just so a tellin' old Tom now and he allows as how she ain't agoin' tu marry me.

JEREMIAH: [*To TOM.*] Ye keep out o' this.

TOM: [*Now near them.*] My son, thee don't mean—[*He gestures toward TOBIAS.*]

JEREMIAH: Well—! What if I do?

TOM: Her mother was—was gentry.

MOLLY: [*Interrupts.*] She wasn't no better'n me or Tobias here. 'Tis yer talks got Bess puffed up like to an adder. Readin' and writin'. [*Sniffs.*] Readin' and writin' for the likes o' her.

JEREMIAH: [*To MOLLY.*] Shut up! [*To TOM.*] Where be she? [*TOM does not answer.*]

MOLLY: A walkin' in the wood with this surveyor lad, and he [*points to TOM*] aidin' and abettin' her.

JEREMIAH: [*To JIM.*] Go fetch her. [*JIM is reluctant to obey his father, but dares not disobey. Goes off at right.*]

TOBIAS: [*Pleased at the turn of affairs.*] I come over t' tell her as how ther's a parson nigh to Winchester; we could make it in two days' travel.

[*WASHINGTON and BESS appear at left. JEREMIAH glares at them.*]

BESS: Evenin', Pa. Git yer supplies?

JEREMIAH: Yer here. Git inside! [*BESS draws to Washington's side and gazes at her father defiantly.*] So—[*He starts for BESS, TOM steps between them.*]

TOM: Easy Jeremiah; say what thee got to afore the girl.

JEREMIAH: [To WASHINGTON.] Who are thee? What thee doin' here?

TOM: Jeremiah, he's——

JEREMIAH: [To WASHINGTON.] What thee doin' walkin' with my darter?

WASHINGTON: We but went in the forest. I would show her——

BESS: [Fearing JEREMIAH'S blind rage.] Pa, if ye'll listen——

JEREMIAH: [Interrupts.] Thee but walked in the forest! [He turns and grabs his rifle leaning against cabin.] Well, now ye'll run in the forest. [TOM follows and reaches out to grab the rifle. JEREMIAH knocks him back against the cabin where he falls. JEREMIAH turns to WASHINGTON with rifle ready.] Run, my fine gentleman. Run as thee never ran afore, 'cause I'm goin' to shoot when thee strikes the trail. [BESS, who is assisting TOM, screams and runs toward WASHINGTON. TOBIAS seizes her. WASHINGTON stands coolly leaning on his rifle watching JEREMIAH.] I fire when I count three, gentleman.

BESS: Don't, Pa! Don't! He's——[TOBIAS puts a hand over her mouth. She struggles to free herself.]

JEREMIAH: One! [Holds rifle at ready.] Two! [He cocks the rifle.]

MOLLY: Don't, Pa! Ye'll be gittin' in trouble! He's only a boy! He's gentry.

WASHINGTON: Don't be concerned, Mistress Jenkins. 'Twould be a much more serious matter to shoot Lord Fairfax's surveyor than to kill an Indian.

JEREMIAH: What means thee? [He takes a step forward, threateningly.]

WASHINGTON: You shall know presently. [He steps toward TOBIAS.] Take your filthy hands from Mistress Jenkins. [TOBIAS lets go of BESS and steps back. To JEREMIAH.] Now I will give you your answer. Graham threatened you—said he saw you kill the Indian——

JEREMIAH: 'Twas an accident.

WASHINGTON: Mayhap, but the price of his silence was the hand of your daughter. More of that later. [He goes to TOM and assists BESS in lifting him to his feet, then to the bench. To MOLLY.] Some water, please. [MOLLY hurries into cabin, brings a gourd of water she gives to BESS. WASHINGTON turns to TOBIAS.] A word of advice, Graham. You are occupying lands owned by my Lord Fairfax; I give you two days to go hence. If I see you here beyond that time, or hear that you are indiscreet in your talks with the Indians, I shall ask my good friend Colin Robert to look in upon you some day. [TOBIAS starts and steps back.] Go!

COLIN: [Steps into view from behind a tree in the forest at left. JIM at his heels. COLIN has his rifle almost at his shoulder.] Afore you go, Tobias, I'd have a word with you. [Strides to TOBIAS, fixes him with a cold eye.] Thee filthy varmint. 'Twas you killed the Delaware.

TOBIAS: I didn't! I didn't! I tell ye!

COLIN: Jenkins shot at a deer. Next day you took him to the spot and showed the Delaware's body.

TOBIAS: Yes. [Points to JEREMIAH.] He did it!

COLIN: Thee lies; I saw thee do it.

TOM: Thunder Bird!

COLIN: Aye, an Injin bent on gettin' the scalp o' the man who slew his brother!

MOLLY: The Injin 'ull kill ye, Tobias!

COLIN: Unless thee leave these parts almighty fast. [TOBIAS nearly sick with fear, his eyes rolling, grasps his rifle, and is about to rush off. COLIN grasps his shoulder.] Here be fifty pounds fer yer belongings. [TOBIAS grabs the money-bag COLIN extends to him and dashes into the forest.]

TOM: Ye made a bad bargain.

COLIN: How? For cattle, a cabin and his property?

TOM: He don't own a foot of the land.

COLIN: What mean you?

TOM: Neither do we this place.

JEREMIAH: Who says we don't?

TOM: Lord Fairfax owns it by grant from the Crown.

[They look at each other in bewilderment, consternation.]

WASHINGTON: Tomorrow I shall survey two hundred acres surrounding this cabin. To be held by a fee paid to Lord Fairfax in the name of Mister Thomas Jenkins.

TOM: [Now recovered, with BESS beside him.] But, Sir, I have no money.

WASHINGTON: That methinks will be provided to Thomas Jenkins.

MOLLY: Ye mean Jeremiah?

WASHINGTON: Not so, Mister Thomas Jenkins. Perchance he will allow his relatives to remain with him—providing——

JEREMIAH: Pervidin' what—Sir?

WASHINGTON: Your daughter can select the man of her choice.

BESS: [Goes to COLIN.] Yer my choice. And, Colin, I care not whether ye own land or no.

COLIN: [Puts an arm about her, smiles ruefully.] Guess ye'll have to take me as I am. Tobias has all my fortune, now.

WASHINGTON: Your claim to his land is a just one, but would have no standing at court——

JEREMIAH: Then what good's his claim?

WASHINGTON: ——it will, however, have standing with my Lord Fairfax. I could survey another two hundred acres.

COLIN: You could arrange with Lord Fairfax?

WASHINGTON: [With a smile.] Mayhap a gift to the bride.

COLIN: You'll arrange it?

WASHINGTON: My Lord Fairfax is always ready to aid the worthy settler. I will speak with him.

COLIN: 'Tis enough for me.

TOM: [Comes forward.] Thee speaks like unto a worthy descendant of John Ball.

WASHINGTON: Mayhap I am his descendant. I would be worthy. [To JIM.] You will walk a ways with me?

JIM: That I will, Sir.

WASHINGTON: Miss Jenkins, I hope for you a long and prosperous life. [To TOM.] You will hear from my Lord Fairfax. [Takes his hand.]

TOM: God bless thee, Sir.

WASHINGTON: Good evening, all. [He bows, turns and goes out trail at left followed by JIM. They all stand, watching him.]

CURTAIN

THE BLUE GOBLET

A GEORGE WASHINGTON PLAY IN ONE ACT

By JAMES K. KNUDSON

TO THE AUDIENCE

Relatively little is known concerning George Washington's first and only journey beyond the shores of America—his trip to the Barbados with his elder half-brother Lawrence. It is recorded in George's diary, however, that during his sojourn in the Barbados he attended dinner meetings of the "Beefsteak and Tripe Club"—a society no doubt composed of many of the prominent men of the island.

It is safe to assume, for the sake of a dramatic plot, that Washington, a keen and perceptive youth at the time, must have noticed together with other things the deplorable conditions existing among the black slaves, who at the time outnumbered the white men on the island, and among the indentured whites, whose lot was even worse than that of the African slaves.

Perhaps it was the recollection of such conditions that later led Washington, as President and plantation owner, to decry the baser side of slavery and hope for the correction of the evils connected therewith, if not for total abolition.

The plot of this play is, of course, for the most part imaginative. The purpose is to portray the character of Washington and his probable reactions under a given set of dramatic circumstances. Whatever departure is made from strict historical accuracy is done with the idea of enhancing the dramatic effectiveness of the play with the mission ever in view.

DRAMATIS PERSONAE

(IN ORDER OF THEIR APPEARANCE)

'AWKINS, *a servant.*

JUDGE NATHANIEL HAGGETT, *host to the "Beefsteak and Tripe Club."*

FOGG, *the gardener.*

LEICESTER, *the headservant.*

HOLLENBERGER, *the cook.*

GEORGE WASHINGTON.

THE PARROT.

CAPTAIN GEORGE JOHN PETRIE, *of Fort Needham, Barbados.*

MAJOR GEDNEY CLARK, *Barbadian merchant.*

DR. LANAHAN.

LAWRENCE WASHINGTON, *elder half-brother to George.*

JAMES CARTER, *member of the Barbadian Council.*

JUDGE SATUS MAYNARD.

JUDGE WILLIAM MAYNARD.

TIME: *An evening in November, 1751.*

PLACE: *The home of Judge Nathaniel Haggett in Bridgetown, Barbados.*

DESCRIPTION OF CHARACTERS

'AWKINS:

A dark servant, more of the appearance of an Indian than a Negro. His movements are quiet and deliberate. He is inoffen-sive, speaks with an accent, using fair English, but having difficulty with the pronunciation. He is dressed as an underservant in a tropical household—barefoot, plain white linen garment short-ened to the knee.

JUDGE HAGGETT:

Past middle-age. A tall man with large frame and wide shoul-ders—a fine type of gentry. He is plainly though richly dressed in smallclothes and coat of dark color. He wears a powdered wig with a queue secured by a black ribbon. As a Master he gives the impression of being somewhat overbearing but quick to forgive.

FOGG:

About thirty-five, nimble and quick, a roguish look on his face; slight of build and almost bald. He speaks with a modified Cockney accent and is a past master at practical jokes. He is dressed in rude civilian smallclothes, somewhat the worse for wear.

LEICESTER:

Somewhat of a gentleman in appearance and manner. Incapable of getting his orders as a headservant taken seriously. He wears the livery of a servant—dark smallclothes with stockings, buckled shoes, full-sleeved shirt and waistcoat.

HOLLENBERGER:

Large and florid, cheeks like apples, beady eyes, a great rotund figure; easily led, but furious when angry. Dressed as a cook—linen shirt with full but short sleeves, short breeches with white hose, large shoes with high tongues and great nickled buckles.

GEORGE WASHINGTON:

Nineteen years of age. Six feet two inches tall, in weight about two hundred pounds, large-boned but well-proportioned. His complexion bronzed by an outdoor life; features strong; hair light brown in color combed back and worn in a queue. Dressed in neat dark smallclothes of the period.

CAPTAIN PETRIE:

A youthful officer about twenty-eight; dressed in uniform of British Army—red coat faced with blue and edged with gold, buff waistcoat and breeches, crimson sash, wears a sword, boots and carries a tricorne hat; wears hair in unpowdered queue.

LAWRENCE WASHINGTON:

Slender and tall, sallow complexion, large eyes; suave but con-vincing manner; quiet in speech. Obviously in ill-health. Wears conservative dark smallclothes.

DR. LANAHAN, MR. CARTER, JUDGES SATUS AND WILLIAM MAYNARD:

Of various ages, dressed in dark smallclothes of the period, with different colored waistcoats.

SET: *The banquet room in the home of* JUDGE HAGGETT. *The kitchen entrance is left and the entrance from the reception room right; backstage there is a large double French door or window, through which can be seen the tropical garden. Palms and other tropical indoor plants are backstage right; and a long, rich-looking table set in buffet fashion backstage left. Downstage from kitchen entrance is a reed or bamboo sofa against wall; and downstage from right entrance is a wine-cabinet or lowboy. A small serving-table is in the center and another near the right entrance. At the former,* JUDGE HAGGETT *sits during the final stage play with* GEORGE WASHINGTON *at his left and* LAWRENCE *on his right.* JUDGE SATUS MAYNARD *sits on the sofa.* DR. LANAHAN, CAPTAIN PETRIE *and* JUDGE WILLIAM MAYNARD, *are grouped about the extra table right. The parrot is between them and* WASHINGTON. *The servants enter from the kitchen.* FOGG *is well down stage when he recites his verses. The guests are seated on comfortable reed or wicker chairs, grouped so as not to seem stilted and to insure visibility of all characters to the audience. Etchings and oil paintings might be hung at discretion about the room. The parrot cage is reed, to harmonize with the furniture.*

NOTE ON PRODUCTION: *The parrot can be imitated by concealing in the cage a microphone which can be operated from off-stage. The cast and script can be cut at pleasure of director.*

[*As the curtain goes up,* 'AWKINS, *the underservant, is discovered polishing the knives and forks on a buffet table which is evidently being prepared to serve several guests. The silver and dishes are arranged indiscriminately. Downstage, right, is a Colonial wine cabinet.* 'AWKINS *looks up toward the entrances, first to the right, then to the left, then carefully puts down the knife he is polishing and tiptoes over to the wine cabinet from which he takes the decanter and several crystal goblets, one conspicuously blue and ornate. All of his movements are furtive and sly. He takes the stopper from the decanter, holds it up to the light, smiles, picks up a goblet, pours out carefully about three fingers, measuring them, places the decanter back on the table, sets his goblet down and reaches to replace the stopper in the decanter. At this moment,* JUDGE HAGGETT, *the master, appears in the room unnoticed by* 'AWKINS, *absorbed in his wine-filching.* 'AWKINS, *with back to the Judge, picks up the goblet he has poured and is about to drink, when the voice of the Judge thunders behind him.*]

JUDGE HAGGETT: Filching my wine, eh? Thou varlet!

'AWKINS: [*Taken off his guard but nevertheless trying to appear innocent.*] Oh—no, sir—just pouring it for the guests, sir. [*He turns to pour out more.*]

JUDGE HAGGETT: So! Thou are a liar and a thief?

'AWKINS: [*Protesting.*] I meant only——

JUDGE HAGGETT: Always thou hast an excuse—I took thee from the plantation and brought thee here thinking thee more trustworthy than a black slave——

'AWKINS: [*In defense.*] And more handy about the house, sir.

JUDGE HAGGETT: I'll have no filchers hereabouts. On the morrow thou shalt go back to the plantation.

'AWKINS: [*Aghast.*] Plantation? Don't send me back there, sir!

JUDGE HAGGETT: Mayhap a little more toil in the sun will bake the dishonesty out o' thee!

'AWKINS: [*Still imploring.*] Don't send me back, sir. **Not** with those greasy niggers. Don't do it, sir! I'll do better, sir. I'll do better.

JUDGE HAGGETT: Silence! Thou meritest twenty stripes. Were I sure this is not thy first offense thou should'st of a certainty get them.

'AWKINS: Spare me, sir!

JUDGE HAGGETT: Thou shalt return to the plantation on the morrow! I have said! Now get thee back to thy work.

[*JUDGE HAGGETT picks up the goblet* 'AWKINS *has poured, empties the wine into the conspicuous blue goblet, drains it in one gulp and walks over to the right wall where he pulls a bell cord. A tinkling bell is heard and* FOGG, *the gardener responds.* 'AWKINS *has returned to the table, where he polishes the knives and forks half-heartedly.*]

FOGG: [*To* JUDGE HAGGETT.] You rang, sir.

JUDGE HAGGETT: I did—but not for a gardener. Where's that rapscallion Leicester.

FOGG: [*Slyly.*] In the kitchen, sir, tantalizin' the cook.

JUDGE HAGGETT: [*Going to the bell cord again and giving it several violent jerks;* FOGG *starts to leave.*] Don't leave Fogg. There's work here for you, also.

FOGG: Aye, sir.

JUDGE HAGGETT: See to it that the parrots are fed and the plants trimmed.

FOGG: Yes, sir.

[LEICESTER, *the headservant, enters hurriedly, buttoning his jacket, which apparently he had taken off.* JUDGE HAGGETT *looks at him impatiently.*]

JUDGE HAGGETT: [*Looking at* LEICESTER, *sternly.*] Know you not that I am expecting guests at the stroke of eight? 'Tis twenty minutes of the hour. [*He looks at his large, key-winding watch, fastened to his waistcoat by a fob and seals.*]

LEICESTER: [*Meekly.*] We 'ave things a' most ready, sir.

JUDGE HAGGETT: A headservant's place is not in the scullery. [FOGG *laughs covertly.*] That, Fogg, applies also to the gardener.

LEICESTER: Yes, sir.

FOGG: Aye, sir.

JUDGE HAGGETT: I expect to find that table well set when I return. [*He starts toward the door.*]

LEICESTER: Yes, sir.

JUDGE HAGGETT: Keep your eye on these louts, Leicester. They're none too trusty. [*Indicating* FOGG *and* 'AWKINS.]

LEICESTER: [*To departing Judge.*] I'll keep both me eyes on 'em, sir.

[LEICESTER *walks over to where* FOGG *is trimming the plants, looks searchingly at him, turns his back and walks toward the table where* 'AWKINS *is still gloomily polishing the silver.* FOGG *makes a face at* LEICESTER *as he turns his back.* HOLLENBERGER, *the cook, enters from the kitchen, whetting a great butcher knife on a flat whet stone. He stands near* FOGG.]

LEICESTER: [*Picking up a knife and holding it up to the light, disgustedly.*] Now, I calls that slovenly. Polish the blades, Bussy! the Master's guests don't cut beefsteak with the 'andles. [*He polishes the blade on the sleeve of his jacket.*]

'AWKINS: [*Glumly.*] I haven't polished that one. [*He takes it from LEICESTER.*]

LEICESTER: 'Ow's a man to tell when they're shined, the way you're doin' it?

FOGG: [*Seriously.*] 'Old the blades up to 't light and look at 'em. If thou see the himage of the jackass on 'em, they're polished.

LEICESTER: [*Gullibly holding another blade up to the light.*] I can't see no jackass.

FOGG: [*Barely able to keep from laughing.*] Look a bit closer.

LEICESTER: This one must not be polished—there's no trace of horse, mule or ass.

FOGG: [*Almost bursting with suppressed mirth.*] 'Tis the same as on a' silver-backed mirror. Look be'ind thyself.

LEICESTER: [*Turning around and looking squarely into the mirror.*] Whoever heard of silver and mirrors hallmarked with the jackass.

FOGG: Look 'arder and thou wilt see the ass in all 'is glory in an 'eadservant's jacket. [*LEICESTER looks and suddenly the joke dawns upon him. HOLLENBERGER and FOGG laugh uproarously. 'AWKINS smiles. LEICESTER is obviously much nonplussed.*]

HOLLENBERGER: Dot vas a goot vun. Vot an ass!

FOGG: Aye, Cook, what an ass.

[*A bright colored parrot in the cage near the buffet table croaks audibly.*] "Vot an ass; hee, hee, vot as ass! Polly want a wafer!"

LEICESTER: [*Seizing path of least resistance for a comeback wheels on the parrot.*] Shut thy pesky beak, thou loquacious popinjay. And thou, likewise, Fogg.

FOGG: Lumme! At thy command, Mr. Jack——

LEICESTER: Enough of this drivel. Have we not guests to prepare for—guests from America?

HOLLENBERGER: From America? The Master told me der Beefsteak und Tripe Club vas meeting here tonight.

LEICESTER: From the Colonies, and who, think you, are the honored guests?

HOLLENBERGER: Honored guests? How should I know?

LEICESTER: The Washingtons from Virginia.

HOLLENBERGER: If der Vashingtons are so honored, vy do ve feed dem sutch rubbish as dripe?

LEICESTER: Rubbish? Fie, man, tripe is the dish o' kings. [*With a look of ecstasy.*] Good old English tripe. A dash of vinegar, a pinch of salt, and a morsel of tripe—and I'll not ask for more. [*He smacks his lips.*]

FOGG: Our minds meet there, me 'earty. Tripe is indeed a royal dish, hespecially when garnished with leek.

LEICESTER: The master had his wits wi' him when he joined such a noble group as the Beefsteak and Tripe Club.

HOLLENBERGER: Dripe, dripe, dripe. Dot's all you Englunders know how to eat!

LEICESTER: The dish o'kings, sirrah!

HOLLENBERGER: Vot der consequence is—physiques like der giraffe—mit long legs, long necks, sharp noses, shriveled up pellies. Gife me mine kraut mit wieners und a stein mit lager froth shpilling over. Dot's food for der gods. Hoch!

LEICESTER: [*By this time having worked around to the other side of the table so it is between him and the cook.*] Tuck in thy swollen stomach, varlet, I'd rather be a giraffe than a hippopotamus.

FOGG: [*To LEICESTER, mockingly.*] 'Oity-toity, giraffe or 'ippopotamus? Now that's what I calls the long and short o' the matter.

LEICESTER: Hold thy tongues, varmits. And thou, Hollenberger forget thy sour cabbage and thy stuffed weiners and get thee into the scullery and cook tripe and beefsteak as thou has never done before—fit to eat.

FOGG: Lumme!

HOLLENBERGER: [*Making a pass at LEICESTER with the long butcher knife. LEICESTER defends himself with a great pewter tray he picks up from the table.*] Ach, Himmel, call me a hippopotamus; call mine cookery no goot! Vy should I not cut from off dy long neck a piece of dripe? [*At this moment JUDGE HAGGETT steps into the room. HOLLENBERGER and LEICESTER are at opposite ends of the table, HOLLENBERGER menacing and LEICESTER cowering. 'AWKINS and FOGG are back stage, right, thoroughly enjoying the scene as their gestures indicate. JUDGE HAGGETT hastily surveys the scene.*]

'AWKINS: [*To FOGG, not seeing JUDGE HAGGETT.*] White man civilization, Fogg. [*Seeing the JUDGE.*] Pst—the Master.

JUDGE HAGGETT: [*Furiously.*] What means this shindig? Thou unspeakable varlets!

[*FOGG hastily retreats to the plants, where he resumes trimming. LEICESTER looks aghast but makes only movements away from the cook's knife. The cook stands transfixed with knife in midair.*]

JUDGE HAGGETT: What would the vistors from America think to walk in on a disgraceful scene like this?

LEICESTER: I was doing my——

JUDGE HAGGETT: You ought all to be striped. Who'se the author of this brawl, Leicester?

LEICESTER: [*Quailing.*] Faith, sir, 'twas yon cook who made the first attack, sir. Beware 'is knife, sir.

HOLLENBERGER: [*Looking menacingly at LEICESTER.*] Ach, dunder! vott a liar! [*To JUDGE HAGGETT.*] He called mine cookery no goot; he——

LEICESTER: 'E threatened me, sir.

HOLLENBERGER: Ach! [*Puffs cheeks out in anger.*]

JUDGE HAGGETT: [*Obviously siding in with LEICESTER.*] Silence, thou scullery knave. Put down that knife. Get thee back into the kitchen—and henceforth keep out of the headservant's precincts.

HOLLENBERGER: [*Protestingly.*] But he——

JUDGE HAGGETT: Forget not that I can turn you over to the law whensoever I choose.

HOLLENBERGER: [*Obviously disturbed.*] You vill not send me to chail?

JUDGE HAGGETT: 'Tis not my liking for your cooking that prompts me to forget what you did to the sailor on the *Corsair*—with that butcher knife of yours.

HOLLENBERGER: Ach!

JUDGE HAGGETT: If you cook another meal as indigestible as the last, I shall not suffer you to remain longer.

HOLLENBERGER: [*Thoroughly awed.*] But nevar hafe I cooked dripe——

JUDGE HAGGETT: Then you must learn—mark you, this night we are to have tripe and beefsteak fit for a king——

LEICESTER: English, not German style.

JUDGE HAGGETT: Anything less, and to jail you go! Remember the *Corsair*.

LEICESTER: [*To* HOLLENBERGER, *sotto voce*.] And don't be drinkin' too much lager tonight.

JUDGE HAGGETT: [*To* LEICESTER, *in tone of mild rebuke as contrasted with the speech to* HOLLENBERGER.] Best not stroke the Prussian eagle too contemptuously, Leicester. His claws are sharp.

LEICESTER: [*Apologetically to the* JUDGE. *Glares at cook*]. Thy pardon, sir. [LEICESTER *and* JUDGE HAGGETT *leave the room; the cook stands sullenly near the table;* FOGG *is chuckling to himself under the palms*.]

FOGG: [*To cook.*] Ho. Ho! Blow me topsails! Asking a German 'ippopotamus to cook English tripe. Now that's irony or I'm a lobster. Ho! Ho! Fit for a king, ho! ho! [HOLLENBERGER *wheels with his butcher knife on* FOGG, *who dashes out through the French window, hat in hand. Just as he leaves, the parrot croaks meaningfully*.]

PARROTT: Vot an ass. Hee, hee, hee! Vot an ass.

HOLLENBERGER: [*A bit out of breath from his chase to the window.*] Blitzen, vot a mess! Me, der cook vot vonce vas for a King, now to cook dripe for a long-necked Englunder.

'AWKINS: Slaves can't choose who they serve.

HOLLENBERGER: Slaves? Dunder! I vas no slave!

'AWKINS: Nor am I, but the master says "do!" and I do; "go!" and I go.

HOLLENBERGER: Jah! He says maybe I go to chail!

'AWKINS: [*His face brightening.*] Jail?

HOLLENBER: Jah! [*A wry smile.*] Dot vas shust a little shoke vot he has mit me.

'AWKINS: A joke?

HOLLENBERGER: Jah! He says I shtuck a knife in a sailor.

'AWKINS: Of the schooner *Corsair*?

HOLLENBERGER: Jah! the *Corsair*.

'AWKINS: And you did?

HOLLENBERGER: Nein, nein! Dot's vot's zo funny! Ha! Ha!

'AWKINS: Funny?

HOLLENBERGER: Jah! Der master don't know der facts enough to send me to chail!

'AWKINS: If someone told him he would know more.

HOLLENBERGER: Dold him?

'AWKINS: Aye, told him!

HOLLENBERGER: Dold him vot?

'AWKINS: Facts.

HOLLENBERGER: [*With worried expression.*] Mein gott! Nobody knows no facts.

'AWKINS: Maybe—I know!

HOLLENBERGER: [*Demandingly.*] Vot you know?

'AWKINS: [*Meaningfully.*] Perchance I know you didn't stab the sailor on the *Corsair*——

HOLLENBERGER: [*Sighing with relief.*] Dunce! Dot's vot I dold you.

'AWKINS: But what I do know——

HOLLENBERGER: Vot!

'AWKINS: —that you did stab the mate on the *Gaspree*!

HOLLENBERGER: [*Horrified.*] You know—!

'AWKINS: [*Suavely.*] Aye, a little bird told me—Beelezebub, the parrot!

HOLLENBERGER: [*Cringing.*] I didn't mean to stab dat fellar!

'AWKINS: Ah—but you did!

HOLLENBERGER: Jah! But I didn't mean to!

'AWKINS: Maybe your knife slipped?

HOLLENBERGER: Jah, slipped, ven he shtruck me first mit a marlin-spike.

'AWKINS: [*Quizzically.*] Then the master could have you hanged for mutiny—killing a mate.

HOLLENBERGER: He shtruck me first.

'AWKINS: If I told him——

HOLLENBERGER: [*Glumly.*] If you told him.

'AWKINS: The master's humor is bad.

HOLLENBERGER: Don't I know!

'AWKINS: He said I go back to the plantation on the morrow.

HOLLENBERGER: [*Shocked.*] Mit dose dirty black men?

'AWKINS: Aye! For crossing his whim.

HOLLENBERGER: I'd rather go to chail! For vy do you go to der plantation?

'AWKINS: For almost takin' a sip o' wine and gettin' caught!

HOLLENBERGER: Dunder! Den vere vould I go if mine cookery vas not to his likeness?

'AWKINS: [*Severely.*] To jail!

HOLLENBERGER: [*Imploringly.*] You vouldn't tell der master?

'AWKINS: No—not if——

HOLLENBERGER: If vot?

'AWKINS: We don't have to go either place.

HOLLENBERGER: Zay, could ve escape?

'AWKINS: We don't have to.

HOLLENBERGER: Ve vill stay here?

'AWKINS: Maybe——

HOLLENBERGER: [*Nervously.*] You shpeak mit riddles. Vot you mean?

'AWKINS: I mean you wouldn't have to go to jail.

HOLLENBERGER: [*Dazed.*] You make mine head to go zum! [*He gestures.*]

'AWKINS: [*Deftly.*] If the master disappeared——

HOLLENBERGER: [*With a question mark written all over his face.*] You vould kidnap him?

'AWKINS: [*Shakes his head negatively.*]

HOLLENBERGER: He vould disappear to another vorld? [*No answer.*] To another vorld?

'AWKINS: [*Smiles.*] To another world—where——

HOLLENBERGER: Vere dead men go. ['AWKINS *smiles.*] You vouldn't dare, [*with determination and stubbornness*] und I vouldn't mit my knife!

'AWKINS: Not with a knife——

HOLLENBERGER: Nein! Because of mine knife I might go to chail already yet.

'AWKINS: [*Confidentially.*] I know a berry what has juice that would make him——

HOLLENBERGER: Sick?

'AWKINS: Maybe he——

HOLLENBERGER: [*Repulsively.*] Vould not lif?—Not dat! Mine knife [*he brandishes it*] is bad enough.

'AWKINS: Maybe to live but—not to remember.

HOLLENBERGER: To forget?

'AWKINS: Everything that is past.

HOLLENBERGER: Der devil's medicine!

'AWKINS: An old Indian poison—those who drink of it forget all.

HOLLENBERGER: You are sure it would make der master to forget everyding?

'AWKINS: [Leering.] Sure, very sure!

HOLLENBERGER: It's too dangerous!

'AWKINS: [Still cautiously.] A little berry juice in the master's wine would make him to forget the taste of the food. Hein?

[They are near the parrot's cage.]

HOLLENBERGER: [Giving in slightly.] He said if der dripe vas bad I vould go to chail. But poison—it might give convulsions.

'AWKINS: [Deftly.] On this devil's island jails are full of vermin.

HOLLENBERGER: Ach, dunder!

'AWKINS: Rats!

HOLLENBERGER: [Shrugs.] Shnakes—dings vot creep! [He shudders.]

'AWKINS: Dead men tell no tales! They send no cooks to jails.

HOLLENBERGER: [Snapping him up.] You said it vouldn't mean a dead man.

'AWKINS: Only dead to memory.

HOLLENBERGER: [With a shudder.] Vell, maybe shust a little of dat berry chuse in his vine vould make him to forget about mine cookery, if it vasn't to his likeness.

'AWKINS: [Quick to sieze the opening.] I'll get the berries.

HOLLENBERGER: [Half-fearfully to the departing 'AWKINS.] You vouldn't tell?

'AWKINS: Wouldst have a pledge?

HOLLENBERGER: Jah! A pledge!

'AWKINS: Give me your knife. [He takes it from the trembling cook and holds the sharp edge to his throat, tilts his head back and draws the knife across his throat.] May a long, sharp blade cut deep in my neck if I ever breathe a word of this. Now you pledge!

HOLLENBERGER: [Takes and holds knife over his heart, pointedly] Should I tell—may der point go to der core of mine heart.

'AWKINS: There's a bush in the garden. I'll get the berries.

HOLLENBERGER: Shust a few—und not real poison.

'AWKINS: [As he departs.] But poison enough. It means our freedom.

[' AWKINS leaves. HOLLENBERGER feels the edge of his butcher knife absent-mindedly, and finding it still dull, begins to whet it vigorously as he walks slowly off toward the kitchen, seeming to gain confidence with every step he takes. As he passes the parrot cage he stops to ruminate.]

HOLLENBERGER: Poison vine—to make him forget der distaste of mine cookery!

PARROT: Vot an ass!

HOLLENBERGER: [Wheeling on the parrot with a startled look and brandishing his knife.] Dunder, vun day I vill smite dot bird dead und speechless! [He starts to go.]

PARROT: Poison vine! Vot an ass! [The cook glowers over his shoulder and closes the door behind him.]

[As he goes out the kitchen door, FOGG'S head is seen to look in at the French door. He looks in carefully, and seeing no one, comes into the room and goes over to the banquet table and pours a glass of wine surreptitiously from the decanter and drinks it down hurriedly, smacking his lips. He filches another. 'AWKINS bursts into the room on the run, catching FOGG in the act of drinking the second glass. FOGG looks sheepish and retreats to the palms, where he continues trimming. 'AWKINS is grasping the berries in his hand.]

'AWKINS: Lucky for thee I am not the master!

FOGG: This is the first sip I've 'ad in months.

'AWKINS: The master caught me sippin' this morning.

FOGG: Faith! Did 'e get 'is 'air off?

'AWKINS: Enow to send me back to slave amongst the blackmen.

FOGG: With the plantation negroes? [He swallows hard.] My eye!

'AWKINS: You would like to go with me? It won't be for long—— [He looks meaningfully at the berries he has in his hand.]

FOGG: What blithering hidiots we be.

'AWKINS: —or worse——

FOGG: Look at me snipping pretty green gee-gaws for a long-'aired Barbados master—master, indeed!

'AWKINS: Aye, master, indeed!

FOGG: Who be I, that I should feed these croaking parrots and snip these tropic whats-its [he snips viciously] for a blasted Cavalier—me a round'ead? [He pats his close-shaven head with a gesture of pride.]

'AWKINS: If thy head was ought else but round and hard thou woulds't not be here.

FOGG: And to think us Round'eads once ruled this cursed hisland!

'AWKINS: Once?

FOGG: Aye, them was the days! [Angrily.] And afore many ships put in at this den o' slaves, they'll be comin' again.

'AWKINS: [With emphasis.] Aye, 'tis a den o' slaves.

FOGG: Then will I snip some o' the long locks from these bloated haristocrats—master, indeed! [As he says "indeed" he gives another vicious snip with the knife and cuts his left forefinger.] Drat that blade! [The parrot behind FOGG in the cage croaks audibly.]

PARROT: Wot an ass! Wot a den o' slaves! Wot an ass!

FOGG: [Wheels on bird and brandishes the knife at the cage, sucking the blood from his finger as he does so.] Shut thy gibbering beak, thou piebald squawker. [' AWKINS smiles. FOGG sucks and spits blood.] Drat thy pretty feathers! I'll eat the like of thee some day. If thy Barbadian brain was as big as thy plutocrat tongue, I'd lay me breeches thou'd tell the master all thou 'earest.

[The bird flutters in the cage. FOGG drops his knife and, holding his wounded finger, approaches 'AWKINS.]

FOGG: Take me kerchief and bind up this scratch.

'AWKINS: Reaching into FOGG'S waistcoat pocket and pulling out a dirty rag, with which he begins to bind the bleeding finger. FOGG winces.] 'Tis a nasty cut. Hold stiller.

FOGG: 'Awkins, 'tis the red blood of a Round'ead you see. Not all the brave men of Cromwell are in their graves.

'AWKINS: [Tersely.] They ought to be!

FOGG: [Startled.] Thy tongue, churl. 'Tis an odious speech you make.

'AWKINS: [Still binding up the wound, looks up slyly at FOGG.] Ought not to be, then—-the grave's too good for 'em. Too good for all whites!

FOGG: [*Pulls his hand away angrily with the bandage dangling.*] How now, varmit! I'll bandage me own wound.

'AWKINS: Methinks 'tis thy temper needs bandaging.

FOGG: [*Struggling with bandage.*] Thou shouldst get twenty stripes for slurring a white man thus!

'AWKINS: Were not the white man slurred also a slave—a slave like me! [*He clenches his fist.*] Maybe thou shall see the day when our master will be a slave—or a dead man.

FOGG: Had I me choice, methinks I'd rather be a dead man. [*Sighs.*]

'AWKINS: Like most slaves. If—[*He looks again at the berries, then at FOGG*]—we could make a plan——

FOGG: What then, 'Awkins?

'AWKINS: Slaves, like thee n' me, might be free——

FOGG: Free?

'AWKINS: Free!

FOGG: You mean?

'AWKINS: I mean we'd have no master.

FOGG: You mean that?

[*Voices are heard approaching from the right.*]

'AWKINS: Just that—quick, the master!

FOGG: Aye, forsooth, we 'ave a master yet!

[*FOGG grabs his knife and starts to trim the palms, having a difficult time keeping the half-tied bandage on his finger. 'AWKINS fusses around the table as the master enters with a tall, handsome youth. The master glances hastily but thoroughly around the room.*]

JUDGE HAGGETT: And this, Master George, is the dining-room, where meets the Beefsteak and Tripe Club.

WASHINGTON: A capital place for a banquet.

PARROT: Polly want a wafer! Polly want a wafer!

WASHINGTON: [*Walking over to the parrot cage.*] A very pretty parrot, Judge Haggett. A Barbadian?

JUDGE HAGGETT: Aye, and I've never seen a more loquacious bird.

WASHINGTON: I wonder whether he'll understand the American tongue?

JUDGE HAGGETT: Where wafers are concerned, he understands all languages.

WASHINGTON: Almost human.

JUDGE HAGGETT: Suppose you look over the terraces and gardens, Master George, while I make ready to welcome the later guests.

WASHINGTON: 'Twill be a pleasure.

JUDGE HAGGETT: You excuse me?

WASHINGTON: Of a surety, Judge Haggett. I have a desire to explore every nook of your delightful estate.

JUDGE HAGGETT: [*Over his shoulder as he leaves.*] Make yourself at home, my boy. The servants are at your command.

WASHINGTON: I thank you. [*He turns to the parrot.*] Polly want a wafer?

PARROT: Vot an ass! Vot an ass! [*WASHINGTON is shocked.*]

FOGG: Yon blasted bird's a terrible tale-bearer, sir. [*FOGG displays his half-bandaged finger, which WASHINGTON sees. FOGG hastily puts his hand behind his back.*]

WASHINGTON: What unspeakable manners!

'AWKINS: He's a devil, sir.

WASHINGTON: [*Looks at parrot, smiling then to FOGG.*] Your hand is wounded?

FOGG: [*Reluctantly.*] Just a bit of a scratch, sir.

WASHINGTON: [*Stepping over to FOGG, who is still struggling with the bandage.*] I will help you with the bandage.

FOGG: [*Surprised.*] 'Tis no gentleman's task, sir.

WASHINGTON: We think not so in America.

FOGG: [*Surrendering his hand to WASHINGTON.*] Then you be one of the guests from America the master was hexpectin'—a Mr. Washington?

WASHINGTON: The younger—and you are——?

FOGG: The gardener, sir; merely the gardener.

WASHINGTON: Your indenture is for long?

'AWKINS: Indenture? 'Tis a slave he is.

WASHINGTON: [*To FOGG.*] But you're white; surely not a slave?

FOGG: The color of a man's skin makes small difference on this cursed isle, sir.

WASHINGTON: 'Tis not plain to me. How come you here?

FOGG: By my own folly, drat the day!

WASHINGTON: Folly?

FOGG: Aye, folly! For years in London Town I was as free as a water rat on Thames' banks.

WASHINGTON: Then you must have seen much of slave trading?

FOGG: Aye, the slave traders I knew by name and face. Oft I told 'em where they might find brawny men and young boys to bring to these parts.

'AWKINS: [*Contemptuously.*] A Roundhead way of makin' an honest living. [*WASHINGTON looks at 'AWKINS, inquiringly.*]

FOGG: [*Retaliating to 'AWKINS.*] That's what a Round-'ead's for, to use and save thy 'ands from gettin' whacked up. [*He gestures at his cut finger.*]

WASHINGTON: And then——?

FOGG: When strange traders'd dock for a load of hindentures, I'd volunteer to sail with 'em for ports unknown. I'd live on their boat, eat their food, and keep me bones warm under their lousy quilts, while they loaded.

'AWKINS: Loaded white slaves for the Barbados!

FOGG: When sailing time'd come, I'd swear to the King's searchers who came aboard I'd been trepanned—meaning kidnapped—and they'd demand my release and I'd go free again the better off—a full belly and a hearty laugh.

WASHINGTON: A novel means of living.

FOGG: Ho! Ho! I'll ne're forget the looks on the faces o' them traders as I'd strut me down the gangplank, all pomp and ceremonious-like. [*He struts.*]

'AWKINS: Always he has what you call a bag of tricks.

FOGG: [*To 'AWKINS.*] But once too often, 'Awkins, did I try this trick. [*To WASHINGTON.*] And I woke up an hundred miles out at sea, with a great welt 'ere [*indicating*] on me shaven pate, pretty as you please, on me way to the Barbados and slavery.

'AWKINS: Forsooth!

FOGG: 'Ere I am now, snipping pretty gee-gaws—and me bloomin' finger. Wot a blithering—— [*He suddenly remembers the parrot and looks at it and cuts his speech short.*]

WASHINGTON: You serve without pay?

FOGG: Oh, mayhap at the hend o' me term—whenever that is—I'll get me a tract of swamp land.

WASHINGTON: From Judge Haggett?

FOGG: Aye, Haggett hain't a bad sort, ['AWKINS *grunts with disapprobation. WASHINGTON looks querulously at him*] save that he expects no foolin'.

WASHINGTON: Methinks 'twere an unlucky day for you when you left England.

'AWKINS: [*Meaningfully.*] 'Twas an unlucky day for these islands when the first Englishman set foot here.

WASHINGTON: [*Finishing bandage.*] Done! [*To 'AWKINS, inquiringly.*] You seem to bear a grudge against Englishmen. ['AWKINS *shrugs.*]

FOGG: I say! you're right 'andy with bandaging.

WASHINGTON: I learned that from the Indians. But pray tell me, which way is the garden? I must see it before the Judge returns.

FOGG: Aye, 'e's mighty proud of 'is garden, sir. I keeps it, sir.

WASHINGTON: I've heard much of the terraces.

FOGG: That way, sir. [*Indicating French doors, WASHINGTON exits.*]

'AWKINS: A dandy young upstart!

FOGG: More considerate than the hislanders, owever dandy. ['AWKINS *grunts a half-hearted approval.*] He did me up nicely. [*Examines his hand.*]

'AWKINS: Aye, he learned that from my race.

FOGG: [*Secretively.*] You were telling me something 'afore the master and the young stranger entered—something about making a plan——?

'AWKINS: [*Elusively.*] There are many plans.

FOGG: You said your plan had to do with [*whispering*] freedom.

'AWKINS: Well! We want freedom, don't we?

FOGG: Lumme! What wouldn't we do with it?

'AWKINS: Aye, but you don't want freedom.

FOGG: Don't want it?

'AWKINS: Aye, don't want it bad enough to get it.

FOGG: Get it? 'Ow could we get it?

'AWKINS: We can't do anything without it. My plan—— [*He hesitates*].

FOGG: Yes—your plan——?

'AWKINS: —wouldn't interest you.

FOGG: [*Curiosity apparent.*] Lumme, bean't I a slave like thee?

'AWKINS: We'll get it when the master dies, methinks?

FOGG: If we don't die first.

'AWKINS: We don't have to die first.

FOGG: [*Gasping.*] You mean——?

'AWKINS: Save your alarm! I ain't said nothing.

FOGG: 'Twould be dangerous——

'AWKINS: Mayhap 'twould be worth the risk.

FOGG: Not to me!

'AWKINS: I have bethought me of a plan, since I talked to thee—a clever plan.

FOGG: I'll not get in any mixups with your plans.

'AWKINS: [*Slyly.*] If the Judge—sickened—it might mean less work for us.

FOGG: Aye, and if all the masters'd die, us slaves'd have a glorious time buryin' 'em.

'AWKINS: Now if our master should die——

FOGG: If he should die at our hands, by 'igh noon we'd both dangle on ropes in the public square.

'AWKINS: —I would get my freedom and you would get your land. My plan takes away the risk.

FOGG: Thy mind is full of evil plans.

'AWKINS: This is a *good* plan.

FOGG: Well—mind thee, I'm no party to it!

'AWKINS: We could have Hollenberger, the cook——

FOGG: [*Surprised.*] Why should he——?

'AWKINS: The master can send 'im to jail.

FOGG: Where learn you all these things?

'AWKINS: [*Mockingly.*] From old Beelzebub, the parrot. [*Smiles.*]

FOGG: That devil bird! [*Looks meaningfully at parrot.*]

'AWKINS: [*Showing FOGG the berries.*] Just a few drops of juice from these berries—in the master's wine——

FOGG: We would be free?

'AWKINS: —placed there by the cook——

FOGG: Free!

'AWKINS: Aye, free! I've planned this much; do you plan our escape. [*At this moment, LEICESTER, the headservant, enters. He observes that 'AWKINS has completely abandoned his work on the table and FOGG his snipping.*]

LEICESTER: Come, come, now; enough of this poppycock. Fogg comes with me, I've a task for thee.

FOGG: A task—me life's full of 'em! Always another task.

LEICESTER: See thou, 'Awkins, that the blades of the knives on the table are whetted for beefsteak. 'Twill take keen edges to cut the meat served by the scullery knave who calls himself a German cook.

FOGG: Calls 'imself!

LEICESTER: Aye, tougher steak than the last one he cooked a dog couldn't gnaw.

FOGG: [*Furtively.*] Did'st try it, sirrah?

LEICESTER: Aye, 'twas too tough for me. [*Suddenly getting the insinuation, he blushes and exits hurriedly, slamming the door in FOGG'S face. FOGG opens it and follows him. As FOGG goes out, he says to 'AWKINS over his shoulder.*]

FOGG: [*Indicating LEICESTER.*] What an ass! [*Seriously.*] Mind you, I'm no party to your dastardly plans!

'AWKINS: [*Reflectively.*] I shouldn't have told him.

[*No sooner are FOGG and LEICESTER out of the room than 'AWKINS goes to the buffet table and selects from among the wine glasses the large and conspicuously colored blue one. He places it on the table where it can easily be seen by the audience. He then goes to the kitchen door and beckons HOLLENBERGER, who comes into the dining-room.*]

HOLLENBERGER: Ach! [*Surprised.*] Back zo zoon?

'AWKINS: With the berries. [*He shows them to the cook.*]

HOLLENBERGER: Ooh! Dot's too many.

'AWKINS: There isn't much juice in 'em.

HOLLENBERGER: Maybe ve better not do dis.

'AWKINS: [*Furtively.*] Some one told me a man was bitten by a rat and died in jail yesterday.

HOLLENBERGER: [*Shuddering.*] But if I cook a goot meal der master von't send me to chail.

'AWKINS: Freedom, yours—and mine. You are 'fraid of freedom?

HOLLENBERGER: Maybe I'm 'fraid ve get caught.

'AWKINS: Afraid? Then you would rather chance the jail?— and snakes?

HOLLENBERGER: [*Desperately.*] Gife dem to me. [*He snatches the berries away from 'AWKINS.*] Now vot?

'AWKINS: You know the master's cup?

HOLLENBERGER: He always uses der vun vot Chudge Maynard gifed him—a fancy blue vun.

'AWKINS: It is on yonder table. [*They approach the buffet table.*]

HOLLENBERGER: Ve'd better hurry.

'AWKINS: Aye, there's no time to dally.

HOLLENBERGER: I squeeze dem?

'AWKINS: With both hands. [*He demonstrates.*]

HOLLENBERGER: Shust squeeze der chuse out like dat? [*He tries squeezing one into his empty hand.*]

'AWKINS: No, with both hands. Not in thy palm, in the blue cup!

HOLLENBERGER: [*Hesitating.*] You are sure ve von't be caught?

'AWKINS: I'm sure we'll get our freedom.

HOLLENBERGER: Freedom! Vot vill I not do mit it?

'AWKINS: Hurry, now; you make my nerves jump.

HOLLENBERGER: [*With decisive movements squeezes the berries one at a time into the cup.*] Dere, ein; dere, zwei; dere, drei— dot's enough.

'AWKINS: Some are left.

HOLLENBERGER: [*Sullenly.*] If ve are caught I'll dook dem mineself.

'AWKINS: Fool, squeeze in the rest of 'em.

HOLLENBERGER: Maybe shust a couple; dere, ein; dere, zwei. Dat's plenty.

[*At this moment the French door opens behind the conspirators and WASHINGTON steps in unconcernedly and opens his mouth as if to speak, but doesn't, when he sees the plotters. He is unobserved and stands looking at them.*]

'AWKINS: Put 'em all in!

HOLLENBERGER: Somevun's coming!

[*A noise is heard of footsteps approaching. WASHINGTON steps back out of the French door and disappears. FOGG enters the room, and LEICESTER calls to him from the other room, "And don't forget to feed the parrots!" FOGG stops abruptly when he sees the two conspirators.*]

HOLLENBERGER: You frightened us.

FOGG: [*To HOLLENBERGER.*] Fright—'tis said fright is the sign of a guilty conscience.

[*HOLLENBERGER blushes and goes hurriedly into his own precincts, the scullery.*]

FOGG: [*To 'AWKINS.*] So you took the risk?

'AWKINS: No, the cook.

FOGG: Aye, the cook——

'AWKINS: [*Assuringly.*] So far everything is all right.

FOGG: [*Looking suspiciously at the wine glasses on the table.*] Aye, but if your plan fails, we'll all rock on the gibbet.

'AWKINS: No fear, Fogg; the cook takes the blame.

FOGG: "There's many a slip twixt cup and lip."

'AWKINS: Be sure 'tis not a slip o' the tongue. [*The French*

door opens and WASHINGTON comes in. The servants are somewhat confused.]

FOGG: [*Hesitating for something to say.*] You saw the garden?

WASHINGTON: Yes, the terraces are beautiful.

FOGG: Think o' the work it took to make 'em.

'AWKINS: Aye, think o' the slaves that toiled at the work.

WASHINGTON: [*To 'AWKINS.*] Still bearing a grudge, my friend?

'AWKINS: [*Sullenly.*] All slaves do. Moreover, I am unjustly a slave.

WASHINGTON: Unjustly? Then thou hast not always been a slave?

'AWKINS: My body, yes! My heart, never! [*He beats on his breast.*]

WASHINGTON: It is not plain to me.

FOGG: [*To WASHINGTON.*] Nor me, sir. [*To 'AWKINS.*] Explain yourself, be or bean't thee a slave?

WASHINGTON: True, you are not black.

'AWKINS: Not I. I'm an Indian——

WASHINGTON: An Indian?

'AWKINS: My people once owned these lands.

FOGG: [*Derisively.*] Lumme, what a puzzle. You are owned with black men; you say you're an Hindian; and you bear an English name.

'AWKINS: A name not of my choosin'.

FOGG: [*To WASHINGTON.*] And now 'e says 'e don't own 'is name!

'AWKINS: [*Vindictively.*] 'Twas the name of an English blackguard.

FOGG: A nasty epithet, that.

WASHINGTON: [*Silencing FOGG with a gesture.*] How came you by this name you bear so grudgingly?

'AWKINS: The man who was grandfather to me was an English sailor—the only one left alive after a fight at sea with the Spaniards.

FOGG: The devil take the Spaniards!

'AWKINS: Aye, the devil take 'em for letting him escape! My grandmother——

FOGG: Lumme! Now 'es blamin' 'is grandmother. [*'AWKINS looks daggers at FOGG, and WASHINGTON motions to FOGG to remain quiet.*]

'AWKINS: —my grandmother found him, cast on shore.

WASHINGTON: Yes?

'AWKINS: She was a beautiful girl named Yariko. Her tribe wanted to scalp the wretch and feed him to the sharks but she saved the life of the varlet!

FOGG: [*Feeling his close-shaven head as if to ascertain whether his own scalp were intact.*] A long-'aired Cavalier coxcomb? They should 'ave scalped 'im.

'AWKINS: A baldish Roundhead he was, sirrah.

FOGG: Lumme!

WASHINGTON: And then?

'AWKINS: And then, when 'im and my grandmother escaped to this cursed island, 'Awkins—that was his name, Sir—sold Yariko into slavery.

WASHINGTON: A dastardly villain, whoever he was.

'AWKINS: A white man, sir. Sometimes methinks they're all alike.

WASHINGTON: Not all, my friend—but the name?

'AWKINS: My father who was also an Indian was born and died a slave.

WASHINGTON: The poor devil!

'AWKINS: They called him 'Awkins. He hated the name. I hate the name!

FOGG: [*With a dig.*] Aye, 'Awkins, a true Round'ead heart beats neath your red 'ide. ['*AWKINS glowers.*]

WASHINGTON: 'Tis a harrowing tale you tell and 'tis small wonder you bear a grudge.

'AWKINS: Aye, small wonder.

FOGG: [*Slyly.*] —a grudge, for whom?

'AWKINS: For the man in the moon! He's white, isn't he?

WASHINGTON: White and watchful; with big ears to hear you and big eyes to watch your doings. ['*AWKINS looks perturbed.*]

FOGG: [*Questioningly.*] Would you perchance look to see the dovecote afore dark?

WASHINGTON: That I would. [*To* 'AWKINS.] Better days, my friend.

[*They exit through the French door. After they have gone out,* 'AWKINS *goes over to the table, picks up the blue glass, looks at it for a long moment, grimaces, puts it down among the others, picks it up a second time, hesitatingly pours contents into another glass and starts toward the kitchen as if repenting of his act; stops suddenly with resolution, walks back to the table, hesitates; voices are heard in the hall; he pours contents back into blue glass, speedily arranges the other glasses and leaves via the kitchen.*

JUDGE HAGGETT *enters with* CAPTAIN PETRIE, DR. LANAHAN, *and* MAJOR GEDNEY CLARKE.]

CAPTAIN PETRIE: [*Jocularly, to* JUDGE HAGGETT.] Judge Haggett, how are you making out with this knife-wielding German cook of yours?

JUDGE HAGGETT: Maybe you'd best ask that to Herr Cook, Captain Petrie.

CAPTAIN PETRIE: Has he convinced you yet that a "stein shpilling over mit lager" is more salutary than a sip of rare old Madeira? [*All chuckle.*]

JUDGE HAGGETT: No, he has not converted me, but he swears my stomach will rust if I don't soon take to drinkin' lager.

MAJOR CLARKE: [*Mockingly philosophic.*] Tush, tush! What matters a mere rusty stomach? We'll all rust sooner or later. What I would know is, can this German scullion cook tripe and beefsteak?

JUDGE HAGGETT: 'Twill be for his best health, Major Clarke, as I have informed him, to serve tripe and beefsteak fit for a king to you gentlemen tonight.

MAJOR CLARKE: A pretty compliment, Sir.

JUDGE HAGGETT: I threatened to send him to jail if he served ought else.

MAJOR CLARKE: When a cook becomes recalcitrant, a jail is a handy weapon.

LEICESTER: [*Appearing at entrance and announcing.*] Judge William Maynard, Judge Satus Maynard, Mr. James Carter, Commodore Francis Hoburn, and Major Lawrence Washington.

[*All shake hands and exchange greetings with each other.*]

JUDGE HAGGETT: [*Bowing.*] Greetings, gentlemen. Especially do we welcome you, our friend from America, Major Lawrence. [*He bows to* LAWRENCE.]

LAWRENCE WASHINGTON: [*Bows in return.*] Your graciousness overwhelms me, gentlemen.—And my brother, George, he is here?

JUDGE HAGGETT: He will be here, anon. He is wandering about in every nook and cranny. I saw him talking with the gardener but a few moments ago.

MAJOR CLARKE: Your health is improving, Major Washington?

LAWRENCE: [*Half hopelessly.*] Sometimes I think so.

DR. LANAHAN: [*Reassuringly.*] A few weeks in this climate will bring you back to your old self again.

MR. CARTER: Ere long you'll feel like faring forth on another Cartagena campaign.

LAWRENCE: [*Remorsefully.*] I fear, Mr. Carter, my soldier days are over.

CAPTAIN PETRIE: If so, you'll have a worthy successor as a soldier, Major Lawrence, in that young brother of yours.

LAWRENCE: You think so?

CAPTAIN PETRIE: [*Enthusiastically.*] Verily! I took him with me to visit Fort Neeham. Nothing escapes his eyes; they're like a hawk's.

LAWRENCE: So they are.

CAPTAIN PETRIE: I'll venture he could draw a plan of the fort now from memory and scarce miss a loophole or a cannon.

LAWRENCE: The lad has in truth a military turn of mind.

MAJOR CLARKE: And, if one can judge by his fencing, a military turn of the wrist.

JUDGE HAGGETT: Suppose we assemble, gentlemen. Major Lawrence, you will kindly occupy the chair to my right. [*The guests seat themselves around the room conveniently.* JUDGE HAGGETT *stands until all are seated.*] Gentlemen, save for our usual pledge to our gracious King, we will dispense with formalities and take up the business of the Club later. You are ready?

ALL: Hear, hear! [*They arise and stand at attention with a salute—right hand over heart.*]

JUDGE HAGGETT: [*Solemnly.*] We hereby pledge allegiance anew to our most sovereign Majesty, King George the Second. May his dominions beyond the seas remain ever faithful; his ministers ever trustworthy; his armies ever powerful; and his navy ever supreme; may a kind and beneficent Providence ever preserve his health, his happiness and his throne!

[*During this toast,* GEORGE WASHINGTON *enters preceded by* LEICESTER. *Sensing the significance of the toast,* GEORGE *also draws himself up to attention with the hand over the heart salute and stands so until the toast is finished.* LEICESTER *makes a belated attempt to come to the salute. After the toast he announces* GEORGE.]

LEICESTER: Mr. George Washington.

JUDGE HAGGETT: Thrice welcome, my lad. A seat awaits you. [*Indicates seat at his left.*]

WASHINGTON: You honor me. I apologize that I am late.

LAWRENCE: [*To* GEORGE.] Judge Haggett tells us you have been frisking about like a colt in a new pasture.

WASHINGTON: I thought I might find a bit of excitement.

CAPTAIN PETRIE: Excitement is difficult to find on this drowsy isle, George.

GEORGE: Not if one hunts for it.

JUDGE WILLIAM MAYNARD: Speaking of excitement—dids't see the hubbub at the wharf this morning?

JUDGE HAGGETT: No, pray tell us of it.

JUDGE WILLIAM MAYNARD: [*All listen.*] It seems that Michael McDonald had bargained with Jasper Rooney, the skipper of the *Negrita*, to trade provisions for one of the wenches Rooney brought on his last trip. [*'AWKINS enters at this moment with a great steaming platter of beefsteak, which he places on the table and then busies himself filling glasses and arranging the silver, thus being able to hear the conversation.*] Said McDonald to Rooney, "If thou'll let me hae some o' thy wench's flesh, thou shalt hae some o' my hog's flesh, a groat a pound for the hog and sixpence a pound for the woman"—as if they were bartering for that beefsteak yonder. [*He points at the beefsteak.*]

JUDGE SATUS MAYNARD: Fie, brother; don't disgrace such sweet-scented meat! [*He draws a deep breath through his nose as if smelling.*]

MAJOR CLARKE: A second Shylock, methinks. [*Chuckles.*]

JUDGE WILLIAM MAYNARD: " 'Tis a bargain," quoth Rooney. The planter placed his largest sow on one side of the scales and the trader brought forth from his evil-smelling ship an extreme fat lassie he called Honor and put her on the other side.

DR. LANAHAN: And the twain were one flesh. [*Laughs.*]

JUDGE WILLIAM MAYNARD: As I live, the sow went up in the air a squealin' like he was stuck, for Honor outweighed the hog by two stone-ten.

JUDGE HAGGETT: A Scotchman's pigs are never overly fat.

JUDGE WILLIAM MAYNARD: McDonald's eyes fair popped out o' his head. He grabbed his hog and would have broken his bargain and fled had not Honor intervened.

MR. CARTER: Intervened?

JUDGE WILLIAM MAYNARD: Aye, she seized the hog by the hind legs, and a crowd gathered and insisted that McDonald go through with the deal—mayhap for Honor's sake. [*All laugh. 'AWKINS, during this story, shows his disdain for the white slave-owners by wicked facial grimaces.*]

MAJOR CLARKE: Methinks 'twas an instance of Rooney's great *Honor* saving the day. [*More laughs.*]

MR. CARTER: One rarely finds honor of such proportions amongst slave traders. [*More laughs.*]

WASHINGTON: [*With youthful impetuosity and sincerity.*] Methinks there is little honor in that kind of slavery.

[*'AWKINS leaves via kitchen.*]

MAJOR CLARKE: [*There is a silence.*] How now, lad? Do you not have slaves on your own Virginia plantations?

WASHINGTON: Aye, but we do not treat them like animals.—Please do not think me personal, gentlemen.

CAPTAIN PETRIE: Slave traders are a rum lot, George.

WASHINGTON: And slave traffic is bad at its best.

CAPTAIN PETRIE: Aye, and 'tis quite different here than in America.

MR. CARTER: Here 'tis necessary that we keep our slaves in fear of our power, lest they rise up and massacre all of us white men.

WASHINGTON: Why should they wish to do that?

JUDGE HAGGETT: One of them told me, 'tis because we feed them nought but lob-lolly. [*Smiles.*]

WASHINGTON: Hunger will drive even beasts to desperation.

JUDGE HAGGETT: But, methinks, that is not the reason——

WASHINGTON: No?

JUDGE HAGGETT: No. Slaves are depraved by nature. God made 'em black so the dirt from white men's fields wouldn't show on 'em.

JUDGE SATUS MAYNARD: And the devil made 'em so low they can't rise.

WASHINGTON: A fallen race can not rise without help.

MAJOR CLARKE: Help! They outnumber us whites three to one, my boy. If we helped them, God help us!

JUDGE SATUS MAYNARD: Aye, some of us still remember the time too well, when a plot almost materialized to exterminate us all and make of this island a Negro haven.

CAPTAIN PETRIE: But for a mulatto woman named Fortuna overhearing the conspiracy and telling her master—

MAJOR CLARKE: And our promptly executing eighteen of the conspirators——

WASHINGTON: 'Tis strange that in this day we should have to live in fear of our servants.

JUDGE SATUS MAYNARD: Strange, but true.

CAPTAIN PETRIE: We have taken care of our fear. If any tumult occurs on one island, a signal gun is fired; the neighboring isle hears the report and likewise fires a volley. In this way, the news of a slave uprising is speedily communicated to every colony.

MAJOR CLARKE: We must and do take precautions.

WASHINGTON: That you must, but is a precaution always a remedy?

MAJOR CLARKE: No, but a precaution is in order until a remedy is found.

WASHINGTON: [*Prophetically.*] Mayhap some future government will legislate against slavery.

LAWRENCE: George never misses an opportunity to comment on the slavery question. Pray do not misconstrue him, gentlemen.

WASHINGTON: Hoity-toity! My volley brought a brother to my defense.

CAPTAIN PETRIE: Methinks you had the situation fairly well in hand yourself.

WASHINGTON: I repeat, I meant not to be personal, gentlemen.

CAPTAIN PETRIE: No fear, George, we did not so regard your comment.

WASHINGTON: The slaves about the island have stirred up my pity with their harrowing tales of hunger and privation.

DR. LANAHAN: There's plenty of both.

[*During this discussion, JUDGE HAGGETT has been carving great chunks of beefsteak. LEICESTER carries the plates to the guests. 'AWKINS enters with a large platter of steaming tripe and places it near the steak. JUDGE HAGGETT proceeds to serve the guests a plate at a time, buffet style. 'AWKINS pours the wine into the glasses and gives each guest a glass, putting the large blue goblet near JUDGE HAGGETT'S place.*]

MR. CARTER: Forsooth, what matter! so long as the Beefsteak and Tripe Club doesn't hunger?

JUDGE WILLIAM MAYNARD: Aye! Heap the plates, sir.

WASHINGTON: 'Tis a tasty-looking dish, Judge Haggett, but would you think me rude if I asked why Englishmen always have their tripe and beefsteak wherever they are?

LAWRENCE: Especially with such rare fruits as you see here. [*He indicates the guavas, pomegranates, etc., on the table.*]

['AWKINS *passes the tripe to the guests, each of whom helps himself.*]

JUDGE SATUS MAYNARD: What Englishman could fare on guavas and sappadillas, Major Washington?

JUDGE WILLIAM MAYNARD: Tripe and beefsteak are national emblems—like the flag, or Westminster, or the Crown jewels. [*Smiles.*]

DR. LANAHAN: Methinks, if St. Peter did not object to such a nationalistic institution, Englishmen would install a tripe shop at the gates of Paradise.

CAPTAIN PETRIE: Mayhap Britain's dominions will extend that far some day, Dr. Lanahan.

DR. LANAHAN: Then St. Peter will have to do as King George dictates. [*More laughs.*]

MR. CARTER: Or fire a volley for help from a neighboring star.

[*GEORGE has turned to the parrot in the cage near him and is offering the bird a broken wafer.*]

WASHINGTON: This bird must be English. He positively scorns wafers—and knows his King's English, too.

JUDGE HAGGETT: Try him again, now. All loquacious beggars will scorn you when they're not hungry.

WASHINGTON: [*To parrot.*] Polly want a wafer? Polly want a wafer? [*No response.*] Evidently his hunger hasn't returned.

CAPTAIN PETRIE: What he needs is an appetizer. Give him a sip of Madiera.

WASHINGTON: [*Reaches for his wine while looking at the parrot and teasing it with a wafer. He inadvertently takes the blue goblet of JUDGE HAGGETT'S just as the JUDGE also is reaching for it.*] Polly want a sip?

PARROT: [*Noisily.*] Poison wine, ass! Poison wine, ass! Polly want a wafer. [*All laugh.*]

WASHINGTON: Faith! Poison wine? I'm glad you told me. I was about to give thee a drink. [*More laughs. GEORGE looks intently at the goblet and sees it is not his own. 'AWKINS looks on with fixed attention.*]

MAJOR CLARKE: A sensible bird, that—a teetotaler.

JUDGE HAGGETT: A regular chatterbox—prim and gossipy as a maiden aunt.

WASHINGTON: [*To JUDGE HAGGETT.*] Thy pardon. I picked up your goblet by mistake.

JUDGE HAGGETT: No pardon due, lad.

[*WASHINGTON replaces the goblet.*]

WASHINGTON: [*Indicating the goblet.*] 'Tis beautiful—the faces on it, especially the Indian on the stem.

JUDGE HAGGETT: [*Reaching for it and holding it up to the light.*] Judge Maynard gave it to me. I seldom drink from any other. [*He then is about to drink when WASHINGTON places his hand on the JUDGE'S arm, obviously to stop him.*]

WASHINGTON: Judge Haggett, I have a request. Woulds't grant it? [*The JUDGE puts his goblet down. 'AWKINS makes a gesture of one who has failed and looks with contempt at WASHINGTON.*]

JUDGE HAGGETT: Of a surety, lad. Name thy wish.

WASHINGTON: Send for Fogg, the gardener.

LAWRENCE: What a strange request, George.

WASHINGTON: A capital entertainer, this man Fogg.

JUDGE HAGGETT: Aye, a merry fool for any court. [*To 'AWKINS.*] Summon Fogg.

'AWKINS: [*Eyes WASHINGTON suspiciously.*] Yes, sir. [*Hesitating.*] Now, sir?

JUDGE HAGGETT: Aye, *now!* Don't stand there pondering!

'AWKINS: Yes—uh—er, sir! [*He departs hurriedly.*]

[*JUDGE HAGGETT again reaches for his goblet. GEORGE diverts his attention this time by coughing rather violently.*]

JUDGE HAGGETT: A nasty cough, lad. The night air?

WASHINGTON: No, sir; my Sunday throat.

JUDGE HAGGETT: 'Tis aggravating how sometimes we get our throats and days confused.

[*He reaches for the blue goblet a third time. GEORGE promptly proffers his own to JUDGE.*]

WASHINGTON: Please honor me by drinking from my cup, Judge Haggett.

[*The JUDGE replaces his own goblet and takes GEORGE'S. 'AWKINS gives WASHINGTON a shrewd, questioning look, which WASHINGTON ignores.*]

JUDGE HAGGETT: You seem to have taken to heart what the parrot said about poison wine, my boy. However, 'tis my pleasure.

[*He drinks from WASHINGTON'S goblet.*]

WASHINGTON: [*At ease.*] Thank you, sir.

JUDGE HAGGETT: Here's Fogg.

JUDGE SATUS MAYNARD: Aye, the fool arrives before the throne.

[*FOGG looks bewildered. He is wringing his hands.*]

JUDGE HAGGETT: [*To FOGG.*] Master George has a favor to ask of thee, Fogg. [*To GEORGE.*] What's your pleasure, lad?

WASHINGTON: [*To FOGG.*] The verses you recited to me in the garden a few moments ago—I would have you say them here.

FOGG: [*Hesitating to frame an answer.*] I forgets which they were, sir.

WASHINGTON: There was one skit with several verses, about tripe.

FOGG: [*Alarmed.*] Oh, sir, I 'ave forgotten that, sir.

WASHINGTON: You said you made up one verse especially for me.

FOGG: That's right, sir. Which one, sir? I forgets easily.

WASHINGTON: You remember, the one about the King and the poison cup.

[*'AWKINS shows increasing uneasiness. He looks wickedly at FOGG.*]

FOGG: Oh, that one! 'Twas but a bit of poppycock to hamuse you, sir.

WASHINGTON: It would, mayhap, amuse us all.

FOGG: You would have me to recite it here, sir?

JUDGE HAGGETT: Addlepate! That's what he's asking you to do.

FOGG: 'Tis but a foolish skit, Master.

JUDGE HAGGETT: More's the reason to speak it.

DR. LANAHAN: Aye, a little foolishness perks up the digestion.

MR. CARTER: —Wakens the slumbering wits——

JUDGE SATUS MAYNARD: —And exalts assininity on dignity's throne.

FOGG: But I merely composed it to tantalize the cook, sir.

JUDGE HAGGETT: Capital! Then the cook shall hear it.

FOGG: [*Seeing his mistake.*] 'E wouldn't like it, sir.

JUDGE HAGGETT: Neither do we like his food sometimes, but we eat it.

FOGG: [*Swallowing hard.*] I am afeared, sir.

JUDGE HAGGETT: Fough! Call Hollenberger, 'Awkins.

'AWKINS: [*Hesitating.*] Now,—sir?

JUDGE HAGGETT: Yes, damme, *now!*

['AWKINS *leaves begrudgingly via kitchen.*]

MAJOR CLARKE: This has promise.

JUDGE SATUS MAYNARD: Aye, mayhap 'twill be as good as the play "George Barnwell" we saw of late.

[HOLLENBERGER *enters timidly.*]

HOLLENBERGER: [*Aside to FOGG*] Vot is dis, Fogg?

FOGG: [*To HOLLENBERGER.*] A bit of a joke, Herr Cook.

JUDGE HAGGETT: Listen closely to Fogg, Hollenberger; 'twill make more of an Englishman out of thee.

WASHINGTON: Aye, the cook must listen closely.

HOLLENBERGER: Ach, am I der object of a shoke?

JUDGE HAGGETT: We shall see. Proceed, Fogg.

WASHINGTON: And mind you, no changes.

FOGG: But faith, I can not remember it word for word.

WASHINGTON: I'll prompt you——

JUDGE HAGGETT: You heard the gentleman; word for word!

WASHINGTON: Prepare for mirth, gentlemen; the poem is most appropriate to the occasion.

MAJOR CLARKE: The occasion?

WASHINGTON: Aye, it concerns the origin of that ancient and honorable dish, tripe.

ALL: Hear! Hear! Etc.

WASHINGTON: Now, Fogg.

[FOGG *hesitates, wrings his hat in his hands, seems to gain a mite of confidence and begins, with a shaky but dramatic voice.*]

FOGG: A king said one day to his cook:
"My stomach craves novel comestibles;
The victuals and broth that you brew
To me are but rank indigestibles.
So bring me this day, if you would, sirrah,
Save your neck from the gibbet for good, sirrah,
A new sustentation, not yet in creation;
Or you'll have no head for your hood, sirrah!"

JUDGE WILLIAM MAYNARD: [*Laughing.*] Sounds as though the King might be our host himself. [*All laugh.*]

FOGG: Oh, no, sir; no, no, sir! This was an early English King, sir.

JUDGE HAGGETT: [*Gesturing.*] Proceed!

FOGG: The cook swore a terrible oath
At the sovereign gormandizer
And vowed he'd prepare a viand—
A toothsome and rare appetizer.
His voice made the scullery ring. Selah.
He'd stir, then he'd beat, then he'd sing, selah.
The new sustentation, not yet in creation,
Would surely be fit for a king. Selah!

ALL: Jolly well done. Hear! Hear! Capital. Etc.

DR. LANAHAN: [*To HOLLENBERGER.*] Herr Cook, this ought to appeal to your sense of humor.

[HOLLENBERGER *looks like a duck out of water, ill at ease, shifting from one foot to the other.*]

JUDGE HAGGETT: Proceed, Fogg.

FOGG: Each pipkin and firkin and crock
Brimmed o'er with ambrosial provender—
Rich compotes and goulash and mince,
Young duckling and terrapin tender.

[*Solemnly.*] But the death raven's screech echoed near, caw, caw,
And the cook quailed and quivered with fear, caw, caw.
A new sustentation defied his creation,
Grim thoughts of the gibbet drown'd cheer. Caw! Caw!

MAJOR CLARKE: Forsooth, the poem was indeed made to tantalize the cook.

HOLLENBERGER: [*Sniffing, with an obvious movement toward the kitchen door.*] Ach! der gravy—I schmell it! [*He starts to leave.*]

JUDGE HAGGETT: The gravy is already on the table, Herr Cook. Remain!

HOLLENBERGER: I schmelled somedink.

'AWKINS: [*To HOLLENBERGER.*] Mayhap you smelled a rat, sirrah.

HOLLENBERGER: Ja! I schmelled somedink. [*He catches the significance of 'AWKINS' speech and eyes him.*]

WASHINGTON: [*Looking at HOLLENBERGER and 'AWKINS.*] Listen closely to the next verse. [*To FOGG.*] Mind you, Fogg, no changes.

JUDGE HAGGETT: Proceed, Fogg.

FOGG: [*Nervously.*]
Then planned he in rancorous grief—
And with him a fellow conspirator—
To poison a potion of wine
And serve to the finicky epicure.
"But first I'll concoct a food vile, ah ha!
And watch his nibs eat it meanwhile, ah ha!
A new sustentation, a horrid creation—
I'll thus lose my head with a smile. Ah! Ha!" [*A wicked laugh.*]

MAJOR CLARKE: Methinks, between the parrot and the poet, we're hearing much of poison wine.

DR. LANAHAN: Aye, the minds of parrots and poets run to such fantasies.

MR. CARTER: And with fools, are equally given to credulity.

JUDGE HAGGETT: Proceed, Fogg.

FOGG: [*Trembling.*]
Once more pots and firkins were filled
With acrid, unsavory dishes.
The cook strove with vigor and zeal
To make one as foul as his wishes.
From a ruminant's belly he tore, fa la!
The white inner lining, not more, fa la!
This vile sustentation, this spongious creation,
The king would be bound to abhor! Fa! La!

HOLLENBERGER: [*No longer able to contain himself.*] Dunder! Und I am der goat! ['AWKINS *looks apprehensive. FOGG quails.*]

FOGG: 'Tis but a joke; contain thyself, Herr Cook.

HOLLENBERGER: A shoke? brrr——

JUDGE HAGGETT: [*Waving cook down.*] On with the story, Fogg.

FOGG: [*With an appealing look at* HOLLENBERGER.]
He garnished it round with fresh leek,
And seasoned with subical flavors.
He carried the dish to the king,
Who laughed at the cook's fears and quavers.
"What is this sop mine eyes now see? Voila!
Thou kitchen knave?" said 'is Majesty. "Voila!"
"The new sustentation—a peerless creation—
Pray taste it, oh king, ere gibbeting me. VOILA!"

CAPTAIN PETRIE: "Beware of the ides of March"—beware of disgruntled cook. [*All laugh.*]

HOLLENBERGER: Ach, disgruntled! [*To* JUDGE HAGGETT.] Fogg said it vas shust a shoke, sir—shust a shoke.

JUDGE HAGGETT: [*Calmly.*] Well, we're laughing, aren't we?

WASHINGTON: And now the last verse, gentlemen.

MR. CARTER: Aye, Fogg, speak it *tripeingly* on the tongue. [*Laughs.*]

FOGG: With sceptical gesture, the king
Did nibble a bit of the pasty mess.
The cook hovered near with the cup
To quench the inimical tastiness.
But lo! the king gulped down the whole! Huzzah!
And forthwith replenished his bowl. Huzzah!
He dubbed the creation—the new sustentation—
"TRIPE."
The epipoetical soul. Huzzah!

[*Exhausted,* FOGG *retires near* 'AWKINS *and* HOLLENBERGER, *who look menacingly at him.*]

ALL: Huzzah! Huzzah! [*There is much mirth.*]

JUDGE HAGGETT: [*Raising his hand for quiet.*] Only one thing remains to be seen, gentlemen; whether the "new sustentation" is all the poet says it is.

[*All laugh.* HOLLENBERGER, FOGG *and* 'AWKINS *are as nervous as can be. They look at each other as if to say,* "*the jig's up!*"]

CAPTAIN PETRIE: [*To* JUDGE HAGGETT.] If you were a king, I'd say, from the looks on Herr Cook's face, that there might be enough poison in your cup to kill ten men. [*All smile and laugh but* WASHINGTON, *who becomes serious.*]

DR. LANAHAN: Thou can not kill an "epipoetical soul," sirrah! It is an eternal entity.

JUDGE HAGGETT: [*Pausing with a giant forkful of tripe half way to his mouth.*] As eternal as tripe. And now, gentlemen, to prove to you that good cooks are made and not born— [*He tastes the tripe, he tastes it more enthusiastically, he fairly gulps down the remainder, and turning to* HOLLENBERGER, *smacking his lips, says.*] The best tripe I have ever eaten, even though it be indelicate to boast of one's own hospitality.

HOLLENBERGER: [*Confusedly pleased.*] Jah! Sehr gut.

ALL: [*Tasting.*] Hear! Hear! Capital, etc.

HOLLENBERGER: [*Humbly.*] Den do I to chail go?

JUDGE HAGGETT: To jail? To cook tripe like this for prisoners and rats? Banish thy fear!

HOLLENBERGER: [*Ecstatically.*] Dankeshoen! sir. Dankeshoen!

JUDGE HAGGETT: If that means, "Thank you"—thank you.

JUDGE SATUS MAYNARD: I propose a toast to your cook.

JUDGE HAGGETT: Capital! We'll let him drink with us—from the inimical cup he himself served to me. [*Laughs.*]

HOLLENBERGER: Not dy blue cup, sir!

JUDGE HAGGETT: An', pray, why not?

HOLLENBERGER: Ach! Der honor is too great.

DR. LANAHAN: Aye, but who so much deserves the high honor of drinking from his master's cup?

HOLLENBERGER: [*Stands as if fixed to the floor.*] Mine pelly vishes it vas lager, mit froth shpilling over. [*All laugh.*]

CAPTAIN PETRIE: Isn't it the Good Book that says "Take thee a little wine for thy belly's sake"?

JUDGE HAGGETT: [*Meaningfully.*] You would spurn my offer?

HOLLENBERGER: Nein! Nein!

JUDGE HAGGETT: Take this, then, and join us. [*He offers the blue goblet to* HOLLENBERGER, *who shrinks back.*]

HOLLENBERGER: It is too muchness. Mine head, he vould go round, zum!

JUDGE HAGGETT: Too much? You shall share it with 'Awkins and Fogg.

FOGG: [*Fairly jumping.*] Oh no, sir. I never touches the stuff.

JUDGE HAGGETT: Except on the sly.

'AWKINS: Nor I, sir, since—since the plantation threat!

JUDGE HAGGETT: We'll forget the plantation.

'AWKINS: [*His face lighting up.*] Forget, sir?

JUDGE HAGGETT: [*Jovially.*] Aye, forget. After all, you're a good servant.

'AWKINS: Thank you, sir. Thy pardon, sir.

JUDGE HAGGETT: We'll all drink, now. Pour a bit in each glass from this, Herr Cook.

FOGG: But I never drinks in the evening, sir. The moon——

JUDGE HAGGETT: [*To* FOGG.] No protests! [*To* HOLLENBERGER.] Take the cup.

[*He offers* HOLLENBERGER *the blue goblet.* HOLLENBERGER *makes a resigned step forward as if to take it.* WASHINGTON *during this repartee sits in thought. Suddenly he seems galvanized into action.*]

WASHINGTON: [*Rising enthusiastically.*] May I have the honor of being the cup-bearer to the one who added new glory to the Beefsteak and Tripe Club? [*He grasps the blue goblet before the* JUDGE *can assent or refuse.*]

JUDGE HAGGETT: Sir George, you are herewith appointed cup-bearer.

[*With mock solemnity,* WASHINGTON *advances, cup in outstretched hands, toward* HOLLENBERGER *and his colleagues. To the Cook,* 'AWKINS *and* FOGG, *the time seems interminable. To the guests, it is as part of a pantomime. When* WASHINGTON *gets within reaching distance of* HOLLENBERGER, *he purposely stumbles and falls headlong.* LAWRENCE *calls, "Save the cup, George!" The wine spills over the floor but he saves the cup.*]

GEORGE gets up, assisted by the cook and 'AWKINS. JUDGE HAGGETT is also on his feet, as are the other guests nearest GEORGE. GEORGE looks from HOLLEN-BERGER to 'AWKINS and both gaze at him in a thankful, relieved way, as if to say, "We have learned our lesson, thanks to you." WASHINGTON starts to brush himself off.]

HOLLENBERGER: [*Concernedly.*] You iss hurted?

　[*'AWKINS stoops and humbly brushes WASHINGTON'S clothes.*]

JUDGE HAGGETT: You are not hurt?

WASHINGTON: No, sir, thank you. [*Still brushing himself off and regaining his composure.*]

FOGG: A lucky fall, methinks—when no one is injured.

WASHINGTON: Aye—at least I saved the precious cup. [*To 'AWKINS, who is facing the same way as JUDGE HAGGETT.*] Not even——

'AWKINS: [*Looking up from WASHINGTON'S knees, which he is brushing.*] Not even the Indian on the stem was injured.

WASHINGTON: [*Looking down at cup which he holds so as to be able to look 'AWKINS in the eyes. In a firm but kindly voice.*] Not even the Indian. Pick yourself up, 'Awkins.

　[*There is a momentary silence.*]

PARROT: Vot an ass! Vot an ass! Polly want a wafer.
　[*All turn and look with jovial surprise at the parrot.*]

CURTAIN

MATCHING WITS

A GEORGE WASHINGTON PLAY IN ONE ACT

DRAMATIS PERSONAE

(IN ORDER OF THEIR APPEARANCE)

CHEVALIER LEGARDEUR DE ST. PIERRE, *Commandant of Fort Le Boeuf.*
JACQUES, *a servant.*
THE HALF-KING *of the Senecas.*
CAPTAIN REPENTIGNY, *second in command of Fort Le Boeuf.*
COMMISSARY LA FORCE, *from Venango.*
McLANE, *a Scotch Trader.*
ALONDAH, *a half-breed Indian girl.*
CHRISTOPHER GIST, *Washington's guide.*
MAJOR GEORGE WASHINGTON.

TIME: *Before sunset, December 16, 1753.*
PLACE: *St. Pierre's headquarters at Fort Le Boeuf.*

DESCRIPTION OF CHARACTERS

ST. PIERRE:

An elderly soldier, with one eye. He is suave, shrewd and a gentleman. He wears a patch over one eye; is dressed in the uniform of a French officer. His white hair worn in a queue. His lines should be spoken with a slight French accent.

JACQUES:

A French servant dressed in small clothes, with stockings, buckled shoes, full-sleeved shirt and waistcoat.

THE HALF-KING:

A fine type of Indian Chief, intelligent, patriotic, proudly tenacious of his territorial right. Wears the full regalia of a Seneca Chief.

REPENTIGNY:

A shrewd, ruthless French officer, about middle age. Dressed in officer's uniform of French army, hair in a queue, wears a sword.

LA FORCE:

Middle-aged, wears breeches of coarse fabric, buckskin leggings, a coat and vest of colonial cut, and a tricorne hat.

McLANE:

A Scotch trader of about middle age. Dresses same as La Force except that he wears a coonskin cap.

ALONDAH:

A beautiful half-breed, winsome but proud and revengeful. Dressed in Indian costume plentifully decorated with beadwork, bedecked with barbaric jewelry.

GIST:

A tall, angular frontiersman, dressed in Indian hunting shirt and leggings, on his head a coonskin cap, at his belt a hunting knife.

WASHINGTON:

Twenty-one years of age. Six feet, two inches tall, in weight about 200 pounds, large boned but well proportioned. His complexion bronzed by an outdoor life, features strong, hair light brown in color, combed back and worn in a queue. He is dressed in a well-fitting uniform of a Colonial Major: red breeches and boots, a red vest, blue coat faced with red, a tricorne hat and long military cape; wears a sword.

SET: *The interior of a log house, part of the fortification of Fort Le Boeuf. To the left of the center of the back wall a window, through which can be seen the sharp-pointed logs forming the outer walls of the Fort, just above them a staff from which waves the Royal Ensign of the King of France. A fireplace on the right with a door in the wall toward rear. At the center of the left wall a heavy oaken door. On the walls hang skins, haversacks, weapons. Over the mantel a musket and powder horn. To the right of the window of rear wall a cabinet; to the left of the door on left wall a bunk covered with skins. Back center, running lengthwise of the room, a rude, heavy table of backwoods manufacture. Before the fireplace a large chair, over its back a fur robe, several other chairs about the room. On the table a decanter and glasses. Seated in the large chair by the table facing right, CHEVALIER LEGARDEUR DE ST. PIERRE, busy writing. He stops, reads a moment, throws a paper toward fireplace. Claps his hands; JACQUES appears.*

ST. PIERRE: [*To JACQUES.*] I am expecting Governor Dinwiddie's messengers at the hour of the sunset-gun.

JACQUES: Mais oui, this Major Washington?

ST. PIERRE: See that he is announced before you admit him.

JACQUES: Certainment, mon Commandant.

ST. PIERRE: Captain Repentigny awaits me?

JACQUES: Mais oui.

ST. PIERRE: Have him in. [*ST. PIERRE turns to letter, JACQUES leaves and CAPTAIN REPENTIGNY enters, bows and stands at attention.*] I am concerned regarding my reply to the message brought by this Major Washington from the English Governor.

REPENTIGNY: The English have ever coveted this territory.

ST. PIERRE: I would you watch the moves of this Washington.

REPENTIGNY: Mais oui, Mon Commandant.

ST. PIERRE: I look to you to keep me informed—ah perhaps—[*A gesture.*] if you cultivate his companions?

REPENTIGNY: [*Knowingly, with a smile.*] I go. [*He leaves at right. ST. PIERRE picks up discarded paper, looks at it, then at Dinwiddie's message. Writes, hesitates and writes again. HALF-KING enters. ST. PIERRE looks up.*]

ST. PIERRE: Who are you that dares to come unannounced into my presence?

HALF-KING: I am Tanacharisson, the Half-King of the Senecas.

ST. PIERRE: Ah, the Half-King. [*Sarcastically.*] Parti-royale.

HALF-KING: I come to protest——

ST. PIERRE: [*Interrupting.*] Protest! Protest! You are ever protesting!

HALF-KING: These hunting grounds are ours.

ST. PIERRE: You talk as a child!

HALF-KING: At a place called Montreal, many moons ago my people kindled a fire and smoked the peace pipe with the French fathers.

ST. PIERRE: [*Impatiently interrupting.*] That is in the past; these lands now belong to his August Majesty, the King of France.

HALF-KING: I say to the French, go! I the chief have spoken.

ST. PIERRE: [*In anger.*] Think you I am afraid of flies or mosquitoes?—the Indians are such as these! You say these lands belong to you—not the black of your finger nails is yours!

HALF-KING: You talk not like a friend, White Father.

ST. PIERRE: We are sworn friends—we have given you a speech belt—the wampum of peace.

HALF-KING: We can give it back to you.

ST. PIERRE: You speak foolish, Half-King—that would mean war.

HALF-KING: The White Father listens to our complaints or we give back the speech belt.

ST. PIERRE: Have a care Half-King, else you anger the French Governor General. [*HALF KING grunts.*] Would you have the French for a foe?

HALF-KING: You build forts on our lands!

ST. PIERRE: We have the right.

HALF-KING: Ugh! The Ingleese will be our brothers.

ST. PIERRE: The English! Always have they been your enemies.

HALF-KING: You take our lands.

ST. PIERRE: Ever we are your friends.

HALF-KING: The Ingleese come but to trade.

ST. PIERRE: [*Contemptuously.*] Think you they come but to trade?

HALF-KING: My brother Conotocarius hath said it.

ST. PIERRE: Conotocarius?

HALF-KING: To the pale-faces he is Washington.

ST. PIERRE: Washington! You dare come with Washington?

HALF-KING: I, Tanacharisson, the Half-King, take the trail with whom I please.

ST. PIERRE: The allies of the French King do not come and go as they please.

HALF-KING: The French Father has but come—he knows not the way of my people.

ST. PIERRE: True, I come but lately to command Fort Le Boeuf—but I know the Indian. [*Laughs sardonically.*]

HALF-KING: You have taken our lands by force, we will take them back the same way.

ST. PIERRE: You are making big talk, Half-King, save it for the morrow, then we will hold council. I now have other matters to attend. [*He goes to cabinet and returns with a bottle of brandy.*] Here, brother, with this to refresh you the time will quickly pass. [*He places bottle in the HALF-KING'S eager hands.*] Go, tomorrow we will hold council. [*The HALF-KING leaves by left door, holding the bottle close to his breast. ST. PIERRE claps his hands, JACQUES instantly appears from right and bows.*] Is Captain Repentigny without?

JACQUES: Mais oui, my Commandant.

ST. PIERRE: Bid him come. [*Picks up a letter and paces back and forth in thought.*]

REPENTIGNY: [*Bowing.*] Monsieur, Le Commandant.

ST. PIERRE: These Indians strain my patience. The Half-King but now comes with complaints.

REPENTIGNY: I trust you settled them satisfactorily?

ST. PIERRE: Settled them, of a certainty not. He had the usual Indian's approach—always a prelude to a request for presents—redress of wrongs!

REPENTIGNY: But Monsieur, this Half-King is an unusual Indian, one of great power in the councils of the tribes.

ST. PIERRE: Not so, Shingees, the Delaware chief, is the real power.

REPENTIGNY: The real leader is the Half King. Shingees is ever swayed by him. I trust you received him with cordiality and respect.

ST. PIERRE: Um—m, of a certainty.

REPENTIGNY: It would be dangerous to anger him lest he join the English.

ST. PIERRE: Oh—! You think the English could win him from us?

REPENTIGNY: I fear ——

ST. PIERRE: [*Now worried.*] I treated him as the usual child of the forest.

REPENTIGNY: Voila! He did not leave in anger?

ST. PIERRE: Oh, no! no! I said I would hear him on the morrow and gave him a bottle of brandy.

REPENTIGNY: Thanks be—a bottle of brandy—fire-water is his one weakness.

ST. PIERRE: How comes it he was allowed to join the entourage of this Monsieur Washington?

REPENTIGNY: I know not. The Commissary La Force is

without. It is possible he could enlighten us. He escorted the English party from *Venango.*

ST. PIERRE: La Force? Have him in. [*REPENTIGNY goes to door at right.*]

REPENTIGNY: [*Opens door.*] La Force, enter, if you please.
[*LA FORCE enters and bows to ST. PIERRE.*]

ST. PIERRE: How comes it the Half-King is with this Englishman?

LA FORCE: He came to Venango with the Major Washington.

ST. PIERRE: Why?

LA FORCE: A grievance—a complaint.

ST. PIERRE: Captaine Joincaire should have settled his complaint.

LA FORCE: Captaine Joincaire took the usual course, mon Commandant—made the Indian drunk.

REPENTIGNY: Had he done likewise to all the Washington party!

LA FORCE: The hospitality of mon Captaine Joincaire is known.

ST. PIERRE: They succumbed to the Captaine Joincaire's hospitality?

LA FORCE: The Dutchman Van Bramm was most convivial, the Monsieur Gist ——

ST. PIERRE: The Major Washington?

LA FORCE: Alas! He alone was sober.

ST. PIERRE: Ah, so the young man refused the cup?

LA FORCE. Methought he drank only because of politeness.

ST. PIERRE: Hah! I see it all! Joincaire in his cups. Washington all ears. Joincaire talks! Talks! Talks!

LA FORCE: I admit the discretion of mon Captaine Joincaire was not of the best.

ST. PIERRE: Sacre Bleu! Damn his French father! Damn his Squaw mother! It is what comes from having a half-breed in command of so important a post. Damn him!

LA FORCE: [*With a shrug.*] Of a certainty he did his best to detain the Half-King.

ST. PIERRE: Bah! his best. He, a French officer, allows this fledgling, Washington, to make ducks and drakes of him!

REPENTIGNY: The young man seems able to exert a strong influence over the aborigines.

ST. PIERRE: Hum—m, we shall see.

REPENTIGNY: Ah—! But he has now to deal with the Chevalier Legardeur de St. Pierre.

ST. PIERRE: He will find he deals with another than a drunken half-breed. I will not be drunk. [*To LA FORCE.*] You may go.
[*Quickly takes a drink.*]

LA FORCE: Merci, mon Commandant. [*Bows, turns to leave.*]

ST. PIERRE: Hold! You had opportunity to study this Major Washington?

LA FORCE: On the long trail from Venango, I was always by his side.

ST. PIERRE: He has perhaps a weakness?

LA FORCE: None that I could fathom. He talks but little.

ST. PIERRE: That is all, La Force. [*LA FORCE bows and leaves. To REPENTIGNY.*] A shrewd young man this Washington. What think you of his mission?

REPENTIGNY: To spy out the land and win over to the English side our Indian allies.

ST. PIERRE: We need the Indians.

REPENTIGNY: The English can put two men in the field to our one.

ST. PIERRE: I know it! I know it! Voila, this Washington—! I thought him, because of his youth, only an adventuresome messenger. I had hoped to—but never mind——

REPENTIGNY: Spoke the Half-King of the speech belt?

ST. PIERRE: [*Casually.*] He spoke of the treaty making at Montreal.

REPENTIGNY: Perchance he threatened to return the belt?

ST. PIERRE: Enough of what is past. We must speed this Washington on his way.

REPENTIGNY: To our governor in Canada?

ST. PIERRE: Of a certainty we must hold the Half-King here.

REPENTIGNY: Would I knew where he and the Englishman met and did they——

[*The face of McLANE, the trader, has appeared at the window, he is in a boisterous mood. He thrusts open the window.*]

McLANE: Hi, Cap. Mon, I hae found ye.

ST. PIERRE: [*In anger.*] Who is that man?

REPENTIGNY: [*In low voice.*] A trader with the Washington party, whom I would question. I left him in my quarters when you sent for me.

McLANE: I hae found ye, Cap.

ST. PIERRE: He was drinking, then?

REPENTIGNY: Aye, mayhap he could tell us of the Half-King.

ST. PIERRE: Have him in.

McLANE: *[*Sings as he leans over window sill.*]
    E'en this wild wood will I range.
      Listen, listen, dearie.
    Nor sigh for towns sa fine ta change
      This forest dreeary.
    Toils an' danger I'll deespise,
      Nevair, nevair weary!
    An' be, while luve is in thine eyes,
      Ever, ever cheery.

REPENTIGNY: McLane, come in and sing for us another verse.

McLANE: That I will, mon. [*He leaves the window.*]

REPENTIGNY: He is quite drunk.

ST. PIERRE: He must be more drunk. Quick, that bottle of brandy in the cabinet. [*REPENTIGNY gets the bottle from cabinet, places it on table as McLANE reels in the door.*] 'Tis a fine voice you have, Monsieur.

McLANE: Aye, yer a mon as ken tell it. Who be ye?

REPENTIGNY: 'Tis Monsieur the Chevalier Commandant Legardeur de St. Pierre.

McLANE: [*Attempts a bow.*] 'Tis glad I am to know ye Monsoor, Commander Letharge—I gie it oop but I gie ye my hand. [*ST. PIERRE grimaces but takes his hand.*] Noo, I'll sing ye the second varse o' me song.

ST. PIERRE: First prepare your throat. Eh—? [*REPENTIGNY is ready with a glass of brandy. McLANE takes it. ST. PIERRE and REPENTIGNY raise wine glasses.*]

REPENTIGNY: To the muses!

---

* See music on page 636.

McLANE: Aye, drink hearty. [*They finish their glasses.*]

REPENTIGNY: Now the second verse.

McLANE: I'll dae my best.

> Ah! wha ta' me air cities gay:
> Listen, listen, dearie.
> If fra me thou wert far away,
> Alas! how dreary!
> Oh! still o'er seas, o'er land I'll rove
> Nevair, nevair weary!
> An' follow on where leads my love,
> Ever, ever cheery.

[*ST. PIERRE and REPENTIGNY clap their hands in applause. JACQUES enters, ST. PIERRE sees him.*]

ST. PIERRE: Jacques, fill up Monsieur McLane's glass, a toast we will have. [*He indicates McLANE'S glass is to be filled with brandy. JACQUES fills glasses.*]

McLANE: 'Tis mickle obliged I am tae ye, monsoor. [*Takes glass from JACQUES.*]

ST. PIERRE: To Monsieur McLane, the singing trader!

REPENTIGNY: May his trading be brisk—profits aplenty.

McLANE: Being a modest mon I canna drink the fairst but tae the second, aye. [*He drinks as do the others.*]

ST. PIERRE: Did you any trading on the journey here, my friend?

McLANE: Na, we came noo tae trade an e'en hae we been o' a mind to, we wudna hae the time ta spend upoon it.

REPENTIGNY: Oh, you made swift progress on your journey!

McLANE: Aye, the Major ever goeth wi' speed. [*Hic.*] A speedin' that gae me noo time for loitering.

ST. PIERRE: Surely you tarried at Logstown?

McLANE: [*With a bleeried leer.*] Where aboot?

REPENTIGNY: At Logstown, where you met the Indians.

McLANE: Aye, the heathen—Logstown—whar wad that be noo?

ST. PIERRE: Come, my man, surely you remember Logstown.

REPENTIGNY: Where the Half-King joined you.

McLANE: Ho! Ho! The Half-King! [*He laughs uproariously.*]

ST. PIERRE: Did not you meet him at Logstown?

McLANE: [*More soberly.*] I dinna recollect.

ST. PIERRE: [*A gesture to JACQUES.*] Have a fresh glass, Monsieur McLane. [*McLANE drains the glass with a grimace and a shudder.*]

REPENTIGNY: [*To ST. PIERRE.*] The Half-King mayhap amuses friend McLane.

McLANE: Betimes, Monsoor, betimes. [*Again he laughs.*]

REPENTIGNY: Did the Half-King appear droll at Logstown?

McLANE: Logstown, ye say? I dinna ken o' Logstown.

[*At a signal from ST. PIERRE, JACQUES offers McLANE another glass of brandy. He takes it, looks at others.*] Air ye na joinin' me? [*ST. PIERRE and REPENTIGNY quickly take from JACQUES glasses of wine. Speculatively.*] Yer na drinkin' the beverage ye air giein' to me?——

REPENTIGNY: We prefer wine.

McLANE: Ye no asked me my preference. I'll na drink brandy whilst ithers drink wine. [*He bangs mug on table.*]

ST. PIERRE: My apologies, Monsieur McLane, 'twas my belief a Highlander drinks only brandy. Wine for Monsieur McLane, Jacques.

McLANE: I'm na daft, wine an' brandy, they gae na tae gither.

ST. PIERRE: Then you to your brandy and we to our wine.

McLANE: Thank ye for yer hoopsitality, Monsoor, I hae enow. [*He staggers to the door, turns and bows; from his hunting shirt falls a bottle of brandy, a counterpart of that on the table. Before he can reach for it, ST. PIERRE quickly places his boot on the bottle neck.*]

ST. PIERRE: [*With heat.*] Where got you that bottle?

McLANE: [*Straightens with drunken dignity.*] There's na use glowerin' at me, Monsoor.

ST. PIERRE: [*With rising anger.*] Answer me!

McLANE: Hold fast yer teemper, Monsoor. [*He laughs.*] I hae it fra' the Half-King.

ST. PIERRE: You took it from him!

McLANE: Na, Monsoor; not. I did but traid fer it. [*Hic.*] I gae him a ring o' brass he envied o' me. [*Hic.*]

ST. PIERRE: [*Turns to REPENTIGNY, takes foot from bottle.*] I neer knew a savage to barter brandy.

REPENTIGNY: An unusual Indian.

McLANE: [*Picks up bottle.*] It grieves me, Monsoor, that the varimant sa lightly conseeders yer gifty. [*Hic.*]

ST. PIERRE: 'Tis of no consequence, they are but children.

McLANE: Aye, an as a teestimonial o' yer fergaeness—[*He seizes the half finished bottle on the table and gaily swinging the two bottles staggers to the door and out, singing.*]

> E'en this wild wood I range:
> Listen, listen, dearie.
> Nor sigh fer towns sa fine tae change
> This forest dreary.
> Toils and danger I'll deespise,
> Nevair, nevair, weary
> An' be, while love is in thine eyes,
> Ever, ever cheery.

ST. PIERRE: [*As McLANE'S song dies away in the distance.*] Sacre Bleu! The Half-King with a clear head!

REPENTIGNY: The speech belt.

ST. PIERRE: [*Laughs bitterly.*] This young Washington doth shrewdly select his companions.

REPENTIGNY: By chance he wins the first trick.

ST. PIERRE: [*Smiles craftily.*] The next may come to me.

REPENTIGNY: Mayhap I might induce the Half-King to partake of my hospitality.

ST. PIERRE: You can but try.

[*REPENTIGNY bows and leaves at right. ST. PIERRE goes to the table, fumbles a bit with papers and then goes to chair by fireplace, picks up a long clay pipe, at fireplace sits in thought. The door, at left, is opened a bit and ALONDAH peeps in, hisses to attract ST. PIERRE'S attention, he looks up and beckons to her. She swiftly enters the door, bars it, runs to ST. PIERRE and stands demurely before him.*]

ST. PIERRE: [*With pipe in hands.*] Ah, La Belle Alondah, I have expected you. [*Makes a gesture toward the floor beside him. She sits down cross-legged, he hands her his pipe. She takes a jar of tobacco from the low table beside his chair. As she fills the pipe he studies her.*] You have spoken to the young man Washington, ma cherie? [*ALONDAH nods her head, gives him the pipe, and taking an ember from the fire, holds it until the pipe is lighted. ST. PIERRE takes a few puffs.*] You were nice to heem?

ALONDAH: Ver nice.

ST. PIERRE: [*With an insinuating leer.*] He was—nice to you?

ALONDAH: He smile at Alondah.

ST. PIERRE: Ah—he smiled. [*Eagerly.*] *And then?*——

ALONDAH: [*Fiercely.*] Turn his back to Alondah—walk on!

ST. PIERRE: Sacre Bleu!

ALONDAH: [*With an appealing gesture.*] Mon ami one-eye, Alondah she veer nice to the tall one—veer lofing one time, two time—by river bank, in shine of moon.

ST. PIERRE: He would have naught to do with you?

ALONDAH: [*Springs to feet.*] No! [*Stamps foot, grasps hilt of her knife.*] I hate heem! I kill heem!

ST. PIERRE: [*Laughs sardonically.*] You hate him—would kill him, so—[*He rises, takes her chin in his hands.*] I wonder, La Belle Alondah, whether 'tis the French or Indian blood now speaking!

ALONDAH: I hate heem! The silent, cold diable!

ST. PIERRE: [*Goes to table, pours himself a drink.*] Ha—a woman scorned—[*Takes a sip of wine.*] Yet, when a woman hates a man—she's near to loving him. [*Another sip of wine.*] Ma petite, I fear you are of no use to me in this direction. [*Steps toward ALONDAH.*] Keep you at a distance from this Major Washington. [*Sternly.*] I command. Go, ma petite. [*ALONDAH meekly goes toward the door, removes bar and leaves. ST. PIERRE looks at his glass.*]

ST. PIERRE: Wine? No! [*Puts down glass.*] Women? No! [*Rubs his chin, thoughtfully.*] All men are vain—[*Thinks for a moment, quickly turns toward the fireplace.*] Especially the young. [*Buckles on his sabre, takes a small mirror from the mantel, arranges his hair and smoothes clothes. Then claps hands. JACQUES enters and bows.*]

ST. PIERRE: Fresh glasses and the best Madeira at hand.

JACQUES: Mais oui, mon Commandant.

[*REPENTIGNY enters hurriedly, nearly upsetting JACQUES as he leaves.*]

REPENTIGNY: [*Excitedly.*] Monsieur Commandant, I fail.

ST. PIERRE: [*Sharply.*] With the Half-King?

REPENTIGNY: Always this Washington holds the Half-King by his side!

ST. PIERRE: Sacre Bleu!

REPENTIGNY: Nothing escapes the eye of the Englishman, he goes about the post noting our defences——

ST. PIERRE: [*A shrug.*] To be expected of a soldier.

REPENTIGNY: ——he will make the most of it—— [*Significantly.*] unless——

ST. PIERRE: [*Quickly.*] Unless what?

REPENTIGNY: [*Tentatively.*] An accident in the forest?

ST. PIERRE: So—you would set the Indians upon him?

REPENTIGNY: Of him I would be apprehensive, were I the Commandant.

ST. PIERRE: [*With dignified severeness.*] 'Tis well for the honor of France you are not in command, Captain Repentigny. Monsieur Washington comes from the Governor of the English Province of Virginia——

REPENTIGNY: [*Hotly.*] He is but a spy.

ST. PIERRE: As an ambassador, his person is sacred. His life shall be protected—understand?

REPENTIGNY: [*Bows.*] I comprehend, Monsieur le Commandant.

ST. PIERRE: Monsieur Washington comes at this hour. This gives you opportunity, make the most of it. See that the Half-King be sodden in drunken slumber on the morrow. [*REPENTIGNY salutes, and leaves. JACQUES enters.*]

ST. PIERRE: [*To JACQUES.*] Am I prepared to entertain Major Washington?

JACQUES: Mais oui, mon Commandant.

[*There is the boom of a cannon. Then a rap on the door at the left.*]

ST. PIERRE: The sunset gun. My guest is prompt. [*JACQUES goes toward the door.*]

GIST: [*Off stage.*] Washington, behind you! Quick! You damned squaw!

[*Off stage there is a piercing scream of pain and anger.*]

WASHINGTON: [*Off stage.*] Don't hurt her, Gist!

ST. PIERRE: Alondah! [*Thrusting JACQUES aside, starts toward door. ALONDAH screams again. The door bursts open. GIST appears with hand grasping the girl's wrist and wrenching the knife from her hand, flings her at the feet of ST. PIERRE, she grasps his coat in supplication and gazes in fear at GIST, standing threateningly with her knife in his hand. WASHINGTON enters.*]

GIST: [*To ST. PIERRE.*] She would have killed Major Washington.

ST. PIERRE: [*Thrusts her aside and quickly draws his sword, stands over her aquiver with rage.*] You carrion! You would soil my honor! [*She shrieks.*]

WASHINGTON: [*Steps between ST. PIERRE and ALONDAH and raises his hand.*] Ah, Sir. She is a woman—an ignorant savage.

ST. PIERRE: She shall die.

WASHINGTON: Nay, Sir!

ST. PIERRE: [*Struck by WASHINGTON'S forbearance.*] But my honor——

WASHINGTON: My honor does not permit it.

ST. PIERRE: You are my guest!

WASHINGTON: As your guest I ask your leniency.

ST. PIERRE: [*Gazes for a long moment at WASHINGTON, then sheaths his sword.*] Your wish is my command. Pardon me, Monsieur, I go to give orders for your safety. [*To ALONDAH.*] Come. [*He goes out the door followed by ALONDAH.*]

WASHINGTON: Heretofore she hath been friendly—too friendly. Strange she should attempt my life.

GIST: Strange? In an alien border post. Think you—

WASHINGTON: [*Quickly.*] Unthinkable! The Commandant is an officer and a gentleman.

GIST: Are they all?

WASHINGTON: At Venango—here—all the arts of a clever foe are arrayed to frustrate my mission—win the Half-King from me.

GIST: 'Tis your wits against theirs. The prize—the Half-King's support.

WASHINGTON: [*Glances about the room.*] Yon window, see. [*GIST nods.*] The Half-King must learn the real aims of the French.

GIST: You would have him hear your conversation?

WASHINGTON: When the Commandant returns you leave, fetch the Half-King—

GIST: The window is closed.

WASHINGTON: 'Tis a warm night for this season. [*He goes to window, opens it a bit.*]

GIST: But if—

WASHINGTON: I will see that it is kept open.

GIST: Ssh! [*ST. PIERRE enters—goes to WASHINGTON.*]

ST. PIERRE: [*Feelingly.*] Oh, Monsieur Washington, words fail me. How can I express my poignant regret for such an occurrence. [*To GIST.*] Thanks to you, Monsieur, for your quickness, or the honor of France would have been besmirched. [*To WASHINGTON.*] Oh, Monsieur! Monsieur! These savages—one can never tell what next they do. But fear not, your person and the people of your entourage shall have the complete protection of Legardeur de St. Pierre.

WASHINGTON: Think no more of it, Sir. I am familiar with the ways of the Indian. [*He takes his glass.*] To his Most Christian Majesty, the King of France. [*ST. PIERRE and GIST take glasses.*]

ST. PIERRE: [*Lifts glass.*] The King.

GIST: [*Lifts glass.*] The King of France. [*They drink.*]

WASHINGTON: And now, my friend Gist, leaves us to our conference.

ST. PIERRE: But ere he goes, permit me— [*He goes to the cabinet, returns with a bottle of brandy. Watches WASHINGTON as he offers bottle to GIST.*]—a testimonial of my regard.

WASHINGTON: I am sure 'twill be most acceptable to my friend. My thanks with his. [*ST. PIERRE is surprised at WASHINGTON'S acquiescence.*]

GIST: [*Takes bottle.*] I thank ye, Sir. [*He bows.*] Good evening, gentlemen.

ST. PIERRE: Good evening, Monsieur Gist. [*GIST leaves.*] Oh, Monsieur Washington, I shudder when I think what disgrace I escape!

WASHINGTON: [*Lifts restraining hand.*] The incident is closed. Have you considered my Governor's message, sir? [*He takes the chair by the table which faces window, forcing ST. PIERRE to sit in the other chair with back to the window.*]

ST. PIERRE: Pardon me, Monsieur. [*He bars the door, goes to window to close it.*]

WASHINGTON: Unless 'tis too cold for you, Sir. [*ST. PIERRE hesitates.*]

ST. PIERRE: My nerves—a bit unstrung.

WASHINGTON: I would have a breath of air.

ST. PIERRE: [*Still hesitates.*] You are a vigorous young man. While I—

WASHINGTON: Methinks, Sir, a tried campaigner who wots not of the elements.

ST. PIERRE: [*Proudly.*] I have ever been one possessed of an iron endurance.

ST. PIERRE: [*Leaves window, comes to table and pours wine.*] I am delighted you deign to honor my humble abode with your distinguished presence, Major Washington. [*He lifts his glass.*] Permit me. His August Majesty, the King of England.

WASHINGTON: [*Raising his glass.*] The King. [*They drink, they sit, ST. PIERRE with back to the window, he fingers the papers.*]

ST. PIERRE: Regarding the message of your Governor, Lord Dinwiddie?

WASHINGTON: Aye, Sir.

ST. PIERRE: My dear Monsieur Washington, 'tis a marvel to me that Governor Dinwiddie should send a message questioning our right to this territory and forsooth, he doth order our departure from it. [*WASHINGTON remains silent.*] These lands were discovered by none other than our peerless explorer, the great La Salle, and dedicated for all time to my sovereign, his Majesty the King of France. Since then our voyagers have traversed these forests and streams trading with the Indians. With them we have made treaties—speech belts they have taken from our hand.

WASHINGTON: [*A quick glance at the window. As ST. PIERRE fills their glasses, the window is moved a bit.*] You have erected forts at Lake Erie, here and Kaskaskia, and also, I gather, will fortify the Forks of the Ohio.

ST. PIERRE: To be frank, Monsieur, we have. [*He sips his wine.*] We shall also take every means possible to hold this territory; such are my orders, and I entreat you, Monsieur, not to doubt for a moment that I am determined to conform to them with all the exactness and resolution which can be expected of a loyal officer. [*WASHINGTON nods his head, his eyes focused upon the window, which opens a bit farther.*]

WASHINGTON: You claim positive sovereignty over these lands, Sir?

ST. PIERRE: We do.

WASHINGTON: You will erect settlements in this territory?

ST. PIERRE: Such are our plans, Monsieur. Should ownership be actively disputed—

WASHINGTON: You would fight to hold them?

ST. PIERRE: With all the power—all the vigor of the greatest Kingdom of Continental Europe.

WASHINGTON: You have imprisoned English citizens who have come here to trade.

ST. PIERRE: I repeat, none other than the French have the right to trade upon these waters or its streams.

WASHINGTON: You forbid the Indians to trade with the English. [*The HALF-KING'S head appears in the window, listening intently.*]

ST. PIERRE: The Indians are subject to the will of his Majesty, my King.

WASHINGTON: You would use force to subject them to your will?

ST. PIERRE: If needs be. [*Strikes table with fist.*] Force to the uttermost—the Indians are the vassals of France. [*The HALF-KING'S face is contorted with rage and disappears from the window.*]

WASHINGTON: This, then, is your reply to Governor Dinwiddie?

ST. PIERRE: In substance, yes.

WASHINGTON: It is a sufficient answer. If you will put it in writing—sir—— Then I may be off on my return journey.

ST. PIERRE: In the interest of the peace and the harmony and the good understanding which my master desires to cultivate and continue with the Crown of England, I entreat you, Monsieur Washington, to extend your journey on to Canada, to the Governor-General, that he, as my superior, may make final reply.

WASHINGTON: I regret, Sir, 'tis not in my orders to go beyond this point.

ST. PIERRE: Ah, Monsieur, what a furore your fine figure would cause among the charming ladies of my Governor's Court.

[*There is a loud knocking on the door at right. ST. PIERRE is surprised at the interruption. He claps his hands. JACQUES enters.*]

ST. PIERRE: Whoever is at the door, send him away. [*JACQUES unbars, opens door, and blocks passage. The HALF-KING thrusts the servant aside and enters.*]

JACQUES: [*With a hand grasping at the HALF-KING'S arm.*] The Commandant—

ST. PIERRE: [*Quickly recovers from his surprise. Rises.*] Silence, my man! 'Tis my brother the Half-King. [*The HALF-KING stands silently watching ST. PIERRE. His blanket held close about him by his left hand. JACQUES closes the door and leaves at right.*] I am most delighted, Chief, that you come. [*HALF-KING grunts. ST. PIERRE quickly pours a glass of wine and takes it to HALF-KING.*] Let us drink to our friendship, my brother, certainly Major Washington will join us. [*The HALF-KING holds off ST. PIERRE with a raised hand, as WASHINGTON rises, a glass in hand.*]

HALF-KING: [*In a harsh voice.*] You are not my brother, you are not a friend!

ST. PIERRE: [*Amazed.*] Half-King, your words are as a knife in my breast.

HALF-KING: Your words are as false as the beckoning of a mirage. Many moons ago we kindled a fire. The French fathers swore they would stay at the place called Montreal—go no farther—yet you built forts in our lands—come settlements. You say Indian shall not trade with the Inglese.

ST. PIERRE: The English would despoil you, Half-King.

HALF-KING: The French rob us of our lands!—build forts—bring settlers!

ST. PIERRE: We do but come to trade.

WASHINGTON: Pardon me, Sir——

ST. PIERRE: [*Quickly turning to WASHINGTON in suppressed anger, interrupts.*] Methinks, Monsieur, 'tis the better part of courtesy that you take no part in this.

WASHINGTON: I regret, Sir, you mistake my motive, I would remove my embarrassing presence. Tomorrow I set out upon my return journey.

ST. PIERRE: I most humbly ask your pardon, Monsieur. Your nice sense of honor does you credit.

WASHINGTON: [*As though there were no interruption.*] I trust by then you will have writ the reply to Governor Dinwiddie's message.

ST. PIERRE: [*Desiring to get rid of him.*] You shall have it early on the morrow.

WASHINGTON: [*Takes hat and cloak, bows.*] Good evening, Sir.

HALF-KING: [*To Washington.*] Wait, my brother, I go with you.

ST. PIERRE: But, Half-King, our council—— I would continue.

HALF-KING: Enough! I, the Half-King of the Senecas, give you back the speech belt. [*He holds forth the speech belt to ST. PIERRE.*]

ST. PIERRE: No! No! I refuse it! [*HALF-KING takes a step toward him, the belt outstretched.*] Never will I accept it!

[*The HALF-KING throws the belt at ST. PIERRE'S feet and haughtily strides out the door as WASHINGTON opens it.*]

WASHINGTON: [*Preparing to follow Indian, bows.*] I bid you good evening, Sir.

ST. PIERRE: [*Bows with a sardonic smile.*] I trust, Monsieur will not be discomfited [*a gesture toward the window*] by the warmth of the night air.

WASHINGTON: [*Bows and smiles.*] I thank you. On the morrow I give you farewell.

CURTAIN.

McLane's Song

Music by J. T. H.

E'en this wild wood will I range. Lis-ten, lis-ten, dear-ie. Nor sigh for towns sa fine ta change This for-est drear-y. Toils an' dan-ger I'll dee-spise, Ne-vair, ne-vair wear-y! An' be while luve is in thine eyes Ev-er, ev-er cheer-y.

Ah! wha ta' me air ci-ties gay: Lis-ten, lis-ten, dear-ie. If fra me thou wert far a-way, A-las! how drear-y! Oh! still o'er seas, o'er land I'll rove Ne-vair, ne-vair wear-y! An' fol-low on where leads my love Ev-er, ev-er cheer-y.

VINDICATED

A GEORGE WASHINGTON PLAY IN ONE ACT

DRAMATIS PERSONAE

(IN ORDER OF THEIR APPEARANCE)

LADY DINWIDDIE, *wife of the Royal Governor of Virginia.*
MRS. OVERTON, *of Brandon Hall.*
MRS. RANSOM.
LIEUTENANT BLAINEY, *aide to the Governor.*
NANCY DINWIDDIE, *daughter of the Governor.*
PHYLLIS OVERTON.
COLONEL GEORGE WASHINGTON.
MAJOR GLENDON, *of the Governor's Staff.*

LORD FAIRFAX, *of Greenway Court.*
MR. ROBINSON, *Speaker of the House of Burgesses.*
COLONEL CARY.
COLONEL WILLIS, *cousin of Washington.*
GOVERNOR DINWIDDIE.
BUTLER.
SERVANT.

TIME: *Late afternoon, August 11, 1754.*

PLACE: *The Governor's Palace at Williamsburg, Virginia.*

DESCRIPTION OF CHARACTERS

LADY DINWIDDIE:

A bit past middle age, very conscious of the rank and position of her husband, the Governor of Virginia. She is credulous yet haughty and inclined to arrogance, can be very gracious on occasion. She wears an elaborate gown with a bodice and skirt of flowered silk. The skirt reaching to the floor is full, hooped, and open in the front, draped back, displaying a fine ruffled silk petticoat. The bodice of the gown is open in front, worn over a stomacher embellished with rows of ribbon down the front. The edges of the square-cut decolletage is decorated with a band of lace. The sleeves elbow length, finished in ruffles and lace. Her white hair is dressed in a high pompadour with a symmetrical arrangement of curls at the side.

MRS. OVERTON:

A handsome middle-aged gentlewoman of a prominent Virginia family, intensely loyal to her friends and spirited in the defense of them. Dressed much the same as LADY DINWIDDIE, *with the addition of a silk cloak of three-quarter length with a hood.*

MRS. RANSOM:

A middle-aged woman of means. She is the fawning, flattering type that enjoys basking in the society of people of rank. Wears the same type of dress and cloak as MRS. OVERTON.

LIEUTENANT BLAINEY:

A mincing, macaroni type of young British officer, with the manners of the Court of St. James. He is of a jealous nature and an unprincipled plotter. Wears the uniform of a Lieutenant in British Army, red coat faced with blue, edged with gold; gold epaulets; buff waistcoat and breeches; crimson sash, and wears dress sword; stockings of white with buckled shoes; wears hair in queue.

NANCY DINWIDDIE:

About eighteen years of age, daughter of GOVERNOR DINWIDDIE. *Elegantly dressed in same style as* LADY DINWIDDIE *except her skirts are about six inches from ground. Her own hair unpowdered, worn in a pompadour with a couple of curls falling over her shoulder in the curve of her neck.*

PHYLLIS OVERTON:

About eighteen years of age, the beautiful daughter of MRS. OVERTON, *and much the same type of character. Handsomely gowned in same style and hair worn same as* NANCY. *Also has a cloak, like* MRS. OVERTON.

COLONEL GEORGE WASHINGTON:

Twenty-two years of age. Six feet two inches tall, in weight two hundred pounds, large boned but well proportioned. His complexion bronzed by an outdoor life; features strong. Hair light brown in color, combed back and worn in a queue. Dressed in uniform of a Colonial Colonel—blue coat faced with red and edged with gold; red waistcoat trimmed with gold; buff breeches, and wears riding boots.

MAJOR GLENDON:

Fine type of British officer, about thirty-five or forty years old, a much different type than BLAINEY. *Wears same type of uniform.*

LORD FAIRFAX:

Sixty-five years; a tall man with a big frame and wide shoulders.

Face deeply lined, of sour visage. He is an irrascible but loyal-hearted man. A fine type of British nobleman. He is plainly though richly dressed in smallclothes and coat of dark color. On his head a grizzled wig worn in a queue. Wears a tricorne hat and carries a cane.

MR. ROBINSON, COLONEL CARY AND COLONEL WILLIS:

Middle-aged Colonial gentlemen, dressed in plain but rich costumes of the period.

GOVERNOR DINWIDDIE:

Sixty-four years of age. A corpulent man with a round, full face. He is irrascible, arrogant, has a fiery temper, withall a gentleman. Dressed richly in costume of the period, wears a large white wig and carries a cane.

BUTLER AND SERVANT:

The butler is an English type, dressed in livery. The servant can be man or maid.

SET: *A richly furnished room of the Governor's palace at Williamsburg, Virginia. Diagonally across the right back corner of the room a beautiful fireplace, with an oil portrait above it. A little to the left of the back wall a door which permits a view of the hall beyond. On the right wall a door between the fireplace and audience leads to music room. On the left wall two windows overlooking the street. Between the door of back wall and left wall a handsome piece of furniture, such as a highboy or cabinet. Near the left wall a davenport with a table beside it. A desk or table at right center, parallel to the fireplace, with a large chair back of it. Tables, chairs, a footstool, etc., about the room.*

LADY DINWIDDIE, MRS. OVERTON, *and* MRS. RANSOM *are sitting grouped at right center taking tea, a man servant stands at a respectable distance in the background.*

MRS. OVERTON: Lady Dinwiddie, in London everybody was talking about our Colonel Washington.

LADY DINWIDDIE: [*With lifted brows.*] Oh—Madam Overton, indeed. [MRS. RANSOM *notices her tone.*]

MRS. OVERTON: That journal of his—the trip to Fort Le Boeuf.

MRS. RANSOM: It was heard of in London?

MRS. OVERTON: 'Twas published in London, you know.

LADY DINWIDDIE: Really?

MRS. OVERTON: 'Twas quite a distinction for us, our acquaintance with Colonel Washington.

LADY DINWIDDIE: Distinction?

MRS. OVERTON: Phyllis was ever talking of him to our English friends.

LADY DINWIDDIE: 'Twas regrettable.

MRS. OVERTON: Regrettable? But Phyllis——

LADY DINWIDDIE: Nay—that the laurels the Colonel won on his Le Boeuf journey should be so withered by his latter experience.

MRS. RANSOM: 'Tis a pity. [*Shakes her head.*] True, nevertheless.

MRS. OVERTON: What mean you?

LADY DINWIDDIE: News of it could not have reached England yet.

MRS. OVERTON: Something untoward chanced to Colonel Washington?

LADY DINWIDDIE: He was in command of the expedition sent to drive the French from the Forks of the Ohio——

MRS. OVERTON: I heard something of it.

LADY DINWIDDIE: —but instead of driving out the French what think you?

MRS. RANSOM: You'd not credit it!

LADY DINWIDDIE: —he surrendered.

MRS. OVERTON: Surrendered! Surrendered to the French!

LADY DINWIDDIE: At a fortified place called Fort Necessity.

MRS. OVERTON: Surrendered! Colonel Washington!

MRS. RANSOM: Forsooth, it ends his military career.

MRS. OVERTON: [To LADY DINWIDDIE.] Surely not! His reputation——

LADY DINWIDDIE: The Governor would not have me to discuss the matter.

MRS. RANSOM: [To MRS. OVERTON.] Lady Dinwiddie's kindness of heart forbids her to speak further upon it.

LADY DINWIDDIE: Governor Dinwiddie is deeply hurt.

MRS. RANSOM: A sorry end to well-laid plans of the Governor.

LADY DINWIDDIE: 'Twas not so much the surrender as the way of it.

MRS. OVERTON: Pray explain.

LADY DINWIDDIE: Methinks I have already said too much.

MRS. RANSOM: My dear lady! You may trust us. [MRS. OVERTON glances inquiringly at MRS. RANSOM.]

LADY DINWIDDIE: Then 'tis for your ears, alone.

MRS. RANSOM: [Eagerly.] Yes, yes, indeed.

LADY DINWIDDIE: No later than this morning, the translations of the articles of surrender were brought to the Governor. Originally they were writ in French.

MRS. RANSOM: La, la! In French.

LADY DINWIDDIE: His Excellency, upon reading the translation, was amazed——

MRS. RANSOM: Oh——!

LADY DINWIDDIE: —amazed and roundly cursed Colonel Washington.

MRS. OVERTON: Cursed Colonel Washington! 'Tis not credible.

LADY DINWIDDIE: [Offended.] Governor Dinwiddie holds that Colonel Washington has brought disgrace on the fair name of Virginia!

MRS. OVERTON: I would believe that of almost anyone save Colonel Washington.

MRS. RANSOM: It must be of great import.

LADY DINWIDDIE: Methinks it be of a very serious nature. The Governor has called together members of the Council Chamber.

MRS. RANSOM: Are they meeting here?

LADY DINWIDDIE: In this very room.

MRS. OVERTON: Is not Colonel Washington also to be here?

LADY DINWIDDIE: He is summoned.

MRS. RANSOM: Every door in the Colony should be closed against him.

LADY DINWIDDIE: [Haughtily.] Needless to say, as long as I am Mistress, Colonel Washington will not find a welcome at the Governor's palace.

MRS. RANSOM: I shall make it very evident that he is not welcome in my home. [To MRS. OVERTON.] You will do the likewise, Sarah?

MRS. OVERTON: [Appraising look at MRS. RANSOM.] I would close my door on any man, no matter how high his station, were I positive he had disgraced the Colony.

MRS. RANSOM: Positive? You have heard Lady Dinwiddie——

MRS. OVERTON: [Interrupting.] With all due respect to my dear Lady Dinwiddie, the charges, whatever they may be, have as yet not been proven.

LADY DINWIDDIE: [Offended.] I can satisfy you as to that, Mistress Overton. [To SERVANT.] Request Lieutenant Blainey to attend me at once. [She takes tea.]

SERVANT: Yes, my Lady. [He leaves.]

MRS. RANSOM: You know Lieutenant Blainey, the Governor's aide, Sarah?

MRS. OVERTON: Yes, I know him.

MRS. RANSOM: Methinks I have heard before you went to England, he was quite attentive to your daughter, Phyllis.

MRS. OVERTON: [Noncommittingly.] I have received him in my home.

LADY DINWIDDIE: Lieutenant Blainey, is he son of an Earl?

MRS. RANSOM: [Sighs.] His manners are those of the Court.

SERVANT: [At door.] Lieutenant, the Honorable Horatio Blainey.

BLAINEY: [Enters and bows to Lady Dinwiddie.] At your service, my Lady. [Bows to ladies.] Madam Overton, Madam Ransom.

MRS. RANSOM: Oh, good afternoon, Lieutenant Blainey.
    [MRS. OVERTON merely bends her head and watches him intently.]

LADY DINWIDDIE: [To BLAINEY.] But yesterday Mistress Overton returned home from England.

BLAINEY: We are all pleased to see Madam Overton and Mistress Phyllis safely returned.

LADY DINWIDDIE: Mistress Overton is but now having opportunity to learn the latest happenings in the Colony.

MRS. RANSOM: Such as the surrender to the French by Colonel Washington.

BLAINEY: Colonel Washington, he is here.

LADY DINWIDDIE: Already here?

BLAINEY: By order of his Excellency—to—ah——

MRS. OVERTON: He will answer any charges.

BLAINEY: [Looks from LADY DINWIDDIE to MRS. OVERTON.] You have learned of it?

LADY DINWIDDIE: These ladies are in my confidence, Sir.

BLAINEY Ah, zounds! I would not be in Colonel Washington's boots.

MRS. OVERTON: The charges against Colonel Washington are——?

BLAINEY: [Looks questioningly at LADY DINWIDDIE, she nods.] I know not what the charges may be, but—— [again looks at LADY DINWIDDIE, she nods permission] he seemed very eager, aye anxious, to surrender Fort Necessity.

MRS. OVERTON: Why should you think that?

BLAINEY: [Now sure of his ground.] So eager was he that he signed articles admitting himself to be a murderer.

MRS. RANSOM: [Gasps.] A murderer!

MRS. OVERTON: There is some error.

BLAINEY: [Shrugs.] Error? With his own signature writ on those articles?

MRS. RANSOM: La, la! His signature!

MRS. OVERTON: No one ever doubted Colonel Washington's mettle.

MRS. RANSOM: But the evidence, Sarah, his signature.

MRS. OVERTON: [*Positively.*] Evidence or no evidence, Colonel Washington is anything but a coward. [*For a moment there is silence. Then from the next room the notes of a piano and a voice singing Ame's "Under the Greenwood Tree."*]

MRS. RANSOM: 'Tis Nancy! [*They listen to the finish of the verse.*] What a charming voice your daughter has.

BLAINEY: 'Tis now charming Colonel Washington.

LADY DINWIDDIE: [*In angry surprise.*] Colonel Washington?

BLAINEY: I left him with Mistress Nancy and Mistress Phyllis.

LADY DINWIDDIE: With my daughter! Lieutenant, do you go to Nancy and bid her come to me at once.

BLAINEY: [*Rises and bows.*] At once, my Lady. [*He leaves, the singing goes on.*]

MRS. RANSOM: How unfortunate! [*The singing ceases in the middle of a word.*]

MRS. OVERTON: [*With rising anger.*] Evelyn Ransom, what is unfortunate?

LADY DINWIDDIE: Mistress Overton, I consider it unfortunate that my daughter is with such a one as this Washington.

MRS. OVERTON: Oh, you do?

MRS. RANSOM: Of course she does, Sarah; who but you wouldn't?

[*MRS. OVERTON rises in anger as NANCY looks in the door and turns to speak to others outside.*]

NANCY: We will have tea with mother and her friends. Come, Phyllis. Come, Colonel Washington.

[*LADY DINWIDDIE gasps, but before she can articulate NANCY enters followed by PHYLLIS and COLONEL WASHINGTON. BLAINEY brings up the rear. WASHINGTON stops and bows. MRS. OVERTON goes at once to WASHINGTON, extends her hand.*]

MRS. OVERTON: George Washington, how pleased I am to see you in such good health.

WASHINGTON: [*Kisses her hand.*] Welcome home to Virginia, Madam Overton.

LADY DINWIDDIE: [*In haughty disapproval.*] Nancy!

NANCY: [*Surprised.*] Mother!

LADY DINWIDDIE: You will come with me.

NANCY: But mother! Our guests?

LADY DINWIDDIE: [*Emphatically.*] You will come with me. [*With haughty mien she strides from the room. MRS. RANSOM, in imitation, elevates her head and follows. PHYLLIS and WASHINGTON are dumfounded; MRS. OVERTON in cold anger; BLAINEY covertly pleased; NANCY shocked, bewildered, stands, amazed, gazing at her mother.*]

MRS. OVERTON: [*Kindly to NANCY.*] Obey your mother, my dear.

NANCY: I don't—I don't understand. Phyllis, Colonel Washington, you'll pardon my absence? I shall return. [*She hurries after her mother, as WASHINGTON bows.*]

PHYLLIS: Mother, why did Lady Dinwiddie——

MRS. OVERTON: [*Interrupting.*] Hush, my dear. Where are your wraps? We are leaving.

PHYLLIS: They are in the hall. But Nancy is returning.

MRS. OVERTON: I think not. [*WASHINGTON goes into the hall.*]

BLAINEY: [*Quickly.*] May I have leave to fetch your wraps, Mistress?

MRS. OVERTON: [*Coldly.*] Lieutenant Blainey, kindly do not trouble yourself.

BLAINEY: 'Tis no trouble, Madam.

MRS. OVERTON: Colonel Washington will fetch them. [*WASHINGTON enters with a bonnet and shawl he gives to PHYLLIS. To WASHINGTON.*] Colonel Washington, I shall consider it a great privilege, indeed an honor, if tomorrow evening you will dine at Brandon Hall with Mr. Overton and myself.

WASHINGTON: I am happy in accepting your kind invitation. [*With meaning.*] My thanks to you, Madam. [*He bows.*]

MRS. OVERTON: Good afternoon, George.

WASHINGTON: Good afternoon, Madam. [*He bows.*]

PHYLLIS: [*To WASHINGTON.*] I shall be happy to see you tomorrow evening. Good afternoon. [*She curtsies.*]

WASHINGTON: Good afternoon, Phyllis. [*He bows.*]

[*MRS. OVERTON and PHYLLIS, without a glance at BLAINEY, sweep from the room. WASHINGTON and BLAINEY bow.*]

BLAINEY: Egad! What a high manner. Were I not the son of an Earl, I vow I'd marry the pretty Phyllis.

WASHINGTON: [*With a look of scorn.*] Methinks were you the Prince of Wales, himself, she would not consider you. [*He starts for the door as NANCY enters, flustered. Stops at sight of WASHINGTON.*]

NANCY: Oh, Colonel Washington. Where is Phyllis?

WASHINGTON: She has gone, Mistress Nancy.

NANCY: Gone! And you——?

WASHINGTON: I await the Governor's pleasure—in another room.

NANCY: [*With a defiant look at BLAINEY.*] May I show you my garden, Colonel Washington?

WASHINGTON: [*Gives her a quizzical look.*] I am interested in horticulture, but——

NANCY: I would have your advice, sir. [*She takes his arm, they leave center door, their voices are heard outside as they meet GLENDON.*]

GLENDON: Ah, Mistress Nancy.

NANCY: Major Glendon.

GLENDON: Colonel Washington, I am happy to see you safely returned.

WASHINGTON: And I am happy to be here, Major Glendon.

GLENDON: I will see more of you anon.

[*BLAINEY kicks the footstool as he listens to the conversation outside, a perplexed frown on his face. GLENDON enters with papers in his hands, looks at BLAINEY, who has turned away, goes and sits at table, arranges papers.*]

GLENDON: Have the gentlemen of the council arrived?

BLAINEY: Not as yet.

GLENDON: [*Busy with papers.*] 'Tis nigh onto the hour.

BLAINEY: Is his Excellency still in anger?

GLENDON: In as black a humor as ever I saw him.

BLAINEY: Good!

GLENDON: [*Looks up.*] Good?

BLAINEY: 'Twill serve the coward aright.

GLENDON: Coward? Who is a coward?

BLAINEY: This boor Washington.

GLENDON: Blainey, why do you so dislike Colonel Washington?

BLAINEY: Bah! I detest these stiff-necked Colonial gentry. They sicken me.

GLENDON: They are men of substance.

BLAINEY: Who give us nothing but sour looks.

GLENDON: I have found Colonel Washington courteous to all.

BLAINEY: The stiff courtesy of a country-bumpkin. To me he is nothing more than a disgraced wilderness rover. [Goes to window, looks out.]

GLENDON: Ah—!

BLAINEY: Here comes the precious members of the council. My Lord Fairfax, the old crab; long-faced Speaker Robinson, and the two backwoods Colonels Cary and Willis.

GLENDON: Colonel Willis is a cousin of Colonel Washington.

BLAINEY: A sickening breed.

GLENDON: I noted, when meeting them in the hall, that one of the breed did not seem sickening to Mistress Nancy.

BLAINEY: Better he make the most of his chance; he will have but small opportunity in the future.

GLENDON: Really?

BLAINEY: But a moment ago Lady Dinwiddie pointedly failed to notice him and left the room.

GLENDON: [Astonished.] Lady Dinwiddie!

BLAINEY: Aye. Lady Dinwiddie cares not for those who disgrace the King's uniform.

GLENDON: Disgrace the uniform! Explain your words.

BLAINEY: The surrender of Fort Necessity. Washington's admitting himself a murderer, and all that.

GLENDON: [Rising. In a severe tone.] How come Lady Dinwiddie by that information?

BLAINEY: [Snddenly flustered.] Why—ah—er——

GLENDON: [In cold anger.] Lieutenant Blainey, you have broken one of the most positive orders of the Governor. You have spoken to others of state matters.

BLAINEY: But Lady Dinwiddie, I thought——

GLENDON: [Severely.] You thought to injure a man who has done nothing to merit your animosity. [He takes an angry stride toward BLAINEY.] You are unworthy of the uniform you wear. You damned cad!

BLAINEY: [Grasping the hilt of his sword.] I demand satisfaction for that insult, sir.

BUTLER: [At door.] My Lord Fairfax, Speaker Robinson, Colonel Cary and Colonel Willis.

[BLAINEY and GLENDON stand for an instant glaring at each other then turn and bow to those entering the door. FAIRFAX is quick to note the tension and attitude of GLENDON and BLAINEY.]

LORD FAIRFAX: [Gazes with shrewd eyes at them.] If our entrance interrupts matters of importance, gentlemen——

GLENDON: [Smiles.] A matter, my Lord, which can be deferred until another time. [To the others.] Good afternoon, gentlemen. [To the BUTLER.] Inform the Governor the gentlemen of the council await his Excellency's pleasure. Colonel Washington is in the garden; my compliments to him, and will he join us now.

BUTLER: Yes, sir. [He exits.]

[FAIRFAX and ROBINSON are together as CARY and WILLIS exchange greetings with GLENDON.]

ROBINSON: Colonel Washington's presence here, mayhap, betokens the Governor has plans for another campaign.

FAIRFAX: 'Od's fish, Dinwiddie knows no more of conducting a campaign than a cow does of architecture.

ROBINSON: Aye, the outcome of the last campaign proves your words. Have you had an opportunity to discuss the surrender of Fort Necessity with Colonel Washington?

FAIRFAX: Nay, I saw him but a moment at Raleigh's Tavern.

ROBINSON: He arrived but last night.

FAIRFAX: By what I know of the lad, he will make no explanation unless requested by the Governor.

BUTLER: [At door.] Colonel Washington.

WASHINGTON: Good afternoon, gentlemen.

ROBINSON: [Goes to WASHINGTON.] Colonel Washington, I am glad to see you in such good health. [They shake hands. CARY and WILLIS greet WASHINGTON. Then FAIRFAX draws WASHINGTON aside.]

FAIRFAX: George, why this meeting?

WASHINGTON: I know nothing about it, my Lord.

FAIRFAX: Perchance to bandy talk on plans for another campaign.

WASHINGTON: Mayhap, but methinks there is an undercurrent that augurs another matter.

FAIRFAX: I have felt—— [Taps cane on floor.]

BUTLER: [At door.] His Excellency the Governor of Virginia.

[They all turn and bow as GOVERNOR DINWIDDIE enters.]

DINWIDDIE: Good afternoon, gentlemen. [He goes to and sits at the table and arranges papers. BLAINEY is at his elbow, the others grouped about. He looks up.] Will you take chairs, gentlemen? [They all sit.] I will to the matter before us at once. You are all familiar with the disastrous outcome of the expedition commanded by Colonel Washington and sent by me to build a fort at the forks of the Ohio. [WASHINGTON, with chin up, looks straight before himself.] This expedition was besieged at a stockade called Fort Necessity, by a company of French and Indians, and surrendered to the enemy. The articles of surrender, written in the French language, have been translated. [His voice rises.] They contain provisions which I could not believe any commander would sign. [They all look at WASHINGTON in surprise. DINWIDDIE fixes WASHINGTON with an accusing eye.] Colonel Washington. [WASHINGTON rises.] Explain, sir—explain how you, an officer of the King's Militia, came to admit over your signature that you were an assassin—a murderer. I consider you disgraced. [They all are amazed. WASHINGTON is dumfounded.]

FAIRFAX: [Hotly.] Your Excellency, it is not the manner among us to condemn a man unheard——

DINWIDDIE: Twice over his signature.

FAIRFAX: —nor, sir, to address a gentleman as you have permitted yourself.

CARY: That, sir, is also my opinion.

WILLIS: [In a low voice to WASHINGTON.] Keep your temper, George.

WASHINGTON: May I see the translation, your Excellency?

DINWIDDIE: [Gives WASHINGTON paper.] Third paragraph, sir. Read it yourself. [*WASHINGTON reads, and is too utterly amazed and confounded to speak.*]

FAIRFAX: [*Kindly.*] Well, Colonel?

WASHINGTON: [*To FAIRFAX.*] 'Tis a fact, my Lord, according to this translation. I have signed an admittance that I am an assassin—that I murdered the French Captain, Jumonville.

FAIRFAX: Jumonville? He was killed in a previous skirmish with the French.

WASHINGTON: On the field of battle, my Lord.

DINWIDDIE: Then why, sir, did you admit murdering the man? Were you so anxious to surrender that you would sign anything?

[*BLAINEY snickers. FAIRFAX is choking with anger. The others are tense. WASHINGTON is calm.*]

WASHINGTON: [*In a cold, stern voice.*] Your Excellency, never before has any man faced me with an accusation of cowardice.

DINWIDDIE: [*Glances uncertainly at the stern faces of the gentry.*] I have not said you were a coward.

FAIRFAX: [*With a bang of his cane on the floor.*] By the eternal, you imputed cowardice.

WASHINGTON: [*To DINWIDDIE.*] Sir, methinks I fail not in understanding your meaning.

FAIRFAX: Nor I.

WASHINGTON: I have long held to the opinion that of all vain things, explanations are the vainest.

DINWIDDIE: Then you refuse to explain why you signed this paper?

WASHINGTON: In this instance I will state facts, you——

DINWIDDIE: Then out with those so-called facts!

WASHINGTON: You may draw your own conclusions. I did not surrender!

DINWIDDIE: You didn't surrender? Then, sir, why did you sign these papers?

WASHINGTON: They are articles of agreement, written in French, translated to me by one of my officers, a Dutchman, Van Braam, whose knowledge of French must have been as faulty as his knowledge of English.

FAIRFAX: So, Van Braam translated this paper?

WASHINGTON: There was no word of assassination mentioned.

DINWIDDIE: Why were these articles not written in English?

WASHINGTON: That I will answer later. As to the facts, we were outnumbered at least three to one. Due to this disparity of numbers I had occupied Fort Necessity, which a month before I had established in the center of a place called Great Meadows.

FAIRFAX: Why did you select that location, Colonel?

WASHINGTON: There were no trees closer than three hundred yards. There I could not be surprised, and a foe, in order to get within rifle range to attack us, would be without cover, must expose themselves to fire upon us. Our enemy fights best behind trees.

DINWIDDIE: Then why did you not hold the fort?

WASHINGTON: We did hold the fort for nine hours of a rainy day—until eight o'clock at night. So effective was the fire of our force that every man accounted for at least one of the foe.

FAIRFAX: They had heavy losses?

WASHINGTON: From my best advices at least three hundred French and Indians were killed and many wounded. All that night they were secretly burying their dead.

DINWIDDIE: Yet you left the field!

WASHINGTON: Twice, under a white flag, the enemy called me to parley.

FAIRFAX: Twice, you say?

WASHINGTON: Aye, and twice I declined, suspecting deceit. The third time I sent officers to discuss the situation with them.

DINWIDDIE: Then you surrendered!

WASHINGTON: Your Excellency, I did not surrender!

DINWIDDIE: Then why——?

WASHINGTON: We were short of ammunition, thirty of my men had been killed—seventy wounded—one hundred sick——

DINWIDDIE: [*Interrupting.*] One hundred sick. Why, sir?

WASHINGTON: Due to lack of supplies.

FAIRFAX: Ah—lack of supplies.

WASHINGTON: We had no medicine. On occupying Fort Necessity we had but two bags of flour and a few slices of bacon.

WILLIS: To feed three hundred men!

FAIRFAX: Humph——

WASHINGTON: Then the enemy, taught by his losses that we could not be easily taken, was eager to quit the field—agreeable to a withdrawal.

DINWIDDIE: [*In anger.*] Then why did you sign these articles?

WASHINGTON: There was no prospect of food, ammunition or reinforcements reaching us.

FAIRFAX: Though they had been promised.

WASHINGTON: Men must eat to live. My only course was to fall back to Wills Creek, where I could obtain provisions.

DINWIDDIE: If the enemy was agreeable to quit the field, then why didn't you both leave? Why was it necessary to sign these articles? [*WASHINGTON and the others are astonished. FAIRFAX smiles. DINWIDDIE is angry.*]

WASHINGTON: Sir, could I march out of a stronghold, under the eyes of a vastly superior foe—half of them savages—without assurance that the enemy would not attack us when we had entered the forest—where he would have a great advantage in numbers?

FAIRFAX: Certainly not!

WILLIS: I believe these articles of agreement were necessary. You took a wise and honorable course, Colonel.

DINWIDDIE: This admission of assassination—murder.

WASHINGTON: The articles were written in the enemy's camp, naturally in their language.

FAIRFAX: Van Braam, in his translation, tricked you.

WASHINGTON: I do not believe it was intentional. He must not have been a well-qualified French scholar.

FAIRFAX: Then, gentlemen, this unfortunate mistake was due to the Governor having failed to provide Colonel Washington with a competent French interpreter.

DINWIDDIE: [*Angry and discomfited.*] Nonsense, My Lord Fairfax. [*To WASHINGTON.*] You should be broke, sir. You are unfit to command.

FAIRFAX: [*In cool anger.*] Be careful of your words, Governor.

WASHINGTON: [*Restrains FAIRFAX with a gesture. Holds DINWIDDIE'S attention with a cold eye and sharp, decisive words.*] If I am unfit to command, this Colonial Government is unfit to wage a campaign. [*DINWIDDIE gasps in anger.*] I was promised men, ammunition, supplies. I was given a fourth of what I was promised.

FAIRFAX: Zounds! 'tis the truth!

WASHINGTON: I did what any commander worthy of the name would do. I obeyed orders. When faced with starvation, surrounded by a superior force, I made terms which I deem amounted to a moral victory. We marched out with all our arms—with the honors of war—we went our way, the enemy the other way—glad to be gone.

FAIRFAX: Drums beating and colors flying, by gad.

WASHINGTON: These are the facts, sir.

FAIRFAX: [*Striking cane on floor.*] Facts, Governor Dinwiddie.

WASHINGTON: I have nothing more to say. Here, sir, is my report. [*He places papers on DINWIDDIE'S desk.*]

DINWIDDIE: I presume, sir, you expect us to accept your statement.

WASHINGTON: [*Glancing at company.*] If any gentleman here doubts it, I——

CARY: [*Interrupting.*] I for one do not, Colonel Washington. I think the matter cleared and I trust his Excellency will see that he has spoken in haste.

[*DINWIDDIE is surprised.*]

FAIRFAX: I know of no man bold enow to doubt Colonel Washington's word. Had the Governor's Council provided the expedition with sufficient supplies and ammunition, there would have been a different tale to relate.

[*DINWIDDIE'S gaze shifts. Looks at his papers in thought, then looks up at next speech.*]

ROBINSON: Your Excellency, as Speaker of the Assembly, I am willing to shoulder my share of the blame. Every one of us from the highest down should do likewise.

WILLIS: I consider Colonel Washington's act as highly honorable in every instance. [*Pauses for effect.*] The people of this Colony understand the circumstances of his withdrawal and are not placing the blame on his shoulders, but on others—where it belongs.

DINWIDDIE: [*Slowly changing face.*] Humph! This Van Braam is a damned traitor.

WASHINGTON: I think you are mistaken, sir.

FAIRFAX: [*Rises and fixes DINWIDDIE with lifted head.*] Governor Dinwiddie——

DINWIDDIE: Well, my Lord.

FAIRFAX: When in the wrong it behooves men of our station to acknowledge our errors.

DINWIDDIE: [*Restlessly; glancing at set faces of others.*] Well—ah. It seems I spoke hastily—Colonel Washington, I—ah—I regret the heat of my words. [*WASHINGTON bows.*]

BLAINEY: May I be excused, sir?

DINWIDDIE: Yes. [*To others.*] Gentlemen, I would consider it a favor if you would all stay to dinner.

FAIRFAX: Thank you, sir; but I must be on my way to Fredericksburg.

ROBINSON: Your excellency, I have guests at home.

CARY: And I likewise, sir.

WILLIS: Thanks, sir; but I have already accepted an invitation to dine with Colonel Byrd.

[*They move to the door. WASHINGTON without replying to DINWIDDIE, with them.*]

DINWIDDIE: Another time then. Colonel Washington, will you remain for a moment? I would have a word with you. [*To others.*] The Council will meet tomorrow. [*They all bow and leave. WASHINGTON has gone to window at left and stands gazing out. DINWIDDIE studies him, a perplexed frown on his face. The door at right opens and NANCY stands on threshold, surveys the two.*]

NANCY: Father, the meeting is ended I take it. [*Both men turn at her words. WASHINGTON bows.*]

DINWIDDIE: Yes, my dear.

NANCY: May I enter?

DINWIDDIE: Come, I need you.

NANCY: Need me?

DINWIDDIE: Yes, to help me to persuade this prideful young Colonel to forgive a hot-headed old fool and accept his invitation to dinner.

NANCY: Why, Father!

WASHINGTON: Your excellency, I hold no ill feelings. 'Twould afford me great pleasure to dine with you and Mistress Dinwiddie but there is a barrier which prevents me.

[*LADY DINWIDDIE hurries in and goes to WASHINGTON, she is all smiles. BLAINEY and MRS. RANSOM follow and stand in back ground.*]

LADY DINWIDDIE: Oh, Colonel Washington, I am happy to hear of your vindication. I hope you will pardon my rudeness.

DINWIDDIE: You—rude to Colonel Washington? When?

LADY DINWIDDIE: Just before the conference.

DINWIDDIE: Why, Madam, were you rude to him?

LADY DINWIDDIE: I thought he had disgraced the Colony.

DINWIDDIE: [*Turns to stare at BLAINEY who is frightened.*] Lieutenant Blainey, you return to England on the next ship.

MRS. RANSOM: [*Frightened.*] La! La!

LADY DINWIDDIE: I regret my act.

WASHINGTON: 'Twas a natural misunderstanding, Madam.

DINWIDDIE: Perhaps you can persuade Colonel Washington to stay to dinner.

LADY DINWIDDIE: You will, Colonel Washington?

WASHINGTON: [*Bows.*] I shall be pleased to, Madam.

NANCY: [*To DINWIDDIE.*] Happily, the barrier is removed.

CURTAIN.

I Follow Washington

A GEORGE WASHINGTON PLAY IN ONE ACT

DRAMATIS PERSONAE

(IN ORDER OF THEIR APPEARANCE)

CAPTAIN CROGHAN, *of the Pennsylvania Militia.*

LEAWANDA.

SIR JOHN ST. CLAIR, *Quartermaster General.*

MAJOR MOORE, *of the Grenadiers.*

COLONEL SIR PETER HALKET, *second-in-command.*

BRIGADIER GENERAL EDWARD BRADDOCK.

BENJAMIN FRANKLIN, *Post-Master General of the Colonies.*

COLONEL DUNBAR, *of the 49th.*

MR. PETERS, *a Colonial.*

CAPTAIN ORME, *Braddock's Aide.*

ENSIGN ALLEN, *of the British Army.*

THE HALF-KING *of the Senecas.*

WHITE THUNDER, *a chief of the Senecas.*

COLONEL GEORGE WASHINGTON.

CAPTAIN JACK GIST, *of the Rangers.*

ORDERLIES, SERVANTS, INDIANS.

TIME: *A day in May, 1755.*

PLACE: *General Braddock's Headquarters at Wills Creek.*

DESCRIPTION OF CHARACTERS

CAPTAIN CROGHAN:

About thirty-four years of age, a fine type of Irishman; a trader for nine years, knows the Indian. Now a Captain of Pennsylvania Militia; wears the uniform of a militia officer, dark blue coat faced with red and edged with gold, red waistcoat edged with gold, red breeches, boots, and tricorne hat; wears his dark hair in a queue.

LEAWANDA:

A beautiful half-breed, niece of the HALF-KING, nearly white in complexion. She is dressed in buckskin Indian garments, beautifully beaded and decorated. About her brow, a beaded band with a single heron's feather; her long hair is worn in two braids; at her belt a knife.

SIR JOHN ST. CLAIR:

About fifty years of age. A pompous, strutting British officer of the beef-eating type. Wears the uniform of the British Army—red coat faced with blue, edged with gold, gold epaulets, buff waistcoat and breeches; crimson sash and sword, boots and tricorne hat; wears hair in queue.

MAJOR MOORE:

A rough, hard-drinking officer of the Grenadiers, dressed the same as ST. CLAIR.

GENERAL BRADDOCK:

Well preserved for all his sixty years of age. A pronounced aristocrat of irritable disposition; he is courageous, impetuous, stubborn. Wears his wealth of white hair tied in a queue with a black ribbon. Immaculately dressed in same type uniform as ST. CLAIR.

BENJAMIN FRANKLIN:

Forty-nine years of age. Of medium height, inclined to stoutness. He has a large head with a kindly look in his eye; his hair is gray, tied in a queue with a black ribbon; he wears gray clothes of a severe Colonial pattern with white hose and buckled shoes.

COLONEL DUNBAR:

About fifty years of age. Dressed same as ST. CLAIR.

MR. PETERS:

About thirty-five or forty years of age. Dressed in plain clothes of Colonial cut.

CAPTAIN ORME:

About twenty-five years of age. Dressed the same as the other officers.

ENSIGN ALLEN:

A youth of twenty-one, the youngest of the officers, dressed as others but without sash.

THE HALF-KING:

A fine type of Indian chief, intelligent, proudly tenacious of his rights. Wears the full regalia of an Iroquois chief.

WHITE THUNDER:

A venerable Indian chief, not dressed quite as elaborately as the Half-King.

WASHINGTON:

Twenty-three years of age. Six feet two inches tall, in weight about 200 pounds, large-boned but well-proportioned. His complexion bronzed by an outdoor life, features strong, hair light brown in color, combed back and worn in a queue. He is dressed in well-fitting uniform of a Colonial Colonel: red breeches and boots, a red vest, blue coat faced with red, a tricorne hat and long military cape. Wears a sword.

CAPTAIN JACK GIST:

A tall, gaunt, middle-aged ranger, dressed in a buckskin Indian hunting shirt and leggings, wears coonskin cap. His hair is long and falls over his shoulders. Carries a rifle, powder-horn slung about his shoulder. In his belt, a tomahawk and knife.

ORDERLIES:

Dressed in red coats of the British private, with white waistcoat and breeches, gaiters calf-high.

SET: *A plain, severe room of Braddock's Headquarters at Wills Creek; the walls are rough plastered and without adornment. In the center of the back wall, a double door. The opening shows the plain, unfinished, narrow hall beyond. To the left of the door, a long, rough sideboard of unmistakable forest manufacture. To the right of the door, a standard with the flag of Great Britain. The right wall has a window about three feet from the back wall; between the window and the audience, a heavy oaken door with a bar across it. The left wall has a door about three feet from back wall; between it and the audience, a huge fireplace; above the mantel a deer's head with wide-spread antlers. In the center of stage, a long table running lengthwise of the room, is littered with maps and papers. A dozen chairs at the table and scattered about the room.*

CROGHAN *is pacing the floor.* LEAWANDA's *head appears at the window.*

LEAWANDA: Captain Croghan!

CROGHAN: [*Starts, turns to her.*] Leawanda!

LEAWANDA: I bring a message for you to give Colonel Washington.

CROGHAN: Come you to the door. [*He hurries to the door, opens it,* LEAWANDA *enters.* CROGHAN *closes the door, bows to her, brings forward a chair.*] Will you be seated?

LEAWANDA: No, my friend. I stay but a moment. My uncle, the Half-King, bids me tell you the attentions of the younger British officers to the squaws must cease.

CROGHAN: I will ask Colonel Washington so to inform General Braddock.

LEAWANDA: 'Tis well, Washington is our friend. Adieu. [*She turns to go.*]

CROGHAN: [*Seizes her hand.*] Leawanda!

LEAWANDA: [*Imploringly.*] Please, my friend! [*She slowly shakes her head.*]

CROGHAN: You love the way of the Indian more than you love me?

LEAWANDA: Nay, 'tis because I love you too well.

CROGHAN: Too well?

LEAWANDA: The white man who marries a squaw loses caste.

CROGHAN: What care I of that? You, who are half white, educated by the French Fathers, you are——

LEAWANDA: —but an Indian.

CROGHAN: —a fit mate for a better man than I.

LEAWANDA: There are none better than you.

CROGHAN: You do love me, Leawanda—and you know I love you. All else is of no consequence.

LEAWANDA: You are on the way to fight those I adore.

CROGHAN: But your uncle, the Half-King, fights with the English against the French.

LEAWANDA: The Half-King is devoted to Colonel Washington. I am but a squaw. I go with my tribe. But my heart——

CROGHAN: I will leave this expedition, for I, like all the Colonials, am disgusted with this Braddock.

LEAWANDA: Is Colonel Washington of that mind?

CROGHAN: Aye, Washington. He is insulted, ignored by the leaders. 'Tis but a question of time when he, too, will have had enough.

LEAWANDA: Then my people will have had enough.

CROGHAN: Come, let us go to a priest, then away to the forest and there live each for the other.

LEAWANDA: Each for the other. [*She stands in thought.* CROGAN *takes her hand.* MAJOR MOORE *and* SIR JOHN ST. CLAIR *enter.*]

MOORE: What ho! Sir John, a love scene in the General's headquarters! [CROGHAN *turns.* LEAWANDA *startled, swiftly runs to the door and exits.* CROGHAN *would follow her, then stops, confronts* MOORE *and* ST. CLAIR.]

ST. CLAIR: Damme! Those squaws ever make mischief with the officers—even invade the General's quarters.

CROGHAN: [*Coldly, with dignity.*] I am here on business. She, Leawanda, the niece of the Half-King, brought from him a message to me.

MOORE: You can't blame the man, Sir John; she is indeed a winsome hussy.

CROGHAN: Have a care, sir, how you speak of a lady.

MOORE: Hoity-toity! A lady! A lady of the pretty gee-gaws, the buckskin dress. Is he not a proud swain? [COL. HALKET *enters, stops in the door.*]

CROGHAN: [*Trembling with anger.*] You keep a civil tongue in your head or you'll regret it.

MOORE: Alack-a-day, when a trader threatens a King's officer.

HALKET: Major Moore, hold your peace. There is trouble enow between our forces and the Colonists.

ST. CLAIR: But the churl threatened him, Colonel.

HALKET: Perchance he had reason to. You cannot treat these people as serfs. [CROGHAN *goes to window and gazes out.*]

ST. CLAIR: Damn the Colonists! They balk us on every hand; I can get neither wagons nor flour.

HALKET: Curses do no good.

ST. CLAIR: Colonel Halket, had I my way, by fire and sword I'd force these Colonists to do the work.

[*Two* ORDERLIES *enter carrying trays of glasses and bottles of wine which they deposit on the sideboard.*]

MOORE: Hear, Hear! [*With a gesture toward the* ORDER-LIES.] The General will soon arrive.

HALKET: Mr. Franklin, the Post-Master of the Colonies, comes with him. Mayhap he can make satisfactory arrangements for supplies.

ST. CLAIR: Benjamin Franklin, a person of low intelligence, seems to take nothing seriously.

MOORE: [*To* ST. CLAIR.] Mayhap we better be more presentable when the General comes.

ST. CLAIR: [*Grumbling.*] The General ever would have us on dress parade. [*They bow to* HALKET *and leave.* HALKET *gazes at* CROGHAN, *then goes to an* ORDERLY.]

HALKET: Pour two glasses of wine.

ORDERLY: Yes, sir. [*He pours wine as* HALKET *studies* CROGHAN.]

HALKET: [*Indicates table.*] There. [ORDERLY *places wine on table.*] Captain Croghan.

CROGHAN: Yes, sir.

HALKET: Will you join me in a glass of wine?

CROGHAN: [*Surprised.*] Thank you, sir. I shall be delighted. [*He goes to* HALKET.]

HALKET: You know me, I take it.

CROGHAN: Sir Peter Halket, Colonel of the 48th.

HALKET: For some time you have been a trader with the Indians?

CROGHAN: Since 1746—nine years.

HALKET: Yet you are an educated man.

CROGHAN: [*Smiles.*] A graduate of Old Trinity, Dublin.

HALKET: Old Trinity—I would toast another Trinity man, a friend and comrade. [*Lifts his glass.*] To Colonel Patrick Croghan.

CROGHAN: [*Lifts his glass.*] My father, sir. [*They drink.*]

HALKET: Your father was a gallant soldier, loyal to his King. And you——

CROGHAN: As my father.

HALKET: Good! Then, as I thought, you will respect my confidence.

CROGHAN: I will, sir, as you do mine.

HALKET: As you know, relations between the Colonists and the King's Regulars are strained.

CROGHAN: Well I know.

HALKET: And the reason?

CROGHAN: There are many reasons—the action of the officers, their assumption of superiority, their impertinences and insults, the disregard, aye, the spurning, of our good offices.

HALKET: 'Tis regrettable.

CROGHAN: And that is not all. Our Indian allies—the chiefs too little considered—their women insulted, or worse.

HALKET: That must be stopped!

CROGHAN: The British officers seem to think it necessary that the Colonials imitate the methods of the regulars.

HALKET: But they should be taught our methods of warfare.

CROGHAN: Not when it comes to fighting in the wilderness. My experience teaches me your officers and men would more need to learn the ways of the rangers.

HALKET: It will be hard so to convince General Braddock.

CROGHAN: He must be convinced.

HALKET: It is so vital?

CROGHAN: The loyal Colonists, our Indian allies, the Rangers, are disgusted with General Braddock for they feel he is heading this expedition to disaster.

HALKET: Disaster! Surely too strong a word!

CROGHAN: General Braddock needs the help of our men and unless he is made to realize the necessity of a change in tactics, they will leave this expedition.

HALKET: As bad as that?

CROGHAN: They only await the word or act of one man——

HALKET: One man?

CROGHAN: Washington.

HALKET: Colonel Washington?

CROGHAN: In him they have implicit confidence.

HALKET: He is very young.

CROGHAN: Not too young to traverse the wilderness and outwit that clever Frenchman, St. Pierre; not too young to be entrusted with command by Governor Dinwiddie.

HALKET: He surrendered Fort Necessity.

CROGHAN: Mismanagement on the part of Dinwiddie—lack of ammunition—provisions. And knowing Washington in no way responsible for the defeat, his reputation grew with the Colonists. They know, would Braddock but take his advice, all would be well.

HALKET: He has so great influence with them as that?

CROGHAN: If he resigns then we will all be quit of this expedition.

HALKET: [*Alarmed.*] You mean he is wavering?

CROGHAN: Can you expect anything else of him?

HALKET: I knew not he was dissatisfied.

CROGHAN: Ah, but you know not this Washington. Beneath his mask of serenity there is a certain noble pride; a high temper—fortunately under control—like unto a devil chained within.

HALKET: [*Speculatively.*] Ah!

CROGHAN: But, tried too far—the devil may break those chains.

HALKET: So—. Much then depends on Washington?

CROGHAN: Methinks the very success of the expedition.

HALKET: [*Voices are heard in hall, the tread of feet.*] The General Braddock comes.

[*BRADDOCK enters with FRANKLIN, followed by ORME, DUNBAR, PETERS, ST. CLAIR, MOORE, and ALLEN.*]

BRADDOCK: [*As they enter the door.*] Rest assured, Mr. Franklin, if the Colonies but do their part, His Majesty's Regulars will take Duquesne.

FRANKLIN: The Colonies can be depended upon to do their best, sir.

BRADDOCK: As yet I have seen no evidence of their doing much of anything. [*Sees HALKET.*] Mr. Franklin, do you know Colonel Sir Peter Halket? [*HALKET moves forward, CROGHAN goes to the window.*]

HALKET: [*Offers his hand.*] 'Tis a pleasure to meet Mister Franklin. Your name is favorably known in Europe.

FRANKLIN: [*Looks at HALKET quizzically, takes his hand.*] I am flattered. [*On the appearance of BRADDOCK, the servants pass about drinks. One stands by FRANKLIN and HALKET, holding tray.*]

BRADDOCK: Gentlemen, I am proposing a toast to a quick victory over our enemy, the French.

ALL: [*Raising glasses.*] To victory!

BRADDOCK: We will dispense with further amenities and consider the matter in hand. [*He sits at center of table. FRANKLIN to his left. DUNBAR at his right, PETERS beyond DUNBAR, ST. CLAIR at FRANKLIN'S left. HALKET at end of table at left. MOORE and ALLEN sit at left center, ORME sits beyond PETERS and ST. CLAIR.*] Sir, how are you getting on with the collection of supplies, wagons and teams?

ST. CLAIR: Getting on? Faith, General, I am not getting on at all. These cursed Colonists balk me at every turn.

BRADDOCK: Mister Franklin, such is the cooperation we secure from these Colonists we come to save from the French and Indians.

FRANKLIN: Sir, 'tis hard to arouse in them a great concern over the enemy.

ST. CLAIR: Or the King's service.

BRADDOCK: Can't you make these Pennsylvania Quakers and Dutchmen understand the King requires their teams?

FRANKLIN: I shall try, sir.

BRADDOCK: Try? 'Tis action we want. Fort Duquesne must be taken ere winter comes. [*Confused mingling of voices are heard off stage. The sharp challenge of a sentry. "Halt! You can't go that way." A rise in the jargon of voices like an infuriated mob. The door at the left is thrust open, the HALF-KING enters, followed by WHITE THUNDER and four or five Indians. Other braves would crowd in but CROGHAN springs to the door, closes and bars it. At the window at left are crowded the heads of Indians, looking in. The officers' hands go to the hilts of their swords; some of them rise.*]

BRADDOCK: [*Coldly angry.*] What means this gross invasion of my quarters?

HALF-KING: White Father, are the Inglees our friends or our enemies?

HALKET: [*To an ORDERLY.*] Fetch Colonel Washington at once. [*ORDERLY rushes out center door.*]

BRADDOCK: Why of a certainty we are your friends, Half-King.

HALF-KING: Then why are we treated as enemies?

BRADDOCK: Who treats you as enemies?

HALF-KING: Your soldiers and officers.

BRADDOCK: My soldiers? You mean the Colonial rangers!

HALF-KING: No. Those who wear red-coats. Are we the dirt beneath your feet? Are our squaws to be the sport of your warriors? Are we a conquered nation?

BRADDOCK: [Lifts a hand.] Make clear your meaning, Half-King. You speak but in riddles.

HALF-KING: A squaw of our tribe, a daughter of the Chief White Thunder [WHITE THUNDER grunts.], beaten unto death because she resisted the attentions of a red coat. The Great Spirit is calling her.

BRADDOCK: The man shall be whipped.

HALF-KING: He dies at our hand.

ST. CLAIR: Give over a British soldier to the savages!

BRADDOCK: No!

HALF-KING: The White Chief speaks without thought. Are we no longer to be friends?

BRADDOCK: [Rises.] Thought? Rather lose your friendship and thousands like you than have one English private die at your hands. [HALF-KING'S and BRADDOCK'S gaze meet in conflict. For a long moment there is silence, broken by a rapping on the door.]

CROGHAN: [At door.] Who would enter?

WASHINGTON: [Outside.] 'Tis I, Washington.

HALKET: [To BRADDOCK.] I sent for Colonel Washington.

[CROGHAN unbars the door. WASHINGTON enters followed by GIST. CROGHAN bars door.]

WASHINGTON: [To BRADDOCK.] I am wanted, sir?

BRADDOCK: Wanted! Yes, if you can control these—these friends of yours. Damme, sir! They demand an English soldier. Want to kill him for attacking a squaw.

WASHINGTON: I have feared this would happen, sir. I have warned——

BRADDOCK: [Interrupts.] Knew you more of camps, Colonel Washington, and soldiers—— [Ends with a gesture.]

CROGHAN: [To WASHINGTON.] The squaw is the daughter of White Thunder. She is near death.

WASHINGTON: [Turns to HALF-KING.] My brother——

HALF-KING: The red coat dies.

WASHINGTON: Or——?

HALF-KING: We go with the French.

[WASHINGTON looks inquiringly at BRADDOCK.]

BRADDOCK: The man will be court-martialed. If found guilty, he will be punished.

WASHINGTON: [To HALF-KING.] 'Tis the law of the white man.

HALF-KING: The law of our nation says—he dies.

HALKET: [To BRADDOCK.] Mayhap, sir; if you will take the matter under advisement. Let Colonel Washington and the Half-King——

BRADDOCK: [Impatiently.] Yes, yes, do that, Colonel. I—I need time to think on it.

WASHINGTON: [To HALF-KING.] You have heard the words of the White Chief, my brother——

MOORE: [To ALLEN, sneeringly.] His brother!

WASHINGTON: —grant me the favor of a council.

HALF-KING: [Looks from WASHINGTON to BRADDOCK.] To no purpose. 'Tis better we go.

WASHINGTON: Anger burns quickly, ashes are bitter. [Sadly.] My brother turns his face from me.

[MOORE laughs. HALF-KING glances contemptuously at MOORE.]

HALKET: [With a scowl at MOORE.] Silence!

HALF-KING: [With dignity.] I will meet my brother in council.

BRADDOCK: Wait here till we are finished, Colonel Washington, then we will talk with the Half-King.

WASHINGTON: [To HALF-KING.] Will you await the pleasure of the White Chief?

HALF-KING: I wait your pleasure, my brother. [At a signal from the HALF-KING, the Indians silently leave. WASHINGTON, CROGHAN and HALF-KING and CAPTAIN GIST form a group at the right.]

BRADDOCK: We will now go on with our conference. [Wine has been distributed, refused by WASHINGTON, CROGHAN, GIST and HALF-KING. BRADDOCK lifts glass.] Your health, Mr. Peters.

PETERS: Thank you, sir. [They drink.]

BRADDOCK: [To PETERS.] When do your wood choppers begin building the road?

PETERS: As soon as a military escort is provided, sir. Until then 'twill not be possible.

BRADDOCK: The Colony must find guards for its own wood-cutters. As to the Indians, His Majesty's Regulars laugh at the idea of danger from them.

ST. CLAIR, MOORE and ALLEN: Hear! Hear!

PETERS: The Indians are not to be despised. Every step of your way will be at the risk of ambuscades.

BRADDOCK: I despise such councils; the Colonists are old women. [PETERS rises in anger.]

HALKET: I am sure, General, you mean not those Colonists present.

BRADDOCK: No; the damned Pennsylvania Quakers. My apologies, Mr. Peters; you shall have your guard. Attend to it, Orme.

ORME: Yes, sir. [Takes notes.]

FRANKLIN: Do I understand, sir, you will build a road all the way to Duquesne?

BRADDOCK: Of a certainty.

FRANKLIN: The trail leads over mountains, through thickly grown forest land, there are deep morasses, steep cliffs.

BRADDOCK: Then we must have a good road.

FRANKLIN: I am conscious of the impropriety of arguing such matters with a military man, but——

BRADDOCK: [Interrupts.] In that you display your usual good sense.

HALKET: [Quickly sensing FRANKLIN'S unfinished sentence.] Captain Washington has had some experience in the irregular warfare of the forest. I should like his opinion.

BRADDOCK: [With a depreciating smile.] Oh, yes; why not? [To WASHINGTON.] You have traversed this trail?

WASHINGTON: I have, sir.

BRADDOCK: How long should it take to build this road?

WASHINGTON: If a road is necessary——

BRADDOCK: [Interrupting.] Necessary? How could we get through without a road?

WASHINGTON: Carry only what we really need. Use our horses for pack animals, sir.

BRADDOCK: [*Laughs.*] Pack animals? What of our artillery?

WASHINGTON: I doubt if artillery will be of sufficient value against the foe to warrant the delay caused by its transport.

BRADDOCK: You have not considered the need of a wagon train, then?

WASHINGTON: We could, with pack animals, carry sufficient food and ammunition.

ST. CLAIR: Preposterous!

MOORE: [*To ALLEN.*] He would have us march as Indians. Crude idea.

BRADDOCK: Methinks, Colonel, you have forgotten 'tis His Majesty's Army traveling on to Duquesne.

WASHINGTON: The road builders could follow us.

BRADDOCK: The British Regulars march with complete camping equipment and not as forest rangers.

ST. CLAIR: Good!

WASHINGTON: I beg leave to add that Duquesne is as yet weakly garrisoned, and the long dry weather will keep the rivers low.

HALKET: A matter of importance?

WASHINGTON: 'Twill make them hard to navigate—difficult for the French to secure reinforcement from Venango and the lake forts.

HALKET: So by dismounting the officers, taking to pack horses and pushing on without encumbrance——?

WASHINGTON: We would be sure of an easy victory.

ST. CLAIR: I would like to ask this young man what he thinks we really need on this expedition.

WASHINGTON: For the men, blankets, an axe, rifle and ammunition, sir.

[*ST. CLAIR, MOORE and ALLEN laugh. BRADDOCK has been paying scant attention, now looks up from papers.*]

ST. CLAIR: How would you carry our food and [*A gesture to his wine glass*] refreshment?

WASHINGTON: The food on pack animals, the rum—I would destroy it.

BRADDOCK: [*Laughs.*] Colonel Washington is not used to the ways of armies. The British soldier must have his rum. But enow of this, we will have a road and a wagon train.

FRANKLIN: But, sir, you must march through a dense forest and your line will be some four miles long. You will, I hope, take Duquesne——

BRADDOCK: [*Impatiently.*] Of a certainty we will take Duquesne.

FRANKLIN: —but you will, I fear, be in constant danger of being cut in two, for the French and Indians are dexterous in ambuscades.

BRADDOCK: [*Ironically.*] Thanks for the advice, Mr. Franklin. But I must remind you that although these savages may be formidable to raw American Militia, they will make no impression on disciplined troops.

HALKET: Still, General, such an eventuality should be considered.

BRADDOCK: Oh, Halket, have you a case of nerves? [*Some of the officers laugh, others are silent.*]

HALKET: Mayhap, sir. Rather would I have them now than later.

BRADDOCK: And what mean you by that?

HALKET: [*With a smile.*] You know, General, Ben Johnson once said: "No man is so foolish but he may sometimes give another good counsel, and no man so wise that he may not easily err if he takes no other counsel than his own."

BRADDOCK: [*Angrily turning on HALKET.*] Your words are nigh onto impertinence, sir.

HALKET: They were not so intended.

BRADDOCK: [*Thinks for a moment.*] I readily take counsel from those who by experience are fitted to give counsel.

ST. CLAIR: [*To BRADDOCK.*] I have heard, sir, that some of our Colonial advisors would send these forest rangers and the Colonial militia on ahead of our column to beat up the wood for lurking redskins. Mayhap our friend Halket would take such advice?

HALKET: I would at least lend an ear to such counsel.

BRADDOCK: Mayhap Colonel Washington's opinion on that matter would be of interest.

WASHINGTON: I fear I have already presumed in stating my opinions.

BRADDOCK: Your opinion was solicited. Come, Colonel, let's have it.

WASHINGTON: It would seem to me advisable to place the Virginia wood-rangers in the advance, to secure the pioneers and road-makers from an ambuscade.

BRADDOCK: Ensign Allen, you have been drilling the Virginia Militia; have you found them worthy of the honor of being placed in the van?

ALLEN: Not so, sir. They are languid, spiritless, unsoldier-like. And their officers—— [*Ends with a gesture of hopelessness.*]

BRADDOCK: What is wrong with the officers?

ALLEN: They are of the same social class as the men, no gentry among them. Why they were selected as leaders I cannot understand.

BRADDOCK: Mayhap Colonel Washington can explain that.

WASHINGTON: Those who know armies in their discipline find it difficult to understand the leadership of the frontier.

BRADDOCK: Why?

WASHINGTON: Such leadership is granted only to those whose force and individuality compel men to obey them.

BRADDOCK: Oh, damn your half-drilled rangers! I shall keep them as a rear guard. [*He lifts his glass.*] A toast to His Majesty's Regulars as an end to this profitless discussion. The Regulars!

ALL: His Majesty's Regulars! [*They drink.*]

[*BRADDOCK rises and WASHINGTON steps toward him.*]

WASHINGTON: Pardon me, sir. I would introduce Captain Jack Gist.

BRADDOCK: In a moment. [*He turns and talks quietly with ST. CLAIR and FRANKLIN.*]

MOORE: [*Drawing near looks GIST up and down.*] You would make a fine grenadier. But who the deuce made you a captain?

GIST: [*Tapping his rifle.*] This.

HALKET: [*Who has drawn near.*] You are well answered, Major.

BRADDOCK: Who have you there, Colonel Washington?

WASHINGTON: Captain Jack Gist, a famous Pennsylvania scout.

BRADDOCK: Let the man wait, I will see him in a day or two.

WASHINGTON: But, sir, he has fifty scouts with him. Their services should be of value.

BRADDOCK: [*To GIST.*] What pay do these men want?

GIST: [*Looking squarely at the General.*] No pay. Nothing.

BRADDOCK: And they will be worth just about that much to us. These men can not be drilled. I have experienced troopers on whom we can rely for such service.

GIST: Good-bye, Colonel Washington. When you have a separate command, send for me. [*Without further words, he turns his back to BRADDOCK and goes out the door at right.*]

BRADDOCK: [*Looks after him with angry astonishment.*] Well, I'll be damned! The ill-bred cur!

WASHINGTON: Sir, will you now talk with the Half-King?

BRADDOCK: Not now, my lad. I have more important matters to attend. Later, perhaps later. [*He turns and goes out door followed by all the officers except HALKET. WASHINGTON'S amazed, angry glance follows BRADDOCK'S retreating form.*]

HALKET: [*Kindly.*] Hold your council with the Half-King. I will go to arrange an audience with the General. [*He glances at CROGHAN, who follows him out into the hall. WASHINGTON and the HALF-KING, when alone, gaze at each other for a moment in silence.*]

HALF-KING: The Inglees, White Chief, is sick of a disease called foolishness. He leads his warriors to their death.

WASHINGTON: Do not be deceived, my brother. About him are wise counselors. A while yet and he will be guided by their words of wisdom.

HALF-KING: My brother speaks only with his lips.

WASHINGTON: My heart is sad, Tanacharisson. My brother would strike his wigwams and take his people over to our enemy.

HALF-KING: The White Chief listens not to my words.

WASHINGTON: He cannot give over to you the man you would have. 'Tis against the law of the whites. [*HALF-KING grunts.*] The White Chief has given his word the man will be tried, then punished.

HALF-KING: His are empty words.

WASHINGTON: Nay, my brother.

HALF-KING: Were you, Conotocarius, in command, I would believe.

WASHINGTON: If I gave you my word, the word of Conotocarius?

HALF-KING: Ever your tongue has spoken truth.

WASHINGTON: My brother, I cannot hide from you what your eyes see. There is confusion, delay. 'Tis always so at the starting, but once under way the English ever conquer. As our friend, your Nation prospers; as our enemy, you will be destroyed. Wait yet a while, and I, Conotocarius, will prevail upon those in command to right your wrongs—stop any disrespect to your women.

HALF-KING: Conotocarius has spoken. I, his brother, listen to his words. I wait.

[*Through the door at center LEAWANDA can be seen in the hall. She hears the HALF-KING'S voice, goes to the door, is about to enter when MOORE lurches out from the hall and seizes her, not noticing WASHINGTON and the HALF-KING.*]

MOORE: Ah, the pretty savage! I'll have a kiss, sweet one. [*LEAWANDA struggles in his arms, before WASHINGTON and the HALF-KING get to the girl. CROGHAN rushes from the hall, pulls MOORE from LEAWANDA and knocks him down. CROGHAN turns to LEAWANDA, who has drawn her knife.*]

CROGHAN: Sheath the blade, dear. No one shall harm you.

[*WASHINGTON is holding back the HALF-KING as MOORE rises, draws his sword, then springs forward to thrust at CROGHAN. LEAWANDA screams. WASHINGTON springs forward, grasps MOORE and hurls him back, drawing his sword and standing between MOORE and CROGHAN.*]

WASHINGTON: You would kill an unarmed man!

[*The HALF-KING, with uplifted tomahawk, stops in his tracks. HALKET and DUNBAR enter door at center, stop on the threshold.*]

MOORE: Get out of my way!

WASHINGTON: [*Coolly.*] Control yourself, sir. You are not helping our cause.

MOORE: To hell with the cause! Get out of my way! [*WASHINGTON does not reply but stands quietly with his sword crossed over MOORE'S, holding its point to the floor. MOORE is livid with rage.*] You would take on his quarrel?

WASHINGTON: Methinks, our swords can better be employed against the French and Indians.

MOORE: A more worthy foe than you. Step aside, I say, or give me satisfaction!

CROGHAN: This is my quarrel. I will give you satisfaction.

MOORE: Me, fight a filthy trader? I'll thrash you with the flat of my sword! I only fight my equals.

HALF-KING: [*Thrusts CROGHAN aside. WASHINGTON steps back, permitting the Indian to face MOORE.*] You would fight only those of rank. I am Tanacharisson, son of a Queen, Aliquippa, Half-King of a great nation. With the white man's weapon, I will fight you. [*MOORE is amazed, steps back at the cold fury of the chief.*]

HALKET: [*Moving forward toward them.*] Nay, Half-King, you are of too high a rank to fight such as he. And I cannot permit the son of Colonel Patrick Croghan so to soil his blade. [*In a stern voice to MOORE.*] Go to your quarters, you are under arrest.

[*MOORE sheathes his sabre, gives CROGHAN a black look. Goes to the door, as the others' eyes follow him. At the threshold turns, bows, and with a sneer on his face, leaves. LEAWANDA goes to stand beside the HALF-KING. An Indian suddenly enters the door, goes quickly to the HALF-KING, speaks a few low words, and as rapidly as he entered leaves.*]

HALF-KING: [*Taking a step toward WASHINGTON.*] Conotocarius, there comes a day when you will lead an army. If till then the Great Spirit suffers the Half-King to live, send thou for me, and I will take your side on the warpath.

WASHINGTON: You will leave us?

HALF-KING: 'Tis better so. I have spoken. [*He turns to LEAWANDA, to whom CROGHAN has gone.*]

CROGHAN: Leawanda, I will meet you on the banks of the Ohio.

LEAWANDA: No, my friend. The ways of your people are not the ways of mine.

CROGHAN: Is it your heart speaking?

LEAWANDA: What the heart says, it is not worth while. I have spoken.

CROGHAN: And yet we meet again.

LEAWANDA: To no purpose, my friend, God be with you. Good-bye. [*HALF-KING and LEAWANDA pass out the door. The others watch them go. As the door closes, CROGHAN turns, smiles ruefully.*]

CROGHAN: 'Tis a day of dupes and fools—nothing is impossible.

[ALLEN distraught, shaken, a wreck of a man, staggers in the center door, goes to the table.]

ALLEN: Brandy! brandy, for God's sake! [He drops in a chair, his head in his hands, moaning. HALKET quickly fills a glass, takes it to him.]

HALKET: Here lad, drink! [ALLEN gulps the wine, shudders.] Pull yourself together, lad. What's wrong with you?

ALLEN: Oh God, what a sight!

DUNBAR: What? What do you mean?

ALLEN: In my tent——

HALKET: What's in your tent?

ALLEN: The body!

DUNBAR: Body?

HALKET: Whose body?

ALLEN: My servant—scalped!—'twas horrible!—he was a good lad—Oh God help me!—I told him to keep away from the squaws.

DUNBAR: Zounds! 'Twas he——

HALKET: The Chief's daughter!

DUNBAR: By the eternal, I'll call out the troops!—the damned redskins! [He starts for the door, WASHINGTON touches his arm.]

WASHINGTON: I would advise against it, sir.

DUNBAR: [Turns.] An Englishman has been foully murdered!

HALKET: Washington is right, Dunbar. Take Allen to your quarters and await my coming.

DUNBAR: [Gazes at HALKET for a moment.] Very well. [He goes to ALLEN, touches his shoulder.] Come lad. [ALLEN shrinks.] Come. [He takes ALLEN'S arm, half lifts him. WASHINGTON assists and ALLEN and DUNBAR leave at center door.]

HALKET: A day of dupes and fools. 'Twas well said, Captain Croghan. [He turns to WASHINGTON.] Colonel Washington, do you realize your importance to this expedition?

WASHINGTON: I seem of little consequence.

HALKET: To some, mayhap. You are appreciated by others.

WASHINGTON: Thank you, sir.

HALKET: You are of a mind to resign? [WASHINGTON says nothing but gazes steadfastly at HALKET.] You do not approve of General Braddock's methods.

WASHINGTON: Who am I to criticize General Braddock?

HALKET: The whole army is not composed of Braddocks.

CROGHAN: Thank God, it isn't!

HALKET: Some of us may disagree with him—take a different course.

CROGHAN: 'Twill be necessary, if Duquesne is to be taken.

WASHINGTON: General Braddock is in command.

HALKET: You are a young man. [WASHINGTON nods acquiescence.] I am old enow to be your father—have seen much of the world—of life. You seem destined for a high place.

WASHINGTON: [Smiles ruefully.] Seem!

HALKET: You can make it certain. [WASHINGTON is silent.] The man who can control himself—keep his head—when others lose control——

CROGHAN: 'Tis not easy.

HALKET: —such a man will go far—if he does his duty.

WASHINGTON: I have never ceased to do what I believe my duty. The hard thing, to know what is one's duty.

HALKET: 'Tis hard for you today?

WASHINGTON: Yes. In what direction does my duty lie?

CROGHAN: To a foolish General or your own people?

HALKET: Not to a person, to a cause. The cause of the Colonies and the Crown are identical.

WASHINGTON: Sometimes, I wonder——

CROGHAN: As do we all.

HALKET: Then cease with vain doubting. Do not distract yourself by looking forward to things you cannot see. Do today's duty. Do not weaken.

[WASHINGTON stiffens, looks at HALKET for a long moment—a direct gaze that seems to go beyond. ORME enters.]

ORME: Pardon me, gentlemen. Colonel Washington, the General has a difficult duty for you to perform, if you will accept it.

[HALKET and CROGHAN narrowly watch WASHINGTON, who for a moment seems deep in thought before he then turns slowly to ORME.]

WASHINGTON: My compliments to the General and say—I will accept. [He bows to HALKET and CROGHAN and goes out the door at center. ORME follows.]

CROGHAN: You win, Colonel. Would that your eloquence may be as potent with General Braddock.

HALKET: Washington does his duty—and you?

CROGHAN: I follow Washington.

CURTAIN.

THAT IS MY ANSWER

A GEORGE WASHINGTON PLAY IN ONE ACT

DRAMATIS PERSONNAE

(IN ORDER OF THEIR APPEARANCE)

JACK STANFORD, Secretary to the Speaker.

LIEUTENANT RAHDEN, Aide to the Governor.

BETTY BYRD, Stanford's sweetheart.

LORD FAIRFAX, of Greenway Court.

CAPTAIN VARDON, Aide to the Governor.

MR. WHIPPLE, a Tory.

THOMAS JEFFERSON.

COLONEL GEORGE WASHINGTON.

MRS. BYRD.

PATRICK HENRY.

TIME: The morning of May 29, 1765.

PLACE: Office of the Speaker, in the Capitol of Virginia, at Williamsburg.

DESCRIPTION OF CHARACTERS

JACK STANFORD:

A fine type of young colonial gentleman, about twenty-one years of age. Dressed plainly but richly in clothes of the period.

LT. RAHDEN:

Aide to Governor Fauquier, a superior acting young soldier in his early twenties; considers himself a wit. Dressed in the British uniform—red coat faced with blue and edged with gold, gold epaulets, buff waistcoat and breeches, crimson sash; wears a sword, boots and tricorne hat of black edged with gold; wears his hair in a queue.

BETTY BYRD:

A beautiful young lady, of seventeen or eighteen years of age, in love with STANFORD. She is bright, witty, and lovable. Richly dressed in a polonaise gown of the period, a bonnet over her curled hair.

LORD FAIRFAX:

Seventy-six years of age; a tall man with a big frame and wide shoulders. Face deeply lined, of sour visage. He is irascible and a loyal-hearted subject of the King. A fine type of English nobleman. He is plainly though richly dressed in smallclothes and coat of dark color. On his head a grizzled wig worn in a queue. Wears a tricorne hat and carries a heavy cane.

CAPT. VARDON:

Of middle age; a shrewd, calculating type of British officer. Dressed in the British uniform as is RAHDEN.

MR. WHIPPLE:

A little past middle-age, the type of Colonial gentry that seeks to curry favor with the British Governor. Dressed in colonial costume; wears his hair in a queue.

THOMAS JEFFERSON:

Twenty-two years of age, tall, thin, raw-boned, has red hair and pointed features. His face intelligent with a kindly expression. His clothes of the period are of good material but plain and indifferently worn.

GEORGE WASHINGTON:

Thirty-three years of age, six feet two inches tall, in weight about two hundred pounds, rather large boned but well proportioned, graceful, dignified, thoughtful, modest in deportment. His complexion rather pale, his features strong, his hair light-brown in color, powdered, worn in a queue tied with a black ribbon. Plainly though richly dressed in dark clothes of the colonial period.

MRS. BYRD:

A buxom woman of middle age; proud, haughty; a confirmed Tory. Plain spoken and forceful. Wears a rich polonaise-fashioned costume of the period and a bonnet.

SET: *Office of the Speaker of the House of Burgesses, a rather plain room in colonial style. In the center of the rear wall, double doors that open on a balcony overlooking the hall where are held the sessions of the House. In the center of the right wall, a door. In the center of the left wall, a fireplace. Before the fireplace, a table, with a litter of books and papers, is on a line with the wall; back of the table is a chair. On each side of the door on the back wall, bookcases. Beside the door of the right wall, a cloak-rack. Portrait paintings of the period can be used to decorate the walls. A half dozen colonial chairs are placed about the room. When the doors of the back wall are opened, two rows of spectators, in seats running lengthwise of the stage, are seen on the balcony, a back drop representing the opposite wall of the hall.*

STANFORD *is at the table sorting and arranging papers. He gives a quick glance at* RAHDEN *as the Governor's Aide enters from left.* RAHDEN *smiles at* STANFORD, *goes to the table and half sits on one end of it.*

RAHDEN: [*Speaks as in soliloquy.*] Ever the faithful secretary—conscientious—industrious—painstaking.

STANFORD: Faugh!

RAHDEN: I marvel that he has the time to pay suit to the fair Elizabeth, daughter of that wealthy Colonel Byrd, of Westover. [*STANFORD for an instant gazes speculatively at RAHDEN and goes on with his work.*] Egad! This Stanford is a sly rogue. [*He slaps STANFORD on the back.*] Aren't you now?

STANFORD: [*Leans back, looks up with a grin.*] It is so strange that such as I should join the admirers that throng about Mistress Byrd!

RAHDEN: Strange, forsooth! Strange there are not more of them.

STANFORD: There are enow as 'tis.

RAHDEN: You know, Stanford, once I doubted you.

STANFORD: [*Gives RAHDEN a quizzical look.*] Doubted me?

RAHDEN: I thought you had a leaning toward these noisy, treasonable, malcontents.

STANFORD: [*Gives him a quick suspicious glance.*] What? You thought me a Whig?

RAHDEN: Aye, until I learned where lay your ambition.

STANFORD: And you doubt me no longer?

RAHDEN: Nay, my lad. If one would gain favor with the daughter he must also cultivate the mother.

STANFORD: And a stauncher Tory never lived.

RAHDEN: Aye—as proof of it, didn't she send packing that red-headed Thomas Jefferson?

STANFORD: [*Smiles.*] She did?

RAHDEN: And she detests this loud declaimer, Patrick Henry. [*Rises and crosses room.*] No, you are a loyal King's man old fellow.

STANFORD: You are sure of that?

RAHDEN: Aye. For did not a charming gossip whisper in mine own ear, that the regal Madam Byrd said you were a man who would go far in the King's service?

STANFORD: 'Tis pleased I am to find favor in her eyes.

RAHDEN: And now, you sly dog, you hope to discover equal favor in the pretty orbs of the charming Betty.

STANFORD: 'Twould be a favor indeed.

RAHDEN: Mayhap, you will soon have the chance.

STANFORD: How so?

RAHDEN: Perchance, she will accompany her mother this morning.

STANFORD: To the meeting of the House?

RAHDEN: No, obtuse one. She will be here to assist in putting the pressure on the austere Colonel Washington.

STANFORD: [*All attention.*] Pressure? Colonel Washington?

RAHDEN: Why, I overheard that master of intrigue, Captain Vardon——

STANFORD: The Governor's confidant?

RAHDEN: —conspiring with our good Tory, Mr. Whipple. They would form a staunch King's party in the House.

STANFORD: I thought there was a King's party.

RAHDEN: Aye, but they are well-nigh overcome by the vaporings of this mad Patrick Henry.

STANFORD: How futile the efforts of the King's party!

RAHDEN: They would have a leader.

STANFORD: Ah——. And they have selected Colonel Washington.

RAHDEN: They think him a good choice?

STANFORD: He has great fame in the Colony.

RAHDEN: Aye. Well they can have him, it concerns me not. But I would be nigh when Vardon dangles the King's dazzling favor before his eyes.

STANFORD: Bribed?

RAHDEN: Bribery and coercion.

STANFORD: Coercion?

RAHDEN: Aye. The weight of the loyal gentry. Lord Fairfax, Madam Byrd, Mr. Whipple and, mayhap, his Excellency himself.

STANFORD: They approach him soon?

RAHDEN: Aye, any moment now, in this very room. Then they send for the doughty Colonel and on the rack he goes. [*Strolls to door at right, turns with hand on knob.*] Luck with the charming Betty. Should I meet her—any message from the lovelorn?

STANFORD: [*Leans back indolently.*] Mayhap she would have some business to transact with the speaker—his secretary can always arrange an interview for her.

RAHDEN: [*With a grin.*] If she first interview the secretary. [*He leaves.*]

[*As the door closes, STANFORD leaps to his feet, paces back and forth, stops in thought, again paces, thinks, goes to table, picks up papers, grabs his hat, starts for door at right. There is a rap on the door. Quickly puts papers back on desk, throws his hat on a chair and sits at desk.*]

STANFORD: [*In composed voice.*] Enter.

BETTY: [*Enters door. In mock bewilderment.*] If you please, where, sir, may I find the speaker's secretary?

STANFORD: [*On his feet, manages a smile.*] I am he. At your service, madam.

BETTY: [*She curtsies deeply.*] 'Tis the first I knew speakers had such gallant and handsome secretaries.

STANFORD: Betty, you rogue! [*Goes to her.*] You just met that worthless Rahden.

BETTY: [*Archly.*] Aren't you glad I did?

STANFORD: This is in proof I am. [*He takes her in his arms. Then is suddenly thoughtful, tense.*]

BETTY: [*Looks up from his shoulder, holds him away from her.*] Jack, you are troubled.

STANFORD: Why, my dear——

BETTY: [*Shakes him.*] Tell me, beloved, what has happened?

STANFORD: Betty, if you loved a man——

BETTY: Why, I love——

STANFORD: —then you discover he is not what, in the world's eyes, he seems to be— [*BETTY looks at him with eyes of fear.*] you discover he stands for that which is anathema to your family——

BETTY: Jack, you would have me understand——

STANFORD: That I am for the Colonies.

BETTY: [*With an intake of her breath.*] Oh——!

STANFORD: For the Colonies—against the King—against the Stamp Act.

[*He avoids her eyes, looks out into space. For a moment she gazes at him in amazement, then a slow smile comes to her face, she goes to him, her arm steals through his, with her other hand she turns his face toward her.*]

BETTY: Jack, is not a promised woman almost a wife?

STANFORD: Why? Mayhap, but——

BETTY: And if 'tis the duty of a wife ever to follow her husband——

STANFORD: What mean you?

BETTY: As Madam Stanford, would it not be my duty to stand beside you for the Colonies?

STANFORD: [*In amazement.*] You—for the Colonies?

BETTY: Even I.

STANFORD: Betty! My beloved. [*He embraces her.*]

BETTY: And I thought you, like mother, blindly following the King. [*Sadly.*] Alack and alas, when married we will have naught to quarrel about.

STANFORD: [*Suddenly he has a thought.*] Betty, you would further the cause?

BETTY: In so far as a woman can.

STANFORD: The Tories are affrighted. They must have a leader.

BETTY: Of a verity, they need one.

STANFORD: They would have Colonel Washington.

BETTY: Colonel Washington!

STANFORD: Vardon, Whipple, your mother——

BETTY: Mother?

STANFORD: —Lord Fairfax, are together here in a moment and will endeavor to persuade him to accept. They will offer him high honors.

BETTY: Much good that will do.

STANFORD: If you can get word to Tom Jefferson, he——

BETTY: Yes, yes——

STANFORD: He will get word at once to Patrick Henry.

BETTY: By fair means or foul——

STANFORD: No one knows how Washington stands. Heretofore he has always been for the King. But mayhap——

BETTY: Ssh——!

[*There is the tap-tap of a cane outside.*]

STANFORD: It must be Lord Fairfax.

FAIRFAX: [*Enters the door, leaning on his cane.*] Lord Fairfax is here. [*They turn at his words. Betty quickly recovers.*] What were you youngsters plotting?

BETTY: [*Drops him an elaborate curtsy.*] My Lord Fairfax. [*STANFORD follows her lead and bows.*]

FAIRFAX: [*Makes a slow and courtly bow.*] What is this I see? The beauty of Westover, alone with this [*he smiles*] scapegrace of a speaker's secretary.

BETTY: [*Hanging her head.*] I'll allow, My Lord, 'tis quite proper.

STANFORD: We are—that is—Mistress Betty has—ah—ah—

FAIRFAX: [*Laughs.*] So—that is how the land lies! Well, well, congratulations, my boy. [*He extends a hand toward Stanford.*]

BETTY: [*Quickly.*] Oh—'tis to be a secret, My Lord. You alone know.

[*STANFORD takes FAIRFAX'S hand and with his other hand signals behind his back for BETTY to go.*]

STANFORD: Thank you, My Lord.

FAIRFAX: [*Wagging a finger at BETTY.*] I have kept many a secret in my time, fair lady, but none more charming than this.

BETTY: I know 'tis safe with you, My Lord. [*At STANFORD'S frantic signal.*] I—I must go now. [*She straightens her bonnet, laughs, and runs to the door, curtsies, throws a kiss to FAIRFAX, then one to STANFORD and leaves as they bow.*]

FAIRFAX: [*Turns to STANFORD.*] Bless 'em! What a beauty she is! Were I two score years younger, my lad. [*He goes to a chair.*]

STANFORD: Methinks I would not be as happy as I am now.

FAIRFAX: [*Sinks into a chair.*] Captain Vardon and John Whipple are here. They requested my presence.

STANFORD: I understand they are to be here presently.

FAIRFAX: I am not of a disposition to be kept waiting.

STANFORD: You have seen Colonel Washington of late, sir?

FAIRFAX: Aye. At the Raleigh Tavern. We had breakfast together.

STANFORD: [*Ill at ease.*] The Colonel is making many experiments in agriculture, I understand.

FAIRFAX: Aye. And if you are interested in them, he will talk aplenty on the subject; though on other matters, these days, he be silent enough.

[*VARDON and WHIPPLE enter from right.*]

VARDON: [*Bows.*] My Lord Fairfax. Ah, you received my request.

FAIRFAX: [*Testily.*] Sir, I am punctual.

VARDON: I trust you were not waiting long.

FAIRFAX: Over long.

WHIPPLE: Good morning, My Lord.

FAIRFAX: Good morning, sir.

VARDON: We will at once take up the matter at hand.

STANFORD: [*Acting on his dismissal.*] Good day, My Lord. [*He bows to FAIRFAX.*]

FAIRFAX: Good day, lad. [*STANFORD exits after weighting down some papers on the desk.*] There is a good lad, his father one of the finest gentlemen in the Colony.

WHIPPLE: Loyal to His Majesty our King?

FAIRFAX: Aye. He stands staunch when others, who should have more sense, are uttering vile words of treason. Would were more like him!

VARDON: Methinks there are plenty, but——

FAIRFAX: Damned cowards, sir; afraid to speak their mind.

WHIPPLE: What they need is a leader.

FAIRFAX: Aye, a leader, one to stand four-square to the world, loyal to the King.

VARDON: A leader, forceful—adroit—faithful.

WHIPPLE: One who can carry out His Excellency's program.

FAIRFAX: Ah, he has a program?

VARDON: Governor Fauquier would adjust all the differences between the Colony and the Motherland.

FAIRFAX: With those two prize fools, the Duke of Grafton and Bané, playing into the hands of the deer-stalker, Patrick Henry, 'tis a matter not so easy to bring about.

WHIPPLE: Methinks with a strong King's party in the House of Burgesses——

FAIRFAX: Aye.

WHIPPLE: —and the right leadership it can be done.

FAIRFAX: Leadership that decent men can look up to and honor. Leadership that wots not of discouragement or reverse. Leadership that's not afraid to lead.

WHIPPLE: Hear! Hear!

FAIRFAX: Leadership that will take the wind out of the sails of that low-country demagogue, Patrick Henry, aigh! [*Strikes cane on floor.*] Point me out such a man.

VARDON: We have one such in mind, sir.

FAIRFAX: Aye? Name the man.

VARDON: Colonel Washington.

FAIRFAX: [*Pleased and surprised.*] My boy, Washington?

VARDON: He has in himself all the qualities for the leadership.

WHIPPLE: He is no orator. But for solid judgment there is no man in the Colony his superior.

FAIRFAX: Aye. [*Sadly.*] If he would——

VARDON: [*Astonished.*] Think you, My Lord, he would not accept this leadership?

FAIRFAX: Humph, I wonder. You have asked him?

VARDON: I sent word to him that the Governor would appreciate it were he to meet with us at this hour.

WHIPPLE: Also that you would be present, My Lord.

FAIRFAX: Well, he may come.

VARDON: He will come. 'Tis practically an order from His Excellency the Governor.

FAIRFAX: [*Looks at VARDON, quizzically.*] Washington, during his public life, has had but small cause to feel kindly toward the governors of this Colony.

[*There is a rap on the door at right.*]

WHIPPLE: Mayhap 'tis Colonel Washington.

[*THOMAS JEFFERSON, followed by STANFORD, enters, with some papers in his hand. STANFORD goes at once to desk, sorts some papers he has left there.*]

FAIRFAX: Oh, 'tis you, Tom Jefferson.

JEFFERSON: Good morning, gentlemen. [*Bows to FAIRFAX.*] I am sorry if we intrude, My Lord.

VARDON: Is there anything I can do for you, Mr. Jefferson?

JEFFERSON: Mr. Stanford has a marked copy of the Gazette for me. [*STANFORD hands him a paper, indicating a marked passage.*] Thank you, ah——

VARDON: More of the Stamp Act, Jefferson?

JEFFERSON: [*Smiles.*] No, sir. Just a matter of a cock-fight. [*To STANFORD.*] Mr. Henry asked me to give you this copy of resolutions he is about to introduce. [*Offers STANFORD papers.*]

FAIRFAX: Bah, resolutions!

STANFORD: For my minutes? Thank you, Mr. Jefferson. [*Takes papers.*]

JEFFERSON: [*To STANFORD.*] The House is about to be called to order.

STANFORD: I am leaving for the hall at once. [*He assembles his papers.*]

JEFFERSON: [*To FAIRFAX.*] My Lord, are you attending the session?

FAIRFAX: Not today, sir.

JEFFERSON: Burgess Henry is to introduce some resolutions of marked significance, sir.

FAIRFAX: I care not what that good-for-nothing introduces!

WHIPPLE: What is the purport of these resolutions?

JEFFERSON: I am not permitted to state, sir, until they are

introduced. [*JEFFERSON goes to the door at right, bows.*] I bid you good morning, gentlemen.

WHIPPLE: Good morning, sir.

[*JEFFERSON leaves.*]

FAIRFAX: Tom Jefferson, a bright young man but a free-thinker. He is pitch and toss with Henry.

WHIPPLE: [*To STANFORD.*] I trust you are not allowing Tom Jefferson to lead you by the nose.

STANFORD: He nor any other man leads me by the nose, sir.

[*STANFORD passes behind them and goes to the door at center to leave.*]

VARDON: Just a minute, Mr. Stanford. [*STANFORD stops.*] I would see those resolutions.

STANFORD: I may not permit them to leave my hand, sir.

VARDON: Damme, sir! I am the Governor's representative.

STANFORD: Sorry, sir.

VARDON: Nevertheless, give them over to me.

STANFORD: [*Coldly.*] I must refuse, sir.

VARDON: [*Rises in anger.*] Give them over to me, sirrah.

STANFORD: 'Tis the law.

VARDON: Unless you do, I will see that you no longer serve as secretary to the speaker.

STANFORD: My resignation will go to the speaker as soon as I can write it.

VARDON: So—you, too, are a traitor to your King!

STANFORD: [*In cold anger.*] For that I expect an apology or——

VARDON: Or what?

STANFORD: —or the satisfaction due one gentleman to another.

VARDON: You whelp. I'll take the flat of my sword to you.

FAIRFAX: Tut! Tut! Captain Vardon. [*Sternly.*] You have no right thus to address a gentleman. [*He rises.*] 'Tis such acts as yours and those of other officers of the Crown that have largely contributed to this bitterness in the Colony. You are in the wrong. [*For a moment there is a tense silence.*] You will apologize.

VARDON: Apologize?

FAIRFAX: 'Tis what I said. Any gentleman would do so.

VARDON: But, My Lord——

FAIRFAX: [*To STANFORD.*] Will you be so kind, Jack, as to have my carriage called?

WHIPPLE: [*Quickly.*] My Lord, I am sure Captain Vardon spoke hastily.

VARDON: [*Realizes he has gone too far.*] I have been so wrought up over treason on every side that my ire rose. I regret my words, sir. [*To STANFORD.*] Mr. Stanford [*bows*], I hope you accept my sincere apology?

STANFORD: I do, sir.

FAIRFAX: Never mind the carriage, Jack. [*He sits. STANFORD opens the door and a confused mingling of voices is heard as though the Burgesses were taking their seats; he exits, and with the closing of the door the noise ceases.*]

VARDON: My Lord, I greatly regret the losing of my temper in your presence.

FAIRFAX: [*Testily.*] A man who cannot command his temper should not think of being a man of affairs.

VARDON: I accept your rebuke, My Lord.

[*There is a rap on the door.*]

WHIPPLE: It should be Colonel Washington. [*Goes to door.*]

FAIRFAX: Ah, if 'tis, there, Captain Vardon, you will see a man with the devil's own temper but ever he is in command of it.

WHIPPLE: [*Opens door.*] Good morning, Colonel Washington.

WASHINGTON: [*Enters.*] Good morning, gentlemen.

VARDON: [*Bows.*] Good morning, Colonel.

FAIRFAX: Good morning, George.

VARDON: Won't you be seated, sir?

WASHINGTON: I have but little time to spare.

VARDON: His Excellency has entrusted to me a very grave mission.

WASHINGTON: The House is about to be called to order, sir.

WHIPPLE: It concerns you, Colonel. [*WASHINGTON silently listens.*]

VARDON: Governor Fauquier is desirous of adjusting the differences between the Colony and the Crown.

WASHINGTON: In the matters at issue, has His Excellency the authority to act?

VARDON: He cannot assume the prerogatives of the King's ministers, still with a better feeling engendered—a saner view taken by many of the Burgesses—a happy solution of our troubles might be effected.

WASHINGTON: I would it could be so.

WHIPPLE: With your assistance, sir, it can be done.

WASHINGTON: My assistance? [*Lifts eyebrows.*]

FAIRFAX: George, the Governor would have you become the leader of the King's party.

WHIPPLE: [*Insinuatingly.*] Your most cordial friends are for the King, Colonel.

FAIRFAX: This is something beyond friendship. 'Tis loyalty to your King.

WHIPPLE: Your forefathers have all been King's men.

VARDON: And the King richly rewards his loyal supporters. [*WASHINGTON takes a long look at VARDON.*]

FAIRFAX: 'Tis time for a strong man to rise in the House of Burgesses, and confound those malcontents whose every breath is an insult to the Crown.

WASHINGTON: My Lord, they but voice their objections to the Stamp Act.

FAIRFAX: Have the Whigs bewitched you? [*WASHINGTON smiles.*] Will you be affected by the vaporings of this Patrick Henry? You, a member of the gentry, cannot associate without contamination with this deer-stalker. He is as mad as a March hare.

WASHINGTON: I have been conscious of no degrading influence in his society, My Lord.

FAIRFAX: Why he used to bring me ale when I passed Hanover Court House. He is a good-for-naught bartender. I tell you, he is a coarse, wench-chucking vagabond.

WASHINGTON: I have not found him so, sir.

FAIRFAX: And now, because he won a dirty damage case against some tuppenny person, he sits in the House of Burgesses and associates with gentlemen!

WHIPPLE: 'Tis he who is causing all this furore over the Stamp Act.

WASHINGTON: There are others who oppose it.

FAIRFAX: Damme, George! 'Tis the will of our King.

WASHINGTON: Pardon me, sir—the King's ministers.

VARDON: The Stamp Act is surely of small consequence in Virginia.

WASHINGTON: It looms large throughout all the Colonies.

FAIRFAX: All the Colonies? What have we Virginians to do with the other Colonies?

WASHINGTON: The Stamp Act will be enforced throughout all the Colonies, and resistance comes from all.

WHIPPLE: Mostly 'tis centered in that den of sedition, Boston Town.

FAIRFAX: Bah! Those Puritan dissenters! Are we to let them lead us around by the nose?

WASHINGTON: Time is passing, sir. I see no profit in such discussion.

FAIRFAX: Humph, 'tis so.

VARDON: [To WASHINGTON.] 'Tis high time that some man, who by his past record has gained the confidence of all elements in the Colony, stem this tide of disloyalty to the Crown by acting as peace-maker, and by his example and precept cause all men to feel that nothing but woe can come from this flagrant defiance of His Majesty's ministers.

WHIPPLE: No man is better fitted to do this than you, Colonel.

FAIRFAX: You would be performing a lasting service to Virginia and to the Crown as well.

VARDON: Your name would be writ large in the history of the Colony.

FAIRFAX: A service beyond price.

WASHINGTON: [To FAIRFAX.] What would you have me do?

VARDON: Draw to your side all the gentry who are loyal—inspire them to use every influence to win over those that hold against the Crown. Pacify the discontented.

WHIPPLE: Even so.

VARDON: We will take care of the firebrands.

WASHINGTON: What do you mean by that, sir?

VARDON: They will destroy themselves.

[The door in the center is opened and MRS. BYRD flounces in. The gentlemen rise and bow.]

MRS. BYRD: Pardon me, gentlemen, for such unceremonious entrance, but that—that low-country demagogue is speaking.

FAIRFAX: You mean Patrick Henry, madam?

MRS. BYRD: Yes, that husband of an inn-keeper's daughter. Half the time he is dressed in buckskins. Times are getting beyond me when such men are allowed to sit as delegates in our House of Burgesses.

WASHINGTON: [With a smile.] I have worn buckskins, madam.

MRS. BYRD: Buckskin has its place in the forest. George Washington, do you presume to defend this Whig leader?

WASHINGTON: He does not need me to defend him, madam.

MRS. BYRD: I can stomach your gentlemen rebels, but your half-baked, bumpkin patriot is too much. Breeding, not to speak of loyalty, seems to count for naught nowadays.

VARDON: I hope, madam, you are not classing Colonel Washington among the rebels.

MRS. BYRD: Well, I would have my doubts about classing you as such, George. You may flirt with these malcontents, but by birth, breeding and training you are a gentleman, and I warrant at heart you are a loyal subject of the King. [WASHINGTON smiles.]

WHIPPLE: Of course he is loyal to the King, madam. He is even now considering the acceptance of the leadership of the King's party in the House.

MRS. BYRD: You are to be congratulated, George.

VARDON: We await his acceptance, do we not, gentlemen?

FAIRFAX: I for one do. George, you have worn with honor the uniform of the King's service, as have your forefathers before you. You are an aristocrat—a man of gentle blood—on the side of law, order and government. The King represents government.

VARDON: The people of this Colony have trust in you, sir. What you do will be regarded as best for all.

WASHINGTON: I doubt that my example would be of much importance in any case.

MRS. BYRD: La! George Washington, you are ever too modest.

VARDON: Your example, your leadership, in the King's cause I veritably believe means future prosperity and happiness to the Colony.

[For a moment there is silence. WASHINGTON is deep in thought.]

FAIRFAX: [With an appealing gesture.] Come, my boy, take your stand on the King's side where you rightfully belong.

VARDON: May I tell His Excellency you accept this honor, Colonel?

[WASHINGTON is silently looking into space. Takes a turn up and down the room, pauses beside the door, listens a moment. Suddenly swings one door to the gallery open. The other door to allow the impassioned voice of PATRICK HENRY to be heard.]

HENRY: [Off stage.] Mr. Speaker, we are free men; we have a right to be so; to enjoy all the privileges and immunities of our fellow-subjects in England. While we retain a just sense of that freedom, and those rights and privileges necessary for its safety and security, we shall never give up the right of representation. Let it suffice to say, once and for all, we will never be taxed but by our own representatives. This is the great badge of freedom. When we see the British Parliament trampling upon that right and acting to destroy it, we wish to see the united wisdom and fortitude of America collected for its defence. Taxation without representation is tyranny!

VOICE: Treason! Treason!

HENRY: Ceasar had his Brutus, Charles I his Cromwell, and George III——

SPEAKER: Treason!

HENRY: [Voice rising above the cries.] —may profit by their example!

OTHERS: Treason! Treason!

HENRY: If this be treason, make the most of it!

[There is a confusion of applause and shouts of treason. WASHINGTON closes the door.]

WASHINGTON: Gentlemen, that is my answer.

CURTAIN

THE INDIAN'S PROPHECY
A GEORGE WASHINGTON PLAY IN ONE ACT

DRAMATIS PERSONAE

(IN ORDER OF THEIR APPEARANCE)

COLONEL ROGERS, *of the British Army.*

DOCTOR CRAIK, *a friend and companion of Washington.*

CRAWFORD, *a woodsman and guide of the party.*

AMES ⎱ *Frontiersmen.*
HARE ⎰

ANUNDAHA, *an Indian, Messenger of the Grand Sachem.*

COLONEL GEORGE WASHINGTON.

THE GRAND SACHEM.

FRONTIERSMEN, INDIANS and SURVEYORS.

The cast can be enlarged to as many Frontiersmen and Indians as desired.

TIME: *Toward evening, late summer of 1770.*

PLACE: *Washington's camp on the Kanawah.*

DESCRIPTION OF CHARACTERS

COLONEL ROGERS:

A middle-aged officer of the British army. May be dressed in the uniform of the English Army or in traveling clothes of the period. He is booted and wears a sword. Hair worn in a queue.

DR. CRAIK:

Forty years of age, staunch friend and admirer of WASHINGTON. *Dressed much the same as* WASHINGTON.

CRAWFORD:

A middle-aged frontiersman, tall, sinewy, bronzed. A fine type of colonial woodsman; crude, sincere, straightforward. He wears doeskin Indian hunting shirt, leggings and a coonskin cap. His own hair worn in a queue. At his belt a hunting knife and tomahawk; in his hands a long rifle.

AMES and HARE:

Men of the type of CRAWFORD, *dressed the same.*

ANUNDAHA:

An Indian, stripped to waist, doeskin leggings, ornamental breech-cloth. Wears amulets, beads, etc. Carries scalping knife and tomahawk.

COLONEL GEORGE WASHINGTON:

Is thirty-eight years of age, six feet two inches tall, in weight about two hundred and ten pounds, large-boned but well-proportioned; dignified and commanding though modest in deportment. His complexion bronzed by an outdoor life, his features strong, his hair light brown in color and tied in a queue. He is dressed in Colonial clothes of a dark serviceable quality, wears boots, three-cornered hat and a military coat.

GRAND SACHEM:

An old Indian chief with a majestic dignity. Noted as an orator. Wears an imposing feathered headdress and handsome bedecked Indian garments, with blanket. Carries tomahawk and scalping knife.

INDIANS:

Dressed in tribal costumes and armed with tomahawks and scalping knives, rifles or bows and arrows. Many of them with blankets.

SURVEYORS and FRONTIERSMEN:

The surveyors are dressed in rough Colonial costumes, some in shirt sleeves with vests, and tricorn hats. Frontiersmen dressed as CRAWFORD, AMES *and* HARE, *and armed with rifles which are always near at hand; at their belts, knives.*

SET: *A wooded glen on the banks of the Ohio River, with a vista through the trees showing the river and the mountains in the distance. At the right an outcropping of rocks forms a higher level about three feet above the level of the stage. In the center the smouldering embers of a camp-fire, over it a kettle suspended on saplings. It is late summer evening and at the end of the scene the sun sinks behind the distant mountains. Blanket-rolls and camp paraphernalia are arranged in an orderly manner. At the extreme left, rear, can be seen a portion of a tent and the prows of birch-bark canoes near the river.*

The woodland setting permits of beautiful scenic effects and the costumes of the frontiersmen and the Indians lend additional color to the picture.

At the right front COLONEL ROGERS *and* DR. CRAIK *are sitting on fallen logs or rocks. The* FRONTIERSMEN *and* SURVEYORS *are gathered in a group at the left rear a bit withdrawn from the fire.*

DR. CRAIK: You leave us on the morrow, Colonel?

ROGERS: I regret that other duties necessitate my going.

DR. CRAIK: Colonel Washington will be sorry to see you depart.

ROGERS: Faith, that pleases me. In this short acquaintance I have acquired a fervent admiration for the man.

DR. CRAIK: 'Tis ever so with those who come in contact with him.

ROGERS: Not many men of his standing would take all this trouble for others.

DR. CRAIK: He believed that the men in the Colonies who fought during the French and Indian war should be rewarded.

[*Noting a stir among the men* DR. CRAIK, ROGERS *and* CRAWFORD *turn and see them gazing at the outcropping where on the higher level stands* ANUNDAHA, *his right arm with open hand held aloft in a token of peace. Some of the men who had grasped their rifles lay them down.* CRAWFORD *rises and steps toward the Indian.*]

CRAWFORD: Who is this that comes with a sign of peace?

ANUNDAHA: Anundaha, of the Iroquois.

CRAWFORD: Anundaha! Methinks we have met before.

ANUNDAHA: By the banks of the Monongahela.

CRAWFORD: Well I remember. Whom do you seek?

ANUNDAHA: The White Chief of the Long-knives.

CRAWFORD: Colonel Washington? [ANUNDAHA nods.] He returns anon. What would you with him?

ANUNDAHA: I am the messenger of the Grand Sachem.

CRAWFORD: [Astonished.] The Grand Sachem?

ANUNDAHA: He would hold talk with the White Chief.

CRAWFORD: Whereabouts the Grand Sachem?

ANUNDAHA: [Points to forest.] He comes.

CRAWFORD: Anundaha, tell the Grand Sachem that Washington, the Chief of the Long-knives, will welcome him to his fire.

[ANUNDAHA nods and disappears into the forest.]

HARE: [To CRAWFORD.] Better I keep an eye on the varlet.

CRAWFORD: Aye, Hare. We're a small party. Ye can't never tell.

[HARE craftily follows ANUNDAHA into the forest.]

DR. CRAIK: [To CRAWFORD.] Is not the Grand Sachem he who commanded the French Indian Allies at the defeat of Braddock?

CRAWFORD: Aye. The same.

[CRAIK, ROGERS and CRAWFORD return to their original places.]

ROGERS: Think you they come in peace?

CRAWFORD: I reckon they do.

ROGERS: But you had a man follow the Indian.

CRAWFORD: If yer wise, ye'll take no chances in the forest.

DR. CRAIK: As Colonel Washington told General Braddock.

ROGERS: Poor Braddock. He would not listen.

CRAWFORD: 'Tis ever the way with British officers.

ROGERS: Ever?

CRAWFORD: They's too stiff-necked to take a Colonial's advice.

ROGERS: I say, now—

CRAWFORD: Lucky fer the rest of Braddock's force that Colonel Washington was in that fight—

DR. CRAIK: Indeed, 'twas fortunate.

CRAWFORD: —ur their scalps 'ud all be curin' in the wigwams of the redskins.

DR. CRAIK: You forget, Crawford, Colonel Rogers is an officer of the King's Army.

CRAWFORD: An I'm hopin' he l'arns sumpthin' from him bein' here. Not many Britishers do.

ROGERS: [Amused.] You speak of me as a Britisher, are you not also a subject of the King?

CRAWFORD: This is a King's Colony. But, Sir, I am an American.

ROGERS: [Laughing.] Well! Well! I say? Doctor, what a spirit of independence is growing in the Colonies!

DR. CRAIK: [Seeking to change the subject.] We were speaking of the battle on the Monongehala, a favorite subject of mine. I was there.

ROGERS: You were?

DR. CRAIK: Yes, I witnessed the gallantry of Colonel Washington.

CRAWFORD: An' there's another amongst us who was there that knows.

ROGERS: I would have speech with him.

CRAWFORD: [Turning to the group of Frontiersmen.] Hi! Jonathan Ames, the Colonel would have speech with thee.

[AMES comes forward and stands silently near the three.]

ROGERS: I hear you were with General Braddock?

AMES: I was with Colonel Washington.

ROGERS: Then you saw the Colonel in action on the Monongahela?

AMES: Aye, so I did.

ROGERS: I am told he has a cool head in action.

AMES: 'Tis more than a cool head he has.

ROGERS: Then he displayed other qualities?

AMES: He had to. I never seed a man that could be in more places at once; trying to rally the scart Britishers who was arunnin' every which-a-way; directin' the fire of us Colonials; chargin' into the red varmints in a tarin' rage; pointin' a cannon and firin' it hisself. I seed one horse shot down under him an they tells me another went down with him a bit later.

ROGERS: I understand 'tis a miracle he lived throughout the day.

AMES: Aye, with them British cowards shootin' at friend as well as foe.

DR. CRAIK: A truce with your tongue, man. 'Tis not beseeming that you, a British subject, should so speak of the King's Regimentals.

AMES: Didn't I seed 'em with my own eyes? Them redcoats that looked down on the likes of us Colonials and laughed at Colonel Washington behind his back.

DR. CRAIK: Tut, Tut, man!

AMES: Didn't I seed 'em turn pale at the first war-whoop of the red varmints, then turn tail and run to save their hair?

ROGERS: They were surprised, ambushed. Indian fighting was new to them.

AMES: An' it was their own fault. Colonel Washington knowed the ways of the savages and he tried to tell 'em.

DR. CRAIK: I, too, was at the Monongahela, Ames. Practically every British officer was killed or wounded in that engagement. They were brave though misguided men.

CRAWFORD: Huh! Brave!

DR. CRAIK: They were bewildered, but remember, man, the King's troops have written too glorious a record on the pages of history———

AMES: So!

DR. CRAIK: —for anyone so to speak of them.

AMES: Uh huh, but I'de bet a hunnerd guineas, if I had it, or

Old Betsy [*Patting the stock of his rifle*] that a company of Colonial Militia under Colonel Washington could give a wallopin' to any three companies of British Regulars.

DR. CRAIK: God grant the time never comes that the Colonies must fight the Motherland!

CRAWFORD: It'll come all right if they don't give us our just dues. This here Stamp Act and the tax on tea's just a sample o' the treatment we git from the King.

ROGERS: You are being treated justly in the granting of lands.

CRAWFORD: Aye, and didn't the ministry oppose the grantin' of lands to us as won the Forks of the Ohio for 'em?

DR. CRAIK: Finally they were granted when Colonel Washington was so insistent in the matter.

CRAWFORD: The Colonel fights fer what he thinks is right, and if the Britishers go too far he'll fight 'em.

ROGERS: Why, Crawford, you are talking sedition. One would believe, from your speech, that you were from Boston Town.

CRAWFORD: Aye, and I stand with the Bostoners against the right of the King to tax the Colonies.

AMES: What right has old fat George to tax the likes of us?

ROGERS: [*Rising in anger.*] I will not allow any man so to speak of His Majesty the King.

DR. CRAIK: Ames, you are going too far!

AMES: I say what I please to any man. And mayhap, if the King hisself was here, I'd say the same to his face.

ROGERS: [*Furious.*] Withdraw those words, man, or I will give you the chastising you deserve. [*Rests his hand on the hilt of his sword.*]

AMES: I withdraw my words fer no man. Chastise me? Try it! [*As they stand glaring at each other, WASHINGTON comes out of the forest, stops on the higher level of the outcropping, and surveys the scene before him. He is followed by HARE. The Frontiersmen and the others have gathered about the belligerents and are not aware of his presence.*]

DR. CRAIK: Ames, your conduct is unwarranted. Colonel, you—

ROGERS: [*To CRAIK*] Don't interfere, Sir! [*To AMES.*] Retract, I say!

AMES: Never!

ROGERS: Then by the Eternal, I'll—! [*Draws his sword.*]

WASHINGTON: Stop! What means this?

[*WASHINGTON steps down from the rocks, strides forward and stands between the combatants. The others draw back to a respectful distance.*]

DR. CRAIK: You have arrived in the nick of time, Sir.

WASHINGTON: Colonel Rogers, why have you drawn the sword?

ROGERS: This ignorant fellow has insulted His Majesty the King. He will not retract. I would chastise the man.

WASHINGTON: Ames, we have been comrades in the service of the King. I have long known you to be a brave man and trustworthy, but you have a ready tongue and a temper not always under control.

AMES: All I sed was: What right had old fat George to tax us? And I bean't going to retract them words.

WASHINGTON: It is not beseeming for one of your known courage so to speak of another when he is not present. Neither do I expect a guest to be insulted by one of my men.

AMES: I didn't insult him, Colonel.

WASHINGTON: You insulted the King of Great Britain. To an Englishman, the King represents his government, an insult to one is an insult to the other.

CRAWFORD: Aye, 'tis true.

WASHINGTON: Could you expect a brave officer, like Colonel Rogers, to sit quietly by and not resent your remark?

AMES: [*A bit crestfallen, scratches his head.*] It bean't my idea to insult your guest, Sir. But the King ain't got no right to tax us Colonials, just the same.

WASHINGTON: Very well, Ames. Remember, we are passing through troublesome times when it is best for every man to keep a close tongue. [*Alters his tone.*] See that the instruments are properly cared for—night will soon be upon us. [*Turns to COLONEL ROGERS as AMES and the others draw away.*] Colonel, I request that you sheath your sword. [*With a smile.*] That is the nearest to an apology anyone can get from a Virginian forester.

ROGERS: Sir, I regret the hastiness of my temper and I should have considered the source of the remark. [*Sheathes his sword.*]

WASHINGTON: Colonel, these men have strong opinions on the rights of the Colonies.

ROGERS: I have noted this growing spirit of sedition.

WASHINGTON: For which I can not help but honor them.

ROGERS: Sir, you don't mean—? You can not mean that you—a man of your position—can be possessed of the same sentiments as Crawford and this fellow Ames?

WASHINGTON: We were all reared in Virginia. We will ever stand on our rights as freeborn citizens.

ROGERS: Nevertheless, you stand for the King against all others.

WASHINGTON: You place me in a position where I am loath to stand. Silence could mean acquiescence and I would not care to deceive by holding my tongue.

ROGERS: You don't mean—!

WASHINGTON: A crisis is fast approaching when every man must take his stand for King or Colony. Sometime the line will be drawn and we must take our respective positions on one side or the other of it. And I am clearly of the opinion that the line ought to be drawn, for the rights of the Colonies must be clearly ascertained.

ROGERS: I can not believe that you would ever oppose the will of your King.

WASHINGTON: Until such time as our freedom is withdrawn, we will be loyal subjects of the King. When the time comes, however, that the rights of Americans, as provided in our charters, are abrogated, then, sir, we Americans will be for our Colonies and against those who would oppress us.

[*ROGERS is astonished, then thoughtfully studies WASHINGTON, as the COLONEL turns to CRAWFORD, who has come up.*]

CRAWFORD: An Indian messenger has been here.

WASHINGTON: So Hare informed me.

CRAWFORD: The Grand Sachem comes. He of the Monongahela.

WASHINGTON: A venerable man, the leader of many tribes.

ROGERS: No doubt the savages consider a visit from this Grand Sachem a signal honor.

WASHINGTON: And so I consider it. There is much in the Indian character that I admire. 'Tis sad to think that he must give up his forests to settlement.

ROGERS: And do you think, Sir, that many settlers will come to these lands of the Ohio?

WASHINGTON: Some day, when you and I have passed away, these hills and dales will be under cultivation and prosperous cities will be built upon the streams, even to the far reaches beyond the Alleghenies and the waters of the Mississippi, and thousands will come, from across the seas, to settle these lands. That, I veritably believe.

ROGERS: You then have greater faith in the people who will make this broad land their home?

[*HARE comes hurriedly into the camp.*]

HARE: The Grand Sachem comes. [*Points to the left wing.*]

[*They all turn as the GRAND SACHEM enters, followed by his tribesmen. He is a striking figure of an Indian, of advanced age and noble mien. He steps toward WASHINGTON and they meet in the center of the stage. For a long moment they gaze at each other.*]

WASHINGTON: I am honored that the Grand Sachem comes to sit by our council fire and partake of the all-too-humble fare we place before him. [*At WASHINGTON'S gesture the GRAND SACHEM seats himself by the fire and WASHINGTON takes his place beside him. One of the men, at a signal from WASHINGTON, offers the GRAND SACHEM a piece of venison taken from the kettle, but the Indian shakes his head.*] Crawford, from the stores, a bottle of claret. [*The Chief refuses to drink.*] A pipe for the Grand Sachem. [*When the pipe is brought the Chief waves it aside.*] Heap fuel upon the council fire. [*Some of the men bring wood for the fire, the flames mount. The GRAND SACHEM finally rises. WASHINGTON also rises and stands with folded arms.*]

GRAND SACHEM: I am a chief and ruler over many tribes. The hunting grounds of my people extend from the thunder of the Onigara and the Great Lakes to the far blue mountains. I have traveled the long and weary path of the wilderness road that I might once again look upon the young warrior of the great battle. By the waters of the Monongahela, we met the soldiers of the King beyond the Seas, who came to drive from the land my French Brothers. They came into the forest with much beating of drums and many flags flying in the breeze. Like a blind wolf they walked into our trap and the faces of these red-clad warriors turned pale at the sound of our war-whoop. It was a day when the white man's blood mixed with the streams of our forests, and 'twas then I first beheld this Chief. [*Points to WASHINGTON.*] I called my young men and said: "Mark yon tall and daring warrior! He is not of the redcoat tribe, he is of the Long-knives. He hath an Indian's wisdom. His warriors fight as we do—himself alone is exposed to our fire. Quick! Let your aim be certain and he dies. Our muskets were leveled—muskets that, for all

but him, knew not how to miss. I, who can bring the leaping squirrel from the top of the highest tree with a single shot, fired at this warrior more times than I have fingers. Our bullets killed his horses, knocked the war bonnet from his head, pierced his clothes, but 'twas in vain; a Power mightier far than we shielded him from harm. He cannot be killed in battle. I am old and soon shall be gathered to the great council fire of the Land of the Shades, but ere I go, there is something bids me speak in the voice of prophecy. Listen! Give ear to my words ye who are gathered here. The Great Spirit protects that man and guides his footsteps through the trails of life. He will become the chief of many nations, and when the sun is setting on the remaining few of my people and the game has departed from our forests and streams, a people yet unborn will hail him as the founder of a mighty empire. I have spoken.

WASHINGTON: [*After a pregnant silence.*] Our destinies are shaped by a mighty Power and we can but strive to be worthy of what the Great Spirit holds in store for us. If I must needs have such a lot in life as our Red Brother presages, then I pray that the Great Spirit give unto me those qualities of fortitude, courage, and wisdom, possessed by our Red Brother. I, the friend of the Indian, have spoken.

GRAND SACHEM: The words, Great Warrior, are as the wisdom of the ages. Thy trust in the Great Spirit shall ever be thy strength. I go now to take the long trail back to the lodges of my people. [*WASHINGTON and the SACHEM grasp hands, then the SACHEM turns away and after a few steps, stops.*] I, the chief of many nations that are fading like yon falling light, salute you. Farewell.

[*Followed by his tribesmen, the GRAND SACHEM exits at left, the white men gazing after him.*]

ROGERS: [*To WASHINGTON.*] Sir, 'tis strange how impressed I am by the words of the savage. Indeed, his prophecy has deeply moved me.

DR. CRAIK: I, too, feel the power of his words.

CRAWFORD: Mayhap, the Great Spirit controls his tongue.

AMES: Sometimes it so happens.

ROGERS: Can it be possible that the differences between England and these Colonies will eventuate in the forming of an independent nation in this new world?

WASHINGTON: We but ask for our rights.

ROGERS: Must the stupidity of a few separate Britannia and her children? No! No! It cannot be! In a few weeks I will be back in England and there I shall let my voice be heard in protest. Would that I possessed the forceful eloquence of that painted savage that I might impress upon the Ministry the folly of their course!

WASHINGTON: William Pitt and many other Englishmen are friends of the Colonies.

ROGERS: I, too, am a friend of America. Come what may, I assure you, Sir, that this sword will never be drawn against those who fight for Liberty.

WASHINGTON: 'Tis such as you, Sir, who gives us hope that the breach between the Motherland and her Colonies will be healed.

AMES: [*Coming to the front.*] Men, three cheers for Colonel Washington and Colonel Rogers.

MEN: Huzzah! Huzzah! Huzzah!

CURTAIN

WASHINGTON GOES IN

A GEORGE WASHINGTON PLAY IN ONE ACT

DRAMATIS PERSONAE

(IN ORDER OF THEIR APPEARANCE)

PATRICK HENRY ⎫
PEYTON RANDOLPH ⎬ Members of the Virginia Convention.
THOMAS JEFFERSON ⎭

GERALD TUCKER (JERRY), a student at William and Mary's College.

MRS. TUCKER, his mother.

LUCY TUCKER, his sister.

JAMES SOUTHALL, landlord of the Raleigh Tavern.

COLONEL GEORGE WASHINGTON.

COLONEL RICHARD BLAND.

MR. TUCKER, Jerry's father.

STUDENTS, FOOTMAN and SERVANTS.

TIME: An August evening in 1774.

PLACE: A room in the Raleigh Tavern, Williamsburg, Virginia.

DESCRIPTION OF CHARACTERS

PATRICK HENRY:

Thirty-eight years of age. A slender man above medium height, stooped and ungainly. A long, thin, saturnine face, cavernous gray eyes. He is dressed carelessly in dull colored Colonial clothes, his dark hair is worn in a queue. Ordinarily, he speaks with a drawl but when aroused, his tones are those of an orator.

PEYTON RANDOLPH:

Aged sixty-four. A heavy-set man in plain Colonial clothes of excellent material, wears a white wig. A solid, dignified, substantial man of the highest circles of Virginia gentry.

RICHARD HENRY LEE:

Forty-two years of age. A tall, spare man with the air of a thinker and an orator. Impetuous, ardent, patriotic. His clothes, of the period, are of good material but plain and indifferently worn.

GERALD TUCKER:

Called JERRY. A pale faced, likeable youth of about twenty. His clothes of a rich quality are disheveled. When first appearing, he has a long cloak about his shoulders. He is a graceful, well-proportioned, young student with a certain air of nonchalance, daring and recklessness, which can change to polite consideration and thoughtful introspection.

MRS. TUCKER:

JERRY'S mother, a trifle past middle age. A haughty, outspoken loyalist, conscious of her family's position. She is dressed in a rich gown of the period, and in her first appearance wears a long cloak of a plain color lined with flowered silk. On her head, a bonnet with long strings tied beneath her chin; on her hands, fingerless mits.

LUCY TUCKER:

JERRY'S twin sister. A beautiful girl about twenty years of age, dressed richly in the same style as her mother.

JAMES SOUTHALL:

The worried, suave, middle-aged landlord of the Raleigh Hotel. Tries to please everybody. Dressed in plain Colonial clothes.

COLONEL GEORGE WASHINGTON:

Forty-two years of age, six-feet two inches tall, in weight about two hundred and ten pounds, large boned but well proportioned, graceful, dignified, commanding though modest in deportment. His complexion bronzed by an outdoor life, his features strong, his hair light brown in color, powdered and worn in a queue. He is dressed in well-fitting clothes of the period made of velvet or broadcloth of a fine texture. Wears a tricorne hat.

COLONEL RICHARD BLAND:

Sixty-four years of age. Much the same type of man and dressed the same as RANDOLPH.

MR. TUCKER:

Past middle age. A staunch supporter of the King. Pompous, haughty, vitriolic, a stern parent. Richly dressed in clothes of the period, wears a tricorne hat and carries a cane.

The SERVANT and FOOTMAN are negroes, the latter in livery.

SET: The reception room at the Raleigh Tavern. A plain Colonial interior. A little to the left of center in the back wall, a broad door, leading to a back room. Diagonally across the corner of the back and right wall, a huge fireplace. Centering the right wall, a door leading to the Apollo room. Centering the left wall, a door leads into a hall. Along the back wall between the fireplace and door, a large settee, between the door and left wall, a highboy or other large piece of furniture. A table at right center and several chairs about the room.

PEYTON RANDOLPH is standing by the table sorting some papers. HENRY is pacing the floor. Their hats are on the table.

HENRY: [Stops beside RANDOLPH.] Mr. Randolph, I tell you it's now or never!

RANDOLPH: I agree with you, Mr. Henry. But can we make the others see is that way?

HENRY: When Governor Dunmore dissolved the House of Burgesses, we organized the Virginia Convention for action——

RANDOLPH: Aye, for action.

HENRY: —there has been nothing but backing and filling, shilly-shallying for the past week.

RANDOLPH: 'Tis true. We have been overlong in reaching a decision.

HENRY: The other Colonies are naming their delegates to the first Continental Congress. 'Tis time to act; we must join them.

RANDOLPH: Would you force the question?

HENRY: Aye, tonight; as soon as we assemble.

[JERRY TUCKER is asleep on the floor behind the settee. He cannot be seen but his voice startles the two.]

JERRY: Ho—o—o—! Hum—m—m!

[RANDOLPH and HENRY gaze at each other in surprise.]

RANDOLPH: What is that?

HENRY: [Smiles] Sounds like some one awakening.

JERRY: Oh Hum—m——m!

[HENRY *looks behind the settee and draws forth* JERRY TUCKER, *who rises, disentangling the cloak from about his head.*]

HENRY: Young man, is this your usual resting place?

JERRY: [*Yawns.*] Why, Mr. Henry. Good evening—or is it good morning?

HENRY: 'Tis evening, you young scapegrace.

JERRY: [*Sees* RANDOLPH, *bows.*] Good evening, Mr. Randolph.

RANDOLPH: [*Sternly.*] Master Tucker, have you been listening to our conversation?

JERRY: I've been sleeping, sir. I received my allowance yesterday. [*Smiles at* HENRY.] I believe it was yesterday.

HENRY: [*Laughs.*] Methinks, then, there are several students of William and Mary who should be in bed.

JERRY: Mayhap, I had better look them up.

RANDOLPH: Better you went to bed, young man. If your father knew of your carrying on——

JERRY: 'Tis my last fling, sir.

HENRY: Ah, you are reforming?

JERRY: Aye, sir. The first of a Tory family to turn Whig.

HENRY: You have indeed reformed.

JERRY: [*Ruefully.*] And like unto all reformers I expect to pay the penalty.

RANDOLPH: When your father learns of the reformation?

JERRY: [*Sighs and shakes his head.*] When he learns, sir.

HENRY: Trouble aplenty ahead.

JERRY: [*Soberly.*] For me and others. May I bid you good day, gentlemen. [*He bows elaborately.*]

RANDOLPH: Good evening, young man.

JERRY: Oh yes, evening. Good evening, gentlemen.

[*Again he bows and walks to the door at rear, opens it and stands upon the threshold. Beyond the door in the back room can be seen a group of convivial students gathered about a table deep in conversation. Espying* JERRY *there are shouts of welcome. "Here's Jerry! Welcome Jerry! Good old Jerry Tucker! Come sing us a song, Jerry!"*]

JERRY: Oh yes, evening. Good evening, gentlemen. ALL *comes forward and again bows.*]

HENRY: Evidently.

[JERRY *passes through the door and closes it.*]

RANDOLPH: He is a wild young blade.

HENRY: But a good lad and he writes some pretty verses not good for loyal ears to hear.

RANDOLPH: I pity the lad when his father learns he has espoused the cause of the Colonies.

HENRY: A stauncher Tory than Adrian Tucker never lived.

[*The door at the left is opened by a servant.* MRS. TUCKER *and* LUCY *enter, followed by a negro footman carrying luggage.*]

RANDOLPH: [*Starts at the sight of* MRS. TUCKER, *then bows.*] Ah, Mrs. Tucker! Good evening, Mrs. Tucker.

[HENRY *looks at* RANDOLPH *with lifted brows, then gazes at the center door and strokes his chin.*]

MRS. TUCKER: Good evening, Mr. Randolph. May I present my daughter Lucy?

RANDOLPH: [*Bows.*] Already I have had the pleasure of meeting the charming Mistress Lucy. [LUCY *curtsies.*] Ladies, may I present my colleague, Mr. Henry?

LUCY: Patrick Henry!

MRS. TUCKER: [*Coldly.*] Oh, Mr. Henry.

HENRY: [*Bows.*] Madam Tucker. Mistress Tucker. [LUCY *curtsies to* HENRY.] I am acquainted with your husband, madam.

MRS. TUCKER: [*With a sniff.*] I have heard him speak of you. [*To the servant.*] Call the landlord at once. [*The servant leaves at left.* MRS. TUCKER *turns her back to* HENRY *and addresses* RANDOLPH.] I trust Madam Randolph is enjoying good health?

RANDOLPH: Yes, madam, she is quite well. I hope you will find time, while in Williamsburg, to call on us.

MRS. TUCKER: I shall be pleased.

SOUTHALL: [*Enters and bows to* MRS. TUCKER.] You sent for me, madam?

RANDOLPH: As Mr. Henry and I have business to attend we must bid you good evening, ladies. [*They bow and leave.* SOUTHALL *comes forward and again bows.*]

MRS. TUCKER: [*Sniffs.*] "Business to attend." Every one knows that Patrick Henry is the very front of these rebel doings.

SOUTHALL: The Virginia Convention is meeting in the Apollo room this evening, madam.

MRS. TUCKER: Faith, then the place is overfull.

SOUTHALL: Oons, madam! There are plenty of beds, though nigh all my tankards are kept well in use.

MRS. TUCKER: Bother your tankards, I want lodgings!

SOUTHALL: Aye, madam. Already they are being prepared for you.

MRS. TUCKER: Mayhap, 'twill be the last time we stay at the Raleigh Tavern.

SOUTHALL: Have you not found comfort at my hostelry?

MRS. TUCKER: I like not the company meeting beneath your roof.

SOUTHALL: Madam, all the gentry stop here.

MRS. TUCKER: You also allow the meetings of members of the so-called Virginia Convention to be held here.

[*While they are talking,* LUCY *has moved toward, and listens at the back door, beyond which sounds of conviviality can be dimly heard.*]

SOUTHALL: The members of the Convention are gentry.

MRS. TUCKER: Gentlemen of birth and wealth forsooth, yet prattling, like the veriest clods, of resisting royal commands. I marvel, Southall, at your allowing sedition to breed beneath your roof.

SOUTHALL: [*Scratching his head in perplexity.*] These be times when 'tis hard to choose betwixt old and the new things, with the Whigs so hot. As for me, though, methinks the old will outlast my time.

MRS. TUCKER: My husband will say, 'Tis not to your credit that you suffer meetings where disloyalty is openly advocated by men like Tom Jefferson and that backwoodsman, Patrick Henry. [*As she speaks the last sentence,* WASHINGTON *enters in time to hear her words.*]

SOUTHALL: [*Bows to* WASHINGTON.] Ah, Colonel Washington.

WASHINGTON: Good evening, Mr. Southall. [*Bows to* MRS. TUCKER *and* LUCY, *who has come forward at his entrance.*] Madam Tucker, Mistress Lucy.

[MRS. TUCKER *bows and* LUCY *curtsies.*]

MRS. TUCKER: Colonel Washington, you here?

WASHINGTON: Aye, madam. Is it strange I should be in Williamsburg?

MRS. TUCKER: I learned that Governor Dunmore dissolved the House of Burgesses.

WASHINGTON: I am attending to the business of the Colony, madam.

MRS. TUCKER: Surely you are not one of this Virginia Convention?

WASHINGTON: Why not, madam? Have not my acts in these matters proclaimed my sentiments?

MRS. TUCKER: Your acts! 'Tis little we know of your acts——

WASHINGTON: So?

MRS. TUCKER: —however, if they are of a stamp with these men who are inflaming the already hot blood of our Virginia youth to rebellion——

WASHINGTON: Why, madam!

MRS. TUCKER: —then my opinion of you has changed.

SOUTHALL: [Entering from left.] Pardon, madam. I can now conduct you to your rooms.

MRS. TUCKER: 'Tis time. My husband will be here directly. [With a curt bow to WASHINGTON, she sweeps out of the door, held open by SOUTHALL. LUCY starts to follow, then swiftly goes to WASHINGTON.]

LUCY: [Perturbed.] Oh, Colonel, have you seen my brother, Jerry?

WASHINGTON: Not for several days, Mistress Lucy. Is anything amiss?

LUCY: Father is seeking him at the College. Father is terribly angry.

WASHINGTON: Some boyish prank, mayhap?

LUCY: Jerry has turned Whig!

WASHINGTON: And his family all Tories.

LUCY: Not I!

WASHINGTON: Not you?

LUCY: Jerry and I are twins. We always think alike.

WASHINGTON: So, you stand for the Colony?

LUCY: With Jerry, for the Colony!

SERVANT: [Enters.] Pahdon, Mis'tes Lucy, your mam wants foh t' go.

LUCY: Oh, I must go, Colonel. If you see Jerry, tell him I am here. [Swiftly she goes out the door; the servant holding it open, follows her; WASHINGTON stands, gazing at her.]

WASHINGTON: [In soliloquy.] Lines sharply drawn—homes disrupted—fathers against sons. [He shakes his head, turns toward the door at right as HENRY, JEFFERSON and RANDOLPH enter from right.] Good evening, gentlemen.

ALL: Good evening, Colonel Washington.

WASHINGTON: The meeting will soon be called to order?

HENRY: Presently, sir.

LEE: Colonel Bland and Colonel Harrison are in the Apollo room. I heard them inquiring for you.

WASHINGTON: Thank you, Mr. Lee. I shall attend them. [He leaves, at right. The others gather about the table.]

RANDOLPH: Gentlemen, I have hastily taken a poll. We haven't enough supporters to carry the resolution.

LEE: There are timid ones in our midst. I count them nigh as dangerous as our foes.

RANDOLPH: They fear to take a step in the dark.

HENRY: Fear! Fear! Temporize—temporize—wait the King's better humor! Bah!

RANDOLPH: [With a smile.] Doth it irk Patrick Henry that some remain cold, untouched by his eloquence?

HENRY: [With a rueful smile.] 'Tis only too true. I have talked until they are wearied of my voice—they are deaf to my arguments, my best turned phrases.

RANDOLPH: Then, mayhap, 'tis time they were swayed by something more potent than oratory.

LEE: What may that be?

RANDOLPH: Reason!

HENRY: Have our pleas been lacking in reason—logic?

RANDOLPH: Nay, Henry. But those you call timid are conservative men; only one of their kind—one in whom they have implicit confidence—can move them.

LEE: You have such a man in mind?

RANDOLPH: He but now passed through this room.

LEE: Colonel Washington?

HENRY: Colonel Washington? The only one who sees!

RANDOLPH: He is no orator.

HENRY: But for solid information and sound judgment he is by far the greatest man in the convention.

LEE: Few are his words, but what a wholesome effect they have on his audience!

HENRY: Aye. The timid ones are swayed by him.

RANDOLPH: Remember that day when he arose and said: "I will raise one thousand men, subsist them at my own expense and march myself at their head for the relief of Boston"?

LEE: Aye. At that very moment we could have passed even an act of independence.

RANDOLPH: If he would speak like that tonight!

LEE: If Washington goes in, Bland, Harrison and all the other conservatives will follow his lead.

HENRY: We must join the other Colonies in this Continental Congress.

LEE: We must also elect delegates, tonight.

HENRY: Washington must speak!

RANDOLPH: If his modesty—his reluctance to speak in public—does not overpower him.

HENRY: You are his close friend, Randolph.

LEE: You should persuade him to speak, tonight.

RANDOLPH: Persuade him! [A gesture of futility.] In a matter such as this he is not swayed by friendship, or by what any man may say.

HENRY: Surely you of all men——

RANDOLPH [Interrupting]: I? Why, Henry. I lack the courage to broach the subject to him. He still hopes for a peaceful adjustment of the differences with the Crown.

LEE: Yet none has been more zealous for maintaining our rights.

RANDOLPH: I have watched him, talked with him. He, like others, is slow to disallegiance, but when certain that our pleas and other efforts are without avail, then Washington will go in.

HENRY: Must we further temporize—await one man's action?

RANDOLPH: Mayhap, already his mind is made up.

HENRY: Then let us find out if it is!

LEE: Why not you two talk it over with him before the meeting? Bring him to this room.

RANDOLPH: And Colonel Bland with him.

HENRY: Aye. A capital idea—the strongest men among the conservatives.

LEE: We will discover how they stand and perchance Washington will speak.

RANDOLPH: He only speaks when greatly moved.

HENRY: Then, God grant he is moved tonight!

[HENRY leads the way and they leave at the right. As they go, SOUTHALL enters from the left, goes to door back center, listens, then opens the door, through which JERRY can be seen and heard declaiming to a crowd of students.]

JERRY: Shall we be ground in the dust, beneath the iron heel of British tyranny?

[Cries of "No! No!" and applause.]

SOUTHALL: Gentlemen! Gentlemen! Quiet, please! [The students turn toward him with derision and shouts. His voice rises above the clamor.] Master Tucker, I must speak to you!

JERRY: After a bit, Southall.

SOUTHALL: 'Tis important! At once!

JERRY: I'll be back gentlemen. [JERRY starts for the door as the students cry: "Come back, Jerry. Good old Jerry." They begin to sing "Three Merry Men of Kent."* JERRY enters, SOUTHALL closes the door, shutting off the song.]

SOUTHALL: Oh, such a din! They will ruin me.

JERRY [Nonchalantly]: Out with it, mine host?

SOUTHALL: Your father!

JERRY [Suddenly sobered]: What of my father?

SOUTHALL: He is here.

JERRY: At the Raleigh Tavern?

SOUTHALL: He has stopped at the college. Come, I warrant, to look into your actions.

JERRY: My actions?

SOUTHALL: 'Tis you who have made the college a pepper-pot, till I doubt not the students would take pleasure in beheading the King.

JERRY: When did my father arrive?

SOUTHALL: Madam and Mistress Tucker are now my honored guests. You father will be here directly.

JERRY [Worried]: He will—my mother—my sister——

SOUTHALL: But now arrived.

JERRY [Grasps SOUTHALL'S arm]: Good Mister Southall, do me a favor?

SOUTHALL [Uncertainly]: Well—now——

---
* For words and music see page 18.

JERRY: Get word to my sister that I await her in this room and don't let mother know of it.

SOUTHALL: 'Tis not to my relish to——

JERRY: Mister Southall, do this one thing for me.

SOUTHALL: I like it not. [JERRY draws him toward door at left.] 'Tis not beseeming in one to—— [They are now at the door.]

JERRY: Have her come at once. There, that's a good fellow. [He pushes SOUTHALL out the door, closes it; for an instant holds his head, walks to a chair by the table and drops into it, with a groan. His head goes forward into trembling hands. He gives way to grief, not noticing RANDOLPH, WASHINGTON, BLAND and HENRY enter.]

WASHINGTON [Sees JERRY, goes to him and places a hand on his shoulders]: My boy——

JERRY [Looks up]: Colonel Washington!

WASHINGTON [Compassionately]: Are you ill?

JERRY: [Pulls himself together, rises.] No, sir. [Smiles manfully.] Not ill at all, sir. I—— [Sees the others.] Excuse me, gentlemen; you would be alone.

BLAND: We have matters to discuss, Master Tucker.

JERRY: Yes, of a certainty. [Looks at door at left, hesitatingly.] I will go, gentlemen. [He bows, starts for the door. Impulsively HENRY overtakes him, places a hand on JERRY'S shoulders as MR. TUCKER enters from left and confronts them.]

TUCKER: [Coldly angry.] So. There is foundation to the tales of your doings. This is the company my son selects!

HENRY: [Smiles, though his glance is hot.] Mr. Tucker, censor not your son for being in my company. 'Tis not his fault that I would speak to him.

[WASHINGTON moves forward, unnoticed by TUCKER, HENRY and JERRY.]

TUCKER: What would such as you have to say to my son, sirrah!

[HENRY stiffens at the insult. WASHINGTON places a restraining hand on HENRY'S arm, steps before TUCKER and bows.]

WASHINGTON: Good evening, Mister Tucker.

TUCKER: [His angry glance rests on WASHINGTON.] Ah, Colonel Washington. [He bows stiffly.] Are you also an associate of this shabby Burgess from Louisa County?

WASHINGTON: I am proud to be so considered, sir.

TUCKER: [Astonished.] 'Tis not in your breed, Colonel Washington, to associate with Whigs.

[As he speaks, and before WASHINGTON can reply, LUCY enters, hesitates for an instant, and gazes on the scene, then runs to JERRY and throws her arms about her brother.]

LUCY: [With a sob.] Oh, Jerry!

JERRY: Lucy, dear!

TUCKER: Lucy, your brother is in disgrace. This is no place for you. Leave the room!

LUCY: If he is in disgrace, he needs me, father.

TUCKER: Am I to be made a public spectacle by my offspring? Leave the room!

[*MRS. TUCKER enters from left, stops in doorway as she hears the last sentence.*]

JERRY: Please go, Lucy.

LUCY: No!

[*WASHINGTON touches HENRY'S arm to draw him away.*]

MRS. TUCKER: [*Highly indignant.*] Colonel Washington, do you enjoy your handiwork—children in rebellion against parental authority!

[*WASHINGTON stops, turns to look at her.*]

TUCKER: Hold your peace, Betsy. Colonel Washington may have been active in the non-importation agreement and misguided in some respects, but he is no malcontent.

WASHINGTON: Madam, I deplore my presence here at this moment. But since you imply responsibility on my part for certain conditions, I must needs answer you.

MRS. TUCKER: [*Angrily interrupting.*] No man can explain disloyalty to the King. I have but now learned you are a leader among the Whigs.

WASHINGTON: A leader?

MRS. TUCKER: To what are we coming! You, George Washington, a rebel!

BLAND: [*Horrified, rushes forward.*] Mrs. Tucker! Oh, Mrs. Tucker! You are unfair. Colonel Washington, like myself, is a Conservative. We are staunch for the constitutional rights of the Colonies but loyal to the king. [*The door at the center is opened; a student, a bit wobbly on his legs, stands on the threshold.*]

STUDENT: Jerry! Your song! The one you wrote! [*He turns, signals to the students behind him and beats the measure as they sing:—*]

*King George the third of his name, tra la.

Will never be known to fame, tra la.

He closes our ports, does away with the courts.

'Tis on him we'll put all the blame, tra la.

TUCKER: [*Rushing to the door.*] Silence! 'Tis treason! Treason to the King!

MRS. TUCKER: Oh, how terrible! Stop them! Stop them! [*The students continue singing the second verse:*]

United Virginians will stand, tra la.

For our rights so noble and grand, tra la.

Beside all the others, for they are our brothers,

Thirteen—for—one, hand-in-hand, tra la.

[*HENRY has gone to the door, and at the end of the verse shoves the student-leader into the outer room and closes the door.*]

MRS. TUCKER: My son wrote that? Oh, the disgrace of it!

TUCKER: [*Beside himself with rage, forgets the others and grasps JERRY by the shoulder.*] Are you the author of that song of treason?

JERRY: Yes, I wrote it.

TUCKER: You! It conveys your sentiments?

JERRY: [*Pulls away from his father.*] It does, sir. Thirteen-for-one. The united Colonies against oppression.

TUCKER: You ingrate! You are no longer my son! Never darken my door again!

[*He raises his cane to strike JERRY. MRS. TUCKER*

* See page 664 for music.

screams. *LUCY springs forward and grasps TUCKER'S arm.*]

LUCY: Father!

[*TUCKER stands with upraised cane, glaring at his defiant son, who makes no move to fend the blow. His face is contorted with rage, injured pride and chagrin; for an instant he gazes at his daughter, lowers his cane, shudders, pulls himself together, turns and with faltering steps goes out the door at left. MRS. TUCKER, in tears, follows her husband. LUCY goes to JERRY.*]

LUCY: Brother, he needs me now. [*They embrace.*]

JERRY: Yes, go to him. [*LUCY follows her father. JERRY fights to control his emotions, looks to the door at left, then to the door beyond which are his companions. His eyes then turn to the men intently watching him. He throws back his shoulders, bows.*] Good evening, gentlemen.

WASHINGTON: [*Strides toward JERRY, puts an arm about the boy's shoulders.*] Methinks 'twas Shakespeare who said: "Be just and fear not; let all the ends thou aimest at be thy country's, thy God's and truth's."

JERRY: [*Looks up at WASHINGTON and smiles.*] Those are good words to live by.

WASHINGTON: Master Tucker, you know the whereabouts of my lodgings?

JERRY: Yes, sir.

WASHINGTON: I would deem it a favor were you to be my guest this night.

JERRY: Thank you, sir. 'Twould be an honor to be your guest. [*He bows and leaves at left.*]

RANDOLPH: The poor lad.

HENRY: From the mouths of babes,—"thirteen-for-one!"

[*WASHINGTON in thought.*]

BLAND: 'Twas an astounding outburst.

RANDOLPH: Most astounding.

BLAND: Colonel Washington, Madam Tucker called you a rebel!

WASHINGTON: [*Turns to gaze at BLAND.*] I am a Virginian—more—an American.

BLAND: An American!

WASHINGTON: The rights of our Country are endangered. We must retain the liberty we have derived from our ancestors. I shall do all in my power to maintain that liberty. If that be rebellion, I am proud to be called a rebel.

BLAND: You mean—you mean you would fight to maintain that liberty?

WASHINGTON: No man should scruple or hesitate a moment to use arms in defense of so valuable a blessing. Yet arms, I beg leave to add, should be the last resort.

HENRY: [*Exchanging glances with RANDOLPH.*] You are for naming delegates to the Continental Congress?

WASHINGTON: Aye. We must form a strong union—thirteen-for-one.

BLAND: There is something grand about those words. By the eternal, I, also, am for it!

SOUTHALL: [*Entering from right.*] Gentlemen, the Convention is about to be called to order.

WASHINGTON: Let us go in.

CURTAIN

Three Merry Men of Kent

[Fast] He that will not mer-ry, mer-ry be, With a gen-er-ous bowl and toast,

Let him be mer-ry mer-ry, mer-ry there, And we will be mer-ry, mer-ry here; For who can know where we may go To be mer-ry an-o-ther

year, brave boys, To be mer-ry an-o-ther year.

Thirteen For One

Rudolf Schramm

Marche héroïque

King George, the Third of his name, tra-la, Will
U-ni-ted Vir-gin-ians will stand, tra-la, For our

nev-er be known to fame, tra-la, He
rights so no-ble and grand, tra-la, Be-

clos-es our ports, Does a-
side all the oth-ers, For

way with our courts, 'Tis on him we'll put all the blame, tra-la!
they are our broth-ers, Thir-teen for one, hand in hand, tra-la!

WASHINGTON TAKES THE RISK

A GEORGE WASHINGTON PLAY IN ONE ACT

DRAMATIS PERSONAE

(IN THE ORDER OF THEIR APPEARANCE)

COLONEL GEORGE WASHINGTON.

MARTHA WASHINGTON.

LORD FAIRFAX

FIELDING LEWIS.

MRS. FIELDING LEWIS, *Betty, sister of Washington.*

JOHN PARKE CUSTIS, *Jack.*

MRS. JOHN PARKE CUSTIS, *Eleanor.*

WILLIAM DIGGES.

MISS DIGGES.

MISS JENIFER.

BEN, *the Washingtons' colored butler.*

GEORGE MASON.

MRS. GEORGE MASON.

CLAIRE MASON, *their granddaughter.*

EDMUND PENDLETON.

JOHN CUNNINGHAM.

JEREMIAH TOWNSEND.

FOUR NEGRO SERVANTS.

TIME: 6.00 P. M., April 27, 1775.

PLACE: *Dining room at Mount Vernon.*

DESCRIPTION OF CHARACTERS

WASHINGTON:

Forty-three years of age, six feet two inches tall; in weight, about 210 pounds; large boned but well proportioned, graceful, dignified; commanding though modest in deportment. His complexion bronzed by an outdoor life; his features strong; his hair light brown in color, powdered, combed back from his forehead and tied in a queue. He is dressed in well-fitted though plain clothes of the period, made of velvet or broadcloth of a fine texture.

MARTHA:

Forty-four years of age; short, inclined to plumpness, with a round placid face; direct, understanding eyes. She is calm, collected, witty; a splendid hostess; she speaks in soft, well-modulated tones. Her powdered hair is worn high on her head, in the mode of Colonial days, embellished by a small lace cap. Her silk gown is of the flowered polonnaise type with a petticoat of frilled white silk; about her shoulders a dainty lace 'kerchief.

LORD FAIRFAX:

Eighty-six years of age, a large man inclined to obesity. He is witty, jolly, but of quick, testy temper. He speaks with all the assurance of a member of the British ruling class. He is dressed handsomely in smallclothes and an elaborately decorated coat of the period; on his head a white wig.

FIELDING LEWIS:

Fifty-eight years of age, tall, slender; enthusiastic; a Virginia gentleman; brother-in-law of WASHINGTON. His hair powdered, his clothes of the best type of the period.

MRS. LEWIS:

BETTY, WASHINGTON'S *only sister, forty-two years of age; a tall, well-built woman, resembles her brother, GEORGE. Her face, though plain, is animated; she radiates good nature, is fun-loving, witty; light-brown hair in Colonial coiffure. She is richly dressed and carries a fan.*

JOHN PARKE CUSTIS:

JACK, MARTHA'S *own son and WASHINGTON'S ward, and beloved by him. He is twenty years old, slender, graceful, dark of complexion; his dark hair is worn in queue and powdered; well dressed in clothes of the period.*

MRS. JOHN PARKE CUSTIS:

ELEANOR, *bride of JACK, eighteen years of age. A beautiful, dark, slender girl; wears own hair done high in mode of day; she is handsomely gowned in clothes of the period.*

WILLIAM DIGGES:

Neighbor and friend of WASHINGTON; about forty-five years of age, dressed as the other men in fine clothes.

MISS DIGGES:

His daughter, richly dressed.

MISS JENIFER:

About nineteen years of age, beautiful girl; friend of the Washingtons, richly dressed. Wears her own hair in mode of the day.

BEN:

WASHINGTON'S *negro butler; a faithful, respected old servant dressed in the livery of the Washingtons—blue breeches, white hose, white coat and vest trimmed with scarlet collar and cuffs and edges, white stock.*

GEORGE MASON:

Fifty years of age; staunch in the cause of liberty; neighbor, friend, and admirer of WASHINGTON; dressed richly, clothes of the period.

MRS. GEORGE MASON:

A middle-aged lady, as richly gowned as the other ladies.

CLAIRE MASON:

Granddaughter of GEORGE MASON; a winsome child six or seven years of age; a great favorite of COLONEL WASHINGTON; her dress, an exact replica of that worn by the ladies; she carries on her arm a silk bag.

EDMUND PENDLETON:

Associate of WASHINGTON as a member of the Continental Congress; about fifty-four years of age; wears a dark wig, unpowdered; well dressed in clothes of the period.

JOHN CUNNINGHAM AND JEREMIAH TOWNSEND:

The messengers; strong-featured men of the yeoman type. Their hair is unpowdered and worn in queue; breeches, vests and coats of rough texture; riding boots to the knee; shirts open at the throat, tricorne hats.

SET: *The dining hall at Mount Vernon. Centered on the back wall, a handsome marble mantel projects eighteen inches into the room; on it are candlesticks and vases of early Spring flowers; above the mantel,* a picture; flanking each side of the mantel are doors centered between the mantel and the side-walls. The door at the right leads into the music room; the one on the left, to the family dining room. Through the right wall, a door; three feet from this door a window opening onto the portico. The left wall has a door and window spaced the same as the right wall. It is a warm April evening and through the outer doors and windows can be seen the blossoms of budding trees.

A long table, placed lengthwise of stage, is handsomely set with fine linen, china and shining silver for ten persons. Against the left wall, between the window and door, a serving table; above it, a handsome gilt mirror; against the right wall beneath the window, a long davenport. A mirror, corresponding to that of left wall, between door and window. Several chairs against the wall. Over the mantel, in a handsome frame, a print of Admiral Vernon's fleet.

COLONEL WASHINGTON *is seated at the head of the table, right; at other end of table, the hostess, MARTHA WASHINGTON. On side of table, back stage, from WASHINGTON to MARTHA, in order, MISS JENIFER, JACK CUSTIS, MRS. LEWIS, LORD FAIRFAX. Opposite them, in order from WASHINGTON to MARTHA, MISS DIGGES, FIELDING LEWIS, ELEANOR CUSTIS, MR. DIGGES. Back of WASHINGTON is BEN, the butler. A male servant in the Washington livery back of MARTHA. Two other servants are also placing wine glasses on table and pouring wine for the party.*

BETTY LEWIS: Now, my Lord Fairfax, do you think that nice?

FAIRFAX: Faith, Mistress Lewis, I but quote our friend Mr. Digges.

DIGGES: Ah, my Lord, you play me false.

LEWIS: No evasion, Digges, my Lord bespeaks you fair. She has ever been a hoyden. I learn it from her own brother. Eh, George? [*Turns to WASHINGTON.*]

BETTY LEWIS: George, hold your peace. Or tales I'll tell of you. [*MISS DIGGES makes an unheard remark to WASHINGTON.*]

WASHINGTON: [*To MISS DIGGES.*] Oh, no, Miss Betsy, we early learned 'twas the better part of wisdom to hold one's peace where Betty was concerned. [*Laughs.*]

FAIRFAX: I ever had the opinion Fielding Lewis was a brave man.

WASHINGTON: Brave but not prudent or he would profit by our example.

BETTY LEWIS: What a reputation my own brother gives me!

MISS JENIFER: Faith, brothers are a terrible trial.

ELEANOR: Wait, my dear, till you're married, then you'll know what real trials some men can be. [*There is much laughter and they all turn to JACK.*]

FAIRFAX: Ah—Jack. What's your latest transgression?

JACK: Transgression? Why, my Lord, a model husband am I, and as Poor Richard says, [*To ELEANOR*] "We can give advice but we cannot give conduct." [*Laughter.*]

ELEANOR: [*To MARTHA.*] Mother, does not Poor Richard list promptness as a virtue?

MARTHA: Jack has not proceeded that far in his reading of the almanac. [*Laughter.*]

JACK: I appeal to you, Miss Jenifer. When you marry, would you censure your husband for being late, when his mare having cast a shoe he must needs stop in Alexandria to have it shod?

MISS JENIFER: I would, if while having the mare shod he visited too long at Gadsby's tavern.

ELEANOR: Aye, listening to the gossip.

JACK: A Major Scathergood of the King's Grenadiers, lately arrived from Boston Town, was there with Esquire Minton.

LORD FAIRFAX: Esquire Minton is a loyal king's man.

MARTHA: Politics will soon be the topic. Better we leave the gentlemen now. [*The ladies prepare to leave; WASHINGTON rises and lifts glass.*]

WASHINGTON: To the ladies, may they in communion find solace and strength to endure sons, husbands, brothers, and lovers! [*There is much laughter, the gentlemen rise, lift their glasses and drink as the ladies retire from the table following MARTHA toward the door at left; they each turn and curtsy as they leave, the men bow. BETTY LEWIS brings up the rear, stops at door.*]

BETTY LEWIS: And may you gentlemen in communion find strength to endure our absence. [*She makes an elaborate curtsy and leaves, the men laugh as they bow to her.*]

LEWIS: [*As she goes.*] 'Tis cruel to deprive us of your charming presence, my dear.

[*BETTY waves her fan over her shoulder.*]

DIGGES: [*To Lewis.*] A last-minute try for forgiveness. [*The laugh is on LEWIS, who strolls around the table and leans against the mantel. DIGGES sits at MARTHA'S place, the servants fill up the glasses and place pipes at the elbows of the men.*]

LEWIS: [*As he reaches mantel.*] Jack, what news did the Major bring of events in Boston?

JACK: The Major, like so many king's officers, assumed an air of superiority. Faith, he was both loud and boastful and to use his own words said, "General Gage has the rebels well tamed."

FAIRFAX: 'Tis good news!

JACK: If 'tis true, sir.

WASHINGTON: My son, in these times one's words should be carefully weighed.

DIGGES: Methinks 'twill take more than General Gage to tame the people of Boston Town.

FAIRFAX: Dammee! England is the mother of these Colonies and she should take a birch rod to them.

LEWIS: But, my Lord, there are other peoples in these Colonies beside English—to them England is but a stepmother and a harsh featured one at best.

DIGGES: I like not that figure of speech that terms England a mother. The ties that bind us to England are strong. From her we secured the tradition of men's rights that shape our lives today.

WASHINGTON: To me England ever seems more like an elder brother, who through inheritance has secured the best of everything, occupying a higher station, and we are perforce prone to look up to that elder brother.

FAIRFAX: As you should!

LEWIS: But when we find that elder brother would deprive us of our rights, tax us against our will, deny us jury-trial——

JACK: Quarter an army upon us at our cost——

LEWIS: ——then, my Lord, it seems high time to sever relations with the elder brother, leave his house and set up our own establishment—our own government.

FAIRFAX: You would have the Colonies break with England for good and all?

LEWIS: I would! And methinks the day approaches when the break will come. [*He steps to the table, picks up a glass of wine.*] And here's to a free America!

FAIRFAX: [*In anger.*] Expect me to drink to such toast!

LEWIS: Not you, my Lord, but others. [*Looks at WASHINGTON.*]

[*DIGGES and CUSTIS raise their glasses. WASHINGTON sits in thought but does not drink.*]

FAIRFAX: George, are you not drinking to the rebel toast?

[*BEN enters and stands respectfully at WASHINGTON'S elbow. WASHINGTON notices BEN.*]

WASHINGTON: Pardon me, gentlemen. [*To BEN.*] What is it?

BEN: Massa Pendleton, Massa Mason, Mistes Mason and little Missy Claire, done called and are wid Mistes Washington, Colonel.

WASHINGTON: Ask the gentlemen to please join us. [*BEN leaves.*]

FAIRFAX: Pendleton and Mason—more rebels.

WASHINGTON: [*With a smile.*] My colleague in the Continental Congress and my very dear friend.

LEWIS: I did not know Pendleton was in the neighborhood.

DIGGES: Nor I.

JACK: [*To servant.*] Fresh glasses for the gentlemen and another bottle of Madeira. [*Servant complies.*]

BEN: [*Opening the door.*] Massa Pendleton and Massa Mason. [*PENDLETON and MASON enter and bow to the company, which has risen.*]

WASHINGTON: Welcome, gentlemen. [*He shakes hands with PENDLETON and MASON who exchange greetings with the others.*]

FAIRFAX: [*As they all take seats.*] Gentlemen, you're just in time; a toast has been proposed. [*His glance is fixed on WASHINGTON.*]

PENDLETON: A toast?

MASON: Let's have it.

[*CLAIRE MASON runs into the room, stops, glances uncertainly at the company, and then runs with outstretched arms to WASHINGTON, who swings her up to his knees.*]

WASHINGTON: Oh, my little dear one. [*She impulsively throws her arms about WASHINGTON'S neck; he embraces her.*]

CLAIRE: I have something for you, Colonel. [*She thrusts a hand into the bag on her arm.*]

WASHINGTON: Something for me?

CLAIRE: Yes, Colonel, I made it all myself.

WASHINGTON: What can it be?

CLAIRE: Guess.

WASHINGTON: Let me see—a sugar image?

CLAIRE: Oh, no—! A hanky! [*Pulls it from bag.*]

WASHINGTON: [*Takes it and examines it.*] 'Tis beautiful——!

MASON: Come, my dear. 'Tis not beseaming for you to take so much of the Colonel's time.

CLAIRE: Yes, father. [*She throws her arms about WASHINGTON'S neck and kisses him.*] I must go now, Colonel. [*WASHINGTON reluctantly releases her. She curtsies to the company; turns to WASHINGTON.*]

WASHINGTON: Ben will take you to my secretary, in the top drawer you will find a package and on it there's writ a name.

CLAIRE: Whose name? Mine?

WASHINGTON: Faith—'tis your name, I believe.

CLAIRE: A present? For me?

WASHINGTON: It must be.

CLAIRE: Oh——!

MASON: Make your grandest curtsy to the Colonel, my dear.

[*She curtsies to WASHINGTON, who has risen; he bows to her and watches as she runs to the door held open by BEN, turns and throws WASHINGTON a kiss; he returns it.*]

CLAIRE: Hurry, Ben. [*She leaves.*]

MASON: And now, the toast!

FAIRFAX: Yes, Lewis, the toast.

LEWIS: [*Raises his glass.*] To—the younger generation!

FAIRFAX: Humph, we can all drink to that.

[*They lift their glasses and drink.*]

WASHINGTON: [*To PENDLETON and MASON.*] You have dined, gentlemen?

MASON: Aye, early at my home, then drove here. Mister Pendleton has an important matter to take up with you; one of deep concern to our cause.

FAIRFAX: If there's rebel plotting to be done here, mayhap I better retire.

MASON: No plotting, my lord. A matter of interest to you, however.

FAIRFAX: Humph!

PENDLETON: [*To WASHINGTON.*] Your many friends, sir, throughout the colony desire that we, of the Virginia delegation to the Continental Congress, propose the name of Colonel Washington as commander-in-chief——

MASON: —Should Britain force war upon us. [*WASHINGTON gazes at PENDLETON in amazed unbelief. FAIRFAX for a moment seems stunned.*]

FAIRFAX: Would you have a man who has worn the British uniform turn traitor?

PENDLETON: Traitor? Would you call William Tell a traitor? The Barons at Runnymede, traitors?

FAIRFAX: [*Hotly.*] Yes, by Heaven, they were!

PENDLETON: Then, my Lord, the word traitor has a vastly more honorable meaning than we are wont to associate with the word.

WASHINGTON: [*Holds up a protesting hand.*] Gentlemen! [*They all turn to him.*] My dear Pendleton, that my friends have thought of me in such a post of honor——

FAIRFAX: Honor——?

WASHINGTON: —is most flattering and I deeply appreciate the implied compliment——

FAIRFAX: Compliment? 'Tis an insult!

WASHINGTON: —but I cannot permit my friends to propose my name for such office.

FAIRFAX: Good!

MASON: There is none better fitted to command.

WASHINGTON: Nay, my friend. Forget not there are others in these Colonies who are much better qualified.

PENDLETON: Who can name one better qualified?

WASHINGTON: In spite of present differences and the acuteness of the situation, I hope it will not be necessary to resort to arms.

FAIRFAX: Well said, George!

MASON: We will never have peace with the present ministry in power.

WASHINGTON: Ministries sometimes fall—we have many friends and advocates in England.

PENDLETON: But if war comes?

WASHINGTON: God forbid!

FAIRFAX: War, bah!

PENDLETON: If war comes, then may we suggest Colonel Washington as commander-in-chief?

WASHINGTON: No.

FAIRFAX: And so speaketh a man of sense!

WASHINGTON: I would not be misunderstood by my friends. Some day America will become an independent nation——

FAIRFAX: Tush, that is tommyrot!

WASHINGTON: —by sheer weight and necessity of circumstances.

LEWIS: Then 'tis your belief, Colonel, that some day the younger brother will become larger, richer, greater?

WASHINGTON: The time will come when the people of this land will say, Why should we be held back by a nation three thousand miles away?

MASON: We say that today.

LEWIS: Aye, then why wait?

DIGGES: Let the break come now!

[*They all look at WASHINGTON, awaiting his answer.*]

WASHINGTON: Better it be left to posterity.

JACK: Poor Richard says, "One today is worth two tomorrows, do it today."

WASHINGTON: And Poor Richard says, "There is a proper time for all occasions."

MASON: You would wait 'till the Colonies grow stronger, have a large population, greater resources?

FAIRFAX: [*Interrupting.*] Fiddlestick! Greater resources—larger population. I doubt if ever there will be more than double the population now in the Colonies.

LEWIS: Forget not, my lord, our population has doubled in fifty years.

FAIRFAX: Think you it will double in the next fifty years?

LEWIS: 'Twould not surprise me.

WASHINGTON: There is a powerful incentive that draws the people of Europe to these shores.

FAIRFAX: What could impel peaceful folk to come to this rebellious land?

WASHINGTON: An irresistible desire—a great hunger.

FAIRFAX: For this liberty that so obsesses all your friends?

WASHINGTON: No, my Lord, I speak of a hunger which is closely allied to the desire for liberty—one more elemental—the great natural hunger men have for land.

FAIRFAX: Land! Forsooth there's plenty of it here, but what can we do with it?

LEWIS: [*Sententiously.*] We have done fairly well, so far.

FAIRFAX: Aye, but the markets for your products are found only in the motherland.

DIGGES: Motherland?

FAIRFAX: [*Hotly.*] Aye, motherland!

WASHINGTON: I have journeyed up and down the wilderness——

FAIRFAX: [*Interrupting.*] Of a truth you have been a great traveller—[*ironically*] in the wilderness.

WASHINGTON: And in the wilderness I have seen men and their families braving the hardships, clearing the forest, establishing homes, winning their way with but a few poor tools made by themselves. They know not of markets abroad.

MASON: Not they.

WASHINGTON: To them England is unnecessary—almost an alien land.

LEWIS: 'Tis God's truth. [*Strikes the table.*]

FAIRFAX: Unnecessary! What could they do without England's protection?

WASHINGTON: Have they not learned that alone they must protect themselves from the incursions of savages and other enemies?

DIGGES: Aye, as after Braddock's defeat.

FAIRFAX: Ah, you speak of adventurers, a class of men fit only for the fringes of society—a brutish lot.

WASHINGTON: A brutish lot, my Lord? Nay. Self-sustaining, self-reliant, brave enough to dare the tomahawk and scalping knife——

FAIRFAX: The hope of the Colonies will be found only in men of gentle blood—gentle blood from England.

WASHINGTON: Without the manners of gentle folk, of humble parentage—true enough; uneducated, mayhap, but they carry the Bible with them into the forest——

FAIRFAX: A passel of non-comformists!

WASHINGTON: [*The others laugh.*] They set up hamlets on the forest edge; they establish some semblance of a school for their children. With ownership of land comes desire for betterment, and, my Lord, there are thousands of just such men in Europe—land hungry—who, wending their way in a great migration to America's shores, will people our wilderness and establish a culture that some day, I verily believe, will rival that of Europe.

[*Galloping hoofs are heard. BEN looks out the window at right and hurries out door.*]

FAIRFAX: Ah, my boy, you amuse me. You are in full gallop on your hobby of the Colonies' great future.

WASHINGTON: More than a hobby, my Lord, a firm conviction.

FAIRFAX: Man, had you but once been in England you would better realize what a long way the Colonies must go before they reach such an estate as you predict.

[*BEN opens door, MARTHA enters; as the door is opened, the strains of "Yankee Doodle" are heard as though picked out with one hand on the harpsichord.*]

[*Without, a feminine call.*] One moment, Madam Washington, tell us, is this the melody of the new tune?

MARTHA: [*Calling back.*] You have it very well. [*Laughter and a voice trills a note or two of the tune. MARTHA turns to the gentlemen.*] Ah, 'tis the new tune from England, "Yankee Doodle." [*To WASHINGTON.*] Two messengers arrived but now from Baltimore; they would see you at once. [*Softly.*] 'Tis momentous news from the north.

WASHINGTON: [*To BEN.*] Have them in. [*BEN leaves, the men look anxiously at one another.*]

PENDLETON: Momentous news!

FAIRFAX: Mayhap from that rebel den of Boston Town.

JACK: Let's have the ladies in. [*WASHINGTON nods his head; MARTHA goes out door, leaving it open. Two or three voices join in a bar of "Yankee Doodle." JACK picks up tune and hums it. BEN ushers in TOWNSEND and CUNNINGHAM, dust-covered, travel-stained, eager to deliver their message. Music stops abruptly. Soft exclamations by ladies are heard.*] Oh!—Messengers!—Here!—News!—What can it be?—From the North! [*Messengers bow to the company.*]

WASHINGTON: I am Colonel Washington. [*Messengers salute WASHINGTON.*]

TOWNSEND: I am Jeremiah Townsend and this is John Cunningham, both members of the committee of safety.

[*As CUNNINGHAM is speaking the ladies excitedly crowd in the door-way with many soft "Pardons" and exclamations.*]

CUNNINGHAM: Mr. Mordecai Gist sent us with tidings from the North, sir.

TOWNSEND: The King's forces have begun the fighting!

LEWIS: Where?

CUNNINGHAM: Lexington, sir.

TOWNSEND: They fired on the Minute Men.

FAIRFAX: You say they fired on the rebels?

TOWNSEND: [*Stiffens.*] They fired on the Minute Men, killing aplenty.

FAIRFAX: [*With heat.*] I said, rebels, sirrah!

CUNNINGHAM: The redcoats got paid in full. They were driven back to Boston Town by our men.

FAIRFAX: [*Striking his cane on the floor.*] Hoity-toity, the King's Regulars routed by a passel of country louts. 'Tis but an idle rumor!

TOWNSEND: [*To WASHINGTON.*] 'Tis the truth, sir. Major Pitcairn and my Lord Percy, with six hundred men, were on their way to seize our powder and take Mr. Hancock.

CUNNINGHAM: The farmers were all up to hinder 'em and the King has lost three hundred men!

TOWNSEND: And we under an hundred!

LEWIS: The first victory!

WASHINGTON: Beaten?—the King's Regulars!

CUNNINGHAM: The Northern Colonies are up in arms, sir.

TOWNSEND: At Baltimore the Liberty Men seized the arsenal.

MASON: The war has begun.

FAIRFAX: [*Aghast.*] War! It can't be true!

WASHINGTON: Mr. Gist sent me a letter?

TOWNSEND: [*Taking a folded paper from inside his coat.*] Yes, Colonel Washington, 'tis here.

WASHINGTON: [*To company as he takes it.*] Pardon me, please. [*WASHINGTON reads the short letter, all stand silently and anxiously watching him. He slowly folds the letter and places it in his pocket.*] On the 19th day of April the King's troops were defeated with heavy loss.

FAIRFAX: George, do you believe this to be true?

WASHINGTON: Beyond a peradventure of a doubt. Mr. Mordecai Gist is a gentleman of honor. I have faith alike in his spoken or written word.

FAIRFAX: [*Aghast.*] War!

WASHINGTON: Mr. Gist has it from Charles Carroll, of Carrollton.

FAIRFAX: It really means war!

JACK: 'Tis come, I knew it would come! Huzzah! Huzzah! Huz——!

WASHINGTON: [*Interrupts the enthusiastic JACK, kindly but seriously.*] My boy, 'tis no time for cheering—'tis time for serious thought. [*To BEN.*] See that Mr. Gist's messengers are given refreshments and proper habitation. [*To Messengers.*] I thank you for the prompt delivery of Mr. Gist's message. You are wearied from your long journey, on the morrow I will have further talk with you.

TOWNSEND: At your pleasure, Colonel Washington. [*They salute WASHINGTON, bow to the others and retire.*]

JACK: [*Grasping a wine glass.*] To the farmers of Lexington.

WASHINGTON: [*Quickly lifts a hand.*] No, my son. Mayhap some present could not drink to such a toast.

FAIRFAX: [*Slowly rises.*] George, I will go. Let not my presence dampen your spirits.

MARTHA: Nay, my Lord. We leave you and Colonel Washington.

[*Both men and women leave, turning at the door, bowing and curtsying. As the last goes and BEN closes the door, FAIRFAX comes to WASHINGTON, lays a hand on his shoulder.*]

FAIRFAX: [*After a silence.*] George, one last appeal from an old man who has lived hard and seen much. I have watched you develop from a silent, lanky stripling to man's estate, and no man has endured more or dared more or striven harder to attain an education, competence. I have seen you grow in stature to a place where none in the Colonies surpasses you in military fame or soundness of judgment. You have won the highest regard of all men. I flatter myself and take pride in the fact that I have had some small part in shaping your career—influencing your life.

WASHINGTON: You have indeed, my Lord.

FAIRFAX: I have loved you as a son. No one, not even your mother, has a keener interest in your welfare.

WASHINGTON: [*Much affected.*] My Lord, I have ever looked upon you as the one who has taken the place of that father I lost so many years ago. Were he standing before me, I could not revere him more or be more affected by his words.

FAIRFAX: And like a father I give you this counsel; think well, my boy, before you make a decision. The war has begun, caused by the folly of His Majesty's ministers and those Massachusetts dissenters who have been rebels since they first set foot on these shores. Your friends would have you commander-in-chief. Congress will call upon you to lead America's armies.

WASHINGTON: That is unthinkable, my Lord.

FAIRFAX: Nay, 'tis a certainty. But, ere you accept this call, think well, I pray, on the consequences. Think you these Colonies can prevail against the might of Britain?

WASHINGTON: I have seen British regulars in action.

FAIRFAX: Be not deceived, George. The armies you encounter will be much larger than Braddock's force, and more ably led.

WASHINGTON: My faith in America's destiny, my knowledge of her people, confirms my conviction that her cause will prevail.

FAIRFAX: At the beginning you may have some successes; but, when the fear of losing this rich heritage strikes deep into the hearts of those who rule England, the whole fury of Britain's power will be loosed against you. Can these Colonies, without manufactures, without munitions, with an army of untrained husbandmen, hope to win against a force that has triumphed over the mightiest powers of continental Europe? Can they?

WASHINGTON: 'Tis not a question of expediency, my Lord.

FAIRFAX: Then what is it?

WASHINGTON: A question of the rights of man.

FAIRFAX: And if you fail?

WASHINGTON: Fail——?

FAIRFAX: What are the penalties that will be visited on the leader? Your estates forfeited, the revenues of your beloved wife confiscated, and as for you, sir, a traitor's hideous doom!

WASHINGTON: Doom——?

FAIRFAX: What a fearful price to pay for the mere attempt to attain a phantom liberty.

WASHINGTON: Can one weigh consequences when honor is at stake?

FAIRFAX: Honor! The honor of Boston tradespeople, of Virginia Redemptioners, of Pennsylvania Quakers, the honor of Georgian debtors—and the whole passel of European peasants that make up this breed you call Americans. Honor, fiddlesticks!

WASHINGTON: They are my countrymen, my Lord.

FAIRFAX: Your countrymen? Bah! You are not of the breed. You come from staunch British gentlefolk.

WASHINGTON: That I have a just pride in my ancestry, I admit. But methinks he who has to look back upon his ancestors to make himself sure he is a gentleman is but a poor sort of a man.

FAIRFAX: In espousing the cause of the Colonies, you become a traitor to your class as well as to your king.—You, sir, who are an aristocrat!

WASHINGTON: If I am, more reason that I be an American aristocrat, one such does not consider caste, nor compromise with honor, when the public weal is menaced.

FAIRFAX: [*Hopelessly.*] You were ever set in your opinion once your mind is made up.

WASHINGTON: [*With a gesture.*] My Lord, I——

FAIRFAX: [*Interrupting.*] Enough! I must retire, and early on the morrow return to Greenway Court. [*WASHINGTON pulls the bell cord by the mantel. BEN enters, immediately.*]

WASHINGTON: Candles for his lordship. [*BEN leaves.*]

FAIRFAX: [*With a gesture of appeal.*] Don't do it, George! Don't do it!

[*MARTHA enters; before she closes the door the strains of "Yankee Doodle" are heard and JACK'S voice saying, "We'll give them back their 'Yankee Doodle.'"*]

WASHINGTON: My Lord retires.

MARTHA: Will your lordship not partake of a hot toddy before retiring?

FAIRFAX: [*With a strained dignity.*] I thank you, no, madam. [*He starts to go, then stops in his tracks, turns abruptly to MARTHA.*] Madam, the war has begun. The Congress will call upon your husband to lead its armies.

WASHINGTON: Mayhap.

FAIRFAX: Doth such a prospect please you?

MARTHA: One's own feelings warrant no consideration at such a time, my Lord.

FAIRFAX: Perchance it would mean years of separation from Mount Vernon—separation from you.

[*WASHINGTON'S hand grasps the back of a chair. He watches MARTHA intently.*]

MARTHA: It might——

FAIRFAX: And in the end, failure.

MARTHA: My Lord—Fairfax——

FAIRFAX: Yes! Failure! And failure means—his estates forfeited, your revenues confiscated, and for him a traitor's hideous doom.

[MARTHA *stiffens, her eyes close for an instant. They open to gaze straight into* WASHINGTON'S *eyes.* FAIR-FAX *watches the effect of his words.*]

FAIRFAX: Madam, he must not take the risk.

MARTHA: [*Bringing her gaze back to* FAIRFAX.] My Lord, my husband will do what is best. George is always right.

FAIRFAX: [*Turns to* WASHINGTON.] George, you have not decided—have you?

WASHINGTON: I have.

FAIRFAX: [*With a long look at* WASHINGTON.] So— you stand against England!

WASHINGTON: Against whoever stands against liberty.

FAIRFAX: And you will lead the rebels!

WASHINGTON: I will serve wherever Congress sees fit to place me.

FAIRFAX: You are mad——!

MARTHA: George?

FAIRFAX: Is it ambition that maddens you?

WASHINGTON: [*Stepping back as though from a blow.*] You of all men should know me better than that. No fame, no position, no power, could tempt me to leave all this [*He spreads his arms in an encompassing gesture.*] I love. [*His eyes rest on* MARTHA. BEN *appears at the door with candles.* FAIRFAX'S *head drops, he walks unsteadily toward the door. Turns and coldly bows.*]

FAIRFAX: Good night, madam. Good night, Colonel Washington. [MARTHA *curtsies.* WASHINGTON *goes toward him.*]

WASHINGTON: I hope, my Lord, we part this night as friends?

FAIRFAX: [*Striving for control.*] Friendship like ours transcends differences of opinion. Though others may heap ignominy upon your head in the troubled future, I shall ever treasure the remembrance of my friendship with George Washington. [*Breaking.*] And damme, George! here's my hand on it! [*They clasp hands.*]

CURTAIN

'TWIXT CUP AND LIP

A GEORGE WASHINGTON PLAY IN ONE ACT

By ELLEN GARRIGUES *and* PAULINE HOPKINS

AWARDED FIRST PRIZE

By DAUGHTERS OF THE AMERICAN REVOLUTION
IN BICENTENNIAL PLAY CONTEST

The Daughters of the American Revolution sponsored a national play writing contest which was approved by the United States George Washington Bicentennial Commission. A considerable number of plays featuring the life and times of General Washington were submitted from all parts of the country. The judges gave the award to " 'Twixt Cup and Lip" for the best one-act play.

PERSONS OF THE PLAY

GENERAL GEORGE WASHINGTON
GENERAL ISRAEL PUTNAM
LORD STIRLING
GENERAL HUGH MERCER
COLONEL JOHN GLOVER
GENERAL NATHANAEL GREENE
SAMUEL FRAUNCES, *Innkeeper*
PHOEBE FRAUNCES, *his daughter*
THOMAS HICKEY, *One of Washington's Body Guard*
BILLY LEE, *General Washington's Negro Body Servant*

SCENE: *Fraunces' Tavern, New York City.*

The banqueting table is set for six people. The furniture is colonial. There are silver candelabra on the table. Above the fireplace is the portrait of Queen Charlotte of England. The shutters at the side windows are open.

TIME: *Very late afternoon, June 20, 1776.*

AT RISE: BILLY, *a tall stalwart Negro servant of about twenty-eight is singing to himself as he arranges the table—a negro spiritual, "Moses, bring back my people."*

PHOEBE: [*Daughter of* SAM FRAUNCES *enters. She is a dark beautiful girl in her twenties. Like her father she is of French extraction. Her dress is of bright rose brocade. She wears a small apron denoting her domestic rank. In her hands is a bunch of roses. She lays down the flowers, unties the ribbons of her hat, draws off her mitts and lays them aside with her hat, the while her glance sweeps the table.*] You have laid for six?

BILLY: Yes, Missy. Yo' father say foh six generals!

PHOEBE: Wine-glasses at each place? I suppose General Washington will want punch as well.

BILLY: Massa George suhtainly do like his punch, Missy.

PHOEBE: Billy, how long have you known the Commander?

BILLY: I was born at Mt. Vernon, Missy. Massa George chose me to go with him when he was made head of the whole army ovah a yeah ago.

FRAUNCES: [*Enters. He is a man in the middle forties, dark, handsome, kindly in manner and with a jovial smile. He wears a powdered wig and his small clothes are of blue velvet embroidered in gold thread. He kisses his daughter on either cheek.*] I am glad you came over, Phoebe. I miss you greatly these days.

PHOEBE: You've no one to gossip with when I am away, Father.

FRAUNCES: That is true. I dare not open my mouth except to say, "I am pleased that you like the flavour of the roast, sir." "Yes, ma'am, it is getting a little late for shad." "You wish Sally Lunn with the tea, ma'am?" It is not safe to venture a political opinion any longer.

PHOEBE: [*With sympathy*] You are really troubled, father?

FRAUNCES: Yes, matters look black. As for the Mayor, he never comes here any longer. I feel he suspects me. A tavern-keeper is not supposed to have any politics, but I am a man and right is right.

PHOEBE: I can't but wonder that his Excellency chose this as a meeting place rather than headquarters.

FRAUNCES: Our situation is near the ferry. General Greene has to cross from Long Island. Each officer is coming alone, after dark, secretly as far as possible. I am using the Long Room because it is upstairs although it is too large for a party of six.

PHOEBE: Why don't you call this tavern the "Patriot's Parlour" instead of "The Queen's Head"? It has earned another name.

FRAUNCES: I'd change the name if I dared. How little I thought fifteen years ago I should come to hate George III. It is not only Mayor Matthews who is unfriendly, but Governor Tryon as well. Another reason the Commander-in-Chief comes here tonight. It may be he hears there is plotting against him. If they could put him out of the way the Tories believe the rebellion would end very quickly.

PHOEBE: Don't be upset over them. Be glad the General has such faith in you. He feels safer here than at headquarters. So many have access to him there.

FRAUNCES: I trust he never has to change that faith. Only you, I and Billy are here tonight. The house is closed to outsiders. No one can attack him here tonight.

PHOEBE: Attack the Commanded-in-Chief. Impossible. He is idolized by his soldiers.

FRAUNCES: The very reason for putting him out of the way, I tell you. The cause would break down without him. But no sword or poison shall reach him here. Better arrange your flowers, my dear. It is getting late.

PHOEBE: Yes. [*Arranges flowers*] Some of his body-guard will watch him tonight as usual.

FRAUNCES: If not too much occupied with you.

PHOEBE: [*Occupied with flowers, hums.*] "Dry your beautiful eyes, Mademoiselle." [*Stops singing*] You are trying to make me cross, father.

FRAUNCES: I'd like to make you sensible. You see altogether too much of one of the members of the body-guard.

PHOEBE: Which one is that?

FRAUNCES: [*Annoyed*] You know whom I mean. He'll be on duty tonight. Trust him for that. Don't try to hoodwink me, Phoebe. I don't like Tom Hickey.

PHOEBE: [*Stopping her work*] You never like any one that likes me, father. Don't you want me to marry?

FRAUNCES: Yes, yes, of course. But a good man. A girl is no judge of a man with a handsome face.

PHOEBE: Can't a man be good-looking and all right? What about you, yourself?

FRAUNCES: Don't try to get around me. I don't like this fellow. I'll wager you are not the only girl he has made love to, since he deserted from the British Army.

PHOEBE: Aren't we all deserters from the British?

FRAUNCES: They drove us to it. But Hickey didn't desert here.

He was on the other side, and not interested in the Colonial cause.

PHOEBE: But he is now. He's one of the Commander-in-Chief's body-guard.

FRAUNCES: His Excellency is one of the least suspicious of men. Your friend, Hickey, is a soldier of fortune and will keep to the winning side.

PHOEBE: Don't you believe that is ours? I can take care of myself. I ought to know men, brought up in this tavern where they all have made up to me as if I were a part of your entertainment.

FRAUNCES: Too true, my dear. But the cleverest woman becomes blind when she is in love.

PHOEBE: You think Tom Hickey loves me?

FRAUNCES: And you, him; I see. It has gone further than I thought.

[*He goes out, passing BILLY entering with the punch glasses on a tray. PHOEBE is still putting the roses in vases.*]

BILLY: Them posies look mighty like those blooming right now at Mt. Vernon, Missy Phoebe. Massa George, he have de finest rose-garden in the world. I presume LADY WASHINGTON keep it up while we gone.

TOM HICKEY: [*Entering with a package in his hand*] I've sought you everywhere. Why are you doing servant's work?

[*BILLY goes out*]

PHOEBE: I'm doing what I like best, arranging flowers. What brings you here?

HICKEY: You! And a bottle of rum. His Excellency wished one brought over, and I maneuvered for the chance. I was to escort him but there are enough for that; so I came a little early to see you. The rum is for the punch tonight. [*He puts the bottle on the table*]

PHOEBE: The General knows we have plenty of good rum.

HICKEY: But you put it in the bill, don't you? This is a gift and especially fine. Shall I put it in the cupboard so that no one can sample it beforehand?

PHOEBE: [*Opening a cupboard, and letting him put the bottle within*] It must be very precious. As for me, one bottle is as good or bad as another. I never touch the stuff.

HICKEY: I know that. That's the reason I brought it straight to you. Better not tell your father about it. He might think the Commander didn't like his liquor. Your father dislikes me anyway.

PHOEBE: He is jealous of his cellar.

HICKEY: And of you. I don't wonder. You are lovelier than any of your roses, Phoebe. But if I had my way you'd have nothing worse to do than to arrange flowers. You're the sweetest girl I ever knew.

PHOEBE: You've known many, I dare say.

HICKEY: [*Standing very close to her*] Never one like you.

PHOEBE: As if I could believe that.

HICKEY: You do! in your heart. I love you more than my life.

PHOEBE: A high saying that. I wonder if I love any one so much.

HICKEY: Not one?

PHOEBE: General Washington, perhaps.

HICKEY: He's old enough to be your father.

PHOEBE: And married these seventeen years. But a cat may look at a king, and that without making eyes at him either.

HICKEY: You are not a cat, although you do try to scratch. And he will never be king.

PHOEBE: You think he is expecting that? Working for himself?

HICKEY: Who isn't? I know you are trying to make me jealous, but I don't want to be loved like a god.

PHOEBE: Never fear, Tom. You never let any one forget you are a man.

HICKEY: Why should I? [*He tries to kiss her*]

PHOEBE: [*Evading him*] No—Wait—wait!

HICKEY: What for? Don't you love me?

PHOEBE: Perhaps. But I don't want to think of us now, with this awful war on. Father and I love this country so much. We have never really had a country and now we hope for one. We are French and you are Irish and we shall both be Americans. Last night I lay awake thinking about it. But then an awful thought came—that you might be killed—and even General Washington. The British fleet is almost here.

HICKEY: You do love me. But don't let the war worry you. I admire these patriots, but I know what they are fighting. It can't last any time. One battle—if they get that far the city may surrender without even one.

PHOEBE: Never. I feel as if it would be a long struggle.

HICKEY: How can it be? Thirteen little settlements that hate one another trying to fight the greatest empire in the world.

PHOEBE: We drove the British out of Boston last year.

HICKEY: That wasn't a real battle. There is only one way for it to end, and soon, too.

PHOEBE: With us defeated.

HICKEY: Call it reconciled. I know.

PHOEBE: How can you talk so? With General Washington at the head? His body-guard ought to have more faith.

HICKEY: Faith has nothing to do with it. He's all you say, except a great general. How can he know anything about strategy? He has never fought except behind trees with rag-tag farmers.

PHOEBE: You sound like the Tories.

HICKEY: No! NO! But how can a man be a general without an army. No one could call what he has an army—without ammunition or proper guns.

PHOEBE: You frighten me. You are not loyal.

HICKEY: I am more so than those who try to get these untrained men to line up in front of the greatest army of the world. You should see those red ranks moving on—and on.

PHOEBE: If you admire them so much, why did you desert them?

HICKEY: Who has been talking to you? I didn't desert. I was left for dead on a field and some country people took me in. When I recovered I had to ship somewhere, and I came here and joined the patriots.

PHOEBE: Oh, I'm so glad, Tom. I hated to think it of you. [*He tries to kiss her again*] But don't talk as you have to any one else. They might not understand. It would sound like treason.

HICKEY: I don't want to talk to any one but you, ever. It's only because I know what the General is fighting against that I am warning you not to hope.

PHOEBE: He knows, too. I believe in him.

HICKEY: But you love me. Will you promise that as soon as the war is over—tomorrow, next month—next year—you'll come with me? Promise.

PHOEBE: Yes. But I want to be a wife, not a widow, Tom.

HICKEY: My dear sweetheart. Believe me the war will soon be over. The city may be lost. The enemy may burn it, but those fire-bells shall be our wedding-bells, and the world well lost. [*He draws her to the window*] When you see it burning I shall be here to snatch you away.

PHOEBE: Oh, don't talk of fire on a night like this—with the wind blowing such a gale.

FRAUNCES: [*Entering, looks angrily at them*] What are you here for, Mr. Hickey?

HICKEY: I am assigned here for the evening, sir. [*He whispers to* PHOEBE] I shall be guarding you, too, sweetheart.

FRAUNCES: [*Much annoyed at his whispering*] Come, come, Phoebe. Light the candles. Wait at the door downstairs, Mr. Hickey.

[*Hickey goes out, passing* COL. GLOVER *coming in*]

GLOVER: [*A bluff man, dressed, as all are, in a Continental uniform*] Good evening, Mr. Fraunces. Your darkey told me to come right up.

FRAUNCES: Quite right, Col. Glover.

COL. GLOVER: You know me?

FRAUNCES: I know every one expected tonight. The house is not open for others. My daughter, Phoebe, Col. Glover.

PHOEBE: Shall I take your cloak, sir?

GLOVER: Thank you, ma'am. [*Takes off his coat and hat and* PHOEBE *places them on a chair. While he directs his talk to* FRAUNCES, *he keeps turning a sailor's eye on* PHOEBE *who does her part in smiling at him*] A fine place, this, Mr. Fraunces. Not much like the taverns I am used to. More pretty women out taking the air here than I have ever seen. There's a dash to them. [PHOEBE, *meeting his glance, makes another curtsy*] Forsooth, I mean it, ma'am.

FRAUNCES: If you will excuse me, sir, I must be at the front door to meet the other gentlemen when they arrive.

GLOVER: I am a bit early. I only arrived today at the order of the Commander. [*As* FRAUNCES *goes out, he addresses* PHOEBE.] Well, ma'am, I take it you're looking out for us.

PHOEBE: I am housekeeper at General Washington's headquarters, sir.

STIRLING: [*The dandy of the army, extremely elegant in appearance, enters*] Good evening, Col. Glover.

GLOVER: How do you do, Lord Stirling.

STIRLING: [*Gives his coat and hat to* PHOEBE *but otherwise takes no notice of her*] Give me my new title of general.

GLOVER: [*Heartily*] Right. It is better than being an earl under a king who has tried to rob his sons of their rights.

STIRLING: The House of Lords did that for me some time ago, but now I feel it was good fortune. I prefer our George to the George across the water.

GLOVER: He is a king among men. The other is not even a man among kings.

STIRLING: You are a maker of epigrams, I see, Col. Glover. King George's mother trained him for a role too great.

GLOVER: Aye, Aye. She should have said, "Be tyrant, George."—But, here is General Mercer.

MERCER: [*Enters. He is slightly older than the other two. He greets* STIRLING *formally,* GLOVER *somewhat lustily, and speaks pleasantly to* PHOEBE] Let me congratulate you on your new title, Lord Stirling. It was deserved. The Commander could have no better aid. We are at the beginning of a long tug, I fear.

STIRLING: There is no doubt of it.

MERCER: Glover, how does New York compare with the Newfoundland Banks?

GLOVER: Better on the whole, though, perhaps not tonight. And we shall soon be fishing in deep waters. I wish we had a navy. I feel safer at sea than on land. Here is Gen. Putnam.

PUTNAM: [*Enters, nods to the three men, speaks to* PHOEBE] Helping your father tonight, Mistress Phoebe?

PHOEBE: [*with a curtsy*] Yes, sir.

PUTNAM: There is one thing we can be sure of here tonight, gentlemen; the food will be good.

PHOEBE: Thank you, sir.

PUTNAM: And safe. I had a queer warning today, gentlemen. A letter from a sergeant in one of the troops begging me to be careful where and what I ate. Is General Washington late? He never is.

GLOVER: [*Pulling out an old-fashioned watch and holding it open in his hand*] He still has one minute.

PUTNAM: Expect him in one minute then. [PHOEBE *goes out*] These are serious days. We have enemies within the city that no fortifications can shut out.

MERCER: Rumors of a Tory plot are rife.

STIRLING: The town is seething.

[WASHINGTON *enters, followed by* HICKEY *and* FRAUNCES. HICKEY *takes* WASHINGTON's *hat and coat and goes out.* FRAUNCES *remains*]

WASHINGTON: [*To the others who are standing*] Good evening. I trust I have not kept you waiting. [*He shakes hands with each of the four.*]

GLOVER: [*Closing his watch with a snap*] On the minute. It is just eight.

WASHINGTON: I'm glad. Where is General Nathanael Greene?

PUTNAM: Not arrived. And this place was chosen for his accommodation.

GLOVER: It's bad crossing the Sound tonight. The tide is running in hard, and a nasty north-easter helps to the current going out. He can not use a sail, and rowing will be none to easy. I'd hate to have to cross tonight.

WASHINGTON: But you would. And so will he. He never

fails me to any one. I never see the Quaker in him. He arrives and most effectively usually. Is your supper ready, Fraunces?

FRAUNCES: Yes, sir.

WASHINGTON: We'll sit and be served, then, and give General Greene a few minutes before we talk of our business here tonight.

[*The men seat themselves,* WASHINGTON *in the center.* PUTNAM *on his right,* STIRLING *on his left,* GLOVER *and* MERCER *together and leaving the place on the extreme left vacant.* BILLY *enters and fills the glasses.*]

WASHINGTON: What are you here for, Billy? I thought you were taking a holiday.

BILLY: Massa Fraunces sent for me, sir.

WASHINGTON: Why?

BILLY: He say you must have all your friends around you tonight, sir.

GLOVER: Like New York better than Mt. Vernon, Billy?

BILLY: Oh, Lordy no. There shore ain't no place like Mt. Vernon on this earth, and heah we have to work for our living.

STIRLING: Sounds like Adam turned out of Eden, General Washington.

[BILLY *goes out*]

WASHINGTON: He almost makes *me* homesick. I missed their dark faces in New England. They have the most genial natures and a talent for leisure, which you Northerners lack, as you discerned from his remarks.

PUTNAM: You are no one to praise leisure, General.

WASHINGTON: Oh, I, too, can loaf in Eden, as Stirling calls it. But it seems long since.

GLOVER: I don't know how you can feel that way toward niggers and keep them as slaves.

WASHINGTON: They are not fit for much else yet. I free them when they are, if they wish their freedom. For the most part they do not. Billy shall choose when the war is over. [*As* BILLY *enters and sets a plate of hot biscuits on the table*] I hope you have something good for us tonight, Billy.

BILLY: Yes, sah, Massa George. I told Massa Fraunces you nevah eat a meal without hot bread.

WASHINGTON: Then you know you've told a lie as black as your skin. I've had cold pie for breakfast in New England for the last year.

GLOVER: And liked it, I trust, General. I do.

WASHINGTON: If I never have worse fare during this war I shall be content.

BILLY: There's floating island, too, like Missus Martha have at Mt. Vernon.

WASHINGTON: That does take me home. But, tonight I'd like to turn Long Island into a floating body and push it out to sea. It is too close to Manhattan. What can be detaining Greene? [*As* PHOEBE *enters with a dish of cold meats*] You are here, too, Mistress Phoebe? I am surrounded by good friends tonight. My housekeeper, you know, gentlemen. Sometimes I feel that my bodyguards obey her more readily than they do me. But I trust her to keep them in order.

STIRLING: Fraunces is a staunch patriot and this place a sanctuary in a city filled by Tories and ruled by them. They grow bolder daily as the fleet nears.

WASHINGTON: Not all Tories. Not half, I think. You ought not to decry your birthplace, Lord Stirling.

[FRAUNCES *fills the wine glasses*]

STIRLING: Aren't you disturbed by the rumors of a Tory plot?

WASHINGTON: I'm trying not to be.

PUTNAM: I had a written warning to beware tonight.

WASHINGTON: Beware of spoiling our digestion now. Let us drink to something pleasant, the Bill of Independence now before Congress.

MERCER: May the Colonies join in passing it. Virginia has already, General.

WASHINGTON: [*As they drink*] Yes, last month.

[GREENE *enters hurriedly, throwing his hat and coat on a chair*]

WASHINGTON: Late again, my youngest Brigadier-General.

GREENE: [*Bowing to all*] My God, General Washington, let me tell you I started hours earlier than necessary to avoid hearing you say that. But such a crossing, driven this way and that by the wind and current. Eddies everywhere. No sail possible. And then on this side the strangest happening. [*Takes his seat at the table*]

WASHINGTON: Eat something and take a glass of wine before you tell us of your troubles. We have just been drinking to our Independence from Great Britain.

GREENE: [*Raising his glass which* FRAUNCES *fills*] Dare I drink? I'll risk anything you have, your Excellency. [*He looks at them, drinks*] Independence from Great Britain.

PUTNAM: What nonsense are you talking?

GREENE: That's what it amounts to, I dare say. But how could I know? As I stepped from the wharf a man, his face muffled in his cloak, seized my arm with a tight grip, whispering, I have waited long for you tonight, Nathanael Greene. Are you loyal to Washington? If you value his life and your own come with me. I thought at first he was threatening me but he had no apparent weapon and as his cloak fell away I saw he was old, very old. I protested I should be late, but he said there were worse offenses. I hope you agree, General. I should have broken away but curiosity let him propel me into a shack by the riverside. Imagine my disgust when he said he was an astrologer. He had read the stars concerning you at your birth on February the eleventh. At that I knew he was mad. You were born on the twenty-second, were you not?

WASHINGTON: By the new calendar. Yes. By the old one he was right. The family Bible says February the eleventh.

GREENE: Umh. That makes it stranger than ever. I was fascinated anyway. Forecasting the future is interesting. He told of your greatness, and I assured him I needed no stars to tell me of that. Then he added, "He will be one of the greatest if he survives the dangers that surround him tonight."

PUTNAM: That is close calculation. But it sounds like my sergeant. The older men call him crazy, too. But he is young. This one was old and an astrologer. Bah.

GREENE: He might have been disguised, now I think of it. He seemed frightened and afraid of being overheard. He hinted that the city might be set on fire tonight. The stars had foretold a conflagration.

MERCER: The rain seems to have got the better of the stars.

GLOVER: No good comes of mocking at the stars.

MERCER: You are a sailor and believe in the old superstitions about the stars?

GLOVER: I sail by them, sir.

GREENE: He told me to induce you to leave this house at once and to eat nothing under this roof.

WASHINGTON: He delayed you too long. We have eaten a goodly amount already.

FRAUNCES: You have not touched one article of food not prepared by me, my daughter or Billy.

WASHINGTON: We all trust you, Sam. Don't worry. You think he may have been disguised? Why?

GREENE: I'm not sure. Suddenly he shoved me out and bade me hasten. Then he pulled me back to say that if we outwitted the evil stars tonight, a great combination pointed to the fourth day of next month as a day of import.

GLOVER: The fourth of July? The fleet may arrive that day.

WASHINGTON: Earlier, I expect. I have no knowledge of astrology and have no desire to know the future.

GLOVER: [*Rising impulsively, goes to the window*] An ugly night. How can one steer without stars?

PUTNAM: [*As* PHOEBE *trims the candles*] We don't need stars. We need plans. Let's to our business.

WASHINGTON: If we knew the future was to be fortunate, we should grow lax in effort to make it so: if we know it was to be evil, we should try to change it. So what benefit is forecasting? Uncertainty makes us do our best.

STIRLING: But there are many rumors of an internal plot. I've heard them myself.

WASHINGTON: One can study what an open enemy can do. That is our business here tonight, but what of the plots of unknown foes! Expecting to be assassinated or poisoned is in itself death, poisoning our faith in every one, even in our food. [*He laughs*] I think I prefer poison to starvation.

[PHOEBE, FRAUNCES, *and* BILLY *leave, carrying out dishes.* HICKEY *paces past the door opening in the passage*]

MERCER: I can't imagine who could plot against you.

WASHINGTON: Certainly, none here tonight. I am as sure of Sam and his daughter as I am of myself, and Billy is one of my own servants. Greene, you have raised a perturbing question. I try to use foresight. It is of the greatest necessity in war. But who can pick out the disloyal. Courage and brains I can judge, but both may be used to cloak treachery. The man on whom you most rely may be the most dangerous.

GREENE: [*With fire*] My life for yours, Commander-in-Chief. [*Raises his glass.*]

MERCER: And mine.

STIRLING: And mine.

PUTNAM: And mine.

GLOVER: [*Nods, drinks*] Yet the Saviour of mankind was sold by one closest to him. I like not ill-boding stars.

WASHINGTON: There is no Judas in this room. We represent a common cause. That cause is our Saviour. Let us now to the business which brings us here.

PUTNAM: So be it.

WASHINGTON: Though it is a year since Lexington, I think we realize that war in earnest is beginning now. Yesterday a fast sloop brought news that Gen. Howe was on his way, presumably to meet his brother, the Admiral with his mighty fleet. Together they can marshal twenty-four thousand men, and we have not half that number. If they can land, take the city, wipe out our army, they believe the war is over.

PUTNAM: Other British troops will move south from Canada.

WASHINGTON: And engage such as we have in the north. As you know, Gen. Putnam has been busy fortifying Manhattan Island and Gen. Greene Long Island. But the stretch from Fort George at the Battery to Spuyten Dyval is fifteen miles. If they can pass the Narrows, and I fear they may, what are our chances of protecting the city?

PUTNAM: They will use Staten Island as a base and sweep up the North and East Rivers with their batteries.

GREENE: They will have to land their troops on Long Island.

WASHINGTON: They may do both.

[FRAUNCES *enters with food*]

MERCER: Only from Long Island can they attack with land forces.

WASHINGTON: So I believe. On Long Island our first battle in the open will take place.

GLOVER: If only we had a navy to meet them at sea.

WASHINGTON: Filled with mariners such as your soldiers from Marblehead it would do much. But we are short even in transportation for ferrying from Fort Lee and Paulus Hook in New Jersey. And in gathering wagons we need, we shall have to leave Kingsbridge short of men. But we must take risks. Men grow more fearful awaiting danger than facing it. What do you think, Greene?

GREENE: Brooklyn Heights is high and well-wooded and fortified. I know the passes between the hills from the shore and can guard them—if I can have men and leaders.

WASHINGTON: You shall have the aid of every officer here and others who can't be present. Sullivan is coming down from Canada. You agree, I trust, gentlemen.

THE OTHERS: Of course. Of course.

GREENE: We'll hold Long Island then.

PUTNAM: [*Rising and walking up and down behind the chairs*] But if we do not we shall have to evacuate all Manhattan.

WASHINGTON: I suppose so. They can fortify and cross all the Sound up to Flushing Bay.

GREENE: There is no use expecting defeat.

WASHINGTON: You are wrong, Greene. Learning to expect defeat is a great part of war—not in order to accept it, only to retreat safely to begin again.

GLOVER: Trust you for that. I wager you can surprise them whatever happens.

WASHINGTON: We must certainly consider every eventuality. I do not wish to seem pessimistic. We have advantages. Their army is in part mercenary and against such poor devils I'll guarantee our men unpaid or only with paper promises. We also know the ground or Greene does, and the others shall. I learned when I was with Braddock, the British do not like to change their methods of fighting.

PUTNAM: [*As he sits down again*] They certainly do not.

WASHINGTON: But they are brave and trained. Never doubt that, and now they will fight in the open and may win. But Congress wants us to risk it.

STIRLING: They will certainly have those among them from this city who know Long Island as well as we do.

WASHINGTON: You may be right. We shall have to know every inch of it, to be able to move quickly in attack or retreat, be awake while they sleep, fast when they feast. We shall have to try Spartan fare and methods.

GLOVER: Not even pie for breakfast, General.

WASHINGTON: Nor floating island for dessert. I fear I have over-eaten. Their numbers and equipment are the real danger. We have too few. They have a great Empire to supply their needs and we not even a united country until the bill in Congress passes. But we have a cause.

GREENE: And we have you, sir. My astrologer was a poor prophet.

Washington: I trust Billy and Mistress Phoebe to outwit evil stars. From you, Greene, we shall want detailed maps of Long Island as soon as you can furnish them.

GREENE: I will have copies ready tomorrow, as many as you want.

WASHINGTON: About twelve, I think. You shall have the pick of the troops. Not much in way of uniforms. We have some good guns, captured from the enemy. Our men know how to train with the old ones, thank God.

[PHOEBE *begins making the punch.*]

GREENE: We can pick out their redcoats and the skirts of the Highlanders and the tall hats of the Hessians. They may take us for just fox-hunting farmers.

GLOVER: Foxes are tricky to hunt.

WASHINGTON: It will be our business to outwit them. I have a task for you, Glover. Will you and your men undertake the transportation? In case of retreat there will be almost no time. You will consider it fully and get your men here as soon as possible.

GLOVER: I don't know the tides or storms that can scare my Massachusetts men. Though a night like this would make it—well, not easy.

WASHINGTON: The fate of the army or of the country may rest with you.

GLOVER: Trust me, sir.

WASHINGTON: I do.

STIRLING: Have you considered. . . . Don't think me too insistent—the foes within the city. While men and officers are on Long Island, might not the Tories burn down the city?

WASHINGTON: Don't think me heedless or indifferent, Stirling. If only I could find one definite bit of information, one person involved. Fraunces, how much do you know of this plot?

FRAUNCES: Only that Governor Tryon and Mayor Matthews are in it or hoping to aid the fleet when it arrives.

WASHINGTON: [*Rises, walks about, opens a window*] How? By burning down the city, which is their own? The British will want to use it if they drive us out. It would be stupid.

GREENE: But men *are* stupid. It was what my astrologer predicted—at a signal—from this house—tonight.

PUTNAM: My message from the sergeant was the same. The two are one and he not worth noting.

FRAUNCES: Who could signal from under my roof? I have closed the place to all strangers tonight. [*He goes out*]

WASHINGTON: It is all beyond my powers, where I cannot

see. I trust God, my friends, to protect us. I can't arrest on rumour—not the Governor of the state or the Mayor.

PUTNAM: You might interne these outspoken Tories.

WASHINGTON: It would make enemies for us among those now wavering.

PUTNAM: You have to fight fire with fire.

GLOVER: But be sure which way the wind is blowing first. You might burn up your own house, Putnam.

WASHINGTON: I promise to act on the first direct evidence I can obtain. Mistress Phoebe, let us have our punch and drown our fears in your good mixture. [*He resumes his chair*]

PHOEBE: It is almost ready, sir. I am stirring in the rum you sent for it.

WASHINGTON: Did I send rum? I do not remember doing so.

PHOEBE: It was a gift, a bottle that one of your body-guard brought.

WASHINGTON: I have some good rum sent by Morris. That must be it. But it is no better than Sam's. However, let's have it.

GREENE: May I have that window closed, General Washington? I must have been chilled by the wetting I received while crossing.

WASHINGTON: By all means. [*As he speaks* FRAUNCES *enters and carries the bowl of punch to the table*] Don't become ill, Greene. You are a very necessary person these days. Hickey, please close the window. [*Calls aloud*]

[HICKEY *enters, notes that the bowl of punch has been placed before Washington who is ladling it into the glasses. Before he closes the window he looks quickly about, sees that no one at the table is watching, leans out and drops a handkerchief.* PHOEBE *alone sees him do this. He returns to his guard at the door.*]

WASHINGTON: Gentlemen, all our friends. [*He passes the glasses*]

PHOEBE: [*Quickly*] Excellency, may I ask a favour?

WASHINGTON: [*Putting cup down*] To be sure. We owe you and your father much for good food and care tonight.

PHOEBE: [*Holding her hand to her heart as if to stop its beating, and speaking so that* HICKEY *cannot hear*] Will you invite your body-guard, Thomas Hickey, to join you in the toast to the great cause?

WASHINGTON: [*Looks sharply at her*] For his benefit or ours?

PHOEBE: God knows. Not I. Do not drink until he does.

WASHINGTON: Gentlemen, rise with your glasses but do not drink unless I tell you to. Hickey, come in.

HICKEY: [*Enters, stands at attention*] Yes, sir.

WASHINGTON: Come forward. We want you to join us here in a toast to the cause for which we are all in arms. [*He hands him a glass.*]

[PHOEBE *moves toward the door, closes it and stands before it.*]

HICKEY: [*Takes the glass and looks at* GENERAL WASHINGTON] I will not. [*He drops the glass and turns to the door, pushing* PHOEBE *roughly out of the way*] Traitorous hussy.

[*He opens the door and falls into the arms of* BILLY *who is just about to enter.* BILLY *seizes* HICKEY *to save himself from falling*]

GREENE: Hold him. Hold him fast, Billy. He's a traitor.

[HICKEY *struggles in vain in the arms of the big black man*]

GREENE: [*Rushes toward* HICKEY] I'll cut you to pieces, you damned poisoner.

WASHINGTON: No! No! A soldier's death is too good for him. Bring him here, Billy. [BILLY *lifts* HICKEY *in his arms and comes in the room. The others disarm him*]

FRAUNCES: Tie his wrists behind him.

BILLY: [*To* WASHINGTON] I was coming to tell you, Massa, someone set fire to this house. I were in time to put it out. It was under the staircase, Massa George.

[*Church bells begin to ring outside*]

GREENE: [*Rushes to the window and flings it open*] Flames near Headquarters, General.

WASHINGTON: There are plenty to attend to that. General Stirling and General Mercer, ride about the city and see if there is danger elsewhere. Gather any soldiers you meet. Hickey, are there others of my guard in this?

[STIRLING *and* MERCER *leave*]

HICKEY: [*Sullenly*] If I tell, do I get off?

WASHINGTON: Never, but I shall find out. Putnam, will you take him to the nearest guard-house? Billy, go with him. We shall have evidence now and give a warning to all traitors.

[PHOEBE *falls, weeping, into a chair*]

WASHINGTON: Why, did you suspect him?

PHOEBE: I'm not sure I did, sir. But you did not seem to know about the rum. Then he signaled from the window. I saw him. You trusted us.

HICKEY: [*Fiercely*] You said you loved me.

PHOEBE: I did. But you would have had me mix death for him and my friends in my father's house. [*A pause*] They called it a sanctuary. Firebells can never be wedding-bells.

GLOVER: They can be funeral bells.

[*They take* HICKEY *out*]

WASHINGTON: [*To* PHOEBE] He is well lost, my girl. The loyalty of this house will never be forgotten. We shall meet here again, Fraunces, if we survive this war. Thank you, Phoebe, for my life and those of my friends. I must go. The war has begun.

[FRAUNCES *stands with his hand on his daughter's head as the curtain falls*]

WASHINGTON DANCED

A GEORGE WASHINGTON PLAY IN ONE ACT

By FRANCE GOLDWATER

Copyright, 1931, by France Goldwater

*Permission was given to produce this play
without royalty fee during 1932.*

DRAMATIS PERSONAE

(IN THE ORDER OF THEIR APPEARANCE)

JED, *General Washington's Negro Butler.*
HARRISON, *General Washington's Secretary.*
GENERAL GEORGE WASHINGTON.
LYDIA CARTWRIGHT, *a visitor from Philadelphia.*
MARTHA WASHINGTON.
LIEUTENANT-COLONEL THOMAS KNOWLTON, *an officer.*
CAPTAIN NATHAN HALE, *of the Colonial Army.*
ANSEL WRIGHT, *Nathan Hale's servant.*
CAPTAIN JOHN HULL
SERGEANT STEPHEN HEMPSTEAD } *Friends of Hale.*
TIME: *Evening of September 14, 1776.*
PLACE: *Headquarters of General Washington, just outside New York*

SET: *Elegantly furnished living room, colonial style. There are two doors, the one at back left leads to the hall, the other, back right, leads to the dining room. The doors are placed so that those entering or leaving are immediately seen. There is a secret door back center hidden by a long table before it, upon which are a Bible and a pair of candlesticks. At the back right is a window with shutters. A fire burns in the fireplace down right. An easy chair stands before it facing the audience. There are a footstool and a small pie-crust table near it. A harpsichord stands right center upstage so placed that the player faces the audience. A bell rope hangs on the wall back left. A colonial secretary stands against the wall left. The desk open and full of papers. Near the front of the stage is a round table and several chairs; three of these are arranged so as to be easy to move to the table.*

COSTUME: *The officers wear the buff and blue uniforms of the Colonial Army. WASHINGTON is dressed in the distinctive garb of Commander-in-Chief. MARTHA and LYDIA are plainly attired in polonaise frocks of the period with hair arranged in Colonial coiffure.*

[*As the curtain rises, JED enters, back left, with a lighted taper; goes fearfully to window and peeps cautiously through the shutter. There is the sound of voices and laughter off back right—WASHINGTON'S and a young girl's—LYDIA'S. HARRISON enters hurriedly, back left, comes quickly to JED, speaks in low tone.*]

HARRISON: Jed, where is General Washington?
JED: [*Indicating back right.*] Still at dinner, Marse Harrison.
HARRISON: [*Impatiently.*] He is dining late.
JED: Hit's on 'count the lil'le Missie Lydia Cartwright jes arriving from Philadelphia.
HARRISON: [*After a moment's indecision.*] Tell General Washington I must see him—and at once. [*As JED stars off back right.*] Be careful not to alarm him. Merely say I'm waiting.
JED: Yes, Suh.
[*He goes out back right. HARRISON quickly brings*

a map from the secretary desk and lays it on the table left. WASHINGTON enters axiously, makes sure the door back right, is closed, comes down quickly to HARRISON.]
WASHINGTON: What did you discover, Mr. Harrison?
HARRISON: Your Excellency, two more spies were caught this evening——
WASHINGTON: [*Clenches his fists and strides center.*] That means the enemy is planning a movement. Any other news?
HARRISON: Five deserters were brought back to camp.
WASHINGTON: [*Angrily.*] They should be meted out severe punishment. [*Paces.*] We must keep up the morale of the army.
HARRISON: I'll make a note of it. [*Writes on a little book which he puts in his vest pocket.*] There is another matter, Your Excellency——
WASHINGTON: Quickly then. [*Looks anxiously toward door back right.*] I dislike remaining away from the ladies too long. It may arouse their fears——
HARRISON: Several men have been apprehended—evidently townspeople—loitering near your headquarters here. There has been word passed through the town, according to them, that you are in hiding, sick with fear——
WASHINGTON: [*Angrily.*] Preposterous!
HARRISON: And that you mean to run away, leaving the army to it's fate——
WASHINGTON: We must stop that rumor!—and at once. [*He strides to fireplace and stands a moment in deep thought.*] Mr. Harrison, have tapers put in the windows of every room in the house, have the shutters opened, to make a show of festivity!
HARRISON: [*In shocked protest.*] But Your Excellency——
WASHINGTON: [*Kindly.*] I know, my boy, it ill becomes us at this serious moment, but it may serve a useful purpose——
HARRISON: [*Bows.*] Very well, Sir. [*Starts off left.*]
WASHINGTON: And Mr. Harrison, send for Lieutenant-Colonel Knowlton. I must know—and immediately—what progress he has made in the matter of securing a spy to send through the British lines.
HARRISON: I shall send a messenger at once.
WASHINGTON: Do.
[*HARRISON goes out, back left.*]
WASHINGTON: [*Opens the door, back right, with a show of gayety.*] Ladies, will you join me now?
[*MARTHA and LYDIA enter, talking together.*]
MARTHA: [*To WASHINGTON.*] I trust you have finished with all matters of business for the day?
WASHINGTON: We can not expect too much, my dear Patsy.

LYDIA: [*Coyly.*] Oh, your Excellency. I have learned the new step that is all the rage in Philadelphia!

WASHINGTON: Can you show us how it is done?

[*MARTHA takes a chair near fireplace.*]

WASHINGTON: [*To MARTHA.*] Are you not joining us?

MARTHA: I would rather watch at first.

LYDIA: Oh, but I must have music to it.

WASHINGTON: Suppose you hum a tune? I have heard you are most aptly inclined toward music.

LYDIA: Oh, Sir, I fear you have been misinformed.

MARTHA: [*Turns, impatiently.*] George, you have ridden among the troops all day. Is it not time you rested?

WASHINGTON: My dear Patsy, this is diversion.

[*He turns expectantly to LYDIA. JED enters, back left, with several lighted tapers, some of which he places in the window, some around the room.*]

MARTHA: Jed, what is the meaning of this?

WASHINGTON: To celebrate the arrival of our charming young guest from Philadelphia.

[*He bows to the girl, who curtsies. MARTHA smiles indulgently. HARRISON enters from back left.*]

MARTHA: Oh, Mr. Harrison, do play a sprightly dance on the harpsichord! Mistress Lydia has promised to show us a new dance.

HARRISON: [*Comes close to WASHINGTON before taking his seat at harpsichord; in low tone.*] I sent a messenger to bring Lieutenant-Colonel Knowlton. [*WASHINGTON nods approval; goes to arrange footstool for MARTHA, who smiles her thanks. LYDIA waits beside harpsichord.*]

LYDIA: [*Humming and beating time.*] In a rhythm like this——

HARRISON: [*Playing a lively jig, Colonial style.*] Now, I have it.

LYDIA: That suits very well. [*Turns to WASHINGTON, who still hovers over MARTHA.*] Your Excellency—we are ready.

MARTHA: [*Shakes a finger.*] Mind you do not dance for an hour—as you did the last time you danced.

WASHINGTON: [*Reaches over to tap her playfully on the cheek.*] You are always understanding, my dear Patsy.

[*He joins LYDIA. HARRISON plays.*]

LYDIA: [*In center of stage, in position to show dance.*] If you attend for a moment, you will catch the rhythm——

LYDIA: Now, Your Excellency—if you are ready. To the right—so—now—to the left—Suppose you try it?

[*They dance the jig as danced in Colonial times. In the middle of the dance, JED enters, back left, excitedly.*]

JED: [*Bowing.*] I beg yo' pardon, Marse——

WASHINGTON: [*Stops abruptly, comes to him.*] Yes, Jed?

[*HARRISON plays softly, tapering off until he stops.*]

JED: An officer gemman to see you, say hit's mos' desprit im-potan'——

WASHINGTON: [*Aside to him.*] Tell him I will see him. I will ring when I am ready to have you bring him in.

[*JED bows and goes out, back left. HARRISON stops playing.*]

MARTHA: [*In alarm.*] What is it, George?

WASHINGTON: [*Goes to her.*] Nothing to be alarmed over. Lieutenant-Colonel Knowlton has brought word.

MARTHA: May not Jed say you will see him in the morning?

WASHINGTON: [*Puts his hands on her shoulders.*] I must hear! [*Crosses to LYDIA.*] I regret, Lydia, that I am forced to postpone the dancing lesson. [*To MARTHA.*] and to ask you both to retire.

LYDIA: [*Pouting.*] We could have had it perfected in a little time!

[*WASHINGTON walks with MARTHA and LYDIA to door, back right.*]

MARTHA: [*Turning at door, playfully stern.*] Mind you do not let him keep you late. These matters of war are making you a mere shadow of your former self.

WASHINGTON: You are kinder to me than I deserve. [*He bows deeply, LYDIA curtsies. They leave. He goes swiftly to pull bell rope. Then joins HARRISON at the table.*] Mr. Harrison, I am very worried. I can scarcely concentrate. Listen closely, let no word escape you. Indicate, if you hear me making decisions that seem counterwise——

HARRISON: You may depend upon me, Sir. [*WASHINGTON puts his hand on HARRISON'S shoulder.*] This is the map captured on one of the spys——[*They bend over the map.*]

KNOWLTON: [*Enters, back left, heartily; he is a six-foot, husky, uncouth.*] Well, your Excellency, what has happened that you call me at this untimely hour? [*He and WASHINGTON shake hands, vigorously.*]

WASHINGTON: I am anxious to know what headway you have made in securing a spy to go through the enemy's lines.

KNOWLTON: [*Sits sprawled on a chair.*] I called the council Your Excellency suggested——[*He hesitates and looks at HARRISON, who sits right with back to audience, facing the Generals.*]

WASHINGTON: [*Impatiently.*] Well? and what came of it?

KNOWLTON: Of the twelve officers I brought together not one offered to go. They felt it beneath their dignity—with certain death, besides.

WASHINGTON: Then we have no one to send?

KNOWLTON: Aye, but wait. I made a powerful speech, pointing out that the man we would send through the British lines must be a man of education, a man who understands the technical side of military plans and can make the necessary drawings.

WASHINGTON: Did not that appeal to them?

KNOWLTON: No one moved. As I finished speaking, young Captain Nathan Hale came forward—he having just arrived. He said, "I will undertake it."

WASHINGTON: [*Much moved.*] Ah, Capt. Nathan Hale——

KNOWLTON: Aye. The meeting broke up in a storm. His friends begged him not to go, then threatened him, but he remained firm.

WASHINGTON: What qualifications has he?

KNOWLTON: You mind, after the army came to New York, that Hale—with only a few of the men from his company—captured a British sloop anchored in the East River? Under the protection of a man-o'-war she was, but young Hale brought her to shore without mishap. Full of clothes and edibles she was too!

WASHINGTON: I remember. It was brave work and showed a cool head.

KNOWLTON: Besides, he's strong, and—[*Looks around to see HARRISON watching him, lowers his voice and leans closer to WASHINGTON*] his loyalty is unquestionable.

WASHINGTON: Has he a suitable disguise?

KNOWLTON: Aye. He taught school at New London and has sent for his schoolmaster's garb.

WASHINGTON: I admire Captain Hale greatly. A fine, clean lad, full of enthusiasm. I hate to sacrifice one of such. For, know ye, this is a perilous undertaking.

KNOWLTON: Better to sacrifice one than a whole army.

WASHINGTON: You say rightly. [*He sits in deep thought for a moment.*] When will he be ready to leave?

KNOWLTON: Immediately. I have asked him to come here for your final instructions.

WASHINGTON: You did well. [*To HARRISON.*] You will bring—from the desk in my bedchamber—a paper upon which I have outlined the objectives——

HARRISON: Yes, your Excellency. [*He bows and goes out, back left.*]

KNOWLTON: [*Watches him leave. After the door closes he wipes his head as if he has been under a great strain.*] He has watched me as if I were the spy meself——

WASHINGTON: You have nothing to fear. I might overlook a detail; Mr. Harrison, never.

KNOWLTON: A fine precaution but damn'd uncomfortable for me, Sir!

WASHINGTON: [*Annoyed.*] I beg your pardon.

KNOWLTON: [*Arises unwillingly and bows.*] And I beg yours, Sir.

[*JED enters, back left.*]

JED: A young gemman say he 'spose to meet Loot-Colon'l Knowlton here.

KNOWLTON: [*Rising.*] That's Captain Hale now!

WASHINGTON: Show him in, Jed.

JED: Yes, Marse. [*He opens the door, back left, for NATHAN HALE, who enters quickly. He is dressed in the uniform of a captain in the Colonial Army. Behind HALE, in the uniform of a private, ANSEL WRIGHT enters, but stops to stand against the wall, back left. He carries a valise. WASHINGTON and KNOWLTON stand facing HALE.*]

HALE: [*Advances and bows.*] Good evening, Your Excellency. [*Bows to KNOWLTON.*] And to you, Sir.

WASHINGTON: [*Acknowledges his greeting.*] Captain Hale, it is indeed a most touching proof of your love for your country that you undertake this perilous mission.

HALE: I am fully sensible of the consequences of discovery and capture in such a situation.

WASHINGTON: Bravely said, but I hope you will not be put to the final test.

HALE: I thank your Excellency for your good wishes but I stand ready to die for my country. [*HARRISON returns with a paper, which he lays on the table before WASHINGTON.*]

WASHINGTON: Please be seated, Gentlemen. [*HARRISON puts three chairs up to the table. WASHINGTON sits center; HALE left; and KNOWLTON right; HARRISON takes his former chair with his back to the audience at left and faces them; he writes constantly. WASHINGTON turns to HALE.*]

WASHINGTON: May I ask what has prompted your act of heroism in undertaking this expedition, beside our country's great need?

HALE: Since I have been in the army, a year and a half by now, I have done little of real worth toward gaining the freedom of my beloved land. It is my motto that, "A man ought never lose a moment." I chafe at my uselessness——

WASHINGTON: Come, my dear Sir, I am sure you underestimate your ability.

HALE: [*Smiling.*] Your Excellency is very kind.

WASHINGTON: [*Raising his hand in protest, sadly.*] This mission may prove your end——

HALE: [*Gets up, takes a turn up stage and back, stands up straight near Washington.*] Sir, the sacrifice of oneself for the benefit and salvation of others, is the worthiest use a man can make of his life.

WASHINGTON: [*With deep feeling, stands near HALE.*] Would that the whole army were made of the stuff that you are! [*KNOWLTON takes a pinch of snuff and sneezes; ANSEL, who still stands back left, drops the valise; the rest turn to look at him; HALE goes quickly to him.*]

HALE: [*To the rest.*] Allow me to introduce my faithful servant, Ansel Wright, who enlisted in my company the better to serve me and my country. [*WASHINGTON and KNOWLTON bow to ANSEL, who is quite overawed; HARRISON keeps his seat.*]

WASHINGTON: [*To HALE.*] You will please ask your Mister Wright to step into the hall until we have had a short conference.

· HALE: Certainly, Sir. [*To ANSEL.*] You will kindly wait until I call.

ANSEL: [*Gets his feet all tangled up as he tries to bow to WASHINGTON; picks up the valise and backs out at the same time.*] Y—yes—S—Sir. [*After he is gone, HALE laughs with the rest and comes back to the table.*]

WASHINGTON: Now, Gentlemen, for the business at hand. [*All three are seated.*] Movements of the enemy's troops started early this evening. We thought it a mere change of camp position, but our messengers inform us they are marching——

KNOWLTON: [*Excitedly.*] Marching? No wonder you are anxious!

WASHINGTON: But we are utterly at a loss to know what their objective is, unless we send a spy through their lines. [*To HALE.*] That is why I have enlisted your aid.

HALE: I understand, your Excellency.

WASHINGTON: [*Spreads out the map; HALE and KNOWLTON bend over it.*] I have marked here the fortifications of the enemy and the strength I feel they have at each place. Make a mental note, Captain Hale, and discover if such is the case.

HALE: I will do so, Sir.

WASHINGTON: It will not be wise to carry papers for reference. All of your findings and drawings should be secreted between the soles of your shoes. You understand?

HALE: I do, Your Excellency.

WASHINGTON: Lieutenant-Colonel Knowlton tells me you have been a schoolmaster. It would be an act of caution to note your findings in Latin.

HALE: I can do it easily.

[*HARRISON writes; HALE notes places on map; KNOWLTON sits back and listens.*]

WASHINGTON: Captain Hale, there are four questions I am desirous of having answered. First;—[*He pauses and holding up his hand checks off the questions on his fingers as he asks them. HALE nods after each one as if letting the question sink into his memory, notes position of places mentioned on map.*] Will the British attack the city of New York directly, or will they cross from Montressor's Island to Harlem? Second;—Will they pass higher up the sound and land at Morrisania, or sail along Long Island and land at some point even further east? Third;—Is it their intention to cut off the communications of the American Army from the whole country? And fourth;—Will they land parties simultaneously in North and East Rivers, stretch across Manhattan Island, and thus hem in the town?

Upon the answers to these questions hangs my future movements. You begin to realize the importance of your mission?

HALE: Yes. And you may rest assured, Your Excellency, I would lay down my life rather than fail you!

WASHINGTON: I believe you. [*Pauses. Bitterly.*] You must realize that we, with but fourteen thousand men, must stand against fully twenty-five thousand. A most unequal match——

HALE: [*Fervently.*] But Oh, Sir, never will the enemy be able to fight with the determination of winning that we have. We are protecting our homes and our beloved country. The Hessians are hirelings of a German king and are not anxious for this war. And winning or losing means naught to the British soldiers.

[*KNOWLTON takes a pinch of snuff and blows his nose loudly; WASHINGTON, greatly moved, rises to stand near HALE.*]

WASHINGTON: Thank you, my son, for reminding me. I have become so accustomed to the hearing of desertions and treason in the ranks, it is as if I had received reenforcements to hear you speak thus!

KNOWLTON: [*Leans back in his chair in know-it-all attitude.*] You will admit I have chosen a fitting person. Haven't I said truly he shows the proper mettle?

WASHINGTON: [*Offended by his attitude.*] He does, indeed. [*To HALE.*] The time draws near for your departure.

HALE: My servant has brought the disguise I shall wear. Does it please Your Excellency to pass upon it?

WASHINGTON: By all means. Mr. Harrison, please to assist Captain Hale to a suitable room where he can change his clothes. [*HALE rises; bows to both men and goes out, left, followed by HARRISON. WASHINGTON watches them go.*] I hesitate to send him.

KNOWLTON: You can not choose but let him go. It would destroy his belief in you if you decided otherwise now.

WASHINGTON: True. [*He paces down stage center and back in deep thought. There is a sound of scuffling in the hall off, left. In a moment JED appears in the doorway, left, excitedly.*]

JED: Begging you' pardon, Master, but hit's two young off'cers 'sistin' to come in! [*KNOWLTON blusters toward door.*]

WASHINGTON: [*Kindly.*] Show them in, Jed.

KNOWLTON: Perhaps, Sir, it were safer for me to see them. You had better retire.

WASHINGTON: [*Quietly.*] No, I will see them.

[*JED opens door, left. CAPTAIN HULL and SERGEANT HEMPSTEAD excitedly appear in door.*]

WASHINGTON: Gentlemen—— [*They advance into the room and bow to him and to KNOWLTON.*]

HULL: Honored Sir, we have come with a protest!

WASHINGTON: Is your protest of such import that we cannot decently greet each other?

HEMPSTEAD: [*Advancing, beseechingly.*] We beg your pardon, your Excellency, but are we too late? Have you already sent Captain Hale?

WASHINGTON: He has not gone as yet. He is preparing in another room.

HULL: [*Eagerly, to HEMPSTEAD.*] Then we yet have time!

HEMPSTEAD: [*To WASHINGTON.*] Believe me, Sir, we do not question your wisdom in sending a spy through the enemy's lines, but we have come to implore you to change your decision about sending Captain Nathan Hale! [*Before he finishes, HALE, dressed as a schoolmaster, appears in door, left. ANSEL and HARRISON are behind him. All stop when they hear HEMPSTEAD.*]

HALE: [*With authority.*] What are you doing here, Sergeant Hempstead? And you, Captain Hull? [*Everyone turns toward him.*] Why have you come to interfere in my affairs?

HULL: But listen, Nathan—— [*HARRISON comes quickly into the room to stand extreme left with his back to the audience so that he may see everyone in the room. ANSEL, frightened by the proceedings, stands against wall, back center. WASHINGTON and KNOWLTON exchange glances over HALE'S changed appearance. They stand right.*]

HALE: A great honor has been bestowed upon me. I am chosen for a delicate mission, which I hope to carry out to the full satisfaction of the one who has entrusted it to me. Nothing you can say, Captain Hull—or you, Sergeant Hempstead, will alter my determination in the least. I intend to go.

HEMPSTEAD: [*Angrily.*] A fine speech, but what of your father, the Deacon? Who will he look to, if you never return? Think of your friends, those of us who were your schoolmates. Does not our sorrow in losing you move you in the least? [*HALE is impressed, but does not move.*]

HULL: [*Following up the advantage Hempstead has gained.*] Only yesterday I brought you the message from Alice Adams. Now that she is a widow, she looks to you, also. She loves you, Nathan. Her whole life is bound up in yours—— [*HALE drops his head; HEMPSTEAD comes to lay a hand on his shoulder.*]

HEMPSTEAD: If you are ruined, if your name is dishonored, her life will be blighted! [*HALE presses his hands over his eyes while he struggles with himself. Suddenly he straightens up to his full height.*]

HALE: I cannot stay, even for her whom I love more than my life. [*He stops, then brokenly.*] Even knowing she will marry no one if I do not return. [*With a brave effort to be calm, to WASHINGTON.*] I am ready, Sir.

WASHINGTON: [*Much moved by what he has witnessed.*] Very good, my son. [*To the others.*] Will you retire for a moment? There are a few parting directions I would say to Captain Hale in private—— [*They go out left. HARRISON offers to stay, but Washington waves him out. He closes the door behind him. WASHINGTON walks seriously to HALE and, laying his hands on his shoulders, looks down at him for a moment before speaking.*] I have the highest admiration for the way in which you have conducted yourself, Captain Hale. If you wish to reconsider the word you have given, it will not offend me.

HALE: Sir, I have no intention of doing so.

WASHINGTON: [*Pleased.*] Then you will proceed at once. Your disguise is perfect. It completely hides your identity. God grant it will insure your safe return!

HALE: I am not afraid, Your Excellency. "How sweet and fitting it is to die for one's country." [*WASHINGTON clasps his hand. They stand silent for a moment.*]

WASHINGTON: The house is being closely watched. I will therefore show you a secret passage out. [*He goes to the wall, back center, and pushing aside the table, opens a small door from which steps lead down.*]

HALE: I have one favor I would ask before I go——

WASHINGTON: Ask it——

HALE: That my servant, Ansel Wright, accompany me on part of the walk before I reach the enemy's lines. I should like to send personal messages to—my dear ones——

WASHINGTON: [*Nods, walks to bell rope left and pulls it. JED appears left.*] Ask a gentleman called Ansel Wright to step in.

JED: Yes, Master. [*Goes out.*]

HALE: Thank you, Sir. [*JED appears with ANSEL. HEMPSTEAD pushes in before they close the door.*]

JED: [*Apologetically.*] I axed de one man an' de odder one come too!

HEMPSTEAD: I could feel you were leaving! Let me accompany you a part of the way, Nathan——

HALE: Would it suit your pleasure, Your Excellency?

WASHINGTON: [*After deliberation.*] It might be a splendid idea to have Sergeant Hempstead and your Ansel Wright wait for you in a boat on the edge of Long Island, so as to quickly convey you thither upon your return.

HALE: [*Bows.*] I shall so arrange it, General.

WASHINGTON: Do make haste to return at the earliest possible moment. Within ten days at the latest—and now, do not tarry, I pray of you! [*JED gives ANSEL a lighted taper. HALE indicates the stairs down the secret passage. ANSEL trembles as he leads the way. HEMPSTEAD goes next. Bows to WASHINGTON before he goes. Before HALE follows, WASHINGTON clasps his hand.*] God be with you!

HALE: And with you, Sir! [*He goes down; JED closes the door and pushes back the table.*]

WASHINGTON: Now you may show the others in. [*JED goes out left. WASHINGTON, much shaken, takes his place at table and assumes attitude of calm and poise. JED opens the door to admit KNOWLTON, HARRISON, and HULL; then goes out.*]

HULL: Where is Nathan?

WASHINGTON: [*Busily looking at map on table.*] He has gone.

HULL: But how? We stood there in the hall.

WASHINGTON: We thought it best to use a secret passage. The house is being closely watched. [*HULL looks bewildered; HARRISON stands with back to audience near fireplace.*]

HULL: With your Excellency's permission, I will retire immediately. Goodnight.

WASHINGTON: [*Kindly.*] Goodnight. [*HULL bows and goes out.*]

KNOWLTON: [*Walks to WASHINGTON, takes his hand with rough affection.*] This was a trying affair for you, Sir, but you need have no fear. That young man will come back, if anyone can.

WASHINGTON: God grant it never be said I have wantonly sacrificed so brave a lad.

KNOWLTON: [*With emotion, huskily.*] Goodnight!

WASHINGTON: [*Trying to hide his emotion.*] Goodnight. [*HARRISON opens the door for KNOWLTON, who gives him a disdainful look and opens the door for himself. Goes out.*]

HARRISON: [*Comes to WASHINGTON, who stands near the fireplace.*] Your Excellency handled the situation masterfully. I have made copious notes, however, if you have cause to refresh your mind on some detail.

WASHINGTON: Thank you, Mister Harrison.

HARRISON: Do you wish to retire now?

WASHINGTON: [*Wearily.*] I think it best. [*JED bursts in, back left.*]

JED: Marse, day's crowds outside watching de house!

HARRISON: [*Delighted.*] Evidently your show of festivity has satisfied them you didn't run away.

WASHINGTON: In that case, Jed, see that the tapers are allowed to burn out.

[*JED hurries out, back left.*]

HARRISON: That will give Captain Hale a fair chance to travel far before his friends miss him.

WASHINGTON: You speak truly. If the ladies have not already retired, ask them to rejoin us.

[*HARRISON goes out, back right. WASHINGTON listens at the secret door, back center, then walks to back right to greet MARTHA and LYDIA as they enter.*]

LYDIA: I thought you would never finish!

WASHINGTON: My impatience for your return was as great as your own.

MARTHA: Apparently those men felt the outcome of the war depended on their seeing you at this particular moment!

WASHINGTON: And perhaps they are right. Who knows?

LYDIA: I hope we are not interrupted again!

WASHINGTON: [*Fervently.*] Would to heaven this one had not been necessary!

[*HARRISON appears at back left and hesitates.*]

LYDIA: Do you, Mister Harrison, hurry and take up the dance where we left off!

[*HARRISON goes to the harpsichord and plays the same jig.*]

WASHINGTON: Suppose, Mistress Lydia, you execute the dance while I look on—I will be better able to dance it later.

[*LYDIA curtsies, begins the dance; dances until curtain. WASHINGTON sits at the table, watches her for a moment, then unrolls the map on the table; traces a course on it with his finger, pauses, sits staring unseeingly into space as the curtain slowly falls.*]

THE VIEW FROM THE WINDOW

A GEORGE WASHINGTON PLAY

(In Three Scenes)

By KATHLEEN READ COONTZ

*Permission was given to produce this play
without royalty fee.*

"The View from the Window" is founded upon an incident which lacks original documentary evidence to render its authenticity probable. However, like all traditional stories, this one of Washington's near-capture was first handed down by word of mouth and later found its way into print, where it has since frequently appeared.

Whether the incident—too rich in dramatic possibilities for the author to pass up—is historic or merely traditional, the background of the play conforms rather closely to history. Washington maintained his headquarters in New York City during the summer of 1776, where he was surrounded by loyalists. There are records of plots to capture the Commander-in-Chief of the American Army. The British began to land June 29. All of the military communications given in the second act of the play are taken from Washington's general orders of 1776.

Colonel Morris campaigned with Washington under Braddock in the French and Indian War and married Mary Philipse, a New York belle whom Washington met on his way back and forth from Boston in 1756 and whom biographers give place in his youthful romances. That Morris was a loyalist and that his home was confiscated by New York is historically true, but again we must fall back upon tradition to uphold his role as the traitor friend of the episode—a part which has been assigned to various loyalists.

So, with the presentation of General Washington true to the author's concept of his justice in punishing wrongdoers, his generosity and esteem of friendship, the play is herewith offered.

CHARACTERS

GENERAL GEORGE WASHINGTON

COLONEL MORRIS, *a country gentleman*

MARY MORRIS, *his wife*

PAT O'REILLY, *the butler*

THE SERGEANT

SIMPSON, *guard at Washington's headquarters*

SECRETARY

HINCKS, *guard*

SOLDIERS

TIME: *A September morning in 1776.*

PLACE: *The drawing room at Morris Mansion, near New York City.*

SET: *The room is furnished in the comfortable style characteristic of colonial estates of the day. Portraits adorn the walls. On the left are great double windows with heavy curtains on either side reaching to the floor and suspended on rings from a rod. Through the windows one catches a glimpse of the Hudson River stretching below, with the rugged woodland of the Harlem region. An old-fashioned sewing basket containing yarn and soldier socks is drawn up beside a low chair, at the right. There is a desk near by. In the background a door opens into the room.*

The COLONEL *and his wife are busy at their tasks as the curtain rises. He sits at the desk writing, she is knitting socks. The* COLONEL *is a distinguished-looking man past middle age with a shock of white hair. He wears a dressing gown of rich material, and glances up affectionately at his wife every now and then.* MRS. MORRIS *is an attractive woman of forty-two or three. She wears a curl over her shoulder and is becomingly gowned in the fashion of the day. She is humming "Liberty Tree" as she knits.* PAT *wears the* MORRIS *livery and is moving around the room dusting the bric-a-brac with a turkey wing, his wooden leg thumping as he goes.*

MRS. MORRIS: [*Laying down her knitting.*] You are writing to England, I know it by the happy look on your face!

COL. MORRIS: [*With quill poised*] It is the lovely sight of you, my love, that brings the happy look.

MRS. MORRIS: [*Rising and going to his side.*] You promised that you would discontinue those letters until the Colonists had won their Independence!

COL. MORRIS: [*Looks up into her face affectionately.*] You speak as though their independence were an assured fact, sweet wife!

MRS. MORRIS: It *is* assured! When the fight is for Liberty it is a fight until it is won.

COL. MORRIS: The Colonists' resources are limited and England's arm is mighty. France claims she is the moon of man's desire, but England is reasonably sure, forsooth, that she is the sun around which the whole earth revolves.

PAT: [*Who has stopped dusting and been listening interestedly.*] And might I ask, sir, whativer is America?

COL. MORRIS: [*Smiling.*] That remains to be seen, Pat.

MRS. MORRIS: [*Turning to* PAT.] You may give my orders to the kitchen, Pat.

[PAT *bows and leaves the room.*]

MRS. MORRIS: [*Laying her hand on her husband's shoulder.*] Don't you see, even the servants feel that you have the interests of the British at heart!

COL. MORRIS: Tut, tut, my love; have I not contributed liberally to the support of the Colonial Army? Is General Washington not a friend of long standing?

MRS. MORRIS: [*A bit impatiently.*] That is just it! We are his friends, and we are American sympathizers, yet you say and do things that awaken suspicion. [*Speaks in a lower voice.*] What business had you with the British colonel the other day?

COL. MORRIS: Did it ever occur to you, my dear, that it is necessary for me to assume a neutral attitude in order that I may be of service to the American Army?

MRS. MORRIS: [*Slowly.*] You mean—in the information you get?

COL. MORRIS: Exactly!

MRS. MORRIS: But he is our friend and a frequent guest in this home, and others are saying——

COL. MORRIS: [*With a twinkle in his eye.*] Heigh-ho, is it the cause of the Colonists or the cause of General Washington you so fervently espouse, pretty puss?

MRS. MORRIS: They are the same. He would not be associated with anything that was not just. He was always the most just person I ever knew, even when he was a very young man and visited these parts.

COL. MORRIS: Pleasant reminiscences, eh? Your friends insist that, once, he proffered his hand and heart to you!

MRS. MORRIS: Nonsense. If General Washington proffered his hand and heart to all who claim it, there would have been no small whit left for Lady Washington, who, in truth, methinks, received it intact.

COL. MORRIS: [*Raising his hand admonishingly.*] We are making too free use of his name. Remember, my dear, the servants have never associated our frequent guest, Colonel Ball, with the Commander-in-Chief of the American Army.

MRS. MORRIS: [*Smiles and goes back to her work.*] Colonel Ball! Didn't we have great sport the evening we selected that title. He was making his first call after establishing his headquarters here. Washington is so honest he even hated to take a disguise name to which he could lay no claim, so he chose his mother's maiden name—Ball.

[*PAT enters and stands at the door.*]

PAT: A soldier outside to see yer, sir.

MRS. MORRIS: An American?

COL. MORRIS: [*Rising.*] To be sure, my love, and who else? [*He leaves the room.*]

PAT: [*Lingering.*] Sure and Americin uniforms aren't after making Americin soldiers, always!

MRS. MORRIS: [*Looking up.*] What do you mean, Pat?

PAT: Perhaps I'm wrong ma'am.

MRS. MORRIS: I believe you'd be fighting in our army today, if it wasn't for your leg, Pat.

PAT: [*With gusto.*] And that I would, my lady! A happy day it will be for Pat, when more Red Coats sport paddies like this. [*Slaps his game leg.*]

MRS. MORRIS: Whenever you see a chance to strike a blow for the cause, you will, won't you, Pat?

PAT: Sure, its achin for the chance I am, Ma'am.

[*The door opens and the COLONEL enters followed by a soldier in the American uniform.*]

COLONEL MORRIS: [*Speaking to his wife.*] A little private business to enact with this soldier, my dear.

[*MRS. MORRIS picks up her knitting and leaves the room. The COLONEL crosses the room and goes to his desk. PAT and the SOLDIER eye each other.*]

SERGEANT: Top of the mawning to you, Mike!

PAT: Me name is Patrick O'Reilly, if it plaze ye.

SERGEANT: I jolly well saw the map of Ireland written on your mug, Patrick O'Reilly!

PAT: The likes of the way the British lion is a-slapping on yer tongue! Mister American Soldier.

[*The SOLDIER starts, glances in the direction of Col. Morris and moves over to the window.*]

SERGEANT: A fine view you have from this window, Patrick O'Reilly.

PAT: Plaze and are you spaking of the bluffs and the river or the British camp yonder?

SERGEANT: Ahem! So you can get a glimpse of the camp!

PAT: Get an eyeful, Mister American! [*They glare at one another.*]

[*COL. MORRIS rises and comes forward with a letter in his hand.*]

COL. MORRIS: Order my horse brought up in an hour, Pat.

[*PAT bows and leaves the room.*]

COL.: [*Speaks in a low voice.*] Did my butler seem suspicious of your uniform?

SERGEANT: He did that, sir.

COLONEL MORRIS: [*Smiles.*] Pat's health will no doubt flourish better on the farm up the river. [*He hands the Soldier the letter.*] Go cautiously, Sergeant. If this letter falls into hands other than Colonel Clinton you may pay for it with your life!

SERGEANT: Of that I am aware, sir.

[*He takes the letter, puts it in an inside pocket, bows to the Colonel and leaves the room. COL. MORRIS walks over to the window and taking out his handkerchief lifts it once or twice above his head. The door is thrown open and PAT appears.*]

PAT: [*Announcing.*] Colonel Ball.

[*COL. MORRIS confusedly puts his handkerchief in his pocket as he turns to greet WASHINGTON, who is dressed in a dark brown suit of the country gentleman.*]

COL. MORRIS: An unexpected pleasure, my friend!

WASHINGTON: I could not refrain from stopping for a brief call on my way by your house.

COL. MORRIS: [*Starts to speak and then turns to PAT.*] Announce the arrival of the Colonel to Mistress Morris.

[*PAT bows and leaves the room.*]

WASHINGTON: As I entered your gate I ran into one of my soldiers. Are my men annoying you in any way?

COL. MORRIS: [*Raising his hand.*] Merely a trifle, General. One of my beef was killed by mistake and the messenger conveyed an apology from the Captain.

WASHINGTON: [*A little wearily.*] I would that a beef were all that the war will cost you, my friend. You have indeed been generous to the cause of liberty.

COL. MORRIS: [*Slowly.*] In the end it will cost me far more than you yourself dream of, General.

WASHINGTON: And yet—no price is too great to bring a country out of travail!

[*MRS. MORRIS enters smilingly and makes a pretty curtsy before WASHINGTON.*]

MRS. MORRIS: We were speaking of you, but a moment ago, General Washington.

WASHINGTON: Not illy, I trust, madam.

COL. MORRIS: [*Laying his hand on WASHINGTON'S arm.*] The praise of you which is heard on every side falls happily on the ears of your friends, sir.

WASHINGTON: [*Apparently moved.*] Friends! What power has that name to lighten the grind of war? What a haven of rest is this home after the turmoil of camp!

COL. MORRIS: [*Steps to the window and leans out.*] Methought I heard footsteps without. Are you attended, General?

WASHINGTON: Merely one of my outriders, sir.

COL. MORRIS: [*Turns to his wife and speaks in a bantering tone.*] He comes to the home of his friends securely guarded. One might deem the General was uncertain of our loyalty!

WASHINGTON: [*Raising his hand in protest.*] Merely the exigencies of war, sir.

    PAT enters bringing in a silver tray containing a tea service. MRS. MORRIS signals him to place the tray on a low tea table near and seats herself beside it.

MRS. MORRIS: I will ring if I need you, Pat. [*PAT bows and leaves the room.*]

MRS. MORRIS: Tea, General my guest, but not the brand that made a seething tea pot of Boston Harbor. My own little brew of sassafras and mint, but 'twill cheer, nevertheless. [*Hands him a cup.*]

WASHINGTON: [*Half rising.*] How could it fail of such a mission when passed by so fair a hand?

MRS. MORRIS: [*Shaking her finger at him.*] Ah, General, would we could subjugate the British with such pretty art!

COL. MORRIS: You have found lead to be a fairer art in that quarter, eh my friend?

    [*WASHINGTON half smiles and nods.*]

MRS. MORRIS: We are expecting you to dine with us on Thursday, as usual.

WASHINGTON: A bright spot in the week, I assure you madam. I have just written Mistress Washington of your frequent kindly hospitality.

MRS. MORRIS: She is well?

WASHINGTON: Quite so, thank you. And busy with soldier knitting.

MRS. MORRIS: [*Sighing, as she waves her hand towards her basket.*] Our needles cannot move swiftly enough to meet the need!

COL. MORRIS: [*Laying his hand on WASHINGTON'S shoulder.*] At such time enforced inactivity is a trifle galling! My age—

WASHINGTON: And your old wound, my friend. I have not forgot those stirring days at the Monongahela twenty years ago, when we fought the French together . . .

COL. MORRIS: Under the British flag. [*Slowly.*] And now you are waging war against that flag!

WASHINGTON: Say *we*, sir. One's service to a cause lies not always on the battle front.

    [*Momentary silence. WASHINGTON consults his watch.*]

WASHINGTON: [*Rising.*] Two minutes lacking the half hour. I must be back by five and have a good hour's ride ahead.

MRS. MORRIS: [*Rises.*] Remember, General. Dinner on Thursday at the usual hour!

COL. MORRIS: [*Who has remained standing.*] It is quite useless to urge promptitude upon one who enjoys so notable a reputa-

tion in that virtue, but might I request, General, that you let nothing detain you beyond the hour. Business in the village may call me away from home at a later hour and I may have important communications for you.

WASHINGTON: I shall be here on the hour of two, sir.

COL. MORRIS: [*Lightly.*] Preceded by an outrider and flanked with guards!

MRS. MORRIS: [*Smiling up into the GENERAL'S face.*] What a way to visit a home whose latchstring hangs on the outside for you. Do you not trust us as friends?

WASHINGTON: All merely a matter of form, I assure you, my dear madam! I would feel myself quite safe in coming to your home unattended.

COL. MORRIS: Such confidence would indeed do honor to my household!

WASHINGTON: [*Slowly and a bit impressively.*] Then as a token of my complete trust in your friendship, I shall come on Thursday next—*alone* . . .

MRS. MORRIS: [*Nervously.*] Is . . . is there any risk . . . General . . .

WASHINGTON: [*Half smiling.*] Our honorable enemy might count me a prize booty, eh Colonel?

COL. MORRIS: Quite so. I merely jested in the matter of the outriders . . .

WASHINGTON: I have considered disposing of them for some time, as liable to excite suspicion from the camp of the enemy.

    [*PAT enters.*]

PAT: Did you ring, ma'am?

MRS. MORRIS: Colonel Ball is leaving.

    [*WASHINGTON bows over MRS. MORRIS' hand and clasps that of the COLONEL. As he moves toward the door PAT who is holding it open makes a step forward.*]

PAT: And sure, sir, is it iver yer luck to lay eyes on Gin'rel Washington?

WASHINGTON: [*With an immobile face.*] I have a mild acquaintance with him, Pat.

PAT: They're after saying down in the village that he's a foine gintleman and cusses like an angel, when tis necessary.

    [*The others laugh.*]

WASHINGTON: His shortcomings may be overlooked, if he only leads the Colonists into victory, Pat.

PAT: [*Warmly.*] Liberty's a grand old wor-rd to put fight in a man, sir. Faith, and if it wasn't for me game leg, I'd be right down there a-lickin the bloomin Red Coats!

WASHINGTON: [*Turning around to the COLONEL and his wife.*] Pat's a real patriot, Colonel. Would we had more like him! [*Bows again, and moves backward until he stands framed in the doorway.*] Again adieu, until we meet again, my friends. [*Leaves followed by PAT, who closes the door.*]

COL. MORRIS: [*His arm around his wife's waist.*] My love, as soon as Pat has escorted Washington to the far gate will you see that he brings the Sergeant who is waiting by the summer arbor?

MRS. MORRIS: [*A little troubled.*] The same trouble about the cattle?

    [*COL. MORRIS half murmurs an assent and goes to his desk. As she reaches the doorway, MRS. MORRIS*] *pauses a moment, one hand on the door knob, the troubled expression still on her face.*]

MRS. MORRIS: The General . . . one feels strangely honored when he says, "My friends."

CURTAIN

SCENE II

TIME. *The next day.*

PLACE. *General Washington's headquarters in New York City.*

[*GENERAL WASHINGTON is writing at one side of the desk, his SECRETARY on the other. HINCKS, personal guard stands nearby. There is a guard at the door.*]

GENERAL WASHINGTON: [*To Secretary.*] Kindly read aloud the copy you have made of the general orders issued at the time of the first landing of the enemy.

SECRETARY: [*Picking up a large sheet.*] The Commander-in-Chief informs General Schuyler that General Howe's fleet from Halifax has arrived in numbers about one hundred and thirty sail. His army is between nine and ten thousand. [*Secretary picks up another communication.*]

By order of the Commander-in-Chief: The unhappy fate of Thomas Hickey executed this day for Mutiny, Sedition and Treachery, the General hopes will be a warning to every soldier in the army to avoid those crimes and all others so disgraceful to the character of a soldier, and pernicious to his country, whose pay he receives and bread he eats. [*Secretary picks up a third paper.*]

The time is now near at hand which must probably determine whether Americans are to be Freemen or Slaves; whether they are to have any property they can call their own; whether their Houses, and Farms, are to be pillaged and destroyed, and they are consigned to a State of wretchedness from which no human efforts will probably deliver them. The fate of unborn millions will now depend, under God, on the courage and conduct of this army. [*Secretary reads another communication.*]

To the Secret Committee of New York.

The necessity of falling upon some measures to remove from the city and its environs persons of known disaffections and enmity to the cause of America is imperative.

[*SECRETARY hands the papers to WASHINGTON who proceeds to seal them. The door at the rear is opened a bit by the guard. From without comes a voice . . . "Who goes there" . . . and "Advance and give the countersign" . . . The SECRETARY springs to the door and stands behind HINCKS, who is speaking to a guard outside.*]

HINCKS [*Handing a letter to the SECRETARY.*] Lord Howe has sent a communication through the lines to the General.

[*The SECRETARY goes over to GENERAL WASHINGTON.*]

SECRETARY: A communication from Lord Howe sent through the lines, General.

[*WASHINGTON takes the letter and scrutinizes the address for a moment, then rises and extends it to the SECRETARY.*]

GENERAL WASHINGTON: [*In a clear cut, cold voice.*] This communication is addressed to George Washington, Esquire. It is therefore intended for a planter in Virginia and not the Commander-in-Chief of the American Army.

[*The SECRETARY salutes, takes the letter and leaves the room. GENERAL WASHINGTON and SECRETARY continue on the correspondence. The door opens and SECRETARY enters into an argument with the guard outside.*]

SECRETARY: He cannot see the General if he comes without a passport.

VOICE FROM WITHOUT: Blast yer, I'll see him if I have to knock down Saint Michael and all his angels.

GENERAL WASHINGTON: [*Looking up.*] Who is causing the disturbance?

[*The SECRETARY closes the door behind him. HINCKS takes his stand by it, hand on his pistol.*]

SECRETARY: [*Addressing the GENERAL.*] A man outside, General, without a passport, demanding to see you.

WASHINGTON: How did he get through the lines?

SECRETARY: Said he squirmed through on his belly, sir.

WASHINGTON: Does he give a name?

SECRETARY: Says his name is Patrick O'Reilly, sir, and says that your friend Colonel Ball knows him well.

[*An enlightened smile half flashes across the GENERAL'S lips.*]

GENERAL WASHINGTON: Admit Patrick O'Reilly, Mr. Secretary.

[*The SECRETARY goes to the door, opens it and speaks to the guards outside. PAT half falls into the room a soldier on either side. PAT is looking decidedly the worst for wear. He is breathing hard and his head is bloody. He struggles loose from the soldiers and crossing the room goes up to the GENERAL, making an awkward attempt at a salute. As he catches his first glimpse of WASHINGTON'S face he starts back.*]

PAT: You, the Gin'rel, sir?

WASHINGTON: [*Smiles.*] Now I recognize you, Pat. Did my soldiers batter you up like that?

PAT: Not your soldiers, sir—I mean Gin'rel—but one a-wearin' the uniform.

WASHINGTON: A spy? [*PAT nods and swallows hard.*]

WASHINGTON: Do you bring a message, Pat?

PAT: [*Looking around at the others.*] Sure and its alone I must see ye sir, I mean Gin'rel.

WASHINGTON: [*To guards.*] This man is known to me. You may remain outside.

[*He includes the others in his orders. The SECRETARY and HINCKS, are loathe to leave, but do so when WASHINGTON again repeats his order.*]

PAT: [*Trying to balance himself on his game leg as he fumbles at his shoe.*] Faith and I've about walked the bloomin letter out! [*Hands the letter to WASHINGTON.*]

[*WASHINGTON takes it and reads the address.*]

WASHINGTON: [*Sternly.*] How comes it that this letter is addressed to General Howe at British headquarters?

PAT: Faith and Colonel, I mean Gin'rel, me hands were only laid on it after I knocked cold the bloke in the American uniform.

WASHINGTON: [*Nods, breaks the seal and reads the letter, then looks up with incredulity written on his countenance.*] This letter is signed by Colonel Morris. Of a certainty it is a forgery!

PAT: And sure Patrick O'Reilly will burn in hell, if he didn't see the Colonel hand the letter to the sojer with his own eyes!

WASHINGTON: The soldier!

[*The whole thing begins to dawn on the GENERAL.*]

PAT: The same, Colonel, I mean Gin'rel, that showed his mug at the house when you were there. Faith, and I didn't like the turn of his eye or the fresh British tongue he wagged. Naither have I liked things I saw a-going on under me nose. Sure and Patrick O'Reilly wasn't born a sivinth child of a sivinth child for nothing.

[*WASHINGTON stands very still, looking down at the letter in his hand, and paying but little attention to PAT'S blusterings.*]

WASHINGTON: [*Speaking slowly.*] Go back to the house, Pat, and say nothing of what has happened. Wait, here is a passport! [*WASHINGTON steps to the desk and writes a few lines which he hands to PAT. PAT takes the letter and half backs toward the door out in deep respect. He pauses for a moment before opening it to give a clumsy salute.*]

PAT: Sure and glad it is am I that you is *you* Colonel—I mean Gin'rel! [*Goes out.*]

[*WASHINGTON stands immovable by the table, his hands slightly clenched, his lips set in a tight line.*]

WASHINGTON: *My friends!*

CURTAIN

SCENE III

PLACE: *The drawing room of the Morris Manor.*
TIME: *The Thursday following.*

[*The COLONEL is pacing restlessly up and down the room. Every now and then he pauses and looks out of the window. MRS. MORRIS enters. She is wearing a becoming gown with frills of lace on the petticoat and at the neck, and wears a rose in her hair.*]

COL. MORRIS: [*Consulting his watch.*] What is detaining our friend?

MRS. MORRIS: The time?

COL. MORRIS: It yet lacks five minutes of the hour we set.

MRS. MORRIS: [*Laughing.*]. He will not be early, he will not be late. . . . The General will be *exactly on* time, of *that* I am sure!

COL. MORRIS: What say you, will he keep his word to come unattended?

MRS. MORRIS: [*Seriously.*] He would keep his word if he knew it meant death.

COL. MORRIS: [*Starting slightly and giving her a quick look.*] What do you mean, my dear?

MRS. MORRIS: [*Rearranging the flowers in a vase on the table.*] Merely that I have never known or heard of him breaking a promise.

[*The door is thrown open and PAT enters announcing the guest.*]

PAT: [*In a ringing important voice.*] General Washington!

[*WASHINGTON steps into the room. He wears the uniform of the Commander-in-Chief of the American army and looks every inch the part. For a moment both COLONEL and MRS. MORRIS stand almost aghast then MRS. MORRIS comes forward with outstretched hand.*]

MRS. MORRIS: Isn't it a bit rash to make your identity known in this way, General?

[*WASHINGTON bows over her hand without answering and turns to the outstretched hand of COLONEL MORRIS which he does not take but instead lays his hand on the COLONEL'S arm.*]

WASHINGTON: I am here, mine host, wearing the uniform of our country's cause and entirely unattended. Could friendship ask more?

COLONEL MORRIS: [*Nervously.*] I should not have made myself known to the servants in this wise, General. One is never assured of their loyalty.

WASHINGTON: Yours appear to espouse the cause of Liberty most heartily, Sir.

[*PATS straightens up proudly and casts a look of disgust at the COLONEL.*]

MRS. MORRIS: I talk it to them constantly, General.

[*There is an air of suppressed excitement. The three cross the room together. The COLONEL waves GENERAL WASHINGTON to a chair on the opposite side of the room and himself moves towards the window. MRS. MORRIS sinks down in her chair and picks up her knitting. GENERAL WASHINGTON remains standing near her.*]

MRS. MORRIS: Dinner will be delayed a bit. The General is to have a pie from our best cherries. Mayhap it will remind him of the cherry trees of his boyhood down on Ferry Farm!

WASHINGTON: [*A bit sadly.*] Both boyhood and Virginia seem far distant today, Madam.

MRS. MORRIS: [*Glancing up into his face.*] Not discouraged, General?

COL. MORRIS: Sir, you have sacrificed much for the cause . . . home . . . personal fortune . . . and . . .

WASHINGTON: [*Looking into his face.*] And friends!

COL. MORRIS AND WIFE: [*Together.*] Friends!?

[*WASHINGTON walks over to the window and looks out.*]

WASHINGTON: A magnificent view this window affords, Sir. Bold fine scenery. Were it not for the mists one might obtain a view of the camp of the enemy.

COL. MORRIS: [*Nervously.*] On clear days the camp is visible.

WASHINGTON: [*Apparently, absent mindedly.*] One might even signal from this advantageous point!

MRS. MORRIS: Accept the home for your headquarters, and you can use it as you will.

[*WASHINGTON again crosses the room and stands over her.*]

WASHINGTON: It may *yet* serve that purpose, Madam. As to your offer, I could swear it emanated from a heart loyal to the cause.

MRS. MORRIS: [*Looking up quickly into his face.*] And one loyal to friendship, also.

WASHINGTON: [*Slowly.*] Treachery to a cause is a grave offense. Treachery to friendship, unforgivable.

[*WASHINGTON joins MORRIS by the window.*]

WASHINGTON: [*Shielding his eyes with his hand.*] Are my eyes deceiving me, sir, or is that not a line of British cavalryman advancing?

MRS. MORRIS: [*Her hand on her heart.*] British cavalrymen!

WASHINGTON: [*To* MORRIS, *in a cold voice.*] And pray, Sir, why may British be crossing your estate?

COL. MORRIS: Have no alarm, my dear friend. I have maintained friendly relations with the British merely as a safeguard. The soldiers will not enter my premises without permission. Stand where you are and I shall shortly send them on their way. [*Leaves the room.*]

WASHINGTON: [*Going to* MRS. MORRIS' *side.*] In the happy days of our youth we were great friends, Mary.

MRS. MORRIS: Are we not still, General Washington?

WASHINGTON: This much I shall say to you now. What you ask of me in friendship's name, shall be granted if possible.

MRS. MORRIS: You are so strange today. Quite as though you were telling us goodbye. Are you moving camp——?

[*Before* WASHINGTON *has time to answer the door is thrown open and* COLONEL MORRIS *enters followed by four or five soldiers dressed in the British uniform.*]

COL. MORRIS: [*In a dramatic voice.*] General Washington, you are my prisoner! [WASHINGTON *stands stock still his hand on his sword.*] It is quiet useless for you to offer resistance, for a company of British soldiers is at the gate to carry out the orders of Lord Howe and accomplish your arrest!

[MRS. MORRIS *half rises and then sinks half fainting in her chair.* PAT *goes over to her and seeks to revive her.* WASHINGTON *stands gazing fixedly at the* COLONEL.]

WASHINGTON: [*Quietly.*] This plot has your approval, Sir?

COL. MORRIS: [*Bows.*] I am first and last a British subject. Sieze him, soldiers!

[*The Soldiers do not move but keep their eyes fixed on* WASHINGTON'S *face.*]

WASHINGTON: [*Drawing himself up and speaking in a cold, hard voice.*] Sir, you are my prisoner! [*The* SOLDIERS *lay hands on the astonished* COLONEL.] It so happens, mine host, that these are my soldiers and the uniforms that gladden your traitor soul in the valley, cover *not* British, but American hearts.

[PAT *advances into the center of the room with a slight swagger.*]

COL. MORRIS: You ornery cur, you are to blame for this!

PAT: And right ye are me lord and proud it is to deliver a turn coat where he belongs.

WASHINGTON: He shall be made an example to other enemies of America, hereabouts!

[MRS. MORRIS, *who has revived and been listening with clasped hands to the conversation, springs to her feet.*]

MRS. MORRIS: [*To* WASHINGTON.] Surely you are not going to allow him to be arrested on the merest suspicion!

[WASHINGTON *looks down kindly at her as he takes the letter from his pocket.*]

WASHINGTON: [*To* COLONEL MORRIS.] Am I mistaken, sir, in accepting this as your signature?

COL. MORRIS: I wrote the letter.

[WASHINGTON *hands the letter to* MRS. MORRIS *who reads it with horror in her face.*]

MRS. MORRIS: [*To* COLONEL MORRIS.] You . . . you planned his arrest in this home!

COL. MORRIS: [*Bows.*]

WASHINGTON: [*To* MRS. MORRIS.] Had the letter not

been intercepted by an American patriot, [PAT *swaggers*] the Commander-in-Chief of the American army might now be a British prisoner. [*Turns to* COLONEL MORRIS.] My erstwhile friend, I merely carried out your capture campaign, with a slight [*ironically*] change in the main character!

COL. MORRIS: [*Sneeringly.*] A master of strategy, what!

[WASHINGTON *makes a mock bow in acknowledgement of the remark.* PAT *steps forward and places himself immediately in front of the* COLONEL.]

PAT: Sure and whativer that master is me fine squire, the Gin'rel is more than that. Faith, and ye was a-talkin about France bein the moon and old England the sun, but maybe ye haven't heerd that Gin'rel Washington is the Joshua who commanded the sun and the moon to stand still, and *they obeyed* him!

[*The soldiers roar and* COLONEL MORRIS *looks as though he will break a blood vessel.*]

WASHINGTON: [*Sternly holding up his hand.*] Silence! Take the prisoner away, and await further orders.

[COLONEL MORRIS *shakes off the soldiers' hands and walks towards the door chin up.* MRS. MORRIS *runs to his side weeping.*]

MRS. MORRIS: How could you, how could you! Now what will happen to you?

COL. MORRIS: Your friend, the General will tell you, my dear!

[SOLDIERS *and* COLONEL *leave the room.* PAT *lingers at the door.*]

PAT: Plaze yer honor, I mean Gin'rel, might there be something in the Americin army for peg-legged Pat? To butler fer the gin'rels or the like?

WASHINGTON: [*Smiling.*] We will see Pat. Wait outside.

[PAT *leaves the room.* MRS. MORRIS *has gone to the window and stands with her handkerchief over her eyes.*]

WASHINGTON: [*Walking over to her side.*] It is these things that put the keenest sting in war, madam.

MRS. MORRIS: How could he! How could he!

WASHINGTON: Then I am right in judging that you were not aware of the plot?

MRS. MORRIS: [*Removing her handkerchief from her face and backing away in indignation.*] So you thought I also betrayed you?

WASHINGTON: I have always looked upon you as a noble patriot to the cause of American liberty, and a staunch friend. I have not changed my opinion.

MRS. MORRIS: What must you do with him?

WASHINGTON: His offense is a grave one, usually punishable by death.

MRS. MORRIS: [*Starting back, her hand on her heart.*] Death!

[WASHINGTON *gravely nods.*]

MRS. MORRIS: [*In a sort of frenzy, catching hold of his arm.*] But you will not allow that, General Washington. Surely you will temper justice with mercy!

WASHINGTON: Mercy walks less frequently on battlefields than elsewhere, Mistress Mary.

MRS. MORRIS: [*In a small quiet voice.*] The Colonel is much older than I, but until this dreadful war, we were very happy together. He is a kind and considerate husband, whatever his other offenses be. If he goes to prison I shall go with him, if he dies I shall die with him!

WASHINGTON: The tolls of war are bitter indeed, madam.

MRS. MORRIS: [*Slowly.*] When we were alone a moment ago, you promised that a request of mine, might find favor from an old friend.

WASHINGTON: You would not ask his release, madam, you are an American.

MRS. MORRIS: In a woman's heart human affection transcends all else, General . . . I shall not ask my husband's release . . . I only ask that his life be spared . . .

[*Silence. WASHINGTON stands arms folded across his breast gaving a bit sadly out of the window.*]

MRS. MORRIS: Is my request granted?

WASHINGTON: It shall be granted under one condition, madam.

MRS. MORRIS: And that?

WASHINGTON: [*Taking her hand and places it on his sword.*] That you will swear on this sword, lifted for the sacred cause of American liberty that your husband leave this country never to return.

MRS. MORRIS: [*Solemnly.*] I swear it. We will both leave.

WASHINGTON: He is the traitor! Your place is by his side, but understand, madam, when you once leave these troubled torn shores you relinquish your rights to return.

MRS. MORRIS: [*Catching her breath in little quick, half hysterical sobs, and speaking rapidly, her head up.*] But every time I hear the name of America I shall thrill to the sound of it. [*Slowly.*] I shall lose my American right but I shall never lose my American heart . . .

WASHINGTON: [*Holding out his hand.*] And now I must bid you adieu.

MRS. MORRIS: One other request . . . it is not a difficult one.

[*WASHINGTON smiles kindly.*]

MRS. MORRIS: Because of all the happy visits we had around this fireside . . . [*Half laughing—half sobbing*] because of the little boy—cherry pie out in the kitchen—untouched . . . say . . . just once again . . . my friend . . .

WASHINGTON: [*Kissing her hand.*] My friend!

CURTAIN.

THE CRISIS AT YORKTOWN

A GEORGE WASHINGTON PLAY IN ONE ACT

DRAMATIS PERSONAE

(IN THE ORDER OF THEIR APPEARANCE)

COLONEL TILGHMAN, *Aide to General Washington.*
MAJOR GREER, *of the Medical Corps.*
TRUMBULL, *Secretary to General Washington.*
SERGEANT OF GUARD.
MAJOR GIBBS, *of Washington's Bodyguard.*
COLONEL HUMPHREYS, *Aide to General Washington.*
MRS. WADE HARRISON.
MAJOR GENERAL THE COUNT DE ST. SIMON, *of the French Army.*
MAJOR GENERAL THE MARQUIS DE LAFAYETTE.
GENERAL WASHINGTON.
MRS. TOM MORGAN.
CAPTAIN AMES.
JOHN DARBY.
MAJOR BYRON.
DR. RUSH.
SERGEANT TOM MORGAN.
BRIGADIER GENERAL WAYNE.
MAJOR GENERAL LINCOLN.
BRIGADIER GENERAL MUHLENBURG.
MAJOR GENERAL THE BARON VON STEUBEN.
BRIGADIER GENERAL KNOX.
LT. GENERAL THE COUNT DE ROCHAMBEAU.
MAJOR GENERAL THE COUNT DE CHASTELLUX.
BRIGADIER GENERAL DU PORTAIL.
LT. DUQUESNE, *Aide to Admiral Count de Grasse.*
COLONEL HAMILTON.

MAJOR GRIMES, *of the British Army.*
AIDES, SOLDIERS AND ORDERLY, *of the American Army.*
OFFICERS AND AIDES *of French Army.*

TIME: *About 8.15 A. M. The morning of October 17, 1781.*

PLACE: *GENERAL WASHINGTON'S headquarters at Yorktown.*

DESCRIPTION OF CHARACTERS

GENERAL WASHINGTON:

Forty-nine years of age, six feet two inches tall, in weight about two hundred pounds; rather large boned, but well-proportioned, graceful; dignified and commanding, though modest in deportment. Complexion rather sallow; his hair light brown in color, worn in a queue, powdered.

BRIG. GENERAL WAYNE:

Thirty-six years of age; above middle size, healthy, strong; fine ruddy complexion, lively expressive eyes; hasty temper; impetuous, daring, resourceful; known as the dude of the army.

BRIG. GENERAL KNOX:

Thirty-one years of age; a large, heavy-set man above middle stature; low forehead, a large face, small gray, brilliant eyes; strong voice. His left hand, having been mutilated at Monmouth, he wears around it a black silk handkerchief, which he unwinds and rewinds when talking but without exposing his hand. Decisive in speech.

MAJ. GEN. BARON VON STEUBEN:

A well-built, handsome man sixty-two years of age; of medium height; erect military bearing, moves with the quick, rigid stride of a drillmaster. *Enthusiastic, generous; speaks English with strong German accent.*

MAJ. GEN. THE MARQUIS DE LAFAYETTE:

Twenty-four years of age; tall, dark, slender; brown eyes, thin face; open, intelligent countenance; reddish hair; of military bearing, light active movements; faultless in dress and manners.

MAJ. GEN. LINCOLN:

Forty-eight years of age; a large man, inclined to stoutness; large head, full face. Limps lightly from an old wound.

BRIG. GEN. MUHLENBURG:

Thirty-two years of age; tall, slender; a strong, lean face, with piercing eyes; black hair worn in a queue. Was a minister before entering the army.

COLONEL HUMPHREYS:

Twenty-six years of age; medium height, a strong, athletic figure; of pleasing address.

COLONEL TILGHMAN:

Thirty-six years of age, slenderly built, above medium height. Speaks in the soft tones of a Marylander.

COLONEL HAMILTON:

Twenty-four years of age; of slight build, five feet seven inches in height. With a face of pleasing expression; quick of speech, dramatic. Reddish brown hair, tied in a queue.

The American officers are all dressed in the well-worn buff and blue of the Continental Army with insignia of their ranks. The soldiers of the American Army in blue Continental uniforms faced with red.

The French officers, in the handsome white uniforms of the French Army; their generals wear orders and decorations contrasting with the more sober uniforms of the Americans.

MRS. HARRISON, *a beautiful woman of middle age, is becomingly gowned for travel; she is a cultured woman of the best social circles of Virginia.*

MRS. MORGAN, *a tall, strong-featured woman, is dressed in plain homespun much the worse for wear, heavy shoes, a Scotch-plaid shawl about her shoulders, without hat; her hair is combed straight back and fastened in a knot at the nape of her neck.*

DARBY *is in rough civilian garb.*

MAJOR GRIMES, *in the red-coated uniform of a British line officer. All the officers carry swords.*

SCENE: *Before General Washington's headquarters at the siege of Yorktown. At the left, the front portion of a headquarters' tent projects into the stage diagonally, a fly extending out from the front of the tent. Under the fly, to the right of the tent opening, a rude table and chair. At the rear, tall trees with an opening in the foliage toward the right, where a sentry can be seen pacing back and forth, silhouetted against the low Virginia hills and the morning sky. In the rear, center, a flagstaff with the Stars and Stripes at the peak showing above the trees. At the right, trees; between those toward the rear, a smaller open tent or marquee, without sides, faced diagonally to the audience. In it several rude camp chairs. Near the right front a crude settee, half facing the audience, made of tree branches, evidently fashioned by some clever soldier. To the left of center, a long table hewn from trees, with four or five crude chairs near by. There is the constant dull boom of distant artillery, inter-*

mittently heavier cannon roar throughout the act, up to the surrender. Orderlies and aides should come and go throughout the act.

A soldier, in a well-fitted Colonial uniform, without a rifle but wearing his bayonet, is acting as orderly and stands at the headquarters tent opening. When anyone enters tent, he holds open the canvas walls. A sergeant of the guard stands by the entrance of the marquee without rifle, wearing bayonet. Colonel TILGHMAN is intently scanning a military map spread out on the long table, left center. TRUMBULL is sitting at table under tent fly busy with papers. While curtain rises, muffled cannon fire is heard. MAJOR GREER of the Medical Corps enters and goes to TILGHMAN and salutes, TILGHMAN returns salute.

GREER: Colonel Tilghman, I understand you are of Philadelphia.

TILGHMAN: I am, Major Greer.

GREER: Know you the celebrated Dr. Rush?

TILGHMAN: Aye, indeed.

GREER: He has lately arrived in camp, and as I am deeply concerned over the condition of Captain Custis, I was wondering——

TILGHMAN: Ah—you would have Dr. Rush in consultation?

GREER: Captain Custis is a very sick man. Knowing that Dr. Rush has ever been opposed to His Excellency, I hesitated to suggest——

TILGHMAN: The welfare of his stepson is very near the General's heart, the pity of it that such a trial should come at this critical hour.

GREER: Then you think——?

TILGHMAN: Aye, but the General must first be consulted.

GREER: Would you——? The matter is urgent.

TILGHMAN: At the earliest opportunity.

[*GREER salutes and leaves. TILGHMAN returns salute and again studies the map. There are two louder detonations of cannon as HUMPHREYS enters and goes to TILGHMAN.*]

HUMPHREYS: Our new batteries have opened fire.

TILGHMAN: I noticed it. What damage to the enemy from them?

HUMPHREYS: I just came from the second parallel. General Knox reports they are doing great execution.

TILGHMAN: Would that we had more! Now that the Count de Grasse withdraws his troops—— [*Shakes his head and returns to the map.*]

HUMPHREYS: [*With a movement of his head toward the tent.*] Is the General in? [*TILGHMAN nods assent and HUMPHREYS enters the headquarters tent. MAJOR GIBBS, escorting MRS. HARRISON, enters at right rear. HUMPHREYS and GIBBS salute as they pass. The SERGEANT OF THE GUARD steps up to them and salutes.*]

GIBBS: [*Returning salute.*] I would have speech with Colonel Tilghman. [*TILGHMAN turns, meets them at right center, returns GIBBS' salute and bows to MRS. HARRISON.*] Good morning, Colonel.

TILGHMAN: Good morning, Major Gibbs.

GIBBS: Mistress Harrison, may I present Colonel Tilghman, aide to General Washington?

TILGHMAN: [*Bows.*] Mistress Harrison. 'Tis a pleasure, indeed.

MRS. HARRISON: [*Curtsies.*] Colonel Tilghman, my husband, Colonel Wade Harrison, has often spoken of you.

GIBBS: Mistress Harrison desires an audience with General Washington.

[*While they are talking an orderly enters hurriedly and goes to TRUMBULL with dispatches, which TRUMBULL looks at, then enters tent.*]

TILGHMAN: His Excellency is extremely busy, madam.

MRS. HARRISON: Nevertheless, I must see him. 'Tis urgent.

TILGHMAN: I will so inform the General, Madam Harrison, but I apprehend he cannot grant you an audience at this hour.

MRS. HARRISON: I am personally acquainted with the General. I am the wife of Colonel Wade Harrison.

[*TILGHMAN bows and enters the tent as TRUMBULL comes out. An orderly comes in, goes to TRUMBULL, salutes, leaves dispatch and hurries out.*]

MRS. HARRISON: What a hurry and ado in a camp, Major.

GIBBS: And what a relief it will be to leave it all when peace comes.

MRS. HARRISON: Ah, the war will end now with the taking of my Lord Cornwallis.

GIBBS: 'Tis what we all have hoped.

MRS. HARRISON: Has anything untoward happened?

[*As they are speaking, the hoofbeats of several horses are heard, the SERGEANT OF GUARD at marquee hurries to orderly at tent, says a few words and goes back to marquee. Orderly enters tent and TRUMBULL appears from tent, followed by orderly, and TRUMBULL goes to right rear to meet a French general and aide. He conducts them to WASHINGTON'S headquarters; MRS. HARRISON notices this.*]

MRS. HARRISON: Oh, Major, who may be that gorgeous French officer?

GIBBS: 'Tis the Marquis de St. Simon, a major general of Count de Rochambeau's army.

MRS. HARRISON: [*Regretfully.*] Oh, then my errand must wait.

GIBBS: Won't you be seated, madam? [*He leads her to the settee as TILGHMAN comes from the tent, approaches them, and bows to MRS. HARRISON.*]

TILGHMAN: His Excellency extends his compliments and begs Mistress Harrison's pardon for being unable to receive her at this time. He suggests you confide your mission to me.

MRS. HARRISON: 'Tis not of my own affairs, sir, but of a poor woman, wanting news of her husband, who has come all these miles from Connecticut afoot.

TILGHMAN: Surely, madam, others could furnish that information. 'Twill not be necessary to trouble His Excellency.

MRS. HARRISON: Aye, but most peculiar circumstances surround the matter. She will only have speech with the General.

TILGHMAN: [*Speculatively.*] Ah-ha-a—secret information.

MRS. HARRISON: Nay. It hath to do with the husband, a private soldier—one Morgan of the Connecticut Line.

TILGHMAN: Morgan?—of the Connecticut Line? Hum-um. And his wife, you say, has come all these miles from Connecticut afoot?

MRS. HARRISON: Yes.

TILGHMAN: Where may she be?

MRS. HARRISON: She waits beyond the sentry.

TILGHMAN: [*To GIBBS.*] Please conduct Madam Harrison to the marquee and have Mistress Morgan fetched there, also. [*To MRS.*

HARRISON.] I will tell the General of Mistress Morgan's coming afoot. [*Bows and turns to tent. GIBBS and MRS. HARRISON enter marquee. As TILGHMAN nears tent ST. SIMON and aide come out, TILGHMAN salutes ST. SIMON and enters tent. ST. SIMON is crossing to right rear, stops as he sees LAFAYETTE enter from right rear saluted by sentry. LAFAYETTE is perturbed— excited. Hurries to ST. SIMON.*]

ST. SIMON: [*Exclaims.*] Oh! Mon ami, Lafayette!

LAFAYETTE: Ah, St. Simon.

ST. SIMON: You have been to the fleet—to Count de Grasse.

LAFAYETTE: Mais oui, I have seen him.

ST. SIMON: No success?

LAFAYETTE: [*Excitedly.*] Non! Non! Non! Nothing I can say—nothing I can urge—moves him.

ST. SIMON: I understand it is our Majesty's orders.

LAFAYETTE: If His Majesty understood, he never would have countenanced the message sent to His Excellency two days ago—that within forty-eight hours the Count would withdraw his troops.

ST. SIMON: Then General Washington's remonstrance is in vain?

LAFAYETTE: Alas! And I, His Excellency's messenger, also a failure——!

ST. SIMON: 'Tis most regrettable—one's countrymen!——

LAFAYETTE: It means Washington's hopes blasted—the raising of the siege!

ST. SIMON: But what can one do?

LAFAYETTE: [*With fire.*] One must do something! [*ST. SIMON gives a shrug of helplessness.*] To have to report failure to my General! [*Without further word he rushes toward WASHINGTON'S tent and enters. ST. SIMON watches him, sighs audibly, turns and goes out with his aide. HUMPHREYS and TILGHMAN come from tent. There is loud huzzahing off stage as an orderly enters on the way to TRUMBULL.*]

TILGHMAN: [*To orderly.*] What means the shouting?

ORDERLY: [*Stops and salutes.*] Some of our men cheering a battalion of French troops, sir.

[*TILGHMAN and HUMPHREYS go to table.*]

TILGHMAN: [*Thinks for a moment.*] I wonder if by nightfall——

HUMPHREYS: [*Looking up.*] Wonder what?

TILGHMAN: —if our men will still be of a mind to cheer the French.

HUMPHREYS: Not by the looks of this map, they won't.

TILGHMAN: Lafayette! What must be his emotion?

HUMPHREYS: It looks as though some of his compatriots are deserting him as well as our cause.

TILGHMAN: Aye, 'tis a big gap to fill—three thousand men out of the line.

HUMPHREYS: Months of planning, of patient diplomacy with our allies, gone for naught!

TILGHMAN: At this critical hour, when the fate of our nation——

HUMPHREYS: God help the General!

TILGHMAN: 'Tis a desperate decision Washington must make!

[*WASHINGTON and LAFAYETTE come from tent and stop.*]

WASHINGTON: [*Puts hand affectionately on LAFAYETTE'S shoulder.*] My dear Marquis, you have done your best, as you always do.

LAFAYETTE: Thank you, my General.

WASHINGTON: As you know, I have called a council of my generals. Will you present my compliments to Count de Rochambeau and ask him to attend?

LAFAYETTE: Most assuredly, Your Excellency. [*Salutes and leaves. WASHINGTON goes toward table. HUMPHREYS steps up to him and salutes.*]

WASHINGTON: [*Gives him a paper he holds in his hand.*] For General Von Steuben—check the details with him.

HUMPHREYS: Yes, Your Excellency. [*Salutes and leaves as WASHINGTON goes to table. MAJOR BYRON enters, approaches WASHINGTON and salutes.*]

BYRON: You sent for me, Your Excellency?

WASHINGTON: Prepare to move post-haste to my home at Mount Vernon. [*Takes a letter from his pocket.*] Give this to Madam Washington; she will take coach at once for Yorktown. You will attend her here, securing an escort from Captain Thomson of the Virginia Militia.

TILGHMAN: [*Before BYRON can take the letter or speak.*] Your Excellency, may I invite your attention to the presence in the camp of Dr. Rush? [*MAJOR BYRON steps back a few paces out of earshot.*]

WASHINGTON: The celebrated Philadelphia physician?

TILGHMAN: Yes, General. Mayhap, by his efforts, Captain Custis might be benefited in so far 'twill not be necessary for Madam Washington to take this fatiguing journey.

WASHINGTON: [*Sadly.*] Think you Dr. Rush would attend my son? He has ever been opposed to me and a supporter of General Gates.

TILGHMAN: Like others, he has undergone a change of mind. I know the doctor well. Have I your permission to send for him?

WASHINGTON: If he would grant me this favor.

TILGHMAN: I will have him here directly. [*Salutes and goes to speak to TRUMBULL, an orderly leaves at once. BYRON steps forward.*]

WASHINGTON: Prepare for the journey; return when you are ready to start. [*BYRON salutes and leaves. WASHINGTON returns letter to his pocket as TILGHMAN comes to him.*]

TILGHMAN: Your Excellency, will you now see Mrs. Harrison and Mrs. Morgan?

WASHINGTON: Yes, at once. [*He looks at map, as TILGH-MAN signals the SERGEANT OF GUARD, who sends MRS. HAR-RISON and MRS. MORGAN to WASHINGTON. MRS. MOR-GAN'S humble garments are travel-stained and tattered, her figure in sharp contrast to MRS. HARRISON'S, a woman of marked southern gentility, well groomed, richly attired.*]

WASHINGTON: [*Bows to MRS. HARRISON.*] You honor me, madam. 'Tis not often one has the pleasure of seeing the wife of an old friend in camp.

MRS. HARRISON: [*Curtsying.*] You are kindness itself, Your Excellency. Allow me to present Mrs. Morgan.

WASHINGTON: [*Bowing.*] Mrs. Morgan, I hope I may be of service.

[*MRS. MORGAN nods her head. Gazes silently at WASHINGTON.*]

MRS. HARRISON: If you will excuse me? [*She takes TILGH-MAN'S arm, they withdraw toward the marquee to stand conversing.*]

WASHINGTON: [*Kindly.*] I hope you have no untoward news of your husband, madam.

MRS. MORGAN: Eet couldna' be worse—letters come ta our veelage fra men o' his company sayin' as Tam's gone o'er ta the Breetish.

WASHINGTON: Deserted to the enemy?

MRS. MORGAN: I would ha' ye gie me the truth. Is Tam Morgan a traitor like ta reenegade Arnold?

WASHINGTON: I know not of the matter. I shall presently have the facts and you the truth.

MRS. MORGAN: Ett's na' like Tam Morgan.

[*LAFAYETTE takes a step toward WASHINGTON but stops as WASHINGTON speaks.*]

WASHINGTON: Should your neighbor's intelligence be proven true, there is nothing I can do for you, madam.

MRS. MORGAN: Aye, ane thing ye ken do.

WASHINGTON: And what may that be?

MRS. MORGAN: An Cornwallis be ta'en, ye can gae Tam Morgan o'er intil ma hand.

WASHINGTON: To be forgiven by a loving wife and escape the penalty of his perfidity?

MRS. MORGAN: [*With passion.*] Naw! I wad hae Tam Morgan ken hoo wife an' bairns scorn him. Theen ye can hang him.

WASHINGTON: [*Looks at her for a long moment.*] Ah— [*To TILGHMAN.*] Conduct Mistress Morgan to the marquee.

[*There is an interruption, COLONEL HUMPHREYS and CAPTAIN AMES enter, hurrying to WASHINGTON, salute.*]

HUMPHREYS: Your Excellency, an enemy messenger trying to effect an entrance to Gloucester was killed by a loyal citizen.

WASHINGTON: Were dispatches on him?

AMES: Dispatches to Cornwallis.

HUMPHREYS: To the effect that Clinton is sailing up the Delaware!

AMES: To attack Philadelphia?

[*At the first words of HUMPHREYS, TILGHMAN leaves MRS. HARRISON, goes to MRS. MORGAN and leads her to MRS. HARRISON. HUMPHREYS takes dispatches from pocket, WASHINGTON holds out his hand.*]

HUMPHREYS: Here, sir. [*WASHINGTON reads.*]

TILGHMAN: Philadelphia is defenseless!

HUMPHREYS: Think you we can get there in time to defend the city?

WASHINGTON: Philadelphia can take care of itself.

HUMPHREYS: And Congress there?

WASHINGTON: Gentlemen, methinks this dispatch was too easily captured.

TILGHMAN: Think you 'twas intended for your hands?

HUMPHREYS: [*To WASHINGTON.*] The man who brought it is here, sir.

WASHINGTON: Have him in.

[*MRS. HARRISON and MRS. MORGAN are at the entrance of the marquee.*]

SERGEANT: [*At WASHINGTON'S command.*] Bring in the citizen. [*Two soldiers, with DARBY between them, immediately enter from the marquee. As MRS. HARRISON would draw MRS. MORGAN away, the latter looks steadfastly at DARBY and stops in her tracks; DARBY does not notice the women.*]

WASHINGTON: [*To DARBY.*] Are you an American?

DARBY: I am Jonathan Talbot, sir, loyal to Congress.

WASHINGTON: When and how came you by these papers?

DARBY: Day come yesterday. A man offered to pay me well to fetch 'im in my boat across the bay.

WASHINGTON: Where from?

DARBY: Cape Charles, sir. 'E said as how 'e must get to thee, sir.

WASHINGTON: Yes; go on.

DARBY: An' being loyal, I fetched him. Nearin' land, come dark, 'e drew a pistol an' threatened me—ordered I should land 'im at Gloucester. [*He wets his lips with tongue.*]

WASHINGTON: Then what?

DARBY: I suspicioned him, sir, so, puttin' the tiller hard aport, sudden-like the boom swung 'round and knocked 'im down. I jumped on 'im—we fought, I knifed 'im, then searched 'im. I found the dispatch to the enemy.

WASHINGTON: Where is he now?

DARBY: 'E's dead, sir. Fearin' meetin' up with the British, I threw 'e's body ower board. Then, come daybreak, ran ashore near our army. I am a loyal Liberty man, sir.

MRS. MORGAN: [*Who has been drawing nearer, disregarding MRS. HARRISON'S half-hearted attempts to hold her back.*] Ye air a liar, ye murthering Tory!

WASHINGTON: Mrs. Morgan, you know this man?

MRS. MORGAN: Yon mon is John Darby, ane o' Captain Fitz's men!

TILGHMAN: Captain Fitz, the Tory leader!

MRS. MORGAN: The same. Wi' a price on his head!

WASHINGTON: Are you positive?

MRS. MORGAN: 'Ta prove eet, d'ye fetch men fra' the Connecticut Line recruited hereaboot Hartford. They'd gae and hang him richt awa'.

WASHINGTON: [*To DARBY, now in terror.*] John Darby, would you be given over to the Connecticut Line——?

DARBY: My God, sir, have mercy! Don't do that! I'll tell the truth, so help me God!

WASHINGTON: You were instructed to see that this dispatch came to my hand?

DARBY: Oh, yes, sir!

WASHINGTON: And when you left New York, Sir Henry Clinton was about to sail for Yorktown?

DARBY: He was, sir.

WASHINGTON: You shall have a fair trial. Take him away, guard him well. [*To MRS. MORGAN.*] I shall at once get news of your husband, madam, and for your sake I hope 'tis of good report. [*To SERGEANT OF GUARD.*] Sergeant, make Mistress Morgan comfortable in the marquee and attend her wants. [*MRS. MORGAN and MRS. HARRISON enter the marquee. TRUMBULL gives WASHINGTON a message just brought by an orderly.*]

WASHINGTON: [*To TRUMBULL.*] Secure news of Morgan; should he be in camp have him brought here at once. [*Something in message attracts his close attention. TRUMBULL speaks with an orderly. Orderly starts to leave. HUMPHREYS goes into tent. TILGHMAN, who has gone to marquee with MRS. HARRISON, returns with DR. RUSH. They go to WASHINGTON.*]

WASHINGTON: [*Bows.*] Dr. Rush, I am indeed pleased to see you.

DR. RUSH: Good morning, General Washington. I am at your service.

WASHINGTON: 'Tis indeed a great service you can do me, Doctor. I hesitated to ask you.

DR. RUSH: I understand. Once I was opposed to you, sir. I was of those duped by General Gates, I thought you had too much power for one man to exercise in a free nation.

WASHINGTON: [*Raising a restraining hand.*] That is all over, now.

DR. RUSH: I wish you to know, sir. I realize I was wrong, and whatever I possess in worldly goods as well as my poor talents are at the disposal of General Washington.

WASHINGTON: I thank you, Doctor; I have one request.

DR. RUSH: You have but to name it.

WASHINGTON: One I love is stricken with a dire malady— my stepson, Madam Washington's own son, Captain Jack Custis. If you will be so kind as to look in on him, and give me a report as to his condition I shall be eternally grateful.

DR. RUSH: I will go to him at once. Would you take my hand, General? [*Extends his hand.*]

WASHINGTON: Why, God bless you, of course. [*They grasp hands, WASHINGTON turns to TILGHMAN.*] Will you see that Dr. Rush is conducted to Captain Custis' quarters?

[*TILGHMAN and RUSH go to marquee. GIBBS enters.*]

GIBBS: [*Salutes WASHINGTON.*] Your Excellency, the man Morgan is here.

WASHINGTON: Request Mrs. Morgan's presence; then bring Morgan here.

GIBBS: [*Salutes.*] At once, Your Excellency.

LAFAYETTE: [*Enters, goes to WASHINGTON.*] I have seen the Count de Rochambeau. He is most charmed to accept your invitation to the conference.

[*MRS. MORGAN and MRS. HARRISON enter escorted by MAJOR GIBBS.*]

WASHINGTON: Thank you, Marquis. I have had brought here a man Morgan of the Connecticut Line.

LAFAYETTE: [*Delighted.*] Morgan. Ah—Sergeant Morgan, you would recognize his——

WASHINGTON: Mistress Harrison, Mistress Morgan, permit me, the Marquis de Lafayette. [*MRS. HARRISON curtsies. MRS. MORGAN just nods her head.*] Marquis, Morgan I take it is of your command?

LAFAYETTE: Of a certainty. Two months ago he went into the enemy's line.

MRS. MORGAN: Ma man—turned traitor!

LAFAYETTE: [*Surprised.*] Ah, madam, you do not understand! He has returned.

MRS. MORGAN: A double-dyed traitor!

[*MORGAN enters between two soldiers, their rifles at carry. As they halt before WASHINGTON, they salute and stand at attention. MORGAN, a strong-visaged man of soldierly bearing, in the uniform of the Continental line, salutes WASHINGTON, his eyes fixed on the General.*]

WASHINGTON: [*To LAFAYETTE.*] Is this the man Morgan of your command?

[*Husband and wife stand gazing steadfastly at each other, MRS. MORGAN'S face is as of steel, MORGAN'S surprised. TILGHMAN enters, goes to MRS. HARRISON.*]

LAFAYETTE: [*Bewildered.*] Of a surety, General.

MORGAN: Henrietta, what do you here?

MRS. MORGAN: I come lookin' ta find a traitor. An' God pity me, it's the truth that ye find wha' ye search for!

LAFAYETTE: No! No! madam. You do not comprehend! Sergeant Morgan is a most honorable man.

MRS. HARRISON: [*Joyously.*] Honorable!

LAFAYETTE: 'Twas at my request he went into the enemy's line.

MRS. HARRISON: But, comrades wrote he had deserted——

LAFAYETTE: 'Twas necessary that his comrades think him a deserter.

MRS. MORGAN: [*Breaking.*] Tam, ye're no a traitor!

MORGAN: Ye believed that o' me, Henrietta?

MRS. MORGAN: I'm no disgraced?

MORGAN: Who says ye are?

MRS. MORGAN: Our bairns need suffer na shame?

LAFAYETTE: Shame—? Voila!

MRS. MORGAN: Ma heart refused ta believe it o' ye. Tam forgie me, ma mon. [*She goes to his side, tearfully.*] Pit ye'er arms aboot ma, an' we'll nair question ainither agin.

[*MORGAN looks uncertainly at WASHINGTON and LAFAYETTE, he is confused. LAFAYETTE is delighted.*]

WASHINGTON: On occasion, Sergeant Morgan, a wife's command supersedes all others. You will obey your wife. [*He takes LAFAYETTE'S arm and draws him away. MRS. HARRISON and TILGHMAN walk toward the marquee. MORGAN takes MRS. MORGAN in his arms. WASHINGTON after a moment turns.*] Sergeant Morgan, you are a brave man, worthy of such a brave wife. You shall have the Order of the Purple Heart.

MORGAN: Oh, thank ye, General. [*Releases his wife, who goes to MRS. HARRISON. They embrace.*]

WASHINGTON: If I can ever grant you a favor——

MORGAN: [*Quickly*] Ye can do so now, sir.

WASHINGTON: What is it?

MORGAN: Whilst I was in the enemy's lines some thief took me rifle. I prized it next to Henrietta and my children.

WASHINGTON: [*Sternly, to LAFAYETTE.*] This camp must be searched for the Sergeant's rifle.

LAFAYETTE: [*With a covert smile.*] Your Excellency——

WASHINGTON: It must be found.

LAFAYETTE: That it shall be, my General.

[*MORGAN, satisfied, salutes and leaves with MRS. MORGAN and MRS. HARRISON, at right rear. During the last part of this dialogue, there can be heard the hoofbeats of many horses arriving.*]

GIBBS: [*Goes to WASHINGTON.*] Generals Wayne, Von Steuben, Knox, Muhlenburg and Lincoln, Your Excellency.

WASHINGTON: Have them enter. [*GIBBS goes to right rear, WASHINGTON goes to the table, stands in thought, orderly brings up chairs to the table, then steps back and salutes as GENERALS WAYNE, VON STEUBEN, KNOX, MUHLENBURG and LINCOLN enter and salute WASHINGTON. WAYNE is limping.*] Good morning, gentlemen. [*They reply and gather about the table. TRUMBULL gives WASHINGTON a message, he stops to read it, then glances up at WAYNE. Please be seated, GENERAL WAYNE. An honorable wound takes precedence over military courtesy.*]

WAYNE: Thanks, your Excellency. [*He sits. WASHINGTON continues to read for an instant. HUMPHREYS comes from tent and leaves. TILGHMAN takes notes of the council of war.*]

WASHINGTON: [*To TRUMBULL.*] We shall attend to that, later. [*TRUMBULL goes back to his table. WASHINGTON takes a chair at the head of the table, the others seat themselves by it.*] Gen-

tlemen, as you know, two days ago the Count de Grasse, who has so generously aided our cause by having his troops in our lines of circumvolution of Yorktown, sent me a message that within forty-eight hours he must withdraw his men from our army. Tonight he will embark the three thousand men of his independent command.

LINCOLN: Sir, will this withdrawal affect Count de Rochambeau's Army? [*WASHINGTON turns inquiringly to LAFAYETTE.*]

LAFAYETTE: General Lincoln, the morale of my compatriots who remain will not be affected.

MUHLENBURG: This means we now must needs shorten our lines to maintain the unbroken ring about Yorktown.

WASHINGTON: Of a certainty, General Muhlenburg.

KNOX: Your Excellency, is there word of Sir Henry Clinton?

WASHINGTON: General Knox, from our latest intelligence, Clinton has been heavily reinforced and is on the way to relieve Yorktown. Admiral Graves' fleet conveying Clinton's army is, we learn, nearing the Capes. [*The Generals are concerned, there is a sudden tenseness in their attitude, they exchange significant glances.*]

KNOX: Count de Grasse believes that, must he fight Graves, 'twould better be at sea.

LINCOLN: Must the result of this campaign hinge on a naval battle?

WASHINGTON: [*Significantly.*] If we await the outcome. [*For a moment there is silence.*]

MUHLENBURG: If fortune favored the enemy Clinton would relieve Cornwallis.

LINCOLN: Then we can but pound away with our artillery until the result of this sea fight is learned.

KNOX: Methinks Cornwallis cannot hold out much longer, our new batteries are most effective.

WAYNE: How long?

KNOX: Not more than a week.

LINCOLN: His morale must be high, or he would not have attempted the sortie last night.

WAYNE: You have a plan, General?

WASHINGTON: We cannot wait a week or more for our artillery to reduce Yorktown. Neither can we risk the outcome of a naval battle.

LINCOLN: [*Springs to his feet.*] Surely, General, you are not considering an attack!

WASHINGTON: Our lines must be shortened at once. Our only recourse is to storm Yorktown. [*They are all amazed.*]

LAFAYETTE: [*Aghast.*] Storm Yorktown!

WASHINGTON: Cornwallis must be taken. [*His fist strikes the table.*]

MUHLENBURG: Think of our losses!

LINCOLN: [*Rising.*] Your Excellency, this army is the only force of any consequence left to carry on the war. Should we fail in this attack, with its attendant loss of life, 'twill be next to impossible to recruit more men. [*He sits. The others are deep in thought.*]

WASHINGTON: What think you, General Knox?

KNOX: The enemy's position is still too strong!

WASHINGTON: Your opinion, General Muhlenburg?

MUHLENBURG: I feel the same as General Knox. The enemy is too strongly intrenched for a frontal attack.

WASHINGTON: Baron Von Steuben, think you we can take Yorktown by storm?

STEUBEN: Vidout our French friends, our boys could take it at de bayonets' point. Dey are de bess fighters in de voild! [*He *leans forward, his fist strikes the table.*] Kill a half of dem, an de udders go on. [*Again he strikes the table.*] Kill annoder half, an dey still go on. [*He strikes the table and rises.*] But before dey all dead, Kornvallis is [*strikes table a harder blow*] taken.

KNOX: Before they are all dead!

STEUBEN: [*Fiercely.*] Yah!

LINCOLN: Without our French allies?

WASHINGTON: Methinks we will need all available troops. Marquis Lafayette, your opinion?

LAFAYETTE: [*Rises.*] Like Monsieur the General the Baron Von Steuben, I, also, have the most fervent admiration for our American soldiers. Their steadfastness—endurance—elan. Voila! I love them! My own compatriots, the soldiers of His Majesty, my King, are they not also superb——?

STEUBEN: I know—I know dem—superb! Magnificent!

LAFAYETTE: —as ready to die, as our own Americans in the cause of liberty!

STEUBEN: Yah!

LAFAYETTE: [*To WASHINGTON.*] Oh, my General, think not I lack courage——

WASHINGTON: Your courage, Marquis? No one could question your courage!

LAFAYETTE: —but I believe the odds too great—the loss of life too appalling. [*He drops into his chair. There are nods of approval from LINCOLN, MUHLENBURG and KNOX. STEUBEN and WAYNE are thoughtful.*]

WASHINGTON: General Wayne?

WAYNE: I am for it, sir.

WASHINGTON: [*Quickly.*] Would you lead the storming party?

WAYNE: If you planned the campaign, sir, I would storm the gates of Hell!

GIBBS: [*Goes to WASHINGTON and salutes.*] The Count de Rochambeau and the Count de Chastellux, Your Excellency.

WASHINGTON: My compliments, ask them to join us. [*GIBBS leaves.*]

LINCOLN: We can order our own men to their death, but mayhap the Count de Rochambeau would not so risk his splendid regiments.

[*GIBBS enters with the French officers.*]

LAFAYETTE: General Lincoln, you will soon know.

KNOX: Was it not planned to use Count de Rochambeau's army in the West Indies, after this campaign?

LAFAYETTE: It was so desired by his Majesty, my King.

[*WASHINGTON and the others rise as the French Generals enter, their aides remain in the background with WASHINGTON'S aides. The French and Americans salute and bow to each other.*]

ROCHAMBEAU: Good morning, General Washington. Good morning, gentlemen.

WASHINGTON: [*Bows.*] Good morning, Count de Rochambeau. Good morning, Count de Chastellux. Will you be seated? [*ROCHAMBEAU and CHASTELLUX take seats.*] The embarkation of Count de Grasse's force——

ROCHAMBEAU: Le Comte must obey his positive orders, Your Excellency.

WASHINGTON: Of a certainty. You of course realize the situation is critical. Our lines must be shortened.

ROCHAMBEAU: Mais oui, mon General.

WASHINGTON: Sir Henry Clinton is nearing Yorktown. Immediate action is necessary. [*ROCHAMBEAU nods his head.*] Cornwallis must be taken before help arrives.

ROCHAMBEAU: Your Excellency, whatever your orders, they will be obeyed.

WASHINGTON: You consider yourself at my order?

ROCHAMBEAU: His Gracious Majesty, my King, has so directed me.

WASHINGTON: And should I order the united armies to storm Yorktown——?

[*ROCHAMBEAU rises in astonishment, CHASTELLUX draws back, aghast.*]

ROCHAMBEAU: [*Quickly recovers, straightens, fixes his eyes on Washington, who has risen.*] 'Tis a soldier's duty to obey. [*His hand rises in salute. Chastellux springs to his feet, his hand at the salute.*]

WASHINGTON: [*Returns their salute, their hands drop to their sides.*] Your Excellencies, I shall never forget this. Your names will be writ large in the future history of my country. [*The French Generals bow. The Americans are on their feet.*] I am loath to sacrifice the lives of gallant soldiers who have ever behaved with so much fidelity and courage.

ROCHAMBEAU: Your Excellency, the decision is in your hands.

WASHINGTON: And that decision you shall soon know.

[*The Generals all bow to WASHINGTON and retire, silently, thoughtfully. WASHINGTON stands as they leave, then he drops into his chair, leans back, his gaze on the horizon, unconscious of the orderly that comes and goes. TILGHMAN, at the entrance to the marquee, stands watching his Commander. DR. RUSH enters from marquee. TILGHMAN looks at him inquiringly. The doctor's glance is fixed on WASHINGTON. TILGHMAN goes to WASHINGTON.*]

TILGHMAN: Your Excellency?

WASHINGTON: [*In a tired voice.*] What is it, Colonel?

TILGHMAN: Dr. Rush.

WASHINGTON: [*For an instant closes his eyes then rises, turns toward RUSH, who advances.*] You have seen my boy?

DR. RUSH: I have.

WASHINGTON: And——?

DR. RUSH: General—. Would I could make a favorable report!

WASHINGTON: I would know his true condition.

DR. RUSH: The young man can live but a few days——

WASHINGTON: A few days——

DR. RUSH: —a week at most.

WASHINGTON: There is no hope?

DR. RUSH: None, sir.

WASHINGTON: Thank you—Dr. Rush.

[*RUSH draws back to TILGHMAN and walks away as WASHINGTON turns falteringly to the table, leans on it for support; his head drops; slowly WASHINGTON draws from his pocket his letter to Martha, unfolds it.*]

WASHINGTON: Col. Trumbull——

TRUMBULL: Yes, your Excellency.

WASHINGTON: —A quill and ink. [*He sits at table.*]

TRUMBULL: Yes, sir. [*Takes quill, ink and some sheets of paper to WASHINGTON, who writes a postscript to Martha's let-*

ter, folds and seals it, then returns it to his pocket. *TRUMBULL has stood by.*]

WASHINGTON: Send for Major Byron, Colonel.

TRUMBULL: Yes, sir. [*Salutes, returns to table and sends orderly for BYRON. WASHINGTON is for a moment in thought, rises and goes to his tent. HUMPHREYS enters and goes to table where TILGHMAN is now writing.*]

HUMPHREYS: The Council of War——? [*TILGHMAN nods.*] What are its conclusions?

TILGHMAN: [*Stops writing, picks up papers and rises.*] His Excellency proposed the storming of Yorktown.

HUMPHREYS: [*Astounded.*] Storm Yorktown!

TILGHMAN: It rests with his Excellency.

HUMPHREYS: And he——?

TILGHMAN: [*With a glance at the tent.*] I think not yet, but——

[*WASHINGTON comes from the tent with maps in his hand, spreads them out on the table and studies them. TILGHMAN goes toward TRUMBULL with papers, then stands watching his chief. HUMPHREYS enters tent.*]

WASHINGTON: [*Without looking up.*] The strength of the 4th Pennsylvania Line, Colonel Tilghman?

TILGHMAN: [*Takes a paper from table, glances at it.*] Four hundred and fifty-six, sir.

WASHINGTON: The 3rd New York?

TILGHMAN: [*Reads.*] Three hundred and ninety-six, sir.

WASHINGTON: The Royal Deux-Ponts of Count de Rochambeau's army?

TILGHMAN: Seven hundred and forty-nine. sir.

WASHINGTON: [*Thinking aloud, his fingers trace the map.*] The 4th Pennsylvania—opposite a redoubt—The Bourbonnois—perchance in reserve—The Virginians, the Marylanders—they could—The 1st New Jersey—over here. [*Thinks for a moment.*] It could be done.

TILGHMAN: [*At WASHINGTON'S words comes forward.*] Did you speak, sir?

WASHINGTON: [*Turns and puts a hand on TILGHMAN'S shoulder.*] You and I have seen much of killing and death, Colonel.

TILGHMAN: We have, Your Excellency.

WASHINGTON: Would that men's differences could be adjusted in some other way! Ever 'tis the statesmen who cause wars—and ever 'tis the soldier who must end them.

TILGHMAN: War takes its terrible toll, sir.

WASHINGTON: I have led these men for six years. [*Turns his head away from TILGHMAN.*] Can I, in the name of humanity, order them to possible death? [*As the last few words are said, approaching hoofbeats are heard, a confused mumble of voices, off stage. A French naval officer enters from right rear, conducted by MAJOR GIBBS. They go to WASHINGTON. Salutes are given and returned.*]

GIBBS: Your Excellency, Lieutenant DuQuesne from the Count de Grasse's flagship. [*WASHINGTON bows.*]

DUQUESNE: [*Bows.*] Les compliments de l'Admiral de Grasse, votre Excellency. Le Captain, an American sheep from across ze bay has just report l'Admiral Graves weeth Clinton armee ees at de Capes.

TILGHMAN: Clinton, at the Capes!

DUQUESNE: Mais oui. [*Extends paper to WASHINGTON.*] My report en writing, Votre Excellency.

WASHINGTON: [*WASHINGTON takes the paper.*] Please convey to the Admiral Count de Grasse my compliments and express my appreciation for the prompt delivery of the intelligence. [*DUQUESNE salutes and leaves. WASHINGTON reads message, crushes it in his hand, paces up and down, stops at table, his hand on the map.*]

WASHINGTON: [*Strikes table with fist.*] It must be done! [*Quickly to TILGHMAN, points to quill and ink.*]

TILGHMAN: Yes, Your Excellency. [*Springs to table, takes quill.*]

WASHINGTON: Draft the necessary orders for the storming of Yorktown. [*Again paces up and down.*]

TILGHMAN: At what hour sir? [*At table, rapidly making notes.*]

WASHINGTON: At two in the morning.

TILGHMAN: Am I to send for General Wayne?

WASHINGTON: My gallant Wayne! [*Shakes his head.*] It can't be Wayne who leads the assault.

TILGHMAN: [*Looks up inquiringly, then with consternation on his face he lifts a restraining hand.*] Not—? You——!

WASHINGTON: 'Tis my right——

TILGHMAN: [*Breathed.*] But, sir——

WASHINGTON: —'Tis my choice.

TILGHMAN: The army would be loath to have you do it. [*He springs to his feet.*] But, by the Eternal, it means victory!

[*The bombardment of Yorktown suddenly ceases, the cannons' fire is stilled. WASHINGTON and TILGHMAN stare at each other in astonishment.*]

WASHINGTON: The guns are stilled!

TILGHMAN: Can it mean—my Lord Cornwallis——

[*Aides, orderlies, guards, gaze to right. The hoofbeats of a horse leaving headquarters. HUMPHREYS comes in with spy glass in hand, goes to WASHINGTON.*]

HUMPHREYS: [*Saluting WASHINGTON.*] Our men in the outer works are standing on the parapets, sir. [*WASHINGTON returns salute. The hoofbeats of a horse are heard rapidly approaching.*]

WASHINGTON: [*Speculatively.*] This very day, four years ago, Burgoyne surrendered at Saratoga.

TILGHMAN: An example I hope, my Lord Cornwallis doth emulate.

[*There is huzzahing off stage. An officer covered with dust rushes in, goes to WASHINGTON and salutes.*]

OFFICER: Sir, I have the honor to report the enemy has raised the white flag. [*WASHINGTON turns to table for a moment, looks into space, slowly folds over a map.*] A British officer comes to arrange the terms of surrender.

[*There is the sound of many horses coming nearer. TILGHMAN, deeply affected, extends his hand.*]

TILGHMAN: May I be the first to extend congratulations, Your Excellency!

WASHINGTON: There is but one other whose hand I would rather take at this hour. [*TILGHMAN'S hand is taken.*]

TILGHMAN: Madam Washington is the only one I would willingly step aside for.

[*COLONEL HAMILTON and several officers enter, leading a British officer who is blindfolded. They quickly remove the handkerchief from his eyes and give it to him as he stands before WASHINGTON.*]

HAMILTON: [*Saluting.*] General Washington, Major Grimes of my Lord Cornwallis' staff.

MAJOR GRIMES: [*Saluting.*] Sir, my Lord Cornwallis' compliments, and he proposes a cessation of hostilities for twenty-four hours, that commissioners may meet to settle terms for surrender. And my Lord has named Colonel Dundas and Major Ross of the British army as his commissioners.

WASHINGTON: My compliments to my Lord Cornwallis. I hope he is in good health. I name as commissioners Colonels Laurens and Viscount De Noailles of Count de Rochambeau's army. [*MAJOR GRIMES salutes, steps back, with a smile places the handkerchief to his eyes. He is led away. Constant hoofbeats of arriving horses. HAMILTON goes to WASHINGTON, bows.*]

HAMILTON: [*They grasp hands, both overpowered by emotion.*] 'Tis victory! [*WASHINGTON takes his hand, so affected he cannot speak. MAJOR BYRON enters, TILGHMAN draws HAMILTON away. BYRON goes to WASHINGTON and salutes.*]

WASHINGTON: [*Returns BYRON'S salute and takes a letter from his pocket, looks at it and slowly extends it to BYRON.*] To Madam Washington. [*BYRON salutes, WASHINGTON'S hand automatically returns salute. BYRON goes. WASHINGTON turns toward table with his hands resting thereon, looks off into space, as in the distance can be heard the huzzahing of the victorious American and French Armies.*]

CURTAIN.

THE DOMINANT FORCE
A GEORGE WASHINGTON PLAY IN ONE ACT

DRAMATIS PERSONAE

(IN ORDER OF THEIR APPEARANCE)

BLAKE, MRS. BINGHAM's *butler.*

MADAME BLAUVELT, *of New Orleans.*

JAMES MADISON, *delegate from Virginia.*

JAMES WILSON, *delegate from Pennsylvania.*

ROGER SHERMAN, *delegate from Connecticut.*

MRS. BINGHAM, *their hostess.*

DARNELL, *a foreign secret agent.*

FENWAY, *a secretary to one of the delegates.*

GEORGE WASHINGTON, *President of the Constitutional Convention.*

GUNNING BEDFORD, *delegate from Delaware.*

LUTHER MARTIN, *delegate from Maryland.*

OLIVER ELLSWORTH, *delegate from Connecticut.*

ELBRIDGE GERRY, *delegate from Massachusetts.*

JOHN RUTLEDGE, *delegate from South Carolina.*

GEORGE MASON, *delegate from Virginia.*

TIME: *A July evening in 1787.*

PLACE: *A room in the home of* MRS. BINGHAM, *at Philadelphia.*

DESCRIPTION OF CHARACTERS

BLAKE:

The usual type of butler, dressed in livery of the period—a profusely braided coat of dark blue or purple velvet, with white breeches and waistcoat, white stockings and buckled shoes.

MADAME BLAUVELT:

A beautiful brunette of about thirty years of age. She is fascinating, secretive, adroit, evidently well born and bred but possessed of all the arts of a courtesan. She is richly dressed in the fashion of the period; wears a lace mantilla over her hair which is dressed high on her head, with curls at the neck.

JAMES MADISON:

A great leader in the making of the Constitution. He is thirty-six years of age, small in stature, neat, refined, courteous and amiable. He is very earnest but reserved in manner. Well dressed in smallclothes of the period.

JAMES WILSON:

One of the strongest men in the Convention; is forty-two years of age, a clear thinker, forceful, logical. Well dressed in clothes of period.

ROGER SHERMAN:

One of the outstanding figures in the Convention, and one of the oldest, being sixty-six years of age. Rather awkward but noted for his common sense and steadfastness to his ideas.

MRS. BINGHAM:

A little past middle age. She is the social leader of Philadelphia. Her parties were very popular with the delegates at the Convention as she was a famous hostess. She is elegantly gowned in the fashion of the late eighteenth century.

DARNELL:

A man of middle age, possessed of elegant manners, and of all of the arts and artifices of a European secret agent. Plainly though richly dressed in smallclothes.

FENWAY:

A young man in his early twenties, enamored of the beautiful MADAME BLAUVELT, *therefore her dupe. He is of fine address and has a likable personality. Richly dressed in colonial smallclothes.*

GEORGE WASHINGTON:

Fifty-five years of age, six feet two inches tall, in weight about two hundred pounds; rather large boned but well proportioned, graceful, dignified, thoughtful, modest in deportment. His complexion rather pale, his features strong, his hair powdered and worn in a queue tied with a black ribbon. Plainly though richly dressed in dark smallclothes of the colonial period.

GUNNING BEDFORD:

Fifty-seven years of age. Opinionated, impatient and intolerant of others' views. Dressed much the same as the other delegates.

LUTHER MARTIN:

Thirty-nine years of age. Irascible, truculent, obstinate. An able lawyer, bitter foe of large States. Slovenly in dress.

OLIVER ELLSWORTH:

Forty-two years of age. Has a fine unaffected presence, courtly, dignified and elegant. Very well dressed in period clothes.

ELBRIDGE GERRY:

Forty-three years of age. A man of high integrity and very persevering. Possesses great self-confidence; rather laborious and hesitating in speech. Plainly though richly dressed.

JOHN RUTLEDGE:

Forty-eight years of age; one of the strong men of the Convention. A man of distinction in the South. Elegantly dressed.

GEORGE MASON:

Sixty-two years of age. Has a lofty bearing and commanding presence; a grave face, dark hair sprinkled with gray.

NOTE: *The descriptions of the delegates are taken from contemporary writers of the time and are given as an index to the characters and attitudes of the delegates, in order to aid the director. The younger men did not wear wigs and few powdered their hair. However, they did wear their natural hair long and tied in a queue. It will be necessary, therefore, to conceal the short hair of the modern day, and in order to lend variety to the characters, it would be well to have the younger delegates wear wigs other than gray or white.*

SET: *An elegantly appointed room in the richest type of colonial architecture and furnishings. Centering the back wall a fire-place with an oil painting hanging above the handsome mantel; to the left of it, a door leading to a drawing room; to the right of the fireplace, a large piece of furniture such as a secretary or bookcase. Centering the left wall, a large French window with handsome drapes. There is a door in the center of the right wall, flanked by handsome pieces of furniture or statuary. Right of center, a library table, at the left, forward, a large davenport or sofa placed at an angle. Beautiful chairs, small tables, footstools, candle sticks, and other furnishings should complete the room.*

[*As the curtain rises BLAKE, the butler, is placing a new quill and ink on the desk, when MADAME BLAUVELT enters hurriedly from right, hesitates when she sees BLAKE.*]

MADAME BLAUVELT: Good evening, Blake. [*At a slower, more aimless pace she goes to window at the left.*]

BLAKE: [*Turns and bows.*] Good evening, Madame Blauvelt.

MADAME BLAUVELT: [*Draws back the curtain, looks out.*] 'Tis a wondrous night.

BLAKE: 'Tis that, Madame.

MADAME BLAUVELT: How beautiful the flowers! Open the window. I would stroll in the garden. [*BLAKE goes to the French window and opens it for her.*] Thank you, Blake.

BLAKE: [*As she exits.*] 'Tis a pleasure to serve you, Madame.

[*He draws the drapes, snuffs a candle on the mantel, starts for the door at right, steps back as MRS. BINGHAM followed by MADISON, WILSON, and SHERMAN, enter.*]

MRS. BINGHAM: Gentlemen, you will not be disturbed; this room is little frequented by my guests.

WILSON: Thank you, Mistress Bingham.

MRS. BINGHAM: [*To BLAKE.*] Attend the gentlemen's desires, Blake, and see that they are not disturbed.

BLAKE: Aye, Madame.

MADISON: We deeply appreciate your hospitality, Mistress Bingham. What would we do without your charming evenings!

SHERMAN: You are kindness itself, Madame.

MRS. BINGHAM: 'Tis little enow. Would I could do more for the members of the convention. [*They bow, she curtsies and leaves as BLAKE opens the door. Then stands beside it.*]

BLAKE: Is there anything I can do, gentlemen?

WILSON: You will not be needed.

MADISON: See that no one enters while we are here.

[*BLAKE nods his head in acquiescence and leaves. WILSON glances about the room.*]

WILSON: So grave is the crisis, gentlemen, I believe 'tis advisable we speak in all frankness.

MADISON: I agree, Mr. Wilson.

WILSON: Are you of a like mind, Mr. Sherman?

SHERMAN: Aye, 'tis best that we do.

WILSON: [*Turns to SHERMAN.*] Though the Connecticut delegation is one of the small State groups, you have ever stood for a strong national government.

SHERMAN: Aye. But also, Mr. Wilson, I stand with my State for equal representation in the senate.

MADISON: The small State group will insist upon it even to the extent of withdrawing from the union.

WILSON: And thereby cause a disruption of these States, which but presages confusion and anarchy.

SHERMAN: Gentlemen, no man would sacrifice more for the establishment of a strong federal government than I.

WILSON: I take it the same cannot be said for certain members of the Committee of Compromise that represents the small States.

SHERMAN: You, as well as I, know the irrepressible Bedford and the obstinate, truculent, Martin.

MADISON: So insistent in their demands that they would wreck the nation.

SHERMAN: We agreed to frankness, Mr. Madison. Who is more determined or obstinate in his stand than Mr. Mason and yourself!

MADISON: Both Mr. Mason and myself have, as members, seen the impotency of the Continental Congress where narrow jealousy and petty State policies have played so conspicuous a role.

WILSON: We are not here to discuss small State or big State claims.

SHERMAN: Aye, 'tis now in the hands of the Committee of Compromise.

WILSON: If they report unanimously, there is naught left for the convention at large but to accept and ratify its report.

MADISON: If they agree on a compromise.

SHERMAN: 'Tis a grave situation, the country—the whole human race will be affected by the Committee's decision.

MADISON: Any one member stubborn in allegiance to his State, concerned but little for the nation at large, may wreck this union.

SHERMAN: The controlling fact is that the country must unite.

WILSON: And what can we do to make certain the agreement of the Committee?

SHERMAN: Who could influence them but Washington?

MADISON: Who but Washington?

WILSON: Ah, if he would speak.

SHERMAN: As President of the Convention, he sits silently through the endless argument.

MADISON: 'Tis his policy to take no part in the discussion.

WILSON: This is an occasion so fraught with dire consequence that he must for once break his rule of silence.

MADISON: Would Bedford and Martin, of the small States, heed his words?

SHERMAN: Would Mason and Gerry, of the large States, do likewise?

WILSON: I can imagine no man who would not be influenced by the words of General Washington.

SHERMAN: Come, Mr. Madison, you are closer to him than any of us, mayhap you can prevail upon him to break his silence.

MADISON: It would be no easy task. Only in a dire emergency would he so act.

WILSON: The emergency is here. This nation has never called on Washington in vain.

MADISON: I can but try.

SHERMAN: The General is to be here this evening. Mayhap he has already arrived.

WILSON: And several members from both groups who are members of the Committee.

SHERMAN: He might speak to them informally.

MADISON: He might.

WILSON: Then go to him, overcome his natural hesitancy to any act that borders on the use of his influence.

SHERMAN: Make him see that he is our only hope for a united nation.

MADISON: I will do my best.

[WILSON starts for the door, SHERMAN follows. MADISON is thoughtful as he goes after them.]

SHERMAN: [As they leave.] I will assist in arranging to get the members of the Committee who are present to gather in this room, later.

[A long moment after they leave, the drapes at window, at left, move, MADAME BLAUVELT'S head appears, then she steps out nonchalantly, smoothes her skirts, arranges her hair, then goes to door at left, opens it a bit, signals to some one, closes door, makes sure there is no one in the room or listening, goes to sofa and sits, arranges her skirts. After a moment DARNELL enters, hurries to her.]

DARNELL: Ah, Madame Blauvelt, I thought you, ah, hem, would never come.

[She gives him her hand; he kisses it rather impatiently.]

MADAME BLAUVELT: Monsieur Darnell, one cannot be impolite to one's hostess.

DARNELL: You were riding with the young secretary this afternoon?

MADAME BLAUVELT: Aye. Monsieur Fenway is a gallant companion.

DARNELL: Is the young cub still infatuated with you?

MADAME BLAUVELT: Ssh! [Her hand raised in admonition. DARNELL looks about.]

DARNELL: What did Fenway tell you?

MADAME BLAUVELT: He had only a few words with his— his employer.

DARNELL: Zounds! Even he, a secretary, is not allowed behind those [rises and looks about the room] closed doors!

MADAME BLAUVELT: Fortunately they—ahem—Monsieur Fenway is such a trusty secretary and is as talkative as is the young man.

DARNELL: Did you learn anything today?

MADAME BLAUVELT: They are at the breaking point.

DARNELL: [Impatiently.] Another impasse!

MADAME BLAUVELT: You are not discouraged, Monsieur?

DARNELL: From the start of the Convention, the reports I sent to my superiors were glowing with accounts of their differences.

MADAME BLAUVELT: It did not seem possible for the States to reach an accord on any issue.

DARNELL: But they have, nevertheless.

MADAME BLAUVELT: Aye, their providing for the popular election of representatives?

DARNELL: I thought they would break on that issue.

MADAME BLAUVELT: 'Twas necessary for you to report to your—ah, superiors, that they overcame that barrier?

DARNELL: Aye, and I received a curt reply that I should have taken some action to have the break actually occur.

MADAME BLAUVELT: Then yours is a mission much more— sinister than the mere securing of information.

DARNELL: When I accepted this mission, I felt certain of success. That these thirteen States with their racial, industrial, agricultural, religious and commercial differences could agree upon any form of a constitution seemed impossible.

MADAME BLAUVELT: So you were satisfied merely to secure information, through me?

DARNELL: Aye, but I must do more. These States must not be united in a strong federal government.

MADAME BLAUVELT: 'Tis not as yet been accomplished, Monsieur.

DARNELL: But with all their wrangling, their bickering, they seem finally to reach an accord on each issue.

MADAME BLAUVELT: True so far.

DARNELL: Some dominating personality seems to hold them to the task.

MADAME BLAUVELT: Ah——

DARNELL: —some inexorable force impels them to give up their pet prejudices and dearest schemes.

MADAME BLAUVELT: At last, you have discovered the personality—the force that is ruling this convention?

DARNELL: Nay. I wish I knew. Can it be Madison?

MADAME BLAUVELT: Madison? I am surprised, Monsieur, that one so clever as you——

DARNELL: Then 'tis not Madison? Who?

MADAME BLAUVELT: Washington!

DARNELL: Washington?

MADAME BLAUVELT: Aye, Washington.

DARNELL: But Madame, if our information is correct——

MADAME BLAUVELT: 'Tis reliable.

DARNELL: —he sits all day, never saying a word, just a figurehead presiding over the Convention.

MADAME BLAUVELT: Washington could never be a figurehead.

DARNELL: You are not serious?

MADAME BLAUVELT: Will your race ever learn to know this man?

DARNELL: Fiddlesticks! So lacking in interest is Washington that he sits before Artist Peale for his portrait. But this evening I heard him jesting about it.

MADAME BLAUVELT: [Earnestly.] Monsieur, I am as desirous of preventing the establishment of a republic as you.

DARNELL: Ah, so you are something more than my paid informant?

MADAME BLAUVELT: Aye, something more.

DARNELL: Would that I knew whom you represent!

MADAME BLAUVELT: [Smiles enigmatically.] Monsieur!

DARNELL: Then 'tis not a fair question?

MADAME BLAUVELT: Suffice that we are allies in a common cause——

DARNELL: That these States shall not form a republic—but be reduced to confusion—anarchy.

MADAME BLAUVELT: I spoke of an impasse.

DARNELL: Also you spoke of Washington.

MADAME BLAUVELT: [Fiercely.] He is an obstacle to my——

DARNELL: To all royalty.

MADAME BLAUVELT: [Fiercely.] The obstacle must be removed.

DARNELL: God, you wouldn't!

MADAME BLAUVELT: Ssh!

[The door at the left opens and FENWAY enters. He is eager to talk to MADAME BLAUVELT but is resentful of DARNELL. He hesitates. DARNELL rises and bows. MADAME BLAUVELT at his appearance hides her impatience at the interruption and smiles.]

DARNELL: Mr. Fenway.

FENWAY: Mr. Darnell. [Bows.]

MADAME BLAUVELT: You are leaving, Monsieur Darnell? [To FENWAY.] Monsieur Darnell has been relating a most amusing incident.

FENWAY: Then I intrude?

DARNELL: Nay. I had completed my narrative and give way to one who, mayhap, is more interesting.

MADAME BLAUVELT: La, La, you men! Come, Monsieur Fenway.

[He eagerly goes to her, kisses her hand.]

DARNELL: [Smiles and from behind FENWAY points toward the door at left. MADAME BLAUVELT nods a crafty assent.] I am eager for a game of cards.

[As DARNELL leaves, MADAME BLAUVELT makes room for FENWAY on the sofa. FENWAY infatuated, seizes MADAME BLAUVELT'S hand.]

FENWAY: Oh, Madame, it seems ages since I saw you!

MADAME BLAUVELT: [Coquettishly.] Fie, Monsieur, and you rode with me this afternoon. So soon am I forgotten?

FENWAY: Forgotten? No one could ever forget you!

MADAME BLAUVELT: Aye.

FENWAY: [Jealously.] This Darnell. He dogs your footsteps. Ever I find him near you.

MADAME BLAUVELT: He is a stranger—a bit forlorn—and——

FENWAY: [Interrupting.] Old!

MADAME BLAUVELT: Well he is a bit——

FENWAY: [Interrupting.] Far too old for you.

MADAME BLAUVELT: [Archly.] I do prefer one with the—ah—the—ah—fire of youth.

FENWAY: [Satisfied.] Of a certainty you would. And if—[Hesitates.]

MADAME BLAUVELT: If what?

FENWAY: —I could always be with you. I am half a mind to give up this stupid position as secretary, so I——

MADAME BLAUVELT: [Interrupting.] Not leave your interesting vocation?

FENWAY: Interesting? Listening to my conceited employer prating about what he said on the floor in reply to what others said.

MADAME BLAUVELT: They tell me you are quite a mimic.

FENWAY: Oh, you have heard that?

MADAME BLAUVELT: Would you? Act for me?

FENWAY: Why—yes—ah, for instance: Mr. Gunning Bedford of Delaware said, after Mr. King of Massachusetts had spoken: [Rising in a declamatory manner.] "Frankly, Gentlemen, I do not trust you! If you possess the power, the abuse of it could not be checked; and what would prevent you from using it to our destruction?"

MADAME BLAUVELT: How amusing? You are, Monsieur, quite the actor.

FENWAY: [Elated at her praise.] Oh, he said more.

MADAME BLAUVELT: Oh, do act again, tell me what he said.

FENWAY: Aye. [Strikes an attitude.] "Sooner than be ruined there are foreign powers who would take us by the hand."

MADAME BLAUVELT: [Starts, but disguises her elation.] Surely he was not serious.

FENWAY: [Impressively.] Oh, he meant it. [Leans toward her.] Do you know, Madame, there are foreign powers that would gladly take over a single State or a group of States.

MADAME BLAUVELT: No?

FENWAY: Yes!

MADAME BLAUVELT: Really. [She looks about the sofa for something mislaid.] Where can it be! [Continues to search.]

FENWAY: What have you lost?

MADAME BLAUVELT: My handkerchief. [Laughs.] I wonder now—the silly man!

FENWAY: [Suspiciously.] Wonder what? What man?

MADAME BLAUVELT: Why I do believe he did.

FENWAY: Who did what?

MADAME BLAUVELT: Mr. Darnell was admiring the perfume I use. Said he could identify the make.

FENWAY: Do you think he took your handkerchief?

MADAME BLAUVELT: I am certain, 'twas only a jest.

FENWAY: [Rises in anger.] I will seek him out at once and fetch it for you.

MADAME BLAUVELT: Now don't be cross with him. If he took it, 'twas in a spirit of jest.

FENWAY: [Sternly.] I will fetch it.

MADAME BLAUVELT: I must go to my room for awhile, 'tis a wondrous night, would you walk with me in the garden?

FENWAY: [Seizes her hand and kisses it.] Will you meet me there?

MADAME BLAUVELT: [Archly.] If you really want me to. Say half an hour.

FENWAY: [Again kisses her hand.] Please don't keep me too long. [He bows, goes to the door at left, looks back and smiles. MADAME BLAUVELT archly returns his smile as she leisurely goes to door at right. As he leaves she opens the door, looks out, nods and returns to center. DARNELL enters and goes to her.]

MADAME BLAUVELT: [*Intensely.*] If you would succeed in your mission, do as I say and act quickly!

DARNELL: As you say?

MADAME BLAUVELT: [*Fiercely.*] As I say!

[*He looks at her intently, tries to read her mind, realizes she is more adroit, far more clever than he. Decides to take orders.*]

DARNELL: Well——

MADAME BLAUVELT: [*Knows she has won and speaks rapidly.*] Washington is President of the Potomac River Company——believes transportation the key to the west and the future development of this nation is in that direction——

DARNELL: Aye.

MADAME BLAUVELT: Such developments need money.

DARNELL: He has plenty of money.

MADAME BLAUVELT: He is land poor. At this moment needs money to pay his taxes.

DARNELL: [*Astonished.*] Really?

MADAME BLAUVELT: Go to him, say you represent large foreign financial interests that could finance his company's plans for a canal he desires to build. His heart is set on it.

DARNELL: I understand.

MADAME BLAUVELT: However, the interests you represent would not consider investments unless a strong national government is founded. They would fear the interference of various States if the new government was not all powerful regarding such matters.

DARNELL: What would that do?

MADAME BLAUVELT: Definitely line up Washington on the side of the large States.

DARNELL: He doesn't take sides.

MADAME BLAUVELT: He believes in a strong federal government. He will make his opinion, whatever it may be, known in this instance. He will do it tonight.

DARNELL: What good will that do?

MADAME BLAUVELT: Strengthen the adherents of big States and antagonize the small ones.

DARNELL: Then the small States will give in.

MADAME BLAUVELT: They will never give in.

DARNELL: How do you know?

MADAME BLAUVELT: There are two small State delegates who even Washington could not influence in this matter. Go! Seek out Washington at once before—if he should speak to the delegates who are here this evening.

DARNELL: Very well. [*He starts for the door at left.*]

MADAME BLAUVELT: Not that way [*goes to the window at left*] here through the garden. [*DARNELL goes to the window, passes out when MADAME BLAUVELT speaks.*] Wait, when that simpering Fenway asks you for my handkerchief give him this, say 'twas taken in jest.

[*She takes a handkerchief from her breast and thrusts it toward DARNELL who as he leaves takes it. WASHINGTON and MADISON enter in time for WASHINGTON, who is ahead of MADISON, to see the passing of the handkerchief. For an instant only she is shaken then coolly goes toward WASHINGTON and MADISON, who bow.*]

MADAME BLAUVELT: [*Curtsies.*] Good evening General Washington, Mr. Madison.

WASHINGTON: Good evening, Madame Blauvelt.

MADISON: Good evening, Madame.

WASHINGTON: I am much interested in your native city, Madame.

MADAME BLAUVELT: [*Uncertain.*] My native city?

WASHINGTON: New Orleans occupies a most favorable commercial situation.

MADAME BLAUVELT: So I have heard it said. However, I know but little of such matters.

WASHINGTON: I shall never rest content until I visit your western country and sail down the great Mississippi to your city.

MADISON: You are seriously contemplating such a journey, General?

WASHINGTON: If all goes well I would make the trip next year.

MADAME BLAUVELT: [*Curtsies.*] And may I be the first citizen of New Orleans to place my home at the disposal of General Washington?

WASHINGTON: [*Bows.*] Thank you, Madame. Mayhap I will accept of your kindness.

MADAME BLAUVELT: [*She goes to door at left.*] What an honor 'twould be to entertain the hero of Trenton and Yorktown. [*She curtsies and leaves.*]

MADISON: A very charming woman Madame Blauvelt.

WASHINGTON: She is making rather a protracted visit to Philadelphia.

MADISON: Came last May.

WASHINGTON: Ah, about the time the Convention started.

MADISON: You will pardon me, General, if I turn the conversation from such a charming subject of conversation as the fair New Orleans lady to a matter not so pleasant.

WASHINGTON: [*With a smile.*] I suspected you had asked me to this room for some purpose.

MADISON: [*Very seriously.*] General, we face a crisis most alarming.

WASHINGTON: Aye. The situation is extremely grave.

MADISON: If the committee, appointed to consider the matter, fails to agree upon a compromise satisfactory to the large and small States, this nation, which you lead to independence, will dissolve into a number of weak States, the prey of any foreign power.

WASHINGTON: [*Deep in thought.*] No morn ever dawned more favorable than ours did; and no day was ever more clouded than the present.

MADISON: The clouds are so dark and menacing that again we must call upon you, sir, to pilot us to a safe shore.

WASHINGTON: You exaggerate my ability, friend.

MADISON: Nay. Your influence must be felt in the committee's deliberations.

WASHINGTON: Sir, as President of the Convention, I have steadfastly refrained from voicing my opinions.

MADISON: [*Earnestly.*] It has not been necessary that you should, for when in session the entire Convention is under your restraining eye. On the deliberations of this Committee the fate of America hangs as by a thread.

WASHINGTON: Aye, true it does.

MADISON: There are present here tonight some of the strongest men of each faction, who are members of the committee, Bedford, Martin and Ellsworth, of the small-State group, Mason, Gerry and Rutledge, of the large States. Through the assistance of our charming hostess and Mr. Sherman of Connecticut, I shall endeavor to maneuver them into this room. If you would join them and for once express your opinion.

WASHINGTON: You are asking me to do something much opposed to my fixed policy of silence in these matters. Forget not I am the presiding officer.

MADISON: 'Twas you who started the movement that resulted in this Convention, sir. [*WASHINGTON is in deep thought. MADISON for a moment watches him intently.*] I leave you to your thoughts, General. America has never called upon Washington in vain. I go to effect my purpose. [*He starts for the door. WASHINGTON lifts a hand to restrain him, which MADISON does not see, WASHINGTON then sits back in deep thought as MADISON leaves at right. WASHINGTON finally slowly shakes his head and as though reaching a decision, he rises. DARNELL enters from right, goes to WASHINGTON and bows.*]

DARNELL: General Washington, may I speak of a matter of considerable moment to me and one in which I believe you will be interested?

WASHINGTON: Shall we be seated, Mr. Darnell? [*They take seats.*]

DARNELL: As President of the Potomac River Company, you are, I understand, interested in the development of water transportation westward.

WASHINGTON: Not only as President of the company am I interested, Mr. Darnell, but as an American citizen who would assist in providing means for the settlement of States that will be formed in our western lands.

DARNELL: I understand, sir, a canal is necessary to circumvent the Great Falls of the Potomac.

WASHINGTON: Aye, a canal must be built.

DARNELL: Such an undertaking would require a vast outlay of money.

WASHINGTON: More than it seems is available, at present.

DARNELL: Mayhap, sir, I could assist in the financing of the venture.

WASHINGTON: [*Studies him.*] Financial assistance would be most welcome.

DARNELL: I represent foreign capital that believes in the future development of this territory. On my word I believe they would invest a considerable amount in the project.

WASHINGTON: Do you feel inclined to advise them to that effect?

DARNELL: If, after investigation, I find the facts are as I now take them to be.

WASHINGTON: We would want you to make a most thorough investigation.

DARNELL: Which I believe, from the character of the men in the Potomac River Company, would but strengthen my already favorable opinion.

WASHINGTON: Mayhap.

DARNELL: However, General, there is a very important consideration which would loom large in the decision of my clients.

WASHINGTON: Please state it.

DARNELL: The present condition of the country and its future government.

WASHINGTON: That would merit their consideration.

DARNELL: If from this Convention comes a strong national government—all powerful—which can assure capital that there will be no interference in such a development by the various State governments.

WASHINGTON: [*Gazes at him fixedly.*] Your clients would fear State interference?

DARNELL: They would.

WASHINGTON: Mr. Darnell, will you tell me now what is the nationality of the men who are so interested in the future of this land?

DARNELL: [*Hesitates.*] In due time, sir, I will.

[*FENWAY'S face appears at the door at right, seeing DARNELL he hurries toward him, then noticing WASHINGTON, he stops.*]

FENWAY: [*Bows.*] Pardon me, General Washington, I was seeking Mr. Darnell. I——

WASHINGTON: Is it a matter that can wait?

FENWAY: A lady asked me to——

DARNELL: [*Impatiently.*] Surely Mr. Fenway, 'tis a matter you can take up with me later.

WASHINGTON: If it concerns a lady's request, Mr. Darnell we can well pardon the interruption.

FENWAY: Madame Blauvelt's handkerchief, sir. She sent me for it.

[*WASHINGTON rises, watches DARNELL, who is controlling his impatience and anger.*]

DARNELL: Madame Blauvelt's handkerchief?

FENWAY: Give it to me!

DARNELL: [*Rises, his hands exploring his pockets.*] Oh, yes. 'Tis here. [*He draws handkerchief from his pocket.*] I took it in jest. Will you please so explain to the charming Madame.

FENWAY: [*Angrily he takes handkerchief.*] You can make your own explanations, sir. [*He bows.*] Please pardon the interruption, General Washington. [*He leaves at left.*]

DARNELL: [*To WASHINGTON.*] Sir, I regret the impetuous young man felt called upon to interrupt us. As he entered I was saying in due time I would name the citizenry of my clients.

WASHINGTON: Mr. Darnell, I must always know with whom I am dealing.

DARNELL: [*Taken aback.*] Why sir, it seems rather——

WASHINGTON: Are you an Englishman?

DARNELL: Why—why, yes, sir?

WASHINGTON: [*Grimly.*] Mayhap. The *Bonaventura* sails from Philadelphia, tomorrow. When you land in Europe, you may convey to your clients or superiors the information that the United States will endure as a nation!

DARNELL: Why, General Washington!

WASHINGTON: You have little time to engage passage Mr. Darnell. [*DARNELL seems to shrink before WASHINGTON'S gaze. Pulls himself together, bows and leaves. WASHINGTON watches him leave. Then stands by the table in deep thought as BEDFORD, MARTIN and ELLSWORTH enter. Surprised to see WASHINGTON alone, they bow to him.*]

BEDFORD: If you are awaiting some one, General, we will leave?

WASHINGTON: Nay, Mr. Bedford, I was but now about to leave, gentlemen. [*He bows, goes to door at right and leaves.*]

MARTIN: Hum! General Washington alone, I wonder what is on his mind.

ELLSWORTH: Mr. Martin, many an hour while the convention is in session I too have wondered what he is thinking.

BEDFORD: Ah, Ellsworth, methinks every delegate has experienced that thought. Ever he sits like a sphinx, with those gray eyes fixed on one man then another.

ELLSWORTH: I must confess 'tis at times most disconcerting.

MARTIN: Recently, when in the heat of debate and for a moment near to anger, I caught his eye upon me and there flashed across my vision Valley Forge and the whole panorama of the Revolution, and for an instant I felt small and ineffectual.

ELLSWORTH: That is a lot for you to admit, Mr. Martin.

[*GERRY, RUTLEDGE, MASON and MADISON, enter; for an instant they hesitate when they see the others. MADISON is quick to take advantage of the situation.*]

MADISON: Ah, Gentlemen, this is a fortunate occurrence. Mr. Gerry, Mr. Rutledge and Mr. Mason, like yourselves, are members of the Committee of Compromise.

MARTIN: What of it, Mr. Madison?

MADISON: Mayhap a calm discussion of the points at issue——

MARTIN: [*Truculently.*] I, for one, am ready to discuss the matter even here, but first I want you gentlemen to understand once and for all that the State of Maryland will have no part in the proposed government unless the representation for all States is equal.

MASON: 'Tis absurd to talk of giving one hundred and eighty thousand men in one section as much weight in the national government as seven hundred and fifty thousand in another section.

BEDFORD: Mr. Mason, Delaware will never consent to be dominated by Virginia nor by Massachusetts, nor by any other powerful State.

MADISON: Let us be tolerant, and not jump to unwarranted conclusions. I am persuaded that no State desires to dominate another. As I am not of this Committee, I withdraw. [*He bows and leaves, the others bow as he passes out the door.*]

RUTLEDGE: I hold with Mr. Madison. Let us be tolerant. Have we no faith in our mutual integrity? Unless it is grounded in faith and confidence, no union is ever possible.

MARTIN: Mr. Rutledge, you hold worthy ideals. But our experience teaches us that "An ounce of prevention is worth a pound of cure." Maryland can never jeopardize her interests by submitting them to a packed jury.

GERRY: These dark suspicions are unworthy. The interest of one is the interest of all. In my own State five counties have a majority of the representatives but the others neither feel nor fear tyranny.

BEDFORD: Mr. Gerry, sovereignty presupposes equality. If the great States wish to unite on such a plan, let them unite, but remember they have no authority to compel the others to unite.

MASON: [*Hotly.*] Then you would wreck all chances of union by a stubborn adherence to this idea of equal representation of States!

GERRY: Which really is not equal representation; our larger population would be submitting to unequal representation.

MARTIN: [*Impatiently.*] The general government is formed for the States rather than for individuals.

ELLSWORTH: The point is well taken.

BEDFORD: If you gentlemen of the large States carry out your plan, Virginia, Massachusetts, New York and Pennsylvania, will certainly dominate the small States. There is no remedy short of a new map that divides our country into equal States.

GERRY: [*In heat.*] That is absurd—ridiculous!

MASON: Not to be considered for an instant!

MARTIN: [*In anger.*] With your attitude, this convention is on the eve of dissolution. Scarcely the strength of a hair holds it together!

[*WASHINGTON enters in time to hear MARTIN'S remark.*]

WASHINGTON: Then, methinks, gentlemen, 'tis time we strengthened the ties that hold it together. [*They are surprised at his*

words, *for a moment confused as they bow to him. He strides to the table, without any formality proceeds.*] It is not my policy to interfere in a committee's deliberations in an informal or formal session.

MASON: We would be pleased to have your views on this matter, sir.

BEDFORD: Those are also my sentiments, sir.

WASHINGTON: My views on this particular question are of secondary importance. [*Their countenances show evidence of disappointment.*] However, I shall for once give voice to my feelings on the future attitude of delegates on any question that is before our body or may come before it. [*He stops, gazes steadfastly at each and every one of them. They are uncomfortable.*] Common danger brought the States into confederation; and on their union our safety and importance depended. We face a present danger as dire as when a foreign foe stood on our soil. The present danger is from within. It should be the highest ambition of every American to extend his views beyond himself. [*He pauses momentarily, the others are thoughtful.*] Methinks 'tis well to bear in mind that your conduct will not only affect yourselves, your country, but your immediate posterity. Remember, gentlemen, you will be judged by your fellow men. What you do today will mean political happiness or misery for ages yet unborn. To establish the government of laws, the union of these States is absolutely necessary—the various and opposite interests must be conciliated; local prejudices must be subdued, diversity of opinions and sentiments must be reconciled; sacrifices must be made on all sides for the general welfare. The future of your country is in your hand.

MARTIN: [*Thinking aloud.*] The future of our country—'tis in our hands. [*There is a long silence, the door at right is opened by a servant. MRS. BINGHAM enters with MADAM BLAUVELT.*]

MRS. BINGHAM: Gentlemen, refreshments are being—oh, I interrupt you, pardon me, gentlemen.

MARTIN: [*As they all bow to her.*] Refreshments, most opportune, Madam; we need refreshment like starved mariners who have passed through a storm and are sailing into a safe harbor.

MASON: Aye, we do.

MRS. BINGHAM: Then, gentlemen, 'tis my pleasure to regale you with a Spanish dish famous in New Orleans.

BEDFORD: Ah, a Spanish dish?

MRS. BINGHAM: — made from one of Madame Blauvelt's own recipes. [*She turns to MADAME BLAUVELT.*] General Washington's table at Mt. Vernon is famous throughout the States. Ever he seeks a new dish. You must copy your recipes for him. Come, gentlemen. [*MADAME BLAUVELT has gone to the table. MRS. BINGHAM passes out followed by the delegates, the late opponents now arm-in-arm. WASHINGTON remains and as the door is closed by the servant turns to MADAME BLAUVELT.*]

MADAME BLAUVELT: Our dear hostess said you desired to speak to me of New Orleans.

WASHINGTON: Aye, Madame.

MADAME BLAUVELT: And would you desire the recipe of the New Orleans dish?

WASHINGTON: Ever I am finding new dishes, Madame.

MADAME BLAUVELT: Are they always palatable, General?

WASHINGTON: Not always palatable, though I have so far been able to digest them.

MADAME BLAUVELT: You will ever find New Orleans dishes palatable.

WASHINGTON: Aye, Madame. Do you find the climate of New Orleans agreeable?

MADAME BLAUVELT: 'Tis exceedingly torrid during the summer months.

WASHINGTON: More so than Philadelphia?

MADAME BLAUVELT: Of a certainty it is.

WASHINGTON: Mayhap you do find the climate of Europe more agreeable?

MADAME BLAUVELT: [For a moment studies WASHINGTON, wonders if she is discovered.] Much more agreeable.

WASHINGTON: I wonder, Madame, that you tarry in such a climate as this when a sojourn in Europe is preferable.

MADAME BLAUVELT: [Now certain of his meaning.] Like unto a physician you are advising a trip to another clime.

WASHINGTON: Not advising.

MADAME BLAUVELT: [Drawing herself up.] Then 'tis a command?

WASHINGTON: Merely a suggestion from a private citizen.

MADAME BLAUVELT: [Grimly.] Yet you have your way with these men who believe they themselves are arranging the destiny of this country. You give no order, yet yours is the will they obey.

WASHINGTON: You unduly flatter me, Madame.

MADAME BLAUVELT: On the morrow I leave Philadelphia.

WASHINGTON: You sail on the Bonaventura?

MADAME BLAUVELT: If I can obtain passage.

WASHINGTON: Bon voyage, Madame.

MADAME BLAUVELT: [Curtsies.] I am dismissed. But ere I go, General Washington, I must exercise a woman's prerogative—have the last word.

WASHINGTON: 'Tis a lady's privilege. [Bows.]

MADAME BLAUVELT: You are the arch-enemy of all royalty.

WASHINGTON: Therefore your enemy, Madame?

MADAME BLAUVELT: [Smiles.] And to think some call you dull.

WASHINGTON: At least, slow of wit.

MADAME BLAUVELT: [Lifts her eyebrows and shakes her head in denial, then laughs.] Oh, the irony of it, the aristocrat, the military genius, the most regal man of the age, the one most fitted to be a king, is busily engaged in establishing a republican government that, should it succeed, will sound the death-knell of all royalty.

WASHINGTON: Constitutional liberty must succeed.

MADAME BLAUVELT: Only by your will. [She curtsies deeply.] Adieu—your—majesty!

CURTAIN

BUILDING A NATION
A GEORGE WASHINGTON PLAY IN ONE ACT

DRAMATIS PERSONAE

EARLY, the handy man of the household.
DANDRIDGE, Secretary to the President.
SAM, the negro butler.
GENERAL HENRY KNOX, Secretary of War.
MRS. KNOX.
COLONEL JAN VAN BRUNT.
PRESIDENT WASHINGTON.
ALEXANDER HAMILTON, Secretary of Treasury.
THOMAS JEFFERSON, Secretary of State.
EDMUND RANDOLPH, Attorney General.
NELLIE CUSTIS.
MARTHA WASHINGTON.
HAYS
LADUE } leaders of the mob.

TIME: July, 1793.
PLACE: A room in President Washington's home in Philadelphia.

DESCRIPTION OF CHARACTERS

EARLY:
A man well past middle age with white hair worn in a queue. He wears homespun breeches and vest, a white shirt open at the neck with sleeves rolled up, buckled low shoes and white hose. He is the handyman of the household, an old soldier, devoted to Washington.

DANDRIDGE:
A man of about middle age, Secretary to the President. Dressed in quiet well fitting clothes of the colonial period. Wears hair in a queue.

SAM:
An ancient negro butler, dressed in dark blue livery trimmed with silver, white stockings and buckled shoes.

GENERAL HENRY KNOX:
A large portly man, a little above middle stature and forty-three years of age. He carries a cane, usually under his arm and uses it when excited in conversation. He is well dressed in black small-clothes of the period. Wears his hair in a queue and powdered.

MRS. KNOX:
A large, jolly, outspoken woman, of middle age. Distinctly well born and a general favorite. Fashionably well dressed in the popular polonaise gown of the period, wears a silken bonnet. Her powdered hair is worn high in the mode of the day.

COLONEL JAN VAN BRUNT:
A man about middle age. Dressed quietly in civilian clothes of a good quality. He has the air of a military man and speaks with a slight accent.

PRESIDENT WASHINGTON:
Sixty-one years of age, six feet two inches tall, in weight about two hundred and ten pounds, rather large boned but well proportioned, graceful, dignified, thoughtful, modest in deportment. His complexion rather pale, his features strong, his white hair worn in a queue. Plainly though richly dressed in dark clothes of the colonial period.

ALEXANDER HAMILTON:
Thirty-eight years of age, five feet seven inches tall, complexion almost womanish, reddish brown hair worn in a queue. He is quick of speech and dramatic.

THOMAS JEFFERSON:

Fifty years of age. A tall man inclined to slenderness. His hair is brownish red, worn in a queue. Wears rich though quiet dress of the period. He has a benevolent, intelligent, placid face. He never shows signs of anger or impatience.

EDMUND RANDOLPH:

Forty years of age. Of a little above medium height. Dressed quietly though richly in the style of the period. Hair black and worn in a queue.

NELLIE CUSTIS:

Fourteen years of age. A vivid dark beauty. Dressed in a gown of light colored material made in the polonaise style of the period with skirt to the ankle.

MARTHA WASHINGTON:

Sixty-two years of age. A round face placid in repose, singularly free from wrinkles. Though short of stature and inclined to stoutness, she has great dignity and poise. She is kindly, tactful, outspoken and decided. She wears a light colored gown in the mode of the day, over her shoulders a lace fichu, on her head a white lace frilled cap holding in place her white hair.

HAYS:

A strong-visaged man a bit past middle age. Dressed in nondescript fashion, homespun breeches and vest, an ill fitting coat, his stock is of a black material; hair black or brown worn in a queue. On his head a red liberty cap.

LADUE:

A foreign type, dark, swarthy, of not quite middle age. Wears clothes of a better quality than HAYS. Black hair worn in a queue. On his head a red liberty cap.

[*EARLY, the carpenter and handy man, is repairing a catch on the window at left. DANDRIDGE is at the table busy with papers. EARLY picks up tools and goes to DANDRIDGE.*]

EARLY: Mr. Dandridge, I've fixed the catch.

DANDRIDGE: Very well, Early. Did you leave the window open?

EARLY: Nay, Sir. [*He goes to the window, opens it, looks out aimlessly, then leans forward as something outside attracts his attention. Then looks uncertainly at DANDRIDGE and goes to him.*] Mr. Dandridge, you think it wise to leave the window open?

DANDRIDGE: [*Without looking up.*] Why not?

EARLY: [*Scratches his head.*] The President's meetin' with the gentlemen of the Cabinet, ain't he?

DANDRIDGE: Yes, after a while. [*Turns and looks at EARLY.*] What of it?

EARLY: I just seen a couple of them red-capped Frenchies goin' by.

DANDRIDGE: There's nothing unusual in that.

EARLY: They're havin' a big meetin' t'-day, Sir.

DANDRIDGE: The Jacobins?

EARLY: Aye, Sir. A lot of asses brayin' for war.

DANDRIDGE: Let them bray, they will not disturb us. [*Returns to his paper.*]

EARLY: But——

DANDRIDGE: [*Impatiently.*] But what?

EARLY: They's paradin', they might come this way.

DANDRIDGE: Not much chance of that.

EARLY: They's gettin' right bold, these daffies, puttin' on red caps, drinkin' confusion to tyrants and sech, callin' each other "Citizen," singin' this here, *Ca Ira*. hollerin' for war with the British.

DANDRIDGE: Don't be disturbed, Early.

EARLY: An this here Citizen Genet—thinkin' he's even a bigger man than the President.

DANDRIDGE: [*Laughs.*] Well, we know differently, Early.

EARLY: 'Deed we do, Mr. Dandridge. Didn't I fight in the General's army from New York to Yorktown?

DANDRIDGE: Then don't worry about Genet. [*Goes back to paper.*]

EARLY: [*Scratches his head, picks up his toolbox, shakes his head.*] I like it not. [*Receiving no answer from DANDRIDGE he leaves at left. SAM enters from left, stops at door.*]

SAM: Gen'l and Mistis' Knox done come, Mr. Dandridge.

DANDRIDGE: The General is early for the meetin'. Show them in, Sam. [*SAM leaves, closing the door. DANDRIDGE leans back in thought. Rises, goes to window at right, looks out for a moment, then comes back to center as Sam opens the door.*]

SAM: [*Sonorously.*] De Hon'able Sec'tary of Wah and his Lady.

[*KNOX and MRS. KNOX enter, the latter is suppressing her mirth.*]

DANDRIDGE: [*Bows.*] General Knox. Madam Knox.

[*MRS. KNOX bursts into laughter. KNOX bows to DANDRIDGE, then looks at MRS. KNOX.*]

KNOX: Why this unseeming mirth, Lucy?

MRS. KNOX: [*Laughs.*] Oh——! Oh——! Pardon me, Mr. Dandridge, but Sam—— [*Laughs.*] Sam, how he loves it! [*Laughs heartily.*]

KNOX: [*Smiling.*] Loves what?

MRS. KNOX: [*Giggling.*] To announce us in this regal manner. [*Laughs.*]

SAM: [*At door.*] A gen'l'man, Sirs, to see the Hon'able Sec'tary of Wah.

KNOX: Who is he, Sam?

SAM: Sed he jest was a old comrade-in-ahms.

KNOX: An old comrade-in-arms!—there are many such.

SAM: De gen'l'man speaks lak he come from foa'en pahts, hon'able sec'tary.

KNOX: Ah! a Frenchman?

SAM: No sah, he doan speak jest like no Frenchman.

KNOX: [*To DANDRIDGE.*] Mayhap one seeking an office.

MRS. KNOX: Oh, see the man, Henry. We are early.

KNOX: I have made up my mind to let Madam Knox have her way, Sam.

SAM: Yessah, yessah.

KNOX: Will we disturb you, Dandridge?

DANDRIDGE: Nay, Sir.

MRS. KNOX: Mayhap Mr. Dandridge will conduct me to Lady Washington?

DANDRIDGE: I shall be delighted, Madam.

KNOX: Have him in, Sam.

SAM: Yessah, Hon'able Sec'tary.

MRS. KNOX: [*Takes DANDRIDGE'S arm, laughs.*] Oh, Sam will be the death of me! Henry, let me know when the Cabinet meeting is ended. [*They leave, at center. SAM opens door at right.*]

SAM: De gen'l'man, you honor.

[*VAN BRUNT enters, bows, smiles at the look of astonishment on KNOX'S face.*]

KNOX: Jan Van Brunt! [*VAN BRUNT steps forward; KNOX with quick strides goes to meet him; they clasp hands.*] A comrade-in-arms!

VAN BRUNT: Ah, my friend, you recognize me.

KNOX: Recognize you? Could I ever forget the man who saved my life at the Brandywine? Come, be seated, Jan. Tell me of yourself. [*They take chairs.*] When did you arrive in America?

VAN BRUNT: I landed two months ago at Boston.

KNOX: And only now you come to Philadelphia!

VAN BRUNT: By slow stages.

KNOX: Where have you been all these years, Jan?

VAN BRUNT: Many places my friend—Poland, France, Germany and my own country.

KNOX: If I mistake not, with your sword drawn in some righteous cause.

VAN BRUNT: Righteous? I was with Kosciuszko.

KNOX: Fighting for Polish liberty! 'Tis like you.

VAN BRUNT: I was in France with the Marquis Lafayette.

KNOX: With Lafayette. You must see the President; he would learn of his friend.

VAN BRUNT: I have seen his Excellency.

KNOX: Oh, you have?

VAN BRUNT: I was a horseback, returning from Valley Forge.

KNOX: Drawn there by memories of other days?

VAN BRUNT: The spirit of the place was upon me. In retrospect, I was again living those icy days of starvation and nakedness, treachery and intrigue. Nearing a cross road, I heard hoof beats and looking up beheld the General.

KNOX: He rides when he has the opportunity.

VAN BRUNT: Aside from his not being in uniform, his attitude, as he sat his mount, was much the same as other days. He was deep in thought, looked careworn, I noted the lines of his face are deeper etches than they were twelve years ago. Methought his shoulders a bit stooped.

KNOX: 'Tis no wonder, Jan. Today he faces troubles as hard to bear as those of Valley Forge.

VAN BRUNT: So I have learned.

KNOX: We are clothed today, we are fed, but as to treachery and intrigue—'tis the same as those days of the Cabal.

VAN BRUNT: With his Excellency still the only one who sees straight.

KNOX: Yes, by Heaven, you are right!

VAN BRUNT: He made this nation.

KNOX: With his sword he won its liberty; with his zeal, courage and foresight he made the union of these States possible; now as President he is steering the Ship of State through the treacherous cross currents of conflicting interests.

VAN BRUNT: There could be no better pilot, friend.

KNOX: But the crew is untrained, some mutinous. The anti-federalists and the Frenchified zealots would ruin his character, destroy his peace and injure his health.

VAN BRUNT: The French zealots—I know them well.

KNOX: The Jacobins are organizing here, and would make a sortie upon him in all the force they could muster—if they dared.

VAN BRUNT: Aye, that I could well believe.

KNOX: They would force us into a war with England—we would be in combat today if 'twere not for his Excellency's wisdom.

VAN BRUNT: He would keep the nation neutral. That is wise.

KNOX: [*Rising.*] I shall ask his Excellency if he has the leisure to see you 'ere the Cabinet meets. [*He goes to center door and raps, as a voice beyond says, "Come in," goes through the door. VAN BRUNT paces the floor and faces door as SAM opens it at left for HAMILTON to enter.*]

SAM: De Hon'able Sec'tary of de Treasury.

[*HAMILTON enters, VAN BRUNT bows, HAMILTON bows but does not recognize him, then turns to SAM.*]

HAMILTON: You said General Knox was here.

SAM: Yessah, he was——[*Scratches his head.*]

VAN BRUNT: He has gone to speak to his Excellency, Colonel Hamilton.

HAMILTON: [*Starts at VAN BRUNT'S words and looks at him keenly.*] Jan Van Brunt! You here! [*Hurries to VAN BRUNT, they clasp hands. WASHINGTON enters from center, stops, gazes for a moment at the meeting of HAMILTON and VAN BRUNT.*]

VAN BRUNT: I called you "Colonel," you have higher letters, and honors, my friend.

HAMILTON: None that I am so pleased with as my old title, Jan.

WASHINGTON: He fills all offices with equal ability, Colonel Van Brunt. [*At WASHINGTON'S words, both men turn and bow. WASHINGTON enters, followed by KNOX, and goes to VAN BRUNT. They clasp hands.*] Your semblance has changed but little since last we met.

VAN BRUNT: [*Pleased.*] Then you have not forgotten me, your Excellency?

WASHINGTON: Could I forget the charge of your regiment at Monmouth and the bravery of its commander! Let us take seats, gentlemen. [*They sit.*] General Knox tells me you were with my dear friend the Marquis Lafayette. Will you tell me of him?

VAN BRUNT: After the defeat of Kosciuszko——

WASHINGTON: Kosciuszko, one of the great souls of this world. When he was imprisoned, liberty lost a glorious champion.

VAN BRUNT: ——I went to France and joined the Marquis early in the French Revolution, was his aide when he commanded the National Guard. I was with him when he denounced the Jacobins.

WASHINGTON: A brave act. 'Twas like him.

VAN BRUNT: But his army stood against him.

HAMILTON: Went over to the Jacobins?

VAN BRUNT: Aye. With Lafayette I fled to Belgium, shared with him imprisonment at Wesel and Madgeburg. When he was sent to that loathsome dungeon at Olmitz, powerful friends in Holland obtained my release.

WASHINGTON: I have appealed to the Emperor of Austria to set the Marquis free, but my appeal was without results. I shall use every effort, consistent with my position, to assist my friend. [*To VAN BRUNT.*] You have no other news of him?

VAN BRUNT: Nay, your Excellency. Two months ago I came to America hoping to find peace.

HAMILTON: And you find a nation clamoring for war.

VAN BRUNT: Many misguided people willing to be an ally of the most despotic government the world has ever known——!

HAMILTON: God's truth!

VAN BRUNT: ——Tyrants and oppressors, traitors to liberty!

WASHINGTON: Can such a government last?

VAN BRUNT: Nay. 'Tis infinitely worse than the despotism of those profligate and degenerate monarchs the French people cast off.

WASHINGTON: 'Twas one of those French Monarchs who sent his troops to our aid during the Revolution.

HAMILTON: To further his own ends, your Excellency.

KNOX: Those who demand war with England say we owe a debt to France.

VAN BRUNT: [Very earnestly.] I am an European, not unfamiliar with the courts of Europe—their intrigues and jealousies—the United States would do well to keep free of their quarrels.

WASHINGTON: [Nods to HAMILTON, speaks to VAN BRUNT.] You have expressed my policy, Colonel.

VAN BRUNT: The French people in their madness are killing or banishing many of those who have their best interests at heart——

HAMILTON: Not unlike Lafayette.

VAN BRUNT: ——from one extreme they have gone to the other. They are now governed by a group of blood-thirsty maniacs.

WASHINGTON: How will it end?

VAN BRUNT: A strong man will arise, a dictator, who will become master of France.

KNOX: Will not a republic, like ours, be formed?

VAN BRUNT: Not for some time. France has no Washington to lead and guide a republican government.

[DANDRIDGE enters from the left. Quietly he goes to WASHINGTON.]

DANDRIDGE: Your Excellency. [WASHINGTON looks up.] Mr. Jefferson and Mr. Randolph await your pleasure.

WASHINGTON: [Rises.] Colonel Van Brunt, 'tis ever a pleasure to meet an old comrade. You will always find a welcome at my home.

[They have all arisen with WASHINGTON.]

VAN BRUNT: Your Excellency, I thank you. In America I shall make my home.

WASHINGTON: And here I hope you will ever find peace.

VAN BRUNT: Like unto the vast majority of the staunch people of America, I have an abiding faith in the President of the United States. [He bows and in a military manner about faces, strides to the door at left, turns and salutes. WASHINGTON, KNOX and HAMILTON, return his salute. He leaves.]

HAMILTON: The truth, from one who knows.

WASHINGTON: One we can trust. [He nods to DANDRIDGE who goes out door at left. WASHINGTON then goes to gaze at some papers neatly arranged on the table, takes a position behind it, facing the audience. SAM opens the door.]

SAM: The Hon'oble Sec'tary of State. The Hon'oble Attorney-Gen'l.

[JEFFERSON and RANDOLPH enter and bow.]

JEFFERSON: Your Excellency, Gentlemen.

RANDOLPH: Your Excellency, Mr. Hamilton, General Knox.

WASHINGTON: Good afternoon, gentlemen. Will you be seated?

[They gather about the table. WASHINGTON sits facing the audience with HAMILTON and KNOX on his left, JEFFERSON and RANDOLPH on his right.]

WASHINGTON: Gentlemen of the Cabinet, for our consideration there are many pressing questions concerning the welfare of our country. However, they must need, for a time, be put aside in order that we may give our attention to a matter which, day by day, is growing to be the most serious problem confronting the nation. I speak of the clamor for war with Great Britain.

KNOX: 'Tis unthinkable, Your Excellency. [Strikes his cane on the floor.]

WASHINGTON: Nevertheless, there are forces at work in our midst that would plunge this nation into war.

HAMILTON: [With fire.] Irresponsible parties who are swayed by the boisterous rantings of this French minister, Genet.

JEFFERSON: I might suggest to the honorable Secretary of the Treasury that such language does not tend toward international amity.

HAMILTON: [In cold anger.] I might and do suggest to the honorable Secretary of State that this is a Cabinet meeting and I do not expect my remarks to be reported to or printed in this scurrilous sheet. [He has taken a "Gazette" from his pocket and thrusts it toward JEFFERSON.]

JEFFERSON: [Calmly.] Do you insinuate, sir, that I have anything to do with that paper?

HAMILTON: I am not in an insinuating mood, Mr. Jefferson. However, this paper is known as an advocate of the anti-Federalist party. In this very issue, its pusilanimous editor dares to attack the motives of the President of the United States!

JEFFERSON: I as sincerely regret and as vehemently denounce such articles as you do, Mr. Hamilton.

WASHINGTON: Gentlemen! [WASHINGTON rises. HAMILTON and JEFFERSON stop and look at WASHINGTON.] I have been called a crocodile, a hyena, a deceiver, a double-dealer, a traitor.

KNOX: [Rising in anger, striking floor with his cane.] By God, General, I would——! [He stops as WASHINGTON raises his hand.]

WASHINGTON: But in what will this abuse terminate? For the results, as it respects myself, I care not, for I have a consolation within that no earthly efforts can deprive me of, and that is that neither ambition nor interested motives have influenced my conduct.

JEFFERSON: Well we know it, sir.

WASHINGTON: The arrows of malevolence, therefore, however barbed and well pointed, never can reach the vulnerable part of me, though whilst I am up as a mark they will be continually aimed.

[WASHINGTON sits; the others for a moment are silent.]

HAMILTON: Freneau and Bache, the editors of these opposition newspapers, are doing their best to drive us into war by influencing the people.

KNOX: —a minority of the people.

JEFFERSON: Perhaps a majority of the people whose instinctive gratitude to France induces them to look with favor on France.

HAMILTON: The character and purpose of France has changed.

WASHINGTON: Neutrality—the strictest neutrality—between England and France seems to me the only rational course.

[*A distant, ominous murmuring of an approaching mob is heard. The members of the Cabinet listen for a moment but continue their discussion.*]

JEFFERSON: But, methinks, Your Excellency, the people will not allow us to achieve neutrality.

[*The mob is coming closer, their cries more distinct. Shouts of "Long live the French Republic!" can be heard.*]

WASHINGTON: Gentlemen, I shall always be guided by the sense of the people upon every matter of great public concern.

[*The mob has come nearer. They are shouting, "Long live the French Republic and damnation to its foes!" "Down with the British!" "Let us help those who helped us!" "We want war with England!"*]

JEFFERSON: The people seem to be speaking in no uncertain voice.

WASHINGTON: Mr. Jefferson, the voice of the mob is not the voice of the people.

[*NELLIE CUSTIS comes in rather timidly from the center.*]

NELLIE: Pardon me, gentlemen.

WASHINGTON: [*Calmly and kindly.*] What is it, my dear?

[*The cries of the mob continue, the noise rises to be almost deafening. The men have risen at NELLIE'S entrance. KNOX is fuming. HAMILTON is coldly angry.*]

NELLIE: [*Points to the window at the left.*] Are you all right, grandpapa?

[*Before he can reply, MARTHA WASHINGTON and MRS. KNOX enter. MARTHA goes to NELLIE.*]

MARTHA: [*Calmly.*] Come, child; 'tis not beseeming in you to disturb the gentlemen.

WASHINGTON: Please, Martha, do not chide her. [*To NELLIE.*] Don't be concerned, dear.

MRS. KNOX: [*Has gone to GENERAL KNOX.*] Are you going to allow that vile rabble to continue that racket?

KNOX: [*Raises a restraining hand.*] I am not in command, Lucy.

[*EARLY enters, his face set in resolute anger, a rifle in his hand, his powder horn across his shoulder. Starts for the window. HAMILTON smiles and grasps his arm, stopping him.*]

MRS. KNOX: [*Points to EARLY.*] There is one man of sense.

WASHINGTON: [*To EARLY.*] Mr. Early, we do not need that sort of protection.

EARLY: [*Salutes.*] Aye, General. But—I'd like to give 'em a taste of the war they're a-wantin'! [*WASHINGTON smiles as EARLY withdraws to the door but can be seen standing beyond with his rifle ready. The mob continues its cries and noise.*]

JEFFERSON: [*To WASHINGTON.*] Mayhap I had better speak to the people. [*Starts for the window at right.*]

WASHINGTON: [*Raises a restraining hand.*] Nay, Mr. Jefferson. [*MR. DANDRIDGE enters with a worried look.*] Mr. Dandridge, is Colonel Van Brunt outside?

DANDRIDGE: Aye, Your Excellency, I saw him talking with some of the mob.

WASHINGTON: I thought so. Will you ask him to conduct the leaders of the demonstration to this room?

DANDRIDGE: At once, Your Excellency. [*Bows and leaves. The noise of the mob has risen in tempo.*]

MRS. KNOX: [*To HAMILTON.*] Will they come?

HAMILTON: Trust Van Brunt, he has never failed to carry out an order.

KNOX: [*Has gone to the window, looks out.*] Van Brunt's bringing them. [*The mob stops its cries, but the mumble of voices can be heard.*] Two men are coming with him.

WASHINGTON: [*Now in his chair. To JEFFERSON.*] Have you taken up the latest matter of the privateers with the French minister?

JEFFERSON: Aye, Your Excellency.

WASHINGTON: And his attitude?

JEFFERSON: He was—ah, rather indignant.

WASHINGTON: We can not allow our harbors to be the haven of French or British privateers. On that our mind is settled.

JEFFERSON: I understand, Your Excellency.

SAM: [*At the door.*] Colonel Van Brunt. [*To some one outside.*] What yo say de name, Sah?

HAYS: [*Gruffly.*] Hays, if ye want to know!

SAM: An' yo' name, Sah?

LADUE: Citizen Ladue.

SAM: Citizen Ladue and Mr. Hays, Your Excellency.

[*VAN BRUNT, HAYS and LADUE enter. As VAN BRUNT salutes, HAYS, a bit embarrassed, follows his example. LADUE is defiant. HAYS takes off his red Liberty cap, then as LADUE does not remove his cap HAYS takes it off LADUE'S head and hands it to him.*]

WASHINGTON: I have asked you gentlemen here to inquire as to the reason for this demonstration.

LADUE: We're for France and we want war with England.

WASHINGTON: Have you ever been in battle?

LADUE: Nay—I was——

HAYS: [*Quickly.*] I served during the Revolution, General. The Second Pennsylvania Line.

WASHINGTON: [*To HAYS.*] The Second Pennsylvania—'twas a brave regiment. And you would again fight the English.

HAYS: The Frenchies are fightin' fer liberty as we were—they helped us.

WASHINGTON: The Second Pennsylvania was at one time part of the Marquis Lafayette's command.

HAYS: Aye, General.

WASHINGTON: The French drove Lafayette from France.

LADUE: He was a traitor to liberty.

WASHINGTON: [*In quick anger.*] Silence! [*To HAYS.*] Do you think the Marquis a traitor, Mr. Hays?

HAYS: [*Scratches his head.*] It seems not like him, sir.

WASHINGTON: Have you any children?

HAYS: Aye, sir; four boys and two lassies.

WASHINGTON: When your boys were four or five years old did you make them do the work of grown men?

HAYS: Nay, sir; I waited till they was full-grown.

WASHINGTON: We have an infant country, Mr. Hays; we must give it a chance to grow to man's estate. Wars stunt the growth of nations as hard work would stunt the growth of a child.

HAYS: I never thought of that, sir.

LADUE: [*To HAYS.*] Ah, he's puttin' it over on ye.

HAYS: Shut yer mouth!

WASHINGTON: A nation must pay its debts.

LADUE: Then pay France by fightin' the British.

WASHINGTON: [*Disregarding LADUE.*] We now owe a debt to men like yourself, Mr. Hays; men who fought for our liberty. Think you we should pay that debt before paying debts to foreigners?

HAYS: Aye, sir.

WASHINGTON: This young nation will never pay any debts if it is continually at war.

HAYS: 'Tis the truth, sir.

WASHINGTON: Have you ever known me to break a promise to the people of this nation, Hays?

HAYS: Nay, General.

WASHINGTON: I say this to you and all others: We must lay a firm foundation on which to build up a strong nation. We need at least twenty years of peace in which to accomplish this task.

HAYS: Aye, sir.

WASHINGTON: We must think as Americans, untainted by foreign influence. [*Turns to LADUE.*] You, I take it, have but recently come to America.

HAYS: He has, sir.

WASHINGTON: Better you learn the true spirit of America before you attempt to tear down what patriotic citizens have built up. Liberty is not license. Thousands who will follow you as immigrants to this country will do well to learn that lesson.

LADUE: I care not for this country. I'm for doing away with all kings!

HAMILTON: And governments, too?

LADUE: Aye!

WASHINGTON: Mr. Hays, you see now the company you keep. [*HAYS looks angrily at LADUE.*] Such men would ruin the nation.

HAYS: [*Throws his red cap on the floor and puts his foot on it.*] I'm through with them, sir.

WASHINGTON: If I understand correctly the spirit of this nation, those of its inhabitants who think of its welfare, and they are in the majority, will ever support its government, even under cir-cumstances in which passions agitated in every direction are liable to mislead, amid appearances sometimes dubious, vicissitudes of fortune often discouraging. This spirit of America will ever prevail as the essential prop of the government.

JEFFERSON: [*With enthusiasm.*] And with it the spirit of democracy.

WASHINGTON: It remains to be seen whether our country will stand upon independent ground or be directed in its political concerns by any other nation. A little time will show who are its true friends.

HAYS: I'm one of its true friends, General, and I'd like to go and tell others that.

WASHINGTON: [*Smiles.*] Mr. Hays, the nation is sound at heart.

HAYS: We have always believed in you, General.

WASHINGTON: Then you can well believe in those who aid me. [*Gestures toward members of the Cabinet.*]

HAYS: Aye, sir; we will. [*He gives a military salute, about faces and strides out the door. LADUE peers about at those in the room, shrugs and follows him. VAN BRUNT bows and leaves. MRS. KNOX, MARTHA and NELLIE leave. WASHINGTON and his Cabinet bow to the ladies who leave. Outside the mob yells as HAYS joins it, then subsides to a low mumble of voices. WASHINGTON turns to JEFFERSON.*]

WASHINGTON: Mr. Citizen Genet must go. We can no longer countenance foreign interference in our political affairs.

JEFFERSON: 'Tis well.

VOICE: [*Outside.*] Three cheers for the United States and President Washington! [*The mob gives three huzzahs.*]

WASHINGTON: [*To his Cabinet.*] Gentlemen, why forego the advantages of our peculiar fortunate situation? Why quit our own to stand upon foreign ground? Why, by interweaving our destiny with that of any part of Europe, entangle our peace and prosperity in the toils of European ambition, rivalship, interest, humor, or caprice?

KNOX: Why, indeed?

CURTAIN

THE WASHINGTONS AT HOME

A GEORGE WASHINGTON PLAY IN ONE ACT

By DWIGHT MARFIELD

Copyright, 1931, by Dwight Marfield

Permission was given to produce this play without royalty fee during 1932.

FOREWORD

The Washingtons at Home was written with the intention of portraying the First President and Martha Washington at a birthday fête at Mount Vernon, in which music rather than dialogue should have the chief part. The dialogue, however, should voice the spirit of the time and of the man Washington who was first in peace as well as in war. The birthday anniversary chosen for the action was President Washington's last. The beautiful Nellie Custis, grand-daughter of Martha Washington, was married at Mount Vernon on that day at "about candle light." Only casual reference is made to this event in the play.

The play does not assume (as is necessarily the case when dramatic action is set on any historic date) to be a literal reproduction of history, save in the spirit which animates it. The historic persons of the cast of characters are General and Mrs. Washington, and General Charles Cotesworth Pinckney of South Carolina, who uttered the immortal retort to the extortionate demands of the French Directory. All other persons of the play are fictitious characters, although they bear names noted in Colonial days.

February 22, 1799, was of necessity chosen as the time of the play. Any earlier date would have precluded references to the historic and epoch making actions and words of Charles Cotesworth Pinckney, John Marshall and Elbridge Gerry, who had been sent to France by President John Adams as envoys to negotiate a peaceful settlement with the French Government of matters in dispute that threatened war.

The ringing reply of Pinckney to French demands demonstrated in striking fashion the wisdom of the theme that was dear to the heart of President Washington, that the people of the United States should never interweave their destiny with that of any part of Europe.

These principles, voiced by President Washington in his Farewell Address, are a legacy of inestimable value. Their importance has immeasurably increased in the years that have passed since dramatic defiance of European intrigue was uttered by an American patriot in words that have come down from that time like a golden tradition——

"Millions for defense but not one cent for tribute."

CHARACTERS

GENERAL GEORGE WASHINGTON.
MARTHA WASHINGTON.
GENERAL CHARLES COTESWORTH PINCKNEY.
COLONEL STUART RANDOLPH.

COLONEL BRAXTON LEE
CAPTAIN GAINES FAIRFAX
CAPTAIN DINWIDDIE SPOTTSWOODE
MR. WASHINGTON CUSTIS
} *Knights of the Golden Horseshoe*

MR. PACE CARROLL
MR. RUSH STOCKTON
MR. HANS STEUBEN
MR. OLIVER RODNEY
MISS PHERABY CUSTIS
MISS BETSY POLLARD
MISS FRANCES LIGHTFOOT
MISS ALINE GWINNETT
MISS FAITH TEMPLETON
MISS ANNETTE HEWES
MISS MARY LOU ROSS
} *Singers, Musicians and Guests.*

M'LLE ROSINA FARRARI, *Italian Diva.*
CHINQUAPEENA, *an Indian maiden.*
JEREMY JACKSON, *the Negro butler.*

TIME: *Evening of February 22, 1799.*
PLACE: *Drawing room of Mount Vernon.*

SET: *The drawing room is decorated with Colonial colors, evergreen, and holly. Buffet against wall at right. Harpsichord at rear center, or any other convenient place. Several card tables at left with candles and decks of cards on them. Door at right near buffet, leading to dining room. Window at rear. Door at left. Comfortable chairs dispersed as in a much-used living room. Open space in center. (Directions are from front of stage.)*

[*As the play opens, GEORGE and MARTHA WASHINGTON, and guests at a birthday dinner, are in the dining room at right. Sounds of happy voices and incidental music and occasional handclapping are heard. At buffet, a negro butler in appropriate uniform of the time, is polishing glasses*

and cups and arranging them about a large punch bowl. Talks to himself. Tiptoes to the door leading to dining room. Eavesdrops.]

JEREMY JACKSON: [*Name always to be pronounced in full.*] Um, um—foh de Lawd sake, ef somebody aint tellin' dat ole story 'bout a cherry tree. Ah hopes dey won't be a comin' in heah foh a long time. [*Tiptoes back to buffet.*] Dis' mah chance. [*Ladles a drink from the punch bowl, holds it up, looks at it, puts in a little more.*] Dat's better. [*Drinks.*] Ah sho' doan b'lieve dat cherry tree story. De General he sho didnt cut down no cherry tree. He done got too much prognostication foh sech foolishness. [*Drains glass, tilting it.*] Um—dats good. [*Smacks his lips. Starts to ladle out another glass. Door right opens. Enter COLONEL STUART RANDOLPH.*]

COLONEL RANDOLPH: Jeremy Jackson! What you doing?

JEREMY JACKSON: Yassuh. [*Drops ladle and slips half filled glass out of sight behind punch bowl.*]

COLONEL RANDOLPH: You old black rascal! Pour me a good long one.

JEREMY JACKSON: Yassuh, dat's what I'se fixin' to do. Ah jist says to mah self, Mars Randolph, he be comin' dis minute. You Jeremy Jackson, you have a glass ready foh Mars Randolph. [*Fills the glass he has just concealed. Hands it to COLONEL RANDOLPH, who drinks, wipes mouth with hanky.*]

COLONEL RANDOLPH: Another, Jeremy Jackson. [*Hands glass to him.*]

JEREMY JACKSON: Yassuh. Another. Dats what I'se jist thinkin'. [*Starts to fill glass.*]

COLONEL RANDOLPH: No! Here they come! [*The Colonel steps toward door to dining room. It opens and first comes BETSY POLLARD, young and vivacious.*]

BETSY POLLARD: You ran away, you bad boy.

COLONEL RANDOLPH: I had to find something to drown my sorrow over seeing the groom so happy, while—I—how long must I wait? [*He bows low to her.*]

BETSY POLLARD: But was it nice to run away?

COLONEL RANDOLPH: I ran away—not from my adorable Miss Betsy. I ran away from my thoughts. [*She curtsies.*]

BETSY POLLARD: Beautifully spoken—but not so loud. Tell me—— [*Other guests are coming through door, laughing and talking. Enter CHINQUAPEENA.*]

COLONEL RANDOLPH: Tell you what?

BETSY POLLARD: [*Indicating CHINQUAPEENA.*] Who is she?

COLONEL RANDOLPH: One of my cousins. You know my cousin, John Randolph of Virginia, is a descendant of Pocahontas, and Chinquapeena also has her blood.

BETSY POLLARD: How wonderful, and she sings?

COLONEL RANDOLPH: But not such a voice as yours, nor such eyes. Come. [*He leads her to the buffet. Addressing JEREMY JACKSON.*] A glass. [*Lifts it in a toast.*] A vos yeux belles. [*Drinks, bows, and kisses her hand, and holding the glass aloft, he recites.*] "Drink to me only with thine eyes, and I will pledge with mine; or leave a kiss but in the cup, and I'll not ask for wine."

BETSY POLLARD: Oh, Colonel! You've brought back with you the charming manners of France.

COLONEL RANDOLPH: My manners are only the reflection of your own charming self. [*She curtsies.*] Some of the French had shocking manners. You know we came back because we were kicked out of the country by the tyrannical government that controls France today.

BETSY POLLARD: Kicked out?

COLONEL RANDOLPH: Yes, literally kicked out. President Adams sent Pinckney and Marshall and that New Englander Gerry over to settle this quarrel with the French Directory in a gentlemanly way.

BETSY POLLARD: That being the case, of course, they needed you with them.

COLONEL RANDOLPH: [Bows low.] Now we are even. Thank you, adorable one.

BETSY POLLARD: And what happened?

COLONEL RANDOLPH: They wouldn't receive Pinckney. But he told them a thing or two. Here he comes now!

[Enter from right, GEORGE WASHINGTON and CHARLES COTESWORTH PINCKNEY. They stop to speak to BETSY.]

GEORGE WASHINGTON: General Pinckney just asked me— "Who is that charming girl?"

BETSY POLLARD: [Curtsying low to both of them.] And we are so proud of you, General Pinckney. You really did tell those scoundrels in Paris "Millions for defense, but not one cent for tribute?"

GENERAL PINCKNEY: I told them! Not a sixpence! Not a sixpence!

BETSY POLLARD: Oh, splendid!

GEORGE WASHINGTON: General Pinckney proved himself a real patriot. His experience with that avaricious Directory gives added weight to my warning to the people, not to interweave our destiny with that of any part of Europe.

GENERAL PINCKNEY: Yes, it shows how quickly friends can become foes.

COLONEL RANDOLPH: No warning in your farewell address was so much needed as that, Mr. President.

GEORGE WASHINGTON: [With a deprecating gesture.] President no longer, Colonel, and thank the good God for it. I'm in the happiest years of my life, freed of the cares of state, and the sky at last cleared of the clouds of war. [JEREMY JACKSON comes to them with a tray of drinks.] And now that our lovely Miss Nellie has been carried away by her splendid husband, I have only my family and faithful old Jeremy Jackson and other loyal servants to care for here at Mt. Vernon.

JEREMY JACKSON: [Bowing and scraping.] Yassuh, Yassuh, de General's good as de Lawd Gawd Jehovah Hisself to us folks.

GEORGE WASHINGTON: That's enough Jeremy Jackson. See that everybody is served.

JEREMY JACKSON: Yassuh, Yassuh. [Goes.]

GEORGE WASHINGTON: This is life at last, Pinckney. You remember Francis Hopkinson, of Philadelphia?

GENERAL PINCKNEY: One of the signers of the Declaration?

GEORGE WASHINGTON: The same. He has written and sent me some beautiful songs.

MARTHA WASHINGTON: [Joining the group and presenting FRANCES LIGHTFOOT to GEORGE WASHINGTON.] George, you recall Frances Lightfoot.

GEORGE WASHINGTON: [Bowing.] I remember her and her beautiful voice. We were just speaking of Hopkinson's songs. Perhaps you can sing some of them?

FRANCES LIGHTFOOT: Gladly—I have one of the songs he dedicated to you with me now, "Beneath a Weeping Willow's Shade."

GEORGE WASHINGTON: [To MARTHA WASHINGTON.] My dear, please ask some one to accompany Frances.

[MARTHA goes with her to the harpsichord and calls for a volunteer to play the accompaniment.]

CAPTAIN GAINES: [Steps to stage center and claps his hands for attention.] Some music, friends. Our gracious hostess has persuaded the charming Miss Frances Lightfoot to sing Francis Hopkinson's touching song "Beneath a Weeping Willow's Shade."

[The guests disperse about the room, some standing, others at the card tables. FRANCES LIGHTFOOT sings. Applause.]

FRANCES LIGHTFOOT: [Curtsying.] I also have with me Mr. Hopkinson's song "My Days Have Been So Wondrous Free." I think it is the first song ever written by a native American composer. Shall I sing it also? The words are so appropriate.

GEORGE WASHINGTON: I shall be delighted. [She sings. WASHINGTON leads in hearty applause.]

GEORGE WASHINGTON: Splendid! That song touches me. Home for the rest of life on this wonderful plantation, with friends about us.

[Encore. The assemblage talks informally; some at the card tables begin to shuffle the decks. MARTHA WASHINGTON goes from one to another. At one table is seated a group made up of BRAXTON LEE, DINWIDDIE SPOTTSWOODE, WASHINGTON CUSTIS, FAITH TEMPLETON, and ALINE GWINNETT.]

MARTHA WASHINGTON: Young ladies! I see you have captured some of the Knights of the Golden Horseshoe.

COLONEL LEE: And we have discovered greater beauty today than the founders of our Order, when they rode over the Blue Ridge into the lovely valley of the Shenandoah.

FAITH TEMPLETON: Colonel Lee has outdone himself with fine speeches.

MARTHA WASHINGTON: Some of these Virginia beaux are wonderful talkers.

ALINE GWINNETT: Wonderful card players, too. The Colonel just found five aces in his hand. I think he must be a member of the Knights of the Golden Fleece.

MARTHA WASHINGTON: Then, it is high time we broke up the game. Let's have some music.

ALINE GWINNETT: May we have something of Mozart?

CAPTAIN FAIRFAX: Attention! [The guests become quiet.] The string quartet will favor us with a composition by Mozart.

[COLONEL BRAXTON LEE, MR. RUSH STOCKTON, MR. HANS STEUBEN, MR. PACE CARROLL, and MISS ANNETTE HEWES render "Theme and Variations from Sonata in A Major" by MOZART. GEORGE WASHINGTON and GENERAL PINCKNEY lead the applause. COLONEL RANDOLPH and MISS BETSY at the buffet with others, drink a toast to the singers. JEREMY JACKSON'S voice is heard rising above everything.]

JEREMY JACKSON: Yassum, 'fore Gawd, he sho' did, Miss Betsy. Ah was dere when General Washington done it. Ah done swim 'cross de ribber and fine de silber dollah after de General t'rowed it 'cross de Rappahannock Ribber. Sho, he done it. Lak he t'rowed ole King George ovah de ocean. He sho' did t'row dat silber dollah ovah de ribber—an' de old King aint come back sence. [*Laughter at the buffet.*]

BETSY POLLARD: Is it true, Stuart?

COLONEL RANDOLPH: Ask the General.

BETSY POLLARD: [*Goes to GENERAL WASHINGTON who has seated himself at one of the card tables.*] Oh, please, General Washington [*WASHINGTON rises*] tell me, did you really, when you were a young man, throw a silver dollar across the Rappahannock River, where it's so terribly wide?

GEORGE WASHINGTON: Well, my dear Miss Betsy, you know a dollar went much farther in those days.

COLONEL RANDOLPH: And Jeremy Jackson says you threw the King over the ocean.

GEORGE WASHINGTON: [*Laughing heartily.*] Did he say that? Well one can throw a sovereign farther than a dollar.

BETSY POLLARD: That's wonderful!

GEORGE WASHINGTON: Youth can do wonderful things. You, for instance, with your charming ways. [*BETSY curtsies.*]

GEORGE WASHINGTON: I understand another charming girl is going to entertain us, with her fiddle.

CAPTAIN FAIRFAX: Everybody attention! [*Silences the guests by clapping his hands. Group at punch bowl is hilariously laughing. As silence falls JEREMY JACKSON'S voice is heard.*]

JEREMY JACKSON: Ah tell you he sho' did—t'rowed de ole king ovah de ocean. [*He suddenly realizes the room is silent, and ducks behind the buffet.*]

GEORGE WASHINGTON: It wouldn't be my birthday if Jeremy Jackson didn't perform for us. But now some more music.

CAPTAIN FAIRFAX: Kamawawa is one of our peaceable and friendly Indian chiefs, and he has a fine looking daughter, Chinquapeena, whom he sent to England for an education. She has come back with a well trained voice, and will now sing for us. Chinquapeena!

[*She sings. Applause. Encore.*]

CAPTAIN FAIRFAX: Pocahontas would be proud of her descendant who has just entertained us. Some of us Virginians are proud of having a dash of her blood in our veins. How about that Colonel Randolph?

COLONEL RANDOLPH: Vastly proud. [*Bows toward CHINQUAPEENA.*]

CAPTAIN FAIRFAX: Now we will have some madrigals by a quartet that has serenaded under the windows of many Virginia mansions.

[*Quartet sings. Applause.*]

CAPTAIN FAIRFAX: General and Mrs. Washington, Ladies and Gentlemen, Guests: A rare treat for you. A diva of song from sunny Italy will sing for us an air from the "*Magic Flute.*" I present the famous Italian diva, Rosina Ferrari!

[*MARTHA WASHINGTON escorts the diva to the harpsichord.*]

MARTHA WASHINGTON: It is gracious of you to come all the way to Mount Vernon and sing for us.

THE DIVA: The whole world would love to sing praise at the shrine of freedom. [*Curtsies toward GEORGE WASHINGTON, who rises and bows. Sings. Encore.*]

CAPTAIN FAIRFAX: Now General, you shall have some music on the fiddle.

MARTHA WASHINGTON: [*At one of the card tables at front is seated alone MISS PHERABY CUSTIS, who is very deaf; a charming elderly woman with white curls. She is playing solitaire. MARTHA WASHINGTON speaks loudly.*] Cousin Pheraby, perhaps you will be able to hear the fiddle.

PHERABY CUSTIS: [*Cupping her hand behind her ear to hear what MARTHA WASHINGTON is saying.*] A riddle? Somebody's going to tell a riddle, Martha?

MARTHA WASHINGTON: [*Loudly.*] The fiddle! the fiddle! Pheraby.

PHERABY CUSTIS: I was never good at guessing riddles, Martha. Thank you just the same. I'll try and finish this hand. [*Plays on.*]

[*MARTHA WASHINGTON motions to CAPTAIN FAIRFAX, who indicates to the violinist to proceed. She plays. Applause. As applause dies, PHERABY CUSTIS eagerly waves her hand.*]

PHERABY CUSTIS: Martha, Martha, come here. [*MARTHA WASHINGTON goes to her.*] I've made it, Martha! Look! [*Holds up a card: speaks very loudly in a high thin voice.*] That king turned up just in time.

JEREMY JACKSON: [*Coming to life at the buffet.*] Lord o' mercy! Is de ole king come back? [*Retires in confusion back of the buffet at the laughter of the guests.*]

CAPTAIN FAIRFAX: Guests and fellow Virginians all—Colonel Randolph and his charming partner, Miss Betsy Pollard. [*They step forward.*] Colonel, when you were in France you must have found time for a little diversion in the land of bold Lafayette, and that upstart Bonaparte who is beginning to play a part over there; or was it all statecraft?

COLONEL RANDOLPH: No, I found the French could play as well as fight. I heard delightful music in Paris and brought some of it home. I have parts of the "*Beggar's Opera*" and one of Martinis' charming songs "*Plaisir d'Amour.*"

CAPTAIN FAIRFAX: What could be more appropriate on an occasion like this, where Cupid has just done his perfect work—and, let me add, still has work to do—what could be more fitting than the song "*Plaisir d'Amour,*" by Colonel Randolph and Miss Betsy? What do you say?

[*COLONEL RANDOLPH and MISS BETSY are greeted with uproarious bravos as they bow acknowledgment and MISS BETSY is for the moment overcome with blushing confusion. They sing "Plaisir d'Amour." After the rendition of their music, there is a short intermission. During this time the party is informal. GEORGE and MARTHA WASHINGTON move among the guests, look over card tables, visit the buffet; talk is spontaneous and natural as at a reception.*]

CAPTAIN FAIRFAX: [*Claps his hands for attention. The hubbub slowly subsides. When silence reigns he speaks.*] General Washington has a word to say. I present our beloved host! [*Applause.*]

GEORGE WASHINGTON: From my heart I thank you for this happy event in the evening of my life. I am more than pleased in noting that many of you bear the names and are of the families of the signers of the charter of our liberties, the Declaration of Independence. Though my name is not upon that immortal document, it enshrines my heart. I gladly gave to the nation it created the full power and devotion of my life. Events that have lately occurred show the world that our country is not lacking in the firm will to retain the liberty so dearly won by the patriots of the war for independence. I have had letters from many who remembered my anniversary. Even from our noble friend Lafayette, who has suffered much of late striving to win real freedom for France, after the bloody excesses that followed her revolution. With the cares of state in able hands, and with a benign Providence restoring Mrs. Washington and myself to our beloved Mt. Vernon, I am content. Let us complete our fête with music by the noble Beethoven, and then dance to the strains of the minuet.

[Applause. After the music of Beethoven. the strains of Boccherini's "Minuet in A" are heard. GEORGE WASH-

INGTON leads MARTHA WASHINGTON in the steps of the stately dance, and all the guests join.]

CURTAIN.

MUSIC: More detailed information as to music called for and suitable for this play may be obtained by consulting the Music Booklet issued by the United States George Washington Bicentennial Commission.

COSTUMES: The characters are to be dressed in costumes appropriate to the period. Military uniforms, smallclothes, wigs, bright colored waistcoats for the men; polonaise frocks, elaborate coiffures, many ruffles and frills for the women. (See the George Washington Play and Pageant Costume Book issued by the Commission for suggestions.)

HAPPINESS DAY

A GEORGE WASHINGTON PLAY IN ONE ACT

DRAMATIS PERSONAE

(IN ORDER OF THEIR APPEARANCE)

MARTHA WASHINGTON.
SALLY, an old negro nurse.
NELLIE CUSTIS LEWIS, Martha's Granddaughter.
A NEGRO NURSE GIRL.
BABY FRANCES, Nellie's firstborn.

TIME: June 5, 1800.

PLACE: Martha Washington's room at Mt. Vernon.

DESCRIPTION OF CHARACTERS

MARTHA WASHINGTON:

Sixty-nine years of age. A round face, placid in repose, singularly free from wrinkles, but on which life has set its marks of sorrow. Though short of stature and inclined to stoutness, she has dignity and poise. She is kindly, tactful but outspoken and decided. She wears a black silk gown in the mode of the late 18th century, over her shoulders a black lace fischu, on her head a white frilled cap holding in place her white hair.

SALLY:

An old negro mammy, dressed neatly in homespun dress, wears an apron, and on her head a bright turban. She is a privileged servant.

NELLIE CUSTIS LEWIS:

Twenty-one years of age. A glowing young matron with a vivid dark beauty. She speaks in a soft voice and has a romantic nature. Dressed in a gown of light colored material made in the empire fashion of the late 18th century.

NURSE GIRL:

A negro nurse in about her middle twenties, dressed in a homespun garment, wears an apron and on her head a small white cap.

FRANCES:

Nellie's baby, six months old.

SET: A small bedroom on the third floor of Mount Vernon, which MARTHA occupied, almost constantly, after the death of WASHINGTON, as its dormer window was the only one in the house permitting a view of WASHINGTON's tomb. A shallow set, showing the plainness and severity of a room which is relieved by the chaste design and beauty of the Colonial furniture. Centering the back wall a door leading to the stairs. The right wall is without opening. The left wall is only four feet high, the slanting roof cutting the angle of ceiling and wall; in the center, a narrow opening about three feet in width projects out, the window can not be seen as the sloping roof and low wall obstruct it. To the right of the door in back wall, a narrow four-poster bed with a canopy, its head resting against the right wall. Between bed and audience, a small Franklin stove. On the left wall between back and dormer, a bureau. To the right of center, a table. A chair placed near the table. A footstool near the window. MARTHA is seated, in a small ladder-backed chair placed at the opening of the dormer window. The strong morning sunlight plays on her face as she gazes off toward the tomb.

The door being open, from the distance can be heard the sound of a few notes on a harpsichord. [A piano can be substituted if played on the treble or a thin sheet of paper can be inserted between the strings and the hammers.] Then a voice singing, "A Wayworn Traveller." * MARTHA listens to the end, then speaks.

MARTHA: "The Wayworn Traveller"—the song he loved. [For a moment she sits in thought, then rises, goes to the bureau, from a drawer takes a large masculine glove; places it lovingly to her cheek, kisses it and returns it to its place. She then takes from a drawer several bundles of letters tied with faded ribbon, holds them to her breast, takes them to the table, carefully lays them down and as she hears footsteps on the stairs, hastily draws a silken scarf over the letters, returns to chair by window. Nellie enters, holding several opened letters. Her face is sad, there are traces of tears on her cheeks.]

NELLIE: Good morning, Grandmama.
MARTHA: Good morning, Nellie.
NELLIE: I bring your personal letters.
MARTHA: They can be of small consequence.
NELLIE: Here is one from the President of the United States.
MARTHA: John Adams, why should he now write to me?

---

* See music on page 715.

NELLIE: Just paying his respects. Alexander Hamilton, James Monroe and Thomas Jefferson also inquire of your health.

MARTHA: 'Tis kind of them to think of me.

NELLIE: [*Looks at a letter.*] The Marquis Lafayette has returned to France—back from exile.

MARTHA: That is good news.

NELLIE: He writes from La Grange.

MARTHA: Near to Paris.

NELLIE: Grandma, he remembers the significance of this day.

MARTHA: Trust the dear Marquis to remember.

NELLIE: Oh, Grandmama! [*Goes to MARTHA, sinks to her knees and buries her face in her grandmother's lap and sobs.*]

MARTHA: [*Patting her head.*] There, there, Nellie. Don't take on so.

NELLIE: Oh, Grandmama! Mount Vernon is filled with his presence today.

MARTHA: It always is, Nellie. Always will be.

NELLIE: If he could come back—'twould be on this day.

MARTHA: [*Her hand goes to her breast, she leans a bit forward, her gaze towards the tomb. Her eyes closed, she leans back.*] Forty-two years ago——

NELLIE: [*Looks up at MARTHA.*] He placed the ring on your finger.

MARTHA: Yes.

NELLIE: And the charming Martha Custis promised to be his bride.

MARTHA: [*With an intake of breath.*] His bride!

NELLIE: [*After a silence.*] Grandmama?

MARTHA: Yes, Nellie.

NELLIE: You were always certain of his love?

MARTHA: [*Looks down at Nellie.*] Certain? As certain as I was that the sun would rise each day and set at eventide.

NELLIE: All his life he was ever as sure of your love.

MARTHA: [*A bit eagerly.*] How know you that?

NELLIE: 'Twas the evening of the day Mr. Lewis asked for my hand in marriage. I was in the garden, lost in dreams——

MARTHA: Rosy dreams.

NELLIE: —Roused by Grandpapa's steps, I looked up. His eyes were upon me——

MARTHA: His understanding eyes.

NELLIE: —He sat beside me, drew me close. "Are you happy, Nellie?" he asked.

MARTHA: You only smiled at him, Nellie?

NELLIE: Aye, then he said, "Are you sure you love Lawrence Lewis?" Some perverse imp caused me to answer, "I believe so."

MARTHA: Believe so?

NELLIE: His face grew serious, as he asked: "Are you not certain?" And I replied, "Can any one be certain?"

MARTHA: Oh, Nellie!

NELLIE: 'Twas then he opened his heart to me.

MARTHA: Yes?

NELLIE: Told me of the beauty of your love. Of your faith in him, those turbulent days before the Revolution. Your steadfastness, loyalty and courage at Valley Forge. How only to you he could unbosom himself in those terrible, dark, despairing days.

MARTHA: Valley Forge!

NELLIE: How with encouraging words and ready wit you helped him over the pitfalls of the first Presidency.

MARTHA: I was ever at his side.

NELLIE: [*She rises.*] Never will I forget his final words that night.

MARTHA: Yes, dear?

NELLIE: There was a certitude in his tones that held me spellbound. A feeling that thrilled my being. "Nellie," he said. "God never gave a man a greater blessing than when he conferred on me the love of my wife. If my countrymen feel grateful to me they should pay homage to her. For no man could have lived through what I have experienced, and achieved what I have done, without the certainty of the love and loyalty of a woman like Martha Washington."

MARTHA: Only the woman that bore him could be as fortunate as I.

NELLIE: [*After a silence.*] Come, Grandmama, let us walk in the garden.

MARTHA: Not yet, Nellie.

NELLIE: Oh, please, Grandmama. All day you sit in this tiny room, ever gazing at his—his last resting place.

MARTHA: And here I shall sit until I join him.

NELLIE: But this is happiness day. Glorious spring. [*She rises, goes to the table with the letter.*] The syringas are in bloom, the garden is a riot of color.

MARTHA: I would spend this day here with my memories. [*NELLIE notices the scarf and lifts it, uncovering the letters.*]

NELLIE: Oh, his letters—letters to you. [*MARTHA turns.*] How I would like to read them.

MARTHA: [*Rises, speaks kindly.*] They were writ for my eyes only.

NELLIE: But some day, Grandmama, when you are——

MARTHA: —are done with them!

NELLIE: You will leave them for me.

MARTHA: No!

NELLIE: [*Surprised at the tone.*] What will you do with them?

MARTHA: They shall be destroyed.

NELLIE: No! No! Not that! Destroy those treasures! They belong to posterity.

MARTHA: They belong to me.

NELLIE: Surely Grandmama——?

MARTHA: Would you have profane eyes pour over those lines?

NELLIE: Then leave them to me. Ever will I treasure them, guard them from others. [*MARTHA'S eyes are on her. A rap on the door interrupts.*]

MARTHA: Come!

[*A Negro nurse enters holding in her arms NELLIE'S six-month-old baby.*]

NURSE: [*Looking at NELLIE.*] I done fetch baby Frances, Missy Nellie; I just done diskevered her first toof.

NELLIE: Her first tooth! My darling!

MARTHA: Give her to me. [*She takes Baby from the nurse, fondles it, places a finger in its mouth.*] 'Tis true, Nellie! [*NELLIE is hovering over the child.*] See, 'tis way through.

NELLIE: I've waited its appearance with anxiety. Think you not its coming over long for the first one?

MARTHA: Nay, my dear. 'Tis better so.

NELLIE: But the hot months are coming?

MARTHA: She is a lusty infant. Oh, you pretty! Yes, you are. [*Looks at NELLIE with astonished pleasure.*] I veritably believe she knows her great grandmother.

NELLIE: 'Tis a good omen, Grandmama. The first tooth—to come this day.

MARTHA: [Holds the child tight to her breast.] Today.

NELLIE: Grandpapa loved her. He held her in his arms.

MARTHA: [To baby.] His arms were once around you, his strong sheltering arms. [Holds the baby toward the nurse.] I would be alone. [The nurse takes the child. Looks in surprise at MARTHA, who has gone to her chair by the window.]

NELLIE: [To nurse.] Yes, go.

[The nurse leaves. NELLIE starts to follow, hesitates as though struck by a thought, and goes to MARTHA, standing back of her chair.]

MARTHA: [Turns.] What is it, dear?

NELLIE: You love my little daughter, Grandmama?

MARTHA: Why bless you child, of a certainty I love her.

NELLIE: When she grows to the age of understanding, I shall proudly tell her of our hero.

MARTHA: Yes. you must do that.

NELLIE: She will open wide her eyes as I unfold the story of him and his great love. [MARTHA'S figure tenses.] I must needs tell the story many times.

MARTHA: Children always ask for many tellings.

NELLIE: And when she is taught to read——

MARTHA: Yes?

NELLIE: —and learns from others of his greatness, she will ask again for the twice told tale.

MARTHA: Mayhap.

NELLIE: When later a Prince Charming comes to her as the gallant, young Virginia Colonel came to you that day at Major Chamberlayne's——

MARTHA: [Living it over.] —forgetting his haste to Williamsburgh.

NELLIE: —forgetting all else, when he looked into your eyes.

MARTHA: He told you of that?

NELLIE: Aye, and many other things. When Prince Charming returns to my Frances, and whispers that which all women love to hear——

MARTHA: From the loved-one's own lips.

NELLIE: —then Grandmama, I would place in her hands letters from the greatest of men to his beloved. [There is an intake of MARTHA'S breath.] I would say, "Read those, my dear, and if you deem your lover as true, as steadfast, and his love as enduring as George Washington's——

MARTHA: No! No! There will never be another love like his!

NELLIE: I implore you, Grandma, keep these letters. Do not destroy them. Were he here today, I feel he would intercede with you to grant my wish.

MARTHA: —as he so often did——

NELLIE: He loved me; he loved my baby. He would want her to have such a part of his past.

[MARTHA'S head is bowed. She is touched by the plea. Her eyes lift, in perplexity. She tilts her head to gaze out at the tomb. Listens as though for a word from the departed. Slowly she rises, walks to the table, picks up a bundle of the letters, gazes at them, holds them to her breast, looks long at NELLIE. Slowly turns and puts the letters back on the table, goes toward her chair by the window.]

MARTHA: You know not what you ask.

NELLIE: You refuse me even one of his letters.

MARTHA: [Stops.] Yea, even one, my dear.

NELLIE: [Desperate.] You have no right!

MARTHA: [Surprised.] I haven't the right?

NELLIE: The world accepts him as the greatest of his time——

MARTHA: I accepted him as that long before the world heard of him.

NELLIE: —mayhap of all time.

MARTHA: I have heard such sentiments expressed many times, my dear. The whole world conspired to keep him from me.

NELLIE: You enjoyed forty years of married life, Grandmama.

MARTHA: Nearly half of those years he was away from Mount Vernon.

NELLIE: His heart was ever here.

MARTHA: But his mind and body were with his country.

NELLIE: He gave for a glorious purpose.

MARTHA: And his constitution was broken by the giving. Oh, Nellie, you are young—only a little over a year married—'tis hard for you to understand.

NELLIE: I want to understand.

MARTHA: How can you understand with all that is beautiful surrounding you—a loving husband ever by your side, your first baby in your arms. You are in the maytime of life. I, who am far into the winter of my time, can look back and feel that of which you as yet happily know nothing.

NELLIE: What mean you, Grandmama?

MARTHA: To see your lover depart from you to lead a forlorn army of untrained husbandmen against the greatest power of Europe. To wait at home, trembling at the hoof beats of every horse that enter our gates, fearing lest his rider bring tidings of disaster. Knowing that your loved one was enduring the bitterness of defeat and, what was worse, disloyalty, ingratitude, jealousy, treason.

NELLIE: But he was victorious.

MARTHA: Victory brought other trials. When the new nation stood on the edge of a precipice ready to take a leap into the abyss of confusion he held America back from anarchy and forged the mighty Constitution.

NELLIE: He made America a Nation.

MARTHA: And, as President he guided an infant republic through the maze of mischief caused by conflicting elements.

NELLIE: His was a splendid achievement!

MARTHA: Splendid to all others.

NELLIE: And to you, Grandmama.

MARTHA: Aye, splendid to me. But I knew the price he paid—those broad shoulders stooping under the load—his magnificent constitution slowly undermined. My dear one aged before his time.

NELLIE: He gave his life for his country. Surely you can give his letters to posterity.

MARTHA: His life to his country—his letters—to me. They are mine! Mine! Mine alone!

NELLIE: Grandma, please!

MARTHA: [Very kindly.] Will you go, dear? I would be alone.

NELLIE: [Stretches out her hands in a gesture of appeal as MARTHA goes to the window.] You won't destroy them? [Getting no response, NELLIE places her handkerchief to her eyes and going out, closes the door. MARTHA slowly sits in the little chair and resumes her vigil. There is a rap on the door.]

MARTHA: Come!

SALLY: [Steps in the door, holding a bowl of flowers.] I done fotched dees hyar s'ringas fom de gahden, Ma'am. Days de firstest ob the yeah.

MARTHA: They are beautiful, Sally. Place them on the table.

SALLY: De gen'l done set a heap ob store on dem blossoms, Ma'am. [*She places flowers on the table, arranges them.*]

MARTHA: The General loved flowers, trees, all growing things.

SALLY: I members well de day he set out dat bush, Ma'am. Jest fifteen years ago.

MARTHA: You have a good memory, Sally.

SALLY: Yessum, I has. 'Spec'ly days like dat—days whut means sumpin'.

MARTHA: You haven't forgotten this day.

SALLY: Lordy, no, ma'am! Dis day, like dat day he set out dis bush, was allus plantin' days. Dat's whut I calls 'em, Ma'am. Case he allus done plant sumpin' choicey dat day.

MARTHA: [*Looks toward the tomb.*] 'Twas ever a special day—a happy day to him.

SALLY: An I done 'spec' it was to you, Ma'am.

MARTHA: You know the meaning of this day?

SALLY: Law, Ma'am. Coas I does. Didn't I heah de Gen'l atellin' Missy Nellie 'bout it de day he done set out dis bush?

MARTHA: He told Nellie?

SALLY: Yessum. I'se her nurse den, ma'am. An she'd follered him 'bout as she allus did, wantin' fo to know whut he was adoin', an why he was adoin' it.

MARTHA: And he told her?

SALLY: Yessum. Said 'twas his hap'ness day case 'twas the anniversity of de day his seed of hap'ness was done planted. An Missy Nellie, she axes him, how 'tis yo plants hap'ness seed an he says, "Yo find some'un yo loves right haad an yo axes em iffen day loves yoall,

an iffen dat some 'un done says, Yessum, yo mahies dem, an yo lives happy evah afta."

MARTHA: —happy ever after.

SALLY: Yessum. [*After a silence.*] Does we have a gran' dinnah today, Ma'am?

MARTHA: No, Sally.

SALLY: Missy!

MARTHA: You may go. Fetch me some tinder.

SALLY: Yoall wantin' a fia in dat contraption? [*Points to the stove.*]

MARTHA: No, Sally. Not now. [*SALLY looks uncertainly at her mistress, and leaves. MARTHA rises, goes to the flowers, buries her face in them, fondles them as she speaks.*] How he loved you, pretty flowers—blooms of love—emblems of faithfulness—seeds of happiness. [*She picks up one of the bundles of letters, goes to the window, gazes at the tomb.*] George, can you hear me? What would you have me do? Your heart dictated them—your hand writ them. Was their message to me alone? Or shall I allow other eyes to gaze upon them? Let others know how you poured out your heart to me waiting, in an agony of suspense, until each one came? Shall I lay bare your soul to the world, as you, in these lines of ink, laid bare your soul to me? Won't you speak, George? [*For a time there is silence.*] Soon I will follow you—be placed beside you. How will you have me come, with these bits of the real you locked in my heart—or leave them for the world to pour over, to dissect? No! no. Not that George! Not that! [*She goes to the table, snatches the letters, takes them to the stove, removes the lid, places them carefully within, returns to the table for a sprig of the syringas, kisses it, places it over the letters; then, slowly—slowly replaces the lid.*]

CURTAIN

The Wayworn Traveller
from the Opera "The Mountaineers"
(1793)

Samuel Arnold (1740-1802)

ANNOUNCEMENTS

Attention is called to the following dramatic material, published by the United States George Washington Bicentennial Commission.

1. GEORGE WASHINGTON PAGEANTS AND PLAYS—a bibliography of all George Washington plays and pageants, with a short synopsis of each, published by the Commission, and a descriptive list of dramatic material on the subject of George Washington, available from publishers throughout the country.

2. GEORGE WASHINGTON COSTUME BOOKLET—a booklet describing the civilian dress and military uniforms of colonial days, with suggestions for costuming plays and pageants.

3. MUSIC FOR PLAYS AND PAGEANTS—including concert pieces, dances, marches and miscellaneous music of the Washington period, together with suggestions as to the adaptability of such music for specific occasions.

4. PAGEANTS AND PLAYS for Bicentennial occasions. (See pamphlet "George Washington Pageants and Plays" for complete list.)

YOUR DRAMATIC PROGRAM

The Commission requests that two copies of the program of any George Washington pageant or play given at any place in the United States or in foreign countries, be sent to the Pageant and Play Department, United States George Washington Bicentennial Commission, Washington Building, Washington, D. C., that the programs may be placed in the Government archives.

It is urged that not only the auspices and the place of presentation—indoor or outdoor—be printed upon the program, but also the date and the name of the city or town and the State.